I/S 10/14

D1102538

Scar
the
Co

THE
RESTAURANT
GUIDE
2015

AA Lifestyle Guides

LIBRARY
NEWCASTLE COLLEGE
NEWCASTLE UPON TYNE

Class 647.95

BARCODE 028b301

Published by AA Publishing, a trading name of AA Media Limited, whose registered office is Fanum House, Basing View, Basingstoke, Hampshire RG21 4EA. Registered number 06112600.

22nd edition published 2014
© AA Media Limited 2014

AA Media Limited retains the copyright in the current edition © 2014 and in all subsequent editions, reprints and amendments to editions. The information contained in this directory is sourced entirely from the AA's information resources. All rights reserved. No part of this publication may be reproduced, stored in a retrieval system, or transmitted in any form or by any means - electronic, photocopying, recording or otherwise - unless the written permission of the Publishers has been obtained beforehand. This book may not be sold, resold, hired out or otherwise disposed of by way of trade in any form of binding or cover other than that in which it is published, without the prior consent of all relevant Publishers.

The contents of this book are believed correct at the time of printing. Nevertheless, the Publisher cannot be held responsible for any errors or omissions, or for changes in the details given in this Guide, or for the consequences of any reliance on the information provided by the same. This does not affect your statutory rights. Assessments of AA inspected establishments are based on the experience of the Hotel and Restaurant Inspectors on the occasion(s) of their visit(s) and therefore descriptions given in this Guide necessarily dictate an element of subjective opinion which may not reflect or dictate a reader's own opinion on another occasion. See page 9 for a clear explanation of how, based on our Inspectors' inspection experiences, establishments are graded. If the meal or meals experienced by an Inspector or Inspectors during an inspection fall between award levels the restaurant concerned may be awarded the lower of any award levels considered applicable. The AA strives to ensure accuracy of the information in this Guide at the time of printing. Due to the constantly evolving nature of the subject matter the information is subject to change. The AA will gratefully receive any advice from our readers of any necessary updated information.

Please contact
Advertisement Sales: advertisingsales@theaa.com
Editorial Department: lifestyleguides@theaa.com

Website addresses are included in some entries as specified by the respective establishment. Such websites are not under the control of AA Media Limited and as such AA Media Limited has no control over them and will not accept any responsibility or liability in respect of any and all matters whatsoever relating to such websites including access, content, material and functionality. By including the addresses of third party websites the AA does not intend to solicit business or offer any security to any person in any country, directly or indirectly.

Photographs in the gazetteer are provided by the establishments. Every effort has been made to trace copyright holders, and we apologise in advance for any unintentional omissions or errors. We would be pleased to apply any corrections in a following edition of this publication.

Typeset and repro by Servis Filmsetting Ltd, Stockport.

Printed in Italy by Printer Trento SRL, Trento

This directory is compiled by AA Lifestyle Guides; managed in the Librios Information Management System and generated by the AA establishment database system.

Restaurant descriptions have been contributed by the following team of writers: Hugh Morgan, Mike Pedley, Allen Stidwill, Stuart Taylor, Andrew Turvil.

AA LIfestyle Guides would like to thank Julia Powers and Sean Callery for their help in the preparation of this guide.

Maps prepared by the Mapping Services Department of AA Publishing. Maps © AA Media Limited 2014.

Contains Ordnance Survey data© Crown copyright and database right 2014.

This is based upon Crown Copyright and is reproduced with the permission of Land & Property Services under delegated authority from the Controller of Her Majesty's Stationery Office.
© Crown copyright and database rights 2014 Licence number 100,363. Permit number 130063

Republic of Ireland mapping based on © Ordnance Survey Ireland/Government of Ireland Copyright Permit number MP000913

Information on National Parks in England provided by the Countryside Agency (Natural England).

Information on National Parks in Scotland provided by Scottish Natural Heritage.

Information on National Parks in Wales provided by The Countryside Council for Wales.

ISBN: 978-0-7495-7617-2

A05153

Contents

Welcome to the AA Restaurant Guide

Welcome to the 22nd edition of The AA Restaurant Guide. As ever, our team of AA hotel and restaurant inspectors have been travelling the length and breadth of the country, making anonymous visits to hundreds of establishments and awarding coveted AA Rosettes to the best of the UK's restaurants.

On the map

For another year, we've been thrilled with the quality of the UK dining scene. This year's guide includes 10 five-rosette, 35 four-rosette and 189 three-rosette restaurants, the elite of what the country has to offer, as well as more than 180 entirely new restaurants to the guide. Though London continues to house the lion's share of destination dining establishments, this is changing; Andrew Turvil highlights the best of Birmingham, Manchester and Edinburgh in our feature on page 20.

Who's in the guide?

We make our selection by seeking out restaurants that are worth making a detour for – the best ingredients, expertly prepared, whether in skilled interpretations of classic dishes or modern, innovative flavour combinations. Some may be part of a high-end chain or attached to an upmarket hotel, others a small family-run business; what they all have in common is excellent food. To learn more about how the AA assesses restaurants for Rosette awards, see page 9.

Unsung heroes

In 2014 we launched the AA Food Service Award in recognition of a frequently overlooked area of the restaurant profession – front-of-house service. After The Waterside Inn in Bray took the inaugural award, this year's winner, seen on page 13, is a worthy successor.

Simon Numphud, Head of AA Hotel Services, also took time to chat to chef Michael Caines – now in his 20th year at Gidleigh Park – about his thoughts on the UK hospitality industry, amongst other topics (see page 28). It's all about playing to your strengths, is the chef's message – which is exactly what the three restaurants singled out for our Wine Awards on page 16 have done. We've also highlighted other restaurants with notable wine lists throughout the guide (🍷 NOTABLE WINE LIST).

Top achievers

You'll find the winner of the AA Chefs' Chef Award, voted for by their peers, on page 10, and our Lifetime Achievement Award winner on page 12 – our congratulations to both. Our team of inspectors have once again nominated their Restaurants of the Year (see page 14) based on their visits. This year they range from a repurposed warehouse to a swanky new London hotel, via a couple of local gems. As always, it's been a strong showing from the UK industry, and we're proud to have these four – alongside the more than 2,000 others you'll find within these pages – featured in this year's guide.

Changing places

The transient nature of the hospitality industry means that chefs move around all the time, and restaurants may change hands. As any change at multi-Rosette level requires a new inspection to verify their award, some of these restaurants appear in the guide with their Rosette level unconfirmed.

Our inspections are ongoing throughout the year however, so once their award is confirmed it will be published in the restaurants section on theAA.com.

Tell us what you think

We welcome your feedback about the restaurants included in this guide, and the guide itself. A readers' report form appears at the back of the book, so please write in, or email us at **AA.Restaurants@theAA.com**.

The restaurants also feature on **theAA.com** and AA mobile apps. You can also follow us on twitter **@TheAA_Lifestyle** or 'like' the AA on facebook at **www.facebook.com/TheAAUK**.

How to use the guide

1.

3.

4.
5.
6.

9.

10.

11.

12.

16.

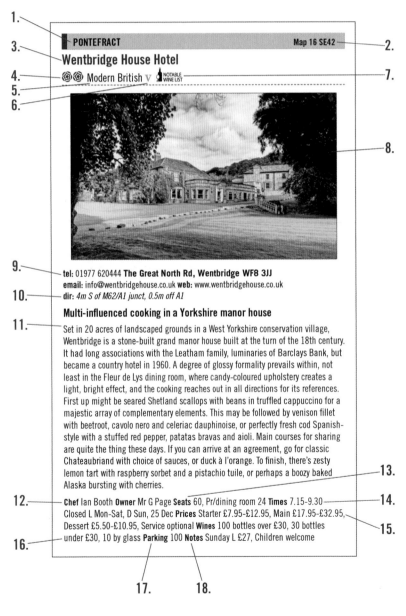

PONTEFRACT   Map 16 SE42

Wentbridge House Hotel

◉◉ Modern British V ❀ NOTABLE WINE LIST

tel: 01977 620444 **The Great North Rd, Wentbridge WF8 3JJ**
email: info@wentbridgehouse.co.uk **web:** www.wentbridgehouse.co.uk
dir: *4m S of M62/A1 junct, 0.5m off A1*

Multi-influenced cooking in a Yorkshire manor house

Set in 20 acres of landscaped grounds in a West Yorkshire conservation village, Wentbridge is a stone-built grand manor house built at the turn of the 18th century. It had long associations with the Leatham family, luminaries of Barclays Bank, but became a country hotel in 1960. A degree of glossy formality prevails within, not least in the Fleur de Lys dining room, where candy-coloured upholstery creates a light, bright effect, and the cooking reaches out in all directions for its references. First up might be seared Shetland scallops with beans in truffled cappuccino for a majestic array of complementary elements. This may be followed by venison fillet with beetroot, cavolo nero and celeriac dauphinoise, or perfectly fresh cod Spanish-style with a stuffed red pepper, patatas bravas and aioli. Main courses for sharing are quite the thing these days. If you can arrive at an agreement, go for classic Chateaubriand with choice of sauces, or duck à l'orange. To finish, there's zesty lemon tart with raspberry sorbet and a pistachio tuile, or perhaps a boozy baked Alaska bursting with cherries.

Chef Ian Booth **Owner** Mr G Page **Seats** 60, Pr/dining room 24 **Times** 7.15-9.30 Closed L Mon-Sat, D Sun, 25 Dec **Prices** Starter £7.95-£12.95, Main £17.95-£32.95, Dessert £5.50-£10.95, Service optional **Wines** 100 bottles over £30, 30 bottles under £30, 10 by glass **Parking** 100 **Notes** Sunday L £27, Children welcome

17.   18.

2.

7.

8.

13.

14.

15.

1. Location
Restaurants are listed in country and county order, then by town and then alphabetically within the town. There is an index by restaurant at the back of the guide and a similar one for the Central & Greater London sections on page 254.

2. Map reference
Each town or village is given a map reference – the map page number and a two-figure reference based on the National Grid. For example:
Map 16 SE42
16 refers to the page number of the map section at the back of the guide
SE is the National Grid lettered square (representing 100,000 sq metres) in which the location will be found
4 is the figure reading across the top and bottom of the map page
2 is the figure reading down at each side of the map page. For Central London and Greater London, there is a map section starting on page 258.

3. Restaurant name
Some details and prices may be omitted from an entry when the establishment has not supplied us with up-to-date information. This is indicated where an establishment name is shown in italics.

4. AA Rosette award
Restaurants are awarded one or more Rosettes, up to a maximum of five. See page 9.

5. Food style
A summary of the main cuisine type(s).

6. Vegetarian menu

V Indicates a vegetarian menu. Restaurants with some vegetarian dishes available are indicated under Notes (see 18, below).

7. Notable wine list

⚑ NOTABLE WINE LIST This symbol, where present, indicates a notable wine list (see pages 16–19).

8. Photograph(s)

Restaurants are invited to enhance their entry with up to two photographs.

9. Contact details

10. Directions

Short directions are given. London locations give the nearest station.

11. Description

Description of the restaurant and the food.

12. Chef(s) and owner(s)

The names of the chef(s) and owner(s) are as up-to-date as possible at the time of going to press, but changes in personnel often occur, and may affect both the style and quality of the restaurant.

13. Number of seats

Number of seats in the restaurant, followed by private dining room (Pr/dining room).

14. Daily opening and closing times

Daily opening and closing times, the days of the week when closed and seasonal closures. Some restaurants offer all-day dining. Note that opening times are liable to change without notice. It is wise to telephone in advance.

15. Prices

Prices are for fixed lunch (2 courses) and dinner (3 courses) and à la carte dishes. Note: Prices quoted are an indication only, and are subject to change. We ask restaurants questions about service charge and their responses appear here too.

16. Number of wines

Number of wines under and over £30, and available by the glass.

17. Parking details

On-site parking or nearby parking.

18. Notes

Additional information as supplied by the restaurants including, for example, availability of vegetarian dishes (not a full menu, see 6, above), Sunday lunch prices and policy towards children.

Smoking regulations

From July 2007 smoking was banned in all enclosed public places in the United Kingdom and Ireland. Internal communal areas must be smoke-free.

Facilities for disabled guests

The Equality Act 2010 provides legal rights for disabled people including access to goods, services and facilities, and means that service providers may have to consider making adjustments to their premises. For more information about the Act see www.gov.uk/government/policies/creating-a-fairer-and-more-equal-society or www.gov.uk/definition-of-disability-under-equality-act-2010.

The establishments in this guide should be aware of their obligations under the Act. We recommend that you phone in advance to ensure that the establishment you have chosen has appropriate facilities.

Website addresses

Where website addresses are included they have been supplied and specified by the respective establishment. Such websites are not under the control of AA Media Limited and as such AA Media Limited has no control over them and will not accept any responsibility or liability in respect of any and all matters whatsoever relating to such websites including access, content, material and functionality. By including the addresses of third-party websites the AA does not intend to solicit business or offer any security to any person in any country, directly or indirectly.

How the AA assesses for Rosette Awards

The AA's Rosette award scheme was the first nationwide scheme for assessing the quality of food served by restaurants and hotels.

A consistent approach

The Rosette scheme is an award, not a classification, and although there is necessarily an element of subjectivity when it comes to assessing taste, we aim for a consistent approach throughout the UK. Our awards are made solely on the basis of a meal visit or visits by one or more of our hotel and restaurant inspectors, who have an unrivalled breadth and depth of experience in assessing quality. They award Rosettes annually on a rising scale of one to five.

What makes a restaurant worthy of a Rosette award?

For our inspectors, the top and bottom line is the food. The taste of a dish is what counts, and whether it successfully delivers to the diner the promise of the menu. A restaurant is only as good as its worst meal. Although presentation and competent service should be appropriate to the style of the restaurant and the quality of the food, they cannot affect the Rosette assessment as such, either up or down. The summaries below indicate what our inspectors look for, but are intended only as guidelines. The AA is constantly reviewing its award criteria, and competition usually results in an all-round improvement in standards, so it becomes increasingly difficult for restaurants to reach an award level. For more detailed Rosette criteria, please visit theAA.com.

⍟ One Rosette

These are excellent restaurants that stand out in their local area featuring:
• Food prepared with care, understanding and skill
• Good quality ingredients
Around 50% of restaurants in this guide have one Rosette.

⍟⍟ Two Rosettes

The best local restaurants, which aim for and achieve:
• Higher standards
• Better consistency
• Greater precision apparent in the cooking
• Obvious attention to the quality and selection of ingredients
Around 40% of restaurants in this guide have two Rosettes.

⍟⍟⍟ Three Rosettes

Outstanding restaurants demanding recognition well beyond their local area. The cooking will be underpinned by:
• Selection and sympathetic treatment of highest quality ingredients
• Consistent timing, seasoning and judgement of flavour combinations
• Excellent, intelligent service and a well-chosen wine list
Around 10% of restaurants in this guide have three Rosettes.

⍟⍟⍟⍟ Four Rosettes

Among the top restaurants in the UK, where the cooking demands national recognition and shows:
• Intense ambition
• A passion for excellence
• Superb technical skills
• Remarkable consistency
• Appreciation of culinary traditions combined with desire for exploration and improvement
• Cooking demands national recognition
Thirty-five restaurants in this guide have four Rosettes.

⍟⍟⍟⍟⍟ Five Rosettes

Where the cooking stands comparison with the best in the world. These restaurants have:
• Highly individual cooking
• Breathtaking culinary skills
• Setting the standards to which others aspire
• Knowledgeable and distinctive wine list
Ten restaurants in this guide have five Rosettes.

AA Chefs' Chef 2014–15

Nathan Outlaw

This year's AA Chefs' Chef Award goes to Nathan Outlaw of Restaurant Nathan Outlaw in Rock, Cornwall

Nathan Outlaw is most associated with the county of Cornwall. It was in the west that this Outlaw made his name, opening his first venture, The Black Pig, aged just 24, but he's actually a man of Kent. His journey to culinary stardom began back in Maidstone, where even as a nipper he helped out his professional chef father with breakfast service. This led to catering college in Thanet and then, aged 18, his first job at the InterContinental Hotel under the late Peter Kromberg.

After stints with Gary Rhodes (another alumni of Thanet) and Eric Chavot, and aged just 20, Nathan headed west to work at Rick Stein's restaurant in Padstow, and a love affair with seafood began. Love was obviously in the air, as it was here that he met his future wife, Rachel, a native of Cornwall, who was working front-of-house.

The couple headed out of the county to work with John Campbell at Lords of the Manor in the Cotswolds before, at the tender age of 23, Nathan was appointed head chef at the Vineyard in Stockcross under Campbell. With experience gained at the cutting-edge of contemporary fine dining, the Outlaws were ready to strike out on their own.

Their first attempt, The Black Pig in Rock, wowed the press, but with only 32 covers and seasonal trade, it was a struggle to make it work. Nathan next opened up in a couple of hotels, before arriving at the St Enodoc (back in Rock as it happens) with the opening of the casual dining Outlaw's, followed by the all-conquering Restaurant Nathan Outlaw in February 2010.

A fixture on TV screens for the last few years, Nathan is the seafood maestro of our times, creating dishes that show respect for the fruits of the sea and their natural flavours, while bringing contemporary flair and creativity to each plate.

A London opening followed to much fanfare – Outlaw's at The Capital Hotel – headed-up by protégé Pete Biggs, and then the Fish Kitchen in Port Isaac. The latest venture is The Mariners pub in Rock, with Paul Ripley as executive chef (an old mucker from the Seafood Restaurant days), so watch this space. The future of British seafood cookery is in safe hands.

On the menu

Cured brill with gooseberries
and horseradish

Turbot on the bone with peas
and green sauce

Raspberry, almond and chocolate
ice cream sandwich

Previous winners

Tom Kerridge
The Hand and Flowers,
Marlow
page 72

Chris and Jeff Galvin
Galvin La Chapelle,
London E1
page 270

Michael Caines
Gidleigh Park,
Chagford, Devon
page 138

Andrew Fairlie
Andrew Fairlie@Gleneagles,
Auchterarder,
Perth & Kinross
page 644

Germain Schwab

Raymond Blanc
Belmond Le Manoir aux
Quat' Saisons, Great Milton,
Oxfordshire
page 437

Shaun Hill
Walnut Tree Inn,
Abergavenny,
Monmouthshire
page 673

Heston Blumenthal
The Fat Duck, Bray,
Berkshire
page 50

Jean-Christophe Novelli

Gordon Ramsay
Restaurant Gordon Ramsay,
London SW3
page 318

Rick Stein
The Seafood Restaurant,
Padstow, Cornwall
page 101

Marco Pierre White

Kevin Viner

Philip Howard
The Square, London W1
page 371

Marcus Wareing
Marcus, The Berkeley,
London SW1
page 307

Martin Wishart
Restaurant Martin Wishart,
Leith, Edinburgh
page 616

Pierre Koffmann
Koffmann's, London SW1
page 305

AA Lifetime Achievement Award 2014–15

Ruth Rogers

When Ruth Rogers and Rose Gray opened The River Café (see page 382) in Ruth's husband's architectural practice, it was out of a need to feed the workers in the Thameside building and an opportunity for them to pursue their own passion for the natural flavours of rustic Italian cooking. Nearly 30 years later it is hard to imagine London's culinary landscape without this landmark restaurant. The restaurant, the books and an inspiring television series had a profound impact on Italian cooking in the UK, not to mention the legacy of all the chefs who have passed through the kitchen. But its impact runs even deeper than that, for The River Café was among the first places to highlight the provenance, seasonality and dazzling freshness of their ingredients. The sheer brilliance of The River Café was always in its simplicity.

Ruth was born in America and attended the London College of Printing, where she studied typography and graphic design, marrying the architect Richard Rogers in 1973. It was Richard's Italian family that first ignited Ruth's passion for the food and flavours of the country (he was born in Tuscany), and five years living in Paris as Richard worked on the Pompidou Centre helped further develop her interest in culinary culture. When The River Café opened its doors in 1987, it was evident that Ruth and Rose (who sadly died in 2010) weren't the only people passionate about the stunning flavours of Italian home cooking.

The River Café's style and attitude has spawned many imitators and inspired countless restaurateurs and home cooks, and though never their intention, Ruth and Rose helped set the tone of future dining habits in the UK. Starchy formality was on the way out and The River Café's relaxed service style and minimalist décor was a template that many followed.

The likes of Theo Randall, Hugh Fearnley-Whittingstall, Jamie Oliver and Sam Clark are just some of the people who have passed through the kitchen over the years, and there are countless others who played a part in its success and have gone on to spread the passion for wonderful ingredients, flavour and simplicity around the globe. And that's a wonderful legacy.

Ruth was awarded the MBE in 2010 for services to the hospitality industry, and it is our privilege to give her our Lifetime Achievement Award in 2014–15.

AA Food Service Award 2014–15

Galvin at Windows, London W1

Customer-facing staff in the UK restaurant industry do not generally get the recognition that they deserve. This award acknowledges the vital role played by service teams across the country. From the 2000-plus AA Rosette restaurants featured in the 2015 Restaurant Guide, the AA inspection team nominated the very best of the best based on the following criteria:

- Consistently delivering excellent standards of restaurant service and hospitality
- Technical service skills and food and beverage knowledge of the highest standard
- Clear commitment to staff training and development

The winner of the 2015 Service Award is Galvin at Windows. Up on the 28th floor of the London Hilton Hotel on Park Lane, Galvin at Windows (see page 344) already has a couple of aces up its sleeve in the form of the stunning 360° views over London and the dynamic modern French cooking of executive chef Joo Won. But when it comes to the art of service, general manager Fred Sirieix has a vision that is realised from the moment you step out of the lift.

It's all about training and attention to detail, with every member of the team participating in regular sessions to ensure they're all in harmony. It's a large restaurant, yet every member of the team manages to remain engaged and show considerable knowledge of the menu and wine list.

The fine balance of when to act and when to stand back so the customer feels cared for, but not smothered, is an area where Galvin at Windows excels. The customer experience is judged just right, from the warm smiles on arrival to the very same smiles as you leave.

The team of sommeliers know their list inside out and are on hand for a sensible recommendation (no chance of a nasty surprise on the bill here), and the fabulous bar area with its table service and delicious cocktails maintains the high standards of customer interaction.

There is no better example in the UK of how to run front-of-house and how to give the customer an experience that is every bit as satisfying as the food on the plate.

The award's two runners-up were Lucknam Park Hotel and Spa, Colerne, and Ormer, Jersey.

AA Restaurants of the Year 2014–15

ENGLAND

THE STICKY WALNUT ❀❀
CHESTER page 88

This is the neighbourhood restaurant that everyone wants in their locality; an accessible, informal and unpretentious restaurant that delivers its food without unnecessary pomp and with a welcome sense of humour. Chef-patron Garry Usher uses Twitter to get the word about this great restaurant out to both the public and the industry, but don't be fooled by the jokes and outrageous comments; Garry and his brigade do actually take cooking very seriously. Consistency is excellent, attention to detail great and the incredible depth of flavour generated from often-simple dishes is a skill that is hard to master.

Last year's winner of the Catey for Menu of the Year, the best-kept secret in Chester is now out and, as it's a small restaurant, it fills up quickly and it can be difficult to get a table. Decor is simple and understated, yet fresh and smart, and the front of house team is equally passionate and knowledgeable. It's a welcome breath of fresh air; every great local restaurant should be like this place.

LONDON

BERNERS TAVERN ❀❀
LONDON page 334

Opening to great acclaim in mid-2013, Berners Tavern, at the new Five Star London Edition Hotel, pushes all the right buttons. From day one the restaurant teams, both front and back of house, have not stopped and on a busy week they will serve approximately 3,000 covers. No mean feat for a hotel restaurant for sure. This is Jason Atherton's latest venture, though not his only plan for the City. Head Chef Phil Carmichael has been with Jason since 2002, most recently at Maze, Cape Town.

Food is honest and ingredients are of the highest quality, with classic roots pervading throughout, and the interesting menus will have you tempted to try everything on offer. The restaurant itself is beautiful; the original ornate plasterwork picked out with subtle coloured lighting and a plethora of paintings and mirrors on the walls. Designed by Ian Shrager (who also designed the hotel interior), it oozes opulence. A large and very busy bar is a feature of one wall, while the egg-shaped chandeliers are supposedly inspired by New York's Grand Central Station. This is certainly one of the hottest tickets in town.

Potential Restaurants of the Year are nominated by our team of full-time inspectors based on their routine visits. We are looking for somewhere that is exceptional in its chosen area of the market; whilst the Rosette awards are based on the quality of the food alone, Restaurant of the Year takes into account all aspects of the dining experience.

SCOTLAND

TIMBERYARD
EDINBURGH page 618

The Radford family, previously renowned for restaurants like Atrium, a former AA Scottish Restaurant of the Year, opened this restaurant in central Edinburgh in 2012. The venue started life quite literally as a timber yard, and diners can still eat al fresco in the central courtyard when the weather permits.

Once inside, you enter what was once a warehouse. The décor remains very minimalistic, with whitewashed walls, rough wooden flooring and a student, punk vibe to proceedings. Friendly young staff with faultless knowledge are simply dressed in jeans, T-shirts and large grey aprons, while modern house music creates a great atmosphere. A large classroom-style revolving blackboard displays drinks, and the open kitchen can be viewed from the dining room.

The ethos of the food is based on seasonal, organic ingredients from small producers, with a menu that allows for 4 courses to be taken; bite, small, large and sweet – though you can miss one course out if you wish. Son Ben Radford heads up the kitchen team of a restaurant that is certainly going places.

WALES

BULLY'S
CARDIFF page 660

Located in the Pontcanna district of Cardiff, Bully's has been developing a reputation as one of the city's little gems for more than 15 years. From the outside this small neighbourhood restaurant is one of a row of shops. On entering however, it transforms to an individual and quirky place. The walls are covered from floor to ceiling with an eclectic mix of framed pictures and articles relating to either food or the family or both, and a canvas of artwork painted by owner Russell Bullimore's two very young children is proudly displayed. Russell is constantly changing the restaurant by adding new things, painting tables or chairs, or changing the cutlery to vintage finds, so it is an ever-changing environment.

The restaurant sources seasonal produce from Welsh providers, and complements it with a unique French wine list from small, passionate growers. Interesting modern food combines with the eclectic atmosphere, and customer satisfaction is paramount. The staff are friendly and unassuming and service is attentive, yet feels relaxed; a true skill in itself.

AA Wine Awards 2014–15

The annual AA wine award, sponsored by Matthew Clark Wines, attracted a huge response from our AA recognised restaurants with over 1,300 wine lists submitted for judging. Three national winners were chosen – the Olive Tree at the Queensberry Hotel, Bath for England and Overall winner; The Peat Inn for Scotland; and The Grove, Narberth for Wales (see overleaf for details of the winners).

All 2,000 Rosetted restaurants in last year's guide were invited to submit their wine lists. From these the panel selected a shortlist of over 260 establishments who are highlighted in the guide with the Notable Wine List symbol ◗ NOTABLE WINE LIST.

The shortlisted establishments were asked to choose wines from their list (within a budget of £80 per bottle) to accompany a menu designed by last year's winner the Witchery, Edinburgh.

The final judging panel included Simon Numphud, Head of AA Hotel Services, John Power, Wine Buyer of The Witchery and Nick Zalinski, Business Director Matthew Clark Wines (our sponsor). The judges' comments are shown under the award winners on the opposite page.

Other wine lists that stood out in the final judging included Llangoed Hall in Llyswen, Fairyhill in Reynoldston, Ellenborough Park in Cheltenham, Donnington Valley in Newbury, Hotel du Vin in Bristol, The Horseshoe Inn in Eddleston and the Ubiquitous Chip in Glasgow.

What makes a wine list notable?

We are looking for high-quality wines, with diversity across grapes and/or countries and style, the best individual growers and vintages. The list should be well presented, ideally with some helpful notes and, to reflect the demand from diners, a good choice of wines by the glass.

Things that disappoint the judges are spelling errors, wines under incorrect regions or styles, split vintages (which are still far too common), lazy purchasing (all wines from a country from just one grower or negociant) and confusing layouts. Sadly, many restaurants still do not pay much attention to wine, resulting in ill-considered lists.

To reach the final shortlist, we look for a real passion for wine, which should come across to the customer, a fair pricing policy (depending on the style of the restaurant) an interesting coverage (not necessarily a large list), which might include areas of specialism, perhaps a particular wine area, sherries or larger formats such as magnums.

Olive Tree at the Queensberry Hotel, Bath – the winning wine selection

Menu	Wine Selection
Canapés	Louis Roederer, Brut, NV
Starter – Tea smoked duck with beetroot sorbet	Art Series Riesling, Leeuwin Estate, Margaret River, 2011
Fish Course – Guy Grieve's scallops, herb baked with smoked Iberico pancetta	Savennieres, Chateau D'epiré, Loire Valley, 2009
Main Course – Côte de Boeuf for two to share served with chophouse butter, salad and triple cooked chips	Ninquen, Mountain Vineyards, Colchagua Valley, 2010
Cheese – Mull cheddar, Lanark Blue and Criffel	Alsace Pinot Noir, Domaine Schleret, 2007
Dessert – Chocolate brioche bread and butter pudding, pistachio ice cream and white chocolate sauce	Warres Otima Tawny Port
Coffee and chocolates	Mortlach, Single Cask Single Malt 2000

The AA Wine Awards are sponsored by Matthew Clark, Whitchurch Lane, Bristol, BS14 Tel: 01275 891 400
email: enquiries@matthewclark.co.uk web: www.matthewclark.co.uk/

AA Wine Awards – the winners

OLIVE TREE AT THE QUEENSBERRY HOTEL ❀❀❀
BATH page 460

Sitting on the gentle rise of Russel Street, the Queensberry is a townhouse hotel of genteel appeal, run with charm by Laurence and Helen Beere. The Olive Tree restaurant is in the basement, and overcomes any sense of subterranean gloom with a light, airy look. The cooking is a confident expression of the contemporary British style; poached and roasted duck liver to start, say, with pickled rhubarb, shiitake mushrooms and candied walnuts, followed by cod with parsnip and vanilla, Alsace bacon and sprouting broccoli. The superb wine list, put together by Laurence Beere, is sorted by style and crosses international borders in search of its wares. Start amongst the 'Wines That Sparkle' and move onto something 'Full Rich Ripe and Toasty' or 'Crisp and Bone Dry'. There are some rarefied clarets to choose from, an excellent choice by the glass, and the pricing is decidedly user-friendly.

Judges' comments: A super list that looks like has evolved around the business and works for both the proprietors and their customers alike. It attempts to engage at all levels and its personality wins through. Its concise format works well and it's easy to navigate.

It's informative and strikes the right balance without being preaching or rambling. It encourages the customer to experiment and try different things. It's very well priced while at the same time not afraid to list some more expensive bottles.

WINNER FOR SCOTLAND

THE PEAT INN ❀❀❀
PEAT INN page 622

Geoffrey and Katherine Smeddle have run this 18th-century coaching inn with professionalism and charm since 2006, and it remains one of the standout destinations in Scotland's culinary firmament. Geoffrey's cooking stands out from the crowd for all the right reasons: he starts from the ground up, using top-quality seasonal ingredients, and takes provenance seriously – locally-landed fish, for example, travels just ten miles to the kitchen. Kick off with braised veal cheek and crisp sweetbreads with roast cauliflower, turnip, and hazelnut dressing, before roast sea bream with poached potatoes, fennel and lobster thermidor sauce. The wine list runs to 400 bottles with a focus on first-rate French producers, sorted by region, plus there are plenty of enticing options from the rest of the world. Small producers compete on the page with the big guns, and red wines are decanted before arriving at the table.

Judges' comments: A cracking, handpicked list which has plenty of interest on every page. Sensibly priced, the list is well balanced and flows really well through each section. Everything has been looked at in detail, a confident list.

WINNER FOR WALES

THE GROVE ❀❀❀
NARBERTH page 680

This pristine white house is surrounded by a gorgeous restored Georgian walled garden, with stunning views of the Preseli Mountains. Inside it's all rather luxurious, with an elegant restaurant looking out over the grounds. The starting point for the seasonally changing menus is tip-top produce; the kitchen knows how to treat superb ingredients with restraint and respect to produce dishes that sing with natural flavours; slow-cooked pork belly and crispy crackling arrive with three langoustine tails, followed by Brecon red deer alongside turnip, glazed shallots and a little venison suet pudding. The wine list has genuine range while displaying evident restraint when it comes to pricing (not too many bottles come in at over £100). There are plenty of French classics, too, and a good choice by the glass and half bottle.

Judges' comments: Nicely put together and a clearly presented list. Fairly priced, good detail in selection with everything handpicked and there for a reason. Clearly gone to some effort to seek out some lesser-known but really delicious wines. Pricing designed to give value even at the top end, priced to move to drink.

No city limits

by Andrew Turvil

It's not just in London that people have an appetite for cutting-edge culinary experiences. As interest in food increases, the market for exciting and positively thrilling restaurants has grown: Birmingham, Manchester and Edinburgh have become major dining destinations in their own right.

Many people reach the conclusion that the UK's greatest culinary exponents are to be found in London and the Home Counties alone. With its huge population, economic clout, global reputation, historic significance etc., the world's focus on London is somewhat inevitable. There are no less than 16 restaurants holding four or more rosettes in London in the *AA Restaurant Guide 2015*, and the city's reputation as a restaurant hotspot has been cemented by firebrand chefs who have become stars on the global stage, as well as a host of international visitors who have opened up global franchises. London is an exciting city to eat these days; the UK finally has a culinary identity of sorts, and the chefs working out of London have had a lot to do with that.

But across the UK things are changing. In fact, the very definition of 'fine dining' is changing, as the formal and rather intimidating ways inherited from the classic European-style of service are washed away. Until relatively recently, restaurants at the top end of the game were formal places where everything was in its place – but attitudes have changed. People want to enjoy themselves. If it ain't fun, why bother?

Awareness of and interest in food culture is more prevalent than it has ever been, too, increasing exponentially over the last ten or twenty years. Those

with a passion can consume *MasterChef*, *The Great British Menu*, *The Taste* and copious other shows. Cookbooks sell like the latest gung-ho thrillers and chick-lit. People want a taste of the new culinary experiences that are being created across the UK.

'Destination dining' addresses *do* exist outside of London. A new brand of restaurants has opened up in cities like Birmingham, Manchester and Edinburgh. London doesn't have it all.

Second city blues

It can't be easy being number two, especially when the number one is eight times bigger. It's not a fair fight – Lennox Lewis versus Amir Khan. Birmingham has already made its mark on the UK's culinary habits with the creation of the balti, and much of the UK's curry-house culture has emanated from the city's vibrant communities. The new-wave of modern British cooking gets a look-in these days, with four chefs in particular impressing with their technical skills and creative ambitions: Glynn Purnell, Steve Love, Adam Stokes and Luke Tipping. These guys (they're all guys – that's another story) produce creative modern food that can hold its own in any city, whether first or second, and they've proven that the residents and visitors to Birmingham have a desire for high-end cooking.

"The new mood in top-end dining suits Manchester. It's not about formality or the 'establishment', it's about the 'wow' factor, maybe even a bit of bling"

attitude and some stunning contemporary food on offer.

Where these four lead, others are sure to follow; fine dining in Birmingham is undeniably on the up.

What's in a number?

Manchester is some way off being England's second city when it comes to population, with Birmingham coming in at just about twice its size. It's not even second, or third, or fourth… but the people of Manchester have never lacked self-confidence. Much has been made of the people of Manchester's resistance to poncey food, to refusing to pay over the odds for dressed-up fancy stuff. The TV show *Restaurant Wars* dealt with that very subject as two top chefs attempted to open restaurants in the city. Well, they're here, in these pages, and still open.

The new mood in top-end dining suits Manchester. It's not about formality or the 'establishment', it's about the 'wow' factor, maybe even a bit of bling. The new fine dining has replaced strict codes of behaviour with a sense of wonder. A bag of chips is always available if that's what you want, but anyone with the money and desire to enter one of Manchester's top-end gaffs is going to get a show. Not one necessarily that astonishes with smoke and mirrors, but a culinary performance that aims to impress with its precision, creativity and maybe a little bit of razzle dazzle.

Step forward Simon Rogan and his head chef Adam Reid, and Aiden Byrne. Rogan took on the old guard at the city's iconic Midland Hotel and shook it up at The French by Simon Rogan with his style of food that revels in provenance and freshness (he has his own farm) and delivers plates of food that are as non-prescriptive as any being produced anywhere in the UK. And Aiden Byrne, hailing from West Kirby on the Wirral (45 miles from Manchester if that matters),

Glynn Purnell must surely be the face of the new wave Birmingham chefs. Cooking divertingly modern stuff at his eponymous restaurant on Cornwall Street, he's a regular on TV, including repeat appearances on *The Great British Menu* and *Saturday Kitchen*. The highlight at Purnell's has to be its themed tasting menus, a collection of witty dishes with a nod to Birmingham's culinary heritage. Luke Tipping, meanwhile, is at the stoves at Simpsons, a star of the local dining scene for over a decade, with owner Andreas Antona credited with helping to ignite the city's interest in fine dining. Check out the fab terrace.

Adam Stokes is the new boy in town, fresh from the four-rosette Glenapp Castle on the Mull of Kintyre. His restaurant, Adam's, another tasting menu-led dining experience around the corner from New Street Station, is already a must-visit address in the city – 'my aim it not to baffle, but to excite and enthuse', says Adam. Steve and Claire Love's place meanwhile, Loves Restaurant, is a powerhouse waterfront address, where there's an unpretentious

> "...they have created a place that has bags of style and food that is as individual and dynamic as you'll get anywhere else in the UK"

heads up the kitchen at Manchester House, a restaurant and bar that aims to impress with some updated northern classics and a showy confidence that attracts the A-list and anyone who wants to get a taste of the high life (it's on the 12th floor after all). Rogan has also opened Mr Cooper's House and Garden in the Midland Hotel, which is the more 'casual' of the bunch, but still has lots of style and a culinary output that aims to bring in the punters for a pork chop with a sage crust and green beans in a creamy tofu sauce.

The incomers have revitalised the Manchester restaurant scene, bringing a much-needed sense of excitement to the city. It's no longer all about the football clubs.

Another capital city

Edinburgh is a city with a global reputation for its festival and as home to the Scottish Parliament, but for food? As it happens three singular and creative chefs lead the way in the city, with a host of Rosettes between them and a passion for Scotland's ingredients. Tom Kitchin and Martin Wishart are Scotsmen who have returned to their home country to

open their restaurants – The Kitchin and Restaurant Martin Wishart respectively – having gained experience at top-end gaffs around the UK and Europe. Kitchen worked at Alain Ducasse's Louis XV in Monte Carlo, and it doesn't get much better than that. The question isn't so much why Edinburgh, as why not?

Tom Kitchin was born in the city and it's the perfect location for his 'from nature to for' philosophy. Scottish ingredients are delivered to the door every day, with Tom and his team undertaking all the filleting and butchery in-house to ensure it's just the way they want it. For Martin Wishart, whose restaurant (like The Kitchin) is located in the booming Leith dockside, the adventure in the city began back in 1999. Also raised in Edinburgh, Martin's cooking has decidedly classic French leanings, but also places fine Scottish produce at the heart of things.

Then there's the singular Paul Kitching and his restaurant with rooms, 21212. Paul is an Englishman who has made the city his home (with partner Katie O'Brien) and together they have created a place that has bags of style and food that is as individual and dynamic as you'll get

"Destination dining is a reality. Head into one of the UK's top cities and you can find some top tucker."

wasn't usually an option. But those chefs passed through great kitchens, learning from master chefs like Pierre Koffmann, Raymond Blanc, Marco Pierre White and a whole host of people called Roux as they went. And now they, and the second and third generation down the line, have the confidence to open up in places where they feel they have an attachment – home, or near home, or anywhere where they fancy living. It doesn't have to be London anymore. Or Paris. That's not to say it isn't a good idea to head off into the wide world and get some experience, but now very good experience can be gained nearer home. As the people of the UK develop more of an interest in eating out and greater curiosity about food, chefs with experience, ambition and imagination are on hand to deliver the product.

Deep pockets

'Most of our people have never had it so good' said Prime Minister Harold Macmillan back in 1957, and it's a relevant mantra for anyone today with an interest in good food. Destination dining is a reality. Head into one of the UK's top cities and you can find some top tucker. We are no longer the laughing stock of the world. But the 'most' element of Macmillan's quote is relevant, too, for this food comes at a price. Eating at the top end has always been expensive, and remains so, but in terms of value for money, there's an argument that a stunning meal made from amazing ingredients is worth every penny if it makes you happy and lingers in the memory. Like great art, it isn't a necessity, but it does enrich the soul.

Next time you're thinking of a city break, don't rule out the cities mentioned above. When it comes to destination dining, the pages of the *AA Restaurant Guide 2015* are filled with amazing addresses from north to south and east to west.

anywhere else in the UK. When it comes to maverick chefs who are as exciting as they are unpredictable, Paul Kitching is your man.

Like any town or city in the UK, there are chain restaurants galore, disappointment awaiting on many a street corner, but go prepared (with a copy of this guide, perhaps) and there are great things to be found. If a measure of success is who else is in town, it's worth noting that the Galvin brothers, who run several storming restaurants in London, have opened in Edinburgh (see entry for Pompadour by Galvin). There are forty-six restaurants in this book in the Edinburgh city area, everything from Indian places to Italian joints and trendy bars. Edinburgh is a culinary destination in its own right.

There should be no element of shock that these restaurants exist. There's a demand for good food all over the country. The cities of Birmingham, Manchester and Edinburgh are examples of how the map of UK dining in changing. But why now? One possible reason is a form of culinary osmosis. Over the last 20 years or so budding chefs left their home towns and cities to seek work in London and mainland Europe. If you wanted to aim for the top, staying near home

Running the empire

An interview with Michael Caines

As Michael Caines achieves a milestone 20 years at Gidleigh Park, he talks to Simon Numphud, Head of AA Hotel Services, about running an ever-expanding business and the state of the UK hospitality industry.

Michael Caines is a busy man. As executive chef at the 5-Rosette Gidleigh Park and Food and Beverage Director of Brownsword Hotels, there aren't too many free hours in his day. The company consists of two distinct groups, owned by Andrew Brownsword – the Gidleigh Collection of top-rank country houses (Gidleigh itself, plus Bath Priory, Amberley Castle, Lower Slaughter Manor, Buckland Manor and The Slaughters Inn), and the ABode group of swish city hotels (six at the last count). Michael has also set up the Michael Caines Academy at Exeter College, and he has a new cookbook on the shelves (his first, remarkably), called *Michael Caines at Home*, which focusses on his first passion – ingredients. Given all those responsibilities, we were lucky to catch up with him.

"20 years on we've achieved a great deal," says Michael, "and we've done that working as a team." Caines is a big personality and a natural leader, but acknowledges that the hospitality industry is all about teamwork: "the greatest lesson I have learnt is to delegate and trust the people who have the right abilities and allow them to shine. The key to any business is the people you employ, the standards you set, and the systems you implement."

Right now he has ten or so executive or head chefs under his stewardship. Michael is proud of his team and part of his role, especially when it comes to the head chefs in the flagship Gidleigh Collection, is to help them achieve their goals while maintaining the ethos of the MC style. "I almost feel like a diplomat sometimes," he confesses. Technical ability and self-discipline are key if you want to make it in Michael's team, but it's not all about being a chef, with the front-of-house training equally as vital – "it's about the pursuit of perfection." And when it comes to his "sheer pace and relentlessness" (his words), Michael takes some keeping up with.

The Michael Caines Academy at Exeter College is something he's rightly very proud of and four years down the line he's implementing the sort of training that can genuinely benefit the industry. One of his aims is a desire to make hospitality a first choice for people, rather than a last resort. Not content just to train the next generation, Michael thinks big and states that he's "looking for the entrepreneurs of the future." The education on offer (over two years) encompasses trips to farms, producers and the like, with the students exposed to the various business models in the industry, with the intention to turn out graduates who are fit-for-purpose for today's industry. It's a terrific opportunity, but as Michael says, "I have to remind young people that it's not a given, to become part of something is one thing, to stay part of it is a commitment that works both ways. No-one gets there without hard work."

"...what you realise after 20 years are the things that matter are the core values, what you're good at... for me that's cooking"

That's a message that resonates very strongly with Michael. He's noticed that chefs are achieving their goals at an earlier age these days and recommends that young people really consider what they're good at. For many at the college that might mean front-of-house rather than the kitchen. But whatever direction they choose, Michael advises they "slow things down and appreciate it's a marathon not a sprint. If you become head chef at 20, you've got the rest of your career as head chef. The more skills you've learned to get to the top the chances are you'll do better when you get there. Longevity is the name of the game."

With longevity in mind, Michael considers his greatest achievement is "still being relevant" after 20 years. And with 5 AA Rosettes to his name, we're not going to argue with that. And on that he muses, "5 AA Rosettes have been won and lost and won back, and that's not a bad thing as you can become complacent or distracted, and what you realise after 20 years are the things that matter are the core values, what you're good at, and for me that's cooking."

Over the past two decades, there have been significant changes in the restaurant industry. "We've long burned the idea that the British can't cook," says Michael. As a long-time advocate of provenance and regional food (from day one at Gidleigh in fact), Michael has been ahead of the curve, but he's a little more cautious when it comes to the sharper end of contemporary cooking – "good technique, great technique, but not at any cost."

Michael sees the environment and health as the two big issues ahead for the hospitality industry: "We'll look back in ten years and see the problems we had with sugar in food in a similar vein to smoking in the 70s," and with the impending crisis on the horizon, "the restaurant industry has a lot of responsibility in terms of sustainable food sources and ensuring we give people healthy options and respond to dietary trends and allergies."

"In terms of restaurant culture, I think the independents will come under pressure from the continued rise and domination of the chain restaurant," he concludes, going on to say "it's hard to offer value for money, but you can't sell food cheaply anymore. That's one thing we've learned from this recession: you can't discount yourself out of a problem. We need to get people to value food."

When it comes to Michael's own future, you might think given his success so far that he'd take it a little easier now, but not likely: "I want to be relevant in 20 years' time," he says with a steely determination. On his wish list is an opening in London – "if you open in London you're at the eye of the storm" – and to find somewhere like Gidleigh that can be all his own. "I think the best years are to come", he concludes, and I don't think anyone would challenge him on that one.

ARTESANO ORIGINAL
PERFECT FOR
PURE BARBECUE PLEASURE.

Authentic, practical, pure. With its original design and mix of premium porcelain, acacia wood and cork,
the ARTESANO ORIGINAL collection is perfect for summer barbecues, making your party a real sensation for all the senses.

Villeroy & Boch
1748

WWW.VILLEROY-BOCH.COM

SPONSORING THE AA AWARDS

Villeroy & Boch are proud to have presented the AA Awards for the past 23 years. Quality and inspiration are the defining qualities of a great restaurant. They are also the values that have made Villeroy & Boch, with its tradition of innovation dating back to 1748, the leading tableware brand in Europe. Dining with friends and family, and enjoying good food and drink together are special to all of us, and these occasions are made all the more special when served on beautiful tableware from Villeroy & Boch. Our distinctive and original designs have consistently set the pace for others to follow and provide the perfect setting chosen by many of the world's leading chefs to frame their award-winning creations. Villeroy & Boch offer a wide range of stunning designs to suit any lifestyle and décor, and create the perfect ambience for successful entertaining and stylish family living.

UK and Ireland customer services line: 0208-871-0011
line open Monday-Friday 9am-5pm

JOIN OUR 1748 CLUB

Subscribe to our FREE 1748 Club email newsletter, and you'll find it packed with:
• Recipes
• New products
• Exclusive Members' offers
• Top tips from our stylist
• Competitions
• Chef's corner
• Table style advice
• Product care
• How to guides
And much more besides. Just register online at
www.1748club.co.uk/newsletter
Incidentally, our 1748Club web site was recently voted 'web site of the week' by a leading women's weekly magazine.

AA MEMBERS SAVE 10%

As an AA member you enjoy **10% off** when shopping online using this link:
www.theaa.com/rewards
In addition, members of the AA also receive **10% off** full price products in any of our Concession Stores on presentation of an AA membership card. For a list of stockists go to www.1748club.co.uk and click on Where Can I See.

Visit our community web site at:
www.1748club.co.uk

The top ten per cent

Each year all the restaurants in the AA Restaurant Guide are awarded a specially commissioned plate that marks their achievement in gaining one or more AA Rosettes. The plates represent a partnership between the AA and Villeroy & Boch – two quality brands working together to recognise high standards in restaurant cooking.

Restaurants awarded three, four or five AA Rosettes represent the top ten per cent of the restaurants in this Guide. The pages that follow list those establishments that have attained this special status.

5 ROSETTES

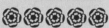

LONDON

Marcus
The Berkeley,
Wilton Place,
Knightsbridge,
SW1
020 7235 1200

Hibiscus
29 Maddox Street,
Mayfair,
W1
020 7629 2999

Sketch
(Lecture Room & Library)
9 Conduit Street,
W1
020 7659 4500

ENGLAND

BERKSHIRE
The Fat Duck
High Street, BRAY
SL6 2AQ
01628 580333

CAMBRIDGESHIRE
Midsummer House Restaurant
Midsummer Common,
CAMBRIDGE
CB4 1HA
01223 369299

CUMBRIA
L'Enclume
Cavendish St,
CARTMEL
LA11 6PZ
015395 36362

DEVON
Gidleigh Park
CHAGFORD
TQ13 8HH
01647 432367

NOTTINGHAMSHIRE
Restaurant Sat Bains
with Rooms
Lenton Lane, Trentside,
NOTTINGHAM
NG7 2SA
0115 986 6566

OXFORDSHIRE
Belmond Le Manoir
aux Quat' Saisons
Church Road,
GREAT MILTON
OX44 7PD
01844 278881

SURREY
Michael Wignall
at The Latymer
Pennyhill Park Hotel
& The Spa, London Road,
BAGSHOT
GU19 5EU
01276 471774

4 ROSETTES

LONDON

Restaurant Story
201 Tooley Street, SE1
020 7183 2117

**Seven Park Place by
William Drabble**
St James's Hotel and Club,
7–8 Park Place, SW1
020 7316 1600

Restaurant Gordon Ramsay
68 Royal Hospital Road,
SW3
020 7352 4441

**Alain Ducasse at
The Dorchester**
The Dorchester,
53 Park Lane, W1
020 7629 8866

Le Gavroche Restaurant
43 Upper Brook Street,
W1
020 7408 0881

The Greenhouse
27a Hay's Mews,
Mayfair, W1
020 7499 3331

**Hélène Darroze at
The Connaught**
Carlos Place, W1
020 3147 7200

Murano
20–22 Queen Street, W1
020 7495 1127

Pied à Terre
34 Charlotte Street, W1
020 7636 1178

Pollen Street Social
8–10 Pollen Street, W1
020 7290 7600

The Square
6–10 Bruton Street, W1
020 7495 7100

Texture Restaurant
DoubleTree by Hilton
Hotel, 34 Portman Street,
W1
020 7224 0028

**Launceston Place
Restaurant**
1a Launceston Place, W8
020 7937 6912

LONDON, GREATER

Chapter One
Farnborough Common,
Locksbottom, BROMLEY
BR6 8NF
01689 854848

ENGLAND

BERKSHIRE

The Waterside Inn
Ferry Road, BRAY
SL6 2AT
01628 620691

L'Ortolan
Church Lane,
SHINFIELD RG2 9BY
0118 988 8500

BRISTOL

Casamia Restaurant
38 High Street, Westbury
Village, Westbury-on-Trym,
BRISTOL BS9 3DZ
0117 959 2884

BUCKINGHAMSHIRE

The Hand & Flowers
126 West Street,
MARLOW SL7 2BP
01628 482277

CHESHIRE

**Simon Radley at
The Chester Grosvenor**
Chester Grosvenor & Spa,
Eastgate, CHESTER
CH1 1LT
01244 324024

CORNWALL

Restaurant Nathan Outlaw
The St Enodoc Hotel,
ROCK PL27 6LA
01208 862737

GLOUCESTERSHIRE

Le Champignon Sauvage
24–28 Suffolk Road,
CHELTENHAM GL50 2AQ
01242 573449

GREATER MANCHESTER

**The French
by Simon Rogan**
The Midland Hotel, Peter
Street, MANCHESTER
M60 2DS
0161 236 3333

LANCASHIRE

Northcote
Northcote Road,
LANGHO BB6 8BE
01254 240555

RUTLAND

Hambleton Hall
Hambleton, OAKHAM
LE15 8TH
01572 756991

SUSSEX, WEST

**The Pass Restaurant
at South Lodge Hotel**
Brighton Road,
LOWER BEEDING
RH13 6PS
01403 891711

WILTSHIRE

**Whatley Manor Hotel
and Spa**
Easton Grey,
MALMESBURY SN16 0RB
01666 822888

CHANNEL ISLANDS

JERSEY

**Ocean Restaurant at
The Atlantic Hotel**
Le Mont de la Pulente,
ST BRELADE JE3 8HE
01534 744101

Bohemia Restaurant
The Club Hotel & Spa,
Green Street,
ST HELIER JE2 4UH
01534 880588

SCOTLAND

CITY OF EDINBURGH

21212
3 Royal Terrace
EH7 5AB
0131 523 1030

The Kitchin
78 Commercial Quay,
Leith
EH6 6LX
0131 555 1755

**Restaurant Martin
Wishart**
54 The Shore, Leith
EH6 6RA
0131 553 3557

HIGHLAND

Boath House
Auldearn, NAIRN
IV12 5TE
01667 454896

PERTH & KINROSS

Andrew Fairlie@Gleneagles
The Gleneagles Hotel,
AUCHTERARDER
PH3 1NF
01764 694267

REPUBLIC OF IRELAND

DUBLIN

**Restaurant Patrick
Guilbaud**
Merrion Hotel,
21 Upper Merrion Street,
01 676 4192

COUNTY WATERFORD

Cliff House Hotel
ARDMORE
024 87800

3 ROSETTES

LONDON

E1
Galvin La Chapelle
St. Botolph's Hall,
35 Spital Square
020 7299 0400

EC1
The Clove Club
Shoreditch Town Hall,
380 Old Street
020 7729 6496

Club Gascon
57 West Smithfields
020 7600 6144

EC2
1901 Restaurant
ANdAZ London,
40 Liverpool Street
020 7618 7000

HKK
Broadgate West, 88
Worship Street
020 3535 1888

NW1
Odette's Restaurant & Bar
130 Regent's Park Road
020 7586 8569

SW1
**Ametsa with
Arzak Instruction**
The Halkin Hotel, 5 Halkin
Street, Belgravia
020 7333 1234

**Apsleys at The
Lanesborough**
The Lanesborough,
Hyde Park Corner
020 7333 7254

**Caxton Grill,
St Ermin's Hotel**
2 Caxton Street,
St James's Park
020 7222 7888

**Dinner by Heston
Blumenthal**
Mandarin Oriental Hyde
Park, 66 Knightsbridge
020 7201 3833

Koffmann's
The Berkeley, Wilton Place
020 7235 1010

Pétrus
1 Kinnerton Street,
Knightsbridge
020 7592 1609

The Rib Room
Jumeirah Carlton Tower
Hotel, Cadogan Place
020 7858 7250

Roux at Parliament Square
Parliament Square
020 7334 3737

**Thirty Six by Nigel
Mendham at Dukes London**
35–36 St James's Place
020 7491 4840

SW3
Outlaw's at The Capital
22–24 Basil Street,
Knightsbridge
020 7591 1202

Rasoi Restaurant
10 Lincoln Street
020 7225 1881

SW4
Trinity Restaurant
4 The Polygon, Clapham
020 7622 1199

SW10
Medlar Restaurant
438 King's Road, Chelsea
020 7349 1900

SW17
Chez Bruce
2 Bellevue Road,
Wandsworth Common
020 8672 0114

SW19
Cannizaro House
West Side, Wimbledon
Common
020 8879 1464

W1
**Alyn Williams at
The Westbury**
Bond Street
020 7183 6426

Arbutus Restaurant
63–64 Frith Street
020 7734 4545

L'Autre Pied
5–7 Blandford Street,
Marylebone Village
020 7486 9696

Brasserie Chavot
41 Conduit Street, Mayfair
020 7183 6425

Canvas
69 Marylebone Lane
020 7935 0858

Chiltern Firehouse
One Chiltern Street,
Marylebone
020 7073 7676

Corrigan's Mayfair
28 Upper Grosvenor Street
020 7499 9943

CUT at 45 Park Lane
45 Park Lane
020 7319 7467

Dabbous
39 Whitfield Street,
Fitzrovia
020 7323 1544

**Galvin at Windows
Restaurant & Bar**
London Hilton on Park
Lane, 22 Park Lane
020 7208 4021

Gauthier Soho
21 Romilly Street
020 7494 3111

Hakkasan Mayfair
17 Bruton Street
020 7907 1888

Kitchen Table
70 Charlotte St
020 7637 7770

Locanda Locatelli
8 Seymour Street
020 7935 9088

Maze
London Marriott Hotel,
10–13 Grosvenor Square
020 7107 0000

The Ritz Restaurant
150 Piccadilly
020 7300 2370

Roka
37 Charlotte Street
020 7580 6464

Roka
30 North Audley St
020 7305 5644

Sixtyone Restaurant
The Montcalm, Great
Cumberland Place
020 7958 3222

Sketch (The Gallery)
9 Conduit Street
020 7659 4500

Social Eating House
58–59 Poland Street
020 7993 3251

**Theo Randall at the
InterContinental**
1 Hamilton Place,
Hyde Park Corner
020 7318 8747

Umu
14–16 Bruton Place
020 7499 8881

Wild Honey
12 Saint George St
020 7758 9160

W4
Hedone
301–303 Chiswick
High Road
020 8747 0377

W6
The River Café
Thames Wharf Studios,
Rainville Road
020 7386 4200

W8
Kitchen W8
1–13 Abingdon Road,
Kensington
020 7937 0120

Min Jiang
Royal Garden Hotel,
2–24 Kensington
High Street
020 7361 1988

W11
The Ledbury
127 Ledbury Road
020 7792 9090

WC2
L'Atelier de Joël Robuchon
13–15 West Street
020 7010 8600

Clos Maggiore
33 King Street,
Covent Garden
020 7379 9696

LONDON, GREATER
La Belle Époque
Sofitel London Heathrow,
Terminal 5, HEATHROW
AIRPORT (LONDON)
TW6 2GD
020 8757 7777

The Glasshouse
14 Station Parade,
KEW TW9 3PZ
020 8940 6777

Bingham
61–63 Petersham Road,
RICHMOND UPON
THAMES TW10 6UT
020 8940 0902

ENGLAND

BEDFORDSHIRE
Paris House Restaurant
London Road, Woburn
Park, WOBURN
MK17 9QP
01525 290692

BERKSHIRE
Hinds Head
High Street, BRAY
SL6 2AB
01628 626151

The Royal Oak Paley Street
Paley Street, Littlefield
Green, MAIDENHEAD
SL6 3JN
01628 620541

The Vineyard
Stockcross, NEWBURY
RG20 8JU
01635 528770

BUCKINGHAMSHIRE
The Artichoke
9 Market Square,
Old Amersham,
AMERSHAM
HP7 0DF
01494 726611

Humphry's at Stoke Park
Park Road,
STOKE POGES
SL2 4PG
01753 717171

Stoke Place
Stoke Green,
STOKE POGES
SL2 4HT
01753 534790

Andre Garrett at Cliveden
Cliveden Estate,
TAPLOW SL6 0JF
01628 668561

CAMBRIDGESHIRE
Restaurant Alimentum
152–154 Hills Road,
CAMBRIDGE
CB2 8PB
01223 413000

CHESHIRE
The Alderley Restaurant
Alderley Edge Hotel,
Macclesfield Road,
ALDERLEY EDGE
SK9 7BJ
01625 583033

**1851 Restaurant at
Peckforton Castle**
Stonehouse Lane,
PECKFORTON
CW6 9TN
01829 260930

CORNWALL &
ISLES OF SCILLY
Hell Bay
BRYHER TR23 0PR
01720 422947

Paul Ainsworth at No. 6
6 Middle Street,
PADSTOW PL28 8AP
01841 532093

The Seafood Restaurant
Riverside, PADSTOW
PL28 8BY
01841 532700

Driftwood
Rosevine, PORTSCATHO
TR2 5EW
01872 580644

Hotel Tresanton
27 Lower Castle Road,
ST MAWES
TR2 5DR
01326 270055

CUMBRIA
**Rogan & Company
Restaurant**
The Square, CARTMEL
LA11 6QD
015395 35917

Hipping Hall
Cowan Bridge,
KIRKBY LONSDALE
LA6 2JJ
015242 71187

Gilpin Hotel & Lake House
Crook Road,
WINDERMERE
LA23 3NE
015394 88818

**Holbeck Ghyll Country
House Hotel**
Holbeck Lane,
WINDERMERE
LA23 1LU
015394 32375

**Linthwaite House Hotel
& Restaurant**
Crook Road,
WINDERMERE
LA23 3JA
015394 88600

The Samling
Ambleside Road,
WINDERMERE
LA23 1LR
015394 31922

DERBYSHIRE
Fischer's Baslow Hall
Calver Road, BASLOW
DE45 1RR
01246 583259

The Peacock at Rowsley
Bakewell Road, ROWSLEY
DE4 2EB
01629 733518

DEVON
The Old Inn
DREWSTEIGNTON
EX6 6QR
01647 281276

**The Elephant Restaurant
and Brasserie**
3–4 Beacon Terrace,
TORQUAY
TQ1 2BH
01803 200044

3 ROSETTES

continued

DORSET
Sienna
36 High West Street,
DORCHESTER
DT1 1UP
01305 250022

**Summer Lodge
Country House Hotel,
Restaurant & Spa**
Fore Street,
EVERSHOT
DT2 0JR
01935 482000

GLOUCESTERSHIRE
Buckland Manor
BUCKLAND WR12 7LY
01386 852626

**The Beaufort Dining Room
Ellenborough Park**
Southam Road,
CHELTENHAM
GL52 3NH
01242 545454

Lower Slaughter Manor
LOWER SLAUGHTER
GL54 2HP
01451 820456

**The Feathered Nest
Country Inn**
NETHER WESTCOTE
OX7 6SD
01993 833030

Cotswolds88Hotel
Kemps Lane,
PAINSWICK
GL6 6YB
01452 813688

Lords of the Manor
UPPER SLAUGHTER
GL54 2JD
01451 820243

GREATER MANCHESTER
**Manchester House
Bar & Restaurant**
Tower 12, 18–22 Bridge
Street, MANCHESTER
M3 3BZ
0161 835 2557

HAMPSHIRE
The Montagu Arms Hotel
Palace Lane,
BEAULIEU SO42 7ZL
01590 612324

36 on the Quay
47 South Street,
EMSWORTH PO10 7EG
01243 375592

Hartnett Holder & Co
Lime Wood, Beaulieu
Road, LYNDHURST
SO43 7FZ
023 8028 7167

JSW
20 Dragon Street,
PETERSFIELD
GU31 4JJ
01730 262030

**Avenue Restaurant at
Lainston House Hotel**
Woodman Lane, Sparsholt,
WINCHESTER SO21 2LT
01962 776088

HERTFORDSHIRE
Colette's at The Grove
Chandler's Cross,
RICKMANSWORTH
WD3 4TG
01923 807807

ISLE OF WIGHT
The Hambrough
Hambrough Road,
VENTNOR PO38 1SQ
01983 856333

KENT
The West House
28 High Street,
BIDDENDEN TN27 8AH
01580 291341

Apicius
23 Stone Street,
CRANBROOK
TN17 3HF
01580 714666

The Marquis at Alkham
Alkham Valley Road,
Alkham, DOVER
CT15 7DF
01304 873410

Thackeray's
85 London Road,
TUNBRIDGE WELLS
(ROYAL) TN1 1EA
01892 511921

LANCASHIRE
**The Freemasons
at Wiswell**
8 Vicarage Fold,
Wiswell, WHALLEY
BB7 9DF
01254 822218

LINCOLNSHIRE
Harry's Place
17 High Street, Great
Gonerby, GRANTHAM
NG31 8JS
01476 561780

Winteringham Fields
1 Silver Street,
WINTERINGHAM
DN15 9ND
01724 733096

MERSEYSIDE
Fraiche
11 Rose Mount,
Oxton, BIRKENHEAD
CH43 5SG
0151 652 2914

**The Dining Room
at Hillbark**
Hillbark Hotel
and Spa, Royden Park,
FRANKBY
CH48 1NP
0151 625 2400

**The Lawns Restaurant
at Thornton Hall**
Neston Road,
THORNTON HOUGH
CH63 1JF
0151 336 3938

NORFOLK
Morston Hall
Morston, Holt,
BLAKENEY
NR25 7AA
01263 741041

**The Neptune Restaurant
with Rooms**
85 Old Hunstanton
Road, HUNSTANTON
PE36 6HZ
01485 532122

**Roger Hickman's
Restaurant**
79 Upper St Giles
Street, NORWICH
NR2 1AB
01603 633522

Titchwell Manor Hotel
TITCHWELL
PE31 8BB
01485 210221

NORTHAMPTONSHIRE
**Rushton Hall Hotel
and Spa**
Rushton, KETTERING
NN14 1RR
01536 713001

OXFORDSHIRE
The Sir Charles Napier
Sprigg's Alley, CHINNOR
OX39 4BX
01494 483011

Orwells
Shiplake Row,
Binfield Heath,
HENLEY-ON-THAMES
RG9 4DP
0118 940 3673

**Fallowfields Hotel
and Restaurant**
Faringdon Road,
KINGSTON BAGPUIZE
OX13 5BH
01865 820416

Macdonald Randolph Hotel
Beaumont Street,
OXFORD
OX1 2LN
0844 879 9132

SHROPSHIRE
Fishmore Hall
Fishmore Road,
LUDLOW
SY8 3DP
01584 875148

SOMERSET
**Allium Restaurant
at The Abbey Hotel**
1 North Parade,
BATH BA1 1LF
01225 461603

**The Bath Priory Hotel,
Restaurant & Spa**
Weston Road,
BATH BA1 2XT
01225 331922

**The Dower
House Restaurant**
The Royal Crescent Hotel,
16 Royal Crescent,
BATH BA1 2LS
01225 823333

**The Olive Tree at the
Queensberry Hotel**
4–7 Russel Street,
BATH BA1 2QF
01225 447928

Little Barwick House
Barwick Village,
YEOVIL BA22 9TD
01935 423902

SUFFOLK
The Packhorse Inn
Bridge Street, Moulton,
NEWMARKET CB8 8SP
01638 751818

SURREY
Stovell's
125 Windsor Road,
CHOBHAM GU24 8QS
01276 858000

Drake's Restaurant
The Clock House,
High Street,
RIPLEY GU23 6AQ
01483 224777

SUSSEX, WEST
Amberley Castle
AMBERLEY BN18 9LT
01798 831992

Langshott Manor
Langshott Lane,
GATWICK AIRPORT
(LONDON) RH6 9LN
01293 786680

Restaurant Tristan
3 Stan's Way, East Street,
HORSHAM RH12 1HU
01403 255688

**AG's Restaurant at
Alexander House Hotel**
Alexander House Hotel,
East Street, TURNERS
HILL RH10 4QD
01342 714914

TYNE & WEAR
Jesmond Dene House
Jesmond Dene Road,
NEWCASTLE UPON TYNE
NE2 2EY
0191 212 3000

WARWICKSHIRE
Mallory Court Hotel
Harbury Lane, Bishop's
Tachbrook, LEAMINGTON
SPA (ROYAL) CV33 9QB
01926 330214

**Restaurant 23
& Morgan's Bar**
34 Hamilton Terrace,
LEAMINGTON SPA
(ROYAL) CV32 4LY
01926 422422

WEST MIDLANDS
Adam's Restaurant
21A Bennetts Hill,
BIRMINGHAM
B2 5QP
0121 643 3745

Loves Restaurant
The Glasshouse,
Canal Square,
Browning Street,
BIRMINGHAM B16 8FL
0121 454 5151

Purnell's
55 Cornwall Street,
BIRMINGHAM B3 2DH
0121 212 9799

Simpsons
20 Highfield Road,
Edgbaston,
BIRMINGHAM
B15 3DU
0121 454 3434

Turners
69 High Street,
Harborne, BIRMINGHAM
B17 9NS
0121 426 4440

WILTSHIRE
**The Bybrook at
The Manor House Hotel**
CASTLE COMBE
SN14 7HR
01249 782206

The Park Restaurant
Lucknam Park Hotel
& Spa, COLERNE
SN14 8AZ
01225 742777

**The Harrow
at Little Bedwyn**
LITTLE BEDWYN
SN8 3JP
01672 870871

Red Lion Free House
East Chisenbury,
PEWSEY SN8 6AQ
01980 671124

WORCESTERSHIRE
**Brockencote Hall
Country House Hotel**
CHADDESLEY
CORBETT DY10 4PY
01562 777876

YORKSHIRE, NORTH
Yorebridge House
BAINBRIDGE DL8 3EE
01969 652060

**The Devonshire Arms
Hotel & Spa**
BOLTON ABBEY
BD23 6AJ
01756 710441

Black Swan Hotel
Market Place,
HELMSLEY YO62 5BJ
01439 770466

The Angel Inn
HETTON BD23 6LT
01756 730263

Samuel's at Swinton Park
Swinton, MASHAM
HG4 4JH
01765 680900

**The Black Swan
at Oldstead**
OLDSTEAD YO61 4BL
01347 868387

**Judges Country
House Hotel**
Kirklevington,
YARM TS15 9LW
01642 789000

YORKSHIRE, WEST
Design House Restaurant
Dean Clough, Arts &
Business Centre,
HALIFAX HX3 5AX
01422 383242

Box Tree
35–37 Church Street,
ILKLEY LS29 9DR
01943 608484

3 ROSETTES

continued

CHANNEL ISLANDS

JERSEY
Grand Jersey
The Esplanade,
ST HELIER JE2 3QA
01534 722301

Ormer
7–11 Don Street,
ST HELIER JE2 4TQ
01534 725100

Longueville Manor Hotel
ST SAVIOUR JE2 7WF
01534 725501

SCOTLAND

ANGUS
Gordon's
Main Street,
INVERKEILOR DD11 5RN
01241 830364

ARGYLL & BUTE
**Isle of Eriska Hotel,
Spa & Golf**
Benderloch, By Oban,
ERISKA PA37 1SD
01631 720371

The Ardanaiseig Hotel
KILCHRENAN
PA35 1HE
01866 833333

Airds Hotel and Restaurant
PORT APPIN PA38 4DF
01631 730236

AYRSHIRE, SOUTH
Glenapp Castle
BALLANTRAE KA26 0NZ
01465 831212

Lochgreen House Hotel
Monktonhill Road,
Southwood, TROON
KA10 7EN
01292 313343

DUMFRIES & GALLOWAY
Knockinaam Lodge
PORTPATRICK DG9 9AD
01776 810471

DUNBARTONSHIRE, WEST
**Martin Wishart
at Loch Lomond**
Cameron House on Loch
Lomond, BALLOCH
G83 8QZ
01389 722504

CITY OF EDINBURGH
Castle Terrace Restaurant
33–35 Castle Terrace,
EDINBURGH EH1 2EL
0131 229 1222

Norton House Hotel & Spa
Ingliston, EDINBURGH
EH28 8LX
0131 333 1275

Number One, The Balmoral
1 Princes Street,
EDINBURGH EH2 2EQ
0131 557 6727

Plumed Horse
50–54 Henderson Street,
Leith, EDINBURGH
EH6 6DE
0131 554 5556

Pompadour by Galvin
The Caledonian, A Waldorf
Astoria Hotel, Princes
Street, EDINBURGH
EH1 2AB
0131 222 8975

**Restaurant Mark
Greenaway**
69 North Castle Street,
EDINBURGH EH2 3LJ
0131 226 1155

CITY OF GLASGOW
**Hotel du Vin at One
Devonshire Gardens**
1 Devonshire Gardens,
GLASGOW G12 0UX
0844 736 4256

FIFE
The Peat Inn
PEAT INN KY15 5LH
01334 840206

Road Hole Restaurant
The Old Course Hotel,
Golf Resort & Spa,
ST ANDREWS KY16 9SP
01334 474371

Rocca Grill
Macdonald Rusacks
Hotel, The Links,
ST ANDREWS KY16 9JQ
01334 472549

HIGHLAND
Station Road
The Lovat, Loch Ness,
Loch Ness Side, FORT
AUGUSTUS PH32 4DU
01456 459250

Inverlochy Castle Hotel
Torlundy, FORT WILLIAM
PH33 6SN
01397 702177

The Torridon Restaurant
TORRIDON IV22 2EY
01445 791242

STIRLING
**Roman Camp Country
House Hotel**
CALLANDER FK17 8BG
01877 330003

SCOTTISH ISLANDS

SKYE, ISLE OF
The Three Chimneys
COLBOST IV55 8ZT
01470 511258

Kinloch Lodge
Sleat, ISLE ORNSAY
IV43 8QY
01471 833214

WALES

ANGLESEY, ISLE OF
Ye Olde Bulls Head Inn
Castle Street,
BEAUMARIS LL58 8AP
01248 810329

CEREDIGION
Plas Ynyshir Hall Hotel
EGLWYS FACH SY20 8TA
01654 781209

CONWY
Bodysgallen Hall and Spa
LLANDUDNO LL30 1RS
01492 584466

MONMOUTHSHIRE
Walnut Tree Inn
Llandewi Skirrid,
ABERGAVENNY
NP7 8AW
01873 852797

The Crown at Whitebrook
WHITEBROOK NP25 4TX
01600 860254

NEWPORT
**Terry M at The Celtic
Manor Resort**
Coldra Woods, NEWPORT
NP18 1HQ
01633 413000

PEMBROKESHIRE
The Grove
Molleston, NARBERTH
SA67 8BX
01834 860915

POWYS
Llangoed Hall
LLYSWEN LD3 0YP
01874 754525

REPUBLIC OF IRELAND

COUNTY CLARE
Gregans Castle
BALLYVAUGHAN
065 7077005

COUNTY KILKENNY
The Lady Helen Restaurant
Mount Juliet Hotel,
THOMASTOWN
056 7773000

AA GUIDES

WE KNOW BRITAIN

▶ THE BEST PLACES TO VISIT

▶ CLEAR TOWN PLANS AND MAPPING

▶ WRITTEN BY LOCAL EXPERTS

▶ RECOMMENDED PLACES TO EAT

▶ TRUSTED LISTINGS

Follow @TheAA_Lifestyle

England

BEDFORDSHIRE

BEDFORD
Map 12 TL04

The Barns Hotel

Modern British **NEW**

tel: 01234 270044 **Cardington Rd MK44 3SA**
email: reservations@barnshotelbedford.co.uk **web:** www.barnshotelbedford.co.uk
dir: M1 junct 13, A421, approx 10m to A603 Sandy/Bedford exit, hotel on right at 2nd rdbt

Modern brasserie-style dining by the river

Samuel Whitbread of brewing fame was born here in the 18th century and today's pub-restaurant-and-hotel combo has plenty of old-world tranquillity about it. The WineGlass Restaurant is the main dining option with a bright and contemporary conservatory-style dining room that opens onto a terrace overlooking the River Great Ouse (there's pub grub in the Riverside Bar, too). The menu favours feel-good modern British combinations, so there might be a black pudding and pork Scotch egg to kick things off, the egg suitably runny, or curried seared scallops with creamed leeks. Main courses such as tender rump of lamb with roasted aubergine, fondant potato and a flavoursome jus show good sense and sound execution, or go for fish and chips with herby batter and 'crushed' peas. To finish, Valrhona white and dark chocolate mousse with salted caramel is properly fashionable. The wine list has a particularly good showing by the glass.

Chef Sean Waskett **Seats** 47, Pr/dining room 80 **Times** 12-2/6.30-9.30 **Prices** Starter £5-£8, Main £12-£25, Dessert £6-£8.50 **Wines** 12 bottles over £30, 26 bottles under £30, 34 by glass **Parking** 90 **Notes** Sunday L £13.50-£17.50, Vegetarian available, Children welcome

The Bedford Swan Hotel

British

tel: 01234 346565 **The Embankment MK40 1RW**
email: info@bedfordswanhotel.co.uk **web:** www.bedfordswanhotel.co.uk
dir: M1 junct 13, take A421 following signs to city centre (one way system). Turn left to The Embankment, car park on left after Swan statue

Re-modelled 18th-century riverside hotel with modish menu

The Georgian Bedford Swan has had a swanky contemporary makeover, but has sacrificed none of its period charm. The 18th-century building's elegant bow windows overlook the River Ouse (where a terrace is the place to be on balmy days) while the interior decor showcases bare stone walls, oak panelling and fancy plaster ceilings as well as contemporary colours and textures. In the River Room restaurant exposed stone walls and burnished wooden tables make an attractive setting for uncomplicated, modern comfort-food cooking. Smoked haddock rarebit tart with dressed lamb's lettuce gets things off the blocks, or ham hock terrine with pickled vegetables could catch the eye. Main course brings a classic combo of seared calves' liver, caramelised onions, mashed potato and red wine jus, or a straight-up steak of 28-day-aged local beef might get your vote. For afters, a tipsy sherry trifle modishly served in a Kilner jar should send you home happy.

Times 12-3/6-10

BOLNHURST
Map 12 TL05

The Plough at Bolnhurst

Modern British **NOTABLE WINE LIST**

tel: 01234 376274 **Kimbolton Rd MK44 2EX**
email: theplough@bolnhurst.com
dir: A14/A421 onto B660 for approx 5m to Bolnhurst village

Classy modern seasonal menu in a lively Tudor pub

The Plough is a classic whitewashed 15th-century country inn which envelops you in a cocoon of Tudor beams and timbers, exposed stone walls, tiny windows, and

welcoming open fires in its cosy bars. A move into the contemporary restaurant brings a striking contrast: the airy extension features lofty oak-beamed ceilings and a wall of full-length windows to flood the room with light. Fizzing with life at lunchtime, the mood mellows into a more intimate, candlelit vibe in the evening. Top-quality local produce is transformed into big-flavoured modern dishes on daily-changing menus that keep an eye on the seasons, opening in summer with Portland crab with Jersey Royal potatoes, spring onion salad and watercress oil. Next up, pork belly is cooked overnight for that melting texture, and matched with roast Bramley apple purée, creamed potato and crushed peas. For pudding, there's vanilla soufflé with strawberry sauce.

Chef Martin Lee **Owner** Martin Lee & Jayne Lee, Michael Moscrop **Seats** 96, Pr/dining room 34 **Times** 12-2/6.30-9.30 Closed 27 Dec-14 Jan, Mon, D Sun **Prices** Fixed L 2 course £16, Starter £4.50-£10.50, Main £15.95-£24, Dessert £1.75-£8.50, Service optional **Wines** 60 bottles over £30, 76 bottles under £30, 15 by glass **Parking** 30 **Notes** Sunday L £21-£25, Vegetarian available, Children welcome

FLITWICK
Map 11 TL03

Menzies Hotels Woburn Flitwick Manor

Modern, Traditional

tel: 01525 712242 **Church Rd MK45 1AE**
email: steven.essex@menzieshotels.co.uk **web:** www.menzieshotels.co.uk
dir: M1 junct 12, follow Flitwick after 1m turn left into Church Rd. Manor 200 yds on left

Contemporary country-house cooking in a Georgian manor

With the classic proportions of the Georgian period, the manor is a small country-house hotel in acres of gardens and woodland. The interior is suitably littered with antiques and period features, while the restaurant is an elegant room, with upholstered seats at clothed tables on a pinky-red carpet. The cooking is more contemporary in tone than the surroundings might suggest, and an element of innovation is apparent. So confit duck terrine is served with gin-pickled rhubarb, and lamb cutlets are crusted with crushed almonds and accompanied by lamb bacon, carrot and maple purée and rosemary dauphinoise. Combinations are well considered and timings spot on: witness correctly made Jerusalem artichoke risotto paired with fillet of red mullet, and duck leg cassoulet, rich and tender, with a selection of vegetables. Desserts make an impact too, among them perhaps spiced crème brûlée and sticky toffee pudding soufflé.

Times 12-3/7-10

LUTON
Map 6 TL02

Adam's Brasserie at Luton Hoo

Modern British

tel: 01582 734437 & 698888 **Luton Hoo Hotel, Golf and Spa, The Mansion House LU1 3TQ**
email: reservations@lutonhoo.co.uk
dir: M1 junct 10A, 3rd exit to A1081 towards Harpenden/St Albans. Hotel less than a mile on left

Brasserie cooking in smartened up stables

The extensive Luton Hoo estate with its golf course and magnificent gardens is home to a luxe spa hotel and two dining options. You'll find Adam's Brasserie in the one-time stables, which operates as a country club and makes a good alternative to the more formal Wernher Restaurant (see entry). A host of films have been shot on the estate and the brasserie walls are adorned with familiar faces who have filmed here over the years. High ceilings and large windows give a sense of space, and some booth seating down one wall boosts the brasserie vibe. The menu fits the bill with a roster of feel-good dishes such as baked baby camembert with toasted home-made walnut bread and red onion marmalade, followed by red mullet with chorizo and black olive, or perhaps a steak or burger cooked on the grill.

Chef Kevin Clark **Owner** Elite Hotels **Seats** 90, Pr/dining room 280 **Times** 12-3/6-10 Closed D Sun **Prices** Starter £6-£8.95, Main £12.95-£28, Dessert £6.75-£8, Service optional **Wines** 26 bottles over £30, 28 bottles under £30, 13 by glass **Parking** 100 **Notes** Jazz Sun L, Sunday L £17.50-£35, Vegetarian available, Children welcome

Wernher Restaurant at Luton Hoo

@@ Modern European

tel: 01582 734437 **Luton Hoo Hotel, Golf and Spa, The Mansion House LU1 3TQ**
email: reservations@lutonhoo.co.uk **web:** www.lutonhoo.co.uk
dir: *M1 junct 10A, 3rd exit to A1081 towards Harpenden/St Albans. Hotel less than a mile on left*

Magnificent country estate with inventive modern cooking

The Wernher is the fine-dining option on the magnificent Luton Hoo estate. The house stately proportions and impeccable credentials – designed by Robert Adam and Sir Robert Smirke (of British Museum fame) and transformed at the turn of the 20th century by one of the richest men in the world. And 'Capability' Brown did the gardens. Today's luxe hotel hosts a couple of dining options, the lavish Wernher the pick of the bunch, with its marble panelling, ornate chandeliers and opulent fabrics. The team in the kitchen deliver bright modern European dishes using high quality ingredients. To start, pan-fried scallops might turn up in the company of roast langoustine and a fennel soubise, or roast venison and partridge terrine with mulled baby beetroot and a Guinness purée. Main course are equally inventive: pan-fried halibut, for example, with mustard and pancetta crust and confit pork belly. There's creativity among desserts, too, with warm beetroot and blackberry chocolate coolant served with a Merlot sorbet.

Chef Kevin Clark **Owner** Elite Hotels **Seats** 80, Pr/dining room 280
Times 12.30-2/7-10 Closed Mon-Tue **Prices** Fixed L 2 course fr £47.50, Fixed D 3 course fr £52.50, Tasting menu fr £62.50, Service optional **Wines** 245 bottles over £30, 8 bottles under £30, 15 by glass **Parking** 316 **Notes** Speciality menu, Sunday L £16-£35, Vegetarian available, Children welcome

See advert below

THE SPECTACULAR SETTING OF
THE WERNHER RESTAURANT

FINE DINING STEEPED
IN HISTORY

THE RELAXED ATMOSPHERE
OF THE ADAM'S BRASSERIE

Luton Hoo Hotel, Golf & Spa,
The Mansion House, Luton, Bedfordshire. LU1 3TQ

01582 734437
www.lutonhoo.co.uk

With two AA Rosettes, Olivier's is The Woburn Hotel's award winning restaurant.

Here, Executive Chef Olivier Bertho provides a superb menu of contemporary English and continental cuisine, served with flair and imagination. Enjoy a wonderful meal in elegant surroundings and a relaxed atmosphere. Booking recommended.

In the heart of the Georgian village of Woburn, The Hotel offers 55 bedrooms and is an ideal base for visitors to Woburn Abbey, Woburn Safari Park and Woburn Golf Club.

OLIVIER'S
RESTAURANT
THE WOBURN HOTEL

Olivier's Restaurant at The Woburn Hotel, 1 George Street, Woburn, Bedfordshire MK17 9PX • Telephone: 01525 290441 • **www.woburn.co.uk/inn**

Paris House Restaurant

WOBURN Map 11 SP93

Modern British v

tel: 01525 290692 **London Rd, Woburn Park MK17 9QP**
email: info@parishouse.co.uk
dir: *M1 junct 13. From Woburn take A4012 Hockliffe, 1m out of Woburn village on left*

Impeccable contemporary cooking in a reassembled timbered house

The house on the Duke of Bedfordshire's Woburn estate was originally built for the International Exhibition in Paris in 1878, where it stood next to the Quai d'Orsay as part of a show entitled 'Streets of Nations'. It was intended to look like a piece of already dated architectural nostalgia, an example of the northern English timbered style of the late medieval era. Following the closure of the exhibition, it was deconstructed and reassembled in Bedfordshire, rather like a Victorian flat-pack. And here it proudly stands, even more at home in the lush parkland than it was on the Rue des Nations. The place has always had aspirations to fine-dining status, maintaining them through changing gastronomic fashion. It comes as no surprise to find that chef/co-patron Phil Fanning has fully absorbed the present-day discipline of using modern culinary techniques creatively to enhance the natural characters of impeccable regional produce. If you've the

time, it's worth going in for the full-on Gourmand experience, a nine-course gastro-pageant that mobilises all the skills and resources at the kitchen's disposal. It may begin modestly enough with a honey-roast fig with dried ham and sourdough bread, followed by a baked scallop in brown onion juice with hazelnuts. Main ingredients are not always the most obvious, so braised snails might turn up next, with salsify and the canonical garlic butter, prior to poached halibut with a shrimp gyoza dumpling in squid broth. And on it goes, via confit loin of Chinese water-deer with haggis and hay, a meat course to conjure with, then a nibble of beetroot and chocolate. Then comes a cheese-plate of artisan British and French items, and a brace of desserts, the finishing note perhaps carrot cake made with goat butter, ginger and walnuts. There are some pretty good wines too.

Chef Phil Fanning **Owner** Phil & Claire Fanning **Seats** 37, Pr/dining room 14 **Times** 12-2/7-9 Closed Xmas, Mon-Tue, D Sun **Prices** Tasting menu fr £39 **Wines** 120 bottles over £30, 4 bottles under £30, 20 by glass **Parking** 24 **Notes** Gourmand menu 6/8/10 course. Chef's table D £200, Sunday L £57, Children welcome

WOBURN
Map 11 SP93

The Inn at Woburn

Modern British, French

tel: 01525 290441 **George St MK17 9PX**
email: inn@woburn.co.uk **web:** www.woburn.co.uk/inn
dir: *5 mins from M1 junct 13. Follow signs to Woburn. Inn in town centre at x-rds, parking to rear via Park St*

High-impact Anglo-French cooking on the Woburn estate

'Inn' is a bit of a misnomer for a substantial hotel where modern-day comforts have been superimposed on the 18th-century core. Olivier's Restaurant is a smart, clubby-looking room, with button-back leather-look seats at polished wooden tables on a boarded floor, and a subdued colour scheme. Olivier Bertho's cooking is a modern interpretation of the classical French repertoire, so chicken, pancetta and tarragon boudin with mushroom and Madeira sauce may be followed by roast cod fillet with clam chowder and spinach. Dishes are carefully put together and never so complicated as to confuse the palate. This is evident in a starter of smoked trout and goats' cheese terrine with pickled beetroot and watercress, then pork, prune and Armagnac hotpot with boulangère potatoes and red cabbage, or pink loin of venison in port jus with sweet potato purée, winter greens and golden beetroot. Puddings are not to be missed, judging by marmalade soufflé with Grand Marnier cream, or chocolate tart with matching sorbet and ginger nut custard.

Chef Olivier Bertho **Owner** Bedford Estates **Seats** 40, Pr/dining room 90
Times 12-2/6.30-9.30 **Prices** Starter £5.20-£8.75, Main £13.50-£18.75, Dessert £6.95-£8.95, Service optional **Wines** 22 bottles over £30, 22 bottles under £30, 18 by glass **Parking** 80 **Notes** Sunday L £20-£25, Vegetarian available, Children welcome

See advert on opposite page

Paris House Restaurant

– *see opposite page*

BERKSHIRE

ASCOT
Map 6 SU96

The Barn at Coworth

British

tel: 01344 876600 **Blacknest Rd SL5 7SE**
email: restaurants.CPA@dorchestercollection.com
dir: *M25 junct 13 onto A30 signed Egham/Bagshot until Wentworth Golf Club. Right at lights onto Blacknest Rd (A329) Hotel on left*

Converted barn with a local flavour

Polo is the game at Coworth Park, a lavish country hotel and spa which is part of the Dorchester group. There's a fine-dining restaurant, of course, but also this converted barn near the stable's where you can tuck into some classy brasserie-style food. It looks great with its open-to-view kitchen, unbuttoned vibe and cheerful service team sporting orange polo tops, and there's a fabulous terrace, too, with gorgeous views over the grounds. There are some good local ingredients on the menu such as trout from the River Test, potted and served with horseradish crème fraîche and lamb's lettuce, or main-course Bramble Farm chicken with creamed potatoes, New Forest mushrooms, cabbage and bacon. There're also the likes of a posh burger and fish and chips. Among desserts, free-range egg custard tart might come with Yorkshire rhubarb in season.

Owner Dorchester Collection **Seats** 75 **Times** 12.30-2.45/6-9.30 **Prices** Fixed L 2 course fr £20, Fixed D 3 course fr £35, Starter £6.50-£10, Main £16.50-£35, Dessert £8-£12.50 **Wines** 44 bottles over £30, 4 bottles under £30, 10 by glass **Parking** 100 **Notes** Fixed L Mon-Fri, D Mon-Thu, Sunday L fr £22.50, Vegetarian available, Children welcome

Bluebells Restaurant & Garden Bar

Modern, International

tel: 01344 622722 **Shrubbs Hill, London Rd, Sunningdale SL5 0LE**
email: info@bluebells-restaurant.co.uk
dir: *From M25 junct 13, A30 towards Bagshot. Restaurant between Wentworth & Sunningdale*

Stylish setting for ambitious contemporary cooking

Bluebells is a delight on the eye: a long room broken up by voile curtains, with a red-brick chimneybreast, pearl-white armchairs in the seating area and matching upholstered dining chairs. Highly worked dishes result in layers of flavours, brought together with intelligence and skill and a good eye for presentation. Seared scallops are partnered by slowly braised belly pork and accompanied by seaweed, butternut squash and dashi, and foie gras adds another dimension to the earthy tastes of rabbit ballotine with bacon, mustard and beetroot. Ingredients are from the top drawer, and treatments vary from poaching (fillet of beef in red wine with oxtail, girolles and carrots, served with a potato and parmesan millefeuille) through frying to roasting (fillet of halibut wrapped in Iberico ham accompanied by winter vegetable ratatouille, tomato chutney and parsnip velouté). Bring proceedings to a successful finale with one of the pretty desserts: perhaps tiramisù with coffee sorbet and a yoghurt and toffee gel.

Chef Adam Turley **Owner** John Rampello **Seats** 90, Pr/dining room 14
Times 12-2.30/6.30-9.45 Closed 25-26 Dec, 1-11 Jan, BHs, Mon, D Sun **Prices** Fixed L 2 course fr £17, Starter £8.90-£16, Main £17-£29, Dessert £8.50-£9.75 **Wines** 74 bottles over £30, 30 bottles under £30, 12 by glass **Parking** 100 **Notes** Sunday L £23.50-£29, Vegetarian available, Children welcome

ASCOT *continued*

Macdonald Berystede Hotel & Spa

◉ British, European

tel: 01344 623311 & 0844 879 9104 **Bagshot Rd, Sunninghill SL5 9JH**
email: general.berystede@macdonald-hotels.co.uk **web:** www.berystede.com
dir: *M3 junct 3/A30, A322 then left onto B3020 to Ascot or M25 junct 13, follow signs for Bagshot. At Sunningdale turn right onto A330*

Up-to-date brasserie cooking near Legoland and the racing

The Berystede is handy for both Legoland and the racing at Ascot, depending on how you get your kicks, and is a handsome red-brick mansion with a rather impressive glassed walkway to the entrance. With spa and business facilities, it's the image of a modern corporate hotel, yet one with some character, and an impressive restaurant, Hyperion, furnished with curving banquettes and quality table appointments. The kitchen brigade brings its creative exertions to bear on seasonal produce in up-to-date brasserie dishes that can look a little busy but deliver on flavour. Start with a poppy-seeded goats' cheese pannacotta with red pepper sorbet and tapenade, which constitutes an artful study in contrasts, before going on to Highland lamb two ways (the tender-as-anything shank getting the vote) with rösti, slow-cooked tomatoes and puréed aubergine in red wine jus. Evenly glazed, pleasantly zesty lemon tart for afters comes with intense raspberry ice cream and coulis.

Chef Jon Machin **Owner** Macdonald Hotels **Seats** 100, Pr/dining room 24
Times 12.30-2/7-9.45 Closed L Sat **Prices** Fixed L 2 course £17.25-£22.95, Fixed D 3 course £38.95 **Wines** 45 bottles over £30, 16 bottles under £30, 12 by glass
Parking 120 **Notes** Sunday L, Vegetarian available, Children welcome

Restaurant Coworth Park

Rosettes not confirmed at time of going to print – see below

BRACKNELL	Map 5 SU86

Coppid Beech

◉ European, Pacific Rim

tel: 01344 303333 **John Nike Way RG12 8TF**
email: sales@coppidbeech.com **web:** www.coppidbeech.com
dir: *M4 junct 10 take Wokingham/Bracknell onto A329. In 2m take B3408 to Binfield at rdbt. Hotel 200yds on right*

Alpine atmosphere and modern food by the Thames

You may think that the Thames Valley is not known for its skiing and Alpine chalets, but that is because you haven't yet discovered the Coppid Beech Hotel. The smart

Restaurant Coworth Park

Rosettes not confirmed at time of going to print

ASCOT	Map 6 SU96

Modern British ⚑ NOTABLE WINE LIST

tel: 01344 876600 **Blacknest Rd SL5 7SE**
email: restaurants.CPA@dorchestercollection.com **web:** www.coworthpark.com
dir: *M25 junct 13 onto A30 signed Egham/Bagshot until Wentworth Golf Club. Right at lights onto Blacknest Rd (A329) Hotel on left*

Pace-setting modern cooking in a cosmopolitan hotel complex

The Rosette award for this establishment has been suspended due to a change of chef. Reassessment will take place in due course under the new chef. It's all happening at Coworth Park, the hotel at the centre of a sprawling 240-acre estate next to Windsor Great Park and the racing at Ascot. Sporting activities abound: tuition in polo is aimed at the newbies, while tennis, riding and croquet may well all be in full swing, and the less outdoorsy may be tucked up under fluffy towels in the spa. It all comes within the aegis of the Dorchester Collection hotel group, so a certain level of cosmopolitan luxury may be taken as standard, but without Park Lane's roaring traffic. A plethora of settings for eating is available too. Nobody will bat an eyelid if you rock up in mud-spattered wellingtons in The Barn, but you might think better of traipsing into the Restaurant in them. Croquettes and poached cheeks of cod in curry foam, or Jerusalem artichoke velouté with chestnut custard are the kinds of thought-provoking dishes that might start you off. Then pedigree meats star in main courses such as slow-cooked Windsor beef fillet with puréed broccoli and baby carrots, or roast loin and braised shoulder of Swaledale lamb with red cabbage and spinach. Supporting elements do just that, support rather than outshine the main items, so a gently poached fillet of Atlantic halibut comes with gem lettuce and chargrilled new potatoes in creamy fish stock, while seaweed gnocchi and pickled baby turnips are the considered accompaniments to gilt-head bream. Ingenious dessert ideas maintain interest, perhaps for mandarin blancmange and mandarin soup with confit cranberries, or dark chocolate parfait with salted caramel and Earl Grey ice cream.

Owner Dorchester Collection **Seats** 66, Pr/dining room 16
Times 12.30-3/6.30-9.30 Closed Mon, D Sun **Prices** Fixed L 2 course fr £20, Fixed D 3 course fr £40, Tasting menu £85 **Wines** 600+ bottles over £30, 4 bottles under £30, 18 by glass **Parking** 100 **Notes** Fixed L Tue-Sat, D Tue-Thu, Tasting menu 7 course, Sunday L £32.95-£39.95, Vegetarian available, Children 8yrs+ D

modern hotel not only has the look of a Swiss chalet, but there's the chance to strap on the planks too as there's a dry-ski slope, an ice rink and toboggan run in the complex. With an appetite suitably sharpened by the year-round winter sports, move on to Rowans, the hotel's upscale dining option. It is an eye-catching space, with plush drapes and linen-clothed tables beneath a soaring timbered ceiling hung with crystal chandeliers as a backdrop to a menu that covers a fair amount of modern European territory. Start with wood pigeon en croûte served with beetroot carpaccio and orange and beetroot jus, followed by sirloin steak with mushrooms, parsnip purée, garlic spinach and marchand de vin sauce. Finish with a Thai-influenced coconut pannacotta with sweet-and-sour pineapple, and basil jelly.

Chef Paul Zolik **Owner** Nike Group Hotels Ltd **Seats** 120 **Times** 12-2/7-9.45 Closed L Sat, D Thu, Sun **Prices** Fixed L 2 course £20-£22.50, Fixed D 3 course £27.50-£33, Starter £4.95-£8.50, Main £14.95-£17.95, Dessert £5.95-£7.25 **Wines** 20 bottles over £30, 20 bottles under £30, 15 by glass **Parking** 350 **Notes** Sunday L £21.50, Vegetarian available, Children welcome

BRAY 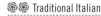 Map 6 SU97

Caldesi in Campagna

◉◉ Traditional Italian

tel: 01628 788500 **Old Mill Ln SL6 2BG**
email: campagna@caldesi.com
dir: M4 junct 8/9, at rdbt exit A308 Bray/Windsor. Continue for 0.5m, left B3028 Bray village, right Old Mill Lane, restaurant in 400yds on right

Refined Italian eatery in Bray

As if to prove that nobody in Bray need be stuck for somewhere to eat out, yet another fine-dining venue springs up, this one a two-handed operation from Italian chef Giancarlo Caldesi and his wife Katie, a food writer specialising in Italy. The restaurant is in a small white house on the outskirts of the village, the refined but simple decor extending to beige tones, parquet flooring, a brick fireplace and quality tableware. There's bar seating too, as well as an outdoor area, and when the Berkshire sun comes out, you might just fancy you were in Tuscany. The more so as Caldesi's cooking pulls off that very 21st-century trick of using British (mainly local) sustainable ingredients to give a convincing impression of the food of somewhere else entirely. The carpaccio is made from Scottish beef, and comes properly dressed with shaved parmesan, rocket, rosemary and balsamic, gaining true succulence from its being served warm. Squid is slow-cooked to tenderness and married with tomatoes and chilli for a fine crostini topping, and the home-made pasta that encases sea bass in ravioli, or tangles up clams, garlic and chilli in spaghetti, is the real thing. Fish cookery is spot-on, the timing of a piece of fried stone bass flawless, while meat might be classic saltimbocca Romana, or Barbary duck breast crusted in pink peppercorns with mashed potato in red grape sauce.

Chef Gregorio Piazza **Owner** Giancarlo Caldesi **Seats** 50, Pr/dining room 12 **Times** 12-2.30/6.30-10 Closed Xmas for approx 5 days, Mon, D Sun **Prices** Fixed L 2 course £14.50-£16.50, Starter £11.50-£16, Main £16.50-£26, Dessert £6.95-£13.50 **Wines** 116 bottles over £30, 19 bottles under £30, 15 by glass **Parking** 8 **Notes** Sunday L, Vegetarian available, Children welcome

Follow the AA on twitter @TheAA_Lifestyle

The Crown

◉◉ Modern British

tel: 01628 621936 **High St SL6 2AH**
email: reservations@thecrownatbray.co.uk
dir: M4 junct 8/9, follow signs for Maidenhead Central, left towards Windsor, right to Bray

Heston's proper pub

With low-beamed ceilings, real fires, leaded windows, secretive little nooks and crannies, and a no-frills bar for drinkers, The Crown is a classic 16th-century inn. However, the location in the gastro-mecca of Bray might set you wondering who owns it, and although there is no obvious clue to that effect, it is indeed owned (along with The Hinds Head) by one Heston Blumenthal. But fear not: a visit to the bank manager is not needed, and the place has not been whizzed upmarket into high-falutin' gastro territory. That said, the food is clearly a cut or two above the average pub grub. Founded on first-class ingredients, you can expect modern British pub classics with added refinement. Chicken liver parfait is served with toasted brioche and sweet-and-sour onions, while fillet of hake is accompanied by charred leeks, celeriac purée, ceps and cep sauce in a simple but perfectly executed main course. Finish with Earl Grey pannacotta with lemon crumble, or flag-waving British cheeses such as Barkham Blue and Lyburn Old Winchester with fig and date chutney and raisin and hazelnut bread.

Times 12-2.30/6-9.30

The Fat Duck

◉◉◉◉◉ – see page 50

Hinds Head

◉◉◉ – see page 51

The Riverside Brasserie

◉◉ Modern European

tel: 01628 780553 **Bray Marina, Monkey Island Ln SL6 2EB**
email: info@riversidebrasserie.co.uk
dir: Off A308, signed Bray Marina

Accomplished cooking by the Thames

If you like to make a grand entrance, why not arrive by boat? This hidden gem is tucked away beside the Thames in Bray Marina; the waterside decked terrace is perfect for alfresco dining, but if summer sets in with its customary severity and drives you indoors, the simple interior oozes understated class and an easygoing ambience. Full-length glass doors mean the river views are still there, while the chefs working in an open-to-view kitchen turn out straightforward yet skilfully cooked brasserie food. Chicken liver and foie gras parfait with onion marmalade and toasted brioche is a classic starter, done right, while splendid ingredients bring lustre to an uncomplicated main course comprising spanking fresh cod with crunchy choucroute, pea purée and crispy Parma ham. Elsewhere, there may be Romney Marsh lamb rump, cooked sous-vide for maximum tenderness, and served with green beans and Sicilian pesto. To finish, a great combo of sweet and salty flavours comes courtesy of a chocolate ganache and salted caramel tart served with milk ice cream.

Times 12-2.30/7-9.30 Closed Mon-Thu (Oct-Mar), L Fri (Oct-Mar)

The Fat Duck

BRAY Map 6 SU97

Modern British V

tel: 01628 580333 **High St SL6 2AQ**
dir: *M4 junct 8/9 (Maidenhead) take A308 towards Windsor, turn left into Bray. Restaurant in centre of village on right*

Mind-boggling culinary creations old and new at Heston HQ

Note: The Fat Duck will be closed from February 2015 for six months while there is an overhaul of the Grade II-listed building. Meanwhile Heston and his team will relocate to The Crown Melbourne Resort, Australia and will return to Bray in Summer 2015. Heston Blumenthal's enthusiasm and passion is seductive. His seemingly tireless curiosity and willingness to push at the boundaries of convention is unyielding. These elements of the man's characteristics have made The Fat Duck what it is today: one of the best restaurants in the world. With the restaurant's 20th anniversary in the offing, it is impossible to imagine the foodie landscape without his innovations. He's a fixture on the telly. His books top the charts. Say 'snail porridge' to just about anyone and they'll have heard about it, but maybe not had a bite. The menu has changed a lot over the years as Heston's mind expanded, high on his discoveries and maybe a sense that he was on the crest of a wave. Just the tasting menu remains these days (just...?), well, only the tasting menu remains, and it's priced at £195 a head, leaping over the 200 quid mark when you add the 12½% service charge. There's no chance of eating here for less, but this is a unique, one-off (for many) experience that really will live long in the memory. When you appreciate the work that goes into each dish, the craft, the passion, the time, the cost seems easier to justify. This is no ordinary restaurant although it looks like one from the outside, where the former pub appears almost humble with its pale-grey walls and swinging sign. No

need to shout after all. Inside, everything is soothingly sophisticated but not overly so, with a genuine feeling of relaxation and anticipation pervading. The stellar staff can cope with eight or so languages so visiting pilgrims can be informed as they go along. The 14-course menu will stimulate every sense – smell, taste, sight and sound – as what follows consumes you as much as you consume it. The nitro-poached aperitifs are a lot of fun, the perfect start, with an espuma flavoured with vodka and lime sour, Campari soda or tequila and grapefruit poached in liquid nitrogen at -196 degrees C, dissolving on your tongue to deliver an intense hit of clean, crisp flavour. The menu does not change but rather evolves, with most of the 'classics' on show as that's what the punters have come for, but new things arrive to keep the interest of seasoned visitors. Three cheers for red cabbage gazpacho with Pommery grain mustard ice cream, and snail porridge with Iberico Bellota ham and shaved fennel, and take a bow the gorgeously seductive roast foie gras rhubarb, confit kombu and crab biscuit. The science and the innovation impresses, but most of all, it is the taste that lingers in the memory. There's the 'Mad Hatters tea party' (as seen on TV), and the 'Sound of the Sea' delivering the aural stimulation (alongside some fab kingfish, abalone and mackerel). Sweet courses are a lot of fun, too, with 'Whisk (e) y wine gums' and a newer addition combining the flavours of rhubarb, sheep's milk yoghurt and bergamot. The wine list is a first-class piece of work befitting of this company.

Chef Heston Blumenthal, Jonny Lake **Owner** Fat Duck Ltd **Seats** 40 **Times** 12-2/7-9 Closed 2 wks at Xmas, Sun-Mon **Prices** Tasting menu £195 **Wines** 500 bottles over £30, 13 by glass **Parking** Two village car parks **Notes** Tasting menu only, Children welcome

BRAY *continued*

Waterside Inn

◉◉◉◉ – *see page 52*

The Crab at Chieveley

◉◉ Modern British V

tel: 01635 247550 **Wantage Rd RG20 8UE**
email: info@crabatchieveley.com **web:** www.crabatchieveley.com
dir: *M4 junct 13, towards Chieveley. Left into School Rd, right at T-junct, 0.5m on right. Follow brown tourist signs*

Singular seafood in rural Berkshire

Restaurants with rooms don't come much more singular in intent than the Crab, a thatched cottage in rural Berkshire where the guest rooms are decorated in homage to famous hotels around the world from Fiji to Scotland, while a warren of interlinked rooms make up the seafood restaurant. In case you've missed the theme, the walls are adorned with fishing scenes in bright colours, and the ceilings hung with laden nets. You could be in a little fishing village, were you not land-bound in Berkshire. Main courses do the freshness and vitality of their prime materials proud, by means of dishes such as sea bass with parmesan gnocchi, mushrooms and artichoke cream, turbot and lobster bouillabaisse with rock samphire, and well-timed scallops with a black pudding beignet and sweetcorn risotto, a dish only slightly unbalanced by over-assertive chorizo. Attention to detail is on reassuring show in starters like duck and foie gras terrine wrapped in Parma ham, with raisin purée and a crisp-fried quail egg, and properly wobbly coconut pannacotta with pineapple granité and soft vanilla meringues.

Chef Dave Horridge **Owner** Heritage Properties & Hotels **Seats** 120, Pr/dining room 30 **Times** 12-2.30/6-9.30 Closed D 25 Dec **Prices** Prices not confirmed **Wines** 15 by glass **Parking** 80 **Notes** Sunday L, Children welcome

The White Oak

◉◉ European

tel: 01628 523 043 **The Pound SL6 9QE**
email: info@thewhiteoak.co.uk
dir: *M4 junct 8/9 onto A308(M) towards Maidenhead Central, continue towards Marlow. Right at lights Switchback Road South to Gardener Road. At rdbt 1st exit B4447 Switchback Road North to Cookham, right at mini-rdbt to The Pound*

Classy food in a charming pub

The red-brick White Oak combines period charm with a bit of contemporary swagger. It's been opened up in the modern manner and decorated with neutral tones to suit the original features, with contemporary artworks and retro light fittings to up the cool stakes. Chef-patron Clive Dixon has managed to maintain the 'pub' feel of the place, with draught ales at the bar and a relaxed vibe, while the kitchen has its sights set a good few notches above the norm. The menu is packed with interesting stuff, follows the seasons, and has a European flavour. This is clear in the fixed-price Auberge Menu option, which pays homage to the French country inns whose dedication to flavour-packed food is something of a template. With dishes that wouldn't be out of place in a big-city brasserie, start with a soup of broad beans and Ibérico ham, followed by Scotch beef burger with gruyère, pickles and chips, or duck bolognese with a garlic crumb and black truffle. Finish with steamed treacle sponge pudding and custard.

Chef Clive Dixon **Owner** Henry & Katherine Cripps **Seats** 80, Pr/dining room 14 **Times** 12-2.30/6.30-9.30 Closed D Sun (winter) **Prices** Fixed L 2 course fr £14, Fixed D 3 course fr £16, Tasting menu fr £45, Starter £6-£14, Main £14-£29, Dessert £6-£9, Service optional **Wines** 26 bottles over £30, 29 bottles under £30, 13 by glass **Parking** 32 **Notes** Tasting menu 5-7 course, Sunday L £14-£25, Vegetarian available, Children welcome

Hinds Head

British ■ NOTABLE WINE LIST
tel: 01628 626151 **High St SL6 2AB**
email: info@hindsheadbray.com
dir: *M4 junct 8/9, at rdbt take exit to Maidenhead Central, next rdbt take exit Bray & Windsor, after 0.5m take B3028 to Bray*

Heston's modern take on old-English fare with bang-on flavours

Heston Blumenthal's vision of an English pub is not as out-there as you might imagine. It's most definitely a pub for a start, with 15th-century beams, open fires and a smart, rustic finish, and there's an honesty and integrity to the food that really fits the bill. That's not to say this is standard pub food – not by a long way – this is Heston after all. The antiquity of the building inspires the menu with historic dishes and classy versions of pub classics peppering the menu. Chef Kevin Love delivers well-crafted dishes that can be as simple as snacks (devils on horseback or a Scotch egg, say) or a starter of beautifully flavoured scallop tartare with a white chocolate and white pepper velouté, chocolate foam, pickled lemon and walnut oil that might sound a little like it comes from the Fat Duck opposite (it is rather on the sophisticated side), but equally you could go for an immaculate salad of cured duck with asparagus, artichoke, crispy bacon and a quail's egg. Everything is presented with a touch of rustic flair and flavours are bang on. Main-course fillet of duck with beetroot, turnips, barley and duck sauce has a stellar piece of meat at the heart of it all, or you could opt for fillet of first-rate bream with spring greens and a mussel broth. For dessert, Quaking pudding comes with a little card describing its origins or you might take refuge in the retro comfort of a rhubarb trifle or an elegant take on peach Melba (with white peaches, blow-torched meringue and crystalized basil). Naturally, the wine list goes way, way beyond the sort of offerings you'd expect in a pub, offering impeccably sourced bottles from small châteaux as well as gilt-edged vintages from around the globe.

Chef Kevin Love **Owner** Hinds Head Ltd **Seats** 100, Pr/dining room 22 **Times** 12-2.30/6.15-9.30 Closed 25-26 Dec, D 1 Jan, BHs, Sun **Prices** Fixed L 2 course fr £17.50, Starter £7.50-£11.75, Main £14.95-£32.95, Dessert £7.95-£9.50 **Wines** 56 bottles over £30, 25 bottles under £30, 14 by glass **Parking** 40 **Notes** Tasting menu 7 course with 24 hrs notice, Sunday L £35.40-£45.75, Vegetarian available, Children welcome

Waterside Inn

BRAY	Map 6 SU97

French · NOTABLE WINE LIST

tel: 01628 620691 **Ferry Rd SL6 2AT**
email: reservations@waterside-inn.co.uk
dir: *M4 junct 8/9, A308 (Windsor) then B3028 to Bray. Restaurant clearly signed*

The Roux family's riverside restaurant four decades on

The Waterside Inn has a prime position on the banks of the majestic River Thames The Roux family's associations with the British dining scene go back to 1967, when the brothers opened Le Gavroche, and they acquired the Waterside in 1972. Today it is the second generation, the sons of the founding fathers, who have carried the mantle into a new century. Alain Roux is chef-patron here in Bray, building on the past to create a bright future. (Le Gavroche and Waterside are separate entities, by the way, the founding fathers going their own way back in the mid-1980s.) The all-pervading luxury is evident from the outset, with valet parking ensuring you have absolutely nothing to worry about from the minute you pull up outside, the duty of care passed to a team who are really and truly second to none. This is the kind of service where the staff know what you want before you do, glasses are filled, plates are cleared, all before your brain registers the necessity for such action. Now, value for money is hard to define, and the Waterside isn't cheap. There are some very big numbers on the menu. But value for money this most certainly is if you're up for an experience you won't forget in a hurry. If the weather is up to scratch the riverside terrace comes into its own, with birds and boats to ponder while sipping a glass of champagne and tucking into some first-class canapés, but on rainy or cold days the lounge and small bar provide comfort enough. The next stage is the seamless move into the classically elegant restaurant, where floor-to-ceiling windows allow lovely river views. Alain Roux still cooks some of the traditional dishes of his father's day, but there are injections of modernity and innovation on the bilingual menu. Céviche of sea bass and octopus, marinated in passionfruit juice and served with a crisp vegetable salad is typical of the new era Waterside – deftly handled flavours, light and punchy. There's also a seasonal game pâté, wrapped in pastry and rich with truffles and foie gras or you can order main course rabbit fillets grilled to tender perfection and served with celeriac fondant, glazed chestnuts and Armagnac sauce. There is also no better treat than watching the Challandais duck expertly carved at the table. Classic desserts such as crème brûlée are refined and dynamic versions, flavoured with pistachio perhaps, and served with vanilla ice cream. The wine list has exemplary credentials, with sommeliers on hand to help you through it.

Chef Alain Roux **Owner** Alain Roux **Seats** 75, Pr/dining room 8 **Times** 12-2/7-10 Closed 26 Dec-29 Jan, Mon-Tue **Prices** Fixed L 2 course fr £45.50, Tasting menu £153, Starter £36-£59, Main £51-£59, Dessert £31-£41 **Wines** 1000+ bottles over £30, 1 bottle under £30, 14 by glass **Parking** 20 **Notes** Tasting menu 6 course, Sun L 3/6 course, Sunday L £79.50-£153, Vegetarian available, No children

FRILSHAM   Map 5 SU57

The Pot Kiln

◉◉ Traditional British, European

tel: 01635 201366 **RG18 OXX**
email: info@potkiln.org
dir: *From Yattendon follow Pot Kiln signs, cross over motorway. Continue for 0.25m pub on right*

Confident country cooking in rural inn

A pub first and foremost, The Pot Kiln is the kind of pub every village deserves: one which serves a proper pint, grows its own vegetables, and sources the rest of the produce used with a good deal of care. And the fact it has a penchant for game, well, that's just a bonus. Of course, it is not the red-brick pub that is doing all this, but the owners, Mike and Katie Robinson. Mike is on the telly a fair bit, usually spreading the good word in support of British game, and he practices what he preaches. So seated at unadorned wooden tables in a thoroughly pubby atmosphere, you might tuck into a salad of Berkshire wood pigeon with black pudding, bacon and Jerusalem artichoke purée, or go your own way with cider-steamed River Fowey mussels. Pavé of Lockinge fallow deer is hard to ignore in this company, but everything is cooked with care and attention and presented with a contemporary touch or two. There's a bar menu too, serving up a cracking ploughman's, sandwiches and the like.

Chef Mike Robinson **Owner** Mike & Katie Robinson **Seats** 48 **Times** 12-2.30/7-9.30 Closed 25 Dec, Tue, D Sun **Prices** Fixed L 2 course fr £13.95, Starter £6.95-£8.50, Main £14.50-£19, Dessert £6-£8 **Wines** 6 by glass **Parking** 70 **Notes** Sunday L £16.50-£18.50, Vegetarian available, Children welcome

HUNGERFORD   Map 5 SU36

Littlecote House Hotel

◉◉ Modern British

tel: 01488 682509 **Chilton Foliat RG17 0SU** **web:** www.warnerleisurehotels.co.uk
dir: *M4 junct 14, A338/A4 Hungerford, follow brown signs*

Appealing modern menu in an historic house

The house in question dates back to the 16th century, but the site is even older than that: a Roman mosaic and the remains of a Roman settlement can be seen in the grounds. Oliver Cromwell's soldiers were said to have been billeted here in the Civil War, an historic fact that's referenced in the name of the most exclusive of the hotel's dining options – Oliver's Bistro. The modern, minimalist dining room looks smart, with views over the immaculate gardens and slick service. An exciting menu showcases local suppliers and dishes are attractively presented. A good range of global wines complements the likes of duo of Cornish mackerel – well-made pâté and pan-seared fillet with a crisp skin-pointed up by gooseberry jam and onion marmalade. Then you might take rump of Gloucester lamb, moist and full of flavour, with garden peas, garlic and salsa verde. Honey crème brûlée with poached rhubarb brings proceedings to a simple but highly effective close.

Chef Matthew Davies **Owner** Warner Leisure Hotels **Seats** 40, Pr/dining room 8 **Times** 6.30-9 Closed Mon, L all week **Prices** Starter £6.50-£7.50 Main £16.50-£22, Dessert £7-£8, Service optional **Wines** 4 bottles over £30, 23 bottles under £30, 13 by glass **Parking** 200 **Notes** L only Oliver's Bistro 12-2, 2/3 course £17.50-£20.50, Sunday L, Vegetarian available, No children

HURLEY   Map 5 SU88

The Olde Bell Inn

◉◉ Modern British

tel: 01628 825881 **High St SL6 5LX**
email: oldebellreception@coachinginn.co.uk
dir: *M4 junct 8/9 follow signs for Henley. At rdbt take A4130 to Hurley, turn right to Hurley Village, 800yds on right*

Classy, creative cooking in a smartly revamped coaching inn

There's no shortage of period character at the 12th-century Bell (very much an olde), with beams, fireplaces etc., but the place is by no means preserved in aspic. In fact, it's done out with a good deal of charm-of the rustic-chic variety-with chunky designer tables and some rather cool fixtures and fittings. There are six acres of fabulous grounds to get lost in, including a kitchen garden that provides plenty of good stuff for the table. The kitchen makes good use of regional produce and serves up some nifty dishes that show sound technical skill and, like the inn itself, a creative and rustic spin. A starter of pressed ham hock terrine comes with apple sauce and rye bread, while roasted quail is partnered with an apple and white cabbage remoulade. Next up, butter-roasted lamb with garlic and cream potato has at its heart a fine piece of meat, correctly cooked, or go for pan-fried plaice served in the classic way with lemon, capers and a nutty brown butter sauce. Sign off in style with an iced mango parfait with caramel popcorn crumb.

Owner Dhillon Hotels Ltd **Times** 12-2.30/6-9.30 **Prices** Fixed L 2 course £13.95-£18.50, Fixed D 3 course £32.50, Starter £5-£7.50, Main £17-£23, Dessert fr £7.50 **Wines** 24 bottles over £30, 33 bottles under £30 **Notes** Sunday L £24.50-£29.50

MAIDENHEAD   Map 6 SU88

Boulters Riverside Brasserie

◉◉ Modern British

tel: 01628 621291 **Boulters Lock Island SL6 8PE**
email: info@boultersrestaurant.co.uk
dir: *M4 junct 7 onto A4 towards Maidenhead, cross Maidenhead bridge, right at rdbt. Restaurant 0.5m on right*

Modern brasserie dining by the river

The to-die-for Thames-side location overlooking Boulters Lock, where the river ambles past Maidenhead Bridge, is a very good reason to head to this buzzy, contemporary brasserie. There may be nothing but glass walls between diners and the river, but Boulters is not a place to let the food take a back seat while the views pull in the punters: the ground-floor fine-dining brasserie is flooded with light and looks stylishly neutral with its bare darkwood tables and wooden floors. The food fits the setting to a T – well-executed contemporary brasserie dishes wrought from quality local produce, all impeccably presented. Roast pumpkin and parmesan risotto gets a herby kick from marjoram and deeper earthy notes from truffle butter, while a main course delivers splendidly fresh baked cod with a cheese crust, fondant potato, wilted spinach and wholegrain mustard sauce. For dessert, only Valrhona's finest will do for a hot chocolate fondant with pistachio parfait.

Chef Daniel Woodhouse **Owner** The Dennis family **Seats** 70, Pr/dining room 12 **Times** 12-9.30 Closed D Sun All-day dining **Prices** Starter £6.95-£9.95, Main £11.95-£19.95, Dessert £5.95-£9.95 **Wines** 78 bottles over £30, 42 bottles under £30, 22 by glass **Parking** 20 **Notes** Brunch 10-11.30am, High tea 3-5pm, Sunday L £12.95-£15.95, Vegetarian available, Children welcome

MAIDENHEAD *continued*

The Royal Oak Paley Street

◎◎◎ *– see opposite page*

– see opposite page

NEWBURY Map 5 SU46

Donnington Valley Hotel & Spa

◎◎ Modern British ⚑ NOTABLE WINE LIST

---

tel: 01635 551199 **Old Oxford Rd, Donnington RG14 3AG**
email: general@donningtonvalley.co.uk **web:** www.donningtonvalley.co.uk
dir: *M4 junct 13, A34 towards Newbury. Take immediate left signed Donnington Hotel. At rdbt take right, at 3rd rdbt take left, follow road for 2m, hotel on right*

Engaging modern cooking in a golfing and spa hotel

There's plenty on offer at Donnington Valley, from tip-top business facilities, golf, a luxurious spa and, in the Wine Press restaurant, some good food to be had, too. It's a smart, modern hotel on a large scale, with no less than 111 bedrooms to choose from. The restaurant is a clear-headed space (no chintz here), set over two levels and decorated in mellow neutral tones, with artworks and fresh flowers adding splashes of colour. The kitchen delivers a slate of broadly modern British dishes based on high quality produce. Ham hock and foie gras terrine, for example, with beetroot chutney and toasted brioche, or from the Market Menu, chicken and duck liver parfait with tomato chutney. There are steaks from the grill, plus modish ideas such as seared monkfish tail with saag aloo, cauliflower beignet, courgette flower and lemon foam, which shows off the sound technical abilities in the kitchen. For dessert, try the rocky road baked cheesecake with hazelnut ice cream. Given the restaurant's name, it's no surprise that the wine list is well worth exploring.

Chef Kelvin Johnson **Owner** Sir Peter Michael **Seats** 120, Pr/dining room 130 **Times** 12-2/7-10 **Prices** Prices not confirmed, Service optional **Wines** 321 bottles over £30, 49 bottles under £30, 36 by glass **Parking** 150 **Notes** Sunday L, Vegetarian available, Children welcome

Newbury Manor Hotel

◎◎ Modern European

tel: 01635 528838 **London Rd RG14 2BY**
email: enquiries@newbury-manor-hotel.co.uk **web:** www.newbury-manor-hotel.co.uk
dir: *M4 junct 13, A34 Newbury, A4 Thatcham, 0.5m on right*

Romantic waterside setting for classically-inspired cooking

Newbury Manor is an elegant Georgian house, set in nine idyllic acres of lush woodland and water meadows that are a haven for wildlife. The short walk through fragrant herb gardens and over wooden bridges to the River Bar Restaurant is a delight, as is the conservatory-style setting in part of an old watermill. Floor-to-ceiling windows look across an alfresco decking terrace to the tranquil pool at the confluence of the Rivers Kennet and Lambourn, where swans sail by in the hope of a treat, and you may catch the electric blue flash of a kingfisher. The cooking suits the comfortable and relaxed tone of the place with its straightforward menus of seasonally-driven dishes. Local produce is the bedrock of unfussy flavour-led ideas, setting out with a country terrine with apple and rhubarb chutney and home-made granary bread, followed by prune-stuffed duck served with red onion purée, mashed potatoes and fine beans. At the end, it's worth finding room for blueberry pannacotta with fruit and nut biscotti and coconut sorbet.

Chef Jan Papcun **Owner** Heritage Properties & Hotels **Seats** 48, Pr/dining room 160 **Times** 12-2.30/6-10 **Prices** Prices not confirmed, Service optional **Wines** 10 bottles over £30, 25 bottles under £30, 12 by glass **Parking** 80 **Notes** Sunday L, Vegetarian available, Children welcome

Regency Park Hotel

◎ Modern European V

---

tel: 01635 871555 **Bowling Green Rd, Thatcham RG18 3RP**
email: info@regencyparkhotel.com **web:** www.regencyparkhotel.co.uk
dir: *M4 junct 13, follow A339 to Newbury for 2m, then take the A4 (Reading), the hotel is signed*

Good brasserie cooking in modern spa hotel

Tucked into the Berkshire hinterland between Newbury and Thatcham, the Regency Park is a modern corporate spa hotel. If you've just hot-footed it from a visit to nearby Highclere Castle (TV's Downton Abbey in its other life), it will look a bit prosaic by comparison, but creature comforts are conspicuous by their abundance, and the Watermark restaurant is kitted out in restful spring-like shades, along with a water feature. The cooking keeps to a simple brasserie formula, but achieves a convincing success rate with the likes of seared scallops and gingered carrots in coriander oil, or duck liver parfait with spiced plum chutney to start, and then perhaps pink-cooked rump of lamb with flageolets and spinach in an outstanding garlic and rosemary jus. A more ambitious fish dish might see hazelnut-crusted turbot turn up with turnips in a red wine and shallot sauce, while dessert could be firm-textured orange cheesecake with sharply contrasting rhubarb compôte.

Chef Laurent Guyon **Owner** Planned Holdings Ltd **Seats** 90, Pr/dining room 40 **Times** 12.30-2/7-10 Closed L Sat **Prices** Prices not confirmed, Service optional **Wines** 21 bottles over £30, 27 bottles under £30, 14 by glass **Parking** 150 **Notes** Sunday L, Children welcome

Looking for a
restaurant by name?
Use the index on page 751

The Royal Oak Paley Street

MAIDENHEAD Map 6 SU88

British, European  NOTABLE WINE LIST

tel: 01628 620541 **Paley St, Littlefield Green SL6 3JN**
email: reservations@theroyaloakpaleystreet.com
web: www.theroyaloakpaleystreet.com
dir: *M4 junct 8/9. Take A308 towards Maidenhead Central, then A330 to Ascot. After 2m, turn right onto B3024 to Twyford. Second pub on left*

First-class modern British cooking in a spruced up country pub

Tucked away down a winding road, the whitewashed 17th-century Royal Oak is rather more than your everyday country pub, although with real ale on the hand-pumps, beams on the ceilings, slate on the floor and a fire in the hearth, it still has bags of country charm, and a lack of pretension throughout. There's an eclectic mix of art on the walls, and when the sun comes out, the contemporary herb garden is a great spot for pre-dinner drinks. Professionalism abounds, and attention to detail ensures everything runs smoothly. It's a foodie destination these days thanks to the appointment of Michael Chapman, who keeps a keen eye on the seasons, and seeking out the very best produce, most of which is British, a significant proportion local, and creating menus filled with things you'll want to eat. The food achieves that holy grail of bringing together earthiness and refinement – sautéed lamb's kidneys with creamed onions, sage and garlic crumbs, for example, or there's all the comfort of foie gras and chicken liver parfait with fig chutney and toasted brioche. At main course stage, wild Berkshire rabbit and bacon pie with mashed potato is a long way from your average pub pie, or you might trade up to the roast turbot with artichokes, Iberico ham and red wine sauce. Don't skip pudding when there's baked Alaska or warm vanilla rice pudding with jam doughnuts up for grabs, otherwise the cheeseboard brims with good stuff from Britain and France. The icing on the cake is a cracking list of 500-odd wines with a good choice by the glass, and the terrace is a lovely spot in the warmer months.

Chef Michael Chapman **Owner** Nick Parkinson **Seats** 80, Pr/dining room 20 **Times** 12-2.30/6.30-9.30 Closed D Sun **Prices** Starter £6.25-£14, Main £16-£34, Dessert £6-£10.50 **Wines** 400 bottles over £30, 80 bottles under £30, 20 by glass **Parking** 70 **Notes** Sunday L £26, Vegetarian available, No children

NEWBURY *continued*

The Vineyard

🏵🏵🏵 *– see below*

The Elephant at Pangbourne

🏵 Modern British, European

tel: 0118 984 2244 **Church Rd RG8 7AR**
email: reception@elephanthotel.co.uk web: www.elephanthotel.co.uk
dir: *A4 Theale/Newbury, right at 2nd rdbt signed Pangbourne. Hotel on left*

Sound contemporary cooking and echoes of the Raj

Echoes of the old British Empire are found at The Elephant, now a boutique hotel, with oriental rugs, Indian furniture and Eastern artefacts littered about. There are two eating options: the bar, with a separate menu (expect upmarket pub food, from sandwiches to cheese and onion omelette with fries, or roast duck breast with a port jus, Savoy cabbage and fondant potato) and the restaurant. The menu here makes a few nods to fashion – a salad of chorizo, potato and tomato for pan-fried salmon steak, for instance – and follows a contemporary line of sound ideas. Game terrine with beetroot and apple chutney can vie for attention with a smoked haddock and salmon parcel with oriental salad and hoi sin dip, preceding venison steak with redcurrant jus, dauphinoise and kale. Puddings have included pear and almond tart with pear sorbet and caramel sauce, and passionfruit crème brûlée.

Chef Mihaela Bratu **Owner** Hillbrooke Hotels **Seats** 40, Pr/dining room 77 **Times** 12-2.30/7-9 **Prices** Starter £5.50-£7.95, Main £12.95-£19.50, Dessert £6.75-£7 **Wines** 10 bottles over £30, 21 bottles under £30, 11 by glass **Parking** 15 **Notes** Sunday L £15.95-£19.50, Vegetarian available, Children welcome

Cerise Restaurant at The Forbury Hotel

🏵🏵 Modern British

tel: 0118 952 7770 **26 The Forbury RG1 3EJ**
email: reception@theforburyhotel.co.uk web: www.theforburyhotel.co.uk
dir: *Telephone for detailed directions*

Sharply delineated brasserie cooking in a cherry-red basement

The hotel frontage is a stolid porticoed affair that does nothing to prepare you for the dramatic ambience of the basement Cerise Restaurant. High side-windows let in plenty of natural light, avoiding the gloomy air that can afflict subterranean dining rooms. Indeed, the restaurant lives up to its name with cherry-red the prevailing tone, while mock-crocodile banquette seating and tub chairs at smartly set tables look the part. Expect a lively menu of pop brasserie food, cooked to order, with sharply delineated flavours and attention to often surprisingly classical detail. A pair of fat croquettes of haddock and mussel arrive on a bed of dill-sauced leeks for a bravura opener, which may be followed by something gamey such as sautéed breast of partridge with a little pie of the confit leg, honey-glazed spicy parsnips, sweet potato and a deeply rich and satisfying game jus. Pastry-work for desserts is top-notch, crisp and brittle for a glazed prune and Armagnac filling, served alongside candied kumquats and a mild-mannered but impressive milk sorbet.

Chef Michael Parke **Seats** 72, Pr/dining room 35 **Times** 12-2/7-10 **Prices** Starter £6-£10.50, Main £14.50-£22.50, Dessert £8.50-£10.50, Service optional **Wines** 70 bottles over £30, 24 bottles under £30, 11 by glass **Parking** 18 **Notes** Sunday L, Vegetarian available, Children welcome

The Vineyard

Modern French V 🍷 NOTABLE
WINE LIST

tel: 01635 528770 **Stockcross RG20 8JU**
email: general@the-vineyard.co.uk web: www.the-vineyard.co.uk
dir: *From M4 take A34 towards Newbury, exit at 3rd junct for Speen. Right at rdbt then right again at 2nd rdbt*

World-class wines and finely tuned modern French cuisine amid five-star splendour

Not one to rest on its thoroughly five-star, contemporary country house laurels, The Vineyard has recently revamped its already luxurious accommodation and chic public areas and added a glossy spa. However, the classy, intelligent French cooking of Daniel Galmiche makes the place a dining destination in its own right. The foodie business goes on in an elegant dining room, where a sweeping staircase sports a balustrade resembling a grapevine coiling between the two levels, tables are dressed in their best whites, and splendid artwork jazzes up the walls. The unstuffy front-of-house team are fully versed in both the menu and – rather impressively – the world-class wine list. The menu concept is to choose four or five dishes and then trust the expert sommelier to match each with a

suitable wine. Alternatively, there are two tasting menus – the seven-course Judgement which pairs dishes up with both Californian and French wines so you can vote for your favourite, or the Discovery with matching wines chosen from lesser-known parts of the world. Whichever route you choose, expect excellent marriages of flavour and texture, and a lot of fun. Lyme Bay skate wing with parsnip, cima di rape greens and capers is an intelligently conceived dish built on ingredients of the highest quality. Next up, there is both artistry and complexity in a composition that works a multitude of textures involving loin of veal, Jerusalem artichoke, rainbow chard and hazelnuts. It all ends on a technically impressive and creative high with white chocolate and passionfruit terrine with exotic purées and coconut. By the way, they don't make wine at The Vineyard – nor do they have any grapevines – but they do serve some pretty amazing wines from a cellar that runs to a staggering 30,000 bottles, with around 100 available by the glass.

Chef Daniel Galmiche **Owner** Sir Peter Michael **Seats** 86, Pr/dining room 140 **Times** 12-2/7-9.30 **Prices** Fixed L 3 course £29, Tasting menu £39-£99, Starter £8-£16, Main £17-£28, Dessert £8-£14, Service optional **Wines** 2800 bottles over £30, 60 bottles under £30, 120 by glass **Parking** 100 **Notes** ALC 2/3 course £62/£72, Tasting menu 5/7 course, Sunday L £39, Children welcome

Forbury's Restaurant

French, European NOTABLE WINE LIST

tel: 0118 957 4044 **1 Forbury Square RG1 3BB**
email: forburys@btconnect.com
dir: *In town centre, opposite Forbury Gardens*

Refined, confident cooking in smartly contemporary venue

Cross the small terrace and enter the smart, warm and inviting interior of Forbury's, with its floor-to-ceiling windows, white-clothed tables, spotlights in the ceiling reflected in mirrors, and young, approachable and friendly staff. The kitchen is a forward-thinking sort of place, stamping its own distinctive style on dishes, turning out pig's cheek broth with root vegetables and roasted sweetbreads, then roast cod fillet with oxtail and mustard sauce and braised red cabbage. An international element is discernible along with variations on classics: tuna céviche, say, with pickled melon and fennel alongside ballotine of foie gras with Sauternes jelly, almonds and toasted brioche, followed by sea bass fillets with salsa verde, green beans and herb-crushed potatoes, or confit duck leg with cassoulet, celeriac mash, figs and marrowbone. Desserts can vary from good old English lemon posset to peanut butter parfait with salted butter caramel.

Chef Chris Prow **Owner** Xavier Le-Bellego **Seats** 80, Pr/dining room 16
Times 12-2.15/6-10 Closed 26-28 Dec, 1-2 Jan, Sun **Prices** Fixed L 2 course £15, Fixed D 3 course £23, Tasting menu £65-£75, Starter £7.25-£13.50, Main £13.50-£28, Dessert £7.50-£9.50, Service optional 12.5% **Wines** 185 bottles over £30, 19 bottles under £30, 12 by glass **Parking** 40 **Notes** Tasting menu 6 course, Vegetarian available, Children 6 yrs+

The French Horn

Traditional French v

tel: 0118 969 2204 **Sonning RG4 6TN**
email: info@thefrenchhorn.co.uk **web:** www.thefrenchhorn.co.uk
dir: *From Reading take A4 E to Sonning. Follow B478 through village over bridge, hotel on right, car park on left*

Classical French dining on the Thames

The riverside setting is a treat rain or shine, but especially in the latter, when the dining room opens up onto the terrace to give views of all the live action on the Thames. The lounge bar ensures all-weather satisfaction, though, perhaps with ducks spit-roasting over the log fire. The family-run French Horn is full of old-school charm and the service is slick and well managed. The menu looks across the Channel for its inspiration, with a classically-minded repertoire, and high prices. A starter of Orkney scallops is a dish alive with vibrant colours – vivid green from the accompanying apples (from their own orchard) and crisp shards of local bacon – with the scallops themselves nicely caramelised. Next up, braised and roasted lamb split with a chive pancake and served with a mint and date sauce, or go for one of those Aylesbury ducks, with apple sauce, sage stuffing and a rich duck sauce. For dessert, rich raspberry soufflé shows the skill in the kitchen, with the sauce poured at the table.

Chef J Diaga **Owner** Emmanuel family **Seats** 70, Pr/dining room 24
Times 12-2/7-9.30 Closed 1-4 Jan **Prices** Fixed L 2 course fr £20.50, Fixed D 3 course £27.50, Starter £14.50-£18, Main £20-£38.90, Dessert £8.90-£12.80
Wines 400 bottles over £30, 7 bottles under £30, 14 by glass **Parking** 40
Notes Sunday L £57.50, Children welcome

Holiday Inn Reading M4 Jct 10

Modern British, Indian

tel: 0118 944 0444 **Wharfedale Rd, Winnersh Triangle RG41 5TS**
email: reservations@hireadinghotel.com **web:** www.hireadinghotel.com
dir: *M4 junct 10/A329(M) towards Reading (E), 1st exit signed Winnersh/Woodley/A329, left at lights into Wharfedale Rd. Hotel on left*

Imaginative modern cooking in a smart new Holiday Inn

It's probably fair to say that the hotel's rather utilitarian moniker wouldn't have you hot-footing it down the M4 for a dinner date, but those in the know are aware that this is a brand-new flagship for the group. Designed with an impressive level of contemporary flair, it's an airy structure with a helical chandelier on the staircase, while the Caprice dining room sports smart linen, fresh flowers, and views of landscaped gardens through full-length windows. Led by a chef with a solid – country house pedigree, the skilled kitchen team delivers well-thought-out menus of modern Mediterranean-inflected ideas built on well-sourced seasonal materials. Lobster ravioli in a light tomato and tarragon cream sauce is the sort of dish you'd love to find all along the motorway network. It is followed by roast rack of lamb with basil potato purée and tomato jam, or there could be a roulade of salmon and sole served with fennel purée and saffron potato. To finish, dark chocolate marquise is paired with spiced banana ice cream.

Chef Graham Weston **Owner** Meridian Reading Ltd **Seats** 120, Pr/dining room 20
Times 12-3/6-11 **Prices** Fixed L 2 course £19.95, Fixed D 3 course £23.95, Service optional **Wines** 7 bottles over £30, 63 bottles under £30, 14 by glass **Parking** 130
Notes Sunday L £19.95-£23.95, Vegetarian available, Children welcome

Malmaison Reading

Modern European, International

tel: 0118 956 2300 & 956 2302 **Great Western House, 18-20 Station Rd RG1 1JX**
email: reading@malmaison.com **web:** www.malmaison.com
dir: *Next to Reading station*

Enlivening brasserie cooking in a restyled railway hotel

The Reading branch of the much-loved Mal chain is a sparkling-white balustraded edifice, formerly the Great Western Railway Hotel, hence its interior proliferation of rail-related memorabilia. Homage duly paid to an era when the trains ran on time, the rest is as breathlessly in-the-moment as can be imagined. A sleek, dark bar is consecrated to premium cocktails and stylistically listed wines, while the street-facing restaurant comes equipped with blinded windows, bare brick walls, exposed ductwork, back-to-back bench seating recalling the old railway couchettes, and lights that look ready to illuminate a Hollywood film-set. A menu of enlivening brasserie food might open with a fun platter of 'lollipops' (chicken satay, prawn tempura, crab spring roll, Thai pork and fishcake bonbon), or a retooled prawn cocktail of admirable simplicity, before moving to coriander-coated rack of lamb with minty yoghurt, or lobster thermidor. A Valrhona chocolate tart brings up the rear.

Chef Marcin Worzalla **Owner** Malmaison Hotels **Seats** 64, Pr/dining room 22
Times 12-2.30/6-10.30 Closed L Sat, D 25 Dec **Prices** Fixed L 2 course £15.95-£39.50, Fixed D 3 course fr £17.95, Starter £4.95-£8.95, Main £12.50-£37, Dessert £5.95-£8.95 **Wines** 45 bottles over £30, 16 bottles under £30, 16 by glass
Parking NCP across road **Notes** Wine D monthly £55, Sunday L £19.95, Vegetarian available, Children welcome

SHINFIELD *continued*

Millennium Madejski Hotel Reading

◉◉ British, International

tel: 0118 925 3500 **Madejski Stadium RG2 OFL**
email: reservations.reading@millenniumhotels.co.uk **web:** www.millenniumhotels.co.uk
dir: *1m N from M4 junct 11. 2m S from Reading town centre*

Modern British dishes in a glam football hotel

The fortunes of Reading FC may not exactly be in the ascendant, but their home, the Madejski Stadium complex, incorporates a winningly contemporary hotel in voguish monochrome and glass. If you're not a supporter, you'll need to know it's junction 11 off the M4. Cilantro is the main restaurant, reached via a stylish champagne bar. With smartly attired tables and staff, it all feels suitably executive-boxish, and there is some vibrant modern British food in prospect. Nanny Williams blue goats' cheese is the ingredient in a starter soufflé, which comes with the fitting companion of a Granny Smith sorbet, looking for all the world like a dessert. Mains might include wonderful seasonal grouse with creamed cabbage, game chips, watercress and gutsy Cumberland sauce, or steamed John Dory with a scallop and wild mushrooms. Finish with orange millefeuille and white chocolate parfait, daringly seasoned with rosemary. There is also a Menu Gourmand taster, in both regular and vegetarian versions.

Times 7-10 Closed 25 Dec, 1 Jan, BHs, Sun-Mon, L all week

Mya Lacarte

◉ Modern British

tel: 0118 946 3400 **5 Prospect St, Caversham RG4 8JB**
email: eat@myalacarte.co.uk
dir: *M4 junct 10, continue onto A3290/A4 signed Caversham. At Crown Plaza Hotel continue over Caversham Bridge, restaurant 3rd left*

Carefully-sourced British produce on the high street

With a love of food that extends to promoting sustainability and environmental conservation, the team behind Mya Lacarte show a good and healthy approach to life. The menu indicates veggie dishes and points out what to go for if you have various allergies and intolerances, and first and foremost the idea is to keep things as local and seasonal as possible. So you might start with local beetroot (puréed, pickled and confit) partnered with Shropshire goats' cheese, or go for Watlington pork belly carpaccio. Follow on with pan-fried Gressingham duck with the accompanying leg, honey-roasted parsnips, red cabbage, cranberry chutney and duck jus, or the fishy catch of the day, finishing with chocolate and beetroot pudding. Situated right in the heart of Caversham, this unpretentious, modish establishment is a fine example of a contemporary neighbourhood restaurant. More power to its elbow.

Chef Justin Le Stephany **Owner** Matthew Siadatan **Seats** 35, Pr/dining room 12 **Times** 12-3/5-10.30 Closed 25-26 Dec, 1 Jan, D Sun **Prices** Fixed L 2 course £14.95, Fixed D 3 course £14.95-£18.95, Tasting menu £50-£65, Starter £5.95-£8, Main £14.95-£23, Dessert £5.95-£8, Service optional **Wines** 10 bottles over £30, 20 bottles under £30, 10 by glass **Parking** NCP **Notes** Sunday L £5.95-£23, Vegetarian available, Children welcome

SHINFIELD	Map 5 SU76

L'Ortolan

◉◉◉◉ *– see opposite and advert below*

l'ortolan

Indulge in the
L'Ortolan Experience

Exquisite contemporary French cuisine by Alan Murchison, exceptional service and a warm welcome

5 minutes from J11 of M4,
L'Ortolan, Church Lane, Shinfield, Reading, RG2 9BY

Reservations and enquiries
0118 988 8500 or book a table online

www.lortolan.com

◉ ◉ ◉ ◉

The L'Ortolan Experience

Chef's Table   Chef's Experience   Cookery Masterclasses   Private Dining   Weddings

L'Ortolan

Modern French V NOTABLE WINE LIST

tel: 0118 988 8500 **Church Ln RG2 9BY**
email: info@lortolan.com **web:** www.lortolan.com
dir: *From M4 junct 11 take A33 towards Basingstoke. At 1st lights turn left, after garage turn left, 1m turn right at Six Bells pub. Restaurant 1st left (follow tourist signs)*

Consummate modern French style in a former vicarage

The handsome red-brick house was built as a vicarage – lucky old vicar – and enjoys a peaceful spot down a quiet lane in the peaceful village (lucky vicar again), with the hubbub of Reading and the M4 not a million miles away. This is very much a destination restaurant, a fine-fining set up with private dining rooms and multi-course tasting menus serving up culinary fireworks. The smart dining room has a conservatory extension giving views over the pretty gardens. Executive chef Alan Murchison is a dynamic restaurateur with a passion for classically – minded modern French cooking, offered via a tasting menu gourmand, a sensibly short à la carte, and a menu du jour at available lunchtime (which is pretty good value as it happens). The full-on gourmand menu might kick things off with a dish of sesame-crusted tuna served with seared scallops, compressed watermelon and radish salad, a dish which depends on pin-point timing and finely judged balancing of flavours, all duly delivered. Another course pairs duck and pineapple, with a ginger jus unifying the dish into a satisfying whole. A fish main course might be stone bass, the fillet cooked just right, and served up with salsify, parsley purée and girolles. Dishes are presented with real style and verve throughout .There's a vegetarian version of the gourmand menu, too, which offers up some classy veggie dishes such as hen's egg and truffle ravioli with artichokes and salsify, and a pumpkin risotto with Amaretto crumb and sage butter. A dessert of salted chocolate mousse partnered with coconut sorbet and confit passionfuit shows the creativity and craft continues through to the finale, as does another of almond pannacotta with poached pears, candied almonds and pear sorbet. As an alternative, or if you've room for more, the cheese trolley is a tantalising option, full up with a British selection served with home-made raisin bread and biscuits. The wine list is a class act, with organic and biodynamic options, and a sommelier on hand to help you through. There are wine flight options, too.

Chef Alan Murchison **Owner** Newfee Ltd **Seats** 58, Pr/dining room 22 **Times** 12-2/7-9 Closed 2 wks Xmas-New Year, Sun-Mon **Prices** Fixed L 2 course £28-£58, Fixed D 3 course £65, Tasting menu £49-£105 **Wines** 200 bottles over £30, 14 bottles under £30, 11 by glass **Parking** 30 **Notes** Chef's table, Children welcome

SLOUGH

Map 6 SU97

Hilton London Heathrow Airport Terminal 5

 British, International NEW

tel: 01753 686860 **Poyle Rd, Colnbrook SL3 OFF**
email: heathrowairportterminal5.info@hilton.com
web: www.hilton.com/heathrowterminal5.com
dir: M25 junct 14, exit onto Horton Rd signed Poyle, Datchet. At 2nd rdbt exit onto Poyle Rd, Heathrow Terminal 5 is 400mtrs on left

Global flavours at Terminal 5

Open all day and located on the mezzanine level of this monolithic hotel by Terminal 5, The Gallery serves up views over the bustling lobby as well offering a long menu that aims to impress with dishes that recall an altogether more pastoral existence. 'From the farm' comes orange- and thyme-crusted rack of Casterbridge lamb served with a potato gratin, spring vegetables and Grand Marnier jus, while 'From the field' there might be Thai vegetable curry with steamed fragrant rice. Start with a good, meaty terrine spiked with apricots served with a Cumberland jelly, or a Cornish crab falafel with beetroot houmous and a pomegranate and chilli salsa. The menu takes a global viewpoint (which seems appropriate in an airport), with a 'From the sea' main course featuring a nicely cooked steamed sea bass fillet perked up with Asian greens and black bean and chilli dressing. Finish with a deconstructed blueberry cheesecake.

Chef Marcus Gregs **Owner** Rishi Sachdev **Seats** 203 **Times Prices** Fixed L 3 course £28.50, Starter £5.95–£12.95, Main £15.95–£32.95, Dessert £6.50–£9.95 **Wines** 20 bottles over £30, 18 bottles under £30, 22 by glass **Parking** 472 **Notes** Sunday L £5.90–£32.95, Vegetarian available, Children welcome

Mr Todiwala's Kitchen

 Modern Pan Asian NEW

tel: 01753 686860 & 766482 **Poyle Rd, Colnbrook SL3 OFF**
email: heathrowairportterminal5.info@hilton.com **web:** www.hilton.com/heathrowt5
dir: M25 junct 14, at rdbt exit Horton Rd signed Poyle, Datchet. 2nd rdbt take 2nd exit onto Poyle Rd

Uplifting pan-Indian cooking at Heathrow's newest terminal

The spanking-new Hilton at Terminal 5 is a classic business-oriented airport hotel, but these days, there is more of an effort to provide distinctiveness in such operations, not least by means of the eating options, which is where TV chef, author and product manufacturer Cyrus Todiwala (he of Café Spice Namaste) comes in. His Kitchen brings pan-Indian style to the scene in a clinically white atmosphere of lime-washed floors and café-style furnishing, with a large wheeled elephant to greet you. Highly spiced, vividly seasoned food is the perfect antidote to corporate anonymity, and is delivered here in the form of tandoori-grilled scallops with their corals alongside hotly spiced peppers and tomato, crab sizzled in mustard seeds and chilli with grated coconut, and mains such as lamb shank bhuna with caramelised onions and yoghurt, pomfret glazed in green coconut chutney and steamed in a banana leaf, and venison tikka singing with star-anise and fennel. Crème brûlée is given thrilling aromatic uplift with saffron, cardamom and ginger.

Chef Cyrus Todiwala, Arun Dev **Owner** Shiva Hotels, Cyrus Todiwala **Seats** 70 **Times** 6–22.30 Closed Xmas, Sun **Prices** Fixed L 2 course fr £19.95, Fixed D 2 course £65, Tasting menu £45–£70, Starter £6.50–£15.50, Main £6.45–£24.50, Dessert £6.50–£8.20 **Wines** 10 bottles over £30, 11 bottles under £30, 10 by glass **Parking** 480 **Notes** Vegetarian available, Children welcome

WINDSOR

Map 6 SU97

The Greene Oak

 Modern British

tel: 01753 864294 **Oakley Green SL4 5UW**
email: info@thegreeneoak.co.uk

Modern pub dining in a welcoming country inn

The Greene Oak probably couldn't be greener if it tried: the exterior of the pub is painted green, and inside the theme continues, with pale green banquettes and chairs, green legs on chunky wooden tables, green panels on some of the walls and splashes of green in the patterned cushions and blinds. It all makes for a very fresh and vibrant look, which is reflected in the waiting staff who are as cheery and welcoming as they come. The modern pub food takes its influences from Europe and beyond, and relies on top-notch, seasonal British ingredients. The carte is supplemented by a daily-changing set menu at lunchtime and some blackboard specials, the latter possibly bringing forth breaded beef rib fingers with braised red cabbage to start: an unusual dish with good textural contrast (moist, tender beef, crispy coating) and great flavour. Main course could be as simple as a sea-fresh roast skate wing with fat-cut chips, seasonal greens and caper and butter sauce, while dessert could end on a fruity note with warm spiced poached plums sitting atop a nicely made pear and almond tart.

Chef Craig Teasdale **Owner** Henry & Katherine Cripps **Seats** 85 **Times** 12–2.15/6–9.15 **Prices** Fixed L 2 course fr £15, Starter £5.50–£7.90, Main £13.20–£17.90, Dessert £5.50–£7 **Wines** 24 bottles over £30, 27 bottles under £30, 21 by glass **Parking** 50 **Notes** Vegetarian available, Children welcome

Macdonald Windsor Hotel

 Scottish, Modern British

tel: 0844 8799101 **23 High St SL4 1LH**
email: gm.windsor@macdonaldwindsor.co.uk **web:** www.macdonaldhotels.co.uk
dir: M4 junct 6 A355, take A332, rdbt 1st exit signed town centre. In 0.7m turn left into Bachelors Acre

Contemporary Scottish dining opposite Windsor Castle

Right opposite the castle, the Macdonald group's boutique hotel was once a branch of John Lewis. The culinary compass in the cool and contemporary Caley's restaurant is set firmly to the north of the border, driven by a Josper charcoal grill to ensure that the kitchen sends out fabulous cuts of prime Scottish beef. Ham hock and parsley terrine with piccalilli get things going in an unfussy manner, ahead of rib-eye steak with thick chips and béarnaise, or Highland lamb cutlets, while more delicate palates might opt for lemon sole with capers and parsley butter. Desserts play unashamedly to the crowd with the nursery comforts of sticky toffee pudding with rich vanilla ice cream, or a fashionably retro knickerbocker glory up for grabs.

Chef Gareth Long **Owner** Macdonald Hotels **Seats** 70, Pr/dining room 24 **Times** 7–10 **Prices** Starter £6.50–£8.50, Main £10.50–£27.50, Dessert £4.50–£8.90, Service optional **Wines** 23 bottles over £30, 18 bottles under £30, 12 by glass **Parking** 30, Pre-booked and chargeable **Notes** Sunday L £19–£23, Vegetarian available, Children welcome

Mercure Windsor Castle Hotel

 Modern British

tel: 0870 400 8300 & 01753 851577 **18 High St SL4 1LJ**
email: h6618@accor.com **web:** www.mercure.com
dir: M25 junct 13 take A308 towards town centre then onto B470 to High St. M4 junct 6 towards A332, at rdbt first exit into Clarence Rd, left at lights to High St

Stimulating contemporary cooking in a regal setting

The handsome, balconied, four-storey hotel, a coaching-inn built in the 16th century, is in distinctly elevated company in Windsor. Just over the road is the Royal Guildhall, and the Queen's Berkshire castle residence and its grounds are only a short stroll. Interiors are done in suave modern style, and the dining-room is named 18 after the hotel's address on the High Street. Chairs upholstered in regal purple look good against white walls and burnished wood tables, while the contemporary cooking is fashioned from conscientiously sourced seasonal materials. Some of the dishes look like familiar modern classics such as pressed ham hock terrine with piccalilli or seared scallops with cauliflower purée. Others set out into new territory, like the stimulating opener of home-cured salmon with orange jelly and fennel, while mains take in slow-cooked pork belly with carrot and vanilla purée, or cod with romanesco and a tangy dressing of apricot and lime. Veg are extra, and desserts smartly bring up the rear with the likes of orange cheesecake and raspberry sorbet.

Chef Damyan Stefanov **Owner** Mercure Hotels **Seats** 60, Pr/dining room 300
Times 12-2.30/6.30-9.45 **Prices** Fixed L 2 course £19.50, Fixed D 3 course £25, Starter £5.25-£7.95, Main £12.50-£19.50, Dessert £6.50-£8.50, Service optional **Wines** 12 bottles over £30, 24 bottles under £30, 14 by glass **Parking** 112 **Notes** Sunday L £19.50-£24.50, Vegetarian available, Children welcome

Oakley Court Hotel

 Modern European V

tel: 01753 609988 **Windsor Rd, Water Oakley SL4 5UR**
email: reservations@theoakleycourthotel.com **web:** www.theoakleycourthotel.com
dir: M4 junct 6 to Windsor. At rdbt right onto A308. Hotel 2.5m on right

Creative modern European cooking amid Victorian Gothic extravagance

The Victorians left the British Isles strewn with a magnificent legacy of Gothic castles. Oakley Court is a prime example, with turrets, stepped gables and 37 acres of well-tended grounds. As you would expect in a hotel of this standing, there's golf, tennis and swimming on tap, or pampering in the treatment rooms. The half-panelled dining room, with its crisply clothed tables and formal service, is the place to head to for creative modern European cooking built on diligently-sourced local ingredients. The contemporary classic pairing of shellfish and pig is celebrated in an opener combining caramelised scallops with Ibérico ham, Cornish crab, and fresh peas, before a big-hearted main course partnering roast rib-eye with the robust flavours of confit oxtail, pan-fried ceps, Maxim potatoes and a meaty jus. Fish might be Loch Duart salmon served with a stew of clams and mussels, with smoked tomato butter and lemon chard potatoes. Finish with a white chocolate and peanut mousse with salted caramel, chocolate soil and peanut sugar.

Chef Kai Taylor **Owner** Vinyl Space Ltd **Seats** 100, Pr/dining room 33
Times 12-2.30/6.30-9.30 Closed L Sat **Prices** Prices not confirmed **Wines** **Parking** 200 **Notes** Sunday L, Children welcome

Sir Christopher Wren Hotel and Spa

 Modern British

tel: 01753 442400 **Thames St SL4 1PX**
email: wrens@sarova.co.uk **web:** www.sirchristopherwren.co.uk
dir: M4 junct 6, 1st exit from relief road, follow signs to Windsor, 1st major exit on left, turn left at lights

Modish cooking by the River Thames

Right next to Eton Bridge, with the river flowing past, there's no quibbling about the name of the Thames View Restaurant-it's a peach of a position, and the windows are expansive enough to give everyone a view. The man himself-Sir Christopher-had connections to Windsor but didn't design the hotel, but that's not to say it isn't a handsome and characterful building, and there's even room for spa and leisure facilities. The restaurant is smart and comfortable, with linen-clad tables and a menu that follows a modern British path. Start with ham hock and foie gras terrine with spiced plums and sakura cress, or oak-smoked salmon with capers, shallots and lemon, before a main course such as sea bass with crab and saffron risotto, confit fennel and saffron cream sauce. To finish, dark chocolate truffle torte with raspberry sorbet hits the spot.

Chef Lee Clarke **Owner** Sarova Hotels **Seats** 65, Pr/dining room 100
Times 12.30-2.30/6.30-10 **Prices** Fixed D 3 course fr £31.50, Starter £6-£10.50, Main £15-£24.50, Dessert £6-£10, Service optional **Wines** 20 bottles over £30, 35 bottles under £30, 10 by glass **Parking** 14, Pre-bookable only, Riverside train station **Notes** Pre-theatre D available, Sunday L £24.95-£26.50, Vegetarian available, Children welcome

BRISTOL

BRISTOL   Map 4 ST57

The Avon Gorge Hotel

 Modern British

tel: 0117 973 8955 **Sion Hill, Clifton BS8 4LD**
email: rooms@theavongorge.com **web:** www.theavongorge.com
dir: From S: M5 junct 19, A369 to Clifton Toll, over suspension bridge, 1st right into Sion Hill. From N: M5 junct 18A, A4 to Bristol, under suspension bridge, follow signs to bridge, exit Sion Hill

Splendid Clifton location and modern British cooking

The Victorian builders of the hotel chose their site well: at one end of Brunel's landmark suspension bridge, overlooking the gorge and the bridge itself. In the restaurant, floor-to-ceiling windows open on to a terrace with some of the city's best views. There's more to the cooking than the self-styled modern British tag would suggest, with the enterprising kitchen turning out grilled sardines with warm tomato vinaigrette, spring vegetable tarte Tatin with rocket pesto and mozzarella, and confit pork belly with cider and brandy sauce and bubble-and-squeak made with black pudding. There's also ham hock terrine with piccalilli and cider jelly, followed by a choice of steaks with béarnaise, or perhaps seared chicken breast with potato and garlic salad and mushrooms. Fish options are worth exploring – pan-fried halibut fillet with broad beans, peas and lemon butter perhaps – and to cap a meal might be steamed nectarine pudding with custard.

Chef Luke Trott **Owner** Swire Hotels **Seats** 50, Pr/dining room 20 **Times** 12-4/6-10 **Prices** Fixed L 2 course £9.95, Starter £5.25-£8.95, Main £9.95-£22.95, Dessert £5.25-£5.95 **Wines** 21 bottles under £30, 24 by glass **Parking** 25 **Notes** Sunday L £15.95-£18.95, Vegetarian available, Children welcome

BRISTOL *continued*

Berwick Lodge

◎◎ Modern British **NEW**

tel: 0117 958 1590 **Berwick Dr, Henbury BS10 7TD**
email: info@berwicklodge.co.uk **web:** www.berwicklodge.co.uk
dir: *M5 junct 17, A4018 (Westbury-on-Trym). At 2nd rdbt 1st left (Westbury-on-Trym). At next rdbt double back on dual carriageway (signed M5 (M4)). Left after brown Clifton RFC sign. At x-rds straight on, follow Berwick Lodge signs*

Top-class contemporary dining in a swankily restored mansion

Lording it on a hilltop in 18 acres of garden and woodland, Berwick Lodge is a grand Victorian country mansion restored to glory in 2009 with 10 plush rooms and a rather swanky restaurant. While the setting is all classic country-house formality, with plasterwork columns and well-spaced tables dressed in their best whites, the kitchen ensures that the food strikes a contemporary pose. Starters such as hand-dived scallops with pumpkin tofu and pine nut praline show creative flair. Even more impressively, a main course of tender hay-baked Somerset Cabrito goat's leg matched with a light beer sauce, smoked onion, braised baby gem and goat's cheese tortellini is evidence of a kitchen that is not scared to deploy unusual ingredients to impressive effect. Top-class, well-sourced and seasonal produce is a mainstay of fishy ideas such as seared line-caught bass with artichoke, braised baby onions, crosnes, and parsley barley, while foraged ingredients turn up in a dessert of wild damson soufflé with honeycomb ice cream.

Chef Ross Marshall **Owner** S & F Arikan **Seats** 80, Pr/dining room 16
Times 12-2.30/6.30-10 Closed D Sun **Prices** Fixed L 3 course £22.50-£25, Fixed D 3 course £35, Tasting menu £55-£65, Starter £10-£12, Main £18-£22, Dessert £8, Service optional 10% **Wines** 350 bottles over £30, 30 bottles under £30, 13 by glass **Parking** 100 **Notes** Sunday L £25, Vegetarian available, Children welcome

Best Western Henbury Lodge Hotel

◎◎ Modern British

tel: 0117 950 2615 **Station Rd, Henbury BS10 7QQ**
email: info@henburyhotel.com **web:** www.henburyhotel.com
dir: *M5 junct 17/A4018 towards city centre, 3rd rdbt right into Crow Ln. At end turn right, hotel 200mtrs on right*

Charming Georgian country-house hotel near Bristol

Henbury Lodge, a white Georgian property in attractive grounds, is an inviting place at which to tarry, with comfortably updated interior, cosy bar and Blaise Restaurant. This is a handsome room, with a wooden floor, creamy-coloured walls hung with gilt-framed mirrors, brown leather chairs at unclothed tables and French doors opening on to a terrace and walled garden. The kitchen sources its ingredients carefully for its monthly-changing menu and works around a contemporary repertory. Starters include goats' cheese baked with honey and thyme on balsamic-dressed leaves with red onion marmalade, and pan-fried fillet of red mullet with chorizo and tomatoes. Dishes tend to be comfortingly reassuring: main courses of grilled sirloin steak with Stilton and rosemary butter, for instance, and roast cod fillet on Savoy cabbage with parsley and lemon dressing. Or there might be more adventurous roast leg of rabbit in Parma ham stuffed with apple and black pudding on sautéed leeks with mustard sauce. Finish with the house 'taster slate' of ice creams, or push the boat out with rich dark chocolate tart with pears poached with lemongrass and thyme.

Chef Paul Bullard **Owner** Tim & Rosalind Forester **Seats** 22, Pr/dining room 12
Times 7-10 Closed Xmas-New Year, Sun, L all week **Prices** Fixed D 3 course £25.95, Service optional 10% **Wines** 1 bottle over £30, 16 bottles under £30, 14 by glass **Parking** 20 **Notes** Vegetarian available, Children welcome

Bordeaux Quay

◎ Modern European

tel: 0117 943 1200 **V-Shed, Canons Way BS1 5UH**
email: info@bordeaux-quay.co.uk
dir: *Canons Rd off the A4, beyond Millennium Square car park*

Modern warehouse conversion covering all bases on the Bristol waterfront

This dynamic set up on Bristol's waterfront takes in a restaurant, brasserie, bar, deli, bakery and cookery school in a stylishly redeveloped dockland warehouse. The operation's eco-credentials mean there's a strong commitment to sustainability and sourcing local, preferably organic, materials which it brings together in well-conceived, daily-changing menus of modern European ideas. The restaurant is on the first floor, with elegant table settings and fine wood alongside industrial pipe work, or you might opt for an alfresco meal on the terrace of the brasserie downstairs. Start with excellent quality artisan charcuterie served with grilled Mediterranean vegetables, mozzarella, rocket and olives. Next up, a classic onglet (skirt) steak with aïoli, caramelised onions, proper fries and a salad, or slow-cooked ox cheek in red wine and spices with rosemary polenta might catch the eye. To finish, a rich dark chocolate torte is served with raspberry coulis, creamy honeycomb ice cream and crunchy honeycomb chunks.

Chef Alex Murray, Andy Pole **Owner** Alex & Luke Murray **Seats** 90, Pr/dining room 28
Times 12-10.30 All-day dining **Prices** Starter £6.50-£11, Main £13.50-£21, Dessert £7-£9.50 **Wines** 40 bottles over £30, 40 bottles under £30, 30 by glass **Parking** Millennium Square **Notes** Breakfast from 8am Mon-Fri, 9 Sat-Sun, Sunday L £13.50-£20.50, Vegetarian available, Children welcome

Casamia Restaurant

◎◎◎◎ – *see opposite page*

Glass Boat Restaurant

◎◎ Modern French

tel: 0117 929 0704 **Welsh Back BS1 4SB**
email: bookings@glassboat.co.uk
dir: *Moored below Bristol Bridge in the old centre of Bristol*

Modern bistro fare on a glamorous barge

Not a mere glass-bottomed boat, please note, but an extensively glazed former barge that floats in the Severn Estuary at the old Bristol docklands, this is one of the city's more individually styled eateries. You may need your sea-legs if the current is high, but the ambience of walnut floors, a beautiful marble bar at the bow end, and pictures that crowd the walls is too glamorous to miss for the sake of a bit of bobbing about. The menu offers modern bistro fare with plenty of imagination, plying a course from smoked trout with pickled fennel, or scallops with salted caramel and Jerusalem artichoke galette, to venison loin with poached pear and caramelised walnuts. Lighter lunchtime dishes are full of appeal too – perhaps something like dill-laced salmon and prawn fishcakes with wilted spinach and hollandaise. Finish with zesty lemon posset and biscotti. Theatre-goers can enjoy a good-value supper until 7pm.

Times 12-2.30/5.30-10.30 Closed 24-26 Dec, 1-10 Jan, L Mon, D Sun

Casamia Restaurant

BRISTOL   Map 4 ST57

Modern British **V**

tel: 0117 959 2884 **38 High St, Westbury Village, Westbury-on-Trym BS9 3DZ**
email: info@casamiarestaurant.co.uk
dir: *Close to Westbury College Gatehouse*

Exciting progressive cooking following the seasons

The name may suggest a cosy neighbourhood Italian, and Casamia may be a family business using the homely name of 'my house', but these days the restaurant is a hotbed of contemporary cooking at the cutting-edge end of the culinary spectrum. It opened its doors in 1999, and with all respect to Paco and Susan Sanchez-Iglesias, things really started to happen when their sons Peter and Jonray took over the kitchen and began to develop their style of bold modern cooking. The entrance is reminiscent of holidays in Spain – wrought iron gate, exposed-brick corridor – and there's a homeliness to the interior, with its beamed ceiling and confident neutrality, and decorative touches to reflect the seasons. And seasonality is the mantra that drives this whole operation: even the decor changes in step with the menu in order constantly to ring the changes and keep all of the senses stimulated. The team in the kitchen brings a touch of theatre to the experience, delivering the food to the table and giving detailed and passionate explanations of each dish. Indeed, the service is charming all round. You don't need to fret over choosing what you want to eat here as there's just the one multi-course dinner menu plus a shorter lunch option, and a tweaked version should you choose to take the chef's table route. Even the menu descriptions give little away, restricting the information to listing a couple of components – 'goats' cheese and beetroot', say, or 'breakfast egg' – so it is very much a case of choosing a bottle of wine and putting your trust in Peter and Jonray. You're in safe hands though: every dish is developed and crafted for maximum flavour impact and dressed to thrill – vivid colours, cocktail glasses, a mix of plates, perfect swipes – but first and foremost it's about taste. Take a dish of spelt, parsley and garlic, for example, a simple enough idea which is executed perfectly, with a deeply intense flavour, or the John Dory with spring greens and cider, the fish topped with a sliver of citrus jelly – this is fantastic fare. There's rainbow trout with variations of cabbage (another stunner), and lamb with an allium stew, mint sauce and potatoes. For dessert you might be treated to a riff on blood orange and rosemary, or rhubarb and vanilla.

Chef Peter & Jonray Sanchez-Iglesias **Owner** Sanchez-Iglesias family **Seats** 40, Pr/dining room 6
Times 12-2/6-9.30 Closed Xmas, New Year, BHs, Sun-Mon
Prices Tasting menu £38-£125, Service optional **Wines** 45 bottles over £30, 9 bottles under £30, 9 by glass
Parking On street **Notes** Children welcome

BRISTOL *continued*

Goldbrick House

 Modern British

tel: 0117 945 1950 **69 Park St BS1 5PB**
email: info@goldbrickhouse.co.uk
dir: *M32, follow signs for city centre. Left side of Park St, going up the hill towards museum*

Modern brasserie cooking in an all-things-to-all-comers venue

You're not exactly stuck for choice when it comes to eating and drinking options at Goldbrick House. In a converted pair of conjoined Georgian townhouses, an informal all-day café/bar, a champagne and cocktail bar, a main restaurant and now the Orangery, a new extension, appear to have all bases covered. That last, formerly the Terrace, is a light-filled space with many windows and bright violet seating, while the main restaurant goes for a mustard-hued look, with Italian chandeliers and large gilt-framed mirrors. Christian Wragg has taken over in the kitchens, but maintains Goldbrick's modern brasserie style in starters such as lamb arancini in redcurrant dressing with minty salad, and mains that mine the heritage cookbook for beef bourguignon with whipped truffle mash, herbed chicken breast with gnocchi and roasted onions, or grilled lemon sole in shellfish broth topped with puff pastry. Fun specials include the de rigueur Scotch egg made with black pudding, and a Bloody Mary version of prawn cocktail, while a nostalgic return to childhood produces finishers like peanut butter crème brûlée with home-made Jammy Dodgers.

Chef Christian Wragg **Owner** Dougal Templeton, Alex Reilley, Mike Bennett **Seats** 200, Pr/dining room 40 **Times** noon-10.30 Closed 25-26 Dec, 1 Jan, Sun All-day dining **Prices** Fixed L 2 course £12, Fixed D 3 course £28.95, Tasting menu £27.50, Starter £5.50-£8.95, Main £14.25-£24.95, Dessert £4.50-£7.50 **Wines** 14 bottles over £30, 22 bottles under £30, 12 by glass **Parking** On street, NCP **Notes** Early D menu 6-6.45pm, Vegetarian available, Children welcome

Hotel du Vin Bristol

 French ▼ NOTABLE WINE LIST

tel: 0844 736 4252 **The Sugar House, Narrow Lewins Mead BS1 2NU**
email: info.bristol@hotelduvin.com **web:** www.hotelduvin.com
dir: *From M4 junct 19, M32 into Bristol. At rdbt take 1st exit & follow main road to next rdbt. Turn onto other side of carriageway, hotel 200yds on right*

Contemporary brasserie fare and exceptional wine list

The HdV formula is familiar enough: the Bristol outpost is found in an 18th-century building near the waterfront and features bare floorboards, banquettes, unclothed wooden tables with candles, and references to wine all over the place (the list is massive). The lively, cheery atmosphere is helped along by well-drilled, friendly staff. Much of the appeal is down to the contemporary take on well-worn brasserie fare, with a good balance between seafood and meat, so expect dressed crab, or devilled kidneys, followed by moules frites, or roast belly pork with Agen prune sauce and mustard dauphinoise. Raw materials are of the top order and the kitchen's care and attention evident in, for instance, tender, lean steak tartare, then a classic example of properly timed lemon sole meunière. Finish with something like rich chocolate pavé offset by crunchy candied pistachios and vanilla ice cream.

Chef Marcus Lang **Owner** KSL Partnership **Seats** 85, Pr/dining room 72 **Times** 12-2.30/6-10.30 Closed L 31 Dec **Prices** Prices not confirmed **Wines** 332 bottles over £30, 18 bottles under £30, 23 by glass **Parking** 8, NCP Rupert St **Notes** Prix Fixe 2/3 course £16.95/£19.95, Sunday L, Vegetarian available, Children welcome

Juniper

 Modern

tel: 0117 942 1744 & 07717 277490 **21 Cotham Road South BS6 5TZ**
email: enq@juniperrestaurant.co.uk

Buzzy neighbourhood place with creative cooking

A neighbourhood restaurant with a good deal of ambition, Juniper serves up some bright and creative food to the people of Cotham and Kingsdown. The vivid blue frontage stands out on Cotham Road South, and once inside all is relaxed and unpretentious-just what you want in a neighbourhood restaurant. The menu pays due respect to the seasons, and the produce of the region, to deliver inventive and full-flavoured dishes. Seared king scallops, for example, nicely caramelised on top, come with a piece of crispy pork belly, sticky coconut rice and oriental stock in a creative twist on a modern classic. Main-course pavé of aged Somerset beef doesn't want for flavour either, partnered with creamed cheddar leeks, baby onions, chorizo- and tomato-flavoured potatoes, and a Cabernet jus. Finish with a warm apple pudding with butterscotch sauce and vanilla bean ice cream.

Chef Nick Kleiner, Simon Line **Owner** Anita & Nick Kleiner **Seats** 70, Pr/dining room 30 **Times** 6.30-12 Closed 26-30 Dec, L all week **Prices** Prices not confirmed **Wines** **Notes** Tasting menu 8 course, Vegetarian available, Children welcome

No.4 Clifton Village

 Modern European

tel: 0117 970 6869 **Rodney Hotel, 4 Rodney Place, Clifton BS8 4HY**
email: bookings@no4cliftonvillage.co.uk **web:** www.no4cliftonvillage.co.uk
dir: *M5 junct 19, follow signs across Clifton Bridge. At mini rdbt turn onto Clifton Down Rd. Hotel 150yds on right*

Bistro cooking in Clifton

With its ever-changing backdrop of local artworks, No. 4 is situated in the smart Rodney Hotel, a spiffing Georgian townhouse in Clifton. The restaurant is a relaxed and unpretentious space, with huge sash windows, ornate ceilings and oak floorboards, and the promise of a table in the secluded garden when the weather allows. There's a decidedly bistro feel to the place, and on the menu, too, where the choice changes daily and the seasons are respected. Start with goats' cheese on thyme crostini with beetroot purée, for example, or crispy duck leg with steamed bok choy and orange. Next up, go for whole grilled plaice, or seasonal vegetable risotto with parmesan and pesto, and for dessert, gooseberry and toffee crunch tart, or summer berry Eton Mess. Side dishes such as hand-cut chips and glazed Chantenay carrots bump up the prices a little.

Chef David Jones **Owner** Hilary Lawson **Seats** 36, Pr/dining room 50 **Times** 6-10 Closed 25 Dec-2 Jan, Sun, L all week **Prices** Starter £4.50-£7.50, Main £12.50-£17, Dessert £5.95-£7.50 **Wines** 5 bottles over £30, 18 bottles under £30, 7 by glass **Parking** On street **Notes** Afternoon tea £15, Vegetarian available, Children welcome

Follow the AA on twitter @TheAA_Lifestyle

The Pump House

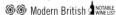 Modern British ⚜ NOTABLE WINE LIST

tel: 0117 927 2229 **Merchants Rd, Hotwells BS8 4PZ**
email: info@the-pumphouse.com **web:** www.the-pumphouse.com
dir: A4 Clevedon to city centre, left before swing bridge

Thriving dockside pub-restaurant with serious approach to food

The one-time hydraulic pumping station on the dockside was ripe for conversion, and chef-proprietor Toby Gritten has judged it just right, creating a buzzy bar and restaurant with a gastro-pub vibe. The scale of the place means there's a place to go whatever mood you're in (or what the weather is like). You can eat downstairs in the pub part of the operation, or sit outside by the water's edge, or head upstairs if you fancy a little less hullabaloo. The kitchen deals in produce from the South West, and it's not just lip-service either, and everything from bread to chutneys are made in-house. Kick off with scallops caught in Lyme Bay and served with celeriac and apple, or maybe rillettes of woodland-reared pork with celeriac and toast. This is robust and hearty stuff, but not without refinement. Main-course beer-battered fish and chips is one way to go, but there's also the likes of tenderloin of pork with celeriac, cavolo nero and apple purée. End on a high with cherry and almond trifle with macaroons, or burnt Cambridge cream with mulled cider sorbet.

Chef Toby Gritten **Owner** Toby Gritten & Dan Obern **Seats** 50 **Times** 12-3.30/6.30-9.30 Closed 25 Dec, Mon-Wed, L Thu, D Sun **Prices** Fixed L 2 course £15, Fixed D 3 course £17.50, Tasting menu £35-£50, Starter £5-£8.50, Main £12-£20, Dessert £6-£8.50 **Wines** 118 bottles over £30, 47 bottles under £30, 22 by glass **Parking** 20 **Notes** Tasting menu 5/8 course, Sunday L £14.50-£18, Vegetarian available, Children welcome

riverstation

⚜ Modern European

tel: 0117 914 4434 & 914 5560 **The Grove BS1 4RB**
email: relax@riverstation.co.uk
dir: On harbour side in central Bristol between St Mary Redcliffe church & Arnolfini

Buzzy riverside setting and modish brasserie food

With its acres of glass and two terraces, it should be possible to see the water wherever you sit. But truth be told, this place is all about the atmosphere and the food. It looks thoroughly modern in the industrial-chic manner-the building was once a river police station-and there's a buzzy café-bar downstairs and cool restaurant on the first floor. The food is serious stuff, based on first-rate seasonal ingredients, and inspiration is drawn from far and wide without ever losing focus. Spice crab börek, for example, come with pickled green tomatoes and sweet chilli dressing, while haricot bean and almond soup is served with mandarin oil and chervil root. These are bright, modish dishes rooted in good culinary sense. Fillet of Cornish gurnard is paired with wild red rice, pak choi and black bean sauce among main courses, and to finish, warm pear and quince crumble with vanilla ice cream is a winning combo.

Chef Toru Yanada **Owner** J Payne & P Taylor **Seats** 120, Pr/dining room 26 **Times** 12-2.30/6-10.30 Closed 24-26 Dec, D Sun **Prices** Fixed L 2 course fr £12.75, Fixed D 3 course fr £18.50, Starter £5.50-£8.50, Main £15.50-£19.50, Dessert £5.50-£7, Service optional **Wines** 34 bottles over £30, 26 bottles under £30, 15 by glass **Parking** Pay & display, meter parking opposite **Notes** Pre-theatre £10 Mon-Fri 6-7.15pm, Fixed D 2/3 course Mon-Fri, Sunday L £16-£19.50, Vegetarian available, Children welcome

The Rockfish Grill & Seafood Market

⚜ Mediterranean, Seafood

tel: 0117 973 7384 **128 Whiteladies Rd, Clifton BS8 2RS**
email: enquiries@rockfishgrill.co.uk
dir: From city centre follow signs for Clifton, restaurant halfway along Whiteladies Rd

Fish and seafood presented fresh and simple

Mitch Tonks' place in the pantheon of latter-day seafood missionaries seems assured. His various establishments, including this portmanteau fish market and restaurant in the Clifton district of the city, maintain a rigorous commitment to freshness and simplicity, all founded on fish and shellfish mostly brought up from the Brixham boats. Piscine artwork and semiology fill the room, and willing, friendly staff make the formula a winning one. How excited is it possible to get about a serving of smoked mackerel mousse on toast? Well, very, when it's this fresh and singing with lemon-zestiness, slathered thickly on grilled ciabatta. The charcoal-burning grill works wonders with sea bass, served with peperonata and basil, monkfish with fennel and watercress, or a crisp-skinned flounder, simply accoutred with boiled potatoes and parsley butter. Rhubarb, meringue, marshmallow and cream owes something to Eton mess, and makes a fine combination, or finish with a selection of European cheeses and roasted quince.

Times 12-2.30/6-10.30 Closed 25 Dec, 1 Jan, Sun-Mon

BRISTOL *continued*

Second Floor Restaurant

◉◉ Modern European ▲ NOTABLE WINE LIST

tel: 0117 961 8898 **Harvey Nichols, 27 Philadelphia St, Quakers Friars BS1 3BZ**
email: Reception.Bristol@harveynichols.com
dir: *Phone for directions*

Lively modern British cooking on the top floor

Other Harvey Nics branches may rise higher (the second-floor home of the restaurant here is the top layer), but only Bristol's Broadmead store overlooks the old Dominican friary of Quakers Friars and the shopping entrepôt of Cabot Circus. Done in gentle umbers and beiges, the dining room is a supremely relaxing place, where Louise McCrimmon offers a menu of lively modern British food. Tea-smoked Creedy Carver duck breast with roast beetroot, poached apple and beetroot jelly makes an attention-seeking opener, or you may be pleasantly surprised by the depth of flavour conjured out of potato and kale soup slicked with chorizo oil. A vegetarian main with broad appeal comes in the form of twice-baked Westcombe Cheddar soufflé with German-style schupfen noodles and pickled oyster mushrooms, or there could be roast sea bass with squid-ink linguini in a cucumber and horseradish emulsion sauce, topped with a crisp-fried oyster. Finish with rhubarb and custard, garnished with rhubarb jelly and mini macaroons, or a plate of West Country and Welsh cheeses with homemade oatcakes and chutney. There are some pretty good wines on offer too.

Chef Louise McCrimmon **Owner** Harvey Nichols Restaurants Ltd **Seats** 60, Pr/dining room 10 **Times** 12-3/6-10 Closed 25 Dec, 1 Jan, Etr Sun, D Sun-Mon **Prices** Fixed L 2 course £17, Fixed D 3 course £20, Starter £6.50-£8, Main £18-£24, Dessert £5-£6.50 **Wines** 310 bottles over £30, 43 bottles under £30, 29 by glass **Parking** NCP/Cabot Circus car park **Notes** Sun brunch 11-4, Afternoon tea daily 3-5, Vegetarian available, Children welcome

BUCKINGHAMSHIRE

■ AMERSHAM	Map 6 SU99

The Artichoke

◉◉◉ – *see opposite page*

The Crown

◉ Modern British

tel: 01494 721541 **16 High St HP7 0DH**
email: reception@thecrownamersham.com **web:** www.thecrownamersham.com
dir: *M40 junct 2 onto A355, continue to Amersham. Onto Gore Hill, left into The Broadway*

Good eating in a modernised coaching inn

This 16th-century timber-framed coaching inn has brushed up nicely after a stylish makeover, and now presents an eclectic rustic-chic look to its 21st-century visitors, mixing ancient period character with a clean-cut modern style. There are Tudor beams, inglenook fireplaces and sloping floors, offset by trendy fabrics and chunky bare wood tables. The unfussy cooking aims for big-hearted natural flavours, serving seared scallops as an opener with crispy cauliflower and a punchy currant and peppercorn vinaigrette, or you might go for home-made balls of hot and crispy breadcrumbed brawn served with piccalilli. Main course brings a well-crafted take on chicken Kiev with truffle butter, braised wing, garlic purée, crispy potatoes and broccoli, while gilthead bream could get a full-flavoured accompaniment of lemon thyme salsify, wild mushrooms, samphire, pommes Anna and red wine jus. After all that richness, crème brûlée gets a lift from lemon verbena, rhubarb and champagne sorbet, and lemon and black pepper shortbread.

Times 12-3/6-9.30

Gilbey's Restaurant

◉◉ Modern British

tel: 01494 727242 **1 Market Square HP7 0DF**
email: oldamersham@gilbeygroup.com
dir: *M40 junct 2, A355 exit Beaconsfield/Amersham*

Imaginative modern cooking in a former school building

A former grammar school building dating from the 17th century is the setting for Gilbey's Old Amersham restaurant and serves its local clientele as a textbook reliable neighbourhood bistro. There are low ceilings, wood flooring and cheerful art on sky-blue walls to create an ambience of stylish, intimate rusticity, while the friendly staff contribute much to the congenial atmosphere that pervades the place. The kitchen makes a virtue of simplicity, working an intelligent vein of appealing modern British ideas that reflects the season's bounty, as in a summery lunch that gets going with a colourful and vibrantly-flavoured starter of seared scallops and crisp pancetta with artichokes, haricot beans, tomato and berries. Next up, the same inventive streak partners an appealingly purple-hued risotto of girolle mushrooms and red wine with radicchio, parmesan, rosemary oil and ciabatta crostini, or there might be rosemary and fennel-braised belly porchetta with crackling, balsamic Puy lentils, broad beans and chicory. To finish, dark chocolate and peanut butter parfait is served to good effect with banana mousse and crystallised chocolate.

Chef Adam Whitlock **Owner** Michael, Bill, Caroline & Linda Gilbey **Seats** 50, Pr/dining room 12 **Times** 12-2.30/6.45-9.45 Closed 24-29 Dec, 1 Jan **Prices** Fixed L 2 course fr £19.50, Fixed D 3 course fr £25.50, Starter £6.50-£10.95, Main £16.95-£25.95, Dessert £7.55-£9.50 **Wines** 7 bottles over £30, 14 bottles under £30, 10 by glass **Parking** On street & car park **Notes** Sunday L £21-£27.50, Vegetarian available, Children welcome

■ AYLESBURY	Map 11 SP81

Hartwell House Hotel, Restaurant & Spa

◉◉ Modern British ▲ NOTABLE WINE LIST

tel: 01296 747444 **Oxford Rd HP17 8NR**
email: info@hartwell-house.com **web:** www.hartwell-house.com
dir: *2m SW of Aylesbury on A418 (Oxford road)*

Ambitious country-house cooking in a rococo stately home

Within 90 acres of parkland in the Vale of Aylesbury, Hartwell House is a majestic property with enough pomp to have served as home to an exiled claimant to the French throne (Louis XVIII, no less). The grand proportions and luxurious features make an ideal setting for an upscale country-house hotel, with the expected spa, meeting rooms and fine-dining restaurant. Decorated in pristine primrose, with ornate mirrors and swags, the dining room is a fine setting for Daniel Richardson's ambitious classically-minded modern cooking. The estate ensures a home-grown flavour to some dishes, but what doesn't come from the grounds is sourced with care and attention. Pan-fried scallops are a fixture on contemporary menus, and here they are partnered with parsley purée, roasted artichoke, smoked bacon foam and pancetta crisp in a well-constructed first course. Everything looks good on the plate and flavours are nicely handled. Main-course pan-roasted loin of venison is a real seasonal warmer, with butternut squash purée and chestnut and bacon gnocchi, while the estate's honey might turn up at dessert stage in the company of a hazel nut and cherry tart.

Chef Daniel Richardson **Owner** Historic House Hotels/National Trust **Seats** 56, Pr/dining room 36 **Times** 12.30-1.45/7.30-9.45 Closed L 31 Dec **Prices** Fixed L 3 course £24.95, Fixed D 3 course £24.95, Tasting menu £72, Starter £8.95-£13.95, Main £25.95-£31.95, Dessert £8.45-£10.95 **Wines** 325 bottles over £30, 11 bottles under £30, 15 by glass **Parking** 50 **Notes** Various D menus 2/3 course £25-£62, Sunday L £26.95-£34.95, Vegetarian available, Children 4 yrs+

The Artichoke

Modern European v  NOTABLE WINE LIST

tel: 01494 726611 **9 Market Square, Old Amersham HP7 0DF**
email: info@artichokerestaurant.co.uk
web: www.artichokerestaurant.co.uk
dir: *M40 junct 2. 1m from Amersham New Town*

Highly creative and technically impressive cooking with a local flavour

Laurie and Jacqueline Gear's property has occupied its prime spot on the market square since the 16th century. It has lots of period charm, of course, some less than precise angles, and the smart paint job and simple, classy signage suggest there's something interesting going on within. And there is! The building was damaged by fire in 2008 forcing it to shut for 18 months, but time spent by Laurie at Noma restaurant in Copenhagen, plus expansion into the next door building (ironically where that fire actually started), has resulted in inspiration all round, from the interior design, to the style of cooking. The decor combines original features such as the huge open fireplace and oak beams, with designer chairs, walnut tables and modern art. The three dining areas look contemporary and stylish and one is home to the open kitchen, bringing even more life and energy to the space. When it comes to the cooking, organic, free range and foraged ingredients lead the way, and the wild food is tamed by a chef with a skilled hand and a keen eye for detail. There's a tasting menu (with wine flight), a veggie version, plus a carte that might begin with caramel-smoked Stockenchurch Farm duck breast, served up with a liver parfait, confit leg beignet, passionfruit jelly and pistachio. This is dynamic stuff, contemporary, full-on and expertly crafted. Next up, roast loin of Cornish cod comes with oxtail and celeriac parcel, lovage pesto and horseradish cream. Desserts are no less creative and appealing; a plum galette, perhaps, with almond purée and almond ice cream, or go for French and English farmhouse cheeses with hand-made crackers. The Artichoke is a class act, and that goes for the wine list, too, with its well-chosen bins covering the globe in style.

Chef Laurie Gear, Ben Jenkins **Owner** Laurie & Jacqueline Gear **Seats** 48, Pr/dining room 16 **Times** 12-3/6.30-11 Closed 1 wk Xmas & Apr, 2 wks Aug/Sep, Sun-Mon **Prices** Fixed L 2 course £21.50, Fixed D 3 course £48, Tasting menu £68, Starter £12-£14, Main £20-£24, Dessert £6.50-£8.50 **Wines** 5 bottles over £30, 5 bottles under £30, 11 by glass **Parking** On street, nearby car park **Notes** Tasting menu 7 course. L Tasting menu 5 course £35, Children welcome

BEACONSFIELD
Map 6 SU99

Crazy Bear Beaconsfield
British, International

tel: 01494 673086 **75 Wycombe End, Old Town HP9 1LX**
email: enquiries@crazybear-beaconsfield.co.uk **web:** www.crazybeargroup.co.uk
dir: M40 junct 2, 3rd exit from rdbt, next rdbt 1st exit. Over 2 mini-rdbts, on right

Bright modern menus in flamboyant setting

The shell of the coaching inn may date from the 15th century, but internally it's been given a flamboyant, even eccentric look, the English-themed restaurant (there are other eating options) featuring chequerboard-patterned cloth walls, chandeliers, cream bench seating, and low light levels. It's a fun, lively place, with a menu that covers a lot of ground, with starters of tuna sashimi with salade Niçoise, steak tartare, and grilled lobster. A global tilt can be detected among main courses too, so tiger prawns 'pil pil', served with Caesar salad, may appear alongside properly timed pan-fried fillet of halibut with crab bisque and a herby potato cake. Finish with classic crêpe Suzette or remain native with English trifle with sloe gin sabayon.

Times 12-12 All-day dining

The Jolly Cricketers
Modern British

tel: 01494 676308 **24 Chalfont Rd, Seer Green HP9 2YG**
email: amanda@thejollycricketers.co.uk
dir: M40 junct 2, take A355 N, at rdbt 1st exit onto A40, next rdbt 2nd exit onto A355, turn right into Longbottom Ln, turn left into School Ln & continue into Chalfont Rd

Assured cooking in village pub with a cricketing theme

Jolly cricketers are indeed depicted on the pub sign outside, a promising indicator of the warm-hearted and congenial atmosphere within this traditional old village pub. A range of real ales and a crowd-pleasing but sensibly concise menu, which underscores the cricketing theme, are all part of the draw. You might start with soft-boiled quail's eggs given a kick from caviar and anchovy mayonnaise, or go for the earthier flavours of pressed ox tongue with pickled shallots and mustard. Traditionalists need look no further than ale-braised ham with colcannon and parsley sauce, or steak and kidney pie, while other main-course offerings may run to fillet of black bream with brown shrimps, caper butter, spinach and crushed ratte potatoes. End with a 'Sticky Wicket': perhaps bread-and-butter pudding with custard, or Valrhona chocolate brownie with cherries and pistachio ice cream.

Chef Matt Lyons **Owner** A Baker & C Lillitou **Seats** 36, Pr/dining room 22
Times 12-2.30/6.30-9 Closed 25-26 Dec, D Sun **Prices** Starter £6-£8.50, Main £10.50-£23.50, Dessert £6-£8.50, Service optional 10% **Wines** 21 bottles over £30, 16 bottles under £30, 16 by glass **Parking** 10, On street **Notes** Sunday L £15-£17, Vegetarian available, Children welcome

BLETCHLEY
Map 11 SP83

The Crooked Billet
Modern British

tel: 01908 373936 **2 Westbrook End, Newton Longville MK17 0DF**
email: john@thebillet.co.uk
dir: M1 junct 14 follow A421 towards Buckingham. Turn left at Bottledump rdbt to Newton Longville. Restaurant on right on entering village

Thatched country pub with city-smart menu

It's a pub with a bar serving up real ales, but this thatched gem of a place is a destination for food- and wine-lovers first and foremost. The 17th-century building has plenty of period charm to be sure – inglenook fireplaces, oak beams and the like – along with a menu that wouldn't look amiss in a chic city brasserie. Mackerel might turn up in a terrine, with caviar crème fraîche, toasted soda bread and sweet-and-sour cucumber, and among main courses there could be grilled Barnsley chop with crispy sweetbreads, fondant potato, minted peas and a creamy thyme reduction. There's some good cooking at dessert stage, too: baked lime tart, for example, with lime posset, a biscuit and a caipirinha sorbet. When it comes to wine, you'll find a staggering 200 choices by the glass, which is pretty much everything except the most expensive bins.

Times 12-2/7-10 Closed 27-28 Dec, L Mon, D Sun

BUCKINGHAM
Map 11 SP63

Villiers Hotel
Modern British

tel: 01280 822444 **3 Castle St MK18 1BS**
email: reservations@villiershotels.com **web:** www.villiers-hotel.co.uk
dir: Town centre - Castle Street is to the right of Town Hall near main square

Straightforward brasserie cooking in the medieval quarter

The white-fronted Villiers Hotel looks a picture in summer, with its overflowing window-boxes. Situated in the medieval district of Buckingham, it makes a good destination for eating out in a generally under-served area. A smart contemporary-styled dining room in rich reds and white overlooks a courtyard, and is clearly popular with in-the-know locals. The straightforward menu of brasserie favourites is not above the odd innovative touch here and there, starting perhaps with roast pigeon and pancetta, garnished with quails' eggs, radicchio and walnuts, and moving on to fillets of lemon sole with crayfish, pea and lemon risotto and spiced cauliflower beignets. More classic offerings lack for nothing in quality, especially the flavourful herb-roasted chicken breast that comes with peas and girolles, smoked bacon, puréed wild mushrooms and thyme-scented jus. More thyme might crop up in an ice cream to accompany tarte Tatin, or there may be bracingly tangy lemon meringue torte with lemon curd ice cream. Good-value market menus at a fixed price are a tempting option.

Chef Paul Stopps **Owner** Oxfordshire Hotels Ltd **Seats** 70, Pr/dining room 150
Times 12-2.30/6-9.30 **Prices** Fixed L 2 course £14-£18, Fixed D 3 course £23-£26, Starter £4.75-£7.95, Main £10.50-£21.50, Dessert £6.95-£7.95, Service optional **Wines** 17 bottles over £30, 32 bottles under £30, 13 by glass **Parking** 52 **Notes** Sunday L £18-£24, Vegetarian available, Children welcome

Looking for a restaurant by name?
Use the index on page 751

BURNHAM
Map 6 SU98

Burnham Beeches Hotel

Modern British, European

tel: 0844 736 8603 & 01628 600150 **Burnham Beeches, Grove Rd SL1 8DP**
email: burnhambeeches@corushotels.com **web:** www.corushotels.com
dir: off A355, via Farnham Royal rdbt

Classically-minded cooking in an early Georgian hotel

A grand Georgian pile in ten acres of pretty grounds, Burnham Beeches is a popular wedding venue, but it is worth checking out the restaurant called Gray's. This consists of two formal interlinked rooms, one rich with oak panels, with tables dressed up in white linen. There are daylight views into the garden through well-proportioned Georgian windows. The kitchen favours sound classical thinking, delivering gently modern dishes that won't scare the horses. Start with a salad of home-smoked chicken breast with crispy pancetta and a soft-poached quail's egg, or pan-fried scallops with creamed leeks and poached baby leeks. Main-course honey-roasted breast of Gressingham duck is an attractively presented plate, the meat nice and pink, with an accompanying croquette and port sauce. Finish with a Yorkshire rhubarb and ginger cheesecake, or the selection of British cheeses.

Chef Rafal Wysocki **Owner** Corus Hotels **Seats** 70, Pr/dining room 120
Times 12-2/7-9.30 **Prices** Tasting menu £30-£60, Starter £6.50-£9.50, Main £16.50-£24.50, Dessert £6.50-£8, Service optional **Wines** 28 bottles over £30, 17 bottles under £30, 9 by glass **Parking** 150 **Notes** Sunday L £22.95-£29.95, Vegetarian available, Children welcome

---

The Grovefield House Hotel

Modern

tel: 01628 603131 **Taplow Common Rd SL1 8LP**
email: info.grovefield@classiclodges.co.uk **web:** www.grovefieldhotel.co.uk
dir: From M4 junct 7, left on A4 towards Maidenhead. Next rdbt turn right under railway bridge. Straight over mini rdbt, garage on right. Continue for 1.5m, hotel on right

Uncomplicated contemporary cooking and splendid garden views

Grovefield House is a splendid-looking Edwardian property, built by the Fuller brewing family, in over seven acres of well-maintained grounds. It's a comfortable, well-fitted-out place, with facilities for weddings and conferences, while classy Hamilton Restaurant is at the heart of things culinary, its white walls hung with images and mirrors and windows giving views of greenery. The kitchen works in the contemporary idiom, and dishes are marked by a lack of fuss or flounce. Proceedings start, for instance, with a simple tomato and onion tart, its pastry good and crisp, or smoked duck breast with a salad of figs, walnuts and rocket. Main courses are in similar vein: an assiette of guinea fowl is accompanied by no more than creamy mash and pancetta and set off by Madeira sauce, and roast codling by Puy lentils and confit of vegetables with red wine sauce. Finish with one of the prettily presented desserts such as iced coffee parfait, or caramelised lemon tart with orange sorbet.

Times 12-2.30/7-10.30 Closed L Sat

CUBLINGTON
Map 11 SP82

The Unicorn

Traditional, Modern British

tel: 01296 681261 **12 High St LU7 0LQ**
email: theunicornpub@btconnect.com **web:** www.theunicornpub.co.uk
dir: 2m N of A418 (between Aylesbury & Leighton Buzzard). In village centre

The kind of pub every village should have

The welcome is warm and sincere, the menu chock-full of the sort of unfussy modern pub food that makes you want a bit of everything, and the 17th-century interior is replete with low beams, open fires, homely mismatched wooden furniture, and old pictures of village life on the walls. The place is the hub of local life too, selling home-made bread, milk, wine, butter, stamps and Cublington greetings cards. And the food lives up to its promise, whether it is a cooked breakfast on Saturday mornings, coffee and afternoon tea with home-made cakes throughout the week – which is rather nice out in the lovely garden – or a doorstop sandwich and a pint of real ale. If you want to put the kitchen through its paces properly, go for the full three-courses: smoked wood pigeon and chicory salad with apple chutney and toasted pumpkin seeds to start, then slow-roast pork belly with mash, braised red cabbage, and sage and cider jus. Wrap it all up with toffee and date pudding with clotted cream and toffee sauce.

Chef Christopher George **Owner** Mr S D George **Seats** 60, Pr/dining room 20
Times 12-2.30/6.30-9 **Prices** Fixed L 2 course £13.95-£16.50, Fixed D 3 course £16.95-£19.50, Starter £5-£8, Main £9-£24.50, Dessert £5-£8, Service optional **Wines** 3 bottles over £30, 26 bottles under £30, 8 by glass **Parking** 20 **Notes** Sunday L, Vegetarian available, Children welcome

Who are the AA's Restaurants of the Year? See page 14

GERRARDS CROSS
Map 6 TQ08

The Bull Hotel

◉ Modern British

tel: 01753 885995 **Oxford Rd SL9 7PA**
email: bull@sarova.co.uk **web:** www.sarova.com
dir: *M40 junct 2 follow Beaconsfield on A355. After 0.5m 2nd exit at rdbt signed A40 Gerrards Cross for 2m. The Bull on right*

Smart hotel restaurant on the high street

The old Bull has borne witness to over 300 years of passing life on the road between London and Oxford, and to prove it isn't all forgotten, the smartly traditional bar is named after a famous highwayman, Jack Shrimpton. The one-time coaching inn is these days a swish four-star hotel with tip-top facilities and a restaurant, Beeches, that has a decidedly contemporary feel: think bold tones of burgundy and cream, and plenty of space between the darkwood tables. The menu is an up-to-date offering, too: parsnip and Cox's apple soup with root vegetable crisp and parmesan might be amongst starters. Follow on with pan-fried sea trout with surf clams, saffron potatoes, samphire and a lemon and chive butter, or pan-seared duck breast with glazed silver skin onion and cherry port jus (among other things). Go home happy after burnt English cream with marinated seasonal berries.

Times 12-2.30/7-9 Closed L Sat

GREAT MISSENDEN
Map 6 SP80

Nags Head Inn & Restaurant

◉ British, French

tel: 01494 862200 & 862945 **London Rd HP16 0DG**
email: goodfood@nagsheadbucks.com **web:** www.nagsheadbucks.com
dir: *N from Amersham on A413 signed Great Missenden, left at Chiltern Hospital onto London Rd (1m S of Great Missenden)*

Charming pub with ambitious Anglo-French cooking

Originally three 15th-century cottages, then a coaching inn, The Nags Head is now a stylishly modernised gastro-pub, with an open fire in the old inglenook under oak beams, and dining areas with a Roald Dahl theme (he was a regular and there's a museum devoted to him nearby). Contemporary Anglo-French cuisine is the attraction, with the kitchen adding its own endlessly inventive – and totally persuasive – touches to dishes. Starters can be as straightforward as a plate of home-smoked fish with lemony coriander butter and tomato chutney and as complicated as pan-fried foie gras on milk bread with red onion and pear jam along with mi-cuit foie gras shavings on rocket. Ever successful main courses follow a similar route, among them fillet of stone bass with green beans and a simple Noilly Prat cream, and roast breast of guinea fowl with a pheasant sausage, liver mousse

feuilleté and thyme jus. To end, sticky toffee pudding seems a fixture, and there might be vanilla crème brûlée as well.

Chef Atilla Jakab, Claude Paillet **Owner** Alvin, Adam & Sally Michaels **Seats** 60 **Times** 12-11.30 Closed 25 Dec, All-day dining **Prices** Prices not confirmed, Service optional **Wines** 95 bottles over £30, 31 bottles under £30, 19 by glass **Parking** 35 **Notes** Sunday L, Vegetarian available, Children welcome

LONG CRENDON
Map 5 SP60

The Angel Restaurant

◉ Modern European, Traditional British ᴠ ⊗ NOTABLE WINE LIST

tel: 01844 208268 **47 Bicester Rd HP18 9EE**
email: info@angelrestaurant.co.uk
dir: *M40 junct 7, beside B4011, 2m NW of Thame*

Confident cooking in 16th-century coaching inn

This one-time coaching inn dates from the 16th century and retains plenty of period charm. It's more restaurant-with-rooms than country pub these days. There is a cosy bar for a pre-dinner drink, plus dining areas filled with original features and a smart conservatory. There are outdoor tables, too, on the heated terrace. The cooking is broadly modern British with a good many Asian influences adding a notion of Pacific Rim to proceedings. Daily specials appear on a blackboard and fish is very much a favourite ingredient in the kitchen. Citrus-cured gravad lax is a starter perked up with crispy fried squid and pickled kohlrabi, with another pairing honey- and soy-glazed duck breast with steamed bok choy and plum and ginger sauce. But there's also char-grilled fillet of beef with classic accompaniments, and desserts such as warm treacle tart with honeycomb ice cream or limoncello pannacotta with rhubarb compôte.

Chef Trevor Bosch **Owner** Trevor & Annie Bosch **Seats** 75, Pr/dining room 14 **Times** 12-2.30/7-9.30 Closed D Sun **Prices** Prices not confirmed, Service optional **Wines** 12 by glass **Parking** 30 **Notes** Sunday L, Children welcome

MARLOW
Map 5 SU88

Crowne Plaza Marlow

◉◉ Modern British

tel: 01628 496800 **Field House Ln SL7 1GJ**
email: enquiries@cpmarlow.co.uk **web:** www.cpmarlow.co.uk
dir: *A404 exit to Marlow, left at mini rdbt, left into Field House Lane*

Modern lakeside dining in this contemporary hotel

A sprawling new build on the edge of a lake, this outpost of the Crowne Plaza marque has all the hoped-for facilities, so there's an indoor pool, all you need to put on a conference or a wedding, and, in the shape of the Glaze Restaurant, somewhere to get some smart, modern food. It's a crisp, contemporary space with raspberry-coloured banquette seating and darkwood tables, and a professional level of service. The fixed-price menu, with some supplements, has plenty of fashionable combinations and cooking shows careful execution. North Atlantic scallops, for example, nicely caramelised, come with smooth pea purée, crunchy pork crackling and vanilla foam, or there might be duck rillettes with a pomegranate dressing. Pressed pork belly stars in a main course with creamed Savoy cabbage and a host of apple-y accompaniments, and there are steaks and a classy burger cooked on the grill. For dessert, sticky toffee pudding with caramel sauce and clotted cream ice cream delivers old-school satisfaction.

Chef Stuart Hine **Owner** Redefine BDL Hotels **Seats** 150 **Times** 6.30-10 **Prices** Prices not confirmed **Wines** 11 by glass **Parking** 300 **Notes** Vegetarian available, Children welcome

The Hand & Flowers

⊚⊚⊚⊚ – see page 72

The Oak Room at Danesfield House

⊚⊚ British ▮ NOTABLE WINE LIST

tel: 01628 891010 **Henley Rd SL7 2EY**
email: reservations@danesfieldhouse.co.uk **web:** www.danesfieldhouse.co.uk
dir: *M4 junct 4/A404 to Marlow. Follow signs to Medmenham and Henley. Hotel is 3m outside Marlow*

Classy, classical dining in a majestic house

Danesfield House seems to defy classification but is in essence a 19th-century architectural pastiche of an Italian Renaissance palazzo. Whatever, it's awesome. Like a fairy-tale castle standing in gardens that have been manicured by Edward Scissorhands, it certainly makes an impression. There are stunning views over the River Thames, and the kind of facilities that are designed to pamper to the maximum – a glorious spa, plush bedrooms, and upmarket business facilities. There are two dining options at the hotel, both now watched over by executive (and experienced hand) Billy Reid. The Orangery offers classy brasserie-style dishes in a room with a wall of glass and a luminous view of open countryside. The main culinary action takes place in The Oak Room restaurant, a space with its eponymous panels coloured in creamy neutrality, and the tables dressed up for the fine dining that follows. The fixed-price menu offers refined modern British/European dishes that have evident classical foundations. A lobster and salmon lasagne with a herb butter sauce is one way to begin a meal, or there might be an escalope of foie gras with brioche and a hen's egg. Main courses might serve up a roast partridge in the company of morels, cavolo nero and a foie gras jus, or sea bass partnered with a bouillabaisse sauce, greens and potato purée. There's no less attention to detail at dessert stage, where, once again, classic combinations win the day. Lemon tart and lemon soufflé is a winning partnership, or go for Bramley and date crumble with vanilla ice cream and double cream. The wine list is an upscale collection, and a classy afternoon tea option is particularly thrilling if it's warm enough to sit on the terrace.

Chef Billy Reid **Seats** 24, Pr/dining room 14 **Times** 12-2.30/7-9.30 Closed 18 Aug-2 Sep, 23 Dec-7 Jan, BHs, Sun-Mon, L Tue-Wed **Prices** Fixed L 2 course £23-£55, Fixed D 3 course £55 **Wines** 350 bottles over £30, 50 bottles under £30, 14 by glass **Parking** 100 **Notes** Vegetarian available, Children 12 yrs+

The Riverside Restaurant

⊚⊚ Modern British

tel: 0844 879 9128 & 01628 405406 **Macdonald Compleat Angler, Marlow Bridge SL7 1RG**
email: compleatangler@macdonald-hotels.co.uk
dir: *M4 junct 8/9 or M40 junct 4. A404 to rdbt, take Bisham exit, 1m to Marlow Bridge, hotel on right*

Modern classic dishes on Izaak Walton's riverside

The Riverside is part of a hotel named after Izaak Walton's indispensable reference, The Compleat Angler (1653), written in and around the Thames at Marlow. It makes the most of its location with a lovely conservatory room overlooking the water, plus formal service from uniformed staff and a helpful sommelier to make apposite recommendations. Cleverly worked modern cooking is part of the attraction, with interesting combinations and attractively presented dishes. Starters might comprise a modern classic presentation of seared scallops with cauliflower and raisin purée, or crab ravioli in langoustine bisque. Mains include loin of Highland lamb and its sweetbreads with crushed minted peas, or monkfish tail with creamed smoked purple potato and shallots. Finish with a twice-baked Stilton soufflé in walnut dressing with port jelly, if your tooth isn't sweet enough for prune tarte Tatin and marzipan ice cream.

Chef Michael Lloyd **Owner** Macdonald Hotels **Seats** 90, Pr/dining room 120 **Times** 12.30-2/7-10 **Prices** Fixed L 2 course fr £22, Starter £9.50-£12.95, Main £21-£34.50, Dessert fr £8 **Wines** 120 bottles over £30, 16 bottles under £30, 17 by glass **Parking** 100 **Notes** Sunday L fr £39.50, Vegetarian available, Children welcome

The Vanilla Pod

⊚⊚ British, French

tel: 01628 898101 **31 West St SL7 2LS**
email: contact@thevanillapod.co.uk
dir: *From M4 junct 8/9 or M40 junct 4 take A404, A4155 to Marlow. From Henley take A4155*

Intelligently constructed dishes in central townhouse

The culinary bar is set high in this well-heeled Thames-side stretch of the stockbroker belt, with stellar competition all around. Happily, The Vanilla Pod has the hand of chef-proprietor Michael Macdonald on the tiller to deliver a sure-footed take on modern British cooking with its roots clearly in the French classics. The setting is a handsome townhouse where TS Eliot once lived, thoroughly refurbished with a chic contemporary look in tones of brown and cream, and the hum of conversation and clued-up service to add to the upbeat feel of the place. Not surprisingly, given the restaurant's name, vanilla is something of a leitmotif, and it might turn up in a starter of seared scallops with truffle-infused butternut squash purée and apple foam. The kitchen extracts clear, robust flavours from top-class ingredients in main courses such as loin of venison with pear and fondant potato, and puddings could press the eponymous pod into service once again in a classic vanilla crème brûlée with butterscotch jelly, condensed milk purée and popcorn ice cream.

Times 12-2/7-10 Closed 24 Dec-3 Jan, Sun-Mon

The Hand & Flowers

MARLOW   **Map 5 SU88**

British, French
tel: 01628 482277 **126 West St SL7 2BP**
email: contact@thehandandflowers.co.uk
web: www.thehandandflowers.co.uk
dir: *M40 junct 4/M4 junct 8/9 follow A404 to Marlow*

Big flavours and traditional techniques in an outstanding gastro inn

There are former pubs turned into restaurants. There are pubs turning out good food. There are plenty of pubs that have closed down and become executive homes. And then there is The Hand & Flowers, a place which keeps to the spirit of what a pub should be, and turns out food that is staggeringly good and sometimes alluringly simple. Tom Kerridge's star has risen, with a TV show to call his own and a reputation firmly made and well earned. In under a decade Tom and Beth Kerridge have taken a jobbing tavern and turned into a destination address, but, perhaps best of all, it still feels relaxed, natural, and geared to good food and good company, which is surely what it's all about. There are bare-boarded floors and rustic furniture, with tables left bare but set with good quality cutlery and glassware. The 'posher' elements of this place are seemingly slipped in unnoticed, so it all feels unpretentious, when in fact there's a lot going on here to deliver a high-end experience in a seemingly easy-going environment. The service team play their part, cheerful and friendly, but entirely on the ball. Tom worked in some top-end kitchens and learned a thing or two about working the ingredients to maximise flavour, but also when to leave well alone. His food has a genuine British flavour and there's smoking, pickling, salt-curing, blowtorching and all sorts going down in the kitchen. That blowtorch comes into its own in a first course which sees Scottish scallops seared to perfection and served with beef and mead bouillon, while another starter has delicious orange chutney to cut through the richness of duck and foie gras parfait (plus some toasted brioche). Main-course slow-cooked duck comes with duck fat chips and Savoy cabbage, or go for Wiltshire venison with Hand & Flowers carrots and game ragout. The produce throughout is first class, often local and always seasonal. There's no slacking at the dessert stage, with glazed apple tart with burnt milk ice cream, or pear soufflé with caraway crumble. The wine list is also on song, offering a good choice by the glass and there are bedrooms, too, in the form of four cottage suites a short stroll from the pub.

Chef Tom Kerridge **Owner** Tom & Beth Kerridge **Seats** 54 **Times** 12-2.45/6.30-9.45 Closed 24-26 Dec, D Sun, 1 Jan **Prices** Fixed L 2 course £15, Starter £8.50-£18.50, Main £25-£36, Dessert £9.50-£11 **Wines** 107 bottles over £30, 16 bottles under £30, 17 by glass **Parking** 20 **Notes** Sunday L £36, Vegetarian available, Children welcome

Humphry's at Stoke Park

STOKE POGES | Map 6 SU98

Modern British

tel: 01753 717171 & 717172 **Park Rd SL2 4PG**
email: info@stokepark.com
web: www.humphrysrestaurant.co.uk
dir: *M4 junct 6 or M40 junct 2, take A355 towards Slough, then B416. Stoke Park in 1.25m on right*

Exciting modern cooking in a country-club hotel

The Stoke Park country club was founded in 1908, but the building and grounds themselves reach considerably further back in time than that. In the 1790s, Humphry Repton was hired to spruce up 'Capability' Brown's landscaped grounds. These cover 300 acres, including soothing parkland and lakes, locations that have appeared in films such as *Dr No*, plus the inevitable golf – all 27 holes of it. It's extensive enough to provide a fine outdoor concert venue, playing host to the likes of Katherine Jenkins and Sir Elton John in 2014. Inside, the place is entirely magnificent, with plenty of notable architectural features and fine oil paintings, and a principal dining room, Humphry's (after the gardener), done in pastel tones of sand and lemon, with seductive views over the grounds. Chris Wheeler has a job-and-a-half on his hands living up to these lavish surroundings, and pulls off an exciting take on modern British gastronomy rather than sticking with tried-and-tested haute cuisine. He is good at relatively delicate constructions, such as an opener of crab and avocado tian with firm cucumber jelly, a soft-boiled quail egg and pink grapefruit. He also masters big belting main-course flavours like those mobilised in roast duck breast with a tranche of foie gras, green beans and parsnip purée in sticky blackberry sauce, or pan-roasted sea bass with creamed cabbage, cauliflower and glazed chestnuts in madeira. A seven-course tasting menu runs the rule over the repertoire, progressing from smoked scallops with watercress niçoise, via cannon of spring lamb with 'osso buco' done in Windsor Ale, to a concluding blackcurrant soufflé with liquorice ice cream. Staying with the carte, a couple might opt to share a freshly made thyme-infused pear Tatin, or consider the wares of the trolley that makes regular stops on its progress round the room, dispensing English and French cheeses in peak condition.

Chef Chris Wheeler **Owner** Roger King **Seats** 50, Pr/dining room 120 **Times** 12-2.30/7-10 Closed 24-26 Dec, 1st wk Jan, Mon, L Tue **Prices** Fixed L 2 course £25, Fixed D 3 course £65, Tasting menu £80 **Wines** 94 bottles over £30, 8 bottles under £30, 15 by glass **Parking** 400 **Notes** ALC L only, Tasting menu 7 course, Vegetarian available, Children welcome

MILTON KEYNES
Map 11 SP83

Mercure Milton Keynes Parkside Hotel

◉ Modern British

tel: 01908 661919 **Newport Rd, Woughton on the Green MK6 3LR**
email: h6627-gm@accor.com **web:** www.mercure.com
dir: *M1 junct 14, A509 towards Milton Keynes. 2nd exit on H6 follow signs to Woughton on the Green*

Modernised traditional dishes in a boutique hotel

In the tranquil rural location of the Ouzel Valley Park, and yet only a short hop from the malls of Milton Keynes, the Grade II listed, white-painted building has been stylishly made over inside to give it a boutique hotel feel. Simply-laid, unclothed tables, framed pictures and a wall papered as a trompe l'oeil library set the tone in the dining room, where the kitchen delivers a repertoire of confidently rendered brasserie favourites. Pan-seared scallops arrive with cauliflower velouté, toasted almonds and white truffle oil ahead of oven-roasted loin of Woburn venison teamed with carrot purée, vegetable rösti, wilted greens and whisky cream sauce. If you're in the mood for fish, cod suprême might be given an exotic spin with a dusting of cumin, and served with pilau rice and curried mussel velouté. For pudding, baked chocolate tart is served with fig ice cream, otherwise an all-British cheeseboard provides a savoury ending.

Chef Jeff Payne **Owner** Mercure Hotels **Seats** 46, Pr/dining room 100
Times 12-2/6.30-9.30 Closed D Sun **Prices** Prices not confirmed, Service optional
Wines 9 bottles over £30, 6 bottles under £30, 11 by glass **Parking** 70
Notes Vegetarian available, Children welcome

STOKE POGES
Map 6 SU98

Humphry's at Stoke Park

◉◉◉ – *see page 73*

Stoke Place

◉◉◉ – *see opposite*

TAPLOW
Map 6 SU98

Andre Garrett at Cliveden

◉◉◉ – *see opposite*

WADDESDON
Map 11 SP71

The Five Arrows

◉◉ Modern European

tel: 01296 651727 **High St HP18 OJE**
email: five.arrows@nationaltrust.org.uk **web:** www.thefivearrows.co.uk
dir: *On A41 in Waddesdon. Into Baker St for car park*

Contemporary dining on the Rothschild estate

The Five Arrows in question are the family emblem of the Rothschilds, each arrow representing one of the five sons who was sent off to establish banking houses in Europe's financial capitals. The rest, as the saying goes, is history. The small Victorian hotel stands at the gates of Waddesdon Manor, and other than a mock-Tudor flourish here and there, has none of the airs and graces of the grand French château-style stately home. The restaurant sports a smartly contemporary look with unclothed darkwood tables and Rothschild wine-related prints on the walls, and a refreshingly relaxed ambience. The repertoire displays a commendable seasonal focus that delivers bright contemporary ideas, starting with a ballottine of chicken and black pudding matched with honey-poached cranberries, cauliflower purée, celery and lemon oil. Next up, the Waddesdon Estate supplies the venison (pan-fried loin and braised haunch) that comes with the hearty accompaniments of herb mash, braised red cabbage, girolles, and redcurrant jus, and for pudding there's hazelnut and vanilla iced parfait with caramelised hazelnuts and hazelnut tuile.

Chef Karl Penny **Owner** Lord Rothschild **Seats** 60, Pr/dining room 30
Times 12-2.15/6.30-9.15 Closed D 25-26 Dec **Prices** Fixed L 2 course fr £14.95, Starter £6.50-£7.95, Main £11.50-£21.50, Dessert £6.95-£7.50 **Wines** 49 bottles over £30, 44 bottles under £30, 18 by glass **Parking** 30 **Notes** Sunday L £15.25-£16.95, Vegetarian available

WOOBURN COMMON
Map 6 SU98

Chequers Inn

◉◉ British, French

tel: 01628 529575 **Kiln Ln HP10 OJQ**
email: info@chequers-inn.com **web:** www.chequers-inn.com
dir: *M40 junct 2, A40 through Beaconsfield Old Town towards High Wycombe. 2m from town left into Broad Ln. Inn 2.5m on left*

French-influenced bistro cooking in an old coaching inn

The Chequers hides its 17th-century pedigree rather well from the outside, but the oak beams and flagstoned floors within tell their own story. Its dining room has been coaxed boldly into the modern era with white-painted walls, contemporary light fixtures and big mirrors, but the crisp white linen remains. A small covered patio is pressed into service on those elusive warmer days. A French-inflected, resourceful bistro cooking style informs the menus, and dishes are turned out well. Sautéed foie gras with roasted fig and cherry syrup makes a bold opening statement, while a reworking of classic cock-a-leekie sees a chicken croquette added to leek fondue, with a compôte of prunes included for good measure. A two-way lamb main course offers roast rack and confit shoulder alongside a mélange of broad beans, peas and baby onions, and dessert might bring a fruity assemblage into play in the form of watermelon and strawberry salsa and rhubarb compôte as accompaniment to traditional vanilla-speckled pannacotta in port syrup.

Chef Pascal Lemoine **Owner** PJ Roehrig **Seats** 60, Pr/dining room 60
Times 12-2.30/7-9.30 Closed D Sun, 25 Dec, 1 Jan **Prices** Fixed L 2 course £13.95-£22.95, Fixed D 3 course £27.95, Starter £6.95-£10.50, Main £14.95-£26.95, Dessert £6.95-£8.50, Service optional **Wines** 11 bottles over £30, 27 bottles under £30, 11 by glass **Parking** 50 **Notes** Afternoon tea £12.95, Sunday L £27.95, Vegetarian available, Children welcome

Follow us on facebook
www.facebook.com/TheAAUK

Stoke Place

STOKE POGES   Map 6 SU98

Modern European NOTABLE WINE LIST

tel: 01753 534790 & 560216 **Stoke Green SL2 4HT**
email: enquiries@stokeplace.co.uk **web:** www.stokeplace.co.uk
dir: *M4 junct 6, A355, right at 1st lights to A4 Bath Rd. At 1st rdbt take 2nd exit onto Stoke Rd. B416 to Stoke Green. Hotel 200mtrs on right*

Finely honed modern creativity in the gastro-hub that is Stoke Poges

Stoke Place is a Queen Anne country home with expansive gardens landscaped by 'Capability' Brown. Extending into 26 acres of parkland abundant with wildlife, it's a rural retreat with knobs on, and yet isn't a million miles from Heathrow and the start of London's sprawl. Inside is a very fresh, updated take on the country-house hotel, where the accommodation comes with carpetless floors and doorless wet-rooms, and the Garden Room restaurant affords views of Brown's handiwork. Craig van der Meer is in charge of culinary affairs, and has at his disposal a well-stocked kitchen garden and herb house, as well as a finely honed creative imagination that is no more limited by traditional expectations of country-house style than is the surrounding decor. Accompaniments are carefully conceived to add surprise, so chorizo, melon and mizuna leaves are the supporting cast for pressed torchon of rabbit and foie gras, while grilled lobster comes with parsnip purée, apple and beetroot. Individual oddities contribute the requisite leftfield cachet, such as a wasabi sphere, onion paper, grapefruit marshmallow. There can be a worry that dishes become subservient to contrivance with this sort of style, and yet van der Meer pulls off his tricks with persuasive aplomb. Main course might be seared cannon of lamb with home-made feta and chakalaka (spicy vegetable relish from chef's native South Africa), or sea bass with vanilla-scented sweetcorn purée, crayfish, samphire and purple potato. A dazzling visual virtuosity distinguishes many dishes, through to desserts such as dark chocolate and olive oil tart with blackberries, pistachio ice cream and blackberry jelly, or a cheese/dessert crossover dish created from a roll of Oxford Blue with kiwi, coffee jelly and a pumpkin-seed biscuit.

Chef Craig van der Meer **Owner** Mr & Mrs Dhillon **Seats** 36, Pr/dining room 30 **Times** 12-2.30/7-9.30 Closed 24 Dec-9 Jan **Prices** Fixed L 2 course £15.50, Fixed D 3 course £45, Tasting menu £55 **Wines** 235 bottles over £30, 41 bottles under £30, 18 by glass **Parking** 120 **Notes** Sunday L £19.50-£23.50, Vegetarian available, Children welcome

Andre Garrett at Cliveden

TAPLOW   Map 6 SU98

Modern British with Classical French Twist V NOTABLE WINE LIST

tel: 01628 668561 **Cliveden Estate SL6 OJF**
email: info@clivedenhouse.co.uk **web:** www.clivedenhouse.co.uk
dir: *M4 junct 7, A4 towards Maidenhead, 1.5m, onto B476 towards Taplow, 2.5m, hotel on left*

Stunning dishes in a stately home with a past

One of England's very stateliest stately homes, Cliveden drips with the sort of history that's anything but stately. It may have played host to all the crowned heads since the first Hanoverians, but during its ownership by the Astors, it became the hub of the cocktail set, and in the 1960s was where John Profumo first laid eyes on Christine Keeler. The dining goes on in the glorious Terrace room, with its squadron of chandeliers, velour banquettes, silk drapes and views over parterre gardens to the Thames. A chef could easily get lost here, but Andre Garrett has his wits about him, and knows how to impress a knowledgeable clientele. Dishes are presented exquisitely, mobilising stunning ingredients: a starter comprises mackerel tartare, smoked eel beignets, black radish, cod roe and caviar for an essay in crisp, fresh flavours. There is fine technique on show amidst all the refinement, with a well-crafted ballottine of foiegras and Cotswold chicken partnered with Cumbrian ham and salt-baked celeriac (plus some golden raisins bringing a sweetness and acidity to the dish). Next might be venison saddle with a panko-crumbed croquette of braised shoulder and puréed quince, with the bitterness of dark chocolate in the sauce, or line-caught Cornish sea bass served on the bone (with squid, clams, potato gnocchi and a parsley velouté). A leisurely wait precedes rice pudding and Agen prune soufflé, into which Earl Grey vanilla sauce is decanted at the table, or slow-cooked Cox's apple with rosemary caramel, raisin purée and walnut ice cream. To accompany coffee the bonbon trolley arrives, with an enticing array served from crystal bowls – pistachio macaroons, dark chocolate ganache and more. There's a tasting menu, including an impressive vegetarian version, and a lunchtime market menu that constitutes very good value indeed. The wine list is a class act, with excellent advice on hand from the sommelier if required.

Chef Andre Garrett **Owner** SRE Hotels **Seats** 78, Pr/dining room **Times** 12.15-2.30/7-9.45 **Prices** Fixed L 3 course fr £28, Fixed D 3 course fr £65, Tasting menu fr £95, Service optional 12.5% **Wines** 575 bottles over £30, 8 bottles under £30 **Parking** 50 **Notes** Sunday L fr £50, Children welcome

CAMBRIDGESHIRE

BALSHAM
Map 12 TL55

The Black Bull Inn

Modern British

tel: 01223 893844 **27 High St CB21 4DJ**
email: info@blackbull-balsham.co.uk **web:** www.blackbull-balsham.co.uk
dir: *A11 Balsham exit, in centre of village*

Thatched country pub with creative team in the kitchen

The old inn is as pretty as a picture with its mop of thatch and neat white-painted façade, and it does not shirk from its pub duties, with real ale on tap and a fabulous garden and terrace designed by a chap with Chelsea flower show medals to his name. Food is a highlight of any visit, with the main event taking place in a barn with a high-vaulted ceiling, a tastefully neutral colour scheme and high quality solid oak tables. The menu takes a broadly modish approach to proceedings, so among first courses there are things like ham hock and foie gras terrine with piccalilli and home-made brioche bun, or beetroot salmon gravad lax with beetroot textures, quail's egg, horseradish jelly and brie ice cream. Follow one of those with roast cod with ruby chard, crushed potatoes, mussel curry and courgettes, and finish with white chocolate and ginger biscuit cheesecake served with a berry sauce.

Chef Peter Friskey **Owner** Alex Clarke **Times** **Prices** Starter £5.50-£10, Main £10-£26, Dessert £2.50-£9, Service optional **Wines** 16 bottles over £30, 38 bottles under £30, 22 by glass **Notes** Tasting menus available, Pudding Club, Sunday L £12-£22, Vegetarian available, Children welcome

CAMBRIDGE
Map 12 TL45

Best Western Plus Cambridge Quy Mill Hotel

Modern European

tel: 01223 293383 **Church Rd, Stow-Cum-Quy CB25 9AF**
email: info@cambridgequymill.co.uk **web:** www.cambridgequymill.co.uk
dir: *exit A14 at junct 35, E of Cambridge, onto B1102 for 50yds. Entrance opposite church*

Confident cooking in a former watermill

The original watermill was built in 1830 and still lies at the heart of Quy Mill, although the place is now a smart contemporary hotel and health club complex set in 11 acres of riverside meadows. Recently refurbished in a contemporary country inn style, the Mill House Restaurant capitalises on its setting in the miller's house, overlooking the waterwheel and mill race: at night it is an intimate place with open fires and candlelight, cool jazz floating in the background, and a friendly, upbeat ambience. The skilled kitchen team likes to keep things imaginative, using spot-on accuracy of timing, careful balance and thoughtful composition to make an impact.

The menu keeps a keen eye on the seasons, cleverly contrasting leek and cauliflower pannacotta with the sharpness of pickled winter vegetables, while roast halibut fillet arrives with scallops, prawn and lobster sauce, and winter greens. Meatier fare might run to pan-roasted beef fillet with slow-cooked oxtail, onions, olive oil mash and spinach mousse. Dessert brings on a faultless baked custard tart with caramel ice cream.

Chef Andrew Walker **Owner** David Munro **Seats** 48, Pr/dining room 80
Times 12-2.30/7-9.45 Closed 25-26 Dec, L Mon-Fri **Prices** Fixed L 2 course £12.50-£25, Fixed D 3 course £30, Starter £6-£10, Main £16-£24, Dessert £6-£10, Service optional **Wines** 25 bottles over £30, 35 bottles under £30, 14 by glass **Parking** 90 **Notes** Complimentary bread & amuse bouche with all ALC, Sunday L £25-£30, Vegetarian available, Children welcome

The Carpenters Arms

Modern British **NEW**

tel: 01223 367050 **182-186 Victoria Rd CB4 3DZ**
email: hello@carpentersarmscambridge.co.uk **web:** www.carpentersarmscambridge.co.uk
dir: *Phone for directions*

Town pub with real ale and classic food

A traditional pub that has had a bit of a makeover, the team behind the Carpenters have maintained the pubby feel of the place, kept its heart and soul intact, and created a family-friendly gastro-pub that serves the community. There's a small courtyard garden for chilling in the sunshine and a wood-fired oven installed to cook-up the people's favourite – pizza. There's live jazz some evenings, too. The menu offers some classic dishes, often with a twist or two (venison burger, for example), and some refinement in the execution. A starter of pan-seared scallops shows the kitchen has a steady hand at the stove – excellent caramelisation – served in the modern classic manner with pea purée and crispy Parma ham, followed by a main course such as confit duck leg with crushed new potatoes and braised red cabbage (another classic). Finish with boozy chocolate truffle cake with clotted cream griottine cherries.

Chef Marco Coelho **Owner** Mike Champion **Seats** 40, Pr/dining room 25
Times 12-2.30/6-10 **Prices** Starter £5-£8, Main £9-£23, Dessert £5-£8, Service optional **Wines** **Parking** 10 **Notes** Sunday L £11-£13, Vegetarian available, Children welcome

Hotel du Vin Cambridge

French

tel: 01223 227330 **15-19 Trumpington St CB2 1QA**
email: info.cambridge@hotelduvin.com **web:** www.hotelduvin.com
dir: *M11 junct 11 Cambridge S, pass Trumpington Park & Ride on left. Hotel 2m on right after double rdbt*

Classic bistro dining in the city centre

The Cambridge branch of the Hotel du Vin chain, bang in the city centre, follows the well-trusted concept of wooden floors, banquettes, unclothed tables, restored fireplaces, plenty of prints and much evidence of viniculture. The kitchen is open to view and the team here put their focus on sourcing top-quality ingredients, with the knowhow to treat them comme il faut. Familiar bistro classics come in the shape of escargots bourguignon, or smoked haddock and leek gougère with gruyère sauce, then cassoulet, or sole Véronique. Dishes are accurately timed and combinations judiciously considered, from seared scallops with Serrano ham and smooth pea purée, through grilled steaks, perhaps with béarnaise, to crisp-skinned, tender roast cod with salsa verde and buttered leeks. To finish? What else but crème brûlée or tarte Tatin?

Times 12-2/6-10

Midsummer House

Modern British 🍾 NOTABLE WINE LIST

tel: 01223 369299 **Midsummer Common CB4 1HA**
email: reservations@midsummerhouse.co.uk
web: www.midsummerhouse.co.uk
dir: *Park in Pretoria Rd, then walk across footbridge.*
Restaurant on left

Stellar cooking from a chef at the top of his game

Daniel Clifford first arrived at Midsummer House in the summer of 1998. An ambitious fellow, he had a vision to take his restaurant to the very top. His competitive edge has been seen on TV shows like the BBC's Great British Menu, where he emerged triumphant. It's easy to imagine what drew him to the location as it's a great spot, right by the River Cam, with cattle grazing on the green, and feels more country than town. The Victorian villa has been gently improved and upgraded over the years, and now the place has a contemporary finish throughout. There are tables in the conservatory area with views over the pretty garden, and a glimpse of the kitchen through a window (just a view, no noise). There's a small bar area upstairs, too, with a terrace that serves up views over the river, plus a private dining room if you fancy separating yourself from the genteel crowd. Daniel has a classical training which is evident in his dishes, although there's no shortage of contemporary flair and flourish, and it perhaps this respect for the foundations of haute cuisine that keeps his food so highly focused and on

song. Attention to detail is a hallmark of the cooking, from the flavours, the presentation, and the sourcing of the produce itself – no stone is left unturned in pursuit of the best. The deal is tasting menus – either five, seven or ten courses – with an optional cheese diversion along the way, and the whole table need to be in agreement regarding which to go for. A meal might begin with a pumpkin velouté with à la grecque mushrooms and parmesan gnocchi, the balance of flavours working together a treat, the skill in the kitchen evident from the off. Roast Cornish cod with Jerusalem artichokes, truffle and sorrel is another winner with harmonious combinations of classic ingredients. There are luxury ingredients such as Wagyu beef, which appears in a dish with braised oxtail, spinach purée, creamed potato and braising juices (another dish with its classical French origins laid bare). There are two sweet courses to look forward to. First off, perhaps, a lemon posset with blueberries and a lemon espuma, followed by a combination of roasted chestnuts, caramel and chestnut frangipane. The service team maintain charm and composure at all times, and everyone plays a role in creating something rather special. That goes for the sommelier as well, the living, breathing face of a fine wine list, featuring plenty of French classics alongside some exciting New World options.

Chef Daniel Clifford **Owner** Midsummer House Ltd **Seats** 45, Pr/dining room 16 **Times** 12-1.30/7-9 Closed 2 wks Xmas, Sun-Mon, L Tue **Prices** Prices not confirmed **Wines** 12 by glass **Parking** On street **Notes** Tasting menu 5/7/10 course £45/£75/£95, Vegetarian available, Children welcome

MIDSUMMER HOUSE

Midsummer House is located in the heart of historic Cambridge. This Victorian Villa encapsulates Daniel Clifford's vision for culinary perfection and is home to some seriously stylish food.

Daniel Clifford's quest for culinary perfection has taken the restaurant to another level over the past 13 years; his cooking has a modern-focus which is underpinned by classical French technique offering seriously sophisticated food with dishes arriving dressed to thrill.

Upstairs there is a private dining room, and a sophisticated bar and terrace for alfresco drinks with river views. Our private dining room is the perfect location for small weddings, lavish birthday celebrations, simple family gatherings or corporate entertaining.

Midsummer Common, Cambridge CB4 1HA
Tel: 01223 369299 • Fax: 01223 302672
Website: www.midsummerhouse.co.uk • Email: reservations@midsummerhouse.co.uk

CAMBRIDGE *continued*

Hotel Felix

◉◉ Modern British

tel: 01223 277977 **Whitehouse Ln, Huntingdon Rd CB3 0LX**
email: help@hotelfelix.co.uk **web:** www.hotelfelix.co.uk
dir: *M11 junct 13. From A1 N take A14 turn onto A1307. At City of Cambridge sign turn left into Whitehouse Ln*

Intricate and inventive modern cooking in a boutique hotel

This lovely bow-fronted Victorian mansion is home to a sleek boutique hotel which artfully combines elegant period features with a contemporary sheen. The Graffiti restaurant sports abstract modern art on battleship-grey walls, burnished darkwood floors, and unclothed tables, while the large terrace is a crowd puller for alfresco aperitifs and fair weather dining. Like the decor, the food is vibrant and sets off along a modern British road with plenty of sunny Mediterranean flavours along the way. It gets off the blocks with a creative juxtaposition of mackerel tartare with celeriac pannacotta, pickled candied beetroot, horseradish cream and smoked sourdough bread. Next out, ballotine of cod shares a plate with salt cod and leek brandade, roasted cauliflower and cauliflower cheese purée, and lemon and caper brown butter, while game season might see roast haunch of venison matched with kohlrabi fondant, rainbow chard, parsley root purée and whisky sauce. The inventive flair is maintained in an enterprising finale of lemon olive oil cake with lemon yoghurt sorbet, raspberry, white chocolate and lavender.

Chef Ashley Bennett **Owner** Jeremy Cassel **Seats** 45, Pr/dining room 60 **Times** 12-2/6.30-10 **Prices** Fixed L 2 course £14.50, Starter £5.50-£10.75, Main £16.25-£24, Dessert £5.50-£8.50 **Wines** 20 bottles over £30, 22 bottles under £30, 19 by glass **Parking** 90 **Notes** Afternoon tea available, Sunday L £14.50-£18.50, Vegetarian available, Children welcome

Menzies Hotels Cambridge

◉ Modern, International

tel: 01954 249988 **Bar Hill CB23 8EU**
email: cambridge@menzieshotels.co.uk **web:** www.menzieshotels.co.uk
dir: *M11 N & S to A14 follow signs for Huntingdon. A14 turn off B1050 Bar Hill, hotel 1st exit on rdbt*

Confident brasserie cooking in a golfing hotel

There's a lot going on at this modern hotel on the outskirts of Cambridge. There's a championship golf course, for a start, and with 200 acres to explore, plus a spa with swimming pool, you'll find plenty to keep just about anyone happy. The Brasserie restaurant is worth a visit, too, an open-plan space with mezzanine floors lit by an atrium-style roof; it's all very relaxed and un-starchy. Kick off with a chicken liver parfait with melba toast and onion marmalade, before moving on to Tuscan chicken with tomato broth, olive and oregano mash or Thai green curry. Wild mushroom and tarragon linguine with garlic ciabatta is a good veggie option, whilst carnivores might go for a steak cooked on the chargrill. For dessert, something like apple crumble with custard or tiramisù is sure to satisfy.

Chef Nick Wilson **Owner** Menzies Hotels **Seats** 170, Pr/dining room 50 **Times** 1-2.30/7-9.30 Closed L Sat (by appt only) **Prices** Fixed L 2 course £9.95-£16.95, Fixed D 3 course £19.95-£29.95, Starter £4.95-£8.95, Main £10.95-£24.95, Dessert £4.95-£8.95 **Wines** 2 bottles over £30, 20 bottles under £30, 11 by glass **Parking** 200 **Notes** Sunday L £9.95-£24.95, Vegetarian available, Children welcome

Midsummer House

◉◉◉◉◉ *– see page 77 and advert opposite*

Restaurant Alimentum

◉◉◉ *– see page 80*

Restaurant 22

◉ Modern European

tel: 01223 351880 **22 Chesterton Rd CB4 3AX**
email: enquiries@restaurant22.co.uk
dir: *M11 junct 13 towards Cambridge, turn left at rdbt onto Chesterton Rd*

Accomplished modish cooking in elegant little restaurant

The converted Victorian townhouse near Jesus Green conceals a discreetly elegant and comfortable dining room done out in shades of fawn, brown and beige. The menu follows a monthly-changing, set-price formula of three courses with a sorbet following the starter, which might be pheasant linguine with toasted pine nuts and sage crisps, or haddock, clam and almond chowder. The cooking is driven by market-fresh ingredients, and dishes are distinguished by a lack of frill and flounce. Consistently accomplished main courses have included griddled swordfish steak, accurately timed, with caper and marjoram sauce, rösti and roast baby vegetables, and a labour-intensive ballotine of three birds wrapped in pancetta served with pearl barley, curly kale and a Calvados reduction. The December menu might feature roast fallow deer with an unusual dark chocolate and sprout salad, a bonbon and sweet potato fondant, and close with Christmas pudding and chocolate fondant with spiced pumpkin ice cream.

Chef Mr Kipping **Owner** Mr A & Mrs S Tommaso **Seats** 26, Pr/dining room 14 **Times** 7-9.45 Closed 25 Dec & New Year, Sun-Mon, L all week **Prices** Prices not confirmed, Service optional **Wines** 26 bottles over £30, 52 bottles under £30, 6 by glass **Parking** On street **Notes** Vegetarian available, Children 10 yrs+

What makes a 5-Rosette restaurant?
See page 9

Get the most out of the AA Restaurant Guide
See page 6

Restaurant Alimentum

CAMBRIDGE
Map 12 TL45

Modern European **NOTABLE WINE LIST**

tel: 01223 413000 **152-154 Hills Rd CB2 8PB**
email: reservations@restaurantalimentum.co.uk
web: www.restaurantalimentum.co.uk
dir: *Opposite Cambridge Leisure Park*

Impeccable ingredients and classy, contemporary cooking

Located in a modern building near the city's leisure park, Alimentum (Latin for 'food': this is Cambridge, after all) has bags of contemporary-cool style, with its black-lacquered tables, walls padded in red above the leather-look banquettes, and smoked glass, plus an open-to-view kitchen giving glimpses of chef-proprietor Mark Poynton and his brigade at work. And work they certainly do, their dedication crystal clear from canapés to petits fours with coffee. Seasonality dictates what appears on the menus, with trusted local suppliers providing top-end raw materials, as the kitchen follows a broadly modern European path of diverting originality. This produces a starter of smoked eel with chicken wing, apple and onion, followed by beef sirloin with carrots and a prune and stout sauce. The terse menu descriptions fail to convey the complexity and multi-layered flavours in dishes: a straightforward-sounding main course of venison, with sweet potato, lentils, Brussels sprouts and pink peppercorn sauce, for instance, is an ideal marriage of complementary flavours. Dishes can be as traditional as a starter of haggis with swede and lentils and as classical as a main course of duck leg confit with cassoulet, and fish is treated inventively, teaming roast halibut fillet, of pinpoint accuracy, with pickled and raw cauliflower, endive and caviar. Admirable breads add to the overall appeal, and dishes are beautifully presented, perhaps to best effect in show-stealing puddings of barbecue orange with parfait, mojito and liquorice, and rhubarb with Muscovado, 'cheesecake mix' and shortbread. As well as the carte, there's a set-price lunch and early-evening menu, a seven-course 'Taste of Alimentum' and a ten-course 'Surprise' menu.

Chef Mark Poynton **Owner** Mark Poynton **Seats** 62, Pr/dining room 34 **Times** 12-2.30/6-10 Closed 24-30 Dec, BHs, L 31 Dec **Prices** Fixed L 2 course £18.50, Fixed D 3 course £24.50, Tasting menu £72-£85, Starter £13, Main £23, Dessert £13 **Wines** 178 bottles over £30, 9 bottles under £30, 22 by glass **Parking** NCP Cambridge Leisure Centre (3 min walk) **Notes** Tasting menu 'surprise' 10 course £85, Sunday L, Vegetarian available, Children welcome

The Anchor Inn

Modern British

tel: 01353 778537 **Bury Ln, Sutton Gault, Sutton CB6 2BD**
email: anchorinn@popmail.bta.com **web:** www.anchor-inn-restaurant.co.uk
dir: *Signed off B1381 in Sutton village, 7m W of Ely via A142*

Local flavours in Fen country

Sitting beside the New Bedford River or 'The Hundred Foot Drain' as locals know it, The Anchor was built around 1650 to house workers digging the canals to drain the Fens. Just seven miles from Ely, and with the big skies of Fenland all around, the setting feels remote, but inside there's the cosy ambience of period oak panelling, low-beamed ceilings and rustic pine tables on quarry tiled floors-all in all a pleasing backdrop for imaginative modern cooking. Using seasonal East Anglian produce-crabs from Cromer, Brancaster oysters and mussels, fresh local asparagus, and venison from the Denham Estate-hearty menus take in the likes of seared scallops with chorizo jam, sweet potato purée and crisps, ahead of pork tenderloin wrapped in Parma ham and filled with sage and onion cream cheese, served with black pudding potato croquette, sautéed leeks and Calvados jus. Chocolate fondant with beetroot sorbet and marshmallow sauce makes an alluring finale.

Chef Maciej Bilewski **Owner** Black Rock Inns **Seats** 70 **Times** 12-3.30/7-11 **Prices** Fixed L 2 course £13.95, Starter £5.50-£10.95, Main £11.50-£24.95, Dessert £5.50-£6.25, Service optional **Wines** 12 bottles over £30, 38 bottles under £30, 10 by glass **Parking** 16 **Notes** Sunday L, Vegetarian available, Children welcome

See advert below

The Anchor Inn

The Anchor Inn has evolved over the last 350 years and now offers every modern facility, but with a timeless charm and character that ensures you still experience a feeling of true antiquity.

Scrubbed pine tables on gently undulating floors, antique prints and roaring log fires in the winter all enhance the cosy, intimate atmosphere of this family run English Inn.

Recognized by all the major food guides, the 17th century *Anchor Inn* offers modern British Cuisine with an emphasis on seasonal and traditional ingredients.

The Anchor is ideally situated for exploring East Anglia; it is only 7 miles from the Cathedral City of Ely and is less than half an hour from the University City of Cambridge. Newmarket and its racecourse are within easy reach.

Why not come and soak up some historic atmosphere.

Sutton Gault, Sutton near Ely, Cambridgeshire CB6 2BD • Tel: 01353 778537 • Fax: 01353 776180
Website: www.anchor-inn-restaurant.co.uk • Email: anchorinn@popmail.bta.com

FORDHAM

Map 12 TL67

The White Pheasant

◎◎ Modern/Traditional British, European NEW

tel: 01638 720414 **21 Market St CB7 5LQ**
email: whitepheasant@live.com

Gastro-pub run by an accomplished chef

After setting out on his culinary career by training at the White Pheasant in 2005, Calvin Holland has returned in triumph as its new chef proprietor following a spell spent honing his craft in some pretty whizzo kitchens. The place ticks all the right boxes for a switched-on modern foodie pub with its simply decorated interior, log fires and plain wood tables, but the cooking sets it a cut above the average. The kitchen has impeccable supply lines to the best materials from local producers, bolstered by freshly-caught fish and seasonal game, and the technical nous to extract full-on flavours from it all. Duck might provide the meat for a starter, served as a crispy croquette, with its liver in a smooth parfait, home-made pickles to cut the richness, and a teriyaki sauce. Main course could see seared rump of lamb partnered with a terrine of shoulder meat and potatoes, crispy sweetbreads, peas and beans, and at the end, lemon drizzle cake comes with lemon curd, violet meringue and ginger beer sorbet.

Chef Calvin Holland **Owner** Gary & Andrea Holland **Seats** 50 **Times** 12-2.30/6.30-9.30 Closed Mon, D Sun **Prices** Fixed L 3 course fr £19.95, Fixed D 2 course fr £22.50, Tasting menu fr £29.95, Starter £6.50-£10, Main £16-£25, Dessert £6.50-£8 **Wines** 15 bottles over £30, 20 bottles under £30, 14 by glass **Parking** 25 **Notes** Sunday L £17.95-£22.95, Vegetarian available, Children welcome

HINXTON

Map 12 TL44

The Red Lion Inn

◎ Modern British

tel: 01799 530601 **32 High St CB10 1QY**
email: info@redlionhinxton.co.uk **web:** www.redlionhinxton.co.uk
dir: M11 junct 10, at rdbt take A505 continue to A1301 signed Saffron Walden/Hinxton for 0.75m & follow signs for Hinxton

Complex modern cookery in a Tudor village inn

The timbered Tudor inn wears its age on its sleeve, with an appealing rustic look both on the pinkish outside and on the beamed and brick-walled interior. Unclothed tables with plenty of space between make for a relaxed feel, and the team do their versatile best to keep everyone happy, both the traditional pub-food customers and the seekers after modern British localist gastronomy. There's much to enjoy in dishes that are often technically quite complex, such as braised pig cheeks with root veg purée, caramelised apple, leek crisps and tomato jus, and mains like truffled turbot with moules marinière, steamed leeks and gnocchi, or maple-glazed goose breast with parsnip variations in horseradish jus, decorated with a blood orange tuile. Home-made ice creams and sorbets, or cheeses with tomato chutney, are simpler alternatives to rather over-involved desserts such as caramelised lemon tart with honey, pistachio praline, mango coulis and a cider and lime sorbet.

Chef Peter Friskey **Owner** Alex Clarke **Seats** 60 **Times** 12-2/6.30-9 **Prices** Starter £5.50-£10, Main £10-£26, Dessert £2.50-£9, Service optional **Wines** 16 bottles over £30, 38 bottles under £30, 22 by glass **Parking** 43 **Notes** Tasting menus available, Pudding Club, Sunday L £12-£22, Vegetarian available, Children welcome

HUNTINGDON

Map 12 TL27

The Abbot's Elm

◎◎ Modern European NEW

tel: 01487 773773 **Abbots Ripton PE28 2PA**
email: info@theabbotselm.co.uk **web:** www.theabbotselm.co.uk
dir: A1(M) junct 13 onto A14 towards Huntingdon. At 1st rdbt straight on (A141 Spittals Way). Left at 2nd rdbt signed Abbots Ripton. 3m in village centre

Thatched inn with confident cooking

A fire a couple of years ago badly damaged this 17th-century pub, but once again the thatch is spruce and the external walls are a warm shade of pinky terracotta. The owners, John and Julia Abbey, took the opportunity to modernise the interior a bit – nothing jarring – keeping the soul of the place, and adding a bit of a contemporary sheen. With exposed oak rafters and a large brick fireplace, The Abbot's Elm has surely never looked so good. There's a lounge bar serving real ales, a cosy snug, a smart restaurant, plus three bedrooms and a cookery school where chef-patron Julia passes on her wisdom and experience. There's a beer garden, too. Expect classy pub classics and sandwiches in the bar (or garden), while the restaurant ups the ante with the likes of seared scallops and red mullet with a crab and scallop sauce. There are classical leanings to the output, with the flavours hitting the mark. Main-course breast of Tiddenham duck arrives perfectly pink, for example, served with its confit leg, dauphinoise potatoes and juniper sauce.

Chef Julia Abbey **Owner** John & Julia Abbey **Seats** 54 **Times** 12-2.15/6-9.30 Closed D Sun **Prices** Fixed L 2 course £13.95, Fixed D 3 course £22.50, Tasting menu £49.50, Starter £4.95-£9.50, Main £8.50-£22.50, Dessert £5.50-£6.75 **Wines** 27 bottles over £30, 21 bottles under £30, 29 by glass **Parking** 50 **Notes** Sunday L £17.95-£22.50, Vegetarian available, Children welcome

The Old Bridge Hotel

◎◎ Modern British ❦ NOTABLE WINE LIST

tel: 01480 424300 **1 High St PE29 3TQ**
email: oldbridge@huntsbridge.co.uk **web:** www.huntsbridge.com
dir: From A14 or A1 follow Huntingdon signs. Hotel visible from inner ring road

Notable cooking and exceptional wines from a popular establishment

The Old Bridge, at one time a bank, combines the function of busy inn, boutique-style hotel and popular, light and airy restaurant overlooking the patio. The kitchen combines Mediterranean and modern British styles with the occasional nod towards the Far East, with seasonality driving its output. One attractively presented and colourful starter is precisely seared scallops served on twigs of rosemary with squash, borlotti beans, capers, sage and chilli, forming a well-considered amalgam of flavours and textures. An alternative might be chicken and shrimp naan roll with sweet chilli dipping sauce and daikon, before main courses such as moist and tender saddle of venison accompanied by potato and beetroot boulangère, artichokes and rosemary sauce, or fillet of bass with crushed new potatoes, purple-sprouting broccoli and another well-wrought sauce, this time salsa verde. Complimentary freshly baked bread is appreciated, and skilfully made puddings could run to chocolate marquise flavoured with salted caramel served with pistachio ice cream and peanut brittle. The extensive wine list is a delight, and there's also a wine shop on site.

Chef James Claydon **Owner** J Hoskins **Seats** 100, Pr/dining room 60 **Times** 12-2/6.30-10 **Prices** Fixed L 2 course £17, Fixed D 3 course £21, Starter £6.95-£9.95, Main £13.95-£25, Dessert £6.95-£7.97, Service optional **Wines** 300 bottles over £30, 75 bottles under £30, 35 by glass **Parking** 60 **Notes** Sunday L £29.50, Vegetarian available, Children welcome

KEYSTON
Map 11 TL07

Pheasant Inn
Modern British

tel: 01832 710241 **Loop Rd PE28 ORE**
email: info@thepheasant-keyston.co.uk
dir: 0.5m off A14, clearly signed, 10m W of Huntingdon, 14m E of Kettering

Imaginative country cooking in a family-owned thatched inn

This pheasant has roosted in a tranquil farming village to the west of Huntingdon, and looks every square inch the image of an utterly charming country inn. It's a low-slung building with a thatched roof, all beams and open fires within, and dotted with tables throughout for the diners, as well as having a more formal dedicated dining room. The place exudes well-managed efficiency and cheer, with some interesting ideas worked into the well-trodden country pub route, seen in a starter of home-cured bresaola with chunks of hot beetroot, a dollop of white bean purée and truffle-oiled saladings. That might be succeeded by crisp-skinned sea bream with saffroned potato gratin in a buttery tiger prawn broth, corn-fed chicken with pancetta and pied de mouton mushrooms, or a pub stalwart like cottage pie. Finish with good artisan cheeses and walnut bread, or raisin ice cream doused in PX sherry.

Chef Simon Cadge **Owner** Simon Cadge, Gerda Koedijh **Seats** 80, Pr/dining room 30 **Times** 12-2/6.30-9.30 Closed 2-15 Jan, Mon, D Sun **Prices** Fixed L 2 course £14.95, Fixed D 3 course fr £19.95, Tasting menu fr £55, Starter £5.95-£8.95, Main £9.95-£21.95, Dessert £5.95-£7.95, Service optional **Wines** 50 bottles over £30, 25 bottles under £30, 12 by glass **Parking** 40 **Notes** Sunday L £15.95-£25, Vegetarian available, Children welcome

LITTLE WILBRAHAM
Map 12 TL55

Hole in the Wall
Modern British

tel: 01223 812282 **2 High St CB21 5JY**
email: hello@holeinthewallcambridge.co.uk
dir: A14 junct 35. A11 exit at The Wilbrahams

Classic country inn with sound seasonal cooking

In a pretty village near Cambridge, this 16th-century inn has bags of character, with open fires, low beams in the ceilings and good-natured atmosphere. Pop in for a drink or join the faithful admirers for a meal: it's easy to see why it is such a popular place, with more than a hint of the cosmopolitan about the daily-changing menu. Scallops are partnered by chorizo and served with cauliflower purée and a novel but effective pickled raisin sauce, and onion and black truffle risotto is perfectly timed to bring out its clear, robust flavours. Often innovative sauces and accompaniments add an extra dimension to sound, well-timed ingredients: a spicy caramel jus adds a touch of sweetness to first-rate roast duck, with rösti, chicory and pickled cucumber, while cod fillet is accompanied by curried granola and raisin agrodolce. Dishes are neatly and appetisingly presented, particularly puddings of lemon and Earl Grey posset, and spiced plum crumble with custard.

Chef Alex Rushmer, Ben Maude **Owner** Alex Rushmer, Ben Maude **Seats** 75, Pr/dining room 40 **Times** 12-2/7-9 Closed 2 wks Jan, Mon, L Tue, D Sun **Prices** Fixed L 2 course £16, Starter £6-£9, Main £13-£20, Dessert £6-£7 **Wines** 10 by glass **Parking** 30 **Notes** Sunday L £23-£31, Vegetarian available, Children welcome

PETERBOROUGH
Map 12 TL19

Best Western Plus Orton Hall Hotel & Spa
Modern British

tel: 01733 391111 **The Village, Orton Longueville PE2 7DN**
email: reception@ortonhall.co.uk **web:** www.bw-ortonhallhotel.co.uk
dir: off A605 E, opposite Orton Mere

Grand old building with well-crafted menu

With a heritage as the former home of the Marquess of Huntly, the old hall doesn't lack for period charm, and that certainly goes for the main restaurant, bedecked with burnished oak panels and mullioned windows. The 20-acre estate boasts a swish spa and former stables turned into an atmospheric pub, but the Huntly Restaurant catches the eye. It's a refined room with smartly dressed tables and a formal service style (drinks in the bar beforehand, for example). The cooking is broadly modern British, with starters such as a terrine of chicken and spicy pork, served with a winter apple chutney, followed by a main of poached Scottish salmon with a smoked haddock velouté and caper and parsley potatoes. To finish there might be glacé cherry and almond parfait with lemon biscuits.

Chef Kevin Wood **Owner** Abacus Hotels **Seats** 34, Pr/dining room 40 **Times** 12.30-2/7-9.30 Closed 25 Dec, L Mon-Sat **Prices** Prices not confirmed, Service optional **Wines** 10 bottles over £30, 37 bottles under £30, 6 by glass **Parking** 200 **Notes** Sunday L, Vegetarian available, Children welcome

Bull Hotel
Modern European, British

tel: 01733 561364 **Westgate PE1 1RB**
email: rooms@bull-hotel-peterborough.com **web:** www.peelhotels.co.uk
dir: Off A1, follow city centre signs. Hotel opposite Queensgate Shopping Centre. Car park on Broadway adjacent to library

Modernised classic dishes in a 17th-century coaching inn

This one-time coaching inn dates from the 17th century and still displays its period credentials out front. There's a contemporary swagger inside, though, not least in the brasserie-style restaurant out back. With its creamy neutrality and darkwood tables, the informal and cheerful vibe is matched by the spiffy staff dressed in trendy black with matching aprons. The menu deals in classic flavours and combinations, comfort food for the 21st century. Chicken liver parfait with balsamic onions and toasted onion bread is a typical first course, or there's the slightly more racy devilled sardine sandwich with tomato and apple chutney. Main-course roast rump of lamb with a fondant potato and Mediterranean-inspired flavours (olives, sun-blushed tomatoes and garlic) hits the spot, or go for chargrilled sirloin steak with parsley mash and Portobello mushrooms. Finish with a hot chocolate fondant with pistachio ice cream and sesame wafer.

Chef Jason Ingram **Owner** Peel Hotels plc **Seats** 80, Pr/dining room 200 **Times** 12-2/6.30-9.45 Closed L Sat **Prices** Fixed D 3 course £24.50-£29.50, Service optional **Wines** 3 bottles over £30, 20 bottles under £30, 8 by glass **Parking** 100 **Notes** Sunday L £10.95-£17.95, Vegetarian available, Children welcome

PIDLEY
Map 12 TL37

The Barn Restaurant
Modern British

tel: 01487 842204 **Fen Rd PE28 3DE**
email: marcello.cambridge@gmail.com
dir: *A141 from Huntingdon to Warboys. At rdbt right into Fenton Rd (B1040). Left into Fen Rd, follow brown signs for Lakeside Lodge Complex. Approx 0.75m, right to restaurant*

Modish cooking in a handsome barn

The premises is indeed a barn-a newly constructed one, built of green oak, extending over two floors and looking pretty fine inside and out. It all takes place on an upmarket caravan and camping site near St Ives, and there's a decidedly modern European spin to the menus, plus plenty of regional produce on show. Start with pan fried scallops and pork belly accompanied by a fennel and apple salad, drizzled with a cider and thyme scented jus, for example, or maybe creamy pancetta, pea and chargrilled asparagus gigli pasta topped with parmesan shavings. Main course serves up the likes of fillet of beef, pear and Roquefort wellington, with herbed parmentier potatoes and a red wine jus, and patience brings its due reward in the form of chocolate and kahlua torte topped with toasted walnuts.

Times 12.15-2.30/6.30-9.30 Closed 1st 2 wks Jan, Mon-Tue, D Sun

ST NEOTS
Map 12 TL16

The George Hotel & Brasserie
Modern British

tel: 01480 812300 **High St, Buckden PE19 5XA**
email: mail@thegeorgebuckden.com web: www.thegeorgebuckden.com
dir: *Off A1, S of junct with A14*

Popular brasserie with well-judged dishes

The heyday of the George may have seemed long gone, but the vision of Furbank family brought the old coaching inn back to life in 2003, successfully creating a venue with a cool and contemporary demeanour while respecting the integrity of the old building. The charming period exterior with its grand columns still exudes old-world solidity, but inside it is opened-up, relaxed and rather stylish. The same forethought and good sense went into the dining option, with the brasserie providing an easy-going environment but not stinting on quality. The chef's Italian background is evident in the menu, which delivers feel-good flavours based on quality ingredients (including some stuff they grow themselves). Pan-roasted scallops with cauliflower purée and punchy salsa is the chef's take on a modern classic, followed perhaps by loin of wild venison with a silky shallot purée, braised

red cabbage, wild mushrooms and a blackberry jus. Pear tarte Tatin with caramel ice cream or almond treacle tart with mascarpone cream end things indulgently.

Chef José Graziosi **Owner** Richard & Anne Furbank **Seats** 60, Pr/dining room 30 **Times** 12-2.30/7-9.30 **Prices** Fixed L 2 course £18-£19, Starter £6.25-£12.95, Main £17.95-£23, Dessert £6.50-£8.50, Service optional **Wines** 42 bottles over £30, 70 bottles under £30, 18 by glass **Parking** 25 **Notes** Sunday L £19-£24, Vegetarian available, Children welcome

STILTON
Map 12 TL18

Bell Inn Hotel
Modern British V

tel: 01733 241066 **Great North Rd PE7 3RA**
email: reception@thebellstilton.co.uk web: www.thebellstilton.co.uk
dir: *A1(M) junct 16, follow Stilton signs. Hotel in village centre*

Modish cooking in rambling old coaching inn

Dick Turpin used to pop into this rambling mellow-stone old coaching inn, and no doubt he'd recognise the fireplaces and rustic beams if he walked in today. The first-floor restaurant might look familiar to him too, with its vaulted ceiling and impressive wooden staircase leading to a gallery. The menus are more cutting edge and cosmopolitan than the surroundings would suggest, though, with seared scallops appearing with black pudding, cauliflower purée and garlic sauce, and a main course of saffron-poached salmon fillet accompanied by herby lemon risotto and a trio of beetroot. The kitchen is led by the seasons, so expect game in winter-perhaps roast breast of guinea fowl with rocket and potato croquettes, tempura broccoli and redcurrant jus-and it comes as no surprise to see no fewer than six stiltons alongside desserts of chocolate tart with pistachio ice cream, or the creative-sounding coconut and lime risotto with chocolate sorbet.

Chef Robin Devonshire **Owner** Liam McGivern **Seats** 60, Pr/dining room 20 **Times** 12-2/7-9.30 Closed 25 Dec, BHs, L Mon-Sat, D Sun **Prices** Fixed D 3 course £29.95-£38.10, Starter £4.95-£7.95, Main £9.95-£18.95, Dessert £5.45, Service optional **Wines** 6 bottles over £30, 36 bottles under £30, 8 by glass **Parking** 30 **Notes** Sunday L £15.95-£18.95, Children welcome

WANSFORD
Map 12 TL02

The Haycock Hotel
Modern British

tel: 01780 782223 & 781124 **London Rd PE8 6JA**
email: phil.brette@thehaycock.co.uk web: www.thehaycock.co.uk
dir: *In village centre accessible from A1/A47 intersection*

Bright, modish cooking in historic inn

This 16th-century coaching inn on the River Nene has been offering up hospitality for travellers for several hundred years and shows no sign of giving up the ghost. Part of the Macdonald group, the 21st-century Haycock matches the period charm of days gone by with the anticipated modern touches, so there are meeting rooms, WiFi and the like, but also a rather nifty dining option. The restaurant has shifted out of the conservatory and into a cosy room not lacking for traditional features. The kitchen is not averse to the occasional contemporary touch and modern cooking technique, so carpaccio of venison might come with a horseradish pannacotta and parmesan wafer, and a main course fillet of beef is served with an oxtail barley risotto and merlot reduction. There's evident ambition on show, although not everything reaches the same heights. For dessert, chocolate and pear brûlée is served with a brandy snap biscuit.

Times 12-2.30/6.30-9.30 Closed D Sun, 24 & 31 Dec

WISBECH
Map 12 TF40

Crown Lodge Hotel
◉ Modern, Traditional

tel: 01945 773391 **Downham Rd, Outwell PE14 8SE**
email: office@thecrownlodgehotel.co.uk **web:** www.thecrownlodgehotel.co.uk
dir: *5m SE of Wisbech on A1122, 1m from junct with A1101, towards Downham Market*

All-comers' hotel menu in a converted car showroom

On the banks of Welle Creek at Outwell, just outside Wisbech, the Crown Lodge is a modern hotel that utilises what were the expansive spaces of a car showroom to resplendent effect. An open-plan bar, lounge and restaurant allows plenty of breathing space, and looks smart and modern. It's a popular local venue, and a glance at the all-encompassing menu, which ranges from light snacks to brasserie dishes of big appeal, reveals why. A salad of goats' cheese and beetroot dressed in red wine vinegar and walnut oil is one modish way to start, three scallops with minted pea purée and hollandaise another. Main course could be mozzarella-glazed gammon steak with a sun-dried tomato and olive salad, or lemon- and thyme-crusted salmon on creamy spinach with asparagus, while comfort is assured at the finishing line in the form of a warm chocolate brownie, offset by raspberry sorbet.

Chef Jamie Symons **Owner** Mr W J Moore **Seats** 40, Pr/dining room 100
Times 12-2.30/6-10 Closed 25-26 Dec, 1 Jan **Prices** Prices not confirmed, Service optional **Wines** 4 bottles over £30, 52 bottles under £30, 10 by glass **Parking** 50
Notes Sunday L, Vegetarian available, Children welcome

CHESHIRE

ALDERLEY EDGE
Map 16 SJ87

The Alderley Restaurant
◉◉◉ – *see page 86*

BROXTON
Map 15 SJ45

De Vere Carden Park
◉ Modern British

tel: 01829 731000 **CH3 9DQ**
email: reservations.carden@devere-hotels.com **web:** www.cardenpark.co.uk
dir: *A41 signed Whitchurch to Chester, at Broxton rdbt turn on to A534 towards Wrexham. After 2m turn into Carden Park Estate*

Contemporary British cooking in a modern golfing hotel

Carden Park's Redmonds Restaurant is a smart, split-level modern setting kitted out with leather armchairs and smart wicker chairs at unclothed dark mahogany tables, and a relaxed ethos that aims for an unbuttoned approach to fine dining. Using top-quality produce to good effect, the kitchen works in a straightforward contemporary idiom, setting the ball rolling with butter-poached salmon terrine with smoked salmon, watercress mayonnaise and sun-blushed tomato and olive salad, ahead of a well-thought-out main course involving slow-braised belly pork with bubble-and-squeak, parsnip purée and crisps, black pudding fritter and root vegetable jus. To finish, vanilla pannacotta gets the exotic treatment with coconut ice cream and mango and pineapple salsa. You'll have no trouble working off the calories here: the sprawling mock-Tudor hotel is lost among 1,000 acres of verdant Cheshire countryside with woodland walks, two championship golf courses, and a spa with 20 treatment rooms.

Times 12.30-2.30/7-10 Closed L Mon-Sat, D Sun

BURWARDSLEY
Map 15 SJ55

The Pheasant Inn
◉ British, European NEW

tel: 01829 770434 **Higher Burwardsley CH3 9PF**
email: info@thepheasantinn.co.uk **web:** www.thepheasantinn.co.uk
dir: *A41 from Chester towards Whitchurch. After 6m turn left for Tattenhall. In village signs for Burwardsley. Top of hill left at PO*

Crowd-pleasing modern pub dining

With a handful of well-kept real ales at the bar, no-nonsense modern pub cooking, and comfy rooms to stay over should you care to take advantage of these twin attractions, the Pheasant is an attractive proposition. There's plenty to tempt on the menu and it's all built on a healthy showing of local produce-perhaps seared scallops with crispy pork belly, cauliflower purée and pickled raisins, ahead of braised shank of Welsh lamb from across the nearby border, Parmentier potatoes, blue cheese dumplings, red cabbage and port sauce, or you could keep it simple with timeless pub classics done well-home-made pies and gravy, or beer-battered haddock and chunky chips with mushy peas and tartare sauce. Puddings take a similarly comforting line with the likes of spotted Dick with golden syrup and real English custard, or go for a savoury finish with artisan cheeses hauled in from a 30-mile radius.

Chef Matt Leech **Owner** Sue & Harold Nelson **Seats** 120 **Times** 12-9.30 All-day dining **Prices** Starter £5-£7.95, Main £8.95-£24.95, Dessert £5.25-£8.95, Service optional **Wines** 13 bottles over £30, 27 bottles under £30, 12 by glass **Parking** 60
Notes Vegetarian available, Children welcome

CHESTER
Map 15 SJ46

Abode Chester
◉◉ Modern British NEW v

tel: 01244 405820 & 347000 **Grosvenor Rd CH1 2DJ**
email: restaurant@abodechester.co.uk **web:** www.abodechester.co.uk

Confident contemporary cooking and stellar views

The Cheshire outpost of the Abode hotel group occupies a shiny, modern rotunda overlooking Chester Racecourse. Like the others in the group (see entries for Exeter and Canterbury), Michael Caines Restaurant is the main dining option, and here it's up on the fifth floor with stellar views over the castle, racecourse and lush countryside. There's a contemporary finish to the space, with stylish fixtures and fittings such as rather glam light fittings. The service team are a well-drilled bunch. The menus – carte, tasting and table d'hôte among them – take a classical approach with contemporary touches along the way. Ham hock terrine comes with an excellent piccalilli and thyme and rosemary focaccia, while a single (and sizable) scallop is partnered with truffled celeriac purée and raisin vinaigrette. Main courses bring slow-cooked venison with sauerkraut, or pan-fried fillet of stone bass with tomato fondue and shellfish bisque. For dessert, there's the likes of pistachio soufflé with the nut also flavouring the accompanying crème anglais and ice cream.

Chef Thomas Hine **Owner** Andrew Brownsword **Seats** 82, Pr/dining room 18
Times 12-2.30/6-9.30 Closed D Sun **Prices** Fixed L 2 course £19.95, Fixed D 3 course £22.95, Tasting menu £50-£65, Starter £7.50-£15, Main £18-£24, Dessert £8.95, Service optional 12% **Wines** 90 bottles over £30, 30 bottles under £30, 10 by glass **Parking** 18 **Notes** Sunday L £14.95-£19.95, Children welcome

The Alderley Restaurant

Modern British v

tel: 01625 583033 **Alderley Edge Hotel,
Macclesfield Rd SK9 7BJ**
email: reservations@alderleyedgehotel.com
web: www.thealderleyedgehotel.com
dir: *A538 to Alderley Edge, then B5087 Macclesfield Rd*

Dynamic modern British cooking amid the Cheshire smart set

On wooded slopes overlooking the well-heeled village, this luxury hotel was built in 1850 in the Gothic-Elizabethan style by a wealthy industrialist. The conservatory restaurant is a room of some splendour, with pillars, pulled-back curtains at the windows and crisp napery on well-spaced tables, while well-informed and amiable staff keep the wheels turning. Chef Chris Holland defines his philosophy as 'modern British food, locally sourced ingredients, fresh clean flavours'. He lives up to all three, judging by what appears on the plate, and he chases innovation not for the sake of it but to make a happy marriage of flavours and textures. Typical of the style is a starter of surf and turf, a casserole of roast scallops, duck and monkfish with crispy duck skin in a delicate sauce, all evenly cooked with clearly discernible flavours. An alternative might be smoked salmon with horseradish cream, red cabbage emulsion and apple and bagel crisps, a prelude to perfectly timed roast sea bass fillets in a rich smoked prawn emulsion accompanied by brown shrimps and a crab doughnut. Dishes can be less lavish and rarefied than the country-house norm, one dinner menu offering slow-cooked beef cheeks with smoked tongue, béarnaise mash and crispy onions, or shoulder of suckling pig with impeccable crackling, apple, shallots and sage. Well-kept cheeses are all patriotically British, and desserts are as well thought out, impressively constructed and attractive as the rest of the show, often with fruit as the base. Choose from 'toffee apple' (parfait and sorbet with dehydrated caramel crumble), or poached kumquats with mandarin sorbet, cheesecake cream and textures of parkin. There's also a brasserie with a separate menu.

Chef Chris Holland **Owner** J W Lees (Brewers) Ltd **Seats** 80, Pr/dining room 130 **Times** 12-2/7-10 Closed 1 Jan, L 31 Dec, D 25-26 Dec **Prices** Fixed L 2 course fr £22.95, Tasting menu £36.95-£69.95, Starter £11.95-£12.50, Main £23.50-£24.25, Dessert £10.95, Service optional **Wines** 300 bottles over £30, 19 bottles under £30, 16 by glass **Parking** 82 **Notes** Sunday L fr £27.95, Children welcome

CHESTER *continued*

La Brasserie at The Chester Grosvenor & Spa

Modern, European

tel: 01244 324024 **Eastgate CH1 1LT**
email: restaurants@chestergrosvenor.co.uk
dir: *A56 follow signs for city centre hotels. On Eastgate St next to the Eastgate clock*

Top-end brasserie dining at landmark hotel

Offering commendable support to its superstar sibling – Simon Radley at The Chester Grosvenor – the brasserie at this landmark hotel is no shrinking violet. With all the swagger of an authentique Parisian outfit, La Brasserie has black-leather banquettes, wooden floors, shimmering brass and a giant hand-painted glass skylight, plus a menu that builds on the classic repertoire with confidence. A first course dish called 'Piglet' turns out some tender pork belly in the company of a squid cassoulet, or go for the simplicity of Severn and Wye smoked salmon. Veal T-bone steak is cooked to delicious smokiness in the Josper grill and comes with Italian ham, artichokes, figs and chestnuts. The Josper is put to good use throughout, with Welsh dry-aged beef cooked over sustainably sourced wood from Kent. Seafood gets a look-in, too, with the likes of Atlantic cod and sea bass cooked as you like and served with a choice of sauces. That leaves desserts such as a terrific Grosvenor chocolate cheesecake with raspberry ice.

Chef Simon Radley, Howard Edwards, Duncan Highway **Owner** Grosvenor - Duke of Westminster **Seats** 80, Pr/dining room 228 **Times** 12-10.30 Closed 25 Dec, All-day dining **Prices** Fixed L 2 course £19.50, Starter £7.95-£13.95, Main £15.95-£28.95, Dessert £6.75-£8.50, Service optional **Wines** 13 bottles over £30, 19 bottles under £30, 32 by glass **Parking** 250, NCP attached to hotel **Notes** Champagne Sun 3 course £35, Vegetarian available, Children welcome

Fifteen Thirty Nine Bar & Restaurant

Modern British

tel: 01244 304611 & 304610 **Chester Race Company Limited, The Racecourse CH1 2LY**
email: restaurant1539@chester-races.com
dir: *Located in Chester racecourse, access via main car park entrance or by foot from Nun's Road*

Ambitious modish cooking overlooking the racecourse

A day at the races can be a very urbane event these days, especially if you head for Chester and grab a table in Restaurant Fifteen Thirty Nine. With its 180 degree views over the racecourse through floor-to-ceiling windows, and contemporary good looks inside, it's a smart setting for some sharp modern food. There's a bar and roof terrace, too. The kitchen rightfully makes a big deal of regional ingredients and there's a good amount of creativity on show. Treacle-cured trout gravad lax with red pepper caramel and 10-hour squid is a starter which demonstrates the ambition here. Move on to a steak from the Vale of Clwyd (rib-eye, perhaps), or butter-poached turbot with a parmesan and basil cream and ratatouille tortellini. And finish with a funky iced buttermilk parfait with rosewater jelly and macerated strawberries. The lunch menu is a steal and the wine list designed to impress.

Chef Darren Boddy **Owner** Chester Race Company **Seats** 160, Pr/dining room 60 **Times** 12-9.30 Closed D Sun All-day dining **Prices** Fixed L 2 course fr £15.39, Fixed D 2 course fr £15.39, Starter £4.95-£12.50, Main £12.50-£28.50, Dessert £4.95-£5.50, Service optional **Wines** 40 bottles over £30, 20 bottles under £30, 14 by glass **Notes** Sunday L £15.39-£19.95, Vegetarian available, Children welcome

Grosvenor Pulford Hotel & Spa

Mediterranean, European

tel: 01244 570560 **Wrexham Rd, Pulford CH4 9DG**
email: enquiries@grosvenorpulfordhotel.co.uk **web:** www.grosvenorpulfordhotel.co.uk
dir: *M53/A55 at junct signed A483 Chester/Wrexham & North Wales. Left onto B5445, hotel 2m on right*

The flavours of the Med in a smart hotel

The sprawling red-brick hotel has a swish spa, luxe bedrooms, and pretty gardens for a stroll or photos (it's a big hit on the local wedding scene), but the main dining option of Ciro's Brasserie really stands out with its classical theme recalling ancient Rome via arches, murals and stucco paintwork. Note that the service team do not wear togas. If it all sounds a little 'theme-y', rest assured it is actually rather charming and fits the bill with its Italian and broadly Mediterranean-inspired menu. Chicken liver parfait with plum and apple chutney and toasted brioche is one way to begin, or go for ravioli filled with oak-smoked salmon and creamed leeks. Main courses are equally well crafted and well considered: Ciro's bouillabaisse, for example, packed with fresh seafood, or blade of beef braised for six hours and served with horseradish creamed potatoes and roasted root vegetables.

Chef Richard Pierce, Paul Prescott **Owner** Harold & Susan Nelson **Seats** 120, Pr/dining room 200 **Times** 12-2/6-9.30 **Prices** Starter £5.95-£9.95, Main £9.25-£28.95, Dessert £6.50-£8.95, Service optional **Wines** 16 bottles over £30, 30 bottles under £30, 12 by glass **Parking** 200 **Notes** Afternoon tea available £24.95 for 2 people, Sunday L £11.95-£22.95, Vegetarian available, Children welcome

What makes a 3-Rosette restaurant? See page 9

CHESTER *continued*

Rowton Hall Country House Hotel & Spa

◉ Traditional British

tel: 01244 335262 **Whitchurch Rd, Rowton CH3 6AD**
email: reception@rowtonhallhotelandspa.co.uk **web:** www.rowtonhall.co.uk
dir: *M56 junct 12, A56 to Chester. At rdbt left onto A41 towards Whitchurch. Approx 1m, follow hotel signs*

Modern and classic menus in a Georgian manor

A grand house with plenty of Georgian period charm and eight acres of grounds, these days Rowton is a big hit on the wedding and conference circuit, with all the usual facilities. It is home to the Langdale restaurant, with its oak-panelled walls and smart linen-clad tables. There's evident classic French culinary influence on the menu and plenty of seasonal British produce on show, while the kitchen is not averse to modern culinary techniques. Start with a sous-vide-cooked loin and leg of rabbit, served with spiced carrot and vanilla foam, for example, or their home-cured gravad lax with a salad of baby chard and beetroot. Main-course rump of lamb might come with minted pea and broad bean cassoulet, plus baby fondants and rosemary jus. Desserts run to blueberry and passionfruit cheesecake with mini passionfruit jellies.

Chef Jamie Leon **Owner** Mr & Mrs Wigginton **Seats** 70, Pr/dining room 120 **Times** 12-2/7-9.30 **Prices** Fixed L 2 course £9.50-£14.50, Fixed D 3 course £19.95-£28.50, Starter £5.95-£14.95, Main £8.95-£28.95, Dessert £4.50-£8.95, Service optional **Wines** **Parking** 200 **Notes** Sunday L £18.50, Vegetarian available, Children welcome

Simon Radley at The Chester Grosvenor

◉◉◉◉ – *see opposite*

AA RESTAURANT OF THE YEAR FOR ENGLAND 2014–15

The Sticky Walnut

◉◉ Modern European **NEW**

tel: 01244 400400 **11 Charles St CH2 3AZ**
dir: *5 mins from Chester train station*

Well-presented high quality seasonal dishes and rustic charm

With its shop-front exterior and rough-and-ready rustic vibe, The Sticky Walnut is a neighbourhood restaurant for the 21st-century-unpretentious, chilled-out and serious about the end product. It is spread over two floors, with chunky wooden tables, blackboards and an open kitchen. On the plate is some seriously good stuff based on excellent seasonal ingredients. There's a broadly European spin to much of the menu and both concept and execution are pretty much bang on. Crispy lamb's tongue with chick pea purée, goats' curd and tomato is a first course that delivers complementary flavours and shows refinement in its presentation. Or choose Jerusalem artichoke soup with focaccia, or sea bream céviche, before a main course of roast grouse with a quenelle of pâté of the same, served with cocotte potatoes, parsnip purée and cavolo nero. With tip-top bread and desserts like blackberry and almond tart with bumper fruits and a perfect thin and crisp pastry base, this is a kitchen that delivers real impact in a relaxed, modern manner.

Chef Gary Usher **Owner** Gary Usher **Seats** 50 **Times** 12-3/6-10 Closed 25-27 Dec, 1-2 Jan, D Sun **Prices** Starter £5-£9, Main £14-£30, Dessert £5-£8 **Wines** 10 bottles over £30, 20 bottles under £30, 11 by glass **Parking** Car park nearby **Notes** Sunday L £16-£20, Vegetarian available, Children welcome

Crewe Hall

◉ Modern European

tel: 01270 253333 & 259319 **Weston Rd CW1 6UZ**
email: crewehall@qhotels.co.uk **web:** www.qhotels.co.uk
dir: *M6 junct 16 follow A500 to Crewe. Last exit at rdbt onto A5020. 1st exit next rdbt to Crewe. Crewe Hall 150yds on right*

Contemporary brasserie in a 17th-century stately home

Crewe Hall is a seriously stately home that truly deserves its Grade I listed status. It is an undeniably magnificent slice of Jacobean architecture, but also manages to pull off a balancing act between displaying its abundant period character and blending seamlessly with 21st-century style, as typified in the Brasserie, located in the contemporary west wing, where its light, fresh, neutral decor makes a complete contrast to the lavish interior of the main building. In tune with the surroundings, the kitchen turns out a straightforward modern repertoire, from openers like confit duck leg rillettes with pistachio purée, red radish cress, and pickled breakfast radish, to main course ideas along the lines of salt-crusted lamb shank with château potatoes, glazed carrots, fine beans and rosemary jus. Presentation is a forte, and flavours stay clean and well balanced through to desserts such as a modishly vegetable-based beetroot pannacotta and sorbet with walnut crisp.

Chef Brian Spark **Owner** QHotels **Seats** 140 **Times** All day All-day dining **Prices** Prices not confirmed, Service optional **Wines** **Parking** 500 **Notes** Sunday L, Vegetarian available, Children welcome

Cottons Hotel & Spa

◉ Mediterranean, International, British

tel: 01565 650333 **Manchester Rd WA16 0SU**
email: cottons.dm@shirehotels.com **web:** www.cottonshotel.com
dir: *On A50, 1m from M6 junct 19*

Broadly appealing menus in modern surroundings

Indulge in a spa treatment before a blowout in the sleekly designed restaurant at Cottons, a large, modern hotel at the edge of town. The menu is an appealing package, with ideas culled from all over. Starters have run to tempura prawns with chilli dipping sauce, and crispy duck with watercress and coriander salad. Alternatively, go for the 'taste of the Cheshire table' and choose a selection of seafood, cured meats and salads, and move on to perhaps fish curry, pancetta-wrapped pork fillet with mustardy sauce, Savoy cabbage and rösti, or something from the chargrill: perhaps rib-eye with barbecue sauce. End with an inventive pudding like white chocolate and raspberry crème brûlée, or toffee apple cheesecake with caramelised popcorn and apple sorbet.

Chef Adrian Sedden **Owner** Shire Hotels **Seats** 80, Pr/dining room 30 **Times** 12-2/7-9.30 **Prices** Prices not confirmed, Service optional **Wines** 15 bottles over £30, 34 bottles under £30, 18 by glass **Parking** 120 **Notes** Afternoon tea, Early bird menu & Supper events available, Sunday L, Vegetarian available, Children welcome

Simon Radley at The Chester Grosvenor

CHESTER | Map 15 SJ46

Modern French V  NOTABLE WINE LIST

tel: 01244 324024 & 895618 **Chester Grosvenor & Spa, Eastgate CH1 1LT**
email: hotel@chestergrosvenor.co.uk
web: www.chestergrosvenor.co.uk
dir: *A56 signs for city centre hotels. On Eastgate St next to the Eastgate clock*

Cooking of grand excitement in Chester's crown jewel hotel

The term 'landmark' is easy to over use, but that's exactly what The Grosvenor is to Chester, holding court since Elizabeth I ruled the roost. It is not, however, just the fabric of the building, standing proud within the ancient Roman walls of the city, that has made this place's reputation, for it can also be called a landmark hotel, and, in the shape of the Simon Radley restaurant, it has one of the North West's landmark restaurants. Part of the Duke of Westminster's property portfolio, the luxurious finish of the interiors and the high-end service would make it stand out in any crowd. (The valet parking sets the tone from the off). The public rooms are lavishly decorated, with a swish bar and classy brasserie among its many riches, plus the de rigueur spa. The jewel in the crown, though, is surely the restaurant, carrying the name of the chef who has done so much to enhance the reputation of the Chester Grosvenor as a serious player on the national stage. The room is suitably refined and classically dignified, while the service maintains a high standard of care and attention all day long. The cooking is contemporary and refined, with a clarity and purity that is not easily found. Modern French, you might say if a label was required. Everything is on the plate for a reason, each ingredient of a very high quality indeed, and all allowed room to be noticed. Needless to say there are all the expected amuses and pre-this and pre-that, and they

may well indeed blow you away, as will the bread – oh the bread – which is a glorious array. A first course snail canapé with frogs' legs bonbons and black and white garlic is full of earthy richness, the balance of each ingredient spot on, or go for another of caramelised veal sweetbread with vanilla-scented lobster tail and avocado purée. Acute technical skills and sound judgement are very much in evidence right the way through. Main-course Yorkshire grouse delivers the tricky bird moist and packed with flavour, served with a gingerbread pain perdu rich with gamey liver, punchy pickled girolles and redcurrant pastilles. Another has Gressingham duck with salt-baked beets, forced rhubarb, fondant liver and pain d'épice. Desserts show no let-up in the craft and creativity: Valrhona chocolate caramel, perhaps, with torched banana, spiced rum and fat raisins. The final piece in the jigsaw is a wine list that is positively A-list.

Chef Simon Radley, Ray Booker **Owner** Grosvenor - Duke of Westminster **Seats** 45, Pr/dining room 228
Times 6.30-9.30 Closed 25 Dec, 1 wk Jan, Sun-Mon, L all week (ex Dec) **Prices** Fixed D 3 course £69, Tasting menu £90 **Wines** 543 bottles over £30, 57 bottles under £30, 15 by glass **Parking** Car park attached to hotel (£10 24hrs)
Notes Tasting menu (incl vegetarian) 8 course No children

KNUTSFORD *continued*

Mere Court Hotel & Conference Centre

◉ Mediterranean, Modern British

tel: 01565 831000 **Warrington Rd, Mere WA16 0RW**
email: sales@merecourt.co.uk **web:** www.merecourt.co.uk
dir: A50, 1m W of junct with A556, on right

Arts and Crafts style and creative modern cooking

Dating from the turn of the 20th century, Mere Court is an Arts and Crafts house with plenty of period swagger – carved wood, metalwork and stained glass included. With seven acres of lush gardens and a lake, this country-house hotel has bags of appeal. The oak-panelled Arboretum Restaurant is an elegant spot, with lake views, and is the setting for some upbeat modern European cooking. Fillet of cold-smoked salmon comes in a first course with soft boiled quails' eggs, beetroot fondant and dill mayonnaise, while main courses might include breast of Gressingham duck with its confit of leg meat turned into a Scotch egg, plus parsnip mash and caramelised chicory. Desserts are similarly creative: white peach parfait, for example, with caramel-roasted white nectarine and peach crisps.

Times 12-2/6.30-9.30

The Mere Golf Resort & Spa

◉◉ International

tel: 01565 830155 **Chester Rd, Mere WA16 6LJ**
email: reservations@themereresort.co.uk **web:** www.themereresort.co.uk
dir: M6 junct 19 or M56 junct 7

Modern Brit brasserie cooking at a Cheshire resort

A golfing resort and health spa not far from Knutsford, the Mere is a must for Cheshire's denizens of the fairways. It's also a good location for accomplished brasserie dining, which takes place in the open-plan Browns, named after a former luminary of the Mere, Max Brown. Linen tablecloths and relatively formal service are slightly at odds with the overall tone, but the food makes some good modern statements. Start perhaps with smoked salmon and salmon rillettes with horseradish cream, beetroot and watercress. Deeply flavoured oxtail roulade with creamed parsnip and a potato scone makes a more robust opener, as a prelude to the likes of well-seasoned grilled John Dory with apple, mussels and pancetta, or slow-cooked venison rump with baby turnips, spiced pear and carrot purée in redcurrant and rosemary sauce. Finish with sticky toffee pudding in butterscotch sauce with vanilla ice cream, or a selection of cheeses with tomato chutney.

Chef Mark Walker **Owner** Mark Boler **Seats** 76, Pr/dining room 60
Times 12.30-4/6-9.30 **Prices** Starter £6.50-£14.50, Main £14.95-£31, Dessert £6.95-£10.95 **Wines** 15 bottles over £30, 2 bottles under £30, 6 by glass
Parking 400 **Notes** Sunday L £18.95, Vegetarian available, Children welcome

Read our interview with chef Michael Caines on page 29

The Church Green British Grill

◉◉ Modern British v

tel: 01925 752068 **Higher Ln WA13 0AP**
email: reservations@thechurchgreen.co.uk
dir: M6 junct 20 follow signs for Lymm along B5158 after 1.5m turn right at T-junct onto A56 towards Altrincham, on right after 0.5m

A class act in a refurbished village pub

Aiden Byrne is a modern media-savvy British chef par excellence. Having made his bones in A-list kitchens-Tom Aikens, Pied à Terre, and The Grill at The Dorchester, among others-he has become a well-known face on the telly, written a cookbook and set up on his own account in The Church Green, a stylishly reinvented old pub in a Cheshire village. Inside is the bare brickwork, natural wood, leather seating and neutral hues you'd expect in a contemporary gastro set-up, and his wife Sarah presides over a switched-on front-of-house team. Byrne stays in touch with the zeitgeist, so in order to chime with the prevailing mood of belt-tightening austerity, he reined in the culinary concept from fine dining to a 'British Grill' with a simplified, more everyman appeal. Be assured, though, that the same uncompromising approach to sourcing the finest local and seasonal ingredients still drives the operation. There are homely classics-steak and kidney pudding, beef hotpot, sausages and mash-or potted Lancashire shrimps, a traditional dish brought bang up to date by adding nutmeg mayonnaise, toasted sourdough bread and apple and watercress salad to the deal. Seared over coconut husk charcoal on the Inka grill, 28-day dry-aged steaks sourced from small Cheshire farms are exemplary, as witnessed in a perfectly-timed and well-rested rib-eye with bonbons of bone marrow and stilton, beef dripping chips and béarnaise sauce.

Chef Aiden Byrne, Ben Chaplin **Owner** Aiden & Sarah Byrne **Seats** 50 **Times** 12-9.30 Closed 25 Dec, All-day dining **Prices** Starter £3-£12, Main £6-£35, Dessert £4-£10, Service optional **Wines** 29 bottles over £30, 28 bottles under £30, 18 by glass **Parking** 25 **Notes** Tasting menu 5 course, Sunday L £15-£25, Children welcome

The Lord Clyde

◉◉ Modern British **NEW**

tel: 01625 562123 **36 Clarke Ln, Kerridge SK10 5AH**
email: hello@thelordclyde.co.uk

Bold contemporary cooking in a charming pub

Something exciting is happening at this charming Victorian inn in a pretty Cheshire village. It's a perfectly pastoral setting, all sweetness and light, but chef Ernst van Zyl is exploding fireworks within (metaphorically speaking). The South African born chef-patron has worked stages at the Fat Duck and Noma and his passion is for contemporary and dynamic cuisine that lingers in the memory. Take a starter of monkish cheeks with lamb's tongue, cucumber and pineapple, which is a vibrant and refreshing combination where a lot of work creates a relatively simple and delicious result. Main-course duck breast with spelt, aubergine and carrot – dish descriptions are minimalistic – is another cracking course, with high quality produce at its heart and lots of harmonious flavours. For dessert, there are more interesting combinations of flavour and texture (showing superb technical skills), with rhubarb and orange in various forms combined with parmesan and nutmeg. It all takes place in a relaxed setting – no stiff linen clothes here – and it goes without saying it is one to watch.

Chef Ernst van Zyl **Owner** Sarah Richmond, Ernst van Zyl **Seats** 24
Times 12-2.30/6.30-9 Closed Mon, D Sun **Prices** Fixed L 2 course £16, Tasting menu £45, Starter £6-£9, Main £12-£19, Dessert £6.50-£8 **Wines** 12 by glass **Parking** 7
Notes Tasting menu 7 course including wine £80, Sunday L £19, Vegetarian available, Children welcome

Shrigley Hall Hotel, Golf & Country Club

Modern British V

tel: 01625 575757 **Shrigley Park, Pott Shrigley SK10 5SB**
email: shrigleyhall@pumahotels.co.uk **web:** www.pumahotels.co.uk
dir: *Exit A523 at Legh Arms towards Pott Shrigley. Hotel 2m on left before village*

Modern British cooking in a stately Georgian hotel

Built in 1825 for William Turner MP, in the days when second homes were less controversial, Shrigley hasn't lost an iota of its grandeur over the past two centuries – the painted domed ceiling above the grand staircase is not to be missed. A spacious, elegant room overlooking the grounds, with the distant Peaks as backdrop, the Oakridge dining room goes for the swagged-curtains-and-chandeliers look as a backdrop to a classical culinary approach. Poached and roasted pork fillet with carrot purée, wilted spinach, and red wine and oregano sauce turns up as a main course, as might chicken roulade with leeks and wild mushrooms, prune purée and red wine jus. Bookending those are the likes of chicken liver parfait with red onion jam and brioche, or a more with-it goats' cheese pannacotta with sun-blushed tomatoes, gem lettuce and black olive bread, and favourite puddings such as raspberry Bakewell tart with ripple parfait.

Chef Colin Gannon **Owner** Puma Hotels **Seats** 130, Pr/dining room 20 **Times** 7-9 Closed L Mon-Sat **Prices** Fixed L 3 course £29, Fixed D 3 course £29, Starter £8-£10, Main £15-£20, Dessert £6-£8, Service optional **Wines** 25 bottles over £30, 15 bottles under £30, 6 by glass **Parking** 250 **Notes** Sunday L £12-£22, Children welcome

---

NANTWICH Map 15 SJ65

Rookery Hall Hotel & Spa

Modern British

tel: 0845 0727 533 **Main Rd, Worleston CW5 6DQ**
email: rookeryhall@handpicked.co.uk **web:** www.handpickedhotels.co.uk/rookeryhall
dir: *B5074 off 4th rdbt, on Nantwich by-pass. Hotel 1.5m on right*

Old-school comforts in an imposing Cheshire mansion

The hall is a solidly imposing bolt-hole from the rigours of the kind of modern living that goes on in nearby Manchester and along the teeming M6. It stands serene amid 38 acres of rolling Cheshire, its late-Georgian magnificence making an impressive backdrop for the spa treatments and contemporary cooking we expect to find-in that order. Enjoy an evening starter perhaps, that looks like breakfast with its runny-yolked warm Scotch egg, black pudding, tomato, brown sauce, and buttered brioche in lieu of a muffin. Otherwise, poached pear has inched its way up the menu from third course to first-though still stained with red wine, it comes with Waldorf salad. Main could be a crisp-skinned rendition of Goosnargh duck confit, along with white bean purée and creamed cabbage in a light reduction sauce of redcurrant and rosemary. Lemon cheesecake comes with an intense cherry sorbet to round it all off.

Chef Michael Batters **Owner** Hand Picked Hotels **Seats** 90, Pr/dining room 160 **Times** 12-2/7-9.30 Closed L Mon-Sat **Prices** Fixed D 3 course £37, Tasting menu £65, Starter £10.75-£14.50, Main £21.50-£34.50, Dessert £11, Service optional **Wines** 81 bottles over £30, 9 bottles under £30, 12 by glass **Parking** 100 **Notes** Tasting menu 8 courses, Sunday L £22.95, Vegetarian available, Children welcome

---

PECKFORTON Map 15 SJ55

1851 Restaurant at Peckforton Castle

— see below

1851 Restaurant at Peckforton Castle

PECKFORTON Map 15 SJ55

Modern British, French
tel: 01829 260930 **Stonehouse Ln CW6 9TN**
email: info@peckfortoncastle.co.uk **web:** www.peckfortoncastle.co.uk
dir: *15m from Chester, situated near Tarporley*

Food fit for a king in a mock-medieval castle

It's not estate agent's blag: Peckforton really has got what it takes to call itself a castle. Admittedly it was built in the Victorian era in the gothic, mock-medieval style, so it has never had to rebuff an onslaught from an invading army, but it looks great. It stands surrounded by lush Cheshire countryside and is a big hit on the wedding scene. The 1851 Restaurant is named after the year the house was constructed and is an opulent room with a deep-pile carpet, thick napery, highly polished glassware and sparkling silverware. Head chef Mark Ellis makes excellent use of the county's produce, serving up dishes that can be creative and thrillingly contemporary, or comforting in their simplicity. In both cases, the quality of the ingredients shines out. If you're in the mood for something straight-up, check out the locally-sourced Angus steaks cooked over charcoal in the Bertha oven (rib-eye, perhaps, or surf 'n' turf with langoustine or scallops joining the party). A first-course of wild duck tenderloin shows technical accomplishment, with the bird served with its poached liver and skin as a 'crumble', plus the flavours of tangerine and gingerbread, as does another starter where sea trout is marinated in treacle for 24 hours, partnered with cockles, pistachios and a hint of liquorice. Main-course fillet of Estate venison doesn't want for va-va-voom either, with accompanying pickled cabbage and young parsnips. For dessert, 'Hive' is a honey-laden ginger biscuit enriched with smooth cream cheese, Cheshire honeycomb and lemon, and 'Almond' is a dish with frangipane, forced winter rhubarb and Amaretto cream, while the cheese selection is a regional bunch kept in tip-top condition.

Chef Mark Ellis **Owner** Naylor family **Seats** 60, Pr/dining room 165 **Times** 6-8.45 Closed L Mon-Sat **Prices** Fixed L 2 course fr £21.95, Fixed D 3 course fr £45, Service optional 10% **Wines** 39 bottles over £30, 27 bottles under £30, 10 by glass **Parking** 100 **Notes** Sun L served all day 12.30-8.45pm, Sunday L, Vegetarian available, Children welcome

PUDDINGTON
Map 15 SJ37

Macdonald Craxton Wood Hotel

@ @ Modern British V

tel: 0151 347 4000 & 347 4016 **Parkgate Rd, Ledsham CH66 9PB**
email: events.craxton@macdonald-hotels.co.uk
web: www.macdonaldhotels.co.uk/craxtonwood
dir: *from M6 take M56 towards N Wales, then A5117/A540 to Hoylake. Hotel on left 200yds past lights*

Smart British cooking and top-notch ingredients

Just a short drive from Chester, this grand-looking hotel is surrounded by 27 acres of peaceful woodland. It's a stylish and relaxed sort of place, with a restaurant done out in muted mauve colours and round-backed padded dining chairs upholstered in striped fabric. The Josper grill comes into its own for main-course meats – rump of Highland lamb, beef sirloin, pork cutlets, all served with traditional accompaniments and a choice of sauces – but the cooking has a lot more going for it. The kitchen has compiled an enterprising, all-embracing menu and turns out some fashionably imaginative dishes, such as starters of black pudding Scotch egg with mustard mayonnaise, apple, watercress and bacon, braised pig's cheek with scallops, squash and date purée, and salads (also available as a main course) such as crayfish tail Caesar with bacon. Quality produce, confidently handled is at the heart of the operation, seen in main courses of crispy pork belly with cranberries, chestnuts and Savoy cabbage, and cod fillet with seared scallops and crispy chicken wing.

Chef David Ashton **Owner** Macdonald Hotels **Seats** 100, Pr/dining room 12
Times 12-11 Closed L Mon-Sat All-day dining **Prices** Service optional **Wines** 32 bottles over £30, 28 bottles under £30, 12 by glass **Parking** 300 **Notes** Sunday L £12-£15, Children welcome

SANDIWAY
Map 15 SJ67

Nunsmere Hall Hotel

@ @ British, European

tel: 01606 889100 **Tarporley Rd, Oakmere CW8 2ES**
email: reservations@nunsmere.co.uk web: www.nunsmere.co.uk
dir: *M6 junct 18, A54 to Chester, at x-rds with A49 turn left towards Tarporley, hotel 2m on left*

Impressive locally based cooking in a glittering Edwardian mansion

Nunsmere was built around the turn of the last century for Sir Aubrey Brocklebank, scion of a Georgian shipping line eventually swallowed up by Cunard, and was the centre of a glittering Edwardian social whirl. Surrounded on three sides by an ornamental lake almost big enough to float a cruise liner, the house is camouflaged in layers of climbing foliage. The Crystal dining room enjoys peeps of the grounds, and is furnished in country-interiors style, with full-length tablecloths and floral adornments. The kitchen tacks to a local and organic course wherever possible, and results are impressive. If you missed breakfast, start with a crispy duck egg, served with black pudding, chorizo, ketchup and breadsticks, before moving on to lemon sole with shrimp risotto and a tempura-battered oyster in cucumber and horseradish sauce, or venison loin in bitter chocolate with red cabbage, roast parsnip and puréed figs. Dessert might be a creative take on crème brûlée with passionfruit sorbet and orange straws, or warm chocolate mousse with mint ice cream and a brownie.

Chef Craig Malone **Owner** Prima Hotels **Seats** 60, Pr/dining room 80
Times 12-2/7-9.30 **Prices** Fixed L 2 course £16.95-£18.95, Fixed D 3 course £34.50-£36.50, Tasting menu fr £49.50, Service optional 12.5% **Wines** 66 bottles over £30, 32 bottles under £30, 15 by glass **Parking** 80 **Notes** Sunday L £27.50-£29, Vegetarian available, Children welcome

TARPORLEY
Map 15 SJ56

Macdonald Portal Hotel Golf & Spa

@ Modern British

tel: 0844 879 9082 **Cobbiers Cross Ln CW6 0DJ**
email: general.portal@macdonald-hotels.co.uk
web: www.macdonaldhotels.co.uk/the portal
dir: *Off A49 in village of Tarporley*

Sophisticated country-club setting for classic cuisine

With three courses spread around its expansive acreages of rolling Cheshire countryside, it is odds-on that most guests are up for a spot of golf at this upscale contemporary hotel, and those not bearing a weighty bag of clubs will no doubt be heading for some serious pampering in the glossy spa. Named after the 12th-century Earl of Chester who built nearby Beeston Castle, the classy Ranulf Restaurant has a clubby feel thanks to a butch decor of sleek contemporary wall panelling, tobacco-hued leather banquettes and bare darkwood tables, softened by romantic candlelight in the evening. The kitchen sources its materials well, and has the sense not to faff around with them, offering among starters Stornoway black pudding with caramelised apple and bacon salad, or fishcakes with caper mayonnaise. Main courses continue the theme of tried-and-true classics – Scottish sirloin or rib-eye steaks sizzling from the grill, or pan-fried fillet of wild sea bass with new potatoes and seasonal greens. Puds are equally comforting – perhaps Eton Mess or a straight-up crème brûlée.

Chef Gary Hazlehurst **Owner** Macdonald Hotels **Seats** 100, Pr/dining room 45
Times 6-9.30 Closed L all week **Prices** Prices not confirmed, Service optional **Wines** 19 by glass **Parking** 200 **Notes** Sunday L, Vegetarian available, Children welcome

 **Learn the latest foodie trends** in Birmingham and Manchester on page 21

WARMINGHAM
Map 15 SJ76

The Bear's Paw
Modern European, British

tel: 01270 526317 **School Ln CW11 3QN**
email: info@thebearspaw.co.uk **web:** www.thebearspaw.co.uk
dir: M6 junct 17, A534, A533 signed Middlewich & Northwich. Continue on A533, left into Mill Ln, left into Warmingham Ln. Right into Plant Ln, left into Green Ln

Northwestern cooking in a modernised village pub

A Victorian pub in the timbered idiom, the Bear's Paw is to be found in a village not far from Sandbach. It's been given a modern makeover inside, with lots of light wood, plenty of space, and library shelves adding a touch of refinement to the dining room. Local farmers and trawlers are called upon to supply the kitchen with quality northwestern produce, with cheeses and ice creams also sourced from within a tightly drawn radius. It all ends up on a lengthy menu of modern country-inn cooking, taking in home-produced black pudding with a poached duck egg and pea purée in mustard sauce, or salmon rillettes with beetroot and chive crème fraîche, to begin. This is followed by the likes of steak-and-ale pie and chips, amaretti-topped Stilton and vegetable lasagne, or hake fillet with a potato and turnip cake and pancetta in clam velouté. Finish with a textbook rendition of Black Forest gâteau, or Bakewell tart with blackcurrant sorbet.

Chef Scott Cunningham **Owner** Harold & Susan Nelson **Seats** 150 **Times** 12-9.30 All-day dining **Prices** Starter £5.50-£7.50, Main £10.95-£23.95, Dessert £5.95-£9.95, Service optional **Wines** 16 bottles over £30, 27 bottles under £30, 10 by glass **Parking** 75 **Notes** Sunday L, Vegetarian available, Children welcome

Who has won our Food Service Award?
See page 13

WILMSLOW
Map 16 SJ88

Stanneylands Hotel
Modern British

tel: 01625 525225 **Stanneylands Rd SK9 4EY**
email: sales@stanneylandshotel.co.uk **web:** www.stanneylandshotel.co.uk
dir: from M56 at airport turn off, follow signs to Wilmslow. Left into Station Rd, onto Stanneylands Rd. Hotel on right

Classically based cooking in a stylish Cheshire hotel

Despite being over the county border in Cheshire, Wilmslow has long been a gentrified refuge from nearby Manchester and the airport, which makes Stanneylands a good bet for the business traveller, as well as those seeking an escape from urban bustle. Way back in the 18th century, it was a simple farmhouse, but gradual evolution has transformed it into a stylish country hotel with a traditional oak-panelled ambience and crisp formality in both the table linen and the service tone. The temptations of modernity are resisted in favour of a classically based repertoire that produces a nicely runny omelette Arnold Bennett topped with watercress, and then sea trout with broad beans, samphire and champ in Thermidor sauce, or roast breast of duck with crisp-fried spinach and a morello sauce, along with an arancino of the confit leg meat and sage. An enormous bowl of under seasoned mash brings us down to earth with a clunk, but a seasonal summer dessert that works strawberries into a mini Pavlova, pannacotta and sorbet is a cheering idea.

Chef Andrew Grundy **Owner** Prima Hotel Group **Seats** 60, Pr/dining room 120 **Times** 12-2.30/7-9.45 **Prices** Fixed L 2 course fr £14.50, Fixed D 3 course fr £31.50, Tasting menu fr £55, Service optional **Wines** 66 bottles over £30, 32 bottles under £30, 15 by glass **Parking** 110 **Notes** Afternoon tea £15, Sunday L fr £24.50, Vegetarian available, Children welcome

CORNWALL & ISLES OF SCILLY

BODMIN
Map 2 SX06

Trehellas House Hotel & Restaurant
Traditional, Modern British, French

tel: 01208 72700 **Washaway PL30 3AD**
email: enquiries@trehellashouse.co.uk **web:** www.trehellashouse.co.uk
dir: Take A389 from Bodmin towards Wadebridge. Hotel on right 0.5m beyond road to Camelford

Bright Cornish cooking at an inn with a past

Trehellas House has come full circle from its early days as the Washaway, the inn to a landed estate, via a period in the Victorian era as a courthouse serving the judicial circuit, to a modern-day country hotel, its guest rooms spread between the inn itself and the coach-house. A low-slung greystone building between Bodmin and Wadebridge, with a beamed, slate-flagged dining room, it makes a homely setting for some bright Cornish cooking that mixes innovation and tradition. Potted St Ives crab with gravad lax and melba toast might be the curtain-raiser for slow-roast lamb shank with crushed minted potatoes and ratatouille in thyme jus, or sea bass with spinach in caper butter sauce. Finish with nutty apple and apricot crumble, served with rhubarb ice cream, or a selection of local cheeses with celery, grapes and chutney. The hotel's proximity to Camel Valley makes that vineyard's benchmark Cornish fizz the obvious aperitif.

Chef Fabrice Gerardin **Owner** Alistair & Debra Hunter **Seats** 40 **Times** 12-2/6.30-9 **Prices** Fixed D 2 course £15, Starter £5.50-£8.50, Main £17-£22, Dessert £6.25 **Wines** 25 bottles under £30, 6 by glass **Parking** 30 **Notes** Sunday L £10-£17, Vegetarian available, Children welcome

BOSCASTLE
Map 2 SX09

The Wellington Hotel

Modern British

tel: 01840 250202 **The Harbour PL35 0AQ**
email: info@wellingtonhotelboscastle.com **web:** www.wellingtonhotelboscastle.com
dir: A30, A395 at Davidstowe follow Boscastle signs. B3266 to village. Right into Old Rd

Creative contemporary cooking in popular fishing village

A coaching inn since the 16th-century, The Wellington was renamed after that business in Belgium in 1815. The views over the harbour have hardly changed in that time, and the building itself stands strong with seeming indifference to the passage of time – it's even got a castellated tower. The restaurant follows the theme (it's called Waterloo) and has plenty of charm with its chandeliers and linen-clad tables, and there's also a traditional bar with real ales and dishes written up on blackboards. The kitchen team seek out regional produce to pepper the restaurant menu. A first-course smoked chicken terrine with pear and honeycomb is a creative construction, or go for the no-less inventive Cornish mussels with curry butter and parsnips. There's plenty of Cornish seafood on show, including a fine piece of cod, cooked just right, and served in a main course with variations of parsnip, vanilla cream, and a crab and basil combo. Finish with a plum tart with poached plums, Armagnac and almonds.

Chef Kit Davis **Owner** Cornish Coastal Hotels Ltd **Seats** 35, Pr/dining room 28
Times 6-10.30 Closed Sun-Mon, L all week **Prices** Fixed D 3 course fr £37.50, Service optional **Wines** 10 bottles over £30, 25 bottles under £30, 7 by glass **Parking** 15
Notes Vegetarian available, Children welcome

BRYHER (ISLES OF SCILLY)
Map 2 SV81

Hell Bay

– see below

CALLINGTON
Map 3 SX36

Langmans Restaurant

Modern British

tel: 01579 384933 **3 Church St PL17 7RE**
email: dine@langmansrestaurant.co.uk
dir: From the direction of Plymouth into town centre, left at lights and second right into Church St

Pedigree local produce on a six-course tasting menu

The Butterys have carved out a glittering reputation for themselves at their highly singular restaurant in this pleasant market town, drawing custom in from Plymouth and beyond. Hung about with work by local artists, and driven by produce from local growers and farmers, it's a distinctively regional operation, and distinctive too in that the format is a six-course tasting menu for all. Most of this is table d'hôte, perhaps opening with a portion of 36-hour pork belly with a strip of crunchy crackling and Cox's apple purée. A soup could be rich and silky butternut squash topped with a halved scallop, before the fish course, a serving of beautifully timed brill with salsify and oyster mushrooms in a creamy sauce. Meat may well offer a choice, maybe chump of lamb sauced with red wine and star anise, or truffled beef sirloin, with a showboat of wonderful vegetables. Pause for some West Country cheeses, and then set about the dessert trio, served on a compartmented glass plate – chocolate tart, passionfruit and chocolate tower, and rhubarb and ginger cheesecake, served with variously complementary ice creams.

Chef Anton Buttery **Owner** Anton & Gail Buttery **Seats** 24 **Times** 7.30-close
Closed Sun-Wed, L all week **Prices** Tasting menu fr £40, Service optional **Wines** 45
bottles over £30, 50 bottles under £30, 11 by glass **Parking** Town centre car park
Notes Tasting menu 7 course, Vegetarian available, No children

Hell Bay

BRYHER (ISLES OF SCILLY)
Map 2 SV81

Modern British V

tel: 01720 422947 **TR23 0PR**
email: contactus@hellbay.co.uk **web:** www.hellbay.co.uk
dir: Access by boat from Penzance, plane from Exeter, Newquay or Land's End

Locally based cooking among the Scillies' smallest community

Hell Bay may sound like somewhere John Wayne made one of his last stands, but the reality could hardly be more blamelessly pacific. Or at least, Atlantic, for lying at the western end of Bryher, it bravely faces the full might of that ocean. Bryher is the smallest of those isles of the Scillies that are inhabited, in this case by some 83 souls. During spring tide, it's possible to squelch intrepidly over to the next nearest islands on foot, but mostly the traffic is by boat, and the reward of the journey is a peach-perfect, unspoiled, gently hilly island with sandy beaches and this white-fronted, low-slung, modern hotel snuggled into its concealing cove. Hung with excellent 20th-century artworks, the place is full of broad ocean daylight and sea air, a bracing backdrop for Richard Kearsley's locally based cooking. Seafood such as crab and lobster is caught off the island itself, and local farmland supplies much of the fresh produce, while mainland west Cornwall contributes scallops, thoroughbred beef and fine cheeses. Dishes are carefully balanced between European tradition and modernity, so a dinner may start out with a perfectly slow-poached duck egg (hailing from the island) with purple sprouting broccoli and lemon hollandaise, or with those scallops, accompanied by apple purée, pancetta and chorizo. Stick with seafood at main, and it could be brill fillet alongside crab risotto Thai-seasoned with lemongrass and ginger. If meat is more your thing, expect shoulder, loin and sweetbread of spring lamb, each element cooked just-so, with a lightly spiced red lentil stew, or pot-roast venison loin with braised red cabbage in chocolate jus. The finale is also likely to be memorable, with chocolate fondant spilling forth its richness alongside hazelnut biscotti and pistachio ice cream, and tiramisù given a touch of refinement in its presentation.

Chef Richard Kearsley **Owner** Tresco Estate **Seats** 70, Pr/dining room 12
Times 12-2/7-9.30 Closed 2 Nov-17 Mar **Prices** Fixed D 3 course £39, Service optional **Wines** 20 bottles over £30, 30 bottles under £30, 11 by glass **Parking**
Notes Children welcome

Falmouth Hotel

British

tel: 01326 312671 **Castle Beach TR11 4NZ**
email: reservations@falmouthhotel.com **web:** www.falmouthhotel.com
dir: *A30 to Truro then A390 to Falmouth. Follow signs for beaches, hotel on seafront near Pendennis Castle*

Seasonal cooking in a great white seafront hotel

Nothing becomes a seaside town like a great white hotel, lording it over the waters from the headland. The eponymous Falmouth went up in the 1860s as the Great Western Railway extended into Cornwall. It did its duty in both wars, and between times, has hosted the crowned heads and pop sensations of the day. The elegant dining room has sweeping views over the bay and a menu that works its way round the seasonal calendar in both British and international modes. Many dishes obligingly come in two sizes, so that you might start imaginatively with roasted ling fillet wrapped in Parma ham in a sweetcorn and potato chowder with prawns and a near-bushel of fresh parsley, while main course might be a rump cut of superb local lamb on well-executed potato rösti. Good pastry is the hallmark of zesty lemon tart, which comes with raspberry coulis and clotted cream.

Times 12-2/6.45-8.45

The Greenbank Hotel

Modern British

tel: 01326 312440 **Harbourside TR11 2SR**
email: reception@greenbank-hotel.co.uk **web:** www.greenbank-hotel.co.uk
dir: *Approaching Falmouth from Penryn, take left along North Parade. Follow sign to Falmouth Marina and Greenbank Hotel*

Dual-purpose menu with panoramic estuary views

Superbly positioned on the estuary, The Greenbank overlooks the backwaters of the Fal towards the marina, as well as the hotel's own private quay, from where a water taxi plies the route into town. Panoramic windows survey the scene from the first-floor restaurant, where a bare wood floor and clothed tables with chairs upholstered in contrasting primary colours set a stripped-down modern tone. The menu divides its wares into Classics and Fusions, depending on whether you're in the mood for smoked chicken pâté and piccalilli, followed by fish in Betty Stogs beer batter with chunky chips, or a more speculative journey that leads from crispy beef tongue with celeriac remoulade in port and orange glaze, to seared breast and confit leg of duck with butternut squash purée and kale. An eclectic mix of culinary styles reinforces the point: smoked bratwurst hot dog with sauerkraut, and lamb loin with ras el hanout, couscous and tzatziki. A technically unimpeachable crème brûlée comes with honeycomb, shortbread and rhubarb sorbet.

Chef Stephen Marsh **Owner** Greenbank Hotel (Falmouth) Ltd **Seats** 60, Pr/dining room 16 **Times** 12-2/6.30-9.15 **Prices** Tasting menu £35-£45, Starter £6-£8, Main £7-£22.50, Dessert £7-£11, Service optional **Wines** 27 bottles over £30, 38 bottles under £30, 14 by glass **Parking** 60 **Notes** Sunday L £16-£20, Vegetarian available, Children welcome

The Royal Duchy Hotel

Modern British

tel: 01326 313042 **Cliff Rd TR11 4NX**
email: reservations@royalduchy.co.uk **web:** www.brend-hotels.co.uk
dir: *On Cliff Rd, along Falmouth seafront*

Well-judged modish dishes overlooking Falmouth Bay

If it is a piece of classic seaside grandeur you're after, The Royal Duchy can deliver. The view across the bay over towards Pendennis Castle and out to sea is magnificent and if you're seated on the terrace, well, you've got the best seat in town. The dining room, with its rich red tones, crisp white linen-clad tables and chandeliers, is a reassuringly traditional setting for some gently contemporary cooking. A first-course ravioli, for example, is filled with fresh crab and ginger and topped with a light ginger foam, or there might be salt-beef terrine with celeriac remoulade and pickled sultanas. A first-rate piece of haddock stars in a main course with watercress purée and lemon sabayon, the balance of flavours just right, whilst vegetarians will find satisfaction in the form of a roasted beetroot risotto with rocket and watercress salad. End on a high with Key lime pie with dark chocolate sorbet.

Times 12.30-2/6-9 Closed L Mon-Sat

St Michael's Hotel and Spa

Modern Mediterranean

tel: 01326 312707 **Gyllyngvase Beach, Seafront TR11 4NB**
email: info@stmichaelshotel.co.uk **web:** www.stmichaelshotel.co.uk
dir: *Follow signs for seafront & beaches*

Seductive sea views and contemporary cooking

If it's a sea view you're after, St Michael's can deliver, and it's all the better when seen from the beautiful sub-tropical gardens, or the terrace. The hotel's Flying Fish Restaurant bags the fabulous vista, but even if the weather prevents you gazing out to sea, there's plenty on the menu to keep you happy. It's a bright, contemporary restaurant, with floor-to-ceiling windows and well-spaced tables dressed in white linen. There's a genuine local flavour to the contemporary menus, with lots of Cornish seafood on offer: whole dressed crab, oysters, Thai-style crabcakes, or the Newlyn seafood grill. There's meat, too, in the form of steaks from Lower Carnebone Farm, or a trio of Cornish pork (slow-cooked belly, seared loin and braised cheek). And for dessert, iced cappuccino parfait with mini doughnuts, chocolate sugar cubes and latte anglaise shows the ambition and skill of the kitchen team.

Chef Andrew Smith **Owner** Nigel & Julie Carpenter **Seats** 90, Pr/dining room 30 **Times** 12-2/6.30-9 **Prices** Prices not confirmed, Service optional **Wines** 12 by glass **Parking** 30 **Notes** Sunday L, Vegetarian available, Children welcome

FOWEY
Map 2 SX15

The Fowey Hotel

◉ Modern European V

tel: 01726 832551 **The Esplanade PL23 1HX**
email: reservations@thefoweyhotel.co.uk **web:** www.richardsonhotels.co.uk
dir: A30 to Okehampton, continue to Bodmin. Then B3269 to Fowey for 1m, on right bend left junct then right into Dagands Rd. Hotel 200mtrs on left

Modish cooking and soothing harbour views

The Fowey Hotel has a good deal of seaside appeal with its grand Victorian façade and position overlooking the Fowey River – the sea is just around the corner. Its restaurant – Spinnakers – has splendid Victorian proportions and features, but does not feel stuck in the past with its smart decor and tables dressed in white linen. There's a good deal of local produce on the menu, not least seafood landed on the nearby quay: pan-seared mackerel, for example, with Niçoise salad and sauce vierge, or pan-seared scallops with belly pork, creamed leeks and cauliflower coulis. Among main courses, West Country lamb might turn up in the company of scallion potato purée, wilted greens, Chantenay carrots, broad beans and a mint and balsamic jus, and to finish, all the exoticism of passionfruit soup with mango parfait and honeycomb ice cream.

Chef Mark Griffiths **Owner** Keith Richardson **Seats** 60, Pr/dining room 22
Times 12-3/6.30-9 **Prices** Prices not confirmed, Service optional **Wines** 17 bottles over £30, 50 bottles under £30, 16 by glass **Parking** 17 **Notes** Sunday L, Children welcome

GOLANT
Map 2 SX15

Cormorant Hotel & Restaurant

◉◉ Modern British V

tel: 01726 833426 **PL23 1LL**
email: relax@cormoranthotel.co.uk **web:** www.cormoranthotel.co.uk
dir: A390 onto B3269 signed Fowey. In 3m left to Golant, through village to end of road, hotel on right

Creative contemporary cooking and glorious estuary views

Built above the Fowey Estuary, this charming small hotel has panoramic views over the water from a terrace as well as from the stylish restaurant, with its wooden floor, pastel colours and mirrors. A glance at the short menu shows that this is a kitchen with its fingers on the culinary pulse, turning out starters like seared scallops with a roe beignet, pear purée and parsnip crisps, and chicken liver and foie gras parfait with grape and balsamic chutney, Madeira jelly and a toasted beetroot brioche. Dishes are thoughtfully constructed to make the most of flavours without too much fiddle, and high culinary standards are applied to quality produce. Poached fillet of local lemon sole, for instance, is accompanied by cockle and mussel chowder, cockle 'scampi', lemon mash, green beans and parsley purée, and roast guinea fowl breast is stuffed with pesto mousse and served with a poached egg and mustard mash. Puddings seem like labours of love if lemon tart is anything to go by: it comes with lemon posset, blood orange sorbet and meringue drops.

Chef Dane Watkins **Owner** Mary Tozer **Seats** 30 **Times** 12-2/6.30-9.30 **Prices** Fixed D 3 course £32.50, Tasting menu £42.50-£65, Starter £7-£11, Main £17-£24, Dessert £7-£10, Service optional **Wines** 22 bottles over £30, 45 bottles under £30, 6 by glass **Parking** 20 **Notes** Tasting menu, incl vegetarian 6 course, Sunday L £10-£30 Children 12 yrs+ D

HAYLE
Map 2 SW53

Rosewarne Manor

◉◉ Modern British

tel: 01209 610414 **20 Gwinar Rd TR27 5JQ**
email: enquiries@rosewarnemanor.co.uk **web:** www.rosewarnemanor.co.uk
dir: A30 Camborne West towards Connor Downs, left into Gwinear Rd. 0.75m to Rosewarne Manor

Ambitious cooking in renovated 1920s manor

After a period when this grand 1920s building had fallen into neglect, the current owners have resurrected Rosewarne as a venue with a keen eye to the weddings and functions market, and with good food to boot. The modern British repertoire is driven by seasonality and local sourcing, and the confident cooking delivers well-defined flavours. The menu gives little away in terms of description or cooking methods, so you will need to quiz the helpful staff about what, exactly, is involved at each stage. You might set the ball rolling with Cornish blue cheese pannacotta, matched inventively with apple textures and gingerbread, then progress to an unusual assemblage of pork belly with dark chocolate, cauliflower and apple, or there could be a modish fish and meat combo involving line-caught sea bass with beef shin, Savoy cabbage and beurre noisette. To finish, egg custard tart with lemon curd and pistachio crumb might catch the eye, or you could round things off on a savoury note with the excellent artisan Cornish cheeses.

Chef Phil Thomas **Owner** Cyril & Gill Eustice **Seats** 60, Pr/dining room 12
Times 12-2.30/6-9 Closed 2 wks at New Year, Mon-Tue **Prices** Tasting menu £45, Starter £6, Main £18, Dessert £6, Service optional **Wines** **Parking** 50 **Notes** Tasting menu 6 course, L Informal dining menu £9.25-£21.50, Sunday L fr £9.85, Vegetarian available, Children welcome

HELSTON
Map 2 SW62

New Yard Restaurant

◉◉ New English

tel: 01326 221595 **Trelowarren Estate, Mawgan TR12 6AF**
email: newyard@trelowarren.com **web:** www.newyardrestaurant.co.uk
dir: 5m from Helston

Modern Cornish cooking on a historic estate

The magnificent Trelowarren estate is a thousand acres of Cornish pasture and woodland that dates back a thousand years, although present owners the Vyvyan family have only been in charge of it for a mere six centuries. It's now in every sense a modern country enterprise, complete with rococo gardens, game park and a restaurant in the old stable yard, refurbished and equipped with a new chef, Max Wilson. With local sourcing a sine qua non, Cornish seafood is allowed star billing for the likes of dressed crab with tomato and basil salsa, or main-course mackerel with tabbouleh and roasted beetroot, while pedigree meats appear in the guises of

Ruby Red beef carpaccio with rocket and parmesan, or Old Spot pork chop with choucroute, bacon and lentils. A Middle Eastern/North African vibe brings on falafels, baba ganoush, houmous, labneh and plenty of that tabouleh, and sweet-tooths may be beguiled at the end by chocolate pudding with lemon yoghurt sorbet. Cheeses are naturally of the West Country finest, and the home-made sourdough bread should not be missed.

Chef Max Wilson **Owner** Sir Ferrers Vyvyan **Seats** 50 **Times** 12-2.15/6.30-9 Closed Jan, Mon (mid Sep-Spring BH), D Sun **Prices** Starter £6-£9.50, Main £12.50-£20, Dessert £3.75-£9, Service optional **Wines** 6 by glass **Parking** 20 **Notes** Sunday L £15, Vegetarian available, Children welcome

LIZARD   Map 2 SW71

Housel Bay Hotel
◉ Modern British

tel: 01326 290417 & 290917 **Housel Cove TR12 7PG**
email: info@houselbay.com **web:** www.houselbay.com
dir: *A30 from Exeter, exit Truro and take A34/A394 to Helston & A3083 to Lizard*

Dramatic clifftop location and compelling cooking

The solid-looking stone property was planned and built as a hotel as long ago as the 1890s, and its founders had a good eye for location: it stands dramatically on top of a cliff looking down over the sea, with the coast path running through the gardens. The kitchen's requirements are met by small Cornish producers, and just about everything is made on the premises. The menu is a slate of interesting ideas, so guinea fowl rillette is given a black Cajun yoghurt dip as well as gherkins, and chargrilled tuna steak comes with a dollop of pineapple salsa and horseradish and a portion of creamy potato and spring onion salad. Elements generally combine or contrast to produce a harmonious end result, as in main-course grilled sea bass fillet with clam and coconut velouté, celeriac rösti, Parma ham snaps, green and broad beans and roast tomatoes, or flavourful, tender rump of lamb with sweetbreads, forestière jus, celeriac fondant, grilled aubergine and samphire. Coconut pannacotta with lemon tart is a refreshing way to end.

Times 12-2.30/7-9.30 Closed Jan

LOOE   Map 2 SX25

Barclay House
◉◉ Modern British V

tel: 01503 262929 **St Martin's Rd PL13 1LP**
email: info@barclayhouse.co.uk **web:** www.barclayhouse.co.uk
dir: *1st house on left on entering Looe from A38*

Inventive coastal cuisine with exquisite views

From its green hillside, surrounded by six acres of gardens and woodland, with an outdoor pool, this white Victorian villa gives spectacular views of the river and harbour below. In the brasserie-style restaurant, French windows open on to a terrace for alfresco dining, and the cooking is based on materials caught and grown in the county, often within 10 miles. There are plenty of enticements on the imaginative menus, with seafood showing up to good effect with perhaps crab and potted shrimps with tomato dressing, followed by baked fillets of brill with cockles, pearl potatoes, tomatoes, white wine and herbs. Meat hardliners may prefer a plate of pork (tenderloin in bacon, crisp roast belly and hog's pudding) served with champ and cider-scented jus. Interest is sharpened by the likes of sautéed squid and tiger prawn chermoula with tabouleh salad, and desserts may run from sticky toffee pudding to chocolate torte with beetroot-flavoured ice cream.

Chef Robert Gibson **Owner** Malcolm, Graham & Gill Brooks **Seats** 60, Pr/dining room 16 **Times** 6.30-9 Closed Sun, L all week (ex by arrangement) **Prices** Fixed D 3 course £19.99, Starter £5.50-£7.95, Main £8.95-£19.50, Dessert £5.50-£8.50, Service optional **Wines** 17 bottles over £30, 36 bottles under £30, 8 by glass **Parking** 25 **Notes** Children welcome

Trelaske Hotel & Restaurant
◉◉ Modern British

tel: 01503 262159 **Polperro Rd PL13 2JS**
email: info@trelaske.co.uk **web:** www.trelaske.co.uk
dir: *B252 signed Looe. Over Looe bridge signed Polperro. 1.9m, hotel signed on right*

Local produce in verdant Cornwall

Run with great charm by hands-on owners, this lovely small-scale hideaway sits in four acres of woodland and pretty, well-tended gardens between Looe and Polperro. Chef-proprietor Ross Lewin is clearly a man who likes to go his own way – self-taught and, to a certain degree, self-sufficient thanks to harvests of fruit, vegetables and herbs grown in the hotel's own poly tunnels, he delivers an accomplished modern British repertoire, built on Cornish materials. Fish fresh from the Looe day boats stars in dishes such as cod fillet with cauliflower couscous and lemon sauce, while Cornish Black pork loin is matched with vanilla mash, hog's pudding and glazed pear. Staying with the local terroir, you could wind proceedings up with Cornish cheeses, crackers and home-made chutney, or go for the comforts of spotted dick with pouring cream.

Chef Ross Lewin **Owner** Ross Lewin, Hazel Billington **Seats** 40 **Times** 12-2/7-9 Closed 22-26 Dec, L Mon-Sat **Prices** Fixed D 3 course £33.50, Service optional **Wines** 8 by glass **Parking** 60 **Notes** Sunday L £19.95, Vegetarian available, Children 5 yrs+

LOSTWITHIEL   Map 2 SX15

Asquiths Restaurant
◉◉ Modern British

tel: 01208 871714 **19 North St PL22 0EF**
email: info@asquithsrestaurant.co.uk
dir: *Opposite St Bartholomews church*

Minimal fuss, maximum flavours

Opposite the medieval church in Lostwithiel, there's a serenity about Asquiths that is wholly inviting. The smart interior is monochrome, except for works by Penzance artist Steve Slimm on the exposed stone walls, and staff are easygoing but nevertheless on the ball. A serious restaurant, then, but not one that takes itself so seriously as to be intimidating. Food-wise, there are no smoke and mirrors here, just well-sourced, cleverly-conceived and skilfully-cooked modern dishes. Cornish credentials are evident throughout, from the beers and wines to the duck livers that appear with a creamy sage and mushroom sauce and potato gnocchi to open proceedings. Next up, crispy-skinned black bream is matched with buttered spinach, crab and chilli potato cake and a well-made citrus beurre blanc, or there might be slow-cooked belly and faggot of local pork with potato purée, white beans and grain mustard. This is confident, mature cooking that shows its final flourish of class with a pannacotta with Monbazillac jelly, raspberry sorbet, and biscotti crumbs.

Chef Graham Cuthbertson **Owner** Graham & Sally Cuthbertson **Seats** 28, Pr/dining room 10 **Times** 7-9 Closed Xmas, Jan, Sun-Mon, L all week **Prices** Starter £5.50-£7, Main £13-£17, Dessert £5.50-£7, Service optional **Wines** 4 bottles over £30, 36 bottles under £30, 6 by glass **Parking** Car park at rear **Notes** Vegetarian available, Children welcome

Mount Haven Hotel & Restaurant

◉◉ Modern British

tel: 01736 710249 **Turnpike Rd TR17 0DQ**
email: reception@mounthaven.co.uk web: www.mounthaven.co.uk
dir: *From centre of Marazion, up hill E, hotel 400yds on right*

Accomplished modern cooking in family-run hotel

The local landmark of St Michael's Mount standing guard in the bay couldn't look finer than when surveyed from the terrace at the Mount Haven, glass of wine in hand of course. The 19th-century coach house is these days a chic hotel with a restaurant that is a cut above the competition. There's good use of natural tones in the decor and a friendly and unpretentious approach to service. The menu shows plenty of local influence, giving a sense of place, and the composition of dishes follows a broadly contemporary path. Pea and ham hock soup, for example, comes with a parsley beignet, and local John Dory is served with celeriac carpaccio among first courses. Main course might bring forth some local venison in a well-balanced partnership with roasted root vegetables, celeriac purée, potato fondant and port jus. If the sea views have whet your appetite, go for pan-roasted pollock with smoked haddock chowder, mussels and crispy leeks, and to finish, apple fritters with cinnamon ice cream and vanilla syrup.

Chef Nathan Williams **Owner** Orange & Mike Trevillion **Seats** 50
Times 12-2.30/6.30-9 Closed 2 Jan-9 Feb **Prices** Fixed L 2 course fr £14.50, Starter £5.50-£8.95, Main £15.50-£25, Dessert £1.50-£7.50, Service optional **Wines** 19 bottles over £30, 23 bottles under £30, 14 by glass **Parking** 30 **Notes** Vegetarian available, Children welcome

The Scarlet Hotel

◉◉ Modern European V

tel: 01637 861800 **Tredragon Rd TR8 4DQ**
email: stay@scarlethotel.co.uk web: www.scarlethotel.co.uk
dir: *A39, A30 towards Truro. At Trekenning rdbt take A3059, follow Newquay Airport signs. Right after garage signed St Mawgan & Airport. Right after airport, right at T-junct signed Padstow (B3276). At Mawgan Porth left. Hotel 250yds on left*

Southwestern clifftop cooking in a soothing eco-hotel

The architecture of the Scarlet, an eco-hotel sitting on the cliff at Morgan Porth, recalls what used to be known as the International Style, with its many windows, exterior staircases and geometric construction, all reflected in a reed-filtered pool in front. Inside is just as cool and soothing, with natural materials in evidence throughout the sparsely furnished spacious interiors. Wide-open spaces separate the tables in a dining room done in browns and aubergine, with clifftop views as standard. Southwestern produce pours forth from artfully composed dishes that achieve a nice balance between tradition and modernity, with wine suggestions appended. Silver mullet with baked beetroot salad and pumpkin seeds dressed in horseradish yoghurt is a bracing way to open the bidding. Then it may be loin and cheek of Cornish beef with fried potato terrine and puréed root veg, or sea trout Thai-style with nam jim dipping sauce, spring onions and coriander. The grand finale could be a sharing wodge of white chocolate cheesecake with rhubarb and honeycomb, or pear and almond tart with pear sorbet and clotted cream.

Chef Tom Hunter **Owner** Red Hotels Ltd **Seats** 70, Pr/dining room 20
Times 12.30-2.15/7-9.30 Closed 3-31 Jan **Prices** Fixed L 3 course £22.50-£25, Fixed D 3 course £42.50, Starter £7-£14, Main £12-£22, Dessert £6-£10, Service optional **Wines** 69 bottles over £30, 19 bottles under £30, 39 by glass **Parking** 37, In village **Notes** ALC menu available L only, Sunday L £25 No children

Budock Vean - The Hotel on the River

◉ Traditional British V

tel: 01326 252100 **TR11 5LG**
email: relax@budockvean.co.uk web: www.budockvean.co.uk
dir: *from A39 follow tourist signs to Trebah Gardens. 0.5m to hotel*

Well-crafted dishes in a traditional country house

Wrapped in 65 unforgettable acres of organically-managed subtropical gardens on the Helford River, and bathed in Cornwall's balmy climate, it's no wonder that Budock Vean has a loyal following of guests who return again and again. Tradition is the watchword at this country house, whose reassuringly formal mood is defined by the jacket-and-tie dress code at dinner. The kitchen hauls in the finest local, seasonal produce as the bedrock of menus that blend traditional and more modern ideas. Things start simply enough with home-smoked breast of Barbary duck with orange fig and toasted pine nuts, then move on to pan-roasted suprême of Cornish turbot served with leeks, crab and parmesan mash, and chive butter sauce; dyed-in-the-wool traditionalists might rejoice at roast sirloin of local beef with duck fat-roasted potatoes, parsnips, onions, Yorkshire pudding and gravy. Dessert delivers the homely comfort of apple and peach crumble with vanilla crème anglaise.

Chef Darren Kelly **Owner** Barlow family **Seats** 100, Pr/dining room 40
Times 12-2.30/7.30-9 Closed 3 wks Jan **Prices** Starter £9.25-£32.50, Main £17.85-£37, Dessert £7.20, Service optional **Wines** 39 bottles over £30, 51 bottles under £30, 8 by glass **Parking** 100 **Notes** 4 course D £41, Sunday L £20.50, Children welcome

Trevalsa Court Hotel

◉ Modern British NEW

tel: 01726 842460 **School Hill, Polstreth PL26 6TH** web: www.trevalsa-hotel.co.uk
dir: *From St Austell take B3273 to Mevagissey. Pass sign to Pentewan. At top of hill left at x-rds. Hotel signed*

Clifftop hotel with a modern menu and good seafood

This is a handsome house built of granite and slate, with some period touches within, including in the smart restaurant. If the weather is kind, a table on the terrace with views across Mevagissey Bay is worth its weight in gold, but fear not, for the view is pretty mint from inside the restaurant, too, particularly if you bag a table by the window. There's a decidedly sub-tropical feel hereabouts – check out the pretty garden –but what appears on the menu is grounded in the local environment, with a decent showing of seafood (crab, lobster and oysters are generally available with a bit of notice). Start with crispy pig's cheek, fennel and apple risotto before a main course of grey mullet perked up with some pickled vegetables, plus squid, mussels, pomegranate and parsley mash. There's also burger, steak or fish cooked on the grill, and desserts such as autumn berry crumble with elderflower and thyme ice cream.

Chef Adam Cawood **Owner** John & Susan Gladwin **Seats** 26 **Times** 12.30-2.30/6.30-9 Closed Dec-Jan **Prices** Prices not confirmed, Service optional **Wines** 7 by glass **Parking** 20 **Notes** Vegetarian available, Children welcome

MULLION
Map 2 SW61

Mullion Cove Hotel

Modern British

tel: 01326 240328 **TR12 7EP**
email: enquiries@mullion-cove.co.uk **web:** www.mullion-cove.co.uk
dir: *A3083 towards The Lizard. Through Mullion towards Mullion Cove. Hotel in approx 1m*

Sea views and accomplished modern cooking

The hotel's location could hardly be bettered: it's perched on the top of cliffs overlooking Mullion's harbour, with spectacular coastal views. There's a timeless elegance to the aptly named Atlantic Restaurant, where window tables are inevitably at a premium, but wherever you sit pleasant and efficient staff ensure guests are well looked after. The menus change daily, with local fishing boats providing the kitchen's seafood stock-in-trade: perhaps a full-flavoured main course of prawn and mussel broth infused with saffron, accompanied by roast fillet of pollock and new potatoes, or bouillabaisse with crab and dill linguine. Combinations are well considered and dishes deliver plenty of punchy flavours, among them a starter of roast guinea fowl with spring onion and chorizo roulade, sweetcorn purée and pickled mushrooms. Meals can end memorably with the likes of raspberry and chocolate pannacotta with fruit salad and lemon ice cream.

Chef Fiona Were **Owner** Matthew Grose **Seats** 60 **Times** 12-2/6.30-8.45 Closed L Mon-Sat **Prices** Fixed D 3 course fr £35, Service optional **Wines** 51 bottles over £30, 44 bottles under £30, 16 by glass **Parking** 45 **Notes** Sunday L fr £15, Vegetarian available, Children 7yrs+

NEWQUAY
Map 2 SW86

Atlantic Hotel

Modern British NEW

tel: 01637 839048 & 872244 **Dane Rd TR7 1EN**
email: info@atlantichotelnewquay.co.uk **web:** www.atlantichotelnewquay.co.uk
dir: *From M5 southbound junct 31, take A30 at Newquay sign. Follow signs Fistral Beach. Hotel at top of Dane Rd*

Modern bistro cooking with a champagne bar attached

Built in 1892 and standing proud on the headland at Newquay, the Atlantic overlooks the stretching expanse of Fistral Beach, Cornwall's surfing central. This is no gloomy Victorian haunt, though, for inside it is alive with daylight and air. The focal point is a bright, modern bistro and champagne bar complex, with zebra-patterned bar-stools, sunburst-styled café chairs and soaring palm trees. In the evenings, candlelight softens the scene as the sun descends into the ocean. Tapas-style appetisers might whet the tastebuds for starters such as Newlyn crab-cakes with lemon and sweet chilli mayo, or classic chicken Caesar. Main courses run the rule over hearty traditionals such as fish stew, crammed with mussels and whatever's fresh that day, simmered in tomato and orange, as well as pork belly with cassoulet and apple sauce. Finishers include vanilla pannacotta with macerated strawberries and crumbled scone, or a crowd-pleasing chocolate brownie with toffee sauce and vanilla ice cream.

Chef Aaron Janes **Owner** Lorraine Stones **Seats** 100, Pr/dining room 24 **Times** All-day dining **Prices** Starter £3.95-£10.50, Main £9.95-£17.95, Dessert £5.95-£6.95, Service optional **Wines** 15 bottles over £30, 24 bottles under £30, 9 by glass **Parking** Car park adjacent **Notes** Sunday L £11.95-£19.50, Vegetarian available, Children welcome

PADSTOW
Map 2 SW97

Margot's

British

tel: 01841 533441 **11 Duke St PL28 8AB**
email: bazbeachdog@aol.com

High-impact bistro cookery amid the Padstow bustle

Amid the brash commercialism that has overtaken Padstow in recent years, Margot's is a haven of appealing modesty, a little bistro with a marine-blue frontage tucked away in the narrow streets of the town centre. Simple wood tables, colourful artworks and a Brains beer flag adorning the ceiling set the tone for some straightforward, direct and high-impact bistro cookery from chef-patron Adrian Oliver. Padstow runs on fresh fish, and just as well when you contemplate a starter of grilled mackerel dressed in cucumber, capers and lemon, or a main such as whole lemon sole in citrus oil. Meats are good too though, perhaps a confit leg of duck with crisped ham and spring onion mash in red wine sauce. A fine finisher is the chocolate pannacotta, its dense richness thrown into relief by the tang of raspberries, with a brandy-snap for added crunch.

Times 12-2/7-9 Closed Nov, Jan, Sun-Mon

The Metropole

Modern British

tel: 01841 532486 & 0800 005 2244 **Station Rd PL28 8DB**
email: reservations@the-metropole.co.uk **web:** www.the-metropole.co.uk
dir: *M5/A30 past Launceston, follow signs for Wadebridge and N Cornwall. Then take A39 and follow signs for Padstow*

Harbourside restaurant with an assured team in the kitchen

This Victorian hotel has commanding views over the foodie town and Camel Estuary, and where better to enjoy them but over a meal in the Harbour Restaurant, with large windows and high-backed upholstered dining chairs at clothed tables on the carpeted floor. The kitchen is driven by local supplies – fish landed in the nearby harbour, for instance – and plays a voguish tune, producing starters of smoked haddock fishcake with curry mayonnaise, creamed leeks, confit egg yolk and crisp black pudding alongside chicken liver parfait with orange and pear salad and red onion marmalade. Sauces and garnishes add depth to main courses: wild mushroom cream for haddock with spring onion mashed potato and wilted spinach, and watercress and mustard café au lait for roast medallions of beef with dauphinoise and crushed root vegetables, for instance. End with one of the attractive desserts, perhaps sticky ginger cake with caramelised banana and vanilla ice cream.

Chef Michael Corbin **Owner** Richardson Hotels Ltd **Seats** 70, Pr/dining room 30 **Times** 6.30-9 Closed L Mon-Sat **Prices** Prices not confirmed, Service optional **Wines** 7 bottles over £30, 24 bottles under £30, 9 by glass **Parking** 50 **Notes** Sunday L, Vegetarian available, Children welcome

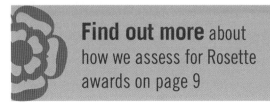

Find out more about how we assess for Rosette awards on page 9

PADSTOW *continued*

Paul Ainsworth at No. 6

 – see opposite

St Petroc's Hotel and Bistro

Traditional, Mediterranean

tel: 01841 532700 **4 New St PL28 8EA**
email: reservations@rickstein.com **web:** www.rickstein.com
dir: *Follow one-way around harbour, 1st left, establishment 100yds on right*

Informal bistro dining from Rick Stein's stable

The bistro is an informal and relaxing sort of place, with simple tables and chairs on worn wooden floorboards, modern paintings on plain white walls, and professional service from attentive staff. There's a cosy bar and a pleasant lounge for pre-dinner drinks and a courtyard and garden for alfresco meals. With Rick Stein at the helm, it comes as no surprise that seafood is the main business, with the kitchen deploying top-quality raw materials to produce dishes of imagination and flair, from well-timed grilled scallops with truffle butter, or salt-cod fritters with aïoli, to grilled lemon sole with brown shrimps and mushrooms, or roast tronçon of turbot with sauce vierge. Steaks from the grill are a feature too, another meaty option perhaps tender, deeply flavoured venison au poivre nicely balanced by salt-baked beetroot and horseradish. End if you can with the bitter-sweet tastes of dense chocolate and marmalade tart with raspberry sorbet, or perhaps warm apple and cider cake.

Chef Nick Evans **Owner** R & J Stein **Seats** 54, Pr/dining room 12
Times 12-2/6.30-9.30 Closed 25-26 Dec, D 24 Dec **Prices** Starter £6.95-£8.95, Main £14.95-£29.50, Dessert £4.80-£7.20, Service optional **Wines** 8 bottles over £30, 15 bottles under £30, 9 by glass **Parking** Car park up hill **Notes** Fixed winter L menu available £10, Vegetarian available, Children welcome

The Seafood Restaurant

 – see opposite

Treglos Hotel

Traditional English with Asian influences **NEW** v

tel: 01841 520727 **Constantine Bay PL28 8JH**
email: stay@treglos-hotel.com **web:** www.tregloshotel.com
dir: *At St Merryn x-rds take B3276 towards Newquay. In 500mtrs right to Constantine Bay, follow brown signs*

Modern Cornish cooking at a smart family hotel

An upscale family hotel overlooking Constantine Bay near Padstow, the Treglos is a late Victorian house converted into a hotel in the 1930s. Wallis Simpson stayed here during the brief reign of Edward VIII, and the sparkling-white frontage and smart interiors certainly look as though they're geared for the glitterati. The dining room is done in maroon and leafy green, with discreet artworks and ceramics here and there, and the menus take a modern approach, with specials built around a solid core repertoire. Proceedings might get under way with a serving of pigeon in delicious blueberry jus, garnished with beetroot purée, potato crisps and pea shoots. This is merely a curtain-raiser for mains such as seafood stew in bouillabaisse sauce with wilted bok choy and saffron aïoli, or tenderloin pork medallions in cider sauce with black pudding and champ. At the end comes flawlessly rendered lemon tart, served with a dollop of incisive lemon curd and the gentling influence of mint crème fraîche.

Chef Gavin Hill **Owner** Jim & Rose Barlow **Seats** 100 **Times** 12-2.30/6.45-8.45 Closed 30 Nov-10 Feb **Prices** Fixed L 2 course £9-£25, Fixed D 3 course £32-£35 **Wines** 8 by glass **Parking** 40 **Notes** Sun L by arrangement £10/£30, Afternoon Tea £5.25 Children 3 yrs+

PENZANCE Map 2 SW43

The Bay@Hotel Penzance

 Seafood, Modern British v

tel: 01736 366890 & 363117 **Britons Hill TR18 3AE**
email: eat@thebaypenzance.co.uk **web:** www.thebaypenzance.co.uk
dir: *From A30 take exit to Penzance at Tesco rdbt. 3rd right onto Britons Hill. Hotel on right*

Splendid seafood-plus and sea views in a stylish setting

With magnificent views over rooftops to Mount's Bay, The Bay is a light and airy restaurant with a stylish, contemporary feel and a relaxed atmosphere in part generated by friendly, professional staff. The kitchen follows a rigorous Cornwall-only policy-seafood from Newlyn and St Ives, specially grown vegetables, meats from local farms-and makes everything in-house, from bread to ice cream, with an assured touch. A separate lobster menu (24 hours' notice needed) might see the crustacean grilled with garlic and herbs, while the carte offers much to entice. Start with rabbit and Parma ham terrine balanced by fig and prune compôte, or seared mackerel fillet interestingly partnered by pickled vegetable salad, capers and shallots. Sea-fresh loin of cod, well timed, in an intense herb crust could be one of the inspired fish main courses, accompanied by spelt risotto, mushroom velouté and curly kale, or there could be classic roast breast of guinea fowl in bacon with dauphinoise, Savoy cabbage and thyme jus. Standards are well matched by puddings like plum jelly with vanilla brûlée and pistachio ice cream.

Chef Steven Mesher **Owner** Yvonne & Stephen Hill **Seats** 60, Pr/dining room 12 **Times** 11-2.30/6.45-9.30 Closed 1st 2 wks Jan **Prices** Fixed L 2 course £13.45-£16, Fixed D 3 course £33.45-£55, Tasting menu fr £49, Service optional **Wines** 26 bottles over £30, 26 bottles under £30, 11 by glass **Parking** 12, On street **Notes** Vegan menu available, menu du Jour, Sunday L £15-£20, Children welcome

Ben's Cornish Kitchen

British

tel: 01736 719200 **West End, Marazion TR17 0EL**
email: ben@benscornishkitchen.com
dir: *On coast road opposite St Michael's Mount*

Free-thinking modern cookery at a family village venue

The epitome of a friendly, big-hearted family operation, Ben Prior's appealing high-street venue is found in the popular little village of Marazion, which is practically a suburb of Penzance. A bright, airy feel pervades the place, enhanced by local artworks, and the real wood floors and raffia chairs keep things agreeably rustic. Locally sourced ingredients pour in fresh each day, allowing the menus to change just as often, but continuity is maintained in the free-thinking contemporary style of the cooking. Begin with an Asian mash-up of curried tempura John Dory fillets with sweet chilli jam and a salad of orange, fennel and capers, before a modern classic pairing of turbot and ox cheek with cep gnocchi and puréed carrot in bourguignon sauce, or smoked loin and faggot of venison with roast salsify and creamed celeriac in damsons and port. Dessert might be burnt honey cream with walnut praline and a pear poached in saffron and Sauternes.

Chef Ben Prior **Owner** Ben Prior **Seats** 45, Pr/dining room 25 **Times** 12-2/6.30-9 Closed Sun, L Mon **Prices** Fixed L 2 course £16, Tasting menu £35-£39, Starter £5-£11, Main £13-£22, Dessert £6-£8, Service optional **Wines** 65 bottles over £30, 65 bottles under £30, 25 by glass **Parking** Across the road **Notes** Vegetarian available, Children welcome

Paul Ainsworth at No. 6

PADSTOW   Map 2 SW97

Modern British v

tel: 01841 532093 **6 Middle St PL28 8AP**
email: enquiries@number6inpadstow.co.uk
dir: *A30 follow signs for Wadebridge then sign to Padstow*

Defining contemporary cooking in a pint-sized townhouse

The little Georgian townhouse with blinds at the windows is hidden away within the narrow streets of the town, though whether anything about Padstow remains entirely concealed these days is open to doubt. A very efficient job of pouring a quart into a pint pot has been made of the interior remodelling here, with three little dining spaces on the ground floor and one upstairs. Tables are squeezed in fairly close, but not half as tightly packed as the tourist throngs outside. In any case, it's the kind of environment where, despite the quirky decorative approach, the surroundings are only a small part of the point. Paul Ainsworth, resident here since 2008 and familiar to viewers of The Great British Menu, is one of the southwest's defining chefs, adroitly marshalling tip-top local produce and technical wizardry in bold, vivid, assertively characterful dishes that get you talking as you taste. Ideas come thick and fast, and don't just remain ideas, but

achieve triumphant vindication on the plate (or board, or whatever their means of conveyance is). A marine spin on a Scotch egg delivers panko-crumbed smoked haddock forcemeat wrapped around a soft-boiled quail's egg (really don't try this at home), garnished with slices of Charles MacLeod's excellent Stornoway black pudding and a couple of blobs of coronation-style mayonnaise. Fish remains supreme at main stage, with cod confit in olive oil alongside 'bubbles' of cod beignet, two shades of cauliflower, and relishes of puréed raisin and curried yoghurt, while meats might offer moorland lamb with hogget pie and salsa verde, or saddleback pork with its crackling, cider apple and a scallop for good measure. Dessert may be more than you bargained for, both for quantity, and for its palette of textures and tastes – perhaps chocolate mousse and sliced banana with spun sugar in pastry layers, with a peanut croquant and passionfruit sorbet rammed solid with concentrated fruit flavour.

Chef Paul Ainsworth **Owner** Paul Ainsworth **Seats** 40, Pr/dining room 22 **Times** 12-3/6-10 Closed 14 Jan-4 Feb, Sun-Mon, L 1 May **Prices** Fixed L 2 course £19, Starter £12-£15, Main £27-£29, Dessert £9-£24, Service optional **Wines** 60 bottles over £30, 18 bottles under £30, 16 by glass **Parking** Harbour car park and on street **Notes** Children 4yrs+

The Seafood Restaurant

PADSTOW   Map 2 SW97

Traditional, International Seafood v   🍷 NOTABLE WINE LIST

tel: 01841 532700 **Riverside PL28 8BY**
email: reservations@rickstein.com **web:** www.rickstein.com
dir: *Follow signs for town centre. Restaurant on left of riverside*

Padstein ahoy!

The place that put Padstow on the gastronomic map a generation ago may have become a gigantosaurus, employing hundreds of people through the year, not least Rick Stein himself, who as you read this, is almost certainly jetting off somewhere new for the BBC, his broadcast mission having broadened imperially from the original remit of teaching Britain to love seafood all over again. When you add the many new converts to those who have always loved it anyway, and factor in the hegemonic power of TV, you come up with something that fizzes like The Seafood Restaurant, a cavernously expansive, white-walled space designed around an altar of shellfish and crustacea, where the press of business barely abates from springtime buds to jingle bells. The Seafood has its detractors, people who regret the handsome cost of fish that is mostly landed in the immediate vicinity, or who nostalgically feel that the executive chef ought to be

cooking their dinner. Some feel that the ventures into foreign waters – Madras fish curry, Singapore chilli crab – don't work as well as the simpler offerings, and it's true that a laden shellfish platter takes some beating, but the judgment is mostly sound. Porthilly mussels are allowed due prominence in a starter that combines them with a high-stakes East Asian liquor of black beans, spring onions, garlic, ginger and coriander. Simpler mains continue to impress, as when a pair of John Dory fillets with girolles, garnished with sun-dried tomatoes and rocket, proclaims its seasonal freshness in ringing tones. Turbot in hollandaise, the menu opines, is 'probably nicer than anything more elaborate', and though there's a lot riding on that 'probably' at the price, many would concur. More than an afterthought, dessert might be full-throttle hot chocolate fondant with on-trend salt caramel and white chocolate mousse. Good breads come with excellent Cornish butter.

Chef Stephane Delourme **Owner** R & J Stein **Seats** 120 **Times** 12-2/6.30-10 Closed 25-26 Dec, D 24 Dec **Prices** Fixed L 3 course £29.95-£38.50, Starter £12.50-£25.50, Main £18-£51, Dessert £8.90-£9.20, Service optional **Wines** 140 bottles over £30, 15 bottles under £30, 21 by glass **Parking** Pay & display opposite **Notes** Children 3 yrs+

PENZANCE *continued*

The Coldstreamer Inn

 Modern British

tel: 01736 362072 **Gulval TR18 3BB**
email: info@coldstreamer-penzance.co.uk **web:** www.coldstreamer-penzance.co.uk
dir: *1m NE of Penzance on B3311, right turn into School Ln in Gulval, opposite church*

Big local flavours in a Cornish village inn

The Coldstreamer is a traditionally run village inn a mile outside Penzance, its participation in the life of the local community extending not just to feeding and watering Gulval and the environs, but showcasing the work of local artists too, a month at a time. Eating takes place in both the bar and a dedicated dining area with foursquare wooden furniture and rough stone walls. Local produce naturally features prominently in menus that offer an uncomplicated style of country-inn cooking with the emphasis on big, belting flavour. Start with chunky fishcakes of salmon, fennel and lemon, then sensitively timed pork loin with brittle crackling, red cabbage and punchy dauphinoise, or a whole plaice with fine beans and tomato in pesto dressing. Pudding could be as light as yoghurt pannacotta with honey-roast figs and blackberry sorbet, if you're not quite up to the sticky toffee and butterscotch route.

Chef Andrew Gibson **Owner** Richard Tubb **Seats** 40 **Times** 12-3/6-9 Closed 25 Dec **Prices** Fixed L 2 course £14.50, Fixed D 3 course £21, Starter £5-£6.95, Main £8-£18.95, Dessert £5-£8, Service optional **Wines** 18 bottles over £30, 27 bottles under £30, 9 by glass **Parking** Village square **Notes** Sunday L £9.95, Vegetarian available, Children welcome

Harris's Restaurant

 Modern European, French, British

tel: 01736 364408 **46 New St TR18 2LZ**
email: contact@harrissrestaurant.co.uk
dir: *Located down narrow cobbled street opposite Lloyds TSB & the Humphry Davy statue on Market Jew St*

Clearly focused, unfussy food just off the high street

The Harris family have been running their restaurant for over 30 years, its success down to professionally prepared and freshly cooked quality produce (local meats, seafood from Newlyn, for instance), with the kitchen taking an unshowy, straightforward line. It's an unpretentious, engaging restaurant on a cobbled side street in the centre. Seafood makes up the bulk of starters, with meat dishes getting a fair showing among mains. Kick off with grilled scallops with a simple herb dressing, or cornets of smoked salmon stuffed with white crabmeat, and proceed to impeccably timed Dover sole grilled with butter and chives, or sole goujons with tartare sauce. Committed meat-eaters could go for pheasant breast stuffed with mushrooms and apple wrapped in filo, and all comers could end with a satisfying pudding like treacle tart, or crème brûlée.

Chef Roger Harris **Owner** Roger & Anne Harris **Seats** 40, Pr/dining room 20 **Times** 12-2/7-9.30 Closed 3 wks winter, 25-26 Dec, 1 Jan, Sun (also Mon in winter), L Mon **Prices** Starter £6.50-£8.95, Main £12.50-£32, Dessert £7.95-£9.50 **Wines** 28 bottles over £30, 17 bottles under £30, 8 by glass **Parking** On street, local car park **Notes** Vegetarian available, No children

The Navy Inn

 Modern British

tel: 01736 333232 **Lower Queen St TR18 4DE**
email: info@navyinn.co.uk
dir: *In town centre, follow Chapel St for 50yds, right into Queen St to end*

Enterprising seafood dishes and more, just off the seafront

The Navy is a small whitewashed pub just off the seafront, with a boarded floor and a nautical theme. It's an atmospheric place, with customers chatting over a pint at the bar, pleasant and willing service, and an enthusiastic and dedicated brigade in the kitchen. Seafood comes from nearby Newlyn fish market and meat from Cornish farms or the local butcher, and it all gets turned into some bright contemporary dishes. Start with well-timed chargrilled John Dory fillet with lime and smoked haddock salad, and move on to seared scallops with black pudding purée and quince paste. Dedicated meat-eaters could opt for duck terrine with rhubarb purée and pickled vegetables, then seared venison loin served with tomato gnocchi, braised shallots and roast tomatoes. All comers could end with an enterprising dessert like a trio of apple (rich curd, fritters and sorbet with cinnamon).

Chef Keir Meikle, Jay Orrey **Owner** Keir Meikle **Seats** 46 **Times** 12-10 Closed 26 Dec, All-day dining **Prices** Starter £2.50-£7.50, Main £11.95-£16.50, Dessert £5.95-£8.95, Service optional **Wines** 10 bottles over £30, 26 bottles under £30, 9 by glass **Parking** 30 mtrs free parking on promenade **Notes** Sunday L £10.45-£11.95, Vegetarian available, Children welcome

---

PERRANUTHNOE   Map 2 SW52

The Victoria Inn

 Modern British

tel: 01736 710309 **TR20 9NP**
email: enquiries@victoriainn-penzance.co.uk **web:** www.victoriainn-penzance.co.uk
dir: *A30 to Penzance, A394 to Helston. After 2m turn right into Perranuthnoe, pub is on right on entering the village*

Clever and accurate top-notch cooking in seaside inn

Reputedly one of the oldest inns in the county, this is in the heart of the village just a minute off the South West Coast Path. It radiates warmth and character, helped along by pleasant and engaging service. Locals gather here for a drink and a chat, but the food draws people from far and near. The kitchen makes the most of good West Country produce, and dishes never fail to interest. Exe mussels go into a risotto with leeks and rocket, and could be followed by roast fillet of local pork with pig's cheek, apple sauce, black pudding and root vegetable mash. Dishes are thoughtfully put together and accurately cooked: a starter of squid and prawns in light, crisp tempura with spicy vegetable salsa and coriander sauce, for instance, and juicy, succulent roast venison steak with roast vegetables, parsnip purée and red wine jus. Puddings can be a star, among them dark chocolate mousse with caramel sauce, Tia Maria cream and coffee ice cream.

Times 12-2/6.30-9 Closed 25-26 Dec, 1 Jan, Mon (off season), D Sun

PORTHLEVEN
Map 2 SW62

Kota Restaurant with Rooms

 British, Pacific Rim

tel: 01326 562407 **Harbour Head TR13 9JA**
email: kota@btconnect.com **web:** www.kotarestaurant.co.uk
dir: B3304 from Helston into Porthleven, Kota on harbour head opposite slipway

Seafood-based fusion food on a Cornish harbour

Perched on the waterfront in a picturesque Cornish harbour town, Kota takes its name from the Maori word for seafood, the linguistic reference giving a clue to one element of chef-patron Jude Kereama's ethnicity. In a spacious beamed room with a tiled floor and unclothed tables, an inspired spin on marine-based fusion food wins many converts. Lively pairings such as Falmouth scallops and pork belly with parsnips and apple and ginger dressing, or a trio of crab presentations (fresh, spring roll and tempura-battered claw) in chilli-tamarind mayo, give way to brightly spiced, generous main dishes like an array of hake, king prawn, scallop and crispy squid in red pepper, ginger and chilli sauce. The meat brigade might look to rump and shoulder of lamb with beetroot, kale and aubergine, dressed with redcurrant jelly and soy jus. Finish up with West Country cheeses and home-made chutneys, or baked lemon mascarpone with lemon curd, ginger crunch and mango sorbet.

Chef Jude Kereama **Owner** Jude & Jane Kereama **Seats** 40 **Times** 5.30-9 Closed Nov-Feb, Sun-Mon, L all week **Prices** Fixed D 3 course fr £21, Starter £6.95-£8.95, Main £11.95-£19.95, Dessert £6.95-£9.50, Service optional 10% **Wines** 13 by glass **Parking** On street **Notes** Vegetarian available, Children welcome

PORT ISAAC
Map 2 SW98

Outlaw's Fish Kitchen

 Modern British, Seafood NEW

tel: 01208 881183 & 880237 **1 Middle St PL29 3RH**
email: fishkitchen@outlaws.co.uk
dir: Please phone for directions

Stunning seafood in a casual setting

'The sea and fishermen dictate our daily menu', declares Nathan Outlaw, a sentiment that ensures freshness and shows due respect to the hard labour that brings the ingredients to the table. Mr Outlaw is a big fish in Cornwall – and on telly these days – with a number of restaurants across the county (plus one in London), the pick of which is Restaurant Nathan Outlaw itself (see entry). The Fish Kitchen is a different kettle of fish, being a rustic little place right on the harbour, with sea views and an easy-going vibe. Inside are whitewashed walls, unclothed tables and a keen service team. The deal is multiple small plates, and what a fab bunch they are too. The menu is straight and true when it comes to the fruits of the sea, so a smoked haddock Scotch egg with curry sauce oozes in all the right places, and seafood and bean stew shows spot-on technique and delivers sparkling flavours. Crispy ling with roasted garlic mayonnaise and pickled carrot and green chilli packs a delightful punch, and, for dessert, there is baked rice pudding with rhubarb and gingerbread. Every seaside town should have one.

Chef Paul Ripley, James Lean **Owner** Nathan Outlaw Restaurants Ltd **Seats** 25 **Times** 12-3.30/6-9.30 Closed Jan, Xmas, Sun-Mon (Nov-Mar), Mon (Apr-May & Oct) **Prices** Starter £3-£14, Dessert £5, Service optional **Wines** 14 bottles over £30, 5 bottles under £30, 6 by glass **Parking** 2 car parks - top of village **Notes** Fish Kitchen for 2 selection menu L & D £56, Children welcome

Driftwood

PORTSCATHO
Map 2 SW83

Modern European
tel: 01872 580644 **Rosevine TR2 5EW**
email: info@driftwoodhotel.co.uk **web:** www.driftwoodhotel.co.uk
dir: 5m from St Mawes off the A3078, signed Rosevine

Accomplished cooking in a stunning coastal setting

From its clifftop position above Gerrans Bay, Driftwood gives unparalleled wide-angle sea views, and within its seven acres a wooded path leads down to its own beach. Soak up the view with a pre-dinner drink from the decked terrace, lit by hurricane lamps after dark, and enjoy the same outlook from vast windows in the restaurant, a predominantly white room with splashes of yellow and blue. Head chef Christopher Eden is his own man, adding distinctive style to everything he produces. Seafood from Cornish waters might appear as a vibrant starter of pan-fried John Dory with cauliflower, vanilla, lime and curry, and whole lobster can be yours for the taking, roasted in the shell with garlic and herb butter, with 24 hours' notice. Dishes never fail to impress with their striking originality, well-judged partnerships and technical accuracy. Crisp lamb belly is a bold first course, served with roasted onion consommé, celery and turnip, while duck goes into a boudin accompanied by braised leg, celeriac, pickled plums and port. Among main courses, roast turbot is successfully partnered by taramasalata and mussels, with kale crisps and broccoli. More humble ingredients are

dealt with no less adroitly: crisp jowl and glazed cheek of pork, for instance, with tenderloin, parsnips, pears and walnuts. Fringe benefits like canapés and breads are first class, as are the carefully constructed puddings.

Chef Christopher Eden **Owner** Paul & Fiona Robinson **Seats** 34 **Times** 7-9.30 Closed early Dec-early Feb, L all week (ex Thu-Sat, Jun-Sep) **Prices** Fixed D 3 course fr £53, Tasting menu fr £85, Service optional **Wines** 40 bottles over £30, 17 bottles under £30, 6 by glass **Parking** 20 **Notes** Vegetarian available, No children

The Lugger

◉◉ European

tel: 01872 501322 **TR2 5RD**
email: reservations.lugger@ohiml.com **web:** www.luggerhotel.com
dir: A390 to Truro, B3287 to Tregony, A3078 (St Mawes Rd), left for Veryan, left for Portloe

Enterprising cooking by the harbour

Dating from the 16th century, now a luxury hotel, The Lugger overlooks the sea and tiny harbour of this picturesque Roseland Peninsula village, with a terrace outside the smart restaurant for summer dining. Local ingredients are the kitchen's linchpin, particularly seafood, which might appear as moules marinière, or crab salad, followed by cod fillet with caper and lemon butter. Elsewhere, look for contemporary treatments of maple-glazed pork belly with a scallop and cauliflower cream, and pigeon with beetroot and pomegranate salad, then pheasant breast with basil polenta, dried tomatoes and game chips, and saddle of venison with bitter chocolate jus, spinach and dauphinoise potatoes. Cornish cheeses are alternatives to puddings like orange pannacotta with poached rhubarb.

Times 12.30-2.30/7-9

Driftwood

◉◉◉ – see page 103

Restaurant Nathan Outlaw

◉◉◉◉ – see opposite

Rose-in-Vale Country House Hotel

◉ Traditional & Modern British

tel: 01872 552202 **Mithian TR5 0QD**
email: reception@roseinvalehotel.co.uk **web:** www.roseinvalehotel.co.uk
dir: Take A30 S towards Redruth. At Chiverton Cross rdbt take B3277 signed St Agnes. In 500mtrs turn at tourist info sign for Rose-in-Vale. Into Mithian, right at Miners Arms, down hill

Modern country cooking in a Cornish valley

The Rose-in-Vale Hotel is a real hideaway, a gorgeous creeper-clad Georgian manor house tucked into the tranquil village of Mithian on the north Cornish coast. Its Valley Restaurant is a bright, traditional space, elegantly accessorised with chandeliers and floral curtains framing the pastoral view, and formal-yet-friendly service. The kitchen makes great use of local produce in gently-updated country-house cooking, starting with ham hock terrine with toasted brioche and home-made piccalilli, or perhaps chilli prawns with rocket salad and lemon and lime crème fraîche. Main courses draw on local fish landed at St Agnes – fillet of turbot is partnered with tomato and lime butter, Cornish asparagus and new potatoes – but there may also be a plate of local lamb, involving cutlet and chump with dauphinoise potatoes and sautéed spinach. To finish, there may be a classic apple tarte Tatin with clotted cream and butterscotch sauce.

Chef Mark Firth, Chris Bailey **Owner** James & Sara Evans **Seats** 80, Pr/dining room 12 **Times** 12-2/7-9 Closed 2 wks Jan, L Mon-Wed (winter) **Prices** Fixed D 3 course fr £25, Tasting menu fr £24.50, Starter £7.95-£8.95, Main £18.95-£35, Dessert £5.95-£6.95, Service optional **Wines** 20 bottles over £30, 25 bottles under £30, 7 by glass **Parking** 50 **Notes** Sunday L £12.95-£19.95, Vegetarian available, No children

Austell's

◉◉ Modern British

tel: 01726 813888 **10 Beach Rd PL25 3PH**
email: brett@austells.co.uk
dir: From A390 towards Par, 0.5m after Charlestown rdbt at 2nd lights turn right. Left at rdbt. Restaurant 600yds on right

Sophisticated dining near the beach

In a small parade of shops on the road to Carlyon Bay, Austell's is a restaurant of cool, uncluttered elegance, with a wooden floor, artwork on plain walls and slatted-back chairs at wooden tabletops; it's split-level, with diners on the raised area so they can see the chefs at work in the open-plan kitchen. Seasonality means the menus change regularly, and everything is made in-house, from breads (among them maybe rosemary and pesto) to petits fours. The cooking, based on contemporary British ideas, is honest, accurate and of clearly defined upfront flavours. Typical of starters is a plate of seared scallops (local, of course) with chorizo, pea mousse and herb salad-a good balance of tastes and textures. Among main courses, peach purée and jus infused with foie gras add an extra oomph to pink, crisp-skinned duck breast, served with wilted spinach and sautéed potatoes. End with a theatrical flourish with basil crème brûlée, served flaming, the sugar still caramelising, accompanied by velvety poached strawberries and punchy strawberry ice cream.

Chef Brett Camborne-Paynter **Owner** Brett Camborne-Paynter **Seats** 48 **Times** 6-9 Closed 1-15 Jan, Mon, L Tue-Sat **Prices** Fixed D 3 course £27.50, Starter £5.50-£8.95, Main £16.50-£19.95, Dessert £5.50-£7.95, Service optional **Wines** 8 bottles over £30, 32 bottles under £30, 11 by glass **Parking** 30 **Notes** Vegetarian available, Children welcome

Boscundle Manor

◉◉ Modern British **NEW** v

tel: 01726 813557 **Boscundle PL25 3TL**
email: reservations@boscundlemanor.co.uk **web:** www.boscundlemanor.co.uk

Country hotel with a local flavour

The 18th-century manor that stands today benefits from the kind of facilities that lure the 21st-century traveller, so expect spa treatments, an indoor pool and a smart restaurant. The hotel is in five acres of grounds, within easy striking distance of the Eden Project, and its restaurant is very much a draw in its own right. The dining room is done out in a traditional and decidedly romantic manner, with candlelight, mellow pinky-red colour tones, and tables dressed up in white linen. Chef Jenny Reed sources much of the produce from the local environment, and everything is made in-house, from bread to ice cream. The à la carte menu is a satisfying blend of classical technique and contemporary touches, with flavours working in harmony. A first course dish of pan-seared scallops sees the bivalves perfectly caramelised and served with roasted butternut squash risotto, crispy pancetta and cumin oil (a winning combo), and for main course there might be breast of honey-glazed duck with potato fondant and a cranberry and orange sauce.

Chef Jenny Reed **Owner** David & Sharon Parker **Seats** 24, Pr/dining room 14 **Times** 6.30-9 **Prices** Fixed D 3 course £25, Tasting menu £49, Starter £5-£9.50, Main £15-£29, Dessert £6-£9.50, Service optional **Wines** 9 bottles over £30, 9 bottles under £30, 3 by glass **Notes** Children welcome

Restaurant Nathan Outlaw

ROCK Map 2 SW97

Modern British, Seafood v ⬥ NOTABLE WINE LIST

tel: 01208 862737 & 863394 **The St Enodoc Hotel PL27 6LA**
email: mail@nathan-outlaw.com
dir: *M5/A30/A39 to Wadebridge. B3314 to Rock*

Refined multi-course seafood dining from a modern master

The Nathan Outlaw brand goes from strength to strength: like many a canny contemporary chef he's not shy of spreading his name far and wide via appearances in the BBC's Great British Menu and other armchair foodie slots on the telly, but the celeb stuff doesn't get in the way of cooking fish in a masterly manner. His empire now encompasses venues in London and Port Isaac, but the serious business goes on in his full-works, namesake flagship in The St Enodoc Hotel. This boutique gem is done out with an understated minimal look involving neutral tones, tasteful art, and an edge of metropolitan chic. Nothing other than sumptuous views over the Camel Estuary distracts from the creative and intelligent work that leaves the kitchen. The concept behind this intimate operation is to let the top-class Cornish materials speak eloquently for themselves, helped along, naturally, with high-flying technique and an innate sense of what works with what. Choosing what to eat is easy: since most diners see this as something of a foodie pilgrimage, there's just a single fish and seafood-only tasting menu, plus a veggie alternative. First off, deliciously plump Porthilly mussels are matched with a smooth cauliflower purée, crisp bacon and black onion seeds in a dish that kicks off proceedings in fine style, before raw scallops pointed up with celeriac purée and a dressing of tarragon oil and roasted celeriac stock. It all looks beautiful on the plate and the quality of the ingredients is never in doubt, with the flavours leaving a lasting impression as one dish follows another. Next up, a superb fillet of lemon sole comes with a crispy breaded oyster, Jerusalem artichoke purée and a warm dill dressing, followed by grey mullet with pickled kohlrabi, a delicate curry sauce and broccoli. Turbot on the bone is roasted to perfection and served with pickled shimeji mushrooms, a smooth mushroom purée and sprout tops – a divine combination. Follow on with a cheese course which is certainly a cut above – Ragstone goats' cheese with various textures of beetroot and candied walnuts – before a brace of desserts such as blood orange curd (rather like a brûlée) with rhubarb and a crunchy crumble, and a clever spin on tarteTatin in the shape of a pear tart with hazelnuts and a stunning yoghurt sorbet. If you're seeking a more unbuttoned alternative, Outlaw's Restaurant serves a 3-course seasonal menu to go with those sublime watery views.

Chef Nathan Outlaw, Chris Simpson **Owner** Nathan Outlaw **Seats** 22 **Times** 7-9 Closed Xmas, Jan, Sun-Mon, L all week **Prices** Tasting menu £99 **Wines** 163 bottles over £30, 1 bottle under £30, 12 by glass **Parking** 30 **Notes** Tasting menu 8 course No children

ST AUSTELL *continued*

Carlyon Bay Hotel

Modern & Traditional British

tel: 01726 812304 **Sea Rd, Carlyon Bay PL25 3RD**
email: reservations@carlyonbay.com **web:** www.carlyonbay.com
dir: *From St Austell, follow signs for Charlestown. Carlyon Bay signed on left, hotel at end of Sea Rd*

Simple traditions on the St Austell clifftop

Surveying the rugged Cornish coast from its clifftop perch above St Austell, the creeper-curtained Carlyon Bay Hotel is an imposing presence above the bay. Within its 250 acres of grounds you'll find a full complement of spa and leisure facilities, including its own championship golf course. Taking care of the gastronomic side of things is the aptly-named Bay View Restaurant, where huge windows allow maximum exposure to the sea views, and everything is smartly turned out, from the linen-swathed tables to the amicable, black-and-white-uniformed staff. The kitchen tacks a pretty traditional course, keeping things simple and relying on the quality and provenance of its ingredients to win plaudits. Cornish mussels with cider, cream and garlic is a good way to start, then follow with roast rump of new season's lamb with pea purée, creamed potato, and rosemary and redcurrant sauce. To finish, vanilla pannacotta gets a lift from tangy poached rhubarb and crunchy pistachio.

Times 12-2/7-9.30

The Cornwall Hotel, Spa & Estate

Modern British, International v

tel: 01726 874050 & 874051 **Pentewan Rd, Tregorrick PL26 7AB**
email: enquiries@thecornwall.com **web:** www.thecornwall.com
dir: *A391 to St Austell then B3273 towards Mevagissey. Hotel approx 0.5m on right*

Smart manor house with modish cooking

If you have a lovely stay here and can't drag yourself away, you could always buy one of the holiday homes in the surrounding 43 acres of parkland. But fear not if your budget won't run to that, for you can simply return to eat here again in either the smart Arboretum restaurant, the more informal Acorns Brasserie, or sit out in the sunshine on the Parkland Terrace. There's a lot going on here. You'll find the Arboretum restaurant in the old White House part of the hotel – once a private mansion – and it's a classy space (two spaces really) done out in fashionably muted colour tones. The menu here takes a broadly contemporary path, drawing inspiration from far and wide whilst making good use of regional ingredients. So you might start with hoisin duck spring rolls with a sweet chilli dip, followed by pan-seared line-caught sea bass with Thai purée and vegetable stir-fry.

Chef Paul Stephens **Owner** Rudrum Holdings **Seats** 40, Pr/dining room 16 **Times** 12.30-2.30/6.30-9.30 **Prices** Fixed D 3 course £25-£35, Starter £6-£12, Main £13.50-£25, Dessert £6-£10, Service optional **Wines** 15 bottles over £30, 18 bottles under £30, 9 by glass **Parking** 100 **Notes** Sunday L £15.95-£19.95, Children welcome

Carbis Bay Hotel

Traditional, Mediterranean

tel: 01736 795311 **Carbis Bay TR26 2NP**
email: info@carbisbayhotel.co.uk **web:** www.carbisbayhotel.co.uk
dir: *A3074, through Lelant. 1m, at Carbis Bay 30yds before lights turn right into Porthrepta Rd to sea & hotel*

Contemporary cooking and panoramic views

Dating from the late 19th century, the family-run Carbis Bay Hotel has stunning views over the eponymous waters from its lofty position. The panoramic view can also be appreciated from the Sands restaurant, a spacious, traditionally decorated room, where the menus are evidence of a kitchen working in the modern vein, with starters encompassing battered haloumi on minted pea purée with beetroot and balsamic dressing, and duck and bean sprout spring roll with hoisin dipping sauce. The same broad sweep of styles is seen in main courses of honey-glazed duck breast with an orange and Cointreau sauce accompanied by patatas bravas and asparagus, and well-timed fried cod served on parmesan mash with creamed leeks and a Noilly Prat reduction. Crème brûlée is a classical rendition, flavoured with Baileys and garnished with raspberries.

Times 12-3/6-9 Closed 3 wks Jan

Garrack Hotel & Restaurant

Modern British

tel: 01736 796199 & 792910 **Burthallan Ln, Higher Ayr TR26 3AA**
email: reception@garrack.com **web:** www.garrack.com
dir: *Exit A30 for St Ives, then from B3311 follow brown signs for Tate Gallery, then brown Garrack signs*

Inventive cooking and stunning views

From its lofty position high above the tourist crowds of the town centre, this ivy-clad granite hotel's show-stopping views over Porthmeor beach and the Atlantic are a diner's dream-ticket. The unstuffy, light-and-airy restaurant's simple design blends traditional and contemporary elements to allow those stunning vistas pride of place, while menus likewise demonstrate a kitchen making the most of Cornwall's natural resources in accomplished modern dishes of creativity and ambition. Seafood rightly scores high in the billing; perhaps seared fillets of red mullet teamed with pea risotto, tapenade of black olives and wilted spinach, while from the land, perhaps another dish with a sunny-climes influence like pan-roasted breast of free-range chicken with chorizo, root vegetable and white bean stew with saffron aïoli. To finish, vanilla pannacotta with forced rhubarb, red berry reduction and fresh strawberries fits the bill.

Times 12.30-2/6-9 Closed 5 days Xmas, L Mon-Sat

Get the most out of the AA Restaurant Guide
See page 6

Who has won our Chefs' Chef award?
Find out on page 10

Porthminster Beach Restaurant

Modern Mediterranean V

tel: 01736 795352 **TR26 2EB**
email: pminster@btconnect.com
dir: On Porthminster Beach, beneath the St Ives Railway Station

Seafood-led fusion cookery on the beach at St Ives

They got there early and bagged themselves a prime spot on the beach at St Ives, beneath the towering eminence of Porthminster Point, the better to look out over the crashing waves breaking on spotless sands. It's a classic contemporary seafood venue, with chilled-out staff, the tiled interior opening onto outdoor decking, where you might sit and set about a dish of crisp-fried salt-and-spice squid with citrus miso under the Cornish sun. An Australian chef ensures there's a lot of knowledgeable fusion thinking going on, as in a main course of baked pollock with smoked pancetta, celeriac, almonds, salsa verde, a razor clam and truffled parcel of egg yolk. Or go with the much simpler crab linguine with Fowey mussels, dressed in chilli, garlic, parsley and lemon. There are good vegetarian dishes too, and sweet treats such as coconut rice pudding with mandarin sorbet, mango and peanut brittle.

Chef M Smith **Owner** Jim Woolcock, David Fox, Roger & Tim Symons, M Smith **Seats** 60 **Times** 12-3.30/6-9.30 Closed 25 Dec, Mon (Winter) **Prices** Starter £5.50-£10.95, Main £9.95-£21.95, Dessert £5.95-£10.95, Service optional **Wines** 16 bottles over £30, 26 bottles under £30, 9 by glass **Parking** 300yds (railway station) **Notes** Children welcome

The Queens

Modern British

tel: 01736 796468 **2 High St TR26 1RR**
email: info@queenshotelstives.com **web:** www.queenshotelstives.com
dir: A3074 to town centre. With station on right, down hill to High St

Upmarket seasonal gastro-pub fare near the harbour

The welcome at this gastro-pub is warmer than the inn sign of an unsmiling Victoria might suggest. Within is a nice jumble of wooden tables and chairs on a boarded floor, with some armchairs and sofas; walls are half-panelled, there's an open fire, and the atmosphere is relaxed and friendly. The kitchen goes to a lot of trouble to source Cornish produce, and its output has more than a hint of urban chic. The short blackboard menu could kick off with tempura prawns with sweet chilli sauce, ling and pickled cucumber and fennel, or partridge with a quail's egg and tomato and bacon jam. Game appears among main courses in season – perhaps roast grouse with cauliflower purée, greens and dauphinoise. Fish is well handled: witness properly timed fillet of hake in a crunchy herb crust hinting of garlic, served with a notable mussel broth and new potatoes. The same attention is paid to moreish puddings, among them perhaps poached pear with home-made coffee ice cream.

Chef Matt Perry **Owner** Neythan Hayes **Seats** 50 **Times** 12.30-2.30/6.30-9 Closed 25 Dec, Mon (Nov-Mar) **Prices** Starter £5-£8, Main £8-£17, Dessert £5-£6, Service optional **Wines** 3 bottles over £30, 20 bottles under £30, 12 by glass **Parking** Station car park **Notes** L menu all mains £10 or under, Sunday L £10, Vegetarian available, Children welcome

Hotel Tresanton

ST MAWES   Map 2 SW83

British, Mediterranean
tel: 01326 270055 **27 Lower Castle Rd TR2 5DR**
email: info@tresanton.com
dir: On the waterfront in town centre

Bright modern cooking in super-stylish seafront hotel

It's easy to breeze on past the Tresanton. This cool and contemporary hotel is set back above the narrow, seafront lane, and once you walk through the secluded entrance, the cluster of smartly revamped former cottages are revealed at the top of the pathway. There's quite a view from the top (the path isn't all that steep), especially from the terrace, with a lovely view out to sea. One of the first of the boutique genre to open up out west, Olga Polizzi transformed the place with a dose of seaside chic back in the late 1990s, and it's still looking good. It has swish bedrooms, a family-friendly attitude, and even a cinema. The restaurant has a Mediterranean-inspired feel, with natural, seaside colour scheme and a smart finish with neatly laid, linen-clad tables. The menu sits nicely with the feel of the place, with a Med attitude and some good local produce. Smoked haddock with a poached egg, spinach and hollandaise is a brasserie-style classic among

first courses, with another beautifully simple dish of San Daniele prosciutto served with rocket. Main course can deliver Red Ruby beef fillet with roast potatoes and Portobello mushrooms, while a fishy main might be wild bass with Fal prawns, mussels and fregola. For dessert, apple tarte Tatin is partnered with prune ice cream, or there's all the indulgence of a maple and pecan ice cream sundae. British cheeses are a good bet if you've room, served with oatcakes and apple chutney. There's afternoon tea, too, with Cornish clotted cream naturally, and children's options such as pan-fried fish with mash and green beans.

Chef Paul Wadham **Owner** Olga Polizzi **Seats** 60, Pr/dining room 45 **Times** 12-2.30/7-9.30 Closed 2 wks Jan **Prices** Fixed L 2 course £22, Starter £8-£12, Main £18-£24, Dessert £7-£8, Service optional **Wines** 47 bottles over £30, 13 bottles under £30, 8 by glass **Parking** 30 **Notes** Sunday L £28, Vegetarian available, Children 6 yrs+ D

ST IVES *continued*

Seagrass Restaurant

Modern British

tel: 01736 793763 **Fish St TR26 1LT**
email: info@seagrass-stives.com
dir: *On Fish Street opposite the Sloop pub*

Splendid seafood straight from the bay

Its location on Fish Street is a serendipitous address for this exciting newcomer to the St Ives foodie scene; Seagrass has already made quite a splash with its modern seafood-orientated cooking. Tucked away just off the seafront, a secretive doorway leads up to the rather cool, stylish first-floor restaurant, where the focus is firmly on top-class seasonal Cornish produce. The kitchen cuts no corners here, making everything – breads, stocks, ice cream – from scratch, and maintaining strong supply lines to local fishermen to ensure the shellfish that make up the platters of fruits de mer are plucked fresh from the bay. Make a start with pan-fried Cornish scallops with cucumber, lime and avocado, then move on to salted cod loin, matched enterprisingly with seafood cannelloni, roast tomato velouté, peas, samphire and crispy sea lettuce, and round off with pink grapefruit tart with candied walnuts and crème fraîche.

Chef Stephen Block **Owner** Scott & Julia Blair **Seats** 32 **Times** 6-9.30 Closed 26 Dec, 1-2 Jan, Sun-Mon (Nov-Apr ex BH), L all week (ex BH), D 25 Dec **Prices** Fixed D 3 course £19.95, Starter £5.95-£9.95, Main £11-£23.95, Dessert £5.95-£9.75, Service optional **Wines** 11 bottles over £30, 23 bottles under £30, 11 by glass **Parking** The Sloop car park **Notes** Vegetarian available, Children welcome

ST MAWES   Map 2 SW83

Hotel Tresanton

– *see page 107*

ST MELLION   Map 3 SX36

St Mellion International Resort

Modern International

tel: 01579 351351 **PL12 6SD**
email: stmellion@crown-golf.co.uk **web:** www.st-mellion.co.uk
dir: *On A388 about 4m N of Saltash*

Accomplished cosmopolitan cooking in large golfing resort

Surrounded by 450 acres of prime Cornish countryside, St Mellion is a modern development complete with golf course, spa and a restaurant – An Boesti – which is well worth a look. The room is spacious and elegant, and the team in the kitchen clearly sets itself high standards. The menu follows a modern cosmopolitan path, offering the likes of carpaccio with wasabi, pickled radish and mustard dressing, and sea bass fillet with a crab bhaji, asparagus, fennel herb, and sea foam. Dishes are intelligently judged –a starter of seared scallops with softly textured pork belly, black pudding and apple is a subtle assembly of flavours – and fine local produce is treated with care: witness a simple and effective main course of roast pigeon, successfully partnered by shallot purée, beetroot and mushrooms. Breads are so good that most people ask for more, but don't overdo it if you want a pudding, such as a trio of chocolate, or deconstructed apple and blackberry crumble with saffron custard and blackberry parfait.

Chef Kevin Hartley **Owner** Crown Golf **Seats** 60, Pr/dining room **Times** 6.30-9.30 Closed Xmas, New Year, Mon-Tue (off season), L all week **Prices** Prices not confirmed, Service optional **Wines** 7 by glass **Parking** 750 **Notes** Sunday L, Vegetarian available, Children 4 yrs+

TALLAND BAY   Map 2 SX25

Talland Bay Hotel

Modern

tel: 01503 272667 **PL13 2JB**
email: info@tallandbayhotel.co.uk **web:** www.tallandbayhotel.co.uk
dir: *Signed from x-rds on A387 between Looe and Polperro*

Vibrant regional cooking on the glorious south Cornwall coast

Beautifully situated between Polperro and Looe on the south Cornwall coast, Talland Bay is about five minutes up from the region's secluded beaches, with the coastal path on hand for when the walking itch strikes you. Needless to say, the views from the long conservatory dining room over the gardens and down to the shoreline are a tonic in themselves. Panelled walls and boldly striped upholstery create a vibrant mood, which does everything to enhance gastronomically. Local supplies feature strongly, especially in seafood starters such as crab linguine with gremolata and nori seaweed and a bisque-flavoured espuma, or simple smoked mackerel pâté with beetroot and Pink Firs in grape dressing, but a good fist is made too of a serving of truffled wild mushrooms on brioche with poached egg. Mains might encompass roasted smoked duck with dauphinoise, chicory and walnuts, or magnificent turbot with watercress purée, crab, radishes and peas. Wonderful Cornish cheeses are a different kind of temptation to dark chocolate crémeux with salt caramel, hazelnuts and crème fraîche.

Times 12.30-2.30/6.30-9.30 Closed L Mon-Sat (Oct-mid Apr)

TRESCO (ISLES OF SCILLY)   Map 2 SV81

New Inn

Modern, Traditional

tel: 01720 423006 & 422867 **TR24 0QQ**
email: newinn@tresco.co.uk **web:** www.tresco.co.uk
dir: *Ferry or light plane from Land's End, Newquay or Exeter; 250yds from harbour (private island, contact hotel for details)*

Simple and direct cooking at a welcoming Scillies inn

This traditional inn looking out to sea makes the most of its location amid the sandy beaches and turquoise waters of the sublime Scilly Isles. Combining old-world character with beachcomber-chic, much of the Driftwood Bar has been fashioned from reclaimed wood from shipwrecks over the years. The airy bistro-style Pavilion restaurant has a New England-style decor, and the sea-facing garden is the place to dine when the weather allows (which is quite often around here). Quality local ingredients, fish and seafood in particular, are the backbone of a crowd-pleasing menu of old favourites and more inventive ideas – popcorn mussels with chilli mayonnaise, for example. Main courses can be as straightforward as a mixed grill that relies on top-class produce and perfectly-timed cooking for its effect. In fitting with the fuss-free tone, dessert is a warm Bakewell tart with fresh raspberries and – what else in these parts? – Cornish clotted cream.

Times 12-2/6.30-9

TRURO   Map 2 SW84

The Alverton Hotel

Modern British **NEW**

tel: 01872 276633 **Tregolls Rd TR1 1ZQ** **web:** www.thealverton.co.uk
dir: *From Truro bypass take A39 to St Austell. Just past church on left*

Grand hotel with upscale brasserie dining using local ingredients

Built in 1830 and designed by the same chap who gave us Truro Cathedral, The Alverton is an impressive construction of granite with manicured gardens and a swish interior – a big hit with wedding planners. Food and drink is a major part of the appeal, whether that's lunch, afternoon tea, cocktails or an evening meal in the upmarket brasserie. There is plenty of period charm and a slick, contemporary finish to the place. The menu takes a modern European path with a good showing of Cornish ingredients. There's an upscale prawn cocktail, while pan-fried scallops with pea purée, crispy angel hair noodles and pancetta dust shows no lack of invention. Wild sea bass gets the pan-fried treatment, too, with crab and saffron risotto, or go for roast loin of venison with wild mushrooms, smoked aubergine purée and a red wine sauce. Finish with lemon tart with thyme crème fraîche or Cornish cheeses.

Chef Damien Uager **Owner** Alverton Hotel Ltd **Seats** 60, Pr/dining room 120 **Times** 12-2/5.30-9.30 **Prices** Fixed L 2 course £15-£20, Fixed D 3 course £28-£45, Starter £6-£9, Main £12-£24, Dessert £6-£9 **Wines** **Parking** 100 **Notes** Pre-theatre menu available, Sunday L £10-£30, Vegetarian available, Children welcome

Bustophers Bar Bistro

 British, French

tel: 01872 279029 **62 Lemon St TR1 2PN**
email: info@bustophersbarbistro.com
dir: Located on right, past Plaza Cinema up the hill

Friendly neighbourhood bistro using good local produce

This longstanding neighbourhood bistro has a loyal following in Truro and it's easy to see why. An infectiously buzzy atmosphere is heightened by an open kitchen and a separate bar area, where some 20 wines are available by the glass. Staff are welcoming and the place holds equal appeal for romantic couples, business suits at lunchtime, and friends grabbing a few drinks for a post work catch-up. The decor is elegant and minimalist, broken up by some bold artwork on the walls, and tables outside are popular in the summertime. Modern bistro food using quality local ingredients is the name of the game here and daily specials are chalked up on the blackboard. You might start with a simple ham hock terrine with piccalilli, following on with turbot with crab risotto and spinach, or perhaps go for a classic moules marinières or the house burger. Custard tart with apple crumble ice cream hits the spot for dessert.

Times 12-2.30/5.30-9.30 Closed 25-26 Dec, 1 Jan

Hooked Restaurant & Bar

Modern British, Seafood

tel: 01872 274700 **Tabernacle St TR1 2EJ**
email: inthecity@hookedcornwall.com
dir: 100yds off Lemon Quay

Consistently good modern seafood cookery with a new look

Formerly known as Indaba Fish, this smart Truro venue on a quiet street in the city centre has moved up a gear, with a modern brasserie look of uncovered tables and floor against voguishly exposed brickwork. There's a palpable sense of new energy about the place, but continuation under the same ownership with executive chef Rob Duncan has ensured consistency where it counts. Seafood is the leading suit still, with tapas dishes available daytime and evening (tempura squid and chilli jam, scallop and black pudding with apple chutney, dill-cured salmon and cream cheese). The main menu incorporates chorizo-stuffed monkfish in pastry with root mash and tarragon sauce, Goa-style seafood curry with jasmine rice and a crab bhaji, and good old fish and chips with mushy peas and tartare. Desserts are intricately worked creations on the themes of orchard fruits, chocolate and nuts, or 'Cream Tea', which comprises clotted cream brûlée, Earl Grey parfait and rose jelly.

Chef Robert Duncan **Owner** Stephen Shepherd **Seats** 40, Pr/dining room 24 **Times** 12-2.30/5.30-9.30 Closed Sun **Prices** Fixed L 2 course fr £13.95, Fixed D 3 course fr £16.95, Starter £3-£7, Main £7.95-£21.95, Dessert £5-£7, Service optional **Wines** 6 bottles over £30, 24 bottles under £30, 12 by glass **Parking** Car park opposite **Notes** Pre-theatre menu 5.30-6.45 Mon-Sat 2/3 course £13.95/£16.95, Vegetarian available, Children welcome

Tabb's

Modern European

tel: 01872 262110 **85 Kenwyn St TR1 3BZ**
email: n.tabb@virgin.net
dir: Down hill past train station, right at mini rdbt, 200yds on left

Skilful contemporary cooking a short stroll from the city centre

London-trained Nigel Tabb forsook the smoke for the pleasant reaches of Cornwall, first in Portreath and latterly at this welcoming venue a short stroll from the centre of Truro. It's a neighbourhood restaurant of considerable charm, from the lavender walls to the cornucopia of local produce on offer, and the formidable range of skill that the chef-patron brings to his essentially simple modern dishes. Thinly sliced ballottine of pork and duck combines superlative meats, with good complements from warm tomato sauce and piccalilli. Mains exhibit similarly fine judgment in the timing of a grilled fillet of hake, bedded on creamed mushroom and leek, in a vanilla-scented tomato dressing, or in offering a pair of venison cuts – fried fillet and pot-roasted shoulder – alongside caramelised orange, shallot cream and shredded parsnips in a port reduction. A burst of vibrant flavour provides a dazzling finale in the form of lime and Earl Grey cheesecake with strawberry and black pepper sorbet and orange sauce. Pedigree southwestern cheeses are the alternative.

Chef Nigel Tabb **Owner** Nigel Tabb **Seats** 30 **Times** 12-2/5.30-9.30 Closed 25 Dec, 1 Jan, 1 wk Jan, Sun-Mon, L Sat **Prices** Fixed L 3 course fr £25, Fixed D 3 course £25, Starter £7.25-£10.50, Main £15.75-£20.50, Dessert £7.50, Service optional **Wines** 17 bottles over £30, 30 bottles under £30, 15 by glass **Parking** 200yds **Notes** Tapas L £12, Pre-theatre menu 5.30-6.45pm bookings only, Vegetarian available, Children welcome

VERYAN

Map 2 SW93

The Quarterdeck at The Nare

Traditional British

tel: 01872 500000 **Carne Beach TR2 5PF**
email: stay@narehotel.co.uk **web:** www.quarterdeckrestaurant.co.uk
dir: From Tregony follow A3078 for approx 1.5m. Left at Veryan sign, through village towards sea & hotel

Overlooking a heavenly sandy beach, The Nare hotel has much to recommend it, including a brace of excellent restaurants. The Quarterdeck has its own entrance and a different, more unbuttoned vibe to its sister venue, the Dining Room. The view is worth going out of your way for, and you get it whether you're out on the idyllic terrace breathing in the salty air, or indoors on a typically severe English summer's day, taking it all in through vast full-length windows in a yachtie-themed setting of polished teak, gingham seats and square rails. The kitchen ensures that peerless piscine produce from the local waters gets star billing in its confident modern dishes – perhaps seared scallops partnered with parsnip purée and truffled mushrooms, then John Dory with cider and thyme mussels, roast garlic and chive mash. Local meat fans will be pleased to learn that the prime protein hasn't clocked up many food miles either – loin of venison is served with butternut squash purée, girolles and potato gnocchi, while two could sign up to a rib of Heligan beef, and wrap things up with Valrhona chocolate fondant, rum ice cream and white chocolate sauce.

Chef Richard James **Owner** Toby Ashworth **Seats** 60 **Times** 12.30-2.30/7-9.30 Closed 25 Dec, D 31 Dec **Prices** Starter £7.50-£9, Main £14.50-£40, Dessert £7.50-£8.50, Service optional **Wines** 150 bottles over £30, 50 bottles under £30, 19 by glass **Parking** 60 **Notes** Afternoon tea available, Vegetarian available, Children welcome

WATERGATE BAY | Map 2 SW86

Fifteen Cornwall

🍽 Italian

tel: 01637 861000 **On The Beach TR8 4AA**
email: restaurant@fifteencornwall.co.uk
dir: M5 to Exeter & join A30 westbound. Exit Highgate Hill junct, following signs to airport and at T-junct after airport, turn left & follow road to Watergate Bay

Italian cooking, Jamie-style, on the beach

Jamie Oliver's Cornish outpost has a sea view that presents an ever-changing colour tone of blue and green, while the interior is more than appealing when darkness has descended. The guiding principle of the place remains to give young people a solid grounding in kitchen skills and experience, and it has been a roaring success. It all takes place in a large, contemporary space with floor-to-ceiling windows serving up that seascape, and although it's an easy-going place, it's no surfer hangout. The classy fixtures and fittings and not-so-low prices mean this is a destination eatery, not necessarily somewhere you'd grab a bite after a day on the beach. There's even a tasting menu. The food follows the Italian principles beloved by Mr Oliver, and the kitchen delivers some good stuff. Creamy burrata with Italian black figs and hazelnuts is one way to begin, or go for a plate of pasta such as radiatore (yes, they look like old school radiators) with Pre Pen Farm ragu and pecorino. Main courses can deliver pan-fried turbot with peperonata.

Times 12-2.30/6.15-9.45

CUMBRIA

ALSTON | Map 18 NY74

Lovelady Shield Country House Hotel

🍽🍽 Modern British 🍷 NOTABLE WINE LIST

tel: 01434 381203 **CA9 3LF**
email: enquiries@lovelady.co.uk **web:** www.lovelady.co.uk
dir: 2m E of Alston, signed off A689 at junct with B6294

Refined modern dining in intimate country house

The seductively situated Lovelady Shield sits among three acres of lush gardens with the River Nent running past, and its charming Georgian features succeed in enhancing further any romantic notions. It looks pretty peachy on the inside, with those generous Georgian proportions and a comfortingly smart and traditional decor. The dining room is suitably elegant with its pastel hues, and service from the friendly and approachable team is just the ticket. The menus follow the seasons and there's a gentle modernism to the output. Seared scallops might come with a poached mousse and trio of cauliflower preparations, for example, or there might be seared pigeon breast with a potato pancake, braised red cabbage, Jerusalem artichoke purée and pancetta crisp. Next up, roast loin of venison with ox tongue, rösti potato gâteau and Scotch quail's egg competes for your attention with poached whiting with smoked haddock brandade and mussel minestrone. There's plenty of modish thinking among desserts, too: Amalfi lemon tart with raspberry 'accompaniments' and gin and tonic gel, for example.

Times 12-2/7-8.30 Closed L Mon-Sat

AMBLESIDE | Map 18 NY30

Waterhead Hotel

🍽 Modern British

tel: 015394 32566 **Lake Rd LA22 OER**
email: waterhead@englishlakes.co.uk **web:** www.englishlakes.co.uk
dir: A591 into Ambleside, hotel opposite Waterhead Pier

Vibrant brasserie cooking on the edge of Windermere

The Waterhead is a townhouse hotel near Ambleside, so named for its strategic siting on the northern edge of Lake Windermere. It hardly needs saying that the surrounding countryside is breathtaking in its quiet majesty, and the hotel is a good place to stay for those on the Lakeland cultural trail. Wordsworth lived nearby, and don't forget Beatrix Potter, readings of whose works are thoughtfully piped into the lavatories for you. Don't get too engrossed in there, though, or you might miss the vibrant brasserie dining going on in the modernist Bar and Grill, with its blue glassware and purple-lit ceiling. Start with a meaty sharing platter of barbecue ribs, chipolata and fell-bred beef carpaccio, or something like sticky-toffee duck leg with wilted greens. Mains might offer a whole poussin with Cumbrian pancetta in red wine jus, or herbed lemon sole in smoked salmon butter, and then there's Grasmere gingerbread cheesecake to finish.

Chef Andrew Caulfield **Owner** English Lakes Hotels **Seats** 70 **Times** 11.30-9.30 Closed Xmas, New Year (only open to residents), L Mon-Sat All-day dining **Prices** Fixed L 2 course £15-£20, Fixed D 3 course £25-£35, Starter £4-£10, Main £13.50-£26, Dessert £6.25-£8.95, Service optional **Wines** 10 bottles over £30, 20 bottles under £30, 12 by glass **Parking** 50, Nearby pay & display **Notes** Vegetarian available, Children welcome

APPLEBY-IN-WESTMORLAND | Map 18 NY62

Appleby Manor Country House Hotel

🍽 Modern British V

tel: 017683 51571 **Roman Rd CA16 6JB**
email: reception@applebymanor.co.uk **web:** www.applebymanor.co.uk
dir: M6 junct 40/A66 towards Brough. Take Appleby turn, then immediately right. Continue for 0.5m

Peaceful rural views and modern country-house cooking

The outlook over Appleby Castle and the Eden Valley towards the fells of the Lake District is a real pastoral treat, and this Victorian sandstone house was put up by someone with an eye for a view. The hotel's newest addition is the 1871 Bistro, named in honour of the year the house went up, and it delivers some breezy feel-good dishes in a charming rustic room with French windows opening onto the garden. The main restaurant takes a more refined approach to proceedings, with tables dressed up in white linen and oak panels on the walls. There's a good amount of regional produce on the menu and the kitchen delivers some smart, upscale food. Double-baked crab soufflé with a seafood velouté is one way to begin, or there might be seared Solway scallops with black pudding and pancetta. Next up, duo of wild mallard (roast breast and slow-cooked leg) is a fine bird, well cooked, and served with vegetable fondants and black cherry sauce. For dessert, try perhaps a lemon tart with Earl Grey sorbet, raspberry syrup and ginger crumble.

Chef Chris Thompson **Owner** Dunbobbin family **Seats** 100, Pr/dining room 20 **Times** 12-2/7-9 Closed 24-26 Dec **Prices** Starter £7.95-£9.50, Main £14.95-£22, Dessert £5.95-£8.95, Service optional **Wines** 10 bottles over £30, 38 bottles under £30, 10 by glass **Parking** 60 **Notes** Sunday L, Children welcome

BARROW-IN-FURNESS
Map 18 SD26

Clarence House Country Hotel & Restaurant

British, International v

tel: 01229 462508 **Skelgate, Dalton-in-Furness LA15 8BQ**
email: clarencehsehotel@aol.com **web:** www.clarencehouse-hotel.co.uk
dir: *A590 through Ulverston & Lindal, 2nd exit at rdbt & 1st exit at next. Follow signs to Dalton, hotel at top of hill on right*

Modern British versatility in an orangery setting

The white-fronted hotel in Dalton-in-Furness, not far from Barrow, is perfectly poised between sandy beaches and the lush green acres of Lakeland. A dining room designed like an orangery, with windows on three sides, affords covetable views over the St Thomas Valley, and terrace tables make the best of the sun. The menus are defined by that resourcefully versatile reach that has come to be the hallmark of the modern British idiom, offering Chinese-style slow-roasted duck in plum sauce with cashews and pomegranate to start, or a tian of Cornish crab set in avocado, tomato and basil. For main, there may be grilled salmon garnished with crisp pancetta and a pea and mint risotto, or roast chump of Cumbrian lamb with provençale accompaniments of aubergine, confit peppers and tapenade. A grill section offers various steaks and chops with a choice of sauces. Friday night is carvery night.

Chef Mr Chris McDonald **Owner** Mrs Pauline Barber **Seats** 100, Pr/dining room 14 **Times** 12-2/7-9 Closed D Sun **Prices** Fixed L 2 course fr £16.95, Starter £5.95-£9.95, Main £14.95-£27.95 **Wines** 28 bottles over £30, 35 bottles under £30, 8 by glass **Parking** 40 **Notes** Fri D carvery £29.95, Sun L 12-3, Sunday L fr £25.95, Children welcome

BASSENTHWAITE
Map 18 NY23

Armathwaite Hall Country House & Spa

British, French v

tel: 017687 76551 **CA12 4RE**
email: reservations@armathwaite-hall.com **web:** www.armathwaite-hall.com
dir: *From M6 junct 40/A66 to Keswick then A591 towards Carlisle. Continue for 7m and turn left at Castle Inn*

Fine dining with lake views

Standing in 400 acres of grounds bordering Bassenthwaite Lake, Armathwaite boasts all of the hoped-for open fires, rich fabrics and acres of oak panelling, and a facelift has brought all the mod cons expected in a 21st-century hotel, including a spa. The Lake View Restaurant is a lovely high-ceilinged room with oak panelling, rich golds and reds and comfortable chairs at formally set tables. Attentive staff are sprucely turned out, as you'd expect of a restaurant with a smart dress code. The kitchen steers a course to keep traditionalists and modernists happy, sending out starters like slow-braised belly of Cumberland pork with buttered spinach and black pudding. Main course might be local game – soy-infused loin of Cartmel venison, say, with marinated red cabbage, sweet potato, pak choi and black pepper jus. For dessert, try perhaps the apple and cinnamon spring roll with vanilla crumble and ice cream and Granny Smith apple purée.

Chef Kevin Dowling **Owner** Graves family **Seats** 80, Pr/dining room **Times** 12.30-1.45/7.30-9 **Prices** Prices not confirmed, Service optional **Wines** 6 by glass **Parking** 100 **Notes** Fixed D 5 course £46.95, Sunday L, Children welcome

The Pheasant

Modern British

tel: 017687 76234 **CA13 9YE**
email: info@the-pheasant.co.uk **web:** www.the-pheasant.co.uk
dir: *M6 junct 40, take A66 (Keswick and North Lakes). Continue past Keswick and head for Cockermouth. Signed from A66*

Interesting contemporary cooking led by Cumbrian ingredients

Dating from the 17th century, this long, low-slung building has a charming, atmospheric bar and a beamed bistro as well as the more formal (think stiff white napery) Fell Restaurant. The kitchen relies on local sources for its ingredients and, while its roots may lie in the great classical techniques and repertoire, it clearly keeps a finger on the culinary pulse to come up with thoroughly modish ideas. It's a busy place too, baking bread, making canapés, pickling grapes and picking sorrel, the last two going into a starter of spiced goats' cheese along with shallots, candied walnuts and celery. If combinations sound overwrought, dishes seem to work, such as perfectly cooked, tender duck breast with chorizo, mushrooms, braised romaine, butternut squash, pearly barley and bacon crisp and truffled hollandaise. Fish might be fillet of cod with shellfish risotto, red pepper velouté and samphire. Puddings are a strength: consider rich dark chocolate terrine cut by griottine cherries and sour cherry ice cream.

Chef Malcolm Ennis **Owner** Trustees of Lord Inglewood **Seats** 45, Pr/dining room 18 **Times** 12-2.30/7-9 Closed 25 Dec, Mon, L Tue-Sat, D Sun **Prices** Prices not confirmed, Service optional **Wines** 12 by glass **Parking** 40 **Notes** Daily changing menu, Sunday L, Vegetarian available, No children

What makes a 4-Rosette restaurant?
See page 9

BASSENTHWAITE *continued*

Ravenstone Lodge

British NEW

tel: 01768 776629 **CA12 4QG**
email: enquiries@ravenstonelodge.co.uk web: www.ravenstonelodge.co.uk
dir: *5m N of Keswick on A591*

Unfussy but imaginative country-house cooking

A country-house hotel on a human scale, the buildings that make up Ravenstone used to be the mews and coach house for the big house across the way. They're not playing second fiddle, though, for this place has plenty going on, including a bar and bistro in the former stables. The main restaurant – the Coach House – is smartly turned out and the team in the kitchen takes good, regional ingredients and doesn't muck about with them too much. There's some good cooking on show, though, and no shortage of good ideas. A starter of mackerel escabèche comes with celeriac remoulade and pickled Chantenay carrots and desserts extend to warm apple tarte Tatin with vanilla ice cream and caramel sauce. In between might come main courses that can be as comforting as roast breast of chicken with celeriac dauphinoise, Savoy cabbage with bacon and wild mushroom jus, or as refined as grilled fillet of brill with basil gnocchi and Cumbrian crab.

Chef James Cooper **Owner** Michael Cornish **Seats** 26 **Times** 6.30-9 **Prices** Starter £4.95-£8.95, Main £13.95-£19.95, Dessert £4.95-£7.95, Service optional 10% **Wines** 10 bottles over £30, 20 bottles under £30, 12 by glass **Parking** 15 **Notes** Vegetarian available, Children welcome

| BORROWDALE | Map 18 NY21 |

Borrowdale Gates Hotel

Modern French NEW v

tel: 017687 77204 & 0845 833 2524 **CA12 5UQ**
email: hotel@borrowdale-gates.co.uk web: www.borrowdale-gates.com
dir: *B5289 from Keswick, after 4m turn right over bridge to Grange. Hotel 400yds on right*

Skilfull modern country house dining with Lakeland views

The fells and rugged countryside of the Borrowdale Valley running down to Derwent Water form a diverting backdrop to dining in this classic Lakeland country house. Pack a copy of one of Wainwright's famous guides and a yomp up Scafell Pike or Catbells should set you up for dinner. The kitchen has ramped up its efforts recently, turning out a confident take on modern British dishes cooked with skill and an eye to local and seasonal materials. Start with a surf and turf combo of crispy pork belly, tiger prawn, chorizo bonbon pointed up with ginger, lemongrass and chilli dressing. Proceed to honey-roasted breast of wild mallard glazed with poached plums, served with a crispy vegetable wonton, celeriac purée, leeks and bacon. End with a dessert that matches the comfort of chocolate fondant with pistachio ice cream.

Chef Christopher Standhaven **Owner** Colin Harrison **Seats** 50 **Times** 12-3/6.30-8.45 Closed Jan **Prices** Service optional **Wines** 19 bottles over £30, 38 bottles under £30, 7 by glass **Parking** 35 **Notes** Sunday L £19.95-£21.50, Children welcome

Leathes Head Hotel

British

tel: 017687 77247 **CA12 5UY**
email: reservations@leatheshead.co.uk web: www.leatheshead.co.uk
dir: *3.75m S of Keswick on B5289, set back on the left*

Traditional country-house cooking and lovely views

There aren't many restaurants in this guide where the food is prepared on an Aga, but that is the case at this former Edwardian gentleman's charming country home. It's a lovely spot with two-and-a-half acres of gardens to call its own and the

rolling fells beyond. The hands-on kitchen team, headed up by David Jackson, show passion for the produce of them thar hills, with a good amount of local food turning up on the plate. The cooking lets the ingredients shine. Kick off with a rich chicken and duck liver parfait, or perhaps a fresh crab salad with king prawns and home-made sweet chilli jam (seafood gets a good look-in here, too). Aga-seared venison steak with plum and venison sausages is a well-balanced dish, with sweet potato champ and port and redcurrant sauce, or there might be pot-roasted guinea fowl with Cumbrian pancetta and curried Bramley apples. For dessert, spiced sticky fig tart is a seasonal warmer.

Chef David Jackson **Seats** 24 **Times** 6.30-8.30 Closed mid Nov-mid Feb **Prices** Prices not confirmed, Service optional **Wines** 23 bottles over £30, 31 bottles under £30, 10 by glass **Parking** 15 **Notes** Coffee incl, Fixed D 4 course £32.50, Vegetarian available, No children

Lodore Falls Hotel

Modern British NEW v

tel: 017687 77285 & 0800 840 1246 **CA12 5UX**
email: lodorefalls@lakedistricthotels.net web: www.lakedistricthotels.net/lodorefalls
dir: *M6 junct 40, A66 to Keswick, B5289 to Borrowdale. Hotel on left*

Plush lakeside modern European dining using local ingredients

This hotel by Derwentwater and the eponymous falls provides a suitably Lakeland vista, with good views served up from the restaurant as well. Its outside tables are a big hit in the warmer months. The Lake View Restaurant has plush, traditional furnishings and pristine white table cloths (along with those views over the water to distant hills), and is the setting for some good modern European dishes. Local ingredients such as lamb and venison turn up in main courses, the latter maybe served up with juniper-flavoured red cabbage compôte, parsnip and vanilla purée and a port and chocolate sauce. Or go for pan-seared gilt head bream with crayfish and parsley mash and a beurre blanc. Start with tiger prawn and crab cakes covered in panko breadcrumbs and expect a sorbet before the main course. Upside-down damson sponge pudding with local damson gin syrup and custard is a dessert to send you home content.

Chef Mike Ward **Owner** Lake District Hotels **Seats** 120, Pr/dining room 24 **Times** 12-2/6.30-9.15 **Prices** Fixed D 3 course £33.95-£39.95 **Wines** 16 bottles over £30, 32 bottles under £30, 12 by glass **Parking** 90 **Notes** Sunday L £13.95-£18.95, Children welcome

| BRAITHWAITE | Map 18 NY22 |

The Cottage in the Wood

Modern British v

tel: 017687 78409 **Whinlatter Forest CA12 5TW**
email: relax@thecottageinthewood.co.uk web: www.thecottageinthewood.co.uk
dir: *M6 junct 40, A66 signed Keswick. 1m after Keswick take B5292 signed Braithwaite, hotel in 2m*

Mountain View at the Cottage in the Wood - the clues are in the name

The Lakeland writer AW Wainwright reckoned that the northwestern fells were the most delectable in the whole district, and there they are, right before your eyes in the view from this 17th-century coaching inn. Despite its faintly fairy tale name, it's a distinctively contemporary place, with spacious, airy rooms and a restaurant called Mountain View for its majestic prospect. Christopher Archer is now in charge of the cooking, maintaining the kitchen's established commitment to sound regional produce in modern British dishes full of sharply honed flavours. Mostarda, smoked apple and gingerbread are the accompaniments to chunky game terrine, or there could be a salad of black figs, goat curd, beetroot and fennel. Neither do the principals for main courses have far to travel: turbot from Whitehaven with brown shrimps, artichoke, wild garlic and lemon, a Cumbrian ham parcel of stone bass in red wine, or Goosnargh duck with orangey carrots and a hint of coffee. That final aromatic twist given to many dishes surfaces again in a dessert of fig Arctic roll with accoutrements of pistachio, lime and green tea.

Chef Christopher Archer **Owner** Liam & Kath Berney **Seats** 36 **Times** 12.30-2.30/6-9 Closed Jan, Sun-Mon **Prices** Fixed L 3 course £25, Fixed D 3 course £45, Tasting menu £60 **Wines** 27 bottles over £30, 23 bottles under £30, 12 by glass **Parking** 16 **Notes** Fixed D 5 course £55 (groups of 7+), Children welcome

BRAMPTON Map 21 NY56

Farlam Hall Hotel

 Modern British

tel: 016977 46234 **Hallbankgate CA8 2NG**
email: farlam@relaischateaux.com web: www.farlamhall.co.uk
dir: On A689, 2.5m SE of Brampton (not in Farlam village)

Anglo-French cooking in a former Victorian family seat

Delightfully situated in the North Pennines, not far from the border country and just a few miles from Carlisle, Farlam Hall is a creeper-covered house with plenty of diverting history. A Victorian family of entrepreneurs and eccentrics, the Thompsons, did most of the decorative work, and were sometime owners of George Stephenson's groundbreaking Rocket, which once careered along a track in the grounds here. A dining room done in peachy tones is divided by a kind of proscenium arch with curtains, and makes a suitably dramatic setting for Barry Quinion's contemporary Anglo-French stylings. Seared scallops with an appetising caramelised surface come with wilted spinach, crisp bacon and a vibrant white wine sauce. This may be followed by loin of local lamb marinated in rosemary, with the classic provençal accompaniment of ratatouille and some creamy parsnip purée. Or there may be salmon fillet fried in butter and dill, served with smoked salmon risotto in sherry sauce. Finish with appealingly light lemon and lime crème fraîche mousse in berry coulis.

Chef Barry Quinion **Owner** Quinion family **Seats** 40, Pr/dining room 20 **Times** 8-8.30 Closed 24-30 Dec, 4-23 Jan, L all week **Prices** Prices not confirmed, Service optional **Wines** 37 bottles over £30, 24 bottles under £30, 12 by glass **Parking** 25 **Notes** Set price D 4 course £47-£49.50 Children 5 yrs+

CARLISLE Map 18 NY35

Crown Hotel

 Modern British

tel: 01228 561888 **Station Rd, Wetheral CA4 8ES**
email: info@crownhotelwetheral.co.uk web: www.crownhotelwetheral.co.uk
dir: M6 junct 42, B6263 to Wetheral, right at village shop, car park at rear of hotel

Modern British cooking in a village hotel

This white Georgian hotel, updated to meet 21st-century requirements, is in a picturesque village a few miles out of Carlisle close to Hadrian's Wall. The

Conservatory Restaurant, overlooking the landscaped gardens, has a striking raftered ceiling, red quarry tiles on the floor and round-backed padded dining chairs at polished wooden tables. The kitchen favours a largely modern British approach and gives dishes their own distinctive identity. Cauliflower, both puréed and pickled, adds extra dimensions to pan-fried scallops with Parma ham, and venison carpaccio is interestingly teamed with Blue Whinnow cheese, pickled walnuts and mushroom pâté. Spirited ways with main courses have seen perfectly cooked curried monkfish with chilli and caper dressing and spiced aubergine, and a mead reduction for Goosnargh duck breast with spicy red cabbage, baby turnips and roast potatoes. For pudding, look no further than glazed lemon tart with lemon ice cream, or pear tarte Tatin with mulled fruit and vanilla cream.

Chef Paul Taylor **Owner** David Byers **Seats** 80, Pr/dining room 120 **Times** 12-2.30/7-9.30 Closed L Sat **Prices** Fixed L 2 course £15.25, Fixed D 3 course £26, Starter £6.50-£11.95, Main £13.95-£24.95, Dessert £5.50-£8.50, Service optional **Wines** 5 bottles over £30, 29 bottles under £30, 12 by glass **Parking** 70 **Notes** Sunday L £18.50, Vegetarian available, Children welcome

CARTMEL Map 18 SD37

Aynsome Manor Hotel

 Traditional & Modern British

tel: 015395 36653 **LA11 6HH**
email: aynsomemanor@btconnect.com web: www.aynsomemanorhotel.co.uk
dir: M6 junct 36, A590 signed Barrow-in-Furness towards Cartmel. Left at end of road, hotel before village

Traditional country-house dining with a daily-changing menu

Once a country residence of the Pembrokes, the manor is an elegant little country house at the head of the Cartmel Valley, looking southwards towards the fabled Norman priory, the stretching meadows and the woods. Inside it has an old-school feel, but in a good way, with clothed tables, silverware and gleaming glasses, deep windows and portraits in oils gazing down from the walls. Pick any number of courses from the daily-changing menu, or go for the full five, perhaps opening with pigeon breast and local black pudding with raspberry-dressed saladings, and then steamed sea trout with samphire, and a sharply contoured sauce of tomato, olives and tarragon. In between comes a soup such as parsnip and apple, and it's all rounded off with a dessert such as impressively fragile vanilla pannacotta with gooseberry compôte, or dark chocolate, pecan and maple syrup tart with minted raspberry coulis, and then perhaps good British cheeses with biscuits.

Chef Gordon Topp **Owner** Christopher & Andrea Varley **Seats** 28 **Times** 7-8.30 Closed 25-26 Dec, 2-28 Jan, L Mon-Sat, D Sun (ex residents) **Prices** Fixed L 3 course £17.95-£18.95, Fixed D 3 course £29-£30, Service optional **Wines** 20 bottles over £30, 45 bottles under £30, 6 by glass **Parking** 20 **Notes** Sunday L £17.95-£18.95, Vegetarian available, Children 5 yrs+

L'Enclume

 – see overleaf

L'Enclume

Map 18 SD37

Modern British V NOTABLE WINE LIST

tel: 015395 36362 **Cavendish St LA11 6PZ**
email: info@lenclume.co.uk **web:** www.lenclume.co.uk
dir: *Follow signs for A590 W, turn left for Cartmel before Newby Bridge*

A world-class dining experience in a little Cumbrian village

From the outside L'Enclume looks a lot like the forge it once was – 700 years old, solid, traditional. Don't go thinking it's all that different on the inside either, for this is the domain of Simon Rogan, a person who appreciates the value of what man and nature can do when they work in harmony. Everything here has vitality and purpose and there is no chintz or fakery, it is certainly not rough-and-ready. The restaurant is done out in neutral tones from natural materials, tables are left unclothed as the wood is beautiful as it is, with any decoration or adornment on the whitewashed walls reflecting the environment, the textures and wildness of the landscape hereabouts. It is possible these days to find out what Rogan is all about without heading to Cumbria (see entries for The French and Mr Cooper's House and Garden by Simon Rogan) – The Midland Hotel in Manchester – is home to a brace of dining rooms run by this most dynamic of chefs. But with stylish bedrooms available at a few places in the village, none more than a short stroll from the restaurant, staying over only extends the pleasure of a visit. Central to everything here are the ingredients. A lot of what you eat will have been picked a short while ago at Rogan's organic farm nearby, or foraged from the local countryside, and the livestock may well have been reared on the farm, too, with what he doesn't produce himself sourced from trusted local suppliers. The service team are on hand to help with the menu, dealing with questions and giving advice with charm and professionalism. There may well be some unfamiliar things on the menu, and in fact such is the drive to deliver absolute perfection that dishes may vary even within a service (the person on the next table may have a slightly different dish to you, but, rest assured, they'll both be brilliant). Everything from the bread onwards is beautifully crafted and stylishly presented, with modern cooking techniques on show, but, more than anything, respect for the produce. Dishes such as oyster pebbles look intriguing and hit the sweet spot for visual appeal and flavour. There might be native lobster with black pudding and parsnip, served with sour cream with roe and chives, and salt-baked beetroot with glazed ox tongue, yoghurt and apple marigold. The colours on the plate make a startling impact, quite beautiful at times, and the flavour combinations are clever, and never a step too far. Suckling Lop comes with mushroom cream, heritage potatoes and pennywort, while a sweet course might deliver sweet clover, pear, walnuts and wild chervil. This is dynamic, contemporary cooking from a chef who has helped the UK gain culinary confidence, delivering British food at its best. To cap it all off, the wine list follows a similar path, championing lesser-seen grape varieties, biodynamic wines, supporting English producers, and giving the customer something different from same old, same old.

Chef Simon Rogan, Mark Birchall **Owner** Simon Rogan, Penny Tapsell **Seats** 50, Pr/dining room 10
Times 12-1.30/6.30-9.30 Closed L Mon-Tue **Prices** Prices not confirmed, Service optional **Wines** 220 bottles over £30, 12 by glass **Parking** 7, On street **Notes** Set price L 6 course £45, Set price D 18-20 course £120 No children

CARTMEL *continued*

Rogan & Company Restaurant

@@@ – *see below*

CROSTHWAITE
Map 18 SD49

The Punchbowl Inn at Crosthwaite

@@ Modern British

tel: 015395 68237 **Lyth Valley LA8 8HR**
email: info@the-punchbowl.co.uk web: www.the-punchbowl.co.uk
dir: *A590 then A5074 signed Bowness/Crosthwaite. Inn within 3m on right*

Fashion-conscious Cumbrian dishes in the damson-rich Lyth Valley

A small country house in the verdant Lyth Valley, where the damsons are nonpareil, the Punchbowl stands next to the parish church of St Mary. It's one of Lakeland's homelier places, run with great civility but without any overly starched formality. A slate-topped bar and modern rustic furniture give the place a fresh look, and the dining room is decorated with interesting pictures and furnished with stylish high-backed chairs. A substantial menu of modern Cumbrian food shows plenty of fashion-conscious technique, as when venison tartare starts proceedings dressed in juniper, hazelnuts, blue cheese, capers and a smoked egg yolk. Mains show off some fine principals, perhaps roast loin and leg croquette of rabbit, with crayfish mousse, apricots and chard, or brill with butternut squash, potato rösti, and smoked salmon and caper butter. Those fabulous damsons might turn up in a posset for pudding, accompanied by lemon jelly and pink peppercorn meringue, or whizzed up as a garnish for the adventurous Anglo-French cheese selection, which also comes with pear chutney and candied walnuts.

Chef Scott Fairweather **Owner** Richard Rose **Seats** 50, Pr/dining room 16 **Times** 12-9 All-day dining **Prices** Service optional **Wines** 74 bottles over £30, 33 bottles under £30, 14 by glass **Parking** 40 **Notes** Sunday L £14.95-£20, Vegetarian available, Children welcome

Who has made the top ten per cent this year?
See page 34

Rogan & Company Restaurant

@@@

CARTMEL
Map 18 SD37

Modern British
tel: 015395 35917 **The Square LA11 6QD**
email: reservations@roganandcompany.co.uk
dir: *From M6 junct 36 follow signs for A590. Turn off at sign for Cartmel village*

Tirelessly inventive pastoral cooking the Rogan way

Simon Rogan is to Cartmel as Heston Blumenthal is to Bray, a towering culinary presence in an unassuming little town. The five-rosette L'Enclume may be the big ticket, but isn't the only Rogan game in town. The secondary place would be a strong contender wherever it was beamed down. As it is, it sits at the riverside watching the ducks, a two-storey Lakeland house of roughcast stone and ineffable charm, surrounded by a rolling soft-focus landscape divided by dry-stone walls, with Cartmel Priory looming in the background. Kevin Tickle has taken over at the stoves, and proves himself another fine exponent of the Rogan genre, offering tirelessly inventive fixed-price menus built from thoroughbred Cumbrian produce, much of it sourced from the Rogan farm a little way down the valley, some of it foraged. Attribution is all: it matters that your slow-poached egg is from a Marans chicken, its richness supported by salt-baked yellow turnip, truffle and toasted seeds, or that your roast ox tongue and smoked bone marrow arrive in a nest of 'spring offerings' from nearby Aynsome Farm. At main, there's Langdale mutton from the fells with roast parsnip, ramsons and capers, as well as suckling British Lop, which may sound like something you were called at school, but is an old native breed of porker, served with hedgerow garlic and carrots glazed in mead. Butter-poached halibut, shrimps and kohlrabi comes with scurvy grass, which you may also have been called at school, unless you know it better as spoonwort, while roasted cod is matched with fermented garlic, salsify and sea greens. Desserts are quite as pastoral and as dazzling, perhaps iced yoghurt with honeycomb, a granola fired up with edible flowers and bee's pollen, or meadowsweet mousse with wild chervil and apple, but spare a thought for the British artisan cheeses and chutney.

Chef Simon Rogan, Kevin Tickle **Owner** Simon Rogan, Penny Tapsell **Seats** 40, Pr/dining room 10 **Times** 12-2.30/6.30-9 Closed Sun, L Mon **Prices** Fixed L 3 course fr £28.50, Fixed D 3 course £40 **Wines** 30 bottles over £30, 18 bottles under £30, 12 by glass **Parking** On street **Notes** Vegetarian available, Children welcome

ELTERWATER

Map 18 NY30

Langdale Hotel & Spa

@ @ Modern British

tel: 015394 37302 & 38080 **The Langdale Estate LA22 9JD**
email: purdeys@langdale.co.uk **web:** www.langdale.co.uk
dir: M6 junct 36, A591 or M6 junct 40, A66, B5322, A591

Well-crafted, modish cooking in a rustic setting

Set in a Victorian former gunpowder factory in a 35-acre estate dotted with streams, ponds, and an original waterwheel and millstones, there's no lack of charm at the Langdale Hotel. Purdey's Restaurant is a smartly rustic venue, with exposed Lakeland stone walls climbing to the raftered roof above wooden tables and chairs; an original cannon used for testing is a talking point, although the only sparks flying around nowadays come from the skilled kitchen team, who make a real effort to keep things seasonal and local. The menus follow a broadly modern British script, starting out with a full-flavoured pairing of seared scallops with crispy veal sweetbreads and salsa verde. Ingredients are well sourced and compositions convincing: a tasting of free-range pork is evidence of sound technical skills, and comes pointed up with pickled apple purée and sage jus. Elsewhere, inspiration may come from far-off shores – perhaps coconut and lemongrass curry to add oomph to spiced monkfish and mussels. For puddings, Yorkshire rhubarb cheesecake is delivered with vanilla-poached rhubarb and gingerbread ice cream.

Chef Gary Auld **Owner** Langdale Leisure Ltd **Seats** 80, Pr/dining room 40 **Times** 6.30-9.30 Closed L ex groups - booking essential **Prices** Tasting menu fr £45, Starter £7-£11, Main £14-£26, Dessert £6-£9, Service optional **Wines** 9 by glass **Parking** 50 **Notes** Tasting menu 7 course, Vegetarian available, Children welcome

GLENRIDDING

Map 18 NY31

The Inn on the Lake

@ @ Modern European V

tel: 017684 82444 **CA11 0PE**
email: innonthelake@lakedistricthotels.net **web:** www.lakedistricthotels.net
dir: M6 junct 40, A66 Keswick, A592 Windermere

Modern cooking on the shore of Ullswater

The lake in question is Ullswater and it is indeed set before you, a beautiful vista that is Lakeland through and through. The hotel has 15 acres of fabulous grounds to explore as well, so there is plenty of opportunity to really connect with this impressive landscape. The interior matches the charming period spaces with some well-chosen furniture, creating smart and comfortable rooms, not least the Lake View Restaurant, which certainly serves up quite a panorama. The team in the kitchen makes good use of the excellent produce available in this region and they don't lack for technical skills and good ideas either. You might start, with confit of Goosnargh duck leg with orange and Cointreau jelly and celeriac purée, or Appleby goats' cheese with textures of beetroot. Bright, modish stuff then. Local lamb might come three ways (fillet, mini-cutlet and shoulder), or try the seared wild sea trout with mussel beignet, shaved fennel and saffron rice broth. Things end on a high with dark chocolate terrine with buttermilk ice cream and marinated blackberries.

Chef Edward Kilty **Owner** Charles & Kit Graves **Seats** 100, Pr/dining room 40 **Times** 12-2/7-9 **Prices** Fixed L 2 course fr £16.95, Fixed D 3 course fr £32, Starter fr £7.95, Main fr £27, Dessert fr £7.95, Service optional **Wines** 20 bottles over £30, 35 bottles under £30, 8 by glass **Parking** 100 **Notes** Sunday L, Children welcome

GRANGE-OVER-SANDS

Map 18 SD47

Clare House

@ Modern British

tel: 015395 33026 **Park Rd LA11 7HQ**
email: info@clarehousehotel.co.uk **web:** www.clarehousehotel.co.uk
dir: Off A590 onto B5277, through Lindale into Grange, keep left, hotel 0.5m on left past Crown Hill & St Paul's Church

Country-house cookery overlooking the bay

The Read family has been running Clare House since the end of the 1960s, and their care and attention is evident at every turn. The beautiful, immaculately tended gardens have a feeling of seclusion from the swirling tourist traffic of the town, and the traditional decor and fittings inside complement the fine views over the bay. Well-spaced tables dressed in crisp linen, attended by smartly turned-out staff, are the order of the day, and the cooking cleaves to an essentially traditional style without straying beyond culinary norms, for all that presentation is as contemporary as can be. That accounts for chicken liver parfait with scrumpy jelly arriving in a Kilner jar. Butter-roasted hake is given resonance with Puy lentils, bacon and herbs, wild mushrooms and a meaty beer sauce, while roast rib-eye comes with balsamic-roasted potatoes and madeira sauce. To finish there could be a well-executed pear frangipane tart with vanilla ice cream.

Chef Andrew Read, Mark Johnston **Owner** Mr & Mrs D S Read **Seats** 36 **Times** 12-2.30/6.30-7.30 Closed Dec-Apr **Prices** Service optional **Wines** 1 bottle over £30, 24 bottles under £30, 3 by glass **Parking** 16 **Notes** Fixed D 5 course £38, Light L menu Mon-Sat, Sunday L £18.50-£23, Vegetarian available, Children welcome

GRASMERE

Map 18 NY30

The Dining Room

@ @ Modern British V

tel: 015394 35217 **Oak Bank Hotel, Broadgate LA22 9TA**
email: info@lakedistricthotel.co.uk **web:** www.lakedistricthotel.co.uk
dir: N'bound: M6 junct 36 onto A591 to Windermere, Ambleside, then Grasmere. S'bound: M6 junct 40 onto A66 to Keswick, A591 to Grasmere

Stylish modern cooking in Lakeland country house

The old Victorian Oak Bank Hotel has lots of Lakeland charm, with pretty gardens that run down to the River Rothay and decor that is smart and comfortable. The Dining Room restaurant – equally comfortable and refined, with a conservatory extension – is perhaps surprisingly, then, among all this civilised conformity, the setting for some ambitious and creative food. Chef Darren Comish clearly has an eye for presentation and enticing combinations, never outlandish, but most certainly contemporary in their execution. A first course, for example, might consist of home-cured gravadlax with a perky lemongrass pannacotta, a creamy caesar cream wrapped in cucumber and roasted melon-a-dish with a good deal going on, a good deal of which is brilliant. Next up, a tasting plate of rare breed pork is among its treasures a succulent cheek and mini black pudding boudin, or go for a fishy option in the form of pan-roasted salt cod with spiced couscous, curry nut crumble and curry velouté. And for dessert, how about a chocolate-fest, including chocolate tart and pistachio cake?

Chef Darren Comish **Owner** Glynis & Simon Wood **Seats** 32 **Times** 12.30-1.30/6.30-8.30 Closed 21-26 Dec, 2-22 Jan, 2-13 Aug, L Mon-Thu **Prices** Fixed L 2 course £21.95-£26.75, Tasting menu £55-£57.50, Service optional **Wines** 14 bottles over £30, 48 bottles under £30, 8 by glass **Parking** 14 **Notes** Fixed D menu 5 course £37.95-£45.45, Sunday L £21.95-£26.75 Children 10yrs+

Macdonald Swan Hotel

Traditional British

tel: 0844 879 9120 **LA22 9RF**
email: sales/oldengland@macdonald-hotels.co.uk **web:** www.macdonaldhotels.co.uk
dir: M6 junct 36, A591 towards Kendal, A590 to Keswick through Ambleside. Hotel on right on entering village

Good honest cooking in smart Lakeland inn

Name-checked in Wordsworth's The Waggoner, the Swan is part of Lakeland history. Sitting at the foot of rolling hills, it dates from the 1650s when it opened its doors as a coaching inn, and today the white-painted building, although much updated, doesn't lack for character. It looks handsome on the inside, with plenty of period details, warming log fires, a bar called Walkers' and a restaurant named The Waggoners. The latter is a smart-looking space with a broad menu that runs from classics such as prawn cocktail and potted shrimps, to the likes of pumpkin ravioli with sage butter. There are steaks cooked on the grill – thickly cut sirloin, for example – served with traditional sauces, and hearty things like beef cheeks with stout and herb dumplings. To finish, there might be Grasmere gingerbread cheesecake with Cumbrian honey ice cream.

Chef Robert Ryan **Owner** Macdonald Hotels & Resorts **Seats** 60, Pr/dining room 20 **Times** 12.30-3.30/6-9 Closed L Mon-Sat **Prices** Prices not confirmed, Service optional **Wines** 11 bottles over £30, 18 bottles under £30, 12 by glass **Parking** 60 **Notes** Sunday L, Vegetarian available, Children welcome

Wordsworth Hotel & Spa

Modern British

tel: 015394 35592 **LA22 9SW**
email: enquiry@thewordsworthhotel.co.uk **web:** www.thewordsworthhotel.co.uk
dir: Off A591 centre of village adjacent to St Oswald's Church

Creative country-house cooking in the heart of the Lakes

What a setting: two acres of riverside gardens with stunning views of Grasmere Vale and the mountains all around mean that before you even sit down to eat, this classic country house – built originally in 1870 as a hunting lodge for the Earl of Cadogan – feels like Lakeland on a plate. The Signature Restaurant – with the bonus of an airy conservatory extension – goes for a plush, rather romantic look, with moody lighting and piano music to set the ambience. The kitchen pulls out all the stops to impress: imaginative ideas appear with colourful presentation, foams and espumas adding gloss to a solid bedrock of fine Cumbrian ingredients. Crisp cod cheeks are winningly matched with salt-cod pannacotta, carrot mousse, red chard and pancetta crumb, ahead of Cumbrian lamb – slow-cooked loin and shoulder and sweetbreads – with broad bean fricassée, rosemary confit potatoes and grelot onions. Macerated strawberries with basil, mascarpone mousse, black pepper sablé biscuit and cinder toffee makes a bright and well-balanced ending.

Chef Jaid Smallman **Owner** Iain & Jackie Garside **Seats** 65, Pr/dining room 18 **Times** 12.30-2/6.30-9.30 **Prices** Fixed L 2 course fr £16.95, Fixed D 3 course £28-£38, Tasting menu £38-£45 **Wines** 40 bottles over £30, 12 bottles under £30, 10 by glass **Parking** 50 **Notes** Sunday L £16.95-£22.95, Vegetarian available, Children 5 yrs+

Sharrow Bay Country House Hotel

British, International

tel: 017684 86301 **Sharrow Bay CA10 2LZ**
email: info@sharrowbay.co.uk **web:** www.sharrowbay.co.uk
dir: M6 junct 40. From Pooley Bridge right fork by church towards Howtown. Right at x-rds, follow lakeside road for 2m

Classically-based cuisine by the majestic tranquillity of Ullswater

If any view is guaranteed to bring out the landscape artist or poet manqué in you, it ought to be the majestic, tranquil prospect over Ullswater enjoyed by Sharrow Bay. The hotel is a venerable old trooper of the country-house movement. At its heart is the defiantly unreconstructed dining room, a place of heavily draped comfort, all pink flounce and cultivated, flawlessly courteous service. The deal here is classically-based cuisine that flies the flag proudly for Cumbrian produce, with a wide range of choice. A trio of seafood makes a compendious opener, offering dressed crab, a seared scallop and lobster tortellino, before the intermediate courses, the first a soup or fish dish (salmon with prawn risotto, perhaps), the second a citrus sorbet. Main course might be best end of Herdwick lamb, or fillet of Matterdale venison, the latter appearing with braised red cabbage, apple and raisins, puréed roast butternut squash, and a strong sauce founded on brandy and port. Some new-fangled thinking-orange polenta cake with blood orange jelly and Cointreau mascarpone cream-inveigles itself among the traditional likes of nougat glacé and toffee pudding for dessert, and then there are fine British cheeses to bring down the curtain.

Times 1-8

Overwater Hall

Modern British

tel: 017687 76566 **CA7 1HH**
email: welcome@overwaterhall.co.uk **web:** www.overwaterhall.co.uk
dir: A591 at Castle Inn take road towards Ireby. After 2m turn right at sign

Creative cooking in splendid Georgian country-house hotel

Overwater Hall is reached by a driveway winding through 18 acres of formal gardens and woodland: try to spot red squirrels and deer. It's a splendid example of 18th-century architecture, with unusual rounded corners, behind one of which is the dining room, styled to reflect the age of the property, with vertically striped wallpaper, swagged curtains and round-backed upholstered chairs at clothed tables. Local produce is everything to chef Adrian Hyde, who proudly lists his suppliers on his daily-changing menus. Dinner runs to four courses, with an intermediate fish dish: perhaps smoked trout fishcake on tartare sauce with pea purée and herbs. Dishes are not without a degree of intricacy, but self-assurance brings them off. Starters have included creamy crab risotto with mustard velouté, a poached egg, asparagus and sun-dried tomato dressing, a masterly combination, and might be followed by pink-roast rack of lamb on dauphinoise served with pan-fried liver, haggis, root vegetables and redcurrant jus, or perhaps classic lobster thermidor. Cheeses are all Cumbrian, and there's a choice of home-made desserts.

Chef Adrian Hyde **Owner** Adrian & Angela Hyde, Stephen Bore **Seats** 30 **Times** 12.30-2/7-8.30 Closed 1st 2 wks Jan, L Sun-Mon **Prices** Fixed D 3 course £45, Service optional **Wines** 30 bottles over £30, 40 bottles under £30, 9 by glass **Parking** 15 **Notes** ALC L only, Light L Tue-Sat 12.30-2, 4 course D £45, Vegetarian available, Children 5 yrs+

KENDAL
Map 18 SD59

Best Western Plus Castle Green Hotel in Kendal
◉◉ Modern British

tel: 01539 734000 **Castle Green Ln LA9 6RG**
email: reception@castlegreen.co.uk **web:** www.castlegreen.co.uk
dir: M6 junct 37, A684 towards Kendal. Hotel on right in 5m

Well-crafted dishes in a smart modern hotel

This substantial hotel sits in 14 acres of gardens and woodland overlooking Kendal Castle and the fells, making it an ideal bolt-hole for exploring Lakeland. The smartly contemporary Greenhouse Restaurant is a light and airy venue where visual entertainment comes two ways: a glass 'theatre window' lets you watch the chefs in action without the inconvenience of noise and smells; look the other way, and sweeping picture windows open onto views of Kendal and its castle. The kitchen bangs the drum for locally-produced ingredients (a Cumbrian tasting menu revolves around supplies from a 55-mile radius), brings an imaginative approach to its work and has a deft touch in its handling of the modern British idiom. A perfectly-timed pan-fried brill fillet with cauliflower fritters, pea purée, watercress, and shellfish sauce makes a fine opening gambit, followed by roast breast and confit leg of mallard matched with swede, chestnuts, red cabbage and an interesting twist from smoked mash. It all concludes with treacle tart with chocolate ice cream and the palate-cleansing sharpness of apricot sauce.

Chef Justin Woods **Owner** James & Catherine Alexander **Seats** 80, Pr/dining room 250 **Times** 12-2/6-10 **Prices** Prices not confirmed **Wines** 8 bottles over £30, 32 bottles under £30, 7 by glass **Parking** 200 **Notes** Tasting menu 3/5 course, Vegetarian available, Children welcome

KESWICK
Map 18 NY22

Morrels
◉ Modern British

tel: 017687 72666 **34 Lake Rd CA12 5DQ**
email: info@morrels.co.uk
dir: Between the market square & the Keswick Theatre by the Lake

Relaxed contemporary dining

Bang in the centre of Keswick between the market and the Theatre by the Lake, the exterior of Morrels may have the look of a classic Lakeland stone-built townhouse, but the stripped-out contemporary interior is a slice of metropolitan style that wouldn't look out of place in a big city. It is a slick act, all pine floors, bare wooden tables, chocolate and cream high-backed chairs, etched glass screens and an eclectic modern menu to match. The kitchen takes its inspiration from around the world, and pulls it all together in simple, contemporary ideas such as pan-fried scallops with chorizo and sweet potato purée, which you might follow with slow-roast pork belly with black mash, apple sauce, crackling and gravy, or steamed sea bass fillet with fennel, tomato and dill ragoût. Friendly staff and a laid-back modern soundtrack make for an easygoing ambience.

Times 5.30-close Closed Mon, L all week

Hipping Hall

KIRKBY LONSDALE
Map 18 SD67

Modern British V

tel: 015242 71187 **Cowan Bridge LA6 2JJ**
email: info@hippinghall.com **web:** www.hippinghall.com
dir: 8.5m E of M6 junct 36 on A65

Accomplished modern cooking with national parks on either hand

What later eras came call stepping-stones were once known as hipping-stones, and a trail of them was laid across Broken Beck, the stream that runs past the old wash-house here. When Hipping's owner married a lawyer's daughter from these parts in the early 1600s, he found himself rising in Kirkby Lonsdale society, and the Hall itself came up in the world too. A three-storey house of local stone, it stands in that lovely land between the Lake District and the Yorkshire Dales, the best of both National Park worlds. There are mature gardens with a water feature to contemplate, but the nerve-centre of the place is the medieval dining room, where young New Zealand chef Brent Hulena creates gastronomic fireworks with the region's seasonal produce. Choose from a three-course menu, or the all-singing, all-dancing seven-course taster. Either way, this is cooking of uncommon acuity and intelligence, bristling with fresh ideas but never departing from a

sense of underlying culinary logic. An opening presentation of quail offers sliced breast, confit leg and an egg, in the company of an array of mushroom variations – dried, pickled and duxelles. Ingredient combinations might seem counter-intuitive, but produce happy discoveries along the way, as when halibut arrives with cauliflower, pine-nuts and samphire, or a fat langoustine with saffron potatoes, red pepper and fennel. Cumbrian pork comes as crackled belly and gelatinous cheek, alongside a black pudding bonbon and choucroute spiked with orange, while a bracing waft of maritime breeze comes across in Morecambe Bay sea bass with a ceviched scallop, sea herbs and ink-dyed farfalle pasta. There is no shyness about incorporating the acid flavours of tart apple into a dessert based on a jelly of caramelised apples with puff pastry and yoghurt sorbet, or how about fig carpaccio doused in mulled wine with redcurrants and liquorice?

Chef Brent Hulena **Owner** Andrew Wildsmith **Seats** 26 **Times** 12-2/7-9 Closed L Mon-Fri **Prices** Prices not confirmed, Service optional **Wines** 58 bottles over £30, 14 bottles under £30, 10 by glass **Parking** 20 **Notes** Tasting menu 7 course, Sunday L No children

Swinside Lodge Country House Hotel

@@ Modern British

tel: 017687 72948 **Grange Rd, Newlands CA12 5UE**
email: info@swinsidelodge-hotel.co.uk web: www.swinsidelodge-hotel.co.uk
dir: *M6 junct 40, A66, left at Portinscale. Follow to Grange for 2m ignoring signs to Swinside & Newlands Valley*

Seasonal set menu amid the brooding fells

A small white-fronted country house in the Newlands Valley, Swinside makes a good job of seeming to be miles from anywhere, despite the nearness of Keswick. Surrounded by brooding fells, its own modest but well-kept gardens look positively friendly, and that's certainly the tone maintained within, where a hands-on approach by the owners makes everyone feel at home. Clive Imber cooks a daily-changing four-course menu. It might begin with a soup such as richly satisfying vine tomato and basil intervening between an impactful fish starter, comprising gravad lax, roast salmon, and crab and horseradish remoulade in beetroot dressing, and a main course of duck breast with potato gratin, sweet shallots and spice-roasted plum sauced in red wine. At the end, there's a choice of desserts, perhaps a traditional sponge pudding such as ginger, or a more adventurous dark chocolate pavé and white chocolate mousse with kirsch-drenched cherries and lots of passion fruit. If you've room, there is always a fine Anglo-French cheese slate, as well as good breads and envelopingly rich petits fours.

Times 7.30-10.30 Closed Dec-Jan, L all week

▌KIRKBY LONSDALE   Map 18 SD67

Hipping Hall

@@@ – *see opposite*

The Sun Inn

@ Modern British v

tel: 015242 71965 **6 Market St LA6 2AU**
email: email@sun-inn.info web: www.sun-inn.info
dir: *From A65 follow signs to town centre. Inn on main street*

Friendly old inn with local ingredients and plenty of flavour

Visitors come to the historic market town of Kirkby Lonsdale, on the borders of the Lake District and the Yorkshire Dales, to revel in the famous 'Ruskin's View' across the Lune Valley. But those with foodie inclinations should also schedule a pit stop in the white-painted 17th-century Sun Inn, a proper pub with oak beams, log fires and cask ales in the traditional bar, and a contemporary feel in the dining room. Wherever you choose to eat, expect a serious commitment to using the best local ingredients, since there are reliable hands in the kitchen to conjure full-flavoured dishes along the lines of breast and braised leg of partridge with figs, wild mushrooms and beef dripping croûtons, followed by a hearty rump of hoggett with butternut squash, mutton and lamb kidney faggot, and rosemary roast potatoes. Finishing with something rib-stickingly traditional like warm treacle tart with nutmeg custard and double Jersey ice cream.

Chef Sam Carter **Owner** Lucy & Mark Fuller **Seats** 36 **Times** 12-5/6.30-9 Closed L Mon **Prices** Fixed D 3 course £24.95-£28.95, Starter £4.50-£6.50, Main £9.95-£21.45, Dessert £5.95-£6.75, Service optional **Wines** 12 bottles over £30, 33 bottles under £30, 9 by glass **Parking** On street & nearby car park **Notes** Sunday L £22.95-£24.70, Children welcome

---

▌LUPTON   Map 18 SD58

The Plough Inn Lupton

@ Modern British

tel: 015395 67700 **Cow Brow LA6 1PJ**
email: info@theploughatlupton.co.uk web: www.theploughatlupton.co.uk
dir: *M6 junct 36 onto A65 signed Kirkby Lonsdale*

Smart contemporary looks and modish pub food

The Plough had fallen on hard times before being given a shot in the arm by the good people behind the Punchbowl Inn in Crosthwaite (see entry). It's surely never looked better. The refurbishment has maintained the best of the pubby elements – wooden floors, beams, real fires and the like – and given the place a classy finish with well-chosen colours, leather sofas, and a Brathay slate-topped bar. There are real ales and a decent slate of wines by the glass alongside a broad menu of Brit-focused food. Start with something like salt and pepper tempura squid, or pan-fried Stornoway black pudding with caramelised apple and a poached hen's egg, and follow on with braised lamb shank with garlic potatoes, spring greens and a rosemary and redcurrant jus. There are old favourites like whole tail breaded scampi and a good burger (8oz Aberdeen Angus), and, for dessert, bread-and-butter pudding with vanilla-poached apricots.

Chef Matt Adamson **Owner** Richard Rose **Seats** 120, Pr/dining room 8 **Times** 12-9 All-day dining **Prices** Prices not confirmed, Service optional **Wines** 28 bottles over £30, 38 bottles under £30, 14 by glass **Parking** 40 **Notes** Sunday L, Vegetarian available, Children welcome

---

▌NEAR SAWREY   Map 18 SD39

Ees Wyke Country House

@ Modern, Traditional British

tel: 015394 36393 **LA22 0JZ**
email: mail@eeswyke.co.uk web: www.eeswyke.co.uk
dir: *On B5285 on W side of village*

Confident country-house cooking in elegant Georgian hotel

A Georgian house above Esthwaite Water, with glorious fell views, Ees Wyke was at one time Beatrix Potter's holiday home, before she bought Hill Top and moved to the village. It's now a comfortable, and comforting, country-house hotel, with dinner served in the dining room overlooking the lake. In typical Lakeland style, everyone takes their seats simultaneously for a daily-changing, five-course menu with a couple of choices per course. Good local sourcing is clear, and the kitchen combines classical ideas with gently modern notions, devising well-balanced meals. Start with seared scallops with balsamic dressing before broccoli and onion quiche, then go on to the main course: pink pan-fried noisettes of lamb with a wine jus hinting of mint and garlic, or gilt head bream fillets grilled with pancetta, thyme and oregano. Puddings might be a toss-up between sticky toffee sponge and pears poached in Muscat with honey and cinnamon, before a choice of local cheeses.

Chef Richard Lee **Owner** Richard & Margaret Lee **Seats** 16 **Times** 7.30-close **Prices** Prices not confirmed **Wines** 18 bottles over £30, 18 bottles under £30, 5 by glass **Parking** 12 **Notes** Fixed D 5 course £43.50, Vegetarian available, No children

NEWBY BRIDGE
Map 18 SD38

Lakeside Hotel Lake Windermere
Modern British V

tel: 015395 30001 **Lakeside LA12 8AT**
email: sales@lakesidehotel.co.uk **web:** www.lakesidehotel.co.uk
dir: M6 junct 36 follow A590 to Newby Bridge, straight over rdbt, right over bridge. Hotel within 1m

Lakeside modern dining with a choice of restaurants

The Lakeside sits, as you might expect, right on the water's edge at the southern shore of Lake Windermere, surrounded by wooded slopes. It started out as a coaching inn in the 17th century, and is now a substantial building, with a lakeside terrace, spa and pool and a brasserie as well as the Lakeview restaurant looking over boats bobbing on the water. Main courses on the interesting menu show that the kitchen has a thoroughly modern outlook, among them halibut fillet with haggis, ceps and mushroom cappuccino, and breast and drumstick of squab pigeon with dates and boulangère potatoes. The bulk of materials are sourced locally, plus seafood from Scotland and Cornwall, going into appealingly assembled starters of white crabmeat with bulgar wheat, avocado and tomato confit, and the full-on flavours of shin of beef with celeriac, beetroot and green mustard. The seasonally-changing menu might conclude with zingy desserts like rhubarb soufflé with eucalyptus parfait and pink grapefruit, or dark chocolate mousse with butterscotch, chocolate soil and double-milk ice cream.

Chef Richard Booth **Owner** Mr N Talbot **Seats** 70, Pr/dining room 30
Times 12.30-2.30/6.45-9.30 Closed 23 Dec-16 Jan **Prices** Starter £5-£8.50, Main £12-£26, Dessert £6-£9 **Wines** 5 bottles over £30, 5 bottles under £30, 12 by glass **Parking** 200 **Notes** Fixed menu D 6 course £48, Children welcome

Follow the AA on twitter @TheAA_Lifestyle

Whitewater Hotel
Modern, Traditional British

tel: 015395 31133 **The Lakeland Village LA12 8PX**
email: enquiries@whitewater-hotel.co.uk **web:** www.whitewater-hotel.co.uk
dir: M6 junct 36 follow signs for A590 Barrow, 1m through Newby Bridge. Right at sign for Lakeland Village, hotel on left

Punchy modern British cooking by the River Leven

The Whitewater is a resort hotel in Lakeland Village, constructed around a converted stone-built mill, offering the latest in spa treatments in an area that's all about tranquil relaxation in its own right. A thoroughly hospitable dining room uses the paradoxically soothing effect of rough stone walls, hung with Lakeland scenes, against a setting of smart table linen, high-backed chairs and views through expansive windows of the cascading River Leven. Whether you feel you need the soundtrack as well is a matter of taste. The modern British food on offer is full of punchy, vivid flavours and subtle technique, teaming goats' cheese and basil pannacotta with beetroot carpaccio, powdered dried olives, pine nuts and honey, for a winning start. Inspiration comes from far and wide, including North Africa for rump of lamb in Moroccan herbs with chick pea purée, preserved lemon, cumined carrots and harissa. Fruit-focused desserts might include raspberry clafoutis with lemon mascarpone.

Times 12-2/7-9 Closed L Mon-Sat

PENRITH
Map 18 NY53

North Lakes Hotel & Spa
Modern British

tel: 01768 868111 **Ullswater Rd CA11 8QT**
email: nlakes@shirehotels.com **web:** www.shirehotels.com
dir: M6 junct 40 at junct with A66

Comfort eating for all the family at a Cumbrian spa hotel

The North Lakes is well placed for those who want to explore the great outdoors, but if hill-walking isn't your bag, there's also a plethora of more sedate spa treatments plus a pool and Jacuzzi to help you let off steam. In the restaurant and bar, oak beams and six real fires help create the feel of a hunting lodge, while the tables are unclothed, adding to the laidback vibe. The crowd-pleasing menus – including children's and early bird – major on comfort food, so you could kick off with heritage beetroot and goats' cheese salad with toasted pine nuts and pomegranate, or baked French onion soup with gruyère cheese. Then go for fish and chips or confit of duck shepherd's pie with slow-braised red cabbage – a rich and warming dish for a cold winter's day. Valrhona chocolate mousse with cherry ice cream pairs classic flavours to good effect. Don't forget to try one of the locally brewed Daniel Thwaites ales before you leave.

Chef Doug Hargeaves **Owner** Shire Hotels **Seats** 112, Pr/dining room
Times 12.15-1.45/6.30-9.15 **Prices** Prices not confirmed, Service optional **Wines** 14 by glass **Parking** 120 **Notes** Vegetarian available, Children welcome

---

RAVENGLASS — Map 18 SD09

The Pennington Hotel
🏵 British

tel: 0845 450 6445 **CA18 1SD**
email: info@penningtonhotels.com **web:** www.penningtonhotels.com
dir: M6, junct 36 to A590 Barrow, right Greenodd A5092, joining A595 Muncaster/ Ravenglass. Located in village centre

Imaginative cooking and estuary views

In the heart of Ravenglass overlooking the estuary, The Pennington Hotel welcomes with its appealing blend of period character (it started life as a 16th-century coaching inn) and smart contemporary style gained from its recent refurbishment. The place is just a stone's throw from the sea and Muncaster Castle, which is a spot of luck since the castle's historic kitchen gardens provide freshly picked seasonal fruit and herbs. The Pennington's kitchen focuses on care and skill rather than convoluted complexity, as demonstrated by a twice-baked soufflé of Blue Whinnow cheese with pear and rocket salad and hazelnut dressing. The same goes for a main course of cod suprême teamed with potato rösti, spinach, Romanesco cauliflower, Chantenay carrots and chervil. For dessert, 'rhubarb and custard' is a well-balanced dish of vanilla pannacotta with poached rhubarb and jelly, and vanilla soup.

Chef Darren Pilling, Kath Steward **Owner** Iona Frost-Pennington **Seats** 36, Pr/dining room **Times** 12-2.30/7-9 **Prices** Starter £6.50-£8.95, Main £12.95-£17.95, Dessert £6.95-£7.95 **Wines** **Parking** 20 **Notes** Sunday L £10.95-£21.95, Vegetarian available, Children welcome

---

SEASCALE — Map 18 NY00

Sella Park House Hotel
🏵 Traditional British

tel: 0845 450 6445 & 01946 841601 **Calderbridge CA20 1DW**
email: info@penningtonhotels.com **web:** www.penningtonhotels.com
dir: From A595 at Calderbridge, follow sign for North Gate. Hotel 0.5m on left

Local supplies and a modern approach

Six acres of lovely gardens running down to the River Calder make this historic 16th-century manor house a popular venue for tying the knot, but you don't have to be heading for a wedding to see what the kitchen can do. There's no faulting the splendid seasonal Cumbrian produce it hauls in as the basis of its up-to-date cooking: vegetables, fruit and herbs are plucked fresh from the kitchen garden at nearby Muncaster Castle, and great care is taken in tracking down the best local meat and fish. The Priory Restaurant makes a traditional setting for ideas that run the gamut from a tried-and-tested pairing of local hand-dived scallops and home-made black pudding lifted by crisp sage and quince jelly, to a main course of Goosnargh duck breast with butternut squash and orange purée, braised red cabbage and spicy duck jus. For dessert, apple tarte Tatin rounds things off nicely.

Chef Jon Fell **Owner** Iona Frost-Pennington **Seats** 34, Pr/dining room 40 **Times** 12-3/6-9 **Prices** Starter £5-£7.50, Main £13-£27.50, Dessert £6.50-£8.50, Service optional **Wines** 14 bottles over £30, 16 bottles under £30, 6 by glass **Parking** 30 **Notes** Sunday L £12.95-£21.95, Vegetarian available, Children welcome

---

TEMPLE SOWERBY — Map 18 NY62

Temple Sowerby House Hotel & Restaurant
🏵🏵 Modern British

tel: 017683 61578 **CA10 1RZ**
email: stay@templesowerby.com **web:** www.templesowerby.com
dir: 7m from M6 junct 40, midway between Penrith & Appleby, in village centre

Imaginative modern cooking in an intimate country-house hotel

Set amid the verdant fells of the Eden Valley close to Ullswater, this small-scale 18th-century country-house hotel overlooks the village green and makes a great base for exploring the northern Lake District. When you come in from hiking the hills, you can warm up by a real fire in the winter, or on balmy days, sip an aperitif in the pretty walled garden before moving indoors to the smart dining room. The skilled kitchen brigade turn out an inventive bang-up-to-date British menu crammed with fine Cumbrian produce and local game – rabbit, for example, which is delivered as lasagne and smoked loin with wild mushrooms and local pancetta. Next up, pan-roasted pollock is perfectly timed and matched with crisp crab cakes, lobster bisque and squid ink gnocchi. Elsewhere, local meat fans might be treated to roast rump and slow-cooked shoulder of Cumbrian lamb with pease pudding, lettuce, smoked onions, and lamb jus. Round things off with the deep comforts of hot chocolate tart, Horlicks ice cream, orange marshmallow, and cookie crumble.

Chef Ashley Whittaker **Owner** Paul & Julie Evans **Seats** 24, Pr/dining room 24 **Times** 7-9 Closed 8 days Xmas, L all week **Prices** Fixed D 3 course £41.50, Service optional **Wines** 10 bottles over £30, 30 bottles under £30, 7 by glass **Parking** 20 **Notes** Vegetarian available, No children

---

WATERMILLOCK — Map 18 NY42

Macdonald Leeming House
🏵 Modern British

tel: 0844 879 9142 **CA11 0JJ**
email: leeminghouse@macdonald-hotels.co.uk **web:** www.macdonald-hotels.co.uk
dir: M6 junct 40, continue on A66 signed Keswick. At rdbt follow A592 towards Ullswater, at T-junct turn right, hotel 3m on left

Ambitious country-house cooking on the shores of Ullswater

This 200-year-old Lakeland manor certainly knows how to capitalise on its splendid location on the edge of Ullswater, offering fishing rights to the rod and line brigade, and making sure that the tables by the French windows of the Regency Restaurant bask in glorious views of the lake. Leeming House takes a traditional approach to the grande-luxe country-house dining experience: a polished front-of-house team deliver correctly formal service, while the kitchen delivers gently modern ideas along the lines of goats' cheese fondue teamed with beetroot in the form of jelly, mousse and caviar. Main courses major in grilled rib-eye and sirloin of Scottish beef, or there might be grilled wild sea bass with creamed potato, broccoli and salsa verde.

Times 12-2/6.45-9

WATERMILLOCK *continued*

Rampsbeck Country House Hotel

◎◎ Modern British

tel: 017684 86442 **CA11 OLP**
email: enquiries@rampsbeck.co.uk **web:** www.rampsbeck.co.uk
dir: *M6 junct 40, A592 to Ullswater, T-junct turn right at lake's edge. Hotel 1.25m, on lake side*

Smart modern cooking in a refined lakeside setting

The white-painted villa sits on a hillside overlooking Ullswater, with 18 acres all to itself, including a piece of valuable shoreline. It delivers a country-house experience which meets expectations in terms combining old world luxury with some contemporary comforts, while the culinary output from the kitchen really catches the eye. There are acres of burnished panels, antiques and ornate ceilings throughout the 18th-century house, and smart lounges where it's easy to lose an hour or two. The dining room itself has all the period details, plus neatly laid tables and a menu with its roots in classical French cooking. But this is bright, modern stuff, presented with a good deal of style. Pan-fried red mullet, for example, comes with a salt-cod mousse, black olive purée and a red pepper crisp in a starter that has evident Mediterranean leanings. Follow on with fillet of English rose veal served with a warm salad of mixed beans, and finish with a modern take on a classic combination of flavours: carrot cake with chocolate soil, yoghurt sorbet and candied carrot.

Chef Ben Wilkinson **Owner** Blackshaw Hotels Ltd **Seats** 40, Pr/dining room 16 **Times** 12-1.45/7-9 **Prices** Fixed L 3 course £32, Service optional **Wines** 100 bottles over £30, 65 bottles under £30, 12 by glass **Parking** 30 **Notes** Fixed D 4 course £59.95, Sunday L £32, Vegetarian available, Children 8 yrs+

Beech Hill Hotel

◎ Modern British V

tel: 015394 42137 **Newby Bridge Rd LA23 3LR**
email: reservations@beechhillhotel.co.uk **web:** www.beechhillhotel.co.uk
dir: *M6 junct 36, A591 to Windermere. Left onto A592 towards Newby Bridge. Hotel 4m from Bowness-on-Windermere*

Appealing modern cooking on the shores of Windermere

After canapés and pre-dinner drinks you can soak up the dramatic views over Lake Windermere to the fells beyond from Burlington's Restaurant. The menu's altogether more catholic than that usually found in such a context, embracing a crispy haggis cake on crushed carrots and turnips topped with a fried egg, and dill-battered sea bass fillet sauced with rouille served with saffron potato purée and tender-stem broccoli. Cumbrian produce is used to good effect, and the kitchen clearly has a solid grounding in the French classics, but adds its own spin on dishes. Morecambe Bay shrimps go into a risotto with dill and parmesan, to be followed perhaps by passionfruit-glazed crispy duck confit served with honey-roast parsnips and carrots. Allow ten minutes for a soufflé-blackcurrant, say, with blueberry sorbet — or order something chilled like mandarin crème brûlée.

Chef Christopher Davies **Owner** Mr F Richardson **Seats** 130, Pr/dining room 90 **Times** 7-9 Closed L all week (ex party booking), D 25 Dec **Prices** Prices not confirmed Fixed D 3 course £32.95, Service optional **Wines** 25 bottles over £30, 25 bottles under £30, 8 by glass **Parking** 60 **Notes** Fixed D 5 course £37.95, Children welcome

Cedar Manor Hotel & Restaurant

◎◎ Modern British

tel: 015394 43192 **Ambleside Rd LA23 1AX**
email: info@cedarmanor.co.uk **web:** www.cedarmanor.co.uk
dir: *From A591 follow signs to Windermere. Hotel on left just beyond St Mary's Church at bottom of hill*

Peaceful small hotel with impressive seasonal cooking

Built of grey stone in 1854, the manor occupies a peaceful spot in attractive gardens, complete with eponymous cedar, on the outskirts of Windermere. It's a small-scale hotel, with a modern look, while the restaurant is well appointed, with leather-look chairs at neatly set tables; well-trained but unbuttoned staff keep the ball rolling. Seasonality leads the kitchen, with its reliance on Lakeland produce, and the cooking is marked out by its technical precision and, given the quintessentially English surroundings, by its wide-ranging scope. Thus, pavé of salmon is marinated in ginger and served with robust wasabi mayonnaise, some pickled vegetables and leaves, and another starter combines the pungency of aubergine, onion and potato bhajis with mint chutney and a coriander and onion dip. Main courses are in similar vein — Moroccan lamb tagine with herby couscous, for instance — although pink-roast duck breast has appeared in autumn with seasonal fruits, sautéed pumpkin and a perfect rendition of dauphinoise. Incidentals like breads and a complimentary soup are well reported, as are puddings such as chocolate millefeuille.

Chef Roger Pergl-Wilson **Owner** Caroline & Jonathan Kaye **Seats** 22, Pr/dining room 10 **Times** 6.30-8.30 Closed Xmas & 6-25 Jan, L all week **Prices** Prices not confirmed, Service optional **Wines** 11 bottles over £30, 26 bottles under £30, 7 by glass **Parking** 12 **Notes** Vegetarian available, Children 9yrs+

Gilpin Hotel & Lake House

◎◎◎ *– see opposite*

Gilpin Hotel & Lake House

Modern British

tel: 015394 88818 **Crook Rd LA23 3NE**
email: hotel@gilpin.co.uk **web:** www.gilpin.co.uk
dir: *M6 junct 36 take A590/A591 to rdbt N of Kendal, then B5284 for 5m*

Dynamic contemporary cooking in fabulous family-run hotel

In 1917 Joseph Cunliffe needed to escape the smog of Manchester after suffering lung damage during World War I, so he bought an Edwardian house in 22 acres of peaceful gardens, moors and woodland near Windermere. Apart from a blip when it left the family ownership for about 20 years, Gilpin Lodge is still run by the Cunliffes who are now well into their third decade of running the place as a country-house hotel done out with a good deal of style and not an iota of chintz. Its original features (built in 1901) remain, but the impression within is of timeless contemporary luxury and comfort. There's also Lake House a short drive away in its own 100 acres, which offers six more beautiful bedrooms, a lakeside vista and spa. As of April 2014 Alan O'Kane is the new man in the kitchen and eating here remains, as ever, a highlight of a stay. The cooking is thrillingly contemporary, but clearly focused at the same

time. There are plenty of creative ideas and preparations on show, everything looks wonderful on the plate, and the ingredients are second to none. Muncaster crab with a crispy battered oyster and heritage carrots in various guises is a storming opener, or things might start with a dish that plays a riff on the textures of broccoli, turbocharged with Stichelton blue cheese and crispy cod cheeks. Follow on with Herdwick mutton – shoulder, belly and a dim sum-style wonton filled with rich meat, partnered with sweet potato crisps and a silky purée, miso and the spring season's last flourish of wild garlic flowers. For pudding there's an exemplary, indulgent take on a classic British sherry trifle. You're welcome to check out the globetrotting bins in the walk-in wine cellar, and the staff run the show with charm and professionalism.

Chef Gordon Cartwright, Alan O'Kane **Owner** Cunliffe family **Seats** 60, Pr/dining room 20 **Times** 12-2/6.30-9.30 **Prices** Fixed L 3 course £30-£35, Starter £7-£10, Main £18-£41.50, Dessert £7-£9, Service optional **Wines** 170 bottles over £30, 11 bottles under £30, 14 by glass **Parking** 40 **Notes** Fixed D 4 course £58.50, Sunday L £30-£35 Children 7 yrs+

WINDERMERE *continued*

Holbeck Ghyll Country House Hotel

❀❀❀ – *see opposite*

Lindeth Fell Country House Hotel

❀ Modern British **NEW**

tel: 015394 43286 **Lyth Valley Rd, Bowness-on-Windermere LA23 3JP**
email: kennedy@lindethfell.co.uk **web:** www.lindethfell.co.uk
dir: *1m S of Bowness-on-Windermere on A5074*

Classic cooking in a refined Lakeland hotel

Built in 1909 as a private residence, Lindeth Fell is these days a classic Lakeland country-house hotel. Its position above Lake Windermere is rather special, surrounded by its own seven acres of lush and colourful gardens. The restaurant is at the front of the house to benefit from the vista through the large windows. It's a traditionally decorated space, with neutral colour tones and a comfortable chintziness, and charming service from the host. The kitchen produces classy plates of food served with a good deal of style. Beetroot gravad lax, for example, with potted salmon and squid ink croute, yellow and red beets, plus a horseradish emulsion, is a colourful combo, followed by haunch of Grizedale venison-nicely tender – with a croquette of braised leg meat and dauphine potatoes. Finish with a top-notch sticky toffee pudding with date purée, salted caramel and rum and raisin ice cream.

Chef Bryon Parsons **Owner** Diana Kennedy **Seats** 50, Pr/dining room 32
Times 12.30-1.30/7-8.30 Closed Jan **Prices** Fixed L 2 course fr £17.95, Fixed D 2 course fr £32.95, Service optional **Wines** 16 bottles over £30, 64 bottles under £30, 6 by glass **Parking** 20 **Notes** Fixed D 4 course £39.95, Afternoon tea £14.50, Sunday L fr £21.95, Vegetarian available, Children 7 yrs+

Lindeth Howe Country House Hotel & Restaurant

❀❀ Modern British **V**

tel: 015394 45759 **Lindeth Dr, Longtail Hill LA23 3JF**
email: hotel@lindeth-howe.co.uk **web:** www.lindeth-howe.co.uk
dir: *1m S of Bowness onto B5284, signed Kendal and Lancaster. Hotel 2nd driveway on right*

Imaginative modern cooking in verdant setting chez Beatrix Potter

There may not be any shortage of delightful Lakeland hotels, nor of any overlooking Lake Windermere, but this is a classic country house with a unique pedigree – it was once home to Beatrix Potter, who wrote a couple of her tales here. So after consuming the delicious views of the lake and mountains beyond, and exploring the verdant grounds, it is back for dinner in the handsomely turned-out dining room. The kitchen team is passionate about regional produce, seeking out first-class ingredients and serving up a menu of contemporary and creative dishes. It all looks as pretty as a picture on the plate and everything is there for a reason. Poached salmon fillet takes centre stage in a starter with broad beans, tomato and pickled samphire, followed by roast corn-fed chicken ballotine with chervil mousse, black garlic mash, carrot purée and a light jus. To finish, warm blackberry clafoutis is matched with tonka bean ice cream, and black pepper and berry jelly.

Chef Robert Taylor **Owner** Lakeinvest Ltd **Seats** 70, Pr/dining room 20
Times 12-2/6.30-9 **Prices** Tasting menu fr £49.50, Service optional **Wines** 8 by glass **Parking** 50 **Notes** Fixed D 5 course £49.50, Table d'hôte menu £46.50, Sunday L Children 7 yrs+

Linthwaite House Hotel & Restaurant

❀❀❀ – *see opposite*

Macdonald Old England Hotel & Spa

❀❀ Traditional British, European

tel: 0844 879 9144 **23 Church St, Bowness LA23 3DF**
email: sales.oldengland@macdonald-hotels.co.uk **web:** www.macdonaldhotels.co.uk
dir: *Through Windermere to Bowness, straight across at mini-rdbt. Hotel behind church on right*

Stylish modern dining and stunning lake views

There is something rather wonderful about dining with a view over water, and with its lakeside setting, the Number 23 Church Street Restaurant at the Macdonald Old England serves up a very nice one indeed. It's Lake Windermere, of course, that you'll see through the floor-to-ceiling windows (or better still the terrace), but there's plenty of other good reasons to come here. The Victorian mansion is much extended these days and includes a spa amongst its many attractions. The restaurant has a good deal to offer, from steaks cooked on the grill, through to some gently contemporary dishes based on top quality regional ingredients. You might start with a ballotine of confit duck leg with honey-pickled vegetables, or a twice-baked cheese soufflé with a fricassée of roasted butternut squash. Those steaks-rib-eye, perhaps-come with plum tomatoes, field mushrooms and hand-cut chips, or go for grilled fillet of grey mullet with fennel purée and poached potatoes. For dessert, chocolate and stem ginger tart with ginger ice cream shows a lightness of touch.

Chef Rohan Nevins **Owner** Macdonald Hotels **Seats** 170, Pr/dining room 60
Times 6.30-9.30 Closed L all week **Prices** Starter £7.25-£12.50, Main £15.95-£32.50, Service optional **Wines** 40 bottles over £30, 15 bottles under £30, 13 by glass **Parking** 100 **Notes** Vegetarian available, Children welcome

Miller Howe Hotel

❀❀ Modern British **V** 🍾 NOTABLE WINE LIST

tel: 015394 42536 **Rayrigg Rd LA23 1EY**
email: info@millerhowe.com **web:** www.millerhowe.com
dir: *M6 junct 36. Follow the A591 bypass for Kendal. Enter Windermere, continue to mini rdbt, take left onto A592. Miller Howe is 0.25m on right*

Romantic lakeside setting and polished country-house cooking

Miller Howe is something of a Lakeland icon, with its landscaped grounds and stunning views over Windermere and the fells. Staying here is an indulgent experience, a new bar area a recent addition, and no less cosseting is dining in the restaurant, with its plush decor and romantic views of the lake. Put yourselves in the hands of chef Andrew Beaton and go for his tasting menu, or make the more difficult choice of something from the carte, with its handful of dishes per course. One way to start is with the extravagance of poached lobster with lobster cream, Jerusalem artichokes and tarragon gnocchi, or the more earthy delight of ham hock ballotine with piccalilli, vegetables and purée. Dishes impress with the technical care applied to quality produce and intelligent balance, whether time-honoured pink-roast saddle of lamb with crispy neck, glazed root vegetables and rosemary jus, or more adventurous baked cod fillet with tandoori-style roast scallops, cauliflower, apples and tandoori oil. Assiettes and tastings are a favoured approach to desserts, perhaps of chocolate or passionfruit.

Chef Andrew Beaton **Owner** Martin & Helen Ainscough **Seats** 80, Pr/dining room 30
Times 12.30-1.45/6.45-8.45 Closed 2 wks Jan **Prices** Fixed L 2 course £21-£25, Tasting menu £55, Starter £8-£14, Main £24-£28, Dessert £10-£14, Service optional **Wines** 100 bottles over £30, 50 bottles under £30, 12 by glass **Parking** 40 **Notes** Set price D 4 course £45, Sunday L fr £27.50, Children welcome

Holbeck Ghyll Country House Hotel

WINDERMERE   Map 18 SD49

Modern British V ⬥NOTABLE WINE LIST

tel: 015394 32375 **Holbeck Ln LA23 1LU**
email: stay@holbeckghyll.com **web:** www.holbeckghyll.com
dir: *3m N of Windermere on A591, right into Holbeck Lane (signed Troutbeck), hotel 0.5m on left*

Breathtaking views and classy modern cooking

Holbeck is reached via a long driveway which reveals a vista that captures Lake Windermere, Scafell Pike, Coniston Old Man and the Langdale Pikes. The house itself, with its solid-stone reliability, positioned to make the best of the view and built on a human scale, avoids any sense of commercialisation. David McLaughlin has been running the kitchen for a dozen years or so and has it all working like clockwork, from the supplies of first-class local growers and producers, to the balance of dishes on the menu. The oak panel and fine artworks add to the high-end feel of the place, with tables dressed up for the business of fine dining, and watched over by a formal service team. Dinner might begin with hand-dived scallops (from the west coast of Scotland) in a modern classic combo with spiced cauliflower and an apple and raisin purée, or a ballotine of ham hock and split peas with celeriac and pickles. Next up, best end of Cumbrian lamb is partnered with shallot purée and rosemary jus, and roasted wild sea bass with aubergine caviar and red pepper sauce. For dessert there might be nougat glacé with exotic fruits

and warm mango parcels, or end with British and French cheeses from the trolley. There's a gourmet tasting menu, if the whole table is on board, and the high-quality wine list is the icing on the cake.

Chef David McLaughlin **Owner** Stephen Leahy **Seats** 50, Pr/dining room 20 **Times** 12.30-2/7-9.30 **Prices** Fixed L 2 course £28-£58, Fixed D 3 course £68, Tasting menu £88, Service optional **Wines** 270 bottles over £30, 29 bottles under £30, 13 by glass **Parking** 50 **Notes** Sunday L £28-£53 Children 8 yrs+

Linthwaite House Hotel & Restaurant

WINDERMERE   Map 18 SD49

Modern British V ⬥NOTABLE WINE LIST

tel: 015394 88600 **Crook Rd LA23 3JA**
email: stay@linthwaite.com **web:** www.linthwaite.com
dir: *A591 towards The Lakes for 8m to large rdbt, take 1st exit (B5284), 6m, hotel on left. 1m past Windermere golf club*

Adventurous contemporary cooking with captivating Lakeland views

The views at this erstwhile Edwardian gentlemen's residence, with over 14 acres of wooded gardens on a hillside looking over Lake Windermere, are rather magical at sunset, whether you're on the terrace basking in fine weather, or hunkered down in the snugness of the conservatory if it's turned a bit blowy. Linthwaite makes an excellent base if you're doing the William Wordsworth and Beatrix Potter trails, and it packs a lot in, with spa treatments and wedding parties in evidence. Style-wise, the place has chucked out the traditional Lakeland chintz and moved up a gear with modish furnishings. The restaurant was restyled by the designer behind Malmaison's chic look, its suite of three dining rooms making an expansive setting for Chris O'Callaghan's contemporary cooking. Drawing on top-class local supplies and novel techniques to craft a more adventurous style

than many Lake District hotel restaurants attempt, you might start with pan-fried foie gras with chicory tart and cherries, or opt for a witty spin on a favourite aperitif, combining gin-cured salmon with a sharply tangy purée of lemon and a tonic sorbet. Ideas are carefully considered and skilfully handled in main courses such as roast leg of lamb with swede Sarladaise, tarragon and goats' cheese, or there may be a take on curry with an exotic Bombay-crusted cod with spiced lentil purée, onion bhaji, and poppadum and lime emulsion. To finish, the inventiveness keeps coming with the likes of tamarind pannacotta with elderflower jelly and carrot sorbet, or cherry parfait with lavender crème anglaise, honeycomb and fennel, while cheese aficionados should head straight to the offerings of artisan cheeses. The wine list is a model of its kind, with helpful, unpretentious tasting notes and an impressive range of choice, from the European heartlands to the southern hemisphere.

Chef Chris O'Callaghan **Owner** Mike Bevans **Seats** 64, Pr/dining room 16 **Times** 12.30-2/7-9.30 Closed Xmas & New Year (ex residents) **Prices** Fixed L 2 course £14.95, Fixed D 3 course £52, Tasting menu £62 **Wines** 25 bottles over £30, 25 bottles under £30, 14 by glass **Parking** 40 **Notes** Sunday L £24.95 Children 7yrs+ D

WINDERMERE *continued*

Porto

Modern British **NEW**

tel: 015394 48242 **3 Ash St, Bowness LA23 3EB**
email: info@porto-restaurant.co.uk

Eclectic modern cookery in a stylish town-centre venue

On a cobbled street in the heart of Bowness-on-Windermere, Porto is well placed to cater to a healthy proportion of the seasonal Lakeland crowds. It's a low-roofed white-fronted old house with seating on two floors, a heated roof terrace and a summer garden, the main room rather dramatically done up in red and gold with mirrors, black napery and crystal light fixtures. Staff are brisk and efficient, and know their onions when it comes to both the menu and the wine list. A voguishly eclectic mix of European and Asian influences amid more obviously straightforward fare indicates a kitchen aiming to please, and David Bewick's dishes are neatly and painstakingly presented. First up could be a classic twice-baked Cumbrian Cheddar soufflé, offset by the sharpness of a white wine and chive sauce, cherry tomatoes and rocket. Mains run a gamut of thematic explorations, from the salmon version that incorporates seared Loch Duart fillet with a mini-fish pie and fishcake to the bluntly named 'pig plate', at which you may feed on slow-cooked belly, pulled pork bubble-and-squeak and pigs in blankets, garnished with apple purée and a creamy mustard sauce. Proceedings end on a crowd-pleasing note with chocolate ganache cake, salted caramel, popcorn and richly flavoured vanilla ice cream.

Chef David Bewick **Owner** Faye Ramsey **Seats** 68, Pr/dining room 50 **Times** 12-2/6-9 Closed 24-26 Dec, 2nd wk Jan-2nd wk Feb, Tue **Prices** Starter £4.95-£8, Main £14.95-£25, Dessert £6.95-£9, Service optional **Wines** 7 by glass **Notes** Vegetarian available, Children welcome

The Samling

– *see below*

Storrs Hall Hotel

Modern British v

tel: 015394 47111 **Storrs Park LA23 3LG**
email: enquiries@storrshall.com **web:** www.storrshall.com
dir: *on A592 2m S of Bowness, on Newby Bridge road*

Creative vision and old-school standards in a creamy-white Windermere mansion

This handsome Georgian mansion on the shores of Lake Windermere epitomises timeless Lakeland beauty. Landscaped gardens look over the lake to wild fells all around – there's even a National Trust-owned temple folly to explore. Inside are the requisite antiques, oil paintings and opulent furnishings of the classic country-house hotel. The ornate solid oak and intricate glass bar is architectural salvage of the highest order: it was recycled from Blackpool Tower. The kitchen has always shown plenty of thought, imagination, and considerable ambition in its contemporary British cooking, and with a new chef taking the helm in March 2014 you can expect plenty of inventive ideas. These may include duck liver parfait matched with Szechuan granola, brioche, pear three ways and Monbazillac syrup, and for main course, perhaps a two-way treatment of beef-slow-roasted Jacob's ladder and sirloin-with potato purée, watercress, and snails in Madeira. Finish with a creative composition involving treacle tart with pickled raisins, crème brûlée ice cream and lemon sorrel.

Chef Conor Toomey **Owner** Storrs Hall **Seats** 82, Pr/dining room 40 **Times** 12.30-2/7-9.30 **Prices** Fixed L 3 course £22-£35, Fixed D 3 course £45, Tasting menu £65 **Wines** 6 by glass **Parking** 50 **Notes** Themed evenings available, Sunday L £22-£35, Children welcome

The Samling

WINDERMERE	Map 18 SD49

Modern British, European v NOTABLE WINE LIST

tel: 015394 31922 **Ambleside Rd LA23 1LR**
email: info@thesamlinghotel.co.uk **web:** www.thesamlinghotel.co.uk
dir: *M6 junct 36, A591 through Windermere towards Ambleside. 2m. 300yds past Low Wood Water Sports Centre just after sharp bend turn right into hotel entrance*

Experimental British cooking in a winsome Windermere retreat

The white-painted house looks pristine against its lush green backdrop, and with 67 acres of grounds and views over the water, it really is a little slice of Lakeland heaven. It's an upscale country-house hotel on a manageable scale, with facilities such as an outdoor hot-tub designed to pamper. The finish within is classy and un-shouty. The restaurant, taking up two separate spaces at either end of the house, has a nicely understated tone, and the service team are a professional and well-drilled bunch. Head chef Ian Swainson turns out smart, contemporary food, the sort of stuff that makes the most of top-rate produce and is happy to mix and match classical and modern ideas to create dishes that feel rather exciting. The suppliers get a name-check on the menu, with local meat and game, and seafood winging it up from Cornwall. There's a tasting menu – lunch and dinner versions – in support of the carte, which offers a sensible four choices per course. Cartmel valley quail might star in a first course with an accompanying prawn and quail ravioli, mango and brown shrimps with soy-roasted seeds, with another starter delivering up a smoked pheasant egg with beef tartare (plus bone marrow croûtons and Oscietra caviar). Main-course roast grouse comes with pan-fried foie gras, cauliflower and prune purée, and peppered loin of venison with roasted butternut squash and salsify, plus goats' curd, chestnuts, walnuts and truffle. Desserts are no less creative; Muscovado sponge, for example, soaked in a lime and Malibu syrup with coconut, honeycomb and coffee. There are British and European cheeses, too, wheeled in on a trolley, and a wine list that does justice to the exciting food.

Chef Ian Swainson **Owner** Mr Danson **Seats** 22, Pr/dining room 8 **Times** 12-2/6.30-9.30 **Prices** Fixed D 3 course fr £60, Tasting menu £45-£80, Service optional **Wines** 198 bottles over £30, 26 bottles under £30, 22 by glass **Parking** 20 **Notes** Tasting menu 7 course, Fixed L menu 5 course £45-£80, Sunday L £45-£80, Children welcome

DERBYSHIRE

ASHBOURNE
Map 10 SK14

Callow Hall Hotel

Traditional British

tel: 01335 300900 **Mappleton Rd, Mappleton DE6 2AA**
email: info@callowhall.co.uk **web:** www.callowhall.co.uk
dir: *A515 through Ashbourne towards Buxton, left at Bowling Green pub, then 1st right*

Classy cooking in family-run country-house hotel

Elaborate ceilings, heavy drapes, an oak staircase, panelling and antiques define the style of this luxury country-house hotel, an ivy-covered Victorian pile in Dovedale. The kitchen does all its own smoking, curing, butchery and baking and fully exploits the finest local produce. It moves with the times too, turning out Indian-spiced gurnard with tomato and chilli chutney and crème fraîche, and another starter of salmon cured in beetroot and vodka, served with caviar, sour cream and pickled cucumber. A self-assured way with materials means that dishes are successfully cohesive, seen in main courses of pan-fried breast and shepherd's pie of duck cut by rhubarb, accompanied by sweet potato purée and chard, and more classically orientated rack of lamb with dauphinoise, roast tomatoes and buttered spinach. Fish is used to good effect: perhaps monkfish fillet, timed to the second, roasted in curry butter served with textures of cauliflower. Desserts such as apricot bread-and-butter pudding with Amaretto ice cream, and chocolate brioche ravioli with vanilla Chantilly cream tick all the right boxes.

Chef Joseph Grayson **Owner** Elyzian Hospitality Ltd **Seats** 70, Pr/dining room 40 **Times** 12-1.45/6.30-9 **Prices** Fixed L 2 course £20, Starter £6.95-£12.50, Main £16-£24.50, Dessert £8.50-£9, Service optional **Wines** 15 bottles over £30, 16 bottles under £30, 6 by glass **Parking** 15 **Notes** Champagne afternoon tea £25.95, Sunday L £28.50-£32, Vegetarian available, Children welcome

Station Hotel

Modern

tel: 01335 300035 **Station Rd DE6 1AA**
email: stationhotel@ashbourne.myzen.co.uk
dir: *Please phone for directions*

Traditional dining room with inventive contemporary menu

A fine example of robust early 20th-century mock-Tudor architecture, the Station Hotel confidently occupies its corner spot, although there is a rather more genteel and feminine tone once you cross the threshold. The decor is on the chintzy side of traditional, while the dining room has plenty of old-school charm and a relaxed service team. The menu is modern and shows plenty of good ideas. Start with braised pork belly with a seared scallop and oriental salad and five spice dressing – a contemporary combination by any standards – or go for the on the money crispy cod cheeks with straw chips and tartar sauce. Among main courses, a fine piece of hake comes in a successful combination with celeriac mash, wild mushrooms and red wine jus, and for dessert there might be baked vanilla custard with rhubarb and star anise compôte and ginger snaps.

Chef James Cornbill **Owner** David & Margaret Dougan **Seats** 28, Pr/dining room 14 **Times** 6-8.30 **Prices** Fixed D 3 course fr £22.95 **Wines** 2 bottles over £30, 10 bottles under £30, 6 by glass **Parking** 16 **Notes** Vegetarian available, Children 5 yrs+

BAKEWELL
Map 16 SK26

Piedaniel's

Traditional French

tel: 01629 812687 **Bath St DE45 1BX**
dir: *From Bakewell rdbt in town centre take A6 Buxton exit. 1st right into Bath St (one-way)*

French bistro dishes with an air of contemporary chic

The stone-built timbered look suggests a traditional country inn, but this appealing venue has an air of contemporary chic about it indoors, with smartly dressed tables, whitewashed stone walls and splashes of spring green in the decor. The order of the day is bistro dishes that reliably deliver to their specifications, starting perhaps with saffron-scented mussel soup, or scallops and tiger prawns provençale, and bringing out the big guns at main-course stage, when best end of lamb is served in its cooking juices with basil couscous and tomato confit, or chicken is swathed in smoked Black Forest ham and served with ratatouille sauce. Finish up with a wodge of chocolate truffle torte with raspberry sorbet.

Times 12-2/7-10 Closed Xmas & New Year, 2 wks Jan, 2 wks Aug, Mon, D Sun

BASLOW
Map 16 SK27

Cavendish Hotel

Modern British V

tel: 01246 582311 **Church Ln DE45 1SP**
email: info@cavendish-hotel.net **web:** www.cavendish-hotel.net
dir: *M1 junct 29 follow signs for Chesterfield. From Chesterfield take A619 to Bakewell, Chatsworth & Baslow*

Modish cooking in historic coaching inn

On the Chatsworth Estate, the Duke and Duchess of Devonshire's country seat, the Cavendish Hotel is a supremely civilised place to stay and eat. There's been an inn on this spot for a good while (even local historians aren't sure when it first opened its doors, but it was a long time ago), and today's incarnation has plenty of period charm. It's been done out with a good deal of style by the Duke and Duchess with lots of antiques and original paintings. The Gallery restaurant is a traditional and elegant room, with smartly laid tables and a service team who are entirely on the ball. On the menu is some ambitious and creative food based on good local ingredients. Start, perhaps, with Gressingham duck in a terrine with foie gras, prunes and Armagnac, its richness cut with the accompanying pineapple, plus pain d'épice. Next up, slow-cooked belly of pork with Thai flavours, seared scallop and satay sauce, and, to finish, glazed lemon tart with raspberry doughnuts, consommé, powder and basil sorbet.

Chef Mike Thompson **Owner** Chatsworth Estates **Seats** 50, Pr/dining room 18 **Times** 12-2.30/6.30-10 Closed D 25 Dec **Prices** Fixed L 2 course £35, Fixed D 3 course £45 **Wines** 34 bottles over £30, 24 bottles under £30, 11 by glass **Parking** 40 **Notes** Sunday L £27.50, Children welcome

Fischer's Baslow Hall

– *see page 128*

Fischer's Baslow Hall

BASLOW Map 16 SK27

Modern European v

tel: 01246 583259 **Calver Rd DE45 1RR**
email: reservations@fischers-baslowhall.co.uk
web: www.fischers-baslowhall.co.uk
dir: *From Baslow on A623 towards Calver. Hotel on right*

Creative cooking in an elegant country house

The house has been here since the Edwardian era, but it seems older, which is in part down to the 17th-century manner of the original design, but also the fact it seems so at home and, in keeping with its environment. It's hard to imagine it hasn't always been here. Max and Susan Fischer set about creating their vision of an individual restaurant with rooms in 1988. They run the place with the same charm and attention to detail that they started out with all those years ago. Arrival is a pleasure – down the tree-lined driveway – and the gardens themselves are clearly well managed and adored, with the kitchen garden supplying plenty of good things for the chefs. The house has lots of period details within and is decorated and furnished in a stylish and decidedly un-corporate manner. The restaurant is suitably well attired with white linen and fine artworks, plus views out to the pretty gardens. Chef Rupert Rowley has been leading the line for a good while now and has built up strong relationships with suppliers, and these top-end British ingredients (including the stuff gown a few yards from the kitchen) help maintain a common thread through the culinary output. There are two menus to choose from, either 'Taste of Britain' or the 'Classic Menu', with neither taking any shortcuts when it comes to delivering intelligent and contemporary food. There's a measured modernity here. Cornish crab sandwich with fennel, wasabi and crab jelly shows an appetite for contemporary flavours, with a pumpkin pannacotta another creative course, partnered with Colston Bassett stilton and pork crackers. Main courses might deliver Dover sole with garden leeks and a garlic and Vermouth sauce, or roast Goosnargh duck with kimchee vegetables and Yorkshire rhubarb. For dessert, perhaps an imaginative combo of treacle sponge and cep ice cream.

Chef Rupert Rowley **Owner** Mr & Mrs M Fischer **Seats** 55, Pr/dining room 38 **Times** 12-1.30/7-8.30 Closed 25-26 & 31 Dec **Prices** Fixed L 2 course fr £20.14, Fixed D 3 course fr £55, Tasting menu £50-£128, Starter £13.50-£14.50, Main £24.50-£25.50, Dessert £9, Service optional **Wines** 110 bottles over £30, 20 bottles under £30, 6 by glass **Parking** 20 **Notes** Sunday L £38 Children 5/8yrs+ L/D

BEELEY
Map 16 SK26

The Devonshire Arms at Beeley

◉◉ Modern British

tel: 01629 733259 **Devonshire Square DE4 2NR**
email: enquiries@devonshirebeeley.co.uk **web:** www.devonshirebeeley.co.uk
dir: *6m N of Matlock & 5m E of Bakewell, located off B6012*

Accomplished cooking in an up-to-date country inn

Set in a charming little village on the Chatsworth Estate, The Devonshire Arms looks for all it's worth the quintessential mellow-stone English country inn. Inside, though, that is not the whole story. The expected classic look of the cosy bar with oak beams, exposed-stone walls and wood-burning fires leads on to a light, modishly-styled brasserie extension rich with bold colours, tub dining chairs and vibrant modern artwork. The estate's produce rightly figures prominently on a repertoire that keeps things intelligently straightforward and seasonal. Start with warm scallop and cockle salad dressed in basil oil, or rabbit and mushroom tortellini with carrot and orange purée. There are classic pub dishes such as bangers (courtesy of one Mr Hancock) served with mash and red wine and onion gravy, or more the more modish tempura skate wing with Russian salad, lobster sauce and duck ham. To finish, Mrs Hill's (the chef's mum) lemon tart with sweet Chantilly cream is a fixture. There's a flexible approach here, with the same menu taken in the bar.

Chef Alan Hill **Owner** Duke of Devonshire **Seats** 60 **Times** 12-3/6-9.30 **Prices** Prices not confirmed, Service optional **Wines** 20 by glass **Parking** 30 **Notes** Sunday L, Vegetarian available, Children welcome

BRADWELL
Map 16 SK18

The Samuel Fox Country Inn

◉◉ Modern British

tel: 01433 621562 **Stretfield Rd S33 9JT**
email: enquiries@samuelfox.co.uk **web:** www.samuelfox.co.uk
dir: *M1 junct 29, A617 towards Chesterfield, onto A619 towards A623 Chapel-en-le-Frith. B6049 for Bradwell, restaurant located on left as you leave Bradwell*

Local produce used in accomplished and unfussy modern cooking

Taking its name from the local Bradwell man whose invention – the folding umbrella – might come in handy while you're up here in the Derbyshire hills, The Samuel Fox looks every inch the well-groomed Peak District country inn with its smart local stone frontage, while indoors it greets visitors with an airy open-plan layout and a fetching blend of rustic charm and clean-cut contemporary looks, with the bonus of lovely views of the Hope Valley. It is certainly a contender in the local foodie stakes, hauling in the best produce from local farms and producers to drive its seasonal menus. Dishes impress with their unfussy attitude and full-on flavours, starting with crumbed cod cheeks with garlic and parsley sauce and pickled mushrooms, before an effective, big-hearted pairing of rare-roasted haunch of venison with pickled beetroot, celeriac, and red wine sauce. Puddings can be as light and palate-cleansing as iced mandarin parfait with mango and passionfruit sauce, or perhaps put a simple but effective spin on sticky toffee pudding by matching it with stout ice cream.

Chef James Duckett **Owner** Johnson Inns **Seats** 40 **Times** 12-2.30/6-9 Closed 2-29 Jan, Mon-Tue (winter), Mon (summer), L Mon-Thu (winter), Mon-Tue (summer), D Sun, 25-26 Dec, 1 Jan **Prices** Fixed L 2 course £19, Tasting menu £45-£70, Starter £6-£8.50, Main £13.50-£22, Dessert £6-£9.50, Service optional **Wines** 8 bottles over £30, 32 bottles under £30, 11 by glass **Parking** 15 **Notes** Sunday L £19-£24, Vegetarian available, Children welcome

BUXTON
Map 16 SK07

Best Western Lee Wood Hotel

◉ Traditional & Modern British

tel: 01298 23002 **The Park SK17 6TQ**
email: reservations@leewoodhotel.co.uk **web:** www.leewoodhotel.co.uk
dir: *M1 junct 24, A50 towards Ashbourne, A515 to Buxton. From Buxton town centre follow A5004 Long Hill to Whaley Bridge. Hotel approx 200mtrs beyond University of Derby campus*

Modish cooking (with nostalgic classics) in a Georgian manor house

Lee Wood can put on an impressive wedding if you're in the market for one, but no matter if not, for the hotel's Elements Restaurant is worth a visit in its own right. The rather handsome Georgian manor house is in a good spot to explore all that the Buxton area has to offer (which is a great deal), while its ambitious restaurant awaits to provide satisfying sustenance at lunch and dinner. The conservatory dining room is the setting for some creative modern cooking. Start, perhaps, with a confit of duck leg with a chilli jelly, spiced bread crisp and pineapple purée. There's more traditional stuff, too, such as first-course cod fishcakes with lemon and parsley sauce, and main-courses range from fish and chips to fillet of sea bass with puréed basil potatoes, peperonata and pesto sauce. Finish with chocolate and hazelnut marquise with caramelised hazelnut and liquorice caviar.

Times 12-2/5.30-9.15 Closed 24-25 Dec

CHESTERFIELD
Map 16 SK37

Casa Hotel

◉◉ Modern European

tel: 01246 245990 **Lockoford Ln S41 7JB**
email: cocina@casahotels.co.uk **web:** www.casahotels.co.uk
dir: *M1 junct 29 to A617 Chesterfield/A61 Sheffield, 1st exit at rdbt, hotel on left*

Celebrate all things Spanish in a lopsided 'pomo' hotel

A hunk of Catalonian postmodernism landed in Chesterfield with the opening of the Spanish-themed Casa, the long blocks of its uneven storeys looking as if assembled by a gigantic five-year-old. Cool, in other words. The interior design counterpoints sober wood tones with splashes of mural colour, including in the second-floor Cocina restaurant, where a dazzlingly illuminated night-time cityscape draws the eye. A tapas repertoire and sharing platters of charcuterie set the compass needle quivering on the menus, with albondigas, pan con tomate and salt-cod croquetas all up to the mark. Mains might tempt by swaddling monkfish in Parma ham and serving it with crab risotto in a sudden eastwards lurch towards Italy, but the star of the show is the charcoal-fired Josper grill, which lends smoky savour to organically reared Belted Galloway rib-eye, sirloin and fillet, hung for four weeks and served with a sauce choice and chips. Finish appropriately with crema catalana and spiced shortbread, or by pondering your selection from the dual-nationality cheese trolley. Spanish wines lead the charge on the list.

Chef Andrew Wilson **Owner** Steve Perez **Seats** 100, Pr/dining room 200
Times 12-2/6-10 Closed L Mon-Sat **Prices** Fixed D 3 course £19.50, Starter £4-£9.50, Main £14-£27, Dessert £5-£7, Service optional **Wines** 31 bottles over £30, 34 bottles under £30, 12 by glass **Parking** 200 **Notes** Early bird menu D 6-7pm Mon-Fri, 5.30-6.30pm Sat, Sunday L £12.95-£20.95, Vegetarian available, Children welcome

CHESTERFIELD *continued*

Peak Edge Hotel at the Red Lion

◎◎ Modern British NEW v

tel: 01246 566142 **Darley Rd, Stone Edge S45 OLW**
email: sleep@peakedgehotel.co.uk **web:** www.peakedgehotel.co.uk
dir: *M1 junct 29, A617 to Chesterfield. At rdbt take 1st exit onto A61, at next rdbt 2nd exit onto Whitecotes Ln, continue onto Matlock Rd (A632) then Darley Rd (B5057))*

Inventive cooking in a Georgian inn next to a brand-new hotel

A new-build stone edifice on the border of the Peak District National Park, the family-owned hotel is handy for the historic houses of Chatsworth and Haddon Hall, as well as the old Derbyshire market towns. Not all is pristine, box-fresh modernity, though, for next door to the new building is the Red Lion, a Georgian coaching inn that is the venue for the hotel's bar and bistro. With the markets and moors to source from, not to mention salad vegetables from its own back garden, there is plenty for the kitchen to go at, and the results are offered in the form of inventive contemporary British dishes. First up might be an assemblage of baked oats, slow-cooked parsnip, egg yolk, pink grapefruit and lettuce, before main courses perform spins on bubble-and-squeak, fillet steak on the bone with horseradish in oxtail bourguignon, or sea bass with pak choi, radishes and oysters. It's all designed to stimulate the imagination as well as the tastebuds, and concludes in like manner with toasted coconut cream, mango, basil sorbet and red chilli, or reimagined Bakewell tart with almond milk ice cream and raspberry jelly.

Chef Daniel Laycock **Owner** Damian & Jo Dugdale **Seats** 80 **Times** 12-9.30 All-day dining **Prices** Fixed L 2 course £17.95-£19.95, Starter £5.50-£8.95, Main £10.50-£25, Dessert £6.50-£7.50, Service optional **Wines** 16 bottles over £30, 27 bottles under £30, 9 by glass **Notes** Afternoon tea, Sunday L £15.95-£20.95, Children welcome

---

| CLOWNE | Map 16 SK47 |

Hotel Van Dyk

◎ Modern British v

tel: 01246 810219 **Worksop Rd S43 4TD**
email: info@hotelvandyk.co.uk **web:** www.hotelvandyk.co.uk
dir: *M1 junct 30, towards Worksop, at rdbt 1st exit, next rdbt straight over. Through lights, hotel 100yds on right*

Sugar-white hotel with appealing modern British cooking

The white-fronted Van Dyk stands on the A619 not far from Chesterfield. Amid the surrounding ruggedness, it looks a little like a sugar-frosting confection, which only adds to its idiosyncratic character. Inside, it's geared up for weddings and business, and the public rooms are all contemporary elegance. That said, there's a hint of old-school formality about the Bowden dining room, with swagged curtains, trio of chandeliers, and a baby grand piano as white as the building itself. Modern northern cooking is the bill of fare, with dishes founded on sound culinary logic. Open with pancetta-wrapped figs stuffed with feta in honey and thyme glaze, as a prelude to roast monkfish in shellfish bisque with saffron mash and parsnip crisps, or chicken and rabbit ballotine with marinated peach and baby carrots. A full vegetarian menu includes the likes of butternut squash stuffed with chestnuts and cranberries in port jus.

Chef Mr Ben Richardson **Owner** Gail & Peter Eyre **Seats** 89, Pr/dining room 16 **Times** 12-9.30 Closed Mon-Tue All-day dining **Prices** Prices not confirmed, Service optional **Wines** 13 by glass **Parking** 80 **Notes** Sunday L, Children welcome

---

| DALBURY | Map 10 SK23 |

The Black Cow

◎ Modern British

tel: 01332 824297 **The Green, Dalbury Lees DE6 5BE**
email: enquiries@theblackcow.co.uk **web:** www.theblackcow.co.uk
dir: *From Derby A52 signed Ashbourne, Kirk Langley; turn into Church Lane, then Long Lane, follow signs to Dalbury Lees*

Good cooking on the village green

The Black Cow looks every inch the rural village pub, complete with pretty hanging baskets. It's a freehouse, so you'll find some interesting ales on tap, including from local breweries with names like Dancing Duck and Peakstone Rock. There are bedrooms, too, if you want to stay over. It's been gently updated inside, so it still feels like a pub, but is done out in muted contemporary tones and, in the dining area, smart high-backed leather chairs stand at chunky darkwood tables. On the menu, the chef takes on British, European and some Asian ideas, starting perhaps with black tiger prawns with peanut, chilli and coconut sauce, and sticky rice, or pressed ham hock and apricot terrine with red onion marmalade. For main course, you might choose a steak or something like pan-fried fillet of sea bass with saffron risotto, roasted butternut squash and sweet pepper dressing.

Chef Jazwant Singh **Owner** Mark & Sean Goodwin **Seats** 30, Pr/dining room 25 **Times** 12-2/6-9 **Prices** Prices not confirmed, Service optional **Wines** 1 bottle over £30, 17 bottles under £30, 8 by glass **Parking** 12, On street **Notes** Sunday L, Vegetarian available, Children welcome

---

| DARLEY ABBEY | Map 11 SK33 |

Darleys Restaurant

◎◎ Modern British v

tel: 01332 364987 **Haslams Ln DE22 1DZ**
email: info@darleys.com **web:** www.darleys.com
dir: *A6 N from Derby (Duffield road). Right in 1m into Mileash Ln, to Old Lane, right, over bridge. Restaurant on right*

Modern British cooking by the water's edge

A table on the terrace is a treat in good weather, but don't make Darleys a fair-weather friend. It looks okay on the inside, too, you see, with stylish contemporary tones of brown and cream, white linen on the tables and a grown-up feel all round. This converted silk mill, right by the River Derwent, is the setting for some bright, modern cooking, with a kitchen team making good use of regional produce. Home-smoked wood pigeon is a thoroughly contemporary way to start a meal, with onion popcorn, pickled cabbage and candied pecans revealing the ambition on show. A main course dish of British venison loin with smoked celeriac purée and a fig reduction shows refinement and endeavour, with another main combining loin of local lamb with a potato gnocchi made with ewes' cheese and finished with a pomegranate sauce. Desserts are no less inventive. Try the cranberry crumble soufflé, perhaps, with white chocolate ice cream. Lunch is a slightly simpler affair, and particularly good value.

Chef Jonathan Hobson, Mark Hadfield **Owner** Jonathan & Kathryn Hobson **Seats** 70 **Times** 12-2/7-9.30 Closed BHs, 1st 2 wks Jan, D Sun **Prices** Fixed L 2 course fr £19.95, Starter £7.20-£8.96, Main £19.75-£22.50, Dessert £7.95-£9.15, Service optional **Wines** 33 bottles over £30, 64 bottles under £30, 15 by glass **Parking** 12 **Notes** Sunday L fr £25, Children welcome

DERBY
Map 11 SK33

Masa Restaurant

 Modern European V

tel: 01332 203345 **The Old Chapel, Brook St DE1 3PF**
email: enquiries@masarestaurantwinebar.com
dir: 8m from M1 junct 25. Brook St off inner ring road near BBC Radio Derby

Modern classic brasserie dishes in a converted chapel

Masa occupies a converted Grade II listed chapel in the city centre, with a lawned garden and rear patio, with the restaurant in what was the gallery overlooking the ground-floor wine bar. It's a stylish, characterful place with a buzzy atmosphere, customers savouring the delights on the versatile brasserie-type menu. The kitchen has a sure touch when it comes to delivering the goods, seen in bright, contemporary ideas such as starters of confit ballotine of duck with glazed chicory, dates, pistachios and orange dressing, and panko-crumbed cod fillet with minted peas, radicchio and pine nuts. There's no doubting the quality of the materials the kitchen deploys: blade of local beef, for instance, with braised oxtail, sautéed swede, celeriac and thyme jus, or pan-fried hake fillet with the exotic accompaniments of marinated cucumber, pickled radish, wasabi and truffle cream. Desserts can be a high point, among them toffee and banana eclair with custard, caramelised banana and Drambuie ice cream.

Chef Adam Harvey **Owner** Didar & Paula Dalkic **Seats** 120 **Times** 12-2/6-9 Closed Mon-Tue **Prices** Tasting menu fr £31.50, Starter £6.50-£8.50, Main £13.50-£24.50, Dessert £6.95-£8.95, Service optional **Wines** 12 bottles over £30, 34 bottles under £30, 11 by glass **Parking** On street (pay & display), Car park Brook St **Notes** Tasting menu 7 course, Sunday L £21, Children welcome

FROGGATT
Map 16 SK27

The Chequers Inn

Modern British

tel: 01433 630231 **S32 3ZJ**
email: info@chequers-froggatt.com **web:** www.chequers-froggatt.com
dir: On A625 between Sheffield & Bakewell, 0.75m from Calver

Rustic Peak District inn with hearty modern dishes

The Tindalls' country inn is a model of Peak District charm, fashioned as it is from a row of Georgian cottages in the Hope Valley. Equipped inside with farmhouse furniture, including old oak settles, and hung with a multitude of framed pictures, it's the kind of place where you can buy a jar of home-made chutney or marmalade to see you on your way. The menu steers a deft course between stalwart dishes to support the inn trade and more modern offerings that nonetheless retain the emphasis on hearty sustenance. Open with grilled mackerel in fennel tea with a salad of mandarin and watercress, ahead of braised pork belly accompanied by a scallop, squid and chorizo in black cider sauce, or monkfish parcelled in Parma ham, with crab arancini and winter roots in veal jus. The giddy pace is sustained into desserts such as chocolate delice with cherry textures and creamed tonka-bean cannelloni.

Chef Carl Riley **Owner** Jonathan & Joanne Tindall **Seats** 90 **Times** 12-2.30/6-9.30 Closed 25 Dec **Prices** Starter £4.95-£8.95, Main £11.95-£18.95, Dessert £5.95-£7.95, Service optional **Wines** 3 bottles over £30, 34 bottles under £30, 10 by glass **Parking** 50 **Notes** Sunday L, Vegetarian available, Children welcome

GRINDLEFORD
Map 16 SK27

The Maynard

Modern British

tel: 01433 630321 **Main Rd S32 2HE**
email: info@themaynard.co.uk **web:** www.themaynard.co.uk
dir: M1/A619 into Chesterfield, onto Baslow, A623 to Calver right into Grindleford

Glorious views, a dash of boutique style and contemporary cooking

The glorious rolling Peak District opens up in front of this rather grand old house, now a decidedly swish boutique hotel. Needless to say, a drink on the terrace is a particularly good idea when the sun is up, laying bare a spectacularly green and pleasant vista, but indoors is no less eye-catching. With clever use of bold colours and artworks, and a mix of textures and materials, the lounge has a good deal of contemporary swagger, whilst the restaurant is done out with hand-painted murals, classy blue tones and smartly dressed tables. The cooking is equally of the moment, with plenty of regional flavours and bags of good ideas. Start, perhaps, with a confit duck and smoked chicken terrine, the luscious richness perfectly cut with rhubarb and pear chutney, or a vibrant Thai hot-and-sour broth with garlicky tiger prawns. Next up, breast of guinea fowl is roasted and comes with creamed Savoy cabbage, butternut squash and potato fondant, while oven-baked sea trout is accompanied by dauphinoise and a chive and caviar cream sauce. To finish, warm chocolate tart comes in a happy union with a red berry sorbet.

Chef Mark Vernon **Owner** Jane Hitchman **Seats** 50, Pr/dining room 140 **Times** 12-2/7-9 Closed L Sat **Prices** Prices not confirmed, Service optional **Wines** 7 by glass **Parking** 60 **Notes** Sunday L, Vegetarian available, Children welcome

HARDSTOFT
Map 16 SK46

The Shoulder at Hardstoft

Modern British

tel: 01246 850276 **Deep Ln S45 8AF**
email: info@thefamousshoulder.co.uk **web:** www.thefamousshoulder.co.uk
dir: Follow signs to Hardwick Hall, take 1st right after turning off B6039

Food-driven pub with passion for local produce

This one-time down-at-heel village boozer has been given a 'more-gastro-than-pub' contemporary makeover. Stone-built and 300 years old, the re-branded Shoulder is essentially a pub and restaurant with rooms, though still with a friendly, relaxed attitude. The restaurant itself is a light, clean-lined space of pale-wood floors and tables, fashionable high-back seating and red, cream or boldly papered walls. There's a snug bar, real fires and leather sofas to chill out on, while the aroma of home-baked loaves (for sale on the bar) heightens anticipation and displays the kitchen's passion for local, home-made, home-smoked and home-grown produce. The cooking takes a modern, precise approach without being too showy: shoulder and loin venison Wellington, perhaps, with foie gras, braised red cabbage, baby leeks and smoked garlic jus. To finish, vanilla crème brûlée, shortbread and freeze-dried raspberries hits the spot. A bar menu is also available, but you can eat whatever you want, wherever you want.

Chef Simon Johnson **Owner** Simon Johnson **Seats** 60 **Times** 12-9 Closed L Mon, D Sun All-day dining **Prices** Prices not confirmed, Service optional **Wines** 5 bottles over £30, 23 bottles under £30, 10 by glass **Parking** 50 **Notes** Sunday L, Vegetarian available, Children welcome

HARTSHORNE
Map 10 SK32

The Mill Wheel

 Modern British

tel: 01283 550335 **Ticknall Rd DE11 7AS**
email: info@themillwheel.co.uk web: www.themillwheel.co.uk
dir: *M42 junct 2, A511 to Woodville, left onto A514 towards Derby to Hartshorne*

Locally-based cooking in a 17th-century mill

An inn only since the 1980s, The Mill Wheel is a converted 17th-century mill, still full of period detail in its stone walls, beamed ceilings and – most majestically of all – the original water-powered wheel, turning sedately in the midst of the bar which has been designed around it. Real ales and comfortable leather sofas are the plus points, and upstairs is a beamed restaurant, done in uncluttered modern style with contemporary artworks and light wooden furniture. Assiduously sourced local produce informs the modern British menus, which take in the likes of a trio of smoked fish with salmon keta and orange salad to start, followed by a pork duo – tenderloin and smoked belly – accompanied by crushed sage potatoes, wild mushrooms and Calvados cream, or sea bass with smoked bacon and peas. An excellent, chunky bread-and-butter pudding with plenty of crème anglaise is the star finale. Pudding Table nights once a month offer a fixed-price three-course dinner with as many puddings as you feel you deserve.

Chef Russel Burridge **Owner** Colin & Jackie Brown **Seats** 52 **Times** 12-2.15/6-9.15 **Prices** Fixed L 2 course fr £6.50, Starter £3.95-£5.95, Main £6.95-£23.95, Dessert fr £5.95, Service optional **Wines** 1 bottle over £30, 15 bottles under £30, 9 by glass **Parking** 50 **Notes** Champagne breakfast 4 course £19.95, Sunday L £13.95-£17.95, Vegetarian available, Children welcome

HATHERSAGE
Map 16 SK28

George Hotel

 Modern British v

tel: 01433 650436 **Main Rd S32 1BB**
email: info@george-hotel.net web: www.george-hotel.net
dir: *In village centre on junction of A625/B6001*

Novel ideas from a hard-working Peak District kitchen

The 500-year-old stone-built hotel looks like a little castle, with its turreted frontage and mullioned windows. Its interiors have been carefully planned to do nothing to obscure the impression of dignified venerability, the hefty stones of the walls offset by a bare wood floor and simple furniture in the smartly attired dining-room. Helen Price presides over a hard-working kitchen, with many of the foundation elements of the menu produced in-house, including breads, pasta and preserves. Most of the rest is sourced from trusted Peak District suppliers, perhaps for a starter of potted beef with Helen's own piccalilli and potato crisps, or there might be soused mackerel, accompanied by the sharp-edged flavours of beetroot, horseradish and a jelly of Granny Smiths. For main, it could be wild boar with blackberries, served with its own sausage and wild mushroom rösti, or sea bream and sweet potato with leeks two ways (caramelised purée and steamed baby ones). Dessert ideas are both novel and enticing, for example rice pudding soufflé with orange and ginger jam, honeycomb, and the entertaining contradiction of a hot toddy sorbet.

Chef Helen Prince **Owner** Eric Marsh **Seats** 45, Pr/dining room 70 **Times** 12-2.30/7-10 Closed D 25 Dec **Prices** Fixed L 2 course £29.95, Fixed D 3 course £36.95 **Wines** 24 bottles over £30, 36 bottles under £30, 11 by glass **Parking** 45 **Notes** Early bird menu Mon-Fri 6.30-7.30pm, Sunday L £20-£25, Children welcome

The Plough Inn

 Modern British

tel: 01433 650319 **Leadmill Bridge S32 1BA**
email: sales@theploughinn-hathersage.co.uk web: www.theploughinn-hathersage.co.uk
dir: *1m SE of Hathersage on B6001. Over bridge, 150yds beyond at Leadmill*

Sustaining modern dishes in a Tudor riverside inn

In a thoroughly restorative setting, the stone-built 16th-century Plough sits in nine acres of grounds that slope gently down to the River Derwent. There's a warm welcome whatever the season, whether out in the courtyard by the babbling brook or before the log fire in winter, and the dining room is always turned out in best bib and tucker. The same might be said of Robert Navarro's cooking, which mixes modern global and homely local to generate its appeal. Starter might be smoked bacon velouté with a black pudding toastie, or mackerel with fennel salad dressed in orange and pomegranate. Follow with sustaining main courses like beef and Guinness pie with honey-roast parsnips and mash, or monkfish with a lobster beignet and wild rice in shellfish cream. Wild mushroom and artichoke pizzetta in tomato and olive fondue is a possible vegetarian main. Given the location, a faithful version of classic Bakewell pudding is only to be expected.

Chef Robert Navarro **Owner** Robert & Cynthia Emery **Seats** 40, Pr/dining room 24 **Times** 11.30-9.30 Closed 25 Dec, All-day dining **Prices** Fixed L 2 course £15-£19, Fixed D 3 course £24-£29, Starter £6.50-£12, Main £15-£27.50, Dessert £6-£7.50, Service optional **Wines** 22 bottles over £30, 23 bottles under £30, 20 by glass **Parking** 40 **Notes** Sunday L £14-£24, Vegetarian available, Children welcome

HIGHAM
Map 16 SK35

Santo's Higham Farm Hotel

◉ Modern International

tel: 01773 833812 **Main Rd DE55 6EH**
email: reception@santoshighamfarm.co.uk web: www.santoshighamfarm.co.uk
dir: *M1 junct 28, A38 towards Derby, then A61 to Higham, left onto B6013*

Italian-influenced cooking in a Derbyshire farmstead hotel

Santo Cusimano runs a highly individual rural retreat. With the rolling Amber Valley all about, it's in a prime slice of Derbyshire walking country, and has been fashioned from an old farmstead. The dining room is designed to soothe the senses, with an air of soft-focus pastel charm, comfortable bucket chairs and smart table settings. Menus mobilise plenty of pedigree local produce, as well as thoroughbred items like steamed Shetland mussels in garlic cream. Given the owner's provenance, Italian influences are never distant, perhaps for parmesan risotto that comes with salt-baked kohlrabi and truffled celeriac purée, or mains such as leg of corn-fed chicken stuffed with wild mushrooms and spinach, alongside a stew of butterbeans and pancetta in red wine sauce. The chargrilled local beef has been aged on the bone for 28 days. For dessert, there's pannacotta and candied pistachios, plus more offbeat proposals, such as sticky ginger cake with pineapple and passionfruit salsa and Pina Colada ice cream.

Chef Cameron Smith **Owner** Santo Cusimano **Seats** 50, Pr/dining room 34
Times 12-3/7-9.30 Closed BHs, L Mon-Sat, D Sun **Prices** Starter £4.50-£6.50, Main £16-£26, Dessert £4.50-£7.50 **Wines** 13 bottles over £30, 37 bottles under £30, 6 by glass **Parking** 100 **Notes** Sunday L £9-£13.95, Vegetarian available, Children welcome

HOPE
Map 16 SK18

Losehill House Hotel & Spa

◉◉ Modern British Ⅴ

tel: 01433 621219 **Lose Hill Ln, Edale Rd S33 6AF**
email: info@losehillhouse.co.uk web: www.losehillhouse.co.uk
dir: *A6187 into Hope. Take turn opposite church into Edale Rd. 1m, left & follow signs to hotel*

Glorious Peak District views and interesting contemporary cooking

Losehill House, built in 1914 in the Arts and Crafts style, is in a secluded spot in the Peak District National Park and has stunning views, also appreciated from the Orangery Restaurant, a light-filled, comfortable room with a contemporary look. The kitchen rounds up Peak District produce and uses it to good effect in its modern, creative style, adding novel and intriguing elements to many dishes. Rolled lamb leg, for instance, is accompanied by leek ash, camomile gel and turnips, and fillet of mackerel by carrot ketchup, carrot purée and sultanas-and those are just starters. Confident techniques and good judgement result in appreciated main

courses of local venison loin with pommes Anna, beetroot, leeks and coco nib crumb, and grilled lemon sole on the bone with a simple lemon sauce, buttered spinach and turnips. Invention marks out desserts: consider chocolate pudding with white chocolate mousse, blackcurrant sorbet and dark chocolate soil, or orange cheesecake with a raspberry bubble, orange jelly and raspberry sorbet.

Chef Darren Goodwin **Owner** Paul & Kathryn Roden **Seats** 50, Pr/dining room 12
Times 12-2.30/6.30-9 **Prices** Prices not confirmed, Service optional **Wines** 6 by glass **Parking** 20 **Notes** Taste of Losehill 7 course £45, Sunday L, Children welcome

MATLOCK
Map 16 SK35

Stones Restaurant

◉◉ Modern British Ⅴ

tel: 01629 56061 **1c Dale Rd DE4 3LT**
email: info@stones-restaurant.co.uk

Modern Mediterranean-influenced dining with a riverside terrace

Stones may be an intimate basement venue, but it has the best of both worlds on fine days thanks to a tiled sun terrace perched above the River Derwent. Fully refurbished after a fire, there's a new conservatory to go with a sophisticated brasserie-style decor that works a mix of subtle earthy tones, with simple art, wooden floors, and seats upholstered with designer fabric to match a Mediterranean-inflected menu of contemporary modern British dishes. Well-judged combinations get under way with a deliciously-scented wild mushroom and spring onion risotto with parmesan and truffle oil. The fish of the day is worth a punt at main course stage, particularly when it is a fine slab of salmon matched with lemon crushed potatoes, creamed leeks and caper velouté, or there might be roasted pork fillet with butternut squash purée, fondant potato, apple gel and crisp pancetta. Dessert is a simple but effective play of well-thought-through textures and tastes involving lemon macaroon, roasted pineapple and raspberry mascarpone.

Chef Kevin Stone **Owner** Kevin Stone, Jade Himsworth, Katie Temple **Seats** 50, Pr/dining room 16 **Times** 12-2/6.30-9 Closed 26 Dec, 1 Jan, Sun-Mon, L Tue **Prices** Fixed L 2 course £16.50, Fixed D 3 course £30-£35.50, Service optional **Wines** 22 bottles over £30, 13 bottles under £30, 9 by glass **Parking** Matlock train station **Notes** Children welcome

MELBOURNE
Map 11 SK32

The Bay Tree

◉◉ Modern British

tel: 01332 863358 **4 Potter St DE73 8HW**
email: enquiries@baytreerestaurant.co.uk
dir: *From M1(N) junct 23A or junct 24 (S) take A453 to Isley Walton, turn right & follow signs to Melbourne town centre*

Modish cooking in a tranquil market town

The charming market town of Melbourne has a gem of a local restaurant in The Bay Tree. And it's a restaurant that takes inspiration from far beyond the Derbyshire countryside-chef Rex Howell has drawn on his experience around the world, especially the Far East, to deliver his style of modern British cooking. There is nothing to scare the horses, though, and flavour combinations are well judged. Cornish crab salad comes with avocado and pickled kohlrabi, for example, or go for Keralan-style green mango and king prawn curry with a spicy home-made tomato chutney. The butternut squash purée that accompanies a rack of English lamb is flavoured with cumin, and star anise infuses the sauce accompanying line-caught sea bass. The village has an old-world feel, but inside The Bay Tree there's a soothing contemporary shimmer and pleasing absence of country chintz.

Times 10.30-3/6.30-10.30 Closed 25 & 31 Dec, BHs, Mon-Tue, D Sun

The Peacock at Rowsley

Modern British v

tel: 01629 733518 **Bakewell Rd DE4 2EB**
email: reception@thepeacockatrowsley.com
web: www.thepeacockatrowsley.com
dir: *A6, 3m before Bakewell, 6m from Matlock towards Bakewell*

Contemporary British cooking in a lustrous Peak District hotel

The solid stone walls of The Peacock were constructed in the 17th century, built to last, and to resist the Peak District weather. Some 400 years later, the place is owned by the keeper of Haddon Hall down the road (one of the country's finest medieval manors) and has been made over by India Mahdavi (one of the hottest designers around). The old-world dependability of the original building plus 21st-century sensibilities is a winning combination because the makeover enhances the charms of the original without ripping out its soul or overwhelming the place with overblown flourishes. It's a tasteful job. The kitchen is under the auspices of Daniel Smith, a man who has evident confidence in the classical culinary traditions and maintains a steady hand on the tiller of experimentalism-modern, well-judged food. There's a definite Britishness to his output, too, with a good showing of high quality regional produce. The main restaurant is a dinner-only job, with the bar serving up lighter stuff during the day (beef, ale and Cropwell Bishop Stilton pie, for example). In the evening, the main dining room (there's a smaller room as well) has tables laid for the serious business of fine dining, with sparkling glasses and burnished table tops. A first course dish of venison tartare with beetroot, charred onion mayonnaise and horseradish has vivid colours and nicely judged flavours, while another delivers Norfolk quail in the earthy company of mushroom purée, salsify and truffle. These are well judged combinations, with flavour to the fore and acute technical skills on show. Main-course breast of Gressingham duck is served with its liver, turnip and blood orange, and sea bass comes with a borscht sauce. Among desserts, Yorkshire rhubarb features in season, perhaps in a custard-rich mousse and partnered with coconut ice cream.

Chef Daniel Smith **Owner** Rutland Hotels **Seats** 40, Pr/dining room 20 **Times** 12-2/7-9 Closed D 24-26 Dec **Prices** Fixed L 3 course fr £17.75, Starter £7.50-£13.50, Main £35.50-£41, Dessert £8.50-£8.95, Service optional **Wines** 44 bottles over £30, 11 bottles under £30, 23 by glass **Parking** 25 **Notes** Sunday L £22.50-£29.50 Children 10 yrs+

The Peacock at Rowsley

The Peacock at Rowsley is a small luxury hotel located in the famous Peak District in the heart of England, and conveniently close to the major towns of Chesterfield, Sheffield, Manchester, Nottingham and Derby.

Owned by Lord Edward Manners, owner of nearby *Haddon Hall*, the hotel has been refurbished throughout and styled by award winning designer India Mahdavi.

Dan Smith, Head Chef, worked with Tom Aikens in London and has since returned to Derbyshire. He has prepared and designed tantalising menus for our restaurant and bar, using, wherever possible, locally sourced ingredients.

We aim to provide a relaxed and comfortable experience whether you are coming for a weekend in the country, a special occasion, or just to eat and drink.

The Peacock at Rowsley, Derbyshire DE4 2EB • **Tel:** 01629 733518 • **Fax:** 01629 732671
Website: www.thepeacockatrowsley.com • **Email:** reception@thepeacockatrowsley.com

MORLEY
Map 11 SK34

The Morley Hayes Hotel
Modern British

tel: 01332 780480 **Main Rd DE7 6DG**
email: enquiries@morleyhayes.com **web:** www.morleyhayes.com
dir: 4m N of Derby on A608

Modern-classic cooking on a converted farm estate

Morley Hayes near Derby has been a farm estate and an orphanage in its time, but has been run as a family hotel since the 1980s. The Dovecote, its principal dining room, is to be found on the raftered first floor of a separate former farm building, overlooking the golf course and surrounding countryside. The cooking is as trend-conscious as can be, with many modern-classic dishes and some novel ideas in evidence. King prawn ravioli with a seared scallop in lemongrass sauce may whet the appetite for Gressingham duck breast with bok choy, radishes, honey-roast carrots and a pastilla of the leg meat. Finish with rhubarb jelly and sorbet, served with buttermilk pannacotta, or else they'll happily deconstruct a Black Forest gâteau for you.

Chef Nigel Stuart **Owner** Robert & Andrew Allsop/Morley Hayes Leisure Ltd **Seats** 100, Pr/dining room 24 **Times** 12-2/7-9.30 Closed 27 Dec, 1 Jan, L Sat, Mon **Prices** Prices not confirmed, Service optional **Wines** 22 bottles over £30, 30 bottles under £30, 12 by glass **Parking** 250 **Notes** Sunday L, Vegetarian available, Children welcome

ROWSLEY
Map 16 SK26

The Peacock at Rowsley
– see page 134 and advert on page 135

DEVON

ASHBURTON
Map 3 SX77

Agaric
Modern British

tel: 01364 654478 **30 North St TQ13 7QD**
email: eat@agaricrestaurant.co.uk
dir: Opposite town hall. Ashburton off A38 between Exeter & Plymouth

Well-judged menu in engaging restaurant with rooms

Nick and Sophie Coiley's restaurant with rooms with its mushroomy name and dedication to the harvest of the local land and sea is a foodies' paradise. Everything is made in-house, much of the produce comes from their own garden, and they've even planted olive trees with the cunning plan to produce their own olive oil in the future. There's a charming rusticity to the interior and a definite lack of stuffiness all round – that goes for the cheerful service team, too – and you can buy some of their preserves, oils and the like to bolster your own store cupboard. The food focuses on flavour and avoids needless over-embellishment. Start with venison, rabbit, pork, prunes and Armagnac terrine, served with their Agaric onion marmalade, followed by breaded fillets of sole with herb and cream sauce and cucumber salad. And to finish, blood orange, vanilla and star anise parfait with blood orange sorbet, mixed berry coulis and an almond biscuit.

Chef Nick Coiley **Owner** Nick & Sophie Coiley **Seats** 30 **Times** 12-2/7-9.30 Closed 1st 2 wks Aug, Xmas, 1 wk Jan, Sun-Tue, L Sat **Prices** Fixed L 2 course £14.95-£16.95, Starter £7.95-£9.50, Main £16.95-£22.50, Dessert fr £6.95, Service optional **Wines** 4 bottles over £30, 27 bottles under £30, 6 by glass **Parking** Car park opposite **Notes** Vegetarian available, Children welcome

AXMINSTER
Map 4 SY29

Fairwater Head Hotel
Modern British

tel: 01297 678349 **Hawkchurch EX13 5TX**
email: info@fairwaterheadhotel.co.uk **web:** www.fairwaterheadhotel.co.uk
dir: A358 into Broom Lane at Tytherleigh, follow signs to Hawkchurch & hotel

Modern classic dishes in a rural Devon retreat

An appealing greystone building covered in climbing foliage, Fairwater Head enjoys panoramic views over the Axe Valley, only five miles from the old carpet town of Axminster. Three acres of manicured lawns and attractive interiors contribute to the restful rural ambience, and the Greenfields dining room boasts smart table linen and friendly, informal service. Devon produce of flawless pedigree flows forth from the kitchen, worked into an extensive choice of modern classic dishes with a refreshing absence of extraneous lily-gilding. Expect wild mushroom risotto with rocket and parmesan, home-cured gravad lax, or chicken liver parfait with onion marmalade in port reduction to start, followed up by sea bass with crushed new potatoes in chive velouté, or lamb rump with dauphinoise and ratatouille. Finish with textbook lemon tart in raspberry coulis with lime sorbet, or crème brûlée wittily served in a cup and saucer. West Country cheeses with home-made chutney are welcome temptations too.

Times 12-2/7-9 Closed Jan, L Mon-Tue, Thu-Fri

BEESANDS
Map 3 SX84

The Cricket Inn
Modern British

tel: 01548 580215 **TQ7 2EN**
email: enquiries@thecricketinn.com **web:** www.thecricketinn.com
dir: From Kingsbridge follow A379 towards Dartmouth, at Stokenham mini-rdbt turn right for Beesands

Quaint seaside inn serving tip-top seafood and more besides

When the crabs, lobster and scallops are hauled in from the sea in front of where you're sitting, you know you're in for a treat. But that's not to say that this gem of an inn on the shingly beach of Start Bay neglects the bounty of the land, which turns up in the shape of locally-reared lamb chop served with cabbage, smoked bacon and black pudding mash. Smartly refurbished, The Cricket Inn still hangs on to its quaint traditional fishing inn character with old photos of Beesands village and fishing paraphernalia in the bar, while the airy restaurant extension is done out in a pared-back New England style. Those diver-caught scallops from the bay might be delivered with shiitaki mushrooms, cauliflower purée, and crispy Parma ham, while lemon sole of the same provenance could turn up simply with lemon and chive butter, or there may be brill with a crab and ginger reduction and deep-fried angel hair noodles.

Chef Scott Simon **Owner** Nigel & Rachel Heath **Seats** 65, Pr/dining room 40 **Times** 12-2.30/6-8.30 Closed 25 Dec **Prices** Prices not confirmed, Service optional **Wines** 2 bottles over £30, 26 bottles under £30, 12 by glass **Parking** 30 **Notes** Sunday L, Vegetarian available, Children welcome

Looking for a restaurant by name?
Use the index on page 751

BLACKAWTON
Map 3 SX85

The Normandy Arms
🏵 British

tel: 01803 712884 **Chapel St TQ9 7BN**
email: info@normandyarms.co.uk **web:** www.thenormandyarms.co.uk
dir: *On A3122 Kingsbridge to Dartmouth road, turn right at Forces Tavern*

Impressive cooking in stylish village inn

Nestled between the fabulous South Hams coast and the rugged expanses of Dartmoor, this long-established village inn is rooted into the fabric of Blackawton. The interior has been reworked with the sort of clean-cut contemporary look you would expect of a switched-on dining pub, blending leather sofas, chunky wooden tables, and colourful art on whitewashed walls with the timeless feel of exposed stone walls and flagstoned floors. Chef-proprietor Andrew West-Letford knows his way around the modern British repertoire and clearly relishes the bounty of local produce on his doorstep – his Salcombe crab tart with marinated cucumber and chive salad is worth the trip alone. Main course brings roast haunch of venison with spiced red cabbage, parsnips and potato galette, another clean, uncluttered dish with subtle contrasts of flavour and texture that shows a confident hand at the stoves. Hazelnut slice with sour cherry sorbet and griottine cherries closes the show on a high note.

Chef Andrew West-Letford **Seats** 50, Pr/dining room 25 **Times** 12.30-2.30/6.30-9.30 Closed Jan, Sun-Mon **Prices** Fixed L 2 course £16, Fixed D 3 course £19, Starter £6-£8.50, Main £16-£19, Dessert £6-£9 **Wines** 5 bottles over £30, 35 bottles under £30, 17 by glass **Parking** 3 **Notes** Menu du jour Tue-Thu D, Vegetarian available, Children welcome

BRIXHAM
Map 3 SX95

Quayside Hotel
🏵 Modern British

tel: 01803 855751 **41-49 King St TQ5 9TJ**
email: reservations@quayside.co.uk **web:** www.quaysidehotel.co.uk
dir: *From Exeter take A380 towards Torquay, then A3022 to Brixham*

The freshest seafood by the harbour

The fish landed in Brixham ends up on menus around the country, but at the Quayside Hotel you can tuck into the fruits of these waters within sight of the fishing boats. The family-run hotel carved out of old fishermen's cottages has views over the harbour and bay beyond and its kitchen makes good use of the bounty on its doorstep. Salt-and-pepper Start Bay squid is one way to begin, or you might fancy their house prawn cocktail, served on chicory leaves. The availability of fish is dependent on the catch of course, so you might find black bream, red mullet and skate, or you might not. Baked monkfish with a citrus beurre blanc stars a fine piece of fish, but there are some meat options if you insist (confit duck, perhaps). River Dart oysters are a treat when available, and the plateau de fruits de mer is a tantalising choice if you can persuade someone to share it with you.

Chef Andy Sewell **Owner** Mr & Mrs C F Bowring **Seats** 40, Pr/dining room 18 **Times** 6.30-9.30 Closed L all week **Prices** Prices not confirmed, Service optional **Wines** 10 by glass **Parking** 30 **Notes** Vegetarian available, Children 5 yrs+

BURRINGTON
Map 3 SS61

Northcote Manor
🏵🏵 Modern British V

tel: 01769 560501 **EX37 9LZ**
email: rest@northcotemanor.co.uk **web:** www.northcotemanor.co.uk
dir: *M5 junct 27 towards Barnstaple. Left at rdbt to South Molton. Follow A377, right at T-junct to Barnstaple. Entrance after 3m, opposite Portsmouth Arms railway station and pub. (NB do not enter Burrington village)*

Tranquil country-house setting and well-sourced modern British food

The old stone manor, dating from the early 1700s, occupies 20 or so acres of lush Devon countryside, and is these days a classy county-house hotel with an impressive restaurant. It's got a reassuringly traditional finish within, with upscale fixtures and fittings, plus a service team who match the charm of the setting. The dining room has the anticipated refinement and formality, with pristine tables and a period feel. The menu makes a play for regional ingredients, ringing the seasonal changes, and there's a good showing of West Country game and seafood. Start, perhaps, with mackerel fillets, which are slow cooked in the oven and served with seared king prawns and sun-blushed tomato risotto, or a mosaic of game from the local moors with winter truffle salad and caramelised pumpkin purée and a red wine reduction. The moor is also the source of a main-course saddle of venison, served with fondant potatoes, baked fig and watercress purée, while dessert might bring forth a hot chocolate fondant or lemon tart with iced lime parfait and orange sorbet.

Chef Richie Herkes **Owner** J Pierre Mifsud **Seats** 34, Pr/dining room 50 **Times** 12-2/7-9 **Prices** Fixed L 3 course £22.50, Fixed D 3 course £45, Tasting menu £90, Starter £12, Main £23, Dessert £10, Service optional **Wines** 22 bottles over £30, 34 bottles under £30, 9 by glass **Parking** 30 **Notes** Sunday L £25.50, Children welcome

CHAGFORD
Map 3 SX78

Gidleigh Park
🏵🏵🏵🏵🏵 – *see page 138*

22 Mill Street Restaurant & Rooms
🏵🏵 Modern British V

tel: 01647 432244 **22 Mill St TQ13 8AW**
email: info@22millst.com
dir: *A382/B3206 enter village into main square, Mill St is on the right*

Lively modern cooking in Dartmoor village

The restaurant is currently closed due to water flood damage, but hopes to reopen later in 2014. Chagford can't have changed all that much in the last several hundred years, except for all the cars. But down a little lane a short stroll from the centre of the village is a restaurant with rooms that definitely feels of these times. It's perfectly traditional on the outside, but within it has a light and gently contemporary finish – lots of pale wood, fashionably neutral colour tones and well-chosen furniture – and makes an appealing setting for the classy cooking. And there is some good cooking going on here. The menu deals in high quality regional ingredients, everything is made in-house, and there are lots of tempting combinations. Start, perhaps, with haddock poached in brown butter with goats' milk, almonds and sorrel, or a whole carrot cooked in dripping and served with warm Sharpham brie, steamed nettles and ale. Next up, braised and roasted pork belly with smoked cockles, sea vegetables and stout and cockle juice, and to finish, warm rice pudding with aired milk and a jam and sloe sorbet. There's a tasting menu, too.

Chef Ashley Wright **Owner** Evision Group **Seats** 28, Pr/dining room 14 **Times** 12-4/6.30-10 Closed 2 wks Jan, Mon **Prices** Prices not confirmed, Service optional **Wines** 8 by glass **Parking** On street **Notes** Tasting menu 5 course, Sunday L Children 5yrs+

Who are the AA's Restaurants of the Year? See page 14

Gidleigh Park

CHAGFORD   Map 3 SX78

Modern European V
tel: 01647 432367 **TQ13 8HH**
email: gidleighpark@gidleigh.co.uk
web: www.gidleigh.com
dir: *From Chagford Sq turn right at Lloyds TSB into Mill St, after 150yds right fork, across x-rds into Holy St. Restaurant 1.5m*

Stunning contemporary cooking in wonderful Dartmoor isolation

As you round the corner on the long, winding drive on the edge of Dartmoor, the sprawling half-timbered mansion heaves into sight against a backdrop of trees, with the River Teign flowing past the front. The shipping magnate who built the property in the Arts and Crafts style (seen in the oak staircase and some specially commissioned hand-made furniture) in the late 1920s obviously intended it to impress his guests, and it still gets jaws dropping today. It's a charming and stylish place of impressively high standards, with the sort of decor entirely appropriate for a luxury country-house hotel. Helpful staff add to a sense of occasion in a series of panelled interconnecting dining rooms with generously spaced, beautifully appointed tables. Michael Caines' cooking is both classical and inspirational, focused on the modern European style, founded on the finest local produce backed up by vegetables, fruit and salad leaves from the hotel's kitchen garden. His dishes never fail to delight for their palate-pleasing compositions, whether langoustine cannelloni with braised fennel, sauce vièrge and shellfish sauce, or another, more classically orientated starter of foie gras terrine with cubes of Sauternes jelly, quince and raisin purée – a remarkably successful marriage of flavours and textures. Technique is flawless, and clever combinations bring out the best of both contrasting and complementary flavours, held together by exemplary sauces.

Rump of local beef, for instance, is accompanied by cheek with a red wine sauce, celeriac purée and wild mushrooms, and veal cutlet with purée of black truffles and celeriac, served with braised baby gem, tomato fondue and sherry sauce. Interesting ways with fish are seen in a full-flavoured but unshowy main course of fillet of sea bass, spankingly fresh and timed to the second, roasted with star anise, served with langoustine and bouillabaisse sauce. Amuse-bouche – perhaps lobster in jelly with caviar and tarragon mayonnaise – are well up to par, as are all other incidentals, while puddings, head-turningly attractive like everything else, are often at the fruitier end of the taste spectrum. Examples include a plate of orange, say (confit, tartlet, mousse and sorbet), or passionfruit mousse with spiced pineapple, mango and lime sorbet and coconut foam. The wine list is enormous, of over 1,300 bins, with over 13,000 bottles in the cellars, but help is on hand from a sommelier.

Chef Michael Caines MBE **Owner** Andrew & Christina Brownsword **Seats** 52, Pr/dining room 22
Times 12-2/7-9.45 **Prices** Fixed L 2 course £44, Tasting menu £125, Service optional **Wines** 1190 bottles over £30, 10 bottles under £30, 16 by glass **Parking** 45
Notes Signature menu 8 course £140, ALC 3 course £115 Children 8 yrs+ D

DARTMOUTH Map 3 SX85

The Dart Marina Hotel

 Modern British V

tel: 01803 832580 **Sandquay Rd TQ6 9PH**
email: reception@dartmarinahotel.com **web:** www.dartmarina.com
dir: A3122 from Totnes to Dartmouth. Follow road which becomes College Way, before Higher Ferry. Hotel sharp left in Sandquay Rd

Confident modern cooking in contemporary riverside hotel

You won't lack for sensory stimulation at the classy waterfront Dart Marina Hotel: if the views over the marina and the watery action on the River Dart aren't enough, there's a spa, plus foodie pleasures courtesy of the recently refurbished and extended River Restaurant. It's a cool, clean-cut space done out with a neutral white, cream and tan palette; full-length windows make the most of its riverfront spot. The seasons are duly noted and South Devon's excellent produce is pressed into service as the foundation of an appealing menu of up-to-date classics. Slow-cooked salmon ballotine with fine herbs, gribiche sauce, and fennel and lemon salad is a well-composed opener, which might be followed by slow-cooked shoulder of Blackawton lamb with cocotte potatoes and roasted root vegetables. Finish with warm cherry Bakewell pudding with passionfruit cream and butternut squash and vanilla ice cream.

Chef Peter Alcroft **Owner** Richard Seton **Seats** 86 **Times** 12-2/6-9 Closed 23-26 & 30-31 Dec, L Mon-Sat **Prices** Fixed D 3 course £37.50, Service optional **Wines** 38 bottles over £30, 26 bottles under £30, 20 by glass **Parking** 100 **Notes** Sunday L £15.50-£18.50, Children welcome

The Seahorse

 Mediterranean, Seafood

tel: 01803 835147 **5 South Embankment TQ6 9BH**
email: enquiries@seahorserestaurant.co.uk

Bountiful fresh seafood by the Dart estuary

Hard to miss in the bustling strip along the Dart waterfront, Mitch Tonks's Seahorse is some kind of flagship for his burgeoning empire of seafood restaurants. Subdued lighting and comfortable banquette seating make the place an inviting evening venue, while big windows let in the Devon light on summer days. The menu evolves rapidly, and is always based, as is only proper, on the day's specials. With a bounty of fresh fish and shellfish virtually on the doorstep, it's easy to see what the attraction is. Mussels cultured in nearby Elberry Cove, summer crustacea, and seasonal veg from the vicinity and from markets just across the Channel, add lustre to menus that take in dressed Dartmouth crab, brill cooked in a paper packet with leeks, fennel and tarragon, roasted turbot steak with hollandaise, and – for the seafood refuseniks – lamb shoulder braised in Chianti with new season's garlic. Many of the dishes are cooked over an open charcoal fire, for anything from sea bass to Angus beef rib. Grilled figs with walnut praline ice cream makes a distinguished finale.

Chef Mat Prowse, Mitch Tonks **Owner** Mat Prowse, Mitch Tonks **Seats** 40
Times 12-2.30/6-9.30 Closed 25 Dec, 1 Jan, Mon, L Tue, D Sun **Prices** Fixed L 2 course £20, Fixed D 2 course £20, Starter £8.50-£13.50, Main £19.50-£32, Dessert £3.50-£6.50, Service optional **Wines** 80 bottles over £30, 20 bottles under £30, 6 by glass **Parking** On street **Notes** Sunday L, Vegetarian available, Children welcome

The Old Inn

DREWSTEIGNTON Map 3 SX79

Modern European V
tel: 01647 281276 **EX6 6QR**
email: enquiries@old-inn.co.uk
dir: A30 W, exit Cheriton Bishop, Drewsteignton, Castle Drogo, turn left at Crockenwell, follow signs to Drewsteignton. A38 to A382 Bovey Tracy, Mortonhampstead, turn right at Sandy Park, continue past Castle Drogo, follow signs to Drewsteignton

Well-judged modern cooking in a Dartmoor village inn

The Old Inn is indeed an old inn, four centuries in age, complete with roughcast whitewashed frontage and three guest rooms. A picture of bucolic charm greets the eye inside, the more so if you're welcomed by one or both of the resident retrievers, with log fires a-crackle when it's filthy outdoors, and a pair of dining rooms – one in mint-green, the other crimson – accommodating fewer than 20 diners. That disinclination to pour a quart into a pint-pot is a heartening indicator that Duncan Walker is concerned to keep things on a manageable scale, an impression reinforced by the compact, pleasingly symmetrical menus, which offer a pair of choices at each stage for lunch, four for dinner. Walker arrived in Devon from the northeast a near-lifetime ago, and has maintained a steady

commitment to locally-based food that has an eye on current trends, without pitching headlong into baffling novelty. Red mullet as a starter is consistently good, perhaps appearing with a quasi-niçoise of fennel, anchovy and quail eggs, or there may be a duck croquette regally got up in full fig and foie gras. Main courses allow principal ingredients their due, as when peppered venison loin is supported by pommes Anna and a cep tart in lustrous port sauce, or turbot is briefly grilled and joined by scallops and artichoke in another fortified wine potion, this one of Madeira. At the richest end of the spectrum, expect roast veal sweetbreads with braised oxtail and smoked bacon, while at the close come celebrations of seasonal fruit, perhaps plum and cardamom tart, or a technically flawless blackcurrant soufflé with liquorice ice cream.

Chef Duncan Walker **Owner** Duncan Walker **Seats** 17, Pr/dining room 10
Times 12-2/7-9 Closed Sun-Tue, L Sun-Thu **Prices** Fixed L 3 course £29.95, Fixed D 3 course £46 **Wines** 24 bottles over £30, 21 bottles under £30, 4 by glass **Parking** Village square **Notes** Service flexible, pre book, tables 6 or more by arrangement No children

DODDISCOMBSLEIGH
Map 3 SX88

The Nobody Inn
Modern English **NEW**

tel: 01647 252394 **EX6 7PS**
email: info@nobodyinn.co.uk **web:** www.nobodyinn.co.uk
dir: From A38 turn off at top of Haldon Hill, follow signs to Doddiscombsleigh

Sophisticated dining in popular country inn

It's worth the drive along narrow twisting lanes to reach this gem of a 17th-century thatched inn, with its blackened beams, low ceilings, inglenook and rustic furniture. It's a winner in many ways, with bedrooms, a hefty wine list, collections of whiskies and cheeses and sophisticated eating. Chef Rob Murray is evangelical about tracking down local produce and uses it compellingly in his stylish modern cooking. Panko-crumbed squid comes with chilli mayonnaise, and game terrine with apple chutney, candied hazelnuts and apple jelly. Dishes are intelligently assembled and ingredients are treated carefully. For example, roast pheasant breast, succulent and full of flavour, is served with confit leg, fondant potato, braised red cabbage and gravy, and steak and ale pie with horseradish mash and seasonal vegetables. There's a fish of the day, and puddings extend to caramel pannacotta with gingerbread, and apple tarte fine with custard and Calvados cream.

Chef Rob Murray **Owner** Susan Burdge **Times** 12-2/6.30-9 Closed 1 Jan, L Sun-Mon, D Sun-Mon **Prices** Starter £4.95-£7.50, Main £12.95-£23.95, Dessert £2.95-£15.95, Service optional **Wines** 102 bottles over £30, 102 bottles under £30, 26 by glass **Notes** Sun L served in the bar, Sunday L £9.95-£11.95

DREWSTEIGNTON
Map 3 SX79

The Old Inn
— see page 139

ERMINGTON
Map 3 SX65

Plantation House
Modern British V

tel: 01548 831100 Totnes Rd PL21 9NS
email: info@plantationhousehotel.co.uk **web:** www.plantationhousehotel.co.uk

Confident cooking in boutique bolt-hole

This Georgian parish rectory looks out over the River Elme with a stately elegance that fits perfectly with its contemporary boutique styling. The interiors are immaculate throughout, and the operation runs with faultless attention to detail that makes the place a heavenly gastro getaway. Dining goes on in a brace of intimate and tasteful rooms with a sun-kissed terrace for summer aperitifs, and the kitchen rightly places carefully-sourced produce at the heart of things, whether it's West Country meats and cheeses, locally-landed sustainable fish, or seasonal foraged materials. This all translates into flavour-driven dishes of real integrity, starting with a modishly retro tian of home-smoked salmon and prawns with avocado and home-made Marie Rose sauce. Next up, roast rump of lamb is matched with Puy lentils, roast shallots, pea purée, and green peppercorn and Merlot jus. The cooking retains undeniable depth through to a dessert of vanilla pannacotta with Campari and orange jelly and orange galette.

Chef Richard Hendey, John Raines **Owner** Richard Hendey **Seats** 28, Pr/dining room 16 **Times** 7-9 Closed L all week **Prices** Prices not confirmed **Wines** 27 bottles over £30, 25 bottles under £30, 6 by glass **Parking** 30 **Notes** 4/5 course D £36/£39.50, Breakfast 7.30-9.30, Children welcome

EXETER
Map 3 SX99

Abode Exeter
Modern British, French **NEW**

tel: 01392 319955 **Cathedral Yard EX1 1HD**
email: tables@abodeexeter.co.uk **web:** www.michaelcaines.com
dir: Town centre, opposite cathedral

Classy cooking chez Michael Caines

Michael Caines made his name in Devon cooking at Gidleigh Park and opened up the first Abode on this site back in 2000. The group has expanded sinceand gone from strength to strength. Just about all the bases are covered here in Cathedral Yard, where the charming hotel occupies a prime spot in the city with a buzzy tavern, café/grill, cocktail bar and the main event, the fine-dining Michael Caines Restaurant set in a handsome room with lots of original features and a smart contemporary finish. There are plenty of regional ingredients on the menu (carte, tasting and an excellent value set lunch option) and the carefully executed dishes are based on a sound classical footing. Start with crab ravioli, say, with grapefruit, ginger and coriander, or a warm salad of Devon quail with smoked bacon, quail's egg and caramelised hazelnuts. Main-course roasted hake is a fine piece of fish, cooked just right, served with River Exe mussels, creamed leeks and saffron sauce. Finish with banana and chocolate parfait.

Chef Michael Caines, Nick Topham **Owner** Michael Caines **Seats** 65, Pr/dining room 80 **Times** 12-2.30/6-9.30 Closed Sun **Prices** Fixed L 2 course fr £14.95, Fixed D 3 course fr £22.95, Tasting menu fr £65, Starter £5.50-£16.95, Main £9.50-£23.95, Dessert £7.95-£12.50 **Wines** 200 bottles over £30, 57 bottles under £30, 30 by glass **Parking** Car park Mary Arches St. **Notes** Afternoon tea available £15, Vegetarian available, Children welcome

Barton Cross Hotel & Restaurant
Traditional British, French V

tel: 01392 841245 & 841584 **Huxham, Stoke Canon EX5 4EJ**
email: bartonxhuxham@aol.com **web:** www.thebartoncrosshotel.co.uk
dir: 0.5m off A396 at Stoke Canon, 3m N of Exeter

Reliably good, well-judged food in thatched hotel

At Barton Cross, a 17th-century thatched longhouse in a delightful rural spot just a few miles from Exeter, low beams and cob walls abound, and while the galleried restaurant looks like it could do service as a medieval banqueting hall, there's nothing archaic about what arrives on the plate. The kitchen deals in straightforward Anglo-European cooking, sending out a gutsy ham hock terrine matched with caramelised apple and red onion chutney, alongside smoked salmon risotto spiked with dill and lemon. Main course sees well-timed beef fillet in a herb crust served with fondant potato, roasted shallot, and sun-blushed tomato and basil sauce. Fish is handled deftly – perhaps fillet of sea bass with tangerine butter and chargrilled fennel, or pan-fried monkfish with coconut and curry sauce. The enterprising desserts run to iced mint and chocolate parfait with hazelnut wafers.

Chef Nicholas Beattie **Owner** Brian Hamilton **Seats** 50, Pr/dining room 26 **Times** 12.30-2.30/6.30-11.30 Closed L Mon-Thu **Prices** Fixed D 3 course £29.50, Starter £6.50, Main £14.50-£20.50, Dessert £6.50, Service optional **Wines** 30 bottles over £30, 60 bottles under £30, 10 by glass **Parking** 50 **Notes** Sunday L, Children welcome

The Olive Tree Restaurant at the Queens Court Hotel

◉◉ Modern British

tel: 01392 272709 **Queens Court Hotel, 6-8 Bystock Ter EX4 4HY**
email: enquiries@queenscourt-hotel.co.uk **web:** www.queenscourt-hotel.co.uk
dir: *Exit dual carriageway at junct 30 onto B5132 (Topsham Rd) towards city centre. Hotel 200yds from Central Station*

Confident, creative cooking in a townhouse hotel

There is much to enjoy at this restaurant in a townhouse hotel on a quiet, leafy square just a short stroll from the city centre. The pared-back monochrome decor – black leather high-backed chairs at linen-clad tables and snow-white walls – has a certain gloss thanks to contemporary chandeliers and Venetian masks on the walls-a nod, perhaps, to the Mediterranean warmth that informs the modern cooking on offer. Sound sourcing lends substance to the whole operation, backed by the kitchen brigade's thoughtful approach and sound technical ability to pull off ideas such as boudin of rabbit mousseline and poached garlic served with lightly-spiced pickled red cabbage and a port reduction. Local roots are celebrated via a herb-crusted rack of West Country lamb, partnered with a slow-braised lamb shank faggot with Lyonnaise potatoes and carrot purée, while creative desserts run to a tiramisù-inspired coffee and mascarpone mousse-filled chocolate macaroon served with miniature jellies and espresso syrup.

Chef Darren Knockton **Owner** C F & B H Bowring **Seats** 28, Pr/dining room 16
Times 12-2/6.30-9.30 Closed Xmas, New Year, L Sun **Prices** Prices not confirmed, Service optional **Wines** 10 by glass **Parking** Public car park in front of hotel
Notes Tasting menu available, Vegetarian available, Children welcome

---

■ EXMOUTH
Map 3 SY08

Les Saveurs

◉ Modern French, International

tel: 01395 269459 **9 Tower St EX8 1NT**
email: lessaveurs@yahoo.co.uk
dir: *A376 to Exmouth, left at rdbt. Right at next rdbt onto Rolle St. Tower St on right*

French fish cookery – and more – near the Exe estuary

On a pedestrianised street near both the centre and the beach, Les Saveurs is everything you could wish for in a small neighbourhood restaurant. It offers a relaxing atmosphere generated by courteous and unobtrusive staff, a pale decor, with some exposed-brick walls, and fine cooking. The kitchen's focus is on seafood, although meat-eaters will find plenty to appeal, from black pudding with a poached egg on green beans, potatoes and sun-blushed tomatoes to a main course of roast rump of lamb with a mushroom and Madeira sauce and dauphinoise potatoes. Otherwise go for pan-fried scallops, accurately timed, with pea purée and minted mussel velouté, followed by crisp-skinned fillet of gilt head bream on chive mash with an exemplary sauce à l'armoricaine, or the modish pairing of cod fillet and chorizo with lentils and lemon and thyme sauce. Puddings reflect the chef's French credentials, among them snow eggs, given a kick with Baileys custard and caramel.

Chef Olivier Guyard-Mulkerrin **Owner** Olivier & Sheila Guyard-Mulkerrin **Seats** 30, Pr/dining room 30 **Times** 7-10.30 Closed Nov-Apr advance bookings only, Sun-Mon, ex by special arrangement, L all week **Prices** Starter £7-£8.50, Main £16.50-£25, Dessert £6.50-£7.95, Service optional **Wines** 10 bottles over £30, 19 bottles under £30, 5 by glass **Parking** On street/council offices **Notes** Vegetarian available, No children

---

■ HAYTOR VALE
Map 3 SX77

Rock Inn

◉ British

tel: 01364 661305 & 661556 **TQ13 9XP**
email: info@rock-inn.co.uk **web:** www.rock-inn.co.uk
dir: *From A38 at Drum Bridges, onto A382 to Bovey Tracey. In 2m take B3387 towards Haytor for 3.5m, follow brown signs*

Simple, honest food at a traditional Dartmoor inn

The 18th-century Rock Inn is a haven of civility and good cheer amid the wild, wind-blasted tors of Dartmoor – the sort of place you should factor in to a day's hiking or car touring in the area. Run by the same family for nigh on 30 years, it's still a proper pub with oak furniture, gleaming brasses and locally-brewed real ales in the bar, and the all-round feelgood factor that comes from roaring log fires, cosy nooks and romantically candlelit tables. The food is simple, effective and flavour-packed, with a good showing of local produce on a menu that gives due credit to suppliers of the principal component of each main course – perhaps pan-fried wild sea bass from Brixham partnered by chorizo risotto and tomato pesto, or for fans of local meat, pan-roasted rump of lamb with fine beans, rosemary fondant potato, beetroot purée and red wine sauce. At the end, West Country cheeses are mighty tempting, or you could go for a vanilla pannacotta with rhubarb compôte and shortbread.

Chef Mark Evans, Mark Tribble, Amy Mitchel **Owner** Mr C Graves **Seats** 75, Pr/dining room 20 **Times** 12-2.15/6.30-9 Closed 25-26 Dec **Prices** Fixed L 2 course £13.50, Fixed D 3 course £24, Starter £6.95-£9.50, Main £10.95-£25, Dessert £5.95-£7.95, Service optional **Wines** 20 bottles over £30, 50 bottles under £30, 16 by glass **Parking** 25 **Notes** Sunday L £9.95-£20, Vegetarian available, Children welcome

---

■ HONITON
Map 4 ST10

The Deer Park Country House Hotel

◉ Modern British NEW

tel: 01404 41266 **Weston EX1 3PG**
email: admin@deerparkcountryhotel.co.uk **web:** www.deerparkcountryhotel.co.uk
dir: *Phone for directions*

Modern cooking in boutique country house

This 18th-century Georgian mansion set in 80 acres of glorious grounds is a quintessentially English set-up brought into the 21st century with a sprinkle of boutique style and great food served in an elegant dining room to seal the deal. Head chef Ian Grant is diligent in his sourcing of local produce, going no further than the kitchen garden for fresh seasonal fruit and veg, and bringing it all together in confidently-cooked modern ideas. Start, perhaps, with wild pigeon breast with confit duck croquette, poached pear and plum purée and follow with a two-way serving of local pork-sage – marinated tenderloin and slow-braised belly – with fondant potato, curly kale, and cider and cracked pepper sauce. Fish might appear in a well-considered composition such as pan-fried Cornish hake with spring onion mash, baby spinach and caviar butter sauce. Finish with a choc-fest dessert of dark chocolate brownie with white chocolate pannacotta and ice cream.

Chef Ian Grant **Owner** Nigel Wray **Seats** 45, Pr/dining room 30
Times 12-2.30/6.30-9.30 **Wines** 17 bottles over £30, 29 bottles under £30, 7 by glass **Notes** Sunday L £24-£28.50, Vegetarian available, Children welcome

HONITON *continued*

The Holt Bar & Restaurant

◎◎ Modern British

tel: 01404 47707 **178 High St EX14 1LA**
email: enquiries@theholt-honiton.com
dir: *At west end of High St*

Imaginative, impressive cooking in a vibrant local pub

With a range of its ales dispensed at the bar, The Holt looks like any other high-street pub from the outside, while the interior has a more contemporary look, with its mixture of seats and sofas and rustic tables and chairs. The main dining area is upstairs: open-plan, with a wooden floor, simple decor, candlelight and pleasant and efficient service. Food is a serious commitment here and standards are consistently high, with the menu a happy blend of the traditional and more modish. The owners run their own smokehouse too, so expect smoked chicken, tarragon and mushroom pie, then oak-smoked pork loin with spice-roast shoulder and a crisp potato cake mixed with black pudding. Elsewhere on the sensibly concise menu might be omelette Arnold Bennett followed by grilled fillet of sea bass with a crabcake, herby crushed potatoes and tartare sauce, concluding with something like a good example of vanilla crème brûlée.

Chef Angus McCaig, Billy Emmett **Owner** Joe & Angus McCaig **Seats** 50
Times 12-2/6.30-10 Closed 25-26 Dec, Sun-Mon **Prices** Starter £5-£7, Main £13-£16.50, Dessert £5.50-£7.50, Service optional **Wines** 6 bottles over £30, 25 bottles under £30, 6 by glass **Parking** On street, car park 1 min walk **Notes** Vegetarian available, Children welcome

---

■ ILFRACOMBE   **Map 3 SS54**

11 The Quay

◎ Modern, Traditional British, European

tel: 01271 868090 & 868091 **11 The Quay EX34 9EQ**
email: info@11thequay.co.uk
dir: *Follow signs for harbour and pier car park. Restaurant on left before car park*

Classic brasserie menu on the harbour front

Perched on the harbour front of this north Devon coastal town, the Quay is a place with a strong sense of identity. Adorned with original artworks by Damien Hirst at his more docile, the Atlantic Room with its vaulted ceiling is a bright and breezy setting for internationally inspired brasserie classics. Crab claws in garlic mayonnaise, native oysters, or mussels from the Exe given the marinière treatment all make the most of the location, while tuna may appear Thai style or niçoise. For main, there are one or two more obviously contemporary ideas, such as roasted cod with pancetta and peas in mussel cream, amid the boeuf bourguignon and mash, or lamb cutlets and mint sauce. Finish with any of a number of chart-topping desserts-tiramisu, lemon posset, chocolate fondant, Eton Mess-or West Country cheeses and pear chutney.

Chef Henry Sowden **Owner** Damien Hirst **Seats** 45, Pr/dining room 26
Times 12-2.30/6-9 Closed 25-26 Dec, 2 wks Jan **Prices** Prices not confirmed, Service optional **Wines** 10 bottles over £30, 19 bottles under £30, 10 by glass **Parking** Pier car park 100yds **Notes** Vegetarian available, Children welcome

Sandy Cove Hotel

◎ Modern British

tel: 01271 882243 **Old Coast Rd, Combe Martin Bay, Berrynarbor EX34 9SR**
email: info@sandycove-hotel.co.uk **web:** www.sandycove-hotel.co.uk
dir: *A339 to Combe Martin, through village towards Ilfracombe for approx 1m. Turn right just over brow of hill marked Sandy Cove*

Simple cooking, local produce, views to die for

The sprawling Sandy Cove Hotel sits on a cliff top with stunning views over the sea and the wild landscape of Exmoor. The best of both worlds. The restaurant is positioned to maximise the vista, with large windows, or if you're really lucky the weather will allow a table on the deck. The hotel itself has a swimming pool with a sliding roof (so indoor or outdoor), and the decor is contemporary. The menu keeps things gently modern, too, with local sea food and steaks from nearby farms, and sticks to familiar and successful combinations. Start with a Thai fishcake, for example, with an accompanying sweet chilli dip, before moving onto roast breast of duck with a fondant potato, red cabbage and a red wine sauce. For dessert, lemon tart gives a good hit of citrus acidity, and is served with a raspberry sorbet.

Chef Oliver Wood **Owner** Dawn Ten-Bokkel **Seats** 150, Pr/dining room 30
Times 12-2/6.30-9 **Prices** Fixed D 3 course £21.95-£30, Starter £4.95, Main £16.95, Dessert £5.95, Service optional **Wines** 3 bottles over £30, 28 bottles under £30, 3 by glass **Parking** 50 **Notes** Sunday L £14, Vegetarian available, Children welcome

---

■ ILSINGTON   **Map 3 SX77**

Ilsington Country House Hotel

◎◎ Modern European

tel: 01364 661452 **TQ13 9RR**
email: hotel@ilsington.co.uk **web:** www.ilsington.co.uk
dir: *A38 to Plymouth, exit at Bovey Tracey. 3rd exit from rdbt to Ilsington, then 1st right, hotel on right in 3m*

Great Dartmoor views and confident cooking

Ilsington presses all the right classy country-house buttons: a Dartmoor bolt-hole set in ten acres of grounds that includes a health club and spa pool. The large airy restaurant maintains the theme, its floor-to-ceiling picture windows offering cracking views across to Haytor Rocks and beyond from well-dressed tables. The kitchen goes the extra mile in its quest for quality ingredients, including using their own eggs, foraging for wild herbs in the grounds and curing fish and meats in their own smokehouse. Otherwise, quality locally-sourced produce forms the basis of the modern approach here, underpinned by a classical French theme. Take seared rump of lamb served with confit shoulder, sweetbreads and a rosemary sauce, for instance, or fillet of sea bream with spring onion and tomato crushed potatoes, root vegetable nage and Avruga caviar chive oil. Finish with lime leaf pannacotta teamed with port braised plum and lemongrass gel.

Chef Mike O'Donnell **Owner** Hassell family **Seats** 75, Pr/dining room 70
Times 12-2/6.30-9 Closed L Mon-Sat **Prices** Fixed D 3 course £36 **Wines** 12 bottles over £30, 32 bottles under £30, 7 by glass **Parking** 60 **Notes** Sunday L £16.95-£20, Vegetarian available, Children welcome

---

Kentisbury Grange

◉◉ Modern Cuisine NEW

---

tel: 01271 882295 **EX31 4NL**
email: reception@kentisburygrange.co.uk web: www.kentisburygrange.com
dir: *From Barnstaple take A3125. At rdbt take 2nd exit onto A39 to Burrington through Shirwell & Arlington. After Kentisbury Ford, follow signs for hotel for approx 0.75m*

Creative modern cooking in a stylish old coach house

This country-house hotel is placed firmly at the boutique end of the spectrum, with decor that is a little bit luxurious but deliberately lived-in. The Coach House restaurant is just that (a former 17th-century coach house), a short scrunch across the gravel from the hotel, and it looks peachy with its rustic-chic oak tables, banquette seating and contemporary artworks. The ingredients are sourced from nearby, including crabs from Lundy Island and ducks from the farm next door. A first course dish of sea bream featuring a superbly cooked piece of fish, red pepper jam, saffron and shellfish sauce and olives is a refined and well-judged combination, or go for the chef's take on a lobster cocktail with smoked Exe mussels. A main course of Waytown fillet of beef comes with Jacob's ladder (short-rib) fritter and roasted shallots, mushroom ketchup and chips. The cheeseboard flies the flag for Devon, while desserts run to lemon tart with frozen yoghurt, lemon curd and meringue.

Chef Jean-Marc Zanetti **Owner** Mark Cushway **Seats** 54, Pr/dining room 22
Times 12-2/6-9 **Prices** Fixed L 2 course fr £14.95, Tasting menu fr £50, Starter £6-£10, Main £12-£22.50, Dessert £6.50-£7 **Wines** **Parking** 70 **Notes** Sunday L £25, Vegetarian available, Children welcome

---

Buckland-Tout-Saints

◉ Modern British V

---

tel: 01548 853055 **Goveton TQ7 2DS**
email: enquiries@bucklandtoutsaints.co.uk web: www.tout-saints.co.uk
dir: *Turn off A381 to Goveton. Follow brown tourist signs to St Peter's Church. Hotel 2nd right after church*

Classic country-house dining with regional accent and period decor

A picture-perfect William and Mary-era house in four acres of gardens and woodland sets the scene for a classy country-house package. The interior is refined and packed with period details such as wood panelling and grand fireplaces, not least in the Queen Anne Restaurant, with one room replete with burnished Russian pine, the other with duck egg blue paintwork. The scene is dressed with white linen and fresh flowers. The kitchen turns out bright modern British cooking with a good showing of regional ingredients. There might be Salcombe crab to start, for example, in a modern dish with pineapple chutney, goats' curd and brown crab purée. Next up, roast rump of lamb with wild garlic and pearl barley risotto, or roasted tail of monkfish with curried lentils and golden raisin purée. Dessert follows the Pan-European pathway, with the likes of vanilla pannacotta perked up with cinnamon beignets and poached raspberries.

Chef Ted Ruewell **Owner** Eden Hotel Collection **Seats** 40, Pr/dining room 40
Times 12-2/7-9 Closed 2-17 Jan **Prices** Fixed L 2 course £17.50, Fixed D 3 course £35, Tasting menu fr £55, Starter £8.50-£11.50, Main £19-£26.50, Dessert £9, Service optional **Wines** 30 bottles over £30, 30 bottles under £30, 10 by glass **Parking** 70 **Notes** Sunday L £22, Children welcome

---

Lewtrenchard Manor

Rosettes not confirmed at time of going to print

Modern British V
tel: 01566 783222 **EX20 4PN**
email: info@lewtrenchard.co.uk web: www.lewtrenchard.co.uk
dir: *Take A30 signed Okehampton from M5 junct 31. 25m, exit at Sourton Cross. Follow signs to Lewdown, then Lewtrenchard*

Inventive modern British cooking in a Jacobean manor house

The Rosette award for this establishment has been suspended due to a change of chef. Reassessment will take place in due course under the new chef. A dignified greystone manor house built in the Jacobean era, Lewtrenchard is not far from Okehampton, overlooked by the rugged hills of north Dartmoor. Its present decorative order stands to the credit of the Victorian hymnist, Sabine Baring Gould, who installed much of the plasterwork, panelling and fireplaces, and the place found its vocation as a country hotel earlier than most, just after the Second World War. A walled vegetable garden supplies new chef Matthew Peryer's kitchen with much of its raw material, and there is a determination to maintain the style of innovative modern British cooking for which the Manor has become noted. A slab of seasonal game terrine with contrasting garnishes of pickled cranberries and candied pistachios makes a satisfying autumnal opener. It may be followed by seared turbot fillet with cheesy wild mushroom risotto and salsify, or two cuts of pork with fondant potato in calvados jus. An elegant dessert turns up in the form of 70% chocolate jelly with banana brûlée and a penetrating passion-fruit sorbet.

Chef Matthew Peryer **Owner** The Murray family **Seats** 45, Pr/dining room 22
Times 12-2/7-9 **Prices** Fixed L 2 course fr £19.50, Fixed D 3 course fr £49.50, Tasting menu fr £69, Service optional **Wines** 50 bottles over £30, 10 bottles under £30, 9 by glass **Parking** 40 **Notes** Purple Carrot Chef's table 8 course £79, Sunday L fr £25 Children 8 yrs+

KNOWSTONE
Map 3 SS82

The Masons Arms

 Modern British

tel: 01398 341231 **EX36 4RY**
email: enqs@masonsarmsdevon.co.uk
dir: *Signed from A361, turn right once in Knowstone*

Strong contemporary cooking in the lush western countryside

A genuinely delightful thatched medieval country inn that maintains strong links to excellent local growers and suppliers, The Masons also manages to retain the atmosphere of a village pub. Deep in the lush countryside on the border between Devon and Somerset, it is surrounded by rolling hills, and is full of cheer on winter evenings when the fire crackles, and in summer too for an outdoor meal. The celestial ceiling mural in the dining room has to be seen to be believed. Mark Dodson once cooked under Michel Roux at Bray (see entry, Waterside Inn, Berkshire), which might explain the flair and precision evident in the dishes here. Good strong contemporary thinking informs a starter of wood pigeon breasts, flash-fried and tender, accompanied by puréed beetroot and pine nuts in blueberry jus, while the main-course pairing of local beef fillet and oxtail in its truffled, Madeira-rich juices continues to be a triumph of timing and seasoning. Fish could be something almost as robust, perhaps sea bass alongside Jerusalem artichoke purée, butter beans and flageolets with smoked garlic in red wine jus, and dessert closes things with a fitting flourish in the form of lemon mascarpone mousse with passionfruit syrup, or an apple trio with Granny Smith sorbet.

Chef Mark Dodson, Jess Thorne **Owner** Mark & Sarah Dodson **Seats** 28 **Times** 12-2/7-9 Closed 1st wk Jan, 1 wk Aug BH, Mon, D Sun **Prices** Fixed L 2 course £20, Starter £8.75-£13.50, Main £18.50-£25, Dessert £6-£9.50, Service optional **Wines** 41 bottles over £30, 17 bottles under £30, 9 by glass **Parking** 10 **Notes** Sunday L £36.50, Vegetarian available, Children 5 yrs+ D

LEWDOWN
Map 3 SX48

Lewtrenchard Manor

Rosettes not confirmed at time of going to print – see page 143

LYNMOUTH
Map 3 SS74

Rising Sun Hotel

 British, French

tel: 01598 753223 **Harbourside EX35 6EG**
email: reception@risingsunlynmouth.co.uk **web:** www.risingsunlynmouth.co.uk
dir: *M5 junct 23 (Minehead). Take A39 to Lynmouth. Opposite the harbour*

Modern British cooking in a convivial harbourside inn

Given its atmospheric location by the harbour and 14th-century walls, it's not surprising that the Rising Sun once had associations with smugglers. Today the place positively rocks with good vibrations. There's a bar that is just that – a proper pub, packed, lively and full of beans – and an oak-panelled dining room that doesn't want for atmosphere either. The food strikes a good balance between hearty generosity and contemporary combinations, with plenty of seafood dishes as you might hope in this setting. Start with a modern classic – seared king scallops with cauliflower cream and crisp pancetta, or an 'old favourite' such as chicken livers

enriched with baby onions, pancetta and a balsamic and Madeira sauce (with brioche to soak up the juices). Next up, a generous portion of wild sea bass with samphire and a bouillabaisse sauce, or char-grilled rib-eye with field mushrooms and twice-cooked chips, and finish with a well-made crème brûlée.

Times 7-9 Closed L all week

Tors Hotel

 Modern

tel: 01598 753236 **EX35 6NA**
email: torshotel@torslynmouth.co.uk **web:** www.torslynmouth.co.uk
dir: *Adjacent to A39 on Countisbury Hill just before entering Lynmouth from Minehead*

Antiques, harbour views and well-judged modern cooking

This long-established hotel in five acres of woodland on the elemental Exmoor coastline has been in the hands of Martin Miller (of Miller's Antiques guides renown) for the last couple of years, during which time he has put his unmistakable signature on the place, stuffing it with antiques and objets d'art. Looking down to Lynmouth straggling along the harbour, the restaurant has glorious bay views as a backdrop to the unfussy repertoire of modern classics. The cooking is accurate, and dishes such as pan-roasted Cornish scallops with pea purée, black pudding crumbs and candied pancetta, have a clear sense of purpose. A well-judged main course sees chicken ballotine with sage, prosciutto and parmesan matched with fondant potatoes, seasonal vegetables, and chicken and grape jus. It all ends with a nicely balanced trio of custard pannacotta pointed up with the tartness of rhubarb and the crunch of vanilla shortbread.

Times 12-2.30/7-9 Closed Nov-Feb, L all week

PLYMOUTH
Map 3 SX45

Artillery Tower Restaurant

 Modern British

tel: 01752 257610 **Firestone Bay, Durnford St PL1 3QR**
dir: *1m from city centre & rail station*

Confident cooking in historic maritime building

Built in the early 1500s to protect the deep water passage into Plymouth Sound, the old Firestone Bay gunnery tower on Plymouth's seafront can certainly claim to be central to the town's history. And it still looks the part. Inside, the circular room is very atmospheric, what with its three-foot-thick exposed stone walls, walnut ceilings, wood-burning stove and neatly laid wooden tables to remind you what you're here for. Peter and Debbie Constable's restaurant is refreshingly focused on the ingredients – superb stuff, sourced locally which are cooked with skill and simplicity, everything made in-house. Start with Devon crab and avocado salad, for example, with Bloody Mary sauce, or roast quail with bacon and lentils. Next up, roast duck breast with confit leg, pear and ginger, or a superb piece of John Dory served with scallops and a tomato and basil sauce. To finish there might be vanilla cheesecake with rhubarb and jelly.

Chef Peter Constable **Owner** Peter & Debbie Constable **Seats** 26, Pr/dining room 16 **Times** 12-2.15/7-9.30 Closed Xmas, New Year, Sun-Mon, L Sat **Prices** Fixed L 2 course fr £12.50, Fixed D 3 course £20-£42, Service optional **Wines** 5 bottles over £30, 20 bottles under £30, 6 by glass **Parking** 20, Evening only **Notes** Vegetarian available, Children welcome

Barbican Kitchen

⊛ Modern v

tel: 01752 604448 **Plymouth Gin Distillery, 60 Southside St PL1 2LQ**
email: info@barbicankitchen.com web: www.barbicankitchen.com
dir: *On Barbican, 5 mins walk from Bretonside bus station*

Convincing brasserie food from the Tanner brothers in a contemporary setting

The renowned Plymouth Gin distillery is home to the Tanner brothers' second dining option in the city, and entering past the huge vats gives a reminder of the esteemed history of the building. You can take a tour if you want. The Barbican Kitchen spreads over two floors and packs a visual punch with its bold colours and contemporary prints (purple and lime chairs and Banksy no less), plus there's an open kitchen to add to the youthful, energetic vibe. The menu is a feel-good foray into contemporary tastes with a West Country flavour. There are burgers and steaks, even beer-battered fish and chips (its accompanying peas 'smashed'), but this is a kitchen that can also turn out rolled lamb shoulder with goats' cheese crumb and salsa verde, or a Chateaubriand for two. Start with chicken liver parfait with apple and cider chutney, and finish with a zesty lemon tart accompanied by raspberry sorbet.

Chef Christopher & James Tanner, Ben Palmer **Owner** Christopher & James Tanner **Seats** 80 **Times** 12-2.30/5-9.30 Closed 25-26 & 31 Dec **Prices** Prices not confirmed **Wines** 5 bottles over £30, 25 bottles under £30, 13 by glass **Parking** Drakes Circus, Guildhall **Notes** Fixed 2/3 course L menu also available pre-theatre, Sunday L, Children welcome

Best Western Duke of Cornwall Hotel

⊛ Modern British, European v

tel: 01752 275850 & 275855 **Millbay Rd PL1 3LG**
email: enquiries@thedukeofcornwall.co.uk web: www.thedukeofcornwall.co.uk
dir: *City centre, follow signs 'Pavilions', hotel road is opposite*

Modern cooking with West Country produce in a Victorian hotel

With its imperious Gothic exterior and impressive Victorian proportions within, the Duke of Cornwall deserves the epithet 'landmark'. You ain't gonna miss it. The restaurant is suitably refined and formal, with its chandelier, patterned carpet and tables dressed with fresh flowers and white linen. The kitchen works a modern European repertoire with a decent showing of West Country ingredients. Pulled Creedy Carver duck might turn up in a warm salad among first courses, with another option being caramelised red onion and goats' cheese tart topped with an abundance of salad leaves. Main course medallion of venison is a good piece of meat, nicely cooked, accompanied by celeriac purée and château potatoes, while

honey-roast duck breast is partnered with sauerkraut. To finish, white chocolate pannacotta is served in a glass with mixed summer berries and crushed almonds.

Chef Darren Kester **Owner** W Combstock, J Morcom **Seats** 80, Pr/dining room 30 **Times** 7-10 Closed 26-31 Dec, L all week **Prices** Starter £5-£7.50, Main £14.95-£21.95, Dessert £4.50-£7.50 **Wines** 8 by glass **Parking** 40, Also on street **Notes** Children welcome

Langdon Court Hotel & Restaurant

⊛⊛ Traditional British, French v

tel: 01752 862358 **Adams Ln, Down Thomas PL9 0DY**
email: enquiries@langdoncourt.com web: www.langdoncourt.com
dir: *signed from A379 at Elburton rdbt*

Impressive regional cooking at a Tudor manor house

The South Hams district of Devon is one of the county's prize assets, and in Langdon Court the area has a country-house hotel fully worthy of it. A 16th-century manor house, it has played host to royal personages and their consorts all the way from Henry VIII and Catherine Parr to Edward VII and the actress Lillie Langtry. A home for sick children to convalesce in style, it returned to private ownership and hotel duties in 1960. Local farm supplies and the Devon catch make their way to Jamie Roger's kitchen, where a dynamic approach has seen the cooking continue on an impressive upward trajectory. Ideas flow thick and fast: an Indian approach to scallops sees them teamed with saag aloo and a cauliflower bhaji, while the Japanese note sounds in a version of gravad lax cured in sake with wasabi crème fraîche. Fish for main might be pollock fillet with clams and leeks in cider, or there could be herb-crusted local lamb provençale. A hugely successful banana version of tarte Tatin comes with rich toffee ice cream.

Chef Jamie Rogers **Owner** Emma & Geoffrey Hill **Seats** 36, Pr/dining room 92 **Times** 12-3/6.30-9.30 **Prices** Service optional **Wines** 26 bottles over £30, 26 bottles under £30, 8 by glass **Parking** 60 **Notes** Sunday L £16.95-£21.95, Children welcome

Rhodes@The Dome

⊛ Modern British

tel: 01752 266600 **Barbican PL1 2NZ**
email: info@rhodesatthedome.co.uk
dir: *On Plymouth Hoe*

Modern bistro dining beneath the dome

The impressive setting for TV chef Gary Rhodes' latest restaurant is a rather glam contemporary affair in a former museum up on Plymouth Hoe. The huge circular bar set beneath the titular glass dome is the obvious place to begin proceedings with nibbles and a cocktail, while taking in the magnificent views of Smeaton's Tower looming above, and Plymouth Sound spread before you. Thankfully, the decor doesn't try to compete with the vista: neutral shades, well-spaced darkwood tables and clean-lined modern style are the order of the day, while the food satisfies current tastes for unbuttoned, ingredients-led bistro dishes. It's a style that allows a croque-monsieur to be turbocharged with warm smoked salmon, or straight-up grilled Devon Ruby sirloin steak with béarnaise, semi-dried tomatoes and mushrooms to share the billing with roast fillet of locally-caught cod served with lemon, capers, shrimps and crushed champ potatoes. Puddings play to the crowd with the likes of glazed lemon tart with local cream.

Chef Gary Rhodes, Kevin Robertson-Wells **Owner** Rhodes@The Dome Ltd **Seats** 150, Pr/dining room 25 **Times** 12-2.30/5.30-10 Closed 25-26 Dec **Prices** Starter £4-£9, Main £12-£28, Dessert £5-£10, Service optional **Wines** 6 bottles over £30, 34 bottles under £30, 7 by glass **Parking** On street **Notes** Sunday L £12-£28, Vegetarian available, Children welcome

PLYMOUTH *continued*

Rock Salt Café and Brasserie

◉◉ Modern British **NEW**

tel: 01752 225522 **31 Stonehouse St PL1 3PE**
email: info@rocksaltcafe.co.uk
dir: *Located between Brittany ferry port & Royal William Yard*

Informal all-day eatery with confident cooking

Open all day and all week from breakfast until late, this former pub with its slate-tiled exterior and easy-going seasidey vibe strikes a relaxed pose but takes the food seriously. There's attention to detail in the likes of smoked salmon and scrambled egg with sourdough toast at breakfast, or a lunchtime king prawn laksa. This is a kitchen that can turn out a classy butter-roasted guinea fowl for lunch, alongside an open sandwich with steak, onion jam and fried egg. If you settle down in the evening for the full three courses you might go from potted shrimps with crayfish, pickles and toast to braised Cornish brill with fennel and anchovies, finishing with a dessert of vanilla pannacotta with passionfruit and honeycomb. It all takes place in a cheery setting of blond wood and tasteful neutral colours, and the service is suitably on the ball.

Chef David Jenkins **Owner** Steve & David Jenkins **Seats** 60, Pr/dining room 25 **Times** 9am-10pm Closed 24-26 Dec, 1-8 Jan, All-day dining **Prices** Tasting menu £45, Starter £3.95-£9.95, Main £8.50-£21.95, Dessert £5.50, Service optional **Wines** 6 bottles over £30, 24 bottles under £30, 6 by glass **Parking** On street **Notes** Sunday L £13.95-£24.95, Vegetarian available, Children welcome

Tanners Restaurant

◉◉ Modern European ◢ **NOTABLE WINE LIST**

tel: 01752 252001 **Prysten House, Finewell St PL1 2AE**
email: enquiries@tannersrestaurant.com **web:** www.tannersrestaurant.co.uk
dir: *Town centre. Behind St Andrew's Church on Royal Parade*

Stimulating modern cookery in a venerable Barbican house

Ancient beams and stone walls are testament to this building's great age, reputedly one of the oldest in the city, while the restaurant has been given a sleek look, with smart claret-coloured high-backed dining chairs at polished wooden tables and contemporary art on the walls. The Tanner brothers certainly know how to keep the punters happy, turning out dishes with some surprising elements. How about duck breast with red sauerkraut, confit leg choux and clementine curd, or seared brill fillet with fennel pollen, mussels and heritage potatoes? That such combinations are such sure-fire winners is down to a deep understanding of what works together, combined with skilful handling of top-grade materials. Starters can seem a lot calmer in comparison: perhaps red mullet, basil and saffron risotto, or guinea fowl and smoked ham hock terrine with salt-baked celeriac and apple. Artisan cheeses, mostly from the West Country, are kept in good condition, alternatives to puddings like vanilla crème brûlée, or marmalade bread-and-butter pudding with vanilla ice cream.

Chef Martyn Compton, Christopher & James Tanner **Owner** Christopher & James Tanner **Seats** 45, Pr/dining room 26 **Times** 12-2/7-9.30 Closed 25 & 31 Dec, 1st wk Jan, Sun-Mon **Prices** Fixed L 2 course fr £14, Fixed D 3 course fr £20, Tasting menu £55-£100, Starter £9.95-£11.95, Main £18.95-£24.95, Dessert £6.95-£8.95, Service optional **Wines** 31 bottles over £30, 29 bottles under £30, 20 by glass **Parking** On street, church car park next to restaurant **Notes** Tasting menu 6 course, Vegetarian available, Children welcome

---

▌PLYMPTON   **Map 3 SX55**

Treby Arms

◉◉ Modern European

tel: 01752 837363 **Sparkwell PL7 5DD**
email: trebyarms@hotmail.co.uk
dir: *A38 Plympton turn off towards Langage & Dartmoor Zoological Park, signed Sparkwell*

Modern cooking of a high order from the 2012 *Masterchef* winner

The trim-looking Treby Arms with its whitewashed front stands in the Dartmoor village of Sparkwell, not far from major routes, but far enough for tranquillity. A small bar with log-fire caters for drinkers, but the greater part of the operation is turned over to dining, as you would expect from a place run by a Masterchef Professional champion. Anton Piotrowski has overseen an upsurge in business since his triumph, and the bookings list has lengthened. Stake your claim early, and be rewarded with locally sourced, energetic modern cookery of a high order. First up might be cider-glazed pig cheek on celeriac and leek fondue, or perhaps roast scallop with a cigar of goose-meat, fennel, lemon and sorrel. Meat is definitely the specialist subject. There's classic fish and chips among the mains, but the stars are cocoa venison, honey-mustard pork, and a serving of superb duck breast, confit and crackling-coated duck heart, with chorizo and some broccoli for greens. Desserts are equally technically skilled, as when a chocolate log oozes yuzu caramel, with caramelised banana and Horlicks adding further richness.

Chef Anton Piotrowski **Owner** Anton & Clare Piotrowski **Seats** 60 **Times** 12-3/6-9.30 Closed 25-26 Dec, 1 Jan, Mon **Prices** Fixed L 3 course £20, Tasting menu £55-£60, Starter £6-£12, Main £14-£26, Dessert £6-£9 **Wines** 19 bottles over £30, 28 bottles under £30, 11 by glass **Parking** 14, Village hall opposite **Notes** Sunday L £14.95, Vegetarian available, Children welcome

Read all about our Wine Award winners on page 17

ROCKBEARE

Map 3 SY09

The Jack In The Green Inn

◉◉ Modern British V

tel: 01404 822240 **EX5 2EE**
email: info@jackinthegreen.uk.com **web:** www.jackinthegreen.uk.com
dir: 3m E of M5 junct 29 on old A30

A creative powerhouse in a Devon country pub

Even when busy-which is frequently the case-The Jack never loses its cool, for this place is run with charm and generosity by Paul Parnell and his team. It looks and feels like a pub, with no airs and graces, just a satisfying mix of old and new throughout its series of atmospheric rooms. Long-term chef Matthew Mason is passionate about Devon produce and his menu is awash with high quality ingredients that reflect the landscape and waters in this beautiful part of the country. There's a refine contemporary polish to the kitchen's output, for everything is presented with style, but flavour is always king. Seared scallops with apple and lime is a modish plateful (and quite a small one), or go for lightly curried cod fillet with tempura mussels. Loin and breast of Whimple lamb is a main course that hits the spot, with boulangère potatoes and an anchovy dressing, and there are updated pub dishes, too, such as venison cottage pie. Finish with lemon mousse with meringues and rhubarb (poached and sorbet).

Chef Matthew Mason **Owner** Paul Parnell **Seats** 80, Pr/dining room 60
Times 12-2/6-9.30 Closed 25 Dec-5 Jan **Prices** Fixed L 3 course £25, Fixed D 3 course £25, Tasting menu fr £39.50, Starter £4.95-£8.50, Main £9.50-£25.50, Dessert £6.50-£8.95, Service optional **Wines** 60 bottles over £30, 40 bottles under £30, 12 by glass **Parking** 120 **Notes** Sunday L £15-£25.75, Children welcome

SALCOMBE

Map 3 SX73

Soar Mill Cove Hotel

◉◉ Modern British

tel: 01548 561566 **Soar Mill Cove, Marlborough TQ7 3DS**
email: info@soarmillcove.co.uk **web:** www.soarmillcove.co.uk
dir: A381 to Salcombe, through village follow signs to sea

Top-notch West Country produce and fab sea views

Few things set you up for a good feed better than salty air and a sea view, and this low-slung hotel is tucked away in 2,000 acres of National Trust-managed coastal heaven with the waves practically lapping at the door. The Serendipity restaurant is looking great after a makeover bringing in a beachcomber-chic, New England-style decor of powder-blue tongue-and-groove wall panelling to match baby-blue seating and polished wood floors; and fear not, the floor-to-ceiling windows are still there, with those uplifting sea views. West Country produce, often organic, anchors the daily-changing menu, and with the fishing fleets of Salcombe and Brixham close to hand, fish and seafood are naturally high on the agenda. Salcombe scallops with spicy chorizo and tomato dressing should stimulate the appetite, while main courses take in the likes of turbot fillet steamed over an infusion of ginger and lemon and teamed with saffron potatoes and citrus sauce. End with a choc-fest of rich chocolate tart with chocolate sauce and sorbet.

Times 10.30-5/7.15-9 Closed Jan, L all week

SAUNTON

Map 3 SS43

Saunton Sands Hotel

◉ Modern, Traditional V

tel: 01271 890212 **EX33 1LQ**
email: reservations@sauntonsands.com **web:** www.sauntonsands.com
dir: Exit A361 at Braunton, signed Croyde B3231, hotel 2m on left

Imaginative and complex cooking beside a beach

The location alone is a draw at this long white art deco hotel, as it overlooks a three-mile stretch of unspoiled sandy beach. It's a popular holiday destination, with a spa and pool and the beach on the doorstep, with rural and seaside pursuits nearby. Watch the sun set from the terrace or soak up the maritime views from the stylish restaurant with its original 1930s chandeliers. The kitchen is impassioned about using only West Country produce and turns out some stimulating dishes in the contemporary mould. The daily-changing menu might open with a complex but effective starter of soused mackerel with smoked mussels, curried mayonnaise, fennel and apple salad, fennel pollen and salted honeycomb, and proceed to pork belly with braised faggot, morcilla, pommes mousseline, quince purée and a cider and sage jus. A fish main-course option might be fillet of bream imaginatively paired with crab and ginger hash, served with braised chicory and shellfish bisque and espuma. Puddings include salted caramel tart with banana ice cream.

Chef D Turland, B Snelling **Owner** Brend Hotels **Seats** 200, Pr/dining room 20
Times 12.30-2/6.45-9.30 **Prices** Fixed L 2 course £19.95, Fixed D 3 course £36, Starter £3.95-£9.95, Main £17-£26.50, Dessert £8.50, Service optional **Wines** 53 bottles over £30, 54 bottles under £30, 15 by glass **Parking** 140 **Notes** Sunday L £19.95-£25, Children welcome

SHALDON Map 3 SX97

ODE dining

 British

tel: 01626 873977 **21 Fore St TQ14 ODE**
email: contact@odetruefood.com
dir: *Cross bridge, 1st right into Shoreside, directly left into car park*

Top-quality local and organic produce in coastal village

This small restaurant, in a Georgian house in an estuary village, gets its name not from anything poetic but more prosaically from its postcode. Ethically sourced and organic produce is the name of the game here, with the kitchen delivering refined and ambitious dishes. Starters can range from salted and slow-cooked cod with granola and bay leaf cream to sugar-cured duck breast with a salad of pickled turnips and pears. Both accuracy and a flair for successful combinations are apparent in the handful of main courses: perhaps a winter offering of guinea fowl with squash, braised lentils and shiitake mushrooms, or steamed sea bass in a rosemary crumb with crispy pork, Savoy cabbage, a blini and cider sauce. Artisan cheeses, served with house-made walnut toast and chutney, are all from the West Country. Otherwise, end with one of the imaginative puddings: walnut and date tart with vanilla and Earl Grey cream, or burnt cream with apple jelly and a rosemary scone. The owners also run a café and micro-brewery.

Chef Tim Bouget **Owner** Tim & Clare Bouget **Seats** 24 **Times** 7-9.30 Closed 25 Dec, BHs, Sun-Tue, L all week **Prices** Fixed D 3 course £40, Service optional **Wines** 10 bottles over £30, 10 bottles under £30, 5 by glass **Parking** Car park 3 mins walk **Notes** Wed reduced price/menu 2/3 course £24/£29, Vegetarian available, Children 8 yrs+

SIDMOUTH Map 3 SY18

Hotel Riviera

 Modern British

tel: 01395 515201 **The Esplanade EX10 8AY**
email: enquiries@hotelriviera.co.uk **web:** www.hotelriviera.co.uk
dir: *From M5 junct 30 take A3052 to Sidmouth. Situated in centre of The Esplanade*

Modern British dining in Regency Sidmouth

The name may suggest Cannes or Las Vegas, but Devon has its very own version of seaside grandeur, and the spotless bow-fronted Riviera is a prime example of it. The future Queen Victoria was brought on holiday here as a little girl, in the days when Sidmouth was all the rage. Tables on an outdoor terrace make the most of the summer weather, and a menu of gently modernised British cooking has something to cater for most tastes. Kick off with duck and blueberry terrine, served with spiced pear and toasted walnut and raisin bread, or perhaps a simple plate of Loch Fyne smoked salmon. Mains encompass bistro-style paupiette of lemon sole stuffed with salmon mousse alongside lemon couscous, as well as roast rack of local lamb with ratatouille, herbed mash and thyme jus. Finish off with the likes of egg custard tart with nutmeg ice cream and blackcurrant coulis.

Chef Matthew Weaver **Owner** Peter Wharton **Seats** 85, Pr/dining room 65 **Times** 12.30-2/7-9 **Prices** Starter £10.50-£14, Main £16-£32, Dessert £6.50-£10.50, Service optional **Wines** 45 bottles over £30, 24 bottles under £30, 10 by glass **Parking** 26 **Notes** Fixed L 5 course £29.50, D 6 course £42, Sunday L, Vegetarian available, Children welcome

The Salty Monk

Modern British V

tel: 01395 513174 **Church St, Sidford EX10 9QP**
email: saltymonk@btconnect.com **web:** www.saltymonk.co.uk
dir: *From M5 junct 30 take A3052 to Sidmouth, or from Honiton take A375 to Sidmouth, 200yds on right opposite church in village*

Gentle modern British food in a former salthouse

The Salty Monk has a new string to its bow – or should that be belt to its habit? – in the form of a brasserie where the old lounge bar used to be (the lounge has moved to the old Gallery Room). It's business as usual, though, in the main restaurant with its warming colour scheme and soothing candle-lit ambience. Andy and Annette Witheridge's charming restaurant with rooms, located in a 16th-century building built to store the salt traded by local monks, has plenty of character and a genuine focus on top-notch regional ingredients: check out the suppliers on the menu. To begin, a smoked fish quiche comes straight out of the oven, or there might be duck liver parfait with melba toast and raisins marinated in Madeira. The splendid West Country produce includes fish such as sea bass, served pan-fried with rösti potatoes and a red wine glaze, and the pork which comes as a trio (roast loin, slow-braised belly and rillettes) with apple fondant and creamed potatoes. Finish with a classic lemon tart.

Chef Annette & Andy Witheridge, Scott Horn **Owner** Annette & Andy Witheridge **Seats** 45 **Times** 12-1.30/6.30-9 Closed 1 wk Nov & Jan, L Mon-Wed **Prices** Fixed L 2 course fr £25, Fixed D 3 course fr £45, Tasting menu fr £65, Service optional **Wines** 22 bottles over £30, 47 bottles under £30, 14 by glass **Parking** 20 **Notes** Tasting menu 7 course, Sunday L £25-£29.50, Children welcome

The Victoria Hotel

Traditional

tel: 01395 512651 **The Esplanade EX10 8RY**
email: reservations@victoriahotel.co.uk **web:** www.victoriahotel.co.uk
dir: *At western end of The Esplanade*

Turn-of-the-century splendour beside the sea

The Victoria's old-world charm and dignity isn't exactly the fashion these days. There's a doorman to usher you inside the handsome building, gents have to put on their jackets and ties in the dining room, and a pianist tinkles away at the ivories. For some, that's just the ticket. The setting at the end of the town's impressive Georgian esplanade is alluring, with the expansive bay offered up in all its shimmering glory. The formal restaurant has pastel tones and spiffy table settings, and what appears on the plate is generally classically-minded and based on local ingredients. Devonshire chicken liver parfait with toasted brioche and piccalilli is one way to begin, or confit of salmon with pickled cucumber, beetroot, and vanilla mayonnaise. Main course fillet of turbot might follow on, or rack of pork with celeriac purée and black pudding, and, for dessert, perhaps a chocolate tart.

Times 1-2/7-9

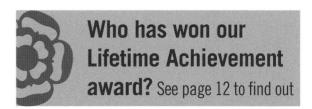
Who has won our Lifetime Achievement award? See page 12 to find out

STRETE

Map 3 SX84

The Laughing Monk

 Modern British

tel: 01803 770639 **Totnes Rd TQ6 ORN**
email: thelaughingmonk@btconnect.com
dir: A38 & follow signs towards Dartmouth, 700yds past Dartmouth Golf Club take right turn to Strete. Restaurant on left just past church

Resourceful and interesting cooking in the South Hams

The South-West Coast Path runs practically outside the front door of this converted old school, and both Slapton and Blackpool Sands are a mere mile or so away. The place has been given a bit of a refurb, and offers a light-filled, airy space with an impressive inglenook and a cheery atmosphere. The kitchen makes enviable use of Devon's resources and turns out carefully composed dishes, often with stimulating touches. Crab and prawn cocktail, for instance, is served with guacamole and lime mayonnaise, and crisp salt-and-pepper squid with Asian salad and sweet chilli dressing. Seafood figures prominently, from roast monkfish and prawns with rösti and pepper confit to sea bass fillet in pancetta with pea purée, roast asparagus and tomato vinaigrette. Carnivores are not overlooked: there might be roast rump of lamb with fondant potato, ratatouille and black raisin sauce. Caramelised apple crumble with custard is a good way to end.

Chef Ben Handley **Owner** Ben & Jackie Handley **Seats** 60 **Times** 6.30-9 Closed Xmas, Jan, Sun-Mon, L all week **Prices** Fixed D 3 course £26, Starter £6.50-£10, Main £14-£24, Dessert £6.50-£9.50 **Wines** 1 bottle over £30, 25 bottles under £30, 5 by glass **Parking** 4, On street **Notes** Early supper menu available Tue-Fri, Vegetarian available, Children welcome

TAVISTOCK

Map 3 SX47

Bedford Hotel

 British

tel: 01822 613221 **1 Plymouth Rd PL19 8BB**
email: enquiries@bedford-hotel.co.uk **web:** www.bedford-hotel.co.uk
dir: M5 junct 31, A30 (Launceston/Okehampton). Then A386 to Tavistock, follow town centre signs. Hotel opposite church

Confident modern cooking in a Gothic hotel

The Gothic building with its castellated walls certainly makes an impression-which is what that style is all about-but those walls were never intended to keep out invaders. This place has always been about hospitality, and so it remains today. There's no lack of character and charm within, including the restaurant with its moulded ceilings and panelled walls. So far, so traditional. The kitchen takes a more contemporary position, but a reassuringly gentle one. A first-course potted rabbit is one way to begin, or go for salmon ballotine in the more modern company of pickled beetroot and wasabi mayonnaise. Devon venison bourguignon is a flavoursome main course, as is a well-judged dish of duck and chorizo. Desserts such as egg custard or treacle tart with Devon clotted cream show off good technical skills, and there are West Country cheeses if you still have room.

Chef Mike Palmer **Owner** Warm Welcome Hotels **Seats** 55, Pr/dining room 24 **Times** 12-2.30/7-9.30 Closed L Mon-Sat **Prices** Fixed L 2 course £20-£25, Fixed D 3 course £30-£35, Service optional **Wines** 18 bottles over £30, 15 bottles under £30, 6 by glass **Parking** 48 **Notes** Sunday L £19.95-£21.95, Vegetarian available, Children welcome

The Horn of Plenty

 Modern British

tel: 01822 832528 **Gulworthy PL19 8JD**
email: enquiries@thehornofplenty.co.uk **web:** www.thehornofplenty.co.uk
dir: From Tavistock take A390 W for 3m. Right at Gulworthy Cross. In 400yds turn left, hotel in 400yds on right

Confident contemporary cooking and glorious valley views

A country-house hotel on a human scale, The Horn of Plenty has views to die for across the Tamar Valley and the kind of cosseting luxury that feels like home (if only home was like this!). It was built in the 19th century for a mine captain, and there's still plenty of period charm inside and out. There are five acres of gardens and wild orchards. The dining room – it does feel more like a hotel dining room than a restaurant, but not in a bad way – has daylight views and a satisfying intimacy, watched over by a soothing service crew. The team in the kitchen are a progressive bunch, headed up by Scott Paton, making good use of local produce (including from the hotel's own garden) and delivering some sharp, contemporary food. Seared scallops with glazed chicken wings and toasted sesame is a fashionable pairing of surf and turf, followed by loin of Exmoor venison with parsnip 'textures' and chocolate jus. There are good skills on show here. Finish with peanut pannacotta and mousse with a sour cherry sorbet and peanut macaroons.

Chef Scott Paton **Owner** Julie Leivers, Damien Pease **Seats** 60, Pr/dining room 16 **Times** 12-2.15/7-10.15 **Prices** Fixed L 2 course £19.50, Fixed D 3 course £49.50, Tasting menu £65, Service optional **Wines** 32 bottles over £30, 31 bottles under £30, 11 by glass **Parking** 25, On street **Notes** Sunday L £19.50-£24.50, Vegetarian available, Children welcome

The Library@Browns

 Modern British

tel: 01822 618686 **80 West St PL19 8AQ**
email: info@brownsdevon.com
dir: B3250 onto A386 to Tavistock

Accomplished contemporary cooking in smart boutique hotel

Dating from the 17th century, the old girl still boasts open fires, oak beams, exposed stone and slate flags, although a makeover gives a contemporary sheen. Dining takes place in The Library, a small and intimate room with soft music, polished oak tables, vivid artwork and an eponymous wall of books. The kitchen hits the spot with modern British and classic dishes, with flavour as king and an eye for presentation. Start with tender, moist quail on a bed of Jerusalem artichoke risotto, with a scattering of girolles and hazelnuts adding depth, while home-made haggis adds a further dimension to a main course of Dartmoor venison paired with bubble-and-squeak and honey-roast roots. West Country produce plays a starring role throughout. Cornish gurnard might appear with mussel and clam chowder, before the likes of local pork with black pudding, bacon, apple, mustard sauce and Savoy cabbage, and, to finish, crème brûlée is a classic. Chocoholics can get their fix with the 'everything chocolatey'.

Times 12-3/7-10.30

Follow us on facebook
www.facebook.com/TheAAUK

THURLESTONE

Map 3 SX64

Thurlestone Hotel

British v

tel: 01548 560382 **TQ7 3NN**
email: enquiries@thurlestone.co.uk **web:** www.thurlestone.co.uk
dir: *A38 take A384 into Totnes, A381 towards Kingsbridge, onto A379 towards Churchstow, onto B3197 turn into lane signed to Thurlestone*

Stunning sea views and well-judged cooking using regional produce

The view across the golf course and subtropical gardens to the sea and distant horizon is a cracker (especially from the terrace), and with its proximity to Salcombe, the Thurlestone is a south Devon hotspot. With a spa and all mod cons, there's plenty to keep you occupied, rain or shine. The Margaret Amelia restaurant is another star attraction, with its formal table setting and glorious views though the floor-to-ceiling picture windows. The menu makes good use of the region's produce in dishes that have classical foundations. Cornish blue cheese pannacotta is an inventive opener, or go for half a grilled lobster. Next up, a sorbet (lemon, maybe) followed by a main course, such as confit of belly pork with crackling, champ, Calvados raisins and Bramley apple purée. For dessert, white chocolate crème brûlée with a compôte of summer berries and shortbread biscuit hits the spot.

Chef Hugh Miller **Owner** Grose family **Seats** 150, Pr/dining room 150
Times 12.30-2.30/7.30-9 Closed 2 wks Jan, L Mon-Sat **Prices** Fixed D 3 course £39.50-£55, Service optional **Wines** 119 bottles over £30, 26 bottles under £30, 9 by glass **Parking** 120 **Notes** 4 course £39.50, Fish tasting menu, Sunday L £19.95-£25, Children welcome

TORQUAY

Map 3 SX96

Corbyn Head Hotel

Modern, Traditional **NEW**

tel: 01803 213611 **Sea Front TQ2 6RH**
email: info@corbynhead.com **web:** www.corbynhead.com
dir: *Follow signs to Torquay seafront, turn right on seafront. Hotel on right with green canopies*

Seafront hotel with imaginative and accomplished cooking

Bang on the seafront, with views over the bay, this white hotel with green awnings above the windows is a blaze of colourful flowers in summer. It's an ideal holiday destination, with an outdoor pool; it also has conference facilities and is a popular wedding venue. It's no poser to guess where the Harbour View Restaurant got its name. The dining area is a pretty room done out in shades of pink, while the kitchen sets itself high standards and turns out dishes in an ambitious, contemporary style. Among starters, ham hock and black pudding terrine is deeply flavoured and tasty, cut by gooseberry relish, or there might be crab and salmon roulade with pickled shredded vegetables and sesame dressing. Main courses are commendably restrained-confit duck leg with vegetable stir-fry and peppercorn sauce, for instance-and fish is a strength, judging by pan-fried cod fillet, of superb quality, fleshy and succulent, with saffron sauce and creamed leeks. End with indulgent clotted cream rice pudding with blueberry compôte.

Chef Wayne Maddern **Owner** Mrs Rew **Seats** 80 **Times** 12-2/7-9 Closed L Mon-Sat **Prices** Service optional **Wines** 37 bottles over £30, 76 bottles under £30, 12 by glass **Parking** 40 **Notes** Fixed D 4 course £29.50, Vegetarian available, Children welcome

The Elephant Restaurant and Brasserie

 – see below

The Elephant Restaurant and Brasserie

TORQUAY

Map 3 SX96

Modern British

tel: 01803 200044 **3-4 Beacon Ter TQ1 2BH**
email: info@elephantrestaurant.co.uk
dir: *Follow signs for Living Coast, restaurant opposite*

Fine dining and brasserie dishes near the harbour

Nowhere on the English Riviera has done as much as the Elephant in laying to rest the ghost of a certain Mr Fawlty and establishing Torquay as a destination on the region's gastronomic map. The yellow façade of the two Georgian townhouses overlooking the marina present a jaunty face to the world and has become a landmark for local foodies. The Elephant offers a two-tier dining experience: go no further than the ground floor if you want uncomplicated brasserie dishes along the lines of slow-cooked pig's cheek with salt-baked celeriac, crispy squid and horseradish cream, or local beef with dauphinoise potatoes, smoked bacon, button onions and Bordelaise sauce. Otherwise, head on upstairs to the first-floor bar and its adjacent dining space, the Room, which opens from April to October for chef Simon Hulstone's full-dress version of contemporary British cooking, delivered via a multi-course tasting menu. Peerless West Country ingredients,

some fashionably foraged, underpin the whole edifice, which might set out with the seasonal simplicity of wild garlic soup with natural yoghurt to get the taste buds standing to attention in readiness for a well-conceived composition of beetroot with Vulscombe goats' cheese, truffle and grain mustard. Subsequent courses could see trout given a lift with tomatoes and chickweed, plaice teamed with almond purée, squid ink and parsley, or guinea fowl partnered with carrot, parsnip and ying yang beans. To finish, soy adds an unusual hit to apple tarte Tatin with crème fraîche, or go for impeccable artisan West Country cheeses from the trolley. The service approach of understated but precisely efficient civility ensures people get treated as the old friends many of them have become. A well-chosen wine list has some attractive selections by the glass.

Chef Simon Hulstone **Owner** Peter Morgan, Simon Hulstone **Seats** 75, Pr/dining room 12 **Times** 12-2/6.30-9 Closed 1st 2wks Jan, Sun-Mon **Prices** Fixed L 2 course £14.50, Tasting menu fr £69.95, Starter £6.50-£8, Main £16-£23.75, Dessert £6-£7.50, Service optional 10% **Wines** 24 bottles over £30, 30 bottles under £30, 8 by glass **Parking** Opposite restaurant **Notes** Vegetarian available, No children

The Headland Hotel

⊛ Modern, Traditional NEW

tel: 01803 295666 **Daddyhole Rd TQ1 2EF**
email: info@headlandtorquay.com **web:** www.headlandtorquay.com

Confident cooking and a sea view

This Victorian villa originally built for royalty (the Romanov's of Russia, no less) has a prime spot overlooking the best the English Riviera has to offer in the form of the promised headland and the sparkling blue sea (some of the time at least). There are two acres of pretty gardens to explore, a heated outdoor pool and an elegant restaurant named after those famous regal former residents. The sea-facing dining room has grand proportions, a great view and a traditional finish. The kitchen turns out well-crafted dishes based on good quality ingredients. Start with a smooth and lightly whipped liver parfait with beetroot chutney and toasted brioche, followed by grilled sea bass with mussels, samphire and a full-flavoured white wine and dill cream.Desserts can be as comforting as a chocolate brownie wheel, accompanied by hot chocolate sauce and whipped cream.

Chef Zibi Klapsia **Owner** Duchy Hotels **Seats** 140, Pr/dining room 20 **Times** 6.30-8.30 **Prices** Prices not confirmed **Wines** **Parking** 45 **Notes** Fixed D 6 course from £24.95, Vegetarian available, Children welcome

The Imperial Hotel

⊛ Modern British

tel: 01803 294301 **Park Hill Rd TQ1 2DG**
email: imperialtorquay@pumahotels.co.uk **web:** www.pumahotels.co.uk
dir: M5 to Exeter, A380 then A3022 to Torquay. Park Hill Rd off Torwood St/Babbacombe Rd, just N of New Harbour

Superb views and well-executed dishes using local produce

The Imperial's Victorian founders couldn't have chosen a better spot for their hotel: from its clifftop position it has wide-ranging views over the bay and Channel. The Regatta Restaurant is housed in a pleasant, spacious room with a sense of grandness, and it is worth getting here before sunset for the full experience of those views. The kitchen chooses its ingredients diligently, making good use of fish and local produce, and turns out well-considered, carefully timed dishes; it clearly has a flair for presentation, too, without over-complicating what appears on the plate. Red mullet escabèche has been a well-executed starter, pearl onions and mustardy chive potato adding contrasting flavours and textures, and may be followed by confit of belly pork with a memorable apple and cider sauce, accompanied by a ham hock 'bonbon', Puy lentils and Savoy cabbage. Puddings end a meal on a high note: witness nougat parfait with smooth, intensely flavoured pistachio ice cream.

Times 7-9.30 Closed L all week

Follow the AA on twitter @TheAA_Lifestyle

Orestone Manor

⊛⊛ Modern, European V

tel: 01803 328098 **Rockhouse Ln TQ1 4SX**
email: info@orestonemanor.com **web:** www.orestonemanor.com
dir: A379 to Shaldon. Follow road through, hotel signed on left (beware sharp turn)

Capable cooking in boutique manor house

This handsome Georgian manor house sits in landscaped grounds overlooking Lyme Bay. Family-run, and with just 11 stylish bedrooms, it combines stylish intimacy with a serious attitude to gastronomy. The views from the smart conservatory-style bistro are of the landscaped gardens and out to sea, while the menu proposes uncomplicated, please-all dishes along the lines of seafood or antipasti platters, local steaks and burgers, bolstered by daily blackboard specials. At dinner, there's a more ambitious à la carte served on linen-clothed tables in the formal restaurant. The kitchen allies sound technique with thorough use of quality local produce, setting out with well-made chicken liver parfait with red onion marmalade and toasted brioche, followed by the comfort of crispy pork belly with Savoy cabbage, lardons and pork jus. If the nearness of the briny puts you in the mood for fish, something like roast Cornish cod fillet with buttered spinach, clams and mussel cream should fit the bill. Finish with a classic vanilla crème brûlée with shortbread.

Chef Tony Carr, Neil & Catherine D'Allen **Owner** Neil & Catherine D'Allen **Seats** 55, Pr/dining room 22 **Times** 12-2.30/6.30-9.30 Closed 3-30 Jan **Prices** Fixed L 2 course £17.95, Fixed D 3 course £22.95, Tasting menu £47.50, Starter £5.50-£12, Main £12.50-£23, Dessert £5.95-£6.95, Service optional **Wines** 22 bottles over £30, 45 bottles under £30, 18 by glass **Parking** 38 **Notes** Tasting menu at wknds or by arrangement, Sunday L £12.50-£23.95, Children welcome

TOTNES

Map 3 SX86

The Riverford Field Kitchen

⊛ Modern British, Mediterranean

tel: 01803 762074 **Riverford TQ11 OJU**
email: fieldkitchen@riverford.co.uk
dir: From A38 Buckfastleigh, take A384 to Totnes. Turn off to Landscove & Woolston Green & follow signs to Riverford Organic Farms

Vegetables take a starring role at this organic Devon farm

If you've sampled the veg boxes, or maybe just seen the vans busying along your road heading to someone else's doorstep, you'll have an idea of what to expect here. This is the hub of the Riverford brand (they have five farms around the country now), delivering organically grown fruit and veg across the land. At Wash Barn you can take a look around the farm, stock up on supplies, or hunker down at communal tables for some good and hearty organic food. It's a fixed deal of whatever is on-the-money that day, with lots of ace organic vegetable and salad accompaniments. Start with a salad packed with beetroot, pickled kohlrabi and Millstone cheese, walnuts and radish sprouts – a winning combination. Next up, a main course of barbecue chicken flavoured with paprika and served up with an array of side dishes – carrots with fennel, rainbow chard with lemon and garlic, potatoes and roasted red peppers, and more. To finish, try an egg custard tart with gooseberry compôte.

Chef Rob Andrew **Owner** Guy Watson **Seats** 72 **Times** 12.30-3/7.30-11.30 Closed D Sun-Wed (winter) **Prices** Fixed L 3 course £22.50, Fixed D 3 course £26.50, Service optional **Wines** 1 bottle over £30, 15 bottles under £30, 6 by glass **Parking** 30 **Notes** Sunday L £22.50, Vegetarian available, Children welcome

TWO BRIDGES

Map 3 SX67

Two Bridges Hotel

Modern British **V**

tel: 01822 892300 **PL20 6SW**
email: enquiries@twobridges.co.uk **web:** www.twobridges.co.uk
dir: 8m from Tavistock on B3357, hotel at junct with B3312

Scenic moorland spot and bold cooking

One bridge (check), two bridges (check), the setting is true Dartmoor, the bridges built of old stone with history in their sturdy frames. The hotel has 60 acres to call its own, but nature is all around. The traditional Tors Restaurant is the setting for some rather daringly contemporary food, the good use of regional produce giving it all a sense of place. Home-made bread, an amuse-bouche and petits fours show the serious intentions of the kitchen crew. Devon rabbit – tender loin, soft confit – with quail's egg, carrot purée, salsify and candied orange is a creative first course, followed perhaps by Crediton chicken with onion bhaji, sag aloo, almonds, dates and apricots, or fillet of sea bass with chorizo, butternut squash, gem lettuce and crab. And to finish, in season you might find rhubarb and custard with meringue, lemon and pistachios.

Owner Warm Welcome Hotels **Seats** 85 **Times** 12–2/6.30–9.30 **Prices** Fixed D 3 course £35–£45, Tasting menu £55, Service optional **Wines** 6 by glass **Parking** 150 **Notes** Sunday L £18.95–£23.95, Children welcome

WOODBURY

Map 3 SY08

Woodbury Park Hotel and Golf Club

Modern British

tel: 01395 233382 & 234735 **Woodbury Castle EX5 1JJ**
email: enquiries@woodburypark.co.uk **web:** www.woodburypark.co.uk
dir: M5 junct 30, take A376/A3052 towards Sidmouth, turn right opposite Halfway Inn onto B3180 towards Budleigh Salterton to Woodbury Common, hotel signed on right

Attractive brasserie food at a golfing and fitness hotel

Exeter is one of those cities that doesn't require too much of a trek outwards in order to come across the rolling acres of the English countryside. There are 550 of them around Woodbury Park, some consecrated to a pair of golf courses, while inside the hotel is a hive of activity, with keep-fit machines, swimming and massages. All of which provide various ways of honing an appetite for the straightforward, aesthetically presented brasserie food on offer in the Atrium Restaurant. Expect grilled mackerel from Brixham, subtly chillied-up and served with tomato jelly and red onion, and then herb-crusted cod with ratatouille and dauphinoise, or a right royal beef platter comprised of a quarter-pound fillet steak, chargrilled rib-eye and oxtail pudding. Vanilla pannacotta has that just-set consistency, its creamy blandness offset with a clutch of sharply balsamic-dressed strawberries. A West Country cheeseboard offers the region's finest, served with membrillo and olives.

Chef Matthew Pickett **Owner** Sue & Robin Hawkins **Seats** 120, Pr/dining room 180 **Times** 12.30–2.30/6.30–9.30 Closed L Mon-Sat, D 31 Dec **Prices** Fixed D 3 course £25–£32, Starter £6.50–£8, Main £16–£18, Dessert £6, Service optional **Wines** 7 bottles over £30, 39 bottles under £30, 10 by glass **Parking** 350 **Notes** Sunday L £10.95–£19.95, Vegetarian available, Children welcome

WOOLACOMBE

Map 3 SS44

Watersmeet Hotel

Traditional British, European

tel: 01271 870333 **Mortehoe EX34 7EB**
email: info@watersmeethotel.co.uk **web:** www.watersmeethotel.co.uk
dir: M5 junct 27. Follow A361 to Woolacombe, right at beach car park, 300yds on right

Superb coastal views and confident cooking

Dramatically perched on the cliffside, this elegant hotel is traditionally decorated throughout and has an old style charm and relaxing ambience. Floor-length windows in the west-facing dining room promise views of incredible sunsets at dinner; every seat in the house enjoys views of the spectacular coastline, sandy beach and across to Lundy Island. The kitchen takes high quality produce and delivers consistently well-executed food with some European influences, with dishes on the daily-changing menu demonstrating an impressive lightness of touch. Home-cured pigeon ham (moist and tender) comes with an appealing combination of celeriac, beetroot, apple and hazelnuts – a dish of nicely contrasting colours and textures – while main-course loin and breast of lamb with flageolet bean purée, sweetbread and balsamic reduction is an equally well-considered plate of food. Caramel pannacotta, honeycomb and poached pear balances all the flavours perfectly or, for the savoury-toothed, the board of English cheeses, seasonal chutney and pickled celery is an alternative way to finish. The newly opened bistro offers more informal dining.

Chef John Prince **Owner** Mrs James **Seats** 56, Pr/dining room 18 **Times** 12–2/7–9 **Prices** Fixed D 3 course £42, Starter £6.25–£9.50, Main £11.75–£18.95, Dessert £6.50–£7.95, Service optional **Wines** **Parking** 40 **Notes** Sunday L, Vegetarian available, Children 8 yrs+

DORSET

BEAMINSTER

Map 4 ST40

BridgeHouse

 Modern International

tel: 01308 862200 **3 Prout Bridge DT8 3AY**
email: enquiries@bridge-house.co.uk **web:** www.beaminsterbrasserie.co.uk
dir: From A303 take A356 towards Dorchester. Turn right onto A3066, 200mtrs down hill from town centre

Up-to-date cooking in a 13th-century building

There's a sense of refinement to BridgeHouse, where the original heritage of the building (all 700 years of it) is respected and maintained, but a sheen of modernity prevents any feeling of stuffiness. It's a class act. That goes for its Beaminster Brasserie, too, which consists of three areas: a slightly more formal panelled and candlelit main room with an Adam fireplace, a conservatory and the terrace overlooking the walled garden. Similarly, the kitchen strikes a good balance between creativity and reassuringly classical thinking, with a good amount of regional produce bringing a sense of place. West Bay crab from down the road turns up in an orientally-inspired first course with samphire spring rolls and bonbons, plus pickled cucumber and sweet chilli. Main course roasted local partridge is a more classical (or classical European) offering with dauphinoise potatoes, braised Savoy cabbage, lardons, baby onions and wild mushrooms. There's a sure hand in the kitchen, with flavours hitting the mark throughout. To finish, warm pistachio cake is perked up by its accompanying poached pear, nifty ginger beer gel and blackberry ice cream.

Times 12–2.30/6.30–9.30

BOURNEMOUTH

Map 5 SZ09

Best Western The Connaught Hotel

◎◎ Modern British

tel: 01202 298020 **30 West Hill Rd, West Cliff BH2 5PH**
email: reception@theconnaught.co.uk web: www.theconnaught.co.uk
dir: *Follow Town Centre West & BIC signs*

Traditionally based British cooking in a grand seaside hotel

The Connaught, as befits its name, is a rather grand old beast, ruling the roost on Bournemouth's West Cliff, with pristine sandy beaches stretching below it. It offers sumptuous prospects all round, and its principal dining room, Blakes, overlooks the hotel's own gardens, where candlelit outdoor tables are a delightful feature on balmy southern evenings. Inside, a curtain divides the room at less busy sessions, the better to create a sense of intimacy, and the lightly formal tone makes an agreeable ambience for carefully considered, traditionally based British dishes. Seared scallops are presented in a delicate bouillabaisse broth with various textural treatments of fennel. That might be followed by roast breast and confit leg of pheasant with Maris Piper mash, pancetta and baby onions in red wine, or seared bream in a saffron-scented nage of mussels. Celebrate the domestic fruit season with a dessert that combines roasted plums and plum and sloe-berry sorbet with silky buttermilk pannacotta. If you're having cheese instead, seek out the local Dorset varieties on the trolley.

Chef Ben Nicol **Owner** Franklyn Hotels Ltd **Seats** 80, Pr/dining room 16 **Times** 6.30-9 Closed L all week (private lunches by arrangement) **Prices** Starter fr £6, Main £15-£26, Dessert £6-£10 **Wines** 23 bottles over £30, 25 bottles under £30, 14 by glass **Parking** 66 **Notes** Pre-theatre menu available must pre-book, Vegetarian available, Children welcome

Bournemouth Highcliff Marriott Hotel

◎◎ Modern British

tel: 01202 557702 **St Michael's Rd, West Cliff BH2 5DU**
email: reservations.bournemouth@marriotthotels.co.uk web: www.highcliffgrill.co.uk
dir: *Take A338 dual carriageway through Bournemouth, then follow signs for International Centre to West Cliff Rd, then 2nd right*

Up-to-date cooking in a colourful clifftop hotel restaurant

As the name pretty much shouts out, it's on a high clifftop overlooking the lush golden sands of Bournemouth beach, and is a majestic old seaside hotel in the grandest vein, with imperious sea views as standard. The dining room has been hauled into the modern era with a stripped-down but colourful look, featuring unclothed tables amid striped and spotted upholstery in candy colours. Up-to-date ingredients and techniques, backed by the provender of local suppliers, distinguish the extensive menus. Smoked mutton 'bacon' with beer-pickled wild mushrooms and onions, zizzed up with horseradish, is an assertive opener, rabbit terrine with date and orange pastilla and pickled carrots perhaps a little overwhelmed by its accompaniments. A partnership of brown crabmeat and quinoa makes an interesting discovery in the context of a main dish of fried hake, while local rose veal comes as roast loin and braised shin with salt-baked celeriac, curly kale and apple. Finish with a rhubarb and custard spin, the former poached and jellied, the latter set into a panna cotta garnished with honeycomb.

Chef Matthew Budden **Owner** Marriott Hotels **Seats** 80, Pr/dining room 14 **Times** 1-3/6-9.30 Closed L Mon-Sat, D Sun (winter) **Prices** Tasting menu £31.50, Starter £7.50-£11, Main £14.50-£27.95, Dessert £6-£7 **Wines** 15 by glass **Parking** 100 **Notes** Tasting menu 4 course, Sunday L £16.50-£23.50, Vegetarian available, Children welcome

The Crab at Bournemouth

◎◎ Seafood

tel: 01202 203601 **Exeter Rd BH2 5AJ**
email: info@crabatbournemouth.com web: www.crabatbournemouth.com
dir: *Follow signs to B.I.C, restaurant opposite*

Seafood specialist on the Bournemouth seafront

The very essence of a seafront venue, the Crab is part of the pristine white-fronted Park Central Hotel, but functions very much as a restaurant in its own right. Recent refurbishment brings a new layout and refitted bar and dining room, and the prevailing tone is of crabshell and sandy hues against a background of dark wood. The seafood theme is reflected in colourful charger plates, but mainly in the menus, where a cornucopia of fresh fish and shellfish spills forth. Preparations are never less than appetising, whether you're starting with John Ross smoked salmon, Caesar risotto and a poached egg, or seared scallops with truffled butternut purée and pancetta. A half-lobster makes a magnificent main, or go large for the whole thing, thermidored, garlic-buttered, or even with Thai-style coconut dressing. Otherwise, there are sea bass with clams, mussels and crab in bouillabaisse, or crab-crusted sole with crayfish potato crush and olive jus. Finish with dark chocolate tart and passionfruit sorbet. A set menu supplements the carte, and there's a namesake sibling restaurant at Chieveley in Berkshire (see entry).

Chef Dave Horridge **Owner** Julie Savage **Seats** 80 **Times** 12-2.30/5.30-10 **Prices** Fixed L 2 course £16.95, Fixed D 3 course fr £20.95, Starter £5.95-£17.95, Main £12.95-£45, Dessert £5.95-£8.50 **Wines** 18 bottles over £30, 24 bottles under £30, 19 by glass **Parking** B.I.C **Notes** Pre-theatre set menu 3 course £20.95 from 5.30-7pm, Sunday L £9.95-£20.95, Vegetarian available, Children welcome

BOURNEMOUTH *continued*

Cumberland Hotel

◎◎ British

tel: 01202 290722 & 556529 **27 East Overcliff Dr BH1 3AF**
email: kwood@cumberlandbournemouth.co.uk web: www.cumberlandbournemouth.co.uk
dir: *A35 towards East Cliff & beaches, right onto Holdenhurst Rd, straight over 2 rdbts, left at junct to East Overcliff Drive, hotel on seafront*

Modern brasserie food and poolside barbecues art deco-style

Sitting proud above Bournemouth Bay, the Cumberland is a beautifully preserved specimen of British art deco, built in 1937. It rises in orderly geometric snowy-white tiers with covered balconies and a sign in elegant period lettering, and retains all its key features inside, with judiciously done recent additions. The Mirabelle Restaurant offers standard hotel cuisine with accompaniment from a grand piano as white as the building itself, while a more obviously contemporary menu is the drill in the Ventana Grand Café, which opens on to a swimming-pool with lido seating, where barbecues and cocktails are the order of many a summer day. Otherwise, expect lively brasserie dishes like salmon fishcake with spinach and sorrel sauce, followed by braised oxtail with champ and cabbage cooked with bacon and cumin, or the house fish pie with a portion of garlic soda-bread. Gourmet burgers won't lack for takers, and nor will the likes of sherry-lashed, Swiss roll-based trifle to finish. Cheese plates show off Dorset's finest. Steak nights and Fish Fridays help to keep the crowds rolling in.

Chef Mateusz Nowatkowski **Owner** Kevin Wood **Seats** 90, Pr/dining room 40 **Times** 12-10 Closed 25 Dec, L 26 Dec, D 31 Dec All-day dining **Prices** Fixed L 2 course £9.95-£19.95, Fixed D 3 course £19.95-£39.95, Starter £4.95-£7.95, Main £9.95-£23.95, Dessert £4.95-£6.95, Service optional **Wines** 4 bottles over £30, 24 bottles under £30, 8 by glass **Parking** 55, On street **Notes** Afternoon tea £12.95, Sunday L £11.95-£18.95, Vegetarian available, Children welcome

The Green House

◎ Modern British

tel: 01202 498900 **4 Grove Rd BH1 3AX**
email: info@thegreenhousehotel.com web: www.thegreenhousehotel.co.uk
dir: *Phone for directions*

Resourceful cooking built on eco-friendly produce

'The greenest hotel in the UK,' claims The Green House, a striking-looking, centrally located property converted and run on sustainable principles. There are beehives on the roof, and the Arbor (Latin for 'tree' to underline its green credentials) Restaurant deals in only organic, Fair Trade and farm-assured, mostly local produce. The seasonally-changing menu might open with Moroccan-spiced chicken wings with couscous studded with apricots, or crab mousse with cauliflower purée topped by zesty caper and tomato salsa. Main courses can be as familiar as beer-battered fish with chips and tartare sauce, and shepherd's pie to accompany slowly braised lamb shoulder, the scope extended by crisp-skinned fillet of sea bream with a spicy chilli-based sauce and saffron potatoes. Local hand-made cheeses, accompanied by home-cooked biscuits and chutney, are a savoury alternative to puddings like summer berry soup with creamy strawberry parfait combined with meringue.

Chef Andrew Hilton **Seats** 50, Pr/dining room 50 **Times** 8am-9.30pm **Prices** Prices not confirmed **Wines** **Parking** 30 **Notes** Sun Jazz L 4 course £22.50, Sunday L, Vegetarian available, Children welcome

Hermitage Hotel

◎ Modern British

tel: 01202 557363 **Exeter Rd BH2 5AH**
email: info@hermitage-hotel.co.uk web: www.hermitage-hotel.co.uk
dir: *Follow A338 (Ringwood-Bournemouth) & signs to pier, beach & BIC. Hotel directly opposite*

Seafront hotel with ambitious and thoughtful cooking

The Hermitage couldn't be in a better location, opposite the beach and pier and a few minutes from the centre. Its restaurant is a large, high-ceilinged room with white linen on properly laid tables where service is on the correct side, with staff formally attired. The interesting menus offer variety aplenty, as they must with residents eating here perhaps every evening. Starters are along the lines of seared scallops with chorizo, cauliflower purée and minted pea dressing, Main courses include steaks, seared duck breast with beetroot jus, fondant potato and wilted spinach, or whole Dover sole. Flavour combinations are straightforward and effective, seen in potted ham hock cut by piccalilli and a pickled duck egg, and crisp-skinned pan-fried fillet of bream in chive butter accompanied by clams and mussels, confit tomatoes and new potatoes. Puddings don't disappoint either: go for clementine and honeycomb parfait with caramelised orange, or even crêpe Suzette.

Times 6-9 Closed L Mon-Sat

Menzies Hotels Bournemouth / Carlton

◎ Traditional & Modern British

tel: 01202 552011 **East Overcliff BH1 3DN**
email: carlton@menzieshotels.co.uk web: www.menzieshotels.co.uk
dir: *M3/M27, follow A338 (Bournemouth). Follow signs to town centre & East Overcliff. Hotel is on seafront*

Sea views and classical cooking

This traditional hotel makes the most of its spectacular location on Bournemouth's East Cliff. The dining room has fab views over the outdoor pool and decking area to the sea beyond, and when the sun shines you might even forget you're in the UK. In Frederick's restaurant, with its high ceilings adorned with chandeliers and swag drapes, a formal dress code applies, which certainly helps maintain that sense of grandeur. Unfussy, classical food is what to expect; smoked haddock and chive ravioli, for example, with a mussel and vegetable broth, or chicken, basil and mint terrine with home-made chutney. Next up, best end of English lamb is served pink with goats' cheese-glazed dauphinoise potatoes and seasonal greens, with chocolate and coffee layer mousse with roasted hazelnut ganache a star turn for dessert.

Chef Richard Allsopp **Owner** Menzies Hotels **Seats** 120, Pr/dining room 180 **Times** 12.30-2/7-9.45 **Prices** Service optional **Wines** 8 by glass **Parking** 76 **Notes** Sunday L fr £16.95, Vegetarian available, Children welcome

What makes a 5-Rosette restaurant?
See page 9

The Print Room & Ink Bar & Brasserie

◉◉ Classic Brasserie

tel: 01202 789669 **Richmond Hill BH2 6HH**
email: info@theprintroom-bournemouth.co.uk **web:** www.theprintroom-bournemouth.co.uk
dir: *Just off town centre in Daily Echo newspaper building. Albert Rd off Richmond Hill*

Cosmopolitan menu in a magnificent art deco venue

The impressive art deco premises of the Daily Echo building make a setting of considerable grandeur for this vast brasserie, cafe and bar. Black-and-white chequerboard floors, maple booths, mirrors, Swarovski chandeliers and black lacquer tables all feed into the Depression-era feel – not that there's anything remotely downbeat about this operation: there's something going on all day here, kicking off with breakfast in the Ink Bar for early birds, until The Print Room takes over with its buzzy brasserie cooking. Modern European ideas appear alongside British classics on a wide-ranging menu built on plenty of local materials. Start inventively with pan-fried scallops with diced chorizo and Bloody Mary butter, ahead of pan-seared free-range chicken breast teamed with sautéed potatoes and pancetta, and white wine and tarragon cream sauce. Elsewhere, a fillet of sea bass might get more exotic treatment with the addition of shiitaki mushrooms, baby sweetcorn, pak choi, bean shoots and an Asian broth. To finish, a well-made, correctly wobbly pannacotta is served with poached figs.

Chef Nick Hewitt **Owner** Print Room Dorset Ltd **Seats** 120, Pr/dining room 22 **Times** 12-3/6-11 Closed 26 Dec, D Sun **Prices** Fixed L 2 course £11.95, Fixed D 3 course £14.95, Starter £4.25-£10.95, Main £8.95-£24.95, Dessert £4.95-£9.50, Service optional **Wines** 18 bottles over £30, 29 bottles under £30, 12 by glass **Parking** NCP - 100yds **Notes** Pre-theatre menu available, Sunday L £10.95, Vegetarian available, Children welcome

Rock Restaurant

◉ Modern British, European v

tel: 01202 765696 **Landseer Rd, Westbourne BH4 9EH**
email: westbourne@rockrestaurants.co.uk
dir: *Exit Wessex Way at County Gates rdbt, follow signs to Westbourne*

Modern British dining in an old Methodist church

A former Methodist church with a Tesco Express on the ground floor and a restaurant above is a rather unusual combination, but so it is here in classy Westbourne. Head up the winding staircase to the first floor and enter Rock to be greeted by the sight of a beautiful stained-glass window plus several other original features of the 18th-century church, such as antique oak panelling and a vaulted ceiling. Providing further visual stimulation is a theatre-kitchen, where you can watch head chef Nick Atkins at work crafting top-notch local and seasonal ingredients into some classics of the modern British idiom, such as plump and juicy seared scallops with pork belly, celeriac purée and apple caramel to start. Main course could be something as simple as a home-made burger in a brioche bun with roasted pepper dressing and all the trimmings, or perhaps a comfort food dish of unctuous slow-cooked featherblade of Dorset beef with a smooth horseradish mash, Savoy cabbage and butter-poached carrots.

Chef Nick Atkins **Owner** Nick Atkins **Seats** 80, Pr/dining room 12 **Times** 12-2.30/6.30-9.30 Closed 25 Dec **Prices** Fixed L 2 course £15, Starter £5.50-£9, Main £11.50-£27.50, Dessert £4-£7, Service optional **Wines** 6 bottles over £30, 6 bottles under £30, 6 by glass **Parking** 100 mtrs away **Notes** High tea £12, Children welcome

West Beach

◉ Modern, Seafood

tel: 01202 587785 **Pier Approach BH2 5AA**
email: enquiry@west-beach.co.uk **web:** www.west-beach.co.uk
dir: *100yds W of the pier*

Sophisticated seafood dishes bang on the beach

For a fish restaurant, the setting is pure gold: it's virtually on the beach, with a sunny terrace even closer to the waves. The full-length glass frontage makes the most of the views, throwing plenty of light into the restaurant whatever the Dorset weather throws your way. It is a bright, modern space of stripped-out beachcomber-chic pastel shades and bleached wood, dealing in spanking fresh seafood simply cooked along modern lines by the chefs beavering away in the open-to-view kitchen. You might set out with roast Portland scallops with carrot purée, pickled raisins and coriander cress, then go for wild sea bass matched creatively with rosemary polenta, chestnut purée, cavolo nero, mushroom duxelles and red wine shallot jus. There are meat dishes if you must – confit pork belly with cabbage and bacon, hash brown, poached apples and Calvados jus, say – and for dessert, perhaps Eton Mess and pannacotta.

Chef Nick Hewitt **Owner** Andrew Price **Seats** 90 **Times** 12-3.30/6-10 Closed 25 Dec, D 26 Dec, 1 Jan **Prices** Starter £6.50-£10.50, Main £12.50-£20, Service optional **Wines** 27 bottles over £30, 42 bottles under £30, 26 by glass **Parking** NCP 2 mins **Notes** Tasting menu available, Pre-theatre 2 course £14.95, Sunday L fr £13, Vegetarian available, Children welcome

 Map 4 SY49

Riverside Restaurant

◉ Seafood, International

tel: 01308 422011 **West Bay DT6 4EZ**
email: neilriverside@hotmail.com **web:** www.riverside-restaurant.com
dir: A35 Bridport ring road, turn to West Bay at Crown rdbt

Long-standing harbourside fish restaurant

When the Watsons acquired this harbourside restaurant no less than 50 years ago, they were continuing a local tradition that stretched back to Victorian days, of serving pearly-fresh fish and seafood from the day's catch with views over the sea. In the 19th century, a humble awning was extended over the spot, whereas now you sit in refreshing splendour behind picture windows, the better to enjoy the prospect. The cooking keeps things as simple as the prime materials require: traditional fish soup with garlicky rouille, grilled lemon sole seasoned with sea salt and lemon, brill in sorrel sauce, whole plaice on the bone. There are occasional forays into the modern cookbook, for seared scallops with truffled celeriac purée, or turbot with banana shallots, mushrooms and pancetta, and these are perfectly sound, but hardly anything beats a seafood platter. Not a fish fan? Then try the crackled pork belly with smoked garlic mash in red wine. Finish with apricot pannacotta and shortbread.

Chef A Shaw, E Webb, N Larcombe **Owner** Mr & Mrs A Watson **Seats** 80, Pr/dining room 30 **Times** 12-2.30/6.30-9 Closed 30 Nov-12 Feb, Mon (ex BHs), D Sun **Prices** Fixed L 2 course £20, Starter £4.95-£10.95, Main £12.95-£25.75, Dessert £4.95-£7.95, Service optional **Wines** 10 bottles over £30, 45 bottles under £30, 12 by glass **Parking** Public car park 40 mtrs **Notes** Sunday L, Vegetarian available, Children welcome

Map 5 SZ19

Captain's Club Hotel and Spa

◎◎ Modern European

tel: 01202 475111 **Wick Ferry, Wick Ln BH23 1HU**
email: enquiries@captainsclubhotel.com **web:** www.captainsclubhotel.com
dir: Hotel just off Christchurch High St, towards Christchurch Quay

Contemporary spa hotel with appealing riverside restaurant

Any skipper should be happy to hang his hat at the Captain's Club, with its position at Christchurch Quay on the River Stour and the seafood offered up on the menu. Whatever your maritime credentials, though, this modern hotel has bags of appeal, including a delicious spa, classy accommodation, and an impressive restaurant. With floor-to-ceiling windows, live music in the piano bar and a large terrace for when the weather is kind, there is a lot of 21st-century style hereabouts. There's an all-day menu which can sort you out with everything from sandwiches (crab,

maybe) to omelette Arnold Bennett, or rib-eye steak with all the expected trimmings. But for lunch and dinner there's also crustacea such as whole crab with lemon and herb mayo, fish main courses such as halibut with crab and asparagus salad and fennel purée, and meaty mains like duck breast served with the confit leg meat mixed into bubble-and-squeak, plus a fried duck egg. Finish with warm spotted dick with custard and berry jam.

Chef Andrew Gault **Owner** Platinum One Hotels Ltd **Seats** 100, Pr/dining room 120 **Times** 11.30-10 All-day dining **Prices** Fixed L 3 course fr £25, Fixed D 2 course fr £35, Starter £6-£12, Main £15-£27, Dessert £3-£10, Service optional **Wines** 64 bottles over £30, 40 bottles under £30, 12 by glass **Parking** 41 **Notes** Sunday L, Vegetarian available, Children welcome

Crooked Beam Restaurant

◉ Modern British

tel: 01202 499362 **Jumpers Corner, 2 The Grove BH23 2HA**
email: info@crookedbeam.co.uk
dir: Situated on corner of Barrack Rd A35 and The Grove

Friendly, family-run restaurant with well-judged menu

'Mind your head' says a sign on the beams, but the slight risk of a bump is a small price to pay for the experience of eating at this delightful little restaurant. The 300-year old building wears its antiquity well and is suitably cosy and traditional within. Husband-and-wife-team Simon and Vicki Hallam run the show-he in the kitchen, she out front-and they know what their customers want. Good quality produce is at the heart of things, with the menu following a broad and crowd-pleasing path. Potted crab, for example, comes with dressed leaves and walnut and raisin toast, and chicken liver and pistachio parfait with a nicely-judged plum chutney and toasted brioche. Main course might deliver sea bass marinated in chilli and coriander served with a warm green bean and tomato salad, and to finish, perhaps a treacle tart with raspberry coulis and Calvados cream.

Times 12-2/7-11 Closed Mon, L Sat, D Sun

The Jetty

◉◉ Modern British

tel: 01202 400950 **95 Mudeford BH23 3NT**
email: dine@thejetty.co.uk
dir: A35/A337 to Highcliffe. Right at rdbt, hotel & restaurant 1.5m on left

Sleek modish venue with sharp, unfussy cooking

If it's a winning waterside location you're after, head on over to The Jetty in the grounds of the Christchurch Harbour hotel. It sits in a glorious position overlooking the water to Mudeford Quay, and the building is a bit of a looker itself: a contemporary carbon-neutral construction built of wood and glass. Every customer is guaranteed the view through the floor-to-ceiling windows, but the terrace has got to be the first choice when the weather is warm. The kitchen is under the auspices of Alex Aitken, a man who knows how to let the ingredients do the talking; the provenance of what appears on the plate is taken very seriously indeed. Start, perhaps, with a Scotch egg, but with a difference: the egg is wrapped in salt-cod brandade and fried in tempura batter. Seafood is king here, so follow on with a fine piece of halibut served with hand-dived Weymouth scallops and tempura Poole Bay rock oyster. There are good meat offerings, too, such as rib-eye steak with hand-cut chips, watercress and béarnaise sauce.

Chef Alex Aitken **Owner** Christchurch Restaurants Ltd **Seats** 70 **Times** 12-2.30/6-10 **Prices** Fixed L 2 course £17.95, Fixed D 3 course fr £21.95, Tasting menu fr £55, Starter £7.50-£15, Main £16.95-£28.50, Dessert £5.95-£7.95 **Wines** 61 bottles over £30, 23 bottles under £30, 24 by glass **Parking** 40 **Notes** Sunday L £24.50-£29.50, Vegetarian available, Children welcome

The Lord Bute & Restaurant

British, Mediterranean

tel: 01425 278884 **179-185 Lymington Rd, Highcliffe BH23 4JS**
email: mail@lordbute.co.uk **web:** www.lordbute.co.uk
dir: Follow A337 to Lymington, opposite St Mark's churchyard in Highcliffe

Consistent cooking in a former castle entrance lodge

What is now an eye-catching boutique hotel was once the entrance lodge to Highcliffe Castle, for a year or two in the 1760s serving as home to the eponymous Lord Bute, one of Britain's lesser-known prime ministers. It's superbly placed for access to the golden beaches and blustery clifftops of the Dorset coast, and has been remade in delightful modern style within, its classical dining room boasts an orangery extension, and on-the-ball, well-drilled service to boot. A loyal local following can't resist the jazz nights, and the long residency of chef Kevin Brown has ensured continuity in the cooking. A broad range of menu choice encompasses modern classic offerings such as seared scallops with black pudding and white bean purée in beurre blanc, herb-crusted lamb loin with asparagus, wilted spinach and a tarragon-spiked red wine sauce, lemon-coated cod in saffron seafood broth, and well-executed passion fruit pannacotta with matching sorbet in caramel sauce.

Chef Kevin Brown **Owner** S Box & G Payne **Seats** 95 **Times** 12-2/7-9.30 Closed Mon, L Sat, D Sun **Prices** Fixed L 2 course £16.95, Fixed D 3 course £25, Starter £6-£10, Main £16-£29.50, Dessert £7.25-£10.25, Service optional **Wines** 13 bottles over £30, 35 bottles under £30, 10 by glass **Parking** 50 **Notes** Sunday L, Vegetarian available, Children welcome

Splinters Restaurant

Modern International

tel: 01202 483454 **12 Church St BH23 1BW**
email: eating@splinters.uk.com **web:** www.splinters.uk.com
dir: Directly in front of Priory gates

Superior cooking in lively neighbourhood restaurant

With over half a century of service now under its belt, Splinters boasts an enviable local following among Christchurch's foodies. The jaunty green frontage stands out on the cobbled street leading to the Priory, and takes its name from the work-related injuries suffered by the carpenters who built the cosy booth seating within. It is a welcoming family-run set-up with a bar-lounge for aperitifs and canapés, and a warren of appealing dining rooms with nooks and corners for a romantic soirée. The kitchen cuts no corners, making everything in house from top-class local materials. The result is a crowd-pleasing repertoire of broadly modern European ideas, starting, perhaps, with a chicken liver parfait served with orange marmalade and toasted brioche. Main course could be honey-roasted duck breast with dauphinoise potato and cranberry compôte, with walnut and caramel tart with vanilla ice cream for pud.

Chef Paul Putt **Owner** Paul & Agnes Putt **Seats** 42, Pr/dining room 30 **Times** 11-2/6.30-10 Closed 26 Dec, 1-10 Jan, Sun-Mon (exc Sun BHs May & Aug) **Prices** Fixed L 2 course fr £13.50, Fixed D 3 course fr £26.50, Service optional **Wines** 30 bottles over £30, 50 bottles under £30, 5 by glass **Parking** Priory car park **Notes** ALC 2/3 course £31.95/£38.95, Vegetarian available, Children welcome

Upper Deck Bar & Restaurant

Modern British

tel: 01202 400954 **Christchurch Harbour Hotel, 95 Mudeford BH23 3NT**
email: christchurch.restaurant@harbourhotels.co.uk
web: www.christchurch-harbour-hotel.co.uk/upper-deck
dir: A35/A337 to Highcliffe. Right at rdbt, hotel & restaurant 1.5m on left

Chic waterside restaurant for local produce and stunning views

Whichever of the two restaurants at this classy hotel you choose, good views over the water are guaranteed, as is a fine showing of regional produce. Chef-patron Alex Aitken is the man behind it all and you are in safe hands with his mantra keeping everything fresh, seasonal and local, The Upper Deck is pretty swanky, featuring a sleek and contemporary bar and an upmarket seaside vibe, or there's the terrace for fine days. It's a quality set up. The cooking takes a modern British route through contemporary tastes, so there are French and British preparations, a few Asian flavours here and there, and, given the setting, plenty of locally-landed fish. Terrine of ham hock, lentils and game comes in the fashionable company of piccalilli to cut through the richness, or there might be Thai fish broth packed with catch of the day. Main course fillet of lemon sole stuffed salmon mousse and served with mashed potato is one way to follow on, or there are steaks cooked on the grill, and crème brûlée for dessert.

Chef Alex Aitken **Owner** Harbour Hotels Group **Seats** 95, Pr/dining room 20 **Times** 12-2.30/6-9.45 **Prices** Fixed L 2 course fr £15.50, Fixed D 3 course fr £19.95, Tasting menu fr £45, Starter £7.50-£11.50, Main £14.50-£24.95, Dessert £5-£7.95 **Wines** 30 bottles over £30, 30 bottles under £30, 12 by glass **Parking** 100 **Notes** Sunday L, Vegetarian available, Children welcome

CORFE CASTLE
Map 4 SY98

Mortons House Hotel

Modern British

tel: 01929 480988 **East St BH20 5EE**
email: stay@mortonshouse.co.uk **web:** www.mortonshouse.co.uk
dir: In village centre on A351

Confident cooking in an Elizabethan manor

There's a lot of history around these parts — Corfe Castle itself had the job of guarding the main route through the Purbeck Hills — and Mortons House has been around to bear witness to over 400 years of it. Built in 1590 or so, these days it's a hotel and restaurant with a good deal of period charm and character. The interior has been done up to meet contemporary needs without affecting the historic integrity of the building. The restaurant is a suitably traditional space with well-dressed tables and a menu that is most definitely not stuck in the past. Start, perhaps, with butternut and sage ravioli with baby spinach and crispy pancetta, or Cornish red mullet with a watercress risotto and romesco dressing. There's a confidence and focus to the kitchen's output, which extends to main courses such as fillet of cod with braised Puy lentils and sautéed wild mushrooms, and fillet of local beef with smoked veal tongue, beetroot dauphinoise potatoes, pickled beetroot, parsnip purée and cavolo nero. For dessert, warm strawberry Bakewell tart with Dorset clotted ice cream ends things in fine style.

Chef Ed Firth **Owner** Mrs Woods, Mr & Mrs Clayton **Seats** 60, Pr/dining room 22 **Times** 12-1.45/7-9 **Prices** Fixed L 2 course £33, Fixed D 3 course £39.50, Starter £6-£11.50, Main £12-£25, Dessert £6.50-£8.50, Service optional **Wines** 17 bottles over £30, 25 bottles under £30, 6 by glass **Parking** 40 **Notes** Sunday L £11.95-£23.50, Vegetarian available, Children 5 yrs+

DORCHESTER
Map 4 SY69

Sienna

◎◎◎ – *see opposite*

EVERSHOT
Map 4 ST50

The Acorn Inn

◎ British

tel: 01935 83228 **28 Fore St DT2 0JW**
email: stay@acorn-inn.co.uk **web:** www.acorn-inn.co.uk
dir: *From A37 between Yeovil & Dorchester, follow Evershot & Holywell signs, 0.5m to inn*

Modern gastro-pub fare in Hardy country

In a pretty village at the heart of Hardy's Wessex, this 16th-century coaching inn is a gem, with a warm and welcoming bar (low ceiling, open fire, brick walls and its own snacky menu) and a stylishly cottagey restaurant with local artwork, antiques and Persian rugs. Scrupulously sourced ingredients bring on locally-smoked venison with classic celeriac remoulade, and Dorset cheddar and walnut soufflé with thyme butter and celery cream. Main courses cover a range of flavours, from chicken, mushroom and tarragon pie with spring onion mash, to a winter hotpot of venison served with caramelised onions and braised red cabbage. Fish might appear as pan-fried hake fillet with salsa verde, and among puddings may be almond tart with a poached pear and vanilla ice cream.

Times 12-2/7-9

George Albert Hotel

◎ Modern British

tel: 01935 483430 **Wardon Hill DT2 9PW**
email: enquiries@gahotel.co.uk **web:** www.georgealberthotel.co.uk
dir: *On A37 (between Yeovil & Dorchester). Adjacent to Southern Counties Shooting Ground*

Uncomplicated cooking in smart modern hotel

There's plenty of scope for working up an appetite at the George Albert since this smart modern hotel is handily placed for exploring the many attractions of Dorset. At its culinary heart is the Kings Restaurant, an expansive open-plan room kitted out in a neutral style, its well-spaced tables swathed in white linen, and tended by friendly, smartly-uniformed staff. The kitchen takes a modern approach to dishes built on good quality, often local, materials, and its strengths lie in the fact that it sticks to tried-and-tested themes – ham hock terrine with home-made piccalilli being a case in point, although you might equally opt to open with beetroot tarte Tatin with horseradish cream. Confit shoulder of Dorset lamb with mini shepherd's pie, pea purée, carrots and lamb jus could turn up for substantial satisfaction at main course stage, before it all concludes on an exotic note with passionfruit pannacotta, pineapple salsa and mango sauce.

Chef Andy Pike **Owner** G Crook & Sons **Seats** 40, Pr/dining room
Times 12-2.30/6.30-9 **Prices** Fixed L 2 course £14-£17.45, Fixed D 3 course £20.50-£23.95, Starter £6.50-£10, Main £19.95-£24.95, Dessert £6.50, Service optional **Wines** 10 bottles over £30, 21 bottles under £30, 14 by glass **Parking** 200 **Notes** Sunday L £5.45-£16.50, Vegetarian available, Children welcome

Summer Lodge Country House Hotel, Restaurant & Spa

◎◎◎ – *see opposite*

FARNHAM
Map 4 ST91

Museum Inn

◎◎ Modern, Traditional British **NEW**

tel: 01725 516261 **DT11 8DE**
email: enquiries@museuminn.co.uk **web:** www.museuminn.co.uk
dir: *12m S of Salisbury, 7m N of Blandford Forum on A354. Signed from A354 Salisbury Blandford Forum Rd*

Fine modern pub cooking in an extended Georgian inn

The celebrated archaeologist General Augustus Pitt Rivers acquired the 17th-century inn and extended it in the 1880s, to provide refreshments for visitors to his museum (which later decamped to Oxford). Standing in the midst of Cranborne Chase, it has a good mix of original and modern to it, with flagstones, alcoves and an endearing jumble of furniture offset by a more up-to-date look in the main dining room, where white walls and light wood tables lift the tone. Jenny Jones casts her net far into the southwest for fine regional produce, from which she constructs the most appealing kind of contemporary pub cooking. Start with a twice-baked soufflé of Blue Vinney and rocket, or scallops with a risotto of Devon crab, prior to venison with a fricassée of ceps in red wine sauce, or well-judged sea bream with cockles and crushed potatoes in saffron sauce. If it's classic pub food you're after, there are steaks and fish and chips on hand. Puddings include a distinctly fragrant tangerine pannacotta with berry and rosewater compôte and crumbled pistachios.

Chef Jenny Jones **Owner** Cirrus Inns **Seats** Pr/dining room **Times** 12-2/6.30-9.30 **Prices** Starter £5.95-£9.95, Main £11.50-£27.95, Dessert £5.95 **Wines** 40 bottles over £30, 24 bottles under £30, 18 by glass **Parking** 14 **Notes** Sunday L £11.95-£16.50, Vegetarian available, Children welcome

LYME REGIS
Map 4 SY39

The Mariners

◎ British, International

tel: 01297 442753 **Silver St DT7 3HS**
email: enquiries@hotellymeregis.co.uk **web:** www.hotellymeregis.co.uk
dir: *S onto B3261 from A35, on left opposite right turn to the Cobb*

Updated old coaching inn with local seafood and more

The former coaching inn dates back to the 17th century and looks the part with its pink-washed façade and period charm. It's looking spruce inside these days, made over with a contemporary finish that matches old and new with a keen eye. There are views from the back over the town and out to sea, which are particularly good from the garden filled with chunky wooden tables on which to sit and ponder. The restaurant with its light and bright feel is the setting for some breezy modern food with a good showing of local seafood. Among starters, for example, might be Lyme Bay scallops with crispy pancetta, butternut squash purée and watercress pesto, or go for an earthy dish of wild mushrooms on toasted brioche. Main course roasted Cornish hake is served with local crab fritters and shellfish paella, while a meaty main might be confit of Creedy Carver duck leg. Finish with a Baileys crème brûlée.

Chef Richard Reddaway, Steve Rainey **Owner** Jerry Ramsdale **Seats** 36 **Times** 12-2/6.30-9 Closed D 25 Dec **Prices** Fixed D 3 course £24.95-£34.95, Starter £4.50-£14.50, Main £9.50-£23.95, Dessert £5-£13.50, Service optional **Wines** 3 bottles over £30, 27 bottles under £30, 9 by glass **Parking** 20, Car park 200mtrs **Notes** Sunday L £9.50-£15.95, Vegetarian available, Children welcome

Sienna

DORCHESTER   Map 4 SY69

Modern British

tel: 01305 250022 **36 High West St DT1 1UP**
email: browns@siennarestaurant.co.uk
dir: *Near top of town rdbt in Dorchester*

Top-class flavour combinations in diminutive restaurant

This small-scale restaurant, uncluttered and plainly decorated, is run by a husband-and-wife double act, with Russell Brown at the stove and Elena running front-of-house with poise, charm and unobtrusive style. The limited number of covers – around 15 – is clearly an advantage, allowing Russell on concentrate on the details of every aspect of his cooking. His confident handling of fine produce, most from the West Country, and innate understanding of what works is apparent in all his dishes. Carefully chosen combinations harmonise effortlessly in terms of appearance as well as flavours and textures, and nothing is irrelevant. Outstanding breads and palate-pleasing canapés (perhaps goats' cheese mousse with truffle, a leek tartlet with superb pastry) set the standard of what will follow: deeply flavoured partridge and wild mushroom terrine with pickled grapes, say, simple-sounding white crabmeat with sweetcorn velouté, or playful 'egg on toast' with ham hock, watercress and mustard. There's no cheffy pretension here, with Russell's respect for his ingredients and pinpoint accuracy evident in well-balanced main courses that can range from fillet of hake with red wine sauce, celeriac and charred mushrooms, to full-on beef, beer and onions (sirloin, braised cheek, onion purée, shallot rings and beer sauce). Desserts are momentous, judging by coffee pannacotta with whisky cream, honeycomb and orange, and a deconstructed sundae consisting of blackberry mousse, apple purée, spiced blackberry jelly, meringue, clotted cream ice cream and red wine jelly, a synergetic combination. All is not over: petits fours with coffee are well up to speed. The tasting menu, with wine recommendations, is worth investigating, and the lunch menu may be considered a snip.

Chef Russell Brown **Owner** Russell & Eléna Brown **Seats** 15 **Times** 12.30-2/7-9 Closed 2 wks Feb/Mar, 2 wks Sep/Oct, Sun-Mon, L Tue **Prices** Fixed L 2 course £25.50, Fixed D 3 course £45, Tasting menu £65, Service optional **Wines** 24 bottles over £30, 15 bottles under £30, 7 by glass **Parking** On street, top of town car park **Notes** Tasting menu 7 course, Vegetarian available, No children

Summer Lodge Country House Hotel, Restaurant & Spa

EVERSHOT   Map 4 ST50

Modern British 🍷 NOTABLE WINE LIST

tel: 01935 482000 **Fore St DT2 0JR**
email: summerlodge@rchmail.com **web:** www.summerlodgehotel.com
dir: *1m W of A37 halfway between Dorchester & Yeovil*

Assured modish cooking in peaceful surroundings

Tucked away in the pastoral heart of Dorset, this country house spa hotel is a hidden gem. Thomas Hardy gave this green and pleasant undulating land an alternative name –Wessex – but the literary giant's talents as an architect are less known, even though he had a hand in designing the Victorian extension to this pretty Georgian dower house. Nowadays it is a luxuriously low-key bolt-hole with a soft-focus take on interior decor that offers a gentle antidote to the harsh modern minimalism favoured by many made-over country houses. With its swagged curtains and elegantly dressed tables, the split-level restaurant exudes the feel of an English rose garden brought indoors, while a light-flooded conservatory extension affords views of the real thing in the four-acre walled garden. The kitchen shows its classical pedigree, injecting flourishes of contemporary flair and refined presentation into the time-honoured country-house idiom. Menus are shot through with superb Dorset produce from the off – perhaps Portland crab with cucumber jelly, yoghurt, chilli, lime and mint, or Lyme Bay scallops with red lentil dhal, roasted cauliflower purée and onion bhaji crisp, to get the ball rolling. Main course might star Dorset lamb-perfectly-timed roast loin paired with a shepherd's pie of braised shoulder, with Savoy cabbage and rosemary jus. Fish, too, is handled deftly-perhaps turbot fillet with wild mushrooms, glazed baby onions, home-cured bacon and red wine jus. The formidable technical abilities of the kitchen team continue to shine in desserts such as chocolate mousse (made with Valrhona's fine products) with passionfruit crémeux and sorbet, or cheese lovers could find nirvana in the trolley loaded with over 20 West Country artisan cheeses. Service from the slick and professional team is a highlight of any visit, including the excellent sommelier on hand to guide you through the top-notch wine list.

Chef Steven Titman **Owner** Bea Tollman **Seats** 60, Pr/dining room 20 **Times** 12-2.30/7-9.30 **Prices** Fixed L 2 course £23, Fixed D 3 course £45, Tasting menu £70, Starter £19, Main £20-£28, Dessert £11-£13, Service optional **Wines** 1450 bottles over £30, 10 bottles under £30, 25 by glass **Parking** 60 **Notes** Tasting menu 8 course available with/out wines, Sunday L £37.50, Vegetarian available, Children welcome

MAIDEN NEWTON   Map 4 SY59

Le Petit Canard

Modern British, French

tel: 01300 320536 **Dorchester Rd DT2 OBE**
email: craigs@le-petit-canard.co.uk **web:** www.le-petit-canard.co.uk
dir: *In centre of Maiden Newton, 8m W of Dorchester*

Honest, accomplished cooking in pretty village restaurant

The location in a cottagey terrace building – once a coaching inn by all accounts – and the traditional, homely decor is not exactly the cutting-edge of restaurant design, but no matter, for this is a delightful place run with passion by Gerry and Cathy Craig. The tables are neatly laid with linen cloths and topped with flowers and candles, and the original features of the property – wooden beams and some exposed stonework-add to its charm. Gerry's cooking does not try to reinvent the wheel, but neither is it stuck in the past. Seared scallops with celeriac purée, for example, is a gently modish construction, or go for the bresaola with rocket, olive oil and parmesan shavings. Main course roast breast of duck comes with a plum and ginger sauce, and loin fillet of local wild venison with pear chutney, while dessert might be a textbook crème brûlée.

Chef Gerry Craig **Owner** Gerry & Cathy Craig **Seats** 28 **Times** 12-2/7-9 Closed Mon, L all week (ex 1st & 3rd Sun in month), D Sun **Prices** Fixed D 3 course £34-£36.95, Service optional **Wines** 4 bottles over £30, 26 bottles under £30, 6 by glass **Parking** On street/village car park **Notes** Sunday L £25, Vegetarian available, No children

Read our interview with chef Michael Caines on page 29

What makes a 3-Rosette restaurant? See page 9

POOLE   Map 4 SZ09

Harbour Heights

Modern European

tel: 0845 337 1550 & 01202 707272 **73 Haven Rd, Sandbanks BH13 7LW**
email: enquiries@harbourheights.net **web:** www.fjbhotels.co.uk
dir: *From A338 follow signs to Sandbanks, restaurant on left past Canford Cliffs*

Spectacular views and modern bistro food

Breathtaking views over Poole Harbour come as standard at this elegant, revamped, 1920s art deco hotel. You can take in the scene either sitting on the south-facing decked terrace whilst sipping a pre-dinner cocktail or a glass of wine, or from the open-plan bistro with its floor-to-ceiling windows. With a new French chef at the helm, you can expect a menu of modern European food with an emphasis on what's local and in season, including fish landed at Poole Quay which is displayed on the fresh fish counter in the restaurant. So you might start with a meaty first course of beef oxtail ravioli with braised onion and consommé, moving on to perfectly cooked lemon sole with a supporting cast of smoked prawn butter, braised Puy lentils, cabbage and sweet-and-sour onions. A rich chocolate marquise, baby poached pear and fromage blanc sorbet is not for the faint-hearted at dessert, or why not try bay leaf pannacotta, passionfruit and crackle crystals?

Chef Loic Gratadoux **Owner** FJB Hotels **Seats** 90, Pr/dining room 120 **Times** 12-2.30/7-9.30 **Prices** Fixed L 2 course £16.50, Fixed D 3 course £29.50, Starter £8-£12.50, Main £15-£25, Dessert £6.50-£9 **Wines** 90 bottles over £30, 48 bottles under £30, 17 by glass **Parking** 50 **Notes** Chef's table, Sunday L £22.50-£29, Vegetarian available, Children welcome

The Haven

 Modern British, International v

tel: 01202 707333 **161 Banks Rd, Sandbanks BH13 7QL**
email: reservations@havenhotel.co.uk **web:** www.havenhotel.co.uk
dir: Follow signs to Sandbanks Peninsula; hotel next to Swanage ferry departure point

Delightful Poole Bay views and confident modern cooking

Dating from the 1880s, this large white hotel is right on the water's edge at the southern end of Sandbanks. La Roche restaurant considerately has its tables tiered, giving more than just window seats a sea view; the room has the feel of a relaxed brasserie, helped along by friendly but informed staff, and two large fish tanks divert the eye. The kitchen buys the best regional produce for the time of year and devises menus with much of interest without confining itself to the fruits of the sea. Start, for instance, with nicely wobbly pannacotta subtly hinting of ginger, with toasted pumpkin seeds, a parmesan crackle and butternut squash purée adding textural and flavour contrasts. Dishes are never too elaborate: a pressing of duck with apple chutney, say, then a well thought out main course of pavé of salmon with curried lentils, salt-cod fritters and raita, or sautéed calves' liver with potato purée and onion sauce. Crème brûlée with banana and passionfruit sorbet and poached pineapple is an ambitious, effective pudding.

Chef Jason Hornbuckle **Owner** Mr J Butterworth **Seats** 80, Pr/dining room 156
Times 12-2.30/7-9.30 **Prices** Fixed D 3 course £29.50, Service optional **Wines** 11 by glass **Parking** 90 **Notes** Sunday L, Children welcome

Hotel du Vin Poole

 Modern British, French

tel: 0844 7489265 **Mansion House, Thames St BH15 1JN**
web: www.hotelduvin.co.uk
dir: A350 into town centre follow signs to Channel Ferry/Poole Quay, left at bridge, 1st left is Thames St

Bistro cooking in an elegant Georgian house

The elegant Virginia-creeper-clad Georgian mansion sits just off the old quayside. In a former life it was the Mansion House hotel, until 2008, when it got the HdV trademark makeover, a winning formula that takes interesting old buildings and reworks them with a smartly-casual wine and bistro food-oriented focus. The Poole outpost offers a smart bar, wine cellar and wine-tasting room, plus the open-plan bistro at its beating heart, which follows the familiar style of banquette seating, unclothed wooden tables, and sunny ochre-washed walls hung with wine-related images. It's an amenable setting for good bistro food backed by an impressive, French-orientated wine list, while the walled outdoor terrace is a major pull on balmy days. Expect good honest cooking that respects the quality of the raw materials – a moules marinière starter is as good as anything you'll find across the nearby Channel. Elsewhere, there's steak tartare or dressed crab with walnut toast, while main course brings seared salmon with warm salad Niçoise and Lyonnaise potatoes.

Chef Darren Rockett **Owner** Hotel Du Vin/SLK **Seats** 85, Pr/dining room 36
Times 12.30-2/5.30-10.30 **Prices** Fixed L 2 course £16.95, Fixed D 3 course £19.95, Starter £3.45-£11.95, Main £12.50-£22.50, Dessert £6.95-£8.50 **Wines** 10 by glass **Parking** 300 **Notes** Pre-theatre 1 course, wine & coffee £12.95, Sunday L £24.95-£34.95, Vegetarian available, Children welcome

---

PORTLAND   Map 4 SY67

The Bluefish Restaurant

◎ Modern

tel: 01305 822991 **15-17a Chiswell DT5 1AN**
email: thebluefish@tesco.net
dir: Take A354 by Chesil Bank, off Victoria Square in Portland, over rdbt towards Chesil Beach, next to 72hr free car park

Well-judged Mediterranean-inspired cooking next to Chesil Beach

On the ground floor of a 400-year-old Portland stone building wedged between Portland Harbour and Chesil Beach, the Bluefish is the epitome of a welcoming neighbourhood eatery. You can sum up this charming operation in two words: simple and unpretentious. Bare, wooden tables and exposed stone walls lit by ceiling spots and tealights conjure a magical setting like a mermaid's cave, while relaxed staff do their bit to foster an unbuttoned ambience. Obviously, food is what you're here for, and the place delivers gutsy, full-flavoured Mediterranean-accented bistro dishes with a strong connection to the sea. Kick off with pan-fried local scallops with sweetcorn purée, black pudding and apple jus. To follow, try grilled mackerel with baked sweet potato, lime pickle, radish and ginger, or there could be a fish and meat pairing of olive oil-poached sea bass with Serrano ham, local faggots, beetroot and port jus. For pudding, there's vanilla pannacotta with prunes and Armagnac.

Times 12-3/7-9 Closed Xmas, Mon-Tue, L Wed-Fri, D Sun (in winter)

POWERSTOCK   Map 4 SY59

Three Horseshoes Inn

◎ British

tel: 01308 485328 **DT6 3TF**
email: threehorseshoespowerstock@live.co.uk **web:** www.threeshoesdorset.co.uk
dir: 3m from Bridport. Powerstock signed off A3066 Bridport to Beaminster

Proper pub, proper pub food

You wouldn't normally go out of your way for Scotch eggs and burgers, but this classic Dorset village inn has elevated pubby classics to a higher plane – that burger being made of Dorset veal and bone marrow, and teamed with barbecue pulled short rib, celeriac slaw and triple-cooked chips. But first, serpentine, skinny lanes have to be negotiated before you arrive to a warm greeting and a fine pint of Palmers ale in the convivial bar – take a table here if you prefer the cheerful country pub vibe, or move through to the cosy restaurant decorated with works (for sale) by local artists, or on fine days, head outside for valley views from the terrace and lovely garden. The kitchen is driven by an enthusiasm for local produce and working with the seasons, and lines up a cast of ideas we'd all like to see in our local: wild boar Scotch egg (a quail's egg, that is) with a venison sausage roll, crispy pig's ears and pickles is a starter that should be on every pub's menu, while mains bring on a proper pub pie – a deep, pastry-topped dish of beef chunks in a rich sauce of Guinness and oysters, served with clotted cream mash, and honey-roasted parsnips and carrots.

Chef Karl Bashford **Owner** Mr K Bashford, Ms Prekopova **Seats** 60
Times 12-2.30/6.30-9.30 Closed L Mon, D Mon (winter only) **Prices** Starter £6-£9, Main £10-£20, Dessert £6, Service optional **Wines** 8 bottles under £30, 8 by glass **Parking** 20 **Notes** Sunday L, Vegetarian available, Children welcome

La Fleur de Lys Restaurant with Rooms

◎◎ Modern French

tel: 01747 853717 **Bleke St SP7 8AW**
email: info@lafleurdelys.co.uk **web:** www.lafleurdelys.co.uk
dir: Junct A350/A30

West Country cooking in a former boarding-school

The former girls' boarding-school that the owners took on in 1991 needed a lot of remedial attention, and has become one of the area's favourite dining destinations, a creeper-covered restaurant with rooms that has something of the feel of a country inn. Smartly linened-up tables are the order in the dining room, where lemon-yellow and exposed stone walls produce a relaxing atmosphere. Fixed-price menus offer an accommodating range of choice, with West Country supplies to the fore. Start with sautéed scallops in zesty lime crumb, served with a cherry tomato and spring onion salad dressed in yoghurt, lime and chilli, or a bowl of hearty broth composed of wild mushrooms, pearl barley and leeks. The main business arrives in the form of hake with king prawns and samphire in coriander sauce, or breast of guinea-fowl with roast parsnips, sauced with grain mustard. Dessert could be as simple as a seasonal cornucopia of strawberries and raspberries with clotted cream, or as 'high-falutin' as a dark chocolate box filled with fudge ice cream, macerated orange and candied nuts in Amaretto sauce.

Chef D Shepherd, M Preston **Owner** D Shepherd, M Preston & M Griffin **Seats** 45, Pr/dining room 12 **Times** 12-2.30/7-10.30 Closed 3 wks Jan, L Mon-Tue, D Sun **Prices** Fixed D 3 course £34-£38, Service optional **Wines** 50 bottles over £30, 50 bottles under £30, 8 by glass **Parking** 10 **Notes** Sunday L, Vegetarian available, Children welcome

Eastbury Hotel

◎◎ Modern British

tel: 01935 813131 **Long St DT9 3BY**
email: enquiries@theeastburyhotel.com **web:** www.theeastburyhotel.co.uk
dir: 5m E of Yeovil, follow brown signs for Eastbury Hotel

Contemporary cooking in an attractive Dorset townhouse

Life changes down a gear or two to a soothingly sedate pace at this boutique Georgian townhouse bolt-hole set in an acre of delightful walled gardens. Hands-on owners lend the operation a family-run feel, while cheery, attentive staff play their part in ensuring friendly and personal service in the dining room, which splits between the main building and a conservatory-style extension. The view looks out over a kitchen garden that does its bit in providing fresh seasonal ingredients, a commendable attitude to provenance that extends to rearing their own pigs and keeping bees. Modern menus are thoroughly in tune with the local market and the seasons, serving up skilfully cooked, well thought out dishes, beginning with a full-flavoured opener involving Lyme Bay scallops, veal tongue, cuttlefish, parsnips and toasted seeds. Fantastic ingredients also distinguish a main course of stone bass matched with crab cannelloni, fennel, charred sea leeks, pollen, and shellfish bisque. At the end, superb, fresh and vibrant raspberry jam makes a perfect foil to the nursery delights of caramelised clotted cream rice pudding.

Times 12-2/7-9.30

The Green

◎◎ Modern British, European v

tel: 01935 813821 **3 The Green DT9 3HY**
email: info@greenrestaurant.co.uk
dir: A30 towards Milborne Port, at top of Greenhill turn right at mini rdbt. Restaurant on left

Creative modern dishes in picture-postcard property

A picture-postcard Grade II listed building, with its heavily beamed interior, offers daily-changing menus that reflect a commitment to local ethically-sourced ingredients. A trio of Dorset crab (landed just the night before) makes a compelling – and popular – starter: with tomato in a Mediterranean-style soup, a savoury crème brûlée and in a parmesan tuile. Duck liver pâté sounds pretty standard but here it's given an extra dimension by beetroot and gherkin 'vinaigrette'. Dishes have a good balance without being too complex, seen in main courses of slowly cooked hogget with Jerusalem artichokes and mint nage, and Lyme Bay gurnard with red pepper and champagne sauce, and the kitchen puts a great deal of effort – and innovation – into its desserts, from meadowsweet mousse with citrus zest and caramelised walnuts, to ginger sticky toffee pudding with lime leaf ice cream and Cointreau caramel sauce.

Chef Alexander Matkevich **Owner** Alexander Matkevich **Seats** 40, Pr/dining room 30 **Times** 12-2.30/7-9.30 Closed Sun-Mon **Prices** Fixed L 3 course fr £20, Fixed D 3 course £20, Starter £5.95-£12.20, Main £12.95-£26, Dessert £5.10-£10.50, Service optional **Wines** 20 bottles over £30, 10 bottles under £30, 8 by glass **Parking** On street, car park **Notes** Children welcome

The Kings Arms

◎ Modern British **NEW**

tel: 01963 220281 **Charlton Herethorne DT9 4NL**
email: admin@thekingsarms.co.uk **web:** www.thekingsarms.co.uk
dir: From A303 follow signs for Templecombe & Sherborne onto B3145 to Charlton Horethorne

Hard-working kitchen in a modernised country inn

Sarah and Tony Lethbridge's stone-built country inn looks rather imposing for a village hostelry, but that is what it has been since it was first licensed way back in the Regency era. Behind that grand façade, the place has been given a thoroughly modern makeover, though not to the detriment of its original charm. There's the usual choice of informal bar eating, or a dedicated dining room, the latter attractively done in wood tones against white walls, with arched panelled mirrors to deepen the space. Sarah Lethbridge heads up the kitchen operation, capitalising on much pedigree West Country produce, as well as drying and curing meats in-house, and making her own breads and ice creams. The style of cooking is unconstrained by national boundaries, bolstering a first course of smoked haddock croquettes with a thick Thai-spiced velouté (scented with coconut and coriander, or serving French-influenced duck leg confit with dauphinoise and Russian kale, alongside a fricassée of wild mushrooms and broad beans. Lusciously rich crème brûlée has its brittle crisp top cleverly echoed with intense wafer-thin ginger biscuits, with a garnish of caramelised plums.

Chef Sarah Lethbridge **Owner** Sarah & Tony Lethbridge **Seats** 120, Pr/dining room 70 **Times** 12-2.30/7-close Closed 25 Dec **Prices** Starter £4.95-£6.95, Main £9.95-£18.95, Dessert £6.50, Service optional **Wines** 18 bottles over £30, 40 bottles under £30, 13 by glass **Parking** 30 **Notes** Sunday L £10.95, Vegetarian available, Children welcome

WIMBORNE MINSTER
Map 5 SZ09

Les Bouviers Restaurant with Rooms
◉◉ French

tel: 01202 889555 **Arrowsmith Rd, Canford Magna BH21 3BD**
email: info@lesbouviers.co.uk **web:** www.lesbouviers.co.uk
dir: *1.5m S of Wimborne on A349, turn left onto A341. In 1m turn right into Arrowsmith Rd. 300yds, 2nd property on right*

Francophile cooking in an elegant restaurant with rooms

A modern, even suburban-looking house in over five acres of land complete with stream and lake is where the Cowards run their restaurant with rooms. The setting for James Coward's elaborate cooking is tastefully decorated and furnished, the restaurant done out in shades of claret and gold, with contemporary artwork hanging on the walls. Cheese soufflé with watercress and horseradish sauce is something of a signature starter, or there might be a salad of local wood pigeon with sautéed tongue and beetroot chutney. Classic Dover sole meunière might appear among main courses, but more typical of the adventurous style is loin of veal with sautéed calves' sweetbreads, tomato confit, buttered spinach and an ivory and wild mushroom sauce, or brill on Puy lentils in saffron sauce with chorizo, courgettes and sun-blushed tomato. Innovative elements are introduced to puddings: chocolate and meringue ice cream for warm dark chocolate fondant, and crème brûlée flavoured with lemongrass, lemon and thyme.

Chef James Coward **Owner** James & Kate Coward **Seats** 50, Pr/dining room 120 **Times** 12-2.15/7-9.30 Closed D Sun **Prices** Tasting menu £58-£72, Service optional 10% **Wines** 24 by glass **Parking** 50 **Notes** ALC 2/3 course £41/£46, Tasting menu 7 course, Sunday L £22.95-£24.50, Vegetarian available, Children welcome

Number 9
◉◉ Modern British

tel: 01202 887557 **West Borough BH21 1LT**
email: no9wimborne@aol.com
dir: *150 yds from The Square before Tivoli Theatre, on West Borough*

Modern European food near the Tivoli Theatre

The late 18th-century townhouse not far from the Tivoli Theatre and the main square has become a supremely stylish restaurant-with-rooms for the modern age. It is designed with today's clean, uncluttered lines and gentle colour palette in mind, as is evidenced by a dining room that features plain walls and unclothed tables flooded with daylight from the French windows. Greg Etheridge cooks to a modern European template, offering a pre-theatre menu for Tivoli-goers, with seafood and fish a notably strong suit. A Niçoise salad of fine chargrilled tuna looks the part, with pinkly meaty fish, crunchy green beans and garlicky olives in two colours. This might be followed majestically by a whole baked sea bass stuffed with lemon and oregano, robustly served with chorizo mash and crunchy seasonal veg. Meat could be a venison steak, served with red cabbage and dauphinoise in a juniper- and rosemary-scented red wine jus, with zesty lemon posset garnished with berry compôte and sugared almonds to finish. A winter spin on Eton Mess adds figs and cinnamon apple to crushed pistachio meringue.

Chef Greg Etheridge **Owner** Roy & Linda Tazzyman **Seats** 50, Pr/dining room 30 **Times** 12-2.30/6-9.30 Closed Xmas, BH Mon, L Mon, D Mon **Prices** Fixed L 2 course fr £19.95, Fixed D 3 course fr £25, Starter £5.50-£8, Main £12.95-£24, Dessert £5.50-£8, Service optional **Wines** 3 bottles over £30, 18 bottles under £30, 9 by glass **Parking** On street or car park **Notes** Pre-theatre menu available, Sunday L £16.95, Vegetarian available, Children welcome

WYKE REGIS
Map 4 SY67

Crab House Café
◉ British, Seafood

tel: 01305 788867 **Ferrymans Way, Portland Rd DT4 9YU**
email: info@crabhousecafe.co.uk **web:** www.crabhousecafe.co.uk
dir: *A354 along Westwey once onto Portland Rd continue for just under a mile, at rdbt take 2nd exit for restaurant*

Fresh seafood in a laid-back beach hut

Situated in a spruced up wooden hut overlooking Chesil Beach, The Crab House Café has natural charms aplenty. Simplicity and freshness is the name of the game, with oysters coming from their own beds out front and everything sourced from within a 40-mile radius. Rustic pub-style benches outside are a treat in the warmer months of the year, but it's all well and good if you've got to eat inside, with an open-to-view kitchen and easy-going attitude. Kick off with some oysters either au naturel or with combos of pesto/parmesan and bacon/cream. A starter of queenie scallops comes topped with a paprika-flavoured gratin and an asparagus purée, or go for Thai fishcakes with sweet chilli sauce. The fresh crabs are hard to ignore – with Chinese spicing perhaps – or go for another main course such as roasted skate with chorizo and spring onions. Finish with a crème brûlée served in a coffee mug.

Chef Nigel Bloxham, Adam Foster **Owner** Nigel Bloxham **Seats** 40 **Times** 12-2/6-9 Closed mid Dec-Jan, Mon-Tue (ex 8 wks in summer), D Sun (Oct-Mar) **Prices** Prices not confirmed, Service optional **Wines** 16 by glass **Parking** 40 **Notes** Sunday L, Vegetarian available, Children welcome

COUNTY DURHAM

BILLINGHAM
Map 19 NZ42

Wynyard Hall Hotel

Rosettes not confirmed at time of going to print – see opposite

DARLINGTON
Map 19 NZ21

Headlam Hall

◎◎ Modern British, French

tel: 01325 730238 **Headlam, Gainford DL2 3HA**
email: admin@headlamhall.co.uk **web:** www.headlamhall.co.uk
dir: *8m W of Darlington off A67*

Country mansion with well-crafted, contemporary food

With its partly creeper-covered façade and elegant period detailing within, Headlam Hall is a rather grand old girl. The main building dates from the 17th century but has moved with the times: there's a swish spa to deliver 21st-century levels of pampering, and a smart restaurant serving up some sparky modern food. The eating takes place in a series of rooms: the Panelled Room is as described, the Orangery a warm and luminous space with well-chosen neutral colours and well-spaced, linen-clad tables. The suppliers of what is to come are listed on the menu – good quality local stuff – and much is produced on their own farm, or comes from the hotel's garden. These fine ingredients are treated with respect by the team in the kitchen and served up in a broadly modern European, good-looking manner. Goats' cheese parfait, for example, with toasted nuts and seeds, red-wine-poached gingerbread and red wine syrup might precede pan-fried haunch of venison with venison ragu, onion purée, fondant potato, roasted shallot and a blueberry and venison jus.

Chef David Hunter **Owner** J H Robinson **Seats** 70, Pr/dining room 30
Times 12-2.30/7-9.30 Closed 25-26 Dec **Prices** Fixed L 2 course fr £14.50, Tasting menu fr £45, Starter £7.50-£9.50, Main £15-£25, Dessert £7-£9, Service optional **Wines** 20 bottles over £30, 38 bottles under £30, 10 by glass **Parking** 80
Notes Sunday L fr £21.50, Vegetarian available, Children welcome

Rockliffe Hall

◎◎◎ Modern British

tel: 01325 729999 **Rockliffe Park, Hurworth-on-Tees DL2 2DU**
email: enquiries@rockliffehall.com **web:** www.rockliffehall.com
dir: *A1(M) junct 57, A66 (M), A66 towards Darlington, A167, through Hurworth-on-Tees. In Croft-on-Tees left into Hurworth Rd, follow signs*

Contemporary and traditional dishes in an ornate dining room

The sturdy redbrick Georgian mansion stands on the River Tees, on the edge of the village of Hurworth, near Darlington. A portfolio of modern country-hotel conveniences is on offer, from championship golf to aromatherapy, and there are no fewer than three restaurant spaces to choose from, depending on whether you're in the market for a light bite, or the full-dress classical and modern cooking of the Orangery. That last has to be seen to be believed: originally the Old Hall of Rockliffe, it has been creatively reconfigured, so that the vaulted Gothic template with its ornate slender columns is offset with gathered blue drapes, the walls crowded with small framed prints. There has been some toing and froing in the kitchens over the past couple of years, but the commitment to the best of contemporary and traditional fine dining, informed by local sourcing, continues. The backbone of the operation is a three-course carte, supplemented by a five-course Signature tasting menu drawn from it, with optional wine pairings. If a pair of you are determined to dine royally, there's the option of a roast for two – rack of lamb or Chateaubriand with béarnaise – carved before your eyes. Otherwise, proceedings might kick off with beetroot-cured salmon with pickled beets, horseradish and seasonal Jersey Royals, or pressed terrine of duck and foie gras with smoked duck breast, figs and

brioche. Main courses run a gamut from old and trusted friends such as lobster thermidor or grilled Dover sole with beurre blanc, to the more obviously new-fangled likes of wood pigeon with herb gnocchi, pak choi and wild garlic in hazelnut vinaigrette. Things become lighter and simpler as the finishing line looms, with mango parfait, rhubarb millefeuille, or tarte Tatin and vanilla ice cream, or the option of a well-laden trolley of British and continental cheeses.

Chef Paul O'Hara, Paul Bussey **Owner** Rockliffe Hall **Seats** 60 **Times** 6.30-9.30 Closed L all week **Prices** Tasting menu £65-£185, Starter £9-£25, Main £17-£42, Dessert £9-£12, Service optional **Wines** 600 bottles over £30, 3 bottles under £30, 35 by glass **Notes** Vegetarian available, No children

DURHAM
Map 19 NZ24

Bistro 21

◎ Modern British V

tel: 0191 384 4354 **Aykley Heads House, Aykley Heads DH1 5TS**
email: admin@bistrotwentyone.co.uk
dir: *Off B6532 from Durham centre, pass County Hall on right & Dryburn Hospital on left. Turn right at double rdbt into Aykley Heads*

Upbeat bistro cooking in a former farmhouse

The bistro tag is on the money: whitewashed walls and pine floors, with the tables covered in white linen to provide the chic bit of the rustic-chic finish. The menu fits the bill, too, traversing the globe in search of winning combinations. It's an easy-going place with a few tables on the terrace for when the mercury rises, and there's a contented buzz about the place when it's busy (which it frequently is). A starter of Asian mussel and prawn broth shows the kitchen's willingness to extend into international waters, but there's also the more regionally inspired salad of kippers, with Pink Fir potatoes and soft-boiled egg. Slow-cooked belly and roast fillet of pork might feature among main courses, with apple and black pudding purée, perhaps, or go for a tart made with heritage beetroots and flavoured with blue cheese. Desserts are creative bunch, for example the hot rhubarb crumble soufflé.

Chef Rauri McKay **Owner** Terence Laybourne **Seats** 65, Pr/dining room 30
Times 12-2/6-10.30 Closed 25 Dec, 1 Jan, D Sun **Prices** Fixed L 2 course fr £15.50, Fixed D 3 course fr £18, Starter £7.50, Main £16.50, Dessert £6.50 **Wines** 6 bottles over £30, 18 bottles under £30, 9 by glass **Parking** 11 **Notes** Early D menu available, Sunday L, Children welcome

Honest Lawyer Hotel

◎ Modern British

tel: 0191 378 3780 **Croxdale Bridge, Croxdale DH1 3SP**
email: enquiries@honestlawyerhotel.com **web:** www.honestlawyerhotel.com
dir: *A1 junct 61*

Something for everybody in a modern city hotel

This wryly-named hotel is a smart, cleanly-designed modern operation with impeccably well-kept guest rooms spread around a courtyard. Food is taken care of by Bailey's Restaurant, a venue with friendly, unpretentious charm, done out in cheering hues of purple and pink. A crowd-pleasing output from the cosmopolitan kitchen ranges from modern European brasserie cooking, to classic Brit comfort food. Local supplies turn up in a starter of ham hock and smoked Ribblesdale cheese terrine with tomato chutney and toasted brioche, while main courses cover a lot of ground from a hearty plateful comprising slow-braised confit duck leg, fondant potatoes, Puy lentils, green beans, a fried duck egg and port wine jus, to slabs of Northumbrian steak, real home-made burgers, or Black Sheep beer-battered haddock with fat chips and minted mushy peas. Finish with a proper home-made pear and frangipane tart with cinnamon ice cream and pear purée.

Chef Harry Bailie **Owner** John Sanderson **Seats** 50, Pr/dining room 60 **Times** 11-9.30 All-day dining **Prices** Prices not confirmed **Wines** 2 bottles over £30, 27 bottles under £30, 7 by glass **Parking** 150 **Notes** Sunday L, Vegetarian available, Children welcome

Ramside Hall Hotel

⚜ International

tel: 0191 386 5282 **Carrville DH1 1TD**
email: mail@ramsidehallhotel.co.uk **web:** www.ramsidehallhotel.co.uk
dir: A1(M) junct 62, A690 to Sunderland. Straight on at lights. 200mtrs after rail bridge turn right

Carnivore heaven in golf-oriented hotel

A grand house has stood on the site of Ramside Hall since Elizabethan times, but the sprawling complex you see today has at its heart a largely Victorian house, beefed up in the late 20th century with lots more rooms and three loops of nine holes to set the emphasis firmly on the pursuit of golf. The crowd-pleasing culinary options run from straightforward carvery and rôtisserie dishes, to the menu in the brasserie-style Rib Room, which 'does what it says on the tin', majoring in slabs of locally-reared 28-day-aged beef. Just choose your cut (there's a 20oz rib-eye if you're feeling particularly peckish) and it arrives with roasted mushrooms, braised onions and a choice of classic sauces; non-carnivores could go for grilled lobster or halibut. Preceding this there might be Provençal fish soup with rouille and croûtons, and to finish, comfort-oriented puddings such as a retro knickerbocker glory or classic crème brûlée.

Times 7am-10pm All-day dining

■ HUTTON MAGNA   **Map 19 NZ11**

The Oak Tree Inn

⚜⚜ Modern British

tel: 01833 627371 **DL11 7HH**
email: claireross67@hotmail.com
dir: 7m W on A66 from Scotch Corner

Confident, creative cooking in a converted village inn

Rough stone and panelled walls, beams, sofas at an open fire and, in the restaurant, high-backed leather-look dining chairs at wooden tables convey a warm and inviting atmosphere at this inn in a sleepy village. Locals pop in for a chat over a drink, but the restaurant is the real business, the appeal due to a sensibly short menu of stimulating ideas based on good-quality produce: turbot fillet, for instance, with steamed Shetland mussels, leeks, olive oil mash and curry sauce, or casserole of Soay lamb and merguez sausage with mashed potato and mushrooms. Dishes are interesting without being overloaded with flavours, seen in starters of Thai-style fish, shellfish and vegetable broth, and a warm salad of pork belly and black pudding with honey and mustard dressing. Salmon is cured in-house (served as a starter with beetroot, lemon cream cheese, fennel and orange), the ice creams to accompany desserts are also home-made: salted caramel for hot chocolate fondant with chocolate mousse, and vanilla for sticky gingerbread pudding.

Chef Alastair Ross **Owner** Alastair & Claire Ross **Seats** 20, Pr/dining room 20 **Times** 6.30-9.30 Closed 24-27 & 31 Dec, 1-2 Jan, Mon, L all week **Prices** Starter £5.50-£8.50, Main £19.50-£25, Dessert £6.50-£8.50, Service optional **Wines** 8 bottles over £30, 45 bottles under £30, 8 by glass **Parking** 3, On street **Notes** Vegetarian dishes & children's portions by prior arrangement, Children welcome

---

Wynyard Hall Hotel

Rosettes not confirmed at time of going to print

BILLINGHAM   **Map 19 NZ42**

Modern British **V**

tel: 01740 644811 **Wynyard TS22 5NF**
email: reception@wynyandhall.co.uk **web:** www.wynyandhall.co.uk
dir: A19 onto A1027 towards Stockton. At rdbt 3rd exit B1274 (Junction Rd). At next rdbt 3rd exit onto A177 (Durham Rd). Right onto Wynyard Rd signed Wolviston. Left into estate at gatehouse

Accomplished cooking in a lavish country mansion setting

The Rosette award for this establishment has been suspended due to a change of chef. Reassessment will take place in due course under the new chef.
A hugely imposing Georgian mansion in 150 acres of grounds with its own lake, Wynyard Hall comes fully loaded with the full spa and pampering package that you'd expect these days in one of the North East's finest hotels. The place is no stranger toliterati, heads of state and royals, listing Charles Dickens, Disraeli, Sir Robert Peel, Churchill, Edward VII, Elizabeth II and the Duke of Wellington among its past guests. As you approach the hall via a long, winding drive and cross over the lion-topped bridge, you get a sense of what's to come: gold-painted interiors, wonderful oil portraits and a lavish rich-red dining room-The Wellington

Restaurant-decorated with magnificent floral displays and plush seating. In surroundings like this the food can fall by the wayside, but executive chef Simon Kelly took the reins in 2014 and his imaginative, contemporary cooking is more than up to the task. The kitchen brings together a love of peerless local produce with some entertaining modern ideas on a menu that reads more like a shopping list than an informative description, so there might be a terrine of ham hock with apple in various guises and sourdough crisps, for example, while the humble pea could head up another starter, appearing in a silky velouté teamed with fine herb-flavoured Chantilly cream and salmon ravioli. Main courses bring together similarly inventive interplays of taste and texture-perhaps starring roast rump of lamb with a supporting cast of butternut squash, beetroot and Parisienne potatoes, or you could go for a delicate combination of pollock with peas, broad beans, Baby Gem and shallot vinaigrette. To finish, pannacotta could arrive with poached rhubarb, strawberry and pear sorbet.

Chef Simon Kelly **Owner** Allison Antonopoulos **Seats** 80, Pr/dining room 30 **Times** 12-3/7-9.30 **Prices** Fixed L 2 course £18, Fixed D 3 course £32, Starter £10-£16, Main £20-£35, Dessert £9-£13, Service optional **Wines** 51 bottles over £30, 30 bottles under £30, 10 by glass **Parking** 200 **Notes** Traditional/Gentleman's afternoon tea £18.95/£24.95, Sunday L £21-£25, Children welcome

Redworth Hall Hotel

Modern British

tel: 01388 770600 **DL5 6NL**
email: redworthhall@pumahotels.co.uk **web:** www.pumahotels.co.uk
dir: *From A1(M) junct 58 take A68 towards Corbridge. At 1st rdbt take A6072 towards Bishop Auckland. At next rdbt take 2nd exit (A6072). Hotel on left*

Modern British cooking in a 17th-century manor

It's a grand looking place – positively stately – dating from the back end of the 17th century and constructed in homage to the earlier Jacobean style. The galleried Great Hall harks back to days of magnificent parties, while today's visitor is as likely to be here for a wedding, a beauty treatment, or the nearby golf courses. The 1774 Restaurant is worth a punt, though, with its classical elegance and posh table settings. The kitchen offers up a gently contemporary repertoire with some good ideas and nothing to scare the horses. Start with chicken and ham terrine, served on a slate, with piccalilli to cut through the richness and some toasted pesto bruschetta. Among main courses, braised blade of beef is served on champ and comes with a red onion tarte Tatin. For dessert, chocolate torte has an accompanying jug of pouring cream.

Times 12–2/6.30–9.30 Closed 25 Dec

The Rose & Crown

Modern British, Continental

tel: 01833 650213 **DL12 9EB**
email: hotel@rose-and-crown.co.uk **web:** www.rose-and-crown.co.uk
dir: *6m NW of Barnard Castle on B6277*

Classically-based cuisine in a lovely old inn

You know you're on to a good thing as soon as you arrive in Romaldkirk: not one, but three village greens complete with Saxon church, village pump and stocks, bracket the Rose & Crown. The 18th-century inn is steeped in tradition, yet bang up-to-date where it matters. With its oak settles and antique chairs, the creaky bar is the sort of place you dream of finding for a pint of Black Sheep by a sizzling log fire-you're welcome to eat here, but at dinner, many guests go for the romantic candlelit vibe of the elegant oak-panelled dining room, where dinner menus are built on local, seasonal produce and inspired by classic and contemporary trends. Slow-braised pressed pork belly with black pudding and a crispy poached egg to give textural contrast shows the style, while main course might be pot-roasted shoulder of local lamb and chorizo with pearl barley, carrot, onion and celery brunoise, sobrasada foam and root vegetable crisps. Creative ideas such as ginger pannacotta with poached rhubarb and hazelnut praline close proceedings.

Chef Henritetta Crosland **Owner** Thomas & Cheryl Robinson **Seats** 24 **Times** 12–2.30/6.30–9 Closed 23–27 Dec **Prices** Starter £5.50–£8, Main £11.50–£21.50, Dessert £6–£8, Service optional **Wines** 22 bottles over £30, 34 bottles under £30, 10 by glass **Parking** 25 **Notes** Sunday L £16.50–£20, Vegetarian available, Children 7yrs+ D

The Ozone Restaurant

Asian Fusion

tel: 0191 516 1400 **Seaham Hall Hotel, Lord Byron's Walk SR7 7AG**
email: hotel@seaham-hall.com
dir: *Leave A1018 onto A19 at rdbt take 2nd exit onto B1285/Stockton Rd. Turn left at Lord Byron Walk in 0.3m turn right*

Asian flavours in a glamorous five-star hotel

The flame-coloured Ozone Restaurant serves up some impressive Pan-Asian food in a cool and chilled-out setting. Located in Seaham Hall, this offers an alternative dining experience to that found in Byron's Bar & Grill (see entry). With great views over the grounds (especially good from the terrace), an open kitchen offers an innovative menu packed with great flavours. Start with confit duck pancake roll,crisp lettuce and cucumber, topped with hoi sin sauce, or a salad of tiger prawns, served with glass noodles and broccoli florets. Sharing and grazing is the best way to approach things. Main-course steamed sea bass fillet with pak choi and nam jim dressing, or go for crispy pork belly with Chinese kale and spring vegetables. For dessert, coconut pannacotta with roasted pineapple.

Chef Sean Wilkinson, Martin Blunos **Owner** Seasons Plc **Seats** 60 **Times** 11–5/6–9 Closed 25 Dec **Prices** Fixed L 2 course £18.50, Fixed D 3 course £24.50, Starter £4–£6, Main £12.50, Dessert £6, Service optional **Wines** 4 bottles over £30, 7 bottles under £30, 11 by glass **Parking** 200 **Notes** Sunday L £14.95–£30, Vegetarian available, Children welcome

Seaham Hall - Byron's Bar & Grill

Modern British NEW

tel: 0191 516 1400 **Lord Byron's Walk SR7 7AG**
email: hotel@seaham-hall.co.uk **web:** www.seaham-hall.co.uk
dir: *A19 at 1st exit signed B1404 Seaham and follow signs to Seaham Hall*

Modern grill dining in luxury hotel

The late 18th-century Seaham Hall now trades as a state-of-the-art spa hotel with luxurious treatment rooms and a brace of stimulating eating options. After complete refurbishment in 2013, the space formerly known as the White Room restaurant is reborn as Byron's Bar and Grill, a swish contemporary space with a glossy sheen, velour banquettes, darkwood flooring and marble-topped tables. The kitchen has kicked the erstwhile fine dining approach into touch and now delivers a crowd-pleasing menu aiming unashamedly at the hearts of carnivores, although well-sourced fish – herb-crusted cod with bacon, Savoy cabbage and carrots, for example – provides meat-free alternatives. Expect the likes of devilled crispy whitebait with caper and parsley mayonnaise to start, followed by top-quality cuts of 28-day-aged beef from the grill – a rib-eye steak with balsamic-glazed onions, confit tomatoes and hand-cut chips, say. Desserts take a similarly uncomplicated approach with the likes of rum baba or chocolate fudge brownie.

Chef Simon Bolsover, Martin Blunos **Owner** Seaham Hall Management Ltd **Seats** 46, Pr/dining room 100 **Times** 11–9.30 All-day dining **Prices** Starter £6–£14, Main £10–£30, Dessert £5–£9, Service optional **Wines** 148 bottles over £30, 22 bottles under £30, 11 by glass **Parking** 120 **Notes** Sunday L £14.95–£30, Vegetarian available, Children welcome

ESSEX

BRENTWOOD
Map 6 TQ59

Marygreen Manor Hotel

Modern European V

tel: 01277 225252 **London Rd CM14 4NR**
email: info@marygreenmanor.co.uk **web:** www.marygreenmanor.co.uk
dir: *M25 junct 28, onto A1023 over 2 sets of lights, hotel on right*

Enterprising modern food in a Tudor mansion

Dating from the early 16th century, when it was built by a courtier of Catherine of Aragon, the manor is a perfect example of a half-timbered building, the restaurant an impressive-looking room with a profusion of oak wall and ceiling timbers and carved stanchions. Classy ingredients are carefully handled by a kitchen that combines them sympathetically to create some stimulating dishes. Start with veal sweetbreads with onions, spinach, rhubarb and radish, or lobster with leeks, ceps and lobster foam, before grilled Dover sole with beurre noisette and capers, or beef fillet with cauliflower purée, mushrooms and pak choi. Vegetarians have a separate menu, and desserts have included banana pudding with caramel fudge sauce and vanilla ice cream, or raspberry and chocolate tart.

Chef Mr Majid Bourote **Owner** Mr S Bhattessa **Seats** 80, Pr/dining room 85 **Times** 12.30-2.30/7.15-10.15 Closed L Mon, D Sun, BHs **Prices** Fixed L 2 course £18, Fixed D 3 course £24, Tasting menu £48-£76, Starter £7.50-£14.50, Main £23.50-£32, Dessert £7.50 **Wines** 72 bottles over £30, 51 bottles under £30, 12 by glass **Parking** 100 **Notes** Tasting menu 6 course, Sunday L £23, Children welcome

CHELMSFORD
Map 6 TL70

County Hotel

Modern European

tel: 01245 455700 **29 Rainsford Rd CM1 2PZ**
email: kloftus@countyhotelgroup.co.uk **web:** www.countyhotelgroup.co.uk
dir: *Off Chelmsford ring road close to town centre and A12 junct 18*

British and Mediterranean flavours in town-centre hotel

A conveniently short stroll from the railway station and town centre, the County Hotel is done out in a cheery modern style, as typified in the County Kitchen restaurant, where oak floors and leather seats in summery pastel hues of mustard, mint and tangerine add colour to neutral contemporary decor. Uncomplicated modern European cooking using local materials is the kitchen's stock in trade, starting along the lines of venison and confit pheasant terrine with celeriac remoulade and toasted walnut bread; mains might bring fillet steak with potato rösti, butternut squash purée, curly kale and red wine jus, or a burst of Mediterranean warmth in the form of Ligurian fish stew. For dessert, there could be dark chocolate fondant with clotted cream ice cream.

Chef Adam Tapia **Owner** Michael & Ginny Austin **Seats** 64, Pr/dining room 135 **Times** 12-2.30/6-10 Closed L Sat **Prices** Fixed L 2 course £14.95-£23.95, Fixed D 3 course £19.95-£19.95, Starter £4.95-£9.75, Main £11.75-£23.95, Dessert £5.25-£6.50 **Wines** 18 bottles over £30, 22 bottles under £30, 6 by glass **Parking** 70 **Notes** Pre-theatre menu available, Sunday L £13.95-£22.95, Vegetarian available, Children welcome

COGGESHALL
Map 7 TL82

Baumann's Brasserie

French, European V

tel: 01376 561453 **4-6 Stoneham St CO6 1TT**
email: food@baumannsbrasserie.co.uk **web:** www.baumannsbrasserie.co.uk
dir: *A12 from Chelmsford, exit at Kelvedon into Coggeshall. Restaurant in centre opposite clock tower*

Gutsy cooking in buzzy brasserie

Originally launched by legendary restaurateur Peter Langan, chef-patron Mark Baumann's buzzy brasserie has been a fixture on the local dining scene for almost 30 years. The setting may be a 16th-century timbered house, and continental-style pavement tables hint at a classic French bistro, but there's nothing stuck in the past about Baumann's inventively-tweaked French and British dishes. Inside, the mood is laid-back and cosmopolitan and the one-off decor is akin to an eclectic art gallery done out with antique linen-clothed tables. Smart, on-the-money food is the deal here, delivered via no-nonsense menus that follow the seasons rather than the vagaries of culinary trends. Beetroot tarte Tatin with chive-whipped goats' cheese and sugar-roasted chestnuts makes a cracking starter, then you might continue with something from the daily French menu-fillet of monkfish, for example, gets the robust flavours of Thai red curry crust and king prawns in garlic and ginger. It all ends on a high note with an excellent traditional marmalade steamed sponge with vanilla custard.

Chef Mark Baumann, John Ranfield **Owner** Baumann's Brasserie Ltd **Seats** 80 **Times** 12-2/7-9.30 Closed 2 wks Jan, Mon-Tue **Prices** Fixed L 2 course fr £14.95, Fixed D 3 course fr £17.95, Tasting menu £49, Starter £7-£10, Main £17-£26, Dessert £7, Service optional **Wines** 11 by glass **Parking** Opposite **Notes** Fixed L plat du jour daily, Changing fish menu daily, Sunday L, Children welcome

COLCHESTER

Map 13 TL92

The North Hill Hotel

◉◉ Modern British

tel: 01206 574001 **51 North Hill CO1 1PY**
email: info@northhillhotel.com **web:** www.northhillhotel.com
dir: *Follow directions for town centre, down North Hill, hotel on left*

Well-prepared food in popular, modern-day hotel bistro

North Hill's sunny yellow façade paints a cheery face onto the exterior of a handsome Georgian building in the historic heart of Colchester, giving a gentle hint at the breezy, rather funky contemporary decor within. Bright and swirly artwork feeds into the cool, pared-back look of the Green Room bistro, where plain wooden tables and chairs are set against sage-green walls, and an unbuttoned vibe completes the setting for the upbeat modern cooking. The kitchen's output is driven by well-sourced local ingredients treated without undue fuss: perhaps warm smoked duck breast with a fig, green bean and grape salad to open the show, ahead of well-timed sea bass fillets with toasted almond and caper butter, wilted spinach, and herb-crushed new potatoes. Meatier fare runs to slow-cooked venison with mushrooms and smoked bacon puff pastry pie. For dessert, there could be elderflower pannacotta served with a warm vanilla doughnut.

Chef John Riddleston **Owner** Rob Brown **Seats** 90, Pr/dining room 30
Times 12-2.30/6-9.30 **Prices** Starter £4.50-£7.50, Main £10.95-£21.95, Dessert £4.50-£10, Service optional **Wines** 14 bottles over £30, 34 bottles under £30, 14 by glass **Parking** NCP opposite **Notes** Pre-theatre 10% discount (Mercury), Sunday L £9.95-£21.95, Vegetarian available, Children welcome

Stoke by Nayland Hotel, Golf & Spa

◉◉ Modern British

tel: 01206 262836 & 265835 **Keepers Ln, Leavenheath CO6 4PZ**
email: winston.wright@stokebynayland.com **web:** www.stokebynayland.com
dir: *From A134, pass through the village of Nayland, ignoring signs to Stoke-by-Nayland. Continue on A134, shortly after Hare & Hounds turn right on to B1068 signed Stoke-by-Nayland Golf Club. In approx 1.5m right*

Complex contemporary cooking overlooking the golf

There's an awful lot going on here on the Suffolk-Essex border. There are two championship golf courses on the 300-acre site for a start, plus the hotel of course, spa facilities, and, in the shape of the Lakes Restaurant, a rather good dining option. A wall of sliding glass doors ensures everyone gets a glimpse of the water

and the greens – better still, bag a table on the terrace – and inside it is a smart and airy space with plenty of room between tables. The menus show a kitchen with a clear fondness for carefully-sourced British ingredients, deployed in a broad-minded European-influenced repertoire. Start with lambs' sweetbreads with purple-sprouting broccoli, potato crisp and wild garlic pesto, or pan-fried cod cheeks with saffron-pickled quail's egg, spiced pear and lotus root. Next up, butter roasted fillet of halibut is topped with a cauliflower and pistachio crust and is served alongside ras el hanout-flavoured carrots, beluga lentils, saffron sauce, rosewater oil and a barbecue date jam.

Chef Alan Paton **Owner** The Boxford Group **Seats** 100, Pr/dining room 60
Times 12.30-2.30/6.30-10 **Prices** Fixed D 3 course £25-£29, Starter £4.60-£6.75, Main £11.50-£18.50, Dessert £6.50-£6.95, Service optional **Wines** 9 bottles over £30, 40 bottles under £30, 14 by glass **Parking** 350 **Notes** Sunday L £4.30-£8.50, Vegetarian available, Children welcome

DEDHAM

Map 13 TM03

milsoms

◉ Modern International

tel: 01206 322795 **Stratford Rd CO7 6HN**
email: milsoms@milsomhotels.com **web:** www.milsomhotels.com
dir: *7m N of Colchester, just off A12. Follow signs to Dedham then brown signs*

Global food in a fuss-free contemporary setting

The village of Dedham is a stronghold of the Milsom mini-empire, home to Le Talbooth and its siblings, including this contemporary bar and brasserie offering pleasingly fuss-free alternatives to the country-house idiom. The laid-back ethos extends to a no-bookings policy, and you order at the well-stocked bar. Together with the stylish textures of wood, stone and leather and colourful artwork in the split-level dining room, it gets its buzz from the 'engine room', as the open-plan kitchen is nicknamed, plus a heated terrace with a huge sail canopy. Add a wide-ranging brasserie menu embracing global influences into the mix, and it's a winning formula. Seared scallops with pineapple carpaccio, carrot spaghetti and sweet chilli dressing is a well-conceived opener, followed by Wester Ross salmon with beetroot, horseradish risotto and kale pesto. To finish, pear tarte Tatin is matched with iced blackberry yoghurt and crème anglaise.

Chef Sarah Norman, Ben Rush **Owner** Milsom family **Seats** 80, Pr/dining room 30
Times 12-9.30 All-day dining **Prices** Starter £5.75-£8.95, Main £11.50-£27, Dessert £5.95-£6.95, Service optional **Wines** 26 bottles over £30, 38 bottles under £30, 20 by glass **Parking** 80 **Notes** Sunday L £29, Vegetarian available, Children welcome

The Sun Inn

Rustic Italian, Modern British NOTABLE WINE LIST

tel: 01206 323351 **High St CO7 6DF**
email: office@thesuninndedham.com **web:** www.thesuninndedham.com
dir: *In village centre opposite church*

A taste of Italy in a village inn

The setting may be in the heart of Constable country, but the Sun Inn's culinary leanings have a distinctly sunny Mediterranean soul. The place is a proper 15th-century village inn, revamped to sit well with modern sensibilities, but not at the expense of its character: there are open fires, doughty timbers and panelling, backed by friendly service and a good range of real ales. Food is taken seriously, combining fresh locally-sourced produce and quality Italian ingredients, such as cured meats, cheeses and oils, in uncomplicated, well-executed dishes. The kitchen is led by an Italian chef, so antipasti are on offer – perhaps a platter of bresaola, Neapolitan salami and Mersea oysters – or take a starter of duck hearts with white onion, sage, broad beans and home-made bread to mop up the juices. A simple main course of top-notch hand-dived scallops with lentils and samphire, is proof that less really can be more, while the Mediterranean theme winds things up in a dessert of elderflower pannacotta with poached apricots.

Chef Ugo Simonelli **Owner** Piers Baker **Seats** 70 **Times** 12-2.30/6.30-9.30 Closed 25-26 Dec, 3-4 Jan **Prices** Fixed L 2 course £14, Fixed D 3 course £17.50, Service optional **Wines** 44 bottles over £30, 46 bottles under £30, 20 by glass **Parking** 15 **Notes** Breakfast available Fri-Sun, Sunday L, Vegetarian available, Children welcome

Le Talbooth

Modern British, European NOTABLE WINE LIST

tel: 01206 323150 **Gun Hill CO7 6HN**
email: talbooth@milsomhotels.com **web:** www.milsomhotels.com/letalbooth
dir: *6m from Colchester follow signs from A12 to Stratford St Mary, restaurant on the left before village*

Classy creative cooking and lovely riverside setting

At the heart of Constable country, Le Talbooth is a half-timbered property in a delightful leafy setting beside the River Stour, with awnings above the waterside terrace for alfresco dining. Well-groomed uniformed staff underline the fact that this is a classy, well-run operation, with the kitchen's shoulder behind a carefully devised menu that combines the familiar with the more contemporary. A trio of

Dingley Dell pork, served with butternut squash, black cabbage and pickled apples, is lifted out of the ordinary by the quality of the ingredients and the accuracy of the cooking. Fish is handled well too, judging by spot-on roast monkfish tail, accompanied by nicely contrasting oxtail tortellini, celeriac, kale and salsify. Starters can vary from an attractively presented pressing of duck liver and locally shot partridge, accompanied by crispy leg and plums, to the wilder shores of tempura of soft-shelled crab with crab mayonnaise, sardine dressing, confit onion and pickled ginger. Puddings hit the mark too: witness textbook vanilla pannacotta served with stewed apple given a kick with lime and coriander.

Chef Andrew Hirst, Ian Rhodes **Owner** Milsom family **Seats** 80, Pr/dining room 34 **Times** 12-2/6.30-9 Closed D Sun (Oct-Apr) **Prices** Fixed L 2 course £24.50, Starter £9.95-£16.50, Main £24.50-£32, Dessert £8.25-£9.75, Service optional **Wines** 250 bottles over £30, 46 bottles under £30, 19 by glass **Parking** 50 **Notes** Sunday L £34.50, Vegetarian available, Children welcome

GESTINGTHORPE   **Map 13 TL83**

The Pheasant

British

tel: 01787 465010 & 461196 **Audley End CO9 3AU web:** www.thepheasant.net
dir: *Telephone for directions*

Foodie satisfaction in charming country inn

Since chef-proprietor James Donoghue took over at The Pheasant in 2006, this mustard-yellow-painted country pub on the Suffolk-Essex border has flourished. The interior has the light and uncluttered look of a switched-on contemporary dining pub, and food is placed passionately at the heart of the operation. There's now a smokehouse, plus a large plot across the road providing organic fruit and vegetables, and the Donoghues also keep bees. The uncomplicated, flavour-driven approach offers plenty to tempt: sweet and tender smoked shell-on prawns are pointed up with saffron aïoli and excellent home-baked brown bread, while a vibrant home-made spicy chicken and tomato pie makes a virtue of simplicity and fresh, flavour-packed raw materials. A pannacotta lifted by delicious strawberry sauce concludes the theme of tried-and-true ideas done really well. Five classy boutique-style B&B rooms mean you can stay over and really loosen the belt at dinner.

Chef James Donoghue **Owner** James & Diana Donoghue **Seats** 40, Pr/dining room 16 **Times** 12-3/6.30-9 **Prices** Prices not confirmed, Service optional **Wines** 5 bottles over £30, 21 bottles under £30, 7 by glass **Parking** 25 **Notes** Sunday L, Vegetarian available, Children welcome

GREAT TOTHAM
Map 7 TL81

The Bull & Willow Room at Great Totham

◎◎ Traditional & Modern British

tel: 01621 893385 & 894020 **2 Maldon Rd CM9 8NH**
email: reservations@thewillowroom.co.uk **web:** www.thebullatgreattotham.co.uk
dir: Exit A12 at Witham junct to Great Totham

Accomplished cooking in made-over pub

The Bull is an Essex pub with lots of period charm and a good deal of contemporary appeal. It really does look the business with its splendid 16th-century façade neatly spruced up, its characterful bar packed with original features, and decorative colours chosen from the favoured neutral and natural palette. There's just the one menu throughout these days, whether you stick in the bar or head into The Willow Room, which offers a touch of refinement in the shape of elegant upholstered chairs and tables dressed in white linen. On the menu is some smart, modish cooking alongside some old favourites. So you could choose to go for prawn cocktail with brown bread and butter followed by steak and kidney pudding, or kick off with smoked ham hock terrine with piccalilli and knacker bread, before moving on to honey-glazed Gressingham duck breast with roasted red plums and endive. To finish, the British artisan cheese platter offers stiff competition to desserts such as chocolate tart with black olive caramel (or you could always have both).

Chef Luke Stevens **Owner** David Milne **Seats** 75, Pr/dining room 20
Times 12-2.30/5-9.45 **Prices** Fixed L 2 course £13.45, Starter £4.95-£7.95, Main £10.95-£49.95, Dessert £5.95-£8.95, Service optional **Wines** 19 bottles over £30, 46 bottles under £30, 9 by glass **Parking** 80 **Notes** Fixed D Mon-Fri, Menus/prices change 8-10 wks, Sunday L, Vegetarian available, No children after 7pm

GREAT YELDHAM
Map 13 TL73

The White Hart

◎◎ British, European

tel: 01787 237250 **Poole St CO9 4HJ**
email: mjwmason@yahoo.co.uk **web:** www.whitehartyeldham.com
dir: On A1017, between Halstead & Haverhill

Characterful old inn with skilful contemporary cooking

As its black-and-white timbered Tudor frontage attests, The White Hart has been in business since the dawn of the 16th century, and as long as folk hanker for this romantic image of Olde England it looks set to prosper. Oak panelling, inglenooks piled with logs, leaded windows, burnished oak tables and head-grazing beams set a suitably historic scene, while the culinary thrust aims at flavour-driven modern British dishes produced from impeccably-sourced materials-home-grown herbs and veg from a nearby field, for instance. This is an intelligent kitchen team firing on all cylinders to deliver well-balanced, technically adept dishes: hand-dived scallops are matched with black pudding fritters, cauliflower purée and bacon foam, ahead of Blythburgh free-range pork (braised belly and slow-roast tenderloin) in a hazelnut and herb crust, with pommes dauphine and Calvados caramel apples. A finale of pear frangipane tart with honeycomb, honey ice cream (from the hotel's own beehives) and pear cider foam is also right on the money.

Chef Mr Wu Zhenjang, Mr K White **Owner** Matthew Mason **Seats** 44, Pr/dining room 200 **Times** 12-12 Closed 25 Dec eve, Mon, L Tue All-day dining **Prices** Starter £6.95-£12.95, Main £16.95-£24.95, Dessert £5.95-£10.95, Service optional **Wines** 19 bottles over £30, 21 bottles under £30, 8 by glass **Parking** 50 **Notes** Sunday L £19.95-£25, Vegetarian available, Children welcome

HARWICH
Map 13 TM23

The Pier at Harwich

◎◎ Modern British, Seafood

tel: 01255 241212 **The Quay CO12 3HH**
email: pier@milsomhotels.com **web:** www.milsomhotels.com
dir: A12 to Colchester then A120 to Harwich Quay

Spankingly fresh seafood and harbour views

What better setting could there be for a restaurant that celebrates the fruits of the sea than Harwich's quay? Watch the boats glide silently by from the first-floor windows of the light and airy Harbourside Restaurant and peruse a menu that takes in the traditional as well as more exotic ideas, so among starters may be deeply-flavoured fish soup with rouille, garlic toasts and parmesan, and crab (from Harwich, naturally) tacos with guacamole and chipotle dressing. Lobster (small, medium or large) gets varied treatments, from thermidor to cold poached, served with celeriac remoulade, truffled potatoes and tomato and watercress salad; Dover sole meunière, perfectly timed, is a classic example, served with lightly cooked green vegetables, and hardliners could always opt for beer-battered fish with triple-cooked chips and pea purée. Meat-eaters are not entirely overlooked, and an imaginative touch with puddings brings on coconut pannacotta with mango, chilli and pineapple salsa, and ginger-braised pineapple with Eccles cake ice cream. The ground-floor Ha'penny Bistro is a more informal but equally popular alternative.

Chef Tom Bushell **Owner** Milsom family **Seats** 80, Pr/dining room 16
Times 12-2/6-9.30 Closed Mon-Tue **Prices** Fixed L 2 course £20, Starter £8.25-£14.80, Main £16.50-£30, Dessert £7.25, Service optional **Wines** 70 bottles over £30, 35 bottles under £30, 16 by glass **Parking** 12, On street **Notes** Sunday L, Vegetarian available, Children welcome

MANNINGTREE
Map 13 TM13

The Mistley Thorn

British, Italian, Mediterranean

tel: 01206 392821 **High St, Mistley CO11 1HE**
email: info@mistleythorn.co.uk
dir: From A12 take A137 for Manningtree & Mistley

Seafood-strong California cool on the Stour estuary

A coaching inn from the early Georgian era, the Thorn is a handsome, creamy-fronted edifice in the picturesque estuarial village of Mistley, not far from the harbour. It's been converted to mostly restaurant business, with bare wood tables offsetting the venerable evidence of gnarled beams and exposed brick. Executive chef Sherri Singleton hails from California, and brings a vibrant West Coast (of America) sensibility to proceedings, with a cookery school, delicatessen and wine store all part of the action. Dishes look simple and zinging-fresh, with fish and seafood the speciality. Salmon turns up in three guises to start: cured, smoked and rillettes, served with dill mustard sauce and toast. Deben mussels get their place in the limelight on 'Moules Madness' nights, every Thursday, but fish is good all round, as shown again in a main course of baked lemon sole, which is timed to a nicety and comes with crayfish butter. There are fine steaks of Red Poll Suffolk beef with beer-battered onion rings to please meat-seekers. Dessert offers intense lemon and rosemary posset with candied zests and a lemon polenta biscuit.

Chef Sherri Singleton, Karl Burnside **Owner** Sherri Singleton, David McKay **Seats** 75, Pr/dining room 28 **Times** 12-2.30/6.30-9.30 **Prices** Fixed L 2 course fr £12.50, Fixed D 3 course fr £15, Starter £4.95-£7.95, Main £10.95-£21.95, Dessert £1.75-£7.95, Service optional **Wines** 4 bottles over £30, 34 bottles under £30, 17 by glass **Parking** 7 **Notes** Sunday L £13.95-£16.95, Vegetarian available, Children welcome

ORSETT
Map 6 TQ68

The Garden Restaurant at Orsett Hall

Modern British

tel: 01375 891402 **Prince Charles Av RM16 3HS**
email: reception@orsetthall.co.uk **web:** www.gardenrestaurant.co.uk
dir: M25 junct 29/A127 Southend, then A128 Tilbury, hotel 3m on right

Inspiring modern cookery in a glassed garden terrace

The hall as it stands today is a painstakingly reconstructed facsimile of the original 17th-century manor house that stood on the same spot, but sadly burned to a shell in 2007. A brisk trade in corporate business and weddings is a mainstay of many such places, but not everywhere boasts such a head-turning dining room as Orsett has. Designed as a glassed terrace overlooking the gardens, it's a riot of bold colours and floral patterns. Coloured glass chandeliers catch the sunlight, while cream wood panelling provides a calming backdrop: an appropriately contemporary and interesting setting in which to enjoy the inspired, intelligent cooking of chef Robert Pearce. A range of flavours and textures distinguishes a starter of pigeon, in which the breast is smoked and the legs served sweet-and-sour, alongside contrasting parsnip purée and crisps. Seafood is showcased in a dazzlingly presented main course of red snapper and spiced scallops in crab bisque, with lemon jelly and lime foam. Aromatically beguiling desserts include rosewater-glazed pineapple with coconut arancini, yoghurt sorbet and lime.

Chef Robert Pearce **Owner** Apex Property Holdings Ltd **Seats** 50 **Times** 12-3/7-9.30 Closed D Sun **Prices** Fixed L 2 course £19.95, Fixed D 3 course £24.50, Tasting menu £49.95, Starter £6.50-£8.25, Main £16-£21.50, Dessert £6.50-£8.95, Service optional **Wines** 14 bottles over £30, 25 bottles under £30, 8 by glass **Parking** 250 **Notes** Sunday L £14.95-£24.50, Vegetarian available, Children welcome

SOUTHEND-ON-SEA
Map 7 TQ88

Holiday Inn Southend

Traditional British NEW

tel: 01702 543001 & 0845 092 1935 **77 Eastwoodbury Crescet SS2 6XG**
email: restaurantmgr@hisouthend.com **web:** www.1935rooftoprestaurant.com
dir: Entrance to Southend Airport

Slick modern dining with aeroplanes in the background

If you're a plane-spotting foodie both of your interests can be indulged in one fell swoop at the fifth-floor 1935 Restaurant overlooking the aviation action at Southend airport. Naturally enough, soundproofing is of the highest order, and there's a real sense of occasion in the slick contemporary space when you look through the full-length glass windows and the runway lights put on a show in the evening. The kitchen deals in unpretentious classic and modern ideas, taking off with game terrine wrapped in pancetta with toasted brioche and red onion marmalade, followed by a three-way serving of duck – leg, breast and confit – matched with beetroot mash, cavolo nero and berry sauce. Elsewhere, there are straight-up steaks from the grill, or fish, in the form, perhaps, of pan-fried hake with pappardelle vegetables, crushed new potatoes and dill cream sauce. Finish with pecan cheesecake with salted caramel ice cream.

Chef Michael Walker **Owner** London Southend Airport Ltd **Seats** 82, Pr/dining room 10 **Times** 12-2.30/6-10 **Prices** Fixed L 2 course £16.95, Fixed D 3 course £25, Starter £4.95-£7.50, Main £9.95-£25.95, Dessert £4.50-£6.95, Service optional **Wines** 5 bottles over £30, 21 bottles under £30, 10 by glass **Parking** 226 **Notes** Afternoon tea available £15.95/£21.95, Sunday L £12.95-£19.35, Vegetarian available, Children welcome

The Roslin Beach Hotel

British

tel: 01702 586375 **Thorpe Esplanade, Thorpe Bay SS1 3BG**
email: info@roslinhotel.com **web:** www.roslinhotel.com
dir: On Thorpe Esplanade 2.5m past Southend Pier towards Shoeburyness

Well-conceived dishes in a buzzy seaside setting

If you do like to be beside the seaside, The Roslin Beach Hotel is for you. It's a popular place and its position looking out across the road to the sea is part of its appeal. With tables outside on the sea-facing heated terrace, and those indoors shielded by glass, it feels seasidey whatever the weather. And it's rather smart, too. Tables are dressed up in white linen and there's quite a buzz about the place when it's busy (which it frequently is). There's a good showing of local seafood on the menu and some of the meat (duck, beef) comes from the owners' farm in Hampshire. Start with locally-caught whitebait with tartare sauce, or gin and tonic smoked salmon, or goats' curd with fig caponata and oatcakes. Among main courses, steaks cooked on the grill are a big hit, but there is also fresh grouse with pickled red cabbage, chestnuts and wild mushroom ravioli. For dessert, try a vanilla and bourbon pannacotta with raspberry 'bombs'.

Chef Wayne Hawkins **Owner** Regis Entertainment Ltd **Seats** 70, Pr/dining room 30 **Times** 12-2.45/6-9.30 **Prices** Fixed L 3 course fr £20, Fixed D 3 course fr £20 **Wines** 18 bottles over £30, 53 bottles under £30, 10 by glass **Parking** 57 **Notes** Sunday L, Vegetarian available, Children welcome

STANSTED MOUNTFITCHET
Map 12 TL52

Linden House

 Modern European **NEW**

tel: 01279 813003 **1-3 Silver St CM24 8HA**
email: stay@lindenhousestansted.co.uk **web:** www.lindenhousestansted.co.uk
dir: M11 junct 8 towards Newport on A120, on right after windmill

Contemporary cooking in a stylish restaurant with rooms

Spruced up with a touch of boutique style, Linden House has designer bedrooms and a bar and restaurant that positively hum when it's busy (which it frequently is). But it isn't all style over substance. The kitchen crew has put together a modern menu of bright ideas, and the service team do their work with a great level of engagement. Seared local wood pigeon with Kentish cobnuts and pan-fried wild mushrooms is a real country dish with a bit of finesse, while vegetarians might be drawn to carpaccio of beetroot with goats' cheese dusted in paprika and dressed with a sweet basil oil. Among main courses, seven-hour pork (slow-cooked collar) sits alongside mixed grill of fish with smoked garlic mayonnaise and hand-cut fat chips, plus Hereford steaks cooked on the grill. Desserts are a comforting bunch ranging from sticky toffee pudding to maple pannacotta with caramelised pineapple.

Chef Sam Smith **Owner** Karl & Sarah Foster **Seats** 50 **Times** 12-3/6-9.30 **Prices** Fixed L 2 course fr £15, Fixed D 3 course fr £20, Service optional **Wines** 38 bottles over £30, 30 bottles under £30, 13 by glass **Parking** Pay & Display 100yds **Notes** Afternoon tea £18.50-£35.50, Brunch available, Sunday L £14.50-£16.50, Vegetarian available, Children welcome

STOCK
Map 6 TQ69

The Hoop

 Modern British

tel: 01277 841137 **High St CM4 9BD**
email: thehoopstock@yahoo.co.uk
dir: A12 Billericay Galleywold junct, on B1007

Assured modern cooking in an old pub

The building was converted to an ale house some 450 years ago and remains in that line of business to this day. The wooden-boarded Hoop has an atmospheric pub on the ground floor – acres of beams, draught ales at the bar – and an upstairs restaurant that is opened up to the rafters to create a slightly more refined setting amid the exposed oak. The kitchen turns out modern food that wouldn't look out of place on the menu of a thrusting big-city brasserie. Chick pea fritters, for example, as a starter with dukkah spice, pomegranate and mango yoghurt, or pheasant tempura with a game gravy to dip them into. Main courses might deliver brined belly of pork with seared scallops and winter cabbage, or slow-roasted Creedy Carver duck leg with black pudding and smoked sausage. Finish with bread-and-butter pudding with candied orange and white chocolate ice cream.

Chef Phil Utz **Owner** Michelle Corrigan **Seats** 40 **Times** 12-2.30/6-9 Closed Beer festival wk, Mon, L Sat, D Sun **Prices** Tasting menu £60, Starter £6-£10, Main fr £12 **Wines** 11 bottles over £30, 33 bottles under £30, 14 by glass **Parking** Village hall **Notes** Sunday L £10-£15, Vegetarian available, Children welcome

Learn the latest foodie trends in Birmingham and Manchester on page 21

TENDRING
Map 7 TM12

The Fat Goose

 Modern British

tel: 01255 870060 **Heath Rd CO16 0BX**
email: eat@fat-goose.co.uk
dir: A120 to Horsley Cross, follow B1035 to Tendring/Thorpe-le-Soken. 1.5m on right

Confident cooking in a charming old pub

The family-run Fat Goose is the kind of place where the kitchen bakes its own bread and local ingredients figure large on the menu. It's a restaurant, not a pub, but it still has an easy-going vibe and it's quite possible to while away a few hours here. The interior blends old and new with aplomb, so expect slate floors, exposed beams and well-spaced wooden tables, and a warming wood-burning stove in the cooler months. The menu ploughs a bistro-like furrow, with twice-baked smoked haddock and cheddar soufflé, followed by a home-made burger (minced from rib-eye, rump and chuck) with hand-cut chips, or pan-roasted haunch of venison with a potato and herb rösti. There's also a daily specials board, plus an extremely good fixed-price menu midweek. For dessert there might be vanilla pannacotta with vanilla and blueberry compôte, or glazed lemon tart with a dark chocolate ganache. There's a children's menu, too.

Times 12-2.30/6.30-9.30 Closed Mon

TOLLESHUNT KNIGHTS
Map 7 TL91

Catch 22 Restaurant

Modern

tel: 01621 868888 **Crowne Plaza Resort, Colchester - Five Lakes, Colchester Rd CM9 8HX**
email: enquiries@cpcolchester.co.uk
dir: From Colchester on A120, then A12, turn onto B1024, then B1023

Super-fresh seafood near the Essex coast

The UK's first Crowne Plaza resort spreads its wings across 320 acres of rolling Essex countryside, an upmarket package that comes fully loaded with country club-style sporting and leisure facilities. The brasserie deals in easy-eating comfort food (see entry below), but when you want something more refined than straight-up steaks, the Catch 22 Restaurant moves into fish mode, since its USP is spanking fresh fish and seafood (the day's 'catch', geddit?) landed in nearby Mersea. The kitchen is right at home when it comes to on-trend contemporary flavours-an opener such as beetroot-cured salmon with wasabi, seaweed, ginger and sake jelly, mizuna and yuzu dressing, for example. Main courses could see a terrine of red mullet and seaweed, smoked artichoke and squid delivered as a foil to grilled gurnard, while more local flavour turns up in the Maldon salt caramel that accompanies warm chocolate fondant with vanilla ice cream.

Owner AB Hotels **Seats** 60, Pr/dining room **Times** 6.30-9.30 Closed Sun-Thu **Prices** Starter £5-£9, Main £16-£25, Dessert £5-£9, Service optional **Wines** 4 bottles over £30, 5 bottles under £30, 9 by glass **Parking** 550 **Notes** Vegetarian available, Children welcome

Crowne Plaza Resort Colchester - Five Lakes

Traditional British

tel: 01621 868888 **Colchester Rd CM9 8HX**
email: enquiries@cpcolchester.co.uk **web:** www.cpcolchester.co.uk
dir: M25 junct 28, then on A12. At Kelvedon take B1024 then B1023 to Tolleshunt Knights, clearly marked by brown tourist signs

Modern British brasserie cooking in a multi-resourced hotel

Following a multi-million-pound refurbishment at this resort hotel – with its two 18-hole golf courses, country club and swish spa – the spacious main restaurant has been re-branded 'Brasserie 1'. In tune with its relaxed, contemporary outlook, the kitchen's classic British comfort food – with emphasis on quality ingredients and freshness – fits the bill to a tee. Expect the likes of a fillet of sea bass teamed with pesto and lemon barley risotto, watercress and a parmesan tuile, or loin of local pork served with mustard mash and a cider sauce, while a range of steaks (21-day dry-aged rib-eye, maybe, with vine tomatoes, flat mushrooms, thick chips and Café de Paris butter) are a perennial favourite. Finish with a warm Bakewell tart and raspberry ripple ice cream.

Owner Mr A Bejerano/AB Hotels **Seats** 80 **Times** 12.30-2/7-10 Closed 26 & 31 Dec, 1 Jan, Sun-Mon **Prices** Starter £3.50-£12, Main £10-£30, Dessert £4-£8, Service optional **Wines** 13 bottles over £30, 11 bottles under £30, 7 by glass **Parking** 550 **Notes** Sunday L £29.95, Vegetarian available, Children welcome

GLOUCESTERSHIRE

ALMONDSBURY
Map 4 ST68

Aztec Hotel & Spa
Modern British

tel: 01454 201090 **Aztec West BS32 4TS**
email: quarterjacks@shirehotels.com **web:** www.aztechotelbristol.com
dir: M5 junct 16/A38 towards city centre, hotel 200mtrs on right

Eclectic globally-inspired modern menu in a vibrant room

A hotel with the full remit of spa activities and business facilities, the Aztec also has a restaurant and bar which is worth a visit. It's a contemporary space with a Nordic feel, with a high-vaulted ceiling, rustic stone fireplace, polished wooden floors, leather seating and bold modern abstract art. The menu takes a broad sweep through global culinary culture, with British 28-day-aged beef cooked on the chargrill a bit of a speciality. You might start with crispy duck with an accompanying coriander salad and pickled ginger, or home-made oxtail soup, the meat slow-cooked for five hours. Main courses take a similar international route, so tiger prawn linguine with chilli and garlic stands alongside Wainwright ale-battered haddock with thick-cut chips, mushy peas and lemon and tartare sauce. Those steaks include Chateaubriand for two, and there's also a steak sandwich on toasted focaccia, with desserts running to warm chocolate brownie with raspberry ripple ice cream.

Times 12.30-2/7-9.30 Closed L Sat, D 25-26 Dec

ALVESTON
Map 4 ST68

Alveston House Hotel
Modern European

tel: 01454 415050 **Davids Ln BS35 2LA**
email: info@alvestonhousehotel.co.uk **web:** www.alvestonhousehotel.co.uk
dir: On A38, 3.5m N of M4/M5 interchange. M5 junct 16 N'bound or junct 14 S'bound

Attractive Georgian hotel with traditionally based menu

A white Georgian hotel with a small portico entrance, set within walled gardens with a restaurant to one side, Alveston House is well worth the short drive out from Bristol. The gardens with their ornamental lily pond are a pleasant spot for a drink, and inside the place is done in calming pastel shades, not the nerve-twanging primary colours favoured by many a boutique hotel. Carriages, the dining room, is all light lemon and cream, a restful neutral backdrop to the gently modernised British fare on offer. Steamed Fowey mussels marinière, or a tartlet of asparagus, leeks and peas with herb salad, could be the curtain-raisers to bacon-wrapped cod with baby greens, sundried tomatoes and olives, or rump and kidney of lamb with red cabbage and mashed potato in grain mustard jus. Finish indulgently with chocolate, almond and hazelnut torte and crème fraîche, or more lightly with lemon tart, mango sorbet and raspberries. Coffee comes with home-made shortbread.

Chef Ben Halliday **Owner** Julie Camm **Seats** 75, Pr/dining room 40
Times 12-1.45/7-9.30 **Prices** Fixed L 2 course £20, Fixed D 3 course £25, Starter

£5.75-£7.75, Main £15.50-£24.50, Dessert £5.75-£7.25, Service optional **Wines** 6 bottles over £30, 29 bottles under £30, 5 by glass **Parking** 60 **Notes** Sunday L £18.50-£22.50, Vegetarian available, Children welcome

ARLINGHAM
Map 4 SO71

The Old Passage Inn
Seafood, Modern British

tel: 01452 740547 **Passage Rd GL2 7JR**
email: oldpassage@btconnect.com **web:** www.theoldpassage.com
dir: M5 junct 13/A38 towards Bristol, 2nd right to Frampton-on-Severn, over canal, bear left, follow to river

Seafood specialities overlooking a bend in the Severn

Set on an ox-bow bend of the Severn where a ford once crossed the river, The Old Passage is a restaurant with rooms done in shimmering green and consecrated to the best of West Country and Welsh seafood. Cornish lobsters and oysters are mainstays of the menu, the latter offered fried, with garlic mayonnaise for dipping, or au naturel. Things get a little exotic when soft-shelled crab comes with kumquat chutney, but old-school classicism is celebrated in main courses such as richly sauced lobster thermidor gratinated under parmesan, while lighter tastes might be served by whole roasted lemon sole in beurre noisette. Good beer-battered fish and hand-sliced chips are a stalwart, and if you're a determined meat eater, there's usually one option, but one that's much more than an afterthought, perhaps saddle of venison with oxtail and spinach arancini, puréed celeriac and braised red cabbage. Treacle tart is respectably gooey and comes with zesty marmalade ice cream. Special breakfasts are held on the days when the Severn is in full bore.

Chef Mark Redwood **Owner** Sally Pearce **Seats** 60, Pr/dining room 12
Times 12-2/7-9.30 Closed 25-26 Dec, Mon, D Sun, Tue-Wed Jan-Feb **Prices** Fixed L 2 course fr £15, Tasting menu fr £68, Starter £7.50-£13.25, Main £18.75-£48, Dessert £7.95-£8.25, Service optional **Wines** 29 bottles over £30, 16 bottles under £30, 15 by glass **Parking** 40 **Notes** ALC menu only, Sunday L, Vegetarian available, Children L only

BARNSLEY   Map 5 SP00

Barnsley House

Modern European

tel: 01285 740000 **GL7 5EE**
email: info@barnsleyhouse.com web: www.barnsleyhouse.com
dir: *4m N of Cirencester on B4425 between Cirencester & Burford*

Uncomplicated country cooking overlooking the kitchen garden

The initials BB engraved above the garden door are the seal of ownership imprinted on the property by the Barnsley village squire for whom it was originally built, one Brereton Bouchier. It dates from the end of the 17th century, and is a slice of soft-focus grandeur in Cotswold stone, its gardens laid out by Rosemary Verey in the 1950s. Contemporary styling within produces a plain-looking long dining room, The Potager, framed in blond wood tones, with views over the kitchen garden from which it takes its name. Dishes are kept simple, the better to celebrate the provenance and quality of their materials. First up could be an assemblage of watermelon, spiced cashews and feta, or grilled cuttlefish with courgette and pepper salad, before mains such as superbly flavoured local chicken, with green beans, dauphinoise and bacon, or salmon from the Wear lightly dressed in fennel, basil and lemon. A side dish of heirloom tomato salad is a must-have in the circumstances. Desserts maintain the straightforward style, matching bitter chocolate tart with praline parfait, or adding plums to glazed rice pudding.

Chef Graham Grafton **Owner** Calcot Health and Leisure **Seats** 40, Pr/dining room 14 **Times** 12-2.30/7-9.30 **Prices** Fixed L 2 course fr £22, Starter £7-£14.50, Main £13-£32, Dessert £7.50 **Wines** 40 bottles over £30, 20 bottles under £30, 10 by glass **Parking** 25 **Notes** Sunday L, Vegetarian available, Children D 12yrs+

Who has won our Food Service Award?
See page 13

Find out more about how we assess for Rosette awards on page 9

The Village Pub

Traditional & Modern British v

tel: 01285 740421 **GL7 5EF**
email: info@thevillagepub.co.uk web: www.thevillagepub.co.uk
dir: *B4425 from Cirencester to Bibury*

Local produce in a delightful Cotswold pub

Located just outside Cirencester, The Village Pub is true to its name at the heart of the community, combining a delightful traditional pub atmosphere with some first-class dining. Owned by the people behind Barnsley House and Calcot Manor (see entries), cosy, yet simple decor with unclothed wooden tables sets the scene inside, while out back there's a small terrace for dining alfresco on warmer days. It's a popular place so it's worth booking, especially at weekends. Local and seasonal produce, including trout from up the road in Bibury, is competently handled on a broadly modern British menu, with some well-executed pub classics for the purists. A punchy shredded Asian confit duck leg with chilli and coriander salad might precede local Ozleworth Estate half grouse wrapped in bacon and sage with dauphinoise potatoes and Savoy cabbage. Finish with chocolate and chestnut torte. A decent range of real ales on tap and some well chosen wines completes the experience.

Chef Graham Grafton **Owner** Richard Ball **Seats** 60 **Times** 12-2.30/6-9.30 **Prices** Starter £4-£13, Main £14-£45, Dessert £6-£11, Service optional **Wines** 5 bottles over £30, 16 bottles under £30, 3 by glass **Parking** 24 **Notes** Sunday L £12-£18, Children welcome

BIBURY   Map 5 SP10

Swan Hotel

Traditional British, European

tel: 01285 740695 **GL7 5NW**
email: info@swanhotel.co.uk web: www.cotswold-inns-hotels.co.uk/swan
dir: *9m S of Burford A40 onto B4425. 6m N of Cirencester A4179 onto B4425. In town centre by bridge*

Modern brasserie in a 17th-century coaching inn

The old Swan is a bucolic place with its riverside setting and creeper-covered walls. The venue can host a swanky wedding, with the lush gardens also available for that purpose, and there are charming bedrooms too – the place has been welcoming guests since the 17th century after all. The dining option is the Brasserie, a rather dashing contemporary space where the cooking doesn't shy away from modern constructions. So scallops come in the fashionable company of pork belly (maple-cured in this instance) and walnut sauce, or there's a more traditional trout roulade with radish and samphire salad. Main courses deliver 31-day aged steaks with hand-cut chips and tempura onions rings, or go for lemon sole with roast fennel and shallots. Dessert brings comfort in the form of cinnamon steamed sponge or banana and toffee mousse with banana cake and rum and coke ice cream.

Chef Shaun Lovegrove **Owner** Mr & Mrs Horton **Seats** 60, Pr/dining room 10 **Times** 12-9.30 All-day dining **Prices** Fixed L 2 course fr £14.50, Fixed D 3 course fr £35 **Wines** 6 bottles over £30, 6 bottles under £30 **Parking** 15, On street **Notes** Sunday L £16.95-£19.95, Vegetarian available, Children welcome

BUCKLAND   Map 10 SP03

Buckland Manor

– see opposite

Buckland Manor

BUCKLAND	Map 10 SP03

British NEW

tel: 01386 852626 **WR12 7LY**
email: info@bucklandmanor.com **web:** www.bucklandmanor.co.uk
dir: *2m SW of Broadway. Take B4632 signed Cheltenham, then take turn for Buckland. Hotel through village on right*

Confident modern cooking in a grand country house

The old stone manor dates from the 13th century and stands alongside the church of St Michael in ten acres of grounds. It's quite a spot, with views that won't have changed a great deal over the centuries, and no shortage of original charm and character within. This country-house hotel of impressive pedigree is home to a rather dynamic restaurant headed up by chef William Guthrie. The formal and traditional dining room has panelled walls and historic portraits hanging on its walls, and they prefer it if gentlemen wear 'a jacket and shirt', although 'smart/casual' is the abiding philosophy. Lunch on the terrace is a summertime treat. This formal atmosphere is the setting for contemporary dishes made from carefully sourced local ingredients and home-grown herbs. A first course confit chicken, duck and foiegras terrine comes with pickled veg to cut

though the delicious richness, plus candied walnuts and apricot purée, or go for a savoury pannacotta made with Oxford Blue cheese. Main-course hake is pan-fried (just right) and served with fennel purée and a creamy caviar sauce, while roast loin of veal is partnered with an oxtail bonbon, pumpkin purée and cavolonero. Desserts are a real treat if a passionfruit mousse with coconut foam and a mango and lime sorbet or blood orange soufflé with jasmine tea foam and white chocolate ice cream are anything to go by. There's attention to detail running right through the kitchen's output, from the amuse-bouche such as a chorizo arancini, to home-made breads and petits fours of white chocolate lollipops. There's a full-on tasting menu which can take you from brown crab bavarois to a selection of British cheeses, plus Sunday lunch and afternoon tea options.

Chef Will Guthrie **Owner** Andrew & Christina Brownsword **Times** 12.30-2/7.30-9 **Prices** Fixed L 2 course £20.50, Fixed D 3 course £65, Tasting menu £85 **Wines** 400 bottles over £30, 6 bottles under £30, 15 by glass **Notes** Tasting menu 7 course, Sunday L £30.50

The Beaufort Dining Room Ellenborough Park

CHELTENHAM	Map 10 SO92

Modern British 🍷 NOTABLE WINE LIST

tel: 01242 545454 **Southam Rd GL52 3NH**
email: info@ellenboroughpark.com **web:** www.ellenboroughpark.com
dir: *A46 right after 3m onto B4079, merges with A435, 4m, over 3 rdbts, left onto Southam Lane, right onto Old Road, right onto B4632, hotel on right*

Culinary alchemy in a traditional Tudor mansion

Ellenborough began life in the early 16th century as Southam House, started by one Thomas Goodman, but sold on before it was finished, somewhat in the manner of a Tudor timeshare. Not that the house lacks anything in historic grandeur, with its Great Hall open to Goodman's original timbered roof, two-storey bay-windowed south wing, and stained-glass tributes to the generally under-loved Henry VII and his queen, Elizabeth of York. It stands on part of the original Cheltenham estate of the sport of kings, and remains handy for the jump-racing today. Refreshingly, no attempt has been made to cosmeticise the public rooms into the modern manner, and the Beaufort dining room is a haven of oak panelling, bone china, window mullions and equestrian paintings. When it comes to the cooking, of course, it's another matter, and an energetically contemporary

intelligence adds its lustre to the scene, courtesy of head chef David Kelman. There is a complexity to the dishes that is brought off in nerveless fashion, making a culinary alchemy of what in lesser hands might be gustatory confusion. Starters encompass king scallops with carrot and quince salsa in coriander and lime mayonnaise, or warm artichoke mousse with a truffled mushroom fritter, artichoke purée and wild mushroom dressing. Following those pump-primers might be brill fillet with a creamed shellfish tartlet, confit fennel, cherry tomatoes and spinach, or roast smoked venison loin with barley and parsnip, salt-baked beetroot and baby onions in chocolate and raspberry jus. An irresistible, extensive menu of helpfully described artisan cheeses is a major lure, but so too are desserts such as white chocolate-coated hazelnut and toffee parfait with banana and pistachio cake and caramelised banana, or pink grapefruit and chocolate baked Alaska in Mandarine Napoléon sauce.

Chef David Kelman **Seats** 60, Pr/dining room 20 **Times** 7-10 Closed Mon, L Mon-Sat, D Sun **Prices** Fixed D 3 course fr £55, Tasting menu fr £65, Service optional **Wines** 510 bottles over £30, 25 bottles under £30, 12 by glass **Parking** 130 **Notes** Sunday L £24-£30, Vegetarian available, Children welcome

CHARINGWORTH   Map 10 SP13

Charingworth Manor Hotel

French, Mediterranean, Traditional British V

tel: 01386 593555 **GL55 6NS**
email: gm.charingworthmanor@classiclodges.co.uk **web:** www.classiclodges.co.uk
dir: M40 exit at signs for A429/Stow. Follow signs for Moreton-in-Marsh. From Chipping
Camden follow signs for Charingworth Manor

Charming country-house hotel with unfussy contemporary cooking

This honey-coloured stone manor has stood on this plot for some 700 years and is a
vision deserving of a place on any biscuit tin. It will come as no surprise to hear the
place is a big hit on the wedding scene – it's romantic, and then some. The interior
matches old and new with a keen eye and there are spa and leisure facilities to
ensure maximum pampering. The business of eating takes place in the John
Greville Restaurant, with its splendid oak beams, shimmering candles, and
fabulous views out over the pretty countryside. The kitchen keeps things relatively
uncomplicated, so you might start with chicken liver pâté with toasted brioche and
apple chutney, or roast parsnip and thyme soup finished with honey and cream.
Next up, main course delivers the likes of roast breast of free-range chicken with
ceps duxelle stuffing and Madeira jus, or honey-roasted belly of pork with crispy
crackling and five spice-scented jus.

Chef Chris Lelliott **Owner** Classic Lodges **Seats** 50, Pr/dining room 50
Times 12-2.30/7-10 **Prices** Fixed L 2 course fr £12.95, Fixed D 3 course fr £39.50,
Tasting menu fr £55, Service optional **Wines** 75 bottles over £30, 25 bottles under
£30, 10 by glass **Parking** 100 **Notes** Fixed D 4 course, Tasting menu available 1st Fri
in month, Sunday L £19.95-£24.95, Children welcome

CHELTENHAM   Map 10 SO92

The Beaufort Dining Room Ellenborough Park

– see page 175

Le Champignon Sauvage

– see opposite

Cheltenham Park Hotel

Modern International

tel: 01242 222021 **Cirencester Rd, Charlton Kings GL53 8EA**
email: cheltenhampark@pumahotels.co.uk **web:** www.pumahotels.co.uk
dir: On A435, 2m SE of Cheltenham near Lilley Brook Golf Course

Classic and contemporary dining beside a lake

Whether you have had a winner or lost your shirt on the horses at nearby
Cheltenham racecourse, the Lakeside Restaurant of this smart country hotel is the
place to end the day with a meal of celebration or consolation. The bright and airy
space is flooded with light from walls of floor-to-ceiling windows overlooking the
gardens and lake, and cheerfully kitted out with tangerine, burgundy, and grey
high-backed seats at bare darkwood tables – a setting that sits well with the
uncomplicated, please-all repertoire of classic and gently modern cooking. The
kitchen sources its materials diligently and delivers well-executed dishes along the
lines of chicken liver parfait with fruit chutney and melba toast, followed by braised
shoulder of lamb with gratin potatoes, spinach, asparagus and roasted parsnips.
End in comfort mode with sticky toffee pudding with butterscotch sauce and
clotted cream.

Chef Mr Sumit Puakrabarty **Owner** Puma Hotels **Seats** 180, Pr/dining room 22
Times 12.30-2.30/7-9.30 Closed L Mon-Sat **Wines** 14 bottles over £30, 47 bottles
under £30, 18 by glass **Parking** 170 **Notes** Sunday L fr £15, Vegetarian available,
Children welcome

The Curry Corner

Bangladeshi, Indian

tel: 01242 528449 **133 Fairview Rd GL52 2EX**
email: info@thecurrycorner.com
dir: From A40 turn right into Hewlett Rd, at mini-rdbt turn left

Genuine Bangladeshi flavours, superbly cooked

On the edge of Cheltenham's main shopping area, The Curry Corner occupies a
Georgian townhouse-style property behind a white façade. It's been given a chic,
contemporary look, with ruby-red wall coverings set off by carvings. Well-dressed
tables are decently spaced, and lighting and music add to the ambience, as do the
relaxed and friendly staff. Genuine Bangladeshi home cooking is the theme, so
spices are flown in from far-flung countries like India, Morocco and Turkey, with
fresh produce sourced locally. This policy, combined with high technical skills and
good judgement, results in dishes that zing with layers of flavours, from starters of
prawn luchi puri (in tomato curry) and shingara (spiced shredded lamb in crisp
pastry) to main courses such as melt-in-the-mouth duck breast in orange-based
curry sauce, and tender hot chilli lamb. Breads, vegetables and chutneys are all of
a standard, as are attractively presented desserts like gulab jamon and coconut
sorbet.

Times 12-2/5.30-11.30 Closed 25 Dec, Mon (open some BHs), L Fri

The Daffodil

British, European

tel: 01242 700055 **18-20 Suffolk Pde, Montpellier GL50 2AE**
email: eat@thedaffodil.com
dir: S of town centre, just off Suffolk Rd, near Cheltenham Boys' College

Chargrilled specialities in a gorgeous art deco cinema

Once Cheltenham's first cinema, opening in 1922 in the days when such venues
were as ostentatious as ocean-liners (check those sweeping staircases), the
Daffodil makes a stunning restaurant venue. Art deco touches abound, including
the majestic light fixtures, and a pair of kissing seats (an undivided double seat for
canoodlers) is preserved in what was once the circle. The open kitchen with its
charcoal oven is the centre of attention nowadays, and the chargrilled dishes are
not to be missed. Calves' liver is tenderly textured and comes in classic fashion
with brittle streaky bacon, fondant potato and mint butter, and the steaks are
among the dazzling ornaments of the town's dining scene. Fish might be sea bass
with clams and cockles in Indian-spiced sauce. Start as you mean to go on with
assertive black pudding and scallops, served with pea purée and truffle honey. The
talking-point dessert is pineapple carpaccio with coconut ice cream and honey
baba in lime and chilli syrup.

Times 12-3/6-10 Closed 1-7 Jan, Sun

Who has won our Chefs' Chef award?
Find out on page 10

Le Champignon Sauvage

Modern French

tel: 01242 573449 **24-28 Suffolk Rd GL50 2AQ**
email: mail@lechampignonsauvage.co.uk
dir: *S of town centre, on A40, near Cheltenham College*

Daring, thoughtful cooking in a supremely civilised setting

Of the many good reasons for a visit to the timelessly beautiful spa town of Cheltenham, the Champignon has to be high on the list. David and Helen Everitt-Matthias have been running the place since the late 1980s, and time hasn't in the least dimmed their enthusiasm. In the case of David's cooking, it has rather refined it to a pitch of sublime accomplishment. This is a place every foodie should have on their bucket list. There is nothing startling in the decor and ambience, just the feeling of stepping straight off the street into a soothingly neutral space enlivened with eye-catching modern artworks setting the relaxing scene over which Helen continues to preside with unflappable aplomb. David's cooking has its roots in the classics but that doesn't mean he's not looking forward; he describes his food as mixing terroir and modern French and this seems a fair assessment of dishes that deal in the humbler cuts of meat alongside the more luxurious, and combine traditional preparations alongside some slightly more modish techniques. Long before it became an over-used buzzword, foraging has been a part of life here, so expect some lesser-known wild ingredients too. Start perhaps with a wonderfully focused dish of butter-poached dabs with new season's peas, onions and wilted ground elder, or seared flank of Dexter beef with Hereford snails and parsley purée. The art of thoughtful combining remains important, as seen in main courses that are all about shining the spotlight on outstanding principal components. This could be a slab of hake poached in beurre noisette and served with both Jerusalem and globe artichokes, so rarely found together despite their deceptively

similar names, or garnet-red wood pigeon, its gamey richness pointed up in a sweet Moroccan pastilla preparation with chermoula paste (think coriander, garlic, olive oil and lemon) and carrot tagine. And when the desire for elevated comfort food strikes, you can't beat the reassuring feeling that comes from a porcine plateful comprising a pavé of Gloucester Old Spot pork, braised cheek and pig's head sweetened with smoked maple and raisin purée . Aromatic herb and spice flavours confer individualism on bewitching desserts such as muscovado parfait with bergamot cream and mandarin jelly, bitter chocolate and olive tart with fennel ice cream, and salted chicory root iced mousse with vanilla rice pudding and rich chocolate sorbet. The excellent wine list focuses on France and the starting prices are very reasonable.

Chef David Everitt-Matthias **Owner** Mr & Mrs D Everitt-Matthias **Seats** 40 **Times** 12.30-1.30/7.30-8.45 Closed 10 days Xmas, 3 wks Jun, Sun-Mon **Prices** Fixed L 2 course £26, Fixed D 3 course £32, Service optional **Wines Parking** Public car park (Bath Rd) **Notes** ALC 2/3 course £48/£59, 4 course inc cheese & dessert £69 No children

CHELTENHAM *continued*

The Greenway Hotel & Spa

🏵🏵 Modern British, French V 🍷 NOTABLE WINE LIST

tel: 01242 862352 **Shurdington Rd GL51 4UG**
email: info@thegreenway.co.uk **web:** www.thegreenwayhotelandspa.com
dir: *3m S of Cheltenham on A46 (Stroud) & through Shurdington*

Refined modern cooking in the Cotswolds

An impeccable Elizabethan manor house of considerable charm, The Greenway has all the initial attributes needed to make a fine country-house hotel, with glorious grounds, original features and the like. Add to those the 21st-century embellishments of a swish spa, elegant bedrooms and a brace of dining options, and you have a place ready to impress the modern day visitor. The Orchard Brasserie is a stylish venue with a cool and contemporary finish, while the main fine-dining Garden Restaurant aims to impress with its take on refined, modern British cooking (with definite evidence of classical French ways). Start with ballotine of rabbit in the company of beetroot 'textures' and a raisin sauce, or scallops with curried lentils and cod cheeks. Main-course might deliver a fillet of pan-seared sea bream with crushed new potatoes and tomato confit, or twice-cooked belly of pork partnered with dauphinoise potatoes. For dessert, expect the likes of orange pannacotta with raspberry sorbet or dark chocolate marquise with honeycomb and passionfruit sorbet.

Chef Robin Dudley **Owner** Sir Peter Rigby **Seats** 60, Pr/dining room 22
Times 12-2.30/7-9.30 **Prices** Prices not confirmed **Wines** 200 bottles over £30, 40 bottles under £30, 11 by glass **Notes** ALC 3 course £49.50, Sunday L, Children welcome

Hotel du Vin Cheltenham

🏵 British, French, European

tel: 01242 588450 **Parabola Rd GL50 3AQ**
email: info.cheltenham@hotelduvin.com **web:** www.hotelduvin.com
dir: *M5 junct 11, follow signs for city centre. At rdbt opposite Morgan Estate Agents take 2nd left, 200mtrs to Parabola Rd*

Bistro dining in Cheltenham's restaurant quarter

The Cheltenham outpost of this popular boutique hotel brand is located in the trendy Montpellier area, and its decorative showpiece is a large spiral staircase down which diners descend from the bar to the busy bistro. Here, the look is as you'd expect: empty wine bottles as decoration, every part of available walls covered with wine related prints and memorabilia, wooden floorboards, simply-laid unclothed tables, black leather chairs and banquettes. Good quality ingredients are treated with care and respect in bistro-style dishes and, of course, the wine list impresses with its mainly French selection, including plenty by the glass. Dressed crab and walnut toast or moules frites start things off on a sound footing, before something like half a Normandy chicken with a jus rôti, or steak haché with fried duck egg and bois bourdain. A classic crêpe Suzette makes a fitting finale.

Chef Paul Mottram **Owner** KSL Leisure **Seats** 92, Pr/dining room 32
Times 12-2/6.30-10.30 **Prices** Fixed L 2 course £17.50-£19.95, Fixed D 3 course £19.95-£24.95, Starter £7-£12.50, Main £15-£32, Dessert £6.50-£7.95 **Wines** 300 bottles over £30, 70 bottles under £30, 20 by glass **Parking** 23 **Notes** Sunday L £24.95-£29.95, Vegetarian available, Children welcome

Lumière

🏵🏵 Modern British V 🍷 NOTABLE WINE LIST

tel: 01242 222200 **Clarence Pde GL50 3PA**
email: info@lumiere.cc **web:** www.lumiere.cc
dir: *Town centre, near bus station*

High-octane modern cooking from masterful chef

Refurbishment has given a clean, elegant and serene ambience to Lumière, with its crisply starched linen, pin-striped carpet, banquettes and gilt mirrors, a bar at one end and a window giving on to the kitchen. Chef Jon Howe brings his own highly distinctive stamp to the style of the cooking, giving dishes a degree of refined complexity witnessed in a pairing of scallops with belly pork served with cumin caramel, carrot, orange and a purée of star anise. His skills and thoughtfulness pay off, producing an attractive, palate-pleasing starter of deep-fried, thinly breaded beef cheek balls, moist and of superb flavour, with corned beef and bresaola, accompanied by wasabi, anchovies and beetroot, each element working well without overpowering the others. Invention extends to desserts along the lines of pineapple carpaccio with stunning kalamansi sorbet, passionfruit, and coconut marshmallows with peanuts, ginger and chilli. Extras like breads and canapés are well up to snuff, and meals end memorably with a selection of petits fours with coffee.

Chef Jon Howe **Owner** Jon & Helen Howe **Seats** 25 **Times** 12-1.30/7-9 Closed 2 wks winter, 2 wks summer, Sun-Mon, L Tue **Prices** Fixed L 3 course £28, Fixed D 3 course £55, Tasting menu £60-£75 **Wines** 58 bottles over £30, 15 bottles under £30, 21 by glass **Parking** On street **Notes** Tasting menu 7/9 course No children

Monty's Brasserie

⚛⚛ Modern British, Seafood v

tel: 01242 227678 **George Hotel, 41 St Georges Rd GL50 3DZ**
email: info@montysbraz.co.uk **web:** www.montysbraz.co.uk
dir: M5 junct 11, follow signs to town centre. At lights (TGI Fridays) turn left onto
Gloucester Rd. Straight on, at lights turn right, Monty's 0.75m on left

Smart seasonal brasserie cooking in stylish Grade II listed hotel

Monty's is part of the Grade II listed George Hotel, built, like much of the spa town,
in the Georgian era. It's a modern and lively brasserie, with a bare boarded floor,
brown leather-look seats at unclothed tables, plain walls and a cheerful
atmosphere. The seasonally-changing menu is exactly right for the place, and what
the kitchen does supremely well with sound ingredients, adding a degree of
complication to dishes without pushing them into a taste too far. Crab, cod and dill
fishcakes, for instance, come with crushed peas, parsley purée, pickled onions and
lemon and caper mayonnaise, and that's just a starter. Roast partridge might
appear in season, stuffed with apricots and cranberries, served with red wine jus,
braised leg, pickled pears and fondant potato. The appeal is broadened by the likes
of Thai crispy duck with chilli and sesame dipping sauce, then seared harissa-
spiced salmon fillet with ras el hanout dressing, chilli and lemon couscous and
cauliflower beignets. To top things off might be sticky toffee pudding with rum and
raisin ice cream.

Chef Renark Cousins **Owner** Jeremy Shaw **Seats** 40, Pr/dining room 32
Times 12-2/6-10 Closed 25-26 Dec **Prices** Fixed L 2 course £13.50, Fixed D 3 course
£15, Starter £7-£10, Main £16-£24, Dessert £5-£8 **Wines** 17 bottles over £30, 25
bottles under £30, 7 by glass **Parking** 30 **Notes** Sunday L £18-£22, Children
welcome

CHIPPING CAMPDEN   **Map 10 SP13**

The Kings

⚛⚛ Modern British v

tel: 01386 840256 **The Square, High St GL55 6AW**
email: info@kingscampden.co.uk **web:** www.kingscampden.co.uk
dir: In centre of town square

Georgian Cotswold townhouse with energetic brasserie cooking

The Kings may be a classic Georgian townhouse built in honey-hued Cotswold stone
right on Chipping Campden's square, but the traditional chintz and twee country
hotel look has been chucked out. Instead, the place wears the style of a smartly
casual modern operation-that's to say comfy banquettes, mismatched furniture and
polished wooden floors in the brasserie, and in the beamed restaurant, unclothed
antique tables, a flagged floor, a log fire and moody lighting. The up-to-date
approach carries through to what appears on the plate: modern food built on
splendid seasonal ingredients. The menus have something for everyone, whether
it's a well-thought-out array of duck-based flavours and textures comprising slices
of duck breast, creamy duck mousse and a duck confit parcel, all mixing well with
sliced cherries, rich cherry sauce and almond biscotti, or a main course of Cotswold
chicken breast with gnocchi, sautéed Mediterranean vegetables, broccoli and
chorizo cream. End with something that adds a clever twist to classic ideas like
elderflower pannacotta with lemon tart ice cream and olive oil biscuits.

Chef Gareth Rufus **Owner** Sir Peter Rigby **Seats** 45, Pr/dining room 20
Times 12-2.30/6.30-9.30 **Prices** Fixed L 2 course £13.50-£18.50, Fixed D 3 course
£32.50-£75, Tasting menu £75, Service optional **Wines** 25 bottles over £30, 22
bottles under £30, 10 by glass **Parking** 12 **Notes** Sunday L £17.50-£22.50, Children
welcome

Three Ways House

⚛ Modern British

tel: 01386 438429 **Chapel Ln, Mickleton GL55 6SB**
email: reception@puddingclub.com **web:** www.threewayshousehotel.com
dir: On B4632, in village centre

More than just desserts at the home of the Pudding Club

You can take it for granted that the Cotswolds home of the famous Pudding Club
won't be serving up any foams, froths or drizzles. As its name hints, the club is
famous for championing Great British Puddings, but there's a lot more to
appreciate here before we get to dessert. The Victorian hotel has oodles of period
character, although the restaurant bucks the trend with a more contemporary look
involving stripy seats and cool blue walls. As you might expect, the food is punchy,
big-hearted British stuff, put together with a flag-waving dedication to local raw
materials. Pressed turkey and bacon terrine with cranberry compôte is a typical
starter, followed by roast pork fillet with black pudding mash and roasted garlic.
And so to pudding, which just has to be a selection of steamed puds-sticky toffee
and date, chocolate, and syrup sponge, anyone?-with lashings of custard.

Chef Mark Rowlandson **Owner** Simon & Jill Coombe **Seats** 80, Pr/dining room 70
Times 12-2.30/7-9.30 Closed L Mon-Sat **Prices** Fixed D 3 course £38.50, Service
optional **Wines** 12 bottles over £30, 31 bottles under £30, 13 by glass **Parking** 37,
On street **Notes** Pudding Club places £3.50, Sunday L £22.50-£26.50, Vegetarian
available, Children welcome

CIRENCESTER   **Map 5 SP00**

Jesse's Bistro

⚛ Modern British

tel: 01285 641497 & 07932 150720   **14 Blackjack St GL7 2AA**
email: info@jessesbistro.co.uk **web:** www.jessesbistro.co.uk
dir: In town centre between the parish church & Roman Museum, behind Jesse Smith
the Butchers

Rustic bistro with local provenance and skilful cookiing

Down a cobbled alleyway alongside a butcher's under the same ownership (Jesse
Smith), this bistro sources its ingredients with due diligence. The meat comes from
the shop of course, and pretty much everything else is sourced locally (except
seafood, which is shipped up daily from Cornwall). It is possible to sit in the small
courtyard on fine days, but it's all tickety-boo inside anyway, with its simple and
smart rustic finish. A starter of pan-seared scallops in the company of celeriac
purée, crisp pancetta and sauce vièrge shows the way, with sound judgement and
careful execution, or try the buttered chicken liver parfait with pear and date

continued

CIRENCESTER *continued*

chutney. Among main courses, there might be whole roasted partridge in season, or loin of English pork with a pistachio crust, served with braised belly, wild mushrooms and Madeira sauce. And to finish, red wine-poached Conference pear with a nicely wobbly vanilla pannacotta and shortbread.

Chef David Witnall, Andrew Parffrey **Owner** Watermoor Meat Supply **Seats** 55, Pr/dining room 12 **Times** 12-3/7-10 Closed Xmas, Sun, D Mon **Prices** Fixed L 2 course £18-£24, Fixed D 3 course £24-£28.50, Starter £6-£15, Main £12.50-£30, Dessert £6.50-£8.50, Service optional **Wines** 35 bottles over £30, 25 bottles under £30, 15 by glass **Parking** Old station car park **Notes** Vegetarian available, Children welcome

---

CLEARWELL Map 4 SO50

Tudor Farmhouse Hotel & Restaurant

◎◎ Modern British

tel: 01594 833046 **High St GL16 8JS**
email: info@tudorfarmhousehotel.co.uk **web:** www.tudorfarmhousehotel.co.uk
dir: Off A4136 onto B4228, through Coleford, turn right into Clearwell, hotel on right just before War Memorial Cross

Clear modern flavours in an ancient farmhouse

In a sleepy village deep in the Forest of Dean this converted farmhouse restaurant, as the name suggests, has inglenooks, wood panelling, venerable beams and exposed stone walls to attest to its origins, but what comes out of the kitchen these days is far from stuck in the past. Driven by seasonal and local ingredients, the menus are full of fresh, modern ideas, among which you might find a terrine of confit chicken, shiitaki mushrooms and pancetta, served with raisin purée, while main courses run to braised shoulder of locally-farmed lamb with poached apple, carrot purée and red wine jus. To finish, head for chestnut and maple tart with vanilla mascarpone cream and orange caramel syrup. This is genuine, unaffected cooking and it's all backed by personable staff who provide efficient, friendly service.

Times 12-2/6.30-9 Closed 2-5 Jan

The Wyndham Arms Hotel

◎ Modern British

tel: 01594 833666 **GL16 8JT**
email: stay@thewyndhamhotel.co.uk **web:** www.thewyndhamhotel.co.uk
dir: Exit B4228. Hotel in village centre on B4231

Polished gastro-pub fare in old village inn

Clearwell is a picturesque village near Offa's Dyke Path between the Wye Valley and the Forest of Dean, and this characterful old inn is at its centre. Local ales and cider are dispensed in the rustic-style bar, and meals are served in the stone-walled, vaulted restaurant. The pub keeps Gloucestershire Old Spot pigs (and sells its own takeaway sausages and burgers), which turn up in pork and ham hock terrine, and as roast loin with apple and potato mash and cider cream. Elsewhere, starters can take in home-smoked duck breast with raspberry vinaigrette, or sardine escabèche in a salad with crayfish and citrus dressing, with pubby main courses like grilled gammon steak with fried eggs and chips, or more classically orientated pan-fried fillet of sea bass with barigoule sauce and saffron-flavoured potatoes.

Times 12-2/6.30-9 Closed 1st wk Jan, L some days in winter, D some Sun

---

CORSE LAWN Map 10 SO83

Corse Lawn House Hotel

◎◎ British, French V ♦ NOTABLE WINE LIST

tel: 01452 780771 **GL19 4LZ**
email: enquiries@corselawn.com **web:** www.corselawn.com
dir: 5m SW of Tewkesbury on B4211, in village centre

Extensive menus in an appealing rural setting

The red-brick house dates from the Queen Anne period of the early 18th century and stands on the village green in front of a large pond that once had the job of cleaning up both coach and horses. It's a lovely spot. The hotel has been run by the Hine family since 1978 and continues to be operated with old-school charm. There's a traditionally decorated bistro (no tablecloths) and a smart restaurant (tablecloths) with the latter serving up a classic modern British menu that makes good use of trusted local supply lines. A simple starter of grilled Cornish sardines (not so local, but lovely and fresh) with tapenade and tomato vinaigrette shows the way, and there are more Mediterranean flavours in a fish soup with all the trimmings. Next up might be pan-fried fillet of pollock with with samphire and saffron sauce, or roast haunch of venison partnered with celeriac and a blueberry sauce. A zingy lemon posset tart makes for a fine finale, and there are cheeses served from the trolley.

Chef Martin Kinahan **Owner** Hine family **Seats** 50, Pr/dining room 28 **Times** 12-2/7-9.30 Closed 24-26 Dec **Prices** Fixed L 2 course £16.50-£22.50, Fixed D 3 course £21.50-£33.50, Starter £6.50-£10.50, Main £14.50-£22.50, Dessert £5.50-£7.50, Service optional **Wines** 220 bottles over £30, 80 bottles under £30, 10 by glass **Parking** 60 **Notes** Sunday L £16.50-£33.50, Children welcome

---

DAYLESFORD Map 10 SP22

Daylesford Farm Café

◎ Modern British

tel: 01608 731700 **GL56 0YG**
email: thefarm@daylesfordorganic.com
dir: From Cheltenham take A40 & A436 through Stow-on-the-Wold, follow signs to Daylesford farmshop

Organic produce cooked with flair in converted barn

The Daylesford brand has grown over the years and it's possible to buy their organic produce in Selfridges and via a major online outlet. Quite a success story. On the Gloucestershire farmland that spawned a mini-empire, the farm shop and café is a little slice of foodie heaven, where shelves are stacked with organic goodies from seafood to veggies, from bread to meat, plus a cook shop and a café. It all takes place in a smartly converted barn with a New England finish and an open-to-view kitchen. The café is busy at lunchtime (it's also open for 'supper' on Friday/Saturday evenings), so arrive early if you want to bag a table. The food makes a virtue of simplicity with the ingredients allowed to shine. A first-course chicken liver and quince parfait, for example, has a fabulous depth of flavour, or go for a salad of pear, quinoa and chick peas with toasted hazelnuts and Daylesford Blue. Wood-roasted shoulder of lamb melts in the mouth, and finish with steamed Seville orange marmalade pudding.

Chef Gaven Fuller **Owner** Carole Bamford **Seats** 75, Pr/dining room 60 **Times** 12-3/7-9.30 Closed 25-26 Dec, 1 Jan, D Mon-Thu, Sun **Prices** Starter £6.50-£10, Main £10-£16, Dessert £4.50-£8 **Wines** 2 bottles over £30, 9 bottles under £30, 6 by glass **Parking** 100 **Notes** Sunday L £10-£16, Vegetarian available, Children welcome

EBRINGTON
Map 10 SP14

The Ebrington Arms
◉◉ Modern British

tel: 01386 593223 **GL55 6NH**
email: reservations@ebringtonarms.co.uk **web:** www.theebringtonarms.co.uk
dir: From Chipping Campden take B4035 towards Shipston-on-Stour, left to Ebrington

Classic village inn with a modern menu

Still very much a pub, and right in the heart of the village by the green, The Ebrington Arms has served its community for several hundred years. The honey-coloured property dates from the 17th century, which is evident from the copious oak beams and flagged floors, and, if you arrive in the cooler months, a roaring fire awaits. It may be a classic pub in the best sense, but the menu takes a contemporary line, with the kitchen turning out bright dishes based on seasonal, local ingredients. There are daily specials and pub classics, too. Ham hock terrine with raisin purée and beef dripping brioche is one way to begin, or dive into Cornish crab cake with garlic aïoli and chilli and coriander salsa. Next up, salt-baked celeriac with cider-braised onions, pearl barley and onion ash is a creative veggie dish, or go for stout-braised ox cheek with creamed potatoes, carrots and kale. There's craft and creativity among desserts, too, with the likes of plum clafoutis with vanilla ice cream.

Chef Andrew Lipp, Jonny Mills **Owner** Claire & Jim Alexander **Seats** 50, Pr/dining room 30 **Times** 12-2.30/6-9.30 Closed 25 Dec **Prices** Starter £5-£7.50, Main £11-£25, Dessert £5.50-£6.50, Service optional **Wines** 22 bottles over £30, 40 bottles under £30, 10 by glass **Parking** 13 **Notes** Sunday L £12.75-£14, Vegetarian available, Children welcome

GLOUCESTER
Map 10 SO81

The Wharf House Restaurant with Rooms
◉ Modern European

tel: 01452 332900 **Over Waterside, Over GL2 8DB**
email: enquiries@thewharfhouse.co.uk **web:** www.thewharfhouse.co.uk
dir: From Over rdbt take A40 westbound to Ross-on-Wye, 1st right in 50 yds

Appealing cooking in a former lockhouse by the Severn

The Wharf House overlooks a canal basin (it's owned by the Herefordshire and Gloucestershire Canal Trust), and there are plenty of watery walks nearby, either along the towpath or by the Severn. Eating out on the terrace may be a possibility, while the restaurant is an inviting prospect, designed along clean, uncluttered lines with modern oak furniture on a parquet floor. 'We strive to work with the best of local suppliers,' declares the menu, and the produce is subjected to modern treatments, often Continental. Herrings are marinated in dill and served with avocado and melon, and carpaccio is plated with fiery horseradish, celery and rocket. Among main courses, venison loin is rolled in walnuts and accompanied by rich redcurrant and chocolate sauce, Savoy cabbage sprinkled with sesame, and chips, and there's normally a fish of the day and a couple of vegetarian options. End with straightforward crème brûlée.

Chef David Penny **Owner** H & G Canal Trust **Seats** 40 **Times** 12-3/6-close Closed 22 Dec-1 Jan **Prices** Tasting menu £45.99-£52.99, Service optional 10% **Wines** 20 bottles over £30, 31 bottles under £30, 7 by glass **Parking** 32 **Notes** Sun L not available in winter, Sunday L fr £15.99, Vegetarian available, Children welcome

LOWER SLAUGHTER
Map 10 SP12

Lower Slaughter Manor
◉◉◉ – see below

Lower Slaughter Manor

LOWER SLAUGHTER
Map 10 SP12

Modern British v
tel: 01451 820456 **GL54 2HP**
email: info@lowerslaughter.co.uk **web:** www.lowerslaughter.co.uk
dir: Off A429, signed 'The Slaughters'. 0.5m into village on right

Classically-based cooking in an elegant Cotswolds hotel

Lower Slaughter Manor epitomises all that the Cotswolds is about: a gorgeous, honey-stoned 17th-century house in a picture-postcard village, it has olde English charm in spades and is a wonderfully relaxing place to stay. The elegant interiors have been brought fully into the 21st century without jarring with the antiquity of the house (although the recent refurb to the restaurant-all grey walls and seating, and grey and red curtains-is said to be a little bit too modern for some older guests), and the staff are as friendly and welcoming as you could hope for. There are several lounges for lounging in before dinner-perhaps with a G&T and a few well-made canapés (plaice goujons with tartare sauce, and ham hock with apricot purée maybe) in hand; it all augurs well for what is to come. And what is to come is some classic, highly skilled cooking from head chef Jamie Raftery, who draws on the abundant local larder for his finely wrought seasonal

dishes. Some warm fresh breads and a little shot of celeriac and truffle velouté are highly enjoyable preludes to a starter of Cornish crab tortellini with stir-fried Enoki and mange tout and lemongrass sauce-a dish of faultless technique and magnificent flavours. Next up, local wild venison saddle is perfectly timed and well seasoned, and accompanied by red cabbage, pear, chestnut, roast parsnip and juniper sauce. A simple but deeply chocolate Valrhona dark chocolate tart with confit orange sorbet and roast hazelnuts is possibly the highlight of the meal. Make sure you draw on the friendly sommelier's expertise when it comes to choosing from the impressive wine list.

Chef Jamie Raftery **Owner** Brownsword Hotels **Seats** 55, Pr/dining room 20 **Times** 12.15-2/7-9.30 **Prices** Fixed L 2 course £20.50-£25.50, Fixed D 3 course fr £65, Tasting menu fr £85, Service optional **Wines** 350 bottles over £30, 20 bottles under £30, 12 by glass **Parking** 30 **Notes** Sunday L, Children welcome

LOWER SLAUGHTER *continued*

The Slaughters Country Inn

◉◉ Modern British **NEW**

tel: 01451 822143 **GL54 2HS**
email: info@theslaughtersinn.co.uk **web:** www.theslaughtersinn.co.uk
dir: *Exit A429 at 'The Slaughters' sign, between Stow-on-the-Wold & Bourton-on-the-Water. In village centre*

Contemporary classic dishes in a Cotswold country hotel

Formerly known as Washbourne Court, this 17th century house, once an Eton crammer, long ago banished all thought of swishing canes for the distinctly lovelier prospect of welcoming guests to the kind of haven of relaxation they might hope for from a hotel on a bank of the River Eye in a peaceful Cotswold village. The riverside terrace is a plum spot for lunch or aperitifs, while memories linger on in the name only of Eton's Restaurant, a stylish venue with fine table appointments and smartly attentive service. Expect a modern British menu that uses an exciting mix of ingredients, in a starter of Hereford salt beef terrine, with mustard mayonnaise and pickled vegetables-alongside contemporary classics. Mains could be grilled sea bream, with artichoke, green beans, shrimps and a lemon butter sauce, or fennel and honey glazed Creedy Carver duck breast, carrots served with a hazelnut and rocket salad. Finish with dark chocolate mousse and pistachio granola, served with caramel ice cream.

Chef Chris Fryer **Owner** Mr & Mrs Brownsword **Seats** 56, Pr/dining room 30 **Times** 12–3/6.30–9 Closed L Mon-Sat **Prices** Starter £5.95–£9.95, Main £12.50–£23.95, Dessert £5.95–£8.50, Service optional **Wines** 15 bottles over £30, 10 bottles under £30, 8 by glass **Parking** 40 **Notes** Afternoon tea available, Sunday L £15.95–£23.95, Vegetarian available, Children welcome

---

MORETON-IN-MARSH	**Map 10 SP23**

Manor House Hotel

◉◉ Modern British ᵥ

tel: 01608 650501 **High St GL56 OLJ**
email: info@manorhousehotel.info **web:** www.cotswold-inns-hotels.co.uk/manor
dir: *Off A429 at south end of town*

Classy modern cooking in a 16th-century gem

On the High Street of the tourist honeypot of a village, this Cotswold-stone hotel dates from the reign of Henry VIII, when he bequeathed it to the Dean and Chapter of Westminster. Careful renovation and updating have brought it squarely into the 21st century while retaining original features – a priest hole, for one – while the Mulberry Restaurant is a carpeted room with generously spaced, dressed tables, comfortable dining chairs and on-the-ball staff. The kitchen demonstrates sound talent and produces appealing dishes without over-complicating things. Foams sometimes embellish starters: redcurrant for venison and game terrine with prune and whisky purée, lemon for another starter of crab exotically flavoured with chilli, coconut, ginger and coriander, served with avocado mousse and Bloody Mary jelly. Well-considered main courses have included a taste of pork (slow-roast belly, braised cheek, pancetta-wrapped tenderloin, all accurately timed), with Calvados sauce, garlicky mash, broad beans and marinated apple, and pan-fried fillets of sole with prawns and scampi, shallot sauce, chive-crushed potatoes and curly kale. End with something like strawberry sponge with sherry ice cream and custard.

Chef Adrian Court **Owner** Michael & Pamela Horton **Seats** 55, Pr/dining room 120 **Times** 12–2.30/7–9.30 Closed L Mon-Sat **Prices** Fixed D 3 course £39, Tasting menu £55 **Wines** 20 bottles over £30, 20 bottles under £30, 12 by glass **Parking** 32 **Notes** Tasting menu 8 course, Sunday L £18.95–£21.50, Children 8 yrs+

Redesdale Arms

◉ British

tel: 01608 650308 **High St GL56 0AW**
email: info@redesdalearms.com **web:** www.redesdalearms.com
dir: *On A429, 0.5m from rail station*

Relaxed dining in historic Cotswold inn

This fine old Cotswold-stone inn has been a part of the bustling, picture-postcard-pretty Moreton scene for centuries, today offering a classy fusion of old and modern. It successfully blends venerable wood panelling, oak floorboards and exposed stone walls with a relaxed contemporary style, using tobacco-hued sofas, modern art and muted colour schemes. Dinner is served in the modern brasserie-styled rear conservatory, with its please-all menus conjured from quality, local and seasonal produce with simplicity and flavour to the fore. Take an opener of warm Cotswold goats' cheese and caramelised red onion tartlet with dressed leaves and balsamic and port wine syrup, and to follow, perhaps pan-seared Cornish sea bass fillet with sautéed potatoes, wilted spinach and a caviar and lemon butter sauce. To close, Greek yoghurt pannacotta with winter berry compôte.

Times 12–2.30/6.30–9

White Hart Royal Hotel

◉ Traditional British

tel: 01608 650731 **High St GL56 0BA**
email: whr@bulldogmail.co.uk **web:** www.whitehartroyal.co.uk
dir: *In town centre*

Modern cooking in a Cotswold coaching inn

Some 370 years ago, Charles I took shelter here after the battle of Marston Moor, and it's not a huge leap of imagination to picture what the place was like back then, with no shortage of period features as reminders of the heritage of the building. Refurbishment has been respectful of all that history, delivering spaces that have original charm alongside a few gently contemporary touches. The Courtyard restaurant – outside tables are a fair-weather treat – is a linen-free zone, the darkwood tables and bold colours creating a smart-casual space that will do for a special occasion or for when no excuse is needed. The menu takes a modern, brasserie-style tack in starters such as barbecue pulled pork croquette with Cajun-spiced baby corn and chipotle purée, or pan-seared scallops with curried lentil salad. Move on to main-course confit chicken thighs with rösti potatoes and desserts such as pistachio crème brûlée.

Chef Carl Chappell **Owner** Bulldog Hotel Group Ltd **Seats** 44, Pr/dining room 12 **Times** 11–10 All-day dining **Prices** Starter £5–£10, Main £12–£23, Dessert £6.50, Service optional **Wines** 7 bottles over £30, 30 bottles under £30, 11 by glass **Parking** 6, On street **Notes** Sunday L, Vegetarian available, Children welcome

Get the most out of the AA Restaurant Guide

See page 6

The Feathered Nest Country Inn

NETHER WESTCOTE
Map 10 SP22

Modern British

tel: 01993 833030 **OX7 6SD**
email: info@thefeatherednestinn.co.uk
web: www.thefeatherednestinn.co.uk
dir: On A424 between Burford & Stow-on-the-Wold, signed

A gem of a country pub in a beautiful Cotswold village

Full of period charm and contemporary appeal, this country pub and restaurant is perfectly situated in an Area of Outstanding Natural Beauty. It's the kind of place that gets the balance just right between servicing the local community as a welcoming pub, offering up swish bedrooms if you want to stay over, and paying a good deal more than passing attention to the food. With open fires and wooden beams alongside well-chosen, country-style furniture, plus a terrace and garden with countryside views, this is a gem of a place, rain or shine. What comes out of the kitchen, though, really puts it on the map, with chef Kuba Winkowski and his team turning out bright, contemporary food made with first-rate local ingredients. There's daily market menu on a blackboard and a seasonally-changing carte, and plenty of imagination and attention to detail on show. Hare might feature in a starter, for example, in a rich, gamey consommé, with agnolotti, salsify and black truffle, or

monkfish with smoked paprika, fennel, avocado and the Asian-inspired flavours of mango, chilli and lime. Main courses keep to the same path, with the likes of stone bass with langoustines and Avruga caviar, topped with a shellfish foam, and veal with oxtail pearl barley, lardo di colonnata mushrooms and a red wine sauce. The blackboard might offer up meaty ribs cooked on the charcoal grill (served with chunky chips and onion rings). Desserts keep on track with some interesting combinations; a soufflé, perhaps, flavoured with blood orange and fennel, or a sticky toffee pudding with lemon curd and pecan nuts. The wine list is a fine piece of work, with a decent choice by the glass, and there are cask-conditioned ales in the bar.

Chef Kuba Winkowski **Owner** Tony Timmer **Seats** 60, Pr/dining room 14 **Times** 12-2.30/6.30-9.30 Closed 25 Dec, Mon, D Sun **Prices** Prices not confirmed, Service optional **Wines** 215 bottles over £30, 29 bottles under £30, 19 by glass **Parking** 45 **Notes** Sunday L, Vegetarian available, Children welcome

NAILSWORTH
Map 4 ST89

Wild Garlic Restaurant and Rooms

 Modern British

tel: 01453 832615 **3 Cossack Square GL6 ODB**
email: info@wild-garlic.co.uk **web:** www.wild-garlic.co.uk
dir: *M4 junct 18. A46 towards Stroud. Enter Nailsworth, turn left at rdbt and then an immediate left. Restaurant opposite Britannia Pub*

Imaginative modern cooking in former blacksmith's

This sweet, small-yet-perfectly-formed modern restaurant is a stylish, relaxed place with enthusiastic staff to match. Chef-prop Matthew Beardshall's kitchen takes an admirable hands-on approach, making everything in-house from organic bread and pasta to sorbets and ice cream, while the concise brasserie-style menu changes monthly to reflect seasonality and make the very best use of the regional larder. On a late spring menu, expect simplicity and flavour from the likes of a fillet of South Coast turbot teamed with a slow-roast tomato salad and samphire, or perhaps Cotswold white chicken Kiev served with wild garlic butter (wild garlic rightly making an appearance on the plate; it's abundant in the area), plus potato, smoked bacon and watercress salad. To finish, maybe rhubarb and custard with champagne and poached rhubarb jelly and almond tuile.

Times 12-2.30/7-9.30 Closed 1st 2 wks Jan, Mon-Tue, L Wed, D Sun

NETHER WESTCOTE
Map 10 SP22

The Feathered Nest Country Inn

 – see page 183

NEWENT
Map 10 SO72

Three Choirs Vineyards

Modern British, European

tel: 01531 890223 **GL18 1LS**
email: ts@threechoirs.com **web:** www.threechoirs.com
dir: *2m N of Newent on B4215, follow brown tourist signs*

Award-winning wines, good food and more

With grape varieties such as seyval blanc and huxelrebe grown on the gently sloping Herefordshire hills, the Three Choirs Vineyard is a reminder, if you need it, that the UK viniculture business is in fine fettle. It makes a good trip out, what with a shop, wine tasting and cookery classes available, and you can even leave with bottles of their own cider and beer if that doesn't seem too heretical. The Vineyard Restaurant and terrace has prime views over the estate and those precious vines, and is the setting for an unfussy menu that deals in well-judged flavour combinations, plus plenty of regional produce. Start with ham hock fritter with celeriac, apples and English mustard, or a crispy free-range egg served up with broad beans and truffle mayonnaise, before 21-day aged Hereford rib-eye or beetroot tarte Tatin, beet purée and Cerney Ash goats' cheese cream. They even have their own dessert wine to accompany the likes of vanilla brulée, Herefordshire raspberries and shortbread.

Chef Siobhan Hartley **Owner** Three Choirs Vineyards Ltd **Seats** 50, Pr/dining room 20 **Times** 12-2/7-9 Closed Xmas, New Year **Prices** Fixed L 2 course fr £24.50, Fixed D 3 course fr £37.50, Starter £6.25-£10.50, Main £13.50-£21.50, Dessert £7-£8.50, Service optional **Wines** 5 bottles over £30, 24 bottles under £30, 14 by glass **Parking** 50 **Notes** Sunday L £24.50, Vegetarian available, Children welcome

PAINSWICK
Map 4 SO80

Cotswolds88Hotel

– see opposite

STOW-ON-THE-WOLD
Map 11 SP12

The Kings Head Inn

British

tel: 01608 658365 **The Green, Bledington OX7 6XQ**
email: info@kingsheadinn.net **web:** www.kingsheadinn.net
dir: *On B4450, 4m from Stow-on-the-Wold*

Refined pub fare in an atmospheric village inn

Picture this: a mellow stone Cotswolds pub looking onto a village green with ducks playing in a meandering brook; inside is a classic bar with wobbly floors – wobblier still after a few pints of Hook Norton – heart-warming log fires, head-skimming beams and an unbuttoned dining room kitted out with solid oak tables on a flagstone floor. All in all, a textbook example of a switched-on village pub where a perfect ratio is struck between food and drink: the place is still the local boozer, while the cooking is a definite notch or two above your average pub. A menu in the modern British idiom showcases local free-range and organic materials, starting with Tamworth ham hock and spinach terrine with artichoke salad and brioche, then perhaps wood pigeon tart with carrot purée, wild mushrooms, rocket and blue cheese. Finish with treacle tart with malt ice cream and raspberry sauce.

Chef Giles Lee **Owner** Archie & Nicola Orr-Ewing **Seats** 32 **Times** 12-2/6.30-9 Closed 25-26 Dec **Prices** Starter £6-£9.50, Main £13-£21, Dessert £6.50-£8.50, Service optional **Wines** 21 bottles under £30, 10 by glass **Parking** 20 **Notes** Sunday L £14.50-£15.50, Vegetarian available, Children welcome

Number Four at Stow Hotel & Restaurant

British, European

tel: 01451 830297 **Fosseway GL54 1JX**
email: reservations@hotelnumberfour.co.uk **web:** www.hotelnumberfour.co.uk
dir: *Situated on A424 Burford Road, at junct with A429*

Stylish modern restaurant serving imaginative food

A building dating from the 17th century is home to this stylish boutique hotel in the heart of the Cotswolds. Number Four is one of those places that gets everything pitch perfect, from the opulent contemporary look, to the sort of prescient service that anticipates guests' needs, and, in the oldest part of the house, light and modern cooking in the characterful beamed and painted wood-panelled Cutler's Restaurant. Head chef Brian Cutler uses local, seasonal produce from a well-chosen network of suppliers to good effect in well-executed dishes. Salad of Cornish crab and smoked salmon, or chicory tarte Tatin with blue cheese and artichoke might open proceedings, while mains extend to well-conceived pairings of flavour and texture – medallions of Cotswold venison with walnut spätzle, or suprême of sea bass with scallop cannelloni, say. Finish with something like strawberry parfait with marshmallow.

Chef Brian Cutler **Owner** Caroline & Patricia Losel **Seats** 50, Pr/dining room 40 **Times** 12-2/7-9 Closed Xmas, D Sun **Prices** Prices not confirmed, Service optional **Wines** 15 bottles over £30, 15 bottles under £30, 10 by glass **Parking** 50 **Notes** Sunday L, Vegetarian available, Children welcome

Cotswolds88Hotel

PAINSWICK Map 4 SO80

Modern British

tel: 01452 813688 **Kemps Ln GL6 6YB**
email: reservations@cotswolds88hotel.com
web: www.cotswolds88hotel.com
dir: *M4 junct 15, follow A419 past Swindon & Cirencester to Stroud. Turn off to Painswick*

Hip boutique hotel with a dynamic kitchen team

If you still associate the Cotswolds with twee little tea rooms and tweedy country-house hotels, think again. There's little to indicate that anything out of the ordinary lies behind the grand greystone façade of the Palladian mansion that is Cotswolds88, yet the interior goes for the chic boutique look, blending off-the-wall vintage pieces and splashes of vibrant colour with a touch of psychedelia. The Juniper Restaurant is an eye-popping exercise in monochrome pyjama stripes, like a set from Tim Burton's *Alice in Wonderland*, with an eclectic soundtrack of chill-out music. There has been a recent change of line-up in the kitchen, with Curtis Stewart heading up the stoves in this dynamic kitchen. This is the kind of creative food that aims to excite the palates of urbanites out for a country weekend, and it fits right in hereabouts. The cooking does not lack ambition, delivering dishes executed with a good deal of skill and understanding of modern techniques. The classic combo of duck and orange appears in a first course of creativity and craft – 'duck and orange salad' consists of cured duck with foiegras bonbons and dinky duck spring rolls, plus orange purée and caramelised pecans. Another starter might be 'veal sweetbread', with the supporting flavours of hazelnuts, lemon and charred leeks. Among main courses, venison comes with smoked hay essence, and Cotswold lamb as rump, tongue and breast with black quinoa, compressed plums and a spring onion purée. A fishy dish might be stone bass partnered with spiced lentils, braised celery, baby carrots and Bonito consommé. Despite the relatively simple dish descriptions, desserts are no less inventive, so tiramisù and apple pie deliver a lot of surprises, while chocolate délice arrives looking rather like a giant Rollo, with a delicious salted caramel and buttermilk centre, plus a bit of crunchy textural contrast from the accompanying cashew nut brittle.

Chef Curtis Stewart **Owner** Mr & Mrs Harris **Seats** 42, Pr/ dining room 14 **Times** 12-2.30/6.30-10 Closed 1 wk Jan, Mon-Tue **Prices** Fixed L 2 course £10-£15, Fixed D 3 course £49.95, Tasting menu £70 **Wines** 60 bottles over £30, 40 bottles under £30, 10 by glass **Parking** 17, Public car park **Notes** Tasting menu 7 course, Sunday L £19.95-£24.95, Vegetarian available, Children welcome

STOW-ON-THE-WOLD *continued*

The Porch House

◉◉ Modern British NEW

tel: 01451 870048 **Digbeth St GL54 1BN**
email: book@porch-house.co.uk **web:** www.porch-house.co.uk

Historic inn with a classy, modern menu

With claims to be the 'oldest inn' in England, the original building has been dated to 947AD, some 100-plus years before the Battle of Hastings. From then on, every century has done its bit to create the atmospheric construction that exits today, and a 21st-century refurbishment has matched the undoubted period charm with a rustic-chic contemporary finish. It's looking good. The bar is stocked with real ales, while the restaurant turns out some impressive modern British dishes. Pan-fried scallops with parsnip purée and smoked bacon is a starter showing spot-on timing and high quality ingredients, followed, perhaps, with a Creedy Carver duck breast with horseradish mash, roasted root vegetables and a thyme and garlic sauce. These are well judged plates of food, with flavour to the fore and a good deal of refinement in the execution. Among desserts there might be a chocolate tart with clotted cream. There are sandwiches and sharing boards, too, alongside bar staples like shepherd's pie and beef and red wine casserole. Upscale en suite bedrooms complete the package.

Chef Rob Chasteauneuf **Owner** Brakspear **Seats** 40, Pr/dining room 12 **Times** 12-2.30/6.30-9.30 Closed L Mon-Sat (Conservatory open), D Sun (Conservatory open) **Prices** Starter £4.50-£9.95, Main £11.50-£19.95, Dessert £5.50-£8.50, Service optional **Wines** 13 bottles over £30, 26 bottles under £30, 11 by glass **Parking** 4 **Notes** Vegetarian available, Children welcome

Wyck Hill House Hotel & Spa

◉◉ Modern British

tel: 01451 831936 **Burford Rd GL54 1HY**
email: info.wyckhillhouse@bespokehotels.com **web:** www.wyckhillhousehotel.co.uk
dir: A429 for Cirencester, pass through 2 sets of lights in Stow-on-the-Wold, at 3rd set of lights bear left signed Burford, then A424 signed Stow-on-the-Wold, hotel 7m on left

Stylish contemporary cooking in smart Cotswolds hotel

Expectations are heightened at first sight of the old Cotswold property with lovely views of the Windrush Valley, expectations fully met by the interior of antique-furnished lounges, an oak-panelled bar, and a smartly kitted-out dining room of neutral-shaded walls, comfortable upholstered chairs and French windows looking over the estate. The menu is in the contemporary idiom, with ideas pulled in from here and there for each dish, so pan-fried king scallops are served with carrot and raisin salsa and wasabi mayonnaise, and warm smoked breast of wood pigeon comes with black pudding, a quail's egg, crisp pancetta and spicy lentils. Interest is well maintained into main courses: crab risotto with sautéed butternut squash might take your fancy, while traditionalists' needs will be well met by roast fillet of beef with béarnaise and the usual accompaniments. A lot of work goes into puddings, with enjoyable results: lemongrass custard and coconut sorbet accompany pineapple sponge pudding, and frosted pecans and plums infused in red wine liven up a vanilla crème brûlée.

Chef Mark Jane **Owner** City & Country Hotels Ltd **Seats** 50, Pr/dining room 120 **Times** 12.30-2/7-9.30 **Prices** Fixed L 2 course £15.95, Fixed D 3 course £25, Starter £6.95-£8.95, Main £14.95-£23.50, Dessert £6.95-£8.95, Service optional **Wines** 40 bottles over £30, 30 bottles under £30, 10 by glass **Parking** 120 **Notes** Sunday L £15.95-£19.95, Vegetarian available, Children welcome

---

Burleigh Court Hotel

◉ British, European

tel: 01453 883804 **Burleigh, Minchinhampton GL5 2PF**
email: burleighcourt@aol.com **web:** www.burleighcourthotel.co.uk
dir: 2.5m SE of Stroud, off A419

Grand old house with refined modern European cooking

Built at the beginning of the 19th century, the grand old house certainly has plenty of Georgian charm, and lush green ivy makes a vivid contrast to the brusque Cotswold stone. The terrace and gardens were put together by Clough Williams-Ellis, the man behind Portmeirion, so there's a lot of pedigree to the place. The restaurant has bags of old-school elegance and refinement, with the service team looking equally spruce. On the menu is some bright European-influenced food, with local produce at the heart of the action. Assiette of duckling consists of a liver parfait, breast and confit, or there might be a trio of Lechlade rainbow trout. Next up, main-course fillet of Mediterranean sea bass comes with an accompanying saffron and mussel velouté, and for dessert, Baileys pannacotta with chocolate and cherries.

Times 12-2/7-9 Closed 24-26 Dec

Calcot Manor

◉◉ Modern British

tel: 01666 890391 **Calcot GL8 8YJ**
email: reception@calcotmanor.co.uk **web:** www.calcotmanor.co.uk
dir: M4 junct 18, A46 towards Stroud. At x-roads junct with A4135 turn right, then 1st left

Charming 14th-century Cotswold retreat with vibrant modern cuisine

The days when Calcot Manor was a lowly farmhouse are long gone: it is now a design-led boutique-style country-house hotel for 21st-century sybarites with pampering on the agenda. A fabulous health spa takes care of the body, while the contemporary rustic chic of the luminous Conservatory Restaurant panders to the palate. The kitchen takes a strong stance on sourcing locally for its repertoire of modern British dishes, and flavours have real punch, helped along by a wood-burning oven that adds an authentically rustic Mediterranean edge. The wide-ranging menu has all bases covered, whether you just want to graze on nibble-sized portions of venison carpaccio with parmesan, blackberries, green chillies and candied chestnuts, or go for the full three course format. Should you prefer the latter, you might set out with turbot tartare with horseradish cream, lobster bisque and crispy potatoes, then look to the wood oven for organic beef from the Calcot estate, with béarnaise sauce, French beans and artichokes, and end with dark chocolate and salted caramel mousse with orange peel sorbet and candied nuts.

Chef Michael Benjamin **Owner** Richard Ball (MD) **Seats** 100, Pr/dining room 16 **Times** 12-2/7-9.30 Closed D 25 Dec **Prices** Fixed L 2 course fr £19, Starter £8-£13, Main £16-£38, Dessert £8, Service optional **Wines** 59 bottles over £30, 26 bottles under £30, 24 by glass **Parking** 150 **Notes** Sunday L £13-£42, Vegetarian available, Children welcome

The Close Hotel

◉◉ Modern British **NEW**

tel: 01666 502272 **8 Long St GL8 8AQ**
email: info@theclose-hotel.com **web:** www.theclose-hotel.com
dir: From M4 junct 17 onto A429 to Malmesbury. From M5 junct 14 onto B4509

Creative cooking in a 16th-century house

Although it's situated in the town, The Close Hotel has the feel of a country-house hotel. It's a handsome pile dating from the 16th century, and within there are period details and a finish of refined, contemporary elegance. There are two dining options in the form of a brasserie and fine-dining restaurant. Any sense of old-school solidity has been avoided by painting the wall panels in a fashionable shade of blue/grey and by keeping the tables free of heavy linen (the Adam ceiling remains to impress traditionalists). The modern British menu strikes the right balance in this setting, with the dishes showing craft and creativity. A first-course goose liver parfait comes with an assiette of rhubarb to alleviate any richness (even an ice cream), plus a slice of pain d'épices. Main courses, such as steamed halibut with broccoli purée and scallop mousse, are equally impressive. Desserts like the hot banana soufflé served with hazelnut ice cream confirm that this is a kitchen on song.

Chef David Brown **Owner** Cotswold Inns & Hotels Ltd **Seats** 54, Pr/dining room 26 **Times** 12-3/6.30-9 **Prices** Fixed L 2 course £12.50, Fixed D 3 course £38 **Wines** 11 bottles over £30, 20 bottles under £30, 6 by glass **Parking** 18 **Notes** Sunday L £16.95-£19.95, Vegetarian available, Children welcome

Hare & Hounds Hotel

◉◉ Modern British **V**

tel: 01666 881000 **Westonbirt GL8 8QL**
email: reception@hareandhoundshotel.com **web:** www.cotswold-inns-hotels.co.uk
dir: 2.5m SW of Tetbury on A433

Charming Cotswold hotel with confident team in the kitchen

The Hare & Hounds has some pretty fancy neighbours in the form of the National Arboretum and the Beaufort Polo Club, but it is quite capable of making an impression on its own merits. The handsome Cotswold-stone house was built in 1928 and cuts quite a dash these days as a country-house hotel, with the Beaufort Restaurant really putting it on the map. The vaulted hammer-beamed ceiling and stone mullioned windows strike an elegant pose, whilst the well-designed chairs and smartly laid tables suggest this place is not stuck in the past. And so it proves on the menu. The well-crafted modern British dishes show adroit technical skills and impressive management of flavours. Start with a carrot velouté in a creative partnership with coconut pannacotta and a sweet and sour ginger relish, moving on to braised shoulder and loin of lamb with choucroute, confit garlic, baby carrots and potato crisp. Everything looks beautiful on the plate, not least desserts such as raspberry and basil vacherin with a lemon and basil parfait and raspberry gel.

Chef David Hammond **Owner** Cotswold Inns & Hotels Ltd **Seats** 60, Pr/dining room 10 **Times** 7-9.30 Closed L Mon-Sat **Prices** Fixed L 2 course fr £15.95, Fixed D 3 course £39 **Wines** 6 by glass **Parking** 40 **Notes** Tasting menu 8 course, Sunday L £18.95-£21.95, Children welcome

---

■ THORNBURY   Map 4 ST69

Ronnie's of Thornbury

◉◉ Modern European

tel: 01454 411137 **11 St Mary St BS35 2AB**
email: info@ronnies-restaurant.co.uk

Modern European cooking in a 17th-century schoolhouse

Tucked away in an unlikely location in the town's shopping precinct, Ronnie's became an instant hit with locals when it opened in 2007. It's easy to see why: whether you pop in for brunch or dinner, the vibe is easygoing, and the modern European cooking keeps things local, seasonal and to the point. The 17th-century building wears its contemporary look well: stone walls, beamed ceilings, wooden floors and neutral hues are pointed up by paintings and photos by West Country artists. Ronnie Faulkner's team will send you away happy if you turn up to kick start the day with coffee and eggs Benedict or round it off with an intelligent, precisely-cooked dinner. This might include potted pork with pistachio and pickled vegetables and fruits, followed by an oriental pairing of sea bass fillets with an aromatic crab broth, enoki mushrooms, crispy wonton and bok choi. For a simple but effective summery pudding, poached peaches are paired with lavender jelly and ricotta , or you could go for a savoury finish with the splendid array of English artisan cheeses.

Chef Ron Faulkner **Owner** Ron Faulkner **Seats** 62 **Times** 12-3/6-10 Closed 25-26 Dec, 1-8 Jan, Mon, D Sun **Prices** Fixed L 2 course £15-£20, Fixed D 3 course £25-£30, Tasting menu £45-£65 **Wines** 33 bottles over £30, 31 bottles under £30, 12 by glass **Parking** Car park **Notes** Menu of the day 2/3 course £10/£13, Sunday L £20-£25, Vegetarian available, Children welcome

---

Thornbury Castle

◉◉ Modern British, European

tel: 01454 281182 **Castle St BS35 1HH**
email: info@thornburycastle.co.uk **web:** www.thornburycastle.co.uk
dir: M5 junct 16, N on A38. 4m to lights, turn left. Follow brown historic castle signs. Restaurant behind St Mary's church

Heritage and modernity side by side in a Tudor castle

Construction work on the castle was well under way in the early 16th century when its intended occupant, Edward Stafford, became one of the many Tudor notables to find himself parting company with his head on the orders of Henry VIII. Thornbury isn't quite the full medieval fortress, more a castellated country house, but is not a whit less grandiose for that. Canopy beds, old tapestries and armour help set the tone, and the hexagonal Tower dining room with its arrow-slits feels secure against the marauding hordes. Supplied in part from Thornbury's own gardens (and vineyard), the menu is in the vein of modern British pastoral, with invention and heritage running side by side. Tomato and shallot tart with pickled samphire and Cerney Ash goat cheese establishes the mood, or there may be wood-pigeon with

continued

THORNBURY *continued*

roasted beetroot and celeriac in caper dressing. Mains may look further afield for roast skrei (Norwegian migratory cod) with crispy oysters, or Devon sea bass with lobster ravioli, but herb-crusted Uley Fields hogget with peas and polenta brings us home to Gloucestershire.

Chef Mark Veale **Owner** LFH **Seats** 72, Pr/dining room 22 **Times** 11.45-2/7-9.30 **Prices** Fixed L 2 course £15, Tasting menu fr £65, Service optional **Wines** 7 by glass **Parking** 50 **Notes** ALC 2/3 course £42/£50, Sunday L, Vegetarian available, Children welcome

| UPPER SLAUGHTER | Map 10 SP12 |

Lords of the Manor
◉◉◉ – *see opposite*

| WINCHCOMBE | Map 10 SP02 |

Wesley House
◉◉ Modern European

fireplace and bare stone walls in the traditional main dining room have been brought up to date with contemporary flair – expect colour-changing lighting and big flower displays. There's also a stylish conservatory with stunning views of the surrounding countryside. The food is certainly rooted in the 21st century, with the kitchen team's modern European output bringing together interesting combinations of ingredients with aplomb. Crab tortellini with coriander and chilli, steamed vegetables and lemongrass cream certainly doesn't stint on the crabmeat, while the ingredients work together a treat. Roasted Loomswood duck breast, balsamic-glazed vegetables, shallot rösti and thyme sauce is equally well-balanced, but save room for the highlight of the meal – properly chewy dark chocolate and nougatine torte with Greek yoghurt sorbet and passionfruit jelly. The wine list features plenty of choice by the glass and bottle and the lunchtime wine flights are a popular way to go.

Chef Cedrik Rullier **Owner** Matthew Brown **Seats** 70, Pr/dining room 24 **Times** 12-2/7-9 Closed Mon, D Sun **Prices** Prices not confirmed, Service optional **Wines** 43 bottles over £30, 48 bottles under £30, 11 by glass **Parking** In the square **Notes** Sunday L, Vegetarian available, Children welcome

See advert below

tel: 01242 602366 **High St GL54 5LJ**
email: enquiries@wesleyhouse.co.uk **web:** www.wesleyhouse.co.uk
dir: *In centre of Winchcombe*

Impressive modern cooking in a period house

The 15th-century merchant's house gets its name from the Methodist preacher who stayed here in the 18th century. Period features like beamed ceilings, an inglenook

Wine Bar & Grill **AA**

AA AA Restaurant with rooms

High Street, Winchcombe, Glos GL54 5LJ

www.wesleyhouse.co.uk
01242 602366

Wesley House Wine Bar & Grill

⚜ European

tel: 01242 602366 **High St GL54 5LJ**
email: enquiries@wesleyhouse.co.uk
dir: In the centre of Winchcombe

Trend-setting brasserie next-door to Wesley House

Historic Wesley House – built for a merchant back in the 15th century – has a few tricks up its sleeve these days, not least its Wine Bar & Grill, which is a delightful 21st-century interloper amid all the antiquity. Next door's fine-dining restaurant (see separate entry) has a rival in the shape of this funky, modern venue, where you can sip on a cocktail and tuck into some sparky brasserie-style food. With mirror-balls, purple lighting, and zebra-skin barstools, there's no lack of contemporary swagger about it. Start with something like steamed Fowey mussels with roasted fennel, coconut and cardamom, before a steak cooked on the grill, or sticky black bean pork belly with coriander mash and stir-fried oriental vegetables. There's a daily tapas selection board, too, plus desserts such as hot chocolate fondant with home-made raspberry sorbet.

Chef Cedrik Rullier **Owner** Matthew Brown **Seats** 50 **Times** 12-2/6-10 Closed 25-26 Dec, 1 Jan, Sun-Mon **Prices** Prices not confirmed, Service optional **Wines** 3 bottles over £30, 24 bottles under £30, 21 by glass **Notes** Vegetarian available, Children welcome

---

WOTTON-UNDER-EDGE   **Map 4 ST79**

Tortworth Court Four Pillars Hotel

⚜ Modern British

tel: 01454 263000 **Tortworth GL12 8HH**
email: tortworth@four-pillars.co.uk **web:** www.four-pillars.co.uk
dir: M5 junct 14. Follow B4509 towards Wotton. Turn right at top of hill onto Tortworth Rd, hotel 0.5m on right

Upmarket brasserie-style menu in striking Victorian mansion

A magnificent Victorian mansion, Tortworth Court is surrounded by 30 acres of grounds including an arboretum. Sympathetic renovation and modernisation in the 1990s have brought all the amenities of a 21st-century hotel, and it's a popular venue for conferences, weddings and other functions, while Moreton's, the main restaurant, has retained the original oak panelling, ornate arches and an impressive fireplace of what used to be the library. The kitchen takes a something-for-everyone approach, an appealing mix of upmarket brasserie-type fare. Dinner could kick off with partridge breast with spicy poached pears, or mussels in saffron and parsley broth, and proceed to hake fillet roasted in chorizo, served with chick peas and new potatoes, or classic navarin of lamb with boulangère potatoes spiked with rosemary. Puddings are a mixed bunch too, taking in lemon posset with mulled berries, and tarte Tatin with cinnamon-flavoured custard.

Chef Nigel Jones **Owner** Four Pillars **Seats** 210, Pr/dining room
Times 12-2.30/6.30-10 Closed L Sat **Prices** Fixed L 2 course fr £22.95 **Wines** 13 by glass **Parking** 250 **Notes** Sunday L fr £13.95, Vegetarian available, Children welcome

Lords of the Manor

UPPER SLAUGHTER   **Map 10 SP12**

Modern British ⚜ NOTABLE WINE LIST

tel: 01451 820243 **GL54 2JD**
email: reservations@lordsofthemanor.com **web:** www.lordsofthemanor.com
dir: Follow signs towards The Slaughters 2m W of A429. Hotel on right in centre of Upper Slaughter

Finely crafted French-inflected cooking in a magical Cotswold hotel

A 17th-century rectory to suit an era when a rector might legitimately expect to live high on the hog, this is the go-to destination for an upscale stay in Upper Slaughter. It's built of the fabled honey-coloured stone, and tucked away within eight acres of landscaped gardens and trim parkland. Glimpsed through the trees, the place looks utterly magical, and it's run with a determination to maintain precisely that ethos. Staff are impeccably professional throughout, and the interiors are decorated with a mix of period style and modern grace. Tramp the Cotswolds during the day if you will (wellingtons are provided for when the going looks soft), but be sure to return in time for dinner in the elegantly appointed dining room, where table settings are pristine and the approach, though formally correct, is also nicely relaxing. Richard Edwards sources in the immediate environs, from local farmers and growers, and brings a delicate touch of contemporary French style to dishes that look finely crafted, colourful and appetising. Quail is modishly anatomised, appearing as the gently poached breast alongside a cannelloni roll of the leg seasoned with sage and onion, not forgetting its egg. A vibrant crustacean treatment produces a pairing of poached lobster and curried crab with avocado and mango, while fish at main course is astonishingly fresh, precision-timed and positively seasoned, as in a tranche of halibut that comes with crab and lettuce salad and farfalle pasta in truffle butter. Game season brings on a well-worked offering of grouse – roast breast and leg croustillant – accompanied by creamed Brussels sprouts, chanterelles, butternut and blackberries. After all the carefully considered experimentation, dessert might return to heritage French gastronomy in the shape of an airily risen raspberry soufflé with matching sorbet, anointed at the table with thick white chocolate sauce.

Chef Richard Edwards **Owner** Empire Ventures **Seats** 50, Pr/dining room 30
Times 12-2.30/7-9.30 Closed L Mon-Sat **Prices** Fixed D 3 course £69, Tasting menu £75, Service optional **Wines** 400 bottles over £30, 95 bottles under £30, 15 by glass **Parking** 40 **Notes** Tasting menu 7 course, ALC menu £69, Sunday L, Vegetarian available, No children

GREATER MANCHESTER

ALTRINCHAM
Map 15 SJ78

Earle by Simon Rimmer

Modern European

tel: 0161 929 8869 **4 Cecil Rd, Hale WA15 9PA**
email: info@earlerestaurant.co.uk
dir: M56 junct 7 onto A556 towards Altrincham, follow signs to Hale

Vibrant modern cooking in village brasserie

Telly chef Simon Rimmer's operation in the busy little village of Hale is a contemporary brasserie that ticks all the right boxes for locally-sourced and seasonal ingredients. The vibe is buzzy yet relaxed and the look is stylish without trying too hard – herringbone wood panelling and floors, exposed red-brick walls and unclothed wooden tables – and you may see the man himself at work in the open-to-view kitchen. A simple approach sees classic comfort dishes alongside bright modern ideas, while the 'Ten-Mile Meal' champions local suppliers. Get going with hot-smoked salmon and spinach frittata with crab mayonnaise, mint and radish, then consider pan-roast rump of lamb with lamb and mint ravioli, braised peas and baby gem lettuce. Rimmer's Manchester establishment, Greens, is vegetarian, so you can expect some creative veggie dishes, such as truffled mushroom and pearl barley stew with pickled red cabbage and celeriac hash. Finish with lemon polenta cake with lemon meringue Eton Mess.

Chef Simon Rimmer **Owner** Simon Rimmer **Seats** 65, Pr/dining room 14 **Times** 12-2/5.30-9.30 Closed 25-26 Dec, 1 Jan, L Mon **Prices** Prices not confirmed, Service optional **Wines** 17 bottles over £30, 20 bottles under £30, 10 by glass **Parking** Station car park **Notes** Sunday L, Vegetarian available, Children welcome

BOLTON
Map 15 SD70

Egerton House Hotel

Modern British

tel: 01204 307171 **Blackburn Rd BL7 9PL**
email: sales@egertonhouse-hotel.co.uk **web:** www.egertonhouse-hotel.co.uk
dir: M61, A666 (Bolton road), pass ASDA on right. Hotel 2m on just past war memorial on right

Well-tuned modern British cuisine in a charming setting

The peaceful position sets the tone here, with its landscaped gardens fringing the lush Lancashire hills, while the house itself has a restorative Victorian charm. Hats off to the textile baron who picked the spot! These days it's a country hotel on a personable scale with a satisfying blend of period comforts and contemporary style. That goes in the restaurant, too, with its garden views in daylight hours, and slick service team. The menu meets modern British expectations, with a good amount of regional produce to the fore. Start with a flavoursome ham hock terrine, with mustard mayonnaise and pickled spring onions, following on with sautéed calves' liver with mustard mash, smoked bacon and a fried duck's egg. For dessert, the likes of peach Melba comes with vanilla ice cream and an almond tuile.

Times 12-3/7-11 Closed BHs, L Mon-Sat, D Sun

DELPH
Map 16 SD90

The Saddleworth Hotel

Modern European NEW

tel: 01457 871888 **Huddersfield Rd OL3 5LX**
email: enquiries@thesaddleworthhotel.co.uk **web:** www.saddleworthhotel.co.uk
dir: A62, located between A6052 & A670

Modern British cooking showing wit and skill

The Saddleworth feels like an assiduous attempt to create a country inn for the modern era. Built of stone, and sitting amid landscaped gardens and woodland with sweeping views over the Lancashire moorland, it's not far from Oldham but feels pleasingly remote from anywhere. The location makes it a popular choice for weddings, and the dramatic decor of Bakers Restaurant, where sparkling glassware gleams against black table linen, exercises its own allure. The opening salvo is some witty little snacking items (including a cucumber mojito and beans on toast). Then the six-course tasting menu ploughs a fascinating furrow through the modern British repertoire, from scallops and cauliflower scented with espresso and adorned with cobnuts and parmesan, through rabbit tortellini with truffled baby artichokes, and turbot with foraged sea flora in shellfish broth, to local free-range pork belly with aubergine purée and celery and Stilton gnocchi. Dessert could be an almond sponge with variations of pear and raspberry.

Chef Wil Regan **Owner** A J Baker **Seats** 30, Pr/dining room 30 **Times** 12-2/7-9.30 **Prices** Prices not confirmed **Wines** 100 bottles over £30, 35 bottles under £30, 6 by glass **Parking** 200 **Notes** Vegetarian available, Children welcome

MANCHESTER
Map 16 SJ89

Abode Manchester

Modern European, British NEW v

tel: 0161 247 7744 **107 Piccadilly M1 2DB**
email: tables@abodemanchester.co.uk **web:** www.michaelcaines.com
dir: in city centre, 2 mins walk from Piccadilly station

Compelling modern cooking in stylish central hotel

On a prime chunk of real estate, this luxury hotel has been converted from a cotton warehouse built in 1898, evidence of which can be seen in the original walnut staircase, tiling and wrought ironwork. The Michael Caines Restaurant is a two-tier room, next to the Champagne Bar, with a glossy designer-led contemporary look and an upmarket vibe. The cooking is exciting and innovative, resting squarely on the classical repertoire. An auspicious amuse-bouche gets the palate ringing before such starters as beautifully made, wafer-thin ravioli stuffed with rich crabmeat in shellfish bisque, topped with tiny pieces of pink grapefruit and ginger for contrast, or a gutsy dish of ox tongue with carrots, a bone marrow galette, and horseradish ice cream. Ambitions are amply met in well-judged main courses: super-fresh and perfectly timed hake fillet under crispy chicken skin in chicken broth with parsnips, or pork fillet with butternut squash, boulangère potatoes and smoked paprika. Puddings alone are worth a visit here, among them the signature chocolate orange confit mousse with orange sorbet and dark chocolate ice cream, and prune and Armagnac soufflé with matching ice cream.

Chef Robert Cox **Owner** Brownsword Hotels **Seats** 80, Pr/dining room 26 **Times** 12-2.30/6-10 Closed Sun **Prices** Fixed L 2 course fr £14.95, Fixed D 3 course fr £22.50, Tasting menu £65-£85, Starter £10-£16, Main £18-£26, Dessert £8.95 **Wines** 200 bottles over £30, 23 bottles under £30, 18 by glass **Parking** NCP opposite **Notes** Prestige 9 course tasting menu, Children welcome

The French by Simon Rogan

– see opposite

What makes a
4-Rosette restaurant?
See page 9

The French by Simon Rogan

MANCHESTER   Map 16 SJ89

Modern British
tel: 0161 236 3333 **The Midland Hotel, Peter St M60 2DS**
email: midlandsales@qhotels.co.uk **web:** www.qhotels.co.uk
dir: *M602 junct 3, follow Manchester Central Convention Complex signs, hotel opposite*

A cutting-edge revolution for The French

The Midland Hotel, a bastion of traditional civility in the heart of Manchester, was injected with a touch of 21st-century dynamism with the arrival of Simon Rogan's restaurant at the beginning of 2013. The old hotel can't have been so cutting-edge since the day it opened its doors to gasps of wonder back in 1903. The oh-so posh 'The French' restaurant in the heart of the hotel has been transformed into a space of intriguing contrasts, keeping the original ornate plasterwork and adding a touch of '60s swing with the fixtures and fittings. Wooden chairs and unclothed tables keep it looking lean and modern, the chandeliers add a touch of glamour, and the bespoke carpet is designed to look like floorboards (brilliant). The food is no longer French, but then again the work of Mr Rogan is so ethereally of-the-moment it is hard to define. Modern British is as good a definition as any, and there is no doubting the Britishness of the ingredients, with much of the produce coming from Rogan's own farms in Cumbria. There is a development kitchen up there, too, where the dishes are devised and refined, and new cooking techniques are perfected. Adam Reid is the man charged with leading the line in the kitchen and he is a sure hand indeed, creating dishes that intrigue and satisfy in equal measure. Multi-course tasting menus are the way to go, perhaps unsurprisingly, with six- or ten-course options. The dishes read well, but nothing can prepare you for the reality – the lightness of touch, the punchy flavours, the refined and delicate presentation. A dish of swede dumplings, for example, delivers fabulous flavours from the humble vegetable, with an egg sauce to elevate it to stellar status, or another of roasted cod with chicken skin, shrimps, broccoli and parsley. The ox in coal oil is already a classic, with the tartare-style rump giving a delicious smokiness to the meat, and another course of caramelised cabbage with scallops, smoked roe and coastal herbs is another stunner. Poached plaice is cooked with a light touch and combined with two ace mussels, cauliflower and seeds, while there's a refined robustness to Cumbrian rose veal two ways with dripping potatoes and turnip purée. The sweet courses are no less creative and thrilling: pears with rocket, rosehips and hazelnuts, maybe, or a sarsaparilla wafer sandwiching an iced parfait and jelly, served with an accompanying soda served in a Kilner jar. It's an inspirational addition to the Manchester dining scene.

Chef Adam Reid, Simon Rogan **Owner** QHotels **Seats** 55
Times 12-1.3/6.3-9 Closed BHs, Sun-Mon, L Tue
Prices Tasting menu £59-£84, Service optional **Wines** 96 bottles over £30, 70 bottles under £30, 75 by glass
Parking NCP behind hotel **Notes** 6/10 course L & D fr £59/fr £84, Children welcome

MANCHESTER *continued*

Greens

 Modern Vegetarian **V**

tel: 0161 434 4259 **43 Lapwing Ln, West Didsbury M20 2NT**
email: simoncgreens@aol.com
dir: *Between Burton Rd & Palatine Rd*

Veggie Mancunian star draws crowds for top flavours

TV chef Simon Rimmer's restaurant is a lively place, drawing crowds with exciting vegetarian cooking. Darkwood tables and chairs, with some banquettes, boarded and tiled floors, some funky wallpaper and spotlights dangling from the ceiling all create a positive impression. Clearly-flavoured cooking is the hallmark of the kitchen, with ideas picked up from around the globe to produce a menu that bursts with bright and appealing dishes. Hits among starters include carrot and sweet potato soup spiked with ginger and chilli, and rich Roquefort, pecan and tarragon cheesecake cut by spicy tomato chutney. Garnishes and sauces give extra depth to dishes, seen in main courses of a generous, well-made spinach, feta and pistachio pie in filo with tomato and cinnamon sauce, and Lancashire cheese and basil sausages with mustard mash, beer gravy and tomato ketchup chutney. Simon's talents extend to puddings along the lines of treacle tart with Earl Grey cream, and textbook lemon tart with raspberry sauce.

Times 12-2/5.30-10.30 Closed 25-26 Dec, 1 Jan, L Mon

Harvey Nichols Second Floor Restaurant

Modern European **V**

tel: 0161 828 8898 **21 New Cathedral St M1 1AD**
email: secondfloor.reservations@harveynichols.com
dir: *Just off Deansgate, town centre. 5 min walk from Victoria Station, on Exchange Sq*

Chic global cuisine with views of the city centre

The Harvey Nics restaurant at the Manchester store is to be found on the second floor, and has the house style familiar from Dublin to Knightsbridge, with the signature emphasis on chic. The leather and wire seats are a triumph of comfort over visual aesthetics, and the pale pastel palette does nothing to detract from the bird's-eye views of the city centre's heritage architecture. Once, the presumption was all for regional French offerings, but present incumbent Sam Everett cooks on-trend renditions of global reference dishes, dressing seared tuna with wasabi, carrot and ginger, garnishing a starter portion of rabbit with sweetcorn purée and pancetta, and then spreading his wings at main course to produce precision-timed lemon sole with wild mushroom risotto and artichoke barigoule, or turning out lamb in three guises — braised shoulder, rump, and a cornet-shaped brik of the sweetbreads — alongside smooth, herb-flecked mash. To finish, there could be properly fragile vanilla pannacotta with rhubarb and ginger, or the crowd-wowing show-stopper of silky chocolate mousse, espresso espuma and hazelnut shortbread.

Chef Sam Everett, Matthew Horsfield **Owner** Harvey Nichols **Seats** 50
Times 12-3/6-9.30 Closed 25-27 Dec, Etr Sun, D Sun-Mon **Prices** Fixed L 2 course £30, Fixed D 3 course £40, Tasting menu £55 **Wines** 20 by glass **Parking** NCP under store opposite **Notes** Menu Gourmand 6 course, Sunday L £30-£40, Children welcome

The Lowry Hotel

Modern International

tel: 0161 827 4000 & 827 4041 **50 Dearmans Place, Chapel Wharf, Salford M3 5LH**
email: hostess@roccofortehotels.com **web:** www.roccofortecollection.com
dir: *M6 junct 19, A556/M56/A5103 for 4.5m. At rdbt take A57(M) to lights, right onto Water St. Left to New Quay St/Trinity Way. At 1st lights right onto Chapel St for hotel*

Well-presented quality dining in super-stylish hotel

The Lowry is a sleek, glamorous, ultra-modern hotel opposite the Trinity Bridge. Diners can enjoy views of the city from the restaurant, a characteristically chic space, with a wooden floor and blue leather-look seats at clothed tables; smartly dressed staff are professional and helpful, contributing to the congenial ambience. The menus feature a few luxuries like lobster thermidor, and the kitchen's supplies are from the top drawer, but the menu is a down-to-earth affair, with influences garnered from here and there to suit each dish. Starters are as varied as shellfish bisque, grilled mackerel with potato and horseradish salad, and salad Niçoise. There are some pasta options too, and attractively presented main courses along the lines of cannon of lamb, served pink, with a tomato and olive jus, spinach and dauphinoise, or seared tuna steak, served rare, with pak choi, shiitaki mushrooms and an oriental-style pickled ginger and soy jus. Steaks from the grill are other possibilities before ending with one of the inventive puddings like lemon balm mousse with rhubarb espuma and ginger ice cream.

Times 12-2.30/6-10.30

Macdonald Manchester Hotel

Modern British, Scottish

tel: 0161 272 3200 **London Rd M1 2PG**
email: general.manchester@macdonald-hotels.co.uk
web: http://www.macdonaldhotels.co.uk/our-hotels/north-england/manchester/
dir: *Opposite Piccadilly Station*

Traditional Scottish fare in the city centre

Dominating the skyline from Piccadilly Station to the Mancunian Way, Macdonald Manchester is an ultra-modern hotel with all the usual amenities of a large city-centre establishment, including a spa and the Scottish Steak Club. As the restaurant's name suggests, the thrust of the menu is on prime beef from accredited farms north of the border, hung for a minimum of 21 days. Josper-grilled rib-eye steak, say, with the traditional accompaniments is pink, succulent and properly seasoned, and the rest of the menu is littered with Scottish classics. But look beyond traditionally smoked salmon from Aberdeen and grilled Highland lamb cutlets to find ham hock and parsley terrine with piccalilli, grilled lemon sole with capers, wild mushroom fettuccine and old favourites like sausages with mash and onion gravy. To finish, sticky toffee pudding with vanilla ice cream seems to be a winning dessert.

Chef Stuart Duff **Owner** Macdonald Hotels **Seats** 140 **Times** 5-10 Closed L all week **Prices** Fixed D 3 course £16.50, Starter £6.50-£12.50, Main £10.50-£27.50, Dessert £4.80-£8.90 **Wines** 24 bottles over £30, 17 bottles under £30, 13 by glass **Parking** 85, Fee for parking **Notes** Vegetarian available, Children welcome

What makes a 3-Rosette restaurant?
See page 9

Learn the latest foodie trends in Birmingham and Manchester on page 21

Malmaison Manchester

Modern International

tel: 0161 278 1000 **1-3 Piccadilly M1 1LZ**
email: manchester@malmaison.com **web:** www.malmaison.com
dir: From M56 follow signs to Manchester, then to Piccadilly

Modern comfort food in the city centre

A prime piece of heritage industrial architecture, Manchester's Malmaison is a former linen warehouse plumb in the city centre, not far from Piccadilly station. The interior scene is all boutiqued to the max, with eye-catching decorative flourishes in a soothing low-lit ambience. Cocktails and upscale brasserie food draw in the buzziest of crowds, and staff cope well with the demand. In the Smoak Bar Grill, the kitchen is open to view, and produces efficient, often surprising versions of modern comfort food, not least the range of steaks that are done on the Josper charcoal grill. Creamed Brie with a wine-poached pear and candied pecans is an attractive opener, while mains run to confit duck with Puy lentils and garlic mash, or calf's liver and pancetta with roasted onions. Chicken tikka with all the Indian trimmings is a crowd-pleaser. Round things off with a vanilla-fragrant crème brûlée.

Chef Kevin Whiteford **Owner** Malmaison Limited **Seats** 85, Pr/dining room 10 **Times** 12-2.30/6-11 **Prices** Prices not confirmed **Wines** 21 by glass **Parking** NCP 100 mtrs **Notes** Sunday L, Vegetarian available, Children welcome

Manchester House Bar & Restaurant

– see below

Mr Cooper's House and Garden by Simon Rogan

International **NEW**

tel: 0161 932 4128 **The Midland Hotel, Peter St M60 2DS**
email: info@mrcoopershouseandgarden.co.uk
dir: From M6 junct 19 join M56. Follow signs city centre (A5103). Follow signs Manchester Central Convention Complex/Bridgewater Hall onto Medlock St. Through lights onto Lower Mosley St. Pass Bridgewater Hall on right, hotel facing you

Cool and contemporary dining

The sister restaurant to the high-flying French (see entry) is named in honour of a coach-making family whose home and gardens were based on this site in the 19th century, and, true to its name, there's a tree in the middle of the dining room. This is the more casual dining option in the hotel, but seeing as this is Simon Rogan's version of casual dining, the culinary output is a cut above the norm. The cool and contemporary venue consists of a number of spaces with a clubby library area with leather-swathed booths and a main room with plants and that 35 foot tree. The menu takes a slightly more global approach than might be expected from Mr Rogan, with his usual attention to detail and passion for provenance, seasonality and flavour. Pork belly with peanut emulsion and black pudding is a starter with winning flavour combinations, followed by confit duck fritter or sea bass with stir-fried corn and a sweet-and-sour sauce. Finish with white chocolate cake with a pineapple and cardamom compôte.

Chef Gareth Jones **Owner** Simon Rogan, QHotels **Seats** 150 **Times** 12-2.30/5-10 Closed 25-26 Dec, 1 Jan **Prices** Fixed L 2 course £15, Fixed D 3 course £23, Starter £4.50-£8.50, Main £13.50-£19.50, Dessert £6-£7 **Wines** 30 bottles over £30, 20 bottles under £30, 10 by glass **Parking** NCP Manchester Central **Notes** Vegetarian available, Children welcome

Manchester House Bar & Restaurant

MANCHESTER	Map 16 SJ89

Modern British **NEW** v
tel: 0161 835 2557 **Tower 12, 18-22 Bridge St M3 3BZ**
email: restaurant@manchesterhouse.uk.com
dir: Located on Bridge St, on edge of Spinning Fields. Entrance is in Tower 12 behind Waitrose

Buzzy new address for contemporary dining

Viewers of BBC2's *Restaurant Wars* will be familiar with the germination of Aiden Byrne's venture in the centre of the city. The show revealed the ups and downs of opening a restaurant at this level of ambition, not to mention the cost of it all. That, though, is all in the past. Manchester has a great addition to its dining scene. There's a clubby and industrial vibe to the place, which seems wholly appropriate in this of all cities, and an open kitchen putting the chefs right in the heart of the action. The lounge and terrace has great 12th-floor views over the city, with bling the order of the day in the shape of a glam cocktail. In the restaurant, Saturday evening makes room for the tasting menu only, but the rest of the time the carte leads the way with the taster an option if the whole table is on board. There's a bit of northern soul to the cooking, with a definite regional flavour and a reinvented classic or too, but the style and presentation is aiming to impress, which it does. Norfolk quail is baked in hay and served with malt-infused celeriac and liver parfait in a first course that requires a lot of technical know-how, or go for charred smoked salmon with goats' cheese and leeks. Next up, another complex number – sea bass (a fine piece of fish) with more of the fish served ceviche-style in little avocado parcels, plus some tempura soft-shelled crab and a couple of pieces of chicken satay. Belted Galloway rib-eye and fillet are hearty plates for the more traditionally minded, and, for dessert, there's Manchester tart or the pretty-as-a-picture warm date sponge with parsnip pannacotta and carrot distillation.

Chef Aiden Byrne **Owner** Living Ventures & Aiden Byrne **Seats** 78, Pr/dining room 8 **Times** 12-2.30/7-9.30 Closed 1st 2 wks Jan, 2wks summer, Sun-Mon **Prices** Fixed L 2 course £22.50, Tasting menu £95, Starter £14-£18, Main £24-£38, Dessert £8.50-£12 **Wines** 193 bottles over £30, 26 bottles under £30, 12 by glass **Notes** Children welcome

MANCHESTER *continued*

Sweet Mandarin

 Chinese v

tel: 0161 832 8848 **19 Copperas St M4 1HS**
email: lisa@sweetmandarin.com
dir: *Top end of High Street opposite Old Smithfield Fish Market façade in Northern Quarter*

Wildly popular Chinese family restaurant run by honoured sisters

The Tse sisters, who run what has become one of the most popular Chinese restaurants for miles around, were awarded MBEs for their services to food in the 2014 New Year Honours list. From humble family beginnings in 1950, Sweet Mandarin has expanded its remit to take in a cookery school, outside catering, a recipe book and a line of products. The foundation for it all is the relaxed and comfortable glass-fronted venue itself, where, against a backdrop of red screens and lanterns, a mix of traditional and less familiar Chinese dishes is offered. Expect chicken and sweetcorn soup, mixed platters of hors d'oeuvres, and well-rendered main dishes like freshly shredded, moistly flavourful Peking duck, Manchurian beef fillet in a sauce of black peppers and onions sizzled on the skillet at your table. Look out for Shanghai-spiced king prawns, and the original General Tse's wok-braised sweet-and-sour tofu cooked with peppers, onions and pineapple.

Chef Lisa Tse **Owner** Helen Tse **Seats** 85 **Times** 5-11 Closed 25-26 Dec, Mon, L all week **Prices** Fixed D 3 course £20-£35, Starter £3.50-£10.95, Main £9.95-£16.95, Dessert £4.95 **Wines** 1 bottle over £30, 13 bottles under £30, 7 by glass **Parking** Shudehill car park **Notes** Children welcome

---

MANCHESTER AIRPORT Map 15 SJ88

Etrop Grange Hotel

 Modern British

tel: 0161 499 0500 **Thorley Ln M90 4EG**
email: reception@etrophotel.co.uk **web:** www.etrophotel.co.uk
dir: *Off M56 junct 5. Follow signs to Terminal 2, take 1st left (Thorley Ln), 200yds on right*

Georgian elegance and modern cooking a stone's throw from the airport

With its elegant red-brick Georgian façade and spacious period rooms, Etrop Grange (Eg for short) makes for an upscale experience. Visitors are attracted by its copious business facilities and proximity to the airport, and the refined restaurant is a draw in itself. The modern British menu shows classical roots, so ham hock terrine comes with a home-made pickle to cut through the richness, and smoked haddock fishcakes are partnered with a caper mayonnaise. Main courses are no less classically-minded, but there are modern touches, too – the compressed melon with roasted duck breast served with broccoli purée and chick peas, for example. Other main courses might be wild mushroom risotto, steak cooked on the grill, or the house burger served with chunky fries. Among desserts a lemon meringue pie gets the deconstruction treatment, or go for a classic Manchester tart with rhubarb and vanilla compôte.

Chef Alan Marshall **Owner** Squire Hotels **Seats** 40, Pr/dining room 20 **Times** 12-2/6.30-9.30 **Prices** Starter fr £5, Main fr £12, Dessert fr £5, Service optional **Wines** 12 bottles over £30, 26 bottles under £30, 4 by glass **Parking** 90 **Notes** Afternoon tea available, Sunday L fr £15, Vegetarian available, Children welcome

---

OLDHAM Map 16 SD90

The Old Bell Inn

 Modern British NEW

tel: 01457 870130 **5 Huddersfield Rd, Delph OL3 5EG**
email: info@theoldbellinn.co.uk **web:** www.theoldbellinn.co.uk
dir: *From M62 junct 22, follow A672 to Denshaw junct signed Saddleworth. Left onto A6052 signed Delph. Through village left at x-rds, 150yds on left*

Up-to-date food with an imaginative edge

This solid 18th-century coaching inn has successfully made the transition to a smart 21st-century operation without losing its soul. Before we get to the table, a gin-based aperitif is in order, since the selection runs to a mind-boggling 230 bottles; thus fortified, the restaurant's high-backed seats and darkwood floors make a suitably contemporary setting for the kitchen's hearty and imaginative modern food. There's much emphasis on local components and plenty to tempt – a velouté of smoked haddock comes in a mini bottle to pour over a Lancashire cheese and leek fishcake paired with a warm leek pannacotta, followed by the porky pleasures of slow-roasted belly, braised shoulder, marinated fillet and sticky rib with cabbage and sweet potato. Fish dishes are worth checking out too – perhaps baked sea bass fillet with braised celery, shellfish risotto and bisque. The creative approach runs through to a dessert of rhubarb and ginger cheesecake with granola nougat and rhubarb sorbet.

Chef Mark Pemberton **Owner** Philip Whiteman **Seats** 65 **Times** 12-9.30 All-day dining **Prices** Service optional **Wines** 5 bottles over £30, 21 bottles under £30, 9 by glass **Parking** 21 **Notes** Signature menu £25-£30, Pre-theatre menu available, Sunday L fr £8.95, Vegetarian available, Children welcome

---

The White Hart Inn

 Modern British v

tel: 01457 872566 **51 Stockport Rd, Lydgate OL4 4JJ**
email: bookings@thewhitehart.co.uk
dir: *M62 junct 20, A627, continue to end of bypass, then A669 to Saddleworth. Enter Lydgate turn right onto Stockport Rd. White Hart Inn 50yds on left*

Modern British cooking in a traditional old inn

The White Hart is a rambling old inn in a moorland setting opposite a church, with real ales served in the friendly bar, and two eating venues: the traditionally styled brasserie with open fires and the more contemporary-looking restaurant. Each has its own menu, and food is a serious commitment in both. The former deals in such fare as rabbit pâté with vegetables à la grecque or marinated tuna with white radish, before braised ox cheek with Serrano ham, potato butter and kale, or pan-fried salmon with spicy oriental-style cabbage. There's not a great deal of difference in the cooking style in the restaurant: perhaps tandoor-roast monkfish with apple and coriander, then slow-roast belly pork with langoustines and shellfish sauce. Lemon soufflé with orange sorbet is be a possibility in the restaurant, with sticky toffee pudding with Guinness ice cream in the brasserie.

Chef Mike Shaw **Owner** Charles Brierley **Seats** 50, Pr/dining room 32 **Times** 12-2.30/6-9.30 Closed 26 Dec, 1 Jan **Prices** Fixed L 2 course £13.50, Tasting menu £47.50, Starter £5-£9.50, Main £11.50-£20.50, Dessert £5.80-£7.50, Service optional **Wines** 70 bottles over £30, 70 bottles under £30, 10 by glass **Parking** 75 **Notes** Tasting menu 7 course, 2 for 1 D 5 course £39.50, Sunday L £22.50, Children welcome

PRESTWICH
Map 15 SD80

Aumbry

◎◎ British v

tel: 0161 798 5841 **2 Church Ln M25 1AJ**
email: enquiries@aumbryrestaurant.co.uk
dir: M60 junct 17, A56 signed Manchester/Prestwich. Turn right into Church Ln

Sharp and terrifically presented modern cooking

If the setting in a pretty cottage in the centre of the village suggests a certain homeliness, think again. There may be a charming simplicity to the small dining room – rustic-chic, you might say – but the cooking takes a thoroughly contemporary tack. That is not too say it's all whizz-bang, techie stuff, but rather the new wave of cooking that gets the most of out the ingredients by maximising their natural flavours. There lots of pickling, curing and clever techniques, with an honesty and purity to what turns up on the plate. And it all looks gorgeous. There's a tasting menu and carte to pick from, plus a bargain tasting menu on Tuesday. A dish of home-smoked mackerel with roast celeriac, pickled beets and mustard cream sums up the style to a T, while another of scallop céviche shows a canny combination of flavours and textures. Slow-cooked kid is a stellar course, packed with rich, goaty flavour, and served with a sour goats' milk gel. Sweet courses such as beetroot and chocolate cakes with bee pollen, hazelnuts, milk and honey are no less compelling.

Chef Laurence Tottingham, Mary-Ellen McTague **Owner** Laurence Tottingham, Mary-Ellen McTague **Seats** 34 **Times** 12-1.30/6.30-9.30 Closed Xmas, 1st wk Jan, Mon, L Tue-Thu, D Sun **Prices** Tasting menu £60-£75, Service optional 10% **Wines** 100 bottles over £30, 25 bottles under £30, 15 by glass **Parking** On street **Notes** Tasting menu 6/9 course, Sunday L £60-£75, Children welcome

ROCHDALE
Map 16 SD81

Nutters

◎◎ Modern British v | NOTABLE WINE LIST

tel: 01706 650167 **Edenfield Rd, Norden OL12 7TT**
email: enquiries@nuttersrestaurant.com
dir: From Rochdale take A680 signed Blackburn. Edenfield Rd on right on leaving Norden

Personality-laden modern British food at a Victorian Gothic manor house

Andrew Nutter's entirely idiosyncratic restaurant is overflowing with character, located as it is in a Victorian Gothic manor house in six acres of parkland on the road between Rochdale and Ramsbottom, and having for its presiding genius the star of screen and stove, Nutter himself. Since acquisition in 2003, the place has been a local beacon for a personality-laden take on modern British food, driven by local supplies and the kind of culinary imagination that scorns boundaries. That explains why you might start a meal with salmon fillet and pickled daikon in ginger and wasabi mayo, or duck leg confit in Caesar dressing, before moving on to lamb rump with a feta fritter and lemon chive mash, or cod with sesame-lime noodles in soy and ginger broth. Business and Sunday lunches, and a six-course menu surprise, add to the various senses of occasion, and it all ends on a high note with desserts like raspberry basked Alaska sauced with white chocolate and Drambuie, or quince and apple crumble with cinnamon custard and cherry flapjack ice cream.

Chef Andrew Nutter **Owner** The Nutter family **Seats** 143, Pr/dining room 100 **Times** 12-2/6.30-9.30 Closed 1-2 days after both Xmas & New Year, Mon **Prices** Fixed L 2 course £13.95-£42, Tasting menu fr £42, Starter £4.80-£9.50, Main £15.60-£23, Dessert £4.40-£7.80 **Wines** 107 bottles over £30, 90 bottles under £30, 9 by glass **Parking** 100 **Notes** Gourmet menu 6 course £42, Sunday L fr £23.50, Children welcome

The Peacock Room

◎◎ Modern British

tel: 01706 368591 **Crimble Hotel, Crimble Ln, Bamford OL11 4AD**
email: crimble@thedeckersgroup.com **web:** www.thedeckersgroup.com
dir: M62 junct 20 follow signs for Blackburn, left onto B6222 (Bury road) contine for 1m Crimble Lane on left

Art deco design and smart modish food

The Peacock Room is a fitting name for this flamboyantly decorated restaurant. Huge gold sculptures of the fowl on the door handles, a mirrored ceiling hung with chandeliers, cornicing picked out in gold, and plush seats on a busily patterned carpet all contribute to the exuberant style, while the birds parade the grounds. Dishes themselves are never over elaborate, the kitchen delivering quail breast with a spicy quail's egg, sweetcorn purée and morels, then butter-poached lemon sole with a fricassee of baby vegetables and time-honoured parsley sauce. Prime ingredients are the norm, and combinations give satisfying results, so foie gras joins ham hock in a terrine, served with poached apples and gingerbread, and poached fillet of halibut is accompanied by snail fricassée, pea purée, green vegetables and smoked butter sauce. Committed meat-eaters could opt for roast cannon of beef fillet with oxtail fritters, foie gras, confit potatoes and celeriac. No need to dither over a pudding when there's a quartet of desserts to order: praline parfait, orange crème brûlée, mango trifle and chocolate delice.

Chef Robert Walker **Owner** The Deckers Hospitality Group **Seats** 80 **Times** 12-2.30/6.30-10 Closed Mon-Tue, L Sat, D Sun **Prices** Fixed L 2 course £13.50, Fixed D 3 course £19.50, Starter £5.05-£9.55, Main £15.95-£23.95, Dessert £5.95-£10, Service optional **Wines** 30 bottles over £30, 71 bottles under £30, 6 by glass **Parking** 120 **Notes** Sunday L £21.50, Vegetarian available, Children welcome

---

Macdonald Kilhey Court Hotel

 Modern British

tel: 01257 472100 **Chorley Rd, Standish WN1 2XN**
email: general.kilheycourt@macdonald-hotels.co.uk web: www.macdonaldhotels.co.uk
dir: *M6 junct 27, through village of Standish. Take B5239, left onto A5106, hotel on right*

Peaceful garden views and sound cooking

The hotel dates from 1884, when it was built by a local brewer, and its Laureate Restaurant occupies a large conservatory on three levels, its atmosphere relaxed and informal, overlooking the hotel's grounds. The kitchen uses fresh seasonal produce to good effect in such tried-and-trusted classics as Stornoway black pudding with caramelised apple and bacon salad, or shrimp cocktail with Marie Rose sauce, then coq au vin, steaks from the grill or pan-fried fillet of sea bass with seasonal vegetables. Vegetarians can go for pumpkin ravioli with sage butter, and to finish, we're all in it together with Eton Mess and crème brûlée.

Times 12.30-2.30/6.30-9.30 Closed L Sat

Wrightington Hotel & Country Club

 Modern International

tel: 01257 425803 **Moss Ln, Wrightington WN6 9PB**
email: info@bennettsrestaurant.com web: www.bennettsrestaurant.com
dir: *M6 junct 27, 0.25m W, hotel on right after church*

Unfussy cooking and top-notch leisure facilities

The leisure and conference facilities place the modern Wrightington Hotel firmly on the local map, with its location close to the M6 (albeit in a quiet countryside setting) delivering a steady flow of business customers and pleasure seekers. Bennett's Restaurant is a large open-plan space with darkwood tables, warm colours and a menu that includes a section called 'Lancashire Classics'. Duck liver parfait with brandied sultanas, tomato chutney and brioche gets the ball rolling, with an individual hotpot with carrot and swede purée flying the regional flag. Finish with a warm melting Belgium chocolate pudding.

Times 6-9.30 Closed Sun, L all week

Grenache

 Modern British **NEW**

tel: 0161 7998181 **15 Bridgewater Rd, Walkden M28 3JE**
email: info@grenacherestaurant.co.uk
dir: *Off Bridgewater Road B5232*

Classy cooking in an upmarket neighbourhood restaurant

Bringing contemporary dining to Walkden, Grenache has sleek modern decor and impresses with its take on modern European food. It's not a stuffy place, for the service team maintain a good balance of welcoming hospitality and professionalism. There's a confident hand in the kitchen, too, in the shape of Mike Jennings. His menu changes on a weekly basis and is packed with good quality ingredients cooked with flair and presented with a great deal of panache. A starter salad consisting of roasted quail and braised lentils brings a touch of refinement to a hearty combination, or go for twice-baked Lancashire cheese soufflé with piccalilli. Next up, main course herb-crusted halibut (a superb bit of fish) is served with asparagus, scallop tortellini and langoustine bisque, while slow-cooked belly pork comes with glazed cheek and smoked mash. Desserts run to rhubarb pannacotta served with a gingerbread and custard ice cream. There are little extras

along the way such as amuse-bouche, pre-dessert and first-class focaccia bread. When they want the table back, head to the lounge bar upstairs.

Chef Mike Jennings **Owner** Hussein Abbas, Yvonne Timms **Seats** 40 **Times** 1-5/5.30-close Closed Mon-Tue, L Wed-Sat, D Sun **Prices** Fixed L 2 course £17.95, Fixed D 3 course £20.95, Tasting menu £45, Starter £5.95-£12.95, Main £10.95-£29.95, Dessert £5.95-£9.95, Service optional **Wines** 13 bottles over £30, 43 bottles under £30, 4 by glass **Parking** On street **Notes** Sunday L £13.95-£20.95, Vegetarian available, Children welcome

---

The Anchor Inn

 British

tel: 01420 23261 **Lower Froyle GU34 4NA**
email: info@anchorinnatlowerfroyle.co.uk web: www.anchorinnatlowerfroyle.co.uk
dir: *From A31, turn off to Bentley*

Masterly and wide-ranging cooking at village inn

The Anchor, dating from the 16th century, has all the elements of a traditional country inn down to its low beams, walls full of pictures and press cuttings, wooden tables and a double-sided bar. It's a popular place, attracting people not just for drinks in the bar but with a wide-ranging menu assembled by a kitchen that clearly has high levels of culinary skill and integrity. Pub stalwarts of sausage and mash are on the menu, but so too is an excellent rack of lamb, served pink in its own juices, with crispy breaded shoulder, pea purée and pommes Anna. Inventive treatments extend to a garlic and thyme sauce for pan-fried fillet of pollock, accompanied by mussels, clams and samphire, and starters of guinea fowl terrine with date and thyme purée, or a purée of avocado, chilli and lime for crab mayonnaise. Desserts are best-sellers, judging by the number on offer, among them pannacotta topped with crumbled nuts served with poached rhubarb.

Chef Kevin Chandler **Owner** The Millers Collection **Seats** 70, Pr/dining room 20 **Times** 12-2.30/6.30-9.30 Closed 25 Dec, D 26 Dec, 1 Jan **Prices** Starter £6-£9.50, Main £11.50-£24, Dessert £5-£10, Service optional 10% **Wines** 18 bottles over £30, 23 bottles under £30, 9 by glass **Parking** 36 **Notes** Sun L 2/3 course, Sunday L £20.50-£26.50, Vegetarian available, Children welcome

---

Esseborne Manor

 Modern British

tel: 01264 736444 **Hurstbourne Tarrant SP11 OER**
email: info@esseborne-manor.co.uk web: www.esseborne-manor.co.uk
dir: *Halfway between Andover & Newbury on A343, just 1m N of Hurstbourne Tarrant*

Confident modern cooking in bucolic country house

In a delicious spot designated an Area of Outstanding Natural Beauty, Esseborne is a dignified Victorian country house on a human scale. The owners have not attempted to wash away all vestiges of the past. There's a traditional finish within – classy rather than chintzy – with an elegant restaurant that is the very model of refined good taste. There's a good chance that if what you eat doesn't come from the garden in the grounds, it won't have travelled very far. Chef Dennis Janssen creates modern dishes that sparkle, showing good technical skills and creativity. It's not all whizz-bang, though, and there is evident classical thinking going on. Chicken liver parfait is simple enough, but the dish is lifted by the accompanying pickled apricot purée. Main course cod with soused vegetables is based around an excellent piece of fish, the accompanying kipper 'essence' bringing a hit of flavourful richness. There's a tasting menu, too, plus desserts such as a contemporary concoction of strawberries, cream and sorrel.

Chef Dennis Janssen **Owner** Ian Hamilton **Seats** 35, Pr/dining room 80 **Times** 12-2/7-9.30 **Prices** Fixed L 2 course £15, Fixed D 3 course £30, Tasting menu £55, Starter £5-£7.50, Main £13-£22, Dessert £5.75-£7.75, Service optional **Wines** 39 bottles over £30, 53 bottles under £30, 12 by glass **Parking** 40 **Notes** Sunday L £23, Vegetarian available, Children welcome

The Plough Inn

@@ Modern British V

tel: 01264 720358 **Longparish SP11 6PB** email: eat@theploughinn.info

Adventurous cooking in a rustic Hampshire pub

Looking for a break from the traffic-clogged stretches of the A303, you might happen upon Longparish nearby, an unmolested Hampshire village that boasts a creeper-clad country pub in the Plough. Serving the locals since the 1720s, it's run these days by London refugee James Durrant, who retains the rustic look of the place with its exposed brickwork, log-burning fires and a snug worthy of the name. The cooking has gradually diverged into two menus, so that the fish and chips and meat pie trade need not feel neglected, but those in the market for something more adventurous are catered for too. First up might be roasted squash with goats' cheese, wild mushrooms and toasted walnuts, before mains head off in the directions of tenderly braised pig cheeks with salt-baked beetroot, smoked mash, spring onions and mint, or a regally served whole grilled plaice in brown shrimp, caper and raisin vinaigrette. Salty caramel continues to rule the roost for afters, appearing here in an ice cream to go with potent chocolate marquise and a more shy and retiring caramel jelly.

Chef James Durrant **Owner** James & Louise Durrant **Seats** 52 **Times** 12-2.30/6-9.30 Closed D Sun **Prices** Starter £7.50-£10.50, Main £14-£22.50, Dessert £6-£7, Service optional **Wines** 19 bottles over £30, 14 bottles under £30, 11 by glass **Parking** 25 **Notes** Sunday L £16.50-£17.50, Children welcome

Pebble Beach

@ British, French, Mediterranean

tel: 01425 627777 **Marine Dr BH25 7DZ** email: mail@pebblebeach-uk.com web: www.pebblebeach-uk.com dir: *Follow A35 from Southampton onto A337 to New Milton, turn left onto Barton Court Av to clifftop*

Upbeat brasserie cooking with a clifftop sun terrace

A clifftop perch gives this modern bar and brasserie a sweeping vista across Christchurch Bay to the Needles and the Isle of Wight. Inside, it is a buzzy split-level venue where high stools at the oyster bar allow you to catch the action in the open-plan kitchen. With a sublime view, plus an irresistible alfresco terrace to bring in the punters, lesser restaurants might slack off in the food department, but with head chef Pierre Chevillard directing culinary efforts, there's a clear Gallic accent in the kitchen's output. Fish and seafood are strong suits – perhaps a Breton-style fish soup with croûtons, garlic mayonnaise and gruyère cheese, followed by grilled sea bass fillet glazed with parmesan, and served with fennel, and orange butter sauce. Meats might encompass wild boar, slow-cooked with juniper and red wine

and matched with sauteéd wild mushrooms, and truffle oil-scented potato mousseline, and proceedings end with lemon crème brûlée and fresh raspberries.

Chef Pierre Chevillard **Owner** Michael Caddy **Seats** 90, Pr/dining room 8 **Times** 11-2.30/6-11 Closed D 25 Dec, 1 Jan **Prices** Starter £6-£11.80, Main £13.60-£25.90, Dessert £6.99-£9.40, Service optional **Wines** 2 bottles over £30, 52 bottles under £30, 16 by glass **Parking** 20 **Notes** Sunday L £14.95, Vegetarian available, Children welcome

Audleys Wood

@@ Modern British

tel: 01256 817555 & 0845 072 7405 **Alton Rd RG25 2JT** email: audleyswood@handpicked.co.uk web: www.handpickedhotels.co.uk/thesimondsroom dir: *M3 junct 6. From Basingstoke take A339 towards Alton, hotel on right*

Local ingredients cooked with classical flair in a grand setting

This striking property was built as a private residence in the 1880s, in seven acres of grounds and woodland, and comes with all the trappings of a luxury country-house hotel. The main restaurant is the grand Simonds Room, the walls covered with heavy oak panelling hung with framed tapestries, with an imposing fireplace and ornate carved oak cornicing. A classical vein runs through the menu of otherwise modern British ideas. Fillet of halibut, for instance, gets the bonne femme treatment in a main course, served with Jerusalem artichoke, and copybook boulangère potatoes accompany a tender, flavourful cut of venison, served rare, along with silky-smooth red cabbage purée. Starters include an up-to-the-minute dish of lightly poached marinated mackerel fillet, served with al dente goats' cheese and potato cannelloni and a pickled clam, the plate dotted with drops of golden and red beetroot purée. The same beautiful balance is seen in deconstructed lemon meringue pie: a crumble base topped by parfait, droplets of curd adding tartness, with individually sculpted pieces of meringue and vanilla ice cream.

Times 7-9 Closed Sun-Mon, L all week

Basingstoke Country Hotel

@ Modern European

tel: 01256 764161 **Scures Hill, Nately Scures, Hook RG27 9JS** email: basingstokecountry.reception@pumahotels.co.uk web: www.pumahotels.co.uk dir: *On A30 between Nateley Scures & Hook*

Good simple cooking in country hotel

A contemporary hotel and country club in four acres of Hampshire countryside just off the M3, the Basingstoke Country Hotel has broad appeal. If you're here for the spa, a business meeting or such like, take time to eat in the hotel's Scures Brasserie. The room won't win any style awards but it is a bright space with a lack of pretension – no starchy tablecloths here. The team in the kitchen takes a classical approach but the food is not stuck in the past. Take a starter of cured salmon and crab, for example, which comes with avocado cream and pickled fennel to bolster its impact. Next up, slow-roasted pork belly, the fat perfectly rendered, comes with soft and tender braised belly and a black pudding bonbon. Dessert might serve up lemon posset complete with a chocolate cookie.

Times 7-10 Closed 23-27 Dec, L all week

BASINGSTOKE *continued*

Oakley Hall Hotel

◉◉ Modern British

tel: 01256 783350 **Rectory Rd, Oakley RG23 7EL**
email: enquiries@oakleyhall-park.com **web:** www.oakleyhall-park.com
dir: M3 junct 7, follow Basingstoke signs. In 500yds before lights turn left onto A30 towards Oakley, immediately right onto unclass road towards Oakley. In 3m left at T-junct into Rectory Rd. Left onto B3400. Hotel signed 1st on left

Modern brasserie cooking and Jane Austen connection

Built in 1795 and extended in the 19th century by Victorian home improvement enthusiasts, Oakley Hall presents a handsome face to the world. It has literary associations, for it was once owned by friends of Jane Austen, who lived in a nearby village and mentioned the place fondly in letters to her sister. These days, huge investment has transformed the old pile into a country-house hotel, offering luxury rooms and a swish contemporary restaurant sporting wall mirrors, cream leather seats, unclothed darkwood tables and stripy carpets. The kitchen turns out some nicely contemporary food, so chicken broth with poached shellfish and chervil dumplings might compete for your attention with pork belly with broad bean fricassée and crispy kohlrabi among first courses. Follow something along the lines of pan-fried duck breast with potato and apricot cake, parsnip and vanilla purée, rainbow chard and Marsala sauce, or roasted hake fillet with lobster ravioli, tarragon and shellfish butter, purple mash and samphire. Finish in the comfort zone with chocolate fondant with home-made brownie ice cream.

Chef Justin Mundy **Owner** Jon Huxford **Seats** 40, Pr/dining room 300 **Times** 12-2/7-9.30 **Prices** Fixed L 2 course £19.95, Tasting menu £49 **Wines** 8 by glass **Parking** 100 **Notes** Afternoon tea daily £19.95, Sunday L £21.95-£27.50, Vegetarian available, Children welcome

---

▌BAUGHURST Map 5 SU56

The Wellington Arms

◉◉ Modern British

tel: 0118 982 0110 **Baughurst Rd RG26 5LP**
email: hello@thewellingtonarms.com
dir: M4 junct 12 follow Newbury signs on A4. At rdbt left signed Aldermaston. Through Aldermaston. Up hill, at 2nd rdbt 2nd exit signed Baughurst, left at T-junct, pub 1m on left

Top pub food crafted from the most local of local produce

The Wellington Arms is a dining pub with a capital D. A good deal of what you eat will have found its way into the kitchen from the garden, and what isn't home-grown or home-reared won't have travelled very far. Jason King and Simon Page are passionate about what they do, and this is reflected in their quest to be as sustainable as possible. The old pub has scrubbed up very nicely indeed and looks as sharp as a pin these days: it is rustic, charming and spruce. There's a fire indoors on cooler days and, with its tiled floor and wooden tables, it's definitely at the rustic-chic end of the spectrum. Blackboards reveal what lies ahead. Twice-baked Marksbury cheddar soufflé sits on braised leeks, finished with a little cream and parmesan, or there might be fine duck liver and organic port parfait with home-made pickled shallots and chargrilled toast. Follow on with Grange Farm rib-eye with hand-cut chips and red wine jus, or baked fillet of cod (from Brixham) with oven-dried tomatoes, black olives and crushed anya potatoes, and finish with chocolate squidgy pudding with espresso ice cream.

Chef Jason King **Owner** Simon Page & Jason King **Seats** 34, Pr/dining room 20 **Times** 12-2.30/6.30-9.30 Closed D Sun **Prices** Fixed L 2 course fr £16, Starter £6-£12, Main £10.50-£24, Dessert £3.50-£7.50 **Wines** 45 bottles over £30, 21 bottles under £30, 9 by glass **Parking** 25 **Notes** Sunday L, Vegetarian available, Children welcome

---

The Montagu Arms Hotel

▌BEAULIEU Map 5 SU30

Modern French 🍷 NOTABLE WINE LIST

tel: 01590 612324 **Palace Ln SO42 7ZL**
email: reservations@montaguarmshotel.co.uk **web:** www.montaguarmshotel.co.uk
dir: From M27 junct 2 take A326 & B3054 for Beaulieu

Resonant contemporary cooking in a New Forest country hotel

The fabulous motor museum at Beaulieu is one of England's great draws, but the Montagu Arms runs it pretty close for an all-round memorable experience. In the heart of the New Forest, it's in a classic location for a country-house hotel. It is also a prime mover in the localism movement, as Matthew Tomkinson sources game, pork and fresh produce from within the national park's environs, including the hotel's own kitchen garden. A suite of dining rooms is kitted out in best country-interiors opulence, with an outdoor terrace for enjoying the traditional English gardens on fine days. Tomkinson's culinary style mixes the excitements and innovations of the modern British idiom with an underpinning of French technique for dishes that are striking in their impact, both on the eyes and on the palate. First up might be a voguish pairing of pig trotter croquette with smoked eel, the different kinds of richness cut with pickled beetroot and tart apple, or

there may be honey-roast quail in wild mushroom consommé with a poached chicken boudin. A lot of work goes into achieving the entrancing resonance in these dishes, and things move up another gear for main courses like Lymington sea bass with cured ham, Jerusalem artichoke purée and watercress in red wine sauce, while intensely flavoured free-range chicken breast is boosted with black truffle, dauphine potatoes and Tunworth cheese. A hungry pair of spring diners might share roast New Forest beef fillet with creamed Jersey Royals, asparagus and sautéed wild garlic, after which a suitable pause is worth taking before the finishing-line comes in sight. The trolley of English and French farmhouse cheeses is a treasure trove of goodies, but so are desserts such as Seville orange soufflé with Szechuan-peppered chocolate ice cream, or passionfruit cheesecake with orange sorbet. For the truly intrepid, Tomkinson offers a seven-course menu surprise.

Chef Matthew Tomkinson **Owner** Greenclose Ltd, Mr Leach **Seats** 60, Pr/dining room 32 **Times** 12-2.30/7-9.30 Closed Mon, L Tue **Prices** Fixed L 2 course £22.50, Fixed D 3 course £70, Tasting menu £85, Service optional **Wines** 258 bottles over £30, 2 bottles under £30, 12 by glass **Parking** 45 **Notes** D 3 course ALC £70, Sunday L £27.50-£32.50, Vegetarian available, Children 8 yrs+

BEAULIEU Map 5 SU30

Beaulieu Hotel
◉ British

---

tel: 023 8029 3344 **Beaulieu Rd SO42 7YQ**
email: beaulieu@newforesthotels.co.uk **web:** www.newforesthotels.co.uk
dir: On B3056 between Lyndhurst & Beaulieu. Near Beaulieu Road railway station

Modern British cooking in the New Forest

Built of warm red bricks, the former coaching inn is in its own landscaped grounds within open heathland on the edge of the village. It's a smartly appointed sort of place, guests' comfort of primary concern, the traditionally styled dining room no exception. Service might be on the formal side, but staff know what they're doing. The kitchen's a busy place, baking bread daily in-house and relying on local and therefore seasonal ingredients. Tea-smoked pigeon and apple salad with beetroot sorbet is something of a signature starter, and might be followed by properly timed, crisp-skinned pan-fried sea bass interestingly complemented by chorizo, olives and pepper relish, or Hampshire lamb cooked two ways served with bubble-and-squeak and pea purée. Pastry work is clearly a forte, judging by a light and fresh base for velvety lemon tart with a novel basil and champagne sorbet.

Chef Michael Mckell **Owner** New Forest Hotels plc **Seats** 60, Pr/dining room 80 **Times** 5.30-9.30 Closed L all week **Prices** Prices not confirmed, Service optional **Wines** 8 bottles over £30, 30 bottles under £30, 8 by glass **Parking** 60 **Notes** Vegetarian available, Children welcome

The Montagu Arms Hotel
◉◉◉ – see opposite

BOTLEY Map 5 SU51

Macdonald Botley Park, Golf & Spa
◉ Modern British, European

---

tel: 01489 780888 **Winchester Rd, Boorley Green SO32 2UA**
email: botleypark@macdonald-hotels.co.uk **web:** www.macdonald-hotels.co.uk/botleypark
dir: M27 junct 7, A334 towards Botley. At 1st rdbt left, past M&S store, over the next 5 mini rdbts. At 6th mini rdbt turn right. In 0.5m hotel on left

Simple, honest cooking in relaxed hotel

Botley Park is a sprawling modern country hotel in 176 acres of landscaped grounds just a short hop from Southampton Airport and the M3. When you have worked up an appetite on its 18-hole championship golf course and steamed away the stress in the spa, the Winchester Restaurant offers a smart contemporary setting for an uncomplicated repertoire of unpretentious cooking. Expect well-sourced, high-quality ingredients in starters such as Stornoway black pudding with caramelised apple and bacon salad, followed by a prime slab of Scottish steak from the grill, or slow-roasted shoulder of lamb with boulangère potatoes and ratatouille. End with the comfort of fig sponge pudding with walnut praline and crème anglaise.

Chef Brian Dixon **Owner** Macdonald Hotels **Seats** 70, Pr/dining room 250 **Times** 12.30-2.30/6.30-9.30 Closed L Sat **Prices** Fixed D 3 course £29.50 **Wines** 42 bottles over £30, 21 bottles under £30, 14 by glass **Parking** 200 **Notes** Sunday L £19, Vegetarian available, Children welcome

---

BRANSGORE Map 5 SZ19

The Three Tuns
◉ British, European

tel: 01425 672232 **Ringwood Rd BH23 8JH**
email: threetunsinn@btconnect.com **web:** www.threetunsinn.com
dir: On A35 at junct for Walkford/Highcliffe follow Bransgore signs, 1.5m, restaurant on left

Appealing varied menu in a traditional thatched inn

Picture this: a picture-postcard 17th-century thatched gem deep in the New Forest National Park which is a delight in summer, festooned with flowers, and cosy in winter, with blazing log fires warming the low beamed bar and dining areas. That's the Three Tuns, which draws foodies and forest visitors for its charm and character, its buzzy atmosphere, the glorious sun-drenched garden, and an eclectic menu that lists pub classics alongside adventurous modern British gastropub dishes. Using game from surrounding estates, locally-shot venison, farm meats and fish delivered to door, the seasonal menu kicks off with a robust Sicilian fish soup full of chunks of sea bass and red mullet and the Mediterranean flavours of fennel, peppers and tomatoes. Follow with Landes chicken roasted with garlic and paired with snails, fondant potato, tomato salad and rocket pesto. To finish, chocolate mousse comes with hazelnut macaroons and popping candy for a bit of fun.

Chef Colin Nash **Owner** Nigel Glenister **Seats** 60, Pr/dining room 50 **Times** 12-2.15/6-9.15 Closed 25-26 & 31 Dec, D 1 Jan, 5 Nov **Prices** Service optional **Wines** 3 bottles over £30, 24 bottles under £30, 11 by glass **Parking** 50 **Notes** Sunday L fr £12.50, Vegetarian available, Children welcome

Follow the AA on twitter @TheAA_Lifestyle

Looking for a restaurant by name?
Use the index on page 751

BROCKENHURST

Map 5 SU30

The Balmer Lawn Hotel

 Modern British

tel: 01590 623116 & 625725 **Lyndhurst Rd SO42 7ZB**
email: info@balmerlawnhotel.com **web:** www.balmerlawnhotel.com
dir: *Take A337 towards Brockenhurst, hotel on left after 'Welcome to Brockenhurst' sign*

Fine dining at grand New Forest hotel

This imposing pavillion-style Victorian hunting lodge turned country hotel has hosted prime ministers and presidents over the years, no doubt drawn by its charming New Forest setting. Reinvented with panache for the modern world, the friendly, family-run operation aims more at pampering or business these days, with its excellent spa, sports and conference facilities. Beresford's restaurant is the fine-dining option, an impressive, grandly-proportioned space done out with understated contemporary style – high-backed black leather seats at unclothed darkwood tables, and a warm palette of toffee and chocolate. The kitchen deals in modern cooking with a healthy showing of prime-quality, often local, materials. Seared scallops matched with breaded Romsey pork belly and black pudding, and apple and vanilla sauce opens the show, ahead of partridge stuffed with Madeira-marinated prunes and chestnuts, and braised Puy lentils, soured white cabbage, and celeriac purée. To round it all off, there's classic apple tarte Tatin with vanilla sauce.

Times 12.30-2.30/7-9.30

Careys Manor Hotel & Senspa

 Modern British

tel: 01590 623551 **Lyndhurst Rd SO42 7RH**
email: zengarden@senspa.co.uk **web:** www.thezengarden.co.uk
dir: *M27 junct 2, follow Fawley/A326 signs. Continue over 3 rdbts, at 4th rdbt right lane signed Lyndhurst/A35. Follow A337 (Lymington/Brockenhurst)*

Imaginative cooking in the New Forest

Careys Manor, the original building dating from 1888, is in a delightful spot in the New Forest. It has three eateries: a French bistro, the Thai Zen Garden (see entry), and the cream of the crop, the Manor Restaurant, where the skilled kitchen team applies some culinary wizardry to fresh seasonal produce. Seared pigeon breast with red wine reduction, sweet potato and cumin purée and rocket sounds mainstream enough, but an alternative may be butter-poached sea trout with seaweed-marinated mooli and cucumber dressing. Technical precision is evident throughout, and combinations thoughtful. Thus, confit pork belly comes with black pudding purée, potato gratin and a sage jus, and slices of roast Dorset rump of veal are plated on spinach and accompanied by pommes Anna, caramelised onion purée and rich thyme-infused gravy. Fish gets a decent showing: perhaps glazed salmon fillet creatively partnered by saffron gratin with kale, caper and raisin purée, prawn shavings and lemon butter. Bread and extras get nods of approval, and desserts are as well made as everything else, among them perhaps honey parfait with raspberry sorbet.

Times 12-2.30/7-10 Closed D Mon

Who are the AA's Restaurants of the Year? See page 14

The Pig

 British **V**

tel: 01590 622354 **Beaulieu Rd SO42 7QL**
email: info@thepighotel.com **web:** www.thepighotel.com
dir: *M27 junct 2, follow A326 Lyndhurst, then A337 Brockenhurst onto B3055 Beaulieu Road. 1m on left up private road*

Home-grown and foraged food in a New Forest hotel

The Pig truly is a restaurant with rooms for our times, where cocktails are served in old jam jars and you can get a massage in the old potting shed. Surrounded by the wilds of the New Forest, the main passion is for home-grown and foraged ingredients, and there's no playing to the gallery here – check out the walled kitchen garden, the wood-fired oven and the 25-mile policy for ingredients on the menu. It's a buzzy place with a retro interior, and the Victorian greenhouse dining room provides an informal setting for the serving of rustic dishes with the focus on flavour. There's simple and careful execution in a starter of Sopley Farm asparagus with pickled quail's eggs, pancetta and a deeply-flavoured lemon dressing. Follow that with rump of Hampshire lamb (a fine piece of meat, too) with broad beans, peas and baby onions, or pollock with Hampshire chorizo and cockles. The careful and considered cooking continues with a dessert of Cox's apple tart with cider apple and Dorset clotted cream ice cream.

Chef James Golding **Owner** Robin Hutson **Seats** 85, Pr/dining room 14
Times 12-2.30/6.30-9.30 **Prices** Starter £5-£9, Main £12-£28, Dessert £7 **Wines** 59 bottles over £30, 38 bottles under £30, 14 by glass **Parking** 40 **Notes** Sunday L, Children welcome

Rhinefield House

 Modern British

tel: 01590 622922 **Rhinefield Rd SO42 7QB**
email: rhinefieldhouse@handpicked.co.uk
web: www.handpickedhotels.co.uk/rhinefieldhouse
dir: *M27 junct, A337 to Lyndhurst, then A35 W towards Christchurch. 3.5m, left at sign for Rhinefield House. Hotel 1.5m on right*

Modern cooking in a stunning Victorian mansion

Rhinefield cropped up on Wordsworth's poetic gazetteer in the 1790s, though he didn't live to see the present magnificencé spring up in the late Victorian era. A Tudor-Gothic hybrid architecturally, the interiors are awash with finely crafted mouldings, copperwork and beautiful examples of the lavatorialist's art, plus Grinling Gibbons carvings, ceilings by Fragonard, and a room modelled on the Alhambra. James Whitesmith steps manfully up to the plate in these surroundings to captivate what remains of your attention with some eye-catching modern cooking. Scallops with sea trout mousse and pickled baby carrots in sauce vierge might set the pace, and be succeeded by cod in Caesar sauce with clams and almonds, or rack of lamb with dauphinoise and rhubarb under a froth of sheep's milk. Dishes can sometimes feel a little over-engineered-you can have all the froths and foams in the world, but getting pork to crackle properly is just as important-but there is no lack of conceptual energy nonetheless. Desserts might include a raspberry version of crème brûlée with raspberry texture variations, served with rhubarb and ginger ice cream.

Chef James Whitesmith **Owner** Hand Picked Hotels **Seats** 58, Pr/dining room 12 **Times** 12-5/7-10 **Prices** Fixed D 3 course fr £24.50, Tasting menu £37, Starter £9.50-£12.50, Main £18.50-£29.50, Dessert £11-£12.50, Service optional **Wines** 151 bottles over £30, 14 bottles under £30, 18 by glass **Parking** 150 **Notes** Sunday L fr £24.50, Vegetarian available, Children welcome

The Zen Garden Restaurant
 Thai **V**

tel: 01590 623219 & 623551 **The SenSpa, Careys Manor Hotel, Lyndhurst Rd SO42 7RH**
email: zengarden@senspa.co.uk
dir: A337 from Lyndhurst signed Lymington, Brockenhurst, within Careys Manor Hotel

Vibrant Thai cooking in a spa

If you go down to the woods today you're in for a big surprise, for within the SenSpa at Careys Manor Hotel in the New Forest is a smart Thai restaurant. Perhaps not a huge surprise these days, but a pleasing one nonetheless. The Zen Garden Restaurant looks the part with its gold columns, bamboo ceiling and darkwood tables and chairs, and there's an ethical approach when it comes to sourcing materials for the traditional menus. Start with something like soft-shelled crab-perfectly cooked-with a Thai salad and a rich, sticky sauce, or taro fritters with a red curry paste and lime leaves. There are soups such as the classic tom yam, and stir-fried dishes such as goong phad prik (tiger prawns with chilli, peppers, red cabbage and spring onion). Beef sirloin comes in a main course with a spicy marinade, crushed roasted rice and a papaya salad with chilli, mint and tamarind.

Chef Thosporn Wongsasube **Owner** Greenclose Ltd **Seats** 50, Pr/dining room 16 **Times** 12-2.30/7-10 Closed D Mon **Prices** Fixed L 2 course fr £22, Fixed D 3 course fr £27.50, Tasting menu £37.50, Starter £6.95-£16.85, Main £9.75-£17.85, Dessert £6.95 **Wines** 10 bottles over £30, 12 bottles under £30, 9 by glass **Parking** 130 **Notes** Sunday L No children

---

BROOK
Map 5 SU21

The Bell Inn
Modern English

tel: 023 8081 2214 **SO43 7HE**
email: bell@bramshaw.co.uk **web:** www.bellinnbramshaw.co.uk
dir: M27 junct 1 onto B3079, hotel 1.5m on right

Gracefully presented modern cooking at a New Forest inn

There can't be many places that can claim to have continued in the ownership of the same family since George III was on the throne, as the Bell can boast. It's in a picturesque New Forest village not far from Lyndhurst, and is a bit more than a simple country inn in that it lays claim to a pair of golf courses. The interior looks the modernised rustic part, with blackboard menus and log fires in winter, and plenty of gracefully presented local produce on offer. A serving of seared scallops with pickled cauliflower and tea-soaked raisins might kick things off, as the preamble to loin, confit belly and crisped hock of local pork, served with mash, greens and pineapple purée. Finish with smoothly textured, sharply zesty lemon cream garnished with crunchy meringue, candied lemon and yoghurt sorbet. A fine selection of cheeses from independent producers, served with biscuits and chutney, is a heartening sight.

Chef Carl France **Owner** Crosthwaite Eyre family **Seats** 50, Pr/dining room 40 **Times** 12-2.30/6.30-9.30 **Prices** Starter £6.50-£6.95, Main £14.50-£28.50, Dessert £5.50-£6.50, Service optional **Wines** 12 bottles over £30, 22 bottles under £30, 10 by glass **Parking** 40 **Notes** Sunday L £14.95-£21.95, Vegetarian available, Children welcome

---

BURLEY
Map 5 SU20

Moorhill House Hotel
Traditional & Modern British

tel: 01425 403285 **BH24 4AG**
email: moorhill@newforesthotels.co.uk **web:** www.newforesthotels.co.uk
dir: Exit A31 signed Burley Drive, through village, turn right opposite cricket pitch

Well-executed British dishes at a New Forest hotel

Penetrating deep into the ancient woodland of the New Forest is as good a start as any for a few days away, or even just a meal, and Moorhill's location, near the pretty village of Burley, admirably fits the bill. Sitting in its own handsome gardens, it's done out in light, attractive country house style within, with log fires for the toasting of toes in winter. In the newly refurbished dining room, straightforward but well-executed British dishes are Ben Cartwright's forte, so expect to start with devilled sardines on fennel-seed toast with cherry tomato and basil compote. Move on to slow-roast pork belly with glazed apple and sautéed Savoy cabbage, sauced with the famous local Burley cider, or grilled haddock with chorizo and chickpea cassoulet. Cockle-warming puddings include a spiced rum parfait with ginger biscuits and coffee sauce, and black treacle and almond tart with orange ice cream.

Chef Ben Cartwright **Owner** New Forest Hotels **Seats** 60, Pr/dining room 40 **Times** 5.30-9.30 Closed L Mon-Sat **Prices** Prices not confirmed, Service optional **Wines** 3 bottles over £30, 28 bottles under £30, 8 by glass **Parking** 50 **Notes** Sunday L, Vegetarian available, Children welcome

---

CADNAM
Map 5 SZ21

Bartley Lodge Hotel
Traditional British

tel: 023 8081 2248 **Lyndhurst Rd SO40 2NR**
email: bartley@newforesthotels.co.uk **web:** www.newforesthotels.co.uk
dir: M27 junct 1, A337, follow signs for Lyndhurst. Hotel on left

Elegant surroundings for country-house cooking

The Grade II listed Bartley Lodge has eight acres of precious Hampshire countryside all to itself, with a croquet on the lawn and an indoor swimming pool among its attractions. The 18th-century house has hung onto many original features, and there's a relaxed and professional attitude all round. The 'flexible dining' approach means the menu is available throughout the hotel, which extends to the Crystal Restaurant with its elegant centrepiece chandelier and delicate Wedgwood blue and gold colour scheme, or the cosy bar. The menu deals in feel-good flavours and simple presentations, so you might start with wild and button mushrooms with bacon and cheese on bruschetta, following on with something as homely as lasagne or Ringwood ale-battered fish and chips, or opt for the more ambitious ballotine of sea trout with horseradish mash and a caviar and leek cream. Finish with a lime and mango pannacotta.

Chef Stuart White **Owner** New Forest Hotels **Seats** 60, Pr/dining room 90 **Times** 5.30-9.30 Closed L Mon-Sat **Prices** Prices not confirmed, Service optional **Wines** 8 bottles over £30, 32 bottles under £30, 8 by glass **Parking** 90 **Notes** Sunday L, Vegetarian available, Children welcome

Read all about our Wine Award winners
on page 17

DOGMERSFIELD
Map 5 SU75

Four Seasons Hotel Hampshire
◉◉◉ Modern French, European v

tel: 01252 853000 & 853100 **Dogmersfield Park, Chalky Ln RG27 8TD**
email: reservations.ham@fourseasons.com **web:** www.fourseasons.com/hampshire
dir: M3 junct 5 onto A287 Farnham. After 1.5m take left to Dogmersfield, hotel 0.6m on left

Modish regionally-inspired cooking in a grand Georgian manor

A grand house on a grand estate, the red-brick Four Seasons is a luxurious outpost of the upscale brand set in lush Hampshire countryside. There's a spa, of course, plus original Georgian features that were built to impress – sweeping staircase, intricate plasterwork and glitzy chandeliers. The dining options include a bistro and café, but the main event is the Seasons restaurant, located in a light-filled room with French windows and an upscale (and gently contemporary) finish. Tables are dressed to the nines and the service team are on hand to treat you like royalty. The team in the kitchen draw on the estate and nearby suppliers to deliver well-crafted and rather dynamic modern French/European food. A starter, for example, of roasted pigeon has pink and tender breast partnered with creamy potatoes, sweet confit shallots and a glossy sauce, followed by a main of roasted turbot atop a rich and smooth broccoli mousseline, and salsify and Jerusalem artichoke fricassée. Desserts such as citrusy lemon tart with blood orange sorbet and glazed meringues are no less on the money.

Chef Cyrille Pannier **Owner** Four Seasons Hotels & Resorts **Seats** 100, Pr/dining room 24 **Times** 6-10.30 Closed Mon, L Tue-Sat, D Sun **Prices** Fixed D 3 course £49 **Wines** 75 bottles over £30, 15 by glass **Parking** 100 **Notes** Sunday L £49 Children 8yrs+ D

DROXFORD
Map 5 SU61

Bakers Arms
◉ Traditional British

tel: 01489 877533 **High St SO32 3PA**
email: adam@thebakersarmsdroxford.com
dir: Off A32

Favourites and fancier in a homely Hampshire pub

Droxford sits in the Meon Valley, within the boundaries of the South Downs National Park, an appealing little village with this equally appealing whitewashed local hostelry at its heart. A stag's head peers down from a wall hung with framed pictures of the place in bygone days, and the rustic furniture, blazing fires and merciful absence of muzak stamp the interior scene with the seal of authenticity. Good local beers and a menu of well-thought out pub favourites such as chicken liver parfait, sausages and mash with onion gravy, and rice pudding with clotted cream seem to guarantee satisfaction. Things can get productively fancier too though, as in pigeon and smoked bacon salad with apple sauce, followed by seared sea bass with curly kale in lentil and herb dressing, with brilliant chips. Chunked-up poached pear on a caramel layer spooned over with creamy yoghurt is a harmonious finale. Don't miss the superb home-made fennel-seed bread.

Chef Adam Cordery **Owner** Adam & Anna Cordery **Seats** 45 **Times** 11.45-3/6-11 Closed D Sun **Prices** Fixed L 2 course fr £13, Fixed D 2 course fr £13, Starter £6-£7.50, Main £9.95-£18.95, Dessert £5.50, Service optional **Wines** 12 bottles over £30, 23 bottles under £30, 13 by glass **Parking** 30 **Notes** Sunday L £15.95-£18.95, Vegetarian available, Children welcome

EMSWORTH
Map 5 SU70

Fat Olives
◉◉ British, Mediterranean

tel: 01243 377914 **30 South St PO10 7EH**
email: info@fatolives.co.uk
dir: In town centre, 1st right after Emsworth Square, 100yds towards the Quay. Restaurant on left with public car park opposite

Locally-inspired inventive modern cooking near the quay

A 17th-century fishermen's cottage just a few steps from the quayside of pretty Emsworth harbour supplies the setting for Lawrence and Julia Murphy's smart brasserie, which ticks all the right boxes for the faithful foodies who have kept it buzzing for over a decade. The stripped-out interior of cream walls, bare wooden floors and unclothed tables is as unvarnished and honest as the food. Lawrence lets the excellent raw materials do the talking, helped by a judicious hand to ensure spot-on accuracy, and a gentle whiff of the Mediterranean. The menu is an appetising fusion of modern, well thought through ideas. It might take in roast breast and confit leg of quail with chorizo-spiked cassoulet, then move on to perfectly-timed silver mullet with Puy lentils, neatly balanced by the tartness of salsa verde. Or you might be tempted by a more Brit-influenced and resolutely local plate of South Downs pork loin teamed with a faggot, quince, and trotter sauce. At the end, vanilla pannacotta comes with raspberry coulis and crunchy oat biscuits.

Chef Lawrence Murphy **Owner** Lawrence & Julia Murphy **Seats** 25 **Times** 12-2/7-9 Closed 1 wk Xmas, 1 wk Mar, 2 wks Jun, Sun-Mon **Prices** Fixed L 2 course fr £18.50, Starter £6.25-£9.50, Main £15.50-£26, Dessert £6.50-£6.75, Service optional **Wines** 23 bottles over £30, 24 bottles under £30, 8 by glass **Parking** Opposite restaurant **Notes** Vegetarian available, No children

36 on the Quay
◉◉◉ – see opposite

FAREHAM
Map 5 SU50

Solent Hotel & Spa
◉ British, European

tel: 01489 880000 **Rookery Av, Whiteley PO15 7AJ**
email: solent@shirehotels.com **web:** www.shirehotels.com
dir: M27 junct 9, hotel on Solent Business Park

Skilful cooking and wide-ranging menus

A modern hotel with spa facilities among meadows and woodland, The Solent's Terrace Restaurant is a dimly lit room, enhanced by candles, separated from the bar by an open fireplace; tables are clothed and correctly set, and the atmosphere is at the same time relaxed and formal. The longish and wide-ranging menu is likely to appeal to all-comers, with starters ranging from crispy Asian duck with watercress, cucumber and coriander salad, to prawn and lobster salad with Marie Rose sauce. Main courses can be reassuringly familiar – exemplary duck leg confit, its meat falling off the bone, with red wine jus, crisp potatoes and honey-infused carrots for instance – although the kitchen also presents more contemporary ideas, among them perhaps roast scallops with black pudding accompanied by pommes purée and red wine sauce. Finish with creamy, light and tangy lemon posset with seasonal berries and a spiced sugar cake, or sticky toffee pudding.

Chef Peter Williams **Owner** Shire Hotels **Seats** 130, Pr/dining room 40 **Times** 12.15-2/7-9.30 Closed L Sat **Prices** Starter £5.95-£10.25, Main £12.95-£57.50, Dessert £4.75-£6.50, Service optional **Wines** 15 by glass **Parking** 200 **Notes** Sunday L £16.95-£19.95, Vegetarian available, Children welcome

FARNBOROUGH Map 5 SU85

Aviator

◉ Modern European V

tel: 01252 555890 **Farnborough Rd GU14 6EL**
email: brasserie@aviatorbytag.com **web:** www.aviatorbytag.com
dir: A325 to Aldershot, continue for 3m. Hotel on right

Innovative food in a monument to wristwatches and flying

The TAG company's contemporary hotel overlooking the airfield at Farnborough is orientated to the twin compass points of luxury timepieces (as in the eponymous wristwatch) and the great days of aviation, when nobody had heard of check-in queues and bag searches. In the glitzed-up surroundings, the decor in the Brasserie is agreeably un-brasserie-like, all aubergine and pigeon-egg in its understatement, though the neatly framed portraits of screen stars add glamour. Steaks of locally farmed, dry-aged beef done on the Josper grill, served with triple-cooked chips, are a centrepiece, but there are some more innovative touches too. Crisp-skinned sea bass in a chowder of clams, fennel and star-anise is singing with aromatic intensity. That might follow a well-built terrine of rabbit and smoked bacon with liver parfait, apple and grape compôte, and crumbled salty pistachios, while the finale could be a bewitchingly scented lavender parfait with matching marshmallow, served with warm poached pear and green apple sorbet.

Chef Luke Wheaton **Owner** TAG **Seats** 120, Pr/dining room 8 **Times** 12-2.30/6-10.30 **Prices** Fixed L 2 course £19-£25, Fixed D 3 course £35-£55, Tasting menu £100, Starter £6-£16, Main £14-£35, Dessert £7-£12, Service optional **Wines** 44 bottles over £30, 18 bottles under £30, 16 by glass **Parking** 169 **Notes** Sunday L £19-£25, Children welcome

HAMBLE-LE-RICE Map 5 SU40

The Bugle

◉ Modern British

tel: 023 8045 3000 **High St SO31 4HA**
email: manager@buglehamble.co.uk
dir: M27 junct 8 to Hamble-Le-Rice. In village follow signs to foreshore

Traditional and modern fare in an ancient riverside inn

Having stood here in one incarnation or another for around 700 years, as ferry-house, cab-hire office and rural inn, the Bugle is staying put, despite an attempt to have it demolished a few years ago. Its carefully restored interiors with their solid brickwork, bare floorboards, low ceilings and beams are exactly what a country inn should look like, while the kitchen offers a clever mix of pub stalwarts and modern dishes that are in tune with present-day requirements. Fish and chips, Sunday roasts and sandwiches will keep traditionalists happy, while the gastro brigade delight in the likes of pressed rabbit and prune terrine with pickled turnip to start, followed by bream fillet with potato salad, creamed leeks and kale, or braised lamb with confit shallots and parsnip purée in rosemary jus. Extras include a tempting bubble-and-squeak cake, and finishers are rewarded with honey-spiced pear with pistachio ice cream and honeycomb, or dark chocolate terrine with boozy cherries and clotted cream.

Chef Tarren Noyce **Owner** Ideal Leisure Ltd **Seats** 28, Pr/dining room 12 **Times** 12-2.30/6-9.30 Closed 25 Dec **Prices** Starter £5.50-£7.50, Main £8-£17, Dessert £5.50, Service optional **Wines** 14 bottles over £30, 26 bottles under £30, 12 by glass **Parking** Foreshore car park 50 yds **Notes** Sunday L, Vegetarian available, Children welcome

36 on the Quay

EMSWORTH Map 5 SU70

Modern British, European

tel: 01243 375592 & 372257 **47 South St PO10 7EG**
email: info@36onthequay.co.uk **web:** www.36onthequay.co.uk
dir: Last building on right in South St, which runs from square in centre of Emsworth

Superlative and beautiful cooking on Chichester Harbour

A fishing village on Chichester Harbour is the location of the Farthings' restaurant with rooms, at its core a smart dining room done out in neutral pastel shades, with local art on the walls and windows giving views of boats bobbing on the water. They make an impressive double act, with Karen running a young, knowledgeable front-of-house team, and Ramon in charge of the stoves. His cooking is consistently innovative, complex and sophisticated, making use of excellent local materials and producing carefully balanced dishes that are big on flavour. Dinner starts with canapés and an amuse-bouche-say, velvety artichoke soup-before perhaps rolled breast of wood pigeon on beetroot purée given extra depth by rosehip, accompanied by pickled mushrooms and beetroot and a red wine dressing. Given the location, it's no surprise that seafood is something of a speciality, seen in a starter of sea bass gravad lax with charred asparagus, pickled baby artichokes and a white balsamic and olive oil dressing. Ramon's care, his remarkable attention to detail and eye for stunning visual appeal are evident in every dish: witness main courses of hake fillet, sparklingly fresh and of exemplary timing, with hazelnut gnocchi, ceps and smoked sausage, all components brought together by fermented rye soup, and a sticky shin and radish salad and hay-baked potatoes as accompaniments for braised Angus cheek with carrots and a meat reduction. Breads are well up to snuff, and a pre-dessert-a shot glass of passionfruit posset with lime jelly-arrives before one of the multi-flavoured, multi-textured puddings. Among them may be orange and macadamia cake with banana ice cream, mandarin pastilles, honeyed cream and sugared macadamias, and apple and vanilla cheesecake with apple foam and gel, blackberry ripple ice cream and toffee popcorn.

Chef Ramon Farthing, Gary Pearce **Owner** Ramon & Karen Farthing **Seats** 45, Pr/dining room 12 **Times** 12-2/7-9.30 Closed 1st 2/3 wks Jan, 1 wk end May & Oct, 25-26 Dec, Sun-Mon **Prices** Fixed D 3 course £57.95, Tasting menu £70, Service optional **Wines** 7 by glass **Parking** Car park nearby **Notes** Tasting menu complete tables only 8 course, ALC menu £57.95, Vegetarian available, Children welcome

HAYLING ISLAND
Map 5 SU70

Langstone Hotel
◎◎ Modern British

tel: 023 9246 5011 **Northney Rd PO11 ONQ**
email: info@langstonehotel.co.uk **web:** www.langstonehotel.co.uk
dir: From A27 signed Havant/Hayling Island follow A3023 across roadbridge onto Hayling Island & take sharp left on leaving bridge

Accomplished, inventive modern cooking in harbourside hotel

On the north of Hayling Island, with estuary and harbour views, The Langstone is a large, modern hotel geared up for conferences and weddings as well as recreational guests. Part of its attraction is the Brasserie Restaurant, a spacious, curved room, with large windows and a terrace giving on to the waters, decked out in shades of beige and brown, plus a menu that shakes a stick at corporate hotel norms. Roast scallops, for instance, are partnered by beetroot-cured salmon and plated alongside yuzu dressing, wasabi cream, nori seaweed and radish, and could be followed by smoked breast and spicy confit leg of duck with red wine cabbage, vanilla potato, pak choi and five spice jus. More orthodox dishes are no less successful: warm haddock and potato salad with smoked cauliflower velouté, and braised blade of beef with bourguignon sauce, horseradish mash, roast carrots and parsnip crisps, and there's also a list of comfort foods and steaks. The kitchen obviously enjoys experimentation: try warm chocolate mousse with chocolate chip and mint ice cream with nitrogen vapour.

Chef James Parsons **Owner** BDL Hotels **Seats** 120, Pr/dining room 120
Times 12.30-2/6.30-9.30 **Prices** Starter £6-£9, Main £12-£23, Dessert £6-£10, Service optional **Wines** 17 bottles over £30, 24 bottles under £30, 7 by glass **Parking** 132 **Notes** Sunday L, Vegetarian available, Children welcome

What makes a 5-Rosette restaurant?
See page 9

What makes a 3-Rosette restaurant?
See page 9

LYMINGTON
Map 5 SZ39

Stanwell House Hotel
◎◎ Modern European

tel: 0844 704 6820 **14-15 High St SO41 9AA**
email: enquiries@stanwellhouse.com **web:** www.stanwellhouse.com
dir: M27 junct 1, follow signs to Lyndhurst into Lymington centre & High Street

Bright, modish cooking in boutique hotel

A classy boutique operation close by Lymington's quay on the edge of the New Forest, Stanwell House occupies a Georgian coaching inn that was once a finishing school for young ladies, and now delivers refinement in a more edible form. Two dining venues – Seafood at Stanwell House and The Bistro – take advantage of excellent Hampshire produce: as its name suggests, the former deals in fishy tapas and piscine pleasures such as seared fillet of brill with shellfish velouté, poached scallops and tomato and basil, or monkfish in Parma ham with squid ink risotto, pickled lemon, and saffron aïoli, while The Bistro's four menus work a more wide-ranging remit of contemporary European dishes in a glossy, modern space overlooking the inviting terrace. Here, you might start with haggis ravioli with braised cabbage, whisky foam and veal jus, and follow with steaks from the grill, or cheek, loin and belly of pork with pickled carrots, haricot beans and orange oil.

Times 12-3/6-10

LYNDHURST
Map 5 SU30

The Glasshouse
◎◎ Modern British

tel: 023 8028 6129 & 8028 3677 **Best Western Forest Lodge, Pikes Hill, Romsey Rd SO43 7AS**
email: enquiries@theglasshousedining.co.uk **web:** www.theglasshousedining.co.uk
dir: M27 junct 1, A337 towards Lyndhurst. In village, with police station & courts on right, take 1st right into Pikes Hill

Contemporary-style restaurant with well-judged cooking

A former dower house built in the Georgian period, this hotel has been given a thoroughly modern look inside, the restaurant with a dramatic decor of black and gold, with striking artwork on the walls. The kitchen prides itself on sourcing ingredients locally and pays due respect to seasonality, so haunch of venison might appear, accompanied by game jus, confit garlic, creamed potatoes and a selection of vegetables. The menus offer plenty of variety, from chicken tikka with pickled cucumber, mango and an onion bhaji, to confit duck with plum sauce and jelly, spring onions, cucumber and a poppadom. Fish is not overlooked – pavé of haddock is poached in red wine and accompanied by crushed new potatoes, roast mooli and beans – and in colder months the kitchen might put winter fruits into a crumble and serve it with juniper pannacotta and clotted cream ice cream.

Chef Darren Appleby **Owner** New Forest Hotels **Seats** 40, Pr/dining room 10
Times 12-2.30/5.30-9.30 **Prices** Prices not confirmed, Service optional **Wines** 16 bottles over £30, 26 bottles under £30, 2 by glass **Parking** 60 **Notes** Sunday L, Vegetarian available, No children

Hartnett Holder & Co
◎◎◎ – see page 206 and advert opposite

HARTNETT HOLDER & CO

Hartnett Holder & Co is a relaxed, stylish and comfortable upscale restaurant - full of character, yet unpretentious. Angela Hartnett and Lime Wood's Luke Holder, with their team, create locally sourced English dishes with a respectful nod to the seasons and to Italian culinary ideologies. This collaboration is reflected in their fresh, confident approach ensuring that this is "fun dining, not fine dining".

Hartnett and Holder's food is out-and-out British yet comes with the much loved Italian approach to eating - where sharing and provenance is everything. Expect a menu of Italian influenced forest dishes with English classics, pulling together both chef's much admired signature styles. Sample dishes include pizzetta with quail egg, taleggio and spinach, whole wild turbot (for two) with fennel, basil & preserved lemon or gnocchi with veal bolognaise.

Lime Wood, Beaulieu Road, Lyndhurst, Hampshire SO43 7FZ
Tel: 02380 287177   Website: www.hhandco.co.uk   Email: info@hhandco.co.uk

Hartnett Holder & Co

British, Italian 🍷 NOTABLE WINE LIST

tel: 023 8028 7167 & 8028 7177 **Lime Wood, Beaulieu Rd SO43 7FZ**
email: info@limewood.co.uk **web:** www.limewood.co.uk
dir: *A35 through Ashurst for 4m, then left in Lyndhurst signed Beaulieu, 1m to hotel*

Italian family cooking in a sophisticated New Forest hotel

Formerly a prep school for the children of the landed gentry, Lime Wood, a Regency manor house hotel in the heart of the New Forest, has been lavishly refurbished with an eye for period detail and a passion for top-notch facilities. There are lodges hidden away in the forest, a classy spa, and attention to detail is evident, from the planting in the grounds to the mix of well-chosen traditional and contemporary fixtures and fittings. The kitchen is a collaborative venture, with Lime Wood's Luke Holder joined by Angela Hartnett (she of London's Murano) to confer a touch of Italianate simplicity on the upscale productions. With the compass point oscillating between Tuscany and Hampshire, you might expect cheerful chaos, but the results are a streamlined blend of honest, clearly focused and genuinely enjoyable dishes that might best be experienced in the form of 'Il Tavolo della Cucina', a surprise menu

where you put your faith in the chefs to conjure a spread of sharing dishes in homage to traditional familial dining. Otherwise, a self-selected dinner might kick off with a trip to the smokehouse for a board of home-smoked meats with pickles, or wild mallard carpaccio with crosnes and Jerusalem artichoke. Given Hartnett's Italian credentials, a dip into the pasta section has to be a good move-perhaps gnocchi with game ragoût, or agnolotti with roasted squash, goats' cheese and sprout leaves-before bringing it all back home again with something as earthily British as partridge with pearl barley and hops, or pork rib-eye from the grill, matched with clams, salami, sherry and parsley. A handful of modern Italian charmers is among the imaginative selection of wines by the glass.

Chef Angela Hartnett, Luke Holder **Owner** Lime Wood Group **Seats** 70, Pr/dining room 16 **Times** 12-11 All-day dining **Prices** Fixed L 2 course £19.50, Starter £8-£12, Main £14-£28.50 **Wines** 565 bottles over £30, 34 bottles under £30, 13 by glass **Parking** 60 **Notes** Tavolo Della Cucina 5 course £55, Sunday L £37.50, Vegetarian available, Children welcome

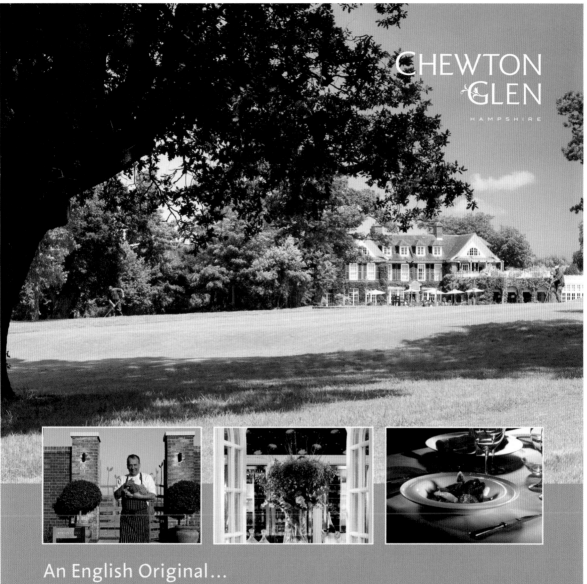

CHEWTON GLEN

HAMPSHIRE

An English Original...

Discover more
www.chewtonglen.com

New Forest Hampshire
BH25 6QS
Telephone (01425) 282212
reservations@chewtonglen.com

★★★★★

NEW MILTON
Map 5 SZ29

Chewton Glen Hotel & Spa

◉◉ Modern British V NOTABLE WINE LIST

tel: 01425 282212 **Christchurch Rd BH25 6QS**
email: reservations@chewtonglen.com **web:** www.chewtonglen.com
dir: A35 (Lyndhurst) turn left through Walkford, 4th left into Chewton Farm Rd

Classy cooking showing great technique in luxury country-house hotel

From the moment you pass through the grand entrance gates and approach the main house along the drive, through 130 acres of golf course and parkland, you know you're in for something special at Chewton Glen. But while the place may be posh, it's not the slightest bit stuffy, doing its utmost to shake off perceptions of tweedy country house formality. Spread across five rooms, the Vetiver restaurant goes for a chic, contemporary look, with lime-green banquettes, black-velvet covered chairs, black and cream walls and large windows looking out onto the lovely gardens. The flexible, crowd-pleasing carte offers everything from a steak, or turbot on the bone served straight from the grill, to the full-blown three courses. Classic French technique and first-class ingredients, many of them sourced locally, underpin every dish, starting perhaps with a twice-baked Emmental soufflé, followed by New Forest venison loin with roast beetroot, vegetables à la Grecque, and chilli chocolate sauce. Well-constructed desserts offer the likes of whisky and Bramley apple delice with hazelnut, and chocolate glaze.

Chef Luke Matthews **Owner** Chewton Glen Hotels Ltd **Seats** 164, Pr/dining room 70 **Times** 12-2.30/6-10 **Prices** Fixed L 3 course fr £25, Tasting menu fr £70 **Wines** 1200 bottles over £30, 27 bottles under £30, 27 by glass **Parking** 150 **Notes** Tasting menu 7 course, Seasonal menu £60, Sunday L fr £35, Children welcome

See advert on page 207

OLD BURGHCLERE
Map 5 SU45

The Dew Pond Restaurant

◉ British, European

tel: 01635 278408 **RG20 9LH**
dir: Newbury A34 South, exit Tothill. Follow signs for Highclere Castle, pass castle entrance on right, down hill & turn left signed Old Burghclere & Kingsclere, restaurant on right in approx 0.25m

Country restaurant with fine views and modern cooking

The Dew Pond is a place that embeds itself forever in the memory if you come to dine alfresco on the decking terrace on a summer's day. The unforgettable view at this idyllic country restaurant in a pair of converted 16th-century drovers' cottages sweeps across the eponymous dew pond to Watership Down and Highclere Castle. But all is not lost should the weather keep you indoors, as the two cosy dining rooms exude the comfort of ancient oak beams, calming pastel shades and colourful local artwork. Chef-patron Keith Marshall looks to the local area for his peerless supplies (including wines from Hampshire) and rejects fads, fashions and fireworks in favour of solid technical ability, turning out appealingly uncomplicated yet thoughtful compositions, along the lines of roasted scallops with chorizo, saffron aïoli, tomato and basil, while saddle of local roe deer is matched with celeriac purée, field mushrooms, shallots, gratin dauphinois and red wine jus. Flavours stay full-throttle for a caramelised lemon tart with meringue and raspberry sorbet.

Times 7-9.30 Closed 2 wks Xmas & New Year, 2 wks Aug, Sun-Mon, L served by appointment only

OTTERBOURNE
Map 5 SU42

The White Horse

◉ Traditional & Modern British

tel: 01962 712830 **Main Rd SO21 2EQ**
email: manager@whitehorseotterbourne.co.uk
dir: M3 junct 12/A335 1st exit at 1st rdbt & 2nd exit at next 2 rdbts, via Otterbourne Hill into Main Rd. Restaurant on left

Modern pub grub done right

When you come down from a hike along the lofty spine of the South Downs – the western end of the South Downs Way is at nearby Winchester – you couldn't ask for a more fortifying pitstop. After a top-to-toe refurb by the team behind The White Star in Southampton and The Bugle in Hamble (see entries) this run-down village boozer now looks every inch the modern dining pub with its wooden and quarry-tiled floors, bare beams, cheerful heritage hues, and mismatched vintage tables. The mood is unbuttoned and family-friendly, while the kitchen is driven by an enthusiasm for local ingredients, served up in a straightforward contemporary vein. This might translate as fried squid with smoked paprika aïoli, followed by beef shin suet pudding paired with seared fillet, braised red cabbage and mash. Puddings take a similarly comfort-oriented route – perhaps Bramley apple syrup sponge with custard.

Chef Keren Atkinson **Owner** Ideal Leisure Ltd **Seats** 90 **Times** 12-2.30/6-9.30 **Prices** Starter £5-£7, Main £8.50-£23, Dessert £5-£6, Service optional **Wines** 14 bottles over £30, 25 bottles under £30, 12 by glass **Parking** 25 **Notes** Sunday L, Vegetarian available, Children welcome

JSW

 – see below

Langrish House

Modern British

tel: 01730 266941 **Langrish GU32 1RN**
email: frontdesk@langrishhouse.co.uk **web:** www.langrishhouse.co.uk
dir: A3 onto A272 towards Winchester. Hotel signed, 2.5m on left

Vigorous modern British cooking at a South Downs house with a past

Langrish House has been home to the Talbot-Ponsonby family for seven generations, and when you see the gorgeous 17th-century mansion in 14 acres of undulating Hampshire countryside it is no surprise that they have never moved on. Frederick's restaurant immortalises an off-the-wall Victorian great uncle who enjoyed the odd game of tennis – very odd, in fact, as he insisted on wearing a skirt. It is a cosy, traditional spot, or for a memorably romantic meal, you could dine in the low-lit intimacy of the old vaults below, which were dug by Royalist prisoners in the Civil War. As far as the food is concerned, it is fast forward to modern times for menus of straightforward up-to-date ideas. Kick off with the likes of roast wood pigeon pointed up with apple and ginger purée, pickled radish, beetroot and wild mushrooms, before moving on to wild sea bass with crushed Jersey Royals, crab, baby leeks and shellfish sauce. Winding up proceedings is a creative combo of honey parfait with popcorn, banana sorbet and toasted marshmallow.

Chef Nathan Marshall **Owner** Mr & Mrs Talbot-Ponsonby **Seats** 24, Pr/dining room 80 **Times** 12-2/7-9.30 Closed 1-17 Jan **Prices** Fixed L 2 course £18.95, Starter £7.50-£10.50, Main £15.50-£26.50, Dessert £7-£10 **Wines** 25 bottles over £30, 24 bottles under £30, 13 by glass **Parking** 100 **Notes** Sunday L £18.95-£21.95, Vegetarian available, Children 7 yrs+

The Old Drum

Modern British

tel: 01730 300544 **16 Chapel St GU32 3DR**
email: info@theolddrum.co.uk **web:** www.theolddrum.co.uk

Robust and creative British cooking in renovated town-centre pub

The Old Drum has the appealing feel of a country pub that's upped sticks and moved to town. Exploratory renovation has uncovered its original beamed and tongue-and-groove ceilings, and it's been decorated with an agreeable mix of fresh, light colours, reconditioned timber flooring and some quirky touches (like a chair upholstered in the Stars and Stripes). Efficient staff and Digby the dog help to radiate as much hospitality as there was when HG Wells used to drink here. Simon Hartnett cooks the kinds of dishes that underpin today's hang-loose British catering. Robust ham hock and brawn terrine with warm pease pudding, parsley jelly and a sage biscuit will put hairs on your chest, and could be followed by 28-day-aged rib-eye steak accompanied by a boozy and spicy Bloody Mary tomato, thick mushroom ketchup and chips cooked in dripping. The world larder is raided for inspiration in dishes such as hake with potato and onion bhaji and spiced lentils in cauliflower velouté. Creative tweaks continue through to desserts such as bread-and-butter pudding made with banana brioche, with a banana fritter and tonka ice cream.

Chef Simon Hartnett **Owner** Simon & Suzi Hawkins **Seats** 45 **Times** 12-2/6-9.30 Closed 1st wk Jan, D Sun **Prices** Starter £5.50-£7.25, Main £10-£19.95, Dessert £6.50-£9, Service optional **Wines** 11 bottles over £30, 19 bottles under £30, 10 by glass **Parking** Adjacent car park **Notes** Sunday L £13.95-£15.95, Vegetarian available, Children welcome

JSW

Modern British V

tel: 01730 262030 **20 Dragon St GU31 4JJ**
email: jsw.restaurant@btconnect.com
dir: A3 to town centre, follow one-way system to College St which becomes Dragon St, restaurant on left

Dynamic contemporary cooking in a made-over old inn

The chef-proprietor's initials provide the name for this relaxed restaurant in an immaculately whitewashed 17th-century former coaching inn. Jake Saul Watkins is a Hampshire lad who has been plying his trade in Petersfield for a dozen years or so, and in this current venue since 2006. He's not the sort of chef who puts his initials above the door then turns up once in a while to oversee the action-you can expect him to be there at the sharp end, giving his all at every service. The dining room has plenty of character, for the antiquity of its exposed oak beams is overlaid with a subtly understated contemporary decor-neutral hues, generously-sized tables dressed in cream floor-length linen. This is a chef who cooks with a passion for his craft, starting with the best materials he can lay his hands on: fish from day boats on the Solent-and the rest from the best local suppliers. The food has a confident modern Anglo-French inflection, underpinned by virtuoso technique and an innate feel for what works together on the plate. Whether you go for the entry-level two-course set menu, the carte, or splurge on the five- or seven-course tasting menus, everything is made in-house with top-level creativity and skills. Fish and seafood are a strong suit-perhaps scallops with cauliflower cheese and ceps, while impeccable timing produces exemplary main courses such as wild sea bass with sea vegetables and a comforting mussel and bacon chowder. Meat offerings might team lamb textures with root vegetables and bergamot, or beef with baked smoked carrot and bone marrow croquette. Flavour is to the fore at dessert stage too – perhaps vanilla cheesecake with ginger beer jelly and rhubarb.

Chef Jake Watkins **Owner** Jake Watkins **Seats** 58, Pr/dining room 18 **Times** 12-1.30/7-9.30 Closed 2 wks Jan, May & summer, Mon-Tue, D Sun **Prices** Fixed L 2 course fr £22.50, Fixed D 3 course fr £32.50, Tasting menu £45-£75 **Wines** 9 by glass **Parking** 19 **Notes** Tasting menu L/D 5/7 course, ALC 2/3 course £32.50/£49.50, Sunday L £32.50-£39.50, Children 7 yrs+ D

PETERSFIELD *continued*

The Thomas Lord

◉◉ Modern British

tel: 01730 829244 **High St, West Meon GU32 1LN**
email: info@thethomaslord.co.uk
dir: *M3 junct 9, A272 towards Petersfield, right at x-rds onto A32, 1st left*

Inventive country pub cooking

A real village pub just off the main road through West Meon, The Thomas Lord is named after the founder of the famous cricket ground in north London. A restoration by new owners has stayed true to the ethos of the place, which is why the good people of West Meon reliably fill it with a convivium of chatter and cheer. Vegetables, salads and herbs are grown in the garden, the eggs come from the pub's own free-range chickens, and the place is under the same ownership as Upham Brewery near Winchester, which supplies its fine ales. The kitchen deals in inventive, dependable country-pub cooking of a high order, starting with a fortifying bowl of creamed cauliflower soup with lardons and cheddar, or chunky chicken and mushroom terrine with artichokes and shallot relish. Mains show off prime materials in the form of sirloin of local beef seared in treacle, its braised shin-meat fashioned into a croquette, in red wine and horseradish jus. Meringue-topped lemon tart comes with resonant star-anise ice cream for afters.

Chef Fran Joyce **Owner** Upham Ales **Seats** 70, Pr/dining room 20
Times 12-2.30/6-9.30 Closed 25 Dec **Prices** Fixed L 2 course £16, Fixed D 3 course £20, Starter £5.50-£8, Main £11.50-£24, Dessert £6.50-£8, Service optional 10%
Wines 16 bottles over £30, 21 bottles under £30, 10 by glass **Parking** 20
Notes Sunday L £11.50-£15.50, Vegetarian available, Children welcome

---

■ PORTSMOUTH & SOUTHSEA   Map 5 SU60

Portsmouth Marriott Hotel

◉ Modern, Seafood

tel: 0870 400 7285 & 023 9238 3151 **Southampton Rd PO6 4SH**
web: www.portsmouthmarriott.co.uk
dir: *M27 junct 12, keep left to lights, turn left. Hotel on left*

Lively hotel restaurant near the marina

Not far from all the main action in Portsmouth, with Gunwharf Quays and the Spinnaker Tower on hand, the Marriott may sport a rather stolid apartment-block look, but inside is a deal more cheering. The Sealevel restaurant is a big open space, furnished with semi-circular booths as well as regular tables, and with an infectiously lively atmosphere. White canvas covers attached to the booths suggest the sails on view in the nearby marina. The cooking nails its colours to a fairly conservative version of modern British, with nothing too startling, but treating quality raw materials with respect. Crab cakes are appetisingly textured and offset with a crisp fennel salad, while well-timed venison comes with a big spinach-topped potato rösti and puréed celeriac in redcurrant jus. For fish-lovers, monkfish is poached in smoked pancetta broth and served with saffron potatoes, and proceedings close with hot chocolate fondant, or pear Bakewell and clotted cream.

Chef Jaap Schep **Seats** 70 **Times** 12-3/6.30-10 **Prices** Fixed L 3 course £15-£24, Fixed D 3 course £29, Starter £5.25-£9.50, Main £13.75-£22.50, Dessert £6, Service optional **Wines** 13 bottles over £30, 28 bottles under £30, 21 by glass **Parking** 196
Notes Sunday L £12.50-£15.95, Vegetarian available, Children welcome

---

Restaurant 27

◉◉ Modern European

tel: 023 9287 6272 **27a South Pde PO5 2JF**
email: info@restaurant27.com
dir: *M27 junct 12, take M275 to A3, follow A288 South Parade, left Burgoyne Rd*

European and Asian modes in a relaxing venue near the seafront

The single-storey whitewashed building a little way off the seafront at Southsea may look a touch prosaic from the outside, but inside has been decorated with some verve. An artist's impression of kitchen scenes hangs over the bar to orientate us, and the darkwood unclothed tables are furnished with simple but stylish implements. Kevin Bingham cooks to a taut, four dishes per course formula, employing European and Asian technique in persuasive synthesis. A spin on crab cocktail offers fine local crabmeat with the sharpening flavours of pickled vegetables, puréed tomato and dill, and may be followed by 30-hour pork belly, which offers beautifully moist but not gelatinous meat of excellent flavour, along with hazelnut gnocchi, roasted sweetcorn and girolles, or a pairing of scallops and king prawns in lemongrass and palm-sugar broth. Crème brûlée is caramelised to order, resulting in a variety of temperature layers beneath, which doesn't please everybody, but its accompaniments of basil meringue, lemon and lime jelly and late-summer berries take it to another dimension altogether.

Chef Kevin Bingham, Annie Smith, Matt Barnes **Owner** Kevin & Sophie Bingham
Seats 34 **Times** 12-2.30/7-9.30 Closed Xmas, New Year, Mon-Tue, L Wed-Sat, D Sun
Prices Fixed L 3 course £29, Fixed D 3 course £44, Tasting menu £39-£50, Service optional **Wines** 29 bottles over £30, 19 bottles under £30, 14 by glass **Parking** On street **Notes** Tasting menu 7 course Wed-Thu/8 course Fri-Sat, Sunday L £29-£39, Vegetarian available, Children welcome

---

■ PRESTON CANDOVER   Map 5 SU64

Purefoy Arms

◉◉ British, Spanish

tel: 01256 389777 **Alresford Rd RG25 2EJ**
email: info@thepurefoyarms.co.uk

A food-focused pub combining Spanish and local flavours

Lurking in a green and pleasant valley, the Purefoy Arms is a smart red-brick pub with a daily-changing menu that reveals the owners' passion for food. Run by a husband-and-wife-team, you'll detect a Spanish flavour, for the chef (and husband), Andres, lived in Spain until he was eight. They've done the place up a treat, keeping the rustic charm, while adding a bit of contemporary polish, and there's a large garden out back where you can eat when the weather allows. The hand-written menu and daily-specials board serves up some refined-meets-rustic dishes which are big on flavour. Cornish sardines on toast is a simple dish put together with a bit of style (a punchy salsa-like accompaniment hits the spot), or you might start with local rabbit terrine with apricot purée and toasted brioche. Main courses are no less on the money: sparklingly fresh skate wing, with mash and black butter, or roast rump of lamb with cauliflower purée, Catalan spinach and Madeira sauce. For dessert, the crema Catalana seems appropriate.

Chef Andres Alemany **Owner** Andres & Marie-Lou Alemany **Seats** 60 **Times** 12-3/6-10 Closed 26 Dec, 1 Jan, Mon, D Sun **Prices** Fixed L 2 course £14.50, Starter £6-£12, Main £10.50-£25, Dessert £5-£12, Service optional 10% **Wines** 50 bottles over £30, 40 bottles under £30, 10 by glass **Parking** 30, On street **Notes** Sunday L £14.50-£16, Vegetarian available, Children welcome

THE WHITE HORSE
HOTEL & BRASSERIE

Welcome to

The White Horse Hotel and Brasserie

Set in the heart of Romsey. The White Horse has been a Coaching Inn for over 600 years. The White Horse Brasserie, opening onto its own delightful court-yard is a wonderful place to enjoy every occasion from a romantic dinner for two to a family lunch. A stay here with us is a time to unwind, savouring some of the finest food in Hampshire in our 2 AA Rosette Brasserie. Relax in one of the hotel's 31 individually designed bedrooms and suites and enjoy a cocktail or Afternoon Tea in the delightful Silks Bar or frescoed Tudor Lounge. The White Horse also offers the most romantic and intimate venue for your Wedding Day. Combining historic charm with modern luxury.

"Small things make perfection but perfection is no small thing"
Sir Henry Royce

The White Horse Hotel, Market Place,
Romsey, Hampshire SO51 8ZJ t:01794 512431
thewhitehorse@silkshotels.com
www.silkshotels.com

ROMSEY — Map 5 SU32

The Three Tuns

Modern British

tel: 01794 512639 **58 Middlebridge St SO51 8HL**
email: manager@the3tunsromsey.co.uk
dir: *A27 bypass on A3030*

Skilful and appealing gastro-pub cooking

Just five minutes from the Market Square, The Three Tuns has all the hallmarks of an old country pub: panelling, bare brick walls, lots of polished wood, slate floors, beams, open fires and real ales. What lifts it out of the country-pub mould is the quality of the cooking; there's no cheffy skulduggery here, just well-considered combinations in carefully cooked dishes using fine local ingredients. Try smoked salmon with celeriac remoulade and a caper and shallot dressing with toasted rye bread, or rustic-sounding black pudding Scotch egg with home-made brown sauce. For main course, the Tuns' pie is a model of its kind – ox cheek slowly cooked with mushrooms and horseradish, rich and full of flavour, in impeccable pastry, served with seasonal vegetables. To top things off may be nicely wobbly vanilla pannacotta with stewed rhubarb, or zingy berry crumble and custard.

Times 12-2.30/6-9 Closed 25-26 Dec

The White Horse Hotel & Brasserie

Modern British

tel: 01794 512431 **19 Market Place SO51 8ZJ**
email: reservations@silkshotels.com **web:** www.silkshotels.com
dir: *M27 junct 3, follow signs for Romsey, right at Broadlands. In town centre*

Modern British classics in an ancient coaching inn

Established as a coaching inn 600 years ago, The White Horse is plumb in the middle of the charming market town of Romsey. Retaining much of its period detail, it offers a boldly decorated bar where orders are taken, as well as a plush dining room with smartly clothed tables. The cooking style is all about modern British classics, delivered with considerable panache. Seared scallops sit on their now canonical cauliflower purée, given texture with crisp-fried shallots and a deeper note of seasoning with curry oil. Duck three ways (breast, confit leg and foie gras) seems the best of all worlds, with its accurately cooked meat and liver, unified with a well-judged white wine jus of orange and grape, while satisfaction is assured in

the sticky department with Jamaica gingerbread chocolate fondant, served with caramelised banana ice cream.

Chef Chris Rock **Owner** Mr Nuttall **Seats** 85, Pr/dining room 40 **Times** 12-3/6-10 **Prices** Fixed L 2 course £15.50, Fixed D 3 course £17.50, Starter £4.50-£9, Main £9.50-£26, Dessert £5-£8.50, Service optional **Wines** 11 by glass **Parking** Car park nearby **Notes** Afternoon tea £18.50-£45, Sunday L £14.50, Vegetarian available, Children welcome

See advert on page 211

ROTHERWICK — Map 5 SU75

Tylney Hall Hotel

Traditional British

tel: 01256 764881 **Ridge Ln RG27 9AZ**
email: sales@tylneyhall.com **web:** www.tylneyhall.com
dir: *M3 junct 5, A287 to Basingstoke, over junct with A30, over rail bridge, towards Newnham. Right at Newnham Green. Hotel 1m on left*

A decorative treasure-house with fine country-hotel cooking

For occasions when only the whole country-house hotel, fine-dining schtick will do, Tylney Hall should hit the spot. The Grade II listed Victorian red-brick pile sits in 66 acres of parkland with gardens designed by Gertrude Jekyll, and the interior is none too shabby either, with its oak panelling and rococo plasterwork. The surroundings scream classical country-house dining, and the Oak Room restaurant duly delivers the goods in a setting involving oak panels, a domed ceiling, and opulent swagged drapes – all accompanied by a tinkling grand piano. What arrives on the plate is a gently-updated take on the classics, with some flourishes of modernity here and there. A coarse terrine of pork and apricot with mangetout, rocket and hazelnut salad gets things off the mark, then for traditionalists, the carving trolley delivers the roast of the evening – rack of local lamb or Angus sirloin maybe. Alternatively, pan-fried breast of free-range chicken comes with turnips, baby leeks and Parmentier potatoes. A chocolate and Bailey's mousse brings down the curtain.

Times 12.30-2/7-10

See advert below

Best Western Chilworth Manor

Modern British **NEW**

tel: 023 8076 7333 **Chilworth SO16 7PT**
dir: *1m from M3/M27 junct on A27 Romsey Rd N from Southampton. Pass Chilworth Arms on left, in 200mtrs turn left at Southampton Science Park sign. Hotel immediately right*

Brasserie-style cooking in a grand Edwardian hotel

A grand Edwardian pile in charming grounds, Chilworth Manor is these days a classy hotel with all mod cons – swish spa, well kitted out meeting rooms and a smart restaurant. There's no shortage of period elegance in the restaurant, with its oak panels and tables dressed in white linen cloths, but the menu takes a slightly less formal approach to proceedings. This is upmarket brasserie-style cooking, with a menu that contains regional ingredients and global influences. Start with pan-seared scallops with parsnip purée and a dressing combining apples and roasted hazelnuts, and follow on with Owtons of Hampshire saddle of venison with fondant potato and a fig and juniper berry sauce. There is a burger, too, and monkfish wrapped in nori. Finish with a fun dessert such as iced prosecco and rhubarb parfait with spiced ginger biscuits and a bag of delicious custard doughnuts.

Chef Chris Keel **Owner** Gavin Elliott **Seats** 80, Pr/dining room 150 **Times** 12-1.45/7-9.30 Closed L Sat **Prices** Fixed L 2 course £22.50, Fixed D 3 course £28.50, Starter £5-£8, Main £15-£21, Dessert £5-£8, Service optional **Wines** 2 bottles over £30, 27 bottles under £30, 11 by glass **Parking** 250 **Notes** Sunday L £17.95, Vegetarian available

Botleigh Grange Hotel

Traditional British

tel: 01489 787700 **Grange Rd, Botley SO30 2GA**
email: enquiries@botleighgrangehotel.net **web:** www.botelighgrangehotel.net
dir: *On A334, 1m from M27 junct 7*

Modern British classics in a stylish spa hotel

A gleaming white spa hotel not far from Southampton, Botleigh Grange has been around since the mid-17th century, yet the place looks pristinely maintained and box-fresh inside, with the Hampshire's dining room bathed in daylight from a glass-domed ceiling, and swagged curtains to frame the garden view. An expansive menu of modern British classics is on offer. The poshing of Scotch eggs (with black pudding and a quail egg here) is right on trend, and fried cakes of either crab or sweet potato and corned beef hash make good starters. After those might come a chicken breast bound in Parma ham and filled with sundried tomatoes and feta in red pepper sauce, or blackened salmon with garlicky crushed potatoes and avocado-mango salsa, before a finale of orange and lemon posset with vanilla shortbread.

Chef Stephen Lewis **Owner** Botleigh Grange Hotel Ltd **Seats** 100, Pr/dining room 350 **Times** 12.30-2.30/7-9.30 Closed L Mon-Sat **Wines** 16 bottles over £30, 29 bottles under £30, 10 by glass **Parking** 300 **Notes** Gourmet break 6 course, Sunday L £14.95-£23.95, Vegetarian available, Children welcome

HAMPSHIRE'S ORIGINAL COUNTRY RETREAT

INNOVATIVE CUISINE WITH A DISTINCTLY BRITISH TWIST

FINE DINING IN THE OAK ROOM RESTAURANT

Tylney Hall, Rotherwick, Hook, Hampshire, RG27 9AZ | 01256 764881 www.tylneyhall.co.uk

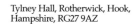

SOUTHAMPTON *continued*

Mercure Southampton Centre Dolphin Hotel

Modern International

tel: 023 8038 6460 **34-35 High St SO14 2HN**
email: H7876@accor.com **web:** www.mercure.com
dir: *A33 follow signs for Docks & Old Town/IOW ferry, at ferry terminal turn right into High Street, hotel 400yds on left*

Historic hotel with crowd-pleasing menu

Formerly a 17th-century coaching inn boasting the likes of Jane Austen, Queen Victoria and Admiral Nelson among its former guests, several million pounds and a takeover from the Mercure chain later, this is a striking and characterful place to stay and to eat. In the Signature Restaurant, contemporary tones abound and it all looks suitably modish and unstuffy – darkwood tables, plenty of period character, and a menu that doesn't stray far from traditional, brasserie-style comforts. Baked ramekin of Hampshire pear with Stilton cream and watercress salad might precede steak and kidney pie, half a roast poussin with bubble-and-squeak and bread sauce, or a Casterbridge steak from the grill.

Chef Tibor Suli **Owner** Longrose Buccleuch **Seats** 80 **Times** 12-2.30/7-9.45 **Prices** Starter £5.50-£6.50, Main £10.95-£19.95, Dessert £5.50-£6.95 **Wines** 8 bottles over £30, 24 bottles under £30, 12 by glass **Parking** 80 **Notes** Vegetarian available, Children welcome

White Star Tavern, Dining and Rooms

British

tel: 023 8082 1990 **28 Oxford St SO14 3DJ**
email: reservations@whitestartavern.co.uk **web:** www.whitestartavern.co.uk
dir: *M3 junct 14 onto A33, towards Ocean Village*

Confident modern dishes in a local hotspot

Bringing a touch of boutique style to Southampton, the White Star – named for the shipping line who commissioned the Titanic – has cool designer bedrooms, a bar/pub that can turn out a nifty cocktail, and a restaurant that delivers feel-good dishes with a local flavour. There's a satisfying blend of period details and contemporary touches in the dining room, and an easy-going attitude that hits the spot. The place is open for breakfast, serves sandwiches until 5pm, and offers classy pub classics such as local beer-battered fish with triple-cooked chips. But this kitchen also produces some strident modern stuff that fits really well with the brasserie-style attitude. Starters include blow-torched smoked salmon with cucumber pickle and crumbed quail's egg, or seared scallops with cauliflower textures and black pudding. Among main courses, cod loin comes with a chestnut crust alongside artichoke purée and dauphinoise potatoes, and Wiltshire partridge with the leg meat in an accompanying raviolo, plus parsnip purée and sticky red cabbage. Finish with Bakewell tart with clotted cream ice cream and drunken cranberries.

Chef Nick O'Hallaran **Owner** Matthew Boyle **Seats** 40, Pr/dining room 10 **Times** 12-2.30/6-9.30 Closed 25-26 Dec **Prices** Starter £5.50-£8.50, Main £12-£23, Dessert £3-£6, Service optional **Wines** 13 bottles over £30, 26 bottles under £30, 16 by glass **Parking** On street or 2 car parks nearby **Notes** Sunday L, Vegetarian available, Children welcome

STOCKBRIDGE Map 5 SU33

The Greyhound on the Test

Modern British

tel: 01264 810833 **31 High St SO20 6EY**
email: info@thegreyhoundonthetest.co.uk **web:** www.thegreyhoundonthetest.co.uk
dir: *9m NW of Winchester, 8m S of Andover. Off A303*

Upmarket town inn with up to date food and local fishing rights

This classily refurbished inn, or restaurant with rooms if you like, has a garden that runs down to the River Test with its own fly fishing beat, so it's well-and-truly on the map for anglers. But The Greyhound has no shortage of appeal, from its upmarket, sumptuous bedrooms to its restaurant with that opened-up, country-chic vibe. Lots of original beams, a mismatched array of chunky wooden tables and warm neutral tones give the place a breezy, relaxed feel, with candles bringing a warm glow all day. The menu is a thoroughly up-to-date affair with regional produce at its heart: pressed lamb croquette with smoked eel among first courses, perhaps, or escabèche of mackerel with pickled shallots, coriander and carrot. For main courses, hake is a super-fresh piece of fish with a good crispy skin, and there might be braised pork belly with celeriac purée and white beans. There are daily specials, too, plus good value set menus and fresh oysters at this highly enterprising establishment. Comforting desserts such as crumble or chocolate fondant will send you home happy.

Times 12-4/7-9 Closed 25-26 & 31 Dec, 1 Jan, D Sun (winter)

The Peat Spade Inn

Modern British

tel: 01264 810612 **SO20 6DR**
email: info@peatspadeinn.co.uk **web:** www.peatspadeinn.co.uk
dir: *M3 junct 8, A303 W approx 15m, then take A3057 Stockbridge/Andover*

Classic British dishes in charming dining inn

Sitting on the banks of the River Test in Hampshire's historic fly fishing country, this dining pub is well-placed for sourcing the area's finest ingredients, even if some of the larger fish specimens might have 'got away' before making it to the kitchen. With simple scrubbed pine tables, bare floorboards, and deep green and burgundy walls hung with old photos and prints, the dining rooms are full of character. The kitchen believes in keeping it simple, relying for its effect on the quality of local produce, including game from the Leckford Estate and wild ingredients from the New Forest. It is the attention to detail that counts here – toasted home-made Guinness bread, for instance, served with chicken liver parfait and onion marmalade. Main courses could see pub classics – beer-battered haddock and triple-cooked chips, or slow-cooked steak and ale pie – alongside ballotine of wood pigeon with crispy black cabbage, creamed potato, beetroot, capers and jus.

Chef Lewis Knight **Owner** Ashley & Tracy Levett **Seats** 49, Pr/dining room 12 **Times** 12-2.30/6.30-9.30 Closed 25 Dec, D 26 Dec, 1 Jan **Prices** Fixed L 2 course fr £15, Starter £6.50-£9.50, Main £13-£22, Dessert £4.50-£9.50 **Wines** 13 bottles over £30, 24 bottles under £30, 10 by glass **Parking** 19 **Notes** Pre-booking strongly recommended, menu changes daily, Sunday L, Vegetarian available, Children welcome

The Three Cups Inn

Traditional & Modern English **NEW**

tel: 01264 810527 **High St SO20 6HB**
email: manager@the3cups.co.uk **web:** www.the3cups.co.uk

Old coaching inn with a modern menu

Dating back to the 1500s, this coaching inn is still very much a pub, offering regularly-changing local ales. It's also a dining destination with low-ceilinged dining room and an orangery extension out back with full-width doors opening up to the garden (eating outside is a fair-weather option). There are en suite bedrooms, too. The kitchen makes good use of local foodstuffs, with local game in season, plus lunchtime snacks and Sunday roasts. From the main restaurant menu, chicken, mushroom and tarragon terrine is perked up with wilted pak choi and soy jus, while among main courses pan-fried calves' liver comes nice and pink with accompanying beetroot dauphinoise, cabbage with pancetta, Chantenay carrots and a red wine jus. Bread is made on the premises and, for dessert, there is a well-made banana and peanut cheesecake with a dark chocolate sauce.

Chef Paul Day **Owner** Mrs L Tickle **Seats** 50 **Times** 12–2.30/6.30–9.30 Closed 25–26 Dec **Prices** Starter £6–£7.95, Main £12.25–£21.95, Dessert £3–£12.50, Service optional **Wines** 10 bottles over £30, 16 bottles under £30, 12 by glass **Notes** Lunch & bar menus available, Sunday L £12.95, Vegetarian available

---

WINCHESTER	Map 5 SU42

Avenue Restaurant at Lainston House Hotel

⊛⊛⊛ – see below

The Black Rat

⊛⊛ Modern British

tel: 01962 844465 & 841531 **88 Chesil St SO23 0HX**
email: reservations@theblackrat.co.uk
dir: M3 junct 9/A31 towards Winchester & Bar End until T-junct. Turn right at lights, restaurant 600yds on left

Former pub serving up seriously good food

A one-time pub, dating from the 18th century, is these days home to a restaurant of distinction. There's a lot of the old pub character remaining on the inside, with beams, brickwork and fireplaces, but that is where the similarity to the old boozer ends, for this place serves up contemporary British food which is as sharp as a pin. There's a lack of pretension to the place – chunky wooden tables to sit at, for example, and a relaxed service style – but it feels smart and comfortable. And what turns up on the plate is high quality ingredients, sourced from (mostly) named regional suppliers or grown on their own allotment, and cooked with precision and imagination. Partridge, foie gras and ham hock are happy bedfellows indeed in a first-course terrine served with crushed egg, fabulous home-made mustard and new potato crisps. Main-course Loch Duart salmon and hand-dived scallop is flavoured with Douglas Fir and comes with crumbled gingerbread, crushed pumpkin and crow garlic, while blood orange and olive oil cake with Pedro Ximenez jelly and toasted almonds is a revelatory finale.

Chef Jamie Stapleton-Burns **Owner** David Nicholson **Seats** 40, Pr/dining room 16 **Times** 12–2.15/7–9.30 Closed 2 wks Etr, 2 wks Oct/Nov, 2 wks Xmas & New Year, L Mon–Fri **Prices** Fixed L 2 course fr £22.95, Starter £9–£11, Main £20–£24, Dessert £8–£9, Service optional **Wines** 6 by glass **Parking** Car park opposite **Notes** Fixed L Sat-Sun only, Sunday L, Vegetarian available, No children

---

Avenue Restaurant at Lainston House Hotel

WINCHESTER	Map 5 SU42

Modern British V NOTABLE WINE LIST

tel: 01962 776088 **Woodman Ln, Sparsholt SO21 2LT**
email: enquiries@lainstonhouse.com **web:** www.exclusivehotels.co.uk
dir: B3049 Stockbridge road, junct with Woodman Ln

Creative modern cooking in 17th-century country-house hotel

Red-brick Lainston House, a charming and cosseting country-house hotel, dates from the 17th century when it was a hunting lodge, and stands in 63 acres of parkland; the ruins of a 12th-century chapel are a short stroll away. It's a stunningly beautiful building in a lovely rural setting, though only a few miles from historic Winchester. A dining area has been added to the kitchen garden, with a wood-fired oven for summer barbecues, and alfresco eating on the terrace is on the cards in warm weather. When the weather isn't being kind, the Avenue Restaurant offers an equally pleasant environment in which to dine. It takes its name from the mile-long stretch of limes glimpsed through its windows. Local produce figures large on the menus, including many fruits and vegetables grown in the hotel's kitchen garden and meat from the resident pigs. Head chef Olly Rouse delivers creative dishes of refinement and focus, where texture and visual impact play their part, but the ingredients remain the star of the show. A first course of beetroot has the vegetable in various forms, with a fondant as the centrepiece, alongside fennel, sprouting broccoli and segments of clementine to invigorate the senses. Another starter matches venison carpaccio with lemon curd, a crisp quail's egg and truffled mayonnaise. Main course duck comes perfectly pink and tender, with rhubarb compôte, roasted potatoes and a single shallot topped with toasted hazelnuts, and accurately timed halibut fillet comes in a fashionable pairing with oxtail, served with parsnips, pickled walnut and pearl barley. British cheeses are an alternative innovative desserts such as dark chocolate pave with coffee beans and a yoghurt and vanilla set foam, or pears poached in orange blossom. The excellent breads are all baked in-house, and the extensive wine list is well worth a moment of your time.

Chef Olly Rouse **Owner** Exclusive Hotels **Seats** 60, Pr/dining room 120 **Times** 12–2/7–10 **Prices** Prices not confirmed **Wines** 302 bottles over £30, 28 bottles under £30, 291 by glass **Parking** 200 **Notes** Sunday L, Children welcome

WINCHESTER *continued*

The Chesil Rectory

◉◉ Modern British

tel: 01962 851555 **1 Chesil St SO23 0HU**
email: enquiries@chesilrectory.co.uk
dir: *S from King Alfred's statue at bottom of The Broadway, cross small bridge, turn right, restaurant on left, just off mini rdbt*

Modernised British dishes in a medieval house

A beautiful half-timbered building dating back to 1450, The Chesil Rectory is the oldest house in Winchester. From the street you enter through a low door – the first of many original features – to be greeted in the cooler months by a roaring log fire warming a brilliantly preserved interior with low ceilings and beams, charming inglenook fireplaces, exposed brickwork and wooden floors, and a quirky collection of taxidermy. The kitchen puts a gently modernised spin onto classic British dishes, bolstered by some that have nothing to do with the native repertoire, as in a starter of creamy white onion risotto with crispy shallots and burnt onion ash. A main course fillet of cod delivers exceptional plump and sea-fresh fish, well-timed and tender, with brown shrimps in chive butter, crushed potatoes and broccoli, or spring might see a pairing of loin and belly of porkwith spätzle and the commendably seasonal accompaniments of asparagus and wild garlic pesto. Finish with an apple tarte fine with salted caramel sauce and Calvados ice cream.

Chef Damian Brown **Owner** Mark Dodd, Damian Brown, Iain Longhorn **Seats** 75, Pr/dining room 14 **Times** 12-2.20/6-9.30 Closed 25-26 Dec, 1 Jan **Prices** Fixed L 2 course £15.95, Fixed D 3 course £19.95, Starter £5.50-£8.95, Main £13.95-£19.50, Dessert £6.95, Service optional **Wines** 42 bottles over £30, 25 bottles under £30, 13 by glass **Parking** NCP Chesil St adjacent **Notes** Set menu Mon-Sat 12-2.20/6-7, Sun 6-9, Sunday L £21.95-£26.95, Vegetarian available, No children

Holiday Inn Winchester

◉ European, International

tel: 01962 670700 **Telegraph Way, Morn Hill SO21 1HZ**
email: info@hiwinchester.co.uk **web:** www.hiwinchester.co.uk
dir: *M3 junct 9, A31 signed Alton, A272 & Petersfield. 1st exit at rdbt onto A31, 1.6m, take 1st exit into Alresford Rd, left into Telegraph Way*

Ambitious cooking at an out-of-town hotel

The out-of-town location can make this Holiday Inn feel a little quiet, but that might come as sweet relief to many. Indeed, everything about the Morn Hill Brasserie on the lower ground floor seems designed to soothe, from the determinedly neutral, coffee-coloured decor to the discreetly attentive approach of service. Some effort is made to feature local produce, which is heartening in a hotel chain, and in the centre of a populist menu of pasta dishes, rib-eye burgers and beer-battered fish and chips is a slate of more ambitious suggestions. From these, a good start can be made with a small New Forest blue cheese soufflé served with apple and chestnut salad, and the cheesy note productively continues in the Gruyère mash that comes with main-course braised beef and red onion marmalade in red wine jus. Fish might be sea bass with braised fennel and parsnip purée, and dessert a trio of crème brûlée variations – vanilla, pistachio and Bailey's.

Chef Robert Quehan **Owner** Zinnia Hotels **Seats** 128, Pr/dining room 200 **Times** 12-2/6.30-9.30 **Prices** Service optional **Wines** 17 bottles over £30, 34 bottles under £30, 10 by glass **Parking** 170 **Notes** Sunday L £11.95-£14.95, Vegetarian available, Children welcome

Hotel du Vin Winchester

◉◉ Traditional British, French 🍷 NOTABLE WINE LIST

tel: 01962 841414 **14 Southgate St SO23 9EF**
email: info@winchester.hotelduvin.co.uk **web:** www.hotelduvin.com
dir: *M3 junct 11, follow signs to Winchester town centre, located on left*

Classic French bistro fare in the first HdV

Here was where the Hotel du Vin (HdV) adventure all began, in the group's first and smallest boutique hotel-cum-winebar-cum-bistro. It's an attractive townhouse dating from the very outset of the Georgian era, not far from the magnificent cathedral. The house decorative style of bare wood floor, unclothed tables and cream walls hung with a multitude of pictures is the ambience here too, and the food is gently modernised classic French bistro fare. Expect to start with chicken liver parfait or French onion soup or, for something a little more enterprising, a successful presentation of seared scallops with artichoke and pistachio purée and pancetta vinaigrette. Mains take in satisfyingly crackled pork belly with mustardy dauphinoise and a sauce incorporating Agen prunes, or there are various cuts of fine 28-day dry-aged beef. Dishes of the day are worth a look, and meals end with the likes of caramel parfait with candied pecans, date-stuffed baked apple, or good old Black Forest gateau. Brunches and afternoon tea bolster the daytime repertoire and, as throughout the HdV group, there is an adventurous, extensive list of French-led fine wines.

Chef Matthew Chorley **Owner** KSL **Seats** 65, Pr/dining room 48 **Times** 12-2.30/5.30-10 **Prices** Starter £6.25-£11.95, Main £15.95-£59.50, Service optional 10% **Wines** 250 bottles over £30, 50 bottles under £30, 20 by glass **Parking** 40, NCP Tower St **Notes** Sunday L, Vegetarian available, Children welcome

Marwell Hotel

◉◉ Modern European

tel: 01962 777681 **Thompsons Ln, Colden Common, Marwell SO21 1JY**
email: info@marwellhotel.co.uk **web:** www.marwellhotel.co.uk
dir: *B3354 through Twyford. 1st exit at rdbt (B3354), left onto B2177 signed Bishop Waltham. Left into Thompsons Ln after 250yds, hotel on left*

Creative cooking in a smart leisure hotel

A short drive from Winchester and all its historic charms, and with Marwell Zoo right on the doorstep, the Marwell Hotel is a good base for exploring this part of Hampshire. There are leisure facilities aplenty on site, including an indoor pool, and the place is a big hit on the wedding scene. Do note, though, that the main restaurant is worth a visit on its own merits. Regional ingredients are given pride of place on the menu and the cooking is contemporary, accurate and really rather good. You might start with squab pigeon, for example, perfectly tender, and served in the company of onion jam, port jus and blackberries. Next up, Hampshire lamb features in a complex dish with the shoulder meat in a pastilla, along with a herb cutlet, an almond-crusted sweetbread, and goats' cheese, black olive mash and port and fig purée. For dessert there might be a creative take on the theme of rhubarb and custard, or a hot Valrhona chocolate fondant with green tea ice cream and cumin caramel.

Chef Scott Foy **Owner** Bastian family **Seats** 80, Pr/dining room 120 **Times** 5.30-10 Closed 25 Dec **Prices** Service optional **Wines** 10 bottles over £30, 10 bottles under £30 **Parking** 100 **Notes** Sunday L £13-£17, Vegetarian available, Children welcome

Running Horse Inn

◎◎ Modern International, British

tel: 01962 880218 **88 Main Rd, Littleton SO22 6QS**
email: runninghorseinn@btconnect.com **web:** www.runninghorseinn.co.uk
dir: B3049 out of Winchester 1.5m, turn right into Littleton after 1m, Running Horse on right

Innovative flavour-packed cooking in informal upgraded inn

A revitalised village inn, with real ales dispensed at the bar, the Running Horse is a relaxed and informal dining environment, with a wood-burning stove in a brick fireplace, some banquette seating, wooden tables and a mixture of artwork adorning the walls. The menu is an enticing read, and the kitchen delivers some stimulating dishes that are full of flavour. Cauliflower pannacotta with capers in a Cajun-spiced parmesan crust has been a skilfully made and tasty starter, offered alongside home-cured gravad lax with cucumber noodles, sour cream and sherry dressing. 'Lighter Bites' are possibilities, among them omelette Arnold Bennett, while main courses run the gamut from sirloin steak with Bordelaise sauce and the usual accompaniments, through Thai green chicken curry with basmati rice to more contemporary ideas like pork belly with a black pudding crumb, buttered leeks, garlic mash and thyme cream. Daily specials extend the range even further, and desserts follow the well-trodden path of crème brûlée and sticky toffee pudding with salted caramel sauce.

Chef Paul Down **Owner** Upham Pub Co **Seats** 60 **Times** 12-2.30/6.30-9.30 **Prices** Starter £5.50-£6.95, Main £9.95-£19.50, Dessert £6-£9, Service optional **Wines** 18 bottles over £30, 22 bottles under £30, 13 by glass **Parking** 40 **Notes** Sunday L, Vegetarian available, Children welcome

The Winchester Hotel and Spa

◎ Modern European

tel: 01962 709988 **Worthy Ln SO23 7AB**
email: info@thewinchesterhotel.co.uk **web:** www.thewinchesterhotel.co.uk
dir: A33 then A3047, hotel 1m on right

Wide-ranging contemporary brasserie fare in a modern hotel

Right in the heart of Winchester, Hutton's Brasserie at the slick modern Winchester Hotel comes with a glossy interior of polished floorboards, darkwood tables, creamy leather chairs and banquettes, shades of purple and pink and chillout music in the background. Switched-on staff look the part, and the kitchen's crowd-pleasing repertoire of classic and modern European ideas has something for everyone, from chargrilled Hampshire steaks and frites to home-made chicken and Stilton pie. Elsewhere, the kitchen's confident, upfront approach can be seen in a starter of seared scallops with celeriac purée and apple and celeriac salad, followed by poached salmon with herb couscous, asparagus, and tomato salsa. Or there may be caramelised Gressingham duck breast with honey mustard, potato and shallot gratin, parsnip purée and port sauce. Bringing up the rear, there's a raspberry riff comprising pannacotta, coulis and fresh raspberries, otherwise local artisan cheeses with home-made breads and chutney might tempt you towards a savoury finish.

Chef Neil Dore **Owner** Quantum Hotels Ltd **Seats** 80, Pr/dining room 40 **Times** 12.30-2/7-9.30 **Prices** Fixed L 2 course £15.50, Fixed D 3 course £24.50, Service optional **Wines** 15 bottles over £30, 25 bottles under £30, 9 by glass **Parking** 47 **Notes** Sunday L £18.50, Vegetarian available, Children welcome

The Wykeham Arms

◎◎ Modern British

tel: 01962 853834 **75 Kingsgate St SO23 9PE**
email: wykehamarms@fullers.co.uk **web:** www.wykehamarmswinchester.co.uk
dir: S out of city along Southgate St. Take 3rd turning L into Canon St, inn on R at end

Rustic, historic pub delivering exciting, crowd-pleasing food

This historic pub is rustically styled: pewter tankards, school caps and pictures adorn the walls, while tables are an eclectic mix of shapes and sizes. Open log fires warm up the traditional, old-style bar, and the garden is a must in the summer months. There's something for everyone on the varied menu. The 28-day aged beef and oyster stew from the 'House Comforts' section is just the job to warm you up on a cold winter's day, while elsewhere there are some technically impressive and exciting dishes, such as an intricate poached and roasted English quail, textures of shallots and parmesan to start. Main course could be roast South Coast hake with coriander-infused shiitaki mushroom, pak choi, spring onion and soy broth, or you might choose juniper and orange-infused venison saddle with dauphinoise potato, beetroot and blackberries. There's a lot going on in coffee and praline pannacotta, cocoa nibs, lime, and salt caramel ice cream to finish. The great selection of high quality wines is accessibly priced.

Chef Gavin Sinden **Owner** Fuller, Smith & Turner **Seats** 90, Pr/dining room 25 **Times** 12-3/6-9.30 Closed D 25 Dec **Prices** Fixed L 2 course £14-£25, Fixed D 3 course £22-£34, Tasting menu £50-£60, Starter £7-£9.50, Main £10-£22.50, Dessert £7.50-£9.50, Service optional 12.5% **Wines** 24 bottles over £30, 41 bottles under £30, 20 by glass **Parking** Town centre car park **Notes** Vegetarian available, Children 14yrs+

WOODLANDS Map 5 SU31

Woodlands Lodge Hotel

◎ Modern British

tel: 023 8029 2257 **Bartley Rd SO40 7GN**
email: reception@woodlands-lodge.co.uk **web:** www.woodlands-lodge.co.uk
dir: M27 junct 2, rdbt towards Fawley, 2nd rdbt right towards Cadnam. 1st left at White Horse Pub onto Woodlands Road, over cattle grid, hotel on left

Kitchen garden produce at a New Forest hotel

When we say this hotel is 'in the New Forest', we mean it. The ancient woodland can be accessed directly from the Lodge's gardens, making it the perfect spot for a walking break. Former service as a hunting lodge is reflected in the name of Hunters restaurant, where an elegant lightness of tone prevails, with chairs and wall panels in delicate forest green to match the view from the swagged windows. A south-facing walled garden supplies vegetables and soft fruits, and all meats are reared locally. It serves capably rendered modern British dishes with plenty of verve, starting perhaps with Lymington scallops and pork belly with butternut purée and parsnip crisps, and proceeding to sea bass en papillote with garlic butter, or a version of that triumphantly returned bistro classic, boeuf bourguignon, served with horseradish mash. Finish off with brioche-and-butter pudding, or Bailey's torte with vanilla ice cream and (no, really) more of those parsnip crisps.

Chef John Oyard **Owner** Robert Anglaret **Seats** 30, Pr/dining room 35 **Times** 12-2.30/7-9 **Prices** Fixed D 3 course £30, Service optional **Wines** 7 bottles over £30, 29 bottles under £30, 5 by glass **Parking** 80 **Notes** Fixed L 3 course, Fixed D 4 course, Sunday L £17.50, Vegetarian available, Children welcome

YATELEY Map 5 SU86

Casa Hotel & Marco Pierre White Restaurant

◉ French, British **NEW**

tel: 01252 873275 & 749142 **Handford Ln GU46 6BT**
email: info@wheelerscamberley.com **web:** www.wheelerscamberley.com
dir: *M3 junct 4a, follow signs for town centre. Hotel signed*

Comforting Anglo-French dining

A sprawling hotel that can sort out your wedding and conference needs, the Casa is home to a Marco Pierre White restaurant, under the Wheeler's umbrella. The restaurant takes over two areas with wooden beams and a real fire to bring a warm glow, and the tables wear white linen cloths to inject a little refinement to proceedings. The menu is classic MPW, that is to say a little bit French, a little bit British, with plenty of things you actually want to eat. King scallops with cauliflower purée is a modern classic, here the bivalves cooked just right, or you might kick off with the comforting familiarity of a prawn cocktail. Move on to pan-roasted breast of guinea fowl with green beans, fondant potato and fine jus is a French brasserie dish of heart and soul, while Wheeler's venison pie with parsnip purée is another deeply satisfying option. Cambridge burnt cream and sticky toffee pudding are typical desserts.

Chef Carlo de Simone, Charles Noorland **Owner** Bobby Obhrai **Seats** 88, Pr/dining room 34 **Times** 12-2.30/6.30-9.30 **Prices** Fixed L 2 course £19.50, Fixed D 3 course £23.50, Tasting menu £45-£65, Starter £6.50-£12.50, Main £14.50-£33, Dessert £6.50-£8.50, Service optional 10% **Wines** 48 bottles over £30, 24 bottles under £30, 16 by glass **Parking** 88 **Notes** Afternoon tea £7.95-£19.95, Sunday L £19.50-£23.50, Vegetarian available, Children welcome

HEREFORDSHIRE

HEREFORD Map 10 SO53

Castle House

◉◉ Modern British

tel: 01432 356321 **Castle St HR1 2NW**
email: info@castlehse.co.uk **web:** www.castlehse.co.uk
dir: *City centre, follow brown signs to Castle House Hotel*

Culinary voyages into modern Britain within sight of Hereford Castle

The house began life as a conjoined pair of elegant villas lording it over Castle Street during the Regency of George IV. Later in the 19th century, two became one, their staircases fusing into one majestic sweep, and the entire edifice embarked on its grand hotel career in the 1940s. Beautifully maintained today, it's owned by a local farmer whose produce finds its way on to the unmistakably modern British menus. The principal dining room overlooks the Hereford Castle moat, and is the refined setting for culinary voyages such as seared scallops with curried cauliflower, pomegranate and shallots, followed perhaps by guinea-fowl with a celeriac rösti and turnips. Reversing the fish and meat order might produce partridge escabèche with pickled veg and spiced plum, and then sea trout with artichokes, braised celery and sweet potato, dressed in raisins and capers, while vegetarian dishes think outside the box for something like open ravioli of goats' cheese, pink grapefruit and spring onions. Then what else to finish with but chestnut and azuki bean galette with matcha green tea granita?

Chef Claire Nicholls **Owner** David Watkins **Seats** 40 **Times** 12-2/6.30-9.30 **Prices** Tasting menu £50, Starter £5-£10, Main £18-£26, Dessert £7-£8, Service optional **Wines** 57 bottles over £30, 41 bottles under £30, 9 by glass **Parking** 12 **Notes** Tasting menu 7 course, Sunday L fr £26, Vegetarian available, Children welcome

See advert on opposite page

Holme Lacy House Hotel

◉◉ Modern British

tel: 01432 870870 **Holme Lacy HR2 6LP**
email: holmelacy@bourne-leisure.co.uk **web:** www.warnerleisurehotels.co.uk
dir: *B4399 at Holme Lacy, take lane opposite college. Hotel 500mtrs on right*

Quality dining in the Wye Valley

Set in the Wye Valley, Holme Lacy House is a listed Georgian mansion in 20 acres of parkland (note the topiary), with an interior boasting ornate ceilings in the lounges, a grand central staircase, and the oak-panelled Orchard Restaurant with its grand fireplace. The menu offers much to interest the palate and the eye, and ingredients are well chosen, with starters like langoustine risotto with tomato fondant and parmesan crisps, and pork faggot with shallot purée, crispy leeks and cider-roast apple. Main courses make an impact too, with nothing too fancy or gimmicky: moist, flavourful roast chicken breast, for instance, served on cabbage, accompanied by confit leg, baby carrots, boulangère potatoes and a well-made jus, or a well-conceived fish alternative of roast halibut fillet with citrus-braised mussels, fennel and dauphinoise potatoes. End with a fruity pudding like pineapple tart with pineapple and Malibu sorbet and coconut mousse, or perhaps the 'quartet of chocolate', or alternatively a plate of top-notch local cheeses.

Chef Douglas Elliman **Owner** Bourne Leisure **Seats** 50 **Times** 6-9 Closed L all week **Prices** Prices not confirmed, Service optional **Wines** 11 bottles over £30, 26 bottles under £30, 11 by glass **Parking** 200 **Notes** Vegetarian available, No children

KINGTON
Map 9 SO25

The Stagg Inn and Restaurant
◉◉ Modern British V

tel: 01544 230221 **Titley HR5 3RL**
email: reservations@thestagg.co.uk
dir: *Between Kington & Presteigne on B4335*

Impeccable regional cooking in an old drovers' inn

Standing at the junction of two drovers' roads, The Stagg is a country inn on a medieval base with Victorian embellishments. It does everything country inns should, offering accommodation to all (not just drovers), refreshing drinkers in the bar with local ales and good wines, and-the absolute essential these days-providing a menu of regionally sourced, impeccably presented British food that works some modern technique into deeply rooted traditional ideas. Hearts and livers of duck with mushrooms on toast is one richly satisfying way to start, while a mackerel fillet comes with smoked bone marrow and pickled cucumber. Locally farmed meats are a joy: rump steak, ox cheek with smoked tongue, shoulder and chop of lamb with caramelised shallots, pheasant with white truffle and parsnip purée. There's room for fish too though, perhaps sea bass with salt-and-pepper squid, and desserts offer an array of seasonal fruits, as well as treats like Pedro Ximénez sherry cheesecake with prunes and coffee ice cream, or there's a trolley freighted with West Country and Welsh cheeses.

Chef S Reynolds, M Handley **Owner** Steve & Nicola Reynolds **Seats** 70, Pr/dining room 30 **Times** 12-2/6.30-9 Closed 2 wks Jan-Feb, 1st 2 wks Nov, Mon-Tue **Prices** Prices not confirmed, Service optional **Wines** 8 by glass **Parking** 22 **Notes** Sunday L, Children welcome

LEDBURY
Map 10 SO73

Feathers Hotel
◉ Modern British

tel: 01531 635266 **High St HR8 1DS**
email: mary@feathers-ledbury.co.uk **web:** www.feathers-ledbury.co.uk
dir: *M50 junct 2. Ledbury on A449/A438/A417. Hotel on main street*

Atmospheric brasserie in a historic inn

Holding court in this historic town since 1564, it is probably fair to call the Feathers an institution. The timbered old coaching inn is these days a smart hotel with two eating options to satisfy the needs of the 21st-century traveller. Quills Restaurant is the smarter of the two spaces, whilst Fuggles Brasserie provides lots of atmosphere and a broadly appealing menu. With its exposed brick walls, chunky wooden tables, and dried hops adorning the ceiling (fuggles is a type of hops), the cooking follows a broadly modern British path where European techniques are fair game and local produce gets a good showing. There are steaks (Herefordshire, of course) from the grill with a selection of sauces, or you might start with baby monkfish tails with chorizo and orange salad and saffron dressing, before moving on to Redmarley pork fillet with a pressing of belly and black pudding, apple and parsnip purée, and spiced red cabbage.

Chef Susan Isaacs **Owner** David Elliston **Seats** 55, Pr/dining room 60 **Times** 12-2/6.30-9.30 **Prices** Fixed D 3 course fr £22, Starter £5.95-£7.50, Main £13.50-£25, Dessert £5.95-£6.50 **Wines** 42 bottles over £30, 97 bottles under £30, 12 by glass **Parking** 30 **Notes** Sunday L £14.25-£17.95, Vegetarian available, Children welcome

LEINTWARDINE
Map 9 SO47

The Lion
◉ Modern British

tel: 01547 540203 & 540747 **High St SY7 0JZ**
email: enquiries@thelionleintwardine.co.uk **web:** www.thelionleintwardine.co.uk
dir: *On A4113. At bottom of High Street by bridge*

Modern British dishes in an idyllic English inn

Set beside the River Teme in a peaceful Herefordshire hamlet, The Lion is a sensitively restored village local with a patio area looking over extensive gardens, and riverside tables under the trees. An English idyll, it was once the local of Sir Banastre Tarleton, who distinguished himself controversially in the American War of Independence, albeit on the losing side. The bare floorboards, leather sofas and beams make all the right noises within, while the kitchen offers a polished repertoire of modern British dishes. A pressed terrine of Devon crab and smoked langoustine has good flavour, and is accompanied by a light watercress pannacotta and baby pear, while prime materials are in evidence in a pairing of best end and herbed breast of spring lamb, which comes with beech mushrooms and mash, or there could be a bracing early summer risotto of green beans, peas and red mint, served with gremolata, lemon yoghurt and pecorino. Modern menus would be lost without their 'textures', here manifesting as doughnut, mousse, ice cream and sherbet sprinkle, composed of different apple varieties.

Times 12-2.30/6-9.30 Closed 25 Dec

Just a two minute walk from Hereford's magnificent Cathedral, Castle House is a unique boutique townhouse hotel and restaurant.

The perfect place for your wedding, and an excellent base from which to explore this truly beautiful and historic area.

Tel: +44 (0)1432 356321
info@castlehse.co.uk
www.castlehse.co.uk
Castle Street, Hereford HR1 2NW, UK

Castle HOUSE

AA ◉◉

Follow us... Like us...

ROSS-ON-WYE
Map 10 SO52

The Chase Hotel

British, Modern European

tel: 01989 763161 **Gloucester Rd HR9 5LH**
email: res@chasehotel.co.uk **web:** www.chasehotel.co.uk
dir: M50 junct 4 onto A449. Take A40 towards Gloucester, turn right at rdbt into Ross-on-Wye. Hotel on left 0.25m

Georgian country-house hotel with modish restaurant

Every bit the contemporary dining room, Harry's Restaurant is named after the owner's grandson, rather than an homage to the iconic Venetian bar. Set in a large Georgian mansion with 11 acres of grounds, its modern shades of cream, tan and black, up-to-date furnishings and silk drapes blend quite happily with the room's original high ceilings, ornate plasterwork and tall windows. The modern European comfort-orientated menu ranges widely, offering something for everyone, built on fresh, quality local ingredients. Things like slow-braised belly pork with black pudding, apple purée and crackling, Puy lentils and creamed potato line up alongside those that speak of sunnier climes-perhaps monkfish wrapped in pancetta and served with silverskin onions, mushrooms and red wine jus. Desserts follow the theme, with a true Brit sticky toffee pudding competing for favour against an almond and apricot tart with Amaretto syllabub.

Chef Richard Birchall **Owner** Camanoe Estates Ltd **Seats** 70, Pr/dining room 300 **Times** 12-2/6-9.30 Closed 24-27 Dec **Prices** Starter £5.50-£9.50, Main £8-£21, Dessert £6-£9.50, Service optional **Wines** 12 bottles over £30, 33 bottles under £30, 13 by glass **Parking** 75 **Notes** Sunday L, Vegetarian available, Children welcome

Glewstone Court Country House Hotel & Restaurant

Modern British, French

tel: 01989 770367 **Glewstone HR9 6AW**
email: info@glewstonecourt.com **web:** www.glewstonecourt.com
dir: From Ross Market Place take A40/A49 (Monmouth/Hereford) over Wilton Bridge. At rdbt left onto A40 (Monmouth/S Wales), after 1m turn right for Glewstone. Hotel 0.5m on left

West Country produce in an attractive Wye Valley Georgian hotel

The location within the Wye Valley is rather gorgeous, with the Forest of Dean in the distance and the hotel's pretty gardens in the foreground. The house can hold its own, though, built in Georgian times to grand proportions and with that impressive aspect. It's kept the best assets to this day, with a curving Regency staircase and fancy plasterwork throughout. The candle-lit dining room has a traditional feel without resorting to excessive chintz. There's a good deal of fine produce in this neck of the woods and the kitchen team at Glewstone make good use of it in classically-minded dishes. A starter of home-smoked rainbow trout might come with an orange and rocket salad with a pomegranate dressing, and main-course tenderloin of local pork, stuffed with Bramley apple farce and wrapped in pancetta, served with a Scotch quail's egg and crackling. For dessert, dark chocolate tart comes in the trendy company of peanut butter ice cream and salted caramel popcorn.

Chef Christine Reeve-Tucker, Vicky Lyons **Owner** C & W Reeve-Tucker **Seats** 36, Pr/dining room 40 **Times** 12-2/7-10 Closed 25-27 Dec **Prices** Fixed L 2 course £15, Tasting menu £40, Starter £5.50-£8, Main £16-£22, Dessert £7, Service optional **Wines** 12 bottles over £30, 31 bottles under £30, 11 by glass **Parking** 28 **Notes** Tasting menu 7 course, Sunday L £21-£22, Vegetarian available, Children welcome

Wilton Court Restaurant with Rooms

Modern British

tel: 01989 562569 **Wilton Ln HR9 6AQ**
email: info@wiltoncourthotel.com **web:** www.wiltoncourthotel.com
dir: M50 junct 4 onto A40 towards Monmouth at 3rd rdbt turn left signed Ross-on-Wye then take 1st right, hotel on right

Intelligent modern cookery on the Wye riverside

A riverside setting on the Wye makes for much natural diversion at Wilton Court. Swans glide, otters splash, kingfishers swoop, and the air is full of birdsong. Wilton itself partly dates back to around 1500 and was once the local magistrate's court. What is now the Riverview dining room rang to the handing down of sentences, while the Mulberry Restaurant is where Martyn Williams' intelligent modern British food is allowed free rein. Full-flavoured soups are a smart bet – perhaps roast tomato and chilli, or celeriac with potato dumplings and bacon foam – or you may opt to start with a vivid risotto of smoked haddock and peas. Then it's local meats to the fore in mains such as mustard- and herb-crumbed lamb loin with dauphinoise and ratatouille, or pedigree Hereford beef fillet on a big flat roasted mushroom, with champ and a sauce of pink peppercorns. West Country and Welsh cheeses (the border is a mere five miles away) get a listing of their own, or there are sweet indulgences like white chocolate parfait with dark chocolate milkshake and a brownie.

Chef Martyn Williams **Owner** Roger & Helen Wynn **Seats** 40, Pr/dining room 12 **Times** 12-2.15/7-9 Closed 1st 2 wks Jan **Prices** Fixed L 2 course fr £16.95, Fixed D 3 course fr £32.50, Tasting menu fr £55, Starter £6.50-£8.95, Main £16-£24, Dessert £6.95-£7.50, Service optional **Wines** 7 bottles over £30, 31 bottles under £30, 8 by glass **Parking** 25 **Notes** Tasting menu 7 course (complete tables only), Sunday L £16.95-£18.95, Vegetarian available, Children welcome

HERTFORDSHIRE

BERKHAMSTED
Map 6 SP90

The Gatsby

Modern European

tel: 01442 870403 **97 High St HP4 2DG**
email: thegatsby@live.co.uk
dir: M25 junct 20/A41 to Aylesbury in 3m take left turn to Berkhamsted following town signs. Restaurant on left on entering High St

Movies and brasserie cooking in a retooled art deco cinema

As the name at the top of the frontage announces, The Gatsby shares these premises with the original Rex cinema, a beautiful piece of 1930s British art deco from the era of Basil Rathbone and Nova Pilbeam, its heritage traced in the screen-stars of the golden age who dot the walls, and the show tunes the restaurant pianist rolls out. The modern brasserie menu feels just right in the glitzy surroundings, and makes a fine prelude or supplement to a film upstairs. Seared pigeon breast with a vegetable pastilla in hazelnut and cumin dressing raises the curtain on a performance that might go on to feature Thai fish broth with red mullet and bok choi, alight with lemongrass and ginger, or roast guinea fowl with truffled parsnip purée in a sauce of ceps. Desserts run to dark chocolate fondant with cherry and lime frozen yoghurt, or there are English and French cheeses.

Chef Matthew Salt **Owner** Nick Pembroke **Seats** 65 **Times** 12-2.30/5.30-10.30 Closed 25-26 Dec **Prices** Fixed L 2 course £14.95, Fixed D 3 course £20.90, Starter £6.95-£9.25, Main £16.25-£28.95, Dessert £7.95, Service optional **Wines** 25 bottles over £30, 27 bottles under £30, 16 by glass **Parking** 10 **Notes** Pre cinema menu Mon-Sat 12-2.30 & 5.30-6.30, Sunday L £14.95, Vegetarian available, Children welcome

DATCHWORTH
Map 6 TL21

The Tilbury

Modern British

tel: 01438 815550 **1 Watton Rd SG3 6TB**
email: info@thetilbury.co.uk
dir: *A1(M) junct 7, A602 signed Ware & Hertford. At Bragbury End right into Bragbury Lane to Datchworth*

Proper village pub serving up well-sourced, carefully-cooked food

The village of Datchworth has a gastro-pub that balances being a good local pub and a place to eat good, proper food. It has been all change at the Tilbury recently, with new owners taking over and a new chef at the helm, but you can be sure that the food is still based on solid foundations. Quality first and foremost is what drives the kitchen's output, starting with carefully-sourced produce, much of it British, and much of it local. Among hearty starters you might encounter oxtail faggot with celeriac purée, while mains span everything from honey-roasted duck leg breast with confit leg, smoked duck lentils and parsnip purée, to roast sea trout with crab mash, samphire and tomato butter sauce. Pudding could be a comforting apple and pear crumble with vanilla ice cream.

Chef Chas Wheeler **Owner** James & Tom Bainbridge, Nicola Brown **Seats** 70, Pr/dining room 36 **Times** 12-2.30/6-9 Closed Closed some BHs, Mon, D Sun **Prices** Fixed L 2 course £15, Fixed D 3 course £19, Starter £6-£9.50, Main £14-£19.50, Dessert £6-£7.50, Service optional **Wines** 15 bottles over £30, 20 bottles under £30, 11 by glass **Parking** 40 **Notes** Sunday L £14-£22, Vegetarian available, Children welcome

FLAUNDEN
Map 6 TL00

Bricklayers Arms

British, French

tel: 01442 833322 & 831722 **Black Robin Ln, Hogpits Bottom HP3 0PH**
email: goodfood@bricklayersarms.com **web:** www.bricklayersarms.com
dir: *M25 junct 20, A451 towards Chipperfield. Into Dunny Ln, 1st right into Flaunden Ln. 1m on single track*

Traditional country inn with well-crafted Anglo-French cooking

The Bricklayers was built in the 18th century and is now a cheery gastro-pub with a cosy atmosphere, rustic oak beams, a log fire and a brick bar, offering plenty of tables in the garden and on the terrace. Food is a serious commitment, with the kitchen sourcing locally and paying due respect to the seasons and complementing the menus with daily fish and vegetarian specials. 'English and French fusion' is the self-described style, so expect to find eggs Benedict to start alongside venison terrine with pear chutney. Among main courses, haunch of venison is cooked in red wine and redcurrants and topped with glazed onions and mushrooms, another full-on meat alternative is ox cheek in ale and honey served with champ. The fish of the day may bring on haddock and red mullet pie in saffron cream, and puddings may run to thin apple tart with vanilla ice cream.

Chef Claude Paillet, Alan Bell, Martin West **Owner** Alvin & Sally Michaels **Seats** 95, Pr/dining room 50 **Times** 12-2.30/6.30-9.30 Closed 25 Dec **Prices** Fixed L 2 course £15, Fixed D 3 course £20, Starter £5.95-£13.95, Main £12.95-£24.95, Dessert £4.95-£6.95, Service optional **Wines** 96 bottles over £30, 34 bottles under £30, 16 by glass **Parking** 40 **Notes** Sunday L £12.95-£16.95, Vegetarian available, Children welcome

Colette's at The Grove

RICKMANSWORTH
Map 6 TQ09

Modern European **NOTABLE WINE LIST**

tel: 01923 807807 **Chandler's Cross WD3 4TG**
email: info@thegrove.co.uk **web:** www.thegrove.co.uk
dir: *M25 junct 19, follow signs to Watford. At 1st large rdbt take 3rd exit. 0.5m, entrance on right*

Avant-garde cooking on a grand country estate

'Groovy and grand' is how The Grove styles itself, appealing to a range of cultural sensibilities, and generations too. The grooviness might take in aromatherapy rituals in the spa, while the grandeur covers everything from the 300 acres of Hertfordshire it stands in, and its historic status as family seat of the Earls of Clarendon, to the fact that the great equestrian painter George Stubbs produced much of his work in the stables here. An air of finely drilled professionalism prevails throughout and, although there is a less formal eating option in those illustrious Stables (see entry), it's in Colette's dining room that Russell Bateman's avant-garde culinary genius is allowed full spate. Bateman has worked with many of the conjurable names of contemporary Anglo-French gastronomy – Nico Ladenis, Marc Veyrat and Marcus Wareing – and settled into his own berth here

in 2009, with a mission to dazzle. It all starts with the raw materials of course, many from the estate's organic walled garden. The simplest approach is to take one of the six- or eight-course taster menus (which include a vegetarian version), and let Bateman weave his magic, but if you're determined to retain a modicum of control, choose from the à la carte Haiku menu. Dishes cross from one to the other anyway, so there may be no need to miss out on Scottish scallops with peanuts, radish and lime, beef tartare with sour cream, horseradish and watercress, or the exploration of cucumber that partners pickled, salted and fresh with smoked anchovies, goats' curd, black olives and mint. Main dishes research the potential of their prime ingredients in terms of seasonings and textures, producing a Jacob's ladder of slow-cooked beef with bone marrow, home-grown onions and pomme purée. Dessert brings Tanzanian chocolate with hazelnuts and grapes.

Chef Russell Bateman **Owner** Ralph Trustees Ltd **Seats** 40, Pr/dining room 24 **Times** 6.30-9.30 Closed Sun-Mon (ex BHs), L all week **Prices** Fixed D 3 course £65, Tasting menu £75-£85, Service optional **Wines** 24 by glass **Parking** 300 **Notes** ALC 3 course £65, Vegetarian available, No children

HATFIELD

Map 6 TL20

Beales Hotel

◉◉ Modern British

tel: 01707 288500 & 288518 **Comet Way AL10 9NG**
email: outsidein@bealeshotels.co.uk **web:** www.bealeshotels.co.uk
dir: On A1001 opposite Galleria Shopping Mall - follow signs for Galleria

Anglo-Med magic in a striking modern hotel

The Hatfield Beales is a striking piece of contemporary design, from its jungle-gym outer packaging to its self-assertively patterned interiors, hung with works by Hertfordshire University students. Not for Beales the monotonous monochrome surfaces of elsewhere; if they could squeeze on a repeating motif, it's got one. The dining room looks unexpectedly small for a hotel, which creates its own aura of exclusivity, and some tables even have couches so you can loll through dinner. The cooking is a mix of modern British classics and Mediterranean magic, with goats' cheese pannacotta in warmly spiced tomato salsa, or a slim slice of chicken and ham terrine in mustard vinaigrette. This sets up the tastebuds for mains such as crisp-fried sea bass with accurately timed saffron risotto and diced chorizo, or perhaps a ribeye steak of local beef with onion rings and peppercorn sauce. A dessert glass of slightly slushy papaya and dragon fruit parfait with excellent passionfruit sorbet is a thing of two halves, raspberry and white chocolate tart with clotted cream and almond brittle may be the better bet.

Times 12-2.30/6-10

RICKMANSWORTH

Map 6 TQ09

Colette's at The Grove

◉◉◉ – *see page 221*

The Stables Restaurant at The Grove

◉ Modern British

tel: 01923 807807 & 296015 **Chandler's Cross WD3 4TG**
email: restaurants@thegrove.co.uk
dir: M25 junct 19, A411 towards Watford. Hotel on right

Creative modern cooking in George Stubbs' favourite stables

The original stable block of the Georgian mansion, where Stubbs spent hours at his easel, has been given a modern makeover under its rafters and is now the informal eatery at The Grove. The open-to-view kitchen is equipped with a wood-fired oven and chargrill, but the menu has a lot more going for it than pizzas and steaks. Imaginative starters have run from chicken liver and foie gras brûlée to beetroot and goats' cheese tarte Tatin with truffled honey. Seafood gets a good airing, from aromatic crab cake to well-timed roast pollock with cockles, pancetta and Jerusalem artichoke purée, and quality produce is apparent throughout. Try roast Banham chicken with Savoy cabbage and chestnuts, say, or roast shoulder of salt marsh lamb with parsley creamed potatoes, mushrooms, roast garlic and confit shallots. Dark chocolate tart and Baileys crème brûlée are popular puddings.

Chef Christopher Mouyiassi **Owner** Ralph Trustees Ltd **Seats** 120, Pr/dining room 16 **Times** 12-3/6-9.30 Closed 25 & 31 Dec **Prices** Starter £8.50-£9, Main £16-£25, Dessert £8, Service optional **Wines** 11 bottles over £30, 10 bottles under £30, 10 by glass **Parking** 300 **Notes** Sunday L £19.50, Vegetarian available, Children welcome

ST ALBANS

Map 6 TL10

Chez Mumtaj

◉◉ French, Asian

tel: 01727 800033 **Centurian House, 136-142 London Rd AL1 1PQ**
email: info@chezmumtaj.com **web:** www.chezmumtaj.com

Franco-Asian fusion food in opulent surroundings

Chez Mumtaj emanates class and style, with its panelled walls and comfortable cream leather-look banquettes at correctly set clothed tables, and an open-to-view kitchen. As the name suggests, the style is a culinary hybrid: what the restaurant itself describes as 'haute cuisine in modern French-Asian dining', with classical techniques applied to tip-top produce. The long menu may open with the signature dish of bird's nest quail Scotch egg – the egg encased in truffle, foie gras and minced chicken, coated in breadcrumbs within crispy kataifi pastry and served with wasabi remoulade – or soft-shelled crab in chilli and garlic tempura with spicy marmalade. Best end of lamb rogan josh sounds familiar enough, and there may also be a main course of seared fillets of sea bass with Keralan-style velouté, garlicky okra, smoked aubergine and chick pea caviar, chive butter, and lemon and chilli rice. End with the more Western-sounding mango and orange crème brûlée.

Chef Chad Rahman **Owner** Chad Rahman **Seats** 100, Pr/dining room 16 **Times** 12-2.30/6-11 Closed 25 Dec, Mon **Prices** Fixed L 2 course £12-£14.95, Fixed D 3 course £14.95-£18.95, Starter £5.95-£12, Main £8.95-£21.95, Dessert £4.95-£6.95 **Wines** 21 bottles over £30, 26 bottles under £30, 14 by glass **Parking** On street & car park nearby **Notes** Tasting & early bird D menus available, Sunday L, Vegetarian available, Children welcome

See advert on opposite page

Sopwell House

◉ Modern British, French

tel: 01727 864477 **Cottonmill Ln, Sopwell AL1 2HQ**
email: enquiries@sopwellhouse.co.uk **web:** www.sopwellhouse.co.uk
dir: *M25 junct 22, A1081 St Albans. At lights left into Mile House Ln, over mini-rdbt into Cottonmill Ln*

Smart country club near historic St Albans

The one-time country residence of Lord Mountbatten is a handsome Georgian house indeed, white-painted, and standing in 12 acres of pretty gardens. It makes an impressive country-house hotel and has all the spa facilities you might imagine. The restaurant is suitably modish in its aspirations, with decoration chosen from the soothing contemporary colour palette and tables dressed up in white linen cloths. A smart setting, then, for some sharp contemporary cooking. Start, perhaps, with quail served with parsley purée, black truffle and pistachio arancini, or king scallop with confit belly of pork, broad beans and sweetcorn purée. Follow on with crab-crusted salmon fillet with a saffron risotto, king prawns and a poppy seed salad, or a duo of Barbary duck with autumn vegetables and orange jus. Dessert might bring forth iced banana parfait with dark chocolate sauce and honeycomb.

Times 12-2/7-9.30 Closed Mon-Tue, L Thu & Sat, D Sun

Thompson@Darcy's

◉◉ Modern British Fine Dining NEW v

tel: 01727 730777 **2 Hatfield Rd AL1 3RP**
email: info@thompsonatdarcys.co.uk
dir: *M25 junct 22, A1081 London Rd to St Albans. At major x-rds right onto St Albans High St, 2nd right onto Hatfield Rd*

Classy contemporary cooking with interesting combinations

Phil Thompson's name is above the door of his restaurant in a row of part-boarded cottages in the centre of town. Having won plaudits at Auberge du Lac down the road, Thompson has struck out on his own in this smartly done out address with local artworks hanging on the walls (for sale if you fancy one) and a stylish contemporary finish. The menu shows classical leanings and plenty of interesting combinations, with the dishes arriving at the table looking fine and dandy. There are set lunch and midweek evening menus (great value) alongside the carte, while Sunday evening is 'Lobster & Steak Night'. A starter of port-marinated foie gras boudin shows off the skill and confidence of this kitchen, with perfect balance of flavours, followed by chargrilled Dingley Dell pork rib-eye partnered with its confit shoulder (plus poached plums and gingerbread crumb). Finish with fromage frais pannacotta with poached Yorkshire rhubarb and delicious little custard doughnuts. A terrific addition to the Hertfordshire dining scene.

Chef Phil Thompson **Owner** Phil Thompson **Seats** 90, Pr/dining room 70
Times 12-2.30/6-10 **Prices** Fixed L 2 course £16.50, Fixed D 3 course £23, Tasting menu £49, Starter £7.50-£14, Main £16.50-£25, Dessert £6.50-£10, Service optional 10% **Wines** 36 bottles over £30, 21 bottles under £30, 16 by glass
Notes Tasting menu 6 course, Lobster & steak night Sun eve, Children welcome

CHEZ MUMTAJ
Modern French-Asian Dining
Restaurant & Saffron Lounge Champagne Bar

Centurian House 136-142 London Road
St Albans, Herts AL1 1PQ

call 01727 800033 for reservations

info@chezmumtaj.com   www.chezmumtaj.com

Opening hours for the Saffron Lounge and Restaurant
12noon - 2.30pm & 6 - 11pm Tues to Sun

■ Modern French-Asian Dining
■ Saffron Lounge & Champagne Bar
■ Private Dining
■ Prix fixe Menus
■ Tasting Menu
■ Open Theatre Kitchen
■ Canapés Parties
■ Corporate Dining

Award Winning Chef Chad Rahman
National And International Chef Of The Year

Pendley Manor Hotel

◉◉ Traditional British

---

tel: 01442 891891 **Cow Ln HP23 5QY**
email: sales@pendley-manor.co.uk **web:** www.pendley-manor.co.uk
dir: M25 junct 20, A41 (Tring exit). At rdbt follow Berkhamsted/London signs. 1st left signed Tring Station & Pendley Manor

Handsome manor house with modern cooking

Although Pendley's history stretches back a thousand years and gets it a mention in the Domesday Book, the current incarnation is part Victorian neo-Tudor, built in 1872 after a fire destroyed the original, and part modern annexe, built to extend significantly its events and conference capacity. The Victorian section offers period grandeur in spades, particularly in the Oak Restaurant where oak flooring, lofty ceilings, colourful patterned wallpaper, and swagged-back drapes at vast bay windows make for an imposing setting. The cooking, however has its feet firmly in the 21st century: 'ham, eggs, chips, peas and ketchup' brings those components together in a rather more refined version than the greasy spoon classic, or you might set out with seared scallops with lobster potato cake, pea salad, plum tomato and lemon verbena sauce. At main course stage, butter-poached halibut fillet is teamed to good effect with chive mash, caramelised veal sweetbreads, gem lettuce, morels, green beans and a chicken stock lifted with sherry vinegar. Finally, peanut parfait arrives with dark chocolate mousse and caramel sauce.

Chef Martin White **Owner** Craydawn Pendley Manor **Seats** 75, Pr/dining room 200 **Times** 12.30-2.30/7-9.30 Closed L Sat **Prices** Fixed L 2 course £20.50, Fixed D 3 course £29.50, Starter £8.50-£11.25, Main £18.75-£32, Dessert £7.50-£9, Service optional **Wines** 13 bottles over £30, 33 bottles under £30, 7 by glass **Parking** 150 **Notes** Sunday L £25.50, Vegetarian available, Children welcome

---

Auberge du Lac

◉◉ French, European, British ᴠ

tel: 01707 368888 **Brocket Hall Estate, Brocket Rd AL8 7XG**
email: auberge@brocket-hall.co.uk **web:** www.brocket-hall.co.uk
dir: A1(M) junct 4, B653 to Wheathampstead. In Brocket Ln take 2nd gate entry to Brocket Hall

Refined and modish cooking in a lakeside hunting lodge

The pretty red-brick Auberge a short stroll from the big house (the magnificent Brocket Hall) used to be a hunting lodge, but these days it has far more leisurely pursuits in mind. Standing by the eponymous lake amidst the 543-acre estate, Auberge du Lac doesn't want for charm, with its 18th-century façade and soothing waterside setting. A table outside is a real treat when the weather allows.Within, all is soothing sophistication, with the tables dressed in pristine white linen. The cooking has its roots in classical French tradition, but a cornucopia of British ingredients and an eye for contemporary culinary goings-on mean the kitchen turns out bright and creative dishes. Pan-roasted Orkney scallops come as a first course in the fashionable company of black pudding and textures of cauliflower, followed by braised pork belly flavoured with five spice and served with a sesame coated spare rib (plus a broccoli purée and pakchoi). Finish with hazelnut, coffee and chocolate dacquoise. The wine list doesn't stint when it comes to offering up stellar French bottles.

Chef Marcus McGuinness **Owner** CCA International **Seats** 70, Pr/dining room 32 **Times** 12-2.30/7-9.30 Closed 27 Dec-17 Jan, Mon, D Sun **Prices** Fixed L 3 course £39.50, Tasting menu £60-£70 **Wines** 14 by glass **Parking** 50 **Notes** ALC fixed 3 course £60, Tasting menu 6/9 course, Sunday L £39.50 Children 12yrs+

See advert on opposite page

Tewin Bury Farm Hotel

◉◉ Modern British

---

tel: 01438 717793 **AL6 OJB**
email: restaurant@tewinbury.co.uk **web:** www.tewinbury.co.uk
dir: A1M junct 6 (signed Welwyn Garden City), 1st exit A1000. 0.25m to B1000 Hertford Rd. Hotel on left

Up-to-the-minute modern cookery on a working farm

A complex of barns on a working farm has been skilfully converted into this characterful modern hotel and restaurant with conference facilities; it's a sought-after venue for weddings too. The restaurant is in what used to be a chicken shed, now a handsome room with a beamed ceiling above rafters, mustard-yellow banquettes, a boarded floor and bare-topped wooden tables. Many of the kitchen's raw materials are produced on-site, with the rest assiduously sourced: Dingley Dell pork from Suffolk, for instance, seen in a gutsy main course of slow-cooked belly with a crisp cake of head in red wine jus with apple purée, celeriac gratin and curly kale. The rest of the menu is a slate of highly original, well-executed ideas, from white bean and chorizo soup to smoked and poached salmon rillettes with nori and a salad of fennel, red endive and orange. The thoughtful approach continues with main courses like spot-on, firm-fleshed fillet of hake with clam chowder, spinach and new potatoes. Glazed orange tart is a rich, creamy way to finish, offset by liquorice ice cream.

Times 12-2.30/6.30-9.30

The Waggoners

◉ French

tel: 01707 324241 **Brickwall Close, Ayot Green AL6 9AA**
email: laurent@thewaggoners.co.uk
dir: A1(M) junct 6 to B197, right into Ayot and 1st left Brickwall Close

Contemporary French cooking in lovely village inn

The Waggoners has all the features associated with a 17th-century village inn: ceiling beams, a brick inglenook and walls hung with prints and mirrors, conveying a cosy, homely image. So it's a bit of a surprise to find a staunchly French menu. The kitchen concentrates on updated classics and bringing a sense of adventure to some dishes, for example lobster cannelloni partnered by slow-roast pork belly served with asparagus and sauce américaine. Well-handled raw materials are of the first order and combined to give vivid combinations of flavours and textures. Start with goats' cheese parfait with mushroom tartare, leeks and truffle dressing, or, for high rollers, a plate of Sévruga caviar with a shot of vodka. Proceed to pink-roast saddle of lamb on rosemary sauce with macaroni cheese, tomato fondue and ceps. End with le chocolat (an assiette with pistachio ice cream) or la tarte (perhaps treacle with caramelised banana).

Chef Paul Ribbands **Owner** Laurent & Aude Brydniak **Seats** 65, Pr/dining room 35 **Times** 12-2.30/6.30-9 Closed D Sun **Prices** Fixed L 2 course £31, Fixed D 3 course £50, Tasting menu £46, Starter £6-£12, Main £13-£25, Dessert £6-£14.50, Service optional **Wines** 40 bottles over £30, 60 bottles under £30, 22 by glass **Parking** 70 **Notes** Sunday L £18-£30, Vegetarian available, Children welcome

The Wellington

◉ Modern British

tel: 01438 714036 **High St AL6 9LZ**
email: info@wellingtonatwelwyn.co.uk **web:** www.wellingtonatwelwyn.co.uk
dir: A1M junct 6, on High Street in Welwyn village across from St Mary's Church

Village inn with an appealing menu

Going strong since 1352, The Wellington, on Welwyn's pretty high street, is an old coaching inn which takes a contemporary approach to the business of hospitality. A makeover a few years ago has opened up the place, seen the addition of some rather cool bedrooms, and put the focus firmly on the gastro side of the pub spectrum. It looks good with its rustic-chic exposed brick walls, real fires and bar stocked with proper beers. The menu keeps things simple and unpretentious, so you might choose to tuck into a hearty beef and Wellington ale pie. If you're up for the full works, however, you might start with crispy duck and hoisin dumpling, or go for one of the daily specials such as crab and tarragon bonbons with samphire, radish, cucumber and tarragon oil. Next up, a fillet burger, fish pie, or something a little more adventurous such as braised ox cheek with an oxtail lollipop.

Chef Tom King **Owner** Christopher Gerard **Seats** 90 **Times** 12-10 All-day dining **Prices** Prices not confirmed **Wines** 10 bottles over £30, 40 bottles under £30, 30 by glass **Parking** 40 **Notes** Sunday L, Vegetarian available, Children welcome

Auberge du Lac

at Brocket Hall

Housed in Brocket Hall's former hunting lodge, Auberge du Lac enjoys an idyllic lakeside setting overlooking the beautiful 543 acre country estate and the Hall itself.

Whether it's al fresco dining in summer at the water's edge or an intimate environment in the winter months, Auberge du Lac provides the right mood for every occasion with a beautiful lounge, picturesque terrace and a host of tastefully decorated private dining rooms

Restaurant | Private Dining | Kitchen Masterclass | Weddings
"The Cloudy Bay Experience"

01707 368888 | auberge@brocket-hall.co.uk | www.brocket-hall.co.uk
Brocket Hall International Ltd | Brocket Hall | Welwyn | Hertfordshire | AL8 7XG

Map 12 TL23

The Fox

Modern British

tel: 01462 480233 **SG6 2AE**
email: info@foxatwillian.co.uk
dir: A1(M) junct 9 towards Letchworth, 1st left to Willian, The Fox 0.5m on left

Creative and accomplished cooking in a smart local pub

If you lived in a pretty village with just the one pub, you'd hope for it to be a stylish gastropub such as the Fox. It ticks all the boxes with its proper bar bristling with well-kept real ales, a smart contemporary open-plan dining room hung with original artwork beneath a glazed atrium ceiling, and a skilled kitchen whose ambition goes way beyond pub grub staples. Under the same ownership as The White Horse in Brancaster Staithe(see entry), supply lines to fish and seafood from the Norfolk coast are strong, so mussels from the beds next to its seaside sibling, served with cider and pancetta cream and freshly-baked bread might open the show, followed by roasted suprême of coley with Parma ham and potato terrine, Savoy cabbage, broad beans, crayfish, and chive beurre blanc. Meaty mains run to pan-fried venison loin with suet pudding, creamed celeriac, roasted beetroot and redcurrant jus.

Chef Sherwin Jacobs **Owner** Anglian Country Inns, The Nye family **Seats** 70 **Times** 12-2/6.30-9.15 Closed D Sun **Prices** Starter £4.95-£10.50, Main £9.95-£22, Dessert £5.95-£7.50, Service optional 10% **Wines** 13 bottles over £30, 28 bottles under £30, 15 by glass **Parking** 40 **Notes** Sunday L £13.50-£14.95, Vegetarian available, Children welcome

ISLE OF WIGHT

Map 5 SZ69

Priory Bay Hotel

Modern British

tel: 01983 613146 **Priory Dr PO34 5BU**
email: enquiries@priorybay.co.uk **web:** www.priorybay.co.uk
dir: B3330 towards Seaview, through Nettlestone. (Do not follow Seaview turn, but continue 0.5m to hotel sign)

Attractive Regency dining room and creative menu

Since the 14th century, medieval monks, Tudor farmers and Georgian gentry have all contributed their bit of character to this sumptuous country house retreat. Buffered from the modern world by a 70-acre estate of gardens, woodlands and even its own beach, the enticing package also comes with a brace of dining options. The Priory Oyster brasserie deals in gutsy dishes along the lines of duck livers on toast with caramelised onions, ahead of fillet and belly of local lamb with sautéed potatoes, kale and wild garlic, or you could trade up to the elegant Regency-style Island Room restaurant with its gilded plasterwork and floor-to-ceiling windows giving views across to the Solent. The fine dining menu is built on local seafood, game and fresh and foraged produce from the gardens and woodlands, and takes in the likes of line-caught sea bass with seaweed, or garden beans in pork broth, and elderberries with Isle of Wight cream to finish.

Chef Oliver Stephens **Owner** Mr R & Mr J Palmer **Seats** 60, Pr/dining room 50 **Times** 12.30-2.15/6.30-9.30 **Prices** Fixed L 2 course £22, Fixed D 3 course £28, Tasting menu £55-£85, Starter £5-£9, Main £10-£22, Dessert £5-£9 **Wines** 88 bottles over £30, 18 bottles under £30, 12 by glass **Parking** 50 **Notes** Tasting menu available (blind tasting), Priory afternoon tea, Sunday L £28, Vegetarian available, Children welcome

The Seaview Hotel & Restaurant

Traditional British

tel: 01983 612711 **High St PO34 5EX**
email: reception@seaviewhotel.co.uk **web:** www.seaviewhotel.co.uk
dir: Take B3330 from Ryde to Seaview, left into Puckpool Hill, follow signs for hotel

Satisfying hotel cooking in a charming fishing village

On the eastern side of the island, the little fishing village of Seaview boasts a namesake hotel, overlooking the waters of the Solent and their hypnotically bobbing boats. Inside, there's quite a complex of bars and dining rooms (two of the latter), but you can pretty much set up camp wherever you like. Fish and seafood specialities are a strong suit, so expect hearty classic fish soup with plenty of rouille, Gruyère and croutons, and mains such as sea bream with roast fennel, chargrilled potatoes, samphire and celery leaf in a gorgeously rich lobster cream sauce. Meats offer a world of satisfaction too though, as with slow-roast pork belly and Savoy cabbage in a grain mustard and shallot sauce, or loin and stew of local venison with braised red cabbage and roasted veg, sauced with red wine. When it comes to the temptation end of the menu, there's properly fragile pannacotta, served with poached rhubarb, rhubarb ice cream and almond crunch.

Chef Alan Staley **Owner** B E F Gardener **Seats** 70, Pr/dining room 25 **Times** 12-2.30/6.30-9.30 Closed 23-27 Dec **Prices** Prices not confirmed, Service optional **Wines** 10 bottles over £30, 16 bottles under £30, 5 by glass **Parking** 8 **Notes** Sunday L, Vegetarian available, Children welcome

Map 5 SZ57

The Hambrough

— see opposite

The Leconfield

Traditional British V

tel: 01983 852196 **85 Leeson Rd, Upper Bonchurch PO38 1PU**
email: enquiries@leconfieldhotel.com **web:** www.leconfieldhotel.com
dir: Situated Upper Bonchurch on A3055, 1m from Ventnor, 2m from Shanklin opposite turning, Bonchurch Shute

Reassuringly homely cooking overlooking the Channel

On the south-facing side of the Isle of Wight, the picture-perfect Leconfield hotel is covered with climbing foliage. It sits above the village of Bonchurch looking out over the Channel, with inspiring views from the Seascape dining room and the conservatory. With service nicely pitched between formal and relaxed, and glass-topped tables on wicker supports, it's the setting for carefully wrought cooking that has a reassuring touch of the homely to it. A bowl of broccoli and Stilton soup delivers the right savoury, salty hit, or there may be mushrooms sautéed in smoked garlic and served on toasted brioche, followed by poached salmon in caper and lemon butter with puréed spinach, or slow-cooked leg of lamb on parsnip mash with redcurrant gravy. A rum-laced chocolate pot comes with matching ice cream and a sweet-and-sour berry compôte to make a satisfying array of flavours. Home-made breads add to the welcome sense of being looked after.

Chef Cheryl Judge **Owner** Paul & Cheryl Judge **Seats** 26 **Times** 6.30-8 Closed 24-26 Dec, 3 wks Jan, L all week (ex by prior arrangement) **Prices** Starter £5.50-£7.50, Main £18.50-£26.50, Dessert £6.50, Service optional **Wines** 3 bottles over £30, 30 bottles under £30, 7 by glass **Parking** 14 **Notes** No children

The Pond Café

Modern European

tel: 01983 855666 & 856333 **Bonchurch Village Rd, Bonchurch PO38 1RG**
email: reservations@robert-thompson.com
dir: *A3055 to Leeson Rd follow Bonchurch signs until village turn off*

Intimate little venue with an eclectic menu

In the tranquil environs of Bonchurch, The Pond is the sister venue to The Hambrough. It's a simpler set-up as the café designation indicates, with candles and intimate proportions adding a romantic charm, and there's an outdoor terrace for those balmier days. The menu offers a pleasing array of rustic Italian dishes and simple stone-baked pizza – anchovies, oregano and capers, anyone? Beef from the island provides the main component for a classic carpaccio served with shaved parmesan and – more unusually – pickled and raw beetroot. Given the proximity to the briny all around, fish has to be a good bet, and here it is in the form of grilled plaice with salsa verde, lentils and sun-blushed tomatoes, or there could be roasted local pigeon with pancetta and cavolo nero. At the end, there's lemon tart with mascarpone sorbet, or pears poached in mulled wine, partnered with zabaglione and crunchy almonds.

Times 12-2.30/6-9.30

The Royal Hotel

Modern British

tel: 01983 852186 **Belgrave Rd PO38 1JJ**
email: enquiries@royalhoteliow.co.uk **web:** www.royalhoteliow.co.uk
dir: *On A3055 (coast road) into Ventnor. Follow one-way system, left at lights into Church St. At top of hill left into Belgrave Rd, hotel on right*

Contemporary cooking in a reassuringly old-fashioned setting

The Royal is a stone-built pile nestling amid sub-tropical gardens on the Isle of Wight's south-eastern coast, a spot that unblushingly styles itself 'the Madeira of England'. It's a formal seaside hotel in the classic manner, with beautifully turned-out interiors and a thoroughgoing professionalism in the service style, best seen in the Appuldurcombe Restaurant, where tied drapes, crisp table linen and little flower vases compose a picture of reassuring civility. The menus are distinctly in the contemporary vein, though, with seafood a particular forte. There is as much intuitive precision in balancing flavours and seasonings in a classical fish soup with rouille as there is in the succeeding dish of roast sea bass accompanied by a portion of moules marinière, saffron potatoes and samphire. Meats are given more traditional treatments, as when roast loin and braised neck of local lamb arrive with baby artichokes and some of the island's celebrated wild garlic, while desserts aim to cosset with the likes of baked almond ricotta cheesecake with roasted peach and nectarine, and raspberry sorbet.

Times 12-1.45/6.45-9 Closed 2 wks Jan or 2 wks Dec, L Mon-Sat

The Hambrough

VENTNOR   **Map 5 SZ57**

Modern British v

tel: 01983 856333 **Hambrough Rd PO38 1SQ**
email: info@thehambrough.com **web:** www.thehambrough.com
dir: *From A3055 follow signs to Ventnor & St Catherine's Church, turn right into Hambrough Rd, restaurant on left*

Creative modern cooking overlooking the sea

The Hambrough is a classy boutique hotel which feels as natural and organic as the gentle sea breeze. It's as if the old Victorian villa was built for such a role in life. The location above the esplanade gives views across the harbour to the open sea, and the decor maintains the seaside-feel with neutral tones and arty touches here and there. The restaurant is made up of two rooms, with sea views to the max and bags of style. The cooking of head chef Darren Beevers is thoroughly contemporary, with a tasting menu and carte to choose from, each packed with a good showing of seafood from local boats. Things get off to a strong start with amuse-bouche such as wild garlic soup with asparagus and Ventor crab with wild garlic flowers, plus excellent breads flavoured with lovage or wild garlic. Pollock is smoked on the island and arrives in a first course with roasted mussels, curry spices and coconut, while a perfectly timed slow-cooked duck egg comes with shredded ham hock and celeriac velouté. Main courses are equally rooted in the environment, with the day boats out of Ventnor providing sea bass, served with roasted cauliflower and chicken wings, or a super-fresh piece of skate partnered with wild rice, crispy kale, a subtle korma sauce and coconut foam. There are good meat options too, with the island's farmers also doing their bit – beef fillet, for example, with braised oxtail, sweet onion, potato fondants and blueberries. The craft and creativity continues into the dessert stage, where custard tart comes with lime and Earl Grey ice cream, and a chocolate tart is topped with imperial mint jelly and comes with an excellent blood orange sorbet. There's a good value lunch menu and even the option of afternoon tea with that sea view.

Chef Darren Beevers **Owner** Kevin Suvismilch **Seats** 32, Pr/dining room 22
Times 12-1.30/6.30-9.30 Closed Sun-Mon **Prices** Fixed L 2 course £25, Fixed D 3 course £55, Tasting menu £55, Starter £8-£12, Main £15-£30, Dessert £8-£12, Service optional **Wines** 70 bottles over £30, 8 bottles under £30, 10 by glass
Parking On street **Notes** Children welcome

YARMOUTH

Map 5 SZ38

The George Hotel

◉◉ British, Mediterranean

tel: 01983 760331 **Quay St PO41 OPE**
email: res@thegeorge.co.uk web: www.thegeorge.co.uk
dir: *Between castle & pier*

Refined seasonal cookery on The Solent

Window seats are at a premium in The George's bright, conservatory-style brasserie – hardly surprising when you look at the location: smack on the water's edge overlooking the yachtie comings and goings on The Solent, the sweeping views extend over immaculate lawns to the castle, quay and pier beyond. Comfy banquettes, bare wooden tables, neutral colours and contemporary art set the scene for bright European-accented brasserie ideas punctuated with materials from the bountiful local larder. Isle of Wight rare-breed pork stars in a terrine served enterprisingly with crisp apple and watercress, raisin purée and cider jelly, or there might be local scallops with roast butternut squash and pancetta risotto. Fish fans will find plenty of interest too: roast organic salmon fillet with crushed new potatoes and smoked bacon and pea velouté scores a hit, or look for locally-landed cod, served with braised fennel, chilli and mint, and tempura oyster. A dessert of poached champagne rhubarb with shortbread biscuit, grenadine crème patissière, and champagne sorbet also passes with flying colours.

Chef Austin Gould **Owner** John Illsley, Jeremy Willcock **Seats** 60 **Times** 12-3/7-9.30 **Prices** Fixed L 2 course fr £22.50, Starter £6-£12, Main £14-£26, Dessert £6-£8, Service optional **Wines** 31 bottles over £30, 12 bottles under £30, 11 by glass **Parking** The Square **Notes** Sunday L £22-£27, Vegetarian available, Children welcome

Looking for a restaurant by name?
Use the index on page 751

Find out more about
how we assess for Rosette awards on page 9

KENT

ASHFORD

Map 7 TR04

Eastwell Manor

◉◉ British, French, European

tel: 01233 213000 **Eastwell Park, Boughton Lees TN25 4HR**
email: enquiries@eastwellmanor.co.uk web: www.eastwellmanor.co.uk
dir: *From M20 junct 9 take 1st left (Trinity Rd). Through 4 rdbts to lights. Left onto A251 signed Faversham. 0.5m to sign for Boughton Aluph, 200yds to hotel*

Creative, classical cooking in a grand manor house

It's a stately pile and no mistake, a breathtaking house with a history that goes back to Norman times. Sure, it has been extended over the years, but it has lost none of its sense of magnificence. The extension means there's room for swish leisure facilities for a start, and it will come as no surprise to hear the place is a popular wedding venue. It stands in over 60 acres of glorious grounds and inside is no less impressive with its ornate plasterwork, carved oak panelling, baronial fireplaces and antiques at every turn. The Manor Restaurant fits in very nicely indeed with its traditional fine-dining finish, and ambitious, well-crafted, gently updated classic cooking. Start with gravad lax with horseradish cream and beetroot purée, or ham hock croquette with carrot and ginger purée and home-made piccalilli, and move on to roast rack of Smarden lamb with braised shoulder confit, red cabbage purée and dauphinoise potatoes. Desserts are equally on the money: warm chocolate fondant, for example, with dark chocolate sauce and tonka bean ice cream.

Chef Gareth Attwell **Owner** Turrloo Parrett **Seats** 80, Pr/dining room 80 **Times** 12-2.30/7-10 **Prices** Prices not confirmed, Service optional 10% **Wines** 163 bottles over £30, 123 bottles under £30, 14 by glass **Parking** 120 **Notes** Gourmet champagne evenings, Sunday L, Vegetarian available, Children welcome

BEARSTED
Map 7 TQ85

Soufflé Restaurant

◉ Modern European

tel: 01622 737065 **31 The Green ME14 4DN**
email: soufflerestaurant@hotmail.co.uk **web:** www.soufflerestaurant.net
dir: M20 junct 7 follow Maidstone signs, bear left towards Bearsted straight over at rdbt, towards Bearsted Green at next mini-rdbt, continue for approx 1.5m to the green. Restaurant on left, turn left just before Soufflé sign & park at rear of restaurant

Updated classics in a friendly and relaxed family-run restaurant

With its quintessentially green and pleasant setting on Bearsted's pretty green, Soufflé is an irresistible prospect, particularly when balmy weather allows alfresco dining on the canopied front terrace. Inside, the 16th-century house is a tangle of low, oak-beamed ceilings and beamed, whitewashed walls; the building was originally a bakery and still has the cast-iron oven set into a bare brick wall. Nick Evenden cooks while his wife Karen takes care of front of house to ensure a friendly and relaxed ambience. It's clearly a formula that works: Soufflé has been a stalwart of the local foodie scene for 15 years, luring in the diners with intelligent cooking that puts a creative spin on classic ideas. Chicken and mushroom terrine with tarragon and mayonnaise dressing sets the ball rolling, followed by baked fillet of pollock topped with tomato fondue and herb crust, with white wine sauce; white chocolate mousse with oranges and Suzette sauce wraps things up in fine style.

Chef Nick Evenden **Owner** Nick & Karen Evenden **Seats** 40, Pr/dining room 25 **Times** 12-2/7-9.30 Closed Mon, L Sat, D Sun **Prices** Prices not confirmed, Service optional **Wines** 20 bottles over £30, 50 bottles under £30, 7 by glass **Parking** 12, On street **Notes** Sunday L, Vegetarian available, Children welcome

BIDDENDEN
Map 7 TQ83

The West House

◉◉◉ – see below

BOUGHTON MONCHELSEA
Map 7 TQ75

The Mulberry Tree

◉◉ Modern British

tel: 01622 749082 & 741058 **Hermitage Ln ME17 4DA**
email: info@themulberrytreekent.co.uk
dir: B2163 turn into Wierton Rd straight over x-rds, 1st left East Hall Hill

Precise, skilful, modern cooking, full of the flavours of Kent

Lost among the back lanes of deepest Kent, the Mulberry Tree's clean-lined modern looks certainly come as a surprise. Inside, the expansive dining area is done out with a light contemporary look – wooden floors, bare wooden tables, and strikingly patterned designer wallpapers. On a mild summer's evening the tranquil garden patio is the place to be. Well-tuned modern British food is what tempts diners out off the beaten track; expect European accents, and staunchly local ingredients from a kitchen that not only bangs the drum for Kent's peerless produce (local suppliers all duly name-checked on the menu), but also tends a kitchen garden and rears its own Kentish Middle White pigs and chickens in a two-acre field behind the restaurant. Skilfully woven flavours and precise timings are the hallmarks of a dinner starting with smoked ham hock and parsley terrine, chicken liver parfait, piccalilli and black pepper crackers, followed by fall-apart tender pork belly with fondant potatoes, apple and kohlrabi salad and apple purée. To finish, vanilla pannacotta comes with almond crumble and a rhubarb-fest of jelly, sorbet and compôte.

Chef Mark Pearson **Owner** Karen Williams & Mark Jones **Seats** 70, Pr/dining room 16 **Times** 12-2/6.30-9.30 Closed 26 Dec, Mon, D Sun **Prices** Fixed L 2 course £15.50, Fixed D 3 course £18.50, Starter £6.95-£8.75, Main £15.95-£21.95, Dessert £6.50, Service optional **Wines** 30 bottles over £30, 31 bottles under £30, 54 by glass **Parking** 60 **Notes** Sunday L £20.50-£23.50, Vegetarian available, Children welcome

The West House

BIDDENDEN
Map 7 TQ83

Modern European v ◖ NOTABLE WINE LIST
tel: 01580 291341 **28 High St TN27 8AH**
email: thewesthouse@btconnect.com
dir: Junct of A262 & A274. 14m S of Maidstone

Vanguard cooking in a charming Kentish village

A generation ago, most of the gastronomic action in the UK took place in the big cities, with grand country-house hotels offering rural retreats when the urge to escape came upon us. These days, country pubs and village restaurants are among the vanguard, being best placed to draw on the local and regional supplies that cutting-edge cookery is all about. Enter the West House, an old beamed edifice in the Kentish wine village of Biddenden, where Flemish weavers' cottages flank the high street, and a sign on the village green commemorates a pair of conjoined twins born in these parts in the twelfth century. If the setting is Old England at its purest, Graham and Jackie Garrett's restaurant-with-rooms is very much a 21st-century operation, for all that the bare floorboards and brick inglenook still speak of centuries gone by. Graham Garrett takes a dynamic

interest in contemporary culinary trends, in which ingredients are explored for the potentialities they might yield when subjected to unusual treatments or brought into interesting alignments with cognate flavours in all sorts of new ways. 'Deconstruction' may be a faintly tedious term now, but as a principle, it works: witness Garrett's take on Caesar salad, with its parmesan pannacotta, scorched lettuce, marinated anchovy and garlic sponge. Fish might appear in voguish 'rockpool' presentation, grilled fillets of white fish alongside squid and pickled seaweed in dashi broth, or in robust Spanish guise, as in roast hake with Ibérico ham, puréed beans and razor-clams. Sika venison with its own little cottage pie is deepened with maple-glazed squash and coffee sauce. Desserts apply the barbecue grill to pineapple, make mousses, ice cream, nuggets and crisps out of milk and honey, or gesture back towards childhood confectionery for a 'Crunchie' of white chocolate and honeycomb parfait.

Chef Graham Garrett, Neil McCue **Owner** Jackie & Graham Garrett **Seats** 32 **Times** 12-2/7-9.30 Closed 24-26 Dec & 1 Jan, Mon, L Sat, D Sun **Prices** Fixed L 3 course £25-£40, Fixed D 3 course £40, Tasting menu £60 **Wines** 54 bottles over £30, 28 bottles under £30, 22 by glass **Parking** 7 **Notes** 6 course £60 (£90 incl wine), Sunday L £35-£40, Children welcome

BRANDS HATCH
Map 6 TQ56

Brandshatch Place Hotel & Spa

◎◎ Modern British

tel: 01474 875000 **Brands Hatch Rd, Fawkham DA3 8NQ**
email: brandshatchplace@handpicked.co.uk
web: www.handpickedhotels.co.uk/brandshatchplace
dir: *M25 junct 3/A20 West Kingsdown. Left at paddock entrance/Fawkham Green sign.*
3rd left signed Fawkham Rd. Hotel 500mtrs on right

Grand location for modern British food

Nothing can disturb the peace at this luxurious and handsome Georgian hotel, not even the iconic racetrack nearby. For here everything is calm, serene and built (by the Duke of Norfolk, no less) with a good deal of panache. It makes a splendid country-house hotel with plenty of room to spread out and forget about the real world. The restaurant is certainly a reason to visit in its own right: with its fine Georgian features, views over the garden, and tables dressed up for the business of fine dining, it's the perfect setting for some smart contemporary cooking. Each dish on the menu comes with an accompanying wine recommendation, and the kitchen sources from Kent where possible. Start, perhaps, with pressed ham hock terrine with home-made piccalilli, or wild garlic and white onion soup. Follow on with a spankingly fresh fillet of hake with kohlrabi fondant, spinach and pancetta, and finish with vanilla pannacotta with a shortbread tuile and blood orange sorbet.

Chef Carl Smith **Owner** Hand Picked Hotels **Seats** 60, Pr/dining room 110 **Times** 12-2/7-9.30 **Prices** Fixed L 2 course £31, Fixed D 3 course £37, Starter £9.95-£12.50, Main £12.95-£26.95, Dessert £7.95-£8.50, Service optional **Wines** 92 bottles over £30, 8 bottles under £30, 18 by glass **Parking** 100 **Notes** Sunday L £23.50, Vegetarian available, Children welcome

CANTERBURY
Map 7 TR15

Abode Canterbury

◎◎ Modern European **NEW** v

tel: 01227 766266 & 826678 **High St CT1 2RX**
email: reservations@abodecanterbury.co.uk web: www.abodecanterbury.co.uk

Boutique hotel with classy cooking

The Abode group of boutique hotels are in a varied mix of buildings, both old and new and here in Canterbury it's most definitely the former – a historic structure within the ancient city walls and only a short distance from the cathedral. There's a pub – The Old Brewery Tavern – plus a glam champagne and cocktail bar, but the main event is the Michael Caines Restaurant. There's a contemporary finish to the room, with polished wooden floors, leather seating and an absence of starchy linen, while the menus run to a carte, tasting versions and a pre-theatre option. The cooking is rooted in classical ways updated for our times. Start with chicken liver and duck liver parfait (pretty as a picture) topped with a Madeira jelly and served with greenbeans in a truffle dressing, before a main course such as a wonderfully flavoured 35-day matured rump of Kentish beef with Anna potatoes and salsify. To finish, the balance of sweet and sharp is spot on in a dish of apple mousse with caramelised apple and green apple sorbet.

Chef Jauca Catalin **Owner** Andrew Brownsword **Seats** 76 **Times** 12-2.30/5.30-9.30 Closed D Sun **Prices** Fixed L 2 course £14.45-£18.50, Fixed D 3 course £19.95-£45, Tasting menu £55-£65, Service optional 12% **Wines Parking** 12 **Notes** Sunday L £16.95-£21.95, Children welcome

The Dove Inn

◎ British, French

tel: 01227 751360 **Plum Pudding Ln, Dargate ME13 9HB**
email: doveatdargate@hotmail.com
dir: *6m NW of Canterbury. A299 Thanet Way, turn off at Lychgate service station*

Attractive food-focused country pub

Head down the evocative-sounding PlumPudding Lane in the village of Dargate and you'll find this splendid Georgian country pub. It's got a lovely rural aspect and a charmingly respectable rusticity to its interior, and the focus is very much on food. Sit at a chunky wooden table, or outside if the weather is playing ball, and tuck into some intelligently put together food, much of it sourced locally (some of it from the pub's own garden), and cooked with flair. You might start with smoked haddock macaroni with a poached duck egg, or pumpkin and sage risotto flavoured with truffle oil, and move on to roasted marsh lamb with black cabbage and pearl barley, or breast of local duck with potato gratin and purple spouting broccoli. The menu shows British and French leanings, not least at dessert stage where you might find a classic crème brûlée with home-made shortbread, or lemon posset with vanilla cream cheese mousse.

Times 12-2.30/7-9 Closed Mon, D Sun, Tue

The Goods Shed Restaurant

◎ British

tel: 01227 459153 **Station Road West CT2 8AN**
email: restaurant@thegoodsshed.co.uk
dir: *Adjacent to Canterbury West train station*

Farmers' market menu at the railway station

The permanent farmers' market that opened next to Canterbury West station in 2002 was a great idea. It has helped to showcase a generation of British artisan farm produce, as well as offering an on-site restaurant elevated above the market floor. Chunky wood tables with views through majestic arched windows over the comings and goings below are a inspired setting for cooking using that market produce to the full, the selections changing with every service. Start with scallops thermidor, or a crab and tarragon 'risotto' of bulghur wheat, before main courses that go the distance with pedigree meats like 24-day ribeye in Colston Bassett Stilton butter, or rack of lamb with prunes and pine nuts. Fish might be hake with curried mussels, and dessert a satisfyingly tart Bramley apple crème brûlée with cinnamon shortbread. Hearty breakfasts incorporate bubble-and-squeak in among all the usual suspects, and are served up to 10.30am.

Chef Rafael Lopez **Owner** Rafael Lopez **Seats** 80 **Times** 12-2.30/6-12 Closed 25-26 Dec, 1-2 Jan, Mon, D Sun **Prices** Starter £6-£10, Main £13-£22.50, Dessert £6.50-£8.50, Service optional **Wines** 10 bottles over £30, 27 bottles under £30, 10 by glass **Parking** 40 **Notes** Banquet menu £35, Sunday L £13.50-£22.50, Vegetarian available, Children welcome

CRANBROOK
Map 7 TQ73

Apicius

◎◎◎ *– see opposite*

DARTFORD
Map 6 TQ57

Rowhill Grange Hotel & Utopia Spa

Modern European V

tel: 01322 615136 **Wilmington DA2 7QH**
email: admin@rowhillgrange.com **web:** www.alexanderhotels.co.uk
dir: M25 junct 3, take B2173 towards Swanley, then B258 towards Hextable. Straight on at 3 rdbts. Hotel 1.5m on left

Soothing modernised dishes in Kentish rural tranquillity

A Georgian house set in acres of trimly manicured grounds, complete with a duck-dotted lake, Rowhill certainly has the virtue of rural tranquillity going for it. Its principal dining room, RG's, is a gently lit space done in mother-of-pearl shades, with quality table linen and modern artworks. The kitchen works to today's best-practice watchwords of seasonality and regionality and modernising takes on bastions of culinary tradition. Thus, green pea soup comes garnished with a poached egg and truffle oil, or smoked salmon with a pickled cucumber salad, for starters. Mains go in for soothing textures and classic combinations, as when butter-poached South Coast lobster is served on linguine with spinach and beetroot purée, or poached and grilled chicken is supported by truffled potatoes and peas and broad beans with pancetta. A slate of grill options for mixing and matching with sauces is a popular feature.

Chef Luke Davis **Owner** Peter & Deborah Hinchcliffe **Seats** 100, Pr/dining room
Times 12-2.30/7-9.30 **Prices** Prices not confirmed **Wines** 37 bottles over £30, 21 bottles under £30, 8 by glass **Parking** 300 **Notes** Sunday L, Children 16 yrs+ D

DEAL
Map 7 TR35

Dunkerleys Hotel & Restaurant

Modern British

tel: 01304 375016 **19 Beach St CT14 7AH**
email: ddunkerley@btconnect.com **web:** www.dunkerleys.co.uk
dir: Turn off A2 onto A258 to Deal - situated 100yds before Deal Pier

Seafood-based menu in a long-running seafront hotel

Run with down to earth friendliness for over a quarter of a century by Ian and Linda Dunkerley, this relaxed and homely seafront hotel in Deal has hit on a winning formula. The place exudes a jauntily inviting air, with its flagpoles and flower-baskets, and the newly refurbed dining room looks the part, with smart white linen and high-backed chairs; on a fine day, the Kentish sunshine might tempt you out on to the terrace. Fuss-free dishes bring fresh local materials together in well-balanced combinations, and in Deal, seafood has got to be the main deal, getting the show on the road with the likes of seared scallops with Bramley apple and sloe gin purée. The main event might star roast sea bass fillet with carrot and star anise purée and shaved fennel, or a whole Dover sole grilled with parsley butter. If you want to get you teeth into something meaty, there's roast rack of herb-crusted lamb with ratatouille and Bordelaise potatoes, and to finish, perhaps cinnamon crème brûlée with praline ice cream.

Chef Ian Dunkerley, Josh Hackett **Owner** Ian & Linda Dunkerley **Seats** 50
Times 12-2.30/7-9.30 Closed Mon, D Sun **Prices** Fixed L 2 course fr £11.95, Fixed D 3 course £28.50-£38.50, Service optional **Wines** 24 bottles over £30, 61 bottles under £30, 9 by glass **Parking** Public car park adjacent **Notes** Sunday L £11.95-£15.95, Vegetarian available, Children welcome

Apicius

CRANBROOK
Map 7 TQ73

Modern European
tel: 01580 714666 **23 Stone St TN17 3HF**
dir: In town centre, opposite Barclays Bank, 50yds from church

Imaginative star quality in a small high-street venue

The high street of a sleepy Kentish village may not seem the most obvious place to set up a high-flying restaurant, but it does mean that the peerless produce of the Garden of England and the hills and coast of Sussex is practically on the doorstep. Tables are booked weeks ahead for weekend dining, so it's clear that chef-patron Timothy Johnson has conjured a winning formula. The name references a Roman gourmet and all-round bon viveur, and the setting is smart and neat and charming. It's an intimate room painted white, the tables neatly draped in white linen and framed menus on the walls showing that the owner's love of the culinary arts runs deep: he's worked with some top chefs in his time. There are only 30 covers so the kitchen can concentrate on squeezing every molecule of flavour from the high quality ingredients that underpin every dish. Expect cooking that is bright, bold, and with a focus and clarity that never fails to impress: a starter of deep-fried lamb's sweetbreads, for example, with celeriac

purée, parsley salad and garlic crisps is a dish with real heart and soul. Ham hock ballotine is another first course packed with flavour, coming with the luxury of seared foie gras, apple purée and pea velouté. Francophile leanings and robust, thrilling flavours are a hallmark – roast and confit wild duck, say, with turnip galette, caramelised ceps, pak choi and soy dressing. Fish is cooked with flair, too: monkfish, perhaps, in a main course with braised Puy lentils, pancetta, artichoke purée and red wine jus. Desserts show no less astute thinking and precise execution: Reblochon cheesecake with poached winter rhubarb and lime sauce anglaise, for example, or dark chocolate ganache with griottine cherries, salted candied walnuts, walnut coulis and tarragon ice cream.

Chef Timothy Johnson **Owner** Timothy Johnson, Faith Hawkins **Seats** 30
Times 12-2/7-9 Closed 2 wks Xmas-New Year, 2 wks summer, Mon-Tue, L Sat, D Sun **Prices** Prices not confirmed **Wines** 19 bottles over £30, 11 bottles under £30, 10 by glass **Parking** Public car park at rear **Notes** Sunday L, Vegetarian available, No children

DOVER
Map 7 TR34

The Marquis at Alkham

@@@ – see below

Wallett's Court Country House Hotel & Spa

@@ Modern British

tel: 01304 852424 **Westcliffe, St Margaret's-at-Cliffe CT15 6EW**
email: dine@wallettscourt.com **web:** www.wallettscourthotelspa.com
dir: M2/A2 or M20/A20, follow signs for Deal (A258), 1st right for St-Margaret's-at-Cliffe. Restaurant 1m on right

Creative cooking in historic manor

The unassuming whitewashed exterior of this family-run country-house hotel hides a 17th-century Jacobean manor, but if staying in a room built of ancient bricks and mortar is too prosaic for your tastes, you could go 'glamping' in a Navajo tipi in the lovely grounds instead. At dinner, though, it's back to the past among the oak beams, inglenook fireplaces and candlelit tables of the romantic restaurant, where the modern British idiom gets a workout to produce dishes based on carefully-sourced materials from Kent and Sussex. The kitchen keeps things straightforward, setting off along the lines of Kentish rabbit terrine with tarragon emulsion and toasted sourdough bread, followed, perhaps, by a 40-day-matured sirloin of Sussex Red beef with roasted salsify, girolles, pommes purées and Madeira jus. In winter, there may be Christmas pudding soufflé with mulled wine sorbet and brandy sauce to wrap things up.

Times 12-2.30/7-9 Closed 25-26 Dec, L Mon-Sat (ex group bookings 10+)

EDENBRIDGE
Map 6 TQ44

Haxted Mill Restaurant

@ Modern French, Mediterranean

tel: 01732 862914 **Haxted Rd TN8 6PU**
email: david@haxtedmill.co.uk
dir: M25 junct 6, A22 towards East Grinstead. Through Blindley Heath, after Texaco garage left at lights, in 1m 1st left after Red Barn PH. 2m to Haxted Mill

A taste of the Med in an idyllic rural English setting

What a setting for a summery meal: the rustic, white-painted weatherboarded building (the stables of a former millhouse) reveals its trump card when you proceed through to the terrace overlooking the mill pond and gently-trickling River Eden. The owners aim to recreate the laid-back ambience of a Mediterranean fish restaurant transposed to the quintessentially English countryside, and it is indeed an irresistible prospect on a balmy summer's evening as the sun sets over the lush Kentish meadows. Shawls are on hand if it gets a bit nippy, or if the season makes alfresco dining a complete no-no, the place is none too shabby indoors, with its beamed ceilings and cosseting, romantic ambience. And as for that summer's day dinner? How about the classic simplicity of super-fresh chargrilled sardines pointed up with tangy sauce vierge, followed by pan-roasted Gers chicken with girolle mushrooms, roast new potatoes and broccoli? To wrap things up an impeccably seasonal note, there's summer pudding with cream.

Times 12-2/7-9 Closed 23 Dec-1 Apr, Mon, D Sun

The Marquis at Alkham

DOVER
Map 7 TR34

Modern British ▮ NOTABLE WINE LIST
tel: 01304 873410 **Alkham Valley Rd, Alkham CT15 7DF**
email: reception@themarquisatalkham.co.uk **web:** www.themarquisatalkham.co.uk
dir: M20 continue to A2. Take A260 exit & turn on to the Alkham Valley Rd

Creative cooking and boutique chic deep in the Kent countryside

This former boozer has left its hard drinking days behind and become a super-smart restaurant with boutique rooms. The bar is still open to non-residents, which is great, but it isn't a pub in the old sense. Right in the heart of the village, there is a terrace and garden serving up views over the Alkham Valley, and once inside expect whitewashed walls broken up with splashes of modern art, wooden floors, stylish furnishings, classy fabrics and subtle lighting. It's smart, contemporary and rather glamorous. There are designer bedrooms, plus accommodation in two cottages at the restaurant's nearby sister business, the Chalksole Estate Vineyard. In the kitchen, Yorkshireman Charles Lakin flies the flag for local Kentish ingredients, producing robust, modern plates of food that really hit the mark. There's a tasting menu if you want to go the whole hog, and a '10 mile' lunch menu which is quite brilliant value for money, comprising produce

drawn from within a ten mile radius of the restaurant. Meanwhile, on the à la carte menu, there's no lack of regional bias and some really creative ideas. Crisp pig's trotter with quail's eggs, piccalilli and creeping Charlie (from the mint family) is a first course with resounding flavours, or go for a veggie dish with a poached duck's egg, celeriac, pickled hedgehog mushrooms and wheat flakes. Main courses are no less assertive and appealing. Try braised leg of Kentish hare, perhaps, with shepherd's pie and fillet, or fillet of pollock with purple potato terrine, mussels and coastal vegetables. This cooking has strident flavours, local influence and a lightness of touch. For dessert, Gadd's ale cake with vintage Ashmore cheese ice cream, apple terrine and mulled raisins confirms the craft and creativity here runs deep.

Chef Charles Lakin **Owner** Tony Marsden & Hugh Oxborrow **Seats** 60, Pr/dining room 20 **Times** 12-2.30/6.30-9 Closed L Mon **Prices** Fixed L 2 course £9.50, Tasting menu £30-£55, Starter £7.95-£14, Main £17.50-£25, Dessert £7-£9.75 **Wines** 173 bottles over £30, 23 bottles under £30, 12 by glass **Parking** 26 **Notes** Sunday L £19.50-£26.50, Vegetarian available, Children 8yrs+

EGERTON
Map 7 TQ94

Frasers
◉ Modern British **NEW**

tel: 01233 756122 **Coldharbour Farm TN27 9DD**
email: lisa@frasers-events.co.uk **web:** www.frasers-events.co.uk
dir: *Phone for detailed directions*

Seasonal eating on an industrious Kentish farm

Adam and Lisa-Jane Fraser are second-generation farmers on a Kentish estate that was founded by Adam's father John, the family being widely known for the House of Fraser group that grew from modest Victorian origins. Where once there was a couple of dairy herds, there is now a large-scale agricultural enterprise supplying many local pubs and turning out its own product lines of breads and preserves. A hotel and cookery school are part of the operation, along with a dining room that hosts regular gourmet evenings, and offers a regular seasonal menu. Proceedings might open with a prawn trio, comprising sautéed, tempura-battered and a mini-cocktail, before moving on to herb-crusted rack of Romney lamb with dauphinoise and cumin and honey carrots, a casserole of local game with a mustardy gratin top, or perhaps teriyaki salmon with oriental salad and rice noodles. To finish, there are Kentish cheeses on hand for those determined to resist the allure of panettone bread-and-butter pudding glazed in vintage marmalade, served with Jersey cream.

Chef Alan Egan **Owner** Lisa-Jane & Adam Fraser **Seats** 30, Pr/dining room 50 **Times** 12.30-3/6.30-9 Closed L subject to private functions, D subject to private functions **Prices** Tasting menu £55-£75, Starter £6.50-£8.50, Main £15.50-£24.95, Dessert £6.95-£11.50 **Wines** 6 bottles over £30, 20 bottles under £30, 5 by glass **Parking** 30 **Notes** Brunch & afternoon tea available, Vegetarian available, Children welcome

FAVERSHAM
Map 7 TR06

Read's Restaurant
◉◉ Modern British ▮ NOTABLE WINE LIST

tel: 01795 535344 **Macknade Manor, Canterbury Rd ME13 8XE**
email: enquiries@reads.com
dir: *From M2 junct 6 follow A251 towards Faversham. At T-junct with A2 (Canterbury road) turn right. Hotel 0.5m on right*

Refined modern British cooking in an elegant Georgian manor

Chef-patron David Pitchford's Georgian manor house has long been a Kentish destination for those in the know. Set in lush grounds, which provide much of the fresh produce used in the kitchen, it feels like a remote country retreat, and is run with the kind of friendly, grown-up affability we hope to find in such places. Old-school refinement is the name of the game, the dining rooms done out with elegant, understated style and flooded with light from floor-to-ceiling sash windows. Read's was doing modern British cooking before many others had cottoned on to it, the dishes carefully composed and based on sound culinary tradition. Haddock fishcakes arrive in a crispy crumb shell with zingy home-made tomato ketchup, followed by a super-fresh pan-fried fillet of locally-caught hake with braised coco beans, salsify and a dry Vermouth sauce. A short wait for dessert is amply rewarded with an apricot soufflé, cooked to order and matched with rich and creamy vanilla ice cream slotted into the centre of the soufflé to melt and mingle. A splendid wine list completes the picture.

Chef David Pitchford **Owner** David & Rona Pitchford **Seats** 50, Pr/dining room 30 **Times** 12-2.30/7-10 Closed BHs, Sun-Mon **Prices** Fixed L 3 course £26, Fixed D 3 course £60, Tasting menu £60, Service optional **Wines** 100 bottles over £30, 45 bottles under £30, 18 by glass **Parking** 30 **Notes** Tasting menu 7 course, Vegetarian available, Children welcome

FOLKESTONE
Map 7 TR23

Rocksalt Rooms
◉◉ Modern British

tel: 01303 212070 **2 Back St CT19 6NN**
email: info@rocksaltfolkestone.co.uk **web:** www.rocksaltfolkestone.co.uk
dir: *M20 junct 13, follow A259 Folkestone Harbour, then left to Fish Market*

Fabulous harbourside setting and a local flavour

The niftily-designed building right on the harbour is actually cantilevered out over the water, so if you're lucky enough to bag a table on the terrace, you're right over the briny. It's a great building, with a huge glass wall to make the most of the view over the boats in the harbour and open sea beyond, and a smart, well-designed interior. Chef Mark Sergeant is a Ramsay protégé with a passion for provenance, and here he's able to grab the freshest possible seafood from local boats and harvest herbs and some vegetables from a farm under the same ownership as the restaurant. Seafood gets a good showing on the menu, but there's also salt marsh lamb shank hotpot or a Boston rib steak to keep all comers happy. Start with potted Dungeness shrimps or Rocksalt fish soup, and move on to herb-crusted Folkestone cod with razor clams and ransoms, or pan-fried red gurnard with cockles and sea purslane. For dessert, a Kentish gypsy tart or lemon meringue pie.

Times 12-3/6.30-10

GRAFTY GREEN
Map 7 TQ84

Who'd A Thought It
◉ Modern British **V**

tel: 01622 858951 **Headcorn Rd ME17 2AR**
email: joe@whodathoughtit.com **web:** www.whodathoughtit.com
dir: *M20 junct 8, A20 towards Lenham. 1m take Grafty Green turn, follow brown tourist signs for 4.5m*

Wacky setting for simple contemporary food

The funky approach to interior design at this restaurant with rooms has resulted in a one-off jungle boudoir look involving sexy shades of caramel, chocolate and cream matched with tigerskin seats and leopard print carpets, plushly padded suede booths and walls studded with rhinestones, and low and moody lighting reflected in gilt-framed mirrors. The place is billed as a champagne and oyster bar, so the requisite bivalves and bubbly are a good way to start – native Colchesters and a good choice of fizz by the glass should hit the spot – otherwise the wide-ranging modern menu kicks off with salt and pepper squid with an Asian-inspired salad of lightly-pickled vegetables, lime emulsion and coriander shoots, followed by pork belly braised in Stowford Press cider with red cabbage, baby onions, diced potatoes, parsnip purée, and crackling. It's all full of flavour and well executed, and standards don't slip at dessert either with a properly comforting sticky toffee pudding with butterscotch sauce and toffee ice cream.

Chef Tim Ward **Owner** Joe Mallett **Seats** 50 **Times** 11.30-3/6-9 Closed 1 Jan **Prices** Prices not confirmed, Service optional **Wines** 80 bottles over £30, 23 bottles under £30, 14 by glass **Parking** 45 **Notes** Tasting small plate menu, Sunday L, Children welcome

LENHAM
Map 7 TQ85

Chilston Park Hotel

 Modern British

tel: 01622 859803 **Sandway ME17 2BE**
email: chilstonpark@handpicked.co.uk **web:** www.handpickedhotels.co.uk/chilstonpark
dir: M20 junct 8

Splendid Georgian mansion with elegant restaurant

Chilston Park has been home to a steady procession of nobility and prominent Kentish families through the centuries. Nowadays, the Georgian mansion does business as an upscale country-house hotel tucked away down leafy lanes in the Garden of England. Secluded in 22 acres of sublime landscaped gardens and parkland, its interior brims with enough period authenticity, antiques and oil paintings that you might be inspired to dress as Jane Austen's Mr Darcy or Elizabeth Bennet for dinner in the unique, sunken Venetian-style Culpeper's restaurant. Here ornate plasterwork ceilings, a grand fireplace and fancy crystal chandeliers certainly build a sense of occasion. The kitchen deals in a style of modern British cooking that is clearly rooted in the classics but has no hesitation in sending out some inventive combinations. A summer vegetable risotto is lifted by a punchy parmesan tuile packed with rocket, followed by an assiette of Sussex pork, involving confit belly, tenderloin, and a porky tortellini, matched with celeriac and potato purée and hickory-smoked jus. To finish, a zingy passionfruit soufflé is turbocharged with a passionfruit shot.

Times 7-9.30 Closed L Mon-Sat

MAIDSTONE
Map 7 TQ75

Fish on the Green

British, French

tel: 01622 738300 **Church Ln, Bearsted Green ME14 4EJ**
dir: N of A20 on village green

Refreshingly simple fish and seafood in a Kentish village

The title says it all: the pretty village green setting is English to the core, while the restaurant occupying a converted stable block near the original coaching house, the Oak on the Green, deals in the finest piscine produce. Fish on the Green has netted a strong local fan base – and what's not to like about its fresh, unpretentious interior of whitewashed brick hung with fishy-themed paintings, the smartly-turned-out and clued-up staff, and, of course, the excellent fish and seafood on the menu? Super-fresh materials are treated simply, setting out with pan-fried crab cakes with crayfish salsa and coriander shoots, or potted crab flavoured with nutmeg and lemon butter. Next up, pan-fried wild sea bass fillet is paired with the Mediterranean flavours of roasted fennel, black olive tapenade and red pepper sauce, and if you just don't fancy fish, something like confit free-range pork belly with seared scallops, sweetcorn purée, black pudding mash and sage jus should fit the bill. Finish with blueberry and frangipane tart with blueberry compôte and clotted cream.

Chef Peter Baldwin **Owner** Alexander Bensley **Seats** 50 **Times** 12-2.30/6.30-10 Closed Xmas, Mon (some), D Sun (some) **Prices** Prices not confirmed **Wines** 7 by glass **Parking** 50 **Notes** Vegetarian available, Children welcome

MARGATE
Map 7 TR37

The Ambrette

Modern Indian

tel: 01843 231504 **44 King St CT9 1QE**
email: info@theambrette.co.uk
dir: A299/A28, left into Hawley St B2055. Restaurant on right corner King St

Modern Anglo-Indian food based on prime Kentish produce

At both his restaurant in Rye and here in Margate, Dev Biswal combines modern British and Indian flavours into something which could be described as modern Indian food, but is probably best labelled Anglo-Indian. The decor is more Anglo than Indian, minimally decorated and filled with wooden tables and chairs. The presentation of dishes is more akin to European food as well. However you choose to define it, the combination is a winning one, with bags of flavour and a good amount of Kentish produce on show (the provenance is written up on the menu). A starter of wood pigeon smoked with cloves and marjoram comes with a rosemary and cinnamon-spiced peach, game pâté, pigeon roulade and a garlic and tomato chutney. Among the main courses, slow-cooked leg of mallard is served with spiced courgette, cauliflower purée and a sauce flavoured with lime leaves and lemongrass.

Chef Dev Biswal **Owner** Dev Biswal **Seats** 52 **Times** 11.30-2.30/5.30-9.30 **Prices** Prices not confirmed **Wines** 15 bottles over £30, 20 bottles under £30, 16 by glass **Parking** 10 **Notes** Pre-theatre menu until 6.30 & after 9pm, Sunday L, Vegetarian available, Children welcome

ROCHESTER
Map 6 TQ76

Topes Restaurant

Modern British

tel: 01634 845270 **60 High St ME1 1JY**
email: julie.small@btconnect.com **web:** www.topesrestaurant.com
dir: M2 junct 1, through Strood High St over Medway Bridge, turn right at Northgate onto High St

An atmospheric gem in historic Rochester

On a corner of Rochester's Dickensian High Street, with the castle and cathedral visible through side windows, Tope's occupies a building spanning the 15th to 17th centuries and could be a set for a period drama with its frontage of wonky, sagging timbers – in fact the place gets a mention in Dickens' last novel, *The Mystery of Edwin Drood*. Inside it's a romantic, cosy space with dark linenfold panels and carved black ceiling beams, far from gloomy and medieval-the patina of age is relieved by light colours, an uncluttered modern decor, and the mood is relaxed. Chef-proprietor Chris Small's cooking taps into the current appetite for ingredients-led, unpretentious dishes with forthright flavours. Excellent Kentish produce underpins a starter of king scallops, truffled cauliflower purée, boudin noir and bacon, and chanterelle cream, before main course brings herb-crusted Romney

Marsh lamb rump, matched with a faggot of braised shoulder, sweet potato fondant, Savoy cabbage, cobnuts, bacon and Jerusalem artichoke purée. A rich and indulgent finale of sticky date pudding, butterscotch sauce and tonka bean ice cream wraps things up in fine style.

Chef Chris Small **Owner** Chris & Julie Small **Seats** 55, Pr/dining room 16 **Times** 12-2.30/6.30-9 Closed Mon-Tue, D Sun **Prices** Fixed L 2 course £16, Fixed D 3 course fr £23, Service optional **Wines** 19 bottles over £30, 35 bottles under £30, 10 by glass **Parking** Public car park **Notes** Sunday L £18.50-£23, Vegetarian available, Children welcome

SANDWICH   Map 7 TR35

The Lodge at Prince's
 Modern British

tel: 01304 611118 **Princes Dr, Sandwich Bay CT13 9QB**
email: j.george@princesgolfclub.co.uk **web:** www.princesgolfclub.co.uk
dir: M2 onto A299 Thanet Way to Manston Airport, A256 to Sandwich, follow sign to golf course

Golf-centric hotel with modern brasserie

This newly-built golf and function-orientated hotel hunkers down among the rolling greensward of its championship golf links, which are, of course, reason enough for many guests to come here. But even if mashies and niblicks aren't your bag, there is much to admire in the views across the wide-open dunes to Sandwich Bay and the white cliffs of Ramsgate. On the food front, the smart, contemporary brasserie-styled restaurant deals in creative modern British dishes founded on well-sourced local materials, served in a clean-cut, rather masculine ambience of neutral shades, pale wooden floors and bare darkwood tables. Crown Prince tortellini are filled with pumpkin and served with velvety sage beurre noisette sauce, while a splendid fillet of beef gets unusual treatment-rolled in ash, and matched with wild mushrooms, meadow grass and milk skin; elsewhere, local fish might get a showing-roast brill, for example, partnered with red wine-poached salsify and chanterelles with a truffle dressing. Desserts run to apple crumble soufflé or banana tarte Tatin with banana ice cream.

Chef Michael Fowler **Owner** Mr M McGuirk **Seats** 55, Pr/dining room 20 **Times** 12-2.30/6.30-9 **Prices** Prices not confirmed, Service optional **Wines** 10 bottles over £30, 30 bottles under £30, 8 by glass **Parking** 100 **Notes** Sunday L, Vegetarian available, Children welcome

SITTINGBOURNE   Map 7 TQ96

Hempstead House Country Hotel
Traditional European

tel: 01795 428020 **London Rd, Bapchild ME9 9PP**
email: info@hempsteadhouse.co.uk **web:** www.hempsteadhouse.co.uk
dir: 1.5m from town centre on A2 towards Canterbury

Modern and classical cooking in a Victorian hotel

Lakes Restaurant at this country-house hotel and spa gets its name from the family who built the original property in the mid-19th century. Elaborate swagged drapes hang at the large windows looking out to the grounds, chandeliers add a bit of glitter, and upholstered dining chairs are pulled up to formally set tables. The kitchen takes its cue from the contemporary British repertoire, with seasonality and local produce to the fore. Scallop and apple tartare, for instance, comes with cider and lemon vinaigrette pearls, and venison carpaccio with saffron and yoghurt dressing and beetroot chutney. Ambitious, well-rounded main courses run to an assiette of lamb-shepherd's pie, braised neck and breaded cutlet-on a celeriac cake with kale, and gurnard fillet on spicy lentil stew served with razor clams and sautéed pickled samphire. Close with chocolate and pistachio fondant with mint chocolate ice cream, or rhubarb custard tart.

Chef Paul Field, Peter Gilbey **Owner** Mr & Mrs A J Holdstock **Seats** 70, Pr/dining room 30 **Times** 12-2.30/7-10 Closed D Sun (non residents) **Prices** Fixed L 2 course fr £14.50, Fixed D 3 course fr £27.50, Starter £7.50-£9.50, Main £18.50-£22.50, Dessert fr £7.50, Service optional **Wines** 16 bottles over £30, 53 bottles under £30, 4 by glass **Parking** 200 **Notes** Sunday L fr £19.95, Vegetarian available, Children welcome

TENTERDEN   Map 7 TQ83

Swan English Restaurant
British

tel: 01580 761616 **Chapel Down Winery, Small Hythe Rd TN30 7NG**
email: booking@swanchapeldown.co.uk
dir: B2082 between Tenterden and Rye

Winning winery with an English flavour on the menu

Make sure there's plenty of room in your boot when you visit the Chapel Down winery so you can head home fully stocked. The Swan is an English restaurant on the first floor of a handsome structure of oak and galvanised steel that houses the wine and food shop, and it's a cool and contemporary space with neutral colour tones and lots of natural wood. It's a sibling to The Swan at West Malling (see entry) and treads a thoroughly English furrow. Start with a lobster and crab chowder, perhaps, packed with shellfish, and follow on with honey-roast pork served with a pudding made with smoked bacon, mashed potatoes and grain mustard. For dessert, rhubarb and custard consists of poached fruit and a set vanilla custard. When it comes to drink, how about some refreshing English rosé to start, followed by a nice cool glass of bacchus?

Chef Paolo Rigolli **Owner** Pete Cornwell **Seats** 65, Pr/dining room 20 **Times** 12-3/6-10.30 Closed D Sun-Wed **Prices** Fixed L 2 course fr £14.95, Starter £6.50-£8.75, Main £11-£23, Dessert fr £5.75 **Wines** **Parking** 100 **Notes** Garden menu 2/3 course Mon-Fri 12-3 advance booking req, Sunday L, Vegetarian available, Children welcome

TUNBRIDGE WELLS (ROYAL)   Map 6 TQ53

Hotel du Vin Tunbridge Wells
French, British NOTABLE WINE LIST

tel: 01892 526455 **Crescent Rd TN1 2LY**
email: reception.tunbridgewells@hotelduvin.com **web:** www.hotelduvin.com
dir: Follow town centre to main junct of Mount Pleasant Rd & Crescent Rd/Church Rd. Hotel 150yds on right just past Phillips House

Anglo-French bistro favourites and a vineyard out back

The HdV group's outpost in Royal Tunbridge Wells is a good-looking sandstone mansion built in 1762. It overlooks the broad acres of Calverley Park from the rear, as well as the hotel's own vineyard. The ambience in the Bistro is classically simple, with dark floorboards, creamy walls, gentle lighting and framed prints, and the food follows suit, with a range of Anglo-French bistro favourites. Fish cookery is impressive, as witness a main course of accurately timed monkfish in a Burgundian-influenced sauce comprised of pearl onions, pancetta and wild mushrooms, or you might opt for the house cassoulet, replete with confit duck and Toulouse sausage. Those might be preceded by devilled lamb's kidneys on toast, or beef carpaccio, watercress and parmesan in horseradish dressing, while tarte Tatin with crème Normande makes a punchy finale. It goes without saying that the wine list offers a wide range of styles and prices to suit all budgets and tastes.

Times 12-2.30/5.30-10

TUNBRIDGE WELLS (ROYAL) *continued*

The Spa Hotel

 Modern, Traditional British

tel: 01892 520331 **Mount Ephraim TN4 8XJ**
email: reservations@spahotel.co.uk **web:** www.spahotel.co.uk
dir: *On A264 leaving Tunbridge Wells towards East Grinstead*

Country-house dining beneath crystal chandeliers

Built in the middle of the 18th century, this handsome mansion first opened its doors as a hotel in the Victorian era to capitalise on the perceived value of the waters around here – an original spa hotel. And today's tip-top spa facilities more than meet contemporary expectations. The house stands in 14 acres of grounds – walking is an alternative fitness therapy after all – and inside the place has a good deal of boutique style to go with the impressive Georgian features. The Chandelier Restaurant is appropriately named and comes dressed up in grand style with well-spaced, well-dressed tables. The menu mixes some traditional and contemporary ideas and is based on good quality ingredients. Start with a risotto of mushrooms with pecorino and truffles, or crispy coconut king prawn with chilli and lime dipping sauce, before a grilled sirloin steak or pan-fried lamb fillets with tarragon cream, parsley sponge, potato cake and soft green cabbage.

Times 12.30-2/7-9.30 Closed L Sat

Thackeray's

 – *see below*

WEST MALLING   **Map 6 TQ65**

The Swan

 Modern British

tel: 01732 521910 **35 Swan St ME19 6JU**
email: info@loveswan.co.uk
dir: *M20 junct 4 follow signs for West Malling, left into Swan St. Approx 200yds on left*

Smart modish cooking in a contemporary Kentish inn

The one-time coaching inn got a millennium makeover back in 2000 and was reborn as a bar and brasserie, and all remains well with the world. The classic-looking 15th-century pub on the pretty high street looks great with its stainless steel, granite and wood, funky modern artworks and mirrors beneath the original oak beams. And in the summer the 'secret garden' – well, it's out back – with its decidedly urban-cool vibe is a great spot to chill and be chilled. The menu matches the good-looking, contemporary attitude with a good deal of swagger of its own, which includes some bright ideas, appealing flavour combinations, and plenty of regional ingredients. Beautifully cooked Rye Bay scallops, for example, might turn up in a first course with pork belly, fennel and a nicely-judged harissa, and main course duck (from just down the road) with crumbed confit leg, beets and a rich Madeira jus. For pud, gypsy tart shows fine pastry work and spot-on balance of sweetness with its accompanying bee pollen ice cream and honeycomb.

Chef Scott Goss **Owner** Swan Brasserie Ltd **Seats** 90, Pr/dining room 20 **Times** 12-3.30/5.30-10 Closed 1 Jan, D Sun **Prices** Fixed L 2 course £18, Fixed D 3 course £22, Starter £6-£11.20, Main £13.60-£29.50, Dessert £5-£7 **Wines** 60 bottles over £30, 32 bottles under £30, 17 by glass **Parking** Long-stay car park **Notes** Fixed menu 2 course 5.30-7pm, Sunday L £12.50-£17.50, Vegetarian available, Children welcome

---

Thackeray's

TUNBRIDGE WELLS (ROYAL)   **Map 6 TQ53**

Modern French, European **v**
tel: 01892 511921 **85 London Rd TN1 1EA**
email: reservations@thackerays-restaurant.co.uk
dir: *A21/A26, towards Tunbridge Wells. On left 500yds after the Kent & Sussex Hospital*

Glossy modern French cooking at the novelist's home

Built around 1660, the traditional Kentish white weatherboarded house is the oldest in town, and was home in the Victorian age, as its name proudly indicates, to the author of *Vanity Fair*. Thackeray loved the town, which features in certain of his writings, notably the lesser-known novel *The Virginians*, reminding us that Tunbridge has other strings to its bow than being the home of vituperative letter-writers. In Richard Phillips, the house has a present-day resident luminary too, a chef who has worked at some of London's smartest addresses, and brings glossy, vigorous French modernity to the kitchens here, enjoyable either in the principal low-ceilinged, floral-wallpapered dining room or on the Japanese terrace. Dishes often look like architectural marvels, complexly and painstakingly constructed, but with expertly captured flavours to the fore. How about a terrine of natural smoked haddock and leeks, served with a portion of fried haddock and a confit egg yolk, or a robust starter of rabbit saddle with medjool dates, Gruyère-boosted bread sauce and jus gras? After either of those might come an assiette of Kent's speciality salt marsh lamb – the braised neck, smoked cannon and roasted sweetbreads – with sheep's curd and almond mousse, sprouting broccoli and red peppers – truly a bravura dish. Or try roast monkfish tail with calamari, lemony fennel purée, poached razor clams and avocado mousse in fish-stock velouté. Cheesecakes remain abidingly popular, and it isn't hard to see why when a white chocolate and vanilla version appears with clementine sorbet, spiced tea jelly and the perfume of tarragon. Otherwise, there may be gariguette strawberry salad with ginger granité and ricotta, dressed in aged balsamic. A six-course taster with a pair of choices at most courses is a winning formula, while Sunday lunch brings on thoroughbred roasts such as venison, guinea-fowl, or 28-day Herefordshire beef in red wine jus.

Chef Richard Phillips, Daniel Hatton **Owner** Richard Phillips **Seats** 70, Pr/dining room 16 **Times** 12-2.30/6.30-10.30 Closed Mon, D Sun **Prices** Fixed L 2 course £16.95, Tasting menu £75, Starter £9.95-£11.95, Main £24.95-£28.95, Dessert £10.95 **Wines** 85 bottles over £30, 18 bottles under £30, 25 by glass **Parking** On street in evening, NCP **Notes** Sunday L £28.95, Children welcome

WHITSTABLE   Map 7 TR16

The Sportsman

◉◉ Modern British

tel: 01227 273370 **Faversham Rd, Seasalter CT5 4BP**
email: contact@thesportsmanseasalter.co.uk
dir: *On coast road between Whitstable & Faversham, 3.5m W of Whitstable*

Bracing freshness and absence of pretension in a Kentish pub

The environs of Seasalter have been in the catering trade, one way or another, since the 12th century, when the land provisioned the kitchens of Canterbury Cathedral, struggling to cope with an influx of pilgrim trade following that unpleasant business in 1170. These days, a member of the productive Harris family looks after the white-fronted inn with its glassed-in terrace and blond wood dining room. Simplicity and honest industry reign throughout, from the churning of butter in-house to the willing, warm-hearted staff. Blackboard menus and a seven-course taster offer local farm-grown and sea-sourced produce via straightforward preparations such as grilled slip-sole in seaweed butter, roast chicken with bread sauce, chestnuts and bacon, and seared thornback ray in brown butter, served with cockles and sherry vinegar. The bracing freshness of it all, coupled with the lack of pretentiousness, exercise a potent allure, and there's chocolate to finish, in the form of a warm mousse, accompanied by salted caramel and milk sorbet.

Times 12-2/7-9 Closed 25-26 Dec, 1 Jan, Mon, D Sun

WROTHAM   Map 6 TQ65

The Bull

◉ Modern British

tel: 01732 789800 **Bull Ln TN15 7RF**
email: info@thebullhotel.com **web:** www.thebullhotel.com
dir: *In centre of village*

Contemporary cooking in old village inn

The Bull, a pub in a peaceful village on the North Downs Way (and just off the M20), has a bit of a past. It dates back to the 14th century, and pilgrims to Canterbury would have stopped here; more recently it was a source of solace for Second World War pilots from nearby airfields. It's still a haven, with a popular bar and a beamed restaurant with two wood-burners. The cooking is more cutting edge than might be

expected in a village inn; starters of beetroot-cured gravad lax, or smoked pigeon breast with apple and celeriac remoulade might be followed by sea bass fillet with pancetta and a tarragon and langoustine sauce. Meats are from local farms – pork chop, say, served with a fried duck egg, black pudding and baby vegetables – and puddings such as champagne syllabub are a highlight.

Chef James Hawkes, Ben Richards **Owner** Martin Deadman **Seats** Pr/dining room 12
Times 12-2.30/6-9 **Prices** Starter £7-£7.50, Main £13-£27.50, Dessert £6.50-£8.50
Wines 28 bottles over £30, 29 bottles under £30, 9 by glass **Parking** 18
Notes Sunday L £13-£27.50, Vegetarian available, Children welcome

LANCASHIRE

BLACKBURN   Map 18 SD62

The Clog & Billycock

◉ Traditional British

tel: 01254 201163 **Billinge End Rd, Pleasington BB2 6QB**
email: enquiries@theclogandbillycock.com
dir: *M6 junct 29/M65 junct 3. Follow signs to Pleasington*

Celebrating northern gastronomy in a Lancashire village inn

Nigel Haworth's pint-sized Ribble Valley pub empire includes this efficiently modernised inn in the village of Pleasington near Blackburn (see also entries for The Highwayman and The Three Fishes). Bench seating supplements the jumble of furniture, while big windows let in plenty of light on the boutiquey interiors, where stone tiles and framed pictures of local food heroes are the order of the day. As at the other venues in the group, a redeveloped version of traditional northern fare produces some novel ideas, founded on thoroughgoing celebration of the region's gastronomic heritage. A starter of Scotch egg made with black pudding comes with straw potatoes and mustard mayonnaise served in an eggbox, while mains run to herb-crusted lamb cutlets with hedgerow fruit jelly, or signature dishes such as hotpot, fish pie, and devilled chicken with dripping chips. You'll rarely find a better bowl of trifle than here, made with proper custard, a lovely, slightly sticky jelly, and fresh raspberries.

Chef Matthew Castelli **Owner** Nigel Haworth, Craig Bancroft, Richard Matthewman
Seats 130 **Times** 12-2/5.30-8.30 **Prices** Fixed L 2 course fr £16, Starter £5.75-£8.50,
Main £9.75-£26, Dessert £3.50-£5.50, Service optional **Wines** 5 bottles over £30, 29
bottles under £30, 11 by glass **Parking** 75 **Notes** Seasonal menu available Mon-Thu,
Sunday L £12.50-£19.50, Children welcome

BLACKBURN *continued*

The Millstone at Mellor

◉◉ Modern British

tel: 01254 813333 **Church Ln, Mellor BB2 7JR**
email: info@millstonehotel.co.uk **web:** www.millstonehotel.co.uk
dir: *4m from M6 junct 31 follow signs for Blackburn. Mellor is on right 1m after 1st set of lights*

Fine Lancashire produce in a smart village inn

It's always a treat to find an inn that puts equal importance on food and drink – such is The Millstone. This Ribble Valley local is owned by Thwaites, the renowned Lancashire brewing company, the founding-father of which is buried in the cemetery next door. If you really want to sample the beers, go for the 'Thoroughly Thirds', which is a taster board of three different ales. And the wine list ain't no slouch either. There is a rustic handsomeness to the bar and eating areas, but rough and ready it most certainly is not. Chef-patron Anson Bolton is passionate about produce and the provenance of what turns up on the plate is never in doubt. There are pub classics (Bowland steak, kidney and Thwaites' Wainwright's ale suet pudding), deli boards (local cheeses among them), steaks cooked on the grill, and seasonally-changing dishes such as grilled Middlewhite pork cutlet with black pudding rösti, pork scratching and apple purée. Start with baked goats' cheese on buttered crumpet and finish with baked ginger parkin with cinnamon ice cream and treacle sauce.

Chef Anson Bolton **Owner** Thwaites Inns of Character **Seats** 90, Pr/dining room 20 **Times** 12-9.30 All-day dining **Prices** Starter £4.95-£7.95, Main £9.50-£24.95, Dessert £2.95-£6.95, Service optional **Wines** 9 bottles over £30, 32 bottles under £30, 9 by glass **Parking** 45, On street **Notes** Sunday L, Vegetarian available, Children welcome

---

BURROW Map 18 SD67

The Highwayman

◉ Traditional British

tel: 01524 273338 **LA6 2RJ**
email: enquiries@highwaymaninn.co.uk
dir: *M6 junct 36 to A65 Kirkby Lonsdale, off A683*

Modern Lancashire pub food chez Haworth

One of the four limbs of Nigel Haworth's Ribble Valley Inns (see also entries for The Three Fishes and The Clog & Billycock), the Highwayman is up in the far north of Lancashire, near Kirkby Lonsdale. The atmosphere here is determinedly rural, with foursquare wooden tables and an open fire, for all that it looks so box-fresh. As at the other inns, pictures of local suppliers hang about the place, and the cooking single-mindedly pursues a celebration of the county's produce. A twice-baked cheese soufflé made with Sandham's Lancashire, dressed with a heap of peppery leaves, is a robust starter. Mains include the house fish pie, lamb hotpot, and battered haddock with beef-dripping chips, and there are excellent showcases for individual farm produce, such as lamb's liver and kidneys with streaky bacon, spring onion mash and onion gravy, a hearty main dish. Portions remain heroic to the end indeed, when a large wedge of almond tart turns up steeped in lemon and wild honey, garnished with clotted cream and strawberry jam.

Chef Simon Tracey **Owner** Nigel Haworth, Craig Bancroft, Richard Matthewman **Seats** 120 **Times** 12-2/5.30-8.30 **Prices** Starter £5.50-£8.50, Main £9.50-£18.50, Dessert £5-£6, Service optional **Wines** 5 bottles over £30, 28 bottles under £30, 11 by glass **Parking** 45 **Notes** Fixed L & D Tue-Thu, Sunday L £16-£19.50, Vegetarian available, Children welcome

---

CHORLEY Map 15 SD51

The Red Cat

◉◉ Modern British V

tel: 01257 263966 **114 Blackburn Rd, Whittle-le-Woods PR6 8LL**
email: enquiries@theredcat.co.uk
dir: *M61 junct 8 signed Wheelton, left off A674*

Intelligent modern British cooking in a relaxed setting

If you care about the provenance of your food, The Red Cat will get you purring. Chef-patron Chris Rawlinson makes good use of the region's bounty and delivers some smart modern British food. It all takes place in a former farmhouse, which later earned its crust as a pub, and is now a thriving restaurant. There's a cool and contemporary rustic-chic vibe within, with neutral tones and darkwood tables. There are sound cooking skills on show and no shortage of good ideas. Start, perhaps, with a Goosnargh duck and apricot terrine, which provides satisfying hits from poached black cherries and Valrhona chocolate. Or go for something like Cornish mackerel with basil and feta dressing. Main courses might see a fashionable surf and turf combo, with cod in hazelnut butter partnered with a piece of pork belly with a crisp layer of crackling, while fillet of British beef is enriched with a truffle mash and seared foie gras. Finish with an orange fest: crème brûlée, lollipop, curd and syrup.

Chef Chris Rawlinson **Owner** Chris & Mike Rawlinson **Seats** 50 **Times** 12-2/6-12t Closed Mon-Tue **Prices** Fixed L 2 course £21.50, Fixed D 3 course £26.50, Tasting menu £55, Starter £6.95-£11.95, Main £16.95-£26.95, Dessert £5.95-£8.95 **Wines** 18 bottles over £30, 34 bottles under £30, 9 by glass **Parking** 100 **Notes** Tasting menu 5 course, Sunday L £21.50-£26.50, Children welcome

---

GISBURN Map 18 SD84

Stirk House Hotel

◉ Traditional, Modern

tel: 01200 445581 **BB7 4LJ**
email: reservations@stirkhouse.co.uk **web:** www.stirkhouse.co.uk
dir: *M6 junct 32, W of village, on A59. Hotel 0.5m on left*

Modern Lancashire cooking in a Tudor manor

Deep in the Ribble Valley, and with the Forest of Bowland and Ribble Hill close by, the wild Lancashire setting of 16th-century Stirk House is a treat in itself. The stone manor house comes with a priest-hole within its ancient walls, but otherwise, the place has been revamped in a tasteful contemporary style. Original plasterwork ceilings, wooden floors and an ornate fireplace add character to the restaurant, where friendly young staff are keen to please and well-briefed on the menu. Relying on splendid Lancashire produce, the cooking keeps things classic and straightforward. Smooth chicken liver parfait comes with red onion jam and toasted sourdough bread, followed by roast duck breast matched with fresh cherry compôte, green beans and colcannon mash. Rounding things off, there's white chocolate pannacotta with fresh raspberries and a glass of sweet botrytis Semillon wine, or a slate of Lancashire cheeses with home-made chutney.

Chef Chris Dobson **Owner** Paul Caddy **Seats** 40, Pr/dining room 50 **Times** 12.30-2.30/7-9 Closed Xmas **Prices** Fixed L 2 course fr £16.50, Starter £4.95-£6.75, Main £10.95-£17.75, Dessert £5.95-£7.50, Service optional **Wines** 9 bottles over £30, 23 bottles under £30, 9 by glass **Parking** 300 **Notes** Sunday L £16.50-£19.50, Vegetarian available, Children welcome

Northcote

Northcote Road, Langho, Blackburn, Lancashire BB6 8BE
Tel: 01254 240555 • **Website:** www.northcote.com
Email: reception@northcote.com

Northcote. *Redefined.*

Renowned country-house hotel and Michelin-starred restaurant Northcote has had an exciting 2014 so far.

Following nearly a year of renovations, Northcote has opened a stunning private dining suite The Louis Roederer Room, a destination Cookery School, a refurbished restaurant and added four fabulous new rooms.

This is the new Northcote, an oasis of food, wine and hospitality but with the same dedication to seasonal menus and British produce diners have come to expect from the kitchen of chef patron Nigel Haworth, Managing Director, Craig Bancroft and head chef Lisa Allen.

Enjoy a gourmet break

- Louis Roederer champagne & canapés
- 5-course gourmet or 7-course tasting menu
- Luxurious overnight stay in one of 18 individually designed guest rooms

Or enjoy a celebration event within the ultra-chic confines of *The Louise Roederer Room* – our new private dining suite

LANCASTER
Map 18 SD46

Lancaster House
◉ Traditional British NEW

tel: 01524 844822 & 0845 850 9508 **Green Ln, Ellel LA1 4GJ**
email: reception.lancaster@englishlakes.co.uk web: www.englishlakes.co.uk
dir: *3m from Lancaster city centre. From S M6 junct 33, head towards Lancaster. Continue through Galgate village, turn left up Green Ln just before Lancaster University*

Regional brasserie cooking in a Lancashire event hotel

A little to the west of the M6, and practically on the doorstep of the Lake District, Lancaster House is an events and leisure hotel with up-to-the-minute spa facilities and all the organisational precision to make anything from a conference to a wedding go swimmingly. Foodworks is the promising name of the restaurant, where a relaxed, hang-loose brasserie feel predominates, with unclothed tables and a bar at one end, ornate light fittings and mural graphics of flat-capped folk going about their Lancashire business. Despite the Cantonese name, Damien Ng is Lancashire born and bred, and cooks a seasonal menu of readily understandable brasserie fare such as starters of scallops and black pudding with pancetta, or duck liver parfait with plum purée and poppyseed toast. To follow, try the chargrilled swordfish with cherry tomato relish and noodles fried in sesame oil, chilli and soy, or minted lamb hotpot with silverskin onions, pickled beetroot and buttered kale, an impeccable regional classic. Finish with plum frangipane tart and Amaretto custard.

Chef Damien Ng **Owner** English Lakes Hotels, Resorts and Venues **Seats** 90, Pr/dining room 150 **Times** 12-2/7-9.30 **Prices** Starter £4.50-£8.95, Main £12.25-£22.95, Dessert £5.50-£8, Service optional **Wines** 11 bottles over £30, 32 bottles under £30, 10 by glass **Parking** 130 **Notes** Please phone to check L openings, Sunday L £13.50-£15.50, Vegetarian available, Children welcome

LANGHO
Map 18 SD73

Northcote
◉◉◉◉ – see opposite and advert on page 239

LYTHAM ST ANNES
Map 18 SD32

Bedford Hotel
◉ Modern British

tel: 01253 724636 **307-313 Clifton Drive South FY8 1HN**
email: reservations@bedford-hotel.com web: www.bedford-hotel.com
dir: *From M55 follow signs for airport to last lights. Left through 2 sets of lights. Hotel 300yds on left*

Clearly-focused cooking in seaside resort hotel

Within walking distance of the town's famous golf course (host of the 2012 British Open) and its genteel seafront with lovely sandy beach, the Bedford is a large Victorian hotel with lots going on, from spa and gym to coffee shop. The Cartland Restaurant has plenty of traditional charm, with decorative plasterwork, warm pastel tones, black-and-white prints of film stars and neatly laid tables. The cooking is classically inspired and makes good use of Lancashire produce, ensuring the place keeps a sense of identity. Thus you might start with Lytham shrimp risotto, or local partridge and pheasant in a terrine served with Bramley apple and pear chutney and warm olive bread. Next up, pot-roasted blade of beef, perhaps, with spring onion mash and red wine sauce, or a traditional salmon en croûte with a chive velouté. The good ideas and careful execution continues at dessert stage with the likes of lemon posset with basil sugar.

Chef Paul Curran **Owner** Baker family **Seats** Pr/dining room 120
Times 10-5/6.30-8.30 **Prices** Fixed L 2 course £10-£14, Fixed D 3 course £23.50, Starter £3.95-£8.95, Main £15.50-£22.50, Dessert £4.95-£7.25, Service optional **Wines** 1 bottle over £30, 22 bottles under £30, 4 by glass **Parking** 20, On street (no charge) **Notes** Sunday L, Vegetarian available, Children welcome

Clifton Arms Hotel
◉◉ British

tel: 01253 739898 **West Beach FY8 5QJ**
email: welcome@cliftonarms-lytham.com web: www.cliftonarms-lytham.com
dir: *On A584 along seafront*

Fun contemporary cooking in a genteel Lytham hotel

The present redbrick building dates from the early Victorian era, and arose on the site of what was a small inn as Lytham ascended to the status of Lancashire gentility. It's a refined spot for an upmarket hotel, all the more so for being not a million miles from the hectic hurly-burly of Blackpool. Chic table settings with good napery and floral adornments look the part against the neutral hues of the main dining room, where Justin Jerome delivers contemporary Anglo-French cooking that keeps a weather eye on the seasons. An autumn menu might kick off with chicken liver and foie gras parfait with truffle-buttered toast and madeira jelly. Mains might include a generous tranche of carefully timed halibut with langoustines and saffron mash in a sweet-sour port reduction, or slow-cooked belly and cheek of Old Spot pork with pease pudding, puréed Bramley and pickled carrots. Dessert presentations are fun: imagine a spooky grassy knoll with a crooked tree growing out of the top, and you've pictured something like the chocolate soil, pistachio sponge and yoghurt offering.

Chef Justin Jerome **Owner** David Webb **Seats** 60, Pr/dining room 140
Times 12-2.30/6.30-9 **Prices** Starter £6, Main £14-£24, Dessert £5, Service optional **Wines** 14 bottles over £30, 36 bottles under £30, 12 by glass **Parking** 50
Notes Sunday L £25, Vegetarian available, Children welcome

Greens Bistro
◉ Modern British

tel: 01253 789990 **3-9 St Andrews Road South, St Annes-on-Sea FY8 1SX**
email: info@greensbistro.co.uk
dir: *Just off St Annes Sq*

Charming basement bistro with Lancashire cooking

Paul and Anna Webster's intimate, basement bistro is a popular neighbourhood venue with plenty of smart rustic character thanks to its low ceilings and plenty of little hideaway nooks and alcoves. It's quite the spot for a cosy tête-à-tête, with the reassuring background hum of contented diners and a good buzz and bustle provided by friendly staff who are happy to engage in a bit of chat with customers. The cooking is straightforward, rustic modern bistro food and unapologetically pro-Lancashire in its sourcing of local ingredients. Get things going on a sound footing with a well-made twice-baked Lancashire cheese soufflé with red onion jam and a green salad, ahead of wild sea trout fillet served with sautéed new potatoes, green summer vegetables and hollandaise sauce. Meatier fare might run to medallions of pork tenderloin with bubble-and-squeak, apple and sauce, sage gravy, and Bury black pudding – the best, locals say, but they would, wouldn't they? Home-spun puddings include baked egg custard with seasonal berries and shortbread.

Chef Paul Webster **Owner** Paul & Anna Webster **Seats** 38 **Times** 6-10 **Closed** 25 Dec, BHs, 2 wks Jan, 1 wk summer, Sun-Mon, L all week **Prices** Prices not confirmed, Service optional **Wines** 7 by glass **Parking** On street **Notes** Vegetarian available, Children welcome

Read our interview with chef Michael Caines on page 29

Northcote

LANGHO   **Map 18 SD73**

Modern British V   🍷 NOTABLE WINE LIST

tel: 01254 240555 **Northcote Rd BB6 8BE**
email: reception@northcote.com **web:** www.northcote.com
dir: M6 junct 31, 9m to Northcote. Follow Clitheroe (A59) signs.
Hotel on left before rdbt

Benchmark modern Lancashire food in a stunningly refurbished country-house hotel

The team behind Northcote has built and burnished a reputation for the place that has elevated it into the highest echelon of the Lancashire scene. Rather than resting on laurels, the partnership of culinary maestro Nigel Haworth and wine expert Craig Bancroft has been tirelessly productive since taking over in the 1980s. The pair of them have been a galvanic force in every aspect of the business, from accommodation to cookery classes to dining, the last entrusted these days to head chef Lisa Allen. The house itself began life as the late-Victorian project of a local lady, who soon relinquished it to the successive ownership of a cavalcade of business bigwigs, and yet it's one of those houses that looks as though it was always destined for country-hotel refinement. Development and refurbing continue apace, and the new decor, installed since 2013, is stunning. A cocktail bar, a new chef's table and private dining rooms, as well as new guest rooms, are all on-stream, and the decorative styling is imaginative and colourful throughout. The restaurant has a new front extension featuring a walled terrace and the many windows look out over the gardens and towards the hills that frame the rolling Ribble Valley, the luxuriant external view complemented by a gentle interior tone, all cream-coloured upholstery, panelled pillars and carpeting striped in two shades of grey. Local farmers and breeders, west-coast fishermen and Northcote's own prodigious kitchen gardens supply Lisa Allen with inspiration and raw materials for menus that are securely in the modern idiom, founded on a pulsing backbeat of pure proud Lancashire. Black pudding and buttered pink trout make a pairing attractive to both eye and palate, sauced as they are with a vivid mustardy watercress potion, while Southport shrimps are the mainstay of an organic porridge with tomato, spring onions and tarragon pesto. Fish is always of exemplary freshness, perhaps John Dory and squid with Ibérico ham and smoked onion, or an ingenious scallop Rossini with seaweed and madeira jelly. You can forgive a chef wanting to blow his own trumpet by showcasing an award-winning main dish, and it gives the rest of us the chance to taste what we've seen on TV – thus Haworth's rare loin and slow-cooked belly of lamb that comes with hotpot potatoes and scorched leeks – or there could be fillet and cheek of rare-breed pork, with pearl barley risotto and chorizo. The hot-ticket pudding is apple crumble soufflé with an ice cream of Kirkham's Lancashire cheese.

Chef Nigel Haworth, Lisa Allen **Owner** Nigel Haworth, Craig Bancroft, Richard Matthewman **Seats** 70, Pr/dining room 60 **Times** 12-2/7-9.30 Closed Food & Wine Festival **Prices** Tasting menu £85, Starter £11-£15, Main £28-£40, Dessert £12-£15 **Wines** 359 bottles over £30, 31 bottles under £30, 12 by glass **Parking** 60 **Notes** Fixed Gourmet D 5 course £60, Sesonal L 3 course £27.75, Sunday L fr £36, Children welcome

| THORNTON | Map 18 SD34 |

Twelve Restaurant and Lounge Bar

@@ Modern British

tel: 01253 821212 **Marsh Mill Village, Marsh Mill-in-Wyre, Fleetwood Road North FY5 4JZ**
email: info@twelve-restaurant.co.uk **web:** www.twelve-restaurant.co.uk
dir: *A585 follow signs for Marsh Mill Complex. Turn right into Victoria Rd East, entrance 0.5m on left*

Stimulating modern cooking in contemporary setting

Virtually under the sails of an 18th-century windmill, Twelve has an ultra-modern, stripped-down sort of look, with exposed air ducts and beams, brick walls, slate flooring, sleek designer furniture and pop art on the walls. Chef-proprietor Paul Moss works in association with regional producers and suppliers, and his bold cooking style is as contemporary as the surroundings. Poached breast of quail with a quail sausage (actually mousse in pancetta), served with light blue cheese gnocchi and textures of pear, is a highly worked starter of clear and clean flavours, as is goats' cheese pannacotta with caramelised walnuts, pickled beetroot and red chard. Main courses are a blend of up-to-date concepts and more traditional ideas. So haunch of venison, with chocolate, beetroot and salsify, might be offered alongside a deconstructed version of fish pie — accurately poached cod fillet with pieces of bacon topped with grilled mash, the plate dotted with green vegetables, all hitting the palate buttons — or 'three bits of pig' (belly, head and fillet) with crackling and apple gel. End with a stylish pudding like vanilla parfait with coffee ice cream and vodka gel.

Chef Paul Moss **Owner** Paul Moss & Caroline Upton **Seats** 90 **Times** 12-3/6.30-12 Closed 1st 2 wks Jan, Mon, L Tue-Sat **Prices** Fixed D 3 course £23-£24.95, Starter £5.95-£10.95, Main £14.95-£24.95, Dessert £5.95-£8.50, Service optional **Wines** 18 bottles over £30, 39 bottles under £30, 12 by glass **Parking** 150 **Notes** Sunday L £17.50-£23, Vegetarian available, Children welcome

See advert below

TWELVE
RESTAURANT & LOUNGE BAR

- Situated beneath a beautifully restored 18th century windmill
- Contemporary- styled restaurant and lounge bar
- 5 minute drive from Blackpool
- Traditional British cuisine with a modern twist using fresh seasonal produce

OPEN
Tuesday – Sunday evenings for dinner
and Sundays 12pm – 2pm

AWARDS
2 AA Rosettes   2007 – 2014

WE ARE LOCATED
Marsh Mill Village
Thornton Cleveleys
Lancashire
FY5 4JZ

TEL 01253 82 12 12 | www.twelve-restaurant.co.uk

WHALLEY
Map 18 SD73

The Freemasons at Wiswell
 – *see below*

The Three Fishes
British

tel: 01254 826888 **Mitton Rd, Mitton BB7 9PQ**
email: enquiries@thethreefishes.com
dir: *M6 junct 31, A59 to Clitheroe. Follow Whalley signs, B6246, 2m*

Village inn celebrating Lancashire food heroes

The whitewashed village inn at Mitton is the flagship venue in a collection of pubs in Lancashire's rolling Ribble Valley (see also entries for The Highwayman and The Clog & Billycock). A lighter decorative scheme than hitherto has lifted the interiors, and the outsized framed map of the county orientates anybody from afar in no uncertain terms. Local food heroes are celebrated with heartening enthusiasm in a style of cooking that represents a building on tradition rather than tweaking it into oblivion. Witness then a prawn cocktail for starter, with nothing avant-garde done to it, just plump, succulent shellfish in a delicately spiced dressing. For main, there may be calf's liver with local bacon, oregano-spiked mash and a courgette fritter in shallot gravy, or a splendid fish pie topped with Butler's Lancashire cheese. Fish and chips is line-caught haddock with dripping-cooked chips and marrowfat peas. And who could resist a finisher of Black Forest gâteau, replete with kirsched-up cherries and layers of Valrhôna chocolate?

Chef Adam Edwards **Owner** Craig Bancroft, Nigel Haworth, Richard Matthewman **Seats** 140 **Times** 12-2/5.30-8.30 **Prices** Starter £4.75-£8.50, Main £9.50-£20.50, Dessert £3.50-£5.50, Service optional **Wines** 5 bottles over £30, 29 bottles under £30, 11 by glass **Parking** 70 **Notes** Fixed L & D 2/3 course Mon, Sunday L £16-£19.50, Vegetarian available, Children welcome

WHITEWELL
Map 18 SD64

The Inn at Whitewell
Modern British

tel: 01200 448222 **Forest of Bowland, Clitheroe BB7 3AT**
email: reception@innatwhitewell.com **web:** www.innatwhitewell.com
dir: *From S M6 junct 31 Longridge follow Whitewell signs. From N M6 junct 33 follow Trough of Bowland & Whitewell signs*

Traditional rural inn with wide-ranging superior food

Overlooking the River Hodder, with stunning views of the Forest of Bowland, this handsome 16th-century inn is a gem of stone floors and ancient beams, open fires, antique furniture and prints. You can eat in the bar areas or in the more formal restaurant. Either way, you'll be spoiled for choice on a diverse menu that encompasses grilled black pudding with cheese mash and apple purée, and a main course of lamb shoulder slowly roasted with rosemary and garlic served with hotpot potatoes, caramelised onions and carrot purée. Much of the produce is local and the kitchen has a confident touch, turning its hands to spicy fried squid in chilli lime and soy dressing with carrot and ginger salad, then seared salmon fillet with smoked haddock, spinach, potato chowder and pea purée, or chargrilled beef sirloin with the usual trimmings. End with one of the traditional puddings or home-made ice cream.

Chef Jamie Cadman **Owner** Charles Bowman **Seats** 60, Pr/dining room 20 **Times** 12-2/7.30-9.30 **Prices** Starter £5.25-£9, Main £16-£27, Dessert £6, Service optional **Wines** 50 bottles over £30, 40 bottles under £30, 20 by glass **Parking** 70 **Notes** Sunday L £5-£14, Vegetarian available, Children welcome

The Freemasons at Wiswell

WHALLEY
Map 18 SD73

Modern British **NOTABLE WINE LIST**
tel: 01254 822218 **8 Vicarage Fold, Wiswell BB7 9DF**
email: steve@freemasonswiswell.co.uk
dir: *A59, located on the edge of Whalley village near Clitheroe*

Exciting virtuoso cooking in an old village inn

Once three small cottages, one of which was a freemasons' lodge, The Freemasons is now a refined gastro-pub, if that's not disparaging of the quality of the food on offer. The interior had a bit of a restyle early in 2014 but what remains is a stylish decor, antique furniture, rugs on the floor, an open fire and even a stag's head, all conveying a welcoming, warm and convivial atmosphere. The kitchen team combs the locality for Lancashire's best produce and combines it with global influences to produce impressive results. Nidderdale lamb, for instance, is served as crisp belly and kofta, accompanied by miso aubergine, charred lettuce, mint and yoghurt. Another starter of monkfish is roasted tandoori-style and plated with sweet potato, apple and amaretti. Pairing seafood with meat is hardly unusual nowadays, but here scorched langoustines come not just with pork belly and rhubarb but with dashi tea too. A playful touch is given to some dishes: velouté of smoked haddock and chargrilled leeks with a fish finger hot dog, followed by Anna's Happy Trotters (roast loin and sausage) with salt-baked pineapple, cabbage, black pudding and pork pie sauce. Fish, meanwhile, might appear as roast loin of cod with a risotto of squid, Jerusalem artichoke and hazelnuts along with chorizo and yuzu, or as plain as the catch of the day simply grilled with lemon and brown butter and accompanied by potted shrimps and chips. The vibrant balance of flavours is as much due to the kitchen's sound techniques as to the thought that goes into compositions and the quality of the raw materials. And attractive presentation is a forte too, with desserts such as passionfruit soufflé with hot chocolate sauce, or caramelised banana tart with rum and raisin ice cream.

Chef Steven Smith, Hywel Griffith **Owner** Steven Smith **Seats** 70, Pr/dining room 14 **Times** 12-2.30/5.30-9 Closed 2 Jan for 2 wks, Mon-Tue **Prices** Fixed L 2 course £19.95-£25.90, Fixed D 3 course £23.95-£29.90, Tasting menu £60, Starter £8.95-£17, Main £19.95-£35, Dessert £7.95-£11.95, Service optional **Wines** 108 bottles over £30, 56 bottles under £30, 30 by glass **Parking** In village **Notes** Fixed L 3 course seasonal menu also offered early supper, Sunday L £21.95-£25.95, Vegetarian available, Children welcome

WREA GREEN
Map 18 SD33

The Spa Hotel at Ribby Hall Village

Modern British

tel: 01772 674484 **Ribby Hall Village, Ribby Rd PR4 2PR**
email: brasserie@ribbyhall.co.uk **web:** www.ribbyhall.co.uk/spa-hotel
dir: M55 junct 33 follow A585 towards Kirkham & brown tourist signs for Ribby Hall Village. Straight across 3 rdbts. Ribby Hall Village 200yds on left

Confident cooking in smart spa hotel

There are some pretty swanky spa facilities at the eponymously named hotel and it's an adult-only venue, so the idea is you leave the kids at home and pamper yourself. So far so good. The Brasserie is another string to its bow, and it is well worth the trip out on its own merits. It occupies a modishly done out space with plenty of room between the darkwood tables, and serves up some smart modern food. There's a good showing of regional ingredients on the menu and a decidedly modern British approach all round. Start, for example, with a soft-boiled duck's egg served with two ham hock croquettes and home-made salad cream, or go for the pressed belly pork with apple, black pudding and Grasmere gingerbread. Follow on with Goosnargh duck breast – the skin nicely rendered – with crystalised turnip, confit fennel and orange, or roast loin of cod with samphire, potted shrimps and shellfish foam. And for dessert there may be treacle tart with orange anglaise, chocolate crumb and clotted cream.

Chef Michael Noonan **Owner** W & G Harrison Ltd **Seats** 46 **Times** 12-2/6-9
Prices Prices not confirmed, Service optional **Wines** 27 bottles over £30, 48 bottles under £30, 14 by glass **Parking** 100 **Notes** Booking advisable, Vegetarian available

WRIGHTINGTON
Map 15 SD51

Corner House

 Modern British

tel: 01257 451400 **Wrightington Bar WN6 9SE**
email: info@cornerhousewrightington.co.uk
dir: 4m from Wigan. From M6 junct 27 towards Parbold, right after motorway exit, by BP garage onto Mossy Lea Rd. On right after 2m

Victorian hostelry with pub classics and modern dishes

Formerly the Mulberry Tree, the whitewashed inn a short tootle from the M6 dates back to the early Victorian era, and has seen service as a wheelwright's and blacksmith's premises over the years. The restaurant is kitted out in dark woods and white walls, and run by friendly, efficient staff, who serve forth an extensive menu of pub classics and more speculative modern dishes. Expect to begin with something like seared scallops on pea, asparagus and lemon risotto, before progressing to a steak from the grill, market-fresh fish such as sea bass or salmon with crushed new potatoes and a choice of sauces, or one of the daily specials that add lustre to the occasion – perhaps rump of lamb with a minty lamb sausage, sautéed potatoes and red wine jus. Vegetarians are properly looked after, as are the sweet of tooth, who might go for Amaretto pannacotta with warm chocolate sauce.

Chef Ross Lawson **Owner** Ross Lawson & Helen Hunter **Seats** 60
Times 12-2.30/5-8.30 Closed 26 Dec, Mon (ex BHs) **Prices** Fixed D 2 course £14.99, Starter £4.95-£8.95, Main £9.95-£21.95, Dessert £5.95-£7.50 **Wines** 9 bottles over £30, 26 bottles under £30, 8 by glass **Parking** 80 **Notes** L menu available from £4.95, Sunday L £14.95-£17.95, Vegetarian available, Children welcome

LEICESTERSHIRE

CASTLE DONINGTON

See East Midlands Airport

EAST MIDLANDS AIRPORT
Map 11 SK42

Best Western Premier Yew Lodge Hotel & Spa

British

tel: 01509 672518 **Packington Hill DE74 2DF**
email: info@yewlodgehotel.co.uk **web:** www.yewlodgehotel.co.uk
dir: M1 junct 24. Follow signs to Loughborough & Kegworth on A6. On entering village, 1st right, after 400yds hotel on right

Peaceful country hotel with creative cooking

Although it sits just minutes from the motorway network and East Midlands airport, the Yew Lodge Hotel is a surprisingly peaceful hideaway. The split-level bistro-style Orchard Restaurant is tended by smartly-uniformed and welcoming staff who play their part in ensuring the place is as well-supported by locals as it is by hotel residents. The skilled kitchen takes classic ideas and adds a contemporary spin here and there, perhaps surprise ingredients such as white chocolate and champagne added to a classic pairing of seared scallops and black pudding, or the sharpness of radish, carrot and citrus to cut the richness of a hay-smoked salmon cheesecake. Mains could bring on pork Wellington with pig's cheek, apple and wild mushrooms, or fish, in the shape of turbot fillet with mussels, curry, coriander, onion and garlic. Dessert could be a playful 'Night at the Movies' assemblage of popcorn, Oreo biscuit, cola, candyfloss, caramel and retro sweets.

Times 12-2/6.30-9.30 Closed L Sat

The Priest House Hotel

Modern British V

tel: 0845 072 7502 **Kings Mills DE74 2RR**
email: thepriesthouse@handpicked.co.uk
web: www.handpickedhotels.co.uk/thepriesthouse
dir: M1 junct 24, onto A50, take 1st slip road signed Castle Donington. Right at lights, hotel in 2m

Confident modern cooking in a riverside country house

Once standing in the vicinity of mills that ground flint for Derby porcelain, the Priest's House survived a fire in the 1920s that destroyed much else around it. Close by the River Trent, its location perfectly fits it for the role of contemporary country-house hotel. A stylish restaurant in neutral tones looks on to a small courtyard, and is decorated with naturally inspired abstract artworks on the stone walls. The kitchen brims with confidence as it sets about furnishing the place with statement examples of modern British cooking. Combinations could be as intuitive as beef carpaccio and horseradish sorbet with pickled turnip, or as off-the-wall as crispy squid, watermelon, dried olives and pumpkin seeds, both highly accomplished openers. Dishes are complex, which always raises the stakes, as when lemon sole is stuffed with crab and served with butternut squash gnocchi in pine nut dressing, but breast of duck with confit leg bonbon, hazelnuts and a skirlie cake oddly doesn't seem greater than the sum of its parts. The bravura dessert is excellent chocolate marquise with a chocolate cylinder of pistachio mousse.

Chef David Humphreys **Owner** Hand Picked Hotels **Seats** 34, Pr/dining room 100
Times 12-2.30/7-9.30 Closed L Mon-Sat, D Sun **Prices** Fixed D 3 course £37, Service optional **Wines** 74 bottles over £30, 11 bottles under £30, 18 by glass **Parking** 100
Notes Sunday L, Children welcome

■ **KEGWORTH**

See East Midlands Airport

■ **LEICESTER** Map 11 SK50

Hotel Maiyango

Modern European

tel: 0116 251 8898 **13-21 St Nicholas Place LE1 4LD**
email: reservations@maiyango.com **web:** www.maiyango.com
dir: M1 junct 21, A5460 for 3.5m. Turn right onto A47 round St Nicholas Circle onto St Nicholas Place

Fab decor and smart modern European cooking

The buzzy rooftop cocktail bar of this city centre boutique hotel is just the spot to soak up an aperitif with the cityscape vista of spires and rooftops. The combo of slick bolt-hole, cool bar and modish restaurant is a winner here, with the restaurant going for an ethnic chic Moroccan and Middle Eastern-inspired look. The food surprisingly veers off from Arabia, taking a more modern European tack, spiked here and there with global influences, while the kitchen's commitment to local sourcing means that supplies come from as close to home as possible. Lobster and crayfish ravioli is matched with carrot and lemongrass broth, then for the main event, chicken breast is wrapped around a punchy pairing of basil mousse and pigeon breast and served with roast sweet potato fondant, smoked beetroot purée and wild mushroom jus. At the end, a blueberry and almond pannacotta comes with caramelised peaches and Bellini sorbet.

Chef Nick Wilson **Owner** Aatin Anadkat **Seats** 55, Pr/dining room 80
Times 12.30-2.30/6.30-9.45 Closed 25 Dec, 1 Jan, L Sun **Prices** Fixed L 2 course £22.50, Fixed D 3 course £32, Tasting menu £35-£45, Service optional **Wines** 19 bottles over £30, 35 bottles under £30, 12 by glass **Parking** NCP **Notes** Pre-theatre menus available, Vegetarian available, Children welcome

■ **LONG WHATTON** Map 11 SK42

The Royal Oak

Modern British

tel: 01509 843694 **26 The Green LE12 5DB**
email: enquiries@theroyaloaklongwhatton.co.uk **web:** www.theroyaloaklongwhatton.co.uk

Skilful modern cooking in a smartly modernised village inn

No longer a pub starved of love and attention, the 21st-century incarnation of The Royal Oak is a thriving gastro-pub in the contemporary manner. The facelift undertaken over the last few years has resulted in a smart interior, the addition of some natty bedrooms, and a focus on food. That said, real ale is all part of the plan, and a few 'pub classics' remain on the menu to ensure the place remains part of the community (a proper pub in other words). The kitchen buys local where possible and turns out bright modish stuff such as chicken liver parfait with red onion jam, or Cullen skink arancini to start. There are sharing platters filled with goodies, and impressive main courses such as grilled fillet of hake with caper and tarragon butter, served with a ham hock bubble-and-squeak and confit egg yolk. To finish, tiramisù with Kahlúa eggnog and cinnamon-infused compôte.

Chef James & Charles Upton, Shaun McDonnell **Owner** Alex & Chris Astwood
Seats 45 **Times** 12-2.30/5.30-9.30 Closed D Sun **Prices** Prices not confirmed, Service optional **Wines** 5 bottles over £30, 23 bottles under £30, 9 by glass **Parking** 30
Notes Early doors menu Mon-Fri 5.30-6.30, Sunday L, Vegetarian available, Children welcome

■ **MELTON MOWBRAY** Map 11 SK71

Stapleford Park

 Modern French, British, International

tel: 01572 787000 & 787019 **Stapleford LE14 2EF**
email: reservations@stapleford.co.uk **web:** www.staplefordpark.com
dir: A1 to Colsterworth onto B676, signed Melton Mowbray. In approx 9m turn left to Stapleford

Aspirational cooking in a grand old Leicestershire house

Stapleford's lineage can be traced back to medieval times, the estate being owned by successive generations of the earls of Harborough for nearly 500 years. Parts of the house itself are of great age, while other bits have been treated to a modernising makeover, the Old Wing having been given a fresher look as recently as 1633. It all comes to a head in the riotously opulent dining room, with its high moulded ceiling, classical paintings and Grinling Gibbons mantelpiece. Impeccable staff keep the elevated tone buoyant, and Martin Furlong's cooking aims high too. Preparations tend to the refined rather than belligerently modern, so expect Cornish crab in lemon mayonnaise, or sea trout rillettes with rocket mousse to start, and then perhaps venison loin with chestnut purée and roast parsnips, or brilliantly judged opalescent halibut, accompanied by a rather prosaic creamy clam chowder. Finish with pistachio cake, comfortingly enriched with chocolate ganache and cherries, or with some inspiring Leicestershire cheeses. The home-made breads arrive in four versions, freshly warmed and yeasty.

Chef Martin Furlong **Seats** 70, Pr/dining room 180 **Times** 11.30-2.30/6-9.30 Closed exclusive use days **Wines** 10 by glass **Parking** 120 **Notes** Tasting menu 7 course, themed monthly gourmet eve £99, Sunday L £27.50, Vegetarian available, Children welcome

■ **NORTH KILWORTH** Map 11 SP68

Kilworth House Hotel & Theatre

Modern British V

tel: 01858 880058 **Lutterworth Rd LE17 6JE**
email: info@kilworthhouse.co.uk **web:** www.kilworthhouse.co.uk
dir: A4304 towards Market Harborough, after Walcote, hotel 1.5m on right

Modern country-house cooking in a luxury hotel

Period authenticity runs through this Italianate 19th-century mansion thanks to a top-to-toe restoration overseen by the eagle eyes of English Heritage. Only two families lived in it for 120 years, before it became an upmarket country-house hotel in the noughties with all the plush style, fittings and furniture befitting a hotel of this standing (including, these days, an open-air theatre in the grounds). If you want to see what the chefs can do, the Wordsworth Restaurant is the fine-dining venue, a truly remarkable confection of stained-glass windows, rich red patterned wallpaper and burnished antique tables beneath a lanterned dome of elaborate plasterwork and twinkling chandeliers; in short, the sort of place you feel that best bib and tucker is required. The scene thus set, what's on the menu is classic country-house cooking brought gently up to date – seared scallops with spiced tomato relish and parsnip purée, for example, while at main course duck is served three ways as breast, confit and rillettes, with pommes Anna, pickled cabbage and orange. If you're in the market for fish, consider brill with sweet potato and coconut curry and red lentil salsa.

Chef Carl Dovey **Owner** Mr & Mrs Mackay **Seats** 70, Pr/dining room 130
Times 12-2.30/7-9.30 **Prices** Fixed L 2 course fr £22.50, Fixed D 3 course fr £29.50, Tasting menu £49, Starter £6.50-£10.95, Main £14.95-£18.95, Dessert £6.95, Service optional **Wines** 44 bottles over £30, 35 bottles under £30, 10 by glass **Parking** 140 **Notes** Theatre menu in season 3 course £28, Tasting menu Wed-Sat, Sunday L £28.95, Children welcome

QUORN
Map 11 SK51

Quorn Country Hotel

◉ Modern British

tel: 01509 415050 **Charnwood House, 66 Leicester Rd LE12 8BB**
email: sales@quorncountryhotel.co.uk **web:** www.quorncountryhotel.co.uk
dir: M1 junct 23/A6 towards Leicester, follow signs for Quorn

Modern British flavours in a stylish country hotel

With manicured gardens and oak-panelled interiors, the Quorn Country Hotel has a 17th-century house at its heart, which has been much extended over the years. The restaurant, Shires, is a useful spot to know about in this neck of the woods, just outside Loughborough, with its formal table settings and professional service team. The menu takes a modern British path, and doesn't stray too far into the outer reaches. You might start with a ham hock terrine with piccalilli and parsnip purée, or seared scallops in the familiar company of cauliflower purée and bacon. Main-course salmon — cooked just right – is partnered with a pea croquette, bubble-and-squeak cake and dressed with a prawn and lemon beurre blanc, or go for breast of Barbary duck with redcurrants and rosemary. Finish with something like lime cheesecake with lemon curd and a brandy snap filled with crème fraîche.

Chef Lloyd Roper **Owner** Mr Walshe **Seats** 112, Pr/dining room 240 **Times** 12-2/7-9 Closed L Sat **Prices** Tasting menu £45, Starter £4.95-£9.95, Main £9.95-£19.50, Dessert £4.95-£6.95, Service optional **Wines** 48 bottles over £30, 12 bottles under £30, 5 by glass **Parking** 120 **Notes** Tasting menu 7 course, Sunday L £14-£19.95, Vegetarian available, Children welcome

WYMESWOLD
Map 11 SK62

Hammer & Pincers

◉◉ Modern European V

tel: 01509 880735 **5 East Rd LE12 6ST**
email: info@hammerandpincers.co.uk

Inventive cooking in smart rural restaurant

Gastro-pub? Country restaurant? It doesn't matter what label you tag onto the Hammer & Pincers – what's beyond argument is that lucky locals in the Leicestershire village of Wymeswold have great food on their doorstep. Run by husband-and-wife team Daniel and Sandra Jimminson who trained in big-name kitchens, this smart rural restaurant is a stylish, contemporary space with bright artworks on exposed brickwork walls. Its serious intent is made clear with keenly-priced multi-course grazing and gourmet menus to bolster a repertoire of creative modern European cuisine. A small card on each table, written with a touch of humour and snippets of personal information, shows the strength of their relationship with local suppliers, and staff are on the ball and happy to chat about the menus, which read like a dream. Chunky ham hock and parsley terrine with piccalilli and toasted walnut and raisin bread is big on flavour, while pan-roasted salmon fillet served with parmesan gnocchi and crayfish velouté makes for a colourful, well-constructed main course. Refined puds include chocolate and orange oil délice with Grand Marnier clementines and milk ice cream.

Chef Daniel Jimminson **Owner** Daniel & Sandra Jimminson **Seats** 46 **Times** 12-2/6-9 Closed Mon, D Sun **Prices** Fixed L 2 course fr £15, Fixed D 3 course fr £18, Tasting menu fr £45, Starter £5-£11, Main £14-£24, Dessert £5-£8, Service optional **Wines** 18 bottles over £30, 26 bottles under £30, 16 by glass **Parking** 40 **Notes** Sunday L £14-£20, Children welcome

LINCOLNSHIRE

GRANTHAM
Map 11 SK93

Harry's Place

◉◉◉ – see opposite

HORNCASTLE
Map 17 TF26

Magpies Restaurant with Rooms

◉◉ British, European

tel: 01507 527004 **73 East St LN9 6AA**
dir: 0.5m from town centre on A158 towards Skegness

Bright, modish cooking in the Lincolnshire Wolds

Andrew and Caroline Gilbert's restaurant with rooms is lovingly formed out of a terrace of 200-year-old cottages. It's all very charming and traditional on the inside, with a log-burning stove in the comfortable sitting room to melt away any winter chill, before you head into the dining room with its neatly laid tables and cool hues of duck egg blue and cream. On the menu you'll find lots of local ingredients and plenty of imaginative and appealing combinations, starting with home-smoked chicken with a baked mini Camembert and a vibrant salad of celeriac, orange and pomegranate seeds. Main course sees loin of Gloucester Old Spot pork stuffed with apricot and hazelnut and served with garlicky potato gratin, fresh veg and a rich, piggy jus, or there might be John Dory partnered with rösti, Chinese greens and scallops lifted with lime and lemongrass beurre blanc. Dark chocolate tart with mocha ice cream hits the spot for pudding or you could waylay the cheese trolley as it does the rounds.

Chef Andrew Gilbert **Owner** Caroline Gilbert **Seats** 34 **Times** 12-2/7-9.30 Closed 26-30 Dec, 1st 2 wks Jan, Mon-Tue, L Sat, 25 & 31 Dec **Prices** Fixed L 2 course £20, Fixed D 3 course £47, Service optional **Wines** 72 bottles over £30, 72 bottles under £30, 7 by glass **Parking** On street **Notes** Magpie menu 3 course D Wed-Thu & Sun £25, Sunday L £20-£25, Vegetarian available, Children welcome

HOUGH-ON-THE-HILL
Map 11 SK94

The Brownlow Arms

◉ British

tel: 01400 250234 **High Rd NG32 2AZ**
email: armsinn@yahoo.co.uk **web:** www.thebrownlowarms.com
dir: Take A607 (Grantham to Sleaford road). Hough-on-the-Hill signed from Barkston

Country-pub cooking in an elegant village inn

A Lincolnshire village inn that has come up in the world, The Brownlow is as elegantly appointed as an interiors magazine country house, with tapestry-backed chairs and gilt-framed mirrors in a panelled dining room. Attentive, friendly service puts everyone at their ease though, and the menu stays within the familiar territory of classic country-pub cooking. Devilled lamb's kidneys in a puff pastry basket make a robust opener, or there might be battered tiger prawns dressed Thai-style in lime, coriander and green chilli. The Asian note might be struck again in a main of sesame-crusted duck with pak choi and a little rhubarb tart, or there may be a fish assemblage of plaice, salmon and scallops, served with crushed peas in lemon and chive beurre blanc. A successful dessert is the griottine cherry frangipane tart, with creamy praline parfait and Frangelico ice cream. Cheeses are served with grapes and membrillo.

Chef Ruarardh Bealby **Owner** Paul & Lorraine Willoughby **Seats** 80, Pr/dining room 26 **Times** 12-2.30/6.30-9.30 Closed 25-26 Dec, Mon, L Tue-Sat, D Sun **Prices** Starter £5.25-£10.50, Main £15.95-£26.50, Dessert £6.95, Service optional **Wines** 8 by glass **Parking** 26, On street **Notes** Sunday L £22.95-£25.95, Vegetarian available, No children

LACEBY
Map 17 TA20

Best Western Oaklands Hall Hotel
Modern British **NEW**

tel: 01472 872248 **Barton St DN37 7LF**
email: reception@oaklandshallhotel.co.uk web: www.oaklandshallhotel.co.uk
dir: *Phone for directions*

Eye-catching, inventive food in a Victorian mansion

The stolid-looking balustraded redbrick mansion, built in 1877, sits in the heart of five acres of landscaped parkland between the Wolds and the Humber, not far from Grimsby. It's a pleasant spot for the full country-house experience, which these days often means a combination of Victorian architectural brio with understated interior styling in the modern idiom. What might once have been called the dining room is, more entertainingly, the Comfy Duck Bistro, a place of unclothed tables, minimal wall adornment, and chairs in alternating beige and blue. Modern food stylings are the norm, with eye-catching presentations of inventive modern British comfort food. A pork pie with salad cream (both home-made) comes with roasted chestnuts as one way to start, while walnut-crumbed pressed smoked salmon is partnered with apple and salted cucumber. Mains comprise multiple technical components – such as duck leg confit with a ham and foie gras croquette, herb-crusted cod with shellfish cannelloni – or else appear in variant guises, as for braised neck and roast rack of lamb with provençal veg, capers and powdered olives. An on-trend dessert is lemon and poppyseed cake with white chocolate cream, salt-baked pineapple and a coconut tuile.

Chef Steven Bennett, Gareth Bartram **Owner** Nigel Underwood, John Lawson **Seats** 80, Pr/dining room 25 **Times** 11.30-2.30/5-9.30 Closed D 25 Dec **Prices** Fixed L 2 course £15-£25, Fixed D 3 course £20-£30, Starter £4.95-£7.95, Main £10.95-£24.95, Dessert £4.95-£6.95 **Wines** 3 bottles over £30, 25 bottles under £30, 12 by glass **Parking** 100 **Notes** Sun evening special offer available, Vegetarian available, Children welcome

LINCOLN
Map 17 SK97

The Lincoln Hotel
Modern British V

tel: 01522 520348 **Eastgate LN2 1PN**
email: jlittle@thelincolnhotel.com web: www.thelincolnhotel.com
dir: *Adjacent to cathedral*

Sharp modern dishes in designer-led hotel

The Lincoln is a modern hotel, hard by the 12th-century cathedral, with a designer-chic interior that's bang up to the minute. The Green Room restaurant is a serenely decorated, chandelier-hung space with drapes over the windows, and a menu that's as sharp and modern an assembly as the surroundings would suggest. Chicken liver and foie gras parfait balanced by mulled cranberry chutney might start you off, followed by monkfish tail wrapped in Parma ham with tomato and merguez sausage cassoulet and butter bean and basil purée. Prime ingredients are cooked with care, and combinations are carefully considered, as in a starter of scallops with apple purée, black pudding crumb and smoked bacon foam, and main-course pan-fried chicken breast, full of flavour, in its own cooking juices accompanied by candied carrots, celeriac purée and hasselback potatoes. Professional but relaxed service, some notable breads, and puddings along the lines of chocolate and pear tart, all add to the pleasure.

Chef Dale Gill **Owner** Christopher Nevile, Lady Arnold **Seats** 30, Pr/dining room 12 **Times** 12-2/6-9.30 Closed L Mon-Sat **Prices** Starter £4-£6, Main £10-£18, Dessert £4-£6, Service optional **Wines** 4 bottles over £30, 21 bottles under £30, 5 by glass **Parking** 40 **Notes** Sunday L £14-£16, Children welcome

Harry's Place

GRANTHAM
Map 11 SK93

Modern French
tel: 01476 561780 **17 High St, Great Gonerby NG31 8JS**
dir: *1.5m NW of Grantham on B1174*

Outstanding quality in a restaurant built for ten

A Georgian house on the outskirts of Grantham is the setting for the Hallams' double act: Caroline runs front-of-house courteously and efficiently, while Harry single-handedly cooks. It's a small-scale operation, catering for up to ten diners at three tables, and clearly a successful one, as the Hallams have been here for around thirty years. Harry's cooking accounts in no small way for that success, evidence of his unerring culinary instinct, well-honed technical skills and top-quality ingredients. The deal is just a pair of alternatives offered at each course, a soup typically one of the starters – celeriac, say – with the other perhaps a gratin of smoked haddock, sweetcorn and chives in a light pastry case. One fish, one meat main course is the norm, and the handwritten menu descriptions fail to convey their complexity of flavours. Try lightly sautéed fillet of wild halibut with julienne of carrots and sugar snaps spiked with garlic and ginger and a sauce of white wine, Pernod, basil and coriander, or pink loin of lamb with an Armagnac

and white wine sauce laced with tarragon, rosemary and thyme, and tomato, olive and caper relish. Breads are freshly baked in-house, and puddings are appreciated for their straightforward, punchy flavours – hot Bramley apple and Calvados soufflé, say, or a signature dish of ice cream such as rhubarb with Cointreau syrup – with a decent choice of well-maintained cheeses the savoury alternative.

Chef Harry Hallam **Owner** Harry & Caroline Hallam **Seats** 10 **Times** 12.30-2.30/7-8.30 Closed 2 wks from 25 Dec, 1 wk Aug, Sun-Mon **Prices** Starter £9.50-£19.50, Main £39.50, Dessert £8, Service optional **Wines** 20 bottles over £30, 7 bottles under £30, 4 by glass **Parking** 4 **Notes** Vegetarian meal on request at time of booking, Vegetarian available, Children 5 yrs+

LINCOLN *continued*

The Old Bakery

◉◉ Modern British

tel: 01522 576057 **26-28 Burton Rd LN1 3LB**
email: enquiries@theold-bakery.co.uk **web:** www.theold-bakery.co.uk
dir: *From A46 follow directions for Lincoln North then follow brown signs for The Historic Centre*

Restaurant-with-rooms in a converted bakery

In the Uphill district of this undulating city, very near the cathedral and castle, Ivano and Tracey de Serio's restaurant-with-rooms is a distinctly homely place, with the feel of a farmhouse kitchen in the tiled dining room. A dresser furnished with produce baskets and a wine rack overlooks proceedings, and the kitchen turns out a fairly lengthy menu of modern British food that has most of the technical tricks of today's culinary fashion at its disposal. Pot-roasted partridge breast with smoked bacon porridge, lemongrass broth and pear and fig chutney is a beguiling mixture of messages to begin, while main courses are multi-layered, richly sauced affairs, running from prune-stuffed rabbit loin in Bateman's Ale with wild mushroom barley risotto and juniper jus, to venison loin and rösti in port and Stilton, via the market fish of the day. A five-course taster menu offers a comprehensive tour. Desserts may take an unconventional Italian approach, adding extra-virgin olive oil to the tiramisù, and an extensive cheese menu contains plenty of top gear.

Chef Ivano de Serio **Owner** Alan & Lynn Ritson, Tracey & Ivano de Serio **Seats** 65, Pr/dining room 15 **Times** 12-1.30/7-9 Closed 26 Dec, 1-16 Jan, 1st wk Aug, Mon, D Sun **Prices** Fixed L 2 course £12.50, Starter £5.95-£11.50, Main £15.50-£25.95, Dessert £5.50-£7.95, Service optional **Wines** 65 bottles over £30, 53 bottles under £30, 9 by glass **Parking** On street, public car park 20mtrs **Notes** Tasting menu 7/10 course, 5/8 course with wine £53-£65, Sunday L £14.50-£18.95, Vegetarian available, Children welcome

Tower Hotel

◉ Modern

tel: 01522 529999 **30 Westgate LN1 3BD**
email: tower.hotel@btclick.com **web:** www.lincolntowerhotel.com
dir: *Next to Lincoln Castle*

Bright modern cooking in the cathedral quarter

The Tower is in the cathedral quarter with the old town on its doorstep and the centre ten minutes down the hill. The restaurant's decor is quite simple, with high-backed wicker chairs at clothed tables, a wooden floor and a mirrored wall on one side. The kitchen exhibits a high level of skill and imagination, turning out starters like Thai-style haddock and tuna fishcake, artistically presented with sweet-and-sour pineapple and lime mayonnaise (a well-considered combination), and a playful rabbit trifle and lollipop with pea custard, celeriac mash and gingerbread. Among main courses, properly timed pan-fried duck breast with maple dressing is complemented by a salty, crumbly goats' cheese bonbon, celeriac fondant, wild mushrooms and baby spinach, while roast bream comes with vanilla mash, leeks braised with fennel seeds, and orange vierge. Lactose- and gluten-free dishes are available, and puddings may extend to Calvados and raisin pannacotta with apple dip and buttermilk ice cream.

Times 12-5/6-9.30 Closed 25-26 Dec, 1 Jan

Washingborough Hall Hotel

◉◉ Modern British

tel: 01522 790340 **Church Hill, Washingborough LN4 1BE**
email: enquiries@washingboroughhall.com **web:** www.washingboroughhall.com
dir: *B1190 into Washingborough. Right at rdbt, hotel 500yds on left*

Modern cooking in Georgian country house

Set in three acres of lovely grounds at the heart of a sleepy Lincolnshire village, and with a garden to provide herbs for the kitchen, Washingborough Hall delivers all you would hope for in a Georgian manor house earning its living as a small but switched-on country-house hotel. The smart Dining Room restaurant exudes quietly understated class with its restrained heritage colours, unclothed tables, pale wooden floors, ornate marble fireplace and floor-to-ceiling Georgian windows overlooking the garden – a suitably unshowy setting for unpretentious modern cooking that aims to soothe rather than challenge. Gently inventive contemporary ideas are underpinned by Lincolnshire produce and keep a keen eye on the seasons, starting with a twice-baked local goats' cheese soufflé with tomato chilli jam, followed by rack of lamb with mustard potato gratin and pan juices. Fish is handled with a similar lack of fuss – perhaps poached paupiette of sole with pea purée and crispy bacon. To finish, try a lemon posset with honeyed nectarines and hazelnut biscuit.

Chef Dan Wallis **Owner** Mr E & Mrs L Herring **Seats** 50, Pr/dining room 50 **Times** 12-2/6.30-9 **Prices** Prices not confirmed, Service optional **Wines** 17 bottles over £30, 37 bottles under £30, 12 by glass **Parking** 40 **Notes** Alfresco summer menu 2/3 course 12-7pm, Sunday L, Vegetarian available, Children welcome

LOUTH   **Map 17 TF38**

Brackenborough Hotel

◉ Modern British

tel: 01507 609169 **Cordeaux Corner, Brackenborough LN11 0SZ**
email: reception@brackenborough.co.uk **web:** www.oakridgehotels.co.uk
dir: *Hotel located on main A16 Louth to Grimsby Rd*

Modish bistro in a rural setting

With its winning location in the open countryside outside Louth, the Brackenborough Hotel takes pole position when it comes to eating, too, with a bistro that has a lot to offer. It's a spacious and contemporary space, with high vaulted ceilings and a chic, modish finish, and views out over the pretty gardens in daylight hours. The menu does not attempt to subvert its bistro moniker, rather it embraces all that is great about the much-loved, unpretentious formula. Start with leek and potato soup served hot or cold as you prefer it, or a traditional Lincolnshire haslet (meatloaf) with apple chutney, and you might follow on with an Aberdeen Angus steak cooked on the grill with a choice of sauces. There's a classic coq au vin, too, and fish and chips, or go for the pan-fried sea bass with parsnip purée and crisps, and caramelised garlic. To finish, perhaps a chocolate and milk tart.

Chef Mike Watts Owner Ashley Lidgard Seats 78, Pr/dining room 120
Times 11.30-2.30/5-9.30 Prices Starter £3.50-£7.50, Main £7.50-£17.95, Dessert
£4.25-£5.95, Service optional Wines 36 bottles over £30, 47 bottles under £30, 11
by glass Parking 80 Notes 2 people 2 course & bottle of wine £33, Sunday L £9.95-
£11.50, Vegetarian available, Children welcome

MARKET RASEN
Map 17 TF18

The Advocate Arms

◉ Modern European, British

tel: 01673 842364 2 Queen St LN8 3EH
email: info@advocatearms.co.uk web: www.advocatearms.co.uk
dir: Located just off Market Place, High Street

Confident cooking in a town-centre restaurant with rooms

This 18th-century restaurant with rooms in the centre of town has a contemporary
finish and aims to impress with its boutique-style attitude and opened-up interior.
The space is cleverly divided up with glass panels to distinguish between the buzzy
bar and lounge and the brasserie-style dining area. The former is the place to head
to for a pint, coffee or something to eat off the bar menu, while breakfast is also
served seven days a week. The main restaurant's output is broadly modern British,
with some inventive combinations and plenty to satisfy traditionalists. Start with a
terrine made with confit belly pork served with a crackling, apple purée and baby
leek, and follow with pan-fried sea bass partnered with mango and crab salsa,
confit potato and a minty pea purée. There are steaks – rib-eye, fillet and sirloin –
served with trad accompaniments, and desserts such as a trendy little number
combining coffee semi-fredo with stem ginger flapjack, coffee sabayon and
popcorn.

Chef Josh Kelly Owner Darren Lince Seats 65, Pr/dining room 16 Times 7am-9.30pm
Closed D Sun (last orders 6.30) All-day dining Prices Fixed D 3 course £16.95-
£23.95, Starter £4.50-£7.95, Main £10.95-£23.95, Dessert £5.50-£5.95, Service
optional Wines 10 bottles over £30, 32 bottles under £30, 12 by glass Parking 6,
Short walk Notes Sun L 2/3 course, Sunday L £12.95-£15.95, Vegetarian available,
Children welcome

SCUNTHORPE
Map 17 SE81

Forest Pines Hotel & Golf Resort

◉ Modern British

tel: 01652 650770 Ermine St, Broughton DN20 0AQ
email: forestpines@qhotels.co.uk web: www.qhotels.co.uk
dir: From M180 junct 4, travel towards Scunthorpe on A18. Continue straight over rdbt,
hotel is situated on left

Sustainable seafood in a country-house hotel

Say the name 'Grimsby' and the port's fishing heritage immediately springs to
mind. The fine-dining restaurant at the swish Forest Pines Hotel & Golf Resort a few
miles inland in the North Lincolnshire countryside is called Eighteen57 in honour of
the year Grimsby's main fish dock opened. Its interior follows a snazzy piscine
theme involving blue mosaic-tiled walls, and pictures, reliefs and murals
celebrating the maritime world. Produced by a kitchen that has an eye to
sustainability in its sourcing policy, local fish and seafood feature prominently, but
by no means exclusively on an enticing modern repertoire, so a meaty starter of
potted pork hock with cider jelly, crackling, and ginger and wholegrain mustard
clotted cream might precede braised ox cheek with confit garlic mash and seasonal
vegetables. On the fish front, citrus batter puts a creative spin on haddock with
triple-cooked chips and pea purée, while pudding brings lemon tart with gin,
cucumber and tonic granita.

Chef Paul Montgomery Owner QHotels Seats 70 Times 6.30-10 Prices Prices not
confirmed, Service optional 10% Wines 7 by glass Parking 400 Notes Vegetarian
available, Children welcome

SLEAFORD
Map 12 TF04

The Bustard Inn & Restaurant

◉ Modern British

tel: 01529 488250 44 Main St, South Rauceby NG34 8QG
email: info@thebustardinn.co.uk
dir: A17 from Newark, turn right after B6403 to Ancaster. A153 from Grantham, after
Wilsford, turn left for South Rauceby

Sensitively refurbished old inn in peaceful village

The local community lost its original boozer when it was demolished in the 19th
century to make way for a new entrance to the Rauceby Hall estate, and it got this
Victorian inn as its replacement in 1860. Now smartly revitalised with a
contemporary country-chic look involving a pared-back decor of dove-grey painted
chairs on a flagstone floor, and a solid oak bar, The Bustard now puts food at the
heart of the operation. Exposed stone walls, ancient timbers and an ornate oriel
window are its original features, which combine with solid ash tables and tapestry
chairs in a smart, relaxed setting for modern cooking with its feet on the ground
and its roots in local, seasonal ingredients. Start out along the lines of pan-fried
scallops with butternut squash purée and chorizo, then move on to loin of Belton
Park venison teamed with potato gratin, carrot purée, blackberries and chestnuts,
and wrap things up with a Lincolnshire plum bread-and-butter pudding with
vanilla ice cream.

Times 12-2.30/6-9.30 Closed 1 Jan, Mon, D Sun

STAMFORD
Map 11 TF00

The Bull & Swan at Burghley

◉ Traditional British

tel: 01780 766412 High St, St Martins PE9 2LJ
email: enquiries@thebullandswan.co.uk web: www.thebullandswan.co.uk
dir: A1 onto Old Great North Rd, left onto B1081, follow Stamford signs

Fuss-free cooking using regional produce in historical inn

The old stone inn used to be a staging post for coaches on the Great North Road
and is nowadays an informal dining pub. Within are beams, stone walls, rugs on
dark wood floors and caramel-coloured leather dining chairs. Regional produce is
the backbone, with meat and vegetables from the nearby Burghley Estate, and the
kitchen balances up-to-date ideas with the more traditional. Ham hock and foie
gras terrine, with apple and celery salad and complementary piccalilli purée, has a
nice balance of flavours, or there might be smoked eel risotto with leeks and
watercress velouté. Main courses embrace gammon steak with chips, egg and
pineapple as well as the wilder reaches of pressed belly pork with cheek and black
pudding tortellini, and sea bass fillet with seaweed, mussel cream, mash and kale.
End with a satisfying pudding like cranberry jam roly-poly with custard.

Times 12-2.30/6-9

Learn the latest foodie trends in Birmingham and Manchester on page 21

STAMFORD *continued*

The George of Stamford

Traditional British NOTABLE WINE LIST

tel: 01780 750750 **71 St Martins PE9 2LB**
email: reservations@georgehotelofstamford.com **web:** www.georgehotelofstamford.com
dir: *From A1(N of Peterborough) turn onto B1081 signed Stamford and Burghley House. Follow road to 1st set of lights, hotel on left*

Historical institution treasured for its traditional values and cooking

History seeps from the pores of every mellow stone of this venerable coaching inn, which once fed and watered passengers from the 40 coaches that stopped here each day on the Great North Road. The oak-panelled restaurant is a magnificent room with an old-world feel, and its menus are steadfastly traditional too: trolleys do the rounds, delivering the signature dish of roast sirloin of English beef, carved at the table. But it's not all about heritage dining, as modernists are kept happy with pan-fried sea bass matched with herb risotto and sun-blushed tomato, or perhaps an up-to-date riff on lamb, comprising roast loin, liver and kidney, and deep fried sweetbreads. Then it's time for the trolleys again, this time to deliver a traditional ending of cheeses and sweets.

Chef Chris Pitman, Paul Reseigh **Owner** Lawrence Hoskins **Seats** 90, Pr/dining room 40 **Times** 12.30-2.30/7.30-10.30 **Prices** Prices not confirmed, Service optional **Wines** 113 bottles over £30, 41 bottles under £30, 19 by glass **Parking** 110 **Notes** Walk in L menu, Sunday L, Vegetarian available, Children 10 yrs+

Jim's Yard

British, European V

tel: 01780 756080 **3 Ironmonger St PE9 1PL**
email: jim@jimsyard.biz

Classic bistro cooking in a conservatory restaurant

It's well worth seeking out Jim's Yard, tucked away as it is behind buildings on Ironmonger Street in this charming old town. French windows in the ground-floor conservatory open on to a secluded courtyard and pretty garden, and there's more space upstairs, where monochrome photographs on brick walls show past times in Stamford. Rich and flavourful goats' cheese risotto studded with cubes of thyme-roasted beetroot gets things off to a flying start, or there might be sautéed prawns thermidor. The kitchen looks towards Europe for its inspiration, so among main courses expect a classic rendition of pan-fried breast of Barbary duck with roast potatoes, seasonal greens and a correctly viscous orange sauce. An alternative might be creamy fish pie with seasonal samphire, and desserts are a class act too, among them pear frangipane tart, its pastry crisp and golden, or chocolate fondant.

Chef Tim Luff **Owner** James & Sharon Trevor **Seats** 55, Pr/dining room 14 **Times** 12-2.30/6.30-9.30 Closed 26 Dec 2 wks, last wk Jul-1st wk Aug, Sun-Mon **Prices** Fixed L 2 course £14.50, Fixed D 3 course £19.50, Starter £5-£9, Main £12.50-£21, Dessert £4.50-£6, Service optional **Wines** 43 bottles over £30, 54 bottles under £30, 13 by glass **Parking** Broad St **Notes** Pre-theatre menu Tue-Thu 6-7pm, Children welcome

Winteringham Fields

❀ ❀ ❀

WINTERINGHAM **Map 17 SE92**

Modern British, European
tel: 01724 733096 **1 Silver St DN15 9ND**
email: reception@winteringhamfields.co.uk **web:** www.winteringhamfields.co.uk
dir: *Village centre, off A1077, 4m S of Humber Bridge*

Rollercoaster cooking on the Humber estuary

Out in the wilds of eastern England on the Humber estuary, Winteringham has long been a destination for culinary excellence and innovation, and remains emphatically so under the aegis of Colin McGurran. The restaurant with rooms is a former farmhouse that incorporates its own working farm, where bees are busy making honey, free-range chickens produce eggs with lustrously coloured yolks, and seasonal fruits pour forth in happy abundance. The soft-focus luxury of the interior is pleasingly at odds with the rugged northern landscape hereabouts; soothing tones of fawn and sienna predominate in the extravagantly curtained main dining room. The private room is a book-lined study, perfect for creating the contemplative mood in which it's best to approach McGurran's culinary productions, many of which have starred on the BBC's *Great British Menu*. If the dishes are not already familiar to you, such as the famous gelatine tomato gravid with gazpacho, served with a crisp garden salad apparently flourishing in black olive soil, they will be fascinating assaults on the expectations. For that reason, the menu surprise is the best route. This rollercoaster ride through gastronomic possibility may start with some homemade crisps and wasabi mayo, and pile on through almond crème brûlée, a roast chicken leg with morels and asparagus in wild garlic velouté, barbecued and tartared mackerel with avocado and cucumber, wood-pigeon with pear and beetroot variations, an explosive basil and pineapple bombe, and an eccentric take on Black Forest gâteau, before the cheese trolley arrives to restore order. A slightly simpler version of the menu appears at lunchtimes, and if you're determined not to be surprised, there is always the option of choosing three courses à la carte. A rarefied list of commendably well-chosen wines has plenty to suit the challenging style of the food.

Chef Colin McGurran **Owner** Colin McGurran **Seats** 60, Pr/dining room 12 **Times** 12-1.30/7-9 Closed 2 wks Xmas, last 2 wks Aug, Sun-Mon **Prices** Prices not confirmed, Service optional **Wines** 20 by glass **Parking** 20 **Notes** Menu surprise 7/9/11 course £69/£79/£89, Vegetarian available, Children welcome

The William Cecil

◉ Modern British

tel: 01780 750070 **High St, St Martins PE9 2LJ**
email: enquiries@thewilliamcecil.co.uk web: www.thewilliamcecil.co.uk
dir: *Exit A1 signed Stamford & Burghley Park. Continue & hotel 1st building on right on entering town*

Stylishly modernised Georgian hotel restaurant with creative flair

The hotel is an interesting amalgam of three Georgian houses built at different times, originally named after one of William Cecil, Lord Burghley's descendants, Lady Anne, but now restored to the Elizabethan statesman himself. Just off the approach road to Stamford, it's a clever blend of old and new inside, the panelling done in lighter colours, with booth seating and a laminate floor in the restaurant. Phil Kent sources locally in the best modern way, and has more than a touch of creative flair at his disposal. That can be seen in a starter of hazelnut-crusted foie gras parfait with truffled cucumber salad and brioche toast, which might be followed by lemon sole and crayfish tails in champagne butter sauce with colcannon, or a meat dish such as Gressingham duck breast and celeriac gratin with a reduction sauce incorporating elderflower and pomegranate. Finish with richly filled chocolate tart, white chocolate honeycomb and vanilla clotted cream.

Chef Phil Kent **Owner** Hillbrooke Hotels Ltd **Seats** 72, Pr/dining room 100 **Times** 12-3/6-9 **Prices** Fixed L 2 course £14.95, Starter £7-£10.95, Main £13.95-£23.95, Dessert £7-£14.95 **Wines** 25 bottles over £30, 23 bottles under £30, 11 by glass **Parking** 70 **Notes** Sunday L £19.50-£24.50, Vegetarian available, Children welcome

---

█ WINTERINGHAM   **Map 17 SE92**

Winteringham Fields

◉◉◉ – *see opposite*

█ WOOLSTHORPE   **Map 11 SK83**

Chequers Inn

◉ Modern British **NEW**

tel: 01476 870701 **Main St NG32 1LU**
email: justinnabar@yahoo.co.uk web: www.chequersinn.net
dir: *From A1 exit A607 towards Melton Mowbray follow heritage signs for Belvoir Castle*

17th-century inn with impeccable modern regional cooking

A beautifully preserved inn from the Stuart era, the Chequers stands cheek by jowl with Belvoir Castle in a pastoral spot where Lincs meets Leics and Notts. The matching of old and new in the decor is a test of many an old country inn, and the Chequers has it just right, with brasserie-style tables and banquettes against imposing stone walls in the dining room, while the pub itself retains its rustic ambience with a big old fireplace and low ceilings to contain the happy babble. There are cask ales and scrumpy, around three dozen wines by the glass, and a menu of impeccably forward-thinking British food built from local supplies. Start with a chicken and stuffing terrine with red onion marmalade and toasted brioche, or Long Clawson Stilton and onion tart. Fish might be a rosette of plaice with brown shrimps and crayfish in saffron velouté, while game season turns up pheasant with pearl barley risotto and roasted roots. For veggies, butternut and aubergine tagine with spiced couscous should appeal. Conclude with dark chocolate and hazelnut marquise and confit kumquats.

Chef Andrew Lincoln **Owner** Justin & Joanne Chad **Seats** 70, Pr/dining room 20 **Times** 12-3/5.30-11 Closed D 25-26 Dec, 1 Jan **Prices** Fixed L 2 course fr £12.50, Fixed D 3 course fr £17.50, Starter £4.95-£9.50, Main £10.95-£19.50, Dessert £4.50-£5.95, Service optional **Wines** 35 bottles over £30, 41 bottles under £30, 33 by glass **Parking** 35 **Notes** Early dining offer all week 6-7pm £7.77, Sunday L £13.95-£17.95, Vegetarian available, Children welcome

London

Index of London Restaurants

This index shows Rosetted restaurants in London in alphabetical order, followed by their postal district or location and plan/map references. Page numbers precede each entry.

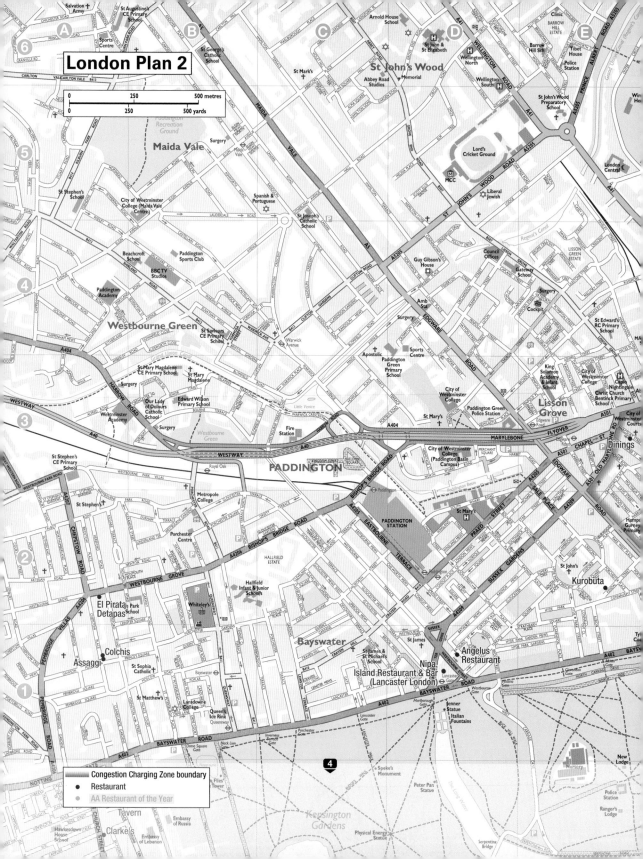

London Plan 2

0 — 250 — 500 metres
0 — 250 — 500 yards

Maida Vale

St John's Wood

Westbourne Green

Lisson Grove

Westway

PADDINGTON

Bayswater

Kensington Gardens

Congestion Charging Zone boundary
● Restaurant
● AA Restaurant of the Year

Dinings

Kurobuta

El Pirata Detapas

Assaggi

Colchis

Island Restaurant & Bar (Lancaster London)

Nipa

Angelus Restaurant

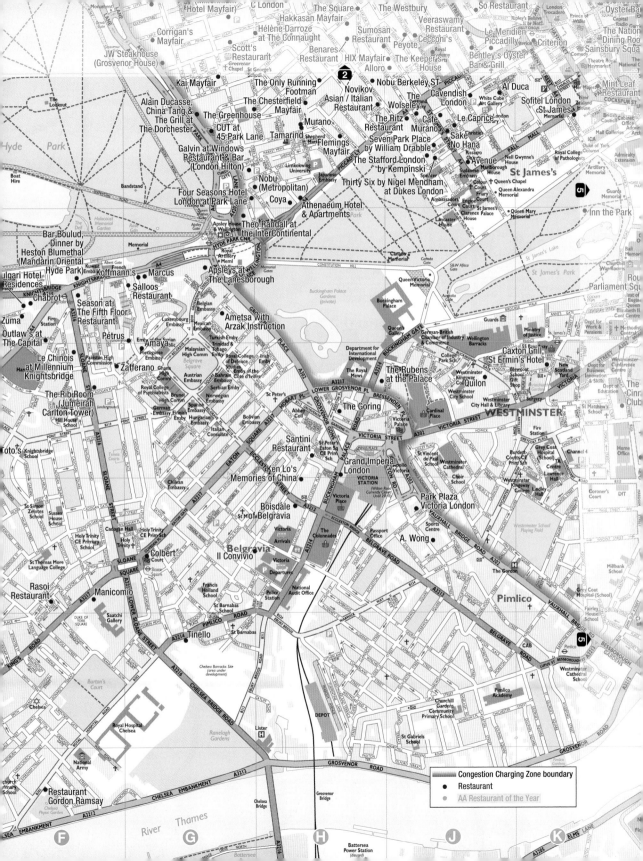

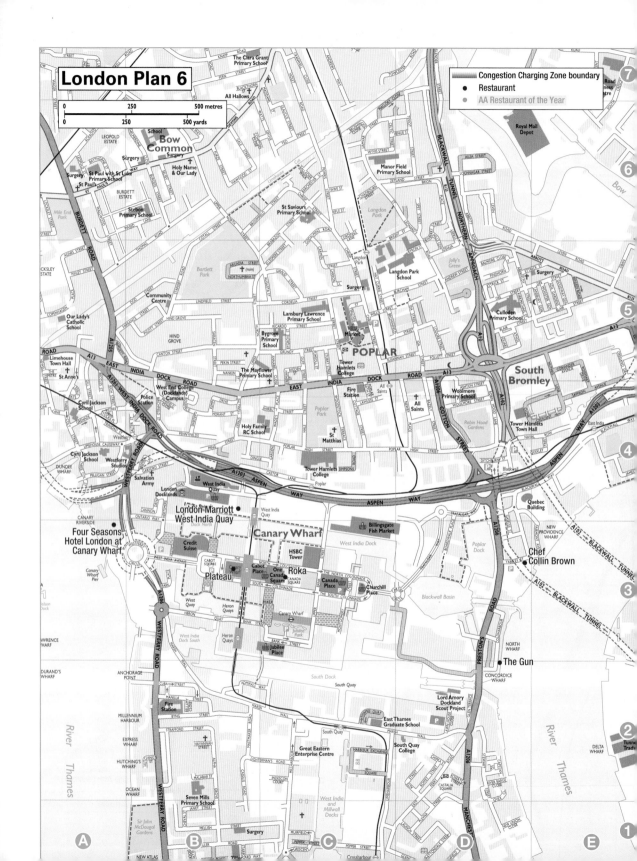

LONDON

Greater London Plans 1-6, pages 258-268: restaurants are listed below in postal district order, commencing East, then North, South and West, with a brief indication of the area covered. Detailed plans 2-6 show the locations of restaurants with AA Rosette Awards within the London postal districts. If you do not know the postal district of the restaurant you want, please refer to the index 254—55 preceding the street plans for the entry and map pages. The plan reference for each restaurant also appears within its directory entry.

LONDON

LONDON E1

Café Spice Namasté
PLAN 3 J1

⊛ Indian

tel: 020 7488 9242 **16 Prescot St E1 8AZ**
email: binay@cafespice.co.uk
dir: *Nearest station: Tower Gateway (DLR), Aldgate, Tower Hill*

Vibrant modern Indian cooking in Whitechapel

This longstanding Indian may be set in an imposing red-brick Victorian block, but its colourful interior is far more Mumbai than Whitechapel. Here, vibrantly-painted walls and colourful fabrics are matched by friendly service headed by the effervescent Pervin Todiwala, while husband Cyrus's refined, confidently spiced, inventive modern cooking draws on his Parsee roots and the best of seasonal British ingredients. From menus with detailed notes, perhaps start with street-food style Dahi Saev Batata Poori (explosive mouthfuls of crisp, wafer-thin puffed poories filled with crushed potato, spiced yoghurt, and tamarind and date chutney, sprinkled with chick pea vermicelli and fresh coriander). Specials up the ante – perhaps sea-fresh line-caught cod fillet for the main event, marinated with tamarind, crushed pepper, yoghurt and garlic, then chargrilled and served with coconut curry sauce. Otherwise, try a traditional Parsee-style chicken curry (Murgh Ni Curry Nay Papaeto): rich and exotic with spiced attitude and cooling coconut in equal parts.

Chef Cyrus Todiwala **Owner** Cyrus & Pervin Todiwala **Seats** 120
Times 12-3/6.15-10.30 Closed Xmas, BHs, Sun, L Sat **Prices** Fixed L 3 course £35-£70, Fixed D 3 course £35-£75, Tasting menu £75, Starter £5.75-£10.50, Main £14.50-£19.50, Dessert £5.95-£7.25 **Wines** 7 by glass **Parking** On street, NCP **Notes** Vegetarian available, Children welcome

Galvin Café a Vin
PLAN 3 H3

⊛⊛ French, Italian

tel: 020 7299 0404 **35 Spital Square E1 6DY**
email: info@galvinrestaurants.com
dir: *Nearest station: Liverpool St*

Bustling City wine café with good bistro cooking

Next door to La Chapelle (see entry opposite), part of the burgeoning empire of the frères Galvin, the clue to this café's true heart is in its name. The interesting, often biodynamic, organic or natural wines on offer come in a variety of measures, and you can sample them sitting at the burnished zinc bar, at a table in the pint-sized interior, or on the heated and covered garden terrace at the back (you can also dine where you wish, too). A jazz pianist plays on Monday and Saturday evenings to boost the already-lively vibe. Jack Boast cooks to an Anglo-French template, doing onion soup with Gruyère croûtons and escargots à la bourguignonne, with perhaps bream fillet in anchovy dressing and purple sprouting broccoli to follow. It's well-wrought modern bistro cooking with the emphasis on hang-loose informality, justifiably popular at lunchtimes and early evening, when a value prix-fixe with a pair of choices at each course might offer soused herrings, then cured pork rib-eye with green beans and mash. Finish with rum baba and Chantilly, or rhubarb cheesecake. Cheeses are from Spitalfields specialists Androuet.

Chef Jack Boast, Jeff Galvin **Owner** Chris & Jeff Galvin **Seats** 47 **Times** 11.30-10.30 Closed 25-26 Dec, 1 Jan, D 24 Dec All-day dining **Prices** Fixed L 3 course fr £19.95, Fixed D 3 course fr £19.95, Starter £5.50-£22, Main £14-£17.50, Dessert £4-£7.50 **Wines** 20 bottles over £30, 11 bottles under £30, 12 by glass **Parking** On street, Spital Square **Notes** Fixed D 6-7pm, Sunday L £16.50-£19.95, Vegetarian available, Children welcome

Galvin La Chapelle
PLAN 3 H3

⊛⊛⊛ – *see page 270*

Marco Pierre White Steak & Alehouse
PLAN 3 H3

⊛ Modern European V

tel: 020 7247 5050 **East India House, 109-117 Middlesex St E1 7JF**
email: info@mpwsteakandalehouse.org
dir: *Nearest station: Liverpool Street*

Quality City steakhouse in bright basement setting

This roll-out brand offers a brasserie-style roster of dishes with timeless English appeal and plenty of ideas from France and Italy. Thus Brit classics like York ham with home-made piccalilli meet tuna steak provençale or wild halibut à la Sicilienne. Meat is the mainstay, with Scottish steaks (from fillet to top-drawer Chateaubriand for two – with the usual choice of sauces) to the likes of calves' liver and dry-cured bacon. Expect well-sourced ingredients and cooking that's not too showy, but factor-in necessary side order veg, while desserts tend to stay on the nursery slopes (Eton Mess to sticky toffee pudding). The basement setting – hidden away from the Bishopsgate mayhem – is a light, clean-cut space, decked out with wooden flooring, red leather chairs, white linen-clad tables and walls lined with JAK cartoons (of Mail on Sunday fame). Throw in well-selected wines and good cocktails and all bases are covered.

Chef Juan Lopez **Owner** James & Rachael Robertson **Seats** 80, Pr/dining room 34 **Times** 12-3/5.30-10 Closed 25 Dec, 1 Jan **Prices** Fixed L 3 course £23.50-£54.50, Fixed D 3 course £23.50-£54.50, Starter £7-£22.50, Main £17.50-£33, Dessert £7.50-£9.50 **Wines** 100 bottles over £30, 23 bottles under £30, 19 by glass **Parking** On street after 6.30pm **Notes** Sunday L £23.50, Children welcome

St John Bread & Wine
PLAN 3 J3

⊛ British

tel: 020 7251 0848 **94-96 Commercial St E1 6LZ**
email: reservations@stjohnbreadandwine.com
dir: *Nearest station: Liverpool Street/Aldgate East*

Gutsy British cooking in Spitalfields

The name sums up the back-to-basics approach to dining in this operation across the street from Spitalfields Market. The younger, smaller sibling of St John is a wonderfully utilitarian, canteen-like space, with whitewashed walls, old wooden furniture and an open-to-view kitchen and bakery, and the focus – like the original – is on the trademark nose-to-tail British food. Expect unfussy and robust dishes, driven by flavour and quality seasonal produce, including those lesser-known cuts and ingredients: where else could you see pig's head stew, or blood cake and duck egg on the menu? There's no truck with three-course convention either, just small and larger plates so sharing is encouraged. Start with devilled duck hearts on home-made toast, or skate cheeks with tartare sauce, and proceed to pheasant and trotter pie. Breads are exceptional, and for pud, there's the likes of Eccles cake and Lancashire cheese, or date loaf and butterscotch sauce.

Chef Tristram Bowden **Owner** Trevor Gulliver & Fergus Henderson **Seats** 60 **Times** 9am-11pm Closed 24 Dec-1 Jan, All-day dining **Prices** Starter £6.90-£9.10, Main £14.10-£17.10, Dessert £6.90-£7.20, Service optional **Wines** 70 bottles over £30, 15 bottles under £30, 12 by glass **Parking** On street **Notes** Vegetarian available, Children welcome

Galvin La Chapelle

French 🍾 NOTABLE WINE LIST

tel: 020 7299 0400
St. Botolph's Hall, 35 Spital Square E1 6DY
email: info@galvinrestaurants.com
web: www.galvinrestaurants.com
dir: *Nearest station: Liverpool Street*

Victorian school chapel with classic and modern French cooking

The Galvin brothers have gone on expanding their London restaurant empire without evidently missing a beat. La Chapelle in Spitalfields was the third in the series, so called because it was once the chapel of a Victorian girls' school, St Botolph's. It's possible to feel fairly small huddled on a chocolate-brown banquette, surrounded by marble pillars that stretch on up to the distant ceiling, some thirty metres above you. But while towering magnificence is fine in the decor, it isn't necessarily what you want in the service approach, and fortunately the Chapelle runs on a mix of friendliness and efficiency. Jeff Galvin's menus, in the hands of head chef Zac Whittle, return us to the magnificent with interpretations of French cuisine both classical and moderne. The flirtation with demotic bistro cooking evident in the earliest iterations of the Galvin formula are sustained here. So you could start with a bowl of wild mushroom consommé laced with pearl barley, or a slab of ham hock and foie gras terrine dressed with red onion marmalade, but then an assemblage of warm smoked eel, Alsace bacon and caramelised pineapple catches the eye. At main course, there are inviting compositions of flavours that are simultaneously unusual and yet wholly intuitive, such as Seville orange-glazed sea bream with endive, pine-nuts, capers and raisins, and others that borrow more obviously from current British modes – loin and faggot of Denham venison with pickled red cabbage and a mingled purée of apple and chestnuts. Other culinary traditions are roped in as appropriate – polenta with the guinea-fowl, or couscous, preserved lemon and harissa to suit a pigeon tagine – reminding us that modern French cooking has been as acquisitive as modern British. At close of business, it could be classic Tatin with Normandy crème fraîche, or poached rhubarb with shortbread, ginger crème patissière and pistachios.

Chef Zac Whittle, Jeff Galvin **Owner** Chris & Jeff Galvin **Seats** 110, Pr/dining room 16 **Times** 12-2.30/6-10.30 Closed 25-26 Dec, 1 Jan, D 24 Dec **Prices** Fixed L 2 course fr £24, Fixed D 3 course fr £29, Tasting menu £70-£120, Starter £9.50-£18.50, Main £22.50-£33.50 **Wines** 271 bottles over £30, 20 bottles under £30, 18 by glass **Parking** On street, NCP **Notes** Fixed price D 6-7pm, Tasting menu 7 course, Sunday L £29-£39, Vegetarian available, Children welcome

LONDON E1 *continued*

Super Tuscan
PLAN 3 H3

◉ Italian

tel: 020 7247 8717 **8A Artillery Passage E1 7LJ**
email: info@supertuscan.co.uk
dir: *Nearest station: Liverpool Street*

An authentic enoteca in Spitalfields

An unassuming entrance leads into a parquet-floored restaurant with brown banquettes along one wall, plain wooden chairs, some booths, and tall stools at a long bar, the sort of functional interior, like many enotecas, that doesn't distract attention from the gutsy Italian food on offer here – or from the intelligently chosen Italian wines. Start with 'sample-sized portions', to use menu-speak: arancini di prosciutto (fried rice balls stuffed with ham, parmesan and béchamel) or polpette di vitello (veal meatballs poached in stock with peas and potatoes), or go for an antipasti platter of assorted meats or regional cheeses for sharing, and proceed to a classic Tuscan dish of chargrilled sausages with fennel seeds. Ingredients, sourced from Italy, are used in authentic Italian recipes, and dishes are big on flavour. Finish with ricotta-stuffed doughnuts with a scoop of outstanding ice cream.

Chef Nick Grossi **Owner** Nick Grossi **Seats** 30 **Times** 12-2.30/5.30-10 Closed Xmas, New Year, Sat-Sun **Prices** Starter £4-£7.95, Main £9.50-£20, Dessert £2.50-£8.50, Service optional **Wines** 35 bottles over £30, 27 bottles under £30, 14 by glass **Notes** Vegetarian available, Children welcome

Les Trois Garçons
PLAN 3 J4

◉◉ French

tel: 020 7613 1924 **1 Club Row, Shoreditch E1 6JX**
email: info@lestroisgarcons.com web: www.lestroisgarcons.com
dir: *Nearest station: Liverpool Street*

Theatrical surroundings for some smart fine dining

An inspired choice for a date or a flamboyant venue for a City business lunch, this one-time Shoreditch pub turned unique French restaurant – just five minutes' walk from Bishopsgate – is a jaw-dropping exercise in chic, high-camp interior design. Sit beneath dangling retro handbags, bejewelled chandeliers or perhaps a stuffed giraffe's head craning from the wall, and yes, that tiger is wearing a necklace and that chimpanzee a tiara. Okay, it might be something of a Marmite venue – you'll either love it or hate it – but it is wonderfully surreal and glamorous, especially by candlelight, and there's no denying the quality and flair of its modern, clear-flavoured and well-dressed French-inspired food. Take rabbit saddle and mushroom roulade with lasagne of its leg, baby carrots and pea shoots to open, and to follow, perhaps Chateaubriand served with roasted potatoes, green beans, Szechuan

pepper jus and béarnaise. Finish with frozen coconut 'nougat' and passionfruit coulis. Charming and knowledgeable service and a French-led wine list complete the picture.

Chef Michael Chan **Owner** Stefan Karlson, Hassan Abdullah, Michel Lassere **Seats** 65, Pr/dining room 10 **Times** 12-2.30/6-9.30 Closed Xmas, New Year, Sun, L Mon-Wed, Sat **Prices** Prices not confirmed **Wines** 90 bottles over £30, 10 bottles under £30, 13 by glass **Parking** On street **Notes** Vegetarian available, No children

Upstairs at The Ten Bells
PLAN 3 J3

◉◉ Seasonal Modern British NEW

tel: 07530 492 986 **First Floor, 84 Commercial St E1 6LY**
email: reservations@tenbells.com
dir: *Nearest station: Shoreditch High St*

In-place Spitalfields gaff for cool, inspired dining

Originally set up as a pop-up by Isaac McHale of the Young Turks chefs' collective, this permanent reincarnation above the high-octane former 'Jack the Ripper' pub is as cool as they come. Hip, pared-back and shabby-chic, the dining room is a trendy confection of mismatched darkwood furniture, scuffed floorboards, retro chandeliers, floor-standing candelabra and edgy contemporary art. The backing track, buzz from downstairs bar and low lighting ride perfectly with the inspiring modern seasonal cooking, marked by flair and layers of flavour, with well-considered dishes delivered with finesse without being overworked. Take a 'wow' dessert of the sweetest roast pineapple, for instance, cleverly teamed with goats' milk rice pudding, yoghurt 'crumb' and skilfully balanced madras sorbet. Ex-Ledbury chef Giorgio Ravelli's compact yet appealing carte starts out with fashionable snacks such as buttermilk chicken and pine salt. The mains feature 'knockout combos' like succulent rolled lamb breast and sweetbreads, accompanied by sweet sandy carrots, caraway and salted lemon. Relaxed and informed service fits the bill, as do the reasonable prices and the excellent wines from France and Italy. Our advice: get here!

Chef Giorgio Ravelli **Owner** Isaac McHale, Johnny Smith, Daniel Willis, Patrick Fawley **Seats** 45, Pr/dining room 15 **Times** 12-2.30/6-10.30 Closed Mon, D Sun **Prices** Fixed L 2 course £17, Fixed D 3 course £39, Tasting menu £45-£55, Starter £7.50-£7.90, Main £15.90-£17.90, Dessert £5-£7, Service optional **Wines** 23 bottles over £30, 11 bottles under £30, 7 by glass **Parking** White's Row car park **Notes** Express L menu 2/3 course £17/£21, Sunday L £6.50-£18.50, Vegetarian available, Children welcome

Brawn
PLAN 3 K5

◉◉ Traditional European 🍷 NOTABLE WINE LIST

tel: 020 7729 5692 **49 Columbia Rd E2 7RG**
email: enquiries@brawn.co
dir: *Nearest station: Liverpool St, Bethnal Green*

Smart, honest cooking in trendy East London

Aside from the vibrant Columbia Road Sunday flower market, Brawn (sibling to Covent Garden's Terroirs) is arguably this edgier quarter of East London's main draw. Set among a run of interesting artisanal shops, the corner-sited restaurant is a fittingly hard-edged and pared-back neighbourhood outfit. The trendy warehouse-like interior of white-painted brickwork, high ceilings and dangling lamps is divided across a pair of rooms separated by a dinky bar. Plain-wood tables and retro wooden chairs foster the chilled look, while the staff are both smiley and informed. The European-focused daily-changing menu (provincial French and Italian with input from Spain) is driven by seasonality and provenance, and the cooking follows a simple path to deliver big-hearted flavours. Three-course formality is dispensed with here in favour of a selection of small plates for sharing. Piggy treats might

continued

LONDON E9 *continued*

take in namesake brawn or rillettes, to prime charcuterie, while gutsy offerings like duck gizzards line up alongside the more conventional, such as a summery risotto of girolles, English peas and parmesan. Top-drawer sourdough and superb wines – from biodynamic and organic producers – demand additional applause.

Chef Owen Kenworthy **Owner** Ed Wilson, Oli Barker **Seats** 70 **Times** 12-3/6-11 Closed Xmas, New Year, BHs, L Mon, D Sun **Prices** Starter £7-£13, Main £10-£16, Dessert £5-£6 **Wines** 98 bottles over £30, 33 bottles under £30, 14 by glass **Parking** On street **Notes** Sunday L £28, Vegetarian available, Children welcome

LONDON E9

The Empress

PLAN 1 G4

 Modern British

tel: 020 8533 5123 **130 Lauriston Rd, Victoria Park E9 7LH**
dir: *Nearest station: Cambridge Heath, Mile End*

Laid-back crowd-pleaser with simple, feisty dishes

With the generous proportions of a Victorian pub and the white walls, bare brickwork, claret Chesterfield banquettes, modern art and canteen-like simplicity of an on-trend contemporary urban eatery, The Empress slots right into the easygoing vibe of its Victoria Park neighbourhood. The kitchen brigade is led by Hackney resident Elliott Lidstone who comes hot-foot from the high-achieving L'ortolan (see entry), and while there's none of that highfalutin' stuff going on here, the emphasis is still firmly on quality produce cooked with care and skill. The simple approach delivers retro ham croquettes, which doesn't sound like it will get your motor running, but they are well-made, creamy and crunchy, or there are similar offerings along the lines of pig's ears, or crab on toast, which you could treat as either bar snacks or nibbly starters. A brace of roasted quails on top of chargrilled spring salad shares the stage with snails with bone marrow and wild garlic, or there might be rainbow trout with Jersey Royals and braised lettuce. End with ginger pannacotta with rhubarb or chocolate mousse with peanut brittle and lime.

Chef Elliott Lidstone **Owner** Michael Buurman **Seats** 49 **Times** 12-3.30/6-10.15 Closed 25-26 Dec, L Mon (ex BHs) **Prices** Starter £4.50-£8, Main £11.50-£23, Dessert £5.60-£5.70 **Wines** 24 bottles over £30, 42 bottles under £30, 14 by glass **Parking** On street **Notes** Brunch available Sat-Sun 10-12, Sunday L, Vegetarian available, Children welcome

LONDON E14

Chef Collin Brown

PLAN 6 D3

 Caribbean

tel: 020 7515 8177 **2 Yabsley St E14 9RG**
email: info@chefcollinbrown.com
dir: *Nearest station: Blackwall*

Authentic Caribbean flavours in the Docklands

Almost in the shadow of Canary Wharf's skyscrapers and with the Thames a few paces away, Chef Collin Brown's Caribbean restaurant is a smart, modern affair yet with a genuine laid-back neighbourhood vibe. A glass-fronted semi-circular space occupying a corner site below an apartment complex, the decor comes with a touch of Caribbean flamboyance. Luxuriant wall-coverings in gold and black meet glitzy chandeliers and gilded mirrors, high-back, plum-coloured dining chairs, parquet flooring and a funky Caribbean soundtrack. The man himself was born in Jamaica and brings his passion for the Caribbean to the table in uncomplicated dishes that are bold and expressive. Witness classic mains like a highly seasoned boneless goat curry, or succulent, high-octane jerk chicken breast, while a light, boozy signature rum, cognac and almond sponge-cake dessert or mango cheesecake finish things off in tropical style. Cocktails take you straight back to holidays in the sun.

Times 5-11.30 Closed Xmas, New Year, L all week

Four Seasons Hotel London at Canary Wharf

PLAN 6 A3

 Italian V

tel: 020 7510 1858 & 7510 1999 **46 Westferry Circus, Canary Wharf E14 8RS**
email: restaurant.quadrato.caw@fourseasons.com
web: www.fourseasons.com/canarywharf
dir: *Nearest station: Canary Wharf*

Traditional northern Italian cooking at Canary Wharf

You may be enveloped within the corporate embrace of Canary Wharf, but the Four Seasons does its best to disavow the setting with its terrace tables looking on to the little courtyard garden and pool. Inside the Quadrato restaurant proper, a slick modern ambience of chocolate-brown banquettes, white cubic pillars and an open kitchen is the setting for a light approach to fairly traditional northern Italian cooking. A soft-boiled duck egg on a potato cake dressed in truffle oil is an appetising starter, and might be followed by one of the customary intermediate risottos or pastas, perhaps creamy-sauced smoked salmon penne with broccoli. A carefully timed slab of grilled tuna with puréed basil is a refreshing main dish, as an alternative to duck breast with figs in balsamic sauce, or grilled lamb cutlets with caponata. Classic tiramisù, or honey pannacotta with an emulsion of orange and pistachio, round things off in style.

Chef Moreno Casaccia **Owner** Four Seasons Hotels & Resorts **Seats** 90 **Times** 12-3/6-10.30 **Prices** Fixed L 2 course £19, Fixed D 3 course £25, Starter £7-£15, Main £13-£28, Dessert £7, Service optional **Wines** 110 bottles over £30, 8 bottles under £30, 35 by glass **Parking** 26 **Notes** Brunch £45, Sunday L £45, Vegetarian available, Children welcome

The Gun

PLAN 6 D2

 Modern British

tel: 020 7515 5222 **27 Coldharbour E14 9NS**
email: info@thegundocklands.com
dir: *Nearest station: South Quay DLR, Canary Wharf*

Gutsy British food in an historic waterside pub

This handsomely remodelled former dockers' boozer comes with a hot-ticket Thames-side setting and is entirely worth the short cab ride from Canary Wharf. Views across the water of the O2 Arena and 2012 Olympic park are part of the package, along with a vibrant, lively atmosphere and big-hearted gastro-pub cooking. There's a smart dining room in the main bar at the front, a smaller bar with two cosy snugs at the back, and it's all decked out with polished wood floorboards, framed naval art on white walls, and burgundy leather seating. Dishes are generous and fashioned from quality ingredients, and the menu runs from classics like beer-battered cod and Wiener schnitzel, to more modish offerings such as curried haddock croquettes or monkfish tail served with smoked bacon and peas, baby gem and a butter sauce.

Times 12-3/6-10.30 Closed 25-26 Dec

Who has won our Food Service Award?
See page 13

London Marriott West India Quay

PLAN 6 B4

Modern International NEW

tel: 020 7517 2808 **22 Hertsmere Rd, Canary Wharf E14 4ED**
email: info@manhattangrill.co.uk **web:** www.manhattangrill.co.uk
dir: *Nearest station: Canary Wharf/West India Quay DLR*

Prime steaks cooked at 650°c overlooking the cityscape

From its soaring waterside tower of shimmering glass, the London Marriott West India Quay's Manhattan Grill restaurant offers a view over the corporate cityscape. It's a modern space on a big scale with large windows, darkwood tables and a calming lilac colour scheme. Steaks are the name of the game, cooked in a Montague broiler at 650°c. Toppings and sides are extra (blue cheese crust and sweet potato fries, maybe), and the meat itself is Creekstone Kansas USDA Black Angus or Scottish Aberdeen Angus in cuts from New York Strip to rib-eye. There are a few starters, too, such as clam chowder or seared scallops with cauliflower purée and crispy pancetta, and a few non-meaty mains such as roasted black cod with bok choy. Finish with sticky toffee pudding or pecan pie.

Chef Damian Trejo **Seats** 100, Pr/dining room 45 **Times** 5-10.30 Closed L all week **Prices** Fixed D 3 course £30, Starter £6.50-£13, Main £12-£34, Dessert £6-£8 **Wines** 49 bottles over £30, 16 bottles under £30, 21 by glass **Parking** Car park 2 mins away **Notes** Vegetarian available, Children welcome

Plateau

PLAN 6 B3

Modern French V NOTABLE WINE LIST

tel: 020 7715 7100 **4th Floor, Canada Place, Canada Square, Canary Wharf E14 5ER**
email: plateaureservations@danddlondon.com
dir: *Nearest station: Canary Wharf DLR/Tube*

Sophisticated, contemporary fine dining in futuristic landscape

There are show-stopping views over Canary Wharf's high-rise cityscape from the aptly named Plateau – a sleek, glass-and-steel roof-top restaurant set four floors up above the shopping mall. The long, lightdrenched space is divided into two zones by a central theatre-style kitchen, each with its own bar and outdoor terrace. The hip Bar & Grill (cocktails and brasserie menu) is up first, while the restaurant on the other side is calmer and more sophisticated. The design mixes retro styling with warm, restrained neutral tones in the restaurant; think funky white plastic 'tulip' swivel dining chairs and curvy upholstered banquettes, white marble-topped tables, huge arching stainless-steel floor lamps, stunning flower arrangements and changing art displays. But it's not all style over substance here, the ambitious, light, well-dressed modern European cooking – underpinned by a classic French theme – shows real pedigree, driven by quality seasonal materials. Take a duo of fine-tuned signature dishes from the carte: English parsley risotto with sauté of snails, garlic butter and red wine jus, and main-course honey-spiced Goosnargh duck with braised endive and port-marinated radish. Desserts keep up the style count, perhaps organic lemon posset with kalamansi crush and jelly, while the wine list is one of distinction.

Chef Allan Pickett **Owner** D & D London **Seats** 120, Pr/dining room 30 **Times** 12-2.30/6-10.15 Closed 25-26 Dec, Sun, L Sat **Prices** Fixed L 2 course fr £22, Fixed D 3 course fr £25, Tasting menu £49-£69, Starter £7.50-£14.50, Main £16.50-£32, Dessert £5-£13.50 **Wines** 400 bottles over £30, 30 bottles under £30, 24 by glass **Parking** 500 **Notes** Tasting menu 6 course with wine, Children welcome

Roka

PLAN 6 C3

Japanese

tel: 020 7636 5228 **1st Floor, 40 Canada Square E14 5FW**
email: infocanarywharf@rokarestaurant.com
dir: *Nearest station: Canary Wharf*

Top-flight Japanese cooking in Canary Wharf

Overlooking Canada Square, Roka is a flavour of the East in Canary Wharf and though times may be hard, it still seems to be pulling in the punters. The interior, like its sister restaurant in Charlotte Street (see entry), has acres of wood offering a pleasing contrast to all that glass and concrete outside, and the robata grill doesn't quite hold centre stage as it does up west. Nevertheless, this is an appealing contemporary space and a fine place to enjoy the divertingly confident Japanese food. Sushi and sashimi remain a highlight and a good way to kick off a meal, but whichever way you go, quality runs right through. The negi toro maki roll is made with first-class tuna, or you might go for a fresh water eel version with avocado and cucumber. From the robata grill, spiced chicken wings are perked up with Sancho salt and lime, and black cod is marinated in yuzu miso. Desserts are no afterthought, and if the weather is up to scratch, there's a terrace from which you might actually be able to smell the money.

Chef Jose Ballesteros **Owner** Rainer Becker, Arjun Waney **Seats** 88 **Times** 12-3.30/5.30-11.30 Closed 25 Dec **Prices** Prices not confirmed **Wines** 152 bottles over £30, 13 by glass **Parking** On street **Notes** Sun brunch £42, with champagne £54, Vegetarian available, Children welcome

LONDON EC1

Bistrot Bruno Loubet

PLAN 3 E4

Modern French

tel: 020 7324 4444 & 7324 4567 **The Zetter Hotel, St John's Square, 86-89 Clerkenwell Rd EC1M 5RJ**
email: info@thezetter.com **web:** www.bistrotbrunoloubet.com
dir: *Nearest station: Farringdon*

Proper bistro cooking in a trendy Clerkenwell hotel

French chef Bruno Loubet has been a mover and shaker on London's dining scene on and off for a couple of decades. He has opened another restaurant in Kings Cross, called Grain Store (see entry) where the humble vegetable is given elevated status on the menu (although it isn't a vegetarian restaurant by any means). Here, at the trendy Zetter Hotel in Clerkenwell, the offering in the laid-back, modern Bistrot is of a much more meaty variety. While dishes may be aesthetically presented, they are at heart proper bistro food, with a pleasantly peasanty undertow. A fat little boudin blanc in a bowl of garbure (ham stew) is the kind of starter Londoners were starved of during the ascendancy of molecular cooking, and is all the more welcome a prospect for its rustic richness. That might be followed by fried grey mullet with salt cod and celeriac, the skin of the mullet singed but the flavour loud and proud, or perhaps the signature hare royale, or a hearty rabbit ragoût with tagliatelle. Flawlessly neat apple tart with crème fraîche and cinnamon sugar makes a fine finish.

Times 12-2.30/6-10.30 Closed 23-27 Dec

Looking for a London restaurant by name?
Use the index on page 254

Find out more about how we assess for Rosette awards on page 9

LONDON EC1 *continued*

The Bleeding Heart
PLAN 3 D3

Modern French NOTABLE WINE LIST

tel: 020 7242 2056 **Bleeding Heart Yard, Off Greville St EC1N 8SJ**
email: bookings@bleedingheart.co.uk
dir: *Nearest station: Farringdon, Chancery Lane*

Revamped French cooking in Hatton Garden favourite

The Yard takes its name from a gruesome 17th-century murder, and nowadays it's the site of a tavern and an informal bistro as well as this smart basement restaurant, a series of rooms with beamed ceilings, fireplaces and panelling. This is the setting for some ambitious French cooking, a fact underlined by bilingual menus. But the kitchen moves with the times, marinating salmon in vodka and beetroot and serving it with salmon caviar, or partnering seared scallops with leek purée, candied lemon and purple shiso leaves. Among main courses, a down-to-earth approach can be given to prime cuts, so tournedos of beef is accompanied by braised cheeks and bourguignon sauce, while a luxury like lobster (in Provençal-style risotto) might be offered on the same day as roast suckling pig with faggots, apple sauce and fondant potato. Among Gallic-inspired desserts of crème brûlée and prune and Armagnac tart there might also be violet-flavoured bread-and-butter pudding.

Chef Julian Marshall **Owner** Robert & Robyn Wilson **Seats** 110, Pr/dining room 40 **Times** 12-3/6-10.30 Closed Xmas & New Year (10 days), Sat-Sun (Bistro open Sat) **Prices** Fixed L 2 course £21, Fixed D 3 course £30, Starter £7-£13, Main £14-£29 **Wines** 360 bottles over £30, 40 bottles under £30, 23 by glass **Parking** 20 evening only, NCP nearby **Notes** Vegetarian available, No children

Le Café du Marché
PLAN 3 E3

French

tel: 020 7608 1609 **Charterhouse Mews, Charterhouse Square EC1M 6AH**
dir: *Nearest station: Barbican*

Rustic, Gallic cooking in a classically converted warehouse

When the urge for Gallic gastronomy strikes, but you don't have time to pop over la Manche, head down a cobbled alley off Charterhouse Square for this authentic slice of France. Set in a rustic-chic converted Victorian warehouse, the place drips classic cross-Channel style with its bare-brick walls, French posters, jazz pianist and bentwood seats at candlelit, starched linen-dressed tables. The scene thus set, you can expect unreconstructed French provincial dishes on an uncomplicated two- or three-course fixed price menu. This honest peasant cooking has stood the test of time, starting with a classic fish soup, or duck salad with Portobello mushrooms and walnut dressing, and progressing to an onglet steak with shallots, parsley and garlic. Two diners might sign up for a grilled leg of milk-fed Pyrenean lamb with flageolet beans and Madeira sauce. Finish with a chocolate and caramel bavarois, or the splendid selection of French cheeses.

Chef Simon Cottard **Owner** Anna Graham-Wood **Seats** 120, Pr/dining room 65 **Times** 12-2.30/6-10 Closed Xmas, New Year, Etr, BHs, Sun, L Sat **Prices** Prices not confirmed **Wines** **Parking** Next door (small charge) **Notes** Vegetarian available, Children welcome

The Clove Club
PLAN 3 H5

– see below

The Clove Club

| LONDON EC1 | PLAN 3 H5 |

British Fine Dining NEW v

tel: 020 7729 6496 **Shoreditch Town Hall, 380 Old St EC1V 9LT**
email: hello@thecloveclub.com
dir: *Nearest station: Old Street*

Magical culinary mystery tour in the old Shoreditch Town Hall

The trend for converting the old banking temples into restaurants has been a familiar one in the most recent generation, but Clove Club goes one grander by setting up camp in the old Shoreditch Town Hall on Old Street, next to Hoxton Square and not far from Liverpool Street station. Built in 1865, it's all porticos and pediments, and while it ceased to be a local government building in the 1960s, it now houses arts venues and this rather chic, trend-conscious eatery. Depending on your style and quantum of free time, you can eat quickly and simply in the bar, or sign up for one of the fixed-price menus in the principal restaurant. These rise to the majesty of a nine-course taster, with new-fangled and revived forgotten ingredients all over the show. The menu specifications eschew the modern tendency to surreal elaboration, and settle instead for a tantalising pared-down approach that leaves you guessing. Grey mullet tartare on rye sounds like something you might buy at a sandwich bar, while buttermilk fried chicken and pine salt is a more robust beginner. Main courses raise eyebrows as well as expectations – try Scottish blood pudding with chicory and overripe pear, Cornish sea bass with smoked roe and spinach, or Hebridean lamb with January king cabbage in seaweed sauce. The Scots note surfaces again in a finisher of peated barley cake and rhubarb compôte, while the house chocolate bar may be presumed to owe something to the machinations of what, until very recently, we used to call molecular gastronomy. Vegetarian dishes are all the more idiosyncratic: radishes, black sesame and gochujang (fermented Korean chilli paste); baked beetroot in apple vinegar and elderberry; leek in Montgomery Cheddar with crystal malt, that last a legal high of sorts. Pre-selected wine pairings only add to the sense of a magical mystery tour.

Chef Isaac McHale **Owner** Isaac McHale, Daniel Willis, Johnny Max Smith **Seats** 47 **Times** 12-2.30/6-10 Closed Xmas, New Year, Sun, L Mon **Prices** Fixed L 3 course £35, Tasting menu £55-£95, Starter £4.50-£9.50, Main £14-£22 **Wines** 40 bottles over £30, 8 bottles under £30, 10 by glass **Notes** Tasting menu 5/9 course £55/£85-£95, Children welcome

Club Gascon
PLAN 3 E3

@@@ – *see below*

Le Comptoir Gascon
PLAN 3 E3

@ Traditional French

tel: 020 7608 0851 **61-63 Charterhouse St EC1M 6HJ**
email: info@comptoirgascon.com
dir: *Nearest station: Farringdon, Barbican, St Paul's*

Gutsy French dishes by Smithfield Market

The casual, bustling, petite bistro-deli sibling of heavyweight Club Gascon (see entry), Comptoir deals in the gutsy food of southwest France. The feel is one of true cuisine terroir, with simple market-driven cooking and full-on flavours: duck confit and garbure béarnaise, for example, or a traditional Toulousain cassoulet. Lighter things might include crispy squid Basquaise with garlic and mixed herbs, while desserts – like lemon tart or a classic chocolate fondant – keep things simple yet show acute technical ability in their making. The decor fits the bill with its modern-rustic vibe; exposed brickwork and ducting, dinky elbow-to-elbow wooden tables, small velour-covered chairs and copious wines tantalising from their cabinets. The fixed-price blackboard lunch menu offers good value, while the miniscule deli counter – with displays of breads, conserves, pastries and the like – offers supplies to takeaway. Well-selected wines are from southwest France... where else?

Times 12-2.30/7-10 Closed 25 Dec-1 Jan, BHs, Sun-Mon

Hix Oyster & Chop House
PLAN 3 E3

@ Modern British V

tel: 020 7017 1930 **36-37 Greenhill Rents, Cowcross St EC1M 6BN**
email: chophouse@restaurantetcltd.co.uk
dir: *Nearest station: Farringdon*

Accomplished ingredient-led Brit cooking in chilled-out Clerkenwell

Mark Hix's first outfit in a now burgeoning portfolio, it perfectly embraces its Smithfield setting. Wooden floors, tiled walls, darkwood and whirring ceiling fans characterise the cool, pared-down space, pepped-up by leather seating, white linen, edgy artwork and a jazz soundtrack.The kitchen takes a similar unfussy approach, the updated British cooking reflecting the Hix credo for quality local, seasonal ingredients (with producers duly name-checked) treated with simplicity, respect and flair. Wild ingredients play their part, as does fish (take sea aster served with sparkling-fresh steamed Torbay hake fillet and Morecambe Bay shrimp), though meats are the main draw; think Boccadon Farm veal chop with sage butter or perhaps well-marbled steaks like South Devon ruby red fillet. It also lives up to its other billing, with great oysters like Blackwater wild or Maldon pearls. Round-off with home-spun desserts (perhaps Wye Valley rhubarb and Bramley apple pie), plus great wines, Brit-brew beers and ciders, and interesting cocktails.

Chef Jamie Guy **Owner** Mark Hix **Seats** 65 **Times** 12-11 Closed 25-26 Dec, BHs, L Sat All-day dining **Prices** Fixed L 2 course £19.50, Starter £7.25-£14.50, Main £16.95-£75, Dessert £1.90-£7.50 **Wines** 56 bottles over £30, 13 bottles under £30, 17 by glass **Parking** On street (meters) **Notes** D served from 5.30pm, Sunday L, Children welcome

Club Gascon

LONDON EC1
PLAN 3 E3

Modern French V NOTABLE WINE LIST

tel: 020 7600 6144 **57 West Smithfields EC1A 9DS**
email: info@clubgascon.com
dir: *Nearest station: Barbican, Farringdon, St Paul's*

Exciting South West French food in a palatial room

Behind the grey facade near Smithfield Market is a grand, high-ceilinged interior of marble walls, oak floors, blue banquettes at closely set tables and giant flower displays, presided over by clued-up, helpful staff and a sommelier offering guidance through the lengthy wine list. The culinary focus is on the cuisine of South West France, Gascony in particular, from where much of the produce is imported, and Pascal Aussignac's cooking remains as vibrant, avant-garde and exciting as it did when it first opened. Meals are constructed around tapas-size dishes, with the menu divided into five sections, from La Route du Sel to Les Pâturages, with Les Foies Gras holding the middle ground. Newcomers can seek help about what and how much to order; they, as well as eager returnees, will find innovative, distinctive dishes, well balanced and technically flawless, using often unfamiliar ingredients of superb quality. A selection could include venison carpaccio with winkles, salted cod and confit ceps; smoked chestnut velouté with pine moss and nasturtium root; and grilled foie gras with grape and shallot chutney. Choosing from the L'Océan section could bring on roast monkfish with wild mushrooms, potted mussels and chestnuts; and cappuccino of black pudding with lobster and asparagus. The style continues into puddings such as blackberry pearls in matcha tea with parsnip ice cream. The two-course set lunch is considered a snip, and there's also a five-course Le Marché menu.

Chef Pascal Aussignac **Owner** P Aussignac & V Labeyrie **Seats** 40 **Times** 12-2/6.30-10 Closed Xmas, New Year, BHs, Sun, L Sat **Prices** Fixed L 2 course £25, Fixed D 2 course £25, Tasting menu £60, Starter £9.50-£16, Main £18.50-£26, Dessert £9-£10 **Wines** 400 bottles over £30, 30 bottles under £30, 15 by glass **Parking** NCP opposite restaurant **Notes** Tasting menu 5 course, Children welcome

LONDON EC1 *continued*

Malmaison Charterhouse Square

PLAN 3 E3

⬡⬡ French, European

tel: 020 7012 3700 **18-21 Charterhouse Square, Clerkenwell EC1M 6AH**
email: athwaites@malmaison.com **web:** www.malmaison.com
dir: *Nearest station: Barbican*

Modern classic brasserie dishes in best boutique surroundings

The London Malmaison occupies a former nurses' home on the edge of Clerkenwell, not far from the Barbican arts complex. Like other hotels in the group, it's done out in best boutique fashion, with dramatic crimson and purple interiors, a sultrily lit bar and a brasserie in deep brown tones. The order of the day is lively modern British dishes with interesting variations here and there. The fritto misto starter comes with sweet chilli and lemon aïoli dips, while creamed Brie has a wine-poached pear and salted and candied pecans. For main, it could be chicken tikka with chutney, raita and naan, lamb forestière, or a chunky smoked haddock fishcake with spinach and poached egg in hollandaise. For something a little off the beaten path, consider sea bass with chorizo in mussel and tomato dressing. There are fine steaks too, dry-aged for 28 days, with a sauce range including piquant blue cheese butter. Crowd-wowing desserts include a spectacular ice cream sundae, or sticky toffee pudding with pecan caramel sauce.

Times 12-2.30/6-10.30 Closed 23-28 Dec, L Sat

The Modern Pantry

PLAN 3 E4

⬡ Modern Fusion

tel: 020 7553 9210 **47-48 St John's Square, Clerkenwell EC1V 4JJ**
email: enquiries@themodernpantry.co.uk
dir: *Nearest station: Farringdon, Barbican*

Creative fusion food in a fashionable part of town

The word 'fusion' is hardly a new term in the foodie firmament these days, but chef-proprietor Anna Hansen has been at the forefront of this particular style of cooking since it first hit these shores in the mid-1990s. The venue is a gem of a conversion of two listed Georgian townhouses in a trendy part of town, and it serves up plenty of options: modish café (and traiteur) on the ground floor and a coolly smart first-floor restaurant where the tables are poshed up with white linen cloths. Food is served all day and flavours come from far and wide. A pear, for example, is roasted with pomegranate molasses and tonka beans and served up in a salad with golden beetroots, Stichelton, bull's blood, sorrel and spiced pecans. Among main courses, roast Gloucestershire Old Spot pork belly might come with mushroom and date purée, choucroute and green pepper relish, and pan-fried cod with smoky red-wine-braised octopus. Matching wines are suggested on the menu.

Chef Anna Hansen **Owner** Anna Hansen **Seats** 110, Pr/dining room 60 **Times** 12-10.30 Closed Xmas, New Year, Aug BH, All-day dining **Prices** Fixed L 2 course £21.50, Starter £6-£9.20, Main £14-£21.50, Dessert £2.80-£7.50 **Wines** 90 bottles over £30, 27 bottles under £30, 19 by glass **Parking** On street (meter) **Notes** Sunday L £21.50-£26.50, Vegetarian available, Children welcome

The Montcalm London City at The Brewery

PLAN 3 G4

⬡ Traditional British

tel: 020 7614 0100 **52 Chiswell St EC1Y 4SB**
email: reservations@themontcalmlondoncity.co.uk
web: www.themontcalmlondoncity.co.uk
dir: *Nearest station: Liverpool St, Barbican, Moorgate*

Smart hotel with a taste of Britain on the menu

The last beer was brewed here in what was originally the Whitbread brewery in 1976. Now the old girl has taken on a new lease of life as a five-star luxury hotel, but you can still get a decent pint in the Jugged Hare gastro-pub or the main restaurant, the Chiswell Street Dining Rooms. The latter has sharp pastel-coloured tones in wood and leather, a cocktail bar if you're up for it, and on the menu some breezy, gently modish food with a definite British streak: baked Dorset crab and Shetland mussels, to start perhaps, with creamed leek gratin, or an Atlantic king prawn cocktail. Follow on with slow-cooked rump of Herdwick lamb with celeriac and parsnip gratin and a shallot and smoked bacon casserole, or 35-day aged Cumbrian rib-eye steak. Finish with an orange and almond sponge with Amaretto ice cream.

Times 11.45-3.30/5.45-11

Moro

PLAN 3 D4

⬡ Islamic, Mediterranean

tel: 020 7833 8336 **34-36 Exmouth Market EC1R 4QE**
email: info@moro.co.uk
dir: *Nearest station: Farringdon, Angel*

Moreish Moorish and Spanish cuisine in a long-stayer

Moro has been a stalwart of the Exmouth Market scene for 16 years. Its popularity is easy to understand: regulars return time and again for the full-on flavours of its vibrant take on Spanish and Moorish cuisine. Diners spill out onto pavement tables in fine weather, while indoors it's a sparsely-furnished, high-decibel venue where you can perch at the bar washing down tapas with the splendid range of sherries and Iberian wines, or sink into a harem-style bolster cushion at one of the closely-packed tables. Get the show on the road with a crispy seafood brik with harissa; next, from the open kitchen might come a straight-talking main course like wood-roasted pork with wilted frisée, pomegranate and migas (pan-fried bacon and breadcrumbs to the uninitiated), or charcoal-grilled sea bass with sprouting broccoli, Seville orange sauce and Canarian-style wrinkled potatoes. For dessert, perhaps sublime chocolate and apricot tart, or exemplary rosewater and cardamom ice cream. Friendly, well-briefed staff keep it all nicely together.

Chef Samuel & Samantha Clark **Owner** Mr & Mrs S Clark **Seats** 90 **Times** 12-2.30/6-10.30 Closed Xmas, New Year, BHs, D Sun **Prices** Starter £8-£9, Main £16.50-£21, Dessert £6.50-£9 **Wines** 72 bottles over £30, 21 bottles under £30, 12 by glass **Parking** NCP Farringdon Rd **Notes** Sunday L, Vegetarian available, Children welcome

Who has won our Chefs' Chef award?
Find out on page 10

Get the most out of the AA Restaurant Guide
See page 6

St John

PLAN 3 E3

◉◉ British

tel: 020 7251 0848 **26 St John St EC1M 4AY**
email: reservations@stjohnrestaurant.com
dir: *Nearest station: Farringdon*

Nose-to-tail eating at its best

Firmly entrenched on the London dining scene (and with a younger brother in the form of St John Bread & Wine), this trailblazer of the 'nose-to-tail' eating approach still packs them in. Set up in 1994 by Fergus Henderson and Trevor Gulliver in a former smokehouse just up from Smithfield Market, its utilitarian look and championing of unglamorous, lesser-used cuts has certainly caught on. A wrought-iron staircase leads up from the bare-bones ground-floor bar and bakery counter to the equally pared-down dining room: here it's all exposed floorboards, coat-hook-lined white walls, ranks of white-paper-clothed tables with café-style chairs, staff dressed in long white aprons and an open kitchen adding to the buzz. On the food front, others may have copied the robust, gutsy style, but few come close to achieving St John's unvarnished, honest simplicity. Roast bone marrow with parsley salad is a menu stalwart, but you might also encounter rabbit offal and radishes, devilled kidneys, or mallard and Jerusalem artichokes. It's not all aimed at meat-eaters though – how about brill with leeks and butter beans, or fennel and Berkswell? Desserts are equally comfort-spun, from the signature Eccles cake and Lancashire cheese, to treacle steamed pudding.

Chef Christopher Gillard **Owner** T Gulliver, F Henderson **Seats** 110, Pr/dining room 18 **Times** 12-3/6-11 Closed Xmas, New Year, BHs, L Sat, D Sun **Prices** Starter £5.50-£11.50, Main £15-£32, Dessert £4.20-£7.50 **Wines** 24 bottles over £30, 10 bottles under £30, 15 by glass **Parking** Meters in street **Notes** Feasting menu groups 10 or more, Vegetarian available, Children welcome

Smiths of Smithfield, Top Floor

PLAN 3 E3

◉◉ Modern British

tel: 020 7251 7950 **67-77 Charterhouse St EC1M 6HJ**
email: reservations@smithsofsmithfield.co.uk
dir: *Nearest station: Farringdon, Barbican, Chancery Lane*

Terrific views, buzzy city-suit vibe and spot-on ingredients

Each of the four floors at SOS (a former Grade II listed meat warehouse now eating and drinking emporium) has its own distinctive style. There's something for everyone, from the high-octane ground floor to the first-level cocktail bar or second-floor brasserie-style Dining Room, the big hitter is the Top Floor. Smack opposite Smithfield Market, it offers show-stopping rooftop views (with the Shard at centre stage) from its long, light-filled room through half-drop sliding glass doors and dream-ticket decked terrace. Also the culinary champion, the Top Floor's kitchen deals in ingredients of quality and provenance in light, modern, refined dishes of flair and flavour. Rare-breed beef steaks fittingly play a starring role (perhaps succulent 28-day dry-aged South Devon sirloin), though fish doesn't play a small part – witness sparkling-fresh pan-fried halibut served with warm tartare sauce, vanilla mash and spinach. For dessert, finish with wobbly buttermilk pannacotta perfection, pepped up by honey roast quince. White linen, funky dining chairs, semi-circular leather banquettes and unstuffy service are spot on, while wines are a serious bunch.

Times 12-3.30/6.30-11 Closed 25-26 Dec, 1 Jan, L Sat, D Sun

LONDON EC2

L' Anima

PLAN 3 H4

◉◉ Italian

tel: 020 7422 7000 **1 Snowden St, Broadgate West EC2A 2DQ**
email: info@lanima.co.uk
dir: *Nearest station: Liverpool Street*

A contemporary take on regional Italian cooking

Occupying part of the ground floor of a large office block, L'Anima is anything but soulless. The name means soul, for a start, and there is nothing bland about the look of the place. There's a stark brilliance to the space, in fact, from its white leather seats and white linen on the tables, to the bar which fizzes with energy and is separated from the restaurant by a glass wall. It's a super-cool, minimalist look which is more Milan than City of London. And so to Francesco Mazzei's menu, which is equally sharp and exciting, founded on the principles of regional Italian cooking, and full of things you really want to eat. A starter of octopus, for example, cooked a la plancha and served with cannellini beans, ricotta mustia and paprika oil is simply perfection. Home-made squid ink cavatelli with clams and peas might follow, or perhaps roast veal with roast potatoes and mammole artichokes. For dessert, raspberry soufflé is a spot-on version, served with vanilla ice cream and raspberry purée.

Chef Francesco Mazzei **Owner** Francesco Mazzei **Seats** 120, Pr/dining room 15 **Times** 11.45-3/5.30-11 Closed BHs, Sun, L Sat **Prices** Fixed L 2 course fr £16.50, Fixed D 3 course fr £19.50, Starter £12-£17.75, Main £15-£36, Dessert £7-£12.50 **Wines** 11 by glass **Parking** On street **Notes** Vegetarian available, Children welcome

Boisdale of Bishopsgate

PLAN 3 H3

◉ Traditional British

tel: 020 7283 1763 **Swedeland Court, 202 Bishopsgate EC2M 4NR**
email: manager@boisdale-city.co.uk
dir: *Nearest station: Liverpool Street*

Cooking showcasing Scotland's best produce

In a narrow alley near Petticoat Lane market, Boisdale's City branch (see also Boisdale of Belgravia) occupies a subtly lit vaulted basement, its vivid red-painted walls hung with a plethora of photographs and prints, with booth seating, upright timbers, and, to underline its Scottish credentials, a tartan carpet; there's also a champagne and oyster bar. The cooking is founded on thoroughbred Scottish meats and seafood, starters including various ways with smoked salmon – perhaps as céviche with pea and avocado purée – the range broadened by the likes of a haggis Scotch egg with piccalilli, and crab with lobster jelly, horseradish and fennel cream. Main courses tend to be safe bets: prime steaks with béarnaise or foie gras and truffle shavings, along with Dover sole meunière with Jersey Royals and spinach, or Hebridean mutton with confit potato, smoked onion purée, and spring greens with pickled raisins.

Times 11-3/6-9 Closed Xmas, 31 Dec, BHs, Sat-Sun

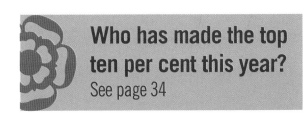

Who has made the top ten per cent this year?
See page 34

LONDON EC2 *continued*

Bonds
PLAN 3 G2

British, European

tel: 020 7657 8088 & 7657 8090 **Threadneedles, 5 Threadneedle St EC2R 8AY**
email: bonds@theetoncollection.co.uk
dir: *Nearest station: Bank*

Ambitious modern cooking in the splendour of a former banking hall

Set in the swish Threadneedles (a former Victorian banking hall turned boutique hotel), the aptly named Bonds is a handsome City bar and restaurant on a grand scale. The look successfully blends the past with the current day: dramatic soaring columns, high decorative ceiling, vast windows and contemporary features like American walnut flooring, oak furnishings, fashionable burgundy leather seating and white linen. The light, well-tuned modern European cooking is rooted in top-notch ingredients and employs a good dose of technical artistry. A smooth and light foie gras parfait with toasted brioche and a fig and watercress salad might start you off, followed by wonderfully tender new-season rump of lamb with crushed Jersey Royals, Puy lentils and a rosemary jus. If fish is more your thing, the steamed halibut teamed with buttered spinach, potato gnocchi tartare, crispy squid, chorizo and a red wine jus should hit the spot, while desserts, like cherry dark chocolate (cherry parfait, dark chocolate mousse and cherry jelly) come dressed to thrill. The daily-changing fixed-price menu is a steal.

Times 12-2.30/6-10 Closed BHs, Sat-Sun

Cinnamon Kitchen
PLAN 3 H3

Modern Indian **NOTABLE WINE LIST**

tel: 020 7626 5000 **9 Devonshire Square EC2M 4YL**
email: info@cinnamon-kitchen.com
dir: *Nearest station: Liverpool St*

Modern Indian cuisine in former spice warehouse

Tucked away in Devonshire Square close to Liverpool Street Station, the 'Kitchen' is the younger, livelier City sibling of Westminster's Cinnamon Club (see entry). Aptly occupying the former East India Company's spice warehouse, the large dining space has a cool, industrial-chic look, kitted out with classy leather seating, polished wooden tables, eye-catching lantern-esque lighting, modern artworks and, at the back, a pewter and black granite tandoor bar. The modern Indian cuisine, fashioned from prime seasonal produce, is as bold as the surroundings, with clean-cut dishes of punchy flavour and well-judged spicing. Witness Kolhapuri-style spiced saddle of Kentish lamb served with pilau rice, or perhaps chargrilled halibut with Rajasthani-style 'kadhi' sauce, while Westernised desserts might take in stem ginger and anise pannacotta with peach compôte. A serious wine list comes with plenty of spice-friendly options, but if cocktails are more your thing, head next-door to the buzzy and coolly sophisticated Anise Bar.

Chef Vivek Singh, Abdul Yaseen **Owner** Indian Restaurant (City) Ltd **Seats** 130, Pr/dining room 16 **Times** 12-2.45/6-10.45 Closed some BHs, Sun, L Sat, D 25 Dec **Prices** Fixed L 2 course £15, Fixed D 3 course £21, Tasting menu £57-£98, Starter £6-£12.50, Main £12.50-£32, Dessert £6-£20 **Wines** 249 bottles over £30, 22 bottles under £30, 21 by glass **Notes** Vegetarian available, Children welcome

City Social
PLAN 3 H2

Rosettes not confirmed at time of going to print

Modern British **NEW**

tel: 020 787703 **Tower 42 EC2N 1HQ**
email: reservations@citysociallondon.com
dir: *Nearest station: Liverpool St*

High-flying cooking in a high-rise city tower

Chef Jason Atherton is on something of a roll these days, with this swanky high-rise restaurant opening hard on the heels of his Pollen Street Social, Little Social and Social Eating House ventures. Up on the 24th floor of Tower 42, the setting is a glamorous contemporary art deco-inspired space with a mirrored ceiling, rosewood panelling, chrome, brass and smoked glass, and a couple of Warhols on the walls, all set against the lights of the city's skyscrapers. When you can tear your attention away from the jaw-dropping vista, the food is equally spectacular stuff – inventive, detailed and bursting with entertaining combinations of taste and texture. A starter brings two crispy breadcrumbed and deep-fried parcels filled with ham hock and pig's trotter, with black pudding encased in fine straw potatoes, apple purée, fresh apple and apple cubes macerated in sweet Madeira. Next up, rack of Romney Marsh lamb is served pink, succulent and imaginatively paired up with a shepherd's pie of braised shoulder meat, three types of carrot, aubergine and miso purée, asparagus and a knockout lamb jus that is full of pure flavours all in perfect balance. The final course is a simple vanilla custard tart with milk sorbet, which might sound humble, but when smooth egg custard, flavoured with nutmeg and set in impeccable crisp pastry, is realised with this degree of technical skill, this old favourite takes on a new life. As you'd expect, the wine list is outstanding, and there's a real pro of a sommelier to steer you through it, as well as a slickly professional service team to keep it all running smoothly.

Chef Jason Atherton **Owner** Jason Atherton & Restaurant Associates **Seats** 90, Pr/dining room 24 **Times** 12-2.45/6-10.30 Closed 25 Dec, 1 Jan, BHs, Sun **Prices** Tasting menu fr £125, Starter £9-£14, Main £18-£38, Dessert £6.50-£8.50, Service optional 12.5% **Wines** 209 bottles over £30, 5 bottles under £30 **Parking** Finsbury Circus NCP **Notes** Tasting menu at Chef's Table, Private dining menu from £65, Vegetarian available

Coq d'Argent
PLAN 3 G2

French

tel: 020 7395 5000 **1 Poultry EC2R 8EJ**
email: coqdargent.co.uk
dir: *Nearest station: Bank*

Traditional French food and rooftop views

With what must be some of the best rooftop views in central London, Coq d'Argent is a smart contemporary setting for some confident French cooking. Divided into a brasserie (food at lunchtimes, lively bar in the evening) and a restaurant with a reception area in between, both have terraces which are a big pull when the sun shines on the City. The restaurant has tables dressed up for serious dining and service which matches the formality without ever taking itself too seriously. Both menus are printed in French with English translations; from the restaurant menu you might kick off with a foie gras parfait with pear and ginger relish, before moving on to baked stone bass with fennel, courgette, tomato and saffron casserole. Desserts to send you home (or back to work) happy include apple tart with roasted cardamom ice cream, and frozen passionfruit and vanilla vacherin.

Times 11.30-3/6-10 Closed BHs, L Sat, D Sun

Follow the AA on twitter @TheAA_Lifestyle

Duck & Waffle

PLAN 3 H2

British, European

tel: 020 3640 7310 **Heron Tower, 100 Bishopsgate EC2N 4AY**
email: dwreservations@sushisamba.com
dir: *Nearest station: Liverpool Street*

Mesmerising views 24/7

Got a head for heights? You might like to look elsewhere if you don't as the Duck & Waffle is on the 40th floor of the City's Heron Tower. The view is amazing. It's actually open all day and all night, so it can sort you out for breakfast, lunch, dinner, cocktails, a late supper, the lot. There are no sharply pressed linen tablecloths here – it's not that sort of place – and the food takes a broad sweep through the UK and mainland Europe. The eponymous dish of duck and waffle is present and correct – confit duck with a fried duck's egg and mustard-maple syrup – but you might prefer to start with pearl barley and wild garlic risotto and move on to whole baked sea bass with warm roasted fennel and chilli. The late night menu is much the same, only shorter, so you can tuck into spicy ox cheek doughnut with apricot jam in the wee small hours.

Times 12-12 All-day dining

Looking for a restaurant by name?
Use the index on page 751

Eyre Brothers

PLAN 3 H4

Spanish, Portuguese

tel: 020 7613 5346 **70 Leonard St EC2A 4QX**
email: eyrebros@btconnect.com
dir: *Nearest station: Old Street Exit 4*

Big, enticing Iberian flavours in the City

Off the beaten track in the City's northern hinterland, this urban-cool outfit looks the authentic Iberian business with its masculine darkwood floors, deep-brown soft leather banquettes, curvy wooden seats, and crisp white tablecloths. A long wooden counter beneath black and white photos of jazz musicians and chalkboards listing gutsy tapas dishes looks onto an open kitchen. Here David Eyre's cooking draws inspiration from across the Iberian Peninsula, delivering full-on flavours wrought from top-class produce treated with integrity and skill. An opener of salt cod brandade with black olives, capers, basil, a soft-boiled egg and crunchy garlic toast evokes the flavours of the Mediterranean, followed by Basque hake and clams in a full-flavoured broth of fresh parsley, green peas and diced potato. If the sizzle of the charcoal grill proves too tempting, you might go for a grilled fillet of acorn-fed Iberico pork marinated with pimentón pepper, thyme and garlic, and served with patatas pobres – potatoes roasted with green peppers, onion, garlic and white wine. Finish with hot caramel and spiced quince tart with vanilla ice cream.

Chef Dave Eyre, Joao Cleto **Owner** Eyre Bros Restaurants Ltd **Seats** 85
Times 12-3/6.30-11 Closed Xmas-New Year, BHs, Sun, L Sat **Prices** Starter £6-£12, Main £14-£24, Dessert £6-£8 **Wines** 42 bottles over £30, 23 bottles under £30, 14 by glass **Parking** On street **Notes** Mixed meat/fish grill Mon-Tue alternate weeks, Children welcome

HKK

– *see below*

HKK

LONDON EC2

PLAN 3 H4

Modern Chinese v NEW

tel: 020 3535 1888 **Broadgate West, 88 Worship St EC2A 2BE**
email: reservations@hkklondon.com
dir: *Nearest station: Liverpool St, Shoreditch High St*

First-class Chinese cooking with borrowings from the West

Just a stone's throw from Liverpool Street Station, this is one Chinese restaurant that really is a cut above. Its modern, minimalist, clean-lined looks – all mushroom-coloured banquettes, black chairs with slate-blue cushions and a glass-walled kitchen – tell you from the off that this is going to be something a bit special, and indeed the various tasting menus (plus set and a la carte menus at lunch) follow classical lines but with some European twists, and ingredients are of the highest possible quality. There's a swish bar for drinks and dim sum, with the dim sum selection – top notch stuff – also served in the restaurant. The 15-course tasting menu (lunch and dinner) might kick off with a poulet de Bresse puff – a light, crisp pastry shell filled with tender chicken, chicken mousse and a nicely contrasting goji berry purée on the side – followed by the 'dim sum trilogy' (a crunchy vermicelli-wrapped and deep-fried lobster tail, a foie gras sweet bun,

and a soft spicy lamb in a tomato dim sum skin). Next up might come cherry wood roasted Peking duck, a classic dish but with a modern presentation, the breast meat moist and full of flavour, with a paper-thin crisp skin, accompanied by a hand-rolled pancake filled with pulled duck meat, cucumber, spring onion and plum sauce, and a delicate salad with more of that crispy duck skin sitting on top. Double boiled chicken soup with pom pom mushroom is slow-cooked for eight hours to produce a deeply flavoured consomme-style broth, ahead of the signature seared Rhug Farm organic lamb with lotus leaf rice – three small pieces of tender, flavoursome lamb with a sweet sticky glaze, some strands of sweet potato and a ball of glutinous rice wrapped in a lotus leaf. Desserts are well and truly of Western persuasion, as in an apple and blackberry jelly with almond crumble and vanilla ice cream as a precursor to a textbook confit orange and macadamia nut parfait.

Chef Tong Chee Hwee **Owner** Hakkasan Group **Seats** 51, Pr/dining room 14
Times 12-2.30/6-9.45 Closed BHs, Sun **Prices** Tasting menu £85-£98, Starter £8-£18.80, Main £6.20-£38, Dessert £8 **Wines** 128 bottles over £30, 2 bottles under £30, 24 by glass **Parking** NCP, On street **Notes** Fixed L 4 course £28.50, Children welcome

LONDON EC2 *continued*

Manicomio, City
PLAN 3 F2

 Modern Italian

tel: 020 7726 5010 **Gutter Ln EC2V 8AS**
email: gutterlane@manicomio.co.uk
dir: *Nearest station: St Paul's*

Contemporary Italian with a cool City vibe

Secreted away on a narrow lane between Cheapside and Gresham Street, the sleek, effortlessly cool modernism of Manicomio's Sir Norman Foster-designed glass building shimmers in the sunlight. Sibling to the Chelsea original (see entry), this three-tiered City version is a resolutely business-suit affair, covering all the bases. A parasol-covered little terrace comes screened from the street, joined at ground-floor level by a lively café-bar/takeaway (open from breakfast). However, for the real culinary action, head upstairs to the more formal yet unstuffy first-floor restaurant: a clean-lined, equally fashionable set up, with high-back leather banquettes or chairs and white-linen-clad tables. The light and fresh modern Italian cooking pays due respect to the provenance, seasonality and quality of its ingredients. Take grilled Cornish turbot teamed with fried artichokes, tomato pulp and green and yellow beans, or perhaps chargrilled Devon rib-eye with roast heritage tomatoes, aubergine and rocket pesto. The Roundhouse on the top floor incorporates a vibrant cocktail bar.

Chef Tom Salt **Owner** Andrew & Ninai Zarach **Seats** 95, Pr/dining room 60 **Times** 11.45-3/6-10 Closed 1 wk Xmas, Sat-Sun **Prices** Starter £8.75-£10.75, Main £14.50-£28.50, Dessert £5-£10.50 **Wines** 101 bottles over £30, 33 bottles under £30, 14 by glass **Parking** Meters in street **Notes** Vegetarian available, Children welcome

Merchants Tavern
PLAN 3 H4

 Modern European **NEW**

tel: 020 7060 5335 & 7033 1879 **36 Charlotte Rd EC2A 3PG**
email: booking@merchantstavern.co.uk
dir: *Nearest station: Liverpool St, Old St*

Crack team, flavours and seasonality at Shoreditch top draw

Don't be fooled by the name, this new City-slick venture in edgy Shoreditch is anything but your standard tavern fodder, especially when you learn it's a collaboration between Angela Hartnett, chef Neil Borthwick (ex-Michel Bras in France, Mayfair's The Square, etc) and the founders of Brit-inspired mini-chain Canteen. It screams serious intent. The converted Victorian warehouse is an on-trend looker; from fashionable bar with giant log burner to the large, low-lit restaurant spread out behind, kitted out with curving green or red leather banquettes, wooden floors, exposed brickwork, giant skylight and 'calm' open kitchen. Service is switched on, while Borthwick's carefully sourced, intensely seasonal, changing menu of British flavours comes underpinned by French influence and a nod to the Med. This is skilled, confident cooking, cleverly woven around balanced layers of flavour and texture that look pretty on the plate. Take a cracking hallmark opener of juicy, tender quail (roasted breast and confit leg) teamed with hazelnut pesto, remoulade and fresh, wobbly pan-fried foie gras. Similarly, mains like sea-fresh roast brill is accompanied by purple sprouting broccoli, toasted almond milk and standout caper and raisin purée. Among the desserts is classic caramelised lemon tart (with 'wow' citrus kick) teamed with basil ice cream.

Chef Neil Borthwick **Owner** A Hartnett, N Borthwick, D Lake, P Clayton-Malone **Seats** 60, Pr/dining room 22 **Times** 12-3/6-11 Closed 25-26 Dec, Mon **Prices** Fixed L 2 course £18, Tasting menu £75-£95, Starter £8-£12, Main £15.50-£24.50, Dessert £7-£12, Service optional 12.5% **Wines** **Notes** Sunday L £5.50-£85, Vegetarian available, Children welcome

1901 Restaurant

LONDON EC2
PLAN 3 H3

British v

tel: 020 7618 7000 **ANdAZ London, 40 Liverpool St EC2M 7QN**
email: london.restres@andaz.com **web:** www.andazdining.com/1901
dir: *Nearest station: Liverpool Street*

Modern British brasserie cooking in hotel's former ballroom

Dating from 1884, when it was built as the Great Eastern Hotel to service Liverpool Street's railway terminus, this large red-brick property has been given a total makeover to create a resolutely 21st-century look. Prime among a number of eating options is 1901 Restaurant, a vast white space, Grade II listed, punctured by soaring columns, frescoes and faux back-lit windows under a magnificent stained-glass skylight (it was protected by mattresses and blankets during the Blitz). The menu is assembled around the best of Britain's native produce, specifying provenance, even potatoes (Desiree, from Kent, for those with an interest in such things), and the cooking is of a standard to match what might be expected of these glossy surroundings. There's real invention behind dishes, and the brigade has clearly investigated some unusual combinations. A winter starter of game terrine of tender meat studded with pistachios and prunes comes with dots of quince chutney and pistachio purée and chunks of mulled wine jelly, a dish marked by its marriage of flavours. Another starter may bring on a trio of salmon (cured, confit and croustillante) with cucumber, sour cream and salmon caviar. Main courses have a degree of complication, with dynamic results: brittle-skinned halibut fillet, for instance, with squid, fregola, Swiss chard and grapes, and a foam of tomato infused with vanilla, and a full-blooded serving of Aberdeenshire beef as braised cheeks and tenderloin with a marrow croquette, carrots and potatoes. Bookending a meal is a complimentary amuse-bouche (perhaps silky-smooth sweet potato and celeriac soup) and desserts that tend towards cakes and tarts, with a deft hand responsible for pastry: rich pecan and hazelnut tart, for instance, and chocolate fudge cut by sour cherry sorbet. A six-course tasting menu is available, afternoon tea is served, and there's a cheese and wine cellar with professional specialist help.

Chef Hameed Farook **Owner** Hyatt **Seats** 100 **Times** 12-2.30/6.30-10 Closed Xmas, New Year, BHs, Sun **Prices** Fixed L 2 course fr £24, Fixed D 3 course fr £30, Tasting menu £60, Starter £10-£14, Main £17-£29, Dessert £7-£9 **Wines** 235 bottles over £30, 16 bottles under £30, 50 by glass **Parking** NCP London Wall **Notes** Tasting menu 6 course, Children welcome

Miyako

PLAN 3 H3

Japanese v

tel: 020 7618 7100 **ANdAZ London, 40 Liverpool St EC2M 7QN**
email: london.restres@andaz.com
dir: *Nearest station: Liverpool Street*

Authentic Japanese dining within the ANdAZ London hotel

Beside Liverpool Street Station, Miyako is within the ANdAZ London hotel, although it has its own entrance on to the street where queues form at lunchtime for takeaway boxes. The restaurant itself has a cool, uncluttered look, thanks to large windows, walls veneered in pale wood and bamboo, and black-lacquered tables and chairs. Traditional Japanese cuisine is the order of the day, with spankingly fresh ingredients cooked just so. The wide-ranging menu takes in sushi (perhaps raw sliced sea bream atop glutinous rice), sashimi (among them tuna with pickled ginger and wasabi) and tempura (say, soft-shelled crab in thin, crisp batter). A bento box is a good introduction to the cuisine, and among the specials may be miso soup with scallops, salmon, sea bass and vegetables, and – dinner only – seafood hoiruyaki consisting of sea bass, scallops, salmon and shiitaki and oyster mushrooms. Finish with a selection of fresh fruit or something more exotic like light, lemony yuzu mousse on a sesame biscuit.

Chef Kosei Sakamoto **Owner** Hyatt **Seats** 30 **Times** 12-5/5-10.30 Closed Xmas, New Year, Sat-Sun **Prices** Starter £3-£7, Main £8-£29, Dessert £5.50 **Wines** 4 bottles over £30, 3 bottles under £30, 9 by glass **Parking** NCP London Wall **Notes** Vegetarian available, Children welcome

1901 Restaurant

PLAN 3 H3

– *see opposite*

Sushisamba London

PLAN 3 H2

Japanese, Brazilian, Peruvian

tel: 020 3640 7330 **Heron Tower, 110 Bishopsgate EC2N 4AY**
email: reservationslondon@sushisamba.com
dir: *Nearest station: Liverpool Street*

Trendy Japanese-meets-South American cuisine with capital views

While the name announces Sushisamba's Japanese-meets-South-American theme, nothing quite prepares you for the Formula 1 speed of the glass elevator ride to its 38th-floor setting in the Heron building. The view from up here is spectacular, and you can enjoy it (and some seriously good people watching too) from a series of cocktail bars (one on the 39th floor), alfresco terraces and a sushi counter. It's a shame the dining room itself looks east, excluding the capital's most historic landmarks, but the decor is pleasingly sleek and contemporary, with tiled floors, a bamboo-covered high ceiling, unclothed tables and funky leather seating, and the kitchen's Japanese/Brazilian/Peruvian fusion food is dressed to thrill and delicious to eat. The menu is in the all-day grazing style, so you might share some superb green bean tempura with rich and powerful black truffle aïoli to begin, moving on to exquisitely fresh black cod miso from the robata (charcoal grill) served with large, sweet Peruvian corn, or maybe succulent duck breast with tangy sansho pepper vinaigrette.

Times 11.30am-mdnt All-day dining

Looking for a London restaurant near you?

Use the maps on pages 258–68

Apex City of London Hotel

PLAN 3 H1

Modern European

tel: 020 7977 9580 & 0845 365 0002 **1 Seething Ln EC3N 4AX**
email: addendum@apexhotels.co.uk **web:** www.apexhotels.co.uk
dir: *Nearest station: Tower Hill*

Smart European flavours in a swanky City hotel

The Apex Hotel's Addendum Restaurant is a softly-lit contemporary-looking space with floor-to-ceiling windows, sleek oak panelling and tables, charcoal granite flooring, and cream leather seats, all enlivened by splashes of colourful artwork – a smart setting that is clearly a big hit with the suited and booted denizens of the Square Mile. The scene thus set, the kitchen delivers seasonally-attuned, straightforward modern European cooking that aims for all-round satisfaction, based on good quality materials brought together in sensibly reined-in combinations. Bath chap terrine is served with the contrasting flavours of apple and grain mustard sauce, ahead of chicken ballotine with pearl barley and roasted leeks, or there might be hearty satisfaction in the shape of pork faggots with parsnip mash and onion rings. To finish, pistachio puts a creative spin on a well-made crème brûlée, pointed up with a tangy cherry sorbet.

Times 12-2.30/6-10

Caravaggio

PLAN 3 H2

Modern Italian

tel: 020 7626 6206 **107-112 Leadenhall St EC3A 4DP**
email: caravaggio@etruscarestaurants.com **web:** www.caravaggiorestaurant.co.uk
dir: *Nearest station: Aldgate, Fenchurch St*

Smart City Italian in former banking hall

There's a hint of 1930s ocean liner about this dapper Square Mile Italian, the former banking hall retaining something of its grand art deco past, with ornate lofty ceilings, splendid light fittings, mellow marble and an imposing staircase leading up to a trump-card mezzanine gallery. The pace is full-on at lunch when the City suits turn up for the pleasing mix of traditional and more modish regional Italian cooking, while the evenings are more chilled. This is food of simplicity, generosity and flavour. Take a classic pasta dish like spaghetti, brimming with the sweet, fresh flavour of a San Murano tomato sauce and buffalo mozzarella, or big-hearted grilled calves' liver paired with luganiga sausage, Italian pancetta and a potato rösti, or even stuffed rabbit leg with Chantenay carrots, baby artichokes and a light parmesan sauce. Desserts fit the mould – think tiramisù to Amalfi lemon cake – while wines are a serious Italian bunch.

Chef Faliero Lenta **Owner** Enzo & Piero Quaradeghini **Seats** 150 **Times** 12-3/6.30-10 Closed Xmas, BHs, Sat-Sun **Prices** Fixed L 2 course £17.50, Starter £7-£12, Main £12.80-£22.90, Dessert £5.80-£9 **Wines** 120 bottles over £30, 30 bottles under £30, 14 by glass **Parking** On street **Notes** Vegetarian available, Children welcome

LONDON EC3 *continued*

Chamberlains Restaurant
PLAN 3 H2

Modern British, Seafood

tel: 020 7648 8690 **23-25 Leadenhall Market EC3V 1LR**
email: info@chamberlains.org
dir: *Nearest station: Bank, Monument*

Super-fresh seafood - and more - in swish City restaurant

Chamberlains has opened an informal brasserie in the basement of its Leadenhall Market premises, with brick walls, a slate floor, wooden tables and its own menu. The restaurant remains the thrust of the operation, three floors done out in great style. Fishmonger Chamberlain and Thelwell is the muscle behind the enterprise, so it's no surprise to find a menu biased towards seafood, all as fresh as can be. The menu offers straightforward preparations and more elaborate renditions. Starters include lobster bisque, roasted scallops garnished with brawn, salsify and sauce gribiche, and smoked eel in apple jelly with parsley sauce and celeriac mayonnaise. Main courses run from perfectly timed grilled Dover sole to multi-flavoured sea bass fillet with samphire, sea vegetables, pickled mussels, crushed new potatoes and seaweed butter. Meat-eaters get a fair share of the billing too – perhaps sautéed foie gras with rhubarb and elderflower, then duck breast with sour cherries, celeriac and cabbage – and to finish off might be homely apple pie with vanilla parfait.

Chef Andrew Jones **Owner** Chamberlain & Thelwell, Andrew Jones **Seats** 115, Pr/dining room 55 **Times** 12-2.30/5.30-9.30 Closed Xmas, New Year & BHs, Sat-Sun **Prices** Starter £9.75-£15.50, Main £16.50-£38, Dessert £6.50-£11.50 **Wines** 41 bottles over £30, 13 bottles under £30, 11 by glass **Notes** Vegetarian available, Children welcome

The Perkin Reveller
PLAN 5 J6

British, Fish

tel: 020 3166 6949 **The Wharf, at The Tower of London EC3N 4AB**
email: info@perkinreveller.co.uk
dir: *Nearest station: Fenchurch Street, Tower Hill*

Seasonal British cooking and stunning Thames views

Don't be put off by the wacky name (a merry character from Chaucer's The Cook's Tale) as this restaurant with show-stopping views of Tower Bridge and the brooding walls of the Tower of London is no touristy pit-stop. Light, contemporary and hard-edged, the glass-walled dining space comes kitted out with solid pale-wood furniture (including long refectory-style tables) set on dark slate-tiled flooring. Of its two bars, one is located in the adjoining tower gatehouse, with its haunting, romantic atmosphere. The kitchen's not stuck in the past though, instead celebrating modern British cooking of flair and panache with a light touch, fashioned from premium seasonal produce. Well-dressed plates might take in signature salt marsh lamb three ways (succulent rump, melt-in-the-mouth slow-cooked shoulder, and crisp fried tongue) served with swede fondant, while desserts could deliver a light, moist carrot cake teamed with marmalade ice cream. The outdoor terrace is a must on a sunny day, and the place is also open for breakfast and afternoon tea.

Chef Andrew Donovan **Owner** Historic Royal Palaces **Seats** 120 **Times** 11.30-3.30/5.30-10.30 Closed 24-26 Dec, D Sun **Prices** Fixed L 2 course £17, Starter £5.50-£11, Main £13.50-£28, Dessert £6-£10 **Wines** 26 bottles over £30, 17 bottles under £30, 19 by glass **Parking** City Key, Arch **Notes** Afternoon tea 3.30-5.30pm, Sunday L £14.95-£16.95, Vegetarian available, Children welcome

Restaurant Sauterelle
PLAN 3 G2

Modern European, French V

tel: 020 7618 2483 **The Royal Exchange EC3V 3LR**
email: pawelk@danddlondon.com
dir: *Nearest station: Bank*

Confident contemporary cooking in landmark building

Sitting beneath glazed arches on the mezzanine floor of the magnificent Royal Exchange, classy Sauterelle certainly has 'wow factor', its best tables looking down on the inner courtyard glistening with high-end jewellers, boutiques and the bustle of the Grand Café below. All carpeted comfort, white linen and modern tub-style chairs or banquettes, the intimate space is lined with wine racks at one end and has an open kitchen 'window' at the other. The vibe is chic, the service slickly professional, and the wines speak with a strong French accent. Avignon-born chef Arnaud Delannay's cooking is inspired by his southern French roots and delivers a light, contemporary touch, clean, fresh flavours and well-dressed presentation. Witness a signature starter of sea-fresh Orkney Isle scallops teamed with a perfectly balanced accompaniment of curried cauliflower purée, sauce vièrge and micro basil, or a main-event top-notch venison haunch of full-on flavour, served with braised red cabbage, celeriac purée and saffron poached quince.

Chef Arnaud Delannay **Owner** D & D London **Seats** 66, Pr/dining room 26 **Times** 12-2.30/6-9.30 Closed BHs, Xmas, New Year, Etr, Sat-Sun **Prices** Fixed L 2 course £20, Fixed D 3 course £23.50, Tasting menu £62, Starter £7.50-£14, Main £21.50-£26, Dessert £7.50 **Wines** 64 bottles over £30, 9 bottles under £30, 17 by glass **Parking** Bell Wharf Lane, Finsbury Sq, Shoe Lane **Notes** Children welcome

■ LONDON EC4

Barbecoa
PLAN 3 F2

Modern

tel: 020 3005 8555 **20 New Change Passage EC4M 9AG**
dir: *Nearest station: St Paul's*

Jamie Olivers buzzing BBQ joint

Expect a backing track of high-energy chatter and throbbing music at Jamie O and Adam Perry Lang's rammed-to-the-rafters City temple to meat, flame and smoke. It's a cool glass-sided venue that offers show-stopping views of St Paul's Cathedral while wrapping itself around a semi-open kitchen. Macho features – polished stone floor and brickwork – mix with low-slung leather banquettes, funky dangling lighting and wine display cabinets. Cooking by fire, smoke and charcoal is the thing, which means some flashy bits of kit like robata grills, tandoor ovens, Texan pit smokers and wood-fired ovens. Impeccably sourced British and Irish meats are prepared in the ground-floor butcher's shop. Tuck into signature dry-aged steaks like rump or T-bone, or try grilled lamb rack or pulled pork shoulder, perhaps with pukka duck-fat chips, while desserts might take in baked vanilla cheesecake with roasted peaches and star-turn Bellini sorbet. A posse of friendly staff help keep the party rolling.

Times 11.30-11 All-day dining

Who are the AA's Restaurants of the Year? See page 14

Bread Street Kitchen

PLAN 3 F2

◉◉ Modern British, European

tel: 020 3030 4050 **10 Bread St EC4M 9AJ**
email: info@breadstreetkitchen.com
dir: *Nearest station: Mansion House*

Vibrant, City-cool brasserie from the Gordon Ramsay stable

The name suggests a homely wholefood co-operative, but the reality is a cavernous, high-decibel, high-octane city-slicker operation, courtesy of Gordon Ramsay Holdings. The huge first-floor restaurant seems to extend as far as the eye can see, a soaring, warehouse-like space that mixes retro and modern looks with art deco references and the feel of a film set from Fritz Lang's Metropolis. Check out the exposed industrial ducting, a wall of full-length glass, black and white chequerboard floors, gold and green banquettes, and classic cafe-style black marble or darkwood tables, plus a mezzanine wine gallery with thousands of bottles in green glass cabinets. Battalions of servers dressed in black ricochet to and fro, all friendly, engaging and on the ball, delivering quick-fire dishes from a lengthy all-day roster (including breakfast weekdays). Try potted salt brisket with grain mustard and piccalilli, then steamed sea bream with braised leeks, brown shrimps, sea purslane and shellfish dressing, or something meaty along the lines of Dingle Dell pork chop or Herdwick lamb cutlets from the Josper grill. End with chocolate fondant with mint chip ice cream.

Times 11-3/5.30-11

The Chancery

PLAN 3 D2

◉◉ Modern British, French

tel: 020 7831 4000 **9 Cursitor St EC4A 1LL**
email: reservations@thechancery.co.uk
dir: *Nearest station: Chancery Lane*

Intimate, fine-tuned dining in legal land

A bijou, understated outfit secreted away in the heart of lawyerland, the aptly named Chancery is a sharp-suited yet unstuffy affair. Effortlessly urbane and dressed as smartly as its clientele with mellow pastel shades, polished-wood floors, white linen, fashionable leather seating, mirrors and modern abstract art, there are two intimate dining rooms on the ground floor and an even cosier eating area in the basement. Alice Churchill's kitchen deals in immaculately presented, inventive modern European dishes such as a starter of seared tuna (accurately timed) with crispy tempura squid, chilli, ginger and spring onions. Mains might turn to the Mediterranean for inspiration, as in roast cod teamed with a stuffed courgette flower, chorizo and heritage tomatoes, or perhaps there might be a more classic roasted rump of new season lamb served with crisp sweetbreads and navarin of baby vegetables. A richly indulgent Amedei mousse with ginger, kumquats and marmalade ice cream hits the spot at dessert. A considered wine list with several by the glass options rounds off a class act.

Times 12-2.30/6-10.30 Closed Xmas, Sun, L Sat

Chinese Cricket Club

PLAN 3 E1

◉ Chinese V

tel: 020 7438 8051 **Crowne Plaza London - The City, 19 New Bridge St EC4V 6DB**
email: loncy.ccc@ihg.com
dir: *Nearest station: Temple, St Paul's, Blackfriars*

Classy Chinese in a modern City hotel

Named after the four-year-old Chinese national cricket team, this restaurant is one of two in the Crowne Plaza London City hotel (see also entry for Refettorio). Cooking-themed images of rural China adorn the neutral modern space, along with plenty of cricket memorabilia and Chinese calligraphy prints. Well-paced service is delivered by smartly dressed staff who are happy to explain the predominantly Szechuan menu, where traditional dishes sit comfortably alongside more contemporary imaginings. You might start with a beautifully balanced hot and sour soup, or prawn and pork sui mai from the dim sum section, before diced chicken with ginger, scallions and sesame, or a signature dish like crispy orange beef or fried perch with garlic chives. Desserts, chawan mushi (steamed egg custard) aside, are more European – try banana toffee cake, or hot chocolate pudding. Various set menus, including a vegetarian version and a chef's tasting menu supplement the carte.

Chef Guanghao Wu **Owner** Blackfriars Hotel Group **Seats** 65, Pr/dining room
Times 12-2.30/6-10 Closed Xmas & Etr, L 10 Jan **Prices** Tasting menu fr £25
Wines 10 by glass **Parking** On street **Notes** No children

Diciannove

PLAN 3 E1

◉ Italian

tel: 020 7438 8052 & 7438 8055 **Crowne Plaza London - The City, 19 New Bridge St EC4V 6DB**
email: loncy.refettorio@ihg.com **web:** www.refettorio.com
dir: *Nearest station: Blackfriars*

Elegant Italian dining in the City

Formerly Giorgio Locatelli's Refettorio, the renamed and relaunched Diciannove in the Crowne Plaza hotel is a masculine, minimalist environment where the deal is slick yet simple Italian cooking prepared from carefully sourced ingredients. Dark wood, sparkling glassware, low-level lighting and booth seating set the tone, and there's a cool bar backlit in yellow where you can perch on a leather stool and take in the atmosphere before dinner. Start with a fresh and flavoursome dish of grilled prawns, rocket leaves, pine kernels and tomatoes – a suitably light option that should leave you room for the home-made pasta: perhaps tagliatelle with beef and pork ragout, or pumpkin filled tortelli with sage, amaretto and butter sauce. Next you might go for calves' liver, braised white onions, pine nuts and raisins, finishing with amaretto parfait with an intense chocolate sauce.

Chef Alessandro Bay **Owner** Crowne Plaza **Seats** 100, Pr/dining room 33
Times 12-2.30/6-10.30 Closed Xmas, 24-30 Jan, Etr & BHs, Sun, L Sat **Prices** Prices not confirmed **Wines** 12 by glass **Parking** NCP - Queen Victoria St **Notes** Vegetarian available, Children welcome

Looking for a London restaurant by name?
Use the index on page 254

What makes a 3-Rosette restaurant?
See page 9

LONDON EC4 *continued*

Lutyens Restaurant

PLAN 3 E2

 Modern European 🍷 NOTABLE WINE LIST

tel: 020 7583 8385 **85 Fleet St EC4Y 1AE**
email: info@lutyens-restaurant.com
dir: *Nearest station: Chancery Lane, St Pauls, Blackfriars*

Accomplished modern brasserie cooking in stylish setting

In the shadow of St Bride's Church, this stylish outfit occupies an elegant Lutyens-designed building that was once home to Reuters and the Press Association. These days its coolly sophisticated interior – pastel tones, pale wood, white linen and towering floral displays – bears the Conran stamp, and the multi-faceted space encompasses a restaurant, all-day bar up front (serving breakfasts from 7.30am), raw bar (for oysters, tartares, carpaccios and céviche) and, in the basement, private dining rooms and a members' club. Chef Henrik Ritzen's cooking is rooted in classic French technique but with a suitably light and sophisticated modern touch. A simple and elegant starter of slow-cooked hen's egg with girolles and lardons shows the style, as does main-course monkfish, clams, samphire and broad beans – a winning dish full of fresh flavours, accurately cooked and stylishly presented. Dessert could be a classic lemon soufflé with the added bonus of some raspberry ripple ice cream and a raspberry Madeleine. Superb breads are freshly baked, and the wine list is an absolute corker.

Chef Henrik Ritzen **Owner** Peter Prescott, Terence & Vicki Conran **Seats** 120, Pr/dining room 26 **Times** 12-3/6-10 Closed Xmas & BHs, Sat-Sun **Prices** Fixed L 2 course fr £22, Fixed D 3 course fr £26, Starter £6-£14, Main £16-£36, Dessert £6-£8 **Wines** 514 bottles over £30, 37 bottles under £30, 40 by glass **Notes** Vegetarian available, Children welcome

28-50 Wine Workshop & Kitchen

PLAN 3 D2

 French, European

tel: 020 7242 8877 **140 Fetter Ln EC4A 1BT**
email: info@2850.co.uk
dir: *Nearest station: Chancery Lane*

Serious about wine, serious about food

Wine steals the show at 28-50, the digits referencing the latitude range within which the world's vineyards are planted. It's a relaxed, uptempo basement affair (from the team behind Texture – see entry) and comes kitted out in a dark-green colour scheme, with wine the theme at every turn (displays of bottles, pictures, corks and boxes). Floorboards, exposed brick, porthole mirrors and knowledgeable service add to the on-cue vibe. Simple French bistro-inspired fare is the name of the game, wrought from premium produce and accessibly priced. Witness succulent rump of lamb served with panisse (chick pea fritter), exemplary ratatouille and basil, or perhaps top-dollar sirloin (28-day aged US grain-fed beef) teamed with braised shallots, watercress and classic béarnaise. And then there are the fairly priced wines, with 30 served by the glass, carafe or bottle on the every-day selection. Alternatively, take your pick from the Collector's List with some starry vintages and more wallet-busting prices. (There's a second branch in Marylebone.)

Chef Imran Rafi **Owner** Xavier Rousset, Agnar Sverrisson **Seats** 60, Pr/dining room 12 **Times** 12-2.30/6-9.30 Closed Xmas, New Year, BHs, Sat-Sun **Prices** Fixed L 2 course £15.95, Starter £6.75-£8.95, Main £12.95-£24.95, Dessert £6 **Wines** 65 bottles over £30, 15 bottles under £30, 30 by glass **Parking** NCP **Notes** Children welcome

Vanilla Black

PLAN 3 D2

Modern Vegetarian ⅴ

tel: 020 7242 2622 **17-18 Tooks Court EC4A 1LB**
email: vanillablack@btconnect.com
dir: *Nearest station: Chancery Lane*

Classy vegetarian cookery in a hidden London location

Andrew Dargue and Donna Conroy's upscale vegetarian restaurant is to be found in an almost hidden location down a side street near Chancery Lane, but the venue itself is expansive and spacious, its clean modern design overlaid with echoes of art deco. There's a good deal of excitement around British vegetarian gastronomy these days, and here's why: interesting, innovative dishes that combine high-quality ingredients, up-to-the-minute technique and a sound approach to texture and flavour contrasts. A brace of Yukon Gold potato cakes start a meal off boldly, gaining plenty of savoury depth from their garnishes of smoked mayonnaise, pickled cucumber ketchup, vinegar dust and crisps. On offer for main may be something strongly redolent of bracing seaside air – seared seaweed, cabbage and pickled potatoes, with soda bread sauce and seaside veg. If something cheesy appeals, try a winning combination of celery pannacotta and blue wensleydale profiteroles, with charred celery and carrots in a precisely and distinctively flavoured apple sauce. The inventiveness doesn't stop there – how about white chocolate and cep tart with a cornflake cake, picpoul wine sorbet and fried tarragon?

Chef Andrew Dargue **Owner** Andrew Dargue & Donna Conroy **Seats** 45 **Times** 12-2.30/6-10 Closed 2wks Xmas & New Year, BH Mons, Sun **Prices** Fixed L 2 course £19.50, Fixed D 3 course £38 **Wines** 10 by glass **Parking** On street (metered) or NCP **Notes** Children welcome

The White Swan Pub & Dining Room

PLAN 3 D3

Modern British

tel: 020 7242 9696 **108 Fetter Ln EC4A 1ES**
email: info@thewhiteswanlondon.com
dir: *Nearest station: Chancery Lane*

City gastro-pub with classy first-floor restaurant

In fair weather, this smart Holborn pub – sibling of The Gun – is picked out by the throng of after-work drinkers pitched up on the pavement outside. The remodelled character panelled bar comes complete with boars' heads and deer antlers mounted on the walls, plus a mezzanine balcony from which to take in the action below. The bar offers more traditional sustenance, while the dapper top-floor dining room is the place to head to for the main culinary action. It's a bright, fashionable room with windows on two sides, a mirrored ceiling, modern leather seating, white linen-clad tables and a patterned-wood floor. The kitchen delivers appropriately modern, well-flavoured dishes with an eye on presentation: witness pan-fried tranche of lemon sole with razor clam, samphire, fennel gratin and clam velouté, or perhaps herb-crusted loin of Herdwick mutton teamed with grilled tongue, violet artichoke, glazed carrots and garlic purée. Check out the sophisticated wine list.

Times 12-3/6-10 Closed Xmas, New Year, BHs, Sat-Sun (ex private parties)

LONDON N1

Almeida Restaurant
PLAN 1 F4

@@ French

tel: 020 7354 4777 **30 Almeida St, Islington N1 1AD**
email: almeida-reservations@danddlondon.com
dir: Nearest station: Angel, Highbury & Islington

Honest French cooking opposite the theatre

A little walk from the hustle and bustle of Islington's busy centre rewards with good honest French food in a contemporary setting. The eponymous theatre is opposite. In the airy room, dressed in fashionable contemporary neutrality, large windows look out onto the street where parasols are set along the pavement for eating outside in the warmer months. White linen tablecloths adorn the tables at the back of the space, whilst up front is a tad less formal; both areas, though, hum with a heartfelt Gallic bonhomie. The food carries its French allegiances lightly, with some standout seasonal British ingredients taking centre stage. Cornish crab ravioli comes with buttered lettuce and beurre blanc in a well-crafted first course, followed by Denham Estate venison à la bourguignon with gratin dauphinoise which is brim full of flavour. Finish with a textbook crème brûlée à la vanille and a warm madeleine.

Owner D & D London **Seats** 90, Pr/dining room 18 **Times** 12-2.30/5.30-10.30 Closed 26 Dec, 1 Jan, L Mon, D Sun **Prices** Prices not confirmed **Wines** 21 by glass **Parking** On street **Notes** Theatre menu 2/3 course £17/£19, Sunday L, Vegetarian available, Children welcome

The Drapers Arms
PLAN 1 F4

@ British

tel: 020 7619 0348 **44 Barnsbury St N1 1ER**
email: info@thedrapersarms.com
dir: Nearest station: Highbury & Islington, Angel

Real gastro-pub serving no-nonsense modern British food

The handsome, Georgian-era Drapers Arms is an inviting neighbourhood pub, tucked away in a leafy, upscale residential quarter of Islington. With real ales on hand-pump, a well-chosen wine list (with an admirable by-glass and carafe selection) and a kitchen that cuts its cloth via truly seasonal ingredients delivered via a daily-changing menu, the Drapers certainly earns the 'gastro-pub' billing so inappropriately used by many other pubs. A light-filled, u-shaped bar with high ceilings and tall windows, scuffed floorboards and retro furniture creates a relaxed environment in which to enjoy the no-nonsense, gutsy British food, such as pigeon and prune pie, bream with cockles, samphire and tarragon butter, or, following the Glorious Twelfth, roast grouse with pâté, toast and blackberries. Puddings, likewise, take the comfort route – maybe a buttermilk pudding with raspberries. Lighter bar snacks are available too, and there's a great little courtyard garden for those sunnier days.

Chef James de Jong **Owner** Nick Gibson **Seats** 80, Pr/dining room 55 **Times** 12-3.30/6-10 Closed 25-26 Dec **Prices** Starter £5.50-£8, Main £11.50-£24, Dessert fr £6.50, Service optional 12.5% **Wines** 30 bottles over £30, 39 bottles under £30, 16 by glass **Parking** On street **Notes** Sunday L £13.50-£17, Vegetarian available, Children welcome

Fifteen London - The Restaurant
PLAN 3 G5

@ Modern British

tel: 020 3375 1515 **15 Westland Place N1 7LP**
dir: Nearest station: Old Street

Turning lives around by means of vibrant seasonal cooking

Sailing into its second decade of operations, the original incarnation of Jamie Oliver's philanthropic restaurant enterprise continues to draw in the punters, though with a completely new look and style. The former warehouse has been completely refurbished to give it more of a neighbourhood vibe, there's a new head chef in place, and gone is the Italian menu and instead the deal is a range of smaller and larger plates for sharing, all based on prime seasonal ingredients and delivering big, fresh flavours. So you might start with devilled egg and smoked anchovy, duck ham and quince, or beef and barley buns and horseradish, moving on to cockles, pig's cheek, butterbeans and laver bread, and braised lamb shoulder with purple sprouting broccoli and new season garlic. The place still continues in its original purpose though – to take in young unemployed people and prepare them for a career in the kitchen – so you can feel good about yourself as you feast on rotisserie Norfolk chicken with violet artichokes and lovage mayo.

Times 12-2.45/6.30-9.30 Closed 25 Dec, 1 Jan, L 26 Dec

Frederick's Restaurant
PLAN 1 F4

@ Modern British

tel: 020 7359 2888 **106-110 Islington High St, Camden Passage, Islington N1 8EG**
email: dine@fredericks.co.uk
dir: Nearest station: Angel

Popular dining spot among Islingtons antique shops

Built in 1789 as a pub, and rebuilt in 1834, Frederick's has been a stalwart of the Islington dining scene since the late 1960s and is still going strong. It's an attractive space, its brick walls hung with abstracts; a recent addition has been the Club Room, a contemporary private dining room. Its appeal lies in its broadly based menu and consistently high-quality cooking. Straightforwardly pleasing starters might take in crab and avocado salad with cucumber jelly, and prawns fried with garlic butter. Among main courses, monkfish gets the bourguignon treatment, served with Charlotte potatoes, while in season may come roast breast of guinea fowl with an onion tart, pepper and cumin purée and purple-sprouting broccoli. Chocoholics could end with rich chocolate fondant cut by cinnamon ice cream, while others could go for something like three ways with rhubarb.

Chef Adam Hilliard **Owner** Nick Segal **Seats** 150, Pr/dining room 50 **Times** 12-2.30/5.45-11.30 Closed Xmas, New Year, BHs, Sun (ex functions) **Prices** Fixed L 2 course £15.50, Fixed D 3 course £19, Starter £7-£14, Main £13-£32, Dessert £6.50-£8.50 **Wines** 125 bottles over £30, 20 bottles under £30, 25 by glass **Parking** NCP Business Design Centre, on street **Notes** Sat brunch available, Vegetarian available, Children welcome

Grain Store
PLAN 1 F4

@@ Modern, European NEW

tel: 020 7324 4466 **Granary Square, 1-3 Stable Square, King's Cross N1C 4AB**
email: eat@grainstore.com
dir: Nearest station: Kings Cross

Classy globe-trotting fare in an industrial landscape

The latest venture from chef Bruno Loubet and the Zetter Group's Michael Benyan, the Grain Store in newly trendy King's Cross blurs the boundary between kitchen and dining room in one massive industrial-looking space. There are ducts snaking across the high ceiling, chunky wooden tables, exposed brickwork and an all-round urban-cool vibe. There's a buzzy bar, too, for a cocktail or something off the all-day menu. The main menu combines the classic cooking of Monsieur Loubet's French roots with something altogether more globe-trotting. Mushroom and duck liver pâté with celeriac remoulade and mulled wine jelly harks of the old country, or go for another starter of mackerel tartare with seaweed and cucumber, green apple purée and pickled redcurrants. Vegetables get top billing (often listed first among ingredients) with grilled leeks and an apple and pickled walnut salsa partnering a gloriously tender confit of pork belly. There's plenty of craft and creativity in desserts, too, such as chocolate and peanut delice, which arrives in the company of slices of eucalyptus- and mint-poached pineapple.

Chef Bruno Loubet **Owner** Zetter Group **Times** 12-2.30/6-10.30 Closed 24-26 Dec, D Sun **Prices** Starter £6-£8.50, Main £14.50-£17, Dessert £5.50-£6.50 **Wines** 41 bottles over £30, 9 bottles under £30, 16 by glass

LONDON N1 *continued*

Smokehouse
PLAN 1 F4

◉◉ International NEW

tel: 020 7354 1144 **63-69 Canonbury Rd, Islington N1 2DG**
email: info@smokehouseislington.co.uk
dir: *Nearest station: Highbury & Islington*

Meat meets fire in an Islington pub

One of a quartet of London pubs forming the Noble Inns group, the Smokehouse is an old Islington boozer that has seen new life as a temple to the simple, primeval principle of subjecting hunks of meat to fire and woodsmoke. In the yard at the back are three giant smokers, fuelled by sustainable English oak, as is detailed on a blackboard above the open kitchen. Neil Rankin doesn't much mind where the culinary influence comes from, as long as smoke can play a part, so expect chunks of French classicism alongside east Asian sizzle and bite – Korean spicy rice cake with mussels, main-course smoked duck with kimchi and potato cake. There is no precious primping here and flavours are primed to explode, as when a lobe of seared foie gras in a reduction of red wine and bourbon is offset by a crisp-shelled apple fritter and a runny duck egg. Following that, short rib bourguignon arrives as though from the barbecue in heaven, its sealed smoky potency supported by a bone-thickened red wine sauce, creamy mash, bacon lardons, girolles and deep-fried shallot rings. There are non-meat dishes, such as roasted aubergine curry, or grilled mackerel with radishes, peanuts and green chilli, but there may be a feeling that shunning the meats is missing the point. If you've room for afters, a hunk of white chocolate cheesecake comes with a properly puckering shot of lemon sorbet as refresher. Book well ahead, for the Smokehouse is playing to packed houses. An extensive list of craft beers is not the least part of the explanation.

Chef Neil Rankin **Owner** Scott & Maria Hunter **Seats** 50 **Times** 6-10 Closed 24-26 Dec, L Mon-Fri **Prices** Starter £6-£10, Main £12.50-£19, Dessert £5-£7 **Wines** 15 bottles over £30, 21 bottles under £30, 11 by glass **Parking** On street **Notes** Sat brunch available, Vegetarian available, Children welcome

Trullo
PLAN 1 F4

◉◉ Italian

tel: 020 7226 2733 **300-302 St Paul's Rd N1 2LH**
email: enquiries@trullorestaurant.com
dir: *Nearest station: Highbury & Islington*

Classic modern Italian cooking near Highbury Corner

Trullo is most people's idea of what a big-city Italian restaurant ought to look and feel like these days. Just off Highbury Corner, it has a pared-down bistro ambience, with bare floorboards, black bentwood chairs, minimal table coverings and an animated atmosphere. More than that, it serves up fast-paced, on-the-ball, fresh Italian dishes, with pasta that is hand-rolled just before start of business, a charcoal grill for adding an aromatic note to fish and meat, and a menu that changes not just with the seasons but daily. Expansion into the basement room has meant more covers, and yet the operation motors on smoothly, with as much unflustered grace and seductive charm as ever. Antipasti full of savoury intensity kick things off – hispi cabbage with Fontina, crab bruschetta – and then you might opt for a pasta primo such as tagliarini with wilted Italian greens and pine-nuts. For main, it could be lamb faggot with slow-cooked porcini and Jerusalem artichokes, or chargrilled cod with puntarelle. Finish up with almond tart and poached rhubarb, or the crowd-pleasing tiramisù.

Chef Tim Siadatan **Owner** Jordan Frieda, Tim Siadatan **Seats** 40, Pr/dining room 30 **Times** 12.30-2.45/6-10.15 Closed 25 Dec-3 Jan, D Sun **Prices** Prices not confirmed, Service optional **Wines** 40 bottles over £30, 11 bottles under £30, 11 by glass **Parking** On street **Notes** Large table menus available £25-£45, Sunday L, Vegetarian available, Children welcome

La Collina
PLAN 1 E4

◉ Modern Italian

tel: 020 7483 0192 **17 Princess Rd, Chalk Farm NW1 8JR**
email: info@lacollinarestaurant.co.uk
dir: *Nearest station: Chalk Farm, Camden Town*

Classy neighbourhood Italian for honest, simple cooking

La Collina is a relaxed and authentic neighbourhood Italian for the boho-chic residents of Primrose Hill, its discreet black frontage slotted into an elegant terrace. Inside, the place is simplicity itself: cream walls without adornment, dark pine floors, black leather seats and white tablecloths, and a small bar in the corner, all flooded with light from large sash windows. A cast-iron spiral staircase coils down to the basement, where you get a ringside seat for the tiny open kitchen – the domain of chef Diana Rinaldo who sends out homespun regional, ingredient-led dishes offering a pleasing mix of tradition and more modish thinking. A starter of home-made pappardelle with cep mushroom sauce is just what Italian food is all about: simple, seasonal and fresh. Next up, spanking fresh sea bass fillets are flavoured with tomatoes, thyme, and white wine, and to finish, the house tiramisù is a paragon of its ilk. All-Italian wines, and friendly Latin service add to the appeal.

Chef Diana Rinaldo **Owner** Patrick Oberto, Diana Rinaldo **Seats** 40 **Times** 12-2.30/6-11 Closed Xmas wk, L Mon **Prices** Fixed L 2 course fr £14.50 **Wines** 35 bottles over £30, 25 bottles under £30, 7 by glass **Parking** Free after 6pm & weekends **Notes** Vegetarian available, Children welcome

The Gilbert Scott
PLAN 3 B5

◉◉ British

tel: 020 7278 3888 **Renaissance St Pancras Hotel, Euston Rd NW1 2AR**
email: reservations@thegilbertscott.co.uk
dir: *Nearest station: St Pancras*

Versatile cooking in Gilbert Scott's majestic St Pancras hotel

Arguably Britain's finest railway hotel when it opened in 1873 as an amenity to St Pancras station, the meticulously restored Midland (now the Renaissance) is once more a London landmark, now witnessing the then unthinkable business of trains that run continuously to the continent. A masterpiece of Gothic Revival, from its magnificent portico entrance to a sweeping double staircase that is broad enough to allow two crinolined ladies to pass each other without unseemly collision, it's the kind of venue that has to be seen to be believed. Dimmed lights and candles create a thrilling ambience in the gorgeous cocktail bar, and the dining room is patrolled by staff whose long aprons match the seating. Traditional and contemporary dishes of imagination and flair complete the alluring picture. Expect roasted beetroot with ricotta, fried onion and beetroot aïoli; beautifully judged Cornish plaice on the bone with mussels, sweet tomatoes and basil; sturdy, well-filled pies such as rabbit, prawn and mushroom. There are indulgeable desserts like toffee cheesecake with salted caramel ice cream, or Lord Mayor's trifle, a concoction of blackberries and coconut sponge.

Chef Nick Ward **Owner** Marcus Wareing Restaurants Ltd **Seats** 110, Pr/dining room 20 **Times** 12-3/5.30-11 **Prices** Fixed L 2 course £21, Fixed D 3 course £25, Starter £6-£13.50, Main £14-£33, Dessert £6.50-£8.50 **Wines** 200 bottles over £30, 2 bottles under £30, 17 by glass **Parking** 12, NCP St Pancras **Notes** Brunch & afternoon tea available, Sunday L £27, Vegetarian available, Children welcome

Gilgamesh Restaurant Lounge

PLAN 1 E4

⚜ Pan-Asian

tel: 020 7482 5757 & 7428 4922 **The Stables Market, Chalk Farm Rd NW1 8AH**
email: reservations@gilgameshbar.com
dir: Nearest station: Chalk Farm, Camden Town

Pan-Asian dishes in a psychedelic re-creation of ancient Babylon

The exotic maelstrom that is Camden's Stables Market is good preparation for a meal here, for Gilgamesh is no ordinary venue. Be prepared for interiors inspired by the excesses of Babylon (the ancient Mesopotamian city, not a nightclub in Ilford). This amounts to hand-carved wooden furniture, extravagant fabrics, a lapis lazuli inlaid 50-metre bar, ornate walls of beaten bronze panels, marble pillars, palm trees, vast windows and nightclub-esque psychedelic lighting. The menu takes its inspiration from the East, serving up a Pan-Asian panoply of ideas: dim sum, sushi, Malaysian curries and more. Start with crispy squid with garlic chips and a sweet-and-sour dipping sauce, or salmon céviche, and move onto rack of organic lamb breaded with oriental herbs and served with an Asian dressing, or beef Penang. Desserts can be as Asian-inspired as an exotic tropical fruit bowl, or as indulgently European as milk chocolate fondant with praline and vanilla ice cream.

Times 12-2.30/6-12

Karpo

PLAN 3 B5

⚜ Modern European

tel: 020 7843 2221 & 7843 2222 **23-27 Euston Rd, St Pancras NW1 2SD**
email: info@karpo.co.uk
dir: Nearest station: King's Cross, St Pancras

Funky all-day restaurant serving up seasonal flavours

Named in honour of the Greek goddess of the fruits of the earth, there's a good deal of modernity on show here, not least at the front of the building (the Megaro Hotel) which is covered in vivid graffiti-style artwork. It's easy to spot at any rate, just opposite St Pancras International station. And it is suitably modern and funky on the inside, too: a mix of contemporary furnishings, colourful artworks, a 'living wall' of plants, and a mixture of canteen-style benches and tables, plus counter dining and an open kitchen. It's a relaxed, easygoing place, with friendly staff and food available all day. The menu shows no particular international allegiances, but is more British than anything else, with the available seasonal produce rightly leading the way. Start with flame-grilled mackerel with oyster and cucumber, before a main course such as Herdwick lamb with pickled carrots and sheep's cheese, with Cox's apple crumble and clotted cream for dessert.

Chef Joe Sharratt **Owner** Antonio Megaro **Seats** 70, Pr/dining room 16
Times 12-3/5.30-10 **Prices** Fixed L 2 course £14-£19, Starter £5-£9, Main £15-£24, Dessert £5-£6 **Wines** 10 bottles over £30, 14 bottles under £30, 8 by glass **Parking** On street **Notes** Brunch, ALC Sat-Sun 8am-4pm, Vegetarian available, Children welcome

Odette's Restaurant & Bar

LONDON NW1	PLAN 1 E4

Modern British **v**
tel: 020 7586 8569 **130 Regent's Park Rd NW1 8XL**
email: info@odettesprimrosehill.com
dir: Nearest station: Chalk Farm

Confident modern British cooking in a long-standing neighbourhood restaurant

A Primrose Hill favourite since the 1970s, Odette's cannot be accused of standing still over that time, but it hasn't chased every passing culinary fashion either. Bryn Williams has run the place since 2008 and it remains a foodie stopover worthy of any postcode. There's a decidedly Francophile feel to the place these days, helped along by the pavement tables out front and the terrace garden out back. A smart finish of cool grey with splashes of yellow from plush leather seats seems to reinforce the Parisian vibe, with the kitchen showing respect for the ways across the Channel. There's plenty of modern British zeal, too, with superb British ingredients on show, with Wales providing a fair share of its bounty (Mr Williams is a Welshman). There's a tasting menu, including a bespoke version if you're sat at the table in the kitchen (yes, that's in the kitchen), an amazing value weekday lunch, plus a full-on carte that offers up five options at each course. Off the latter menu, a starter of marinated scallops resonates with clarity and freshness, with the flavours and textures of pear, mooli and Carmarthen ham, while glazed pork cheek is matched with an apple and lobster bisque. Main courses are equally well-crated and finely tuned; roasted monkfish, say, with asparagus, gem lettuce and salted grapes, or beef braised in ale and served with smoked mash potatoes and ceps. Welsh cheeses served with bara brith and quince jelly make a satisfying interlude before desserts if you want to go the French way. And when it comes to puds, Odette's Jaffa cake with orange cream and marmalade shows affection for a childhood favourite, or go for Yorkshire rhubarb with a yoghurt pannacotta and brown sugar meringue. There's a vegetarian version of the tasting menu available on Mondays.

Chef Bryn Williams, Jamie Randall **Owner** Bryn Williams **Seats** 70, Pr/dining room 10 **Times** 12-2.30/6-10.30 Closed 25-26 Dec, 1 Jan **Prices** Fixed L 2 course £13, Fixed D 3 course fr £20, Tasting menu £50-£80, Starter £7-£10, Main £16-£20, Dessert £7-£9 **Wines** 36 bottles over £30, 16 bottles under £30, 16 by glass **Parking** On street **Notes** Tasting/Vegetarian menu 6/10 course, Sunday L £25-£30, Children welcome

LONDON NW1 *continued*

Meliá White House

PLAN 2 H4

◉◉ Spanish, Mediterranean

tel: 020 7391 3000 **Albany St, Regent's Park NW1 3UP**
email: melia.white.house@melia.com **web:** www.melia-whitehouse.com
dir: *Nearest station: Great Portland St, Regent's Park, Warren St*

Ambitious Spanish cooking in an art-deco hotel

Close to Regent's Park, and an easy stroll from Oxford Street, the Iberian-owned art-deco hotel pays homage to its national cuisine in the elegant fine-dining Spanish restaurant, L'Albufera. It is a glossy space, all polished wooden floors, black-clothed tables and cream upholstered chairs as a backdrop to vibrant cooking that straddles both traditional and modern Spanish schools. Materials are sourced from the homeland for maximum authenticity, so Serrano ham is carved from a trolley, and there are tapas dishes – crab croquettes, or cod tongues in pilpil sauce with shiitaki mushrooms, say – if that's the route you want to take, otherwise you might start with in-house-smoked sea trout with marinated baby beetroot and citrus dressing, then move on to slow-cooked turbot in a crab crust with fondant potatoes and fennel consommé. For dessert, a mojito could be deconstructed as brown rum parfait with mint sorbet and lime foam, or finish instead with exemplary Spanish cheeses served with figs and tarragon oil.

Times 7-10.30 Closed Sun, BHs, L all week

Michael Nadra Primrose Hill

PLAN 1 E4

◉◉ Modern European

tel: 020 7722 2800 **42 Gloucester Av NW1 8JD**
email: primrose@restaurant-michaelnadra.co.uk
dir: *Nearest station: Chalk Farm, Camden Town*

Classy modern food, with surroundings to match, by the canal

Chef-patron Michael Nadra made his name in Chiswick before branching out with this second, more ambitious canal-side venue in leafy Primrose Hill. Scoring high in the cool stakes, the interior ranges over different levels, with a martini bar at its centre, along with a subterranean vaulted-and-cobbled area (formerly a tunnel for barge horses), and there's a terrace for alfresco dining. Dark slate floors, fashionable leather seating, exposed brick and large windows all add up to some seriously good looks, while service is slickly professional but friendly. The cooking fits the contemporary style of the place: light, clean, bold-flavoured, skilful dishes that aren't overworked and allow prime ingredients to sing. Combinations are creative and everything is founded in well-honed classical technique. Thinly sliced roast rib-eye with cauliflower purée, rocket, parmesan and truffle jus is a starter that's big on flavour, and might be followed by succulent lamb rump teamed with sautéed sweetbreads, swede fondant, Savoy cabbage and cracking rosemary jus. A first-class fishy alternative could be grilled halibut accompanied by sautéed scallops, celeriac purée, truffled leeks and bisque sauce. If you can't wait 20 minutes for a classic apple tarte Tatin finale, go for wobbly vanilla pannacotta perfection.

Chef Michael Nadra **Owner** Michael Nadra **Seats** 100, Pr/dining room 40
Times 12-2.30/6-10 Closed 24 Dec, 1 Jan **Prices** Tasting menu £44-£55, Starter £8-£12, Main £18-£25, Dessert £7-£10 **Wines** 150 bottles over £30, 25 bottles under £30, 16 by glass **Parking** On street **Notes** Tasting menu 6 course, L 20% discount ALC menu, Sunday L £19, Vegetarian available, Children welcome

Odette's Restaurant & Bar

PLAN 1 E4

◉◉◉ – *see page 287*

Pullman London St Pancras

PLAN 3 A5

◉ Modern European

tel: 020 7666 9000 & 7666 9038 **100-110 Euston Rd NW1 2AJ**
email: h5309@accor.com **web:** www.accorhotels.com/5309
dir: *Nearest station: King's Cross, Euston, St Pancras Int*

International menu in a contemporary railway hotel

The hotel is ideally placed to receive weary travellers debouching from the Eurostar at St Pancras International, five minutes off. A major refurbishment has generally glitzed things up, though the main restaurant has gone for the anonymous feel of an astronautical control centre, with grey seating at regulation-spaced tables and dark nets screening the street view. The global menu is flagged with international wine suggestions for each dish, and the neatly presented items encompass enjoyable risotto nero with ink and flesh of chargrilled calamari, sautéed skate with roast beets in beurre noisette, and Josper-grilled rib-eye with hefty pont-neuf chips and vigorously seasoned portobello mushroom. 'Timeless Specialities' include a beef and oyster pie made with ox cheek, smoked oysters and caramelised onions in puff pastry. A slim slice of Valrhôna chocolate tart served warm is nicely contrasted with a scoop of milky ice cream, or there may be crema catalana garnished with caramelised ginger.

Chef Michael Penn **Owner** Accor UK **Seats** 92 **Times** 12-2.30/6-11 Closed L Sat-Sun **Prices** Fixed L 2 course £20-£25, Fixed D 3 course £35-£45, Tasting menu £45, Starter £8-£12, Main £12-£24, Dessert £7-£9 **Wines** 46 bottles over £30, 12 bottles under £30, 310 by glass **Notes** Vegetarian available, Children welcome

St Pancras Grand Brasserie

PLAN 3 B5

◉ British

tel: 020 7870 9900 **St Pancras International NW1 9QP**
email: stpg@searcys.co.uk
dir: *Nearest station: King's Cross, St Pancras*

French-inspired brasserie cooking at the Eurostar terminal

They weren't kidding when they named it the Grand Brasserie. Part of the regeneration of St Pancras station that accompanied its elevation to a Eurostar terminal, alongside the rebirth of Giles Gilbert Scott's old station hotel, the stunning restaurant designed by Martin Brudnizki is all burnished reflective surfaces and braced globe light fittings. Situated opposite a busy champagne bar, it looks for all the world as though it boarded the Eurostar at Montparnasse and alighted here last week. Quality ingredients presented with flair and care underpin modern French-inspired dishes, as in a starter of black pudding and foie gras with apple caramelised in calvados. Main courses take in truffled artichoke risotto, roast pheasant with Savoy cabbage and smoked parsnip purée, and an impressively well-timed herb-crusted cod fillet with watercress pesto and baby carrots. Finish with dark chocolate tart and pistachio ice cream with honeycomb, and then totter into the champagne bar, probably.

Chef Chris Dines, Jack Norman, Chris Leaves **Owner** Searcys **Seats** 160, Pr/dining room 2 **Times** 11am-mdnt Closed 25 Dec, All-day dining **Prices** Fixed L 2 course £12-£25, Fixed D 3 course £20-£35, Starter £5-£10.50, Main £6.50-£25, Dessert £5.50-£13.50 **Wines** 39 bottles over £30, 29 bottles under £30, 24 by glass **Notes** Sunday L £20-£25, Vegetarian available, Children welcome

The Winter Garden
PLAN 2 F3

◉◉ British, Mediterranean

tel: 020 7631 8000 & 7631 8230 **The Landmark London, 222 Marylebone Rd NW1 6JQ**
email: restaurants.reservation@thelandmark.co.uk **web:** www.wintergarden-london.com
dir: *Nearest station: Marylebone*

Classical cooking under a soaring glass roof

The Winter Garden is open all day for breakfast, lunch, afternoon tea and dinner, and the mood changes as does the hour (and the weather), for this dining room is in the heart of the eight-storey glass-covered atrium that forms the central focus of The Landmark Hotel. A grand railway hotel of the old school, it is these days an upscale address and its atrium is an impressive spot to sit and tuck into some classically-minded modern European food. Start, for example, with crab and sweetcorn cannelloni or roasted wood pigeon with a foie gras ballotine, spiced figs and pistachio. Denham Estate venison might feature among main courses as pan-fried loin and a separate pie (with salsify and Cumberland chutney), while a fish option might be wild halibut with mild curried gnocchi and trompette mushrooms. Desserts are equally well put together with sticky toffee pudding cranking up the comfort factor, and iced tarragon parfait showing the inventive streak runs right through.

Chef Gary Klaner **Owner** Khun Jatuporn Sihanatkathakul **Seats** 90
Times 12-2.30/6.30-10.30 **Prices** Prices not confirmed, Service optional **Wines** 25 by glass **Parking** 40, On street **Notes** Sun Champagne brunch, Theatre/Opera D available, Sunday L, Vegetarian available, Children welcome

Read all about our Wine Award winners on page 17

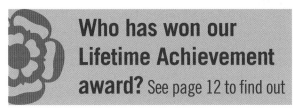

Who has won our Lifetime Achievement award? See page 12 to find out

Manna
PLAN 1 E4

◉ International Vegan

tel: 020 7722 8028 **4 Erskine Rd, Primrose Hill NW3 3AJ**
email: inquires@mannav.com
dir: *Nearest station: Chalk Farm*

Long-running neighbourhood vegetarian in leafy Primrose Hill

A forerunner of gourmet vegetarian and vegan dining when it opened in the 60s, Manna is still going strong with regard to ethical principles and organic values. The attractive shop front in a residential street in well-heeled Primrose Hill opens onto a rather modish decor with wooden floors and furniture given a touch of class with designer wallpaper featuring silhouetted trees and birds and silver wreath-style light fittings. Carefully-sourced produce is turned into vibrantly colourful dishes that are step with the times, taking inspiration from far and wide. The menu globetrots from Greek-style spanikopita tart with a salad of fennel, rocket, preserved lemon and dill salad, to a main course of wild mushroom ragù with chestnut polenta, seared kale, beetroot and horseradish slaw and parsnip crisps. For dessert, there's a light vegan take on sticky toffee pudding with vanilla ice cream and caramel sauce.

Owner R Swallow, S Hague **Seats** 50 **Times** 12-3/6.30-11 Closed Xmas & New Year, Mon, L variable **Prices** Tasting menu £14-£22, Starter £7-£8, Main £14-£15, Dessert £8 **Wines** 8 by glass **Parking** On street **Notes** Sunday L £14-£40, Children welcome

XO
PLAN 1 E4

◉ Pan-Asian

tel: 020 7433 0888 **29 Belsize Ln NW3 5AS**
email: xo@rickerrestaurants.com
dir: *Nearest station: Swiss Cottage, Belsize Park*

Asian variety act in well-heeled Belsize Park

This northern outpost of Will Ricker's stable of trendy bar-restaurants brings a touch of big-city cool to a leafy enclave of Belsize Park. The fashionably minimalist space is divided between bar and dining room and dotted with modern oriental touches: think black lacquered surfaces, funky chandeliers, decorative ironwork, low-slung booth-style leather seating and under-lit wall mirrors so you can check out who's in the house as you graze through the menu of voguish Pan-Asian dishes. The kitchen's repertoire is designed for sharing and takes in everything from dim sum (roast pumpkin and spinach gyoza, perhaps) to sashimi and sushi (salmon and avocado maki maybe), tempura (such as tiger prawn, lime and salt), curries, barbecued dishes and roasts (including the ever-popular black cod with sweet miso). Eye-catching cocktails, well-chosen wines and up-tempo music complete a polished package.

Chef Rodrigo Colombo **Owner** Will Ricker **Seats** 92, Pr/dining room 22
Times 12-3/6-11 Closed 25-26 Dec, 1 Jan **Prices** Fixed L 2 course fr £15, Starter £5.50-£16, Main £9.50-£30, Dessert £5-£6 **Wines** 33 bottles over £30, 19 bottles under £30, 16 by glass **Parking** On street **Notes** Sunday L, Vegetarian available, Children welcome

LONDON NW4

Hendon Hall Hotel

PLAN 1 D5

◉◉ Modern/Traditional British

tel: 020 8457 2200 **Ashley Ln, Hendon NW4 1HF**
email: hendonhall@handpicked.co.uk **web:** www.handpickedhotels.co.uk/hendonhall
dir: *Nearest station: Hendon Central*

Historic North London mansion with contemporary cooking

The impressive North London mansion dates from the 16th century and has earned a crust as a hotel since 1911. Nowadays, the place has a light contemporary look that blends well with a host of period features, including crystal chandeliers, a grand staircase and handsomely-proportioned rooms. Named after the 18th-century actor and manager of the eponymous Drury Lane theatre, who once owned the hall, the fine-dining Garrick Restaurant works an upmarket modern look with contemporary art on the walls and smart russet and gold high-backed chairs at formally-laid tables. The kitchen continues to score palpable hits with its up-to-date cooking, setting out with a well-made terrine of confit duck, guinea fowl and foie gras matched creatively with red wine pear purée and parsnip. Next up, roast fillet of hake comes with capers and leek fondue, and jus noisette. The modern, creative thinking continues at dessert stage too with a well-thought-out composition of flavours and textures involving whipped lemon curd, meringue, citrus jelly and lemonade granita.

Chef Richard Walker **Owner** Hand Picked Hotels **Seats** 60, Pr/dining room 18 **Times** 12.30-2.30/6.30-9.30 **Prices** Fixed L 2 course £30, Fixed D 3 course fr £37, Starter £9-£12, Main £15.50-£25.50, Dessert £7.50-£9.50 **Wines** 60 bottles over £30, 6 bottles under £30, 17 by glass **Parking** 150 **Notes** Seasonal market menu 2/3 course £30-£37, Sunday L £30-£37, Vegetarian available, Children welcome

LONDON SE1

The Anchor & Hope

PLAN 5 E5

◉◉ British

tel: 020 7928 9898 **36 The Cut SE1 8LP**
email: anchorandhope@btconnect.com
dir: *Nearest station: Southwark, Waterloo*

Thrilling gastro-pub with big-hearted cooking

This tumultuous Waterloo gastro-pub is a roaring success – roaring being the operative word when it is rammed and you're in the high-decibel bar with a pint of real ale waiting your turn for a table in the eating area (you can't book to eat, except for Sunday lunch). The Anchor & Hope still looks and feels like a pub with its pared-back, no-frills interior – oxblood walls hung with modern art, and well-worn wooden tables and mismatched chairs. The food suits the mood of the place: flannel-free, unpretentious dishes built on quality seasonal ingredients. The menu changes each session, and descriptions rarely go beyond a handful of words, so forget three-course formality and just order whatever grabs your attention – warm snail and bacon salad or grilled razor clams might get the juices flowing, followed by roast Swaledale beef rump with dripping potatoes and horseradish. Otherwise three of you (or a greedy pair) could sign up for roast kid's leg 'saltimbocca' with chips and aïoli. Puds stay on message, perhaps raspberry Bakewell tart with clotted cream.

Times 12-2.30/6-10.30 Closed BHs, 25 Dec-1 Jan, L Mon, D Sun

Brigade

PLAN 5 H6

◉ British

tel: 0844 346 1225 **The Fire Station, 139 Tooley St SE1 2HZ**
email: info@thebrigade.co.uk
dir: *Nearest station: London Bridge*

Turning up the heat in an old fire station

Brigade isn't only so-called because of its location in an old fire station. The name also references the brigade in the kitchen as they're mostly apprentices who have been at risk of homelessness or have lived on the streets, and are on a six-month chef training scheme aimed at giving them the skills, qualifications and confidence to turn their lives around. The scheme is being run in conjunction with Southwark College and the Beyond Food Foundation charity, founded by Brigade chef-patron Simon Boyle. The restaurant has a contemporary look with leather high-backed chairs and banquettes, and black lacquered tables, and the lively atmosphere is helped along by the sounds, sights and smells of the centrally positioned open kitchen (grab a seat at the counter if you want to be really close to the action). The menu is broadly modern British, using plenty of top-notch seasonal, British ingredients. Hand-dived Scottish scallops with beetroot and chilli risotto is one way to start, perhaps followed by one of the best burgers in town, made from rump steak and with shredded oxtail sitting on top.

Times 12-3/5.30-10 Closed Sun, L Sat

Cantina Vinopolis

PLAN 5 F6

◉ Modern Mediterranean

tel: 020 7940 8333 **1 Bank End SE1 9BU**
email: cantina@vinopolis.co.uk
dir: *Nearest station: London Bridge*

Dining underneath the arches at the South Bank's wine emporium

The soaring arches of a Victorian railway viaduct near London Bridge Station make an impressive cathedral-like space for worshipping the grape in its multifarious forms. Part of the Vinopolis complex, Cantina is the place to head for Mediterranean-accented dining in a modish setting of oak tables and leather banquettes beneath cavernous vaulted brick ceilings, with the rumble of overhead trains as an evocative soundtrack. It's run by staff who are passionate about food and wine, and in case you had forgotten that this is a temple to good wines, there are displays of bottles and a splendid list to jog the memory. Expect straight-talking ideas along the lines of duck foie gras terrine with home-made bread, followed by pheasant served with potato fondant, braised black cabbage, green lentils and vegetable stew, or if you fancy fish, perhaps lemon sole with spinach, new potatoes, capers and passionfruit marinière. Stay with the wine theme and treat yourself to a glass of something sticky to go with prune and almond tart served with vanilla ice cream.

Chef Moges A Wolde **Owner** Claudio Pulze **Seats** 200, Pr/dining room 100 **Times** 12-3/6-10.30 Closed Xmas, BHs, L Mon-Wed, D Sun **Prices** Fixed L 2 course £14.95, Fixed D 3 course £29.95, Starter £6.50-£9.50, Main £12.50-£22.50, Dessert £5.25-£7.50 **Wines** 50 by glass **Parking** On street **Notes** Sunday L £15-£19.95, Vegetarian available, Children welcome

Chino Latino London

PLAN 5 C3

◉◉ Modern Pan-Asian V

tel: 020 7769 2500 **Plaza on the River London, 18 Albert Embankment SE1 7TJ**
email: london@chinolatino.co.uk web: www.chinolatino.co.uk
dir: *Nearest station: Vauxhall*

Asian and Latin American spice and fire on the South Bank

Pan-Asian food with Latin inflections is the best-of-both-worlds approach at this rocking international chain that has pitched its London tent in the Park Plaza hotel complex on the South Bank, not far from Vauxhall station. A cocktail bar to be seen in, where the fiery Latino potions come with lashings of chilli and crushed mint, a sushi bar, and a sexy main dining room all in black, offset with light-panels in shimmering cherry, add up to a potently heady style mix. The food delivers too, with exquisitely presented dishes bursting with freshness, heat and umami. A maki roll of soft-shell crab, avocado and Japanese rice comes with tomato-chilli mayo, or you might kick off with chicken, foie gras and shiitake shu mai in teriyaki sauce. Main courses mix and match the house influences, as when duck breast is dressed in both miso marinade and aji Amarillo yellow chilli, while bracing seafood flavours feature in the shape of a pairing of yuzu-gratinated lobster and king crab with

chilli-garlic hollandaise. The eye-catching finisher is a chocolate dome of salted banana toffee, served with vanilla ice cream.

Chef Sebastian Francis, Werner Seebach **Owner** Park Plaza Hotels **Seats** 85 **Times** 12-2.30/6-10.30 Closed 1 Jan, L Sat-Sun **Prices** Prices not confirmed **Wines** 29 bottles over £30, 18 bottles under £30, 12 by glass **Parking** Q-park at Waterloo station **Notes** Children welcome

See advert below

H10 London Waterloo Hotel

PLAN 5 E5

◉ Modern Mediterranean, Spanish

tel: 020 7928 4062 **384-302 Waterloo Rd SE1 8RQ**
email: h10.london.waterloo@h10hotels.com web: www.hotelh10londonwaterloo.com
dir: *Nearest station: Waterloo, Lambeth North*

Cool Mediterranean food in a new Waterloo hotel

The freshly minted H10 in Waterloo is a prime piece of London new-build from a dynamic international hotel group, a sharp-edged wedge of a building close to the station. Interior styling is as up-to-the-minute as can be, with postmodern graphic panels in the clinically white lobby, and a design tone in the first-floor Three O Two restaurant that recalls an upmarket cafeteria, with its geometrically perfect lines of

continued

Chino Latino

Modern Pan-Asian Cuisine and Latin Bar

18 Albert Embankment, London, SE1 7TJ
0207 769 2500
www.chinolatino.eu

Chino Latino at Plaza on the River serves some of the finest and most imaginative Pan-Asian cuisine in the capital. Sample subtle flavours of the far east complemented by our lively Latino cocktails. Signature dishes include the award winning Black Cod in spicy miso, freshly caught sushi, sashimi and a wide selection of tempura and dim sum.

LONDON SE1 *continued*

unclothed tables for two. Grab a window table for the best views of what's happening down on Waterloo Road. Light Mediterranean brasserie food is what to expect, perhaps starting with an attentively timed dried tomato and asparagus risotto, dressed in olive oil and balsamic, moving on to lamb confit, cooked at a laid-back temperature for ideal tenderness, and bedded on sweet potato dauphinoise with glazed shallots, and concluding with assertively nutmegged crema catalana of authentic texture (ie a shade looser than crème brûlée).

Chef David Ovejo **Seats** 100, Pr/dining room 50 **Times** 6.30-10.30 **Prices** Starter £2.80-£16.60, Main £11-£19.90, Dessert £5.10-£9.50 **Wines** 9 bottles over £30, 37 bottles under £30, 16 by glass **Parking** NCP Library St or Elephant & Castle **Notes** Vegetarian available, Children welcome

Hutong
PLAN 5 G6

◉◉ Northern Chinese **NEW** v

tel: 020 3011 1257 **Level 33 The Shard SE1 9RY**
email: hutongreservations@aqua-london.com
dir: *Nearest station: London Bridge*

Top-end Chinese dining on the 33rd floor

Hutong pays homage to the cuisine of Northern China, the cooking based on the Shandong cuisine that was served up in the Imperial Palaces of old Peking. It's not exactly located in a palace as such, but a shrine to London's international standing, for it's located on the 33rd floor of The Shard. Yes, the view is stunning, particularly at night with the shimmering lights below, and it goes without saying there's maximum glass to enable everyone to get full impact. The room is a bit of a looker itself, with red lanterns and an open-to-view wood-fired oven where the ducks – a big part of the menu – can be seen cooking and drying. The kitchen turns out some classy dim sum at lunchtime, but the carte is also available lunch and dinner. Start with spiced razor clams or Szechuan peppered cuttlefish before tucking into the classic Peking duck, served in two waves – the crispy skin with pancakes and hoi sin sauce, then the meat with onions, peppers and chilli in a rich, flavoursome sauce. Fried prawns with jasmine tea leaves is a typically impressive main course, and there are sweet custard buns for dessert.

Chef Xiazhong Zhang **Owner** David Yeo, Aqua Restaurant Group **Seats** 130, Pr/dining room 24 **Times** 12-3/6-11 Closed 25 Dec, 1 Jan **Prices** Tasting menu £68, Starter £8-£14, Main £9-£29, Dessert £5.50-£6 **Wines** 57 bottles over £30, 4 bottles under £30, 13 by glass **Notes** Dim Sum L menu 5 course £28, Sunday L, Children welcome

Follow us on facebook
www.facebook.com/TheAAUK

What makes a 5-Rosette restaurant?
See page 9

Magdalen
PLAN 5 H6

◉◉ British, European

tel: 020 7403 1342 **152 Tooley St SE1 2TU**
email: info@magdalenrestaurant.co.uk **web:** www.magdalenrestaurant.co.uk
dir: *Nearest station: London Bridge*

Vibrantly flavoured and thoughtful cooking near London Bridge

Magdalen, on a corner site hard by London Bridge, is a classy place, with burgundy-coloured walls hung with contemporary artwork, bentwood chairs at white-clothed tables covered with paper liners and a darkwood floor. Dishes are marked by their simplicity and judicious combinations (which belies the kitchen's technical skill and careful choice of ingredients), so clear flavours are allowed to speak for themselves. Perfectly timed, tender pieces of cuttlefish are cooked in ink and simply accompanied by whole chickpeas with a squeeze of lemon and a sprinkling of parsley, and chopped suckling pig comes with spiced clementines and toast. Main courses follow a similar mould: one beautifully presented dish is rare, melt-in-the-mouth roast haunch of venison with braised red cabbage and a gratin of potatoes and Gubbeen (an Irish cheese), or there is baked sea bass fillet with fennel, chard and anchovy dressing. Puddings make an impact too – perhaps decadent, dense chocolate pot, its richness cut by preserved cherries, or classic tarte Tatin.

Chef James & Emma Faulks, David Abbott **Owner** Roger & James Faulks **Seats** 90, Pr/dining room 30 **Times** 12-2.30/6.30-10 Closed Xmas, BHs, Sun, L Sat **Prices** Prices not confirmed **Wines** 58 bottles over £30, 15 bottles under £30, 12 by glass **Parking** On street **Notes** Vegetarian available, Children welcome

Oblix
PLAN 5 G6

◉ American **NEW**

tel: 020 7268 6700 **Level 32, The Shard, 31 St Thomas St SE1 9RY**
email: info@oblixrestaurant.com
dir: *Nearest station: London Bridge*

Steaks and more 32-floors up

If it's not a little trite to say so, the views are terrific. This is the 32nd-floor of The Shard after all, and the Oblix takes up the entire space with its slick, brasserie vibe, open kitchen, cool lounge bar, luxe cocktails and live music (they have their own house band – really). When it comes to food, the grill and Josper oven are the stars of the show, with veal chop and gremolata and Wagyu tenderloin waiting to provide a satisfying hit of protein. It's not all about the red stuff, though, for this is a kitchen that turns out nifty starters such as grilled diver-caught scallops with lime and tamarind cream or wood-fired roasted beets with rye bread and goats' curd. Among main courses, too, there are alternatives to the meaty offerings, with barbecue black cod with coriander salsa catching the eye. Finish with a pecan nut and chocolate bar with bourbon ice cream, and then hit the bar. It's a seriously glamorous spot.

Chef Fabien Beaufour **Owner** Rainer Becker **Times** 12-2.30/6-10.30 **Prices** Starter £9-£24, Main £14.50-£92, Dessert £6-£42 **Wines** 300+ bottles over £30, 3 bottles under £30, 22 by glass **Notes** Sunday L

The Oxo Tower Restaurant

PLAN 3 D1

@@ Traditional, Modern British V

tel: 020 7803 3888 **8th Floor, Oxo Tower Wharf, Barge House St SE1 9PH**
email: oxo.reservations@harveynichols.com web: www.harveynichols.com
dir: *Nearest station: Blackfriars, Waterloo, Southwark*

Captivating views and modish food

The view is 24-carat gold. Up on the eighth floor of the old Oxo building, this bar, brasserie and restaurant combo overlooks the river and St Paul's Cathedral, a position which never ceases to impress, day or night. A table on the outdoor terrace is a prized possession indeed (when the weather's right, of course), but it's impressive enough from behind the vast wall of glass. The contemporary cooking matches the modish neutrality of the decor, while the well turned-out staff deliver slick and clued-up service. Gourmet burgers are all the rage these days, and here we have a venison version served with Caesar salad, brioche crumbs and a fried egg, but the cooking is more broadly focused on European preparations. John Dory, for example, with gratinated razor clams, chestnut and garlic purée and ceps, or wild duck breast with slow-cooked rillettes, pear and walnut jam, spiced walnuts, radicchio and salsify. To finish, quince tart Tatin with Calvados pannacotta, or caramel soufflé with rum baba and chestnut ice cream should hit the spot.

Chef Jeremy Bloor **Owner** Harvey Nichols **Seats** 250 **Times** 12-3/6-11.30 Closed 25 Dec, D 24 Dec **Prices** Fixed L 3 course £50-£65, Fixed D 3 course £80, Tasting menu £120, Starter £14.50-£20, Main £19.50-£35, Dessert £7.50-£19.50 **Wines** 650 bottles over £30, 8 bottles under £30, 14 by glass **Parking** On street, NCP **Notes** Pre-theatre menu 2 course £35, Children welcome

Park Plaza County Hall London

PLAN 5 C5

@ Italian

tel: 020 7021 1919 & 7021 1800 **1 Addington St SE1 7RY**
email: ppchres@pphe.com web: www.parkplazacountyhall.com
dir: *Nearest station: Waterloo, Westminster*

Italian favourites in Thames-side landmark building

This snazzy modern hotel is next to County Hall on the South Bank, so right in the heart of the central London action. L'Italiano restaurant is on a mezzanine level, looking down on the buzzy first-floor bar, and it has got bags of style. There's a great view of the capital through the large wall of glass. At the heart of the culinary action is a wood-fired oven, which given the Italian focus of the place, means great pizzas (picante, perhaps, with salami, red onion and chill, or rustica with Parma ham and artichokes). But there lots more going on. Beef carpaccio is a good version, or you might start with deep-fried squid with lemon mayonnaise. Pasta and risotto are traditional choices such as lasagne or seafood linguine, but there's also slow-roasted pork belly and whole sea bass poached in a light, spicy broth. Desserts are a familiar bunch: pannacotta with wild berries, or tiramisù.

Chef Mark Dancer **Owner** Park Plaza Hotels **Seats** 104, Pr/dining room 50 **Times** 5.30-10.30 Closed L all week **Prices** Prices not confirmed **Wines** 12 bottles over £30, 18 bottles under £30, 13 by glass **Parking** U Park Ltd **Notes** Vegetarian available, Children welcome

Park Plaza Westminster Bridge London

PLAN 5 C5

@ Modern French

tel: 020 7620 7200 **SE1 7UT**
email: ppwlres@pphe.com web: www.parkplaza.com
dir: *Nearest station: Westminster, Waterloo*

Vibrant modern brasserie dishes on the South Bank

In a perfect riverside location near to the South Bank's attractions (London Eye, London Aquarium, National Theatre, etc) and just across the bridge from Big Ben and the Houses of Parliament, the Park Plaza Westminster Bridge is a contemporary colossus with over 500 stylish rooms, and is also home to French-style Brasserie Joël. It is a clean-cut, darkly minimalist space with bare black-lacquered tables, black and cream banquettes, moody red lighting, and a huge showpiece olive tree as a nod to the culinary style. Uncomplicated modern brasserie dishes aim to please, so dig in and start with blue cheese tart with caramelised shallots and lamb's lettuce, then move on to roast rack of lamb with garlic confit and watercress, or if you're in the market for fish, go for a whole sea bass chargrilled in the Josper oven and served with fennel confit and bouillabaisse sauce. End with roast pear millefeuille with chestnut cream.

Chef Walter Ishizuka **Owner** PPHE Hotels **Seats** 180, Pr/dining room 80 **Times** 12-2/5.30-10.30 Closed L Sat **Prices** Fixed L 2 course £11.95, Fixed D 3 course fr £19.95, Starter £6.50-£11.50, Main £10.50-£26.50, Dessert £6.50 **Wines** 23 bottles over £30, 14 bottles under £30, 10 by glass **Parking** NCP **Notes** Pre-theatre menu available, Sunday L fr £12.50, Vegetarian available, Children welcome

What makes a 3-Rosette restaurant?
See page 9

Restaurant Story

LONDON SE1   PLAN 5 J5

Modern British v

tel: 020 7183 2117 **201 Tooley St SE1 2UE**
email: dine@restaurantstory.co.uk
web: www.restaurantstory.co.uk
dir: *Nearest station: London Bridge, Tower Hill*

White-hot opening from a rising global talent

If you want to eat at Restaurant Story, you need to be quick off the mark: a table at this new addition to every foodie's must-visit list is so in demand, bookings are only being taken on a month-by-month basis. So why the big fuss? Well, word has got round that chef-patron Tom Sellers is a real star who honed his skills with some of the greats of the industry (Tom Aikens in London, Thomas Keller at Per Se in New York and René Redzepi at Noma in Copenhagen) and is turning out some truly stunning food at his first solo venture. The setting is a Nordic-styled wood-clad building at the Tower Bridge end of Tooley Street (easy to spot then), where floor-to-ceiling windows offer views of The Shard. Inside it's all clean-lined modernity, with polished concrete floors, chocolate-brown leather chairs and blonde-wood tables, and, thank heavens, an open kitchen. The menu — presented inside an old book as a first hint at the 'story' theme — follows the tasting format (either six or ten courses), with each stage designed to reflect Sellers' journey through life, with some clever plays on childhood memories. The signature opener of 'bread and dripping' — a Wee Willie Winkie-style candle made of beef dripping that melts so you can dip the fresh, warm sourdough roll in — is followed swiftly by a succession of clever, playful 'snacks', including an afternoon-tea-style rabbit finger sandwich, Oreo biscuit (a savoury biscuit coloured with squid ink), and corn on the cob with corn custard. Next up might be 'onion, apple and Old Tom' (caramelised onions with sliced and slow-cooked plums, with a stunning onion and Old Tom gin essence poured over the dish at the table that simply lifts it to another level), then 'heritage potato, asparagus and coal' (incredibly smooth mashed potato topped with asparagus, a wicked butter sauce and a charcoal oil dressing to temper the richness of the dish). Ingredients are of the highest possible quality and seasonal, as in 'raw beef, apple and Périgord truffle' a theatrical dish serving the beef and truffle in an apple with swirling dry ice smoke. The creativity and intrigue continues into sweet treats like 'almond and dill', a sublime almond ice cream, 'snow' and milk married with dill oil and dill salt. This is highly innovative, technically brilliant cooking that thrills with its intriguing combinations, big, bold flavours, and awe-inspiring presentation.

Chef Tom Sellers **Owner** Tom Sellers **Seats** 40
Times 12-2.30/6.30-9.30 Closed 2wks Aug, 2 wks Xmas, Sun-Mon **Prices** Fixed L 3 course fr £35 **Wines Parking** On street **Notes** Fixed menu L/D 6/10 course £60/£80, No children

LONDON SE1 *continued*

Pizarro

PLAN 5 H4

◎◎ Traditional Spanish

tel: 020 7378 9455 **194 Bermondsey St SE1 3TQ**
email: management@pizarrorestaurant.com
dir: *Nearest station: Bermondsey, Borough, London Bridge*

Spanish cooking at its best in foodie Bermondsey

If you've fallen in love with the tapas served at José at 104 Bermondsey Street, then you might want to hotfoot it down to number 194 where the eponymous José Pizarro has opened a stylish and casual restaurant serving a full menu of authentic and modern Spanish cuisine. Floor-to-ceiling windows fill the room with natural light, while the open kitchen adds to the buzz and you can take your pick of places to sit (on a stool at the bar, beside the window for some people watching, or a more intimate booth at the back). The regularly-changing menu is bolstered by daily specials, and the kitchen deals in top-notch ingredients put together in simple, unfussy combinations. Lamb's sweetbreads with PX sherry is one way to begin, the sweetbreads moist and rich and served with an intense but well balanced sauce, while Iberico pork presa with Jerusalem artichokes and pear purée makes a fine main course (precisely cooked meat complemented perfectly by sweet pear and earthy artichokes). Round things off with a textbook vanilla cheesecake with fresh raspberries.

Chef José Pizarro **Owner** José Pizarro **Seats** 75, Pr/dining room 10 **Times** 12-3/6-11 Closed 4 days over Xmas **Prices** Prices not confirmed, Service optional **Wines** 20 bottles over £30, 15 bottles under £30, 27 by glass **Parking** On street, NCP car park **Notes** All day menu Sat, Sun brunch 10am-2pm, Sunday L, Vegetarian available, Children welcome

Le Pont de la Tour

PLAN 5 J6

◎◎ Modern French 🍷NOTABLE WINE LIST

tel: 020 7403 8403 **The Butlers Wharf Building, 36d Shad Thames SE1 2YE**
email: lepontres@danddlondon.com **web:** www.lepontdelatour.co.uk
dir: *Nearest station: Tower Hill, London Bridge*

Great views and assured French cooking

In the league table of London's restaurants with a view, Le Pont de la Tour is definitely in the Premiership. The name translates as Tower Bridge, and that's what lies before you, whether you're dining out on its planter-lined terrace, or indoors taking in the scene through vast floor-to-ceiling windows. The setting owes a debt to the gracious lines of art deco style and everything is just right – correctly-paced service, a chic ambience that evokes 1930s Paris, and food that is rooted in the French classics. The spotlight is always on seafood here and luxury ingredients are liberally pressed into service, as in a generously filled lobster raviolo served with spinach and sauce Nantua. A wintery dish of venison comes in a spicy peppery crust with salsify, braised red cabbage and sauce poivrade, or you might go for roasted wild sea bass with tomato fondue, courgette ribbons and olive crumb. Sticking with the Gallic theme, apple tarte Tatin is served with vanilla ice cream and honeycomb tuile. If your wallet can stand the strain, the place is well known for its cracking wine list.

Chef Tom Cook **Owner** Des Gunewardena **Seats** 140, Pr/dining room 24 **Times** 12-3/6-11 **Prices** Prices not confirmed, Service optional 12.5% **Wines** 150 bottles over £30, 20 bottles under £30, 35 by glass **Parking** On street & car park **Notes** Sunday L, Vegetarian available, Children welcome

Restaurant Story

PLAN 5 J5

◎◎◎◎ – *see opposite*

Roast

PLAN 5 G6

◎ British V 🍷NOTABLE WINE LIST

tel: 0845 034 7300 **The Floral Hall, Borough Market, Stoney St SE1 1TL**
email: info@roast-restaurant.com **web:** www.roast-restaurant.com
dir: *Nearest station: London Bridge*

Great British produce overlooking Borough Market

There's no doubting the foodie credentials of the location, right in the heart of Borough Market, even if the place is more of a tourist attraction these days. The one-time Floral Hall is a cracking setting for a restaurant, perched above the market with views across London taking in St Paul's Cathedral. There's a bar serving up seasonal cocktails, and a top-notch Scotch egg if you're feeling peckish. The restaurant is the setting for some British-focused food, sourced with due diligence, and in true market fashion, it's open for breakfast. Maldon sweetcorn and smoked haddock chowder is a starter packed full of flavour, or go for gamekeeper's terrine with cranberry compôte. Next up, pan-fried fillet of Cornish sole is a generous serving, with accompanying smoked sea trout and chive butter sauce. For dessert, there's chocolate and clementine trifle, or an excellent Dorset blueberry and almond tart with yoghurt cream.

Chef Marcus Verberne **Owner** Iqbal Wahhab **Seats** 120 **Times** 12-3.45/5.30-11 Closed 25-26 Dec, 1 Jan, D Sun **Prices** Fixed L 3 course £30, Fixed D 3 course £30, Starter £7-£10.50, Main £15.75-£35, Dessert £6.75-£8.50 **Wines** 310 bottles over £30, 20 bottles under £30, 21 by glass **Parking** NCP Kipling St **Notes** Sunday L £35, Children welcome

LONDON SE1 *continued*

RSJ, The Restaurant on the South Bank
PLAN 5 D6

◉ Modern European

tel: 020 7928 4554 **33 Coin St SE1 9NR**
email: tom.king@rsj.uk.com
dir: *Nearest station: Waterloo*

Pleasingly unfussy food and notable Loire wines

RSJ's proximity to the National Theatre and other delights of the ever-improving South Bank makes it a big hit with culture vultures stopping by for the pre- and post-theatre menus. The wine list is a big draw too, and quite rightly so, with its focus on the Loire – many of the wines are organic and have been selected by the owner who's been visiting France for 'research purposes' for more than 30 years. In the kitchen, simple food is elevated by intelligent flavour combinations and sound cooking in the likes of salted ox cheeks with a duck egg, horseradish and pea shoots, or a main-course roast rump of lamb partnered with saffron butter beans, piquillo peppers and baby artichokes. If you're in the mood for fish, there could be pan-fried sea bass fillet with crushed peas, white asparagus and crab dressing. To finish, try an invigorating trio comprising lime tart, mango ice cream and passionfruit sauce.

Times 12-2.30/5.30-11.30 Closed Xmas, 1 Jan, Sun, L Sat

Skylon
PLAN 5 C6

◉ Modern British v

tel: 020 7654 7800 **Royal Festival Hall, Southbank Centre SE1 8XX**
email: skylonreservations@danddlondon.com
dir: *Nearest station: Waterloo Station*

Smart riverside dining at the Royal Festival Hall

With a name that may suggest an empire in a galaxy, far, far, away, Skylon is in fact in the Royal Festival Hall on the Southbank of the River Thames. There's a cool bar, a swish grill, and a restaurant headed up by executive chef Adam Gray. The restaurant occupies a large, high-ceilinged space facing the water, and there's a vast wall of glass so you won't miss a thing. It looks very sharp with its well-spaced (there is plenty of room after all), linen-clad tables, muted colour tones and impressive designer light fittings. On the menu are some smart classical ideas gently updated in places, based on good quality produce, and with a modern British flavour. Start, perhaps, with pressed duck foie gras and Lincolnshire smoked eel terrine with apple jelly and warm brioche, and follow on with pan-fried halibut with creamed celeriac, wild mushrooms, smoked bacon and red wine gravy.

Chef Adam Gray **Owner** D & D London **Seats** 100, Pr/dining room 33
Times 12-2.30/5.30-10 Closed 25 Dec, D Sun **Prices** Fixed D 3 course fr £29, Tasting menu fr £59 **Wines** 260 bottles over £30, 16 bottles under £30, 18 by glass
Notes Pre-theatre menu available, Fixed menu 2/3 course £42/£48, Sunday L £27-£32, Children welcome

Read our interview with chef Michael Caines on page 29

Union Street Café
PLAN 5 E6

◉◉ Italian, Mediterranean NEW

tel: 020 7592 7977 & 7592 1701 **47-51 Great Suffolk St SE1 0BS**
email: unionstreetcafe@gordonramsay.com
dir: *Nearest station: Southwark*

Ramsays new warehouse-styled urban-chic Southwark/Borough Italian

David Beckham may have pulled out of backing this new venture with his pal Gordon Ramsay at the last moment, but it didn't do the opening's media frenzy any harm. The casual, urban-chic warehouse sheen makes it a big hit with the thirtysomethings, while switched-on casually clad staff fit the bill too. Trendy background music, funky lighting, buffed concrete, striking artwork and fashionable leather seating, keep it right on white-linen-free vogue, with an elevated open kitchen and cool vibe to boot. The cooking is Italian from chef Davide Degiovanni, and menus (in Italian) change daily to keep things fresh driven by the best market produce. Skilled simplicity and a confident light modern touch keep the food high on flavour. Take the crispiest fritto rammed with the freshest salt cod and teamed with silky peppers and vibrant salsa verde to open, while pasta might feature big-hit flavoured tagliatelle with rabbit, caciocavallo (cheese) and olives, or wobbly pannacotta perfection with 'wow' Yorkshire rhubarb compôte at dessert. The basement bar has an equally casual-chic, arty vibe, and the cocktails are a big draw.

Chef Davide Degiovanni **Owner** Gordon Ramsay Group **Seats** 125, Pr/dining room 18 **Times** 12-3/6-11 Closed 25-26 Dec, 1 Jan **Prices** Fixed L 2 course £19, Fixed D 3 course £25, Starter £7-£12, Main £16-£28, Dessert £6-£8 **Wines** 116 bottles over £30, 23 bottles under £30, 20 by glass **Parking** NCP, Ewer St **Notes** Events menu 3/4 course £35/£45, Vegetarian available, Children welcome

Zucca
PLAN 5 H5

◉◉ Modern Italian

tel: 020 7378 6809 **184 Bermondsey St SE1 3TQ**
email: reservations@zuccalondon.com
dir: *Nearest station: London Bridge*

Vibrant, compelling modern Italian cooking and a lively atmosphere

Zucca woos both the critics and crowds with its vibrant modern Italian cooking and prime people-watching through its large, floor-to-ceiling windows. The emphasis here is on tip-top seasonal ingredients, simply but accurately cooked with passion to deliver light, fresh, clean dishes that sing with flavour. The compact menu changes daily, and the pricing is commendably reasonable for food of this quality. Antipasti (set for sharing) includes namesake zucca fritti (zucca meaning pumpkin in Italian) or perhaps sea bass carpaccio, while a smattering of unmissable home-made pasta might feature taglierini with new-season mushrooms and parmesan. For mains, try grilled swordfish with Sicilian aubergines and chick peas, or a veal chop with spinach and lemon, while desserts – like pistachio and raspberry tart with vanilla ice cream – shouldn't be overlooked. Super home-baked breads, informed service and some corking Italian wines all add up to a class act, while the minimalist surroundings – an open kitchen, white walls broken up by a few abstracts, wooden flooring and white Formica-style tables and chairs – fit the relaxed café-style vibe.

Chef Sam Harris **Owner** Sam Harris **Seats** 64, Pr/dining room 10 **Times** 12-3/6-10 Closed 25 Dec, 1 Jan, Etr, Mon, D Sun **Prices** Starter £4.95-£10, Main £15-£18.50, Dessert £5-£9, Service optional **Wines** 141 bottles over £30, 11 bottles under £30, 12 by glass **Parking** On street **Notes** Sunday L, Vegetarian available, Children welcome

Chapters All Day Dining
PLAN 1 H3

◎◎ Modern British

tel: 020 8333 2666 **43-45 Montpelier Vale, Blackheath Village SE3 OTJ**
email: chapters@chaptersrestaurants.co.uk **web:** www.chaptersrestaurants.com
dir: *Nearest station: Blackheath*

Blackheath Village eatery buzzing all day long

With a super location overlooking the heath from its alfresco pavement tables or through floor-to-ceiling windows, Chapters (relaxed sibling of big-hitting big-brother restaurant Chapter One – see entry) is an all-round hot ticket. Fashionable good looks (floorboards, banquettes, exposed brick, mirrors, dangling globe lights and a zinc-topped bar) pull in an appreciative young and young-at-heart crowd to the two-floored dine-all-day outfit at the heart of trendy Blackheath Village. It covers all the bases, from breakfast to weekend brunch, morning coffee to modern brasserie classics at lunch and dinner. Throw in daily specials, a fixed-price lunch option, kids' dishes, well-chosen wines (with plenty by glass or pichet) and accessible prices and everyone's happy. Conjured from quality ingredients, well-presented, clean-flavoured dishes might take in slow-roasted belly of Gloucestershire Old Spot pork with colcannon, caramelised apple and a cider velouté, or perhaps smoked haddock fishcake with creamed spinach, beurre blanc sauce and frisée salad, while from the Josper grill there might be rib-eye steak or Kentish double Barnsley lamb chop. Comfort desserts (Eton Mess, baked vanilla cheesecake) round off an accomplished, neighbourhood-restaurant act.

Chef Alex Tyndall **Owner** Selective Restaurants Group **Seats** 100 **Times** 8am-11pm Closed 2-3 Jan, All-day dining **Prices** Fixed L 2 course £12.95, Fixed D 3 course £17.50, Starter £4.95-£9.95, Main £10.95-£16.95 **Wines** 24 bottles over £30, 40 bottles under £30, 17 by glass **Parking** Car park by station & on street **Notes** L set menu Mon-Thu 2/3 course £12.95/£14.95, Sunday L, Vegetarian available, Children welcome

Franklins
PLAN 1 F2

◎ Seasonal British

tel: 020 8299 9598 **157 Lordship Ln, East Dulwich SE22 8HX**
email: info@franklinsrestaurant.com
dir: *Nearest station: East Dulwich*

Hearty British cooking on East Dulwich high street

Among the shops, pubs and coffee bars on busy Lordship Lane, Franklins stands out from the crowd with its in-vogue rendition of gutsy British cooking. It divides into a pubby front bar and a pared-back small bistro at the rear, all exposed brick, bare floorboards, big Victorian mirrors, paper-clothed tables and an open window into the kitchen. The daily-changing concise menu deals in seasonal British produce, with provenance and simplicity the key. There's small-plate snacking (black pudding on toast, for example) to top-end blow-outs like roast grouse with bread sauce and liver pâté, while, in between, starters like chicken hearts with sweet dumpling squash, or mains such as calves' faggots and rainbow chard, further illustrate the hearty, no-frills style. Puds stay in the treacle tart and chocolate truffle cake comfort zone.

Chef Ralf Wittig **Owner** Tim Sheehan, Rodney Franklin **Seats** 42, Pr/dining room 24 **Times** 12-12 Closed 25-26 & 31 Dec, 1 Jan, All-day dining **Prices** Fixed L 2 course fr £13.95, Starter £6-£9, Main £14-£21.50, Dessert £5-£7, Service optional **Wines** 16 bottles over £30, 30 bottles under £30, 15 by glass **Parking** Bawdale Road **Notes** Sat brunch available, Sunday L £14.50-£21, Vegetarian available, Children welcome

The Palmerston
PLAN 1 F2

◎ Modern British, European

tel: 020 8693 1629 **91 Lordship Ln, East Dulwich SE22 8EP**
email: info@thepalmerston.co.uk
dir: *Nearest station: East Dulwich*

Modern cooking in a traditional East Dulwich pub

The venerable corner pub in East Dulwich looks like suburban hostelries used to, with loads of dark wood panelling inside, chunky undressed tables and blackboards. It makes a fine inviting environment for modern pub cooking based on seasonal British produce, overlaid with Mediterranean and Asian influence, and full of honest upstanding flavours. A quarter of Colchester rock oysters come dressed in lime, chilli, ginger and coriander butter, or you might start adventurously with grilled ox heart, served with beetroot and horseradish purée. A wide choice of mains takes in whole baked plaice in béarnaise with caramelised lemon, or a brace of quail with prosciutto in truffled madeira sauce. Seasonal veg servings are charged extra, perhaps Brussels sprouts with almond butter in winter. Finish with lemon tart and raspberry sorbet, or be patient for 15 minutes while the team rustles up a luxurious chocolate pithivier, accompanied by chocolate mint ice cream.

Chef Jamie Younger, James Donnelly **Owner** Jamie Younger, Paul Rigby, Remi Olajoyegbe **Seats** 70, Pr/dining room 26 **Times** 12-2.30/7-12 Closed 25-26 Dec, 1 Jan **Prices** Fixed L 2 course fr £13.75, Starter £5-£9, Main £12-£44, Dessert £5-£12 **Wines** 40 bottles over £30, 20 bottles under £30, 30 by glass **Parking** On street **Notes** Light menu available daily 3-6pm, Sunday L £15.50, Vegetarian available, Children welcome

Looking for a London restaurant near you? Use the maps on pages 258–68

Babur

PLAN 1 G2

@@ *Modern Indian*

tel: 020 8291 2400 **119 Brockley Rise, Forest Hill SE23 1JP**
email: mail@babur.info **web:** www.babur.info
dir: *Nearest station: Honor Oak Park*

Modern Indian cuisine in a cool brasserie-style setting

With a prowling, life-size tiger on the roof, newcomers could be forgiven for thinking this is just another flock-wallpapered curry house, but Babur takes a thoroughly creative approach to cuisine as well as decor. Inside the look is classy and modern: walnut veneer, exposed brickwork and blue limestone flooring meets brown-leather banquettes and industrial ducting – throw in a gallery of striking ethnic artworks and funky pendant lighting and the place really comes to life. The cooking certainly doesn't hold back either, delivering a colourful blend of traditional and contemporary thinking. Quality ingredients – many not widely encountered in Indian cooking – and judicious spicing are joined by well-dressed presentation. Witness ostrich (clove-smoked and marinated in Rajasthani spices) or goat patties (with tamarind and raisin chutney) to start, followed by mains like well-spiced Kerala-inspired coconut lamb with tomato rice. Desserts follow the East-meets-West theme – perhaps a spiced chocolate fondant or mango brûlée – while wines are spice-friendly and the menu includes recommendations to match each main course.

Chef Jiwan Lal **Owner** Babur 1998 Ltd **Seats** 72 **Times** 12-2.30/6-11.30 Closed 26 Dec, L 27 Dec, D 25 Dec **Prices** Tasting menu £29.95-£49.95, Starter £6.75-£8.50, Main £11.95-£16.95, Dessert £4.75-£5.95, Service optional **Wines** 3 bottles over £30, 46 bottles under £30, 13 by glass **Parking** 15, On street **Notes** Vegetarian tasting menu also available, Sunday L £12.95, Vegetarian available, Children welcome

See advert below

A smart, comfortable, space with fantastic food

119 Brockley Rise, Forest Hill SE23 1JP
mail@babur.info   www.babur.info

020 8291 2400

LONDON SW1

Al Duca

PLAN 4 J6

Modern Italian

tel: 020 7839 3090 **4-5 Duke of York St SW1Y 6LA**
email: alduca@btconnect.com
dir: Nearest station: Green Park

Buzzy, fairly priced Italian in St James

Contemporary good looks, a buzzy ambience and sensible pricing all add up to a package that keeps happy customers returning to this eternally popular St James's Italian. A modern interior provides a quick trip to the Med with its stone floors, light oak furniture, and Italian tones of olive and terracotta, the mood of well-being boosted by a roll-back glass frontage for alfresco eating on fine days; smartly turned-out, chatty and knowledgeable staff and a spot-on all-Italian wine list play their part too. The kitchen's repertoire of uncomplicated classic and gently-modernised Italian dishes built on top-class ingredients has stood the test of time: home-made pasta is as good as you'd hope, particularly if pappardelle with venison ragoût and seasonal mushrooms is up for grabs. Next up, pan-fried duck breast benefits from the bittersweet tones of grilled radicchio, pumpkin sauce and a Marsala reduction, before a textbook tiramisù winds things up on top form.

Chef Giovanni Andolfi **Owner** Cuisine Collection, Claudio Pulze **Seats** 56 **Times** 12-11 Closed Xmas, BHs, Sun All-day dining **Prices** Fixed L 2 course £23.50, Fixed D 3 course £28 **Wines** 160 bottles over £30, 20 bottles under £30, 13 by glass **Parking** Jermyn St, Duke St **Notes** Pre & post theatre menu 2/3 course £16.50/£19.50, Vegetarian available, Children welcome

Amaya

PLAN 4 G4

Modern Indian  NOTABLE WINE LIST

tel: 020 7823 1166 **Halkin Arcade, Motcomb St SW1X 8JT**
email: amaya@realindianfood.com
dir: Nearest station: Knightsbridge, Hyde Park, Sloane Square

Fine Indian cuisine with plenty of kitchen theatre

As befits its Halkin Arcade address, Amaya is a stylish, sophisticated restaurant, with a glazed ceiling, leather chairs at wooden tables, modern artwork on the walls and an open-to-view kitchen where the cooking is based on three methods: the tandoor, tawa (flat griddle) and sigri (charcoal grill). Ingredients are of the first order, dishes are accurately timed, and spicing and seasoning are spot on. The menu explains the restaurant's USP: to select a succession of 'grilled delicacies' and end with a 'grandstand dish'. Dishes arrive as and when, so get grazing. First up may be scallops in a herby sauce, minced chicken wrapped in lettuce with coconut and lime dressing, and wok-tossed spinach, followed by perhaps tandoori prawns with tomato and ginger, or cross-cultural lamb osso buco slowly cooked in the tandoor. The culmination, and the pièce de résistance, might be boned tandoori quail with apricots, herbs and spices, masala lobster, or tandoori half duck in tamarind glaze, before the curtain comes down on perhaps coconut and pineapple brûlée.

Chef Karunesh Khanna **Owner** R Mathrani, N&C Panjabi **Seats** 99, Pr/dining room 14 **Times** 12.30-2.15/6.30-11.30 **Prices** Fixed L 3 course £21-£32.50, Tasting menu £43-£110, Starter £11-£25.50, Main £21.50-£26, Dessert £8-£9.50 **Wines** 19 by glass **Parking** NCP **Notes** Fixed D 2 course, Vegetarian tasting menu, Vegetarian available, No children

Ametsa with Arzak Instruction

PLAN 4 G5

– see page 300

Apsleys at The Lanesborough

PLAN 4 G5

– see page 300

Avenue

PLAN 4 J6

Modern British

tel: 020 7321 2111 **7-9 St James's St SW1A 1EE**
email: avenuereservations@danddlondon.com
dir: Nearest station: Green Park

Buzzy modern restaurant and bar with its heart in New York

The address may be quintessentially English, but the re-launched Avenue has been transformed into a stylish American gaff. Okay, there are elements of its voguish past, with its high ceilings and eclectic modern art, but today's soundtrack is Manhattan glam. The long bar sets a classy tone, while the restaurant spreads out behind around a centrepiece 'wine-glass' chandelier and decanting bar, instantly confirming wine as a key player. The big-city-cool look comes with semi-circular banquettes, trendy low-back chairs and funky 'tilting' lamps, while service is equally switched on. Chef Michael Bizzard (ex-Bar Boulud) delivers his take on modern American fare with a light, fresh, clean-flavoured touch characterised by a pinch of spice. Take signatures like clam chowder (served in hollowed-out sourdough with littleneck clams and paper bag 'crumbled' bay crackers) or desserts like 'donut holes' (with cinnamon sugar, raspberry jam and bourbon chocolate). In between, perhaps sea-fresh stone bass mains (with old bay spice pepping up a spring vegetable succotash) to Black Angus hamburgers or grain-fed beef steaks.

Times 12-3/5.45-11 Closed 25-26 Dec, 1 Jan, BHs, Sun, L Sat

A. Wong

PLAN 4 J3

Chinese **NEW**

tel: 020 7828 8931 **70 Wilton Rd, Victoria SW1V 1DE**
email: info@awong.co.uk
dir: Nearest station: Victoria

Adventurous Chinese regional cooking

The 'A' stands for Andrew, the new broom who has taken the helm of the Wong family's restaurant in the unpromising hinterlands of Victoria station. But in case the 10-course tasting menu isn't enough of a hint, this is a long way from your average Cantonese takeaway. The setting is pared-back and contemporary, with an open kitchen if you want to get up close and personal with the chefs as they give the repertoire of Chinese regional cuisines a thorough workout. The menu covers all bases from meticulously detailed dim sum – a dumpling of Yunnan mushroom, pork and truffle, or crab, seafood and bean curd canelloni with pickled cockles, perhaps – to inventive contemporary ideas such as glazed Brixham monkfish cheeks with a Uighur pomegranate salad from Northwest China, or beef rump with salsify, preserved plum powder and oyster sauce. You might not expect much from the dessert possibilities in a Chinese restaurant, but think again: there's snowball meringue with lychee granita, mango purée and lime sorbet up for grabs.

Chef Andrew Wong **Owner** Andrew Wong **Seats** 65, Pr/dining room 12 **Times** 12-2.30/5.30-10.30 Closed Xmas, Sun, L Mon **Prices** Fixed L 2 course £13.95, Tasting menu £45, Starter £4.95, Main fr £6, Dessert £6.50 **Wines** **Parking** On Street **Notes** Vegetarian available, Children welcome

Ametsa with Arzak Instruction

LONDON SW1 PLAN 4 G5

New Basque 🍷 NOTABLE WINE LIST

tel: 020 7333 1234 **The Halkin Hotel, 5 Halkin St, Belgravia SW1X 7DJ**
email: ametsa.thehalkin@comohotels.com **web:** www.amestsa.co.uk
dir: *Nearest station: Hyde Park Corner*

Flavourburst Basque cuisine for a new age

The name of the restaurant might not roll off the tongue, but the Arzak name carries a lot of weight, with the family restaurant in San Sebastian a global foodie destination. 'New Basque cuisine' is the name of the game back in Northern Spain, which amounts to molecular techniques matched with the region's natural resources. Here in London, the 'Amesta' bit means 'dream', so you get the drift: the inspiration is the homeland and this is modern Basque cooking in London. The restaurant is located in the super-cool Halkin, a minimalist mecca with an impeccable address. The dining room looks pristine in brilliant white, with an impressive ceiling fashioned from 7,000 golden glass test tubes filled with spices (more contemporary art installation than ceiling). There's a flourish to the service and presentation of dishes here, the science very much on show, the performance captivating from start to finish. An à la carte menu supports the tasting menu, both packed with first-class ingredients, many of which are sourced from these shores. Among starters on the carte might be a dish of scallops partnered with a cassava soufflé, the craft and technique of the kitchen evident from the off. These are delicate plates of swipes and vivid colours, with the ingredients respected, but flavours maximised. Sea bass comes with leek 'ash', John Dory with a red root 'mojo', and venison is fired up with red chillies. Things carry on in the same vein among desserts, where clever combinations and finely judged flavours win out – a chocolate fondant with piquillo ice cream, for example, or a wooden board filled with chocolate treats. There are Spanish and English cheeses, too, appropriately enough.

Chef Sergio Sanz **Owner** Halkin by COMO **Seats** 68, Pr/dining room 24
Times 12-2.30/6.30-10.30 Closed 25 Dec, L Sun, Mon **Prices** Fixed L 2 course
£24.50, Tasting menu £52-£145, Starter £13-£38, Main £26-£39, Dessert £12.50
Wines 126 bottles over £30, 13 by glass **Parking** On street (after 6pm)
Notes Fixed L 4 course £52, Tasting menu 7 course, Vegetarian available,
Children welcome

Apsleys at The Lanesborough

LONDON SW1 PLAN 4 G5

Modern Italian, Mediterranean

tel: 020 7333 7254 & 7333 7645 **The Lanesborough, Hyde Park Corner SW1X 7TA**
email: apsleys@lanesborough.com **web:** www.apsleys.co.uk
dir: *Nearest station: Hyde Park Corner*

Outstanding modern Italian cooking from top team in luxury hotel

At the time of going to press, we were advised of a major refurbishment to this elegant and iconic Hotel. Highest of international standards of comfort, quality and security are unlikely to change and bedrooms will reflect the historic nature of the property, offering high levels of comfort and a superb range of complimentary facilities. London is hardly short of impressive relics of empire, but this grand old mansion on Hyde Park Corner is in the Premier League. The Lanesborough is the kind of place offering the world-class level of luxury and service that's a magnet for celebs and oligarchs. But if you're not in the market for stratospherically-priced rooms – personal butler included – you can get a glimpse of the hotel's plush glamour by booking a table at Apsley's, the conservatory-style restaurant named after the Duke of Wellington's former residence Apsley House, which lords it across the road. The space is as opulent and luxurious as any Venetian palazzo, with modern chandeliers, a glass atrium, deep carpets, a striking mural and tables resplendent with top-class crystal and chinaware. Modern Italian cuisine is the kitchen's thing, cooked with top-level skill and authenticity under the aegis of stellar German chef Heinz Beck, a professional at the top of his game, with his La Pergola restaurant in Rome winning plaudits galore. Delivering the Beck style with flair and top-level skills is head chef Heros De Agostinis. The bilingual menu kicks off with antipasti as you might imagine: duck foie gras terrine with quail breast lifted by the tart intensity of frozen raspberry dust and coulis, and wild mushrooms. The ingredients are first-class and the excellent technical abilities of the team in the kitchen bring the very best out of them. Pasta is as good as you might hope, with pillowy carbonara fagottelli providing a clever take on a classic, followed by secondi of grouse in a bread crust, its drumsticks served separately and delivered with more seasonal wild fungi, celeriac, and pepper sauce. Dessert follows the same modern Italian path, with a tiramisu sphere providing impact and a bravura display of technical proficiency.

Chef Heinz Beck, Heros De Agostinis **Owner** St Regis Hotels and Resorts
Seats 100, Pr/dining room 14 **Times** 12.30-2.30/7-10.30 **Prices** Prices not
confirmed **Wines** 27 by glass **Parking** 25 **Notes** Tasting menu 5/7 course,
Vegetarian available, Children welcome

LONDON SW1 *continued*

Bar Boulud

PLAN 4 F5

◉◉ French, American 🍷NOTABLE WINE LIST

tel: 020 7201 3899 **Mandarin Oriental Hyde Park, 66 Knightsbridge SW1X 7LA**
email: barboulud@mohg.com
dir: *Nearest station: Knightsbridge*

Very classy bistro cooking from superstar chef

Lyon via New York, Daniel Boulud is a big-name stateside and his London restaurant doesn't lack for glitz and glamour. This is bistro food, albeit high cost bistro food with a bit of New York swagger, and it is a winning formula judging by the contented buzz in the room. Tables are turned, staff whizz about...it is terrific fun. The long zinc-topped bar is a cool spot to linger, and there's a charcuterie counter overlooking the open kitchen, or you might prefer to sink into one of the red leather banquettes in one of the inter-connected dining rooms. The menu speaks French with English translations and offers up high-quality ingredients, prettily presented. An array of charcuterie, terrines and pâtés served with pickles and mustards is a great way to start, if you want to share. Or you might fancy the classy sausages (the spicy lamb merguez, perhaps with mint tabouleh and pepper stew). Main-course coq au vin or sea bass cooked a la plancha are classy rustic-chic main courses, and for dessert, pomme Bretonne or gâteau Basque await. Burgundy and the Rhône are the stars of the stellar wine list.

Chef Dean Yasharian, Daniel Boulud **Owner** Daniel Boulud **Seats** 168, Pr/dining room 20 **Times** 12-11 All-day dining **Prices** Fixed L 3 course £24, Fixed D 3 course £24, Starter £8-£18, Main £12-£32, Dessert £5-£17 **Wines** 500 bottles over £30, 6 bottles under £30, 27 by glass **Parking** NCP Sloane St **Notes** Sunday L, Vegetarian available, Children welcome

Boisdale of Belgravia

PLAN 4 H3

◉ Traditional British

tel: 020 7730 6922 **15 Eccleston St SW1W 9LX**
email: info@boisdale.co.uk
dir: *Nearest station: Victoria*

A bit of Scotland imported to London

A combination of jazz venue, bar and restaurant, Boisdale of Belgravia is spread over a number of rooms in a handsome townhouse, with a clubby decor and red walls hung with a profusion of pictures. As at its sibling in Bishopsgate (see entry), the cooking is built on fine Scottish produce, skilfully and accurately worked. Seared scallops with haggis and saffron-mashed potatoes are a happy blend of flavours, an alternative to another starter of seasonal asparagus with a poached duck egg and truffle vinaigrette. Top-quality Aberdeenshire steaks with a choice of sauces may vie for attention with the luxury of grilled lobster with garlic and parsley butter, although a gutsy dish of sautéed lamb's sweetbreads and braised kidneys, served with mustard and tarragon sauce, mash, and Savoy cabbage mixed with bacon, may be an option too.

Chef Colin Wint **Owner** Mr R Macdonald **Seats** 140, Pr/dining room 40 **Times** 12-3/6-11.15 Closed Xmas, New Year, Etr, BHs, Sun, L Sat **Prices** Fixed L 2 course fr £19.75, Fixed D 3 course £29.50-£55, Starter £8.50-£22.50, Main £16.50-£38, Dessert £6.25-£7 **Wines** 22 by glass **Parking** On street, Belgrave Sq **Notes** Vegetarian available, Children welcome

Cafe Murano

PLAN 4 J6

◉◉ Italian NEW

tel: 020 3371 5559 **33 St James's St SW1 1HD**
email: reception@cafemurano.co.uk
dir: *Nearest station: Green Park*

Celebrated chef Angela Hartnett's relaxed new St James's Italian

Little sister to grown-up Murano, this Angela Hartnett newcomer is anything but a 'café', rather a sophisticated, albeit relaxed, St James's take on a 'pop-in-every-day' Italian. It comes with in-place credentials and pizzazz, and service doesn't miss a beat. The snazzy, voguish, art deco-esque slim room is a looker from its marble-topped bar (decked out for bar dining) to wooden floors, brown leather banquettes and eye-catching lighting and mirrors. The cooking – under Hartnett's protégé Sam Williams – is equally on-cue, embracing that relaxed 'Murano' theme, with a northern Italian menu of simple, rustic (if refined, well-executed and presented) lightly portioned dishes conjured from top-notch produce. Witness classics like cichetti (big-hit truffle arancini) to freshly-made signature pasta, perhaps wonderful pappardelle with the meaty kick of a hogget ragu and olives. Fish might feature sparkling-fresh cod teamed with earthy castelfiorito lentils and a vibrant salsa verde. Desserts, such as prune and almond bake with lemon cream, hold-up afters form, likewise peripherals such as fabulous focaccia, while cracking Italian wines (and cocktails) also tempt. The set menu is particularly good value.

Chef Sam Williams **Owner** Angela Hartnett **Times** 12-2.45/5.30-10.45 **Prices** Fixed L 2 course £18, Fixed D 3 course £22, Starter £3-£17.50, Main £15.50-£20, Dessert £5.50-£6.50 **Wines** 37 bottles over £30, 4 bottles under £30, 13 by glass **Notes** Fixed D available 10-11pm, Sunday L

Le Caprice

PLAN 4 J6

◉ Modern European V

tel: 020 7629 2239 & 7016 5220 **Arlington House, Arlington St SW1A 1RJ**
email: reservations@le-caprice.co.uk
dir: *Nearest station: Green Park*

Renowned Mayfair favourite

A 30th-anniversary refurb (September 2011) has kept the iconic revolving front doors at this glam Mayfair classic – tucked away behind The Ritz – with a terrace, cool bar, and sleek new floor and windows ringing the changes. The monochrome retro-cool '80s look remains, including its celebrated gallery of black-and-white David Bailey photographs. The much-loved simple classic dishes – like salmon fishcakes or Caprice burger – haven't gone anywhere either. Service is slick and professional, with the charm offensive commencing as soon as you enter through those doors. The please-all roster of reliable European-brasserie comfort dishes includes the likes of deep-fried fish with minted pea purée, chips and tartare, plus seasonal specials like whole grilled Cornish monkfish tail with béarnaise, or the more modish Thai-baked sea bass with fragrant rice. Nursery desserts (aka, lemon curd steamed sponge pudding) and a short afternoon menu (served 3-5.30pm) keep the fun rolling all day, and note the cover charge remains.

Chef Andy McLay **Owner** Caprice Holdings **Seats** 86 **Times** 12-12 Closed 25-26 Dec, L 1 Jan, D 24 Dec All-day dining **Prices** Fixed D 3 course £24.25, Starter £8.75-£17.50, Main £15.75-£34.50, Dessert £3.50-£9.50 **Wines** 110 bottles over £30, 6 bottles under £30, 29 by glass **Parking** On street, NCP **Notes** Wknd brunch menu, Sunday L, Children welcome

LONDON SW1 *continued*

Cavendish London

PLAN 4 J6

 British

tel: 020 7930 2111 **81 Jermyn St SW1Y 6JF**
email: info@thecavendishlondon.com **web:** www.thecavendishlondon.com
dir: *Nearest station: Green Park, Piccadilly*

Lively cooking in a smart hotel behind Fortnum's

Among the gentlemen's outfitters and boutique emporia of Jermyn Street, the Cavendish lurks opposite the back entrance of Fortnum and Mason. The location is as chic as can be then, and the hotel interiors rise to the occasion with a plethora of striking modern paintings, and a first-floor dining room that may look out on St James's, but conjures in its name – Petrichor – the scent of freshly moistened earth after the first rains. Staff are acutely attentive and professional, as befits the ethos. Nitin Padwal's cooking draws on thoroughbred suppliers for materials such as Wicks Manor pork, perhaps served as a croquette of the cheek meat, alongside a trio of garlic purées – white, black and wild green. After that, it may be fillets of salmon given extra depth with an accompaniment of crushed potatoes laced with smoked haddock and a vivid green pea velouté. Dessert produces the upstanding zestiness of lemon and orange posset with citrus salad, a tuile of popping candy and a scattering of tiny basil leaves.

Chef Nitin Padwal **Owner** Ascott Ltd **Seats** 80, Pr/dining room 70 **Times** 12-2.30/5.30-10.30 Closed 25-26 Dec, 1 Jan, L Sat-Sun & BH Mon **Prices** Fixed L 2 course fr £22.50, Fixed D 3 course fr £29, Starter £8-£9.50, Main £15.50-£22.50, Dessert £6.50-£9.50 **Wines** 31 bottles over £30, 12 bottles under £30, 10 by glass **Parking** 60, Secure on-site valet parking **Notes** Pre-theatre menu Sun-Thu 5.30-6.30/Fri-Sat 5-6.30pm, Vegetarian available, Children welcome

Caxton Grill, St Ermin's Hotel

PLAN 4 K4

 – *see below*

Chabrot

PLAN 4 F5

 French

tel: 020 7225 2238 **9 Knightsbridge Green SW1X 7QL**
email: info@chabrot.co.uk
dir: *Nearest station: Knightsbridge*

Authentic French bistro in Knightsbridge

'Bistrot d'amis' heads up the menu, and indeed Chabrot has the sort of friendly atmosphere typical of a bistro du coin, helped along by characteristic bentwood chairs, closely set tables covered by red and white cloths, and friendly, informal service. The cooking is based on the cuisine of southern France, the menu ranging from grazing-sized plates of, for example, smoked herrings with warm potato salad, or foie gras terrine with green beans, to duck confit with a salad of potatoes, beans and shallots. The kitchen puts tip-top French produce to good effect: Brittany oysters with baby chorizo, andouille and jambon de Bayonne in a platter of charcuterie, Périgord truffle with poached Landais chicken breast, served with vegetables, and, for two to share, Pyrenean lamb shoulder roasted with spices, dried fruit and couscous. Wave the tricolore at the end with prunes and Armagnac syrup.

Times 12-3.30/6.30-11 Closed Sun

Caxton Grill, St Ermin's Hotel

LONDON SW1   **PLAN 4 K4**

Modern European, British
tel: 020 7222 7888 **2 Caxton St, St James's Park SW1H 0QW**
email: reservations@sterminshotel.co.uk **web:** www.caxtongrill.co.uk
dir: *Nearest station: Victoria, St James's Park*

Confident modern cooking in a luxury hotel

St Ermin's is one of those grand London hotel's that oozes sophistication right from the off – the sweeping staircase in the lobby suggests more glamorous and refined times. It's the sort of place that can put on a pretty swanky event, whether for business or pleasure, and it's a good spot for either a nifty cocktail or afternoon tea. The restaurant, Caxton Grill, is well worth a visit in its own right, with the kitchen headed up by MasterChef: The Professionals finalist Adam Handling. The smart dining room has a contemporary finish and modish neutrality, with splashes of colour from original artworks on the walls. Given the grill moniker the Josper is a key bit of kit, but there's a lot more going on besides. A first course of Orkney scallops come with the flavours of ponzu (the citrusy Japanese sauce) and seaweed butter, while a salad of celeriac is enriched with truffles and dates. Everything looks attractive on the plate and flavours hit the

mark. There are some more Japanese flavours in main courses, too, such as monkfish yakitori with scallop toast and turnip, while it's back to Europe for fillet of beef rolled in ash and served with garlic, barley and parmesan. The grill delivers first-class meats including Wagyu from the Scottish Highlands, plus dry-aged strip loin, veal sirloin on the bone, and saddle of lamb with gremolata and smoked aubergine. Side dishes such as hand-cut chips with garlic and parsley and Chantenay carrots with honey and mustard are extra. For dessert, char-grilled pear is served with chocolate fondant, or go for various 'textures and temperatures' of chocolate and passionfruit. There's an outdoor terrace overlooking the courtyard for a champagne cocktail or two, plus food such European and Asian bento boxes, while the bar stocks whiskies galore.

Chef Adam Handling, Sylvan Chevereau **Owner** Amerimar **Seats** 72, Pr/dining room 10 **Times** 12-2/6-10.30 Closed L Sat-Sun, 26 & 31 Dec **Prices** Fixed L 2 course £18-£27, Fixed D 3 course £35-£63, Tasting menu £70-£110, Starter £8-£16, Main £19-£35, Dessert £8-£12 **Wines** 45 bottles over £30, 16 bottles under £30, 25 by glass **Parking** Valet parking **Notes** Vegetarian available, Children welcome

Le Chinois at Millennium Knightsbridge
PLAN 4 F4

Chinese

tel: 020 7201 6330 **17 Sloane St, Knightsbridge SW1X 9NU**
email: lechinois@millenniumhotels.com web: www.millenniumhotels.com/knightsbridge
dir: *Nearest station: Knightsbridge, Victoria*

Refined Chinese cooking in modern hotel

The restaurant at this modern Sloane Street hotel has morphed into Le Chinois, which has taken as its inspiration Singapore's Orchard Hotel. The deal is now a long carte of Chinese dishes, gently tempered to appeal to refined Western palates. Vegetable spring rolls and pan-fried chicken dumplings are conventional enough starters, and there could also be sesame prawns on toast. Among main courses, prime cuts and luxuries jostle for attention with lesser ingredients, all handled with the same high levels of skill: lobster comes with ginger and spring onions on a bed of noodles, rib-eye is sautéed in black bean sauce, and minced pork and tofu are cooked in a clay pot. Vegetables are properly timed à la minute – mushrooms stir-fried with seasonal greens, say – and among desserts red bean pancake with ice cream competes for your attention with more westernised options like a classic tarte Tatin.

Chef Anthony Robinson **Owner** Millennium & Copthorne Hotels **Seats** 65 **Times** 12-10.30 All-day dining **Prices** Prices not confirmed **Wines** 16 bottles over £30, 10 bottles under £30, 9 by glass **Parking** 8, NCP Pavilion Rd **Notes** Sunday L, Vegetarian available, Children welcome

The Cinnamon Club
PLAN 5 A4

Modern Indian **NOTABLE WINE LIST**

tel: 020 7222 2555 **The Old Westminster Library,
30-32 Great Smith St SW1P 3BU**
email: info@cinnamonclub.com
dir: *Nearest station: Westminster, St James Park*

Inventive Indian food in a grand listed building

Former public buildings tend to make good venues, particularly ones built with a bit of empire pomp. Such is the old Westminster Library, with its handsome façade and galleried interior (including some shelves stacked with books in homage to days gone by). Tables are neatly laid, nicely spaced apart, and there's a high-end feel all round. On offer is some well-worked, classy modern Indian cooking that combines Asian and European techniques to deliver bang-on flavours. Bengali-style cod cakes with kasundi mustard, shrimp and coriander mayonnaise, for example, is a starter showing fine balance of flavours, the cake packed with fish, the cooking skills flying high. Ingredients are top quality, too, such as a generous main-course portion of chargrilled halibut with Kashmiri fennel, ginger sauce and curry leaf quinoa, while roasted loin of Oisin red deer might turn up with fenugreek potatoes, Indore korma and wild venison pickle. There are daily specials and desserts which tend more to the European perspective, such as lemon tart with bergamot sorbet and iced lemon mousse.

Chef Vivek Singh, Rakesh Ravindran **Owner** Indian Restaurant Ltd **Seats** 130, Pr/dining room 60 **Times** 12-2.45/6-10.45 Closed BHs (some), Sun, D 25 Dec **Prices** Fixed L 2 course £22, Fixed D 3 course £30, Tasting menu £75-£150, Starter £9.50-£15, Main £16-£35, Dessert £7.50-£12.50 **Wines** 305 bottles over £30, 18 bottles under £30, 19 by glass **Parking** Abingdon St **Notes** Tasting menu D 7 course, with paired wines £115-£150, Vegetarian available, Children welcome

Colbert
PLAN 4 G3

French V

tel: 020 7730 2804 **50-52 Sloane Square, Chelsea SW1W 8AX**
email: info@colbertchelsea.com
dir: *Nearest station: Sloane Square*

France comes to Sloane Square

Occupying a prominent corner site on Sloane Square, Colbert is owned by the same team behind The Delaunay and The Wolseley (see entries) and runs along a similar all-day dining concept to the latter. Inspired by a classic Parisian café, it's a trip back to the France of the Belle Epoque or 1930s inside, with burgundy leather banquettes, mirrors, wood panelling, artworks and chessboard tiles. Except for the absence of Gauloises smoke and stripy jumpers, the scene could hardly be more Gallic – even the blackboard specials are written in French. Expect fish soup with rouille and gruyère to taste just as hearty and punchy as it would across the Channel, before moving on to old friends such as chicken paillard, steak tartare, navarin of lamb, or Toulouse cassoulet with confit duck. Beret-wearing desserts feature the likes of tarte fine aux pommes, crème caramel and chocolate mousse.

Chef David Collard **Owner** Corbin & King **Times** 8am-11.30pm All-day dining **Prices** Prices not confirmed **Wines** 37 by glass **Notes** Cover charge £1.75 L & D in dining rooms, Children welcome

Dinner by Heston Blumenthal
PLAN 4 F5

– *see page 304*

The Goring
PLAN 4 H4

Traditional British V **NOTABLE WINE LIST**

tel: 020 7396 9000 **Beeston Place SW1W OJW**
email: diningroom@thegoring.com web: www.thegoring.com
dir: *Nearest station: Victoria*

Refined, classical English cooking in a grand hotel

Run by the Goring family since 1910, this Edwardian treasure remains one of London's most luxurious and alluringly English hotels. The place is practically an annexe to Buck House, so home-grown and foreign royals have popped in and out over the years – the Middletons stayed in 2011, and the Queen's nephew David Linley designed the dining room, a lavish space with grand proportions, ornate plasterwork, Swarovski chandeliers and precisely laid tables. It is all kept running as smoothly as a Swiss watch by a skilled service team. There's never any doubt about the kitchen's skill and use of top-quality ingredients, delivered via a menu that's reassuring rather than challenging, encompassing posh and peasant combos such as fried pig's trotter with seared foie gras and barbeque lentils, followed by oxtail bun with grilled beef rib, malted parsnip purée, and ale jus. Fish-wise, fillet of halibut might come with smoked eel pearl barley, and parsley and garlic purée, and for pudding, egg custard tart with Earl Grey ice cream and orange marmalade.

Chef Shay Cooper **Owner** Goring family **Seats** 70, Pr/dining room 50 **Times** 12-2.30/6-10 Closed L Sat **Prices** Fixed L 3 course fr £42.50, Fixed D 3 course fr £52.50 **Wines** 450 bottles over £30, 5 bottles under £30, 22 by glass **Parking** 7 **Notes** Pre-theatre 2 course £35, Sunday L, Children welcome

LONDON SW1 *continued*

Grand Imperial London
PLAN 4 H4

Cantonese, Chinese **NEW** v

tel: 020 7821 8898 **The Grosvenor, 101 Buckingham Palace Rd SW1W OSJ**
email: reservations@grandimperiallondon.com **web:** www.grandimperiallondon.com
dir: *Nearest station: Victoria*

Upscale Chinese dining in a Victorian setting

Classic and modern Cantonese cooking in a grand Victorian building is the USP of the Grand Imperial. The two elements combine very well indeed in the stylish and refined restaurant with the room's splendid proportions and period details enhanced by some smart oriental touches. There's a dim sum menu at lunchtime, with some impressive upscale options such as chicken sui mai with black truffle, or a black cod dumpling with saffron. There's a dim sum option among first courses on the carte, too, or else you might kick off with crispy duck salad or golden king prawns with wasabi mayo. Soups such as a beef broth with mushroom are an option before main courses of baked black cod with miso, deep-fried duck with lemon sauce, or pork ribs with barbecue and honey sauce. Set menus can make ordering a breeze, and there's a swanky tasting version, too.

Chef Rand Cheung **Owner** Grand Imperial & Guoman Hotels **Seats** 140, Pr/dining room 26 **Times** noon-11 Closed 25-26 Dec, All-day dining **Prices** Fixed L 2 course £12.80-£58, Fixed D 3 course £20-£45, Tasting menu fr £58, Starter £4-£12, Main £10-£45, Dessert £3.50-£8 **Wines** 60 bottles over £30, 10 bottles under £30, 12 by glass **Parking** NCP **Notes** Meal deals available, Sunday L, Children welcome

House of Ho
PLAN 2 K1

Modern Vietnamese **NEW**

tel: 020 7287 0770 **55-59 Old Compton St, Soho W1D 6HR**
email: info@houseofho.co.uk
dir: *Nearest station: Piccadilly Circus*

Buzzy Vietnamese joint with a fusion flavour

Bobby Chinn is quite the star in Asia with TV shows, books and a restaurant in Hanoi to his name, and now he's in Old Compton Street with a lively, buzzy place that fits right into the Soho scene. Tables are close together, cocktails rule, and the food is a mix of traditional and contemporary Vietnamese. There are evident influences from France as the two countries' food cultures are very much entwined (former colony and all), plus Bobby's time in London, Egypt and San Francisco. From the 'Light & Raw' section comes duck 'a la banana' blossom salad or spicy salmon tartare, while 'Hot & Grilled' delivers barbecue baby back ribs with a light Asian slaw. Sharing is the way to go, with apple-smoked pork belly with braised cabbage and chicken potato curry coming in generous portions. Finish with lemon-scented crème brûlée.

Chef Bobby Chinn **Owner** Bobby Chinn **Seats** 90, Pr/dining room 12 **Times** Closed 25 Dec, New Year, All-day dining **Prices** Fixed D 3 course £45, Starter £4-£9, Main £5-£14, Dessert £4.50-£6.50, Service optional 12.5% **Wines** 27 bottles over £30, 11 bottles under £30, 12 by glass **Parking** Metered parking **Notes** Pre-theatre menu 1/2 course £19.50/£23.50, Vegetarian available, Children welcome

Dinner by Heston Blumenthal

LONDON SW1   PLAN 4 F5

British

tel: 020 7201 3833 **Mandarin Oriental Hyde Park, 66 Knightsbridge SW1X 7LA**
email: malon-dinnerhb@mohg.com **web:** www.dinnerbyheston.com
dir: *Nearest station: Knightsbridge*

Heston looking back to move forward, with top quality results

If you're after a taste of Heston in the capital, you need to head on over to the swanky Mandarin Oriental Hotel. The restaurant occupies a capacious space backing onto Hyde Park, serving up a five-star finish with swish neutral tones, lots of leather and light fittings that on closer inspection are designed like jelly moulds. The jewel in the crown, though, is the open-to-view kitchen, where Ashley Palmer-Watts and his team can be observed doing their thing. And what a thing it is. The name 'Dinner' is inspired by Heston's curiosity about food culture, something very much reflected here, with each dish on the menu given a date of its approximate arrival on the culinary scene – roast marrowbone (c. 1500), spiced pigeon (c. 1780) – ranging from 1390 to 1940. If you were hoping for the future, not the past, rest assured there is nothing ancient about the cuisine here, for this is modern stuff, inspired by the past but delivering contemporary

satisfaction in spades. There is a Josper grill to precisely time the cooking, and a clockwork rotisserie grill which is a design feature in itself. 'Frumenty' is a first course headlined as dating from 1390, and consists of tender octopus in a deliciously smoky broth with pickled dulse (a red seaweed) and lovage, while the 'Meat Fruit' (circa 1500) has pretty much been the signature dish from day one. Main-course Hereford rib-eye with triple-cooked chips and mushroom ketchup is a crowd pleaser, or head into the 1940s for cod in cider with chard, onions and smoked artichokes. The high quality of the produce is a stand-out feature throughout. For dessert, time travel to the Georgian era for caramelised apple tart, or a little earlier for baked Sussex pond pudding. Attention to detail runs right through the place, from the slick service to the classy wine list.

Chef Ashley Palmer-Watts **Owner** Mandarin Oriental Hyde Park **Seats** 138, Pr/dining room 10 **Times** 12-2.30/6.30-10.30 **Prices** Fixed L 3 course £38, Starter £16-£17.50, Main £28-£42, Dessert £12-£14.50 **Wines** 500 bottles over £30, 1 bottle under £30, 20 by glass **Parking** Valet parking, NCP **Notes** Vegetarian available, Children welcome

Il Convivio

PLAN 4 G3

◎◎ Modern Italian

tel: 020 7730 4099 **143 Ebury St SW1W 9QN**
email: ilconvivio@etruscarestaurants.com **web:** www.ilconvivio.co.uk
dir: *Nearest station: Victoria, Sloane Square*

Modish Italian in smart Belgravia

Named after Dante's poem which translates as 'a meeting over food and drink', Il Convivio offers creative modern Italian food based on high quality ingredients. Entering the Georgian townhouse restaurant on moneyed Ebury Street, the feeling is one of light and space, thanks to a glass frontage, a skylight in the main restaurant and the conservatory out back with a fully retractable roof to cope with the UK's

unpredictable seasons. A deep red wall amongst the white continues the theme with inscriptions of Dante's poems, while limestone-tiled floors, cedar wooden panels and white linen add to the romantic atmosphere. The large Italian wine list has plenty to choose from by the glass. Start with all the simplicity of beef carpaccio with celery and basil infused olive oil, before moving on to tagliatelle with Cornish crab, rocket and black olive, and a main course such as monkfish fillet wrapped in courgette and Parma ham, served with fennel and mint salad.

Chef Marco Tozzi **Owner** Piero & Enzo Quaradeghini **Seats** 65, Pr/dining room 14 **Times** 12-3.15/6-11.15 Closed Xmas, New Year, BHs, Sun **Prices** Fixed L 2 course £17.50, Fixed D 2 course £23.50, Starter £8.50-£17.50, Main £14-£24, Dessert £6-£9.50 **Wines** 142 bottles over £30, 28 bottles under £30, 14 by glass **Parking** On street **Notes** Vegetarian available, Children welcome

Koffmann's

LONDON SW1

PLAN 4 G5

French ⬛NOTABLE WINE LIST

tel: 020 7235 1010 **The Berkeley, Wilton Place SW1X 7RL**
email: koffmanns@the-berkeley.co.uk
dir: *Nearest station: Knightsbridge, Hyde Park Corner*

Top-grade regional French cooking from a virtuoso

From the early days of haute cuisine at La Tante Claire (over 35 years ago!) to today's slightly less haute approach, Pierre Koffmann has always remained true to his roots in South-West France and the focus here is the hearty, robust flavours of the region. But this being PK, it is done with phenomenal attention to detail, and he remains one of the finest exponents in the country. The Berkeley makes a classy home for some smart – sometimes homely, sometimes luxurious – seasonal French cooking. The other side of the building from Marcus Wareing's operation, Koffmann's has its own entrance and feels very much like a stand-alone restaurant. It's a mellow space with neutral, natural tones, comfortable chairs, tables laid with crisp white cloths, and foodie prints on textured walls, all supported by a formal French service team. Expect classical favourites alongside some of the great man's signature dishes, based on fabulous ingredients. The

bilingual menus offer up snail ravioli with Bayonne ham and garlic croûtons bringing a delightful textural contrast to get the ball rolling, or there might be a classic lobster bisque with great depth of flavour. Next up, those hankering for the bygone days of Tante Claire could hit the jackpot with pig's trotter stuffed with sweetbreads and morels, or go for a homely dish of beef cheeks braised in red wine. Traditional ideas executed with great attention to detail run to fish dishes such as Dover sole, pan-fried and served with a Grenobloise sauce of tomato, caper and parsley noisette butter. Desserts deliver some old favourites such as crêpes Suzette and lemon tart with lemon sorbet, but if you can wait for 15 minutes, pistachio soufflé with pistachio ice cream is up for grabs. The wine list is packed full of interesting selections to match the French regional cooking.

Chef Pierre Koffmann **Owner** Pierre Koffmann **Seats** 120, Pr/dining room 16 **Times** 12-2.30/6-10.30 **Prices** Fixed L 2 course £21.50-£22.50, Fixed D 3 course fr £28, Tasting menu fr £100, Starter £11-£16, Main £18-£34, Dessert £9-£15 **Wines** 250 bottles over £30, 10 bottles under £30, 14 by glass **Parking** Knightsbridge car park **Notes** Pre/post theatre menu 2/3 course £24/£28, Sunday L £22.50-£26, Vegetarian available, Children welcome

LONDON SW1 *continued*

Inn the Park
PLAN 5 A5

British

tel: 020 7451 9999 **St James's Park SW1A 2BJ**
email: reservations@innthepark.com
dir: *Nearest station: St James's Park, Charing Cross, Piccadilly*

Honest, seasonal British cooking in the heart of a London park

In a fantastic location by the lake in St James's Park beneath a verdant canopy of stately plane trees, this curving wooden building is just the spot to enjoy Central London's park life in a happy, bustling atmosphere. Thanks to full-length walls of sliding glass, the interior is a striking, light-flooded space with a clean-lined, Scandinavian-feeling decor of tubular steel chairs, tooled black leather banquettes and apricot-topped tables. But it's the covered wooden terrace that is the hot ticket when warm weather strikes and you're in the market for fresh, impeccably seasonal British produce prepared with pleasing simplicity. Grilled squid, maple-cured bacon and blistered tomatoes is a bright and cheerful dish bursting with the feel of summer, followed by whole Cornish megrim sole partnered with crab vinaigrette and crushed new potatoes with diced tomato, green herbs and white crab meat, or you might go for honey-glazed, herb-fed chicken with smoked potatoes, broad beans, peas and bacon.

Times 12-3.30/5.30-9.30

Ken Lo's Memories of China
PLAN 4 H3

Chinese

tel: 020 7730 7734 **65-69 Ebury St SW1W ONZ**
email: moc@londonfinedininggroup.com
dir: *Nearest station: Victoria*

Classy Chinese dishes at a long-standing Belgravia venue

A generation of well-heeled Belgravia custom has trooped through the sumptuous upscale restaurant created by the late Kenneth Lo, one of modern Chinese gastronomy's early movers and shakers in the capital. Oriental screen dividers, smartly clothed tables and a bottle-store create a fine-dining ambience for classy Chinese cooking from all the regions. A gargantuan menu in the classical idiom features delights such as Pekingese guo-tie fried dumplings filled with chicken, garlic, ginger and spring onion with a vinegary dipping sauce, as well as pepperpot fish soup, luxurious stir-fried lobster with noodles. Look out for guo da chicken in omelette batter sauced in rice vinegar and garlic, iron-plate sizzling dishes of salmon or beef, and sides such as Yangchow fried rice with shrimp, chicken and peas. Fixed-price set menus offer a traditional way of experiencing the range, and there is even the odd tempting dessert such as spun-sugar glazed apple and banana with vanilla ice cream.

Chef Peter Shum Tsui **Owner** A-Z Restaurants **Seats** 120, Pr/dining room 27
Times 12-2.30/6-11 Closed 25-26 Dec **Prices** Prices not confirmed **Wines** 6 by glass
Parking On street **Notes** Sunday L, Vegetarian available, Children welcome

Koffmann's
PLAN 4 G5

– *see page 305*

Marcus
PLAN 4 G5

– *see opposite*

Mint Leaf Restaurant & Bar
PLAN 5 A6

Modern Indian

tel: 020 7930 9020 **Suffolk Place, Haymarket SW1Y 4HX**
email: reservations@mintleafrestaurant.com web: www.mintleafrestaurant.com
dir: *Nearest station: Piccadilly, Charing Cross*

Inspired modern Indian food at a seductive West End address

A contemporary Indian eaterie to grace the West End, the Mint Leaf is on a corner of one of the side-streets off Haymarket. Its interiors are svelte and seductive, a dimly lit mood prevailing in the dramatic cocktail bar and the main restaurant, where angled spots enhance the varnished tabletops and quality glassware, as well as the colourful, assertively spiced dishes. The menu teems with original and inspired preparations, from lime- and garlic-marinated tiger prawns in mango salsa, or beetroot and potato cake with papaya chutney, to mains such as sea bass steamed in a banana leaf with ginger, coriander and coconut, or the sublimely fiery duck and pepper stir-fry with red onions, curry leaves, garlic, star anise and black cardamom. Vegetarian dishes are full of imagination too, for example stuffed romero peppers with spiced potato, corn and aubergine, dressed with tomato and coriander chutney. Finish with blueberry kulfi, served with a warm compote of summer berries.

Chef Rajinder Pandey **Owner** Out of Africa Investments **Seats** 144, Pr/dining room 66
Times 12-3/5.30-11 Closed 25-26 Dec, 1 Jan, L Sat-Sun **Prices** Fixed L 2 course fr
£13.95, Fixed D 3 course £35-£50, Starter £7-£13, Main £13.50-£20 **Wines** 100
bottles over £30, 17 bottles under £30, 13 by glass **Parking** NCP, on street
Notes Pre-theatre menu 5-7pm 2/3 course £13.95/£17.95, Vegetarian available,
Children welcome

Looking for a London restaurant near you?
Use the maps on pages 258–68

Who has won our Food Service Award?
See page 13

Marcus

LONDON SW1   PLAN 4 G5

Modern European **NOTABLE WINE LIST**

tel: 020 7235 1200 **The Berkeley, Wilton Place, Knightsbridge SW1X 7RL**

email: reservations@marcuswareing.com

web: www.marcus-wareing.com

dir: *Nearest station: Knightsbridge, Hyde Park Corner*

Impeccable benchmark modern European cooking with a new look

Major changes have been afoot here. Wareing's venue has long been an autonomous business within the Berkeley, but such is the stellar reputation and televisual familiarity of the presiding genius that the abbreviation to the forename alone can be risked. The address hasn't changed, but in March 2014 a brand-new look was unveiled. Gone is the old claret and oxblood, with its intimation of gentlemen's clubbery, and in comes a lighter style that aims for a homelier look with seats in striking duck-egg blue, but with the deep oak panelling retained. There has been a little productive refunctioning in the service too, with the punctilious formalities of old-school service now giving place to a more interactive, voluble, personal style. Despite the fact that head chef Mark Froydenlund is in charge, Marcus himself remains intimately involved with the planning and supervision of operations here, and the happy result is benchmark modern European cooking. Some restructuring of the menu format also allows those pressed for time to take a one-course lunch. Quality produce remains the sine qua non, with intricacies of technique and artistry playing supporting roles to impeccable prime ingredients. A pairing of Dorset snails and rabbit in a first course is enhanced by the sharpness and pungency of watercress and wild garlic, while for another, foie gras has its buttery-smooth richness offset by the crunch of granola and the twang of mango. Seafood and fish are handled with supreme care, producing an assemblage of pollock and lobster with a razor clam in a medium of coco beans and chicory. Meats are of the finest, for example the favoured Herdwick suckling lamb (loin and shoulder) has unimaginable tenderness and depth, accompanied by black olive soil, radish and mint. Pork is from Denbigh's Rhug estate – a serving of the belly with pease pudding, fennel and glazed apple – and beef is Galloway. It may well be hard to resist a side-order of sublimely fluffy mash, which comes in a sauce of Lincolnshire Poacher cheese. Dessert deconstructions continue to be much favoured as ways of elevating their enjoyment from mere indulgence into something more thoughtful and rewarding. Lemon meringue pie served with delicate tea sorbet is a case in point, as is the counter-factual take on tiramisù. Pain perdu makes the base for an exploration of the Caribbean reference-points of pineapple and coconut. Or consider the resources of the faithful cheese chariot, which rolls around the new room as sedately as it did the old, dispensing exquisite wares in prime condition.

Chef Marcus Wareing, Mark Froydenlund **Owner** Marcus Wareing Restaurants Ltd **Seats** 90, Pr/dining room 16 **Times** 12-2.30/6-11 Closed 1 Jan, Sun **Prices** Fixed L 2 course £30, Fixed D 3 course £85, Tasting menu £120 **Wines** 700 bottles over £30, 13 by glass **Parking** NCP, on street **Notes** Children welcome

LONDON SW1 *continued*

Osteria Dell'Angolo

PLAN 5 A4

Italian

tel: 020 3268 1077 **47 Marsham St SW1P 3DR**
email: osteriadell_angolo@btconnect.com
dir: *Nearest station: St James's Park, Westminster*

Italian classics in the heart of Westminster

The kitchen of this contemporary Italian in the heart of Westminster near to the Houses of Parliament has its finger firmly on the regional pulse of Tuscan cuisine. After a glass of prosecco in the smart darkwood bar, take a seat in the dining room where butch burgundy leather contrasts with white linen and the Mediterranean warmth of a yellow and amber colour scheme. Well-sourced artisan produce from Italy and splendid true-Brit materials work together in dishes such as grilled Cornish squid filled with Swiss chard, capers, pine kernels, stracciatella Pugliese cheese and black olives, while home-made gnocchi are stuffed with goats' cheese and served with wild mushrooms, pumpkin and sage sauce. Full-flavoured mains run to roast monkfish with osso buco sauce, sautéed radicchio, and toasted almond and red wine sauce, or grilled Galloway beef fillet with turnip tops and a timbale of borlotti beans and leeks.

Chef Massimiliano Vezzi **Owner** Claudio Pulze **Seats** 80, Pr/dining room 22 **Times** 12-3/6-10.30 Closed Xmas, New Year, last 2 wks Aug, BHs, Sun, L Sat **Prices** Fixed L 2 course fr £17.50, Starter £7.50-£11.50, Main £16-£25, Dessert £5.50 **Wines** 200 bottles over £30, 8 bottles under £30, 12 by glass **Parking** 6 **Notes** Vegetarian available, Children welcome

Park Plaza Victoria London

PLAN 4 J3

Venetian-Italian cicchetti

tel: 020 7769 9771 & 0844 415 6754 **TOZI Restaurant & Bar, 239 Vauxhall Bridge Rd SW1V 1EQ**
email: reservations@tozirestaurant.co.uk **web:** www.parkplaza.com
dir: *Nearest station: Victoria*

Venetian sharing plates in a contemporary space

The Fiat 500 at the entrance of the TOZI Restaurant & Bar of the swanky Park Plaza is a clue to what lies ahead. Venetian Cichetti is the name of the game, those fashionable sharing plates of punchy Italian flavours, and it all takes place in a snazzy modern room with an open kitchen and full-length windows. With lots of natural wood and neutral colours, this is a classy and chilled-out environment with a bar that can turn out a nifty Bellini or spritz. Veal ravioli with girolles shows that the kitchen can cook, as the dish provides a nicely judged delicate earthiness, and there is soft-shelled crab, too, with red chilli and parsley sauce. There are good meats such as wild boar salami from Umbria, and aged Parma ham, plus pizetta and piadina cooked in the wood-fired oven. Berries and Limoncello millefoglie is a well-balanced finish.

Times 6-10

Pétrus

PLAN 4 G5

– *see below*

Pétrus

| LONDON SW1 | PLAN 4 G5 |

Modern French **v**
tel: 020 7592 1609 **1 Kinnerton St, Knightsbridge SW1X 8EA**
email: petrus@gordonramsay.com
dir: *Nearest station: Knightsbridge, Sloane Square, Hyde Park*

Immaculate modern French cooking from the Ramsay stable

Gordon Ramsay's Pétrus bears the hallmarks of a high-achieving chef with a carefully burnished brand to protect.The place displays all the meticulous attention to detail that goes into the sought-after Pomerol wine after which it's named, though dinner here will set you back considerably less than even a young bottle of Château Pétrus would (unless, of course, you drink the eponymous wine with it). The room is striking in its design, orientated as it is around a central walk-in glass wine store. Tables arc around it to either side, and the predominant tone is crème fraîche white, with splashes of claret-red in the seating. A large service team attends assiduously to the niceties, the tone all dignified formality. The talented Sean Burbidge's kitchen turns out modern French cooking based on first-class seasonal produce, with menu luxuries liberally dispersed throughout, presented immaculately in finely detailed arrangements that enhance the impact of the dishes themselves. Casterbridge beef appears in an opening tartare, served with crisped veal sweetbreads, slivered foie gras, a quail egg and toasted brioche, a dish of great resonance, which might be followed by precision-timed pan-roasted cod with mussels, Puy lentils and puréed cauliflower in a lightly Indian-spiced velouté. Or another route might be an almost classical lobster and salmon raviolo with creamed leeks in champagne and chives, as a prelude to breast and confit leg of Goosnargh duck with trendy granola in a Szechuan pepper jus with spring onions. Explosive finales include star-anise crème brûlée with caramelised pear and liquorice, or a hefty cylinder of blackberry parfait with chocolate ganache and lime and vanilla cream. The five-course tasting menu (with a choice of main) is a good way to experience the repertoire, and the vegetarian menu shows plenty of imagination.

Chef Sean Burbidge **Owner** Gordon Ramsay Holdings **Seats** 55, Pr/dining room 8 **Times** 12-2.30/6.30-10.30 Closed 22-26 Dec, Sun **Prices** Prices not confirmed **Wines** 428 bottles over £30, 2 bottles under £30, 16 by glass **Parking** On street (free after 6.30)/NCP Park Towers **Notes** Chef's menu 5 course, Children welcome

Quilon

PLAN 4 J4

◎◎ Indian ▮ NOTABLE WINE LIST

tel: 020 7821 1899 **41 Buckingham Gate SW1E 6AF**
email: info@quilonrestaurant.co.uk **web:** www.quilon.co.uk
dir: *Nearest station: St James's Park, Victoria*

Upmarket decor and south-west traditional and contemporary Indian cuisine

Quilon has the sort of designer-led, ultra-modern interior that looks as if it had money thrown at it, with a predominantly gold colour scheme, some wooden latticed screens and comfortable chairs and banquettes. It's no surprise to know that a parliamentary division bell rings here when MPs need to vote. The cooking concentrates on the cuisine of India's south-west coastal region, mixing traditional and more progressive recipes, with tip-top materials the backbone of the kitchen's output. Masala dosai filled with 'tempered' potatoes and vegetables is subtly spiced with ginger, garlic and turmeric, served with rich and flavoursome sambhar, while seafood broth spiked with coriander is an authentic dish of the area. Main courses are well up to snuff too, among them roast quail stuffed with minced meat flavoured with chilli, ginger, onion and spices served with mustard sauce, and equally judiciously spiced baked black cod. The kitchen pays the same care and attention to rice and breads, there's a decent showing of vegetarian dishes, and desserts may run to caramelised banana pudding with parfait.

Chef Sriram Aylur **Owner** Taj International Hotels **Seats** 90, Pr/dining room 16 **Times** 12-2.30/6-11 Closed 25 Dec **Prices** Fixed L 3 course £24-£43, Tasting menu £48-£63, Starter £8-£14, Main £15-£31, Dessert £8-£9 **Wines** 130 bottles over £30, 4 bottles under £30, 16 by glass **Parking** On street, NCP **Notes** Sunday L £24-£45, Vegetarian available, Children welcome

See advert below

The Rib Room

PLAN 4 F4

◎◎◎ *— see page 310*

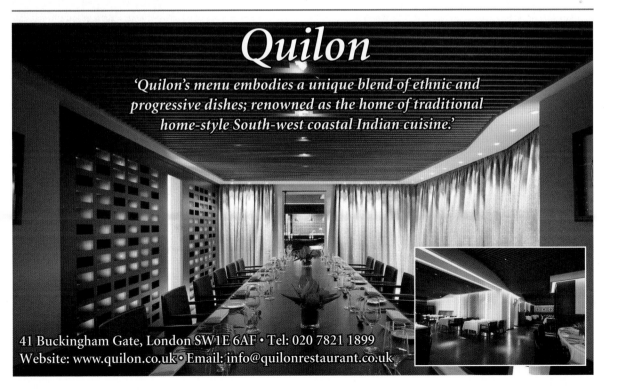

Quilon

'Quilon's menu embodies a unique blend of ethnic and progressive dishes; renowned as the home of traditional home-style South-west coastal Indian cuisine.'

41 Buckingham Gate, London SW1E 6AF • Tel: 020 7821 1899
Website: www.quilon.co.uk • Email: info@quilonrestaurant.co.uk

The Rib Room

LONDON SW1　　　　　　　　　　　　**PLAN 4 F4**

British V

tel: 020 7858 7250 & 7858 7181 **Jumeirah Carlton Tower Hotel, Cadogan Place SW1X 9PY**
email: JCTinfo@jumeirah.com **web:** www.jumeirah.com
dir: *Nearest station: Knightsbridge*

Old stalwarts and seasonal modernity in a plutocrats' Sloaneland hotel

The Carlton Tower in Sloaneland is one of the district's premier addresses for five-star sparkle. A clientele of international plutocrats sashays to and fro, some of them chomping on cigars on the outdoor terrace, adding to the bewitching scent of money. The gazillions spent on periodic refurbishments maintain the lustrous opulence of it all, and among the varied dining options, the Rib Room – established over 50 years, as they say – is the beacon of tradition. That said, its current look is relatively understated, with deeply cushioned leather upholstery in the seating, heavy dark-wood plantation blinds at the windows, and a smart wine-store establishing the clubbable tone. Ian Rudge oversees a menu that is founded on classical lines, with some more modern flourishes to appeal to the adventurous. Dishes are treated with reverence by waiting staff, who announce them at table as though they were titled people arriving at a soirée. Classicists will feast on Loch Fyne smoked salmon, beef tartare, Dover sole meunière, and calf's liver with bacon and onion sauce for years to come, but the seasonal specialities are where things get a sight more interesting. Gently seared Orkney scallops with spiced butternut compôte and chargrilled spring onions in lime caramel, is a well-worked opener. It might be followed by dry-aged beef sirloin with slow-cooked oxtail, smoked shallots and sweet-and-sour pumpkin, or roast monkfish with octopus curry, spiced cauliflower purée and toasted almond sauce. Sides of parsnips roasted in honey and thyme or silky mash are worth the extra. Light desserts are in vogue, so expect coconut and white rum mousse with pineapple jelly and kalamansi curd, or a serving of luscious vanilla ice cream topped with raisins and chocolate sticks, glopped with PX sherry by the waiter.

Chef Ian Rudge **Owner** Jumeirah **Seats** 88, Pr/dining room 16
Times 12.30-2.45/6.30-10.45 **Prices** Fixed L 2 course £28-£49, Fixed D 3 course £58, Starter £15-£19, Main £26-£30, Dessert £8.50-£12 **Wines** 400 bottles over £30, 30 bottles under £30, 17 by glass **Parking** 70 **Notes** ALC Seasonal or Classic menu available, Sunday L £55, Children welcome

Roux at Parliament Square

LONDON SW1　　　　　　　　　　　　**PLAN 5 b5**

Modern European

tel: 020 7334 3737 **Parliament Square SW1P 3AD**
email: roux@rics.org **web:** www.rouxatparliamentsquare.co.uk
dir: *Nearest station: Westminster*

High-flying candidate on Parliament Square

Whichever way you look at it, this is a restaurant with serious pedigree. Just a few paces from the Houses of Parliament, it's on the ground floor of a listed building designed by Alfred Waterhouse, architect of London's Natural History Museum no less. The Roux in the name needs no introduction, although it isn't Michel Roux jnr who's cooking here on a daily basis – he's over at Le Gavroche, of course, while Steve Groves is in charge of the kitchen in Westminster. The restaurant may not be well-known to the masses, but those in the know – and that includes a good deal of politicians and architects from the local environs – keep on coming back for the clean, precise, classically based cooking that keeps a keen eye on the seasons. If cocktails are your thing, a pit-stop at the bar upstairs is a must before moving on into one of the two dining rooms, each done out in soothing neutral tones with crisp linen, fine glassware and sparkling silverware, where the service is polished but by no means fussy. Excellent brown sourdough bread and a silky smooth amuse of spiced butternut squash velouté gets an autumn meal off to a fine start, before an opener of charred Cornish mackerel (accurately timed) with heritage beetroots bringing contrasting colours and textures, and a mackerel tartare bound with horseradish cream. Roast partridge with haggis, neeps and tatties and Balvenie Doublewood whisky (the latter in the form of a spray from an atomiser to add a nice bit of table theatre) is a wintery main that demonstrates a solid grasp of technique, while dessert continues the form, bringing on a delicately poached pear with well-made fennel pollen ice cream, a warm and light almond sponge and a pear gel. It all looks beautiful on the plate, and the balance of flavours is well judged throughout. The wine list is all that you'd expect from a Roux-influenced selection.

Chef Steve Groves **Owner** Restaurant Associates **Seats** 56, Pr/dining room 10
Times 12-2/6.30-10 Closed Xmas, New Year, BHs, Sat-Sun **Prices** Fixed L 3 course £35, Tasting menu £79, Starter £12-£16, Main £17-£27, Dessert £8-£14
Wines 4 bottles under £30, 14 by glass **Parking** NCP Semley Place
Notes Vegetarian available, Children welcome

Roux at Parliament Square

PLAN 5 B5

◉◉◉ – *see opposite*

The Royal Horseguards

PLAN 5 B6

◉◉ Modern, Traditional British

tel: 0871 376 9033 & 020 7451 9333 **2 Whitehall Court SW1A 2EJ**
email: royalhorseguards@guoman.co.uk **web:** www.theroyalhorseguards.co.uk
dir: *Nearest station: Embankment, Charing Cross*

Enterprising cooking near Whitehall

This regal Victorian pile was once home to the Secret Service in the First World War and now makes a suitably grand Thames-side hotel. The upmarket postcode is about as central as things get, handy for the London Eye, and a stone's throw from the Houses of Parliament and Trafalgar Square. The detectives of Scotland Yard were once based next-door, and their number – Whitehall 1212 – which was dialled in many a black-and-white noir thriller, now lives on in One Twenty One Two, the hotel's fine dining restaurant. The kitchen sources its materials from far and wide to ensure quality is always of the highest order, delivering well-crafted food in a gently modern vein, while never losing sight of its French roots. Dinner starts out with diver-caught scallops with truffle and cauliflower soup and garlic crisps, before moving on to buttered guinea fowl with pears, shallot purée, chestnut cream and grilled salsify. To finish, Valrhona's Dulcey blond chocolate stars in a mocha parfait, partnered by espresso cream, milk sorbet and home-made doughnut.

Times 12-3/5.30-10

The Rubens at the Palace

PLAN 4 H4

◉◉ Modern British

tel: 020 7834 6600 **39 Buckingham Palace Rd SW1W OPS**
email: bookrb@rchmail.com **web:** www.redcarnationhotels.com
dir: *Nearest station: Victoria*

British food in a hotel with history

The Library Restaurant at the Rubens, opposite the Royal Mews at Buckingham Palace, has a whiff of old-fashioned gentility, with richly upholstered winged armchairs at the dining tables, wall lights and standard lamps, and a gilded mirror above the fireplace, where a stove may be lit. The kitchen puts a lot of effort into finding its materials, with fish from the West Country and beef from the Buccleuch Estate, among others, and turns out appealing and unpretentious dishes, such as starters of duck and foie gras terrine with fig compôte, and prawn and lobster cocktail in Marie Rose sauce. Combinations are sensibly thought out to provide interest without jarring the palate, so breast of Gressingham mallard comes with Puy lentils, Savoy cabbage mixed with bacon, and sloe jus, and lamb cutlets with confit shoulder, crushed peas and rosemary-flavoured fondant potato. Fish comes in the shape of, say, John Dory fillets with clam chowder, cavolo nero and champagne velouté. To cap off a meal there might be spiced caramel parfait with apple sorbet and compôte.

Chef Nelson Linhares **Owner** Red Carnation Hotels **Seats** 26, Pr/dining room 60 **Times** 7.30-10.30 Closed 24-27 Dec, L all week **Prices** Fixed D 3 course £32.50, Starter £8-£13, Main £16-£35, Dessert £7-£10 **Wines** 93 bottles over £30, 17 bottles under £30, 16 by glass **Parking** NCP at Victoria Coach Station **Notes** Vegetarian available, Children welcome

Sake No Hana

PLAN 4 J6

◉◉ Traditional Japanese

tel: 020 7925 8988 **23 Saint James's St SW1A 1HA**
email: reservations@sakenohana.com
dir: *Nearest station: Green Park, Piccadilly Circus*

Sophisticated Japanese cooking in a smart part of town

Just round the corner from the Ritz, you can expect a touch of class in posh St James's, and this sleek contemporary Japanese certainly delivers the goods. In the airy first-floor dining room, blinds ressembling sushi rolling mats screen full-length windows, and a wooden lattice structure suspended from the soaring ceiling helps to make the room feel more intimate as well as more authentically Japanese. The kitchen deploys a range of traditional styles and every dish is based on superb, fresh ingredients, whether you perch for the ringside action at the sushi bar, or sit at a low-slung leather banquette. Charmingly attentive staff are happy to talk you through a menu which combines imported Japanese produce and UK ingredients to good effect in traditional and fusion dishes. Seared tuna with mooli, wasabi and a tangy yuzu sauce is a dish full of flavour, ahead of sukiyaki – sliced rib-eye beef with vegetables, tofu and mushrooms, cooked at the table. Matcha green tea pannacotta with kumquat, yuzu sorbet and pistachio makes for an imaginative fusion finale.

Times 12-2.30/6-11 Closed 24-25 Dec, Sun

Salloos Restaurant

PLAN 4 G5

◉ Pakistani

tel: 020 7235 4444 **62-64 Kinnerton St SW1X 8ER**
dir: *Nearest station: Knightsbridge*

Authentic Pakistani cooking in Knightsbridge mews house

Discreetly tucked away in a flower-decked corner mews house just across from The Berkeley hotel, Salloos is a genuine, family-run Pakistani outfit plying its trade here since 1976. Climb the stairs from the tiny bar to the intimate first-floor dining room to enjoy some of the Capital's most consistently sound Pakistani cooking. White linen, warm authentic colours and latticework-screened windows blend with modern seating, crystal chandeliers and contemporary artwork, while the atmosphere is traditional and the service formal (some might judge poker-faced). The kitchen's authentic, well-tuned Mughlai cuisine (the chef has been here almost 40 years so confident spicing is assured) is fashioned from quality produce on a repertoire that sees little change. Salloos is renowned for its tandooris like lamb chops or chicken or lamb shish kebab, and its house specialities such as a Khyber region chicken karahi (de-boned chicken cooked in fresh tomatoes, ginger, green chillies and fragrant coriander), while salan (curries) could include jheenga masala (small prawns cooked with onions, tomatoes and spices).

Chef Abdul Aziz **Owner** Mr & Mrs M Salahuddin **Seats** 65 **Times** 12-11 Closed Xmas, Sun All-day dining **Prices** Prices not confirmed **Wines** 37 bottles over £30, 11 bottles under £30, 2 by glass **Parking** Meters, car park Kinnerton St **Notes** Vegetarian available, No children

Looking for a London restaurant by name?
Use the index on page 254

Seven Park Place by William Drabble

LONDON SW1   **PLAN 4 J6**

Modern French  NOTABLE WINE LIST

tel: 020 7316 1600 **St James's Hotel and Club, 7-8 Park Place SW1A 1LS**
email: info@stjameshotelandclub.com
web: www.stjameshotelandclub.com
dir: *Nearest station: Green Park*

Assured classical French cooking in a riotously decorated St James's club

Following some unpleasantness at a rival establishment in 1857, Earl Granville and a minister of the Sardinian government, the Marchese d'Azeglio, decided to found their own London club where they would be made welcome. The St James was the result, and instantly became a magnet not just for the idle rich, but for the more discerning artists of the day, and has since been a haunt for many a celeb. The place was relaunched in 2008 as a club-hotel with a refit that brought Murano chandeliers and cashmere-lined walls to a London about to be plunged into the financial crisis, followed the year after by William Drabble to head up a self-named restaurant. Drabble was for over a decade the man holding the reins at Aubergine in Chelsea, which he brought back to premier-league status following Gordon Ramsay's departure, and as such he represented a stellar signing for the St James. The dining room decor is something of an acquired taste, it must be said, being a riot of geometric patterning in carpets and upholstery, with broad swathes of art deco-ish foliage advancing up the brown walls. While not for the hung-over, it at least makes a refreshing change from the ubiquitous greige minimalism of modern restaurants. It's perhaps all the more reassuring in the circumstances that Drabble's food is not about jarring sensory assault, but achieves wondrous results from dishes that make a show of themselves where it counts: on the palate. There is exquisite concentration and intensity in the cooking, which is impeccably seasonal in its use of ingredients, and in terms of the kind of weighting that works best, so lighter food in summer, more heartily rustic when the chill sets in. A seam of assured French classicism runs through the menus, which might open with baked fillet of red mullet with courgette and basil purée and sweet red pepper, or a partnership of seared foie gras with confit vegetables, raisin purée and Muscat sauce. Next up, perhaps the subtle satisfaction of roasted fillet of turbot with braised peas and lettuce, smoked bacon lardons and Italian lardo, or breast of Rhug Estate chicken with mousseron mushrooms, broad beans, morels and foie gras. At the end you might take a plate of Paxton and Whitfield cheeses or finish sweetly with something like creamed rice with mango and lime syrup, or there may be banana parfait with set chocolate custard and honeycomb.

Chef William Drabble **Seats** 34, Pr/dining room 40 **Times** 12-2/7-10 Closed Sun-Mon **Prices** Fixed L 2 course fr £25.50, Fixed D 3 course fr £61, Tasting menu fr £72 **Wines** 257 bottles over £30, 16 bottles under £30, 11 by glass **Parking** On street and NCP **Notes** Fixed 6 course Menu Gourmand, Vegetarian available, Children welcome

LONDON SW1 *continued*

Santini Restaurant

PLAN 4 H4

@ Italian

tel: 020 7730 4094 & 7730 8275 **29 Ebury St SW1W 0NZ**
email: santini@santinirestaurant.com **web:** www.santinirestaurant.com
dir: *Nearest station: Victoria*

Faithful Italian cooking in ritzy surroundings

Santini has been a glamorous Belgravia darling since the early 1980s, much in demand with the glitterati for its romantic alfresco terrace discreetly bordered by glass screens, potted Mediterranean herbs and olive trees, and an airy pastel-hued interior with marble floors, leather banquettes and low-slung chairs. The traditional values of a family-run Italian restaurant underpin this glossy set-up, and Latin style runs all the way from the waiters to the wine list. Impeccably sourced seasonal ingredients treated with a light touch are at the centre of things, starting with the likes of fried courgette flowers stuffed with mozzarella and herbs; if you prefer to start with classic pasta, you can't get much more simple and authentic than cappellini with fresh tomato and basil. Main courses take in poached sea bass with lentils and herb and balsamic dressing, or grilled beef fillet with Barolo butter, with – what else? – classic tiramisú to finish.

Chef Christian Gardin **Owner** Mr G Santin **Seats** 65, Pr/dining room 30 **Times** 12-3/6-11 Closed Xmas, 1 Jan, Etr Sun-Mon, L Sat-Sun **Prices** Starter £10-£20, Main £14-£35, Dessert £7.50-£11 **Wines** 55 bottles over £30, 2 bottles under £30, 15 by glass **Parking** Meters (no charge after 6.30pm) **Notes** Pre-theatre menu, Vegetarian available, Children welcome

Season at The Fifth Floor Restaurant

PLAN 4 F5

@@ Modern International

tel: 020 7235 5250 **Harvey Nichols, 109-125 Knightsbridge SW1X 7RJ**
email: reception@harveynichols.com
dir: *Nearest station: Knightsbridge, Hyde Park Corner*

Market menus on the top floor at Harvey Nics

It's all about great food and wine up on the top floor at Harvey Nics, with a classy food store, a café and the flagship restaurant, the forerunner of all the various First, Second, Fourth, and indeed Forth Floors in branches of the swish department store around the country. As one might hope, the Season restaurant delivers bright contemporary dishes that do indeed follow the seasons avidly, setting out with the likes of pan-fried Rye Bay scallops with marinated carrots, smoked haddock croquette, buttered samphire and carrot and orange gel. At main course stage, the cooking remains accurate, delivering clean-cut flavours in easy-on-the-eye dishes. Sautéed cuttlefish, red pepper purée, Provençal beans and marjoram jus provide a perfect supporting cast for a pancetta-wrapped roast loin of Kentish rabbit, or you

might prefer halibut poached in Barolo wine with salt cod brandade, smoked eel, and radish and red wine butter. Kiss the diet goodbye with a white chocolate and ricotta cheesecake with poached rhubarb and champagne sorbet.

Chef Chris Bower **Owner** Harvey Nichols **Seats** 120 **Times** 12-3/6-11 Closed Xmas, Etr Sun, D Sun **Prices** Fixed L 2 course £18.95, Fixed D 3 course £21, Starter £9.95-£12.95, Main £23.95-£27.50, Dessert £8.50 **Wines** 30 by glass **Parking** On street, NCP Cadogan Place **Notes** Sunday L, Vegetarian available, Children welcome

Seven Park Place by William Drabble

PLAN 4 J6

@@@@ – *see opposite*

Sofitel London St James

PLAN 4 K6

@ French, British

tel: 020 7968 2900 **6 Waterloo Place SW1Y 4AN**
email: thebalcon.london@sofitel.com **web:** www.sofitelstjames.com
dir: *Nearest station: Piccadilly Circus*

A touch of French style on Pall Mall

The hotel is an imposing piece of London real estate in an upmarket part of town, and The Balcon restaurant is suitably capacious and stylish (and rather glamorous with it). It's done out in the grand Parisian manner with double-height ceiling, soaring columns, a show-stopping duo of matching spiral staircases, plus a charcuterie and champagne bar. The menu ploughs a brasserie furrow with British and French influences along the way, and some excellent British ingredients on show. There are tarts and tartines (Welsh rarebit, for example) and superb charcuterie from Trealy Farm in Monmouthshire and Mas le Rouget in Cantal (south-central France). Start with a salad – perhaps roasted and pickled beetroots with Roquefort, candy walnuts and frisée – follow on with Label Anglais chicken cooked on the rotisserie, or beer-braised ox cheeks, and finish with a lemon pudding with lemon sauce.

Times 11-11 All-day dining

The Stafford London by Kempinski

PLAN 4 J6

@ Traditional British, European

tel: 020 7493 0111 **16-18 St James's Place SW1A 1NJ**
email: info@thelyttelton.com **web:** www.thelyttelton.com
dir: *Nearest station: Green Park*

Luxurious hotel dining in exclusive location

It's easy to forget you're in central London when you're safely ensconced in The Stafford. Hidden away down a discreet street by Green Park, it is a luxurious St James's address that is worth knowing about. The American Bar, for a start, should put it on any map; head on down for a damn fine martini. If it is something more sustaining you're after, The Lyttelton restaurant does a nice line in classy British food, where fine UK produce gets treated with due diligence and turned into smart, gently refined dishes. It all takes place in a rather swanky room with tones of ivory and grey, smart contrasting floral fabrics, commissioned artwork and chandeliers. Start with tartare of beef with melba toast and quail's egg, move on to best-end of Daphne's lamb with celeriac dauphinoise and mint sauce, or risotto of wild mushrooms. End in style with Seville orange marmalade sponge with Grand Marnier custard.

Chef Carlos Martinez **Owner** B H L **Seats** 52, Pr/dining room 44 **Times** 12.30-2.30/6-10.30 **Prices** Fixed L 2 course £19.12, Starter £11.50-£23, Main £24.50-£34, Dessert £9-£12 **Wines** 340 bottles over £30, 5 bottles under £30, 11 by glass **Parking** NCP on Arlington Street **Notes** Pre-theatre menu 5.30-7pm 2/3 course £19.12/£24.12, Sunday L £19.12-£24.12, Vegetarian available, Children welcome

LONDON SW1 *continued*

Thirty Six by Nigel Mendham at Dukes London PLAN 4 J6

⚜⚜⚜ – see below

Tinello PLAN 4 G2

⚜⚜ Italian

tel: 020 7730 6327 & 7730 3663 **87 Pimlico Rd SW1W 8PH**
email: info@tinello.co.uk
dir: *Nearest station: Sloane Square*

Classy Italian cooking in stylish restaurant

Run by brothers Federico and Max Sali and backed by their mentor, celeb chef Giorgio Locatelli, you're in good hands at Tinello. The place lives up to its posh Belgravia location with a classy, rather masculine decor of bare bricks, dark oak floors and brown banquettes at linen-swathed tables beneath low-slung brass lampshades. It strikes a discreet and serious pose to go with straightforward modern Italian cooking built on a clear dedication to superb ingredients. There are 'small eats' – roast bone marrow with celery, capers and rocket salad, say, or you might launch straight into skilfully-made pasta from the seasonal repertoire: a classic pairing of herb pappardelle with duck ragù, or spaghetti with gurnard and black olives. Main courses take an equally gimmick and fuss-free line. A splendid slab of perfectly-timed roast Cornish cod with sliced razor clams and cannellini beans is a pitch-perfect combination, or you might enjoy the meaty delights of chargrilled quail with the simple accompaniments of sautéed broccoli, almonds and chilli. Finish with pannacotta with intensely-flavoured preserved amarena cherries.

Chef Federico Sali **Owner** Giorgio Locatelli **Seats** 75, Pr/dining room 25 **Times** 12-2.30/6.15-10.30 Closed BH Mon, Sun **Prices** Starter £1.95-£18, Main £13-

£26.50, Dessert £3.90-£13.50, Service optional **Wines** 189 bottles over £30, 50 bottles under £30, 23 by glass **Parking** On street, single yellow from 6.30pm **Notes** Vegetarian available, Children welcome

Zafferano PLAN 4 F4

⚜⚜ Modern Italian

tel: 020 7235 5800 **15 Lowndes St SW1X 9EY**
email: zafferano@londonfinedininggroup.com
dir: *Nearest station: Knightsbridge*

Refined but authentic Italian cooking in Knightsbridge

Italian cooking has gone through a productive evolution in the capital over the past 20 years, with greater regional awareness, integrity of ingredients and the learning of a whole new lexicon undergirding it all. Knightsbridge's Zafferano has been one of the prime movers in that development, offering refined, authentic food that doesn't lose sight of the foundational principle of simplicity, in a room that adopts the moneyed rustic look of candy-striped upholstery against stolid brickwork. The output has occasionally wavered with each new change of kitchen regime, but the menus still inspire confidence: seared scallops in saffron vinaigrette are a signature opener, or there may be richly deliquescent burrata with aubergine and sun-dried Piennolo tomatoes. After an interlude for pasta, gnocchi, or perhaps langoustine risotto, it's on to corn-fed chicken with cavolo nero in textbook peverada (a sauce combining the richnesses of chicken livers, sausage and anchovy), or maybe turbot in walnuts and capers. The lightest finish is mulberry pannacotta decorated with dried figs, and there are fine Italian cheeses, too.

Chef Miles Nixon **Owner** A-Z Restaurants-London Fine Dining Group **Seats** 140, Pr/dining room 28 **Times** 12-11 Closed 25 Dec, All-day dining **Prices** Fixed L 2 course fr £22.50, Starter £11.50-£18.50, Main £19.50-£55 **Wines** 600 bottles over £30, 5 bottles under £30, 6 by glass **Parking** NCP behind restaurant **Notes** Vegetarian available, Children welcome

Thirty Six by Nigel Mendham at Dukes London

LONDON SW1	PLAN 4 J6

Modern British
tel: 020 7491 4840 **35-36 St James's Place SW1A 1NY**
email: thirtysix@dukeshotel.com **web:** www.dukeshotel.com
dir: *Nearest station: Green Park*

Refined contemporary cooking in luxe Mayfair hotel

Dukes is a hotel with an impeccable pedigree and postcode, and a correspondingly luxurious, moneyed sheen. This Mayfair institution flaunts its boutique status with pride and delivers the sort of glossy, cossetting embrace one expects in this neighbourhood. An aperitif in the rather fab bar is an absolute must, and with its connections to James Bond creator Ian Fleming, Martinis are a bit of a house speciality. The man whose name is pinned to the restaurant is Nigel Mendham, a chef who does not quiver at the thought of every new gadget or slavishly buy the latest piece of technological wizardry, preferring tried-and-true cooking methods to smoke and mirrors trickery. And his food is no less dynamic and contemporary for that, arriving with a spectacular look on the plate. It all takes place in the luxe Thirty Six restaurant, a magic number that relates in part to its address, but also has associations with the solar square of ancient Western

tradition, and is a favoured number in Chinese astrology. All that good fortune has resulted in a smart, modish dining room with fine artworks and high comfort levels. There's a showpiece tasting menu in support of the carte, plus an early evening menu if you're in a hurry, or on a budget, and a good-value set lunch. The cooking is refined, intelligent and captivating, starting with a visually striking dish of goat's cheese tart and croquettes matched with a colourful riff on a beetroot theme, and celery sorbet. Next up, John Dory is teamed with spiced mussels, aubergine and herb quinoa, or there could be salt marsh lamb with braised lettuce, goats' curd, broad beans and mustard seeds. Apples get a contemporary workout at dessert stage, appearing as a tart and sorbet with gingerbread parfait.

Chef Nigel Mendham **Seats** 36 **Times** 12-2.30/6-9.30 Closed L Mon, D Sun **Prices** Prices not confirmed **Wines** 13 by glass **Parking** Holiday Inn, Britannia car park **Notes** Tasting menu 6 course, Sunday L, Vegetarian available, Children welcome

LONDON SW3

Bibendum Restaurant
PLAN 4 E3

@@ British, French V NOTABLE WINE LIST

tel: 020 7581 5817 **Michelin House, 81 Fulham Rd SW3 6RD**
email: reservations@bibendum.co.uk web: www.bibendum.co.uk
dir: *Nearest station: South Kensington*

Modern classics at a Chelsea institution

With its sexy Art Nouveau looks, the landmark Michelin building merits a visit for the iconic surroundings, let alone the classic food. At ground floor level is the casual oyster bar, a busy, high-ceilinged space with tiled wall friezes and mosaic floors, but it's the first-floor dining room that has a magic about it, especially when it's a bright day and the Michelin man stained glass windows light up an amazingly luminous space. It is a bastion of Frenchness, starting with the smooth Gallic service that imparts an air of quiet refinement to the place, through to the traditional French dishes that rub along nicely with modern British ideas. You might start with snails then move on to steak au poivre — after all they have been fixtures on the menu since the 1980s. Otherwise, feuillette of chicken livers and bone marrow with trompette de la mort mushrooms and sauce poivrade sets the ball rolling, ahead of roast wood pigeon with spinach and quince croustade, and juniper sauce. To finish, there's exemplary tarte Tatin with Jersey cream.

Chef Matthew Harris **Owner** Sir Terence Conran, Simon Hopkinson, Michael Hamlyn **Seats** 80 **Times** 12-2.30/7-11 Closed 25-26 Dec, 1 Jan, D 24 Dec **Prices** Fixed L 2 course fr £27.50, Starter £11-£25, Main £18.50-£29, Dessert £8-£9.75 **Wines** 516 bottles over £30, 20 bottles under £30, 18 by glass **Parking** On street **Notes** Sun D 3 course £33.50, Sunday L £33.50, Children welcome

Bo Lang Restaurant
PLAN 4 E3

@ Chinese **NEW**

tel: 020 7823 7887 **100 Draycott Av SW3 3AD**
email: reservations@bolangrestaurant.co.uk
dir: *Nearest station: South Kensington*

Enterprising dim sum in Chelsea

This is the Chelsea hangout for lovers of dim sum, a dimly lit space with grey leather sofas, charcoal velvet chairs, wooden-topped tables, cut-out wooden screens and a load of lanterns dangling from the ceiling. The short menu is helpfully divided into sections (dim sum steamed, dim sum baked/fried, main courses and so on). Standards are high, and dishes never less than interesting. Three rolls of honey-glazed rib wrapped in puff pastry, tender shui mai of chicken minced with black truffle, and soft-shelled crab with chilli and lime have all been mentioned in dispatches. No less accomplished are main courses: stir-fried diced beef in rich black bean and pepper sauce, slivers of chicken with noodles and cashew nuts, and baby pak choi steamed with garlic and goji berries all make an impact. There's even a short choice of desserts, among them frozen lemongrass and ginger yoghurt.

Chef Kai Wang **Owner** Aytan Eldarova **Seats** 60 **Times** noon-11.30 All-day dining **Prices** Fixed L 2 course fr £22, Starter £5-£20, Main £13-£28, Dessert fr £7.20 **Wines** 22 bottles over £30, 9 by glass **Parking** On street **Notes** Afternoon tea Mon-Sat 3-5pm £35, Vegetarian available, Children welcome

Cassis Bistro
PLAN 4 E4

@@ French

tel: 020 7581 1101 **232-236 Brompton Rd SW3 2BB**
email: reception@cassisbistro.co.uk
dir: *Nearest station: Knightsbridge, South Kensington*

Modern Mediterranean bistro with lashings of contemporary style

Cassis brings a certain Mediterranean panache to bustling Brompton Cross and, befitting its chic postcode, is at the luxury end of the bistro genre. A roll-back

frontage and pavement tables seduce in fair weather, while the interior is glossily done out with striking in-vogue artworks, pale grey tiling, glass wine display cabinets and a zinc-topped bar. The menu embraces the modern Mediterranean theme; southern France meets Italy with gusto via tip-top produce, full-on flavours and skilled simplicity. Set off with a terrine of foie gras and peach, or swordfish carpaccio with a nicely balanced citrus dressing, or perhaps a pasta dish like homemade fettuccine pepped up with mushrooms and confit duck. Veal cutlet Milanese (with Sicilian orange and fennel salad) or sea-fresh roasted turbot (teamed with crushed new potatoes, Swiss chard and salsa verde) might feature at main course, while desserts continue the theme — perhaps strawberry semi-fredo or rich ricotta and bitter chocolate soufflé. The awesome wine list (over 700 bins) captures the mood, as does the bar, with its separate menu and booth-style seating.

Times 12-11 Closed 25 Dec, All-day dining

Le Colombier
PLAN 4 D2

@ Traditional French

tel: 020 7351 1155 **145 Dovehouse St SW3 6LB**
email: lecolombier1998@aol.com
dir: *Nearest station: South Kensington*

Classic authentic French bistro décor and cooking in Chelsea

An old-school French corner restaurant with a flower-bedecked terrace under a blue awning, a little way from the Fulham Road, the Dovecote could have been transported here from some provincial town across the water. Café chairs and linened tables make a simple but thoroughly agreeable setting for a classic French bistro menu in both languages, where the options open with seafood specials comme il faut (blue lobster, langoustines, oysters, crab), before heading off towards foie gras terrine and oeufs pochés en meurette territory. Mains encompass the traditional likes of grilled sole in parsley butter, veal sweetbreads with wild mushrooms, or roast corn-fed chicken with bacon and petits pois, or wander off-piste for scallops with ginger and spring onions dressed in sesame and soy. At pudding stage, get set for crêpe Suzette, oeufs à la neige, or rum baba. There are tempting sorbets doused in liqueurs, or else go for a cheese plate featuring Brie de Meaux, Comté and Roquefort.

Chef Philippe Tamet **Owner** Didier Garnier **Seats** 70, Pr/dining room 28 **Times** 12-3/6.30-10.30 **Prices** Fixed L 2 course £19.50-£23, Starter £8.50-£14.50, Main £19-£35, Dessert fr £7.90 **Wines** 195 bottles over £30, 32 bottles under £30, 10 by glass **Parking** Metered parking **Notes** Sunday L £23, Vegetarian available, No children

Eight Over Eight
PLAN 4 D1

@ Pan-Asian

tel: 020 7349 9934 **392 King's Rd SW3 5UZ**
email: eightovereight@rickerrestaurants.com
dir: *Nearest station: Sloane Sq, South Kensington*

Pan-Asian cooking in a cool, buzzy Chelsea favourite

The King's Road branch of Will Ricker's oriental fusion trio (also see E&O and XO), Eight Over Eight is a fashionable assemble of bar and understatedly sexy restaurant. Effortlessly cool, the corner-sited, high-ceilinged outfit is flush with light from huge windows by day and large dangling oriental-style lights by night. Wide floorboards, paper-clothed tables, slick banquettes and black lacquered chairs complete the on-trend, up-tempo vibe. But it's not all style over substance, with well-conceived pan-Asian grazing plates the kitchen's raison d'être. All the classics appear on a well-honed roster, from dim sum to classy sushi and sashimi, through to pukka tempura (like soft-shell crab and zesty jalapeno), Asian salads, curries (think high-octane dry red barramundi with green beans) and specials like black cod and sweet miso. And it's all prepared with skill and presented with plenty of style to match the surroundings and switched-on service. Eye-catching Asian-influenced cocktails are a good way to kick-off proceedings.

Times 12-3/6-11 Closed 24-29 Dec, Etr

Outlaw's at The Capital

LONDON SW3　　　　　　　　　　　　　PLAN 4 F5

British, Seafood v

tel: 020 7591 1202 **22-24 Basil St, Knightsbridge SW3 1AT**
email: outlaws@capitalhotel.co.uk **web:** www.capitalhotel.co.uk
dir: *Nearest station: Knightsbridge*

The best of Cornish seafood in London

Nathan Outlaw may hail from Kent but he has made a name for himself flying the Cornish flag of St Piran's at his restaurant in Rock. And now he's opened in London in the ultra-smart setting of The Capital. This magnificent townhouse hotel just around the corner from Harrods is a little piece of five-star heaven: discreet, chic and refined – you know you're somewhere special when the liveried doorman ushers you inside. Outlaw's restaurant occupies the smart dining room which has shed some of its formality since the arrival of the new incumbent, but still retains an understated art deco-esque civility and glamour with its blond wood panelling, paintings of seahorses, wall mirrors and unclothed tables, supported by a service team out of the top drawer. With his flagship St Enodoc moored out on the Cornish coast, you can't expect Outlaw to be regularly at the stoves here so he has put his right-hand man, Pete Biggs, in charge of the kitchen. The concept behind this operation mirrors that of the mothership: to let the top-class Cornish materials speak eloquently for themselves, helped along, naturally, with high-flying technique and an innate sense of what works with what. The kitchen also looks west for the predominantly Cornish seafood that is the mainstay of the output. Take a starter of scallops with hazelnuts, Jerusalem artichoke and watercress – simply perfection – or perhaps baked crab pointed up with the flavours of curry, celeriac, fennel and lime. Mains might shine the spotlight on an immaculate tranche of turbot which comes with the umami-rich flavour of crispy oysters, oyster sauce, cabbage and bacon, or monkfish on the bone with shellfish sauce, leeks and green olives. This is a kitchen that is strong in all areas, through to a dessert of quince and ginger cheesecake with quince and cider sorbet.

Chef Nathan Outlaw, Pete Biggs **Owner** Mr D Levin **Seats** 35, Pr/dining room 24 **Times** 12-2/6.30-10 Closed Sun **Prices** Prices not confirmed **Wines** 37 by glass **Parking** 8 **Notes** Children welcome

Rasoi Restaurant

LONDON SW3　　　　　　　　　　　　　PLAN 4 F3

Modern Indian v ♦ NOTABLE WINE LIST

tel: 020 7225 1881 **10 Lincoln St SW3 2TS**
email: info@rasoirestaurant.co.uk
dir: *Nearest station: Sloane Square*

Chelsea townhouse with leading-light Indian cooking

Rasoi is one of the leading lights among groundbreaking Indian eateries in the capital. The location in a side-street off the Sloane Square end of the King's Road is counter-intuitive enough. It's a Chelsea townhouse complete with tiled path and window-box. Previously, the premises were devoted to modern English cooking in an atmosphere that felt like an upscale private home. Rasoi, for all that the Hindi name means simply 'Kitchen', has carefully maintained and nurtured that sense of gracious living, albeit with subcontinental artefacts in place of the English chintz. What could be more elevated than having to ring a bell to get in? Vineet Bhatia's menus are structured in the western three-course format, with prestige and vegetarian taster deals on offer, the former with the option of pre-selected wine matches. The cooking is characterised by finely honed acuity in its handling of flavours, as well as great originality, producing starters such as salmon cooked in a smoky tandoor with herb mash and raita, or lamb and apricot kofta on aubergine couscous with a samosa of goats' cheese and smoked cashews. A certain cross-fertilisation of Indian and western technique lends personality to main dishes like rogan josh lamb shank à la bordelaise with beetroot and coconut thoran and kidney-bean and saffron pulao, or achari tomato chicken with fennel-seeded potato crush in mushroom chicken jus. But there is no mistaking the compass-bearings in Maharashtra sea bass with beetroot moilee, lemon and peanut rice and coconut-coriander chutney. Intriguing desserts might include glazed carrot fudge with carrot kulfi in set smoked cardamom milk, as well as a copiously stocked plate consecrated to 'Chocolate Cravings'.

Chef Vineet Bhatia **Owner** Vineet & Rashima Bhatia **Seats** 35, Pr/dining room 14 **Times** 12-2.30/6-10.30 Closed Xmas, New Year, BHs, Mon, L Sat **Prices** Fixed L 2 course £23, Fixed D 3 course £65-£75, Tasting menu £79-£89, Starter £21, Main £32-£40, Dessert £12-£22 **Wines** 300 bottles over £30, 10 bottles under £30, 10 by glass **Parking** On street **Notes** Tasting menu 7 course incl wine, Sunday L £23-£33, Children welcome

LONDON SW3 *continued*

Manicomio
PLAN 4 F3

Modern Italian

tel: 020 7730 3366 **85 Duke of York Square, Chelsea SW3 4LY**
email: info@manicomio.co.uk
dir: *Nearest station: Sloane Square*

Bustling modern Italian just off Sloane Square

Built as the military asylum of the Duke of York barracks, Manicomio presents a cool, calming image, with its planked floor, wall banquettes and vivid artwork. Contemporary Italian cooking is the draw, with many ingredients imported from the Motherland: perhaps speck d'Aosta in a starter with mozzarella and baby artichokes, and lentils from Umbria to accompany roast hake fillet, parsley pesto and spinach. The menu is evenly divided between fish and meat, the latter extending to chargrilled quail skewered with chicken livers on polenta with vin cotto sauce, followed by a winter main course of grilled sirloin with bone marrow, braised ox cheek and roast squash. Finish with the tiramisù or treacle and lemon tart.

Chef Tom Salt **Owner** Ninai & Andrew Zarach **Seats** 70, Pr/dining room 30 **Times** 12-3/6.30-10.30 Closed Xmas & New Year, D Sun (winter) **Prices** Fixed L 2 course £22.50 **Wines** 78 bottles over £30, 23 bottles under £30, 18 by glass **Parking** On street **Notes** Sunday L, Vegetarian available, Children welcome

Nozomi
PLAN 4 E4

Contemporary Japanese V

tel: 020 7838 1500 & 7838 0181 **14-15 Beauchamp Place, Knightsbridge SW3 1NQ**
email: enquiries@nozomi.co.uk
dir: *Nearest station: Knightsbridge*

Contemporary Japanese cooking in slick setting

The fashionable good looks of the front bar of this contemporary Japanese make it a darling of the see-and-be-seen crowd, though for foodies the real draw is the dining room behind. This is a rather more soothing space with cream walls and leather seating, subdued lighting, and black-clad waiting staff combining with a trendy backing track to create an upbeat, modern space for some equally in-vogue cooking. Authentic contemporary Japanese cuisine is the deal, with the long menu covering a lot of ground. A selection of sushi is a good way to start – perhaps turbot and salmon nigiri – or choose from an extensive list of maki rolls and temaki, or small dishes such as soft shell crab with spicy red pepper sauce, or grilled eel in unagi sauce. Not surprisingly in this postcode, luxuries are strewn liberally around, among them whole tempura lobster with ponzu and daikon, pan-fried foie gras marinated in whisky, and chargrilled Wagyu beef steaks.

Seats 170, Pr/dining room 30 **Times** 12-3/6.30-11.30 Closed L Mon **Prices** Prices not confirmed **Wines** 10 by glass **Parking** 10, Valet parking & on street **Notes** Pre-theatre menu, D 4 course £59-£99, Sunday L, Children welcome

Outlaw's at The Capital
PLAN 4 F5

– see opposite

Racine
PLAN 4 E4

Traditional French

tel: 020 7584 4477 **239 Brompton Rd SW3 2EP**
email: bonjour@racine.com
dir: *Nearest station: Knightsbridge, South Kensington*

An authentic French brasserie opposite Brompton Oratory

When you long for the French bourgeois cooking of the neighbourhood bistros and brasseries of Paris and the elbow-to-elbow bouchons of Lyon, Racine comes up with the goods: this is timeless dining built on the solid foundations of diligently-sourced, seasonal produce. The look is spot-on too, with wooden floors, chocolate leather banquettes, wall mirrors, soft-focus lighting and an easygoing vibe, all kept ticking over by correctly courteous staff. Slacken your belt and be prepared for big-hearted, robust, gutsy cooking. Seared foie gras with caramelised apple and Calvados makes a classic opener, or you might go for a visceral plate of calf's brains with black butter and capers. Mains plough a similarly Gallic furrow – grilled rabbit with mustard sauce and smoked bacon, or veal kidneys with creamed Fourme d'Ambert cheese, Espelette pepper jus and pommes purée.

Chef Henry Harris **Owner** Henry Harris **Seats** 60, Pr/dining room 22 **Times** 12-3/6-10.30 Closed 25 Dec **Prices** Fixed L 2 course £17.75-£19.50, Fixed D 3 course £19.50-£21.50, Starter £7-£14.75, Main £12.50-£29.50, Dessert £6.50-£9.50 **Wines** 100 bottles over £30, 14 bottles under £30, 20 by glass **Parking** On street **Notes** Sunday L £19.50-£21.50, Vegetarian available, Children welcome

Rasoi Restaurant
PLAN 4 F3

– see opposite

Restaurant Gordon Ramsay
PLAN 4 F1

– see page 318

Tom's Kitchen
PLAN 4 E2

British, French

tel: 020 7349 0202 **27 Cale St, South Kensington SW3 3QP**
email: info@tomskitchen.co.uk
dir: *Nearest station: South Kensington, Sloane Square*

First-class brasserie food from top-class chef

With its utilitarian good looks, Tom's kitchen fizzes with life and bonhomie. The ethos is there for all to see: 'food for everyone and anyone' it says engraved on a piece of slate, and that's a fair statement, just as long as that 'someone' can pay seventeen quid for fish and chips. But this is Chelsea (just around the corner from Tom's flagship restaurant) and the prices are not unreasonable, and perhaps most important of all, the quality is high. Covering three floors of this handsome townhouse, there's a space to suit your mood, and it is the all-day, ground-floor brasserie where most of the action takes place at tightly packed wooden tables. Spicy crabcake, perked up with a tomato salsa and packed with a goodly amount of crab, shows the way, or go for something along the lines of baked scallops with garlic and lemon. Top-notch produce is sourced with due diligence throughout. Chicken, leek and bacon pie is a real cracker, and desserts run to apple and blackberry crumble with toasted almond ice cream. There's a second branch in Somerset House in the West End.

Chef Robert Stephens, Tom Aikens **Owner** Tom Aikens Group Ltd **Seats** 75, Pr/dining room 62 **Times** 12-3.30/6-10.30 Closed 25-26 Dec, D 24 Dec **Prices** Starter £7.80-£17.25, Main £13.90-£30, Dessert £7.50 **Wines** 24 bottles over £30, 23 bottles under £30, 13 by glass **Parking** On street **Notes** Sunday L £21.50, Vegetarian available, Children welcome

Looking for a London restaurant near you? Use the maps on pages 258–68

Restaurant Gordon Ramsay

LONDON SW3	PLAN 4 F1

French, European **V**

tel: 020 7352 4441 **68 Royal Hospital Rd SW3 4HP**
email: reservations@gordonramsay.com
dir: *Nearest station: Sloane Square*

The mothership of the Gordon Ramsay empire

There are more than a dozen Ramsay restaurants in the UK, a host of addresses Stateside (from New York to West Hollywood), plus France, Italy and Qatar. It all started back here at Royal Hospital Road in 1998, when a then 31-year-old Mr Ramsay got the keys to his first place. Clare Smyth has been in charge of the kitchen at Restaurant Gordon Ramsay since 2008, and now has the title chef-patron. Ramsay has a long history of nurturing talent, giving his chefs the scope to develop, and Clare Smyth has made RGR her own. It's a plush room with an art deco finish, and despite the relatively small scale of the space, there's enough room between tables and an air of exclusivity all round. The service, led by Jean-Claude Breton, has long been a stand-out feature of a visit, and it remains charming, gracious and extremely proficient. There are a host of menus to choose from, starting with the set lunch (not so much a bargain as a decent entry point), and extending up to the 'Seasonal Inspiration' tasting menu, which consists of seven inspired courses. Ramsay's favoured cooking style has always come under the modern French banner, which continues under Clare Smyth, with lots of luxury ingredients of quite outstanding quality. From the carte, a first course dish of poached Scottish lobster tail with lardo di Colonnata, pickled vegetables and coral vinaigrette is a stunning combination, the flavours judged just right, while another consists of a pressing of foie gras with green apples, turnips and smoked duck. Everything is presented with visual impact, every flavour and texture plays its part in creating the complete dish. Main-course Cornish turbot is baked on the bone and served with seaweed and Palourde clams, while another main puts Cotswold lamb at the centre of things, with its best end, braised shank, confit breast and shoulder. There are cheeses from the trolley – perfect, truly – and desserts like an English peppermint soufflé with a bitter chocolate sorbet display the same level of technical virtuosity and spectacular presentation. To cap it all off, the wine list, under the auspices of sommelier Jan Konetzki, is a serious piece of work packed with goodies from the world's top producers (at a price of course).

Chef Gordon Ramsay, Clare Smyth **Owner** Gordon Ramsay Holdings Ltd **Seats** 45 **Times** 12-2.15/6.30-10.15 Closed 1 wk Xmas, Sat-Sun **Prices** Fixed L 3 course £55, Tasting menu £135-£185 **Wines** 1300 bottles over £30, 5 bottles under £30, 22 by glass **Parking Notes** ALC 3 course £95, Tasting menu 7 course, Children welcome

LONDON SW4

Bistro Union

PLAN 1 E2

◉ ◉ British

tel: 020 7042 6400 **40 Abbeville Rd, Clapham SW4 9NG**
email: eat@bistrounion.co.uk
dir: *Nearest station: Clapham South*

True-Brit food in neighbourhood bistro

Chef-proprietor Adam Byatt certainly seems comfortable in Clapham. His Trinity operation (see entry), which opened in 2006, has gone from strength to strength to be the top dog in the postcode, and it is now joined by this new, more informal neighbourhood venture. A simple, de-cluttered brasserie-style decor sits well with the local clientele in the trendy Abbeville enclave: there are stripped wood floors, chunky unclothed tables, and a central bar where you can perch on wooden stools with your cutlery and menu in individual drawers under the counter, perusing a bar menu of on-trend nibbles (pork scratchings, pickled quail's eggs, winkles and pickled shallots, to name but three) hand-written onto a roll of brown paper. The food is in the day-to-day hands of Karl Goward who comes from Fergus Henderson's St John Bread and Wine (see entry), so you can expect a no-nonsense approach with a nod to the 'nose-to-tail' eating style. What leaves the kitchen is creative, fun, and built with British-led ingredients – perhaps beer and onion soup with Welsh rarebit, or baked aubergine with cow's curd and mint to start, then more of the same butch, true-Brit ideas, along the lines of Cumberland toad in the hole with Guinness onions.

Chef Karl Goward, Adam Byatt **Owner** Adam Byatt **Seats** 40 **Times** 12-3/6-10 Closed 24-27 Dec, 1-2 Jan, D Sun **Prices** Starter £4-£7, Main £11-£24, Dessert £5-£6 **Wines** 27 bottles over £30, 12 bottles under £30, 13 by glass **Parking** On street **Notes** D Sun 6-8pm 3 course £27, Brunch available wknds, Sunday L £11-£24, Vegetarian available, Children welcome

The Dairy

PLAN 1 E2

◉ ◉ Modern British V

tel: 020 7622 4165 **15 The Pavement, Clapham SW4 0HY**
email: bookings@the-dairy.co.uk
dir: *Nearest station: Clapham Common*

Relaxed bar-bistro serving innovative modern food

Its central Clapham location – looking out over the common just a few paces from the tube – isn't The Dairy's only draw, as this relaxed, on-cue outfit is home to some seriously fine cooking at accessible prices. From the outside it looks unremarkable, but step inside and you'll find it a friendly, welcoming and popular place, with a dinky bar up front and a bistro behind with a pared-back look of recycled and reclaimed furniture and fittings, flag-stoned floors and an open kitchen. The cooking is clever and innovative, producing well-crafted dishes that are light and colourful with clean flavours and modern presentation. Some of the seasonal ingredients used come from The Dairy's own urban garden. Kick off with some fresh sourdough bread with home-made smoked bone marrow butter, then choose a selection of small plates from the varied menu. You might begin with a plate of potted salmon with Guinness soda bread, or some slices of excellent salumi, moving on to garden-fresh peas with celery, mint and fried bread, and perhaps sea-fresh West Coast lemon sole teamed with maple pancetta and ember oil buttermilk. For dessert, how about Lincolnshire rhubarb (nicely tart) with contrasting sweet hibiscus meringue, pumpkin seeds and rhubarb ice cream?

Chef Robin Gill **Owner** Robin & Sarah Gill, Matt Wells **Seats** 40 **Times** 12-11 Closed Xmas, Mon, L Tue, D Sun All-day dining **Prices** Tasting menu £35-£45, Starter £5-£8, Main £8.50-£10, Dessert £6 **Wines** 20 bottles over £30, 18 bottles under £30, 7 by glass **Notes** Fixed L 4 course £25, Seasonal menu changes, Sunday L, Children welcome

Trinity Restaurant

LONDON SW4

PLAN 1 E2

British, European V

tel: 020 7622 1199 **4 The Polygon, Clapham SW4 0JG**
email: dine@trinityrestaurant.co.uk
dir: *Nearest station: Clapham Common*

Dynamic modern cooking in Clapham

Adam Byatt is a singular kind of chef who has bought a run-down gaff in Clapham and turned it into a hot-house of creative culinary endeavour, showing confidence and a good deal of nous. Where others might run a neighbourhood restaurant to bring easy comfort to the locals, Byatt dazzles with inventive contemporary cuisine. The food does the talking. That's not to say it isn't a nice place to pass time but the energies of this chef are focused on the food on the plate. There are white linen cloths on the tables, a trendy zinc-topped bar, modern artworks and windows that open up when the sun shines on Clapham. There's a tasting menu and carte available lunch and dinner, plus a good-value lunch, and even a Sunday lunch menu which might serve up a powerhouse roast of 40-day-aged Dexter beef with Yorkshire pudding, among other things. Everything looks amazing on the plate – if indeed it comes on a plate – and the evident skill and

attention to detail of the food never fails to impress. Sweetcorn soup with chicken confit and summer truffles demonstrates real depth of flavour, while another first course of crispy trotters with gribiche, quail's egg and crackling reveals classical leanings. The menu evolves through the seasons with a new dish arriving every week or so. Main course begins new season lamb is another plateful of superbly judged flavours, with sweet and sour peppers and smoked goats' cheese knitting together to form a satisfying whole. Among desserts, lemon sponge is as delicate as can be, with fresh ricotta, crisp honeycomb and crème fraîche sorbet, or there might be prune and Armagnac soufflé with spiced bread ice cream. Lucky, lucky Clapham.

Chef Adam Byatt, Graham Squire **Owner** Angus Jones & Adam Byatt **Seats** 61, Pr/dining room 12 **Times** 12.30-2.30/6.30-10 Closed 24-27 Dec, 1-2 Jan, L Mon, D Sun **Prices** Fixed L 2 course £22, Tasting menu £50-£55, Starter £7-£13, Main £25-£34, Dessert £7-£9 **Wines** 205 bottles over £30, 22 bottles under £30, 15 by glass **Parking** On street **Notes** Sunday L £32, Children welcome

LONDON SW4 *continued*

Trinity Restaurant
PLAN 1 E2

@@@ – *see page 319*

Tsunami
PLAN 1 F2

@ Japanese

tel: 020 7978 1610 **5-7 Voltaire Rd SW4 6DQ**
email: clapham@tsunamirestaurant.co.uk
dir: *Nearest station: Clapham North*

Cool minimalism and Japanese fusion food

This original branch of the two Tsunami outlets (the other is on Charlotte Street in the West End) has been making waves in Clapham's hinterland for a dozen years and still gets rammed with crowds of thirty-somethings eager for first-class sushi and sashimi and slick modern Japanese fusion food. A confection of grey, black and gold hues – including faux crocodile-skin banquettes, an open-to-view kitchen and clubby cocktail bar – hits all the fashionable notes, while pavement-side tables offer alfresco dining. Okay, the open-planned space may be hard-edged and high-decibel, but it's really sociable, with the kitchen delivering fresh, skilful, smart-looking classic-meets-contemporary dishes designed for sharing and grazing. Witness unagi (freshwater eel) and foie gras nigiri to seafood tempura, or mains like top-dollar grilled black cod in sweet miso, to truffle rib-eye, while crossover desserts could feature a lemongrass and lime pannacotta.

Chef Ken Sam **Owner** Ken Sam **Seats** 90 **Times** 12.30-3.30/5.30-11 Closed 24-26 Dec, 1 Jan, L Mon-Fri **Prices** Fixed L 2 course £15, Starter £4.65-£12.50, Main £9.75-£28, Dessert £3.95-£6.50 **Wines** 23 bottles over £30, 11 bottles under £30, 11 by glass **Parking** On street **Notes** Fixed D 5 course £37/£42, Sunday L £4.65-£12.50, Vegetarian available, Children welcome

LONDON SW5

The Abbeville Kitchen
PLAN 4 A3

@ British, European

tel: 020 8772 1110 & 3163 0699 **47 Abbeville Rd SW5 9QN**
email: food@abbevillekitchen.com
dir: *Nearest station: Clapham Common, Clapham South*

Top-notch cooking with a nod to the Med in a buzzing restaurant

The Abbeville Kitchen is the kind of neighbourhood restaurant every neighbourhood should have. Squeezed in amongst the shops and restaurants in a residential street near Clapham Common, it looks rather café-like from the outside, but behind that unassuming frontage there's an awful lot going on. The menu changes daily, so you can be assured the ingredients are always super-fresh, and everything, including some drinks, is made in-house. You can sit up at the small bar at the front or head for one of the wooden tables in the buzzy restaurant with its semi-open kitchen. The menu is mostly Spanish, with a bit of Italian and some British dishes thrown into the mix, so you might start with anticuchos – grilled skewers of herb-marinated ox heart, the meat wonderfully tender and full of flavour – or perhaps minestrone soup, or Hampshire pork and prune terrine. Main course could be as simple as a whole roast bream served with superb home-made chunky chips and aïoli, or roast lamb rump with chick peas and wild garlic. Torta de Santiago with crème fraîche and blood orange is a textbook version of the Spanish classic.

Chef Kevin McFadden **Owner** Kevin Hastings, Kevin McFadden, Tom Burchfield **Seats** 42 **Times** 12-3/6.30-11 Closed Xmas, 31 Dec, L Mon-Wed **Prices** Fixed L 2 course fr £10, Starter £5-£8, Main £12-£17, Dessert £5-£6, Service optional **Wines** 19 bottles over £30, 23 bottles under £30, 10 by glass **Parking** On street **Notes** Breakfast available Sat-Sun, Sunday L £16-£30, Vegetarian available, Children welcome

Cambio de Tercio
PLAN 4 C2

@@ Spanish V

tel: 020 7244 8970 **163 Old Brompton Rd SW5 0LJ**
email: cambiodeterciogroup@btconnect.com
dir: *Nearest station: Gloucester Road*

Vibrant modern Spanish cooking in a setting to match

With tapas joints Capote y Toros (see entry) and Tendido Cero, owner Abel Lusa has created a 'Little Spain' enclave on this bend in Old Brompton Road. In flagship Tercio, folding full-length glass windows open the place up to the street for a Mediterranean vibe, and there's a G&T bar with over 80 gins to tackle. Inside it has a dark, intimate, sexy Spanish feel – black slate floors and big and bold hues of mustard yellow and deep fuchsia pink hung with striking modern artworks. The modern Spanish food is equally colourful and good looking, ranging from traditional tapas done right, to innovative signature dishes with a homage to the legendary El Bulli here and there. Oxtail caramelised in red wine matched with apple and lemon-thyme air is a star turn, while more substantial mains run to Basque-style hake casserole with parsley sauce, razor clams, mussels and cockles, or grilled skate with crunchy pig's trotters, Burgos morcilla terrine and orange vinaigrette. Desserts keep the creativity on stream with the likes of crispy Cuban mojito in a caramel ball.

Chef Alberto Criado **Owner** Abel Lusa **Seats** 90, Pr/dining room 18 **Times** 12-2.30/6.30-11.30 Closed 2 wks at Xmas, New Year **Prices** Fixed D 3 course £40-£55, Tasting menu £39, Starter £3.75-£22.95, Main £19.50-£28, Dessert £7.50-£12 **Wines** 6 by glass **Parking** 10, Paid parking **Notes** Sunday L £23-£27, Children welcome

Capote y Toros
PLAN 4 C2

@ Spanish V

tel: 020 7373 0567 **157 Old Brompton Rd SW5 0LJ**
email: cambiodeterciogroup@btconnect.com
dir: *Nearest station: South Kensington, Gloucester Road*

Authentic tapas plus interesting specialities

A few doors away from sibling Cambio de Tercio, Capote y Toros describes itself as a tapas, ham and sherry bar. It has vivid decor with photographs of matadors and hams hanging from the ceiling above the bar. Live flamenco music and a friendly team providing attentive levels of service add to the laid-back sense of fun. More than 100 sherries and a patriotic wine list play a part too. Ask the staff about how much and what to order and jump in. Soft and tender chorizo cooked in fino, Galician-style octopus with potato and paprika, five pork meatballs with oloroso sauce and patatas bravas should see you right, being of exceptional quality and all cooked exactly as they would be back home. Don't overlook the specialities, among them loin of venison with baked apple and Pedro Ximénez sauce, and home-made cod sausage with peppers and vegetables. Among the puddings, try perhaps tipsy Spanish bread pudding with amontillado.

Chef Luis Navacerrada Lanzadera **Owner** Abel Lusa **Times** 6-11.30 Closed Xmas, Sun-Mon, L all week **Prices** Fixed D 3 course £12.75-£46, Starter £4-£22, Main £4.25-£10.50, Dessert £5.75-£6.90 **Wines** 110 bottles over £30, 35 bottles under £30 **Parking** On street **Notes** Children welcome

Find out more about how we assess for Rosette awards on page 9

New Lotus Garden

PLAN 4 B3

 Chinese V

tel: 020 7244 8984 **15 Kenway Rd SW5 ORP**
email: jiang.hubert@gmail.com
dir: *Nearest station: Earl's Court*

Neighbourhood Chinese that really hits the spot

Down a residential street in Earl's Court, the white-painted New Lotus Garden is a little powerhouse of Pekinese and Cantonese cooking. This is the domain of Hubert Jiang and it's only little and rather humble, but that's a good thing, and the warm red decor gives a comforting glow. The menu is long and doesn't really stand out from the crowd, but execution is good and the flavours sing out. Start with salt and pepper asparagus, or succulent barbecue spare ribs, or mussels in black bean sauce. There are dim sum dishes, too, plus crispy aromatic duck and soups like a classic chicken and sweetcorn version. Among main courses, twice-cooked belly of pork with preserved vegetables hits the spot, or try the spicy crispy shredded beef. Vegetarians get a decent amount of choice with things like aubergines braised in black bean sauce, and there is a good range of noodle dishes.

Chef Hubert Jiang **Owner** Hubert Jiang **Seats** 40 **Times** 12-2.30/5-11.30 Closed 24-26 Dec **Prices** Fixed L 2 course fr £12, Fixed D 3 course fr £15, Starter fr £4, Main fr £5.90, Dessert fr £2 **Wines** 2 by glass **Notes** Sunday L fr £10, Children welcome

---

LONDON SW6

Blue Elephant

PLAN 1 E3

 Thai V

tel: 020 7751 3111 **The Boulevard, Imperial Wharf, Townmead Rd SW6 2UB**
email: london@blueelephant.com
dir: *Nearest station: Imperial Wharf*

Lavish riverside setting for old Thai favourite

In its swanky new home since 2012, The Blue Elephant (originally on Fulham Broadway) pulls in an adoring crowd to the plush Thames-side development of Imperial Wharf. Some might find it a bit Footballers' Wives with its extravagant decor inspired by the Saran Rom palace in Bangkok: think wood carvings, warm colours, a forest of green foliage, chandeliers and drapes, and a gilded bar modelled on the Royal Barge of Thailand. The lengthy menu is a complicated beast, focusing on Thai cooking of 'the past', 'today' and 'tomorrow', while throwing in a couple of tasting options and a separate vegetarian section along the way. From the old days, perhaps lamb shank yellow curry, and, for something new, try wild-catch black pepper prawns (stir-fried with garlic and black pepper and topped with lemongrass). Service is charming and authentic and there's also a riverside alfresco terrace.

Chef Nooror Somany **Owner** Blue Elephant International Group **Seats** 150, Pr/dining room 8 **Times** 12-2.30/7-10.30 Closed 25-26 Dec, 1 Jan, L Mon **Prices** Fixed L 2 course fr £14, Tasting menu £38-£55, Starter £9-£15, Main £18-£30, Dessert £6.50-£9 **Wines** 100 bottles over £30, 5 bottles under £30, 13 by glass **Parking** Car park next to Imperial Wharf tube station **Notes** Sunday L fr £30, Children welcome

The Harwood Arms

PLAN 1 E3

  British

tel: 020 7386 1847 **27 Walham Grove, Fulham SW6 1QR**
email: admin@harwoodarms.com
dir: *Nearest station: Fulham Broadway*

Supplier-led British cooking in smart gastro-pub

On an unassuming backstreet in trendy Fulham, the stylish Harwood Arms is one of Britain's top gastro-pubs, all the more so as it remains true to its roots as a cracking community local – Tuesday night is quiz night, there's a raft of real ales on tap, and the overall vibe is relaxed and informal. With Brett Graham of The Ledbury (see entry) and The Pot Kiln's (see entry) Mike Robinson as owners, you've a right to have high expectations. And they are duly met. Inside you could almost forget you're in London with photos of outdoor country pursuits hung on grey and cream walls, and rustic wooden tables. On the menu, first class, carefully-sourced English produce is cooked with confidence; Berkshire rabbit faggots, for example, with split peas, smoked bacon and pickled mushrooms, a robust way to start, before moving on to Gloucestershire Old Spot pork belly with root vegetable broth and ribs glazed in ginger beer, or wild sea bass with cauliflower, oat-crusted mussels and preserved lemon. And neither do desserts miss a beat: baked stem ginger custard with honeycomb ice cream is an unerringly satisfying finale.

Times 12-3/6.30-9.30 Closed 24-28 Dec, 1 Jan, L Mon

Marco Grill

PLAN 1 E3

  British Grill

tel: 020 7915 2929 **M&C Hotels At Chelsea FC, Stamford Bridge, Fulham Rd SW6 1HS**
email: info@marcogrill.com
dir: *Nearest station: Fulham Broadway*

MPW brasserie-style dishes at Stamford Bridge

Yes, it is that Marco who is the man behind this high-gloss operation, so rest assured that MPW's signature style of tried-and-tested French brasserie dishes is stamped all over the carte, and it is all driven by top-class ingredients, sharply-defined flavours and classy execution. Although the Blues' supporters would no doubt appreciate the excellent range of ales on offer, this is a world a long, long way from the pies and hotdogs that traditionally fuel footie fans: a chic decor brings together charcoal-grey walls, smoked mirrors, low-level lighting, and leather banquettes and velour seats at linen-swathed tables. A charcuterie platter with cornichons and silverskin onions sets out in fine Gallic style, then roast cod is served with buttered spinach, cucumber and brown shrimps. However, top-class 35-day-aged steaks are the main culinary thrust here, or meaty fare such as roast rack of lamb with Mediterranean vegetables, gratin dauphinoise and sauce Paloise. The menu comes back across the Channel to end with flag-waving puddings along the lines of champagne rhubarb crumble with vanilla ice cream.

Chef Roger Pizey **Owner** C.F.C **Seats** 70 **Times** 6-10.30 Closed 2 wks Jul-Aug, Sun-Mon, L all week **Prices** Starter £7-£11, Main £13-£31, Dessert £5.50-£7 **Wines** 20 bottles over £30, 7 bottles under £30, 8 by glass **Parking** 10 **Notes** Steak club Thu, Vegetarian available, Children welcome

---

Follow the AA on twitter @TheAA_Lifestyle

What makes a 3-Rosette restaurant?
See page 9

Baglioni Hotel
PLAN 4 C5

 Modern Italian

tel: 020 7368 5700 **60 Hyde Park Gate, Kensington Rd SW7 5BB**
email: brunello.london@baglionihotels.com web: www.baglionihotels.com
dir: *Nearest station: Kensington High Street*

Modern Italian cooking in swish hotel

The Baglioni's Brunello restaurant is an open-plan bar-lounge and stylish dining room with plush seating, rich fabrics, chandeliers and charming and attentive staff, mostly Italian. Ingredients are diligently sought out, many from the motherland, to re-create the modern Italian cooking style, as in a richly flavoured starter of caponata and burrata cheese drizzled with olive oil, and smoked swordfish with exotic fruit salad in a grape reduction. Pasta dishes are given their due – perhaps pappardelle with veal ragù and broad beans – and main courses have included pink and succulent veal chop with creamy mash and sautéed spinach, and chargrilled prawns and squid with baby seasonal vegetables. There's a great range of home-made breads, and among dolci might be vanilla cheesecake with cherry sorbet.

Chef Claudio Milani **Owner** Baglioni Hotels **Seats** 70, Pr/dining room 60 **Times** 12.30-3/5.30-11 **Prices** Fixed L 2 course £18-£65.50, Fixed D 3 course fr £29, Starter £12-£21, Main £18.50-£34.50, Dessert £8 **Wines** 4 bottles under £30, 8 by glass **Parking** 2, On street Kensington Rd/De Vere Gardens **Notes** Pre-theatre menu 5.30-7pm all wk £25-£29, Sunday L £18-£22.50, Vegetarian available, Children welcome

Bombay Brasserie
PLAN 4 C3

 Indian

tel: 020 7370 4040 **Courtfield Close, Courtfield Rd SW7 4QH**
email: info@bbrestaurant.co.uk
dir: *Nearest station: Gloucester Road*

Long-running stylish address with modern Indian cooking

It's hard to believe that the Bombay has been feeding London with authentic, carefully crafted Indian food for over 30 years, but so it is. The Kensington location ensures a lot of plutocratic custom, but the place has always had wide appeal. There are two stylish dining rooms, one of deep-pile banquettes under statement chandeliers, the other a lighter conservatory-roofed space. The food is presented as elegantly as contemporary western cuisine, its spices and seasonings guaranteed to make the palate sit up and take notice. Start with crisp-fried spinach in evanescently thin batter, dressed with date and tamarind chutney and yoghurt, or with cakes of shredded duck meat stuffed with red onions in yoghurt and mint. Those might be followed by corn-fed chicken tikka marinated in cardamom, coriander and garlic, masala sea bass with mushrooms, or a majestic seafood platter that includes, among other items, prawns with green mango, soft-shell crab and tandoori monkfish. Keep on going to dessert stage, and don't miss the almond and date pudding, with fennel and cracked pepper sauce and rose ice cream.

Chef Prahlad Hegde **Owner** Taj International Hotels **Seats** 185, Pr/dining room 16 **Times** 12-3/6.30-11.30 Closed 25 Dec **Prices** Fixed L 3 course £24, Fixed D 3 course £43-£60, Tasting menu £48-£56, Starter £7-£12, Main £16-£31 **Wines** 97 bottles over £30, 7 bottles under £30, 18 by glass **Parking** Millennium Gloucester Hotel next door **Notes** Sunday L £29, Vegetarian available, No children

Bulgari Hotel & Residences
PLAN 4 F5

Rosettes not confirmed at time of going to print

Modern French

tel: 020 7151 1010 & 7151 1025 **171 Knightsbridge SW7 1DW**
email: reservations@rivealondon.com web: www.rivealondon.com
dir: *Nearest station: Knightsbridge*

Franco-Italian cooking in incomparably stylish surroundings

Alain Ducasse has already made an impact in London at the Dorchester and as we go to press he's opened Rivea in the swish Bulgari Hotel. Too late for the award of Rosettes this year, the legendary chef has protégé Damien Leroux heading up the kitchen on Knightsbridge. Despite the postcode, Rivea is about informal and relaxed dining. The Riviera is the inspiration for the menu (that's the one in the Med, not Devon), with the flavours of Italy and France combining to create dynamic and classic flavour combinations. Small plates are the deal, for sharing or keeping to yourself, with the dishes arriving from the kitchen as and when they are ready. Red mullet with confit tomatoes and olives captures the essence of the cuisine to a T, as does another dish of warm octopus and potato salad. There are pasta courses such as ravioli filled with artichoke and borage, or another with Sicilian casareccia pasta served with raw and cooked courgettes. Corn-fed chicken comes with macaroni au gratin, and roasted duck with tender turnips and beetroots, with chocolate tart or tiramisù for dessert.

Chef Damien Leroux **Seats** 80, Pr/dining room 12 **Times** 12-2.30/6.30-10.30 **Prices** Fixed L 3 course £35, Starter £7-£11, Main £8-£23, Dessert £5-£6 **Wines** 200 bottles over £30, 5 bottles under £30, 15 by glass **Parking** NCP Pavillion Road **Notes** Sunday L £35, Vegetarian available, Children welcome

L'Etranger
PLAN 4 C4

French, Japanese ■ NOTABLE WINE LIST

tel: 020 7584 1118 & 7823 9291 **36 Gloucester Rd SW7 4QT**
email: etranger@etranger.co.uk
dir: *Nearest station: Gloucester Road*

A happy marriage between France and Japan in a swanky setting

Decked out in soothing shades of silver-grey with oak flooring, fashionable dark-leather seating, mirrors, striking floral displays and windows screened with sparkling beads, intimate L'Etranger delivers a classy calmness that fits with its modern French credentials and flirtation with Japanese cooking. The private dining area has similar good looks and wine-bottle-lined walls. The kitchen's fine-tuned roster is driven by tip-top produce, a hint of luxury, flavour and well-dressed presentation. Take Scottish John Dory fillet say, perhaps teamed with a clam risotto, baby leeks and Riesling sauce, or an Asian-inspired caramelised Alaskan black cod with miso, sushi rice and pickled ginger. Desserts take up the theme too, running from a classic apple tarte Tatin to chocolate fondant with green tea ice cream. The location ensures some gold-card prices, though this is tempered by good-value lunch, early bird and weekend brunch offerings, and service is thoroughly professional and eager to please (including a sommelier for an absolute corking tome of a wine list). Downstairs, evenings-only venue Meursault offers a more casual take on the L'Etranger theme.

Chef Jerome Tauvron **Owner** Ibi Issolah **Seats** 64, Pr/dining room 20 **Times** 12-3/5.30-11 Closed 26-27 Dec **Prices** Fixed L 2 course £17.50, Fixed D 3 course £48-£58, Starter £8.50-£16.50, Main £18.50-£96, Dessert £7.50-£12.50 **Wines** 1400 bottles over £30, 60 bottles under £30, 12 by glass **Parking** NCP **Notes** Degustation 5/6 course £65/£95, Early bird Mon-Fri 6-6.45pm, Sunday L £95, Vegetarian available, Children welcome

Millennium Bailey's Hotel London Kensington

PLAN 4 C3

Italian

tel: 020 7331 6308 **140 Gloucester Rd SW7 4QH**
email: olives.baileys@millenniumhotels.co.uk web: www.millenniumhotels.co.uk
dir: *Nearest station: Gloucester Road*

Italian cooking in smart townhouse hotel

The setting may be a blue-blooded, beautifully restored Victorian townhouse in Kensington, but the language changes to Italian in the Olives Restaurant. Waiting staff bring an authentic Italian buzz to a modern setting of bare darkwood tables and contemporary artwork on rich blue walls, while an open kitchen adds a further dynamic element to proceedings. A glass of prosecco in the stylish bar should cement the feel-good mood before tucking into a mix of classic and updated dishes all made with well-sourced materials. Get going with excellent bread and olive oil, then follow with risotto of wood pigeon and artichokes, or venison ragoût with red wine and juniper berries. Main courses offer classic osso buco Milanese alongside oven-baked monkfish served with spelt and olives in clam guazzetto. Check out the keenly-priced lunch special and pre-theatre menus too.

Times 12-10.30

Zuma

PLAN 4 F5

Modern Japanese

tel: 020 7584 1010 **5 Raphael St, Knightsbridge SW7 1DL**
email: info@zumarestaurant.com
dir: *Nearest station: Knightsbridge*

Buzzy modern Japanese in fashionable Knightsbridge

With a network of branches spanning the planet from Miami to Hong Kong as well as Knightsbridge, Zuma is an expanding global brand. Its aim is to spread the word on the informal Japanese dining style, known as izakaya. The venue uses all the contemporary textures of blond wood, granite blocks, steel and glass you might expect in an über-chic, minimally Zen-like setting, but the vibe is the polar opposite of calm and relaxation when the crowds turn up (often in chauffeur-driven Bentleys – it's that sort of place) and fuel up on the 40 different types of sake in the buzzing bar. It is certainly not a case of style over substance: whether you are dining in the main restaurant or at the open robata grill and sushi counter, the cooking is defined by superb fresh ingredients, razor-sharp flavours and magnificent presentation. The sushi is exemplary and you could go about things tapas-style and graze through yellowtail sashimi with soy dashi, shallot and crispy garlic, then seared beef with soy, ginger, lime and coriander alongside pork skewers with yuzu mustard miso. Desserts can be a weaker element of the Japanese idiom, but a parfait-like caramelised chocolate saikoro with cocoa crumble holds its own.

Times 12-2.30/6-11 Closed 25 Dec

LONDON SW10

Chelsea Riverside Brasserie

PLAN 1 E3

Traditional British, French

tel: 020 7823 3000 **Wyndham Grand London, Chelsea Harbour SW10 0XG**
web: www.chelseariversidebrasserie.co.uk
dir: *Nearest station: Fulham Broadway, Imperial Wharf*

Marina dining in the heart of London

The boats in Chelsea harbour form the backdrop to the brasserie dining room of the Wyndham Grand. The vivid royal blue seats provide a luminosity the Thames river water is never likely to match, and floor-to-ceiling windows and terrace tables ensure what natural light is available is fully absorbed. The menu keeps on the straight and narrow with some familiar offerings jazzed up for the Chelsea set – prawn cocktail with a virgin bloody Mary jelly and celery oil, for example. A char-grilled artichoke and gruyère tart is a well-made opener, followed by seared turbot

with a garlicky potato purée and prawn bisque. There are pasta dishes and steaks cooked on the grill and served with French fries and a choice of sauces. Among desserts, a classic tarte Tatin comes with vanilla ice cream, and a flourless chocolate fondant is partnered with a pear sorbet.

Chef Imthiaz Kader **Seats** 75, Pr/dining room 12 **Times** 12-10.30 All-day dining **Prices** Fixed L 2 course £18, Fixed D 3 course £32-£42, Starter £7-£15, Main £16-£30, Dessert £7-£9, Service optional 12.5% **Wines** 40 bottles over £30, 20 bottles under £30, 24 by glass **Parking** NCP **Notes** Vegetarian available, Children welcome

Chutney Mary Restaurant

PLAN 1 E3

Indian

tel: 020 7351 3113 **535 King's Rd, Chelsea SW10 0SZ**
email: chutneymary@realindianfood.com
dir: *Nearest station: Fulham Broadway*

Stunning venue for Indian cooking that's a cut above

This glamorous Chelsea Indian has been going strong for more than two decades, and when you descend the staircase from the reception and first set eyes on the glittering spectacle that is the basement restaurant, you start to understand why. The place looks simply stunning, and the tricky decisions start before you've even looked at the menu: do you take a table in the opulently decorated split-level dining room, with its mirrored walls, rich orange hues, framed crystal-studded silk hangings and Raj-era sketches, or in the spacious conservatory, decked out greenhouse-style with trees and plants soaring towards the high ceiling? Wherever you sit, expect flickering candles on the linen-clad tables and friendly, professional service. The authentic Indian cooking is brought bang up-to-date with attractive, modern presentation, and the ingredients are top-notch. Start, perhaps, with tokri chaat, a crispy straw potato basket filled with traditional Indian street foods and topped with strained yoghurt and chutneys – a dish full of contrasts in texture, flavour and colour. Roast shoulder of tender lamb in a brown onion based sauce with fine green beans is a suitably modern take on a lamb curry. Round things off in a slightly more Western vein with a first-class coconut pannacotta with black cherry sorbet. The restaurant will relocate to St James from November 2014.

Chef Mr Manar Tulli **Owner** R Mathrani, N & C Panjabi **Seats** 110, Pr/dining room 24 **Times** 12.30-2.45/6.30-11.30 Closed L Mon-Fri, D 25 Dec **Prices** Starter £7.75-£11, Main £17.50-£26, Dessert £3-£7 **Wines** 18 by glass **Parking** Parking meters outside **Notes** Sunday L £26, Vegetarian available, Children welcome

Medlar Restaurant

PLAN 4 D1

– *see page 324*

The Painted Heron

PLAN 1 E3

Modern Indian

tel: 020 7351 5232 **112 Cheyne Walk SW10 0DJ**
email: thepaintedheron@btinternet.com
dir: *Nearest station: South Kensington*

First-rate modern Indian near the river

Rather secreted away on the north bank of the Thames close to Battersea Bridge, this Chelsea Indian is a thoroughly modern affair. The clean-lined interiors – think black lacquered leather upholstered chairs, white linen-clothed tables and plain walls dotted with modern art – deliver a stylish, on-vogue edge to the deceptively roomy dining area. The cooking is equally smart and modern, underpinned by seasonality and judicious spicing, and making use of produce not readily encountered on many Indian repertoires: take tandoor grilled squab pigeon breasts in tamarind to open, followed by the likes of diced rabbit in a hot Kajasthani jungle curry, or perhaps guinea fowl supreme in Karahi masala with chick peas and fried green chillies. Otherwise try black cod (spice roasted) in a Malabari curry, or lamb neck fillet in a Pakistani 'nihari' curry with kholrabi. The dessert list looks to the west

continued

LONDON SW10 *continued*

for something like a spot-on chocolate and pistachio fondant, while ancillaries (like naan or poppadoms and pickles) maintain the good form. There's plenty of spice-friendly wines too, and cigar smokers have the luxury of their own lounge out back.

Times 12-3/6.30-11 Closed Xmas, Etr, L Sat

The Butcher & Grill

PLAN 1 E3

Modern British

tel: 020 7924 3999 **39-41 Parkgate Rd, Battersea SW11 4NP**
email: info@thebutcherandgrill.com
dir: *Nearest station: Clapham Junction, Battersea*

A carnivore's delight in relaxed, modern warehouse-style setting

This all-day combo of butcher's shop, deli, coffee bar, and no-frills grill restaurant ticks all the modern lifestyle boxes in its warehouse setting. Its butcher's-apron-style striped awning makes it easy to spot, while inside the look is all exposed floorboards and brick, modern wood furniture, leather banquettes and big monochrome photos of livestock to reinforce the meaty theme. Top-grade ethically-reared meat is the mainstay of the brasserie-style menu, which majors around the grill, offering fab dry-aged and big-flavoured steaks, or the likes of Gloucestershire Old Spot pork chops; it's all handled simply but with skill. And there's much more besides, including classics like pie and mash or blackboard specials such as day-boat fish – maybe whole plaice simply served with sautéed potatoes, spinach and a lemon butter sauce. Non-carnivores aren't forgotten either, with decent veggie options like roasted butternut squash with cep and parmesan Wellington and a balsamic glaze. A rear terrace overlooks a disused Thames wharf, and there's a sibling branch in Wimbledon.

Chef Abbas Abbas **Owner** Dominic Ford **Seats** 64 **Times** 12-3/5.30-11 Closed 25-26 Dec, D Sun **Prices** Fixed L 2 course fr £13.95 **Wines** 16 by glass **Parking** On street -

some restrictions apply **Notes** Fixed L available Mon-Fri, Brunch available wknds & BHs, Sunday L, Vegetarian available, Children welcome

---

Entrée Restaurant and Bar

PLAN 1 E2

Modern European

tel: 020 7223 5147 **2 Battersea Rise, Battersea SW11 1ED**
email: info@entreebattersea.co.uk
dir: *Nearest station: Clapham Junction, Clapham Common*

Buzzing neighbourhood restaurant and bar

It's easy to see why this smart but relaxed venue – complete with bijou low-lit cocktail bar and jazz piano on the lower floor and atmospheric dining room above-is such a big hit with the Battersea/Clapham set. There's an on-cue open kitchen, while wooden floors, black leather banquettes and unclothed tables create a laid-back fashionable tone. Thoughtfully presented food-on a regularly changing menu-comes prepared from fresh, seasonal, quality Brit ingredients, with the cooking influenced by France. Ambition is apparent yet it's skilfully restrained, with light, refined, eye-catching dishes the kitchen's forte. Take a duo of lamb (succulent rump and full-flavoured shoulder) teamed with a Med-inspired combo of tomato, chargrilled courgette and olive and pommes purées, or for fish lovers, perhaps sea bass, the fillet seared and served with braised baby gem, crushed new potatoes and cauliflower. Do save room for desserts like a classy bitter chocolate délice with pistachio ice cream and a wow-inducing blood orange purée to cut through the richness. Relaxed small-plate dining is offered in the bar.

Chef Ian Owen **Owner** Jayke Mangion, Gerry O'Keefe **Seats** 55 **Times** 12-4/6-10.30 Closed 1 wk Xmas, Mon, L Tue-Fri, D Sun **Prices** Fixed L 2 course £19.50, Fixed D 3 course £23.50, Tasting menu £55-£75, Starter £6.50-£11, Main £15.50-£21.50, Dessert £5-£7 **Wines** 19 bottles over £30, 19 bottles under £30, 10 by glass **Parking** On street **Notes** Sun Brunch available, Sunday L £15-£22.50, Vegetarian available, Children welcome

---

Medlar Restaurant

LONDON SW10   PLAN 4 D1

Modern European **NOTABLE WINE LIST**

tel: 020 7349 1900 **438 King's Rd, Chelsea SW10 0LJ**
email: info@medlarrestaurant.co.uk
dir: *Nearest station: Sloane Square, Earl's Court, Fulham Broadway*

Highly skilled cooking and a refreshing lack of pretension

It can be a fine line between success and failure in the restaurant game, but some people manage to make success look very easy indeed, and these include Joe Mercer Nairne and David O'Connor. Medlar is one of those restaurants that goes about its business with a quiet confidence: the menu reads (and eats) like a foodie's dream, the service is slick but not overbearing, and the prices are reasonable, particularly considering the trendy King's Road location looks good from the street with cool, muted colour tones, awning, and doors that open up to give that European vibe in the warmer months (there are actually a few tables outside as well). Inside it is simply elegant, not casual, but not over-conceptualised either – sage-green banquettes, mirrored walls and tables dressed in white linen, the designer touches are present but not in your face. It is

restrained and confident – a bit like the cooking. The food has a rustic charm about it, but it is far from unsophisticated: the only fly in the ointment is having to choose what to eat when you want to eat it all. What food lover could pass up the chance to kick off with duck egg tart with red wine sauce, turnip purée, lardons and sautéed duck heart, or slow-cooked cuttlefish with Morteau sausage, saffron, sherry, soft white polenta and gremolata? And that's just the starters. Next up, duck breast and confit leg with Puy lentils, beetroot, mustard fruits and paysanne salad competes for your attention with roast cod with boulangère potatoes, Jerusalem artichoke purée, Swiss chard and salmoriglio sauce. For dessert, lemon curd beignet with lemon sorbet and Chantilly cream and chocolate tart with salted caramel and praline parfait maintain the high standards to the very end.

Chef Joe Mercer Nairne **Owner** Joe Mercer Nairne, David O'Connor **Seats** 85, Pr/dining room 28 **Times** 12-3/6.30-10.30 Closed Xmas, New Year **Prices** Fixed L 2 course £22-£30, Fixed D 3 course £35-£45 **Wines** 400+ bottles over £30, 35 bottles under £30, 15 by glass **Parking** On street (may be difficult during lunch) **Notes** Prix Fixe menu available, Sat L 2/3 course £25/£30, Sunday L fr £35, Vegetarian available, Children welcome

London House

PLAN 1 E3

◉◉ Modern European NEW

tel: 020 7592 8545 & 7592 7952 **7-9 Battersea Square, Battersea Village SW11 3RA**
email: londonhouse@gordonramsay.com
dir: Nearest station: Clapham Junction

Classy neighbourhood restaurant and bar-lounge from the Ramsay stable

Smack on the corner of Battersea Square, Gordon Ramsay's latest offering has an unmistakable touch of 'classy neighbourhood outfit' about it. The buff lounge looks more Mayfair than SW11 (great for cocktails, as is the copper-topped bar), while white linen and smartly dressed, switched-on staff look the part too. A series of light, interconnecting rooms (with large 'window-like' openings set into the walls) offer an uptempo vibe and score high in the good-look stakes, the striking artwork and stylish seating (baguettes and voguish chairs) blending with fashionable dark wood floors. Chef Anna Haugh-Kelly's fixed-priced market-driven menus fit the bill too, influenced by her international career (think gremolata-crusted yellow fin tuna, golden beetroot and anchovy) and displays real talent. Light (almost 'tasting' size), fresh, of-the-moment dishes show her impressive credentials, alongside precision and flair. Take an opener of tortellini rammed with crab and served with black radish and a tableside jug of shellfish broth, or signature mains like succulent Cumbrian beef fillet teamed with 'wow' broad bean purée and 'knock-out' braised cheek stuffed potato gnocchi and requisite mini-saucepan of jus to add theatre.

Chef Anna Haugh-Kelly **Owner** Gordon Ramsay **Seats** 63 **Times** 12-3/6-10 Closed Mon (exc BHs), L Tue-Thu **Prices** Fixed L 3 course £28, Fixed D 3 course £40, Service optional 12.5% **Wines** 180 bottles over £30, 22 bottles under £30, 13 by glass **Parking** On street **Notes** Vegetarian available, Children welcome

LONDON SW12

Harrison's

PLAN 1 E2

◉ Modern British

tel: 020 8675 6900 **15-19 Bedford Hill, Balham SW12 9EX**
email: info@harrisonsbalham.co.uk
dir: Nearest station: Balham

Casual all-day brasserie for simple cooking and a friendly vibe

The Balham crowd have taken this cool and relaxed all-day brasserie and bar into their hearts. And no wonder: with its cheery vibe, upbeat music and smiling staff, it's the sort of place you'd like on your manor for easygoing, reliable dining. Full-length windows fold back to open the place up to the pavement tables; indoors, the action revolves around a central stainless steel open kitchen with low-slung lights and a bar on one side, and two dining areas with the modern good looks of bright-red banquettes, grey tiled walls, industrial-style wall lights, bare darkwood tables and booths. The menu delivers simple, robust ideas – ham hock and black pudding fritters with celeriac purée to get things off the blocks, then mains as simple as whole Cornish plaice with new potatoes and brown caper butter. To finish, it's worth the short wait for chocolate fondant baked to order and matched with salted caramel ice cream.

Chef Greig Hunter **Owner** Sam Harrison **Seats** 80, Pr/dining room 40 **Times** 12-12 Closed 24-27 Dec, All-day dining **Prices** Fixed L 2 course £13.50, Fixed D 3 course £16.50, Starter £5.50-£9.50, Main £11.50-£23.50, Dessert £4.50-£8.50 **Wines** 24 bottles over £30, 32 bottles under £30, 22 by glass **Parking** On street **Notes** Fixed L Mon-Fri, D Sun-Thu, Sunday L £14.50-£16.50, Vegetarian available, Children welcome

Lamberts

PLAN 1 E2

◉◉ Modern British

tel: 020 8675 2233 **2 Station Pde, Balham High Rd SW12 9AZ**
email: bookings@lambertsrestaurant.com
dir: Nearest station: Balham

Top-notch produce treated with respect in a smart, modern setting

Just a minute's stroll from the tube station, this smart eatery makes the idea of a foray into Balham a more inviting prospect than might otherwise be the case. The compact space wears an inoffensively neutral modern look with mustard yellow walls, chocolate brown banquettes, bare darkwood tables and dark hardwood flooring – nothing to stand out from many an urban brasserie, perhaps, but it is apparent when the food arrives that the place is driven by a passion for sourcing top-class ingredients, and a chef who knows how to make their flavours shout out loud. There's certainly much more going on than the dishes' minimal menu descriptions would suggest: confit trout with potato salad and watercress bursts with subtle notes, while a main course of Herdwick lamb with peas, wilted gem lettuce and mash gains lustre from the sheer quality of the produce. For dessert, a textbook chocolate fondant mingles wickedly with stout ice cream.

Chef Ryan Lowery **Owner** Mr Joe Lambert **Seats** 50 **Times** 12.30-2.30/6-10 Closed 25 Dec, BHs (except Good Fri), Mon, D Sun **Prices** Fixed L 2 course £17, Fixed D 3 course £20, Starter £7-£10, Main £15-£25, Dessert £6-£9 **Wines** 33 bottles over £30, 25 bottles under £30, 13 by glass **Parking** On street **Notes** Sunday L £28, Vegetarian available, Children welcome

LONDON SW13

Sonny's Kitchen

PLAN 1 D3

◉◉ Modern British, French

tel: 020 8748 0393 & 8741 8451 **94 Church Rd, Barnes SW13 0DQ**
email: manager@sonnyskitchen.co.uk
dir: Nearest station: Barnes

Popular and highly regarded neighbourhood restaurant

Sonny's, part restaurant, part food store, has occupied its premises in a parade of shops for a generation. Chefs may come and go, but constant updating and reinvention keep the place ahead of the game, and changes in decor make for a comfortable, relaxing and welcoming space. The sensibly concise menu offers enough variety and sunny Mediterranean accents to keep regulars returning again and again. Standards are consistently high, whether it's a neatly tweaked classic – grilled asparagus with a deep-fried bantam's egg and wild garlic aïoli, say – or foie gras and chicken liver parfait with pickles and toasted sourdough bread. Otherwise, start with the likes of nettle and lovage soup with poached haddock and Jersey Royals before main courses like pan-fried sea bass with prawn and saffron risotto or a veggie offering of roast artichoke and cauliflower with duck egg, wild mushrooms and truffle. Puddings end on a satisfying note: vanilla pannacotta with passionfruit and lime shortbread, or rice pudding with rhubarb compôte, or lavender cheesecake with Eton mess.

Chef James Holah **Owner** Rebecca Mascarenhas, Phil Howard **Seats** 100, Pr/dining room 18 **Times** 12-2.30/6.30-10.30 Closed Xmas, New Year **Prices** Fixed L 2 course £16.50, Fixed D 3 course £18.50, Starter £6.50-£10.50, Main £11.50-£19.50, Dessert £6-£8.50, Service optional 12.5% **Wines** 36 bottles over £30, 24 bottles under £30, 20 by glass **Parking** On street **Notes** Brunch available Sat-Sun 10-noon, Sunday L £21-£25, Vegetarian available, Children welcome

LONDON SW14

The Depot
PLAN 1 D3

Modern European, British

tel: 020 8878 9462 **Tideway Yard, 125 Mortlake High St, Barnes SW14 8SN**
email: info@depotbrasserie.co.uk
dir: *Nearest station: Barnes Bridge*

Popular, relaxed, neighbourhood-style riverside brasserie

Thames-view tables in the dining room and bar are The Depot's principle draw-card, while a sunny terrace in the cobbled courtyard out front offers alfresco opportunities without the watery vista. The interior is relaxed and unstuffy rather than big-city cool: banquette seating and café-style chairs combine with pastel tones, simple wooden tables and herringbone-patterned floorboards. The service fits the unpretentious, upbeat vibe, while the kitchen's modern, simply constructed, please-all, brasserie-style roster comes with an occasional nod to sunnier climes. A classic bouillabaisse might start you off, followed by stone bass and scallops served with crayfish, tarragon and baby spinach risotto, or a grilled leg of lamb steak teamed with baby carrots, borlotti bean stew and spinach. Comfort-zone desserts might offer Eton Mess or the ubiquitous sticky toffee pudding. Fixed-price options and bar and children's menus help keep the Barnes locals returning.

Chef Gary Knowles **Owner** Tideway Restaurants Ltd **Seats** 120, Pr/dining room 60 **Times** 12-3.30/6-10 **Prices** Fixed L 2 course £13.50, Fixed D 3 course £18, Starter £5-£8.50, Main £10.95-£21.95, Dessert £5.95-£6, Service optional 12.5% **Wines** 13 bottles over £30, 33 bottles under £30, 20 by glass **Parking** Parking after 6.30pm & at wknds **Notes** Brunch available Sat & BH Mon 11-1pm, Sunday L £5-£21.95, Vegetarian available, Children welcome

LONDON SW15

Bibo
PLAN 1 D2

Modern Italian **NEW**

tel: 020 8780 0592 **146 Upper Richmond, Putney SW15 2SW**
email: info@biborestaurant.com
dir: *Nearest station: East Putney*

Relaxed, high-energy East Putney Italian with bags of pedigree

Rebecca Mascarenhas, London restaurateur with the Midas touch when it comes to neighbourhood outfits (think Kitchen W8, Sonny's, etc), launched this cracking local Italian back in March 2014 and it hit the ground running. Head chef Chris Beverley has pedigree too (ex Theo Randall at The InterContinental and Chez Bruce) and it shows on the menu and plate. In classic Italain style, and, with a strong regional accent, simple seasonal combinations allow prime ingredients to shine. Pasta is a forte, perhaps spot-on taglierini nero teamed with octopus and pepped up by chilli and garlic, while mains, like sparkling-fresh sea bream, deliver brilliantly with squeaky-fresh asparagus and spinach. Desserts (pannacotta with poached rhubarb), in-house breads, all-Italian wines and sunny service maintain stellar form. The fashionable pared-back surroundings fit the neighbourhood billing, with street-side terrace and bar up front (and all-day small-plate dining), while the two-tiered dining room behind comes with vibrant Bruce McLean prints, and the upper-level with conservatory-style overhead windows. Otherwise, white-washed brickwork, small waxed-oak tables, banquettes or café-style chairs and high decibels complete the on-cue look.

Chef Chris Beverely **Owner** R Mascarenhas **Seats** 70 **Times** 12-2.30/6-10.30 Closed 24-26 Dec, BHs, L Good Fri, D Etr Sun **Prices** Starter £5-£8, Main £15-£17, Dessert £5.50-£12.50, Service optional 12.5% **Wines** **Parking** On street **Notes** Vegetarian available, Children welcome

Enoteca Turi
PLAN 1 D2

Italian **NOTABLE WINE LIST**

tel: 020 8785 4449 **28 Putney High St SW15 1SQ**
email: info@enotecaturi.com
dir: *Nearest station: Putney Bridge*

Regional Italian food and wine in Putney

Occupying its corner plot since 1990, EnotecaTuri is an Italian restaurant of heart and soul. Run by the same family for all that time, the focus remains on regional Italian flavours, with the menu highlighting the origins of each dish (Piedmont, Puglia, etc.). It's the kind of place that buzzes with life when it's busy, which is often the case. The wine is another element that makes it stand out from the crowd, with more than 300 bins offering some really interesting stuff, sorted by region with matches for every dish. The menu doesn't lack for refinement, but the focus is on high quality, seasonal ingredients. Among antipasti, braised cuttlefish might come with chick pea purée and deep-fried pasta, or grilled fillet of mackerel with fennel and blood orange salad and a citrus dressing. Next up, a duck dish with a punchy sauce flavoured with liver, served with polenta gnocchi and cavolonero.

Chef Baldo Amodio **Owner** Mr G & Mrs P Turi **Seats** 85, Pr/dining room 18 **Times** 12-2.30/7-10.30 Closed 25-26 Dec, 1 Jan, Sun, L BHs **Prices** Prices not confirmed **Wines** 300 bottles over £30, 15 bottles under £30, 13 by glass **Parking** Putney Exchange car park, on street **Notes** Vegetarian available, Children welcome

LONDON SW17

Chez Bruce
PLAN 1 E2

– *see opposite*

LONDON SW19

Cannizaro House
PLAN 1 D1

– *see opposite*

The Fox & Grapes
PLAN 1 D2

Traditional British

tel: 020 8619 1300 **9 Camp Rd, Wimbledon SW19 4UN**
email: reservations@foxandgrapeswimbledon.co.uk
dir: *Nearest station: Wimbledon*

Pub food à la Claude Bosi

It may sound like a cosy old-fashioned boozer, but The Fox & Grapes has been transformed into a contemporary food-oriented pub with a cavernous open-plan interior of parquet floors, wood panelling, and chunky bare wooden tables and mismatched chairs wrapped around a central island bar. The man behind this radically reinvented gastro-pub on the edge of Wimbledon Common is none other than Claude Bosi of Mayfair restaurant Hibiscus fame (see entry), so if the prices at the West-End flagship are a bit rich for your blood, you can buy into his flavour-driven take on pub classics via crispy ox tongue with watercress and sauce gribiche, then mains taking in brown ale-battered hake and chips with mushy peas, or Cumberland sausage with chive mash and red onion gravy. For pudding, generous satisfaction might come in the shape of apple and rhubarb crumble with custard, or a platter of fine artisan British cheeses.

Times 12-3/6-9.30 Closed 25 Dec

Chez Bruce

LONDON SW17   **PLAN 1 E2**

Modern **NOTABLE WINE LIST**

tel: 020 8672 0114 **2 Bellevue Rd, Wandsworth Common SW17 7EG**
email: enquiries@chezbruce.co.uk
dir: *Nearest station: Wandsworth Common, Balham*

Supremely accomplished cooking in an understated white room

Bruce Poole has been enough of a mover and shaker on the London restaurant scene to have clocked up very nearly 20 years at his venue opposite Wandsworth Common, and to be able to sell a signature cookbook at the reception desk. It isn't easy to forge a gold-standard reputation from one of the outlying London districts, yet Poole's unostentatious, but supremely accomplished, cooking has taken the place from top-of-the-range neighbourhood eatery to a destination on the gastronomic satnav. The place itself has always seemed to reflect the studied absence of showboating: a purple exterior fronting a white-walled room set with linen-clad tables, adorned with representational and abstract pictures. Tables are comparatively snugly fitted in, yet the room never feels cramped or rowdy, and staff run it with unflappable aplomb and keen attention. Poole's cooking has a yen for the Mediterranean, those bright, sunny, savoury flavours that stand as the antidote to the richnesses of haute cuisine, with dishes that are built from an array of harmonising ingredients that taste supremely of themselves. Warm cod brandade in anchovy and orange dressing, garnished with mackerel and monk's beard, is a typically forthright opener. It might be followed by risotto milanese with stickily glazed veal shin, dressed in soffrito and gremolata, or crisped sea bream with sweet potato gnocchi in sherry vinegar and thyme. There are excursions southwards for chickpea pastilla with stuffed aubergine and houmous, eastwards for ox cheek rendang with Asian salad, peanuts and coriander, and into the heritage cookbook for a serving of côte de boeuf with chips and béarnaise. The menu returns to southern Europe for stracciatella ice cream and dulce de leche. Otherwise, tarts, puddings and pies make for comfort-factor desserts, the last perhaps a passion-fruit meringue version with pistachios and lime.

Chef Bruce Poole, Matt Christmas **Owner** Bruce Poole, Nigel Platts-Martin **Seats** 75, Pr/dining room 16 **Times** 12-2.30/6.30-10 Closed 24-26 Dec,1 Jan **Prices** Fixed L 2 course £23.50-£29.50, Fixed D 3 course fr £45 **Wines** 750 bottles over £30, 30 bottles under £30, 15 by glass **Parking** On street, station car park **Notes** Sunday L £35, Vegetarian available, Children L only

Cannizaro House

LONDON SW19   **PLAN 1 D1**

Modern British, European
tel: 020 8879 1464 **West Side, Wimbledon Common SW19 4UE**
email: info@cannizarohouse.com **web:** www.cannizarohouse.com
dir: *Nearest station: Wimbledon*

Creative cooking in a parkland setting

Cannizaro House is one of those hidden gems, a Georgian mansion within Wimbledon Common that provides boutique-style bedrooms in a soothingly tranquil setting. It's looking spruce these days after one of those makeovers where money was seemingly no object. The addition of the modern and trendy Orangerie for all-day dining brings a bit of Mediterranean glamour to the place, serving up Italian artisan ingredients. The main restaurant is looking good, too, with funky pink flamingo wallpaper (a lot better than it sounds) and a classy, contemporary sheen, especially in the conservatory side extension. The kitchen turns out creative, modern stuff these days, with top-rate produce at the heart of proceedings. A first course might see a courgette flower filled with a scallop and Scottish lobster mousse, while another partners breaded lamb's sweetbreads with celeriac remoulade and truffle mayonnaise. The craft and creativity continues into main course such as plaice tronçon with beef shin cannelloni, chanterelles and Highland Burgundy potatoes, and a perfectly cooked fillet of stone bass with a quinoa 'beach', Welsh sea vegetables and a cockle and bacon dressing. Meaty main courses might be confit of sirloin beef partnered with an oyster and bone marrow croquette and Avruga caviar, or lamb cutlet with Stichelton cheese mousse, crispy liver and polenta. There's no imagination amongst desserts: chocolate gel with minted marshmallows, black sesame meringue and tonka bean ice cream, say, or warm Bramley apple frangipane tart with a cider purée and fennel ice cream. The cheeses hail from these shores. There's a stylish bar, too, serving an impressive range of cocktails, and afternoon tea is an appealing option, particularly with a glass of champagne and fresh strawberries (Wimbledon is just down the road after all).

Chef Christian George **Owner** Bridgehouse Hotels **Seats** 60, Pr/dining room 120 **Times** 12-2.30/7-9.30 **Prices** Fixed L 2 course £24.50, Fixed D 3 course £29.50, Tasting menu £50-£80, Starter £8-£12, Main £17-£26, Dessert £7-£9.50, Service optional **Wines** 12 by glass **Parking** 55 **Notes** Sunday L £27-£32, Vegetarian available, Children welcome

LONDON SW19 *continued*

The Lawn Bistro
PLAN 1 D2

◉◉ British, European

tel: 020 8947 8278 & 8944 1031 **67 High St, Wimbledon SW19 5EE**
email: info@thelawnbistro.co.uk
dir: *Nearest station: Wimbledon*

Modern French pedigree in stylish neighbourhood bistro

Well-heeled locals pack this modern French bistro in the heart of Wimbledon village, and it's not hard to see why: the setting has the charm you'd expect of a bourgeois neighbourhood venue, with its light oak flooring, unclothed wooden tables and olive-green leather-clad chairs and banquettes looking as sleek and chic as the trendy boutiques all around, while the food, courtesy of head chef Ollie Couillaud, is a blend of rusticity and refinement that doesn't miss a beat. Staff turned out smartly in long aprons, white shirts and dark ties run a tight ship, serving up a repertoire that is Franco-centric, with occasional brushstrokes of British, Spanish and Italian. Seared scallops and black pudding are matched with apple purée and lentil and hazelnut vinaigrette in a gutsy starter, then main course partners a top-class breast of free-range chicken with white asparagus, spring cabbage, Jersey Royals and a bowl of frothy truffle velouté. To finish, the flavours and textures of a Valrhona chocolate and caramel pot with salted pistachio praline are a match made in heaven, or two could sign up for a retro baked Alaska, flambéed at the table.

Chef Ollie Couillaud **Owner** Akbar Ashurov **Seats** 70, Pr/dining room 24
Times 12-2.30/6.30-10.30 Closed Xmas, 1 Jan, Mon, D Sun **Prices** Fixed L 2 course £14.95-£42, Fixed D 3 course £27.95-£49, Starter £7-£11.50, Main £14-£32.50, Dessert £5-£9.95 **Wines** 78 bottles over £30, 32 bottles under £30, 11 by glass **Notes** Early D menu £23.95-£27.95, Sunday L £15.50-£22.50, Vegetarian available, Children welcome

The Light House Restaurant
PLAN 1 D1

◉ British, International

tel: 020 8944 6338 **75-77 Ridgway, Wimbledon SW19 4ST**
email: info@lighthousewimbledon.com
dir: *Nearest station: Wimbledon*

Cheerful neighbourhood restaurant with appealing cooking

Light streams into this popular neighbourhood restaurant, adding to a bright and breezy atmosphere created in part by friendly service and a decor of pale wood floors and modern art hung on plain walls. There's more than just a hint of the Mediterranean to the broad-based menu, so there's plenty to interest regulars and newcomers alike. How about starting with harissa mackerel with aubergine and tahini dip and piquillo peppers, or squid with chorizo, saffron, spinach risotto and gremolata? If they don't appeal there may be ham hock terrine with mustard pickles. The kitchen hauls in choice produce and handles it with skill to bring out distinctive flavours: roast duck breast, for instance, with Sarladaise potatoes and spinach and kumquat sauce, and spot-on wild sea bass with mussels and coconut red curry with jasmine rice. Finally, who could fail to be won over by puddings like blueberry frangipane tart with crème fraîche?

Chef Chris Casey **Owner** Mr Finch & Mr Taylor **Seats** 80, Pr/dining room 12
Times 12-3/6-10.30 Closed 24-26 Dec, 1 Jan, D Sun **Prices** Fixed L 2 course fr £14.50, Starter £5.50-£12.50, Main £12.75-£21.50, Dessert fr £6 **Wines** 53 bottles over £30, 21 bottles under £30, 18 by glass **Notes** Fixed D 3 course Mon-Thu & early eve £18.50/£22.50, Sunday L, Vegetarian available, Children welcome

LONDON W1

Alain Ducasse at The Dorchester
PLAN 4 G6

◉◉◉◉ – *see opposite*

Alloro
PLAN 2 J1

◉ Modern Italian ⬧ NOTABLE WINE LIST

tel: 020 7495 4768 **19-20 Dover St W1S 4LU**
email: alloro@londonfinediningroup.com
dir: *Nearest station: Green Park*

Honest, full-flavoured cooking in a chic Mayfair Italian

The exterior is the very picture of understated Mayfair discretion: frosted window panels etched with the restaurant's name ensure privacy from the street; inside, the space is split into a smart, busy bar and the sober, neutral tones of the dining room, where Alloro's bayleaf motif (the name means bayleaf in Italian) is engraved into marble panels above brown leather and oatmeal fabric banquettes, white linen-clothed tables, burgundy leather chairs and a chequerboard hardwood floor. The menu might read quite plainly, but the emphasis is on top-class ingredients and the kitchen displays the confidence and skill to bring out their full flavours, as in a starter of home-made black ink taglierini with fresh, tender squid. Flavours are similarly clean and clear in a main course of impeccable pan-fried fillets of John Dory with potato purée and purple sprouting broccoli, then a masterful tiramisú ends on a high note. All breads and pasta are made in-house, and service never misses a beat.

Times 12-2.30/7-10.30 Closed Xmas, 4 days Etr, BHs, Sun, L Sat

Alyn Williams at The Westbury
PLAN 2 H2

◉◉◉ – *see page 330*

Andrew Edmunds
PLAN 2 J1

◉ Modern European

tel: 020 7437 5708 **46 Lexington St, Soho W1F 0LW**
dir: *Nearest station: Oxford Circus*

Evergreen, rustic, Soho favourite

The tiny ground-floor dining room of this bistro stalwart is one of the West End's most intimate and romantic venues. With its simple rustic decor-wood floors and church pews, elbow-to-elbow tables with paper tablecloths, all low-lit by candles in wine bottles-it has an Old Soho feel of a Dickensian tavern. The kitchen takes an equally uncomplicated and honest approach, producing seasonal, ingredients-driven dishes on a daily-changing handwritten menu that has its feet firmly in the modern European idiom. Slow-cooked octopus and chorizo in tomato sauce with gordal olives and capers arrives straight from the Iberian tapas repertoire, followed by a splendid slab of snow-white wild halibut partnered simply with buttered new potatoes, spinach, and a zingy home-made tartare sauce. Carnivores might be tempted by roast spatchcock grouse with duck fat potatoes, watercress, and bread sauce, while puddings bring the nursery comforts of warm treacle tart with cream.

Chef Roberto Piaggesi **Owner** Andrew Edmunds **Seats** 46 **Times** 12-3.30/5.30-10.45 Closed Xmas, Etr **Prices** Starter £3.50-£9.50, Main £12.50-£25, Dessert £5-£6.75 **Wines** 100 bottles over £30, 70 bottles under £30, 5 by glass **Notes** Sunday L, Vegetarian available, Children welcome

Alain Ducasse at The Dorchester

LONDON W1   PLAN 4 G6

Contemporary, Modern French **V** ♦ NOTABLE WINE LIST

tel: 020 7629 8866 **The Dorchester, 53 Park Ln W1K 1QA**
email: alainducasse@thedorchester.com
dir: *Nearest station: Hyde Park Corner, Marble Arch*

Unashamedly classical French haute cuisine

Ducasse, a French maître cuisinier with a rep undisputed from Monte Carlo to London, is not one of the avant-gardistes of the present-day international culinary scene, and given that nowadays it can feel as though contemporary cooking is all avant and no garde, that ought to come as a breath of fresh air. Ducasse is a classicist, a chef who may once have been surprised that there was still an understanding, let alone an appetite, for the repertoire of French haute cuisine in a capital city often intent on standing aloof from continental habits. There is some seriously good cooking going on here that remains an object-lesson in finely judged refinement. The main menu barely alters from one season to the next, although there is always a seasonal prix-fixe: winter offers a scallop in lettuce cream with caviar, foie gras raviolo in duck consommé with chestnuts, a serving of lobster tail in its own stunningly rich sauce, sea bass adventurously cooked in lapsang souchong with chanterelles, corn-fed Landes chicken albuféra, a portion of truffled Brie de Meaux, and an ad-lib dessert choice, perhaps a vacherin of what the menu still sweetly calls 'exotic' fruits. This kitchen stands proud on the strengths of classic mainstays such as halibut in shellfish marinière, veal loin blanquette, and saddle and rib of Welsh venison with pumpkin and cranberries. Everything is translated and the dishes are expertly described by the

legions of flawlessly professional staff. Do leave space for one of the grander final flourishes, whether it be dallying over the cheese chariot (as an alternative to the sublime pre-paired Colston Bassett Stilton with a tot of liquorous Arbois vin de Paille), or a customised rum baba, which will be doused to order in your choice from half-a-dozen rums.

Chef Jocelyn Herland, Angelo Ercolano, Jean Philippe Blondet **Owner** The Dorchester Collection **Seats** 82, Pr/dining room 30 **Times** 12-1.30/6.30-9.30 Closed 1-7 Jan, 18-21 Apr, 26-30 Dec, Sun-Mon, L Sat **Prices** Fixed L 2 course fr £65, Fixed D 3 course fr £90, Tasting menu fr £125 **Wines** 15 by glass **Parking** 20 **Notes** Tasting menu 7 course, Seasonal menu £180, D 4 course £105 No children

LONDON W1 *continued*

Antidote
PLAN 2 J2

◎◎ Modern European NEW

tel: 020 7287 8488 **12a Newburgh St W1F 7RR**
email: contact@antidotewinebar.com
dir: *Nearest station: Oxford Circus*

Relaxed restaurant and wine bar with food and wine of pedigree

Trendily tucked away in a cobbled, 'off-the-radar' lane behind Carnaby Street, Antidote offers the perfect fix for organic/biodynamic wine lovers and foodies alike. A makeover and re-launch in March 2014 grabbed the attention, not least because Mikael Jonsson (aka, Chiswick's Hedone) owned up to being its consultant. Upstairs, above its bustling wine bar, the dining room is a relaxed oasis, with a fashionable pared-back look of grey walls, floorboards, funky silver bistro chairs, wooden tables and dangling Edison-style light bulbs. Chef Chris Johns provides the colour (alongside cheery French service) and takes on Jonsson's ethos for perfection and carefully-sourced ingredients with aplomb. Thus simplicity reigns on changing set-course menus of light, delicate, understated, clear-flavoured, 'pretty' dishes. Standouts might include sparkling Cornish turbot teamed with wonderful rainbow chard, monk's beard and a light shellfish emulsion, while succulent guinea fowl might come served with green asparagus, cracking wild garlic and spinach purée and spot-on sauce vin jaune. A rich, high-gloss dark chocolate moelleux is another winner, with passionfruit ice cream the perfect partnership. Sourdough bread (from Hedone's kitchen) is to die for, while the wine list is a corker.

Chef Mikeal Jonsson, Chris Johns **Owner** Thierry Bouteloup, Guillaume Siard **Seats** 45 **Times** 12-2.30/6-10.30 Closed Xmas, BHs, Sun **Prices** Fixed L 2 course £19, Tasting menu £60 **Wines** 188 bottles over £30, 12 bottles under £30, 21 by glass **Parking** On street **Notes** Fixed D 4 course £40, Tasting menu w/ends only 7 course, Vegetarian available, Children welcome

Aqua Kyoto
PLAN 2 J2

◎◎ Japanese

tel: 020 7478 0540 **240 Regent St W1B 3BR**
email: reservation@aqua-london.com
dir: *Nearest station: Oxford Street*

Classy Japanese food in super-cool roof-top setting

From the smart lobby entrance, you're whisked by lift to the 5th floor and the über-chic world of Aqua. The super-sexy Spirit cocktail bar is up first; it's shared by twin restaurants Aqua Nueva (Spanish tapas — see entry) and this modern Japanese outfit, and covers the top floor of the former Dickins & Jones building. There's great rooftop views from the terrace, while, like everything else here, Kyoto's ultra-designed dining room shimmers with contemporary style and teems with beautiful people, especially in the evenings when it becomes a high-energy 'destination' (lunch is quieter). Moody black, red and gold complement the theatre of a sunken centrepiece sushi bar, charcoal grill and jaw-dropping lantern-style light fitting. It's not design over substance: the cooking deserves serious attention, while friendly staff are happy to advise on the menus. Visually striking, well-constructed dishes and top-drawer ingredients are the thing; take king crab tempura with crab miso, or perhaps twice-cooked crispy pork belly with langoustine and yuzu pepper to high-rolling Wagyu beef with garlic ponzu and grape icicles. Otherwise there's cracking sushi and sashimi, fashionable wines and super cocktails.

Times 12-3/6-11.15 Closed 25-26 Dec, BHs, D Sun

Alyn Williams at The Westbury

LONDON W1   PLAN 2 H1

French, European ᴠ ⚜ NOTABLE WINE LIST

tel: 020 718 36426 **Bond St W1S 2YF**
email: alynwilliams@westburymayfair.com **web:** www.alynwilliams.com
dir: *Nearest station: Oxford Circus, Piccadilly Circus, Green Park*

Innovation, top-flight skills and heaps of glamour

After serving his time in other people's kitchens (chez Gordon Ramsay and Marcus Wareing, no less) Alyn Williams has been rewarded with his own name over the door of the top-end dining venue of The Westbury Hotel. Williams brings an unquestionable pedigree to the table, and a couple of years down the line, continues to cook at a rarefied level, displaying highly-refined, French-accented contemporary cooking and a commitment to technical excellence without resorting to flashy effects to grab attention. The Westbury is firmly entrenched among the A-list playground of Mayfair's hotels, so you can expect an interior of self-conscious glamour and opulence. A cocktail amid the chic, art deco-inspired Swarovski crystal fittings and Fendi-designed look in the Polo Bar is de rigueur, while the restaurant wears an understated yet unmistakably glossy decor of oatmeal-hued chairs at linen-swathed tables, set against softly burnished

darkwood panels, huge mirrors, and romantic, subtly-backlit alcoves. Sparse menu descriptions do more to pique the interest than to inform, as in a starter of langoustine, mackerel, cuttlefish, watermelon, almonds, and spicy flowers, which unleashes top-flight technical skills on an intriguing juxtaposition of components, textures and flavours. It is all audacious and visually exciting stuff, yet it is anchored by finely-honed discipline. Meaty dishes gain lustre through the pedigree of their components – Rhug Estate poussin is pointed up with fennel in various guises, wilted lettuce, and pumpernickel crisps filled with Chaource cheese, while fish dishes offer super-fresh John Dory with clams, courgette, fresh peas, sumac sauce and lovage purée. Desserts also provide endless pleasure, from a re-invented walnut whip involving walnut mousse and ice cream and chocolate discs, to chocolate cake with Marsala-infused mascarpone and passionfruit coulis. Vegetarians are invited to the party too, with an equally inventive meat-free tasting menu and carte to explore.

Chef Alyn Williams **Owner** Cola Holdings Ltd **Seats** 65, Pr/dining room 20 **Times** 12-2.30/6-10.30 Closed 1-17 Jan, 18 Aug-4 Sep, Sun-Mon **Prices** Fixed L 3 course £28, Fixed D 3 course £58, Tasting menu £65 **Wines** 450 bottles over £30, 6 bottles under £30, 12 by glass **Parking** 20 **Notes** Fixed ALC 3 course, Tasting menu 7 course, Children welcome

Aqua Nueva
PLAN 2 J2

◎◎ Spanish

tel: 020 7478 0540 **5th Floor, 240 Regent St W1B 3BR**
email: reservation@aqua-london.com
dir: *Nearest station: Oxford Circus*

Fashionable restaurant for Spanish wines and top-notch tapas

A lift whizzes you up from ground-floor street life to jet-set high life on the fifth floor, where a huge bull's head sculpture looms from a dimly-lit corridor, and you emerge in the nightclubby bling of the super cool Aqua Spirit cocktail bar. Slurp a cocktail with the beau monde then move into the slick restaurant, a designer-led space hung with thousands of wooden spindles. Two roof terraces and a Cava bar add to the upbeat vibe. This is the sort of place where people come to see and be seen as much as for the contemporary renditions of tapas based on top-end Spanish ingredients, so take your pick from a bilingual menu full of good-sounding ideas. Old favourites abound, from salt cod croquettes to morcilla blood sausage with roasted peppers, or lamb shoulder confit. Otherwise, a 3-course format might start with ox cheek cannelloni with tomato confit, potato purée and guacamole, then continue with black cuttle fish rice with aïoli, and conclude with coffee sponge with Amaretto jelly.

Times 12-3/6-11.30 Closed Xmas, New Year, BHs, Sun

Arbutus Restaurant
PLAN 2 K2

◎◎◎ – *see page 332*

Athenaeum Hotel & Apartments
PLAN 4 H6

◎◎ Modern British

tel: 020 7499 3464 **116 Piccadilly W1J 7BJ**
email: info@athenaeumhotel.com **web:** www. athenaeumhotel.com
dir: *Nearest station: Hyde Park Corner, Green Park*

Classy British cooking in a luxurious Mayfair hotel

The eye-catching vertical garden that spans the ten floors of the Athenaeum has helped make the place a bit of a landmark (watch as first-timers stare in amazement). But the hotel is no less impressive on the inside, with a luxurious five-star finish and bags of style. The place is also renowned for its afternoon teas, whilst the Whisky Bar is a favoured haunt of lovers of the grain. The restaurant with its cool black and white photos and discreet seating arrangements makes for a classy venue for some sharp, contemporary cooking. First-class ingredients feature in starters such as venison terrine with red onion marmalade, mixed seed toast and micro leaves, and mains such as saddle of rabbit wrapped in cured ham and served with wild garlic and woodland mushrooms, beetroot purée, truffle onions and crispy potatoes. For dessert, lemon posset with strawberry coulis and home-made shortbread biscuit, or chocolate marquise with milk sorbet hit the spot.

Chef David Marshall **Owner** Ralph Trustees Ltd **Seats** 46, Pr/dining room 70 **Times** 12.30-2.30/5.30-10.30 **Prices** Fixed L 2 course £19, Fixed D 3 course £32, Tasting menu £99, Starter £8-£14, Main £20-£32, Dessert £9, Service optional 12.5% **Wines** 28 bottles over £30, 10 bottles under £30, 15 by glass **Parking** Close car park **Notes** Sunday L £26.50-£32, Vegetarian available, Children welcome

L'Autre Pied
PLAN 2 G3

◎◎◎ – *see page 332*

Avista
PLAN 2 G1

◎◎ Italian

tel: 020 7596 3399 & 7629 9400 **Millennium Hotel Mayfair, 39 Grosvenor Square W1K 2HP**
email: reservations@avistarestaurant.com **web:** www.avistarestaurant.com
dir: *Nearest station: Bond Street*

Authentic Italian cooking in Grosvenor Square

When Michele Granziera wanted to move on from Zafferano to set up on his own, only the best would do: as a home to Avista, the Millennium Hotel fits the bill. It is the very image of moneyed Mayfair elegance, although the restaurant also has its own equally posh entrance on Grosvenor Square. The high-gloss setting fits the swanky postcode: marble floors, vast interstices between linen-swathed tables, and soft-focus tones of ivory, honey and beige. A granite-topped workstation where chefs primp dishes in readiness for presentation adds a touch of drama to the hushed refinement. Granziera cherry-picks his way around the Italian repertoire, bringing together rustic and contemporary ideas that are taken to higher level by the sheer quality of the ingredients. In winter, a robust fish stew of salmon, prawns and squid comes in the hearty company of fregola and croûtons rubbed with garlic and fresh parsley. Next up, a full-flavoured dish of venison loin with roast polenta, quince, pears and red wine jus, while fish could be represented by roast monkfish with crispy Parma ham and celeriac purée.

Chef Michele Granziera **Owner** Millennium & Copthorne Hotels **Seats** 75, Pr/dining room 12 **Times** 12-2.30/6-10.30 Closed 1 Jan, Sun, L Sat **Prices** Fixed L 2 course fr £19.99, Fixed D 3 course fr £25, Starter £9.50-£20, Main £17-£29.50, Dessert £4.20-£10.80 **Wines** 103 bottles over £30, 7 bottles under £30, 14 by glass **Parking** On street/NCP **Notes** Vegetarian available, Children welcome

Barnyard
PLAN 2 K3

◎ Farmhouse **NEW**

tel: 020 7580 3842 **18 Charlotte St W1T 2LZ**
email: info@barnyard-london.com
dir: *Nearest station: Goodge Street*

Country cool with plenty of flavour on Charlotte Street

With corrugated iron on the walls, an abundance of chunky planks of wood and staff dressed as farm hands, the theme runs deep, but this place is the brainchild of Ollie Dabbous, and there's substance to the style. It looks great, with a cool, rustic bar and tables up on a mezzanine level. Sharing is the name of the game, with the menu full of full-flavoured stuff with broad appeal and the comfort factor. Dishes are listed in sections which reflect a country-style honesty – 'pig', 'cow' and 'chicken', plus 'egg', 'vegetables & sides' and 'pudding'. Lard on toast is decidedly old school, but this is a 21st-century version, while chicken in a bun is another plate that needs no introduction. Barbecued grain-fed short rib with home-made pickle, mustard and black treacle sums up what this place is all about – great ingredients cooked to maximise flavour and served in a straight-up, no-nonsense manner. Finish with a classic lemon posset with marjoram.

Chef Joseph Woodland **Owner** Joseph Woodland, Charlie Bolton **Seats** 40 **Times** 12-3/5-10.30 Closed 25-26 Dec, Etr BH, D Sun **Prices** Fixed L 3 course fr £18, Fixed D 3 course fr £24, Service optional **Wines** 4 by glass **Notes** Sunday L

Arbutus Restaurant

LONDON W1 PLAN 2 K2

Modern French

tel: 020 7734 4545 **63-64 Frith St W1D 3JW**
email: info@arbutusrestaurant.co.uk
dir: *Nearest station: Tottenham Court Road*

Adventurous cooking with interesting combinations off Soho Square

Pass the greeter and the bar (counter-top dining possible here) and a small back room to reach the main dining room, which has a pared-down, minimalist look: wooden floor, plain walls hung with artwork and photographs, and a picture window giving on to Frith Street, from where passers-by gawp at what's on the plates. Anthony Demetre's cooking style is sophisticated and uncomplicated, modern and inventive, and he changes his menus every day. He follows the nose-to-tail philosophy espoused by Fergus Henderson of St John, seen in a signature starter of warm crisp pig's head with potato purée, pickled turnips and pistachios, and another of seared lamb heart unusually partnered by ewes' curd, with wild mushrooms and mint. Otherwise, dishes impress with the quality of their ingredients and their sensible but interesting combinations: a starter of Dorset crab with guacamole, peanuts and mango, for instance, and a main course of Elwy Valley lamb breast with Iranian aubergine, lemon and spinach. Diners reach for the bread basket to mop up the eloquently flavoured sauces such as chicken juices for roast cod fillet with boneless chicken wings and sweetcorn, and blood orange sauce for Cornish silver mullet with caramelised endive and curly kale. Don't pass on the wizard desserts: there might be a rich treacle tart with crème fraîche, or Yorkshire rhubarb crumble with vanilla ice cream. All the bottles on the 50-strong wine list also sold by the 250-millilitre carafe, so diners can mix and match. Prices are eminently fair throughout, given the context, with a pre-theatre deal, a working lunch and plat du jour all part of the package. Wild Honey and Les Deux Salons, both London, are in the same stable (see entries).

Chef Anthony Demetre, Tom Duffil **Owner** Anthony Demetre, Will Smith **Seats** 75 **Times** 12-2.30/5-11.30 Closed 25-26 Dec, 1 Jan **Prices** Fixed L 2 course £17.95, Fixed D 3 course £20.95, Starter £6.50-£11.50, Main £15.50-£19.50, Dessert £4.50-£8 **Wines** 40 bottles over £30, 10 bottles under £30, 50 by glass **Parking Notes** Pre-theatre D 5-6.30pm 2/3 course £18.95/£20.95, Sunday L £19.95, Vegetarian available, Children welcome

L'Autre Pied

LONDON W1 PLAN 2 G3

Modern European V NOTABLE WINE LIST

tel: 020 7486 9696 **5-7 Blandford St, Marylebone Village W1U 3DB**
email: info@lautrepied.co.uk
dir: *Nearest station: Bond St, Baker St*

Exciting contemporary cooking off Marylebone High Street

L'Autre Pied, sister of Pied à Terre, smacks of sophistication, with textured flower motifs on the walls, rosewood tables at brown leather chairs and burgundy-coloured banquettes, a wooden floor and flower arrangements. Professional and considerate staff contribute to a sense of occasion in a relaxing and comfortable environment. Andrew McFadden's cooking goes from strength to strength as he comes up with exciting new ideas for his dishes, combining a starter of flame-grilled mackerel with hazelnuts, apple tapioca, celery and miso, for instance, and a main course of loin of sika deer with Douglas fir, parsley roots, carrots, kohlrabi and pine nuts. But there's no chasing after novelty for its own end; every component has been carefully chosen and road-tested to ensure dishes burst with flavours. This results in roast breast and confit leg of quail appearing with black garlic, dried grapes and mushrooms, then squab pigeon with toasted hay, black pudding, beetroot and peanut crumble. This is a kitchen firing on all cylinders, with flawless techniques applied to first-class produce. Fish is timed to the second, seen in well-composed main courses of roast cod fillet with squid ink, caramelised salsify and brassicas, brown butter and almonds, and monkfish wrapped in Serrano ham accompanied by butternut squash, celeriac and soya beans. The momentum is well maintained in artfully contrived puddings, among which might be stem ginger mousse with chestnuts and clementines, or coconut pannacotta with toasted marshmallow and banana and passionfruit sorbet.

Chef Andrew McFadden **Owner** David Moore **Seats** 53, Pr/dining room 15 **Times** 12-2.45/6-10.45 Closed 4 days Xmas, 1 Jan, D Sun **Prices Wines** 200 bottles over £30, 6 bottles under £30, 10 by glass **Parking Notes** Sunday L £30-£35, Children welcome

LONDON W1 *continued*

Barrafina
PLAN 2 K2

Spanish

tel: 020 7813 8016 **54 Frith St W1D 4SL**
email: jose@barrafina.co.uk
dir: *Nearest station: Tottenham Court Rd*

Classic Spanish tapas at a marble counter in Soho

In a city that hasn't always got time to linger over dining, tapas is often the answer, and while the term has been elasticated nowadays to cover anything that comes in undersized portions, the original Spanish article remains the bedrock. With a new branch open from April 2014 on Adelaide Street, Charing Cross, Barrafina is a prime exponent of the genre. A long marble counter facing an open kitchen is the setting for vigorous, piquant, often gorgeous mouthfuls of strong savoury satisfaction, such as pimientos de Padrón, Ibérico de Bellota, prawn and piquillo tortilla, octopus with capers, chicken in romanesco, chorizo with potato and watercress, or baby gem salad with anchovies and smoked bacon. It's all served efficiently and with dispatch, though the no-bookings policy means you may have to wait your turn. What better opportunity to kick back with a glass of manzanilla? If you've time, finish with canonical tarta de Santiago, or a mouthful of gum-coating turrón.

Chef Nieves Barragán-Mohacho **Owner** Sam & Eddie Hart **Seats** 23 **Times** 12-3/5-11 Closed BHs **Prices** Starter £3-£6, Main £8-£12.50, Dessert £4.70-£8 **Wines** 26 bottles over £30, 19 bottles under £30, 34 by glass **Parking** On street **Notes** Sunday L, Vegetarian available, Children welcome

Bellamy's
PLAN 2 H1

French

tel: 020 7491 2727 **18-18a Bruton Place W1J 6LY**
email: gavin@bellamysrestaurant.co.uk
dir: *Nearest station: Green Park, Bond St*

Classy brasserie just off Berkeley Square

Resolutely Mayfair, with its mews setting just off Berkeley Square, its effortlessly classy good looks and slickly professional service, Bellamy's epitomises the chic, timeless French brasserie genre. Dark-green leather banquettes, pale-yellow walls (lined with vibrant French posters and mirrors), white linen and staff in bow ties and waistcoats add to the authentic look, while the classic brasserie cooking is conjured from premium seasonal produce. Simple, ungimmicky, clear-flavoured dishes are the kitchen's raison d'être, with menus written in franglais and sporting luxury at every turn – foie gras terrine, oysters, or caviar to start, Dover sole or Castle Mey beef entrecote to follow. Otherwise, try poached sea-fresh skate Grenobloise (set atop spinach and served with croûtons, capers and a buttery lemon sauce), and finish with a classic tarte Tatin. Fabulous all-French wines and an interconnecting oyster bar and food store complete the experience.

Chef Stephane Pacoud **Owner** Gavin Rankin and Syndicate **Seats** 70 **Times** 12-3/7-10.30 Closed Xmas, New Year, BHs, Sun, L Sat **Prices** Fixed L 2 course £19.75, Fixed D 3 course £24.75, Starter £6-£16, Main £14.50-£29.50, Dessert £6.50 **Wines** 58 bottles over £30, 7 bottles under £30, 17 by glass **Parking** On street, NCP **Notes** Vegetarian available, Children welcome

Looking for a London restaurant by name?
Use the index on page 254

Benares Restaurant
PLAN 2 H1

Modern Indian V

tel: 020 7629 8886 & 7514 2805 **12a Berkeley Square W1J 6BS**
email: reservations@benaresrestaurant.com
dir: *Nearest station: Green Park*

New-wave Indian cooking on Berkeley Square

Atul Kochhar is a busy man these days, what with a new venture in Kent and outposts in Dublin and on P&O cruise ships, but he remains adamant that this upscale Mayfair address on Berkeley Square is where his attention is most closely focused. A broad staircase sweeps up to the stylish first-floor bar and dining room, complete with chef's table, and the place retains the feel of the sort of nightclub one probably couldn't afford to be a member of. Well-drilled staff take a serious approach, and the flash and fire of the new-wave Indian cooking is not one bit bedimmed. Start with a trio of crisp-shelled venison samosas with tamarind and pear chutney for a palate-priming overture, before going on to cumin-roasted monkfish with green pea upma (a kind of South Indian porridge) and saffron sauce, or tandoori blackleg chicken supreme stuffed with forest mushrooms, accompanied by fine biryani and raita. A subtle westernising inflection is discernible in certain dishes, notably a dessert such as apple crumble with Armagnac custard, though even here the crumble is fragrant with spices.

Chef Atul Kochhar **Owner** Atul Kochhar **Seats** 120, Pr/dining room 34 **Times** 12-2.30/5.30-11 Closed 23-31 Dec, Sun **Prices** Fixed L 2 course £29, Fixed D 3 course £35, Tasting menu £82, Starter £11-£25, Main £25-£36, Dessert £8.50-£12 **Wines** 300 bottles over £30, 10 bottles under £30, 17 by glass **Parking** On street **Notes** Fixed D available until 6.30pm, Children before 7pm

Bentley's Oyster Bar & Grill
PLAN 2 J1

Modern British, Seafood

tel: 020 7734 4756 **11-15 Swallow St W1B 4DG**
email: reservations@bentleys.org **web:** www.bentleys.org
dir: *Nearest station: Piccadilly Circus*

Lovingly restored seafood bar and restaurant in London's Piccadilly

The ground floor oyster bar in the heart of London's Piccadilly originally opened in 1916. A mere eight years ago it was taken over by celebrated restaurateur Richard Corrigan (see entry for Corrigan's Mayfair), who has restored the old girl to all of her former glory. Enter through a nightclub-style curtain and pull up a stool at the original marble oyster bar or one of the red leather banquettes. Peruse a menu of oysters, cév005iches and simple seafood dishes, or head upstairs to the restaurant for a more full-blown meal from the wider menu. Striking William Morris wallpaper, blue leather chairs and bold artwork set the tone for traditional comfort food or more modish dishes. Start with a flavoursome fish soup or homely macaroni of lobster and basil, before something like seared fillet of hake with roast shallot,

LONDON W1 *continued*

bacon and razor clams. Save room for a perfectly oozing chocolate fondant with blood orange sorbet, honey and grapefruit.

Chef Michael Lynch **Owner** Richard Corrigan **Seats** 90, Pr/dining room 60 **Times** 12-3/6-11 Closed 25 Dec, 1 Jan, L Sat (Grill only) **Prices** Starter £9.75-£32, Main £19-£49, Dessert £6.50-£8.50 **Wines** 40 bottles over £30, 40 bottles under £30, 16 by glass **Parking** 10 yds away **Notes** Pre-theatre menu 2/3 course £26/£29, Sunday L, Vegetarian available, Children welcome

---

AA RESTAURANT OF THE YEAR FOR LONDON 2014–15

Berners Tavern
PLAN 2 J2

@@ Contemporary British **NEW** &NOTABLE WINE LIST

---

tel: 020 7908 7979 **The London Edition, 10 Berners St W1T 3NP** **email:** bernerstavern@editionhotels.com **web:** www.bernerstavern.com **dir:** *Nearest station: Oxford Circus*

Glam all-day dining chez Jason Atherton

The main restaurant at the London Edition Hotel is under the auspices of Jason Atherton, and there's not a hotter chef in town. With Pollen Street Social and its off-shoots pulling in the punters, the Berners Tavern is following suit. It's a breath-taking room adorned with hundreds of pictures in gilded frames, swish chandeliers and ornate plasterwork that would have doubtless impressed Louis XVI. Open all day from breakfast until late in the evening, the menu offers a modern British cast that can sort you out for a barbecue-pulled Gloucestershire Old Spot pork sandwich or grass-fed British steak cooked on the chargrill. Native lobster and prawn cocktail with avocado and crispy shallot is a classy number among starters, followed perhaps with an excellent main of braised Atlantic halibut with squid ink risotto. A dessert of caramel apple and Calvados éclair with salted caramel ice cream looks stunning on the plate, and there are cocktails aplenty, too. This is a seriously glamorous addition to the London dining scene.

Chef Phil Carmichael, Jason Atherton **Seats** 114, Pr/dining room 14 **Times** 12-2.30/6-10.30 **Prices** Starter £8.50-£14.50, Main £14.50-£36, Dessert £4.50-£12 **Wines** 330 bottles over £30, 25 bottles under £30, 19 by glass **Parking** On street, NCP & car park **Notes** Sunday L £6-£22.50, Vegetarian available, Children welcome

Blanchette
PLAN 2 J2

@ French Tapas **NEW**

---

tel: 020 7439 8100 **9 D'Arblay St, Soho W1F 8DR** **email:** info@blanchettesoho.co.uk **dir:** *Nearest station: Oxford Circus*

Homely French bistro dining in the hinterland of Soho

A trio of French brothers established Blanchette in the hinterland of Soho, with a mission to bring back the prospect of homely French bistro cooking to the seen-it-all West End. The tiled murals of ducks flying through a pastoral landscape make an attempt to spirit you away to a world of peace and quiet, and in the kitchens is Tam Storrar, son of a countryside ranger, who learned all about foraging in his boyhood, almost as though he knew it would one day be indispensable to running a modern restaurant kitchen. First up, there's a snacks and starters menu for the grazers, featuring the likes of croque-monsieur, crispy frog legs, charcuterie and cheese. But it's the main dishes that most evocatively conjure up happy memories of bistro dining across the Channel. Peppered tuna with garlic greens and piperade, a baked scallop in Café de Paris butter, chou farci filled with braised beef shin, or lamb shoulder slow-cooked with anchovies and rosemary in sauce soubise, all hit the spot, with side-dishes of fennel à la grecque or leeks vinaigrette.

Chef Tam Storrar **Owner** Maxime, Yannis & Malik **Times** 12-3/5.30-11 **Prices** Fixed L 3 course fr £25, Fixed D 3 course fr £25 **Wines** 17 bottles over £30, 7 bottles under £30, 15 by glass **Notes** Charcuterie & cheese platters available when kitchen closed, Sunday L

Bocca di Lupo
PLAN 2 K1

@ Italian &NOTABLE WINE LIST

---

tel: 020 7734 2223 **12 Archer St W1D 7BB** **email:** info@boccadilupo.com **dir:** *Nearest station: Piccadilly Circus*

Regional Italian sharing plates in the heart of Soho

Tucked away as it is behind a modest red-brick façade in a quiet Soho side street, you wouldn't imagine that the atmosphere inside Bocca di Lupo would be so electric. But it's a highly popular place, buzzing at lunch and from early evening (with the pre-theatre crowd) and until late. You can perch on a stool at the long marble bar, or head on into the restaurant proper, with its bare wood tables, contemporary brown leather chairs and bright art on the walls. On the long Italian menu everything is regionally name-checked and comes in small or large portions to encourage sharing. Standout dishes include hot and salty sage leaves filled with anchovy, a sweetly moreish rabbit, pearl barley and wild garlic orzotto, and comforting cime di rapa with garlic and chilli. Desserts are particularly strong, be it gelato from their own ice cream parlour – Gelupo – across the road, or torta Caprese 'bilivello' (chocolate and blood orange tart from Capri).

Times 12.15-3.45/5.15-22.45 Closed Xmas

Looking for a London restaurant near you?
Use the maps on pages 258–68

Looking for a restaurant by name?
Use the index on page 751

Brasserie Chavot

LONDON W1   **PLAN 2 H1**

Modern French

tel: 020 7183 6425 **41 Conduit St, Mayfair W1S 2YF**
email: reservation@brasseriechavot.com
dir: Nearest station: Bond Street, Green Park

Classy brasserie from a French master

The eponymous Monsieur Chavot has been around the London dining scene for long time. He worked at Harveys with Marco back in the day, with Koffman at La Tante Claire, and his own star shone at The Capital for a decade. After a couple of years out of London, he returned in 2013 to open Brasserie Chavot, and, on this evidence, he'll be around for a while yet. Attached to the high-end Westbury Hotel, the room is a real bobby-dazzler with its mosaic floor, mirrors, dark wood panels, chandeliers and flashes of rich red from the leather on the chairs and banquettes. The glamorous finish is not matched by crazy prices, though, and given the quality of the cooking, it's actually pretty good value given the competition in Mayfair. The premise is an entente cordiale of British and French ingredients, whatever is at its best, with plenty of classic brasserie preparations to justify the moniker. The craft of the cooking puts this place on a higher level than many other brasseries. Chicken liver parfait with prune and fig chutney, céviche of scallops, beef carpaccio with pickled mushrooms... these are honest, traditional things done very well indeed. It's all in the detail. Main course might see roasted cod served with lentils and ventrèche bacon, or go for the filet de canette à l'orange (the menu flits about between English and French). There's a grill section, too, offering up new season rump of lamb, or tiger prawns with harissa. Desserts are an equally classic bunch, so Ile flottante or crème brûlée lead the way. The wine list is mostly French with a few global interlopers.

Chef Eric Chavot **Owner** Eric Chavot **Seats** 76 **Times** 12-2.30/6-10.30 **Prices** Starter £10-£12.50, Main £17.50-£26, Dessert £7.50-£9 **Wines** 23 by glass **Parking Notes** Sunday L, Vegetarian available, Children welcome

Canvas

LONDON W1   **PLAN 2 G3**

Modern European NEW v

tel: 020 7935 0858 **69 Marylebone Ln W1U 2PH**
email: info@michael-riemenschneider.com
dir: *Nearest station: Bond St, Baker St*

Dynamic modern cooking in Marylebone

Swiss-born Michael Riemenschneider's restaurant on Marylebone Lane is only a little place – just 20 covers – but it's making its mark with feisty cooking that is at the sharp end of contemporary culinary fashion. The diminutive dining room in two sections has bare-brick walls, no table cloths, no unnecessary adornments, and it looks good for it. The service team are as bright as a button and sometimes positively effusive. Riemenschneider's menu is of the tasting variety, with a difference, of sorts; the dishes are small-ish tasting plates and it's up to the customer to pick which of the 16 or so items they fancy going for, up to the full-on ten course. So everyone's tasting menu can be different. There are freebie canapé, amuse-bouche and the like as well (a pea and artichoke velouté maybe). Wine flight options include 'Classic' and 'Iconic' options, with glasses matched to the food, and every featured wine is also available by the bottle if you fancy sticking with one. An opening course of raw scallops, thinly sliced and partnered with pickled radish and cucumber and topped with frozen yoghurt infused with horseradish, makes for a fine beginning, the flavours, fresh, vivid and harmonious. Next up, sea bass comes with a fondue (a foamy one) with tart caper berries and turnip, before a meat dish of sirloin, rib and tail of beef, the latter in a little pot on the side (soft and tender and topped with mash), with carrots and rich, beefy purée. Duck and orange are familiar enough, but here it's a nicely pink bird with an intense orange purée, and among sweet courses there might be a mousse infused with beetroot and chocolate, plus raspberry 'leather' and basil jelly. This is a welcome addition to the Marylebone (and London) dining scene.

Chef Michael Riemenschneider **Seats** 20, Pr/dining room 10 **Times** 12-2.30/6-10 Closed 12 Aug-2 Sep, 22 Dec-6 Jan, Sun-Mon **Prices** Fixed L 2 course £20, Fixed D 3 course £25, Tasting menu £50-£95, Starter £18-£20, Main £30-£34, Dessert £10-£16, Service optional 12.5% **Wines** 35 bottles over £30, 2 bottles under £30, 35 by glass **Parking** On street, Cavendish Square car park **Notes** Fixed D menu only available 6pm, Tasting menu 5/7/10 course, Children welcome

LONDON W1 *continued*

Brasserie Chavot
PLAN 2 H1

◉◉◉ – *see page 335*

Brasserie Zedel
PLAN 2 J2

◉ French V

tel: 020 7734 4888 **20 Sherwood St W1F 7ED**
email: reservations@brasseriezedel.com
dir: *Nearest station: Piccadilly Circus*

Authentic brasserie dining in the heart of Piccadilly

From seasoned restaurateurs Corbin and King (see entries for The Wolseley, The Delaunay and Colbert) comes Brasserie Zedel – an authentic Parisian brasserie in the heart of Piccadilly. The grand art deco interior boasts high ceilings, marble pillars and period lighting with deep red seating. The food is equally authentic. All in French (an English version is available on request), the extensive all-day menu is supplemented by a good value prix-fixe and plats du jour. Start with a simple and light foie gras parfait or fish soup with rouille, before a perfectly cooked and nicely presented spatchcock chicken supported by a tarragon vinaigrette, sautéed potatoes and green beans. Finish with a textbook tarte au citron. There's plenty of opportunity to explore the all-French wine list, as each wine is available by the glass and carafe. For some after dinner entertainment, The Crazy Coqs cabaret and jazz venue is also on site.

Chef Andrew Parkinson **Owner** Chris Corbin, Jeremy King **Seats** Pr/dining room 40 **Times** 11.30-mdnt Closed 25 Dec, All-day dining **Prices** Fixed L 2 course fr £8.95, Fixed D 3 course £11.75-£19.75, Starter £2.75-£13.50, Main £8.75-£29.50, Dessert £3.50-£6.75 **Wines** 55 bottles over £30, 13 bottles under £30, 34 by glass **Parking** NCP Brewer St **Notes** Pre-Fixe menu 2/3 course, Sunday L fr £8.95, Children welcome

---

Canvas
PLAN 2 G3

◉◉◉ – *see page 335*

Cecconi's
PLAN 2 J1

◉◉ Traditional Italian

tel: 020 7434 1500 **5a Burlington Gardens W1X 1EP**
dir: *Nearest station: Piccadilly Circus, Oxford Circus*

Swanky Mayfair address for top-class seasonal Italian cooking

Cecconi's works a glossy Mayfair look with its discreet dark glass frontage. Black-suited waiters swish in and out bearing trays of aperitifs and cicchetti (Venetian tapas) to the pavement tables; inside, the vibe is low-lit, old-school glamour – a magnet for the well-heeled international crew raising the decibels at green-leather high stools round the marble-topped island bar. All around are linen-clad tables, mirrored walls, blue velour banquettes and black-and-white diagonal-striped marble floors. Waiters are real pros, working the room with professional slickness but still chatty and friendly, and they know the all-day menu inside out. The trump card here is dedication to top-class seasonal produce, prepared simply to deliver clear, full-on flavours. Kickstart the taste buds with the cicchetti – ox tongue and salsa verde, say – then move on to pasta of unimpeachable class: crab ravioli in a delicate tomato and fish stock broth with fresh basil and tomatoes. Main course brings an intensely-flavoured casserole of baked cod with clams, mussels and capers, or you might go meaty with a simple pairing of lamb cutlet and caponata.

Times 7am-1am Closed Xmas, New Year, All-day dining

The Chesterfield Mayfair
PLAN 4 H6

◉◉ Traditional British

tel: 020 7491 2622 **35 Charles St, Mayfair W1J 5EB**
email: bookch@rchmail.com web: www.chesterfieldmayfair.com
dir: *Nearest station: Green Park*

Cosseting luxury, Mayfair style

The Chesterfield Mayfair goes all out to bathe guests in upmarket warmth with plenty of antiques and plush fabrics throughout, and if this puts you in the mood for a spot of old-school fine dining, Butler's restaurant delivers the goods. The setting is appropriately formal with crimson chairs at white linen-swathed tables, and traditional carving and flambéing trolleys working the room. Naturally, the cooking isn't trying to push the culinary envelope, but well-honed technical skills and the splendid quality of the produce work together to pull off a class act. A surf and turf starter of Orkney king scallops with pork cheek, sweetcorn and baby carrots might start you off, while for mains you could stick with the familiarity of a fine Scottish steak or Dover sole from the grill, or go down the modernist route with herb-crusted loin of lamb with potato and goats' cheese terrine, artichokes, fennel purée and olives. Finish with the theatre of crêpes Suzette, or carrot cake with Earl Grey tea ice cream.

Chef Ben Kelliher **Owner** Red Carnation Hotels **Seats** 65, Pr/dining room 40 **Times** 12-2.30/5.30-10 Closed L Sat-Sun **Prices** Fixed L 2 course £19.50, Fixed D 3 course £25.50, Starter £9-£17.50, Main £18.50-£38.50, Dessert £8.50-£12.50 **Wines** 60 bottles over £30, 12 bottles under £30, 20 by glass **Parking** NCP 5 minutes **Notes** Pre-theatre menu, Afternoon tea available, Vegetarian available, Children welcome

---

Chiltern Firehouse
PLAN 2 G3

◉◉◉ – *see opposite*

China Tang at The Dorchester
PLAN 4 G6

◉◉ Classic Cantonese ♣ NOTABLE WINE LIST

tel: 020 7629 9988 **53 Park Ln W1K 1QA**
email: reservations@chinatanglondon.co.uk
dir: *Nearest station: Hyde Park Corner*

Glamorous Cantonese cooking in five-star Park Lane surroundings

There are basements and basements. Needless to say, the basement of The Dorchester is not a bad place to be, in fact, it looks incredible, and its home to China Tang. The bar is opulent and old school, the restaurant itself a celebration of refined Chinoiserie with contemporary fish-themed Asian art and art-deco mirrored columns. There's a reassuring confidence and professionalism to the service team. The menu won't be unfamiliar to anyone used to eating Cantonese food in the UK, but there are more than enough luxury items to act as a reminder that this is the Dorchester. Soft-shelled crab fried with egg yolk shows this to be a kitchen that doesn't waste time with unnecessary embellishments, likewise the salt-and-pepper squid. There is classic lobster braised in bouillon, plus whole suckling pig if you give 24-hour's notice, but equally there's the humble lamb brisket cooked in a clay pot. Desserts such as warm chocolate pudding with vanilla ice cream can have a Western flavour, and dim sum is served all day.

Times 12-12 Closed 25 Dec, All-day dining

C London

PLAN 2 H1

◎◎ Italian

tel: 020 7399 0500 **23-25 Davies St W1K 3DE**
email: london@crestaurant.co.uk
dir: *Nearest station: Bond Street*

Venetian elegance and celeb spotting in Mayfair

Formerly named (and still known to its faithful as) Cipriani, C London is sibling to Venice's famous Harry's Bar and is beloved by the international glitterati. Don't be surprised if the paparazzi are waiting outside as you arrive at the glass-fronted restaurant with its revolving door, such is its popularity on the celeb circuit. Once inside, meeter-greeters from a battalion of white-jacketed, slickly professional staff commence the charm offensive no matter what your status, and the large, snazzy dining room looks appealing with its impeccable art-deco styling complete with Murano glass chandeliers. It's certainly not all style over substance – the straightforward classic Italian cooking is founded on tip-top produce and doesn't disappoint. Take sea-fresh Dover sole simply partnered by zucchini, or from the grill, moist, full-flavoured corn-fed chicken with lovely crispy skin, served simply with mixed vegetables. Breads are fabulous, a Bellini aperitif is almost a requisite, and for dessert you might choose something like lemon meringue pie from the 'selection of home-made cakes'. Factor in a buzzing atmosphere, 15% service and prices that are certainly determined with the celebrity in mind.

Times 12-3/6-11.45 Closed 25 Dec

Cocochan

PLAN 2 G2

◎ Chinese, Japanese

tel: 020 7486 1000 **38-40 James St, Marylebone W1U 1EU**
email: info@cocochan.co.uk **web:** www.cocochan.co.uk
dir: *Nearest station: Bond Street*

Pan-Asian fusion cooking in vibrant West End setting

Not far from the craziness of Oxford Street, Cocochan offers an escape to far away continents, for your taste buds at least, for this is Pan-Asian country, where the flavours of China, Japan, Vietnam, Thailand and Korea come together harmoniously. There's an eye-catching Eastern modernism to the three dining spaces (one of which is the outdoor terrace) in the form of metallic and mirrored latticework on the walls and bamboo tables, and it's all good fun. Crabcakes with jalapeño mayo and Thai salad sums it all up pretty nicely, but there's straight-up sushi and sashimi if you wish to keep it simple. Chargrilled lamb cutlets with kimchee and nashi pear

continued

Chiltern Firehouse

LONDON W1

PLAN 2 G3

Modern American **NEW**
tel: 020 7073 7676 **1 Chiltern St, Marylebone W1U 7PA**
email: reservations@chilternfirehouse.com
dir: *Nearest station: Baker Street, Bond Street*

Stunning food in a high-gloss setting

As the name hints, the Chiltern Firehouse is indeed a former fire station, built with Victorian grandeur and cavernous proportions, and now entered through a courtyard garden which comes into play for alfresco dining on balmy days. The place occupies part of the swish designer Andre Balasz hotel, so inside, the space has been reworked with serious wow factor: the high-ceilings are lined with woven chair webbing and the textures are of brass and wood against a neutral cream backdrop. For sure, it's a see-and-be-seen sort of gaff, but more impressive still are the two chefs behind this high-gloss venture: Nuno Mendes brings his cutting-edge approach from Viajante, and Dale Osborne comes from Dinner by Heston Blumenthal, which has to raise expectations skyward. Luckily the food lives up to its promise with razor-sharp execution to deliver pure, clear flavours – this is food cooked with love and that will make you smile. The action

all goes on in full view in an open kitchen at the back of the room, with counter tables and high stools for those who really want to get up close and personal with the culinary theatre. Remarkable depth of flavour is clear from the outset with a starter of marinated cod paired simply with tomatoes, salmorejo, toasted tomato flatbread and enhanced with parsley oil. Main-course monkfish is cooked over pine to add a smoky resinous edge to enhance its firm and meaty flesh, while smooth pearl barley and crunchy puffed barley, fennel purée and crisp braised fennel add excellent variety to the dishes textural interest. Dessert delivers another knockout idea with a frozen apple pannacotta covered in toasted meringue in the manner of baked Alaska and paired up with diced apple and apple jelly, and herb granité.

Chef Nuno Mendes **Owner** Andre Balazs **Seats** 120, Pr/dining room 12
Times 12-2.30/5-10.30 **Prices** Prices not confirmed **Wines** 250 bottles over £30, 20 bottles under £30, 14 by glass **Notes** Vegetarian available, Children welcome

LONDON W1 *continued*

shows textbook meat cookery, or go for calamari salad with shiitaki mushrooms, shallots, Thai basil and yuzu soya. End European style with the likes of pannacotta with mixed berry compôte.

Chef Ethan Musico **Owner** Hrag Darakjian **Seats** 80, Pr/dining room 35 **Times** 12-12 Closed 25 Dec, 1 Jan, All-day dining **Prices** Starter £3.50-£22, Main £13-£27, Dessert £4.50-£7 **Wines** 40 bottles over £30, 15 bottles under £30, 15 by glass **Parking** On street **Notes** Sharing menu group 10 £30-£65, Bento box L min £13.50, Sunday L, Vegetarian available, Children welcome

Corrigan's Mayfair

PLAN 2 G1

◎◎◎ – *see opposite and advert below*

Coya

PLAN 4 H6

◎◎ Modern Peruvian NEW

tel: 020 7042 7118 **118 Piccadilly, Mayfair W1J 7NW**
email: info@coyarestaurant.com
dir: *Nearest station: Hyde Park Corner*

Peruvian cooking and bags of style

With three open kitchens, a céviche counter, an open charcoal grill, and a pisco bar stocking trendy infusions and over 40 tequilas, Coya is a hive of Peruvian-inspired activity. It's seriously cool. The kitchen delivers classy plates of food that are rich with South American flavours and a contemporary swagger. The strong visual impact of the restaurant extends to the food, too, such as a classic plate of that céviche – sea bass, cut with precision and sparklingly fresh, with red onions, sweet potato and white corn. The ingredients are spot-on throughout, such as a plate of octopus cooked on the Josper grill and partnered with Peruvian olives. The meat

cookery is equally impressive; corn-fed baby chicken, for example, with aji panca (a dark red pepper) and coriander, or lamb chops with crushed aubergines. The signature dessert is the corn sundae, consisting of sweetcorn ice cream and popcorn, or go for the salted caramel ganache with blood orange and pisco. The tasting menu is a good option (at a price).

Chef Sanjay Dwiveve **Owner** Mr Wanyan **Times** 12-2.45/6-10.45 **Prices** Fixed L 2 course £19.50, Tasting menu £75, Starter fr £8, Main fr £15, Dessert fr £7 **Wines** **Notes** Tasting menu 17 course, Groups tasting menu 10+ £55-£75

Criterion

PLAN 2 K1

◎ Modern British, European

tel: 020 7930 0488 **224 Piccadilly W1J 9HP**
email: reservations@criterionrestaurant.com
dir: *Nearest station: Piccadilly Circus*

Well-produced brasserie fare in spectacular-looking restaurant

Byzantium comes to Piccadilly Circus with the Criterion's spectacular interior, a large, long room of marble, mosaics, gold and mirrors. The kitchen deals in modern British brasserie-style cooking based on the great French traditions. Expect starters of mussels, served in a pot, cooked in a well-made creamy cider-based sauce with garlic and shallots, or ham hock and black pudding terrine with apple purée and pickled vegetables. Accurate timing and sound technique are evident in main courses: pink, juicy and tender lamb chop accompanied by smooth mashed potato and broccoli, and pan-fried salmon fillet (from Loch Duart) with beetroot and horseradish purée, samphire and chive beurre blanc. Breads – and butter – are made in-house, and a creative talent is behind such puddings as brioche and Calvados baba with custard foam and blackberry sorbet, or orange posset with spicy poached clementines and lemon verbena gratin.

Times 12-2.30/5.30-11.30 Closed 25 Dec

Richard Corrigan's eponymous restaurant, located in the heart of Mayfair. Generous portions, Irish influences and a mecca for wild and foraged ingredients. Game is highly regarded in this establishment and is presented in every shape and variety.

· 6 course tasting menu
· Four private dining rooms seating from 2 – 30
· Cookery Classes

· Private hire of the restaurant 85
· Picnic Hampers
· Nearest station – Marble Arch

020 7499 9943
RESERVATIONS@CORRIGANSMAYFAIR.COM
www.corrigansmayfair.com

28 Upper Grosvenor Street, London, W1K 7EH

Corrigan's Mayfair

LONDON W1 PLAN 2 G1

Modern British, Irish v 🍷 NOTABLE WINE LIST

tel: 020 7499 9943 **28 Upper Grosvenor St W1K 7EH**
email: reservations@corrigansmayfair.com
web: www.corrigansmayfair.com
dir: *Nearest station: Marble Arch*

Finely crafted gutsy cuisine and top service in Mayfair

The man from Dublin, via County Meath, is quite the celeb chef with a host of TV appearances and books under his belt. It's a bit disingenuous perhaps to say he has the common touch at these prices, but Corrigan is a chef who likes to feed, to satisfy, and here, just off Park Lane, he does just that. And his name is written in gold above the door. There's a real sense of style here, of old-school grandeur, and playfulness, too (note the ostrich lamps), and if it is indulgence you're after, just wait until the Cognac trolley comes trundling by. The 25-foot marble topped bar is the place to head for if you want to perch and tuck into crispy fillets of sole with tartare sauce, or if the main restaurant is jammed to the gills. Beyond lurks the club-like luxury of the art-deco-style restaurant with lots of burnished wood, plush leather seats and banquettes. The service team scoot about with professional zeal and all the required discretion. The food is refined and robust, classical certainly, and rarely short on flavour. To kick off, if you can bear to pass on the Carlingford oysters, there are the likes of white pudding with parsnip purée and grated truffle and a salad of crab and artichokes waiting in the wings. Main-course slow-cooked rib of beef falls off the bone as you hope it might, and is served with spinach purée, crisp marrow toast, wild leeks and a flavoursome jus, but if you want spuds with it, that'll be an extra few quid for double-cooked chips or mash. Fish main courses are equally on the money – whole Dover sole, perhaps – and so too are desserts such as chocolate délice with a dark and white chocolate sorbet. With a tasting menu, plus a lunchtime daily market menu, and a stellar wine list, Corrigan's is a class act from top to bottom.

Chef Richard Corrigan, Chris McGowan **Owner** Richard Corrigan **Seats** 85, Pr/dining room 25 **Times** 12-2.30/6-11 Closed 23-27 Dec, L Sat **Prices** Fixed L 2 course £25, Tasting menu £75, Starter £9-£24, Main £24-£34, Dessert £7.50-£11 **Wines** 40 bottles over £30, 40 bottles under £30, 12 by glass **Parking** On street **Notes** Tasting menu 6 course, Chef's table available, Sunday L £29, Children welcome

CUT at 45 Park Lane

LONDON W1   PLAN 4 G6

Contemporary American V NOTABLE WINE LIST

tel: 020 7319 7467 & 7493 4545   **45 Park Ln W1K 1BJ**
email: restaurants.45L@dorchestercollection.com **web:** www.dorchestercollection.com
dir: Nearest station: Hyde Park Corner, Green Park

Stunning steaks from a king of Californian cuisine in Mayfair

Austria via Beverly Hills, Wolfgang Puck hasn't taken a particularly traditional route to the London dining scene, but here he is with a dynamic version of a steakhouse, and it's all going very well indeed. He's a big fish in the USA and at Spago helped define what we now know as Californian cuisine. The hotel location under the Dorchester marque is darn swanky, with the restaurant on the ground floor making a good first impression. It's a long, narrow room with six striking chandeliers of the modern variety, plus modern wooden panels and a glamorous, upscale vibe. All this for steaks? Well, just you wait. Let a humble tomato salad do the talking: Heirloom tomato, Neal's Yard goats' curd, shaved onions, white anchovies, basil aïoli and 50-year-aged balsamic is something to behold. The dish is lifted by the quality of the ingredients and indeed the confidence of the kitchen to let those flavours shine. There's also main courses such as pan-roasted poulet noire 'Label Rouge', which is a wonderful piece of meat, deep with flavour, served with chanterelles, creamy potato purée and a delicious thyme jus. But onto the steaks. The quality of the meat is second to none, and they come from all over the world to your plate: Black Angus from Creekstone Farms in Kansas, South Devon Angus from the West Country, and Wagyu from Queensland in Australia. They aren't cheap, but you guessed that, right? Sides are extra, but you guessed that too, right? It's a good idea to leave room for dessert for the skilled kitchen team does not lower its guard: vanilla and tonka bean pannacotta, for example, with strawberries, basil and a dash of aged balsamic, and a razor thin arlette.

Chef David McIntyre **Owner** Dorchester Collection **Seats** 70, Pr/dining room 12 **Times** 12-2.30/6-10.30 **Prices** Fixed L 2 course £34, Fixed D 3 course £90, Tasting menu £160, Starter £12-£26, Main £21-£92, Dessert £11, Service optional 12.5% **Wines** 600 bottles over £30, 7 bottles under £30, 20 by glass **Parking** 40 **Notes** Brunch ALC menu available, Children welcome

Dabbous

LONDON W1   PLAN 2 J3

Modern British

tel: 020 7323 1544 **39 Whitfield St, Fitzrovia W1T 2SF**
email: info@dabbous.co.uk
dir: Nearest station: Goodge Street

Highly innovative, natural cooking with a wholly urban backdrop

Dabbous went down a storm when it opened its doors in 2012, as much for its industrial-chic design as anything: all bare brick and concrete, metal grille, exposed pipes and even unshaded light bulbs dangling on bare wires. Entirely in keeping, staff come across as cool and trendy. Central to the cooking style are fresh, fresh herbs, fruit and vegetables, and foraged wild foods. The eponymous Ollie Dabbous eschews the classical school's reliance on dairy produce for sauces and garnishes and has an unfailing grasp of successful combinations, turning out some highly original dishes. A starter of avocado, basil and almonds in chilled fig leaf broth is a triumph of accurate flavours, and might be followed by tender barbecued octopus with a contrasting violet and mustard emulsion and Jerusalem artichokes. Smoked halibut with pickled celeriac sounds positively run of the mill in comparison, but main-course offerings after it soon induce the surprise factor: cod wrapped in wood shavings with honey and turnip dressing, say, or roast goose with birch sap and white miso. Dishes are remarkable for their palate-pleasing clean flavours and attractive rustic presentation, and staff are happy to explain any unfamiliar items: kinome, for instance, in a main course of braised veal cheek with toasted spelt and celery. Seeded bread is served in a brown-paper bag, and puddings make an impact in the form of hot cashew nut butter with ginger beer and lime, served in a tankard, or rhubarb with lavender and ice lettuce, while the savoury of tooth could opt for truffled cheese on toast.

Chef Ollie Dabbous **Owner** Ollie Dabbous **Times** 12-2.15/6.30-9.30 Closed 1 wk Etr, 2 wks Aug, 3 wks Xmas, Sun-Mon **Prices** Tasting menu £59, Service optional 12.5% **Wines** 110 bottles over £30, 10 bottles under £30, 16 by glass **Parking** **Notes** 4 course set L/D £28/£48, Tasting menu whole tables only

LONDON W1 *continued*

CUT at 45 Park Lane

PLAN 4 G6

◎◎◎ – *see opposite*

Dabbous

PLAN 2 J3

◎◎◎ – *see opposite*

Degò

PLAN 2 J2

◎◎ Modern Italian

tel: 020 7636 2207 **4 Great Portland St W1W 8QJ**
email: info@degowinebar.co.uk
dir: *Nearest station: Oxford Circus*

New-wave Italian a few paces from Oxford Circus

Tucked away just a stone's throw from the maddening crowds at Oxford Circus, this contemporary Italian may easily be overlooked, but it certainly stands out from the crowd with its full-flavoured cooking and cracking Italian wines. Kitted out in red and darkwood, it comes with a trendy ground floor wine bar (including pavement tables) and a sleek basement restaurant with suede- and leather-textured wall tiles, snazzy lighting and booth-style leather banquettes. The kitchen takes an equally modern approach, while staying true to the Italian philosophy of simplicity and letting prime ingredients shine. Dine on fashionable small or large plate dishes, choose a sharing platter, or go down the more conventional three-course route. Take succulent redcurrant glazed pork belly (cooked for 12 hours), its sweetness balanced by balsamic and endive, while fresh home-made pasta is a must, perhaps big-flavoured smoked ricotta and spinach ravioli offset by sweet braised red onions. A high-octane hot chocolate cake finale is a chocoholic's dream.

Chef Massimo Mioli **Owner** Massimo Mioli **Seats** 45 **Times** 12-3/5.30-11.30 Closed Xmas, Etr, Sun, L Mon **Prices** Fixed L 2 course £15-£45, Fixed D 3 course £25-£60, Starter £6.70-£11.80, Main £9.80-£26.50, Dessert £7.40-£12.30 **Wines** 250 bottles over £30, 30 bottles under £30, 16 by glass **Notes** Pre-theatre & tasting menus available, Vegetarian available, Children welcome

Dehesa

PLAN 2 J1

◎ Spanish, Italian

tel: 020 7494 4170 **25 Ganton St W1F 9BP**
email: info@dehesa.co.uk
dir: *Nearest station: Oxford Circus*

First-rate tapas in Soho

Dehesa comes from the same stable as Salt Yard and Opera Tavern (see entries) and, like them, is a charcuterie and tapas bar dedicated to the cuisines of Spain and Italy. It's a small place and it's easy to see why it gets so busy: quality ingredients are handled professionally, following authentic recipes, to bring the flavours of those two countries to life in London. Bar snacks of house-cured duck breast, or jamón ibérico, with a glass of fino make pleasing partners, or select from the full list of unfussy hot and cold dishes. Venetian-style sardines with sautéed onions, sultanas and pine nuts, and piquant salt-cod croquettes with sauce romesco are among the fish options, with tender confit pork belly with rosemary-scented cannellini beans, and fried lamb cutlet with broad beans, chilli and mint among the meat. You might not need extra vegetables like patatas fritas, but leave room for tempting puddings like chocolate cake with cappuccino ice cream.

Chef Giancarlo Vatteroni **Owner** Simon Mullins, Ben Tish **Seats** 40, Pr/dining room 12 **Times** 12-3/5-11 Closed 24-26 & 31 Dec, 1-2 Jan **Prices** Prices not confirmed **Wines** 25 bottles over £30, 15 bottles under £30, 11 by glass **Parking** NCP **Notes** Sunday L, Vegetarian available, Children welcome

Dinings

PLAN 2 E3

◎◎ Japanese, European

tel: 020 7723 0666 **22 Harcourt St W1H 4HH**
dir: *Nearest station: Edgware Rd, Marylebone*

Pint-sized basement room doing dazzling Japanese tapas

Exquisitely-crafted miniatures are a Japanese strong point, so the concept of Japanese tapas shows the savvy culinary synergy going on here at Dinings, where the creative kitchen fuses Japanese and modern European dishes into some extremely productive ideas. There's still a bonsai-sized traditional sushi bar on the ground floor where just six diners get to share elbow-to-elbow space, up close and personal with the chefs, but it is down in the utilitarian basement that a city-chic clientele turns up to be led through the hot, sour, sweet and savoury spectrum. Concrete floors, walls painted blue and cream, bare tables and leatherette seating amount to a pretty spartan setting, but you're not here for the interior design: check out the blackboard specials, then tackle the lengthy menu in the true tapas spirit by sharing a bunch of small dishes. Pan-fried padron peppers with garlic and shichimi pepper, tar-tar chips (home-made potato crisps filled with avocado, seafood, meat, vegetables and sauces) and – heading upmarket – seared Wagyu beef with chilli miso is a typical trio.

Chef Masaki Sugisaki, Keiji Fuku **Owner** Tomonari Chiba, Masaki Sugisaki **Seats** 28 **Times** 12-2.30/6-10.30 Closed Xmas, 31 Dec-1 Jan, Sun **Prices** Prices not confirmed **Wines** 24 bottles over £30, 6 bottles under £30, 9 by glass **Parking** On street & NCP **Notes** Fixed L menu available, Vegetarian available, Children welcome

Downtown Mayfair

PLAN 2 J1

◎◎ Italian

tel: 020 3056 1001 **15 New Burlington Place W1S 2HX**
email: info@downtownmayfair.com
dir: *Nearest station: Charing Cross, Oxford Circus*

Italian glamour in Mayfair

From the owners of C London (see entry) and Harry's Bar (see the wonderful city of Venice) comes Downtown Mayfair. Located in a modern building between Regent Street and Savile Row, the interior is a smart recreation of 1940s London, updated through the prism of 21st-century fashion. It looks good with its burnished panels, engraved glass, mosaic marble floors, chandeliers and linen-clad tables, and there's even a little 'library' area which forms an inviting booth. The menu, like its siblings, looks to Italy, and in particular the north of the country. Before you tuck in, though, there's the small matter of a Bellini, taken on the terrace if you're lucky. Start with king crab salad – no-one said it was cheap – and move onto something like calves' liver alla Veneziana or tagliolini with prosciutto. For dessert, the tiramisù is not obligatory, but it is always likely to be a favourite.

Times 12-11.45 Closed BHs, Sun All-day dining

DSTRKT

PLAN 2 K1

◎◎ Modern American

tel: 020 7317 9120 **9 Rupert St W1D 6DG**
email: reservations@dstrkt.co.uk
dir: *Nearest station: Piccadilly Circus*

Nightclub-style dining at the cutting edge

With a name that looks like it's written in Klingon, this restaurant/nightclub hybrid is high on concept, but determined to prove that being seen with beautiful people and eating well don't have to be mutually incompatible endeavours. It all happens down a dark staircase in a cavernous, high-decibel witches' grotto in black and gold, interlaced with botanical forms. Georgi Yaneff, an American chef of major

continued

LONDON W1 *continued*

repute, brings a forceful West Coast sense of sass with him, boldly melding continental cuisines with Pan-Asian modes into a gigantic global fusion. Starters are sized for pick'n'mixing: flash-fried cubes of tuna are topped with soy foam and supported by avocado purée, while a single tentacle of grilled octopus is matched with an earthy caramelised chickpea purée, fresh peas and preserved orange. At main-course stage, ostrich skewers come with a mustard and Guinness dipping sauce, and grilled lamb cutlets arrive with lamb pancetta, smoky aubergine purée and piquillo pepper coulis. Finish with caramelised apple frangipane tart with apple purée and ice cream and Cognac cream.

Chef Georgi Yaneff **Owner** Deyan Dobrev **Seats** 90 **Times** 6pm-3am Closed Sun-Mon, L all week **Prices** Fixed D 3 course £20-£200, Tasting menu £45-£80, Starter £6-£14, Main £11-£35, Dessert £6-£9 **Wines** 62 bottles over £30, 14 bottles under £30, 15 by glass **Parking** NCP 100mtrs **Notes** Tasting menu 12 course, pre-theatre menu £25, Vegetarian available, Children welcome

L'Escargot
PLAN 3 A2

@@ Traditional French

tel: 020 7439 7474 & 7494 1318 **48 Greek St W1D 4EF**
email: sales@lescargotrestaurant.co.uk **web:** www.lescargotrestaurant.co.uk
dir: *Nearest station: Tottenham Court Rd, Leicester Square*

Classic French bistro cookery at an old Soho stager

The dear old Snail of Soho has seen some changes since its inception in 1927, and the pattern continued in 2014. New owners Brian Clivaz and Laurence Isaacson began transforming the place room by room at the beginning of the year, and a new man, Oliver Lesnik, arrived to head up the kitchen. The Escargot's many firm friends need have no fear that some wrenching gear-change in the style is under way; the kitchen continues to produce sleekly worked renditions of classic French bistro food for an appreciative audience. Bilingual menus open with pork and veal terrine grande-mère, onion soup slicked with Gruyère, and baked haddock with quail eggs, before launching off into fortifying comfort-food territory for devilled sweetbreads in mustard, lobster thermidor, coq au vin, and grilled veal cutlet with lemon and thyme. Rest assured that snails, oysters and caviar still ornament the menu, and that you won't be deprived of a crème brûlée, a Grand Marnier soufflé, or even a startlingly trendy némésis au chocolat, at the end of it all.

Chef Oliver Lesnik **Owner** Brian Clivaz **Seats** 80, Pr/dining room 60
Times 12-2.30/5.30-11.30 Closed 25-26 Dec, 1 Jan **Prices** Fixed L 2 course £17.50, Fixed D 3 course £19.50, Starter £5-£12, Main £14-£36, Dessert £5-£12, Service optional 12.5% **Wines** 168 bottles over £30, 25 bottles under £30, 8 by glass **Parking** NCP Chinatown, on street parking **Notes** Fixed L & D 2/3 course available pre & post theatre, Sunday L, Vegetarian available, Children welcome

Fera at Claridge's
PLAN 2 H1

Rosettes not confirmed at time of going to print

Modern British **NEW** V

tel: 020 7107 8888 **Brook St W1K 4HR**
email: reservations@feraatclaridges.co.uk **web:** www.feraatclaridges.co.uk
dir: *Nearest station: Bond Street, Green Park*

Dynamic modern cooking courtesy of Simon Rogan

The man of the moment in the UK's culinary firmament is surely Simon Rogan, with L'Enclume long appreciated as one of the best in the land, and The French in Manchester hitting its stride. And now Fera at Claridge's. 'Fera' means wild, so it is an appropriate moniker for a restaurant in the dominion of Rogan, with his farm supplying a good deal of the produce. It all takes place in a room that once housed Ramsay's place and is rich with art-deco style. The designers worked their magic on the room, bringing colours that follow nature's lead – slate grey and green – and there are some shapely branches rising up to the gloriously adorned ceiling. There is no need for tablecloths on the walnut tables. The team in the kitchen is headed up by executive chef Dan Cox, with the à la carte menu supported by a ten- or 16-course tasting menus. The cooking is driven by the seasons and the ingredients are allowed room to breathe and leave a lasting impression. Clay-baked asparagus comes with savory and onions, pork skin, mead and ramson shoots, and raw beef is served with smoked broccoli cream, scallop roe and an acidic apple juice. Among main courses, plaice is braised in nettle butter and partnered with cockles and salsify, and dry-aged Herdwick hogget arrives with pickled tongue and hen of the woods (a mushroom). Desserts deliver iced beech leaf with nitro sweet cheese, apple and sorrel, or outdoor rhubarb with aerated honeycomb, gingerbread and sorrel. The wine list is a fine piece of work.

Chef Simon Rogan, Dan Cox **Owner** Simon Rogan **Seats** 94, Pr/dining room 12 **Times** 12-2/6.30-10 **Prices** Fixed L 2 course £45, Tasting menu £95-£125, Service optional 12.5% **Wines** 500 bottles over £30, 7 bottles under £30, 17 by glass **Parking** On street, NCP **Notes** Fixed ALC menu £85, No Children

Fino
PLAN 2 J3

@@ Spanish

tel: 020 7813 8010 **33 Charlotte St W1T 1RR**
email: info@finorestaurant.com
dir: *Nearest station: Goodge St, Tottenham Court Rd*

Stylish buzzy basement restaurant serving classy authentic tapas

Once you've found the place, down a narrow side road just off trendy Charlotte Street (it's just behind Roka), take the stairs down to this airy, buzzy basement room. Fino serves tapas of the highest order, the authentic and inventive Spanish dishes made from top quality ingredients. Take a ringside seat on a high stool at the bar in front of the semi-open kitchen, or on red leather banquettes or rattan-backed chairs at one of the well-spaced tables, and take on the concise listing of first-rate contemporary and classic tapas dishes. Ingredients, many imported, are the real McCoy, and are honestly and confidently handled to deliver full-on flavours. Start with a take on tortilla, turbo-charged with salt cod, piquillo peppers and spinach, then go for seafood from the plancha – cuttlefish with pancetta and ink, anyone? – or a timeless meat dish: crisp pork belly that's as rich and piggy as you could wish for. There are textbook Spanish puddings too, like Santiago tart, or a Moorish fusion of dates poached in coffee and cardamom.

Chef Nieves Barragan Mohacho **Owner** Sam & Eddie Hart **Seats** 90 **Times** 12-2.30/6-10.30 Closed Xmas, BHs, Sun, L Sat **Prices** Starter £4-£12, Main £11-£25, Dessert £4-£8 **Wines** 78 bottles over £30, 18 bottles under £30, 12 by glass **Notes** Menu Del Dia L 6 tapas £17.50, Vegetarian available, Children welcome

Flemings Mayfair

PLAN 4 H6

Modern European

tel: 020 7499 0000 **Half Moon St, Mayfair W1J 7BH**
email: thegrill@flemings.co.uk **web:** www.flemings-mayfair.co.uk
dir: Nearest station: Green Park

Luxury hotel with top-notch steaks and more

This luxury boutique hotel in well-heeled Mayfair has an entirely appropriate glossy restaurant, with a striking rich colour scheme of red, brown and gold, a soft swirly-patterned carpet and comfortable dining chairs and button-back banquettes. TV chef Rosemary Shrager has had some input, with half a dozen dishes on the menu attributed to her. These include smoked duck with chicory marmalade, hazelnuts and beetroot, and halibut fillet with cockles and mussels, salsify and lobster essence. Otherwise, the main thrust is on steaks from the grill with a choice of sauces: say, rib-eye with mustard and tarragon butter. The rest of the menu is a relatively humble bunch, although produce is of the best quality and high levels of technical skill are clear. Start with smoked salmon with watercress dressing, capers and lemon, go on to chicken or beef burger or the fish of the day. Conclude with pears poached in white wine with chocolate sauce.

Chef Brian Henry **Seats** 60, Pr/dining room 22 **Times** 12-2/5.30-10 Closed L Sat-Sun **Prices** Starter £7.50-£12.50, Main £17.50-£25, Dessert £8.50-£12.50 **Wines** 18 bottles over £30, 9 bottles under £30, 14 by glass **Notes** Afternoon tea available, Vegetarian available, Children welcome

Four Seasons Hotel London at Park Lane

PLAN 4 G6

International, British, Italian V

tel: 020 7319 5206 **Hamilton Place, Park Ln W1J 7DR**
email: amaranto.lon@fourseasons.com **web:** www.fourseasons.com/london/dining
dir: Nearest station: Green Park, Hyde Park Corner

Innovative Italian cooking in red-and-black splendour

It is hard to imagine a more unapologetically opulent look than that sported by the Amaranto restaurant after its dramatic interior makeover in 2011. The grand old Four Seasons by Hyde Park has never been short of sultry, high-gloss glamour, and the Amaranto concept, comprising an interlinked bar, lounge and restaurant does not disappoint. The decor involves theatrical hues of blood-red and jet-black, mirror-shined marble flooring, deep-pile carpets, onyx and burnished dark-wood tabletops, and abstract artworks, as well as a light-flooded conservatory and alfresco terrace. The cooking offers a contemporary nuova cucina take on the Italian idiom using authentic ingredients driven by creative, up-to-date flavour combinations. Antipasti show the style with dishes such as roasted octopus with spicy pork 'Nduja pâté, warm ratte potato foam and salsa verde, or 21-day-aged organic beef tartare with porcini. Pasta and main course dishes can be as classic as spaghetti with tomato and basil, or a perfectly-judged platter of grilled fish, shellfish and vegetables, marinated in extra virgin olive oil and lemon.

Chef Adriano Cavagnini **Owner** Four Seasons Hotels & Resorts **Seats** 58, Pr/dining room 10 **Times** 12-2.30/6.30-10.30 **Prices** Prices not confirmed **Wines** 200 bottles over £30, 17 by glass **Parking** 10 **Notes** Tasting menu 6 course, Sunday L, Children welcome

Galvin at Windows Restaurant & Bar

PLAN 4 G6

– see page 344

Galvin Bistrot de Luxe

PLAN 2 G3

French NOTABLE WINE LIST

tel: 020 7935 4007 **66 Baker St W1U 7DJ**
email: info@galvinrestaurants.com **web:** www.galvinrestaurants.com
dir: Nearest station: Baker Street

Well-crafted French cooking in stylish bistro

The Galvin brothers' consistently rammed bistrot on Baker Street is so Parisian, it almost makes a trip on Eurostar redundant. The place looks the part, with its smart 1930s style, the mahogany interior offset by mirrors, dangling globe lights, whirling ceiling fans and leather bentwood chairs and banquettes at crisply-clothed tables, while attentive, sunny natured staff (donning white aprons and black bow ties and waistcoats) add to the theatre and authenticity of it all. The seasonally-inspired menus (including a great value lunch and early evening prix fixe) are spot on too, delivering exceptionally well-executed French bistro classics fashioned from fine produce and with a light modern touch. Witness a generous pavé of sea-fresh cod served with crushed garden peas, girolles, rich boudin noir and light and creamy mashed potato, or perhaps succulent rump of lamb with bouillon of new season vegetables. Desserts continue the theme: take a spot-on signature tarte Tatin (with crème fraîche) or blueberry soufflé (supported by milk ice cream), while the extensive wine list is a Francophile's dream.

Chef Chris Galvin, Kevin Tew **Owner** Chris & Jeff Galvin **Seats** 110, Pr/dining room 22 **Times** 12-2.30/6-10.30 Closed 25-26 Dec, 1 Jan, D 24 Dec **Prices** Fixed L 3 course £19.50, Fixed D 3 course £21.50, Starter £7.50-£15.50, Main £16.50-£29.50, Dessert £6.50-£11 **Wines** 157 bottles over £30, 19 bottles under £30, 15 by glass **Parking** On street, Portman Square car park **Notes** Prix Fixe D available 6-7pm, Sunday L, Vegetarian available, Children welcome

Gauthier Soho

PLAN 3 A1

– see page 344

Who has won our Chefs' Chef award?

Find out on page 10

Get the most out of the AA Restaurant Guide

See page 6

Galvin at Windows Restaurant & Bar

LONDON W1   **PLAN 4 G6**

Modern French 🍷 NOTABLE WINE LIST

tel: 020 7208 4021 **London Hilton on Park Ln, 22 Park Ln W1K 1BE**
email: reservations@galvinatwindows.com
dir: *Nearest station: Green Park, Hyde Park Corner*

Stunning bird's eye views and compelling French cooking

It's been open for nearly a decade now, but a table in Galvin at Windows is still one of the hottest tickets in town. The view of the capital from the 28th floor of the Park Lane Hilton is enough of a draw in itself, and while the window tables are the prize spots, the restaurant's clever split-level design allows everyone a share of that stunning panorama. Chef-patron Chris Galvin is renowned for his bold, creative take on French haute cuisine, and while he doesn't man the stoves here on a daily basis, newly installed head chef Joo Won is fully versed in the signature style. If you haven't managed to bag a window table in the restaurant, your luck might be in the bar, where spectacular views and equally impressive cocktails go hand in hand. In the restaurant itself, the look is all 1930s glamour, with tables dressed up to the nines, and service that's on the ball whether or not the master, Fred Sirieix (you may have seen him on the telly), is on duty. The cooking eschews butter, cream and rich sauces in favour of clean, vibrant, natural flavours, with seasonality a watchword. Seared Scottish king scallops are timed to perfection to start and matched with succulent slow-cooked pork belly, a sweetcorn puree and an intensely flavoured shellfish reduction, while main-course breast of Landes pigeon comes nicely pink and tender, sitting on a bed of couscous, with an excellent pastilla of the leg meat, finished with blobs of aubergine puree and a harissa jus for an injection of spice. A first-class rum baba with a golden raisin compote and crème fontainebleu (a very creamy cream cheese) might turn up for dessert, or perhaps a multi-dimensional dark chocolate mousse on a crunchy hazelnut and chocolate base, with a flavour-packed griotte cherry sorbet, a pool of saffron anglaise and some thin chocolate and nut wafers. The wine list is well worth a moment or two of your time.

Chef Joo Won, Chris Galvin **Owner** Hilton International **Seats** 130
Times 12-2.30/6-10.30 Closed BHs, 26 Dec, 9 Apr, 7 May, L Sat, D Sun, 25 Dec
Prices Fixed L 2 course fr £25, Fixed D 3 course fr £68, Tasting menu fr £95
Wines 248 bottles over £30, 36 bottles under £30, 31 by glass **Parking** NCP
Notes Tasting menu 6 course, Dégustation menu available, Sunday L £25-£29, Vegetarian available, Children welcome

Gauthier Soho

LONDON W1   **PLAN 3 A1**

French v 🍷 NOTABLE WINE LIST

tel: 020 7494 3111 **21 Romilly St W1D 5AF**
email: info@gauthiersoho.co.uk
dir: *Nearest station: Leicester Square*

Outstanding modern French cooking in the heart of Soho

Gauthier takes up a Georgian townhouse (ring the doorbell to get in), with two restaurant rooms and five private dining rooms spread over three floors. A clean, uncluttered look is produced by white walls and table covers, beige dining chairs, mirrors, and spotlights in the high ceilings, with splashes of colour from fresh flowers, while slick and tuned-in staff keep the wheels turning. 'You won't find any recipe books, measuring equipment or timing devices in this kitchen' declares the restaurant; rather, M Gauthier relies on his instincts, intuition and taste buds, and the results can be stunningly good. The menus follow a set-price formula, with two or three courses at lunch, up to five at dinner, priced according to number taken (trois plats £40, and so on). Excellent canapés and breads are an impressive foretaste of the main business to come, underlined by a first course of fine black truffle ravioli with mascarpone and brown butter. Impeccable sourcing is a hallmark, with ingredients imaginatively mixed and matched and treated with a high level of both artistry and respect, serving roast scallops, for instance, with turnips in a light ginger cream, with crunchy green apples and coral dressing. Spot-on cod fillet is given a boost by its accompanying toasted salsify with wild mushroom marmalade, and lettuce and fish velouté, while among meat options loin of venison gets lifted out of the ordinary by an unusual pumpkin and pepper jus and Williams pear and celeriac purée. Sure-footedness continues into not-to-be-missed desserts like passionfruit soufflé with yoghurt sorbet, and mandarin curd with a matching sorbet.

Chef Gerard Virolle, Alexis Gauthier **Owner** Gerard Virolle, Alexis Gauthier
Seats 60, Pr/dining room 32 **Times** 12-2.30/6.30-10.30 Closed Xmas, BHs, Sun-Mon **Prices** Fixed L 2 course fr £18, Fixed D 3 course fr £40, Tasting menu fr £70
Wines 150 bottles over £30, 30 bottles under £30, 20 by glass **Parking** On street, NCP Chinatown **Notes** ALC fixed L/D menu, Children welcome

LONDON W1 *continued*

Le Gavroche Restaurant PLAN 2 G1

@@@ – *see next page*

Goodman PLAN 2 J1

@ British, American 🍷 NOTABLE WINE LIST

tel: 020 7499 3776 **26 Maddox St W1S 1QH**
email: reservations@goodmanrestaurants.com
dir: *Nearest station: Oxford Circus*

American-style Mayfair steakhouse serving prime cuts

Goodman is every bit the upmarket New York-style steakhouse (though it's actually part of a Russian chain with outlets in the City and Canary Wharf too). The interior looks the part with its polished darkwood walls and floors, combined with liver-brown leather seating (including some booths). A meal here gets underway with a generous array of prime, aged-in-house cuts from traceable herds (perhaps 150-day-aged corn-fed USDA Angus, or Irish grass-fed) brought to your table by informed, friendly staff. There are extra daily cuts to choose from on the blackboard, and although it's by no means cheap, depth of flavour is priceless. Rib-eye, T-bone, sirloin and fillet (priced by weight) all find their place, each accurately cooked over charcoal, and served with a choice of sauces. For non-meat eaters there's the likes of lobster cocktail or Caesar salad, while desserts continue the theme, with baked New York cheesecake a fixture. The corking wine list is unsurprisingly big on beefy reds.

Chef John Cadieux, Phil Campbell **Owner** Michail Zelman **Seats** 95 **Times** noon-10.30 Closed Xmas, New Year, BHs, Sun All-day dining **Prices** Starter £7.50-£16, Main £15-£45, Dessert £3.50-£12 **Wines** 252 bottles over £30, 4 bottles under £30, 23 by glass **Parking** On street **Notes** Children welcome

Great British Restaurant PLAN 2 G1

@@ British

tel: 020 7741 2233 **North Audley St W1K 6WE**
email: reservations@eatbrit.com
dir: *Nearest station: Bond Street, Marble Arch*

Top-notch British food at accessible prices in Mayfair

The capital's hardly awash with eating places serving classy British food, but Mayfair's relaxed Great British Restaurant sets about filling the void. Located just around the corner from all the Oxford Street mayhem, the narrow, darkwood-panelled room has something of a nostalgic clubby vibe, with its black-and-white tiled floor, tables topped with Victorian reclaimed tiles, and dark-green leather upholstered bench seating and café-style chairs, while walls are lined with monochrome photos of '70s and '80s Brit Pop icons. The kitchen champions the best of British too, with seasonality, sourcing and traceability key, while menus include refined classic fare alongside more modern light, clear-flavoured dishes. Go for something traditional like signature shepherd's pie or standout fish and chips, or a more modish day-boat Cornish turbot (super-fresh) served with shrimp butter and parsley. Top and tail that with Maize Farm salt beef, mustard pease pudding, radicchio and pickles, and a comfort pud like textbook Cox apple and fruit crumble with proper custard. British cheeses and English wines and ales stay true to the home-grown ethos. Brunch is available at the weekend.

Chef Pete Taylor **Owner** George Hammer **Seats** 39, Pr/dining room 14 **Times** 12-3/5.30-10.30 Closed Xmas, New Year & BHs, D Sun **Prices** Starter £5.50-£8, Main £12.75-£23, Dessert £5.75-£7.50 **Wines** 4 bottles over £30, 8 bottles under £30, 7 by glass **Parking** On Street **Notes** Non fixed menu available L & D, Brunch menu Sat-Sun 9-3, Sunday L, Vegetarian available, Children welcome

The Greenhouse PLAN 4 H6

@@@@ – *see page 347*

Le Gavroche Restaurant

LONDON W1	PLAN 2 G1

French

tel: 020 7408 0881 **43 Upper Brook St W1K 7QR**
email: bookings@le-gavroche.com
dir: *Nearest station: Marble Arch*

Unwavering commitment to classical French gastronomy

The winsome logo of the Gavroche references the restaurant's naming in honour of a street-urchin in Hugo's Les Misérables. Its location since 1967 in a redbrick terrace townhouse on the fringes of Mayfair, not far from Park Lane, may not look to have anything like the brash glitz or the understated sleek-finished gleam of today's gastro hotspots, but the Gavroche has never particularly seen the need to muscle its way into the vanguard – except where it finally matters, in the commitment to impeccable quality, fastidious correctness in service, and a massive wine list full of French classics to beguile the old-school connoisseur. Michel Roux Jr does a lot more these days than preside over the kitchens here, as anyone who ever watches TV will know, but he nonetheless manages to maintain a standard of excellence forged and maintained over many years by his father Albert. A brief closure over the winter of 2014 to fit new kitchens saw the introduction of a private room called the Chef's Library, but the tenacious insistence on classical French gastronomy remains undimmed. Longstanding dishes like lobster mousse with caviar and champagne butter sauce will surely never disappear from the menu, and nor should they, but there are excursions into more contemporary modes. Braised and smoked pork cheeks delivers stunning, intense flavours, with the meat melting in the mouth, supported by a raviolo filled with belly meat and red cabbage condiments, while another first course sees perfectly cooked langoustines combined with air-dried Bayonne ham and peas, dressed with a light shellfish foam. Roast saddle of rabbit with crispy potatoes and parmesan

delivers so much more than the dish description, with the moist and flavour-packed loin joined by kidneys and legs, each element cooked just right (with a bit of service theatre to boot), Rejoice in classic dishes burnished by tradition: roast breast and confit leg of duck in port; darne of turbot in chive butter; saddle of rabbit with potato galette. There are pedigree cheeses (or cheese in the singular, such as aged Mimolette with rocket and walnut oil), and desserts can raise the roof, judging by a hot passionfruit soufflé with white chocolate ice cream (an essay in the balance of sweetness and fruity acidity). In this exalted company, the canapés and petit fours seem a little pedestrian, but the wine list is anything but – a grandiose tome indeed with advice on hand from the expert sommeliers.

Chef Michel Roux Jnr **Owner** Le Gavroche Ltd **Seats** 60, Pr/dining room 6 **Times** 12-2/6-10 Closed Xmas, New Year, BHs, Sun, L Sat **Prices** Fixed L 3 course £54.80, Tasting menu £124-£194, Starter £19.80-£60.80, Main £26.40-£68.60, Dessert £16.40-£40.20, Service optional 12.5% **Wines** 2500 bottles over £30, 25 bottles under £30, 25 by glass **Parking** NCP - Park Lane **Notes** Tasting menu 8 course, Vegetarian available, Children welcome

The Greenhouse

LONDON W1   **PLAN 4 H6**

French, European

tel: 020 7499 3331 **27a Hay's Mews, Mayfair W1J 5NY**
email: reservations@greenhouserestaurant.co.uk
dir: *Nearest station: Green Park, Bond St*

Gastronomic delights in a discreet Mayfair location

The thinking behind the name becomes apparent as you stroll down the decked pathway, lined with bamboo plants, box hedges, bay trees, sculptures and little fountains on the way to the front door – a lovely, tranquil garden setting, tucked away down a wide Mayfair mews, that instantly puts you in a relaxed mood. Alfresco dining isn't an option, but you do get views of the garden from the serenely stylish dining room, where the extremely professional yet very friendly service plays its part in creating an oasis of calm and refinement. Natural, restful shades of beige and ivory are offset by modern darkwood floors, avocado-coloured leather banquettes and chairs, tables dressed in their finest white linen, and a feature wall taken up by a filigree display of tree branches to emphasise the garden theme. Many great chefs have run the stoves at the Greenhouse over the years, and today's incumbent, Arnaud Bignon, is not about to let the side down. He cooks from the heart, starting with the best ingredients money can buy and combining techniques old and new to produce dishes with clean, precise flavours that look beautiful on the plate. The arrival of canapés on sticks and forks protruding from a small rectangular block signals that you're in for something rather special: the presentation is fun, while the flavours and textures are remarkable. After some fabulous artisan-style fresh breads (parmesan, sunflower seed and a baguette) might come a signature starter of Cornish crab with mint jelly, cauliflower, Granny Smith apple and curry, a delightful dish that's light, fresh, beautifully balanced and full of textural contrasts. Next up might be one of the eastern-inflected fish dishes, perhaps nori-wrapped monkfish in dashi with cockles and razor clams, or turbot with coconut, tamarind and ginger, or you might choose Welsh organic lamb from the Rhug Estate, given a similarly oriental twist with miso and mooli, as well as Anya potato and puntarelle (winter chicory). A skilled hand at pastry is evident in a dessert that encases the North African notes of orange, dates and saffron in ruffles of filo, while cheeses come from unimpeachable suppliers in France, Switzerland and Neal's Yard. Make sure you don't skip coffee as the petits fours are something else. The wine list is a serious piece of work which may require a little help from the knowledgeable sommelier, and perhaps a little from the bank manager too.

Chef Arnaud Bignon **Owner** Marlon Abela Restaurant Corporation **Seats** 60, Pr/dining room 12
Times 12-2.30/6.30-11 Closed Xmas, BHs, Sun, L Sat
Prices Prices not confirmed **Wines** 3222 bottles over £30, 20 bottles under £30, 30 by glass **Parking** On street
Notes Vegetarian available, Children welcome

LONDON W1 *continued*

The Grill at The Dorchester

PLAN 4 G6

◉◉ British ▮ NOTABLE WINE LIST

tel: 020 7629 8888 **The Dorchester, Park Ln W1K 1QA**
email: restaurants.TDL@thedorchester.com **web:** www.thedorchester.com
dir: *Nearest station: Hyde Park Corner*

Top quality eating at a world-class hotel

My goodness, there is some good eating to be had at The Dorchester this century. The hotel is all you'd hope it to be and simply walking through the front door for the first time is a bit of a thrill. If Monsieur Ducasse will forgive us for a moment (see separate entry), we're here to talk about The Grill, a restaurant that is an essential part of The Dorchester package. It's an eye-catching room filled with rich fabrics and murals on a Scottish theme (so lots of tartan), looked over by exceptional staff, for whom gueridon service (carving from the trolley, etc.) is a specialty of the house. The quality of the produce is second to none, and the menu mixes tradition with more contemporary touches. Start with sardine cannelloni, grilled cucumber and dill juice (a fabulously punchy dish), or some home-smoked Loch Duart salmon and gravad lax carved at the table. Among main courses, grilled Dover sole and fabulous Black Angus beef sit alongside Romsey lamb with aubergine purée, watercress and potato risotto, and to finish, expect the likes of hazelnut and chocolate moelleux.

Times 12–2.30/6.30–10.30

Hakkasan

PLAN 2 K2

◉◉ Chinese

tel: 020 7927 7000 **8 Hanway Place W1T 1HD**
email: reservation@hakkasan.com
dir: *Nearest station: Tottenham Court Rd*

New-wave Chinese cooking in a see-and-be-seen basement setting

Discretely hidden from the maddening crowds just off Tottenham Court Road and Oxford Street, this original Hakkasan still rocks (there's a sister restaurant in Mayfair). Descend to the moody basement and you're immediately captivated by the effortlessly cool, modern Chinoiserie design and night-clubby vibe: think darkwood latticing, black and gold traditionally drawn panels, and low-slung leather seating, plus a backlit cocktail bar and open kitchen. To match the up-tempo vibe, an innovative repertoire of new-wave meets classic Cantonese dishes covers all bases, and everything is exquisitely presented. You might start with some first-rate dim sum (XO scallop dumplings perhaps) or jasmine tea smoked organic pork ribs from the 'small eat' section of the menu, before moving on to something like stir-fried Chilean sea bass with white truffle and black bean sauce, or maybe sweet and sour Duke of Berkshire pork with pomegranate. Desserts lean heavily on the West: witness a deconstructed apple tart Tatin with blackberry, almond and vanilla. A heavyweight wine list and an exciting cocktail selection completes the picture.

Times 12–3/6–12 Closed 25 Dec

Hakkasan Mayfair

PLAN 2 H1

◉◉◉ *– see below*

Hakkasan Mayfair

LONDON W1   PLAN 2 H1

Chinese
tel: 020 7907 1888 & 7355 7701 **17 Bruton St W1J 6QB**
email: mayfairreservation@hakkasan.com
dir: *Nearest station: Green Park*

Upmarket Chinese cooking in luxury surroundings

A doorman at the entrance and, inside, welcoming greeters at the end of the corridor sets the tone for this upmarket Chinese restaurant, sibling to the Hanway Place branch. No surprise for Mayfair, it's been expensively decorated and fitted, with a marble floor, comfortable banquettes, polished wooden panels and subdued lighting; staff are slick, friendly and speedy – and they need to be, given the number of covers, as the place always seems busy. The menu is littered with top-end ingredients and luxuries, with prices to match, among them Peking duck with Beluga caviar, braised lobster with noodles in royal supreme sauce, and Wagyu beef with enoki mushrooms and soya and garlic dipping sauce. The rest of the menu is a roll-call of interesting, often unusual and original dishes, a far cry from the usual Chinatown staples, and the cooking is marked out by its accurate timing, judicious combinations and well-judged spicing and seasoning. Salt-

and-pepper squid with sweet chilli sauce is a classic example of the dish, and another starter from the 'small eat' section could be tender braised beef shank wrapped in lotus root. Sauces and garnishes are exemplary: one of rice wine and garlic for steamed cubes of lobster wrapped in glass vermicelli, royal broth for Cantonese-style watercress with clams and shimeji mushrooms, and Szechuan sauce for stir-fried sea bass and leeks served in a potato basket. Incidentals like rice and side orders of vegetables, such as crisp and vibrant gai lan (Chinese broccoli), all get a thumbs up. Desserts, surprisingly for this cuisine, can be highlights, such as a light banana soufflé with blobs of salted caramel, served with a 'feast' (a lollipop of ice cream, nuts and chocolate), for instance, and lemon pot (curd, meringue and crumble). The menu also recommends appropriate pudding wines.

Chef Tong Chee Hwee, Koon Chuen Liang **Owner** Tasameem **Seats** 220, Pr/dining room 14 **Times** 12–3.15/6–11.15 Closed 24–25 Dec, L 26 Dec, 1 Jan **Prices** Prices not confirmed **Wines** 9 by glass **Parking** NCP **Notes** Afternoon menu available 3.15–5pm, Vegetarian available, Children welcome

Hélène Darroze at The Connaught

Modern French **V**

tel: 020 3147 7200 **Carlos Place W1K 2AL**
email: creservations@the-connaught.co.uk
web: www.the-connaught.co.uk
dir: *Nearest station: Bond Street, Green Park*

Stellar cooking from a French chef in a British institution

This is one serious piece of real estate. The hotel has been on this spot since 1815, with a serious makeover occurring in the 1890s, and the place has been a by-word for luxury ever since. It really isn't stuck in the past, though, with the most recent interior design effort including a softening of the hotel's famous restaurant, run by Hélène Darroze since 2008. There is all the grandeur you might imagine at such an iconic address, with places to sip champagne, tuck into a magnificent afternoon tea, or dine pretty much any time of the day in the Espelette dining room. The Hélène Darroze restaurant is very much the main event, though, with the culinary action taking place in a swish room where designer India Mahdavi has introduced softer tones amid the original burnished oak panelling. Darroze used to work under the great Alain Ducasse and then went on to make her own mark at her eponymous restaurant in Paris, and she currently spends her time between the two cities. The cooking has its roots in her native South-Western France, but the overall impression is of well-crafted, dynamic, modern food, and everything looks stunning on the plate. The fixed-price menu follows the tasting format, with five-, seven- or nine-course options, plus an additional cheese course. Things begin impressively with amuse-bouche (foie gras crème brûlée with hazelnut foam, if you're lucky), and bread that delivers a beautiful aroma to the table. Given the chef's own provenance, there's more foie gras among first courses, in a dish with the liver given the confit treatment (with sangria), and accompanying figs (poached and fresh) and date purée to cut through the delicious richness of it all. The quality of the ingredients is a stand-out feature of a visit. There's a lot going on in each dish, such as a fallow venison main course, with its roasted saddle and rack (both succulent and bursting with flavour) in the company of civet cannelloni, celeriac mousseline, stilton Chantilly, William pear and a glossy grand veneur sauce. Terrific stuff. Desserts are equally creative, modern and refined, for example praline mousse made with hazelnuts from Piedmont, with candied fennel and a lemon foam giving a satisfying sharpness. The service team strike a really pleasing balance, with the slick professionalism expected at this level measured by a relaxed confidence. The wine list meets expectations at this level, with plenty of big-hitters and big prices.

Chef Hélène Darroze **Owner** Maybourne Hotel Group **Seats** 64, Pr/dining room 20 **Times** 12-2.30/6.30-10.30 Closed 1 wk Jan, 2 wks Aug, Sun-Mon **Prices** Prices not confirmed **Wines** 550 bottles over £30, 14 by glass **Parking** Valet parking **Notes** ALC Fixed menu £80, Signature menu 6/9 course, Children welcome

LONDON W1 *continued*

Haozhan

PLAN 3 A1

Modern Chinese

tel: 020 7434 3838 **8 Gerrard St W1D 5PJ**
email: info@haozhan.co.uk
dir: *Nearest station: Trafalgar Square, Piccadilly Circus*

Chinatown restaurant serving exciting oriental fusion food

Haozhan stands out from the opposition in the heart of Chinatown by virtue of its simple contemporary looks and a creative kitchen that fuses elements of Far Eastern styles – Thai, Malaysian, Japanese, among others – to create some truly original dishes. Statement lampshades hang above simple black wooden tables and a wall of illuminated green and black, and the buzzy ambience is a testament to the popularity of its cooking. A broad-minded roster of dim sum dishes now bolsters an already extensive menu, so start with steamed dumplings of spanking-fresh scallops and spinach, then look beyond the comfort of staples such as aromatic crispy duck for the full-bore flavours of braised eel, pork and garlic hotpot. Elsewhere, stir-fried rib-eye beef with red wine sauce vies for attention with chicken with lemongrass and lime sauce, mint leaves, chilli and lemon zest. End with something like black sesame ice cream with fresh mint.

Chef Heng Thiang **Owner** Jimmy Kong **Seats** 80, Pr/dining room 40 **Times** 12-11.30 Closed 24-25 Dec, All-day dining **Prices** Fixed D 2 course £10-£30, Tasting menu £30-£45, Starter £6-£33.20, Main £9.70-£46.10, Dessert £5.80-£7.70 **Wines** 18 bottles over £30, 44 bottles under £30, 13 by glass **Parking** Chinatown **Notes** Tasting menu for 2, Pre-theatre menu from £16.50, Vegetarian available, Children welcome

Hélène Darroze at The Connaught

PLAN 2 H1

– *see page 349*

Hibiscus

PLAN 2 J1

– *see opposite*

Looking for a London restaurant by name?
Use the index on page 254

Looking for a London restaurant near you?
Use the maps on pages 258–68

HIX

PLAN 2 J1

British

tel: 020 7292 3518 **66-70 Brewer St W1F 9UP**
email: reservations@hixsoho.co.uk
dir: *Nearest station: Piccadilly Circus*

A celebration of British ingredients

You could easily pass by the giant wooden door on Soho's Brewer Street without ever knowing there's a bustling restaurant on the other side. The red neon 'HIX' sign leads the way, for this is one of Mark Hix's gaffs – the burgeoning empire now running to eight venues (seven in the capital). Here in Soho, the spacious dining room has an air of art-deco style about it, with reeded glass panels, white-tiled floor, mirrors, brown leather banquettes and a long silver-topped bar running the whole length of one wall. Colourful mobiles and neon signs by Hix's artist chums (including Damien Hirst and Tim Noble) hang from the high ceiling. No-nonsense, modern British cooking utilising excellent seasonal ingredients is what to expect, and first impressions are good, with a small loaf of hot sourdough bread brought to the table fresh from the oven. Spring herb soup with Ticklemore goats' cheese is a delightfully earthy starter, while herb roasted Loch Duart salmon and spring vegetable salad is as fresh as fresh can be. Yorkshire rhubarb pie, served hot with a great big dollop of cold, creamy custard on top, makes a smile-inducing finish. For drinks (and small plates of simple food) check out Mark's Bar in the basement.

Times 12-12 Closed 25-26 Dec, 1 Jan, All-day dining

HIX Mayfair

PLAN 2 J1

Traditional British V NOTABLE WINE LIST

tel: 020 7518 4004 **Brown's Hotel, Albemarle St W1S 4BP**
email: hixmayfair@roccofortehotels.com **web:** www.roccofortehotels.com
dir: *Nearest station: Green Park*

Modern cooking of traditional ingredients with contemporary art on show

The dining at Brown's Hotel has undergone a fair few manifestations in recent years, but the present one, under the aegis of in-demand modern Britishist Mark Hix, is undoubtedly one of the most inspired. Against a backdrop of work by British artists of various generations – Tracey Emin and Bridget Riley among them – Hix's menus are given dazzling execution by Lee Streeton. Hix himself drops in to give the occasional workshop on such essentials as carving. Thoroughbred British produce and foraged materials pour forth on menus that take in Dorset snails with Cumbrian black pudding and bacon, crispy Goosnargh duck with chickweed and marinated cherries, and a salad of vibrantly coloured Dorset Blue lobster with sea-purslane. These fine prime ingredients are treated with respect, not muddled into a crowd of supporting characters, so that main courses such as chargrilled Torbay sole, and roast mallard with gamekeeper's pie and spiced red cabbage, make perfect sense. So does an apple pie made with juicy, aromatic Cox's and served with real custard.

Chef Mark Hix, Lee Streeton **Owner** Rocco Forte Hotels **Seats** 80, Pr/dining room 70 **Times** 12-3/5.30-11 **Prices** Fixed L 2 course £27.50, Fixed D 3 course £32.50, Starter £6.95-£30, Main £17.50-£42.50, Dessert £6-£10.95 **Wines** 280 bottles over £30, 2 bottles under £30, 18 by glass **Parking** Valet/Burlington St **Notes** Pre-theatre bookings 5.30-7.30pm Mon-Sat, Sunday L, Children welcome

Hibiscus

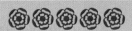

Modern French V NOTABLE WINE LIST
tel: 020 7629 2999 **29 Maddox St, Mayfair W1S 2PA**
email: enquiries@hibiscusrestaurant.co.uk
dir: *Nearest station: Oxford Circus, Marble Arch*

Top-class modern French cooking from a master of his art

Claude Bosi moved to the UK in the mid-'90s having worked with some stellar French chefs in Paris. French culinary traditions run deep with Monsieur Bosi, with a childhood spent at his parents' restaurant in Lyon. On arrival in Shropshire, first off, it was the UK's lack of appreciation of the nation's superb produce that caught his eye. And he did something about it. To this day, Bosi uses trusted independent suppliers to keep his kitchen fuelled with prime seasonal ingredients, and his menu is based on a thorough appreciation of French classical cooking alongside fabulous creativity. His food is refined, but never over-blown, and flavour is king. When moving to London in 2007, Bosi (and his wife, Claire) didn't open up in a fancy hotel, but opted instead for a discreet place in Mayfair, nothing too flash, somewhere rather dignified. A recent refurbishment has resulted in a contemporary and civilised space, with muted tones and modern art. Tables are dressed up in brilliant white cloths, and a statement floral display holds court in the centre of the room. The front-of-house is run with charm and professionalism by Claire Bosi, with the mood satisfyingly free of stuffiness. The menu needs a little explaining. First off, lunchtime is terrific value, three choices at each course and even a plat du jour dish available Monday to Friday, in honour, perhaps, of chef's childhood in Lyon. The main menu consists of three options: three, six or eight courses, which is straightforward enough. But what follows depends on what is red-hot that day, and what suppliers have delivered to the door. But fear not, for you are in very safe hands. You will be served artfully constructed dishes that look beautiful to the eye but never lack for punchy flavours. On the lunch menu might be a warm pike quenelle with new season chestnuts and 'quiche Lorraine', with each dish much more than the sum of its parts. Claude Bosi is a chef capable of maximising the impact of every ingredient, bringing together combinations that meld together as a whole while maintaining the integrity of each individual element. The courses on the tasting menus tantalise with brief descriptions that give no clue as to the craft and technical know-how on display: Devonshire crab, Yorkshire venison, Amalfi lemon, each one, though, living long in the memory. It's back to the lunch menu for Scottish partridge with roasted cauliflower, curried capers and raisins, followed by an impressive dessert that combines sweet potato and clementine in a 'cheesecake'. Just as Bosi seeks out the very best ingredients for the table, the wine list gets the same attention to detail, with natural growers to the fore.

Chef Claude Bosi **Owner** Claude Bosi **Seats** 48, Pr/dining room 18 **Times** 12-2.30/6.30-10.30 Closed 10 days Xmas, New Year, Sun-Mon **Prices** Fixed L 2 course £29, Fixed D 3 course £87.50, Tasting menu £95-£105 **Wines** 345 bottles over £30, 4 bottles under £30, 20 by glass **Parking** On street **Notes** Tasting menu D only 3/6/8 course, Children welcome

LONDON W1 *continued*

Iberica Marylebone
PLAN 2 H4

@ Modern Spanish

tel: 020 7636 8650 **195 Great Portland St W1W 5PS**
email: reservations@ibericalondon.co.uk web: www.ibericalondon.co.uk
dir: *Nearest station: Great Portland St, Regent's Park*

An authentic taste of Spain in the heart of Marylebone

With a particular focus on the Asturias region of Northern Spain, Ibérica occupies a sizable corner plot in Fitzrovia/Marylebone border country. There's a decidedly Ibérian feel to the interior, with a marble-topped bar in the double-height space, plus tiles, huge lanterns and a deli section with hanging hams. A mezzanine level adds even more tables. Tapas and pinchos are the name of the game, and there is an authenticity to the output. A simple plate of asparagus, Manchego and onion confit on a truffle oil toast is a classy little toastie, the cheese soft and melting, the aroma of truffle nicely judged. There are all the anticipated cured meats, too, and croquettes such as a classic ham version served in a generous portion. Twice-cooked lamb comes with an almond purée and tomatoes and pepper from El Bierzo (near Léon), while cuttlefish and prawns star in a risotto made with black rice and served with a zingy aïoli. Desserts run to apple tart with crema catalana, and there are Spanish wines and sherries to help you on your way.

Chef Miguel Garcia, Nacho Manzano **Owner** Iberica Food & Culture Ltd **Seats** 100, Pr/dining room 30 **Times** 11.30-11 Closed 25-26 Dec & BHs, D Sun All-day dining **Prices** Prices not confirmed **Wines** 43 bottles over £30, 24 bottles under £30, 21 by glass **Notes** Vegetarian available, Children welcome

JW Steakhouse
PLAN 2 G1

@ American

tel: 020 7499 6363 & 7399 8400 **Grosvenor House, 86 Park Ln W1K 7TN**
email: info@jwsteakhouse.co.uk web: www.jwsteakhouse.co.uk
dir: *Nearest station: Marble Arch*

Prime steaks and cocktails on Park Lane

There is and ever shall be a reliable market for prime steak. Offer the luxy surroundings of a Park Lane hotel, and few would pass up the opportunity. The expansive JW brings steakhouse dining, American style, to the Grosvenor House, in an ambience of black and white ceramic floor tiles and parquet, dark wood dressers, and a big blackboard menu offering all the permutations of cuts, sauces, cooking degrees and provenance. There's a cocktail bar on hand to wet your whistle, before getting stuck into the protein. The beef is all thoroughbred USDA-approved gear, from Josper-grilled New York strip steak in béarnaise, with superb hand-cut chips and organic salad, to the house Tomahawk ribeye, for which the indispensable partner is Tomahawk Vineyard Napa Valley Cabernet Sauvignon. Start

with a bowl of earthy, creamy truffled wild mushroom soup, and finish with a gooey-centred, freshly baked chocolate brownie and vanilla ice cream, and it's hard to know what more you could wish for.

Times 12-2.30/6-10.30

Kai Mayfair
PLAN 4 G6

@@ Modern Chinese

tel: 020 7493 8988 **65 South Audley St W1K 2QU**
email: reservations@kaimayfair.co.uk
dir: *Nearest station: Marble Arch*

Vibrant Chinese cooking in opulent Mayfair setting

Spread over two floors, this swanky Chinese restaurant is decorated in rich hues, with arty Chinese photographs on the walls. Kai aims to show the diversity of Chinese cuisine and the cooking is noted for its accurate timing, judicious use of spicing and seasoning, and its subtle combination of flavours and textures. You could take refuge in the comfort of classics such as crispy duck and sweet and sour pork, but why not get off to a flying start with deep-fried soft-shelled crab, in a crisp batter spiked with garlic, chilli and shallots, and pointed up with green mango julienne, or a decadent fusion idea pairing pan-fried foiegras with caramelised cashews, white pepper, spring onions, their richness cut with grapes and passionfruit dressing? Next up, top-class Iberico pork loin comes with bean and shrimp crumble, Washington apple compôte and Granny Smith jelly. The menu opens unusually with a page of desserts, showing how seriously they are taken here, and Amadei chocolate fondant with pistachio ice cream, crumbs and powder shows the creative approach.

Chef Alex Chow **Owner** Bernard Yeoh **Seats** 85, Pr/dining room 12 **Times** 12-2.15/6.30-10.45 Closed 25-26 Dec, 1 Jan **Prices** Starter £12-£85, Main £18-£75, Dessert £11 **Wines** 342 bottles over £30, 14 by glass **Parking** Directly outside **Notes** Sunday L, Vegetarian available, Children welcome

The Keeper's House
PLAN 2 J1

@ Modern British, French NEW

tel: 020 7300 5881 **Royal Academy of Arts, Burlington House, Piccadilly W1J OBD**
email: keepershouse@peytonandbyrne.co.uk
dir: *Nearest station: Piccadilly Circus*

Appealing European cooking in a newly opened section of the Royal Academy

Tucked away in one corner of the courtyard, the Keeper's House was installed in the 19th century as a grace-and-favour apartment for the resident steward of the Royal Academy collections. A strikingly attractive restaurant has been fashioned from it, the recessed rooms imitating those of the galleries upstairs, with bare contemporary light fittings and jade-green walls hung with small casts of classical reliefs. As well as inspiring cocktails and English wines, there's a menu of spruce European cooking. Start boldly with snail ravioli, or a bowl of refreshing gazpacho with red pepper sorbet, and then consider the likes of roast lamb saddle in tomato ragoût and gnocchi, turbot and prawns with kale and glazed pumpkin, or pedigree sirloin aged for four weeks and dressed with bone marrow and browned onions. Round things off with a serving of rhubarb rice pudding and matching sorbet, or brown bread mousse. It's members only until 4pm, and then all are welcome.

Chef Morgan Meunier **Owner** Oliver Peyton **Seats** 65, Pr/dining room 45 **Times** 12-3/5.30-10 Closed Sun **Prices** Fixed L 2 course fr £28.50, Starter £9.50-£12.50, Main £16.50-£28.50, Dessert £8.50-£12.50 **Wines** 45 bottles over £30, 15 bottles under £30, 14 by glass **Parking** On street **Notes** Pre-theatre menu 5.30-7pm 2/3 course £19/£24, Vegetarian available, Children welcome

Kitchen Table

PLAN 2 J3

@ @ @ – see below

Latium

PLAN 2 J3

@ @ Italian

tel: 020 7323 9123 **21 Berners St W1T 3LP**
email: info@latiumrestaurant.com
dir: *Nearest station: Goodge St, Oxford Circus*

Regional Italian cooking with ravioli a speciality

Latium, an L-shaped room with black chairs and banquettes at clothed tables, its plain walls covered with some vibrant artwork, gets its name from the Italian region Lazio (Latium). Much of the produce is imported direct, and the kitchen makes everything else, including pasta and bread each day. Such is chef Maurizio Morelli's dedication to his native shores that he has a separate ravioli menu: one of mushrooms in snail and tomato sauce, for instance, or mixed fish with bottarga, and sweet versions like chocolate pasta stuffed with ricotta, candied peel and pistachios in orange sauce. Elsewhere, the kitchen delivers the authentic goods in the shape of prosciutto with burrata cheese and mixed leaves, followed by seared scallops wrapped in pancetta with pearl barley cooked in squid ink and red pepper purée, and beef cheek braised with radicchio in red wine accompanied by seared polenta and baby onions. Flag-waving desserts may include wobbly pannacotta with apple and cinnamon sauce and figs poached in red wine.

Times 12-3/6.30-10.30 Closed BHs, Sun, L Sat

Levant

PLAN 2 G2

@ Lebanese, Middle Eastern v

tel: 020 7224 1111 **Jason Court, 76 Wigmore St W1U 2SJ**
email: reservations@levant.co.uk
dir: *Nearest station: Bond Street*

The scents and flavours of the Middle East

Secreted away in a basement just behind Oxford Street, the exotic fantasy world of Levant is reminiscent of a scene from Arabian Nights. Think brass lamps, flickering candles, incense, richly-coloured fabrics and carved wood, with nightly belly dancing and, at the weekends, a live Middle Eastern band and DJs to bring the place even more alive. Lunch is better for a quiet repas à deux, but whatever the time of day, the food is no afterthought: set up for sharing, the kitchen sends out an array of uncomplicated, warmly-spiced Middle Eastern food – with a strong Lebanese leaning – via fixed-price feast or meze menus and a carte. Kick off with some excellent falafel, or perhaps baba ghanoush or sambusak bil laham (spiced lamb and pine nuts in pastry), then move onto roasted sea bass fillet with citrus-scented rice, or cubed lamb marinated in lemon juice and spices grilled on skewers. Exotic cocktails and a range of Moroccan and Lebanese wines complete the experience.

Chef David Jones **Owner** Tony Kitous **Seats** 150, Pr/dining room 12 **Times** 12-3am Closed 25-26 Dec, L 1 Jan All-day dining **Prices** Fixed L 2 course £10, Fixed D 3 course £10-£40 **Wines** 25 bottles over £30, 20 bottles under £30, 20 by glass **Parking** Welbeck St **Notes** Sunday L £10, Children welcome

Kitchen Table

LONDON W1	PLAN 2 J3

Modern British NEW
tel: 020 7637 7770 **70 Charlotte St W1T 4QG**
email: kitchentable@bubbledogs.co.uk
dir: *Nearest station: Goodge Street*

Cutting-edge market-led dining at the kitchen counter

Increasingly, for those in search of cutting-edge dining, it seems an anachronism to be expected to sit at a linen-clad table under glittering chandeliers amid reverential hush. The boundary between consumer and producer has been eroded to invisibility. Charlotte Street, arguably the scene of London's most exciting eating, feels exactly the right location for Kitchen Table. Lurking behind an upfront operation called Bubbledogs (champagne and hot dogs), it offers 19 counter seats at point-blank range to the sizzle and clatter of the engine-room. The kitchen at some chef's tables may be no more than a finishing-station, but here you're up close to the real thing, though the retro mood lighting makes for a curiously calm, warming environment. Menus are decided on the hoof daily, according to what looks good to buy that morning, dishes designated by a one-word identifier. Pig is sublime crackled pork sprinkled in powdered shrimp with a brown crab dip; Cod offers a crisp-shelled profiterole filled with smoked roe, brushed with brown butter and dressed in dill; Scallops are raw and heaped with kohlrabi, radish, cucumber and seaweed, then bathed in warm Icelandic seaweed beer. In a city athirst for novelty, it's some achievement to produce one surprise after another, and all so resonantly successful. Even the less bizarre elements are superb, as witness sea-trout in wild garlic sauce with scorched spring onions. Some items come in two instalments, as when duck appears first as the creamed liver with maple syrup and cocoa-nibs, and then in glorious profusion as breast, heart and olive-coated terrine, with fennel purée and damson jam. Pause for cheese, perhaps Vacherin cooked in its little wood box with champagne, patanegra, walnuts and honeycomb, before the train rattles on down the track with desserts such as meringue-topped blood-orange and matcha green tea powder, or coconut jelly, mango purée and creamy yoghurt zizzed up with lime juice.

Chef James Knappett **Owner** James Knappett, Sandia Chang **Seats** 19 **Times** 6-11 Closed Sun-Mon, L all week **Prices** Tasting menu £88 **Wines** 50 bottles over £30, 8 by glass **Parking** On street

LONDON W1 *continued*

Lima
PLAN 2 K3

◉ Modern Peruvian

---

tel: 020 3002 2640 **31 Rathbone Place, Fitzrovia W1T 1JH**
email: enquiry@limalondon.com
dir: *Nearest station: Goodge Street, Tottenham Court Rd*

Buzzy, contemporary setting for a genuine taste of Peru

Unless you've been to South America you're unlikely to have come across much Peruvian cuisine, but that's about to change: Lima is at the head of a new wave of London restaurants showcasing the unique melting pot of cultures (native Peruvian, European and Asian) that make up modern Peruvian cuisine. There's a fair chance you'll need a little help with the menu, which has been put together by one of Peru's most celebrated chefs, Virgilio Martinez, and covers all the bases from raw ('crudo') dishes such as céviches and tiraditos, to starters and mains from the 'mar' and the 'tierra'. Sea bass causa with yellow pepper potato purée, crushed avocado and red shiso is a neatly presented and vibrantly colourful opener, full of fresh, clean flavours. Main course could be a precisely cooked confit of suckling pig in a well balanced dish with roasted Amazonian cashew, lentils and pear. Chocolate fans can't go wrong with the cacao porcelana 75 per cent, mango and hierbabuena granita and blue potato crystal – a rich chocolate parfait, partnered with a mango and mint granita and potato crisps, to you and me.

Chef Robert Ortiz, Virgilio Martinez **Owner** Gabriel Gonzalez, Virgilio Martinez, Jose Luis **Seats** 60, Pr/dining room 25 **Times** 12-2.30/5.30-10.30 Closed Xmas, Sun **Prices** Fixed L 2 course £20, Tasting menu £48, Starter £9-£14, Main £20-£29, Dessert £6.50-£8, Service optional 12.5% **Wines** 31 bottles over £30, 9 bottles under £30, 12 by glass **Parking** On street **Notes** Pre-theatre 2/3 course 5.30-6pm £20/£23, pre-bkg recommended, Vegetarian available, Children welcome

---

Little Social
PLAN 2 H2

◉◉ French, Modern European

---

tel: 020 7870 3730 **5 Pollen St W1S 1NQ**
email: reservations@littlesocial.co.uk
dir: *Nearest station: Oxford Circus*

Jason Atherton's take on a Parisian bistro

Across the road from its big brother – Pollen Street Social – le petit social is a dose of Parisian bistro-style in London. And it isn't all that small by the way. It looks the part with vintage pictures cramming the walls, ox-blood-coloured banquette seating, darkwood tables, and a cocktail bar at the front. It fairly fizzes with bonhomie. The menu is a heady mix of French classics and more esoteric Atherton creations, and all based on tip-top (mostly) British ingredients. There's steak tartare, for example, steak frites, too, and a Côte de boeuf for two to share (at a price). But equally you might start with crab, tomato and radish salad with miso tomato dressing and marinated beetroot, and follow on with pork chop with butternut squash purée, pine nut dressing and endive. Atherton has always been a dab hand at desserts, so save room for a classic tarte Tatin (for two again), or pink peppercorn meringue with lemon and lime curd and passionfruit.

Chef Carey Docherty **Owner** Jason Atherton **Seats** 55, Pr/dining room 8 **Times** 12-2.30/6-10.30 Closed 25-26 Dec, 1-2 Jan, Sun **Prices** Fixed L 2 course £21, Starter £9.50-£14.50, Main £15-£25.50, Dessert £4.50-£16 **Wines** 60 bottles over £30, 3 bottles under £30, 23 by glass **Parking** Burlington Car Park, Cavendish Square **Notes** Exclusive hire & Pre Fixe menu available, Vegetarian available, Children welcome

---

Locanda Locatelli
PLAN 2 G2

◉◉◉ – *see opposite*

The Mandeville Hotel
PLAN 2 G2

◉ Modern British

---

tel: 020 7935 5599 **Mandeville Place W1U 2BE**
email: info@mandeville.co.uk **web:** www.mandeville.co.uk
dir: *Nearest station: Bond St, Baker St*

Brasserie food in a stylish boutique hotel

What is now known as Marylebone village has always been an oasis of civility for those prepared to venture a block or two north of the permathronged Oxford Street, and a boutique hotel like the Mandeville suits the district to a T. Understated contemporary decor and a calming ambience are the hallmarks, while the cumbersomely named Reform Social and Grill emulates the London gentlemen's club, albeit one where women are allowed. Unclothed tables and bottle-green banquettes set the tone, and the food follows on with plenty of hang-the-diet protein in the form of steaks and quality burgers. A starter of chunky roast chicken terrine and smooth chicken liver pâté mobilises the best of both worlds, and a Josper-grilled lobster burger with chips is an interesting variant. Otherwise, expect braised ox cheeks with horseradish mash, or 'seaside pie' made with smoked haddock, coley, cockles and samphire, before getting down to the serious end of things with jam roly-poly or sticky toffee.

Times 12-3/7-11

Maze
PLAN 2 G1

◉◉◉ – *see opposite*

Maze Grill
PLAN 2 G1

◉◉ American

---

tel: 020 7495 2211 **London Marriott Hotel, Grosvenor Square, 10-13 Grosvenor Square W1K 6JP**
email: mazegrill@gordonramsay.com **web:** www.gordonramsay.com
dir: *Nearest station: Bond St*

Gordon Ramsey's steakhouse overlooking Grosvenor Square

With New York's establishments as a template and its swish address on Grosvenor Square, Maze Grill is a fusion of British and American favourites, plus some top-notch sushi for good measure. Its sister restaurant next door may get the lion's share of the plaudits, but the Grill is a good-looker, too, with a sleek, contemporary design and a menu that is true to its USP. The beef tends to steal the show – Aberdeen Angus rib-eye, perhaps, cooked medium rare as requested in the Josper char-grill, and served with half a roasted garlic bulb, roasted sweet potatoes and a side order of mac 'n' cheese. There is Dedham Vale beef, too, aged for 31 days, USDA Prime from the US of A, and Wagyu 9th grade at a whacking 130 quid for a 12oz rib-eye. Starters include excellent sushi and more trad stuff like devilled whitebait and salt water prawn cocktail, and if you're really not in the mood for red meat, main courses such as pan-fried sea bream and fried buffalo chicken are handy alternatives. Finish with treacle and bourbon tart.

Times 12-10.30 All-day dining

Locanda Locatelli

LONDON W1   **PLAN 2 G2**

Italian 🍷 NOTABLE WINE LIST

tel: 020 7935 9088 **8 Seymour St W1H 7JZ**
email: info@locandalocatelli.com **web:** www.locandalocatelli.com
dir: *Nearest station: Marble Arch*

Fabulous top-class Italian cooking of daring simplicity

Before Giorgio Locatelli carved out a TV career for himself, his name was already beloved of London foodies for serving up Italian food that your Mamma couldn't make in her wildest dreams (probably). He's very good on the telly, and he's shifted a few books over the years, too. But you can still eat his food. Admittedly it isn't at the budget end of Italian dining in the capital, but it is just about as good as it gets. It's a delicious room, attached to a hotel but you wouldn't know it, with parquet floors, textured wooden walls, beige leather bucket chairs, and booths divided by etched glass screens – classy and just a little glamorous. The service team are smart, informed and light on their feet. The cooking has traditional Italian values at its core – freshness and simplicity – and there's an earthy heartiness to it, alongside a bit of contemporary panache. Tortellini in brodo (a clear broth) kicks things off with clarity and simplicity, the pasta packed with chicken and pork filling, the broth balanced somewhere between intensity and subtlety. Another starter sees pan-fried scallops paired with celeriac purée and saffron vinaigrette, or there's a classic ox tongue with salsa verde. Main-course roast monkfish with walnut and caper sauce and samphire is straight and true, the fish as fresh as can be, the cooking timed just right. Or go for the slow-cooked Scottish beef with black cabbage and parsnips. Desserts can deliver a tiramisù, or a ricotta mousse with a pistachio sponge, chocolate chips and pistachio ice cream. To cap it all off, the wine list is a virtuoso performance, with plenty of choice by the glass.

Chef Giorgio Locatelli **Owner** Plaxy & Giorgio Locatelli **Seats** 70, Pr/dining room 50 **Times** 12-3/6.45-11 Closed Xmas, BHs **Prices** Starter £9-£20, Main £18-£32.50, Dessert £6.50-£12.50, Service optional **Wines** 30 bottles under £30, 18 by glass **Parking** NCP adjacent, parking meters **Notes** Vegetarian available, Children welcome

Maze

LONDON W1   **PLAN 2 G1**

French, Asian

tel: 020 7107 0000 **London Marriott Hotel, 10-13 Grosvenor Square W1K 6JP**
email: maze@gordonramsay.com **web:** www.gordonramsay.com/maze
dir: *Nearest station: Bond Street*

Exciting fusion cooking in Grosvenor Square

Viewed from the landmark square, the building hosting Maze could be an embassy, or a Government building, but inside is a vision of cool modernity that couldn't be further from ministerial austerity. There's a swish bar for a nifty cocktail, plus a sushi bar which turns out some seriously classy plates of top-notch stuff. The main restaurant has hand-crafted screens designed to give a maze like sense, creating little private corners, and increasing the sense of exclusivity. The menu takes its inspiration from the Far East and France, predominantly, with the small-plate set-up meaning you get to try a lot of things. The mixed sushi platter is a tempting opener, given the skill set of the team just across the way: a fab California roll with snow crab, for example, plus some first-rate nigiri. Ingredients are excellent throughout and there is real skill and craft in the kitchen. A dumpling packed with lobster, tiger prawns and salmon sits in a pungent pool of lemongrass broth is a signature dish that lives up to its reputation. Brill with brown shrimps, lemon, salsify and horseradish sauce is a dish that looks more to Europe, while another of duck breast, steamed bun, sweetcorn and miso most definitely has its focus on the east. This fusion style is handled with good sense and a light touch, so flavours are mostly on song. There's a touch of theatre when a dessert of lemon meringue pie with a blackberry sorbet arrives, with aromas of lemon released tableside to engulf the senses. Another dessert serves up a cider-glazed apple with an apple cake and custard ice cream. There's attention to detail from start to finish here, with excellent bread and a wine list that covers the globe with impunity.

Chef Alex Thiebaut, Matthew Pickop **Owner** Gordon Ramsay Holdings Ltd **Seats** 108, Pr/dining room 40 **Times** 12-3/6-11 **Prices** Tasting menu fr £75 **Wines** 400+ bottles over £30, 3 bottles under £30, 23 by glass **Parking** **Notes** Fixed L/D 4 course £30, Vegetarian available, Children welcome

LONDON W1 *continued*

Mele e Pere
PLAN 2 J1

 Italian

tel: 020 7096 2096 **46 Brewer St, Soho W1F 9TF**
email: info@meleepere.co.uk
dir: *Nearest station: Piccadilly Circus*

Rustic Italian food in modish surroundings

The name means 'apples and pears', which explains why the plate glass window of this Soho Italian is full of Murano glass renditions of the fruits. You also have to descend the 'apples and pears' to reach the buzzy, modishly minimal basement restaurant – all chunky bleached wood tables lit by wall-mounted anglepoise lamps – a decor that perhaps prepares diners for the fact that this is not a comfort-food Italian serving the usual spag bol suspects. The chef-patron hails from northern Italy, and his repertoire takes the path of well-rendered rusticity, as typified in an unusual Italian take on a classic beef tartare accompanied by shaved parmesan and yellow Castelfranco radicchio. The concise menu continues with tagliatelle with rabbit and fresh peas, while mains run to sea bream with fregola and fennel, or pork belly with lentils and bean sprouts. Finish with a classic pannacotta or excellent Italian cheeses.

Chef A Mantovani **Owner** P Hughes, A Mantovani **Seats** 90 **Times** 12-11 Closed 25-26 Dec, 1 Jan, All-day dining **Prices** Prices not confirmed **Wines** 16 by glass **Parking** NCP **Notes** Pre-theatre menu until 7pm £15.50-£17.50, Vegetarian available, Children welcome

Le Meridien Piccadilly
PLAN 2 J1

British

tel: 020 7734 8000 **21 Piccadilly W1J 0BH**
email: piccadilly.terrace@lemeridien.com **web:** www.lemeridienpiccadilly.com
dir: *Nearest station: Piccadilly Circus*

Grills, and a lot more, at a top-end hotel

Le Meridien, among the capital's top-end hotels, occupies a prime site on one of central London's most famous thoroughfares. Within is a series of vast public rooms, with the impressive Terrace Grill and Bar a futuristic atrium-style space with a curved glass ceiling, columns and darkwood tables; a terrace looking over Piccadilly is a possibility for alfresco dining. In this context, it's no surprise that the kitchen deploys prime ingredients – Carlingford oysters, Denham Estate venison (served as carpaccio), native lobster (paired with anchovy and shallot butter), and red-poll beef steaks. Although grills – all accurately timed – abound, from lamb rack to lemon sole, a contemporary approach is taken for some dishes. For instance, chicken and duck liver parfait with beetroot and spiced oranges could be followed by a steamed sea bass parcel with mussels in Pernod. In-house bread is excellent, and among puddings could be banoffee sundae with home-made vanilla ice cream or retro knickerbocker glory.

Times 12-2.30/5.30-10.30 Closed L Sun

Mews of Mayfair
PLAN 2 H1

Modern British V

tel: 020 7518 9388 **10-11 Lancashire Court, New Bond St, Mayfair W1S 1EY**
email: info@mewsofmayfair.com
dir: *Nearest station: Bond Street*

Fashionable setting for modern brasserie cooking

The fashionable Mayfair set converge on this stylish bar and restaurant, delightfully hidden from the maddening Bond Street crowds on a narrow cobbled alleyway. With its terrace tables and roll-back doors, on a warm day it feels more Mediterranean than West End. The lively street-level cocktail bar and cool basement lounge make a glam statement, while the first-floor brasserie is a light, airy space decorated in pastel tones, with cream leather banquettes, exposed floorboards and chunky wooden tables, and a relaxed, easy vibe. The kitchen delivers a please-all brasserie roster of seasonal dishes driven by prime, responsibly sourced produce. There are comfort classics like fish and chips (with mushy peas and tartare) alongside the likes of Cornish cod with parsley crumb and a fabulous crab mash, or perhaps 35-day dry-aged steaks (South Devon rib-eye maybe) cooked on the Josper grill. Well-made desserts continue the theme, such as banoffee pie or treacle tart.

Chef Michael Lecouteur **Owner** James Robson & Robert Nearn **Seats** 70, Pr/dining room 28 **Times** 12-4/6-12 Closed 25 Dec, D Sun **Prices** Starter £3-£25, Main £6.50-£42, Dessert £5-£10 **Wines** 50 bottles over £30, 13 bottles under £30, 16 by glass **Parking** On street, NCP **Notes** Sunday L £18, Children welcome

The Montagu
PLAN 2 F2

Modern British

tel: 020 7299 2037 **Hyatt Regency London, The Churchill, 30 Portman Square W1H 7BH**
email: montagu.hrlondon@hyatt.com
dir: *Nearest station: Marble Arch*

Modern comfort food in smart West End venue

The swanky five-star hotel has many riches, not least Locanda Locatelli (see entry), which has its own entrance and a life of its own. The hotel's Montagu restaurant has plenty to offer, too, with a menu of smart, modern British ideas and views over Portland Square. There are liveried doormen out front and elegant proportions within. An open kitchen ensures a buzz in the room and the food takes an up-beat brasserie approach with grills, lunchtime specials and comforting puddings. You might start with a ham hock, pistachio and chestnut terrine, in the company of a Cumberland sauce, or an upmarket prawn cocktail with avocado. Main-course fillet of Sussex black bream comes with a scallop céviche and a potato and Jerusalem artichoke millefeuille, or there's a beer-battered cod served in the traditional manner. Banoffee pie with honey ice cream competes for attention with chocolate and raspberry delice among desserts, and there are the artisan British cheeses, too.

Chef Felix Luecke **Owner** Hyatt Regency London-The Churchill **Seats** 60 **Times** 12-3/6-10.45 **Prices** Fixed L 2 course £20, Fixed D 3 course £25, Tasting menu £45, Starter £6-£12, Main £15.50-£36, Dessert £6.50 **Wines** 43 bottles over £30, 5 bottles under £30, 13 by glass **Parking** 48 **Notes** Chef's table 3/5 course £55/£75 incl wine, Sunday L £65, Vegetarian available, Children welcome

Murano
PLAN 4 H6

– *see opposite*

Murano

LONDON W1   PLAN 4 H6

Modern European, Italian influence V NOTABLE WINE LIST

tel: 020 7495 1127 **20-22 Queen St W1J 5PP**
email: muranorestaurant@angela-hartnett.com
dir: *Nearest station: Green Park*

Top-drawer Italianish cooking in smart white surroundings

The namesake Venetian glass features as a specially-commissioned chandelier, a statement from the off, perhaps, that this restaurant is all about Italian refinement. Angela Hartnett is a flag-bearer for upscale Italian dining in London these days, with perhaps only a few other places getting anywhere near. The Mayfair location is reflected in the upscale decor (and the prices, you might say, although the lunch is very good value at this level), with white leather seats, crisp linen on the tables, and funky, contemporary lights around an atrium. There's a swanky chef's table, too. The menu is not entirely Italian in focus, with an evident broader modern European influence, but Italian ingredients and preparations are very much on show. Service is slick and entirely on the ball. The bread and all the little extras hit the mark, with grissini and focaccia flying the flag for the motherland. Roasted scallops with curried parsnip purée, apple chutney and macadamia nuts is a first course with decidedly contemporary credentials, the timing spot on, the flavours deftly handled. Another starter featuring a purée partners a fine apple and shallot version with some roasted sweetbreads, served with toasted walnuts. It might be a mistake to skip pasta, with the signature pumpkin tortelli with sage butter and crushed amaretti on offer, or pheasant agnolotti with shallot purée and rosemary. When it comes to main courses, the dilemma is meat or fish, with sea bass with baby artichokes, smoked cod's roe and confit lemon competing with fillet of Cumbrian beef in a broth with curly kale, bone marrow and Jerusalem artichoke. Desserts

are equally well-made and appealing, with a feel-good choice of caramelised Amalfi lemon tart sitting alongside pistachio soufflé with a hot chocolate sauce. The set lunch menu doesn't lack for impact either, kicking off with something like rabbit and Swiss chard tortelli with marjoram butter and pancetta, before a main of Cornish sole with baby gnocchi, puntarelle and wild mushrooms, finishing with a vanilla rice pudding with Yorkshire rhubarb. The wine list, like the food, is Italian-ish, with a good showing from France.

Chef Diego Cardoso **Owner** Angela Hartnett **Seats** 46, Pr/dining room 12 **Times** 12-3/6.30-11 Closed 25-26 Dec, Sun **Prices** Fixed L 2 course £25, Fixed D 3 course £65, Starter £15, Main £35, Dessert £15 **Wines** 8 bottles under £30, 17 by glass **Parking Notes** 4/5 course £75/£85, Children welcome

LONDON W1 *continued*

Newman Street Tavern　PLAN 2 J3

🏵 Modern British

tel: 020 3667 1445 **48 Newman St W1T 1QQ**
email: info@newmanstreettavern.co.uk
dir: *Nearest station: Goodge Street*

Revamped pub with a passion for ingredients

More restaurant than boozer these days, the Newman Street Tavern places food at the top of the agenda, and everything is sourced when at its very best – seasonality is the watchword. It's all very charming and relaxed on the inside with copious pictures of that produce from land and sea covering the walls, banquette seating in the windows, darkwood tables, and a marble-topped bar. There's a pleasing clarity and focus to the menus and a definite lack of fuss, so you might kick off a meal with country pâté with cornichons and silver skin onions and toast, or sweet-cured wild trout, before moving on to cottage pie, or Galloway beef with beetroot and horseradish. Helford fish and shellfish gratin is packed with the fruits of the sea, or there might be all the simplicity of ray wing with lemon and watercress. For dessert, Ayrshire cardamom kulfi competes for your attention with apple crumble and vanilla ice cream.

Times 12-11 Closed D Sun All-day dining

Nobu　PLAN 5 H6

🏵🏵 Japanese

tel: 020 7447 4747 **Metropolitan London, 19 Old Park Ln W1K 1LB**
email: london@noburestaurants.com **web:** www. noburestaurants.com
dir: *Nearest station: Hyde Park Corner, Green Park*

Top-end Japanese dining with views over Hyde Park

From Miami to Milan, globe-trotting foodies are never too far away from a Nobu. Here, overlooking Hyde Park, is where in 1997 Londoners' first got a glimpse of Nobu Matsuhisa's brand of Japanese precision and South American spice. It was staggeringly fashionable and super-cool back then, and – do you know what? – it can still hold its own. They come, they look cool, they nibble. The prices were eye-watering back then, now the place just seems as expensive as everywhere else. The quality remains high, the seafood sparklingly fresh – the tuna, halibut and sea urchin linger long in the memory. South American street food is the inspiration for anticucho spicy salmon skewer, or tea-smoked lamb, and there are straight-up Japanese dishes such as sushi and sashimi. There are luxury ingredients such as an indulgent Wagyu and foie gras gyoza with spicy ponzu, and the pretty much iconic black cod with miso. It all looks beautiful on the plate and the staff are extremely helpful. Desserts maintain the fusion theme – Fuji apple crumble, for example – and there are cocktails and sake, too.

Chef Mark Edwards **Owner** Nobuyuki Matsuhisa **Seats** 160, Pr/dining room 40
Times 12-2.15/6-10.15 **Prices** Prices not confirmed **Wines** 8 by glass **Parking** Car park nearby **Notes** Pre-theatre Bento box £35, Fixed L 6 course, D 7 course, Sunday L, Vegetarian available, Children welcome

Nobu Berkeley ST　PLAN 4 H6

🏵🏵 Japanese, Peruvian

tel: 020 7290 9222 **15 Berkeley St W1J 8DY**
email: berkeleyst@noburestaurants.com
dir: *Nearest station: Green Park*

Super-cool Mayfair hot-spot for great Japanese food

With a globe-spanning empire stretching from the Bahamas to Beijing, the Nobu brand still ranks among the A-list players on the Japanese cuisine scene. The über-chic Berkeley Street outpost is a high-energy, high-decibel magnet for Mayfair fashionistas who come for the see-and-be-seen buzz of the ground-floor bar, before winding up the spiral staircase to the cool David Collins-designed restaurant, where the decor plays a riff on an autumnal woodland theme. Black-clad staff aren't just there to look good either – they know their way around the menu, whose concept puts a lively spin onto classical high-end Japanese dining by applying the heat of Latin American fusion ideas. For traditionalists, there's a sushi bar, and a sunken hibachi table for fun DIY dining supervised by the chefs. Whichever path you take, expect first-rate ingredients, exquisite presentation, and the typical cleanness and precision of Japanese cooking. Open with a hybrid lobster taco, or perfect rock shrimp tempura, then move on to Wagyu rump tataki with ponzu and sansyo zuke salsa cooked in the wood oven.

Chef Mark Edwards **Owner** Nobu Matsuhisa, Robert de Niro **Seats** 180
Times 12-2.30/6-1am Closed 25 Dec, 1 Jan, BH Mon, L Sun (ex Mother's Day)
Prices Tasting menu £70-£90 **Wines** 200 bottles over £30, 10 by glass
Parking Mayfair NCP **Notes** Tasting menu 6 course, Bento box available L £35-£45, Vegetarian available, Children welcome

NOPI　PLAN 2 J1

🏵 Mediterranean

tel: 020 7494 9584 **21-22 Warwick St W1B 5NE**
email: contact@nopi-restaurant.com
dir: *Nearest station: Oxford Circus, Piccadilly Circus*

A buzzing atmosphere and creative cooking with flavour to the fore

Owner Yotam Ottolenghi's cooking is built on the sun-drenched cuisines of the Middle East, North Africa and the Mediterranean with some global input. This translates as a menu packed with creativity and bursting with punchy flavours, served in an all-white brasserie-style space with white marble floors, white-topped tables edged with brass and Levantine-style hemispherical brass ceiling lights. Down in the basement are two large communal tables with ringside seats for the action in the open-to-view kitchen. Whichever you choose, the vibe is a chatty hubbub of people enjoying themselves while tucking into dishes made for sharing; if ingredients sound alien ask the clued-up staff for explanation. Kick off with cod, crispy pancetta, pistachio, and lovage vichyssoise, or go veggie with roasted aubergine, feta, coriander pesto and walnut. Main course brings twice-cooked baby chicken with lemon myrtle salt and chilli sauce, and desserts such as caramel and roasted peanut ice cream, chocolate sauce and peanut brittle come with equally vigorous flavours.

Chef Yotam Ottolenghi, Ramael Scully **Owner** Yotam Ottolenghi **Seats** 100
Times 12-2.45/5.30-10.15 Closed D Sun **Prices** Prices not confirmed, Service optional 12.5% **Wines** 16 by glass **Notes** Pre-theatre menu 2/3 course £21.50/£24.50, Vegetarian available, Children welcome

Looking for a London restaurant by name?
Use the index on page 254

Novikov Asian Restaurant

PLAN 4 H6

◉ Chinese & Pan Asian

tel: 020 7399 4330 **50a Berkeley St W1J 8HA**
dir: *Nearest station: Charing Cross, Green Park*

Style-conscious Pan-Asian dining in Mayfair

Arkady Novikov's Mayfair food emporium is the dernier cri of hot-button, style-drenched dining. As well as an Italian section (see entry), there is an Asian Room, where Japanese, Chinese, Thai and Malaysian dishes coexist in perfect harmony. Granite walls and a lacquered ebony and jade bar counter create a busy but cool impression, while the glass-fronted kitchen is like watching a giant TV. Croissant-shaped dumplings of beef and foie gras, served on a banana leaf, are a fittingly stylish start, as are the unimpeachable sushi and maki rolls. They might be succeeded by Malay-style soft-shelled crab, classic Singapore noodles with pork and prawns, or spectacular meat dishes such as seared Wagyu rib-eye in ponzu, or roast duck with oriental mushrooms in truffle sauce. An unmoulded brûlée of green tea with guava sorbet keeps the taste buds humming at dessert stage, and there are more obviously western chocolate creations like semi-fredo with pear sorbet.

Chef Jeff Tyler **Owner** Arkady Novikov **Seats** 160 **Times** 12–4/5.30–12 Closed 25 Dec, D 24 Dec **Prices** Prices not confirmed **Wines** 13 by glass **Parking** NCP Carrington Street **Notes** Vegetarian available, Children welcome

Novikov Italian Restaurant

PLAN 4 H6

◉ Italian

tel: 020 7399 4330 **50a Berkeley St W1J 8HA**
email: reservations@novikovrestaurant.co.uk
dir: *Nearest station: Green Park*

Jaw-dropping temple of Italian (and Asian) gastronomy

Arkady Novikov is an internationally known Russian restaurant entrepreneur with the resources to realise grandiose projects. The present complex is on the scale of a biblical temple, incorporating a sleek lounge-bar lit like a nightclub, a ground-floor Asian venue (see entry) and an Italian venue in the basement. Security-staff are on hand to ensure there are no sudden moves, and everywhere you look, there are shrines devoted to food and drink – mountains of oranges in wicker baskets, panniers of fresh produce in front of a long service counter, bottles of grappa crowded on to the top of a wine barrel. Once you get down to it, the Italian cooking is convincing, surprisingly rustic and honest, with some southern and Sardinian dishes for depth. Gossamer-thin slices of beef carpaccio with parmesan strips and rocket is the real deal, as is the asparagus salad with broad beans and Sardinian stone-dried red mullet bottarga. Calves' liver is top-drawer gear, lightly sautéed for melting texture, dressed in butter and sage.

Chef Marco Torri **Owner** Arkady Novikov **Seats** 180, Pr/dining room 40 **Times** 12–12 Closed 25 Dec, D 24 Dec All-day dining **Prices** Prices not confirmed **Wines** 10 by glass **Notes** Fixed L 4 course £26, Vegetarian available, Children welcome

10 Greek Street

PLAN 3 A2

◉◉ Modern British

tel: 020 7734 4677 **W1D 4DH**
email: info@10greekstreet.com
dir: *Nearest station: Charing Cross, Tottenham Court Rd*

Soho cool and good cooking too

There's no showboating here – not even a sign outside – but you should find it easy enough. The place has the fashionable insouciance that is endearingly all the rage in Soho these days – neutral colours, darkwood tables, old tiles, blackboards, some seating right on the pass, and simple food done really, really well. You gotta love it. The food is the star of the show, the ingredients take all the plaudits, but be assured the skill is to make this look easy. A starter of grilled asparagus with egg yolk ravioli and truffle oil says it all really, the yolk perfectly runny, the asparagus

as fresh as a daisy. There's the likes of potted Dorset crab, too, with cucumber, mint and chilli, and main courses such as a whole lemon sole on the bone (wonderfully fresh) with samphire, fennel and sea radish, or Welsh Black beef with root vegetable mash, broccoli and horseradish. For pud, the chocolate pot with poached pear and vanilla cream is another winning dish.

Chef Cameron Emirali **Owner** Luke Wilson, Cameron Emirali **Seats** 30, Pr/dining room 12 **Times** 12–2.30/5.30–10.45 Closed Xmas, Sun & some BHs **Prices** Starter £6–£10, Main £12–£21, Dessert £5–£7, Service optional **Wines** 10 bottles over £30, 21 bottles under £30, 20 by glass **Parking** China Town, NCP Upper St Martins Lane **Notes** Vegetarian available, Children welcome

The Only Running Footman

PLAN 4 H6

◉ Traditional British

tel: 020 7499 2988 **5 Charles St, Mayfair W1J 5DF**
email: manager@therunningfootmanmayfair.com
dir: *Nearest station: Green Park*

Smart Mayfair pub with commitment to great food

It looks like a pub, which indeed it is, but there's more than meets the eye to The Only Running Footman. The distinctive red-brick corner building in Mayfair has a ground-floor bar where you can have a drink and pick something off the all-day bar menu (from a sandwich to chargrilled Longhorn rib-eye steak), plus a smarter and quieter upstairs restaurant, where closely-packed tables are done-out in crisp white linen and all is a little more refined. (There's also a chef's table in a separate room which doubles up as a cookery school.) Upstairs you might start with sautéed Cornish squid and chorizo salad, followed by pan-fried sea bass with caramelised salsify and sauce vierge, finishing off with a berry Pavlova or cheeses from the Bath Cheese Company with pear chutney and pain aux fruits.

Chef Eddie Kouadio, Peter Pereira **Owner** Barnaby Meredith **Seats** 30, Pr/dining room 40 **Times** 12–2.30/6.30–10 Closed D 25 Dec **Prices** Fixed L 3 course £35–£42, Fixed D 3 course £35–£42, Starter £5.50–£17.50, Main £11.95–£29.95, Dessert £6–£6.50 **Wines** 49 bottles over £30, 28 bottles under £30, 12 by glass **Parking** On street **Notes** Chef's table available £80, Sunday L £16.95–£17.95, Vegetarian available, Children welcome

Orrery

PLAN 2 G3

◉◉ Modern French V ▮ NOTABLE WINE LIST

tel: 020 7616 8000 **55-57 Marylebone High St W1U 5RB**
email: orreryreservation@danddlondon.com
dir: *Nearest station: Baker St, Regent's Park*

Stylish, elegant restaurant above designer store

The Orrery may be a Marylebone old-timer, but it cuts a contemporary swagger with its classy good looks, polished service and skilful, modern take on classical French cuisine. On the first floor above the Conran store, the long, narrow room is a fashionably clean-lined space, filled with light from its large arched windows and ceiling skylight. Pastel tones blend with pale wood, mirrors and white linen, while a glass wine cellar signals a dazzling list. Menus are driven by prime ingredients and seasonality, and come dotted with luxuries (attracting the odd supplement here and there), with dishes showing a lightness of touch, matched by refined presentation. Fish delivers strongly, perhaps a seafood ravioli opener in a rich lobster bisque, while to follow, sea-fresh turbot is served with braised celery and gnocchi and complemented by a fabulous mussel velouté. There's no let up at dessert stage either: witness honey-glazed poached pineapple with a light-as-a-feather pistachio sponge and yoghurt sorbet. An intimate bar, summer roof terrace and street-level epicerie add further appeal.

Chef Igor Tymchyshyn **Owner** D & D London **Seats** 80, Pr/dining room 18 **Times** 12–2.30/6.30–10.30 Closed 1 Jan, 26–27 Dec **Prices** Fixed L 2 course £24.50, Fixed D 3 course £30, Service optional 12.5% **Wines** 300 bottles over £30, 40 bottles under £30, 18 by glass **Parking** NCP, 170 Marylebone Rd **Notes** ALC menu, Gourmand menu £65, Potager menu £65, Sunday L fr £29.50, Children welcome

LONDON W1 *continued*

Park Plaza Sherlock Holmes
PLAN 2 F3

British, Modern European

tel: 020 7486 6161 **108 Baker St W1U 6LJ**
email: info@sherlockholmeshotel.com **web:** www.sherlockholmeshotel.com
dir: *Nearest station: Baker Street*

Modern grill near the home of Holmes

Located accurately in the fictional Edwardian sleuth's postcode, this slick Baker Street operation eschews the period theme in favour of a chic contemporary boutique hotel look. Polished wood floors and cream leather seats at black quartz inlaid tables set a smart, modern, city-slicker tone in the open-plan space of Sherlock's Bar & Grill. Holding centre stage is the kitchen team, hard at work over charcoal grills and a wood-burning oven in the open-to-view kitchen. From a broadly European menu comes a generous serving of pan-fried king scallops with butternut squash purée and crispy bacon to set the ball rolling, then hot off the charcoal grill there might be veal escalope in breadcrumbs with roasted plum tomato and rocket, or from the wood-fired oven, Gressingham duck breast with caramelised plums and Swiss chard. For pudding, how about a good honest and homely version of apple and sultana crumble with cinnamon ice cream?

Chef Rachid Hammoum **Owner** Park Plaza Hotels **Seats** 44, Pr/dining room 50 **Times** 12-2.30/6-10.30 Closed D Sun, BHs **Prices** Fixed L 2 course £15-£18, Fixed D 3 course £18-£22, Starter £5-£11, Main £12-£20, Dessert £5.50 **Wines** 6 bottles over £30, 11 bottles under £30, 10 by glass **Parking** Chiltern St, NCP **Notes** Sunday L £15-£18, Vegetarian available, Children welcome

La Petite Maison
PLAN 2 H1

French, Mediterranean

tel: 020 7495 4774 **54 Brooks Mews W1K 4EG**
email: info@lpmlondon.co.uk
dir: *Nearest station: Bond St*

The flavours of the Midi in Mayfair

Modelled on and named after its sister restaurant in Nice, the light, open-plan, sunny room exudes a breezily Mediterranean vibe transposed to an ultra-posh postcode. The Riviera-cool look takes in creamy walls with large frosted-glass windows, an open-to-view kitchen and an up-tempo, see-and-be-seen atmosphere. A battalion of skilful staff respond without hovering at closely-set tables, while the cooking shows a light modern touch, keeping things simple and fresh, driven by top-notch produce in a procession of skilfully delivered dishes designed for sharing. You're never far from the sun-drenched flavours of the Côte d'Azur and its Italian neighbours over the border in Liguria with starters like an authentique salade Niçoise, a pissaladière tart of onions and anchovies, or burrata cheese with tomatoes and basil. Pasta dishes could offer home-made tagliolini with clams, while mains proceed along the lines of sea bream baked en papillote with lemon, herbs and olive oil, or grilled lamb cutlets with smoked aubergine. The Gallic focus runs through to a finale of marinated Agen prunes with gingerbread ice cream.

Times 12-3/6-11 Closed 25-26 Dec

Peyote
Mexican **NEW**

tel: 020 7409 1300 **13 Cork St, Mayfair W1S 3NS**
email: info@peyoterestaurant.com
dir: *Nearest station: Green Park*

Modern Mexican food good for sharing in Mayfair

That it's named after a cactus native to the Chihuahuan desert is a pointer to this restaurant's Mexican theme, and indeed it has called on some of that country's finest chefs to give London modern interpretations of its cuisine. It's been given an ultra-modern, stylish makeover, over two levels, with closely set wooden tables and artistic skulls making a bold design statement. Well-informed staff are on hand to offer guidance through the menu of mainly tasting-sized platters for sharing, so it's sensible to come in a group and order a variety. Ensalata de nopales (cactus salad), hot, fresh and spicy, sums up the style, along with lobster céviche subtly flavoured with chilli, and soft-shelled crab tacos. Dishes are distinctly flavoured without being swamped, seen in main courses of veal chop with onion and jalapeño salsa, and sea bass with pineapple sauce spiked with coriander. Finish by trying churros with chocolate sauce or play safe with whisky crème brûlée.

Chef Hili Sharabani **Owner** Tarun Mahrotri **Seats** 110, Pr/dining room 12 **Times** 12-3/6-1 Closed Xmas, New Year, Sun, L Sat **Prices** Prices not confirmed **Wines** 88 bottles over £30, 7 bottles under £30, 11 by glass **Notes** Vegetarian available, Children welcome

Picture
PLAN 2 H3

Modern European **NEW** v

tel: 020 7637 7892 **110 Great Portland St W1W 6PQ**
email: info@picturerestaurant.co.uk
dir: *Nearest station: Oxford Circus*

Top-call for small-plate dining with a touch of pedigree

This happening outfit's name reflects its setting in the shadow of the BBC, yet it is anything but a corporate diner and has a refreshingly cool neighbourhood vibe. There are classy credentials from the off, as it is set up by three talented young deserters from the acclaimed Arbutus/Wild Honey stable (a manager and two chefs). The stylishly stark long room presses all the so-now buttons, with grey-washed walls, floorboards, retro furnishings and warehouse-style bulkhead lighting, while a rear atrium allows daylight to flood in. The food is also more cheffy than its trendy brown-paper menus, tea-towel napkins, accessible pricing, or casually dressed staff (switched-on and cheery) might suggest. The kitchen deals in fresh, clean, prettily dressed, fashionable 'small-plates' spiked with flavour and flair and put together with skill and confidence. Take ravioli of Italian greens pepped up by ricotta and chilli, while succulent 28-day-aged beef gets the 'Picture' treatment teamed with heritage carrots, Swiss chard and a hit of cumin. Desserts might feature vanilla pannacotta topped with wonderful champagne rhubarb and zingy gingerbread 'crisps'. Well-selected wines are offered by-glass, carafe or bottle.

Chef Alan Christie, Colin Kelly **Owner** Tom Slegg, Alan Christie, Colin Kelly **Seats** 55 **Times** 12-2.30/6-10.30 Closed Xmas, BHs, Sun **Prices** Tasting menu £35, Starter £7, Main £9, Dessert £4-£5 **Wines** 12 bottles over £30, 14 bottles under £30, 21 by glass **Parking** On street **Notes** Tasting menu 6 course, Children welcome

Pied à Terre
PLAN 2 J3

– *see opposite*

Looking for a London restaurant near you?
Use the maps on pages 258–68

Pied à Terre

Modern French, European **V** NOTABLE WINE LIST

tel: 020 7636 1178 **34 Charlotte St W1T 2NH**
email: info@pied-a-terre.co.uk
dir: *Nearest station: Goodge Street*

Art on a plate in one of London's finest and longest-standing restaurants

If it looks rather like an art gallery from the outside, then all well and good, for within is an ever-changing panoply of contemporary art, with owner David Moore instigating an 'artist in restaurant' concept which ensures there's always something rather exciting on the walls. David Moore has always been a singular kind of restaurateur, not someone to chase fashion or follow others, which is why this restaurant has remained at the very top of London's culinary listings. An ability to pick a winner among chefs is another of Moore's skills, with the current incumbent (the prodigiously talented Marcus Eaves) following the standard set previously by Richard Neat, Tom Aikens and Shane Osborn. The restaurant itself takes up several floors of a townhouse, with a roof garden at the apex, from which herbs and flowers find their way to the table, plus a private dining room and bar above the ground-floor main restaurant. It's a comfortable space with a chic, contemporary finish watched over by an impeccable, highly professional service team. The set-lunch menu remains terrific value, and there is also the full-on ten-course tasting menu if you're in for a penny in for a pound. The dishes arrive looking stunning on the plate, every ingredients there for good reason, every flavour standing up to be counted. A first course from the à la carte, for example, consists of seared fillet of red mullet with South Coast squid, the seafood as fresh as you'll find anywhere, served with courgette, smoked sardine and dressed with vinaigrette made from Minus 8 vinegar. Main-course best end of Cornish lamb comes with confit wet garlic and a ragout of peas and smoked bacon, finished with a mint jus, while pan-fried halibut with a delicious heritage carrot and anise purée is a fish dish of class and control. Desserts match the visual impact of what has come before, with seasonal, high-quality ingredients to the fore once again — Yorkshire rhubarb and cardamom millefeuille, for example, with vanilla cream and rhubarb sorbet. There's a vegetarian version of the tasting menu which must surely be one of the very best in the country, and the wine list is a class act brimming with mighty classics and new discoveries.

Chef Marcus Eaves **Owner** David Moore **Seats** 40, Pr/dining room 12 **Times** 12-2.45/6.15-11 Closed 2 wks Xmas & New Year, Sun, L Sat **Prices** Fixed L 2 course fr £27.50, Fixed D 3 course fr £80, Tasting menu £105-£145 **Wines** 700 bottles over £30, 25 bottles under £30, 15 by glass **Parking** Cleveland St **Notes** ALC 2 course menu £65, Children welcome

LONDON W1 *continued*

Plum Valley
PLAN 2 K1

Chinese

tel: 020 7494 4366 **20 Gerrard St W1D 6JQ**
dir: *Nearest station: Leicester Square*

Contemporary Cantonese cooking and cool decor in Chinatown

There's a cool confidence to Plum Valley, standing out on Gerrard Street with its sleek black frontage. Like a lot of the restaurants in Chinatown, there are multiple rooms and stairs to be negotiated, but unlike a lot of the opposition, it's got a dark, contemporary finish. Service is brisk. The kitchen has kicked MSG into touch and instead gets the best out the ingredients by handling them with skill and respect. The mainstay of the menu is classic Cantonese stuff, with plenty of familiar dishes and some perky modern stuff, too. Vietnamese vegetable spring rolls are as crisp and golden as you might hope, while veggies might opt for spicy tofu in a light batter. There's a dim sum platter and main courses such as braised lobster with ginger and spring onion (at the pricier end of the spectrum), or braised pork belly with rice wine and sweet vinegar, or even pan-fried ostrich.

Times noon-11.30 Closed 25 Dec, All-day dining

Pollen Street Social
PLAN 2 J2

— *see opposite*

Polpo
PLAN 2 J1

Italian

tel: 020 7734 4479 **41 Beak St W1F 9SB**
dir: *Nearest station: Piccadilly Circus*

Bustling Venetian-style bacaro in the heart of Soho

An ultra casual take on the bacaros of Venice, Polpo is almost too cool for its own good, with the diminutive outfit constantly rammed and tables hard to come by. You can't book in the evenings, so expect to queue beside the bar with its high stools for dining (even this feels part of the fun though). The decor is pared-back and distressed, all elbow-to-elbow tables, dangling light bulbs, exposed-brick and floorboards. So what's all the fuss about? It's Italian-style tapas (cichetti) ordered from brown-paper menus (doubling as placemats) and sent out quick-fire by the kitchen as affordably priced small plates to graze on. It's authentic, simple, bold-flavoured stuff hewn from more modest cuts: think spicy pork and fennel meatballs with a good anise note, cod cheeks with lentils and piquant salsa verde, or perhaps grilled mortadella with celeriac and apple slaw. Italian wines come by glass (tumblers in this case), carafe and bottle, while a basement Campari bar kicks off at 5.30pm. There are sibling Polpo's in Covent Garden, Smithfield and Notting Hill.

Chef Tom Oldroyd **Owner** Polpo Ltd **Seats** 60 **Times** 12-11 Closed 25 Dec-1 Jan, D Sun All-day dining **Prices** Prices not confirmed **Wines** 12 bottles over £30, 15 bottles under £30, 18 by glass **Notes** Cicheti - small plates based on Venitian bacaros, Vegetarian available, Children welcome

The Providores and Tapa Room
PLAN 2 G3

International NOTABLE WINE LIST

tel: 020 7935 6175 **109 Marylebone High St W1U 4RX**
email: anyone@theprovidores.co.uk
dir: *Nearest station: Bond St, Baker St, Regent's Park*

Twin-faceted venue for inventive fusion cooking

There's always plenty to keep the palate entertained on Kiwi Peter Gordon's inventive menus of Asian-accented fusion food. The place occupies two floors: if the downstairs Tapa Room doesn't bring tapas to mind, that's because the name comes not from tapas, but from the traditional Rarotongan tapa cloth that covers a whole wall of the buzzy casual cafe-style space. Upstairs on the first floor is where the cooking gets more serious in the formal Providores dining room, a minimal, neutral space with white tablecloths, black leather banquettes, pale grey and white walls, arched windows, and one large, striking modern artwork. Menu descriptions stimulate the taste buds with their esoteric ingredients and off-the-wall combinations, and it all comes together in plates of colourful, well-conceived food. Starters could run to creative meat-free combos such as herby quinoa salad with girolles, goats' curd, chargrilled courgettes and pomegranate ginger dressing, while fishy ideas take in pan-fried sea bass with watermelon panzanella, wakame, samphire and sesame. Meatier fare could see roast English lamb chump matched with spelt, globe artichoke, rooibos-infused cranberries, mint and sumac labne.

Chef Peter Gordon **Owner** P Gordon, M McGrath **Seats** 38 **Times** 12-2.30/6-10 Closed 24 Dec-3 Jan, Etr Mon **Prices** Tasting menu £33-£65, Starter £8.80-£13.80, Main £18-£25.50, Dessert £9.80-£12 **Wines** 88 bottles over £30, 10 bottles under £30, 18 by glass **Notes** Fixed D 5 course £63, Tasting menu available 6 nights a week, Vegetarian available, Children welcome

Quo Vadis
PLAN 2 K2

Modern British

tel: 020 7437 9585 **26-29 Dean St W1D 3LL**
email: reception@quovadissoho.co.uk
dir: *Nearest station: Tottenham Court Road, Leicester Square*

Smart British cooking at a Soho institution

Safe in the capable hands of the Hart brothers, Quo Vadis has an illustrious culinary history. Jeremy Lee leads the line with his take on British cuisine; a little bit modern, certainly, but also recalling heartier times. The art deco building has some tables outside if you fancy a cigarette and a slice of Soho life, but it's looking pretty fine inside these days, with tan leather banquettes, modern art on the walls, and original stained-glass windows, wall mirrors and wooden floors in appreciation of the building's heritage. There's a cocktail bar, private rooms, and even a bakery turning out some quality stuff. Squid with puntarella, fennel and bergamot is a simple starter with a spot-on sweet and sour hit, followed perhaps with a dish of beautifully tender and pink venison, with roasted apples and cranberries. Desserts run to an indulgent apple, almond, mincemeat and crumble tart sitting in a pool of crème anglaise. The service team are a friendly bunch, adding greatly to the charm of the place.

Chef Jeremy Lee **Owner** Sam & Eddie Hart **Seats** 80, Pr/dining room 32 **Times** 12-2.30/5.30-11 Closed 24-25 Dec, 1 Jan, BHs, Sun **Prices** Fixed L 2 course £17.50, Fixed D 3 course £20, Starter £4-£9, Main £12.50-£22.50, Dessert £6.50-£8.50 **Wines** 131 bottles over £30, 14 bottles under £30, 10 by glass **Parking** On street or NCP **Notes** Pre-theatre menu available, Vegetarian available, Children welcome

Follow the AA on twitter @TheAA_Lifestyle

Pollen Street Social

LONDON W1 PLAN 2 J2

Modern British **V** NOTABLE WINE LIST

tel: 020 7290 7600 **8-10 Pollen St W1S 1NQ**
email: reservations@pollenstreetsocial.com
dir: *Nearest station: Oxford Circus*

Refined bistro cooking and a buzzing atmosphere at Atherton's flagship

With Social Eating House, Little Social, Berners Tavern, plus restaurants in Singapore, Hong Kong and Shanghai, Jason Atherton is a chef with the Midas touch. The empire-building started here in a small road south of Oxford Street that's easy to miss. There's an evident eye for the theatre of restaurant dining, hence the 'social' moniker perhaps, with an open kitchen (glass-fronted to reduce noise but keeping the visual impact), a bar area with its own grazing menu and cocktail list, and the now famous dessert bar. There's a contemporary neutrality to the space, where wooden floors and tables and white walls broken up by modern artworks that are anything but an afterthought. 'A contemporary bistro offering deformalised fine dining' is how Atherton describes the place, with a distinction between the 'social' bar, the restaurant and the dessert bar. If this is bistro cooking, Lionel Messi is a man who plays around with a football. Like the great Argentinian with the ball at his feet, Atherton is playing a game that not many can master. His knack is creating deconstructed masterpieces, with pace-setting invention and riveting combinations of taste and texture. His dishes look pretty amazing on the plate, too. There's an eight-course tasting menu, the à la carte, a dedicated vegetarian menu, and a set lunch offering that is well worth heading over for. The ingredients are sought from top British farmers and producers, with the menu listing the distances travelled (winkles from Skegness, 149 miles). There are plenty of modern techniques used in Atherton's cooking, bags of contemporary ideas, and clever twists and turns along the way. This is exciting stuff. Line-caught Devon squid, for example, cooked in cauliflower, with roasted squid juices, ink rice and sea herbs is one hell of a creative first course, with another a smart pairing of hay-smoked quail 'brunch', with cereals, toast and tea. Main-courses maintain the intensity of flavours and the enticing combination such as loin of Highland venison with honey-spiced beetroots, quince purée and pickled pear. When it comes to pud, the choice is yours whether to head over to the dessert bar or stay at your table, and, whichever you choose, the result is a magnificent finale. There might be chestnut, pumpkin sorbet and jam, with hazelnut sponge, or the PBJ (peanut parfait, cherry yuzu sorbet and nitro peanut). It's a treat and no mistake.

Chef Jason Atherton **Owner** Jason Atherton **Seats** 52, Pr/dining room 14 **Times** 12-2.45/6-10.45 Closed BHs, Sun **Prices** Fixed L 2 course £26, Tasting menu £85, Starter £13.50-£16, Main £29.50-£38.50, Dessert £9-£10 **Wines** 800 bottles over £30, 8 bottles under £30, 20 by glass **Parking** On street, car park Mayfair, Park Lane **Notes** Tasting menu 8 course, Children welcome

LONDON W1 *continued*

The Red Fort
PLAN 2 K2

Traditional Indian V

tel: 020 7437 2525 **77 Dean St, Soho W1D 3SH**
email: info@redfort.co.uk
dir: *Nearest station: Leicester Square, Tottenham Court Road*

Authentic modern Indian in the heart of Soho

This stylish red-fronted Indian has a surprisingly restrained demeanour for bustling Soho, with its white linen, smartly attired staff, leather seating and walls of inlaid sandstone and Mogul arch motifs. Opened back in 1983, it was one of the early modern Indian restaurants, and today continues to deliver a mix of classic Mogul court cooking and more contemporary dishes, successfully combining fine British produce with authentic sub-continental flavours, albeit at fairly hefty prices. From the open kitchen at the rear, expect a traditional Hyderabadi bhuna gosht (chunks of Herdwick lamb with a rich, aromatic spicing hit of ginger, black pepper, coriander seed and red chilli simply served with a cooling peach raita), while for seafood lovers, there's Samundari rattan (a Neptune's supper of scallops, squid, stone bass and king prawn in a spicy fennel, coconut and carom sauce). Below stairs, the more trendy Zenna Bar is the place to head for after-work cocktails and lighter bites.

Chef M A Rahman **Owner** Amin Ali **Seats** 84 **Times** 12-3/5.30-11.30 Closed L Sat-Sun **Prices** Fixed L 2 course £15-£25, Fixed D 3 course £18-£59, Tasting menu £49, Starter £6-£14, Main £18-£38, Dessert £7-£16 **Wines** 173 bottles over £30, 29 bottles under £30, 11 by glass **Parking** NCP Brewer St **Notes** Tasting menu 4 course, Fixed pre-theatre D, Children welcome

The Riding House Café
PLAN 2 J3

Modern British

tel: 020 7927 0840 **43-51 Great Titchfield St W1W 7PQ**
email: info@ridinghousecafe.co.uk
dir: *Nearest station: Oxford Circus*

Buzzy all-day brasserie near Oxford Street

If you're shopping on Oxford Street and looking for a pit-stop, then take a short diversion up Great Titchfield Street to The Riding House Café, where a fashionable all-day dining menu – everything from breakfasts to afternoon teas – is served in a lively, buzzing environment. Much more restaurant than café, The Riding House stands out from the crowd with its striking art-deco design (think large, 1930s-style windows all around, affording its diners great street views and plenty of light), whilst inside it is all parquet flooring and clubby wood panelling. You can perch on a swivel seat at the bar and watch the chefs at work or take an old wooden cinema seat at the long communal table to eat refectory-style; there are plenty of regular tables too if communal ain't your thing. Classic brasserie dishes are the order of the day at lunch and dinner: start with a couple of 'small plates', such as beautifully flavoured braised rabbit with soft polenta and parmesan, and crispy salt-cod fritters with red pepper aïoli, before tucking into a very fine fish and chips. The apple and sultana crumble for two with vanilla ice cream and custard is a very happy ending.

Chef Paul Daniel **Owner** Clive Watson, Adam White **Seats** 115, Pr/dining room 14 **Times** 12-3.30/6-10 Closed 25 Dec **Prices** Prices not confirmed **Wines** 15 bottles over £30, 15 bottles under £30, 20 by glass **Parking** On street **Notes** Sunday L, Vegetarian available, Children welcome

The Ritz Restaurant
PLAN 4 J6

– *see below*

The Ritz Restaurant

LONDON W1   PLAN 4 J6

British, French V   NOTABLE WINE LIST

tel: 020 7300 2370 **150 Piccadilly W1J 9BR**
email: ritzrestaurant@theritzlondon.com web: www.theritzlondon.com
dir: *Nearest station: Green Park*

Arresting dining in sumptuous formal restaurant

Not an establishment to hide its light beneath a bushel, the Ritz announces itself as 'The world's greatest hotel, as conceived by the world's greatest hotelier'. And it would be a brave person indeed who tried to argue The Ritz wasn't the most famous hotel on the planet. The place has a weight of history and expectations to live up to, a task which it pulls off with aplomb. Entering the grand dining room often provokes a sharp intake of breath, as if you had taken a wrong turn and ended up in Versailles Palace, with its floor-to-ceiling windows looking over Green Park, and rich Louis XVI-inspired decor of murals, statues and glittering chandeliers, reflecting from mirrored walls. It's an extravagantly opulent space that requires gentlemen to turn up in jacket and tie. An army of waiting staff (four sommeliers, no less) set the scene for theatrical dining with classic tableside service which, while knowledgeable and skilful, is not at all stuffy.

Harking back to the days of Auguste Escoffier, the menu explores the classical repertoire with classics such as goose liver terrine with Sauternes and peaches, but executive chef John Williams has created his own distinctively contemporary repertory, so a starter matches veal sweetbread with grated and puréed parsnip, truffles, and rich veal jus. Given the surroundings, and the prices, luxury ingredients abound, among them lobster as a main course with carrot fondant, ginger and lime. Elsewhere, ingredients are of the highest order, as in a superb fillet of turbot served in a walnut crust with ceps, roasted celeriac and brown butter sauce. At dessert stage, a light and perfectly risen banana soufflé comes with banana and rum ice cream, or you could invoke the spirit of Escoffier and bow out with crêpes Suzette flambéed theatrically at the table.

Chef John T Williams MBE **Owner** The Ritz Hotel (London) Ltd **Seats** 90, Pr/dining room 60 **Times** 12.30-2/5.30-10 **Prices** Fixed L 3 course £49-£59, Fixed D 3 course £59-£95, Tasting menu £95-£130, Starter £18-£24, Main £38-£42, Dessert £14-£36, Service optional **Wines** 450 bottles over £30, 15 by glass **Parking** 10, NCP **Notes** Menu surprise 6 course £95, 'Live at the Ritz' menu £95, Sunday L fr £59, Children welcome

Roka

LONDON W1   **PLAN 2 J3**

Modern Japanese

tel: 020 7580 6464 **37 Charlotte St W1T 1RR**
email: info@rokarestaurant.com
dir: *Nearest station: Goodge St, Tottenham Court Rd*

Exquisite robata-grill cookery in London's Medialand

The robata grill is the focal point of this flourishing Japanese restaurant, where its live action fills the room with fiery energy. With waiting staff turned-out in spiffy designer outfits, Roka is cool from top to bottom. There are others in Canary Wharf and Hong Kong, but it is here in Charlotte Street that it feels most at home, among the cutting-edge media businesses that pervade this part of town. There are tables outside, protected by an army of potted plants, and the full-length glass windows open up to create an outdoor-vibe in the summertime. Exotic hardwoods dominate the interior, and their swirling grains bring texture to the minimalist space. Sharing is the way to go, with a tasting menu on offer for those that find choosing too much to bear, but rest assured the service team are adept at helping first-timers through the menu. The quality of the ingredients shines out, presentation is clean and sharp, and flavours really hit the spot. Soft-shelled crab is pretty much a must-eat dish here, perhaps with roasted chilli dressing, and you won't go wrong with the range of sushi and sashimi either. Fillet of sea bream with ryotei miso and red onion is a dish with a wonderful glaze, the fish as fresh as can be, while the robata grill delivers scallop skewers with wasabi and shiso, or lamb cutlets with Korean spices. Desserts manage a tantalizing fusion of East and West, such as yoghurt and almond cake with mango toffee and caramel miso ice cream, or honey custard with pink guava, lychee granita and marshmallow. The basement Shochu Lounge is a moody spot for Japanese-influenced cocktails and also serves the full menu.

Chef Hamish Brown **Owner** Rainer Becker, Arjun Waney **Seats** 90 **Times** 12-3.30/5.30-11.30 Closed Xmas, New Year **Prices** Prices not confirmed **Wines** 150 bottles over £30, 24 by glass **Parking** On street, NCP in Brewers St **Notes** Vegetarian available, Children welcome

---

Roka

LONDON W1   **PLAN 2 G1**

Modern Japanese NEW

tel: 020 7305 5644 **30 North Audley St W1K 6ZF**
email: infomayfair@rokarestaurant.com
dir: *Nearest station: Bond Street*

Dazzling robata grill cuisine in Mayfair

The third and latest addition to Roka's über-cool operations in Canary Wharf and Fitzrovia (see entry) opened its substantial glass doors in 2014, and couldn't have landed in a more upmarket postcode. In fitting with the ultra-posh Mayfair location, Japanese designer Noriyoshi Muramatsu has come up with a drop-dead cool interior of exotic hardwoods and hard industrial textures of steel, concrete and copper, with walls of floor-to-ceiling windows to ensure that the see-and-be-seen factor is sufficiently high. The robata grill is the pulsing heart of the operation, holding centre stage in the super-slick dining room and driving the soul of the menu, which takes the fashionable route of sharing plates with dishes whizzed to the table as soon as they are ready. There's also sushi and sashimi, and a tasting menu should you choose to submit to a journey of the chef's choosing, or you could steer your own course with the help of the well-briefed service team, and you can rest assured that everything is made with real skill using wonderfully fresh and flavourful ingredients. Yellowfin tuna of exceptional quality opens the show, lightly seared to seal in the freshness of its garnet red interior, matched with crunchy shredded white radish and pointed up with the spicy notes of a punchy dressing involving apple, mustard, vinegar and sesame. Next up, plump scallops are skewered and seared to perfection on the barbecue and delivered with the simple accompaniments of wasabi mayonnaise and shiro, or you could opt for cedar-roasted baby chicken with the bracing flavours of chilli, lemon and garlic soy. The craft and creativity carries on into desserts as well, with the rich, nutty flavour of sobacha buckwheat giving depth to a well-crafted crème brûlée served with the contrasting textures of toasted hazelnuts and Yamazaki whisky ice cream. An extensive list with tasting notes means sake fans are in for a treat too.

Chef Cristian Brauaccini **Owner** Rainer Becker, Arjun Waney **Seats** 113 **Times** 12-3.30/5.30-11.30 **Prices** Tasting menu £55-£79, Starter £5.60-£16.90, Main £13.90-£36.90, Dessert £6.90-£9.60 **Wines** 100 bottles over £30, 3 bottles under £30, 13 by glass **Notes** Vegetarian available, Children welcome

LONDON W1 *continued*

Roka
PLAN 2 J3

◎◎◎ – *see page 365*

Roka
PLAN 2 G1

◎◎◎ – *see page 365*

Roti Chai
PLAN 2 G2

◎◎ Modern Indian

tel: 020 7408 0101 **3 Portman Mews South W1H 6HS**
email: infowala@rotichai.com
dir: *Nearest station: Bond Street, Marble Arch*

Vibrant Indian street-food close to Oxford Street

Roti Chai is a restaurant of two halves that takes its inspiration from the street stalls, roadside and railway cafés of the Indian sub-continent. The ground-floor Street Kitchen is a bright, casual canteen-style venue serving homely 'street food', while the basement Dining Room deals in more refined nouveau Indian cooking. The look is part industrial – exposed ducting and spotlights and black-painted breezeblock walls – mixed with smart contemporary darkwood floors, chunky oak tables, black leather seats, and railway carriage references in wall-mounted luggage racks and brass-framed, smoked mirrors. Staff are all young, keen, and well-briefed on the menus. Expect a vibrant, modern take on Indian flavours wherever you sit. Bengali crab & fish cakes with onion seeds and cumin gets things under way in the Dining Room, followed by a posh version of classic saagwala gosht – slow-cooked Elwy Valley Welsh lamb in a smooth and spicy spinach sauce. For dessert, chai brûlée puts a twist on an old friend by flavouring it with cardamom, cloves and cinnamon.

Times 12-11.45 All-day dining

Roux at The Landau
PLAN 2 H3

◎◎ Modern European, French V

tel: 020 7636 1000 **The Langham London, Portland Place W1B 1JA**
email: reservations@thelandau.com web: www.thelandau.com
dir: *Nearest station: Oxford Circus*

Highly polished modern cuisine à la Roux

The Roux dining room at the elegant Langham Hotel opposite the BBC building is a haven of traditional values. If things have gone dressed-down and laid-back elsewhere, here the elevated tone of the panelled oval room does justice to the highly polished cooking of the Roux ethos. Chris King is its vicar on earth, and having worked at Le Gavroche, not to mention for New York hotshot Thomas Keller, may be presumed a confident hand on the tiller. Attentive timing and precise balance distinguish a first-course trio of caramelised scallops with braised pork jowl, chickpea purée and cracked spices, ahead of a serving of richly flavoured milk-fed lamb and kidneys, accompanied by buckwheat salad and diced feta. A creamy, lemon-spiked sauce arrives almost as an afterthought. Gigha halibut appears in a Japanese study, with miso-glazed white asparagus, Tokyo turnips and grapefruit. Comice pear soufflé with lightly poached whole pear is an essay in airy delicacy, the dish given depth by the kid-glove insertion at the table of a bitter chocolate sorbet.

Chef Chris King **Owner** Laneham Hospitality Group **Seats** 100, Pr/dining room 18
Times 12.30-2.30/5.30-10.30 Closed BHs, Sun, L Sat **Prices** Fixed L 3 course £35-£45, Fixed D 3 course £35-£45, Tasting menu £65-£115, Starter £9.25-£24, Main £25-£56, Dessert £8.50-£15 **Wines** 200 bottles over £30, 12 bottles under £30, 20 by glass **Parking** On street, NCP **Notes** Children welcome

Salt Yard
PLAN 2 J3

◎◎ Italian, Spanish

tel: 020 7637 0657 **54 Goodge St W1T 4NA**
email: info@saltyard.co.uk
dir: *Nearest station: Goodge St*

Top-notch tapas just off Tottenham Court Road

Spain and Italy unite harmoniously in this buzzy restaurant in fashionable Fitzrovia. The ground-floor bar is a top place for a glass of prosecco or cava, or a nifty Bellini and some charcuterie. But if you're here for a while, and looking for something more substantial, head downstairs to the main dining room, with its leather banquette seating and views into the kitchen. The winning combination of two great European nations results in an appealing mix of feel-good flavours and ideas. Salt-cod croquetas with bravas sauce are an irresistible classic, but there might be the less commonly seen marmitako of tuna (a Basque stew), or confit of Gloucestershire Old Spot pork belly with rosemary-scented cannellini beans. The idea is to share, tapas-style, and the mix of the familiar and creative works a treat. There are good technical shows on show, too: crispy baby squid, for example, cooked perfectly, and served with a perky squid ink aïoli and baby chard, or the chargrilled chorizo with chick pea, cumin and garlic.

Times 12-3/5.30-11 Closed BHs, 10 days Xmas, Sun

Sartoria
PLAN 2 J1

◎ Italian

tel: 020 7534 7000 & 7534 7030 **20 Savile Row W1S 3PR**
email: sartoriareservations@danddlondon.com
dir: *Nearest station: Oxford Circus, Green Park, Piccadilly Circus*

Smart setting for modern Italian cooking

Named in honour of its location in the fine suiting and booting world of Savile Row (the name is Italian for tailor's shop), Sartoria is an immaculately turned-out operation with a chic, Milanese-inspired interior and switched-on, upbeat service from staff dressed to look the part. On the menu is an earthy, uncomplicated roll-out of creatively re-imagined modern Italian ideas. Antipasti could take the shape of capon broth with cappellacci 'Bishop's hat' ravioli, pumpkin and chestnut, while pasta dishes run to Piemontese ravioli with sheep's milk ricotta, spinach, walnuts and sage. Among main courses might be braised lamb shank with celeriac purée, or baked red mullet with spinach and gremolata, while the dolci department offers layered Amedei chocolate cake with passionfruit.

Chef Lukas Pfaff **Owner** D & D London **Seats** 100, Pr/dining room 48
Times 12-3/5.30-11 Closed 24-26 Dec, 1-2 Jan, Etr Mon, Sun (open for private parties only), L Sat **Prices** Fixed L 2 course £25, Fixed D 3 course £30 **Wines** 119 bottles over £30, 23 bottles under £30, 13 by glass **Parking** On street
Notes Vegetarian available, Children welcome

Looking for a London restaurant by name?
Use the index on page 254

Scott's Restaurant
PLAN 2 G1

◉◉ British

tel: 020 7495 7309 **20 Mount St W1K 2HE**
dir: *Nearest station: Bond Street, Green Park*

Bags of style and first-rate seafood

With its Mayfair address and art-deco good looks, Scott's is quite the glamour puss. There are mosaics, huge mirrors, oak-panelled walls, leather seats, and impressive modern British artworks to catch the eye, plus a menu brimming with top-notch seafood to enjoy. The onyx-topped central crustacea bar sets the scene and champagne is most definitely on the cards. There are some meat and vegetarian choices on the menu, but seafood is the thing. Those oysters might include Lindisfarne rocks or West Mersea natives, whilst among starters fried squid with chilli relish and lime shows the style – fine fresh produce and careful execution. Seared sea bass with lemon and herb butter hits the spot, or you might push the boat out and go for lobster thermidor. Among desserts, the Bakewell pudding with almond ice cream is a bit of a show-stopper, as is the pear tarte Tatin (if you've got a friend to share it with you). The service is a bit of a highlight too.

Times 12-10.30 Closed 25-26 Dec, 1 Jan, D 24 Dec All-day dining

Shogun, Millennium Hotel Mayfair
PLAN 2 G1

◉ Japanese

tel: 020 7629 9400 **Grosvenor Square W1K 2HP**
email: reservations.mayfair@millenniumhotels.co.uk
dir: *Nearest station: Bond Street, Green Park*

Traditional Japanese in a posh Mayfair hotel

Oddly secreted away in the rear courtyard of Grosvenor Square's swanky Millennium Hotel, Shogun is an unapologetically traditional Japanese outfit set in a somewhat dated cellar. It does have a certain old-world charm though, with its faux-stone wine cellar look accessorised with heritage touches like a life-size Samurai warrior statue, traditional prints and lantern lighting, while unclothed tables are divided by display racks of kyudo archery arrows. The simple, straight-up traditional cooking fits the surroundings, the lengthy roster fronted by a series of set house menus (perhaps based around sashimi or tempura), otherwise, mains step out with teriyaki of tuna, salmon, duck and Scotch sirloin, or perhaps sliced pork fried with ginger or deep-fried chicken. Among the Millennium's other dining options, classy Italian Avista – see entry – is off the main foyer.

Times 6-11 Closed Mon, L all week

Sixtyone Restaurant
PLAN 2 F2

◉◉◉ *– see below*

Sixtyone Restaurant

◉◉◉

LONDON W1   **PLAN 2 F2**

Modern British **NEW**

tel: 020 7958 3222 **The Montcalm, Great Cumberland Place W1H 7TW**
email: reservations@sixtyonerestaurant.co.uk **web:** www.sixtyonerestaurant.co.uk
dir: *Nearest station: Marble Arch*

Boldly flavoured deconstructive food amid southern Marylebone glitz

Sixtyone aims to be a neighbourhood restaurant, albeit in a neighbourhood of glossy hotels. Technically, it's part and parcel of the Montcalm, but functions very much as an autonomous business, with a champagne bar next door for wetting the whistle. From humble beginnings amid the seafood treasures of Devon, our host, Anglo-French chef Arnaud Stevens, went on to work under many of the capital's headline names (including Gordon Ramsay, Pierre Koffman and Jason Atherton). The look of the place could be anywhere, frankly, a pastel-beige dining room with banquette seating and big mirrors, unclothed tables and quality glassware, with structured service in the old-school manner. Any hint of the ordinary, though, is banished by what emerges from the kitchen. Seasonal menus furnished by artisan suppliers are compiled from boldly flavoured dishes presented in the deconstructive fashion, but with a refreshing avoidance of smears and froths. Big impact is conjured from a meaty starter serving of roast partridge, wrapped in bresaola and filled with foiegras, the whole offset with the tartness of puréed dates. At main, moistly flaky cod comes in garbure (the hearty southern French soup), garnished with pancetta and a chickpea croquette, or there may be beef rump in a silky onion emulsion with the tang of sea-veg. Vegetarian dishes don't stint on forthright richness either: try marinated beetroot salad with Cashel Blue and walnuts, then pea risotto with Baby Gem and burrata. For dessert, banoffee pie lights out into new territory when it turns into crisp-coated toffee parfait, caramelised banana and caramel popcorn with banana sauce, while other reimaginings are applied to lemon meringue pie and a drizzle cake fragranced with elderflower.

Chef Arnaud Stevens **Owner** Searcys **Seats** 61, Pr/dining room 16
Times 12-2.45/5.30-10.30 Closed 24-26 Dec, D Sun **Prices** Fixed L 2 course £15, Fixed D 3 course £24, Tasting menu £55-£85, Starter £7-£12, Main £16-£24, Dessert £7-£9 **Wines** 170 bottles over £30, 8 bottles under £30, 12 by glass
Notes Pre-theatre menu £19/£24, Wknd brunch £22/£28, Sunday L £22-£28, Vegetarian available, Children welcome

Sketch (The Gallery)

LONDON W1   PLAN 2 J1

Modern European **NOTABLE WINE LIST**

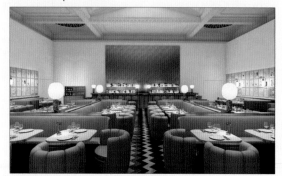

tel: 020 7659 4500 **9 Conduit St W1S 2XG**
email: info@sketch.uk.com **web:** www.sketch.uk.com
dir: *Nearest station: Oxford Circus*

Virtuoso cooking in artist-designed restaurant

It's all change at The Gallery, with the Martin Creed design replaced by the works of David Shrigley (and the touch of designer India Mahdavi). It's a striking space one again, this time with a pink hue and some funky barrel chairs, plus 293 (to be precise) humorous cartoons by Shrigley. The crockery has been designed by the artist too, so expect a few thought-provoking additions to the glossy white ceramics. The service remains a highlight of a visit, with the well-informed staff positively brimming with enthusiasm. Pierre Gagnaire's food continues to impress with its vibrancy, creativity and sheer sense of joy of life (joie de vivre indeed). This is the brasserie option in Sketch's culinary canon, but it's not like any other you'd have been to. A starter of 'Chantilly lace' is Gagnaire's version of a lobster bisque, with a tower of rice (black, basmati and white) topped with a horseradish cream, around which the waiter pours a delicious bisque, while another of tuna sashimi, creamy avocado and black olive gelée is presented as a homage to the artist in residence. Main-course delivers a full-flavoured, corn-fed chicken in a fricassée with pearl onions and an indulgent macaroni, or go for Sketch fish and chips (pollock) with straw potatoes, peaches, mushy peas and tartare sauce. There's no lack of creativity when it comes to desserts either, with a stunning looking cheesecake that lives up to expectations in the eating – cream cheese, hazelnut praline, caramelised pear and pear velouté combining to maximum effect. Afternoon tea is another treat on offer in The Gallery dining room, with some spectacular cakes and more of Mr Shrigley's tableware to help the conversation flow. The wine list is a divertingly spectacular thing, too, with lots of good things available at a price. It's not the cheapest brasserie in town by a long way, but it is most certainly unique.

Chef Pierre Gagnaire, Herve Deville **Owner** Mourad Mazouz **Seats** 150 **Times** 12-2/6.30pm-2am Closed Xmas, New Year, BHs, L all week **Prices** Starter £12-£25, Main £16-£39, Dessert £8.50-£10 **Wines** 85 bottles over £30, 9 bottles under £30, 15 by glass **Parking** On street, NCP **Notes** Vegetarian available, Children welcome

Sketch (Lecture Room & Library)

PLAN 2 J1

Modern European V NOTABLE WINE LIST

tel: 020 7659 4500 **9 Conduit St W1S 2XG**
email: info@sketch.uk.com **web:** www.sketch.uk.com
dir: *Nearest station: Oxford Circus*

Multiform dishes of exhaustive complexity in a Mayfair 'experience' venue

The multi-faceted Sketch offers a number of what can only be called 'experiences' within one Mayfair package and the Lecture Room and Library is the nerve-centre of the whole operation. From the street entrance, you may feel a little as though as you are entering the kind of nightclub where the friends of Prince Harry might be seen, but what unfolds within is a darn sight kookier altogether. It was once said of a painting by James Whistler that he had thrown a pot of paint in the public's face. Things have gone a little further than that here, and at the top of the stairs, your attendant flings wide the doors to reveal a room of throbbing, red-hot colour. Geometric panels of pink and orange advance across the carpet, the walls are padded in cream leather, while gigantic Ali Baba vases stand in alcoves decorated with Vorticist sunbursts. When it comes to the business of eating, you're in for the ride of a life, courtesy of French modern maître Pierre Gagnaire. His favoured dining format is multiform dishes that are served as a circular array of little plates, to be progressed through in a prescribed order. A mere hint of the exhaustive complexity can be gleaned from a starter of langoustines that consists of a tartare with grapefruit juice, lemon granita and vodka; consommé with grated daikon; mousseline with manzanilla, enoki mushrooms and green pepper;

gingerbread-crumbed langoustine with apple-cinnamon compôte and cuttlefish in cider; and a grilled one on chicory and barberry fondue. Barely have you taken all that in than a main course poses another set of gustatory challenges, perhaps by means of roast and poached breast of guinea-fowl with green tea and almond cream stuffing, Swiss chard, Golden Delicious apple, blood orange semolina and French bean salad. Certain of the dishes seem to be straining at their moorings in the conventional menu classifications, so a listing that begins with mace-rubbed, oregano-roasted veal with sweetbread curry ends by wandering off into the realms of an ice cream version of burrata, while an artichoke ice cream finds its way into the company of grilled beef in Sarawak-peppered beurre noisette. Neal's Yard cheeses are the straightforward alternative (though even these come with white beetroot purée and Roquefort-pear ice cream) to desserts such as vanilla soufflé with poached pear, almond paste, dragon fruit and aloe vera, or the show-stopping Pierre Gagnaire Grand Dessert selection. Choose three or seven from the likes of peppered apple and dried fruit sablé with avocado in pomegranate and blackcurrant syrup; chocolate consommé with ganache and prune confit; kumquats with mango and red pepper confit and Campari-and-orange granita, and more, much more.

Chef Pierre Gagnaire, Romain Chapel **Owner** Mourad Mazouz **Seats** 50, Pr/dining room 24 **Times** 12-2.30/6.30-11 Closed 18-29 Aug, 23-30 Dec, 1 Jan, BHs, Sun-Mon, L Sat **Prices** Fixed L 2 course fr £35, Tasting menu £75-£95, Starter £35-£48, Main £46-£55, Dessert £16-£17 **Wines** 730 bottles over £30, 70 bottles under £30, 20 by glass **Parking** NCP Soho, Cavendish Sq **Notes** Tasting & Vegetarian tasting menu 6 course, Children welcome

Sketch (The Gallery)   PLAN 2 J1

@@@ – see page 368

Sketch (Lecture Room & Library)   PLAN 2 J1

@@@@@ – see page 369

Sketch (The Parlour)   PLAN 2 J1

@@ Modern European

tel: 020 7659 4500 **9 Conduit St W1S 2XG**
email: info@sketch.uk.com **web:** www.sketch.uk.com
dir: *Nearest station: Oxford Circus, Green Park, Bond St*

Eccentric, arty setting for casual dining and drinking

This Parisian-esque salon's sexy boudoir look may appear a little Laurence Llewelyn-Bowen, with its quirky array of Louis XV antique chairs, sofas and divans, atmospheric lighting and bold retro colours and objets d'art, but it all fits the bill perfectly. The Parlour is the entry-level option at Sketch, the funky collaboration between French super-chef Pierre Gagnaire and Mourad 'Momo' Mazouz that spans various eating and drinking spaces (see also Lecture Room & Library and The Gallery) in this arty, theatrical and glam Mayfair playpen. An all-day café to see and be seen, The Parlour serves breakfasts, afternoon teas and informal comfort food (from noon) before morphing into a lively evening cocktail bar (members only after 9pm). Enjoy haddock soufflé or croque monsieur to larger plates like chicken cocotte or steak and pommes sautés. Desserts and cakes are to die for, as in 'royal peach' (sweet wine poached peach with kirsch mousseline, rose ice cream and almond and redcurrant sponge cake), and first-class macaroons like rose and raspberry or lemon.

Chef Pierre Gagnaire, Herve Deville **Owner** Mourad Mazouz **Seats** 50 **Times** 12-10 Closed Xmas, 1 Jan, All-day dining **Prices** Starter £8.50-£24, Main £14-£24, Dessert £2-£5 **Wines** 23 bottles over £30, 4 bottles under £30, 12 by glass **Parking** NCP Soho **Notes** Vegetarian available, Children welcome

Social Eating House

LONDON W1   PLAN 2 J2

Modern British **v**
tel: 020 7993 3251 **58-59 Poland St W1F 7NS**
email: reservations@socialeatinghouse.com
dir: *Nearest station: Oxford Circus*

Vintage chic and classy cooking with flavours galore

Jason Atherton's empire has expanded eastwards to Hong Kong, Singapore and Shanghai, and with Berners Tavern and Pollen Street Social in London to attend to as well, there's a need for trusted lieutenants. Step forward Paul Hood. In Soho, right in the heart of medialand, the Social Eating House is run by the said Mr Hood as chef-patron, which means there's a keen eye on proceedings at all times. The place is designed to fit right into the Soho vibe, so it's casual (social, if you like), with a pared-back, vintage retro decor over three floors consisting of the main restaurant, the oh-so-cool Blind Pig bar, and a 15-seater chef's bar. The menu doesn't hold a candle for any particular style of cuisine, but it's a little bit British, a touch French, and more about flavour than anything else. Simplicity is a virtue indeed when it comes to a first course plate of smoked Black Angus tartare, with radishes, horseradish and mustard leaf, and soup is anything but humble if a Jerusalem artichoke and trompette mushroom enriched with Scottish scallop and crispy pork skin version is anything to go by. Main courses continue in the same vein, with some robust flavours on the plate and the acute technical skill in the kitchen plain for all to see. Roasted Cornish cod comes with toasted chestnuts and the house's own smoked bacon, plus cavolo nero and sprouts, while another combines roast Scottish venison with smoked ricotta, pear, Brazil nuts and 12-year-old balsamic. There's lots of fun to be had at dessert stage, with a nostalgia hit on offer in the form of the 'Wagon Wheel' (toasted meringue with salted caramel and raspberry), or an apple pie with Calvados ice cream, cinnamon custard and toffee apple. There are sharing jars designed to fortify drinkers.

Chef Paul Hood **Owner** Paul Hood, Jason Atherton **Seats** 75, Pr/dining room 8 **Times** 12-2.30/6.30-10.30 Closed 25-26 Dec, BHs, Sun **Prices** Fixed L 2 course £19, Starter £9.50-£11.50, Main £16-£77, Dessert £7.50-£8.50 **Wines** 111 bottles over £30, 9 bottles under £30, 14 by glass **Parking** Soho or Broadwick masterpark **Notes** Chef's experience £110, Children welcome

The Square

LONDON W1   PLAN 2 H1

Modern French V

tel: 020 7495 7100 **6-10 Bruton St, Mayfair W1J 6PU**
email: reception@squarerestaurant.com
dir: *Nearest station: Bond Street, Green Park*

Shining star bursting with intelligence and technique in the heart of Mayfair

The Square has remained at the top of the London dining scene since it opened its doors back in 1991. That is no mean feat. It's down to the hard work and talent of Philip Howard, in charge from day one. He's surrounded himself with talented people, of course, with Gary Foulkes heading the kitchen team. Change has come, slowly, deliberately, but never revolution or change for its own sake. The room was never a show-stopper, but it is refined and gently contemporary: abstract art on pearlescent walls, polished wooden floors and generously-spaced tables dressed up in pristine linen cloths. This is Mayfair after all. The cooking is broadly modern French with the emphasis on flavour rather than showy technique, but, that said, the cooking is precise and certainly contemporary. The set lunch remains a good entry point, while the tasting menu with wine flight is well worth a punt if the whole table is with you. Langoustine claw and ceps gratin with hand-rolled macaroni and autumn truffle is a refined dish from the lunchtime menu that delivers satisfying flavours. The carte might offer up a warm salad of Cornish mackerel with leek, celery, Linzer potatoes, sour cream and rhubarb. The impeccable quality of the ingredients is a signature of Philip Howard's cooking, with a devotion for provenance and seasonality that pays dividends. Main-course roast breast of mallard is a superb bird, the breast and accompanying leg (croustillant – wrapped in potato) tender and rich with flavour, served with creamed cabbage, bacon and pickled blueberries. The bang-on technical ability and intelligent thinking of this team continues at desserts stage; a dish of blackberry and hibiscus, for example, with mousse, jelly and sorbet packing a punch. Bread is classic French-style baguette that is as good as it gets, and there are all the freebie courses you expect at this level. The service team glide about with efficiency and grace, and the wine list is a mighty tome packed with amazing stuff, and a particularly remarkable showing from Burgundy.

Chef Philip Howard **Owner** N Platts-Martin & Philip Howard **Seats** 75, Pr/dining room 18 **Times** 12-2.30/6.30-10.30 Closed 24-26 Dec, 1 Jan, L Sun, BHs **Prices** Fixed L 2 course £32.50-£35, Fixed D 3 course £90, Tasting menu £115 **Wines** 14 by glass **Parking Notes** ALC 2/3 course £65/£90, Children welcome

LONDON W1 *continued*

Social Eating House

PLAN 2 J2

@@@ – *see page 370*

So Restaurant

PLAN 2 J1

@@ Japanese

tel: 020 7292 0767 & 7292 0760 **3-4 Warwick St W1B 5LS**
email: info@sorestaurant.com
dir: *Nearest station: Piccadilly Circus*

Modern Japanese with some top-notch European ingredients

Tucked away in Soho's hinterland just behind Piccadilly Circus, So is an unassuming but authentic, smart, modern Japanese. It spreads over two floors; a busy café-like ground floor with sushi bar and a more intimate, low-lit basement room. Laminate tables, an open-plan kitchen and a yobanyaki grill (where items are cooked over volcanic rocks imported from Mount Fuji) tick all the design boxes. The menu has a broad scope, from tempura (soft-shelled crab or squid), to sushi and sashimi, plus some European-inspired dishes; the kitchen makes good use of quality European produce, too, such as pan-fried foie gras served with Japanese mushrooms and teriyaki sauce, or half lobster meunière. There's fashionable stuff like black cod marinated in saikyo miso, too, plus good value West End lunch and bento box deals.

Chef Kaoru Yamamoto **Owner** Tetsuro Hama **Seats** 70, Pr/dining room 6
Times 12-3/5.30-10.30 Closed Xmas-New Year, Sun **Prices** Prices not confirmed
Wines 25 bottles over £30, 16 bottles under £30, 8 by glass **Parking** On street
Notes Pre-theatre menu 3 course £19.95, Tasting menu 3 course, Vegetarian available, Children welcome

The Square

PLAN 2 H1

@@@@ – *see page 371*

Sumosan Restaurant

PLAN 2 H1

@@ Japanese Fusion

tel: 020 7495 5999 **26B Albemarle St, Mayfair W1S 4HY**
email: info@sumosan.com
dir: *Nearest station: Green Park*

Glossy backdrop for first-class contemporary Japanese cooking

The glossy contemporary interior – a large open-plan room in dark shades, with padded purple panels on brown walls, pale wood floors, and deeply-lacquered exotic tiger-striped macassar wood tables – is a suitably high-end modern backdrop for the up-to-date Japanese cooking that draws in crowds of international jet-setters and well-heeled denizens of Mayfair. The vibe is bustling and always on the boil as well-briefed, uniformed staff work the room, whisking the kitchen's output of precisely-cooked, immaculately-presented dishes built on top-class ingredients efficiently to their destination. To get things rolling, there's spot-on crispy salt and pepper squid, or excellent sushi – yuwaku roll with king crab, super-fresh raw tuna, wasabi mayonnaise, spring onion, sesame seeds and bottarga-type fish roe, say – prepared by chefs at an open marble-topped counter, as well as sashimi dishes and teppan grilling The wide-ranging menu runs to fusion ideas such as steamed Chilean sea bass with orange sauce, or lamb chops furikaki presented in a salty, nutty, crunchy coating of sesame seeds, almonds, and spices.

Times 12-3/6-11.30 Closed 26 Dec, New Year, L Sat-Sun

Tamarind

PLAN 4 H6

@@ Indian

tel: 020 7629 3561 **20 Queen St, Mayfair W1J 5PR**
email: manager@tamarindrestaurant.com **web:** www.tamarindrestaurant.com
dir: *Nearest station: Green Park*

Classy, contemporary Indian cooking with a European touch

Discreetly tucked away in a quiet Mayfair street, Tamarind was in the vanguard of design-led new-wave Indians when it opened in 1995. The expansive basement still works a glamorous contemporary chic with shimmery hues of bronze and black leather, and linen-clad tables tended by formally dressed, charming staff. The cooking takes its cue from the rich Mogul dishes of the Indian north-west, which makes ample use of the tandoor, but Chef Alfred Prasad likes to experiment and keep things fresh by tossing modern European ideas into the mix, using top-drawer ingredients enhanced by subtle spicing. A light-touch starter of seafood salad brings steamed shrimps, tilapia, squid and black olives with a fennel and ginger dressing, ahead of a remarkably tender Hyderabadi lamb shank with a velvety sauce of turmeric, yoghurt and freshly-ground spices. Elsewhere there may be a creative partnership of sea bass fillet with fine beans, raw mango and a tamarind and tomato sauce, and to finish, tandoori-grilled spiced pineapple is drizzled with honey and matched with rose ice cream.

Chef Alfred Prasad, Peter Joseph **Owner** Indian Cuisine Ltd **Seats** 90
Times 12-2.45/5.30-11 Closed 25-26 Dec, 1 Jan, L Sat **Prices** Fixed L 2 course fr £21, Fixed D 3 course fr £60, Starter £7.50-£16.50, Main £16.50-£39.50 **Wines** 134 bottles over £30, 2 bottles under £30, 14 by glass **Parking** NCP **Notes** Pre-theatre D £28.50 5.30-7pm, Sunday L fr £32, Vegetarian available, No children

Texture Restaurant

PLAN 2 F2

@@@@ – *see opposite*

Texture Restaurant

LONDON W1   PLAN 2 F2

Modern European v NOTABLE WINE LIST

tel: 020 7224 0028 **DoubleTree by Hilton Hotel, 34 Portman St W1H 7BY**
email: info@texture-restaurant.co.uk
web: www.texture-restaurant.co.uk
dir: *Nearest station: Marble Arch, Bond St*

Creative and dynamic cooking with Icelandic soul

Raymond Blanc played inadvertent matchmaker when chef Agnar Sverrisson met whizz-kid sommelier Xavier Rousset while both were working at Le Manoir. In 2007, the pair combined their considerable talents to open Texture, and they have developed a mini-empire over the last few years, their trio of 28 to 50 wine bars bringing a welcoming presence to the London dining scene. Situated in the grand Georgian hotel, the partnership is built on putting equal importance on food and wine. There's an extraordinary list of 110 Champagnes to choose from in the cool and sophisticated Champagne Bar, and the wine list is a serious piece of work, too. The room itself is a grand space with high ceilings, ornate plasterwork, large windows and polished wooden floors, overlaid with effortlessly cool Scandinavian looks. The cooking is distinguished by clear and harmonious flavours, textures (of course) and creativity, and the lightness of touch in first and main courses is in part down to the absence of cream and butter (they are unleashed when you get to dessert), and the technical skills on show are impressive. Start, perhaps, with Norwegian king crab with textures of Jerusalem artichoke and black Périgord truffle, or a more or less textbook serving of gravad lax, albeit one in which the salmon comes in one juicily delicious hunk. New season's beetroot with goat cheese and pistachios offers a light but vibrant spin on a modern classic. Main-course Anjou pigeon is stunning, the bird chargrilled on the outside but lividly pink within, the richly tender meat supported by sweetcorn and shallots, as well as bacon popcorn, in a red wine essence, while fish might be lightly salted Icelandic cod and prawns with delightful garnishes of quinoa and cauliflower. The dairy products arrive at dessert stage, as promised: Icelandic skyr (a strained yoghurt) comes with vanilla ice cream, rye breadcrumbs and clementine for a harmonious combination, or there could be a French-meets-Scandi idea involving Valrhôna white chocolate mousse and ice cream in a thought-provoking marriage with dill and cucumber. Incidentals are top-notch too, from the sourdough bread with olive oils, to a pre-dessert of crushed sorbet and mint, and the petits fours, which include a witty variant on the Fisherman's Friend (should clear any blocked passages), as well as a cardamom-spiked chocolate truffle. The set-lunch menu is terrific value and there are three tasting menus, including Scandinavian seafood and vegetarian versions.

Chef Agnar Sverrisson **Owner** Xavier Rousset, Agnar Sverrisson **Seats** 52, Pr/dining room 16
Times 12-2.30/6.30-11 Closed 2 wks Xmas, 2 wks Aug, 1 wk Etr, Sun-Mon **Prices** Fixed L 2 course £24.90, Tasting menu £79, Starter £14.50-£32, Main £27.50-£37.50, Dessert £10.50-£13.50 **Wines** 500 bottles over £30, 6 bottles under £30, 14 by glass **Parking** NCP Bryanston St
Notes Scandinavian fish tasting menu £78, Children welcome

LONDON W1 *continued*

Theo Randall at the InterContinental   PLAN 4 G5

✿✿✿ – *see below*

Trishna   PLAN 2 G3

✿✿ Modern Indian v

tel: 020 7935 5624 **15-17 Blandford St W1U 3DG**
email: info@trishnalondon.com
dir: *Nearest station: Bond St, Baker St*

The distinctive flavours of southwest India brought to Marylebone

A real gem of a restaurant in the heart of chic Marylebone village, Trishna takes a minimalist line with its decor in two dining rooms done out with oak floors and tables, painted brickwork, mirrored walls, and hues of cream and duck-egg blue. On sunny days, floor-to-ceiling windows open onto the street. The kitchen celebrates the coastal cuisine of southwest India in fresh, flavour-packed contemporary dishes, although equal attention is given to meat and vegetarian ideas, and it's all built on well-sourced British seasonal produce. Nandu Varuval – crispy soft shell crab deep-fried in tempura batter spiked with green chilli and garlic, and matched with white crab chutney – makes a cracking starter, followed by a Keralan tiger prawn curry distinctively flavoured with coconut and fresh curry leaves. Carnivores could go for duck seekh kebab then tandoori lamb chops with chilli, ginger and mooli radish, or guinea fowl tikka with masoor lentils, star anise and fennel. Desserts end creatively with carrot halva and samosa with masala chai ice cream.

Chef Karam Sethi **Owner** Karam Sethi **Seats** 65, Pr/dining room 12 **Times** 12-2.45/6-10.45 Closed 24-29 Dec, 1 Jan **Prices** Fixed L 2 course £17.50, Tasting menu £40-£55, Starter £6.25-£13, Main £12-£25, Dessert £6.75-£8 **Wines** 150 bottles over £30, 15 bottles under £30, 13 by glass **Parking** On street, NCP **Notes** Early D menu 4 course £25 & incl wines £45, Sunday L £17.50-£32.50, Children welcome

---

Umu   PLAN 2 H1

✿✿✿ – *see opposite*

Vasco & Piero's Pavilion Restaurant   PLAN 2 J2

✿✿ Modern Italian

tel: 020 7437 8774 **15 Poland St W1F 8QE**
email: eat@vascosfood.com
dir: *Nearest station: Oxford Circus*

Seasonal Umbrian cooking in hospitable Soho favourite

If you're after some authentic Italian cooking and atmosphere, V & P's intimate, family-run restaurant won't disappoint. It's been a firm favourite in Soho for over 40 years now. Both the sunny Mediterranean decor and food are suitably unpretentious and to the point, with the unfussy Umbrian cooking concentrating on good quality ingredients (often imported from Italy) and allowing the flavours to shine through. Seasonality is celebrated with gusto here, so expect great things in the truffle season, and the likes of spring lamb will feature when at its best. Pasta is made in-house and the menus change twice daily, with good value early menus for post-work or pre-theatre brigades. Hand-made sea bass tortellini with fresh tomato, zucchini, carrots and celery is a fine version indeed, while strips of calves' liver and onions with sautéed cabbage also hits the spot. Finish with panettone bread-and-butter pudding with grappa-soaked raisins.

Chef Vasco Matteucci **Owner** Tony Lopez, Paul & Vasco Matteucci **Seats** 50, Pr/dining room 36 **Times** 12-3/5.30-10 Closed BHs, Sun, L Sat **Prices** Starter £6.50-£11.50, Main £17.50-£26.50, Dessert £3.50-£7 **Wines** 35 bottles over £30, 19 bottles under £30, 12 by glass **Parking** NCP car park opposite **Notes** Tasting menu on request, Vegetarian available, Children 5 yrs+

Theo Randall at the InterContinental

LONDON W1   PLAN 4 G5

Italian v ⬥ NOTABLE WINE LIST

tel: 020 7318 8747 **1 Hamilton Place, Hyde Park Corner W1J 7QY**
email: reservations@theorandall.com
dir: *Nearest station: Hyde Park Corner, Green Park*

Exciting and authentic Italian cooking in landmark hotel

Theo Randall's restaurant at the InterContinental is a spacious, light and airy room with a sophisticated decor of cool, neutral tones. The walls feature artwork and mirrors, while green leather-look and darkwood chairs at white-clothed tables create the impression of a stand-alone restaurant rather than an impersonal hotel dining room. It's a relaxed, unstuffy environment too, with even a kids' menu. The daily-changing (adult) menu is a celebration of Italian regional cooking, with fresh produce flown in, often from small artisan producers, including Sardinian bottarga and San Marzano tomatoes. Given that, and the fact that this is a prime chunk of London real estate, prices seem remarkably reasonable. The intention is to replicate the simple rustic dishes of Theo Randall's inspirational cuisine, and he achieves impressive results, coaxing

mouthfuls of flavours from even simple-sounding dishes – insalata mista, for instance, a plate of mixed Italian leaves with caprino (goats' cheese), datterini tomatoes, cucumber and basil – as well as gutsier combinations such as another starter of smoked eel with red and golden beetroot and horseradish. Freshly made pasta is worth a punt for those with hearty appetites – perhaps tagliatelle with beef sauce slowly cooked in Chianti – while main courses exemplify what makes Italian food so unique. Roast sirloin, of superb quality, perfectly cooked rare, as requested, is served simply with earthily flavoured artichokes and a deeply flavoured red wine jus. Good use is made of the wood-fired oven, from roast guinea fowl stuffed with Parma ham and mascarpone, with cavolo nero braised with chestnuts and rosemary, to Dover sole, impeccably timed, enhanced by Swiss chard and roasted red peppers. A dab hand is responsible for pastry, seen in tarts – almond with prunes and crème fraîche, and Amalfi lemon – otherwise fly the flag with a classic tiramisù.

Chef Theo Randall **Seats** 124, Pr/dining room 24 **Times** 12-3/5.45-11 Closed 25-26 Dec, New Year, BHs, Sun, L Sat **Prices** Fixed L 2 course fr £27, Fixed D 3 course fr £33, Tasting menu fr £65, Starter £12-£23, Main £27-£36, Dessert £7-£12.50 **Wines** 147 bottles over £30, 1 bottle under £30, 13 by glass **Parking Notes** Sharing menu £60, Children's menu £8-£16, Children welcome

Umu

LONDON W1   PLAN 2 H1

Japanese 🍷 NOTABLE WINE LIST

tel: 020 7499 8881 **14-16 Bruton Place W1J 6LX**
email: reception@umurestaurant.com
web: www.umurestaurant.com
dir: *Nearest station: Green Park, Bond St*

First-class Japanese dining off Berkeley Square

Umu is consistently busy and you might say there's a
contented purr to the place. Hit the button to open the
sliding door and you enter a room where Kyoto is the guiding
light, natural wood is the dominant feature, and the charm
and sincere hospitality of the hosts rings true. If you care
about such things, note that it is a little on the dark side.
Chef Yoshinori Ishii has a pedigree at the top-end of this
style of modern Japanese cooking and no stone is left
unturned in the search for super-fresh produce; the
ingredients come from all over the world, but Britain has a
good showing. Chef turns his hands to other things as well,
so if you're admiring the plates or the watercolours on the
menu, those are his handywork, too. There's a rare sort of
integrity to Umu. The food is not cheap, in fact it's rather
expensive, but it is seriously good, and the people, they do
come. The traditional kaiseki set menu is a good way to go if
you're on unfamiliar territory, with its multi-courses
including the likes of nimonowan (a clear soup with Scottish
lobster, coral egg tofu, sea lettuce and kinome), and
charcoal-grilled guinea fowl thigh with the breast steamed
in sake, plus an accompanying foie gras quinoa. There's
also a sushi kaiseki menu. Everything is beautifully
presented, including a first-course dish of Scottish
langoustines with tomato jelly, providing bursts of
harmonious fresh flavours, followed perhaps by grade six
Wagyu beef served in a large magnolia leaf, sitting on a
charcoal burner as it is brought to the table. There's a set
lunch menu, fabulous sushi and sashimi options, and over
160 varieties of sake to choose from, including a sparkling
version. The wine list confirms the seriousness of this
venture.

Chef Yoshinori Ishii **Owner** Marlon Abela Restaurant
Corporation **Seats** 64, Pr/dining room 12
Times 12-2.30/6-11 Closed Xmas, New Year, BHs, Sun, L Sat
Prices Prices not confirmed **Wines** 860 bottles over £30, 25
by glass **Parking** On street, NCP Hanover Hill **Notes** Kaiseki
menu £115, Vegetarian available, Children welcome

LONDON W1 *continued*

Veeraswamy Restaurant

PLAN 2 J1

Indian NOTABLE WINE LIST

tel: 020 7734 1401 **Mezzanine Floor, Victory House, 99 Regent St W1B 4RS**
email: info@realindianfood.com
dir: *Nearest station: Piccadilly Circus*

Stylish subcontinental cooking in Britain's oldest Indian restaurant

The granddaddy of all Indian restaurants in Britain, this lavishly elegant first-floor venue just off Regent Street threw open its doors in the year of the General Strike. It has served London durably and stylishly all through the generations, introducing adventurous palates to the cooking of the various regions of the sub-continent, from the humblest street-snacks to the grand dishes of the Raj culinary repertoire. The rich reds and oranges of the decorative scheme seem to reflect the vivid spicing of dishes such as crab cakes vibrant with ginger, lime and chilli, or Kerala prawn curry with green apple. Scallop moilee is a popular starter, its gingery aromatics a preparatory boost to the tastebuds, but there are also tried-and-true classics such as Kashmiri rogan josh (very much a signature dish here), the soft shank meat enhanced with crimson cockscomb flowers and saffron, Malabar lobster curry with coconut and green mango, and biryani variations. Favoured sweets include benchmark gulab jamun, as well as seductive caramelised banana kulfi. Impeccable service enhances the experience.

Chef Uday Salunkhe **Owner** R Mathrani, C & N Panjabi **Seats** 114, Pr/dining room 24 **Times** 12-2.30/5.30-11.30 Closed D 25 Dec **Prices** Fixed L 2 course £20, Tasting menu £55, Starter £6.75-£16.50, Main £20-£38.50, Dessert £7-£7.50 **Wines** 18 by glass **Parking** On street after 8pm/wknds, NCP **Notes** Business L 2 course £27.50, ALC D only, Sunday L, Vegetarian available, No children

Villandry

PLAN 2 H3

French, European

tel: 020 7631 3131 **170 Great Portland St W1W 5QB**
email: contactus@villandry.com
dir: *Nearest station: Great Portland Street, Oxford Circus*

Appealingly simple cooking in a foodie emporium

Thanks to new owners who have given the place a smart refurb, Villandry has voguish good looks. Billing itself as a grand café, it's an on-trend all-day food emporium, combining a café-bar with takeaway, a shop and patisserie counter, the 'red room' full of wines to drink in or take home, and a more formal restaurant at the rear. The flexible nature of the place means you can grab breakfast (eggs Benedict, say), have coffee and a pastry (salted caramel and walnut tart perhaps), moules frites with wine, or a full blown meal in the restaurant. Here, simple, sunny natured, French-Mediterranean dishes are prepared with a lightness of touch from seasonal produce. Tuck into something like cod with a high-impact chorizo crust, with wilted spinach, white beans and fresh tomatoes, or big-hearted Galloway fillet steak (28-day dry-aged) with chips and béarnaise. Dessert might deliver a pukka classic like apple tarte Tatin or warm chocolate fondant.

Times 12-3/6-10.30 Closed 25 Dec, Sun, BHs

Wild Honey

PLAN 2 H1

– *see below*

Wild Honey

LONDON W1

PLAN 2 H1

Modern European
tel: 020 7758 9160 **12 Saint George St W1S 2FB**
email: info@wildhoneyrestaurant.co.uk
dir: *Nearest station: Oxford Circus, Bond St*

Classy bistro cooking and great wines

The Mayfair outpost of Anthony Demetre and Will Smith opposite the landmark St George's Church, is a swish and stylish restaurant with wood-panelled walls and comfortable red wall banquettes facing yellow leather-look chairs on the opposite side of well-dressed tables. Well-oiled staff deliver the goods efficiently if a tad formally. As at Arbutus, Anthony Demetre's balanced menu is restricted to a handful of dishes per course, and he brings his own highly individual cooking style to the kitchen. He takes his inspiration from France, although influences from elsewhere are also detectable: a salad of buffalo mozzarella with Italian tomatoes and broad beans among the starters, for instance. More typical of his unpretentious, down-to-earth approach, and a fondness for using humble cuts of meat, are slices of classic tête de veau with sauce gribiche, simple and a delight

to eat, and another starter of the full-on flavours of smoked eel with turnips and pickled shiitaki. An overlap with Arbutus is discernible in some dishes – crab with guacamole, for instance, here accompanied by mango, and a main course of grilled 'piece of beef' with dauphinoise, roasted onions and beetroot. Otherwise look for moist and succulent roast chicken with morels and peas, Marseilles-style bouillabaisse, or stunningly good cod fillet, perfectly timed, with earthy, herby spiced lentils and onion fritters. Breads get high praise, and puddings can be a tour de force, among them tarte Tatin (for two to four people) and a sphere of peanut butter parfait dotted with nibs of dark chocolate and roasted peanuts , with a slice of roasted banana, a splotch of intense lime gel and light and creamy caramel espuma. As at Arbutus, all 50 or so bottles on the wine list are available in 250-millilitre carafes, making it easy to match wines and food.

Chef Anthony Demetre, Patrick Leano **Owner** Anthony Demetre, Will Smith **Seats** 65 **Times** 12-2.30/6-11 Closed 25-26 Dec, 1 Jan, Sun **Prices** Fixed L 2 course £29, Tasting menu fr £75, Starter £8-£18, Main £24-£32, Dessert £7-£8 **Wines** 45 bottles over £30, 6 bottles under £30, 50 by glass **Parking** On street **Notes** Vegetarian available, Children welcome

The Wolseley

PLAN 4 J6

Traditional European V

tel: 020 7499 6996 **160 Piccadilly W1J 9EB**
email: reservations@thewolseley.com
dir: *Nearest station: Green Park*

Bustling landmark brasserie stylishly serving all day

They describe themselves as a 'café-restaurant in the grand European tradition', which is exactly what it feels like, particularly the 'grand' part. A doorman ushers you inside, The Ritz is a near neighbour, and there are soaring pillars and marble floors, but there's nothing stuffy about The Wolseley. This place fair fizzes with energy. Staff rush about, customers chatter, and that's the case all day long, from breakfast, brunch, lunch and afternoon tea, through to evening meals. Expect timeless brasserie classics, from soupe de poisson or Severn and Wye oak-smoked salmon to kick off, followed by seared duck livers with girolles, spinach and Madeira jus, or grilled rib-eye with pommes frites. Desserts carry on in the same classic vein, with crème brûlée and lemon meringue tart. Breakfast is a large choice from full English to grilled kipper with mustard butter, and the all-day concept fits the bill whether you're after savoury satisfaction or a sweet treat.

Chef Lawrence Keogh, Marc Benzimra **Owner** Chris Corbin, Jeremy King **Seats** 150, Pr/dining room 12 **Times** 7am-mdnt Closed D 24 Dec All-day dining **Prices** Starter £7.25-£24.50, Main £11.25-£34.75, Dessert £3.95-£8 **Wines** 44 bottles over £30, 7 bottles under £30, 37 by glass **Parking** NCP Arlington St **Notes** Afternoon tea available, Sunday L, Children welcome

Yauatcha

PLAN 2 J2

Modern Chinese NOTABLE WINE LIST

tel: 020 7494 8888 **15 Broadwick St W1F 0DL**
email: reservations@yauatcha.com
dir: *Nearest station: Tottenham Court Rd, Piccadilly, Oxford Circus*

Skilful dim sum in a trendy Soho address

A contemporary dim sum tea house, is how Yauatcha describes itself, and the tea house side of things greets you on the ground floor with an amazingly colourful array of pâtisserie. Down in the basement, however, things take a more glamorous turn, with bare brick walls studded with crucifix-shaped candle-lit mirrors, low-slung green leather banquettes at darkwood tables and a long, slim, illuminated fish tank (its occupants are not on the menu). Staff are well versed in the extensive menu, which impresses with its excellent ingredients and intriguing blend of traditional Cantonese favourites and more esoteric contemporary compositions. Venison puffs are Wellington-style flaky pastry dim sum with notes of hoi sin, chilli and sesame, while more hardcore foodies might go for chicken feet in chilli black bean sauce. Larger plates also deliver full-throttle flavours – witness braised Somerset lamb with black pepper sauce, or for fish fans, there may be braised sea bass with shiitaki, bamboo shoots and wolfberry. Tea smoothies, unusual iced tea combinations and off-the-wall cocktails are the on-trend tipples of choice.

Times noon-11.45 Closed 24-25 Dec, All-day dining

YMing Restaurant

PLAN 3 A1

Traditional Chinese V

tel: 020 7734 2721 **35-36 Greek St W1D 5DL**
email: info@yming.co.uk
dir: *Nearest station: Piccadilly Circus, Leicester Square*

Chinese regional specialities in theatreland

The frantic bustle of Chinatown is close by this smart Soho Chinese, but Christine Yau's operation runs on helpful and friendly service that is a welcome change from the infamously curt treatment meted out to diners across the other side of Shaftesbury Avenue. The setting is neat and clean, and the Cantonese and regional Chinese cooking reliably good, with a biblical carte from which to make your selection. Big mouth-filling flavours are driven by fresh, top-quality ingredients, while modern health-oriented sensibilities are assuaged by the use of leaner cuts and light oils. Authentic regional dishes start out with Beijing-style spare ribs spiced with cumin, black pepper, fennel seeds, garlic and fiery chillies, then move on to Shanghai with a 'treasure hunt' of pork, chicken, prawns and air-dried sausage. Elsewhere there's anise-flavoured gansu duck, or Tibetan garlic lamb.

Chef Liang Liang Lin **Owner** Christine Yau **Seats** 60, Pr/dining room 25 **Times** noon-11.45 Closed 25-26 Dec, 1 Jan, Sun (ex Chinese New Year) All-day dining **Prices** Fixed L 3 course £12-£23.90, Fixed D 3 course £18.50-£23.90, Starter £4.50-£11, Main £8.20-£30, Dessert £3-£6.80 **Wines** 20 bottles over £30, 20 bottles under £30, 8 by glass **Parking** Chinatown car park **Notes** Pre-theatre 3 course £12, Children welcome

Zoilo

PLAN 2 G2

Argentine NEW

tel: 020 7486 9699 **9 Duke St W1U 3EG**
email: info@zoilo.co.uk
dir: *Nearest station: Bond Street*

Authetnic flavours of Argentina and an easy-going atmosphere

South American cuisine may well be flavour of the month right now, but that's for a very good reason. This previously un-mined cooking-style has a lot to offer, the authentic, full-on version available at Zoilo inspired by the regions of Argentina, from Patagonia to Mendoza. Over two floors in classy Duke Street, another big part of its appeal is the rustic, easy-going vibe, with exposed brick walls and darkwood tables, plus basement counter seats right in front of the open kitchen. It's contemporary and buzzy and fun. The wine list is 100% Argentinian, with carafe options on most bins. Sharing is the name of the game, so get ready for satisfying plates such as crab on toast with humita and pickled turnips or sweetbreads with onions, hazelnuts and preserved lemons. There are empanadas, too, with fillings such as braised beef skirt, potatoes, onions and olives, or a veggie version with spinach, goats' cheese raisins and pine nuts. Asado (flank steak with celeriac and bone marrow) is a classic, and to finish, there might be milk cake with passionfruit sorbet and toasted almonds.

Chef Diego Jacquet **Owner** Diego Jacquet, Alberto Abbate **Seats** 48, Pr/dining room 10 **Times** 12-3/5.30-10.30 Closed Xmas, Sun **Prices** Fixed L 2 course £9.95 **Wines** 42 bottles over £30, 19 bottles under £30, 22 by glass **Parking** On street **Notes** Vegetarian available, Children welcome

Looking for a London restaurant by name?
Use the index on page 254

Looking for a London restaurant near you?
Use the maps on pages 258–68

LONDON W2

Angelus Restaurant
PLAN 2 D1

◉◉ Modern French ⌑ NOTABLE WINE LIST

tel: 020 7402 0083 **4 Bathurst St W2 2SD**
email: info@angelusrestaurant.co.uk
dir: *Nearest station: Lancaster Gate, Paddington Station*

Classy French brasserie with modish cooking

A former pub which was transformed into a classy Parisian-style brasserie by renowned sommelier, Thierry Tomasin, Angelus Restaurant continues to impress with its luxe, art nouveau-inspired finish and ambitious, modern French cooking. It looks smart with its darkwood panelling and red leather banquettes, and with its wine list offering up some seriously good drinking, this is a place worth knowing about. The kitchen turns out some rather ambitious stuff, rooted in French tradition perhaps, but with plenty of bright, modern ideas on show. Fried and poached scallops, for example, might come in a first course with dehydrated scallop roe and langoustine foam, while another starter serves up duck liver in a luscious crème brûlée alongside caramelised almonds and toasted bread. For main course, coq au vin comes with smoked mash, and pan-fried gurnard with char-grilled white asparagus, caper butter and a crab beignet. The bright, modern ideas continue into dessert stage with the likes of compressed English apples and pears partnered with salted caramel and a ginger and oat crumble.

Chef Joe Howley **Owner** Thierry Tomasin **Seats** 40, Pr/dining room 22 **Times** 10am-11pm Closed 23 Dec-4 Jan, All-day dining **Prices** Fixed L 2 course fr £22 **Wines** 600 bottles over £30, 16 bottles under £30, 4 by glass **Parking** On street **Notes** Brunch menu available, Sunday L fr £22, Vegetarian available, Children welcome

Assaggi
PLAN 2 A1

◉ Italian

tel: 020 7792 5501 **39 Chepstow Place W2 4TS**
email: nipi@assaggi.demon.co.uk
dir: *Nearest station: Notting Hill Gate*

Straightforward Italian dishes in relaxed surroundings

Assaggi occupies a first-floor room above Georgian restaurant, Colchis (see entry). It may be possible to confuse the two entrances, though hardly the cuisine styles, since Assaggi has for years traded in the simple, straightforward Italian food that became popular with the first wave of Mediterranean cooking in Britain in the 1990s. The decor is minimal, rough-and-ready even, but by no means uncomfortable, and the relaxed air of contentment that pervades the place tells its own story. Simple classics are done with consummate brio, such as oozy burrata sandwiched by slices of grilled aubergine, or tip-top fritto misto comprised of mullet, sole, prawns and squid on straw potatoes and greens. The day's selection of desserts might furnish forth impressive, high-octane chocolate torte, served warm with vanilla ice cream. Carta di musica crispbread and focaccia with good olive oil start things off well, and the wine list is teeming with fine Italian choices.

Chef Nino Sassu **Owner** Nino Sassu, Pietro Fraccari **Seats** 35
Times 12.30-2.30/7.30-11 Closed 2 wks Xmas, BHs, Sun **Prices** Prices not confirmed, Service optional **Wines** 6 by glass **Notes** Vegetarian available, Children welcome

Colchis
PLAN 2 A1

◉ Modern European

tel: 020 7221 7620 **39 Chepstow Place W2 4TS**
email: info@colchisrestaurant.co.uk
dir: *Nearest station: Notting Hill Gate, Bayswater*

A taste of Georgia in trendy Notting Hill

A revamped pub below the well-known Italian restaurant Assaggi (see entry) is home to this newcomer exploring the food and wine of Georgia – that's the East European country, not the US state. It's a stylish, light, contemporary place with little to announce its Georgian influences until you view the menu. Up front is an all-day bar with feature wine wall display and brass-topped bar counter, plus a mix of low and high tables, chairs and banquettes. Colours are neutral, seat coverings leather, suede and fabric, while quirky lighting catches the eye. The dining room (to the rear) follows the theme and colour palette, with the dinner carte delivering authentic staples like khinkali (Georgian dumplings with mince beef and pork, eaten by nibbling a small hole in one side then sucking out the warm broth before eating the filling) or lobio mchadit (black-eyed bean stew with corn cakes), to the more Western-inspired sea bass with grilled vegetables. The small plates and sharing platters are a hit, and the wine list includes some Georgian numbers.

Times 12-2/6-11 Closed L Mon-Fri

El Pirata Detapas
PLAN 2 A2

◉ Modern Spanish

tel: 020 7727 5000 & 7229 1520 **115 Westbourne Grove W2 4UP**
email: info@elpiratadetapas.co.uk
dir: *Nearest station: Notting Hill Gate*

Classy, creative tapas and a good buzz

This offshoot of El Pirata in Mayfair gives off infectiously buzzy vibes in a long, sleek room done out with elbow-to-elbow darkwood tables, and a bar counter at the back that hits the spot for the trendy Westbourne Grove and Notting Hill crew. Things are buzzing away in the kitchen too, which serves up authentic Spanish flavours in its cracking repertoire of on-trend tapas dishes. Iberian hams are hanging in the basement just waiting to be carved, and if everyone at the table is up for it, there are keenly-priced tasting menus. You could stay with tried-and-tested sunny Spanish flavours – charcuterie and cheese platters, grilled prawns with garlic olive oil and parsley – or go for something more contemporary like pork cheeks with braised shallots and carrot purée, or wood pigeon with fig purée, red cabbage and red wine jus.

Chef Rafael Rodriguez **Owner** Detapas Restaurant Ltd **Seats** 90, Pr/dining room 30 **Times** 12-3/6-11 Closed 25-26 & 31 Dec, D 24 Dec **Prices** Fixed L 2 course £9.95-£11.45, Tasting menu £21-£25, Starter £3-£9, Main £11-£13, Dessert £4.50-£6.50 **Wines** 15 by glass **Parking** Queensway **Notes** Chef's menu £25, Degustation menu £21, Vegetarian available, Children welcome

Island Restaurant & Bar
PLAN 2 D1

◉◉ Modern European

tel: 020 7551 6070 **Lancaster London Hotel, Lancaster Ter W2 2TY**
email: eat@islandrestaurant.co.uk **web:** www.islandrestaurant.co.uk
dir: *Nearest station: Lancaster Gate*

Polished brasserie-style cooking with Hyde Park views

The Island Grill at this modern hotel cocoons diners from the roar of the traffic on the one-way system outside. It's a well-groomed sort of place, with a smart contemporary decor, floor-to-ceiling windows looking over Hyde Park (and the traffic) and a brasserie-style menu. Influences are plucked from near and far: chargrilled smoked chicken breast, for instance, is served in a salad with avocado, pomegranate, baba ganoush and flatbread, and crisp-fried squid with tomato and chilli jam and preserved lemons. Traditionalists will be pleased with a retro main course of veal Holstein, but more representative of what the kitchen is capable of in terms of imagination and skill is perhaps a braised faggot and haggis mash to accompany grilled pork cutlet, and crabcake with red pepper salsa and a salad of pequillo peppers, radicchio and pickled shallots. To crown a meal might be home-made Eccles cake with maple custard, or the enticement of baked vanilla custard with coffee bavarois, Valrhona chocolate sorbet and crushed amaretti.

Chef Eibhear Coyle **Owner** Khun Jatuporn Sihanatkathakul **Seats** 68 **Times** 7am-10.30pm All-day dining **Prices** Fixed L 2 course £9.50, Starter £4.95-£15.95, Main £12.50-£21.95, Dessert £4.50-£6 **Wines** 10 bottles over £30, 8 bottles under £30, 6 by glass **Parking** Hotel or on street **Notes** Brunch Sat-Sun 12-6pm, Sunday L £12.50-£21.95, Vegetarian available, Children welcome

Kurobuta

PLAN 2 E2

◉◉ Japanese NEW

tel: 020 3475 4158 **17-20 Kendal St, Marble Arch W2 2AW**
email: info@kurobuta-london.com
dir: *Nearest station: Marble Arch, Edgeware Road*

On-trend Japanese fusion cooking

The man at the culinary reins of this upbeat Japanese fusion operation is Scott Hallsworth, former head chef at Nobu, so there's no question about his familiarity with the genre. Inspired by Japan's izakaya taverns, the interior goes for a stripped-down look of white walls and wooden benches, and a trendy soundtrack adds to the high-decibel vibe. A vibrant opener of salmon gravlax and avocado tartare with dill mayonnaise, crunchy rice crackers and a citrussy hit of yuzu zest has the tastebuds all standing to attention in readiness for a pair of fluffy steamed buns filled with full-flavoured barbecued pork belly and a thick, sticky soy and chopped peanut dressing. The à la mode robata grill provides tea-smoked lamb with smoky nasu and Korean miso, or on the lighter side, there's crisp-coated squid kara-age with a punchy green jalapeño dipping sauce. Desserts don't let you down either. Yuzu tart puts an oriental spin on an old western favourite with a topping of soft meringue on a lush citrus filling.

Chef Scott Hallsworth **Owner** Scott Hallsworth **Seats** 85 **Times** 9am-11.30pm All-day dining **Prices** Prices not confirmed **Wines** 17 bottles over £30, 4 bottles under £30, 10 by glass **Parking** On street, NCP nearby **Notes** Average spend per head £40-£50, Vegetarian available, Children welcome

Nipa

PLAN 2 D1

◉◉ Thai

tel: 020 7551 6039 **Lancaster London Hotel, Lancaster Ter W2 2TY**
email: nipa@lancasterlondon.com
dir: *Nearest station: Lancaster Gate*

Precise Thai cooking in an authentic setting overlooking Hyde Park

Twinned with the homonymous Nipa at The Landmark Hotel in Bangkok, The Lancaster's version is one of fewer than 20 Thai restaurants in the UK to receive its home country's Thai Select award. A panoramic window overlooks Hyde Park, while the decor does its best to persuade you, via carved wooden artefacts, orchids and chopsticks, that you've been beamed to Southeast Asia. The impression is helped along by the uniformly excellent Thai staff, standing ready to offer unpatronising guidance through the menus for non-initiates. Fire up the taste buds with pancake-wrapped balls of minced chicken and peanuts, served with mango salad, or crisp-fried prawn cake with chilli plum sauce, before progressing to a bowl of scorching-hot tom yum kai soup. Main dishes are timed and spiced with flawless precision, as in roast duck with pineapple and holy basil in coconut broth, and stir-fried chicken with chilli and basil. A range of set menus offers a good introduction, and meals can end with the unexpected, such as a steamed banana cake with sugared flaked almonds and ginger ice cream.

Chef Nongyao Thoopchoi **Owner** Lancaster London **Seats** 55 **Times** 5-10.30 Closed L all week **Prices** Starter £11-£24, Main £16-£30, Dessert £9 **Wines** 23 bottles over £30, 8 bottles under £30, 21 by glass **Notes** 4 course D £35-£40, Khantok menu 5-7pm £19.95, Vegetarian available, Children welcome

LONDON W4

Hedone

PLAN 1 D3

◉◉◉ *– see below*

Hedone

LONDON W4

PLAN 1 D3

Modern European
tel: 020 8747 0377 **301-303 Chiswick High Rd W4 4HH**
email: Aurelie@hedonerestaurant.com
dir: *Nearest station: Chiswick Park, Gunnnersbury*

Chiswick temple to superb produce cooked with flair

The open kitchen takes centre stage at the ever-buzzing Hedone, and that's only right, as it really is the nerve centre of the operation; ingredients at the pinnacle of freshness and quality arrive daily, informing what lands on the ever-evolving menus (as certain ingredients run out, so one table may not get exactly the same dishes as another). In short, it's all about the ingredients, and that's not surprising when you learn that the man behind it all is food blogger and ingredient-expert-turned-chef Mikael Jonsson. Almost everything is cooked to order, and there's a great deal of skill and creativity on show. There's a three-course option for a very reasonable £35, but if you can push the boat out and go for the tasting menu or 'carte blanche' (chef's surprise menu) then do it – you won't regret it. The home-baked sourdough bread is so moreish it's hard to hold back, but with so much good eating to come you'd be wise to. Poached Cornish

rock oysters are plump, juicy and faultlessly cooked, lifted with a delicate apple foam and a hint of shallot, while a single hand-dived scallop cooked in its own juices needs no more than a hint of salt and dried seaweed powder to intensify its natural flavours. Liquid parmesan ravioli with onion consommé, mild horseradish and pancetta is an inventive, warming, comforting dish, the pasta beautifully made and the flavours nicely judged, while next up might come roasted breast and leg of squab (well timed and with excellent flavour and texture), with silky-smooth smoked potatoes, a deeply-flavoured blackcurrant puree, a vivid green puree made from rocket and lemongrass, and a foie gras sauce. Dessert stage might bring on fresh English blueberries with an intense blueberry syrup, topped with a tiny crisp meringue and a beautifully-made lemon and rosemary sorbet, and then a warm chocolate mousse with powdered raspberry, a flavour-packed passion fruit jelly, and Madagascan vanilla ice cream.

Chef Mikael Jonsson **Owner** Mikael Jonsson **Seats** Pr/dining room 16 **Times** 12-2.30/6.30-9.30 Closed Sun-Mon, L Tue-Wed **Prices** Prices not confirmed

LONDON W4 *continued*

High Road Brasserie

  European

PLAN 1 D3

tel: 020 8742 7474 **162 Chiswick High Rd W4 1PR**
email: cheila@highroadhouse.co.uk
dir: *Nearest station: Turnham Green*

Buzzy brasserie serving good, honest food all day

A Soho House Group outfit (see also entry for Cecconi's), the High Road Brasserie is a typically stylish, on-trend hotspot on Chiswick's main drag. Awnings shield plenty of pavement tables for alfresco dining, while inside the fashionable brasserie look is brought together with darkwood panelling, a patchwork of coloured floor tiles, marble-topped bar and smart lighting. The place is open all day, from breakfast to dinner and everything in-between, and the please-all modern European menu takes simplicity and good quality ingredients as its watchwords. Get started with a small plate or two (perhaps salt cod croquettes), moving on to a straightforward chicken, bacon and avocado salad, or mackerel Niçoise. Then, for the main event, cod, fine beans and café de Paris butter, or perhaps another classic done well in the form of fillet steak with béarnaise and fries.

Times 7-mdnt All-day dining

Restaurant Michael Nadra

PLAN 1 D3

 Modern European

tel: 020 8742 0766 **6/8 Elliott Rd, Chiswick W4 1PE**
dir: *Nearest station: Turnham Green*

Classy modish cooking in Chiswick

An Edwardian villa with shop-front windows looking onto the road is home to Michael Nadra's restaurant. You might describe it as a neighbourhood restaurant, but don't go thinking it is parochial in any way, for this is a classy address with some well-crafted food on offer. Burnished wooden tables come set with crisp white linen napkins, and leatherette banquettes and chairs give a touch of urban chic. The menu is packed with good ideas that manage to be sophisticated and clearly focused at the same time. Black tiger prawn, scallop and chive dumplings, for example, come with a delicious spinach and broccoli velouté and crisp red onions to start, whilst for main course roasted cod is partnered with ratte potatoes, samphire, fennel salad and chervil cream. The quality of the ingredients and the composition of dishes is spot on. And there's no less craft and creativity at dessert stage: blueberry and almond sponge, perhaps, with Greek yoghurt sorbet and blueberry granité. There's a sister Restaurant Michael Nadra in Primrose Hill (see entry).

Chef Michael Nadra **Owner** Michael Nadra **Seats** 55 **Times** 12-2.30/6-10 Closed Xmas, 1 Jan, D Sat **Prices** Fixed L 2 course fr £20, Fixed D 3 course fr £36, Tasting menu £44-£55 **Wines** 16 by glass **Parking** On street **Notes** Tasting menu 6 course, Sunday L, Vegetarian available, Children welcome

Sam's Brasserie & Bar

PLAN 1 D3

 Modern European, International

tel: 020 8987 0555 **11 Barley Mow Passage, Chiswick W4 4PH**
email: info@samsbrasserie.co.uk **web:** www.samsbrasserie.co.uk
dir: *Nearest station: Chiswick Park, Turnham Green*

All-day brasserie in a factory conversion

Exposed girders, pipes and bare brickwork are a nod to this buzzy neighbourhood brasserie's former life as a paper factory. Of course, the postcode is rather des-res these days, tucked away just off Chiswick High Road, so the look goes for a loft-style urban edge in its bare pale wood tables and menus with something for all-comers printed on brown paper table mats. It's easy to see the appeal of the place: the big bar provides a tempting diversion on entering the large, open-plan space before moving on to the mezzanine dining area, where chatty staff dressed sharply in long black aprons and white shirts keep things ticking over nicely, and the kitchen is open to view. Quality ingredients are deployed with aplomb in a starter of lambs' belly fritters with pumpkin purée and salsa verde, then a splendid crisp-skinned slab of line-caught Atlantic cod arrives with buttered leeks, clams, and chervil pesto. Two- and three-course set menus deliver top value for the bargain hunter.

Chef Mack Baines **Owner** Sam Harrison **Seats** 100 **Times** 9am-10.30pm Closed 24-26 Dec, All-day dining **Prices** Fixed L 2 course £13.50, Fixed D 3 course £16.50, Starter £6.50-£12, Main £11.75-£23.50, Dessert £6-£12.50 **Wines** 18 bottles over £30, 36 bottles under £30, 22 by glass **Parking** On street & car park **Notes** Fixed L Mon-Fri, Early bird D all week before 7.30pm, Sunday L £21.50-£25.50, Vegetarian available, Children welcome

Who has won our Chefs' Chef award?

Find out on page 10

La Trompette
PLAN 1 D3

 Modern European NOTABLE WINE LIST

tel: 020 8747 1836 **5-7 Devonshire Rd, Chiswick W4 2EU**
email: reception@latrompette.co.uk
dir: *Nearest station: Turnham Green*

Assured modern French cooking in Chiswick

One of the trio of high-achieving operations that takes in Wandsworth's Chez Bruce and Kew's Glasshouse, La Trompette has been delighting the residents of this well-heeled Chiswick enclave for over a decade. The place is looking smart as a button after a recent refurb, the cooking is still firmly rooted in France, and while there may be a degree of rusticity to it, it's neither clumsy nor prissy. Ravioli of suckling pig with grilled turnip tops, pickled walnuts and creamy bacon sauce sets out in fine style, delivering balance and full-bore flavours, before main course brings on an equally intensely flavoured and perfectly cooked slow-roasted short rib of beef with smoked bone marrow, scorched shallots, and field mushrooms. Fish main courses come in for similarly robust treatments, perhaps pairing roast John Dory with black rice, broccoli, Dorset crab and tarragon. Attention to detail is impressive all the way through to a dessert of chocolate millefeuille with salted caramel mousse and roast pear.

Chef Rob Weston **Owner** Nigel Platts-Martin, Bruce Poole **Seats** 88, Pr/dining room 16 **Times** 12-2.30/6.30-10.30 Closed 24-26 Dec, 1 Jan **Prices** Fixed L 2 course fr £23.50, Fixed D 3 course fr £45 **Wines** 450 bottles over £30, 100 bottles under £30, 16 by glass **Parking** On street **Notes** Sunday L £27.50-£32.50, Vegetarian available, Children welcome

Le Vacherin
PLAN 1 D3

 French

tel: 020 8742 2121 **76-77 South Pde W4 5LF**
email: info@levacherin.com
dir: *Nearest station: Chiswick Park*

French classics in smart, relaxed neighbourhood bistro

There's plenty of Gallic bonhomie over in Chiswick in the form of Le Vacherin, a restaurant named in honour of a fine French cheese or an iconic dessert, depending, perhaps, on which is your favourite. It looks the part with its polished-wood floors, burgundy leather banquettes and mirror-friezes on cream walls hung with French-themed posters, and the kitchen's output doesn't let the side down either. If a judge of a good restaurant is doing the simple things well, a plate of sautéed new season's ceps with garlic and parsley is a very good sign indeed. There's Bayonne ham with remoulade and classic onion soup, too, and main courses such as confit duck leg with Puy lentils and fillet of sea bass with salsify and samphire. Wild rabbit with Morteau sausage and Dijon mustard is a good dose of rustic authenticity, and, for dessert, iced prune and Armagnac parfait or a good old crème brûlée hit the spot. The prix-fixe menu is particularly good value in any language.

Chef Malcolm John **Owner** Malcolm & Donna John **Seats** 72, Pr/dining room 36 **Times** 12-3/6-11 Closed New Year & BHs, L Mon **Prices** Fixed L 2 course £18.50, Starter £17-£14.50, Main £16-£23, Dessert £7.50-£9.50 **Wines** 200 bottles over £30, 15 bottles under £30, 12 by glass **Parking** On street (metered) **Notes** Steak & wine offer £9.95 Mon-Thu/Sun before 8pm, Sunday L £25, Vegetarian available, Children welcome

Charlotte's Place
PLAN 1 C3

 Modern European

tel: 020 8567 7541 **16 St Matthews Rd, Ealing Common W5 3JT**
email: restaurant@charlottes.co.uk
dir: *Nearest station: Ealing Common, Ealing Broadway*

Splendid seasonal food in a neighbourhood gem

This sparkling neighbourhood bistro has impeccable ethical credentials, sourcing its materials from like-minded local suppliers and working in tune with the seasons to ensure there's always something to catch the interest on its breezy modern menus. The setting suits the food: an unpretentious yet stylish blend of black leather seats at unclothed darkwood tables on well-trodden wooden floors, all framed by plain cream walls hung with colourful prints. Top-notch pastry skills distinguish a splendid tart of line-caught mackerel matched with a lively accompaniment of olives, peppers, parmesan, anchovy and balsamic. A Mediterranean warmth infuses a main course of well-timed hake teamed with braised octopus, sautéed potatoes, chorizo and croûtons cooked in chorizo oil, all rounded off with a punchy salsa verde; meat comes in for robust treatment – perhaps onglet skirt steak with bone marrow fritter, celeriac, roast onions and sauce Bordelaise. In summer, English raspberries are showcased fresh and as a coulis to go with a wobbly pannacotta pointed up with mint, Moscato d'Asti jelly and a Breton biscuit.

Chef Lubos Vaskanin **Owner** Alex Wrethman **Seats** 54, Pr/dining room 30 **Times** 12-3/6-9.30 Closed 26 Dec, 1 Jan, D 25 Dec **Prices** Fixed L 2 course fr £17.95, Fixed D 3 course fr £32.95 **Wines** 141 bottles over £30, 38 bottles under £30, 6 by glass **Parking** On street **Notes** Early D daily 6-7pm 3 course & aperitif £26.95, Sunday L £20.95-£24.95, Vegetarian available, Children welcome

Crowne Plaza London - Ealing
PLAN 1 C4

 Modern European

tel: 020 8233 3278 & 8233 3226 **Western Av, Hanger Ln, Ealing W5 1HG**
email: west5@cp-londonealing.co.uk **web:** www.cp-londonealing.co.uk
dir: *Nearest station: Hanger Lane*

Alluring British brasserie dishes in a stylish (on the inside) hotel

If the Hanger Lane gyratory system can be said to have a distinguishing feature, the Crowne Plaza Ealing would be it. To be fair, it's a bit of an anonymous lump from the outside, but the public rooms are considerably more stylish than you may be led to expect. A dripping chandelier in the lobby and a bar upholstered in lavender lead on to the neutral but smart West 5 Brasserie, where modern dishes in the British idiom make up an alluring menu that doesn't just stick to the tried-and-tested. A crab terrine is served warm to emphasise its Gruyère content, and is offset by a pleasant cloudy citrus jelly, while mains run to whole baked mackerel with fennel and lemongrass citrus butter, or rosemary-crusted rack of lamb with a faggot of the shank meat, celeriac rösti, steamed cabbage and redcurrant jus. Fruity notes continue into desserts such as passionfruit brûlée tart with coordinating sorbet.

Chef Ross Pilcher **Owner** Pedersen (Ealing) Ltd **Seats** 106, Pr/dining room 60 **Times** 12-9.45 Closed D 31 Dec All-day dining **Prices** Prices not confirmed, Service optional **Wines** 7 bottles over £30, 17 bottles under £30, 9 by glass **Parking** 82 **Notes** Vegetarian available, Children welcome

LONDON W6

Anglesea Arms   PLAN 1 D3

 Modern British

tel: 020 8749 1291 **35 Wingate Rd, Ravenscourt Park W6 0UR**
dir: *Nearest station: Ravenscourt Park, Goldhawk Rd, Hammersmith*

Superior cooking in pioneering gastro-pub

The Anglesea was one of the pioneering London gastro-pubs, and its successful formula means it's as popular today as it ever has been: a buzzy, laid-back atmosphere, a flexible approach (eat as much or as little as you like) and good, honest, unfussy but appealing cooking that bats well above the weight of other establishments. The daily-changing menu is brimful of interesting ideas, sending people into dithering over starters like cured trout with fennel and watercress salad, or a tartlet of sautéed lamb's kidneys with Swiss chard. Technical accuracy and well-judged combinations mark out the cooking, seen in main courses like cod fillet with sautéed bacon, Cornish mids and turnip tops, and lamb loin and shepherd's pie with carrots and cabbage. Finish with traditional apple crumble with custard or something like rhubarb trifle.

Times 12.30-2.45/7-10.30 Closed 25-27 Dec

Novotel London West   PLAN 1 D3

 Modern British

tel: 020 8741 1555 **1 Shortlands W6 8DR**
email: H0737@accor.com **web:** www.novotellondonwest.co.uk
dir: *Nearest station: Hammersmith*

Modern comfort food in a contemporary hotel

This is the kind of modern hotel that can satisfy the needs of business folk in need of meeting space or accommodation , or families with children looking for somewhere to cut loose in West London. When it comes to eating, it's a 24/7 kind of place, with the Artisan Grill restaurant being the hub of the culinary output. The modern space with a glass facade offers views of the hotel's comings and goings, and the menu does its best to cover most bases. The eponymous grill turns out steaks in familiar formats, and there's also all the comfort of traditional steak and kidney pie in a rich gravy with colcannon, or mussels marinière with chips. Desserts continue to raise the comfort factor with something like chocolate fondant, which has a light sponge and oozing liquid centre.

Chef Roy Thompson **Owner** Accor UK **Seats** 42, Pr/dining room 10 **Times** 12-2.30/5.30-10.30 Closed L Sat-Sun **Prices** Starter £6-£9, Main £16-£40, Service optional **Wines** 38 bottles over £30, 29 bottles under £30, 32 by glass **Parking** 240 **Notes** Vegetarian available, Children welcome

The River Café   PLAN 1 D3

 – see below

Sagar   PLAN 1 D3

 Indian Vegetarian V

tel: 020 8741 8563 **157 King St, Hammersmith W6 9JT**
email: info@sagarveg.co.uk
dir: *Nearest station: Hammersmith*

Cracking-value South Indian vegetarian dining

Set on Hammersmith's main shopping drag, to the uninitiated Sagar might appear like just another modern-look high-street curry house rather than a well-regarded Southern Indian vegetarian outfit. Behind the full-drop glass frontage, pale-wood walls dotted with brass figurines (backlit at night), and tightly packed tables set the tone. Expect well-crafted dishes, smartly attired service and some recession-busting prices. The roster focuses on the crisp paper-thin dosas (rice and lentil pancakes with various fillings) and uthappams (lentil 'pizzas'), while starters include idli (fluffy rice and lentil steamed dumplings) and Bombay chowpati (street snacks) like crispy puri (perhaps a pani puri version, served with chick peas and sour-and-spicy

The River Café

LONDON W6   **PLAN 1 D3**

Italian

tel: 020 7386 4200 **Thames Wharf Studios, Rainville Rd W6 9HA**
email: info@rivercafe.co.uk
dir: *Nearest station: Hammersmith*

Outstanding Italian cooking from one of the prime movers and shakers

The River Café's success over the quarter-century of its Hammersmith residency has been remarkable from whichever angle you look at it. It participated in starting the vogue for Mediterranean cooking in the capital when the last twitchings of nouvelle cuisine were still upon London. Its kitchen has produced a generation of not just restaurant chefs, impressive though they be in themselves, but important voices and forces within British food culture, pre-eminently Jamie Oliver and Hugh Fearnley-Whittingstall. The gamble, as co-founder Ruth Rogers has said, was not just that Italian food would stick when the tempests of food fashion started blowing in alternative directions, but that people would continue to come out to a riverside location in London W6 to find it. That the place is

internationally sought out by aficionados of its style of cooking answered both those caveats years ago, and still does. That 'Café' tag remains as tongue-in-cheek as ever. There may be a relaxed, unrestauranty mood to the big light-filled room with its waterside views, but the menu has always been a bells-and-whistles tour of Italian foodways, presented in the traditional four-part structure. Antipasti such as meltingly tender beef fillet carpaccio crusted in thyme and black pepper, and served with violet artichoke, are succeeded by carb dishes based on impeccable pasta (viz spaghetti and mussels in Soave, or pappardelle with a game-hunter's bagful of pheasant, pigeon, rabbit and pancetta in Vernaccia). Main courses brilliantly spotlight the excellence of their prime ingredients: wood-roasted whole Dover sole with sea-kale; marinated lamb leg with spiced salsa rosso, chickpeas and turnip-tops; veal shin simmered in Barolo. The freshness and lightness of it all are what sustain the appeal, all the way from the first blood-orange Prosecco to the last scoop of stracciatella gelato or nibble of thoroughbred Italian cheese.

Chef Joseph Trivelli, Ruth Rogers, Sian Owen **Owner** Ruth Rogers **Seats** 120, Pr/dining room 18 **Times** 12.30-3/7-11 Closed 24 Dec-1 Jan, BHs, D Sun **Prices** Starter £15-£26, Main £35-£45, Dessert £9-£12 **Wines** 230 bottles over £30, 14 by glass **Parking** 29, Valet parking evening & wknds, Pay & display **Notes** Sunday L, Vegetarian available, Children welcome

consommé). Curries (maybe bhindi bhajee – fresh okra cooked in fresh tomato with South Indian spices) and all-inclusive thalis add to the lengthy output, while the menu also helpfully indicates vegan options, plus nut, onion and garlic, and wheat-free dishes. (Sibling branches in Covent Garden and Bloomsbury.)

Chef S Sharmielan **Owner** S Sharmielan **Seats** 60 **Times** 12-3/5.30-10.45 Closed 25-26 Dec **Prices** Prices not confirmed, Service optional **Wines** 911 bottles under £30, 8 by glass **Parking** On street **Notes** No children

LONDON W8

Babylon

PLAN 4 B5

◉◉ Modern British

tel: 020 7368 3993 **The Roof Gardens, 99 Kensington High St W8 5SA**
email: babylon@roofgardens.virgin.com **web:** www.roofgardens.virgin.com
dir: *Nearest station: High Street Kensington*

South London skyline views and modern British cooking

There's no shortage of restaurants boasting skyline views in the capital these days, but Babylon has something different to offer as well – views over the famous roof-top gardens one floor below. With a chic finish and a wall of glass serving up those views, plus tables on a terrace, Babylon is a seventh-floor hotspot for modern British dining. The menu deals in classic combinations with a contemporary spin here and there. Start, for example, with an open lasagne made with smoked chicken and leeks, while treacle-cured salmon and smoked Gigha halibut is an option if you fancy something a little lighter. Next up, scallop and squid comes with black tagliolini and roasted rump of lamb with aligot potato gnocchi and a mushroom and Madeira reduction. Desserts show plenty of ambition, too, judging by baked lemon cheesecake with jasmine latte foam, ginger custard and dule de leche ice cream, or an almond financier with salted caramel, passionfruit cream and Granny Smith purée.

Times 12-2.30/7-10.30 Closed D Sun

See advert on page 384

Belvedere

PLAN 1 E3

◉◉ British, French

tel: 020 7602 1238 **Abbotsbury Rd, Holland House, Holland Park W8 6LU**
email: sales@belvedererestaurant.co.uk **web:** www.belvedererestaurant.co.uk
dir: *Nearest station: Holland Park*

Modern brasserie-style dishes in upscale Holland Park

A dream-ticket location in lovely Holland Park – surrounded by primped lawns, flower gardens and fountain, and the odd peacock or two – ensures Belvedere is a year-round hit. Dating back to the 17th century and once the summer ballroom of Holland House, the dining room is a real looker too. High ceilings and bags of art deco glitz with giant shell-like lampshades, bevelled mirrors, parquet flooring and cloister-style windows bring the va-va-voom, while white linen and modern leather seating provide the comforts. A marble staircase sweeps up to a mezzanine and a much-sort-after terrace overlooking the gardens, and a slinky bar adds further kudos. The room and setting may be the real draw, but the accomplished Anglo-French brasserie cooking certainly plays its part. Take the freshest Cornish pollock served on curly kale and crushed new potatoes with star-turn shrimp beurre noisette, or succulent roast lamb rump with classic pommes boulangère, haricots verts and rosemary jus. A top-value jour menu delivers all the glam at lunch and early evening without gold-card pricing.

Times 12-2.30/6-10.30 Closed 26 Dec, 1 Jan, D Sun

Clarke's

PLAN 4 A6

◉◉ Modern British, Mediterranean

tel: 020 7221 9225 **124 Kensington Church St W8 4BH**
email: restaurant@sallyclarke.com
dir: *Nearest station: Notting Hill Gate*

Full-on flavours chez Sally

Sally Clarke's eponymous restaurant is on two levels: a light-filled ground-floor room and a larger basement with an open-to-view kitchen. Her cooking is founded on the best, freshest produce available in the markets each day, which means the menu changes at each session, and focuses on the integrity of that produce. Vegetables, herbs and salad leaves are often brought from Sally's own garden, the last going into a typical, clear-tasting starter with mozzarella, pears and blood orange with citrus dressing, or a heartier one of rare roast duck breast and grilled heart with balsamic and beetroot dressing. Main-course meats and fish are often chargrilled or roasted to bring out the maximum flavour: a large veal chop, precisely grilled, for instance, with well-chosen vegetables, or roast monkfish tail with anchovy salsa verde, baked artichoke and Désirée potatoes. Imaginative puddings could run to rhubarb trifle or chocolate tart, its pastry light and crisp.

Chef Sally Clarke **Owner** Sally Clarke **Seats** 90, Pr/dining room 40 **Times** 12.30-2.30/6.30-10 Closed 8 days Xmas & New Year, Sun **Prices** Starter £7.50-£12, Main £19-£28, Dessert £7-£8.75 **Wines** 80 bottles over £30, 10 bottles under £30, 8 by glass **Parking** On street **Notes** Vegetarian available, Children welcome

LUNCH WITH A VIEW

Enjoy fabulous sky high views, without the sky high prices. Join us for a set-menu lunch and enjoy 2 delicious courses from £23.00 or 3 courses from £26.00 Monday – Sunday 12pm – 2.30pm

THE BABYLON TERRACE

You don't have to be dining in the restaurant to take in the dazzling views of London's skyline; why not come down for a few drinks on the heated terrace and indulge in a cocktail or two?!

LIVE JAZZ EVERY TUESDAY

Babylon comes alive on Tuesday nights from 7.30pm with the smooth tunes of live jazz. Sit back and enjoy a delicious menu against a backdrop of live music.

CONTACT: 0207 368 3993   babylon@roofgardens.virgin.com   www.roofgardens.virgin.com
Babylon 7th Floor   99 Kensington High Street (Entrance Off Derry Street)   London W8 5SA
Terms and conditions apply. Subject to availability.

the·roof·gardens

Kitchen W8

LONDON W8 **PLAN 4 A4**

Modern British

tel: 020 7937 0120 **11-13 Abingdon Rd, Kensington W8 6AH**
email: info@kitchenw8.com
dir: *Nearest station: High Street Kensington*

Exciting complex modern cooking off the High Street

At Kitchen W8, Rebecca Mascarenhas and Philip Howard have brought to life their vision of a neighbourhood restaurant, and the place looks pretty cool and upmarket with its smart black façade and awning hinting that you're in for something a bit special. Expectations are borne out by the equally slick interior: vibrant art on the walls, designer wall lights, good-looking upholstered chairs at linen-swathed tables and an all-round attractive decor. 'Integrity and simplicity' are the buzz words behind the kitchen's output, although dishes have a higher level of ambition and complexity than the second of those nouns would suggest. But let's not quibble over semantics when dishes are as well conceived and precisely cooked as they are here. This menu is a treasury of bright modern ideas, ingredients are of the first order, and the amount of effort that goes on in the kitchen is clear. Deeply satisfying starters might include smoked eel, thinly sliced and partnered with grilled mackerel, leek hearts and sweet mustard for instance, or there could be caramelised Orkney scallop with wilted chanterelles, roast chicken skin, celeriac and truffle. Roast Cornish cod with octopus, squid ink dumplings, seaweed oil, sea beet and brassicas, and aged beef sirloin with turnips, horseradish, black cabbage, bone marrow and shiitake mushrooms are the sort of main courses that will surely send you home happy. And the momentum extends into desserts that might range from salt caramel parfait with roast peanut ice cream, chocolate milk purée, praline and lime, to warm rice pudding mousse with Cox's apple, Medjool dates, walnuts and oats. The intelligent wine list has around 20 choices by the glass and 250ml carafe and on Sunday there is an amnesty on corkage for BYO-ers.

Chef Mark Kempson **Owner** Philip Howard, Rebecca Mascarenhas **Seats** 75 **Times** 12-2.30/6-10 Closed 25-26 Dec, BHs **Prices** Fixed L 2 course fr £21, Fixed D 3 course fr £25, Tasting menu fr £60, Starter £10.50-£16.50, Main £19.95-£29.50, Dessert £5.95-£7.95 **Wines** 89 bottles over £30, 20 bottles under £30, 14 by glass **Parking** On street, NCP High St **Notes** Fixed D 6-7pm 2/3 course £22/£25, Sunday L fr £32.50, Vegetarian available, Children welcome

Launceston Place Restaurant

LONDON W8   PLAN 4 C4

Modern European  NOTABLE WINE LIST

tel: 020 7937 6912 **1a Launceston Place W8 5RL**
email: lpevents@danddlondon.com
dir: *Nearest station: Gloucester Road, High Street Kensington*

Dynamic modern cooking in a genteel Kensington mews

At first glance, a passer-by might think Launceston Place to be a steady neighbourhood restaurant, albeit one upmarket enough for this postcode. The truth is, it's more than that. Launceston Place has long been a place with ambition and it has maintained a reputation as a serious player for many years. These days, under head chef Tim Allen, it's gone intergalactic. Made up of four Victorian houses on the corner of a posh mews, inside it is all sober neutrality, with the series of spaces decked out with charcoal walls and statement modern art. Tables are dressed up for the occasion, and the service team keep it all running along nicely. Chef hails from Yorkshire and is clearly passionate about British ingredients, but quality is sought wherever it exists, so there's top produce from across the channel, too. His cooking is modern, creative and dynamic, but with a subtle touch, and the contemporary flourishes are well judged. There's a Tasting Menu alongside a Market Menu, which is the à la carte by another name, plus a set lunch. A starter of leveret hare (a young animal) with lightly-pickled red cabbage, baked potato cream, caramelised bacon and 100% pure cacoa, draws on classic combinations and delivers the chef's own vision. Another starter has Cornish mackerel, cold-smoked and grilled, partnered with gooseberries, charred cucumber and iced grain mustard. The high skill level and bold, exciting cooking continues into main courses such as English veal served three ways, with mushroom purée, truffle linguine and Madeira jus. A fishy main course of wild sea bass comes with a crab and leek cannelloni, confit lemon and black truffle. These dishes are characterised by an informed sense of what works with what, with the technical finesse adding another level of interest all together. Desserts impress in the same way, with a passionfruit soufflé powered up with grated fresh lime and served with coconut ice cream, and a caramel chocolate sphere partnered with Williams pear and caramelised walnuts. The wine list is a fine piece of work, with an ace team of sommeliers on hand to help you through.

Chef Timothy Allen **Owner** D & D London **Seats** 50, Pr/dining room 10 **Times** 12-2.30/6-10.30 Closed Xmas, New Year, Etr, L Mon **Prices** Fixed L 2 course fr £25, Tasting menu fr £70, Service optional 12.5% **Wines** 395 bottles over £30, 15 bottles under £30, 15 by glass **Parking** On street & Car park off Kensington High St **Notes** Market menu 3 course £52, Tasting menu 6 course, Sunday L fr £35, Vegetarian available, Children welcome

LONDON W8 *continued*

Kensington Place

PLAN 4 A6

British

tel: 020 7727 3184 **201-209 Kensington Church St W8 7LX**
email: kensingtonplace@danddlondon.com
dir: *Nearest station: Notting Hill Gate*

Buzzy brasserie starring seafood

It's over a quarter of a century since Kensington Place first made a splash on the London dining scene. Now part of the D&D London restaurant group, KP concentrates on the fruits of the sea (there's even a wet fish shop next door), serving up seafood from Billingsgate market or direct from the Cornish coast. The setting on Kensington Church Street remains a cracker, with its floor-to-ceiling windows and bright and breezy vibe. The daily market menu might deliver a tranche of turbot or skate wing (add extras such as triple-cooked chips and green beans), or stick to the carte and choose from the likes of Cornish mackerel tartare with beetroot and anchovy caviar, followed by marinated squid and prawn salad, or confit organic salmon. There are meat and veggie options too. Finish with plum and almond tart with iced orange curd.

Chef Daniel Loftin **Owner** D & D London **Seats** 110, Pr/dining room 40 **Times** 12-3/6.30-10.30 Closed 24-25 Dec, 1 Jan, BHs, L Mon, D Sun **Prices** Fixed L 2 course £25, Fixed D 3 course £30, Starter £5.50-£11, Main £12.50-£21.50, Dessert £5.50-£6.25 **Wines** 50 bottles over £30, 13 bottles under £30, 28 by glass **Parking** On street **Notes** Sunday L £17-£18.50, Vegetarian available, Children welcome

Kitchen W8

PLAN 4 A4

— *see page 384*

Launceston Place Restaurant

PLAN 4 C4

— *see page 385*

The Mall Tavern

PLAN 4 A6

Traditional British

tel: 020 7229 3374 **71-73 Palace Gardens Ter, Notting Hill W8 4RU**
email: info@themalltavern.com
dir: *Nearest station: Notting Hill Gate*

Appealingly innovative gastro-pub cooking near the tube

A Victorian pub a stone's throw from Notting Hill Gate tube station, The Mall Tavern has a bar for drinkers but the majority of people troop into the light and airy dining room – a clean, uncluttered space of bare wooden floor, wall banquettes and plain wooden tables. There's also a tiny enclosed garden for sunny lunches. Friendly and relaxed staff deliver menus – including a good value fixed-price lunch – of sparklingly fresh ideas. How about dandelion salad with ricotta, a pheasant egg and black pudding, followed by the signature cow pie? The cooking is marked out by its lack of fuss and gimmick but dishes are intelligently composed to allow flavours to shine, with the kitchen not averse to a bit of innovation. Chestnut hummus with rosemary pitta bread is an unusual but effective starter, offered alongside chicken liver pâté with pickled red onions, while main courses might take in 'pork-o-bucco' with braised lentils, and smoked salmon fishcakes with broccoli and sauce maltaise. Desserts are an irresistible bunch, among them chocolate caramel tart with orange salad.

Chef Asher Abramowitz **Owner** Perritt & Perritt Ltd **Seats** 45, Pr/dining room 15 **Times** noon-10 Closed 24 Dec-2 Jan, All-day dining **Prices** Fixed L 2 course £10, Fixed D 3 course £25, Starter £4-£10, Main £10-£30, Dessert £3.50-£6 **Wines** 8 bottles over £30, 8 bottles under £30, 17 by glass **Notes** Sunday L £12-£45, Vegetarian available, Children welcome

The Milestone Hotel

PLAN 4 B5

Modern British

tel: 020 7917 1000 **1 Kensington Court W8 5DL**
email: bookms@rchmail.com **web:** www.milestonehotel.com
dir: *Nearest station: High St Kensington*

Elegant hotel dining with a taste of luxury

This Grade II listed boutique hotel with 24-hour butler service in Kensington prides itself on its professionalism and luxurious interior and aims to pamper guests unreservedly. The ornate Cheneston's restaurant (deriving its name from an early spelling of Kensington) doesn't break the mould: it's an intimate space with traditional, cosseting service. An open fireplace, one of several original features, and candles on the tables at night lend a cosy air, while mahogany furniture and correctly laid tables add to the formal feel. The broadly modern British menu includes some of Bea Tollman's (founder and president of the Red Carnation Hotel Collection, of which The Milestone is part) favourite dishes. Wild sea trout with pickled cucumber, apple and radish salad makes a fine start to a meal, and might be followed by moist and flavoursome roast cannon of Welsh lamb with shallot purée, baby beetroot and potato fondant. Signature puddings include The Milestone quartet of desserts and Milestone rice pudding – vanilla rice pudding, Chantilly cream, salted caramel and candied nuts. The excellent wine list showcases many bottles from the owner's estate in South Africa.

Chef Kim Sjobakk **Owner** The Red Carnation Hotels **Seats** 30, Pr/dining room 8 **Times** 12-3/5.30-11 **Prices** Fixed L 3 course £26.50-£27.50, Fixed D 3 course £26.50-£27.50, Starter £10.50-£21, Main £18-£42, Dessert £8-£12 **Wines** 200 bottles over £30, 10 bottles under £30, 12 by glass **Parking** NCP Young Street off Kensington High Street **Notes** Vegetarian available, Children welcome

Min Jiang

PLAN 4 B5

— *see opposite and advert on page 388*

Min Jiang

Chinese

tel: 020 7361 1988 **Royal Garden Hotel, 2-24 Kensington High St W8 4PT**
email: reservations@minjiang.co.uk
web: www.minjiang.co.uk
dir: *Nearest station: High Street Kensington*

Stylish and authentic Chinese cuisine overlooking Hyde Park

The Royal Garden may look box-fresh, but has actually been standing on its site in Kensington High Street since 1965. It's a favoured bolthole of visiting sports stars, and its proximity to the Royal Albert Hall means that you may well find yourself going up in the lift with some distantly recognisable musical veteran. It's still privately owned, and is therefore free of what can often be the dead hand of corporatism, and the view from the top over Kensington Gardens and Hyde Park is rapturous. Upscale Chinese cuisine in five-star hotels is not always the best idea (the risk is that you find yourself eating sweet-and-sour pork at about ten times what it would cost in Chinatown), but in Min Jiang, the Garden has an emphatic riposte to the doubters. A strikingly stylish design job features blue-and-white Chinese porcelain against a contemporary interpretation of red lacquered walls, tables are laid up with stiff white linen, and the service is proficient and helpful, with unpatronising explanations of dishes for anybody still getting their bearings. The menus inevitably take a tour d'horizon of the vast Chinese landmass, but authenticity in ingredients, seasonings and timings is assured. A platter of steamed dim sum makes a fine introduction, including scallop and pumpkin dumpling, and blue swimmer crab xiao long bao, all perfectly textured and feather-light. A bowl of soup, say sweetcorn and snow fungus, might then precede main items such as Alaskan black cod with sha cha sauce, or Sichuan double-cooked pork belly with Chinese leek, with a side-dish perhaps of gai lan in ginger sauce, or fried mushrooms with pickle chilli and mustard greens. Desserts are so often not the point, and yet some creative modern thinking here produces jackfruit cheesecake with cashew and pandan ice cream, or fruity Sichuan pancake with Cornish vanilla ice cream.

Chef Lan Chee Vooi, Wong Wen Han **Owner** Goodwood Group
Seats 100, Pr/dining room 20 **Times** 12-3/6-10.30
Prices Prices not confirmed, Service optional **Wines** 133 bottles over £30, 4 bottles under £30, 15 by glass
Parking 200 **Notes** Sunday L, Vegetarian available, Children welcome

ROYAL GARDEN HOTEL

LONDON

ELEVATE YOUR SENSES...
EXPERIENCE THE AUTHENTIC,
TASTE CHINA AT MIN JIANG

Lunch and Dinner, Open Daily

2-24 KENSINGTON HIGH STREET LONDON W8 4PT
TEL +44 (0)20 7361 1988 FAX +44 (0)20 7361 1991
WWW.ROYALGARDENHOTEL.CO.UK
WWW.MINJIANG.CO.UK

LONDON W8 *continued*

Park Terrace Restaurant   PLAN 4 B5

⊛⊛ Modern British

tel: 020 7361 1999 **Royal Garden Hotel, 2-24 Kensington High St W8 4PT**
email: reservations@parkterracerestaurant.co.uk **web:** www.parkterracerestaurant.co.uk
dir: *Nearest station: High Street Kensington*

Sophisticated modern British cuisine overlooking Kensington Gardens

On the ground floor just off the marble-floored foyer of the swanky Royal Garden Hotel, the aptly-named Park Terrace comes with leafy views over Kensington Gardens through floor-to-ceiling windows running the full length of the room. Okay, it may not have the glamour of the hotel's other dining option, Min Jiang, up on the 10th floor (see entry), but it doesn't disappoint either. The contemporary decor cleverly reflects the park-life theme, with a natural colour palate, wood veneer and large black-and-white images of trees. Steve Munkley's modern British cooking is light, clear-flavoured and uncomplicated, and shows a strong commitment to local British suppliers and seasonality. Expect a duo of daily fish (perhaps salmon and scallop) served with cocotte potatoes and a tomato and olive salsa at lunch, while dinner ups the ante with lavender-and-herb crusted Essex lamb rump teamed with French beans, pea purée and confit potato, and desserts like a hot chocolate and cherry soufflé with cherry sorbet. Service is smartly attired and friendly, while the value lunch keeps the Kensington ladies on-side.

Chef Steve Munkley **Owner** Goodwood Group **Seats** 90, Pr/dining room 40
Times 12-3/6-10.30 **Prices** Service optional **Wines** 70 bottles over £30, 6 bottles under £30, 13 by glass **Parking** 200 **Notes** Pre-theatre menu daily, Afternoon tea available, Sunday L £21-£26, Vegetarian available, Children welcome

See advert below

LONDON W10

The Dock Kitchen   PLAN 1 D4

⊛ Modern International

tel: 020 8962 1610 **Portobello Docks, 342/344 Ladbroke Grove W10 5BU**
email: reception@dockkitchen.co.uk
dir: *Nearest station: Ladbroke Grove, Kensal Rise, Kensal Green*

Appealingly eclectic cooking beside the canal

Stevie Parle's former pop-up restaurant in Tom Dixon's furniture design gallery has gone from strength-to-strength since becoming a permanent fixture called The Dock Kitchen. Set in a new building smack beside the Grand Union Canal, the restaurant is a cool and contemporary dining space, with an open-to-view, glass-walled kitchen at its heart, and floor-to-ceiling glass on the water-facing side giving great canal views. Tom Dixon's furniture still gets a showing in the dining area, the wooden and metal tables un-clothed and accessorised with flowers and tea lights. Parle's cooking is influenced by his travels around the world, and so the menu offers an eclectic mix of dishes ranging from Middle Eastern to Italian to Indian. Norfolk cod roe on toast with raw peas, broad beans, dill and crème fraîche is typical of the simple approach, as is a main of hake roasted in white wine and herbs with samphire, lentils, Marinda tomatoes and mayonnaise.

Chef Stevie Parle **Owner** Stevie Parle **Seats** 80, Pr/dining room 56
Times 12-2.30/7-9.30 Closed Xmas, BHs, D Sun **Prices** Fixed L 2 course £18, Tasting menu £30-£50, Starter £7-£10, Main £15-£26, Dessert £7-£8 **Wines** 40 bottles over £30, 10 bottles under £30, 10 by glass **Parking** On street **Notes** Tasting menu themed 4 course, Vegetarian available, Children welcome

PARK TERRACE
RESTAURANT, BAR AND LOUNGE

Enjoy fresh, seasonal British cuisine
at Park Terrace restaurant.

Lunch and dinner, open daily.

2-24 KENSINGTON HIGH STREET LONDON W8 4PT
TEL +44 (0)20 7361 1999 FAX +44 (0)20 7361 1991
WWW.ROYALGARDENHOTEL.CO.UK
WWW.PARKTERRACERESTAURANT.CO.UK

DISTINCTIVE
DINING

LONDON W11

Chakra
PLAN 1 E3

Indian

tel: 020 7229 2115 **157-159 Notting Hill Gate W11 3LF**
email: reservations@chakralondon.com
dir: *Nearest station: Notting Hill Gate*

Smart Indian restaurant in Notting Hill

Named after the energy points of the body according to Hindu and Buddhist tradition, the chakras are vital in aligning mind, body and soul. Chef Andy Varma has similar plans to invigorate and energise you with his food. It all takes place in a smart room a million miles from curry-house cliché, where the walls and banquettes are covered in cream-coloured leather, crisp white linen adorns the tables, and chandeliers hang from the ceiling. The cooking is most definitely a cut-above, too. The menu serves up lots of less familiar ideas and flavours are nicely judged throughout. Start with venison galouti, yam chaat, or masala asparagus, and move on to main courses such as chicken Jalandhar, which is a version of the Punjabi classic – tandoor grilled chicken with fine tomato and masala sauce, served with a roti. There's Chakra black cod, roasted quail, and Bengal fish curry, too, plus vegetarian dishes such as kadhai paneer and black dhal.

Chef Andy Varma **Owner** Chakra London Ltd **Seats** 75, Pr/dining room 30
Times 12-3/6-11 Closed 1 Jan, 25-26 Dec **Prices** Fixed L 2 course £9.95-£19.95, Fixed D 3 course £45-£85, Tasting menu £60-£75, Starter £7.95-£16.95, Main £4.95-£29, Dessert £6.50-£8.50 **Wines** 30 bottles over £30, 9 bottles under £30, 11 by glass **Notes** Sunday L £14.95-£65, Vegetarian available, Children welcome

E&O
PLAN 1 D4

Pan Asian

tel: 020 7229 5454 **14 Blenheim Crescent, Notting Hill W11 1NN**
email: eando@rickerrestaurants.com
dir: *Nearest station: Notting Hill Gate, Ladbroke Grove*

East Asian grazing plates for the Notting Hill cognoscenti

The joint still jumps at E&O, one of the central supports of Will Ricker's era-defining restaurant group, providing Pan-Asian mini-plates to the grazers and hangers-out of Notting Hill. It's more than proved itself a winning formula since opening in 2001: people pack the place whatever the weather for finely honed, highly spiced, cleanly presented food sourced from the principal East Asian traditions. Chilli salt squid and crispy pork belly in black rice vinegar, the latter upholstered with an eye-popping layer of fat, are as authentic-seeming as anything in Chinatown, and a paper cone of tempura soft-shelled crab with creamy jalapeño dipping sauce is fun. The westernmost extremities of Pan-Asia are drawn with sufficient elastic to allow Ibérico pork a look-in, in the form of a firm pre-sliced chop with shimeji mushrooms and soba noodles, or you might choose whole crispy sea bass with chilli jam and spiced mango. Desserts head west too for mango pannacotta and lime granita, or banoffee pie.

Chef Simon Treadway **Owner** Will Ricker **Seats** 86, Pr/dining room 18
Times 12-3/6-11 Closed 25-26 Dec, 1 Jan, Aug BH **Prices** Fixed L 3 course £20, Tasting menu £39-£59, Starter £3.50-£13, Main £7.50-£33, Dessert £4.50-£6 **Wines** 37 bottles over £30, 13 bottles under £30, 15 by glass **Parking** On street **Notes** Fixed price D available reserved private dining only, Sunday L, Vegetarian available, Children welcome

The Ledbury

LONDON W11
PLAN 1 E4

British, French V NOTABLE WINE LIST

tel: 020 7792 9090 **127 Ledbury Rd W11 2AQ**
email: info@theledbury.com
dir: *Nearest station: Westbourne Park, Notting Hill Gate*

Imaginative cooking from a supremely talented, tirelessly focused chef

Brett Graham has been at The Ledbury for almost a decade, and in that time he's developed the place into a serious player in the London dining scene. From the team behind the Square, where Brett cut his teeth after arriving in the UK from his native Australia, The Ledbury serves up pin-sharp contemporary cooking in W11. It looks smart from the outside, exclusive even, with a few tables on the street protected by a veritable rainforest of greenery. Once through the door, clever use of mirrors gives the impression of a sizable space, but that's a clever illusion, as there are just 50 or so covers. The service team play their part in making a visit a high-end experience, with not a step out of place, but there's nothing stuffy about The Ledbury. There's a tasting menu, set lunch and a carte (available lunch and dinner) that is set out to encourage a four-course option,

which is well worth the punt if you've room. Course one gets the ball rolling with an inspired cured duck and foie gras with a salad of Chinese, violet and Jerusalem artichokes and hazelnuts. Brett's food is presented with real flair, the plates promising much and delivering a great deal. If you're on track for the full four courses, move on to roast turbot with broccoli stems, black quinoa and crab, or a curd made from Hampshire buffalo milk served with aged Comté, truffle toast and a broth of grilled onions. The third course might deliver breast and confit leg of pigeon, with quince, red vegetables and leave. These are technically stunning dishes. For dessert, passionfruit soufflé with Sauternes ice cream maintains the standard, and the wine list is put together with the same care and attention as the food.

Chef Brett Graham **Owner** Nigel Platts-Martin, Brett Graham, Philip Howard **Seats** 55 **Times** 12-6.30 Closed 25 Dec, Aug BH, L Mon-Tue **Prices** Prices not confirmed **Wines** 819 bottles over £30, 10 bottles under £30, 16 by glass **Parking** Talbot St **Notes** Fri-Sun eve tasting menu only, Sunday L, Children welcome

Edera
PLAN 1 D3

Modern Italian

tel: 020 7221 6090 **148 Holland Park Av W11 4UE**
email: roberto@edera.co.uk
dir: *Nearest station: Holland Park*

Well-liked neighbourhood Italian in leafy Holland Park

Decked out on tiered levels, with blond-wood floors, light walls hung with big mirrors and linen-dressed tables, this minimally-styled Holland Park eatery pulls in a well-heeled crowd for its fashionable Sardinian-accented Italian cooking. Pavement tables fill early on warm sunny days despite traffic passing close by. The kitchen certainly knows its stuff, keeping things simple and straightforward, allowing the excellent ingredients to speak for themselves. There is much that is familiar from the Italian mainland, bolstered by a daily specials list featuring the likes of chargrilled sea bream with courgettes and basil oil, and baked salted sea bass with potato salad, but the chef is Sardinian, so there might be spaghetti with grey mullet roe, and Sicilian cannoli for pudding.

Chef Carlo Usai **Owner** A-Z Ltd/Mr Pisano **Seats** 70, Pr/dining room 20 **Times** 12-11 Closed 25-26 & 31 Dec, All-day dining **Prices** Prices not confirmed **Wines** 13 by glass **Parking** On street **Notes** Black truffle menu all year, white truffle menu in season, Children welcome

The Ledbury
PLAN 1 E4

– *see opposite*

Lonsdale
PLAN 1 E4

Modern British

tel: 020 7727 4080 **48 Lonsdale Rd W11 2DE**
email: info@thelonsdale.co.uk
dir: *Nearest station: Notting Hill, Ladbroke Grove*

Trendy Notting Hill lounge bar dining

Tucked away on a residential street, this hip Notting Hill/Westbourne Grove hangout is an up-tempo evenings-only affair. The lively front bar gets rammed on busy nights, with cocktails and fizz de rigueur before moving on to the equally funky lounge-style dining area behind. Red mock-croc, low-backed banquettes, darkwood tables, gold walls and a centrepiece light feature deliver a low-lit night-club vibe for a backing track of trendy music, youthful service and high decibels. The equally well-dressed but straightforward modish cooking is driven by quality ingredients and suits the mood; perhaps haunch of venison with juniper and chocolate sauce or pan-roasted sea bass with a fricassée of mussels, samphire and sorrel. Steaks from the Lake District (35-day hung) and starters such as black figs with Gervic goats' cheese fit the bill.

Times 6-12 Closed 25-26 Dec, 1 Jan, Sun-Mon, L all week

LONDON W14

Cibo
PLAN 1 D3

Italian

tel: 020 7371 2085 **3 Russell Gardens W14 8EZ**
email: ciborestaurant@aol.com
dir: *Nearest station: Olympia, Shepherds Bush*

W14's Italian flagship

In a parade of shops on a small side street off busy Holland Road, Cibo is a small and unpretentious restaurant, a destination for lovers of Italian food. A bar dominates the room, decoration is provided by nude reliefs, ornaments and ceramic pots, and Italian staff are knowledgeable and helpful. Bread – focaccia, carta di musica – and nibbles like olives are promising openers before starters along the lines of smooth polenta topped with a tomato-based ragù of fennel-infused luganega sausage, or crudo di tonno with capers. Pasta is the real thing – perhaps ravioli, cooked al dente, stuffed with smooth minced pheasant in wild mushroom sauce, a well-balanced dish – and the kitchen's care with quality ingredients, some imported, shines throughout, from whole sea bass plainly grilled with lemon and herbs, to pan-fried venison fillet served with agnolotti pasta filled with apple in venison sauce. Puddings are convincing renditions of the classics, from tiramisù to zabaglione.

Chef Piero Borrell **Owner** Gino Taddei, C Pertini **Seats** 50, Pr/dining room 14 **Times** 12.15-3/6.15-11 Closed Xmas, Etr BHs, L Sat, D Sun **Prices** Starter £9-£12.50, Main £14-£24.50, Dessert £5-£8 **Wines** 26 bottles under £30, 4 by glass **Parking** On street **Notes** Sunday L fr £19.50, Vegetarian available, Children welcome

LONDON WC1

The Montague on the Gardens
PLAN 3 B3

British

tel: 020 7612 8416 & 7612 8412 **15 Montague St, Bloomsbury WC1B 5BJ**
email: pbradley@rchmail.com web: www.montaguehotel.com
dir: *Nearest station: Russell Square, Holborn, Tottenham Court Rd*

Stylish hotel bistro with modern comfort classics

The bowler-hatted doorman at the entrance posts notice that this is a classy boutique hotel, on a quiet street around the corner from the British Museum. Its Blue Door Bistro is a welcoming and informal dining room, decorated on three sides by a frieze depicting London in around 1850. There's mahogany panelling, with contemporary wall lights and good use of mirrored glass and flowers on clothed dining tables. Simplicity is the kitchen's byword, producing starters such as a signature bowl of chicken noodle soup, and a portion of smoked salmon with beetroot salad and horseradish cream. Quality produce is treated with good judgement, seen in main courses like haddock fillet in crisp and golden beer batter, served with mushy peas, chips and notably good tartare sauce, and ham-wrapped chicken breast accompanied by olives, green beans and cherry tomatoes. End with an upbeat dessert like pear and chocolate tart.

Chef Martin Halls **Owner** Red Carnation Hotels **Seats** 40, Pr/dining room 100 **Times** 12.30-2.30/5.30-10.30 **Prices** Fixed L 2 course £22.50, Fixed D 3 course £27.50, Starter £5.90-£12.50, Main £12.50-£38, Dessert £6-£7 **Wines** 61 bottles over £30, 25 bottles under £30, 24 by glass **Parking** On street, Bloomsbury Sq **Notes** Pre-theatre 2/3 course £16.50/£19.50, Sunday L £12.50-£38, Vegetarian available, Children welcome

Paramount
PLAN 3 A2

Modern European

tel: 020 7420 2900 **Centre Point, 101-103 New Oxford St WC1A 1DD**
email: reservations@paramount.uk.net
dir: *Nearest station: Tottenham Court Rd*

Amazing views and appealing menu

Thirty-two-floors up in the Centre Point building, the panorama is paramount. Once you've stepped out of the lift you're confronted with spectacular views across the capital which are worth the trip on their own, but there's some good eating and drinking to be had whilst you're up here. The Paramount restaurant and bar have fabulous views day and night through huge windows. The cool decor has darkwood floors, funky-ish lime green upholstered seating and copper tables (matching its copper cocktail bar) inlaid with black lacquered tops. And on the menu is some broadly appealing, gently contemporary food. You might start for instance with carrot and coriander soup, but equally there's smoked eel risotto with sorrel and soft herbs, or seared scallop with black pudding and cauliflower purée. Next up, pan-fried whole plaice comes in traditional guise with caper and brown shrimp butter, and braised pork belly with Morteau sausages, lentils and carrots.

Times 12-3/5.30-11 Closed Xmas, 1 Jan

LONDON WC1 *continued*

Rosewood London
PLAN 3 C3

🏵🏵 Modern European **NEW**

tel: 020 3747 8620 & 3747 8621 **252 High Holborn WC1V 7EN**
email: mirrorroom@rosewoodhotels.com **web:** www.rosewoodhotels.com/london
dir: *Nearest station: Holborn*

British heritage cookery in a magnificently restored building

Once the headquarters of the Pearl Assurance company, the magnificent building on High Holborn was begun on the eve of the Great War, and gradually took shape over half a century. In consultation with English Heritage, its fine façades, original banking halls and grand staircase have been restored to glory, and the entrance into a domed courtyard would have been suitable for the horse-drawn carriages of the Georgian era. It's a fitting venue for a Rosewood hotel, the old East Banking Hall with its soaring marble pillars now seeing service as a modernistically grand restaurant, with bars at either end for counter dining. A brasserie menu of traditional British dishes that have been gently coaxed into the present day offers the likes of Dublin Bay prawns in mayonnaise, Marie Rose shellfish cocktail with avocado, or fried squid with Gentleman's Relish to start. Majestic follow-ups follow, such as roast beef rib, served with a fine, deeply flavoured gravy and crisp onion rings, or perfectly timed, garlic-buttered grilled lobster with sea vegetables and chips. There is the odd surprise – a shrimp burger with jalapeño tartare – but the essential repertoire contains nothing that would have baffled Mrs Beeton. Baked rice pudding with a blob of blackcurrant jam, sherried-up trifle, or banana with custard, are the pleasantest ways of harking back.

Chef Jerome Voltat , Bjorn van der Horst **Owner** Rosewood Hotel London **Seats** 70, Pr/dining room 20 **Times** 12-3/6.30-10.30 **Prices** Fixed L 2 course £28, Starter £11-£22, Main £19-£34, Dessert £7-£9 **Wines** 350 bottles over £30, 4 bottles under £30, 16 by glass **Parking** 12 **Notes** Afternoon tea available, Vegetarian available, Children welcome

▮ LONDON WC2

L'Atelier de Joël Robuchon
PLAN 3 A2

🏵🏵🏵 – **see below**

Balthazar
PLAN 3 B1

🏵 French, European

tel: 020 3301 1155 **4-6 Russell St WC2B 5HZ**
email: info@balthazarlondon.com
dir: *Nearest station: Covent Garden*

All-day French brasserie fare and an electric atmosphere

The hottest ticket in Covent Garden right now, the much-hyped Balthazar – set in the old Theatre Museum just off the piazza – has played to packed houses ever since it opened in spring 2013. The London outpost of Keith McNally's legendary New York brasserie, it's a real looker, a large, elegant, high-ceilinged room decked out with mosaic floors, darkwood panelling, impressive art deco lighting, red-leather banquette seating and giant antique mirrors. And with an army of sunny natured staff, a swanky bar, and a constant turnover of animatedly enthusiastic diners, the place really rocks. The all-day offer takes in breakfast, lunch, afternoon tea and dinner (plus weekend brunch), with menus delivering a wide range of classic French brasserie fare, from fruits de mer to salad Niçoise, moules frites to steak au poivre. Some dishes get a more modish treatment, such as roasted cod fillet with crushed potatoes, superb olive tapenade and pistachios, while desserts are mostly comfort classics like apple tarte Tatin and profiteroles.

Times 7.30am-mdnt All-day dining

L'Atelier de Joël Robuchon

LONDON WC2
PLAN 3 A2

Modern French **V** 🍷 **NOTABLE WINE LIST**

tel: 020 7010 8600 **13-15 West St WC2H 9NE**
email: info@joelrobuchon.co.uk
dir: *Nearest station: Leicester Sq, Covent Gdn, Tottenham Court Rd*

Concept dining with a clubby feel from a French master-chef

Las Vegas, Paris and Tokyo aren't the latest tour dates for Lady Gaga, but some of the locations of the L'Atelier brand, for like the good lady, Monsieur Robuchon is a global superstar. (Albeit with a more mellow dress sense). 'Atelier' means workshop and the London operation is as much like a workshop as Harrods is like, well, a corner shop. This is glam territory, where Robuchon lets out his inner Gaga over three floors of a handsome townhouse on the fringes of Covent Garden. There's the dark and brooding L'Atelier with an open-view kitchen area on the ground floor, the monochrome La Cuisine one floor up, and the Salon Bar and Terrace on top, and you can eat what you want where you want. If it all sounds like too much fun, the cooking is a serious business and there is no doubting the culinary chops of Joël Robuchon. Staff deal with all questions with great charm (advice on the menu might be required) and the Franco-Mediterranean dishes

come with a good dose of Japanese umami. Small-plated multi-course eating is the way to go downstairs if you really want to get a taste of the place or share, while the first floor offers a more regular restaurant experience. So to the food. The bi-lingual menu might offer seared 'mildly spiced' Scottish scallops which are certainly mild, but the two plump bivalves are fresh as can be and cooked just right. Veal escalope with crunchy vegetable medley with heart of Romaine lettuce and tonnato sauce again shows spot-technical skills and the dish combines into a satisfying whole. A spectacular vision arrives for desserts in the form of a coconut caramel bonbon with vanilla ice cream and crunchy praline. It doesn't come cheap, but there are pre- and post-theatre menus, while the veggie carte is sure to impress non-meat eaters.

Chef Xavier Boyer **Owner** Joel Robuchon **Seats** 43 **Times** 12-3/5.30-11 Closed Aug BH, 25 Dec, 1 Jan **Prices** Fixed L 2 course £31-£45, Tasting menu £129-£214, Starter £9-£40, Main £19-£49, Dessert £11 **Wines** 250 bottles over £30, 4 bottles under £30, 16 by glass **Parking** Valet parking service **Notes** Pre-theatre menu 2/4 course £31/£41, Sunday L, Vegetarian available, Children welcome

Clos Maggiore

LONDON WC2   PLAN 3 B1

Modern French, Mediterranean v **NOTABLE WINE LIST**

tel: 020 7379 9696 **33 King St, Covent Garden WC2E 8JD**
email: enquiries@closmaggiore.com
web: www.closmaggiore.com
dir: *Nearest station: Covent Garden, Leicester Sq*

An intimate oasis in the heart of Covent Garden

It is with good reason that the two words most associated with Clos Maggiore are 'romantic' and 'oasis.' Right in the middle of the Covent Garden hubbub, the jewel in the crown of this classy outfit is the courtyard garden, with its retractable roof opening up to reveal the twinkling sky (or as much as the sky twinkles over major conurbations). It's a delightful spot, reminiscent of an upscale auberge in Provence or Tuscany, with foliage adding to the natural, garden vibe. The internal dining rooms don't lack for romantic appeal either, though, with an open fire, plush fabrics, elegantly laid tables and soft-focus lighting. Given the location, there's not surprisingly a prix-fixe, pre-theatre menu, with suggested pre-dinner cocktails if you're really pushing the boat out, plus a tasting menu backing up the sizable à la carte menu. The cooking is modern French in direction with some broader Pan-European influences, and dishes are refined and elegantly presented. A roasted

pumpkin and pine nut soup comes with a clever truffle croquet-monsieur among first courses, with another partnering braised shoulder of Loire Valley rabbit with sweet-and-sour black radish and wholegrain mustard mousseline. There's a good choice for vegetarians (including a veggie tasting menu), with dishes such as roasted English beetroot and red onion tart (with soft gorgonzola and endive) catching the eye. Slow-cooked belly of Limousin veal is served as a main course with autumn vegetable étuvée, Pommery mustard and tarragon sauce. For dessert there might be soft almond and dark chocolate cake with glazed Corsican clementines and a Napolean clementine sorbet, or finish with the selection of European cheeses. The wine list is very well put together indeed, with some seriously good stuff from first-rate producers, plus a decent choice under £30 a bottle.

Chef Marcellin Marc **Owner** Tyfoon Restaurants Ltd, Paul Corrett **Seats** 70, Pr/dining room 23 **Times** 12-2.30/5-11 Closed 24-25 Dec **Prices** Fixed L 2 course £15.50, Fixed D 3 course £19.50-£22.50, Tasting menu £49, Starter £6.90-£14.90, Main £17.50-£29.50, Dessert £6.90-£8.90 **Wines** 1900 bottles over £30, 10 bottles under £30, 21 by glass **Parking** On street, NCP **Notes** Pre & post theatre menus Mon-Sat 5-6, Sun 5-11pm, Sunday L £22.50-£39 Children L only

LONDON WC2 continued

Christopher's

PLAN 3 C1

Contemporary American

tel: 020 7240 4222 **18 Wellington St, Covent Garden WC2E 7DD**
email: reservations@christophersgrill.com
dir: *Nearest station: Embankment, Covent Garden*

Lively Stateside eating in an elegant Covent Garden room

The long-running Christopher's, an American eatery on the fringes of Covent Garden, can hardly ever have looked so elegant as it has since its refurb in early 2013. High, elaborately corniced ceilings tower over the expansive main room, where chairs in grey and lemon are offset by purple drapes, not to mention stylishly attired staff. Executive chef Francis Agyepong oversees a menu of lively Stateside food, including the likes of blackened salmon and jambalaya risotto, BBQ-rubbed tip steaks of USDA beef, and pork belly with creamed corn and plantain blinis, with perhaps a side of Boston baked beans, or mac and cheese, optionally ritzed up with lobster. More off-piste dishes work well too, as in caramelised scallops with chorizo in orange-cardamom dressing, or an Italianate sea bass main, served with roasted figs, ricotta and prosciutto, before all are reunited for embroilingly gooey chocolate and peanut butter tart with salty caramel ice cream.

Chef Francis Agyepong **Owner** The Hon Ambar Paul **Seats** 110, Pr/dining room 40 **Times** 12-3/5-11.30 Closed Xmas, 1 Jan **Prices** Fixed L 2 course fr £18, Fixed D 3 course fr £22, Starter £8-£14, Main £16-£68, Dessert £7-£9 **Wines** 100+ bottles over £30, 5 bottles under £30, 12 by glass **Notes** Fixed D theatre Mon-Sat 5-6.15 & 10-11.30, Sun Supper menu, Vegetarian available, Children welcome

Cigalon

PLAN 3 D2

French

tel: 020 7242 8373 **115 Chancery Ln WC2A 1PP**
email: bookings@cigalon.co.uk
dir: *Nearest station: Chancery Lane, Temple*

Friendly, relaxed and classy Provençal paradise in legal land

Blink and you could almost be on a sun-drenched Provençal veranda rather than the dusty legal world of Chancery Lane, courtesy of Cigalon's inspired design that brings the outside indoors via an atrium-like glass ceiling and open patio-style kitchen. Embellishing the illusion, pastel-striped banquettes, silver bamboo and curving lavender-coloured central booths come set to a soundtrack of chirpy birdsong and cicada. But it's not all good looks over substance: the operation – backed by some former Club Gascon folk – scores on all fronts. The kitchen itself focuses on the grill to deliver its sunny, seasonal Provençal menu of simple, robust, punchy flavoured classics. Witness an opener cassoulet of snails and anchovies, or perhaps blowsier beef onglet teamed with baby onions, gnocchi and full-throttle red wine jus. Desserts might feature a warm black chocolate and nuciola tart with quenching pear sorbet to cut through its richness, while wines are exclusively French, focusing on Provence (with a nod to Corsica) like the food. (Baranis, their trendy bar, sits in the basement.)

Chef Julien Carlon **Owner** Vincent Labeyrie **Seats** 60, Pr/dining room 8 **Times** 12-2.15/5.45-10 Closed Xmas, New Year, BHs, Sat-Sun **Prices** Fixed L 2 course £19.50, Fixed D 3 course £24.50, Starter £8.50-£13.50, Main £8.50-£19.50, Dessert £6.50-£8.50 **Wines** 83 bottles over £30, 20 bottles under £30, 10 by glass **Parking** On street **Notes** Vegetarian available, Children welcome

Clos Maggiore

PLAN 3 B1

– see page 393

The Delaunay

PLAN 3 C2

European

tel: 020 7499 8558 **55 Aldwych WC2B 4BB**
email: reservations@thedelaunay.com
dir: *Nearest station: Holborn, Covent Garden*

All day brasserie dining in the grand European tradition

If the Wolseley (see entry) is your bag, then you'll adore its Aldwych sibling. The Delaunay, like the ever-popular Piccadilly original, gets its inspiration from the grand café-restaurants of central Europe. The David Collins' design follows the same winning formula, as does the extensive all-day dining repertoire, though the Delaunay's swish interior has a rather warmer tone. Darkwood panelling, marble surfaces, green leather upholstered banquettes and chairs, linen-clothed tables, brass lighting and white-and-grey tiled floors set a classy tone, alongside a roomy bar-café area. It's an equally vibrant, glamorous spot, great for people watching and with slick, well-pitched service. And the show never stops; from breakfast and an all-day carte, plus afternoon tea, you can expect the likes of omelette Arnold Bennett, moules frites or croquet-monsieur to more substantial things such as roasted rump of lamb with spinach fregola or Wiener schnitzel. Not leaving room for desserts – like apple and marzipan strudel or baked vanilla cheesecake – would be a mistake. The Delaunay Counter – with separate entrance – offers a takeaway service, including fabulous patisserie.

Times 11.30-mdnt All-day dining

Les Deux Salons

PLAN 3 B1

French

tel: 020 7420 2050 **40-42 William IV St WC2N 4DD**
email: info@lesdeuxsalons.co.uk
dir: *Nearest station: Charing Cross, Leicester Square*

Authentic French brasserie menu in the heart of theatreland

Anthony Demetre and Will Smith's little London group (see also Arbutus and Wild Honey) continues to demonstrate that its finger is firmly on the pulse of big-city dining with this attractive Montparnasse-style brasserie in the heart of Covent Garden theatreland. Complete with menu formule, two-course prix-fixe, and pre- and post-theatre deals, the ethos is right too, and the offering of salade niçoise, foie gras terrine, chicken with lemon and garlic, sea bass in caper butter, and profiteroles could scarcely be more authentic. That said, if your tastes tend to the modern dissenting, the kitchen can also turn out well-wrought crab cakes with chilli jam to start, and sugar-dusted lemon curd doughnuts to finish. Prime materials, such as those on show in the slow-cooked Welsh lamb in a viscous reduction sauce with root veg, are unimpeachable, and the properly apposite aperitifs include Lillet and Floc de Gascogne.

Chef Colin Layfield **Owner** Will Smith, Anthony Demetre **Seats** 160, Pr/dining room 34 **Times** 12-11 Closed 25-26 Dec, 1 Jan, D Sun All-day dining **Prices** Fixed L 2 course fr £12.95, Starter £3.95-£9.95, Main £7.50-£19.50, Dessert £3.95-£6.50 **Wines** 37 bottles over £30, 11 bottles under £30, 28 by glass **Parking** On street **Notes** Prix Fixe £12.95, Formule £22.95, Sunday L, Vegetarian available, Children welcome

Great Queen Street

PLAN 3 B2

◉ British, European

tel: 020 7242 0622 **32 Great Queen St WC2B 5AA**
email: greatqueenstreet@googlemail.com
dir: *Nearest station: Covent Garden, Holborn*

Best of British at bustling gastro-pub

Younger stablemate of Waterloo's Anchor & Hope (see entry), Great Queen Street rocks week long. The long pub-like room – with a bar down one side (set for bar dining) and an open kitchen at the back – comes decked out in dark red walls, while elbow-to-elbow wooden tables (constantly being turned) and mismatched chairs fit with its back-to-basics ethos and high-decibel atmosphere. Wines are served in tumblers and specials get chalked -up, while the twice-daily-changing menu deals in quality produce where seasonality, sourcing and provenance are king. Intelligently simple, unfussy Brit fare with gutsy, big flavours is the kitchen's preference. There's no three-course formality, with dishes laid out in ascending price order, so mix-and-match with smaller plates or large dishes like smoked Gloucestershire Old Spot and choucroute or braised hare with polenta.

Chef Tom Norrington-Davies, Sam Hutchins **Owner** R Shaw, T Norrington-Davies, J Jones, M Belben **Seats** 70 **Times** 12-2.30/6-10.30 Closed last working day in Dec-1st working day in Jan, BHs, D Sun **Prices** Prices not confirmed **Wines** 13 by glass **Notes** Sunday L, Vegetarian available, Children welcome

Green Man and French Horn

PLAN 3 B1

◉◉ French

tel: 020 7836 2645 **54 St Martins Ln WC2N 4EA**
email: enquiries@greenmanfrenchhorn.co
dir: *Nearest station: Leicester square*

Gutsy Gallic food matched with Loire wines

This newcomer to the Covent Garden foodie scene takes its inspiration from France, or to be more precise, dishes associated with the lands along the River Loire that are a match made in heaven when paired with the wines of the region. The operation occupies an old pub done out unfussily with bare brick walls, well-worn parquet floors, wooden tables and banquettes, and the formula works a treat: plates of rich, robust food matched with interesting, sensibly-priced wines, including an excellent choice by the glass. You might go for a plat du jour – grilled sardines with lemon, garlic and parsley, say – with a glass of wine for a mere tenner, or set out with a hearty slab of terrine made from pork belly, shoulder and liver served with cornichons and excellent sourdough bread, then move on to rabbit matched with salsify and cider. For dessert, a splendid tarte vigneronne – winemaker's tart – is another treat from the Loire, a slim puff pastry tarte fine of apple set in red wine jelly.

Chef Ed Wilson **Owner** Ed Wilson, Oliver Barker **Seats** 55 **Times** 12-3/5.30-11 Closed Xmas, New Year, BHs, Sun **Prices** Starter £5-£11, Main £11-£24, Dessert £6-£7 **Wines** 271 bottles over £30, 34 bottles under £30, 15 by glass **Parking** On street **Notes** Pre-theatre menu 2/3 course £14.50/£16.50, Vegetarian available, Children welcome

The Ivy

PLAN 3 A1

◉ British, International

tel: 020 7836 4751 **1-5 West St, Covent Garden WC2H 9NQ**
dir: *Nearest station: Leicester Square*

Old and new brasserie cooking at a Theatreland institution

A long-running old stager on a corner site in the heart of London Theatreland, the Ivy has seen stars of stage, screen and Westminster come and go within its hallowed portals. Despite the close cramming of tables, it requires booking well ahead, and if you can break off from the star-gazing for five minutes, there's a menu of ancient and modern brasserie dishes to choose from. The modernist forays are best seen in starters like popcorn shrimp with piri-piri ketchup and burnt lime, and a Japanese-inspired main course of perfectly timed baked sea bass dressed in white soy, edamame, mirin and cucumber, but the compass-needle has always tended towards stolid traditionalism. Steak tartare, dressed crab with celeriac remoulade, and the various roasts, grills and hamburgers are what keep the crowds returning. To finish, there could be banoffee cheesecake with candied brazils, or nicely balanced prosecco and blood orange jelly with rippled ice cream.

Times 12-11.30 Closed 25-26 Dec, 1 Jan, All-day dining

Jamie's Italian

PLAN 3 B1

◉ Modern Italian

tel: 020 3326 6390 **11 Upper St Martin's Ln, Covent Garden WC2H 9FB**
email: covent@jamiesitalian.com
dir: *Nearest station: Covent Garden, Leicester Square*

Jamie does the West End

In a prime position between Covent Garden and Leicester Square, Jamie Oliver's West End gaff (the group grows and grows) packs them in; avoid peak times to beat the queues. The place fairly buzzes from noon to midnight, the closely-set tables leading to quite a chorus. Jamie's hallmark Italian food is the name of the game, with good quality seasonal produce featuring in unfussy, fresh and vibrant dishes brimful with chilli, lemon and herby flavours. Pasta is made in-house and bread is baked twice daily in their artisan bakery next door. From the seasonal menu and chalkboard specials, perhaps kick-off with carpaccio of braised octopus with olives, rocket and herbs, then follow with a tender, full-flavoured feather steak, flash-grilled with sage and prosciutto, and served with a spicy tomato, basil and chilli salsa and a side dish of excellent polenta chips flavoured with rosemary and parmesan. Finish with a text-book smooth, creamy and precisely-flavoured vanilla pannacotta with fruit compôte.

Chef Matt Burgess **Owner** Jamie Oliver **Seats** 190 **Times** noon-11.30 Closed 25-26 Dec, All-day dining **Prices** Fixed L 3 course fr £29.95, Fixed D 3 course fr £29.95, Service optional 10% **Wines** 10 bottles over £30, 15 bottles under £30, 15 by glass **Notes** Vegetarian available, Children welcome

J. Sheekey & J. Sheekey Oyster Bar

PLAN 3 B1

◉ Seafood

tel: 020 7240 2565 **32-34 St Martin's Court WC2N 4AL**
dir: *Nearest station: Leicester Square*

Renowned theatreland fish restaurant

Very much London legend, this enduring and much-loved seafood restaurant in the heart of theatreland began life as a seafood stall in the 19th century. J Sheekey expanded the business into adjoining properties and it has been a haunt of the great and the good ever since, including theatrical types who ply their trade on the surrounding boards. Inside is a warren of snug wood-panelled dining rooms, plus a seafood and oyster bar, and a menu listing relatively straightforward fish and shellfish dishes prepared from superb quality raw ingredients. Start with a classic Catalan-inspired dish of razor clams with chorizo and broad beans, or a choice of oysters if you want to keep it simple, followed by a superb cod fillet on buttered leeks with meaty Isle of Mull mussels and wilted sea aster. A-listers might go for Beluga with blinis and sour cream (£195 for 30g), but everyone else can take comfort in a plum and almond tart.

Times 12-3/5.30-12 Closed 25-26 Dec, 1 Jan, D 24 Dec

LONDON WC2 *continued*

Kaspar's Seafood Bar & Grill
PLAN 3 C1

◉◉ Seafood

tel: 020 7836 4343 **The Savoy, Strand WC2R OEU**
email: savoy@fairmont.com **web:** www.fairmont.com/savoy
dir: *Nearest station: Embankment, Covent Garden, Charing Cross*

Super-fresh seafood and more in a stunning art deco setting

When The Savoy reopened after its multi-million-pound overhaul a few years back, The River Restaurant was preserved exactly as it was: a formal, traditional, old-school hotel dining room. But that's all changed now. It still overlooks the river, but every trace of the original has been erased and replaced with an informal, buzzy seafood bar and grill. Named Kaspar's after the legend of Kaspar the cat (ask one of the friendly staff for the full story), the room looks stunning with its central seafood bar and 1920s-inspired decor of gold and black patterned tiling, blue leather banquettes and tub-style chairs, mirrors, decorative glass panels and unusual light fittings. You can sit up at the seafood bar and watch as the chef prepares you a fruit de mer platter or a plate of smoked fish, or head to a table and order something from the extensive and varied carte – perhaps smoked sand shrimp and eel cocktail (a brilliant take on the classic prawn cocktail) to start, followed by a simple lobster club sandwich with fries, or monkfish kebabs from the grill.

Chef James Pare **Owner** Fairmont **Seats** 114, Pr/dining room 12 **Times** 12-11.30 All-day dining **Prices** Fixed D 3 course £26, Starter £9-£19, Main £15-£38, Dessert £9-£15 **Wines** 40 bottles over £30, 40 by glass **Notes** Fixed D is only available during pre-theatre 5-6.30pm, Vegetarian available, Children welcome

Kopapa
PLAN 3 B2

◉◉ Fusion

tel: 020 7240 6076 **32-34 Monmouth St, Seven Dials, Covent Garden WC2H 9HA**
email: information@kopapa.co.uk
dir: *Nearest station: Covent Garden*

Culinary Covent Garden alchemy from a master of fusion cuisine

The Seven Dials sister of Providores in Marylebone (see entry), Kopapa is another piece of fusion heaven from Kiwi trail-blazer Peter Gordon. It can pretty much sort you out any time of the day – breakfast, brunch, lunch, dinner, small plates, big plates, sharing (or not), it's up to you. And it has a chilled out vibe, too, with a marble-topped bar (bar snacks available, of course), and a relaxed attitude that keeps the customers coming back. On the menu is some creative fusion food, which means anything from Europe and Asia is fair game: deep-fried sesame and Urfa chilli-salted squid with sumac mayonnaise (small plate), or twice-cooked Middlewhite pork belly with sweet potato purée, cucumber lychee salad, peanuts and sweet chilli coconut sauce, for example. To finish, apple and quince Charlotte with preserved lemon custard competes for your attention with peanut butter parfait served with a délice made with Original Beans 75% Piura Criolla chocolate, plus sea salt caramel and chocolate crumble.

Chef Peter Gordon, Thomas Sturrock **Owner** Peter Gordon, Adam Willis, Brandon Allan, Michael McGrath **Seats** 66 **Times** 12-11 All-day dining **Prices** Fixed D 3 course fr £21.95, Starter £6.50-£9, Main £16.50-£23.50, Dessert £6.50-£8.50 **Wines** 25 bottles over £30, 12 bottles under £30, 21 by glass **Parking** On street **Notes** Pre-theatre menu until 7pm Mon-Sat, Sun 9.30pm, Vegetarian available, Children welcome

Massimo Restaurant & Oyster Bar
PLAN 5 B6

◉ Modern Italian

tel: 020 7998 0555 **10 Northumberland Av WC2N 5AE**
email: tables@massimo-restaurant.co.uk
dir: *Nearest station: Embankment, Charing Cross*

Grand Roman style in the West End

The David Collins' designed interior certainly makes an impression with its soaring striped columns, magnificent light fittings, striking artworks and tables dressed up in white linen. It's a bold and exhilarating space to tuck into high quality seafood with an Italian flavour. There's a cool oyster bar where you can dive into Maldon, Loch Fyne, Irish Rock and Natives and accompany them with an oyster martini if it takes your fancy. There's loads of choice on the menu, so choosing may take a while: seared and peppered tuna with courgette fritters, or langoustines with rocket and Ligurian olive oil? Follow on with black tagliatelle with squid, carrot and courgette, and among 'carni' options you might find braised beef cheek with creamed potatoes. Top-quality seafood is the thing, though, such as a whole monkfish served with that Ligurian olive oil and Amalfi lemon, or lemon sole with tomato and anchovy sauce. To finish, Massimo's tiramisù is one way to go.

Chef Garry Hollihead **Owner** Corinthia Hotel London **Seats** 140, Pr/dining room 20 **Times** 12-3/6-11 Closed Sun **Prices** Fixed L 2 course £25, Fixed D 3 course £30, Starter £8-£20, Main £11-£45, Dessert £8-£11 **Wines** 10 by glass **Parking** Car park **Notes** Vegetarian available, Children welcome

Mon Plaisir
PLAN 3 B2

◉ Traditional French

tel: 020 7836 7243 **19-21 Monmouth St WC2H 9DD**
email: monplaisirrestaurant@googlemail.com **web:** www.monplaisir.co.uk
dir: *Nearest station: Covent Garden, Leicester Square*

Appealing French bistro food since the 1940s

The long-running Mon Plaisir near Seven Dials has been feeding London with deeply appealing French bistro food since not long after General de Gaulle departed his London exile. You might still imagine you'd been beamed up to the Boulevard St-Germain at sight of its only lightly reconstructed interior, although the bar was imported here from a house of ill repute in Lyon. The old modes often proving to be the best, the bilingual menu still deals in the likes of pork and chicken liver terrine, snails in garlic and pastis butter, and prawn and crayfish cocktail on herb salad to start, with follow-ups of plaice florentine in mornay, or casseroled wild boar with a tangle of tagliatelle. There is the odd swerve these days, to gather in salmon marinated in lime and coconut, or scallops with cauliflower puree and bacon, but the piste is firmly regained by the finish-line, with tarte Tatin, or rum baba with red fruit salad.

Chef Francois Jobard **Owner** Alain Lhermitte **Seats** 100, Pr/dining room 25 **Times** noon-11.15 Closed Xmas, New Year, BHs, Sun All-day dining **Prices** Fixed L 2 course £14.95, Fixed D 3 course £24.95, Starter £5.95-£18.95, Main £16.45-£22.95, Dessert £5.75-£6.95 **Wines** 50 bottles over £30, 21 bottles under £30, 20 by glass **Notes** Fixed D pre-theatre 2/3 course incl coffee £13.95/£15.95, Vegetarian available, Children welcome

The National Dining Room Sainsbury Square PLAN 3 A1

British **NEW**

tel: 020 7747 2525 **The National Gallery, Trafalgar Square WC2N 5DN**
email: ndr.reservations@peytonandbyrne.co.uk
dir: *Nearest station: Charing Cross*

Simple, seasonal cooking in a prime spot

The Peyton and Byrne team have bagged a dream location for this sleek modern all-day operation. Overlooking Trafalgar Square from the National Gallery, the place would never struggle to fill its tables, but there's a lot more to the cooking than a simple pit stop when you're checking out the art. The unfussy modern British repertoire is built on well-sourced materials and keeps an keen eye on the seasons, starting with a Cornish crab salad with Jersey Royals, gem leaves, wild herbs and cocktail sauce that has 'Spring' written all over it. Main course could be a superior take on an old friend – slow-cooked gammon with peppered pineapple, chips, a quails egg with crisp pancetta and home-made brown sauce – or you might trade up to John Dory with lentils, salsify, horseradish and Savoy cabbage. It all ends with a fun 'broken' lemon pie with crisp pastry atop the lemon curd filling and peaks of soft meringue all around.

Chef Gillan Kingstree **Owner** Oliver Peyton **Seats** 84 **Times** 10-5.30/5.30-8.30 Closed 24-26 Dec, 1 Jan, D Sat-Thu **Prices** Fixed L 2 course £27.50 **Wines** 8 bottles over £30, 14 bottles under £30, 13 by glass **Notes** Vegetarian available, Children welcome

The Northall PLAN 5 B6

Modern British **v**

tel: 020 7321 3100 **Corinthia Hotel London, 10A Northumberland Av WC2N 5AE**
email: northallenquiry@corinthia.com **web:** www.thenorthall.co.uk
dir: *Nearest station: Charing Cross, Embankment*

Quality ingredients impeccably cooked in stylish hotel

The Northall restaurant at the Corinthia, a luxury hotel just off Whitehall, is a vast designer-led space of high ceilings, tall windows, orange banquettes at correctly set unclothed tables, and plenty of flowers in evidence. The kitchen showcases the best of British produce (suppliers are named under each dish) and has assembled a crowd-pleasing menu of modern ideas as well as established classics like crab bisque and steaks from the Josper grill. Kick-off with an indulgent starter of pan-fried foie gras well complemented by roast mango and sauce Jacqueline, or something more unusual like céviche of scallops dressed with fermented lemons and edible flowers. Timings are spot on and combinations well thought out, so roast haunch of venison comes nicely caramelised outside, pink inside, served with spicy red cabbage and rich, sticky gravy. The kitchen's not too proud to turn its hand to burgers and beer-battered haddock, but its full creative talents are seen in puddings like a visually pleasing plate of vanilla parfait offset by a flawless cherry compôte and mint jelly.

Chef Garry Hollihead **Owner** Corinthia Hotel London **Seats** 185, Pr/dining room 30 **Times** 12-3/5.30-11 **Prices** Fixed L 2 course £25, Fixed D 3 course £30, Starter £6-£15, Main £12-£42, Dessert £8-£12 **Wines** 16 bottles over £30, 16 by glass **Parking** Valet parking **Notes** 3 course incl glass of champagne, Sunday L £45-£75, Children welcome

The Opera Tavern PLAN 3 C1

Spanish, Italian

tel: 020 7836 3680 **23 Catherine St, Covent Garden WC2B 5JS**
email: info@operatavern.co.uk
dir: *Nearest station: Covent Garden*

Knock your socks off Spanish and Italian tapas

When busy, which it usually is, The Opera Tavern hits all the right notes like a soprano in full flow at the nearby Opera House. From the team behind Salt Yard and Dehesa (see entries), the winning idea of combining the best of the tastes of Italy and Spain in dishes to share brings in the crowds. The one-time pub in the heart of theatreland has a vibrant ground-floor bar and grill (feel the heat at the far end of the room), with a little more refinement in the upstairs dining room; wherever you sit, the place positively throbs with energy. Friendly, clued-up staff will steer you through the entertaining fusion of Spanish and Italian ideas. The mini Ibérico pork and foie gras burger must surely be considered a classic by now, and the charcuterie and cheeses should not be ignored either. Smoked eel and pancetta brandade with free-range egg and horseradish velouté demonstrates the mettle of this kitchen. If tapas isn't your way, it's possible to stick to three-course convention.

Chef Jamie Thickett, Ben Tish **Owner** Simon Mullins, Sanya Morris, Ben Tish **Seats** 75 **Times** 12-3/5-11.30 Closed 25-26 Dec, some BHs, D Sun **Prices** Prices not confirmed **Wines** 24 by glass **Notes** Fixed Tapas menus 3 course over 7 people £35-£40, Vegetarian available, Children welcome

Orso PLAN 3 C1

Modern Italian

tel: 020 7240 5269 **27 Wellington St WC2E 7DA**
email: info@orsorestaurant.co.uk
dir: *Nearest station: Covent Garden*

Regional Italian food in a lively basement

Since 1975, savvy crowds have been flocking downstairs to this relaxed, all-day Covent Garden Italian tucked away in an expansive basement that was once an orchid warehouse. The place buzzes with conversation, clinking glasses and unstuffy, quick-fire service. It is all classic Italian from the herringbone-patterned wood floors, white tiled columns, terracotta walls and black-and-white photos, with their nod to Milan of the '50s, through to crowd-pleasing menus showcasing simple regional Italian cooking. A concise handful of pasta dishes offers the likes of tagliatelle with braised lamb, rosemary and tomato, while mains bring Tuscan 'cacciucco' – a seafood stew with hake, king prawns, cuttlefish, mussels, chilli & tomato – or slow-roasted crispy pork belly with cavolo nero and roast potatoes. At dessert, rhubarb makes a zingy foil to a textbook creamy vanilla pannacotta with candied fennel. A fixed-price pre-theatre option and all-Italian wine list add to the all-round appeal.

Times 12-12 Closed 24-25 Dec, L Sun (Jul-Aug) All-day dining

Get the most out of the AA Restaurant Guide

See page 6

LONDON WC2 *continued*

Savoy Grill
PLAN 3 C1

◉◉ British, French

tel: 020 7592 1600 **1 Savoy Hill, Strand WC2R OEU**
email: savoygrill@gordonramsay.com
dir: *Nearest station: Charing Cross*

Classically inspired cooking at a Premier League address

The Savoy's iconic Grill didn't escape the interior designer's hand in the zillion-pound makeover of the hotel, and quite frankly it looks drop-dead gorgeous. It's always been the place to see and be seen; from the Victorian literati to movie stars and the international jet-set, the handsome, low-lit art deco room inspires with its walnut panelling, mirrors and plush banquettes set beneath the glitter of chandeliers. The cooking is international, with classic foundations, yet it doesn't feel in the least bit old-fashioned. From the fish and shellfish section of the menu might come lobster Thermidor or Dover sole (grilled or meunière), while top-dollar grills from the wood charcoal oven take in British steaks (rib-eye to chateaubriand). There are 'roasts, braises and pies', such as steak-and-ale pudding or pot au feu of Hereford beef. Desserts adhere to the theme too, perhaps profiteroles or raspberry soufflé. Pricing is high, portions on the smaller side, and there's a £2 cover charge to factor in. However, the simpler lunch/pre-theatre option delivers good value. A heavyweight wine list fits the bill.

Times 12-3/5.30-11

Terroirs
PLAN 3 B1

◉◉ Mediterranean, European ◈ NOTABLE WINE LIST

tel: 020 7036 0660 **5 William IV St, Covent Garden WC2N 4DW**
email: enquiries@terroirswinebar.com
dir: *Nearest station: Covent Garden, Charing Cross*

French provincial cooking with flavours to the fore

Head to the ground floor, which takes its inspiration from Parisian wine bars, and have a glass of something good with a plate of charcuterie (perhaps pork and pistachio terrine), or one of the plats du jour (rump of lamb with cime di rapa and anchovies) – or spread out at one of the tables downstairs. Either way, the inspiration is the cooking of a provincial grand-mère, with ideas pulled in from the Mediterranean and even further afield: lamb kofta, for instance, with the punch of harissa softened by mint and yoghurt, a careful balance of heat and fragrance. Dishes are carefully considered so the integrity of each ingredient is clear. A salad of beetroot, lentils and ricotta is a lovely blend of flavours, at the same time earthy and delicate. Equally impressive is the stronger taste of braised oxtail with gnocchi, while main courses may take in full-on cassoulet, or cod fillet with monk's beard and brown shrimps. Puddings are appreciated for their simplicity, among them perhaps rhubarb tarte fine with custard, or rich chocolate pot.

Chef Sandy Jarvis **Owner** Ed Wilson, Oli Barker, Eric Narioo **Seats** 120 **Times** 12-11 Closed Xmas, New Year, Etr, BHs, Sun **Prices** Prices not confirmed **Wines** 200 bottles over £30, 30 bottles under £30, 18 by glass **Notes** Fixed 1 course L £10, Vegetarian available, Children welcome

BARNET Map 6 TQ29

Savoro Restaurant with Rooms

◉ Modern European, British

tel: 020 8449 9888 **206 High St EN5 5SZ**
email: savoro@savoro.co.uk **web:** www.savoro.co.uk
dir: *M25 junct 23 to A1081, continue to St Albans Rd, at lights turn left to A1000*

Contemporary good looks and well-judged menu

Set back from Barnet's bustling high street, the traditional frontage of this snazzy neighbourhood restaurant with rooms belies its contemporary good looks. Done out in clean-cut fashionable manner, with neutral tones, etched glass screens, mirrors and cream tiled floors, it provides the perfect backdrop for the kitchen's modern approach. The cooking encompasses British classics with the flavours of the Med and Asia. A well-conceived starter brings beetroot and cranberry relish as a foil to a full-flavoured baked goats' cheese soufflé, while a main-course pan-fried fillet of sea bass is matched to good effect with chargrilled calamari, warm tomato and fennel salad, crispy samphire and Chardonnay dressing. Or you might go for something meatier such as roast rump of lamb with boulangère potatoes, broccoli and rosemary gravy. A range of steaks and fish from the grill covers all the bases, while desserts continue the style with vanilla pannacotta with rhubarb and mango jelly.

Chef Jozef Konco, Jameer Bhatkar **Owner** Jack Antoni, Dino Paphiti **Seats** 68 **Times** 12-3/6-11 Closed 1 Jan, 1 wk New Year, D Sun **Prices** Fixed L 2 course £11.95-£14.95, Fixed D 3 course fr £27.95, Starter £5-£7, Main £18-£25, Dessert £6-£7 **Wines** 12 by glass **Parking** 9 **Notes** Early eve menu Mon-Thu 2 course £11.95, Sunday L £19.95-£22.95, Vegetarian available, Children welcome

BROMLEY

Chapter One
PLAN 1 H1

◉◉◉◉ – *see opposite*

Chapter One

BROMLEY   PLAN 1 H1

Modern European V

tel: 01689 854848 **Farnborough Common,
Locksbottom BR6 8NF**
email: info@chaptersrestaurants.com
web: www.chaptersrestaurants.com
dir: *On A21, 3m from Bromley. From M25 junct 4 onto A21
for 5m*

Strikingly refined cooking in out-of-town hotspot

To prove that central London is not the be all and end all of
dining within the M25, step forward Chapter One. And when
it comes to culinary luminaries working within striking
distance of the bright lights, but pointedly away from the
hubbub, no one shines brighter than Andrew McLeish. It all
takes place in a rather unassuming landscape, but once
you're through the contemporary entranceway, it starts to
make sense. The Tudor house has been made over with a
good deal of style and there's plenty of on-site parking if
you're concerned about the practical stuff. The decor meets
contemporary expectations when it comes to its colour
palette (neutral tones of coffee and cream) and its level of
refinement (tables dressed to impress), and it's all watched
over by a professional service team. It must be considered
very good value, too, for the pricing is considerably below

what you'd pay for similar quality food a few miles to the
north west, and the Menu du Jour (available at lunchtimes
from Monday to Friday), is an absolute bargain. Expect
beautifully crafted dishes that have at their heart superb
ingredients, with lots of creative touches and finely tuned
flavours. A starter of quail Kiev, for example, is a delightful
plate, with the bird's roasted leg, herb mayonnaise,
dandelion leaf and gruyère, while another first course
combines a fricassée of wild rabbit with roast gnocchi and
butternut purée. The craft and creativity continues into main
courses such as poached Loch Duart salmon, partnered with
an étuvée of leeks, baby artichokes and vanilla mayonnaise,
and another that consists of poached and roasted haunch of
venison (from Chart Farm) with confit shoulder and a shallot
tarte Tatin. If you're in the mood for something comfortingly
direct and to the point, the Josper grill works its magic on
USDA prime rib-eye served with twice-cooked chunky chips
and béarnaise sauce. The quality is maintained when it gets
to dessert stage, where baked lemon tart with blood orange
sorbet and orange sherbet, or hot Valrhona chocolate
fondant with chocolate soil and griottines cherries await.
Like everything else at Chapter One, the wine list has been
put together with care and attention, with the bottles visible
behind tempered glass, where temperature and humidity are
controlled to ensure they reach you in tip-top condition.

Chef Andrew McLeish **Owner** Selective Restaurants Group
Seats 120, Pr/dining room 55 **Times** 12-2.30/6.30-10.30
Closed 2-4 Jan **Prices** Fixed L 3 course fr £19.95, Starter
£5-£9.25, Main £17-£21, Dessert £5.50-£8.25 **Wines** 20
bottles over £30, 20 bottles under £30, 13 by glass
Parking 90 **Notes** Brasserie menu light lunches available
Mon-Sat 12-3pm, Sunday L £22.95, Children welcome

ENFIELD

Map 6 TQ39

Royal Chace Hotel

Modern British

tel: 020 8884 8181 **162 The Ridgeway EN2 8AR**
email: reservations@royalchacehotel.co.uk **web:** www.royal-chace.com
dir: *3m from M25 junct 24, 1.5m to Enfield*

Imaginative cooking in an elegant setting with rural views

There's some bright, modern cooking going on at this large hotel that caters for weddings and conferences, and it's a useful spot to know about in the outer-reaches of North London. There are pretty gardens – good for those wedding photos – and some rather splendid function spaces, while The Kings Restaurant puts the venue on the culinary map. It's a rather elegant room with a large skylight and an swish finish (linen cloths, fresh flowers, that sort of thing), and what comes out of the kitchen is some smart modern British fare. Seared hand-dived scallops might come with a white fish and Puy lentil mousse, a trendy golden raisin purée and crustacean broth, or how about Gressingham duck confit with sweet pickled candy beetroot and foie gras ravioli? Main-course delivers the likes of a trio of Saddleback pork, and dessert a Hertfordshire rhubarb fool with toffee popcorn and sesame crisp.

Times 12-9.30 Closed D Sun All-day dining

HADLEY WOOD

Map 6 TQ29

West Lodge Park Hotel

Modern British

tel: 020 8216 3900 **Cockfosters Rd EN4 OPY**
email: westlodgepark@bealeshotels.co.uk **web:** www.bealeshotel.co.uk
dir: *On A111, 1m S of M25 junct 24*

Polished cooking in a parkland setting

The restaurant at this imposing white mansion takes its name from the portraitist Mary Beale, an ancestor of the owners, whose works hang on the walls. This is a stylish room, given a contemporary look, with well-spaced tables and light streaming in from huge windows looking over the surrounding parkland, and there's summer dining on the terrace. The kitchen makes good use of local produce and cooks in a confidently unfussy style. Game terrine balanced by home-made tomato and onion chutney is an impressive starter, and there could be a more modish pairing of seared scallops and oxtail sauce with cauliflower purée. Main courses run from boeuf bourguignon through Madras chicken curry to accurately cooked sea bass fillets with lemon butter, croquette potatoes, carrots and spinach. To finish a soufflé – perhaps spicy apple and sultana with blackberry custard – is well worth the 20-minute wait.

Times 12.30-2.30/7-9.30

HARROW ON THE HILL

Incanto Restaurant

PLAN 1 B5

Modern Italian NOTABLE WINE LIST

tel: 020 8426 6767 **The Old Post Office, 41 High St HA1 3HT**
email: info@incanto.co.uk **web:** www.incanto.co.uk
dir: *M4 junct 3 at Target rdbt, follow signs A312 Harrow. Continue through South Harrow, turn right at Roxeth Hill, turn left at top of hill*

Ambitious regional Italian cooking with a refined light modern touch

While Incanto's enticing street-side deli-café would make an inspired tuckshop choice for students of the famed Harrow school (just yards away), it's the clean-lined restaurant stretching out behind that's the culinary big hitter at this former Victorian post office turned vibrant modern Italian. Inside the long loft-like, split-level space boasts a glass skylight, bold beams, darkwood tables and fashionable seating, while distinctive artwork provides colour. Southern Italian-inspired dishes are the thing (alongside a more general nod to the Med), the ambitious kitchen delivering light, fresh, refined dishes that look pretty on the plate and are conjured from prime produce. Think Scottish lobster lasagnetta (its delicate pasta layers rammed with succulent lobster meat) served with a lobster sauce and Prosecco foam for a hit of luxury. Mains follow suit, perhaps sparkling-fresh brill fillet teamed with monk's beard, Jersey Royal potato 'crisps', fennel purée and squeaky fresh English asparagus and the refreshing crunch of breakfast radishes. Desserts, like a top-call wobbly vanilla pod pannacotta, might come with smoky pineapple and big-hit pineapple sorbet. There's a classy Italian-dominated wine list and genuinely friendly, informed service.

Chef Ciprian Marginean **Owner** David & Catherine Taylor **Seats** 64, Pr/dining room 30
Times 12-2.30/6.30-10.30 Closed 24-26 Dec, 1 Jan, Etr Sun, Mon, D Sun
Prices Fixed L 2 course £17.95, Fixed D 3 course £23.95, Tasting menu £42.50-£55, Starter £6.50-£9, Main £14.50-£22.50, Dessert £5.50-£7.50 **Wines** 82 bottles over £30, 28 bottles under £30, 14 by glass **Parking** On street **Notes** Sunday L £20-£37, Vegetarian available, Children welcome

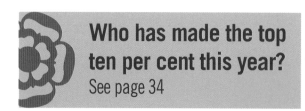

Who has made the top ten per cent this year?
See page 34

Looking for a London restaurant by name?
Use the index on page 254

HARROW WEALD

Best Western Plus Grim's Dyke Hotel   PLAN 1 B5

British, European

tel: 020 8385 3100 **Old Redding HA3 6SH**
email: reservations@grimsdyke.com **web:** www.grimsdyke.com
dir: 3m from M1 between Harrow & Watford

Modern British cooking in a country setting

The former home of Sir William Gilbert of 'and Sullivan' fame, Grim's Dyke is a rather grand house standing in 40 acres of grounds, including primped gardens and natural woodland. The hotel has made good use of the capacious features of the house, not least in Gilbert's Restaurant, which occupies the space that was once the great man's billiard room. Traditional decor remains in keeping with the building, the formal tone maintained by the uniformed service team. The chef trained under Gary Rhodes and displays evident affection for English classics such as fish and chips and Lancashire hotpot, but there's a lot more going on here, expanding into the modern British repertoire which itself entails some global flavours and broader European influences. Ham hock terrine with piccalilli and toast, or a crispy oriental duck salad are two possibilities when it comes to first courses, followed perhaps by calves' liver, creamed potato and razor thin shards of crispy pancetta. There is a classic roast option for Sunday lunch, and desserts such as a tangy lemon tart.

Chef Daren Mason **Owner** Skerrits of Nottingham Holdings **Seats** 60, Pr/dining room 88 **Times** 12.30-2/7-9.30 Closed 24 Dec, 1 Jan, L Sat, D 25-26 Dec **Prices** Fixed D 3 course fr £28.50, Starter £5-£8.50, Main £10-£25, Dessert £5-£7.50, Service optional **Wines** 25 bottles over £30, 20 bottles under £30, 10 by glass **Parking** 100 **Notes** Sunday L fr £24.95, Vegetarian available, Children welcome

HEATHROW AIRPORT (LONDON)

La Belle Époque   PLAN 1 A3

– see below

The Continental Hotel   PLAN 1 B2

Modern European

tel: 020 8572 3131 & 8538 5883 **29-31 Lampton Rd TW3 1JA**
email: f&b@thecontinental-hotel.com **web:** www.thecontinental-hotel.com
dir: A4, right onto A3006, left onto A3005 then left onto Lampton Rd

Modern European brasserie cooking near Heathrow

A spa hotel near Heathrow Airport will look like an essential resource if you've just spent nine hours in an economy seat, but is a useful addition all-round to the gastronomically impoverished Hounslow area. A stylish cocktail bar with gigantosaurus TV screen showing live sport is only the half of it. Youthful staff contribute to the vivacious ambience, and the menu in the Twentynine restaurant draws on modern European brasserie style to good effect in a rollcall of on-trend dishes. Start with venison ravioli topped with shaved parmesan, or seared scallops with beignets and purée of cauliflower or butternut squash. Flavourful lamb shank comes with apposite garnishes of roast garlic mash, honeyed parsnip and a Madeira jus, while fish might be grilled salmon with creamed leeks in caviar beurre blanc. Finish with coconut and vanilla pannacotta and orange coulis, classic tiramisù, or an Anglo-European cheese selection with tomato relish.

Chef Palash Roy **Owner** Vistastar Leisure Plc **Seats** 36 **Times** 12.30-10.30 All-day dining **Prices** Fixed L 2 course £12-£20, Fixed D 3 course £15-£22, Starter £4.95-£7.95, Main £8.95-£16.95, Dessert £4.50-£5.95 **Wines** 5 bottles over £30, 9 bottles under £30, 6 by glass **Parking** 19 **Notes** Pre-theatre 2/3 course £20/£25, Sunday L, Vegetarian available, Children welcome

La Belle Époque

HEATHROW AIRPORT (LONDON)   PLAN1 A3

French

tel: 020 8757 7777 **Sofitel London Heathrow, Terminal 5, London Heathrow Airport TW6 2GD**
email: H6214-FB9@sofitel.com
dir: M25 junct 14, follow signs to Terminal 5

Fine dining only a short walk from Terminal 5

The Heathrow branch of this international chain of hotels is an ultra-modern building, with a covered walkway linking to Terminal 5. There are seemingly eating and drinking options every which way you look, from cocktails in Sphere to champers in the Perrier-Jouët Bar, and from an open-kitchen venue to a tea salon. The whole place indeed seems designed to make you forget you're in an airport, or at least induce you to cancel your flight and get bedded in for a longer stay. La Belle Epoque restaurant is the hot ticket, a capacious room of strikingly contemporary design, with generously spaced tables and banquette seating. The name alone is a proclamation of the kitchen's culinary orientation, but the style is anything but preserved in aspic. Tea-smoked mallard is sliced and rolled, and comes with balled rillettes of confit leg, lightly dusted with pistachios and served with wafer-thin slices of subtly pickled poached nashi pear. Main courses are notable for their clarity and balance of flavours, as well as the outstanding quality of prime materials, seen in mint-crusted, pink-cooked rack of lamb, perfectly timed, served with a crisp, golden spring roll tightly packed with shredded shoulder meat, and two squares of confit belly, accompanied by an intense tomato emulsion, a swipe of vibrant pea purée, a scattering of petitspois, roasted garlic and a viscous, deeply flavoured red wine sauce. Standards of desserts are just as high, perhaps a mango sorbet and pistachio bonbon with smooth and delicate mango mousse and a rather more assertive citrus compôte aromatised with rose tea. Incidentals are up to the mark, too, as in an appetiser of richly concentrated langoustine bisque with a dollop of crabmeat on a finger of toasted brioche.

Chef Daren Pavey **Owner** Surinder Arora **Seats** 88, Pr/dining room 20 **Times** 12-2.30/6-10 Closed Xmas, New Year, BHs, Sun **Prices** Fixed L 2 course £29-£40, Fixed D 3 course £37-£53, Starter £8.50-£11.50, Main £20-£33, Dessert £8.50 **Wines** 10 by glass **Parking** 400 **Notes** Vegetarian available, Children welcome

HEATHROW AIRPORT (LONDON) *continued*

Vivre Restaurant
PLAN 1 A3

◉ International NEW

tel: 020 8757 5027 & 8757 7777 **Sofitel London Heathrow, Terminal 5,
Wentworth Dr, London Heathrow Airport TW6 2GD**
email: vivre@sofitelheathrow.com
dir: *M25 junct 14, follow signs to Terminal 5*

Assured international cooking from an open-to-view kitchen

The Heathrow Sofitel boasts more decent eating than many an airport hotel. Head for Terminal 5 and walk through. As an alternative to the fine French goings-on in La Belle Époque, Vivre is the place to repair for a more informal dining experience. It's an open-plan room full of vibrantly colourful contemporary design, the kitchen team on view at their wokking, pizza-throwing and grilling, and service that aims to put everyone at their ease. The large menu changes seasonally, but is built around a core of stalwarts cooked with assurance. Among the international offerings of note are tempura-battered king prawns with tonkatsu sweet chilli dip and a crunchy salad, mildly spiced Indian butter chicken with a side of spinach, served with the full monty of naan bread, poppadums and fluffy basmati rice, and French-style glazed apple frangipane tart with light puff pastry, served with rip-roaringly rich clotted cream ice cream.

Chef Daren Pavey **Seats** 235 **Times** 6-10.30 **Closed** L all week **Prices** Fixed L 2 course £24.50, Starter £7.25-£8.50, Main £13.75-£29.50, Dessert £7-£7.50 **Wines** 24 bottles over £30, 6 bottles under £30, 19 by glass **Notes** Vegetarian available, Children welcome

Herbert's
◉◉ Modern European

tel: 01689 855501 **6 Commonside BR2 6BP**
email: info@thisisherberts.co.uk
dir: *M25 junct 4, follow A21 Bromley*

Ambitious modern fare and a relaxing atmosphere

A white property on Keston Common is the home of Herbert's, an oak-floored space with oval-backed chairs at wooden-topped tables and a warm and relaxing atmosphere. A new chef is at the helm, continuing to cook in the modern European mode and to devise menus with headings such as 'stream and sea' and 'four legs (or two)'. Imaginative starters may run to prawns in white wine with gremolata, or pheasant ballottine with mushroom and beetroot dressing. Ingredients are well chosen and handled confidently so flavours are clear. Pork belly, served with apple sauce, red cabbage and pommes purée, is the sort of mainstream main course to expect, and fish is properly treated, seen in pan-fried mackerel partnered by pancetta, accompanied by cockle dressing, roast onions and new potatoes, and cod fillet given a kick from Madeira jus accompanied by ham hock mash. Finish with a comforting dessert like cinnamon-flavoured rice pudding with poached plums, or lemon curd tart with crème fraîche ice cream and passionfruit coulis.

Chef Angela Herbert-Bell **Owner** Angela Herbert-Bell **Seats** 48, Pr/dining room 32 **Times** 12-3/6.30-10 **Closed** Mon-Tue (ex BHs), D Sun **Prices** Prices not confirmed **Wines** 12 bottles over £30, 12 bottles under £30, 10 by glass **Parking** Free car park 1min walk away **Notes** Fixed L 2/3 course includes tea/coffee, D 3 course Wed-Fri, Sunday L, Vegetarian available, Children welcome

The Glasshouse

KEW
PLAN 1 C3

Modern International
tel: 020 8940 6777 **14 Station Pde TW9 3PZ**
email: info@glasshouserestaurant.co.uk
dir: *Just outside Kew Gardens underground station*

French-based cooking of exemplary consistency in a modern setting

This perennially popular neighbourhood restaurant's name comes from the floor-to-ceiling plate glass windows that stand out in the village-like parade of shops near Kew Gardens tube station, and make for a luminous, unbuttoned and slickly neutral contemporary setting. With Bruce Poole and Nigel Platts-Martin (the team behind the equally in-vogue Chez Bruce in Wandsworth and La Trompette in Chiswick) at the helm, you can rest assured that this place is all about seasonally driven modern European cooking that hits the high notes without seeming to try too hard, built upon the solid foundations of classical French cuisine bourgeoise (rather than the posturing of the haute variety). A rich, simple and sumptuous opening dish of rabbit lasagne is layered with green spinach pasta, spiked with fresh tarragon and given extra depth by the addition of parmesan velouté and pickled mushrooms, or there might be a warm salad of smoked eel with salt-baked beetroot, apple and salsify and a beignet of cod. It takes formidable technical skills to make these ideas seem effortless, and main course brings a similarly accomplished layering of flavours and textures in a dish of sea-fresh Cornish cod, supported by poached prawns, parsley gnocchi, charred fennel and a deeply flavoured lobster bisque. Meatier ideas could see breast and stuffed leg of guinea-fowl accompanied by potato gratin into which curry-leaves have been inveigled, the Indian note accentuated with black lentil sauce and coriander pesto. At dessert stage, a pannacotta-like baked white chocolate custard with crunchy honeycomb, damson syrup and gin sauce shows a firm grasp of how flavours work together, or pastry skills might come into play for painstakingly constructed apple tarte fine with ginger ice cream and caramel sauce. Conscientious and clued-up staff are the icing on the cake, and there's a serious wine list to support the kitchen's efforts.

Chef Berwyn Davies **Owner** Nigel Platts-Martin, Bruce Poole **Seats** 60 **Times** 12-2.30/6.30-10.30 **Closed** Xmas, New Year **Prices** Fixed L 2 course £23.50-£27.50, Fixed D 3 course fr £42.50 **Wines** 397 bottles over £30, 29 bottles under £30, 15 by glass **Parking** On street (metered) **Notes** Sunday L £22.50-£32.50, Vegetarian available, Children welcome

The Glasshouse

PLAN 1 C3

⚜⚜⚜ – *see opposite*

Friends Restaurant

PLAN 1 B5

⚜ Modern British

tel: 020 8866 0286 **11 High St HA5 5PJ**
email: info@friendsrestaurant.co.uk **web:** www.friendsrestaurant.co.uk
dir: *In centre of Pinner, 2 mins walk from underground station*

Heartwarming French bistro fare in an old timbered house

In the 20 years or so since chef-patron Terry Farr established Friends in a picture-postcard black-and-white timbered 400-year-old cottage, it has become a fixture on the local foodie scene. The interior is similarly monochrome, but with a sharp, contemporary look – black leather seats at white linen tables, and modern Provençal artwork that hints at where the kitchen's heart lies. After two decades in business, local supply lines are strong, while top-grade meat and fish comes from Smithfield and Billingsgate markets. Tried-and-true French bistro cooking jazzed up with sound modern thinking is the deal here. To start, wild mushroom risotto is supercharged with porcini oil and parmesan tuile, followed by a classic trio of sautéed South Downs lamb fillet with creamy dauphinoise potatoes and flageolet beans. At the end, a compôte of rhubarb and balsamic and hazelnut biscotti prove the perfect foil to rhubarb pannacotta.

Chef Terry Farr **Owner** Terry Farr **Seats** 40, Pr/dining room 30 **Times** 12-3/6.30-10.30 Closed 25 Dec, BHs, Mon, D Sun **Prices** Fixed L 2 course £19.50-£20.50, Fixed D 3 course £33.50-£34.50, Starter £7.50-£8.75, Main £17.50-£25, Dessert £7.50-£8.50 **Wines** 21 bottles over £30, 23 bottles under £30, 16 by glass **Parking** Nearby car parks **Notes** Pre-jazz season D 3 course (incl wine) £20 Oct-Apr from 6pm, Sunday L £24-£29.50, Vegetarian available, Children welcome

Bacco Restaurant Italiano

PLAN 1 C2

⚜ Italian

tel: 020 8332 0348 **39-41 Kew Rd TW9 2NQ**
email: bookings@bacco-restaurant.co.uk
dir: *A316 towards Richmond Station or town centre, 2 min walk from tube*

Family hospitality and traditional Italian cooking

There is a thoroughly charming air of family hospitality to this Italian eatery opposite Richmond Station and near to the Orange Tree Theatre. Linen-clothed tables look smart, and there is much to divert the eye in the shape of the colourful prints and paintings that crowd the pale yellow walls. Italian simplicity is the hallmark of the bilingual menus, although this isn't a kitchen to rest on its laurels. The pasta is freshly made in-house every day, perhaps for spaghetti served in a parmesan basket dressed in truffle oil. That might follow a bowl of traditional fish and shellfish soup with chick peas and garlic crostino, while mains run to calves' liver in sage butter with stewed cabbage, and well-seasoned sea bass with cherry tomatoes, black olives and capers in white wine sauce. Traditional tiramisù is a satisfying way to finish, or there may be vanilla pannacotta with mango coulis. A range of quality Italian wines completes the picture.

Chef Vito Fanara **Owner** Stefano Bergamin **Seats** 50, Pr/dining room 27 **Times** 12-2.30/5.45-11 Closed Xmas, New Year, BHs, D Sun **Prices** Fixed L 2 course £15-£18, Fixed D 2 course £15-£35, Starter £7-£11, Main £12-£24.50, Dessert £4.50-£6 **Wines** 20 bottles over £30, 30 bottles under £30, 16 by glass **Notes** Sunday L £15-£30, Vegetarian available, Children welcome

Bingham

PLAN 1 C2

⚜⚜⚜ – *see page 404*

La Buvette

PLAN 1 C2

⚜ French, Mediterranean ∇

tel: 020 8940 6264 **6 Church Walk TW9 1SN**
email: info@labuvette.co.uk
dir: *3 mins from train station, opposite St Mary Magdalene Church, off main High St on corner of Tesco Metro*

Cheery bistro serving French classics and more

If the sun is shining on Richmond-upon-Thames, La Buvette's courtyard tables come into their own, but this place is a winner all-year-round when it comes to classic, bistro-style dining. It's a real neighbourhood joint, down a leafy walkway of the main high street, with closely packed tables and a menu of familiar dishes backed up by daily specials. A starter of rabbit and pork terrine with onion marmalade is one way to kick off, or go for scallops in a flavour-packed plateful with broad beans, bacon and persillade. Main-course braised shin of pork comes with black pudding and hispi cabbage, and there's roast salmon with crushed new potatoes and sorrel cream sauce. There's steak, too, in the form of chargrilled onglet, served rare, with garlic butter, chips and salad, and a plate of artisan French cheeses if you're more. Dessert delivers old favourites such as crème brûlée and a charlotte made with Yorkshire rhubarb.

Chef Buck Carter **Owner** Bruce Duckett **Seats** 50 **Times** 12-3/5.45-10 Closed 25-26 Dec, 1 Jan, Good Fri, Etr Sun **Prices** Fixed L 2 course £16.50, Fixed D 3 course £22, Starter £5.25-£9.50, Main £13.50-£18.50, Dessert £5.25-£6.75 **Wines** 16 bottles over £30, 18 bottles under £30, 11 by glass **Parking** NCP - Paradise Road **Notes** Sunday L, Children welcome

RICHMOND UPON THAMES *continued*

The Dysart Petersham

PLAN 1 C2

◉◉ Modern British **v**

tel: 020 8940 8005 **135 Petersham Rd, Petersham TW10 7AA**
email: enquiries@thedysartarms.co.uk
dir: *Opposite the pedestrian gate to Richmond Park*

Fantastic ingredients used creatively in an Arts and Crafts setting

The decor at The Dysart is neutrally simple the better to show off the original details in the 1904 Arts and Crafts building like the leaded windows and wooden window frames. The oak bar is even older, bought in 1850 from decommissioned French warships. The building faces south over Richmond Park, so sunshine streams in in summer and a log-burning stove adds cheer on gloomy winter days. Kenneth Culhane is a confident cook whose experimental approach results in some deeply flavoured dishes. How about hand-dived scallops with fennel, wakame and roasted popcorn dashi broth for starters, or charred mackerel with kombu-braised daikon, ginger and champagne? Not everything is unfamiliar, and a classical training is evident, with a spotlight on top-end raw materials. Perhaps start with veal sweetbreads with black truffle vinaigrette and candied walnuts. Proceed to wild halibut fillet in a Viennese crust with well-made vin jaune sauce, or roast mallard with classic bigarade (orange) sauce and celeriac croustillante. Meals end strongly with such puddings as tonka bean crème brûlée, or burnt honey custard with Chablis apple.

Chef Kenneth Culhane **Owner** Mr & Mrs W N Taylor **Seats** 50, Pr/dining room 40 **Times** 11.30-3/5.30-11.30 Closed D Sun **Prices** Fixed L 2 course £18.50, Fixed D 3 course £22.50, Tasting menu £60, Starter £7.50-£15, Main £15.95-£31.95, Dessert £6.50-£9.50, Service optional **Wines** 122 bottles over £30, 42 bottles under £30, 16 by glass **Parking** 30 **Notes** Sun L Prix Fixe 3 course £32, Sunday L £20.50-£23.95, Children welcome

The Petersham Hotel

PLAN 1 C2

◉◉ British, European **v**

tel: 020 8939 1084 & 8940 7471 **Nightingale Ln TW10 6UZ**
email: restaurant@petershamhotel.co.uk **web:** www.petershamhotel.co.uk
dir: *From Richmond Bridge rdbt A316 follow Ham & Petersham signs. Hotel in Nightingale Ln on left off Petersham Rd*

Classic cookery overlooking a bend of the Thames

Built on the side of Richmond Hill in 1865, the Petersham is master of all it surveys, which takes in a stretch of the Thames and its surrounding meadows, the view best enjoyed from the terrace. Sports fans note: it's not too far from the rugby at Twickenham either. The dining room capitalises on the location with its own views over the river bend, and with comfortable banquette seating and smartly dressed tables, a sense of high-toned relaxation is assured. Alex Bentley divides the culinary operations between a slate of Petersham classics, which run from potted shrimps in lobster butter to ribeye steaks, veal escalope with pasta, and Dover sole in beurre noisette, and a seasonal specials deal. In winter, the latter might turn up pork and smoked ham terrine with pickled veg, followed by a ritzy take on coq au vin with ox tongue, choucroute and a braising liquor fragrant with orange and juniper. Finishers include rum baba with rum and raisin compôte, or classic rhubarb pavlova.

Chef Alex Bentley **Owner** The Petersham Hotel Ltd **Seats** 70, Pr/dining room 26 **Times** 12.15-2.15/7-9.45 Closed 25-26 Dec, 1 Jan, D 24 Dec **Prices** Fixed L 2 course £22.95, Fixed D 3 course £26.95, Starter £10.50-£14.50, Main £16.50-£34, Dessert £8-£12.50 **Wines** 93 bottles over £30, 34 bottles under £30, 8 by glass **Parking** 45 **Notes** Degustation menu 5 course £95, Sunday L £34.50, Children welcome

Bingham

RICHMOND UPON THAMES

PLAN 1 C2

Modern British **v** ⚑ NOTABLE WINE LIST

tel: 020 8940 0902 & 8940 8009 **61-63 Petersham Rd TW10 6UT**
email: info@thebingham.co.uk **web:** www.thebingham.co.uk
dir: *On A307, near Richmond Bridge*

Peerless produce cooked with intelligent simplicity beside the river

With so many chain restaurants dominating the centre of town, this little independently run boutique hotel just a short stroll along the river is a breath of fresh air. It occupies a rather handsome pair of Georgian townhouses, with gorgeous Thames views from the covered balcony (the hot ticket for alfresco dining during the summer months), and an interior that could have come straight out of a glossy design magazine. The chosen colour palette is one of easy-on-the-eye neutral hues, with statement teardrop chandeliers and cleverly recessed lights softly illuminating the glamorous dining rooms – a sexy boudoir scene of velvety curvaceous banquettes and chairs in pale gold, feature mirrors and silk curtains. It's a glamorous setting indeed, but it certainly doesn't upstage the cooking of Mark Jarvis, a talented chef who has the good sense to source

impeccable, sustainably produced ingredients, mostly from the local area, and to do as little as possible to them so their natural flavours just sing out. Thus a starter of Cornish mackerel offers crisp-skinned grilled fillet alongside vibrantly fresh tartare, accompanied by poached and puréed William pear, while violet artichoke salad comes with duck egg, mint and aged balsamic – a lovely, light, fresh dish that's a joy to eat. Main-course line-caught cod is perfectly timed and well-served by plump mussels, samphire and puréed parsnip, with curry-spiced sabayon on the side, while tender venison is paired classically with chestnut, pickled celery and bitter chocolate. The technical skill on show here is without question, and that extends to desserts like bitter chocolate with marzipan, sorrel and chocolate mousse, or sliced apple cooked in cinnamoned beurre noisette, with hazelnuts and stunning barley malt ice cream. The excellent cheeses come from Teddington Cheese just down the road, and if cocktails are your thing, it's worth stopping off at the bar before you leave.

Chef Mark Jarvis **Owner** Ruth & Samantha Trinder **Seats** 40, Pr/dining room 90 **Times** 12-2.30/7-10 Closed D Sun **Prices** Fixed L 2 course fr £25, Fixed D 3 course fr £25, Tasting menu fr £65, Starter £12.50-£16.50, Main £22.50-£30, Dessert £8.50-£12.50 **Wines** 14 by glass **Parking** 8, Town centre **Notes** Tasting menu 8 course, Pre-theatre 2 course menu, Sunday L £38, Children welcome

Petersham Nurseries Café

PLAN 1 C2

Modern British, Italian

tel: 020 8940 5230 **Church Ln, Petersham Rd TW10 7AG**
email: info@petershamnurseries.com
dir: Adjacent to Richmond Park & Petersham Meadows. Best accessed on foot or bicycle along the river

Fresh, vibrant cooking from garden to plate

Having gained a foodie following under Skye Gyngell ('til her departure in 2012), this charmingly ramshackle glasshouse restaurant still packs in the crowds. It's a romantically eccentric, shabby-chic place, best enjoyed on sunny days when it feels more Tuscany than Richmond, with its dirt floor, mismatched tables and chairs and riot of leafy fronds. It's a dress-down affair (old shoes rather than heels), but then that's all part of the fun. The kitchen's modern European approach is inspired by the seasons and the bounty of fresh produce that flows from the garden (including edible flowers and herbs straight from the walled potager). Witness simple, light dishes like a roast pepper and fennel salad (with basil aïoli) to accompany sea-fresh halibut, or a wild garlic, garden bean, and crème fraîche and almond partnership for a more gutsy flavoured lamb shoulder. Be warned though, prices are high and parking tricky. (The adjacent glasshouse is a more accessibly priced all-day teahouse.)

Chef Cat Ashton **Owner** Franceso & Gael Boglione **Times** 12-2.45 Closed Etr Sun, 25 Dec, Mon, D all week **Prices** Prices not confirmed **Wines** 11 by glass **Parking** Town Centre, Paradise Road or The Quadrant **Notes** Vegetarian available, Children welcome

Richmond Hill Hotel

PLAN 1 C2

Modern European

tel: 020 8939 0265 **144-150 Richmond Hill TW10 6RW**
email: info.richmond@kewgreen.co.uk **web:** www.richmondhill-hotel.co.uk
dir: A316 for Richmond, hotel at top of Richmond Hill

Riverside dining in Richmond

The oldest part of this upmarket hotel dates from the 1720s and while the Georgian charm of its period features abounds inside and out, and its position overlooking the Thames and Richmond Park is positively idyllic, the chintz has been definitively chucked out here. The place sports a pleasingly unshouty contemporary finish, particularly in the Pembrokes Restaurant and Bar, where smart pastel tones mingle with burnished darkwood floors and tables. The menu deals in the familiar comforts of uncomplicated modern European dishes, spiked with occasional Eastern influences, opening with the likes of ham hock terrine with piccalilli and crostini, followed by confit lamb shoulder and grilled rump with boulangère potatoes and creamed broad beans. That Eastern edge might appear in grilled salmon with sweet teriyaki sauce, noodles and Asian greens, or a mini prawn spring roll to accompany grilled sea bass with samphire and chargrilled new potatoes.

Times 10.30am-10.30pm All-day dining

Read all about our Wine Award winners
on page 17

The Barn Hotel

PLAN 1 A5

Modern French

tel: 01895 636057 **West End Rd HA4 6JB**
email: info@thebarnhotel.co.uk **web:** www.thebarnhotel.co.uk
dir: A40 onto A4180 (Polish War Memorial) exit to Ruislip. 2m to hotel entrance at mini-rdbt before Ruislip tube station

Assertive modern cooking at a Middlesex boutique hotel

An expansive modern boutique hotel handy for inward-bound travellers at Heathrow, the Barn might sound rather agricultural, but stands in fact in three acres of attractive landscaped gardens, and has all the business facilities you might need. A Jacobethan effect has been created in the dark-panelled dining room, Hawtrey's, where classical music plays, and the scene is set with chandeliers, spotlit oil paintings, and painstaking descriptions of the dishes as they're delivered. Chef Vic Ramana cooked his way around the Indian Ocean before arriving in Middlesex, and there's a refreshing breadth of appeal to the menus. Langoustine in squid-ink tortellini with pak choi is a dramatic starter, and big, convincing flavours distinguish potted duck with cranberry jelly and pickled veg, as well as slow-cooked pork belly with black pudding crushed potatoes, an onion bhaji and raisin purée. An assertive approach to fish sees roast brill and calamari offset with red pepper tapenade, a ragout of mange-tout and clam-flavoured foam. Technically impressive desserts include a chocolate sponge roll filled with pistachio parfait, served with clearly defined Bailey's ice cream.

Chef Vic Ramana **Owner** Pantheon Hotels & Leisure **Seats** 44, Pr/dining room 20 **Times** 12-2.30/7-10.30 Closed L Sat, D Sun **Prices** Prices not confirmed **Wines** 9 by glass **Parking** 50 **Notes** Sunday L, Children welcome

The French Table

PLAN 1 C1

French, Mediterranean NOTABLE WINE LIST

tel: 020 8399 2365 **85 Maple Rd KT6 4AW**
email: enquiries@thefrenchtable.co.uk
dir: 5 min walk from Surbiton station, 1m from Kingston

Contemporary French dining with panache in the suburbs

The French Table is a class act. The setting in a parade of shops might lead you to thinking this is a humble neighbourhood place, when in fact Eric and Sarah Guignard's restaurant is a little power-house of contemporary French cooking. It serves the neighbourhood, for sure, but Eric's food can hold its own in most company. There's a café/patisserie next door, too, with the French Tarte serving fabulous pastries, baguettes and quiches. Meanwhile, back at the main event, the decor is all pristine neutrality with linen on the tables. There's a tasting menu if you fancy going the whole hog, while the fixed-price lunch menu and à la carte are bolstered by daily specials. The cooking has a light, contemporary touch, with a classic French theme and some inspiration drawn from the broader Mediterranean (including North Africa). A starter of ox cheek cannelloni with onion pickle and hazelnut foam is packed with perfectly balanced flavours, followed by a main course piece of hake, roasted just-so and served with champagne risotto, queen scallops, samphire and a crustacean sauce. With excellent bread, classy desserts and a wine list that embraces the world and highlights organic and biodynamic wines, The French Table goes from strength to strength.

Chef Eric Guignard **Owner** Eric & Sarah Guignard **Seats** 48, Pr/dining room 32 **Times** 12-2.30/7-10.30 Closed 25-26 Dec, 1-3 Jan, Sun-Mon **Prices** Prices not confirmed Tasting menu fr £45 **Wines** 66 bottles over £30, 32 bottles under £30, 10 by glass **Parking** On street **Notes** Tasting menu whole table only (with wine £75), Children welcome

TEDDINGTON

Retro

PLAN 1 C1

◉◉ French V

tel: 020 8977 2239 **114-116 High St TW11 8JB**
email: retrobistrot@aim.com
dir: *A313 Teddington High St*

French bistro with bags of style and provincial cooking

This highly individual bistro certainly brings a taste of France to suburbia, standing out from the crowd not just for its bold-flavoured cooking and sassy avant-garde decor, but for the charming, flamboyant service of owner and front-of-house impresario Vincent Gerbeau. Bold-patterned wallpaper, glitzy chandeliers and vibrant-coloured banquettes and drapes deliver the retro-chic backdrop, along with Parisian café-style tables and chairs, bare floorboards, exposed brick and big mirrors. Appropriately, the kitchen turns out some retro French classics like moules marinière, grilled snails, Chateaubriand and hot chocolate fondant, alongside more à la mode dishes like sea-fresh halibut fillet teamed with a striking risotto nero, piquant confit red peppers and naturally salty samphire, or perhaps melt-in-the-mouth braised pork belly with cavolo nero, root vegetables and a liquoricey anise jus. The flavours are simple and big-hearted and it's all fashioned from prime seasonal ingredients. Accompanying wines fittingly all speak with a patriotic French accent.

Chef Michael Collins **Owner** Vincent Gerbeau **Seats** 110, Pr/dining room 50 **Times** 12-3.30/6.30-11 Closed Xmas, 1 Jan, BHs, D Sun **Prices** Fixed L 2 course £10.95, Fixed D 3 course £19.95-£22.50, Starter £6.20-£12.50, Main £13.50-£27.50, Dessert £6.50-£7.95 **Wines** 56 bottles over £30, 30 bottles under £30, 26 by glass **Parking** On street **Notes** Fixed D 2/3 course min price applies Mon-Thu, max Fri-Sat, Sunday L, Children welcome

TWICKENHAM

A Cena

PLAN 1 C2

◉ Modern Italian

tel: 020 8288 0108 **418 Richmond Rd TW1 2EB**
email: acenarichmond@gmail.com
dir: *100yds from Richmond Bridge*

Reliable Italian cooking near Richmond Bridge

An informal neighbourhood Italian smartly kitted out in bistro style, A Cena is certainly not your average pizza-pasta joint. True, pasta might make an appearance, but a thoughtful one: perhaps spaghetti con gamberoni (tiger prawns, chilli, rocket and lemon). The cooking reliably follows the seasons whilst speaking of sunnier climes. Take a fish main like pan-fried Sicilian-style marinated hake with its accompaniment of capers, white wine, lemon and green beans, or a veggie option like polenta fritters with Swiss chard, tomato and parmesan. For dessert there might be pannacotta (perhaps served old-school-style in a cocktail glass) with a brûlée-esque topping of salted peanut brittle and coffee caramel, while cheeses and wines all speak with an Italian accent. The dining room is a stylish mix of darkwood (floorboards, furniture and bar) and white walls hung with feature mirrors. Note that the restaurant is on the Twickenham side of Richmond Bridge.

Chef Nicola Parsons **Owner** Camilla & Tim Healy **Seats** 55 **Times** 12-2/7-10 Closed Xmas & BHs, L Mon, D Sun **Prices** Starter £6.50-£8.50, Main £10.50-£23.50, Dessert £6-£9, Service optional 12.5% **Wines** 60 bottles over £30, 13 bottles under £30, 16 by glass **Parking** On street **Notes** Fixed L 3 course available pre-rugby match £50, Sunday L £21-£25, Vegetarian available, Children welcome

MERSEYSIDE

BIRKENHEAD

Map 15 SJ38

Fraiche

◉◉◉ – *see opposite*

FRANKBY

Map 15 SJ28

The Dining Room at Hillbark

◉◉◉ – *see opposite*

LIVERPOOL

Map 15 SJ39

The London Carriage Works

◉◉ Modern European

tel: 0151 705 2222 **Hope Street Hotel, 40 Hope St L1 9DA**
email: eat@hopestreethotel.co.uk **web:** www.thelondoncarriageworks.co.uk
dir: *Follow cathedral & university signs on entering city, at the centre of Hope St between the two cathedrals*

Regionally-focused menu in a trendy hotel conversion

The stripped-back interior of the one-time carriage workshop is a very modern sort of dining room, with shards of floor-to-ceiling glass and lots of exposed bricks, plus large windows to give a view of the street action. There's plenty of room between the light-wood tables and the young service team are attentive. The menu makes much of provenance and there's a satisfying regional flavour to the menu. Grilled fillet of Menai mackerel might kick things off, or breast of Lakeland wood pigeon with a beetroot and green peppercorn sauce. There are sharing platters, too, with vegetarian, seafood and meaty options, plus salads such as one with marinated herring fillets and new potatoes. Main-course assiette of Blackface Suffolk lamb consists of loin, shoulder and kidney, or go for roast breast of Gressingham duck with jasmine tea, pink grapefruit and root ginger jus. Desserts run to Sicilian lemon and raspberry tart – good and zesty – with raspberry sorbet and sesame tuile, and there's a good selection of British cheeses.

Chef David Critchley **Owner** David Brewitt **Seats** 100, Pr/dining room 50 **Times** 12-3/5-10 Closed D 25 Dec **Prices** Fixed L 2 course £17.50, Fixed D 3 course £22.50, Starter £5-£14.50, Main £9.50-£30, Dessert £6.50-£13.50, Service optional **Wines** 143 bottles over £30, 42 bottles under £30, 21 by glass **Parking** On street, car park opposite **Notes** Pre-theatre & tasting menus available, Sunday L £17.50-£58.50, Vegetarian available, Children welcome

Fraiche

BIRKENHEAD
Map 15 SJ38

Modern French, European v

tel: 0151 652 2914 **11 Rose Mount, Oxton CH43 5SG**
email: contact@restaurantfraiche.com
dir: *M53 junct 3 towards Prenton. In 2m left towards Oxton. Fraiche on right*

Cutting-edge cooking on the Wirral peninsula

Marc Wilkinson's wholly idiosyncratic Wirral restaurant has been a shining light on the peninsula for a decade now. When he opened here in April 2004, it's fair to say there wasn't much to lift the gastronomic heart in the area. Fraiche feels like somewhere that could sit as the jewel in the crown of a renovated quayside development after the manner of Edinburgh's Leith. As it is, the conservation village of Oxton near Birkenhead has proved a congenial home for the tireless researches and discoveries of which Wilkinson's menus are composed. Make no mistake: this is cutting-edge food, blending contrasts of flavour, seasoning, texture and temperature to the greater good of making food new all over again. It's somehow all the more dazzling for taking place in a decidedly understated room that reflects the topography of the local shoreline, with striking contemporary glass artworks. Marc Wilkinson's career developed from classical French foundations, which inform ingredients, techniques and the presentation of the dishes. These are succinctly summarised in the menu specifications. A fixed six-course dinner menu is the heart of the operation, and might open with a cucumber granita with pineapple and mint, followed by textures of artichoke with a chicken crisp in white port. A scallop pops up next, in lime butter with a serving of wild rice, then Anjou pigeon with varicoloured beetroots and lettuce. Lunch is a shorter affair, but no less creative, perhaps built around monkfish cheeks with olives and orange, before Suffolk lamb with shallot purée and parsley root. Flexibility extends to the option of a menu of salty snacks (the Salt Bench), concluding with the siren temptations of the cheese trolley. Among the sweeter offerings might be this year's must-have dessert, an éclair fashioned from celery and rhubarb, and there's also a head-turning take on lemon meringue pie.

Chef Marc Wilkinson **Owner** Marc Wilkinson **Seats** 16, Pr/dining room 20 **Times** 12-1.30/7-9.30 Closed 25 Dec, 1 Jan, Mon-Tue, L Wed-Thu **Prices** Prices not confirmed, Service optional **Wines** 260 bottles over £30, 30 bottles under £30, 6 by glass **Parking** On street **Notes** Sunday L, Children 8 yrs+

The Dining Room at Hillbark

FRANKBY
Map 15 SJ28

Modern British v NOTABLE WINE LIST

tel: 0151 625 2400 **Hillbark Hotel and Spa, Royden Park CH48 1NP**
email: enquiries@hillbarkhotel.co.uk **web:** www.hillbarkhotel.co.uk
dir: *M53 junct 3, A552 (Upton), right onto A551 (Arrowe Park Rd). 0.6m at lights left into Arrowe Brook Rd. 0.5m on left*

Experimental cooking in a Victorian medieval hall

Hillbark has to be seen to be believed. It's one of England's many works of Victorian architectural pastiche, in this case of a medieval timbered manor house, but an astonishingly precise one, all intricately beamed façade and panelled halls. It was built in 1891 by a soap magnate, and was acquired in the 1920s by the Royden family, shipbuilders to the Cunard line. They moved it, panel by panel, to Frankby, and here it remains, complete with its William Morris stained windows, a Robert Adam fireplace, and another that once belonged to Sir Walter Raleigh. The proximity of Premier League football clubs has some influence on the starry clientele the place attracts, and if they know anything at all about contemporary British cooking, they'll be in for a treat. New chef Richard Collingwood took up the reins in late 2013, and bold experimental combinations and cutting-edge technique now distinguish the output. Expect to start with something like rabbit loin on a soil of morel mushrooms, with purple sprouting broccoli, bacon and a poached egg yolk, or with a more vigorous jolt to the tastebuds in the form of seared mackerel with dill pickle, white chocolate and wasabi, and dill ice cream – a shock-of-the-new dish if ever there was. Main courses accord star billing to their principals, the spotlight shone on halibut with its supporting cast of kohlrabi, burnt leeks and crisp-skinned chicken confit, venison with beetroot, quince and cocoa-nib granola, or perhaps a king oyster mushroom with more of that blackened leek, 'aerated' potato and black quinoa. It all finishes with either a dessert such as delicately cooked Yorkshire rhubarb with its own firm jelly, baked yoghurt, pistachio olive oil cake and a full-flavoured yoghurt tuile, or a cheese course like truffledTunworth (a soft cow's-milk cheese from Hampshire) with Sauternes jelly, walnut crunch and celery granita.

Chef Richard Collingwood **Owner** Contessa Hotels **Seats** 36, Pr/dining room 30 **Times** 12-2.30/7-10 Closed Sun-Mon **Prices** Fixed L 2 course £18.50, Fixed D 3 course £60, Tasting menu £95, Service optional 12.5% **Wines** 600 bottles over £30, 3 bottles under £30, 560 by glass **Parking** 160 **Notes** Champagne afternoon tea £33, Sunday L, Children welcome

LIVERPOOL *continued*

Malmaison Liverpool

Modern British

tel: 0151 229 5000 **7 William Jessop Way, Princes Dock L3 1QZ**
email: liverpool@malmaison.com web: www.malmaison.com
dir: *Located on Princes Dock near the Liver Building*

Modern brasserie food on the Princes Dock

Right on the water's edge, with the Liver Birds as near neighbours, the Liverpool Mal is in the heart of the action. It's a purpose-built hotel with the brands trademark luxe bedrooms, some of which pay homage to Liverpool legends. The double-height brasserie references the industrial heritage of the city, and the docks in particular, with a stripped-down, industrial look of exposed bricks and pipework. Modern brasserie cooking is the name of the game, with plenty of global flavours on show. Fritto misto recalls sunnier climes, with the tempura of squid, tiger prawn and courgette served up with a lemon aïoli and sweet chilli sauce, or there's a classic Caesar salad available as either a starter or main course. Steak frites is another old favourite, served with a red wine and shallot sauce, while chicken tikka with a masala sauce shows the global reach of the kitchen. Finish with pear tarte Tatin with Calvados mascarpone.

Times 12-2/6.30-10.30 Closed L Sat

60 Hope Street Restaurant

Modern British V

tel: 0151 707 6060 **60 Hope St L1 9BZ**
email: info@60hopestreet.com web: www.60hopestreet.com
dir: *From M62 follow city centre signs, then brown tourist signs for cathedral. Hope St near cathedral*

Confident modern cooking near the cathedrals

The Georgian townhouse restaurant on Hope Street has been a presence on the Liverpool dining scene for over a dozen years now. It's in a good spot, close to the Philharmonic Hall and the two cathedrals, and it keeps pulling in the crowds. There's a relaxed bistro vibe on the ground floor, with a metal staircase leading to the restaurant and private dining room upstairs. It looks smart and contemporary, but remains a reassuringly friendly place to eat and drink. Ham fritters with peach salad shows the style, as does goats' cheese and beetroot trifle – two modish starters full of flavour. Next up, perhaps, roast rump of Cumbrian lamb with confit potatoes, squash purée and sautéed wild mushrooms, or pan-seared fillet of turbot topped with a potato crust and served with Jerusalem artichoke and white wine velouté. Finish with cherry Bakewell with strawberry ice cream.

Chef Neil Devereux **Owner** Colin & Gary Manning **Seats** 90, Pr/dining room 40
Times 12-2.30/5-10.30 Closed 26 Dec, 1 Jan **Prices** Fixed L 2 course £20.95, Fixed D 3 course £24.95, Starter £7.25-£12.95, Main £13.95-£31.95, Dessert £6.95-£9.50, Service optional **Wines** 60 bottles over £30, 9 bottles under £30, 6 by glass
Parking On street **Notes** Pre-theatre daily 5-7pm, Sunday L, Children welcome

Spire

Modern British, European

tel: 0151 734 5040 **Number One Church Rd L15 9EA**
email: spirerestaurant@btinternet.com

Contemporary bistro comforts

The name might lead you to think that this relaxed modern bistro lies in the shadow of one of Liverpool's two cathedrals, but it is actually a cab ride away in the Wavertree area, right by the one-and-only Penny Lane. The trip out of the centre is amply rewarded though: the friendly neighbourhood bistro venue has an unbuttoned vibe and looks the part too, with its well-trodden floorboards, bare brick and white-painted walls hung with colourful abstract art, and unclothed wooden tables. The kitchen deals in simple contemporary brasserie-style classics with a Mediterranean slant – chicken liver parfait with elderflower jelly and toasted brioche, say, while mains deliver the comforts of braised belly pork with swede purée, crispy black pudding, baby carrots and apple sauce, or roast mustard and herb-crumbed chump of salt marsh lamb partnered with ratatouille, lemongrass and oregano, and baby carrots. Chocolatey puddings – white chocolate pannacotta with chocolate ice cream, perhaps – will win friends, but there might also be apple tarte Tatin with caramel and vanilla sauce.

Chef Matt Locke **Owner** Matt & Adam Locke **Seats** 70, Pr/dining room 40
Times 12-1.45/6-9.30 Closed BH Mon, 2 wks from 2 Jan, Sun, L Sat, Mon
Prices Fixed L 2 course £11.95-£14.95, Fixed D 3 course £14.95-£17.95, Starter £4.45-£9.95, Main £13.95-£21.95, Dessert £5.95-£8.95, Service optional 10%
Wines 30 bottles over £30, 30 bottles under £30, 12 by glass **Parking** On street, local pub car park **Notes** Vegetarian available, Children welcome

---

PORT SUNLIGHT   Map 15 SJ38

Leverhulme Hotel

Modern International

tel: 0151 644 6655 & 644 5555 **Central Rd CH62 5EZ**
email: enquiries@leverhulmehotel.co.uk web: www.leverhulmehotel.co.uk
dir: *From Chester: M53 junct 5, A41 (Birkenhead) in approx 4m left into Bolton Rd, on at rdbt, 0.1m right into Church Drive. 0.2m hotel on right. From Liverpool: A41 (Chester), 2.7m, 3rd exit at 3rd rdbt into Bolton Rd (follow directions as above)*

Locally sourced natural flavours amid art deco philanthropy

The whiter-than-white interiors of the Leverhulme are fitting for a building that has its origins in cleanliness. One of the Edwardian era's great philanthropists, Lord Leverhulme, opened the place in 1907 as a cottage hospital for soapworks employees at his Port Sunlight garden village, and who wouldn't find their health restored amid such exquisite art deco surroundings? Maintaining the ethical standards in which its history is steeped, the hotel now boasts a dining venue called Twenty-Eight Miles, which is the distance, as the crow flies from Port Sunlight, within which most of the supplies are garnered. John Wilkins took over as chef in August 2013. He has broadened the menu's base to take in celebrations of natural bounty as Hedgerow Platter (pigeon terrine, blackberry jelly, pickled mushrooms), Wirral Rock Pool (crayfish in bisque with an egg yolk simmered at 62 degrees), cod loin in a borrowed coat of chicken skin with caramelised onion purée, and a dessert array of sweet vegetables – pea pannacotta, carrot and vanilla purée, beetroot jelly and honeyed parsnip.

Chef John Wilkins **Owner** Contessa Hotels **Seats** 60, Pr/dining room 20
Times 12-2.30/6-10 **Prices** Starter £7-£9, Main £17-£35, Dessert £6-£9, Service optional 12.5% **Wines** 136 bottles over £30, 15 bottles under £30, 126 by glass **Parking** 70 **Notes** Champagne afternoon tea £28, Sunday L, Vegetarian available, Children welcome

SOUTHPORT

Map 15 SD31

Bistrot Vérité

🌸 French

tel: 01704 564199 **7 Liverpool Rd, Birkdale PR8 4AR**

Traditional French cooking in Birkdale village

Marc Vérité's self-named bistro in Birkdale village flies the tricolour proudly for the old French culinary traditions, with the benefit that much of what he produces is based on prime Lancashire ingredients. Crammed-in tables, chalkboard menus and a friendly, breezy buzz characterise the operation, as does some accomplished cooking. A wooden board of hors d'oeuvres variés encompasses a generous range of hot and cold items, including a scallop with pickled veg, duck and game terrine, battered frogs' legs, a snail simmered in Pernod, a goats' cheese croquette, and more. Main-course wood pigeon served with foie gras and wild mushrooms sautéed in garlic and parsley is a richly satisfying dish, and meals may end with a thickly caramelised classic crème brûlée.

Chef Marc Vérité **Owner** Marc & Michaela Vérité **Seats** 45 **Times** 12-1.30/5.30-late Closed 1 wk Feb & 1 wk Aug, Sun-Mon **Prices** Starter £4.95-£8.25, Main £9.95-£26.95, Dessert £5.95, Service optional **Wines** 12 bottles over £30, 29 bottles under £30 **Parking** Birkdale station **Notes** Vegetarian available, Children welcome

Gusto

🌸 Italian

tel: 01704 544255 **58-62 Lord St PR8 1QB**
email: info@gustotrattoria.co.uk
dir: *Located centre Southport*

A taste of Italy in Southport

Gusto is a trattoria with a nice line in cheerful bonhomie and some good and proper Italian cooking. The two rooms are looked over by the charming service team and the open kitchen adds to the buzz of the place. The food does not attempt to reinvent the wheel, just to do things properly. The pizzas are very good – the 'boscaiola', for example, with ham and mushrooms, or the 'Gusto', fired up with anchovies and chilli. Vegetali parmigiana is a first course filled with the flavours of the Med, or go for polpette piccanti (meatballs in a spicy Arrabiata sauce). Pasta is made in-house and should not be ignored: pappardelle al carciofo, maybe, which is cooked perfectly, or try the gnocchi al pesto. Desserts such as frutta caramellata and home-made tiramisù hit the spot, too, and it all comes at a very reasonable price.

Chef Giorgio Lamola **Owner** Giorgio Lamola **Seats** 38 **Times** 12-3/5-10 Closed Mon (excl BH) **Prices** Starter £3.95-£7.45, Main £6.50-£9.25, Dessert £3.95-£5.25, Service optional **Wines** **Parking** On street **Notes** Open all day Sat-Sun 12-10, Vegetarian available, Children welcome

The Lawns Restaurant at Thornton Hall

THORNTON HOUGH

Map 15 SJ38

Modern European V

tel: 0151 336 3938 **Neston Rd CH63 1JF**
email: reservations@thorntonhallhotel.com **web:** www.lawnsrestaurant.com
dir: *M53 junct 4 onto B5151 & B5136, follow brown tourist signs (approx 2.5m) to Thornton Hall Hotel*

British modernism in a Victorian Wirral mansion

Situated amid the rolling golf courses of the Wirral peninsula, Thornton Hall is an august Victorian manor house turned modern country hotel. Virtually anything you can think you might want to do on an away-break is available here, from golf itself (at the Heswall club) to wallowing under scented muds in the spa and getting married. The public rooms are generously expansive, and the temptation to disguise their 19th-century grandiosity with modernisingaccoutrements has largely been resisted, so you're still seeing the Hall as it was intended to be seen. In the Lawns dining room, bay windows gaze over the grounds, a chandelier glitters, and the intricately worked wood carvings in the half-panelling and on the magnificent ceiling should not be missed. Not that there's anything Victorian about the cooking, of course, which speaks a language that would have entirely

baffled Isabella Beeton. It's British modernism with knobs on, as meals open with stuffed rabbit saddle alongside salt-baked parsnip and watercress pannacotta, or grilled fillet and tartare of Cornish mackerel, thrown into relief with spring onions, radishes and pink grapefruit. Mains look to local meats such as rose veal or pork, but also further afield for Lincolnshire roe deer, the loin and a croquette of the leg accompanied by turnips and wild garlic in a sweet-sour jus, or there may be turbot and clams in chicken juices with Brussels sprouts and celeriac. Mutton is good to see on a menu, the rosemaried loin and treacled rib served with aubergine, goat curd and charred kale. New takes on favourite finishers include blueberry cheesecake with almonds and lemon curd, or the blackberry, white chocolate and violet remake of Viennetta. Cheeses from the trolley are served with membrillo. If choosing seems an imposition, relax with the ten-course taster.

Chef David Gillmore **Owner** The Thompson family **Seats** 45, Pr/dining room 24 **Times** 12-2.30/7-9.30 **Prices** Service optional **Wines** 100 bottles over £30, 34 bottles under £30, 11 by glass **Parking** 250 **Notes** Tasting menu available Mon-Sat, Sunday L £21, Children welcome

SOUTHPORT *continued*

Vincent Hotel

 British, European, Japanese

tel: 01704 883800 **98 Lord St PR8 1JR**
email: manager@thevincenthotel.com **web:** www.thevincenthotel.com
dir: *M58 junct 3, follow signs to Ormskirk & Southport*

Skilful cooking in a stylish hotel

The V-Café and Sushi Bar at this stylish contemporary hotel is the place to be in the evening, when lights are dimmed and candles are lit. Tables are closely packed and floor-to-ceiling windows look onto bustling Lord Street, where there are tables for alfresco dining. The menu roams around Britain and Europe before arriving in Japan with some platters of authentic sushi and sashimi, maki and temaki, with a section of 'gringo sushi for non-fish-lovers' – roasted crispy duck and mango maki for example, or barbecue pulled pork maki. Choosing from the European side of the fence, you might start with uncomplicated classics along the lines of duck liver parfait with toasted brioche, or smoked haddock and salmon fishcake with tartare sauce and endive salad. A main course suprême of cod matched with spring onion mash and brown shrimp beurre noisette stands out for its freshness, accurate cooking and balanced combinations. Those with a taste for rhubarb could finish with the tart vegetable served as ice cream and compôte with custard foam and spicy ginger crumb.

Chef Andrew Carter **Owner** Paul Adams **Seats** 85, Pr/dining room 12 **Times** 7.30am-9.30pm All-day dining **Prices** Fixed D 2 course £14.95, Starter £2.95-£12.95, Main £4.50-£25.95, Dessert £5.95-£14.95, Service optional **Wines** 8 bottles over £30, 12 bottles under £30, 5 by glass **Parking** 50, Valet parking **Notes** Fixed D 3 course available Sun-Thu, Sunday L £12.95, Vegetarian available, Children welcome

Warehouse Kitchen & Bar

 International

tel: 01704 544662 **30 West St PR8 1QN**
email: info@warehousekitchenandbar.com
dir: *M58 junct 3, then A570 Southport*

Cool warehouse setting and smart modish cooking

The stylish New York-esque Warehouse has white linen-clad tables against the bare-brick walls in a light and airy space and, up the stairs, a chic bar. Co-owned these days by Liverpool footballer Steven Gerrard, this town centre venue has been going strong for 15 years, its modern international cooking, cool design and relaxed vibe proving popular with the locals. Typical dishes include Ribble Valley pork croquettes with sweet honey mustard, crackling salad and baby pickles, followed perhaps by a trio of Cumbrian beef – steak and ale pie, fillet and oxtail sauce – and finishing with Wakefield rhubarb 'mayhem' – rhubarb Bakewell tart, tonka bean pannacotta and rhubarb sorbet.

Chef Matthew Worswick **Owner** Paul Adams, Steven Gerrard **Seats** 95, Pr/dining room 20 **Times** 12-2/5.30-10 Closed 26 Dec, 1 Jan, Sun **Prices** Fixed L 2 course £12.95, Fixed D 3 course £16.95, Starter £4.95-£11.95, Main £12.50-£27.95, Dessert £5.50-£14.95, Service optional **Wines** 10 bottles over £30, 14 bottles under £30, 9 by glass **Parking** On street **Notes** Fixed D 2/3 course Tue-Thu all evening, Fri-Sat 5.30-6.30pm, Vegetarian available, Children welcome

THORNTON HOUGH
Map 15 SJ38

The Lawns Restaurant at Thornton Hall

– see page 409

NORFOLK

ALBURGH
Map 13 TM28

The Dove Restaurant with Rooms

 Modern European V

tel: 01986 788315 **Holbrook IP20 OEP**
email: info@thedoverestaurant.co.uk **web:** www.thedoverestaurant.co.uk
dir: *On South Norfolk border between Harleston & Bungay, by A143, at junct of B1062*

Classic cooking in charming restaurant with rooms

Robert and Conny Oberhoffer have been running their restaurant with rooms for 15 years, although it's been in Robert's family since 1980. The restaurant is a prettily decorated room, long and thin, with two rows of dining tables on a lightwood floor, the scene for some classy honest-to-goodness cooking. Hits among starters include home-made pork and game terrine with onion chutney, and potted smoked mackerel pâté with piri-piri sauce. Typical of the straightforward style of main courses is venison casserole with creamed potatoes, red cabbage and ham, and roast whole sea bass finished with a balsamic reduction served with peppers, capers and sun-dried tomatoes. Breads are made in-house, as are puddings of Valrhona chocolate terrine with meringue, whipped cream and mango coulis, and cherry and confectioner's custard flan with home-made ice cream.

Chef Robert Oberhoffer **Owner** Robert & Conny Oberhoffer **Seats** 60 **Times** 12-2/7-9 Closed Mon-Thu, L Fri-Sat, D Sun **Prices** Fixed L 2 course £16.50, Starter £5.95-£8, Main £14.95-£19.95, Dessert £5.95, Service optional **Wines** 1 bottle over £30, 31 bottles under £30, 5 by glass **Parking** 20 **Notes** Sunday L, Children welcome

BACTON
Map 13 TG33

The Keswick Hotel

British

tel: 01692 650468 **Walcott Rd NR12 OLS**
email: margaret@keswickhotelbacton.co.uk **web:** www.keswickhotelbacton.co.uk
dir: *On B1159 coast road*

Unpretentious dining in small and friendly seaside hotel

Smack on the seafront in Bacton, this charming small hotel punches above its weight in culinary matters thanks to a kitchen that takes carefully sourced seasonal and local materials – Cromer crab, Brancaster mussels, rare-breed meats – as the starting point for its vibrant modern cooking. No-one is trying to reinvent the wheel here: expect simple, classic combinations in unpretentious but skilfully cooked dishes, starting out at its most emphatically seasonal with a summery idea such as crab cake with wasabi mayonnaise, pea shoots and a salad of micro leaves and herbs. Next, crisp-skinned, pan-fried sea bass arrives with rösti, wilted spinach, chorizo and brown shrimp butter, and for pudding there's condensed milk pannacotta with strawberry coulis and fresh strawberries.

Times 12-3/6-9 Closed L Mon-Sat

Who has won our Lifetime Achievement award? See page 12 to find out

BARNHAM BROOM
Map 13 TG00

Barnham Broom

 Modern British, European

tel: 01603 759393 **Honingham Rd NR9 4DD**
email: enquiry@barnhambroomhotel.co.uk web: www.barnham-broom.co.uk
dir: *A11/A47 towards Swaffham, follow brown tourist signs*

Contemporary and disciplined cooking with views across the greens

This luxury country hotel, surrounded by acres of countryside, boasts two golf courses, plus a gym, indoor pool and spa facilities. There are two bars and The Brasserie, a spacious room looking on to greenery, which used to be called Flints Restaurant. The kitchen takes a creatively modern approach with its quality local produce, and keeps dishes fairly straightforward. The menu might kick off with seared scallops modishly paired with black pudding and Chablis bisque, or ham hock with a poached egg and Madeira broth. Steaks from the grill feature among main courses, with a choice of marinades and sauces, with others as classical as coq au vin, or Cromer mussels cooked in white wine and cream, the range extended by the likes of monkfish wrapped in pancetta served with roasted fennel. Tempting desserts include traditional treacle tart with bay-flavoured ice cream, and cheesecake with cherry compôte.

Chef Erling Rugsten **Owner** Barnham Broom **Seats** 100, Pr/dining room 50 **Times** 12.30-2/7-9.30 Closed L Mon-Sat **Prices** Starter £5.75-£8.95, Main £12.95-£24.95, Dessert £5.75-£8.45 **Wines** 27 bottles over £30, 29 bottles under £30, 9 by glass **Parking** 500 **Notes** Afternoon tea available £10.95, Sunday L £10.95-£18.95, Vegetarian available, Children welcome

BLAKENEY
Map 13 TG04

The Blakeney Hotel

 Modern British **V**

tel: 01263 740797 **The Quay NR25 7NE**
email: reception@blakeneyhotel.co.uk web: www.blakeneyhotel.co.uk
dir: *From A148 between Fakenham & Holt, take B1156 to Langham & Blakeney*

Accomplished modern cooking in a quayside hotel

Those who like to be by the sea need look no further: this hotel is in a perfect spot on the quay, with magnificent views over the estuary to Blakeney Point. Well-sourced raw materials underpin the operation, while a sure-footed handling of ingredients gives dishes layers of flavours. Seared pigeon breast, for instance, comes with a salad of cracked wheat, hazelnuts and pistachios in mint and quince dressing, and a stew of peppers, chick peas and orange is the accompaniment for squid seared with chorizo. To follow, roast breast of guinea fowl in bacon gets the familiar partners of roast roots, potato gratin and bread sauce. Well-timed grilled Dover sole comes on pommes Anna with pickled vegetables and caper and lemon butter. Puddings are in the mould of sherry trifle and lemon tart.

Chef Martin Sewell **Owner** Stannard family **Seats** 100, Pr/dining room 80 **Times** 12-2/6.30-9 Closed 24 Dec D, 25-26 Dec, 31 Dec D **Prices** Fixed D 3 course £29-£38.50, Starter £5.50-£10.25, Main £10.25-£15.75, Dessert £5.50-£9.50, Service optional **Wines** 25 bottles over £30, 75 bottles under £30, 16 by glass **Parking** 60 **Notes** ALC 3 course £29-£38.50, No high chairs after 6.45pm, Sunday L £21.50, Children welcome

Morston Hall

 – *see below*

Morston Hall

BLAKENEY
Map 13 TG04

Modern British, European **V** | NOTABLE WINE LIST

tel: 01263 741041 **Morston, Holt NR25 7AA**
email: reception@morstonhall.com web: www.morstonhall.com
dir: *On A149 (coast road) between Blakeney & Stiffkey*

Revelatory cooking in a country hotel on the human scale

Galton and Tracy Blackiston's place is a large, but not grandiloquent, 17th-century country house a couple of miles outside Blakeney on the covetable north Norfolk coast. True, there's a conservatory extension for dining in, for you wouldn't want to miss the bracing views, and there are cookery demonstrations as well as actual cooking, as befits the prolific author of recipes that Galton has been since his Lake District days. The whole package, though, manages to remain on the human scale, with an air of unforced hospitality prevailing amid the uncluttered but colourful elegance of the interiors. The drill is admirably simple in its structure – a seven-course set menu with optional wine flight – though the food itself is full of revelations, many of them arising from novel combinations of excellent materials. A soup of white cabbage floated with sage oil might open the batting, ahead of a thought-provoking hors d'oeuvre of fallow venison in 96%

chocolate and liquorice. Fish might be black bream in raspberry vinegar jus, but the colder months might well see a pair of meat courses – say, pencil fillet of lamb with broccoli and pearl barley, before ox cheek with smoked blueberries and beetroot. A teasing little dessert, perhaps brown bread ice cream, might tempt you to follow it with another, frozen winter berries in white chocolate with celery granita, or there are thoroughbred British cheeses with walnut-sultana bread. Those who sign up for the selected wines will be treated to an imaginative journey through Mendoza, Bolgheri, the Côte de Beaune and Piedmont, with a traditional glass of port to go with the cheese.

Chef Galton Blackiston **Owner** T & G Blackiston **Seats** 50, Pr/dining room 26 **Times** 12.30-7.30 Closed 2 wks Jan, L Mon-Sat (ex party booking) **Prices** Tasting menu £66, Service optional **Wines** 129 bottles over £30, 24 bottles under £30, 18 by glass **Parking** 40 **Notes** Champagne tea £26, Sunday L £33, Children welcome

The White Horse

 Modern British

tel: 01485 210262 **PE31 8BY**
email: reception@whitehorsebrancaster.co.uk web: www.whitehorsebrancaster.co.uk
dir: *On A149 (coast road) midway between Hunstanton & Wells-next-the-Sea*

Seafood-led cooking on the Norfolk coastal marshes

There's always somewhere good to eat in north Norfolk, and the White Horse is stabled in one of the more gorgeous coastal locations. Surveying the broad sweep of salt marshland, the tidal wash and stretching sandy beaches, it's a restorative prospect indeed, the more so for those who choose to stay. Even if you don't, the conservatory dining room offers panoramic views of the coastline, complete with fishing-boats and mussel-growers going about their business. It isn't surprising that what they gather in forms a strong suit on Avrum Frankel's menus. Those mussels reliably turn up in garlicky white wine cream, and the local Brancaster oysters are tempura-battered or simply spritzed with shallot vinegar. If you're sticking with the theme, look then to grilled whole megrim in cockle and avruga cream, or to hake in Spanish livery, with Norfolk chorizo, mussel and bean stew and saffron foam. Alternatives take in lamb rump with parsnips, kale and smoked mash, or butternut and sage risotto with a parmesan crisp. Ingenious desserts include cherry Bakewell 'arancini' with cherry mousse and vanilla anglaise.

Chef Avrum Frankel **Owner** Clifford Nye **Seats** 100 **Times** 12-2/6.30-9 **Prices** Starter £5.95-£7, Main £11.95-£17.95, Dessert £5.50-£6.95, Service optional **Wines** 12 bottles over £30, 31 bottles under £30, 13 by glass **Parking** 85 **Notes** Sunday L £13.95, Vegetarian available, Children welcome

The Lavender House

 Modern British **v**

tel: 01603 712215 **39 The Street NR13 5AA**
email: lavenderhouse39@aol.com
dir: *A47 E, 4m from Norwich city centre*

Enterprising restaurant and cookery school in a Tudor cottage

The thatched Tudor cottage to the south of Norwich began its career as a restaurant in 1962, when it was known as Old Beams. Richard Hughes has been careful to maintain the core of the building's character, with its exposed brickwork and simple tiled floors, and the place is a hive of industry, hosting themed evenings and cookery classes, some aimed at getting teens into the kitchen (good luck with that). An eclectic melting-pot of influences is evident on the enterprising menus, which deal in starting combinations like seared mackerel with salted kohlrabi, green tea and yoghurt sorbet. The mains include venison loin crusted in juniper and pepper, with roast beets, cinnamon plums and smoked chestnuts, or a VIP gathering of fish – cod, monkfish and red mullet – in saffron-scented mussel and leek chowder. A pause for pre-dessert precedes something like warm spiced Bramley cake with nougatine glacé.

Chef Richard Hughes **Owner** Richard Hughes **Seats** 50, Pr/dining room 36 **Times** 12-4/6.30-11 Closed Mon-Wed, L Thu-Sat, D Sun **Prices** Tasting menu £28, Service optional **Wines** 8 by glass **Parking** 16 **Notes** Fixed D £45, Willi Opitz Table, Sunday L £49.95-£65, Children welcome

The Hoste

 Modern British

tel: 01328 738777 **The Green PE31 8HD**
email: reservations@thehoste.com web: www.thehoste.com
dir: *2m from A149 between Burnham & Wells*

Straightforward modern dishes in a historic Norfolk inn

A couple of miles back from the heritage North Norfolk shoreline, Burnham Market has acquired the kind of gentrified reputation that has seen it nicknamed Little-Chelsea-on-Sea. The Hoste is a historic whitewashed inn, partially covered in climbing foliage in the shape of a trident. Recent extensive refurbishment has introduced a lodge dining area influenced by New Zealand restaurant style, and an open kitchen. Great emphasis is laid on sourcing as much produce from within a 30-mile Norfolk radius as possible and that avoids unnecessary frippery. Brancaster oysters thus come in straightforward options (red wine vinegar, garlic and parsley, tempura or Bloody Mary), as an appetising prelude to herb-crusted cannon of succulently pink lamb with curly kale and dauphinoise, or roast salmon with lemon tabbouleh, a tiger prawn in filo, and honey and mustard cream sauce. The on-the-money finisher is beautifully moist sticky toffee pudding with caramel sauce, a pecan tuile and nutmeg ice cream, and there are fine Norfolk cheeses with date and apple chutney.

Chef James O'Connor **Owner** Mr Brendan Hopkins **Seats** 250, Pr/dining room 24 **Times** 12-2.30/6-9.15 Closed D 25 Dec **Prices** Starter £7-£12, Main £13-£26, Dessert £6-£9, Service optional **Wines** 34 bottles over £30, 28 bottles under £30, 22 by glass **Parking** 45 **Notes** Sunday L £16, Vegetarian available, Children welcome

Norfolk Mead Hotel

 Modern British

tel: 01603 737531 **Church Ln NR12 7DN**
email: info@norfolkmead.co.uk web: www.norfolkmead.co.uk
dir: *From Norwich take B1150 to Coltishall village, go right with petrol station on left, 200 yds church on right, go down driveway*

Cooking with a local flavour in a charming small country-house hotel

This handsome old house in the heart of the beautiful Norfolk Broads has never looked so dapper. Refurbishment by new owners has given the Norfolk Mead a contemporary, country-chic look, none more so than in the restaurant, where period features combine with white walls broken up with abstract artwork, wooden floors and tables decorated with simple flower arrangements. Windows look out over the pretty gardens – a must for a pre- or post-prandial stroll down to the river – while the charming small bar offers a range of whiskies and real ales, with the bonus of a delightful sun-trap terrace. And so to the food: chef Anna Duttson sources the finest, freshest local ingredients for her attractively presented modern British cooking. Start, perhaps, with a well-made double-baked cheese soufflé, followed by something like black bream, perfectly cooked, served with a potato and crab cake. Apple tarte Tatin with vanilla pod ice cream and caramel shard rounds things off nicely.

Chef Anna Duttson, Dave Potter **Owner** James Holliday, Anna Duttson **Seats** 40, Pr/dining room 22 **Times** 12-2.30/6.30-9 Closed L Mon-Sat **Prices** Fixed D 3 course fr £30, Service optional **Wines** 22 bottles over £30, 31 bottles under £30, 8 by glass **Parking** 45 **Notes** Afternoon tea £13.50, Sunday L, Vegetarian available, Children welcome

CROMER
Map 13 TG24

The Grove Cromer
◎◎ Modern British NEW

tel: 01263 512412 **95 Overstrand Rd NR27 0DJ**
email: enquiries@thegrovecromer.co.uk web: www.thegrovecromer.co.uk
dir: *Into Cromer on A149, right at 1st mini rdbt into Cromwell Rd. At double mini rdbt straight over into Overstrand Rd, 200mtrs on left*

Polished and passionate cooking on the coast

A white creeper-covered Georgian property, with an indoor pool and self-catering cottages in barn conversions, is the setting for this charming restaurant of well-appointed wooden tables, high-backed dining chairs and views over the garden. Chef Charlie Hodson, who often emerges to chat to guests, is passionate about his cooking, and creates dishes from the best Norfolk produce. A meal might start with his signature dish of lightly seared scallops with bacon, pea purée and herb dressing or his novel take on prawn cocktail: crayfish and shell-on prawns in Marie Rose sauce with beetroot purée. No less impressive is pheasant terrine with fig chutney, followed by a labour-intensive main course of belly pork, marinated for 36 hours before being slowly cooked, served with herby potato purée, piquant apple sauce and red wine jus, a well-balanced and nicely portioned dish. Fish comes in the guise of beer-battered fillet with tartare sauce and the usual trimmings, as well as seared sea bass fillet with pesto, dauphinoise and braised red cabbage. End with deeply flavoured, rich coffee crème brûlée.

Chef Charlie Hodson **Owner** The Graveling family **Seats** 48, Pr/dining room 30 **Times** 12-2/6-9 Closed Jan (phone to check), L Mon-Sat (winter) **Prices** Fixed L 2 course £14.95-£19.95, Fixed D 3 course £24.95-£45, Starter £5.95-£11.95, Main £10.95-£25.95, Dessert £5.95-£9.95, Service optional **Wines** 30 bottles over £30, 9 bottles under £30, 10 by glass **Notes** Sunday L £19.95-£24.95, Vegetarian available, Children welcome

Sea Marge Hotel
◎◎ Modern British

tel: 01263 579579 **16 High St, Overstrand NR27 0AB**
email: seamarge@mackenziehotels.com web: www.mackenziehotels.com
dir: *A140 to Cromer, B1159 to Overstrand, 2nd left past Overstrand Church*

Appealing modern menus on the North Norfolk coast

Terraced lawns lead down to the coast path and beach from this 1908-built mansion. The property has been lovingly restored, with many original features retained, a notable one being a minstrels' gallery. It's a friendly and relaxing hotel, with professional, helpful staff serving in the restaurant. The menu, with a handful of choices per course, is an appealing package of contemporary ideas, running from marinated wood pigeon with duck liver ravioli, parsnip purée and roast hazelnut dressing, to poached fillet of sea bass with a chowder of smoked haddock, brown

shrimps and vegetables. Goats' cheese soufflé, served with apple and walnut salad, rises to the occasion, and may be followed by flavourful rump of local lamb with thyme jus and well-considered accompaniments of minted pea purée, smoked bacon mash and roast green beans. Puddings include a memorable chocolate torte with pineapple sorbet and peanut brittle.

Chef Rene Ilupar **Owner** Mr & Mrs Mackenzie **Seats** 80, Pr/dining room 40 **Times** 12-2/6.30-9.30 **Prices** Fixed D 3 course £21, Service optional **Wines** 4 bottles over £30, 24 bottles under £30, 7 by glass **Parking** 50 **Notes** Full afternoon tea, Sunday L £9.95-£16.95, Vegetarian available, Children welcome

The White Horse Overstrand
◎◎ Modern European

tel: 01263 579237 **34 High St, Overstrand NR27 0AB**
email: enquiries@whitehorseoverstrand.co.uk web: www.whitehorseoverstrand.co.uk
dir: *From A140, before Cromer, turn right onto Mill Rd. At bottom turn right onto Station Rd. After 2m, bear left onto High St, White Horse Overstrand on left*

Great Norfolk produce cooked with flair

The family-run Victorian inn in the village of Overstrand goes from strength to strength, with food occupying an ever-prominent place at the heart of the operation, whether it is glammed-up old favourites in the bar, themed grill, Spanish or Italian nights, or vibrant modern dishes in the recently converted Barn restaurant. Large wrought-iron chandeliers hang from ceilings with original oak roof trusses, above rustic Norfolk flint walls and solid oak tables in a clean-cut contemporary setting that suits the switched-on modern food. Top-class local and seasonal produce underpins the repertoire, whether it is a starter trio of Cromer crab remoulade, brown shrimp rillettes, and shallow-fried Cajun squid, or mains of pan-roast rump of Norfolk lamb with rösti potato, garden pea purée, sautéed baby leeks and lamb jus. Don't skip pudding, as bittersweet chocolate fondant with home-made coconut ice cream is a real treat.

Times 12-3/6-9.30 Closed D 25 Dec

GREAT BIRCHAM
Map 13 TF73

The Kings Head Hotel
◎ Modern British

tel: 01485 578265 **PE31 6RJ**
email: info@thekingsheadhotel.co.uk web: www.the-kings-head-bircham.co.uk
dir: *A148 to Hillington through village, 1st left Bircham*

Classic and modern food in an revamped old inn

Bringing a bit of boutique style to Great Bircham, The Kings Head is a charming old inn with a swish interior that incorporates a smart, open-plan bar and lounge area and a restaurant that aims to please with a menu of classic and more ambitious dishes. There are plenty of Norfolk ingredients on the menu, plus traditional Sunday lunches and bar meals including a classy burger and fish and chips. The main restaurant menu runs to starters such as lightly poached smoked haddock with New England-style sweetcorn chowder and soft-boiled quails' eggs, and a bumper prawn cocktail which combines tiger prawns, cold water Atlantic prawns and brown shrimps. Among main courses, confit of English lamb is served with roasted sweet potatoes and buttered curly kale, while slow-braised local port cheeks come with Agen prunes poached in cider. Finish with Baileys brûlée with biscotti.

Chef Nicholas Parker **Owner** Craig Jackson **Seats** 80, Pr/dining room 30 **Times** 12-3/6.30-9 **Prices** Fixed L 2 course £13.95-£25, Fixed D 3 course £17.95-£35, Starter £5-£9.50, Main £9-£25, Dessert £5-£8, Service optional **Wines** 8 bottles over £30, 46 bottles under £30, 14 by glass **Parking** 25 **Notes** Sunday L £10-£20, Vegetarian available, Children welcome

GREAT YARMOUTH
Map 13 TG50

Andover House

◉◉ Modern British

tel: 01493 843490 **28-30 Camperdown NR30 3JB**
email: info@andoverhouse.co.uk **web:** www.andoverhouse.co.uk
dir: *Opposite Wellington Pier, turn onto Shadingfield Close, right onto Kimberley Terrace, follow onto Camperdown. Property on left*

Breezily contemporary cooking in townhouse

A touch of boutique styling has been sprinkled over the white-painted Victorian terrace that is Andover House, and these days it's a rather cool hotel, restaurant and bar, with a spruce look of fashionable muted pastel tones and a distinct lack of chintz. The restaurant is filled with blond wood with nary a tablecloth in sight and is a bright and breezy environment for the cooking, which fits the bill to a T. There's a daily specials board in support of the à la carte menu. The cooking treads a modish path and there are plenty of global flavours on show: first-course crispy beef and spring onion salad with a sweet chilli and pimento dressing, for example, or a vegetarian main course tajine. It's back to Europe for a pasta starter – linguini with pan-fried squid, chorizo, ginger, chilli and lime – and main-courses such as tournedos Rossini or rack of English spring lamb with ratatouille, Parmentier potatoes, minted pears and rosemary jus. For dessert, the tasting plate removes any indecision.

Times 6-9.30 Closed Xmas, Sun-Mon, L all week

Imperial Hotel

◉ Modern British

tel: 01493 842000 **North Dr NR30 1EQ**
email: reception@imperialhotel.co.uk **web:** www.cafecrurestaurant.co.uk
dir: *Follow signs to seafront, turn left. Hotel opposite waterways*

Modern brasserie classics in a grand old seaside hotel

Successive generations of the Mobbs family have been running the grand old Imperial since the 1930s, when one of the attractions that lifted it above the common run of seaside hotels was that guests were seated at separate tables. Its physiognomy has changed somewhat in modern times with the addition of a glassed-in terrace for watching the tide roll in, and the Café Cru restaurant, where frosted glass panels divide the seating booths as though to demonstrate that separate tables are still the elevated norm. Classic dishes from the present-day brasserie repertoire are the stock-in-trade, opening perhaps with lime and chilli scallops and smoked pancetta with minted pea purée, and following on with pesto-crusted cannon of local lamb with puréed parsnip and balsamic courgette ribbons in red wine and rosemary, or sea bass with a risotto of beetroot, mushrooms and Merlot. Finish exotically with spiced coconut rice pudding and caramelised pineapple.

Chef Simon Wainwright **Owner** Mr N L & Mrs A Mobbs **Seats** 60, Pr/dining room 140 **Times** 12-2/6.30-10 Closed 24-28 & 31 Dec, L Sat, Mon, D Sun **Prices** Starter £5-£9, Main £10-£25, Dessert £6-£9, Service optional **Wines** 10 bottles over £30, 30 bottles under £30, 12 by glass **Parking** 45 **Notes** Sunday L £17-£22, Vegetarian available, Children welcome

GRIMSTON
Map 12 TF72

Congham Hall Country House Hotel

◉◉◉ Modern British, European V

tel: 01485 600250 **Lynn Rd PE32 1AH**
email: info@conghamhallhotel.co.uk **web:** www.conghamhallhotel.co.uk
dir: *6m NE of King's Lynn on A148, turn right towards Grimston. Hotel 2.5m on left (do not go to Congham)*

Creative contemporary cooking in charming Georgian house

The Georgian house was built in the 1780s by a wealthy merchant from King's Lynn, which is about the time that the nearby royal residence of Sandringham House was constructed. If an invite to the latter is not forthcoming, fear not, for Congham Hall can provide plenty of cossetting luxury, with gorgeous gardens, a swish spa and a restaurant that has genuine Georgian charm. The dining room has French windows looking onto the garden and pristine, linen-clad tables. There's a herb garden in the grounds with an amazing 400 varieties finding their way to the table, plus a kitchen garden and orchards, and what ingredients don't hail from the grounds are sourced with care from the local environs. The cooking is gently modern and shows allegiance to both the crown and our European partners. Start, perhaps, with a tart of local feta, leek and artichoke, or a duck and chicken liver terrine with garden chutney. For main course, a trio of local pheasant or roasted fillet and liver of Sandringham beef, and for dessert, hot chocolate fondant with popcorn ice cream.

Chef Nick Claxton Webb **Owner** Nicholas Dickinson **Seats** 50, Pr/dining room 18 **Times** 12-2/7-9 **Prices** Starter £6.50-£10.95, Main £13.95-£29.50, Dessert £6.50-£9.50, Service optional **Wines** 78 bottles over £30, 38 bottles under £30, 16 by glass **Parking** 50 **Notes** Gourmand menu L £36, D £71.50 (with wines £101.50), Sunday L, Children welcome

HEACHAM
Map 12 TF63

Heacham Manor Hotel

◉ Modern European

tel: 01485 536030 & 579800 **Hunstanton Rd PE31 7JX**
email: info@heacham-manor.co.uk **web:** www.heacham-manor.co.uk
dir: *On A149 between Heacham & Hunstanton. Near Hunstanton rdbt with water tower*

Fine local produce by the Norfolk coast

The wide-open skies of Norfolk's fabulous coast make Heacham Manor an attractive prospect; the place even comes with its own coastal golf course if you're a player. Originally built as an Elizabethan manor, the hotel has been brought smartly up-to-date by complete renovation in recent years, and its airy conservatory-style Mulberry Restaurant is reason enough to pay a visit. The kitchen's output is simple, staunchly seasonal and driven by a sincere belief in local sourcing – salt marsh lamb comes from Wells-next-the-Sea, and the locally-landed fish and seafood racks up very few food miles on its way to the table. Goats' cheese cheesecake with red onion marmalade and mizuna leaf salad gets things off the blocks, followed by Gressingham duck breast teamed with grain mustard mash, Savoy cabbage, celeriac purée, and blackberry jus. At the end, rhubarb compôte provides a tangy foil to crème brûlée with fennel seed biscotti.

Times 12-2.30/6.30-9

HETHERSETT Map 13 TG10

Park Farm Hotel

Modern British

tel: 01603 810264 **NR9 3DL**
email: enq@parkfarm-hotel.co.uk **web:** www.parkfarm-hotel.co.uk
dir: 6m S of Norwich on B1172

Unfussy modern cooking in a spa hotel

The hotel, with spa and conference facilities, is in a rural location surrounded by 200 acres of countryside. The restaurant looks over the gardens, an open-plan-style room with ceiling spotlights, tall-backed padded chairs at clothed tables and potted plants. The kitchen has a comprehensive outlook, turning out starters of tempura red mullet fillet with lemon and lime salsa, and tender pigeon breast on confit garlic mash with cranberry and onion chutney, pea purée and port jus. Ingredients are of good quality and timings accurate, seen in nicely presented main courses of baked halibut fillet on fennel purée with wasabi mash, diced smoked salmon, braised chicory and pickled raspberries, and partridge roasted with bacon and thyme served on rösti with baby vegetables and red wine sauce. For a notable conclusion, perhaps try hazelnut and Muscovado tart topped with clotted cream on a mixed berry coulis.

Times 12-2/7-9.30

HOLT Map 13 TG03

The Lawns Wine Bar

Modern European

tel: 01263 713390 **26 Station Rd NR25 6BS**
email: info@lawnshotelholt.co.uk **web:** www.lawnshotelholt.co.uk
dir: A148 (Cromer road). 0.25m from Holt rdbt, turn left, 400yds along Station Rd

Populist cooking in a Georgian townhouse

A small hotel dating from Georgian times, The Lawns offers a number of dining options: bar, conservatory, restaurant and south-facing garden. It's a warm and friendly place, reflected in a menu of largely comfortingly reassuring dishes pinned on East Anglian produce. Thai-style beef curry with coconut rice and prawn crackers is about as exotic as things get; more typical are main courses of beer-battered haddock with chips, or braised oxtail with bubble-and-squeak and root vegetables. Bookending them might be prawn and crayfish cocktail, or sautéed pigeon breast with chorizo, red cabbage and mini roast potatoes, and resourceful puddings of Tunisian sticky orange cake with Chantilly cream, or plum crumble cheesecake with raspberry coulis.

Chef Leon Brookes, Adam Kobialka **Owner** Mr & Mrs Daniel Rees **Seats** 24
Times 12-2/6-9 **Prices** Starter £4.95-£7.50, Main £9.95-£18.95, Dessert £5, Service optional **Wines** 2 bottles over £30, 32 bottles under £30, 13 by glass **Parking** 18
Notes Sunday L fr £11.50, Vegetarian available, Children welcome

The Pheasant Hotel & Restaurant

Modern, Traditional **NEW**

tel: 01263 588382 & 588540 **Coast Rd, Kelling NR25 7EG**
email: enquiries@pheasanthotelnorfolk.co.uk **web:** www.pheasanthotelnorfolk.co.uk
dir: On A149 coast road, mid-way between Sheringham & Blakeney

Modern British dining in a smart country house

A smart country-house hotel owned by the Kelling Estate, the Pheasant is within easy reach of the coast, a fact which has not gone unnoticed by the team in the kitchen – Taste of the Sea Night being a particular highlight. The restaurant has a traditional finish with pristine linen, twinkling tea lights and sparkling glasses. It's not only the Norfolk waters that provide their bounty for the table, for the estate plays its part, too, with meat and seasonal game. The modern British output has classical French foundations. Thus jellied ham hock is served as a starter with home-made piccalilli, and Kelling Estate lamb is slow-braised and comes with honey and garlic butter, pommes mousseline and sea purslane. For dessert, lemon posset is partnered with an Eton Mess made with English raspberries. Lunch in the garden is a fair-weather treat and there's a cocktail menu to up the glam stakes.

Chef Simon Holman Marsh **Owner** Mr G Widdowson **Seats** 78, Pr/dining room 30
Times 12-2.30/6-9 **Prices** Starter £6-£7.50, Main £11-£16, Dessert £6-£8.50, Service optional **Wines** 13 bottles over £30, 24 bottles under £30, 12 by glass **Parking** 50 **Notes** Sunday L £20-£26, Children welcome

---

The Watermark Wine Bar & Restaurant

Modern International **V**

tel: 01263 710790 & 07833 392584 **9 Appleyard NR25 6BN**
email: reservations@watermarkholt.com
dir: Just off High Street, signed Appleyard

Eclectic all-day eating and a lovely courtyard garden

What used to be Butlers Restaurant is now The Watermark, with new owners, a new chef, new menus and a fresh look, although the copper beech still stands in the courtyard garden. It's possible to eat at any time of day, while the dinner menu is a wide-ranging affair, with the kitchen, which buys only the best local produce, hijacking global cuisines for inspiration. Starters have included confit duck salad with chilli, spring onion and a sesame and hoisin dressing, and tempura pork with Asian vegetables and sweet chilli dipping sauce. Traditionalists will be pleased to see, among main courses, beef and mushroom pie and rib-eye steak with the usual trimmings, while halibut fillet gets a Thai-style treatment, served with vegetable stir-fry, egg noodles and chilli sauce. Return to base with Bakewell tart partnered by raspberry coulis and clotted cream.

Chef Gemma Arnold **Owner** Mike & Cissy Millsopp **Seats** 55 **Times** 12-5.30/6-9.45
Prices Starter £5.95-£7.25, Main £12.75-£21.95, Service optional **Wines** 5 bottles over £30, 14 bottles under £30, 8 by glass **Parking** On street (free after 6pm)
Notes Italian Tue with live music, Sunday L, Children welcome

Follow us on facebook
www.facebook.com/TheAAUK

HUNSTANTON | Map 12 TF64

Caley Hall Hotel

 Modern British V

tel: 01485 533486 **Old Hunstanton Rd PE36 6HH**
email: mail@caleyhallhotel.co.uk **web:** www.caleyhallhotel.co.uk
dir: *located on A149, Old Hunstanton*

Well-judged menus on the Norfolk coast

Built around a manor dating from 1648, Caley Hall is a short walk to the wide beaches on The Wash, a twitcher's paradise. Its restaurant, in a former stable block, is a relaxing-looking room with a tartan carpet and high-backed leather-look seats at well-spaced tables. It's a popular place, part of the attraction the consistently precise cooking of quality East Anglian produce. The short menu is unlikely to rock any boats, starting with perhaps crayfish cocktail in Marie Rose sauce with avocado purée and tomato confit, followed by beef braised in red wine and rosemary served with celeriac mash, carrots and greens. Look to the specials for more vim: perhaps seared scallops with cauliflower purée, bacon crisps, sorrel and shallot butter, then three ways with pork (slow-cooked belly, herb-crusted fillet, fried liver) with a thyme jus, potato terrine and roasted baby parsnips. Finish with peanut butter parfait with salted peanut brittle, a truffle and griottes.

Chef Amos Burrows **Owner** Caley Hall Hotel Ltd **Seats** 80 **Times** 12-9 **Closed** 22-26 Dec, 5-11 Jan, All-day dining **Prices** Fixed L 2 course £15.95, Fixed D 3 course £17.95, Starter £4.50-£9, Main £10-£19.50, Dessert £6.50-£7, Service optional **Wines** 23 bottles under £30, 6 by glass **Parking** 50 **Notes** Sunday L £10.95, Children welcome

The Neptune Restaurant with Rooms

⊕⊕⊕ *– see below*

KING'S LYNN | Map 12 TF62

Bank House Hotel

⊕ Modern British

tel: 01553 660492 **King's Staithe Square PE30 1RD**
email: info@thebankhouse.co.uk **web:** www.thebankhouse.co.uk
dir: *Follow signs to Old Town and onto quayside, through floodgate, hotel on right opposite Custom House*

Breezy brasserie cooking at the birthplace of Barclays Bank

A Grade II Georgian townhouse on the quayside, handily placed for the Corn Exchange theatre, Bank House is so named because it once housed a bank (Gurney's, which would in due course become Barclays). An outdoor terrace

The Neptune Restaurant with Rooms

⊕⊕⊕

HUNSTANTON | Map 12 TF64

Modern European V
tel: 01485 532122 **85 Old Hunstanton Rd PE36 6HZ**
email: reservations@theneptune.co.uk **web:** www.theneptune.co.uk
dir: *On A149*

Precision-tuned cooking in a smartly converted Norfolk inn

The move from the Isle of Wight to North Norfolk that Kevin and Jacki Mangeolles undertook in 2007 was a bold but hugely productive one. With a prescient eye for the coming fashionability of this glorious region, and an appreciation of the rich natural bounty it offers, the Neptune always had a head start. It may seem as though you can toss up a coin anywhere around here, and it will come down on somewhere good to eat, but if it lands on the Neptune, you really have hit the jackpot. The place is a Georgian coaching inn that has been delicately coaxed into the smart but uncluttered form of a modern restaurant with rooms. Catering for only 24 covers at a time keeps the kitchen precision-tuned, and this is nothing if not intensely focused food. There is a multi-course taster menu, naturally, that begins with the bracing simplicity of a glass of iced tomato juice and builds to the final emergence of a sphere of chocolate doused in warm sauce, with many extraordinary discoveries along the route. The hits are legion: a starter of Brancaster lobster and star anise mousse that comes with chunky lobster salad and fresh pea purée and pea shoots is an exercise in finely judged refreshment of the palate. Afterwards might come Cumbrian rose veal with thin slices of the tongue, alongside diced turnip and smoothly puréed sweetcorn, producing wonderful contrasts of sweet and bitter, or haunch and loin of darkly rich hare, served with creamed celeriac and dauphinoise. Combining the elements of a dessert that comprises damson parfait, apple sponge, apple sorbet and crisp caramel produces sweet alchemy on the taste buds, or there are superb British and French cheeses with grape chutney. Breads are great, as are the petits fours, which may include airily irresistible cinnamon doughnuts with hot chocolate for dipping.

Chef Kevin Mangeolles **Owner** Kevin & Jacki Mangeolles **Seats** 24 **Times** 12-1.30/7-9 **Closed** Jan, 2 wks Nov, 26 Dec, Mon, L Tue-Sat (except by arrangement) **Prices** Starter £12.95-£15.75, Main £25.50-£29.75, Dessert £9.50, Service optional **Wines** 70 bottles over £30, 22 bottles under £30, 14 by glass **Parking** 6, On street **Notes** Sunday L £31.50, Children 10 yrs+

supplements the various indoor eating areas, and the style is laid-back, breezy modern brasserie – as is the food, which aims to please by incorporating sun-splashed Mediterranean style into some traditional British fare. Expect to start by slathering Turkish flatbread with hummus, before gliding on with salmon terrine and tartare sauce, or a sharing platter of antipasti or mixed seafood. Mains run to robust fish dishes such as roast cod with mussels, spinach and gnocchi in curry sauce, or button-pushing meats like confit duck leg with sweet potato gratin, braised red cabbage and buttered peas, with butternut and pepper risotto for the veggies. Close with mango jelly and spiced crème fraîche, or a plate of 'mini-puds'.

Chef Stuart Deuchars **Owner** Jeannette & Anthony Goodrich **Seats** 100, Pr/dining room 40 **Times** 12-2.30/6.30-9 **Prices** Starter £5.25-£7.95, Main £7.95-£17.95, Dessert £3.25-£6.95, Service optional **Wines** 17 bottles over £30, 26 bottles under £30, 15 by glass **Parking** On quayside or Baker Lane car park **Notes** Pre/post theatre menu, Sunday L fr £12, Vegetarian available, Children welcome

NORTH WALSHAM
Map 13 TG23

Beechwood Hotel

@@ Modern British V

tel: 01692 403231 **20 Cromer Rd NR28 OHD**
email: info@beechwood-hotel.co.uk **web:** www.beechwood-hotel.co.uk
dir: From Norwich on B1150, 13m to N Walsham. Left at lights, next right. Hotel 150mtrs on left

Charming hotel with good local ingredients on the menu

This handsome creeper-clad Georgian hotel should exert a strong pull for murder and mystery fans, since Agatha Christie came here frequently to visit when it was owned by family friends, and her framed letters are hung in the hallway. It is a lovely personal touch that sums up the exemplary attitude to service and attention to detail that is the hallmark of this charming small hotel. It all helps you to change down a gear into relaxation mode before settling into an elegantly traditional dining room, which is the setting for some well-crafted, contemporary cooking, delivered by a kitchen with a passion for sourcing top-grade Norfolk produce – much of it from within a ten-mile radius. A perfectly crisp and golden haddock and prawn fishcake with a poached egg, hollandaise sauce and pea shoot salad opens on fine form, ahead of loin of Aylsham lamb partnered simply by rosemary roast potatoes, parsnip purée, carrots and Savoy cabbage. Finally, a textbook crème brûlée is pointed up with vibrant raspberry compôte and coulis.

Chef Steven Norgate **Owner** Don Birch & Lindsay Spalding **Seats** 60, Pr/dining room 20 **Times** 12-1.45/7-9 Closed L Mon-Sat **Prices** Fixed L 3 course £25, Fixed D 3 course £39, Service optional **Wines** 50 bottles over £30, 26 bottles under £30, 11 by glass **Parking** 20 **Notes** Sunday L, Children welcome

NORWICH
Map 13 TG20

Best Western Annesley House Hotel

@@ Modern International

tel: 01603 624553 **6 Newmarket Rd NR2 2LA**
email: annesleyhouse@bestwestern.co.uk **web:** www.bw-annesleyhouse.co.uk
dir: On A11, close to city centre

Georgian hotel with modish menu

Georgian and Grade II listed, Annesley House is a pretty property a short walk from the centre of the city. It's got three acres of gardens to call its own, so really does feel like a little oasis. There are views over the garden from the conservatory restaurant, which has a decidedly contemporary finish with its wood-affect flooring, leather seats and darkwood tables. The kitchen matches the decor with its equally modish approach, which consists of sourcing good quality East Anglian ingredients and subjecting them to some fashionable Pan-European preparations. Thus hand-dived scallops, wrapped in smoky streaky bacon, are served with crisp pork belly, roast shallot purée and chicken jus. Next up, perhaps roast chump of lamb with fondant potato and chargrilled Mediterranean vegetables, or pan-fried salmon with fresh tagliatelle, braised baby gem, sautéed asparagus, broad beans and girolles. And to finish, Tunisian orange cake comes with a prune and orange compôte, stem ginger ice cream and crème anglaise.

Chef Steven Watkin **Owner** Mr & Mrs D Reynolds **Seats** 30 **Times** 12-2/6-9 Closed Xmas & New Year, L Sun **Prices** Prices not confirmed, Service optional **Wines** 10 bottles under £30, 7 by glass **Parking** 29 **Notes** Pre-theatre menu available from 6pm by arrangement, Vegetarian available, Children welcome

Best Western George Hotel

@ Modern British, Mediterranean

tel: 01603 617841 **10 Arlington Ln, Newmarket Rd NR2 2DA**
email: reservations@georgehotel.co.uk **web:** www.arlingtonhotelgroup.co.uk
dir: From A11 follow city centre signs, becomes Newmarket Rd. Hotel on left

Brasserie classics in a stylish Victorian hotel

The large white Victorian hotel is a brisk ten-minute trot from the city centre if you're on foot, in a peaceful conservation area of Norwich. Decorated out front with climbing plants and flowers, it presents a more obviously contemporary look inside, with elegant modern styling in the public rooms, including the Arlington Grill and Brasserie, where tan banquettes and half-clothed tables furnish a long, mirrored room. Simple classic brasserie dishes with something of a Mediterranean slant are the order of the day, beginning with filo parcels of spinach and dolcelatte served with red onion relish, or salmon, crayfish and rocket cocktail with citrus mayo, proceeding to chicken breast with ratatouille, beer-battered haddock and chips, or loin of lamb with caraway cabbage and parmentier potatoes in red wine jus. Desserts aim to please the naughty-but-nice brigade with chocolate mousse cake, tiramisù, or sticky toffee pudding and vanilla ice cream.

Chef Paul Branford **Owner** David Easter, Kingsley Place Hotels Ltd **Seats** 44, Pr/dining room 80 **Times** 12-2/6-10 **Prices** Fixed L 2 course fr £8.95, Starter £4.50-£5.95, Main £10.95-£18.50, Dessert £4.25-£5.95, Service optional **Wines** 18 bottles under £30, 10 by glass **Parking** 40 **Notes** Sunday L £9.50-£16.50, Vegetarian available, Children welcome

NORWICH *continued*

Brasteds

◎◎◎ Modern European

tel: 01508 491112 **Manor Farm Barns, Fox Rd, Framingham Pigot NR14 7PZ**
email: enquiries@brasteds.co.uk **web:** www.brasteds.co.uk
dir: *A11 onto A47 towards Great Yarmouth, then A146. After 0.5m turn right onto Fox Rd, 0.5m on left*

Exciting skilful cooking in a stylish barn conversion

In the village of Framingham Pigot, four miles from the city centre, Brasteds occupies a converted barn, a charming room of raftered ceiling, oak floor and brick walls. Chris 'Buzz' Busby is a skilful and confident chef, compiling seasonally-changing menus that are big on canny ideas, all based on impressive Norfolk produce. Dishes are not without a degree of complexity, but sure-footed experience brings everything together. Starters might be poached ray wing with grape gel, steamed clams and a chorizo and truffle cream, or a terrine of smoked chicken, foie gras and Parma ham with grilled garlic snails and tomato and chive caviar. Main courses are generally in the same vein, although classic bouillabaisse might also make an appearance. Accurately sautéed sea bass, for instance, is plated with creamed potato, artichoke purée spiked with chervil, sticky red cabbage and lemon butter sauce, while lamb fillet gets the Wellington treatment, accompanied by confit of shoulder, minted pea and potato crumble and a rich jus. Welsh rarebit is on offer alongside puddings of cherry Bakewell tart with cherry sorbet and caramelised cherries.

Chef Chris Busby **Owner** Nick Mills, Chris Busby & Michael Zouvani **Seats** 40, Pr/dining room 16 **Times** 12-2.30/7-10 Closed Sun-Wed, L Sat, Thu **Prices** Starter £7.85-£12.95, Main £19.50-£28, Dessert £8.50-£10.25, Service optional **Wines** 8 by glass **Parking** 50 **Notes** Vegetarian available, Children welcome

Brummells Seafood Restaurant

◎ International, Seafood

tel: 01603 625555 **7 Magdalen St NR3 1LE**
email: brummell@brummells.co.uk **web:** www.brummells.co.uk
dir: *In city centre, 2 mins walk from Norwich Cathedral, 40yds from Colegate*

Venerable seafood restaurant in a 17th-century building

A blue-fronted, beamed, 17th-century building in the historic heart of Norwich is home to chef-patron Andrew Brummell's seafood restaurant. Venerable beams and standing timbers, round-backed wooden chairs at the tables, and candlelight in the evenings create a romantic atmosphere, but it's the uncomplicated approach to seafood cookery that attracts the loyal crowds. Preparations vary from classics like pan-fried skate with black butter, lobster (thermidor or Mornay) if you're in a spendy mood, or Dover sole Véronique, baked with Vermouth and cream, to the more modern: monkfish fritters with roast tomato relish, or steamed sea bass with prawn butter, ginger and leeks. Starters show the same broad sweep, from Brancaster mussels with creamy Champagne sauce, to squid stewed with ink and red wine. There are meat dishes too – local venison steak with Marsala and juniper berry sauce, say, and to finish there might be iced pear parfait with nutmeg mascarpone and caramelised pear.

Chef A Brummell, J O'Sullivan **Owner** A Brummell **Seats** 25 **Times** 12-flexible/6-flexible **Prices** Prices not confirmed, Service optional **Wines** 39 bottles over £30, 42 bottles under £30, 6 by glass **Parking** On street after 6.30pm & Sun, Car park nearby **Notes** Sunday L, Vegetarian available, Children welcome

Roger Hickman's Restaurant

◎◎◎

Modern British
tel: 01603 633522 **79 Upper St Giles St NR2 1AB**
email: info@rogerhickmansrestaurant.com
dir: *In city centre, from A147 at rdbt into Cleveland Rd, 1st left into Upper St Giles St*

Finely calibrated modern British cooking at a destination address

The premises just off Grapes Hill have long been one of the destination addresses, the pre-eminent one indeed, on the Norwich restaurant scene. A warren of intricately knocked-through rooms with stripped floors, the place has subtly altered in ambience over the years from a rough-and-ready bistro feeling to the present, distinctly upmarket look. Pale walls with a hint of lemon, floor-length napery, arched windows and near-abstract landscape prints create a soothing, almost neutral backdrop, but one not lacking in hospitable warmth. Norfolk and East Anglian produce informs Roger Hickman's culinary practice, and his style, while unmistakably in the current British idiom, feels lighter, fresher, less exhaustively worked than can be the case. Dishes look texturally striking as well as appetising, as when a fillet of blowtorched mackerel appears with puffed wild rice, beetroot and nasturtiums, or the various incarnations of quail – its leg, breast and egg – arrive in the company of celeriac and apple for bite and watercress to add a peppery, savoury note. Reference vegetable ingredients of the new British cooking – kale, sprout tops, cavolo nero, salsify – are distributed throughout the main courses, the last two with a serving of crackled pork belly that also comes with salt-baked turnip and raisins for a full range of counterpointing flavours, while pickled cucumber and dill add their acerbity and fragrance to simply grilled sea bream. A pre-dessert allows a moment's pause before multi-layered desserts such as a poached pear with mascarpone mousse, thyme frangipane and milk snow, or rice pudding with poached prunes and Earl Grey mousse. Everything is finely calibrated, with combinations delicately judged and yet striking in their impact. Optional wine choices on the taster menu are inspired, running perhaps to Picpoul de Pinet, Chilean Gewürztraminer, Pinot Noir from Romania and California Black Muscat, among others.

Chef Roger Hickman **Owner** Roger Hickman **Seats** 40 **Times** 12-2.30/7-10 Closed 1 wk Jan & Aug, Sun-Mon **Prices** Prices not confirmed, Service optional **Wines** 95 bottles over £30, 14 bottles under £30, 12 by glass **Parking** On street & St Giles multi-storey **Notes** Pre-theatre menu £20/£24, Vegetarian available, Children welcome

The Maids Head Hotel

⊛ Modern British

tel: 01603 209955 **Tombland NR3 1LB web:** www.maidsheadhotel.co.uk
dir: A147 to north of the city. At rdbt for A1151, signed Wroxham, follow signs for Cathedral and Law Courts along Whitefriars. Hotel is approx 400 mtrs on right along Palace St

Sound modern cooking in city-centre hotel

This part-timbered, part-brick building opposite the cathedral has its roots in the 13th century, although nowadays it provides conference facilities as well as all the other amenities expected of a modern hotel. Its restaurant is in a splendid room, once a courtyard, now glassed over with a pitched roof; it's airy and spacious, with a terracotta floor and well-appointed darkwood tables. Well-presented, modern British dishes are the kitchen's stock in trade. A trendy starter like properly cooked scallops with pancetta crisps and cauliflower purée may be followed by something old-fashioned and hearty like a game pie – its meat tender, its pastry perfectly crisp, with a rich gravy – served with roasted root vegetables. Finish with a lively, exotic pudding like smooth-textured coconut pannacotta with seared mango and caramel.

Times 12-3/6.30-9.30

The Old Rectory

⊛⊛ Modern British V

tel: 01603 700772 **103 Yarmouth Rd, Thorpe St Andrew NR7 0HF**
email: enquiries@oldrectorynorwich.com **web:** www.oldrectorynorwich.com
dir: From A47 southern bypass onto A1042 towards Norwich N & E. Left at mini rdbt onto A1242. After 0.3m through lights. Hotel 100mtrs on right

Georgian rectory hotel with a local flavour

Creepers cover the large Georgian house giving the impression the garden is attempting to reclaim the land – but the red-brick former rectory is here to stay, built to last back in the day and thriving in the 21st century as a country hotel. The centre of Norwich is only a couple of miles away, but you'd never know it once ensconced in the drawing room. The dining room has a traditional finish, a room of generous proportions and period details, and is the setting for candle-lit dinners (afternoon tea is also available). The daily-changing menu has a good showing of regional produce and keeps to a sensibly manageable choice of three dishes per course. Starters of potted dressed Cromer crab or beetroot- and dill-cured organic salmon are typical of the output. Among main courses, roasted fillet of brill is served with a warm vegetable and potato salad and a saffron and brown shrimp dressing, and Gressingham guinea fowl might feature as marinated breast and slow-roasted thigh (served with buttery Savoy cabbage).

Chef James Perry **Owner** Chris & Sally Entwistle **Seats** 18, Pr/dining room 16 **Times** 7-9 Closed Xmas, New Year, Sun, L all week **Prices** Fixed D 3 course £27-£30, Service optional **Wines** 5 bottles over £30, 16 bottles under £30, 5 by glass **Parking** 16 **Notes** Children welcome

Roger Hickman's Restaurant

⊛⊛⊛ – see opposite

St Benedicts Restaurant

⊛ Modern British, French

tel: 01603 765377 **9 St Benedicts St NR2 4PE**
email: stbenedicts@rafflesrestaurant.co.uk
dir: Just off inner ring road. Turn right by Toys-R-Us, 2nd right into St Benedicts St. Restaurant on left by pedestrian crossing

Imaginative accomplished cooking in the heart of Norwich

This popular city-centre restaurant has been going strong for more than 20 years. A blond-wood floor, pale wooden tables and chairs and pale blue tongue-and-groove panelling all combine to give it a light, airy feel, a convivial place in which to enjoy some consistently accomplished cooking based on indigenous produce. Starters of duck rillettes with home-made plum chutney, and hot-smoked salmon with green beans, red onion and crayfish set the standards. The main courses have a good balance of flavours without being over-complicated: slow-cooked crispy duck, say, with mustard sauce, caramelised apple, bubble-and-squeak and glazed carrots, or well-timed grilled sea bass fillet with pea purée, Jerusalem artichokes and waxy new potatoes. End with one of the moreish desserts like dark chocolate délice with raspberries, or lemon buttermilk pudding with candied zest.

Chef Nigel Raffles **Owner** Nigel & Jayne Raffles **Seats** 42, Pr/dining room 24 **Times** 12-2/6-10 Closed 25-31 Dec, Sun-Mon **Prices** Prices not confirmed **Wines** 8 by glass **Parking** On street, Car parks nearby **Notes** Prix Fixe menu 6-7pm Tue-Sat 2 course £10, Vegetarian available, Children welcome

St Giles House Hotel

⊛⊛ Modern British

tel: 01603 275180 **41-45 St Giles St NR2 1JR**
email: reception@stgileshousehotel.com **web:** www.stgileshousehotel.com
dir: A11 into central Norwich. Left at rdbt signed Chapelfield Shopping Centre. 3rd exit at next rdbt. Left onto St Giles St. Hotel on left

Classic and modern dishes in an architectural gem

You could punctuate your perusal of Norwich city centre's retail opportunities with a pitstop in St Giles House for coffee, a massage, cocktails or something more gastronomically satisfying in the SGH Bistro. The grand Edwardian pile is worth a gander in its own right – beyond its magnificent pillared facade is a palatial interior of marble floors, oak panelling and elaborate plaster ceilings, all sharpened with a slick contemporary makeover. The art-deco bistro restaurant is a slick setting for the kitchen's appealing repertoire of uncomplicated modern dishes, as witnessed in a smooth and well-flavoured chicken liver parfait served with celeriac remoulade, tomato chutney and melba toast, ahead of pan-fried chicken breast teamed with a leek and wild mushroom pie, olive oil mash, sautéed baby carrots and Marsala sauce. To finish, there's peanut butter and chocolate parfait served with chocolate biscotti, peanut brittle and salted caramel sauce. Smartly turned-out in black, the front-of-house team are a polished act who keep everything running smoothly.

Chef Stewart Jefferson **Owner** Rachel Roofe **Seats** 50, Pr/dining room 48 **Times** 11-10 All-day dining **Prices** Fixed D 3 course £32.50, Starter £5.25-£9, Main £13.50-£24, Dessert £5-£8, Service optional **Wines** 23 bottles over £30, 37 bottles under £30, 19 by glass **Parking** 30 **Notes** Afternoon tea available £13.50, Sunday L £17.50-£21.50, Vegetarian available, Children welcome

NORWICH *continued*

Sprowston Manor, A Marriott Hotel & Country Club

 Traditional British, International

tel: 01603 410871 **Sprowston Park, Wroxham Rd NR7 8RP**
email: mhrs.nwigs.frontdesk@marriotthotels.com
web: www.marriottsprowstonmanor.co.uk
dir: *From A47 take Postwick exit onto Norwich outer ring road, then take A1151. Hotel approx 3m and signed*

Grand manor house serving cleverly modernised classics

The centre of Norwich isn't all that far away, but this elegant step-gabled manor feels countrified though-and-through. The full country-house package is on offer, with a championship golf course to call its own, plus a swanky spa and a couple of dining options. The Restaurant 1559 is the smarter of the two restaurants, but there's nothing stuffy about the place. It takes a brasserie-style approach and the menu trades in bright, contemporary presentations. Basil-roasted peach partnered with vodka and cranberry jelly is an inventive first course, or there might be battered cod cheeks with caramelised orange. Main-course duo of Norfolk pork (belly and cheek) comes with braised red cabbage and fondant potato, and there are local steaks cooked on the grill. Finish with warm treacle tart with clotted cream or raspberry cheesecake.

Chef Martin Ng **Owner** Marriott International Inc **Seats** 70, Pr/dining room 150 **Times** 12.30-3/6-10 Closed L Mon-Sat **Prices** Fixed L 2 course £17, Starter £6-£11, Main £14-£21, Dessert £6, Service optional **Wines** 3 bottles over £30, 22 bottles under £30, 10 by glass **Parking** 170 **Notes** Vegetarian available, Children welcome

Stower Grange

 Modern British

tel: 01603 860210 **40 School Rd, Drayton NR8 6EF**
email: enquiries@stowergrange.co.uk **web:** www.stowergrange.co.uk
dir: *Norwich ring road N to ASDA supermarket. Take A1067 (Fakenham road) at Drayton, right at lights into School Rd. Hotel 150yds on right*

Eclectic dining in a Norfolk rectory

The creeper-covered former rectory a few miles out of Norwich makes a relaxing rural retreat, and is decorated in classic country-house style, with a dining room done in restful pastel shades looking out through full-drop windows on to the well-tended gardens. Menus offer a broad range of choice, from the oriental mash-up that is Thai-spiced duck with mango and chilli chutney and duck wonton, to mains such as slow-cooked belly of Blythburgh pork with sweet potato fondant, spiced chick peas and preserved lemon purée, or roast hake with braised lentils, salsa verde and wilted spinach. It's good to see sharper flavours being celebrated in desserts like lemon sponge with lemon curd sauce and gooseberry ice cream.

Chef Lee Parrette **Owner** Richard & Jane Fannon **Seats** 25, Pr/dining room 100 **Times** 12-2.30/6.30-9.30 Closed 26-30 Dec, D Sun **Prices** Starter £5.50-£7.50, Main £12.95-£19.50, Dessert £6.50, Service optional **Wines** 6 bottles over £30, 37 bottles under £30, 8 by glass **Parking** 40 **Notes** Light bite menu £5.50-£9.50, Sunday L fr £25, Vegetarian available, Children welcome

The Sugar Hut

 Thai

tel: 01603 766755 **4 Opie St NR1 3DN**
email: lhongmo@hotmail.co.uk
dir: *City centre next to Castle Meadow & Castle Mall car park*

Vibrant Thai food near the castle

Leelanooch Hongmo's expanding empire now incorporates four restaurants: this venue near the castle, plus two others in Norwich, and one in Coltishall. The ethos throughout combines the famed courtesy of Thai service with a menu dealing in the sweet, hot-and-sour currents of classic cooking from that country. A yellow and blue colour scheme offsets the black-clad staff to a T, and the food is as bracing and vibrant as you would hope. Khanom jeep – dumplings of steamed marinated minced pork and prawns, deep-fried in wonton pastry – are a good way to set about things, or you could kick start the palate with lime-sharp tom yam gung soup. Main course curries – fiery beef gang ped red curry, for example – are the real deal, while roast duck with seaweed and tamarind sauce offers an excursion beyond the usual Thai staples. Good pad Thai, drunken noodles, or fried rice with crabmeat provide a fragrant accompaniment.

Chef Chartchai Fodsungnoen, Saowanee Hongmo **Owner** Leelanooch Hongmo **Seats** 40 **Times** 12-2.30/6-10.30 Closed Sun, L Mon **Prices** Fixed L 2 course £8.95-£9.95, Fixed D 3 course £27.50, Starter £4.95-£6.50, Main £8.95-£16.95, Dessert £2-£4.95, Service optional **Wines** 3 by glass **Parking** Castle Mall **Notes** Vegetarian available, Children welcome

Thailand Restaurant

 Thai V

tel: 01603 700444 **9 Ring Rd, Thorpe St Andrew NR7 0XJ**
email: siamkidd@aol.com
dir: *From Southern bypass, follow airport signs. Located at top of hill past Sainsbury's*

True flavours of Thailand in busy out-of-town restaurant

Plants and colourful hanging baskets add some dash to the exterior of this well-established restaurant. Inside, the decor is as busy on the eye as the bamboo-framed upholstered seats are as busy with customers: drapes over the windows, statues in niches, friezes on the ceiling beams and lots of greenery. What marks out the cooking is the sourcing of authentic ingredients, the accurate use of spicing and seasoning and spot-on timing to replicate the true flavours of Thailand's cuisine in the suburbs of Norwich. From the long menu comes namoo – deep-fried minced pork within a bread base served with plum and chilli sauce – alongside the more commonplace chicken satay, followed by tender spare ribs marinated in curry sauce, beef musaman – braised steak stewed with red curry paste, roasted peanuts and new potatoes – and prawns stir-fried with garlic in oyster sauce and coriander. Finish with a refreshing sorbet or go back to base with bananas in creamy coconut milk sauce.

Chef Anan Sirphas, Sampoin Jukjan **Owner** Richard & Onuma Kidd **Seats** 55 **Times** 12-3/6-10 Closed 25 Dec, L Sat-Sun **Prices** Prices not confirmed, Service optional **Wines** **Parking** 25 **Notes** No children

SHERINGHAM   Map 13 TG14

Dales Country House Hotel

British, European

tel: 01263 824555 **Lodge Hill NR26 8TJ**
email: dales@mackenziehotels.com **web:** www.mackenziehotels.com
dir: *On B1157, 1m S of Sheringham. From A148 Cromer to Holt road, take turn at entrance to Sheringham Park. Hotel 0.5m on left*

Smart modern cooking in rural Norfolk

Handy for a stopover if you've been ogling the spectacular rhododendrons and azaleas in Humphry Repton's Sheringham Park gardens next door, you'll find that the grounds of the Dales Country House Hotel are no slouch either. Just a couple of miles from the big skies of the North Norfolk coast, the step-gabled Victorian house has heaps of period charm, although the cooking in Upchers restaurant takes a rather more contemporary European view of things. With the briny so near, fish and seafood is always going to be a good idea – perhaps gratin of local mussels with brown shrimps and Cromer crab velouté to start, then a delicate millefeuille of sea bass and lobster with fennel, chicory rösti potato, and girolles. Local meat plays its part too – maybe cannon of lamb partnered by confit lamb hash cake, butternut squash ratatouille, aubergine caviar and thyme sauce. To finish, try a sweetshop array of cinnamon doughnuts, strawberry jelly, chocolate sauce and caramel ice cream, or go savoury with a plate of Norfolk's finest cheeses.

Chef Rene Ilupar **Owner** Mr & Mrs Mackenzie **Seats** 70, Pr/dining room 40 **Times** 12-2/7-9.30 **Prices** Fixed D 3 course £23, Service optional **Wines** 6 bottles over £30, 26 bottles under £30, 7 by glass **Parking** 50 **Notes** Full afternoon tea, Sunday L £16.95, Vegetarian available, Children welcome

---

SNETTISHAM   Map 12 TF63

The Rose & Crown
 British

tel: 01485 541382 **Old Church Rd PE31 7LX**
email: info@roseandcrownsnettisham.co.uk **web:** www.roseandcrownsnettisham.co.uk
dir: From King's Lynn take A149 N towards Hunstanton. After 10m into Snettisham to village centre, then into Old Church Rd towards church. Hotel 100yds on left

Consistently popular village inn with hearty cooking

The stone-built whitewashed country inn stands in a north Norfolk village a little way from King's Lynn. Inside is all twisty passageways and lowering beams, with a crackling fire to warm the winter away, and the full array of hand-pumped ales, flagged floors and hearty cooking. It isn't unknown for locals to dine here three or four times a week, which should tell you something, and what they return for are fried sardines in arrabbiata sauce, crisp-skinned salmon in seafood chowder, and sterling meat dishes from the environs, such as pigeon with a black pudding and mushroom tart and sprouting broccoli, or duck breast with bubble-and-squeak and green beans in red wine jus. House classics include exemplary fish and chips and Lincolnshire sausages and mash in a gravy of Adnams bitter. Finish with eggnog pannacotta, served with a poached pear and biscotti.

Chef Jamie Clarke **Owner** Anthony & Jeanette Goodrich **Seats** 160, Pr/dining room 30 **Times** 12-2/6.30-9 **Prices** Starter £4.95-£7.95, Main £11.50-£18.25, Dessert £3.95-£6.25, Service optional **Wines** 10 by glass **Parking** 70 **Notes** Sunday L £13.95, Vegetarian available, Children welcome

---

STALHAM   Map 13 TG32

The Ingham Swan
◎◎ Modern European **NEW**

tel: 01692 581099 **Sea Palling Rd, Ingham NR12 9AB**
email: info@theinghamswan.co.uk **web:** www.theinghamswan.co.uk

14th-century thatched foodie inn with daily-changing menu

Originally part of Ingham priory, the 14th-century Swan survived Henry VIII's attempts to demolish it, and still presents the timeless face of a thatched chocolate box inn to the 21st-century world. Like many a country pub, the old place has traded up these days – if you fancy a pint, there's a cosy bar serving Woodforde's ales, but the driving force is the stylish rustic restaurant where exposed Norfolk flint walls, oak parquet floors, beams and an inglenook are overlaid with modern art. Daily-changing menus are built on local materials handled skilfully and without fuss to deliver a repertoire offering plenty to tempt. Seared pigeon breast with earthy wild mushroom and truffle oil risotto, crispy pancetta and swede purée is strong opener, followed by a confidently-cooked main course of pan-fried wild sea bass with crispy Cromer crab cakes, buttered local asparagus, samphire and watercress velouté. The kitchen continues to deliver the goods right through to a seriously impressive pudding showcasing seasonal rhubarb as sorbet, poached, and in a pannacotta with vanilla, and ginger syrup.

Chef Daniel Smith **Owner** Daniel Smith **Seats** 55 **Times** 12-2/6-9 Closed 25-26 Dec **Prices** Fixed L 2 course £15, Fixed D 3 course fr £26.95, Tasting menu fr £47.50, Starter £6.50-£9.50, Main £14.50-£24.95, Dessert £6-£8.50, Service optional **Wines** 27 bottles over £30, 21 bottles under £30, 9 by glass **Parking** 12, On street **Notes** Sunday L £20.95-£26.95, Vegetarian available, Children welcome

---

THETFORD   Map 13 TL88

Elveden Café Restaurant
◎ Traditional British

tel: 01842 898068 **London Rd, Elveden IP24 3TQ**
email: lucy.wright@elveden.com
dir: On A11 between Newmarket & Thetford, 100 mtrs from junct with B1106

Fresh seasonal cooking in a busy farm shop

The 10,000 acres of the Guinness estate in Norfolk are the base for a modern agricultural enterprise, supplying a formidable annual tonnage of fresh produce to East Anglia and beyond, with a raftered farm shop at its heart. The all-day café it incorporates is a bright, open space with granite tables and a wall of deep windows. At lunchtimes, it hosts quite a press of enthusiastic regular business, but service remains attentive and focused, and the weekend pre-Christmas party nights are a blast. A weekly-changing menu of sensitively cooked seasonal dishes, precisely seasoned and neatly presented, might open with smoked salmon and prawn potato cakes in mango-chilli dressing, and continue with braised pig cheeks on celeriac purée with smoked mash, or pan-roasted Loch Duart salmon on pasta with artichokes and peas in a vivid, sharp watercress sauce. Finish with a bravura version of lemon meringue pie, served with clotted cream and seasonal berries.

Chef Scott Taylor **Owner** The Earl of Iveagh **Seats** 80 **Times** 9.30-5 Closed 25-26 Dec, D all week **Prices** Starter £5.50-£7.50, Main £10.95-£13.95, Dessert £5.50-£5.95, Service optional **Wines** 6 bottles under £30, 6 by glass **Parking** 200 **Notes** Sunday L £10.95-£11.95, Vegetarian available, Children welcome

---

THURSFORD   Map 13 TF93

The Old Forge Seafood Restaurant
◎ Seafood

tel: 01328 878345 **Fakenham Rd NR21 0BD**
email: sarah.goldspink@btconnect.com **web:** www.seafoodnorthnorfolk.co.uk
dir: On A148

Rustic seafood cooking in a historic former forge

The whitewashed former coaching station and forge used to be a resting place for pilgrims heading to Walsingham, and even merits a name-check in The Pilgrim's Progress. A sympathetic refurbishment means beams, York stone floor and walls; even the original iron hooks where the horses were shod are in evidence in the cosy, buzzy restaurant. It's all about the seafood here, and why not, when you can get it in fresh every day from nearby Blakeney and Wells-next-the-Sea? Expect good, honest, rustic cooking, often with Spanish influences and using spices grown in the forge's garden. There might be sizzling tiger prawns in the Spanish way, served with chunks of bread, lobster grilled with garlic and parsley butter, or a zarzuela of fish – another Spanish dish with white fish and shellfish cooked in white wine, cream and tomatoes, served in a large paella-style pan.

Chef Colin Bowett **Owner** Colin & Sarah Bowett **Seats** 28 **Times** 6.30-10 Closed Mon, L all week, D Sun **Prices** Fixed D 3 course £19.50, Starter £3.95-£10.50, Main £14.50-£34, Dessert £3.95-£5.95, Service optional **Wines** 1 bottle over £30, 12 bottles under £30, 5 by glass **Parking** 12 **Notes** Opening times vary (phone to check), no late bkgs Jan-Feb, Vegetarian available, Children 5 yrs+

Find out more about how we assess for Rosette awards on page 9

TITCHWELL
Map 13 TF74

Titchwell Manor Hotel
@@@ – *see opposite*

WIVETON
Map 13 TG04

Wiveton Bell
@ British, European

tel: 01263 740101 **The Green, Blakeney Rd NR25 7TL**
email: wivetonbell@me.com **web:** www.wivetonbell.co.uk
dir: *1m S of Blakeney on the Holt road*

Flying the regional flag in a north Norfolk country inn

An authentic Georgian country pub on the village green next to a fine old church, the Bell is near Blakeney and the salt-marshes of north Norfolk. Done up in light and airy modern fashion, it's perfectly placed to capitalise on the pick of regional seasonal produce, which of course includes fine seafood from local boats. There's even work by local artists on display to orient you even more securely. The cooking has a pleasingly traditional air about it, with the odd splash of Mediterranean sunshine for such as gilt-head bream poached in olive oil with escabèche vegetables. Otherwise, expect smoked haddock fishcake with spinach and sorrel in saffron velouté, then treacle-cured beef blade with a horseradish beignet and mash. Bringing up the rear might be an Eton Mess made with winter fruits, or orange and star-anise blancmange with candied orange and roast almonds. Norfolk cheeses include Walsingham Cheddar and Temple's wonderful Binham Blue.

Chef Dean Horgan **Owner** Berni Morritt & Sandy Butcher **Seats** 60
Times 12-2.15/6-9.15 Closed 25 Dec **Prices** Prices not confirmed **Wines** 6 bottles over £30, 22 bottles under £30, 13 by glass **Parking** 5, village green 50yds away
Notes Sunday L, Vegetarian available, Children welcome

See advert opposite

WYMONDHAM
Map 13 TG10

Number Twenty Four Restaurant
@@ Modern British

tel: 01953 607750 **24 Middleton St NR18 0AD web:** www.number24.co.uk
dir: *Town centre opposite war memorial*

Relaxed dining and market fresh produce

Jonathan and Isobel Griffin's restaurant in the heart of the historic market town doesn't want for period charm. The row of Grade II listed cottages dates from the 18th century and once you cross the threshold all is soothingly refined and genteel. The mood is relaxed and hospitable. In the kitchen, Jonathan creates dishes that strike a good balance between fine-dining sparkle and hearty satisfaction. There's evident care in the sourcing of ingredients, with local and seasonal produce to the fore, and a good deal of skill in the execution. The modern British output might see pheasant hotpot rich with cider, apple and bacon, or a fashionable pairing of seared tiger prawns with crispy pork belly (served on Thai-spiced cauliflower). Main-course seared loin of venison might follow, or grilled breast of duck with celeriac purée and confit fennel, or a twice-baked Comté soufflé with creamy cauliflower. Among desserts, spotted dick with vanilla custard competes with a Pavlova perked up with warm spiced rum.

Chef Jonathan Griffin **Owner** Jonathan Griffin **Seats** 60, Pr/dining room 55
Times 12-2/7-9 Closed 26 Dec, 1 Jan, Mon, L Tue, D Sun **Prices** Fixed L 2 course fr £15.95, Fixed D 3 course fr £26.50, Service optional **Wines** 3 bottles over £30, 30 bottles under £30, 7 by glass **Parking** On street opposite, in town centre car park
Notes Sunday L £15.95-£17.95, Vegetarian available, Children welcome

Follow the AA on twitter @TheAA_Lifestyle

What makes a 3-Rosette restaurant?
See page 9

Titchwell Manor Hotel

TITCHWELL

Map 13 TF74

Modern European

tel: 01485 210221 **PE31 8BB**
email: margaret@titchwellmanor.com **web:** www.titchwellmanor.com
dir: On A149 (coast road) between Brancaster & Thornham

Assertive contemporary cooking in majestic North Norfolk

Margaret and Ian Snaith and their son Eric set up here back in 1988, in a Victorian farmhouse near Brancaster, a wee hop from the majestic coast. What they have achieved here is testament to their own sound judgment, genuine enthusiasm and, of course, hard work. It's a consummate operation, run with avoidance of undue ceremony, but welcoming guests and diners in with understated warmth. The conservatory dining room with its fairy-lights and smart table appointments looks just right as a backdrop for the younger Mr Snaith's cooking. With a relatively large brigade for such a place, Eric Snaith offers an assertive, bold-as-brass style of contemporary cooking that draws on pedigree East Anglian produce and wild ingredients, presented in the form of a seven-course 'Conversation' menu, which can be taken in an edited four-stage version for the more abstemious. Ideas flow freely, the presentations are bewitching, and the impact on the palate dynamic. The whole event might open with tender lobster tail, partnered with crab-apple purée and solferino balls of seasoned cucumber, prior to a serving of truffled sweetcorn with sea purslane and popcorn. The principal fish may be cod cooked in charcoal oil with sea buckthorn berries, duck-fat carrots and cobnuts in dashi stock, following which comes white fallow venison en ragoût with baby beetroots and puréed parsley root. After a cheese course, and perhaps a little salted yoghurt with grapefruit and honeycomb, the show closes with barbecued pineapple, pineapple meringue and coconut cake, all fragrant with lemon verbena.

Chef Eric Snaith **Owner** Margaret & Ian Snaith **Seats** 80 **Times** 12-5.30/6.30-9.30 **Prices** Tasting menu £45-£60, Starter £6-£13, Main £9-£27, Dessert £7-£10, Service optional **Wines** 9 by glass **Parking** 50 **Notes** Tasting menu D 5/8 course, Sunday L £23-£27, Vegetarian available, Children welcome

The Wiveton Bell Pub with Rooms

• Stylish Interiors, Open Fire, Service Second to none
• Newly refurbished Rooms with Private Balconies
• South facing Garden Terrace. Candle Lit by Night

www.wivetonbell.com

AA Rosette Award

Reservations **01263 740101** or book online at
www.wivetonbell.com

NORTHAMPTONSHIRE

DAVENTRY
Map 11 SP56

Fawsley Hall
◎◎ Modern British

tel: 01327 892000 **Fawsley NN11 3BA**
email: info@fawsleyhall.com **web:** www.fawsleyhall.com
dir: *A361 S of Daventry, between Badby & Charwelton, hotel signed (single track lane)*

Assertive modern British cooking in a grand setting

Plantagenets, Tudors and Georgians all had a go at Fawsley Hall over the centuries, resulting in the beguiling architectural mishmash we see today. It screams 'grand', with oak panels, stone arches and the fabulous Equilibrium dining room, where a 25-foot-high beamed ceiling and huge inglenook, flagstone floor and flickering candlelight create a real sense of occasion. That said, the number of covers is kept low, so that a proper feeling of intimacy pervades the place, and the kitchen deals in imaginative 21st-century ideas with clever flavour combinations and impeccable ingredients. Start perhaps with pressed Landes foie gras with apricot granola and sour apples, or yellow fin tuna sashimi pointed up by lime oil, pressed tomatoes, wasabi rouille and basil caviar. Main courses might offer seared halibut with vegetable tajine, confit squid, chickpeas and lemon oil, or a pairing of smoked belly pork with langoustines, supported by cocotte potatoes, carrot purée and sorrel and watercress sauce. Desserts stay creative with the likes of poached pear with pickled walnuts, and Roquefort ice cream.

Times 7-9.30 Closed Xmas/New Year, Sun-Wed, L all week

EASTON-ON-THE-HILL
Map 11 TF00

The Exeter Arms
◎ Modern British

tel: 01780 756321 **21 Stamford Rd PE9 3NS**
email: reservations@theexeterarms.net **web:** www.theexeterarms.net
dir: *From A43 enter village, inn 300yds on left*

Smartly revamped old inn with a local flavour

The Exeter Arms is an old inn that seems entirely in tune with its environment, which must be down to the fact it's owned by a local farming family. The place combines rustic charm with an opened-up modernity, so there lots of natural surfaces and real ales at the bar, but also some contemporary, muted colour tones and well-chosen country-style fixtures and fittings. The family farm provides food for the table in the form of beef, lamb and pork, and what isn't grown or produced by this industrious team is sourced with care and attention (quite often locally, too). Whether you eat in the restaurant, snug or Orangery, expect to begin with simple, carefully-crafted starters such as goats' cheese fritters with basil and sweet pepper chutney, or wild mushroom and spinach risotto. Next up, Grasmere Farm pork belly with a potato cake vies with a burger with home-made chips, or go for classic beer-battered fish and chips.

Chef Nigel Fish **Owner** Michael Thurlby, Sue Olver **Seats** 80, Pr/dining room 24
Times 12-2.30/6-9.30 Closed D Sun **Prices** Starter £5-£8.50, Main £12.50-£19.95, Dessert £5.25-£7.95, Service optional **Wines** 3 bottles over £30, 38 bottles under £30, 19 by glass **Parking** 30 **Notes** Sunday L £14.50-£20.50, Vegetarian available, Children welcome

KETTERING
Map 11 SP87

Kettering Park Hotel & Spa
◎ Modern British

tel: 01536 416666 **Kettering Parkway NN15 6XT**
email: kpark.reservations@shirehotels.com **web:** www.ketteringparkhotel.com
dir: *Off A14 junct 9 (M1 to A1 link road), hotel in Kettering Venture Park*

International classics in a characterful hotel restaurant

A member of the Shire spa hotels group, Kettering Park belies its location in a business park by having a degree of charming personality about it. The restaurant boasts a real open fire in winter for a start, and is a multi-tiered room with an appealing look of the modern brasserie, with views over the gardens at the back. The menu deals in the international stalwarts of today, but turned out with proficiency and style, and there is a buffet featuring a selection of local produce, from Melton Mowbray pies to Leicestershire cheeses. Kickstart the taste buds with coriander-laced salad of crispy duck and pickled ginger in sesame oil and soy, or salt-and-pepper squid with aïoli, before building up to a mighty steak and mushroom suet pudding with greens and mash in thyme-scented red wine and shallot gravy. Finish nostalgically with apple and blackberry crumble, or warm treacle tart and custard.

Chef Jamie Mason **Owner** Shire Hotels **Seats** 90, Pr/dining room 40
Times 12-1.45/7-9.30 Closed Xmas, New Year (ex residents & pre-booked), L Mon-Sat **Prices** Fixed D 3 course £20.95, Starter £5.95-£14.95, Main £11.95-£27.95, Dessert £5.95-£6.95, Service optional **Wines** 27 bottles over £30, 49 bottles under £30, 16 by glass **Parking** 200 **Notes** Sunday L £16.95-£19.95, Vegetarian available, Children welcome

Rushton Hall Hotel and Spa
◎◎◎ – see opposite

NASSINGTON
Map 12 TL09

The Queens Head Inn
◎◎ Modern British

tel: 01780 784006 **54 Station Rd PE8 6QB**
email: info@queensheadnassington.co.uk **web:** www.queensheadnassington.co.uk
dir: *A1M N exit Wansford, follow signs to Yarwell & Nassington*

Inviting riverside inn with treats from the grill

Standing on the banks of the River Nene in the postcard-pretty village of Nassington, the Queens Head is a delightful mellow stone inn with a relaxed vibe and a solid line in muscular modern cooking built on locally-sourced ingredients. The 200-year-old hostelry still functions as a pub if you fancy a jar, but it is food that really drives the action these days. When you have a serious piece of kit such as a charcoal-fired Josper grill and oven in the kitchen, it makes sense to focus on unfussy meat and fish dishes sizzled to perfection on the flames. If you're up for some serious meat action, the steaks are impeccably sourced, and even extend to a rib-eye of Wagyu beef. Otherwise, you might take on hickory-smoked rump of lamb with rosemary croquettes, wild garlic, Chantenay carrots and wine jus, and end with salted caramel doughnuts with maple-glazed peanuts, ginger powder and orange ice cream.

Chef Erran Buckingham **Owner** Complete Hotels Ltd **Seats** 40, Pr/dining room 70
Times 12-2.30/6-9 **Prices** Fixed L 2 course £12.50, Starter £4.95-£8.50, Main £10.95-£15.75, Dessert £5.95-£7.50, Service optional **Wines** 6 bottles over £30, 23 bottles under £30, 14 by glass **Parking** 45 **Notes** Sunday L, Vegetarian available, Children welcome

OUNDLE
Map 11 TL08

Oundle Mill

◎◎ Modern British NOTABLE WINE LIST

tel: 01832 272621 **Barnwell Rd PE8 5PB**
email: info@oundlemill.co.uk
dir: *Located just outside Oundle off A605*

Confident cooking in comfortably converted mill

The River Nene that fueled the old mill for so many years wrought havoc in 2012, forcing the restaurant to close for four months until March 2013, but rest assured, the old mill is back. Oak beams, standing timbers and stone walls bring a rustic-chic character to the space, while the kitchen follows suit to some degree, with a successful rustic-chic style of its own. Country farmhouse terrine, for example, is a first course with accompanying spiced fruit chutney and toasted sourdough bread, or there might be squid ink risotto with fried squid and squid crackers. There's a good deal of technical ability in the kitchen and some good modish thinking. Thus North Atlantic cod appears in a main course with saffron polenta, chorizo tempura, Norfolk spinach and red sorrel cress, and wood pigeon turns up in Wellington guise, with chicory and orange marmalade, thatched potatoes and sloe gin. Finish in style with a lemon sherbet jelly, lemon curd and lemon meringue ice cream.

Chef Gavin Austin **Owner** Mark & Sarah Harrod **Seats** 50, Pr/dining room 45 **Times** 12-2.30/6.30-9.30 Closed 25-26 Dec, 1 Jan, Mon-Tue, D Sun **Prices** Fixed L 2 course £15, Fixed D 3 course £18, Tasting menu £38.50-£46, Starter £6-£7.50, Main £15.50-£21, Dessert £4.95-£7, Service optional **Wines** 175 bottles over £30, 47 bottles under £30, 18 by glass **Parking** 60 **Notes** Thu offer ALC 3 course £18.95, Sunday L £19.50-£22.50, Vegetarian available, Children welcome

The Talbot Hotel

◎ British

tel: 01832 273621 **New St PE8 4EA**
email: talbot@bulldogmail.co.uk **web:** www.thetalbot-oundle.com
dir: *A605 Northampton/Oundle at rdbt exit Oundle A427 - Station Road turn onto New Street*

Brasserie favourites in an ancient hostelry

There has been a hostelry of some sort on this site since the seventh century, and the current manifestation of The Talbot certainly looks the ancient part. In the centre of charming Oundle, it now appears as a multi-faceted package, offering a hotel, eatery and coffee-house. The small dining room has been given a minimalistic modern makeover, with bare tables and fine cutlery, and is a comfortable space, although you are actually welcome to eat wherever you like, including the paved courtyard and garden. A long menu is comprised of today's brasserie favourites – smoked haddock and salmon fishcake, steak, ale and mushroom pie – as well as some more off-piste dishes. A generous bowl of crab linguine seasoned with chilli, dill and lemon in crème fraîche starts things off well, and may be succeeded by roast breast of Goosnargh duck with sweet potato in a distinctly retro raspberry dressing. Finish with a slice of bracingly tangy lemon tart sauced with blueberry coulis.

Chef David Simms **Owner** Bulldog Hotel Group **Seats** 48, Pr/dining room 64 **Times** 12-2.30/6.30-9.30 **Prices** Starter £6-£13, Main £12-£20, Dessert £1.75-£7, Service optional **Wines** 9 bottles over £30, 30 bottles under £30, 16 by glass **Parking** 30 **Notes** Sunday L £12-£29, Vegetarian available, Children welcome

Rushton Hall Hotel and Spa

❀❀❀

KETTERING
Map 11 SP87

Modern British
tel: 01536 713001 **Rushton NN14 1RR**
email: enquiries@rushtonhall.com **web:** www.rushtonhall.com
dir: *A14 junct 7, A43 to Corby then A6003 to Rushton, turn after bridge*

Innovative British cooking in a magnificent old hall

Rushton Hall looks to all intents and purposes like a stately home. There are 25 acres of gorgeous grounds to wander through, while, on the inside, the hotel does not fail to impress. The restaurant, under the auspices of head chef Adrian Coulthard, is an oak-panelled panoply with a huge fireplace and smartly turned out tables. Chef brings a touch of 21st-century innovation to the menu. He delivers the most striking platefuls that make an impression, with two plump scallops arriving atop a piece of grey slate, with textures of cauliflower and raisins, and a nicely judged aroma of curry, or seared breast of squab pigeon served up with its crisp confit leg, Puy lentils and fig jam. These are successful combinations, with the execution well up to the mark. Main courses might deliver 28-day-aged rump of Aberdeenshire beef, partnered with its slow-cooked shin and root vegetables, or steamed fillets of plaice with crab tortellini. The creative flourishes and well-judged flavours extend into desserts such as a cheesecake – goats' cheese and lemon version, with candied walnuts and fizzy grapes – or a soufflé made with mango and arriving at the table with a banana and passionfruit sorbet. Save room for the British cheeses if you can, for a fine selection is on offer including, perhaps, Wode Hill from Bedfordshire and Bosworth Ash from Tamworth in Staffordshire. There's a lounge menu and afternoon tea on offer, too.

Chef Adrian Coulthard **Owner** Tom & Valerie Hazelton **Seats** 40, Pr/dining room 60 **Times** 12-1/7-9 Closed L Mon-Sat **Prices** Service optional **Wines** 62 bottles over £30, 30 bottles under £30, 11 by glass **Parking** 140 **Notes** Fixed L 3 course only available Sun, ALC 3 course £55, Sunday L £30, Vegetarian available, Children 10yrs+ D

ROADE
Map 11 SP75

Roade House Restaurant

Modern British

tel: 01604 863372 **16 High St NN7 2NW**
email: info@roadehousehotel.co.uk
dir: M1 junct 15 (A508 Milton Keynes) to Roade, left at mini rdbt, 500yds on left

Much-loved village restaurant with rooms serving interesting fare

With Silverstone race track and the M1 in the vicinity, the Roade House is just the ticket, slowing down the frenetic pace and delivering soothing hospitality in a village setting. It's a family-run place with ten bedrooms and a restaurant where chef-patron Chris Kewley and his team take the time and effort to make everything on the premises. The dining room is decorated in a traditional manner, with pastel tones and the tables topped with white linen, and there's no truck with 21st-century affectations. The food is not stuck in the past, though, for flavour is always at the forefront and inspiration drawn from far and wide. Portuguese chorizo and kale soup might stand alongside rillettes of fresh and smoked salmon among the starters, with main courses running to Hungarian goulash or grilled fillet of halibut with crab tortellini and chive butter sauce. For dessert there might be a pannacotta with rhubarb syrup. There are regular themed nights.

Chef Chris Kewley **Owner** Mr & Mrs C M Kewley **Seats** 50, Pr/dining room 16 **Times** 12-2/7-9.30 Closed 1 wk Xmas, BHs, L Sat, Mon, D Sun **Prices** Fixed L 2 course £20.50, Starter £5.75-£9, Main £16.50-£23.25, Dessert £6.50, Service optional **Wines** 20 bottles over £30, 20 bottles under £30, 4 by glass **Parking** 20 **Notes** Sunday L £20.50-£23.50, Vegetarian available, Children welcome

WEEDON
Map 11 SP65

Narrow Boat at Weedon

Modern British NEW

tel: 01327 340333 **Stowe Hill, A5 Watling St NN7 4RZ**
email: info@narrowboatatweedon.co.uk **web:** www.narrowboatatweedon.co.uk
dir: M1 junct 16 follow signs Flore. At A5 junct turn south towards Towcester. Located on Grad Union Canal

Canalside eatery serving classic and modern fare

The place is not an actual narrowboat, but plenty of them moor up for this popular dining inn's modern British cooking. Easy to find on the A5, it's an enticing spot for alfresco meals in summer with watery views and fields all around, while the kitchen caters to all comers with menus taking in everything from pub classics – home-made pies, burgers made from top-grade beef, say – to stone-baked pizzas, and more up-to-date ideas in the restaurant. Start with pressed ham hock with minted pea purée, a ham and cheese bonbon and English mustard mayo before going on to main business such as pan-seared duck breast with a cottage pie of confit leg meat with baby veg and red wine jus. The finale is a reworking of the good old rhubarb and custard theme: custard pannacotta with the rhubarb element appearing as ice cream, poached and jelly with ginger biscotti.

Chef Daniel Turner **Owner** Richard & Karen Bray **Seats** 100, Pr/dining room 40 **Times** 12-2.30/6-10 Closed 26 Dec, All-day dining **Prices** Fixed L 2 course £13.50, Starter £4.75-£7.95, Main £8.95-£22.95, Dessert £5-£7.50, Service optional 10% **Wines** 4 bottles over £30, 25 bottles under £30, 20 by glass **Parking** 40 **Notes** Sunday L £11.95-£14.50, Vegetarian available, Children welcome

WHITTLEBURY
Map 11 SP64

Whittlebury Hall

Modern British, European

tel: 01327 857857 & 0845 400 0002 **NN12 8QH**
email: reservations@whittleburyhall.co.uk **web:** www.whittleburyhall.co.uk
dir: A43/A413 towards Buckingham, through Whittlebury, turn for hotel on right (signed)

Contemporary and creative fine dining and motor-racing

Whittlebury Hall, a plush neo-Georgian hotel with a Rolls Royce of a spa, lies just a Ferrari's roar away from Silverstone. The much-loved Formula 1 commentator Murray Walker lends his name to its sophisticated fine dining restaurant, where some of his celebrated gaffes are immortalised on the walls, together with F1 memorabilia. While the slick front-of-house team ensures diners can relax in the slow lane, the kitchen shifts into top gear with its modern British cooking underpinned by finely-tuned classical techniques. A starter entitled 'ham, egg and chips' grabs the attention, delivering ham hock and Serrano ham with truffled scrambled egg and golden raisin jus, while line-caught sea bass with garlic, sauce basquaise, mussels and grapes turns up at main course stage. Meatier offerings might run to veal sirloin with lentils, celeriac root, pied bleu mushrooms and baby turnips, and for pudding, a take on millefeuille is served with raspberries, with champagne and lemon sorbet.

Chef Craig Rose **Owner** Whittlebury Hall and Spa Ltd **Seats** 32, Pr/dining room 10 **Times** 7-9.30 Closed selected dates at Xmas, 31 Dec, Sun-Mon, L all week **Prices** Starter £10-£14, Main £19-£28, Dessert £10-£12.50, Service optional **Wines** 34 bottles over £30, 18 bottles under £30, 7 by glass **Parking** 460 **Notes** Tasting menu available, Vegetarian available, No children

Read our interview with chef Michael Caines on page 29

Learn the latest foodie trends in Birmingham and Manchester on page 21

NORTHUMBERLAND

BAMBURGH
Map 21 NU13

Waren House Hotel

◉ Modern British

tel: 01668 214581 **Waren Mill NE70 7EE**
email: enquiries@warenhousehotel.co.uk **web:** www.warenhousehotel.co.uk
dir: Exit A1 on B1342, follow signs to Bamburgh. Hotel in 2m in village Waren Mill

Local supplies for country-house cooking

Handily placed for exploring the coast by Bamburgh Castle and Lindisfarne Island, Waren House is a Georgian mansion set in six acres of landscaped grounds with sea views. Everything cries out classic country-house style, from the grandfather clock and log fires to the oil paintings and soothing blue-and-gold hues of the restaurant, where burnished tables and gleaming glassware reflect the candlelight at dinner. Tradition is the watchword in the kitchen, too, starting with diligent sourcing of the region's finest ingredients, which are brought together in a broadly modern British style. A well-made Doddington cheese soufflé is served simply with sweet beetroot chutney, followed by a more involved main course of pavé of halibut with wilted spinach, yellow pea purée, and mussels in leek, cream, and vermouth sauce with bacon crumbs. A dark chocolate fondant, its centre soft and oozing, is a good way to finish, especially when it comes with white chocolate sorbet, crème fraîche, and chocolate streusel.

Chef Steven Owens **Owner** Mr & Mrs Laverack **Seats** 28 **Times** 6.30-8.30 **Prices** Prices not confirmed, Service optional **Wines** 83 bottles over £30, 126 bottles under £30, 8 by glass **Parking** 20 **Notes** Vegetarian available, No children

BERWICK-UPON-TWEED
Map 21 NT95

Magna

◉ Indian NEW

tel: 01289 302736 & 306229 **39 Bridge St TD15 1ES**
email: oliul.khan@gmail.co.uk
dir: A1 Berwick next to the old bridge

Skilled tandoori cooking and local ingredients at a popular restaurant

Since firing up the tandoor in 1982, Magna has earned a reputation for top-notch Indian cooking. It occupies a rather grand Victorian building close to the original bridge over the Tweed, and inside bright red chairs add a cheery glow to the space. The menu has plenty of familiar curry-house standards on the menu, but the thing that sets the place apart is its use of local meats (including game) and locally-grown vegetables. Start with bhuna prawns on puri, a dish with sensitively balanced spicing and good, plump prawns, or maybe lamb tikka cooked in the tandoor. The main course of horeen makhani is succulent pieces of venison in a creamy sauce with almonds, fresh tomatoes and subtle spicing, or go for a sagwala dish made with fresh spinach leaves. Incidentals like naan and rice are on the money, and lucky locals can get a takeaway if they wish.

Chef Oliul Khan **Owner** The Khan family **Seats** 85, Pr/dining room 40 **Times** 12-2/5-11.30 **Prices** Fixed L 2 course £5.95, Fixed D 3 course £22.95-£34.95, Starter £3.95-£8.95, Main £6.95-£15.95, Dessert £2.95-£4.95 **Wines** 2 bottles over £30, 16 bottles under £30, 6 by glass **Parking** 60 **Notes** Sunday L £5.95-£9.95, Vegetarian available, Children welcome

CHATHILL
Map 21 NU12

Doxford Hall Hotel & Spa

◉◉ Modern British V

tel: 01665 589700 **NE67 5DN**
email: info@doxfordhall.com **web:** www.doxfordhall.com
dir: 8m N of Alnwick just off A1, signed Christon Bank & Seahouses. B6347 then follow signs for Doxford

Modish treatments of local supplies

A continuous programme of investment and generous dollops of TLC in recent years have brought food and rooms fully up to 21st-century spec at Doxford. Entered through a classic period portico, the late-Georgian pile is framed in ten acres of landscaped grounds (including a maze) just a short drive from Alnwick and the Northumbrian coast. For those intent on pampering and rejuvenation, there's a classy spa and leisure club, while gastronomes will find no fault with the elegant restaurant, where a huge stone fireplace, white linen, burnished wood panelling and full-length windows make for a luminous setting. Fresh, local and seasonal are clearly buzz words, and the kitchen takes a gently modern approach that sits comfortably alongside tried-and-tested classics. Seared rabbit and prawn with braised paella rice, chorizo, mussels and rabbit beignet is an intelligent reworking of the paella theme, while casserole of pheasant served with steamed suet and leek pudding, thyme and pancetta impresses with the quality of produce and power of its flavours. Warm pear and almond tart with pistachio ice cream is a good way to finish.

Chef Paul Blakey **Owner** Robert Parker **Seats** 60, Pr/dining room 200 **Times** 12-2/6.30-9.30 **Prices** Starter £8.50-£9.50, Main £15.50-£23.95, Dessert £7.95, Service optional **Wines** 25 bottles over £30, 47 bottles under £30, 15 by glass **Parking** 100 **Notes** Afternoon tea available, Sunday L £23.95, Children welcome

CORNHILL-ON-TWEED
Map 21 NT83

Tillmouth Park Country House Hotel

◉ Modern British

tel: 01890 882255 **TD12 4UU**
email: reception@tillmouthpark.force9.co.uk **web:** www.tillmouthpark.co.uk
dir: A698, 3m E from Cornhill-on-Tweed

Seasonal cooking in a splendid mansion

Close to the Scottish border, this lovely old mansion, originally built in 1882 as a family home, is set in 15 acres of landscaped gardens. It's a peaceful and atmospheric place to stay, where real fires, comfy sofas and oil paintings abound. Dining here is leant a sense of occasion before you even sit down, as entry to the elevated Library Dining Room — with candlelit tables and views over the grounds — is via a beautiful wooden staircase around the edge of the tower. The kitchen turns out some classically-based modern British food with menus informed by the best of local produce. Prawn cocktail or duck leg confit with orange chutney and chocolate and balsamic syrup might start you off, followed, perhaps, by pork fillet Wellington with an indulgent creamed mushroom sauce. Cinnamon and apple strudel with vanilla ice cream is another classic done well to bring things to a close.

Chef Piotr Dziedzic **Owner** Tillmouth Park Partnership **Seats** 40, Pr/dining room 20 **Times** 7-9 Closed 26-28 Dec, Jan-Mar, L all week **Prices** Starter £4.95-£7.50, Main £12.50-£18.95, Dessert £5-£8.25, Service optional **Wines** 18 bottles over £30, 33 bottles under £30, 7 by glass **Parking** 50 **Notes** Vegetarian available, Children welcome

HEXHAM
Map 21 NY96

Barrasford Arms

 Traditional & Modern British

tel: 01434 681237 **NE48 4AA**
email: contact@barrasfordarms.co.uk
dir: A69 at Acomb onto A6079 towards Chollerton. Turn left at church and follow signs to
Barrasford

Modern English cooking in a genuine country inn

Not far from the heritage landmark of Hadrian's Wall, surrounded by the undulating
grandeur of the Northumberland hills, the Barrasford is an authentic country inn
with ivy climbing over its facade. A suite of three dining rooms is kitted out with
rustic furniture, the walls hung with pictures of the place in bygone days. Tony
Binks works to a modern English template, with the emphasis firmly placed on
regional supplies and big flavours. Ham hock terrine with pease pudding and toast
is a characteristically earthy start, but if you're after something lighter, a twice-
cooked Cheddar soufflé should fit the bill. Moving on, there may be full-flavoured
grilled sea bass in lobster sauce with crunchy spring cabbage, or tenderest lamb
shank in red wine, garlic and rosemary, served with a cloud of fluffy champ. Finish
with a slice of plum and almond tart with vanilla sauce, or a lemon posset
scattered with summer berries.

Chef Tony Binks **Owner** Tony Binks **Seats** 60, Pr/dining room 10 **Times** 12-2/6.30-
close Closed 25-26 Dec, BHs, Mon (Nov-Mar), L Mon, D Sun **Prices** Fixed L 2 course
£13, Starter £5-£7.50, Main £9.50-£17, Dessert £6, Service optional **Wines** 1 bottle
over £30, 19 bottles under £30, 7 by glass **Parking** 30 **Notes** Sunday L £11-£17.50,
Vegetarian available, Children welcome

De Vere Slaley Hall

 Modern & Classic British

tel: 01434 673350 **Slaley NE47 OBX**
email: slaley.hall@devere-hotels.com **web:** www.devere.co.uk
dir: A1 from S to A68 link road follow signs for Slaley Hall. From N A69 to Corbridge then
take A68 S and follow signs to Slaley Hall

Old and new in a grand Northumbrian manor

From its elevated position, the imposing Edwardian pile of Slaley Hall looks out over
1,000 acres of parkland, and beyond to the wild and rugged Northumberland
countryside. There's plenty going on at Slaley – luxury accommodation, two
championship golf courses, a spa and fitness centre, and three dining venues.
Duke's Grill is the top dining option, a bay-windowed dining room done in tasteful
Edwardiana, with wing-backed chairs in claret upholstery, lit framed pictures and
mirrors, and an air of unruffled calm. The cooking balances old and new, setting out
with a simple but effective combo of fried duck egg with Stornoway black pudding,
crispy pancetta and truffle dressing. Next up, prime cuts of meat and fish are
cooked on the Josper grill – perhaps a whole rack of Ingram Valley lamb for two to
share, or monkfish wrapped in Bayonne ham and delivered with squid céviche.

Chef Michael Eames **Owner** De Vere Hotels **Seats** 40, Pr/dining room 30
Times 6.30-9.45 Closed L all week **Prices** Starter £6-£9, Main £18-£65 **Wines** 54
bottles over £30, 20 bottles under £30, 15 by glass **Parking** 200 **Notes** Afternoon tea
available, Vegetarian available, Children welcome

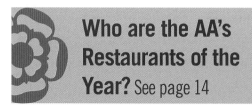

Who are the AA's Restaurants of the Year? See page 14

Langley Castle Hotel

 Modern British

tel: 01434 688888 **Langley on Tyne NE47 5LU**
email: manager@langleycastle.com **web:** www.langleycastle.com
dir: From A69 S on A686 for 2m. Hotel on right

Modern European cooking in a genuine medieval castle

The word 'castle' often appears to cover a multitude of extravagances and follies in
Britain, but Langley is the real thing, a fortified pile dating from Edward III's reign
in the mid-14th century, complete with battlements and seven-foot-thick walls. As
the centuries rolled, it weathered the Jacobite rising and ownership by the
Admiralty, and enters the modern age as one of England's most diverting hotels.
The Josephine dining room has something of the feel of a particularly opulent
country inn, with its heavy beams and sturdy stone walls, but Andrew Smith brings
things up to date with modern European dishes of nice judgment and flair. Twice-
cooked belly of piglet sounds a little medieval, to be sure, but partnered with black
pudding crumble, cauliflower purée and whisky sauce and the time-machine
hurtles us forward. The same is true of main courses such as baked cod in a pine-
nut and lemon crust, served with cockle and parsley risotto in langoustine bisque,
and what could be more 'now' than bread-and-butter pudding made with
panettone, garnished with Cointreau butterscotch and vanilla mascarpone?

Chef Andy Smith **Owner** Dr S Madnick **Seats** 48, Pr/dining room 28
Times 12-2.30/7-9 **Prices** Fixed L 2 course fr £17.95, Fixed D 3 course £42.50,
Starter £5.95-£10.50, Main £18.95-£26.50, Dessert £9.95, Service optional
Wines 21 bottles over £30, 33 bottles under £30, 10 by glass **Parking** 57 **Notes** 4
course D £42.50, Sunday L £24.95, Vegetarian available, Children welcome

LONGHORSLEY
Map 21 NZ19

Macdonald Linden Hall, Golf & Country Club

 Modern British

tel: 01670 500000 **NE65 8XF**
email: lindenhall@macdonald-hotels.co.uk **web:** www.macdonaldhotels.co.uk/lindenhall
dir: 7m NW of Morpeth on A697 off A1

Appealing mainstream cooking in a grand Georgian manor

The late-Georgian manor house of Linden Hall sits in 450 acres of park and mature
woodland amid uplifting views of the Cheviots and wild Northumberland
landscapes. As one might expect, a hotel of this standing comes with its own
championship golf course and a full complement of spa and health and fitness
facilities to sharpen the appetite. At its culinary heart is the upscale Dobson
Restaurant, a plush venue done out in warm autumnal tones of russet and brick-
red, with linen-clothed tables and relaxed, professional service. It makes a suitably
refined setting for well-conceived dishes based on carefully-sourced raw materials.
Tried-and-tested themes aim to comfort rather than challenge diners, so ham hock

terrine is accompanied by mustard mayonnaise, then main course brings roasted corn-fed chicken breast stuffed with sun-blushed tomato mousse and matched with sweet potato fondant, braised red cabbage and red wine jus. Otherwise, there may be braised pork belly with vegetable dauphinoise, caramelised apple and cider jus. To finish, there's a classic lemon meringue pie with raspberry sorbet.

Times 12.30-2/6.45-9.45 Closed Mon-Thu (winter), L Mon-Sat, D 31 Dec

---

MATFEN
Map 21 NZ07

Matfen Hall

Modern British

tel: 01661 886500 & 886400 **NE20 0RH**
email: info@matfenhall.com **web:** www.matfenhall.com
dir: *A69 signed Hexham, leave at Heddon-on-the-Wall. Then B6318, through Rudchester & Harlow Hill. Follow signs on right for Matfen*

Dinner in the library at an ancestral home

Ancestral home of the Blacketts since the reign of George II, the hall we see at Matfen today is a creation of the Victorian era. Only 15 miles out of Newcastle, but wrapped in 300 acres of rolling northern parkland, it's an oasis of pastoral calm, with all the modern amenities from spa treatments to golf. The library, still replete with shelves of old volumes, does duty as the dining room, and has taken to the role well, with plenty of natural light by day and a romantic air in the evenings. Chris Delaney's extensive contemporary menus make a neat counterpoint to the surroundings, offering a crab salad with pea purée, crab pannacotta and the jolt of chilli jam to start, and then fantastic local beef tournedos under a bone marrow crust with braised leeks in a sauce of the sublimely fruity Magic Ale brewed by nearby High House Farm. Fish could be seared stone bass with rainbow chard, kale and samphire in bouillabaisse. A well-executed glazed lemon tart with raspberry sorbet makes a fine finish.

Times 12-2.30/6.45-9.30 Closed L Mon-Sat

MORPETH
Map 21 NZ18

Eshott Hall

British, European

tel: 01670 787454 **Eshott NE65 9EN**
email: info@eshotthall.co.uk **web:** www.eshotthall.co.uk
dir: *Eshott signed from A1. N of Morpeth*

Ambitious cooking of Northumbrian produce

Between Morpeth and Alnwick, Eshott Hall is a compact boutique hotel in a handsome Georgian property, its front covered with wisteria, within lovely gardens and woodland. It makes a perfect base from which to explore the Northumberland National Park and end the day with dinner in the elegantly appointed restaurant, with its moulded plasterwork on the walls, a soothing gold colour scheme and a fire in cooler weather. Chris Wood is a creative chef who takes full advantage of the natural bounties of the area, with some vegetables and fruit from the hotel's kitchen garden. Pork belly wonton with apple jelly and crackling, and Craster smoked salmon with Seahouses crab, celeriac remoulade and watercress salad are the sort of lively starters to expect. Main courses maintain his style, seen in well-crafted dishes of seasonal roast saddle of venison with braised ox cheek, pommes Anna, baby shallots and veal jus, and halibut fillet with an accomplished tarragon cream sauce, heritage potato, roast squash and fennel. End on a sweet note such as tiramisù mousse with coffee and vanilla cream.

Chef Chris Wood **Owner** Rev Robert Parker **Seats** 30, Pr/dining room 30
Times 1-2.30/6-9.30 Closed private functions **Prices** Fixed L 2 course £25, Fixed D 3 course £25, Service optional **Wines** 12 bottles over £30, 20 bottles under £30, 14 by glass **Parking** 60 **Notes** Sunday L £22.50, Vegetarian available, Children welcome

---

WARENFORD
Map 21 NU12

The White Swan

Modern British

tel: 01668 213453 & 07500 080571 **NE70 7HY**
email: dianecuthbert@yahoo.com
dir: *100yds E of A1, 10m N of Alnwick*

Rural pub serving fine local food

Warenford is only a couple of miles off the A1, and yet it feels reassuringly remote, hiding away amid the rolling countryside. The White Swan is a locals' favourite, with a good reputation for its locally supplied meat, served in a raised dining area with unclothed chunky wood tables and a properly rustic feel. Staff are relaxed enough to chat, and what they bring you is hefty portions of carefully presented modern pub cooking. Salmon and dill fishcakes are generously constructed and offset with the nice surprise of a mango mayonnaise, while main might be well-crackled pork belly on a heap of parsnip, apple and black pudding, sauced powerfully with Calvados, or maybe a whole lemon sole with asparagus in vermouth and elderflower hollandaise. Cocoa potency is the selling point of a hunk of chocolate and Amaretto torte with vanilla ice cream.

Chef Mark Poole **Owner** Andrew & Diane Hay **Seats** 65, Pr/dining room 30
Times 12-2.30/6-9 **Prices** Starter £4.85-£8.95, Main £10.25-£18.95, Dessert £4.95, Service optional **Wines** 3 bottles over £30, 31 bottles under £30, 10 by glass **Parking** 50 **Notes** Sunday L £8.95-£9.25, Vegetarian available, Children welcome

---

NOTTINGHAMSHIRE

FARNDON
Map 17 SK75

Farndon Boathouse

Modern European, International

tel: 01636 676578 **Off Wyke Rd NG24 3SX**
email: info@farndonboathouse.co.uk
dir: *From A46 rdbt (SW of Newark-on-Trent) take Fosse Way signed Farndon. Turn right into Main St signed Farndon. At T-junct turn right into Wyke Lane, follow Boathouse signs*

Up-to-date brasserie cooking in a riverside setting

The leafy banks of the meandering River Trent make an interesting contrast to the contemporary exposed ducting, industrial-style lighting, stone floors and glazed frontage of the stylish Boathouse. The kitchen is driven by the guiding principles of sourcing locally and seasonally, and using modern cooking techniques such as sous-vide to squeeze every molecule of flavour from the ingredients. Uncomplicated contemporary brasserie dishes run the gamut from starters such as in-house-smoked duck breast with marinated feta cheese, compressed melon and lamb's lettuce, and cashew crumb, to seared sea bass with home-made pesto and parmesan gnocchi, squash purée and roast tomatoes; meaty ideas are along the lines of pan-fried pheasant breast with potato terrine, crispy ham, confit garlic and peas and roasting juices. Finish with the home comforts of sticky toffee pudding with milk ice cream and caramel sauce.

Chef Dan Garner **Owner** Dan Garner, Nathan Barton **Seats** 120 **Times** 12-3/6-9.30 **Prices** Fixed L 2 course £14.95, Fixed D 3 course £17.95, Starter £4.95-£11.95, Main £9.95-£27.50, Dessert £6.50-£8.50, Service optional **Wines** 20 bottles over £30, 10 bottles under £30, 18 by glass **Parking** 18 **Notes** Early bird menu L & 6-7pm daily, Sunday L, Vegetarian available, Children welcome

GUNTHORPE Map 11 SK64

Tom Browns Brasserie

◉◉ Modern International

tel: 0115 966 3642 **The Old School House, Trentside NG14 7FB**
email: info@tombrowns.co.uk **web:** www.tombrowns.co.uk
dir: A6097, Gunthorpe Bridge

Creative cooking in an old Victorian schoolhouse

The rather fashionable retro decor at Tom Browns Brasserie suits the Victorian space – once a schoolhouse, and hence the name – with a clever mix of old and new creating a spot-on dining space for the 21st century. There are natural colour tones on the walls, wooden floors and fixtures and fittings such as old chandeliers and modern lampshades. Best of all, though, is the setting by the River Trent, and the mezzanine deck with its delicious watery vista. The cooking matches the mood of the place with contemporary inclinations and creative thinking. Scottish king scallops might feature in a first course with crispy squid and avocado purée, chorizo and Pepperdew salad, with another partnering a stilton soufflé with fig jam and candied walnuts. The upscale brasserie-vibe continues in main course such as the char-grilled Scottish steaks or roasted loin of cod with an onion tart, and a dessert of passionfruit pannacotta with coconut mousse and brandy snaps.

Chef Tom Franiuk **Owner** Adam & Robin Perkins **Seats** 100, Pr/dining room 20 **Times** 12-2.30/6-9.30 Closed D 25-26 Dec **Prices** Starter £5.50-£12.95, Main £12.95-£25.95, Dessert £6.95-£8.95, Service optional **Wines** 15 bottles over £30, 43 bottles under £30, 16 by glass **Parking** 28, On street **Notes** Early bird L 12-3pm, Fixed D 6-7pm, Sunday L, Vegetarian available, Children welcome

LANGAR Map 11 SK73

Langar Hall

◉◉ Modern British

tel: 01949 860559 **Church Ln NG13 9HG**
email: info@langarhall.co.uk **web:** www.langarhall.com
dir: Signed off A46 & A52 in Langar village centre (behind church)

A unique country house with a local flavour

It was never originally in the owner's game plan to run this handsome saffron-washed Victorian mansion as a hotel, but after dipping a toe into the water, she dived in with great enthusiasm and has infused the place with a one-off character.

An avenue of lime trees runs past croquet lawns, a 12th-century church, and carp-filled medieval fishponds; inside, is an elegant scene of statues, crystal chandeliers, antiques and oil paintings, while dining takes place in a romantic marble-pillared dining room lit by silver candelabra, or in an airy conservatory. The kitchen's repertoire is built on ingredients from the garden, game from local estates and top-class stuff from local producers, and veers eclectically from simple classics – a twice-baked cheese soufflé, perhaps – to elaborate modern ideas, such as pan-fried brill with crème fraîche crushed new potatoes, braised fennel, brown shrimp and tarragon. Elsewhere, pig's cheek croquette might be partnered by smoked eel, salt-baked beetroot, pickled apple and mustard, while potato gnocchi, home-made ricotta, wild garlic and green olives could be the supporting cast for an assiette of Langar lamb.

Times 12-2/7-10

NOTTINGHAM Map 11 SK53

Cockliffe Country House

◉◉ Modern European

tel: 0115 968 0179 **Burntstump Country Park, Burntstump Hill, Arnold NG5 8PQ**
email: enquiries@cockliffehouse.co.uk **web:** www.cockliffehouse.co.uk
dir: M1 junct 27, follow signs to Hucknall (A611), then B6011, right at T-junct, follow signs for Cockliffe House

Intelligent flavour combinations in an elegant country setting

It's hard to believe Cockliffe is a mere seven miles from the vibrant city centre of Nottingham, set as it is in three acres of garden with its own wood. Nevertheless, the grey-stone building has been here since the 17th century and is a lovely place to enjoy a peaceful break with some aesthetically pleasing cooking. The intimate dining room seats around 20 and is tastefully decorated with gilt mirrors, striking artwork and luxurious gold swag curtains framing the windows that look out over the gardens. Home-made individual brioche served with cep butter paves the way for a well-executed confit quail leg with seared breast, foie gras and white peaches, while another starter of Scottish scallops, pork pie purée, apples and trotter nuggets is typical of the kitchen's creative style. A sure hand at balancing contrasting flavours is evident in saddle of spring lamb, salsa verde, polenta cake and red pepper purée with a red wine jus. Lemon tart with crème anglaise and raspberry sorbet ends things on a high.

Times 6-9.30 Closed Sun, L all week

Restaurant Sat Bains with Rooms

NOTTINGHAM   Map 11 SK53

Modern British V ◆ NOTABLE WINE LIST

tel: 0115 986 6566 **Lenton Ln, Trentside NG7 2SA**
email: info@restaurantsatbains.net
web: www.restaurantsatbains.com
dir: *M1 junct 24, A453 for approx 8m. Through Clifton, road divides into 3 - take middle lane signed 'Lenton Lane Industrial Estate', then 1st left, left again. Follow brown Restaurant Sat Bains sign*

Analytical dining from a quicksilver creative intellect

Sat Bains' professional life is lived in the spotlight. You'd expect a bit of TV work here and there and a book launch every now and then, par for the course at this level, but these days modern chefs find themselves on view in their own kitchens. For today, the customer wants to get right into the heart of the action. Here in Nottinghamshire, you can sit at the Chef's Table, The Kitchen Table (not the main kitchen, but a working kitchen nonetheless), and the Kitchen Bench (which has a bird's eye view of the new pastry kitchen). Mr Bains has embraced the demand for interaction, sated the thirst for knowledge, for few chefs are more passionate about the craft. A new development kitchen opened in 2014, where the next wave of dishes is planned and perfected, for that's another thing about Sat Bains: he doesn't stand still. This restaurant with rooms is in the business of delivering surprises, confounding expectations and delivering memorable experiences. The location itself, on the edge of an out-of-town industrial estate and near a flyover is not what you'd expect, perhaps, but it matters not, for once ensconced in the converted Victorian farmhouse all is soothing neutrality and cossetting professionalism. What follows is a quite breath-taking journey through cutting-edge cooking that is more than anything driven by taste. The menu, in fact, uses colour charts to show the balance of flavours in each dish, and his mastery of sweet, sour, salt, bitter and umami has placed the chef at the very top of the UK's culinary firmament. Taste, texture and temperature work in harmony to stunning effect, the kitchen's endeavours backed up by the exemplary service team who don't seem to put a foot wrong. Seven- and ten-course tasting menus chart the journey, which might begin with a dish of perfect scallops, the balance of sweetness and umami ensuring a comforting hit to get the ball rolling, with fennel, vanilla and Belotta ham. Chicken muesli is a menu description that leaves a lot to the imagination, but this is a clever construction with creamy liver at its heart. Lamb's sweetbreads with Puy lentils and mint is another firecracker of a dish, followed by another of roe deer 'Salisbury Plain' that shows acute technical accomplishment and flavours that positively thrill. There's a 'crossover' dish that hits the perfect balance between sweet and sour before the sweet courses themselves, such as one that combines the flavours of chocolate, mandarin and cardamom. The ingredients throughout are as good as they get, everything in season and in song. To cap it all, the vegetarian menu breaks new ground, and the exceptional wine list includes drinks 'packages' to go with each menu.

Chef Sat Bains **Owner** Sat & Amanda Bains **Seats** 40, Pr/dining room 14 **Times** 12-1.30/7-8.30 Closed 2 wks Jan, 1 wk May, 2 wks Aug, Sun-Mon, L all week **Prices** Prices not confirmed **Wines** 30 by glass **Parking** 22 **Notes** Chef's table L Tue-Sat 7 course £75, No children

NOTTINGHAM *continued*

Hart's Restaurant

◉◉ Modern British

tel: 0115 988 1900 & 911 0666 **Hart's Hotel, Standard Court, Park Row NG1 6GN**
email: ask@hartsnottingham.co.uk **web:** www.hartsnottingham.co.uk
dir: *At junct of Park Row & Ropewalk, close to city centre*

Smart modish cooking from a skilled team

Next to the boutique hotel of the same name, Hart's Restaurant is owned by Tim Hart, who also owns Hambleton Hall Hotel in Oakham, Rutland. With its contemporary good looks and booth seating, it's a welcoming restaurant with an approachable, daily-changing menu of neatly devised dishes in the modern British idiom. The kitchen's with-it approach is seen in main courses of accurately pan-fried cod fillet with a cassoulet of tomatoes, beans and chorizo and roast vegetables, and sticky glazed pork belly with a mushroom sauce infused with lemongrass, accompanied by compressed vegetables and noodles. Bookending them might be classic lobster bisque with brandy cream, or ham hock croquette with pickled onions and a mustard and sherry dressing, and apple soufflé with vanilla ice cream, or pecan tart with clotted cream. Tim Hart compiled the interesting wine list, which is arranged by style.

Chef Daniel Burridge **Owner** Tim Hart **Seats** 80, Pr/dining room 100
Times 12-2/6-10.30 Closed 1 Jan, L 31 Dec, D 25-26 Dec **Prices** Fixed L 2 course £15.95, Fixed D 3 course £24, Starter £5.95-£12.95, Main £14.95-£24.95, Dessert £7.25-£8.50 **Wines** 6 by glass **Parking** 15, Mount Street NCP **Notes** Pre-theatre menu 3 course £18, Sunday L £23, Children welcome

Park Plaza Nottingham

◉ Pan-Asian

tel: 0115 947 7444 & 947 7200 **41 Maid Marian Way NG1 6GD**
email: ppnconf@pphe.com **web:** www.chinolatino.eu
dir: *A6200 (Derby Rd) into Wollaton St. 2nd exit into Maid Marian Way. Hotel on left*

Vibrant, contemporary atmosphere and Pan-Asian flavours

The Park Plaza is a modern hotel with all mod-cons and a cool and contemporary restaurant in the form of Chino Latino. The winning formula has been tried-and-tested in the group's London outpost, and it fits the bill in Nottingham, too. There's a moody club-like vibe to the space (set over two levels), views through to the kitchen, and the focus is on Latino cocktails and Pan-Asian food. Start with dim sum such as chicken sui mai dumplings with foie gras and shiitaki mushrooms, or go Japanese with some sushi like spicy tuna roll with bonito flakes and chilli miso. Main-course duck breast toban-yaki arrives full of sizzle, or try the black cod with spicy miso. Desserts are no afterthought: banana spring roll, for example, with chocolate fudge sauce and vanilla ice cream.

Chef Paul Thacker **Seats** Pr/dining room 70 **Times** 12-10.30 Closed Xmas, Sun All-day dining **Prices** Fixed D 3 course £45, Starter £4-£11, Main £14-£29, Dessert £5-£13, Service optional **Wines** 28 bottles over £30, 7 bottles under £30, 11 by glass **Parking** On street, NCP **Notes** 4 course L £9.95, Vegetarian available, Children welcome

Restaurant Sat Bains with Rooms

◉◉◉◉◉ *– see page 431*

World Service

◉◉ Modern British 🍷 NOTABLE WINE LIST

tel: 0115 847 5587 **Newdigate House, Castle Gate NG1 6AF**
email: info@worldservicerestaurant.com **web:** www.worldservicerestaurant.com
dir: *200mtrs from city centre, 50mtrs from Nottingham Castle*

Sharp cooking and idiosyncratic surroundings

Renaissance-styled Newdigate House was built in 1675, but what leaves its kitchen since it became home to World Service is distinctly contemporary work. The idiosyncratic interior mines a colonial vein, the warm orange and copper hues of the main dining room offset with Oriental artefacts: Buddha heads, Indian statuary and objets d'art in glass cases. It all combines to create a laid-back Zen ambience, but the staff are super-slick, smartly-suited and sharp on the uptake, while bassy background beats add a funky urban edge to proceedings. If the restaurant's name isn't enough of a hint, the cooking has a gentle East-meets-West theme, although western influences hold sway. This is a kitchen that thinks about textures, putting an imaginative spin onto classic ideas, as seen in a starter matching braised ox tongue with gremolata and parmesan – a clever twist on classic carpaccio – followed by accurately-timed sea bass served with Korean sticky rice cakes, spring onion and bok choy. Carnivores might go for rump and shoulder of local lamb with potato terrine, butternut squash purée and shallot rings. At the end, banana parfait with banoffee caramel and palm sugar sorbet keeps the good ideas coming.

Chef Valentin Petiteau **Owner** Daniel Lindsay, Phillip Morgan, Ashley Walter **Seats** 80, Pr/dining room 34 **Times** 12-2.15/7-10 Closed 26 Dec, 1-7 Jan, D Sun (ex Dec & BH Sun) **Prices** Fixed L 2 course £14.95, Fixed D 3 course £24.95, Starter £5-£15.50, Main £14.95-£26.50, Dessert £5.50-£8.50 **Wines** 113 bottles over £30, 58 bottles under £30, 17 by glass **Parking** NCP **Notes** Sunday L £14.95-£19.95, Vegetarian available, Children welcome

Who has won our Food Service Award?
See page 13

OLLERTON
Map 16 SK66

Thoresby Hall Hotel

Modern British

tel: 01623 821000 & 821008 **Thoresby Park NG22 9WH**
email: thoresbyhall@bourne-leisure.co.uk **web:** www.warnerleisurehotels.co.uk

Accomplished modern cooking in a grand Victorian pile

If you're weary of the identikit greige conformity of contemporary minimal restaurants, beat a path to Thoresby Hall for a jaw-dropping antidote. Its imposing creeper-hung façade beckons you to a Victorian fantasy of turrets and gables, and within are tapestries, chandeliers, weapons and family portraits. The Blue Room is the top-end dining option, a room of soaring ceilings, ornate plasterwork and blue walls, but the kitchen's style is rather more up-to-date, reworking French classics in the modern British idiom. It starts with the likes of seared king scallops with chorizo, sweetcorn purée and roasted macadamia nuts, or butternut squah velouté with rabbit tortellini, haricots blancs and sherry. Good quality produce is again treated without too much fuss or elaboration in main courses such as a fish and meat combo involving roast turbot with crispy belly pork, langoustines, baby beetroot and leeks, and lemongrass. Otherwise, go for braised shin of beef with Bourguignon sauce, crispy dumpling and oxtail. Finish with cherry clafoutis paired with pistachio ice cream and Amaretto sauce anglaise.

Chef Mark Maris, Gary Griffiths **Owner** Warner Leisure **Seats** 50, Pr/dining room 50 **Times** 12-2/6.30-9 Closed Mon **Prices** Prices not confirmed, Service optional **Wines** 15 by glass **Parking** 140 **Notes** Sunday L, Vegetarian available, No children

OXFORDSHIRE

ASTON ROWANT
Map 5 SU79

Lambert Arms

Modern British

tel: 01844 351496 **London Rd OX49 5SB**
email: info.lambertarms@bespokehotels.com **web:** www.bespokehotels.com
dir: *M40 junct 6, at T-junct right towards Chinnor (B4009), back under motorway. 1st left to Postcombe/Thame (A40)*

Timbered coaching inn a stone's throw from the M40

The Lambert is a Georgian timbered coaching inn not far from Oxford, and a mere 500 yards from the M40. It works as a pub, if you're in the market for nothing more than a pint of real ale, but it's also a tastefully furnished modern hotel with a light and airy dining room. Pub food stalwarts like sausages and mash with onion gravy form the backbone of the menus, and there are some brasserie favourites such as chicken Caesar salad and steak burgers, but the kitchen also has a confident way with more contemporary classics. Goats' cheese and herb pannacotta with walnut dressing might be the prelude to Barbary duck breast with bok choi in five-spice jus, or sea bream with crab and parsley risotto in caper sauce. Round things off with pear and almond tart, served with anglaise sauce and white chocolate ice cream, or a selection of West Country cheeses.

Times 12-2.30/6.30-9

BANBURY
Map 11 SP44

Best Western Plus Wroxton House Hotel

Modern British

tel: 01295 730777 **Silver St, Wroxton OX15 6QB**
email: reservations@wroxtonhousehotel.com **web:** www.wroxtonhousehotel.com
dir: *From M40 junct 11 follow A422 (signed Banbury, then Wroxton). After 3m, hotel on right*

Modern brasserie dishes in a thatched hotel restaurant

Partly dating back to the days of the Commonwealth, the stone-built Wroxton House is a honey-stone beauty in a photogenic thatched village near Banbury. Its restaurant occupies what was a terraced row of cottages, and is all oak beams and columns with an inglenook fireplace. Table settings are smart, service is a matter of well-judged formality, and the kitchen team, headed by Steven Mason-Tocker, turns out thoughtfully composed modern brasserie dishes founded on classic combinations. A starter might be poached cod, served with crayfish risotto in chorizo oil, or more simply a bowl of butternut and sweet potato soup. Duck for main course comes two ways – roast breast and confit leg – with wilted kale and puréed carrots in blackcurrant sauce, while fish might be gilt-head bream with new potato, spinach and chorizo salad. Finish with pear frangipane tart and clotted cream. English and French cheeses come with outstanding home-made chutney.

Chef Steve Mason-Tocker **Owner** John & Gill Smith **Seats** 60, Pr/dining room 80 **Times** 12-2/7-9 Closed L Mon-Sat **Prices** Service optional **Wines** 7 bottles over £30, 35 bottles under £30, 10 by glass **Parking** 70 **Notes** Sunday L £21.95, Vegetarian available, Children welcome

BURFORD
Map 5 SP21

The Angel at Burford

Modern British

tel: 01993 822714 **14 Witney St OX18 4SN**
email: enquiries@theangelatburford.co.uk **web:** www.theangelatburford.co.uk
dir:

Creative cooking in a charming old pub

The Angel is a gem of a pub in historic Burford, a town with more than its fair share of chocolate-box charm. It's a proper pub, albeit an upmarket one, with a row of Hook Norton ales on the pumps and a roaring fire during the cool months of the year. It's the kind of place where your dog is made welcome. There's a serious approach to food, too, with due respect paid to local suppliers and the seasons. A first course such as beetroot tarte Tatin with frozen broad bean crème fraîche, micro herb salad and beetroot powder demonstrates that this is a kitchen of ambition, with lots of good ideas. Pickled red mullet and baby squid with red pepper bavarois and black olive tapenade is another creative starter, followed by pan-fried South Coast plaice with parsley pearl barley risotto, baby red chard and parsley foam. End with lemon tart with pistachio ice cream and raspberry coulis.

Chef Andrew Frost **Owner** Terence King, Gemma Finch **Seats** 28, Pr/dining room 14 **Times** 12-3/6-9.30 **Prices** Fixed L 2 course £17.50, Fixed D 3 course £23, Starter £6.50-£9.75, Main £13.50-£21.50, Dessert £7.55-£10.50, Service optional **Wines** 4 bottles over £30, 32 bottles under £30, 6 by glass **Parking** On street, car park **Notes** Sunday L £15.95-£23, Vegetarian available, Children welcome

BURFORD *continued*

The Bay Tree Hotel

 Modern British

tel: 01993 822791 **Sheep St OX18 4LW**
email: info@baytreehotel.info **web:** www.cotswold-inns-hotels.co.uk/baytree
dir: *A40 or A361 to Burford. From High St turn into Sheep St, next to old market square. Hotel on right*

Modern British pub food in an elegant Cotswold inn

A Cotswold country inn smothered in wisteria with flagstone floors and leaded windows overlooking a garden is an appealing prospect, and The Bay Tree fills the bill. Candlelit in the evenings, and professionally run, the dining room is a cream-coloured space with high-backed chairs and cooking that takes a modern approach to its task. Accompanying cured salmon with excellent crab jelly and watercress cream works a treat, ahead of duck breast with the leg meat rolled in cannelloni, served with confit celeriac and braised, subtly spiced red cabbage. When rhubarb and custard got deconstructed, it got deconstructed for good, and here is a prime example, incorporating rhubarb jelly and custard mousse with almond crumble.

Times 12-2/7-9.30

The Bull at Burford

 Modern French, Traditional British

tel: 01993 822220 **105 High St OX18 4RG**
email: info@bullatburford.co.uk **web:** www.bullatburford.co.uk
dir: *On A40 between Cheltenham & Oxford, in town centre*

Confident cooking in a former coaching inn

The High Street of Burford is rich with historic buildings, including The Bull, which first opened its doors in 1610 as a coaching inn. The façade maintains the period character, of course, but inside there's a little more leeway to bring in a contemporary touch or two. There's still charm and traditional features aplenty, but there's a satisfying modernity, too, with the restaurant offering up bare Cotswold-stone walls, age-blackened beams, original artwork, and butterscotch-hued seats at linen-swathed tables. The kitchen turns out bright, contemporary stuff, inflected with modern European ideas. Among starters, lemon and parsley fishcake comes with Provençal vegetables and a tomato and thyme sauce, for example, and a fish platter is filled with the likes of salmon tartare, herring salad and gravadlax. A main course pan-seared fillet of Bibury trout is served with an accompanying pea and asparagus risotto, while sirloin steak comes with a choice of classic sauces. Desserts might deliver a baked Vienna cheesecake with caramelised peaches and passionfruit sorbet.

Chef Peter Juszkiewicz **Owner** Mr & Mrs J-M Lauzier **Seats** 40, Pr/dining room 12
Times 12-2.30/7-9.30 **Prices** Starter £5.95-£9.75, Main £14.95-£20.75, Dessert £6.75-£9.75, Service optional **Wines** 36 bottles over £30, 39 bottles under £30, 12 by glass **Parking** 6, On street **Notes** Sunday L £21.95, Vegetarian available, Children welcome

The Lamb Inn

 Modern British v

tel: 01993 823155 **Sheep St OX18 4LR**
email: info@lambinn-burford.co.uk **web:** www.cotswold-inns-hotels.co.uk/lamb
dir: *Exit A40 into Burford, down hill, take 1st left into Sheep St, hotel last on right*

Contemporary cooking in a medieval Cotswold inn

The Lamb is on (where else?) Sheep Street in a charm-laden Cotswold village. Built of local stone in the early 15th century, it was once a set of weavers' cottages, and the flagstone floor was once trodden by those medieval artisans. As a modern country inn, the place has been sensitively converted to give a sense of soft-focus creature comforts amid the big stone fireplaces and ancient beams, nowhere more so than in the elegantly appointed, raspberry-coloured restaurant. Sean Ducie echoes the surroundings with food that has a classic British foundation, but builds some contemporary ideas on top of it. Scallops and langoustines come with de rigueur cauliflower purée, but also a crisp-textured seaweed salad, or there may be ox tongue pastrami with horseradish cream, pickled radish and brioche croutons. Mains produce an inspired take on the pork and beans idea, paprika-cured tenderloin in cannellini bean fricassée with black pudding mash, and if you want to keep things light at dessert, look no further than yoghurt parfait with nutmegged apple compôte and an ingenious crumble tuile.

Chef Sean Ducie **Owner** Cotswold Inns & Hotels **Seats** 40, Pr/dining room
Times 12-2.30/7-9.30 **Prices** Fixed L 2 course £20, Fixed D 3 course £39, Tasting menu £55 **Wines** 60 bottles over £30, 40 bottles under £30, 12 by glass
Parking Care of The Bay Tree Hotel **Notes** Tasting menu 8 course, with Dégustation wines, Sunday L £18.95-£23.95, Children welcome

| CHECKENDON | Map 5 SU68 |

The Highwayman

 Modern & Traditional British

tel: 01491 682020 **Exlade St RG8 OUA**
dir: *Exlade St signed off A4074 (Reading/Wallingford road), 0.4m*

Nice mix of menus in a welcoming country local

This Highwayman is a switched-on country dining pub that stands and delivers with its good honest cookery. A hike on the wooded Chiltern Hills nearby should bring on a keen appetite, and the setting is a rambling, 17th-century inn done out with exposed brickwork and beams and a wood-burner in a huge inglenook. Fine ales are on tap in the pubby bar, and all bases are covered in the food department by slabs of 28-day-aged Windsor Estate beef from the grill, home-made pies – venison, game, or wild boar, perhaps – and if you're in the market for something more contemporary, a carte with plenty of seasonal focus. Cod and crab cakes with garlic mayonnaise are a great way to start, followed by roast corn-fed chicken with chorizo risotto and seasonal vegetables. Round off with a trio of crème brûlée flavoured with coffee, vanilla and pistachio.

Chef Paul Burrows **Owner** Paul Burrows **Seats** 55, Pr/dining room 40
Times 12-2.30/6-10 Closed 26 Dec, 1 Jan, Mon, D Sun **Prices** Service optional **Wines** 5 by glass **Parking** 30 **Notes** Sunday L £11.95-£19.95, Vegetarian available, Children welcome

CHINNOR
Map 5 SP70

The Sir Charles Napier

 – see below

CHIPPING NORTON
Map 10 SP32

The Chequers

 British

tel: 01608 659393 **Church Rd, Churchill OX7 6NJ**
email: reservations@thechequerschurchill.com
dir:

Pub classics done right in village gastro-pub

Once you're inside, this unassuming stone pub in a pretty Cotswolds village has modern gastro-pub style in spades, but that's not to say you can't just have a pint in the cosy bar. The ambience is relaxed and unforced and there are plenty of interesting objets to catch the eye, as well as a small oyster bar that is also home to delicious arrays of charcuterie and cheese. The kitchen has an eye for top-notch local produce, which it turns into direct and purposeful dishes with clear, punchy flavours. The menu divides helpfully into starters, classics, steaks, and roasts, so begin with grilled squid with gremolata, rocket and lemon, then go for calves' liver and bacon with mashed potatoes and spinach from the classics section, which is a perfect example of what this place is all about: simple dishes done well. To finish, a well-made raspberry and almond tart comes with vanilla ice cream.

Times 12-3/6-9.30 Closed D Sun

The Kingham Plough

Modern British

tel: 01608 658327 **The Green, Kingham OX7 6YD**
email: book@thekinghamplough.co.uk **web:** www.thekinghamplough.co.uk
dir: *B4450 from Chipping Norton to Churchill, 2nd right to Kingham. Left at T-junct, Plough on right*

Revamped pub with creative cooking

An idyllic inn on the green of a chocolate-box-pretty Cotswolds village, the Plough presents a quintessentially English face to the world. Inside, the place has been reinvented with a stylish rustic-chic decor to go with its venerable beams and exposed stone walls. In the bar there are large comfy armchairs and sofas, real ales and scrumpy, and proper bar food such as Scotched quail's eggs or home-made pheasant sausage and mash. But if you want to see what the kitchen brigade can really do, head for the stylishly informal restaurant where exec chef Emily Watkins, who used to work at Heston's Fat Duck, happily deploys traditional and up-to-the-minute cooking techniques to deliver intelligent interpretations of the modern British idiom. Spot-on pastry skills are evident in a starter of penny bun and girolle mushroom tart with tarragon butter sauce and pickled girolles, while rump and sweetbreads of Cotswold rose veal benefit from a well-matched accompaniment of runner beans and foraged mushrooms, exemplary mash and mustard sauce. Puddings show a similar vein of clever comfort cooking with a bitter chocolate and salted caramel tart with popcorn ice cream.

Chef Emily Watkins, Ben Dulley **Owner** Emily & Miles Lampson **Seats** 54, Pr/dining room 20 **Times** 12-2/6.30-9 Closed 25 Dec, D Sun **Prices** Starter £8-£10, Main £15-£22, Dessert £6-£8 **Wines** 7 by glass **Parking** 30 **Notes** Sunday L, Vegetarian available, Children welcome

The Sir Charles Napier

CHINNOR
Map 5 SP70

Modern British, European

tel: 01494 483011 **Sprigg's Alley OX39 4BX**
email: info@sircharlesnapier.co.uk **web:** www.sircharlesnapier.co.uk
dir: *M40 junct 6, B4009 to Chinnor. Right at rdbt to Sprigg's Alley*

Inspired seasonal cooking in a professionally run Chilterns inn

A little to the southwest of Chinnor proper, is Julie Griffiths' consummately professional and appealing village inn, which features a vine-shrouded summer terrace overlooking the herbaceous borders and the herb gardens, with the Chiltern Hills and the beech woods beyond. Any tendency to twee is firmly resisted, with exposed brick walls, bare floors and modern furniture, not to mention characterful modern sculptures. The cooking is informed by seasonal local materials, with foraged wild garlic and nettles, as well as woodland mushrooms, playing their respective parts in spring and autumn. Chris Godfrey's cooking celebrates the cycles of the year with offerings such as citrus-dressed lobster salad with asparagus in spring, or crab ravioli with pickled vegetables in bisque, perhaps followed by rack and pressed shoulder of local lamb with shallot and garlic purée and broad bean salsa verde, in summer. The seven-course tasting menu makes ample gastronomic sense, and there are more straightforward two-course fixed-price deals that might offer beetroot-cured salmon with horseradish cream, before confit duck with flageolet bean cassoulet and cavolo nero. If it's still summer by the time you reach dessert, go for strawberry and cucumber salad with Pimm's sorbet.

Otherwise, there may be an admirably gooey terrine of chocolate, peanut and salted caramel.

Chef Chris Godfrey **Owner** Julie Griffiths **Seats** 75, Pr/dining room 45 **Times** 12-3.30/6.30-10 Closed 25-27 Dec, Mon, D Sun **Prices** Fixed L 2 course £17.50-£19.50, Fixed D 2 course £17.50-£19.50, Starter £10.50-£15.50, Main £22.50-£30, Dessert £8.50-£10.50 **Wines** 10 by glass **Parking** 60 **Notes** Sunday L £21.50-£27.50, Vegetarian available, Children welcome

CHIPPING NORTON *continued*

Wild Thyme Restaurant with Rooms

◉◉ Modern British

tel: 01608 645060 **10 New St OX7 5LJ**
email: enquiries@wildthymerestaurant.co.uk web: www.wildthymerestaurant.co.uk
dir: *A44 Evesham, through Market Place. On left opposite Sainsbury's car park*

Contemporary style and well-presented modish cooking

Grade II listed and 400 years old, Wild Thyme is located in a building that doesn't want for character. The interior of this smart little restaurant with rooms (just 35 covers and three bedrooms) has original features on show, but the place feels bright and contemporary just the same. That's down to the easy-going look of exposed stone walls and white-painted woodwork, with the wooden tables left unclothed. There's modern art, too, matching the modernity of the kitchen's output. Chef-patron Nick Pullen seeks out top-notch seasonal regional produce and turns out smart, contemporary British food that deals in intelligent flavour combinations, revealing a respect for classical culinary traditions. A double-baked goats' cheese soufflé arrives in the company of gold beetroots, hazelnuts and red onion marmalade, and Cornish mackerel with parsnip purée, shiitake mushrooms and crispy pancetta. Among main courses, local rabbit stars three ways in one dish as puff pastry pie, steamed loin and wonton (served with wild mushrooms, Puy lentils and winter roots). For dessert, there's the likes of crispy apple tart with rosemary ice cream, or a riff on rhubarb with crumble, quince brulée and ice cream.

Chef Nicholas Pullen **Owner** Nicholas & Sally Pullen **Seats** 35, Pr/dining room 14 **Times** 12-2/7-9 Closed Mon, L Tue **Prices** Fixed L 2 course fr £18, Starter £6-£11, Main £14-£22, Dessert £6.50-£11.50, Service optional **Wines** 11 by glass **Parking** Public car park 3 min walk **Notes** Sun L winter only, Vegetarian available, Children welcome

---

DEDDINGTON   Map 11 SP43

Deddington Arms

◉ Modern British

tel: 01869 338364 **Horsefair OX15 0SH**
email: deddarms@oxfordshire-hotels.co.uk web: www.deddington-arms-hotel.co.uk
dir: *From S: M40 junct 10/A43. 1st rdbt left to Aynho (B4100) & left to Deddington (B4031). From N: M40 junct 11 to hospital & Adderbury on A4260, then to Deddington*

Good country-pub fare in a 16th-century inn

Things continue to evolve at this 16th-century black-and-white coaching inn, with the addition of a range of old pasta and pizza favourites to its crowd-pleasing output of good, honest country-pub fodder. Kitted out with the requisite low beams, stone floors and cosy fireplaces, it remains a local watering hole with plenty of period allure in the bar, and a pared-back modernised sheen in the dining room. The kitchen sources its produce diligently from the local area, but it doesn't have to cast its net much wider than the front door when the farmers' market is in full swing on the village square. Home-made corned beef with Dijon mustard remoulade and rocket salad might start you off, before something like chicken breast with dauphinoise potato, woodland mushrooms and shallot and red wine sauce. Sticky date pudding with butterscotch sauce and vanilla ice cream ends things squarely in the comfort zone.

Chef Nick Porter **Owner** Oxfordshire Hotels Ltd **Seats** 60, Pr/dining room 30 **Times** 12-2.30/6-9.30 Closed 25 Dec **Prices** Fixed L 2 course fr £14, Fixed D 3 course fr £23, Starter £4-£8, Main £10-£22, Dessert £5-£8, Service optional **Wines** 9 bottles over £30, 37 bottles under £30, 10 by glass **Parking** 36 **Notes** Sunday L £18-£23, Vegetarian available, Children welcome

---

FARINGDON   Map 5 SU29

The Eagle

◉◉ Modern European

tel: 01367 241879 **Little Coxwell SN7 7LW**
email: eaglelittlecoxwell@gmail.com web: www.eagletavern.co.uk
dir: *A420, follow signs for 1m to Little Coxwell village*

Accomplished cooking in revamped village inn

With chef Marcel Nerpas at the stoves, The Eagle is no ordinary local. A revamp has transformed the traditional country pub into a clean-lined contemporary operation furnished with chunky unclothed wooden tables lit by fat church candles, and art hung on soothing pastel-hued timbered walls. The ales are well kept in the casual bar, and the kitchen ensures the food toes a modern line, drawing on excellent local produce combined with hints of European influences (chef Nerpas hails from Slovakia). A lively streak of invention lifts the repertoire above the tried-and-tested category, scoring palpable hits with the likes of a deceptively simple sounding 'goats' cheese and beetroot' starter – a composition of goats' cheese spheres, roasted beets, brioche croûtons, and honey and truffle oil. Next up could be haunch of venison with Jerusalem artichoke purée, turned potatoes and wild mushroom sauce. A reinvented banoffee pie is presented with a touch of theatre: a globe of white chocolate on a biscuit base dissolves to reveal a filling of chopped banana and caramel sauce when a jug of hot milk chocolate sauce is poured onto it at the table.

Chef Marcel Nerpas **Owner** Marcel Nerpas **Seats** 28 **Times** 12-2.30/5.30-11 Closed Mon, D Sun **Prices** Fixed L 2 course fr £11.95, Starter £3-£6.50, Main £11-£16.50, Dessert £6-£7, Service optional **Wines** 4 bottles over £30, 21 bottles under £30, 8 by glass **Parking** On street **Notes** Sunday L £9.95-£19.95, Vegetarian available, Children welcome

---

The Trout at Tadpole Bridge

◉ Modern & Traditional British

tel: 01367 870382 **Buckland Marsh SN7 8RF**
email: info@troutinn.co.uk web: www.troutinn.co.uk
dir: *A415 from Abingdon signed Marcham, through Frilford to Kingston Bagpuize. Left onto A420. 5m, right signed Tadpole Bridge. Or M4 (E'bound) junct 15, A419 towards Cirencester. 4m, onto A420 towards Oxford. 10m, left signed Tadpole Bridge*

Classy inventive cooking in a traditional Thames-side inn

The 17th-century stone inn in an idyllic spot on the upper reaches of the Thames, with berthing for up to six boats and a waterside garden, has the expected rural charm of open fires and beams. It hasn't forgotten it's a pub, with real ales dispensed at the bar, but the main attraction is a menu sparkling with bright ideas. Sourcing is a strength (Hereford beef, Kelmscott pork, for instance) and dishes are created to bring out forthright and often bold flavours. Fishcakes with buttered spinach and tartare sauce is a signature starter, and rabbit and quail pâté with fig chutney is typical. Apricot and rosemary jus gives a lift to pink-roast rack of lamb with dauphinoise and red cabbage purée, an alternative to confit rabbit Wellington with roasted salsify, garlicky spinach and port sauce. Invention doesn't tail off among desserts; there may be limoncello jelly, or mango and vodka cheesecake.

Chef Pascal Clavaud **Owner** Helen & Gareth Pugh **Seats** 50, Pr/dining room 40 **Times** 12-2/7-9 Closed 25-26 Dec **Prices** Prices not confirmed, Service optional **Wines** 60 bottles over £30, 50 bottles under £30, 12 by glass **Parking** 40 **Notes** Sunday L, Vegetarian available, Children welcome

Belmond Le Manoir aux Quat' Saisons

GREAT MILTON   Map 5 SP60

Modern French V NOTABLE WINE LIST

tel: 01844 278881 **Church Rd OX44 7PD**
email: lemanoir@blanc.co.uk **web:** www.manoir.com
dir: *M40 junct 7 follow A329 towards Wallingford. After 1m turn right, signed Great Milton and Le Manoir aux Quat' Saisons*

Benchmark French cooking of rare excellence

Now part of the worldwide Belmond hotels and leisure group, the Manoir remains nonetheless serenely itself, an enduring monument to the achievement of a young French chef who arrived in Oxford a generation ago, with nary a cookery lesson under his belt. The place looks a little like one of the smaller Oxford colleges in its gabled and mullioned demeanour, but the catering is a bit better. It's always worth a stroll around the grounds, where a Japanese tea-garden pops up one minute, a row of well-stocked greenhouses the next. Have a peep: a cornucopia of vegetables and more herb varieties than most of us are capable of naming are in production, providing Gary Jones' kitchen team with the backbone of his monthly-changing seasonal menus. Localism, and therefore seasonality, were a touchstone of the Manoir long before they became shibboleths of serious restaurants the world over, but that was never the whole story. Blanc fulfilled his mission here within a year of opening, attracting top ratings just about everywhere, but the meteoric rise didn't betoken any self-satisfied flatlining. The Manoir has gone on achieving through the decades with ultra-refined French cooking that manages complex intricacy without befuddlement, extraordinary delicacy without blandness, and mesmeric intensity without overstatement. The bilingual menu specifications are precise, yet only hint at the finished product. The truffled wild mushroom risotto is an object-lesson in hugely rich, savoury potency, pungent with the waft of Périgord earth, while great depth is conjured from a pasta such as agnolotti with butternut squash and hazelnuts in a powerful blue cheese sauce of Fourme d'Ambert. Fish is boldly but not roughly treated, as when tenderly flavourful monkfish tail is gently spiced and accompanied by mussels in a saffron-scented Gewürztraminer sauce, while meats are perfectly aged, trimmed, timed and rested to produce main courses such as roast venison loin with celeriac and kale, or squab baked in a salt crust in an unabashedly old-school sauce of truffled madeira. The only way to resist the temptations of the cheese chariot is not to let it anywhere near you. If you do, you'll be regaled by a protean array of fine European specimens, all in prime nick. And just in case things are all getting a little precious, Blanc and Jones have always enjoyed a fun dessert (who remembers the witty chocolate cup of coffee mousse invented here in the 1980s?). These days, there's a house take on millionaire shortbread that puts to shame what they sell on the trains, and yet is more or less constructed on the same principle – soft toffee with bitter chocolate on crumbly shortbread, with the added allure of salty butter ice cream. Go for the seven-course Menu Découverte for the full unforgettable journey.

Chef Raymond Blanc, Gary Jones **Owner** Mr R Blanc & Belmond **Seats** 100, Pr/dining room 50
Times 12-2.30/7-10 **Prices** Starter £40-£42, Main £48-£54, Dessert £24-£28, Service optional **Wines** 850 bottles over £30, 40 by glass **Parking** 60 **Notes** Fixed L 5 course Mon-Fri, 7 course daily, D 6/9 course daily, Sunday L £124-£154, Children welcome

FYFIELD
Map 5 SU49

The White Hart
◎◎ Modern British

tel: 01865 390585 **Main Rd OX13 5LW**
email: info@whitehart-fyfield.com
dir: *A420 Oxford-Swindon, 7m S of Oxford A34*

Confident cooking in a tranquil village inn

This historic Tudor coaching inn is a former chantry house, built during the reign of Henry VI, and sold to St John's college in Oxford after the Dissolution. Its many charms include a secret tunnel to Fyfield Manor (not so secret any more, then), and a minstrels' gallery – eat up here if you like, or stay down below with the cosy, pubby vibe of flagstoned floors, inglenooks, and enough timbers to build a galleon. Chef-proprietor Mark Chandler's appealing contemporary gastro-pub cooking draws in foodies from miles around with its impressive technical proficiency and ingredients that are local, fresh, seasonal, and may even be freshly plucked from the aromatic herb garden outside. A three-course approach gets going with goats' cheese and red onion tarte Tatin, followed by pan-fried duck breast and smoked duck spring roll pointed up with a tangy rhubarb and anise sauce, and a three-way treatment of sweet potato, served as purée, crisps and potato Anna. Finally, there's dark and white chocolate brownie with salted caramel ice cream and honeycomb.

Chef Mark Chandler **Owner** Kay & Mark Chandler **Seats** 65, Pr/dining room 32 **Times** 12-2.30/7-9.30 Closed Mon (ex BHs), D Sun **Prices** Fixed L 2 course £17, Starter £6.50-£9, Main £12-£25, Dessert £6.50-£7.50, Service optional **Wines** 28 bottles over £30, 26 bottles under £30, 11 by glass **Parking** 60 **Notes** Chef's tasting menu available on request, Sunday L £23-£26, Vegetarian available, Children welcome

GORING
Map 5 SU68

The Leatherne Bottel
◎◎ British, French

tel: 01491 872667 **Bridle Way RG8 OHS**
email: leathernebottel@aol.com web: www.leathernebottel.co.uk
dir: *M4 junct 12 or M40 junct 6, signed from B4009 towards Wallingford*

Anglo-French cooking by the Thames

The Bottel floats serenely on the Thames with the Chilterns as a backdrop. If you're arriving by your own launch, you can step straight on to the sun-dappled or windswept terrace, depending on the season. It's a lovely spot, and the place is a dining destination of long repute, weathering the vicissitudes of culinary fashion without getting stuck in any ruts. The accent is Anglo-French, perfectly seen in a meal that follows a petit crottin goats' cheese, roast fig and chestnut purée with beef Wellington, a beautifully moist recollection of the victory at Waterloo, complete with a porty reduction but rather uneven pastry. Lighter fish dishes might include seared turbot with shallot gratin in smoked haddock chowder, and meals come to a satisfying conclusion with something like a pear poached in pinot noir served with clotted cream and toasted almonds. The radio blaring out from the kitchen can make one wish all the more wistfully that someone would step up to the plate and give us something on the grand piano that stands in the centre of the dining room.

Times 12-2/7-9 Closed D Sun

GREAT MILTON
Map 5 SP60

Belmond Le Manoir aux Quat' Saisons
◎◎◎◎◎ – *see page 437*

HENLEY-ON-THAMES
Map 5 SU78

Hotel du Vin Henley-on-Thames
◎◎ European NOTABLE WINE LIST

tel: 01491 848400 **New St RG9 2BP**
email: info.henley@hotelduvin.com web: www.hotelduvin.com
dir: *M4 junct 8/9 signed High Wycombe, take 2nd exit and onto A404 in 2m. A4130 into Henley, over bridge, through lights, up Hart St, right onto Bell St, right onto New St, hotel on right*

French bistro specials in a Georgian brewery

One of the unique selling points of the HdV chain is the interesting buildings in which the various hotels have taken root. In Henley, the setting is the Georgian headquarters of the Brakspear brewery, making a perhaps counter-intuitive context for an operation consecrated to wine, but hard to argue with when you survey the wondrous beamed interiors. The Bistro here is particularly atmospheric, with claret-coloured pillars and recreations of eye-catching paintings beneath the brick arches. Efficient renditions of French bistro food are the drill, with one or two modern English touches creeping discreetly in. Smoked salmon dressed with egg, capers and gherkins, or mushrooms sautéed in butter and garlic on toasted brioche, are pleasantly informal ways to start. Then it might be bouillabaisse of red mullet, monkfish, sea bass and prawns, minted rack of lamb, or a veggie special such as gnocchi, tomato and butter bean ragoût. Dry-aged steaks emerge sizzling from the grill, perhaps with a side of petits pois à la française, and desserts maintain the tone with tarte Tatin, or crêpes suzette flamed in Grand Marnier.

Chef Rob Lacey **Owner** KSL **Seats** 90, Pr/dining room 72 **Times** 12-2.30/5.30-10 **Prices** Fixed L 2 course fr £14.95, Fixed D 3 course £16.95-£19.95, Starter £5.45-£11.95, Main £12.50-£28.95, Dessert £6.95-£8.50 **Wines** 120 bottles over £30, 20 bottles under £30, 19 by glass **Notes** Sunday L £22.95, Vegetarian available, Children welcome

Orwells
◎◎◎ – *see opposite*

KINGSTON BAGPUIZE
Map 5 SU49

Fallowfields Hotel and Restaurant
◎◎◎ – *see opposite*

MILTON COMMON
Map 5 SP60

The Oxfordshire
◎ Modern British

tel: 01844 278300 **Rycote Ln OX9 2PU**
email: info@theoxfordshire.com web: www.theoxfordshire.com
dir: *From S M40 junct 7 onto A370 towards Thame. Hotel on right in 2m*

Modern British cooking in golfing hotel

The championship golf course is the main attraction at this new-built hotel in the Chilterns. Leisure facilities, a spa and indoor pool add to the pleasure of a stay here, along with stylish bedrooms, while the first-floor restaurant has stunning views from its picture windows of the course and countryside, with friendly and efficient staff adding to the congenial atmosphere. The menu is built broadly around the modern British repertory with some European influences, so to start may be rich, smooth chicken liver parfait with nicely contrasting fruit chutney. Presentation is a strength, judging by blade of local beef braised in red wine, served with woodland mushrooms, carrots, spinach and mash – a commendably good marriage of flavours and textures. But you might find the kitchen saves the best till last, with vanilla pannacotta with sherbet-sprinkled mixed berries and raspberry coulis turning out to be the star of a meal.

Times 6-9.30 Closed Xmas, New Year, D Sun

Orwells

Modern British

tel: 0118 940 3673 **Shiplake Row, Binfield Heath RG9 4DP**
email: eat@orwellsatshiplake.co.uk
dir: *A4155 to Binfield Heath, take Plough Lane to Shiplake Row, restaurant on left*

Creativity and classics in a Georgian country pub

The location on Binfield Heath, not far from Henley, couldn't be more appropriate for the kind of operation that Ryan Simpson and Liam Trotman had in mind when they opened here in 2010. Surrounded by rolling farmland near the Oxon-Berks border, they have plugged into local supply-lines for their brand of sleekly modern British cooking informed by natural flavours and seasonal wild ingredients. The Georgian pub looks unassuming enough from the outside, black-framed windows offsetting a clean whitewashed frontage. Inside, bare boards and exposed brick set the tone, with plain white walls and unclothed tables keeping things as straightforward as can be. The place is very much consecrated to dining, both classically and creatively, and a new venture is a tapas-style lunch offering of small plates for mixing and matching across a table. These include wagyu salad with piccalilli and horseradish, crab fritter with red pepper and apple, and more oddball permutations such as foie gras with liquorice lentils and rhubarb. Main menu dishes in the evenings bring on extra layers of complexity, adding smoked eel, tamarind, apple, barley and marinated mushrooms to the foie gras, and introducing pork belly and monkfish to each other with an alliterative audience of pea, piccalilli and peanuts. Those on-trend fish-meat pairings work sublimely well in a main course of halibut and veal, with parsnip, radishes, spring onions and grapes, or keep it pure with poached plaice and cockles, or lamb rump with asparagus, chickpeas, aubergine and tomato. If it's pub classics you're after, look to chicken liver parfait on toast, then a rib-eye steak, or beer-battered haddock and chips. Seasonal sides such as Jerusalem artichokes with Stilton and almonds, or buttered wild garlic, add to the appeal, and meals end with either a simple chocolate brownie, or the more off-the-wall likes of pink praline tart and sorrel sorbet.

Chef Ryan Simpson, Liam Trotman **Owner** Ryan Simpson, Liam Trotman **Seats** 60, Pr/dining room 20 **Times** 11.30-3/6.30-9.30 Closed 2 wks beg Jan, 1 wk Apr, 2 wks beg Sep, Mon-Tue, D Sun **Prices** Tasting menu £60-£75, Starter £5.50-£13, Main £13-£26, Dessert £6.50-£9, Service optional **Wines** 129 bottles over £30, 31 bottles under £30, 23 by glass **Parking** 40 **Notes** Tasting menu with/without wines, Tapas available L, Sunday L £18-£29.95, Vegetarian available, Children welcome

Fallowfields Hotel and Restaurant

Modern British v

tel: 01865 820416 **Faringdon Rd OX13 5BH**
email: stay@fallowfields.com web: www.fallowfields.com
dir: *A34 (Oxford Ring Rd) take A420 towards Swindon. At junct with A415 left for 100yds then turn at mini rdbt. Hotel on left after 1m*

Ultra-local ingredients cooked with flair and imagination

When it comes to sourcing raw ingredients for the kitchen, they don't have to go far from the front door at Fallowfields. The family-run hotel may be small – just ten bedrooms – but there's so much land surrounding the delightful, honey-stoned building that as well as an orchard and kitchen garden, they keep Tamworth pigs, chickens, sheep, quail and their own herd of Dexter cattle. With produce as fresh and local as this, Matt Weedon must be the envy of many a chef in these parts. The restaurant is as lovely as you could hope for, housed in a conservatory with views of the lawns and paddocks, and candlelit at night. It's a light and airy setting by day, romantic in the evenings, although it's clearly the assured modern British cooking of Matt and his team that make people travel great distances. The excellent canapés, amuse-bouche and freshly-baked breads get things off to a flying start, before a first course of confit and cured salmon, the fish simply melting in the mouth, served with a delightful, vibrant garden salad with beetroot and a quenelle of savoury ice cream. Fallowfields pork seems like a wise way to go at main course, and what arrives on the plate is just exquisite: a three-way serving of roast pork loin, braised belly and confit shoulder, all precisely cooked and beautifully presented. Prune, apple and armagnac soufflé is as good as it gets at dessert, the soufflé itself faultless in execution and the flavours clearly defined and brilliantly balanced, or you might go for garden rhubarb with a vanilla and goose egg custard, granola and pistachio – a clever, winning combination of flavours and textures. With such a skilled hand at pastry at work in the kitchen, it would be a crime to skip the coffee and fantastic selection of petits fours.

Chef Matt Weedon **Owner** Anthony & Peta Lloyd **Seats** 42, Pr/dining room 14 **Times** 12-2.30/7-9.30 **Prices** Fixed L 2 course £25, Starter £15-£20, Main £28-£35, Dessert £9-£16 **Wines** 70 bottles over £30, 20 bottles under £30, 14 by glass **Parking** 50 **Notes** Tasting menu 7 course must be taken by the whole table, Sunday L £30, Children welcome

MURCOTT
Map 11 SP51

The Nut Tree Inn

Modern European V NOTABLE WINE LIST

tel: 01865 331253 **Main St OX5 2RE**
dir: *M40 junct 9. A34 towards Oxford, take 2nd exit for Islip. At Red Lion pub turn left, then 3rd right signed Murcott*

Confident cooking in a pretty village inn

You can prop up the bar with a jar of real ale in this whitewashed and thatched 15th-century inn surveying the village pond deep in the idyllic Oxfordshire countryside, but it's the food that is the big draw now that chef-proprietor Mike North's skilful modern European cooking has turned the inn into a local foodie destination. Stone walls, gnarled beams and wood-burning stoves provide a cosy pubby backdrop for dishes that are unfussy, precise and assured, and designed to tease maximum flavour from exemplary ingredients. Those Gloucestershire Old Spot and Tamworth pigs roaming the acreages of garden are destined for the table in the company of excellent raw materials from local artisan producers. Foie gras, ham hock and chicken terrine with sauce gribiche is a typically straightforward starter, while roast saddle and faggot of Oxford Downs lamb with fondant potato and sauce Niçoise is the sort of main event that satisfies with deep flavours and satisfying textures. To finish, passionfruit features both in a zingy hot soufflé and the accompanying ice cream.

Chef Michael & Mary North **Owner** Michael & Imogen North **Seats** 70, Pr/dining room 36 **Times** 12-2.30/7-9 Closed 27 Dec-3 Jan, Mon, D Sun **Prices** Fixed L 2 course £18, Fixed D 2 course £18, Tasting menu £55, Starter £7.50-£15, Main £17-£30, Dessert £7.50-£10.50, Service optional **Wines** 104 bottles over £30, 17 bottles under £30, 14 by glass **Parking** 30 **Notes** Sunday L £17-£24, Vegetarian available, Children welcome

OXFORD
Map 5 SP50

Gee's Restaurant

Mediterranean

tel: 01865 553540 **61 Banbury Rd OX2 6PE**
email: info@gees-restaurant.co.uk
dir: *N off A4165, from city centre right onto Banbury Rd, located just past Bevington Rd*

Med-influenced brasserie cooking in a glasshouse

The long-running Gee's continues to delight townies and gownies alike on the northern edge of the city centre. Not the least attraction is the glasshouse setting, where silvery-green potted olive trees and lightweight café-style furniture in a room flooded with natural light are an uplifting prospect on a bright day. Weekend brunches and inexpensive lunch deals remain popular, as does the Med-influenced modern brasserie cooking, now in the hands of Richard Allen. A newly installed wood-fired oven turns out pizzetti and sharing ribs of beef, while a charcoal grill does its stuff to steaks, burgers and chops of lamb, pork or venison, served with creamed spinach. Crab mayonnaise or artichoke fritters are good starters, while fish-lovers may be tempted by the prospect of a whole sea bass dressed in the simple homespun of lemon and parsley. Finish with blood orange tart, or a serving of prune ice cream glooped with treacly PX sherry.

Chef Richard Allen **Owner** Jeremy Mogford **Seats** 74 **Times** 12-10.30 All-day dining **Prices** Fixed L 2 course fr £13, Starter £5.50-£10.50, Main £11-£17.50, Dessert £5-£6.50 **Wines** 7 bottles over £30, 13 bottles under £30, 14 by glass **Parking** On street **Notes** Sat-Sun brunch 10-11.45am, Sunday L £14.50-£16.50, Vegetarian available, Children welcome

Macdonald Randolph Hotel

– see below

Macdonald Randolph Hotel

OXFORD
Map 5 SP50

Traditional British
tel: 0844 879 9132 & 01865 256400 **Beaumont St OX1 2LN**
email: foodservice.randolph@macdonald-hotels.co.uk
web: www.macdonaldhotels.co.uk
dir: *M40 junct 8, A40 towards Oxford, follow city centre signs, leads to St Giles, hotel on right*

Adventurous cookery in grand city-centre hotel

The Randolph is the city of Oxford's runner in the grand hotel stakes, an imposing stone-built edifice tucked in among the dreaming spires, readily familiar to viewers of ITV's detective drama *Lewis*. A commissionaire waits to bid you into the golden glow of the lobby, through which heads of state have sashayed over the years, and the Inspector Morse theme is acknowledged in a bar named after that indefatigable sleuth. An air of refined civility prevails in the dining room, where all is crisp napery, rose-coloured upholstery and sparkling glassware. Full-drop windows look out over Beaumont Street and the Ashmolean Museum, and the walls are adorned with the crests of Oxford's colleges. Simon Bradley arrived in 2013 with the intention of giving the menus here an adventurous uplift, and the

results are plain to see. He draws resourcefully on modern techniques for a good-humoured starter called 'fish and chips', comprised of velvety cod mousse, wafers of beer batter, lemon sole tartare, dried tomatoes and capers, while seasonal game features strongly in openers such as partridge and ham hock terrine, or grouse with venison 'ham' in bread sauce. Those may be followed by an all-singing, all-dancing presentation of Highland lamb in the various forms of roast saddle, crisp breast, sweetbreads and a steamed kidney dumpling, a versatile and powerful dish that only needs a lighter hand with the mint. Fish is subjected to the sorts of robust treatments that can often be good for it, as when chargrilled turbot appears with pennybun mushrooms and Jerusalem artichokes in sherry and thyme. Exciting contrasts inform a dessert of apple mousse that comes with superlative hot apple fritters and blackberry ripple ice cream, or there may be classic crème brûlée garnished with strawberries and an almond biscuit.

Chef Simon Bradley **Owner** Macdonald Hotels **Seats** 90, Pr/dining room 30 **Times** 12-2.30/6.30-10 Closed L Mon-Fri **Prices** Tasting menu fr £60, Starter fr £10, Main fr £27.50, Dessert fr £7.50 **Wines** 120 bottles over £30, 20 bottles under £30, 15 by glass **Parking** 50, Chargeable (pre-booking essential) **Notes** Pre-theatre menu 2 course & glass of wine £21, Sunday L £23.95-£32.95, Vegetarian available, Children welcome

Malmaison Oxford

◉ Modern British, French v

tel: 01865 268400 **Oxford Castle, New Rd OX1 1AY**
email: oxford@malmaison.com **web:** www.malmaison.com
dir: *M40 junct 9 (signed Oxford/A34). Follow A34 S to Botley Interchange, then A420 to city centre*

Egalitarian menu in the city's one-time prison

With a knack for finding good properties, the Mal group hits the mark here in Oxford with none other than the city's former prison. It's a glamorous spot these days, with a sprinkle of boutique dust sorting it out a treat. The brasserie is in the basement, with vaulted ceilings and the trademark mood lighting and rustic-chic vibe; there are tables outside, too, where prisoners used to stretch their legs. The cooking is a little bit French, a little bit British, and a little bit global. This results in chicken liver parfait, burgers, steaks and even a curry, and a feel-good bunch they are too. Pork and prune terrine with walnut loaf and pickles will sort out the Francophiles, while prawn cocktail will bring comfort to many. Next up, a steak, aged for 28 days (minimum, they say) and cooked on the grill, or pan-fried sea bass with chorizo, samphire and cockle vinaigrette. And for dessert, perhaps a classic crème brûlée.

Chef Daniel Bell **Owner** KSL **Seats** 100, Pr/dining room 35 **Times** 12-2.30/6-10.30 **Prices** Prices not confirmed **Wines** 45 bottles over £30, 10 bottles under £30, 18 by glass **Parking** Worcester St, Westgate **Notes** Tasting menu with wine 5 course, pre-theatre menu available, Sunday L, Children welcome

Mercure Oxford Eastgate Hotel

◉ Modern British

tel: 01865 248695 **73 High St OX1 4BE**
email: h6668-fb1@accor.com **web:** www.thehightableoxford.co.uk
dir: *A40 follow signs to Headington & city centre, over Magdalen Bridge, stay in left lane, through lights, left into Merton St, entrance to car park on left*

Vibrant brasserie in an historic building

The 17th-century building doesn't want for period charm with its mullioned windows and sandstone façade, but on the inside it's rather swanky in the contemporary manner – well-designed fixtures and fittings and a decidedly cool restaurant called the High Table Brasserie & Bar. Old regulars such as C.S. Lewis and J.R.R. Tolkien wouldn't recognise the place. It's a large open-plan space with whitewashed walls, white-tiled flooring, bare wooden tables and grey banquette seating; a perfect setting for its menu of British and Mediterranean-influenced food. Start with a single salmon fishcake served with a micro herb salad, follow on with a home-made burger with chips fried in duck fat, or roasted Cornish bass with braised Puy lentils, celeriac and pear remoulade. To finish, expect something like sticky toffee pudding with clotted cream ice cream and caramel sauce. And note it's close to all the city-centre action.

Times 12-2.30/6-9.30

Find out more about how we assess for Rosette awards on page 9

The Oxford Hotel

◉ Modern British

tel: 01865 489988 **Gidstow Rd, Wolvercote Roundabout OX2 8AL**
email: oxford@pumahotels.co.uk **web:** www.pumahotels.co.uk
dir: *A34 Peartree junct, follow signs to A40, take 4th exit at rdbt*

Brasserie-style menu in modern hotel restaurant

Within easy striking distance of the city centre, this modern hotel has conference and leisure facilities aplenty, plus a number of options for unwinding before or after said activities. There's the Medio Bar for a cocktail and bar snack, the Cappuccino Lounge for a light meal or afternoon tea, and, up on the first floor, the smart and modish restaurant. The menu here has a lot to offer and satisfies contemporary expectations with its breadth and depth. You might start with ham hock terrine, for example, with a counter-pointing grape and apple chutney, or go for an Asian flavour with mussels steamed in a Thai sauce. The grill does its work on the steaks – 8oz rib-eye, maybe – served up in the traditional manner with a choice of sauces. And there are main courses like slow-cooked pork belly with bubble-and-squeak, or battered haddock fillet, or roasted artichoke and pea risotto. Finish with a pear and almond tart with clotted cream and caramel sauce.

Chef Gavin Chapman **Owner** Puma Hotels Collection **Seats** 180 **Times** 7-9.30 Closed L all week **Prices** Prices not confirmed, Service optional **Wines** 8 bottles over £30, 20 bottles under £30, 18 by glass **Parking** 250 **Notes** Sunday L, Vegetarian available, Children welcome

STADHAMPTON Map 5 SU69

The Crazy Bear

◉◉ Modern British

tel: 01865 890714 **Bear Ln OX44 7UR**
email: enquiries@crazybear-stadhampton.co.uk **web:** www.crazybeargroup.co.uk
dir: *M40 junct 7, A329. In 4m left after petrol station, left into Bear Lane*

Rebooted Tudor inn with brasserie classics and more offbeat stuff

We often say that the modern conversion of an English Tudor inn has been carried out so as carefully to preserve its original character, but the epithet 'crazy' (unknown in the sense of 'mad' in Tudor English) is the clue that a different approach, to put it mildly, has been adopted here. Pink cushioned walls, a leopard-print carpet, big steel mirrors and a kind of herringbone overhead wine store set the scene for what's on offer in the English arm of the operation (see entry below for the Asian room). It's an exhaustively long list of contemporary brasserie food, with lots of push-button classics, such as tuna tartare and wasabi mayo, scallops and black pudding with pea purée, and chicken and mushroom pie with triple-cooked chips, mingling in among the more offbeat likes of squid pil-pil with pancetta, coriander and chilli, or crispy pork belly and smoked eel with baby beets and horseradish cream. You could even kickstart an evening with honey-glazed Old Spot whizzers, if you knew what they were, and ensure contentment at the end with a white chocolate cone of hazelnut semi-fredo.

Chef Martin Picken **Owner** Jason Hunt **Seats** 40, Pr/dining room 140 **Times** 12-10 All-day dining **Prices** Fixed L 2 course fr £14.95, Fixed D 3 course fr £19.95, Starter £9.50-£18.25, Main £14.75-£26.75, Dessert £8.95-£12.50 **Wines** 235 bottles over £30, 21 bottles under £30, 20 by glass **Parking** 100 **Notes** Sunday L, Vegetarian available, Children welcome

STADHAMPTON *continued*

Thai Thai at The Crazy Bear

@@ Modern Thai

tel: 01865 890714 **The Crazy Bear, Bear Ln OX44 7UR**
email: enquiries@crazybear-stadhampton.co.uk
dir: M40 junct 7, A329. In 4m left after petrol station, left into Bear Lane

Southeast Asian cooking in a Tudor village inn

The original incarnation of the expanding Crazy Bear group occupies a Tudor inn in a rural Oxfordshire village. As well as a modern British dining room, it also boasts a head-turning Thai restaurant with crimson velvet beams, scatter-cushions and tables that give the thrown-together impression of brass platters balanced on boxes. If it all looks at first like a concept that has run away with itself, the extensive menus are replete with authentically fresh, hot, bracing southeast Asian dishes. There are forays beyond the Thai borders, for Peking duck rolls dipped in hoisin, salt-and-pepper Japanese tofu with spring onions and habanero chillies, and stunning vegetarian compositions such as Penang aubergine with lychees, cherry tomatoes and grapes. The core of the repertoire, though, is accurately seasoned, palate-priming Thai classics, from pork satay to vermicelli glass noodles with black mushrooms, duck breast red curry with pineapple to steamed red snapper in a firestorm of chillies, galangal, lemongrass, lime leaves, garlic, coriander and lemon juice. Finish with bitter chocolate soup.

Chef Chalao Mansell **Owner** Jason Hunt **Seats** 30, Pr/dining room 140
Times 12-3/6-12 Closed L Sun **Prices** Tasting menu £29.95-£49.95, Starter £3.95-£11.95, Main £10.95-£39.95, Dessert £8.95-£10.95 **Wines** 235 bottles over £30, 21 bottles under £30, 20 by glass **Parking** 100 **Notes** Vegetarian available, Children welcome

| SWINBROOK | Map 10 SP21 |

The Swan Inn

@@ Modern British

tel: 01993 823339 **OX18 4DY**
email: info@theswanswinbrook.co.uk **web:** www.theswanswinbrook.co.uk
dir: A40 towards Cheltenham, turn left to Swinbrook

Historic village inn with locally-sourced ingredients

On the borders of Oxfordshire and Gloucestershire, this quintessential village pub, with an apple orchard to the rear and the Windrush River running by, takes the food-side of the operation seriously. It's owned by the Dowager Duchess of Devonshire and there is interesting memorabilia around the place relating to the Mitford sisters, including canvas prints of family portraits. Seasonal ingredients are sourced with care (traceability is a big deal here), and the fine produce turns up in dishes such as plum tomato and mozzarella tartlet with rocket and pesto, followed by confit belly of Cotswold lamb with spring vegetables, capers and mint, or locally-reared Aberdeen Angus steaks served with horseradish cream, green beans and skinny chips.

Times 12-2/7-9 Closed 25-26 Dec

| TOOT BALDON | Map 5 SP50 |

The Mole Inn

@@ Modern European

tel: 01865 340001 **OX44 9NG**
email: info@themoleinn.com
dir: 5m S of Oxford, restaurant 15 mins from M40 junct 7

Med-influenced country cooking in the pride of Toot

There are two Baldons, but only Toot boasts the Mole Inn. Lying about five miles out of Oxford, the place is testament to the Witchalls' unwavering vision of what a

country inn should be. A mix of roughcast walls, exposed beams and terracotta tiles, it's adorned with framed mirrors and staff whose hospitable politesse adds to the charm. A small conservatory to one side makes a pleasant summer retreat. Hearty portions of Mediterranean-influenced cooking are the leading card: calamari with lemon and tartare, crab risotto with chilli, ginger and lime, wild mushroom, garlic and parmesan linguine. More obviously pubby specials are great too though, as in a ginormous helping of smoked mackerel pâté with balsamic fig and onion chutney and toasted ciabatta, or lamb's liver and kidney with bacon, rosemary mash and onion gravy. The timing of a piece of crisped sea bream inspires confidence, as does its accompanying prawn and lime risotto. To finish, what could be better than treacle tart with ice cream made from Carnation milk?

Chef Gary Witchalls **Owner** Gary Witchalls **Seats** 70 **Times** 12-2.30/7-9.30 Closed 25 Dec **Prices** Fixed L 2 course £19.50, Fixed D 3 course £25, Starter £6.95-£8.50, Main £12.95-£18.50, Dessert £6.50, Service optional **Wines** 7 bottles over £30, 24 bottles under £30, 8 by glass **Parking** 40 **Notes** Sunday L £13.95-£16.50, Vegetarian available, Children welcome

| WANTAGE | Map 5 SU38 |

The Star Inn

@@ Modern British NEW

tel: 01235 751873 **Watery Ln, Sparsholt OX12 9PL**
email: info@thestarsparsholt.co.uk **web:** www.thestarsparsholt.co.uk

Reinvented inn with accomplished food

This solid 300-year-old inn in the quintessentially English village of Sparsholt has had a stylish makeover since being taken over by a partnership between a local interior designer and chef-patron Dave Watts. Inside, all is decluttered and open plan with chunky wooden furniture and plain white walls beneath venerable blackened beams, and the food has a suitably modern accent. The kitchen sets great store by local produce and Dave's cooking gets straight to the point: an impressive starter balances the richness of foie gras and duck liver parfait with pear chutney and granola, and it comes with a buttery home-made brioche bun. Mains partner pan-fried halibut with sweet millet, purple sprouting broccoli, samphire, and a buttermilk cream sauce laden with squid, mussels and cockles. Elsewhere, loin of new season lamb is served with its sweetbreads, peas, broad beans, scorched baby gem lettuce and salsa verde. Dessert takes mango as a theme to play with, serving it in an iced parfait with nougat, and as a purée, powder and frozen carpaccio with rose sorbet.

Chef David Watts **Owner** Caron Williams **Seats** 45, Pr/dining room 40
Times 12-2/6.30-9 Closed 2nd wk Jan 2 wks, Mon, D Sun **Prices** Fixed L 2 course £16.50, Fixed D 3 course £19.95, Starter £5.50-£11.50, Main £9.95-£22.95, Dessert £4.95-£6.95 **Wines** 20 bottles over £30, 21 bottles under £30, 12 by glass **Parking** On Street **Notes** Sunday L £18.50, Vegetarian available, Children welcome

| WATLINGTON | Map 5 SU69 |

The Fat Fox Inn

@ British

tel: 01491 613040 **13 Shurburn St OX49 5BU**
email: info@thefatfoxinn.co.uk
dir: M40 junct 6 onto B4009 S for 2.5m. On right in village

Characterful inn with a local flavour

Right at the heart of this small market town, The Fat Fox is a proper inn with an unreconstructed bar, comfortable bedrooms and a serious approach to local food, cooked with flair and without fuss – hurrah! There's even a piano by the front door alongside some comfy sofas. It doesn't matter if you eat in the bar or the dining area, with its warm colour tones and laid-back service, and there's no background music, just the happy hubbub of the contented customers. Local farmers and producers get name-checked on the daily-changing menu, which keeps things fresh, seasonal and unpretentious. Britwell Farm ox tongue, carrot and raisin salad, for example, is just the ticket, or try the excellent duck liver parfait with port jelly and red onion marmalade. Follow on with bavette steak with slow-roasted tomatoes, anchovy butter and chips, or its thanks again to Britwell Farm for its lamb belly, cooked with lentils and leeks.

Chef Stewart Lennox **Owner** John Riddell **Seats** 26, Pr/dining room **Times** 12–3/6.30–10 **Prices** Prices not confirmed **Wines** 2 bottles over £30, 21 bottles under £30, 12 by glass **Parking** 20 **Notes** Sunday L, Vegetarian available, Children welcome

WESTON-ON-THE-GREEN — Map 11 SP51

The Manor Restaurant
⊛⊛ Modern European **NEW**

tel: 01869 350621 **Weston Manor Hotel OX25 3QL**
email: house@themanorweston.co.uk **web:** www.westonmanor.co.uk
dir: *M40 junct 9, exit A34 to Oxford then 1st exit on left signed Weston-on-the-Green/Middleton Stony B4030. Right at mini rdbt, hotel 400yds on left*

Grand period room and modern cooking

Dating back some 900 years, The Manor certainly doesn't lack period character. A grand pile in glorious gardens, these days the house operates as a swish hotel with elegant bedrooms and a restaurant in the 11th-century Baron's Hall. As far as dining rooms go, this one is rather special, with a 30 foot high ceiling, acres of panels and a giant chandelier. The room has been dressed for the business of fine dining with crisp white linen and sparkling glassware, while the kitchen turns out some bright, modern British food via tasting or à la carte menus. A fashionable surf 'n' turf combo turns up amongst the starters – Native lobster cooked à la plancha, with chicken wing, leek purée and a truffle-flavoured sauce – while main course brings forth spiced Herdwick mutton with pickled grapes and ratte potatoes. Flavours hit the mark in a dessert of Yorkshire rhubarb sorbet with fromage blanc and almonds.

Chef Larry Jayasekara **Owner** Oxon Investments **Seats** 50, Pr/dining room 80 **Times** 12–2.30/7–9 **Prices** Fixed L 2 course £21, Tasting menu £60, Starter £11–£16, Main £24–£32, Dessert £9–£10, Service optional 12.5% **Wines** **Parking** 100 **Notes** Tasting menu 7 course, wine pairing available £45, Sunday L, Vegetarian available, Children welcome

WITNEY — Map 5 SP31

Old Swan & Minster Mill
⊛ Traditional British

tel: 01993 774441 **Old Minster OX29 0RN**
email: reception@oldswanandminstermill.com **web:** www.oldswanandminstermill.com
dir: *Exit A40 signed Minster Lovell, through village right T-junct, 2nd left*

Charming country pub by the River Windrush

In a wonderful English setting, the Old Swan is a smart country pub (the more modishly done-out Minster Mill is next-door) with a good deal of rustic charm and a serious approach to food. It's very cosy on the inside, with lots of spaces to tuck yourself away, and there's real ale on tap if that's what you're after. There's a local flavour to the menu, a refreshing lack of pretension, and even ingredients grown in their own kitchen garden. At lunchtime there's a range of tip-top ploughman's, whilst there's always the option of going for broke and settling down for three courses: Wychwood Forest duck terrine, perhaps, with citrus salad and aged port dressing, followed by Oxfordshire farm steak and Hobgoblin ale pie with King Edward mash and Old Swan garden vegetables, with old fashioned treacle tart with vanilla seed custard for pudding. The garden is a gem.

Chef David Mwiti **Owner** DeSavary family **Seats** 110, Pr/dining room 55 **Times** 12.30–3/6.30–9 **Prices** Starter £5.50–£9, Main £11.40–£22.50, Dessert £6.95–£9, Service optional **Wines** 33 bottles over £30, 19 bottles under £30 **Parking** 70 **Notes** Sunday L £16.95, Vegetarian available, Children welcome

The Restaurant at Witney Lakes Resort
⊛ Modern European

tel: 01993 893012 & 893000 **Downs Rd OX29 0SY**
email: restaurant@witney-lakes.co.uk
dir: *2m W of Witney town centre, off B4047 Witney to Burford road*

Popular brasserie cooking in a resort hotel

The sprawling modern resort in west Oxfordshire caters for iron-pumpers, niblick-swingers and the nuptial trade, as well as offering contemporary brasserie cooking in a destination restaurant that has acquired a dedicated local following. Regular champagne evenings and gourmet Thursdays are all part of the drill, and there are tables on a lakeside terrace in the sunnier months, but the core attraction is a menu of consistently dependable modern classic dishes. Opening with game terrine and pickled pear with sourdough toast, you might go on to gilt-head bream in sauce vierge, or ox cheek and kidney suet pudding. In among these are one or two more speculative offerings, such as baby squid with chickpeas, chorizo and aïoli, while two of you might sign up for a rendition of sinew-stiffening cassoulet. Fifteen minutes' wait at dessert stage is rewarded with a chocolate fondant, served with salted caramel ice cream, or opt instead for a selection of local cheeses.

Chef Sean Parker, Owen Little **Owner** Sean Parker **Seats** 75 **Times** 12–3/6.30–9 Closed 25 & 31 Dec, 1 Jan, L Sat, D Sun-Mon **Prices** Fixed L 2 course £13, Starter £4.50–£6.25, Main £12–£17.25, Dessert £4.95–£7.50, Service optional 10% **Wines** 9 bottles over £30, 38 bottles under £30, 11 by glass **Parking** 400 **Notes** Themed evenings, Sunday L £17–£19, Vegetarian available, Children welcome

WOODCOTE — Map 5 SU68

Woody Nook at Woodcote
⊛ Modern British

tel: 01491 680775 **Goring Rd RG8 0SD**
email: info@woodynookatwoodcote.co.uk
dir: *Opposite village green*

International flavours and top-notch Australian wines

Given the quintessential English setting opposite the village green, with creepers and hanging baskets serving up a riot of foliage, you might be surprised to discover that there's a decidedly antipodean flavour at this pretty cottage restaurant. Named after the owners' award-winning boutique winery in the Margaret River region of Western Australia, you can sample the full range of wines here, plus tuck into a menu of dishes that draws inspiration from Australia, the UK, and a few places in between. So, king crab bound in ginger, chilli, lemon and coriander mayonnaise is one way to start a meal, or go for traditional Provençal fish soup with all the regulation accompaniments. There are fish specials such as cod with vine tomato sauce and parmesan fettuccine, and wild Pacific tiger prawns grilled with garlic and herb butter. Finish with vanilla and mango crème brûlée with ginger shortbread.

Chef Stuart Shepherd **Owner** Jane & Peter Bailey **Seats** 50 **Times** 12–2.30/7–9.30 Closed Xmas, Mon-Tue, D Sun **Prices** Fixed L 2 course £15.95, Starter £5.95–£8.95, Main £11.95–£17.95, Dessert £5.95–£7.95, Service optional **Wines** 8 by glass **Parking** 25 **Notes** Sunday L £17.95, Vegetarian available, Children welcome

Who has won our Chefs' Chef award?
Find out on page 10

WOODSTOCK
Map 11 SP41

The Feathers Hotel

◎◎ Modern British

tel: 01993 812291 **Market St OX20 1SX**
email: enquiries@feathers.co.uk **web:** www.feathers.co.uk
dir: *From A44 (Oxford to Woodstock), 1st left after lights. Hotel on left*

Modern British cooking in a colourfully boutiqued hotel

A brick-built inn in a Cotswold market town not far from Oxford, the Feathers has long been a local fixture. There can be no doubt about its having been coaxed into the boutique hotel era when you get inside. Get a load of those eye-popping colours: rooms turned out in appetising collisions of lime and cherry, a dining room with raspberry-red banquettes and a mixture of bold graphic and abstract artworks. A copiously stocked gin bar is in the record-books for having the most varieties on offer. Thoroughly modern British cooking is the order of the day, with organics and locals among the menu ingredients, as well as seafood from the distant coasts. That last might be on-trend seared scallops with pickled fennel and roasted scallop roe, full of sea-fresh appeal and natural sweetness, while mains bring along cod in tomato-herb dressing with bubble-and-squeak. A meatier route might produce braised pig cheeks with pearl barley in thyme sauce, then roast rump, smoked shoulder and curried sweetbreads of lamb. If you missed a G&T earlier, it could turn up as dry flakes decorating a lemony crème brûlée.

Chef Simon Kealy **Owner** Empire Ventures Ltd **Seats** 40, Pr/dining room 24 **Times** 12.30-2/7.10-9.30 **Prices** Tasting menu £55, Starter £7.50-£11.50, Main £12.50-£27.50, Dessert £7.50-£9.50 **Wines** 80 bottles over £30, 10 bottles under £30, 16 by glass **Parking** On street **Notes** Sunday L £24.95, Vegetarian available, Children welcome

Kings Arms Hotel

◎ Modern British

tel: 01993 813636 **19 Market St OX20 1SU**
email: stay@kingshotelwoodstock.co.uk **web:** www.kingshotelwoodstock.co.uk
dir: *In town centre, on corner of Market St & A44*

Stylishly revamped Georgian hotel

The white-painted Georgian Kings Arms fits in perfectly in well-to-do Woodstock with its air of distinction and handsome country decor within. It's only a short stroll from the splendour of Blenheim Palace after all. For all its period charm, there's a good deal of contemporary polish to the place, not least in the Atrium Restaurant with its sharp, modern good looks: think chunky wooden tables and black high-backed chairs on a black-and-white chequerboard floor, plus original artworks and huge antique mirrors with rococo frames. The menu is a happy mix of old and new, too, with lots of gently modish things to choose from. Game terrine with pear chutney and rustic toast to start, perhaps, followed by Kelmscott Farm ham with free-range egg and chips, or go for the more upmarket braised duck leg with rich plum sauce, celeriac dauphinoise and buttered chard. Finish with a treacle and roast walnut tart.

Chef Simon Cottrell **Owner** David & Sara Sykes **Seats** 80 **Times** 12-2.30/6.30-9.30 **Prices** Prices not confirmed, Service optional **Wines** 12 bottles over £30, 27 bottles under £30, 13 by glass **Parking** On street **Notes** Sunday L, Vegetarian available, Children welcome

Macdonald Bear Hotel

◎◎ Traditional & Modern British

tel: 01993 811124 & 08448 799143 **Park St OX20 1SZ**
email: general.bear@macdonald-hotels.co.uk **web:** www.macdonaldhotels.co.uk/bear
dir: *M40 junct 9 follow signs for Oxford & Blenheim Palace. A44 to town centre, hotel on left*

Accomplished modern cooking in medieval hotel

Woodstock is not without its complement of attractive old buildings, and this creeper-covered hotel is one of them. Inside, evidence of the great age of the property is seen in the beams, stone walls and fireplaces in the traditional-looking dining rooms. The kitchen, though, keeps abreast of matters culinary, producing starters of ham hock roulade and crispy Stornoway black pudding with piccalilli vegetables and garlic ciabatta crisp, and Smoked John Ross Jr haddock fish cake with herb hollandaise. Beef is naturally reared in Scotland and aged for a minimum of 21 days, so perhaps you might go for a grilled rib-eye steak with Carroll's heritage hand-cut chips and your choice of sauce (red wine, béarnaise or peppercorn), or if fish is more your thing, pan-fried fillet of skrie cod with saffron potatoes and mussel vinaigrette. Traditional lemon tart with crème fraîche provides a simple but effective finale, or there's all the comfort of rhubarb crumble with fresh egg custard.

Chef Cameron Weyers **Owner** Macdonald Hotels **Seats** 65, Pr/dining room 26 **Times** 12.30-2.30/7-9.30 **Prices** Fixed L 2 course £19.95, Fixed D 3 course £39, Starter £7-£9.75, Main £10.95-£15.75, Dessert £7-£11.25, Service optional **Wines** 30 bottles over £30, 20 bottles under £30, 16 by glass **Parking** 50 **Notes** Sunday L, Vegetarian available, Children welcome

WOOTTON
Map 11 SP41

The Killingworth Castle

◎◎ Modern British **NEW**

tel: 01993 811401 & 01386 593223 **Glympton Rd OX20 1EJ**
email: reservations@thekillingworthcastle.com
dir: *M40 junct 9, 2m outside Woodstock on Glympton Road, on edge of Wootton*

Inspired pub cooking in a reborn country inn

Jim and Claire Alexander acquired the venerable village inn in only 2012, but have comprehensively re-transformed it back into what it always was, the heart of its local community in the countryside near Woodstock. Dating back to the reign of Charles I, its kitchen and brew house are being renovated to become part of the dining area, the gardens are undergoing a revival, and it's hoped to recommence the home-brewing that was once an integral part of the Castle's remit. Executive chef Andrew Lipp oversees operations both here and at the owners' other venue, the Ebrington Arms, and the results are offered in the form of a menu that provides plenty of choice while keeping things within sensible bounds. It all looks and tastes good, whether it be confit pork rillettes with prunes and cider-apple purée, or a haddock and crab Scotch egg in curried bisque, to start, or main courses such as butter-poached chicken breast with girolles and tarragon pistou, or grilled Cornish plaice served with roasted new potatoes and anchovy, artichoke barigoule and salsa verde. Finish with translucently light buttermilk pannacotta, honey-poached plums and gingerbread.

Chef Andrew Lipp, Phil Currie **Owner** Jim & Claire Alexander **Seats** 68, Pr/dining room 12 **Times** 12-2.30/6-9 **Closed** 25 Dec **Prices** Starter £5-£7.50, Main £11-£25, Dessert £5.50-£7, Service optional **Wines** 22 bottles over £30, 40 bottles under £30, 10 by glass **Parking** 40 **Notes** £7 L special Mon-Thu, Monthly food night, Sunday L £12.75-£14, Vegetarian available, Children welcome

RUTLAND

CLIPSHAM
Map 11 SK91

The Olive Branch

◎◎ British, European V

tel: 01780 410355 **Main St LE15 7SH**
email: info@theolivebranchpub.com **web:** www.theolivebranchpub.com
dir: 2m from A1 at Stretton junct, 5m N of Stamford

Refined modern pub dishes in a charming village inn

The Olive Branch is the kind of pub many a village would die for. Like many local inns, it closed its door (in 1997) and was lost for a while, but it came back firing on all cylinders thanks to a bunch of guys who saw its potential, and they have created a little oasis in pretty Clipsham. First and foremost it is still a pub (hurrah!) and can deliver a decent pint and provide space for locals to chew the fat. But, just as the serving of food saved many pubs from extinction, it was instrumental in the phoenix-like resurrection of The Olive Branch. This is a kitchen with a passion for seasonal and local stuff, for food that is big on flavour and fits the easy-going atmosphere of the great British pub. A steak, kidney and bone marrow pie, for example, served with crushed buttered swede and carrots is full of rich flavours and hearty intentions, or go for the more genteel beetroot risotto with watercress and local Colwick cheese.

Chef Sean Hope **Owner** Sean Hope, Ben Jones **Seats** 45, Pr/dining room 20 **Times** 12-2/7-9.30 Closed D 25 Dec, 1 Jan **Prices** Fixed L 2 course £16.95-£20.50, Fixed D 3 course £24.50, Starter £6.50-£11.50, Main £14.75-£24.50, Dessert £6.75-£6.95, Service optional **Wines** 67 bottles over £30, 24 bottles under £30, 16 by glass **Parking** 15 **Notes** Sunday L £20.50-£25.50, Children welcome

LYDDINGTON
Map 11 SP89

The Marquess of Exeter

◎ Modern European V

tel: 01572 822477 **52 Main St LE15 9LT**
email: info@marquessexeter.co.uk **web:** www.marquessexeter.co.uk
dir: M1 junct 19, A14 to Kettering, then A6003 to Caldecott. Right into Lyddington Rd, 2m to village

Welcoming village inn with appealing menus

Chef-proprietor Brian Baker has done a lovely job of transforming this village pub into the sort of local we would all like on our patch. It is a relaxed and informal place with a fresh rustic look; in the cosy bar there are head-skimming gnarled beams, flagstoned floors and baskets of logs ready to go on the open fire – just the spot for a pre-dinner drink. The restaurant has a completely different feel: the open-plan layout is decluttered, and decorated with white walls and scrubbed pine tables; friendly, chatty staff jolly things along with an upbeat mood. Menus make the most of seasonal ingredients and local produce in good honest dishes: chicken liver parfait with fig chutney and grilled bread, for example, makes a triumphant start, ahead of rosemary and garlic roasted chicken with herb crushed potatoes, peas and mustard jus. For pudding, crème brûlée is made as per the textbook and served with buttery shortbread.

Chef Brian Baker **Owner** Brian Baker **Seats** 90, Pr/dining room 14 **Times** 12-2.30/6.30-9.30 Closed 25 Dec **Prices** Fixed L 2 course fr £14.95, Fixed D 3 course fr £17.50, Starter £5.50-£9.50, Main £12.95-£19.50, Dessert £6.25, Service optional **Wines** 11 bottles over £30, 30 bottles under £30, 12 by glass **Parking** 40 **Notes** Sunday L £12.95-£19.50, Children welcome

OAKHAM
Map 11 SK80

Barnsdale Lodge Hotel

◎ Modern British

tel: 01572 724678 **The Avenue, Rutland Water, North Shore LE15 8AH**
email: enquiries@barnsdalelodge.co.uk **web:** www.barnsdalelodge.co.uk
dir: Turn off A1 at Stamford onto A606 to Oakham. Hotel 5m on right. (2m E of Oakham)

Simple British cooking at an ancestral family seat

The Noel family have lived at Barnsdale since the accession of George III, and they aren't going anywhere soon. To one side of the Earl of Gainsborough's Exton estate, it's a handsome country seat on the north shore of Rutland Water, with a conservatory dining room decorated in idiosyncratic taste. Surveying the patio gardens, it's festooned with parasols and animal objets d'art, and plays host to the simple modern British cooking of Stephen Conway, who uses the produce of the vegetable garden and of a plethora of local suppliers in his menus. A meal might follow an inspired and satisfying course from seared scallops with orange and fennel salad and watercress, through accurately timed marinated rump of local lamb with Chantenay carrots and garlic and rosemary dauphinoise, to a final sweet treat of reticently flavoured honey and yoghurt pannacotta with warm poached figs. Very fine breads add to the overall sense of quality.

Chef Steve Conway **Owner** The Hon Thomas Noel **Seats** 120, Pr/dining room 200 **Times** 12-2.15/6.30-9.30 **Prices** Fixed L 2 course £13.50, Starter £4.50-£9.50, Main £13.95-£19.95, Dessert £4.95-£6.95 **Wines** 27 bottles over £30, 58 bottles under £30, 17 by glass **Parking** 250 **Notes** Sunday L fr £21.95, Vegetarian available, Children welcome

Hambleton Hall

British V ♦ NOTABLE WINE LIST

tel: 01572 756991 **Hambleton LE15 8TH**
email: hotel@hambletonhall.com
web: www.hambletonhall.com
dir: *8m W of A1 Stamford junct (A606), 3m E of Oakham*

Superb fine dining in majestic country-house hotel

The magnificent house first appeared amid the lush rolling landscape in 1881. The landmark reservoir was opened in 1976. So when Tim and Stefa Hart arrived in this lovely part of Rutland in 1979, they were the final piece of the jigsaw, possessing the vision to create the little slice of heaven that is Hambleton Hall today. First off, the grounds, with the shimmering reservoir as a backdrop, are as formal and beautiful as many a stately home, an ideal place to wander in wonder. The house itself was built as a hunting lodge for a Victorian brewer, and its grandness is on a human scale. This place was built for entertainment and the pursuit of pleasure, which continues today with elegant bedrooms, chic public rooms and a restaurant that lives up to the billing of such a classically classy country-house hotel. The two dining rooms are filled with chandeliers, oil paintings and tables dressed with reassuring formality, and the service throughout is charming, professional and engaging. Aaron Patterson leads the line in the kitchen, and he has done so since 1992 – staff tend to stick around here, which is a very good sign indeed.

Chef has had plenty of time to gather together the very best of the region's growers and producers, and he ensures everything that comes to the tables is as fresh (and therefore seasonal) as it can be. Bread is baked in the in-house bakery, proving attention to detail runs deep here. There's a tasting menu, plus a terrific value set lunch, and if you opt for the former do consider splashing out on the accompanying wine flight, for another of Hambleton's little treasures is the magnificent wine list, and top-drawer sommelier. The dining experience begins with well-crafted canapés and the fabulous breads before moving onto first courses such as pan-fried foie gras with candied aubergine and pimento. The cooking is creative and contemporary, everything looks stunning on the plate, and, best of all, it tastes great. Main-course loin of fallow venison comes with spiced lentils, caramelised endive and celeriac, or go for the assiette of rabbit with its accompanying pearl barley risotto and liquorice-flavoured sauce. A fishy main might be pan-fried fillet of line-caught sea bass with wild mushrooms, artichokes and clams. When it comes to desserts the technical dexterity of the team in the kitchen remains to the fore: a terrine of rhubarb, for example, with lime leaf flavoured ice cream, or a mint chocolate pavé with yoghurt sorbet.

Chef Aaron Patterson **Owner** Mr T Hart **Seats** 60, Pr/dining room 20 **Times** 12-2/7-9.30 **Prices** Fixed L 2 course fr £25.50, Fixed D 3 course fr £65, Tasting menu fr £75 **Wines** 30 bottles under £30, 10 by glass **Parking** 40 **Notes** Sunday L fr £48, Children welcome

OAKHAM *continued*

Hambleton Hall

 – *see opposite*

see opposite

UPPINGHAM
Map 11 SP89

The Lake Isle

 British, French

tel: 01572 822951 **16 High Street East LE15 9PZ**
email: info@lakeisle.co.uk **web:** www.lakeisle.co.uk
dir: *M1 junct 19 to A14 Kettering, at rdbt take A43 signed Corby and then A6003 to Rockingham/Uppingham. Continue to pedestrian lights Uppingham, right onto High St, Lake Isle on right after the square*

Georgian townhouse hotel with confident cooking

Named for W. B. Yeats' Lake Isle of Innisfree, the hope is that visitors will experience a similar feeling of tranquillity in this Georgian townhouse with rooms in the lovely market town of Uppingham. On a pleasingly intimate scale, with a large window looking out onto the high street, inside there are panelled walls and original mahogany fittings, plus simply laid, heavy wooden tables attended by the friendly and efficient service team. French influences are in evidence on the broadly British menu, which changes every six weeks to keep flow with the seasons. There are some smart flavour combinations on show; take a starter of grilled medallion (well, fillet) of South Coast mackerel with crispy ham, bitter leaves, sautéed potatoes and a punchy piccalilli dressing. The quality of the lamb is indisputable in a duo including pan-roasted rack and medallion of braised shoulder, served with creamed celeriac, Savoy cabbage and pancetta. Then, sit back and wait while the dark chocolate and baby pear fondant pudding (served with stem ginger ice cream) is cooked to order.

Times 12-2.30/7-9 Closed 26 Dec-1 Jan, L Mon, D Sun

WING
Map 11 SK80

Kings Arms Inn & Restaurant

Modern British

tel: 01572 737634 **13 Top St LE15 8SE**
email: info@thekingsarms-wing.co.uk **web:** www.thekingsarms-wing.co.uk
dir: *1m off A6003, between Oakham & Uppingham*

Enterprising supplier-led cooking in a traditional inn

Stone walls, beams and flagstones are reminders that this village inn dates from the 17th century. Real ales are dispensed in the bar, where comfortable seating is arranged around an open fire, and there's an informal and friendly dining room. 'Good food takes time to source, prepare and serve,' trumpets the menu, and the kitchen is evangelical about all three, with everything delivered from within about 30 miles and even charcuterie and ketchup made in-house. Such integrity is amply demonstrated by what appears on the plate. Farmhouse pâté is deeply flavoured, topped with sautéed onions and mushrooms on a slice of toast, making a satisfying starter, and there could be a bold assembly of smoked eel (from the pub's smokehouse), black pudding, pancetta and apple sauce. Main courses are equally strong: pheasant hotpot with accurately timed green vegetables, say, or sea bass fillet with crab and fennel risotto and a tempura oyster. Portions tend to be generous but puddings are not to be missed, judging by vanilla and lavender pannacotta cut by Kirsch-soaked cherries.

Chef James Goss **Owner** David, Gisa & James Goss **Seats** 32, Pr/dining room 20 **Times** 12-2.30/6.30-9 Closed Mon, D Sun **Prices** Prices not confirmed, Service optional **Wines** 30 bottles over £30, 20 bottles under £30, 33 by glass **Parking** 20 **Notes** Sunday L, Vegetarian available, Children welcome

SHROPSHIRE

BRIDGNORTH
Map 10 SO79

The Old Vicarage Hotel

British, European

tel: 01746 716497 **Hallow, Worfield WV15 5JZ**
email: admin@oldvicarageworfield.com **web:** www.oldvicarageworfield.com
dir: *Off A454, approx 3.5m NE of Bridgnorth, 5m S of Telford on A442, follow brown signs*

Classic combinations in a conservatory-style hotel dining room

Set in two acres of pleasant gardens in green-and-pleasant Shropshire countryside, and handily close to Bridgnorth and Telford, The Old Vicarage is an Edwardian house which earns its keep these days as a smart country-house hotel. The airy conservatory-style dining room looking out over the gardens is one of its many charms. Flooded with sunlight on fine days and smartly done out with linen-clad tables, it is an agreeable spot for cooking that aims high and delivers a repertoire of classic and contemporary combinations based on top-class materials, much of it sourced from the local area. A well-presented starter matches ham hock ravioli with crushed peas, baby onions and pea mousse, ahead of free-range chicken breast teamed with spiced cauliflower purée, cardamom carrots and chicken cream. Local beef fillet might show up with parsley crust and jelly, crispy snails and red wine jus, while fish fans might find poached cod with River Exe mussels, marinière velouté and brandade bonbons. It all ends on a high note with bitter chocolate cream with lavender ice cream and candied flowers.

Times 12-2.30/7-9.30 Closed L Mon-Tue, Sat-Sun (by reservation only), D 24-26 Dec

CHURCH STRETTON
Map 15 SO49

The Studio

British, French

tel: 01694 722672 **59 High St SY6 6BY**
email: info@thestudiorestaurant.net
dir: *Off A49 to town, left at T-junct onto High St, 300yds on left*

Inspired home cooking in a former artist's studio

Tony and Sheila Martland's personable neighbourhood restaurant is housed in a former artist's atelier in a little town on the route from Shrewsbury to Ludlow. As befits its origin, it's hung with good local artworks, and there's a feeling of genuine warmth in the approach. The Martlands work side-by-side in the kitchen, producing as much as they can in-house, from ingredients sourced along the West Country supply-lines. The fixed-price dinner menu comes with certain items as standard (bread and olives to kick things off, dauphinoise and veg selections with the mains), and there are some inspired modern ideas. Start with duck leg confit alongside pomegranate and cashew salad, and then consider roast cod with prawns in lemon and caper brown butter, or venison steak with pickled pear and puréed celeriac in blackcurrant and red wine jus. Sheila's parkin with ginger and vanilla ice cream remains the signature dessert, but raspberry crème brûlée might tempt too.

Chef Tony Martland **Owner** Tony & Sheila Martland **Seats** 34 **Times** 7-9 Closed 2 wks Jan, 1 wk Apr, 1 wk Nov, Sun-Wed, L all week **Prices** Fixed D 3 course fr £29.50, Service optional **Wines** 6 bottles over £30, 33 bottles under £30, 6 by glass **Parking** On street parking available **Notes** Vegetarian available, Children welcome

The Inn at Grinshill

 Modern British

tel: 01939 220410 & 07730 066451 **High St SY4 3BL**
email: info@theinnatgrinshill.co.uk **web:** www.theinnatgrinshill.co.uk
dir: *7m N of Shrewsbury towards Whitchurch on A49*

Village coaching inn with inventive modern British cooking

Handily placed for stocking its larder with Shropshire's splendid bounty, this Georgian coaching inn now trades as a switched-on 21st-century restaurant with rooms. It's something of an inn for all seasons, welcoming all comers, whether you're piling into the pubby Elephant and Castle Bar with muddy boots off the local hills, or looking all sophisticated with a glass of pre-dinner fizz in the slick Bubbles Bar. The mood in the contemporary-styled restaurant is unbuttoned, and an open hatch lets you keep tabs on the talented young kitchen team as they turn out imaginative, up-to-date country-pub cooking. Staff are helpful and clued-up, which is a boon since the laconic menu merely lists the components of each dish, so a quail starter arrives as a pasty-like Wellington served with confit leg and wilted spinach, while crayfish risotto is enriched with creamy lobster bisque and pointed up with lemon and coriander. It all stays inventive through to a deconstructed Black Forest gâteau dessert involving chocolate mousse, cherries and cubes of cherry jelly.

Times 12-2.30/6.30-9.30 Closed Mon, D Sun

Saracens at Hadnall

 Modern British

tel: 01939 210877 **Shrewsbury Rd SY4 4AG**
email: reception@saracensathadnall.co.uk **web:** www.saracensathadnall.co.uk
dir: *M54 onto A5, at junct of A5/A49 take A49 towards Whitchurch. Follow A49 to Hadnall, diagonally opposite church*

Modish cooking at village restaurant with rooms

This rather fine looking red-brick Georgian coaching inn is on good form these days. It's surely never looked better. There's a traditional bar with lots of burnished oak and leather sofas to sink into, but the pièce de résistance is the fine-dining restaurant, headed up by David Martin. There are two dining rooms, both modishly done out, one being a conservatory with a 40-foot-deep well. The food is ambitious, creative and confidently executed, and there's a good deal of regional produce on the menu, including meat from the owners' south Shropshire farm. The presence of two tasting menus shows the get-up-and-go of the kitchen, whilst the carte is sensibly short and focused. Start, perhaps, with Cornish mackerel tartar with yoghurt, lime, sesame and soy, or a luscious soup such as one of parsley velouté with thyme jelly and truffled cream cheese. Main-course belly of Welsh pork comes with Jerusalem artichokes, red-wine infused scallop, prune and Armagnac jus and, for dessert, Irish stout might turn up in a pannacotta with accompanying blackcurrant sorbet.

Chef David Martin **Owner** Ben & Steve Christie **Seats** 45 **Times** 12-2.30/7-9.30 Closed D Sun **Prices** Fixed L 2 course £16.50, Fixed D 3 course £21.50, Tasting menu fr £35, Starter £5.95, Main £12.95-£19.95, Dessert £5.95, Service optional **Wines** 10 bottles over £30, 28 bottles under £30, 7 by glass **Parking** 20 **Notes** L Mon-Fri £7.75-£12.95, Sunday L £12.95-£15.95, Vegetarian available, Children welcome

La Bécasse

Rosettes not confirmed at time of going to print

Modern French v

tel: 01584 872325 **17 Corve St SY8 1DA**
email: info@labecasse.co.uk
dir: *In town centre opposite Feathers Hotel, at bottom of hill*

Modernist and traditional cooking in an oak-panelled cocoon

The Rosette award for this establishment has been suspended due to a change of chef. Reassessment will take place in due course under the new chef.
These premises, on one of Ludlow's principal thoroughfares, have been part of the town's emergence to culinary greatness since the beginning of the last decade. Once home to Hibiscus, prior to its move to the West End of London, it became in 2007 a player in Alan Murchison's squad, as the chef-patron of L'Ortolan expanded his operations into a range of classy venues across the country. Here in Ludlow, the restaurant inhabits a low-lit, oak-panelled and stone-walled, cocoon-like room with the feeling of a fine-dining grotto. A change of chef and team in January 2014 prevented us from being able to award a rating this time, but what seems certain is that new incumbent Chris O'Halloran will bring the same high

degree of creative lustre to the menus as his predecessors did. This is a man whose passion for cooking extends back to a boyhood in which he would greet his Mum home from work with a tray of freshly baked flapjacks. These days, it's a little more elaborate, with inspired, original ideas abounding. Starters encompass a curry-spiced crab and Gruyère quiche, or scallop and sweetcorn with a quail egg in truffled cream sauce. At main course, there's a willingness to explore the arc from modernist to traditional that many chefs have embraced, from cod with chicken wings and snails alongside spinach risotto. Escoffier himself could hardly have taken issue with a deeply intuitive braise of Angus beef, with smoked mash, wild mushrooms, caramelised shallots and foie gras in its own jus. Finish with a homage to rice pudding, copiously adorned with apricots, prunes, cherries and pistachios. Otherwise, look to the trolley for blue-riband cheeses, served with the full array of jellies, crackers, chutneys and fruity bread.

Chef Chris O'Halloran **Owner** Ludlow Restaurant Ltd **Seats** 40, Pr/dining room 14 **Times** 12-1.30/7-8.30 Closed Sun-Mon **Prices** Tasting menu £65 **Wines** 120 bottles over £30, 8 bottles under £30, 8 by glass **Parking** 6 **Notes** ALC L 2/3 course £28/£32.50, ALC D 2/3 course £45/£55, Children welcome

IRONBRIDGE
Map 10 SJ60

Restaurant Severn
◉◉ British, French

tel: 01952 432233 **33 High St TF8 7AG web:** www.restaurantsevern.co.uk
dir: *Travelling along High St pass Restaurant Severn on right, to mini rbdt, take 3rd exit onto Waterloo St, continue 50mtrs to car park on left*

Country cooking beside the Ironbridge gorge

Eric and Beb Bruce's small neighbourhood restaurant blends in unobtrusively with the terrace of souvenir and tea shops facing Abraham Darby's World Heritage cast iron bridge. Inside, however, sunny yellow walls, bare wooden floors, unclothed tables and high-backed toffee leather chairs make for an intimate brasserie look. The supply lines to local producers are good in these parts, and full advantage is taken of the local larder, supplemented by home-grown organic seasonal materials from their own smallholding. Classical French influences are evident in starters such as a smooth chicken liver and malt whisky parfait served with red onion marmalade and melba toast, while mains plough a similarly simple and unfussy furrow, partnering medallions of Shropshire venison saddle with braised red cabbage, and Cognac and sun-dried cranberry sauce. Puddings are Beb Bruce's domain – perhaps dark Belgian chocolate délice with chocolate cannelloni – or you might be tempted by a platter of Shropshire cheeses served with home-made chutney and Beb's spiced bread.

Chef Eric & Beb Bruce **Owner** Eric & Beb Bruce **Seats** 30 **Times** 12-2/6.30-8.30 Closed BHs, Mon-Tue, L Wed-Sat, D Sun **Prices** Service optional **Wines** 15 bottles over £30, 30 bottles under £30, 6 by glass **Parking** On street & car park opposite **Notes** Sun lunch once mthly, Wed-Thu 2/3 course £24.95/£26.95, Sunday L £18.95-£20.95, Vegetarian available, No Children

LUDLOW
Map 10 SO57

La Bécasse
Rosettes not confirmed at time of going to print – see opposite

The Clive Bar & Restaurant with Rooms
◉◉ Modern British

tel: 01584 856565 & 856665 **Bromfield SY8 2JR**
email: info@theclive.co.uk **web:** www.theclive.co.uk
dir: *2m N of Ludlow on A49, near Ludlow Golf Club, racecourse & adjacent to Ludlow food centre*

Assured regional cooking in Clive of India's former residence

The name memorialises Major-General Robert Clive (he of India), who once lived in this brick-built house on the Earl of Plymouth's estate. Just outside Ludlow, in the village of Bromfield, it became a pub for estate workers in recent times, and has been imaginatively refurbished to form the present day restaurant-with-rooms. West Country produce abounds on the seasonally informed menus, which feature a stunning opener of Dorset crab raviolo, the white meat sharing its pasta parcel with a soft-poached quail egg, accompanied by a salad of preserved lemon and fennel dressed in lemon purée. That might be succeeded by Herefordshire beef fillet with potato galette, creamed spinach and honey-roast carrots, a triumphantly traditional marriage of local ingredients in a rich bourguignon sauce, or perhaps sea bass with roasted salsify and sweet button onions in saffron vinaigrette. To finish comes a pretty textbook rendering of Bakewell tart, given contemporary twists with creamy apricot ice cream and a little pouring jug of Seville orange syrup, or there's a good selection of local cheeses served with fruit chutney.

Chef Krisztian Balogh **Owner** Ludlow Food Centre **Seats** 90 **Times** 12-3/6.30-10 Closed 25-26 Dec **Prices** Prices not confirmed, Service optional **Wines** 19 bottles over £30, 36 bottles under £30, 9 by glass **Parking** 80 **Notes** Sunday L, Vegetarian available, Children welcome

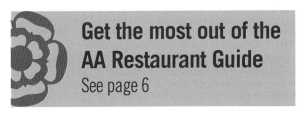

Get the most out of the AA Restaurant Guide
See page 6

What makes a 4-Rosette restaurant?
See page 9

LUDLOW *continued*

Dinham Hall Hotel

 Modern British

tel: 01584 876464 **By the Castle, Dinham SY8 1EJ**
email: info@dinhamhall.com **web:** www.dinhamhall.com
dir: *Town centre, off Market Place, opposite Ludlow Castle*

Ambitious modern British cooking opposite the castle

This three-storey house dates from the Georgian period and stands in the town centre opposite the castle. Open fires in the lounge are a welcoming touch in winter, there's a pretty terrace for summer dining, and the restaurant itself is in two sections, one under a large skylight, the other in the original building. The kitchen's an enthusiastic place, building its output on a solid bedrock of local suppliers and turning its hands to starters such as sweet, well-timed seared scallops served with deeply flavoured black truffle and roast pumpkin as well as a more familiar-sounding salad of black pudding, smoked bacon and Jersey Royals. Moving on, you may come across fillet of silver mullet with pickled spring vegetables, saffron and coriander. Another option may be pink, tender and succulent venison steak, from Mortimer Forest, with a textbook version of red wine sauce, accompanied by braised endive, pumpkin purée, sautéed mushrooms and roast potatoes. Finish with a classic tiramisù or pistachio and griottine cherry crème brûlée with cherry sorbet.

Chef Wayne Smith **Owner** Metzo Hotels Ltd **Seats** 36, Pr/dining room 60 **Times** 12.30-2.30/6.30-9.30 **Prices** Fixed L 2 course fr £19.95, Fixed D 3 course fr £34.95, Service optional 10% **Wines** 8 by glass **Parking** 16, On street **Notes** Sunday L, Vegetarian available, No children

The Feathers Hotel

 British, European

tel: 01584 875261 **Bull Ring SY8 1AA**
email: enquiries@feathersatludlow.co.uk **web:** www.feathersatludlow.co.uk
dir: *from A49 follow town centre signs to centre. Hotel on left*

Gentle modern British cooking in a venerable much-timbered inn

'That prodigy of timber-framed houses,' Pevsner called it, and it isn't hard to see what he meant. The place was converted to an inn by a Royalist veteran of the Civil War in around 1670, though its oldest parts hark back to the reign of James I. It has been sensitively decorated throughout to retain its true identity, as witness the dining room, where dark brown upholstery and crisp white linen blend in with the roughcast stone walls and venerable beams. Stuart Forman essays a gentle take on the modern British idiom. He partners scallops with the components of a BLT and vanilla mayonnaise to start, then adding a wild mushroom and tarragon mousse to saddle of rabbit with green beans in hazelnut butter, or pan-roasted halibut on fennel slaw with purple potatoes in lemon oil. Proceedings close with Valrhona fondant and pistachio ice cream, or with artisan cheeses, served with membrillo and walnut bread.

Chef Stuart Forman **Owner** Ceney Developments **Seats** 50, Pr/dining room 30 **Times** 7-9 Closed L all week **Prices** Fixed D 3 course £39.95, Service optional

Wines 7 bottles over £30, 30 bottles under £30, 10 by glass **Parking** 36 **Notes** Vegetarian available, Children welcome

Fishmore Hall

 – *see opposite*

Overton Grange Hotel and Restaurant

Modern British

tel: 01584 873500 **Old Hereford Rd SY8 4AD**
email: info@overtongrangehotel.com **web:** www.overtongrangehotel.com
dir: *M5 junct 5. On B4361 approx 1.5m from Ludlow towards Leominster*

Classic-meets-modern cooking and attentive service in Ludlow

Whether it's a stroll in the Shropshire Hills, exercise in the indoor pool, or a chill in the spa, Overton Grange is positioned to offer a wealth of possibilities in preparation for dinner. The dining room in this Edwardian house has an elegant finish, with warm lavender-coloured walls, high-backed leather chairs and tables dressed up for the business of fine dining. The menu is classically minded, with an Anglo-French focus, and carefully sourced ingredients. Presentation is on the contemporary side – a slate here and there – and there are canapés and amuse-bouche in true country-house style. Seared scallops with apple tapioca and black pudding bonbon looks impressive on the plate, with another starter stuffing chocolate ravioli with game and serving it with a girolles velouté. Main-course seared duck breast – nicely pink – is partnered with parsnip purée, nutmeg gnocchi and Cassis jus, or there might be grilled sea bass with herb polenta and fennel pollen cream sauce. For dessert, dark chocolate fondant oozes in all the right places, and comes with cinnamon ice cream.

Chef Thomas Jacks **Owner** Metzo Hotels Ltd **Seats** 40, Pr/dining room 24 **Times** 12-2.30/7-9.30 **Prices** Fixed L 3 course fr £32.50, Fixed D 3 course fr £42.50, Tasting menu fr £59.50, Service optional 10% **Wines** 12 by glass **Parking** 50 **Notes** Sunday L fr £32.50, Vegetarian available, No children

---

MARKET DRAYTON   Map 15 SJ63

Goldstone Hall

Modern British

tel: 01630 661202 **Goldstone Rd, Goldstone TF9 2NA**
email: enquiries@goldstonehall.com **web:** www.goldstonehall.com
dir: *4m S of Market Drayton off A529 signed Goldstone Hall Hotel. 4m N of Newport signed from A41*

Modern British ideas in a manor-house hotel

The Georgian house is handsome enough – with traditional features and an elegant interior – but the two stand-out elements to Goldstone Hall are its magnificent gardens and ambitious restaurant. The kitchen garden is a major part of the operation, providing fresh, seasonal produce for the table, and it's a good idea to make time to explore the grounds during a visit. Dining takes place in either a grandly panelled dining room with an Arts and Crafts fireplace, or in the more informal Orangery. The kitchen turns out some bright, modern dishes while avoiding jumping on the bandwagon of every contemporary fashion (foams are avoided, for example), and the flavours of these carefully sourced (and home-grown) ingredients are given room to make an impression. Start with pan-fried scallops with pickled Cox's apples and a purée, plus air-dried ham, followed by rack of local lamb served with spinach from the garden, asparagus and an apple mint purée. Finish with smooth chocolate delice with nibbed praline and rosemary ice cream. Excellent amuse-bouche gets things off to a flying start, as do the excellent home-made breads.

Chef Steven Blackshawe **Owner** John Cushing & Helen Ward **Seats** 60, Pr/dining room 14 **Times** 11-3/7-10 **Prices** Starter fr £7, Main fr £14.50, Dessert fr £8.95, Service optional **Wines** 30 bottles over £30, 70 bottles under £30, 15 by glass **Parking** 70 **Notes** Garden L menu available, Sunday L fr £30, Vegetarian available, Children welcome

Fishmore Hall

Modern European v

tel: 01584 875148 **Fishmore Rd SY8 3DP**
email: reception@fishmorehall.co.uk
web: www.fishmorehall.co.uk
dir: *A49 from Shrewsbury, follow Ludlow & Bridgnorth signs. 1st left towards Bridgnorth, at next rdbt left onto Fishmore Rd. Hotel 0.5m on right after golf course*

Renovated country house with fresh, thoughtful cooking

Fishmore was rescued from near-dereliction in 2007 by its present owners, although you'd scarcely guess as much to look at it now. Situated just outside the gastro-hub that is Ludlow, it surveys the undulating acres of Shropshire farmland and landscape all around, with Clee Hill in the distance. You can just make out the turrets of the castle poking their heads above the treeline. A recent orangery extension forms the venue for Fishmore's dining operation, named Forelles after the variety of pear-trees planted in the garden. Neutral decor and minimalist artworks establish a gentle background, and tables are dressed to impress, with smart napery and quality stemware. David Jaram cooks a modern European menu, founded on pedigree British materials, focusing on straightforward flavours and freshness, with nothing making a confrontational challenge

for the sake of it. There's thoughtfulness and delicacy to a starter of scallop carpaccio seasoned with a touch of chilli and bundles of Thai basil, as well as diced cucumber and a lime jelly. That might be followed by loin of local lamb with Herefordshire snails, onion purée and spring veg in salsa verde and wild garlic, a fresh green study if ever there was, or turbot with braised celery, crosnes and purslane. There's a wickedly rich finisher of dark chocolate ganache, alongside blackberry sorbet in a thin chocolate shell and crushed pistachios. At the summit of the kitchen's productivity is a nine-course tasting menu (ten if you take a local cheese selection too) that puts all Jaram's creativity and ingenuity on glittering show, the itinerary starting out with a salmon pavé, anise-glazed beetroot, goats' curd and red chard, and coming to its journey's end with chocolate fondant, prunes and Earl Grey ice cream.

Chef David Jaram **Owner** Laura Penman **Seats** 40, Pr/dining room 20 **Times** 12-2.30/7-9.30 Closed D Sun, BHs **Prices** Fixed L 2 course fr £20, Fixed D 3 course fr £49, Tasting menu £59-£69, Service optional **Wines** 52 bottles over £30, 16 bottles under £30, 12 by glass **Parking** 36 **Notes** Tasting menu 6/9 course, Vegetarian 2/3/6/9 course £30-£60, Sunday L £25, Children welcome

MARKET DRAYTON *continued*

Ternhill Farm House & The Cottage Restaurant

◉◉ Modern International

tel: 01630 638984 **Ternhill TF9 3PX**
email: info@ternhillfarm.co.uk **web:** www.ternhillfarm.co.uk
dir: *On junct A53 & A41, archway off A53 to back of property*

Ambitious cooking in homely Georgian farmhouse

Mike and Jo Abraham have been hard at work for the last decade, unleashing a top-to-bottom facelift on their red-brick Georgian farmhouse and giving the place a new lease of life as a smart restaurant with rooms. The dining room occupies the old kitchen, complete with Aga, where they have pulled off a clean-cut modern look, blending original oak beams and pine flooring with leather seats and bare wooden tables, and custard yellow walls hung with mirrors and eclectic art. The cooking takes a hearty, crowd-pleasing approach, relying on the excellent quality of the local and home-grown ingredients for its effect. A complex beetroot medley delivers chilli-spiced beetroot soup with chive cream, chilled beetroot and orange-cured salmon with mustard and lime dressing, and goats' cheese and beetroot bruschetta, while main course is another multi-faceted dish involving pan-fried partridge breast wrapped in honey-cured bacon, slow-braised leg, pheasant confit, rabbit, venison and pigeon with plum jus, spiced red cabbage, thyme dauphinoise potato and quince jelly.

Chef Michael Abraham **Owner** Michael & Joanne Abraham **Seats** 22, Pr/dining room 14 **Times** 6.30-12 Closed Sun-Mon, L all week **Prices** Prices not confirmed, Service optional **Wines** 6 bottles over £30, 37 bottles under £30, 6 by glass **Parking** 16 **Notes** Fixed D 2 course available Tue-Fri, Credit cards 2% charge, Vegetarian available, No children

---

MUCH WENLOCK   Map 10 SO69

Raven Hotel

◉◉ Modern British

tel: 01952 727251 **30 Barrow St TF13 6EN**
email: enquiry@ravenhotel.com **web:** www.ravenhotel.com
dir: *10m SW from Telford on A4169, 12m SE from Shrewsbury. In town centre*

Ambitious cooking in a 17th-century coaching inn

The former coaching inn has held court in Much Wenlock since the 17th century and remains in the same line of business to this day. The place still has period charm, with venerable beams, log fires and hand-pulled ales available in the bar. On the dining front, though, things are a little more contemporary, positively 21st-century in fact. The kitchen makes excellent use of the plentiful (and top quality) produce available in this neck of the woods, and the menu turns them into smart, modern European constructions. It all takes place in a traditional room which is ear-marked for a revamp as we go to press. A starter soup shows the ambition in the kitchen, with a slow-roast celeriac version topped with chorizo beignet and parmesan emulsion. Main course might bring forth a surf 'n' turf number, pairing roast fillet of Mortimer Forest venison with lobster, plus haricot blanc, pancetta and lobster espuma. There's a tasting menu, too, serving up 68°C loin of cod. Desserts run to Granny Smith pannacotta with warm apple cake and apple ice cream, and the cheese selection is first class.

Chef Jason Hodnett **Owner** Kirk Heywood, Sheila Hartshorn **Seats** 40, Pr/dining room 14 **Times** 12-2.30/6.45-9.30 Closed 25-26 Dec **Prices** Fixed D 3 course £39, Tasting menu £45-£59, Service optional **Wines** 10 bottles over £30, 48 bottles under £30, 12 by glass **Parking** 30 **Notes** Vegetarian available, Children welcome

---

MUNSLOW   Map 10 SO58

Crown Country Inn

◉◉ Modern British

tel: 01584 841205 **SY7 9ET**
email: info@crowncountryinn.co.uk **web:** www.crowncountryinn.co.uk
dir: *On B4368 between Craven Arms & Much Wenlock*

Classy modern cooking in old village inn

In an Area of Outstanding Natural Beauty, the Crown has some history behind it: it dates from Tudor times and was first licensed in 1790. The first-floor restaurant, a courtroom in the 17th century, is a beamed, cottagey-looking room with an impressive open fireplace. The kitchen follows the 'Local to Ludlow' precepts, thus sourcing its ingredients within the locality, and produces food in the up-to-the-minute culinary idiom. Apple and hazelnut salad is the accompaniment for a starter of crisp-crumbed blue cheese fritters with hazelnut and orange dressing, and pickled vegetables for duck liver and orange parfait. Inspirational main courses offer plenty of variety, from home-made venison meatloaf wrapped in pancetta served with wild mushroom sauce, braised red cabbage and dauphinoise potatoes, to accurately grilled fillet of sea bass with shellfish beurre blanc, red wine syrup and saffron-infused mash. Chocoholics will be delighted to find among puddings hot chocolate quenelle with Baileys parfait, pistachio crumble and coffee syrup, and other indulgences include orange pannacotta and pears poached with tonka beans and orange jelly.

Chef Richard Arnold **Owner** Richard & Jane Arnold **Seats** 65, Pr/dining room 42 **Times** 12-2/6.45-8.45 Closed some days during Xmas, Mon, D Sun **Prices** Starter £6-£8, Main £15-£20, Dessert £6.50, Service optional **Wines** 2 bottles over £30, 29 bottles under £30, 5 by glass **Parking** 20 **Notes** Sunday L £19.95-£22.95, Vegetarian available, Children welcome

---

NORTON   Map 10 SJ70

The Hundred House

◉◉ Traditional British, French

tel: 01952 580240 **Bridgnorth Rd TF11 9EE**
email: reservations@hundredhouse.co.uk **web:** www.hundredhouse.co.uk
dir: *Midway between Telford & Bridgnorth on A442. In village of Norton*

Hands-on family hotel where quirky charm meets skilled modern cuisine

Run by the Phillips family since the mid-1980s, The Hundred House is brimful of character and personality, a breath of fresh air in a world of corporate blandness. The rather handsome Georgian coaching inn has stylish bedrooms which fall into the boutique end of the spectrum by contemporary classifications, a bar serving some pretty nifty pub grub, and a brasserie and restaurant producing some classy dishes based on tip-top regional ingredients. A first course of griddled scallops is served with a risotto cake and stir-fried vegetables, with another offering a plate of meze including falafel and aubergine purée. Next up, a main course of roast rack of Shropshire lamb with creamed garlic mash, or chicken breast stuffed with ricotta, spinach and pine nuts. Desserts can deliver all the comfort of a hot treacle tart with home-made custard, or sticky toffee pudding with vanilla ice cream, or go for the English cheeses with home-made chutney and biscuits.

Chef Stuart Phillips **Owner** Mr H Phillips, Mr D Phillips, Mr S G Phillips **Seats** 80, Pr/dining room 34 **Times** 12-2.30/6-9.30 Closed D 25 Dec **Prices** Starter £5.95-£8.95, Main £12.95-£22.95, Dessert £5.95-£6.95, Service optional **Wines** 9 bottles over £30, 36 bottles under £30, 12 by glass **Parking** 60 **Notes** Gourmet evenings, Sunday L £5.95-£13.95, Vegetarian available, Children welcome

OSWESTRY Map 15 SJ22

Pen-y-Dyffryn Country Hotel

 Modern British

tel: 01691 653700 **Rhydycroesau SY10 7JD**
email: stay@peny.co.uk **web:** www.peny.co.uk
dir: *3m W of Oswestry on B4580*

Locally based cooking on the cusp of England and Wales

An enterprising construction company built the rectory, church and village school here in 1840 for £1,260 all in – quite a bargain. We can only shudder at the planning procedures that would be provoked today by the fact that the church is on the Welsh side of the border and the rectory, now a country hotel, on the English. With sweeping views over the valley, it's a relaxing place indeed, traditionally furnished in country-house style, with table linen, floral decorations and candles gracing the dining room, not to mention some fetching near-abstract paintings suggestive of the local landscape. David Morris's cooking is firmly in the modern Anglo-Welsh (to hedge our bets) idiom, with organic materials and upstanding flavours on show. King scallops in verjus cream with tomato, basil and spinach delivers appetising sweetness and fragrance, and may be succeeded by well-seasoned lamb rump with a meat-stuffed tomato, creamed cabbage and pancetta. Fish could be a pairing of halibut and crab with red pepper risotto. The finale might be a properly vanillary crème brûlée strewn with raspberries.

Chef David Morris **Owner** MJM & AA Hunter **Seats** 25 **Times** 6.45-11 Closed 20 Dec-21 Jan, L all week **Prices** Fixed D 3 course £32-£39, Service optional **Wines** 40 bottles over £30, 40 bottles under £30, 6 by glass **Parking** 18 **Notes** Vegetarian available, Children 3 yrs+

Sebastians

 International, French

tel: 01691 655444 **45 Willow St SY11 1AQ**
email: sebastians.rest@virgin.net **web:** www.sebastians-hotel.co.uk
dir: *From town centre turn into Willow St signed Selatyn. Hotel on left in 400yds*

Skilled French cooking in boutique venue

Mark and Michelle Fisher have run their boutique restaurant with rooms for a couple of decades, and it shows in the well-polished professionalism and amiability that pervades the place. The building is a 16th-century inn, full of quaint beamed character, but not stuck in the past. For drinks and canapés, choose between a dinky bar or a comfy lounge with sofas and a roaring fire, before moving on to the oak-panelled, apricot-hued dining room with its tobacco leather chairs and crisp white linen. Orient Express-themed artwork hints at the French theme running through the menus: dinner takes you through five courses of well-crafted, Gallic-influenced ideas, or there's a great value market menu for tighter budgets. Pan-fried scallops with haricot cassoulet, red peppers, micro salad and raisin dressing is a cracking starter, followed by lamb (loin and ballottine of braised leg) matched to great effect with smoked aubergine purée, aubergine crisp, and rich jus spiked with goats' cheese. Of-the-moment techniques appear too, as in the sous-vide-cooked strawberries served with lemon pistachio cake and lemon verbena ice cream.

Chef Mark Fisher **Owner** Mark & Michelle Fisher **Seats** 35 **Times** 6.30-9.30 Closed 25-26 Dec, 1 Jan, Etr Mon, Sun-Mon, L all week **Prices** Prices not confirmed, Service optional **Wines** 18 bottles over £30, 31 bottles under £30, 7 by glass **Parking** 6, On street **Notes** 5 course D £44.50, Vegetarian available, No children

Wynnstay Hotel

 Modern European

tel: 01691 655261 **Church St SY11 2SZ**
email: info@wynnstayhotel.com **web:** www.wynnstayhotel.com
dir: *In town centre, opposite church*

Modern dishes in a Georgian setting complete with bowling-green

Standing proud in the heart of town, the hotel is an august redbrick edifice, fronted by a portico entrance with flags flying above. Like many such places, it began life as a coaching-inn in the early Georgian era, and is still privately owned and maintained with impressive attention to detail. There are the expected spa and gym facilities, but a major attraction of the Wynnstay is a magnificent crown bowling-green. The Four Seasons restaurant is hung with depictions of the pleasures of the table, and service is flawlessly professional. A gentle style of modern British cooking produces favourites such as ham hock terrine with piccalilli, mussels simmered in cider, grilled mackerel with cockles and leeks, and thyme-roasted chicken breast with Anna potatoes and a good stock sauce. Desserts might include blackberry cheesecake or a pear poached in red wine, served with ginger ice cream, and there are local cheeses for the savoury-minded.

Times 12-2/7-9.30 Closed 25 Dec

SHIFNAL Map 10 SJ70

Park House Hotel

 Modern European

tel: 01952 460128 **Park St TF11 9BA**
email: reception02@parkhousehotel.net **web:** www.parkhousehotel.net
dir: *From M54 junct 4 take A464 through Shifnal; hotel 200yds after railway bridge*

Modern cooking in singular market town hotel

Two 17th-century country houses, one red-brick, one faced with white stucco have been pasted seamlessly together to make Park House, an upmarket venue in a pleasant Shropshire market town. Period oak panelling and ornate plasterwork combine with a dramatic contemporary colour scheme to provide a classy backdrop in the brasserie-style Butlers restaurant. The kitchen doesn't try to reinvent the wheel here, focusing instead on good quality local produce in a repertoire of straightforward modern European ideas. King scallops with pancetta and pea purée might lead the way, followed by rump of lamb served with Puy lentil and root vegetable cassoulet. At the end, local cheeses compete for your attention with crowd-pleasers such as hot chocolate fondant with pistachio ice cream.

Chef Chris Davies **Owner** Andrew Hughes **Seats** 50, Pr/dining room 180 **Times** 12-10 All-day dining **Prices** Fixed L 2 course £19.95, Fixed D 3 course £24.95, Tasting menu £20, Starter £4.95-£8.50, Main £10.95-£19.95, Dessert £5.50-£7, Service optional **Wines** 7 bottles over £30, 24 bottles under £30, 10 by glass **Parking** 100 **Notes** Afternoon tea £9.95, Steak night Fri-Sat £35 (2 people), Sunday L £16.95-£24.95, Vegetarian available, Children welcome

Who has made the top ten per cent this year?
See page 34

SHREWSBURY   Map 15 SJ41

Albright Hussey Manor Hotel & Restaurant

◉◉ Modern British

tel: 01939 290571 **Ellesmere Rd, Broad Oak SY4 3AF**
email: info@albrighthussey.co.uk **web:** www.albrighthussey.co.uk
dir: 2.5m N of Shrewsbury on A528, follow signs for Ellesmere

Confident modern cooking in a fascinating Tudor house

The Subbiani family's Tudor hotel is one of the more architecturally arresting 16th-century English buildings. It may look rather crudely extended to the untutored eye, but the two entirely unmatching wings – one brown-timbered, the other taller half of stone-faced brick – were built only 35 years apart. The place is stocked with fascinating antiques, both martial and domestic, the guest-rooms have canopy beds, and dining takes place in a beamed room with mullioned windows and a pleasing coral-pink colour scheme. Confident contemporary cooking is the day's order, starting perhaps with gently spiced ham hock terrine dressed with raisin relish and Baby Gem and apple salad, or home-cured salmon with beetroot, before mains such as crisply seared sea bass with scallops and vegetable 'spaghetti' in a rich beurre blanc containing sorrel, or medallion of local beef with oxtail ravioli, fondant potatoes and spinach. Finish with proudly risen amaretto soufflé laced with honey, accompanied by intensely flavoured matching ice cream, or else a fine local cheese such as Wrekin Blue, served with rhubarb chutney.

Times 12-2.15/7-10

Drapers Hall

◉◉ Modern, Traditional

tel: 01743 344679 **10 Saint Mary's Place SY1 1DZ**
email: goodfood@drapershallrestaurant.co.uk **web:** www.drapershallrestaurant.co.uk
dir: From A5191 (St Mary's St) on one-way system into St Mary's Place

Updated classic cooking in a medieval dining room

Dating back to 1556, Draper's Hall restaurant with rooms is situated in the heart of Shrewsbury and offers the chance to dine in a lovingly restored period building. It's proud to be one of the oldest buildings in the market town, as evinced by its grand inglenook fireplaces, old wooden beams, medieval floors and wood-panelled walls. Striking candelabras dominate white-clothed tables with their tartan wool chairs. Ella Fitzgerald playing softly in the background adds to the civilised vibe. When it comes to the menu, tried-and-tested combinations benefit from some additional fashionable touches, so foams and jellies may crop up here and there. Roast quail, celeriac and vanilla purée and game jus is brimming with earthy flavours and might come before Cornish black bream with crab risotto and fish velouté, or a rib-sticking tartiflette with Reblochon cheese, potatoes and cream. Finish with a decadent dessert of baked dark chocolate, frangipane, cherries and Amaretto ice cream.

Times 11-3.30/6-9.30 Closed D Sun

Follow the AA on twitter @TheAA_Lifestyle

Lion & Pheasant Hotel

◉◉ British v

tel: 01743 770345 **49-50 Wyle Cop SY1 1XJ**
email: info@lionandpheasant.co.uk **web:** www.lionandpheasant.co.uk
dir: From S & E: pass abbey, cross river on English Bridge to Wyle Cop, hotel on left. From N & W: follow Town Centre signs on one-way system to Wyle Cop. Hotel at bottom of hill on right

Classic modern brasserie cooking in a townhouse hotel

This was a coaching inn back in the 16th-century and the period façade still fits right in on Wyle Cop. It's a different picture inside, where contemporary style takes over, but in a restrained, easy-on-the-eye New England manner. Neutral tones and tongue-and-groove-panelling combine with the ancient beams and natural brick to create a very engaging space built for the business of hospitality. There are boutique bedrooms, a rather cool bar with a real fire and some cocktails, and a smart but relaxed restaurant that focusses on British ingredients. The menu shows a modern British spin to classic, brasserie-style combinations. Dill-cured salmon gravad lax, for example, with horseradish crème fraîche, beetroot and capers is a simple enough dish, the flavours all pulling together, or there might be white onion soup with smoked cheese beignets. Main-course whole roasted partridge comes with confit potato, trompettes and a nicely intense jus, and slow-roasted belly of pork with mustard mash and braised red cabbage and glazed carrots.

Chef Matthew Strefford **Owner** Jim Littler **Seats** 35, Pr/dining room 45
Times 12-2.30/6-9.30 Closed 25-26 Dec **Prices** Prices not confirmed, Service optional **Wines** 105 bottles over £30, 70 bottles under £30, 14 by glass **Parking** 14, NCP opposite **Notes** Sunday L, Children welcome

Porter House SY1

◉ Modern British, International v

tel: 01743 358870 **15 St Mary's St SY1 1EQ**
email: info@porterhousesy1.co.uk **web:** www.porterhousesy1.co.uk
dir: In Shrewsbury town centre, on the one-way system, almost opposite St Mary's Church

Trending brasserie food with upscale burgers a speciality

The place used to be known as Mad Jack's, in homage to a Georgian roustabout, but has had an image makeover and gone distinctly saner, with a 21st-century monochrome look, all white walls and charcoal-grey furniture under the atrium ceiling. Local sourcing is a sine qua non, with Shropshire beef a particularly proud boast. It turns up, along with a little wagyu for luxury, in many of the upscale burger variations that form the theme element of Monday nights, and the rest of the menu maintains the pace with trending brasserie preparations such as Maryland crabcakes and chipotle mayo, sticky ribs, fish or beef tacos with spicy rice, and creamy carbonara. It all creates a breezy mid-Atlantic feel in unassuming Shrewsbury, through to a slate of hipster desserts like sticky maple pecan pie with cream soda float. Brunchers, start your tastebuds with one of the Bloody something hangover cocktails, before moving on to a fishfinger sandwich and skinny fries.

Chef Idris Hughes Owner Ann & Danny Ditella Seats 60, Pr/dining room 45 Times 10-10 Closed 25-26 Dec, All-day dining Prices Fixed L 2 course fr £12, Fixed D 3 course fr £15, Starter £5.50-£9, Main £11-£27, Dessert £5-£6.50, Service optional 10% Wines 13 bottles over £30, 37 bottles under £30, 14 by glass Parking Town centre Notes Sunday L £14-£26, Children welcome

TELFORD
Map 10 SJ60

Chez Maw Restaurant
◎◎ Modern British V
----
tel: 01952 432247 Best Western Valley Hotel, Buildwas Rd, Ironbridge TF8 7DW
email: info@thevalleyhotel.co.uk web: www.chezmawrestaurant.co.uk
dir: M6/M54 from junct 6 take A5223 to Ironbridge for 4m. At mini island right, hotel 80yds on left

Modern British cooking in a hotel near the Iron Bridge

Right on the bank of the Severn in the UNESCO World Heritage Site of Ironbridge, barely a rivet's throw from the eponymous first iron construction in the world, the Valley Hotel was once owned by Arthur Maw and his family, suppliers of ceramic tiles to the notability. Hence the name of its restaurant, which is quite as fully occupied in supplying modern British cooking to a discerning local present-day clientele. A broad range of choice brings an array of different reference-points on to the menus, so starter might be a salmon and spring onion fishcake with chana dal in coconut-coriander cream sauce, or a spiced poached pear with dolcelatte mousse, melon and candied walnuts, before the main attraction arrives in the form of honey-glazed confit duck leg with celeriac, red cabbage and orange and onion marmalade in madeira jus. A Chinese approach to fish sees sea bream accompanied by pak choi in sweet-and-sour dressing. Finish with chocolate and peanut délice and chocolate ice cream, or carrot, date and sultana cake with mascarpone sorbet and orange syrup.

Chef Barry Workman Owner Philip & Leslie Casson Seats 50, Pr/dining room 30 Times 12-2/7-9.30 Closed 26 Dec-2 Jan, L Sat-Sun Prices Starter £4.95-£7.50, Main £13.50-£18.95, Dessert £6.50, Service optional Wines 2 bottles over £30, 37 bottles under £30, 7 by glass Parking 100 Notes Children welcome

Hadley Park House
◎ Modern British
----
tel: 01952 677269 TF1 6QJ
email: info@hadleypark.co.uk web: www.hadleypark.co.uk
dir: M54 junct 5, A5 (Rampart Way), at rdbt take A442 towards Hortonwood, over double rdbt, next rdbt take 2nd exit, hotel at end of lane

Locally based cooking at a well-maintained Georgian manor

The origins of Hadley Park remain shrouded in mystery, but it seems likely to have been built in the mid-Georgian era, the 1770s perhaps. An august redbrick manor house in a couple of acres of lovely gardens, it makes a target venue for summertime country weddings. The conservatory extension dining room in the form of Dorrells is dedicated to the elegant pursuit of regionally sourced modern British cooking. Dishes are well-conceived, with a tendency to big, rich flavours, as in a starter of black pudding Scotch egg with pancetta crisps and mushroom ketchup, the sort of thing you could happily set about at breakfast, and mains like honey-glazed pork belly with peppery potato rösti in a shiny red wine jus. The showcase dessert is a layered parfait of white chocolate and raspberry, served with textural variations on raspberry – dried, gel and sorbet. Good home-made breads are a credit to the kitchen too.

Times 12-2/6.30-9.30 Closed 25-26 Dec D

UPTON MAGNA
Map 10 SJ51

Basils@The Haughmond
◎ Modern British NEW
----
tel: 01743 709918 SY4 4TZ
email: contact@thehaughmond.co.uk web: www.thehaughmond.co.uk
dir: Phone for directions

Multi-component dishes at the relocated Basil's

Martin Board has relocated his restaurant, to this long white-fronted roadside inn not far from Shrewsbury. Modernised inside, the oak beams painted chalky-white, walls washed in pale greens and greys, with exposed brickwork and mismatched furniture, it's a proper rural hostelry, but dressed up in crisp linen and fine glassware in the dining room. Multi-component dishes indicate a labour-intensive approach, as in a starter dish combining red onion and goats' cheese tart, smoked haddock chowder and chicken Caesar. Extending into the suggested four-course format avails you of a fish course such as sea trout with new potato and spinach salad in brown shrimp and lemon sauce, while meaty mains bring on beef fillet with haggis dauphinoise and celeriac-horseradish purée in peppercorned whisky sauce. Finish with a citrus job comprising sharp lemon tart, orange posset and lemon sorbet.

Chef Martin Board, Tanja Dale-Jensen Owner Melanie & Martin Board Seats 20, Pr/dining room 20 Times 12-3/5.30-11 Prices Fixed L 3 course £12-£15, Fixed D 3 course £30-£35, Tasting menu £35-£40, Starter £6-£8, Main £10-£19, Dessert £5-£8, Service optional Wines 12 bottles under £30, 12 by glass Parking 30 Notes Tasting menu 4 course, Sunday L £10-£20, Vegetarian available, Children welcome

SOMERSET

AXBRIDGE
Map 4 ST45

The Oak House
◎◎ Modern British
----
tel: 01934 732444 The Square BS26 2AP
email: info@theoakhousesomerset.com web: www.theoakhousesomerset.com
dir: M5 junct 22 onto A38 north, turn right to Axbridge, signed

Adventurous combinations in a rustic restaurant-with-rooms

A lovely old house (old as in partly 11th-century) on the square in tranquil Axbridge is the setting for the Sayers' friendly restaurant-with-rooms. A farmers' market sets up on the village square the first Saturday of every month, while inside the ambience of rustic traditionalism is only thrown into relief by the toasting of marshmallows rather than muffins on the open fire. The cooking keeps things briskly up-to-date, though, with much West Country produce and Cornish seafood underpinning the adventurous combinations. Start, for example, with grilled mackerel, pickled turnips and avocado. A pairing of red mullet and Bath chap (pork cheek) with fennel and capers works a treat, and may be followed by a version of kedgeree that has undergone a modish disassembling, including a potato and rice croquette with an egg in the middle, but is fun nonetheless. Otherwise, game season brings on roast partridge with ham hock, beetroot, cabbage, chestnuts and raisins, before the grand finale of chocolate malt parfait in ale and caramel sauce with malt ice cream.

Chef Newstead Sayer Owner Hannah Brown Seats 22 Times 12-2/6-9 Closed 2-3 Jan, Mon, L Tue-Wed, D Sun Prices Starter £6-£10, Main £14-£20, Dessert £7-£8.50, Service optional Wines 4 bottles over £30, 21 bottles under £30, 7 by glass Parking 100mtrs Notes Sunday L £12-£14, Vegetarian available, Children welcome

BATH

Map 4 ST76

Allium Restaurant at The Abbey Hotel

◉◉◉ – *see opposite*

The Bath Priory Hotel, Restaurant & Spa

◉◉◉ – *see opposite*

The Chequers

◉◉ Modern British

tel: 01225 360017 **50 Rivers St BA1 2QA**
email: info@thechequersbath.com **web:** www.thechequersbath.com
dir: *City centre near The Royal Crescent and The Circus*

Exciting dedicated cooking in a Georgian gastro-pub

George III was on the throne when The Chequers opened its doors, a gastro-pub a short walk from the Royal Crescent and The Circus. Much wood is in evidence amid its calming pale colour scheme, from parquet floor to cushioned benches and plain tables, and sunshine streams in through large windows. Food is the core of the operation, with a serious kitchen sourcing all ingredients locally and making everything from spelt bread to stocks and sauces (plum and orange, for instance, for a starter of Scotch egg of chicken liver wrapped around a lightly poached quail's egg: what's that but a labour of love?). Swashbuckling (and labour-intensive) dishes have included seared scallops with smoked pork belly, cauliflower, candied lime and cumin velouté, and main courses of tender, soft braised ox cheek on smoked garlic mash with salt-baked carrots and mushrooms on duck fat toast, and more straightforward roast plaice with capers and brown butter. End on a high with burnt custard flavoured with mango, passionfruit and coconut.

Chef Leigh Evans **Owner** Joe Cussens, Justin Sleath **Seats** 60, Pr/dining room 20
Times 12-2.30/6-9.30 Closed 25 Dec **Prices** Starter £6.50-£11.50, Main £14.50-

£23.50, Dessert £6.95-£8.50, Service optional **Wines** 23 bottles over £30, 41 bottles under £30, 26 by glass **Parking** On street **Notes** Sunday L £13.50-£15.50, Vegetarian available, Children welcome

The Circus Café and Restaurant

◉ Modern British

tel: 01225 466020 **34 Brock St BA1 2LN**
email: ali@allgolden.co.uk
dir: *From West side of The Circus turn into Brock St, second building on right heading towards the Royal Crescent*

Impressive upmarket cooking near the Royal Crescent

In a prime location between the Circus and the Royal Crescent stands this upmarket all-day eatery, done out in a soothing shade of green, with modern art hung on the walls under a moulded ceiling. Chef Ali Golden builds her monthly-changing menus on fine West Country produce and takes inspiration from such culinary British greats as Jane Grigson and Joyce Molyneux. Lunch might bring on grilled field mushrooms under cheddar and cider rarebit on toast, or a modern interpretation of kedgeree, with a full menu operating in the evening. Start perhaps with thick and rich smoked haddock chowder, or, in summer, samphire with salmon tartare and watercress sauce, and go on to a well-composed main course of soft and tender loin of boar with apple purée and mustard sauce, or rabbit pie. There's always a fish option, and among puddings might be seasonal raspberry crème brûlée or whim-wham, an 18th-century version of trifle.

Chef Alison Golden **Owner** Alison & Geoffrey Golden **Seats** 48, Pr/dining room 32
Times 10am-10.30pm Closed 3 wks from 24 Dec, Sun All-day dining **Prices** Starter £6.50-£7.30, Main £16.50-£18.50, Dessert £4.70-£6.50, Service optional **Wines** 9 bottles over £30, 27 bottles under £30, 3 by glass **Parking** On street, NCP Charlotte St **Notes** ALC D, Vegetarian available, No children

Combe Grove Manor Hotel

◉◉ British, European

tel: 01225 834644 **Brassknocker Hill, Monkton Combe BA2 7HS**
email: combegrovemanor@pumahotels.co.uk **web:** www.pumahotels.co.uk
dir: *Exit A36 at Limpley Stoke onto Brasknocker Hill. Hotel 0.5m up hill on left*

Well-judged and inventive country-house cooking

A beautifully proportioned Georgian manor of mellow stone with 69 acres of gardens and woodland, Combe Grove boasts a driving range, tennis, a health club and both indoor and outdoor pools. There's also a brasserie and The Georgian Room restaurant, where pale blue walls, white-painted half-panelling and swagged curtains give a fresh and calming look. Consistently high standards from the kitchen are what to expect, with quality apparent in the raw materials. A warm Scotch egg with crispy bacon, grilled tomatoes and London (i. e. home-made brown) sauce is a novel starter, rather like a mini breakfast, but more typical of the style is smoked haddock brandade with a quail's egg and curried mayonnaise. Main courses are generally updated versions of tried-and-tested combinations: perhaps tender haunch of venison with rich chocolate sauce accompanied by sweet potato purée, beetroot game chips and juniper-flavoured cabbage, or pan-fried fillet of red mullet with chorizo, saffron arancini, parsnip purée and pak choi. Incidentals like bread get nods of approval as do puddings like orange and cardamom crème brûlée.

Times 12-2/7-9.30

Allium Restaurant at The Abbey Hotel

BATH   Map 4 ST76

Modern British 🍷 NOTABLE WINE LIST

tel: 01225 461603 **1 North Pde BA1 1LF**
email: reservations@abbeyhotelbath.co.uk **web:** www.abbeyhotelbath.co.uk
dir: *M4 junct 18/A46 for approx 8m. At rdbt right onto A4 for 2m. Once past Morrisons stay in left lane & turn left at lights. Over bridge & right at lights. Over rdbt & right at lights. Hotel at end of road*

Stunning modern brasserie cooking in a Georgian hotel

Ian and Christa Taylor, previously Cotswold country-house specialists, bought the Abbey in 2012, finding the lure of Georgian Bath as irresistible as it proves to its legions of tourists. The pedimented portico entrance leads into a clean-lined boutique ambience, where a fine collection of modern artworks, including one of Warhol's Marilyns, is on prominent view in the Artbar. The nerve-centre of culinary operations is the Allium Brasserie, where Chris Staines produces streamlined contemporary dishes to a menu formula that may look fairly straightforward, but which belies a wealth of creativity and stunningly direct impact. Nothing in these dishes is superfluous or makeweight and every element has been carefully considered for what it can contribute. Starters are all assertive confidence: glazed chicken wings teamed with Jerusalem artichokes, smoked onions and an egg yolk and sauced with roasting juices; poached smoked haddock with curried mussels and beignets of kedgeree. Main courses are similarly constructed of interlocking layers, as when sea bass and squid turn up with miso butternut, chorizo jam and a purée of cauliflower and almonds, and there is a playful way with tradition that results in an Angus beef daube of robust intensity, its bacon, baby onions, eryngii mushrooms and creamy mash all pulling together for the greater good. The same understanding of flavour contrasts makes desserts magical too – perhaps a toffeeish brown sugar tart with date and tamarind purée, green apple sorbet and candied walnuts. Cocktails are a big thing at the Abbey, cropping up as stimulating aperitifs (a swizzle of Tanqueray gin, Cornish pastis, lemon and soda) or dreamy digestifs (milk vodka, Mozart liqueur and crème de cacao – you know you want to).

Chef Chris Staines **Owner** Ian & Christa Taylor **Seats** 60, Pr/dining room 14 **Times** 12-3/5.30-9 **Prices** Fixed L 2 course fr £15.95, Fixed D 3 course fr £21, Starter £7-£12, Main £16.50-£23.50, Dessert £8, Service optional **Wines** 82 bottles over £30, 4 bottles under £30, 16 by glass **Parking** Manvers St, Southgate Centre (charge made) **Notes** Fixed L/D daily 12-7, Afternoon tea 3-5.30, Sunday L, Vegetarian available, Children welcome

The Bath Priory Hotel, Restaurant & Spa

BATH   Map 4 ST76

Modern European v 🍷 NOTABLE WINE LIST

tel: 01225 331922 **Weston Rd BA1 2XT**
email: info@thebathpriory.co.uk **web:** www.thebathpriory.co.uk
dir: *Adjacent to Victoria Park*

Impeccable modern cooking in a gorgeously decorated house

Although only a short stroll from the city centre, The Bath Priory has the air of a country retreat, as it's in four acres of well-maintained grounds. The Regency Gothic mansion is the epitome of a luxurious country-house hotel, sumptuously decorated, with deep sofas, antiques, chandeliers, and artwork on the walls. Executive chef Sam Moody is in charge of the kitchens, and his culinary style is exactly right for this context: elegant and refined, innovative without being needlessly complex. It employs classical repertory and techniques without resorting to pyrotechnics, and uses ingredients of the highest order, some produce coming from the hotel's kitchen garden. A restrained approach brings out the clear flavours of first courses, among them perhaps goats' cheese mousse with heritage beetroots and baked apple compôte, or duck liver terrine with apricot and caraway chutney and almonds. Seasonality also dictates what may appear, winter bringing on cod confit with local truffles and cauliflower and hazelnut couscous. Exemplary sauces and gravies are a feature of intelligently composed main courses: Armagnac sauce is a perfect foil for slowly cooked wild duck, served with pâté en croûte, roast chicory and dates, and red wine sauce for roast and braised rare-breed beef, accompanied by truffled mashed potato and roasted leeks. The menu is sensibly restricted to around half a dozen dishes per course, with one of the fish options perhaps roast wild sea bass fillet boosted by chicken and vanilla jus partnered by ginger-spiked parsnip purée. The momentum is carried unfalteringly into desserts, which look as appealing on the eye as everything else, among them perhaps pistachio soufflé with matching ice cream, and dark chocolate delice with diced mango and passionfruit sorbet.

Chef Sam Moody **Owner** Mr A Brownsword **Seats** 64, Pr/dining room 64 **Times** 12.30-2.30/6.30-9.30 **Prices** Fixed L 2 course £22.50, Fixed D 3 course £80, Tasting menu £95-£110, Service optional **Wines** 14 by glass **Parking** 40 **Notes** Tasting menu D 7 course, Menu surprise 11 course, Sunday L £37, Children 12 yrs+

BATH *continued*

The Dower House Restaurant

@@@ – *see below*

The Hare & Hounds

@ Modern British

tel: 01225 482682 **Lansdown Rd BA1 5TJ**
email: info@hareandhoundsbath.com **web:** www.hareandhoundsbath.com
dir: M4 to A46 Bath for 4m, right A420 Bristol. After 0.8m take left to Bath Racecourse for 1.5m, then left towards Bath. Hare & Hounds on left in 2.5m

Impressive committed cooking with glorious views

A mile and a half north of Bath, The Hare and Hounds is an enticing bolt-hole away from the city's bustle, with glorious views from its hilltop location. Huge leaded windows look over the terrace and catch the views in the neat interior, where wood proliferates: tables, chairs, panelling and floor. Relaxed and informal it may be, but the kitchen has a serious commitment to food and draws on top-grade produce. Starters include a slab of exemplary duck terrine, served with hazelnut salad and fig chutney, and crab and cod fishcakes with mango and chilli salsa. Main courses run the gamut from beer-battered haddock with chips and tartare sauce, through twice-baked cheese soufflé with pear and watercress salad and braised chicory, to full-blooded braised ox cheek with bourguignon garnish plus potato creamed with horseradish and root vegetables. Desserts are a strong suit too: try salted caramel tart with mandarin gel.

Chef Emma Carpenter **Owner** Joe Cussens, Justin Sleath **Seats** 70, Pr/dining room 14 **Times** 12-3/5.30-9 **Prices** Starter £5.50-£7.50, Main £11.50-£15.95, Dessert £4.95-£6.50, Service optional **Wines** 15 bottles over £30, 42 bottles under £30, 28 by glass **Parking** 30 **Notes** Sunday L £13.50-£15.50, Vegetarian available, Children welcome

The Dower House Restaurant

BATH	Map 4 ST76

Modern British V ⬦ NOTABLE WINE LIST

tel: 01225 823333 **The Royal Crescent Hotel, 16 Royal Crescent BA1 2LS**
email: info@royalcrescent.co.uk **web:** www.royalcrescent.co.uk
dir: From A4, right at lights. 2nd left onto Bennett St. Continue into The Circus, 2nd exit onto Brock St

Stimulating modern dishes in the newly refurbished dower house

The 2000 years of history that Bath comes wrapped up in makes the city one of England's best-loved tourist destinations, but it's the elegant Georgian architecture, the row upon row of immaculate honey-coloured terraces that mostly indelibly fix its identity in the mind. The Royal Crescent is surely the most famous curving stretch of houses in the country, and the boutique hotel named after it is tucked in discreetly near the centre. This has always been an elegant destination for eating and staying, but it has hardly ever looked more so than it does after its recent refit. The new incarnation of the Dower House restaurant opened in 2013, in its old spot within the dower house overlooking the gardens at the back. With outdoor dining in summer and warming log-fires in winter, it's a treat either way, and the ambience of dark seating against pristine white napery is enhanced by features such as a blue-blossomed branch snaking along one wall and a mural design of theatre-goers sitting in their boxes. Continuity is assured by David Campbell's enduring presence in the kitchen. His cooking is founded on carefully sourced local materials of impeccable quality, fashioned into dishes that are full of stimulating flavours and textures, without losing their principal focus. A slow-cooked duck egg, rich as Croesus, is garnished with a roast cep, Ibréico ham, leeks and duck-fat soldiers for a sturdy, fortifying opener. Next, maybe try spiced turbot with creamed cauliflower, pressed apple and coco beans, dressed two ways (a vanilla-scented brown shrimp vinaigrette and a coriander emulsion), or magnificent fallow deer in the company of Stilton and parsley quinoa, Stilton beignets, wet walnuts and juniper jus. Chocolate is often the medium nowadays for architecturally ingenious constructions, as when a sphere of Valrhona with a mousse centre turns up with malt ice cream and blowtorched banana.

Chef David Campbell **Owner** Topland (Royal Crescent Hotel) Ltd **Seats** 60, Pr/dining room 20 **Times** 12.30-2/7-9.30 **Prices** Fixed L 2 course £22.50, Starter £14-£16, Main £26.95-£29.95, Dessert £12.50-£14, Service optional **Wines** 200 bottles over £30, 18 bottles under £30, 10 by glass **Parking** 17, Charlotte St (charge for on site parking) **Notes** Pre-theatre & tasting menu available, Sunday L £27.50-£34.50, Children welcome

Jamie's Italian

◉ Modern Italian

tel: 01225 432340 **10 Milsom Place BA1 1BZ**
email: bath.office@jamiesitalian.com
dir: *From A4 follow signs to city centre. Opposite Jolly's department store*

Jamie's winning way with real Italian food

The formula is a simple one: find a nice building (a Georgian one in the case of Jamie's Bath branch), fit it out with a trendy rustic look and run it with a wholesome lack of formality. It's a format that clearly works, judging by the queues that build at busy times (bookings are taken for large groups only). This popularity brings a surefire buzz to both floors of the place, matched by the energy and enthusiasm of the staff. As elsewhere in the chain, fresh, rustic Italian dishes are what the kitchen deals in, built on well-sourced raw materials. Sharing planks of excellent cured meats, Italian cheeses, pickles and vegetables make a popular opener. Then it's on to pasta, which is made fresh each day – wild rabbit casarecce, say, or a main-course of herb-stuffed porchetta with crispy crackling. End on chocolate fudge brownie with Amaretto ice cream and popcorn.

Chef Eric Bernard **Owner** Jamie's Italian **Seats** 180 **Times** 12-11 **Closed** 25-26 Dec, All-day dining **Prices** Prices not confirmed, Service optional **Wines** 16 by glass **Parking** Podium car park Walcot St (A3039) **Notes** Vegetarian available, Children welcome

Macdonald Bath Spa

◉◉ Modern British V

tel: 0844 879 9106 & 01225 444424 **Sydney Rd BA2 6JF**
email: sales.bathspa@macdonald-hotels.co.uk
web: www.macdonald-hotels.co.uk/bathspa
dir: *From A4 follow city centre signs for 1m. At lights left signed A36. Turn right after pedestrian crossing, left into Sydney Place. Hotel 200yds on right*

Well-judged menu in grand Georgian hotel

The city of Bath has been about spa treatments and self-indulgence since Roman times, and the Bath Spa hotel keeps the tradition alive with an array of hydro-therapy facilities for 21st-century sybarites. Its majestic Georgian façade sets a grand tone, and it all looks over landscaped gardens. The classy Vellore Restaurant is in the original ballroom, with a high-domed ceiling, pillars and all round stately air. There's also a canopied outdoor terrace, plus engaging staff and a helpful sommelier keep things on track. The kitchen extracts the best from carefully-sourced ingredients, delivering well-conceived and unfussy dishes. Grilled mackerel comes with compressed cucumber cannelloni filled with crab and horseradish cream, or the seasonal approach may bring wild garlic soup with truffle oil. Next up, saddle of Highland lamb with an olive stuffing arrives with velvety sweetbreads, rosemary polenta and red pepper piperade, or there might be roast cod with salt cod brandade, asparagus, vanilla raisins and confit chicken wing. To finish, chocolate marquise is served with lavender ice cream and cherries.

Chef Giles Stonehouse **Owner** Macdonald Hotels **Seats** 80, Pr/dining room 120 **Times** 12-10 **Closed** L Mon-Sat All-day dining **Prices** Fixed D 3 course fr £45 **Wines** 140 bottles over £30, 20 bottles under £30, 12 by glass **Parking** 160 **Notes** Children welcome

Marlborough Tavern

◉◉ Modern British

tel: 01225 423731 **35 Marlborough Buildings BA1 2LY**
email: info@marlborough-tavern.com **web:** www.marlborough-tavern.com
dir: *200mtrs from W end of Royal Crescent, on corner of Marlborough Buildings*

Seasonal cooking and proper beer

The 18th-century Marlborough is built of mellow Bath stone and is only a short stroll from the iconic Royal Crescent. As for its credentials as a proper pub, there are local ales and ciders on tap, a pleasingly unstuffy atmosphere, and food that is decidedly 'gastro'. Seated at unadorned wooden tables you can tuck into some pretty impressive seasonal dishes which remain unpretentious and understated but with bags of good ideas on show. A first course among the daily specials might be a ballottine of pheasant and pistachio, served with the nicely pink breast in a salad with celeriac and apple, for example, or keep it simple with a half pint of prawns. The butcher who provides the steaks gets a name-check, and his locally-reared beef is available as sirloin, rump or rib-eye. Pistachio cake with lemon curd and sorbet, or West Country cheeses, are equally good ways to bring proceedings to a close. There's a good value set lunch available mid-week.

Chef Sam Coltman **Owner** Joe Cussens, Justin Sleath **Seats** 60 **Times** 12-2.30/6-10 **Closed** 25 Dec, D Sun **Prices** Fixed L 2 course £12, Starter £6.25-£10.50, Main £11.95-£21.95, Dessert £5.90-£6.95, Service optional **Wines** 23 bottles over £30, 42 bottles under £30, 26 by glass **Parking** On street opposite **Notes** Sunday L £13.50-£15.50, Vegetarian available, Children welcome

BATH *continued*

The Olive Tree at the Queensberry Hotel

@@@ – *see below*

Woods Restaurant

@ Modern British, French

tel: 01225 314812 & 422493 **9-13 Alfred St BA1 2QX**
email: woodsinbath@gmail.com
dir:

Contemporary bistro cooking in a Georgian setting

First opening its doors in 1979, Woods has stood the test of time, showing perhaps that quality lasts. It's a very 'Bath' setting, occupying the ground floor of five Georgian townhouses, and the comfortable bistro-look is pretty much timeless. They're not adverse to change, though, with a bar menu a useful addition to the repertoire. The cooking is broadly European, with French and Italy to the fore, and a British flavour here and there. A first course dish of grilled Whitelake goats' curd with red pepper confit, crushed hazelnuts and vanilla honey is a vibrant construction, or go for home-cured peppered salmon with beetroot yoghurt and baby curd. Confit of chicken leg with peas, Dijon mustard and a herby cream sauce is a bistro classic, or there might be Brixham crab linguine with a red Thai curry sauce and baby coriander. Finish with New York-style cheesecake with raspberry sauce.

Times 12-2.30/5-10 Closed 25-26 Dec, D Sun

The Pilgrims

@@ Modern British V

tel: 01963 240597 **Lovington BA7 7PT**
email: jools@thepilgrimsatlovington.co.uk **web:** www.thepilgrimsatlovington.co.uk
dir: *On B3153, 1.5m E of lights on A37 at Lydford*

Impeccable West Country produce in a stone-built village inn

The name honours those brave souls who passed this way in centuries gone by on their quest to find King Arthur's tomb. How times change: the stone-built inn has been reinvented these days as a welcoming restaurant with rooms, run with cheerful bonhomie by the Mitchisons – Sally taking care of front of house and Jools running the kitchen with the eminently sound ethos that the most important quality in a chef is restraint. The place is a hive of activity, and a showcase for excellent local suppliers, thus Lyme Bay crabmeat forms the flavour-packed filling for crisp-crumbed deep-fried crab cakes with bagnarotte sauce, followed by an exemplary slab of fresh turbot, whose sheer quality is allowed to do the talking alongside the simple accompaniments of asparagus, white sprouting broccoli, Jersey Royals and saffron crème fraîche. Meatier fare runs to pork in a blanket – full-flavoured tenderloin stuffed with Toulouse sausage, alongside black pudding and prunes macerated in cider brandy. Dessert is a simple but effective pear frangipane tart with vanilla ice cream.

Chef Julian Mitchison **Owner** Julian & Sally Mitchison **Seats** 25 **Times** 12-3/7-11 Closed Mon, L Tue, D Sun **Prices** Fixed L 2 course £17, Starter £5-£9, Main £17-£25, Dessert £5-£9, Service optional **Wines** 7 bottles over £30, 21 bottles under £30, 15 by glass **Parking** 40 **Notes** Sunday L £15-£18, Children welcome

---

The Olive Tree at the Queensberry Hotel

| **BATH** | **Map 4 ST76** |

WINNER OF THE AA WINE AWARD FOR ENGLAND AND OVERALL WINE AWARD WINNER 2014–15

Modern British V 🍷 NOTABLE WINE LIST

tel: 01225 447928 **4-7 Russel St BA1 2QF**
email: reservations@olivetreebath.co.uk **web:** www.olivetreebath.co.uk
dir: *100mtrs from the Assembly Rooms*

Confident modern British cooking in a Georgian townhouse hotel

Run with warmth and charm by Laurence and Helen Beere, The Olive Tree restaurant is in the basement, of the Queensberry Hotel, in a series of interconnecting rooms that overcomes any sense of subterranean gloom with a light, airy look. Tables are crisply dressed in their whites, against chocolate-brown upholstery to the seating, and abstract artworks adorn the walls. Chris Cleghorn's cooking is a confident expression of the contemporary British style, in which main ingredients are often given different stages of treatment, then deepened with arrays of aromatic and assertively flavoured accompaniments in thoughtful combinations. Poached and roasted duck liver to start comes with pickled rhubarb, shiitake mushrooms and candied walnuts for a nice medley of sour and sweet elements, or there may be slow-cooked cured Loch Duart salmon with beetroot and horseradish cream. Main course might be robustly treated fish, perhaps cod with parsnip and vanilla, Alsace bacon and sprouting broccoli, or else a brace of meat cuts – fillet and shin of beef with roasted shallots and wholegrain mustard, or loin and smoked haunch of venison with toasted quinoa, chestnuts and fig. Capably marshalled textures lend interest to desserts like peanut butter mousse with banana bread, caramelised sorbet and aerated chocolate, or Earl Grey soufflé with spiced bread ice cream. The multi-course tasting menu gives virtually nothing away in its specifications, which amount to a tantalising shopping-list of scallops, quail, halibut, venison, rhubarb and yoghurt.

Chef Chris Cleghorn **Owner** Mr & Mrs Beere **Seats** 60, Pr/dining room 30
Times 12-2/7-10 Closed L Mon-Thu **Prices** Fixed L 2 course £18.50, Tasting menu £60, Starter £8.50-£14.50, Main £18-£26.50, Dessert £7.50-£9.50 **Wines** 320 bottles over £30, 17 bottles under £30, 34 by glass **Parking** On street pay & display **Notes** Sunday L £25-£45, Children welcome

The Pony & Trap

 Modern British

tel: 01275 332627 **Knowle Hill BS40 8TQ**
email: info@theponyandtrap.co.uk
dir: *Take A37 S from Bristol. After Pensford turn right at rdbt onto A368 towards Weston-Super-Mare. In 1.5m right signed Chew Magna & Winford. Pub 1m on right*

Big-hearted modern food in a country cottage inn

The Pony & Trap looks like a traditional enough pub from the outside: a classic 200-year-old country cottage in lush Chew Valley countryside. Inside, there's a classic pubby bar with a relaxed and welcoming ambience, but a quick glance over the menu will tell you that chef Josh Eggleton has transformed the place into an up-to-date inn driven by its switched-on, hearty cooking. Whether you go for the no-nonsense bare wooden tables in the bar, or trade up to the restaurant area with its slate floors, white linen and countryside views, the menu stays the same: punchy food with a big heart. High quality native ingredients are at the core of a culinary philosophy that delivers precise flavours and combinations that work, coming up with starters of devilled duck livers and hearts with mushrooms on toast, and main-course marinated pork fillet with Parma ham, rich braised shoulder, hodge podge, home-made black pudding, apple and celeriac. Apple and blackberry crumble with vanilla ice cream is a textbook example.

Chef Josh Eggleton **Owner** Josh Eggleton **Seats** 60 **Times** 12-2.30/7-9.30 Closed Mon **Prices** Tasting menu £50-£55, Starter £7.50-£9.50, Main £12.50-£22, Dessert £4-£7, Service optional **Wines** 14 bottles over £30, 45 bottles under £30, 26 by glass **Parking** 40 **Notes** Tasting menu 7 course, Sunday L £13.50-£15.50, Vegetarian available, Children welcome

The Wheatsheaf Combe Hay

 Modern British **NEW** v

tel: 01225 833504 **BA2 7EG**
email: info@wheatsheafcombehay.com **web:** www.wheatsheafcombehay.com
dir: *A367 towards Shepton Mallet, left at park & ride rdbt, follow signs Combe Hay Village*

Popular country inn with accomplished cooking

'Contemporary rustic chic' is how the proprietors describe the style of their 16th-century pub in large gardens overlooking the village, borne out by sofas in front of an inglenook, bare wooden tables on the boarded floor and vibrant artwork on plain walls, some half-panelled, some of rough stone. The kitchen has a generally modern British outlook and adds a dash of ingenuity to its dishes, turning out starters like wild rabbit ravioli with carrot and star anise, and seared scallops with fennel purée and a matching bhaji. Quality is clear at every turn, and the kitchen delivers successful main courses with the minimum of fuss: breast of guinea fowl, for instance, is poached in Sauternes and partnered by truffled mash and wild mushroom cassoulet. Fillet of brill is given an added zing from chorizo-crushed potatoes and watercress pesto. Meals end cheerfully with the likes of treacle tart, or chocolate delice with exotic fruit salad.

Chef Eddy Rains **Owner** Ian Barton **Seats** 55 **Times** 12-2/6.30-9 Closed Xmas, 1st wk Jan, Mon, D Sun **Prices** Fixed L 2 course fr £14, Fixed D 3 course fr £21, Starter £6-£9, Main £12-£22, Dessert £6-£10.50 **Wines** 113 bottles over £30, 33 bottles under £30, 13 by glass **Parking** 100 **Notes** Sunday L £19.50-£24.50, Children welcome

The Queens Arms

 Modern British

tel: 01963 220317 **DT9 4LR**
email: relax@thequeensarms.com **web:** www.thequeensarms.com
dir: *A303 exit Chapel Cross signed South Cadbury & Corton Denham. Follow signs to South Cadbury. Through village, after 0.25m turn left up hill signed Sherborne & Corton Denham. Left at top of hill, pub at end of village on right*

Enterprising West Country cooking in a charming country pub

Tucked away on the Somerset-Dorset border, a little way north of Sherborne, the Queen's Arms dates from the late 18th century, and these days comes in a fetching shade of primrose on the outside. Inside might be an object-lesson in how to modernise a country pub without tearing its heart out. Local people drop in for a pint, while their labradors find it all a tail-wagging treat, a wood-burning stove is fired up for business, and the mismatched furniture is perfect for cosying up in. Plus, there's some enterprising cooking going on. Dishes look slick and well-finished and are built on fine West Country produce: an autumnal starter might be a slice of pheasant ballottine with caramelised quince in warm bread sauce, before main course delivers sublime cod fillet with romesco sauce and earthy chorizo and leek risotto. Spoiled for choice at dessert stage, you may opt for a trio comprising lavender crème brûlée, salted caramel pannacotta and strawberry ice cream.

Chef Ben Abercombie, Sam McKean, Ben Green **Owner** Jeanette & Gordon Reid **Seats** 40, Pr/dining room 30 **Times** 12-3/6-10 Closed D 1 Jan **Prices** Tasting menu fr £34.50, Starter £5.95-£8.50, Main £13.95-£22.50, Dessert £6.25-£8.95, Service optional **Wines** 25 bottles over £30, 33 bottles under £30, 20 by glass **Parking** 20 **Notes** Weekly menu L 2 course, Meal deal film offer, Sunday L £5.95-£13.95, Vegetarian available, Children welcome

Tarr Farm Inn

 Modern British

tel: 01643 851507 **Tarr Steps, Liscombe TA22 9PY**
email: enquiries@tarrfarm.co.uk **web:** www.tarrfarm.co.uk
dir: *6m NW of Dulverton. Off B3223 signed Tarr Steps, signs to Tarr Farm Inn*

Exmoor riverside inn with appealing brasserie menu

The Exmoor location deep in the Barle Valley, near the famous thousand-year-old Tarr Steps bridge over the river, feels as timeless and bucolic as just about anywhere in the UK. And the wild landscape turns provider when it comes to the menu at this 16th-century inn. The bar has bags of rustic charm but there's a nicely contemporary edge to the place these days, not least in the dining room which has a brasserie vibe going on. The kitchen keeps things relatively simple, seasonal and local. River Fowey mussels with cider and cream is one way to begin, the high quality of the regional ingredients speaking for themselves. Next up, supreme of guinea fowl with wild mushroom rice, a pasta dish such as penne carbonara, or a Devon Ruby steak cooked on the grill (12oz T-bone, for example). Crème brûlée is a classic dessert done well.

Times 12-3/6.30-12 Closed 1-10 Feb

DULVERTON *continued*

Woods Bar & Dining Room

Modern British, French

tel: 01398 324007 **4 Banks Square TA22 9BU**
email: woodsdulverton@hotmail.com
dir: *From Tiverton take A396 N. At Machine Cross take B3222 to Dulverton. Establishment adjacent to church*

Locally sourced cooking in a rural Somerset inn

On the edge of Exmoor, Woods is a pub cunningly disguised on the outside to look like a café. The interior scene is cheered with a log fire in winter, and wooden partitions roughly divide the place between the drinking of local ales and the eating of locally sourced food. There are light lunches and bar-snacks in the daylight hours, and in the evenings the kitchen takes wing with intricately worked modern British cooking. Start with a tart of seasonal woodcock, garnished with prosciutto and puréed dates in madeira sauce, ahead of roast ling fillet with mussels, clams, almonds, bacon and broccoli. Or try a protean trio of lamb – shoulder, loin and faggot – with Jerusalem artichoke purée, cavolo nero, spiced onion fondue and thyme sauce. At meal's end, it could be classic sticky toffee pudding with clotted cream, or a choice from home-made ice cream and sorbet flavours such as liquorice, white peach, and apple and star anise.

Chef Ed Herd **Owner** Paddy Groves **Seats** 38 **Times** 12-2/7-9.30 Closed 25 Dec **Prices** Prices not confirmed, Service optional **Wines** **Parking** On street **Notes** Sunday L, Vegetarian available, Children welcome

Crown Hotel

Modern British

tel: 01643 831554 **Park St TA24 7PP**
email: info@crownhotelexmoor.co.uk **web:** www.crownhotelexmoor.co.uk
dir: *From Taunton take A38 to A358. Turn left at B3224 & follow signs to Exford*

Good full-flavoured cooking in a handsome coaching inn

The 17th-century Crown sits at the heart of pretty Exford Village, in three acres of grounds surrounded by countryside and moorland – huntin', shootin' fishin' territory, where horses clip-clop by and every other vehicle seems to be a 4x4. Naturally, then, this is a dog- and horse-friendly establishment, where the bar (complete with stag's head) makes an appealingly rustic spot for a pre-dinner drink, or you could tuck into hearty pub classics. But in the elegant dining room the kitchen cranks things up a notch or two. Free-range and organic local meat and fish get a good showing in full-flavoured dishes cooked with flair and precision. First out is pan-fried scallops with pancetta and cauliflower and pea purée, followed by crispy-skinned confit duck leg with Savoy cabbage, fondant potato, roasted root vegetables and port sauce. Raspberry pannacotta with a zingy exotic fruit salad and lime sorbet brings it all to a satisfying close.

Chef Raza Muhammad **Owner** Mr C Kirkbride, S & D Whittaker **Seats** 45, Pr/dining room 20 **Times** 6.45-9.15 Closed L all week **Prices** Prices not confirmed, Service optional **Wines** 20 bottles over £30, 12 bottles under £30, 19 by glass **Parking** 30 **Notes** Sunday L, Vegetarian available, Children welcome

Follow the AA on twitter @TheAA_Lifestyle

Homewood Park Hotel & Spa

British **V**

tel: 01225 723731 **Abbey Ln BA2 7TB**
email: info@homewoodpark.co.uk **web:** www.homewoodpark.co.uk
dir: *6m SE of Bath on A36, turn left at 2nd sign for Freshford*

Bright modern cooking in a grand Georgian house

Overlooking the Limpley Stoke valley not far from Bath, Homewood is a spiffing country house in the classic mould, with trimly manicured grounds and a dining room that looks out over them. The cooking is broadly contemporary and avoids undue showboating. Smoked ham tortellini with parmesan foam and rocket sounds an Italian note at the outset, as does the outstandingly flavourful beetroot and blue cheese risotto with pea shoots. Rump of local lamb with thyme mash and parsnip purée and pork three ways (loin, belly and ears) are typical of the style. Fish could be a pavé of salmon in saffron-scented mussel and potato broth, and you might finish with the likes of an enthusiastically nutmegged egg custard tart, which boasts superb pastry and offsetting tang from a rhubarb sorbet.

Chef Wojciech Nawalka **Owner** Longleat Hotels **Seats** 70, Pr/dining room 40 **Times** 12-2.30/6.30-9.30 **Prices** Fixed L 2 course £18, Starter £7-£11, Main £14-£25, Dessert £7-£10 **Wines** 107 bottles over £30, 10 bottles under £30, 20 by glass **Parking** 40 **Notes** Afternoon tea available, Sunday L £22-£26, Children welcome

The Holcombe Inn

British, International, French

tel: 01761 232478 **Stratton Rd BA3 5EB**
email: bookings@holcombeinn.co.uk **web:** www.holcombeinn.co.uk
dir: *From Bath or Shepton Mallet take A367 (Fosse Way) to Stratton. Follow inn signs*

Characterful inn with broad appeal

A genuine country inn with good food, real ales and comfortable bedrooms, The Holcombe is just what the doctor ordered. The whitewashed 17th-century property, near Downside Abbey, has plenty of character with oak beams, panelled walls and open fireplaces, and, if you visit when the weather is mild, outside tables with fabulous views. Indoors, eat in the bar or separate dining room and choose from a menu that follows a broad sweep of culinary thinking. Start with the likes of salt-and-pepper squid or devilled kidneys on toast, before moving on to the home-made pie of the day, a ploughman's, or pan-seared John Dory with baby vegetables and beurre blanc. There are steaks from a local farm – choose from rib-eye, fillet and rump – with accompanying sauces including chilli butter or Stilton. For dessert, crème caramel with toasted nuts and thyme is an appealing way to end a meal.

Chef David Beazer **Owner** Julie Berry **Seats** 65 **Times** 12-2.30/6.30-9 Closed D 25-26 Dec **Prices** Prices not confirmed, Service optional **Wines** 9 bottles over £30, 30 bottles under £30, 16 by glass **Parking** 30 **Notes** Sunday L, Vegetarian available, Children welcome

The Vobster Inn

British, European

tel: 01373 812920 **BA3 5RJ**
email: info@vobsterinn.co.uk **web:** www.vobsterinn.co.uk
dir: *4m W of Frome, between Wells & Leigh upon Mendip*

Spanish-influenced menus in a country pub

The Vobster is a friendly and welcoming stone-built inn dating from the 17th century surrounded by four acres of rolling countryside. Food is an important part of the operation, with the lively bar serving baguettes, sausage and mash and cheese omelette with chips. A blackboard lists tapas (the chef-proprietor is Spanish) along the lines of chorizo, patatas bravas, and chick pea and beetroot houmus, while a full menu operates in the quieter dining room. Start with onion soup twirled with truffle oil, or seared pigeon breast with white pudding, and go on to tender rib-eye with garlic butter, crisp onion rings and a fried egg, roast sea bass with pesto, or roast chicken breast flavoured with thyme and saffron served with braised red cabbage and truffled potatoes. Finish with a straightforward dessert like crema catalana with orange sorbet, or chocolate mousse.

Times 12-3/6.30-11 Closed 25 Dec, Mon (check at BHs), D Sun

| MIDSOMER NORTON | Map 4 ST65 |

Best Western Plus Centurion Hotel
 Traditional British NEW

tel: 01761 417711 & 412214 **Charlton Ln BA3 4BD**
email: enquiries@centurionhotel.co.uk **web:** www.centurionhotel.co.uk
dir: Phone for directions

Golfing hotel with careful but confident cooking

When it comes to R&R, this Best Western Hotel has a nine-hole golf course and spa facilities among its offerings, but there are conference rooms if you're intent on serious business. The main dining option is the Cubros Restaurant (there are snacks and light bites in the bar, too), where views over the garden are served up in the daylight hours. It's a contemporary looking space, with a conservatory extension and a Mediterranean vibe. Regional ingredients figure on menus that have broad appeal and show careful, confident cooking. Start with an Asian-inspired dish of home-smoked duck with a hot Asian salad, steamed pak choi and hoisin sauce, before moving on to a main course of 30-day aged Ashdale steak – rib-eye, perhaps, served as requested in the company of triple-cooked chips (in duck fat no less), roasted cherry tomatoes and horseradish beignet. Well-kept cheeses include British and European options, served with crackers, quince jelly and fresh apple.

Chef Tom Bally **Owner** L&F Jones Holdings Ltd **Seats** 60, Pr/dining room 120 **Times** 12-2/6-9.30 Closed 25-26 Dec, D Sun **Prices** Starter £5.50-£8, Main £12-£23, Dessert £6-£10, Service optional 10% **Wines** 7 bottles over £30, 18 bottles under £30, 6 by glass **Parking** 100 **Notes** Sunday L £12-£26, Vegetarian available, Children welcome

---

| MILVERTON | Map 3 ST12 |

The Globe
 Modern British

tel: 01823 400534 **Fore St TA4 1JX**
email: adele@theglobemilverton.co.uk **web:** www.theglobemilverton.co.uk
dir: M5 junct 26 onto A38, then B3187 to Milverton

Modern culinary thinking in a country pub

The Globe looks every inch the traditional red-brick coaching inn from the outside, but these days the village hostelry is more of a 'glasses of wine' rather than 'jars of ale' sort of place. Easy-on-the-eye good looks take in an airy and light modern decor – white paint and blond wood, local artwork on the walls – while the kitchen has its finger on the pulse of what people want to eat: unpretentious, up-to-the-minute ideas delivered via a constantly updated main menu and daily-changing specials. River Fowey mussels with cider and cream is a great example of letting the sheer quality of the ingredients shine, followed by guinea fowl suprême with wild mushroom sauce. Don't even think of passing on the home-made desserts when there's classic crème brûlée or sticky toffee pudding with toffee sauce and West Country clotted cream up for grabs.

Times 12-3/6-11.30 Closed L Mon, D Sun

| MONKSILVER | Map 3 ST03 |

The Notley Arms Inn
 Classic British NEW

tel: 01984 656095 **Front St TA4 4JB**
email: notleyarmsinn@hotmail.com
dir: Please telephone for directions

Stimulating well-flavoured cooking in village inn

A refurb has given a bright, fresh look to this whitewashed village inn. There are chesterfields at an open fire and a mix of dining chairs and pew-style seating at sturdy wooden tables; attentive staff genuinely engage with customers, adding to the enjoyable experience. The kitchen makes a virtue of its location by using local produce, and turns out some eloquently flavoured dishes, among them starters of ham hock terrine with mustard mayonnaise, pressed apples and pickled mushrooms, and goats' cheese mousse with candied walnuts and beetroot and celery salad. Dishes are assembled in the modern idiom and well executed: seared sea bass fillet, for instance, with a subtle saffron sauce, Bombay potatoes and buttery spinach, and confit duck leg with sticky red cabbage, curly kale and five-spice sauce. Some pub stalwarts like fish and chips might be added to the mixture, and to finish there may be smooth and silky lemon tart with raspberry sauce and passionfruit sorbet.

Chef Barrie Tucker **Owner** Simon & Caroline Murphy **Seats** 55 **Times** 12-2.30/6-9.30 **Prices** Starter £4.50-£7, Main £5-£18, Dessert £2.50-£7 **Wines** 7 bottles over £30, 25 bottles under £30, 12 by glass **Parking** 20 **Notes** Sunday L £4.50-£18, Vegetarian available, Children welcome

---

| NORTH WOOTTON | Map 4 ST54 |

Crossways
 Modern British, French NEW

tel: 01749 899000 **Stocks Ln BA4 4EU**
email: enquiries@thecrossways.co.uk **web:** www.thecrossways.co.uk
dir: Exit M5 junct 22 towards Shepton Mallet, 0.2m from Pilton

Classy country inn with local ingredients and a Mediterranean twist

A thoroughly contemporary kind of inn these days, the 18th-century Crossways looks much the same as it always has from the outside, but a 21st-century makeover within has opened-up the place, bringing soothing neutrally-toned modernity. There's a splash of terracotta in the floor-tiles of the dining area, though, (after all, the place is Italian owned). It's the kind of place where you can eat what you want where you want, and there's a children's menu, too. The chef, who isn't Italian as it happens, makes a big play for local and regional ingredients, with Somerset's finest on show, but there's a Mediterranean spin to proceedings. Sautéed tiger prawns with sweet chilli, chorizo garlic, coriander and cream is a splash of southern sunshine and comes with the excellent home-made bread. Follow on with roasted breast of pheasant with its leg cooked confit, or honey-glazed ham with triple cooked chips from the Pub Classics section. To finish, banana and walnut bread is the star of a busy dessert menu.

Chef Nick Cooper **Owner** Mr M & Mr A Ambrosini **Seats** 100, Pr/dining room 86 **Times** 12-2/6-9 Closed 25-26 Dec **Prices** Starter £5.25-£8.50, Main £11.50-£17.50, Service optional **Wines** 2 bottles over £30, 24 bottles under £30 **Parking** 120 **Notes** Sunday L £8.45-£16.45, Vegetarian available, Children welcome

Follow us on facebook
www.facebook.com/TheAAUK

Map 4 ST64

OAKHILL   Map 4 ST64

The Oakhill Inn
 Traditional British

tel: 01749 840442 **Fosse Rd BA3 5HU**
email: info@theoakhillinn.com **web:** www.theoakhillinn.com
dir: On A367 between Stratton-on-the-Fosse & Shepton Mallet

Well-judged menu in a country inn

A country inn on the A367, The Oakhill gazes out over the undulating Mendips, with the village church for company. Inside, the stone interiors present a mix of sofas and tables in the main bar, where locals knock back Orchard Pig cider and cask ales, and a quieter dining area with unclothed wooden tables and candles and a log fire. The kitchen uses quality regional produce in an uncomplicated way for pub cooking that's a cut above the norm. Tiger prawns dressed in sweet chilli sauce on a crisp salad with coriander fires up the taste buds, as a prelude to a venison steak with dauphinoise and seasonal greens in gin sauce, or roast salmon with Jersey Royals and kale in caper butter. Puddings include apple and pear crumble, bread-and-butter pudding with banana, and a fine, thin-shelled treacle tart served with excellent vanilla ice cream.

Chef Neil Creese **Owner** JC & AJ Digney **Seats** 30 **Times** 12-3/6-9 Closed 25-26 Dec **Prices** Starter £5-£8, Main £9-£22, Dessert £5-£7.50, Service optional **Wines** 7 bottles over £30, 24 bottles under £30, 10 by glass **Parking** 12 **Notes** Sunday L £9-£15, Vegetarian available, Children welcome

PORLOCK   Map 3 SS84

The Oaks Hotel
 Traditional British

tel: 01643 862265 **TA24 8ES**
email: info@oakshotel.co.uk **web:** www.oakshotel.co.uk
dir: From E of A39, enter village (road narrows to single track) then follow hotel sign. From W: down Porlock Hill, through village, hotel sign on right

Traditional cooking in the Exmoor National Park

This Edwardian country-house hotel is the kind of place where the genuine hospitality of the hands-on, husband-and-wife-team who run the place keeps the customers coming back. It helps that it's in a lovely spot, of course, on the outskirts of a village in the Exmoor National Park. The cheery yellow-walled restaurant has panoramic views and a short daily-changing dinner menu of unfussy, traditional dishes, cooked by Anne Riley. There's plenty of local produce and a genuine regional flavour; start with a delicious bacon, mushroom and cheese savoury, moving on to a tender breast of guinea fowl with morels, and finish with a flavoursome banana and ginger ice cream.

Times 7-8 Closed Nov-Mar, L all week

Looking for a restaurant by name?
Use the index on page 751

SHEPTON MALLET   Map 4 ST64

Charlton House Spa Hotel
 Modern British

tel: 01749 342008 **Charlton Rd BA4 4PR**
email: enquiries.charltonhousehotel@bannatyne.co.uk **web:** www.bannatyne.co.uk
dir: On A361 towards Frome, 1m from town centre

Contemporary cooking in a smart country house

Charlton House aims squarely at the corporate market, with business facilities and spa pampering all part of the package. And its approach to dining is no mere afterthought. The decor in the restaurant keeps step with the classic country-house theme, kitted out in best country-house chintz, with swagged curtains framing a view over the gardens. Owned by *Dragon's Den* star Duncan Bannatyne, you can expect the whole operation to be run on sharply professional lines, so service is from a keen, well-drilled young team, who maintain a relaxed atmosphere. The kitchen treats top-class, well-sourced produce with due respect to produce simple-but-effective contemporary dishes, starting out with tortelli of Brixham crab with bok choi, lotus root and lemongrass, while mains deliver well-timed Salisbury Plains venison in the company of red cabbage, apples, wild mushrooms and sage. If you're in the market for fish, there might be line-caught sea bass fillet with cannelloni of Cornish lobster, oven-fried tomatoes and salsa verde. Good technical skills keep everything on a high note to a fruity finale involving banana parfait, mango sorbet and pineapple salsa.

Chef Michael Sharp **Owner** Bannatyne Hotels Ltd **Seats** 60, Pr/dining room 80 **Times** 12.30-2.15/7-9.15 **Prices** Fixed L 2 course £14.95, Fixed D 3 course £36.95, Service optional **Wines** 22 bottles over £30, 25 bottles under £30, 9 by glass **Parking** 70 **Notes** Sunday L £19.95-£24.95, Vegetarian available, Children welcome

The Thatched Cottage Inn
 Modern British, European

tel: 01749 342058 **Thatched Cottage, 63-67 Charlton Rd BA4 5QF**
email: enquiries@thatchedcottageinn.com **web:** www.thatchedcottageinn.com
dir: 0.6m E of Shepton Mallet, at lights on A361

Smart old inn with an industrious kitchen

The 17th-century Thatched Cottage Inn has the requisite chocolate-box appearance you would expect given its name, and a strong local fan base who come for its straightforward modern cooking based on good local produce, and the knowledge that its kitchen makes just about everything in-house. The interior looks the part too, made over with a gently contemporary polish without detracting from the intrinsic charm of its wooden beams and panelling, and vast stone fireplaces. You can do no wrong by starting with something as simple as mushrooms on toast, especially when the excellent fungi are served on garlic toast and pointed up with truffle oil. A well-thought-out main course brings pot-roast chicken breast with pearl barley and sage risotto, wilted spinach and lemon and thyme jus, while dessert winds proceedings up with a classic Bakewell tart served with marinated dried cherries and a dollop of clotted cream as an excellent foil to the tart.

Times 12-2.30/6.30-9.30

SOMERTON
Map 4 ST42

The Devonshire Arms
 Modern British NEW

tel: 01458 241271 **Long Sutton TA10 9LP**
email: mail@thedevonshirearms.com **web:** www.thedevonshirearms.com
dir: *Off A303 onto A372 at Podimore rdbt. After 4m, left onto B3165, signed Martock and Long Sutton*

Good, honest cooking by the village green

Set on a picturesque village green, The Devonshire Arms is a Georgian former hunting lodge turned restaurant with rooms. A spruce makeover has given the interior a smart contemporary look involving unclothed darkwood tables and hues of burgundy and grey; it's a convivial sort of place where people pop in for a jar of the village's own ale or cider in the bar, or for a full meal in the restaurant; on a balmy day, the courtyard and walled garden offer alfresco options. The cooking seeks to comfort rather than to challenge, so expect locally-sourced materials brought together in well-considered combinations, along the lines of partridge breast with pancetta, quince and caramelised walnuts, followed by haunch of venison with red onion potato cake, curly kale and port jus. Finish in the comfort zone with sticky toffee pudding with Somerset cider brandy ice cream, or go out on a savoury note with the West Country cheeseboard.

Chef Max Pringle **Owner** Philip & Sheila Mepham **Seats** 40, Pr/dining room 16 **Times** 12-2.30/7-9.30 Closed 25-26 Dec, 1 Jan **Prices** Starter £5.95-£10.95, Main £12.95-£19.95, Dessert £5.95-£7.50, Service optional 10% **Wines** 9 bottles over £30, 20 bottles under £30, 9 by glass **Parking** 6, On street **Notes** ALC menu served D, Sunday L £12.95-£14.50, Vegetarian available, Children welcome

STON EASTON
Map 4 ST65

Ston Easton Park Hotel
 Modern British

tel: 01761 241631 **BA3 4DF**
email: info@stoneaston.co.uk **web:** www.stoneaston.co.uk
dir: *A39 from Bath for approx 8m. Onto A37 (Shepton Mallet). Hotel in next village*

Properly memorable cooking at a Palladian manor

A splendid snapshot of the early-Georgian Palladian style, Ston Easton is a treat. The 36 acres of grounds include gardens landscaped by Humphry Repton, as well as an 18th-century icehouse and a fountain in a ruined grotto, plus the babbling waters of the River Norr. There's also a Victorian walled kitchen garden that serves the Chefs well with organic fruit and veg, herbs and even edible flowers. You're positively invited to have a wander round, and get some green-fingered tips from the head gardener. It all ends up being transformed into the carefully worked-out menus of The Sorrel Restaurant, where intense flavours and pin-sharp presentations are the order of the day. A first-course plate bravely teams up poached salmon, Brixham crab, merguez sausage and heritage tomatoes from the garden for a stimulating composition, followed perhaps by a cleverly modulated take on classic French cuisine, as in the lapin aux pruneaux that features the fruit-stuffed saddle with braised lentils and a bubble-and-squeak croquette. Desserts bring on garden berries in the season, perhaps loaded on to a Pavlova and accompanied by a raspberry sorbet.

Times 12-2/7-9.30

TAUNTON
Map 4 ST22

Brazz
 Modern British NEW

tel: 01823 252000 **Castle Green TA1 1NF**
email: restaurant@the-castle-hotel.com
dir: *From M5 junct 25, follow signs for Town Centre/Castle Hotel*

Buzzy brasserie in renowned hotel

The landmark Castle Hotel has a bold and contemporary neighbour in the shape of Brazz, the hotel's brasserie dining option. It has a life of its own, really, with a separate entrance and a decor that defies its 12th-century heritage. A fish tank occupies the space between interior design and art form, plus vivid colours and a buzzy atmosphere. The menu takes a defiantly brasserie-style stance, with lots of British and broader European ideas. Chicken liver parfait with apple chutney and toasted sourdough bread is a classic done well, or go for the warming comfort of curried parsnip soup. They make a big play of burgers here, so you can expect something a little above the average, and there are steaks, hung for 28 days before chargrilling. Whole mackerel with brown butter and lemon is a simple alternative to the red meat, the fish shipped up from Brixham. Finish with Cambridge burnt cream.

Chef Liam Finnegan **Owner** Chapman family **Seats** 60, Pr/dining room 80 **Times** 12-3/6-9.30 Closed 25 Dec **Prices** Fixed L 2 course £10, Fixed D 2 course £10, Starter £5-£9.50, Main £10-£17.50, Dessert £5-£8, Service optional **Wines** 3 bottles over £30, 20 bottles under £30, 20 by glass **Parking** 40 **Notes** Sunday L, Vegetarian available, Children welcome

Castle Hotel
 Modern British NEW

tel: 01823 272671 **Castle Green TA1 1NF**
email: restaurant@the-castle-hotel.com **web:** www.castlebow.com
dir: *M5 junct 25, follow signs for town centre/castle.*

Local, seasonal produce cooked with skill

This particular castle has been around in one form or another since the 12th century, and although it can't lay claim to being a foodie destination for 900 years, a couple of celeb chefs (a young Gary Rhodes, then Phil Vickery) have shone the spotlight on the old place in the last couple of decades. The man directing the action at the stoves these days is Liam Finnegan, who is no stranger to stellar kitchens, and aims to provide all-round satisfaction via confidently-cooked modern dishes. Chicken liver parfait topped with Madeira jelly is served with the classic accompaniments of toasted brioche and home-made chutney, or wild Quantock Hills rabbit might provide the filling for ravioli, served with peas, blewit mushrooms and tarragon. Main course sees top-class Lyme Bay sea bass partnered with mussels, chard, salsify, parsnip purée and ginger, while local meat fans might go for loin and braised shoulder of lamb with boulangère potatoes and roast fennel. Dessert is a splendid zesty caramelised lemon tart with raspberry sorbet and lemon jelly.

Chef Liam Finnegan **Owner** Chapman Family **Seats** 36, Pr/dining room **Times** 7-9.30 Closed Sun-Tue **Prices** Starter £5.50-£8.50, Main £13.50-£21.50, Dessert £6-£10 **Wines** 69 bottles over £30, 22 bottles under £30, 14 by glass **Parking** 50 **Notes** Children welcome

TAUNTON *continued*

The Mount Somerset Hotel & Spa

@@ British v

tel: 01823 442500 **Lower Henlade TA3 5NB**
email: info@mountsomersethotel.co.uk **web:** www.mountsomersethotel.co.uk
dir: M5 junct 25, A358 towards Chard/Ilminster, right in Henlade (Stoke St Mary), left at
T-junct. Hotel 400yds on right

Luxurious cooking in a luxurious hotel

The surroundings of Mount Somerset have an undeniable serenity that is
guaranteed to lift the spirits. The handsome Regency building sits in four acres of
grounds in an elevated position between the Blackdown and Quantock Hills, and
still tacks to a classic country-house style, its period features – high ceilings,
ornate plasterwork, polished wooden floors, open fireplaces, and a sweeping spiral
staircase for when you feel the need to make a grand entrance – all contributing to
an air of luxury and refinement. Taking its name from the peacocks roaming the
grounds, the dining room is a suitably formal setting for the kitchen's accomplished
modern cooking. Golden raisin purée and apricot and chamomile jelly are a well-
judged foil to duck liver parfait with smoked Creedy Carver breast, while an
impressive main course sees boneless whole quail matched with sweet potato,
ceps, baby onions and sherry vinegar jus. Seasonal fruits cascade forth from the
dessert listings, offering the likes of a simple but effective pairing of poached
pears with vanilla bean and apple mousse.

Chef Stephen Walker **Owner** Eden Hotel Collection **Seats** 60, Pr/dining room 50
Times 12-2/7-9.30 **Prices** Fixed L 2 course £17.50, Fixed D 3 course £35-£55,
Tasting menu £60-£75, Starter fr £5.95, Service optional **Wines** 56 bottles over £30,
30 bottles under £30, 8 by glass **Parking** 100 **Notes** Sunday L £18.95-£22.50,
Children welcome

The Willow Tree Restaurant

@@ Modern British

tel: 01823 352835 **3 Tower Ln, Off Tower St TA1 4AR**
email: willowtreefood@hotmail.co.uk
dir: 200yds from Taunton bus station

Pin-sharp cooking in a 17th-century townhouse

Tucked away down a little lane beside a stream, The Willow Tree is a cosy and
intimate sort of restaurant, beamed and tastefully furnished and decorated, with
well-chosen artwork on the walls and high-backed chairs at clothed tables. Darren
Sherlock applies his distinctively precise, thoughtful cooking style to tip-top
produce to give it the maximum impact with the minimum of fuss. Cheddar soufflé
is a light, well-risen classic of great flavour balanced by a creamy sauce of walnuts
and celery, and another starter, of confit duck gizzard, served with Puy lentils,
bacon, smoked celeriac purée and a pear and quince jelly, impresses for its well-
thought-out marriage of flavours and textures. Main courses include pan-fried
venison, tender and succulent, served simply with pan-fried root vegetables and
contrasting sweet potato purée, and seared hake fillet topped with brandade
sauced with chive beurre blanc. Baking skills are evident in breads, and thought
and workmanship are behind even straightforward-sounding desserts like
Muscovado crème brûlée with spicy fig compôte.

Chef Darren Sherlock **Owner** Darren Sherlock & Rita Rambellas **Seats** 25
Times 6.30-9 Closed Jan, Aug, Sun-Mon, Thu, L all week **Prices** Fixed D 3 course
£27.95-£32.95, Service optional 10% **Wines** 20 bottles over £30, 27 bottles under
£30, 6 by glass **Parking** 20 yds, 300 spaces **Notes** Vegetarian available, No children

Crown & Victoria

@ British

tel: 01935 823341 **14 Farm St BA22 8PZ**
email: info@thecrownandvictoria.co.uk **web:** www.thecrownandvictoria.co.uk
dir: W'bound off A303 follow signs for Tintinhull

Good, honest cooking in a lovely village pub

It's the kind of country pub that spurs urbanites to up sticks and make a move to a
rural idyll. It's a proper pub, for a start, with a changing rota of ales at the bar and
a serious approach to food. There's a fabulous garden, too, and a large conservatory
dining room which can hold its own against the worst of the weather. The kitchen
keeps things as local as possible, seeking out organic and free-range ingredients to
treat with simplicity and integrity. So, duck liver parfait with red onion jam and
sourdough toast is just the ticket, simple and well made. Half-pint of prawns with
garlic mayonnaise harks back to pub dining of the 1970s, but fried duck's egg with
foie gras and toasted brioche wasn't likely to be on the menu back in the day. The
'hodge podge' of Christopher Batstone's pork is a hearty serving, or go for battered
Lyme Bay fish of the day with chips.

Chef Steven Yates **Owner** Isabel Thomas, Mark Hillyard **Seats** 100, Pr/dining room 45
Times 12-2.30/6.30-9.30 Closed D Sun **Prices** Prices not confirmed, Service optional
Wines 8 by glass **Parking** 50 **Notes** Sunday L, Vegetarian available, Children
welcome

Ancient Gate House Hotel

@ Modern Italian

tel: 01749 672029 **20 Sadler St BA5 2SE**
email: info@ancientgatehouse.co.uk **web:** www.ancientgatehouse.co.uk
dir: 1st hotel on left on cathedral green

A touch of Italy opposite the cathedral

Ancient the hotel certainly is; the building even incorporates the 15th-century Great
West Gate, once part of the city's defensive walls. The Rugantino Restaurant looks
the part too, with its large brick fireplace and ceiling beams. While it may look like
something from England's yesteryear, its menu is resolutely Italian, with the kitchen
focusing on quality ingredients and producing commendably unfussy dishes.
Properly made risotto is a good way to start, perhaps with crab, smoked salmon and
scallops, or wild mushrooms and parmesan, and there could also be classic
carpaccio. Home-made pasta is a speciality – rigatoni with meatballs stuffed with
dolcelatte, say – or follow with rump of lamb, served pink, successfully combined
with lamb tortellini, minted pea purée and a rosemary and fennel jus. Puddings fly
the flag with lightly textured vanilla pannacotta with fruit compôte, and plum and
Amaretto semi-fredo with first-rate cantucci.

Chef Jamie Cundill **Owner** Nicholas & Jonathan Rossi **Seats** 40, Pr/dining room 20
Times 12-2.30/6-10 Closed 25-29 Dec **Prices** Fixed L 2 course £10.90-£13.90, Fixed
D 3 course £14.70-£25, Starter £3.25-£7.25, Main £9.95-£18.95, Dessert £1.95-
£5.95 **Wines** 11 bottles over £30, 23 bottles under £30, 8 by glass **Parking** On street
Notes Tasting menu & pre/post cathedral concert menu available, Sunday L £14-
£18, Vegetarian available, Children welcome

Best Western Plus Swan Hotel

◎◎ Modern British

tel: 01749 836300 **Sadler St BA5 2RX**
email: info@swanhotelwells.co.uk **web:** www.swanhotelwells.co.uk
dir: *A39, A371, on entering Wells follow signs for Hotels & Deliveries. Hotel on right opposite cathedral*

An ancient inn with creative full-flavoured contemporary cooking

Hard by the cathedral, The Swan started life as a coaching inn and is now a sizable hotel with a health suite. One of its attractions is the quality of the food in the restaurant, a pleasant room with antiques, panelling and upholstered dining chairs at properly laid tables. The menu offers only a handful of choices per course but it's been assembled with some ingenuity to produce scope. Broccoli soup is a good rendition, deeply flavoured and served with cheese nuggets, or there might be seared Brixham scallops with grilled chorizo and white bean purée. Sirloin steak with well-made béarnaise seems to be a fixture, but other main courses include an accurate interpretation of lamb (from Launceston) kleftiko with couscous, and cod fillet in a herby crab crust served with pea and clam soup, leeks and mashed potato. There's a decent selection of breads, and desserts might run to crème brûlée or an unusual chocolate and beetroot torte with raspberry crème fraîche.

Chef Leigh Say **Owner** Kevin Newton **Seats** 50, Pr/dining room 90 **Times** 12-2/7-9.30 **Prices** Fixed L 2 course fr £12, Fixed D 3 course fr £27, Starter £5.95-£12.75, Main £14.75-£24.95, Dessert £6.95-£8.95, Service optional **Wines** 14 bottles over £30, 21 bottles under £30, 7 by glass **Parking** 30 **Notes** Sunday L £17.95-£19.95, Vegetarian available, Children welcome

Goodfellows

◎◎ Mediterranean, European

tel: 01749 673866 **5 Sadler St BA5 2RR**
email: goodfellows@btconnect.com **web:** www.goodfellowswells.co.uk
dir: *Town centre near Market Place*

Creative fish restaurant with a café attached

Look for the plum-coloured façade in the centre of town, and you can't go far wrong. If it's first thing in the morning, breakfast is on hand in the café, or you might have a Danish and cappuccino for elevenses. Otherwise, sign up for some distinguished seafood cookery in the adjoining restaurant, where fish is handled with confidence

and care by a small, intensely focused brigade at work in the central open kitchen. There's a six-course tasting menu that reads like a shopping list (perhaps Crayfish, Salmon, Crab, Turbot, Scallops, Coconut), while the three-course format begins with poached ballotine of salmon with couscous salad and spicy tomato coulis, followed by a sunny southern composition of seared tuna loin with saffron-braised fennel, Mediterrenean vegetables and tapenade. Meat eaters might go for a venison haunch steak with roasted root vegetables, confit potato, and prunes soaked in Armagnac. Don't skip dessert – the on-site patisserie means puddings and bread are ace, so end with iced almond parfait with fresh strawberries and strawberry coulis.

Times 12-2/6.30-9.30 Closed 25-27 Dec, 1 & 7-20 Jan, Sun-Mon, D Tue

The Old Spot

◎◎ Italian, French

tel: 01749 689099 **12 Sadler St BA5 2SE**
email: theoldspotwells@googlemail.com
dir: *On entering Wells, follow signs for Hotels & Deliveries. Sadler St leads into High St, Old Spot on left opposite Swan Hotel*

Confident Anglo-French cooking with regional ingredients

Back in the 1990s, Ian Bates was working in some of London's hottest addresses, and now it is the lucky people of Wells who get the benefit of all his experience. Hanging baskets outside suggest the mellow tone within, and indeed it is an easy-going place where the focus is on good food and good company. Chef also trained with the French master Michel Guérard, so there's a Gallic influence on show, but, most of all, it's all about the fabulous (and seasonal) produce of the South West. Twice-cooked gruyère soufflé with thyme and cream is light and full of flavour, or another starter might be potted mackerel with pickled cucumber, apple and sour cream. Rabbit might surface among courses, sautéed with cavolo nero, bacon and a parsnip purée, or try roast line-caught cod with mussels, cucumber and tarragon. Sunday lunch turns out a cracking roast chicken. For dessert, bitter chocolate mousse with praline parfait is a winning combo.

Chef Ian Bates **Owner** Ian & Clare Bates **Seats** 50 **Times** 12.30-2.30/7-10.30 Closed 1 wk Xmas, Mon, L Tue, D Sun **Prices** Fixed L 2 course fr £15.50, Starter £5.50-£12, Main £12.50-£21, Dessert £6.50-£8.50, Service optional **Wines** 33 bottles over £30, 30 bottles under £30, 12 by glass **Parking** On street, Market Square **Notes** Sunday L £19.50-£22.50, Vegetarian available, Children welcome

WESTON-SUPER-MARE
Map 4 ST36

The Cove
Modern British

tel: 01934 418217 **Marine Lake, Birnbeck Rd BS23 2BX**
email: info@the-cove.co.uk
dir: *From Grand Pier on Royal Parade N onto Knightstone Rd. Left into Birnbeck Rd. Restaurant on left*

Cool seaside brasserie with Mediterranean influence in rejuvenated Weston

Bucket-and-spade Weston-super-Mare is trading up these days, and this smartly revamped bistro-style restaurant on the seafront near Birnbeck Pier fits in admirably with the town's new image. The outdoor terrace perched above the water is the place to be on a balmy day, while full-length picture windows make for a light-flooded space where everyone still gets a view of the bay, and chunky pale wood tables combine with oak floors in a pared-back contemporary look that wouldn't look out of place in a big city. Spanking-fresh fish and seafood landed by dayboats in Newlyn and Brixham is the mainstay of an unpretentious, Mediterranean-accented menu that starts with the likes of steamed Cornish mussels with smoked bacon, kale and cider sauce, followed by poached sea bream fillet with Bombay potatoes, spinach and spiced cream. There's plenty to keep carnivores happy too — perhaps confit duck leg with Toulouse sausage and mash.

Chef Richard Tudor, Gemma Stacey **Owner** Heath Hardy, Gemma Stacey **Seats** 65 **Times** 12-9.30 Closed 25 Dec, Mon (Oct-Mar) All-day dining **Prices** Fixed L 3 course £14.50, Fixed D 3 course £19.50, Service optional **Wines** 2 bottles over £30, 25 bottles under £30, 6 by glass **Parking** On street/car park **Notes** Sunday L £19.50, Vegetarian available, Children welcome

WINCANTON
Map 4 ST72

Holbrook House
Modern British

tel: 01963 824466 **Holbrook BA9 8BS**
email: enquiries@holbrookhouse.co.uk **web:** www.holbrookhouse.co.uk
dir: *From A303 at Wincanton, turn left on A371 towards Castle Cary & Shepton Mallet*

Diverting modern cooking in a house with a history

Close by the intersection of Somerset, Dorset and Wiltshire, Holbrook is a handsome Georgian manor house on an estate that can trace its history back to the 13th century — inquisitive guests can study the records of its venerable lineage. Set amid acres of woodland and clad in red creeper, it makes a classic country-house hotel, complete with spa treatments and a health club, and in James Forman it has

Little Barwick House

YEOVIL
Map 4 ST51

Modern British NOTABLE WINE LIST

tel: 01935 423902 **Barwick Village BA22 9TD**
email: reservations@barwick7.fsnet.co.uk **web:** www.littlebarwickhouse.co.uk
dir: *Turn off A371 Yeovil to Dorchester opposite Red House rdbt, 0.25m on left*

Simple but powerful dishes amid West Country heritage

Just outside Yeovil, Little Barwick makes a fine base-camp for exploring the cultural riches of Somerset and Dorset. Forde Abbey and Montacute lie close to hand, as does the thatched cottage where Thomas Hardy was born. None of which is to detract from the house itself, which is one of the half-hidden gems of the West Country. Tim and Emma Ford have pitched the tone to perfection, both in terms of the country decor, which is elegant without tumbling headlong into frou-frou, and for the front-of-house approach, where everybody — and this is very much a family concern, with sons and pets all doing their bit — behaves as though we're all on the same side. It's the kind of location in which you would expect a fair proportion of local produce, and Tim Ford doesn't disappoint. Not the least impressive aspect of what the kitchen turns out is that nothing looks or tastes overworked. Dishes are stylish and carefully composed, to be sure, but

there is a refreshing lack of extraneous intricacy. Rolling up lobster mousse into a paupiette of lemon sole, and saucing it with a concentrated essence of lobster, isn't the most straightforward procedure, and yet the effect on the palate is powerful in its directness. A pressed terrine of guinea fowl and foie gras, served with pineapple chutney, achieves the same impact of potency through simplicity. At main course, there may be local meats such as beef fillet, lamb rump or pork belly, the last roasted in five-spice and honey, and sauced with calvados. Fish is again finely judged, as in a fillet of crisp-skinned sea bass with basiled-up crushed new potatoes, baby vegetables and a full-flavoured red wine sauce. Desserts tend to the lighter side, for blackberry mousse with blackberry and apple compôte and calvados ice cream, or there could be two-tone chocolate terrine with griottine cherries.

Chef Timothy Ford **Owner** Emma & Timothy Ford **Seats** 40 **Times** 12-2/7-9 Closed New Year, 2 wks Jan, Sun-Mon, L Tue **Prices** Fixed L 2 course £25.95, Fixed D 3 course £47.95, Service optional **Wines** 6 by glass **Parking** 25 **Notes** Vegetarian available, Children 5 yrs+

a formidably gifted chef. Don't rush things – there's a plethora of different spots for pre-dinner drinks – but take in the consummate professionalism of the surroundings, where staff are knowledgeable about the menus and there's a serious wine list to contemplate. Diverting dishes include a finely wrought tian of Salcombe crab with salmon tartare, cucumber jelly and almonds, dressed with assertively spicy pickle, and mains such as duckling breast with glazed beetroot and kohlrabi fondant in red wine jus. A visually striking chocolate tube is the dessert vehicle for tiramisù with mascarpone mousse and figs, as well as crunchy amaretti ice cream.

Times 12.30-2/7-9 Closed L Mon-Thu, D Sun

YEOVIL
Map 4 ST51

Little Barwick House
◉◉◉ – *see opposite*

The Yeovil Court Hotel & Restaurant
◉◉ Modern European

tel: 01935 863746 **West Coker Rd BA20 2HE**
email: unwind@yeovilhotel.com **web:** www.yeovilhotel.com
dir: *2.5m W of town centre on A30*

Modern hotel with stimulating brasserie cooking

On the outskirts of town, the sparkling white Yeovil Court has been kitted out with a modern makeover. It's all expansive, light-filled, airy spaces these days, and is run with a relaxed approach by a young team. The entire ground floor is given over to eating and drinking in one form or another, from the bar where lighter bites are served to the large restaurant with its black-and-white window blinds and elegant table settings. The cooking offers a stimulating version of modern brasserie food, influences drawn from far and wide for the likes of marinated tuna with Thai noodle salad dressed in chilli and sesame oil, followed by fillet of Dorset beef with satisfyingly textured pearl barley risotto and parsnip crisps, or grilled monkfish with red onion couscous and rocket. A classic combination of flavours and temperatures distinguishes a finisher of hot chocolate fondant with pistachio ice cream.

Times 12-1.45/7-9.30 Closed 26-30 Dec, L Sat

STAFFORDSHIRE

LEEK
Map 16 SJ95

Three Horseshoes Inn & Country Hotel
◉◉ Modern British

tel: 01538 300296 **Buxton Rd, Blackshaw Moor ST13 8TW**
email: enquiries@threeshoesinn.co.uk **web:** www.threeshoesinn.co.uk
dir: *M6 junct 15 or 16 onto A500. Exit A53 towards Leek. Turn left onto A50 (Burslem)*

Grills and much more in a Peak District country inn

The stone-built inn overlooked by lowering gritstone outcrops in the southern stretches of the Peak District does a good job of covering many bases. It's a country pub, a smart rural hotel and a chic brasserie and grill all in the one package. The original oak beams in the brasserie and grill are offset by contemporary styling, with an open-to-view kitchen augmenting the dynamic atmosphere. The odd Southeast Asian dish appears on the menu among the western stuff, so that chicken, rabbit and pigeon terrine must take its chances amid the excitements of three Thai ways with crab (spring roll with tamarind, in noodle salad, and crabcake) to start, followed by Penang red curry on pineapple fried rice, or a steak from the Inka charcoal grill served with beef dripping chips, roasted tomato, herb butter, roasted mushroom and your choice of sauces. Intensive labours pay off in a dessert that offers white chocolate and raspberry in the various manifestations of trifle, cheesecake, doughnut and Eton mess.

Times 6.30-9 Closed 26-30 Dec, 1-2 Jan, Sun, L all week

LICHFIELD
Map 10 SK10

Netherstowe House
◉ Modern British **NEW**

tel: 01543 254270 **Netherstowe Ln WS13 6AY**
email: reception@netherstowehouse.com **web:** www.netherstowehouse.com
dir: *A38 onto A5192, 0.3m on right into Netherstowe Ln. 1st left, 1st right down private drive*

Local produce presented well in a boutique setting

With origins in the 12th century, Netherstowe is a characterful house that has been given the boutique treatment. It's not got one of those stark, modern interiors, however, boasting instead an altogether more genteel and refined finish. There are two dining options in the hotel. First off, The Steak Cellar Restaurant is a moodily-lit basement brasserie serving up 28-day aged beef from local farms, while the alternative is the fine-dining option, where the tables are dressed in white linen. There's passion for provenance and food miles throughout (locations and distances appear on the menu), and the fine-dining output is modern and attractively presented. Start with Staffordshire beef tartare with a confit duck egg yolk and move on to a main course such as braised shoulder of Bretby lamb, served with its hay-smoked loin, or a fish dish of pan-roasted Cornish hake with wild nettle and spinach risotto. Finish with a pistachio and olive oil cake.

Chef Stephen Garland **Owner** Ben Heathcote **Seats** 30, Pr/dining room 14
Times 12-2.30/6-9 **Prices** Fixed L 2 course £14.95-£29, Fixed D 3 course £19.95-£35, Service optional **Wines** 75 bottles over £30, 27 bottles under £30, 9 by glass
Parking 50 **Notes** Vegetarian available, No children

LICHFIELD *continued*

Swinfen Hall Hotel

◉◉ Modern British

tel: 01543 481494 **Swinfen WS14 9RE**
email: info@swinfenhallhotel.co.uk **web:** www.swinfenhallhotel.co.uk
dir: *2m S of Lichfield on A38 between Weeford rdbt & Swinfen rdbt*

Opulent country-house cooking in a Georgian mansion

Built as a grandiose businessman's residence in the reign of George II, Swinfen Hall was extended to the south by a later scion of the family who had in turn married into the Eno's Liver Salts fortune. An Edwardian oak-panelled ballroom with a properly sprung dance floor was only the half of it, but the daughter whose 21st birthday it was all in aid of eloped just before the party. Although very much a mod-cons country-house hotel these days, it maintains an air of gracious civility, from the valet parking to the opulent dining room with its sky-high hand-painted ceiling. The kitchen team draw on the produce of the estate, including a deer farm and walled kitchen gardens, for menus that combine modern presentational style with classical culinary understanding. That produces a fashion-conscious pairing of scallops and deep-fried battered chicken wing, with further interest from mascarpone-rich broad bean mousse. Main might be ballotine of quail with a shallot tarte fine and creamy cider sauce, and then a finisher of well-made pear frangipane tart with fine brown bread ice cream.

Chef Paul Proffitt **Owner** Helen & Vic Wiser **Seats** 45, Pr/dining room 20
Times 12.30-2.30/7.30-9.30 Closed 1 Jan, D Sun **Prices** Tasting menu £60-£90, Service optional **Wines** 98 bottles over £30, 31 bottles under £30, 9 by glass **Parking** 80 **Notes** ALC D 3 course £48, Vegetarian tasting menu available, Sunday L £28-£35, Vegetarian available, Children welcome

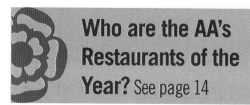

Who are the AA's Restaurants of the Year? See page 14

| STAFFORD | Map 10 SJ92 |

The Moat House

◉◉ Modern British

tel: 01785 712217 **Lower Penkridge Rd, Acton Trussell ST17 0RJ**
email: info@moathouse.co.uk **web:** www.moathouse.co.uk
dir: *M6 junct 13 towards Stafford, 1st right to Acton Trussell, hotel by church*

Confident, creative cooking by a canal

This Grade II listed moated manor house dating back to the 14th century has a lovely waterside location; diners in the Conservatory Restaurant get to watch the narrow boats wend their way along the canal from the comfort of their linen-clad tables, where candles flicker in the evening. The hotel competes in the wedding and business markets, while its restaurant is a hit for its ambitious contemporary cooking. The presence of a tasting menu nails their ambition to the mast (there's a veggie one too), with matching wines available if you wish to go the whole hog. From the à la carte, start with a decidedly modish Jerusalem artichoke velouté with caper and sultana purée, cauliflower beignet and micro coriander, before moving on to a flavoursome slow-cooked blade of beef with Savoy cabbage and bacon, creamed potatoes, chestnut mushrooms, glazed shallots and Guinness sauce. The creative thinking continues at dessert stage, too: banana and caramel parfait, perhaps, with toffee popcorn and bitter chocolate sorbet.

Times 12-2/6.30-9.30 Closed 25 Dec

| UTTOXETER | Map 10 SK03 |

Restaurant Gilmore at Strine's Farm

◉◉ Modern British

tel: 01889 507100 **Beamhurst ST14 5DZ**
email: paul@restaurantgilmore.com
dir: *1.5m N of Uttoxeter on A522 to Cheadle. Set 400yds back from road along fenced farm track*

Farmhouse cooking in a Staffordshire village

Paul and Dee Gilmore upped sticks from Birmingham in 2003, having always rather fancied the idea of running a farmhouse restaurant out in the country. And here they are, off the A522 in the peaceful village of Beamhurst near Uttoxeter, As farmhouses go, it's on the grandish scale, with luxuriant foliage climbing over the front, an attractive garden, and a restaurant operation that extends informally across a set of ground-floor rooms. The menu format is fixed-price for anything from two to five courses at dinner. Assuming you won't want to miss out on anything, the five will take you perhaps from a grilled salmon sausage with peas in crab bisque, through an intermediate salad of scallops, bacon and wild mushrooms dressed in blackcurrant butter, or boozy fruit sorbet if you prefer, to a main course of roasted locally shot partridge with braised cabbage and potato gratin. After farmhouse British cheeses with celery and chutney, things come to a supremely satisfying close via warm treacle tart in caramel chocolate sauce.

Chef Paul Gilmore **Owner** Paul & Dee Gilmore **Seats** 24 **Times** 12.30-2/7.30-9 Closed 1 wk Jan, 1 wk Etr, 1 wk Jul, 1 wk Oct, Mon-Tue, L Sat, Wed, D Sun **Prices** Fixed L 2 course £25, Fixed D 3 course £35, Service optional **Wines** 13 bottles over £30, 32 bottles under £30, 5 by glass **Parking** 12 **Notes** Fixed D 4/5 course £40/£45, Sunday L £25-£30, Vegetarian available, Children welcome

ALDEBURGH
Map 13 TM45

Brudenell Hotel

 Modern British, European

tel: 01728 452071 **The Parade IP15 5BU**
email: info@brudenellhotel.co.uk **web:** www.brudenellhotel.co.uk
dir: A12/A1094, on reaching town, turn right at junct into High St. Hotel on seafront adjoining Fort Green car park

Sunny brasserie cooking in a beachfront hotel

The elegant hotel stands proud on the Aldeburgh seafront, just a few steps from the shingle beach. As you might hope and expect, there are lovely panoramic marine views, especially from the terrace and the spacious, light-filled restaurant, attired in sunny yellow and sky-blue. A major refurbishment has enhanced the atmosphere of breezy freshness, and the casual approach of the service feels just right. James Barber steps up to the plate with bright modern brasserie dishes using good ingredients, many of them local. Start with potted venison and spiced apricot chutney, or a retro courgette flower stuffed with crab mousse, served in rich crab bisque. Mains range from classic British fare with a delicate twist, such as panko-crumbed plaice, mushy peas, chips and tartare sauce, to more cross-Channel offerings like duck leg with sauté potatoes in peppercorn sauce. The retro-styling resurfaces in desserts such as textbook peach Melba, properly made with meringue, vibrant raspberry coulis, flaked almonds and a local vanilla ice cream.

Chef James Barber **Owner** TA Hotel Collection **Seats** 100, Pr/dining room 20 **Times** 12-2.30/6-9 **Prices** Starter £6-£13, Main £12-£22, Dessert £5-£6, Service optional **Wines** 87 bottles over £30, 37 bottles under £30, 31 by glass **Parking** 15, Fort Green car park **Notes** Sunday L £15-£16, Vegetarian available, Children welcome

Regatta Restaurant

Modern British

tel: 01728 452011 **171 High St IP15 5AN**
email: rob.mabey@btinternet.com
dir: Middle of High St, town centre

Buzzy bistro, local seafood the stars

A nautical-themed mural and piscine prints leave no doubt that fresh local seafood, often landed on the beach, is the main thrust of the Mabeys' restaurant on the High Street. It's a cheery, relaxed sort of place, with brown leather-look banquettes and upholstered dining chairs at plain wooden tables, and a blackboard of daily specials padding out the carte. Oak-smoked salmon (from the smokery in the back garden) is appealingly partnered by Thai-style cucumber salad as a starter, contesting for attention with perhaps crayfish cocktail with basil and lemon. Dishes are timed just so and sensibly composed without swamping the main event, so griddled scallops are served on pea purée with crispy bacon, and, for meat-eaters, breast of chicken on roast sweet potatoes with piri-piri sauce and chips. Round things off with apple sorbet with a shot of Calvados, or malted bread-and-butter pudding with salted caramel sauce.

Chef Robert Mabey **Owner** Mr & Mrs R Mabey **Seats** 90, Pr/dining room 30 **Times** 12-2/6-10 Closed 24-26 & 31 Dec, 1 Jan, D Sun (Nov-Feb) **Prices** Starter £4.50-£10.75, Main £11-£22, Dessert £4.25-£6 **Wines** 6 bottles over £30, 30 bottles under £30, 12 by glass **Parking** On street **Notes** Gourmet evenings, Sunday L, Vegetarian available, Children welcome

Wentworth Hotel

Modern British

tel: 01728 452312 **Wentworth Rd IP15 5BD**
email: stay@wentworth-aldeburgh.co.uk **web:** www.wentworth-aldeburgh.com
dir: From A12 take A1094 to Aldeburgh. In Aldeburgh straight on at mini rdbt, turn left at x-roads into Wentworth Rd. Hotel on right

Family-run hotel with impeccable traditional cooking

The Wentworth is in a peaceful spot on Aldeburgh's seafront. Its restaurant has claret-coloured walls hung with portraits, a thickly carpeted floor, crisp napery and sea views. The cooking has its roots in the traditional English repertory, with local produce the mainstay: meats from Suffolk farms, fish landed on the beach that morning. There may not be many modern culinary fireworks, but techniques are sound and tried-and-tested combinations mean that dishes hit the spot. Starters range from prawn and crayfish salad with Marie Rose sauce to baked mushrooms in a Stilton crust with roast red pepper and rocket salad, while main courses take in perhaps guinea fowl casseroled with root vegetables and bacon, served with mash and kale, beef bourguignon, or beautifully fresh, perfectly grilled Dover sole. A separate seafood listing may offer pan-fried skate wing with caper and lemon butter, and among puddings could be zesty lemon tart.

Times 12-2/7-9

The White Lion Hotel

British, French

tel: 01728 452720 **Market Cross Place IP15 5BJ**
email: info@whitelion.co.uk **web:** www.whitelion.co.uk
dir: M25 junct 28 to A12 onto A1094, follow signs to Aldeburgh at junct on left. Hotel on right

Modern brasserie dining on the Aldeburgh seafront

The White Lion is the famous Suffolk festival town's oldest hotel, sitting in prime beachfront splendour by the shingle banks of Aldeburgh's strand. Bathed in a dramatic cobalt-blue light by night, the sparkling-white building revels in a fresh contemporary look inside, with its beautifully-carved inglenook in the bar and oak panels in the restaurant still holding pride of place. Unpretentious brasserie dining is the deal here, and it's all built on fine Suffolk ingredients. In fact, sourcing doesn't get more local than the fish landed but a few steps away on the beach, which turns up on the plate as exemplary haddock in Adnams beer batter with crisp golden chips and chunky tartare sauce. Topping and tailing this fine main course are cranberry and goats' cheese beignets with candied onions and pickled beetroot salad to start, and a moresome finale of white and dark chocolate brownie with Baileys ice cream and bitter chocolate sauce.

Times 12-3/5.30-10

BILDESTON
Map 13 TL94

The Bildeston Crown
◉◉ Modern British **NEW**

tel: 01449 740510 **104 High St IP7 7EB**
email: alice@thebildestoncrown.co.uk **web:** www.thebildestoncrown.com
dir: *A12 junct 31. B1070 to Hadleigh, B1115 to Bildeston*

Creative, skilfull cooking in revamped coaching inn

This part of Suffolk is full of enough charming period properties to satisfy a chocolate-box maker for a lifetime, and The Bildeston Crown is such a place, its walls etched with 600-odd years of life. The former coaching inn is very much the 21st-century version these days, which means boutique bedrooms, a smart, atmospheric bar, and some classy cooking. There's a posh dining room – Ingrams – or you can eat in the more relaxed pub-style area, or outside on the terrace. New chef Zack Deakins cooks some refined and creative modern dishes, with a good deal of technical know-how and a fair amount of regional produce. There's a 'Classics' menu – with smart, updated versions, mind you, such as potted shrimps with melba toast – and the full-throttle 'Tasting' and 'Crown Select' menus. From the latter, lobster tortellini with braised pork belly, pickled cauliflower and crispy capers is a slick contemporary starter, with main-course smoked halibut fillet following on (served with roasted chervil root and red wine-poached salsify). Desserts are no less impressive: try the apple and walnut tarte Tatin with vanilla pannacotta and maple syrup.

Chef Zack Deakins **Owner** Mrs G & Mr J K Buckle **Seats** 100, Pr/dining room 18 **Times** 12-3/7-10 Closed D 25-26 Dec, 1 Jan **Prices** Prices not confirmed, Service optional **Wines** 11 by glass **Parking** 36, Market Sq (overflow) **Notes** Fixed L Mon-Sat, D 5 course £50, Tasting 8 course, Sunday L, Vegetarian available, Children welcome

BRANDESTON
Map 13 TM26

The Queen's Head Inn
◉ Modern, Traditional British

tel: 01728 685307 **The Street IP13 7AD**
email: brandestonqueen@gmail.com
dir: *Signed from A1120 at Earl Soham, follow signs to village, on left*

Superior pub cooking in relaxing village inn

In the heart of a lovely historic village, the old red-brick Queen's Head is a cracking local, drawing a loyal crowd for its well-kept Adnams ales and straight-talking modern pub food. It's the sort of place that hosts the village fête, beer festivals and summer's day hog roasts. Inside, expect heaps of character, log fires crackling in winter, smart contemporary style, and a friendly service team. Whether you're in the market for something straightforward from the blackboard menus or more gastronomically ambitious ideas from the carte, you can be sure it has all been cooked from scratch using tip-top Suffolk ingredients. Keeping things simple, French onion soup is a fine example of its ilk, especially when it's served with crusty bread and melted cheese; next comes beer-battered haddock and chips with tartare sauce and salad, then apple crumble and home-made custard rounds it all off to perfection.

Chef Freddie Footer **Owner** Anna Cornford, Tim Johnson **Seats** 65 **Times** 12-2/6-9 Closed Mon, D Sun **Prices** Starter £4.95-£6.95, Main £9.50-£15.95, Dessert £4.95-£6.50, Service optional **Wines** 1 bottle over £30, 11 bottles under £30, 10 by glass **Parking** 25, On street **Notes** Sunday L £13.50, Vegetarian available, Children welcome

BROME
Map 13 TM17

Best Western Brome Grange Hotel
◉ Traditional British **NEW**

tel: 01379 870456 **Norwich Rd, Nr Diss IP23 8AP**
email: info@bromegrangehotel.co.uk **web:** www.bromegrangehotel.co.uk
dir: *2m S of Diss on A140 between Ipswich & Norwich*

Former coaching inn with carefully presented classic cooking

It's easy to imagine horse-drawn carriages sweeping into the central courtyard of this 16th-century former coaching inn, with plenty of period details remaining inside and out. It's a sprawling series of buildings with red pantiles on the roof and four acres of gardens. The restaurant is a traditional affair with lots of character – beams, fireplaces, leaded windows and wooden panelling – and leads into a conservatory. The service team are a cheerful bunch. The menu takes a broadly classical approach with some sound thinking going on and an eye for presentation. Start with a smoked salmon roulade, brought to the table with an accompanying sunflower and honey loaf, and move on to roast loin of cod in the sensible company of dill butter and sauté potatoes. To finish, bread-and-butter pudding is perfectly moist and comes flavoured with dates and orange.

Chef Neil Gainsbrye **Owner** Brian & Kelly Keane **Seats** 40, Pr/dining room 120 **Times** 12-2/6.30-9 Closed D 25 Dec **Prices** Fixed L 2 course £16.95, Fixed D 3 course £21.95, Service optional **Wines** **Parking** 100 **Notes** Sunday L £9.95-£12.95, Vegetarian available, Children welcome

BURY ST EDMUNDS　　　　　　Map 13 TL86

The Angel Hotel

 Modern British

tel: 01284 714000 **Angel Hill IP33 1LT**
email: staying@theangel.co.uk **web:** www.theangel.co.uk
dir: From A134, left at rdbt into Northgate St. Continue to lights, right into Mustow St, left into Angel Hill. Hotel on right

Med-influenced brasserie dining in creeper-covered hotel

With a prime position overlooking the cathedral and the old abbey walls, The Angel meets all expectations of a quintessential Georgian coaching inn. Its brickwork façade is suitably handsome and curtained with creepers, and inside, the generous Georgian spaces have been overlaid with a contemporary boutique look, especially in The Eaterie, where artworks, bare pale wood tables, high-backed chairs and a statement chandelier make for a pleasingly up-to-date setting. The kitchen shows equally 21st-century sensibilities in its repertoire of Mediterranean-influenced brasserie food, sourcing top-notch local produce and bringing it all together in appealing flavour combinations with no unnecessary embellishment. Start with grilled quail with panzanella salad, or ox cheek braised in red wine matched with white onion and garlic risotto, then follow on with peppered leg of lamb with a salad of sautéed new potatoes, warm green beans, red onion and pecorino cheese. Finish with chocolate fondant with pistachio ice cream, or a true Brit classic such as sticky toffee pudding with vanilla ice cream.

Chef Arron Jackson **Owner** Robert Gough **Seats** 85, Pr/dining room 16 **Times** 12-9.45 All-day dining **Prices** Fixed L 2 course £13.95-£17.95, Starter £6-£9.50, Main £12.95-£29.50, Dessert £4.95-£8.95 **Wines** 51 bottles over £30, 24 bottles under £30, 40 by glass **Parking** 20 **Notes** Sunday L £17.95-£21.95, Vegetarian available, Children welcome

Best Western Priory Hotel

 Modern British, International

tel: 01284 766181 **Mildenhall Rd IP32 6EH**
email: reservations@prioryhotel.co.uk **web:** www.prioryhotel.co.uk
dir: From A14 junct 43 take Bury St Edmunds W slip road. Follow signs to Brandon. At mini-rdbt turn right. Hotel 0.5m on left

Brasserie cooking in a tranquil priory

The Priory is a Grade II listed building a couple of miles from Bury St Edmunds town centre, making the most of its tranquil setting with landscaped gardens bounded by the old priory walls, as well as a thoroughly relaxing ambience inside. The dining room is divided into three areas, including a conservatory, where smartly clothed tables confer an air of gentility for inspired brasserie-style dishes from the modern cookbook. Pigeon and guinea fowl terrine with toasted brioche, or Manchego parfait with tomato and basil salsa, are sterling openers, setting the scene for something like roast monkfish with chorizo and sultanas in chardonnay vinegar, or Denham Estate venison loin with horseradish rösti and parsnip purée, in a sauce enriched with bitter chocolate. The ever-dependable way to finish is with properly sticky toffee pudding, served with caramel sauce and good vanilla ice cream, but the local farmhouse cheeses, served with quince jelly, are tempting too.

Chef Steve Aves **Owner** Peter Hobday **Seats** 72, Pr/dining room 28 **Times** 12-2/7-10 **Prices** Starter £5.25-£7.50, Main £9.50-£18.95, Dessert £5 **Wines** 3 bottles over £30, 23 bottles under £30, 7 by glass **Parking** 60, On street **Notes** Pre-theatre D £50 inc transfer to theatre, Sunday L £13-£15, Vegetarian available, Children welcome

Clarice House

 Modern European

tel: 01284 705550 **Horringer Court, Horringer Rd IP29 5PH**
email: bury@claricehouse.co.uk **web:** www.claricehouse .co.uk
dir: From Bury St Edmunds on A143 towards Horringer and Haverhill, hotel 1m from town centre on right

Well-crafted, modish cooking at a spa retreat

Sybaritic spa pampering is the first item on the agenda for many of the guests at Clarice House. After a restorative hit of massage and manipulation, followed by an appetite-stimulating stroll through the splendid grounds of the Jacobean-style country house, a table awaits in the smart oak-panelled restaurant, a suitably sumptuous backdrop for uncomplicated modern European cooking. Start with goats' cheese pannacotta served with hot and sour cherry tomatoes, confit pepper and parmesan tuile, followed by a more substantial minced venison ragù with horseradish mash, roasted carrots and parsnips. With that under your belt, you might as well throw caution to the wind and finish with an orange and Grand Marnier crème brûlée with clementine jam and pistachio madeleine.

Chef Steve Winser **Owner** King family **Seats** 70, Pr/dining room 20 **Times** 12-2/7-9 Closed 25-26 Dec, 1 Jan **Prices** Prices not confirmed, Service optional **Wines** 4 bottles over £30, 15 bottles under £30, 14 by glass **Parking** 110 **Notes** Sunday L, Vegetarian available, Children welcome

The Grange Hotel

 Modern British

tel: 01359 231260 **Barton Rd, Thurston IP31 3PQ**
email: info@grangecountryhousehotel.com **web:** www.grangecountryhousehotel.com
dir: A14 junct 45 towards Gt Barton, right at T-junct. At x-rds left into Barton Rd to Thurston. At rdbt, left after 0.5m, hotel on right

Charming country-house with ambitious kitchen

Three miles outside of Bury St Edmunds, the faux-Tudor Grange is a Victorian hotel with lots of period charm inside and out. It has lovely gardens to explore and a reassuringly traditional decor within, and, to confirm its country-house credentials, there's a spa here too. The dining room is suitably elegant and refined, with a good deal of period character, and tables smartly set for what is to come. And what is to come is some well-crafted, bright, contemporary cooking. Start, perhaps, with tea-smoked chicken and foie gras terrine with pickled walnuts and a tarragon yoghurt dressing, or a red onion tarte Tatin with glazed Crottin goats' cheese and a balsamic and basil ice cream. For main course, seared Barbary duck comes with dauphinoise potatoes, Savoy cabbage, bacon and red wine jus, and, for dessert, there's chocolate textures (tart, fondant and gin-flavoured bonbon), or sticky toffee pudding with gingerbread ice cream and caramel sauce.

Owner Sortpad Limited **Seats** 32, Pr/dining room 40 **Times** 12-2/7-9 Closed 1 Jan **Prices** Prices not confirmed, Service optional **Wines** 15 bottles over £30, 20 bottles under £30, 11 by glass **Parking** 60 **Notes** Afternoon tea, Sunday L, Vegetarian available, Children welcome

BURY ST EDMUNDS *continued*

The Leaping Hare Restaurant & Country Store

◉◉ Modern British

tel: 01359 250287 **Wyken Vineyards, Stanton IP31 2DW**
email: info@wykenvineyards.co.uk
dir: *8m NE of Bury St Edmunds, 1m off A143. Follow brown signs at Ixworth to Wyken Vineyards*

Vineyard restaurant with accomplished modern cooking

The Leaping Hare occupies a splendid 400-year-old barn, with a high beamed and raftered ceiling and polished wooden floor, on a 1,200-acre farm complete with a flock of Shetland sheep and Red Poll cattle, plus a vineyard. What the farm doesn't provide is grown or farmed locally too, often within five miles, with fish landed at Lowestoft. The kitchen follows a straightforward, uncomplicated route along classical lines, so expect starters of River Deben moules marinière, and roast pigeon breast with pancetta and artichoke and garlic purée. Accomplished main courses are distinguished by accurate timings and clearly discernible flavours, seen in a hearty dish of game and ale steamed pudding, served with mash and roasted root vegetables, and roast rack of estate lamb and confit shoulder with roast garlic jus, pommes Anna and purple-sprouting broccoli. Fish isn't entirely overlooked – there might be smoked salmon fillet with celery hearts and white beans with chorizo – and puddings end on an upbeat note with, say, ginger, passionfruit and white chocolate trifle.

Chef Jon Ellis **Owner** Kenneth & Carla Carlisle **Seats** 55 **Times** 12-2.30/7-9 Closed 2 wks Xmas, D Sun-Thu **Prices** Fixed L 2 course fr £18.95, Starter £5.95-£7.95, Main £13.95-£18.95, Dessert £5.95-£6.50, Service optional **Wines** 6 bottles over £30, 11 bottles under £30, 13 by glass **Parking** 50 **Notes** Fri D 3 course £25.95, Sunday L, Vegetarian available, Children welcome

Maison Bleue

◉◉ Modern French

tel: 01284 760623 **30-31 Churchgate St IP33 1RG**
email: info@maisonbleue.co.uk
dir: *A14 junct 43 (Sugar Beet, Central exit) to town centre. Follow signs to the Abbey Gdns, Churchgate St is opposite cathedral*

Classical French seafood specialities in historic Bury

The Blue House is secreted amid the backstreets of the historic part of town, an outpost of French seafood celebration in East Anglia. Any blueness is gently sponged away by the colour-free interiors, where black pillars, wood tones and cream upholstery take over, and even the pictures of roiling seascapes are easy on the eye. Subdued lighting helps to soften the scene still further. Thus cocooned, you should be perfectly primed for the classically-based French dishes on offer, which might begin with deboned frogs' legs in garlic velouté with broad beans and asparagus, or textbook Provençal-style fish soup with all its accoutrements, before main courses like roast turbot with aubergine caviar in sage sauce, or wild salmon seasoned with grain mustard in parsley sauce. Meat dishes are available too, perhaps guinea fowl breast stuffed with almonds and sultanas, and sauced with Amaretto. Probably the best note to end on is with seasonal fruits such as local strawberries in their own soup, served with strawberry yoghurt ice cream.

Chef Pascal Canevet **Owner** Pascal & Karine Canevet **Seats** 65, Pr/dining room 35 **Times** 12-2/7-9 Closed Jan, 2 wks summer, Sun-Mon **Prices** Fixed L 2 course £18.50, Fixed D 3 course £33.50, Starter £7.95-£13.95, Main £17.95-£29.95, Dessert £7.95-£9.95, Service optional **Wines** 12 by glass **Parking** On street **Notes** Vegetarian available, Children welcome

Pea Porridge

◉◉ Modern Bistro

tel: 01284 700200 **28-29 Cannon St IP33 1JR**
email: enquiries@peaporridge.co.uk
dir: *Off A14 towards town, in Northgate St turn left into Cadney Lane. Restaurant opposite Old Cannon Brewery*

Technically accomplished cooking of upbeat modern ideas

Originally two cottages, then a bakery (the oven still in situ), Pea Porridge is now a homely and unpretentious three-roomed restaurant with wooden floors, pine tables, exposed bricks and an open fire. A strong streak of invention and innovation runs through the menu, taking in as it does Lebanese-style lamb broth (with merguez, apricots, chick peas, coriander and harissa), and sea bream fillet with chorizo, braised cocoa beans, spinach, peppers and root vegetables. Dishes can be as forthright of flavours as starters of lamb sweetbreads in curry sauce, accompanied by roast sweet potato and spinach, and black pudding and crispy pigs' ears with cavolo nero and chanterelles. Raw materials are carefully chosen, timings are impressively accurate and if dishes can seem overladen with different elements they nonetheless work well: witness a main course of hake fillet – an excellent piece of fish, perfectly timed – with tempura cod cheek (a triumph), olive oil mash, samphire, fennel, saffron and chives. Desserts can seem quite ordinary in comparison, among them perhaps silky-smooth vanilla yoghurt and mango pannacotta.

Chef Justin Sharp **Owner** Justin Sharp **Seats** 46, Pr/dining room 20 **Times** 12-2.30/6.30-10 Closed 2 wks Sep, 2 wks Xmas, Sun-Mon, L Tue **Prices** Prices not confirmed, Service optional **Wines** 15 bottles over £30, 25 bottles under £30, 9 by glass **Parking** On street **Notes** Vegetarian available, Children welcome

The White Horse

◉ Modern British

tel: 01284 735760 & 07778 996666 **Rede Rd, Whepstead IP29 4SS**
dir: *5m from Bury St Edmunds, 2m off A143 Bury/Haverhill*

Well-crafted, unfussy cooking in country gastro-pub

Stylishly made over in recent years, this mustard-yellow village inn now sits comfortably at the gastro-pub end of the spectrum, but without losing any of the features one hopes for – the interior is a series of smart and cosy rooms with a copper-sheathed bar serving Suffolk ales, and there are exposed beams, a huge inglenook, country-style tables and chairs, artwork on the walls, and soothing Farrow & Ball colour schemes. The kitchen here appreciates the value of top-class local ingredients, follows the seasons keenly, and cuts no corners, making everything from scratch (including their own bangers – how about pork, paprika and sun-dried tomato sausages?). The blackboard menu lists joyously simple ideas: country pâté with home-made chutney and French bread, followed by a North African-influenced slow-braised shoulder of Ickworth lamb with tomatoes and black olives. Finish with baked apricot cheesecake, or bow out on a savoury note with a plate of East Anglian cheeses.

Chef Gareth Carter **Owner** Gary & Di Kingshott **Seats** 50, Pr/dining room 25 **Times** 12-2/7-9.30 Closed 25-26 Dec, D Sun **Prices** Starter £2.25-£6.25, Dessert £4.95-£5.95, Service optional **Wines** 7 bottles over £30, 18 bottles under £30, 8 by glass **Parking** 30 **Notes** Sunday L fr £13.50, Vegetarian available, Children welcome

CAVENDISH
Map 13 TL84

The George

 Modern British

tel: 01787 280248 **The Green CO10 8BA**
email: thegeorgecavendish@gmail.com **web:** www.thecavendishgeorge.co.uk
dir: A1092 into Cavendish, The George next to village green

Modish Med-inflected cooking in characterful inn

The handsome timbered George dates from the 16th century and is rooted into the fabric of its ancient Suffolk village. These days, as is often the case, it's more of a restaurant with rooms than a village boozer – apart from a few bar stools there's not much pubbiness left: there are beams and bare-brick walls, but the understated Farrow & Ball neutral shades and classy cream seats combine in a tastefully made-over, thoroughly modern interior. The man cooking up a storm in the kitchen is chef-patron Lewis Bennet, who deals in no-nonsense modern comfort food with big, bold Mediterranean-inflected flavours that keep a keen eye on the seasons. You might start with ballotine of quail partnered with foie gras parfait, poached grapes and truffled mushroom toast, and follow with roast duck breast supported by Jerusalem artichoke puree, wild mushroom duxelle, and baked new potatoes, or turbot fillet with saffron and spinach risotto, crab mousse and squid ink. Pudding could be a deliciously summery elderflower pannacotta with wild rose jelly.

Times 12-2/6-9.30 Closed 25 Dec, 1 Jan, D Sun

CHILLESFORD
Map 13 TM35

The Froize Freehouse Restaurant

 British, European

tel: 01394 450282 **The Street IP12 3PU**
email: dine@froize.co.uk
dir: On B1084 between Woodbridge & Orford

Popular inn with cracking menu

Converted from a brace of red-brick gamekeepers' cottages, The Froize is a welcoming Suffolk inn that is in fine shape after a contemporary makeover, and the mood is dressed-down and relaxed. Chef-proprietor David Grimwood is a local lad who likes to bang the drum for local materials, so his food taps into the current appetite for ingredients-led, honest-to-goodness dishes with clean-cut flavours – it's all so driven by what's in season locally that there are no menus at lunch, just blackboards with the day's specials. This is food straight from the heart – roast shoulder of locally-reared Gloucestershire Old Spot pork is served with proper pan juice gravy, fresh apple sauce, crisp crackling and stuffing, or there might be slow-cooked hare with chestnuts, ceps and blackberry brandy. Starters could see Orford crab cakes pointed up with sweet chilli sauce, whilst desserts are comfort classics along the lines of marmalade bread-and-butter pudding.

Chef David Grimwood **Owner** David Grimwood **Seats** 48, Pr/dining room 20
Times 12-2/7-close Closed Mon (ex BHs) **Prices** Fixed L 2 course fr £20, Starter fr £6.75, Main fr £17.50, Dessert fr £6.50, Service optional **Wines** 14 bottles under £30, 14 by glass **Parking** 40 **Notes** Vegetarian available, Children welcome

DUNWICH
Map 13 TM47

The Ship at Dunwich

 Modern British

tel: 01728 648219 **Saint James St IP17 3DT**
email: info@shipatdunwich.co.uk **web:** www.shipatdunwich.co.uk
dir: From N: A12, exit at Blythburgh onto B1125, then left to village. Inn at end of road. From S: A12, turn right to Westleton. Follow signs for Dunwich

Locally based cooking in an ideally located coastal pub

Climbing foliage in the form of a trident is the distinguishing outer feature of the redbrick pub in an East Anglian coastal village surrounded by wild heathland and nature reserves, with a beach on hand and Southwold nearby. It's got the lot, including an expansive garden with an ancient fig tree. Foursquare rustic furniture inside and a courtyard for sunny outdoor dining set the tone for a menu that takes in pork, apricot and pistachio terrine with pickled courgette, or salmon cured in Adnams' vodka and beetroot, to start, with follow-ups of chicken breast served with a pearl barley risotto of butternut, bacon and sage, or leg of local lamb with lamb cobbler, carrot and swede mash, and braised red cabbage in rosemary gravy. Your reward for finishing up your greens may well be chocolate nut torte with boozy blackberries, or there are fine East Anglian cheeses and home-made chutney.

Chef Sam Hanison **Owner** Agellus Hotels Ltd **Seats** 70, Pr/dining room 35
Times 12-3/6-9 **Prices** Starter £4.95-£6.95, Main £10.90-£14.50, Dessert £4.50-£5.75, Service optional **Wines** 3 bottles over £30, 19 bottles under £30, 8 by glass **Parking** 20 **Notes** Open all day for food Jul-Aug, Sunday L £9.95-£13.95, Vegetarian available, Children welcome

FRESSINGFIELD
Map 13 TM27

Fox & Goose Inn

 Modern British

tel: 01379 586247 **Church Rd IP21 5PB**
email: foxandgoose@uk2.net
dir: A140 & B1116 (Stradbroke) left after 6m - in village centre by church

Village restaurant and bar with modish cooking

Abutting Fressingfield's medieval church, this one-time timber-framed Tudor guildhall turned local inn – set at the heart of a small chocolate-box village – ticks all the quintessential English boxes. But appearances can be deceiving; inside the place sports a thoroughly pared-back modern look, and, while there's a wealth of character in its old beams and open fires and the bar still serves real ales tapped straight from the barrel, it's much more a restro-pub these days. Accomplished and creative European ideas pepper the kitchen's modern cooking driven by Suffolk's abundant larder. Take lemon sole fillets served with crab and potato tempura, English asparagus, chervil mayo, micro greens and a hazelnut vinaigrette, or perhaps beef bourguignon with horseradish mash, glazed carrots and parsnip purée. Finish in classic style with vanilla crème brûlée accompanied by an oatmeal tuile and blackcurrant sorbet. The more formal evenings-only restaurant is upstairs, while downstairs there's a smaller dining room in the old lounge as well as the bar area.

Chef P Yaxley, M Wyatt **Owner** Paul Yaxley **Seats** 70, Pr/dining room 35
Times 12-2/7-8.30 Closed 25-30 Dec, 2nd wk Jan for 2 wks, Mon **Prices** Prices not confirmed, Service optional **Wines** 9 bottles over £30, 43 bottles under £30, 8 by glass **Parking** 15 **Notes** Tasting menu 8 course, Sunday L, Vegetarian available, Children 9 yrs+ D

HINTLESHAM
Map 13 TM04

Hintlesham Hall Hotel

◎◎ Modern European V

tel: 01473 652334 **IP8 3NS**
email: reservations@hintleshamhall.com **web:** www.hintleshamhall.com
dir: *4m W of Ipswich on A1071*

Polished cooking in top-ranking country-house hotel

Hintlesham Hall never fails to impress, a beautifully proportioned building of three wings, the façade a 1720 addition to the 16th-century core. The interior is equally impressive, with all the elements expected in a grand country-house hotel, from oil paintings to antiques. The Salon dining room is truly stunning, with ruched drapes at the windows, an ornate fireplace, and portraits on white walls contrasting with a red carpet. The kitchen works around a slate of contemporary ideas and displays a level of originality not commonly seen in such surroundings. Thus, pan-fried scallops are served with spicy cauliflower dhal and coriander dressing, and peppered haunch of venison comes with aubergine, caramelised onion chutney and cranberry bonbons. Main courses show a level of restraint to allow flavours to be clearly defined: monkfish is studded with garlic and accompanied by chilli mash and a tarragon infusion, and slow-cooked belly pork by pork cheeks with chorizo and braised root vegetables. Desserts are as well constructed and attractively presented, among them pear and walnut frangipane tart with butterscotch ice cream.

Chef Alan Ford **Owner** Has Modi **Seats** 80, Pr/dining room 80 **Times** 12-2/7-9.30
Prices Prices not confirmed, Service optional **Wines** 100 bottles over £30, 64 bottles under £30, 9 by glass **Parking** 80 **Notes** Sunday L, Children 12 yrs+ D

INGHAM
Map 13 TL87

The Cadogan Arms

◎ Traditional British

tel: 01284 728443 **The Street IP31 1NG**
email: info@thecadogan.co.uk **web:** www.thecadogan.co.uk
dir: *A134 4m from Bury St Edmunds*

Well-executed dishes in stylish gastro-pub

The interior of this former coaching inn has been reworked and spruced up with a stylish decor, subdued lighting, upholstered sofas and chairs and a curved bar dispensing real ales. Flexibility is the name of the game, with grazing boards for snackers and a lunch menu of sandwiches and dishes like local ham, eggs and chips. The kitchen moves up a couple of gears in the evening, its skills and nifty presentation evident in smoked chicken with home-made chorizo and a crisp poached egg, followed by confit shoulder of mutton with fondant potato and root vegetable purée. Seafood gets the modern treatment: battered shrimps cut by sweet chilli jam, and smoked coley fillet in Welsh rarebit with pea velouté and new potatoes.

Chef Michael Bell **Owner** David Marjoram **Seats** 72 **Times** 12-2.30/6-9.30
Closed 25-26 Dec **Prices** Starter £4.50-£6.50, Main £8.50-£17, Dessert £5.50, Service optional **Wines** 8 bottles over £30, 37 bottles under £30, 12 by glass **Parking** 39 **Notes** Sunday L £8.50-£16, Vegetarian available, Children welcome

IPSWICH
Map 13 TM14

Best Western Claydon Country House Hotel

◎ Modern British

tel: 01473 830382 **16-18 Ipswich Rd, Claydon IP6 0AR**
email: enquiries@hotelsipswich.com **web:** www.hotelsipswich.com
dir: *A14, junct 52 Claydon exit from rdbt, 300yds on left*

Modern British cooking close to Ipswich

Two old village houses were joined seamlessly together to form this friendly, small-scale hotel to the north west of Ipswich. The Victorian-style restaurant overlooks the gardens through a conservatory extension, although the classic look has been given a gentle update by ditching the cloths on its darkwood tables and adding high-backed leather chairs. Staff are smartly turned out to create a professional, welcoming vibe, and the kitchen draws on splendid locally-sourced produce as the bedrock of its unfussy European-accented modern British dishes. Expect starters along the lines of seafood risotto with rocket and parmesan, while mains could turn up roast rack of lamb with chive mash, wilted greens, and red wine and rosemary glaze. End with a warm Belgian chocolate muffin with chocolate sauce and vanilla ice cream.

Times 12-2/7-9.30

Best Western Gatehouse Hotel

◎ Modern British V

tel: 01473 741897 **799 Old Norwich Rd IP1 6LH**
email: reception@gatehousehotel.com
dir: *A14 junct 53 take A1156 Ipswich, left at lights onto Norwich Road, hotel on left*

Unfussy modern food in Regency-style country house

This small and friendly country-house hotel on the outskirts of Ipswich offers a pleasant juxtaposition of town and country in a handsome Regency building. Three acres of immaculately-kept mature gardens provide seclusion as well as pleasant pre-dinner strolls to sharpen the appetite before settling into the easygoing ambience of the restaurant, where an elegant centrepiece fireplace and heaps of period character are set against a more contemporary look of smart high-backed leather seating and bare darkwood tables. The kitchen doesn't try to reinvent the wheel here, preferring to keep things simple and put its faith in the quality of local produce. You might set the ball rolling with something as straightforward as king prawns in crispy filo pastry with sweet chilli dipping sauce and baby leaf salad, followed by pan-seared rump steak with sautéed new potatoes, roasted red onions and wilted spinach. To finish, there's the comfort of steamed spotted dick with home-made custard.

Chef Frankie Manners **Owner** Khurram Saeed **Seats** 40 **Times** 12-2/7-9.30 **Prices** Fixed D 3 course fr £24.95, Service optional **Wines** 5 by glass **Parking** 30 **Notes** Sunday L fr £15.95, Children welcome

Mariners

🌐 French, Mediterranean

tel: 01473 289748 **Neptune Quay IP4 1AX**
email: info@marinersipswich.co.uk
dir: *Accessed via Key St. Follow brown tourist signs to waterfront*

Honest Gallic brasserie fare afloat in Ipswich

A French brasserie on a Belgium gunboat in Ipswich... you've got to love it! Moored on Neptune Quay, the boat dates from 1899, but once you're on board, you could well be in Paris, and that could be the Seine through the window rather than Ipswich Marina. The brainchild of local hero, Regis Crepy ('local' via France), owner of The Great House in Lavenham and Maison Bleue in Bury St Edmunds, Mariners is no gimmick. There's a decidedly classy finish to the brasserie-style decor, with polished original brass, chandeliers, lots of burnished wood and tables laid with white linen cloths. Kick-off with a well put together carpaccio of beef with whole grain mustard sauce and green leaves, or a Mediterranean soup with the traditional accompaniments. Main-course grilled fillet of halibut with chive and shrimp sauce competes for your attention with a 36-hour-roasted belly of pork confit. Finish with French apple tart with vanilla ice cream and crème anglaise.

Times 12-2.30/7-9.30 Closed Jan, Sun-Mon

Milsoms Kesgrave Hall

🌐 Modern International v

tel: 01473 333741 **Hall Rd, Kesgrave IP5 2PU**
email: reception@kesgravehall.com **web:** www.kesgravehall.com
dir: *A12 N of Ipswich/Woodbridge, rdbt onto B1214*

Relaxed dining in a contemporary setting

A buzzy bistro is at the culinary heart of Kesgrave Hall, a Georgian mansion in thick woodland just north of Ipswich. Inside, however, a boutique makeover in recent years has reinvented the place as a stylish boutique hotel with a pared-back modern look involving oak floors, pine tables, leather chairs and muted shades of cream and sage; outdoors, there's a spacious terrace with a retractable awning that keeps the place on the boil whatever the weather. The crew in the open kitchen are nicely in tune with the surrounding landscape, serving modern brasserie dishes along the lines of smoked haddock fishcake with a soft-boiled egg, pickled

cucumber and lemon mustard mayonnaise, followed by braised Dedham Vale beef featherblade with carrot purée, cavolo nero and crispy bone marrow. Wrap it all up with pineapple tarte Tatin, with coconut sorbet, candied noodles and rum syrup.

Chef Stuart Oliver **Owner** Paul Milsom **Seats** 80, Pr/dining room 24 **Times** 12-9.30 All-day dining **Prices** Starter £3.75-£10.50, Main £11.50-£26.50, Dessert £5.95, Service optional **Wines** 38 bottles over £30, 43 bottles under £30, 18 by glass **Parking** 150 **Notes** Brunch daily 10-11.45am, Sunday L £14.95-£25, Children welcome

Salthouse Harbour Hotel

🌐🌐 Modern British

tel: 01473 226789 **1 Neptune Quay IP4 1AX**
email: reservations@salthouseharbour.co.uk **web:** www.salthouseharbour.co.uk
dir: *A14 junct 53, A1156 to town centre & harbour, off Key St*

Well-executed, modish dishes on the waterfront

Smack on the waterfront overlooking the marina, Salthouse Harbour is a converted warehouse reinvented as a design-led contemporary boutique hotel. Ablaze with vivid colours and with its rich red-brick walls hung with an eclectic collection of striking modern art and installations and eye-catching kitsch curiosities, The Eaterie rather undersells itself with such a self-effacing name. It is an expansive, well-thought-out space kept ticking over by a switched-on young service team. The name of the game is clearly to combine good-quality, local and seasonal ingredients with lively contemporary treatments to produce a Mediterranean-accented menu with broad appeal. Plump scallops are teamed with a crisp sweet potato and chorizo croquette and roasted tomato salsa, while loin of venison wrapped in bacon stars in a main course with beetroot and blackberry purée, braised red cabbage, Parisienne potatoes and red wine venison jus. The flavours keep on coming right through to a dessert of affogato – vanilla ice cream with hot espresso poured over – with cinnamon doughnuts.

Chef Chris McQuitty **Owner** Robert Gough **Seats** 70 **Times** 12-10 All-day dining **Prices** Fixed L 2 course £13.95-£17.95, Starter £6-£9.95, Main £12.95-£29.50, Dessert £5.95-£8.95 **Wines** 51 bottles over £30, 24 bottles under £30, 36 by glass **Parking** 30 **Notes** Sunday L, Vegetarian available, Children welcome

---

IXWORTH Map 13 TL97

Theobalds Restaurant

🌐🌐 Modern British

tel: 01359 231707 **68 High St IP31 2HJ**
dir: *7m from Bury St Edmunds on A143 (Bury to Diss road)*

Seasonal modern British food in a beamed Tudor inn

Simon and Geraldine Theobald converted this whitewashed Tudor inn into a restaurant for our times back in 1981 and the place is a testament to tenacity and commitment. Ancient beams abound, with tables got up in pristine white, and out back is a pretty little garden awash with trellised plants. Simon was in the forefront of the seasonal revolution in British cooking in the 1980s, which is more of a claim than it may sound now that everybody's at it, but the principle shines brightly. Late spring brings poached asparagus with basil-scented hollandaise, followed perhaps by spring lamb with celeriac purée in rosemary and madeira, while the winter menu trades in monkfish wrapped in Serrano ham with braised leeks in white wine sauce, and peppercorned rump steak flamed in cognac. Locally reared meats and East Anglian fish are the mainstays, and the quality of raw materials is indisputable. Desserts aim to indulge by means of brioche bread-and-butter pudding with apple and sultanas, or lemon and lime tart with matching sorbet.

Chef Simon Theobald **Owner** Simon & Geraldine Theobald **Seats** 42, Pr/dining room 16 **Times** 12.15-1.30/7-9 Closed 10 days in spring/summer, Mon, L Tue-Thu, Sat, D Sun **Prices** Fixed L 2 course £22.95, Fixed D 3 course £32.50, Starter £7.50-£9.95, Main £15.95-£20.95, Dessert fr £7.50, Service optional **Wines** 16 bottles over £30, 34 bottles under £30, 7 by glass **Parking** On street **Notes** Fixed L menu available Fri, Fixed D midwk & Fri, Sunday L, Vegetarian available, Children 8 yrs+ D

LAVENHAM
Map 13 TL94

Lavenham Great House 'Restaurant with Rooms'

◉◉ Modern French

tel: 01787 247431 **Market Place CO10 9QZ**
email: info@greathouse.co.uk **web:** www.greathouse.co.uk
dir: In Market Place (turn onto Market Lane from High Street)

Modern French cooking in a medieval building

Opposite the 16th-century timber-framed Guildhall, owned by the National Trust, The Great House is itself pretty ancient behind its Georgian façade, though its dining room has been given a thoroughly modern look. It's a calm and soothing room, done out in soft tones, with a darkwood floor and comfortable upholstered chairs at white-clothed tables set with flowers and sparkling glasses. The cooking has its roots in the great French repertoire, so a pressing of pork belly and duck foie gras with marinated grapes, port jelly and balsamic reduction may be followed by confit lamb shoulder, cooked for 36 hours and partnered with aubergine caviar roulade and olive, cognac and basil jus. That's not to say there aren't some more global influences at play though: wasabi and mustard sauce adds an oriental twist to roasted fillet of Suffolk pork with celeriac, while yellow fin tuna is grilled and accompanied by steamed pak choi, tomato and vanilla chutney. Finish off with beetroot and basil pannacotta with apple jelly and beetroot caramelised with honey.

Chef Regis Crepy **Owner** Mr & Mrs Crepy **Seats** 40, Pr/dining room 15 **Times** 12-2.30/7-9.30 Closed Jan & 2 wks summer, Mon, L Tue, D Sun **Prices** Fixed L 2 course £18.50, Fixed D 3 course £33.50, Starter £9.95-£12.95, Main £15.50-£26.95, Dessert £6.95, Service optional **Wines** 65 bottles over £30, 75 bottles under £30, 10 by glass **Parking** Market Place **Notes** Sunday L £33.50, Vegetarian available, Children welcome

Find out more about how we assess for Rosette awards on page 9

Read all about our Wine Award winners on page 17

The Swan

◉◉ Modern British V ⚑ NOTABLE WINE LIST

tel: 01787 247477 **High St CO10 9QA**
email: info@theswanatlavenham.co.uk **web:** www.theswanatlavenham.co.uk
dir: From Bury St Edmunds take A134 (S) for 6m then take A1141 to Lavenham

Modernist cooking beneath a medieval minstrels' gallery

The asymmetrical timbered white building on the main street through the medieval East Anglian village of Lavenham gives evidence of its own great age. Dating back to the 15th century, it's an endearing maze of crannies and beams within, beautifully maintained and bursting with character. There's informal dining in the Brasserie, but the main restaurant is the Gallery. Here the high vaulted ceiling and minstrels' gallery, and polished and attentive service from smartly uniformed staff add to the sense of occasion. The modernism of the cooking is productively at odds with the venerability of its surroundings, opening perhaps with truffled goats' cheese and lightly pickled beets in pea-shoot salad, and progressing to cod with spiced lentils and tempura sprouting broccoli, guinea-fowl breast with gingered potato rösti and cumin-spiced pumpkin purée or, for vegetarians, an open lasagne of Mediterranean veg with chargrilled halloumi and pesto. An exhaustive deconstruction of tiramisù results in vanilla pannacotta, coffee meringue, vanilla foam, hazelnut crumb and coffee jelly, and very pleasing it is too.

Chef Justin Kett **Owner** Thorpeness & Aldeburgh Hotels Ltd **Seats** 90, Pr/dining room 32 **Times** 12-2.30/7-9.30 **Prices** Fixed L 2 course £16.95, Starter £8-£12.95, Main £21-£24, Dessert £6.95-£10.45, Service optional **Wines** 111 bottles over £30, 32 bottles under £30, 11 by glass **Parking** 50 **Notes** Sunday L, £26.95 Children 5 yrs+

LOWESTOFT
Map 13 TM59

The Crooked Barn Restaurant

◉◉ Modern British

tel: 01502 501353 **Ivy House Country Hotel, Ivy Ln, Oulton Broad NR33 8HY**
email: aa@ivyhousecountryhotel.co.uk **web:** www.ivyhousecountryhotel.co.uk
dir: A146 into Ivy Lane

Locally-based cooking in a thatched barn

On the banks of Oulton Broad, in 20 acres of grounds, the Ivy House Country Hotel has an ace up its sleeve in the form of The Crooked Barn Restaurant. The hotel's destination eatery is located in a 16th-century barn which has an abundance of character with the ceiling exposed to the rafters. There's plenty of room within for the smartly set tables, dressed in white linen and generously spaced around the room, plus views over the pretty garden. The kitchen makes excellent use of the region's produce in dishes that smack of Pan-European eclecticism. Start with a modern combo such as pan-fried scallops with parsnip purée and crispy bacon, or go for the globally-inspired home-cured salmon with tempura king prawns with cucumber and sweet chilli dip. Main-course fillet of beef is served in a classical manner with dauphinoise potatoes, honey-roasted vegetables and cracked black pepper sauce, while fillet of plaice is filled with a crayfish mousse and partnered with potato galette and a creamy saffron sauce. Finish with hot chocolate fondant.

Times 12-1.45/7-9.30 Closed 19 Dec-6 Jan

MILDENHALL   Map 12 TL77

The Bull Inn
Modern British

tel: 01638 711001 **The Street, Barton Mills IP28 6AA**
email: reception@bullinn-bartonmills.com **web:** www. bullinn-bartonmills.com
dir: Off A11 between Newmarket & Mildenhall, signed Barton Mills. Hotel by Five Ways rdbt

Local produce and appealing modern menus

The Bull has dropped the 'olde' from its name and gone back to its original moniker, which seems appropriate given the forward-thinking, boutique approach that's going down in Barton Mills. There are spiffing designer bedrooms, a bar where you can drink a pint and eat some smart bar food, and a brasserie-style restaurant with a nifty menu that's big on local ingredients. Kick-off a meal with Suffolk ham hock with wholegrain mustard and tarragon and home-made chutney, or brie fritters with a winter berry purée, watercress and caramelised walnuts. Move on to roast rump of Norfolk lamb with sweet potato Parmentier, charred broccoli, rosemary and red wine jus, or a locally-farmed steak cooked on the chargrill and served with smoked garlic

mash or hand-cut chips, plus a field mushroom, plum tomato and watercress salad. Dessert might be a spring berry Eton tidy (the clue is in the title).

Chef Cheryl Hickman, Shaun Jennings **Owner** Cheryl Hickman & Wayne Starling **Seats** 60, Pr/dining room 30 **Times** 12-9 Closed 25 Dec, All-day dining **Prices** Starter £6.50-£10, Main £13-£27, Dessert £6.50-£8, Service optional **Wines** 16 bottles over £30, 24 bottles under £30, 11 by glass **Parking** 60 **Notes** Sunday L £13-£22, Vegetarian available, Children welcome

See advert below

NEWMARKET   Map 12 TL66

Bedford Lodge Hotel
Modern International

tel: 01638 663175 **Bury Rd CB8 7BX**
email: info@bedfordlodgehotel.co.uk **web:** www.bedfordlodgehotel.co.uk
dir: From town centre take A1304 towards Bury St Edmunds, hotel 0.5m on left

Classy brasserie dishes near the famous racecourse

This extended one-time Georgian hunting lodge has a prime position near the racecourse and enough top-end facilities to satisfy a 21st-century epicure. There are spa treatments aplenty, the hotel is a big hit for weddings and business get-togethers, and there's a rather spruce restaurant called Squires, named in honour of a notorious former owner of the house. The split-level dining room has a comfortable finish and lots of local artworks to give a sense of place. The menu is packed with enticing brasserie-style dishes with decidedly modern British leanings and some creative combinations. Start with Earl Grey-smoked duck breast sharing

continued

THE FRESHEST SEASONAL INGREDIENTS COMBINED WITH FABULOUS LOCAL SUPPLIERS EQUALS FANTASTIC FOOD.

AWARD WINNING AA DINING ROOMS
GREAT BRITISH BREAKFASTS & ROASTS
PUB WITH REAL ALES & LOG FIRE
PRIVATE DINING
15 BOUTIQUE & FUNKY BEDROOMS
MURDER MYSTERY & LOTS MORE...

HOMEMADE FOOD SERVED ALL DAY

AA Gold Star Award Inn 2014

T: 01638 711001 E: reception@bullinn-bartonmills.com www.bullinn-bartonmills.com The Street, Barton Mills, Nr Mildenhall, Suffolk IP28 6AA

NEWMARKET *continued*

space with a blood orange gel, celeriac and maple syrup, or the equally imaginative goats' mousse and bonbons with walnuts, bitter leaves and pomegranate gel. Main-course seared calves' liver comes with a roasted fig and smoked garlic-flavoured potatoes, and there are meats such as Norfolk-reared rib-eye cooked on the grill. Finish with a chocolate sphere plus hot chocolate sauce and white chocolate foam.

Chef James Fairchild **Owner** Review Hotels Ltd **Seats** 60, Pr/dining room 150 **Times** 12-2/7-9.30 Closed L Sat **Prices** Fixed L 2 course £23, Fixed D 3 course £28.50, Starter £6-£9, Main £17-£29, Dessert £6-£9 **Wines** 71 bottles over £30, 30 bottles under £30, 16 by glass **Parking** 120 **Notes** Sunday L £26.50, Vegetarian available, Children welcome

The Packhorse Inn

@@@ – *see below*

Tuddenham Mill

@@ Modern British

tel: 01638 713552 **High St, Tuddenham St Mary IP28 6SQ**
email: info@tuddenhammill.co.uk **web:** www.tuddenhammill.co.uk
dir: *M11 junct 9 towards Newmarket, then A14 exit junct 38 in direction of Norwich. Turn right at Herringswell road*

Imaginative cooking of unusual ingredients in a converted watermill

The mill still looks as if it could put in a hard day's craft, but look more closely and you'll see it's had a makeover. The riverside setting is positively serene and the contemporary decor within matches those views with original features and a clean, modern look. The water-wheel has been encased in glass to form a fine feature in the bar, while the restaurant has heavy oak beams and views over the millpond. There's a new head chef in 2014 in the form of Lee Bye, who was sous chef here a few years ago, and the bright, contemporary-style cooking continues. Local and regional produce figures large in creative dishes that utilise lots of modern culinary techniques. From the carte, for example, organic salmon is cooked at 40 degrees and comes with plum emulsion and crispy rice, with another starter pairing a crispy skinned chicken wing with squash purée and roasted peanuts. These clever constructions are soundly thought through and carefully executed. Main-course hake has a well-judged cumin coating, served with Norfolk coppa with a flavourful leek and clam ragu, and another pairs lamb rump with its barbecued shoulder, soured red cabbage and mint. Desserts are no less creative: parsnip cake with celery ice and parsnip toffee, for example (a cracking combo), or lemon curd with goats' milk, hazelnut and mint oil.

Chef Lee Bye **Owner** Agellus Hotels **Seats** 54, Pr/dining room 18 **Times** 12-2.15/6.30-9.15 **Prices** Service optional **Wines** 141 bottles over £30, 32 bottles under £30, 13 by glass **Parking** 40 **Notes** Sunday L £24.50, Vegetarian available, Children welcome

Who has won our Lifetime Achievement award? See page 12 to find out

The Packhorse Inn

NEWMARKET   Map 12 TL66

Modern British **NEW**

tel: 01638 751818 **Bridge St, Moulton CB8 8SP**
email: info@thepackhorseinn.com **web:** www.thepackhorseinn.com
dir: *A14 junct 39 onto B1506. After 1.5m turn left at x-rds onto B1085 (Moulton Rd). In Moulton, left into Bridge St*

Classy modern pub food in a gracious country inn

The old village pub has been spruced up to meet 21st-century expectations in terms of its decor and its culinary output, with Chris Lee at the stoves (once of the Bildeston Crown). The place has scrubbed up very nicely indeed, with a good balance of original rustic charm and upmarket country style. The mostly bare-boarded floors are strewn with occasional rugs, flowers adorn the tables, vividly coloured ornithological prints the cream and aubergine walls, and there's a general air of gracious country-living serenity about it all. It still operates as a pub with a relaxed attitude and welcoming approach, but it's also serious about its food, for everything is sourced with care and attention, and the menus regularly change to respect the seasons. Gentrified pub-food nibbles might whet the appetite with Scotched quail eggs and salad cream, or cheese and onion croquettes with piccalilli, and then it's into the main menu. The ambitious output includes a fabulous Suffolk venison pie with smoked potato served in a Kilner jar, and rather ritzy seared foiegras with pain d'épices and glazed pineapple. Main-course roast Suffolk chicken breast with sage and onion and bread sauce might sound old-fashioned but is nothing of the sort, while respectfully treated fish dishes might include stone bass with carrots, artichokes and red chicory, or whole grilled plaice with wild garlic and mash. The Kilner jar gets another outing for a delicious dessert of coconut rice pudding with passionfruit jelly, or there could be summery strawberry pannacotta, or the benchmark indulgence of chocolate tart and orange sorbet. The Anglo-French cheese selection comes with port jelly. Attention to detail extends to variously fruit-flavoured pastilles, or doughnuts with contrasting fillings of custard, chocolate or apple, to round it all off.

Chef Chris Lee **Owner** Phillip & Amanda Turner **Seats** Pr/dining room 32 **Times** 12-2.30/7-9.30 Closed D 25 Dec **Prices** Starter £7-£11, Main £15-£22, Dessert £7-£9, Service optional **Wines** 74 bottles over £30, 36 bottles under £30, 18 by glass **Parking** 30 **Notes** Sunday L £15-£19, Vegetarian available

The Crown & Castle

 Italian, British V NOTABLE WINE LIST

tel: 01394 450205 **IP12 2LJ**
email: info@crownandcastle.co.uk **web:** www.crownandcastle.co.uk
dir: Off A12, on B1084, 9m E of Woodbridge

Very good eating in a chic old Suffolk inn

There has been a hostelry on this site for 800 years and the tradition of hospitality is in particular good heart in the 21st century. It's co-owned by Ruth Watson (she's also executive chef) who was TV's Hotel Inspector once upon a time, and the combination of stylish bedrooms and an easy-going, rustic-chic restaurant is a winning one. There's genuine character to the spaces within, where beams, unclothed wooden tables and comfortable burgundy-velvet cushioned chairs and benches help create a relaxed vibe. The place is still an inn popular with the locals up for a pint, but it's also something of a foodie destination. The daily-changing menu has an Italian accent these days, featuring the fashionable Venetian small plates, cicchetti, alongside flavour-driven dishes that showcase the region's excellent ingredients. Grilled octopus with nduja sausage and potato salad is one way to kick off a meal, followed perhaps with duck breast with warm borlotti beans and morels, or a proper shortcrust steak and kidney pie. Finish with zabaglione or treacle tart.

Chef Ruth Watson, Charlene Gavazzi **Owner** David & Ruth Watson, Tim Sunderland **Seats** 60, Pr/dining room 10 **Times** 12.15-2.15/6.30-9.15 **Prices** Starter £5.25-£9.95, Main £15.50-£25, Dessert £6.95 **Wines** 65 bottles over £30, 66 bottles under £30, 16 by glass **Parking** 17, Market Sq, on street **Notes** Pre-concert supper available (prior booking essential), Sunday L £23-£28, Children 8 yrs+ D

Sibton White Horse Inn

Modern British

tel: 01728 660337 **Halesworth Rd IP17 2JJ**
email: info@sibtonwhitehorseinn.co.uk **web:** www.sibtonwhitehorseinn.co.uk
dir: From A12 in Yoxford take A1120 signed Sibton & Peasenhall. 3m, in Peasenhall right opposite butcher's shop. White Horse 600mtrs

Charming Tudor pub with modern global cooking

In the heart of Suffolk at its sleepiest, among villages full of candy-coloured cottages, though only a few minutes' drive from the A12 and Saxmundham, the White Horse is a beamed Tudor inn dating back to the 16th century. The place is reliably abuzz with local custom, chatter and laughter filling the low-ceilinged, quarry-tiled rooms. James Finch draws on regional produce to craft menus that display the global influences of modern cooking, but don't take off on a one-way trip to La-La Land either. Tea-smoked salmon makes a diverting starter, the deeply fragrant fish set off with grape and walnut salad and horseradish crème fraîche. That might be followed by pot-roast breast of first-class Gressingham duck with dauphinoise, roast baby onions and pak choi, a lovely balance of weight and flavour, or sea bass with Asian-spiced sticky rice and sweet chilli jam. Pear and pistachio millefeuille with mulled wine sorbet rounds things off in style.

Chef Gill Mason, James Finch, Emma Pearson **Owner** Neil & Gill Mason **Seats** 40, Pr/dining room 18 **Times** 12-2/6.45-9 **Closed** Xmas, L Mon **Prices** Starter £5.50-£6.50, Main £11.50-£19.50, Dessert £4.75-£7.50, Service optional **Wines** 3 bottles over £30, 31 bottles under £30, 7 by glass **Parking** 35 **Notes** Sunday L £11.25-£12.95, Vegetarian available, Children 6yrs+ D

The Blyth Hotel

Modern British

tel: 01502 722632 **Station Rd IP18 6AY**
email: reception@blythhotel.com **web:** www.blythhotel.com
dir: Follow A1095 from the A12, signed Southwold. Hotel on left after bridge

Edwardian hotel dining a few minutes from the beach

The Ashwells' attractively restored Edwardian hotel augments the range of options in trendy Southwold, and benefits from being only a five minute walk down to the golden sands and gaily painted beach-huts on the shore. Like many another coastal place, it's a good setting for fresh fish, and you can't go far wrong with a starter of mackerel fillet served with Serrano ham and celeriac remoulade, followed by cod with crushed new potatoes, pea-shoots and a chorizo and pea fricassée. The range is wider, though, encompassing well herb-crusted pork fillet with braised leeks, poached apple and butternut purée in sage jus, and veggie offerings such as fried falafel with spiced couscous and harissa. Dessert options may include white chocolate pannacotta with strawberry sorbet, apple and rhubarb crumble with custard, or a minutely detailed take on key lime pie. The celebrated Adnams ales are on tap in the bar.

Chef Lee Walding **Owner** Richard & Charlie Ashwell **Seats** 38, Pr/dining room 14 **Times** 12-2/6.30-9 **Closed** L Mon-Wed **Prices** Starter £6.50, Main £10.95-£17.95, Dessert £6.50-£8.50, Service optional **Wines** 10 bottles under £30, 10 by glass **Parking** 8, On street **Notes** Pre-theatre/Family dining from 5.30 Jul & Aug, Sunday L £9.95, Vegetarian available, Children welcome

Sutherland House

Modern British, Seafood

tel: 01502 724544 **56 High St IP18 6DN**
email: enquiries@sutherlandhouse.co.uk **web:** www.sutherlandhouse.co.uk
dir: A1095 into Southwold, on High St on left after Victoria St

Neighbourhood fish restaurant with diligent sourcing

The original parts of the building date from the 15th century, with the Georgians and Victorians chipping in along the way, to create a period house of genuine charm. There are wooden beams from ships that fought in the battle of Sole Bay (and that was in 1672!) and ornate ceilings, coving and real fireplaces throughout. The fixtures and fittings cut a more contemporary dash, giving a decidedly chic finish. Likewise, the cooking impresses with its modern ambitions, passion for seafood, and loyalty to local ingredients (fruit and veg come from their own allotment, and there's a local flavour all round – 'food yards', as they say). Start with Debden mussels in classic marinière style, or English snails with a parmesan and asparagus soufflé. Main-course roasted cod loin comes with champ, clams and brown shrimps, and a meaty option might be 28-day-aged fillet steak with sweet potato skinny fries. Dessert stage might deliver bread-and-butter pudding with a

continued

SOUTHWOLD *continued*

brûlée topping and vintage marmalade ice cream, or lemon and ginger cheesecake with candied lemon.

Chef Jed Tejada **Owner** Peter & Anna Banks **Seats** 50, Pr/dining room 60 **Times** 12-2.30/7-9 Closed 25 Dec, 2 wks Jan, Mon (Oct-Mar) **Prices** Starter £5.50-£11.50, Main £18-£23, Dessert £5-£6.50, Service optional **Wines** 10 bottles over £30, 20 bottles under £30, 10 by glass **Parking** 1, On street **Notes** Sunday L £12-£24, Vegetarian available, Children welcome

Swan Hotel

◉◉ Modern British

tel: 01502 722186 **High St, Market Place IP18 6EG**
email: swan.hotel@adnams.co.uk **web:** www.adnamshotels.co.uk
dir: *A1095 to Southwold. Hotel in town centre. Parking via archway to left of building*

Smart British cooking at Adnams' flagship hotel

The Adnams empire has things pretty tied up in Southwold, where it is the seaside town's brewer, main publican, wine merchant and hotelier. Just in front of the brewery, the Swan – a handsome bay-fronted Victorian façade occupying pole position among the boutiques – is the epicentre of operations. Inside, its 17th-century origins are revealed: there are wall panels, genuine 18th-century oil paintings and gilt chandeliers, but time has not stood still, so it is all leavened with smart contemporary styling. Afternoon tea in the drawing room is something of a local institution, but don't spoil your appetite for dinner in the smart dining room. As one would hope from a set-up with its roots deep into the local area, provenance of raw materials is emphatically regional, and the cooking is confident, full-flavoured stuff. That old stalwart of seared scallops and black pudding is matched here with celeriac, apple purée and pea shoots, and followed by a dish of confit duck leg with bubble-and-squeak, roast parsnips, plum compôte and port jus.

Times 12-2.30/7-9.30

The Crown

◉◉ Modern British

tel: 01206 262001 **CO6 4SE**
email: info@crowninn.net **web:** www.crowninn.net
dir: *Stoke-by-Nayland signed from A12 & A134. Hotel in village off B1068 towards Higham*

Boutique hotel and village inn serving modern British food

Perfectly placed for exploring Constable country – the soaring tower of nearby St Mary's Church is immortalised in the artist's works – and with unspoilt views across the peaceful Box Valley, the classy 16th-century Crown has been spruced up with style and panache, morphing into a classy boutique inn with the addition of 11 swish bedrooms. The rambling beamed bar and dining areas sport a smart contemporary look, with cockle-warming log fires, cosy corners, and an in-house wine shop. Monthly-changing modern British menus, supplemented by daily fish dishes – landed by local fishing boats working from the Blackwater Estuary – on the chalkboard, reflect the seasons and show flair, imagination, and sound use of quality local ingredients. A summer's dinner sets out with guinea fowl terrine with bacon, garlic toast and apricot chutney, then the kitchen's confident creative spirit continues with pan-fried rainbow trout fillet with cauliflower and almond purée, wilted gem lettuce, a fried egg and thick-cut chips. For pudding, a deliciously retro Black Forest gâteau comes with fresh cherries.

Chef Dan Hibble **Owner** Richard Sunderland **Seats** 125, Pr/dining room 14 **Times** 12-2.30/6-9.30 Closed 25-26 Dec **Prices** Starter £5.25-£7.50, Main £9.95-£21.95, Dessert £2.75-£6.50, Service optional **Wines** 244 bottles over £30, 76 bottles under £30, 22 by glass **Parking** 49 **Notes** Sunday L, Vegetarian available, Children welcome

The Case Restaurant with Rooms

◉ Modern British **V**

tel: 01787 210483 **Further St, Assington CO10 5LD**
email: restaurant@thecaserestaurantwithrooms.co.uk
web: www.thecaserestaurantwithrooms.co.uk
dir: *Located on A134 between Sudbury & Colchester. 0.5m past Newton Golf Club*

Characterful Suffolk inn with brasserie-style menu

Located in deepest Suffolk countryside, this great little property has bags of character. Dating back to about 1700, the whitewashed country inn used to be a private home and now there are beautiful bedrooms and a cosy little restaurant to attract paying customers. It's a little like eating in someone's front room (in a nice way), with a wood-burning stove, darkwood tables and low ceiling beams. Brasserie cooking is the name of the game and a highlight of the meal may well be the mini-beef Wellington that is a first-course option, but what follows on the daily-changing menu is sure to appeal too – a meaty Dingley Dell pork chop and sausage, perhaps, with apple tartlet, jacket potato, green vegetables and Suffolk Aspall cider sauce, or poached fillet of plaice filled with salmon mousse.

Chef Barry & Antony Kappes **Owner** Barry Kappes **Seats** 40 **Times** 6.30-9 Closed L Mon-Sat, D Sun **Prices** Starter £5.95-£9.95, Main £10.95-£31, Dessert £5.95-£17.95, Service optional **Wines** 10 bottles over £30, 23 bottles under £30, 11 by glass **Parking** 30 **Notes** Children welcome

Thorpeness Hotel

◉ Modern British

tel: 01728 452176 **Lakeside Av IP16 4NH**
email: info@thorpeness.co.uk **web:** www.thorpeness.co.uk
dir: *A1094 towards Aldeburgh, take coast road N for 2m*

Simple but sound cookery next to Britain's greenest golf course

A golfing hotel by the sea, Thorpeness boasts Britain's greenest course, laid out in 1922 and now replete with new bunkers and swales. If you're the understanding partner of a golfer, be it noted that there are fine walks hereabouts, the beach is only five minutes' stroll, and Aldeburgh beckons in the middle distance. Understated modern styling makes the hotel interiors look trim, and there are of course grand views of the fairways from the main restaurant, the covered patio bar and terrace. The food on a daily-changing menu doesn't aim for too much distraction from the main business, but achieves sound satisfaction by means of ham hock with melba toast, chutney and salad, followed perhaps by lamb shank with bubble-and-squeak and roasted winter veg in a richly assertive gravy, with solid comfort arriving at the final hole in the form of sticky toffee pudding, served with gooey toffee sauce and vanilla ice cream.

Chef Mark Knowles **Owner** T A Hotel Collection Ltd **Seats** 80, Pr/dining room 30 **Times** 12.30-3/7-9.30 Closed L Mon-Sat **Prices** Starter £4.50-£7.50, Main £12.50-£19.95, Dessert £4.95-£7.25 **Wines** 3 bottles over £30, 27 bottles under £30, 15 by glass **Parking** 80 **Notes** Sunday L, Vegetarian available, Children welcome

WALBERSWICK
Map 13 TM47

The Anchor
 Modern British

tel: 01502 722112 **Main St IP18 6UA**
email: info@anchoratwalberswick.com
dir: On entering village The Anchor on right, immediately after MG garage

Globally influenced food in an eco-conscious village inn

The Dorbers took over The Anchor in 2004, and set about restoring it to its rightful place at the heart of the time-warp seaside village of Walberswick. Solar panels, eco-timber and rainwater butts hint that The Anchor has been not only spruced up but conscientiously greened in the process, but you can rest assured that plenty of the original character remains, as well as great sea views and a relaxed atmosphere. The owners' vast knowledge of beer and wine is apparent with each dish matched with one or the other, and the kitchen deals in the freshest local and seasonal produce using many ingredients from the owners' allotment. Excellent home-made breads are a prelude to a menu that casts its net far and wide for influences, starting in Europe with scallops matched with parsnip purée, and fennel and pancetta salad, before zooming to Asia for a main course of oriental belly pork with crunchy crackling, bok choy, sweet soy reduction and crispy lotus root. A nicely wobbly vanilla and rosemary pannacotta makes a fine end to proceedings.

Times 11-11 All-day dining

WESTLETON
Map 13 TM46

The Westleton Crown
 Modern British V

tel: 01728 648777 **The Street IP17 3AD**
email: info@westletoncrown.co.uk **web:** www.westletoncrown.co.uk
dir: A12 N, turn right for Westleton just after Yoxford. Hotel opposite on entering village

Vibrant modern cooking in an ancient inn

This textbook red-brick Suffolk coaching inn may date from the 12th century, but there's nothing archaic about the gastronomic side of the operation. The Crown is still an endearingly cosy local with well-kept real ales, a log fire and ancient beams in the bar, while the modern conservatory restaurant is done out in a clean-cut style with mismatched scrubbed wood tables and a wall of sliding glass doors that opens up to the lovely terraced gardens. The food also keeps its feet planted in the present with some cleverly-honed modern ideas wrought from first-rate local produce. Orford smoked haddock might provide the foundations for a puff pastry tart made with spinach and free-range eggs, ahead of main courses running from steamed halibut with cocotte potatoes, wilted red chard and a vegetable and herb nage, to a more gutsy four-way workout of local Suffolk chicken, in the form of poached breast, roasted thigh, confit leg, and breaded wing with pasta, parsley sauce and braised lettuce.

Chef Robert Mace **Owner** Agellus Hotels Ltd **Seats** 85, Pr/dining room 50 **Times** 12-2.30/6.30-9.30 **Prices** Starter £5.50-£9.95, Main £13.25-£23.50, Dessert £5.75-£6.50, Service optional **Wines** 23 bottles over £30, 21 bottles under £30, 9 by glass **Parking** 50 **Notes** Afternoon tea, Sunday L £12.50-£14.95, Children welcome

WOODBRIDGE
Map 13 TM24

The British Larder Suffolk
 Modern British **NEW**

tel: 01394 460310 **Oxford Rd, Bromeswell IP12 2PU**
email: info@britishlardersuffolk.co.uk
dir: From A12 take exit onto Woods Lane A1152 towards Melton/Orford. Continue over railway crossing onto Wilford bridge, take 1st exit at rdbt on A1152, 0.8m on right

Food-focused pub with a local flavour and great technical skills

The clue is in the name: this Suffolk pub is all about food (but that's not to say you can't enjoy a pint of real ale). Maddy Bonvini-Hamel and Ross Pike are two professional chefs who are passionate about the region's produce and they have created a fabulous little slice of foodie heaven in the Suffolk countryside. Settle down into one of the many cosy little areas within the red-brick pub – or outside on the terrace – and peruse a menu packed full of organic, local and seasonal ingredients. There's a good deal of culinary nous on display here and a steady hand at the stove. Pan-fried Blaxhall wood pigeon is an autumnal dish that hits the right notes, with its accompanying roasted golden and ruby beetroot, pine nuts and a watercress emulsion. Or go fishy with the Orford Smoke House platter. Next up, pan-fried hake is a great piece of fish, cooked just right, and served with celeriac, baby onions, chard and sauce vièrge. To finish, plum and almond tart with almond ice cream shows off high-level technical skills.

Chef Madalene Bonvini-Hamel, Ross Pike **Owner** Madalene Bonvini-Hamel, Ross Pike **Seats** 62 **Times** 12-3/6-10 Closed Mon Jan-Mar, D Sun Jan-Mar **Prices** Fixed L 2 course £17, Tasting menu £45-£48.50, Starter £6-£14, Main £14-£22, Dessert £6.50-£7.50, Service optional **Wines** 21 bottles over £30, 18 bottles under £30, 28 by glass **Parking** 40 **Notes** Sunday L fr £16, Vegetarian available, Children welcome

The Crown at Woodbridge
 Modern European

tel: 01394 384242 **2 Thoroughfare IP12 1AD**
email: info@thecrownatwoodbridge.co.uk **web:** www.thecrownatwoodbridge.co.uk
dir: A12 follow signs for Woodbridge onto B1438, after 1.25m from rdbt turn left into Quay Street & hotel on right, approx 100 yds from junct

Distinguished brasserie cooking in a market town

A dramatic no-expense-spared facelift relaunched the Crown as a stylish 21st-century inn back in 2009. The look is decidedly boutique, combining 16th-century features with a fresh, contemporary design ethos in four dining areas. One has glowing paprika red walls, another is done out in cool shades of grey and features an etched glass mural screen, while a Windermere skiff hangs above the glass-roofed bar. The vibe is suitably urbane and relaxed, and the kitchen raids the Suffolk larder for its unfussy, big-hearted modern British cooking. Local fish and seafood make a good showing on a wide-ranging menu. Start with seared scallops with taramasalata, crispy pancetta and oven-dried tomatoes, and follow with roasted Orford cod with a cassoulet of chorizo, chickpeas and piquillo peppers, or seared loin and confit leg of local rabbit with black pudding, apples and Savoy cabbage. Desserts can be as creative as baked vanilla cheesecake with elderflower meringues, pan-fried strawberries with black pepper and basil cress, or as classic as sticky toffee pud with clotted cream.

Chef Luke Bailey **Owner** Thorpeness & Aldeburgh Hotels **Seats** Pr/dining room **Times** 12-2.15/6.15-9 Closed D 25 Dec (available for residents only) **Prices** Fixed L 3 course fr £13, Fixed D 3 course fr £13, Starter £6-£8, Main £12.50-£22, Dessert £6.50, Service optional **Wines** 30 bottles over £30, 15 bottles under £30, 14 by glass **Notes** Sunday L £12.50, Vegetarian available, Children welcome

WOODBRIDGE *continued*

Seckford Hall Hotel

◉◉ Modern European, British

tel: 01394 385678 **IP13 6NU**
email: reception@seckford.co.uk web: www.seckford.co.uk
dir: *Hotel signed on A12 (Woodbridge bypass). Do not follow signs for town centre*

Characterful multi-influenced cooking in a Tudor mansion

The Tudor hall was built around an even earlier structure, and stands amid 34 acres of Suffolk just outside Woodbridge. Its reboot as a country-house hotel offers a sight more individuality than can often be the case, the original panelled walls blending well with more modern fixtures. The 1530 restaurant emphasises these contrasts well, the colourful decor sets off monochrome photographs of the hall, with discreet jazz schmoozing away in the background. Here, Messrs Durrant and Oakenfull, joint head chefs, oversee a menu of strong, characterful contemporary British food with the accent frequently falling on Asian seasoning. That last point is successfully seen in a starter of sautéed scallops with spiced papaya purée and chilli and coriander salad, or the trio of local pork – tenderloin, cheek, and twice-cooked belly – in fragrant star anise jus. Influences are drawn from all over, from Morocco for spiced lamb rump with chickpea cassoulet, or Italy for poached halibut and tagliatelle with braised gem in crayfish and fennel velouté. A dessert to rejoice in features grilled pineapple and deep-fried coconut ice cream with gingerbread in caramel sauce.

Chef Liam Oakenfull, Ashley Durrant **Owner** Mr & Mrs Pankhurst **Seats** 85, Pr/dining room 150 **Times** 12.30-1.45/7-9.30 **Prices** Starter £5.95-£10.95, Main £12.95-£20.95, Dessert £5.45-£8.95, Service optional **Wines** 11 by glass **Parking** 100 **Notes** L menu 2/3 course £19/£40, Sunday L £23, Vegetarian available, Children welcome

YAXLEY   Map 13 TM17

The Auberge

◉◉ Traditional, International

tel: 01379 783604 **Ipswich Rd IP23 8BZ**
email: aubmail@the-auberge.co.uk web: www.the-auberge.co.uk
dir: *5m S of Diss on A140*

Well-crafted dishes in a medieval Suffolk inn

The ancient beams, panelling and exposed brickwork dating back to medieval times are clear evidence that this was a public house for many centuries, but its name serves notice that it is now reincarnated as a modern restaurant with rooms. The room is still darkly intimate; tables are crisply laid with linen, embellished with bowls of fresh lemons, limes and chillies and lit by candles. As the name would suggest, French influences underpin the cooking, but the kitchen relies on good supply lines to local materials for modern, skilfully rendered food that makes a virtue of simplicity. Start perhaps with smoked haddock fishcakes with pea shoots and lime and thyme mayonnaise, or a twice-baked three-cheese soufflé, before moving to slow-roasted pork belly with Aspall cider, crackling, and caramelised Pink Lady apples, or one of the speciality steaks – rib-eye, perhaps, with garlic and balsamic butter or pink peppercorn sauce. Puddings go unashamedly for the populist vote, with a pyramid of dark chocolate and nuts served with Cointreau ice cream, or cappuccino cheesecake.

Chef John Stenhouse, Mark Bond **Owner** John & Dee Stenhouse **Seats** 60, Pr/dining room 20 **Times** 12-2/7-9.30 Closed 1-7 Jan, Sun, L Sat-Mon **Prices** Fixed L 2 course £14.95, Fixed D 3 course £19.95, Starter £5.30-£7.50, Main £12.80-£21.50, Dessert £6.95-£8.95, Service optional **Wines** 22 bottles over £30, 28 bottles under £30, 13 by glass **Parking** 25 **Notes** Vegetarian available, Children welcome

YOXFORD   Map 5 TM36

Satis House Hotel

◉◉ Modern British

tel: 01728 668418 **Main Rd IP17 3EX**
email: enquiries@satishouse.co.uk web: www.satishouse.co.uk
dir: *off A12 between Ipswich & Lowestoft. 9m E Aldeburgh & Snape*

Piquant flavours in rural Suffolk

Satis House is a Grade II listed building dating from the 18th century with connections to Charles Dickens (it gets a name-check in *Great Expectations*). Today's incarnation has lost none of its period charm and it is decorated in such a way as to enhance the period features without seeming chintzy or dated. The restaurant has a decidedly contemporary sheen to it, with its polished wooden floor, bold red-flowered wallpaper and darkwood unclothed tables. Carefully-sourced local produce features prominently on the menu, which might take you from chicken liver parfait with onion marmalade to veal cutlet with olive and caper butter, or the more Eastern-inspired pan-fried scallops with crème fraîche and sweet chilli jam to Thai duck leg curry with pickled plums and duck spring roll. For dessert, chocolate mousse comes with a peanut parfait and brittle, while the seasonal celebration of rhubarb brings forth jelly, brulée and pudding (with ginger).

Times 12-3/6.30-11 Closed L Mon-Tue

SURREY

BAGSHOT   Map 6 SU96

The Brasserie at Pennyhill Park

◉◉ Modern British V ◈ NOTABLE WINE LIST

tel: 01276 471774 **Pennyhill Park Hotel & The Spa, London Rd GU19 5EU**
email: enquiries@pennyhillpark.co.uk
dir: *M3 junct 3, through Bagshot, left onto A30. 0.5m on right*

Relaxed and airy brasserie with punchy contemporary cooking

The Brasserie is the more informal and relaxed alternative to Pennyhill Park's trailblazing Latymer. This large, colourful, stone-walled room, with bright banquettes and lots of windows, overlooks the pool and the huge spa complex. It makes a swish setting for some lively modern cooking, and the kitchen accordingly puts a fresh spin on the brasserie repertoire, aiming for punchy, tightly-defined flavours in creations that are contemporary without being outlandish. Poached crab roulade is matched with cured trout and basil jelly. Main courses bring the comfort of classic grilled steaks, or you might strike out towards more enterprising dishes – perhaps braised shoulder and loin of lamb teamed with haricot bean fricassée, spring cabbage, smoked celeriac purée and lamb caper jus, or pollock fillet baked in squid ink with pearl barley, pak choi, tapioca crisp, shiitaki mushrooms and coconut jus. To finish, lime parfait is a zingy counterpoint to strawberry marshmallow and sorbet.

Chef Ram Jalasutram **Owner** Exclusive Hotels and Venues **Seats** 120, Pr/dining room 30 **Times** 12-2.30/6-10 Closed L Sat **Prices** Fixed L 2 course £30-£45, Fixed D 2 course £28-£35, Starter £7.50-£12.50, Main £16.50-£33, Dessert £6.50-£10.50 **Wines** 45 bottles over £30, 15 bottles under £30, 13 by glass **Parking** 500 **Notes** Fixed D Mon-Sat 2 course before 7pm, Sunday L £37, Children welcome

Michael Wignall at The Latymer

◉◉◉◉◉ – *see opposite*

Michael Wignall at The Latymer

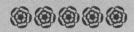

BAGSHOT Map 6 SU96

Modern European **V** NOTABLE WINE LIST

tel: 01276 471774 **Pennyhill Park Hotel & The Spa, London Rd GU19 5EU**
email: enquiries@pennyhillpark.co.uk
web: www.exclusivehotels.co.uk
dir: *M3 junct 3, through Bagshot, left onto A30. 0.5m on right*

Stunningly-crafted contemporary cooking in a luxurious hotel

Pennyhill Park is the ideal place for a perfectionist like Michael Wignall, because everything about the place is precise and refined. The original building was constructed for a 19th-century businessman and everything within is either classically elegant or cutting-edge modern. The spa alone covers 45,000 square feet, then there's the 123 acres of wooded parkland, a golf course and even a rugby pitch, which is a favoured training ground of the England squad, and an elegant brasserie restaurant. The shining star, though, is Michael Wignall at The Latymer, the landmark restaurant and holder of five of our rosettes. Located in the main Victorian house, looking out over the beautiful grounds, The Latymer is an intimate room full of period character with oak panelling and stained-glass windows, given a gentle modernity by the contemporary colour palette. The menu options depend on the day you visit, with the carte offering up six choices per course on Tuesday to Wednesday evenings, and the full-whack tasting menu with ten courses up for grabs on Tuesday to Saturday evenings. Lunch is a good entry point if you want to get a measure of the place for pretty much half the price. The cooking is technically precise, clever without ever losing its way, and everything looks perfect on the plate. The ten-course tasting menu might get things rolling with a mosaic of Goosnargh corn-fed chicken and duck, the flavours and textures singing in harmony, with baked celeriac, couscous and a liquorice powder. Each flavour and texture on the plate plays its part in making an impact. Warm pastrami of Anjou squab comes with poached and roasted foie gras, cocoa granola, Stilton, spiced apple and a Pedro Ximenez jelly in a highly creative course that balances strong flavours with a subtle hand. Another savoury course puts together razor and Palourde clams with cockles in a cassoulet, with cuttlefish gnocchi and poached quail's egg. There's a cheese course before the sweets – Vacherin Mont d'Or, perhaps, with Manchego sablé and quince. Expect plenty of craft and creativity among desserts, too, not least in a dish of Jerusalem artichoke cheesecake, which is served with a salted caramel ganache, white chocolate namelaka (a Japanese term meaning 'creamy texture') and peanut butter powder. The service team are a class act, and you can put yourself in the heart of the culinary action if you wish, by booking the chef's table (a funky bubble-glass one with adjustable lighting). To cap it all off, the wine list is a stellar piece of work, and there is a wine flight option for every dish.

Chef Michael Wignall **Owner** Exclusive Hotels and Venues **Seats** 50, Pr/dining room 16 **Times** 12.30-2/7-9.30 Closed 1-14 Jan, Sun-Mon (open Sun BHs but closed following Tue), L Tue, Sat **Prices** Fixed L 3 course £38-£39.50, Fixed D 3 course £88, Tasting menu £88-£106 **Wines** 300 bottles over £30, 20 by glass **Parking** 500 **Notes** Tasting menu L 8 course, D 10 course, No children

CAMBERLEY | Map 6 SU86

Macdonald Frimley Hall Hotel & Spa

◉◉ Modern European

tel: 0844 879 9110 **Lime Av GU15 2BG**
email: gm.frimleyhall@macdonald-hotels.co.uk **web:** www.macdonaldhotels.co.uk
dir: M3 junct 3, A321 follow Bagshot signs. Through lights, left onto A30 signed Camberley & Basingstoke. To rdbt, 2nd exit onto A325, take 5th right

Smart modern cooking in peaceful setting

Readers of a certain age who remember Wright's Coal Tar Soap might be interested to know that this creeper-clad manor house ensconced in pretty gardens and unspoilt woodland was once the soap baron's family home. Nowadays, the country-house hotel has scrubbed up well: its grand looks – magnificent oak staircase and panelling, ornate plasterwork – are leavened with a pared-back modern style, plus the obligatory spa and health club are present and correct. The Linden Restaurant goes for a soothing, minimal look with a neutral colour scheme, deploying simple table settings as a backdrop to its modish cooking. The kitchen shows a solid focus on flavour whilst throwing some daredevil components into the mix, as in a starter of goats' cheese mousse teamed with poppy seed wafer, apple purée and olive tapenade. Next out, a porcine trio of pork fillet, pork belly and black pudding is served with vanilla-infused apple sauce, green beans and fondant potato, whilst the simplicity of a well-made classic crème brûlée is all that's needed for a satisfying finish.

Times 12.30-2/7-9.30 Closed L Sat, D 25-26 Dec

CHERTSEY | Map 6 TQ06

Hamilton's

◉ Modern European, British

tel: 01932 560745 **23 Windsor St KT16 8AY**
email: bookings@hamiltons23.com **web:** www.hamiltons23.com
dir: M25 junct 11 St Peters Way (A317). At rdbt 1st exit, Chertsey Rd (A317), next rdbt 2nd exit into Free Prae Rd, then Pound Rd. Left into London St, opposite church

Skilful modern cooking in a charming restaurant with rooms

Occupying a corner site in the town centre, Hamilton's is a small and intimate restaurant with rooms, with a warm and welcoming feel from its hands-on proprietors. Semi-frosted windows look out onto the street, allowing for a spot of people-watching as you take in the ambience in the stylishly done out space. Chef-patron Carter Williamson deals in thoughtfully presented modern European dishes using top-notch seasonal ingredients. Smoked venison carpaccio with mizuna cress salad, quail's egg, parsnip crisps and truffle oil is a simple starter done well, or you might go for seared king scallops (precisely timed) with wasabi potato purée, pickled cucumber and lotus root. Scallops turn up again in a main-course pairing with oriental belly pork, along with bok choy, sweet soy reduction and crispy lotus root – a winning combination of tastes and textures. Raspberry vodka jelly with raspberry and mint salad and vanilla bean ice cream ends things on a high.

Chef Carter Williamson **Owner** Carter & Kerry Williamson **Seats** 30 **Times** 6-9.30 Closed Sun-Tue, L all week **Prices** Fixed D 3 course £23, Tasting menu £55-£75, Starter £6-£9, Main £15-£26, Dessert £6-£9, Service optional **Wines** 6 bottles over £30, 5 bottles under £30 **Parking** 3, On street **Notes** Vegetarian available, Children welcome

Stovell's

CHOBHAM | Map 6 SU96

Modern European

tel: 01276 858000 **125 Windsor Rd GU24 8QS**
email: enquiries@stovells.com
dir: M25 junct 11. Join A317 then take A320 towards Chobham, A319 turn right Windsor Road

Exhilarating modern food in a Tudor farmhouse

The Stovells' move in 2012 from catering to the celeb circuit of London's private clubs to renovating a 16th-century Tudor farmhouse in deepest Surrey must have been something of a culture shock, but clearly a welcome one, since their self-named restaurant bears all the hallmarks of a passionate enthusiasm for food. Retaining its physiognomy of gnarled old age, it's all beams and low ceilings inside, with open fires in winter. There are contemporary-styled pictures of mushrooms to look at, and a rose-red Ibérico ham waiting on its slicer for the starter orders. The pairing of unusual flavours and textures is clearly a passion, requiring an arsenal of skills to prepare and luckily there's some serious technical ability in the kitchen, so what is promised is delivered. An exhilarating virtuoso opening dish brings Salcombe crab spiked with almonds and apple beneath a single sheet of lasagne and a wafer-thin disc of squid ink bread alongside a battered oyster in a shellfish broth with remarkable depth of flavour that takes the dish to a higher plane. Next up, superb butter-roasted cod comes on a comforting broth of diced potato and celeriac. Carnivores are in for a treat too: there might be loin, leg and saddle of local rabbit partnered with fermented turnips, pistachio, yarrow and parsley purée. A wood-fired clay oven does its bit too, chargrilling a big old rib of beef over vine cuttings from nearby Hush Heath vineyard, or adding smoky savour to the elements of an ovine mixed grill – rump, best end, belly and sweetbreads – served with grilled polenta, artichokes and toasted gorse flowers. Impressive desserts are peppered with good ideas – a light-as-air baked dark chocolate mousse arrives on a fudgy salted caramel base with a thrilling blood orange sorbet – or finish on a savoury note with perfectly ripened artisan cheeses.

Chef Fernando & Kristy Stovell **Owner** Fernando & Kristy Stovell **Seats** 60, Pr/dining room 14 **Times** 12-3.30/6-10.30 Closed Mon, L Sat, D Sun **Prices** Fixed L 2 course £15.50-£28, Fixed D 3 course £38-£52, Tasting menu £60-£90 **Wines** 87 bottles over £30, 16 bottles under £30, 14 by glass **Parking** 20 **Notes** Sunday L £21-£25, Vegetarian available, Children welcome

CHIDDINGFOLD
Map 6 SU93

The Swan Inn

 British, International

tel: 01428 684688 **Petworth Rd GU8 4TY**
email: info@theswaninnchiddingfold.com **web:** www.theswaninnchiddingfold.com
dir: M25 junct 10, A3 to Milford junct. At rdbt 1st exit onto A283, left at lights. At next rdbt 2nd exit, 5m to Swan Inn

Wide-ranging menus in a former coaching inn

Expect to see lots of exposed brickwork, stripped floors, logs burning, and a comfortable and inviting dining room, with flowers on wooden tables, at this former coaching inn in a quintessential English village. The kitchen turns its hands to a principally British menu with some input from further afield, so roast chicken breast with merguez sausage and white bean cassoulet might appear next to rump of lamb with roast root vegetables, braised red cabbage and red wine jus. An innovative soup could kick things off – perhaps white onion, cider and sage – or go for soused mackerel with potato, cucumber and dill salad. End with a creditable trio of English cheeses or with passionfruit pannacotta with a kick of lime.

Chef Graham Digweed **Owner** Annemaria & Stuart Boomer Davies **Seats** 40, Pr/dining room 40 **Times** 12-3/6.30-10 **Prices** Starter £5-£12.25, Main £11.75-£19.95, Dessert £4-£6 **Wines** 22 bottles over £30, 30 bottles under £30, 15 by glass **Parking** 35 **Notes** Sunday L £11.75-£19.95, Vegetarian available, Children welcome

CHOBHAM
Map 6 SU96

Stovell's

 – see opposite

CHURT
Map 5 SU83

Best Western Frensham Pond Hotel

 Modern British

tel: 01252 795161 **Bacon Ln GU10 2QB**
email: info@frenshampondhotel.co.uk **web:** www.frenshampondhotel.co.uk
dir: A3 onto A287. 4m left at 'Beware Horses' sign. Hotel 0.25m

Modernised classic brasserie dishes overlooking a truly great pond

The house is originally 15th century, but only got into its stride in the hospitality game in the Georgian era. Sitting by the eponymous Great Pond, not far from Farnham, it's in a picturesque spot, and offers keep-fit facilities and all mod cons to the Home Counties traveller. The Watermark dining room enjoys a sweeping prospect of the pond, and is handsomely kitted out with crisp linen, fresh posies and well-upholstered seating. Modernised classic brasserie dishes are the order of the day, and soup fans are well served with a rotating list of changes being rung through the days of the week. Start, perhaps, with baked goats' cheese with salad leaves and croûtons, then a well-timed pork loin steak with celeriac purée and caramelised onions in port and thyme reduction, before coming to rest with a good mixed berry cheesecake, or lemon tart with minty crème fraîche.

Times 12.30-2.30/7-10 Closed D Sun

Follow us on facebook
www.facebook.com/TheAAUK

DORKING
Map 6 TQ14

Mercure Box Hill Burford Bridge Hotel

 British, European

tel: 01306 884561 **Burford Bridge, Box Hill RH5 6BX**
email: h6635@accor.com **web:** www.mercure.com
dir: M25 junct 9, A245 towards Dorking. Hotel within 5m on A24

Traditionally-based hotel cooking in rural Surrey

At the foot of Box Hill by the River Mole, the Burford Bridge is in a peaceful spot (though not far from the A24), as may be appreciated by those availing themselves of the outdoor pool or the croquet lawn. A beige-hued modern dining room, the Emlyn, is the setting for some gently tweaked, traditionally-based cooking, along the lines of oxtail soup with herb dumplings, grilled haddock with shrimp butter and parsley mash, or breast and cabbage-wrapped confit leg of duck in sloe gin sauce. Interesting ideas for pudding include chocolate and rosemary soufflé with orange biscotti, or praline parfait with wine- and cinnamon-poached pear.

Times 12-2.30/7-9.30 Closed D Sun

Two To Four

 Modern European V

tel: 01306 889923 **2-4 West St RH4 1BL**
email: two_to_four@hotmail.co.uk **web:** www.2to4.co.uk
dir: M25, exit at Leatherhead junct, follow signs to town centre

Modern cooking in a thriving neighbourhood venue

Occupying a period building in the town centre, this is the sort of friendly and welcoming neighbourhood restaurant we would all like on our manor. The decor goes in for a smart-casual look with unclothed tables, creaky floors and a blackboard specials menu that underlines the informal tone. First-class ingredients are the name of the game in a repertoire of uncomplicated modern European-style dishes; much of the meat is sourced from within a five-mile radius, and organic produce is used liberally. Seared scallops with artichoke purée, toasted hazelnuts and honey truffle vinaigrette is one way to start, while main courses take in roasted pork chop with parsnip mash, braised red cabbage and red wine jus, or perhaps pan-fried fillet of black bream with black olives, anchovy mayonnaise, Serrano ham and lemon gel, all realised with technical verve and presented with a modern flourish. For dessert, bread-and-butter pudding could be jazzed up with the addition of banana and peanut, and served with peanut butter ripple ice cream.

Chef Rob Gathercole **Owner** Restaurant 2to4 Ltd **Seats** 70, Pr/dining room 12 **Times** 12-2.30/6.30-10 Closed Xmas, Mon (subject to change) **Prices** Fixed L 2 course £12, Fixed D 2 course £19, Tasting menu £55, Starter £7.25-£9.95 **Wines** 21 bottles over £30, 19 bottles under £30, 8 by glass **Parking** West St car park **Notes** Sun L Oct-Mar, Sunday L £14.95-£24.95, Children welcome

EGHAM
Map 6 TQ07

The Estate Grill
◎◎ Modern British

tel: 01784 433822 **Great Fosters, Stroude Rd TW20 9UR**
email: reception@greatfosters.co.uk **web:** www.greatfosters.co.uk
dir: *A30 (Bagshot to Staines) right at lights by Wheatsheaf pub into Christchurch Rd. Straight on at rdbt (pass 2 shop parades on right). Left at lights into Stroude Rd. Hotel 0.75m on right*

Ingredient-led contemporary cooking with British artworks

With its chapel-like beams and displays of contemporary British artworks, The Estate Grill is the brasserie alternative to the more high-falutin Tudor Room here at Great Fosters. They share a commitment to sourcing prime seasonal ingredients from regional suppliers, including Old Spot pigs reared in the grounds, supplemented by kitchen garden and greenhouse produce, and honey from the apiary, as well as Cumbrian fell-bred lamb and Label Anglais chicken from Essex. It all works its way into dishes such as home-cured gravad lax carved at the table, served with apple, juniper and horseradish salad, or cauliflower cheese risotto, to start. Then try slow-cooked beef suet pudding, whole baked sea bass with fennel and anise, or charcoal-roasted chicken with lemon, garlic and thyme, for main. Sharing platters can be for starters or main (the seafood version looks hard to resist), and meals end with the likes of roast pineapple with yuzu savarin, mango and coconut.

Chef Simon Bolsover **Owner** Great Fosters (1931) Ltd **Seats** 44, Pr/dining room 20 **Times** 12.30-9.30 All-day dining **Prices** Starter £8-£15, Main £16-£36, Dessert £9-£10 **Wines** 80 bottles over £30, 10 bottles under £30, 15 by glass **Parking** 200 **Notes** Sunday L £34, Vegetarian available, Children welcome

The Tudor Room
Rosettes not confirmed at time of going to print – see below

GODALMING
Map 6 SU94

La Luna
◎◎ Modern Italian 🍷 NOTABLE WINE LIST

tel: 01483 414155 **10-14 Wharf St GU7 1NN**
email: info@lalunarestaurant.co.uk **web:** www.lalunarestaurant.co.uk
dir: *In town centre, at junct of Wharf St & Flambard Way*

Stylish modern Italian venue

There's a satisfying modernity to La Luna, a place which deals in Italian dishes that are both familiar and a cut above. The space is on the sophisticated side, with

The Tudor Room

Rosettes not confirmed at time of going to print

EGHAM
Map 6 TQ07

Modern European v
tel: 01784 433822 **Great Fosters, Stroude Rd TW20 9UR**
email: reception@greatfosters.co.uk
dir: *A30 (Bagshot to Staines) right at lights by Wheatsheaf pub into Christchurch Rd. Straight on at rdbt (pass 2 shop parades on right). Left at lights into Stroude Rd. Hotel 0.75m on right*

Contemporary cooking in an historic house

The Rosette award for this establishment has been suspended due to a change of chef. Reassessment will take place in due course under the new chef. The stately-looking Great Fosters has a history going back 500 years and has original features and character galore, as well as meeting (and exceeding) contemporary expectations for comfort and facilities. There are two dining options: the Estate Grill is the more easy-going venue, with an upscale brasserie-style menu, and then there is the Tudor Room, where a large 17th-century tapestry takes pride of place. It's a grandly formal space (seating only 24) with rich, elegant decor and tables dressed up for the business of fine dining. The cooking is broadly modern European in approach, with the estate providing its

considerable bounty, including fruit, vegetables and meats, and what isn't home-produced doubtless won't have travelled too far. New chef Nik Chappell demonstrates a real understanding of flavour and a keen instinct for innovating in dishes such as an opening wholegrain mustard macaroon on truffled goats' cheese, served with confit tomatoes, nuts and balsamic caviar. He is equally at home with the more obviously classical approach of pressed duck confit and foie gras terrine, albeit one served with pistachio custard, ribbons of rhubarb and vivid pink rhubarb ice cream. Main courses look to traditional French ways for poached lemon sole, which comes in a broth of clams, cockles, white beans and garlic with a serving of fennel, while crisp-skinned Goosnargh duck breast is sauced with a rich, sticky reduction and accompanied by sweet salsify and turnips. Well-judged compositions are also the hallmark of desserts such as crème caramel, caramel jelly and honeycomb, served with a Thai-spiced lemongrass and lime leaf ice cream, or a pavé of high-quality white chocolate with salt-baked pineapple and passionfruit sorbet.

Chef Nik Chappell **Owner** Great Fosters (1931) Ltd **Seats** 24, Pr/dining room 20 **Times** 12-2/7-9.30 Closed 2 wks Jan, 2 wks Aug, Sun-Mon, L Sat **Prices** Fixed L 3 course fr £29.50, Tasting menu £60-£75 **Wines** 245 bottles over £30, 12 by glass **Parking** 200 **Notes** L de jour menu, Tasting menu D 6/8 course & L 8 course, Children welcome

fashionable muted earthy tones to the fore, and the service team go about their business with charm and confidence. The bilingual menu follows a traditional format, so things kick off with antipasti such as a plate of charcuterie to share, or smoked tuna tartare served with semi-dried cherry tomatoes and pickled artichoke hearts. Next up, a primipiatti of first-rate pasta or risotto; paccheri with monkfish and gaeta olives and capers, for example, or squid ink risotto with seared scallop and gremolata. Then it's on to the main event, secondi piatto, such as baked sea bream with herby new potatoes and smoked aubergine purée, or Shackleford pork fillet with smoked ham and a potato and Jerusalem artichoke millefoglie. There is a good value lunch menu, plus a tasting version with wine flight. For dessert there might be Sicilian blood orange tart or chocolate and orange tiramisù.

Chef Valentino Gentile **Owner** Daniele Drago **Seats** 58, Pr/dining room 24 **Times** 12-2/7-10 Closed 2 wks Aug, BHs, Sun-Mon **Prices** Fixed L 2 course fr £13.50, Tasting menu fr £85, Starter £5.50-£10.95, Main £11.95-£19.50, Dessert £4.50-£6.25, Service optional **Wines** 141 bottles over £30, 37 bottles under £30, 8 by glass **Parking** Public car park behind restaurant **Notes** Tasting menu 7 course incl wine, Vegetarian available, Children welcome

---

HASLEMERE
Map 6 SU93

Lythe Hill Hotel & Spa
Modern British, French

tel: 01428 651251 **Petworth Rd GU27 3BQ**
email: lythe@lythehill.co.uk **web:** www.lythehill.co.uk
dir: *1m E of Haslemere on B2131*

Inspired British modernism in a 15th-century farmhouse

The listed ancient farmhouse dates back to the near-end of the Plantagenet era in 1475, and some of the guest rooms retain architectural features from those times. The oak-panelled dining room at the front is of the same age, while the supplementary room, though of distinctly more modern provenance, overlooks the attractive grounds and ornamental lake. A changing of the guard in the kitchen brings David Quinn to the stoves. He maintains the house style of innovative modern British dishes interlaced with populist classics, but with a slightly more pared-down look, which is all to the good. A spin on a traditional provençal dish, artichoke barigoule, is served cold in a truffle emulsion with goats' cheese mousse, and may be succeeded by pan-roasted monkfish tail with romanesco and champ, the fish wrapped in chicken skin that needs crisping more to achieve the intended effect, with charred spring onions adding their own smoky note. Tonka pannacotta is a lovely dessert idea, sharply counterpointed by poached rhubarb and sorbet and sweetened with honeycomb.

Chef David Quinn **Owner** Simon Drake (GM) **Seats** 70, Pr/dining room 34 **Times** 12-2.30/7-9.30 **Prices** Prices not confirmed **Wines** 23 bottles over £30, 25 bottles under £30, 9 by glass **Parking** 65 **Notes** Fixed L all week, Sunday L, Vegetarian available, Children welcome

---

HORLEY
For restaurant details see Gatwick Airport (London), (Sussex, West)

OCKLEY
Map 6 TQ14

Bryce's The Old School House
Modern British, Seafood

tel: 01306 627430 **The Old School House, Stane St RH5 5TH**
email: fish@bryces.co.uk
dir: *From M25 junct 9 take A24, then A29. 8m S of Dorking on A29*

Enterprising seafood in a smart country inn

Serving up South Coast seafood in the Surrey countryside for over 20 years now, Bryce's is a restaurant and country pub with a lot going on. Once upon a time it was a boys' boarding school and the beamed restaurant served time as its gym, but these days you can expect to tuck into seafood landed at Shoreham Harbour or bought at Billingsgate. Trio of Devon crab comes as a pan-fried cake, quenelle of mousse and twice-baked soufflé, or try their home-cured gravadlax with dill and mustard sauce. Among main courses, red snapper gets an Eastern flavour with bok choy, soy, ginger and sesame dressing, while fillets of plaice are stuffed with smoked salmon and chive mousse and served with champagne sauce. There's a bar menu too with scampi, fish pie and the like, plus a vegetarian menu and steaks as an alternative to all the fishy things.

Chef B Bryce, Steve Cave **Owner** Mr W & Mrs E Bryce **Seats** 50 **Times** 12-2.30/7-9.30 Closed 25 Dec, 1 Jan, Mon (Nov & Jan-Feb), D Sun (Nov & Jan-Feb) **Prices** Starter £6.95-£8.95, Main £12.95-£16.95, Dessert £5.25-£6.50, Service optional **Wines** 9 bottles over £30, 20 bottles under £30, 13 by glass **Parking** 35 **Notes** ALC 2/3 course £25.15/£32.40, Sunday L, Children welcome

---

OTTERSHAW
Map 6 TQ06

Foxhills Club and Resort
Traditional & Modern British

tel: 01932 704480 **Stonehill Rd KT16 0EL**
email: marketing@foxhills.co.uk **web:** www.foxhills.co.uk
dir: *From M25 junct 11 take A320 to Woking. At 2nd rdbt take last exit Cobham Rd, turn R into Foxhills Rd, follow until T-junct, turn L into Stonehill Rd*

Contemporary and classic dining in a Victorian manor

It's hard to believe that this 19th-century manor house is just a short hop from the frenzy of Heathrow, but you certainly don't need to think of leaving the country when there's a championship golf course, a spa and all manner of sporting pursuits spread around its 400-acre estate. That lot should help you work up an appetite for dining in the Manor Restaurant, an impressive setting with lofty vaulted ceilings within the oldest part of the building. Driven by locally-sourced ingredients – South Downs lamb and Surrey-bred beef, for example – the food belongs mostly to the contemporary idiom. Seared parsley and garlic-crusted scallops with lemon purée and shaved parmesan opens the show, ahead of a trio of Blythburgh pork (braised cheek, slow-roasted belly, and poached fillet) teamed with sweet potato and apples. For dessert, there's hot chocolate soufflé with chocolate cream sauce.

Times 12-2.30/6.30-9

REDHILL
Map 6 TQ25

Nutfield Priory Hotel & Spa
Modern British

tel: 0845 072 7486 & 01737 824400 **Nutfield Rd RH1 4EL**
email: nutfieldpriory@handpicked.co.uk **web:** www.handpickedhotels.co.uk/nutfieldpriory
dir: *On A25, 1m E of Redhill, off M25 junct 8 or M25 junct 6, follow A25 through Godstone*

New classic dishes in a Victorian Gothic house

Standing in 12 acres on Nutfield Ridge, the Priory is a piece of classic Victorian neo-Gothic, finished in the 1870s as a homage to Pugin's Westminster. Despite the restfulness of the setting, it's not far from Gatwick, ideally placed to embrace the weary air-traveller. A dining room named Cloisters feels just right in the circumstances, its mullioned windows offering expansive views over the grounds and lake. Roger Gadsden is clear about his intentions: to recreate classic dishes, as well as adding some new ones. Duck rillettes thus come tricked out with beetroot arancini and Puy lentils, or you might start with Asian-spiced pollock, with crisp-fried mussels and citrus-dressed samphire. Chateaubriand of 35-day dry-aged beef for two will prove hard to resist for the high rollers, but there are also fine, vibrantly pink duck with truffled mash, creamed hispi cabbage and bacon in oloroso sauce, or spicy monkfish with butternut squash purée. Keen interest is maintained through to the many-layered desserts, which may include raspberry delice with elderflower granita, lemon curd, elderflower custard and brilliant pink peppercorn meringue.

Times 12.30-2/7-9.30 Closed L Sat

REIGATE
Map 6 TQ25

The Dining Room
◉◉ Modern British V

tel: 01737 226650 **59a High St RH2 9AE**
dir: M25 junct 8/A217 follow one way system into High St. Restaurant on left

Stimulating cooking on the High Street

Tony Tobin may have TV chef status but he still heads up the brigade at his first-floor restaurant on the High Street. It's a smart-looking place, easy on the eye, with pictures on the walls and correctly set tables. A fixed-price deal pulls in the punters at lunchtime, drawn equally by a roster of bright contemporary ideas. Starters can vary from cauliflower soup enhanced by vanilla and curry oil, to a nicely presented dish of wild boar terrine with pear chutney, pistachios and truffle oil. There's no stinting on quality: fillet steak goes into meatballs (in tomato, pepper and chorizo sauce), and fillet of turbot comes roasted, moist and full of flavour, and served with Parmentier potatoes, girolles, broad beans and a complementary kick from smoked haddock foam. Breads are first rate, home-made chocolates come with coffee, and ingenuity extends to puddings such as lemon verbena Arctic roll with jelly-like balls of lemon syrup, or orange and lemon tart with blackcurrant sorbet.

Chef Tony Tobin **Owner** Tony Tobin **Seats** 75, Pr/dining room 28 **Times** 12-2/7-10 Closed Xmas, BHs, L Sat, D Sun **Prices** Prices not confirmed **Wines** 70 bottles over £30, 20 bottles under £30, 10 by glass **Parking** On street, car park **Notes** Tasting menu available, Sunday L, Children welcome

RIPLEY
Map 6 TQ05

The Anchor
◉◉ Modern British **NEW**

tel: 01483 211866 **High St GU23 6AE**
email: info@ripleyanchor.co.uk
dir: M25 junct 10 onto A3 towards Guildford, exit at junct for Ripley

Relaxed dining pub with a side order of pedigree

Though sibling to its renowned mother-ship restaurant Drake's just over Ripley village's bustling High Street, The Anchor is no pretentious gastro-pub annexe, but is rather a relaxed, friendly dining pub in the modern idiom with a dusting of pedigree. Okay, Drake's head chef Mike Wall-Palmer has moved across to man the stoves, but the Anchor delivers simple dining-pub fare with a touch of creativity and panache using quality produce. Dishes cover all the bases with a light modern touch, for example so 'now' snacks like crispy Pollock croquettes with seaweed mayo, and mains such as sea-fresh cod fillet with piquant chorizo purée and mushrooms. Afters hold form, perhaps caramelised apple custard (brûlée perfection) with intense-flavoured Granny Smith sorbet and 'wafers'. The Grade-II listed property itself (former almshouses) comes as well dressed as the food, with voguish good looks and hard surfaces. It has fashionable darkwood furniture, slate floors and Venetian blinds melded around original features, while armchairs by the log-burner add cosier, warming touches. Well-selected wines (and local ales) plus lovely in-house sourdough showcase add class.

Chef Michael Wall-Palmer **Seats** 38, Pr/dining room 8 **Times** 12-2.30/6-9.30 Closed Mon, D Sun **Prices** Starter £6-£9.50, Main £12-£25, Dessert £6-£9, Service optional **Wines** 49 bottles over £30, 26 bottles under £30, 11 by glass **Parking** 14 **Notes** Sunday L £14-£17, Vegetarian available, Children welcome

Drake's Restaurant

RIPLEY
Map 6 TQ05

Modern British V

tel: 01483 224777 **The Clock House, High St GU23 6AQ**
email: info@drakesrestaurant.co.uk **web:** www.drakesrestaurant.co.uk
dir: M25 junct 10, A3 towards Guildford. Follow Ripley signs. Restaurant in village centre

Thoughtful modern cookery in a listed Georgian house

A wholly delectable Home Counties village dating back to Norman times, Ripley is a little way off the A3. The somewhat improbable birthplace of Eric Clapton, it's crammed with listed buildings, in one of which, the Georgian redbrick Clock House, Steve and Serina Drake made their restaurant home a decade ago. The large Roman-numeralled timepiece above the door should orient you. Recent refurbishment has refined the look of the place, with a light, understated feel offset by the rustic wood of doors and window frames, and views on to a pretty walled garden with a terrace for aperitifs. Steve Drake is a big figure in the Slow Food movement, which promotes and celebrates the virtues of real food, thoughtful eating and sustainability. Prime materials are sourced throughout the kingdom, not just locally, and Drake's cooking style is very much led by considerations of flavour. Yes, there are unusual juxtapositions here, but they work in alliance with each other, and the overall effect is one of accessible simplicity. Discovery and Journey are the two menu options, the latter being the shorter. Cornish crab tortellini with spiced butternut, apple and sorrel may be the aromatic opener, before a pair of pork cheeks cooked in vermouth, alongside cockles and crab-apple. After a fish course such as lemon sole in chicken jus with salt-baked celeriac, it may be roast duck with elderberry onions, sweet potato and Douglas fir. A pre-dessert of passionfruit, coconut and grapefruit prepares the way for the grand finale of pistachio cake with banana and black olive ice cream. The seriously good wine list is no more than the food deserves.

Chef Steve Drake **Owner** Steve & Serina Drake **Seats** 40 **Times** 12-2/7-9.30 Closed 1 wk Jan, 2 wks Aug, 1 wk Xmas, Sun-Mon, L Tue **Prices** Prices not confirmed **Wines** 245 bottles over £30, 9 bottles under £30, 12 by glass **Parking** 2, 2 local car parks **Notes** Discovery menu £80, Journey menu £60, Tasting menu 9 course, Children welcome

Drake's Restaurant

◉◉◉ – *see opposite*

Woodlands Park Hotel

◉◉ Modern European

tel: 01372 843933 **Woodlands Ln KT11 3QB**
email: woodlandspark@handpicked.co.uk
web: www.handpickedhotels.co.uk/woodlandspark
dir: *A3 exit at Cobham. Through town centre & Stoke D'Abernon, left at garden centre into Woodlands Lane, hotel 0.5m on right*

Formal dining in a grand Victorian country house

A fortune built on matches allowed Victorian industrialist William Bryant (of Bryant and May fame) to build this red-brick mansion, and simultaneously dispense with the need for his own products to light the gas lamps, by being one of the first houses in the UK to have electric lighting. He picked a lovely spot, set in landscaped gardens and grounds, and these days anyone with the cost of a meal to spend can enjoy it from the Oak Room restaurant, a period piece, all beautiful oak-panelled walls and splendid coffered oak ceilings, and well-padded leather seats at linen-swathed tables. It all adds up to an impressive scene for some vibrant modern cooking, along the lines of crab ravioli teamed with seared scallops and shellfish bisque, followed by daube of Chanctonbury Estate venison with thyme fondant potato and horseradish cream. Desserts might be as creative as mint and chocolate millefeuille with a white chocolate sorbet shot and chocolate orange bonbon.

Times 12-2.30/7-9.30 Closed Mon, L Tue-Sat, D Sun

Brooklands Hotel

◉◉ British, European

tel: 01932 335700 **Brooklands Dr KT13 0SL**
email: brasserie@brooklandshotelsurrey.com **web:** www. brooklandshotelsurrey.com
dir: *Telephone for detailed directions*

Striking modern hotel where British motor-racing began

This thrillingly modern structure is built on a grand scale overlooking the first purpose-built car racing circuit in the world, opening back in 1907. You get a great view of the track while slurping a cocktail in the stylish art deco-inspired bar, before heading into the 1907 Restaurant, where cool colour tones of charcoal and aubergine and darkwood surfaces give a moody club-like vibe to the space. There's a creative modern brasserie feel to the food, with the kitchen team keen to deploy adventurous cooking techniques in dishes that arrive dressed to thrill. Salt cod brandade comes with watercress mayonnaise, a slow-poached egg and beurre noisette powder, followed by pink and tender duck breast with a spring roll of confit leg meat, bok choy, sesame and pine nut purée, pickled shimeji mushrooms and an aromatic jus. A dessert on a rhubarb theme ends on a high note with the tart vegetable arriving poached, in a crème brûlée and a sorbet, with walnut and cream cheese in a deconstructed carrot cake.

Times 12.30-2.30/6.30-10

Deans Place

◉◉ Modern British V

tel: 01323 870248 **Seaford Rd BN26 5TW**
email: mail@deansplacehotel.co.uk **web:** www.deansplacehotel.co.uk
dir: *off A27, signed Alfriston & Drusillas Zoo Park. Continue south through village*

Modern country cooking on the edge of the South Downs

On the southern fringe of the South Downs national park, and once part of an extensive farming estate, Deans Place has been a hotel of one sort or another for the past century. Scarcely can it have been quite such an alluring prospect as it is today, its elegant modern decor making a refreshing backdrop to the Victorian gardens and charming riverside location. The principal dining room is Harcourts, with the full-dress experience of fine table linen and glassware, while weekday lunches are served in the primrose-hued Terrace Room, with its gentle views over the croquet lawn. A distinctive style of updated country cooking is on offer in many formats: grills, seafood, vegetarian, and the principal dinner menu. That last might open with smoked haddock chowder and quail eggs, or scallops with a tempura-battered oyster, and then move to local lamb with olive gnocchi, goats' cheese and romesco sauce, or sea bass with parsnip-vanilla purée, lemon potatoes and bok choy in vermouth cream. Finish with chocolate and bayleaf tart on pistachio anglaise.

Chef Stuart Dunley **Owner** Steyne Hotels Ltd **Seats** 60, Pr/dining room 50
Times 12.30-2.30/6.30-9.30 **Prices** Prices not confirmed, Service optional **Wines** 25 bottles over £30, 47 bottles under £30, 10 by glass **Parking** 100 **Notes** Sunday L, Children welcome

BATTLE
Map 7 TQ71

Powder Mills Hotel
◉◉ Modern British V

tel: 01424 775511 **Powdermill Ln TN33 0SP**
email: jcowpland@thepowermills.com **web:** www.powdermillshotel.com
dir: *M25 junct 5, A21 towards Hastings. At St Johns Cross take A2100 to Battle. Pass abbey on right, 1st right into Powdermills Ln. 1m, hotel on right*

Appealing modish cooking near the 1066 battlefield

Powder Mills was once the site of a major gunpowder making operation (good stuff, apparently, which helped defeat Napoleon), but these days it is about a tranquil a setting as you can imagine. The pretty Georgian house stands in 150 acres of glorious Sussex countryside with lush parkland, woods and a seven-acre fishing lake. It's the kind of place where country pursuits are on offer and the owner's Springer Spaniels sometimes welcome new arrivals. Wining and dining takes place in the Orangery Restaurant with its bright and traditional demeanour (wicker chairs, linen-clad tables and marble floors. The kitchen turns out broadly contemporary dishes with a good showing of regional ingredients to ensure a local flavour. Start with wild mushroom and tarragon soup enriched with truffle Chantilly, or smoked pigeon breast with Madeira jelly and balsamic pearls. Move on to a main course that partners Gressingham duck breast with ravioli made from the confit leg meat, plus cauliflower purée and roasted salsify. Finish with pistachio soufflé with a pistachio and thyme ice cream.

Chef Callum O'Doherty **Owner** Mrs J Cowpland **Seats** 90, Pr/dining room 16 **Times** 12-2/7-9 **Prices** Fixed L 2 course £17.50, Fixed D 3 course £29.95, Tasting menu £59.95 **Wines** 4 by glass **Parking** 100 **Notes** Library menu £5-£21, Tasting menu 8 course, Sunday L £21.95-£24.95, Children 10 yrs+

BODIAM
Map 7 TQ72

The Curlew Restaurant
◉◉ Modern British V

tel: 01580 861394 & 861202 **Junction Rd TN32 5UY**
email: enquiries@thecurlewrestaurant.co.uk
dir: *A21 south turn left at Hurst Green signed Bodiam. Restaurant on left at end of road*

Sharply focused modern cooking

A mere few years is all it has taken to resurrect this simple white-painted clapboard coaching inn and transform it into one of East Sussex's foodie hotspots. The clean-cut decor would not look out of place in a chic urban venue, while cow motif wallpaper, antler coat hooks and stag's head mirrors serve as a playful reminder that you're out in the sticks. The vibe is suitably easygoing, helped along by a service team who are well-briefed on the innermost workings of the menu — they need to be, since it merely lists the components of each dish rather than giving any elucidation as to what has actually been done to them. Local produce drives the output, including foraged herbs and mushrooms, while line-caught fish travels a short way from the south coast. The result is clever, of-the-moment, technically accomplished food: wood pigeon carpaccio with truffle custard, salt-baked artichoke and Madeira to get things going, followed by rump of Romney Marsh lamb teamed with grilled little gem lettuce, crispy lamb bacon and a dollop of sour cream. Finish with strawberry shortcake with buttermilk custard.

Chef Tony Parkin **Owner** Mark & Sara Colley **Seats** 64 **Times** 12-2.30/6.30-9.30 **Prices** Fixed L 2 course £20, Fixed D 3 course £25, Starter £8-£11, Main £15.50-£23, Dessert £8-£8.50, Service optional **Wines** 66 bottles over £30, 13 bottles under £30, 19 by glass **Parking** 16 **Notes** Sunday L £17.50-£39, Children welcome

BRIGHTON & HOVE
Map 6 TQ30

Chilli Pickle
◉◉ Regional Indian

tel: 01273 900383 **17 Jubilee St BN1 1GE**
email: info@thechillipickle.com **web:** www.thechillipickle.com
dir: *From the Steine (A23) right into Church Lane & right into Jubilee St. Next to myhotel Brighton, opposite Library*

Vibrant Indian flavours in buzzy venue

The Chilli Pickle has gone from strength to strength since it moved into capacious premises on a pedestrianised square in the regenerated North Laine quarter. Its full-length glass walls create the impression of dining alfresco whatever the weather, offering ringside seats for Brighton's ever-colourful street life. The interior works a contemporary rustic look with chunky wooden tables, blond-wood floors, and vivid splashes of blue and yellow to jazz up the almost Scandinavian minimalism of the place. The menu gives sub-continental clichés and curry house standards a swerve, dealing in smartly reworked thalis, dosai and Indian street-food-inspired dishes at lunchtime — fried coconut and coriander balls coated in potato and served with smoked red pepper, for example, ahead of Rajasthani mutton shoulder curry. At dinner, the kitchen cranks things up a gear, making good use of a brace of tandoors to produce the likes of a whole sea bream coated in green peppercorn chutney served with lemon rice and coconut chutney, or you could go all-out with a platter involving tandoor-roasted chicken, quail, clove-smoked venison, and spiced lamb chop.

Chef Alun Sperring **Owner** Alun & Dawn Sperring **Seats** 115 **Times** 12-3/6-10.30 Closed 25-26 Dec, 1 Jan **Prices** Prices not confirmed, Service optional **Wines** 14 bottles over £30, 29 bottles under £30, 12 by glass **Parking** NCP Church St **Notes** King Thali menu daily £13.50, Sunday L, Vegetarian available, Children welcome

What makes a 5-Rosette restaurant?
See page 9

The Foragers

⚜ Modern European

tel: 01273 733134 **3 Stirling Place BN3 3YU**
email: info@theforagerspub.co.uk **web:** www.theforagerspub.co.uk
dir: A2033 Sackville Rd, left Stirling Place, restaurant 200m on left

Foraged ingredients and more in a popular Hove pub

This buzzy backstreet pub tucked away behind Hove's main drag hums with a casual upbeat vibe. Refreshingly free of designer gastro pretensions, the dining area goes for a likeable shabby-chic look: simple pine-topped pub tables set against funky shades of turquoise and fuchsia pink, and a large mural in blocks of vivid paintbox colours inspired by a Brazilian favela scene that turns the brightness factor up to 11. This, however, has nothing whatsoever to do with the culinary theme, which celebrates splendid seasonal Sussex produce. As its name suggests, the kitchen likes to use wild and foraged ingredients, so wood pigeon breast might start the show, together with sautéed Portobello mushrooms and parsnip purée, before a main course of tender duck breast with confit leg, potato fondant, red cabbage purée and orange jus. Dessert could be an intriguing and eclectic trio of ginger parkin with local Flower Marie cheese, and rosemary and hogweed seed honey.

Chef Patrick Calf **Owner** Paul Hutchison **Seats** 74 **Times** 12-3/6-10 **Prices** Fixed L 2 course fr £12, Fixed D 2 course fr £12, Starter £5-£6.50, Main £12-£20, Dessert £3.50-£6.50, Service optional **Wines** 1 bottle over £30, 24 bottles under £30, 14 by glass **Parking** On street **Notes** Sunday L £11-£14, Vegetarian available, Children welcome

The Gingerman Restaurant

⚜⚜ Modern British

tel: 01273 326688 **21A Norfolk Square BN1 2PD**
email: info@gingermanrestaurants.com
dir: A23 to Palace Pier rdbt. Turn right onto Kings Rd. At art-deco style Embassy building turn right into Norfolk Sq

Modern European cooking and a buzzing atmosphere near the seafront

The original mothership of chef Ben McKellar's Ginger-themed stable of restaurants is tucked away on a side-street close by the seafront. It's a cosy, bistro-style venue decorated in neutral hues and hung with artworks for sale – perhaps paintings of cows and sheep on the South Downs to put you in mind of the kitchen's sound local sourcing ethos. A loyal local fan base keeps the place jam-packed, but on-the-ball staff run it with admirable cool, and it has the unbuttoned vibe that is par for the course in Brighton. Assured modern European ideas kick off with pork cheek with chargrilled leeks, apple, sesame seeds and miso crisps, followed by rump of Sussex lamb with a pistachio and herb crust, confit potatoes, peas and mint jelly – a simple well-conceived combination of flavours which comes together in a lovely, seasonal, vibrantly-coloured dish. Daily fish specials might encompass lemon sole with scallop ravioli, spinach, and horseradish and cucumber sauce. Desserts maintain the standard with another admirably summery pairing: a textbook, well-risen strawberry soufflé with clotted cream ice cream.

Chef Ben McKellar, Dan Kenny **Owner** Ben & Pamela McKellar **Seats** 32 **Times** 12.30-2/7-10 Closed 2 wks from New Year's eve, Mon **Prices** Fixed L 2 course £15, Fixed D 3 course £35, Service optional 12.5% **Wines** 14 bottles over £30, 23 bottles under £30, 14 by glass **Parking** Regency Square NCP **Notes** Sunday L £14.50-£22.50, Vegetarian available, Children welcome

The Grand, Brighton

⚜ Modern European, British, International

tel: 01273 224300 **King's Rd BN1 2FW**
email: reception@grandbrighton.co.uk **web:** www.devere.co.uk
dir: On A259 (seafront road between piers) adjacent to Brighton Centre

Fish specialities in the stylishly remodelled Grand

Following an extensive makeover in 2013, gone is the slightly frowsy air of formality that served The Grand well in Victorian and Edwardian times, and in has come a stylish champagne and oyster bar, while the main dining room is now remodelled as GB1, a fish and seafood venue. The views along the south coast's most well-known seafront, with the spindly ruin of the West Pier standing ankle-deep in the sea, are continuing fixtures, but the menu now feels more in tune with Brighton's gastro-universe. Expect fried whitebait dusted in smoked paprika with garlic mayo, as well as crowd-pleasers like beer-battered pollock and triple-cooked chips, or classic fish pie. A strand of inventiveness also produces perfectly timed sea bass with confit celery, gnocchi and merguez, and there are fine local meats too. Dessert could be sensuously oozy Valrhona chocolate fondant with spiced plum and star anise ice cream.

Chef Alan White **Owner** De Vere **Seats** 140, Pr/dining room 80 **Times** 12.30-2/7-10 **Prices** Fixed L 2 course £12.95, Starter £1.50-£8, Main £12.50-£34, Dessert £5-£7 **Wines** 41 bottles over £30, 17 bottles under £30, 19 by glass **Parking** 43, NCP **Notes** Sunday L £15.95-£23.70, Vegetarian available, Children welcome

BRIGHTON & HOVE *continued*

Graze Restaurant

◉◉ Modern British V

tel: 01273 823707 **42 Western Rd BN3 1JD**
email: info@graze-restaurant.co.uk
dir: *Along A2010 Queens Rd, from clock tower head W on B2066 Western Rd. Restaurant on S/side of road just beyond Brunswick Sq*

Grand Regency setting for inventive, seasonally-inspired modish food

Just a hop away from the Regency grandeur of Hove's Brunswick Square, this smart contemporary venue references the period's style with its crystal chandeliers, mirrors, red flock wallpaper and hues of burgundy and grey. But that's the only nod to the past: the kitchen takes a thoroughly modern approach, setting about its task in an open-to-view space bordered by an ornate gilt frame. Local, seasonal supplies drive the menus, and there's certainly no lack of ambition in seven-course tasting menus that unload the arsenal of foams, purées, gels and powders in support of inventive combinations. A conventional three-course format sets out with cured beef carpaccio with parmesan, shaved truffle and truffle emulsion, Pedro Ximenez vinegar gel and baby artichokes. Next up, rack and belly of salt marsh lamb are supported by almond milk barley, olive purée, confit tomato and fennel; if the nearby briny brings fish to mind, you might go for monkfish with green tea and beetroot broth, beetroot carpaccio, crab foam and crab ravioli. For pudding, caramelised white peach and sorbet sits atop rosemary and white chocolate pannacotta.

Chef Adrian Hawkins **Owner** Kate Alleston, Neil Mannifield **Seats** 50, Pr/dining room 22 **Times** 12-2/6.30-9.30 Closed 1-9 Jan **Prices** Fixed L 3 course £18-£21, Fixed D 3 course £35-£43, Tasting menu £45-£50 **Wines** 34 bottles over £30, 18 bottles under £30, 11 by glass **Notes** Vegetarian tasting menu £45, Tasting menu 7 course, Sunday L £14-£17, Children welcome

Hotel du Vin Brighton

◉ Traditional British, French

tel: 01273 718588 **2-6 Ship St BN1 1AD**
email: info@brighton.hotelduvin.com **web:** www.hotelduvin.com
dir: *A23 to seafront, at rdbt right, then right onto Middle St, bear right into Ship St, hotel at sea end on right*

Upmarket bistro cooking off the seafront

The Brighton branch of the chain, just off the seafront, has all the expected Francophile touches, its walls adorned with wine and spirit posters and risqué pictures, leather-look banquettes running back to back down the centre, and small wooden tables (easily pushed together by nifty staff for larger groups). A glance at the menu shows that this is more than your average bistro fare, with potted crab with caper berries and egg salad followed by ox cheek bourguignon, alongside chicken terrine and bouillabaisse. Evidently the kitchen orders great-quality raw materials, often locally, and treats them with care and respect at the stoves. A simple starter of salmon ballotine with herbed fromage blanc might precede main-course chicken Dijonnaise, moist and full of flavour, with mousseline potatoes. Momentum doesn't falter at the final stretch, with light and tasty pistachio parfait with chocolate ice cream, the plate dotted with thick caramel sauce.

Times 12-2/7-10

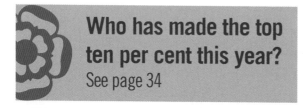

Who has made the top ten per cent this year?
See page 34

The Little Fish Market

◉◉ Modern Fish **NEW**

tel: 01273 722213 **10 Upper Market St BN3 1AS**
email: info@thelittlefishmarket.co.uk
dir: *Just off Western Rd Upper Market St past Co-op. Restaurant on right*

Virtuoso seafood cooking in a simple setting

Opening its doors in early 2013, chef-patron Duncan Ray's first solo venture in a highly promising career has certainly raised the bar for the Brighton and Hove dining scene. Tucked away in a little side street near the seafront, the setting is an open, light-filled space done out with a bare-bones contemporary look: neutral colours, pale wood tables, rustic chairs, quarry-tiled floors, and fish-related art. As the restaurant's name suggests, the focus is on fresh, sustainably-sourced fish and seafood, and with just 20 diners to attend to, Ray's food displays a high degree of technical skill, with tip-top materials raised by a well-considered creative edge. To start, plump and juicy scallops share a plate with caramelised cauliflower and come sharply dressed with an exciting mix of golden raisin, pomegranate, capers and coriander. Next up, more big flavours come courtesy of a super-fresh slab of monkfish matched with pork belly, carrot and star anise purée, squid and pine nuts. To finish, there's a masterclass in the flavours and textures of chocolate, paired with caramel fleur de sel ice cream, caramel sauce and hazelnuts.

Chef Duncan Ray **Owner** Duncan Ray **Seats** 22 **Times** 12-2/7-10 Closed 1 wk Mar, 2 wks Sep, Xmas, Sun-Mon, L Tue **Prices** Starter £7-£10, Main £18-£22, Dessert £7-£10, Service optional **Wines** 10 bottles over £30, 6 bottles under £30, 14 by glass **Parking** On street **Notes** Vegetarian available, No children

Terre à Terre

◉ Modern Vegetarian V

tel: 01273 729051 **71 East St BN1 1HQ**
email: mail@terreaterre.co.uk **web:** www.terreaterre.co.uk
dir: *Town centre, close to Brighton Pier & The Lanes*

Ground-breaking vegetarian and vegan cooking

Terre à Terre is a vegetarian restaurant of ambition which sets the bar for creative, classy veggie-vegan food. It's just up from the seafront, not far from the pier, and generates a happy buzz within. The dining area is bigger than it looks from the outside, stretching back to a small terrace, and the service team are a professional and cheerful bunch and happy to help with the menu. The food has made its mark with its highly creative combinations – and long, detailed dish descriptions – and everything is listed as to its status (gf = no gluten, v = vegan, etc.). Congee shiso yuzu and tempura shiitaki is a satisfying hit of Japanese flavours, whilst main-course Terre à Tiffin includes cauliflower and ginger bhaji and confit brinjal pickle among its delights. The puds are a highlight: Moorish merlot molten mouthful (a take on a chocolate fondant, served with a merlot poached pear), for example.

Chef A Powley, P Taylor **Owner** A Powley, P Taylor **Seats** 110 **Times** 12-10.30 Closed 25-26 Dec, All-day dining **Prices** Fixed L 3 course £26, Fixed D 3 course £26,

Starter £6.10-£8.95, Main £13.95-£14.95, Dessert £6.20-£9.20, Service optional **Wines** 14 bottles over £30, 40 bottles under £30, 14 by glass **Parking** NCP, on street **Notes** Promotional fixed price L & D menus available, Children welcome

Twenty Four St Georges

◉◉ Modern European **NEW**

tel: 01273 626060 **24-25 St Georges Rd, Kemp Town Village BN2 1ED**
email: reservations@24stgeorges.co.uk
dir: *A23 Brighton, left onto Edward St to Eastern Rd, right onto College Place, left onto St George's Rd*

Creative cooking in relaxed neighbourhood venue

Tucked away in the quiet end of Kemp Town village, just back from the seafront, chef-proprietors Dean Heselden and Jamie Everton-Jones have been quietly carving themselves a niche in the local foodie scene. The dining room is a relaxed and unshouty space, and the culinary deal is straightforward, well-executed dishes with an emphasis on local, seasonal produce – as you might hope when the splendid bounty of the Sussex coast and South Downs is on the doorstep. A starter of lobster cannelloni with Sussex blue cheese, tarragon, lemon gel and apple sets the tone, before a main course starring free-range chicken – breast and ballotine with chorizo stuffing – with a truffled croquette, oyster mushrooms, spring greens and Rioja jus. Fish might appear in the shape of pan-fried brill with Parmentier potatoes, seasonal vegetables, squid, and cider and tarragon sauce. Desserts range from chocolate and orange sponge with a crunchy piece of honeycomb, and the tang of mango bavarois and sorbet, to lemon drizzle cake with rhubarb ice cream, poached rhubarb, caramelised apple and meringue tuile.

Chef Dean Heselden **Owner** Jamie Everton-Jones, Dean Heselden **Seats** 52, Pr/dining room 12 **Times** 6-9.30 Closed 25-26 Dec, 1-2 & 11-19 Jan, Sun-Mon, L Tue-Fri **Prices** Fixed L 2 course £18.95, Fixed D 3 course £36-£44, Tasting menu £50, Starter £6.95-£10.50, Main £11.95-£23.95, Dessert £6.95-£7.95, Service optional **Wines** 29 bottles over £30, 21 bottles under £30, 8 by glass **Parking** On street voucher **Notes** Vegetarian available, Children welcome

---

CAMBER Map 7 TV91

The Gallivant

◉◉ Modern & Traditional British

tel: 01797 225057 **New Lydd Rd TN31 7RB**
email: mark@thegallivanthotel.com **web:** www.thegallivanthotel.com
dir: *M29 junct 10 to A2070, left Camber Road before Rye. Hotel located on left in Camber Village*

Local meats and seafood with New England style

Overlooking the Camber shoreline near Rye, the Gallivant has its heart in New England, where that laid-back eastern seaboard style translates as oceans of space, light wood, café furniture and a feeling that you might have stepped accidentally onto a small cruise-liner. Sourcing from within a 30-mile radius is an especially good idea when the radius takes in impeccable bay seafood, Sussex charcuterie and salt marsh lamb. Ben Fisher sensibly keeps things simple, offering a brasserie menu that opens with half-pints of prawns, and oysters in shallot vinegar, as well as sharing boards of shellfish or meaty stuff like rillettes, chorizo and Scotch egg. Once you get into the main menu, there are classics such as devilled crab with melted cheese and soldiers, then catch of the day with hollandaise or salsa verde, or rump and ribs of local beef in red wine, and that all-important salt marsh lamb, served with truffle-oiled green beans, garlic aubergine and buttery mash. Sides include a salad of caramelised orange and fennel, and the closer could be warm chocolate doughnuts with thick cream for dunking.

Chef Ben Fisher **Owner** Harry Cragoe **Seats** 55, Pr/dining room 100 **Times** 12-3/6-9.30 Closed L Mon-Wed **Prices** Fixed D 3 course £27, Starter £6-£9, Main £12-£22, Dessert £6-£8 **Wines** 41 bottles over £30, 38 bottles under £30, 20 by glass **Parking** 20 **Notes** Sunday L £27-£29, Vegetarian available, Children welcome

---

EASTBOURNE Map 6 TV69

The Grand Hotel

◉◉ Modern, Classic ⟡ NOTABLE WINE LIST

tel: 01323 412345 **King Edward's Pde BN21 4EQ**
email: reservations@grandeastbourne.com **web:** www.grandeastbourne.com
dir: *Western end of seafront, 1m from Eastbourne station*

Grand seafront hotel with confident modern cooking

Built in 1875, Eastbourne's Grand Hotel – the 'White Palace' to its friends – embodies glorious Victorian Empire pomp like few other British seaside hotels. The grande dame of the seafront has hosted some famous faces over the years including Winston Churchill, Charlie Chaplin, Elgar, and Debussy who composed La Mer on his hols here in 1905. Naturally, the old girl has had a facelift to keep her 21st-century guests sweet, but some things don't change, such as that fine institution of afternoon tea, served in the marble-columned majesty of the Great Hall. The fine dining Mirabelle restaurant is an equally ritzy old-school setting, but there's nothing passé about the kitchen's contemporary take on flavour combinations and textures. When the silver cloches are lifted, the plates beneath reveal modern European thinking: to start, a crabmeat, tomato and saffron brûlée with soused cucumber, pickled ginger and toasted brioche, followed by slow-braised shin of beef with creamed potatoes, Tête de Moine cheese, and goulash sauce. A Granny Smith apple crumble with Calvados ice cream and custard makes a fine finale.

Chef Keith Mitchell, Gerald Roser **Owner** Elite Hotels **Seats** 50 **Times** 12.30-2/7-10 Closed 2-16 Jan, Sun-Mon **Prices** Fixed L 2 course fr £21, Fixed D 3 course fr £39, Tasting menu £61-£93, Starter £5.50-£8.75, Main £8-£16, Service optional **Wines** 237 bottles over £30, 26 bottles under £30, 17 by glass **Parking** 70 **Notes** Fixed L/D supplements added to price, Tasting menu 5 course, Sunday L fr £29, Vegetarian available, No children

See advert on page 496

EASTBOURNE *continued*

Langham Hotel

 Modern British

tel: 01323 731451 **43-49 Royal Pde BN22 7AH**
email: neil@langhamhotel.co.uk web: www.langhamhotel.co.uk
dir: *A22 follow signs for seafront Sovereign Centre, take 3rd exit onto Royal Pde. Hotel on corner Royal Pde & Cambridge Rd*

Enterprising modern cooking on the seafront

The Langham is composed of three knocked-through Victorian houses on the seafront, with wide views over the bay towards the pier. Standards are high, in terms of both comfort levels and the quality of the cooking in the Conservatory restaurant, which has the same expansive sea views. The short menu is a stylish assembly, the cooking based on fresh local produce: fish landed locally, lamb from the South Downs, for instance. Quail, from Wilmington, is roasted and served with pancetta, Brussels sprouts and a redcurrant jus, and roast monkfish comes with mussels and clams flavoured with saffron. Starters, meanwhile, can be as sophisticated as seared scallops with black pudding, creamed leeks and apples, or salade Niçoise with tuna mousse and a quail's egg. Desserts are often updated versions of the familiar given a novel flourish, for instance pear baked in caramelised filo, served with custard, or ginger and honey ice cream for sticky toffee pudding.

Chef Michael Titherington **Owner** Neil & Wendy Kirby **Seats** 24 **Times** 12-2.30/6-9.30 **Prices** Service optional **Wines** 1 bottle over £30, 29 bottles under £30, 15 by glass **Notes** Sunday L £15-£20.95, Vegetarian available, Children welcome

What makes a 3-Rosette restaurant?
See page 9

Ashdown Park Hotel & Country Club

 Modern British | NOTABLE WINE LIST

tel: 01342 824988 **Wych Cross RH18 5JR**
email: reservations@ashdownpark.com web: www.ashdownpark.com
dir: *A264 to East Grinstead, then A22 to Eastbourne. 2m S of Forest Row at Wych Cross lights. Left to Hartfield, hotel on right 0.75m*

Grand hotel dining in an upmarket country house

Everything about the swanky Ashdown Park Hotel and Country Club is done in the high-flown style you would expect of an upscale Victorian country house: its 186 acres of landscaped gardens and parkland are secluded in the depths of Ashdown Forest, and there's an 18-hole golf course and a fitness and spa complex. Gents will need to pack a jacket and tie, and everyone can expect old-school formality in the Anderida Restaurant, where the front of house staff deliver all the precision of silver service. On the plate comes flamboyantly-presented classical cuisine, glossed up with modern takes on time-honoured ideas and fashionably-deconstructed dishes: a starter of smoked haddock fish 'pie', for example, presented in a Kilner jar with a scallop on top, pea purée, prawn toast and a tranche of fish terrine. Main course brings roasted rump of lamb with a pastilla of shoulder teamed with sweet

FIVE STAR OPULENCE
BY THE SEA…

DELIGHTFUL CREATIONS IN THE
MIRABELLE RESTAURANT

THE INVITING AMBIENCE OF
THE GARDEN RESTAURANT

The Grand Hotel, King Edwards Parade,
Eastbourne, East Sussex, BN21 4EQ

01323 412345
www.grandeastbourne.com

tomato risotto and pesto, then a final flourish of brown sugar parfait with banana rice pudding, exotic foam and honeycomb brings down the curtain.

Chef Andrew Wilson **Owner** Elite Hotels **Seats** 120, Pr/dining room 160 **Times** 12-2/7-10 **Prices** Prices not confirmed, Service optional **Wines** 250 bottles over £30, 16 bottles under £30, 12 by glass **Parking** 120 **Notes** Tasting menu 8 course, Sunday L, Vegetarian available, Children welcome

See advert below

HASTINGS & ST LEONARDS   Map 7 TQ80

Jali Restaurant

◎ Traditional and Modern Indian

tel: 01424 457300 & 720188 **Chatsworth Hotel, 7-11 Carlisle Pde TN34 1JG**
email: info@chatsworthhotel.com **web:** www.jalirestaurant.co.uk
dir: *On Hastings seafront, near railway station*

An Indian flavour by the seaside

The original in a small chain that now includes Crewe and Blackpool amongst its number, Jali is in the Chatsworth Hotel, with a prime seafront position close to the old town and the pier. It's all very civilised inside, with some Indian artefacts and artworks dotted around but resisting clichés, with tables smartly dressed in white linen cloths. The menu also avoids the typical curry house standards; start, perhaps, with gin-fried chicken, the meat marinated in the said booze and stir-fried

with fresh herbs, and from the long kebab section there might be noorani seekh (minced lamb kebab) or salmon sula (grilled in the tandoor with a lime and herb crust). There's plenty for vegetarians, too, such as a main-course khumb kaju curry (mushrooms and cashew nuts in a spicy tomato, onion and yoghurt gravy) and meat course might be dal gosht (lamb cooked with lentils).

Times 6-10.30 Closed Sun, L all week

LEWES   Map 6 TQ41

Jolly Sportsman

◎◎ Modern British, European

tel: 01273 890400 **Chapel Ln, East Chiltington BN7 3BA**
email: info@thejollysportsman.com
dir: *From Lewes A275, East Grinstead road, left onto the B2116 Offham, 2nd right into Novington Lane. In approx 1m first left Chapel Lane*

Rustic-chic inn serving up hearty food with a true Sussex flavour

Tucked away among the meadows and rural lanes of the Sussex hinterland, chef-patron Bruce Wass's weatherboarded country inn is well worth hunting down. Inside, there's an inviting and cosy bar area with casks on trestles, but the place is clearly much more than a simple rustic boozer: sage-green walls hung with colourful works from local artists, mellow oak flooring and great rough-hewn oak slab tables add up to the tastefully uncluttered country-chic look of a switched-on modern dining inn. The kitchen delivers vibrant, contemporary cooking with a spot-on feel for sourcing the freshest, local and seasonal produce. Smoked ham hock terrine with celeriac remoulade and pickled shallot makes a robustly rustic opener, while superb, meltingly-tender slow-cooked pork belly with home-made sausage roll, quince aïoli, cider gravy, colcannon and green beans is a superior version of an old favourite. Fans of local fish might find roast brill (landed in Newhaven) with chive sauce, white beans and salsa verde. Gingerbread pudding with rich sea salt butterscotch sauce and vanilla ice cream makes a richly comforting finish.

Chef Bruce Wass **Owner** Bruce Wass **Seats** 80, Pr/dining room 20 **Times** 12-3/6.30-10 Closed 25 Dec, Mon (ex BHs), D Sun **Prices** Fixed L 2 course fr £14.50, Fixed D 2 course fr £19.85, Starter £5.85-£9.85, Main fr £13.75, Dessert fr £5.75, Service optional 10% **Wines** 80 bottles over £30, 40 bottles under £30, 13 by glass **Parking** 35 **Notes** Sunday L fr £16.45, Vegetarian available, Children welcome

SITUATED IN THE HEART OF
THE ASHDOWN FOREST

WE USE ONLY THE FINEST AND
FRESHEST INGREDIENTS

THE GRAND SETTING OF THE
ANDERIDA RESTAURANT

Ashdown Park Hotel & Country Club,
nr Forest Row, East Sussex, RH18 5JR

01342 824988
www.ashdownpark.co.uk

RYE

Map 7 TQ92

The George in Rye

Modern Mediterranean

tel: 01797 222114 **98 High St TN31 7JT**
email: stay@thegeorgeinrye.com **web:** www.thegeorgeinrye.com
dir: *M20 junct 10, then A2070 to Brenzett then A259 to Rye*

Stylish modern brasserie in a 16th-century building

It may have a venerable history, having taken root on this spot back in 1575, but The George is not stuck in the past. It's a smart and stylish boutique hotel that blends period features with contemporary good taste, and offers brasserie-style dining in The George Grill. There's no old-school stuffiness here. The menu is equally of the moment, featuring lots of local produce and making good use of the kitchen's charcoal grill. Start with salt and pepper squid with a home-made green chilli and coriander mayonnaise, but it's hard to skip the Rye Bay scallops (with cauliflower purée and vegetables à la grecque, perhaps). Main-course oven-baked cod has a soft herb crust and accompanying tomato fondue, or go for Romney March lamb or rib-eye steak. For dessert you could try a baked vanilla rice pudding with berry compôte and almond biscotti.

Chef Robert Wright **Owner** Alex & Katie Clarke **Seats** 60, Pr/dining room 100 **Times** 12-3/6.30-9.30 **Prices** Starter £7-£10, Main £12-£22, Dessert £6 **Wines** 12 bottles over £30, 9 bottles under £30, 17 by glass **Parking** On street **Notes** Vegetarian available, Children welcome

Mermaid Inn

British, Traditional French v

tel: 01797 223065 **Mermaid St TN31 7EY**
email: info@mermaidinn.com **web:** www.mermaidinn.com
dir: *A259, follow signs to town centre, then into Mermaid St*

Atmospheric medieval inn with modish menu

The cellars at the Mermaid Inn date from the 12th century, the inn itself from a mere 1420, so it is only 600 years old. In a town filled with spellbinding period buildings, this old inn has lots of historic charm and atmosphere. Check out the giant inglenook fireplace in the bar with its priest's hole, and the linenfold panels in the restaurant. The food takes an Anglo-French path and there are some appealingly contemporary dishes on the menu. You might start with the modish salt and pepper squid (from the south coast) with sweet chilli and coriander, or the more Francophile pressed duck leg terrine with toasted brioche, fruit chutney and watercress salad. Main course might serve up braised shoulder of Romney Marsh lamb (local ingredients get a good showing here) with chestnut mushrooms, baby onions, parsley creamed potatoes and pancetta. Finish with winter berry soufflé with orange crème anglaise and white chocolate ice cream.

Chef Kyle Tatner **Owner** J Blincow & G Kite **Seats** 64, Pr/dining room 14 **Times** 12-2.30/7-9.30 **Prices** Fixed L 2 course £21, Fixed D 3 course £38.50-£48.50 **Wines** 15 bottles over £30, 22 bottles under £30, 15 by glass **Parking** 26 **Notes** Sunday L £22-£26, Children welcome

Webbes at The Fish Café

Modern British

tel: 01797 222226 **17 Tower St TN31 7AT**
email: info@thefishcafe.com
dir: *100mtrs before Landgate Arch*

Local seafood in an informal converted warehouse

This three-storey converted warehouse in Rye's centre is home to a ground floor restaurant, above which is a private function room, with cookery demonstrations held on the top floor. There's a lively informal vibe in the restaurant making it popular with families and tourists alike. An open-plan kitchen provides some entertainment and red-brick walls showcase sea related artwork. Excellent quality fish and seafood, confidently prepared, comes mainly from Rye and Hastings ports, but meat eaters and veggies won't feel left out. Begin with a shellfish platter, or mackerel fritters with mirin and lime dressing, vegetable salad and chilli jam, or pork and wild mushroom rillette with red onion marmalade. Roast fillet of wild sea bass, brown shrimps, leek risotto and shellfish sauce hits the spot. Puddings might include vanilla pannacotta with strawberry ice cream and fresh strawberries. An affordable global wine list adds to the appeal.

Chef Paul Webbe, Matthew Drinkwater **Owner** Paul & Rebecca Webbe **Seats** 52, Pr/dining room 60 **Times** 11.30-2.30/6-9.30 Closed 24 Dec-10 Jan **Prices** Prices not confirmed, Service optional **Wines** 10 by glass **Parking** Cinque Port Street **Notes** Sunday L, Vegetarian available, Children welcome

TICEHURST

Map 6 TQ63

Dale Hill Hotel & Golf Club

Modern European

tel: 01580 200112 **TN5 7DQ**
email: info@dalehill.co.uk **web:** www.dalehill.co.uk
dir: *M25 junct 5/A21. 5m after Lamberhurst turn right at lights onto B2087 to Flimwell. Hotel 1m on left*

Imaginative modern European menu in a golfing hotel

With its duo of 18-hole courses, golf may be the signature dish at this hotel and country club in a fabulous location high on the Sussex Weald, but for non-players, uplifting views over the hills of East Sussex, a heated indoor pool and gym, and a brace of dining options are reasons enough to come. Of the two restaurants, the expansive fine-dining Wealden Restaurant is the star attraction, and it comes –

perhaps inevitably – with vistas of the 18th green. Modern European cooking is par for this particular course, and it appears in some appetising ideas. You might tee off with pan-fried scallops with crisp pig's cheeks, celeriac purée and chestnut pesto, and follow on with a Barnsley lamb chop with watercress, confit shallots, pommes frites and Bordelaise sauce, or wild mushroom tagliatelle with parmesan and truffle oil. Finish with pistachio and white chocolate mousse with pomegranate foam and lemon sorbet.

Chef Mark Carter **Owner** Mr & Mrs Paul Gibbons **Seats** 60, Pr/dining room 24 **Times** 12–2.30/6.30–9 Closed 25 Dec, L Mon-Sat **Prices** Fixed D 3 course £25, Starter £5.50–£8, Main £12.95–£18.95, Dessert £6.50–£7.50, Service optional **Wines** 8 bottles over £30, 29 bottles under £30, 7 by glass **Parking** 220 **Notes** Sunday L £9–£16, Vegetarian available, Children welcome

---

UCKFIELD	Map 6 TQ42

Buxted Park Hotel

◉◉ Modern European V

tel: 01825 733333 **Buxted TN22 4AY**
email: buxtedpark@handpicked.co.uk **web:** www.handpickedhotels.co.uk/buxtedpark
dir: From A26 (Uckfield bypass) take A272 signed Buxted. Through lights, hotel 1m on right

Pace-setting modern British cooking in a pristine Palladian mansion

Buxted is the full country-house package, a graceful white Palladian mansion rising above immaculately laid gardens, with a pillared portico entrance and deep windows. It was built in the early Georgian era for Thomas Medley, who had made a fortune as a port shipper during Britain's periodic hostilities with France. A striking layout in the dining room features a mix of booth and table seating, with lilac upholstery against a pristine white backdrop. Steve Cole arrived at the end of 2013 to take over the pace-setting modern British operation here, and produces an entertaining and carefully composed version of the style. Crispy pork bonbons with pickled apple, rocket and grain mustard might provide a way into main courses such as sea bass with crushed thyme potatoes and glazed fennel in caviar butter, or stuffed rabbit saddle with confit leg, puréed carrot and braised red cabbage in blackberry jus. A gentle finale is offered by the straightforward approach to desserts: expect lemon tart with clotted cream, or vanilla pannacotta with cherry sorbet.

Chef Steve Cole **Owner** Hand Picked Hotels **Seats** 40, Pr/dining room 120 **Times** 12–2/7–9.30 **Prices** Fixed L 2 course fr £16.50, Fixed D 3 course £38, Tasting menu £64–£99, Starter £12.50–£15.50, Main £23.50–£33.95, Dessert £6.50–£10.50, Service optional **Wines** 95 bottles over £30, 5 bottles under £30, 18 by glass **Parking** 100 **Notes** Dégustation 7 course with/without wine, Sunday L £25.95, Children welcome

---

East Sussex National Golf Resort & Spa

◉ British, French

tel: 01825 880088 **Little Horsted TN22 5ES**
email: reception@eastsussexnational.co.uk **web:** www.eastsussexnational.co.uk
dir: M25 junct 6, A22 signed East Grinstead & Eastbourne. Straight on at rdbt junct of A22 & A26 (Little Horsted). At next rdbt right to hotel

Well-executed modern cooking and golf

The name nails this sprawling, purpose-built operation's colours to the mast. And if it would appear that you must be here for its two obvious core attractions – the fairways of its two championship golf courses and spa pampering treatments – there is a very good third reason to be here, and that is the fine dining on offer in the Pavilion restaurant. The setting is on the minimal end of the contemporary spectrum, and looks through a wall of full-length windows onto the greens and the rolling South Downs countryside. The kitchen has the bountiful produce of Sussex close to hand, which it deploys in appealing ideas along the lines of pan-seared

rabbit loin with bacon and leek risotto balls and béarnaise sauce, followed by roast venison from the estate served with Lyonnaise potatoes, buttered curly kale, broad beans and wild mushroom jus.

Times 12–2.30/7–9 Closed L Sun

Horsted Place

◉◉ Modern British

tel: 01825 750581 **Little Horsted TN22 5TS**
email: hotel@horstedplace.co.uk **web:** www.horstedplace.co.uk
dir: From Uckfield 2m S on A26 towards Lewes

Unpretentious country-house cooking in Victorian Gothic masterpiece

When you're in the mood for a hit of Victorian Gothic splendour, Horsted Place delivers in spades: the house was built in 1850 by George Myers, with Pugin taking care of the details. It sits in 1,000 acres of verdant Sussex countryside with, oh yes, two championship golf courses, a tennis court and croquet on the lawn. Inside is as ornate as is to be expected, with well-spaced tables dressed in floor-length linen, and pictures of landscapes and horses in the dining room. Despite a few modernist tweaks, the country-house cooking does nothing to frighten those horses, but sticks to tried-and-true combinations, achieved with assured technical ability. Chargrilled baby squid appear with braised fennel, mangetout and aïoli dressing, while a main course brings beef fillet with shallot and potato rösti, creamed leeks, girolles, green beans and red wine sauce. On the fish front, there might be pan-seared stone bass fillet with olive oil mash, provençal tomato and gremolata. Finish with limoncello cake with vanilla pannacotta and brandy-roasted peach.

Chef Allan Garth **Owner** Perinon Ltd **Seats** 40, Pr/dining room 80 **Times** 12–2/7–9.30 Closed 1st wk Jan, L Sat **Prices** Fixed L 2 course £18.95, Starter £9.50, Main £20, Dessert £8.50, Service optional **Wines** 74 bottles over £30, 24 bottles under £30, 9 by glass **Parking** 50 **Notes** Afternoon tea £18.50, Sunday L £28.50, Vegetarian available, Children 7 yrs+

WESTFIELD	Map 7 TQ81

The Wild Mushroom Restaurant

◉◉ Modern British

tel: 01424 751137 **Woodgate House, Westfield Ln TN35 4SB**
email: info@wildmushroom.co.uk
dir: From A21 towards Hastings, left onto A28 to Westfield. Restaurant 1.5m on left

Modern British cooking in a charming converted farmhouse

A converted 19th-century farmhouse surrounded by countryside just a short drive from Hastings, Paul and Rebecca Webbe's restaurant is part of a mini-empire that includes Webbe's at The Fish Café in Rye and Rock-a-nore in Hastings Old Town. The restaurant takes up the whole of the ground floor, with a conservatory bar overlooking a small garden at the rear. There are original features like flagged floors and low beams, and a smart country feel to the place, helped along by the friendly service. Sharp, contemporary cooking is the name of the game, with ingredients shipped in locally from trusted suppliers and due heed paid to the seasons. There are set lunch, à la carte and tasting menus to choose from, with canapés, an amuse-bouche and home-made breads all part of the package. Pork and wild mushroom rillette served with toasted granary bread and home-made piccalilli is a switched on starter, with slow-cooked ox cheek with garlic mash and Shiraz jus a hit among main courses.

Chef Paul Webbe, Christopher Weddle **Owner** Mr & Mrs P Webbe **Seats** 40 **Times** 12–2.30/7–10 Closed 25 Dec, 2 wks at New Year, Mon-Tue, D Sun **Prices** Fixed L 2 course £16.95, Tasting menu fr £34, Starter £5.95–£8.95, Main £12.95–£19.95, Dessert £7, Service optional **Wines** 6 by glass **Parking** 20 **Notes** Tasting menu 6 course, Sunday L £24, Vegetarian available, Children welcome

WILMINGTON
Map 6 TQ50

Crossways

 Modern British

tel: 01323 482455 **Lewes Rd BN26 5SG**
email: stay@crosswayshotel.co.uk **web:** www.crosswayshotel.co.uk
dir: On A27, 2m W of Polegate

Country-house dining in relaxed restaurant with rooms

Crossways, a Georgian house below the South Downs Way, was at one time the home of Elizabeth David's parents, and foodies can pay their respects to the writer as her grave is a short distance away. A monthly-changing four-course dinner is served in the small and comfortable dining room, with its private party vibe created in part by relaxed service from the proprietors. The well-balanced menu could kick off with seafood pancake, or smoked duck and Asian pear salad, with a soup of the day to follow. Main courses reflect the kitchen's straightforward, uncluttered approach to its output – perhaps game pie in a rich gravy – and sauces and garnishes are well considered: wild mushroom sauce for sautéed loin of local venison, say, mango, ginger and cranberry for roast breast of Gressingham duck, and a maple glaze for pork tenderloin in a parmesan crumb coating.

Chef David Stott **Owner** David Stott, Clive James **Seats** 24 **Times** 7.30-8.30 Closed 24 Dec-24 Jan, Sun-Mon, L all week **Prices** Prices not confirmed, Service optional **Wines** 11 bottles over £30, 28 bottles under £30, 10 by glass **Parking** 20 **Notes** 4 course D £42.50, Vegetarian available, No children

WEST SUSSEX

ALBOURNE
Map 6 TQ21

The Ginger Fox

 Modern British

tel: 01273 857888 **Muddleswood Rd BN6 9EA**
email: gingerfox@gingermanrestaurants.com
dir: On A281 at junct with B2117

Classy country gastro-pub

Part of a small Brighton-based group, The Ginger Fox is a country pub with the South Downs as its backyard and food very much at its heart. Done out in modern gastro-pub fashion, it blends neutral tones, unclothed oak tables, black tiled floors and enough original features to remind you of the antiquity of the old thatched building. The kitchen deals in up-to-the-minute dishes conjured from locally-sourced ingredients and is not afraid to travel the globe for inspiration. Roasted harissa spring chicken with pea and mint tabouleh, baba ganoush and coriander yoghurt sits alongside pork and cider pie with mash, spring greens and gravy, and to finish, perhaps a tropically influenced passionfruit posset (with mango jelly and coconut tapioca) or crowd-pleasing dark chocolate brownie. There's a garden with views of the Downs too.

Chef Ben McKellar, James Dearden **Owner** Ben & Pamela McKellar **Seats** 50, Pr/dining room 24 **Times** 12-2/6-10 Closed 25 Dec **Prices** Prices not confirmed, Service optional **Wines** 18 bottles over £30, 25 bottles under £30, 20 by glass **Parking** 60 **Notes** Fixed L 2 course Mon-Fri until 7pm, Sunday L, Vegetarian available, Children welcome

AMBERLEY
Map 6 TQ01

Amberley Castle

 – see opposite

ARUNDEL
Map 6 TQ00

The Town House

 Modern V

tel: 01903 883847 **65 High St BN18 9AJ**
email: enquiries@thetownhouse.co.uk **web:** www.thetownhouse.co.uk
dir: Follow A27 to Arundel, onto High Street, establishment on left at top of hill

Classy bistro cooking facing Arundel Castle

The next best thing to dining with the Duke of Norfolk in Arundel Castle itself is to bag a table at the Regency townhouse restaurant with rooms that sits on a town-centre hill facing it. It's a place of enormous charm and heart, topped off with a superb gilt carved ceiling originally transported from Florence. Tables are quite tightly packed, making for a sense of affable esprit de corps, and staff manage that elusive balance of amiability and polish that ensures a classy operation. Lee Williams takes the best of Sussex produce as his inspiration for dishes that have sound bistro appeal. Sautéed foie gras with red onion chutney and home-made brioche is a simple but well-executed starter, and may be followed by turbot with basil mash and spinach, or the signature South Downs venison fillet with wild mushrooms, baby onions and crisp roast potato. It's all very carefully timed and presented with aplomb, and when a dessert like intense chocolate tart with smoothly rich vanilla ice cream turns up to seal the deal, happiness is assured.

Chef Lee Williams **Owner** Lee & Kate Williams **Seats** 24 **Times** 12-2.30/7-9.30 Closed 2 wks Etr, 2 wks Oct, Xmas, Sun-Mon **Prices** Fixed L 2 course fr £17.50, Fixed D 3 course fr £29.50, Service optional **Wines** 53 bottles over £30, 29 bottles under £30, 9 by glass **Parking** On street or nearby car park **Notes** Children welcome

BOSHAM
Map 5 SU80

The Millstream Hotel & Restaurant

 Modern British

tel: 01243 573234 **Bosham Ln PO18 8HL**
email: info@millstreamhotel.com **web:** www.millstreamhotel.com
dir: 4m W of Chichester on A259, left at Bosham rdbt. After 0.5m right at T-junct signed to church & quay. Hotel 0.5m on right

Stylish inventive cooking in a charming quiet setting

Built of red brick and flint, the building was originally three 17th-century workmen's cottages, and has since earned a crust as a charming hotel. On a balmy evening, the fabulous lawned gardens with ducks quacking along the millstream make an idyllic spot for drinks, or you could join the yachtie crew in the convivial bar. The kitchen stays abreast of modern trends while keeping traditionalists happy with crowd-pleasing menus that bring new dishes each day. Starters can be as classic as warm chicken terrine with Caesar salad and grilled sourdough, or might push the boundaries a touch with the likes of smoked haddock and leek tart with a crispy egg yolk and crème fraîche. Quality is clear in the raw materials, and combinations are intelligently thought through, so fillet of sea bass is partnered by shellfish bisque, crab beignets and Jersey Royals, and fillet of beef by truffle mash, morels, and smoked bone marrow. Puddings are worth exploring: perhaps basil pannacotta with strawberry jelly and Champagne granita.

Chef Neil Hiskey **Owner** The Wild family **Seats** 60, Pr/dining room 40 **Times** 12.30-2/6.30-9 **Prices** Fixed L 2 course fr £21, Fixed D 3 course fr £34, Tasting menu fr £55, Service optional **Wines** 28 bottles over £30, 34 bottles under £30, 13 by glass **Parking** 40 **Notes** Tasting menu with wine 6 course, Pre-theatre menu, Sunday L £21.50-£26.50, Vegetarian available, Children welcome

---

CHICHESTER
Map 5 SU80

Crouchers Country Hotel & Restaurant

 Modern British

tel: 01243 784995 & 07887 744570 **Birdham Rd PO20 7EH**
email: crouchers@btconnect.com **web:** www.croucherscountryhotel.com
dir: From A27 Chichester bypass onto A286 towards West Wittering, 2m, hotel on left between Chichester Marina & Dell Quay

Imaginative cooking in stylish hotel

A fixture on the Chichester area's dining scene for many a year, Crouchers has morphed from a simple B&B to a smart modern hotel with an inviting wine bar and stylish oak-beamed restaurant looking over open green countryside near to Dell Quay and the marina. What keeps this well-run operation perennially popular is a pleasing lack of airs and graces, and a kitchen that takes a serious approach to its work – that means bringing out the best from splendid locally-sourced raw materials to produce well-composed, imaginative modern ideas, as in a starter of wild mushroom and white truffle risotto matched with deep-fried blue cheese beignets and garlic pesto. The main course brings an ambitious composition of rabbit loin stuffed with spinach and tarragon mousse, partnered by braised Puy lentils, butternut squash purée and tarragon reduction. Desserts are no mere afterthought either, as shown by the well-balanced flavours and textures of a salted

caramel and white chocolate fondant served with a nibbed cocoa tuile and raspberry sorbet.

Times 12-2.30/7-9.30

Earl of March

 British

tel: 01243 533993 & 783991 **Lavant Rd PO18 0BQ**
email: info@theearlofmarch.com
dir: On A286, 2m N of Chichester towards Midhurst, on the corner of Goodwood Estate

Classy cooking in revamped old pub

The view represents this part of Sussex through-and-through: the South Downs and Goodwood racecourse form the backdrop. This traditional 18th-century coaching inn has been made-over for modern times, on the inside at least, and has an opened-up, smart finish which is very easy on the eye, with darkwood tables and swish leather chairs. During the summer months there's a seafood and champagne shack in the former bakehouse. The menu can sort you out with some classic pub dishes such as Sussex ham with free-range eggs and hand-cut chips, but equally you might go for 'double duck', which is honey-glazed breast with a faggot made from the leg meat, fondant potato and spiced plum sauce. Or you might start with a fillet of red mullet with scallop mousseline, prawn tempura and Bloody Mary mayonnaise, and finish with white chocolate and rhubarb pannacotta with black pepper and chocolate crumb.

Chef Giles Thompson, Luke Gale **Owner** Giles & Ruth Thompson **Seats** 60, Pr/dining room 16 **Times** 12-2.30/5.30-9.30 **Prices** Fixed L 2 course £17.50-£19.50, Fixed D 3 course £19.50, Starter £6.50-£8.50, Main £13.50-£25, Dessert £6.50-£7, Service optional **Wines** 42 bottles over £30, 33 bottles under £30, 24 by glass **Parking** 30 **Notes** Pre-theatre/Early bird menu 2/3 course, Sunday L fr £15.50, Vegetarian available, Children welcome

---

Amberley Castle

AMBERLEY
Map 6 TQ01

Modern British NEW v
tel: 01798 831992 **BN18 9LT**
email: info@amberleycastle.co.uk **web:** www.amberleycastle.co.uk
dir: Off B2139 between Storrington & Houghton

Confident cooking in a one-off historical setting

Arriving here along the drive through 12 acres of grounds where peacocks and alpacas roam transports you back 900 years to a bygone age. This Norman castle is the real deal with a portcullis and twin-tower gatehouse, imposing battlements running along a 60-foot-high curtain wall, and sweeping views of the South Downs as a backdrop; within are stone vaults, lancet windows, Norman arches and enough medieval weaponry to re-enact the Battle of Agincourt, all opulently swathed in the ultra-plush decor of a top-flight modern hotel. The Queen's Room restaurant is no less grand with its 12th-century barrel-vaulted ceiling, open fireplace, murals and tapestries, and a front-of-house team that defuses any suggestion of stuffiness. The kitchen brigade is led by Robby Jenks who is no stranger to posh country house kitchens and highly skilled at delivering big flavours in a contemporary European style with lots of twists along the way,

without losing sight of the basic elements of seasonality and local sourcing. Proceedings open with pan-fried foiegras matched with rhubarb purée as a foil to its richness, and hazelnuts and pain d'épice crumb to add crunch, or you might opt for a more delicate chicken mousse with herb purée, wild mushrooms and seasonal vegetables. Combinations are built up with apposite logic, so main-course sees perfectly-timed pan-fried cod partnered with saffron, mussels and leek fondue, or pork tenderloin might be partnered with its belly, black pudding, pickled white cabbage and broad bean purée. Dessert is an inventive finale involving wild strawberry mousse with sweet woodruff granita, and olive oil and vanilla soil, and a similarly creative approach might see sea buckthorn soufflé alongside camomile ice cream and crystallised coconut. The wine list is a country-house heavyweight ably supported by a switched-on sommelier.

Chef Robby Jenks **Owner** Andrew Brownsword **Times** 12-2/7-9 **Prices** Fixed L 3 course £25.50-£30.50, Fixed D 3 course £65, Tasting menu £85, Service optional **Wines** 171 bottles over £30, 15 by glass **Parking** 40 **Notes** Sunday L £30.50, Children 8yrs+

CHICHESTER *continued*

Halliday's

 Modern British

tel: 01243 575331 **Watery Ln, Funtington PO18 9LF**
email: hallidaysdinners@aol.com
dir: *4m W of Chichester, on B2146*

Quality local produce cooked with flair

With its thatched roof and red-brick and flint exterior, Halliday's presents a decidedly traditional face to the world. Inside, everything remains respectful to its 13th-century origins, whilst setting the scene for some smart, well-crafted cooking. Andy Stephenson goes that extra mile when it comes to sourcing first-rate produce from the local area, including home-smoking and foraging in the woodland, and everything is made in-house with a good deal of finesse. Begin with a terrine packed with pigeon, veal and pistachios, with accompanying spiced oranges and sourdough toasts, or go for Selsey crabcakes with rocket leaves, lemon and caper dressing. Fish from the South Coast might include sea bass (served with steamed samphire and mussels) or turbot baked on the bone with seafood bouillabaisse. Among meaty options, pot roast rabbit with Serrano ham, aubergine and basil ragout is a bit of a treat, and, to finish, fine apple tart with cinnamon sugar and cinnamon ice cream shows off the sound technical abilities of the chef.

Chef Andrew Stephenson **Owner** Mr A & Mrs J Stephenson **Seats** 26, Pr/dining room 12 **Times** 12-2.15/7-10.15 Closed 1 wk Mar, 2 wks Aug, Mon-Tue, L Sat, D Sun **Prices** Fixed L 2 course fr £16, Fixed D 3 course fr £27.50, Starter £8.25-£10.50, Main £17.50-£22, Dessert £6.75-£7.25, Service optional **Wines** 26 bottles over £30, 36 bottles under £30, 8 by glass **Parking** 12 **Notes** Sunday L £24, Vegetarian available, Children welcome

Richmond Arms

 Eclectic **NEW**

tel: 01243 572046 **Mill Rd, West Ashling PO18 8EA**
email: richmondarms@gmail.com

Village pub serving local produce with real style

Situated in a pretty Sussex village, the Richmond Arms is a pub with a good deal of rustic charm and a serious approach to food. Locally-sourced ingredients figure large in a menu of contemporary country-style dishes that really hit the spot. A suitably informal vibe pervades, so open fires, unclothed wooden tables and flickering candles set the mood, and a Parma ham slicer further endorses its foodie credentials. It's an enterprising place, too, as seen in the shape of the bright and sleek-looking Skittle Alley, where wood-fired pizza is served from an old Citroen van outside. On the main menu, hot and runny venison Scotch egg with pickled fennel is pretty classy, or go for local pigeon in a pastilla with dried plum dressing. Whole baked Selsey crab or slow-braised English lamb are what to expect among main courses, and, to finish, try hot chocolate and peanut butter fondant with salted caramel ice cream.

Chef William Jack **Owner** William & Emma Jack **Seats** 36, Pr/dining room 60 **Times** 12-3/6-11 Closed Mon-Tue, D Sun **Prices** Starter £4.95-£10.95, Main £14.95-£21.95, Dessert £6.75-£6.95, Service optional **Wines** **Parking** 9, On street **Notes** Sunday L £14.95-£15.95, Vegetarian available, Children welcome

The Royal Oak Inn

 Modern British, European

tel: 01243 527434 **Pook Ln, East Lavant PO18 0AX**
email: info@royaloakeastlavant.co.uk **web:** www.royaloakeastlavant.co.uk
dir: *From Chichester take A286 towards Midhurst, 2m to mini rdbt, turn right signed East Lavant. Inn on left*

Imaginative modern menu in a charming village inn

Food is high on the agenda at this village inn, but The Royal Oak also fits the bill if you're looking for a pint of cask ale, a table by the fire, or a seat out on the terrace to enjoy Sussex views. In short, it's a 200-year-old pub that has managed to strike a good balance. There's satisfying rusticity to the interior with exposed brick walls, beams, leather-look chairs and wooden tables. The kitchen's output has a modern flavour with lots of British and European ideas, and daily specials on the blackboard. Start with ox cheek ravioli with roast shallot purée, buttered leeks and red wine reduction, or seared Scottish scallops with home-cured bacon and cauliflower as both purée and beignet. Main courses are just as intelligently put together: slow-cooked local venison, maybe, or sage- and honey-glazed pork cheeks with a lightly curried parsnip purée and bubble and squeak.

Chef Daniel Ward **Owner** Charles Ullmann **Seats** 55 **Times** 10-3/6-10.30 **Prices** Fixed L 2 course £16.95, Starter £6.50-£12.95, Main £13.90-£27.90, Dessert £5.95-£8.95, Service optional **Wines** 54 bottles over £30, 26 bottles under £30, 20 by glass **Parking** 25 **Notes** Pre-theatre menu from 5.30pm, Sunday L, Vegetarian available, Children welcome

See advert opposite

"One of our favourite places"

Harpers Bazaar

Why not talk to Charles or one of the team about providing a special menu with carefully chosen wines for your party or anniversary . . .

Or if you have a business occasion why not let us make it a particular success . . .

If you would like to stay with us we have five luxurious en suite rooms and three charming Sussex Cottages please don't hesitate to ask!

THE ROYAL OAK
EAST LAVANT

Pook Lane, East Lavant, Chichester, West Sussex, PO18 0AX
Telephone: (+44) (0) 1243 527434   Email: Info@royaloakeastlavant.co.uk   www.royaloakeastlavant.co.uk

---

The Ship Hotel

Modern British

tel: 01243 778000 **57 North St PO19 1NH**
email: enquiries@theshiphotel.net **web:** www.theshiphotel.net
dir: *From A27 follow signs for town centre and Chichester Festival Theatre. Restaurant signed from Northgate rdbt*

Modern brasserie cooking in a boutique city-centre hotel

In the heart of historic Chichester, The Ship presents a sober, red-brick Georgian face to the world, but inside it's another story altogether. The designers have been unleashed, and the place is now a riot of boutique style. Murray's Restaurant is a split-level dining room that works a classy colonial look with palm trees, touchy feely fabrics, exposed floorboards and unclothed dark wood tables. Brasserie-style menus tick the right boxes, opening with the likes of game terrine with cranberry relish and chargrilled sourdough bread, or scallops and belly pork with celeriac and apple purée and pancetta crumb. To follow, there are straight-up slabs of beef from the grill, or comforting old favourites such as steak and kidney pudding, while fish might be halibut with saffron fondant potatoes, celeriac, fennel remoulade and roasted beetroot. Simple but effective finishers include classic apple tarte Tatin with cinnamon and pecan ice cream, or chocolate ganache with orange oil and spices.

Chef Jon Lander **Owner** Chichester Hotel Company LLP **Seats** 120, Pr/dining room 48 **Times** 10-10 All-day dining **Prices** Fixed L 2 course fr £16.50, Fixed D 3 course fr £19, Starter £5.25-£7.95, Main £8.50-£24.95, Dessert £6, Service optional **Wines** 6 bottles over £30, 20 bottles under £30, 12 by glass **Parking** 25 **Notes** Pre-theatre Prix Fixe plus full ALC, Sunday L £19.50-£24.50, Vegetarian available, Children welcome

---

EAST GRINSTEAD Map 6 TQ33

The Felbridge Hotel & Spa

Modern British

tel: 01342 337700 **London Rd RH19 2BH**
email: info@felbridgehotel.co.uk **web:** www.felbridgehotel.co.uk
dir: *From W: M23 junct 10, follow signs to A22. From N: M25 junct 6. Hotel on A22 at Felbridge*

Inventive modern food in a spa hotel

The Felbridge Hotel had a swish makeover back in 2007 making it fighting fit for the modern market. There's a snazzy spa, for a start, and a brace of dining options, the pick of the bunch being the Anise restaurant. There's an upmarket sheen to the

continued

EAST GRINSTEAD *continued*

room, with tones of brown and cream, and the tables are set for the business of fine dining. This is a kitchen turning out bright, contemporary food, with a keen eye on the provenance of the ingredients, a good amount of which comes from the south east. Modern techniques are used to maximise flavour and visual impact. A starter dish of scallops sees the bivalves partnered with mussels, chorizo, peas and wild rice, with the flavour of saffron deftly handled. Another first course puts Sussex ham hock centre stage, with pineapple, fennel and pistachio. Main-course breast of duck comes with parsnips, rhubarb and hazelnuts in a dazzling construction, and, for dessert, there's humour in the naming of 'Gone Nuts', which has baklava and almond pannacotta amongst its little treasures.

Chef Richard Simmonds **Owner** New Century, East Grinstead Ltd **Seats** 34, Pr/dining room 34 **Times** 6-10 Closed L all week **Prices** Fixed D 3 course £37.50-£45.50 **Wines** 50 bottles over £30, 35 bottles under £30, 16 by glass **Parking** 200 **Notes** Vegetarian available, Children welcome

See advert below

Gravetye Manor Hotel

Rosettes not confirmed at time of going to print – see opposite

---

GATWICK AIRPORT (LONDON) Map 6 TQ24

Langshott Manor

@ @ @ *– see page 506*

Sofitel London Gatwick

@ @ British, French

---

tel: 01293 567070 & 555000 **North Terminal RH6 OPH**
email: h6204-re@accor.com **web:** www.sofitel.com
dir: M23 junct 9, follow to 2nd rdbt. Hotel straight ahead

Smart brasserie cooking by the North Terminal

An impressive central atrium makes a massive impact at this smart hotel in a hefty new building in close proximity to Gatwick's North Terminal. Around this central space are three dining options: a café, Chinese restaurant, and La Brasserie, where the two rosettes are duly lodged. La Brasserie has a rather upscale finish, given the moniker, with neatly laid tables and prominent modern artworks. The menu takes a modern British path, with lots of good ideas and a sure hand at the stove. Start with a terrine of rabbit, ham hock and foie gras, for example, which is packed with flavour and comes in the company of a croquette, pickled carrot and punchy Pernod purée. Next up, sea bass fillet is cooked in a vacuum to maximise the flavour and precision, and is cooked just-so, with the flavours of lemon and dill well judged, plus a warm Pink Fir potato salad, lardons and citrus salad. The dessert menu offers a satisfying blueberry cheesecake with white chocolate sorbet and blueberry gel.

Chef David Woods **Owner** S Arora **Seats** 70, Pr/dining room 40 **Times** 6.30-10.30 Closed L all week **Prices** Fixed D 3 course £29.90, Starter £6.75-£10.95, Main £17.95-£26.95, Dessert £6.15-£7.90 **Wines** 29 bottles over £30, 12 bottles under £30, 19 by glass **Parking** 565 **Notes** Vegetarian available, Children welcome

---

ANISE
@ @ RESTAURANT

felbridge
HOTEL & SPA
★★★★

The stunning AA 2 Rosette Anise Fine Dining Restaurant at The Felbridge Hotel and Spa provides a flavour of the West End with its unique selection of dishes that complement the elegant surroundings and quality service.

Our Award Winning Executive Chef is continuously preparing a selection of innovative dishes; each beautifully presented and well balanced with a combination of classical techniques and culinary flair. Make a reservation by calling 01342 337700.

Anise Restaurant at The Felbridge Hotel and Spa
London Road, East Grinstead, West Sussex, RH19 2BH. T: 01342 337700 W: www.felbridgehotel.co.uk

Gravetye Manor Hotel

Rosettes not confirmed at time of going to print

EAST GRINSTEAD   Map 6 TQ33

Modern British V NOTABLE WINE LIST

tel: 01342 810567 **Vowels Ln, West Hoathly RH19 4LJ**
email: info@gravetyemanor.co.uk
web: www.gravetyemanor.co.uk
dir: *From M23 junct 10 take A264 towards East Grinstead. After 2m take B2028 to Haywards Heath. 1m after Turners Hill fork left towards Sharpthorne, immediate 1st left into Vowels Lane*

Superb dining in Elizabethan country-house hotel

The Rosette award for this establishment has been suspended due to a change of chef. Reassessment will take place in due course under the new chef. A stunning mellow-stone Elizabethan manor, Gravetye is surrounded by acres of parkland and beautiful gardens perfect for an appetite stimulating stroll. Within are comfortable lounges furnished in-keeping with the style of the property, and an oak-panelled dining room hung with oils, with plenty of well-trained and attentive staff on hand to add to the pleasure of a visit. Canapés — perhaps arancini with pea and herbs, and anchovy sticks with houmous — get things off to a flying start, and a glimpse at the menu shows a highly motivated kitchen with serious culinary ambition, clearly met by what appears on the plate. Some dishes get lavish country-house treatments, with luxuries appearing as a ballotine of foiegras with sherry jelly, salted grapes, caramelised hazelnuts and brioche, followed by juniper-marinated local venison loin with salsify, romanesco, red wine-poached pear and venison jus. Dishes are intelligently composed, the results always impressive: for instance, a starter of pancetta-wrapped quail with smoked potato purée, pickled shimeji mushrooms and light quail sauce, all beautifully presented and a good balance of flavours and textures, or a main course of tender beef fillet with beer-braised ox cheek, pearl barley, garlic purée and malt foam. Fish is timed to the second, perhaps seared John Dory fillets with baby squid and cauliflower risotto with squid ink purée and ginger beurreblanc. 'All of our desserts are prepared to order' warns the menu, but that's okay because a first-class pre-dessert arrives to fill the gap — perhaps peach granita with marinated blackberries — and when the main event does arrive it's well worth the wait: a dark chocolate pavé, say, with crisp plum cannelloni, coffee ice cream and honeycomb. Excellent bread rolls with superb butter and all the extras contribute to a truly memorable dining experience.

Chef Andy Robertson **Owner** Jeremy & Elizabeth Hosking
Seats 40, Pr/dining room 20 **Times** 12-2/6.30-9.30
Prices Fixed L 2 course £25, Tasting menu £75, Starter £17-£22, Main £29-£32, Dessert £12 **Wines** 5 bottles under £30, 10 by glass **Parking** 25 **Notes** 4 course D £40, All day menu 10am-10pm, Afternoon tea 3-5pm, Sunday L £35, Children 7 yrs+

Langshott Manor

Modern European V

tel: 01293 786680 **Langshott Ln RH6 9LN**
email: admin@langshottmanor.com **web:** www.langshottmanor.com
dir: *From A23 take Ladbroke Rd, off Chequers rdbt to Langshott, after 0.75m hotel on right*

Modern global cooking in an Elizabethan country hotel

Langshott is something of an architectural jewel, an Elizabethan manor house of timber and herringbone brick in the Surrey countryside. It's only a short cab-ride from Gatwick, if you're intent on fleeing the country, but the surrounding ambience is more safely grazing sheep than jumbo-jet. Inside, the place wears its 500 years on its sleeve, with inglenooks of exposed brickwork and mullioned windows framing the restful view over manicured lawns. In the Mulberry restaurant, Langshott's principal dining room, Phil Dixon plies a modern British line that, as is only to be expected nowadays, makes use of local ingredients in season, including those that pour forth from the hotel's own kitchen garden. Dishes hover indeterminately in that overlapping space where France and southern Europe meet east Asia, producing crab with smoked chicken, coconut and avocado in yuzu dressing, or a tian of hare with blue cheese, chocolate and pear, for stimulating starters. Meat and fish partnerships are all the rage, perhaps introducing halibut and rabbit to each other in the company of chorizo and lemon. A more obviously traditional furrow is ploughed for a serving of poached truffled pheasant breast with cabbage and prunes. Desserts continue to cast the net wide with Granny Smith and cinnamon terrine with rice pudding espuma, or cannelloni of pineapple and Szechuan pepper with roast coconut and coriander. Artisan cheeses are served with pear and tomato chutney and bread studded with pickled walnuts. A six-course taster with pre-selected wines covers the spectrum from white onion consommé to dark chocolate custard, in the company of a vinous parade that starts with French Colombard-Chardonnay and comes to rest with a tot of sublimely toffeeish ten-year-old tawny port. The vegetarian version looks just as tempting, perhaps built around a main course of butternut squash Tatin with mango and chilli salsa.

Chef Phil Dixon **Owner** Peter & Deborah Hinchcliffe **Seats** 55, Pr/dining room 22 **Times** 12-2.30/7-9.30 **Prices** Fixed L 2 course fr £15, Fixed D 3 course fr £49.50, Tasting menu £65-£95, Starter £8.50-£12.50, Main £14.50-£27.50, Dessert £8.50-£12.50 **Wines** 76 bottles over £30, 8 bottles under £30, 16 by glass **Parking** 25 **Notes** Sunday L £27.50, Children welcome

Restaurant Tristan

Modern British, French

tel: 01403 255688 **3 Stan's Way, East St RH12 1HU**
email: info@restauranttristan.co.uk
dir: *Phone for directions*

Clever, creative cooking in a historic beamed building

The 16th-century building in a pedestrianised street in the heart of Horsham is a bit of a historic gem. It looks gorgeous from the outside, and once inside the first-floor restaurant (downstairs is a casual seating area for daytime light bites, coffees and cakes) it's a real mix of original features like exposed wooden beams and bare floorboards, with a contemporary decor of cream-painted walls broken up with some feature black-and-cream floral wallpaper. The pale-wood tables are simply set with olive-green place mats and crisp linen napkins, while chocolate-brown leatherette seating completes the modern look. Chef-patron Tristan Mason's food is certainly from the modern end of the spectrum too, but that's not to say he doesn't draw on his solid grounding of classic French technique (having trained with Marco Pierre White you'd expect nothing less). An amuse-bouche of ham hock and white bean velouté shows off some impressive skills from the word 'go', while the freshly baked breads with two butters – unsalted and a mushroom, onion and truffle flavoured version – are hard to stop eating. Foie gras three ways – hot (a perfectly seared slice), cold (an excellent parfait) and iced (an ice cream) – with rhubarb and oat crumble is a starter that wows with its contrasting temperatures, textures, and richness juxtaposed with fruity tartness. Line-caught sea bass might be next up, beautifully cooked and partnered by some nicely golden salsify chips, a whole deep-fried duck egg rolled in herbs with a satisfyingly gooey yolk, and Oscietra caviar to add a salty hit. Things are brought to a playful close with a dessert entitled 'twigs, nuts and berries' – a crushed brownie to give the impression of soil, a pistachio and almond crumb to replicate moss, some chocolate tuile 'twigs' and a mixture of fresh, colourful berries around an iced berry parfait. This is innovative, creative, technically skilful cooking presented with panache and all founded on ingredients out of the top drawer.

Chef Tristan Mason **Owner** Tristan Mason **Seats** 40 **Times** 12-2.30/6.30-9.30 Closed 2 wks after Xmas, 2 wks summer, Sun-Mon **Prices** Prices not confirmed **Wines** 30 bottles over £30, 20 bottles under £30, 20 by glass **Parking** **Notes** Tasting menu 5 course (with wine £90), Vegetarian available, No children

GOODWOOD
Map 6 SU80

The Goodwood Hotel

 Contemporary British

tel: 01243 775537 **PO18 0QB**
email: reservations@goodwood.com **web:** www.goodwood.com
dir: Off A285, 3m NE of Chichester

Masterly cooking on the Goodwood Estate

The luxury hotel, complete with health club and spa, is at the heart of the 12,000-acre Goodwood Estate, with the home farm, certified as organic, providing the kitchens of its various restaurants with pork, lamb and beef. The main dining option, the 17th-century Richmond Arms, is elegantly kitted out, with an adjoining character bar serving a range of drinks from cask ales to cocktails. The menu follows a contemporary British path, offering dishes unlikely to startle with any newfangled and flashy innovation, but well-conceived and holding plenty of interest. Cheese soufflé, served with apple, chicory and caramelised walnuts, seems to be something of a signature starter, and may be offered alongside smoked salmon with horseradish slaw and pickled lemons, or a seasonal salad of winter vegetables with blood orange, yoghurt and seeds. Among main courses you might find pork belly with chive mash, pickled red cabbage and apple and rhubarb sauce, or confit duck and flageolet bean cassoulet. Vegetarians are not entirely overlooked, and a couple of fish options may include roast fillet of halibut with seafood and vegetable broth.

Chef Simon Wills **Owner** The Goodwood Estate Company Ltd **Seats** 85, Pr/dining room 120 **Times** 12.30-2.30/6.30-10.30 Closed L Mon-Sat **Prices** Starter £6.50-£12, Main £17-£32, Dessert £6.50-£10, Service optional 12% **Wines** 50 bottles over £30, 29 bottles under £30, 12 by glass **Parking** 150 **Notes** Sunday L £22.50-£25.50, Vegetarian available, Children welcome

HAYWARDS HEATH
Map 6 TQ32

Jeremy's at Borde Hill

 Modern European, Mediterranean

tel: 01444 441102 **Balcombe Rd RH16 1XP**
email: reservations@jeremysrestaurant.com **web:** www.jeremysrestaurant.com
dir: 1.5m N of Haywards Heath, 10mins from Gatwick Airport. From M23 junct 10a take A23 through Balcombe

Confident flavoursome cooking in idyllic garden setting

It is hard to imagine a more idyllic setting for summer dining than this contemporary restaurant in the quintessentially English Borde Hill Gardens. Jeremy's occupies a stylishly converted stable block overlooking the Victorian walled garden (which comes up trumps with fresh herbs and seasonal produce) and a dreamy south-facing terrace basking in the Sussex sun. Indoors, it's a wide-open, bright space with wooden floors, smart high-backed leather chairs and modern art on the walls. Chef-patron Jeremy Ashpool has a well-established network of small

local producers to supply the best ingredients the bounteous Sussex larder has to offer, and knows how to extract the best from them. Expect big, bold flavours and colourful platefuls of thoroughly modern, vibrant, Mediterranean-inflected food, starting with grilled sea bass with red pepper, smoked aubergine purée and chargrilled fennel. Next up, rump and belly of South Downs lamb stars in a main course with smoked sheep's cheese, confit potatoes, carrots and tarragon jus. For dessert, bitter dark chocolate pavé is matched with white chocolate popcorn and salted caramel ice cream.

Chef Jimmy Gray, Jeremy Ashpool **Owner** Jeremy Ashpool **Seats** 55 **Times** 12-3/7-9.30 Closed after New Year for 7 days, Mon, D Sun **Prices** Fixed L 2 course fr £17, Fixed D 3 course fr £20, Tasting menu fr £60, Starter £8-£9.50, Main £15-£24, Dessert fr £7.50 **Wines** 10 by glass **Parking** 15, Overspill car park **Notes** Tasting menu 6 course, Fixed D midweek, Sunday L, Vegetarian available, Children welcome

HORSHAM
Map 6 TQ13

Restaurant Tristan

 – see opposite

Wabi

 Japanese v

tel: 01403 788140 **38 East St RH12 1HL**
email: reservations@wabi.co.uk
dir: Corner Denne Rd & East St

Trendy venue for top-class Japanese in Horsham's restaurant quarter

There's no trace of Wabi's former life as a street-corner boozer: stylish to the hilt, the ground floor is a trendy, upbeat cocktail bar with copper pendant lights hanging from the raftered roof, a modern waterfall curtain behind the mixologists, plus a sushi bar/grill counter. Up on the first floor, the restaurant has a more minimal, cool and calming Zen garden vibe, with tatami-screened booths above spotlit beds of white pebbles, and darkwood everywhere. Japanese flavours are clearly the kitchen's primary inspiration, but that doesn't rule out input from the modern European idiom, while impeccable ingredients are sourced locally. If the menu terminology is alien, knowledgeable staff will penetrate the language barrier, and it's all designed for a sociable, tapas-style sharing approach. Get going with crispy chilli squid kara-age in crisp and light tempura batter, paired with mirin-sweetened daikon pickle and chilli dipping sauce, or roast duck bun with spicy peanut soy, red onions and chilli. For a knockout dish of head-spinning flavours, try tea-smoked lamb chops with smoky Japanese aubergine and spicy Korean red miso sauce. **Due to a fire in May 2014, the restaurant will be closed for several months.**

Owner Paul Craig **Seats** 90, Pr/dining room 14 **Times** 12-2.30/6-10.30 Closed BHs, Sun-Mon **Prices** Fixed L 2 course £7.50-£14.50, Tasting menu £33-£45, Starter £4-£13, Main £11.50-£22.50, Dessert £2.50-£6, Service optional 12.5% **Wines** 7 bottles over £30, 8 bottles under £30, 8 by glass **Parking** Car park **Notes** Fixed L & D 6 course £33-£45, Children welcome

LODSWORTH
Map 6 SU92

The Halfway Bridge Inn

@ Modern British

tel: 01798 861281 **Halfway Bridge GU28 9BP**
email: enquiries@halfwaybridge.co.uk **web:** www.halfwaybridge.co.uk
dir: *From Petworth on A272 towards Midhurst, 3m on right*

Updated pub classics in renovated old inn

With the South Downs National Park all around, and the famous stately home and antique emporia of Petworth close by, you won't be short of ideas to fill the day when staying at this classy 18th-century roadside inn. Recently renovated from top to bottom, the interior works a cosy yet smartly-contemporary look, with muted tones set against its dark beams, exposed brickwork and herringbone parquet floors; wood burners and roaring fires boost the feel-good factor still further in winter. The ambience is friendly and unbuttoned, while the kitchen deals in traditional pub classics brought up-to-date, and built on materials that reflect the local area and what's in season. Kick off with the full-throttle flavours of duck liver faggots with wilted greens and bordelaise sauce, then follow with another rib-sticking idea – whole roast partridge with game jus, bread sauce, and pommes Anna. To finish, toffee apple crumble tart comes with excellent cinnamon ice cream.

Chef Gavin Rees **Owner** Sam & Janet Bakose **Seats** 55, Pr/dining room 16 **Times** 12-2.30/6-10 **Prices** Starter £6.50-£9.50, Main £12.50-£29, Dessert £6.50-£8, Service optional **Wines** 24 bottles over £30, 23 bottles under £30, 22 by glass **Parking** 30 **Notes** Sunday L £15.50-£17.50, Vegetarian available, Children welcome

LOWER BEEDING
Map 6 TQ22

Camellia Restaurant at South Lodge Hotel

@@ British V ❡ NOTABLE WINE LIST

tel: 01403 891711 **Brighton Rd RH13 6PS**
email: enquiries@southlodgehotel.co.uk **web:** www.southlodgehotel.co.uk
dir: *On A23 left onto B2110. Turn right through Handcross to A281 junct. Turn left, hotel on right*

Contemporary cooking in comfortable hotel dining room

Camellia is the second dining option at South Lodge (see entry for The Pass), a neo-Jacobean pile dating from 1883. It's a smartly kitted-out room, with some panelling and camellia-patterned wallpaper, smartly set tables and views over the extensive grounds. The menus are built around contemporary renditions of traditional seasonal dishes, reflecting the culinary style of the day; vegetables, fruit and herbs come from the hotel's kitchen garden and supplies from local producers. Moist and flavoursome boned chicken leg is spiked with Cajun spices and served alongside a sweet and juicy seared scallop and sweetcorn purée, a nicely balanced starter that might be followed by loin of Rusper lamb with pearl barley, salsify and roast shallots. Seasonal game may appear as roast partridge breast with a chicory tart, pickled walnuts and quince, and seafood gets a decent showing: dressed crab with cauliflower, lime and peanuts, say, followed by skate wing with Jerusalem artichokes, capers and parsley. Desserts range from vanilla crème brûlée with orange sorbet, to warm chocolate fondant with coffee ice cream.

Chef Steven Edwards **Owner** Exclusive Hotels **Seats** 100, Pr/dining room 140 **Times** 12-2.30/7-10 **Prices** Fixed L 2 course fr £18, Fixed D 3 course £37.50, Starter £12-£18, Main £24-£28, Dessert £9-£12 **Wines** 179 bottles over £30, 14 bottles under £30, 193 by glass **Parking** 200 **Notes** Sunday L £29.50, Children welcome

The Pass Restaurant at South Lodge Hotel

@@@@ – *see opposite*

PETWORTH
Map 6 SU92

The Leconfield

@ Modern British

tel: 01798 345111 **New St GU28 0AS**
email: reservations@theleconfield.co.uk

Lots of creative energy in a lively and popular restaurant

The Leconfield's lively ground-floor restaurant, with its bar and white walls hung with artwork, opens on to a light and airy orangery leading to a cobbled courtyard; there's also a splendidly beamed room upstairs. All sorts of ideas find their way on to the menus, from foie gras parfait with cherry fluid gel and pickled walnuts, to crab salad with pickled daikon, pea shoots and crab mayonnaise. Crab and lobster bisque is a convincing rendition, and may be followed by accurately timed sesame-crusted tuna steak accompanied by ginger-flavoured glass noodles and a blob of wasabi, or herb-coated rack of lamb with white bean purée and tomato and garlic fondue. Good home-made breads come with dripping, and among interesting puddings may be rhubarb cheesecake with apple sorbet.

Chef David Craig Lewis **Owner** Nicola Jones **Seats** 60, Pr/dining room 30 **Times** 12-3/6-9.30 Closed Mon, D Sun **Prices** Fixed L 3 course £25-£29, Fixed D 3 course £25-£29, Starter £8-£17, Main £19-£25, Dessert £9-£12 **Wines** 7 by glass **Parking** On street, car park **Notes** Fixed D early evening, Sunday L £25-£30, Vegetarian available, Children welcome

ROWHOOK
Map 6 TQ13

The Chequers Inn

@ British

tel: 01403 790480 **RH12 3PY**
email: thechequersrowhook@googlemail.com
dir: *From Horsham A281 towards Guildford. At rdbt take A29 signed London. In 200mtrs left, follow Rowhook signs*

Ambitious modern cooking in village inn

The Chequers may well have been around since the 15th century, but it has stayed in tune with modern tastes. It is a proper village local, and with flagstones, oak beams, chunky wooden tables, welcoming open fires and a battery of well-kept real ales on handpump – what's not to like? Chef-proprietor Tim Neal clearly loves to haul in the best Sussex ingredients he can find, some of them supplied as locally as from the pub's garden, as well as foraged goodies and game in season. There are no pretensions or gimmicks, just bang-on-the-money modern ideas, from pan-fried scallops with parsnip and vanilla purée, to crispy confit duck with Puy lentil and merguez ragoût, spinach and French beans. If you're up for fish, there may be crispy hake fillet with curried mussel and leek cream, new potatoes and buttered spinach, and you could end with sticky toffee pudding with caramel sauce and vanilla ice cream.

Chef Tim Neal **Owner** Mr & Mrs Neal **Seats** 40 **Times** 12-2/7-9 Closed 25 Dec, D Sun **Prices** Starter £5.50-£9.95, Main £14.95-£21.50, Dessert £6.25-£8.50, Service optional **Wines** 7 bottles over £30, 26 bottles under £30, 8 by glass **Parking** 40 **Notes** Sunday L £9.95-£21.50, Vegetarian available, Children welcome

The Pass Restaurant at South Lodge Hotel

LOWER BEEDING　　　　　　　　　　　Map 6 TQ22

Modern British **V** NOTABLE WINE LIST

tel: 01403 891711 **Brighton Rd RH13 6PS**
email: enquiries@southlodgehotel.co.uk
web: www.southlodgehotel.co.uk
dir: *From A23 turn left onto B2110 & then right through Handcross to A281 junct. Turn left, hotel on right*

Cutting-edge cooking before your very eyes

We've become familiar with the chef's table concept, and South Lodge has taken the theme a step further and inserted a whole restaurant into the kitchen. For the uninitiated, the pass is the part of the kitchen where the head chef gives the final okay to dishes before waiting staff whisk them away. Here, it's decked out in hyper-modern style – lime green and cream leather seats at tables running along the edge of the pass, with the industrial stainless steel of the kitchen as a backdrop and plasma screens to zoom in on the action out of view. It can be genuinely enlightening to see dishes being put together, the panoply of technique ranging from jaw-dropping to 'I could do that' (not very often for the latter, admittedly). Matt Gillan and his team work in near silence, assembling dishes that mobilise all the tricks of the contemporary gastronomic trade. The format is tasting menus only of 6, 8 or 10 courses with a vegetarian choice and optional wine flights – and the wines are stunning, worth the extra outlay if you're going for broke. The menus offer little enlightenment as each course is described with either three words or a single component, but rest assured that it's full of lively invention, based on first-class produce and sent out dressed to thrill. Contrasting textures are a big theme, so clams are matched with kiwi and radish, while the fish course might see cod with the more mainstream accompaniments of aubergine and tomato. Meaty ideas could see venison partnered with leeks and walnut, while the vogue for offering different cuts of meat brings on oxtail and tongue of beef with radish. The selection of artisan cheeses may take in Somerset's unpasteurised Rachel goats' cheese and the full-flavoured Admiral Collingwood, washed with Newcastle Brown ale. Desserts burst forth with further complexes of flavour, from yuzu with sourdough and chocolate, to rhubarb and liquorice tart with popcorn and fennel. The vegetarian menu may encompass beetroot tartare and sorbet with blue cheese and orange; salted charred leek with watermelon, pickled apple and olive; caramelised swede with butternut squash, clementine and grain mustard; and a main course of vegetable Wellington. The Camellia Restaurant is the hotel's alternative dining option.

Chef Matt Gillan **Owner** Exclusive Hotels **Seats** 26
Times 12-2/7-9 Closed 1st 2 wks Jan, Mon-Tue
Prices Fixed L 3 course £25 **Wines** 185 bottles over £30, 6 bottles under £30, 181 by glass **Parking** 200 **Notes** Fixed L 5/7 course £35/£55, Fixed D 6/8 course £65/£75, Sunday L, No children

RUSPER
Map 6 TQ23

Ghyll Manor

 Traditional British

tel: 0845 345 3426 & 01293 871571 **High St RH12 4PX**
email: reception@ghyllmanor.co.uk **web:** www.ghyllmanor.co.uk
dir: M23 junct 11, A264 signed Horsham. Continue 3rd rdbt, 3rd exit Faygate, follow signs for Rusper, 2m to village

Country-house cooking amid 40 acres of prime Sussex countryside

A timbered manor house in 40 acres of picture-perfect Sussex countryside, Ghyll Manor is an obvious candidate for a retreat from the hurly-burly of the southeast. Inside, an appealing mixture of period features and modern styling creates a harmonious impression, and there's a terrace overlooking the gardens for summer aperitifs. Graham Digweed became head chef in late 2013, and maintains a steady hand at the tiller for country-house cooking that has its finger on the pulse of current tastes, without going all out for gasp-inducing avant-garderie. Beetroot-cured salmon with pickled fennel and cucumber is a modern classic dish, without question, but other starters are more traditional, perhaps ham hock terrine with Bramley apple compôte, before main courses arrive to deliver slow-roasted pork cheeks with white beans and chorizo, or rosemary-scented chicken breast with lentils, mushrooms and smoked bacon. Finish up with bread-and-butter pudding, or a passionfruit parfait garnished with toasted meringue.

Chef Graham Digweed **Owner** Civil Service Motoring Association **Seats** 48, Pr/dining room 40 **Times** 12–2/6.30–9.30 **Prices** Fixed L 2 course fr £20, Fixed D 3 course fr £32, Service optional **Wines** 9 by glass **Parking** 50 **Notes** Sunday L £15.95–£19.95, Vegetarian available, Children welcome

SIDLESHAM
Map 5 SZ89

The Crab & Lobster

 Modern British

tel: 01243 641233 **Mill Ln PO20 7NB**
email: enquiries@crab-lobster.co.uk **web:** www.crab-lobster.co.uk
dir: A27 S onto B2145 towards Selsey. At Sidlesham turn left onto Rookery Ln, continue for 0.75m

Switched-on modern menu in a waterside restaurant with rooms

The 17th-century, white-painted pub is these days more upscale restaurant with rooms than boozer, and it's looking spruce from top to bottom. On the edge of the Pagham Harbour nature reserve, The Crab & Lobster offers smart bedrooms and a stylish restaurant that aims to impress with its fine-dining ambitions. The period features of the building remain to bring character to the spaces, while the furnishings take a more contemporary line. The kitchen team supply upscale modern British food that looks good on the plate and delivers bang-on flavours. Potted rabbit with toasted brioche and shallot marmalade is a classy first course, and there is a good showing of seafood, too, with the likes of Selsey crab cakes with mango, sesame and chilli jam. Main courses can be as populist as loin of beer-battered hake with hand-cut chips and tartare sauce (a swish fish and chips indeed), or as refined as Jerusalem artichoke and Oxford Blue risotto with artichoke crips and parsley oil. Finish with apple and rhubarb parfait.

Chef Sam Bakose, Clyde Hollett **Owner** Sam & Janet Bakose **Seats** 54 **Times** 12–2.30/6–10 **Prices** Fixed L 2 course £21.50, Starter £7.50–£13.50, Main £16.50–£31, Dessert £6.95–£8.95, Service optional **Wines** 25 bottles over £30, 25 bottles under £30, 23 by glass **Parking** 12 **Notes** Sunday L £16.50–£18.50, Vegetarian available, Children welcome

TANGMERE
Map 6 SU90

Cassons Restaurant

 Modern British

tel: 01243 773294 **Arundel Rd PO18 0DU**
email: cassonsresto@aol.com
dir: On Westbound carriageway of A27, 400mtrs from Tangmere rdbt

Good eating near Goodwood

Chef-patronne Viv Casson is a Kiwi who has run a successful restaurant across the water in France, so you can expect clear Gallic culinary influences to her work. The setting is a couple of farm cottages beside the A27 handily close to Goodwood, reinvented with a rustic simplicity that gains character from the huge inglenook and low-beamed ceilings, while the modern menu takes in straightforward, classically-influenced ideas as well as some more daring forays into innovative territory. Opting for the great-value fixed-price lunch menu offering five choices at each stage, a crisp pastry parcel of smoked haddock with spinach and curry foam gets things off the mark, ahead of belly of suckling pig teamed with wilted greens, shallot mash, caramelised apples, black pudding and cider jus. Things get quite avant-garde at dessert, when good technical skills bring together a composition involving blackcurrant gel, fresh blackberries, apple compôte, honeycomb, crème anglaise, and apple crisps.

Chef Viv Casson **Owner** Viv & Cass Casson **Seats** 36, Pr/dining room 14 **Times** 12–1.30/7–10 Closed between Xmas & New Year, Mon, L Tue, D Sun **Prices** Fixed L 2 course £16.95–£28.90, Starter £8–£11, Main £23, Dessert £8–£11, Service optional **Wines** 41 bottles over £30, 33 bottles under £30, 6 by glass **Parking** 30 **Notes** Gourmet & special events, Sunday L £22.50–£28, Vegetarian available, Children welcome

TILLINGTON
Map 6 SU92

The Horse Guards Inn

 Traditional British

tel: 01798 342332 **Upperton Rd GU28 9AF**
email: info@thehorseguardsinn.co.uk **web:** www.thehorseguardsinn.co.uk
dir: On A272, 1m west of Petworth, take road signed Tillington. Restaurant 500mtrs opposite church

Enterprising pub cooking near Petworth House

On the edge of Petworth Park, opposite the parish church, The Horse Guards is a relaxed, friendly and informal pub dating back 350 years, with open fires, plain wooden tables and seats, beams and a boarded floor. It's very much a foodie destination, the attraction a menu that changes daily, depending on what's been bought or foraged locally or dug up from the garden. Wide-ranging, contemporary ideas include starters of straightforward game terrine with rowan jelly, and more complex smoked eel with a potato cake, treacle, bacon, beetroot and horseradish. Main courses are equally varied, from a mainstream pairing of pork loin cutlet with apple sauce and gravy, served with fondant potato, celeriac purée and kale, to the vibrant flavours of mussels steamed in chilli, lemongrass, coconut milk and coriander. Diehards can opt for a pudding like steamed treacle suet sponge with custard, and there might also be chocolate, cherry and pistachio torte.

Chef Mark Robinson **Owner** Sam Beard & Michaela Hofirkova **Seats** 55, Pr/dining room 18 **Times** 12–2.30/6.30–9 **Prices** Starter £5–£9.50, Main £9.50–£21, Dessert £5.50–£7, Service optional **Wines** 25 bottles over £30, 17 bottles under £30, 14 by glass **Parking** On street **Notes** Sunday L £10–£17, Vegetarian available, Children welcome

TROTTON
Map 5 SU82

The Keepers Arms

British, Mediterranean

tel: 01730 813724 & 07506 693088 **Love Hill, Terwick Ln GU31 5ER**
email: sharonmcgrath198@btinternet.com
dir: *A272 towards Petersfield after 5m, restaurant on right just after narrow bridge. From Midhurst follow A272 for 3m, restaurant on left*

Upmarket country pub with appealing menu

The red tile-hung exterior of this 17th-century country inn is an inviting prospect on its perch above the A272, with a lovely garden and terrace that have plenty of alfresco appeal, and once inside, it is a gem of a pub. There's a proper friendly bar with a range of well-kept real ales, and the whole space has been opened out and given an easy-on-the-eye decluttered modern look, without sacrificing the inherent character in its plentiful beams and timbers. The stylish dining room looks out over the South Downs and aims for a contemporary hunting lodge look involving blond-wood tables, warm colours and funky tartans. Go for pubby classics from the chalkboards, or trade up to the carte of easy-eating contemporary ideas, and start with chicken liver and port parfait, followed by pan-fried sea bass fillet with truffle oil, crushed new potatoes, spinach and vanilla butter, and finish with chocolate fondant.

Chef Sharon McGrath, James Nelson **Owner** Sharon McGrath **Seats** 56, Pr/dining room 8 **Times** 11-3/6.30-9.30 **Prices** Fixed L 2 course £15.50-£18.50, Fixed D 3 course £20-£25, Starter £3.50-£7.50, Main £10.95-£21.50, Dessert £4.50-£6.50, Service optional **Wines** 8 by glass **Parking** 25, On street **Notes** Sunday L £13.50, Vegetarian available, Children welcome

TURNERS HILL
Map 6 TQ33

AG's Restaurant at Alexander House Hotel

– *see below*

Reflections at Alexander House

Modern International V

tel: 01342 714914 **Alexander House Hotel, East St RH10 4QD**
email: admin@alexanderhouse.co.uk **web:** www.alexanderhouse.co.uk
dir: *6m from M23 junct 10, on B2110 between Turners Hill & East Grinstead*

Modern brasserie cooking in an elegant spa hotel

The setting is impressive inside and out: 120 acres of gardens, woodland and parkland surround a handsome 17th-century mansion which has had a thoroughly modern makeover, moving it into boutique territory. Spa enthusiasts will be delighted by the restorative facilities at Alexander House, but there's also a buzzy brasserie – Reflections – to lift the spirits still further (the fine-dining option is AG's Restaurant). Expect sleek chocolate-coloured leather banquettes, slate floors and subtle grey and peach tones on the walls, plus there's a champagne bar and tables in the courtyard for eating outdoors. Start with something like terrine of foie gras and ham hock with sourdough toast, pig fritter and apricots, or gazpacho with avocado and cucumber, moving on to a classic beer-battered fish and chips or a more adventurous Telmara duck breast with gooseberry compôte and crisp radish salad. Banana parfait with toffee sauce and caramelised bananas makes for a richly indulgent pud, but then so does traditional warm sticky toffee pudding with rum and raisin ice cream.

Chef Mark Budd **Owner** Peter & Deborah Hinchcliffe **Seats** 70, Pr/dining room 12 **Times** 12-3/6-10 **Prices** Starter £8-£12, Main £16-£32, Dessert £8.50 **Wines** 25 bottles over £30, 5 bottles under £30, 12 by glass **Parking** 100 **Notes** Children welcome

AG's Restaurant at Alexander House Hotel

TURNERS HILL
Map 6 TQ33

British, French V
tel: 01342 714914 **Alexander House Hotel, East St RH10 4QD**
email: admin@alexanderhouse.co.uk **web:** www.alexanderhouse.co.uk
dir: *6m from M23 junct 10, on B2110 between Turners Hill & East Grinstead*

Modern Anglo-French inventiveness in the Sussex countryside

With 120 acres of Sussex countryside all to itself, Alexander House is a beautifully situated mansion, close enough to Gatwick Airport to be useful for anyone coming or going, but really it's a destination in its own right. The handsome red-brick hotel has glam bedrooms, a spa that can pamper you to within an inch of your life, and two rather smart dining options. Reflections brasserie is the more informal choice, with AG's serving up some dynamic modern food in a dining room boasting an upscale and rather refined finish, with tables dressed up in white linen. The menu takes its inspiration from contemporary French cooking, with the South Downs and the waters off the South Coast providing a good deal of the wares on show. These are modern constructions, showing acute technical skills and some intelligent thinking. A first course combines Dorset crab and line-caught mackerel, for example, with pickled apple, peanuts and an apple

jelly, with another a rather clever deconstructed rabbit dish in its own consommé, with prune and parfait on toast. Among main courses, hay-smoked rib of beef comes with whisky-glazed cheek, violet gnocchi and maple-roast squash, and a fishy main might be wild brill with clams, cockles and an oyster emulsion. Desserts are equally as inventive; a caramelised pear and prune terrine, for example, with Muscat sorbet, quince and mulled wine, or another of hot banana soufflé with malt toffee ice cream and toasted corn ice cream. There's a tasting menu with optional wine flight, and everything including the bread is made with craft and attention to detail.

Chef Mark Budd **Owner** Alexander Hotels Ltd **Seats** 30, Pr/dining room 18 **Times** 12-2.30/7-9.30 Closed Mon, L Tue-Sat **Prices** Tasting menu £75-£110, Starter £16-£22, Main £28-£30, Dessert £9.50-£13.50 **Wines** 13 by glass **Parking** 100 **Notes** Tasting menu with wine 8 course, Sunday L £24-£30, No children

TYNE & WEAR

Eslington Villa Hotel

◉ Modern British

tel: 0191 487 6017 **8 Station Rd, Low Fell NE9 6DR**
email: home@eslingtonvilla.co.uk **web:** www.eslingtonvilla.co.uk
dir: *off A1(M) exit for Team Valley Trading Estate. Right at 2nd rdbt along Eastern Av. Left at car show room, hotel 100yds on left*

Simple modern cooking in a Victorian villa

A restyled Victorian villa with a pair of flights of steps sweeping up to the front has become a family-owned contemporary hotel of great character. It's run with a genuine sense of bonhomie by Nick and Melanie Tulip, and its popularity as a wedding venue isn't hard to fathom. Dining goes on mainly in a conservatory extension with tiled floor and commanding views over the lawns, as well as in the interior room behind it. Some ambitious ideas are tried out, as in a three-bird terrine with fine bean salad and sticky raisins, the last element rather dominating the whole, but the simpler things perhaps work best. Steamed salmon with mash in a dilled-up root vegetable nage is one way with fish, or there might be tender, flavourful braised venison with beetroot in a sweet jus. The vanilla pannacotta wobbles good and proper, and comes with luscious Italian amarena cherries.

Chef Jamie Walsh **Owner** Mr & Mrs N Tulip **Seats** 80, Pr/dining room 30
Times 12–2/5.30–9.45 Closed 25–26 Dec, 1 Jan, BHs **Prices** Fixed L 2 course £13.95, Fixed D 3 course £27.50–£30.50, Service optional **Wines** 9 bottles over £30, 36 bottles under £30, 8 by glass **Parking** 30 **Notes** Early bird D 2/3 course £14.95/£17.95 from 5.30–6.45pm, Sunday L £16.75–£19.75, Vegetarian available, Children welcome

Blackfriars Restaurant

◉ Traditional & Modern British

tel: 0191 261 5945 **Friars St NE1 4XN**
email: info@blackfriarsrestaurant.co.uk **web:** www.blackfriarsrestaurant.co.uk
dir: *Take only small cobbled road off Stowell St (China Town). Blackfriars 100yds on left*

Productive brasserie cooking in the old Dominican refectory

The Dominican friary at the heart of medieval Newcastle is an integral part of the city's heritage, and a thriving modern restaurant has arisen on the site where they began serving food to the monks in 1239. Plenty of natural wood, exposed stonework and medieval artefacts establish the venerable tone, but the clientele is more mixed these days, with students and tourists mingling with football supporters fortifying themselves early, before setting off to St James's Park. The brasserie classics of today are given some productive twists, as in a dish of hand-rolled pasta with Northumberland oxtail in sage butter, or peppered mackerel with goats' cheese and chive soufflé and horseradish cream. Mains constructively pair well-timed cod with a haggis cake, alongside pea purée, spinach and a poached egg, and roasted gammon steak with pease pudding, while crowd-pleasers among desserts include dark chocolate torte with hazelnut brittle and Horlicks ice cream.

Chef Dan Duggan **Owner** Andy & Sam Hook **Seats** 80, Pr/dining room 50
Times 12–2.30/5.30–12 Closed Good Fri & BHs, D Sun **Prices** Fixed L 2 course fr £15, Fixed D 3 course fr £18, Starter £5–£11, Main £12–£25, Dessert £5–£9 **Wines** 14 bottles over £30, 31 bottles under £30, 8 by glass **Parking** Car park next to restaurant **Notes** Fixed menu available 5.30–7pm, Sunday L £12–£18, Vegetarian available, Children welcome

Café 21 Newcastle

◉ Modern British V

tel: 0191 222 0755 **Trinity Gardens, Quayside NE1 2HH**
email: enquiries@cafetwentyone.co.uk
dir: *From Grey's Monument, S to Grey St & Dean St towards Quayside, left along the Quayside, 3rd left into Broad Chare. 1st right then 1st left into Trinity Gdns, restaurant on right*

Brasserie buzz on the Newcastle quayside

The spacious, glass-fronted brasserie, with its polished wooden floor, leather banquettes and neatly clothed tables, remains as buzzy as ever, with slick and smooth service ensuring that all is as it should be. Part of the attraction is the ambitious cooking, with the longish menu an appealing mix of modern British brasserie-style dishes. Cheddar and spinach soufflé, perfectly cooked and nicely presented, is a great way to start, and there might be scallops grilled with chilli and garlic, or foie gras terrine. Main courses offer variety aplenty, from skewered tiger prawns on coconut curry risotto, through grilled calves' liver with bacon and onions, to roast cod fillet with boulangère potatoes, brown shrimps and red wine sauce. Crusty white bread is appreciated, and puddings can be a highlight, among them chocolate and salted caramel macaroons, and passionfruit soufflé with chocolate sorbet.

Chef Chris Dobson **Owner** Terry Laybourne **Seats** 90, Pr/dining room 44
Times 12–2.30/5.30–10.30 Closed 25–26 Dec, 1 Jan, Etr Mon, D 24 Dec **Prices** Fixed L 2 course £16.50, Fixed D 3 course £21, Starter £7.60–£14.80, Main £16–£29.80, Dessert £6.20–£9.20 **Wines** 54 bottles over £30, 32 bottles under £30, 15 by glass **Parking** NCP/Council **Notes** Fixed L/D 2/3 course available Mon-Fri D 5.30–7pm, Sunday L £18.50–£22, Children welcome

House of Tides

Rosettes not confirmed at time of going to print

NEWCASTLE UPON TYNE   Map 21 NZ26

Modern British **NEW**
tel: 0191 230 3720 **28-30 The Close NE1 3RF**
email: info@houseoftides.co.uk

Virtuoso cooking with a touch of fun

The Rosette award for this establishment has been suspended due to a change of chef. Reassessment will take place in due course under the new chef.
Local lad made good, Kenny Atkinson, a veteran of telly cheffery with appearances in *The Great British Menu* et al, is the talk of the toon these days, firing on all cylinders in his new gaff, a 16th-century merchant's town house by the River Tyne. The old quayside building flaunts its industrial heritage flagstone floors, exposed beams and cast-iron columns, while the kitchen is not only open to view for diners, but to anyone who walks by outside the restaurant. Things begin on the ground floor with aperitifs before diners proceed up to the restaurant proper on the first floor for a bravura show of creativity and technical wizardry. Produce is resolutely British, often locally sourced, and delivered via two nine-course tasting menus, one of which is a veggie option – this is a chef who clearly prefers to show you what he can do rather than let you choose what you would

like to eat, although if you're counting the pennies, you might come mid-week for a cheaper fixed menu, or a 3-course option that allows diners to cherry-pick items off the tasting format. Luckily the whole edifice is supported by excellent technical skills, a thoughtful approach, and a fun element that aims to defuse the stuffiness of 'faine daining'. Baby leeks are steamed, deep-fried and served in black truffle to look like soil, with an onion purée for dipping. Lindisfarne oysters spiked with cucumber, lime and ginger come on a bed of pebbles while a dry ice mist wafts the smell of seaweed across the table. Further ideas include scallops on sliced celeriac with braised and rolled pig's head, smoked eel beignet and white truffle, or a posh Craster fish pie filled with smoky kippers, mussels and lobster. Splendid cheeses intervene before puddings such as a dark bitter chocolate pavé balanced by meringue, pistachio, red wine syrup and lemon ice cream.

Chef Kenny Atkinson **Owner** Kenny Atkinson **Times** 5.30-9.30 Closed 2 wks Xmas-New Year, Sun-Mon, L all week **Prices** Tasting menu £50-£65 **Wines** 35 bottles over £30, 25 bottles under £30, 20 by glass

Jesmond Dene House

NEWCASTLE UPON TYNE   Map 21 NZ26

Modern British, European
tel: 0191 212 3000 **Jesmond Dene Rd NE2 2EY**
email: info@jesmonddenehouse.co.uk **web:** www.jesmonddenehouse.co.uk
dir: *From city centre follow A167 to junct with A184. Turn right towards Matthew Bank. Turn right into Jesmond Dene Rd*

Imaginative modern cooking in an Arts and Crafts stately home

Not the least aspect of Jesmond Dene's allure is that it has always felt like a splendid country house that ought to be standing in the midst of rolling English countryside somewhere, and yet is actually within the city limits of Newcastle. Its original Georgian architect, John Dobson, was responsible for much of the look of the old city centre, but the present incarnation of the house dates largely from the 1870s, when its new owner, Andrew Noble, had it extended and enhanced in the Arts and Crafts style to act as a magnet to the glitterati of Tyneside society and beyond. The plasterwork, stone carvings and stained glass are all worthy of your scrutiny, while the restaurant conveys a mix of design messages, with striped carpeting, russet and ivory-coloured walls, dark wood dresser, paintings and prints. The full panoply of modern British culinary techniques is on display in

menus that show plenty of Michael Penaluna's imagination, building to a multi-course taster with optional wine flight, where all the stops are pulled out. A serving of tenderly flavourful chicken breast poached in Earl Grey comes with accompaniments of lemon marmalade and romanesco, along with a clutch of sesame seeds. Following it might come judiciously timed monkfish with Serrano ham, sea kale and al dente wild garlic risotto, or fillet of locally reared Belted Galloway beef crusted in bone marrow and parsley, garnished with beetroot and chard. A performance dessert with high visual impact consists of a sphere of dark chocolate that melts before your eyes to reveal a disc of shortbread with salted caramel and roasted peanuts, or there might be a sablé made with roast plums and served with Sichuan pepper espuma. All the incidentals, from appetisers to pre-dessert, combine to make this an all-round classy experience.

Chef Michael Penaluna **Owner** Peter Candler, Tony Ganley, Terry Bayliff, Paul Morrisey **Seats** 80, Pr/dining room 24 **Times** 12-2/7-9.30 **Prices** Tasting menu fr £75, Starter £13.50-£15.50, Main £19.50-£35, Dessert £5-£9.50 **Wines** 99 bottles over £30, 42 bottles under £30, 24 by glass **Parking** 64 **Notes** Sunday L £25-£26, Vegetarian available, Children welcome

NEWCASTLE UPON TYNE *continued*

David Kennedy's Food Social

◉ Modern British

tel: 0191 260 5411 **The Biscuit Factory, 16 Stoddart St, Shieldfield NE2 1AN**
email: info@foodsocial.co.uk

Brasserie dining in a stylish commercial art gallery

The synergy between art and food is laid bare here in The Biscuit Factory (where Food Social is based). There's plenty to inspire, whether it is the artworks on display in the industrial heritage building, or the bright, modern cooking of Andrew Wilkinson. The easy-going restaurant and bar has exposed brickwork and ducting as remnants of the past, and leather sofas from which you can admire the art. The menu reflects the region with warm appreciation and offers some appealing dishes which are both rustic and refined. Chicken liver parfait is full of flavour among first courses, or there might be a pressing of locally-shot game with quince, root vegetables and lentils. Main courses are no less robust and hearty: blade of beef, perhaps, braised in red wine and served with creamed potatoes, or a veggie suet pudding packed with leeks. Among desserts, chocolate delice shows a light touch, served with ginger ice cream and a lime granita.

Times 12-2/5.30-9 Closed 25-26 Dec & 1 Jan, D Sun

Hotel du Vin Newcastle

◉◉ British, French

tel: 0191 229 2200 **Allan House, City Rd NE1 2BE**
email: reception.newcastle@hotelduvin.com **web:** www.hotelduvin.com
dir: *A1 junct 65 slip road to A184 Gateshead/Newcastle, Quayside to City Rd*

French brasserie fare in designer hotel with superb wine list

As ever with this chain, the building itself is a feature, in this case the converted red-brick Edwardian warehouse of the Tyne Tees Steam Shipping Company. Its riverside location gives the hotel commanding views of the city's many bridges, and the centre is just moments away. In keeping with other branches, the restaurant has the look of a French bistro, with its darkwood floor and wooden-topped tables; patio doors open on to a courtyard for alfresco eating and drinking. Trademark French brasserie fare is the deal, prepared from fresh seasonal produce, with starters taking in simple onion soup to more ambitious pan-seared scallops with artichoke and pistachio purée and pancetta vinaigrette. Old faithful boeuf bourguignon and moules frites show up among main courses, the range extended by the likes of well-presented roast halibut fillet nicely complemented by a robust langoustine bisque. Light and moist Black Forest gâteau is a good example of the beast.

Chef Stuart Donaldson **Owner** KSL Capital **Seats** 86, Pr/dining room 22
Times 12-2.30/5.30-10 **Prices** Starter £6.25-£11.95, Main £12.50-£29.50, Dessert fr £6.95 **Wines** 350 bottles over £30, 15 bottles under £30, 18 by glass **Parking** 15, On street (pay & display) **Notes** Sun brunch 4 course, Vegetarian available, Children welcome

Read our interview with chef Michael Caines on page 29

Hotel Indigo Newcastle

◉ Traditional British **NEW** v

tel: 0191 300 9222 **2-8 Fenkle St NE1 5XU**
email: info@mpwsteakhousenewcastle.com **web:** www.hotelindigonewcastle.com
dir: *Tyne Bridge, take 1st right St Nicholas St, 1st left Westgate Rd, right Scotswood Rd, continue onto Clayton St, hotel on right*

Boutique styling and a modern-meets-classical menu

A new-build hotel with a bit of boutique swagger, Indigo aims to make an impression, and its Marco Pierre White Steakhouse, Bar & Grill certainly helps to lay down a marker as a serious address in the city. As you'd expect with anywhere bearing the MPW name, there's a high-end finish to the ground-floor room, with plush leather chairs, and some banquette seating, plus pristine white tablecloths and good design all-round. The open kitchen brings even more energy to the space. The menu combines British and European classical thinking and there's a decidedly comfort-orientated spin to proceedings. Potage of Mussels Billy by or potted duck with Agen prunes are good choices to kick-off a meal, or there's all the clarity and simplicity of smoked salmon with brown bread and butter. There are pies (Wheeler's of St James's fish version, for example), classy fish and chips, or something like pan-fried duck with the leg slow-roasted and French-style peas.

Chef Paul Amer **Owner** Interstate Hotels **Seats** 96 **Times** 12-3/6.30-10 **Prices** Fixed L 2 course £18.50, Fixed D 3 course £28.50, Starter £5.75-£9.50, Main £13.50-£28.75, Dessert £6.25 **Wines** 36 bottles over £30, 19 bottles under £30, 12 by glass **Parking** 120 **Notes** Pre-theatre 3 course Fri-Sat £25, Paul Amer menu Fri-Sat D, Sunday L £15-£18.50, Children welcome

House of Tides

Rosettes not confirmed at time of going to print – see page 513

Jesmond Dene House

◉◉◉ *– see page 513*

Malmaison Newcastle

◉ French, British

tel: 0844 6930658 **104 Quayside NE1 3DX**
email: newcastle@malmaison.com **web:** www.malmaison.com
dir: *A1 junct 65 to A184 signed Gateshead/Newcastle. Follow signs for city centre, then for Quayside/Law Courts. Hotel 100yds past Law Courts*

Brasserie dining with bright modern food by the quay

Facing the Gateshead Millennium Bridge, the Newcastle branch of the urban-cool Mal group has a top spot in the heart of the quayside action. Its rich and glamorous decor brings in the crowds for a cool cocktail in the Malbar, or some feel-good dining in the brasserie restaurant. The kitchen team are an industrious lot, turning out some bright modern food that doesn't challenge too much, but doesn't lack for good ideas. Chicken lollipops is a fun dish that involves little spears of satay, Thai bonbon and more, served with a sweet chilli and aïoli dipping sauces, or you might start with a classic Caesar salad (also maxed up to a main course). There are posh burgers and steaks cooked on the grill, or the likes of pan-fried sea bass with chorizo, samphire and cockle vinaigrette. Finish with a iced cream parfait with drunken cherries.

Chef Jim Hall **Owner** KSL Group **Seats** 68, Pr/dining room 20 **Times** 12-2.30/6-11 **Prices** Prices not confirmed **Wines** 62 bottles over £30, 47 bottles under £30, 42 by glass **Parking** 60, Sandgate (chargeable) **Notes** Brunch available, Sunday L, Vegetarian available, Children welcome

Vujon

 Indian NEW

tel: 091 2210601 **29 Queen St, Quayside NE1 3UG**
email: mahtab@vujon.com

Fine dining Indian style at the trendy quayside

Set in the trendy quayside area, Vujon has been the smart place to go for new-wave Indian cuisine since the 1990s. A stylish contemporary-looking dining room and switched-on service are the backdrop to a creative mix of classic and up-to-date Indian dishes. Spicing is expert and can be delicate, particularly in a main course of boneless pheasant tarkari, cooked in a mildly spicy sauce that shows its French origins from the Pondicherry region, while fusion dishes such as Jaipur-style pan-seared venison fillet, scented with cloves and served with spicy tomato and chilli jam, appear among old favourites along the lines of lamb saag gosht and chicken tikka masala. Rice and naan breads are exemplary, and the tandoor naturally plays its part too, turning out grilled tiger prawns marinated in chilli, lemongrass, kaffir lime and garlic. Super-sweet gulab jamun dumplings soaked in rose and cardamon syrup make for a classic finale.

Chef Ataur Rahman, Anhar Mohammed **Owner** Mr Miah **Seats** 80
Times 12–2/5.30–11.30 Closed 25 Dec, L Sun **Prices** Starter £4.90–£7.90, Main £9.90–£15, Dessert £3.50–£5.90, Service optional **Wines** 13 bottles over £30, 27 bottles under £30, 2 by glass **Notes** Fixed L & D menu available, Vegetarian available

WARWICKSHIRE

ALCESTER Map 10 SP05

Number 50

 Modern British

tel: 01789 762764 **50 Birmingham Rd B49 5EP**
email: info@numberfifty.co.uk
dir: From town centre towards Birmingham & M42. Restaurant is opposite Alcester Grammar School

Unfussy cooking in a friendly modern bistro

A 17th-century cottage on the outside, Number 50 opens onto a scene of clean-cut contemporary style that mixes up ancient oak beams with cream-washed walls hung with modern art, and leather chairs at darkwood tables and slate placemats. The place has a strong local fan base, and no wonder: the vibe exudes the relaxed, friendly bustle of a well-loved neighbourhood eatery. The kitchen deals in cooking to suit the surroundings – unpretentious modern British dishes that are big on flavour, cooked accurately and without fuss, using a rock-solid base of locally-sourced produce. Set-price menus offer great value, setting out with seared scallops with green pea pannacotta, pea purée and crispy pancetta, while main-course roasted duck breast gets spicy Szechuan treatment and is matched with potato terrine and liquorice jus. To finish, a simple classic is given a novel spin: rhubarb crumble soufflé comes with custard ice cream.

Times 10–2.30/6.30–10 Closed Mon, D Sun

ALDERMINSTER Map 10 SP24

Ettington Park Hotel

 Traditional & Modern British

tel: 01789 450123 **CV37 8BU**
email: ettingtonpark@handpicked.co.uk **web:** www.handpickedhotels.co.uk/ettingtonpark
dir: M40 junct 15/A46 towards Stratford-upon-Avon, then A439 into town centre onto A3400 5m to Shipston. Hotel 0.5m on left

Confident contemporary cooking in a Gothic mansion

A magnificent example of mid-Victorian Gothic architecture, Ettington Park stands in 40 acres of grounds in the picturesque Stour Valley (the river runs through the estate). The interior is in keeping with the style, all antiques and walls hung with paintings; look out too for a number of friezes. The Oak Room restaurant takes its name from its panelled walls under a moulded ceiling. Staff are friendly and well drilled and deliver some surprisingly – given the surroundings – contemporary cooking. A deconstructed club sandwich is something of a signature starter, a successful amalgam of flavours consisting of chicken tortellini, tomato confit and aïoli, bacon foam, quail's eggs, little gem and breadcrumbs. If dishes seem to pile on the ingredients they nonetheless come off: witness a main course of seared scallops wrapped in smoked bacon served with apple and fennel coleslaw, deep-fried brie and cranberry sauce. An exotic element is sometimes seen – curry-crusted loin of monkfish with dhal and an aubergine and onion bhaji – and puddings continue the labour-intensive approach, among them an attractive assiette of chocolate (millefeuille, cannelloni and lime-flavoured ganache).

Times 12–2/7–9.30 Closed L Mon-Fri

ANSTY Map 11 SP48

Macdonald Ansty Hall

 British

tel: 0844 879 9031 **Main Rd CV7 9HZ**
email: ansty@macdonald-hotels.co.uk **web:** www.macdonald-hotels.co.uk/anstyhall
dir: M6/M69 junct 2 through Ansty village approx 1.5m

Tried-and-tested modern dishes not far from Stratford

Whether you're up in the area for the cultural enlightenment of the Shakespeare trail, or doing business in nearby Brum, Ansty Hall makes a rather classy base. The handsome, red-brick 17th-century mansion house sits in eight acres of landscaped grounds amid the rolling farmland and thatched cottages of Warwickshire. Within, all is elegantly furnished and replete with period character, not least in the classy Shilton dining room, where lavishly-draped sash windows offer views of the surrounding landscape. Tables are clothed in their best white linen, and the emphasis is firmly on British food wrought from good-quality seasonal produce, cooked without pretension and served without undue fanfare and fuss. Ham hock and leek terrine with chilled pease pudding gets things off the mark, followed by braised ox cheeks with toasted root vegetables and mash. Warm hazelnut and walnut sponge with home-made Muscovado ice cream and sweet pickled plums makes for a great finale.

Chef Paul Kitchener **Owner** Macdonald Hotels **Seats** 60, Pr/dining room 40
Times 12.30–2.30/6.30–9.30 Closed D 25 Dec **Prices** Prices not confirmed, Service optional **Wines** 12 by glass **Parking** 100 **Notes** Sunday L, Vegetarian available, Children welcome

ARMSCOTE
Map 10 SP24

The Fuzzy Duck
 Seasonal British **NEW**

tel: 01608 682635 **Ilmington Rd CV37 8DD**
email: info@fuzzyduckarmscote.com **web:** www.fuzzyduckarmscote.com
dir: M40 junct 5

Creative modern food in a swish gastro-pub

This upmarket gastro-pub with boutique bedrooms is looking pretty swanky these days after a makeover that made the most of the original character of the place (it's been doing the business as a coaching inn since the 18th century) and injected a bit of contemporary style. There's a serious approach to food and a pleasing lack of pretention. The modern British menu reads like a dream with lots of local ingredients on show and no lack of imagination or creativity. Hand-dived scallops come with confit duck, summer turnip and smoked hazelnuts in a thoroughly modern dish that strikes a good balance, and that might be followed by Scottish Red stag with heritage carrots, sweet cicely purée, blackcurrant and a potato fondant. A meat-free main course might be pearl barley risotto with mushrooms, duck yolk and truffle. Desserts such as stout and chestnut pudding have no less appeal and invention as witnessed in the accompanying cherry sorbet, stout ice cream and pork scratchings (yes, that's right: pork scratchings).

Chef Joe Adams **Owner** Tania & Adrian Slater **Seats** 35, Pr/dining room 20 **Times** 12-2.30/6.30-9 **Closed** Mon **Prices** Starter £4.50-£9.50, Main £9.95-£29, Dessert £4.25-£6.95, Service optional **Wines** 22 bottles over £30, 21 bottles under £30, 6 by glass **Parking** 15, On street **Notes** Sunday L £14.50-£15.95, Vegetarian available, Children welcome

BRANDON
Map 11 SP47

Mercure Coventry Brandon Hall Hotel & Spa

 International

tel: 024 7654 6000 **Main St CV8 3FW**
email: h6625@accor.com **web:** www.mercure.com
dir: A45 towards Coventry S. After Peugeot-Citroen garage on left, at island take 5th exit to M1 South/London (back onto A45). After 200yds, immediately after Texaco garage, left into Brandon Ln, hotel after 2.5m

Confident, unfussy cooking in a smart manor-house hotel

Set in 17 acres of green-and-pleasant Warwickshire countryside, Brandon Hall is a smartly-revamped 19th-century manor that has something for everyone, whether you're in the area for business, or enjoying a spot of down time in the spa and fitness centre. Tones of chocolate and green predominate in the smart, contemporary-styled Clarendon restaurant, while service is as keen as mustard and the kitchen follows the seasons, drawing on conscientiously-sourced supplies for its straight-and-true menu of uncomplicated ideas. Well-made ham hock terrine is served with apple and celeriac salad and home-made piccalilli, or you could kick off with sautéed wild mushrooms in creamy white wine sauce on toasted brioche. Mains can be as straightforward as a 28-day-aged rib-eye steak with herb-roasted field mushrooms, plum tomatoes, chips and pesto hollandaise, or there might be cod fillet with Dorset crab risotto and lobster sauce. For pudding, a chocolate fondant releases the requisite hot sauce when cut open, and comes with raspberry ripple ice cream and marshmallows.

Times 7-9.30 **Closed** L Sat

HENLEY-IN-ARDEN
Map 10 SP16

The Bluebell
British

tel: 01564 793049 **93 High St B95 5AT**
email: info@bluebellhenley.co.uk
dir: M4 junct 4, A3400 (Stratford Rd) to Henley-in-Arden

Exciting globally-influenced food in a Tudor coaching inn

The Bluebell occupies a half-timbered coaching inn dating from the Tudor period on Henley's uncommercialised High Street. Within are uneven flagged floors, beams in the low ceilings, lots of white plaster, draught beers in the bar and an enterprising restaurant menu that pulls in the punters. The kitchen taps into local supply lines for its produce and travels further afield for some ideas, so expect Moroccan-style lentils with roast, spiced neck fillet of lamb along with a shallot, anchovy and parsley salad, and a cassoulet of orzo, cockles and vegetables with roast fillet, juicy and moist, of stone bass. Dishes are intelligently thought out and technique is never in doubt. A lovely, rich celeriac and pear velouté is served with a ramekin of crisp and cheesy gougères, and a pressing of duck and foie gras is enhanced by spicy plum purée and a helping of baby onions and beans. Home-baked sourdough bread gets rave notices, and desserts are well regarded: perhaps apricot, cranberry and sultana brioche-and-butter pudding with white chocolate ice cream.

Chef James Devonshire **Owner** Leigh & Duncan Taylor **Seats** 46, Pr/dining room 10 **Times** 12-2.30/6-9.30 **Closed** Mon (ex BHs), D Sun **Prices** Fixed L 2 course £15, Fixed D 3 course £18, Starter £6.45-£8.95, Main £12.95-£24.95, Dessert £6-£6.95, Service optional **Wines** 13 bottles over £30, 19 bottles under £30, 13 by glass **Parking** 20 **Notes** Afternoon tea £18, Sunday L £20-£25, Vegetarian available, Children welcome

LEA MARSTON
Map 10 SP29

Lea Marston Hotel & Spa
Modern British

tel: 01675 470468 **Haunch Ln B76 0BY**
email: info@leamarstonhotel.co.uk **web:** www.leamarstonhotel.co.uk
dir: From M42 junct 9/A4097 signed Kingsbury Hotel, 2nd turning right into Haunch Lane. Hotel 200yds on right

Modern seasonal cooking in a golf and spa hotel

The modern Lea Marston Hotel sits in the tranquil Warwickshire countryside buffered by 54 acres of grounds, and is handy for doing business or exploring all that the rejuvenated centre of Birmingham has to offer. There's a spa, of course, to sort out the de rigueur 21st-century pampering requirements, as well as a golf course and a good eating option in the shape of The Adderley Restaurant. Decked out in shades of aubergine and greys it's a swish, modish, low-lit and romantic space with an unbuttoned vibe. The kitchen deals in unpretentious contemporary ideas, with a clear focus on seasonal, local ingredients – pink and tender pigeon is balanced thoughtfully by raspberry vinaigrette and orange salad and makes a fine precursor to wild sea bass with scallops, peas and vanilla foam. Otherwise, you might go for confit rump of lamb with fondant potato, chickpea and chorizo cassoulet, and red wine jus. Finish with a wobbly coconut pannacotta partnered with pineapple and vanilla salsa and cardamom ice cream.

Chef Richard Marshall **Owner** Blake family **Seats** Pr/dining room 120 **Times** 1-3/7-9 **Closed** L Mon-Sat, D Sun **Prices** Fixed D 3 course £27.50, Starter £4.25-£9.50, Main £16.95-£29.95, Dessert £5.25-£6.50, Service optional **Wines** 6 bottles over £30, 23 bottles under £30 **Parking** 220 **Notes** Sunday L £13.95-£15.95, Vegetarian available, Children welcome

LEAMINGTON SPA (ROYAL)   Map 10 SP36

The Brasserie at Mallory Court

◎◎ Modern British v

tel: 01926 453939 & 330214 **Harbury Ln, Bishop's Tachbrook CV33 9QB**
email: thebrasserie@mallory.co.uk
dir: M40 junct 13 N'bound left, left again towards Bishop's Tachbrook, right onto Harbury Ln after 0.5m. M40 junct 14 S'bound A452 to Leamington, at 2nd roundabout left onto Harbury Ln

Casual brasserie dining in an elegant hotel

As well as the main dining room, Mallory Court also boasts a more contemporary looking brasserie a short stroll from the main house. No mere adjunct to the main action, this is a fine venue in its own right, with glass-topped wicker tables, soothing neutral decor, and a backdrop of gentle jazz, a nice counterpoint to the formal refinement of the principal restaurant. A proper sectioned-up brasserie menu is offered, covering a range from ham and potato croquette with piccalilli, through beef medallions in Madeira sauce, to chocolate marquise and pistachio ice cream. Dishes are given careful consideration, so that skilful technique produces a tempura-battered soft-shell crab with pungent aïoli, as well as intensely flavourful chicken rillettes with green beans. A layered dessert in a glass is always fun, and may consist here of blueberry and apple compôte topped with blueberry and vanilla pannacotta, granola, and apple sorbet. Or sign up for a selection of five pedigree cheeses from England, Ireland and France.

Chef Jim Russell **Owner** Sir Peter Rigby **Seats** 80, Pr/dining room 24
Times 12-2.30/6.30-9.30 Closed D Sun **Prices** Starter £4.25-£9.50, Main £11.50-£19.50, Dessert £5.95, Service optional **Wines** 42 bottles over £30, 30 bottles under £30, 10 by glass **Parking** 100 **Notes** Sunday L £22.50, Children welcome

Mallory Court Hotel

◎◎◎ – see below

Queans Restaurant

◎ Modern European

tel: 01926 315522 **15 Dormer Place CV32 5AA**
email: laura@queans-restaurant.co.uk

Charming restaurant with well-sourced menu

You'd never guess from her cheerful and welcoming demeanor that chef-proprietor Laura Hamilton works alone in the kitchen-there are no outward signs that she feels any pressure! This is a delightful establishment with a good deal of genteel charm, where a smartly neutral decor meets an appealing menu of unpretentious dishes based on high-quality regional produce. You might start with a vegetarian tart such as one filled with roasted beetroot and butternut squash, served with an accompanying walnut salad, or maybe a brie and hazelnut bake with a smoky bacon jam. Clearly a dab hand at vegetarian cookery, chef can also turn out some impressive meat and fish options, too, such as a main-course grilled whole black bream (marinated in coriander and lime mustard), or roast loin of lamb with caramelised onion and fig stuffing. Finish with strawberry and pink champagne cheesecake. Somehow Laura finds the time to produce her own ice cream which is sold locally (and here, of course).

Times 12-2.30/6-10 Closed L Sat-Tue, D Sun-Mon

Mallory Court Hotel

LEAMINGTON SPA (ROYAL)   Map 10 SP36

Modern British v NOTABLE WINE LIST

tel: 01926 330214 **Harbury Ln, Bishop's Tachbrook CV33 9QB**
email: reception@mallory.co.uk **web:** www.mallory.co.uk
dir: M40 junct 13 N'bound. Left, left again towards Bishop's Tachbrook. 0.5m, right into Harbury Ln. M40 junct 14 S'bound, A452 for Leamington. At 2nd rdbt left into Harbury Ln

Innovative modern seasonal cooking in a late-Victorian manor

Close by Royal Leamington Spa and Warwick, and also handy for the Shakespeare trail, Mallory Court was built for a cotton magnate at the close of the Victorian era. Since nothing is ever quite as it seems in Victorian architecture, the place is some kind of homage to a Georgian manor house, but looking lovely, whatever its age, in its luxuriant coat of climbing foliage. A mix of styles within spans an arc from the art deco hints of the informal Brasserie to the Lutyens idiom of the main house and its principal dining room. Paul Foster became head chef at Mallory in early 2014, and upholds the lively, innovative cooking style for which the place has been noted for many years now. Innovation may be a totem, and yet menus don't scorn the seasons, hunting out asparagus and the first soft fruits in late spring, on to autumn game and winter preserves. That said, not everything comes from Warwickshire, particularly when you begin withsalmon cooked at 40 degrees, its richness balanced with apple, cucumber, oyster emulsion, and Alexander leaves plucked fresh from the herb garden. Indeed the landlocked location happily doesn't preclude a plethora of fish and seafood, from shellfish tortellini in bisque to a main course of Cornish stone bass with chicory, cauliflower and sea vegetables. Meatier ideas come up trumps in a dish of roast venison with its own bolognaise in peppery port sauce. Dessert is a deconstructed take on a whipped egg custard tart with crisp brown butter pastry, lifted by the tartness of fresh apple julienne and apple sorbet; alternatively go for a savoury finish with a plate of pedigree British and continental cheeses dressed with plum chutney.

Chef Simon Haigh, Paul Foster **Owner** Sir Peter Rigby **Seats** 56, Pr/dining room 14
Times 12-1.45/6.30-8.45 Closed L Sat **Prices** Prices not confirmed, Service optional **Wines** 200 bottles over £30, 25 bottles under £30, 12 by glass **Parking** 100 **Notes** Tasting menu 7 course, Sunday L, Children welcome

LEAMINGTON SPA (ROYAL) *continued*

Restaurant 23 & Morgan's Bar

◉◉◉ – *see below*

SHIPSTON ON STOUR   Map 10 SP24

The Red Lion

◉ Traditional British

tel: 01608 684221 **Main St, Long Compton CV36 5JJ**
email: info@redlion-longcompton.co.uk web: www.redlion-longcompton.co.uk
dir: *5m S on A3400*

Well-presented modern pub food in a traditional country inn

Settle into a settle by the inglenook fireplace on a winter's evening, and prepare to be regaled by tales of the Long Compton witches, or the history of the Neolithic Rollright stone circle nearby. In an area drenched in ancient folklore, not far from Shipston-on-Stour, the Red Lion is a textbook country inn, down to the real ales, log-fired dining room and locally based seasonal cooking. The bill of fare is amped-up pub food, with the emphasis on eye-catching presentations and unimpeachable raw materials. A meal might progress from smoked haddock and sweetcorn chowder to chargrilled Barnsley lamb chop with crushed cannellini beans, maple-roasted shallots and rosemary jus, or from pork and chicken terrine with Bramley apple chutney to pesto-crusted salmon with spinach in garlicky provençale dressing. Look to the blackboard for daily specials, and make room for lemon and ginger cheesecake with lime syrup to close the deal.

Chef Sarah Keightley **Owner** Cropthorne Inns **Seats** 50, Pr/dining room 20
Times 12-2.30/6-9 Closed 25 Dec **Prices** Fixed L 2 course fr £13.95, Fixed D 3 course

---

fr £16.95, Starter £5.50-£6.95, Main £12.95-£16.95, Dessert £5.95-£6.95, Service optional **Wines** 2 bottles over £30, 24 bottles under £30, 10 by glass **Parking** 70 **Notes** Pre Fixe 2/3 course £12.50-£15.50 Mon-Thu L & 6-7pm, Sunday L fr £13.95, Vegetarian available, Children welcome

---

STRATFORD-UPON-AVON   Map 10 SP25

The Arden Hotel

◉◉ Modern British

tel: 01789 298682 **Waterside CV37 6BA**
email: enquiries@theardenhotelstratford.com web: www.theardenhotelstratford.com
dir: *M40 junct 15 follow signs to town centre. At Barclays Bank rdbt left onto High St, 2nd left onto Chapel Lane (Nash's House on left). Hotel car park on right in 40yds*

Enterprising modern cooking opposite the theatre

Directly facing the theatre complex of the Royal Shakespeare Company, the Arden has been coping with the tides of business generated by the Swan of Avon for many a long year. Overseas tourists and school parties of A-level students alike have trooped through its dining room, though these days a modern brasserie with big picture windows looking out over the river is the order of the day. Outdoor tables and a champagne bar play their parts in rising to the occasion, as does the enterprising contemporary cooking on offer from a skilled team. A favoured starter is the pot-roast pigeon with Scotch quail egg, oyster mushrooms and quinoa, a modern reference dish if ever there was. Mains take in the likes of roast cod with coco beans, spicy squid, chargrilled courgette, roast pepper and brandade, or duck breast with a little pie of the confit leg, braised chicory and orange purée. On-trend rhubarb gets a dessert look-in when it turns up in a moist cake strongly flavoured with orange and a crunchy garnish of almond brittle.

Times 12-5

Restaurant 23 & Morgan's Bar

LEAMINGTON SPA (ROYAL)   Map 10 SP36

Modern European
tel: 01926 422422 **34 Hamilton Ter CV32 4LY**
email: info@restaurant23.co.uk
dir: *M40 junct 13 onto A452 towards Leamington Spa. Follow signs for town centre, just off Holly Walk, next to police station*

Accomplished modern cookery in a handsome Victorian building

Peter Knibb's extravagantly stylish restaurant and bar operation is the cynosure of Leamington Spa's dining and drinking scene. Housed in a splendid, white-fronted Victorian building in the town centre, with steps leading up to a portico entrance, it's done out inside in best contemporary fashion. Apple and aubergine are the principal tones in Morgan's Bar, where Leamington sophisticates repair for galvanising cocktails and quality wines, and the dining room is done in more muted tones, with gathered drapes and lighting from outsized haloes. Knibb is a local boy, whose career began with a placement at Claridges in London, and has been in the steady ascendant ever since. His accomplished cooking is distinguished by a determination to work with the grain of top-drawer raw materials, producing worlds of satisfaction from dishes that are multi-faceted

without falling into the everything-but-the-kitchen-sink tendency. Crab and salmon ravioli with pressed cucumber in lemongrass bisque, dressed with herring roe, makes an uplifting sea-savoury starter, or there could be rabbit loin parcelled in pancetta with Agen prunes and pistachios, a distinctly French-inspired dish that acquires further depth from its accompaniments of a rabbit croquette and the seared liver. At main, roasts and sautés do prime components proud: cod comes with butternut squash, Jerusalem artichokes and Puy lentils in red wine, while venison rump is teamed with a pithivier of the meat, as well as Savoy cabbage, salsify and puréed ceps. The same intensive attention is lavished on desserts such as Brillat-Savarin cheesecake with gingerbread, poached rhubarb, ginger-beer jelly and rhubarb sorbet, or perhaps chocolate delice with hazelnut polenta cake, roasted pear and popcorn ice cream, and there are fine British and French artisan cheeses. The seven-course taster menu with its wine options is worth pre-booking for an occasion.

Chef Peter Knibb **Owner** Peter & Antje Knibb, Richard Steeves **Seats** 65, Pr/dining room 25 **Times** 12-2/6.15-9.45 Closed 26 Dec, 1 Jan, Mon, D Sun **Prices** Fixed D 3 course fr £18.95, Tasting menu fr £60, Starter £10-£15, Main £18-£27, Dessert £7.95-£12.50, Service optional **Wines** 200 bottles over £30, 26 bottles under £30, 11 by glass **Parking** On street opposite **Notes** Afternoon tea all week 3-5pm, Sunday L £24-£26, Vegetarian available, Children welcome

Billesley Manor Hotel

◉◉ Modern European

tel: 01789 279955 **Billesley, Alcester B49 6NF**
email: billesleymanor.reservations@pumahotels.co.uk **web:** www.pumahotels.co.uk
dir: *M40 junct 15, A46S towards Evesham. Over 3 rdbts, right for Billesley after 2m*

Traditional Anglo-French cooking in Tudor manor house

Set in 11 acres of primped and preened grounds in deepest Shakespeare country, Billesley Manor is a charming mellow-stone Elizabethan country mansion dating from the time of the Bard. A further attraction for those on the Shakespeare trail is a library reputedly used by the literary legend himself, but for those with culinary rather than literary matters in mind, the classic oak-panelled Stuart Restaurant is a more relevant venue. It is the quintessential English country-house setting-all plushly-upholstered comfort and formal service-and the kitchen has no intention of rocking this particular boat, sending out classically-inspired dishes with a nod to modern trends and presentation, and a keen eye on seasonal ingredients. A rich terrine of confit chicken and foie gras with quince jelly and pork scratchings gets things off to a flying start, ahead of cod fillet served atop curried lentils, and framed by baby samphire and minted yoghurt. Standards remain high through to dessert – a well-made chocolate fondant with lush triple chocolate ice cream.

Times 12.30-2/7-9.30

The Legacy Falcon Hotel

◉ British

tel: 0844 411 9005 **Chapel St CV37 6HA**
email: res-falcon@legacy-hotels.co.uk **web:** www.legacy-hotels.co.uk
dir: *M40 junct 15, follow town centre signs towards Barclays Bank on rdbt. Turn into High Street, between Austin Reed & WH Smith. Turn 2nd right into Scholars Lane & right again into hotel*

Tudor inn with pre- and post-theatre menus

The old Falcon looks the period Tudor part, a heavily timber-ribbed building with original windows that sit a few degrees off the perpendicular. It's only a short totter from the Royal Shakespeare Theatre, so the pre- and post-theatre menus are a reliably popular draw. An expansive beamed room with modern varnished bare tables is named Will's Place (no guessing in whose honour), and is a hospitable setting for contemporary pub food built on a foundation of fresh seasonal ingredients. Dishes are ambitious enough to please both eye and palate without resorting to undue gilding of the lily, producing main courses such as tenderly braised lamb shoulder with dauphinoise, buttered cabbage and a purée of carrots and elderflower, and properly indulgent desserts such as rich chocolate marquise.

Times 12.30-2/6-9

Macdonald Alveston Manor

◉ Modern British

tel: 01789 205478 **Clopton Bridge CV37 7HP**
email: events.alvestonmanor@macdonald-hotels.co.uk
web: www.macdonald-hotels.co.uk/alvestonmanor
dir: *6m from M40 junct 15, (on edge of town) across Clopton Bridge towards Banbury*

Classically based cooking in a charming Tudor manor

A Tudor manor house only a few minutes' walk from the centre of the Shakespeare action in Stratford, Alveston brims with old-school charm. When you've wearied of minimalism in glass and steel, the gnarled oak beams and mullioned windows of the Manor dining room suddenly look luxurious. Traditional service from table-side trays is the vehicle for the subtly modernised British dishes that emerge from a classically rooted kitchen. The limitless variations on Scotch egg see another twist, with a breadcrumbed smoked mackerel pâté outer casing to a runny egg, the plate

swiped with horseradish cream for good measure. Next up might be a pair of fine lamb cutlets alongside a pasty of minced lamb and pearl barley, with braised red cabbage and mash, or salmon fillet with crushed potato in herbed broth. Finish with a benchmark rendition of cherry Bakewell blobbed with clotted cream.

Chef Paul Harris **Owner** Macdonald Hotels plc **Seats** 110, Pr/dining room 40
Times 6-9.30 Closed L all week **Prices** Prices not confirmed **Wines** 15 bottles under £30, 15 by glass **Parking** 120 **Notes** Pre-theatre menu available, Vegetarian available, Children welcome

Menzies Welcombe Hotel Spa & Golf Club

◉◉ Modern British, French

tel: 01789 295252 **Warwick Rd CV37 0NR**
email: welcombe@menzieshotels.co.uk **web:** www.menzieshotels.co.uk
dir: *M40 junct 15, A46 towards Stratford-upon-Avon, at rdbt follow signs for A439. Hotel 3m on right*

Modern Euro-cuisine in a refurbished Victorian hotel

The mid-Victorian Welcombe Hotel is a gabled quasi-Jacobean confection which the Menzies group has recently treated to a comprehensive £2 million refurbishment. Thankfully the integrity of features such as the magnificent oak-panelled lounge with its open fireplace remain undisturbed, while the dining room has been done in corporate beige, with swagged brown drapes to frame the view over a section of the 150 acres of grounds. The kitchen pilots a course through the busy waters of modern European cuisine, dressing spicy squid with tomato, cucumber and red onion salsa, or savouring up silky-smooth pea velouté with salty ham hock and mustard grains. A bells-and-whistles main course sees loin of local venison teamed with vanilla-poached pear, puréed celeriac, baby leeks and chocolate oil, or there's a more classical skate wing with brown shrimps dressed in lemon and parsley. Pear and vanilla dispensed with at main-course stage, dessert must mean time for parsnips, turning up in the form of ice cream and crisps to accompany chocolate tart.

Chef Matt Workdon **Owner** Topland No 14 **Seats** 70, Pr/dining room 150
Times 12.30-2/7-10 Closed L Sat **Prices** Prices not confirmed, Service optional **Wines** 10 bottles over £30, 10 bottles under £30, 8 by glass **Parking** 150 **Notes** Pre-theatre D menu available from 5.30pm, Sunday L, Vegetarian available, Children welcome

Mercure Stratford-upon-Avon Shakespeare Hotel

◉ Modern British

tel: 01789 294997 **Chapel St CV37 6ER**
email: h6630@accor.com
dir: *Follow signs to town centre. Round one-way system, into Bridge St. At rdbt turn left. Hotel 200yds on left*

Modish cooking in historic Tudor building

From the outside, this link of the Mercure chain is all you'd hope for given the location-the historic, black-and-white timbered building is a real good looker. It's no slouch on the inside either, with a well-judged contemporary finish blending in nicely with the original features. That goes for Othello's Bar Brasserie, too, with its darkwood furniture, fireplace, smart table settings, and splashes of colour from the upholstered chairs. On the menu, modern British nicely sums up the aspiration, with plenty of good British ingredients and some preparations from farther afield. Thus chicken liver parfait is perked up with an accompanying vodka jelly, plus raspberry foam and toasted brioche, and among main courses you might go for a 28-day aged Casterbridge steak or wild mushroom tortellini with spinach and parmesan. There is a good choice of wines by the glass and the likes of lemon tart with passionfruit soufflé to bring down the curtain.

Times 12-10 All-day dining

STRATFORD-UPON-AVON *continued*

The Stratford

 British **NEW**

tel: 01789 271000 **Arden St CV37 6QQ**
email: thestratfordreception@qhotels.co.uk **web:** www. qhotels.co.uk
dir: *A439 into Stratford. In town follow A3400/Birmingham, at lights left into Arden Street, hotel 150yds on right*

Creative, well-presented cooking in contemporary hotel dining room

The sprawling Stratford hotel with its mod cons and state-of-the-art business facilities is also home to Quills Restaurant, a thoroughly contemporary place with a menu that shows a good degree of creativity. The part-wood-panelled walls give a sense of maturity to the space, joined by tones of purple, red and cream to maintain that urbane hotel-dining feel. The youthful service team set a pleasing, relaxed tone. The kitchen likes to deal in contemporary combinations and shows a keen eye for presentation. A scallop starter comes with pork belly 'nuggets', apple and rehydrated sultanas in a dish with a good balance of sweetness and sharpness, or go for chilled watermelon gazpacho with cured ham. The main course rump of lamb gets a Mediterranean spin in the company of feta, broad beans, peas and mint from the garden. For dessert, warm carrot cake comes with cardamom custard and stem ginger ice cream.

Chef Ben Tynan **Owner** QHotels **Seats** 70, Pr/dining room 120 **Times** 5.30-9.30 Closed L all week **Prices** Starter £5.50-£12.50, Main £13-£24.50, Dessert £6-£10 **Wines** 12 bottles over £30, 18 bottles under £30, 16 by glass **Parking** 90 **Notes** Pre-theatre menu available, Sunday L, Vegetarian available, Children welcome

WARWICK
Map 10 SP26

Ardencote Manor Hotel & Spa

Modern British

tel: 01926 843111 **The Cumsey, Lye Green Rd CV35 8LT**
email: hotel@ardencote.com **web:** www.ardencote.com
dir: *Off A4189. In Claverdon follow signs for Shrewley & brown tourist signs for Ardencote Manor, approx 1.5m*

Confident, creative cooking by a lake

Ardencote Manor occupies a prime piece of Warwickshire countryside with a golf course, pretty gardens and shimmering lakes to call its own. It's a popular wedding venue for obvious reasons, but The Lodge Restaurant, located in a separate building next to one of the lakes, is a venue of ambition in its own right. A table outside is a real fair-weather treat, but it looks great indoors, too, with its high quality finish (leather seats, neutral tones, linen tablecloths and glistening glassware). The cooking is contemporary stuff and shows a good deal of craft and creativity. A starter terrine of duck leg, for example, with confit gizzards, quince jam, roast pistachios and gingerbread shows classical sensibilities and a thorough understanding of taste and texture. Follow on with roast Atlantic turbot with vanilla-poached potatoes, cobnuts, Salcombe cock crab, apple, sea kale and wild chervil, or roast quail with pearl barley, artichokes, salted plums, ransoms and bread sauce. The confident cooking continues with desserts such as peanut butter cheesecake with salted peanuts, caramel popcorn and sweetcorn ice cream.

Times 12.30-2/6-10

Learn the latest foodie trends in Birmingham and Manchester on page 21

WELLESBOURNE
Map 10 SP25

Walton Hall

British

tel: 01789 842424 **Walton CV35 9HU**
web: www.thehotelcollection.co.uk/hotels/walton-hall-warwickshire
dir: *A429 through Bradford towards Wellesbourne, right after watermill, follow signs to hotel*

Carefully crafted cooking with a sense of fun

Seven miles from Stratford-upon-Avon, Walton Hall, which stands in 65 acres of Warwickshire amid lush gardens and a lake, is usefully placed to offer a breather from the hurly-burly of the Shakespeare trail. Interiors have been gently coaxed into modernity, the Moncreiffe dining room going for a light, airy feel with white walls, recessed floral displays and moderately sized chandeliers. Staff take a formal but friendly line, and Adam Bateman carefully crafted cooking is not without a sense of fun. Scallops and cauliflower purée is familiar enough, but achieves added depth here with a pungent emulsion sauce of oyster and garnishes of apple, leek and sorrel. That sets the tone for artfully considered main courses such as pink-cooked duck breast on a gingerbread base with foie gras, its richness and mellow spice counterpointed by the sweetness of beetroot and carrot, with artichoke to add edge. The textural approach to desserts makes an organised mess of rhubarb and custard, with granola, rhubarb ice cream, honeycomb and ginger, only the unnecessary space-dust seeming like a joke that has worn a bit thin.

Chef Adam Bateman **Owner** Puma Hotels **Seats** 60, Pr/dining room 40 **Times** 7-9.30 **Prices** Prices not confirmed, Service optional **Wines** 9 bottles over £30, 40 bottles under £30, 10 by glass **Parking** 240 **Notes** Vegetarian available, Children welcome

WEST MIDLANDS

BALSALL COMMON
Map 10 SP27

Nailcote Hall

Modern European

tel: 024 7646 6174 **Nailcote Ln, Berkswell CV7 7DE**
email: info@nailcotehall.co.uk **web:** www.nailcotehall.co.uk
dir: *On B4101 towards Tile Hill/Coventry, 10 mins from NEC/Birmingham Airport*

Traditional and modern in a 17th-century house

A half-timbered 17th-century house sitting in 15 acres of Warwickshire, Nailcote Hall became a hotel in 1990. It's a country house on a human scale, not far from the Midlands business hubs, and there's a golf course on hand. The low-ceilinged Oak Room restaurant with its inglenook fireplace and darkwood tables provides an atmospheric ambience in the evenings especially, when a resourceful repertoire of traditional British and more modern dishes is tried out. You might begin with well-seasoned asparagus velouté with a parmesan gougère and hazelnut oil, before tackling tender marinated loin of venison with spiced caramelised red cabbage and roast celeriac, finishing with prune and Armagnac soufflé with Earl Grey ice cream.

Times 12-2.30/7-9.30 Closed L Sat

BIRMINGHAM
Map 10 SP08

Adam's Restaurant

 – see opposite

Adam's Restaurant

BIRMINGHAM Map 10 SP08

Modern British V

tel: 0121 643 3745 **21A Bennetts Hill B2 5QP**
email: info@adamsrestaurant.co.uk
dir: *Located in Birmingham City Centre, 2 mins walk from New Street Station*

Dynamic contemporary cooking in the city centre

The Adam in question is Adam Stokes, a chef with bags of experience at the top of the culinary firmament, and now he has his name above the door. He's chosen a former sandwich shop just around the corner from New Street Station, which might sound great news in the passing trade front, but this is no everyday eatery: this is destination dining. The old snack bar has become a rather refined room, with a satisfying mix of old and modern, almost like a movie set in some near-future adventure-hard to place, but classic somehow. There are just 35 covers-they could have squeezed in many more-but that leaves plenty of space to relax and enjoy your meal. The service team are a confident bunch, matching the seriousness of the venture. Adam says 'my aim is not to baffle, but to excite and enthuse', which he readily achieves, for this is dynamic, modern cooking that makes perfect sense-balanced, creative and beautiful on the plate. Tasting

menus are the thing here, with five- or nine-course options (the latter only on Saturday night), plus a decent value lunchtime option which is a very good entry point. To kick things off, there are some pretty nifty amuse-bouches such as a fab goats' cheese and beetroot macaroon, for example. The five-course tasting menu might start with a dish of sea bream with sea vegetables and orange buckwheat, the fish as fresh as a daisy and cooked just right, followed by another refined and intelligent dish of Jerusalem artichoke, chorizo and egg yolk. The evident technical skills in the kitchen remain consistently high throughout, as seen in a course which matches pheasant breast with celeriac and a crispy mushroom fritter, the plate dressed with a Sauternes and grape sauce, or in a dessert which combines whisky and cream with chocolate and honey.

Chef Adam Stokes **Owner** Adam & Natasha Stokes **Seats** 35 **Times** 12-2/7-9.30 Closed 2 wks summer, 3 wks Xmas, Sun-Mon **Prices** Fixed L 3 course fr £32, Tasting menu £50-£80 **Wines** 66 bottles over £30, 4 bottles under £30, 19 by glass **Parking** On street **Notes** Tasting menu 5/9 course, Children welcome

Loves Restaurant

BIRMINGHAM Map 10 SP08

Modern British V

tel: 0121 454 5151 **The Glasshouse, Canal Square, Browning St B16 8FL**
email: info@loves-restaurant.co.uk
dir: *Turn off Broad St towards NEC & Sherbourne Wharf then left to Grosvenor St West & right into Sherbourne St, at end take right into Browning St*

Starry cooking on the Birmingham waterside

One of the heavyweights of the ever-improving Birmingham dining scene, Loves delivers a contemporary version of fine dining that impresses on the plate and palate while managing to maintain a happy mood in the dining room. There is no reverential hushed silence at Loves, simply the sound of happy customers. Steve and Claire Love opened their restaurant by one of the city's canals in 2009 and hit the ground running, which was not all that surprising given Steve's experience (he's a former Roux Scholarship winner, which won him a stint with the legendary Alain Ducasse) and Claire's knowledge and passion for wine and skills front-of-house. There's a satisfying lack of starchiness to the interior, with a chic minimalism that looks the part but doesn't distract, and there are floor-to-ceiling windows giving views over the watery urban landscape. Tasting menus of five or

ten courses stand alongside a concise à la carte menu (three choices per course), and there are top-drawer veggie versions of all of them. The provenance and quality of the ingredients is at the heart of the cooking, and everything that is brought to the table meets Steve's rigorous standards. His cooking is refined, beautifully crafted and everything looks glorious on the plate. They taste good, too, and there's enough of a British flavour to give this restaurant a genuine sense of place. A starter of Herefordshire beef carpaccio has a fine piece of meat at its heart, with pickled vegetables and a corned beef croquette elevating this often simple dish to a level of delicious refinement. Next up, Cotswold lamb, maybe, the slow-cooked belly, braised cheek and tongue served with lentils and gnocchi made with sheep's milk. Finish with a treatise on vanilla and apple, or tuck into the regional cheeses. The wine list is put together by Claire with heart and soul.

Chef Steve Love **Owner** Steve & Claire Love **Seats** 32, Pr/dining room 8 **Times** 12-1.45/6-9.30 Closed 1 wk Etr, 2 wks Aug & Xmas, Sun-Mon (excl last Sun of each month) **Prices** **Wines** 240 bottles over £30, 30 bottles under £30, 20 by glass **Parking** Brindley Place car park **Notes** ALC 2/3 course £40/£48, Sunday L £35, Children 10 yrs+ D

BIRMINGHAM *continued*

Hotel du Vin Birmingham

British, French | NOTABLE WINE LIST

tel: 0121 200 0600 **25 Church St B3 2NR**
email: info@birmingham.hotelduvin.com **web:** www.hotelduvin.com
dir: *M6 junct 6/A38(M) to city centre, over flyover. Keep left & exit at St Chads Circus signed Jewellery Quarter. At lights & rdbt take 1st exit, follow signs for Colmore Row, opposite cathedral. Right into Church St, across Barwick St. Hotel on right*

Bistro dining in converted former eye hospital

The former eye hospital is a grandiose Victorian red-brick edifice on a corner site in the regenerated Brummie hotspot of the Jewellery Quarter. A perfect location then, and thoroughly in keeping with the stylish brand's penchant for taking architecturally distinguished buildings to convert into its trademark boutique bolt-holes. The second city's branch of HdV retains oodles of period detail alongside cool modern styling. There's a classy champagne bar just off the central courtyard, and a clubby Pub du Vin serving up local ales in the former cellar bar. The bistro is an impressive space with lofty ceilings, bare floorboards, unclothed wooden tables, leather upholstered period chairs, and yellow ochre walls hung with framed, wine-themed pictures. Top-notch local produce drives the straightforward Anglo-French cooking – expect simple crowd-pleasers such as French onion soup, steak tartare and moules-frites, or you might take a classic opener like creamy chicken liver parfait with toasted brioche and raisin chutney ahead of monkfish grand-mère, garnished with pearl onions, pancetta and wild mushrooms and served with potato rösti. Sticking with the Gallic theme, finish with apple tarte Tatin with crème Normande. The outstanding wine list is up to the usual HdV standards.

Chef Mark Nind **Owner** KSL **Seats** 85, Pr/dining room 108 **Times** 12-2/6-10 **Prices** Fixed L 2 course £16.95, Fixed D 3 course £19.95, Starter £5-£11.95, Main £12.50-£29.50, Dessert £6.95 **Wines** 220 bottles over £30, 62 bottles under £30, 21 by glass **Parking** NCP Livery St **Notes** Sun brunch 4 course, Sunday L £12.95-£24.95, Vegetarian available, Children welcome

Lasan Restaurant

Indian

tel: 0121 212 3664 & 212 3665 **3-4 Dakota Buildings, James St, St Paul's Square B3 1SD**
email: info@lasan.co.uk
dir: *Near city centre, adjacent to Jewellery Quarter*

Contemporary Indian cooking in the Jewellery Quarter

Lasan is a Premier League contender in the new order of Brum's contemporary Indians. It has the de rigueur postcode in the trendy Jewellery Quarter, and minimal good looks in its expansive split-level layout – in fact, there's nothing obvious to suggest this is an Indian restaurant except for a sitar on the wall and ethnic background music. The vibe is up-tempo and high-decibel, but the service team are on the case, while the kitchen brigade hails from all corners of the sub-continent to ensure pukka regional authenticity. What arrives on the plate is contemporary fusion thinking applied to top-class raw materials. Goan mackerel recheado is pan-fried fillets spiced with chilli and garlic, served with fresh cucumber and mooli salad, while Wiltshire Downs lamb is showcased in lamb lababdar, a trio of marinated cutlet, ten-hour confit shoulder, and braised shin pattie pointed up with spicy lentils and smoked bone marrow jus spiced with nutmeg and cinnamon.

Chef Aktar Islam, Gulsher Khan **Owner** Jabbar Khan **Seats** 64 **Times** 12-2.30/6-11 Closed 25 Dec, L Sat **Prices** Starter £5.45-£12.95, Main £12.95-£21.95, Dessert £4.95-£7.95 **Wines** 14 bottles over £30, 12 bottles under £30, 7 by glass **Parking** On street **Notes** Sunday L, Vegetarian available, No children

Loves Restaurant

– *see page 521*

Purnell's

BIRMINGHAM Map 10 SP08

Modern British | NOTABLE WINE LIST
tel: 0121 212 9799 **55 Cornwall St B3 2DH**
email: info@purnellsrestaurant.com
dir: *Close to Birmingham Snow Hill railway station & junct of Church St*

Superbly accomplished and inventive cooking in a conservation area of the city

It's fair to say that Birmingham once lagged behind in the gastronomic stakes, but the second city now has a range of dining options to compete in the first division. Glynn Purnell's place in a conservation area of the financial district, not far from St Philip's cathedral, is a resounding case in point. It comes with the imprimatur of a TV celebrity chef, and has been expensively and stylishly fashioned out of a redbrick and terracotta corner site, the interior bathed in plenty of natural light during the day, the better to set off the cool blue and mushroom tones of the decor. The drill is tasting menus, a smaller seasonal one supplementing the bells-and-whistles nostalgia or ultra-mod offerings, labelled respectively Reminisce and Now. Technical wizardry and diverting presentations are much in evidence, and the all-important fun element of modern cooking is

borne in mind. Reminiscences include a skit on cheese and pineapple, with goats' curd cubes and a quarter of pineapple set amid micro-grissini cocktail sticks, and a nod to Birmingham's rich south Asian food heritage in the form of monkfish in masala with red lentils, pickled carrots and coriander chutney. Move into the Now with a whole range of oddball technical tricks and combinations, including curry-cured salmon with wasabi crumble and cucumber ketchup, Balmoral venison with liquorice, leeks and lettuce, and waffles in foie gras butter with crispy chicken skin and maple syrup. Combinations throughout are capable of bemusing, as when beef carpaccio with salt beef and sour cream arrives with octopus stewed in red wine. It all comes to a head in desserts such as the medley of whole, moussed and meringued rhubarb, with burnt English custard served in the two halves of an eggshell in a hay-lined basket, to ring down the curtain on a superbly accomplished performance.

Chef Glynn Purnell **Owner** Glynn Purnell **Seats** 45, Pr/dining room 12 **Times** 12-1.30/7-9 Closed 1 wk Etr, 2 wks end Jul-early Aug, Xmas, New Year, Sun-Mon, L Sat **Prices** Fixed L 3 course £32, Tasting menu £65-£85 **Wines** 284 bottles over £30, 20 bottles under £30, 20 by glass **Parking** On street, Snow Hill car park nearby **Notes** Tasting menu 6/12 course, Wine tasting fr £60, Vegetarian available, No children

Simpsons

Modern British V [NOTABLE WINE LIST]

tel: 0121 454 3434 **20 Highfield Rd, Edgbaston B15 3DU**
email: info@simpsonsrestaurant.co.uk
dir: *1m from city centre, opposite St George's Church, Edgbaston*

Outstanding beautifully-presented cooking in classy Edgbaston favourite

Chef-patron Andreas Antona's restaurant with rooms occupies a white Georgian house, with a verandah, in the genteel, leafy suburb of Edgbaston. The restaurant is a tastefully kitted-out space, with quality napery on formally set tables, and a conservatory extension looking over the landscaped garden (alfresco dining possible here under large parasols). The cooking is of the first order, with dishes displaying a high degree of sophistication built on top-class ingredients. Fillet of turbot, for instance, is partnered by oxtail and served with pickled shimeji mushrooms, grilled lettuce, salsify and red wine jus, a main course commendable for its skillful marriage of flavours and textures. The kitchen applies its own contemporary, imaginative and innovative approach to the classical French repertoire, showing a meticulous eye for detail and superb technical skills.

Smoked haddock appears as a starter with potato espuma, leeks and black pudding, or try duck confit with a duck egg, mushrooms, parsley roots and cep and chestnut velouté. Main-course combinations are just as intelligently thought through, showing a number of influences, with outstanding results. Lamb shank is paired with a samosa, yellow lentil dhal, burned aubergine, yoghurt and curry oil, and venison with haggis bolognese, celeriac and pear, while a more muted treatment is seen in some dishes: cod fillet in a pine nut crust hinting of vanilla, with potato terrine and cabbage. Well-crafted and attractive-looking desserts may run to passionfruit soufflé with coconut sorbet, and chocolate mousse with popcorn ice cream. As well as the carte and set-price lunch, there's an eight-course tasting menu with and without the sommelier's choice of wines.

Chef Andreas Antona, Luke Tipping **Owner** Andreas & Alison Antona **Seats** 70, Pr/dining room 20 **Times** 12-2.30/7-9.30 Closed BHs, D Sun **Prices** Fixed L 3 course fr £40, Tasting menu fr £90 **Wines** 20 bottles over £30, 10 bottles under £30, 11 by glass **Parking** 12, On street **Notes** Tasting menu 8 course, Sunday L, Children welcome

Turners

Modern French
tel: 0121 426 4440 **69 High St, Harborne B17 9NS**
email: info@turnersrestaurantbirmingham.co.uk

Cooking up a gastronomic storm in a Birmingham suburb

The days when Brum's culinary scene went about as far as a good night out for a few quid in the balti belt are long gone, and Turner's easily holds its own in the premier league of the new wave of stellar gastronomic offerings. The classy operation is tucked away in an unprepossessing row of shops on des-res Harborne's high street, but it stands out with its smart gunmetal-grey frontage, and you certainly won't forget where you are once inside, as chef-patron Richard Turner's name is etched all over the striking mirrors lining the walls of the bold, dark and moody charcoal-grey dining room. Equally unforgettable is the refined, confident and creative modern French cooking conjured from top-notch seasonal ingredients, and well-judged professional service boosts the quality factor still further. There's a lot of work going on in that kitchen, producing stunning-looking dishes with remarkable attention to detail, and it is all presented with due ceremony. Excellent home-made breads and meticulously-wrought amuses (a

pig's head croquette with a black squid ink cracker, apple purée and seafood emulsion, for example) precede stuffed pig's trotter with ham hock, piccalilli and Lincolnshire Poacher cheese fritters, a dish of punchy, clearly defined flavours all working together. A vibrant composition of red mullet and langoustine comes with courgette flowers (stuffed enterprisingly with prawns and prawn mousse), a rich and tasty ratatouille, crisp samphire and bouillabaisse sauce. Elsewhere, a tasting of new season lamb is a delightful workout of flavour and texture, delivered with the faultlessly seasonal accompaniments of wild garlic and asparagus. Finally, variations on chocolate is a masterclass in razor-sharp technique involving fondant, dark chocolate sauce and milk chocolate crisp, partnered with smooth and silky banana ice cream, and pointed up with intense swipes of lime and miso.

Chef Richard Turner **Owner** Richard Turner **Seats** 30 **Times** 12-2.30/6-9.30 Closed Sun-Mon, L Tue-Thu **Prices** Fixed L 2 course £25-£40, Fixed D 3 course £50-£80, Tasting menu £85 **Wines** 89 bottles over £30, 1 bottle under £30, 13 by glass **Parking** 50 **Notes** ALC 3 course £50, Tue Taste of Turners £35, Vegetarian available, Children welcome

BIRMINGHAM *continued*

Malmaison Birmingham

◉ Traditional, Modern

tel: 0121 246 5000 **1 Wharfside St, The Mailbox B1 1RD**
email: birmingham@malmaison.com **web:** www.malmaison.com
dir: *M6 junct 6, follow the A38 (city centre), via Queensway underpass. Left to Paradise Circus, 1st exit Brunel St, right T-junct, Malmaison directly opposite*

Buzzy setting and smart brasserie-style cooking

Housed in the former Royal Mail sorting office, the groovy Mailbox development is a flagship of Brum's sexy new image. The city's outpost of this stylish metropolitan hotel and brasserie chain has bagged the ideal location, with designer boutiques and a branch of Harvey Nic's as neighbours. The Mal brasserie pulls off its trademark look using a classic clubby blend of darkwood and chocolate leather, while old pictures of Birmingham's canal heritage give a sense of place. Staff are on the ball-there are no airs and graces here-and the menu matches the mood with unfussy modern brasserie classics. So you might start with chicken liver parfait with tomato chutney and toasted brioche, then move on to a straight-up grilled steak served with crispy frites and béarnaise sauce, or pan-fried sea bass with chorizo, heritage potatoes, samphire and cockle vinaigrette. Finish with an iced hazelnut parfait with praline and Valrhona chocolate sauce.

Times 12-2.30/6-10.30

Opus Restaurant

◉◉ Modern British

tel: 0121 200 2323 **54 Cornwall St B3 2DE**
email: restaurant@opusrestaurant.co.uk **web:** www.opusrestaurant.co.uk
dir: *Close to Birmingham Snow Hill railway station in the city's business district*

Smart city favourite for modern British cooking

Opus has bags of big-city attitude and a vibrant buzz in a cavernous open-plan space. An eye-catching, full-length, girder-framed glass frontage references the city's industrial heritage, while inside it's a stylish, cosmopolitan setting: darkwood floors, linen-clothed tables, olive green suede and black leather banquette seating, and earthy red ochre walls to relieve the muted palette. The menu has broad appeal, drawing in suited and booted execs from the financial and legal chambers nearby, as well as style-led shoppers doing lunch. Top-quality seasonal British produce anchors the whole operation, and it's all brought together in straightforward modern treatments – you'll find nothing fussy, over-complex or speculative in either composition or presentation of dishes. From the great-value market menu, a free-range ham hock and potato roulade might start you off, followed by cod with roasted artichokes, wild mushrooms, and wilted greens. Trade up to the carte, and pan-fried breast and herb-crusted leg of quail with leeks and bacon could get you going, followed by turbot fillet with spiced cauliflower purée, crushed potatoes and cod brandade.

Chef David Colcombe **Owner** Ann Tonks, Irene Allan, David Colcombe **Seats** 85, Pr/dining room 32 **Times** 12-2.45/6-10 Closed between Xmas & New Year, BHs, L Sat, D Sun **Prices** Fixed L 2 course £14, Fixed D 3 course £16, Tasting menu £75, Starter £4.75-£10.50, Main £15-£24, Dessert £2.25-£7, Service optional 12.5% **Wines** 29 bottles over £30, 30 bottles under £30, 11 by glass **Parking** On street **Notes** Tasting menu 5 course, Sunday L £25, Vegetarian available, Children welcome

Purnell's

◉◉◉ – *see page 522*

Simpsons

◉◉◉ – *see page 523*

Turners

◉◉◉ – *see page 523*

HOCKLEY HEATH   **Map 10 SP17**

Nuthurst Grange Hotel

◉◉ Modern British

tel: 01564 783972 **Nuthurst Grange Ln B94 5NL**
email: info@nuthurst-grange.co.uk **web:** www.nuthurst-grange.com
dir: *Exit A3400, 0.5m S of Hockley Heath. Turn at sign into Nuthurst Grange Lane*

Inventive cooking in classy country-house hotel

It may come as no surprise, given the beautiful gardens and the handsomeness of the house inside and out, that Nuthurst Grange is a big hit for weddings. As for non-conjugal visitors, there's still plenty of reason to come, not least for the food. There's a bistro in the orangery where you can order from the fine-dining carte if you wish, or you can choose to eat the same in the smart and elegant main dining room, with its country views, linen-clad tables and well-drilled service. The menu is a decidedly contemporary affair with lots of good ideas, carefully executed and based on fine produce. A starter of quail three ways, for example, has the breast cooked at 64 degrees, the leg crisped up and the egg pickled, whilst venison carpaccio comes with red cabbage slaw, endive salad, and a Valrhona chocolate oil. Caraway-roasted pork tenderloin stars in a main course with crushed purple potato cake, curly kale and Dijon mustard cream, and there's a touch of sunshine in a dessert of tropical fruit soufflé with coconut ice cream and exotic fruit smoothie.

Times 12-2.30/7-9 Closed D Sun

See advert opposite

MERIDEN   **Map 10 SP28**

Best Western Plus Manor NEC Birmingham

◉◉ Modern British, French

tel: 01676 522735 **Main Rd CV7 7NH**
email: reservations@manorhotelmeriden.co.uk **web:** www.manorhotelmeriden.co.uk
dir: *M42 junct 6, A45 towards Coventry then A452 signed Leamington. At rdbt take B4102 signed Meriden, hotel on left*

Smart modish cooking in a Midlands manor

The elegant Georgian Manor Hotel in the village of Meriden strikes a neat balance between town and country: the rural setting is charming, yet the National Exhibition Centre and Brum are close to hand if you're doing business in the area. The Regency Restaurant has carved itself a niche in the local foodie scene with its up-to-date takes on classic dishes; it is an airy, traditionally styled space hung with paintings of English country scenes above smartly dressed tables laid with sparkling glasses and fresh flowers, and young, upbeat staff ensure it all ticks along with nicely. Assured and unpretentious modern British cooking is the order of the day, starting with crab and scallop ravioli teamed with samphire and prawn bisque, followed by a piggy trio of pork tenderloin medallions, smoked pig's cheek and a trotter bonbon partnered with apricot and sage compôte, carrots, dauphinoise potato and thyme jus. The show closes with another well-matched trio-salted caramel parfait, white chocolate popcorn and a mini crème brûlée.

Chef Darion Smethurst **Owner** Bracebridge Holdings **Seats** 150, Pr/dining room 220 **Times** 12-3/6-10 Closed L Mon-Sat **Prices** Fixed L 3 course £19.50, Fixed D 3 course £27, Starter £7.25-£8.25, Main £16.75-£16.95, Dessert fr £4.25, Service optional **Wines** 1 bottle over £30, 34 bottles under £30, 16 by glass **Parking** 190 **Notes** Sunday L £19.50, Vegetarian available, Children welcome

Forest of Arden Marriott Hotel & Country Club

Modern British v

tel: 01676 522335 **Maxstoke Ln CV7 7HR**
email: nigel.parnaby@marriotthotels.com **web:** www.marriottforestofarden.co.uk
dir: M42 junct 6 onto A45 towards Coventry, over Stonebridge flyover. After 0.75m left into Shepherds Ln. Left at T-junct. Hotel 1.5m on left

Good eating at a smart golfing hotel

A big hotel with lots going on – golf and spa for a start – the Forest of Arden Marriott is well-positioned for the East Midlands hub, and its Oaks Bar and Grill is a restaurant of note in its own right. There's a bold carpet, leather banquettes, straight-backed chairs and scatter cushions giving it a bright and breezy modish feel, and views over the grounds are an added bonus. On the menu, straightforward grills rub shoulders with more inventive things; a classic combination of warm figs and Parma ham is paired with bucks fizz jelly and sweet saffron syrup, followed perhaps by baked fillet of haddock with a poached egg, curried sauce and sautéed greens. To finish, strawberry Arctic roll, vanilla pannacotta and compôte is a good bet.

Chef Darcy Morgan **Seats** 192, Pr/dining room 18 **Times** 1-2.30/6.30-9.45 **Prices** Fixed D 3 course fr £32, Service optional **Wines** 16 by glass **Parking** 300 **Notes** Children welcome

---

OLDBURY | Map 10 SO98

Saffron Restaurant

Modern Indian

tel: 0121 552 1752 **909 Wolverhampton Rd B69 4RR**
email: info@saffron-online.co.uk
dir: M5 junct 2. Follow A4123 (S) signs towards Harborne. Restaurant on right

Smart modern setting for up-to-date Anglo-Indian fusion cooking

This contemporary Indian in the heart of the Black Country goes for a bold colour scheme involving scarlet and black chairs arranged in a chequerboard pattern at darkwood tables, plushly padded booths and statement wallpaper, tempered by minimally white walls and dark wooden flooring. If you're not the adventurous type, tandoori staples and classics such as lamb rogan josh or chicken korma feature on a wide-reaching menu. But dig deeper, and you'll find more refined, delicately spiced ideas built on quality, fresh ingredients. Among the seafood section, perhaps nilgiri machli, a traditional Parsee fish curry with garlic, green herbs and poppy paste. Catching the eye among starters is rabbit varuval, a South Indian speciality teaming tender rabbit with onion, curry leaves, mustard seeds and a palate-tingling hit of chilli. Choosing from the signature dishes reaps rewards too, in the shape of achari venison-meltingly tender pan-fried venison steak served with spiced potato gâteau and sauced with the bittersweet citrus tang of achaar pickle.

Chef Sudha Shankar Saha **Owner** Abdul Rahman, A Momin **Seats** 96 **Times** 12-2.30/5.30-11 Closed D 25 Dec **Prices** Prices not confirmed, Service optional **Wines** 38 bottles under £30, 8 by glass **Parking** 25, On street **Notes** Sunday L, Vegetarian available, Children welcome

Learn the latest foodie trends in Birmingham and Manchester on page 21

Superb Cuisine ...

From A La Carte, Lunch, Banqueting and traditional Sunday Roast Menus to choose from, Nuthurst Grange has much to offer the discerning guest. Our AA two rosettes restaurant offers a warm welcome to both residents and non-residents alike!

nuthurst grange COUNTRY HOUSE HOTEL & RESTAURANT

Hockley Heath, Warwickshire B94 5NL www.nuthurst-grange.co.uk **Call: 01564 783972**

SOLIHULL
Map 10 SP17

Hampton Manor

◉◉ Modern British NEW v

tel: 01675 446080 **Swadowbrook Ln, Hampton-in-Arden B92 0EN**
email: info@hamptonmanor.eu **web:** www.hamptonmanor.eu
dir: *M42 junct 6 follow signs for A45 (Birmingham). At 1st rdbt, 1st exit onto B4438 (Catherine de Barnes Ln). Left into Shadowbrook Ln*

Imaginative contemporary dishes with a sense of theatre

A charming stone-built castellated manor house in the countryside not far from Solihull, Hampton saw service for a long while as a nursing home, but looks as though it had always been waiting to slip into its current role as a luxurious country house hotel. The guest-rooms are mostly named after historic personages, and the founder of the modern police force is honoured. Peel's Restaurant, situated in the main manor house and over-looking the clock tower gardens, is the former dining room of the manor, with, impressive original fire place, and recently decorated in a stunning chinoiserie style. Ryan Swift has a sizeable kitchen brigade at his side, with a fantastic collective CV, and the menus are straight out of the contemporary top drawer, with plenty of home-grown ingredients coming together in dishes full of intense flavours and creative textures, and a touch of theatrics thrown in. It's on the tasting menus, though, that the cooking really takes wing, for mains such as stone bass with a scallop, chorizo and parsley root, or a transcendent presentation of Scottish venison, served pink with a gently spiced, cabbage-wrapped kofta too, garnished with home-grown beetroot and dollops of goat curd. A plate of apple variations at dessert comprises a crumble parfait, a terrine of baked apple, juicy sorbet and an ice cream rendered to popcorn texture with liquid nitrogen.

Chef Ryan Swift **Owner** Jan & Derrick Hill **Seats** 26, Pr/dining room 14
Times 12-3/7-9.30 Closed L Mon-Sat (ex tasting rooms), D Sun **Prices** Tasting menu £45-£75, Starter £8-£16, Main £16-£35, Dessert £8-£14, Service optional 10%
Wines 226 bottles over £30, 38 bottles under £30, 12 by glass **Parking** 30
Notes Tasting menu 4/7 course, Afternoon tea available, Sunday L £30, Children welcome

SUTTON COLDFIELD
Map 10 SP19

Best Western Premier Moor Hall Hotel & Spa

◉ Modern British NEW

tel: 0121 308 3751 **Moor Hall DRive, Four Oaks B75 6LN**
email: mail@moorhallhotel.co.uk **web:** www.moorhallhotel.co.uk
dir: *A38 onto A453 towards Sutton Coldfield, right at lights into Weeford Rd. Hotel 150yds on left*

Appealing well-delivered modern cooking in country-house hotel

Although part of the Best Western stable, Moor Hall is a family-run country-house hotel within parkland. It has two restaurants, prime of which is the panelled Oak Room in what was the dining room when the property was privately owned. The cooking is based on a repertory of contemporary ideas, producing starters of goats' cheese with beetroot textures (dust, crisps, purée and balls), rocket and toasted pine nuts, and seared scallops with black pudding bonbons and celeriac purée. Sound technique is applied to good-quality raw materials (the menu flags items produced within a 40-mile radius). This is evident in a full-bodied trio of meats-pork belly, duck and deconstructed beef Wellington-all correctly cooked and tender, with creamy mash and a selection of vegetables, and well-timed steamed brill with mussel chowder. The same care goes into puddings such as unctuous dark chocolate tart, its pastry wafer-thin, with honeycomb and vanilla ice cream.

Chef Charlotte Foster **Owner** Michael Webb **Seats** 70, Pr/dining room 30
Times 12-3.30/7-9.30 Closed L Mon-Sat, D Sun **Prices** Starter £6-£9, Main £14.50-£23, Dessert £4.50-£5, Service optional **Wines** 13 bottles over £30, 38 bottles under £30, 10 by glass **Parking** 170 **Notes** Sunday L fr £19.50, Vegetarian available, Children welcome

New Hall Hotel & Spa

◉◉ Modern British

tel: 0121 378 2442 & 0845 072 7577 **Walmley Rd, Walmley B76 1QX**
email: newhall@handpicked.co.uk **web:** www.handpickedhotels.co.uk/newhall
dir: *On B4148, E of Sutton Coldfield, close to M6 & M42 junct 9*

Modern fine dining in historic house

It is hard to imagine, but before Birmingham's suburban sprawl engulfed the village of Sutton Coldfield, this 800-year-old moat house stood in empty countryside. The hall hasn't actually been 'new' since the 14th century, and does business nowadays as an upmarket operation that on one hand flaunts its age in medieval beams, flagstones, and heraldic crests, and on the other, supplies 21st-century spa pampering with all the bells and whistles. It is all cushioned from the hurly-burly of modern Brum by 26 acres of fabulous grounds. The Bridge Restaurant is the top-end dining option, where mullioned stained-glass windows blend with a gently modern neutral decor as a setting for cooking that is rooted in the classics but tweaked for today's tastes with modern techniques and presentation. Smoked mackerel is matched with Serrano ham, aubergine purée and samphire, ahead of steamed hake with Jerusalem artichoke, broccoli, crispy chicken wings and white port sauce. A vibrant finale delivers quenelles of vanilla cheesecake with a riff on rhubarb (purée, ice cream and poached) and black olive tuile.

Chef Paul Soczowka **Owner** Hand Picked Hotels **Seats** 24, Pr/dining room 14
Times 7-9.30 Closed L all week, D Mon-Wed **Prices** Fixed D 3 course fr £45, Service optional **Wines** 14 by glass **Parking** 60 **Notes** Vegetarian available, Children welcome

WALSALL   Map 10 SP09

Fairlawns Hotel & Spa

 Modern British V

tel: 01922 455122 **178 Little Aston Rd, Aldridge WS9 0NU**
email: reception@fairlawns.co.uk **web:** www.fairlawns.co.uk
dir: *Outskirts of Aldridge, 400yds from junction of A452 (Chester Rd) & A454*

Modern cooking in a characterful family-run hotel

Well placed for virtually anywhere you may need to be in the West Midlands, the spa hotel near Walsall is family-owned and run with plenty of individual character, a refreshing antidote to corporate anonymity. A sense of humour is in evidence in the interior signposting, while the dining room is a stylish venue, decorated with vivid paintings, wooden blinds and globe light fittings. An extensive Market Menu is supplemented by seafood specialities, and the style is modern British, but without too many oddball combinations. First up might be a twice-baked cauliflower cheese soufflé garnished with pancetta, its Mornay sauce perhaps overdoing the cheese note, or mussels in penne with a poached egg. Mains bring on well-timed roast stone bass on parsnip purée with onion rings, peas and baby gem in balsamic saucing, or a beef duo of slow-cooked shin and seared fillet with creamed celeriac and port-glazed shallots. Indulge yourself at the finishing line with a luscious treacle tart, served with mascarpone, lemon curd and a lemon and ginger coulis.

Chef Steve Kirkham, Paul Ingleby **Owner** John Pette **Seats** 80, Pr/dining room 100 **Times** 12-2/7-10 Closed 25-26 Dec, 1 Jan, Good Fri, Etr Mon, May Day, BH Mon, L Sat **Prices** Prices not confirmed, Service optional **Wines** 20 bottles over £30, 40 bottles under £30, 12 by glass **Parking** 120 **Notes** Sunday L, Children welcome

WOLVERHAMPTON   Map 10 SO99

Bilash

 Indian, Bangladeshi

tel: 01902 427762 **2 Cheapside WV1 1TU**
email: m@thebilash.co.uk
dir: *Opposite Civic Hall & St Peter's Church*

A happy mix of new and old ideas in longstanding Indian

In a quiet corner of the pedestrianised square overlooking St Peter's Church, Bilash has been pushing beyond the confines of mere curry for 30 years. The stylishly clean-cut interior works a colourful decor of caramel and burgundy high-backed leather seats at wooden tables set against pale lemon walls hung with modern Indian-themed pastel prints, a smart contemporary setting that reflects the kitchen's approach to its creative roll call of Bangladeshi and Indian regional dishes. Start with maacher shami kebab, a flat fishcake with lime, herbs and garam masala, served with tamarind sauce and excellent home-made chutneys, then follow with Goan tiger prawn masala – enormous tiger prawns marinated in spicy tomato paste and cooked with cumin, coriander, green chillies, roasted onions, curry leaves, mint and spring onions. Don't miss pukka Indian desserts such as rasmalai-an über-sweet dumpling made from Indian paneer (cottage cheese) flavoured with cardamom and saffron, poached in sweetened cardamom-flavoured milk and served with chopped almonds, pistachios and saffron.

Chef Sitab Khan **Owner** Sitab Khan **Seats** 48, Pr/dining room 40 **Times** 12-2.30/5.30-10.30 Closed 25-26 Dec, 1 Jan, Sun **Prices** Fixed L 2 course £9.95-£12.95, Fixed D 3 course £22.50-£45.95, Starter £5.90-£7.95, Main £10.90-£22.90, Service optional **Wines** 5 by glass **Parking** 15, Civic car park **Notes** Pre-theatre D, Tasting menu with wine, Vegetarian available, Children welcome

WILTSHIRE

AMESBURY   Map 5 SU14

Holiday Inn Salisbury - Stonehenge

 Modern International, British

tel: 0845 241 3535 & 01980 677466 **Midsummer Place, Solstice Park SP4 7SQ**
email: reservations@hisalisbury-stonehenge.co.uk
web: www.hisalisbury-stonehenge.co.uk
dir: *Exit A303, follow signs into Solstice Park. Hotel adjacent to service area*

Wide-ranging brasserie menus near Stonehenge

First sight of this huge glass hotel soaring up from the A303 comes as a bit of a surprise, given its location. The Solstice Bar and Grill, so named because of its proximity to Stonehenge, is a large, light and airy room, curving around the contour of the building, with black and white dining chairs and floor-to-ceiling windows affording views of the countryside. The lengthy menu runs from sandwiches and light meals through chargrills, among them steaks and salmon fillet in citrus dressing, to the full works, with the kitchen taking an eclectic approach. So expect chicken dopiaza and Thai-style fishcakes as well as beer-battered cod and chips. Start with perhaps a classic prawn and crab cocktail in Marie Rose sauce, then proceed to roast loin of venison with potato and beetroot mash, parsnip crisps and Brussels sprouts crushed with onion. End with flavourful bread-and-butter pudding with vanilla ice cream and raspberries.

Chef Matthew Bills **Owner** Armani Hotels Ltd **Seats** 80, Pr/dining room 18 **Times** All-day dining **Prices** Fixed L 2 course £12.95-£33, Fixed D 3 course £19.95-£42, Starter £5.50-£10, Main £13-£23, Dessert £5-£9, Service optional **Wines** 3 bottles over £30, 22 bottles under £30, 22 by glass **Parking** 200 **Notes** Sunday L £13.95, Vegetarian available, Children welcome

BEANACRE   Map 4 ST96

Beechfield House Hotel, Restaurant & Gardens

 Modern British

tel: 01225 703700 **SN12 7PU**
email: reception@beechfieldhouse.co.uk **web:** www.beechfieldhouse.co.uk
dir: *M4 junct 17, A350 S, bypass Chippenham, towards Melksham. Hotel on left after Beanacre*

Contemporary country-house dining

Beechfield House, built in 1878 as a private residence in the Venetian style, became a hotel in the 1960s and gently updated to meet 21st-century requirements. Soft classical music is just right for the handsome restaurant, with its chandelier, rug on the wooden floor, a large gilded mirror above the mantelpiece and Roman blinds at the windows. The expressive cooking follows a contemporary theme and keeps things fairly simple, turning out ham hock and cider terrine with pear and apricot chutney, then slowly roast shoulder of local lamb with root vegetables and a gratin of potato and sweet potato. A masterful handling of seafood brings on the likes of sautéed scallops with pancetta, cauliflower purée and truffle butter, and a main course of fish stew with mussels, chorizo and parmesan. There's a dab hand at desserts behind such offerings as pear and almond tart with deeply flavoured chocolate and single-malt ice cream.

Chef Paul Horrell **Owner** Chris Whyte **Seats** 70, Pr/dining room 20 **Times** 12-2/7-9 Closed 23-26 & 31 Dec, 1 Jan **Prices** Fixed L 2 course £15-£18.50, Fixed D 3 course £27.20-£42.50, Starter £5.75-£10, Main £15.50-£24, Dessert £5.95-£8.50, Service optional **Wines** 15 bottles over £30, 27 bottles under £30, 5 by glass **Parking** 70 **Notes** Sunday L £18.50-£21.50, Vegetarian available, Children welcome

BRADFORD-ON-AVON

Map 4 ST86

The Muddy Duck

Modern British **NEW**

tel: 01225 858705 **Monkton Farleigh BA15 2QH**
email: dishitup@themuddyduckbath.co.uk **web:** www.themuddyduckbath.co.uk
dir:

Hearty modern dining in revamped pub

This wisteria-clad, stone-built 17th-century inn has been transformed in recent years from a simple local boozer into a switched-on dining pub. The traditional feel remains untouched-a walk-in inglenook, exposed beams and wooden floors make for a bar you'd be happy to perch at with a pint and some nibbles-but food is more of a driving force here these days. The kitchen deals in hearty modern pub grub, built on a bedrock of local produce and cooked with confidence to deliver well-defined flavours, as in a starter of confit chicken terrine and pâté with frozen grapes and sourdough toast, followed by slow-cooked, maple-glazed Wiltshire pork belly with pan-seared scallops and braised fennel. Fish might appear in the form of skate wing with braised butter beans, chorizo and salsa verde, while puddings can be as simple as good old rhubarb and custard or perhaps plum tarte Tatin with vanilla ice cream.

Chef Josh Roberts **Owner** Simon Blagden, Nigel Harris **Seats** 70
Times 12-2.30/6-9.30 Closed Xmas, D Sun **Prices** Starter £4-£8, Main £10-£22, Dessert £4-£8, Service optional **Wines** 19 bottles over £30, 32 bottles under £30, 12 by glass **Parking** 30 **Notes** Sunday L £4-£16, Vegetarian available, Children welcome

The Three Gables

 Modern European V NOTABLE WINE LIST

tel: 01225 781666 **St Margaret St BA15 1DA**
email: info@thethreegables.com
dir: M4 junct 18, A46 towards Bath, A363 Bradford-on-Avon, restaurant over Tower Bridge

Mediterranean-influenced menu in a venerable greystone inn

The name reflects the trio of architectural eminences that surmount the facade of this venerable greystone inn opposite the town bridge. It's had an extensive restoration throughout, with a contemporary feel to the first-floor dining room, which extends across the three gable windows, where a mixture of exposed stonework and washed walls and a wood floor look the part. There's also a delightful raised terrace at the back for alfresco dining. Co-owner (and wine expert-hence the fantastic list) Vito Scaduto takes care of things out front with unfailing Italian charm, while chef Marc Salmon beavers away in the kitchen producing some highly refined Mediterranean-influenced cuisine. A first-class terrine of Wiltshire pork with piccalilli and egg bhajee is an inventive take on a classic, or you might go for Cornish mackerel and horseradish pastry with cucumber oyster velouté. Cornish brill-a first-class piece of fish, perfectly cooked-comes with a crispy soft-shelled crab, rouille and samphire in an inspired main course, while dessert might actually be three puds in one: a rich dark chocolate mousse with moist pistachio polenta cake and moreish beetroot ice cream.

Chef Marc Salmon **Owner** Marc Salmon, Vito Scaduto **Seats** 55 **Times** 12-2/6.30-10 Closed 1-12 Jan, Sun-Mon **Prices** Fixed L 2 course £12-£18, Fixed D 3 course fr £29.50, Service optional **Wines** 200 bottles over £30, 50 bottles under £30, 16 by glass **Parking** Public car park **Notes** Children welcome

CALNE

Map 14 ST97

The White Horse

Modern British

tel: 01249 813118 **Compon Bassett SN11 8RG**
email: info@whitehorse-comptonbassett.co.uk
web: www.whitehorse-comptonbassett.co.uk
dir: M4 junct 16 onto A3102, after Hilmarton village turn left to Compton Bassett

A warm welcome and local produce

Set in the Wiltshire countryside in the village of Compton Bassett, this freehouse guarantees a warm welcome from its hands-on owners. You can eat wherever you choose in the refurbished pub – be it in the modern and comfortable restaurant with its unclothed wooden tables, or in the bar which is well stocked with local ales and made cosy with a log burner. The kitchen supports local suppliers, both big and small, so if you've got good quality produce to spare, you're encouraged to bring it in and head chef Danny Adams will use it on the menu. Expect simple, honest cooking with some contemporary techniques on show, as in a superbly gamey seared breast of pigeon with celeriac purée, wild mushrooms and red wine jus. Roasted corn-fed chicken supreme supported by sweet potato mash, roasted root vegetables, chorizo and red wine jus makes a fine main course, while sticky toffee pudding with malted vanilla ice cream hits the spot for pud.

Chef Danny Adams **Owner** Danny & Tara Adams **Seats** 45, Pr/dining room 45
Times 12-2.15/6-9 Closed Mon, D Sun **Prices** Prices not confirmed, Service optional **Wines** 7 bottles over £30, 34 bottles under £30, 8 by glass **Parking** 45 **Notes** Sunday L, Vegetarian available, Children welcome

CASTLE COMBE

Map 4 ST87

The Bybrook at The Manor House Hotel

– see opposite

COLERNE

Map 4 ST87

The Brasserie

Modern British

tel: 01225 742777 **Lucknam Park Hotel & Spa SN14 8AZ**
email: brasserie@lucknampark.co.uk
dir: M4 junct 17, A350 towards Chippenham, then A420 towards Bristol for 3m. At Ford left to Colerne, 3m, right at x-rds, entrance on right

Smart, modish brasserie in majestic country-house hotel

The second string to Lucknam Park's bow, The Brasserie offers a modernist, informal alternative to The Park Restaurant's fine-dinery. Located within the walled garden, with a wall of glass of its own, and right next-door to the spa, The Brasserie has a classy finish and serves up some pretty classy food, too – and there are 'healthy options' for those taking the spa detox thing seriously. There's an open kitchen, a wood-burning oven to confirm those brasserie credentials, and a team that knows what it's aiming for and keeps things simple and appealing. Start with crisp parmesan beignets, for example, with tomato salsa, avocado and herbs from the Lucknam Park gardens, or a Brinkworth blue cheese mousse with parsnip fritters, pear and walnut salad, and truffled honey vinaigrette. Slow-cooked pork belly might come in a main course with cumin sauerkraut, carrot purée, roast apple and sage, and to finish, there's the likes of satsuma, mango and pistachio in a creative trifle, or local farmhouses cheeses with chutney and crackers.

Chef Hywel Jones **Owner** Lucknam Park Hotels Ltd **Seats** 40 **Times** 7.30am-10pm All-day dining **Prices** Fixed L 2 course £19, Starter £6.50-£8, Main £12.50-£28, Dessert £7, Service optional **Wines** **Parking** 80 **Notes** Sunday L, Vegetarian available, Children welcome

The Park Restaurant

⚜⚜⚜ – see page 530 and advert on page 531

– see page 530 and advert on page 531

CORSHAM Map 4 ST87

Guyers House Hotel

⚜⚜ Modern European

tel: 01249 713399 **Pickwick SN13 OPS**
email: enquiries@guyershouse.com **web:** www.guyershouse.com
dir: A4 between Pickwick & Corsham

Creative ideas in a traditional country house

Set in six acres of lovely English gardens with a tennis court and croquet lawn, Guyers House is a classic country-house hotel that is equally as happy to sort out your wedding or business needs as it is to put you up in serene comfort. When it comes to dining, the kitchen keeps fruitful connections with the local food network, as well as furnishing the larder with fresh, seasonal ingredients from its own vegetable and herb garden. Although the setting is resolutely traditional, the menu can come up with some surprising compositions that work well, as in a starter that sees creamy fennel velouté poured over a roll of smoked salmon with crème fraîche and mixed cress at the table, or an unusual dessert involving spiced chocolate and sweet potato dauphine matched with chestnut ice cream and a dark chocolate pavé. Sandwiched between these delicious ideas, there's a fashionable multi-cut tasting of top-quality local Biddestone pork, consisting of roast belly and fillet, braised shoulder and a full-flavoured faggot matched with caramelised onion purée and crispy shallots.

Chef Gareth John **Owner** Mr & Mrs Hungerford **Seats** 66, Pr/dining room 56 **Times** 12.30-2.30/7-9 Closed 30 Dec-3 Jan **Prices** Fixed L 2 course £20-£30, Fixed D 3 course £25-£50 **Wines** 9 bottles over £30, 24 bottles under £30, 5 by glass **Parking** 60 **Notes** Sunday L £20-£25, Vegetarian available, Children welcome

The Methuen Arms

⚜⚜ British, European

tel: 01249 717060 **2 High St SN13 OHB**
email: info@themethuenarms.com **web:** www.themethuenarms.com
dir: M4 junct 17 onto A350 towards Chippenham, at rdbt exit onto A4 towards Bath. 1m past lights, at next rdbt turn sharp left onto Pickwick Rd, 0.5m on left

Gimmick-free appealing modern cookery in a Georgian building

The Methuen Arms doesn't look in the least like a pub, being a Georgian building over three floors with a portico over the front door. Inside, though, real ales are dispensed at the bar, there are elm floorboards, rugs, log fires and softly neutral walls hung with local prints and etchings. 'No foams, towers or swipes,' declares the inn, promising instead simple, well-sourced and tasty food, aims it amply fulfils. Well-timed pan-fried scallops with saffron and parmesan risotto garnished with red watercress has been a notably accomplished starter, with another risotto, of leek and thyme, for chargrilled wood pigeon. Deep-fried haddock and chips and a burger are among main courses, but look elsewhere for more interest, a confident touch bringing on whole roast lemon sole complemented by a rich lobster and prawn sauce with crunchy broccoli tempura, and unusual pork Wellington with Jerusalem artichoke purée and wild mushrooms. Desserts can look as pretty as a picture, with a martini glass layered with vanilla pannacotta, poached rhubarb and Prosecco and rhubarb jelly, and there may also be quince frangipane tart with cinnamon ice cream.

Chef Piero Boi **Owner** The Still family **Seats** 60, Pr/dining room 20 **Times** 12-3/6-10 **Prices** Fixed L 2 course £15.50, Fixed D 2 course £18.50-£21.50, Starter £5.95-£9, Main £13.50-£26, Dessert £6.50-£8.50, Service optional **Wines** 29 bottles over £30, 37 bottles under £30, 14 by glass **Parking** 40 **Notes** Party menu 3 course £29.50, Sunday L £22.50-£26.50, Vegetarian available, Children welcome

The Bybrook at The Manor House Hotel

CASTLE COMBE Map 4 ST87

Modern British v 🍷 NOTABLE WINE LIST

tel: 01249 782206 **SN14 7HR**
email: enquiries@manorhouse.co.uk **web:** www.manorhouse.co.uk
dir: M4 junct 17, follow signs for Castle Combe via Chippenham

Complex contemporary cooking in a pretty medieval village

The Manor has held court in the village since the 14th century and remains at the centre of the action to this day, with its golf course and fine-dining restaurant among its armoury to lure the 21st-century adventurer. The soaring structure, knitted with verdant climbers, looks handsome from the outside, while the interior has been given a gentle contemporary sheen but remains traditional and classic where it counts. The hotel's restaurant, The Bybrook, is headed up by Richard Davies, as seen in the BBC's *Great British Menu*. The room is rich with period detail and pristine tables await. The kitchen's output is based on high quality ingredients, a good deal of which are sourced from the vicinity, and what doesn't carry the 'local' tag is tracked with due diligence. The hotel's garden provides herbs and flowers to bring a dash of seasonal colour to proceedings. A classical foundation to the dishes is matched by some nicely controlled modern culinary

techniques. First-course flame-grilled mackerel partners the fish with celeriac remoulade and pink grapefruit, with an accompanying smoked eel beignet, while another combines hand-dived scallops with the assorted flavours and textures of apple, walnut, cauliflower and pickled shallot. Everything looks beautiful on the plate and every flavour and texture plays its part in creating the whole. Next up, slow-cooked loin of Brecon venison comes in the company of chestnuts, sautéed sprouts, roast salsify and blackberry jus, and Cornish pollock (caught by line) with chorizo risotto and smoked Palourde clams. The impressive technique and creativity continues with desserts such as a burnt butter parfait with green apple sorbet and apple crisp, or lemon cheesecake with anise ice cream and candied fennel. The 1,000-bin wine list contains lots of exciting things, and each dish on the menu has a recommended accompaniment.

Chef Richard Davies **Owner** Exclusive Hotels and Venues **Seats** 60, Pr/dining room 120 **Times** 12.30-2/7-9.30 Closed L Mon-Tue **Prices** Fixed L 2 course £25, Fixed D 3 course £60, Tasting menu £74, Starter £16, Main £35, Dessert £12 **Wines** 300 bottles over £30, 25 bottles under £30, 20 by glass **Parking** 100 **Notes** Tasting menu 7 course, Sunday L £30, Children welcome

The Park Restaurant

COLERNE   Map 4 ST87

Modern British V   🍷 NOTABLE WINE LIST

tel: 01225 742777 **Lucknam Park Hotel & Spa SN14 8AZ**
email: reservations@lucknampark.co.uk
web: www.lucknampark.co.uk
dir: *M4 junct 17, A350 to Chippenham, then A420 towards Bristol for 3m. At Ford left towards Colerne. In 4m right into Doncombe Ln, then 300yds on right*

Adventurous refined cooking in a stately home

The tree-lined driveway increases expectation which is met when the house comes into view; the late 17th-century Palladian mansion is a gem of a building, surrounded by 500 acres of prime Wiltshire countryside. Today's country-house hotel has maintained the traditional feel, avoiding the temptation to strip away the past, instead filling the spaces with antiques, oil paintings and opulent fabrics. There is a modern spa within the old walled garden, which is also home to The Brasserie, the pair offering a splash of contemporary living amid the period charm. The main restaurant is called The Park, and occupies the one-time ballroom, a room built for entertainment, with swagged curtains, shimmering chandeliers and tables dressed for the business of fine dining. It all starts with a nibble and sip in the drawing room or library before heading into the dining room itself, where the cooking of Hywel Jones and his team awaits. Mr Jones has been leading the line for a decade now and has finely tuned the output and the supply chain, with the kitchen garden also providing a host of tip-top ingredients for the table. The cooking is refined, complex and smart. A first course dish of confit of citrus-cured Loch Duart salmon is partnered with a cobnut praline and glazed autumn vegetables in a winning combination, or go for poached fillet of Devonshire rose veal served with sweetbreads glazed in pancetta, marinated salsify and Wiltshire truffles. Loin of Brecon lamb stars in a main course with butternut squash and cumin purée, a pastilla, violet artichokes and plum tomato confit. There's a lot going on, but the clever combinations of flavours and acute technical skills in the kitchen ensure everything works in balance. For dessert, banana soufflé with bitter chocolate sauce and salted caramel ice cream ends things on a high.

Chef Hywel Jones **Owner** Lucknam Park Hotels Ltd **Seats** 80, Pr/dining room 30 **Times** 1-3/6.30-10 Closed Mon, L Tue-Sat, D Sun **Prices** Fixed D 3 course £75-£90, Tasting menu £75-£90, Service optional **Wines** 15 by glass **Parking** 80 **Notes** Gourmand menu available from £90, Sunday L £39, Children 5 yrs+

LUCKNAM PARK
HOTEL & SPA, BATH

1720

World Class Spa · Award-winning Gourmet Restaurant · Equestrian Centre
Cookery School · Well-being House

A Palladian Mansion set within 500 acres of private parkland just
6 miles from the historic City of Bath, a World Heritage Site

Lucknam Park Hotel & Spa, Colerne, Chippenham, Wiltshire SN14 8AZ
Tel: +44 (0)1225 742777 reservations@lucknampark.co.uk www.lucknampark.co.uk

RELAIS &
CHÂTEAUX

CRICKLADE
Map 5 SU09

Cricklade House
◉◉ Modern British

tel: 01793 750751 **Common Hill SN6 6HA**
email: reception@crickladehotel.co.uk **web:** www.crickladehotel.co.uk
dir: A419 onto B4040. Left at clock tower. Right at rdbt. Hotel 0.5m up hill on left

Country-house dining in a Wiltshire conservatory

Built at the turn of the last century, Cricklade is a handsome country house on the edge of the Cotswolds. A flight of steps sweeps up from the lawns towards an original conservatory that runs across the full extent of the facade, its elevated position ensuring panoramic views over the acres of rolling golf course and Wiltshire downland. It's a delightful prospect for a light evening, and if the decor looks a touch retro, that's all in keeping with the period style. The menus are not about retro nostalgia at all but more the tried-and-true formula of gentle country-house cooking, which scores some notable successes. The in-vogue pairing of goats' cheese and beetroot produces fine contrast and visual appeal, garnished as it is with celeriac remoulade and dressed in aged balsamic. The main course might turn up simply cooked fish, such as a whole grilled lemon sole with prawn butter sauce, or pedigree meat like slow-cooked pork belly with a crisp-fried beignet, creamed potato and thyme-scented jus. Great citric zing brings a dessert of traditional key lime pie with lemon sherbet ice into pin-sharp focus.

Chef Ross Hastings **Owner** Ambienza Ltd **Seats** 60, Pr/dining room 120 **Times** 12-2/7-9.30 Closed D 25 Dec **Prices** Fixed L 2 course £12.50, Fixed D 3 course £34.50, Service optional **Wines** 7 bottles over £30, 20 bottles under £30, 7 by glass **Parking** 100 **Notes** Sunday L £17.50-£19.50, Vegetarian available, Children welcome

The Red Lion Inn
◉ Modern British

tel: 01793 750776 **74 High St SN6 6DD**
email: info@theredlioncricklade.co.uk **web:** www.theredlioncricklade.co.uk
dir: Just off A419 between Swindon & Cheltenham

Hearty food in a beer-oriented inn

Let's give a big cheer for beer, for The Red Lion is a temple to all things hoppy. This place really takes beer seriously: it has its own Hop Kettle micro brewery (where plans are afoot to install a chef's table), and offers dozens of hand-pulled and bottled artisan beers, which come with tasting notes and food matching suggestions. Choose between the traditionally pubby bar for pub classics done right, or the contemporary country-chic look of the dining room, where the kitchen deals in the sort of switched-on, ingredients-led dishes that make you want to eat it all. Starters such as terrine of locally-shot game, quince purée, and toasted home-made bread, or locally-foraged pied bleu and grey oyster mushrooms with garlic butter on toast, show the style-and as the pub rears its own pigs, why not follow with a pork chop with grain mustard mash, broccoli, and honey-glazed carrots?

Chef Chris White **Owner** Tom Gee **Seats** 40, Pr/dining room 18 **Times** 12-2.30/6.30-9 **Prices** Starter £5-£7.95, Main £9.95-£22.95, Dessert £5-£7.95 **Wines** 7 bottles over £30, 24 bottles under £30, 9 by glass **Parking** On street **Notes** Sunday L £12.95-£18.95, Vegetarian available, Children welcome

FOXHAM
Map 4 ST97

The Foxham Inn
◉ Modern British NEW

tel: 01249 740665 **SN15 4NQ**
email: info@thefoxhaminn.co.uk **web:** www.thefoxhaminn.co.uk
dir: Off B4069 between Sutton Benger & Lyneham

Local pub with imaginative menu based on local produce

The family behind the Foxham are an industrious bunch, producing a range of jams, chutneys and sauces, as well as running this red-brick country inn and restaurant with its locally-sourced food and B&B accommodation. A passion for provenance runs right through the menu, and dishes list producers and regional affiliations. There are some bright ideas on the menu, too, with an appealing rusticity, and lots of big flavours. Start with Dorset snails with pancetta, chorizo and lentils in a dish guaranteed to quicken the pulse of a trencherman or woman, or there might be a savoury crème brûlée to catch the eye (made with leeks and Brinkworth blue cheese). Main courses might see breast of Tiddenham duck in a classic combo with braised red cabbage and dauphinoise potatoes, or pea risotto enriched with brie and elevated by shavings of Wiltshire truffles. Finish with bread-and-butter pudding with prune and Armagnac parfait.

Chef Neil Cooper, Ben Reid **Owner** Neil & Sarah Cooper **Seats** 36 **Times** 12-2.30/7-11 Closed 1st 2 wks Jan, Mon **Prices** Fixed L 2 course £17, Fixed D 3 course £24-£30, Tasting menu £65-£75, Starter £6-£9, Main £12-£19, Dessert £6-£9 **Wines** 10 by glass **Parking** 16 **Notes** Sunday L £17-£22, Vegetarian available, Children welcome

HINDON
Map 4 ST93

The Lamb at Hindon
◉ Traditional British

tel: 01747 820573 **High St SP3 6DP**
email: info@lambathindon.co.uk **web:** www.lambathindon.co.uk
dir: M3 junct 8 onto A303. Exit towards Hindon 4m after Salisbury exit & follow signs to Hindon

Modern pub food in a centuries-old village inn

The Boisdale group's heterogeneous restaurant portfolio extends from the cityscape of Canary Wharf to this ancient village inn near Salisbury. There has been a hostelry on the site since the start of Plantagenet era, and the sense of venerability is enhanced by antique beams and flagstones, old oil paintings and an open fire. The catering of course is rather more up-to-date, offering hot-smoked mackerel with pickled beetroot and pea-shoots in honey-mustard vinaigrette with horseradish cream as an assertive opener. Gourmet burger variations (anyone for truffle mayo or chipotle ketchup?) are the mood of the moment for mains, but there may also be a casserole of local game in Butcombe ale with sage and onion dumplings, or baked salmon with Jansson's temptation (the fishy Swedish version of dauphinoise). Finish with apple, pear and walnut crumble and custard, or marmalade crème brûlée with almond shortbread.

Owner Ranald Macdonald (Boisdale plc) **Seats** 52, Pr/dining room 32 **Times** 12-2.30/6-9.30 **Prices** Prices not confirmed **Wines** 9 by glass **Parking** 16 **Notes** Sunday L, Vegetarian available, Children welcome

The Harrow at Little Bedwyn

LITTLE BEDWYN   Map 5 SU26

Modern British v ⚑ NOTABLE WINE LIST

tel: 01672 870871 **SN8 3JP**
email: office@theharrowatlittlebedwyn.com
web: www.theharrowatlittlebedwyn.com
dir: *Between Marlborough & Hungerford, well signed*

A shining beacon of quality food and wine in deepest Wiltshire

From the outside, The Harrow looks like many Victorian country pubs, its brick facade covered with creeper. The interior, though, has been tastefully modernised and its appearance leaves no doubt that this is a place where food is a serious commitment. Pale walls are hung with artwork, high-backed upholstered dining chairs are pulled up to white-clothed tables on the polished floorboards, and a double-sided wood-burner adds a homely touch to the interconnecting rooms. Roger Jones has built up an admirable network of suppliers over the years, buying only natural and free-range produce, much of it from artisan growers and traders. He has also set himself high culinary aspirations, pulling off some surprising combinations, such as a starter of foie gras, scallop and black pudding. Exotic touches can give depth to often classical ideas-enhancing lobster with chilli, ginger and spicy salt, for instance-and

other cuisines can be plundered to suit a particular dish, seen in another starter of yellowtail tuna sashimi with bass and turbot céviche. Main courses on the short carte are normally evenly divided into fish and meat, the former perhaps fillet of line-caught turbot, of spot-on accuracy, served simply with hen-in-the-woods mushrooms and local truffles, the latter by pork fillet and belly with black pudding, a faggot and apple sauce. This apparently straightforward approach produces dishes of clear, assertive flavours, and conceals the kitchen's high technical strength and the level of consideration it puts into combinations, seasoning and accompaniments. Puddings do the trick in the shape of custard tart with rhubarb compôte, or a mini platter of parfaits, sorbets and chocolate. Every item comes with a wine recommendation, and the full list, assembled with expertise and enthusiasm, is a joy.

Chef Roger Jones, John Brown **Owner** Roger & Sue Jones **Seats** 34 **Times** 12-3/7-11 Closed Xmas & New Year, Sun-Tue **Prices** Tasting menu fr £75, Starter £15, Main £30, Dessert £10, Service optional **Wines** 750 bottles over £30, 250 bottles under £30, 20 by glass **Parking** On street **Notes** Fixed L 5 course & wine £40, Gourmet menu 8 course £75, Children welcome

Whatley Manor Hotel and Spa

MALMESBURY　　　　　　　　　　　Map 4 ST98

Modern French 🍷 NOTABLE WINE LIST

tel: 01666 822888 **Easton Grey SN16 0RB**
email: reservations@whatleymanor.com
web: www.whatleymanor.com
dir: *M4 junct 17, follow signs to Malmesbury, continue over 2 rdbts. Follow B4040 & signs for Sherston, hotel 2m on left*

Technically brilliant contemporary French cooking in a luxury spa hotel

This Cotswold-stone manor hotel has a delicious blend of historic charm and new-world luxury. The finish is luxurious sure enough, but there is a lot of personality to the place, and it doesn't take very long to feel at home. As well as 12 acres of utterly charming grounds-manicured gardens, flower-filled meadows, wild woodland-there's a first-class spa, even a cinema, and a couple of dining options that put the hotel on the national culinary map. Martin Burge is the man behind the output of both Le Mazot (the brasserie choice) and The Dining Room (the fine-dining hot seat). He has worked with some big-name players over the years, including a stint as Raymond Blanc's right-hand-man at Le Manoir, and has been leading the line here for over a decade now. Le Mazot is going for the Swiss chalet vibe with lots of blond wood and a roaring fire, plus tables on the terrace when the weather allows. With a menu going from moules

marinière to fillet of salmon in a Thai broth, or a steak cooked on a hot stone at the table, Le Mazot offers sterling support to the headlining Dining Room. The Dining Room is a quietly refined space with a pale bamboo floor, buttermilk walls and subtle lighting, while the cooking is French-focused, contemporary, and looks beautiful on the plate. The produce is top-notch, such as a first-course loin of local hare, roasted and dressed with a smoked shallot purée, and served with lightly confit red cabbage and poached raisins. There are acute technical skills on display among main courses; roasted loin of venison, for example, partnered with game sausage, confit chestnuts and a peppered brandy sauce, or dish of pan-fried sea bass with caramelised langoustine tail, truffle and shellfish macaroni. There's real finesse in desserts, too, like a chocolate and praline soufflé with an accompanying lemongrass ice cream, or a show-stopping black truffle ice cream with lightly creamed Roquefort, deep-fried Crottin and candied walnuts. There's a tasting menu option of course, plus a wine list containing lots of interesting options, with the sommelier on hand to help you find just what you fancy.

Chef Martin Burge **Owner** Christian & Alix Landolt **Seats** 40, Pr/dining room 30 **Times** 7-10 Closed Mon-Tue, L all week **Prices** Tasting menu £110 **Wines** 350 bottles over £30, 5 bottles under £30, 16 by glass **Parking** 120 **Notes** ALC menu £85, Wine matching with tasting menu £65 extra, Vegetarian available, No children

HORNINGSHAM
Map 4 ST84

The Bath Arms at Longleat

◉◉ Modern, Traditional British

tel: 01985 844308 **Longleat Estate BA12 7LY**
email: enquiries@batharms.co.uk **web:** www.batharms.co.uk
dir: *A36 Warminster. At Cotley Hill rdbt 2nd exit (Longleat), Cleyhill rdbt 1st exit. Through Hitchcombe Bottom, right at x-rds. Hotel on the green*

Charming boutique hotel with accomplished cooking

A solid-looking stone property covered in creepers, The Bath Arms is in a peaceful village within the Longleat Estate. The hotel's aim is to create an atmosphere of 'informality, fun, friendliness and efficiency' and it seems to succeed on all counts, from a welcoming bar with its own popular menu and local ales on handpump to a dining room with chandeliers and king-sized candles where young staff are friendly and eager. Local supplies are at the heart of the operation, the menu focusing on game in season: game sausage (actually more akin to partridge mousse) with deeply flavoured apple jelly, followed by roast pigeon with wild mushrooms and braised chicory, say. Dishes are marked by an absence of fuss and frills but the results hit the spot: duck pudding with pickled cherries and walnuts, followed by pan-fried sea bass with brown shrimps and white bean cassoulet, and, to finish, rhubarb and coconut crumble with coconut ice cream.

Times 12-2.30/7-9

LITTLE BEDWYN
Map 5 SU26

The Harrow at Little Bedwyn

◉◉◉ *– see page 533*

LOWER CHICKSGROVE
Map 4 ST92

Compasses Inn

◉ Modern British

tel: 01722 714318 **SP3 6NB**
email: thecompasses@aol.com **web:** www.thecompassesinn.com
dir: *Off A30 signed Lower Chicksgrove, 1st left onto Lagpond Ln, single-track lane to village*

Broadly-appealing menu in an ancient inn

Approach down narrow lanes and catch sight of the thatched roof: it's a pub and no mistake. And it won't disappoint on the inside either: beams, standing timbers, open fires, nooks and crannies and high-backed wooden booths, and menus written up on blackboards. It's a friendly sort of place, very much used and appreciated by the local community, and food-wise it is most definitely a cut above. Whether you eat in the bar or the adjacent dining area, you can expect a mix of traditional favourites and more modish things, with local produce figuring prominently, including vegetables from nearby Rowswell's Farm. Start with pan-fried pigeon breast with a parsnip gratin, beetroot mousse and red wine glaze, and follow on with a traditional lamb hotpot or something like pan-fried fillets of sea bass with mussel and saffron cream sauce. Strawberry tart with Pimm's sorbet is a summertime treat among desserts.

Chef Dave Cousin, Dan Cousins **Owner** Alan & Susie Stoneham **Seats** 50, Pr/dining room 14 **Times** 12-3/6-11 Closed 25-26 Dec, L Mon (Jan-Mar) **Prices** Starter £5.50-£8.95, Main £7.95-£21.50, Dessert £5.50-£6.25, Service optional **Wines** 2 bottles over £30, 28 bottles under £30, 8 by glass **Parking** 35 **Notes** Sunday L £10.95-£14.95, Vegetarian available, Children welcome

MALMESBURY
Map 4 ST98

Old Bell Hotel

◉◉ Traditional & Modern British, French

tel: 01666 822344 **Abbey Row SN16 0BW**
email: info@oldbellhotel.com **web:** www.oldbellhotel.com
dir: *M4 junct 17, follow A429 north. Left at 1st rdbt. Left at T-junct. Hotel next to Abbey*

Nearly eight centuries of service to Malmesbury

In 1220 a guest house was established here to accommodate visitors to the nearby abbey, and The Old Bell has been providing hospitality ever since. It's a substantial old building, its mellow stone frontage hung with wisteria, and there are charming and comfortable public rooms and an elegant restaurant, recently redecorated. The kitchen demonstrates sound techniques and avoids over-complication, demonstrating a keen sense of what works with what. So crab and salmon fishcakes come with no more than chilli and lime, and a main course of lamb rump with creamed potatoes and mushrooms. If prime cuts and luxury ingredients are the norm (lobster with garlic mayonnaise, côte de boeuf with béarnaise),it's equally confident with earthier materials, turning out crispy pig's head with pancetta and apple, and partnering cod brandade with pan-fried halibut and broccoli. Desserts are an enticing lot, among them lemongrass crème brûlée with confit lime and lemon, and, for the old school, rice pudding with poached clementines.

Chef Richard Synan **Owner** The Old Bell Hotel Ltd **Seats** 60, Pr/dining room 48 **Times** 12.15-2/7-9.30 **Prices** Fixed L 2 course £19.50, Starter £6-£7.50, Main £15.50-£21.50, Dessert £6.75, Service optional **Wines** 89 bottles over £30, 71 bottles under £30, 13 by glass **Parking** 35 **Notes** Sunday L £25, Vegetarian available, Children welcome

Whatley Manor Hotel and Spa

◉◉◉◉ *– see opposite*

PEWSEY
Map 5 SU16

Red Lion Free House

◉◉◉ *– see page 536*

Learn the latest foodie trends in Birmingham and Manchester on page 21

Who has won our Food Service Award?
See page 13

PURTON
Map 5 SU08

The Pear Tree at Purton
◉◉ Modern British

tel: 01793 772100 **Church End SN5 4ED**
email: stay@peartreepurton.co.uk web: www.peartreepurton.co.uk
dir: *From M4 junct 16, follow signs to Purton. Turn right at Best One shop, hotel 0.25m on right*

Charming conservatory setting in a former vicarage

It may sound like a humble pub, but this former Cotswold-stone vicarage on the edge of an old Saxon village is actually a country-house hotel with fabulous grounds which include a flower meadow, wetlands and a vineyard (three of their wines are on offer in the restaurant). Having reached a landmark 25 years here, owners Francis and Anne Young have made their mark and the hotel has lots to offer, from comfortable rooms to conference and wedding facilities,to the Conservatory Restaurant with its pleasing garden views and ambitious, gently modern menus. Smooth duck liver parfait is served as a first course with brioche and cauliflower pickle, followed perhaps by breast of wood pigeon in red wine flavoured with juniper and black treacle. A fish main course might be paupiettes of lemon sole served with a salmon and lemongrass mousseline and vegetable spaghetti, and among desserts, lemon and basil cheesecake with limoncello ice cream hits the spot.

Chef Alan Postill **Owner** Francis & Anne Young **Seats** 50, Pr/dining room 50 **Times** 12-2/7-9.15 Closed 26 Dec **Prices** Starter £6.95-£7.50, Main £14-£22.50, Dessert £6.95-£8.95, Service optional **Wines** 18 bottles over £30, 21 bottles under £30, 12 by glass **Parking** 30 **Notes** Sunday L £23, Vegetarian available, Children welcome

RAMSBURY
Map 5 SU27

The Bell at Ramsbury
◉ Modern British, European

tel: 01672 520230 **The Square SN8 2PE**
email: reservations@thebellramsbury.com web: www.thebellramsbury.cim
dir: *M4 junct 14, A338 to Hungerford. B4192 towards Swindon. Left to Ramsbury*

Ambitious cooking in made-over country inn

New owners have rung in a new era for the 300-year-old Bell. Dazzlingly whitewashed outside, and revamped in an almost Scandinavian-looking, pared-back modern style, the interior is what you'd expect from a smart contemporary food-oriented inn. Ramsbury Brewery ales, hand-pulled at the bar, go nicely with pub classics like daily pies, burgers, and fish and triple-cooked chips, or you could trade up to the more formal restaurant, where the deal is an ambitious output of dishes built on local materials, bolstered by home-grown produce from the kitchen

Red Lion Free House

PEWSEY
Map 5 SU16

British
tel: 01980 671124 **East Chisenbury SN8 6AQ**
email: enquiries@redlionfreehouse.com web: www.redlionfreehouse.com
dir: *Exit A303, at rdbt take A345 to Enford, right into East Chisenbury. Pub located on right*

Exciting modern cooking in the Wye Valley

The setting, in the densely-wooded Wye Valley near to Tintern Abbey, may be Welsh through and through, but this upscale restaurant with rooms seems to model its modus operandi on the classic upmarket French country auberge. Originally a drovers' inn dating from the 17thcentury, its venerable beams are the only clue to the building's age once you're inside. A well-drilled team of staff get things off on the right foot with aperitifs served at leather sofas in the cosy lounge area, then it is time to move through to the classy dining room, a modern space of soft-focus coffee and cream hues, with original artwork on the walls. The kitchen here is firing on all cylinders under head chef Chris Harrod, whose rock-solid technical abilities are the foundations of a dazzling repertoire of modern ideas, marked by flavours profiles that are never less than fascinating, their scope widened by fashionably foraged ingredients from the surrounding woodlands. Roast Jerusalem artichokes with goat's cheese cream, the woody notes of oyster mushrooms and rosemary all add up to a simple but impactful starter of light flavours and textures. Fresh flavours and razor-sharp timing are similarly to the fore in main courses that might see pan-fried halibut fillet partnered with parsley root, nasturtium tubers and cured pork back fat, while those seeking more robust things will find no fault with a marriage of locally-farmed suckling pork with soft and sticky caramelised celeriac, pear and sorrel. A dessert described tersely as 'pear, almond' delivers soft poached pears and pear sorbet partnered with almond mousse and marzipan crumble, or there could be chocolate and cinnamon parfait with Ashmead Kernel apple and Ty Gwyn cider jelly.

Chef Guy & Brittany Manning **Owner** Guy & Brittany Manning **Seats** 45, Pr/dining room 25 **Times** 12-2.15/6-9 **Prices** Fixed L 2 course £16, Tasting menu £75, Starter £7-£10, Main £17-£30, Dessert £7-£10 **Wines** 26 bottles over £30, 27 bottles under £30, 13 by glass **Parking** 14 **Notes** Prix Fixe menu 2 course £20, Sunday L £17-£25, Vegetarian available, Children welcome

garden and game from the Ramsbury Estate. Pan-fried foie gras with apricot and hazelnut crunch, mini brioche loaf and Sauternes gel is a typical starter that might be followed by bacon-wrapped tenderloin of free-range pork with celeriac and smoked bacon gratin, and pear and vanilla sauce. For dessert, there could be lemon meringue parfait with basil sorbet.

Times 12-3/6-9.30 Closed D Sun

ROWDE
Map 4 ST96

The George & Dragon
◉◉ Modern British V

tel: 01380 723053 **High St SN10 2PN**
email: thegandd@tiscali.co.uk **web:** www.thegeorgeanddragonrowde.co.uk
dir: On A342, 1m from Devizes towards Chippenham

Tudor inn with modern seafood-led menu

This Tudor coaching-inn stands on the main road through the unassuming village of Rowde, not far from Devizes. It's long had a solid reputation as a destination dining venue for the area, and is an attractively traditional country inn with lots of bare wood in furniture and floors. The daily-changing menu of modern pub food makes a fitting speciality of seafood hauled in from the boats at St Mawes, Cornwall. A simply grilled kipper on toast will satisfy anyone who skipped breakfast, but Cajun-spiced fishcakes with chilli dipping sauce are on hand too. A brochette of chargrilled scallops and black pudding slices may be taken as either starter or main, while the principal listing gets stuck into whole grilled lemon sole, mackerel with anchovy butter, or swordfish with rocket and parmesan. If seafood isn't your bag, beef fillet or rack of lamb may fit the bill, and it all finishes with chocolate and raspberry roulade, or 'ye olde lemon posset', its qualifier referring, we trust, to the historic nature of its recipe.

Chef Christopher Day **Owner** Christopher Day, Philip & Michelle Hale **Seats** 35 **Times** 12-3/7-11 Closed D Sun **Wines** 9 by glass **Parking** 14 **Notes** Sunday L £13.75-£19.50, Children welcome

SALISBURY
Map 5 SU12

Salisbury Seafood & Steakhouse
◉ Modern, International

tel: 01722 417411 & 424110 **Milford Hall Hotel, 206 Castle St SP1 3TE**
email: info@salisburyseafoodandsteakhouse.co.uk
web: www.salisburyseafoodandsteakhouse.co.uk
dir: From A36 at rdbt on Salisbury ring road, right onto Churchill Way East. At St Marks rdbt left onto Churchill Way North to next rdbt, left in Castle St

More than surf and turf in a stylish setting

The restaurant is part of the Milford Hall Hotel, an extended Georgian mansion in pretty gardens. It's a smartly appointed room, with a blond-wood floor, brown and cream high-backed dining chairs and one wall occupied by bottles of wine. You can dine very well on a seafood starter of pan-fried scallops with minted pea purée, crisp pancetta and balsamic syrup before a 28-day dry-aged steak with a choice of sauces: perhaps rib-eye with garlic and lime mayonnaise. But there's more to enjoy on the menu than surf and turf. Start with carpaccio with parmesan and rocket and go on to chargrilled butterflied chicken breast with lime and herb butter, chips, herb-grilled tomatoes and watercress, or pork, green pepper and mushroom stroganoff. Bring a meal to a happy conclusion with a dessert like apricot and frangipane tart with custard, or Baileys and orange cheesecake dusted with chocolate.

Chef Chris Gilbert **Owner** Simon Hughes **Seats** 55, Pr/dining room 20 **Times** 12-2/6-10 **Prices** Fixed L 2 course £11.50, Fixed D 3 course £19.95, Starter £5.95-£12.50, Main £9.95-£26.50, Dessert £4.95-£7.25, Service optional **Wines** 4 bottles over £30, 25 bottles under £30, 12 by glass **Parking** 60 **Notes** Sunday L £8.50-£14.50, Vegetarian available, Children welcome

SWINDON
Map 5 SU18

Chiseldon House Hotel
◉ Modern European, British

tel: 01793 741010 **New Rd, Chiseldon SN4 ONE**
email: welcome@chiseldonhouse.com **web:** www.chiseldonhouse.com
dir: M4 junct 15, A346 signed Marlborough. After 0.5m turn right onto B4500 for 0.25m, hotel on right

Unfussy fine dining in a Regency manor house

The grand Regency manor house is a popular wedding venue, with the Marlborough Downs and attractive gardens providing a stunning backdrop, and the M4 handy for ease of access. The restaurant is a bright, opened-up dining room with smartly laid tables (white linen and all) and a cheerful service team. The cooking takes a fine-dining stance, with lots going on and an eye for presentation. A starter of pan-fried wood pigeon comes with rhubarb purée, crispy lardons and black pepper sauce, another pairing is poached pear with pickled walnuts and Oxford Blue cheese. Main-course stuffed neck of lamb is served with cannellini bean and leek confit and a minted jus, fishy mains depend on what has been landed at Brixham. For dessert, bitter chocolate tart comes with an Amaretto-flavoured pannacotta and toasted almonds.

Chef Robert Harwood **Owner** Mark & David Pennells **Seats** 100, Pr/dining room 32 **Times** 12-2/7-9 **Prices** Fixed L 2 course fr £16.95, Fixed D 3 course fr £19.95, Starter £5.50-£8.25, Main £15.25-£22.95, Dessert £5.95-£7.95, Service optional **Wines** 7 by glass **Parking** 40 **Notes** Brunch served BHs, Champagne afternoon tea £22.45, Sunday L £10.95-£14.95, Vegetarian available, Children welcome

WARMINSTER
Map 4 ST84

The Bishopstrow Hotel & Spa
◉ Modern British V

tel: 01985 212312 **Boreham Rd BA12 9HH**
email: info@bishopstrow.co.uk **web:** www.bishopstrow.co.uk
dir: From Warminster take B3414 (Salisbury). Hotel signed

Modish British cooking in a light-filled elegant Regency house

Surrounded by 27 acres of grounds alongside the River Wylye, Bishopstrow is a creeper-clad Regency mansion that has been discreetly reinvented as a glossy country house hotel with a cool contemporary spa. The tone throughout is airy and elegant, with neutral tones and light from full-length windows suffusing the dining rooms. Chef Andy Britton has cooked in glam hotels all over, from the Caribbean to the Channel Islands, and offers a style of modish cooking, supported by top-class ingredients from the estate and local area. Pork and pigeon terrine with red onion marmalade, pickled beets and radishes is a typical starter. The main course might see Wiltshire lamb given a workout in the form of cutlet, shoulder and sausage matched with cumin cauliflower, and chard and Gruyère gratin. Bailey's pannacotta with chocolate fondue provides a suitably luscious finale, or you could go savoury with West Country cheeses.

Chef Andrew Britton **Owner** Longleat Enterprises Ltd **Seats** 65, Pr/dining room 30 **Times** 12-2/7-9.30 **Prices** Starter £5.50-£9.50, Main £14-£25, Dessert £6.50-£8.50 **Wines** 50 bottles over £30, 5 bottles under £30, 8 by glass **Parking** 70 **Notes** Sunday L £17.50-£22.70, Children welcome

Find out more about how we assess for Rosette awards on page 9

WARMINSTER *continued*

The Dove Inn

British, European

tel: 01985 850109 **Corton BA12 OSZ**
email: info@thedove.co.uk **web:** www.thedove.co.uk
dir: *Off A36, Salisbury to Bath road, signed to Corton. Follow Station Road for 3m, pub on right*

Good simple pub cooking in the Wylye Valley

A Victorian pub in the village of Corton, The Dove retains its bucolic appeal, with oak and flagstone floors inside, and an atmosphere of happy banter. A conservatory-style restaurant is as mod as the cons get, and outdoor tables make the most of fine days. Cask ales and decent wines lift the spirits of drinkers, and the approach to food is exactly what we expect – locally based, nice and simple, and cooked with care and attention. Blackboard fish specials supplement the printed menu, which also features beer-battered haddock with minty peas as a stalwart. A brace of giant field mushrooms stuffed with port-laced Stilton on toasted ciabatta might set the ball rolling, and be followed by tender-as-anything lamb shank braised in spiced red wine, served with garlic mash and buttered greens. A lighter-than-usual strawberry cheesecake has a pleasing moussey texture and crumbly biscuit base, and comes with vibrant strawberry coulis.

Chef Bruno Fitas, Sarah Hoddinott **Owner** William Harrison-Allan **Seats** 60
Times 12-2.30/6-9 Closed 25 Dec **Prices** Prices not confirmed, Service optional
Wines 11 bottles over £30, 15 bottles under £30, 7 by glass **Parking** 20
Notes Sunday L, Vegetarian available, Children welcome

Who has won our Chefs' Chef award?

Find out on page 10

Get the most out of the AA Restaurant Guide

See page 6

█ **BEWDLEY** **Map 10 SO77**

The Mug House Inn

Modern British

tel: 01299 402543 **12 Severnside North DY12 2EE**
email: drew@mughousebewdley.co.uk **web:** www.mughousebewdley.co.uk
dir: *B4190 to Bewdley. On river, just over bridge on right*

Inventive modern British pub cookery

Bewdley once boasted 71 licensed premises, and while the drinking scene may be somewhat curtailed these days, it nonetheless retains this old charmer. A mug house was the unvarnished name for a boozer in centuries gone by, and this Georgian example is an entirely pleasing place, with its hanging baskets adorning the white facade, and tranquil views of river traffic floating past on the Severn. Temptations include duck and orange terrine with fennel and pomegranate salad, and mains such as featherblade steak with roast roots, horseradish dumplings and champ, or halibut with buttered spinach in a chowder of clams, leeks and laverbread. Don't let the creative urge dip at dessert stage, when dark chocolate and cardamom mousseline with raspberry 'caviar' and Bailey's ice cream is in the offing.

Chef Drew Clifford, Zac Birchley **Owner** Drew Clifford **Seats** 26, Pr/dining room 12
Times 12-2.30/6.30-9 Closed D Sun **Prices** Fixed L 2 course fr £12.95, Fixed D 3 course fr £15.95, Starter £3.95-£7.50, Main £12-£30, Dessert £5.95-£7.95, Service optional **Wines** 1 bottle over £30, 26 bottles under £30, 10 by glass **Parking** Car park 100mtrs along river **Notes** Fixed D Mon-Thu only, Fixed L Mon-Sat only, Sunday L, Vegetarian available, No children

Royal Forester Country Inn

Modern European

tel: 01299 266286 **Callow Hill DY14 9XW**
email: royalforesterinn@btinternet.com **web:** www.royalforesterinn.co.uk
dir:

Contemporary dining in medieval inn

A sympathetic makeover has brought 21st-century comforts to this 15th-century inn while retaining the best of its venerable features. There's a bar with sofas and a baby grand, and a meandering restaurant full of nooks and crannies, with bare-brick walls and ancient timbers. The menus change daily on the basis of that morning's deliveries, with fish brought up from Cornwall (perhaps grilled tranche of turbot with clams and Parmentier potatoes) and game a speciality in season: perhaps a starter of guinea fowl and tarragon ballotine with pickled carrots and a verjus reduction. Consistently high standards can be seen throughout the wide-ranging menu, from mackerel three ways (pan-seared fillet, spicy tartare and pâté) to monkfish tails roasted with pancetta, served with tomato and herb sauce, or roast duck breast with a damson gin jus, with chocolate bread-and-butter pudding to finish.

Chef Mark Hammond **Owner** Sean McGahern, Maxine Parker **Seats** 60, Pr/dining room 18 **Times** 12-3/6-9.30 **Prices** Fixed L 2 course fr £13.99, Fixed D 3 course fr £16.99, Starter £5-£9.50, Main £12.50-£25, Dessert fr £4.95, Service optional **Wines** 14 bottles over £30, 34 bottles under £30, 6 by glass **Parking** 25
Notes Gourmet menu with 4 glasses of wine £30 1st Tue of month, Sunday L £7.99-£12.99, Vegetarian available, Children welcome

BROADWAY Map 10 SP03

The Broadway Hotel
Traditional British **NEW**

tel: 01386 852401 **The Green, High St WR12 7AA**
email: info@broadwayhotel.info web: www.cotswold-inns-hotels.co.uk/broadway
dir: *Follow signs to Evesham, then Broadway. Left onto Leamington Rd, hotel just off village green*

Nifty modern cooking in a brand new atrium

The Broadway Hotel, overlooking the village green, has its roots in the 16th century, so Tattersalls Brasserie, in a contemporary, light-filled atrium, is a stark contrast to its traditional surroundings. The kitchen focuses on quality seasonal produce and has an assured sense of what will work, turning out appealing starters of seared scallops with chickpea and cauliflower curry and pickled cucumber, and seared mackerel fillet on crab bisque with diced roasted celeriac. Main courses maintain the momentum with Lighthorne lamb three ways (roast rump, slow-cooked shoulder and devilled kidney, all tender and full of flavour) with root vegetable gratin and rosemary sauce, a selection of steaks, and perhaps pan-fried hake fillet winningly accompanied by langoustine risotto and mousse, orange-braised fennel and a parsley fritter. Ambition doesn't falter with puddings of caramelised pineapple tart served with basil and mint syrup and basil ice cream.

Chef Eric Worger **Owner** Mr & Mrs Horton **Seats** 60 **Times** 12-3/7-9.30 **Prices** Fixed L 2 course fr £14.50, Starter £5.50-£7.50, Main £14.50-£25.50, Dessert £5.50-£6.50, Service optional **Wines** 3 bottles over £30, 23 bottles under £30, 13 by glass **Parking** 15 **Notes** Prix Fixe 2/3 course £14.50/£17.50, Sunday L £17.50-£19.95, Vegetarian available, Children welcome

Dormy House Hotel
Modern British **v**

tel: 01386 852711 **Willersey Hill WR12 7LF**
email: reservations@dormyhouse.co.uk web: www.dormyhouse.co.uk
dir: *2m E of Broadway off A44, at top of Fish Hill turn for Saintbury/Picnic area. In 0.5m turn left, hotel on left*

Creative cooking in an impressive Cotswold house

Dormy House, a honey-stone property perched above Broadway with views of the Cotswolds, has all the comforts of a contemporary hotel, with oak beams and panelling reminders of its 17th-century origins. The restaurant, an open-plan, airy room, has been given a modern look, and large windows give stunning views over the flower garden and beyond. Under new chef Jon Ingram, the kitchen delivers full-flavoured, well-composed and uncluttered dishes that are distinctly in the contemporary British idiom. Watercress velouté is silky-smooth, rich and peppery, garnished with air-dried ham and a poached egg, or there may be treacled smoked salmon with Guinness bread and caviar cream for a touch of posh. At mains, roasted cod is a well-timed piece of fish, served on wilted cabbage in an excellent mussel and bacon jus, while beef fillet is gently poached and comes with salt beef hash and smoked onion marmalade for deeply resonant savoury and sweet notes. Dessert ideas are resoundingly successful too: unctuous honey and almond parfait sits on a thin layer of cobnut sponge with a spiced half plum.

Chef Jon Ingram **Owner** Sorensen family **Seats** 75, Pr/dining room 14 **Times** 12.30-2.30/7-9.30 **Prices** Main £40, Service optional **Wines** 125 bottles over £30, 65 bottles under £30, 30 by glass **Parking** 70 **Notes** Sunday L £28, Children welcome

The Lygon Arms
Modern British

tel: 01386 852255 **High St WR12 7DU**
email: thelygonarms@pumahotels.co.uk web: www.pumahotels.co.uk
dir: *From Evesham take A44 signed Oxford, 5m. Follow Broadway signs. Hotel on left*

Majestic Tudor hotel with 21st-century comforts

Fans of period dramas can live the dream at The Lygon Arms. This historic place has been offering up hospitality to weary travellers since the 16th century and has included Oliver Cromwell and Charles I as former visitors (doubtless not at the same time). The glorious honey-coloured exterior can't have changed much in all that time, but the interior – while keeping hold of a host of original features – is fit and ready for the modern traveller, whether that's for business or pleasure. The main restaurant occupies the Great Hall, an impressive space with a minstrels' gallery and no shortage of period charm, but rest assured a smart finish ensures comfort all round. The menu takes a contemporary approach while showing evident respect for classical ways. Start with breast of wood pigeon in the earthy company of Puy lentils, wild mushrooms and pancetta and move on to hake with lobster and razor clams, or a duo of mallard with a fig tarte Tatin. Finish with an intricate and elegant chocolate dessert.

Chef Ales Maurer **Owner** Puma Hotels Collection **Seats** 80, Pr/dining room 80 **Times** 12-2/7-9.30 Closed L Mon-Sat **Prices** Fixed L 2 course fr £15, Fixed D 3 course fr £39.50, Starter fr £7.50, Main fr £23.50, Dessert fr £8.50, Service optional **Wines** 14 bottles over £30, 48 bottles under £30, 24 by glass **Parking** 150 **Notes** Sunday L £15-£19.95, Vegetarian available, Children welcome

Russell's
Modern British

tel: 01386 853555 **20 High St WR12 7DT**
email: info@russellsofbroadway.co.uk web: www.russellsofbroadway.co.uk
dir: *A44 follow signs to Broadway, restaurant on High St opposite village green*

Modern cooking in a paradise of honey-coloured stone

With its honey-coloured stone facade, Russell's is a restaurant with rooms that sits comfortably in the centre of Broadway. The traditional exterior hides a more contemporary interior, with the space opened up to create a tasteful modernity that confirms this is indeed the 21st century. The food has taken sides and chosen the modern path. There is an evident passion for regional ingredients here, with the daily-changing menu including a local flavour, and the food is delivered to the table looking fine and dandy (be that on plate or slate). Among first courses might be an Asian-inspired dish of monkfish with wilted pak choi, soused radish and wasabi mayonnaise, followed by main course such as wild mallard (roast breast and confit leg) with cavolo nero and blackberry sauce, and, for dessert, a pineapple tarte Tatin with rum ice cream and marinated raisins.

Chef Neil Clarke **Owner** Andrew Riley **Seats** 60, Pr/dining room 14 **Times** 12-2.30/6-9.30 Closed BH Mon, D Sun **Prices** Fixed L 2 course £15.95-£21.95, Fixed D 3 course £18.95-£22.95, Starter £6-£14, Main £16.50-£28, Dessert £6-£10.95, Service optional **Wines** 18 bottles under £30, 12 by glass **Parking** 7 **Notes** Sunday L £21.95-£24.95, Vegetarian available, Children welcome

BROMSGROVE
Map 10 SO97

The Vernon

Modern European, British

tel: 01527 821236 **Hanbury B60 4DB**
email: info@thevernonhanbury.com web: www.thevernonhanbury.com
dir: *A38 onto B4091 Hanbury Road, on junct with B4090*

Enticing cooking in revamped 18th-century inn

The Vernon reopened in mid-2012 after an extensive – and expensive – revamp, giving a stylishly contemporary sheen to the whole place. There's a good-looking bar with lightwood furniture, a classy restaurant with a wooden floor and chairs upholstered in different-coloured fabrics, and an extensive outdoor area. Food is a serious preoccupation, with the kitchen basing its modern style on fresh local produce. Asparagus in this area is not to be missed, served here with a deep-fried duck egg, parmesan shavings, watercress and truffle oil, an alternative to the full-on flavours of 'cheeky pig terrine' with blood orange, rum-soaked sultanas, carrots and toasted sourdough. Confident handling brings on, among well-judged main courses, succulent pan-fried chicken breast served with broad beans, baby gem, fondant potato and tarragon sauce, and seared sea bass fillets with clams, crushed potatoes, spring onion, mushrooms and lemon oil. Leave room for puddings like chocolate mousse with cherries and pistachio ice cream.

Chef Sarah Sheen **Owner** Vernon Leisure Ltd **Seats** 73, Pr/dining room 24 **Times** 12-2.30/6-9.30 **Prices** Fixed L 2 course £13.50-£15.95, Fixed D 3 course £16.95-£19.95, Starter £6.95-£10.95, Main £10.95-£25.95, Dessert £6.50-£8.95, Service optional **Wines** 22 by glass **Parking** 50 **Notes** Sunday L £15.95-£19.95, Vegetarian available, Children welcome

CHADDESLEY CORBETT
Map 10 SO87

Brockencote Hall Country House Hotel

⚜⚜⚜ *– see below*

KIDDERMINSTER
Map 10 SO87

Best Western Stone Manor Hotel

Modern British

tel: 01562 777555 **Stone DY10 4PJ**
email: enquiries@stonemanorhotel.co.uk web: www.stonemanorhotel.co.uk
dir: *2.5m from Kidderminster on A448, hotel on right*

Traditional comforts and good, modish eating with interesting combinations

Built in 1926 on the burnt-out ruins of the original manor house, today's sprawling structure is popular for weddings and conferences, and is also home to Fields Restaurant. It's a traditionally decorated room with plenty of space between the linen-clad tables, and offers simply presented modern British dishes. Flavour combinations are well considered; chicken liver parfait, for instance, with red onion jam and toasted brioche – simple, honest food – or a bold starter of potted shrimps with melba toast and a mango purée. Main-course pan-fried fillet of sea trout comes with samphire and a caper and cream sauce, and rack of lamb with celeriac purée, fondant potato, red cabbage and red wine jus. Desserts might include a dark chocolate roulade with white chocolate sauce and vanilla cream, or a warm poached pear and almond tart with crème anglaise and caramel apple ice cream.

Times 12-2/7-10

Brockencote Hall Country House Hotel

CHADDESLEY CORBETT
Map 10 SO87

Modern British v
tel: 01562 777876 **DY10 4PY**
email: info@brockencotehall.com web: www.brockencotehall.com
dir: *M5 junct 4 to A38 Bromsgrove, then A448 just outside village, between Kidderminster & Bromsgrove*

Authoritative modern cookery in a grand Victorian manor house

The distinctly palatial Victorian manor house looks most striking when reflected in the waters of its ornamental lake, a principal feature of the 70 acres of landscaped gardens and parkland in which the house stands. Adam Brown is in charge of the gastronomic show, and takes Worcestershire as his palette, combining and transforming quality prime materials, including foraged wild ingredients, with cutting-edge culinary technique. Brockencote's own hives supply the honey. If the modern British movement has been about anything, it's been the juxtaposition of long-forgotten methods and ingredients with revelatory innovation, so Brown's menus might offer soused mackerel with apple and mouli, or wild mushroom varieties such as yellow-foot chanterelles with stone bass and cockles, alongside voguish textural variations for items such as beetroot, to accompany goat cheese pannacotta, or pear with cured salmon and horseradish mousse. The construction of dishes generally works with the grain of expectation rather than cutting across it, partnering duck confit terrine with blood orange and chicory, or serving a blade of beef with nothing more outré than truffled mash and carrots. Vegetarian dishes on their own menu manage to think outside the tart and risotto boxes for chestnut and cranberry pastilla with honey-roast parsnips, or pressed potato terrine with beetroot and chicory. More textures may surface at dessert stage, perhaps of rhubarb with warm pistachio cake, while a chocolate statement pairs a dark delice with bitter sorbet. English and French artisan cheeses are of the best-bred, and there's a wine list of reassuring magnificence to fantasise over.

Chef Adam Brown **Owner** Eden Hotel Collection **Seats** 80, Pr/dining room 20 **Times** 12-3/6.45-9.45 **Prices** Fixed L 2 course £22.95, Fixed D 3 course £42.95-£59.95, Tasting menu fr £75, Service optional **Wines** 132 bottles over £30, 18 bottles under £30, 12 by glass **Parking** 60 **Notes** Tasting menu 7 course, Sunday L £32.95, Children welcome

The Granary Hotel & Restaurant

◎◎ Modern British

tel: 01562 777535 **Heath Ln, Shenstone DY10 4BS**
email: info@granary-hotel.co.uk **web:** www.granary-hotel.co.uk
dir: *On A450 between Worcester & Stourbridge. 2m from Kidderminster*

Smart, seasonal contemporary cooking in a boutique hotel

Close to the Midlands motorway arteries, yet nicely set in the countryside on the fringes of Kidderminster, the boutique-style Granary Hotel boasts its own market garden to supply the kitchen with the ultimate in low-mileage fruit and veg. The key players in the kitchen brigade have worked together for the best part of a decade, developing contemporary style of cooking that is all about working with the seasons and bringing great ingredients together in well-considered compositions. Given that the restaurant is about as far from the coast as it is possible to be in the UK, the team displays impressive dedication to sourcing fresh fish and seafood, and it is presented without fuss in a starter of sautéed king scallops in a classic pairing with crispy belly pork, sweet potato and apple. Main course brings a well-balanced combination of Barbary duck breast with glazed Parmentier potatoes, creamed cabbage, redcurrants and red wine jus. To finish, vanilla pannacotta gets a lift from fresh strawberries and crunchy honeycomb.

Times 12-2.30/7-11 Closed L Mon, Sat, D Sun

See advert below

❙ MALVERN   **Map 10 SO74**

L'Amuse Bouche Restaurant

◎◎ Traditional French, British

tel: 01684 572427 **The Cotford Hotel, 51 Graham Rd WR14 2HU**
email: reservations@cotfordhotel.co.uk **web:** www.cotfordhotel.co.uk
dir: *From Worcester follow signs to Malvern on A449. Left into Graham Rd signed town centre, hotel on right*

Modern Anglo-French cuisine in the Bishop of Worcester's old place

In the days when bishops were entitled to summer residences to escape to when the charm of the episcopal palace began to pall, the Victorian Gothic house that is now the Cotford Hotel was the preserve of the incumbent of Worcester. Tucked against the Malvern foothills, it wears its air of refinement nonchalantly, with high-ceilinged rooms and deep windows, and what was once its private chapel is these days L'Amuse Bouche. Against a background of pink wallpaper depicting climbing foliage in gold, and smartly attired tables, Chris Morgan offers a French-based modern cuisine that incorporates elements of contemporary British thinking. How else to characterise a menu that might as easily begin with scallops, wild mushrooms and samphire with pancetta dust as with escargots normande? Main courses feature quality prime cuts – Herefordshire beef fillet, Barbary duck breast, Highland venison haunch – in attractive preparations, the last in elderflower and port jus as well as béarnaise. Finish with classic crème brûlée, or a version of tarte Tatin made with banana and rosemary.

Chef Christopher Morgan **Owner** Christopher & Barbara Morgan **Seats** 40, Pr/dining room 12 **Times** 12-1.30/6-8 Closed L Mon-Sat **Prices** Prices not confirmed, Service optional **Wines** 6 by glass **Parking** 15 **Notes** Pre-theatre menu available, Sunday L, Vegetarian available, Children welcome

THE GRANARY
HOTEL & RESTAURANT

Heath Lane, Shenstone, Kidderminster, Worcestershire DY10 4BS
Tel: 01562 777535 • Fax: 01562 777722
Website: www.granary-hotel.co.uk • **Email:** anchorinn@granary-hotel.co.uk

Dine – Our 2 AA Rosette Restaurant, offering our premium daytime carvery and acclaimed a la carte dining in the evenings, offers something for everyone.

Explore – The hotel is perfectly situated for exploring a rich variety of attractions, from museums to historic buildings, leisure facilities and areas of outstanding natural beauty.

Stay – The hotel bedrooms are all refurbished and well equipped. Two luxury Executive Suites, with modern contemporary 4 Poster beds and luxurious bathrooms, are also available.

MALVERN *continued*

Colwall Park Hotel

 Modern British

tel: 01684 540000 **Walwyn Rd, Colwall WR13 6QG**
email: hotel@colwall.com **web:** www.colwall.co.uk
dir: *On B4218, off A449 from Malvern to Ledbury*

Fine local produce in the lee of the Malvern Hills

On the western side of the Malvern Hills, Colwall Park is a large, half-timbered tribute to the country-house hotel idiom. Decorated in gracious style within, its dining room pushes the right buttons with light oak panelling, wrought-iron chandeliers and bespoke artworks. A local farmer, rearing livestock in the eighth generation of his family, supplies the kitchen with dry-aged beef, hill-grazed lamb and free-range poultry and pork. Brixham fish and own-grown herbs and saladings help to undergird the modern British dishes with solid quality, and James Garth is a chef very much in the contemporary mould. Gently toasted scallops arrive with their present-day accoutrements of crisped Parma ham and a silky-smooth sweet potato purée, with some faintly extraneous bits of orange and a vanilla-scented froth. Next up might be local venison casseroled to melty richness, served with butternut mash and braised red cabbage, as well as some parsnip crisps that need eating quick before the cooking liquor gets at them, and then perhaps a zesty lime cheesecake with gin-and-tonic sorbet.

Chef James Garth **Owner** Mr & Mrs I Nesbitt **Seats** 40, Pr/dining room 100 **Times** 12-2/7-9 Closed L all week (ex by arrangement) **Prices** Starter £5-£8, Main £13-£24, Dessert £5-£8, Service optional **Wines** 22 bottles over £30, 66 bottles under £30, 9 by glass **Parking** 40 **Notes** Sunday L £19-£24, Vegetarian available, Children welcome

The Cottage in the Wood Hotel

 Modern British ⬛ NOTABLE WINE LIST

tel: 01684 588860 **Holywell Rd, Malvern Wells WR14 4LG**
email: reception@cottageinthewood.co.uk **web:** www.cottageinthewood.co.uk
dir: *3m S of Great Malvern off A449, 500yds N of B4209, on opposite side of road*

Ambitious cooking in charming hotel

A visit during daylight hours has its own reward, for this is some view – a 30-mile sweep across the Severn Valley, in fact. Perched on a wooded hillside, the former Georgian dower house is a smart hotel and restaurant with appeal that goes beyond the undoubted beauty of its geographical situation. The Outlook Restaurant has the

vista – as you might have guessed – and the space is suitably smart and comfortable. The family-run hotel's kitchen is headed up by one of the clan (Dominic Pattin), and his cooking is based on sound seasonal thinking. Start with confit shoulder of lamb with slow-roasted tomato, confit garlic, sweet tomato purée and thyme jus, or one of a choice of home-made soups. Next up, whole Cornish lemon sole is done in the classic manner, or go for pan-roasted guinea fowl with caramelised fennel gnocchi and shallot purée. Finish with a star anise flavoured crème brûlée with a poached pear given a liquorice lift. The wine list is exceptional.

Chef Dominic Pattin **Owner** The Pattin family **Seats** 70, Pr/dining room 20 **Times** 12.30-2/7-9.30 **Prices** Starter £5.45-£10.45, Main £12.55-£19.95, Dessert £5.95, Service optional **Wines** 203 bottles over £30, 138 bottles under £30, 12 by glass **Parking** 40 **Notes** Pre-theatre D from 6pm, L menu Mon-Sat, Sunday L £18.95-£23.95, Vegetarian available, Children welcome

The Malvern

 Modern British

tel: 01684 898290 **Grovewood Rd WR14 1GD**
email: enquiries@themalvernspa.com **web:** www.themalvernspa.com
dir: *A4440 to Malvern. Over 2 rdbts, at 3rd turn left. After 6m, left at rdbt, over 1st rdbt, hotel on right*

Contemporary brasserie dining in the Malvern Hills

The very first spa resort in the town, The Malvern opened its doors back in 1910 to satisfy the demands of the Edwardian public. It's changed a bit since then. In fact, the interior is spellbindingly modern and capacious. The spa has all the bells and whistles you might imagine, and there's also a brasserie restaurant if you're seeking fulfillment of a different kind. It's a fresh-looking contemporary space with muted neutral tones, wooden tables and local artworks on the walls. The menu follows a bright and breezy brasserie-style format, so you might start with something very of the moment such as slow-cooked pork belly with black pudding, cauliflower purée, spaghetti crackling and sage jus, or go for the Asian flavours of Thai green mussels. Main-course baked lemon sole is served on the bone, and for dessert, caramel, banana and rum pannacotta comes with raisin purée, banana sorbet and vanilla-poached prunes.

Chef Steve Rimmer **Owner** Huw Watson **Seats** 34, Pr/dining room 24 **Times** 12-3/7-9.30 **Prices** Starter £5.85-£9, Main £13-£16.50, Dessert £6.50-£8, Service optional **Wines** 8 bottles over £30, 12 bottles under £30, 9 by glass **Parking** 82 **Notes** Brunch every Sun, Themed menus every month, Vegetarian available, No children

OMBERSLEY — Map 10 SO86

The Venture In Restaurant

 British, French

tel: 01905 620552 **Main Rd WR9 0EW**
dir: *From Worcester N towards Kidderminster on A449 (approx 5m). Left at Ombersley turn. Restaurant 0.75m on right*

Exceptional cooking in a crooked medieval house

Behind the half-timbered facade of this 15th-century property is a small bar with a welcoming open fire, comfortable sofas and low tables and a restaurant with bags of ancient character from its ceiling beams and standing timbers, with large brown leather-look dining chairs at the tables. Chef Toby Fletcher stamps his own style on a modern Anglo-French repertory, carefully sourcing quality produce and handling it confidently and imaginatively. Chicken, guinea fowl and foie gras terrine has been a startlingly successful starter, its richness cut by oven-dried grapes, with a sherry vinegar and shallot dressing, with another option steamed home-smoked haddock fillet with spinach, leeks and Mornay glaze. Effective, well-balanced combinations are also evident in main courses: perhaps pan-fried hake fillet on leek, saffron and tarragon risotto with an intense shellfish sauce, or seared pork fillet and confit belly with a modish Tatin of beetroot and goats' cheese and sage sauce. Extras like breads and petits fours are all of a standard, as are moreish puddings of Valrhona chocolate parfait with a delightful mango and passionfruit crumble.

Chef Toby Fletcher **Owner** Toby Fletcher **Seats** 32, Pr/dining room 32
Times 12-2/7-9.30 Closed 25 Dec-1 Jan, 2 wks summer & 2 wks winter, Mon, D Sun
Prices Fixed L 2 course £25, Fixed D 3 course £39, Service optional **Wines** 38 bottles over £30, 35 bottles under £30, 6 by glass **Parking** 15, on street **Notes** Sunday L £29, Vegetarian available, No children

UPTON UPON SEVERN — Map 10 SO84

White Lion Hotel

 Modern British, European

tel: 01684 592551 **21 High St WR8 0HJ**
email: info@whitelionhotel.biz **web:** www.whitelionhotel.biz
dir: *From A422 take A38 towards Tewkesbury. After 8m take B4104 for 1m, after bridge turn left to hotel*

Historic hotel with contemporary feel and flavour

The author Henry Fielding put up here while writing *Tom Jones*, and the White Lion also played a booze-fuelled part in the Civil War, but fascinating as the 16th-century inn's history may be, the place has stayed in tune with current trends without impacting on its immense character. Nowadays, the interior works a cheerfully-updated look in the Pepperpot Brasserie, blending black timbered walls filled with blocks of yellow ochre, apricot, and terracotta colour with bare chunky oak tables and high-backed chairs. Food-wise, the deal is straightforward combinations and big-hearted flavours on a menu that has something for all-comers. Seared scallops are skewered on a rosemary sprig and matched with roast butternut squash purée and chorizo, ahead of a hearty plate of mustard- and herb-crusted roast rump of lamb served with bubble-and-squeak, celeriac purée and rosemary jus. Baked apple crème brûlée with butterscotch sauce is a properly indulgent pudding.

Chef Jon Lear, Richard Thompson **Owner** Mr & Mrs Lear **Seats** 45 **Times** 12-2/7-9.15 Closed 31 Dec-1 Jan, L few days between Xmas & New Year, D 24 Dec **Prices** Fixed L 2 course fr £13, Starter £6.50-£8.50, Main £12-£19, Dessert £6.50, Service optional **Wines** 2 bottles over £30, 20 bottles under £30, 7 by glass **Parking** 16 **Notes** Sunday L fr £15.75, Vegetarian available, Children welcome

EAST RIDING OF YORKSHIRE

BEVERLEY — Map 17 TA03

The Pipe and Glass Inn

Modern British V ⬥ NOTABLE WINE LIST

tel: 01430 810246 **West End, South Dalton HU17 7PN**
email: email@pipeandglass.co.uk
dir: *Just off B1248*

Superior modern cooking in stylish country inn

The P and G's dedication to high quality food has not been at the expense of its pub credentials: pop in and have a pint to find out for yourself. It would be a shame not to stay and eat, though, for there is some exceptionally good stuff on offer. The 15th-century village pub is looking good in the 21st, with its rustic charms enhanced by smart and rather classy decoration and furniture; there's a new private dining room upstairs, too. Chef-patron James Mackenzie runs an industrious kitchen, cooks with a good deal of care and creativity, and seeks out high-quality ingredients. A little jar of Gloucestershire Old Spot potted pork comes in a starter with sticky apple, crackling salad and spelt toast, or there might be fresh salmon pastrami with Jerusalem artichokes, horseradish crème fraîche, crispy quail's egg and coriander. Follow on with slow-cooked crispy shoulder of lamb with spiced green lentils, cumin carrots, mint yoghurt and cucumber pickle, and end happily with a pear and almond tart with pear sorbet and Poire William custard.

Chef James Mackenzie **Owner** James & Kate Mackenzie **Seats** 70, Pr/dining room 28
Times 12-2/6.30-9.30 Closed 25 Dec, 2 wks Jan, Mon (except BHs), D Sun
Prices Prices not confirmed, Service optional **Wines** 13 by glass **Parking** 60
Notes Sunday L, Children welcome

WILLERBY — Map 17 TA03

Best Western Willerby Manor Hotel

Modern European

tel: 01482 652616 **Well Ln HU10 6ER**
email: willerbymanor@bestwestern.co.uk **web:** www.willerbymanor.co.uk
dir: *M62/A63, follow signs for Humber Bridge, then signs for Beverley until Willerby Shopping Park. Hotel signed from rdbt next to McDonald's*

Extensive brasserie menu in countryside setting

Four miles out of Hull, Willerby Manor is a modern spa hotel in the East Yorkshire countryside. Its fine dining goes on in Figs Brasserie, a relaxing room done in avocado and coffee tones, which extends on to a paved outdoor terrace on balmy evenings. An extensive menu of brasserie dishes incorporates some neat ideas, such as a starter of goats' cheese pannacotta with red-wine-poached pear and gingerbread, but also features many classic ideas like Whitby scampi and chips, chicken breast with black pudding, chestnuts, sprouts and mash in red wine sauce, and apple and blueberry crumble with vanilla cream.

Chef David Roberts, Ben Olley **Owner** Alexandra Townend **Seats** 40, Pr/dining room 40 **Times** 10-10 Closed 25 Dec, All-day dining **Prices** Starter £6-£6.20, Main £10.40-£19.50, Dessert £4.50-£5.20, Service optional **Wines** 16 bottles under £30, 14 by glass **Parking** 200 **Notes** Sunday L £12-£15, Vegetarian available, Children welcome

NORTH YORKSHIRE

ALDWARK
Map 19 SE46

The Aldwark Arms
 Modern

tel: 01347 838324 **YO61 1UB**
email: peter@aldwarkarms.co.uk

Characterful Yorkshire country pub refitted under new management

Under the ownership of the Hardisty family since December 2013, the Aldwark has had a smart refit, including a new wood-burning stove. The welcoming character of this timbered pub in the Vale of York remains, with log-fires in winter, a kitchen garden terrace in kinder weather, hand-pumped ales and a plethora of locally sourced produce. New chef David Sandford cooks an ambitiously extensive menu, bolstered by weekly specials, and there is much to entice. Seafoodies will be drawn to a starter of prawns, crayfish and white crabmeat stuffed into smoked salmon cornets, or there might be a tartlet of Mediterranean vegetables and goats' cheese with salad dressed in walnut oil. Main courses encompass favourites such as Thai green chicken curry or pasta carbonara, as well as sea bass in a Moroccan vibe with chickpeas, courgettes and spinach. Game season turns up breast and confit leg of locally shot pheasant with bacon in port and juniper jus. Desserts are chalked up on the blackboards, and may include banoffee pie with vanilla ice cream.

Chef David Sandford **Owner** Peter, Ian & Andrew Hardisty **Seats** 60 **Times** 12-2/5.30-9 Closed Mon, D Sun **Prices** Starter £4.95-£8.95, Main £9.95-£22.95, Dessert £4.75-£5.25, Service optional **Wines** 3 bottles over £30, 27 bottles under £30, 8 by glass **Parking** 30 **Notes** Early bird 5.30-7pm 1-3 course £8.95-£16.95, Sunday L £10.95-£18.95, Vegetarian available, Children welcome

ARKENGARTHDALE
Map 18 NY90

Charles Bathurst Inn
British **NEW**

tel: 01748 884567 **DL11 6EN**
email: info@cbinn.co.uk **web:** www.cbinn.co.uk
dir: B6270 to Reeth, at Buck Hotel turn N to Langthwaite, pass church on right, inn 0.5m on right

Seasonal contemporary menus in a Dales inn

The CB, as it's familiarly known, is in Arkengarthdale-a tributary valley of celebrated Swaledale, five miles down the road from the lively market village of Reeth. It's named after a Georgian parliamentarian, and is done out with today's preferred light wood, with plenty of space between tables in the raftered dining room. Local farmers and fishermen supply much of the larder, which results in seasonally changing menus of modern Yorkshire cooking. It's shown off to best effect on the Mirror Menu, where Whitby crab and avocado tian with lime and shallots comes with vivid saffron dressing, or a fine Scotch egg accompanied by home-made piccalilli and mustard-dressed saladings. After that, there may be a heartily sustaining casserole of local beef and Masham's Black Sheep ale, with a suet dumpling and leek mash, or salmon fillet with puréed celeriac and braised fennel. Look out for classically garnished roast grouse in the game season, and make space for desserts such as baked vanilla cheesecake with cranberry compôte.

Chef Gareth Bottomley **Owner** Charles Cody **Seats** 70, Pr/dining room 60 **Times** 12-2.30/6-9 Closed 25 Dec **Prices** Starter £4.35-£9, Main £9.95-£21.95, Dessert £5.20-£7.25 **Wines** 15 bottles over £30, 20 bottles under £30, 10 by glass **Parking** 25 **Notes** Sunday L £10.50, Vegetarian available, Children welcome

ASENBY
Map 19 SE37

Crab Manor
Modern British, European

tel: 01845 577286 **Dishforth Rd YO7 3QL**
email: enquiries@crabandlobster.co.uk **web:** www.crabandlobster.co.uk
dir: A1(M) junct 49, on outskirts of village

Idiosyncratic restaurant with a strong line in seafood

At first sight, this thatched and creeper-clad Georgian inn could be the template for a classic Yorkshire country pub, although an observant eye might spot the old enamelled advertising signs that are a hint to the Aladdin's cave of esoteric odds and ends that fills the interior with endless visual entertainment. In case the name isn't enough of a clue, fish and seafood is the kitchen's main culinary focus, whether you choose to eat in the sun-trap garden, the airy pavilion, the main restaurant or the convivial bar. The choice is vast, taking in starters such as seared hand-dived scallops with confit belly pork, crisp black pudding and roast butternut squash cream, or fishcakes of local cod, pollock, and cured fish served with creamed greens and a poached egg. Next up, a chunk of local cod could come with spicy sausage boulangère potatoes, buttered greens and gravy, or you might take a meatier route with the likes of herb-crusted roast rump of Faceby lamb with cumin-roasted carrots, gratin potatoes, rosemary and redcurrant. To finish, go for something like chilled Valrhona chocolate fondant with honeycomb and caramelised banana yoghurt ice cream.

Chef Steve Dean **Owner** Kymel Trading **Seats** 85, Pr/dining room 16 **Times** 12-2.30/7-9 **Prices** Fixed L 2 course fr £18.95, Starter £7.50-£14, Main £14-£30, Dessert £8-£15, Service optional **Wines** 12 bottles over £30, 27 bottles under £30, 8 by glass **Parking** 80 **Notes** Sunday L, Vegetarian available, Children welcome

AUSTWICK
Map 18 SD76

The Traddock
Modern British

tel: 015242 251224 **Settle LA2 8BY**
email: info@thetraddock.co.uk **web:** www.thetraddock.co.uk
dir: From Skipton take A65 towards Kendal, 3m after Settle turn right signed Austwick, cross hump back bridge, hotel 100yds on left

Local and seasonal cooking at a Georgian house in the Dales

The stone-built house in the Yorkshire Dales is bountifully endowed with charm. It's a Georgian country hotel on the human scale with peaceful lawns for sitting and contemplating. A soothingly designed dining room with William Morris wallpaper and darkwood chairs (and muzak, sad to say) is the setting for cooking built on relationships with local artisan producers. Honey-roasted baby beetroot and goats' cheese with Burgundy jelly and black pepper toast is one way to start, or there may be crab from Whitby, properly dressed, served with Russian salad, capers and red caviar. The modish two-way serving of suckling pig-shoulder and belly-features fine Middlewhite meat alongside Parmentier potatoes and spiced quince compôte, sauced with cider. Main courses come with a plethora of those local vegetables, but look a little further afield for the chorizo and red pepper coulis that comes with baked codling. Honey-roasting is a favoured technique, applied as enthusiastically to summer veg as to the plums in a tarte Tatin with a difference.

Chef John Pratt **Owner** The Reynolds family **Seats** 36, Pr/dining room 16 **Times** 12-2.30/6.30-11 **Prices** Fixed D 3 course £30, Starter £4.95-£7.25, Main £14.75-£25.95, Dessert £5.25-£7.95, Service optional **Wines** 24 bottles over £30, 26 bottles under £30, 16 by glass **Parking** 20, On street **Notes** Afternoon tea 3-5pm, Sunday L £9.95-£17.95, Vegetarian available, Children welcome

Yorebridge House

British, European V
tel: 01969 652060 **DL8 3EE**
email: enquiries@yorebridgehouse.co.uk **web:** www.yorebridgehouse.co.uk
dir: *A648 to Bainbridge. Yorebridge House N of centre on right before river*

Creative but uncomplicated cooking in a Victorian riverside schoolhouse

Yorebridge was a school in the Victorian era, but what a charmingly sited one. Sitting by the river's edge in a little Dales village not far from Wensleydale, it's become a modern boutique hotel that makes the most of its rugged remoteness, welcoming you to guest rooms that are named after exotic locations a long way from Yorkshire. A contemporary restaurant with simple clean lines, an exposed wood floor and tables, and restorative views over the surrounding countryside also affords peeps into Dan Shotton's kitchen. New to Yorebridge in 2013, he offers regionally based dishes full of skill and creativity without complication, as when a serving of pink, thinly sliced local venison is garnished with blackberries and nasturtium leaves in a light sauce of chocolate as a thought-provoking opener. Mains might take in flawlessly timed sea bream with a langoustine, cherry tomatoes and salsify to add sharpness, sweetness and vibrant colour, and lentils and red wine to add a more earthy dimension to the layerings of flavour, or duck breast might be partnered more simply with boulangère potatoes and broccoli. Seasonality is a strong point in all dishes and local suppliers are duly namechecked on the menu. Finish with delicately glazed apple and almond tart, scattered with caramelised apple balls and served with excellent vanilla ice cream, or a dark chocolate pavé with pear, honeycomb and praline ice cream. All of the peripheral items are crafted with the same thoughtful approach and attention to detail, whether it's an oven-fresh Wensleydale cheese and thyme roll, an amuse-bouche of velvety parsnip velouté with parsnip crisps and shimeji mushrooms, or a pre-dessert of vanilla pannacotta with a tiny quenelle of strawberry. The wine list sources some imaginative choices from the New World as well as doing justice to the classic regions of Europe.

Chef Dan Shotton **Owner** Damien Fort (GM) **Seats** 35, Pr/dining room 20 **Times** 12-2/7-9 **Prices** Fixed L 2 course £17.50, Fixed D 3 course £45, Starter £7-£9.50, Main £17-£22, Dessert £7.50 **Wines** 43 bottles over £30, 32 bottles under £30, 8 by glass **Parking** 30 **Notes** Tasting menu can be arranged by reservation, Sunday L £17.50-£22.50, Children welcome

The Devonshire Arms Hotel & Spa

Modern French
tel: 01756 710441 & 718111 **BD23 6AJ**
email: res@devonshirehotels.co.uk **web:** www.burlingtonrestaurant.co.uk
dir: *On B6160 to Bolton Abbey, 250 yds N of junct with A59 rdbt*

Top-flight cooking in a tranquil Yorkshire Dales setting

There's no two ways about it, The Devonshire Arms is a fantastic country-house hotel. Right in the heart of the Yorkshire Dales, surrounded by 30,000 acres of land making up the Duke of Devonshire's Bolton Abbey Estate (the ruined abbey is a stone's throw away), this one-time coaching inn dating back to the 17th century is in a fabulous location. Yet it has a lot more going for it besides its geography, with welcoming log fires in the numerous quiet and comfortable lounges, luxurious bedrooms, a swish spa and two restaurants-the more informal Devonshire Brasserie & Bar, and the jewel in the crown, the Burlington Restaurant. The dress code has been relaxed in recent times (smart casual is now the required attire), but the room remains as elegant and traditional in style as ever, with its pale aubergine walls decorated with classical architectural drawings (borrowed from the Devonshire collection at Chatsworth, no less), soft lighting, and antique tables dressed with designer silverware and sparkling crystal. Here, head chef Adam Smith presents his individual take on modern British cooking with dishes that impact on both the eye and the palate in equal measure, and are honed largely from the estate's excellent produce, as well as herbs, vegetables and fruits from the kitchen garden. Superb canapés and amuse-bouche might precede a nicely balanced starter of super-fresh crabmeat wrapped inside finely sliced apple, with bergamot jelly, pressed fennel and radish. Game from the estate is a real highlight here, as in main-course peppered venison, the meat accurately timed and tender, with a welcome injection of sweetness from some glazed and pureed chestnut, pear and celeriac; this is certainly a chef who knows just what works with what. Presentation is a strong point throughout, and that flows right through to a wickedly indulgent dessert of Amedei chocolate ganache with salted caramel and tonka. If you need a little help choosing from the 2,500-bin wine list, as well you might, do call on the knowledge of cellar master Nigel Fairclough.

Chef Adam Smith **Owner** Duke & Duchess of Devonshire **Seats** 70, Pr/dining room 90 **Times** 7-9.30 Closed Xmas, New Year, Mon, L all week **Prices** Tasting menu fr £75 **Wines** 2000 bottles over £30, 20 bottles under £30, 30 by glass **Parking** 100 **Notes** ALC menu £65, Vegetarian available, Children welcome

BAINBRIDGE
Map 18 SD99

Yorebridge House
◎◎◎ – *see page 545*

BOLTON ABBEY
Map 19 SE05

The Devonshire Arms Hotel & Spa
◎◎◎ – *see page 545*

The Devonshire Brasserie & Bar
◎ Modern British V

tel: 01756 710710 & 710441 **Bolton Abbey BD23 6AJ**
email: res@devonshirehotels.co.uk
dir: *On B6160, 250yds N of junct with A59*

Smart brasserie cooking in a top-class country hotel

The Devonshire Arms has a lot going for it, from its fabulous position on the 30,000-acre estate, the luxe bedrooms and high-end restaurant, but don't forget about the Brasserie & Bar. It sets the pace for a more informal experience, with its colourfully upholstered chairs and local artworks displayed on the whitewashed walls, and it generates a happy hum. There are tables on the terrace, too, to increase the feel-good-factor. The menu deals in upscale modern brasserie food, with a Yorkshire flavour, so you might tuck into a 'classic' such as sausage (from Lishmans of Ilkley) with mash and onion gravy, or go for pork tenderloin with crisp pancetta and Yorkshire Blue dauphinoise. Starters run from black pudding, bacon and soft-boiled egg salad, to Thai-spiced Whitby crab cake with wasabi mayonnaise and tamarind ketchup, and there's creativity among desserts, too: baked ginger parkin with pickled plum purée, goats' milk sorbet and granola, for example.

Chef Charlie Murray **Owner** The Duke & Duchess of Devonshire **Seats** 60
Times 12-2.30/6-9.30 **Prices** Starter £6-£9, Main £14-£18, Dessert £5.50-£7.50
Wines 16 by glass **Parking** 40 **Notes** Sunday L, Children welcome

BOROUGHBRIDGE
Map 19 SE36

The Crown Inn
◎ Modern British V

tel: 01423 322300 **Roecliffe YO51 9LY**
email: info@crowninnroecliffe.com **web:** www.crowninnroecliffe.com
dir: *A1(M) junct 48, follow brown sign*

Old coaching inn with modish cooking

The Crown is an old coaching inn which still radiates charm and hospitality within its 16th-century walls, with the hoped for stone-flagged floors, chunky oak beams and roaring log fires all present and correct. It's been revamped with a keen eye by owners Karl and Amanda Mainey, blending traditional and contemporary touches into a pleasing whole. A good deal of local produce finds its way into the kitchen and is turned into brasserie-style dishes which have a regional flavour, and a bit more besides. Start with Whitby crab soup perked up with brandy, or a terrine of local rabbit studded with pickled walnuts and served with Wakefield rhubarb chutney and granary toast. Next up, there might be fish pie, or steak and kidney pie made with local ale, or the more outré spiced monkfish with chilli-spiked Puy lentils and a crab and coriander bhaji.

Chef Steve Ardern **Owner** Karl & Amanda Mainey **Seats** 60, Pr/dining room 20
Times 12-3.30/6-11 **Prices** Fixed L 2 course £17.95, Fixed D 2 course £17.95, Starter £4.50-£9.95, Main £13.50-£19.95, Dessert £6.50-£7.95, Service optional **Wines** 20 bottles over £30, 20 bottles under £30, 19 by glass **Parking** 30 **Notes** Sunday L £17.95-£19.95, Children welcome

The Dining Room Restaurant
◎◎ Modern British, French

tel: 01423 326426 **20 St James Square YO51 9AR**
email: chris@thediningroom.co.uk
dir: *A1(M), Boroughbridge junct, follow signs to town. Opposite fountain in town square*

Assured cooking in stylish neighbourhood restaurant

Housed within a bow-fronted Queen Anne building The Dining Room is the sort of personable neighbourhood restaurant that attracts a strong local following. Inside, it's a bright white contemporary affair, with artworks to inject colour, or when the weather plays ball, you can move outside to the walled terrace for relaxed alfresco dining or pre-dinner drinks. Husband-and-wife-team Christopher and Lisa Astley run it with hands-on verve, chef Chris calling the shots in the kitchen while Lisa takes care of the front-of-house team. The cooking steers clear of over-complication, sticking to a repertoire of well-thought-out combinations that leave the top-class local materials tasting honestly and forthrightly of themselves. Wild venison terrine with gherkins, redcurrant jelly and Melba toast make reliable bedfellows as a starter, followed perhaps by slow-cooked duck confit with black pudding and cider apple compôte and creamy grain mustard mash. Fish is deftly handled too, delivering the likes of pan-fried sea bass with samphire, lemon and thyme. Puddings stick to classic themes such as crème brûlée or glazed lemon tart.

Chef Christopher Astley **Owner** Mr & Mrs C Astley **Seats** 32 **Times** 12-2/7-9.30
Closed 26-28 Dec, 1 Jan, BHs, Mon, L Tue-Sat, D Sun **Prices** Fixed D 3 course fr £18.95, Starter £4.95-£9.50, Main £11.50-£29.50, Dessert £4.95-£7, Service optional **Wines** 12 bottles over £30, 19 bottles under £30, 16 by glass **Parking** On street/Private on request **Notes** Early bird set menu from 6pm, Sunday L, Vegetarian available, Children 5 yrs+

Grantham Arms
◎ Contemporary British **NEW**

tel: 01423 323980 & 07809 757461 **Milby YO51 9BW**
email: info@granthamarms.co.uk **web:** www.granthamarms.co.uk
dir: *A1 junct 48*

Stylish pub with creative and beautifully presented cooking

An old inn with a swish modern makeover, the Grantham Arms boasts contemporary bedrooms, a plush bar serving cocktails and a restaurant headed-up by a runner-up in BBC's *MasterChef–The Professionals*. It's all very 'boutique' with lots of designer touches and the restaurant decorated in purple and grey. The kitchen aims to impress with its fine-dining output, with prettily presented plates of classically-inspired with a contemporary flourish. North Sea cod appears as a starter with lightly spiced mussel chowder, with another matching smoked local duck breast with Caesar salad and an orange reduction. There's a good showing of regional ingredients throughout. Main-course roasted rump of lamb comes with parmesan gnocchi, sautéed little gem and caper and raisin purée, and, for dessert, Yorkshire rhubarb makes a seasonal appearance in a deconstructed cheesecake with a vodka and rhubarb jelly and popping candy.

Chef Dan Graham **Owner** Richard Sykes **Times** 12-2.30/6-9 **Prices** Fixed L 2 course £15.95, Fixed D 3 course £19.95, Starter £6.95-£8.95, Main £15.95-£21.95, Dessert £6.95-£12.95, Service optional **Wines** 20 bottles over £30, 31 bottles under £30, 8 by glass **Notes** Fixed D menu available 6-7pm, Sunday L £15.95-£21.95

What makes a 4-Rosette restaurant?
See page 9

BURNSALL
Map 19 SE06

The Devonshire Fell
◉◉ Modern British V

tel: 01756 729000 **BD23 6BT**
email: manager@devonshirefell.co.uk **web:** www.devonshirefell.co.uk
dir: On B6160, 6m from Bolton Abbey rdbt A59 junct

Modern cooking in a made-over old building

The traditional stone exterior belies the contemporary makeover within at The Devonshire Fell, all vibrant colours, bold fabrics and attractive artwork. Part of the Devonshire Hotels & Restaurants group, which also includes The Devonshire Arms at Bolton Abbey, it's more of a boutique hotel than anything else these days, with attractive accommodation and a modern, funky-looking bistro, bar and conservatory all designed by the Duchess of Devonshire (who owns the group with her husband). The bright, airy and welcoming feel of the place is aided by informal, friendly service, while on the food front, the modern British cooking is based on top-notch local ingredients brought together in unfussy, appealing combinations by a small kitchen team. A starter of 'velouté-tomato, chilli and lime crème fraîche'-is full of fresh, clean flavours, while main-course honey-glazed duck breast comes perfectly cooked and accompanied by a smooth spring onion mash, buttered spinach, glazed baby carrots and blackberry jus. Home-made bread-and-butter pudding with clotted cream and apricot compôte is as good as it gets.

Chef Oliver Adams **Owner** Duke & Duchess of Devonshire **Seats** 40, Pr/dining room 70 **Times** 12-2.30/6.30-9.30 **Prices** Starter £4.50-£11.50, Main £12.95-£22.50, Dessert £4.50-£7.50 **Wines** 8 by glass **Parking** 40 **Notes** Fixed D 5 course £50, Sunday L, Children welcome

CRATHORNE
Map 19 NZ40

Crathorne Hall Hotel
◉◉ Modern British

tel: 01642 700398 **TS15 0AR**
email: crathornehall@handpicked.co.uk **web:** www.handpickedhotels.co.uk/crathorne-hall
dir: Off A19, 2m E of Yarm. Access to A19 via A66 or A1, Thirsk

Contemporary British style with clever combinations

A grandiose Edwardian pile built in 1906, Crathorne Hall was the largest and last to be built in North Yorkshire in the swan-song years of stately homes. While the decor and furnishings of the Leven Restaurant are a trip back to the early 20th century-oak half-panelled walls, heavy drapes at tall windows, oil paintings, and a gilt-edged coffered ceiling-it's fast forward to the 21st century in the kitchen. Here the style tends towards modern British sensibilities, with plenty of sound, classical technique on display. Tip-top produce, much of it sourced locally, is put to good use in well-considered dishes, starting with perfectly-timed scallops matched with chorizo, compressed apple and caper dressing. Next up, loin of lamb appears in a simple partnership with sautéed Jersey Royal potatoes and a fricassée of seasonal vegetables, or there might be pan-fried sea bass with red wine risotto, garlic purée and samphire. Puddings bring on more carefully considered combinations of flavour and texture, delivering velvety bitter chocolate tart with chocolate soil, pistachio ice cream and cherries.

Times 12.30-2.30/7-9.30

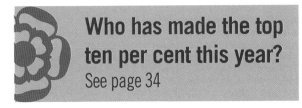

Who has made the top ten per cent this year?
See page 34

GRASSINGTON
Map 19 SE06

Grassington House
◉◉ Modern British

tel: 01756 752406 **5 The Square BD23 5AQ**
email: bookings@grassingtonhousehotel.co.uk **web:** www.grassingtonhousehotel.co.uk
dir: A59 into Grassington, in town square opposite post office

Inventive cooking in boutique surroundings

In the heart of Wharfedale in the Yorkshire Dales National Park, this charming three-storey Georgian restaurant with rooms has been stylishly modernised. Its location makes it ideal for walkers looking for a touch of luxury, or for couples on special breaks. A boutique feel dominates the small bar and cosy reception area and extends to the smart No. 5 Restaurant (part of which is in the conservatory), with its red tones and birdcage-print wallpaper. Informal service comes courtesy of a young team. The modern European cooking puts the emphasis on local produce, including pigs home-reared by chef-patron John Rudden and his wife Sue. Expect inventive combinations such as local pheasant and prune cannelloni with brown onion and wild mushroom dressing, or pigeon breast roasted in potato crisps with a textbook beetroot risotto, followed by pan-roasted Yorkshire venison haunch, Savoy cabbage faggot and juniper beetroot, or perhaps fillet of plaice with crab and lobster ravioli and sambuca shellfish sauce. To finish, you might treat yourself to date soufflé cooked to order and served with salted caramel ice cream.

Chef John Rudden **Owner** Susan & John Rudden **Seats** 40 **Times** 12-2.30/6-9.30 **Prices** Fixed L 2 course £13.50-£14.50, Fixed D 3 course £16.50-£17.50, Tasting menu £39.50, Starter £4.50-£7.95, Main £12.95-£23.50, Dessert £5.95-£6.25, Service optional **Wines** 17 bottles over £30, 28 bottles under £30, 12 by glass **Parking** 20 **Notes** Fixed D 4 course Sun-Tue £39.50 per couple, Sunday L £14.50-£17.50, Vegetarian available, Children welcome

GUISBOROUGH
Map 19 NZ61

Gisborough Hall
◉◉ Modern British

tel: 0844 879 9149 & 01287 611500 **Whitby Ln TS14 6PT**
email: general.gisboroughhall@macdonald-hotels.co.uk **web:** www.gisborough-hall.co.uk
dir: A171, follow signs for Whitby to Waterfall rdbt then 3rd exit into Whitby Lane, hotel 500yds on right

Well-crafted interesting dishes in a Victorian mansion

On the edge of the North York Moors, the hall is an imposing Victorian-built, creeper-covered country-house hotel within well-kept grounds. Chaloner's restaurant is in what used to be the billiard room, a large space with pillars, a fireplace, white-patterned burgundy-coloured carpet and white upholstered seats at wooden-topped tables. The kitchen works around the abundance of Yorkshire's produce and puts a lot of effort into dishes that never seem overwrought. Roast breast of guinea fowl, for instance, perfectly cooked, is accompanied by a creditable Scotch egg made with fowl meat, together with mushroom ketchup, confit potatoes, kale and carrots, all elements working well together. A fish alternative might be steamed plaice fashionably partnered by chicken wings and quinoa, served with winkles, chicory and garlic. For starters, expect straightforward game terrine, or tea-smoked confit of mackerel with pickled cucumber and fennel. The kitchen clearly has an eye for presentation and an understanding of the balance of textures and flavours, seen in a theme on apple: mousse, strudel, poached and caramel.

Chef Dave Sotheran **Owner** Gisborough Estates Ltd **Seats** 90, Pr/dining room 33 **Times** 12.30-2.30/6.30-9.30 Closed L Mon-Sat **Prices** Fixed D 3 course £35-£48, Starter £6.75-£9.75, Main £18.50-£23.50, Dessert £6.75-£8.75, Service optional **Wines** 41 bottles over £30, 30 bottles under £30, 19 by glass **Parking** 180 **Notes** Sunday L £18.95-£21.95, Vegetarian available, Children welcome

HAROME
Map 19 SE68

The Star Inn
◉◉ Traditional British

tel: 01439 770397 **YO62 5JE**
email: reservations@thestaratharome.co.uk
dir: From Helmsley take A170 towards Kirkbymoorside, after 0.5m turn right towards Harome. After 1.5m, inn 1st building on right

Exhilarating Yorkshire cooking in a thatched country inn

The thatched country pub in a moorland village just outside Helmsley is a perfect crooked house: it's hard to get pictures to hang straight on 14th-century walls, as you'll see. Comprising a comfortable rustic bar with candles, an old dining room with chunky tables, a real fire and knick-knacks galore, and a newer one with a bright, opulent, contemporary feel, The Star has it all, not forgetting genuinely friendly staff and Andrew Pern's Yorkshire-rooted country cooking, which places a high premium on big, rugged flavours. It doesn't come much more rugged than Stinking Bishop, the prime ingredient in a twice-baked soufflé served with smoked bacon salad and red wine shallots. That could be followed by roast rump of Ryedale lamb, pink and tender, with pan haggerty and pearl barley, all hedged about with rosemary-scented pan juices, or breaded Scarborough woof with brown shrimps, buttered samphire and duck egg gribiche. The exhilarating sense of novelty extends into desserts such as spiced fig Bakewell with superb chestnut and honey ice cream and a little jug of almond anglaise.

Chef Andrew Pern, Steve Smith **Owner** Andrew Pern **Seats** 70, Pr/dining room 10 **Times** 11.30-3/6.30-11 Closed L Mon, D Sun **Prices** Fixed L 2 course £20, Fixed D 3 course £25, Tasting menu £70, Starter £6-£14, Main £18-£27, Dessert £6-£15 **Wines** 70 bottles over £30, 30 bottles under £30, 24 by glass **Parking** 30 **Notes** Chef's table for 6-8 people, tasting menu 6-8 course, Sunday L, Vegetarian available, Children welcome

HARROGATE
Map 19 SE35

Hotel du Vin Harrogate
◉ British, Mediterranean

tel: 0844 7364257 **Prospect Place HG1 1LB**
email: reception.harrogate@hotelduvin.com **web:** www.hotelduvin.com
dir: A1(M) junct 47, A59 to Harrogate, follow town centre signs to Prince of Wales rdbt, 3rd exit, remain in right lane. Right at lights into Albert St, right into Prospect Place

Fine food and wine in chic Georgian townhouse setting

The senses have always been well catered for by the renowned tea shops and Victorian spa in Harrogate, a tradition continued 21st -century-style by the local outpost of the HdV chain in a luxuriously converted terrace of eight Georgian townhouses opposite the 200-acre Stray common. As its name suggests, the Hotel du Vin brand takes a serious approach to the grape, so a snifter of one of the impressive array of wines available by the glass in the bar is a good move before settling into the slick Gallic-style bistro. The kitchen makes a virtue of simplicity and restraint, leaving the quality and freshness of the ingredients to speak for themselves. Chicken liver parfait with raisin chutney and toasted brioche makes a well-rendered version of a tried-and-tested starter, while superb steaks from the grill grab carnivores' attention at main course stage. On the fish front, there could be lemon sole Véronique, served with shallot and grape sauce.

Times 12-2/5.30-10

Read all about our Wine Award winners on page 17

Nidd Hall Hotel
◉◉ Modern British ᵥ

tel: 01423 771598 **Nidd HG3 3BN web:** www.warnerleisurehotels.co.uk
dir: A1(M) junct/A59 follow signs to Knaresborough. Continue through town centre & at Bond End lights turn left, then right onto B6165 signed Ripley & Pateley Bridge. Hotel on right in approx 4m

Graceful modern cooking in a grand late-Georgian manor house

Built in the 1820s for a Bradford wool magnate, Nidd Hall is an early example of 19th-century pastiche, a glorious hodge-podge of architectural and stylistic references that take in everything from stained window panels to Tuscan columns. The colossal double-height fireplace and distant copper ceiling in the dining room give notice that the place was once grand enough to host the first meeting between Edward VIII and Mrs Simpson – possibly. Ancestral paintings and antlered heads surround you in the Terrace restaurant, the fine-dining option, which nonetheless manages a light decorative tone in keeping with the graceful version of modern British cooking on offer. Expect to find mandarin and camomile fragrancing the confit duck and foie gras terrine, and then perhaps crispy noodles in seafood broth as a medium for main-course sea bass with mussels, or beetroot dauphinoise and black pudding teaming up with a pair of pork cuts, gingery fillet and slow-roasted belly. Desserts are just as inventive, serving date and port clafoutis with an apple and brandy shot, rum and raisin ice cream and mint foam.

Chef Kiran Selevarajan, Dan Saddler **Owner** Bourne Leisure **Seats** 42 **Times** 6.30-9.30 Closed Tue-Wed, L Mon, Thu-Sat **Prices** Service optional **Wines** 11 by glass **Parking** 300 **Notes** No children

Rudding Park Hotel, Spa & Golf
◉◉ Modern British

tel: 01423 871350 **Follifoot HG3 1JH**
email: reservations@ruddingpark.com **web:** www.ruddingpark.co.uk
dir: A61 at rdbt with A658 follow signs 'Rudding Park'

Brasserie menu in an elegant Regency era hotel

When you're ready for the whole country house pampering package, Rudding Park fits the bill. It has its own golf course, glossy spa, and food that's worth a detour in the Clocktower Restaurant. The interior designer has come up trumps here to create vibrant, colourful spaces, from the long limestone bar, to the grand conservatory with a 400-year-old Catalonian olive tree, and the dining room with its eye-catching pink glass chandelier and elegantly understated contemporary looks. The kitchen team delivers skilful modern British cooking and local flavour via the 'food heroes' menu, which hauls in produce from a 75-mile radius, and a brasserie-style main menu setting out with seared scallops with salt and pepper squid, chorizo and roast red pepper gel. Next comes local venison with crispy bone marrow, chicory tart Tatin and pommes Anna, while two could sign up for an eight-bone rack of lamb with celeriac dauphinoise, watercress and paloise sauce from the grill section. To finish, there could be apple and blackberry mousse with apple jelly and blackberry sorbet.

Chef Eddie Gray **Owner** Simon Mackaness & family **Seats** 170, Pr/dining room 16 **Times** 12-2.30/7-9.30 **Prices** Fixed L 2 course fr £29.50, Fixed D 3 course fr £38.50, Starter £9-£12.95, Main £19.50-£34, Dessert £9-£9.50, Service optional **Wines** 71 bottles over £30, 44 bottles under £30, 17 by glass **Parking** 350 **Notes** Sunday L £25-£32, Vegetarian available, Children welcome

Studley Hotel

 Pacific Rim

tel: 01423 560425 **28 Swan Rd HG1 2SE**
email: info@studleyhotel.co.uk **web:** www.orchidrestaurant.co.uk
dir: Adjacent to Valley Gardens, opposite Mercer Gallery

Smart hotel restaurant giving culinary tour of Asia

Mango and darkwood interiors divided by Japanese lattice-style screens are the setting for the Studley Hotel's Orchid restaurant, where the chefs give an eclectic Pan-Asian array of cuisines from China, Indonesia, Japan, Korea, Malaysia, the Philippines, Thailand and Vietnam a thorough workout. A friendly team of attentive staff who know their way around the menu is a big plus, as is the large TV screen showing all the live action going on in the kitchen. Food miles are sacrificed in the name of authenticity as key ingredients are flown in regularly from Asia. A starter of aromatic Szechuan lamb brings slow-cooked lamb belly with cucumber, leek, red pepper, pancakes and yellow bean and honey dip, ahead of pan-fried chicken with Szechuan black pepper sauce and garlic cucumber. Desserts tend to be more successful when they stay within the Asian idiom-say Thai-style steamed banana cake cooked in a banana leaf and served with coconut ice cream.

Chef Kenneth Poon **Owner** Bokmun Chan **Seats** 72, Pr/dining room 20 **Times** 12-2/6-10 Closed 25-26 Dec, L Sat **Prices** Fixed L 2 course £11.50, Fixed D 3 course £24.95-£32.50, Starter £5.30-£7.60, Main £8.40-£19.90, Dessert £4.50-£8 **Wines** 15 bottles over £30, 26 bottles under £30, 12 by glass **Parking** 18, On street **Notes** Sunday L £16.90, Vegetarian available, Children welcome

van Zeller

 Modern British v

tel: 01423 508762 **8 Montpellier St HG1 2TQ**
email: info@vanzellerrestaurants.co.uk

Impressively creative cooking in Montpellier

On two levels, with tables on the lower looking out onto fashionable Montpellier, van Zeller is a smartly done-out restaurant, with brown leather-look chairs and banquettes at clothed tables, a dark wooden floor and subdued lighting providing a pleasant glow in the evening. Tom van Zeller has handed over the kitchen reins to his head chef, Neil Bentinck, and between them they've created a range of menus that are bursting with innovative ideas, from roasted onion 'tea' with peas, radish and spelt to a main course of roast Suffolk lamb with young nettles, celeriac dumplings, buttermilk and borage. Masterly technique is evident throughout, and a confident approach means that even unexpected compositions succeed, often using wild ingredients. Try pig's head with sorrel, dandelion, turnips and smoked eel, and go on to Goosnargh duck pie with lovage mash, roast onions, artichoke and lettuce. Seafood receives similar treatments, seen in halibut fillet with salt-baked beetroot, turnips, charred spring onions and brown shrimp and smoked butter, and for pudding there might be chocolate and peanut brownie with liquorice and raspberry.

Chef Tom van Zeller/Neil Bentinck **Owner** Tom van Zeller **Seats** 34 **Times** 12-2/6-10 Closed 10 days Jan, Sun-Mon **Prices** Fixed L 3 course fr £35, Fixed D 3 course fr £50, Tasting menu fr £85, Service optional 12.5% **Wines** 9 by glass **Parking** Montpellier Hill **Notes** 10 course chef's menu from £85, Children welcome

The White Hart Hotel

 British

tel: 01423 505681 **2 Cold Bath Rd HG2 0NF**
email: reception@whitehart.net **web:** www.whitehart.net
dir: A59 to Harrogate. A661 3rd exit on rdbt to Harrogate. Left at rdbt onto A6040 for 1m. Right onto A61. Bear left down Montpellier Hill

Modern brasserie dishes in a Georgian landmark

Not far from the Valley Gardens park, The White Hart is something of a Harrogate landmark, having been a comfortable resort of the discerning traveller since the Georgian era. The old dining room is now a trendy pub called the Fat Badger, while the main eating space is a light room done out in on-trend sandy neutral colours with a checkered pattern in curtains and seating. They call it a Brasserie, the logic of which is revealed at sight of a menu that deals in the likes of grilled scallops with leeks, bacon and cheddar, or oxtail risotto with a crisp-fried quail's egg and horseradish bubbles. An interesting fish offering is goujons of Scarborough woof (a catfish, despite its name) with baby clams in Cullen skink, and there's also a voguish three-way serving of pork – belly, fillet and cheek – seasoned with vanilla and purple sage. Puddings include the regional delicacy, Yorkshire curd tart, dolled up with cinnamon ice cream and blood orange, as well as peanut butter crumble with caramel.

Times 11.30-3.30/6-10

| HAWNBY | Map 19 SE58 |

The Inn at Hawnby

 Modern British

tel: 01439 798202 **YO62 5QS**
email: info@innathawnby.co.uk **web:** www.innathawnby.co.uk
dir: From the S, A1 to Thirsk & Teeside exit A19/A168 for Scarborough onto A170. 1st left through Felixkirk. Through Boltby into Hawnby

Local cooking in an old grey moorland inn

The Youngs' old greystone country inn near Helmsley has the sweeping majesty of the North York Moors all around it, an inspiringly remote setting for walkers and gastronomes. A homely village pub atmosphere, complete with log fire, makes a cheering prospect, while the dining room looks more high-toned, with tables got up in double cloths, laid with quality settings and glassware. Jason Reeves keeps things on a local leash as far as possible, beginning with a pairing of ham hock terrine and a Scotched quail egg with pickled carrots and caper mayonnaise, and following with roast salmon, salade niçoise and salsa verde, or a porcine assemblage of honeyed pork belly and porkfat potatoes dressed in pomegranate and chimichurri. It can sometimes feel as though dishes would be more successful if they weren't striving so intently for complexity, but the prime materials are impeccable, and nobody is complaining at the arrival of textbook vanilla crème brûlée with a blowtorched top.

Chef Jason Reeves **Owner** Kathryn & David Young **Seats** 32, Pr/dining room 30 **Times** 12-2/7-9 Closed 25 Dec, L Mon-Tue (limited opening Feb-Mar please phone) **Prices** Starter £5.50-£7.50, Main £10.95-£17.50, Dessert £5.50-£9.95, Service optional **Wines** 11 bottles under £30, 12 by glass **Parking** 22 **Notes** Sunday L £10.75-£15, Vegetarian available, Children welcome

Find out more about how we assess for Rosette awards on page 9

Black Swan Hotel

Modern British v

tel: 01439 770466 **Market Place YO62 5BJ**
email: enquiries@blackswan-helmsley.co.uk
web: www.blackswan-helmsley.co.uk
dir: *A170 towards Scarborough, on entering Helmsley hotel at end of Market Place, just off mini-rdbt*

Art on a plate in a gallery restaurant

The Black Swan has been right at the heart of this lovely little market town for centuries, and in the 21st it's looking rather dapper both outside and in. It's full of old-world charm, with open fires and antiques aplenty, alongside bags of contemporary swagger. There's an award-winning tearoom should you fancy treating yourself to a cream tea or a Yorkshire parkin, while the newly refurbished and relaunched Gallery restaurant is the place to head for something more substantial – and rather more special. Paul Peters cooks with a high level of skill and a good deal of creative flair, sourcing the finest Yorkshire ingredients and turning them into dishes that wow with their clearly defined flavours and beautiful presentation. The restaurant doubles up as a gallery during the day, showcasing original artworks available to buy, while during the evenings the focus switches to dining, with the elegant tables dressed in their finest white linen, with sparkling glassware and soft music playing in the background. The front of house staff are well versed in the menus, and they've got a lot to remember given that they include a six-course tasting menu and a ten-course 'gastronomic' option. Things get off to a flying start with an opener entitled 'piggy in a garden' (a pressing of local ham hock with black pudding, baby vegetables, quail egg and soft herbs) which is a lesson in how a simple assembly of super-fresh, immaculately prepared ingredients can taste mind-blowingly good. Pan-fried turbot with lobster minestrone, soft herbs, ravioli of lobster and garlic croutons has superb depth and clarity of flavour, every component expertly handled, while a dessert of 'flavours and textures of pistachio' stars a wonderfully moist and light pistachio cake complemented by a vibrant and tangy quenelle of cherry sorbet (amongst other things). All the peripherals-homemade breads, amuse-bouche, petits fours-maintain the standard, while the wine list is certainly worth exploring if your budget allows.

Chef Paul Peters **Owner** John Jameson **Seats** 65, Pr/dining room 50 **Times** 12.30-2.30/7-9.30 Closed L Mon-Sat **Prices** Prices not confirmed, Service optional **Wines** 134 bottles over £30, 59 bottles under £30, 15 by glass **Parking** 40 **Notes** Tasting menu 6/10 course, Market menu available, Sunday L, Children welcome

| **HELMSLEY** | Map 19 SE68 |

Black Swan Hotel

◎◎◎ – *see opposite*

Feversham Arms Hotel & Verbena Spa

◎◎ Modern British V

tel: 01439 770766 **1-8 High St YO62 5AG**
email: info@fevershamarmshotel.com **web:** www.fevershamarmshotel.com
dir: *A1 junct 49 follow A168 to Thirsk, take A170 to Helmsley. Turn left at mini rdbt then right, hotel on right past church*

Modern spa hotel with equally modern culinary ideas

The Feversham Arms has oodles of contemporary style behind its old stone frontage, with a restaurant of dark walls under its vaulted atrium and banquettes and designer-style seating at correctly set tables, an appropriate setting for sharp and sophisticated cooking built on fine regional ingredients. Pan-fried foie gras with mulled pears and brioche seems entirely appropriate for a hotel in an affluent market town, and there might also be accurately made ravioli stuffed with scallops and shrimps. Seasoning and timings are just so and flavour combinations well considered, seen in pan-fried cod loin with fish velouté, parmesan dumplings and parsnip purée, and roast duck breast with green peppercorn sauce, shallot tarte fine and celeriac purée. Good breads are all part of the package, and tempting desserts have included figs poached in red wine with parkin and yoghurt sorbet, and vanilla parfait with blueberry compôte.

Chef Jason 'Bruno' Birkbeck **Owner** Feversham Arms Ltd **Seats** 65, Pr/dining room 24 **Times** 12-2/6.30-9.30 **Prices** Tasting menu fr £55, Starter £9-£12.50, Main £21-£30, Dessert £4.95-£12.50, Service optional **Wines** 38 bottles under £30, 18 by glass **Parking** 50 **Notes** Tasting menu 5 course whole tables only, Sunday L £19.50-£25, Children welcome

The Pheasant Hotel

◎◎ Modern British NEW V

tel: 01439 771241 **Mill St, Harome YO62 5JG**
email: reservations@thepheasanthotel.com **web:** www.thepheasanthotel.com
dir: *Exit A170 signed Harome, hotel located opposite church*

Skilful cooking by the village duck pond

Overlooking the duck pond in the pretty village of Harome, The Pheasant has been carved out of a blacksmith's, village shop and barns, all set around a courtyard of fruit trees. The flagstone-floored conservatory is mainly used for dining, with candles on neatly clothed tables lit after dark and where service is on the formal side. The cooking style is an updated British version of the classical French repertory, with an expert's skills behind judicious combinations. Expect dressed crab with a matching velouté, lemon sabayon, cucumber and seaweed sticks, followed by roast rump of beef with duxelle, pommes Anna and spinach purée. Dinner kicks off with an amuse-bouche – perhaps root vegetable velouté with ginger beer foam – before starters along the lines of seared scallops, perfectly cooked and seasoned, with rich braised lamb neck and cauliflower and truffle purée, or classic steak tartare with a hen's egg and beetroot, then braised pig cheeks boosted with squid, served with Alsace bacon and smoked butter mash. Satisfying puddings include rice pudding with damson jam.

Chef Peter Neville **Owner** Peter Neville, Jacquie Pern **Seats** 60, Pr/dining room 30 **Times** 12-2/6.30-9 **Closed** D 25 Dec **Prices** Fixed L 2 course £23.50-£28.50, Fixed D 3 course £36-£45, Tasting menu £55-£65, Starter £9-£15, Main £20-£24, Dessert £9-£13, Service optional **Wines** 67 bottles over £30, 20 bottles under £30, 12 by glass **Parking** 15 **Notes** Afternoon tea available, Sunday L £22-£34, Children welcome

| **HETTON** | Map 18 SD95 |

The Angel Inn

◎◎◎ – *see below*

The Angel Inn

| **HETTON** | Map 18 SD95 |

British

tel: 01756 730263 **BD23 6LT**
email: info@angelhetton.co.uk **web:** www.angelhetton.co.uk
dir: *6m N Skipton, follow B6265 towards Grassington, left at duck pond & again at T-junct. The Angel up the hill on right*

Culinary delights in well-established Dales dining inn

A granddaddy of the gastro-pub movement, The Angel Inn places good food at the heart of the operation. It all takes place in a creeper-covered inn with origins dating back to the 15th century, with later generations adding a bit here and there-the majority of the current structure dates from the 18th century. It occupies a charming spot in a diminutive village in the Yorkshire Dales National Park. The interior is brimful of oak beams, nooks, crannies and roaring open fire-a real charmer. There are two dining options to choose from, with the bar/brasserie keeping it easy-going and cosy, with orders taken at the bar and real ales on tap. The main restaurant takes a more refined approach, with a genteel atmosphere and tables dressed up in white linen cloths. There's a tasting menu if you want to go the whole hog, or an à la carte that offers five choices per course. There's a genuine local flavour all round, with meat and game from the Dales and Lancashire, fish from the two coasts that are within striking distance, and everything made in-house. Kick off with a wild mushroom risotto, say, topped with a truffled rape seed foam, or go for the winning combination of crispy pork belly with a Granny Smith reduction and Parma ham crisps. Roasted haunch of fallow deer comes with a bitter chocolate sauce among main courses, and pan-seared fillet of brill with parsley root, wild mushrooms and roasted baby parsnips. A classic dessert such as bread pudding is jazzed up with accompaniments that include whisky jelly and marmalade ice cream, and the British cheese selection is well worth a punt.

Chef Bruce Elsworth **Owner** Juliet Watkins **Seats** 65, Pr/dining room 24 **Times** 12-2.30/6-10 **Closed** 25 Dec & 1 wk Jan, L Mon-Sat, D Sun **Prices** Tasting menu £55, Starter £6.95-£7.50, Main £12.95-£26.95, Dessert £6.95-£10.95, Service optional **Wines** 107 bottles over £30, 46 bottles under £30, 26 by glass **Parking** 40 **Notes** Sat D 3 course £42, Sunday L £19.95-£24.50, Vegetarian available, Children welcome

KIRKBY FLEETHAM
Map 19 SE20

The Black Horse
@@ Traditional & Modern

tel: 01609 749010 & 749011 **7 Lumley Ln DL7 0SH**
email: gm@blackhorsekirkbyfleetham.com **web:** www.blackhorsekirkbyfleetham.com
dir: Exit A1 to Kirkby Fleetham, follow restaurant signs

Stylish pub cooking in a stone-built village inn

A short spin from the whirling traffic at Scotch Corner brings you to the north Yorkshire hamlet of Kirkby Fleetham, and its stone-built traditional inn, which pushes all the right buttons for a northern country hostelry, complete with stylishly furnished guest-rooms. The main dining room, an elegant, ivory-coloured space under a low beamed ceiling, looks out over the back garden and lifts the Horse to an altogether higher level. A range of globally inspired modern dishes is offered, and if you find it hard to choose, the recommended way to begin is with one of the sharing-boards of 'bits and bobs', comprising different elements from the starter menu. There may be home-smoked mackerel with apple, beetroot and horseradish, chicken liver parfait with clementine marmalade, garlic and chilli king prawns with sesame toast, and more. Main courses span a range from Parma-wrapped chicken breast filled with smoked applewood Cheddar in wild mushroom sauce, or pork belly with black pudding and mustard mash in cider jus. Finish with rhubarb and vanilla pannacotta with a pistachio tuile.

Chef Marc Lomas **Owner** HRH Group **Seats** 40, Pr/dining room **Times** 12-2.30/5-9 **Prices** Starter £4.95-£7.95, Main £10.95-£44.95, Dessert £5.50-£9.95, Service optional **Wines** 21 bottles over £30, 27 bottles under £30, 10 by glass **Parking** 40 **Notes** Sunday L, Vegetarian available, Children welcome

KNARESBOROUGH
Map 19 SE35

General Tarleton Inn
@@ Modern British

tel: 01423 340284 **Boroughbridge Rd, Ferrensby HG5 0PZ**
email: gti@generaltarleton.co.uk **web:** www.generaltarleton.co.uk
dir: A1(M) junct 48 at Boroughbridge, take A6055 to Knaresborough. 4m on right

Polished cooking in a refined old coaching inn

This 18th-century coaching inn, in open countryside, is a characterful place, with low beamed ceilings, rustic walls, log fires and cosy corners. It has a private dining room and separate cocktail bar – sure indicators of its market – as well as a smart restaurant in what was the stable. 'Food with Yorkshire Roots' is emblazoned on the menu, and indeed a taste of Nidderdale salmon (smoked, mousse, and seared with pickled fennel, accompanied by horseradish ice cream) may precede chargrilled fillet of Dales beef with foie gras tortellini and veal consommé. Locally sourced or not, dishes are well rendered and combinations intelligent: chilli-spiced crispy squid on a julienne of peppers and coriander, say, then roast pheasant breast rolled in sage and pancetta accompanied by confit leg, Savoy cabbage, and boulangère potatoes. The kitchen's momentum continues into the final straight, with puddings like chocolate fondant with orange ice cream and mandarin jelly, and classic lemon tart with raspberry sorbet.

Chef John Topham, Marc Williams **Owner** John & Claire Topham **Seats** 64, Pr/dining room 40 **Times** 12-1.45/5.30-9.15 Closed L Mon-Sat, D 25-26 Dec, 1 Jan **Prices** Fixed L 2 course £15, Fixed D 3 course £18.50, Starter £5.95-£9.50, Main £13.50-£22.50, Dessert £5.75-£7.25, Service optional **Wines** 57 bottles over £30, 25 bottles under £30, 12 by glass **Parking** 40 **Notes** Sunday L £21-£28.50, Vegetarian available, Children welcome

MALTON
Map 19 SE77

The Talbot Hotel
@@ British

tel: 01653 639096 **Yorkersgate YO17 7AJ**
email: reservations@talbotmalton.co.uk **web:** www.talbotmalton.co.uk
dir: A46 Malton

Highly accomplished local cooking from a local chef

The Talbot is a foursquare Yorkshire house that has been in the Naylor-Leyland family since 1739, and they've looked after it well over the centuries, from the landscaped gardens to the light-toned contemporary elegance with which today's hotel is furnished. If localism is a virtue in food sourcing, it's surely all the more so in the provenance of the chef himself, and James Martin was born in Malton, so has Yorkshire blood and Yorkshire pride flowing through him. The style of cooking he delivers (in an executive capacity) rises to the occasion of the smart, sophisticated dining room, where crisp white linen, silver cutlery and formal service play their part. Modern British thinking is to the fore, with a mix of classical and up-to-date technique brought to bear on the fine ingredients the kitchen has at its disposal. A kind of croquette of lightly smoked kipper starts things off with a flourish, accompanied as it is by seasonal Sand Hutton asparagus and a capery Cambridge butter sauce. That's followed by superb lamb from Terrington, roasted in lavender and hay and partnered by braised shallots, peas and celery cress, with daringly savoury notes creeping into desserts too – dark chocolate fondant with caramel ice cream and black salt praline, for example.

Chef James Martin, Craig Atchinson **Owner** Fitzwilliam Estate **Seats** 40, Pr/dining room 40 **Times** 12.30-2.30/6.30-9.30 **Prices** Fixed L 2 course £18, Tasting menu £55, Starter £7.50-£11.50, Main £15-£24, Dessert £6.25-£8, Service optional **Wines** 200 bottles over £30, 40 bottles under £30, 14 by glass **Parking** 40 **Notes** Thu Supper Club 2 main course & wine £25, Sunday L £20-£25, Vegetarian available, Children welcome

MASHAM
Map 19 SE28

Samuel's at Swinton Park

◎◎◎ – see below

Vennell's

◎◎ Modern British

tel: 01765 689000 **7 Silver St HG4 4DX**
email: info@vennellsrestaurant.co.uk
dir: 8m from A1 Masham exit, 10m N of Ripon

Lively modern cooking in stylish surroundings

Vennell's is a smartly appointed restaurant, with a small bar and split-level dining room done out in plum and taupe, with rich fabrics and crisp white napery. Jon Vennell's cooking is marked out by the high quality of the produce he uses, his eye for presentation and an unfussy approach that makes for well-defined flavours. Thus venison carpaccio (melt-in-the-mouth stuff) is accompanied simply with pickled carrots and courgettes and parmesan strips in an attractive-looking, clear-flavoured starter, while main course might bring forth braised ox cheek, cooked to perfection, with creamy mash, wild mushrooms and shallots and a smattering of gremolata. The short menu normally encompasses a few seafood options: perhaps slowly poached salmon fillet enhanced by watercress sauce and crisp leeks, and well-timed, pan-fried sea bream inventively accompanied by mussels, broccoli, beetroot gnocchi and masala sauce. An impressive line-up of Yorkshire cheeses is a possibility for those who want to pass on a pudding like rich dark chocolate terrine with smooth white chocolate sauce.

Chef Jon Vennell **Owner** Jon & Laura Vennell **Seats** 30, Pr/dining room 16 **Times** 12-4/7.15-12 Closed 26-29 Dec, 1-14 Jan, 1 wk Sep, Mon-Tue, L Wed-Sat, D Sun **Prices** Fixed L 2 course £22.50, Fixed D 3 course £27.99-£34.50, Service optional **Wines** 27 bottles over £30, 28 bottles under £30, 11 by glass **Parking** On street & Market Sq **Notes** Sunday L, Vegetarian available, Children 4 yrs+

MIDDLESBROUGH
Map 19 NZ41

Chadwicks Inn Maltby

◎◎ Modern British V

tel: 01642 590300 **High Ln, Maltby TS8 OBG**
email: info@chadwicksmaltby.co.uk
dir: A19-A174(W)/A1045, follow signs to Yarm & Maltby, left at the Manor House, inn 500yds on left through village

Ambitious modern cooking in a moorland country inn

Formerly known as The Pathfinders, in honour of World War II flying aces, one of whom owned the place after hostilities were over, the country inn on the edge of the North York Moors still features a quantity of aviation memorabilia among its Victorian beams and stonework. A discreet boutique feel has crept in latterly, bringing hurricane lamps with church candles, banquette seating and swinging Sinatra coming from the speakers, and there is a partially open-to-view kitchen. The carte is all ambitious modern fare, offering scallops and clams with Avruga in fennel beurre blanc, and venison with a cherry Bakewell suet roll and bubble-and-squeak croquette. A menu of simpler bistro fare deals in velvety-rich chestnut mushroom soup with crispy shallots, and free-range chicken breast with béarnaise and chips. Wednesday night is grill night, when sirloins and rib-eyes, spatchcocked chicken and butterflied sea bream come into play. To finish, caramelised lemon syllabub with dots of meringue looks very pretty on its slab of black slate, and there are fine northern cheeses.

Chef Matthew Beadnall **Owner** Gary & Helen Gill, Lee Tolley **Seats** 47 **Times** 12-2.30/5-9.30 Closed 26 Dec, 1 Jan, Mon, D Sun **Prices** Fixed L 3 course £17.95, Starter £6.50-£7.95, Main £16.95-£26, Dessert £4.95-£6.95, Service optional **Wines** 22 bottles over £30, 22 bottles under £30, 6 by glass **Parking** 50 **Notes** Steak & grill night fr £30 for 2, Bistro menu L & early eve, Sunday L £11.95-£17.95, Children welcome

---

Samuel's at Swinton Park

MASHAM
Map 19 SE28

Modern British V
tel: 01765 680900 **Swinton HG4 4JH**
email: enquiries@swintonpark.com **web:** www.swintonpark.com
dir: Please telephone for detailed directions

Exciting contemporary techno-cuisine

Swinton Park is an ancestral home re-imagined as a castle, the forbidding façades softened with climbing foliage, launched into the modern grand-hotel arena by present owners, the Mashams, in 2001. An earnest of the modernising intent can be had from the dining room, where the laminate floor offsets a light-filled space with chairs in contrasting cream and violet, and tables laid up in full linen fig. It would be something of a disappointment nowadays if there weren't also a menu of exciting contemporary techno-cuisine to go with it all, and Simon Crannage is a master of the genre. Not just the combinations and methodology of the dishes are inspired, but the ingredients themselves stray productively beyond the usual prime cuts. Start with glazed monkfish cheek teamed with a pig's head croquette and artichoke purée in red wine, or perhaps cured trout from the estate with a squid cracker, pickled veg and wasabi. Those sharply honed arrangements prepare the palate for mains that are constructed from multiple layers of flavour and texture: stone bass with spiced mussels, sautéed greens and soused fennel; poached estate pheasant breast with charred leeks, mushrooms and garden kale in truffled poultry butter; a double-act of oxtail and halibut with barley, root veg, red wine shallots and puréed garlic. Individually garnished Yorkshire cheeses then look tempting, if

the sweetness of your tooth doesn't extend to roast pineapple with almond cake and anise ice cream.

Chef Simon Crannage **Owner** Mr & Mrs Cunliffe-Lister **Seats** 60, Pr/dining room 20 **Times** 12.30-2/7-9.30 Closed L Mon (only Castle menu in bar) **Prices** Fixed L 2 course £22, Fixed D 3 course £52, Tasting menu £60, Service optional **Wines** 132 bottles over £30, 30 bottles under £30, 13 by glass **Parking** 80 **Notes** Sommelier pairing £28.50, Garden produce menu £52, Sunday L £28, Children 8 yrs+ D

NORTHALLERTON
Map 19 SE39

Solberge Hall
◉ Modern British NEW

tel: 01609 779191 **Newby Wiske DL7 9ER**
email: reservations@solbergehall.co.uk **web:** www.macdonaldhotels.co.uk/solberge
dir: A1(M) junct 51, follow A684 to Northallerton. After village of Ainderby Steeple turn right (signed Solberge Hall) for 2m

Skilful contemporary cooking in a Georgian manor

A spiffing Georgian manor with a charming pastoral outlook, Solberge Hall, with its country-house decor, is a big hit on the wedding scene and business function circuit. It also has a restaurant that makes it a useful place to know about in this neck of the woods. The elegant dining room — more casual eating is available in the lounge bar — is the setting for some ambitious contemporary cooking that matches classical techniques with bright, modern ideas. A pressed guinea fowl terrine comes as a first course with a Scotch quail's egg and piccalilli, or there might be scorched line-caught mackerel with curried mussels, coriander and fennel bhaji and a golden sultana purée. Move on to haunch of venison with dauphinoise and parsnip textures, or a classic Yorkshire sirloin steak, and finish with a Yorkshire rhubarb and custard pannacotta.

Chef Mark Wilson **Owner** West Register Hotels **Seats** 35, Pr/dining room 22 **Times** 12-2/7-9 **Prices** Fixed L 2 course fr £13.95, Fixed D 3 course fr £32, Service optional **Wines** 12 bottles over £30, 23 bottles under £30, 10 by glass **Parking** 95 **Notes** Sunday L fr £19.95, Vegetarian available, Children welcome

OLDSTEAD
Map 19 SE57

The Black Swan at Oldstead
◉◉◉ — see below

OSMOTHERLEY
Map 19 SE49

Cleveland Tontine
◉ Modern European NEW

tel: 01609 882671 **Staddlebridge DL6 3JB**
email: bookings@theclevelandtontine.co.uk **web:** www.theclevelandtontine.co.uk

Modern bistro cooking in revamped roadside restaurant-with-rooms

Built in 1804 to put up travellers on the Yarm to Thirsk turnpike, this characterful roadside stopover is an enticing prospect after a contemporary refurbishment, and its atmospheric candlelit dining room with a monumental stone fireplace has lost none of its charm. The culinary style might best be described as modern British-meets-French-bistro, opening effectively with pan-seared scallops with black squid ink risotto, chorizo and squid tempura, followed by pan-fried pollock with potted shrimp tortellini, lemon mayonnaise and breaded whitebait. If you're up for something more meaty, open with a terrine of local rabbit and foie gras with crispy black pudding and broad bean and morel salad, ahead of smoked fillet and crispy belly of local pork with a salted toffee apple. At dessert stage, duck eggs are used to add extra richness to a crème brûlée which is balanced with the tartness of Yorkshire rhubarb and a ginger crumble biscuit.

Chef James Cooper **Owner** Charles & Angela Tompkins **Seats** 88, Pr/dining room 50 **Times** 12-2.30/6.30-9 Closed D 25-26 Dec, 1 Jan **Prices** Fixed L 2 course £17.50, Fixed D 3 course £22, Starter £6.50-£12.95, Main £14.95-£35, Dessert £5.95-£10.95 **Wines** 17 by glass **Parking** 40 **Notes** Sunday L £26.95-£29.95, Vegetarian available, Children welcome

The Black Swan at Oldstead

OLDSTEAD
Map 19 SE57

Modern British V
tel: 01347 868387 **YO61 4BL**
email: enquiries@blackswanoldstead.co.uk **web:** www.blackswanoldstead.co.uk
dir: A1 junct 49, A168, A19 S (or from York A19 N), then Coxwold, Byland Abbey, Oldstead

Exciting cooking in a charming family-run restaurant with rooms

In a lovely, quiet little village in the North York Moors National Park, the quaint old building of The Black Swan (it's been here for some 500 years) is run as a restaurant with rooms by the Banks family, who have lived and farmed here for generations. It's a real family affair, with Tom and Anne Banks working in the bar and restaurant, son James managing front of house and his brother Tom heading up the kitchen. It's no wonder the place has such a homely, friendly feel. For the restaurant, head upstairs where you'll find a charming, uncluttered room with an oak floor, Persian rugs, an open fire, and candles on the tables giving a gentle, soothing glow. Chef Tom cooks with the seasons and with a great deal of passion and flair, and his menus are full of interesting and exciting combinations. Smoked scallops to start are plump, juicy, subtly smoky and perfectly timed, and need no further embellishment than their simple accompaniments of butternut squash, shiitake, and pumpkin seeds for some contrasting crunch. Main-course venison, served as perfectly cooked saddle and in a superb sausage, shows some real classic skills, the accompanying blackberries, celeriac and hazelnut complementing the flavour of the meat well whilst adding contrasting colours. Black Forest gateau may sound rather ordinary for dessert, but what arrives on the plate is something else: an individual gateau on to which is poured (at the table) a hot fruit compote which melts its way through the cake, creating a taste explosion that really takes you back.

Chef Tommy Banks **Owner** The Banks family **Seats** 40, Pr/dining room 12 **Times** 12-2/6-9 Closed 1 wk Jan, L Mon-Wed **Prices** Fixed L 3 course fr £28, Fixed D 3 course fr £28, Tasting menu fr £75, Starter £11-£15, Main £24-£29, Dessert £9-£10, Service optional **Wines** 121 bottles over £30, 12 bottles under £30, 11 by glass **Parking** 25 **Notes** L Tasting menu 6 course £48, D Tasting menu 9 course, Sunday L £38-£48, Children welcome

PICKERING
Map 19 SE78

Fox & Hounds Country Inn

Modern British

tel: 01751 431577 **Main St, Sinnington YO62 6SQ**
email: fox.houndsinn@btconnect.com **web:** www.thefoxandhoundsinn.co.uk
dir: *In Sinnington centre, 3m W of Pickering, off A170*

Quality fare in village gastro-pub

The bar is a popular place at this 18th-century inn, originally three separate cottages (count the front doors), with its log burner, settles and beams. Just as popular with diners is the stylish restaurant, where upholstered chairs are pulled up at oak tables. Light lunches run from black pudding with sautéed potatoes, a poached egg and crispy bacon to fish pie, while the kitchen sets out its stall with a more ambitious evening menu. First-course sea bass fillet accompanied by chilli and ginger scallops, stir-fried shiitaki mushrooms and Chinese greens might precede beef brisket slowly braised with red wine, bacon and shallots, served with croquette potatoes and roast root vegetables. Diehards could go for a steak with the usual trimmings, and desserts are a satisfying lot, among them perhaps apple and plum crumble with custard.

Chef Mark Caffrey **Owner** Mr & Mrs A Stephens **Seats** 40, Pr/dining room 10 **Times** 12-2/6.30-9 Closed 25-27 Dec **Prices** Starter £4.95-£8.25, Main £12.25-£22.95, Dessert £5.95-£11.95, Service optional **Wines** 9 bottles over £30, 32 bottles under £30, 9 by glass **Parking** 35 **Notes** Early D menu Sun-Thu 5.30-6.30pm £9.95, Sunday L £22.65-£28.45, Vegetarian available, Children welcome

The White Swan Inn

Modern British V

tel: 01751 472288 **Market Place YO18 7AA**
email: welcome@white-swan.co.uk **web:** www.white-swan.co.uk
dir: *Just beyond junct of A169/A170 in Pickering, turn right off A170 into Market Place*

Proud Yorkshire produce in a Tudor coaching inn

The Swan is a venerable stone-built coaching inn, older than many as it dates from the Tudor period, in a historic market town on the edge of the North York Moors. It's run with a clear eye to its role in the community, being a welcoming hostelry for locals, and a prime destination for regionally sourced eating. Darren Clemmit's kitchen regime is all about feeding patrons on good Yorkshire produce that isn't overly mucked about with ('we don't do froths and smudges,' he says). Rare-breed meats from the celebrated Ginger Pig butcher in nearby Levisham, local cheeses, fish from Whitby and veg from the allotment all feature proudly. Expect to start with venison carpaccio, pickled red onion and Yorkshire Blue, or scallops and black pudding with sour apple purée, before being spoiled for main-course choice. Will it be pork belly with braised red cabbage and mash, a dressed whole crab, or a chargrilled item such as bacon chop, lamb rump, or even hake? Puddings bring on sticky toffee or rhubarb crumble, or maybe lemon tart with prunes in armagnac.

Chef Darren Clemmit **Owner** The Buchanan family **Seats** 50, Pr/dining room 18 **Times** 12-2/6.45-9 **Prices** Starter £5.95-£9.95, Main fr £12.95, Dessert £6.95-£10.95, Service optional **Wines** 31 bottles over £30, 32 bottles under £30, 19 by glass **Parking** 45 **Notes** Fixed L & D menu on request, ALC sharing main course £42.95, Sunday L £7.95-£16.95, Children welcome

PICKHILL
Map 19 SE38

Nags Head Country Inn

Modern British

tel: 01845 567391 **YO7 4JG**
email: reservations@nagsheadpickhill.co.uk **web:** www.nagsheadpickhill.co.uk
dir: *Leave A1 junct 50 (travelling N) onto A6055; junct 51 (travelling S) onto A684, then A6055*

Ambitious cooking in country inn

In a quiet village just off the A1, the Nags Head is a civilised, welcoming inn, dating from the 17th century. The taproom dispenses real ales and has a separate menu, with the restaurant menu focused on seasonal ingredients, with game prominent in season: seared breast of wood pigeon with apple and blue cheese salad and mustard dressing, say, followed by game pie. New season's asparagus may appear in late spring, with a fried egg and ham shavings, alongside a more exotic starter of tempura king prawns with salt-and-pepper squid, wasabi and pickled ginger. Prime ingredients are sometimes given a surprising twist-foie gras terrine with pease pudding, for instance, in a starter with ham hock, tomato relish and crumbled crackling-and flavours can be piled up, although the results are normally successful, as when seared loin of lamb with confit breast and sautéed sweetbreads is joined by beetroot risotto, broad bean and lovage stew and nettle purée.

Times 12-2/6-9.30 Closed 25 Dec

RIPON
Map 19 SE37

The George at Wath

Modern British

tel: 01765 641324 **Main St, Wath HG4 5EN**
email: reception@thegeorgeatwath.co.uk **web:** www.thegeorgeatwath.co.uk
dir: *From A1 (dual carriageway) N'bound, left signed Melmerby & Wath. From A1 S'bound, exit at slip road signed A61. Right at T-junct signed Ripon. Approx 0.5m, right for Melmerby & Wath*

Revamped country inn with enterprising cooking

The George sports the spruced-up and decluttered look of a modern hostelry and opens its doors to all-comers: drinkers are as welcome as foodies in the traditional bar with its log-burner and oak and flagstone floors, while the restaurant is smartly done out with mellow tones and white tablecloths, and helpful and genuinely friendly staff provide a good level of service. The food is simple, seasonal and locally sourced, with daily specials boosting the carte, which might open with pan-fried scallops with rocket salad and sweet chilli jam, then move on to classic mains along the lines of beer-battered haddock with proper chips, minted mushy peas and home-made tartare sauce, or a rib-sticking steak and ale pie with mash. If you'd like to make the father, and, son team at the stoves work harder, consider grilled loin of cod wrapped in Parma ham with lemon risotto, topped with a seared scallop.

Times 12-2.30/5.30-9 Closed D Sun

Follow the AA on twitter @TheAA_Lifestyle

Looking for a restaurant by name?
Use the index on page 751

RIPON *continued*

The Royal Oak

 Modern British

tel: 01765 602284 **36 Kirkgate HG4 1PB**
email: info@royaloakripon.co.uk **web:** www.royaloakripon.co.uk
dir: *In town centre*

Modernised traditional inn with food to suit

The old coaching inn stands in the centre of this small cathedral city, with all the historic sights to hand and the famous racecourse only a short canter away. The old place has been opened up within and has an uncluttered contemporary feel with wooden floors, real fires and leather sofas. It's still very much a pub, though, with real ales on tap, a separate dining area, and a small patio out back. The menu has broad appeal and plenty of old favourites among some perkier ideas. You might start, for example, with crabcake with potted shrimp butter and Bloody Mary ketchup, or chicken liver parfait with toasted spiced fruit loaf and Landlord ale chutney. Main courses include classic fish and chips, local steaks from Wateredge Farm, and Yorkshire Dales lamb with potatoes, red cabbage and garden peas, but you might also go for sticky Ripon beef with beetroot gnocchi, Paris mushrooms, horseradish cream and parmesan crackling.

Chef Jonathan Murray **Owner** Adrian Sykes **Seats** 50 **Times** 12-9.30 All-day dining **Prices** Fixed D 2 course £13.50-£16.95, Starter £5-£9, Main £9-£20, Dessert £5-£6, Service optional **Wines** 18 bottles under £30, 10 by glass **Parking** 4, Market car park **Notes** Quarterly seasonal tasting menu, Sunday L fr £10, Vegetarian available, Children welcome

---

SCARBOROUGH | Map 17 TA08

Lanterna Ristorante

 Italian

tel: 01723 363616 **33 Queen St YO11 1HQ**
email: ralessio@lanterna-ristorante.co.uk
dir: *Phone for directions*

Convivial long-running Italian with classic cooking

It has been honoured by Italian newspaper La Stampa as 'the English temple of Italian cuisine', which seems an extraordinary accolade for an unassuming, albeit heartily convivial, place in Scarborough, but then Lanterna has been here for nigh on 40 years. Its present chef-patron, the tireless Giorgio Alessio, has been here since 1997, and undertook a major redecoration of the place in 2013, bringing in warm contrasting colour-schemes of reds and oranges, and sunny yellow and sky-blue, in the two dining rooms. The menu continues to fly the flag for simple, well-handled Italian cooking of the classic school: carpaccio in olive oil and shaved parmesan; venison ravioli with egg and spinach; porcini risotto; fresh fish and lobster; veal in marsala cream; and the likes of baked pears in Barbera syrup, or copybook zabaglione, to finish. The winter season sees white truffles shaved over everything from pasta dishes and risottos to fillet steak.

Chef Giorgio Alessio **Owner** Giorgio & Rachel Alessio **Seats** 35 **Times** 7-9.30 Closed 2 wks Oct, 25-26 Dec, 1 Jan, Sun **Prices** Starter £7.95-£30, Main £14.25-£45, Dessert £7.50-£11.50, Service optional **Wines** 35 bottles over £30, 36 bottles under £30, 5 by glass **Parking** On street, car park nearby **Notes** Vegetarian available, Children welcome

Palm Court Hotel

 Modern British **NEW**

tel: 01723 368161 **St Nicholas Cliff YO11 2ES**
email: generalmanager@palmcourt-scarborough.co.uk
web: www.palmcourtscarborough.co.uk

Modern dining in a Victorian hotel

Scarborough is enjoying something of a Renaissance these days, and this grand old Victorian hotel has also moved with the times with a modern makeover sitting comfortably beside its elegant period features. Run by the same family for 30 years, it's a popular spot for the impeccably British institution that is afternoon tea, which should keep you ticking over until dinner in the elegant, neutral-toned restaurant, where tables swathed in floor-length linen sit beneath chandeliers. The kitchen doesn't try to reinvent the wheel here, relying on top-class local produce allied with tried-and-true culinary principles for its effect. Ham hock terrine with plum chutney and toasted brioche is a capably executed starter, followed by the simple comforts of roast belly pork with red cabbage, grain mustard mash and honey-glazed parsnips. Or there might be locally-landed cod matched with chorizo and red pepper vinaigrette, seafood pudding and spinach. Dessert is a refreshing duo of lemon tartlet and lemon curd sorbet.

Chef Will Howes, Mike Stead **Owner** Mrs G Braithwaite, Mrs J Owen **Seats** 85, Pr/dining room 60 **Times** 6-8.45 Closed 25 Dec, L all week **Prices** Fixed D 3 course £24.95-£35.95 **Wines** **Parking** Palm Court NCP **Notes** Pre-theatre 2 course £19.75, Vegetarian available, Children welcome

---

SKIPTON | Map 18 SD95

The Bull at Broughton

 Traditional British

tel: 01756 792065 **Broughton BD23 3AE**
email: enquiries@thebullatbroughton.com
dir: *M65/A6068 (Vivary Way) for 1m, turn left onto A56 (Skipton Rd) for 7m, then right onto A59. Restaurant on right*

Regional cooking from an experienced team in charming village inn

Traditional old pubs don't get much more robust than The Bull, with its solid stone walls and flagged floors. The 21st-century sees the place in the safe hands of Nigel Haworth and Craig Bancroft of Northcote fame as part of their mini-empire of gastro-boozers. That means there's a nicely balanced modernity to the interior and lots of local food and drink on offer. It's still very much a pub, with all the easy-going associations you'd expect, including outside tables for when the weather is good. The menu shows hearty respect for British tradition, but doesn't get bogged down in the past. Start with twice-baked Wensleydale cheese soufflé served with beetroot relish and foraged leaves, or a Scotch egg made with venison and black pudding. Lancashire hotpot is a staple on the menu, or you might go for a local steak cooked on the grill.

Chef Lee Unthank **Owner** Craig Bancroft, Nigel Haworth, Richard Matthewman **Seats** 101 **Times** 12-2/5.30-8.30 **Prices** Starter £5-£10.50, Main £9.50-£19.50, Dessert £5-£6, Service optional **Wines** 6 bottles over £30, 30 bottles under £30, 11 by glass **Parking** 41 **Notes** Fixed L & D Tue-Thu only 2/3 course £11.50/£15, Sunday L £16-£19.50, Vegetarian available, Children welcome

SUTTON-ON-THE-FOREST
Map 19 SE56

The Blackwell Ox Inn

◉ British

tel: 01347 810328 **Huby Rd YO61 1DT**
email: enquiries@blackwelloxinn.co.uk **web:** www.blackwelloxinn.co.uk
dir: Off A1237, onto B1363 to Sutton-on-the-Forest. Left at T-junct, 50yds on right

Broadly appealing menu in a picturesque North York village

Named in honour of a legendary Shorthorn Teeswater ox that stood six feet at the crop before it met its fate, this Regency-era village inn is well placed for exploring the city of York and the wilds of the North York Moors. It's smartly done out with period colours and traditional furniture in both the bar and restaurant. The kitchen keeps a keen eye on what is in season locally and serves up a menu of classic and slightly more adventurous stuff. Thus you might start with a 'proper' prawn cocktail, Whitby crab salad, or the more trendy seared scallops with pulled pork and shallot purée. Among main courses a steak cooked on the grill seems fitting (rib-eye, maybe, served with chunky chips and onion rings), but there's also beef and ale pie, or chargrilled monkfish with confit duck, creamed cabbage and Puy lentils.

Chef Christopher Moscrop **Owner** Blackwell Ox Inns (York) Ltd **Seats** 50, Pr/dining room 20 **Times** 12-2/6-9.30 Closed 25 Dec, 1 Jan, D Sun **Prices** Prices not confirmed, Service optional **Wines** 20 by glass **Parking** 19 **Notes** Sunday L, Vegetarian available, Children welcome

The Rose & Crown

◉ Modern British V

tel: 01347 811333 **Main St YO61 1DP web:** www.theroseandcrownyork.co.uk
dir: 8m N of York towards Helmsley on B1363

A local flavour in a 200-year-old inn

There's no shortage of period charm at The Rose & Crown, with the 200-year-old inn still packing a punch when it comes to period features (wooden floors, low-beamed ceilings and the like), but it is looking pretty spruce these days, fit-for-purpose as a 21st-century dining pub. The culinary output is focused on seasonal and local ingredients. Start, perhaps, with pan-seared king scallops with celeriac purée and truffle oil sitting on rocket leaves and thinly sliced Granny Smith apples, or a crispy pork croquette made with Gloucestershire Old Spot pork, served with a shot of local cider. Main-course Yorkshire Dales lamb consists of braised confit and mint-glazed cutlet, partnered with minted new potatoes and an apple crisp, while a meat-free main course might be vegetable strudel. Local rhubarb is a seasonal treat, perhaps in a crème brûlée, with Yorkshire lemon curd ice cream. And if you want to end on a savoury note, what else but three local cheeses with biscuits?

Chef Mark Young **Owner** Stuart & Sarah Temple **Seats** 70, Pr/dining room 30 **Times** 12-2.30/6-9 Closed Jan, Mon, D Sun **Prices** Fixed L 2 course £26, Tasting menu £27.50, Starter £4.65-£9.95, Main £14-£55, Dessert £6-£13, Service optional **Wines** 10 bottles over £30, 23 bottles under £30, 20 by glass **Parking** 12 **Notes** Afternoon tea 2-5pm, Sunday L £17.50-£19.50, Children welcome

Who has won our Food Service Award?
See page 13

THIRSK
Map 19 SE48

The Black Lion & Bar Bistro

◉ Modern British **NEW**

tel: 01845 574302 **8 Market Place YO7 1LB**
email: info@blacklionthirsk.co.uk **web:** www.blacklionthirsk.co.uk
dir: Phone for directions

Traditional and modernist cooking in a revamped Yorkshire pub

A dramatic up-tick in the old Black Lion, easily found in the centre of the moorland market town of Thirsk, has produced an unmistakably modern venue. Rustic wood tables, plain half-panelled walls and a slate-tiled floor form a neutral backdrop to the well-supported buzzy ambience of the place. Menus change seasonally and are supplemented by blackboard specials, and the style mixes indelible British tradition with what is now equally indelible British modernism. A hearty bowl of Shetland mussels with smoked bacon in a cider broth with toasted sourdough is a good start, or there may be a modern reference dish such as scallops with pork belly and pea purée. For mains, daily fish specials and fine meats are treated with respect, as for thickly carved roast duck breast with Savoy, black pudding, duck-fat potatoes and a Chinese-spiced orange glaze. The homelier things are done well too, with Black Sheep ale going into the cod batter, and Sunday roasts arriving with all the required trimmings. Pannacotta in a Kilner jar is an improbable idea that works, its vanilla intensity counterpointed by sharp apple jelly, caramelised pistachios and a cloud of candyfloss.

Chef Harrison Barraclough **Owner** Paul Binnington **Seats** 100, Pr/dining room 8 **Times** 11.30-2.30/6.30-9 Closed D Sun, Mon **Prices** Starter £4.95-£6.95, Main £10.95-£17.95, Dessert £5.95-£8.95 **Wines** 2 bottles over £30, 20 bottles under £30, 10 by glass **Parking** 10 **Notes** Sunday L £10.95-£13.95, Vegetarian available, Children welcome

WEST WITTON
Map 19 SE08

The Wensleydale Heifer
Modern British V

tel: 01969 622322 **Main St DL8 4LS**
email: info@wensleydaleheifer.co.uk web: www.wensleydaleheifer.co.uk
dir: *On A684 (3m W of Leyburn)*

Top-notch seafood and more in the heart of the Yorkshire Dales

This whitewashed 17th-century coaching inn in the heart of the beautiful Yorkshire Dales National Park combines period atmosphere with a bit of boutique style in a winning combination; stay overnight and you can really get to know the place. There are two dining options: the more casual fish bar, with rattan chairs, wooden tables and pictures of seafaring cows as a nod to the heifer theme, and a smart restaurant done out with stylish chocolate leather chairs, linen-clothed tables and Doug Hyde artwork. There's a seafood focus here, but much more besides, and a desire to keep things local and relatively unfussy. So you will find good quality fish and chips, but you might also start with chilli-salt squid with Asian herb and noodle salad and sweet chilli dressing. Main-course roast Atlantic halibut competes for your attention with roast shoulder of lamb with goats' cheese and garlic gratin potatoes.

Chef David Moss **Owner** David & Lewis Moss **Seats** 70 **Times** 12-2.30/6-9.30 **Prices** Fixed L 2 course £19.75, Fixed D 3 course £22.75, Starter £8.75-£11.50, Main £16.25-£44, Dessert £5.50-£9.75 **Wines** 31 bottles over £30, 26 bottles under £30, 13 by glass **Parking** 30 **Notes** Sunday L, Children welcome

WHITBY
Map 19 NZ81

The Cliffemount Hotel
Modern British

tel: 01947 840103 **Bank Top Ln, Runswick Bay TS13 5HU**
email: info@cliffemounthotel.co.uk web: www.cliffemounthotel.co.uk
dir: *Exit A174, 8m N of Whitby, 1m to end*

Simple but effective cooking in a clifftop hotel

Visitors to the ruined 13th-century abbey at Whitby, note that a mere five miles outside the town is the petite fishing village of Runswick Bay, where overlooking said bay from a windy perch is the Cliffemount. Indeed, the bluster off the sea is about as turbulent as things get in this sublimely peaceful spot, and the plainly decorated dining room enjoys the best of the views. The cooking keeps things reasonably simple but very effective. A large glass plate bearing a starter of grilled mackerel caught in the bay, with curried mussels and spring onion, makes the point eloquently, or there could be pork and apricot terrine with cranberry-clementine chutney. Fish is just as strong a suit at main, perhaps for well-timed hake with a croquette of brown shrimps in scampi bisque, while meat may be Gressingham duck breast with butternut purée and dauphinois. Mulled plums are a delightful accompaniment to warm orange cake and vanilla ice cream, while local cheeses come with home-made Cheddar biscuits and Black Sheep ale cake.

Chef David Spencer **Owner** Ian & Carol Rae **Seats** 50 **Times** 12-2.30/6-9 **Prices** Fixed D 3 course £25-£32.50, Tasting menu £32.50-£35, Starter £5.95-£12.95, Main £14.95-£23.95, Dessert £6.95-£8.25, Service optional **Wines** 3 bottles over £30, 24 bottles under £30, 10 by glass **Parking** 25 **Notes** Sunday L £12.95, Vegetarian available, Children welcome

Judges Country House Hotel

YARM
Map 19 NZ41

Modern British V | NOTABLE WINE LIST

tel: 01642 789000 **Kirklevington TS15 9LW**
email: enquiries@judgeshotel.co.uk web: www.judgeshotel.co.uk
dir: *1.5m from junct W A19, take A67 towards Kirklevington, hotel 1.5m on left*

Well-conceived modern British cooking in a Victorian country house

Standing in more than 20 acres of meticulously maintained grounds a little to the south of Middlesbrough, the hotel's in a fine location, which it makes the most of with the aid of a conservatory-style dining room. Tables are double-clothed, muzak is banished, and staff are well-versed both in the professional requirements of the job at this level, and in John Schwarz's inspiring take on modern British cooking. The incidentals are to be noted: great opening canapés (including a haggis beignet); a cleverly judged winter appetiser of ham and sausage broth; excellent home-made breads of immpeccable texture and flavour; and fun petits fours, including the (in)famous bubblegum jelly. In among all that, there are some fine, well-conceived principal dishes too. A first course might involve setting perfectly timed scallops in herby broth with winter veg and mussels, before fillet of locally reared beef turns up with oxtail and confit potato cut into chips, in red wine and marrow jus. Fish shows up well in the earthy truffled treatment given to halibut, which comes with Brussels sprouts and celeriac, while loin of venison gains from the modern classic accompaniments of black pudding, red cabbage and pumpkin. To finish, there may be an admirably rich and smooth fondant made with Michel Cluizel chocolate, served with hazelnut ice cream, or a new manifestation of Arctic Roll constructed of prunes and pear and scented with Earl Grey. Premium cheeses come with home-made walnut bread. The extremely well-tended wine list is

illustrated with oenological maps to orient you, and starts with an imaginative selection by the glass.

Chef John Schwarz **Owner** Mr M Downs **Seats** 60, Pr/dining room 50 **Times** 12-2/7-9.30 **Prices** Fixed L 2 course £27.45-£30.45, Fixed D 3 course £39.50, Starter £11.95-£17.95, Main £34.50-£42.50, Dessert £11.95-£18.95, Service optional **Wines** 107 bottles over £30, 28 bottles under £30, 12 by glass **Parking** 110 **Notes** Early bird menu available, Sunday L £29.50, Children welcome

Estbek House

◉◉ Modern British

tel: 01947 893424 **East Row, Sandsend YO21 3SU**
email: info@estbekhouse.co.uk **web:** www.estbekhouse.co.uk
dir: *From Whitby follow A174 towards Sandsend. Estbek House just before bridge*

Fresh seafood by the sea near Whitby

Overlooking the North Sea just north of Whitby, Estbek House is perfectly positioned to source its materials from the chilly waters out front and the rolling moors behind (the North Yorks Moors National Park no less), and that's exactly what the kitchen team does. It all takes place in a handsome Regency house (Grade II listed) that operates as a restaurant with rooms of considerable charm. The smart restaurant has a soothing modernity and the staff are on the ball. Wild fish is the main passion here, hauled from local waters and prepared simply. Start with pan-seared scallops (from Shetland, but they grow 'em good up there) with pea purée and crisp Parma ham, and then it's into the main event, lemon sole, perhaps, expertly filleted and served with watercress sauce (or another sauce if you prefer) and dauphinoise potatoes and mixed veg. There's fish pie, too, plus local fillet steak glazed with Shiraz, and, for dessert, plum soup with ginger sorbet.

Times 6-9

YARM	Map 19 NZ41

Judges Country House Hotel

◉◉◉ – *see opposite*

YORK	Map 16 SE65

Best Western Plus Dean Court Hotel

◉ Modern British

tel: 01904 625082 **Duncombe Place YO1 7EF**
email: sales@deancourt-york.co.uk **web:** www.deancourt-york.co.uk
dir: *City centre, directly opposite York Minster*

Contemporary Yorkshire cooking next to the Minster

Sitting on the corner of Petergate, the original principal thoroughfare through Roman York, Dean Court is an amalgam of Victorian buildings originally put up to house clergy at the celebrated Minster, adjacency to which is a powerful selling-point for today's privately run boutique hotel. Neither Gothic medievalism nor Victorian interior design have been carried through to the DCH dining room, which

is a clean-lined, light-coloured contemporary haven adorned with decorative twigs. The modern styling gives a clue to the orientation of the cooking, where Yorkshire produce is put to effective use in offerings such as pigeon breast on beetroot risotto in blackcurrant jus, followed by sea bass and wilted spinach in shellfish bisque, or roast breast of guinea-fowl with braised red cabbage in madeira jus. The show-stopping sharing dish is rib of beef carved at the table and served with dauphinoise, and the show closes with variations on a theme of mango – brûlée, cheesecake and jelly.

Chef Patrick Franklin **Owner** Mr B A Cleminson **Seats** 60, Pr/dining room 40
Times 12.30-2/7-9.30 Closed 25 Dec eve, L Mon-Fri **Prices** Fixed L 2 course £18.50-£19.50, Fixed D 3 course £24.50, Starter £5.95-£8.95, Main £14.25-£21.50, Dessert £6.50-£9.50 **Wines** 30 bottles over £30, 47 bottles under £30, 19 by glass
Parking Pay & display car park nearby **Notes** Sunday L £21.50-£24.50, Vegetarian available, Children welcome

Cedar Court Grand Hotel & Spa

◉◉ Modern British

tel: 01904 380038 **Station Rise YO1 6GD**
email: dining@cedarcourtgrand.co.uk **web:** www.cedarcourtgrand.co.uk
dir: *A1 junct 47, A59 signed York, Harrogate & Knaresborough. In city centre, near station*

Smart Edwardian hotel with grill and fine-dining options

Built as the headquarters of the North Eastern Railway (NER) and opening at the turn of the 20th century, this grand Edwardian structure was ripe for conversion to a hotel. It overlooks the historic walls of the city and today offers a host of 21st-century facilities, from a swish spa to smart meeting rooms, plus a couple of dining options. Hudsons is the brasserie-style choice, a grill room that serves up steaks sourced from a Yorkshire farm, with 14oz T-bone, for example, served with hand-cut chips and Portobello mushrooms and confit tomato. There's langoustine cocktail to start, and plenty of alternatives to the steaks including duck leg with sweet potato, or aubergine cannelloni with spiced lentils. Finish with a classy version of apple crumble. The second dining option is the newly opened HQ, a fine-dining restaurant that aims to impress with its contemporary cooking. A tasting menu – plus optional wine flight – delivers handsomely constructed dishes such as rabbit with veal sweetbread and foie gras, turbot with red chicory, samphire and orange.

Chef Martin Henley **Owner** Cedar Court Hotels **Seats** 45, Pr/dining room 32
Times 12.30-2.30/6.30-10 **Prices** Service optional **Wines** 113 bottles over £30, 23 bottles under £30, 7 by glass **Parking** NCP Tanner Row **Notes** Sunday L £19.95-£24.95, Vegetarian available, Children welcome

YORK *continued*

The Churchill Hotel

 Modern British

tel: 01904 644456 **65 Bootham YO30 7DQ**
email: info@churchillhotel.com **web:** www.churchillhotel.com
dir: *On A19 (Bootham), W from York Minster, hotel 250yds on right*

Imaginative food and piano music

The set-up is all rather civilised in this Georgian mansion in its own grounds just a short walk from York Minster. The Churchill blends the airy elegance of its period pedigree with the sharp looks of a contemporary boutique city hotel in a dining room that looks through those vast arching windows (that the Georgians did so well) into the garden, where the trees are spangled in fairy-lights. Laid-back live music floats from a softly-tinkling baby grand piano as the soundtrack to cooking that hits the target with its imaginative modern pairings of top-grade regional produce. Local wood pigeon, for example, is paired with black pudding bonbons, bitter chocolate and espresso jelly, while main-course saddle of venison might share a plate with Morteau sausage, choucroute, parsley root, and red wine salsify. To finish, duck eggs add extra oomph to a custard tart served with clementine, apricot, and vanilla ice cream.

Times 11-2.30/5-9.30

The Grange Hotel

 Modern

tel: 01904 644744 **1 Clifton YO30 6AA**
email: info@grangehotel.co.uk **web:** www.grangehotel.co.uk
dir: *A19 (York/Thirsk road), approx 400yds from city centre*

Classy brasserie in a city-centre hotel

A short walk from the Minster, The Grange is an elegantly proportioned townhouse dating from the 1830s. The interior has all the style and comfort of a country-house hotel – open fires, deep sofas, antique paintings, swagged curtains – while the Ivy Brasserie has a more modish design, the most striking feature a mural of horseracing. The cooking is a cut above the brasserie norm, the kitchen clearly a creative and skilful powerhouse. Pressed ham hock and guinea fowl is vivified by zingy pineapple chutney, and curried crab goes into a salad with apple, almonds and cauliflower fritters to make another lively starter. Braised beef cheeks with parsnip purée and bourguignon sauce is a gutsy winter main course, and at other times there may be a lighter dish of pan-fried salmon fillet with shellfish chowder, creamed sweetcorn and baby leeks. Grilled steaks are possibilities, and proceedings can close with lemon and thyme pannacotta topped with lemon curd, meringue and blackberry jelly.

Chef Will Nicol **Owner** Jeremy & Vivien Cassel **Seats** 60, Pr/dining room 75
Times 12-2.30/6.30-9.30 Closed L Mon-Sat, D Sun **Prices** Starter £5.95-£7.95, Main £15.50-£20.95, Dessert £5.25-£7.25 **Wines** 17 bottles over £30, 25 bottles under £30, 11 by glass **Parking** 26 **Notes** Sunday L £14.95-£17.95, Vegetarian available, Children welcome

Guy Fawkes Inn

 Traditional British

tel: 01904 466674 **25 High Petergate YO1 7HP**
email: reservations@gfyork.com **web:** www.gfyork.com
dir: *A64 onto A1036 signed York & inner ring road. Over bridge into Duncombe Place, right into High Petergate*

Historic city centre inn serving classic British food

The Gunpowder Plotter was born on this spot in 1570, in the shadow of York Minster, a fact which adds a frisson to the pub that has done business here for centuries. It is a darkly atmospheric, history-steeped den with an interior akin to stepping into an Old Master painting, with roaring log fires, wooden floors, gas lighting, cosy nooks and crannies, and cheerful service that suits the buzzy vibe. Menus change regularly to keep step with the seasons and daily chalkboard specials follow a hearty modern pub grub course, treating great local produce with honest, down-to-earth simplicity. Expect hearty main courses such as a porcine plateful of braised belly and seared loin of pork with a pig's cheek, black pudding and braising jus, pan-fried salmon with mussel and cockle chowder, or North Sea pollock with minted crushed peas and proper chips. And for afters, it's sticky toffee pudding with clotted cream.

Times 12-3/6-9 Closed D Sun

Hotel du Vin York

 European, French

tel: 01904 557350 **89 The Mount YO24 1AX**
email: info.york@hotelduvin.com **web:** www.hotelduvin.com
dir: *A1036 towards city centre, 6m. Hotel on right through lights*

Winning bistro fare and an outstanding wine list

Not surprisingly for the Hotel du Vin chain, its York outpost is done out in the style of a French bistro, with wooden floors and tables softened by lighter-coloured walls hung with horsey images, reminders of the proximity of the city's racecourse. It's a smoothly run, easygoing sort of operation, with clued-up staff keeping wheels turning and offering advice about the wines on the outstanding list, and a menu of winning bistro fare, like escargots and cassoulet. Kick off a meal with rich and intense chicken liver parfait served with toasted brioche and raisin chutney, a fine starter if ever there was one, and go on to properly timed roast rack of lamb partnered by a seasonal fricassée of broad beans, peas and baby onions. Quality doesn't falter when it comes to desserts, among which could be chocolate pavé (layers of ganache and sponge) sprinkled with candied pistachios.

Times 12-2.30/6.30-10.30

The Lamb & Lion

 Traditional & Modern British

tel: 01904 654112 **2-4 High Petergate YO1 7EH**
email: reservations@lambandlionyork.com **web:** www.lambandlionyork.com
dir: *A64 onto A1036. 3.5m, at rdbt 3rd exit, continue on A1036. 2m, right into High Petergate*

Good honest cooking in a historic city-centre pub

Built quite literally into the ancient city walls and sitting in the shadow of York Minster, The Lamb & Lion offers everything you could reasonably ask of a historic pub: a labyrinth of cosy little rooms takes in a bar bristling with hand-pulled real ales and kitted out with church pews, bare wooden tables and a real fire, while skinny corridors lead to the back snugs and parlour dining room. Straight-talking traditional food aims to please all comers, and you can rest assured that the quality of the ingredients is up to scratch. Pub classics such as home-made steak pie with mash and real gravy, or fish and chips with mushy peas and tartare sauce sit alongside unpretentious ideas-perhaps lamb shank with garlic and rosemary jus, or wild mushroom risotto with parmesan crisp. Finish with the comforting simplicity of chocolate brownie and ice cream or a retro knickerbocker glory.

Chef Katie Hoskins **Owner** Phil Barker **Seats** 40 **Times** 12-3/6-9 **Prices** Starter £4.25-£5.60, Main £11.20-£14.90, Dessert £4.50-£6.10, Service optional **Wines** 15 bottles under £30 **Parking** Marygate car park **Notes** Sunday L, Vegetarian available, Children welcome

Melton's Restaurant

◎ Modern British

tel: 01904 634341 **7 Scarcroft Rd YO23 1ND**
email: greatfood@meltonsrestaurant.co.uk
dir: South from centre across Skeldergate Bridge, restaurant opposite Bishopthorpe Road car park

Long-running favourite with a well-judged menu

Melton's remains as popular as ever, and it's been going for over 20 years. It's bright and modern, with mirrors and murals on the walls, a wooden floor, banquettes and unclothed tables – all very unpretentious, with friendly but efficient service. The kitchen conscientiously uses Yorkshire produce, name-checking suppliers for dishes that are well thought out and carefully cooked. The menu of modern ideas offers plenty to enjoy – cep and field mushroom parfait with herb custard, parsley and garlic purée, say, or coley brandade with celeriac and truffle oil to start, followed by the full-throttle piggy flavours of belly pork, ham hock terrine, and pork and cep ballotine with soured cabbage and boulangère potatoes. If you're in the mood for fish, smoked haddock is matched with warm artichoke mousse, poached egg yolk, and leek and potato. The regional approach extends to cheeses and Yorkshire rhubarb with sablé biscuits and vanilla sabayon.

Chef Calvin Goddard, Michael Hjort **Owner** Michael & Lucy Hjort **Seats** 30, Pr/dining room 16 **Times** 12-2/5.30-10 Closed 23 Dec-9 Jan, Sun-Mon **Prices** Fixed L 2 course fr £22.50, Tasting menu fr £38, Starter £7-£9, Main £16-£21, Dessert £6.80-£7, Service optional **Wines** 40 bottles over £30, 73 bottles under £30, 6 by glass **Parking** Car park opposite **Notes** Pre-theatre D, early evening 2/3 course £22.50/£26, Vegetarian available, Children welcome

Middlethorpe Hall & Spa

◎◎ Modern British ⬛ NOTABLE WINE LIST

tel: 01904 641241 **Bishopthorpe Rd, Middlethorpe YO23 2GB**
email: info@middlethorpe.com **web:** www.middlethorpe.com
dir: A64 exit York West. Follow signs Middlethorpe & racecourse

Seasonal modern British cooking in a 17th-century mansion

Homes don't come much more stately than Middlethorpe Hall, a handsome William and Mary country house just a short canter away from York racecourse-in fact, after a big win on the gee-gees, a stay with a blow-out meal here would be an appropriate way to celebrate. Perhaps the ultimate accolade for its splendour is the fact that the National Trust took over the management of the place in 2008, but that's not to say Middlethorpe is a museum preserved in aspic. This is a grand hotel complete with a 21st-century luxury spa, and an elegant, candlelit, oak-panelled restaurant that aims high and moves with the times. To start, confit duck and a duck liver compression are given further depth with Yorkshire rhubarb, gingerbread and orange, ahead of a slow-cooked fillet of 40-day-aged beef partnered with braised oxtail ballotine, carrots, pickled onions and beer mustard. Desserts keep those full-on flavours coming with a decadent composition of warm millionaire's chocolate tart with salted butter caramel mousse and a velvety bitter chocolate sorbet.

Chef Nicholas Evans **Owner** The National Trust **Seats** 60, Pr/dining room 56 **Times** 12.30-2/6.30-9.45 **Prices** Fixed L 2 course fr £19.90, Fixed D 3 course fr £43, Tasting menu £69-£99, Starter £11-£14.50, Main £21.50-£28.50, Dessert £7.50-£13 **Wines** 194 bottles over £30, 38 bottles under £30, 15 by glass **Parking** 70 **Notes** Gourmet menu 6 course, Sunday L £28, Vegetarian available, Children 6 yrs+

Oxo's on The Mount

◎◎ Modern European V

tel: 01904 619444 **The Mount Royale Hotel, 119 The Mount YO24 1GU**
email: info@oxosrestaurantyork.com
dir: W on A1036, 0.5m after racecourse. Hotel on right after lights

Yorkshire produce in modern French guise

Sitting proud on top of the Mount, one of the ancient approaches to medieval York, the Mount Royale Hotel does a very good job of creating the atmosphere of a country-house venue within the confines of a city. Cobbled ingeniously together from a pair of 1830s houses, its main dining room, formerly known as Burbridge's, extends into an outdoor terrace called the Gazeover. Here, Russell Johnson celebrates fine Yorkshire produce in menus that display plenty of lightly-borne French influence, so expect rabbit confit with white beans, pickled girolles, macadamias and garlic mayonnaise, or seared scallops with artichoke purée in a reduction of cider. Try mains such as poached sea bass with clams and trompettes in caviar butter, or perhaps venison loin with braised sweet potato and a purée of smoked celeriac in hedgerow berry jus. Finish in bravura style with tonka pannacotta served with cinnamon-roasted figs, popcorn, honeycomb and cherries in Kirsch syrup.

Chef Russell Johnson **Owner** Richard Stuart Oxtoby **Seats** 70, Pr/dining room 18 **Times** 6-9.30 Closed L Mon-Sat **Prices** Starter £5.25-£10.95, Main £14.25-£28.95, Dessert £6.50-£7 **Wines** 6 bottles over £30, 23 bottles under £30, 12 by glass **Parking** 15 **Notes** Sunday L £19.95, Children welcome

SOUTH YORKSHIRE

ROSSINGTON Map 16 SK69

Best Western Premier Mount Pleasant Hotel

◎ Modern British

tel: 01302 868696 & 868219 **Great North Rd DN11 0HW**
email: reception@mountpleasant.co.uk **web:** www.mountpleasant.co.uk
dir: S of Doncaster, adjacent to Robin Hood Airport, on A638 between Bawtry & Doncaster

Sound country-house cooking in a tip-top hotel

This smart 18th-century country-house hotel squirrelled away in 100 acres of beautiful woodland feels miles from anywhere, yet it is on the outskirts of Doncaster. While the grand old house is traditional in many aspects of its cosy decor and formal-yet-friendly service, Mount Pleasant comes fully geared for the 21st century with a full complement of glossy spa, leisure and conference facilities. The kitchen sources its raw materials diligently and takes a broadly modern British line in its well-thought-out repertoire of comfort-oriented classics. A twice-baked Yorkshire cheese soufflé is well-rendered, ahead of slow-cooked shoulder of lamb with buttery mashed potato, roast Mediterranean vegetables and tomato jus, or you might go for fish in the shape of sea bass with minted fritters and garden pea broth. For pudding, salted caramel chocolate torte with caramel ice cream is as rich and indulgent as anyone could reasonably ask for.

Chef Dave Booker **Owner** McIlroy family **Seats** 72, Pr/dining room 200 **Times** 12-2/6.45-9.30 Closed 25 Dec **Prices** Starter £5.95-£9.95, Main £12.95-£27.50, Dessert £4.95-£7.50 **Wines** 10 bottles over £30, 50 bottles under £30, 7 by glass **Parking** 140 **Notes** Sunday L £19.95, Vegetarian available, Children welcome

ROTHERHAM

Map 16 SK49

Hellaby Hall Hotel

Modern British **NEW**

tel: 01709 702701 **Old Hellaby Ln, Hellaby S66 8SN**
email: reservations@hellabyhallhotel.co.uk **web:** www.hellabyhallhotel.co.uk
dir: 0.5m off M18 junct 1, onto A631 towards Maltby. Hotel in Hellaby - NB do not use postcode for Sat Nav

Enterprising modern British cooking in a tasteful hotel

This hotel in pretty gardens has at its core a distinctive 17th-century manor of grey stone over three floors. The Carnelly Restaurant, spacious and airy, has white beams in the vaulted ceiling and floral yellow wallpaper on one wall contrasting with the otherwise subdued decor and darkwood furniture. A grounding in the classical French repertoire shines out of the cooking, with the kitchen following a more or less modern British route. Chicken and thyme ballotine is a first-rate rendition, complemented by pickled vegetables, another starter perhaps smoked haddock rillettes with arancini and pickled fennel salad. Clearly defined flavours are hallmarks, seen in main courses of tender honey-glazed pork shoulder in a rich sauce with apple purée, caramelised red cabbage and buttery mash, and pan-fried grey mullet with pancetta, mushroom risotto and confit shallots. For dessert, go for retro steamed syrup sponge with custard, or classic lemon tart with raspberry sorbet.

Chef Craig Tyrrell **Owner** Prima Hotel Group Limited **Seats** 56 **Times** 6-9.15 Closed L all week **Prices** Fixed D 3 course £24.95, Service optional **Wines** 1 bottle over £30, 16 by glass

SHEFFIELD

Map 16 SK38

Copthorne Hotel Sheffield

Modern European

tel: 0114 252 5480 **Sheffield United Football Club, Bramall Ln S2 4SU**
email: trevorvels@millenniumhotels.co.uk
web: www.millenniumhotels.co.uk/copthornesheffield
dir: M1 junct 33, A57 Sheffield, A61 Chesterfield Rd, follow brown tourist signs for Bramall Lane

Contemporary cooking near the home of the Blades

The 18Fifty5 Restaurant at the Copthorne, a large modern hotel adjacent to Sheffield United's football stadium not far from the centre, is a striking room, with a decor of dark colours. The kitchen relies on local produce for its materials, organic whenever possible, and its seasonally changing menu is a cross-cultural affair, with tandoori salmon fishcakes served with roast cumin and coriander yoghurt and sweet mango chutney, and a platter of antipasti among starters. Among main courses, some vivid combinations may bring on Parma ham-wrapped chicken breast stuffed with mozzarella, accompanied by lime and coriander couscous and a bean casserole flavoured with chilli and oregano. Or try accurately timed whole sea bass baked with soy and tamarind, with sesame linguine, peanuts and spring onions. Round off a meal with Baileys brioche-and-butter pudding with vanilla sauce, or chocolate and orange pudding with Cointreau sauce.

Chef Mark Jones **Owner** Millennium Copthorne Group **Seats** 100, Pr/dining room 300 **Times** 12.30-2.30/6.30-10 **Prices** Starter £6-£7, Main £14-£20, Dessert £6-£6.50, Service optional **Wines** 4 bottles over £30, 16 bottles under £30, 12 by glass **Parking** 250 **Notes** Vegetarian available, Children welcome

Nonnas

Modern Italian v **NOTABLE WINE LIST**

tel: 0114 268 6166 **535-541 Ecclesall Rd S11 8PR**
email: info@nonnas.co.uk
dir: From city centre onto Ecclesall Rd, large red building on left

Italian mini-chain with exceptional modern cooking

Nonnas is a bustling, good-natured Italian restaurant with friendly staff, café-style marble-topped tables and green walls. Many of the staples are made in-house, from pasta to ice cream, using Yorkshire produce and ingredients flown in from the homeland, and the menu is a celebration of modern Italian cooking. This is an imaginative kitchen turning out properly cooked, highly original dishes. Rigatoni is sauced with duck leg braised in vin santo, with sausage and sage, and linguine with crab, chilli and fennel. Among accomplished 'secondi' there might be the vivid combinations of Merlot-braised oxtail with beetroot mash and horseradish canederli (bread dumplings) and grilled sea bass fillet with borlotti bean and tomato stew and rosemary aïoli. Inspired puddings have included chocolate and beetroot cake with sweet beetroot and balsamic ripple ice cream alongside classic tiramisù.

Chef Jamie Taylor **Owner** Gian Bohan, Maurizio Mori **Seats** 75, Pr/dining room 30 **Times** 12-3.15/5-9.45 Closed 25 Dec, 1 Jan **Prices** Fixed D 3 course £25-£30, Starter £5-£15, Main £10-£20, Dessert £4-£17, Service optional **Wines** 28 bottles over £30, 21 bottles under £30, 22 by glass **Parking** On street **Notes** Brunch Sun 9am-1pm, Sunday L, Children welcome

Rafters Restaurant

Modern British, European

tel: 0114 230 4819 **220 Oakbrook Rd, Nethergreen S11 7ED**
email: bookings@raftersrestaurant.co.uk **web:** www.raftersrestaurant.co.uk
dir: 5 mins from Ecclesall road, Hunters Bar rdbt

Creative cooking in a leafy neighbourhood

After over 20 years as a dining hotspot in the city, Rafters is under new ownership and continues to go from strength to strength. That seems to be the way with Rafters; the city won't be without it. Located on the first floor of a shop in a green part of Sheffield, there are leafy views to be had and some seriously good cooking to be enjoyed. The room has capacious windows and a smart finish, with richly upholstered, high-backed chairs and tables laid with white linen cloths. The cooking is modern and the menu is packed with interesting combinations. A starter of cumin-spiced scallops with cauliflower and golden raisins is the kitchen's version of a modern classic, or go for celeriac risotto with compressed apple and roasted hazelnuts. Main courses are equally on the money, with a duo of pork (fillet and belly) with butternut squash purée and sage gnocchi, or fillet of sea bass with courgette purée, crushed ratte potatoes and tapenade. Finish with an egg custard tart with forced rhubarb.

Chef Thomas Lawson **Owner** Alistair Myers, Thomas Lawson **Seats** 38 **Times** 12-2/6-10 Closed 25-26 Dec, Mon-Tue, L Wed-Sat **Prices** Fixed D 3 course £39-£44, Service optional **Wines** 15 bottles over £30, 24 bottles under £30, 12 by glass **Parking** On street **Notes** Sunday L £28-£34, Vegetarian available, Children 5 yrs+

Whitley Hall Hotel

◉◉ Modern British

tel: 0114 245 4444 **Elliott Ln, Grenoside S35 8NR**
email: reservations@whitleyhall.com **web:** www.whitleyhall.com
dir: A61 past football ground, then 2m, right just before Norfolk Arms, left at bottom of hill. Hotel on left

Imaginative British cooking in a stunning country hotel

Surrounded by rolling countryside, Whitley Hall is a solid stone mansion dating from the 16th century (it has a priest's hole) with 20 acres of grounds including lakes and immaculate gardens. In surroundings like these, it's no wonder the place is a popular wedding venue. The restaurant may have a whiff of formality, but the kitchen keeps ahead of the game with a thoroughly modern menu, with gratifying results. Juxtaposing fruit with meat seems to be a favoured device, so pressed rabbit terrine comes with poached grapes and apricot purée and could be followed by duck breast with peaches, caramelised fennel purée, vanilla-infused mash and a lavender reduction. The team's confidence brings off even some unconventional-sounding combinations: fried pig's cheek, for instance, with a coriander pudding, fine beans and a devilled quail's egg, then seared monkfish liver accompanying tournedos of Shetland salmon served with spicy Puy lentils, braised vegetables and fig and apple chutney. Originality doesn't dry up among puddings, either: try vanilla crème brûlée with roast plums, plum ripple ice cream and gingerbread.

Times 12-2/7-9.30

WORTLEY
Map 16 SK39

The Wortley Arms

◉◉ Modern British v

tel: 0114 288 8749 **Halifax Rd S35 7DB**
email: enquiries@wortley-arms.co.uk
dir: M1 junct 36. Follow Sheffield North signs, right at Tankersley garage, 1m on right

Up-to-the-minute brasserie food in a Georgian pub

A two-pronged operation consists of The Wortley Arms, a traditional Georgian pub with panelled walls, a jumble of furniture and oak beams, and a more obviously modern urban-style restaurant upstairs that tends only to open at weekends now. The up-to-the-minute brasserie stylings of the menu are on offer throughout, though, so there's no need to miss out on tian of crab, squid and crayfish, or ham hock terrine with piccalilli and salad, to start, followed by cod with garlic mash and walnut pesto, or a special such as breast of duck with a confit leg croquette, braised cabbage and puréed carrot. Treacle tart comes with cream to anoint it with, or there may be good sharp lemon posset with lavender shortbread.

Chef Andy Gabbitas **Owner** Andy Gabbitas **Seats** 80, Pr/dining room 12 **Times** 12-2.30/5-9 Closed D Sun **Prices** Starter £3.50-£8.50, Main £10.50-£18.50, Dessert £5.25-£7.50, Service optional **Wines** 5 bottles over £30, 24 bottles under £30, 8 by glass **Parking** 30 **Notes** Sunday L £10.50-£12.50, Children welcome

WEST YORKSHIRE

ADDINGHAM
Map 19 SE04

Craven Heifer

◉◉ Modern British

tel: 01943 830106 **Main St LS29 0PL**
email: info@wellfedpubs.co.uk **web:** www.thecravenheifer.com
dir:

Switched-on cooking in an ambitious gastro-pub

This stylishly refurbished pub lies not far from Skipton and the wild moors, and offers seven luxurious rooms themed on Yorkshire characters should you want to stay over and take full advantage of the place's gastronomic possibilities-and a quick glance over the menu suggests this might be a good idea, as the output here aims way beyond pub staples. The kitchen team are certainly out to make an impact with an inventive roster of lively, flavour-driven modern ideas hauling in top-drawer local ingredients, including daily fish specials, to supplement the weekly market menu and carte. Choosing from the latter, you might open with a tongue-in-cheek 'ham, egg and chips', which turns out to be a rather more involved assemblage of ham hock ballottine with home-made brown sauce, slow-cooked egg yolk, confit potatoes, and Pickering watercress. Main course could bring a similarly creative streak, matching butter-roasted John Dory with cauliflower (poached and purée) a mini fishcake, and chive velouté. End with baked stem ginger cheesecake with Yorkshire rhubarb (sorbet, poached and sherbet).

Chef Mark Owens **Owner** Craig Minto **Seats** 41, Pr/dining room **Times** 12-2/5.30-9 **Prices** Prices not confirmed, Service optional **Wines** **Parking** 20 **Notes** Early bird menu 2/3 course £12/£15, Sunday L, Vegetarian available, Children welcome

BINGLEY
Map 19 SE13

Five Rise Locks Hotel & Restaurant

◉ Modern British v

tel: 01274 565296 **Beck Ln BD16 4DD**
email: info@five-rise-locks.co.uk **web:** www.five-rise-locks.co.uk
dir: From A650 signed Bingley centre, turn right Park Rd. Beck Lane 300mtrs on left

Unfussy cooking in a family-run hotel

Built by a successful Victorian businessman in 1875, this one-time mill owner's family home is now a family-run hotel on a pleasingly intimate scale (just nine bedrooms), with a restaurant that's worth knowing about. Done out in a smart manner with high-backed leather chairs, linen-clad tables and a splendid burgundy and cream paint job, it offers views in daylight hours over the garden and Aire Valley. On the menu you'll find some appealing combinations such as warm goats' cheese and red onion confit served en croûte, or pigeon breast with rocket and beetroot salad to start. Next up, perhaps pan-fried calves' liver with crushed new potatoes, cabbage and onion confit, and, to finish, lemon posset or a selection of British cheeses.

Chef Steven Heaton, Richard Stoyle **Owner** Richard & Margaret Stoyle **Seats** 40, Pr/dining room 20 **Times** 12-2/6.30-9.15 Closed L Mon-Sat, D Sun (ex residents) **Prices** Prices not confirmed, Service optional **Wines** 4 bottles over £30, 26 bottles under £30, 10 by glass **Parking** 15 **Notes** Early bird menu 2 course, Mon-Sat 6.30-7.30pm, Sunday L, Children welcome

BRADFORD
Map 19 SE13

Prashad
◉ Indian Vegetarian V

tel: 0113 285 2037 **137 Whitehall Rd, Drighlington BD11 1AT**
email: info@prashad.co.uk
dir: *Follow A650 Wakefield Road then Whitehall Road*

Indian vegetarian food of the highest order

When it comes to pukka Indian cooking, the competition in Bradford is strong, but Mrs Kaushy Patel's take on the vegetarian repertoire ensures a zealous local following beats a path to her door in new premises after a relocation in late 2012. The new venue goes for a bright and cheerful look, with one wall taken up by a huge mural of a tumultuous Indian street scene. The all-in-one thali platter is a splendid way in to the vegetarian cuisine of the Gujarat, or you could head south for a spicy uttapam or masala dosa pancake served with spicy lentil soup and coconut chutney. Curries include chole-chick-peas cooked with whole cumin seeds in a tomato and onion sauce, which goes great with light-as-air puri bread-and classic tarka dhal. Spicing is spot on throughout, and breads are cooked fresh to order.

Chef Kaushy & Minal Patel **Owner** Mohan Patel **Seats** 75, Pr/dining room 10 **Times** 12-5/6-11.30 Closed 25 Dec, Mon, L Tue-Thu **Prices** Starter £5-£8.95, Main £9.20-£13.40, Dessert £2.99-£6.25, Service optional **Wines** 6 bottles over £30, 12 bottles under £30, 4 by glass **Parking** 26 **Notes** Children welcome

CLIFTON
Map 16 SE12

Black Horse Inn Restaurant with Rooms
◉ Modern British, Mediterranean

tel: 01484 713862 **Westgate HD6 4HJ**
email: mail@blackhorseclifton.co.uk **web:** www.blackhorseclifton.co.uk
dir: *M62 junct 25, Brighouse, follow signs*

Bold British flavours in a Yorkshire inn

This whitewashed 17th-century inn has the look of a traditional pub with its down-to-earth beamed bar with a real fire, and – more to the point – real ales. But give the menu a quick once-over, and it's clear that the Black Horse is more about food these days. A brace of stylish dining rooms offers different settings: one is more casual with high-backed leather chairs and bare darkwood tables, the other more formally dressed in white linen; on a fine day, the courtyard is an appealing spot too. Wherever you choose, the kitchen turns out contemporary ideas with a modish flourish here and there, all built on locally-sourced ingredients. Ox cheek croquette with onion purée, pickled chestnut mushrooms and blue cheese foam makes a punchy impact, followed by confit Gressingham duck leg with sticky red cabbage, bubble-and-squeak and plum jus. Dessert ends impressively with popcorn pannacotta with caramel popcorn and chocolate tuile.

Chef Richard Barrett **Owner** Andrew & Jane Russell **Seats** 70, Pr/dining room 60 **Times** 12-2.30/5.30-9.30 Closed D 25-26 Dec, 1 Jan **Prices** Fixed L 2 course £16.95, Fixed D 3 course £19.95, Starter £6-£10, Main £14-£20, Dessert £6-£8, Service optional **Wines** 20 bottles over £30, 40 bottles under £30, 12 by glass **Parking** 60 **Notes** Sunday L, Vegetarian available, Children welcome

HALIFAX
Map 19 SE02

Design House Restaurant
◉◉◉ – *see below*

Design House Restaurant

HALIFAX
Map 19 SE02

Modern British, European
tel: 01422 383242 **Dean Clough, Arts & Business Centre HX3 5AX**
email: info@designhouserestaurant.co.uk
dir: *Telephone for detailed directions*

Inventive modern cooking in a buzzy former mill house

It may be in a converted old mill, but inside it's a thoroughly modern affair, with white-topped tables, back-lit wall panels in caramel and cream, and framed prints bringing splashes of colour to the white walls. Halifax's food-loving inhabitants of all ages have really taken this place to their hearts, and it's not surprising given its buzzy vibe, friendly, welcoming and knowledgeable staff, and contemporary, inventive cooking. You can soak up the atmosphere perched on a tall white-leather stool at the central bar before moving to your table to dine from either the à la carte or tasting menu (or if it's the middle of the day perhaps the two-course lunch menu at an incredible £10). Chef-proprietor Lee Marshall is a Halifax lad who, together with head chefs Ben Varley and Dave Duttine, is keen to promote the best of the local larder; the cooking from the open-plan kitchen follows the seasons faithfully, as in a starter of Ripon Estate pigeon with cherry wood, cobnuts, elderberries and beetroot. A fishy alternative to begin might be crab served as white crabmeat surrounded by a lime-flavoured jelly, brown meat in cannelloni, with apple and nasturtium flowers – an outstanding dish in terms of technical ability, flavour balance and stunning presentation. Suckling pig might be next up, timed to perfection and complemented brilliantly by the flavours of smoked eel and potato, smoked yoghurt, and the crunch of pork 'granola' – a very clever dish. Broken tart for dessert sounds like a mishap but it's actually a deliberate deconstruction of a bitter chocolate tart, accompanied by bee pollen and 'ice cream cone flavoured ice cream' – what else? The chefs' playful approach continues through to coffee, when a dish filled with what appears to be soil arrives at the table: dig deep and you'll find some faultless chocolate truffles hidden underneath a layer of chocolate crumb.

Chef Lee Stevens Marshall, Ben Varley, Dave Duttine **Owner** Lee Stevens Marshall **Seats** 70 **Times** 12-2/5.30-9.30 Closed 26 Dec-9 Jan **Prices** Fixed L 2 course £12, Tasting menu £48-£55, Service optional **Wines** 12 by glass **Parking** 100 **Notes** ALC 3 course £42, Vegetarian available, Children welcome

Shibden Mill Fold
Shibden, Halifax

West Yorkshire HX3 7UL
Tel: 01422 365840
Fax: 01422 362971
Email: enquiries@shibdenmillinn.com
Website: www.shibdenmillinn.com

For over 350 years *The Shibden Mill Inn* has been at the heart of life in West Yorkshire's Shibden Valley. It's a magical place where generation after generation of locals have enjoyed time well spent with friends and family, sharing in life's special moments and shaping memories to last a life time.

The Inn's reputation for warm hospitality, premier 2 Rosette gastro dining and 4 Star Inn accommodation draws people to the Shibden Valley from far and wide, and the Mill has naturally become a popular choice for those wishing to savour a sumptuous weekend break or mid-week stay.

Stunning countryside walks are in easy reach, as too the bright lights and city centre shopping on offer in Leeds. From its unique location, The Shibden Mill offers easy access to the very best to be found in this delightful part of West Yorkshire.

Opening times for breakfast, morning coffee & cake, afternoon teas, lunch and dinner can be found on the food page of the website www.shibdenmillinn.com

HALIFAX *continued*

Holdsworth House Hotel

◉◉ Traditional British V

tel: 01422 240024 **Holdsworth Rd, Holmfield HX2 9TG**
email: info@holdsworthhouse.co.uk **web:** www.holdsworthhouse.co.uk
dir: *From Halifax take A629 (Keighley road), in 2m right at garage to Holmfield, hotel 1.5m on right*

Secluded manor house with well-crafted cooking

It's little wonder that Holdsworth House is so popular with wedding parties – it really is a fairytale setting in secluded gardens. The oak-panelled rooms and roaring fires will certainly win you over, and the three inter connecting rooms that make up the restaurant have oodles of period charm too (the building dates back to 1633), with low beams and mullioned windows, plus super views of the gardens. Yorkshire ingredients are much in evidence in traditional British cooking which is not adverse to some contemporary thinking. Start with sautéed black pearl scallops and marinated squid with pea purée and roasted red pepper sabayon, before Holme Farm venison Wellington with buttered spinach, gratin potatoes and juniper jus. Sarsaparilla and peanut butter cheesecake and honeycomb ice cream is a creative finish.

Chef Simon Allott **Owner** Gail Moss, Kim Wynn **Seats** 45, Pr/dining room 120 **Times** 12-2/7-9.30 Closed D 25-26 Dec **Prices** Tasting menu £45, Starter £5.95-£12.95, Main £15.95-£24.50, Dessert £7-£7.95, Service optional 10% **Wines** 47 bottles over £30, 37 bottles under £30, 13 by glass **Parking** 60 **Notes** Tasting menu 5 course, Sunday L £16.95-£22.50, Children welcome

Shibden Mill Inn

◉◉ Modern British V

tel: 01422 365840 **Shibden Mill Fold, Shibden HX3 7UL**
email: enquiries@shibdenmillinn.com **web:** www.shibdenmillinn.com
dir: *From A58 into Kell Lane, after 0.5m left into Blake Hill. Inn at bottom of hill on left*

Adventurous flavours in a renovated corn mill

Converted from a 17th-century mill, the inn consists of a series of rooms connected by steps and stairs, with a rustic look generated by beams, exposed stone, and mismatched tables and chairs. Service is friendly but polished, and the whole place has a warm, good-humoured atmosphere. The kitchen's a hive of industry, judging by an assiette of pork: potted belly, a miniature pie, and crispy cheek, all accompanied by black pudding bread, beetroot and orange coleslaw, and beetroot chips – and that's just a starter. Another one combines pan-fried scallops with caramelised pistachio crumble and truffle and Jerusalem artichoke. The compositions of dishes may sound far-fetched, but the results are successful: Wellington-style baked salt cod, for instance, comes with spinach and mushrooms, smoked kippers and curried mussels. Cheeses are all made by Yorkshire artisan

producers, or you could end with a plate of banana – crème brûlée, fritter and cake with salted toffee sauce.

Chef Darren Parkinson **Owner** Simon & Caitlin Heaton **Seats** 50, Pr/dining room 8 **Times** 12-2/6-9.30 Closed Xmas, D 24-26 Dec, 1 Jan **Prices** Service optional **Wines** 32 bottles over £30, 54 bottles under £30, 22 by glass **Parking** 60 **Notes** Sunday L fr £12.95, Children welcome

See advert on page 565

▌ **HAWORTH**   Map 19 SE03

Ashmount Country House

◉ Modern British V

tel: 01535 645726 & 07814 536044   **Mytholmes Ln BD22 8EZ**
email: info@ashmounthaworth.co.uk **web:** www.ashmounthaworth.co.uk
dir: *M65 junct 13A Laneshaw Bridge, turn right over moors to Haworth. Turn left after car park on right onto Mytholmes Lane, 100yds on right*

Confident cooking in the Brontë village

A solid Victorian house with open fires and antique furniture, Ashmount is a short stroll from the Brontës' famous parsonage. Elegantly laid tables set the tone in the dining room, with its views over the hillside. The sensibly short menu, which changes every few days, is well planned to offer plenty of scope, the style set by a well-conceived main course of pan-fried sea bass fillet with tomato velouté, English asparagus, spinach and saffron-flavoured new potatoes. Equally, there may be honey-roast duck breast with blackberry jus, sweet potato dauphinoise and baked vegetables, with starters like a chunky galantine of duck and chicken with fruity marmalade, and puddings tend to the hearty: sticky toffee, say, or apple and raspberry crumble.

Chef Alastair Bowling **Owner** Ray & Gill Capeling **Seats** 26, Pr/dining room 20 **Times** 6-9 Closed Mon, L all week **Prices** Starter £4.95-£7.95, Main £12.95-£24.95, Dessert £4.95-£6.75, Service optional **Wines** 10 bottles over £30, 17 bottles under £30, 11 by glass **Parking** 12, On street **Notes** Afternoon tea £13.50, No children

▌ **HUDDERSFIELD**   Map 16 SE11

315 Bar and Restaurant

◉ Modern V

tel: 01484 602613 **315 Wakefield Rd HD8 0LX**
email: info@315barandrestaurant.co.uk **web:** www.315barandrestaurant.co.uk
dir: *M1 junct 38 to Huddersfield*

Ambitious city-smart cooking in a reborn Yorkshire pub

Out in the sumptuous Yorkshire countryside not far from Huddersfield, 315 is a refurbished pub reborn as a city-smart restaurant and bar, with a fine conservatory room and a chef's table, which is pretty much all bases covered. Chairs upholstered in silver velvet and orchids on the tables make an aspirational statement, as does Jason Neilson's cooking, which is based on industrious in-house production of everything from breads to ice creams, and represents a successful alliance of English ingredients with modern French technique. A tall, thin, twice-cooked goats' cheese soufflé is an architectonic masterwork, and comes with a pecorino salad, the plate squiggled with sun-dried tomato sauce and pesto, while salmon and haddock are fashioned into a sausage that comes with warm potato salad and cauliflower cream. Local lamb gets a good outing, the best end crusted in garlic and rosemary, the liver sautéed, accompanied by fennel and red onion purée, or there might be sea bass with green-lip mussels and saffron potatoes. Desserts such as treacle apple tart with apple crumble ice cream on shortbread are a strength.

Chef Jason Neilson **Owner** Jason Neilson, Terry Dryden **Seats** 90, Pr/dining room 115 **Times** 12-9 Closed D Sun All-day dining **Prices** Fixed L 2 course £15, Starter £5-£7.50, Main £12.50-£23.50, Dessert fr £6.25, Service optional **Wines** 18 by glass **Parking** 97 **Notes** Sunday L £17.50-£19.95, Children welcome

ILKLEY
Map 19 SE14

Box Tree

 – see below

LEEDS
Map 19 SE23

De Vere Oulton Hall

◉◉ British

tel: 0871 222 4690 **Rothwell Ln, Oulton LS26 8HN**
email: Oulton.hall@devere-hotels.com **web:** www.devere-hotels.co.uk
dir: 2m from M62 junct 30, follow Rothwell signs, then 'Oulton 1m' sign. 1st exit at next 2 rdbts. Hotel on left. Or 1m from M1 junct 44, follow Castleford & Pontefract signs on A639

Modern British cooking in a splendid mansion

The De Vere group's Oulton Hall is a magnificent country mansion off the M62 to the south of Leeds. It's the kind of place that's grand enough to have staff swishing about the grounds on golf buggies, though ever mindful not to interrupt the outdoor Shakespeare that goes on in the summer. A stylish contemporary refurbishment has produced dashing interiors, and a strikingly elegant dining room done in black and crimson, with rich fabrics and lots of dark wood, and lighting low enough for an undercover rendezvous. The chosen culinary idiom is modernised classic British, with a fair bit of table side theatre if you don't mind the company, mixing up salads, slicing smoked salmon and carving the Chateaubriand before your very eyes. Baked cod with mushrooms, peas and pea shoots is an example of one of the attractively presented mains, or venison loin with poached pear and cocoa nibs in port. In the season, you could opt for a three-course rhubarb menu.

Times 7-9.45 Closed L all week

Box Tree

ILKLEY
Map 19 SE14

Modern British, French V ◥ NOTABLE WINE LIST
tel: 01943 608484 **35-37 Church St LS29 9DR**
email: info@theboxtree.co.uk
dir: On A65 from Leeds through Ilkley, main lights approx 200yds on left

Outstanding cooking in a landmark Yorkshire venue

The Box Tree has been a culinary leader since it opened it's doors in 1962, nowadays in the capable hands of chef-proprietor Simon Gueller and wife Rena. It occupies a refurbished 300-year-old building, with an elegant interior defined by art and antiques, rich fabrics and deeply comfortable furniture, while service is correct but unstuffy. Simon handles his top-quality ingredients sensitively and intelligently, his modern French style underscored by the classical repertoire and techniques. An amuse-bouche – perhaps Wensleydale cheese foam with pickled onion – and other incidentals are indicators of his serious approach, to be followed by glazed veal sweetbreads with caramelised onion and a Madeira and truffle jus, or tartare of mackerel with pickled cucumber, radish and lemon dressing. There's no chasing wild combinations for the sake of originality. Dishes make an impact with their uncluttered mixtures of flavours and textures, seen in

daube of local grass-fed beef with no more than a portion of wild mushrooms and red wine sauce, and loin of venison with braised red cabbage, roasted parsnips, apple and blackcurrant. A fish option may be a perfectly timed tranche of wild turbot complemented by servings of truffled white beans and cauliflower with garlic sauce. Good culinary judgement is applied to desserts too: dark chocolate ganache and salted caramel, for instance, with a novel but effective sorbet of cucumber and lime, or light and fluffy prune and Armagnac soufflé with rum ice cream.

Chef Mr S Gueller, Mr L Yates **Owner** Mrs R Gueller **Seats** 50, Pr/dining room 20 **Times** 12-2/7-9.30 Closed 27-31 Dec, 1-7 Jan, Mon, L Tue-Thu, D Sun **Prices** Fixed L 3 course £30, Fixed D 3 course £60, Tasting menu £70 **Wines** 11 bottles over £30, 12 bottles under £30, 7 by glass **Parking** NCP **Notes** Fixed L Fri & Sat only, Sunday L £35, Children welcome

LEEDS *continued*

Jamie's Italian, Leeds

 Italian

tel: 0113 322 5400 **35 Park Row LS1 5JL**
email: leeds@jamiesitalian.com
dir: *300mtrs from station*

Italian tradition à la Jamie in a bank-turned-warehouse

A thoroughgoing makeover has transformed a once-grand banking temple into a warehouse eatery in the modern idiom, its original features still visible amid the girdering, tiling and brickwork. Sit up on high stools at a counter, or around cafeteria-style booth tables, for the Jamie-goes-to-Italy experience. Should the British affection for simple Italian food ever pall, the empire may come juddering to a halt, but thankfully no such disaffection is in evidence. And why would it be when a bowl of beautifully timed wild truffle risotto with aged parmesan is on hand, as well as pasta dishes built on luxuries like local lamb ragu, slow-cooked for 20 hours in red wine and rosemary, mixed into what the menu calls 'wriggly' pappardelle? With planks of antipasti, chillified arancini, or baked salmon with balsamic-roasted veg, there is plenty of versatility to the range, and nobody minds deserting Italian tradition to finish with a lump of chocolate brownie, amaretto ice cream and caramelised amaretti popcorn.

Chef Jimmy Carr **Owner** Jamie Oliver **Seats** 200 **Times** 12-11 Closed 25-26 Dec, All-day dining **Prices** Fixed L 2 course £12, Fixed D 3 course £29.95-£39.95, Starter £3.75-£6.85, Main £9.75-£24, Dessert £4.95 **Wines** 14 bottles over £30, 20 bottles under £30, 17 by glass **Parking** On street **Notes** Vegetarian available, Children welcome

Malmaison Leeds

 Modern British

tel: 0113 398 1000 **1 Swinegate LS1 4AG**
email: leeds@malmaison.com **web:** www.malmaison.com
dir: *City centre. 5 mins walk from Leeds railway station. On junct 16 of loop road, Sovereign St & Swinegate*

Vibrant cooking with global influences in a stylish city brasserie

The Malmaison group's Leeds branch has been carved out of an impressive building that used to be the headquarters of a tram company. In common with other hotels in the group, it is decorated and furnished to a high standard, creating the atmosphere of a contemporary boutique hotel. The brasserie is no exception, with plush leather booths and open fireplaces under its elegant ceiling. The cooking is built on a framework of quality ingredients, and talented professionals are clearly at work. So mushroom soup with croûtons, smooth and deeply flavoured, might be followed by properly timed calves' liver, its centre just pink, with buttery mash, crisp pancetta and roasted onions. Influences have been gathered from around the globe to add to the broad appeal, so fritto misto might appear next to another starter of chicken lollipops, a fusion dish if ever there was one: satay, Moroccan-spiced croquette, Thai bonbon, tandoori and barbecue. End on a calmer note with pear tarte Tatin with Calvados-flavoured mascarpone.

Chef Andrew Lawson **Owner** Malmaison **Seats** 85, Pr/dining room 12
Times 12-2.30/6.30-9.30 **Wines** 25 by glass **Parking** Criterion Place car park, Q Park **Notes** Sunday L fr £19.95, Vegetarian available, Children welcome

The New Ellington

 Modern British

tel: 0113 204 2150 **23-25 York Place LS1 2EY**
email: info@thenewellington.com **web:** www.thenewellington.com

Stylish boutique hotel with hearty modern cooking

The name references the late, great Duke who played the Leeds Music Festival in 1958, and there's a definite New Orleans, jazz-age vibe going on here. It's all very tasteful though and the hotel wears its 'boutique' billing very well indeed. If you're a fan of gin, head to The Gin Garden bar to take your pick from a head-spinning 100 or so varieties, before moving on down to the lower-ground floor to the plush Digby's Restaurant, where you'll find low-lit booths with smart velour banquette seating and tables dressed up in crisp white linen. On the menu are unpretentious modern ideas and classic brasserie-style dishes. Start, perhaps, with slow-braised oxtail with mini Yorkshire puddings and horseradish sauce, and choose from main courses along the lines of pan-fried red mullet fillet with creamed leeks, peas, broad beans and dry-cured bacon. Desserts deliver traditional comforts in the shape of marmalade bread-and-butter pudding with vanilla custard.

Times 12-2/5.30-10 Closed 25-26 Dec, D Sun

Salvo's Restaurant & Salumeria

 Italian

tel: 0113 275 5017 & 275 2752 **115 Otley Rd, Headingley LS6 3PX**
email: dine@salvos.co.uk
dir: *On A660 2m N of city centre*

Popular Italian with a salumeria (deli-café)

Since it first opened its doors back in 1976, Salvo's has served the local Headingley community and built a deserved reputation. It's lively, family-friendly and family-run and will sort you out for some rustic and hearty regional Italian cooking. The Salumeria, which is a café-deli during the day and opens in the evening for musical soirees and the like, lies a few doors down from the restaurant. If you've come for a pizza because nothing else will do, the classics are all present and correct and you won't leave disappointed. But there is so much more: antipasti such as buffalo mozzarella with tomatoes and fresh basil, or Puglian sea bream fishcake layered with potatoes and pecorino cheese, pasta-perhaps tagliatelle with slow-cooked pork and beef ragù-and main courses run to the likes of twice-cooked belly pork with a sweet-and-sour confit of red peppers and capers.

Chef Giuseppe Schirripa, Geppino Dammone **Owner** John & Geppino Dammone **Seats** 88, Pr/dining room 20 **Times** 12-2/5.30-10.30 Closed 25-26 Dec, 1 Jan, L BHs **Prices** Fixed L 2 course £11.50-£14.50, Fixed D 3 course £17.50, Starter £3.95-£8.50, Main £8.50-£19.50, Dessert £3.95-£14.75, Service optional **Wines** 9 bottles over £30, 33 bottles under £30, 6 by glass **Parking** On street, Pay & display nearby **Notes** Sunday L £14.50-£17.50, Vegetarian available, Children welcome

Who are the AA's Restaurants of the Year? See page 14

Thorpe Park Hotel & Spa

🏵 Modern British

tel: 0113 264 1000 **Century Way, Thorpe Park LS15 8ZB**
email: thorpepark@shirehotels.com **web:** www.shirehotels.com
dir: M1 junct 46, follow signs off rdbt for Thorpe Park

Accomplished contemporary cooking in Thorpe Park

On the edge of the city, convenient for the motorway, Thorpe Park is a smart hotel with popular leisure facilities and a spa. The restaurant is an open-plan, split-level room with a pale wooden floor, artwork on the walls, and black leather-type chairs. The menu cleverly combines familiar with more contemporary ideas, so expect roast scallops with black pudding, potato purée and red wine sauce alongside sirloin steak with béarnaise. Tempura tiger prawns with chilli dipping sauce is a popular starter, or go for something like Asian-style duck with watercress, cucumber and coriander salad. Fish is confidently handled, seen in grilled salmon, sea bass and scallops with salsa verde and thin fries, and a commitment to local produce is evident: belly pork from Bacup, for instance, is slowly cooked and served with black pudding, champ, apple chutney and cider sauce, a satisfying combination of flavours and textures.

Times 12-2/6.45-9.30

Town Hall Tavern

🏵 Modern British

tel: 0113 244 0765 **17 Westgate LS1 2RA**
email: info@townhalltavernleeds.co.uk
dir: Located in city centre, opposite the Law Courts

Refined pub fare in the city centre

Located between the law courts and the Park Square Business Centre, this city-centre inn was at one time the haunt of policemen and solicitors. It dates from the 1920s, its more recent makeover creating a comfortable and homely atmosphere while retaining the building's original look. The menu sets out the pub's stall, emphasising that it buys from ethical local producers, and the kitchen's output is well up to the mark. Pub standards include gammon, egg and chips, and home-made burger, while a short 'perfect for lunch' section of the menu runs to omelettes and corned-beef hash. Those wanting the full works could go for salt-and-pepper squid with tempura prawns and honey and soy sauce, then slow-roast belly pork with passionfruit, braised fennel and mustard mash, and end with vanilla and ginger cheesecake with rhubarb.

Chef Gordan Mann **Owner** Jon & Sam Carter **Seats** 26 **Times** 11.45-9 Closed 25-26 Dec, BH Mon, All-day dining **Prices** Prices not confirmed, Service optional **Wines** 17 bottles under £30, 7 by glass **Parking** On street at rear **Notes** Sunday L, Vegetarian available, Children welcome

Read all about our Wine Award winners on page 17

Healds Hall Hotel & Restaurant

🏵 Modern British

tel: 01924 409112 **Leeds Rd WF15 6JA**
email: enquire@healdshall.co.uk **web:** www.healdshall.co.uk
dir: M1 junct 40, A638. From Dewsbury take A652 signed Bradford. Left at A62. Hotel 50yds on right

International favourites in a family-owned historic hotel

A short tootle from the M62, the stone-built Healds Hall is a family-owned hotel on the quietly grand scale, run with genuine Yorkshire hospitality and charm. Choose from a pair of eating spaces, the more informal Bistro with its conservatory extension, and Harringtons, the full-dress restaurant done in today's neutral tones. An extensive menu looks hither and thither for international favourite dishes such as crispy salt-and-pepper squid with garlic-lemon mayo, or Jamón Iberico de Bellota with chorizo and Manchego. The best of the English repertoire turns up in the form of mains like pork and leek sausages with creamy mash, and salmon and herb fishcake with tartare, or you may wander into the realms of venison medallions with truffled artichoke risotto and morels in red wine sauce. A vegetarian tart comes laden with tomato, roast pepper, goats' cheese and basil, dressed in aged balsamic. Simple but satisfying puddings include treacle tart, and lemon crème brûlée with stewed rhubarb.

Chef Andrew Ward, David Winter **Owner** Mr N B & Mrs T Harrington **Seats** 46, Pr/dining room 30 **Times** 12-2/6-10 Closed 1 Jan, BHs, L Sat, D Sun (ex residents) **Prices** Fixed L 2 course £10.95, Fixed D 3 course £18-£21, Starter £4.65-£8.95, Main £11.50-£25.50, Dessert £4.95-£5.50, Service optional **Wines** 14 bottles over £30, 34 bottles under £30, 8 by glass **Parking** 90 **Notes** Sunday L £18.95-£24.95, Vegetarian available, Children welcome

Chevin Country Park Hotel & Spa

🏵 Modern British

tel: 01943 467818 **Yorkgate LS21 3NU**
email: gm.chevin@crerarhotels.com **web:** www.crerarhotels.com
dir: A658 towards Harrogate. Left at 1st turn towards Carlton, 2nd left towards Yorkgate

Modern cooking in a Scandinavian-style log cabin

Tucked away in 40 acres of private Yorkshire woodland complete with three lakes, extensive gardens and abundant wildlife, it's seems hard to believe that Leeds/Bradford Airport is just a short drive away from this rather unusual, purpose-built hotel. The restaurant is housed in one of the UK's biggest log cabins (bedrooms are mostly scattered around the grounds in chalets) and it's all charmingly old fashioned with smartly dressed tables and lovely lakeside views through the picture windows. The modern menus — including a carte and steak and grill menu — are full of crowd-pleasers and local produce features strongly. Start, perhaps, with a well-made, smooth chicken liver parfait served with toasted brioche and red onion marmalade, before Scottish scallops sautéed with butter and pancetta lardons. Lemon tart with almond and ginger ice cream is a satisfying end to a meal.

Chef Liam Stringwell **Owner** Crerar Hotels **Seats** 80, Pr/dining room 30 **Times** 12-2.30/6-9 **Prices** Fixed L 2 course £9.95, Tasting menu £32.95, Starter £4.95-£8.95, Main £14.95-£19.95, Dessert £5.95-£7.95, Service optional **Wines** 39 bottles over £30, 34 bottles under £30, 9 by glass **Parking** 100 **Notes** Sunday L £9.95-£12.50, Vegetarian available, Children welcome

PONTEFRACT
Map 16 SE42

Wentbridge House Hotel
◉◉ Modern British V ▮ NOTABLE WINE LIST

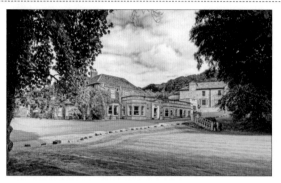

tel: 01977 620444 **The Great North Rd, Wentbridge WF8 3JJ**
email: info@wentbridgehouse.co.uk web: www.wentbridgehouse.co.uk
dir: *4m S of M62/A1 junct, 0.5m off A1*

Multi-influenced cooking in a Yorkshire manor house

Set in 20 acres of landscaped grounds in a West Yorkshire conservation village, Wentbridge is a stone-built grand manor house built at the turn of the 18th century. It had long associations with the Leatham family, luminaries of Barclays Bank, but became a country hotel in 1960. A degree of glossy formality prevails within, not least in the Fleur de Lys dining room, where candy-coloured upholstery creates a light, bright effect, and the cooking reaches out in all directions for its references. First up might be seared Shetland scallops with beans in truffled cappuccino for a majestic array of complementary elements. This may be followed by venison fillet with beetroot, cavolo nero and celeriac dauphinoise, or perfectly fresh cod Spanish-style with a stuffed red pepper, patatas bravas and aioli. Main courses for sharing are quite the thing these days. If you can arrive at an agreement, go for classic Chateaubriand with choice of sauces, or duck à l'orange. To finish, there's zesty lemon tart with raspberry sorbet and a pistachio tuile, or perhaps a boozy baked Alaska bursting with cherries.

Chef Ian Booth **Owner** Mr G Page **Seats** 60, Pr/dining room 24 **Times** 7.15-9.30 Closed L Mon-Sat, D Sun, 25 Dec **Prices** Starter £7.95-£12.95, Main £17.95-£32.95, Dessert £5.50-£10.95, Service optional **Wines** 100 bottles over £30, 30 bottles under £30, 10 by glass **Parking** 100 **Notes** Sunday L £27, Children welcome

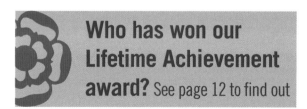

Who has won our Lifetime Achievement award? See page 12 to find out

WAKEFIELD
Map 16 SE32

Waterton Park Hotel
◉ Traditional & Modern British V

tel: 01924 257911 **Walton Hall, The Balk, Walton WF2 6PW**
email: info@watertonparkhotel.co.uk web: www.watertonparkhotel.co.uk
dir: *3m SE off B6378. Exit M1 junct 39 towards Wakefield. At 3rd rdbt right for Crofton. At 2nd lights right & follow signs*

Sound flavour-packed cooking by a huge lake

The location of the Georgian hotel must be unique, as it stands on an island in a 26-acre lake, with a modern extension on the shore accessed via a bridge, which explains where the attractive Bridgeman restaurant gets its name from. Dishes are admirably understated and flavours are to the fore, with starters running from a salad of seared scallops with black pudding, poached apples and cauliflower foam, to carpaccio with parmesan shavings and horseradish dressing. Raw materials are conscientiously chosen and carefully cooked, demonstrated by main courses of Whitby cod steak in a walnut crust served with parsnip purée and white wine beurre blanc, and seared Gressingham duck breast with caramelised orange, pickled red cabbage and port-based gravy. Puddings make a fine finale, among them Yorkshire rhubarb crème brûlée with vanilla ice cream, and a duo of chocolate with espresso custard and chocolate drizzle.

Chef Armstrong Wgabi **Owner** The Kaye family **Seats** 50, Pr/dining room 40 **Times** 7-9.30 Closed D Sun **Prices** Service optional **Wines** 10 by glass **Parking** 200 **Notes** Sunday L £21-£30, Children welcome

WETHERBY
Map 16 SE44

Wood Hall Hotel
◉◉ Modern British V

tel: 01937 587271 **Trip Ln, Linton LS22 4JA**
email: woodhall@handpicked.co.uk web: www.handpickedhotels.co.uk/woodhall
dir: *From Wetherby take A661 (Harrogate road) N for 0.5m. Left to Sicklinghall/Linton. Cross bridge, left to Linton/Woodhall, right opposite Windmill Inn, 1.25m to hotel (follow brown signs)*

Classy cooking using local produce in an elegant country-house hotel

High on a hill, with fine views, this is the sort of country-house hotel where you'll want to linger. Dating from 1750, the property retains a number of original details, while furnishings and decor have been chosen with guests' comfort and well-being in mind. The Georgian Restaurant is as elegant as the other rooms, with its relaxing colour scheme, upholstered chairs and drapes at the windows. Chef Neal Birtwell is rigorous in his pursuit of Yorkshire produce – beef from local farms, lamb from the moors, produce from the garden – and eschews over-elaboration and unnecessary garnishes in favour of a simple approach, so his cooking is marked out by clear, distinct flavours. Raviolo of rabbit confit, with a sautéed scallop and gingery consommé is characteristic, as is duck terrine with fig and port jelly. A trio of beef (roast fillet, braised cheek and marrowbone croquette) with a rich jus is a typically well-conceived main course, with a fish option perhaps salmon 'pastrami' with beetroot and radish. End with an upbeat pudding like banana bavarois with caramelised fruit and peanut ice cream.

Chef Neal Birtwell **Owner** Hand Picked Hotels **Seats** 40, Pr/dining room 100 **Times** 12-2.30/7-9.30 Closed L Mon-Sat **Prices** Prices not confirmed, Service optional **Wines** 50 bottles over £30, 10 bottles under £30, 18 by glass **Parking** 100 **Notes** Sunday L, Children welcome

CHANNEL ISLANDS
GUERNSEY

CASTEL — Map 24

Cobo Bay Hotel

 Modern, Traditional

tel: 01481 257102 & 07781 156757 **Cobo Coast Rd, Cobo GY5 7HB**
email: reservations@cobobayhotel.com **web:** www.cobobayhotel.com
dir: *From airport turn right, follow road to W coast at L'Erée. Turn right onto coast road for 3m to Cobo Bay. Hotel on right*

Superb views and admirable use of local produce

The view across the eponymous bay is seen at its best if you time it right for a sunset dinner at this west-facing beachside hotel. If you're lucky you can dine alfresco on the beach terrace, but if not it's no hardship to grab a table indoors in the smart contemporary restaurant. As you might hope in this wave-lapped setting, seafood is a strong suit here, arriving slithery fresh from local boats, and it is presented in straightforward contemporary combinations, along with a cornucopia of other top-quality locally-sourced produce. Courgette and red pepper soup is a well-made opener, or you might prefer to head straight for the fish – perhaps tempura monkfish or fritto misto with lemon and caper mayonnaise – then move on to pan-fried sea bass with pea and prawn risotto, garlic king prawns, and crab and lobster bisque. Banana tarte Tatin with caramel ice cream presses the comfort button at the end.

Times 12-2/6-9.30

ST MARTIN — Map 24

The Auberge

Modern International

tel: 01481 238485 **Jerbourg Rd GY4 6BH**
email: dine@theauberge.gg
dir: *End of Jerbourg Rd at Jerbourg Point*

Seafood-led menu on a Guernsey clifftop

Its clifftop position, overlooking the Channel and the neighbouring islands through floor-to-ceiling windows, certainly draws people to this sleek contemporary restaurant near St Peter Port. The garden and terrace for alfresco dining are a further attraction, but the main reason for a visit must of course be the food. Chef Daniel Green's cooking takes a lively and imaginative approach to the island's top-quality seasonal produce, and the resulting dishes are full of interest. The menu is big on fish and seafood, with locally-caught red mullet getting the escabèche treatment, served with sardine rillettes and toasted hazelnuts, or scallop tempura amongst the appealing starter options. Main courses run to roasted turbot with a cassoulet of haricot beans, basil, chorizo and mussels, or meatier fare along the lines of a 3-way composition of local pork, involving twice-cooked belly, sweet and sour cheeks, and roasted fillet, with chargrilled broccoli, shiitake mushrooms and butternut squash. End with a local version of cranachan – Guernsey cream, raspberry parfait, toasted oats, and honey and whisky sponge.

Chef Daniel Green **Owner** Liberation Group **Seats** 70, Pr/dining room 20 **Times** 12-2/7-9.30 Closed 25-26 Dec, D Sun **Prices** Fixed L 2 course £17.50, Fixed D 3 course £22.50, Starter £5.95-£8.50, Main £12.95-£25, Dessert £5.75, Service optional **Wines** 30 bottles over £30, 26 bottles under £30, 12 by glass **Parking** 25 **Notes** Sunday L £16.50-£29, Vegetarian available, Children welcome

La Barbarie Hotel

British, French

tel: 01481 235217 **Saints Rd GY4 6ES**
email: reservations@labarbariehotel.com **web:** www.labarbariehotel.com
dir: *At lights in St Martin take road to Saints Bay. Hotel on right at end of Saints Rd*

Unpretentious country-house cooking in a charming setting

The hotel's name comes from the story that, back in the 17th century, the owner of the house was kidnapped by Barbary Coast pirates. There is no such drama nowadays, the former priory transformed into a comfortable hotel with a soothing vibe and a restaurant that puts to good use the cornucopia of peerless fresh produce – fish, seafood, meat, cream and butter – supplied by Guernsey's coasts and meadows. La Barbarie's kitchen team clearly look to the nearby French mainland for their inspiration in the repertoire of simply cooked and presented dishes. A simple pairing of pan-fried scallops with black pudding, pancetta and apple sauce gets things off the blocks, followed by a classic combo of roast rack of new season lamb with shallot, port and rosemary sauce, dauphinoise potatoes, and fine green beans. Caramelised apple tart with a sharp palate-refreshing green apple sorbet brings things to a zingy close.

Times 12-1.45/6-9.30 Closed mid Nov-mid Mar

Bella Luce Hotel, Restaurant & Spa

Modern European **NEW** v

tel: 01481 238764 **La Fosse GY4 6EB**
email: wakeup@bellalucehotel.com **web:** www.bellalucehotel.com
dir: *From airport, turn left to St Martin. At 3rd set of lights continue 30yds, turn right, straight on to hotel*

Sharp, modern cooking in a classy boutique hotel

With its 12th-century granite walls, bags of period charm and luxe boutique finish, Bella Luce really leaves a lasting impression. It's a class act. The Bar & Grill is the place for a cocktail or an upmarket sandwich or steak seared on the grill, but the main culinary action takes place in the restaurant where there's some sharp, classically-minded contemporary cooking going down. It's an elegant space with pristine tables and lots of character, looked over by a slick, professional team who leave nothing to chance. There's a good showing of local produce on the menu and a good deal of skill in the execution of dishes. Everything looks beautiful on the plate, too. Dressed Chancre crab comes with a Bloody Mary shot and coconut, while another starter sees belly of pork braised for eight hours and served with watercress salad and flavoured with lavender and honey. For mains, ox cheeks also get the braising treatment, served with creamed horseradish potato and sprouting greens, or go for plaice roasted on the bone and classically served with brown shrimps and a beurre noisette. Desserts are equally on the money.

Chef Seb Orzechowski, Seb Laskowy, Richard Waller, Chris Harworth **Owner** Luke Wheadon **Seats** 70, Pr/dining room 20 **Times** 12-2.30/6.30-9.30 Closed 2-22 Jan **Prices** Fixed L 2 course £22.50, Fixed D 3 course £27.50, Tasting menu £39-£85, Starter £6-£9.50, Main £13-£29, Dessert £5.50-£8.50 **Parking** 38 **Notes** Sunday L £21-£26, Children welcome

ST MARTIN *continued*

Hotel Jerbourg

 Modern British

tel: 01481 238826 **Jerbourg Point GY4 6BJ**
email: stay@hoteljerbourg.com **web:** www.hoteljerbourg.com
dir: *From airport turn left to St Martin, right at filter, straight on at lights, hotel at end of road on right*

Ocean views and classic seafood dishes

Magnificent views are a major pull at this modern hotel in lovely grounds out on the tip of the Jerbourg Peninsula. With the Atlantic lapping all around, thoughts are bound to turn to fish, so you will not be disappointed to see that the classic French repertoire is weighted in that direction. The kitchen resists the temptation to gild the lily, letting the sheer freshness and quality of prime piscine produce do the talking, serving Guernsey chancre crab with prawn and apple cocktail, ahead of turbot with crayfish and caviar butter sauce, or grilled brill fillet with sauté potatoes, spinach, and martini beurre blanc. Straight-up chargrilled steaks (entrecôte with dauphinoise potatoes and Roquefort sauce, say), or something requiring a touch more input from the kitchen – perhaps honey-glazed Barbary duck breast with potato rösti, asparagus and sherry vinegar jus – should keep the carnivores quiet. End with a classic crème brûlée.

Chef Paul Scambler **Owner** Ess Ltd **Seats** 80, Pr/dining room 40
Times 12-2.30/6.30-9.30 Closed 5 Jan-Mar **Prices** Service optional **Wines** 6 by glass
Parking 30 **Notes** Sunday L £17.50, Vegetarian available, Children welcome

---

ST PETER PORT   Map 24

The Absolute End

 Mediterranean

tel: 01481 723822 **St Georges Esplanade GY1 2BG**
email: the-absolute-end@cwgsy.net
dir: *Less than 1m from town centre. N on seafront road towards St Sampson*

Italian-accented fish restaurant overlooking the harbour

Any faint note of exasperation in the name is entirely misleading. Peppe Rega's welcoming harbourside seafood place, formed from the knocking together of two former fishermen's cottages, is perfectly positioned to enjoy views over the sea, and draws in locals and holiday-makers for its softly Italian-accented menus of straightforward fish and shellfish. A light-filled ground-floor room in olive-green and white is supplemented by a terrace upstairs, and staff ensure a friendly tone to the proceedings. Reliable renditions of crisp-fried crab cakes with sweet chilli sauce, oysters alla fiorentina, and mains such as grilled sea bass with bitingly lemony meunière, all come up to snuff, but meat-eaters are not forgotten either. Fillet steaks, rack of lamb or veal saltimbocca should keep them happy. A slate of pasta and risotto variations provides carbs, and energetically garnished dessert plates feature the likes of milk chocolate fondant with Greek yoghurt and strawberry compôte.

Times 12-2.30/6.30-10 Closed Sun

Best Western Hotel de Havelet

 Traditional British, International NEW v

tel: 01481 722199 **Havelet GY1 1BA**
email: stay@dehaveletguernsey.com **web:** www.dehaveletguernsey.com
dir: *From airport follow signs for St Peter Port through St Martins. At bottom of 'Val de Terres' hill turn left at top of hill, hotel on right*

Sea views and classic no-nonsense cooking

The Georgian hotel is in a quiet spot surrounded by trees with sea and castle views and picture windows in the two restaurants to make the most of the vista. Both of the dining options are in the converted coach house (although there is bar food, too), with the Havelet Grill on the ground floor and the main Wellington Boot above. The latter is the main event, decorated in a traditional manner with neat tables and formal settings. There's nothing complicated about the food on offer, no bandwagons being jumped on, just classical cooking with a sure hand, and plenty of local ingredients. Start with beef carpaccio, which has at is heart some excellent meat, cut just right, and served with a rocket pesto. Next up, chargrilled lamb cutlets perfectly prepared, line-caught local sea bass, or perhaps an Egyptian-style beef ragout showcasing the chef's roots. Finish with a well-made crème brûlée.

Chef Mohammed Ekamy **Owner** Mrs Karel Harris **Seats** 100, Pr/dining room 20
Times 12-2/7-9.30 Closed L Mon-Sat **Prices** Fixed L 2 course £15.95, Fixed D 3 course £20-£25, Starter £5.95-£8.95, Main £14.95-£18.95, Dessert £5.95-£7.25
Wines 10 bottles over £30, 20 bottles under £30, 5 by glass **Parking** 35
Notes Sunday L £15.95-£18.50, Children welcome

The Duke of Richmond Hotel

 Modern International

tel: 01481 740866 & 726221 **Cambridge Park GY1 1UY**
web: www.dukeofrichmond.com
dir: *Opposite Cambridge Park*

Leopard-spotted style in one of Guernsey's oldest hotels

A historically fascinating site once housed Guernsey's first hotel, Grover's, and subsequently the Richmond, the island's premier boarding-house. Following the rude interruption of occupation by the Nazis during wartime, the place once more became a hotel, but one that had come up in the world. An ennoblement of the name paved the way for the present incarnation, and what an incarnation it is. A rather fetching leopard-spotted theme has been introduced to the bar and dining room, and a screened-off kitchen provides the now de rigueur voyeur's eye on the culinary action, rivalled for visual attention only by the views from the conservatory extension. Simple brasserie cooking is the chosen mode, with Caesar salad and excellent chicken liver pâté to start things off, followed by very mild lamb curry with basmati, classic fish and chips, or pasta primavera. Finish with a hefty wodge of baked American cheesecake. The concise list features the wines of Bouchard-Finlayson, one of South Africa's reference producers.

Chef Jack Darbyshire, Stamatis Loumousiotis **Owner** Red Carnation Hotels **Seats** 80, Pr/dining room 260 **Times** 12-2/6-10 Closed D 31 Dec **Prices** Starter £6-£9.50, Main £12-£21, Dessert £6-£9 **Wines** 30 bottles over £30, 20 bottles under £30, 25 by glass **Parking** On street **Notes** Sunday L £19.50, Vegetarian available, Children welcome

---

Fermain Valley Hotel

 Modern European

tel: 01481 235666 **Fermain Ln GY1 1ZZ**
email: info@fermainvalley.com **web:** www.fermainvalley.com
dir: *From town centre on Fort Rd follow St Martin signs. Fermain Ln on left. Hotel 0.5m on left*

Brasserie-style dishes in a beautiful Guernsey valley

In a spectacularly sylvan setting, the white-painted Fermain Valley Hotel is close to the bay of the same name, the bright blue water glimpsed from the terrace over the treetops. It stands in beautiful gardens, too, so there's plenty of opportunity to unwind. The Valley Restaurant is the main dining option here – refurbished in 2013 – and makes a smart setting for some bright and gently contemporary cooking. Start with lemon sole and a fried oyster with cucumber and lemon, for example, or local Guernsey crab with tomato consommé jelly, avocado purée and brown crab toastie. There's a French and Italian flavour to the menu, thus a pork chop might come with Tuscan beans and a roast garlic and fennel crust, and the entrecôte steak with ceps pudding, oven-roasted tomatoes and parsley and garlic sauce.

Finish with a rhubarb and champagne jelly with scorched meringue, or on a savoury note with potted cheddar with celery pickle and raisin toast.

Times 12-2.30/6.30-9.30

Mora Restaurant & Grill

Traditional European, British, Mediterranean

tel: 01481 715053 **The Quay GY1 2LE**
email: eat@mora.gg
dir: Facing Victoria Marina

Contemporary cooking in a stylish venue by the marina

Creative restyling has made Mora a more obviously engaging venue, without losing any of the firmly loyal local custom. There's an easygoing ground-floor brasserie, while a sweeping metal staircase leads up to the full dining experience in a stylish room with a vaulted ceiling and an open kitchen to add to the sense of theatre. The cooking puts the focus sharply on local produce and deals in unfussy combinations with European leanings and some contemporary flourishes to contrast with a solid foundation of tradition. Main-course hits might be slow-cooked lamb shank with minted mashed potatoes and flageolet bean sauce, or brill fillet with calamari, spicy tomato sauce and saffron mash. Preface either of those with smoked duck breast with anise-poached pear, or seared scallops with black pudding and creamed cauliflower, and the whole deal looks very attractive. Vodka pannacotta with raspberry sorbet and milkshake is a good way to end.

Chef Trevor Baines **Owner** Nello Ciotti **Seats** 90 **Times** 12-2.15/6-10 Closed 24 Dec, Jan, L 25 Dec **Prices** Fixed L 3 course £24.95-£35, Fixed D 3 course £24.95-£35, Starter £5-£8.95, Main £13-£25, Dessert £5.95-£6.95, Service optional **Wines** 30 bottles over £30, 40 bottles under £30, 11 by glass **Parking** On pier **Notes** Brasserie menu available, Sunday L, Vegetarian available, Children welcome

The Old Government House Hotel & Spa

Indian

tel: 01481 724921 **St Ann's Place GY1 2NU**
email: governors@theoghhotel.com **web:** www.theoghhotel.com
dir: At junct of St Julian's Av & College St

Indian cooking at the old governor's residence

The beautiful white Georgian building was once the island governor's harbourside residence, though that's going back a fair while, as it was converted into a hotel as long ago as 1858. The red carpet that rolls out down the front steps sets the tone, and the magnificent interiors culminate in a dining room done in warm fuchsia tones and decorated with martial memorabilia and paintings. It's known now as the Curry Room, and serves authentic subcontinental food from an Indian chef, Arun Singh. Expect marinated tandoori tiger prawns with cherry tomatoes, or a set of aubergine variations with minted yoghurt, to start, followed by dynamically spiced main courses bursting with flavour, such as white fish and squid curry with mushroom and pea masala, butter chicken, or baby vegetable coconut curry for the veggies. Aromatic desserts include rosewater rice pudding with ginger snaps, or banana cake with coconut ice cream and masala caramel.

Times 12-2/7-11 Closed 25 & 31 Dec

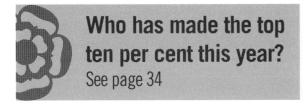

Who has made the top ten per cent this year?
See page 34

See page 34

The Farmhouse Hotel

Modern British

tel: 01481 264181 **Route des bas Courtils GY7 9YF**
email: enquiries@thefarmhouse.gg **web:** www.thefarmhouse.gg
dir: From airport turn left. Approx 1m left at lights. 100mtrs, left, around airport runway perimeter. 1m, left at staggered junct. Hotel in 100mtrs on right

Boutique hotel with resourceful cooking

The same family has owned this 15th-century farmhouse, now a boutique hotel, for three generations. Beams, stone floors and granite are reminders of the property's antiquity, superimposed today with a modern decor and comfortable furnishings. Eating outside is an attractive proposition, while the restaurant is in the oldest part of the building. Seasonality is central to the kitchen's output, bringing on shellfish in summer: perhaps scallops with a simple white wine sauce. Game is abundant in the colder months: partridge tortellini, say, with confit leg, leeks and basil, followed by roast goose with leg meat stuffing cut by spot-on orange sauce. Otherwise, there might be boar's head with truffles, mushrooms and sauce gribiche, or fried fillet of cod with a smoked cod beignet, greens, fondant potatoes and parsley and caper beurre blanc, with a finale of chocolate and hazelnut tart, its pastry exemplary, with a hazelnut shard and vanilla crème fraîche.

Chef Darren Curson **Owner** David & Julie Nussbaumer **Seats** 60, Pr/dining room 160 **Times** 12-2.30/6.30-9.30 **Prices** Fixed L 2 course £23.95, Fixed D 3 course £28.45-£31.90, Starter £5.95-£9.95, Main £11.95-£22, Dessert £4.50-£7.95, Service optional **Wines** 43 bottles over £30, 30 bottles under £30, 12 by glass **Parking** 80 **Notes** Sunday L £19.50-£23.95, Vegetarian available, Children welcome

White House Hotel

European, Traditional British V

tel: 01481 750000 **GY1 3HR**
email: hotel@herm.com **web:** www.herm.com
dir: Close to harbour. Access by regular 20 min boat trip from St Peter Port, Guernsey

Simple cooking and sea views in an island retreat

If you hanker for a simpler, slower pace of life, how about the pocket-sized, car- and pollution-free island of Herm? The island's only hotel – the White House – even takes the concept of getting away from it all a step further by dispensing with TVs, phones and clocks, but that doesn't mean you can totally kick back and relax in the restaurant, since old-school values require gentlemen to wear jackets and/or ties. As its name suggests, the Conservatory Restaurant is light and airy, and every table has a sea view. The kitchen doesn't try to reinvent the wheel, sticking to unfussy dishes that rely on the sheer quality of the raw materials and simple, accurate cooking for their effect. The contemporary European menu opens with an easy-on-the-eye composition of seared Guernsey scallops with Puy lentil and pancetta casserole, and truffled celeriac purée, before reaching out into the realms of duck breast teamed with Waldorf croquettes, roasted figs, Chantenay carrots and whisky jus. To finish, there's classic apple tarte Tatin with vanilla crème anglaise.

Chef Nigel Waylen **Owner** Herm Island Ltd **Seats** 100 **Times** 12-2/7-9 Closed Nov-Apr **Prices** Service optional **Wines** 60 bottles over £30, 100 bottles under £30, 12 by glass **Notes** D 4 course £30, Sunday L £18.50, Children welcome

JERSEY

GOREY
Map 24

The Moorings Hotel & Restaurant

◉◉ Traditional

tel: 01534 853633 **Gorey Pier JE3 6EW**
email: reservations@themooringshotel.com **web:** www.themooringshotel.com
dir: *At foot of Mont Orgueil Castle*

Local food on the quayside

Right on the waterfront with the magnificent Mont Orgueil Castle looming large above it, The Moorings truly is at the centre of things. The wonderful beach is just a stroll away, there are outdoor tables for that continental vibe, and there's a passion for seafood within. It's not all about fish and shellfish, though, for both the bistro and Walkers Restaurant deliver the fruits of both land and sea. The restaurant is a pretty space with neatly laid tables and a warm, summery colour scheme. There's a Gallic imprint on the menu, with the kitchen making good use of the first-class ingredients in unfussy, clearly-focused dishes. Start, perhaps, with picked white chancre crab with a vegetable and miso soup, or pan-fried scallops with artichoke purée, wild rocket and truffle dressing. Next up, pan-fried fillet of sea bass with crushed potatoes, scallops and sauce vierge, or braised lamb fillets with parmesan risotto and stuffed Savoy cabbage. There's a great value fixed-price menu in support of the carte. Finish with a classic vanilla crème brûlée.

Chef Simon Walker **Owner** Simon & Joanne Walker **Seats** 65, Pr/dining room 35 **Times** 12-2/7-8.30 **Prices** Fixed L 2 course fr £12.50, Fixed D 3 course £23-£27, Service optional **Wines** 26 bottles over £30, 36 bottles under £30, 8 by glass **Notes** Sunday L, Vegetarian available, Children welcome

Sumas

◉◉ Modern British Ⅴ

tel: 01534 853291 **Gorey Hill JE3 6ET**
email: info@sumasrestaurant.com **web:** www.sumasrestaurant.com
dir: *From St Helier take A3 E for 5m to Gorey. Before castle take sharp left. Restaurant 100yds up hill on left (look for blue blind)*

Inventive cooking and marina views

If beachside-chic is in your restaurant vocabulary, you'll have an idea what to expect here. Overlooking Gorey Bay, the vista changes with the ebb and flow of the tide, so you might be watching the boats bobbing in the harbour or locals digging for clams in the sands. The tables on the terrace have the best of those views.

Inside is pretty peachy too, mind you, with whitewashed walls and plenty of splashes of blue giving a feeling of seaside bonhomie. There's a goodly amount of seafood on the menu, but not exclusively so, for this is a kitchen which also seeks out the best the local land has to offer. Expect well-crafted, modish dishes along the lines of local crab and pumpkin risotto with lemongrass and coriander, that's assuming you can resist the Royal Bay oysters. Main courses might deliver Angus rib-eye steak with hand-cut chips and Madeira sauce, or pan-fried local brill with crushed Charlotte potatoes mixed with crab, topped with a fish foam. For dessert, lemon tart with honey and Earl Grey ice cream will send you home content.

Chef Patrice Bouffaut **Owner** Mrs Bults, Paul Dufty **Seats** 40 **Times** 12-2.30/6-9.30 Closed late Dec-mid Jan (approx), D Sun **Prices** Fixed L 2 course £15-£19, Fixed D 3 course £23, Starter £6.75-£12, Main £14.50-£25.50, Dessert £5.75-£14, Service optional **Wines** 30 bottles over £30, 27 bottles under £30, 12 by glass **Parking** On street **Notes** Sunday L £19-£23, Children welcome

ROZEL
Map 24

Chateau la Chaire

◉◉ Traditional British, French Ⅴ

tel: 01534 863354 **Rozel Bay JE3 6AJ**
email: res@chateau-la-chaire.co.uk **web:** www.chateau-la-chaire.co.uk
dir: *From St Helier NE towards Five Oaks, Maufant, then St Martin's Church & Rozel. 1st left in village, hotel 100mtrs*

Locally based cooking at the Pulpit

A chaire in French is a pulpit, this property having been named after an ecclesiastical-looking rock overhang. It was built for the botanist Samuel Curtis in the 1840s, after he'd earmarked the spot as a perfect location to establish a tropical garden. The interiors are all lush Victorian rococo, with cherubs sporting in the mouldings and walls of oak panelling in what are now the bar and dining room, though eating also extends into the conservatory and on to the terrace. The best of local materials — scallops, crab, pork, rabbit — are the backbone of Marcin Ciechomski's menus, which are squarely in the modern British mainstream. That crab turns up in cucumber gazpacho with lime sorbet and a crab-flavoured cracker, before chargrilled fillet and 'sticky shin' of Jersey beef, served with a hash brown and broccoli in Dijon mustard jus, or perhaps monkfish tail marinated in Merlot, with saffron risotto, aubergine purée and sauce vierge. Stay local for ice creams and cheeses, or wander off in the direction of peanut butter pannacotta and blackberry jam with berry sorbet.

Chef Marcin Ciechomski **Owner** Hatton Hotel Group **Seats** 60, Pr/dining room 28 **Times** 12-2/7-9.30 **Prices** Fixed L 3 course £16.95, Fixed D 3 course £30, Tasting menu £65-£75, Starter £7.95-£10.25, Main £16.25-£21.95, Dessert £6.95-£10.25 **Wines** 24 bottles over £30, 18 bottles under £30, 7 by glass **Parking** 30 **Notes** 'Taste of Jersey' tasting menu with/out wines available, Sunday L £21.95, Children welcome

Follow us on facebook
www.facebook.com/TheAAUK

ST AUBIN — Map 24

The Salty Dog Bar & Bistro

Modern International V

tel: 01534 742760 **Le Boulevard JE3 8AB**
email: info@saltydogbistro.com web: www. saltydogbistro.com
dir: *Walking from centre of St Aubin Village along harbour, approx halfway along, slightly set back*

Vibrant seafood cooking (and more) by the harbour

Nowhere is out of bounds for this salty dog, with a menu that happily globetrots around the Med, across the Indian Ocean, and back home to the English Channel. The harbourside location sets the tone, with the outside seating – plenty of it – coming into its own in the summer. Whenever you visit, though, this one-time smugglers' residence is a fun place to eat. Thai beef salad gets those Asian flavours spot on, there might be crab and crayfish risotto, or the Salty's tasting platter for two to share if you can't decide which way to go. Next up, from the 'spice kitchen', Malaysian Penang curry, or, from the grill, classic beef fillet cooked straight up or with an aged mustard and black pepper sauce. It's back to the Med for Spanish churros with a rich dark chocolate dipping sauce, or the crème brûlée of the day.

Chef Damon James Duffy **Owner** Damon & Natalie Duffy **Seats** 60 **Times** 12.30pm-1.30am Closed 25-26 Dec, 1 Jan, L Tue-Thu (Nov-Apr) All-day dining **Prices** Fixed L 2 course fr £17.50, Fixed D 3 course £24-£35, Starter £8.25-£9.95, Main £14-£30, Dessert £5.20-£6.50 **Wines** 16 bottles over £30, 33 bottles under £30, 8 by glass **Parking** Car parks & on street parking nearby **Notes** Sunday L, Children welcome

ST BRELADE — Map 24

L'Horizon Beach Hotel and Spa

Modern British

tel: 01534 743101 **La Route de la Baie JE3 8EF**
email: lhorizon@handpicked.co.uk web: www.handpickedhotels.co.uk/lhorizon
dir: *From airport right at rdbt towards St Brelade & Red Houses. Through Red Houses, hotel 300mtrs on right in centre of bay*

Creative cooking and a touch of luxury on the beach

Built by a Victorian colonel who clearly knew a good spot when he saw one, L'Horizon has a contemporary finish within and offers maximum pampering in its spa and treatment rooms. Overlooking the bay, with pristine sand and shimmering sea out front, the view is a big draw, but it's the Grill restaurant that really puts this place on the map. It's a smart room with neutral colours and white linen on the tables, and a menu that makes excellent use of the island's bounty in bright, modern dishes. This is creative, contemporary stuff, with first courses such as scallops partnered with pig's cheek and lobster and crayfish tortellini, or garden and golden beets with ripple and crème fraîche. Among mains, turbot is served with gherkins and clams, and sea bass with a crab and vanilla sauce. Everything is presented with panache, and, given they call themselves the Grill, there's steak in the form of 28-day aged fillet with burnt shallot purée and horseradish creamed potatoes. Finish with apple soufflé with crumble and sorbet.

Chef Byron Hayter **Owner** Julia Hands **Seats** 44, Pr/dining room 300 **Times** 6.30-10 Closed L Mon-Sat **Prices** Fixed D 3 course £47.50, Starter £8-£13.50, Main £24-£27.50, Dessert £8-£12, Service optional **Wines** 25 bottles under £30 **Parking** 100 **Notes** Sunday L £27.50, Vegetarian available, No children

Hotel La Place

Modern British

tel: 01534 744261 & 748173 **Route du Coin, La Haule JE3 8BT**
email: andy@hotellaplacejersey.com web: www. hotellaplacejersey.com
dir: *Off main St Helier/St Aubin coast road at La Haule Manor (B25). Up hill, 2nd left (to Red Houses), 1st right. Hotel 100mtrs on right*

Modern bistro cooking near the harbour

A short walk from St Aubin's harbour, the hotel is a collection of country cottages centred on an original 17th-century farmhouse in a particularly tranquil district of Jersey. Dining goes on in a pale beige and white room known as the Retreat, where modern bistro dishes in a light style are on the menu. Bresaola with fennel slaw, or crab fritters with beetroot and apple salsa, fire the starting gun, and may be followed by the likes of pollock on wilted spinach in parsley sauce, or braised ox cheeks on celeriac purée, served with braised leeks and rosemary roast potatoes. Finish up with lemon tart and blueberry compôte, or a canonical version of Eton Mess.

Times 6.30-9 Closed L Sat-Sun

Ocean Restaurant at The Atlantic Hotel

– see page 576

Oyster Box

Modern British

tel: 01534 850888 **St Brelade's Bay JE3 8EF**
email: eat@oysterbox.co.uk
dir: *On the beach just east of Fishermen's chapel*

A beachside setting for spankingly fresh seafood

With views during the day of kids building sandcastles, windsurfers, sand-yachters and the like, The Oyster Box's position right on lovely St Brelade beach really does take some beating, and a seat on the terrace is a prized position. At night, it's lit up and decidedly cool, with its open-to-view kitchen, slate floors and high-backed wicker chairs at wooden tables. The large menu is packed with fabulous seafood – Jersey Rock oysters, of course, served as you like them – plus plenty of non-fishy choices. You might start with confit duck spring rolls with celery, fennel and popcorn shoot salad, or squid a la plancha, before moving on to a risotto or pasta dish. There's sushi, too, plus whole lemon sole served on the bone with wilted spinach and garlic butter, Oyster Box fish and chips with pea purée and tartare sauce, or braised Irish ox cheek with smoked mashed potatoes and oxtail and bone marrow sauce. Attention to detail runs right the way through to desserts such as Frangelico pannacotta with fresh raspberries.

Chef Patrick Tweedie **Owner** Jersey Pottery **Seats** 100 **Times** 12-2.30/6-9.30 Closed 25-26 Dec, Mon (Jan-Mar), L Mon, D Sun (winter only) **Prices** Starter £6-£13.50, Main £11.50-£28, Dessert £6-£8.50, Service optional **Wines** 55 bottles over £30, 50 bottles under £30, 25 by glass **Parking** Car park opposite **Notes** Sunday L, Vegetarian available, Children welcome

Ocean Restaurant at The Atlantic Hotel

ST BRELADE   **Map 24**

Modern British **V** 🍷 **NOTABLE WINE LIST**

tel: 01534 744101 **Le Mont de la Pulente JE3 8HE**
email: info@theatlantichotel.com **web:** www.theatlantichotel.com
dir: *A13 to Petit Port, turn right into Rue de la Sergente & right again, hotel signed*

Top-class Jersey produce treated with skill in a breathtakingly beautiful location

With exotic palm trees, white louvred shutters, a deep blue pool straight out of a Hockney painting and a whiff of art deco in the clean lines of its low-slung white facade, this could be Miami, but luckily the Atlantic Hotel overlooks the stunning Jersey coast. The Ocean Restaurant has views out over the gardens towards the sea, and a colour palette of blues, whites and beiges, comfortable hand-crafted furniture and modern artwork on the walls. It's a wonderfully light and airy setting, and the exciting cooking of Mark Jordan has turned this place into a real Channel Islands destination. Having served his time with a stellar cast of mentors in top-drawer restaurants, he brings a wealth of effervescent ideas, backed by masterful techniques, to produce good-looking results. There's a mix of classic and visionary dishes here, all headlined with their main ingredient. Superb goats' cheese and olive bread, and an amuse-bouche of a parsnip espuma with real depth of flavour, accompanied by a perfectly timed roasted scallop, might begin proceedings. Next, a starter entitled 'sea shore' is something of a signature, comprising a mixture of local fish (extremely high quality and precisely cooked) presented on a plate alongside foraged seaweed and anchovy 'sand', with a tomato essence poured over at the table. Main course might be a posh combo of fish and meat, matching pan-roasted fillet of Jersey brill (exemplary quality again) with melt-in-the-mouth braised oxtail, salsify and wild mushrooms and parmesan shavings, or there could be an assiette of Jersey beef – all accurately cooked and full of rich natural flavour – with lobster ravioli and beef consommé. Vegetarians are admirably well catered for here, with a dedicated vegetarian menu alongside the regular carte, offering the likes of goats' cheese bonbon with pickled beetroot, candied walnuts and beetroot sorbet to start, followed by a full-flavoured risotto of truffles and morel mushrooms with shaved parmesan and crème fraîche. Decisions get really tough at dessert time, when ideas display the same thought-provoking flavours spiked with a sense of fun – a blueberry snowball with lemon granité and white chocolate ice cream, for example, vying for your attention with a colourful and creative cream cheese crémeux with mandarin pearls and carrot cake ice cream. The sommelier is a real pro too, pointing you in the right direction with a globetrotting list that offers a good choice by the glass.

Chef Mark Jordan **Owner** Patrick Burke **Seats** 60, Pr/dining room 60 **Times** 12.30-2.30/7-10 Closed Jan **Prices** Fixed L 2 course £20, Fixed D 3 course £55, Tasting menu £80 **Wines** 509 bottles over £30, 41 bottles under £30, 35 by glass **Parking** 60 **Notes** Fixed ALC 2/3 course £55/£65, Tasting menu 7 course, Sunday L £30, Children welcome

Bohemia Restaurant

Modern French, British v

tel: 01534 880588 & 876500 **The Club Hotel & Spa, Green St JE2 4UH**
email: bohemia@huggler.com **web:** www.bohemiajersey.com
dir: *In town centre. 5 mins walk from main shopping centre*

Free-thinking creative cooking at a boutique spa hotel

As befits its senior status, Jersey has, more than any of the other Channel Islands, outgrown the region's reputation as a perfectly preserved vision of bygone days and entered the modern mainstream. Its most innovative hotels and restaurants wouldn't look out of place in any of the big mainland urban hubs, and yet of course they come with all the marine views and island landscapes that you don't tend to get in Clerkenwell. The Club Hotel is one such. Sitting in the centre of St Helier, it's a stunning boutique hotel, full of uncluttered, understated space inside, where natural tones create a soothing impact, at its best in the burnished wood and tiled floor of the Bohemia dining room (the restaurant is due to be refurbished in early 2015). Head chef Steve Smith's CV includes a lavishly garlanded stint in Melbourne, and something of the free-thinking creativity of Pacific Rim cuisine characterises his productions here. There are set menus galore, depending on whether your orientation is pescatarian, vegetarian or whadda-ya-got. Dinner might commence for all with a serving of rocket dressed in lemon and ginger, before diverging. The fish menu may go on with smoked haddock velouté and mustard ice cream, with an egg yolk dropped into it at the table, before a scallop and some truffled smoked eel turn up with celeriac and apple, and later a piece of turbot with shrimps, cauliflower and grapes. An omnivore table, meanwhile, might be setting about duck salad with rhubarb, walnuts and foiegras cream, prior to a take on coq au vin with chanterelles and Cévennes onions, with interludes for a langoustine with

parsnip and sea herbs in smoked butter, and a tasting of beetroot with verjus and lemon thyme. It should be clear that there is plenty of experimentation going on here, but dishes are carefully thought through, and the combinations work soundly and impressively, not least for the array of technical expertise marshalled in their construction or deconstruction. A re-imagined kirroyale acts as pre-dessert to compositions such as blackberries and pressed apple in black butter, or sour cherry soufflé with chocolate sorbet. The vegetarian menu is just as dynamically inventive: expect cauliflower with curried raisins, carrots and coriander, before a Jerusalem artichoke risotto enriched with St Maure de Touraine goats' cheese. Wine flights to match lead you boldly away from the realms of Sauvignon towards Chilean Gewürztraminer, New Zealand Gamay and Austrian Grüner Veltliner.

Chef Steve Smith **Owner** Lawrence Huggler **Seats** 60, Pr/dining room 24 **Times** 12-2.30/6.30-10 Closed 24-30 Dec, Sun -ex BH, BH Mon **Prices** Fixed L 2 course fr £19.95, Fixed D 3 course fr £59, Tasting menu £75-£85 **Wines** 24 by glass **Parking** 20, Opposite on Green Street **Notes** ALC 3 course £59, Surprise L/D menu 6 course £45/£49, Children welcome

ST CLEMENT   Map 24

Green Island Restaurant

British, Mediterranean

tel: 01534 857787 **Green Island JE2 6LS**
email: info@greenisland.je

Great local seafood in bustling beach café

This laid-back beach café and restaurant stakes its claim to the title of most southerly eatery in the British Isles, so kick back and bask in its sun-kissed views over sandy Green Island bay. As you'd hope in this briny location, the emphasis is firmly on fish and shellfish, and the kitchen has the nous to treat them with a light touch to let the freshness and quality do the talking, as in an ultra-simple dish of freshly-landed sole meunière with Jersey potatoes and salad. If it's meat you're after, tarragon-crusted roast rack and braised shank of lamb with boulangère potatoes, garlicky flageolet beans and baby carrots, roasted root vegetables and garlic might be up for grabs, and to finish, a classic crème brûlée with sablé biscuits should strike a suitably Gallic note.

Chef Paul Insley **Owner** Alan M Winch **Seats** 40 **Times** 12-2.30/7-9.30 Closed Xmas, New Year, Jan, Mon, D Sun **Prices** Fixed L 2 course fr £16.50, Fixed D 3 course fr £23.50, Starter £8.50-£9.75, Main £17.50-£26.95, Dessert £6-£6.95, Service optional **Wines** 20 bottles over £30, 20 bottles under £30, 5 by glass **Parking** 20, Public car park adjacent **Notes** Fixed D £23.50 Tue-Thu, Sunday L £18.50-£21.50, Vegetarian available, Children welcome

ST HELIER   Map 24

Best Western Royal Hotel

Modern European

tel: 01534 726521 **26 David Place JE2 4TD**
email: manager@royalhoteljersey.com **web:** www.morvanhotels.com
dir: Follow signs for Ring Rd, pass Queen Victoria rdbt keep left, left at lights, left into Piersons Rd. Follow one-way system to Cheapside, Rouge Bouillon, at A14 turn to Midvale Rd, hotel on left

Trendily presented food in a smart hotel

The Royal has been accommodating guests since the early Victorian era, when it was more humbly known as Bree's Boarding House. A wide stone-coloured frontage makes a bright and fresh impression, as does the light-filled white dining room known as Seasons, where smartly clothed tables and comfortable leather upholstery make for a relaxing ambience. Trendy presentations on black slate distinguish beginners such as tea-smoked duck with a salad of celeriac, apple, raisins and hazelnuts, while scallops get paired modishly with chorizo in red pepper coulis. Main courses up the ante for classic luxuries such as tournedos Rossini in wild mushrooms and Madeira with potato and bacon gratin, or sea bass with shellfish risotto in chive beurre blanc. Tarte Tatin with Jersey butter ice cream is a beautifully rendered dessert, only thrown off balance by the addition of no fewer than three sauces where one would do perfectly well, or there may be black cherry clafoutis.

Chef Alun Williams **Owner** Morvan Hotels **Seats** 90, Pr/dining room 12 **Times** 6.30-9 Closed L all week **Prices** Fixed D 3 course fr £23.95, Service optional **Wines** 3 bottles over £30, 38 bottles under £30, 7 by glass **Parking** 14 **Notes** Vegetarian available, Children welcome

Bohemia Restaurant

– see page 577

Grand Jersey

– see opposite

Ormer

– see opposite

Restaurant Sirocco@The Royal Yacht

Modern British

tel: 01534 720511 **The Weighbridge JE2 3NF**
email: reception@theroyalyacht.com **web:** www.theroyalyacht.com
dir: Adjacent to Weighbridge Park overlooking Jersey Harbour

Cool, contemporary hotel with confident team in the kitchen

Bringing a touch of glamour to the harbourside, The Royal Hotel is a slick, modern place with high-end facilities including a swish spa and a host of eating options. Pick of the bunch is the Sirocco restaurant, which had a recent makeover to bring even more designer chic to proceedings, with tones of magenta and funky light fittings, while keeping the views over the harbour. The team in the kitchen are dedicated to delivering local ingredients and the menus – à la carte and tasting versions – showcase the kitchen's ambition. These are pin-sharp modern dishes, with successful flavour combinations and plenty of technical ability on display. A first-course dish of seared scallops brings some fashionable surf 'n' turf to the table, accompanied by barbeque pork cheek (plus parsnip purée), while another starter combines slow-cooked organic salmon with its smoked roe and black pudding. Main-course roast turbot has a pine nut crust and comes with lobster cannelloni, and, for dessert, there is rhubarb pannacotta and crisps with strawberry meringue and sorbet.

Chef Steve Walker **Owner** Lodestar Group, The Royal Yacht **Seats** 65, Pr/dining room 20 **Times** 12-4/7-10 Closed L Mon-Sat **Prices** Fixed D 3 course £27.50, Starter £8.50-£10.50, Main £16-£31, Dessert £8.50, Service optional 10% **Wines** 108 bottles over £30, 49 bottles under £30, 20 by glass **Parking** Car park **Notes** Tasting menu available, Weekly rotating Table d'hôte menu, Sunday L £24.50, Vegetarian available, Children welcome

See advert on page 580

Grand Jersey

ST HELIER   Map 24

Modern British   NOTABLE WINE LIST

tel: 01534 722301 **The Esplanade JE2 3QA**
email: reservations@grandjersey.com **web:** www.grandjersey.com
dir: *Located on St Helier seafront*

Luxurious island cooking in an understated bayfront hotel

The Grand Jersey doesn't look especially palatial from the outside, at least not if you're expecting a towering temple of Victorian splendour. Inside, however, a different prospect emerges, of modern plush enhanced by subdued lighting, a bright white pilastered foyer, a spacious lounge given over to the consumption of champagne and, in Tassili, an elegantly understated modern dining room. Simple table settings, wall-recess glass stores and nouveau presentations on slate plates and such establish the tone, while the prospect over St Aubin's Bay is bound to gentle the senses to a state of serenity. Local and therefore seasonal island produce is, as one would hope, the backbone of Richard Allen's culinary production, with a range of fixed-price menus to lure you in. If you can't bear the suspense of a menu surprise, there are itemised tasters, including pescatarian and vegetarian versions, as well as the carte. With so much choice, it's hard to know where to start, but Jersey lobster Caesar-style with lobster jelly and avocado can't be a bad place. For an equally luxurious alternative, consider foie gras parfait with smoked duck, in a complicated but happy medium of chocolate, pine nuts, chamomile and Ximénez sherry vinegar. At main course, there may be variations on lamb, featuring a serving of the best end alongside a casserole and a haggis bonbon, simply dressed in rocket and tomato, or turbot with chancre crab and quinoa, aromatised with saffron and pennywort. On the vegetarian slate, you'd have got to a sea-vegetable risotto with poached quail egg by now, to follow your truffled cep espuma, while desserts produce intricate but indubitably comforting combinations like warm ginger cake with gingerbread mousse, poached rhubarb and black butter ice cream. Cheeses from the trolley are served with Lavoche crispbread and fruit-and-nut loaf.

Chef Richard Allen **Owner** Redefine BDL Hotels **Seats** 25 **Times** 12-2.30/7-9.30 Closed Sun-Mon, L Tue-Thu **Prices** Prices not confirmed, Service optional 10% **Wines** 14 by glass **Parking** 32, NCP **Notes** Tasting menu 6 course, Chef's surprise menu 9 course, Sunday L, Vegetarian available, No children

Ormer

ST HELIER   Map 24

British, French **v NEW**

tel: 01534 725100 **7-11 Don St JE2 4TQ**
email: book@ormerjersey.com
dir: *Phone for directions*

Shaun Rankin's welcome return to St Helier's restaurant scene

It was a sad day for St Helier's foodies when Shaun Rankin announced he was leaving Bohemia restaurant at the swish Club Hotel, but thankfully he didn't go far: here he is, running his own place in the centre of town, and it's a real gem. The site on Dom Street has been lavishly done out with hints of art deco style (the refurb totalled £1.4 million, apparently) and it looks stunning with its wooden floors, chandeliers, plush blue velvet and mustard yellow leather seating, and darkwood tables simply decorated with small lamps. There's a lively bar on the ground floor, a fab terrace on the street out front – prime for a spot of people watching – and upstairs a smart private dining room and a roof garden and cigar terrace for those balmier Jersey days. And so to the food: Rankin is a firm believer in the superlative quality of Jersey's produce from land and sea, and thus his menus showcase the best the island has to offer in dishes that impress with their depth of natural flavour and beautiful presentation; seasonality and freshness are the watchwords here. Take a starter of Jersey lobster, the meat served along with scallop and crab in a single large ravioli (perfectly cooked pasta), with a fresh-tasting tomato bisque, flavours of ginger and coriander, and some puffed black rice for textural contrast – a hugely enjoyable opener. Pork belly with calamari, Teruel ham, parmesan custard, butternut squash, chorizo and apple dressing might be the inventive follow on, the calamari lightly chargrilled and maintaining its moistness, and the pork accurately timed and singing with flavour. More treats follow, with desserts like popcorn brownie with malted ice cream and salted caramel, and some excellent petit fours served, cleverly, in a wooden trug on a base of (chocolate) soil, designed to resemble some freshly pulled Jersey Royal potatoes.

Chef Shaun Rankin **Owner** Shaun Rankin, Nick Bettany **Seats** 70, Pr/dining room 14 **Times** 12-2.30/6.30-10 Closed 25 Dec, Sun **Prices** Fixed L 2 course fr £19, Fixed D 3 course fr £29, Tasting menu fr £75, Starter £10-£16, Main £22-£30, Dessert £9 **Wines** 196 bottles over £30, 48 bottles under £30, 15 by glass **Parking** On street, Sand Street car park **Notes** Spring Market D menu available 3 course, Children welcome

★ ★ ★ ★
HOTEL • SPA • RESTAURANTS

Great food on another level

FIRST FLOOR
THE ROYAL YACHT

DISCOVER DELECTABLE FOOD, EXQUISITE WINES
AND A RELAXED FRIENDLY ATMOSPHERE

RESERVATIONS RECOMMENDED PLEASE CALL 720511

Sirocco

THE ROYAL YACHT WEIGHBRIDGE ST HELIER • TEL 01534 720511 • WWW.SIROCCOJERSEY.COM

ST PETER — Map 24

Greenhills Country Hotel

Mediterranean, British, French

tel: 01534 481042 **Mont de L'Ecole JE3 7EL**
email: reserve@greenhillshotel.com **web:** www.greenhillshotel.com
dir: A1 signed St Peters Valley (A11). 4m, turn right onto E112

Contemporary cooking of Jersey's fine produce

A riot of colour, the hotel's garden is a treat, but then again, there is a lot to like about Greenhills. Dating from the 17th century, the building has traditional charm inside and out, and a restaurant where the tables are dressed in white linen ready and waiting for the Anglo-European output from the team in the kitchen. The ambitious repertoire might see Jersey Bay scallops served with a pancetta crisp, caper berries, sweetcorn purée and a garnish of fresh raspberries, before main-course lamb Wellington or pan-fried sea bass with asparagus salad, warm potatoes, baby vegetables, tomato concasse, tarragon vinegar and champagne sauce. There's no less endeavour in the desserts, with yoghurt and mango tart served on a raspberry coulis with blackcurrant sorbet and fresh fruit garnish.

Chef Marcin Dudek **Owner** Seymour Hotels **Seats** 90, Pr/dining room 40 **Times** 12.30-2/7-9.30 Closed 21 Dec-12 Feb **Prices** Fixed L 2 course £13, Fixed D 3 course £29.50, Starter £5.50-£9.50, Main £11.50-£24.50, Dessert £4.25-£7.50, Service optional **Wines** 19 bottles over £30, 62 bottles under £30, 8 by glass **Parking** 45 **Notes** ALC specialities, Sunday L £21, Vegetarian available, Children welcome

Mark Jordan at the Beach

Anglo French

tel: 01534 780180 **La Plage, La Route de la Haule JE3 7YD**
email: bookings@markjordanatthebeach.com
dir: A1 W from St Helier, left mini-rdbt towards St Aubins, follow sign 50mtrs on left

Anglo-French fish dishes next to the beach

A suave, sea-breezy feel imbues the Atlantic Hotel, which is hardly surprising as only the promenade road separates it from the beach at St Peter. On sunny days when the sea sparkles, it comes into its own, the more so for having a dining room where a signature chef gets to strut his stuff. It's a pleasant white-walled space with wicker chairs and fish pictures, which gives you all the clue you need as to what the forte is. The style is contemporary Anglo-French, as befits the location, seen in a starter quartet of delicately seared scallops with a wedge of improbably successful roasted cucumber in chive beurre blanc. Next up might be a piece of sea bass, its scored skin crisp, the flesh properly opalescent, served amid a ring of steamed mussels, alongside crushed new potatoes mixed with crabmeat. If you're dead set on meat, you won't be neglected, either for lamb rump with dauphinoise, or Jordan's take on coq au vin. Dessert brings the sweet simplicity of an apple tarte fine with sticky apple sauce and toffee ice cream.

Chef Mark Jordan, Benjamin Crick **Owner** Mark Jordan, Patrick Burke **Seats** 50 **Times** 12-2.30/6-9.30 Closed Jan, Mon (winter), D Sun (winter) **Prices** Fixed L 2 course £19.50, Fixed D 3 course £27.50, Starter £7.50-£13.50, Main £14.50-£21.50, Dessert £6-£9.50, Service optional **Wines** 27 bottles over £30, 23 bottles under £30, 6 by glass **Parking** 16 **Notes** Sunday L £27.50, Vegetarian available, Children welcome

ST SAVIOUR — Map 24

Longueville Manor Hotel

— see below

Longueville Manor Hotel

ST SAVIOUR — Map 24

Modern Anglo-French V NOTABLE WINE LIST
tel: 01534 725501 **JE2 7WF**
email: info@longuevillemanor.com **web:** www.longuevillemanor.com
dir: From St Helier take A3 to Gorey, hotel 0.75m on left

Accomplished country-hotel cooking in an ancient house

There's history in the stones, as one of Jersey's most venerable buildings dates in part all the way back to the Norman era, although the facade is a mere 16th-century stripling. Longueville stands in 17 acres of immaculately maintained gardens, perfect for strolling in, and has been the destination place for the full country-house hotel package on the biggest Channel Island since its transformation into a hotel just after the second world war. There's history in the panelling too, the wood that furnishes the Oak Room restaurant having been carved from oak chests lifted as spoils of war from the Spanish Armada. And it's almost tempting to say there's history in the kitchen too, since Andrew Baird has been in residency here for over 20 years. His culinary style has moved judiciously with the times over that longue durée, without ever chasing global trends for their own sake. A kitchen garden supplying vegetables, herbs and salad leaves was a fixture here long before it became fashionable everywhere else, and local fish and shellfish and island livestock provision the menus too. An Anglo-French orientation suits the geography of the place, producing a starter range that takes in goats' cheese fondant with caramelised red onion, apple and pecans, as well as scallops with pork belly and black pudding, while main courses draw on classical culinary modes for wrapping a saddle of rabbit in Parma ham, presenting flavourful deep-water halibut in a lightly curried mussel ragoût with sea asparagus, or adding a tortellino of oxtail to grilled Angus fillet and woodland mushrooms. At close of business, there may be passionfruit soufflé with raspberry ripple sorbet, or a modish sphere of Valrhona, served with Bailey's ice cream, hazelnut mousse and banana. French and British artisan cheeses perambulate the room on a trolley of 180-year-old French oak.

Chef Andrew Baird **Owner** Malcolm Lewis **Seats** 65, Pr/dining room 22 **Times** 12.30-2/7-10 **Prices** Fixed D 3 course £60-£64.50 **Wines** 300 bottles over £30, 69 bottles under £30, 25 by glass **Parking** 45 **Notes** Discovery menu with/without wine £80-£110, ALC 2/3 course, Sunday L, Children welcome

TRINITY
Map 24

Water's Edge Hotel

🏵 Modern British

tel: 01534 862777 **Bouley Bay JE3 5AS**
email: info@watersedgejersey.com **web:** www.watersedgejersey.com
dir: 10-15 mins from St Helier, A9 N onto A8 then onto B31, follow signs to Bouley Bay

Sea views and cooking that aims high

Tucked into the cliffs of Bouley Bay a wave's lap from the briny, the Water's Edge is aptly named. The view from the restaurant is hard to beat, looking across an unbroken expanse of sea to the distant coast of France, and the food also merits serious attention. A new kitchen team took the reins in April 2013 and is keen to stamp its mark on the local foodie scene, hauling in the finest local produce and delivering it in well-executed, easy-on-the-eye dishes. Fish and seafood are naturally a strong suit – perhaps salmon tartare to start, ahead of braised shin of Jersey Angus beef which arrives with slices of fillet and foie gras, roasted baby beets, glazed carrots, sautéed leeks and horseradish duchesse potatoes. The ambition continues to a well-crafted finale involving pear tarte Tatin and an unusual yet effective ice cream of Jersey Blue cheese and walnuts.

Times 12-2.30/6.30-9

SARK

SARK
Map 24

La Sablonnerie

🏵 Modern, Traditional International

tel: 01481 832061 **Little Sark GY10 1SD**
email: reservations@sablonneriesark.com **web:** www.sablonneriesark.com
dir: On southern part of island. Horse & carriage transport to hotel

Uncomplicated ways with home-grown produce on a special island

Visiting this charming whitewashed 400-year old former farmhouse on the tiny island of Sark is a step back in time. Even the journey there is medieval: the island is car free, so the hotel sends a vintage horse-drawn carriage to pick you up from the ferry and trundle down the single lane track to an idyllic haven. Beautiful gardens are perfect for dining alfresco and taking in the unpolluted air, and inside, low beams, exposed stone walls and a coal fire make for a cosy dining experience.

Just-landed lobster is a speciality, and other seafood is treated without fuss, perhaps roasted scallops with garlic butter, or halibut ravioli with hollandaise. Much of the produce comes from the hotel's own farm and gardens, guaranteeing freshness and seasonality. Look for caramelised duckling breast with green peppercorn sauce, or veal with Madeira sauce and wild mushrooms. To finish there might be cappuccino crème brûlée, or lemon tart with Sark cream.

Chef Colin Day **Owner** Elizabeth Perrée **Seats** 39 **Times** 12-2.30/7-9.30 Closed mid Oct-Etr **Prices** Fixed L 2 course £26.50, Fixed D 3 course £34.50, Tasting menu £39.50, Starter £9.80, Main £17.50, Dessert £9.50 **Wines** 16 bottles over £30, 50 bottles under £30, 6 by glass **Notes** Sunday L, Vegetarian available, Children welcome

Stocks Hotel

🏵🏵 Modern British **NEW**

tel: 01481 832001 & 832444 **GY10 1SD**
email: reception@stockshotel.com **web:** www.stockshotel.com
dir: From Jersey or Guernsey via ferry to Sark harbour. Transfer to hotel approx 20 mins by foot, bicycle or carriage

Fine classically focused dining in a secluded valley

Sitting in a quiet and picturesque valley – but then again just about everywhere on Sark is quiet and picturesque – Stocks is a smart hotel built around a farmhouse dating from the mid-1700s. It's done out in a traditional manner, and that goes for the fine-dining restaurant, too. There's also a bistro by the swimming pool and an atmospheric bar. The main restaurant serves up plenty of local ingredients in bright, classically-focused modern dishes, with traditional lunches on Sundays. Rabbit loin is wrapped in Parma ham and roasted as a first course, served with apple and celeriac purée, and among main courses might be local sea bass partnered with braised celery, lobster sauce and chervil foam. Honey and Drambuie parfait is a dessert that shows good technical skills, served with a praline biscuit, and meals are preceded by canapés and breads served with excellent (and strong) local butter.

Chef Pascal Lemoine **Owner** Alex & Helen Magell **Seats** 60, Pr/dining room 12 **Times** 12-2.30/7-9 Closed Jan-Mar **Prices** Fixed L 2 course £26.25, Fixed D 3 course £35, Tasting menu £70, Starter £10.50-£13.95, Main £17.95-£26.95, Dessert £8.75-£12.95, Service optional **Wines** 57 bottles over £30, 24 bottles under £30, 6 by glass **Parking** 36, Bicycle spaces only **Notes** Champagne afternoon tea £49.50 for 2, Ride & Dine £95 for 2, Sunday L £15-£24.50, Vegetarian available, Children welcome

ISLE OF MAN

DOUGLAS Map 24 SC37

JAR Restaurant

 Modern, International, Pacific Rim

tel: 01624 663553 & 629551 **Admiral House Hotel, 12 Loch Promenade IM1 2LX**
email: jar@admiralhouse.com **web:** www.jar.co.im
dir: *Located 2 mins from Douglas Ferry Terminal. 20 mins from airport*

Sharp cooking using prime Manx produce in grand hotel

Set within the Victorian Admiral House Hotel, in a prime site on the promenade, JAR Restaurant has been given a clean, modern, spruced-up look. The menu opens with a selection of grazing-size dishes for sharing. Strong among them are sashimi, sushi and tempura rolls, taking in yellowfin tuna, teriyaki beef, smoked duck and squid with lime. Those who prefer the more conventional three-course route can opt for one of the 'small plates' for first course: perhaps beetroot-cured salmon and fennel salad, chicken, lime and coconut salad, or beef tartare. The kitchen buys only the best Manx produce and turns out dishes of bold combinations and vibrant flavours. Main courses have included roast cod fillet with squid ink, quinoa, spring onions and chilli, and roast monkfish with razor clams, chorizo and squid as well as more conventional roast duck breast with a parcel of leg meat, shallots and pak choi. End with familiar-sounding lemon crème brûlée with raspberry sorbet.

Chef Noel Breaks **Owner** Branwell Ltd **Seats** 48 **Times** 12-2/6-10 Closed 26-30 Dec, Sun-Tue, L Sat **Prices** Starter £4-£21.50, Main £14.50-£28, Service optional **Wines** 34 bottles over £30, 12 bottles under £30, 7 by glass **Parking** Free parking opposite **Notes** Tasting menu available, Vegetarian available, Children welcome

What makes a 5-Rosette restaurant?
See page 9

Get the most out of the AA Restaurant Guide
See page 6

Read our interview with chef Michael Caines on page 29

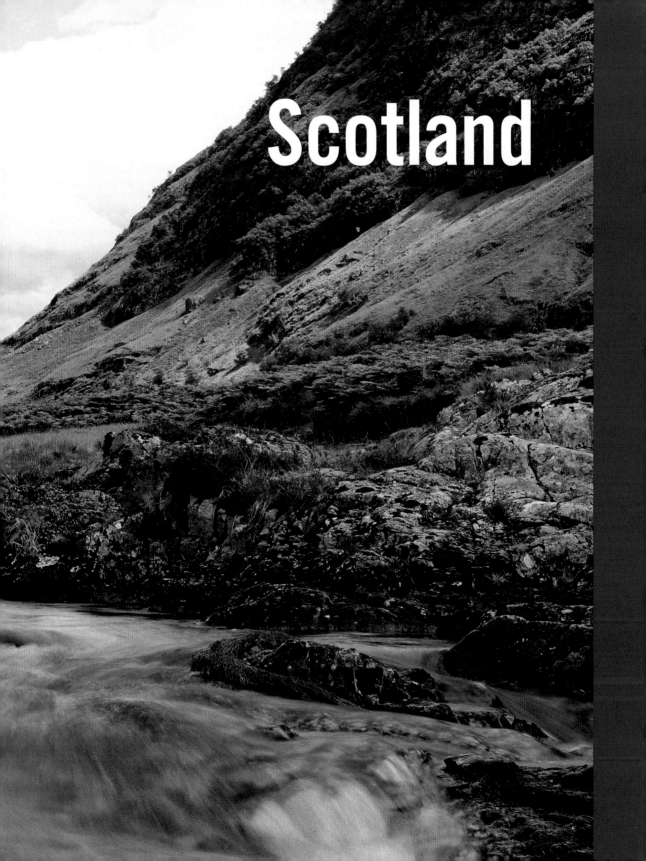

Scotland

CITY OF ABERDEEN

ABERDEEN Map 23 NJ90

The Adelphi Kitchen

 Modern British

tel: 01224 211414 & 07912 666256 **28 Adelphi AB11 5BL**
email: hello@theadelphikitchen.co.uk
dir: Off Union St

Switched-on barbecue restaurant with an upbeat vibe

Chris and Lynsey Tonner's restaurant in the Adelphi district of the city took a radical departure from its previous incarnation in 2013, emerging with the new monicker and a reinvented culinary concept. The latter has installed an open-pit barbecue in the kitchen to deliver impeccably-sourced local meat and seafood cooked 'dirty' – that's to say directly on the hot charcoal – with clear influences from those good ol' stateside barbecue-meisters and their racy Tex-Mex flavours . The place still has a buzz about it, with young, cheery staff keeping the mood casual and upbeat, and the kitchen sending out pan-fried scallops with tempura roe, asparagus, and smoked tomato and shellfish bisque sauce, followed by venison loin alongside potatoes with crispy chorizo, a mix of beetroots, confit cherry tomatoes and tomato jus. At dessert stage, sour cherry sorbet is a clever idea to cut through the richness of a double chocolate, bourbon and ginger brownie.

Times 12-2.30/5-9.45 Closed 1st 2 wks Jan, Sun

Malmaison Aberdeen

 Modern British

tel: 01224 327370 **49-53 Queens Rd AB15 4YP**
email: info.aberdeen@malmaison.com **web:** www.malmaisonaberdeen.com
dir: A90, 3rd exit onto Queens Rd at 3rd rdbt, hotel on right

Cool contemporary brasserie with theatre kitchen

Built from the solid granite that gives the city its moniker, the Aberdeen branch of the Malmaison group is suitably dashing, with boutique allure and a cool industrial-chic finish. The brasserie is at the heart of the operation, literally at the centre in this case, with exposed pipework on the high ceiling, and the rustic colours are moody, chic and reminiscent of the Scottish Highlands. The open-to-view kitchen reveals the Josper Grill, the source of a good deal of what follows. When it comes to red meat, you can pick out what you fancy through the glass partition. Start with chicken liver parfait with fig chutney and toasted brioche, or maybe a Thai roast pumpkin soup (there are no borders here). Next up, something from that Josper: a whopping T-bone, perhaps, or rib-eye, but there are other options such as smoked haddock fishcake with a warm poached egg, or a veggie risotto with pumpkin, tallegio, walnuts and sage. There are tasty-sounding burgers, too.

Chef John Burns **Owner** Malmaison **Seats** 90, Pr/dining room 30
Times 12-2.30/5.30-10.30 Closed D 25 Dec **Prices** Fixed L 2 course £15.95-£35, Fixed D 3 course £19.95-£60 **Wines** 26 bottles over £30, 16 bottles under £30, 27 by glass **Parking** 30 **Notes** Brunch available £22.95, Sunday L, Vegetarian available, Children welcome

Maryculter House Hotel

 Modern British

tel: 01224 732124 **South Deeside Rd, Maryculter AB12 5GB**
email: info@maryculterhousehotel.com **web:** www.maryculterhousehotel.com
dir: Off A90 to S of Aberdeen and onto B9077. Hotel is located 8m on right, 0.5m beyond Lower Deeside Caravan Park

Classical cooking in a characterful setting beside the River Dee

The location has connections to the Knights Templar and the house itself has bags of charm and character, standing on the banks of the River Dee (with fishing rights). The hotel's Priory restaurant doesn't lack period charm either, with stone walls and flickering candles, plus tables formally dressed for fine dining. There's an informal brasserie, too. The main event sees a menu of classically-minded dishes that might start with a confit duck and pear terrine served with a celeriac remoulade and mixed leaves dressed in a honey and mustard vinaigrette. Next up, main course might see salmon (as you might hope around here), pan-fried and partnered with wilted greens, fondant potato and a fishy chive cream. For dessert, a slice of dark chocolate tart with perfectly thin pastry comes with pistachio ice cream and chocolate truffles. There's a tasting menu, too, plus a slate of well-kept cheeses.

Chef Adam McKenzie **Owner** James Gilbert **Seats** 58, Pr/dining room 30 **Times** 6-9 Closed L all week **Prices** Starter £5.50-£6.50, Main £14.95-£16.95, Dessert £5.50-£6.95, Service optional **Wines** 19 bottles over £30, 13 bottles under £30, 3 by glass **Parking** 60 **Notes** 7 course gourmet menu on certain dates, Sunday L, Vegetarian available, Children 4 yrs+

Mercure Aberdeen Ardoe House Hotel & Spa

 Modern Scottish, French

tel: 01224 860600 **South Deeside Rd AB12 5YP**
email: h6626-dm@accor.com **web:** www.mercure.com
dir: 4m W of city off B9077

19th-century hotel with 21st-century cooking

The soaring towers and grand gables of this old greystone house give a fine impression of an ancient castle, but actually it was built as a family home back in the 1870s. Three miles from the city centre and surrounded by 30 acres of grounds, these days it's a smart hotel with a spa and all mod-cons. The exterior may speak of traditional comfort, elegance and old-world grandeur, but indoors the designers have revamped the old girl with a jazzy contemporary look that carries through to the sleek new lines of Blair's Restaurant. The kitchen takes a modish path, turning out suitably unbuttoned and up-to-date dishes. These go from crispy salt and pepper-battered whitebait with lime and confit garlic aïoli, to main-course cod, crusted with chorizo and pimento and matched with spring onion and pea risotto and fennel and orange cream. Finish with rhubarb and custard pannacotta with poached rhubarb and shortbread.

Times 12.30-3.30/6.30-9.30

Norwood Hall Hotel

Modern British

tel: 01224 868951 **Garthdee Rd, Cults AB15 9FX**
email: info@norwood-hall.co.uk **web:** www.norwood-hall.co.uk
dir: *Off A90, at 1st rdbt cross Bridge of Dee, left at rdbt onto Garthdee Rd (B&Q & Sainsburys on left) continue to hotel sign*

Victorian mansion showcasing fine Scottish produce

Built in 1881 on the site of 15th-century Pitfodels Castle, Norwood is a magnificent Victorian mansion with all of its period grandeur still present and correct. A sweeping oak staircase, stained-glass windows and ornate fireplaces are all as impressive as you might expect, while the restaurant is a suitably grand oak-panelled room hung with tapestries. Friendly and efficient service sets the right tone to banish any trace of starchiness, and the menu takes an accessible modern approach based on top-class seasonal produce. You might open proceedings with venison, black pudding and pork terrine with honey pickled beetroot and date purée, then move on to something like pan-fried fillet of wild sea bass with curried lentils and spicy carrot salad. Meat eaters could tackle navarin of lamb with root vegetables, potato purée and red wine jus, and for pudding, a please-all approach takes in sticky toffee pudding with vanilla ice cream or cranachan cheesecake with raspberry coulis.

Chef Kenny McMillian, Neil Ireland **Owner** Monument Leisure **Seats** 48, Pr/dining room 180 **Times** 12-2.30/6-9.45 **Prices** Prices not confirmed, Service optional **Wines** 46 bottles over £30, 24 bottles under £30, 12 by glass **Parking** 140 **Notes** Sunday L, Vegetarian available, No children

The Silver Darling

French, Seafood

tel: 01224 576229 **Pocra Quay, North Pier AB11 5DQ**
email: silverdarling@hotmail.co.uk
dir: *At Aberdeen Harbour entrance*

Interesting ways with superbly fresh seafood

As befits its quayside location at the mouth of Aberdeen harbour, The Silver Darling has a firm focus on the bounty of the sea. The name is a colloquial reference to the herring that were once the bedrock of the local economy, and you can watch the trawlers come and go once you have ascended the spiral staircase to the luminous conservatory-style dining room perched atop a stocky granite building. The appetite for fish and seafood duly stimulated, the kitchen fulfills its part of the deal via a menu of French-accented contemporary ideas, with the odd foray into far-Eastern flavours. A clever starter sees mackerel served three ways – rillettes on toast, a little fishy burger, and pickled – accompanied by a stimulating mix of cucumber, fennel and dill, and apple and celery remoulade. Main course brings a splendid fillet of sea trout with Jerusalem artichoke purée, asparagus, and a turbocharged hit of vibrant Bois Boudran dressing. Desserts are impressive too – pannacotta is infused with vanilla seeds and served with rhubarb that has been poached or flavours a vibrant sorbet.

Chef Didier Dejean **Owner** Didier Dejean, Karen Murray **Seats** 50, Pr/dining room 8 **Times** 12-1.45/6.30-9.30 Closed Xmas-New Year, Sun, L Sat **Prices** Fixed L 2 course fr £19.50 **Wines** 26 bottles over £30, 14 bottles under £30, 10 by glass **Parking** On quayside **Notes** Vegetarian available, Children welcome

ABERDEENSHIRE

BALLATER Map 23 NO39

Darroch Learg Hotel

Modern Scottish **NOTABLE WINE LIST**

tel: 01339 755443 **56 Braemar Rd AB35 5UX**
email: enquiries@darrochlearg.co.uk **web:** www.darrochlearg.co.uk
dir: *On A93 at the W end of village*

Country house with modern Scottish cooking and wonderful views

Darroch Learg means 'the oak wood on the sunny hillside' in old Gaelic, and this small country-house hotel, which has been in the Franks family for over 40 years, is every bit as appealing as its name suggests. There are lovely walks from the hotel grounds to the top of the hill, where you're rewarded with a fantastic view over Ballater. Originally built as a country residence in 1888, the hotel is no less special inside: oak panelling and antiques abound, and diners can soak up the views across the valley in the restaurant, which extends into a conservatory. The kitchen team proudly uses the best of the local larder in its modern Scottish cooking, presented on daily-changing menus. Pan-fried Loch Fyne scallops are perfectly cooked and come with curried cauliflower purée, apple shallot vinaigrette and pakora, while breast of Gressingham duck is pan-seared and served with celeriac purée, pak choi and Puy lentil jus in a beautifully presented main course. Finish with classic lemon tart and berry sauce.

Chef John Jeremiah **Owner** The Franks family **Seats** 48 **Times** 12.30-2/7-9 Closed Xmas, last 3 wks Jan, L Mon-Sat **Prices** Fixed D 3 course £45-£51, Tasting menu fr £55 **Wines** 98 bottles over £30, 33 bottles under £30, 4 by glass **Parking** 15 **Notes** Sunday L fr £27.50, Vegetarian available, Children welcome

Follow the AA on twitter @TheAA_Lifestyle

BALLATER *continued*

Loch Kinord Hotel

◉ Modern British

tel: 01339 885229 **Ballater Rd, Dinnet AB34 5JY**
email: stay@lochkinord.com **web:** www.lochkinord.com
dir: *Between Aboyne & Ballater, on A93, in Dinnet*

Classical cooking in Royal Deeside

Built in rock-solid granite in the Victorian period, Loch Kinord is well placed for maximising time spent in Royal Deeside, whether that's the renowned fishing, a wee spot of whisky tasting, or simply walking in the glorious hills. There are homely lounges within where real fires keep you toasty, a small bar and a dining room newly done out with tartan wallpaper and plush red and gold carpets. There's a classical leaning to the kitchen's output, evident understanding of culinary ways, and a good showing of regional produce to inject a sense of place. Game terrine with red onion marmalade and toasted brioche is a typical starter, followed perhaps by rack of lamb with mustard and herb crust, the meat perfectly pink and tender, served with braised red cabbage and black pudding mash. Chocolate fondant oozes in all the right places and comes with a scoop of intensely flavoured vanilla ice cream.

Times 6.30-9 Closed L all week

BALMEDIE Map 23 NJ91

Cock & Bull

◉ Modern Scottish, British **V**

tel: 01358 743249 **Ellon Rd, Blairton AB23 8XY**
email: info@thecockandbull.co.uk **web:** www.thecockandbull.co.uk
dir: *6m N of Aberdeen on A90*

Big flavours at a distinctive country inn

The Cock & Bull is a pub of the gastro variety, a low-slung establishment built in the 19th century with all the incumbent character. There are wooden beams and

real fires, but there's nothing stuck in the past about this particular pub: modern food and local artworks ensure that a visit is very much of our time. The art is for sale if it takes your fancy. Eat in either the conservatory dining room, cosy lounge in front of the fire, or the main restaurant, where traditional decor is gently updated to meet modern expectations. There's an all-day menu containing a good amount of regional goodies and modern-leaning ideas: black pudding Scotch egg, for example, with home-made brown sauce, or king scallops with autumn squash and coal oil. Next up, Gressingham duck leg confit, or the gourmet hot dog made with pulled pork, and, for dessert, dark chocolate fondant with honeycomb ice cream.

Chef Ryan Paterson **Owner** Rodger Morrison **Seats** 80, Pr/dining room 30 **Times** 10.30-late Closed 26 Dec, 2 Jan, All-day dining **Prices** Starter £5.95-£6.95, Main £9.95-£18.95, Dessert £7, Service optional **Wines** 11 bottles over £30, 24 bottles under £30, 7 by glass **Notes** Sunday L £21.95-£24.95, Children welcome

BANCHORY Map 23 NO69

Cow Shed

◉◉ Modern Scottish

tel: 01330 820813 **Beamoir Rd AB31 5QB**
email: info@cowshedrestaurant.co.uk
dir: *A93 from Aberdeen, right at Tesco on Hill of Banchory East, at T-junct right onto A980, second left*

Regional Scottish cuisine in a converted dairy

You won't actually be eating in the old cowshed here – that's still standing in the neighbouring field – but Graham Buchan's enterprising contemporary brasserie stands on the site of the old dairy. It's as pastoral a Highland setting as you could wish, in other words, with views over ploughed fields towards the Hill of Fayre. Any hint of twee rusticity has been banished though, thanks to an interior design featuring a viewable kitchen behind a sliding glass panel, an extensive wine store, and natural wood tones throughout. The infectious buzz that animates the place drifts up to the high ceiling, and the modern Scottish dishes do the rest. Deeside partridge is an impeccable example of the local bounty, the caramelised breast served with confit leg in an alternating stack along with sliced potato, puréed parsnip, crispy kale and a 'scorched' poached pear. That may follow a bowl of celeriac and mushroom velouté containing a fat raviolo stuffed complicatedly with ham hock, ricotta and black garlic purée. The technically skilful desserts include an unmoulded pumpkin brûlée topped with nougatine, garnished with cocoa nibs in syrup and coffee ice cream.

Chef Neil Hudson **Owner** Graham & Joy Buchan, David Mutter **Seats** 62 **Times** 12.30-3/6.30-9.30 Closed 1st wk Jan, Mon-Tue (Jan-Feb & Nov-Dec), L Mon-Sat, D Sun **Prices** Starter £5-£7.75, Main £15-£28, Dessert £5-£7.50, Service optional **Wines** 46 bottles over £30, 17 bottles under £30, 6 by glass **Parking** 36 **Notes** Sunday L £21.50-£26.50, Vegetarian available, Children welcome

Raemoir House Hotel

◎◎ Modern & Traditional British ▮NOTABLE WINE LIST

tel: 01330 824884 **Raemoir AB31 4ED**
email: hotel@raemoir.com **web:** www.raemoir.com
dir: A93 to Banchory then A980, hotel at x-rds after 2.5m

Modern country-house cooking in Royal Deeside

Raemoir House is set in 11 acres surrounded by the hills and forests of Royal Deeside. It was built in the Georgian period, its restaurant in what was the Oval Ballroom – all dark flocked velvet, 19th-century portraits and mirrors, a chandelier hanging from the corniced ceiling, and fires blazing in winter. Dinner is a set-price deal of four courses, plus coffee, with around four choices per course. A soup – perhaps spiced parsnip, with moreish breads – normally follows the starter, which might be something like a plate of smoked salmon with lemon curd, compressed cucumber and Keta caviar. Main courses are updated classical ideas: four slices of pink venison in rich gravy on a fricassee of wild mushrooms and shallots with green beans, parsnip purée and golden-topped dauphinoise, or perhaps smoked pollock fillet with sauce vierge, polenta and wilted greens. Dishes are artfully presented, as seen in puddings like white chocolate mousse sandwiched by sponge with a scoop of vivid passionfruit sorbet studded with cocoa nibs, the plate drizzled with rhubarb syrup and butterscotch sauce.

Chef Alexandria Hay **Owner** Neil & Julie Rae **Seats** 40, Pr/dining room 16
Times 12-2.30/5.30-9.30 **Prices** Service optional **Wines** 62 bottles over £30, 22 bottles under £30, 12 by glass **Parking** 50 **Notes** Tasting menu available, 4 course D £45, Sunday L £27-£32, Vegetarian available, Children 12yrs+

▮ CRATHES   Map 23 NO79

The Milton Brasserie

◎ Traditional British

tel: 01330 844566 & 844474 **AB31 5QH**
email: jay@miltonbrasserie.com
dir: On the A93, 15m W of Aberdeen, opposite Crathes Castle

Modern brasserie cooking in a cottage near the castle

Picturesquely sited near the castle at Crathes, not far from the Royal Deeside railway, The Milton is hardly a brasserie in the big-city sense. From the outside a charming whitewashed stone cottage, it has a countrified air within, complete with log-like pillars supporting a beamed ceiling and leathery, tweedy tones in the upholstery. The bill of fare, though, is more obviously in the modern idiom, starting with the likes of a fish and crab cake with fennel and dill chutney and russet-hued partan bree, as a prelude perhaps to lightly charred Barbary duck breast in Amarena cherry jus with cider fondant potato, or hake wrapped up in prosciutto with parsley risotto and a reduction of Noilly Prat. An individual cheesecake incorporating stewed rhubarb on a ginger biscuit base with rich custard ice cream is a neat way of combining two favourite dessert ideas, and there are Celtic cheeses with homemade oatcakes.

Chef Bob Miller **Owner** Jay Emmerson **Seats** 70, Pr/dining room 25 **Times** 12-2.30/6-9 Closed 25-26 Dec, 1-2 Jan, D Sun-Tue **Prices** Fixed D 3 course £25-£30, Service optional **Wines** 6 bottles over £30, 21 bottles under £30, 11 by glass **Parking** 70 **Notes** Sunday L £12-£20, Vegetarian available, Children welcome

---

▮ ELLON   Map 23 NJ93

Eat on the Green

◎◎ Traditional British, Scottish

tel: 01651 842337 **Udny Green AB41 7RS**
email: enquiries@eatonthegreen.co.uk **web:** www.eatonthegreen.co.uk
dir: A920 towards Udny Green/Ellon

Bright, modern cooking in a starry village inn

Craig Wilson is an enterprising chef and he's passionate about sharing his appreciation for fine Scottish ingredients. Ever fancied being a chef for the day? You can here, hands-on, as part of the team. There's also a champagne club, a chef's table (via a video link), and a private room on the first floor. And they even do afternoon tea. The two charming dining rooms are rich with local colour, with pictures of hereabouts and the chef in action, and tables dressed in sharp white linen. It's an atmospheric spot. The kitchen turns out some impressive modern dishes, presented with style, and delivering some spot-on flavours. A first-course tart has ultra-thin pastry and is packed with chorizo, pickled mushrooms and Mull cheddar, or there might be a pea risotto with crispy shallots and parmesan. Main-course Aberdeenshire pork hits the mark in a dish featuring both belly and fillet, served with a potato and pancetta terrine, plus an apple emulsion, confit of soya tomato and mushroom jus. Desserts such as vanilla pannacotta with strawberries and lemon curd are no less impressive.

Chef Craig Wilson **Owner** Craig & Lindsay Wilson **Seats** 82, Pr/dining room 28 **Times** 12-2/6-9.30 Closed 1st wk Jan, Mon-Tue, L Sat **Prices** Fixed L 2 course £23.95-£26.95, Fixed D 3 course £55, Tasting menu £85-£115, Starter £5.50-£9, Main £19-£28, Dessert £6.50-£10, Service optional **Wines** 9 by glass **Parking** 7, On street **Notes** Tasting menu 8 course 48hrs notice required, Sunday L £31.95, Vegetarian available, Children welcome

---

▮ INVERURIE   Map 23 NJ72

Macdonald Pittodrie House

◎◎ Traditional, Modern Scottish

tel: 0870 194 2111 & 01467 622437 **Chapel of Garioch, Pitcaple AB51 5HS**
email: pittodrie@macdonald-hotels.co.uk **web:** www.macdonald-hotels.com/pittodrie
dir: From A96 towards Inverness, pass Inverurie under bridge with lights. Turn left & follow signs

Gently modern cooking in a pastoral setting

A few miles off the main road, Pittodrie House has a wonderfully peaceful position, plus 2,000 acres to call its own. The building has its roots in the 15th century and there's a rugged grandeur to the place. Inside all is rich, warm decor and period detail, including the restaurant with its classical proportions and large oil canvases on the walls. It's a smart, classical setting for some gently modern Scottish cuisine. There's plenty of fine regional produce on the menu to add to the local flavour. Start with West Coast wild salmon and lobster tortellini with a frothy lobster bisque and spinach dressed with lobster oil, or there might be cream of cauliflower soup with truffle cream. Follow on with loin of Highland venison, the meat pink and tender, and served with celeriac both roasted puréed, plus chestnuts and silky juniper-flavoured jus. Finish with blackberry parfait or a selection of British cheeses.

Chef Graham Campbell **Owner** Monument Leisure **Seats** 28 **Times** 12-3/7-9.30 **Wines** 103 bottles over £30, 29 bottles under £30 **Parking** 300 **Notes** Sunday L fr £29.50, Vegetarian available, Children welcome

OLDMELDRUM Map 23 NJ82

Meldrum House Country Hotel & Golf Course

 Modern British

tel: 01651 872294 **AB51 OAE**
email: enquiries@meldrumhouse.co.uk **web:** www.meldrumhouse.com
dir: *11m from Aberdeen on A947 (Aberdeen to Banff road)*

Smart country-house hotel with a local flavour

Even if you're not a whizz with a niblick, Meldrum House is a good place to marinate in the luxury of a turreted baronial pile that has been around since the 13th century. It is a deeply traditional country-house hotel in 350 acres of wooded parkland, so there's plenty of breathing space to work up an appetite. The dining room strikes a traditional pose with its splendid proportions, ancestral portraits, real fire and burnished darkwood tables, and makes a grand setting for modern Scottish country-house cooking that puts local produce firmly on the agenda. You might set out on a rich note with wood pigeon paired with game confit and game sauce, or keep things light with a duo of scallops, langoustine and chilli ravioli. Next up, ballottine of slow-roasted pheasant with barley risotto, sweet potato purée and foie gras sauce is hard to resist in season, and, to finish, banoffee soufflé with spiced banana ice cream and toffee sauce is one alternative to Scottish cheeses with oatcakes and grape chutney.

Chef Walter Walker **Owner** Peter Walker **Seats** 40, Pr/dining room 16
Times 12-2/6.30-9 **Prices** Service optional **Wines** 8 by glass **Parking** 70
Notes Afternoon tea available, Sunday L fr £31.50, Vegetarian available, Children welcome

PETERHEAD Map 23 NK14

Buchan Braes Hotel

Modern Scottish, European

tel: 01779 871471 **Boddam AB42 3AR**
email: info@buchanbraes.co.uk **web:** www.buchanbraes.co.uk
dir: *From Aberdeen take A90, follow Peterhead signs. 1st right in Stirling signed Boddam. 50mtrs, 1st right*

Bright, modern cooking in a contemporary hotel

The low-slung Buchan Braes won't win any architectural prizes, but it makes a spiffy contemporary hotel with its rural aspect (views of Stirling Hill), and up-to-date facilities that make it a hit for weddings and conferences. There's also the Grill Room restaurant, with its open kitchen, funky chandeliers, and warmly colourful decor. The modern Scottish cooking isn't all about the grill, although you might well opt for the chargrilled fillet with horseradish mash and oxtail and root vegetable broth. The kitchen also turns out pan-seared pigeon breast – nicely pink – with a potato and onion cake and claret jus, followed by baked loin of cod with baby spinach, creamy mash and Cullen skink sauce, or fillet of pork with slow-cooked belly. There's a pretty good showing of local ingredients all round. For dessert, perhaps a honeycomb Pavlova or rhubarb crumble with custard.

Chef Gary Christie, Paul McLean **Owner** Kenneth Watt, Tony Jackson **Seats** 70, Pr/dining room 80 **Times** 11.45-2.30/6-9.30 **Prices** Prices not confirmed, Service optional **Wines** 10 bottles over £30, 24 bottles under £30, 7 by glass **Parking** 100 **Notes** Sunday L, Vegetarian available, Children welcome

STONEHAVEN Map 23 NO88

Carron Art Deco Restaurant

Modern British

tel: 01569 760460 **20 Cameron St AB39 2HS**
email: jacki@cleaverhotels.eclipse.co.uk
dir: *From Aberdeen, right at town centre lights, 2nd left onto Ann St, right at road end, 3rd building on right*

Seasonal brasserie food in an art deco masterpiece

The Carron is an impressive piece of Highlands art deco, with its sleek white bow-fronted rear facade. This was once solely the restaurant entrance (there were shops on the other side), and is preserved today pretty much as it looked in the 1930s, with steps like overlapping ripples ascending amid a floral rockery. Inside it feels expansive and properly stylish, with 500 lightbulbs (hang the electricity bill) and a tall mirror gorgeously etched with a naked female form in the Picasso idiom. A carte of seasonally-evolving brasserie food is supplemented by blackboard specials, and there is a distinctive Scottish note to proceedings. Start, perhaps, with the abidingly popular beetroot and red onion bhaji with matching jelly and coulis and chunky mango salsa, moving on to a thoroughly hearty game casserole: venison, pheasant and rabbit enriched with Marsala, smoked bacon and button mushrooms, with a herby suet dumpling floating in it. Crumbly-textured pastry appears in a very grown-up bitter chocolate tart with orange compôte and a creamy white chocolate sorbet.

Chef Robert Cleaver **Owner** Robert Cleaver **Seats** 80, Pr/dining room 30
Times 12-2/6-9.30 Closed 24 Dec-10 Jan, Sun-Mon **Prices** Starter £4.35-£7.25, Main £11.95-£26.95, Dessert £6.25, Service optional **Wines** 6 bottles over £30, 21 bottles under £30, 6 by glass **Parking** Town Square **Notes** Vegetarian available, Children welcome

The Tolbooth Restaurant

Modern British, Seafood

tel: 01569 762287 **Old Pier, Stonehaven Harbour AB39 2JU**
email: enquiries@tolbooth-restaurant.co.uk
dir: *15m S of Aberdeen on A90, located in Stonehaven harbour*

Speciality seafood restaurant overlooking the harbour

There can't be many better spots than this in the UK for tucking into seafood. It's right on the harbour wall, with a local museum on the ground floor and the upstairs restaurant gives views over the boats coming and going from the safety of Stonehaven. The open-plan layout is contemporary and easy-going with the tables smartly dressed in linen cloths and a pleasing lack of airs and graces. What you eat depends on what has been landed that day, what's at its best, and everything is made on the premises. To start, crayfish mornay, a daily special, is packed with flavour, or there might be hot-smoked monkfish with white asparagus and bois boudran dressing, or steamed Shetland mussels with a chunk of focaccia. Main-course hake is poached in cabernet sauvignon and served with sesame prawn bonbons, Puy lentils, pancetta and curly kale, and, for dessert, there is a fashionable salted-caramel tart with stem ginger ice cream and crème anglaise.

Chef Craig Somers **Owner** J Edward Abbott **Seats** 46 **Times** 12-4/6-12 Closed 1st 3 wks Jan, Sun (Oct-Apr) & Mon **Prices** Fixed L 2 course £15.95, Starter £6.95-£9.50, Main £16.95-£23.95, Dessert £6.25-£7.95, Service optional **Wines** 21 bottles over £30, 13 bottles under £30, 6 by glass **Parking** Public car park, 100 spaces **Notes** Sun L & D (May-Sep), Sunday L £20-£25, Vegetarian available, Children welcome

ANGUS

FORFAR
Map 23 NO45

Drovers

Modern British

tel: 01307 860322 **Memus By Forfar DD8 3TY**
email: info@the-drovers.com
dir: *Forth Road bridge onto A823 then M90. Dundee through to Forfar onto A90, then B9128 Memus, Cortachy, The Glens*

Country inn serving rustic modern Scottish cooking

The Drovers Inn is the kind of place you want to be stranded when the weather closes in. It's has a rural aspect amid the beautiful glens and a rustic solidity that suggests it's been around for a few years and the animal horns and antlers on the walls remind you that this is wild country. It's a very modern kind of pub that is as happy to serve you a pint as sit you down and serve up some smart, modern food. The restaurant positively buzzes with life at times and the service team cope with an easy charm. The menu makes good use of what lives and grows hereabouts and turns these fine ingredients into some rustic, modern Scottish food. Seared king scallops with roast pork belly, shallot and garlic purée and chestnut mushrooms is a positively contemporary first course, with the scallops cooked just-so and the balance of flavours spot on. Next up, roast monkfish is wrapped in Serrano ham and comes with Puy lentils, and venison steak is served in the company of celeriac and truffle purée.

Chef Eden Sinclair **Owner** John Dodd **Seats** 60, Pr/dining room 16
Times 12-2.30/5.30-9 **Prices** Fixed L 2 course £15-£30, Fixed D 3 course £20-£45,

Starter £4-£8.50, Main £10-£20, Dessert £4.50-£7, Service optional **Wines** 11 bottles over £30, 18 bottles under £30, 7 by glass **Parking** 35 **Notes** Sunday L £10-£15, Vegetarian available, Children welcome

INVERKEILOR
Map 23 NO64

Gordon's

– *see below*

ARGYLL & BUTE

ARDUAINE
Map 20 NM71

Loch Melfort Hotel

Modern British

tel: 01852 200233 **PA34 4XG**
email: reception@lochmelfort.co.uk **web:** www.lochmelfort.co.uk
dir: *On A816, midway between Oban & Lochgilphead*

Ambitious contemporary cooking and stellar views

There is something very special about the West Coast of Scotland and the Loch Melfort Hotel presents it to you on a plate – the landscape (metaphorically speaking) and the wonderful ingredients (quite literally). The position of the hotel is nothing short of magnificent, on the shore of Asknish Bay, with views over the loch to copious islands, and the famous Arduaine Gardens right next door. The Asknish Bay Restaurant is positioned to make the best of the view, and note it is first-come-first-served at the best positioned tables. The team in the kitchen serve up

continued

Gordon's

INVERKEILOR
Map 23 NO64

Modern Scottish

tel: 01241 830364 **Main St DD11 5RN**
email: gordonsrest@aol.com **web:** www.gordonsrestaurant.co.uk
dir: *From A92 exit at signs for Inverkeilor (between Arbroath & Montrose)*

Striking modern Scottish cookery in a coastal hamlet

On the eastern littoral between Arbroath and Montrose, Inverkeilor is a coastal hamlet with a sandy beach, a little high street and not much else – unless you overlook the Watsons' hugely distinguished restaurant with rooms, which would be a grave mistake. It's a family affair, in the hands of Gordon and Maria and their son Garry, the boys running the kitchen side of things between them. The place is hard to miss, with its russet-coloured frontage, offset with blue-violet window frames and diamond-patterned stained glass. Exposed stone walls and a wood-burning stove lend the place an aura of welcoming rusticity inside, but Messrs Watson are a cut above the rustic norm when it comes to sourcing, menu designing and cooking. Fixed-price formats at lunch and dinner keep things simple, and the template is high-definition modern Scottish. Dinner might open with a voguish pairing of roast scallops and crisp-fried chicken wings garnished

with Jerusalem artichokes and hazelnuts, or perhaps roast quail breast in beetroot jus, with a boudin of the leg-meat, as well as celeriac and apple. An intermediate soup course offers the silky charms of a velouté of carrot and orange with smoked eel, and then mains offer a threeway choice from, maybe, venison, duck or monkfish. The last is crusted in fennel and served on spiced couscous with bok choy and mussel beignets in curry dressing, for a composition hovering tantalisingly somewhere between Morocco, China and India, while the duck is Gressingham, and arrives in the familiar double-act of breast and confit leg, alongside herb gnocchi and shallot purée in honey and cracked pepper jus. Desserts offer a gentle coda to the performance, in the form of crisp apple tarte fine with Calvados ice cream and toffee sauce.

Chef Gordon & Garry Watson **Owner** Gordon & Maria Watson **Seats** 24, Pr/dining room 8 **Times** 12.30-1.45/7-9 Closed 2 wks Jan, Mon, L Sat, Tue, D Sun (in Winter) **Prices** Fixed L 3 course £29, Fixed D 3 course £55, Service optional **Wines** 11 bottles over £30, 33 bottles under £30, 5 by glass **Parking** 6 **Notes** All bookings essential, Vegetarian available, No children

ARDUANE *continued*

ambitious contemporary dishes based on first-class regional produce, thus pan-fried rabbit loin is served with a plump langoustine, girolles and chicory, and roast Barbreck marrow bone with caper and shallot relish and toasted soda bread among first courses. Follow on with steamed pavé of halibut with Puy lentils, artichoke purée, foie gras, kale and port sauce, finishing with glazed lemon curd tart with raspberry sorbet. The Chartroom II Bistro is another dining option.

Chef Peter Carr **Owner** Calum & Rachel Ross **Seats** 60, Pr/dining room 14 **Times** 6.30-9 Closed mid 2 wks Jan, midwk Nov-Mar, 1st 2wks Dec, L all week, D Tue-Wed (Nov-Mar) **Prices** Prices not confirmed, Service optional **Wines** 21 bottles over £30, 54 bottles under £30, 8 by glass **Parking** 65 **Notes** 4 course D £39.50, Vegetarian available, Children welcome

---

ERISKA   Map 20 NM94

Isle of Eriska Hotel, Spa & Golf

@@@ – *see opposite*

KILCHRENAN   Map 20 NN02

The Ardanaiseig Hotel

@@@ – *see opposite*

Taychreggan Hotel

@@ Modern British

tel: 01866 833211 & 833366 **PA35 1HQ**
email: info@taychregganhotel.co.uk **web:** www.taychregganhotel.co.uk
dir: *W from Crianlarich on A85 to Taynuilt, S for 7m on B845 (single track) to Kilchrenan*

Inventive cooking with sublime loch views

This plush 17th-century country-house hotel is a million miles from the primitive drovers' inn that once put up herders who swam their cattle across Loch Awe. Although not far from Oban, it also feels a very long way from anywhere, standing in glorious isolation in 40 acres of well-kept grounds freckled with colourful rhododendrons on a peninsula jutting into Loch Awe, and with wrap-around views of timeless Highland scenery – views that can be soaked up at leisure from the floor-to-ceiling arched windows of the low-slung restaurant. On the food front, the kitchen delivers a well-judged and inventive fusion of contemporary Scottish and French influences. The chefs forage for wild herbs and flowers, as well as putting great care into sourcing the prime ingredients for five-course set dinner menus. It all begins with an espresso cup of onion and star anise soup with bacon and chives, then progresses via pressed pork belly with apples, horseradish cream, celeriac remoulade, herbs and flowers, to a main course of slow-cooked Argyll beef with almonds, sorrel, and potato fondant in chicken stock. Dessert brings pistachio and dried apricot tart with yoghurt sorbet, spiced mascarpone and caramelised walnuts.

Times 7-8.45 Closed 3-21 Jan

LUSS   Map 20 NS39

The Lodge on Loch Lomond

@@ Traditional British, International

tel: 01436 860201 **G83 8PA**
email: res@loch-lomond.co.uk **web:** www.loch-lomond.co.uk
dir: *N of Glasgow on A82*

Fine Scottish dining above the loch

Perched on the edge of the loch, The Lodge could hardly be more guaranteed to induce a sense of tranquillity, the effect best enjoyed from Colquhoun's restaurant, which occupies a balcony built out on struts to give the impression that you are floating above the pristine glassy surface of the water. Glass-topped tables and tartan carpeting comprise the decorative order, and staff offer a discreetly attentive approach that exactly suits the surroundings. That must-have accoutrement of the modern restaurant kitchen, a Josper charcoal grill, rules the roost, turning out great Scotch sirloin accompanied by truffled mash and the likes of creamy peppercorn or paprika butter sauces. Prior to that could be monkfish tempura dressed in coconut, lime and ginger, or seared wood-pigeon with shallot purée and an intense demi-glace dressing. Combinations of meat and shellfish, such as pork belly with garlic prawns, are less convincing, but desserts like chocolate and hazelnut brownie and toffee ice cream, or mango parfait with pineapple relish and coconut sorbet, are impressive, as are the Scottish cheeses served with chutney, apple and grapes.

Chef Stephen Gedman **Owner** Niall Colquhoun **Seats** 100, Pr/dining room 100 **Times** 12-5/6-9 **Prices** Fixed D 3 course £30, Tasting menu £17.95-£19.95, Starter £4.95-£6.25, Main £12.95-£22.95, Dessert £4.95-£8.95, Service optional **Wines** 7 by glass **Parking** 70 **Notes** Sunday L, Vegetarian available, Children welcome

---

OBAN   Map 20 NM82

Best Western The Queens Hotel

@ Scottish

tel: 01631 562505 & 570230 **Corran Esplanade PA34 5AG**
email: thequeenshoteloban@hotmail.co.uk **web:** www.thequeenshotel-oban.co.uk
dir: *Entering Oban on A85 take 2nd exit rdbt to seaside, next rdbt Ganavan Sands, hotel 0.4m on right*

Creative modern dishes in revamped seafront hotel

The Queens Hotel is an unmissable presence along the esplanade with its high-gabled frontage looking rather like a trio of bishops in a meeting. After refurbishment it's all looking spick and span inside, with the grandly-proportioned Glen Campa Restaurant perfectly positioned to make the most of the seafront vistas. Bare darkwood tables on a colourful tartan carpet make a smart setting for well-conceived contemporary dishes. Diligent sourcing of fine Scottish ingredients is clearly on the agenda of a kitchen that deals in starters such as gruth dhu mousse – translation courtesy of the knowledgeable and friendly staff reveals this to be black crowdie cheese which is served with marinated beetroot, fennel pollen oatcakes, and salted caramel walnuts. Main course stars Argyll pork, delivered as a trio of cured fillet, cannelloni of braised collar, and roasted belly with wilted spinach; with the briny just a few steps away, you might be tempted by Oban-landed wild sea bass with sea spinach, plantain purée, chick pea and chorizo, and fried baby squid.

Chef Gary Goldie **Owner** Raymond & Susan Hyams **Seats** 32 **Times** 12-2/5.30-9 Closed Xmas & Jan **Prices** Fixed L 2 course £15-£20, Service optional **Wines** 2 bottles over £30, 24 bottles under £30, 5 by glass **Parking** 16 **Notes** Fixed D 3/5 course from £27.50/£32, Sunday L £19.50-£25, Vegetarian available, Children welcome

Looking for a restaurant by name?
Use the index on page 751

Isle of Eriska Hotel, Spa & Golf

ERISKA   **Map 20 NM94**

Modern British v

tel: 01631 720371 **Benderloch, By Oban PA37 1SD**
email: office@eriska-hotel.co.uk **web:** www.eriska-hotel.co.uk
dir: *Exit A85 at Connel, onto A828, follow for 4m, then follow hotel signs from N of Benderloch*

Culinary modernity in splendid Scots baronial isolation

In terms of exclusivity, the Isle of Eriska hotel is hard to beat. It sits alone on the little island after which it is named, which was in medieval times a church sanctuary. The architect Hipployte Blanc built the present manor house in the 1880s, at the height of the Victorian vogue for Scots baronial. The rickety-sounding little bridge was only added at the turn of the last century; otherwise, you would need to wade across at low tide to reach Eriska. The whole domain was acquired in 1973 by the Buchanan-Smith family, who have turned it into a gracious and sumptuously decorated country hotel, complete with log fires, a snug little bar and stunning sea views. If the cooking for a while languished in the shallows of the unadventurous country-house idiom, it is now swimming vigorously with the currents of culinary modernity, in the confines of a striped and panelled dining room under the aegis of the recently appointed Ross Stovold. Wild marine vegetation plays a strong part, whether in appetiser nibbles of seashore crackers with seaweed mayonnaise, or the sea vegetables and pickled seaweed that come with a starter serving of Loch Creran smoked salmon and burnt sour cream. A meatier start might be had with braised beef cheek in mushroom bouillon, grilled kale and bone-marrow, as a possible prelude to fully-flavoured mature chicken – roasted breast and braised leg – with toasted grains and watercress, or skate with baby turnips in tartare sauce and ham fat. Meat and fish come together productively well in Mallaig turbot with cured pork neck, accompanied by grilled Gem lettuce and sour leek. It all builds up to intensely concentrated, squishy chocolate and hazelnut cake, served with sea-salt caramel, malt ice cream and dark chocolate mousse, or perhaps poached plums with whipped custard, hibiscus and pistachios.

Chef Ross Stovold **Owner** Mr Buchanan-Smith **Seats** 50, Pr/dining room 20 **Times** 7.30-9 Closed Jan, L all week **Prices** Prices not confirmed, Service optional **Wines** 10 by glass **Parking** 50 **Notes** Children welcome

The Ardanaiseig Hotel

KILCHRENAN   **Map 20 NN02**

Modern British v

tel: 01866 833333 **PA35 1HE**
email: marcel@ardanaiseig.com **web:** www.ardanaiseig.com
dir: *From A85 at Taynuilt onto B845 to Kilchrenan. Left in front of pub (road very narrow) signed 'Ardanaiseig Hotel' & 'No Through Road'. Continue for 3m*

Well-tuned food and high comfort in a stunning lochside hotel

Hidden away down a single-track road, Ardanaiseig is ensconced in the sort of jaw-dropping scenery that has graced a million shortbread tins. Such seclusion means tranquillity is guaranteed at this Victorian baronial country house set in miraculously lush gardens where Ben Cruachan rises from the clear waters of Loch Awe. The interior is tailor-made for holing up over a weekend with a good book amid antiques and fine art, but this is no starchy tartan-and-antlers museum. The colour scheme is bold-and-funky designer-Gothic and staff are young and the opposite of stuffy. The icing on the cake is that this gem of a hotel is a sanctuary for food-lovers. The wonderful views glimpsed through the generously-proportioned windows beat any artwork, and that goes for the dining room, too, which is the setting for some rather splendid modern Scottish cooking built on diligently sourced regional ingredients – a policy that extends to foraging in the surrounding landscape, with no stone left unturned in the search for a local flavour. It is all delivered via a four-course dinner menu (make that five-course if you fit in cheese as well as pudding) that is punctuated by all the little intermediaries you might expect at this level, plus some pretty fine breads. An amuse of wild mushroom risotto sets the ball rolling, ahead of Mull scallops with salmon, saffron potatoes, tomato and sweetcorn, then a soup course intervenes – perhaps a velvety cream of Jerusalem artichoke – before the main event, an impeccably-cooked saddle of venison pointed up with beetroot purée, blackberries, roast potatoes and crosnes. And whichever way you choose to finish – sweetly with a splendid interplay of flavour and textures involving quince crumble with iced double cream and granola, or a savoury plate of French or Scottish cheese – you're sure to feel a warm glow of satisfaction.

Chef Cornel Uys **Owner** Bennie Gray **Seats** 38, Pr/dining room **Times** 12-2.30/7-11 **Prices** Tasting menu £50-£59.50, Service optional **Wines** 46 bottles over £30, 20 bottles under £30, 10 by glass **Parking** 20 **Notes** Tasting menu 6 course, Sunday L £35, Children 5 yrs+

OBAN *continued*

Coast

◉ Modern British

tel: 01631 569900 **104 George St PA34 5NT**
email: coastoban@yahoo.co.uk
dir: *On main street in town centre*

Vivacious brasserie cooking in a converted bank building

Next door to the art gallery, Coast is the very image of a modern brasserie, its granite frontage and expansive windows looking distinctly stately (it used to be a bank). Inside, it all looks clean-lined and sharp, the unclothed tables simply laid, with a seasonally changing menu of vivacious brasserie dishes offering something for everyone. Start with generously constructed salmon fishcakes with aïoli and balsamic-dressed salad leaves, or richly pungent Cullen skink, before going on with beautifully tender guinea fowl breast, served with Stornoway black pudding and chive mash, wilted baby leeks and spiced carrots in red wine jus, or a winning duo of halibut and kedgeree risotto, garnished with a fennel and apple parcel and sauced with chervil cream. Flavours can sometimes be a touch shy, as when white chocolate and cardamom mousse doesn't quite deliver on its promise of spice, but there are also good Scottish cheeses, served with oatcakes and grapes.

Chef Richard Fowler **Owner** Richard & Nicola Fowler **Seats** 46 **Times** 12-2/5.30-9.30 Closed 25 Dec, 2 wks Jan, Sun (Nov-Mar), L Sun **Prices** Fixed L 2 course £14.50, Fixed D 3 course £17.50, Starter £4.50-£8.95, Main £13.50-£22.95, Dessert £5.95, Service optional **Wines** 13 bottles over £30, 33 bottles under £30, 5 by glass **Parking** On street **Notes** Vegetarian available

Manor House Hotel

◉ Scottish, European

tel: 01631 562087 **Gallanach Rd PA34 4LS**
email: info@manorhouseoban.com web: www.manorhouseoban.com
dir: *Follow MacBrayne Ferries signs, pass ferry entrance for hotel on right*

Traditional country-house dining by Oban harbour

Built for the Duke of Argyll in 1780, the Manor House sits in a suitably commanding position overlooking the harbour at Oban. Half-panelled walls and original oil paintings set the heightened tone in the low-ceilinged dining room, and a lighting level to encourage intimacies prevails. Fine regional Scottish produce receives its due celebration in menus that aim for a soft-focus country-hotel approach (including intermediate courses of a soup such as celery and leek, then lemon sorbet) rather than anything too wacky. Brilliantly timed salmon fillet (crisp outside, soft within) comes on a chunky salsa of tomato, fennel and capers for an inspired first course, after which the choice may take in guinea fowl breast with pommes Parisienne and an assertively truffle-oiled jus gras, or rack of lamb with honey-glazed veg and wilted spinach. A brisk chocolate kick is administered by a hefty warm brownie with glossy fudge glaze and vanilla ice cream.

Times 12-2.30/6.45-8.45 Closed 25-26 Dec

Airds Hotel and Restaurant

◉◉◉ – *see opposite*

The Pierhouse Hotel

◉ Modern, International

tel: 01631 730302 & 730622 **PA38 4DE**
email: reservations@pierhousehotel.co.uk web: www.pierhousehotel.co.uk
dir: *M8, A82 to Crianlarich & Fort William. At Ballachulish take A828 towards Oban. Turn right in Appin for Port Appin & Lismore Ferry*

Top-notch fish and seafood with stunning views

Tucked away on a quiet arm of Loch Linnhe where the little foot passenger ferry shuttles across to Lismore Island, this waterside restaurant specialises in fish and seafood. The brasserie-style dining room is a simple, magnolia-painted space – after all, there's no point fretting over interior design when all eyes are turned towards the peaks marching across the skyline above the loch. Oysters are hand-picked from the Lismore oyster beds, mussels and langoustines come from Loch Linnhe, and lobsters are kept in creels at the end of the pier where day boats drop off fish at the door. There's no point faffing about with produce like that, so the kitchen keeps it all simple: who could resist seared local scallops with artichoke purée and Stornoway black pudding to start things off? The glorious simplicity and freshness of the seafood platters is hard to ignore, and there's Drambuie crème brûlée to send you home happy.

Chef Laura Milne **Owner** Nicholas & Nicolette Horne **Seats** 45, Pr/dining room 25 **Times** 12.30-2.30/6.30-9.30 Closed 25-26 Dec **Prices** Starter £4.95-£12.50, Main £14.95-£39.95, Dessert £5.95-£9.95, Service optional **Wines** 8 bottles over £30, 27 bottles under £30, 5 by glass **Parking** 25 **Notes** Vegetarian available, Children welcome

Rosslea Hall Hotel

◉ Modern British

tel: 01436 439955 **Ferry Rd G84 8NF**
email: enquiries@rossleahallhotel.co.uk web: www.rossleahallhotel.co.uk
dir: *From Erskine Bridge A82 to Dumbarton to junct with A814 follow to Helensburgh. Along water front 2m on left*

Well-executed modern dishes and wonderful Clyde views

Views over the Firth of Clyde offer a stunning backdrop to this substantial, solid-looking Victorian property, now a comfortable, stylish hotel. In the equally smart restaurant, friendly but informed staff cut through any hint of formality projected by correctly set clothed tables complete with candles and flowers. The kitchen works around a tranche of modern ideas, producing, for instance, a well-conceived, tasty starter of ham hock, parsley and potato terrine, served on a sliver of parsnip purée with punchily spiced plums and port jelly. This might be followed by red onion tarte Tatin successfully partnered by roasted beetroot and beetroot essence, or returning to the classics for duck leg confit with Parmentier potatoes. Seasonality is seen in a summery main course of pan-fried sea bass with a fricassee of peas, broad beans and asparagus, served with gnocchi and vanilla cream, as it is in raspberry sorbet as an accompaniment for raspberry and white chocolate cheesecake.

Chef James Quinn **Owner** BDL Select Hotel **Seats** 48, Pr/dining room 40 **Times** 12-3/6.30-9.30 **Prices** Fixed L 2 course £12.95-£16.50, Fixed D 3 course £24.95, Starter £4.50-£5.50, Main £14.95-£18.75, Dessert £4.75-£6.95, Service optional **Wines** 8 bottles over £30, 28 bottles under £30, 6 by glass **Parking** 60 **Notes** Afternoon tea £8.50, Sunday L £9.95-£14.95, Vegetarian available, Children welcome

STRACHUR
Map 20 NN00

The Creggans Inn
◉◉ Modern British, French

tel: 01369 860279 **PA27 8BX**
email: info@creggans-inn.co.uk **web:** www.creggans-inn.co.uk
dir: *A82 from Glasgow, at Tarbet take A83 towards Cairndow, left onto A815 to Strachur Or by ferry from Gourock to Dunoon onto A815*

Locally-sourced cooking on the shore of Loch Fyne

On the shores of Loch Fyne with pan-fried scallops, pea purée and a Parma ham crisp on the menu – this must be heaven. The Creggans Inn is a whitewashed hotel just across the road from the chilly waters of the loch, family run and full of life. There's a bar and bistro with roaring fires and real ales, plus a restaurant – named in honour of the loch, of course – which delivers a menu packed with gently modern constructions, the ingredients drawn from local the waters and hills. Dinner is a smart affair, with spruce waiting staff and classical music. If those scallops don't catch your eye, start with slow-roast pork belly with apple purée and thyme jus, or caramelised Golden Cross goats' cheese with beetroot carpaccio and pickled walnuts. There's a soup or sorbet/granita next, followed by a main course such as herb-crusted rack of Scotch lamb, or baked fillet of halibut, and desserts extend to iced banana parfait with caramelised banana and chocolate sauce, or warm date pudding with toffee sauce and coffee Chantilly cream.

Chef Robbie Hutchinson **Owner** The MacLellan family **Seats** 35 **Times** 7-9 Closed 25-26 Dec, L all week **Prices** Prices not confirmed, Service optional **Wines** 6 by glass **Parking** 25 **Notes** Vegetarian available, Children 8 yrs+

TIRORAN
Map 20 NM42

Tiroran House Hotel
◉◉ Modern Scottish **NEW** v

tel: 01681 705232 **PA69 6ES**
email: info@tiroran.com **web:** www.tiroran.com
dir: *Phone for directions*

Outstanding cooking in secluded country house

The white-painted hotel perches on a wooded hillside in a remote spot with spectacular loch views that transport you instantly from the cares of 21st-century life. Inside, it's an intimate place with a classic, lived-in country-house feel, perfect to settle into after a day spent walking the hills and spotting Mull's abundant wildlife, with the promise of skilfully-cooked local produce to end on a high note. Provenance is key here, with only the finest regional materials, bolstered by organic fruit and veg from Tiroran's orchard and gardens making it into the kitchen. These prime ingredients are handled with due respect and top-class technical skills, thus dinner begins creatively with local creel-caught crab and lobster pointed up with lemon purée, shellfish powder, mizuna and amaranth. Next up, perfectly-judged saddle of venison is matched with baby turnip and leeks, parsley root purée, wild garlic and millefeuille potatoes, and dessert is an indulgent workout of textures and flavours on a theme of white chocolate and caramel mousse. Wine lovers should note that the owner takes justifiable pride in the impeccably composed wine list.

Chef Craig Ferguson, Alex Dashwood-Baker **Owner** Lawrence & Katie Mackay **Seats** 26 **Times** **Prices** Prices not confirmed **Wines** 10 bottles over £30, 18 bottles under £30, 7 by glass **Parking** 16 **Notes** ALC menu 5 course £48, Pre-booked L menu available, Children welcome

Airds Hotel and Restaurant

PORT APPIN
Map 20 NM94

Modern British v
tel: 01631 730236 **PA38 4DF**
email: airds@airds-hotel.com **web:** www.airds-hotel.com
dir: *From A828 (Oban to Fort William road), turn at Appin signed Port Appin. Hotel 2.5m on left*

Accomplished modern seasonal cooking by Loch Linnhe

The Argyll coast is one of Scotland's many natural assets, a rugged and lovely stretch of western littoral incorporating a great variety of seductive prospects. The little hamlet of Port Appin sits on the shore of beautiful Loch Linnhe in a setting of sublime tranquillity, with the brooding Morvenmountains as backdrop. Not far from the old ferry-point, the Airds is a country hotel on the restrained scale, although its interiors have quite as much inviting comfort as many a grand old pile. Landscape pictures by contemporary British artists are hung all over the show, and the dining room is a long, tastefully furnished space with views over the narrow road towards the loch – worth nabbing a window table for. High-class tableware, including napkins in tartan ties and crisp linen, looks the part, and so does the seasonal modern Scottish cooking, in the hands since 2013 of new chef

Jordan Annabi. Wafts of Asian and Mediterranean influence are evident in first courses such as cured salmon and nori roulade with daikon, pickled cucumber, lime, cucumber and wasabi sorbet, or a bold combination of seared scallops with apple and ginger purée, confit ginger and apple caramel. The cooking may draw on an eclectic palette, but everything makes sense, and prime Scottish produce is always at the heart of it, as may be seen in mains like Highland venison loin with spiced red cabbage purée, parsnips in several forms and blackberry jus. The relative complexity of dishes doesn't overshadow the quality of prime ingredients, which shine boldly through, as in poached lemon sole with pommes soufflées, spinach royale, Muscat grapes, smoked hazelnuts and Vermouth cream. To finish, there could be an interesting spin on tiramisú, or a bracing passionfruit soufflé with coconut and mango délice and an exotic fruit salad.

Chef Jordan Annabi **Owner** Mr & Mrs S McKivragan **Seats** 32 **Times** 12-1.45/7.15-9.15 **Prices** Fixed L 3 course £18.95, Tasting menu £74, Starter £3-£7, Main £7.50-£21, Dessert £4-£6, Service optional **Wines** 225 bottles over £30, 10 bottles under £30, 12 by glass **Parking** 20 **Notes** 5 course D £55, Tasting menu 7 course, Sunday L £17.50, Children 8 yrs+

NORTH AYRSHIRE

DALRY
Map 20 NS24

Braidwoods

@@ Modern Scottish

tel: 01294 833544 **Drumastle Mill Cottage KA24 4LN**
email: keithbraidwood@btconnect.com
dir: 1m from Dalry on Saltcoats road

Creative cooking from a gifted husband-and-wife-team

In a cottage in the middle of a field near Dalry, Braidwoods is a small, unpretentious restaurant, its two rooms split by a central fireplace, with beams in the low ceilings, close-set tables, an informal, relaxed atmosphere, and young and helpful staff. Dinner, of three or four courses, could open with a well-balanced dish of seared scallops on pea purée along with crispy chicken wings, or perhaps even more modish beetroot-cured gravad lax on beetroot and clementine salad with a potato cake. Main courses impress with their timing and presentation: melt-in-the-mouth roast best end of local lamb on wilted spinach, with a mound of cauliflower purée topped with confit neck fillet and a square of dauphinoise, all complemented by rosemary jus, or grilled turbot fillet crowned with tapenade served on herb risotto and a rich shellfish jus. Canapés make a great introduction to a meal, and puddings impress too, among them Valrhona truffle cake with prune and Armagnac ice cream.

Times 12-1.45/7-9 Closed 25-26 Dec, 1st 3 wks Jan, 1st 2 wks Sep, Mon, L Tue (Sun Etr-Sep), D Sun

SOUTH AYRSHIRE

AYR
Map 20 NS32

Enterkine Country House

@@ Modern British V

tel: 01292 520580 **Annbank KA6 5AL**
email: mail@enterkine.com **web:** www.enterkine.com
dir: 5m E of Ayr on B743

Well-crafted contemporary cooking in an elegant 1930s country house

Enterkine, dating from the 1930s, when it was built in the art-deco style, is approached via a tree-lined avenue running through its 300 acres. Three sides of the restaurant have huge windows giving views of the estate; it's a handsome room, with high-backed upholstered chairs at clothed tables, a polished floor and swagged curtains. The menus have been carefully designed to maximise Ayrshire produce, although some items come from further afield: fillet of Orkney beef, for instance, with foie gras, parsnips, chanterelles and spinach. The kitchen adds a contemporary spin, producing starters of a tian of smoked salmon and langoustines with a quail's egg and chilli pineapple, and pork and ham hock terrine with wild mushrooms, red cabbage purée and truffled bean salad. Well-conceived main courses manage to balance traditional ideas with the more modish, so alongside loin of venison with red cabbage, shallots, celeriac and salsify might be halibut fillet with pancetta, brown shrimps, mousserons and samphire. Puddings make a satisfying conclusion: perhaps chocolate marquise with caramel ice cream.

Chef Paul Moffat **Owner** Mr Browne **Seats** 40, Pr/dining room 14 **Times** 12-2/7-9 **Prices** Fixed L 2 course £16.95, Fixed D 3 course £35, Tasting menu £70, Service optional **Wines** 37 bottles over £30, 19 bottles under £30, 4 by glass **Parking** 20 **Notes** Sunday L £16.95-£19.95, Children welcome

Fairfield House Hotel

@@ Modern International

tel: 01292 267461 **12 Fairfield Rd KA7 2AS**
email: reservations@fairfieldhotel.co.uk **web:** www.fairfieldhotel.co.uk
dir: From A77 to Ayr South. Follow signs for town centre. Left into Miller Rd. At lights turn left, then right into Fairfield Rd

Modern Scottish food overlooking the Firth of Clyde

Built as a seaside retreat for a Glasgow merchant whose fortune was in tea, Fairfield enjoys seafront views over the firth towards the Isle of Arran. The interiors are a mix of trad and mod, with the latter prevailing in Martin's Bar and Grill, where orange and yellow tones, and a vividly stripy carpet, add a sense of bounce to the atmosphere. A conservatory opens on to an outdoor terrace when the sun's out. Confident modern Scottish cooking is Liam Murphy's forte, with stylishly presented dishes fashioned from pedigree Scots produce and big flavours. A black slate slab bears a starter of three Orkney scallops with cubes of roasted celeriac, pig's head croquettes and a two-tone purée swipe of celeriac and apple. Mains are equally eye-catching, as when sliced lamb saddle is teamed with its slow-cooked belly and a pastilla of the shoulder, alongside boulangère potatoes and puréed broccoli in a garlicky jus. Finish on a Caribbean note with coconut crème brûlée and variations on pineapple – jelly, sorbet and whole roasted chunks.

Chef Liam Murphy **Owner** G Martin **Seats** 80, Pr/dining room 12 **Times** 11-9.30 All-day dining **Prices** Prices not confirmed, Service optional **Wines** 6 by glass **Parking** 50 **Notes** Vegetarian available, Children welcome

See advert below

Refreshingly Different

The Fairfield House Hotel's guests enjoy excellent cuisine and comfort in our atmospheric, award-winning Martin's Bar & Grill.

Our head chef uses fresh local seasonal produce cooked in a traditional manner but with a modern theme. In the warmer months, al fresco dining and drinking is available on our new terrace which has stunning views over to Arran

fairfield house hotel

email/ reservations@fairfieldhotel.co.uk
www.fairfieldhotel.co.uk • Tel 01292/267461

AA 2 Rosette Restaurant

Glenapp Castle

BALLANTRAE Map 20 NX08

Modern British v

tel: 01465 831212 **KA26 0NZ**
email: info@glenappcastle.com **web:** www.glenappcastle.com
dir: *S through Ballantrae, cross bridge over River Stinchar, 1st right, castle gates in 1m, use entry system*

Inventive contemporary cooking in a Victorian castle

Built in 1870 in the Scottish baronial style, Glenapp Castle is a pretty impressive sight, with towers and turrets rising above the battlements. It's surrounded by 36 acres of lawns, a lake, woods and vegetable gardens and gives views over the Irish Sea to Arran and the granite rock of Ailsa Craig. The interior is in keeping with the style of the castle, with a magnificent panelled entrance hall, richly decorated and furnished public rooms, oil paintings on the walls, and a restaurant with oak-panelled walls and sea views. Meanwhile the six-course dinner menu looks set to continue, deploying the very best Scottish produce and showing judicious restraint with combinations. Dinner might open with mussel and clam chowder with bacon and chives, and proceed to rich ballotine of foiegras cut by Sauternes jelly flavoured with chamomile before the third course,

normally seafood: perhaps lobster ravioli with shellfish consommé and leek fondue. There's no choice until main course, when a pair are offered: feather blade of beef braised in red wine with sautéed wild mushrooms and onion purée, or poached breast of guinea fowl with thigh roulade and mustard velouté. A pre-dessert arrives before the real thing – caramel soufflé, say, with roasted banana ice cream – with a selection of Scottish cheeses an alternative.

Chef Tyron Ellul **Owner** Graham & Fay Cowan **Seats** 34, Pr/dining room 20 **Times** 12.30-2/7-10 Closed 3 Jan-25 Mar, Xmas **Prices** Prices not confirmed, Service optional **Wines** 9 by glass **Parking** 20 **Notes** Fixed Gourmet D 6 course £65, Sunday L, Children 5 yrs+ D

Lochgreen House Hotel

TROON Map 20 NS33

Modern French

tel: 01292 313343 **Monktonhill Rd, Southwood KA10 7EN**
email: lochgreen@costley-hotels.co.uk **web:** www.costley-hotels.co.uk
dir: *From A77 follow Prestwick Airport signs, take B749 to Troon, hotel on left, 1m from junct*

Modern cooking in a stunningly restored manor house

Say 'Troon' and golf probably springs to mind. Lochgreen House pays due homage to the sport from its setting in 30 acres of spotlessly-kept gardens and woodland looking over the famous Royal Troon links and out to sea along the glorious Ayrshire coastline. Built in 1905 for a wealthy lace mill owner and bought by the Costley family back in 1989, the handsome white-painted mansion is as immaculately presented as its grounds, carefully restored and sympathetically extended to provide oceans of space in the Tapestry restaurant, an expansive venue with a lofty beamed roof, drenched with light from huge windows, and smartly done out with plush high-backed chairs, a trio of chandeliers, tables dressed in their best whites and tartan carpets to remind you of the location. Head chef Andrew Costley likes to wave the flag for Scotland's peerless produce,

which he puts to good use in his thoroughly accomplished modern cooking, delivering punchy, clearly delineated flavours and clever texture contrasts. Well-crafted canapés get the ball rolling – haggis bonbon , perhaps – before a first course of cauliflower risotto with crumbled cheddar and a poached hen's egg wrapped in crisp potato, or there may be the luxury of pan-seared foie gras with kumquat and orange jam, dark chocolate and pistachio. Next up, a fabulous breast of corn-fed chicken is the star of the show, matched with a haggis Scotch egg, turnip purée, potato and thyme rösti and whisky sauce, or try something like poached fillet of sole with textures of cauliflower, grapes, mussels and pommes Maxim. There's sharp technique at dessert stage, too, in a complex confection of coconut pannacotta with caramelised pineapple, mango meringue, white chocolate and rum sorbet and coconut shavings, or a classic apple tarte Tatin with the double whammy of vanilla ice cream and sauce anglaise.

Chef Andrew Costley, Ian Conway **Owner** Mr W Costley **Seats** 80, Pr/dining room 40 **Times** 12-2/7-10 **Prices** Fixed L 2 course £17.95, Fixed D 3 course £42.50, Service optional **Wines** 95 bottles over £30, 25 bottles under £30, 12 by glass **Parking** 70 **Notes** Sunday L £20-£25, Vegetarian available, Children welcome

BALLANTRAE
Map 20 NX08

Glenapp Castle

@@@ – see page 597

TROON
Map 20 NS33

Lochgreen House Hotel

@@@ – see page 597

MaccCallums of Troon

@ Seafood

tel: 01292 319339 **The Harbour KA10 6DH**

Simple, fresh seafood on the harbourside

Watching the waves crash against Troon's harbour wall as the fishing fleet lands its catch, thoughts turn inescapably to the prospect of dining on fish and seafood. And this harbourside restaurant in an attractively converted pump house is guaranteed to come up with the goods. Inside it is a businesslike space of high rafters, exposed brick walls liberally layered with maritime memorabilia, and bare, rustic wooden tables set in a simple manner that echoes the unfussy treatments meted out to the spanking-fresh seafood (whose journey from boat to table can be measured in feet). What has just come in on the quayside gets star billing on the chalkboard. The Cullen skink delivers a creamy, smoky opener filled with chunks of haddock, potatoes and leek, while a splendid fillet of halibut is showcased in a main course beside a supporting cast of baked ratatouille, saffron potatoes and fish fumet. Dessert is no mere sideshow either, as seen in a light bitter chocolate mousse with orange and white chocolate ice cream.

Chef Philip Burgess **Owner** John & James MacCallums **Seats** 43
Times 12-2.30/6.30-9.30 Closed Xmas, New Year, Mon, D Sun **Prices** Prices not confirmed, Service optional **Wines** 1 bottle over £30, 20 bottles under £30, 4 by glass **Parking** 12 **Notes** Sunday L, Children welcome

The Marine Hotel

@@ Modern British, Seafood

tel: 01292 314444 **Crosbie Rd KA10 6HE**
email: marine@pumahotels.co.uk **web:** www.pumahotels.co.uk
dir: A77, A78, A79 onto B749. Hotel on left after golf course

Colourful cooking and fantastic coastal views

The tripartite, split-level Fairways dining room at the Troon Marine enjoys fantastic views over the Firth of Clyde towards the Isle of Arran; the sunsets are amazing. Formally dressed tables and formally drilled service establish a civilised tone, with colourful artworks on the warm orange walls and a wine store that seems to invite exploration. Equally as colourful as the surroundings is a starter of beetroot-stained mackerel with red onion confit in orange and tomato dressing, seasoned with sesame oil and soy. A brace of pork servings – roast fillet and cider-braised belly – with a smear of garlic and chive mash makes for an elegant main course, its creamy cider sauce adding to the dish, or there could be salmon with aubergine purée, king scallop and sesame-fried pak choi. The filling of a slice of dark chocolate tart is thickly luxurious, and is partnered with vanilla ice cream and a garnish of orange.

Owner Puma Hotels Collection **Seats** 120, Pr/dining room 50 **Times** 12.30-2.30/5-10 **Prices** Fixed L 2 course fr £16.50, Starter £5.50-£9.50, Main £17.95-£24.50, Dessert £6.50, Service optional **Wines** **Parking** 220 **Notes** Early evening menu 2/3 course £16.50/£19.50, Vegetarian available, Children welcome

TURNBERRY
Map 20 NS20

Turnberry Resort, Scotland

◉◉ Traditional French

tel: 01655 331000 **Maidens Rd KA26 9LT**
email: turnberry@luxurycollection.com web: www.turnberryresort.co.uk
dir: *From Glasgow take A77, M77 S towards Stranraer, 2m past Kirkoswald, follow signs for A719/Turnberry. Hotel 500mtrs on right*

Classical dining at renowned coastal golf resort

The 1906 Restaurant of this luxurious golf-centric hotel is named after the year it opened. But before we get to food, there's a lot more to take in: the Turnberry sits on the glorious Ayrshire coast, with sweeping views across greens and fairways to the hump of Ailsa Craig. For those not bitten by the golfing bug, there's pampering in a top-notch spa, and the Grand Tea Lounge is resurrected for genteel afternoon teas. For the full-on dining experience, however, it's back to 1906, where the setting resembles a giant wedding cake, and the kitchen puts a luxury modern spin on Escoffier's classics. Foie gras gets its own section, starting perhaps with a brûlée with Sauternes-poached fruit, pumpernickel granola and gingerbread, then follow that with something from Escoffier's recipe book – perhaps honey-glazed duck suprême with braised chicory, baby turnips and pan juices. Finish with a Grand Marnier-flambéed crêpe Suzette with orange and vanilla ice cream.

Chef Munur Kara **Owner** Leisurecorp **Seats** 120, Pr/dining room 10 **Times** 7.06-10 Closed 8-22 Dec, L all week **Prices** Service optional **Wines** 198 bottles over £30, 21 bottles under £30, 16 by glass **Parking** 200 **Notes** Brunch 1st & 3rd Sun of month, Sunday L £28, Vegetarian available, Children welcome

DUMFRIES & GALLOWAY

ANNAN
Map 21 NY16

Del Amitri Restaurant

◉ Modern European

tel: 01461 201999 **95a High St DG12 6DJ**
email: enquiries@del-amitri.co.uk web: www.del-amitri.co.uk
dir: *Located above the Cafe Royal*

Creative cooking in the Borders

The name might have an Italian ring about it, but this stylish first-floor restaurant on Annan High Street is definitely not in the business of Italophile cuisine. The venue is a long, narrow room in tones of chocolate and plum, with wooden floors and brown leather seats at clothed tables. The vibe is relaxed – the table is yours for the evening, so no need to watch the clock – while the kitchen turns out well-executed modern Scottish dishes with a French accent. The fine produce of Scotland is well to the fore, as in a starter of smoked haddock kedgeree with soft-boiled quail's eggs and curried mayonnaise. Next out, North Sea halibut is baked under a

layer of herb crumb and served with crushed new potatoes, butternut squash cream and buttered kale. Chocoholics are well catered for by an assiette comprising dark chocolate brownie, white chocolate ice cream and milk chocolate mousse.

Times 12-2/6-10 Closed Mon, L Tue-Sat, D Sun (Nov-May)

AUCHENCAIRN
Map 21 NX75

Balcary Bay Hotel

◉◉ Modern French, European

tel: 01556 640217 & 640311 **Shore Rd DG7 1QZ**
email: reservations@balcary-bay-hotel.co.uk web: www.balcary-bay-hotel.co.uk
dir: *on A711 between Dalbeattie & Kirkcudbright. In Auchencairn follow signs to Balcary along shore road for 2m*

Modern country-house cooking on the Solway coast

The solid-looking white hotel stands on the shore of the Solway Firth with views across the water to Heston Isle and the Lake District beyond. Soak up the views from the restaurant, with its predominantly blue and yellow colour scheme, a pleasant environment in which to enjoy some snappy cooking. The hotel might be in a secluded spot, but the kitchen team proves to be a forward-looking lot, turning out starters of hot-smoked trout with fennel and orange salad and a shallot and broad bean confit, and rolled pig's cheek in Parma ham with black pudding and cider jus. The daily-changing, set-price menu offers around five choices per course, with main courses extending from roast pheasant breast on Puy lentil stew with glazed shallots, carrot purée and game sauce to pan-fried beef fillet with spring onion mashed potato, roasted roots and gravy. Fish is imaginatively treated – perhaps grilled salmon fillet on a charred potato cake with candied beetroot and herb sauce – and to end might be lemon rum baba with thyme-poached apricots.

Chef Craig McWilliam **Owner** Graeme A Lamb & family **Seats** 55 **Times** 12-2/7-8.30 Closed Dec-Jan, L Mon-Sat **Prices** Service optional **Wines** 54 bottles over £30, 43 bottles under £30, 12 by glass **Parking** 50 **Notes** Sunday L £25.25, Vegetarian available, Children welcome

GATEHOUSE OF FLEET
Map 20 NX55

Cally Palace Hotel

◉ Traditional V

tel: 01557 814341 **Cally Dr DG7 2DL**
email: info@callypalace.co.uk web: www.callypalace.co.uk
dir: *From A74(M) take A75, at Gatehouse take B727. Hotel on left*

Formal dining using Scottish produce on the Solway coast

A Georgian country manor in 150 acres of parkland on the Solway coast, Cally Palace aims squarely at the golfing market, but you don't have to set off with the clubs to enjoy a stay. There's a full complement of leisure facilities, with 600 acres of the Fleet Oak Woods bordering the estate, plus hiking and biking trails in the area. Old-school opulence is the deal here, while the feeling of a bygone age extends to the formal tone in the restaurant – that means jacket and tie. The kitchen delivers gently-modernised country-house cooking built on soundly-sourced Scottish produce – perhaps white onion velouté with shaved parmesan and elderflower sorbet, ahead of pan-fried pork fillet matched with Stornoway black pudding, apple purée, potato fondant and Calvados jus. End with apple and frangipane tart partnered by almond and Amaretto ice cream.

Chef Jamie Muirhead **Owner** McMillan Hotels **Seats** 110, Pr/dining room 25 **Times** 12-1/6.45-9 Closed 3 Jan-early Feb **Prices** Fixed L 2 course £14-£22, Starter £4.95-£6.95, Main £9.95-£18.95, Dessert £3.95-£6.95, Service optional **Wines** 35 bottles over £30, 55 bottles under £30, 11 by glass **Parking** 70 **Notes** Afternoon tea £14.50, Sunday L, Children welcome

GRETNA
Map 21 NY36

Smiths at Gretna Green

◉◉ Modern British

tel: 01461 337007 **Gretna Green DG16 5EA**
email: info@smithsgretnagreen.com **web:** www.smithsgretnagreen.com
dir: *From M74 junct 22 follow signs to Old Blacksmith's Shop. Hotel opposite*

Inventive cooking in a striking modern hotel

Gretna's sterling service to the wedding industry continues unabated, an island of romance in a cynical world, and Smiths hotel doesn't stint when it comes to hosting some of the brisk nuptial business. Not surprisingly, the place is always turned out in its special-occasion best, not least in the fascinating chainmailed area of the restaurant, where a floor-to-ceiling cordon marks off a striking mirrored space. Concept starters set the tone, perhaps an artist's impression of ham, egg and chips incorporating 'liquid peas', or a 'winter picnic' comprised of a chunk of hot-smoked salmon, a smoked salmon sandwich, a quail Scotch egg, champagne jelly and caviar. Fish and meat combinations, often a risk, are handled persuasively, mixing pork belly, turbot, scallops and black pudding in one majestic main-course dish that manages not to lose any of its component flavours, and dessert could be well-executed orange and lemon tart with razor-sharp gin-and-tonic sorbet. And with that, you'll be ready to depart on your honeymoon.

Chef Phillip Woodcock **Owner** Alasdair Houston **Seats** 60, Pr/dining room 18 **Times** 12-9.30 Closed 25 Dec, All-day dining **Prices** Service optional **Wines** 31 bottles over £30, 37 bottles under £30, 12 by glass **Parking** 115 **Notes** Tea time menu 3 course £10.95 4.30-6pm, Sunday L £15.95, Vegetarian available, Children welcome

MOFFAT
Map 21 NT00

Brodies

◉ Modern British

tel: 01683 222870 **Holm St DG10 9EB**
email: whatscooking@brodiesofmoffat.co.uk **web:** www.brodiesofmoffat.co.uk
dir: *M74 junct 15 towards Selkirk, take 2nd right turn*

Smart modish cooking in contemporary setting

Brodies is open all day from 10am (10.30 on Sundays) and aims to satisfy with everything from coffee and cakes through to a full-on evening meal. This all-encompassing approach works a treat, making the place a valued asset just off the high street. The interior is bright and contemporary and quite easily flits between its roles of coffee shop and restaurant. There's confidence in the kitchen's output, with everything cooked in-house and made with good quality produce (some of it local). An evening meal might kick off with salmon, leek and carrot spring roll served with a sweet yellow chilli and ginger dipping sauce, or smoked duck salad with a raspberry vinaigrette. Main courses might deliver slow-roasted rump of lamb with braised red cabbage and sautéed pak choi, or salmon fillet with chorizo. Desserts are an equally international bunch, with treacle tart or chocolate and Amaretto cheesecake.

Chef Russell Pearce **Owner** Russell & Danyella Pearce **Seats** 40 **Times** 10am-11pm Closed 25-27 Dec, D Tue-Wed (Oct-Mar) All-day dining **Prices** Service optional **Wines** 15 bottles under £30, 7 by glass **Parking** On street **Notes** Early door menu available 5.30-7pm, Sunday L £13.95-£16.95, Vegetarian available, Children welcome

---

Hartfell House & The Limetree Restaurant

◉ Modern British

tel: 01683 220153 **Hartfell Crescent DG10 9AL**
email: enquiries@hartfellhouse.co.uk **web:** www.hartfellhouse.co.uk
dir: *Off High St at war memorial onto Well St & Old Well Rd. Hartfell Crescent on right*

Confident global cooking in a Victorian house

In a peaceful setting in an area of Outstanding Natural Beauty, Hartfell House is built of local stone and dates back to around 1850. Its period features are all perfectly intact, both outside and in. The resident's lounge is the place to linger over drinks either before or after dinner in the intimate Limetree Restaurant, which dazzles with gold cornices and ceiling roses. Non-residents would do well to book as this is a popular place to eat thanks to its eclectic menus informed by top-quality local produce. Malaysian spiced coconut milk soup with prawns, rice noodles, lime and coriander could precede loin of roe deer and Barony venison sausage with mushroom gratin dauphinoise, roast celeriac and carrots with thyme, and braised shallot sauce. For dessert you might well return to home territory with something like sticky gingerbread pudding with vanilla ice cream and treacle toffee sauce.

Chef Matt Seddon **Owner** Robert & Mhairi Ash **Seats** 26 **Times** 12.30-2.30/6.30-9 Closed Xmas, Mon, L Tue-Sat, D Sun **Prices** Fixed L 2 course £19.50, Fixed D 3 course £27.50, Service optional **Wines** 7 bottles over £30, 20 bottles under £30, 4 by glass **Parking** 6 **Notes** Sun L by arrangement, Vegetarian available, Children welcome

NEWTON STEWART
Map 20 NX46

Kirroughtree House
◉◉ Modern British

tel: 01671 402141 **Minnigaff DG8 6AN**
email: info@kirroughtreehouse.co.uk **web:** www.kirroughtreehouse.co.uk
dir: *From A75 take A712, entrance to hotel 300yds on left*

Historic mansion serving up fine Scottish produce

Built in the early 18th century by a chap who called Rabbie Burns a friend, Kirroughtree House is a grand pile indeed, set in bucolic gardens within the Galloway Forest Park. The traditionally elegant interior is rich with period panels, antique furniture and plush upholstery, while the formal service ensures everything remains tickety-boo. The restaurant matches the rest of the house with its classical proportions and sophisticated decor, but there is no longer a requirement for gents to wear a jacket at dinner. The formal, four-course dinner has at its heart excellent regional produce, sourced with due diligence by the kitchen team. Start perhaps with a game terrine, served at just the right temperature to maximise the flavours, with beetroot and orange chutney. Next up, a soup course such as broccoli and Stilton, followed by a main course such as breast of guinea fowl with rösti potato and rosemary jus, or salmon with a shallot butter sauce. Finish with a good looking warm plum clafoutis with crème fraîche sorbet.

Times 12-1.30/7-9 Closed 2 Jan-1 Feb

PORTPATRICK
Map 20 NW95

Knockinaam Lodge
◉◉◉ – see below

SANQUHAR
Map 20 NS70

Blackaddie House Hotel
◉◉ Modern British

tel: 01659 50270 **Blackaddie Rd DG4 6JJ**
email: ian@blackaddiehotel.co.uk **web:** www.blackaddiehotel.co.uk
dir: *300mtrs off A76 on north side of Sanquhar*

Traditional country-house hotel with engaging modern cooking

A veteran of many a stellar kitchen, chef-patron Ian McAndrew has been busily establishing the restaurant at Blackaddie as a dining destination for fans of locally-sourced, vibrant modern cooking – some of it as local as the seasonal veg, herbs and fruit that come but a few steps from the kitchen garden. The honey-hued stone hotel was once a rectory and sits in heavenly tranquil grounds alongside the River Nith, a renowned salmon fishing spot, and while its smart restaurant may be small, it certainly punches above its weight with such an experienced hand directing the action in the kitchen. The daily-changing menus fizz with good ideas and dishes impress with their depth of flavour and elegant presentation, such as a starter of seared diver-caught scallops with Parma ham, spiced apples, smoked Cairnsmore cheese, macadamia nuts and red wine dressing. Main course could bring roast monkfish with red wine rice, parsnip purée and bacon dust, then more well-conceived intricacy in a finale of white chocolate cheesecake with caramel-poached pineapple and Amaretto sorbet.

Chef Ian McAndrew **Owner** Ian McAndrew **Seats** 20, Pr/dining room 20 **Times** 12-2/6.30-9 **Prices** Tasting menu fr £64, Service optional **Wines** 10 by glass **Parking** 20 **Notes** Gourmet tasting menu 7 course, Fixed D 4 course £52, Sunday L, Vegetarian available, Children welcome

Knockinaam Lodge

PORTPATRICK
Map 20 NW95

Modern Scottish V ⬗ NOTABLE WINE LIST

tel: 01776 810471 **DG9 9AD**
email: reservations@knockinaamlodge.com **web:** www.knockinaamlodge.com
dir: *From A77, follow signs to Portpatrick, then tourist signs to Knockinaam Lodge*

Well-judged, classically based cooking in splendid Galloway isolation

The Victorian hunting lodge is now a luxury boutique hotel, in a remote spot accessed via a single-track lane, surrounded by 30 acres of grounds running down to a private beach. A warm family welcome awaits, with log fires, a relaxing lounge and a choice of more than 120 single malts in the oak-panelled bar hung with a stag's head. The dining room has a homely feel, with curtains at the windows, a wooden fireplace complete with coal scuttle, and shelves of decorative plates in alcoves. The daily-changing four-course menu is a no-choice affair except for a selection of British and French cheeses as an alternative to dessert. Tony Pierce cooks with assurance, his classically based approach entirely appropriate for the style of the operation. He sources ingredients locally, with some produce from the gardens or foraged in the woods and sometimes fished with his own hands. Meals are well balanced, and dishes are strong on flavour and short on fuss and gimmick. Dinner might kick off with simple but effective ideas such as seared Skye scallops and garlic butter, or grilled salmon fillet with pesto. Next up is a soup – perhaps oyster mushroom with truffles – before the main course, always a well-conceived combination of flavours. For example, dishes include slowly roasted fillet of Aberdeen Angus with pommes Pont-Neuf, a trio of onions and a port reduction, or noisette of lamb with a port and bell pepper reduction, a haggis beignet, parsnip purée and seasonal vegetables. A soufflé, always perfectly executed, may well round things off, perhaps clementine and Grand Marnier with green apple sorbet for contrast, or there may be an imaginative assembly of pear tarte Tatin with vanilla ice cream, ginger caramel and lime custard.

Chef Anthony Pierce **Owner** David & Sian Ibbotson **Seats** 32, Pr/dining room 18 **Times** 12.30-2/7-9 **Prices** Service optional **Wines** 7 by glass **Parking** 20 **Notes** Fixed L 4 course £40, D 5 course £65, Sunday L fr £30, No children

STRANRAER
Map 20 NX06

Corsewall Lighthouse Hotel

Modern Scottish v

tel: 01776 853220 **Corsewall Point, Kirkcolm DG9 0QG**
email: info@lighthousehotel.co.uk web: www.lighthousehotel.co.uk
dir: *Take A718 from Stranraer to Kirkcolm, then follow B718 signed Lighthouse*

A unique location with a true local flavour

Corsewall still earns its keep as a beacon for passing mariners heading into Loch Ryan, but it's also a hotel and restaurant. Needless to say the setting is something special, reached via a winding single-track road, with fabulous sea views towards Arran and Ailsa Craig waiting at the end. The accommodation and restaurant are in what used to be the keeper's living quarters and stores. There's a maritime theme in the restaurant, a traditionally-decorated room with bare wooden tables and a friendly, relaxed vibe. The menu keeps things relatively simple, so you might start with goats' cheese and red onion tartlet with a pesto dressing, before moving on to smoked haddock with a creamy Tobermory cheddar cheese sauce, or roast rack of Galloway lamb with a rich sherry, redcurrant and thyme reduction. Dessert extends to Amaretto and vanilla cheesecake with raspberry coulis.

Chef Andrew Downie **Owner** Kay & Pamela Ward **Seats** 28 **Times** 12-2.15/7-9.15 **Prices** Fixed L 2 course £12.60-£28.50, Fixed D 3 course £31.95-£36.70, Starter £3.85-£8.75, Main £8.75-£19.75, Dessert £7.25, Service optional **Wines** 9 bottles over £30, 24 bottles under £30, 2 by glass **Parking** 20 **Notes** Fixed D 5 course £35-£39.75, Sunday L £15.95-£19.50, Children welcome

THORNHILL
Map 21 NX89

The Buccleuch and Queensberry Arms Hotel

Modern Scottish NEW

tel: 01848 323101 & 330215 **112 Drumlanrig St DG3 5LU**
email: info@bqahotel.com web: www.bqahotel.com
dir: *On A76 in centre of Thornhill*

Hotel dining with a local flavour

The BQA to its friends, this family-run hotel has undergone an extensive refurbishment and emerged looking good and fit for purpose in the 21st century. There's a satisfying Scottish-ness to the place, which extends to the culinary output. The region's produce figures large on menus which show Pan-European leanings and no lack of ambition. A starter of smoked Solway haddock and butternut squash ravioli hits the spot, or go for the more exotic sesame prawn toast with pickled cauliflower mushroom and nori. Main-course local wild rabbit arrives in Wellington form, with truffle mash and roasted root vegetables, while Penrith chicken Kiev is enriched with black truffle and garlic butter. To finish, single origin chocolate fondant with salted caramel and vanilla ice cream competes with local cheeses (or you could have both). There's a classy bar menu, too, with ploughman's and a posh burger.

Chef Will Pottinger **Owner** The Sweerts de Landas family **Seats** 42, Pr/dining room 22 **Times** 10-10 All-day dining **Prices** Starter £4-£8, Main £14-£25, Dessert £4-£8, Service optional **Wines** 25 bottles over £30, 21 bottles under £30, 10 by glass **Parking** 100 **Notes** Sunday L £25, Vegetarian available, Children welcome

WEST DUNBARTONSHIRE

BALLOCH
Map 20 NS38

The Cameron Grill

Modern British

tel: 01389 722582 & 755565 **Cameron House on Loch Lomond G83 8QZ**
email: reservations@cameronhouse.co.uk web: www.devere.co.uk
dir: *M8 (W) junct 30 for Erskine Bridge. A82 for Crainlarich. 14m, at rdbt signed Luss, hotel on right*

Classy grill in grand lochside hotel

Cameron House sits in a great location on the banks of Loch Lomond, pulling off a classy act with its stylish blend of tartans and sybaritic contemporary looks. The decor in The Cameron Grill typifies the style with its dark and clubby masculinity – tobacco-brown leather chairs and banquettes, burnished darkwood, and a huge mural showing how clansmen caroused back in the day. It's not all about steak, but they are truly exceptional slabs of protein, cooked on a Josper grill, and the locally-reared stuff is joined by American grain-fed USDA Creekstone and Casterbridge from Devon. If you're a touch peckish and up for some red meat action, take a man-sized 500g rib-eye (we're in metric land here), from Angus-Limousin cattle bred at Cairnhill Farm in Ayrshire. Otherwise, start with ham hock and foie gras terrine with pineapple, parsley purée and dried tomato, then move onto Gressingham duck with leg meat pastilla, creamed Savoy cabbage, blackberries, and vanilla foam. The hotel is also home to the fine-dining Martin Wishart at Loch Lomond (see entry).

Times 6.30-10 Closed L all week, D 26 Dec

Martin Wishart at Loch Lomond

– *see opposite*

CLYDEBANK
Map 20 NS47

Beardmore Hotel

Modern British

tel: 0141 951 6000 **Beardmore St G81 4SA**
email: info@beardmore.scot.nhs.uk web: www.thebeardmore.com
dir: *M8 junct 19, follow signs for Clydeside Expressway to Glasgow road, then A814 (Dumbarton road), then follow Clydebank Business Park signs. Hotel on left*

Gently modish cooking on the banks of the Clyde

Handy for the M8 and overlooking the River Clyde, the Beardmore is a hive of activity. The large, modern hotel does a roaring business trade and has a health club (yin and yang, perhaps), a bar with its own menu, and a fine-dining restaurant. The latter is an intimate space lacking in natural light but not in charm, with abstract artworks, darkwood tables and a well-drilled service team. Respect is shown to the producers (some of whom are name-checked on the menu), there's a general appreciation of healthy living, and gluten-free dishes are clearly marked as such. Start, perhaps, with mosaic of Scottish game with spiced pear chutney and sourdough croûton served prettily on a black slate. Next up, braised cheek and roast tail of monkfish with rösti potato, creamed cabbage and tomato and chive beurre blanc, and, to finish, vanilla crème brûlée with flapjack biscuits.

Times 6.30-10 Closed Sun, L all week

CITY OF DUNDEE

DUNDEE
Map 21 NO43

DoubleTree by Hilton Dundee

Modern British

tel: 01382 641122 **Kingsway West DD2 5JT**
email: reception@doubletreedundee.co.uk **web:** www.doubletreedundee.co.uk
dir: A90 at Landmark rdbt, west Dundee city centre

Contemporary setting for modish and trad food

The original stone baronial mansion bristling with turrets was built to impress, but the whole place has been brought up to 21st-century spec with modern extensions, a smart leisure club, spanking new bedrooms and a classy conservatory restaurant. Looking into the hotel's six acres of lovely grounds and mature gardens, The Maze is named for the box hedge planting you see before you; it's an upmarket setting with linen-swathed tables and moody lighting at dinner. The kitchen steers a crowd-pleasing course with appealing menus of tried-and-trusted modern ideas. You could encounter spaghetti with prawns, basil, red peppers and lobster cream, ahead of an assiette of lamb comprising confit breast, cutlet and shoulder with dauphinoise potatoes, wild garlic, peas and broad beans. Ending it might be a deconstructed banoffee pie, in the shape of banana mousse and jelly, toffee parfait and Chantilly cream.

Chef Raymond Sterpaio **Owner** BDL Management **Seats** 100, Pr/dining room 50
Times 12-10 All-day dining **Prices** Starter £4.95-£8.95, Main £14.95-£18.25, Dessert £4.95-£6.95, Service optional **Wines** 14 bottles over £30, 26 bottles under £30, 9 by glass **Parking** 150 **Notes** Fixed L & D on request only, Sunday L, Vegetarian available, Children welcome

Malmaison Dundee

British, French NEW

tel: 0844 693 0661 **44 Whitehall Crescent DD1 4AY**
email: brasseriemgr.dundee@malmaison.com **web:** www.malmaison.com
dir: Phone for directions

Modern brasserie cooking in boutique style

The latest branch of the boutique Mal chain takes the score sheet to 13, and in this case it's a lucky number for the Dundonian dining scene. The setting is a majestic old hotel with a domed ceiling above a central wrought-iron staircase, reinvented with the Malmaison trademark sexy looks, which run through to the intimate candle-lit brasserie's velour seats and darkly atmospheric colour scheme. The menu plays the modern brasserie game too, but isn't scared to step outside the European classics to set out with tuna tartare with avocado, pickled ginger, soy and lime dressing and wasabi. A main-course grilled double chicken breast is pointed up with a punchy lemon and caper dressing, while fans of red meat will no doubt be overjoyed to hear that there's a gold-standard Josper grill to make sure those dry-aged steaks are sizzled to perfection. A vanilla crème brûlée wraps things up on a classic note.

Chef Steven Frei **Owner** Malmaison **Seats** 90, Pr/dining room 12
Times 12-2.45/5.30-10.30 **Prices** Fixed L 2 course £19.95, Fixed D 3 course £24.95, Starter £5-£9, Main £13-£36, Dessert fr £6, Service optional 10% **Wines** 25 bottles over £30, 16 bottles under £30, 41 by glass **Parking** Greenmarket multi-storey
Notes Sunday L £19.95-£24.95, Vegetarian available, Children welcome

Martin Wishart at Loch Lomond

BALLOCH
Map 20 NS38

Modern French V NOTABLE WINE LIST

tel: 01389 722504 **Cameron House on Loch Lomond G83 8QZ**
email: info@mwlochlomond.co.uk
dir: From A82, follow signs for Loch Lomond. 1m after Stoneymullan rdbt on right

Refined, intelligent cooking on the shores of Loch Lomond

Scottish culinary superstar Martin Wishart's first venture outside his eponymous Leith restaurant HQ has been a key address on the foodie itinerary north of the border since it opened in 2009, and the stately castellated mansion of Cameron House is a suitably five-star setting for the expansion of the Wishart brand. The loch-side restaurant looking over the bonnie, bonnie banks of Loch Lomond has always been a sybaritic setting worthy of a glossy interiors magazine, and a recent makeover has given the place a funky new look with lime-green banquettes, Regency-striped seats and an air of all-round refinement, presided over by a highly polished front-of-house team that makes sure everything happens at the right pace. Leith is still the centre of operations, so don't expect Wishart to be at the stoves: the man charged with interpreting the boss's contemporary take on French classics is head chef Graeme Cheevers, who keeps faith with the house style of hyper-precise, refined modern cooking. He likes to paint a pretty picture on the plate, and delivers assured flavours. Underpinning it all is spanking fresh, conscientiously sourced Scottish produce. There's a tasting menu, of course, and a vegetarian version that might even convert a hardened carnivore. From the carte, tartare of Borders roe deer is partnered with pear, chestnuts and smoked crème fraîche in a compelling first course, while mains could see a surf 'n' turf combo of braised pig's cheeks and langoustines with choucroute, parsley root purée, and parsley and garlic sauce. Other ideas might star turbot crusted with Comté cheese and delivered with caramelised onion, walnuts, pommes boulangère and sauce vin jaune. Nothing is out of place on the plate, and all the flavours work in harmony. Finish with Valrhona chocolate and orange mousse with Sacher sponge, and be sure not to leave without appreciating the magnificent wine list.

Chef Graeme Cheevers **Owner** Martin Wishart **Seats** 40 **Times** 12-2.30/6.30-10 Closed 25-26 Dec, 1 Jan, Mon-Tue, L Wed-Fri **Prices** Fixed L 3 course £28.50, Fixed D 3 course £70, Tasting menu £75 **Wines** 240 bottles over £30, 12 bottles under £30, 12 by glass **Parking** 150 **Notes** Tasting menu 6 course, Du Jour L 3 course, Sunday L £28.50, Children welcome

CITY OF EDINBURGH

EDINBURGH Map 21 NT27

Apex City Hotel

 Scottish

tel: 0845 365 0002 & 0131 243 3456 **61 Grassmarket EH1 2HJ**
email: agua@apexhotels.co.uk **web:** www.apexhotels.co.uk
dir: *Into Lothian Rd at west end of Princes St, 1st left into King Stables Rd. Leads into Grassmarket*

Modern brasserie cooking in a contemporary hotel

With its position on the Grassmarket and contemporary good looks, there's plenty to like about Edinburgh's branch of the Apex group. The Agua restaurant cuts quite a dash too, with its modernist clean lines, banquette seating and mellow contemporary colour tones. No starchy linen tablecloths here. The menu keeps in step with its brasserie-style offerings which match broad appeal with an inventive streak. Crab and lime bonbon with mango and basil is one way to kick off, or there may be rabbit terrine with cabbage and ceps, pea purée and pickled carrot. Main-course duo of lamb (seared rump and slow-cooked shoulder) is cooked with skill, and comes with aubergine, goats' cheese and potato bake. There's a market fish dish of the day and steak, too, plus desserts such as home-made Jaffa cake, which consists of syrup-spiked sponge, marmalade jelly filling, chocolate ganache and orange anglaise.

Chef James McCann **Owner** Norman Springford **Seats** 60, Pr/dining room 50 **Times** 12-4.30/5-9.30 Closed 20-26 Dec, All-day dining **Prices** Fixed L 2 course £14.95, Fixed D 3 course £19.95, Starter £5.50-£6.50, Main £14.50-£19.95, Dessert £5.95-£9.95 **Wines** 3 bottles over £30, 16 bottles under £30, 11 by glass **Parking** On street & NCP **Notes** Eat early 12.30-6.30 wkdays 2 course £9.95, Vegetarian available, Children welcome

Apex International Hotel

 Modern Scottish

tel: 0845 365 0002 **31-35 Grassmarket EH1 2HS**
email: heights@apexhotels.co.uk **web:** www.apexhotels.co.uk
dir: *Into Lothian Rd at west end of Princes St, then 1st left into King Stables Rd, leads into Grassmarket*

Accomplished modern cooking and views of the Castle

Enter the ground floor of this modern hotel and take the lift to the top to reach the Heights Restaurant, a large room with a pale colour scheme and floor-to-ceiling windows giving spectacular views over to nearby Edinburgh Castle. The kitchen makes good use of Scotland's abundant larder in a modern, international style of cooking. Start perhaps with cured Loch Etive trout, served with oyster mayonnaise and pickled cucumber, or pig's cheek and ham hock terrine with home-made piccalilli. Main courses are never too complicated to confuse the palate, among them maybe roast rump of lamb, cooked pink, with a pastille of the neck, smoked aubergine and pine nut purée, with the sea represented by roast cod fillet, properly timed, well matched by a clam and mussel broth and noodles. Desserts are variations of classics: perhaps coconut pannacotta with salt-baked pineapple, or pistachio sponge with matching ice cream.

Chef John Newton **Owner** Norman Springford **Seats** 120 **Times** 5.30-9.45 Closed Jan, Sun-Mon, L all week **Prices** Starter £6.50-£8.25, Main £14.95-£18.75, Dessert £7.50-£9.25, Service optional **Wines** 11 bottles over £30, 13 bottles under £30, 7 by glass **Parking** 65 **Notes** Pre-theatre Tue-Sat 2 course £30 for 2 people, Vegetarian available, Children welcome

Apex Waterloo Place Hotel

 Modern Scottish NEW

tel: 0845 365 0000 & 0131 523 1819 **23-27 Waterloo Place EH1 3BH**
email: edinburgh.reservations@apexhotels.co.uk **web:** www.apexhotels.co.uk

Clever contemporary food in slick setting

Grand Georgian proportions and elegant period features blending with a slick contemporary look give this hotel a classy edge, and the feel-good factor gets a further boost from a glossy spa and accomplished modern cooking in Elliot's Restaurant. The setting looks the part, mixing wooden floors, unclothed tables and curvy cream leather seats with corniced ceilings and soaring windows that flood the space with light. The kitchen deals in modern food that makes imaginative use of high-quality ingredients to come up with starters of Lanark Blue cheese pannacotta with roast pear purée, chicory, candied walnuts and walnut dressing, followed by Gressingham duck breast pointed up with satay glaze, pineapple purée, toasted cashews and hispi cabbage. Or you might go for a fish and meat combo of poached skate wing with glazed pork belly, cauliflower purée, salsify, morels and jus gras. Finish with burnt lemon custard with filo crisps and morello cherry sorbet.

Chef Simon Rush **Owner** The Springford family **Times** 12-3/5.30-9.30 **Prices** Fixed L 2 course £12, Fixed D 3 course £18, Starter £5-£9, Main £14-£22, Dessert £4.50-£5 **Wines** 11 bottles over £30, 13 bottles under £30, 13 by glass **Parking** On street (metered) **Notes** Pre-theatre 5.30-7pm 2/3 course £14/18, Vegetarian available, Children welcome

Bia Bistrot

 British, French NEW

tel: 0131 452 8453 **19 Colinton Rd EH10 5DP**
email: info@biabistrot.com
dir: *From city centre at Holy corner turn right onto Colinton Rd*

Classy bistro fare that is tasty and well-crafted

The 'Bia' element of the name is the Gaelic for food, the 'Bistrot' part perhaps rather more self-evident, and it's the winning setting for the cooking of husband-and-wife-team Roisin and Matthias Llorente. Their Irish/Scottish and French/Spanish ancestry seems to be a winning combination, too, with their bistrot serving up well-crafted and satisfying plates of food. It all takes place in a charming and easy-going environment, where wooden tables and smart leather seats stick to the 'bistrot' ethos. Lobster bisque of great depth of flavour comes with a salmon tortellini among first courses, or go for smoked haddock brandade with toasted rye bread. Main-course roasted rump of lamb is served with carrot purée and a textbook potato gratin, while a fishy main might be hake with broccoli purée and pan-fried polenta. Finish with a crêpe with caramelised apples and Chantilly cream, or British cheeses. There's a good value set lunch and early evening menu, too.

Chef Roisin & Matthias Llorente **Owner** Roisin & Matthias Llorente **Seats** 60, Pr/dining room 24 **Times** 12-2.30/5-10 Closed 1st 2 wks Jan, 2nd wk Jul, Sun-Mon **Prices** Fixed L 2 course £9.50, Starter £4-£6.50, Main £12.50-£19.75, Dessert £2-£7, Service optional **Wines** 5 bottles over £30, 15 bottles under £30, 9 by glass **Notes** Pre-theatre available 5-6pm, Vegetarian available, Children welcome

Bistro Provence

 French NEW

tel: 0131 344 4295 **88 Commercial St EH6 6LX**
email: reservations@bistroprovence.co.uk
dir: *Phone for directions*

Traditional Provençal cooking in the city centre

Michael Fons began his career, inauspiciously enough, working in a pizzeria in Marseille in the 1990s, but there has always been rather more to the British affection for Provence than pizza, and in 2013 he left a post at Gidleigh Park, Chagford to open a restaurant hommage to his native region in the Scottish capital. The city-centre venue, with its wide-windowed frontage, is done in impeccable modern style, with unclothed tables and white seating making a clean, neutral background for the provençal specialities to come. You'd have something to say about it if there were no fish soup with rouille and garlic croutons, and it's a relief to find there is, alongside baked scallops à la provençale, among 'Les Starters'. 'Les Mains' take in flambéed red mullet with braised fennel and peppers, and rosemaried lamb cutlets with polenta cake and piperade, sauced with sweet red Maury. To finish, there's traditional crème brûlée with cumin-flavoured langue de chat biscuits, or chocolate bavarois.

Chef Paul Malinen, Michael Fons **Owner** Michael Fons **Seats** 45, Pr/dining room 12 **Times** 12-3/6-10.30 Closed 1-10 Jan, Mon **Prices** Fixed L 2 course fr £12.50, Fixed D 3 course fr £26, Tasting menu £36 **Wines** 16 bottles over £30, 11 bottles under £30, 11 by glass **Parking** 20 **Notes** Tasting menu 4 course, Special offer L menu £9.50, Vegetarian available, Children welcome

Learn the latest foodie trends in Edinburgh and Manchester on page 21

Café Royal

 Modern Scottish

tel: 0131 556 1884 **19 West Register St EH2 2AA**
email: info@caferoyal.org.uk
dir: *Just off Princes St, close to Waverley Station*

Brasserie food in a heritage Scots-Parisian landmark

A Victorian plumber, one Robert Hume, put up this exquisite slice of Parisian rococo in the 1860s, with the intention of taking Edinburgh's breath away with the latest designs in bathroom furniture. Alas (though it's only a small alas), the washbasins and bathtubs never saw the light of day, as the place was commandeered to become the latest venue for the recently demolished Café Royal, which had once stood across the road. The stained glass, plaster mouldings and ceramic murals are as gasp-inducing now as they must have been when horse-drawn carriages clattered along outside, and the place was saved from the indignity of being sold to Woolworths (who remembers them now?) in 1969. This remarkable venue is thus preserved as a setting for modern brasserie cuisine, of the likes of accurately cooked mussels in a Thai broth of coconut, ginger, coriander and chilli, generous crab linguine with tiger prawns and chorizo, prosciutto-wrapped lamb with garlic mash in red wine, and warm chocolate and raspberry torte with vanilla ice cream.

Times 12-2.30/5-9.30

Castle Terrace Restaurant

@ @ @

EDINBURGH Map 21 NT27

Scottish, French V 🍷 NOTABLE WINE LIST

tel: 0131 229 1222 **33-35 Castle Ter EH1 2EL**
email: info@castleterracerestaurant.com
dir: *Close to Edinburgh Castle, at the bottom of Lady Lawson St on Castle Terrace*

Refined, intelligent modern cooking with style near the Castle

Castle Terrace is a modern, stylish and bright restaurant, nestling under the Castle, with a predominantly purple and brown colour scheme, darkwood tables and a gold ceiling. The switched-on staff are efficient and knowledgeable. Chef-patron Dominic Jack set up the restaurant in conjunction with Tom Kitchin, and the two establishments share the same culinary 'from nature to plate' philosophy, as printed on the menus, which means that a great deal of effort is spent on sourcing impeccable Scottish raw materials and some from further afield. The cooking is rooted in the classical French repertoire (Dominic spent many years in restaurants in France), and he creates some exiting, innovative dishes. Pâté en croûte of roe deer, with pear, prune and port, may be reminiscent of a French cookery book, but this is no slave to any one cuisine or style, so other starters may include sushi-style salmon tartare, and lightly curried seared scallops. 'Sea' and

'land' get equal billing among main courses and show an equally catholic approach as well as a well-considered balance of flavours and textures and accurate timings. So there may be paella with spelt risotto alongside roast monkfish wrapped in ham served on brandade with crisp potato and black olives, and saddle of venison with celery, celeriac, apple and caramelised walnuts as an alternative to pork fillet with braised fennel, smoked aubergine purée and basil gnocchi. Dishes are plated carefully and attractively, particularly when it comes to imaginative puddings of caramel soufflé with vanilla ice cream, chocolate sauce and honeycomb, and mango and lime marshmallow with pistachio profiteroles and mango sorbet.

Chef Dominic Jack **Owner** Dominic Jack **Seats** 65, Pr/dining room 16 **Times** 12-2.30/6.30-10 Closed Xmas, New Year (subject to change), Sun-Mon **Prices** Fixed L 3 course £28.50, Tasting menu £75, Starter £13-£19, Main £25-£42, Dessert £10-£12, Service optional **Wines** 260 bottles over £30, 6 bottles under £30, 18 by glass **Parking** NCP, on street **Notes** Tasting menu 6 course, Children 5yrs+

EDINBURGH *continued*

Calistoga Restaurant

◉ Modern American **NEW** ♦ NOTABLE WINE LIST

tel: 0131 225 1233 **70 Rose St, North Ln EH2 3DX**
email: bookings@calistoga.co.uk
dir: *In North Lane off Rose St, between Frederick St & Castle St*

The tastes and easy vibe of California with plenty of wine choices

If California was an independent country its economy would make it the 12th richest nation in the world (give or take), and here on a cobbled lane it is possible to reach across the Atlantic and get a taste of the great state's food and wine. It feels a bit like a wine merchant's because there's a choice of more than 100 bins from the region – reasonably priced, with a fixed mark-up so the better the wine you drink, the better value you are getting. There's a gently Californian feel to the decor, and an easy-going vibe all round – smart, but relaxed. Some of the dishes really suggest the USA (a starter of smoked turkey with citrus fruit and crisp bacon salad and cranberry chutney, for example), while others would seem equally happy with a modern European label. Main-course halibut has a broad bean coating and comes with herb couscous and tomato salsa, and there are steaks cooked on the grill.

Chef Alex MacKenzie **Owner** Gordon Minnis **Seats** 45, Pr/dining room 32
Times 12-2.30/5-10 Closed 26 Dec **Prices** Fixed L 2 course £12, Fixed D 3 course £25, Tasting menu £68, Starter £5-£12, Main £14-£28, Dessert £6-£8 **Wines** 27 bottles over £30, 86 bottles under £30, 13 by glass **Notes** Pre-theatre 5-6pm daily 2 course £12, Vegetarian available, Children welcome

Castle Terrace Restaurant

◉◉◉ – *see page 605*

Chop Chop

◉ Traditional Chinese

tel: 0131 221 1155 & 440 4708 **248 Morrison St, Haymarket EH3 8DT**
email: yin@chop-chop.co.uk
dir: *From Haymarket Station, restaurant 150 yds up Morrison St*

Reliable Manchurian café dining

Specialising in the culinary ways of China's Manchurian northeast (Dongbei) region, this enjoyable venue is effectively a Chinese café. The menu makes a courteous point of explaining the format to newbies, but basically anyone familiar with dim sum ordering will understand the drill. Choose from a slate of jiaozi or guo tie dumplings (boiled and fried, respectively), and get stuck in as the dishes arrive. The main menu deals in many well-rendered northern Chinese standards, among them crispy beef in ginger and vinegar, Changchun hotpot, and pork with ginger and coriander. Boiled and stir-fried noodle dishes are also highly reliable. The DIY dessert of sugar-string apple or pancake, which you crisp up for yourself by dunking them in iced water, is an entertaining way to finish, or there are yet more dumplings to ponder, of mixed fruits or peanuts. There's a sister branch in Leith (see entry).

Chef Xuwei Ku **Owner** Jian Wang **Seats** 80 **Times** 12-2/5.30-10 **Prices** Starter £2.95-£5.45, Main £4.45-£10.50, Dessert £1.70-£7.50, Service optional 10% **Wines** 11 bottles under £30, 6 by glass **Parking** NCP **Notes** Unlimited banquet £20.25, Business L 4 dishes £7.50, Sunday L £2.95-£10.50, Vegetarian available, Children welcome

Chop Chop Leith

◉ Traditional Chinese

tel: 0131 553 1818 & 440 4708 **76 Commercial St, Commercial Quay, Leith EH6 6LX**
email: yin@chop-chop.co.uk
dir: *From Ocean Terminal follow Commercial St for 400 yds*

Chop Chop's highly rated cooking to share in Leith

Leith is not without its share of eateries, and this is the pick of the Chinese crop. It's justifiably popular: a coolly elegant interior, everything prepared in-house, including noodles and dumplings, with no artificial additives, accurately timed and seasoned cooking, and an owner who visits China annually to keep abreast of culinary trends. The intention is for tables to order collectively and share dishes whenever they arrive. Order a banquet or start with a selection of flavour-bursting dumplings – perhaps beef, chicken and prawn – with dipping sauces, and go on to spiced-up fillets of tilapia, strips of lamb stir-fried with cumin seeds, and a bowl of noodles with vegetables in a piquant sauce hinting of chillies. Snow-white boiled rice is exemplary, prawn crackers are a mile above the average, and puddings are not overlooked: try dumplings stuffed with peanut butter, raisins and sesame seeds.

Chef Haiping Yang **Owner** Jian Wang **Seats** 100, Pr/dining room 10
Times 12.30-2.30/6-10 Closed L Mon-Fri **Prices** Starter £2.95-£5.45, Main £4.45-£10.50, Dessert £1.70-£7.50, Service optional 10% **Wines** 11 bottles under £30, 6 by glass **Notes** Unlimited banquet £20.25, Sunday L £2.95-£10.50, Vegetarian available, Children welcome

Dalmahoy, A Marriott Hotel & Country Club

◉ Modern, Traditional

tel: 0131 333 1845 **Kirknewton EH27 8EB**
email: mhrs.edigs.frontdesk@marriotthotels.com **web:** www.marriottdalmahoy.co.uk
dir: *Edinburgh City bypass (A720) turn onto A71 towards Livingston, hotel on left in 2m*

Golfing hotel with imaginative modern menu

An attractive stone-built country hotel near Livingston, Dalmahoy is dedicated to the single-minded pursuit of golf. Its dining room looks out over the greens, so there's no need to miss a single swing, and the split-level layout capitalises on the view. The style of cooking is modern British, with local produce to the fore and a certain stateliness to the presentations. An imaginative spin on the pea and ham theme turns up in a starter of gently set pea pannacotta with wafers of crisp pancetta and a pea salad dressed in white truffle oil, or there may be gravad lax with Scotch whisky in the marinade, served with a potato scone and biting horseradish cream. Main course might produce a monkfish steak in haricot casserole, or quality Perthshire lamb rump with spiced beetroot purée, Lyonnaise potato and pearl barley risotto. If you've started with a pannacotta, finish with pasta, as in ingenious chocolate ravioli in red berry consommé.

Chef James Thomson **Owner** Marriott Hotels **Seats** 150, Pr/dining room 18
Times 7-10 Closed L all week **Prices** Prices not confirmed, Service optional **Wines** 15 by glass **Parking** 350 **Notes** Sunday L, Vegetarian available, Children welcome

Divino Enoteca

◉ Modern Italian, International

tel: 0131 225 1770 **5 Merchant St EH1 2QD**
email: info@divinoedinburgh.com
dir: *Near National Museum of Scotland and The Grassmarket*

Exemplary Italian cooking and wines

Leave the cobbled street and descend the stairs leading into Divino Enoteca's stygian gloom punctured by candles and spotlights picking out the artwork on the bare-brick walls, a number of wine displays underlining that this is 'not just a wine bar but a wine library', to quote the restaurant. Clued-up staff are as knowledgeable about the wines as they are about the all-Italian menu, with the cooking based on the very best Italian produce. Pan-fried scallops on a bed of salad drizzled with sweet chilli sauce is a simple but effective starter, an alternative to one of the hand-made pastas: perhaps gnocchi with crisp Italian bacon, peppers and courgettes topped with parmesan and balsamic. Main courses can be as straightforward as pan-fried fillet of sea bream on orange-flavoured risotto with a julienne of vegetables, or as complex as baked quail wrapped in pancetta, stuffed with sausage meat and chestnuts, on a bed of spinach and honey-glazed butternut squash. The tiramisù here is in a league of its own.

Chef Leandro Crolla **Owner** Tony Crolla **Seats** 85, Pr/dining room 14 **Times** 4-mdnt Closed Sun, L Mon-Fri All-day dining **Prices** Fixed D 3 course £30-£40, Starter £5.95-£9, Main £10-£19, Dessert £4-£5, Service optional **Wines** 200 bottles over £30, 40 bottles under £30, 34 by glass **Parking** On street **Notes** Vegetarian available, Children welcome

The Dungeon Restaurant at Dalhousie Castle

◉◉ Traditional European

tel: 01875 820153 **Dalhousie Castle & Aqueous Spa, Bonnyrigg EH19 3JB**
email: info@dalhousiecastle.co.uk **web:** www.dalhousiecastle.co.uk
dir: *From A720 (Edinburgh bypass) take A7 south, turn right onto B704. Castle 0.5m on right*

Creative cuisine in a truly unique setting

Dalhousie Castle is a pukka 13th-century fortress in acreages of wooded parkland on the banks of the River Esk, so you know you're in for something a bit special when you're heading for the Dungeon Restaurant. And the reality does not disappoint: the barrel-vaulted chamber comes with a full complement of romantic medieval candlelit vibes and enough weaponry – suits of armour, battleaxes and broadswords – to sort out the French all over again. Mentioning our cross-Channel cousins, the cooking here has its roots in French classicism, and is built on top-class ingredients with plenty of luxury factor. But the kitchen doesn't rely on the one-off setting and posh ingredients for its effect: a spirit of eclectic creativity reworks it all with a clever contemporary spin that might see wild garlic and cream cheese terrine matched with roast plum tomato jelly and Bloody Mary foam, ahead of lavender and honey-glazed pork fillet served with artichoke barigoule and onion textures. To finish, consider date and walnut soufflé with coffee mocha sauce and honey madeleines.

Chef Francois Giraud **Owner** Robert & Gina Parker **Seats** 45, Pr/dining room 100 **Times** 7-10 Closed L all week **Prices** Prices not confirmed, Service optional **Wines** 52 bottles over £30, 43 bottles under £30, 10 by glass **Parking** 150 **Notes** ALC 5 course £49.50, Vegetarian available, Children welcome

La Favorita

◉ Modern Italian, Mediterranean

tel: 0131 554 2430 & 555 5564 **325-331 Leith Walk EH6 8SA**
email: info@la-favorita.com
dir: *On A900 from Edinburgh to South Leith*

Vibrant Leith Italian venue with more than just giant pizzas

The Vittoria group's Leith pizzeria aims to provide upscale Italian food for a vibrant city crowd, seated at booth tables amid aquamarine walls. The menu core is an inspiring list of 14-inch pizza variations, from Zia Rosa (topped with chicken, sweet peppers and cherry tomatoes) to truffle-oiled sausage and mushroom Montanara, all made freshly in wood-fired ovens. A vast list of cured meats or vegetable antipasti, multi-ingredient pasta dishes and arborio risottos broadens the choice. Snack on polenta chips dipped in spicy salsa, or perhaps seafood bruschetta, to start. Those not in the market for pizza may opt for pancakes of scampi, prawns and crab in Cognac cream sauce, or a sweet-savoury risotto made with caramelised pears and Taleggio. Traditional mains include steaks, veal chops and surf-and-turf options. Finish classically with pannacotta, tiramisù or ice creams. Cocktail pitchers help to get the party started, and there is a series of fixed-price deals for celebrations.

Chef Jareck Splawski **Owner** Tony Crolla **Seats** 120, Pr/dining room 30 **Times** 12-11 Closed 25 Dec-1 Jan, All-day dining **Prices** Fixed L 2 course £11.95, Fixed D 3 course £25-£27, Tasting menu fr £33, Starter £3.50-£7.25, Main £6.50-£25.75, Dessert £2.95-£5.95 **Wines** 4 bottles over £30, 26 bottles under £30, 7 by glass **Parking** On street **Notes** Sunday L, Vegetarian available, Children welcome

Galvin Brasserie de Luxe

◉ French

tel: 0131 222 8988 **The Caledonian, A Waldorf Astoria Hotel, Princes St EH1 2AB**
email: brasserie.reservations@waldorfastoria.com
dir: *On Rutland St off Lothian Rd at Caledonian Hotel*

Timeless French brasserie dishes à la Galvin

The well-composed menu at the more accessible of the Galvin brothers' Edinburgh operations (see also entry for The Pompadour) pleases diners hankering for a hit of cross-Channel classicism built on top-class Scottish produce. Housed in the luxurious Caledonian Waldorf Astoria, the setting also aims straight at the heart of Francophiles with its Parisian brasserie-styled looks: there are navy-blue banquettes, darkwood flooring and tables around a circular island seafood bar, and waiting staff in time-honoured black-and-white uniforms. As for the food, it's a trip to France without needing to fly: steak tartare, Burgundian snails, terrine of chicken, ham hock and foie gras with sauce gribiche are all present and correct, while mains take in the rich flavours and textures of duck confit with boudin noir and red wine sauce, or pork cutlet with pommes mousseline and Agen prunes. Classic desserts take in tarte Tatin with crème fraîche and rum baba with Chantilly.

Chef Craig Sandle **Owner** Chris & Jeff Galvin **Seats** 120, Pr/dining room 20 **Times** 12-2.30/6-10 **Prices** Fixed L 2 course fr £16.50, Fixed D 3 course fr £18.50, Starter £6-£11.50, Main £12.50-£28.50, Dessert £5.50-£7.50 **Wines** 35 bottles over £30, 31 bottles under £30, 16 by glass **Notes** Prix Fixe menu available until 7pm, Sunday L £15, Vegetarian available, Children welcome

EDINBURGH *continued*

The Gardener's Cottage
@ British **NEW**

tel: 0131 558 1221 **1 Royal Terrace Gardens, London Rd EH7 5DX**
email: eat@thegardenerscottage.co
dir: *Access from London Road*

Seasonal cooking in a sociable setting

This quirky restaurant is housed in a building dating from 1836 that was indeed once a gardener's cottage, The approach along the path through the kitchen garden past the poly tunnels that supply fresh veg and herbs will hearten any foodie keen on local provenance, and once inside, there's a funky retro vibe extending to old vinyl LPs providing the soundtrack. You need to be the gregarious type as seating is at long communal tables, so if such snugness with strangers is not a deal breaker, you're in for some irreproachably fresh, seasonal and local food delivered via a lunchtime carte and six-course set dinner. The former sets out with crisp pieces of Stornoway black pudding and hazelnuts tossed together with tagliatelle, followed by tender pink roe deer with heavenly roast potatoes, cauliflower purée, wilted garden greens and beetroot. At the end, moist carrot cake comes with nettle ice cream and hazelnut meringue.

Chef Edward Murray, Dale Mailley **Owner** Edward Murray, Dale Mailley **Seats** 30, Pr/dining room 10 **Times** 12-2.30/5-9.30 Closed Xmas & New Year, Tue-Wed **Prices** Starter £5-£7, Main £17-£19, Dessert £5-£6, Service optional **Wines** 13 bottles over £30, 9 bottles under £30, 11 by glass **Parking** On street (charges apply 8.30-5) **Notes** Fixed D 6 course £30, Vegetarian available

La Garrigue
@@ Traditional French, Mediterranean 🍷 NOTABLE WINE LIST

tel: 0131 557 3032 **31 Jeffrey St EH1 1DH**
email: reservations@lagarrigue.co.uk **web:** www.lagarrigue.co.uk
dir: *Halfway along Royal Mile towards Holyrood Palace, turn left at lights into Jeffrey St*

Charming bistro with authentic South of France menu

La Garrigue is the name given to the wild, herb-scented expanses of scrubland in Provence and Languedoc in the south of France and chef-patron Jean-Michel Gauffre (who hails from down that way) has brought the honest rustic cooking of this region to his smart neighbourhood restaurant in Edinburgh's old town. Inside, there are vibrant artworks on lavender and purple walls, and chunky wooden tables and chairs made by the woodcarver and artist Tim Stead. The regional cooking style delivers full-bore flavours, using good local produce in authentic French country dishes done properly. The menu is a list of things you want to eat, starting with a fish soup with croûtons and rouille, tasting as if it has been flown in straight from the quayside of Marseille. Gauffre was born in the heartlands of cassoulet so you can rest assured that his take on the rich stew of belly pork, duck confit, Toulouse

sausage and white beans is the real deal. Finish with baked cheesecake and cherry compôte, or a lavender crème brûlée.

Chef Jean-Michel Gauffre **Owner** Jean-Michel Gauffre **Seats** 48, Pr/dining room 11 **Times** 12-3/6.30-10.30 Closed 26-27 Dec, 1-2 Jan **Prices** Fixed L 2 course £12.50-£13.50, Fixed D 3 course £25-£35 **Wines** 33 bottles over £30, 30 bottles under £30, 12 by glass **Parking** On street, NCP **Notes** Sunday L £12.50-£16, Vegetarian available, Children welcome

Hadrian's
@ Modern Scottish

tel: 0131 557 5000 & 557 2414 **The Balmoral Hotel, 1 Princes St EH2 2EQ**
email: hadrians.balmoral@roccofortecollection.com
dir: *Follow city centre signs. Hotel at E end of Princes St, adjacent to Waverley Station*

Classy brasserie in landmark hotel

Not to be outfaced by its fine-dining sibling at the landmark Balmoral Hotel (see entry for Number One), Hadrian's, the more casual venue, is a useful address in its own right. The handsome art-deco styling of the chic brasserie is quite a head turner with its walnut floors, darkwood tables and subtle shades of violet and lime, while nattily turned-out staff in long white aprons and black waistcoats set the right tone for its repertoire of European-accented, yet unmistakably Scottish, dishes. Tuna carpaccio with oriental salad, sesame and coriander dressing is a starter that could pop up anywhere in the world, but move on to loin of Perthshire venison, served tender and pink, with red cabbage and gnocchi, or Isle of Gigha halibut with crab brandade and dill sauce, and you're clearly knee-deep in Scottish terroir. Awaiting at the finale are classic ideas – tiramisù with Baileys ice cream, or classic vanilla crème brûlée.

Times 12-2.30/6.30-10.30

Harvey Nichols Forth Floor Restaurant
@ British, Modern, International 🍷 NOTABLE WINE LIST

tel: 0131 524 8350 **30-34 St Andrew Square EH2 2AD**
email: forthfloor.reservations@harveynichols.com
web: www.harveynichols.com/restaurants
dir: *Located on St Andrew Square at the east end of George Street, 2 min walk from Princes Street*

City views and sharp modern Scottish cooking

Views of the castle – check. The Forth Bridge – check; the vista from the top floor of Harvey Nic's Edinburgh restaurant really does serve up the city on a plate. On the top floor, of course, there's the usual brasserie and bar, and the more refined restaurant itself. The latter offers a slick contemporary dining room with white linen on the tables and burgundy-coloured leather seats to sink into, and on the menu is some sharp, contemporary cooking. The kitchen turns out smart seasonal dishes that don't lack for contemporary finesse and Scottish ingredients. Duck roulade with Calvados-soaked apricots, piccalilli purée and melba toast is a typically creative first course, grounded in classical technique, but not adverse to a bit of fun. Next up, perhaps venison cooked sous-vide and partnered with a shallot Tatin, or a superb piece of North Atlantic hake with creamed leeks and parsley potatoes (the ingredients really do the talking with that one). Finish with blackberry and apple soufflé.

Chef Stuart Muir **Owner** Harvey Nichols **Seats** 47, Pr/dining room 14 **Times** 12-3/6-10 Closed 25 Dec, 1 Jan, D Sun-Mon, 24 & 26 Dec, 2 Jan **Prices** Fixed L 2 course £25, Fixed D 3 course fr £30, Tasting menu £65-£95, Starter £9-£13, Main £17-£25, Dessert £7-£10 **Wines** 266 bottles over £30, 46 bottles under £30, 16 by glass **Parking** 20 **Notes** Tasting menu 6 course, Afternoon tea £20 Sun-Fri 3-4pm, Sunday L £25-£30, Vegetarian available, No children

The Honours
 Modern French

tel: 0131 220 2513 **58a North Castle St EH2 3LU**
email: info@thehonours.co.uk
dir: In city centre

Classic French brasserie food Wishart style

Martin Wishart is a shining star of the Scottish (and indeed national) restaurant firmament, with his eponymous restaurant in Leith collecting awards aplenty. Here, though, he's bought his dedication to high quality and his attention to detail to the world of the French brasserie. There's a contemporary sheen to the place and a dedication to Scottish produce that delivers some feel-good food that proves the auld alliance is alive and well. A starter of crab cappuccino with rouille, croûtons and parmesan is a classy bowlful, or go for pressed duck and pistachio terrine with Morello cherries. Next up, there's grass-fed Scottish steaks cooked on the charcoal grill (T-bone, for example, with garlic and soy marinade), or ox cheeks à la Bordelaise. There are shellfish, too (Cornish oysters, or hand-dived Orkney scallops), and fishy mains such as monkfish tail with crisp potato and Puy lentils. For dessert, rum cake competes with the soufflé du jour, and there are after dinner cocktails if you're in for the long haul.

Chef Paul Tamburrini **Owner** Martin Wishart **Seats** 65 **Times** 12-2.30/6-10 Closed Xmas, 1-3 Jan, Sun-Mon **Prices** Fixed L 3 course £18.50, Fixed D 3 course £19.50, Starter £7.50-£18, Main £17-£34.50, Dessert £2.50-£7.95, Service optional **Wines** 34 bottles over £30, 22 bottles under £30, 20 by glass **Parking** On street **Notes** Fixed D Tue-Fri 6-7pm, Vegetarian available, Children welcome

Hotel du Vin Edinburgh
Modern British, French

tel: 0131 247 4900 & 0844 736 9255 **11 Bristo Place EH1 1EZ**
email: reception.edinburgh@hotelduvin.com **web:** www.hotelduvin.com
dir: M8 junct 1, A720 (signed Kilmarnock/W Calder/Edinburgh W). Right at fork, follow A720 signs, merge onto A720. Take exit signed A703. At rdbt take A702/Biggar Rd. 3.5m. Right into Lauriston Pl which becomes Forrest Rd. Right at Bedlam Theatre. Hotel on right

Bags of HdV style and sound brasserie cooking

The former city asylum is the setting for HdV's Edinburgh outpost. These days the setting is considerably more cheerful thanks to the group's trademark clubby look of well-worn leather seats and woody textures. There's a splendid tartan-clad whisky snug, plus a buzzy mezzanine bar overlooking the bistro, which offers the usual nods to France with its wine-related paraphernalia and hearty, rustic contemporary brasserie cooking that the group specialises in everywhere from Royal Tunbridge Wells to the Scottish capital. An Isle of Mull cheese soufflé is the signature starter, which you might follow with a classic plate of haggis, neeps and tatties, or perhaps hake paella.

Chef Gavin Lindsay **Owner** Hotel du Vin, Malmaison **Seats** 88, Pr/dining room 26 **Times** 12-2.30/5.30-10.30 Closed D 25 Dec **Prices** Fixed L 2 course £14.95-£16.95,

Fixed D 3 course £16.95-£19.95, Tasting menu £89.95-£129.95, Starter £6.25-£15.95, Main £12.95-£69.50, Dessert £6.95-£14.95 **Wines** 150 bottles over £30, 75 bottles under £30, 18 by glass **Parking** NCP **Notes** Sun brunch from £22.95, Sunday L £22.95-£29.95, Vegetarian available, Children welcome

Hotel Missoni Edinburgh
 Italian

tel: 0131 220 6666 & 240 1666 **1 George IV Bridge EH1 1AD**
email: info@gandvhotel.com **web:** www.quorvuscollection.com
dir: At corner of Royal Mile & George IV Bridge

Modern Italian cucina in a glamorous Royal Mile hotel

As we go to print we have been advised this establishment is now called the Q & V Royal Mile Hotel. This luxurious style-slave hotel delivers a colourful hit of in-your-face Italian glamour amid the Royal Mile's dour grandeur. The boutique bolt-hole oozes contemporary chic, with loud and proud design touches throughout-check out those gigantic vases sitting in the lobby windows-and its rooms come fully loaded with all the latest gizmos. The food, obviously enough, is Italian too, served in the bustling, light-flooded Cucina, where la dolce vita is enthusiastically celebrated amid a lively decor of bold slabs of paintbox colours and psychedelic abstract art. Chef Mattia Camorani comes from the Locatelli stable and offers a gently-modernised take on Italian cooking. Pasta and risotto dishes hit the spot – linguine with octopus, chilli and tomato is simple but oh-so good. Elsewhere, risotto with nettles and Gorgonzola might catch the eye, followed, perhaps, by saddle of rabbit with polenta and grilled radicchio, or steamed halibut with lentil stew. For pudding, how about a boozy baba soaked in Grand Marnier and served with orange sauce and yoghurt ice cream?

Chef Mattia Camorani **Owner** G&V Royal Mile Hotel **Seats** 90, Pr/dining room 40 **Times** 12.30-3/6-10 Closed D 25 Dec **Prices** Prices not confirmed, Service optional **Wines** 14 by glass **Notes** Pre-theatre 2/3 course 6-7pm £16/£19, Vegetarian available, Children welcome

The Howard
Modern Scottish

tel: 0131 557 3500 **34 Great King St EH3 6QH**
email: reception@thehoward.com **web:** www.thehoward.com
dir: E on Queen St, 2nd left, Dundas St. Through 3 lights, right, hotel on left

Quality Scottish cooking in an intimate hotel dining room

The Howard is very much in its Edinburgh element, a conversion of three 1820s townhouses on Great King Street in the heart of the New Town. Its 18 rooms are named after streets in the locality, and where other hotels have room service, the Howard has butlers, if you please. That the Atholl Restaurant seats a mere 14 covers is somehow in keeping with the tone of personalised solicitude, and its marble fireplace, smart table accoutrements and fresh flowers are a joy to behold. The modern Scottish cooking on offer is all about quality prime materials. Sautéed scallops are accompanied by black pudding, celeriac purée and a dressing of peppery rocket oil, or there might be velvety Jerusalem artichoke and leek soup garnished with cinnamon foam and garlic crisps. At main, delectably rich braised lamb shank comes with skirlie cake and puréed carrots in a rich, succulent jus, while Loch Etive salmon gets Shetland black potatoes and wilted spinach in a classic beurre blanc. Dessert is a highlight with correctly caramelised tonka bean crème brûlée.

Chef William Poncelet **Owner** Ricky Kapoor **Seats** 14, Pr/dining room 40 **Times** 12-2/6-9.30 **Prices** Fixed L 2 course £21-£26, Fixed D 3 course £27.50-£32, Tasting menu £55-£85, Starter £7.50-£14.75, Main £15.50-£28.95, Dessert £7.50-£9.95, Service optional **Wines** 50 bottles over £30, 10 bottles under £30, 10 by glass **Parking** 10 **Notes** Pre-theatre menu available, Sunday L £21-£26, Vegetarian available, Children welcome

EDINBURGH *continued*

Iggs

◉ Modern Spanish

tel: 0131 557 8184 **15-19 Jeffrey St EH1 1DR**
email: info@iggs.co.uk **web:** www.iggs.co.uk
dir: *In heart of Old Town, 0.5m from castle, just off Royal Mile*

Enterprising modern Spanish cooking in the city centre

Consisting of a restaurant and adjacent barioja (tapas bar), Iggs is the lifetime work of Ignacio Campos (Iggy to one and all) and 2014 saw it celebrate its 25th year. The restaurant has contemporary good looks and a fun, positive approach to life: there are no starchy tablecloths, black and white photos hang on the walls, and the music has a Latin vibe. The menu is full of Spanish heart and soul. Start with sopa de judias blanca (white bean soup – the menu is bilingual), which is full of flavour, or go for grilled sardines with black olive tapenade and cauliflower couscous. The famous acorn-fed Ibérian pigs might feature in a main course with spinach and olive oil purée and Rioja jus – the meat as tender and delightfully sticky as can be – or go for deep-fried hake served on the bone. Desserts can be as traditional as churros with a warm chocolate sauce.

Times 12-2.30/6-10.30 Closed Sun

The Indian Cavalry Club

◉ Indian

tel: 0131 220 0138 **22 Coates Crescent EH3 7AF**
email: info@indiancavalryclub.co.uk
dir: *Few mins walk from Haymarket Railway Station & the west end of Princes St*

The West End's Indian star serving authentic flavours

Just a few minutes from the city's hub, this Indian restaurant has been going strong since it opened its doors in 1986. It's a comfortable, good-looking sort of place, with a contemporary decor of creamy tones and a wooden floor, with well-appointed tables and professional, well-drilled staff. The kitchen deploys sound techniques and quality ingredients to produce the authentic flavours of the sub-continent, taking great care with spicing and seasoning. Start with a lamb crêpe stuffed with tender meat in a sauce that bursts with flavour, or perhaps seafood soup, before tandoori chicken in a rich, piquant sauce with spicy yoghurt. Try chargrilled fillet of sea bass and a sauce of your choice: one of lime and coconut, say, lightly sour and hot, from Goa. Vegetarian options, among them paneer palak (spinach and cottage cheese), get the thumbs up, as do naan and light and fluffy pilau rice, while desserts might run to gulab jamon in fruit syrup.

Chef M D Qayum, Biplob **Owner** Shahid Chowdhury **Seats** 120, Pr/dining room 50
Times 12-5/5.30-11.30 **Prices** Prices not confirmed **Wines** 9 bottles over £30, 23 bottles under £30, 2 by glass **Parking** On street **Notes** Sunday L, Vegetarian available, Children welcome

Jamie's Italian Restaurant

◉ Italian

tel: 0131 202 5452 **The Assembly Rooms, 54 George St EH2 2LR**
dir:

Backslapping Italian bonhomie Jamie-style

Housed in the historic Assembly Rooms, Jamie's Italian empire extends into the capital with all its backslapping bonhomie. Subdued lighting lends softness to the deep reds and ornately lofty ceilings of the room, and seating is a mix of booths, freestanding tables, banquettes, and counter seating at the bar, where whole hams and salsicce are suspended. Napkins are virtually big enough to act as tea-towels. For anybody who doesn't yet know the drill, it's laid-back Italian cooking stripped down to the essentials of hearty commensality, with sharing platters of antipasti

setting the ball rolling. After that might come crisp-fried squid seasoned with lemon and chilli, served with garlic mayo, then prawn linguine with fennel and tomato ragù and bundles of rocket, or truffled turkey milanese stuffed with prosciutto and Fontal, topped with a fried egg. Finish with Jamie's 'epic brownie', a warm fudge wodge still gooey in the middle, complemented by Amaretto ice cream. And caramelised amaretti popcorn. And chocolate sauce.

Times 12-11 All-day dining

Kanpai Sushi

◉ Japanese

tel: 0131 228 1602 **8-10 Grindlay St EH3 9AS**
dir: *Joined to Lothian Road behind Usher Hall*

Classic Japanese food in Edinburgh's culture zone

Just around the corner from the Usher Hall and the Traverse Theatre, Kanpai is a diminutive but elegant sushi place that takes its name from the Japanese expression for 'Bottoms up!' As well as the sushi bar itself, there is an open kitchen counter where you can watch the kitchen brigade setting about its well-drilled artistry, and there is a soothing absence of the staff shouting that often animates Japanese venues. Attention to fine detail, and naturally exemplary freshness, are the hallmarks of offerings such as seared tuna in home-made miso, delicately battered squid tempura, melt-in-the-mouth nigiri scallops, maki rolls of teriyaki salmon and avocado, and the moreish Tokyo roll – strips of breaded chicken with avocado wrapped in sticky rice with a light sweet dressing and a garnish of orange fish roe. Specials may include snow crab with onions in ponzu. To finish, the ice creams come flavoured with black or white sesame or green tea.

Chef Jack Zhang **Owner** Monica Wang **Seats** 45, Pr/dining room 8
Times 12-2.30/5-10.30 Closed Mon **Prices** Starter £2.50-£9.90, Main £8.90-£20.90, Dessert £4.20-£6.50, Service optional **Wines** 3 bottles over £30, 8 bottles under £30, 9 by glass **Parking** On street **Notes** Vegetarian available, Children 6 yrs+

The Kitchin

◉ ◉ ◉ ◉ – *see opposite*

Malmaison Edinburgh

◉ British, French

tel: 0844 693652 **One Tower Place, Leith EH6 7BZ**
email: edinburgh@malmaison.com **web:** www.malmaison.com
dir: *A900 from city centre towards Leith, at end of Leith Walk through 3 lights, left into Tower St. Hotel on right at end of road*

Dockside brasserie in the Mal boutique style

The first of the Malmaison boutique brand, Edinburgh's Mal occupies a renovated seamen's mission on the Forth waterfront in the old part of Leith. It's a perfect spot as the dockyards have been resurrected to house a trendy restaurant and bar zone, so there's a buzzy vibe about the place. The brasserie is a dark, clubby space with brown leather seating, ornate ironwork, deep burgundy walls, bold artwork, unclothed tables and candles and it all overlooks the Port of Leith (there's outdoor eating on the terrace too when the weather allows). On the menu is an impeccably contemporary and simple take on French brasserie food, which might start as classically as chicken liver parfait with spiced pear chutney and toasted brioche. The main course can be as unreconstructed as steaks or burgers, or those in the mood for fish could see immaculately-timed sea bass matched with chorizo, new potatoes and tomato and mussel dressing.

Chef Andrew McQueen **Owner** Malmaison Hotels Ltd **Seats** 60, Pr/dining room 60
Times 12-2.30/6-10.30 **Prices** Starter £4.95-£8.95, Main £12.50-£37, Dessert £5.95 **Wines** 33 bottles over £30, 9 bottles under £30, 42 by glass **Parking** 45
Notes Sunday L £19.95, Vegetarian available, Children welcome

The Kitchin

EDINBURGH   Map 21 NT27

Scottish, French V  NOTABLE WINE LIST

tel: 0131 555 1755 **78 Commercial Quay, Leith EH6 6LX**
email: info@thekitchin.com
dir: *In Leith opposite Scottish Executive building*

Benchmark modern Scottish cooking of great impact

A former whisky warehouse in Leith's dockside is home to one of Scotland's most dynamic chefs, whose name seems wholly suited to the trade. Tom Kitchin's star has risen since he (and wife Michaela) opened here in 2006, with TV appearances and cookery books to his name. With a CV that boasts time with Alain Ducasse and Pierre Koffmann, Kitchin's wealth of classical training and experience meant he hit the ground running. The 'nature to plate' philosophy is adhered to here with fervent passion, no mere lip service, but a dedication to the best ingredients at the very best time of the year. The restaurant itself reflects the wild colours of Scotland's countryside, with tones reminiscent of heather and granite, and an upscale sheen that befits the inspiration of the kitchen and the aspirations of the clientele. Those supreme ingredients arrive at the door in pristine condition and are turned into beautiful looking plates of food that spark with clever ideas and technical virtuosity, yet never compromise the integrity of the produce itself. The à la carte is the mainstay of the menu options, with a tasting version available if the whole table is up for it, plus a set lunch menu that amounts to pretty decent value at this level. From the carte, a starter of crispy Highland ox tongue lays down a marker, served with pearl barley risotto, pumpkin and sage, while another might see hand-dived Orkney scallops seared and partnered with a ragout of sea kale from Eassie Farm in Angus. Among main courses a splendid piece of turbot, landed at Peterhead, might steal the show, served with shellfish ravioli and a green crab consommé, but, then again, there's also sea bass poached in red wine with leek à la crème, squid, winkles and sea purslane. Difficult choices must be made. A meaty main course might be crispy veal sweetbreads served with roasted seasonal vegetables from St Andrews, or roasted mallard with endive Tatin and an orange sauce. This is contemporary cooking with clever twists and turns, but everything is so perfectly judged it simply seems timeless. Desserts maintain the excitement. A baked cheesecake with poached rhubarb and a jelly and sorbet of the same, competes for attention with a glazed lemon tart with a lemon macaroon and frozen yoghurt, and there are British cheeses in perfect condition served from the trolley.

Chef Tom Kitchin **Owner** Tom & Michaela Kitchin **Seats** 50 **Times** 12.15-3/6.45-10 Closed Xmas, New Year, 1st 2 wks Jan, Sun-Mon **Prices** Fixed L 3 course £28.50, Tasting menu £75-£90, Starter £16.50-£24, Main £28-£45, Dessert £11-£14, Service optional **Wines** 250 bottles over £30, 20 by glass **Parking** 30, On site parking evening only, all day Sat **Notes** Tasting menu 6 course, Game tasting menu £90 (autumn/winter), Children 5 yrs+

Norton House Hotel & Spa

EDINBURGH   Map 21 NT27

Modern Scottish, French

tel: 0131 333 1275 **Ingliston EH28 8LX**
email: nortonhouse@handpicked.co.uk **web:** www.handpickedhotels.co.uk/nortonhouse
dir: M8 junct 2, off A8, 0.5m past Edinburgh Airport

Proficient modern Scottish cooking near the airport

Outside the city, nor far from the international airport, Norton House was
nonetheless considered sufficiently close to the capital to be acquired in the
1880s by the Usher family, Edinburgh brewers, staunch Unionists and occasional
rugby players. It was built at the beginning of the Victorian age, and its interior
aspects show much of the Victorian designer's fondness and flair for stylistic
quotation. There are moulded ceilings in the manner of Robert Adam, and
Jacobean touches all over the ground floor. There's a choice of dining styles too,
with informal goings-on in the Brasserie, while Ushers restaurant, done in
modern neutrals with light brown napery and a wall feature of framed mounted
stones, is where Graeme Shaw gets to show his culinary paces. A nine-course
taster menu is certainly the hot ticket for those determined to test the range. The
array of technical proficiency, sensitive judgment and fecund imagination

produces dishes that are perfectly balanced: white onion and parmesan velouté
with a foie gras 'sandwich'; corn-fed chicken tortellini with Brussels sprouts and
chanterelles; Indian-spiced turbot, mussels, cauliflower and almonds; Perthshire
roe deer with cabbage, pancetta, baby onions and pear; apple trifle with
blackberry sorbet; and more. If it all sounds quite complex, the evidence on the
plate is refreshingly direct, with every component earning its place, as in a main
course of sea bass with Jerusalem artichokes, quinoa, puréed parsley root and a
razor clam. Nor is there any bashfulness about making a populist appeal at
dessert stage with Valrhona chocolate, salted caramel, peanuts and a malted
sorbet. Cheeses are accorded their own menu listings with detailed descriptions.
The nucleus is benchmark Scottish artisan varieties with one or two from France
and Italy, served with walnut bread and honeycomb.

Chef Graeme Shaw, Glen Bilins **Owner** Hand Picked Hotels **Seats** 22, Pr/dining
room 40 **Times** 7-9.30 Closed Jan-Feb, Sun-Tue, L all week **Prices** Tasting menu
fr £65, Starter £9.50-£11.50, Main £20.50-£38, Dessert £7.50-£8.95, Service
optional **Wines** 80 bottles over £30, 15 bottles under £30, 12 by glass
Parking 100 **Notes** Tasting menu 8 course, Vegetarian available, Children
welcome

Number One, The Balmoral

EDINBURGH   Map 21 NT27

Modern Scottish v 🍷 NOTABLE WINE LIST

tel: 0131 557 6727 **1 Princes St EH2 2EQ**
email: numberone@roccofortehotel.com **web:** www.restaurantnumberone.com
dir: Follow city centre signs. Hotel at E end of Princes St, adjacent to Waverley Station

Exquisite modern cooking at Number One Edinburgh

Number One Princes Street, the address of the sumptuous Balmoral Hotel, may as
well be Number One Edinburgh, such a landmark is it and so strategically placed
for the start of every memorable visit to the Scottish capital. Looming over
Waverley station, it is one of the country's grand old railway hotels, though that
classification rather belies its modern-day opulence. The august pilastered public
rooms establish a lavish tone, and in the Number One restaurant itself, its
interior designed by Olga Polizzi, an ambience of gold-coloured banquettes and
red lacquered walls hung with artworks on loan from the Royal College of Art, the
Balmoral offers a go-to dining experience fit for discerning international custom.
Jeff Bland's mum once told a careers adviser he was a dab hand at the
scrambled eggs, and the rest is history, though not a history set in stone, but one
that comports a tirelessly inventive culinary intelligence. Dishes are boldly but

carefully conceived, so that, although they may appear to be full of assertive
flavours, the central element always shines forth. That's exquisitely demonstrated
in a first course scallop trio surrounded by oxtail, lentils and parsley root in
Indian-spiced masala oil, in which the sweetness and freshness of the shellfish
exercises the greatest claim on the palate. Main courses might produce Loch
Duart confit salmon with an oyster, cauliflower purée and citrus-zesty
hollandaise, or perfectly timed Barbary duck in the company of turnips, hazelnuts
and pickled pear. Imaginative vegetarian outings have included truffled celeriac
spelt risotto with a crisp egg yolk and mushroom foam, and desserts maintain
the pace for a many-layered pastry millefeuille of pineapple and coconut with
rum-sozzled banana sorbet. All the incidentals, including stunning breads and
luxurious petits fours, are up to the mark as is the compendious, quality-driven
wine list.

Chef Jeff Bland, Brian Gringer **Owner** Rocco Forte Hotels **Seats** 55 **Times** 6.30-10
Closed 3-15 Jan, L all week **Prices** Fixed D 3 course fr £68, Tasting menu fr £75,
Service optional **Wines** 10 bottles over £30, 8 by glass **Parking** NCP & on street
Notes Children welcome

EDINBURGH *continued*

Mithas

◎◎ Modern Indian V

tel: 0131 554 0008 **7 Dock Place EH6 6LU**
email: dine@mithas.co.uk
dir: *Commercial St, Commercial quay, near to Scottish executive building*

Modern Indian cooking at the docks

The Leith dock area does not want for good places to eat, but Mithas is a great addition to the community – a modern Indian restaurant with real va-va-voom. It avoids clichés in the decor and on the menu, whilst respecting tradition. The kitchen is open to view so the tantalising sight and smells of the searing grill and tandoori ovens gets you in the mood. The quality of the ingredients deserves a mention, as does the fact that they have a BYO policy with no corkage charge for table wine or fizz. The à la carte menu is supported by tasting versions that are worth checking out. Start with partridge, marinated in honey and mustard and cooked in the tandoor, served with three sauces (plum chutney, sweet chilli and a dried spice), followed by samudri khazana, which is scallops, monkfish, mussels, clams, sea bass and langoustines served in a spring onion and coconut gravy – superb seafood and a great flavour. The carrot taster dessert makes a fabulous finale.

Chef Pramod Nawani **Owner** Islam Mohammed **Seats** 72, Pr/dining room 14 **Times** 12-2.30/5.30-10 Closed 26 Dec, Mon, L 1 Jan, D 25 Dec **Prices** Fixed L 2 course £9.95-£11.95, Tasting menu £29.95-£49.95, Starter £4.95-£24.95, Main £9.95-£29.95, Dessert £5.95-£7.95, Service optional **Wines** 39 bottles over £30, 34 bottles under £30, 11 by glass **Parking** On street **Notes** Sunday L £9.95-£19.95, No children

Norton House Hotel & Spa

◎◎◎ – *see opposite*

Number One, The Balmoral

◎◎◎ – *see opposite*

Ondine Restaurant

◎◎ Seafood ⚑ NOTABLE WINE LIST

tel: 0131 226 1888 **2 George IV Bridge EH1 1AD**
email: enquiries@ondinerestaurant.co.uk
dir: *In Edinburgh City Centre, just off the Royal Mile*

Contemporary seafood restaurant with ethical outlook

Ondine has earned a loyal following in a few short years, and it's not hard to see why: just off the Royal Mile, on George IV Bridge, it's a modish space with great views out over the old town, but sustainable seafood served amid an atmosphere of cheerful bustle is the main draw, and the sustainability ethos is not empty marketing speak. You could take a high seat at the central horseshoe-shaped crustacea bar, or park on a stripy banquette and get things under way with oysters – 4 types, no less, either as they come or cooked (tempura or grilled with Charentais sausage, perhaps) – or something like a classic fish and shellfish soup with the time-honoured accompaniments of rouille, gruyère and croûtons. Chef Roy Brett

takes a sensibly restrained approach, so nothing is overworked and every molecule of flavour is extracted from the first-class piscine produce at his disposal. Thus main course might be simple crab gnocchi with lemon and garlic, sea bream curry, or good old-fashioned deep-fried haddock and chips with minted pea purée.

Chef Roy Brett **Owner** Roy Brett **Seats** 70, Pr/dining room 8 **Times** 12-3/5.30-10 Closed 1st wk Jan, Sun **Prices** Fixed L 2 course £22, Starter £8-£12, Main £14-£49, Dessert £8-£11, Service optional **Wines** 60 bottles over £30, 6 bottles under £30, 25 by glass **Parking** On street or Castle Terrace car park **Notes** Pre-theatre menu 2/3 course £22/£25 5.30-6.30pm, Vegetarian available, Children welcome

One Square

◎ Modern British

tel: 0131 221 6422 **The Sheraton Grand Hotel & Spa,**
1 Festival Square EH3 9SR
email: info@onesquareedinburgh.co.uk **web:** www.onesquareedinburgh.co.uk
dir: *Off Lothian Road. Entrance to hotel behind Standard Life building*

Modern regional cooking in a trendy setting

The views of Edinburgh Castle certainly give a sense of place to One Square, a slick, modern dining option in The Sheraton Grand hotel. The menu plays its part, too, serving up a good number of traditional dishes, albeit spruced up for the modern consumer. The restaurant and bar are sleek, contemporary spaces, with floor-to-ceiling windows and a cool, classy finish. The broad menu aims to satisfy all day long, so there are steak sandwiches, BLT, a posh burger and the like, but this kitchen can turn its hand to many things. Their version of partan bree is rich with crab and comes topped with fritters made from the brown meat, or go for monkish 'scampi' with a citrus mayonnaise. Next up, lamb Wellington with spiced carrot purée and burnt leek has the meat nicely pink, the pastry cooked just right, while a fishy main course sees sea bream partnered with Madras-spiced mussel broth. Finish with a warm apple and bramble tart.

Chef Craig Hart **Owner** Sheraton Grand **Seats** 90, Pr/dining room 40 **Times** 7am-11pm All-day dining **Prices** Fixed L 2 course £16, Fixed D 3 course £20, Tasting menu £60-£80, Starter £5-£13, Main £9-£31, Dessert £2-£8.50 **Wines** 29 bottles over £30, 23 bottles under £30, 11 by glass **Parking** 125 **Notes** Unique Dining Experiences at The Pass or The Kitchen Table, Sunday L £29, Vegetarian available, Children welcome

Plumed Horse

◎◎◎ – *see page 614*

Pompadour by Galvin

◎◎◎ – *see page 614*

Restaurant Mark Greenaway

◎◎◎ – *see page 615*

Restaurant Martin Wishart

◎◎◎◎ – *see page 616*

Plumed Horse

EDINBURGH
Map 21 NT27

Modern European 🍷 NOTABLE WINE LIST

tel: 0131 554 5556 **50-54 Henderson St, Leith EH6 6DE**
email: contact@plumedhorse.co.uk **web:** www.plumedhorse.co.uk
dir: *From city centre N on Leith Walk, left into Great Junction St & 1st right into Henderson St.*

Consistently impressive contemporary cuisine near the Leith dockland

The smart frontage on a street corner in Leith confirms that this is a classy restaurant, with an upmarket modern decor, high-backed cream leather dining chairs at neatly set tables and abstracts hanging on muted green walls. Tony Borthwick has a magician's touch, turning out consistently original dishes, and painstaking attention to detail and high levels of workmanship define the kitchen's output. Anyone for a potage of oyster, scallop and plaice flavoured with apple, ginger and herbs accompanied by caviar? Canapés and an amuse-bouche post notice of the kitchen's serious intentions. They are followed by some daring but memorable combinations such as carpaccio of wood pigeon with pickled baby vegetables, smoked apple, black radish and truffle mayonnaise, or pavé of smoked salmon and trout with crab salad, crab bisque purée, pink grapefruit and a quail's egg. The cooking showcases the finest native produce, and main courses can be masterpieces of multiple flavours: witness veal kidneys with Black Forest ham accompanied by sautéed scallops, shallot purée, salsify, artichoke and sauce diable. Fish is given the same adventurous treatment, so expect bacon-wrapped roast fillet of monkfish with smoked eel, white bean cassoulet and parsley and truffle sauce. That such combinations succeed so well is down to Borthwick's intelligence and masterly

understanding of what will work, exemplified by puddings of pineapple tarte fine with jasmine and lemongrass pannacotta, coriander purée and rum and coconut sorbet.

Chef Tony Borthwick, William Grubb **Owner** The Company of The Plumed Horse Ltd **Seats** 40 **Times** 12-2/7-9 Closed Xmas, New Year, 2 wks summer, 1 wk Etr, Sun-Mon **Prices** Fixed L 2 course £21-£43, Fixed D 3 course £55, Tasting menu £69, Service optional **Wines** 229 bottles over £30, 32 bottles under £30, 16 by glass **Parking** On street **Notes** Tasting menu 8/9 course, Vegetarian available, Children 5 yrs+

Pompadour by Galvin

EDINBURGH
Map 21 NT27

Modern French V 🍷 NOTABLE WINE LIST

tel: 0131 222 8975 & 222 8777 **The Caledonian, Waldorf Astoria Hotel, Princes St EH1 2AB**
email: pompadour.reservations@waldorfastoria.com **web:** www.galvinrestaurants.com
dir: *Situated on east end of Princess St, on Rutland St & Lothian Rd*

Haute cuisine Galvin-style comes to Edinburgh

The Caledonian Waldorf Astoria is a grand Victorian railway-era hotel restored to its full glory after a megabucks refurbishment, and The Pompadour, its grande dame of a restaurant, has been a byword for opulence since it opened its doors in 1925. The old girl was always considered to be the hottest ticket in town before the culinary opposition over in the rejuvenated Leith docks upped the ante, and it is still up there as a contender now the empire-building Galvin brothers have come to town and set up their high-end gastronomic HQ in its palatial environs. 'The Pomp' – as locals affectionately know this belle époque extravaganza – still provokes sharp intakes of breath from awe-struck diners as they take in its wedding cake plasterwork, delicate hand-painted panelling and peerless views of Edinburgh Castle perched upon its lofty crag. They've certainly nailed the

luxurious service vibe with a full-works, classical French hierarchy as professional, charming and efficient a team as you're ever likely to encounter, including a seriously knowledgeable sommelier to guide you through the oh-so French listings. Naturally, The Pompadour shows the same Francophile culinary direction as the Galvins' celebrated London establishments, delivering rich seasonal ingredients that sit together happily, prepared with razor-sharp technical ability and realised with haute cuisine flair. A procession of intricately presented dishes might begin with roast John Dory, partnered with pig's trotter and veal sweetbreads, parsnip purée and apple fondant, or a wood pigeon pot au feu with cavolo nero and truffle macaroni. Next up, roast monkfish 'osso buco' might arrive with the robust flavours of smoked potato purée and Bourguignon garnish. Finally, an impeccable apple tarte Tatin with vanilla ice cream shows there's nothing quite like a classic done right.

Chef Craig Sandle **Owner** Chris & Jeff Galvin **Seats** 60, Pr/dining room 20 **Times** 6.30-10 Closed 2 wks Jan, Sun-Mon, L all week **Prices** Fixed D 3 course £30-£58, Tasting menu fr £68, Starter fr £18, Main fr £30, Dessert fr £10 **Wines** 229 bottles over £30, 6 bottles under £30, 28 by glass **Parking** 42 **Notes** Tasting menu 7 course, Children welcome

EDINBURGH *continued*

Rhubarb at Prestonfield House

◉◉ Traditional British ⚑ NOTABLE WINE LIST

tel: 0131 225 1333 **Priestfield Rd EH16 5UT**
email: reservations@prestonfield.com **web:** www.rhubarb-restaurant.com
dir: *Exit city centre on Nicholson St, onto Dalkeith Rd. At lights turn left into Priestfield Rd. Prestonfield on left*

Opulent surroundings for high-impact cooking

Amateur food historians might like to take note that this restaurant has more right than most to name itself after the eponymous Asian vegetable, since it was the former owner of Prestonfield, Sir Alexander Dick, who brought the exotic rarity to Scotland in 1746. The blue-blooded 17th-century mansion wears a rather different set of clothes these days: the designers have done their stuff, kitting out the old girl with a decadent, theatrical and rather glam boudoir look that delivers all the wow-factor you'd expect from Regency rooms done out with chandeliers and oil paintings set against darkly opulent shades of blood red and burgundy. The food is no wallflower either, thanks to a kitchen that makes its own luxurious contribution, blending old-school classicism with an eclectic contemporary spirit. Hand-dived scallops appear with a supporting cast of cauliflower purée, lovage, chorizo, apple and truffle dressing and confit lemon, all staged to make maximum visual impact. Next up, roast loin of Strathspey venison with black pudding crumble, red cabbage purée, and Arran mustard and potato mousse. An intricate dessert brings together top-notch chocolate flavoured with extra-virgin olive oil with financiers, coconut ice cream, and a sphere of Earl Grey tea-flavoured gel.

Times 12-2/6.30-10

Restaurant Mark Greenaway

EDINBURGH	Map 21 NT27

Modern British **NEW**
tel: 0131 2261155 **69 North Castle St EH2 3LJ**
email: bookings@rmgedinburgh.com
dir: *Phone for directions*

Tautly controlled, imaginative dishes from a Scottish food ambassador

Having represented Scotland on *The Great British Menu*, and cooked at such stellar establishments as One Devonshire Gardens, Glasgow, and Kilcamb Lodge, Strontian, Mark Greenaway is one of the prime movers and shakers north of the border. He opened his self-named restaurant on the corner of North Castle and Queen Streets in 2011, and with Martin Wishart's Honours on the opposite side of the road, is clearly in good company. A few steps lead up to the entrance, allowing the place an elevated view of Queen Street gardens, and the scene inside is one of classy, understated civility. Dark grey walls and smartly clothed tables with bistro-style chairs are offset with a partition decorated in a geometric design. Greenaway is an ambassador for fine Scots produce, showing off thoroughbred ingredients in dishes brimming with flair and imagination, and although there is undeniably a lot going on, everything feels tautly controlled and cohesive. A starter of sweet-savoury components comprises millet grains, popcorn, tarragon porridge, pickled beetroot, radicchio and labneh with saffron mayonnaise, or there could be citrus-cured sea trout with mandarin gel, roast langoustine, brioche tuile and sweet capers. Main courses offer counter-intuitive spins on classic preparations, so counter indeed that they all but leave intuition behind, as for monkfish bourguignon, where the beautifully timed tail cut appears with chargrilled octopus, crisp pancetta and puréed carrot, plus the bourguignon elements of mushrooms and baby onions and buttery red wine sauce. Clash Farm pork belly is roasted for 11 hours, and served alongside blackened fillet and a pig cheek pie in toffee apple jus. Complex variations are conjured in a dessert of rich chocolate tart with custard jelly, frozen cookies, crème fraîche parfait, salted caramel and kumquat purée, with occasional explosions of popping candy going off here and there for good measure.

Chef Mark Greenaway **Owner** Mark Greenaway, Nicola Jack **Seats** 60
Times 12-2.30/5.30-10 Closed 24-26 Dec, 1-2 Jan, Sun-Mon **Prices** Fixed L 2 course £17-£30, Tasting menu £65.50-£100, Starter £8-£13, Main £21-£29, Dessert £8-£10.50, Service optional **Wines** 67 bottles over £30, 25 bottles under £30, 13 by glass **Parking Notes** Vegetarian available, Children 5 yrs+

Restaurant Martin Wishart

EDINBURGH　　　　　　　　　　　　　Map 21 NT27

Modern French **V**  NOTABLE WINE LIST

tel: 0131 553 3557 **54 The Shore, Leith EH6 6RA**
email: info@martin-wishart.co.uk
dir: *off the A199*

Contemporary French cooking from Scotland's darling of the restaurant scene

Martin Wishart opened the doors of his eponymous restaurant in 1999, which put him at the forefront of the regeneration of the Leith dock area. Others have followed. Having trained with many of the great and the good of the British culinary scene (names such as Albert Roux, Michel Roux jnr and Marco Pierre White), his experience was in modern French cuisine, and that, combined with a passion for Scotland's superb produce, has resulted in a restaurant that is a benchmark for culinary excellence. Wishart hasn't let the grass grow under his feet, with openings at Cameron House in Loch Lomond and a classy brasserie in the centre of Edinburgh (it is called The Honours). The elegant dining room overlooking the water has a gently contemporary finish – refined and civilised – with tables dressed in pristine linen and set with sparkling glassware, and a mellow colour palette of creams and shades of natural wood. The service team match the slickness of the surroundings with their professionalism and are well informed regarding the culinary output from the kitchen. There is an underlying intelligence to the cooking here, everything is on the plate for a reason, each element contributing to the whole, and flavour very much to the fore. Everything looks beautiful on the plate, the precision in the execution really quite remarkable. There is an à la carte menu but it isn't much cheaper than the tasting menu, so this is perhaps a good time to settle in and let the chef lead the way. There's also a fish, shellfish and crustacean-only tasting menu. Dish descriptions are brief, but the excellent service team can

help expand where necessary. From the tasting menu, partridge ravioli might get the ball rolling, served with cabbage flavoured with sage and a truffle sauce. Next up, a céviche of halibut, the fish as fresh as you're likely to find anywhere, with mango and passionfruit, and then Loch Fyne crab 'Marie Rose', with a tartare of rose veal, tomato and crab mayonnaise. These are dishes that positively resound with flavour. Roasted veal sweetbreads are served in the company of chestnuts and potato, and roast loin of Ayrshire hare with a pastilla made from the braised leg meat. A sweet course Bramley apple soufflé with apple butter sauce ends things on a high. The superb breads, canapés, amuse-bouche and a first-class wine list complete a truly class act.

Chef Martin Wishart, Joe Taggart **Owner** Martin Wishart **Seats** 50, Pr/dining room 10 **Times** 12-2/6.30-10 Closed 25-26 Dec, 1 Jan, 2 wks Jan, Sun-Mon **Prices** Fixed L 3 course £28.50, Fixed D 3 course £70, Tasting menu £75, Service optional **Wines** 250 bottles over £30, 9 bottles under £30, 17 by glass **Parking** On street **Notes** Tasting menu 6 course, Children welcome

EDINBURGH *continued*

The Scran & Scallie

🏵 Traditional British **NEW** v NOTABLE WINE LIST

tel: 0131 332 6281 **1 Comely Bank Rd EH4 1DT**
email: info@scranandscallie.com
dir: *Phone for directions*

Classy pub grub from two stellar chefs

From the local maestros behind The Kitchin and Castle Terrace, Tom Kitchin and Dominic Jack's pub is done out in a fashionable shabby-chic, with exposed brick walls and heritage artworks and fabrics. It's a popular place with bags of style and a chilled-out vibe, just the right sort of setting for a menu of rustic dishes combining classy modern classics with traditional preparations that might have previously fallen out of favour. 'From nature to plate', the restaurant says. Newhaven crab and coriander ravioli shows rather more refinement than you might be expecting, the little parcels packed with flavour, or else you can start with game terrine with pear chutney and toast. Main-course pheasant ballottine is another classy little number, or go for the house burger or steak pie. The feel-good factor continues with desserts in the shape of a chocolate brownie with stout ice cream.

Chef David Umpherson **Owner** Tom Kitchin, Dominic Jack **Seats** 138 **Times** 12-3/6-10 Closed 25 Dec **Prices** Fixed L 3 course £15, Starter £5.50-£9, Main £9.50-£19, Dessert £5.50-£8.50, Service optional **Wines** 25 bottles over £30, 19 bottles under £30, 44 by glass **Parking** On street **Notes** Sunday L £14-£23, Children welcome

The Sheep Heid

🏵 British

tel: 0131 661 7974 **43-45 The Causeway EH15 3QA**
email: enquire@thesheepheidedinburgh.co.uk
dir: *A1 from city centre towards Musselburgh, right at lights into Duddingston Road West, take 4th or 5th right into The Causeway*

Hearty dining in the city's oldest pub

Said to be Edinburgh's oldest pub, The Sheep Heid has fed and watered the residents of Duddingston village since 1360. After an appetite sharpening ramble in nearby Holyrood Park, it makes for a convivial pitstop with its relaxed, shabby-chic decor of olive-green painted panelling, traditional pews and mismatched chairs at bare wooden tables. If you prefer the pubby setting, complete with antique skittle alley, stay downstairs; alternatively, go up to the eclectically-furnished first-floor restaurant. Wherever you settle, expect straight-talking food with generous portions, big flavours and splendid ingredients. Sautéed Portobello and oyster mushrooms in Marsala cream sauce on toasted ciabatta is a good way to start, followed by smoked loin of cod served with spiced Puy lentils, wilted greens and a salt-cod fritter. For pudding, rich Columbian chocolate provides the oomph in a glazed brownie with vanilla ice cream.

Times 12-10 All-day dining

Stac Polly

🏵 Scottish

tel: 0131 556 2231 **29-33 Dublin St EH3 6NL**
email: bookings@stacpolly.com
dir: *On corner of Albany St & Dublin St*

City centre cellar with Franco-Scottish flavour

In the New Town area of Edinburgh, Stac Polly occupies a labyrinthine cellar and serves up Scottish dishes with the twang of a French accent. Housed in a 200-year-old building, the place has loads of character thanks to stone floors, bare-brick walls, linen-clad tables, and there's even a small outside courtyard if you fancy a bit of alfresco eating. The well-judged cooking sees some interesting flavour combinations and a few firm favourites such as haggis filo pastry parcels stay on the menu by popular demand. Start perhaps with queen scallops grilled in the shell and topped with a smoked salmon and citrus butter, followed by a multi-component main course such as suprême of halibut with a parsley crust, citrus and dill mash, broccoli and creamy curry sauce with fresh mussels. There's another branch in St Mary's Street.

Times 12-2/6-10 Closed L Sat-Sun

The Stockbridge Restaurant

🏵🏵 Modern European

tel: 0131 226 6766 **54 Saint Stephen St EH3 5AL**
email: jane@thestockbridgerestaurant.com **web:** www.thestockbridgerestaurant.com
dir: *From A90 towards city centre, left Craigleith Rd B900, 2nd exit at rdbt B900, straight on to Kerr St, turn left onto Saint Stephen St*

Spirited flavours and assured cooking in distinctive surroundings

The Stockbridge is a charming restaurant, accessed down a flight of steps, in the affluent area it's named after. Dark-grey walls, some stone, are hung with vivid modern artwork and mirrors, and spotlights in the low ceiling create pools of light on crisply-clothed tables with upholstered chairs. The cooking goes from strength to strength, with the kitchen producing consistently well-conceived dishes from fine Scottish produce. Seared scallops with Serrano ham, butternut squash purée, apple salsa and caramelised walnuts, or chorizo and red pepper risotto flaked with parmesan are the sort of modern ideas that crop up among starters. A lot can go on in main courses, but an assured touch means flavours are clean and well defined. Try perfectly cooked grilled halibut fillet served with crayfish and scallop mousse, braised beef cheeks, crushed potatoes, spinach and red wine jus, for instance, or roast duck breast with a foie gras boudin, a confit spring roll, chicory and potato terrine. A pre-dessert arrives before the real thing, which might be a theme on chocolate: rich brûlée, brownie, mousse and ice cream.

Chef Jason Gallagher **Owner** Jason Gallagher, Jane Walker **Seats** 40 **Times** 7-9.30 Closed 1st 2 wks Jan, Mon, L all week (open on request only min 6 people) **Prices** Fixed L 2 course fr £14.95, Fixed D 3 course fr £23.95, Starter £7.95-£11.95, Main £17.95-£24.95, Dessert £4.95-£8.95, Service optional **Wines** 5 by glass **Parking** On street **Notes** Pre-theatre Aug only, Vegetarian available, Children welcome

EDINBURGH *continued*

AA RESTAURANT OF THE YEAR FOR SCOTLAND 2014–15

Timberyard

◉◉ Modern Scottish **NEW** 🍷 NOTABLE WINE LIST

tel: 0131 221 1222 **10 Lady Lawson St EH3 9DS**
email: eat@timberyard.co **web:** www.timberyard.co
dir: *From Princes St, Lothian Rd (A700) left onto Castle Terrace, right at rdbt, left onto Lady Lawson St, restaurant on right*

Exciting modern Scottish cookery in a lumber yard

The Timberyard is very much a family concern of the Radfords, with five members of two generations taking part in an exciting new addition to Edinburgh's dynamic restaurant scene. It is of course a former lumber yard, and the south-facing yard itself makes a fine al fresco space, with a wood-burning stove to warm the cockles when it's time to retreat to one of the indoor spaces. Ben Radford runs the kitchen in accordance with impeccable current thinking, sourcing from small growers, breeders and foragers, and the place has its own in-house butchery and smokehouse. Water is filtered on the premises, and there's even a herb patch. Menus are sorted according to dish size, from Bites – buttered langoustine with fennel in tarragon cream – through the intermediate Smalls, which might include a duck egg smoked over hay with kohlrabi, burnt onion, malt, rye and lichen, to the Large main dishes, when smoked sea trout and squid come with leeks and a dollop of lumpfish roe, or red deer with a harvest festival of cabbage, squash, beetroot, cauliflower, potato and salsify. Ingredients surprise – and may baffle – throughout. Sea purslane may be familiar enough now, but anyone for scurvy grass? How would you like your ramps (wild leeks)? It all concludes with desserts assembled from more familiar components such as chocolate, marshmallow, oats, milk and figs.

Chef Ben Radford **Owner** The Radford family **Seats** 72, Pr/dining room 10
Times 12-2/5.30-9.30 Closed 1 wk Apr, Oct, Xmas, Sun-Mon **Prices** Fixed L 2 course

£19, Fixed D 3 course £24, Tasting menu £27, Starter £9-£10, Main £16-£21, Dessert £8-£9, Service optional **Wines** 52 bottles over £30, 25 bottles under £30, 30 by glass **Parking** Castle Terrace NCP **Notes** Vegetarian available, Children welcome

21212

◉◉◉◉ – *see opposite*

The Witchery by the Castle

◉ Traditional Scottish 🍷 NOTABLE WINE LIST

tel: 0131 225 5613 **Castlehill, The Royal Mile EH1 2NF**
email: mail@thewitchery.com **web:** www.thewitchery.com
dir: *Top of Royal Mile at gates of Edinburgh Castle*

Confident Scottish cooking in magnificent surroundings

This place is the real deal. Where so many strive for individuality by adding 'boutique' character, The Witchery is as strikingly unique, intriguing and lavish as they come. The higgledy piggledy collection of 16th-century buildings in the old town right by the castle has a slate of glamorous rooms and a restaurant that really takes the biscuit. The two dining rooms (Witchery and Secret Garden) leave a lasting impression: the former with its fabulous oak panelling and tapestries, the latter with its ornately painted ceiling and French windows onto a secluded terrace with great views. On the menu is some smart Scottish cooking, rooted in tradition but with a contemporary sheen. Haggis, neeps and tatties is blended into a chicken mousse to begin, followed by a seafood platter, slow-cooked monkfish with an Asian broth, or steamed saddle of rabbit served with a suet pudding filled with braised shoulder and kidney.

Times 12-4/5.30-11.30 Closed 25 Dec

21212

Modern French **NOTABLE WINE LIST**

tel: 0131 523 1030 & 0845 222 1212 **3 Royal Ter EH7 5AB**
email: reservation@21212restaurant.co.uk
web: www.21212restaurant.co.uk
dir: *Calton Hill, city centre*

Intense flavours and fun, creative cooking from a true culinary genius

At first glance 21212 might seem like a fairly standard high-end restaurant. It's in a rather handsome Georgian terraced house, for example – Royal Terrace no less – and there's a decidedly plush finish to the interior. But look more closely and you'll spot some quirkier design touches – yes, those are giant moths on the carpet – and the menu itself is far from typical of anything you're likely to have seen before. This is the domain of Paul Kitching and Katie O'Brien, a couple who go their own way to stunning effect. The name of the place needs some explanation: 21212 is the menu format, or at least it was until it changed. The deal is five courses with a choice of two starters, two mains and two desserts, with one soup course and a cheese course in between. That's the deal for lunch, anyway, with the dinner menu now adding another choice at each course – 31313. But, hey, they go their own way. What's in a number? The high-ceilinged restaurant retains its original ornate plasterwork and has been given a classy finish with curvaceous banquettes, muslin-draped walls and windows looking out over Royal Terrace and the gardens beyond, while at one end a patterned glass partition separates diners from the open-to-view kitchen. Katie manages the front of house with charm and professionalism while Paul and his team beaver away in the kitchen crafting some technically astounding food. This is modern, creative stuff. Menu descriptions can seem a little overwhelming as every element of each dish gets a name-check, but the service team can help bring enlightenment, and you're in safe hands anyway. There's some humour too, as in a first course on the dinner menu called 'chick, chick, chicken', which consists of breast of the corn-fed bird with butterbeans, smoked mackerel and red tipped chicory, plus French plum tomatoes and pommes dauphinoise sauce. It is remarkable at this level that the menu changes so frequently – weekly in fact – with dishes coming and going at a pace that reflects the inventive energy of Paul Kitching. A main course dish of 'well pruned beef, breaded prawn & coleslaw' is another thrilling combination, while another is called 'grilled mixed thrill' and puts together tender pork fillet with smoked duck, corned beef, bacon, haggis, lamb's kidney and gammon. Expectation is high by dessert stage and they don't disappoint: lemon curd cheesecake tart, for example, with pineapple juice and creamed cheese. The wine list is a class act, too.

Chef Paul Kitching **Owner** P Kitching, K O'Brien, J Revle **Seats** 36, Pr/dining room 10 **Times** 12-1.45/6.45-9.30 Closed 2 wks Jan, 2 wks summer, Sun-Mon **Prices** Fixed L 2 course fr £20, Fixed D 3 course fr £48, Tasting menu fr £68, Service optional **Wines** 245 bottles over £30, 9 bottles under £30, 6 by glass **Parking** On street **Notes** Fixed D Tue-Thu 4/5 course £58/£68, Fri-Sat 5 course only, Vegetarian available, Children 5 yrs+

FALKIRK

BANKNOCK
Map 21 NS77

Glenskirlie House & Castle
◎◎ Pan-European

tel: 01324 840201 **Kilsyth Rd FK4 1UF**
email: macaloneys@glenskirliehouse.com **web:** www.glenskirliehouse.com
dir: *Follow A803 signed Kilsyth/Bonnybridge, at T-junct turn right. Hotel 1m on right*

Pan-European cooking next to a photogenic modern castle

As castles go, Glenskirlie's is a little more Disney World than medieval, but it makes a fine backdrop for wedding photos and a good setting for a private bash. The dining room – in the house next door – has a small conservatory for aperitifs, while the low-ceilinged room itself is done in faintly retro glam, with elaborate wallpaper in cream and black, large mirrors and low lighting. The cooking incorporates elements of the modern technical repertoire for a Pan-European style that embraces confit chicken and wild mushroom ravioli with sharply pungent balsamic foam, and mains such as baked sea trout with Cullen skink risotto and pancetta, or brilliantly executed roast saddle and panko-crumbed shoulder of venison with parsnip purée, Chantenay carrots and spinach in a glossy juniper jus. The chocolate creations can be a little under-powered – better look to the zestier likes of lemon meringue torte with lime and cucumber sorbet, or blackberry and vanilla parfait with violet sorbet and a poppy seed tuile.

Times 12-2/6-9.30 Closed 26-27 Dec, 1-4 Jan, D Mon

POLMONT
Map 21 NS97

Macdonald Inchyra Hotel and Spa
◎ Modern, Traditional **NEW**

tel: 01324 711911 & 0844 879 9044 **Grange Rd FK2 OYB**
email: inchyra@macdonald-hotels.co.uk **web:** www.macdonald-hotels.co.uk
dir: *2 mins from M9 junct 5*

Brasserie-style cooking in a popular hotel

The solid-stone Inchyra is a smart hotel with a plush spa and all mod cons, making it a big hit on the wedding scene. It's also home to The Scottish Steak Club, a modern brasserie-style dining option done out in swathes of rich leather, animal prints and dark wood. They've got the relaxed mood just right, too, and the presence of a Josper grill in the kitchen suggests that detail has been attended to. The menu is a fashionable foray into brasserie-land, so prawn cocktail or shallot and goats' cheese tart might kick things off. Next up, a steak seems the way to go: rib-eye on the bone, perhaps, cooked pink as requested, and served with the classic accompaniments of fat-cut chips, vine tomatoes, watercress and a béarnaise sauce. There are plenty of non-steak options like pie of the day or jumbo scampi, plus more of that red meat fashioned into a burger. Finish with sticky toffee pudding or suchlike.

Seats 90, Pr/dining room **Times** 12-9.45 All-day dining **Prices** Prices not confirmed **Wines** 32 bottles over £30, 13 bottles under £30, 15 by glass **Notes** Sunday L, Vegetarian available, Children welcome

FIFE

CUPAR
Map 21 NO31

Ostlers Close Restaurant
◎◎ Modern British V

tel: 01334 655574 **Bonnygate KY15 4BU**
dir: *In small lane off main street, A91*

Fabulous seasonal produce and skilled hand in the kitchen

Down a narrow alley just off the main street, this one-time scullery of a 17th-century Temperance hotel has been a favoured foodie bolt-hole since 1981. That's when James (Jimmy) and Amanda Graham bought the place, and their passion and dedication has put it well and truly on the map. With red-painted walls and linen-clad tables, it's an intimate space (just 26 covers), which is watched over by Amanda with a good deal of charm and enthusiasm. Jimmy's pleasingly concise, hand-written menus make the most of fruit, veg and herbs from the restaurant's garden (and polytunnel), and at the right time of year he can be found gathering wild mushrooms from the local woods. Seasonal Scottish produce takes centre stage, and you might spot an occasional Spanish influence amid the well-crafted modern repertoire. Dishes are packed with flavour, never over worked, with the ingredients given room to shine. Start, perhaps, with roast breast of Perthshire partridge with Stornoway black pudding mash and pork belly confit, before moving on to fillet of wild Scottish halibut (perfectly cooked) served with Pittenweem prawns, winter greens and saffron sauce. Vanilla pannacotta with a compôte of fruits, damson gin coulis and damson sorbet makes a fine and refreshing finale.

Chef James Graham **Owner** James & Amanda Graham **Seats** 26 **Times** 7-9.30 Closed 25-26 Dec, 1-2 Jan, 2 wks Apr, 2 wks Oct, Sun-Mon, L all week **Prices** Starter £7.75-£13, Main £22-£26, Dessert £7.95, Service optional **Wines** 23 bottles over £30, 44 bottles under £30, 6 by glass **Parking** On street, public car park **Notes** Fixed D 3 course only available Tue-Fri, Nov-May £30 Children 6 yrs+ D

ELIE
Map 21 NO40

Sangsters
◎◎ Modern British

tel: 01333 331001 **51 High St KY9 1BZ**
dir: *From St Andrews on A917 take B9131 to Anstruther, right at rdbt onto A917 to Elie. (11m from St Andrews)*

Modern cooking on the village high street

Bruce and Jackie Sangster set up shop plumb in the middle of the main street of this unassuming Fife village, and set about wowing the locals with finely-crafted modern Scottish cooking that showcases plenty of local produce, including apples and herbs from the back garden. It all takes place in a smart dining room hung with landscape pictures, and furnished with crisply dressed tables and high-backed chairs. Dinner follows a four-course, fixed-price format, kicking off perhaps with seared Ross-shire scallops in a Thai-fragrant dressing of chilli, ginger, galangal and lemongrass, before an intermediate fish course, which could be steamed stuffed Loch Duart salmon, teamed with Arbroath smokie and Finnan haddock, in Sauternes and ginger sauce. Main course might be pork two ways, braised cheek and fillet stuffed with black pudding and apricot, with fennel, cabbage and braising juices, while mango and white chocolate parfait with tropical fruits and a sesame and poppy seed biscuit brings things to a close in style.

Times 12.30-1.30/7-8.30 Closed 25-26 Dec, Jan, 1st wk Nov, Mon (also Tue winter), L Tue-Sat, D Sun

PEAT INN Map 21 NO40

The Peat Inn

◉◉◉ – *see page 622*

ST ANDREWS Map 21 NO51

The Adamson

◉◉ British **NEW**

tel: 01334 479191 **127 South St KY16 9UH**
email: info@theadamson.com

Confident cooking in a classy modern brasserie

Once home to the pioneering photographer and physician, Dr John Adamson (hence the name), the handsome building is these days home to a chef who was runner-up in the 2013 edition of the BBC's *MasterChef – The Professionals* (well, it's not his home as such, but it is his place of work). The restaurant has a cool, rustic-chic finish, with exposed bricks, darkwood tables and a bar that serves up a nifty cocktail. The menu brings vim and vigour to the brasserie format with more than a touch of contemporary style and some high quality ingredients. Parmesan crème brûlée is a winning starter showing the ambition of this kitchen, with chargrilled Scottish squid with chorizo jam an appealing alternative. Braised blade of beef stars in a main course with haricot purée and sauce diablo, while a fishy option might be Atlantic sole with wilted spring greens and cockle burnt butter. The standard does not falter with desserts such as a great looking (and tasting) dish of bitter dark chocolate with salted caramel and banana.

Chef Scott Davies **Owner** Ken Dalton, Julie Lewis **Seats** 68 **Times** 12-3/5-10 Closed 25-26 Dec **Prices** Fixed L 2 course fr £13, Fixed D 3 course fr £16.50, Starter £4.95-£9.50, Main £11.50-£29.50, Dessert £3.50-£7.50, Service optional **Wines** 16 bottles over £30, 14 bottles under £30, 11 by glass **Parking** On street **Notes** Chateaubriand to share £65, Sunday L fr £15.50, Vegetarian available, Children welcome

Esperante at Fairmont St Andrews

◉◉ Modern Mediterranean

tel: 01334 837000 & 837021 **KY16 8PN**
email: standrews.scotland@fairmont.com **web:** www.fairmont.com/standrews
dir: *1.5m outside St Andrews on A917 towards Crail*

Mediterranean flavour at a coastal golf resort

The sprawling Fairmont resort stands in 520 acres in a grand coastal setting. There are all the facilities you could wish for, including golf, massages, and a butler to run your bath for you, as well as the Esperante dining room, named after a classic racing car. Done in autumnal hues of terracotta, brown and olive, it's a relaxing venue for cooking that makes a virtue of healthy eating. A terrine of smoked salmon and caper butter is fruitily garnished with poached apple and peach jelly, and there's mango purée with the duck rillettes. Mediterranean influences waft over mains such as cod with chorizo fricassée, sun-blush tomatoes and beans, while a winning pasta combination offers goats' cheese cannelloni with sweet potato tortellini in sauce vierge. Finish with a dark chocolate and Frangelico mousse with praline ice cream, perhaps with a glass of Muscat de Beaumes-de-Venise.

Times 6.30-9.30 Closed L all week, D Mon-Tue

The Inn at Lathones

◉◉ Modern European

tel: 01334 840494 **Largoward KY9 1JE**
email: innatlathones.com **web:** www.innatlathones.com
dir: *5m SW of St Andrews on A915. In 0.5m before Largoward on left, just after hidden dip*

Imaginative, switched-on cooking in a characterful coaching inn

A cottagey white property in the hills above St Andrews, the 400-year-old former coaching inn is now a much-expanded hotel, its rooms around a central courtyard. A fireplace separates the bar from the restaurant in the original building. It is simply decorated, with plain walls, a beamed ceiling and bare wooden tables, vivid blue-upholstered dining chairs adding a colourful contrast. The cooking brings a switched-on, metropolitan-chic style to the area, seen in subtly flavoured crab crème brûlée with laverbread crisps and cucumber, then fillet of pork atop Savoy cabbage accompanied by confit belly and braised cheek, the plate dotted with bonbons of black pudding, baby apples, broad beans and carrots and a swipe of glossy Calvados sauce. More straightforward ideas work equally well: smoked ham hough, say, with a quail's egg, piccalilli and cheese, followed by seasonal roast partridge with red cabbage, Puy lentils, fondant potato and red wine jus. The pastry work is a strength too, judging by chocolate tart with a scoop of delicately flavoured parsnip ice cream, rich caramel sauce and cubes of banana bread.

Times 12-2.30/6-9.30 Closed 26 Dec, 1st 2 wks Jan

Nahm-Jim & the L'Orient Lounge

◉ Japanese, Thai

tel: 01334 470000 & 474000 **60-62 Market St KY16 9NT**
email: manager@nahm-jim.co.uk
dir:

Authentic flavours of Thailand in the town centre

This family-run Thai and Japanese restaurant in St Andrews has a fanatical local fan base, who come for its pukka dishes in an upbeat setting of red and white walls, wooden floors and Southeast Asian decorations. Taking its name from the hot, sour and salty paste of chilli, coriander, garlic, galangal and lime juice used in Thai dishes, Nahm-Jim deals in authentic Thai cooking using fresh herbs and spices flown in weekly from the markets of Bangkok, as well as Japanese bento boxes, sushi and sashimi. Dim sum are the real deal here, so kick off with flavour-packed parcels of minced pork, shrimp and crab meat, then move on sea bass fillets deep-fried in tempura batter and served with sweet-and-sour sauce and coconut milk, or a curry (lamb massaman, perhaps, slowly braised with shallots and potatoes in a non-fiery sauce). End on an authentic note with pandan-flavoured pancakes with sweet coconut and coconut ice cream.

Chef Bunonerd Mayoo, Bee Mitchell **Owner** Sandy & Bee Mitchell **Seats** 85, Pr/dining room 8 **Times** 12-10 Closed 25-26 Dec, 1 Jan, All-day dining **Prices** Prices not confirmed **Wines** 5 bottles over £30, 17 bottles under £30, 2 by glass **Notes** Vegetarian available, Children welcome

Road Hole Restaurant

◉◉◉ – *see page 623*

Who has made the top ten per cent this year?
See page 34

Who has won our Chefs' Chef award?
Find out on page 10

The Peat Inn

PEAT INN   Map 21 NO40

**WINNER OF THE AA WINE AWARD FOR SCOTLAND
2014–15**

Modern British 🍾 NOTABLE WINE LIST

tel: 01334 840206 **KY15 5LH**
email: stay@thepeatinn.co.uk **web:** www.thepeatinn.co.uk
dir: *At junct of B940/B941, 6m SW of St Andrews*

Virtuoso skills in village institution

Geoffrey and Katherine Smeddle have run this 18th-century coaching inn with professionalism and charm since 2006, and it remains one of the stand-out destinations in Scotland's culinary firmament. It may look humble from the outside, but that belies the sybaritic set-up within, where luxurious bedroom suites mean you can settle in for dinner and forget about getting home afterwards. It's the kind of place where you study the menu in the comfort of a plush lounge, aperitif in hand, with a roaring log fire adding to the cossetting feel. Then it's into one of the trio of smart, beamed dining rooms which reflect the cottagey feel of the original building while maintaining the fine-dining factor. Geoffrey's cooking stands out from the crowd for all the right reasons: he starts from the ground up, using top-quality seasonal ingredients, and takes provenance seriously — locally-landed fish, for example, travels just 10 miles to the kitchen. Dishes are often multi-layered, but never overwrought, and there are no speculative ideas or smoke and mirrors trickery. Flavours are clearly delineated so that they work together rather than fight it out on the plate. Things kick off with canapés and an amuse-bouche — cauliflower pannacotta with parmesan crisps and foam, say — before a first course such as braised veal cheek and crisp sweetbreads with roast cauliflower, turnip, and hazelnut dressing, or langoustine tempura with crisp basil, oyster pannacotta and avocado wasabi purée. Next up, perhaps roast sea bream with poached potatoes, fennel and lobster thermidor sauce, or loin of Cairngorm venison, served in earthy partnership with Savoyarde potatoes, hispi cabbage, venison haggis and quince. To finish, prune and Armagnac soufflé and ice cream rises to the occasion. There is a tasting menu, with optional wine flight, and while we're on the subject, the cellar runs to 400 bins.

Chef Geoffrey Smeddle **Owner** Geoffrey & Katherine Smeddle **Seats** 40, Pr/dining room 14 **Times** 12.30-1.30/7-9 Closed 25-26 Dec, 1-14 Jan, Sun-Mon **Prices** Fixed L 3 course fr £19, Fixed D 3 course fr £45, Tasting menu fr £65, Service optional **Wines** 350 bottles over £30, 10 bottles under £30, 16 by glass **Parking** 24 **Notes** Tasting menu 6 course D, Chef's menu 4 course L, Vegetarian available, Children welcome

Road Hole Restaurant

ST ANDREWS Map 21 NO51

Modern Scottish 🍷 NOTABLE WINE LIST

tel: 01334 474371 **The Old Course Hotel, Golf Resort & Spa KY16 9SP**
email: reservations@oldcoursehotel.co.uk
web: www.oldcoursehotel.co.uk
dir: M90 junct 8 then A91 to St Andrews

Stylish modern Scottish cooking overlooking the 17th hole

The Old Course Hotel is in a spectacular location, towering above the famous golf links, specifically the 17th hole, the 'Road Hole', with views of West Sands beach and the coastline. The restaurant is due for a makeover but what will remain are the open-plan kitchen, top-class, unfussy service and inspiring views from large windows over the course to the coast beyond. The kitchen takes full advantage of the region's natural larder from both land and sea and works in a modern Scottish style, adding enough twists and turns to dishes to maintain novelty and interest without going over the top. Given the surroundings it's no surprise to find luxuries of lobster and foie gras among the starters, the former in a signature gratin with parsley purée and mustard mayonnaise, the latter as a multi-flavoured dish of roulade with duck confit, accompanied by orange and chicory marmalade, duck ham, verjus and pistachio. Techniques and timings are spot on: witness moist and succulent belly pork given extra dimensions from a langoustine and Morteau sausage, served with burned leeks, parsley root purée and pommes Anna, and pink venison Wellington with pearl barley, parsnips and kale. Fish is handled confidently too, seen in fillet of Gigha halibut intriguingly served with spicy squid, fregola, Jerusalem artichoke and Madras oil. Perhaps surprisingly in the context, vegetarians get a good deal, with confit of celeriac and goats' cheese salad, with apple and candied walnuts, preceding pithivier of squash and chickpeas served with kohlrabi, red onion, tahini and pickled cucumber. Impressive-looking puddings include a pyramid of intense chocolate mousse flanked by a fine example of pistachio crème brûlée and marzipan ice cream, and cheesecake soufflé with blackcurrant sorbet.

Chef Martin Hollis **Owner** Kohler Company **Seats** 70, Pr/dining room 16 **Times** 12.30-2.30/7-10 Closed Sun-Mon (Jan-Mar), Mon-Tue (Apr-Oct), L Mon-Fri (Jan-Mar), Mon-Wed (Apr-Oct), D Sun-Mon & Mon-Tue (Mar-Oct) **Prices** Fixed L 3 course £18.50, Tasting menu £55, Starter £7-£14.50, Main £14-£36, Dessert £6-£8, Service optional **Wines** 185 bottles over £30, 15 bottles under £30, 11 by glass **Parking** 100 **Notes** Sunday L £18.50, Vegetarian available, No children

ST ANDREWS *continued*

Rocca Grill

◉◉◉ – see below

Rufflets Country House

◉◉ British, European ▮ NOTABLE WINE LIST

tel: 01334 472594 **Strathkinness Low Rd KY16 9TX**
email: reservations@rufflets.co.uk **web:** www.rufflets.co.uk
dir: *1.5m W of St Andrews on B939*

Appealing up-to-date menus in tasteful country-house hotel

Built in the Roaring Twenties for the widow of a Dundee jute baron, Rufflets is a turreted mansion in ten acres of fabulous landscaped gardens just a few minutes' drive from the centre of St Andrews. The Terrace Restaurant looks over those lovely grounds. It has a richly-hued contemporary look, with bold fabrics and vibrant artworks as a setting for up-to-date menus of inventive Mediterranean-accented modern Scottish dishes. The kitchen takes a creative approach to its output, offering locally-reared lamb and venison, plus fish and seafood landed nearby. These are bolstered by interesting combinations of flavour and texture through the seasonal bounty of the hotel's own garden. Breast of wood pigeon is paired with a raviolo of leg meat and supported by chestnut mushrooms, Puy lentil and pancetta sauce, before a creative surf and turf marriage of grilled sea bass with crispy pork belly, a twice-baked soufflé of lobster and dill, and lobster bisque. Desserts work alluring combinations too, as in bitter chocolate and salt caramel tart with Bramley apple sorbet and chocolate crémeux.

Owner Ann Murray-Smith **Seats** 60, Pr/dining room 130 **Times** 12.30-2.30/7-9.30 Closed L Mon-Sat **Prices** Prices not confirmed, Service optional **Wines** 70 bottles over £30, 40 bottles under £30, 9 by glass **Parking** 50 **Notes** Sunday L, Vegetarian available, Children welcome

Russell Hotel

◉ Scottish, International

tel: 01334 473447 **26 The Scores KY16 9AS**
email: enquiries@russellhotelstandrews.co.uk **web:** www.russellhotelstandrews.co.uk
dir: *From A91 left at 2nd rdbt into Golf Place, right in 200yds into The Scores, hotel in 300yds on left*

Scottish-Italian cooking in an intimate hotel dining room

A Victorian terraced townhouse on The Scores overlooking the bay makes a wonderfully relaxing bolthole for anyone, though golfing fanatics will particularly relish its proximity to the Old Course. A couple of minutes' walk and you're at the first tee. The small dining room is done in a mixture of sober grey and thistled wallpaper, with framed prints of the local scenery. It's a very intimate room, with low lighting in the evenings, and staff who aim to soothe with friendly conversation and assured knowledge. The cooking is modern Scottish with Italian inflections, with no alarming combinations. Smoked haddock with leek and goats' cheese croquettes and a salad of rocket, basil and walnuts is a gentle enough opener. Main courses include lemon- and herb-crusted cod in garlicky tomato sauce, pot-roasted pheasant with chestnut mushrooms and lardons, or roast loin of Grampian venison with pearl barley risotto, shaved parmesan and pesto.

Times 12-2/6.30-9.30 Closed Xmas

What makes a 3-Rosette restaurant?
See page 9

Rocca Grill

◉◉◉

ST ANDREWS   **Map 21 NO51**

Modern Italian, Scottish ⱽ

tel: 01334 472549 **Macdonald Rusacks Hotel, The Links KY16 9JQ**
email: info@roccagrill.com **web:** www.roccagrill.com
dir: *M90 junct 8, A91 to St Andrews. Turn left onto Golf Place, then right onto the links*

Smart, modish food with top-class golfing views

For many people, particularly the hordes of international pilgrims who jet in from the States and Asia, St Andrews is all about golf. If you happen to be a golf-smitten foodie, you can indulge both of your passions in the Macdonald Rusacks Hotel, where front-row balcony seats for the golfing action taking place at the 18th hole of the Old Course are available for the cost of a meal in the Rocca restaurant. This chic contemporary operation deals in splendid Scottish ingredients subjected to Italian-accented contemporary treatments, served in an expansive, well-lit space with high ceilings, statement lights, and a chic decor of richly-coloured fabrics and darkwood tables. The mood is friendly and relaxed thanks to staff who dispel any whiff of stuffiness, and under the guidance of executive chef Davey Aspin, the kitchen fires on all cylinders. 'Classical Scottish cooking with a creative Italian twist' is the restaurant's mantra, and it delivers the goods via a five-course tasting menu, a grill menu featuring prime slabs of Aberdeen Angus beef, while a vegetarian menu keeps things sweet for non-carnivores. Things begin with a contemporary juxtaposition of meat and seafood – hand-dived West Coast scallops with ox tongue, celeriac and horseradish risotto. The kitchen's technical skills don't miss a beat, as witnessed in the spot-on timing of a main course comprising venison served with a supporting cast of quince, espresso, chocolate and pistachio, its flavours and colours

delivered with head-turning presentation. Rounding things off in style is a perfectly executed version of that old classic, tiramisù.

Chef Davey Aspin **Owner** APSP Restaurants Ltd **Seats** 80, Pr/dining room 34 **Times** 6.30-9.30 Closed L all week, D Sun (Oct-Mar) **Prices** Fixed L 2 course £18.50-£30, Fixed D 3 course £35-£58.50, Tasting menu £55, Starter £6.50-£12.75, Main £15.90-£34.70, Dessert £6-£11.50, Service optional 10% **Wines** 10 by glass **Parking** 23 **Notes** Market menu Oct/Apr 3 course £35, Children welcome

Sands Grill

 Steak, Seafood

tel: 01334 474371 & 468228 **The Old Course Hotel, Golf Resort & Spa KY16 9SP**
email: reservations@oldcoursehotel.co.uk
dir: M90 junct 8 then A91 to St Andrews

Locally-inspired brasserie-style cooking

The Old Course Hotel occupies an enviable spot overlooking the world-famous golf course and the coast beyond. It's a luxurious five-star affair with a spread of dining options, Sands Grill being the informal (relatively speaking) option, a contemporary brasserie-style venue done out with lots of butch black leather and dark wood, and kept ticking over by a slick and unstuffy service team. The kitchen plays a straight bat, delivering simple Mediterranean-inflected ideas. This could be a gratin of crab and prawn rigatoni to start, before excellent locally-sourced meats from the charcoal-fired Josper oven – Scotch Black Isle beef fillet, say, or rack of lamb with cottage pie, peas and broad beans. In the seafood department, high-rollers could splash out on grilled lobster with garlic and hazelnut butter, or tighter budgets could go for a more down-to-earth fishy main course such as breaded goujons of coley with hand-cut chips and brown shrimp butter.

Chef Martin Hollis **Owner** Kohler Company **Seats** 75, Pr/dining room 40 **Times** 6-9.30 Closed L all week **Prices** Starter £7-£55, Main £10.50-£59.50, Dessert £6.50-£8.50, Service optional **Wines** 35 bottles over £30, 19 bottles under £30, 11 by glass **Parking** 100 **Notes** Vegetarian available, Children welcome

The Seafood Restaurant

 Modern Seafood

tel: 01334 479475 **Bruce Embankment KY16 9AB**
email: standrews@theseafoodrestaurant.com
dir: On A917 turn left along Golf Place

Enlivening fish cookery between golf and sea

Less than 200 yards from the Old Course at St Andrews, the restaurant sits precariously balanced over the edge of the sea wall, with breathtaking views of the distant North Sea rollers. When the tide turns, the sea suddenly rushes in and rapidly submerges the rocks below. All of which explains why the internal decor of The Seafood contains next to nothing to distract the eye from the marine activity. Nothing, that is, except an open kitchen, where Colin Fleming and his team work assiduously at producing fish and seafood dishes that are as fresh and enlivening as the sea spray. Soused mackerel with charred cucumber, broccoli, almonds and buttermilk gives evidence of thinking outside the box, while a main course of herb-crumbed mustardy hake comes with earthy accompaniments of smoky Morteau sausage, shredded sprouts and sautéed potatoes. A perennially popular starter is smoked haddock rarebit with creamed leeks and pancetta in mustard dressing. This might set you up for an adventurous foray into the realms of gilt-head bream and braised squid with foie gras in truffle cream. Simple satisfaction is delivered in a dessert pairing of coconut crème brûlée with lime sorbet.

Times 12-2.30/6.30-10 Closed 25-26 Dec, 1 Jan

Who are the AA's Restaurants of the Year? See page 14

Craig Millar@16 West End

 Modern Scottish 🍷 NOTABLE WINE LIST

tel: 01333 730327 **16 West End KY10 2BX**
email: craigmillar@16westend.com
dir: Take A959 from St Andrews to Anstruther, then W on A917 through Pittenweem. In St Monans to harbour then right

Eclectic cooking with sweeping harbour views

Sweeping views of the Firth of Forth and St Monans harbour can get dramatic when winter waves surge over the sea wall, but all of the briny turmoil just serves to remind you of the business in hand here: serving fabulous fish and seafood with an exciting, modern spin. Large windows flood the uncluttered space with natural light, while unbuttoned service enhances the chilled out vibe. Chef-patron Craig Millar succeeds in blending fabulous Scottish produce with well-honed technique to deliver precise, Asian and European-influenced dishes in the modern idiom. Hand-dived scallops with Jerusalem artichoke purée, smoked bacon, nuts and seeds opens the show with a burst of intense flavour, while simplicity is the key in a main course of top-quality stone bass matched with couscous and satay sauce. Of course, it's not all about fish – braised ox cheek with Puy lentils and root vegetables should satisfy the carnivores at main course. On-the-money flavour combinations see chocolate tart matched with banana ice cream and salt caramel to finish.

Chef Craig Millar **Owner** Craig Millar **Seats** 35, Pr/dining room 25 **Times** 12.30-2/6.30-9 Closed 25-26 Dec, 1-2 Jan, 2 wks Jan, Mon-Tue **Prices** Fixed L 2 course £18-£22, Fixed D 3 course £42, Tasting menu £60-£85, Service optional **Wines** 77 bottles over £30, 11 bottles under £30, 7 by glass **Parking** 10 **Notes** Sunday L £18-£26, Vegetarian available, Children 12yrs+ D

Blythswood Square

 Modern British

tel: 0141 248 8888 **11 Blythswood Square G2 4AD**
email: reserve@blythswoodsquare.com **web:** www.blythswoodsquare.com
dir:

Contemporary and classic cooking in former automobile headquarters

Built in 1821 as the grand headquarters for the Royal Scottish Automobile Club on leafy Blythswood Square, this imposing building has been injected with a good dollop of boutique style, plus a luxurious 21st-century spa for good measure, resulting in a hotel of real verve. A drink in the palatial Salon Lounge among fluted columns topped with gilt capitals makes a fine first impression, before heading into the restaurant in the former ballroom, where a stylish contemporary decor works a treat with the high ceilings and ornate plasterwork. The setting says switched-on and modern, and the good-looking food follows suit. Chicken liver parfait with prune chutney and toasted brioche sets out on a classic note, ahead of roast fillet of turbot with creamed spinach, grape fluid gel and white wine cream sauce. They've got a Josper grill too, which does justice to the excellent Scottish steaks (guest breeds are sourced from local farms), and it all ends with a creative spin on carrot cake, matched with crème fraîche sorbet, fizzy whipped lemon curd cream and ginger crumb.

Chef Derek Donaldson **Owner** Peter Taylor **Seats** 120, Pr/dining room 80 **Times** 12-2.30/6-10 **Prices** Fixed L 2 course £18.50, Starter £5.95-£11.95, Main £15.95-£36, Dessert £3.50-£6.95 **Wines** 40 bottles over £30, 10 bottles under £30, 14 by glass **Parking** On street **Notes** Pre-theatre menu available, Sunday L, Vegetarian available, Children welcome

GLASGOW *continued*

La Bonne Auberge

 French, Mediterranean

tel: 0141 352 8310 & 352 8300 **Holiday Inn Theatreland, 161 West Nile St G1 2RL**
email: info@higlasgow.com **web:** www.labonneauberge.co.uk
dir: *M8 junct 16, follow signs for Royal Concert Hall, hotel opposite*

Parisian style with imaginative menu in theatreland

This ever-popular venue looks for all the world like a French brasserie, with a predominantly red decor, lamps on wooden tables, banquettes and attentive and friendly staff wearing black waistcoats and long white aprons. The cooking might be based on the classic French repertoire, but the kitchen adds its own imaginative twists and turns to dishes, making a sauce of prawns, tomatoes, peas and lemon, for instance, to embellish fillet of sea bass served with sautéed new potatoes and spinach. There's a high degree of integrity and effort behind the output, seen in distinctly flavoured twice-baked cheese soufflé on sautéed mushrooms topped with pea shoots, and crisp-skinned pan-fried duck breast on a bed of creamed cabbage and pine nuts hinting of nutmeg, with a well-made cherry sauce and a textbook version of dauphinoise potatoes. Desserts might include vanilla pannacotta with cherry compôte, and iced banana parfait with rum and raisin ice cream and chocolate sauce.

Chef Gerry Sharkey **Owner** Chardon Leisure Ltd **Seats** 90, Pr/dining room 100 **Times** 12-2.15/5-10 **Prices** Prices not confirmed **Wines** 10 by glass **Parking** NCP opposite **Notes** Pre-theatre menu £16.95 from 5pm, Sunday L, Vegetarian available, Children welcome

Cail Bruich

 Modern British

tel: 0141 334 6265 **752 Great Western Rd G12 8QX**
email: info@cailbruich.co.uk

Artful modern cookery using the best of regional produce

The Charalambous brothers' Glasgow bistro is in the West End, adjacent to a stretch of the Botanical Gardens and not far from the university. The interior scheme emphasises bare wood, softened by leather upholstery and colourful artwork, as well as a floor-to-ceiling wine store. There is imagination at work throughout the menu, which utilises artful modern technique in ways that underline the unquestioned quality of the produce. Arran crab with a salad of fennel, tomato and cucumber keeps things simple enough, but there is also smoked Perthshire pigeon tricked out with pickled veg and dressed in raisins and capers. A more classical foie gras ballottine comes with dots of sublime almond milk, compressed plum and a napkin-swaddled slice of warm gingerbread. The seafood dishes are cause for celebration: a rolled fillet of Scrabster lemon sole on shredded leek set about with smoked haddock and potato, together with garlicky potato purée and an emulsion of smoked butter is a hauntingly aromatic dish. The finale might be an exotic chiboust of mango and sea-buckthorn with mango curd, candied carrots and carrot sorbet for a ravishing study in gold.

Chef Chris Charalambous **Owner** Paul & Chris Charalambous **Seats** 48 **Times** 12-2.30/5.30-9.30 Closed Xmas, New Year, Mon **Prices** Fixed L 2 course fr £14.95, Fixed D 3 course fr £20, Tasting menu £35-£45, Starter £7-£11, Main £14-£24, Dessert £6-£8, Service optional **Wines** 18 bottles over £30, 24 bottles under £30, 16 by glass **Parking** On street **Notes** Pre-theatre offer Tue-Sun, Tasting menu 5/7 course, Sunday L, Vegetarian available, Children welcome

Central Market

 Modern British **NEW**

tel: 0141 552 0902 **51 Bell St G1 1PA**
email: info@centralmarketglasgow.com
dir: *Telephone for directions*

Imaginative bistro-style cooking in buzzing ambience

Central Market, a combination of café, restaurant and deli, makes a big impression with its black and white decor, horseshoe-shaped bar, with its display of oysters on ice, an open-to-view kitchen and mezzanine floor where guests can see what's going on downstairs. It's a must-visit destination, a crowd-pleasing menu of modern bistro-style cooking accountable for its popularity. Pop in for breakfast, sandwiches or the full deal. A starter of duck confit with pickled mushrooms, Puy lentils and port vinaigrette is a great example of how to construct a dish, its flavours jumping off the plate. Alternatively, there might be chargrilled squid with panzanella, then steak tartare with cornichons, capers and shallots. Fish is well handled, judging by crisp-skinned, flaky fillet of pollock in an inventive creamy oyster sauce with salt-baked celeriac, and puddings tick all the right boxes too, from light clementine sponge cake with fig jam and mascarpone to blueberry tart.

Chef Neil Palmer, Andrew Lambert **Owner** David Leishman **Seats** 50, Pr/dining room 20 **Times** 11-10 Closed 26 Dec, 1 Jan, All-day dining **Prices** Starter fr £5.50, Main fr £15, Dessert fr £5, Service optional **Wines** 12 bottles under £30, 12 by glass **Parking** On street, NCP **Notes** Vegetarian available, Children welcome

Gamba

⊛⊛ Scottish, Seafood

tel: 0141 572 0899 **225a West George St G2 2ND**
email: info@gamba.co.uk
dir: *On the corner of West Campbell St & West George St, close to Blythswood Sq*

Top-notch vibrant fish and seafood in the West End

This basement restaurant certainly wears its heart on its sleeve, with its name dropping a strong hint about its culinary raison d'être, gamba being Spanish for fat and juicy king prawns. This perennial favourite enjoys a well-deserved reputation as the go-to place for top-notch fish and seafood in the fashionable West End of the city. Warm colours, floors of dark wood and terracotta tiles, stylish fish-themed artwork and polished-wood tables create a decidedly warm feel, perfect for the Mediterranean- and Asian-influenced cooking. The kitchen is passionate about sourcing the best seasonal produce from the Scottish larder, with fish from sustainable stocks cooked with simplicity and flair. The menu might get under way with an oriental twist on fish soup with crab meat, stem ginger, coriander and prawn dumplings. It follows with a resolutely Scottish pairing of Isle of Gigha halibut with peat-smoked haddock, garden peas, leek, and a creamy sauce of scallops and chives. Standards stay high through to a dessert of frozen chocolate cake with mascarpone, caramel, and chocolate sauce.

Chef Derek Marshall **Owner** Mr D Marshall **Seats** 66 **Times** 12-2.30/5-10 Closed 25-26 Dec, 1st wk Jan, L Sun **Prices** Fixed L 2 course fr £18, Fixed D 3 course fr £22, Starter £7.50-£14.50, Main £11-£32, Dessert £6-£9.50, Service optional **Wines** 21 bottles over £30, 14 bottles under £30, 6 by glass **Parking** On street **Notes** Pre-theatre menu, 3 course winter menu incl wine £25, Vegetarian available, Children welcome

The Gannet

◎ Modern Scottish NEW

tel: 0141 204 2081 **115 Argyle St G3 8TB**
email: info@thegannetgla.com
dir: *Phone for directions*

Buzzy, trendy joint with a rustic Scottish menu

The Gannet has dived straight into the Glasgow dining scene. There's something about the urban-rustic vibe that fits right in with the city's West End, and the place has quite the buzz about it. The cool, easy-going attitude fits the bill and the food manages the nifty trick of being both rustic and refined at the same time. With its lively bar to the front, exposed brick walls, darkwood tables and fashionably minimalist light fittings, the Gannet is packing them in. There's passion in the provenance here, too, and a real Scottish flavour. Stornoway black pudding stars in a first course in Scotch egg form, served with a sauce gribiche, or go for the house cold-smoked salmon with crab and fennel salad. It is good, simple stuff, cooked with care and attention. Slow-cooked pork comes in a main course with champ and apple purée, while, for dessert, pannacotta is served with poached rhubarb and a crumble topping.

Chef Peter McKenna, Ivan Stein **Owner** Peter McKenna, Ivan Stein **Seats** 45, Pr/dining room 12 **Times** 12-2.30/5-9.45 Closed 1-8 Jan, 1-8 Jul, Mon **Prices** Fixed L 2 course £15, Fixed D 3 course £19, Starter £5-£10, Main £10-£22, Dessert £5-£9, Service optional **Wines** 15 bottles over £30, 17 bottles under £30, 12 by glass **Parking** On street **Notes** Sunday L, Vegetarian available, Children welcome

The Hanoi Bike Shop

◎ Vietnamese

tel: 0141 334 7165 **8 Ruthven Ln G12 9BG**
email: pho@thehanoibikeshop.co.uk **web:** www.thehanoibikeshop.co.uk

Stirring Vietnamese street food

Garage-chic, you might say, as this vibrant venture uses the machines as decoration alongside hanging lanterns which bring vivid colour to the space. It's the brainchild of the good people behind the long-running Ubiquitous Chip and its sister restaurant, Stravaigin. Down a little lane you'll find a hit of dazzling Vietnamese flavours, the joint spread over two buzzing floors, with staff in branded T-shirts working like troopers. It's got a chilled-out, canteen-style vibe which suits the authentic street food menu, and sharing is the way to go. The menu gives the Vietnamese names of dishes followed by a detailed English translation, thus bahn

thit lon trung are pork and coriander dumplings with a runny egg centre – packed with flavour – and ga nuong sua va xuai is a jelly fish salad with chargrilled chicken and mango. There are classic pho dishes, too, and a 'from the pot' section perhaps chargrilled chicken leg in a Kaffir lime leaf and ginger sauce. Great fun.

Chef Tad McLean **Owner** Colin Clydesdale, Carol Wright **Seats** 75, Pr/dining room 35 **Times** 12-12.30 Closed 25 Dec, 1 Jan, L 26 Dec All-day dining **Prices** Starter £4.95-£5.95, Main £6.25-£10.50, Service optional **Wines** 2 bottles under £30, 4 by glass **Parking** On street **Notes** Sun brunch 11-5, Sunday L £4.95-£10.50, Vegetarian available, Children welcome

Hotel du Vin at One Devonshire Gardens

◎◎◎ – *see page 628*

Malmaison Glasgow

◎ Modern French, Scottish, International

tel: 0844 693 0653 **278 West George St G2 4LL**
email: reception.glasgow@malmaison.com **web:** www.malmaison.com
dir: *From George Square take St Vincent St to Pitt St. Hotel on corner with West George St*

Reliable brasserie food in a former church

You can rely on the Malmaison chain to come up with out-of-the-ordinary settings for their design-led boutique hotels: the Glasgow Mal occupies the old Greek Orthodox church and its brasserie lies at the bottom of a spiral staircase in the original crypt. With its vaulted ceilings, comfy banquettes, darkly atmospheric colour scheme, and low lighting to lend the place an intimate vibe, it's a memorable setting for modern brasserie food. The eclectic menu takes in comfort classics from the grill – the burger stack, say, which comes with foie gras, celeriac slaw and onion rings – otherwise, start with beef consommé with braised oxtail, celeriac, field mushrooms and orzo pasta, followed by coriander-crusted rack of lamb with spiced potatoes and mint yoghurt. Also look for blackboard specials driven by what's available locally and in season. For pudding, treacle tart with clotted cream provides a typically comfort-oriented finale.

Chef Colin Manson **Owner** Malmaison Hotels Ltd **Seats** 85, Pr/dining room 12 **Times** 12-2.30/5.30-10.30 **Prices** Fixed L 2 course £15.95, Fixed D 3 course £19.95, Starter £5-£9.50, Main £12-£36, Dessert £2-£9 **Wines** 26 bottles over £30, 16 bottles under £30, 27 by glass **Parking** Q Park Waterloo St **Notes** Pre-theatre menu available, Sunday L fr £19.95, Vegetarian available, Children welcome

GLASGOW *continued*

Mother India

🏵 Indian NEW

tel: 0141 2211663 & 2211832 **28 Westminster Ter, Sauchiehall St G3 7RU**
email: info@motherindia.co.uk
dir: *From Kelvingrove Museum located on corner of Sauchiehall St & Kelvingrove St*

Long-running Indian landmark serving smart, interesting curries

This landmark restaurant has spawned a chain of outlets across Glasgow and Edinburgh since it launched here in 1990, and it continues to draw the crowds with its inventive, flavour-packed Indian food. Spread over three floors of a corner property near Kelvingrove Park, Mother India avoids cliché in its decor with prints of the city on the walls, wood panelling in the first-floor room, and an atmospheric cellar. Similarly, the menu takes a step away from curry-house standards to deliver some smart, broadly appealing dishes, with a few names and preparations that will be familiar to curry regulars. Start with chicken tikka pakoras, for example, which really hit the spot, served with spicy tomato chutney, following on with lamb mussalam with baby turnips and leeks, a dish slow-cooked to maximum effect. Desserts don't let the side down either; gulab jamun, perhaps, with an accompanying scoop of cardamom ice cream.

Chef Amar Kumar Maurya **Owner** Monir & Smeena Mohammed **Seats** 145, Pr/dining room 8 **Times** 12.30–2.30/5.30–10.30 Closed Xmas, New Year, L Mon-Thu **Prices** Fixed L 2 course £11–£25, Starter £4.50–£5.80, Main £7.50–£14.50 **Wines** 2 by glass **Parking** On street **Notes** Pre-theatre menu available £11.50, Sunday L fr £11.50, Vegetarian available, Children welcome

Number Sixteen

🏵 Modern International

tel: 0141 339 2544 & 07957 423615 **16 Byres Rd G11 5JY**
dir: *2 mins walk from Kelvinhall tube station, at bottom of Byres Rd*

Buzzy neighbourhood venue mixing interesting flavour combinations

This dinky neighbourhood restaurant on Glasgow's vibrant Byres Road has a strong local fan base who appreciate its unbuttoned vibe and the kitchen's creative approach to modern Scottish cooking. It is an elbow-to-elbow sort of space with a pocket-sized downstairs area, and a mini-mezzanine above, all decorated with colourful artwork, and kept ticking over by casually dressed, on-the-ball staff. The chefs beavering away in the open-to-view kitchen aren't scared to experiment with novel flavour combinations, without losing sight of the seasons and the local supplies that come with them. A summer's lunch starts conventionally enough by bringing together a chicken liver and foie gras parfait with peach chutney and herb croûtons, before deploying a vibrant barrage of flavours in a main course of sea bream fillet with fennel, cucumber and olive salad, basil and almond gremolata, and pesto. Pudding delivers a subtly-flavoured combo of lavender pannacotta, poached plums and rhubarb.

Chef Gerard Mulholland **Owner** Gerard Mulholland, Joel Pomfret **Seats** 36, Pr/dining room 17 **Times** 12–2.30/5.30–9.30 Closed 25-26 Dec, 1-2 Jan **Prices** Fixed L 2 course £11.95, Fixed D 3 course £17.95, Starter £4.95-£8, Main £13.95-£21, Dessert £6.50-£8.50, Service optional **Wines** 2 bottles over £30, 31 bottles under £30, 6 by glass **Parking** On street **Notes** Sunday L £11.95-£14.95, Vegetarian available, Children welcome

Hotel du Vin at One Devonshire Gardens

GLASGOW	Map 20 NS56

French, European

tel: 0844 736 4256 **1 Devonshire Gardens G12 0UX**
email: bistro.odg@hotelduvin.com web: www.hotelduvin.com
dir: *M8 junct 17, follow signs for A82 after 1.5m turn left into Hyndland Rd*

Smart, creative cooking in an elegant townhouse hotel

One Devonshire Gardens must be the jewel in the crown of the Hotel du Vin chain of boutique hotels, a terrace of porticoed Victorian houses on a tree-lined street. It's been furnished and decorated with a great deal of panache, with the Bistro – as the restaurant is named, in keeping with the rest of the group – a panelled room with large bay windows, a rich carpet and good-quality napery and clued-up, friendly staff. The short menu manages to span a decent range of options, from roulade of Dunkeld smoked salmon, with lemon jelly and avocado, to a ballottine of wood pigeon and foiegras with damson, and fig and almond bread. The cooking reflects prime supplies and high levels of technical skills, with sharp, modern ideas the norm. Perfectly-seared pan-fried scallops are served with squid ink noodles, poached Cornish oysters, cucumber and caviar, and is followed by an assiette to celebrate the joys of pork – the gold-standard acorn-fed Iberico variety to be precise – comprising shoulder meat wrapped in spinach with a potato fritter and shards of crackling, slices of loin with braised cabbage, and slow-cooked belly with black pudding, served with a rich, glossy jus and vanilla and apple purée. Wild mushroom ravioli, with excellent parmesan cream sauce, topped with shavings of truffle and garnished with pea shoots, has been an exemplary version, and Chateaubriand has been spot on, served with sautéed potatoes and creamed spinach. Dishes have a good balance of flavours and textures, seen in a truffle salad with pickled and raw vegetables, micro herbs and seeds, and perfectly cooked halibut fillet on crab velouté incorporating clams, mussels and balls of courgettes and carrots. Attention to detail extends to fine breads, petits fours and puddings of amarena cherry soufflé with Valrhona chocolate sauce poured in at table, accompanied by Kirsch ice cream.

Chef Barry Duff **Owner** KSL **Seats** 78, Pr/dining room 70 **Times** 12–2/5.30–10 Closed D 25 Dec **Prices** Fixed L 2 course £21.95, Fixed D 3 course £26.95, Tasting menu £69, Starter £10.50-£13.95, Main £16.50-£26.50, Dessert £6.50-£14.50 **Wines** 12 by glass **Parking** On street **Notes** Tasting menu 7 course, Sunday L £24.95, Vegetarian available, Children welcome

Opium

🏵 Chinese, Oriental fusion

tel: 0141 332 6668 **191 Hope St G2 2UL**
email: eat@opiumrestaurant.co.uk

Asian fusion from a Hong Kong masterchef in the heart of the city

The name might evoke memories of a low point in Anglo-Chinese politics, but east and west are reconciled here in this pin-sharp, contemporary-styled Asian fusion restaurant in the pulsing heart of Glasgow. Big picture-windows allow light to flood into a slick space done out with dark wood and muted brown tones, where communal tables with high chairs share the space with conventional restaurant seating. Kwan Yu Lee learned his skills from virtual boyhood in Hong Kong, but has honed an on-trend mélange of classical and modern Asian fusion dishes. An array of dim sum shows basic skills are not forgotten, with steamed chicken shu mai dumplings full of evocative aromas and clear flavours. Next up, a huge bowl of shrimp noodles incorporates king prawns, mussels, squid and crab with fresh noodles in a rich pork broth flavoured with roasted garlic, miso and fried shallots. Finish with banana fritters with butterscotch sauce and vanilla ice cream.

Chef Kwan Yu Lee **Owner** Trevor Lee **Seats** 54 **Times** 12-2.30/5-10 **Prices** Prices not confirmed, Service optional **Wines** 2 bottles over £30, 19 bottles under £30, 8 by glass **Notes** Pre-theatre 2/3 course menu, Sunday L, Vegetarian available, Children welcome

La Parmigiana

🏵 Italian, Mediterranean

tel: 0141 334 0686 **447 Great Western Rd, Kelvinbridge G12 8HH**
email: sgiovanazzi@btclick.com **web:** www.laparmigiana.co.uk
dir: *Next to Kelvinbridge underground*

West End institution serving superior Italian fare

The blue-painted exterior of this West End stalwart conceals a calm and refined interior of red walls, bare wooden floor and purple-padded wooden seats at white-clothed tables, with friendly and knowledgeable staff adding to the congenial atmosphere. Bog-standard Italian fare this isn't, although fresh home-made pasta is a good bet – perhaps spinach and ricotta tortelli. Go for one of the shellfish starters like lobster ravioli with basil sauce, or chargrilled scallops with Jerusalem artichoke and beurre blanc. Progress perhaps to a well-rounded dish of tender, pink roast fillets of venison on polenta croûtons with a sauce of porcini and Italian sausage. The kitchen works its magic on top-drawer materials and treatments are never too complicated, so fillet of salmon is encased in puff pastry and served with lemony mustard sauce, and beef fillet is roasted and accompanied by a rich Barolo sauce. Fly the Italian flag with desserts like tiramisù, or vanilla pannacotta with matching ice cream.

Chef Peppino Camilli **Owner** Sandro & Stefano Giovanazzi **Seats** 50
Times 12-2.30/5.30-10.30 Closed 25-26 Dec, 1 Jan, D Sun **Prices** Fixed L 3 course fr

£17, Starter £6.20-£12.50, Main £18.30-£29.95, Dessert £5.90-£8.50, Service optional **Wines** 35 bottles over £30, 15 bottles under £30, 8 by glass **Parking** On street **Notes** Pre-theatre 2/3 course 5.30-7pm £17.10/£19.90, Sunday L, Vegetarian available, Children welcome

Rogano

🏵🏵 Scottish, Seafood v

tel: 0141 248 4055 **11 Exchange Place G1 3AN**
email: info@roganoglasgow.com

Modern cooking with a sense of occasion in an art deco masterpiece

Fast approaching its 80th birthday, it's fair to call Rogano a Glasgow institution. The art-deco look of the place never fails to leave an impression, particularly the oyster bar, and there's a sense of bygone sophistication running right through. The charming service team plays a big part in maintaining a sense of occasion. Some classic seafood dishes have been on the menu since 1935 – platefuls of Scottish fruits de mer, for example, and lobster thermidor – but you might also start with haggis, neeps and tatties with an Arran mustard cream, and follow up with rabbit wrapped in Parma ham. But seafood is king here. Langoustines en croûte with aïoli is a starter featuring wonderfully fresh shellfish, or go for Scottish oysters from Cumbrae. Among main courses, grilled fillets of red mullet with couscous, chargrilled vegetables and harissa dressing competes for your attention with lemon sole, either grilled or meunière, and served on or off the bone. And for dessert there might be vanilla and honeycomb parfait with butterscotch sauce.

Chef Andy Cumming **Owner** Lynnet Leisure **Seats** 70, Pr/dining room 16
Times 12-2.30/6-10.30 Closed 1 Jan **Prices** Fixed L 2 course £16.50, Fixed D 3 course £21.50, Tasting menu £45-£80, Starter £6.50-£14.50, Main £19.95-£40, Dessert £6.75-£13.95 **Wines** 100 bottles over £30, 30 bottles under £30, 14 by glass **Parking** NCP car parks **Notes** Tasting menu 4 course, Sunday L £16.50-£21.50, Children welcome

Shish Mahal

🏵 Indian

tel: 0141 339 8256 **60-68 Park Rd G4 9JF**
email: reservations@shishmahal.co.uk
dir: *From M8/A8 take exit towards Dumbarton. On Great Western Rd 1st left into Park Rd*

Long-standing Indian in a quiet part of the city

A Glaswegian institution since the '60s, the Shish Mahal has seen generations of curry fans pass through its doors to sample Mr Ali's reliable classic Indian cooking. The house motto may be 'unspoilt by progress', but the decor has moved with the times – there's a smart modern feel to its warm Asian colour scheme, while leather seating and linen-clad tables do their bit to bolster the feel-good factor, and service is friendly and knowledgeable. The extensive menu explores familiar regional variations, taking in old favourites from the Madras, vindaloo and bhuna stables, but there are plenty of intriguing ideas to broaden your horizons too. Murgh tikka achari is chicken breasts in a tikka-spiced marinade, pan-fried with onion seeds and cracked coriander, while mains head north to the Punjab for an aromatic nashedar banjara – succulent lamb in a rich sauce of ginger, garlic, coriander, tomato and green pepper.

Chef Mr I Humayun **Owner** Ali A Aslam, Nasim Ahmed **Seats** 95, Pr/dining room 14
Times 12-2/5-11 Closed 25 Dec, L Sun **Prices** Prices not confirmed, Service optional **Wines** 2 bottles over £30, 18 bottles under £30, 1 by glass **Parking** Side street, Underground station car park **Notes** Fixed L 4 course, Vegetarian available, Children welcome

GLASGOW *continued*

Stravaigin

◎◎ Modern International

tel: 0141 334 2665 **28-30 Gibson St, Kelvinbridge G12 8NX**
email: stravaigin@btinternet.com **web:** www.stravaigin.com
dir: *Next to Glasgow University. 200yds from Kelvinbridge underground*

Popular eatery with creative, multi-national flavour

The tagline of this switched-on stalwart of the Glasgow foodie scene – 'Think global, eat local' – neatly sums up its culinary ideology. Spread over two floors of café-bar and a basement restaurant, the operation goes for a quirky contemporary look. Reclaimed and reinvented pieces of modern art and interesting objets are set against rough stone walls, and beamed ceilings. This is the perfect foil to the consistently imaginative, flavour-driven cooking. The kitchen plunders Scotland's magnificent larder for its raw materials, which are allied with an eclectic approach to the world's cuisines. A starter of West Coast crab partnered with haddock wrapped in cucumber 'canneloni', an apple and celeriac take on a Waldorf salad, and a spicy Indian-accented Vadouvan oil all prove the point. Korean braised ox cheek with brown rice cake, kimchi, tempura oyster, and sesame-dressed cucumber and beansprouts makes a similarly full-frontal attack on the taste buds, while desserts keep exploring interesting combos of flavour and texture with vanilla-poached rhubarb with pecan and brioche crumble and heather honey ice cream.

Chef Kenny Mackay **Owner** Colin Clydesdale, Carol Wright **Seats** 50, Pr/dining room 50 **Times** 11-11 Closed 25 Dec, 1 Jan, L 26 Dec All-day dining **Prices** Fixed L 2 course £12.95, Starter £5.25-£8.95, Main £8.95-£18.95, Dessert £4.65-£9.95, Service optional **Wines** 6 bottles over £30, 40 bottles under £30, 23 by glass **Parking** On street, car park 100yds **Notes** Pre-theatre menu 2/3 course £13.95/£15.95, Sunday L, Vegetarian available, Children welcome

Ubiquitous Chip

◎◎ Scottish V ☐ NOTABLE WINE LIST

tel: 0141 334 5007 **12 Ashton Ln G12 8SJ**
email: mail@ubiquitouschip.co.uk **web:** www.ubiquitouschip.co.uk
dir: *In West End, off Byres Rd. Adjacent to Hillhead underground station*

Iconic address for modern Scottish cooking

Part of the West End scene since 1971, the Chip is many things to many people. First and foremost it represents the best of Scotland, flying the flag for Scottish ingredients (and culture even), and it matters not if you just want to pop in to drink in one of the three bars or dine heartily under the glassed-over roof of the courtyard restaurant. Inside it's a warren of four dining areas, including a brasserie, the courtyard and a mezzanine, and all around are sprawling colourful murals and the buzz of contented customers. The cooking is more sophisticated than you might imagine, but it is always clear-headed and based on superb Scottish ingredients. You might start with the long-running favourite, venison haggis, but equally you could go for torchon of foie gras with pain d'épice, Gewürztraminer jelly and apple. Main course might deliver fillet of sole with squid ink spätzle, grilled leek and langoustine sauce, or a fabulous Aberdeen Angus steak, and for dessert, there's always the Caledonian oatmeal ice cream to tempt you.

Chef Andrew Mitchell **Owner** Colin Clydesdale **Seats** 100, Pr/dining room 50 **Times** 12-2.30/5-11 Closed 25 Dec, 1 Jan, L 26 Dec **Prices** Fixed L 2 course £15.95, Starter £5.95-£13.95, Main £15.95-£35, Dessert £5.95-£7.95, Service optional **Wines** 215 bottles over £30, 58 bottles under £30, 37 by glass **Parking** Lilybank Gardens (50mtrs) **Notes** Pre-theatre 2/3 course fr £15.95/£19.95 5-6.30pm, Sunday L £15.95-£23.95, Children welcome

Urban Bar and Brasserie

 Modern British

tel: 0141 248 5636 **23-25 St Vincent Place G1 2DT**
email: info@urbanbrasserie.co.uk
dir: *In city centre between George Sq & Buchanan St*

Updated and interesting brasserie fare in a former bank

This sleek and modern bar-brasserie has capitalised on the grandiose architecture of a former bank (the erstwhile Scottish HQ of the Bank of England, no less), throwing in brown leather banquettes and chairs, smartly laid tables, and huge canvases of modern art to bring vibrant splashes of colour into the mix. Add in black-clad staff wearing long white aprons, and a bustling vibe, and you might be in a classic Parisian brasserie. The kitchen knows its stuff, producing a menu of Scotland-meets-Mediterranean ideas sprinkled with Asian flavours – a spirited starter of fish soup spiked with ginger and prawn dumplings being typical of the style. Main courses can be as unreconstructed as Scotch beef sirloin with button mushrooms, pepper gravy and chips, or head into the francophile realms of duck confit with Toulouse sausage, borlotti beans and rosemary jus. To finish, the addition of lemon and thyme puts a novel spin on a crème brûlée.

Chef David Clunas **Owner** Alan Tomkins **Seats** 110, Pr/dining room 20 **Times** 12-10 Closed 25 Dec, 1 Jan, All-day dining **Prices** Fixed L 2 course fr £13.95, Starter £4.95-£11, Main £9-£23, Dessert £5.50-£6.50, Service optional **Wines** 19 bottles over £30, 26 bottles under £30, 13 by glass **Parking** NCP West Nile St **Notes** Pre-theatre, Fixed D menu available, Sunday L, Vegetarian available, No children

La Vallée Blanche

 French

tel: 0141 334 3333 **360 Byres Rd G12 8AW**
email: enquiries@lavalleeblanche.com

Confident Franco-Italian cooking in a Glasgow ski lodge

Up a small staircase off the Byres Road is a little piece of the Haute-Savoie in Glasgow. The ski-chalet vibe is good fun, but this place is no novelty act – they can cook. The food is inspired by French and Italian ways, with fine Scottish ingredients at the heart of the action. There's a brasserie feel to the place as far as the service goes – relaxed, approachable – but the dishes arrive dressed to thrill. Seared scallops with confit pork belly and salted brandy caramel is a modern starter with two ace bivalves (cooked just right) as the star attraction, followed by fillet of sea bream with Stornoway black pudding and a crispy poached egg, or rump of lamb with dauphinoise, ratatouille and a brandy-flavoured morel jus. Banana soufflé with custard ice cream or a whisky and pine nut parfait with rosemary syrup end things in style.

Chef Andrew Temple **Seats** 78 **Times** 12-2.15/5.30-10 Closed 25 Dec, 1 Jan, Mon **Prices** Fixed L 2 course £12.95, Starter £5.95-£8.95, Main £12.95-£24.95, Dessert £5.95-£8.95, Service optional **Wines** 14 bottles over £30, 21 bottles under £30, 8 by glass **Notes** Brunch available, Vegetarian available, Children welcome

Read all about our wine award winners on page 17

Wee Lochan

 Modern Scottish

tel: 0141 338 6606 **340 Crow Rd, Broomhill G11 7HT**
email: eat@an-lochan.com

Polished contemporary cooking in the West End

You could keep things as simple as coffee and a scone at this welcoming family-run operation, but you would be missing out if you didn't stay for the lively, modern Scottish cooking. Bag a seat at one of the pavement tables outside if the weather is being kind, but no matter if it's not, for it's lovely inside too: simple and inviting, with white walls hung with bright artwork and white leather-look chairs at wooden tables. The local-is-best philosophy reigns in the kitchen, finding its expression in seared scallops with Jerusalem artichoke purée, chorizo and vinaigrette, followed by crispy panko-crumbed fillet of hake given an Asian spin by coconut rice, pak choi, and soy and ginger dressing, or there may be roast crown of partridge wrapped in Parma ham with pan-fried foie gras, bubble-and-squeak and red wine sauce. Finish with vanilla pannacotta with poached rhubarb and ginger crumble.

Chef Rupert Staniforth **Owner** Aisla & Rupert Staniforth **Seats** 50 **Times** 12-3/5-10 Closed 25 Dec, 1-2 Jan **Prices** Fixed L 2 course £11.95, Fixed D 3 course £17.95, Starter £3.90-£9, Main £12.60-£22, Dessert £4.50-£6.20, Service optional **Wines** 6 bottles over £30, 30 bottles under £30, 18 by glass **Parking** On street (no charge) **Notes** Pre-theatre set menu available, Sunday L £12.95-£15.95, Vegetarian available, Children welcome

HIGHLAND

DORNOCH Map 23 NH78

Dornoch Castle Hotel

 Modern Scottish

tel: 01862 810216 **Castle St IV25 3SD**
email: enquiries@dornochcastlehotel.com **web:** www.dornochcastlehotel.com
dir: *2m N of Dornoch Bridge on A9, turn right to Dornoch. Hotel in village centre opp Cathedral*

Medieval castle hotel with a true Scottish flavour

Situated on Dornoch's quaint Market Square, opposite the 12th-century cathedral, this dramatic 15th-century castle turned hotel and restaurant flies the flag for Scottish good looks and a happy mix of modern and traditional cooking. There's a small, internal courtyard and cosy bar complete with a fire and exposed brick castle walls, while the conservatory style dining room embraces its Scottish heritage: think tartan table runners over burgundy tablecloths, burgundy napkins and some interesting Tain Pottery (plates, cruets and vases). Tea lights and soft music create a relaxing atmosphere, and black-clad staff display good knowledge of a menu that sees some Scottish tradition amongst the mainly modern British, well-presented dishes. Start with pressed ham hock terrine, prune purée and chargrilled focaccia before a fantastic pan-fried fillet of John Dory, vegetables, new potatoes, caper and herb butter sauce. Deconstructed cranachan – raspberry jelly, whisky parfait and oatmeal cream – works well as a modern take on an old favourite.

Chef Mikael Helies **Owner** Colin & Ros Thompson **Seats** 75, Pr/dining room 25 **Times** 12-3/6-9.30 Closed 25-26 Dec, 2nd wk Jan **Prices** Starter £5.75-£9.50, Main £18-£24, Dessert £5.75-£7.75, Service optional **Wines** 10 bottles over £30, 20 bottles under £30, 6 by glass **Parking** 12, On street (free) **Notes** Early D special menu, Sunday L £9.50-£18, Vegetarian available, Children welcome

FORT AUGUSTUS — Map 23 NH30

Inchnacardoch Lodge Hotel

Modern Scottish

tel: 01456 450900 **Inchnacardoch Bay PH32 4BL**
email: happy@inchhotel.com **web:** www.inchhotel.com
dir: *On A82. Turn right before entering Fort Augustus from Inverness*

Hearty regional cooking overlooking Loch Ness

A mid-Victorian hunting lodge overlooking Loch Ness, the Inch (as it's more monosyllabically known) did war service as an RAF base, but found its métier as a country-house hotel in the 1950s. Its hauntingly memorable location is on show through the picture windows, and is echoed in the pictures that adorn the dining room walls. The kitchen furnishes the kinds of hearty dishes to sate those of an outdoor persuasion, so a generous smoked salmon starter is further bolstered with a salmon fishcake, lime-spiked crème fraîche and tomato salsa. Main course might be roast rack of local lamb alongside a shepherd's pie, amid a plethora of vegetables and a handful of parsnip crisps, in redcurrant and rosemary gravy. Another option may be breast of corn-fed chicken glazed in Orkney cheddar and smoked bacon in an old-school creamy sauce of leeks, mushrooms, white wine and thyme. The final fortification arrives in the form of hot chocolate fondant with raspberry sauce and vanilla ice cream.

Seats 24, Pr/dining room 6 **Times** 7.30-10 Closed L all week **Prices** Prices not confirmed **Wines** 4 bottles over £30, 5 bottles under £30, 3 by glass **Parking** 15 **Notes** Vegetarian available, Children welcome

Station Road

⚅⚅⚅ – *see opposite*

FORT WILLIAM — Map 22 NN17

Inverlochy Castle Hotel

⚅⚅⚅ – *see opposite*

GLENFINNAN — Map 22 NM98

The Prince's House

⚅⚅ Modern British

tel: 01397 722246 **PH37 4LT**
email: princeshouse@glenfinnan.co.uk **web:** www.glenfinnan.co.uk
dir: *From Fort William N on A82 for 2m. Turn left on to A830 Mallaig Rd for 15m to hotel*

Regionally based cooking in a gorgeous historic region

Glenfinnan is where Bonnie Prince Charlie raised the Jacobite standard in 1745, as is attested by the stone monument that stands within its little walls against a gorgeous backdrop of loch, hills and viaduct. It would be hard to imagine a more splendid, or historically poignant, spot for a retreat hotel, and Kieron and Ina Kelly's white-fronted house has charm in bucketloads. The dining room is hung with the Kellys' fine art collection, and extends into a small conservatory section with ravishing views over the glen. Kieron Kelly's cooking steps up to the regional plate with locally grown produce, fish from Mallaig and venison from the surrounding hills. The four-course set menu might start with butternut squash soup, poured at the table over buttered leeks, beetroot crisps and crème fraîche, before salmon and halibut with asparagus in prawn butter, and then that venison, perhaps paired with wood-pigeon in red wine and rowanberry jus. Dessert might transport you to sunnier climes with caramelised pineapple in passionfruit syrup, alongside lime and ginger sorbet and candied chillies.

Chef Kieron Kelly **Owner** Kieron & Ina Kelly **Seats** 30 **Times** 7-9 Closed Xmas, Oct-Mar, L all week **Prices** Prices not confirmed **Wines** 40 bottles over £30, 30 bottles under £30, 3 by glass **Parking** 18 **Notes** 4 course D £45-£50, Vegetarian available, Children welcome

INVERGARRY — Map 22 NH30

Glengarry Castle Hotel

Scottish, International

tel: 01809 501254 **PH35 4HW**
email: castle@glengarry.net **web:** www.glengarry.net
dir: *1m S of Invergarry on A82*

Traditional fare in a grand lochside hotel

If your knowledge of the lochs is a little shaky, note that Loch Oich, which the Glengarry overlooks, is situated between Loch Ness and Loch Lochy. The present building is a consummate slice of Victorian Scots baronial, built in the 1860s, and furnished throughout in the grand manner. Spotless white linen and quality glassware glow beneath the chandelier in the opulent dining room, where lightly modernised traditional fare is the order of the day. Pigeon breast and caramelised onion in port jus, all indulgent sticky-sweetness, could be the prelude to baked sea bass in a fragrant sauce of tomato, saffron and white wine, or chargrilled venison strip loin in juniper jus, served with a skirlie cake, the meat properly black-striped on the surface while pink in the middle. No whim need go unpandered to when there are desserts such as dark chocolate and ginger tart with white chocolate ice cream, and there are fine Scottish cheeses too.

Chef John McDonald **Owner** Mrs MacCallum & Sons **Seats** 40 **Times** 12-1.45/7-8.30 Closed mid Nov-mid Mar **Prices** Fixed D 3 course £34 **Wines** 14 bottles over £30, 35 bottles under £30, 9 by glass **Parking** 30 **Notes** Vegetarian available, Children welcome

INVERGORDON

The Birch Tree

British, French **NEW** v

tel: 01349 853549 **Delny IV18 ONP**
email: thebirchtree@live.co.uk
dir: *2m north of Tomich junct on left. Located at Delny Riding Centre*

Classy Scottish cookery at the Riding Centre

About a mile off the A9, amid fields crowded with horses from his parents' Delny Riding Centre, Barry Hartshorne's rural bistro lies in a village near Invergordon. The whole complex looks like the family home it is, the dining room smartly done in dark brown and cream, the kitchen on view through a small pass. Hartshorne mostly goes it alone back there, and the results are all the more impressive for that. Scottish ingredients predominate in cooking of distinct accuracy and class. A starter soufflé of Strathdon Blue stands in a pool of cheese and chive sauce, or there may be king scallop soup with squid-ink croutons. At main, there's zingingly fresh fish, perhaps John Dory in smoked haddock velouté with brown shrimps and dill mash, as well as rump and belly of Ross-shire lamb, with broad beans and asparagus and minted pea croquette. Lemon tart is creamier than the norm, with a burnt sugar topping, and sharply offset with lemon parfait.

Chef Barry Hartshorne **Owner** Barry Hartshorne **Seats** 32 **Times** 12-2/6-10 Closed Mon-Tue, D Sun **Prices** Fixed L 2 course fr £12.95, Fixed D 3 course fr £26.95, Starter £4.95-£8.95, Main £12.50-£19.50, Dessert £6, Service optional **Wines** 5 bottles over £30, 17 bottles under £30, 4 by glass **Parking** 18 **Notes** Children welcome

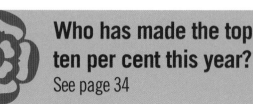

Who has made the top ten per cent this year?

See page 34

Station Road

FORT AUGUSTUS
Map 23 NH30

Modern British v

tel: 01456 459250 & 0845 450 1100 **The Lovat, Loch Ness, Loch Ness Side PH32 4DU**
email: info@thelovat.com **web:** www.thelovat.com
dir: *On A82 between Fort William & Inverness*

Clever, creative cooking with loch views

The house has been here, in an elevated position at the southern tip of Loch Ness, since Victorian times, and it's been given a major overhaul by the current owners. Today's hotel not only has a glossy sheen – a successful combination of period charm and mdoern style – but it's run on sound eco-friendly principles (ask about the biomass wood chip boiler), so you can be sure everything you're served in the restaurant is as local and sustainable as possible. In fact, there's a lot going on in chef Sean Kelly's world, for as well as being extremely choosy about the ingredients he uses in his five-course dinner menus, he's also incredibly imaginative and creative, producing dishes that never fail to bring a smile to your face. The restaurant (there's a more informal brasserie too) is an elegant room with high ceilings, wood-panelled walls and views across the grounds to Loch Ness through large bay windows, while the friendly staff are fully versed in the intricacies of each dish. 'Venison, liver, garden beets' to begin turns out to be carpaccio and tartare of superb quality venison, with a well-made parfait secreted inside a cannelloni of beetroot jelly, with a horseradish cream adding further depth. 'Shellfish, seaweed, shells' might be next up: crab ravioli with a lobster bisque, mussels, langoustine and razor clams, all singing with the flavours of the sea and technically impressive in its execution. A take on steak and kidney pie – perfectly cooked fillet alongside a mini pie with fabulous pastry, smooth parsley potato puree, carrots, parsnips and wild mushrooms – is another joyous dish to eat at main course stage, the flavours finely balanced. 'Cheese on toast' may sound like a savoury snack but reveals itself to be a lemon cheesecake (shaped as emmental) with toast ice cream and toast biscuit, which is followed by 'not banoffee pie', a highly inventive and skilful dessert involving chocolate jelly spaghetti, nougatine cannelloni filled with an iced banana parfait, whipped cream, fresh banana and a chocolate crumb.

Chef Sean Kelly **Owner** Caroline Gregory **Seats** 24, Pr/dining room 50 **Times** 7-9 Closed Nov-Mar, Sun-Wed, L all week **Prices** Tasting menu £45-£50, Service optional **Wines** 25 bottles over £30, 35 bottles under £30, 13 by glass **Parking** 30 **Notes** Children 8yrs+

Inverlochy Castle Hotel

FORT WILLIAM
Map 22 NN17

Modern British v NOTABLE WINE LIST

tel: 01397 702177 **Torlundy PH33 6SN**
email: info@inverlochy.co.uk **web:** www.inverlochycastlehotel.com
dir: *3m N of Fort William on A82, just past Golf Club, N towards Inverness*

Exceptional cooking combines technique and imagination in a grand castle

Near the ruins of its 13th-century namesake, Inverlochy is a magnificent Victorian castle, surrounded by 500 green acres overlooking its own loch. Luxuriant furnishings and fittings, paintings, crystal chandeliers and open fires all add to an ambience of grandeur and opulence. Some of the furniture in the three dining rooms was a gift from the King of Norway and dining here without a jacket and tie, gentlemen, is not permitted. Given all this, the food served is surprisingly modern, based on the finest native produce. A colourful starter of sparklingly fresh Isle of Barra crab with celery, walnuts, apple and pomegranate is a masterly contrast of flavours and textures, offered alongside a multi-flavoured dish of pan-fried skate wing with crisp pork belly, butternut squash and wild mushrooms. High aspirations are met by Philip Carnegie's technical expertise and his unerring confidence about palate-pleasing combinations. Truffles add an unexpectedly successful dimension to a main course of loin on monkfish with parmesan gnocchi and romanesco, and deeply flavoured, flawlessly made sauces and gravies are a particular strength. Check out the sauce poivrade for a winter main course of melt-in-the-mouth loin of Lochaber venison with creamed Brussels sprouts, pickled quince and chestnuts, and bordelaise sauce for fillet of Aberdeen Angus with an oxtail croustillante. Attractive-looking desserts present an agonising choice: whether to go for banana crumble soufflé, with malted milk chocolate ice cream, and wait 10 minutes, or plump for tonka bean crème with poached Yorkshire rhubarb and ginger wine jelly; either way, everyone leaves the table delighted.

Chef Philip Carnegie **Owner** Inverlochy Hotel Ltd **Seats** 40, Pr/dining room 20 **Times** 12.30-1.45/6.30-10 **Prices** Fixed L 2 course £28, Fixed D 3 course £67, Tasting menu £85 **Wines** 240 bottles over £30, 4 bottles under £30, 11 by glass **Parking** 20 **Notes** Children 8yrs+

INVERGORDON *continued*

Kincraig Castle Hotel

◎◎ Modern British

tel: 01349 852587 **IV18 OLF**
email: info@kincraig-castle-hotel.co.uk **web:** www.kincraig-castle-hotel.co.uk
dir: *Off A9, past Alness towards Tain. Hotel is 0.25m on left past church*

Classy modern cooking in a traditional setting

Built in the early part of the 19th century, Kincraig does have turrets and some impressive gables, but it's a genteel kind of castle, rather too refined to repel invaders. Situated in a delightful spot with views over the Cromarty Firth, the white-painted house has elegant rooms and a restaurant dressed in formal attire (white linen and all), for the business of fine dining. In the cooler months a fire adds its glow to the room, while the local service team bring a cheery professionalism to the table. The menu makes good use of the fine produce available around these parts, following the seasons, and what appears on the plate shows classical influences and intelligent thinking. Things get off to a good start with preliminaries such as a freebie seafood cocktail topped with a lemon and thyme sorbet, plus excellent bread. A first course dish of Scottish scallops has the bivalves cooked just right and served in the fashionable company of cauliflower as purée and fritters, and a caper and raisin dressing. Main-course Scottish pork plate is a stunning looking dish, with crispy monkfish cheeks adding a surf 'n' turf element. For dessert, strawberries and cream is presented as a clever and creative finale.

Times 12-2/6.30-9

▮ INVERNESS   Map 23 NH64

Abstract Restaurant & Bar

◎ Modern French, European V

tel: 01463 223777 **Glenmoriston Town House Hotel, 20 Ness Bank IV2 4SF**
email: reception@glenmoristontownhouse.com **web:** www.glenmoristontownhouse.com
dir: *2 mins from city centre, on river opposite theatre*

Top Scottish produce in intimate restaurant by the river

The contemporary Glenmoriston Town House Hotel sits on the banks of the River Ness, close to Inverness city centre. The piano bar, with live music on Fridays and Saturdays, is the place to head to for a pre- or post-dinner drink (perhaps your choice from the impressive list of 200-plus malt whiskies), while the Abstract Restaurant is an atmospheric place to dine, with tea lights on the tables and modern artwork on the walls. There's a tasting menu should you wish to splash out on a seat at the chef's table, otherwise the carte offers prettily presented, French-influenced dishes based on top Scottish produce. Start with seared hand-dived scallops from the West Coast with celeriac and white truffle purée, before a duo of Ross-shire lamb – roasted rack and braised shoulder – with aubergine purée, fondant potatoes and balsamic jus.

Chef Stuart Thomson **Owner** Larsen & Ross South **Seats** 30, Pr/dining room 15
Times 6-10 Closed Sun-Mon, L all week **Prices** Prices not confirmed, Service optional
Wines 11 by glass **Parking** 50 **Notes** Children welcome

Bunchrew House Hotel

◎◎ Scottish

tel: 01463 234917 **Bunchrew IV3 8TA**
email: welcome@bunchrewhousehotel.com **web:** www.bunchrewhousehotel.com
dir: *3m W of Inverness on A862 towards Beauly*

A touch of Scottish baronial splendour

With 400 years of history to its name, Bunchrew is a baronial-style country-house hotel in a glorious position on the banks of Beauly Firth. Spires rise into the Highland sky, 20 acres of gardens and woodlands await to be explored, and the sunsets over the distant hills may well leave a lasting impression. The dining room, resplendent with its wood-panelled walls, old portraits and smartly laid tables, serves up some excellent Scottish produce, including the harvest of the hotel's own gardens. Slices of salt-roasted duck might come in a first course with caramelised red onion tartlet and a sloe gin sauce, followed by local salmon with a Savoy cabbage parcel and shellfish sauce, or go for breast and thigh of guinea fowl with Stornoway black pudding. To finish, pannacotta gets perked up with blueberry and orange.

Times 12-1.45/7-9 Closed 23-26 Dec

Loch Ness Country House Hotel

◎◎ Modern British

tel: 01463 230512 **Loch Ness Rd IV3 8JN**
email: info@lochnesscountryhousehotel.co.uk **web:** www.lochnesscountryhousehotel.co.uk
dir: *On A82 (S), 1m from Inverness town boundary*

Asian-influenced modern cooking for the monster-hunters

The greystone, bay-windowed Georgian house may not be on the lochside but, situated three miles out of Inverness, makes a good operational base for monster-hunters nonetheless. Its interiors are very classy, all stripes and tartan in the grand domestic manner, with dining going on in a pair of interlinked rooms done in restrained buffs and browns. Adam Dwyer is certainly plugged into modern food currents, and amalgamates an array of European and east Asian influences into his contemporary Scottish style. Dishes look crisply composed and full of appeal, as when a circle of home-made black pudding arrives topped with pink chicken liver and foie gras parfait, in turn crowned with apple and vanilla compôte. That could be followed by poached and fried sea bass with crab, samphire and pink fir-apples in lemongrass consommé. Another Asian-inspired offering is shiitake-coated roast pork loin and soy-braised shoulder with sesame pork toast, spiced crackling, puffed pork and pak choi in Chinese-spiced jus. The fragrant notes continue in desserts like basil pannacotta on gingerbread crumble with spiced toffee apple chunks and a ginger beer sorbet.

Chef Adam Dwyer **Owner** Loch Ness Hospitality Ltd **Seats** 42, Pr/dining room 16
Times 12-2.30/6-9 **Prices** Fixed L 2 course £9.95-£18.95, Fixed D 3 course £30-£39, Tasting menu £55-£75, Starter £5.50-£10.50, Main £13.50-£27.50, Dessert £6.50-£9.95, Service optional **Wines** 10 bottles over £30, 20 bottles under £30, 9 by glass **Parking** 50 **Notes** Sunday L £9.95-£18, Vegetarian available, Children welcome

The New Drumossie Hotel

◉◉ Modern Scottish

tel: 01463 236451 **Old Perth Rd IV2 5BE**
email: stay@drumossiehotel.co.uk **web:** www.drumossiehotel.co.uk
dir: *From A9 follow signs for Culloden Battlefield, hotel on left after 1m*

Confident, seasonal cooking at an art deco hotel

A few miles out of Inverness, the hotel is a sparkling-white art deco beauty, in acres of well-tended grounds framed by the Scottish Highlands – a setting that is balm to the soul. Its charm is due in no small part to the staff who treat guests with engaging politeness and feed them in a setting of well-oiled serenity in the Grill Room, where intricately-presented modern Scottish dishes are built on top-class raw materials. A starter of wood pigeon breast, seared nicely pink and matched with Stornoway black pudding, puréed and pickled beetroot, pickled vegetables and game jus shows the style. Mains include crispy pork belly with kale and leek mash, sweetcorn and aubergine purées, and apple and mirin jus. If something simple and sizzling from the grill appeals, there are impeccable Scottish rib-eye and sirloin steaks, with a choice of sauces that includes Arran mustard or whisky cream. Form stays true to the end with a confection of espresso pannacotta, dark chocolate and orange cream, toasted hazelnuts and banana bread mousse.

Chef Stewart Macpherson **Owner** Ness Valley Leisure **Seats** 90, Pr/dining room 30
Times 12.30-2/7-9.30 **Prices** Fixed L 2 course £18, Fixed D 3 course £30-£35,
Starter £6.50-£9, Main £16-£24, Dessert £6-£9 **Wines** 13 by glass **Parking** 200
Notes Sunday L, Vegetarian available, Children welcome

Rocpool

◉◉ Modern European

tel: 01463 717274 **1 Ness Walk IV3 5NE**
email: info@rocpoolrestaurant.com **web:** www.rocpoolrestaurant.com
dir: *On W bank of River Ness close to the Eden Court Theatre*

Riverside setting and smart modern cooking

This buzzy contemporary brasserie operation capitalises on its corner site on the banks of the River Ness, with sweeping windows on two sides to open up floodlit views of the river and castle at night. The interior is a cool exercise in contemporary design flair featuring lots of wood and a decor of natural tones. On the menu is an appealing cast of crowd-pleasing modern European dishes built on top-class Scottish produce, starting with hand-dived West Coast scallops with chorizo, its heat softened by spring onion crème fraîche and lemon, garlic and parsley butter. Next up, accurately-timed sirloin of rose veal arrives pink to celebrate early spring in the commendably seasonal company of pea and spinach risotto, asparagus and a warm dressing of feta cheese, mint and lemon. Elsewhere, there might be roast fillet of halibut with clams, cotechino sausage and polenta, spinach and fresh tomato confit. Dessert delivers a perfectly wobbly yoghurt and vanilla pannacotta with the refreshing tropical flavours of roasted pineapple, and passionfruit and Malibu syrup.

Chef Steven Devlin **Owner** Steven Devlin **Seats** 55 **Times** 12-2.30/5.45-10
Closed 25-26 Dec, 1-3 Jan, Sun **Prices** Fixed L 2 course £14.95, Fixed D 2 course
£16.95, Starter £3.95-£9.95, Main £12.95-£23.95, Dessert £6.95, Service optional
Wines 15 bottles over £30, 26 bottles under £30, 11 by glass **Parking** On street
Notes Early D 5.45-6.45pm 2 course £16.95, Vegetarian available, Children welcome

Who has won our Lifetime Achievement award? See page 12 to find out

Follow us on facebook
www.facebook.com/TheAAUK

KINGUSSIE
Map 23 NH70

The Cross

 Modern Scottish V **NOTABLE WINE LIST**

tel: 01540 661166 **Tweed Mill Brae, Ardbroilach Rd PH21 1LB**
email: relax@thecross.co.uk **web:** www.thecross.co.uk
dir: *From lights in Kingussie centre along Ardbroilach Rd, 300yds left onto Tweed Mill Brae*

Modern Scottish cooking in an old water mill

Originally a water-powered tweed mill built in the late 1800s, The Cross sits in a secluded enclave of the town of Kingussie, in the heart of the Cairngorm National Park. The old building is surrounded by four acres of woodland and garden beside the Gynack Burn, and if the weather is kind there's a terrace beside the river where you can take in the tranquillity of the setting – and, if you're lucky, spot a red squirrel or two. Inside, the small restaurant seats around 20 and is full of period features including exposed beams, white-painted stone walls and an open fireplace. The set menu of modern Scottish dishes changes daily depending on what produce is at its peak. An imaginative starter of local grouse chipolatas, parsley root purée, cobnuts, and caper and sherry vinegar jus is typical of the style, and might be followed by Scottish beef fillet, pan-fried duck foie gras, chef's foraged mushrooms and Madeira jus. End on a high with Alvie Estate raspberry soufflé, tarragon crème anglaise and honey ice cream, or a selection of artisan cheeses with hand-made Ullapool oatcakes and apple, pear and fig chutney.

Chef Ross Sutherland **Owner** Derek & Celia Kitchingman **Seats** 30 **Times** 12-2.30/7-8.30 Closed Xmas & Jan (ex New Year) **Prices** Fixed L 2 course fr £23, Tasting menu fr £58, Service optional **Wines** 81 bottles over £30, 48 bottles under £30, 5 by glass **Parking** 12 **Notes** Afternoon tea £17, ALC D 3 course £55, Tasting menu 6 course, Children welcome

KYLE OF LOCHALSH
Map 22 NG72

The Waterside Seafood Restaurant

Modern, Traditional Seafood

tel: 01599 534813 **Railway Station Buildings, Station Rd IV40 8AE**
email: seafoodrestaurant@btinternet.com
dir: *Off A87*

Popular fish restaurant in the old railway waiting room

Located in the old railway station waiting room, with original carved British Rail chairs (you weren't expecting Rennie Mackintosh, were you?), the nautical-hued blue and yellow restaurant is simple and informal. Fish and seafood specials are the name of the game, the menu updated as items sell out, the staff doing their efficient best to cope with the press of business. Among the popular dishes are lightly spiced crabcakes with red pepper and coriander salsa, smoked mackerel with sour cream and dill, and mains such as fat scallops complete with their roe, fried in herb butter and served in the shell with rice, red Thai seafood curry replete with hot spice and coconut milk, and the all-important seafood platters with salads and dips. Finish straightforwardly with a chunky and nutty chocolate brownie, served with vanilla ice cream.

Times 5-9.30 Closed end Oct-early Mar, Sun (please phone to confirm opening hrs), L Sat

LOCHALINE
Map 20 NM64

The Whitehouse Restaurant

Modern British, Scottish V

tel: 01967 421777 & 07866 586698 **PA80 5XT**
email: info@thewhitehouserestaurant.co.uk
dir: *Phone for directions*

Vibrant, ingredient-led modern Scottish cooking

In a remote spot near the ferry crossing to Mull, this restaurant does indeed occupy an unassuming white house overlooking Lochaline bay. Inside, it looks every inch the unpretentious modern eatery, from its pale wooden tables and flooring to the whitewashed walls hung with maritime and food-themed art. Blessed with a remarkable natural larder close to hand, the kitchen is passionate in its local sourcing ethos, and skilled when it comes to wringing every molecule of flavour from the peerless produce. Daily-changing chalkboards reference the provenance of the main element of each dish, starting with Lochaber chicken liver parfait served with spiced apple chutney and toasted raisin and walnut bread. Next out, a vibrantly colourful dish sees Gigha halibut poached in sea water and matched with Creran oysters, sweet cicely, and caper butter. Dessert brings a clever take on pear Belle Hélène: rich chocolate marquise layered with spiced poached pears and quenelles of chocolate sorbet.

Chef Michael Burgoyne, Lee Myers **Owner** Jane Stuart Smith, Sarah Jones **Seats** 26 **Times** 12-3/6-9.30 Closed Nov-Mar, Sun-Mon **Prices** Prices not confirmed, Service optional **Wines** 9 bottles over £30, 17 bottles under £30, 5 by glass **Parking** 10 **Notes** Children welcome

MUIR OF ORD
Map 23 NH55

Ord House Hotel

British, French

tel: 01463 870492 **Ord Dr IV6 7UH**
email: admin@ord-house.co.uk **web:** www.ord-house.co.uk
dir: *Off A9 at Tore rdbt onto A832. 5m, through Muir of Ord. Left towards Ullapool (A832). Hotel 0.5m on left*

Comforting bistro cooking in a 17th-century house

A Stuart country house in its own expansive and manicured gardens not far from Inverness, Ord House is popular among local anglers and country sports people. Log fires and a snug bar make a comforting scene in winter, and the first-floor dining room is small enough to feel intimate, with views over the grounds. Residents may make the acquaintance of the lady ghost who stalks the place after dark. A vegetable garden supplies much of the kitchen's fresh produce, and local suppliers the bulk of the rest. The culinary style is modern bistro, starting with the likes of tempura king prawns and sweet chilli dip, or foie gras with baked egg, and then going on to well-judged baked halibut in dill hollandaise, or Highland pheasant with crumble-topped leeks and mushrooms. Finish with defiantly textbook crème brûlée.

Chef Eliza Allen **Owner** Eliza & John Allen **Seats** 26 **Times** 12-2/7-9 Closed Nov-end Feb **Prices** Starter £6.25-£9.50, Main £15.75-£21.25, Dessert £4.75-£6.95 **Wines** 9 bottles over £30, 37 bottles under £30, 4 by glass **Parking** 24 **Notes** Vegetarian available, Children welcome

NAIRN
Map 23 NH85

Boath House

– *see opposite*

Boath House

Modern British V NOTABLE WINE LIST

tel: 01667 454896 **Auldearn IV12 5TE**
email: wendy@boath-house.com
web: www.boath-house.com
dir: *2m E of Nairn on A96 (Inverness to Aberdeen road)*

Astonishing culinary intricacy in a restored Georgian manor house

This lovely Regency property was on Historic Scotland's endangered list when the Mathesons bought it in the 1990s and restored it to its original splendour as a luxury country-house hotel. It's surrounded by over 20 acres of impressive grounds (Wendy is a garden designer) that include a trout lake, streams, parkland and formal walled gardens which are occasionally open to the public but accessible to all guests. Behind the porticoed front door is a plush interior of deep sofas and antiques, with the circular dining room, candlelit at night, strikingly decorated a shade of raspberry. There are rugs on the wooden floor, artworks hanging on the walls, sculptures on pedestals and floor-to-ceiling windows framing the willow on the lake. Charles Lockley's cooking is founded on top-quality ingredients, with others foraged and some from the kitchen gardens, and he follows a generally contemporary approach without being a slave to culinary fads and fashions. His set-price dinner menu, of up to six courses, is topped and tailed by an impressive array of canapés and petits fours, with a meal normally opening with a demi-tasse of soup: perhaps unorthodox parsley root with chestnut crackers. Dishes are marked out by pin-point precision, clarity of flavours and virtuoso mastery of techniques, with a strong element of innovation. Game galantine, flavoured with mace, is a classic example, served with celeriac, with a seafood course to follow: perhaps langoustines with orange and burned butter, barley providing a contrast of textures, or a seared scallop topped with shellfish foam, alongside a small mound of quinoa in squid ink under grated celery and fennel. Typical of main courses is blade of veal with a rich jus, onion, crosnes and thyme, while December might bring on turkey with bacon and the expected cranberries and the unexpected chervil root. Cheeses are kept in good condition – perhaps Hebridean Blue, served with port and apple jelly – breads are wonderful, and dessert might be stem ginger cake with dates and pearl barley one day, and on the next plum pudding with quince, cinnamon and lemon.

Chef Charles Lockley **Owner** Mr & Mrs D Matheson
Seats 28, Pr/dining room 8 **Times** 12.30-1.15/7-7.30
Prices Fixed L 2 course £24, Fixed D 3 course £45, Tasting menu £70, Service optional **Wines** 120 bottles over £30, 20 bottles under £30, 15 by glass **Parking** 25 **Notes** Tasting menu 6 course, Sunday L £24-£30, Children welcome

NAIRN *continued*

Golf View Hotel & Spa

 Modern Scottish V

tel: 01667 452301 **Seabank Rd IV12 4HD**
email: golfview@crerarhotels.com **web:** www.golfviewhotel.co.uk
dir: *Off A96 into Seabank Rd & continue to end*

Modern Scottish cooking with golfing and sea views

The clue is in the name at a hotel that's another of Scotland's numerous places consecrated to the swinging of five-irons. In case you were under the impression there was only golf to look at, though, it enjoys a bracing seaside location, looking out over the Moray Firth not far from Inverness. Dining is in a choice of settings – the informal Links Brasserie with views of the greens, or the Fairways Restaurant, a more traditional half-panelled space with chandeliers and stripy drapes. A six-course fixed-price menu of modern Scottish food looks the best route to take, essaying a course from quail's egg hollandaise, through beetroot carpaccio with goats' cheese, to a demi-tasse of wild mushroom velouté, then on to a double-act of Highland venison and wood-pigeon with rösti in game jus. A dessert such as plum crumble with ginger ice cream is followed by a taster serving of a single cheese, perhaps Dunsyre Blue with grape jelly.

Chef Darren Munro **Owner** Crerar Hotels **Seats** 70 **Times** 6.45-9 Closed L Mon-Sat **Prices** Tasting menu £32.95, Starter £4.95-£12.75, Main £10.95-£44.25, Dessert £4.95-£7.95, Service optional **Wines** 11 bottles over £30, 35 bottles under £30, 8 by glass **Parking** 30, Next to hotel on street **Notes** Steak night Thu, Tasting menu 6 course, Sunday L £9.95-£12.95, Children welcome

SHIEL BRIDGE Map 22 NG91

Grants at Craigellachie

 Modern Scottish

tel: 01599 511331 **Craigellachie, Ratagan IV40 8HP**
email: info@housebytheloch.co.uk **web:** www.housebytheloch.co.uk
dir: *A87 to Glenelg, 1st right to Ratagan opposite the Youth Hostel sign*

Well-crafted cooking in charming setting

A great little restaurant with rooms in a splendid location just off the main road to Skye, Grants is run by a hands-on husband-and-wife-team. There are (perhaps unsurprisingly in this neck of the woods) superb views from the white-painted house (over Loch Duich as it happens, across to the Five Sisters of Kintail mountains). The conservatory restaurant has just four tables so booking is advisable to say the least. It's a charming and elegant place to eat, with tables laid with crisp white linen and fresh flowers. Co-owner Liz Taylor runs front of house with relaxed charm while hubby Tony works his magic in the kitchen, championing local producers as he goes. Warm mousse of Loch Hourn queen scallops with Corran Red Velvet crab and squat lobster bisque is a beautifully flavoured first course, followed perhaps by braised tongue of Highland beef with glazed baby onions and an Amontillado sherry and rosemary reduction. To finish, a pear poached in mulled wine comes with banana crème caramel and mascarpone, almond and Amaretto ice cream.

Chef Tony Taylor **Owner** Tony & Liz Taylor **Seats** 12 **Times** 7-11 Closed Dec-mid Feb, L all week, D Sun, Mon **Prices** Fixed D 3 course £25.25-£44.25, Starter £5.50-£9.75, Main £15-£25, Dessert £4.75-£9.75, Service optional **Wines** 7 by glass **Notes** Restaurant open only by reservation, Vegetarian available, No children

SPEAN BRIDGE Map 22 NN28

Russell's at Smiddy House

 Modern Scottish

tel: 01397 712335 **Roy Bridge Rd PH34 4EU**
email: enquiry@smiddyhouse.com **web:** www.smiddyhouse.com
dir: *In village centre, 9m N of Fort William, on A82 towards Inverness*

Seasonal cooking amid elegant pastoral surroundings

Occupying a corner spot on the main road through the heart of Spean Bridge, the low-roofed, whitewashed building offers four smart bedrooms to stop over and spoil yourself with Glen Russell's modish seasonal Scottish cooking. Russell's, located on the ground floor in the 'Smiddyhouse', (once the village blacksmith's, hence the name) is an intimate, candelit spot where crisp linen-clothed tables are decked with sparkling glasses, quality china and fresh flowers. Well-presented modern Scottish cuisine makes good use of top-notch local materials, as in a starter of seared West Coast scallops partnered by Stornoway black pudding and two contrasting sauces of orange and butter. This paves the way for a well-wrought main course of saddle of Highland venison with a black pudding bonbon, mashed turnip, curly kale, carrots and a punchy whisky cream sauce, the whole dish dusted with toasted oatmeal. Exotic flavours are mustered at dessert stage for a finale involving marinated pineapple carpaccio layered with toasted coconut meringues, matched with vanilla ice cream and orange syrup.

Times 6-9 Closed 2 days a wk (Nov-Apr), L Mon-Sat

STRONTIAN Map 22 NM86

Kilcamb Lodge Hotel & Restaurant

Modern European, Scottish V

tel: 01967 402257 **PH36 4HY**
email: enquiries@kilcamblodge.co.uk **web:** www.kilcamblodge.co.uk
dir: *Take Corran ferry off A82. Follow A861 to Strontian. 1st left over bridge after village*

Imaginative modern Scottish cooking on a remote lochside

Reputedly one of the oldest stone houses in Scotland, the Lodge found itself acting as a billet for government soldiers during the Rising in 1745, but the scene today is one of unruffled tranquillity. Standing on the shore of Loch Sunart in 22 acres of sumptuous grounds, the place is worth a journey that includes a crossing on the car ferry from Ardgour. Continuing development of the hotel includes the addition now of an informal venue, the Driftwood Brasserie, to complement the gleaming silver and crisp linen of the upscale Restaurant. Gary Phillips provisions the latter with contemporary Scots cooking of imagination and verve. Proceedings might kick off with a chicken and goats' cheese boudin, served with tomato and apple relish and caramelised red pepper sauce, or a tower of brown crab and butternut risotto with a scallop and pancetta, accompanied by pea and pistachio salad. Gressingham duck as a main course is well served by its roasting at low temperature, producing tender pink meat cut by caramelised plum and celeriac slaw, while populist desserts include crumble-topped Baileys chocolate mousse.

Chef Gary Phillips **Owner** Sally & David Fox **Seats** 40 **Times** 12-2/5.30-9.30 Closed 1 Jan-1 Feb **Prices** Fixed D 3 course £52, Tasting menu £65, Starter £6-£11, Main £16.50-£24, Dessert £7, Service optional **Wines** 53 bottles over £30, 16 bottles under £30, 10 by glass **Parking** 28 **Notes** Sunday L £18.50, No children

TAIN
Map 23 NH78

The Glenmorangie Highland Home at Cadboll
◎◎ British, French

tel: 01862 871671 **Cadboll, Fearn IV20 1XP**
email: relax@glenmorangie.co.uk **web:** www.theglenmorangiehouse.com
dir: *N on A9, at Nigg Rdbt turn right onto B9175 (before Tain) & follow signs for hotel*

Dinner party dining in a magnificent Highland location

Set in fantastic grounds with a large walled garden and a tree-lined walk down to its own private beach, The Glenmorangie has appeal in spades: the namesake Distillery is nearby, making it something of a whisky lover's paradise (whisky tasting weekends prove a big pull), and as if that weren't enough, the French-influenced cuisine is out of the top drawer. Guests dine dinner-party-style here, at the long oak table. Seasonal produce might come straight from the walled garden to take a star turn in technically impressive creations on four-course, no-choice menus. Poached fillet of halibut with razor clams and mussels partnered with bok choy and champagne broth precedes a main course with real wow factor – a workout of local Peking duck involving truffled honey-glazed breast, leg rillettes and liver parfait with shallot purée, 'tattie' terrine, baby veg and duck jus. Dessert brings another tour de force of flavours and texture via banana (caramelised and parfait), dark chocolate and tonka bean ganache, peanut butter mousse, chocolate and peanut purée and passionfruit gel.

Chef David Graham, John Wilson **Owner** Glenmorangie Ltd **Seats** 30, Pr/dining room 12 **Times** 8-close Closed L ex by prior arrangement **Prices** Prices not confirmed, Service optional **Wines** 43 bottles over £30, 10 bottles under £30, 15 by glass **Parking** 60 **Notes** 4 course D £55, D single sitting guests seated 7.30 for 8, Vegetarian available, No children

THURSO
Map 23 ND16

Forss House Hotel
◎◎ Modern Scottish, British

tel: 01847 861201 **Forss KW14 7XY**
email: anne@forsshousehotel.co.uk **web:** www.forsshousehotel.co.uk
dir: *On A836, 5m outside Thurso*

Gentle country cooking in a Highland Georgian hotel

You can't get much further away from urban bustle in the mainland British Isles than the northern Highlands, where this Georgian country-house hotel luxuriates in splendid tranquillity below a waterfall on the River Forss, amid 20 acres of woodland. It was once the seat of the Radclyffe family, whose portraits hang in the dining room, many of them dating from before the house itself was built. Views of the gardens and riverside soothe the soul, even as the gentle Scottish country cooking seduces the taste buds. Plenty of pedigree Highland produce is on parade, naturally, with Scrabster scallops to start, in a winning combination with sweet shallot purée and parsley and caper dressing, while the main course might see Caithness lamb teamed with root veg dauphinoise and glazed red cabbage, or pan-roasted lemon sole accompanied by crushed potatoes mixed with Scrabster crab. Finish up with locally gathered mixed berries to garnish frozen strawberry mousse and crushed meringue, or with liquid-centred chocolate fondant with salt caramel ice cream and a coulis made from more of those berries.

Chef Paul Ruttledge **Owner** Ian & Sabine Richards **Seats** 26, Pr/dining room 14 **Times** 7-9 Closed 23 Dec-4 Jan, L all week **Prices** Starter £6-£7.50, Main £18.50-£24.50, Dessert £6.50-£7.50, Service optional **Wines** 6 bottles over £30, 19 bottles under £30, 4 by glass **Parking** 14 **Notes** Vegetarian available, Children welcome

TORRIDON
Map 22 NG95

The Torridon Restaurant
◎◎◎ – see below

The Torridon Restaurant

TORRIDON
Map 22 NG95

British, French V ◊ NOTABLE WINE LIST

tel: 01445 791242 **IV22 2EY**
email: info@thetorridon.com **web:** www.thetorridon.com
dir: *From Inverness take A9 N, follow signs to Ullapool (A835). At Garve take A832 to Kinlochewe, take A896 to Torridon. Do not turn off to Torridon Village. Hotel on right after Annat*

A piece of loch-side Highland luxury

By a sea loch and surrounded by soaring trees, Torridon certainly delivers a Highland vista, matched only by the splendid turreted house itself, built in Victorian times as a shooting lodge, with 58 acres of grounds to wander through and work up an appetite. There's magnificent period detailing within the house, with swish furnishings that are entirely in keeping. This place is a class act. There are more than 350 malts waiting at the whisky bar, too, if you really want to get into the spirit of the place. The restaurant takes up two interconnecting rooms, each elegantly attired with acres of oak panels, ornate plasterworks on the ceilings, and pristine white linen on the tables, and, during daylight hours, fantastic views. With the hotel's kitchen garden at its disposal, plus the fruits of the local hills and waters, the industrious kitchen turns out some smart, impeccably seasonal modern Scottish dishes that impress. The fixed-price, five-course menu might kick off in springtime with garden leek velouté with potato espuma and a crispy smoked haddock beignet. Next up, Highland lamb might be the star, arriving in the forms of pan-roasted chump, braised shoulder and a mini shepherd's pie, together with soubise purée, caramelised red onions and lamb jus. Otherwise, go for the fishy option: seared hake fillet with Isle of Ewe smoked salmon, confit onion and Savoy cabbage blanquette. The presentation of dishes impresses, as do the service team, with their formally constrained enthusiasm. There's a pre-dessert such as banoffee pie before the main sweet event, when forced rhubarb from the garden arrives in a sorbet with lemon cream, macaroons and an almond wafer, or go for the selection of British and French cheeses. The wine list is good enough to act as a serious distraction from the view out of the window.

Chef David Barnett **Owner** Daniel & Rohaise Rose-Bristow **Seats** 38, Pr/dining room 16 **Times** 12-2/6.45-9 Closed 2 Jan for 5 wks **Prices** Prices not confirmed, Service optional **Wines** 8 by glass **Parking** 20 **Notes** Fixed D 5 course £55, Children 10 yrs+

NORTH LANARKSHIRE

CUMBERNAULD
Map 21 NS77

The Westerwood House & Golf Resort

Modern Scottish

tel: 01236 457171 **1 St Andrews Dr, Westerwood G68 OEW**
email: stewartgoldie@qhotels.co.uk **web:** www.qhotels.co.uk
dir: A80 junct signed Dullatur, from junct follow signs for hotel

Confident modern cooking and top-drawer service

Westerwood House is a stylish contemporary golf and spa-oriented hotel in extensive grounds overlooking the Campsie Hills, yet only a 15-minute drive from the bright lights of Glasgow city centre. On the food front, Fleming's Restaurant fits the bill with its clean-cut modern look, all darkwood tables and seats upholstered in warm hues of tangerine and sage green, while a switched-on professional team make sure it all goes with a swing. The kitchen follows a broadly modern Scottish path, enlivened with a splash of well-considered creativity here and there. Pan-fried scallops with chorizo and sweetcorn salsa and sweetcorn purée is a typical starter, while mains might run to roast rump of Perthshire lamb with Provençal vegetables, pan juices and pesto. To round things off, an irresistibly Scottish Irn Bru baked Alaska should hit the spot.

Times 6.30-9.30 Closed Sun-Mon, L all week

SOUTH LANARKSHIRE

EAST KILBRIDE
Map 20 NS65

Macdonald Crutherland House

British

tel: 01355 577000 **Strathaven Rd G75 OQZ**
email: general.crutherland@macdonald-hotels.co.uk **web:** www.macdonald-hotels.co.uk
dir: Follow A726 signed Strathaven, straight over Torrance rdbt, hotel on left after 250yds

Elegant hotel dining room with accomplished cooking

With the original parts of the building dating from the early 1700s, Crutherland House stands in nearly 40 acres of peaceful grounds. There are conference facilities aplenty these days, plus a spa in which to unwind and detox. The hotel is done out in a traditional manner, not least in the restaurant, with its panelled walls, paintings and well-spaced, burnished darkwood tables. The menu takes a comforting classical approach to culinary matters, with plenty of Scottish ingredients on show. Start with traditional smoked salmon from John Ross Jnr of Aberdeen, for example, or smoked haddock and leek fishcakes with lemon and parsley mayonnaise. Among main courses there are steaks cooked on the grill (21-day hung Scottish sirloin, maybe), or the likes of pan-roasted venison with dauphinoise potatoes, honey-glazed parsnips and blackberry jus. Among desserts, citrus tart competes with dark chocolate truffle cake with coffee anglaise and chocolate ice cream. There are Scottish cheeses, too.

Times 7-9 Closed L all week

Looking for a restaurant by name?
Use the index on page 751

STRATHAVEN
Map 20 NS74

Rissons at Springvale

Modern Scottish

tel: 01357 520234 & 521131 **18 Lethame Rd ML10 6AD**
email: info@rissons.co.uk **web:** www.rissonsrestaurant.co.uk
dir: M74 junct 8, A71, through Stonehouse to Strathaven

Modern Scottish bistro cooking in a comfortable restaurant with rooms

A bright, airy restaurant with rooms in the small town of Strathavan near East Kilbride, Rissons caters to an enthusiastic local crowd. The main dining room is a fairly intimate space overlooking the gardens, with linen-clad tables and subdued lighting in the evenings, and wooden blinds to mitigate the glare through conservatory-style windows on sunny days. The modern Scottish bistro cooking makes a good fist of utilising local supplies, with respectable portion sizes and unfussy presentations. Scott Baxter can turn out a well-executed twice-baked goats' cheese soufflé with interesting fruity 'winter coleslaw', or produce a hearty fish casserole of sea bream and scallops in the robust company of chorizo, beans and tomato. Properly crackled pork belly of tip-top flavour comes with assertive haggis croquettes and creamed cabbage in port sauce, and satisfaction is guaranteed for fans of both chocolate and salty caramel in the form of a softly bitter terrine accompanied by crunchy honeycomb ice cream.

Chef Scott Baxter, Evan Munro **Owner** Scott & Anne Baxter **Seats** 40
Times 1-close/6-9.30 Closed New Year, 1 wk Jan, 1st wk Jul, Mon-Tue, L Wed-Sat, D Sun **Prices** Prices not confirmed, Service optional **Wines** 6 by glass **Parking** 10
Notes Early evening menu Wed-Fri, Sunday L, Vegetarian available, Children welcome

EAST LOTHIAN

ABERLADY
Map 21 NT47

Ducks at Kilspindie

Modern British

tel: 01875 870682 **EH32 ORE**
email: kilspindie@ducks.co.uk **web:** www.ducks.co.uk
dir: A1 (Bankton junct) take 1st exit to North Berwick. At next rdbt 3rd exit onto A198 signed Longniddry, left towards Aberlady. At T-junct, facing river, right to Aberlady

Inventive modern cooking in smart restaurant with rooms

In the heart of golfing country with no less than 21 courses within striking distance, Ducks has a lot to offer. Here on the high street of an East Lothian village, Malcolm Duck offers relaxation and fortification in the form of restaurant, bistro and bedrooms. The main culinary attraction is the diminutive main restaurant – just ten tables – with its charming mix of objets and artworks, and a menu based around good quality local ingredients. There's lots of craft and imagination on display throughout. Start, perhaps, with a winter soup flavoured with pumpkin and ginger, or steak tartare with a lime cure, pear, and mustard seasoning. Next up, cannelloni of sea fish with chick pea and rosemary sauce and seaweed competes for your attention with a duo of quail with a cider-cooked apple, a filo pastry nest and tempura vegetables. White chocolate cheesecake with raspberry jelly brings things to a close. Donald's Bar Bistro serves up real ale and whisky (over 50) alongside the likes of sandwiches and 40-day aged steaks.

Chef David Towand **Owner** Malcolm Duck **Seats** 22, Pr/dining room 22
Times 12-3/6-10 Closed 25 Dec, Mon-Tue **Prices** Starter £6.50-£8.65, Main £12.50-£18.50, Dessert £6.70-£12, Service optional **Wines** 121 bottles over £30, 48 bottles under £30, 9 by glass **Parking** 15 **Notes** Sunday L £8.30-£14.95, Vegetarian available, Children welcome

EAST LINTON
Map 21 NT67

The Linton
 Traditional NEW

tel: 01620 860202 **3 Bridgend EH40 3AF**
email: infolinton@aol.com **web:** www.thelintonhotel.co.uk
dir: *From A1, follow signs for East Linton, 3m*

Pub-style but inventive comfort food in a smart setting

There's a comforting robustness to The Linton, with is brisk stone facade and warm, inviting interior. There's a proper pub bar which has been dishing out ale since the 18th century (three regularly-changing draught beers to choose from), while the bistro with its smart country-style decor plays its part by delivering some rather nifty updated pub-style food. Try smoked haddock and leek fishcake topped with a poached egg and an accompanying tomato and herb sauce, and there's haggis, too, but in a trendy bonbon form, with roasted neeps, herb mash and whisky sauce. The fish and chips is a stonking version, or go for slow-roasted belly of pork with a black pudding and chorizo potato cake. For dessert, there's the exoticism of caramelised lemon tart with mango and passionfruit sorbet, or a slightly tongue in cheek (but tasty) Irn Bru and cream soda sorbet with deep-fried Mars Bar.

Chef George Kelso, Dawn Ritchie **Owner** Michelle Kelso **Seats** 24, Pr/dining room 30 **Times** 12-2.30/6-9 **Prices** Starter £4-£8, Main £9-£21, Dessert £5-£7, Service optional **Wines** 15 bottles under £30, 15 by glass **Parking** On street **Notes** Sunday L, Vegetarian available, Children welcome

GULLANE
Map 21 NT48

La Potinière
 Modern British

tel: 01620 843214 **Main St EH31 2AA**
dir: *5m from North Berwick on A198*

Well-considered cooking on the high street

A raspberry-painted exterior, with net curtains hanging in the windows, conceals a must-visit restaurant. It's a double-act operation with both Mary Runciman and Keith Marley at the stoves, and the small scale of the operation allows them to oversee every last detail, produce everything in-house and time each dish to the second. Scrupulous sourcing means the menus change regularly, depending on what's best seasonally, with some produce grown in their own garden. The deal is just a couple of choices per course, kicking off perhaps with warm truffle and brie salad with truffle and honey dressing, or more modest but no less successful beetroot pannacotta with horseradish crème fraîche. A sense of balance and high levels of skill are evident in main courses: perhaps steamed sea bass set off by a light vanilla fish sauce, with scallops and nutmeg-scented mash, or braised lamb shank with lamb sauce and parsnip mash, both served with seasonal vegetables. Contrasting flavours are given to puddings: perhaps coffee parfait with prune and almond tart, mandarin compôte and orange sorbet.

Chef Mary Runciman, Keith Marley **Owner** Mary Runciman **Seats** 24 **Times** 12.30-1.30/7-8.30 Closed Xmas, Jan, BHs, Mon-Tue, D Sun **Prices** Fixed L 2 course £20, Fixed D 3 course £38, Service optional **Wines** 31 bottles over £30, 26 bottles under £30, 7 by glass **Parking** 10 **Notes** Fixed D 4 course £43, Sunday L, Vegetarian available, Children welcome

NORTH BERWICK
Map 21 NT58

Macdonald Marine Hotel & Spa
 European

tel: 01620 897300 **Cromwell Rd EH39 4LZ**
email: sales.marine@macdonald-hotels.co.uk **web:** www.macdonaldhotels.co.uk/marine
dir: *from A198 turn into Hamilton Rd at lights then 2nd right*

Impressive Victorian pile with confident and accomplished cooking

On Scotland's majestic East Coast, the Marine Hotel is an upscale Grade II listed Victorian manor overlooking the East Lothian golf course. Named after the man at the stoves, John Paul McLachlan, its restaurant surveys the action on the links through sweeping bay windows, while oak panelling, plush fabrics and chandeliers suspended from lofty ceilings convey a distinct sense of occasion. The service keeps things suitably friendly and relaxed. The kitchen is proud of what's on its doorstep and puts this splendid regional produce to good use, keeping up to speed with contemporary culinary goings on, while showing respect for classical thinking. Braised pork belly with white bean and chorizo casserole has a satisfyingly well-balanced richness, followed by an impeccably-timed fillet of sea bass partnered with king prawn and sweetcorn broth. Otherwise, the uncomplicated appeal of slow-braised beef cheeks with creamed potatoes and rosemary jus should hit the spot. To finish, classic crème brûlée is served with mango sorbet, or there might be the deep comfort of warm treacle tart with clotted cream.

Times 12.30-2.30/6.30-9.30

WEST LOTHIAN

LINLITHGOW
Map 21 NS97

Champany Inn
 Traditional British

tel: 01506 834532 & 834388 **Champany Corner EH49 7LU**
email: reception@champany.com
dir: *2m NE of Linlithgow. From M9 (N) junct 3, at top of slip road turn right. Champany 500yds on right*

Upmarket steakhouse in a characterful old mill

The Champany Inn deals in the polar opposite of fussy, faddy food and sticks to what it knows best: this is the destination of choice for fans of properly-hung, expertly-butchered and chargrilled slabs of Class-A meat. The rambling cluster of buildings dates from the 16th century, and focuses on the main circular restaurant in a former horse-powered flour mill, with its candlelit burnished wooden tables and bare-stone walls beneath a vaulted roof. Chicken liver parfait is a classic they do to perfection here, and it is all the better for a sharp Gewürztraminer jelly to cut its richness. Or you might start with hot-smoked salmon or cod from the Champany smokepot. But this is a mecca for beef, so the main event offers up your favourite cut – T-bone, porterhouse, rib-eye, Chateaubriand and all points in between – whacks it on a charcoal grill, and delivers the result timed to perfection. Quality of the raw materials is second to none, and consequently expensive. If you're on a budget, go for the more wallet-friendly Chop and Ale House.

Chef C Davidson, D Gibson **Owner** Mr & Mrs C Davidson **Seats** 50, Pr/dining room 30 **Times** 12.30-2/7-10 Closed 25-26 Dec, 1-2 Jan, Sun, L Sat **Prices** Fixed L 2 course £25.50, Fixed D 3 course £42.50, Starter £9.50-£18, Main £31-£45, Dessert £8.95 **Wines** 450 bottles over £30, 24 bottles under £30, 8 by glass **Parking** 50 **Notes** Vegetarian available, No children

LINLITHGOW *continued*

Livingston's Restaurant

@@ Modern European v

tel: 01506 846565 **52 High St EH49 7AE**
email: contact@livingstons-restaurant.co.uk **web:** www.livingstons-restaurant.co.uk
dir: *On high street opposite old post office*

Modern European cookery at a family-run place

Accessed via a sweet little alley off the main high street, which opens up into a pretty garden with a summer house, Livingston's is a family-run restaurant with a good deal of traditional charm. There's plenty of period character on the inside with stone floors in two of the dining areas (the third being a conservatory extension with views over the garden). The menu treads a modish path with a good showing of Scottish ingredients and some bright, Pan-European ideas. Start, for example, with braised Tamworth pork cheek with pickled apple, apple jelly and maple bacon, or a pea velouté with coconut foam. Among main courses, Shetland monkfish tail is roasted with Bayonne ham and served with fennel and leek purée and spiced lentils, or go for the poached loin of Highland venison with beetroot rösti, celeriac milk gel, syboes (spring onions) and port-glazed baby beetroot. There's no less creativity at dessert stage: strawberry and elderflower cannelloni, for example, with honeycomb, strawberry bonbon and balsamic ice cream.

Chef Martin Connor **Owner** The Livingston Family **Seats** 60, Pr/dining room 15 **Times** 12-2.30/6-9.30 Closed 1 wk Jun, 1 wk Oct, 2 wks Jan, Sun-Mon (ex Mothering & Etr Sun) **Prices** Fixed L 2 course fr £18.75, Fixed D 3 course fr £41.75, Service optional **Wines** 32 bottles over £30, 29 bottles under £30, 6 by glass **Parking** NCP Linlithgow Cross, on street **Notes** Mid-wk menu offer, Children welcome

What makes a 5-Rosette restaurant?
See page 9

Macdonald Houston House

@@ Traditional British, Modern Scottish

tel: 0844 879 9043 **EH52 6JS**
email: houstoun@macdonald-hotels.co.uk
web: www.macdonaldhotels.co.uk/houstoun.house
dir: *M8 junct 3 follow Broxburn signs, straight over rdbt then at mini-rdbt turn right towards Uphall, hotel 1m on right*

Scottish cooking in an atmospheric tower restaurant

The white-painted house sits in a secluded spot surrounded by 22 acres of peaceful woodlands to the west of Edinburgh. It dates from the 16th century and Mary, Queen of Scots is said to be a past visitor. Recently redecorated, up in the tower the four rooms that make up the restaurant – Jeremy Wares at Houstoun House – sport deep burgundy walls, grand chandeliers and elegant unclothed tables lit by a single tall candle. The kitchen relies heavily on quality Scottish ingredients and presents them in a modern, unfussy style. You might start with thin onion and thyme tart and beetroot relish, or seared Skye scallops with red wine risotto and tomato pesto, before moving on to a traditional ashet (a pie) of ox cheek with creamy mash and root vegetables. The patriotic mood continues with a rich Caledonia burnt cream with rhubarb, or seasonal cranachan mess, amongst the desserts.

Chef Jeremy Wares, Chris Hazelton **Owner** Macdonald Hotels **Seats** 65, Pr/dining room 30 **Times** 6.30-9.30 Closed L all week **Prices** Prices not confirmed, Service optional **Wines** 13 by glass **Parking** 200 **Notes** Sunday L, Vegetarian available, Children welcome

---

The Sun Inn

@ Traditional, Modern

tel: 0131 663 2456 & 663 1534 **Lothian Bridge EH22 4TR**
email: thesuninn@live.co.uk **web:** www.thesuninnedinburgh.co.uk
dir: *Opposite Newbattle Viaduct on the A7 near Eskbank*

Winning menus in a popular gastro-pub

'Eat, drink, relax' exhorts the motto of this gastro-pub, and it's easy to comply, the last helped along by friendly, obliging staff and the conversion in 2008 of the old building that combines fabulous boutique bedrooms, and a good dose of rustic chic style with the original oak beams, exposed stone and panelling. Expect welcoming log fires in winter, a bright patio in summer, and whatever the season, Scotland's larder forms the backbone of the kitchen's output. An eclectic menu, supported by blackboards namechecking local suppliers, delivers pub classics as well as inventive but not over-blown contemporary dishes. Pig's cheek with celeriac and cider purée with a baby toffee apple, for example, while mains could bring Scotch game pie with confit and rolled rabbit, pan-seared pigeon breast, prune purée, sprouts and bacon and horseradish mash. There's beer from the independent Stewart's of Edinburgh and a well-chosen wine list to complete the picture.

Chef Ian Minto, Barry Drummond **Owner** Bernadette McCarron **Seats** 90 **Times** 12-2/6-9 Closed 26 Dec, 1 Jan **Prices** Fixed L 2 course £11-£15, Starter £5-£9, Main £10-£23, Dessert £5-£7, Service optional **Wines** 21 bottles over £30, 17 bottles under £30, 28 by glass **Parking** 125 **Notes** Set menu 2/3 course £15/£18, Sunday L £15-£18, Vegetarian available, Children welcome

LASSWADE	Map 21 NT36

The Paper Mill

British, Scottish

tel: 0131 663 1412 **2-4 Westmill Rd EH18 1LR**
email: info@thepapermill-lasswade.co.uk
dir: *In centre of Lasswade village*

Eclectic brasserie cooking overlooking the Esk

A former paper mill beside the River Esk, boasting a large waterside terrace, is now an all-day bar and brasserie with an oak-clad bar, one section of the restaurant decorated with paper lanterns and leather booths and another reached via steps. Staff are relaxed and informal and the place hums, creating a striking environment for the beguiling crowd-pleasing brasserie menu. Haggis wontons with sweet-and-sour sauce is a cross-cultural dish if ever there was one, an alternative perhaps to parmesan monkfish with cocktail sauce. Well-sourced raw materials are carefully cooked whatever style the kitchen chooses for a particular dish. Main courses are a mixed bag, among them yakitori salmon kebab with wild rice, roast duck breast with a Cassis and green peppercorn sauce, and game casserole with herb dumplings. A talent for desserts is behind such delights as chocolate marquise with coffee sauce, and sticky toffee pudding with vanilla ice cream.

Chef Campbell Cameron **Owner** Karen Calvert, David Johnston **Seats** 140, Pr/dining room 14 **Times** 12-10 Closed 25 Dec, All-day dining **Prices** Fixed L 2 course £16, Fixed D 3 course £26, Starter £4.95-£7.50, Main £7.95-£20.95, Dessert £4.95-£5.95 **Wines** 13 bottles over £30, 35 bottles under £30, 16 by glass **Parking** 25 **Notes** Sunday L fr £10.95, Vegetarian available, Children welcome

MORAY	

FORRES	Map 23 NJ05

Cluny Bank

Traditional European NEW

tel: 01309 674304 **69 St Leonards Rd IV36 1DW**
email: info@clunybankhotel.co.uk **web:** www.clunybankhotel.co.uk
dir: *From Torres High St turn down Tolbooth St beside Clocktower. At rdbt take 2nd exit (B9010), 500yds on left*

Sophisticated classical cooking and warm hospitality in a smart setting

A substantial Victorian mansion in lush, green gardens, Cluny Bank has traditionally-styled decor and a small, smart restaurant called Franklin's. It's the domain of chef-patron Lloyd Kenny, who is the sole hand in the kitchen (and the soul of the place, along with wife Julia out front). There is a lot of period charm to the restaurant and a definite air of sophistication. The menu is suitably classically focused, with the local Moray suppliers duly name-checked. You might kick off with mini oxtail suet pudding with a rich gravy, or pan-fried monkfish cheeks with shimeji mushroom fricassee and salsa verde, and follow on with a duo of pork – slow-cooked Iberian black pig's cheek and Gables Farm loin – or grilled whole Dover sole. Chef likes to come out of the kitchen and his bonhomie is very welcome indeed, as are his desserts such as chocolate and rosemary pot with burnt caramel ice cream.

Chef Lloyd Kenny **Owner** Lloyd & Julia Kenny **Seats** 24 **Times** 6.30-20.45 Closed Sun, L all week **Prices** Starter £4.95-£9.50, Main £17.50-£28.95, Dessert £6.25, Service optional **Wines** 29 bottles over £30, 41 bottles under £30, 7 by glass **Parking** 10 **Notes** Vegetarian available, Children 8yrs+

PERTH & KINROSS	

AUCHTERARDER	Map 21 NN91

Andrew Fairlie@Gleneagles

 – *see page 644*

The Strathearn

British, French NOTABLE WINE LIST

tel: 01764 694270 **The Gleneagles Hotel PH3 1NF**
email: gleneagles.restaurant.reservations@gleneagles.com **web:** www.gleneagles.com
dir: *Off A9 at exit for A823 follow signs for Gleneagles Hotel*

Classical and modern cooking in art deco dining room

The vast hotel has a worldwide reputation for its championship golf courses and it has quite a reputation for cooking too, with Andrew Fairlie@Gleneagles as well as The Strathearn, a splendid art deco room with grand columns and moulded ceilings. A sense of drama is generated by the number of trolleys wheeled to the tables: fillet steak is flambéed, whole Dover sole is taken off the bone, roast meats are carved. If this creates the impression that the restaurant is in some time warp, think again: the kitchen is sharp enough to embrace the contemporary as well as the classics. Start with dressed crab accompanied by green apple jelly and tagliatelle, or wood pigeon with mooli choucroute, cherry purée and cocoa sesame crisp. Products are from the top drawer, and dishes are appealingly composed, main courses ranging from properly timed roast cod with black truffle, salsify and braised baby gem to guinea fowl ballottine with leg confit, girolles, sweetcorn, beetroot and potato espuma. Puddings could run to Grand Marnier soufflé with marmalade ice cream.

Chef Paul Devonshire, Jean Philippe Dupas **Owner** Diageo plc **Seats** 322 **Times** 12.30-2.30/7-10 Closed L Mon-Sat **Prices** Prices not confirmed, Service optional **Wines** 15 by glass **Parking** 300 **Notes** Sunday L, Vegetarian available, Children welcome

COMRIE	Map 21 NN72

Royal Hotel

Traditional British

tel: 01764 679200 **Melville Square PH6 2DN**
email: reception@royalhotel.co.uk **web:** www.royalhotel.co.uk
dir: *In main square, 7m from Crieff, on A85*

Luxury small hotel with confident modern cooking

The 18th-century stone building on the main street of this riverside village is now a plush small-scale luxury hotel, with a peaceful library and lounge for pre-dinner drinks, where youthful staff take food orders, and a restaurant split into two areas linked by double doors. The kitchen's in the capable hands of David Milsom, who gives a gently modern tilt to his output without sacrificing tried-and-tested favourites. The seasonally-changing menu might open with fettuccine, cooked al dente, with a sauce of butternut squash, mushrooms and chestnuts, served with sage butter and parmesan shavings, or reassuringly familiar potted shrimps. Trustworthy sourcing is clear in pink slices of venison, of excellent quality, with black pudding clapshot, buttery spring greens and a port and redcurrant sauce, and in sea bass fillet with tomato tagliatelle. Standards are well maintained in puddings of vanilla pannacotta with chopped pineapple, and Eton Mess.

Times 12-2/6.30-9 Closed 25-26 Dec

Andrew Fairlie@Gleneagles

Modern French V 🍷 NOTABLE WINE LIST

tel: 01764 694267 **The Gleneagles Hotel PH3 1NF**
email: reservations@andrewfairlie.co.uk
dir: *From A9 take Gleneagles exit, hotel in 1m*

Franco-Scottish cooking at the hermetic heart of a golfing hotel

This hotel is used to being the centre of attention, built in 1924 in the style of a French chateau, it's no shrinking violet. The place is vast, the grounds are vast, the building is vast, and regardless of the weather there are vantage points aplenty within the hotel from which to admire the gorgeous Perthshire countryside, or the lush green fairways. There are plenty of places to refuel, drink and dine, but this is the jewel in the crown, a restaurant right in the heart of the hotel where one of Scotland's brightest chefs cooks world class food. It's a blissfully serene room, windowless, but none the worse for it, with a vaguely art deco resonance that is by turns classic and contemporary. This upmarket setting is a fitting environment for Andrew Fairlie's cooking, with no view to detract from the dynamic kitchen's output. With a CV showing time served in some top restaurants across the Channel, Fairlie's food reflects equal passion for the French culinary arts and the fine ingredients of Scotland's natural larder. This amounts to contemporary dishes of balance and integrity that deliver some exciting elements while never losing their way. There's a tasting menu that is just the ticket if all of the table are up for it, while the à la carte offers some half-dozen choices per course if you want to go your own way. A first course of roasted hand-dived scallops delivers the bivalves timed to perfection in the company of grilled squid and confit chicken, with a winter starter partnering roast pheasant with grilled foie gras and seasonal vegetables. The technical dexterity and pin-point accuracy continues with main courses such as slow-cooked beef cheek with confit onions, carrots and salsify, or fillet of sea bass with Jerusalem artichoke purée, wild mushrooms and smoked eel. Everything looks wonderful on the plate, not least desserts like a Bramley apple soufflé with accompanying ginger beer sauce and crème brûlée ice cream, or quince mousse with poached quince and walnut ice cream. The wine list is put together with the same sort of attention to detail and passion as the menu, with wine flight options available.

Chef Andrew Fairlie **Owner** Andrew Fairlie **Seats** 54 **Times** 6.30-10 Closed 24-25 Dec, 3 wks Jan, Sun, L all week **Prices** Prices not confirmed **Wines** 12 by glass **Parking** 300 **Notes** ALC 3 course £95, 6 course Degustation £125/Du Marché £95, No children

FORTINGALL   Map 20 NN74

Fortingall Hotel

◉◉ Modern Scottish

tel: 01887 830367 & 829012 **PH15 2NQ**
email: enquiries@fortingall.com **web:** www.fortingall.com
dir: *B846 from Aberfeldy for 6m, left signed Fortingall for 3m. Hotel in village centre*

Well-balanced menu in Arts and Crafts village

Fortingall Hotel, near Loch Tay with views down Glen Lyon, is a solidly built property, and within is a lounge bar that serves pub-style food and a choice of two dining rooms, one in Arts and Craft style, the other slightly less formal; staff are knowledgeable and approachable throughout. Set dinners offer a trio of choices at each course, the kitchen utilising as much local produce as it can; Perthshire lamb, for example, as a main course of pink-roast loin with thyme jus, creamed cabbage, artichoke purée and pommes en cocotte. Meals might kick off with a platter of smoked salmon, quail's eggs and Avruga caviar adding touches of luxury, or foie gras and game terrine complemented by Sauternes jelly, Cumberland sauce and poached figs. Fish is well handled, judging by pan-fried fillet of halibut served on two balls of saffron-flavoured noodles with caviar butter and pak choi. Go for cranachan if offered – the real thing, served with whisky jelly.

Times 12-2/6.30-9

KILLIECRANKIE   Map 23 NN96

Killiecrankie Hotel

◉◉ Modern British V

tel: 01796 473220 **PH16 5LG**
email: enquiries@killiecrankiehotel.co.uk **web:** www.killiecrankiehotel.co.uk
dir: *off A9 at Pitlochry, hotel 3m along B8079 on right*

Satisfying country-house cooking in tranquil Perthshire

There's a sense of splendid isolation at Killiecrankie, and you'd never guess the A9 was so handy if you hadn't come that way yourself. The charming early Victorian house was built for a church minister, but these days administers a different type of absolution – a chance to escape from the real world and get a little taste of comfort and joy. It's in a plum spot, surrounded by soaring trees, with four acres of grounds to call its own and the River Garry flowing past. There's a soothing and smart traditionalism to the interior, including the dining room, with its linen-clad tables, one of which is yours for the night. The menu features plenty of regional ingredients and does not attempt to rock the boat. You might start with sautéed wild mushroom and chorizo tartlet with a leek cream sauce, followed by monkfish wrapped in Parma ham with seared king scallops, potato and sunblushed tomato rösti, and a roasted garlic and parsley butter sauce. Warm frangipane and pear flan with crème fraîche hits the spot at dessert.

Chef Mark Easton **Owner** Henrietta Fergusson **Seats** 30, Pr/dining room 12
Times 6.30-8.30 Closed Jan-Feb, L all week **Prices** Service optional **Wines** 32 bottles over £30, 47 bottles under £30, 9 by glass **Parking** 20 **Notes** Pre-theatre menu from 6.15pm Mon-Sat, 4 course D £42, Sunday L £15-£20, Children welcome

KINCLAVEN   Map 21 NO13

Ballathie House Hotel

◉◉ Classic V

tel: 01250 883268 **PH1 4QN**
email: info@ballathiehousehotel.com **web:** www.ballathiehousehotel.com
dir: *From A9, 2m N of Perth, take B9099 through Stanley & follow signs, or from A93 at Beech Hedge follow signs for Ballathie, 2.5m*

Modern country-house cooking by the Tay

The Glasgow to Aberdeen train used to deliver anglers to this turreted Scottish mansion by the River Tay, and although Ballathie is still a prime spot for the rod and line brigade, you don't need to dangle your fly into frigid waters to enjoy a stay here. The gastronomically inclined will appreciate the elegant buttercup-hued restaurant, and a kitchen team that takes native produce – much of it from the surrounding estate – as its starting point. Cooking is unapologetically in the tried-and-tested modern country-house idiom, and succeeds thanks to its superb ingredients and refusal to veer off course into faddish trends. Judicious balance and luxury touches combine in a starter of confit duck croustillant with seared foie gras, macerated apricots and carrot and orange purée, ahead of loin and truffled haunch of Sutherland venison with thyme rösti, red wine salsify, celeriac purée and praline sauce. Dessert wraps things up with a melting chocolate fondant with cherry compôte and pistachio ice cream.

Chef Scott Scorer **Owner** John Milligan **Seats** 60, Pr/dining room 35
Times 12.30-2/7-9 **Prices** Service optional **Wines** 151 bottles over £30, 36 bottles under £30, 14 by glass **Parking** 100 **Notes** Sunday L £29, No children

MUTHILL   Map 21 NN81

Barley Bree Restaurant with Rooms

◉◉ British, French V

tel: 01764 681451 **6 Willoughby St PH5 2AB**
email: info@barleybree.com **web:** www.barleybree.com
dir: *A9 onto A822 in centre of Muthill*

Franco-Mediterranean cooking in a conservation village

This early 19th-century inn in a Perthshire conservation village, which once provided stabling for coach horses plying the Highland roads, has gone through a number of incarnations and names over the years, and settled into its present manifestation with the arrival of Fabrice and Alison Bouteloup in 2007. Now a modern day restaurant with rooms, its ancient brick and stone walls enhance the pleasingly come-as-you-are feel of the dining room. French and Mediterranean food traditions inform Fabrice's cooking, expressed through the medium of pedigree Scots produce. First up might be chicken and chorizo terrine with puréed trompettes and saffron-pickled cucumber, or peat-smoked haddock and a seared scallop with a gratin of courgette and potato in gremolata. Those lively openers lead on to saddle of venison with charred cabbage in truffle emulsion, or orientally inspired East Neuk monkfish tail dressed in red chilli and coriander, with orzo pasta and choi sum in Asian-spiced lobster bisque. For afters, seasonal berries come with white peach sorbet, rosé wine jelly and mint cream, while the crème brûlée is fragranced with rosemary.

Chef Fabrice Bouteloup **Owner** Fabrice & Alison Bouteloup **Seats** 35
Times 12-2/6.45-9 Closed Mon-Tue, D Sun **Prices** Prices not confirmed **Wines** 23 bottles over £30, 50 bottles under £30, 15 by glass **Parking** 12 **Notes** Sunday L, Children welcome

PERTH

Map 21 NO12

Deans@Let's Eat
◎◎ Modern Scottish

tel: 01738 643377 **77-79 Kinnoull St PH1 5EZ**
email: deans@letseatperth.co.uk web: www.letseatperth.co.uk
dir: On corner of Kinnoull St & Atholl St, close to North Inch & cinema

Dazzling cooking in stylish restaurant

Deans really is a family-run joint, with Willie and Margot joined by their two sons at their ever-popular restaurant. It's right in the centre of town, in the heart of the action, and it delivers modern Scottish flavours in a vibrant and easy-going atmosphere. The red room provides a soothing respite if the weather is grim, with colourful prints adorning the walls and the darkwood tables left free of formal white linen. Willie Deans is a highly accomplished chef and his kitchen turns out some skilfully executed dishes such as a first course twice-baked Isle of Mull cheese soufflé of perfect consistency, with McSween's haggis, neeps and a whisky cream – a beautifully presented plate, too. A main course dish of loin of Ochil venison comes next, with a turnip and potato swirl, braised red cabbage, pear purée and a glossy, sticky jus. A fishy main might be fillets of halibut and sole with a leek and champagne sauce, and, for dessert, tuck into a caramel pannacotta with chocolate and orange truffle and caramel ice.

Chef Willie Deans **Owner** Mr & Mrs W Deans **Seats** 70 **Times** 12-3/6-10 Closed 1st 2 wks Jan, Sun-Mon **Prices** Fixed L 2 course £12.50, Fixed D 3 course £21, Starter £4.50-£10.50, Main £13.50-£23.95, Dessert £2.50-£8.95, Service optional **Wines** 23 bottles over £30, 36 bottles under £30, 14 by glass **Parking** Multi-storey car park (100 yds) **Notes** Pre-theatre 2 course inc glass wine £20 Tue-Fri 6-9pm, Vegetarian available, Children welcome

Murrayshall House Hotel & Golf Course
◎◎ Modern British

tel: 01738 551171 **New Scone PH2 7PH**
email: info@murrayshall.co.uk web: www.murrayshall.co.uk
dir: From Perth A94 (Coupar Angus) turn right signed Murrayshall before New Scone

Polished cooking amid the rolling Lowland acres

With a brace of 18-hole courses woven into its densely-wooded 350-acre estate, it's fair to say that most of Murrayshall's guests have golf in mind, but there are other attractions too, not least the fine dining to be had in its Old Masters restaurant. Bag a window table to soak up the views which stretch all the way to the city of Perth, and take in the leaded windows, original artworks and faultlessly elegant tone of the room. Menus bang the drum for Scottish produce and offer much to please traditionalists, plus a few creative flourishes to assuage modern tastes. The fatty richness of a duck liver pâté is offset with the acid twang of tart gooseberries and smoked bacon salad, while main course brings layers of pork belly and black pudding atop crushed apple purée spiked with Calvados and served with Savoy cabbage, mushrooms and rich jus. Puddings take refuge in classily-tweaked old

favourites – cherry Bakewell tart with cherry ice cream and a shot glass of cranberry punch, for example.

Chef Craig Jackson **Owner** Old Scone Ltd **Seats** 55, Pr/dining room 40 **Times** 12-2.30/7-9.45 Closed 26 Dec, L Sat-Mon **Prices** Fixed L 2 course £16.95, Fixed D 3 course £29.50, Tasting menu £60, Starter £5.75-£6.95, Main £15.25-£23.95, Dessert £5.95-£6.95, Service optional **Wines** 17 bottles over £30, 27 bottles under £30, 8 by glass **Parking** 120 **Notes** Sunday L £21.95, Vegetarian available, Children welcome

The New County Hotel
◎◎ Modern British v

tel: 01738 623355 **22-30 County Place PH2 8EE**
email: enquiries@newcountyhotel.com web: www.opusone-restaurant.co.uk
dir: A9 junct 11, Perth. Follow signs for town centre. Hotel on right after library

Modish cooking in city-centre boutique hotel

Part of the boutique New County Hotel in Perth centre, the Opus One restaurant is a hotspot for business lunches, while culture vultures turn up to refuel on forays to the city's theatre, concert hall and galleries. The hotel goes for a cosmopolitan city-slicker look in Opus One that brings together bare darkwood tables and floors with chocolate-brown high-backed leather seats, soft lighting, and cool jazz burbling in the background. On the food front, the kitchen clearly reads from a French-influenced script and has the necessary technique and creativity to make the most of the top-drawer ingredients from Perthshire's larder. A switched-on menu kicks off with goats' cheese soufflé with cauliflower, served both pickled and as a curried purée, and Grana Padano crisp; next up, slow-cooked beef blade comes with a bone filled with marrow and garlic snails, pearl barley and parsley, or there might be braised pork neck with Jerusalem artichoke, hazelnut, apple and red wine reduction. The good ideas keep coming to the end with a mincemeat pithivier matched with a nutmeg tuile and vanilla bean ice cream.

Chef Rory Lovie **Owner** Mr Owen, Mrs Sarah Boyle **Seats** 48 **Times** 12-2/5.30-9 Closed Sun-Mon, L Tue-Thu **Prices** Fixed D 3 course £22.95-£32.95, Tasting menu £42-£49, Service optional **Wines** 20 bottles over £30, 19 bottles under £30, 7 by glass **Parking** 10, plus opposite on street **Notes** Early bird menu available, Children 10 yrs+

Pig'Halle
◎ French NEW

tel: 01738 248784 **South St PH2 8PG**
email: info@pighalle.co.uk
dir: Beside Salutation Hotel

Pork, and more, in buzzy French bistro

On a busy street in the centre of Perth, Pig'Halle has been given a Parisian look, with a map of the Métro embossed on a large mirror, wine memorabilia, some banquette seating and red-upholstered round-backed chairs at darkwood tables. It's an atmospheric, buzzy sort of place, people drawn by the bistro-style cooking and the France-inspired menu. As its punning name suggests, pork is a theme, from a starter of melt-in-the-mouth belly with black pudding, sautéed spiced pear and apple and tomato salsa, a beautifully composed dish, to a full-blooded main course of confit trotter with spinach, celeriac remoulade and chips. Elsewhere, seek out Gallic classics such as frogs' legs, or sole Véronique with wilted spinach and crushed potatoes, and don't ignore the board of specials: there could be a flavour-packed duo of venison (braised shoulder pie, and collops fanned over a rich ragout of pancetta and Puy lentils). Well-executed desserts might include tarte Tatin and creamy chocolate and Amaretto tart.

Chef Herve Tabourel **Owner** Herve & Paula Tabourel **Seats** 40 **Times** 12-3/5.30-9.30 Closed 26 Dec, 1 Jan, Mon **Prices** Fixed L 2 course £10.90, Starter £3.90-£6.45, Main £9.90-£41.90, Dessert £4.90-£7.90, Service optional **Wines** 6 bottles over £30, 26 bottles under £30, 11 by glass **Parking** Canal St car park **Notes** Pre-theatre 5.30-6.45pm 2/3 course £13.90/£16.90, Vegetarian available, Children welcome

The Roost Restaurant

◉ British, European NEW

tel: 01738 812111 **Forgandenny Rd, Bridge of Earn PH2 9AZ**
email: enquiries@theroostrestaurant.co.uk
dir: M90 junct 9, Bridge of Earn. Follow brown tourist signs

Impressive regional cooking in an unassuming-looking village venue

Tim and Anna Dover's place in the village of Kintillo, just outside Perth, hides itself well. A single-storey building of red stone, it looks altogether grander inside, with tartan carpeting, framed prints, low-hanging bright green rafters, and many little hens and roosters here and there to emphasise the brand. Staff are superb, full of helpful, friendly chatter and good advice, and Tim Dover runs the kind of operation that has him going out fishing and foraging, as well as cultivating local suppliers. The results are impressive, as is demonstrated by a starter plate of rabbit rillettes, pickled carrot and celeriac, and toasted home-made crostini. Main courses can be labour-intensive, as when halibut is stuffed with langoustines and served with saffron risotto and braised baby leeks in a ritzy sauce of vermouth and champagne, or when a fat leg of proper confit duck comes with thin, brittle rösti scented with thyme, braised red cabbage, chantenay carrots and a delicate thyme jus. Nothing could be more satisfying than to finish with a wedge of moistly fresh plum frangipane scattered with flaked almonds and served with a little jug of orange anglaise.

Chef Tim Dover **Owner** Tim & Anna Dover **Seats** 24 **Times** 12-2/6.45-9 Closed 25 Dec, 1-18 Jan, Mon, D Tue-Wed, Sun **Prices** Prices not confirmed, Service optional **Wines** 19 bottles over £30, 20 bottles under £30, 7 by glass **Parking** 6 **Notes** Sunday L, Vegetarian available, Children 10 yrs+ D

63@Parklands

◉◉ Modern European V

tel: 01738 622451 **Parklands Hotel, St Leonards Bank PH2 8EB**
email: info@63atparklandshotel.com **web:** www.63atparklands.com
dir: Adjacent to Perth station, overlooking South Inch Park

Smart contemporary cooking in a chic hotel

Sister restaurant to 63 Tay Street (see entry), 63@Parklands is located in a smart hotel near the river, and comes complete with a lovely patio area for alfresco dining. It offers the same style of technically adept, well-focused and creative cooking from chef Graeme Pallister as its ever-popular sibling. Fixed-price menus with choices of two at the principal stages are the business, opening perhaps with Loch Nevis langoustine fricassée with shimeji mushrooms and penne. A soup is interposed before the main-course alternatives of Kirriemuir lamb rump crusted in olives and pine nuts, with tomato, basil and garlic, or salmon roasted in Hebridean salt and herbs with smoked salmon noodles in salmon roe butter sauce. Cheeses are followed by creative desserts such as rhubarb burnt cream with a salty ginger ice cream doughnut.

Chef Graeme Pallister **Owner** Scott & Penny Edwards **Seats** 32, Pr/dining room 22 **Times** 7-9 Closed 25 Dec-5 Jan, Tue-Wed, L all week **Prices** Fixed D 3 course £39.50, Service optional **Wines** 30 bottles over £30, 40 bottles under £30, 8 by glass **Parking** 25 **Notes** Children welcome

63 Tay Street

◉◉ Modern Scottish V ◆NOTABLE WINE LIST

tel: 01738 441451 **63 Tay St PH2 8NN**
email: info@63taystreet.com
dir: In town centre, on river

Attractive, imaginative cooking by the river Tay

Graeme Pallister's popular local restaurant occupies part of the ground floor of an imposing stone building on the Tay riverside. A shipboard feel is created by means of porthole mirrors, and the decor is all about stripped-back elegance, with an uncovered floor, good napery and claret-hued seating. 'Local, honest, simple' is the stated motto, although a restaurant chef's idea of 'simple' may not necessarily accord with yours. Dishes look attractive, as with a shallow, crisp-coated, twice-baked Roquefort soufflé, with sweetly poached pear and cobnuts, or a fish main course such as Scrabster cod and West Coast mussels bedded on gently curried green lentils, a dish that has enough innate sea-fresh flavour to throw a red wine sauce into relief. Meat might be an imaginative fusion assemblage of spatchcock quail with pickled plum, cavolo nero and merguez sausage, while the highly original garnish for sublime white chocolate and pistachio mousse and vanilla ice cream is a hot sweet wonton filled with soft banana, the whole garnished with candied orange peel. Don't miss the fine breads.

Chef Graeme Pallister **Owner** Scott & Penny Edwards, Graeme Pallister **Seats** 38 **Times** 12-2/6.30-9 Closed Xmas, New Year, 1st wk Jul, Sun-Mon, L Tue-Wed **Prices** Fixed L 2 course £19-£26, Fixed D 3 course £39.50-£45, Tasting menu £50, Starter £8-£10, Main £23.50-£29, Dessert £8-£10, Service optional **Wines** 123 bottles over £30, 49 bottles under £30, 7 by glass **Parking** On street **Notes** Pre theatre 2/3 course £19.50/£25 Tue-Fri 5.45-6.15pm, Children welcome

Tabla

◉ Indian V

tel: 01738 444630 **173 South St PH2 8NY**
email: thirmalreddy@yahoo.com

Zesty Indian home cooking in the city centre

'The guest is God,' declares the menu, but don't let it go to your head. Start nibbling on ambrosia, and you'll miss out on the richly satisfying, traditional Indian home cooking of the Kumar family's central Perth eatery. The ambience has more personality than many a formula Indian, with exposed stone walls, full-drop windows and a glass panel looking into the kitchen. Indian music featuring the eponymous tabla drums is played softly. The menu deals in standards that are full of freshness and zest, starting with hara bhara tikki, little fried patties of mashed potato, peas and spinach, seasoned with green chillies, coriander, garlic and ginger, as an appetiser for mains such as lamb bhuna, slow-cooked and served in a thick masala, or kadhai jhinga, king prawns tossed in onions, tomatoes and peppers. A full listing of vegetarian dishes is given due prominence on the menu. Finish with glutinous gulab jamun, or kulfi sprinkled with pistachios.

Chef Praveen Kumar **Owner** Praveen Kumar & Saroo **Seats** 42 **Times** 12-2.30/5-10.30 Closed L Sun **Prices** Fixed L 2 course fr £8.95, Fixed D 3 course fr £14.95, Starter £4.45-£6.95, Main £7.95-£13.95, Dessert £3.45-£3.95 **Wines** 4 bottles over £30, 4 bottles under £30, 3 by glass **Parking** On street **Notes** Pre-theatre 2 course fr £11.95, Wine & Dine 2 people £34.95, Children welcome

Find out more about how we assess for Rosette awards on page 9

PITLOCHRY
Map 23 NN95

Fonab Castle Hotel

Modern Scottish, British NEW

tel: 01796 470140 **Foss Rd PH16 5ND**
email: reservations@fonabcastlehotel.com **web:** www.fonabcastlehotel.com
dir: Pitlochry A9 take Foss Rd junct. Hotel 1st on left

Creative modern cooking in a stylish hotel

With its gables and turrets, Fonab's castle credentials are not in dispute, although it's not so much an intimidating monolith as a grand manor house, and it's in a glorious position, too, overlooking wooded hillsides and a loch. Once home to the Sandeman family (of port and sherry fame), the place is now a swish hotel with a contemporary finish and bags of style. There are two dining options: the brasserie in a stylish modern extension of glass and wood (with a bar and lounge above) and the smart Sandemans fine-dining restaurant with an impressive gin and whisky display. In the latter, the kitchen turns out some classy modern food based on top quality regional produce via a tasting menu. A little taster of langoustine with radish and curry foam makes a great impression from the off, followed by the likes of hand-dived scallops with lobster and tomato velouté, and a meat course of poached and roasted Aberdeen angus (acute technical skills and balancing of flavours and textures all round). A sweet course might be chocolate praline with lime and pistachio crème fraîche.

Chef Graham Harrower **Owner** Mr & Mrs Clark **Times Prices** Tasting menu £75, Starter £5.50–£12.95, Main £13.95–£29.50, Dessert £5.25–£7.50 **Wines** 114 bottles over £30, 36 bottles under £30, 15 by glass **Parking** 50 **Notes** Fixed menu 5 course £55, Sunday L £16.95–£19.95, Vegetarian available, Children welcome

Green Park Hotel

 British

tel: 01796 473248 **Clunie Bridge Rd PH16 5JY**
email: bookings@thegreenpark.co.uk **web:** www.thegreenpark.co.uk
dir: Turn off A9 at Pitlochry, follow signs for 0.25m through town, turn left at Clunie Bridge Rd

Country-house cooking with magnificent views

The Green Park has one of those dining rooms where the injunction to 'bag a table by the window' is worth heeding, the reward being prime views over Loch Faskally, with the forests and mountains as backdrop. It's a long room with a chintzy feel, where tables are clad in floor-length coverings, respectably spaced and individually adorned with blooms. A gentle version of country-house cooking is in the offing, so avocado mousse is garnished with Serrano ham, shaved parmesan and dried tomato, while main courses run to braised rose veal osso buco with basil mash, in a dressing of tomatoes, olive oil and herbs, or a seafood assemblage of poached salmon, prawns, mackerel and anchovies with saffron mayonnaise and salad. Finish up with moreish gingerbread pudding served with a moat of caramel sauce and a garnish of banana ice cream.

Times 12–2/6.30–8.30

Knockendarroch House Hotel

Traditional British

tel: 01796 473473 & 07802 878231 **Higher Oakfield PH16 5HT**
email: bookings@knockendarroch.co.uk **web:** www.knockendarroch.co.uk
dir: On entering town from Perth, 1st right (East Moulin Road) after railway bridge, then 2nd left, last hotel on left

Resourceful cooking at elegantly appointed hotel

A handsome sandstone house in a wooded setting, Knockendarroch has country-house comforts and a diminutive restaurant that delivers classy modern Scottish food. It's all very traditional within, with warming fires in the cooler months, ornate cornicing, chandeliers and the like, and a genuine hospitality runs right through the place. The kitchen makes good use of high quality regional produce to deliver well-crafted and refined dishes. A starter of wood pigeon, for example, its breast beautifully pink, comes with parsnip purée and a smoked bacon rösti, while main courses might see loin of Perthshire lamb partnered with pommes dauphinoise, Jerusalem artichoke purée and an excellent haggis samosa. A fishy main might be hake with a sweetcorn pancake and zingy sun-blushed tomato and chorizo salsa, and, for dessert, there might be lemon meringue pie with nicely zesty lemon curd, toasted marshmallows and golden pastry crumb.

Times 5.30–8.30 Closed mid Nov–mid Jan, L all week

ST FILLANS
Map 20 NN62

The Four Seasons Hotel

Modern British

tel: 01764 685333 **Lochside PH6 2NF**
email: info@thefourseasonshotel.co.uk **web:** www.thefourseasonshotel.co.uk
dir: From Perth take A85 W, through Crieff & Comrie. Hotel at west end of village

Breathtaking loch views and appealing modern cooking

Perched on the edge of Loch Earn, The Four Seasons has a location to die for with its breathtaking south-westerly views over the water and wooded hills. The hotel dates from the 19th century, with modifications made over the years to fine tune the place for modern sensibilities. Country-house chintz has definitely been chucked out in this stylish bolt-hole, particularly in the waterside Meall Reamhar restaurant, where colourful seats contrast with cool white walls hung with original artwork and those stunning views as a backdrop to a modern British menu built on spectacular Scottish ingredients brought together in inventive pairings. Grilled West Coast scallops partnered with crispy black pudding, sweet potato and cumin purée and sweet chilli vinaigrette, or lamb Wellington with ceps duxelles, mousseline potatoes, minted greens and game jus are typical main courses. These might be book-ended by savoury Mediterranean bread and butter pudding with sun-blushed tomato reduction and Kalamata olive tapenade, and creative desserts such as damson pannacotta with thyme shortbread, and elderflower and mint crystals.

Chef Mathew Martin, Didier Nemesien **Owner** Andrew Low **Seats** 40, Pr/dining room 20 **Times** 12–2.30/6–9.30 Closed Jan–Feb & some wkdays Mar, Nov & Dec **Prices** Fixed D 2 course £28–£39.90, Service optional **Wines** 61 bottles over £30, 52 bottles under £30, 8 by glass **Parking** 30 **Notes** 4 course D £38–£49.90, Sunday L £15.95, Children welcome

EAST RENFREWSHIRE

UPLAWMOOR
Map 10 NS45

Uplawmoor Hotel

Modern Scottish

tel: 01505 850565 **66 Neilston Rd G78 4AF**
email: info@uplawmoor.co.uk **web:** www.uplawmoor.co.uk
dir: M77 junct 2, A736 signed Barrhead & Irvine. Hotel 4m beyond Barrhead

Modern and traditional cooking in a former coaching inn

This long whitewashed building has been greatly expanded and upgraded since its humble 1750 beginnings as a one-room coaching inn. Nowadays it's very much the hub of the village, with its popular restaurant in a rectangular blue-carpeted room with white walls and darkwood furniture under a beamed ceiling. The kitchen bakes its own bread and works around fresh local produce, steering a course between the traditional and more esoteric notions. Starters of Cullen skink or chicken liver pâté with onion and orange marmalade might appear next to seared scallops with black pudding and crispy bacon in balsamic dressing. Main courses come from the familiar mould of chicken Kiev, beef Stroganoff, and seared salmon fillet in a creamy leek and white wine sauce with Lyonnaise potatoes and green beams. End with a tried-and-tested dessert like banana split or sherry trifle.

Chef Paul Brady **Owner** Stuart & Emma Peacock **Seats** 30 **Times** 12-3/6-9.30 Closed 26 Dec, 1 Jan, L Mon-Sat **Prices** Prices not confirmed, Service optional **Wines** 8 by glass **Parking** 40 **Notes** Early evening menu available 5.30-7pm Sun-Fri, Sunday L, Vegetarian available, No children

SCOTTISH BORDERS

EDDLESTON
Map 21 NT24

The Horseshoe Restaurant with Rooms

Modern Scottish NOTABLE WINE LIST

tel: 01721 730225 **Edinburgh Rd EH45 8QP**
email: reservations@horseshoeinn.co.uk **web:** www.horseshoeinn.co.uk
dir: On A703, 5m N of Peebles

Voguish Scottish cookery in a roadside restaurant with rooms

Centuries ago, the single-storey, cottage-like roadside premises housed a blacksmith's, but time transformed them into a village inn, and now distinctly more upmarket restaurant with rooms. Beneath low ceilings, a striking decorative approach features mottled wallpaper, Romanesque interior pillars and dark red carpeting. Soft lighting in the main dining area creates an intimate feel, with smartly dressed staff doing their descriptive bit as dishes are delivered. They carry voguish Scottish cookery founded on top-drawer ingredients. First up could be a marbled terrine of rabbit, prune and potato with a serving of Stornoway black pudding and rather assertive piccalilli, before mains such as poached cod with mussels, chervil gnocchi and artichokes, or roast haunch of Highland red deer with cavolo nero and parsnips in black pepper jus, with a mini-cottage pie full of Morteau sausage. Dessert might be dark chocolate délice with orange purée and honeycomb. Cheeses come with apricot chutney, quince and oat biscuits.

Chef Alistair Craig **Owner** Border Steelwork Structures Ltd **Seats** 40, Pr/dining room 14 **Times** 12-2.30/7-9 Closed 2 wks Jan, Mon-Tue **Prices** Fixed L 2 course £16-£20, Fixed D 3 course £30, Tasting menu £50, Service optional **Wines** 118 bottles over £30, 44 bottles under £30, 12 by glass **Parking** 20 **Notes** ALC 3 course £40, Sunday L £22.50-£27.50, Vegetarian available, Children welcome

KELSO
Map 21 NT73

The Cobbles Freehouse & Dining

Modern British

tel: 01573 223548 **7 Bowmont St TD5 7JH**
email: info@thecobbleskelso.co.uk
dir: A6089 from Edinburgh, turn right at rdbt into Bowmont St. Restaurant in 0.3m

Appealing menu in lively pub setting

Festooned with hanging baskets in the summer, this 19th-century inn is just off the town's main square. It's the brewery tap for the Tempest Brewing Co just up the road, so a pint or two should hit the spot, but there are plenty of other good reasons to visit. The beamed bar has bags of atmosphere with a roaring log fire in winter, there's live music on Friday nights, plus no shortage of nice things to eat. You might opt for a home-made burger off the bar menu, or settle down in the cosy restaurant and choose something like seared breast of wood pigeon with crumbled Stornoway black pudding, red cabbage and port jus, followed by crispy-skin sea bass with pea purée, crushed lemon new potatoes, confit cherry tomatoes and tomato Choron sauce. There's a good showing of regional ingredients, and the beer might even sneak into dessert in the form of Tempest mocha porter ice cream served with a chocolate fondant and poached blueberries.

Owner Annika & Gavin Meiklejohn **Seats** 35, Pr/dining room 30 **Times** 12-2.30/5.45-9 Closed 25-26 Dec **Prices** Starter £4-£7.50, Main £9.95-£20.95, Dessert £5-£7, Service optional **Wines** 4 bottles over £30, 26 bottles under £30, 7 by glass **Parking** Free parking behind restaurant **Notes** Sunday L £12.95-£20.95, Vegetarian available, Children welcome

The Roxburghe Hotel & Golf Course

Modern British NOTABLE WINE LIST

tel: 01573 450331 **TD5 8JZ**
email: hotel@roxburghe.net **web:** www.roxburghe-hotel.com
dir: From A68, 1m N of Jedburgh, take A698 for 5m to Heiton

Impressive country setting for fine modern Scottish cooking

Owned by the Duke of Roxburghe, who takes a hands-on approach to running this grand Jacobean country-house hotel, the turreted pile is tucked in woodland close to the River Teviot on the Duke's vast estate. If you're not a roughy toughy outdoor type, there's pampering on hand in the health and beauty salon. But first and foremost, this is prime huntin' shootin' fishin' territory, so the estate provides a good deal of what turns up on the menu. The impressive dining room delivers ducal finery in spades, with its views over the manicured lawns, plush fabrics, horse-racing prints, crisp linen tablecloths, and a tartan carpet to remind you that you're north of the border. Thankfully the kitchen is not stuck in the past, turning out modernist ideas starting with a risotto of Orkney girolles and goats' cheese, followed by Eyemouth with saffron and squid ink linguine, langoustines and trompette de mort mushrooms. To finish, green apple sorbet makes a zingy foil to moist pumpkin cake with crunchy pumpkin seeds.

Chef Gordon Campbell **Owner** Duke of Roxburghe **Seats** 40, Pr/dining room 16 **Times** 12.30-2/7-9.30 **Prices** Fixed L 2 course £17, Fixed D 3 course £39.50, Starter £7-£14.50, Main £19.50-£29.50, Dessert £7-£14, Service optional **Wines** 91 bottles over £30, 42 bottles under £30, 10 by glass **Parking** 150 **Notes** Sunday L £17-£25, Vegetarian available, Children welcome

MELROSE
Map 21 NT53

Burt's Hotel
Modern Scottish, British NOTABLE WINE LIST

tel: 01896 822285 **Market Square TD6 9PL**
email: enquiries@burtshotel.co.uk **web:** www.burtshotel.co.uk
dir: *A6091, 2m from A68, 3m S of Earlston. Hotel in market square*

Contemporary cooking at an old favourite

Owned and run by the Henderson family for over 40 years, this handsome 18th-century inn is rooted into Melrose life. It stands on the picturesque market square, a short stroll from the River Tweed, and sports a hunting, shooting and fishing theme that extends through the traditionally decorated restaurant and the bustling bar, where you'll find winter log fires, hearty grub, Scottish ales, and a mere 90 malt whiskies to work your way through. The kitchen moves with the times, turning out modern Scottish dishes prepared from quality locally-sourced produce. Crisp belly pork comes with caramelised apples, hazelnut salad and apple purée, and game and pistachio terrine is served with cranberry and pear compôte and warm brioche. This being Scotland, you're never far from game, so follow with saddle of venison served with the time-honoured accompaniments of potato fondant, caramelised red cabbage and juniper, or roast salmon fillet with Lyonnaise potatoes, crushed peas, and tomato and chive butter sauce. Finish with a palate-tingling passionfruit mousse with caramelised pineapple and clementine sorbet.

Chef Trevor Williams **Owner** The Henderson family **Seats** 50, Pr/dining room 25 **Times** 12-2/7-9 Closed 26 Dec, 5-12 Jan, L Mon-Fri **Prices** Starter £7.95-£12, Main £16.95-£25, Dessert £7.95-£8.95, Service optional **Wines** 33 bottles over £30, 27 bottles under £30, 8 by glass **Parking** 40 **Notes** Sunday L £20-£29, Vegetarian available, Children 10 yrs+

Who are the AA's Restaurants of the Year? See page 14

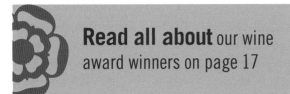

Read all about our wine award winners on page 17

PEEBLES
Map 21 NT24

Cringletie House
Rosettes not confirmed at time of going to print – see opposite

Macdonald Cardrona Hotel, Golf & Spa
Modern British

tel: 0844 879 9024 & 01896 833600 **Cardrona EH45 8NE**
email: general.cardrona@macdonald-hotels.co.uk **web:** www.macdonald-hotels.co.uk
dir: *From Edinburgh on A701 signed Penicuik/Peebles. Then A703, at 1st rdbt beside garage turn left onto A72, hotel 3m on right*

Modish cooking and ravishing country views

Amassed on the banks of the River Tweed, the Cardrona is a swish modern hotel with a championship golf course and luxe spa. It's also home to Renwicks restaurant, where a wall of glass serves up views of the green fairways and rolling Border Hills beyond. There's a good deal of regional produce on the menu and the cooking is straightforward and gently modern. A roulade of confit duck leg with Asian slaw and oriental dressing looks beyond the border county for its inspiration, but equally there might be locally-smoked haddock with a savoury pannacotta and lemon and caper dressing. Main course might see outdoor reared pork (fillet and braised belly) partnered with Stornoway black pudding and an apple purée, or seared rib-eye with a red onion and feta tart. Desserts run to warm chocolate brownie with caramelised pistachio and pistachio ice cream.

Times 12.30-2/6.30-9.45

STIRLING

ABERFOYLE
Map 20 NN50

Macdonald Forest Hills Hotel & Resort
Modern Scottish

tel: 01877 389500 **Kinlochard FK8 3TL**
email: general.forest-hills@macdonald-hotels.co.uk
web: www.macdonald-hotels.co.uk/foresthills
dir: *4m from Aberfoyle on B829*

Modern cooking in a happening resort hotel

Loch Ard forms a stunning backdrop to this white hotel in a peaceful location, with its grounds running down to the shore from its elevated position. A refurb of the restaurant was rumoured as this guide went to press, but what's certain to remain is the curved wall of floor-to-ceiling windows taking in the view. 'The beauty of the dish is in the greatness of the ingredients with a focus on simplicity,' states the menu. The claim is met by what appears on the plate, judging by starters of salmon, prawn and pepper tian, and a pressing of lamb and foie gras complemented by carrot and mint chutney. Main courses maintain the equilibrium: crisp-skinned, flaky butter-basted cod fillet on creamy mash in a pool of fish sauce accompanied by a stew of mussels and spinach, and another well-composed dish of seared rump of beef with a ragout of oxtail, pancetta and mushrooms. End on a high note with chocolate fondant with chocolate and Kirsch ice cream.

Chef David Robertson **Owner** Macdonald Hotels **Seats** 70, Pr/dining room 20 **Times** 6.30-9.30 Closed L Mon-Sat **Prices** Fixed D 3 course £25-£35, Service optional **Wines** 42 bottles over £30, 15 bottles under £30, 13 by glass **Parking** 50 **Notes** Sunday L £15-£19, Vegetarian available, Children welcome

CALLANDER
Map 20 NN60

Roman Camp Country House Hotel
– see opposite

Cringletie House

Rosettes not confirmed at time of going to print

PEEBLES   Map 21 NT24

Modern French **v**
tel: 01721 722510 **Edinburgh Rd EH45 8PL**
email: enquiries@cringletie.com **web:** www.cringletie.com
dir: *2.5m N of Peebles on A703*

Creative modern cooking in baronial-style country house

The rosette award for this establishment has been suspended due to a change of chef. Reassessment will take place in due course under the new chef.
A grand baronial house with gables and turrets galore, Cringletie (built in 1861) stands in rolling countryside some 30 minutes from Edinburgh. There are 28 acres of grounds to explore, while within all is period grandeur and elegant refinement. The restaurant – recently extended – is up on the first floors to maximise the views, with an ornate ceiling and tables dressed up to the nines. The à la carte menu is called 'Indulgence', there's a 'Temptation' menu, plus a full-on 'Tasting' version with six courses and an optional wine flight. The cooking is modern, refined and French-influenced, with local and regional produce to the fore. Lemon and thyme risotto is a first course enriched with roasted ceps, while another combines gurnard and mussels in a dish with aromatic vegetables and herbs. Seafood is handled well, with the likes of John dory and langoustine partnered by white bean purée with baby leeks and herb jus, and vegetarians are well looked after when a tarte Tatin of chicory, blue cheese and walnuts is on the menu. Roast haunch of venison is served with glazed carrots and spätzle, and roast pigeon with foie gras and grilled figs. Desserts are equally creative: spiced pineapple doughnuts, for example, with gingerbread ice cream, or Valrhona chocolate soufflé with a truffle centre and minted caramel ice cream.

Chef Wayne Smith **Owner** Jacob & Johanna van Houdt **Seats** 60, Pr/dining room 14 **Times** 12.30-2.30/6.30-9 Closed 2-23 Jan **Prices** Fixed D 3 course fr £37.50, Tasting menu fr £55, Service optional **Wines** 50 bottles over £30, 17 bottles under £30, 8 by glass **Parking** 30 **Notes** ALC 3 course £47.50, Sunday L £22.50-£28.50, Children welcome

Roman Camp Country House Hotel

CALLANDER   Map 20 NN60

Modern French **v**
tel: 01877 330003 **FK17 8BG**
email: mail@romancamphotel.co.uk **web:** www.romancamphotel.co.uk
dir: *N on A84 through Callander, Main St turn left at East End into drive*

Ritzy luxury and immaculate modern cooking

Roman Camp, which takes its name from nearby Roman earthworks, was built in the 17th century as a shooting lodge for the Earls of Moray. It's a charming small hotel tucked away in extensive grounds adjacent to the river but Callander's high street is only moments away. There's a whiff of opulence to the interior, with yards of sumptuous fabrics, plush sofas, ornate plasterwork and oak panelling, and skilled and attentive service in the large, oval-shaped restaurant with its crisp white napery and sparkling silverware and crystal reflecting the candlelight. Scotland's hills, seas and lochs provide the kitchen with its raw materials, and the cooking is certainly technically accomplished. Moist and flavourful loin of rabbit, with confit leg, a perfectly cooked kidney, chard and jus, has been a memorable starter, an alternative perhaps to the more contemporary notion of breast of squab pigeon with goats' cheese risotto and pickled walnut jelly. Meat and seafood pairings are a characteristic: langoustines with slow-cooked pork belly and parsnip remoulade, say, then a main course of roast turbot fillet, timed to the second, with braised ox cheek and pungent horseradish cream. Meatier main courses are equally well considered, seen in caramelised sweetbreads, full of natural flavours, with Clonakilty black pudding and gnocchi, and a rare sighting of hare, as roast loin with leg and shoulder pastilla and an accomplished sauce of port and raisins. Peripherals like breads are well up to the mark, and puddings end strongly, among them perhaps dark and white chocolate gâteau, and a modish trio of caramelised pineapple, coconut parfait and avocado and mint sorbet.

Chef Ian McNaught **Owner** Eric Brown **Seats** 120, Pr/dining room 36 **Times** 12-2/7-9 **Prices** Fixed L 3 course £25-£28.50, Tasting menu £55, Starter £14.50-£21, Main £28.50-£34.50, Dessert £9.50-£15.50, Service optional **Wines** 16 by glass **Parking** 80 **Notes** Tasting menu 4 course dishes change daily, Sunday L £25-£30, Children welcome

STIRLING

Map 21 NS79

The Stirling Highland Hotel

British, European

tel: 01786 272727 **Spittal St FK8 1DU**
email: stirling@pumahotels.co.uk **web:** www.pumahotels.co.uk/stirling
dir: *In road leading to Stirling Castle - follow Castle signs*

Commanding valley views and confident cooking in an old school

Perched high up on the hillside next to Stirling Castle, this former 1850s high school boasts panoramic views across the Forth Valley. Don't feel nervous about being asked to the Headmaster's Study, it's actually a rather relaxing place to enjoy a drink before your meal in the Scholar's Restaurant. Consisting of three grand rooms with vaulted ceilings, it's a bit like eating in Hogwarts. The confident modern cooking makes the most of fine Scottish produce, so you might start with an earthy dish of caramelised pan-fried pigeon breast with black pudding, watercress salad and beetroot dressing, moving on to a technically impressive fillet of steamed sea bass with pancetta mousse, bean purée, confit tomato and asparagus. Dessert might be something a little more classic, such as a crème brûlée with some wonderfully buttery home-made shortbread just to remind you where you are.

Chef Mark Bain **Owner** Puma Hotels Collection **Seats** 96, Pr/dining room 100
Times 7-9.45 Closed L all week **Prices** Prices not confirmed **Wines** 20 by glass
Parking 106 **Notes** Vegetarian available, Children welcome

STRATHYRE

Map 20 NN51

Creagan House

French, Scottish

tel: 01877 384638 **FK18 8ND**
email: eatandstay@creaganhouse.co.uk **web:** www.creaganhouse.co.uk
dir: *0.25m N of village, off A84*

17th-century Trossachs farmhouse with good food

The views alone make a visit worthwhile to this welcoming 17th-century farmhouse in a village at the head of Loch Lubnaig. Dinner is served in the stately baronial-style dining room, with its vaulted ceiling and grand stone fireplace. The surroundings contrast with the contemporary-style country-house cooking, built on irreproachable local produce – meat from Perthshire farms, fish from Scottish ports, eggs from their own hens, and as much fruit and vegetables as possible grown in the garden. Typical starters are seared Mull scallops topping creamed clams, leeks and mushrooms, and a filo parcel of braised oxtail with Jerusalem artichoke crostini, mushrooms and truffle. Ingredients are sensibly and skilfully handled, so dishes are never short of interest: fillet of turbot, for instance, comes with a pan-fried pâté of lobster, scallop and crab and vermouth sauce, and loin of local venison on beetroot and pearl barley risotto gets a gin and juniper sauce. Finish with a selection of well-kept Scottish cheeses or one of the home-made desserts.

Chef Gordon Gunn **Owner** Gordon & Cherry Gunn **Seats** 15, Pr/dining room 6
Times 7.30-8.30 Closed 29 Oct-26 Mar, Wed-Thu, L all week (ex parties) **Prices** Fixed D 3 course fr £35, Service optional **Wines** 40 bottles over £30, 27 bottles under £30, 7 by glass **Parking** 15 **Notes** Vegetarian available, Children 10 yrs+

Find out more about how we assess for Rosette awards on page 9

SCOTTISH ISLANDS

ISLE OF ARRAN

BRODICK

Map 20 NS03

Kilmichael Country House Hotel

Modern British

tel: 01770 302219 **Glen Cloy KA27 8BY**
email: enquiries@kilmichael.com **web:** www.kilmichael.com
dir: *Turn right on leaving ferry terminal, through Brodick & left at golf club. Follow brown sign. Continue past church & onto private drive*

Classical cooking in a refined country-house hotel

This small country-house hotel is run by hands-on proprietors, and sits in its own secluded gardens – home to 14 friendly peacocks running free, rolling lawns, water features and attractive flowerbeds. It's by no means all for show, for they grow all their own fruit, vegetables, salad leaves, herbs and edible flowers here, as well as keeping chickens and ducks. Inside is no less beguiling, as antiques and artwork abound in the tastefully decorated rooms (no wonder guests return again and again). Co-owner Geoffrey Botterill looks after guests – only around 16 at a time – in the small and intimate, red-hued dining room, while chef-patron Antony Butterworth takes care single-handedly of the classic country-house cooking. The daily-changing, no-choice menu might feature salmon tartare with avocado and coriander sorbet followed by a full-flavoured prime fillet of lamb spiked with garlic and fresh lavender and baked with Scottish heather honey. A trio of autumnal desserts – damson and soured cream brûlée, wild bramble cobbler, and a 'wee' toffee apple with home-made toffee and walnut ice cream – makes a smile-inducing finale.

Chef Antony Butterworth **Owner** G Botterill, A Butterworth **Seats** 18 **Times** 7-8.30 Closed Nov-Mar, L all week, D Mon-Tue **Prices** Prices not confirmed, Service optional **Wines** 3 by glass **Parking** 12 **Notes** 4 course D £45, Vegetarian available, No children

ISLE OF HARRIS

SCARISTA (SGARASTA BHEAG)

Map 22 NG09

Scarista House

Modern Scottish

tel: 01859 550238 **HS3 3HX**
email: timandpatricia@scaristahouse.com **web:** www.scaristahouse.com
dir: *On A859 15m S of Tarbert*

Assured regional cooking in Harris's only hotel

If you've made landfall on the Isle of Harris and are looking for somewhere to stay, this is the only option. Fortunately, it's an absolute jewel, worth the journey in itself. The whitewashed house overlooks the glorious beach, with the heather-clad mountains as backdrop, and is run by Tim and Patricia Martin with assured professionalism. Tim's cooking makes its way into a pair of dining rooms at 8pm sharp, and the format is a four-course set menu based on superlative Highland and island produce. Proceedings might open with a terrine of Uist salmon, both hot-smoked and cold-smoked over peat, garnished pertly with pink grapefruit and Campari and mint vinaigrette, as a prelude to a more traditional pink-roasted Angus fillet in a burgundy reduction with roasted roots and mash. Another day might deliver Jerusalem artichoke soup with smoked scallops and lentils, before Stornoway halibut in champagne chive sauce. Dessert follows, perhaps textbook floating islands, or chocolate sorbet spiked with peaty Lagavulin single malt, before the finale brings a serving of thoroughbred Scottish cheeses.

Chef Tim Martin **Owner** Tim & Patricia Martin **Seats** 20, Pr/dining room 14
Times 7.30-8 Closed 25 Dec, Jan-Feb, L all week **Prices** Fixed D 3 course £43.50-£48.50, Service optional **Wines** 37 by glass **Parking** 10 **Notes** Vegetarian available, Children 7 yrs+

TARBERT (TAIRBEART) — Map 22 NB10

Hotel Hebrides

 Modern Scottish

tel: 01859 502364 **Pier Rd HS3 3DG**
email: stay@hotel-hebrides.com **web:** www.hotel-hebrides.com
dir: *To Tarbert via ferry from Uig (Isle of Skye); or ferry from Ullapool to Stornaway, A859 to Tarbert; or by plane to Stornaway from Glasgow, Edinburgh or Inverness*

Traditionally-based cooking opposite the harbour

Just across from the ferry terminal on the Isle of Harris in the Outer Hebrides is a modern family-owned hotel with a distinct boutique feel, run with impressive attention to detail by the Macleods. One corner of the ground floor is occupied by the Pierhouse restaurant, where full-drop windows look on to the working harbour, and black-clad staff bustle efficiently. The cooking has a traditional base, but isn't shy of building some up-to-date ideas on top of it, so expect haggis, neeps and tatties to appear in a towering stack, sauced with malt whisky cream, or pigeon with pickled chanterelles and toasted hazelnuts. Mains might see local scallops teamed with smoked Gigha cheese mash and pea purée, or Lewis lamb come with creamed cabbage and bacon in rosemary jus. Finish with strawberry cheesecake in its own coulis, topped with toasted marshmallows, or lemon meringue délice with raspberries and basil ice cream.

Chef Richard Agnew **Owner** Mr & Mrs Macleod **Seats** 35 **Times** 12-4/6-9 **Closed** Nov-Mar **Prices** Fixed L 2 course £12.95-£16.95, Fixed D 3 course £30-£35, Starter £5-£15, Main £15-£30, Dessert £5-£12, Service optional **Wines** 8 bottles over £30, 10 bottles under £30, 4 by glass **Parking** 30 **Notes** Sunday L, Vegetarian available, Children welcome

ISLE OF ISLAY

BOWMORE — Map 20 NR36

The Harbour Inn and Restaurant

Scottish, International **NEW**

tel: 01496 810330 **The Square PA43 7JR**
email: info@harbour-inn.com **web:** www.harbour-inn.com
dir: *Bowmore approx 8m from both ports (Port Ellen & Port Askaig)*

Bold, creative cooking in a traditional inn with sea views

Right by the harbour and with the renowned distillery as a neighbour, The Harbour Inn looks traditional enough. Indeed it is in many ways – a spot for a dram and a dreamy gaze out of the conservatory windows – but you can also get stuck into some dynamic modern Scottish cuisine. The kitchen brigade here pushes the envelope to deliver some smart, appealing contemporary food – nothing bonkers, but really rather good. A visually stunning first course dish of ham hock terrine is a very good start, in the busy company of pickled quail's egg, broad bean and shallot salad, rye crumbs and apple gel – a classy dish. Good Scottish ingredients are at the heart of everything. Loin of Scottish lamb, for example, superbly tender, is served with amongst other things a Violetta potato terrine and a little haggis pie filled with a light mousse, finished with a rich, glossy jus. There's no less craft and invention at dessert stage: look out for carrot cake with cream cheese 'snow', carrot jam, candied walnuts, sweet cucumber and black pepper salad and carrot 'dust'.

Chef Paul Lumby **Owner** Carol & Neil Scott **Seats** 44 **Times** 12-2.30/6-9.30 **Prices** Prices not confirmed, Service optional **Wines** 8 by glass **Notes** Children 10 yrs+

ISLE OF MULL

TOBERMORY — Map 22 NM55

Highland Cottage

Modern Scottish, International

tel: 01688 302030 **24 Breadalbane St PA75 6PD**
email: davidandjo@highlandcottage.co.uk **web:** www.highlandcottage.co.uk
dir: *Opposite fire station. Main St up Back Brae, turn at top by White House. Follow road to right, left at next junct into Breadalbane St*

Inspired local cooking in a charming island hotel

The Curries' salmon-hued small hotel in Tobermory's conservation area, not far from the fishing pier, is a jewel of a place. The charming interiors, replete with squashy sofas, interesting books and well-chosen ornaments, are a delight, and the place is cleverly laid out to lead you from the bar and conservatory into the suavely furnished dining room. Jo Currie cooks, and does a splendid job of showcasing Mull produce, as well as much from the mainland. A starter risotto is a demonstration dish, both for its flawless timing and the savoury intensity of its locally smoked haddock, topped for the final flourish with a perfect poached egg. Loin of superlative lamb might come next, the tender, richly flavoured meat supported by potato and turnip gratin and a concentrated redcurrant and rosemary gravy, or there may be bracingly fresh sea bass with braised leeks, in tomato, olive and caper butter. Cranachan gains from a peaty malt flavour to the oatmeal, as well as an intense raspberry hit, or go for the tang of lemon posset, served with buttery homemade shortbread.

Chef Josephine Currie **Owner** David & Josephine Currie **Seats** 24 **Times** 7-9 **Closed** Nov-Mar, L all week **Prices** Fixed D 3 course £39.50-£42 **Wines** 12 bottles over £30, 21 bottles under £30, 11 by glass **Parking** On street in front of establishment **Notes** Vegetarian available, Children 10 yrs+

SHETLAND

SCALLOWAY — Map 24 HU43

Scalloway Hotel

Modern Scottish **v**

tel: 01595 880444 **Main St ZE1 OTR**
email: info@scallowayhotel.com **web:** www.scallowayhotel.com
dir: *7m from Lerwick on west mainland on A970*

Creative cooking in an unpretentious setting in the far north

A family-run hotel on the waterfront in the islands' former capital, the proximity to the water imbues the menu at this thriving establishment. It's not all about seafood, though, with beef and lamb playing starring roles in many dishes. It's an unpretentious place, with bedrooms, a bar, and an all-round community feel. The bar offers up a more informal dining option, although the restaurant isn't exactly posh (it presents itself very nicely with linen tablecloths and quality glasses). There are some bright ideas on the menu. Start with Saat whiting in a Scotch egg, for example, served with piccalilli, or a tian of smoked ham hock (or hough as they say in these parts). Slow-cooked beef cheeks with celeriac, leek and potato dauphinoise is a warming main course, or go for pan-fried scallops and panko-breaded monkfish in a Red Thai curry sauce. Desserts are no less creative: chocolate tart with caramelised salted pecans, pomegranate and chocolate ice cream.

Chef Ciaran Lack **Owner** P McKenzie **Seats** 36 **Times** 12-3/5-9 **Closed** Xmas, New Year **Prices** Starter fr £4.50, Main fr £13.95, Dessert fr £5.95, Service optional **Wines** 10 bottles over £30, 16 bottles under £30, 10 by glass **Parking** 10 **Notes** Sunday L, Children welcome

ISLE OF SKYE

COLBOST
Map 22 NG24

The Three Chimneys
◉◉◉ – *see opposite*

ISLEORNSAY
Map 22 NG71

Duisdale House Hotel
◉◉ Modern Scottish

tel: 01471 833202 **Sleat IV43 8QW**
email: info@duisdale.com **web:** www.duisdale.com
dir: *7m N of Armadale ferry & 12m S of Skye Bridge on A851*

Modern Scottish seasonal cooking in remotest southern Skye

With bags of boutique style and a dreamy location by the Sound of Sleat, Duisdale House has a lot going for it. The garden is a treat, too, especially if you're a fan of rhododendrons, but it's the restaurant that really catches the eye. Occupying a conservatory and a rich-red room with a real fire and stylish fixtures and fittings, the restaurant focuses on seasonal, regional ingredients and the cooking is in the modern vein. It's the kind of place that likes to satisfy with additional bits and bobs, such as canapés, including a haggis bonbon, and amuse-bouche such as smoked ham hock with piccalilli. Hand-dived scallops are familiar enough in these parts, but here they come in a first course with white onion purée, grapefruit, syboes (spring onion) and bacon (or at least a bacon 'dust'). Main-course fillet and cheek of Lochaber pork is an equally satisfying construction, with potato fondant, Savoy cabbage, celeriac and a rich, glossy jus. To finish, enjoy another complex array of flavours in a dish of banana mousse with dark chocolate, pineapple and yoghurt.

Chef Peter Cullen **Owner** K Gunn, A Gracie **Seats** 50 **Times** 12-2.30/6.30-9
Prices Prices not confirmed, Service optional **Wines** 30 bottles over £30, 30 bottles under £30, 6 by glass **Parking** 30 **Notes** Sunday L, Vegetarian available, Children welcome

Hotel Eilean Iarmain
◉◉ Traditional Scottish

tel: 01471 833332 **Sleat IV43 8QR**
email: hotel@eileaniarmain.co.uk **web:** www.eileaniarmain.co.uk
dir: *Mallaig & cross by ferry to Armadale, 8m to hotel or via Kyle of Lochalsh*

Spectacular sea views and consummate cooking

The whitewashed old building in well-maintained grounds looks across the waters of the Sound of Sleat to the mainland's Knoydart Hills, and the restaurant – a panelled room hung with works by a local artist, with a log fire in winter and a conservatory extension – takes full advantage of the spectacular views. The lack of

fuss and artifice in the decor extends to the kitchen's output, with its reliance on the island's glorious resources: venison from the estate, for instance, and langoustines landed at the pier outside. The cooking is not without a high level of refinement and ambition, though: chicken ballottine is stuffed with mushrooms and spinach, wrapped in Parma ham and served on a dollop of walnut mayonnaise, with blobs of red onion marmalade around the square glass plate. Main courses are as well composed, seen in accurately grilled salmon fillet with crayfish risotto, grilled fennel and saffron velouté, or fanned slices of roast breast of guinea fowl, cooked just so, straightforwardly accompanied by silky parsnip purée, fondant potato, Savoy cabbage and red wine jus.

Chef Alistair Kelly **Owner** Lady Lucilla Noble **Seats** 40, Pr/dining room 22
Times 12-2.30/6.30-8.45 **Prices** Fixed D 3 course £40-£55, Service optional
Wines 14 bottles over £30, 21 bottles under £30, 7 by glass **Notes** Sunday L, Vegetarian available, Children welcome

Kinloch Lodge
◉◉◉ – *see page 656*

Toravaig House Hotel
◉◉ Modern Scottish

tel: 01471 820200 **Knock Bay, Sleat IV44 8RE**
email: info@skyehotel.co.uk **web:** www.skyehotel.co.uk
dir: *From Skye Bridge, left at Broadford onto A851, hotel 11m on left. Or from ferry at Armadale take A851, hotel 6m on right*

Plush island retreat with modern Scottish cooking

With views over the 14th-century Knock Castle and the Sound of Sleat, the whitewashed Toravaig House serves up an enviable Skye vista. The hotel has classy interiors, with high quality fixtures and fittings, and it's run with passion and attention to detail by owners Anne Gracie and Ken Gunn. The restaurant – the Iona – is an equally smart space, with candlelight bringing a cosy glow in the evenings. The cooking takes a modern Scottish path, in keeping with the majestic surroundings, and makes good use of regional produce. Island scallops, for example, come in a creative combination with confit carrot, mustard dressing and smoked cheddar, with another option being roast breast of quail with a Mediterranean spin with polenta and chorizo. There's a soup course next, or rather a nifty wild mushroom velouté, followed by a main course such as West Coast turbot with razor clams, or Barbary duck breast with pearl barley and caramelised shallots. These are well-crafted plates of food. Finish with Blairgowrie raspberries with white chocolate and oregano oil.

Chef Joel Kirby **Owner** Anne Gracie & Ken Gunn **Seats** 25 **Times** 12.30-2.30/6.30-9.30
Prices Fixed L 2 course £15-£28, Fixed D 3 course £45-£48, Starter £5-£10, Main £14-£24, Dessert £4-£7.50, Service optional **Wines** 40 bottles over £30, 25 bottles under £30, 6 by glass **Parking** 20 **Notes** Sunday L, Vegetarian available, Children 10yrs+

PORTREE
Map 22 NG44

Cuillin Hills Hotel

 Modern Scottish

tel: 01478 612003 **IV51 9QU**
email: info@cuillinhills-hotel-skye.co.uk **web:** www.cuillinhills-hotel-skye.co.uk
dir: 0.25m N of Portree on A855

Creative dining and breathtaking views

Built originally as a hunting lodge, this splendid country-house hotel perches above Portree Bay in 15 acres of mature grounds – a jaw-dropping location where views unfurl endlessly across the bay to the Sound of Raasay and the dragon's back crags of the Cuillin Mountain range. And it is with just cause that the restaurant is named 'The View' since it is visible from all tables. The split-level room is none too shabby either, decked out in classic ivory and white tones, with cream leather chairs at linen-swathed tables and regularly-changing works by local artists. Ingredients from the sea and hills all around get pride of place on the European-accented modern menu, perhaps braised shoulder of Skye lamb with shallot purée, Savoy cabbage, potato almondine and caper jus, followed by pan-fried John Dory with spoots (that's razor clams in the local lingo), apple and fennel salad, chorizo and red pepper salsa, and watercress sauce. If you need any further reminder that you're in Scotland, a 'deconstructed cranachan' pulls off an exciting array of flavours and textures for dessert.

Chef Daniel Flemming **Owner** Wickman Hotels **Seats** 40 **Times** 12-2/6.30-9
Prices Prices not confirmed, Service optional **Wines** 25 bottles over £30, 36 bottles under £30, 8 by glass **Parking** 56 **Notes** Sunday L, Vegetarian available, Children welcome

STAFFIN
Map 22 NG46

The Glenview

 British, French

tel: 01470 562248 **Culnacnoc IV51 9JH**
email: enquiries@glenviewskye.co.uk **web:** www.glenviewskye.co.uk
dir: 12m N of Portree on A855, 4m S of Staffin

Skilled cooking with local ingredients

On the wild Trotternish Peninsula in the north of the Isle of Skye, where snow-dusted peaks march across the skyline, this delightful whitewashed restaurant with rooms certainly lives up to its name. Housed in a Victorian croft that was once the Culnacnoc village shop, it now deals in unpretentious modern cooking built on splendid materials, many of which have travelled but a short distance from producers and fishermen on the island. These prime ingredients are then handled with due confidence and care, as in a simple but perfectly-executed starter of braised and glazed Staffin pork belly with pickled carrot salad and sweet chilli dressing. Next out, the venison from MacLeod's Table – a hill range near the hotel – couldn't be more local, and it appears with roast garlic and rosemary sauce, gratin potatoes and spring greens. A chocolate fudge tart with crème fraîche sorbet and sugared macadamia nuts ends on a note of splendid indulgence.

Times 7-8.30 Closed Jan, 8 Feb, Sun-Mon, L all week

The Three Chimneys

COLBOST
Map 22 NG24

Modern British 🍷 **NOTABLE WINE LIST**

tel: 01470 511258 **IV55 8ZT**
email: eatandstay@threechimneys.co.uk **web:** www.threechimneys.co.uk
dir: 5m W of Dunvegan take B884 signed Glendale. On left beside loch

Exceptional cooking in a wild, romantic setting

Crofters' cottages are as firmly rooted in the terroir as it is possible to be, synonymous with the island and its rugged and wild landscape. Two such crofts form the basis of Eddie and Shirley Spear's restaurant, which over the last 30 years has made its mark, too, on both the local economy and on the island's culinary reputation. This is destination dining. There are also classy bedrooms next door as staying over is a good option given the location. The decor reflects the natural environment, too, being proud of its origins, adding refined touches here and there but guaranteeing a sense of place. That sense of place is enhanced by the stunning views over land and loch. Michael Smith has been here for a decade in 2015, in which time he has cemented the reputation of the place and become a champion for Scottish produce. His is the kind of cooking that impresses with its technique and precision but somehow leaves the ingredients room to speak for themselves. There's a sensibly short carte – three or so options per course – alongside a tasting menu that packs quite punch. There's a bit of the local lingo on the menu, but the proficient service team are on hand: Colbost skink (smoked haddock) with marag dubh (black pudding) and a Talisker (whisky) crumb, served with an oozing egg yolk, for example. Blackface lamb from the Black Isle comes as a haggis pasty, and Lochalsh venison (saddle and haunch) with layered roots and crowdie and ginger. Sweet courses are no less creative and thrilling; hot marmalade pudding soufflé, for example, with Drambuie syrup and mealie ice cream. There's a table in the kitchen so diners' can get close to the action. The wine list is a fine piece of work, and even more reason to book one of those charming bedrooms.

Chef Michael Smith **Owner** Eddie & Shirley Spear **Seats** 40, Pr/dining room 12
Times 12.15-1.45/6.15-9.45 Closed 1 Dec-23 Jan, L Sun & Nov-Mar **Prices** Fixed L 2 course fr £28.50, Fixed D 3 course fr £60, Tasting menu £90-£110, Service optional **Wines** 105 bottles over £30, 12 bottles under £30, 25 by glass **Parking** 12 **Notes** Tasting menu 7 course, Sun L Jun-Aug, Sunday L £37, Vegetarian available, Children 5yrL/8yrD

Kinloch Lodge

ISLEORNSAY   Map 22 NG71

French, Scottish v 🍷 NOTABLE WINE LIST

tel: 01471 833214 & 833333 **Sleat IV43 8QY**
email: reservations@kinloch-lodge.co.uk
web: www.kinloch-lodge.co.uk
dir: *1m off main road, 6m S of Broadford on A851, 10m N of Armadale*

Accomplished Scottish cooking in the Macdonald ancestral home

The spotless white house stands above Na Dal sea-loch on the fringes of Skye. Kinloch is home to Godfrey, high chief of Clan Donald, and his wife, Lady Claire, a prolific food writer. They threw open the doors of Kinloch as a hotel nearly 40 years ago, and if you wanted an object lesson in how to run an ancestral home with genuine hospitality and cheer, look no further. The public rooms are imbued with all the elegant splendour you may anticipate, with log fires ablaze in the island winters, but the tone has always been one of gratifying informality, with Claire's cookery classes adding to the occasion. With all the remote beauty of the Skye landscape about you, the highly accomplished cooking of Marcello Tully comes as icing on the cake. Dinner is a daily-changing, five-course affair, with a choice of fish or meat at main, and suggested wine, beer or whisky flights to match the dishes. First up might be a sip of Jerusalem artichoke soup, as a prelude to roast quail with a mousse of fresh vegetables and Perthshire honey in port and orange jus, and then Marcello's special in-betweenie, squid-ink tortellini filled with crab. Depending on which route you're taking, main could be Mallaig sea bass on a nest of crisp vegetable julienne, in aromatic coriander and vanilla sauce, or Speyside beef fillet, matured for three weeks, served in traditional haute cuisine fashion with shallots and wild mushrooms and sauced with brandy, accompanied by a mousse of Strathdon Blue. Finish with either apple crumble parfait with a little cinnamon doughnut, or Scottish and French cheeses from the trolley. A seven-course taster allows Tully to spread his wings, flitting from seared scallop in Parma ham with peanuts, via herb-crusted Black Isle lamb, to dark chocolate melt with vanilla espuma, doused in crème de menthe.

Chef Marcello Tully **Owner** Lord & Lady Macdonald **Seats** 40, Pr/dining room 20 **Times** 12-2.30/6.30-9 **Prices** Fixed L 2 course £32.99, Tasting menu £80, Service optional **Wines** 150 bottles over £30, 25 bottles under £30, 16 by glass **Parking** 20 **Notes** Fixed D 5 course £70, Sunday L fr £9, Children welcome

STEIN

Map 22 NG25

Loch Bay Seafood Restaurant

British Seafood

tel: 01470 592235 **MacLeod Ter IV55 8GA**
email: lochbay@gmail.com
dir: *4m off A850 by B886*

Satisfying straightforward seafood cookery by the bay

With room only for a couple of dozen diners at a time, Loch Bay is a diminutive institution around these parts, a place of simplicity and integrity. Its position right by the loch shore, in a row of 18th-century fishermen's cottages, sets the tone for the fishy delights that lie within. David and Alison Wilkinson run the place with hands-on enthusiasm and passion – she's out front, he's at the stoves – and the menu is driven by what comes out of the local waters. It's humble and rustic within, with a wood-burning stove, pictures of the area and wooden tables. Start with razor clams – or spoots as they call them round these parts – fresh as a daisy and grilled with garlic and herb sauce, or the lobster and leek risotto might catch your eye. Main-course Dover sole comes with excellent triple-cooked chips, and Loch Bay king prawns are a good choice if they're available. Vanilla and Drambuie pannacotta with passionfruit ends things on a high.

Chef David Wilkinson **Owner** David & Alison Wilkinson **Seats** 23 **Times** 6.30-9 Closed mid Oct-Etr, Sun-Tue, L all week **Prices** Fixed D 3 course £33-£41.50, Service optional **Wines** 10 bottles over £30, 30 bottles under £30, 8 by glass **Parking** 6 **Notes** Vegetarian menu on request, Vegetarian available, Children 8 yrs+ D

What makes a 3-Rosette restaurant?
See page 9

STRUAN

Map 22 NG33

Ullinish Country Lodge

Rosettes not confirmed at time of going to print

Modern French V

tel: 01470 572214 **IV56 8FD**
email: ullinish@theisleofskye.co.uk **web:** www.theisleofskye.co.uk
dir: *9m S of Dunvegan on A863*

Electrifying cooking in a Skye hideaway

The rosette award for this establishment has been suspended due to a change of chef. Reassessment will take place in due course under the new chef.
The breathtaking views alone make the journey to this white-painted hotel worthwhile, with lochs on three sides and the rugged beauty of the Black Cuillins and MacLeod's Tables. The interior is comfortingly traditional, with tartan used in moderation in the panelled restaurant, where service is relaxed, friendly and polished. A daily 'link van' collects meat, seafood and garden produce from a network of the island's small suppliers and delivers them to the kitchen, where the team works its wizardry. Dishes can sound convoluted, but there's clearly considerable talent at play here when it comes to the art of balancing flavours. Dinner menus offer 2 courses at each stage, so a starter of quail breast arrives perfectly cooked, with full-flavoured confit leg, sweetcorn in various guises, pickled shallots, mushrooms and golden raisins, all beautifully presented and working in harmony, or there could be heather-roasted scallops with gooseberry pearls, apple sorrel, and nettle and duck egg purée. Among main courses, spanking-fresh Mallaig turbot is matched with truffle gnocchi, cauliflower purée and crisps, sharp little hits of crispy fried capers, fennel and onion ash – another resounding success, while the meaty alternative might see black-faced lamb partnered with baked potato skins and potato purée, spinach milk and sea lettuce . Extras like canapés are not only plentiful but exemplary – smoked trout with a miniaturised take on the old classic trio of haggis, neeps and tatties, say – as are puddings, among which is a stunning hot cranachansoufflé with an exhilarating raspberry sorbet.

Chef Richard Massey **Owner** Brian & Pam Howard **Seats** 22 **Times** 7.30-8.30 Closed 24 Dec-31 Jan, L all week **Prices** Prices not confirmed, Service optional **Wines** 36 bottles over £30, 40 bottles under £30, 16 by glass **Parking** 10 **Notes** 4 course D £49.50, No children

Wales

ISLE OF ANGLESEA

BEAUMARIS — Map 14 SH67

Bishopsgate House Hotel

◉ Traditional Welsh

tel: 01248 810302 **54 Castle St LL58 8BB**
email: hazel@bishopsgatehotel.co.uk web: www.bishopsgatehotel.co.uk
dir: *from Menai Bridge onto A545 to Beaumaris. Hotel on left in main street*

Reliable cookery on the Beaumaris waterfront

The cheery mint-green facade of Bishopsgate House stands out from the neighbours along the Georgian terrace overlooking Beaumaris Green and the peaks of Snowdonia across the Menai waterfront. The intimate, low-ceilinged restaurant is full of old-world charm and enjoys a strong following with locals who know they can rely on the kitchen's quietly confident cooking, as well as a healthy showing of top-class local produce. Straightforward crowd-pleasing menus set out with braised pork belly with apple purée and white pudding, while brandy and herbs add extra interest to a chicken liver pâté served with onion marmalade and brioche. Next up, a fresh piece of hake is crusted with lemon and herbs and served with creamed leeks, or if you're in the mood for a meaty main course, there might be pan-fried loin of lamb with a mustard and herb crust and honey and rosemary jus. Finish with pecan tart and honeycomb ice cream.

Times 12.30-2.30/6.30-9.30 Closed L Mon-Sat

Ye Olde Bulls Head Inn

◉ ◉ ◉ – *see opposite*

BRIDGEND

BRIDGEND — Map 9 SS97

Bokhara Brasserie

◉ Indian, Welsh ⅴ

tel: 01656 720212 **Court Colman Manor, Pen-y-Fai CF31 4NG**
email: experience@court-colman-manor.com web: www.bokhararestaurant.com
dir: *M4 junct 36/A4063 in direction of Maesteg, after lights take 1st exit at rdbt to Bridgend continue under motorway, take next right & follow hotel signs*

A salute to Indian cuisine in a country-house hotel

Within the grand Court Colman Manor country-house hotel, the Bokhara brasserie comes as quite a surprise, decked out in warm colours, with an open-to-view kitchen, and a wall of slate. The menu concentrates on the regional cuisine of the sub-continent, with many a dish inspired by the rich cooking of the old Northwest frontier. The kitchen prides itself on not using colourings or ghee and on buying only locally grown and reared produce and meat. Thus Welsh lamb could appear as a fiery Punjabi rara gosht, as a whole leg (for six people) cooked in aromatic spices, or in a hot and sour mutton Madras curry. The tandoor pulls its weight too, turning out everything from authentic naan, kulcha and roti breads to skewers of marinated king prawns flavoured with ajwain, red chillies, turmeric and garam masala. The hotel carte, meanwhile, offers 'a taste of Wales', including Glamorgan sausages, cawl, and Welsh faggots.

Chef Sarvesh Jadon **Owner** Sanjeev Bhagotra **Seats** 80, Pr/dining room 120 **Times** 7-10 Closed 25 Dec, L all week **Prices** Starter £2.50-£9.95, Main £4.95-£16.95, Dessert £3.95, Service optional **Wines** 11 bottles under £30, 3 by glass **Parking** 100 **Notes** All you can eat buffet Sun, Children welcome

CARDIFF

CARDIFF — Map 9 ST17

AA RESTAURANT OF THE YEAR FOR WALES 2014–15

Bully's

◉ ◉ French, European

tel: 029 2022 1905 **5 Romilly Crescent CF11 9NP**
email: info@bullysrestaurant.co.uk
dir: *5 mins from city centre*

Lively modern cooking in busy but relaxed restaurant

Bully's is a busy-looking restaurant, virtually every inch of its walls covered with pictures, mirrors and other paraphernalia, and Russell Bullimore tirelessly adds and changes things. The kitchen relies on Welsh providers for its materials and devises menus that show a clear grounding in the French repertoire while pulling in ideas from near and far. Timing is ever well judged, seen in starters of seared scallops fragrant with vanilla essence, accompanied by Puy lentils and fine beans, and pan-fried foie gras cut by caramelised pineapple. Sauces are well considered: a glossy one of marjoram for a main course of pink rump of lamb with rainbow chard, creamed leeks and sautéed potatoes, one of peanuts and star anise for succulent pork tenderloin with pak choi and Parmentier potatoes. Puddings are worth a punt too, among them crisp-based mango tarte Tatin with peach and vanilla ice cream, and canonical honey and orange crème brûlée.

Chef Gareth Farr **Owner** Russell Bullimore **Seats** 40 **Times** 12-2/6.30-9 Closed 22-27 Dec, 1st wk Jan, D Sun **Prices** Fixed L 2 course £14, Fixed D 3 course fr £20, Tasting menu £35, Starter £5-£9.50, Main £14-£26, Dessert £6.50-£9.50 **Wines** 19 bottles over £30, 15 bottles under £30, 10 by glass **Parking** On street **Notes** Gourmet menu 7 course every 2 mths, Sunday L £16-£19.50, Vegetarian available, Children welcome

Ye Olde Bulls Head Inn

BEAUMARIS Map 14 SH67

Modern British 🍷 NOTABLE WINE LIST

tel: 01248 810329 **Castle St LL58 8AP**
email: info@bullsheadinn.co.uk
web: www.bullsheadinn.co.uk
dir: *Town centre, main street*

Brilliant modern Welsh cookery in a Plantagenet inn

The Bull's Head has been sitting in the centre of whatever there has been of Beaumaris since the end of the Plantagenet epoch. So long a tenure in so prime a location means it has seen some history, having variously headquartered the Roundhead General Thomas Mytton during the Civil War, been the first Quaker meeting-house in Anglesey in the Georgian era, and opened its hospitable doors to the discriminating intelligences of Dr Johnson and, later, Charles Dickens. There is today a very 21st-century blend of heritage and modernity about the place, encompassing a beamed pub with hanging jugs and armoury pieces, and a chic contemporary dining room in the Loft, where sloping ceilings mean you'll need to mind your head as you take your seat. Gentle lighting and a soothingly neutral colour scheme allow Hefin Roberts' modern Welsh cooking to shine. The menu is quite a read, with fairly lengthy descriptions giving you more of a clue than the staccato bullet-points favoured elsewhere. Influences are drawn from southern Europe with a little east Asian sass for the likes of yellowfin tuna tartare, celeriac remoulade, tempura mussels and wasabi crème fraîche. Seafood is a strong suit all round, including colourful mains such as monkfish with brown shrimps, split yellow peas and black kale, but there are pedigree meats too, from cured pork belly with garlic snails and chorizo risotto to start, to venison loin glazed in sloe gin with a venison rissole, red cabbage, parsnip-cumin purée, a thyme and garlic hash brown and creamed leeks. There's certainly a lot going on in these dishes, but the overall effect is of carefully considered balance. The thirst for novelty produces dessert choices like spiced beer cake with butternut-vanilla purée and caramelised milk pannacotta, as well as lemon mousse with Cointreau savarin, blood orange curd and ginger arlette (a thin crisp biscuit of puff pastry).

Chef Hefin Roberts **Owner** D Robertson, K Rothwell **Seats** 45
Times 7-9.30 Closed 25-26 Dec, 1 Jan, Sun-Mon, L all week
Prices Fixed D 3 course £45, Service optional **Wines** 65
bottles over £30, 35 bottles under £30, 4 by glass
Parking 10 **Notes** Vegetarian available, Children 8 yrs+

Park House

◉◉ British, International V NOTABLE WINE LIST

tel: 029 2022 4343 **20 Park Place CF10 3DQ**
email: bookings@parkhouseclub.com
dir: Opposite Cardiff Museum

Contemporary cooking in a gothic revival architectural masterpiece

Once a private club, Park House is one of the Welsh capital's finest pieces of architectural extravagance. Designed by William Burges, one of the premier practitioners of the gothic revival, it overlooks the gardens of the National Museum of Wales. The architect is celebrated in the name of the restaurant, which is done out in gently clashing tones of pinks and peaches against a background of solid oak panelling, and offers the added bonus of a pianist and singer at the weekends. Chef Jonathan Edwards offers an ambitiously lengthy menu that features much prime produce. A mastery of contemporary technique is exhibited in a classic pairing of scallop and black pudding which gains depth from seared foie gras and a sparse swipe of treacle-rich PX caramel. Meanwhile, peas and butter beans form the base for a composition of oriental mushrooms, apple and crispy konbu with beetroot jelly and dashi consommé, and top-quality Shorthorn beef fillet appears with St Brides Bay lobster alongside a mound of vigorously spiced tarka dhal and mushroom and sherry sabayon. Desserts like buttermilk ice cream and honeycomb with sherry caramel and puréed apple round off a polished act.

Chef Jonathan Edwards **Owner** Adam & Claire Pledger **Seats** 80, Pr/dining room 40 **Times** 11-4/6-11 Closed 25-26 Dec & some BHs, Mon-Tue, D Sun **Prices** Fixed L 2 course £16, Fixed D 3 course £45-£47, Tasting menu £69, Starter £12, Main £26, Dessert £7-£10, Service optional 8% **Wines** 450 bottles over £30, 60 bottles under £30, 10 by glass **Parking** NCP 50mtrs away **Notes** Pre-theatre ALC D menu 25% discount, No children

Park Plaza Cardiff

◉ British, European V

tel: 029 2011 1111 & 2011 1103 **Greyfriars Rd CF10 3AL**
email: lagunarestaurant@parkplazahotels.co.uk **web:** www.lagunakitchenandbar.com
dir: Located on Greyfriars Rd inside Park Plaza Hotel

Efficient classic cooking in a chic city-centre hotel

In the centre of the city, and therefore handy for just about everything that's going on in the Welsh capital, the Park Plaza offers contemporary comfort with plenty of imaginative design features. Ring-form chandeliers and bright upholstery in the bar give way to a more neutral look in the restaurant, where darkwood boards, cream banquettes, a wine store, and big windows giving on to a decked area are the order of the day. The kitchen offers efficient classic cooking with some modern touches. Expect to start with a fishcake of smoked Grimsby haddock and spring onion with Indian accoutrements, or strongly flavoured duck liver and foie gras parfait with spiced plum and ginger chutney, before the main part of the show brings on rump and shoulder of lamb with caponata, celeriac purée and Kalamata olive jus, or well-handled sea bass with gnocchi, wild mushrooms, peas and tarragon. Dessert could be a rich dark chocolate and Penderyn whisky torte with apple and pear sauce and vanilla mascarpone.

Chef Justin Llewellyn **Owner** Martin Morris **Seats** 110 **Times** 12-2.30/5.30-9.30 Closed 25-26 Dec **Prices** Fixed L 2 course fr £12.95, Fixed D 3 course fr £18.95, Starter £4.95-£7.95, Main £12.95-£26.95, Dessert £4.95-£8.95 **Wines** 44 bottles over £30, 38 bottles under £30, 9 by glass **Parking** NCP **Notes** Pre-theatre fr £12.95, Champagne afternoon tea £21, Sunday L, Children welcome

The Thai House Restaurant

◉ Thai

tel: 029 2038 7404 **3-5 Guildford Crescent, Churchill Way CF10 2HJ**
email: info@thaihouse.biz **web:** www.thaihouse.biz
dir: At junct of Newport Rd & Queen St turn left past Queen St station, before lights turn left into Guildford Crescent

Long-standing Welsh Thai trailblazer

When Noi Ramasut and Arlene Thomas opened The Thai House Restaurant in 1985, there were only five Thai restaurants in London, let alone Wales, which was virgin territory. The Thai-Welsh alliance of their marriage is reflected in the orientation of this well-supported, long-standing venue not far from Queen Street station, where Welsh ingredients (supplemented by imports from Bangkok) go into the vivaciously spicy, diamond-bright cooking of southeast Asia. Classic gung sarong, king prawns deep-fried in a thin batter with sweet chilli dipping sauce and artistically carved vegetables are a surefire winner to start with. Then there are trout fillets in rich red curry with ginger, the locally celebrated duck in tamarind, and hot pork curry with pumpkin and galangal in richly creamy coconut and chilli sauce. It all comes with fluffy jasmine rice, and the best way to finish is with 'The Beach', a refreshing array of coconut ice cream, mango sorbet and coulis, sliced kiwi and strawberries.

Times 12-2.30/5.30-10.30 Closed Xmas, 1 Jan, Sun

Woods Brasserie

◉◉ Modern European

tel: 029 2049 2400 **Pilotage Building, Stuart St CF10 5BW**
email: woods@knifeandforkfood.co.uk
dir: In heart of Cardiff Bay. From M4 junct 33 towards Cardiff Bay, large stone building on right

Modern brasserie fare in trendy Cardiff Bay

A vast expanse of full-length windows capitalises on the views over Cardiff Bay from the Victorian grey-stone Pilotage Building. Inside, a grey-tiled floor, lime-green banquettes and bare pale wood tables give the place a thoroughly contemporary look, while the kitchen has strong supply lines to local farms, butchers and fishermen, so you can take top-quality ingredients and a healthy approach to seasonality as read. Modern brasserie ideas form the backbone of a crowd-pleasing, great-value table d'hôte menu and an imaginative carte. You might start with steamed Gower coast mussels with chorizo and olive oil, or caramelised ox cheek and foie gras ballotine with star anise pickle and crispy bread, then follow with pan-fried fillet of hake with wilted spinach, saffron potato mousse, and bouillabaisse sauce. Carnivores can head straight to the grill for slabs of prime Welsh protein with thick-cut chips and flavoured butters. Desserts such as bitter chocolate tart with salted caramel and cappuccino ice cream end the meal on a high note.

Times 12-2/5.30-10 Closed 25-26 Dec & 1 Jan, D Sun (Sep-May)

Follow the AA on twitter @TheAA_Lifestyle

CARMARTHENSHIRE

LAUGHARNE
Map 8 SN31

The Cors Restaurant

◉◉ Modern

tel: 01994 427219 **Newbridge Rd SA33 4SH**
email: nick@thecors.co.uk
dir: A40 from Carmarthen, left at St Clears & 4m to Laugharne

Charming restaurant in Dylan Thomas country

Chef-proprietor Nick Priestland has taken a lovely Victorian rectory and transformed it into a one-off, idiosyncratic restaurant with rooms. Just off Laugharne's main street in Dylan Thomas country, the trees, shrubs, ponds, and modern sculptures in the magical bog garden ('cors' is Welsh for bog) are unmissable when lit up at night, while the moody interior has a gothic edge with its deep claret-hued walls, wrought-iron seats and stained-glass windows; an atmospheric setting for unaffected, precise cooking that trumpets the virtues of excellent local ingredients. Full-on flavours are more important here than fancy presentation, thus smoked haddock brûlée certainly grabs the attention at the start of a summer's dinner, before roast rack of Welsh lamb arrives with the punchy flavours of a rosemary and garlic crust, dauphinoise potatoes and caramelised onion gravy, and it all ends happily with a summer fruit Pavlova.

Times 7-9.30 Closed 25 Dec, Sun-Wed, L all week

LLANDEILO
Map 8 SN62

The Plough Inn

◉ Modern International

tel: 01558 823431 **Rhosmaen SA19 6NP**
email: info@ploughrhosmaen.com **web:** www.ploughrhosmaen.com
dir: On A40 1m N of Llandeilo towards Llandovery. From M4 onto A483 at Pont Abraham

Modern and traditional dishes in a refurbed boutique hotel

The contemporary boutique hotel is in the beautiful Towy Valley, on the edge of the Brecon Beacons and not far from the National Botanic Garden of Wales. It's recently had a new refurbishment, with light tones predominating in both the inviting bar and the raftered dining room. Informal, warm-hearted service sets the tone, and there's a menu of modern Welsh cooking to supplement the more obvious favourites such as beer-battered fish and chips, or peppered steaks with onion rings. Slow-cooked pig cheeks with roasted shallots in pearl barley broth is a particularly warming way to start, with mains such as bream fillet alongside pea and coriander risotto, or pot-roasted, locally shot partridge with creamed Savoy cabbage in rosemary jus, to follow. Desserts to fire the imagination include a spin on baked Alaska, with mixed berry ice cream and peach sauce, or pannacotta with tonka biscotti, blood-orange sorbet and pistachio soil.

Chef Chris Lovell **Owner** Andrew Roberts **Seats** 190, Pr/dining room 30
Times 11.30-3.30/5.30-9.30 Closed 26 Dec **Prices** Fixed L 2 course £14.25, Fixed D 3 course £23-£29, Starter £4.95-£8.50, Main £10.95-£23.95, Service optional
Wines 6 bottles over £30, 32 bottles under £30, 11 by glass **Parking** 70
Notes Sunday L £16.70-£18.95, Vegetarian available, Children welcome

LLANELLI
Map 8 SN50

Sosban Restaurant

◉◉ British, French

tel: 01554 270020 **The Pumphouse, North Dock SA15 2LF**
email: ian@sosbanrestaurant.com **web:** www.sosbanrestaurant.com
dir: Phone for directions

Informal brasserie cooking in a former hydraulic station

The contemporary British restaurant scene is all about offbeat, talking-point locations, and in Sosban, Llanelli has a beauty. A majestic paean to late-Victorian engineering, the building once supplied hydraulic power to the town's docklands, and after a long interregnum in which it was put to various light-industrial uses, it has re-emerged triumphantly today as a fantastic modern brasserie venue. If you can see its 90-foot tower on the horizon, you're heading in the right direction. With an outdoor terrace for light evenings, and plenty of room to breathe amid the stolid stone walls inside, it's an inspired setting indeed for informal, but carefully conceived, on-trend dishes such as Monmouth ham with celeriac remoulade, shellfish gratin, or poached pear and Perl Las salad, for starters, followed by the likes of sea bass with gnocchi in garlic cream, pork belly in madeira with braised cabbage and mash, or rich cheese soufflé with chive beurre blanc. A modern brasserie isn't complete without crowd-pleasing puddings, so get set for tarte Tatin with vanilla ice cream, mixed berry cheesecake, or sumptuous gâteau opéra.

Chef Sian Rees, Ian Wood **Owner** Robert Williams & Partners **Seats** 90, Pr/dining room 20 **Times** 12-2.45/6-9.45 Closed 25 Dec, 1st Jan, D Sun **Prices** Fixed L 2 course £16, Fixed D 3 course £19, Starter £2-£15, Main £14-£48, Dessert £4.50-£6.50
Wines 49 bottles over £30, 34 bottles under £30, 14 by glass **Parking** 100
Notes Fixed D available until 6.45pm, Sunday L £16-£19, Vegetarian available, Children welcome

Looking for a restaurant by name?
Use the index on page 751

NANTGAREDIG
Map 8 SN42

Y Polyn
◉◉ Modern British

tel: 01267 290000 **SA32 7LH**
email: ypolyn@hotmail.com
dir: *Follow brown tourist signs to National Botanic Gardens, Y Polyn signed from rdbt in front of gardens*

Unpretentious cooking from an industrious country-pub kitchen

Mark and Sue Manson make no bones about the approach at their hospitable country pub: 'we're not trying to win any prizes for innovative cooking'. On the other hand, they do deserve plaudits for their single-minded commitment to hard graft. Virtually everything on the menu is something that has been produced in the kitchen here, much of it from excellent local prime materials, and while Sue may disavow any striving for modish novelty in her cooking, there is nonetheless a pleasing freshness to the menus. Start with pig brawn, roasted cauliflower purée and pickled red cabbage, or mackerel escabéche with soused veg. For mains, try the pairing of local beef ribeye with cured ox tongue, chestnut mushrooms and shallots in red wine, or maybe a whole lemon sole, assertively dressed in anchovy, caper and parsley butter. At the end comes a rollcall of everybody's favourite puddings – chocolate brownie with salty caramel, pannacotta ritzed up with pomegranate, clementine and candied pistachios, or egg custard tart. Fine Welsh cheeses come with oatcakes and walnut chutney.

Chef Susan Manson **Owner** Mark & Susan Manson **Seats** 40 **Times** 12-2/7-9 Closed Mon, D Sun **Prices** Fixed L 2 course £12, Fixed D 3 course £32.50, Starter £6-£8.50, Main £12.50-£17.50, Dessert £6.50-£7.50, Service optional **Wines** 25 bottles over £30, 51 bottles under £30, 9 by glass **Parking** 25 **Notes** ALC prices for L only, Sunday L £18.50-£23.50, Vegetarian available, Children welcome

NEWCASTLE EMLYN
Map 8 SN34

Gwesty'r Emlyn Hotel
◉ Welsh **NEW**

tel: 01239 710317 **Bridge St SA38 9DU**
email: reception@gwestremlynhotel.co.uk **web:** www.gwestremlynhotel.co.uk
dir: *In town centre*

Welsh ingredients in a revamped coaching inn

This 300-year-old one-time coaching inn looks the part with its four-square facade and archway, and there is plenty of period charm within, but it's had a bit of a makeover to sport a gently contemporary look, albeit one which won't scare the horses. The restaurant, called Bwyty'r Bont, has warm, neutral tones and smartly upholstered chairs and nary a stiff linen tablecloth in sight. The menu is short and to the point and offers up a good amount of Welsh produce, while the relaxed and friendly service team suit the mood to a tee. Start with a slice of barbecue pork belly served on thin slices of crusty bread and pea purée, or a trio of Welsh 'tasters' that includes Glamorgan sausage and cockles with bacon and laverbread. Next up, medallions of Welsh beef with roasted root veg and garlic mash, or grilled fillet of turbot with sauce vierge.

Chef Ian Williams, Italo Veritis **Seats** 60, Pr/dining room 8 **Times** **Prices** Fixed L 2 course fr £9.95, Fixed D 3 course fr £28.50, Starter £7.20-£8.50, Main £18.20-£20.95, Dessert £4.50-£6.50 **Wines** **Parking** 120 **Notes** Sunday L £10.95-£18, Vegetarian available, Children welcome

CEREDIGION

ABERAERON
Map 8 SN46

Ty Mawr Mansion
◉◉ Modern British, Welsh

tel: 01570 470033 **Cilcennin, Lampeter SA48 8DB**
email: info@tymawrmansion.co.uk **web:** www.tymawrmansion.co.uk
dir: *4m from Aberaeron on A482 to Lampeter road*

Food from within ten miles of a handsome Georgian mansion

In a lofty position above the Aeron Valley, this stone-built Georgian mansion is tucked away in 12 acres of gorgeous grounds. Inside, it is an authentically-restored gem right down to its heritage colour schemes – sunny yellows lighten the feel, while lavender walls combine with darkwood floors and blue and white Regency-striped chairs at bare wooden tables in the rather splendid restaurant. Lots of hotels go on about their organic and local ingredients, but in this case it is not empty bluster: most of the materials come from within a ten-mile radius, including organic produce from Cilcennin village's farms on the doorstep, while the coast (four miles distant) supplies the fishy stuff. Start, perhaps, with seared Cardigan Bay scallops with cauliflower risotto, chorizo and tempura caper berries, then move on via a sorbet, to pan-seared fillet and confit belly of local pork served with crackling, parsnip purée and pan juices. For pudding there may be duck egg tart with garden rhubarb in the form of compôte and sorbet.

Chef Geraint Morgan **Owner** Martin & Catherine McAlpine **Seats** 35, Pr/dining room 12 **Times** 7-9 Closed 26 Dec-7 Jan, Sun, L all week, D Mon **Prices** Fixed D 3 course £39, Service optional **Wines** 5 bottles over £30, 23 bottles under £30, 6 by glass **Parking** 20 **Notes** ALC 5 course available, Vegetarian available, Children welcome

EGLWYS FACH
Map 14 SN69

Plas Ynyshir Hall Hotel
◉◉◉ *– see opposite*

LAMPETER
Map 8 SN54

The Falcondale Hotel & Restaurant
◉◉ Modern British v

tel: 01570 422910 **Falcondale Dr SA48 7RX**
email: info@thefalcondale.co.uk **web:** www.thefalcondale.co.uk
dir: *1m from Lampeter take A482 to Cardigan, turn right at petrol station, follow for 0.75m*

Fine Welsh produce cooked in a lovely rural setting

An Italianate mansion built in verdant countryside, Falcondale has 14 acres all to itself. It's the kind of country-house hotel that delivers peace and quiet and that getting-away-from-it-all vibe, with elegant and refined public spaces that bring about nothing more than the desire for another G&T and a read of the paper. The dining room has a traditional finish, but a dash of contemporary style, too, so the tables are left unclothed and a happy hum pervades. The cooking reveals classical roots, but this is gently modernised stuff, and good use is made of the regional bounty. Haloumi cheese from the Cothi Valley is served in a first course with salted beet, horseradish and a cabernet sauvignon dressing, while another starter might be pork belly with black pudding and caramelised apple. Loin of venison stars in a main course with Gorwydd cheese gnocchi, enoki mushrooms and a chocolate and onion sauce, and a fishy main might be fillet of plaice with dauphine potatoes, braised fennel and lemongrass sauce. Finish with fig tarte Tatin.

Chef Michael Green **Owner** Chris & Lisa Hutton **Seats** 36, Pr/dining room 20 **Times** 12-2/6.30-9 **Prices** Fixed L 2 course fr £15.95, Fixed D 3 course fr £40, Tasting menu fr £67.50, Service optional **Wines** 49 bottles over £30, 60 bottles under £30, 21 by glass **Parking** 60 **Notes** Tasting menu 7 course (pre-booked), Sunday L £27.50-£29.50, Children welcome

CONWY

ABERGELE
Map 14 SH97

The Kinmel Arms
Modern Welsh

tel: 01745 832207 **The Village, St George LL22 9BP**
email: info@thekinmelarms.co.uk **web:** www.thekinmelarms.co.uk
dir: *From A55 junct 24a to St George. E on A55, junct 25. 1st left to Rhuddlan, then 1st right into St George. Take 2nd right*

Sophisticated cooking in the Elwy Valley

In a village near the coast, this 18th-century stone coaching inn is a combination of bar, with a wood-burning stove and real ales, and restaurant with rooms. The restaurant itself has a conservatory feel, with light wooden furniture and exposed brickwork and a lively bustle. The kitchen focuses on the best quality ingredients it can find in Wales and the Marches and turns out accomplished, imaginative dishes. A pressing of belly pork, for instance, is served with braised turnips, pickled carrots and rhubarb compôte, and another starter may be scallops sautéed with smoked paprika accompanied by lemon purée and chorizo foam. Influences are culled from here and there to create some adventurous, palate-pleasing compositions – accurately grilled sea bass fillet, for instance, on a bed of sautéed pak choi and steamed mooli with saffron tempura mussels, chilli and spring onion dressing and galangal chips – although pink-roast sirloin gets a more mainstream treatment, served with red wine purée and Madeira jus. Pudding fanciers can end with rum baba or apple tarte Tatin.

Chef Heddwen Wheeler **Owner** Tim & Lynn Watson **Seats** 88 **Times** 12-3/6-11.30 Closed 25 Dec, 1-2 Jan, Sun-Mon **Prices** Prices not confirmed, Service optional

Wines 49 bottles over £30, 49 bottles under £30, 20 by glass **Parking** 60 **Notes** Vegetarian available, Children welcome

BETWS-Y-COED
Map 14 SH75

Craig-y-Dderwen Riverside Hotel
Traditional, International

tel: 01690 710293 **LL24 0AS**
email: info@snowdoniahotel.com **web:** www.snowdoniahotel.com
dir: *A5 to Betws-y-Coed, cross Waterloo Bridge, take 1st left*

Modern Welsh cooking in a beautiful riverside setting

Built in the 1890s for a Midlands industrialist, the partly timbered house became a favourite bolthole, and perhaps inspiration too, for Sir Edward Elgar. A hotel since the twenties, it has been carefully restored to offer the full country-house package, complete with conservatory dining room views of a riverside teeming with wildlife (do look out for the otters). Dishes mix and match ingredients in the bold modern idiom, and while the performance is not perfectly consistent, there is plenty to celebrate. Black pudding and Carmarthenshire ham add lustre to a seared scallop starter, which may be the preamble to a leg of duck served with fine dauphinoise, spinach and pak choi, or a piece of hake crusted in marjoram and lemon on chive beurre blanc. A benchmark version of bread-and-butter pudding with vanilla ice cream is where the smart money is at dessert stage. Cheeses from the current generation of Welsh specialists are worth a punt too.

Chef Paul Goosey **Owner** Martin Carpenter **Seats** 82, Pr/dining room 40 **Times** 12-2.30/6.30-9 Closed 2 Jan-1 Feb **Prices** Prices not confirmed, Service optional **Wines** 50 bottles over £30, 60 bottles under £30, 7 by glass **Parking** 50 **Notes** Sunday L, Vegetarian available, Children welcome

Plas Ynyshir Hall Hotel

EGLWYS FACH
Map 14 SN69

Modern British V NOTABLE WINE LIST

tel: 01654 781209 **SY20 8TA**
email: ynyshir@relaischateaux.com **web:** www.ynyshir-hall.co.uk
dir: *On A487, 6m S of Machynlleth*

Daring contemporary cooking amid birdsong and ancient trees

The term 'destination hotel' is particularly apt for this tranquil country house: secreted away in splendid gardens within a 1,000-acre RSPB reserve on the Dovey Estuary, Plas Ynyshir Hall is not the sort of place you simply stumble upon. It's no exaggeration to say that Rob and Joan Reen have contributed in their own way to the illustrious history of the hall, making it one of the gastronomic magnets of west Wales, and running the whole show with solicitous care and attention. These days, the place is balm to the soul, with the sound of birdsong to help soothe away modern life's nerve-frazzling effects, and masterful cooking to boost the feeling of spiritual well-being further still. A lavender-hued dining room is easy on the eye, with owner Rob Reen's vibrant landscape paintings adorning the walls, and new head chef Gareth Ward's culinary magic playing its part. Fish from Cardigan Bay and the local rivers, produce from the hall's own gardens and

foraged wild ingredients, as well as pedigree meats from the valleys, form the basis of 8 and 11-course tasting menus that weave complex combinations of flavour and texture. Opening the show, mackerel comes in a vibrant sea-fresh partnership with pork belly, oyster and seaweed, then the national vegetable of Wales is paid due honour in a composition involving barbecued, puréed and fermented leeks. That might be counterpointed by the full-bore savoury impact of a main course of a roe deer loin and a burger served atop smoking pine with mushrooms and wild garlic, while seafood ideas might see prawns in a thought-provoking ménage with melt-in-the-mouth Wagyu beef (farmed up the road in Hereford) and the contrasting sour edge of fermented red cabbage. Ynyshir ricotta with pickled pineapple, ham and rocket provides a crossover dish before the intriguing flavours of yeast porridge with hazelnuts, maple syrup and verjus.

Chef Gareth Ward **Owner** Rob & Joan Reen, John & Jen Talbot **Seats** 30, Pr/dining room 16 **Times** 12.30-2/7-9 Closed Jan **Prices** Tasting menu £72.50-£90, Service optional **Wines** 291 bottles over £30, 35 bottles under £30, 17 by glass **Parking** 15 **Notes** 5 course L £29.50, Sunday L fr £29.50, Children welcome

BETWS-Y-COED *continued*

Llugwy River Restaurant@Royal Oak Hotel

🏵 Modern British, Welsh

tel: 01690 710219 **Holyhead Rd LL24 0AY**
email: royaloakmail@btopenworld.com **web:** www.royaloakhotel.net
dir: *on A5 in town centre, next to St Mary's church*

Former coaching inn with quality Welsh cuisine

Cappuccino-coloured walls with yellow sconces and ceiling chandeliers characterise the restaurant at this Victorian coaching inn, with dining chairs in a stripy fabric pulled up at lightwood tables on a patterned carpet, all brightly comfortable. The kitchen staunchly supports local suppliers and assembles a concise menu that buzzes with interest, often displaying Eastern influence. As well as chicken liver parfait with red onion marmalade, starters may run to scallop carpaccio with lime sabayon, mango jelly and pea shoots. Main courses vary from a duo of lamb (roast rump and faggot) with bubble-and-squeak, ratatouille and red wine jus to grilled sea bass with Thai-spiced risotto and green curry cream. Game shows up in season – perhaps whole roast partridge with parsnip purée, red cabbage and fig tart – and to end there may be tiramisù with coffee ice cream.

Chef Dylan Edwards **Owner** Royal Oak Hotel Ltd **Seats** 60, Pr/dining room 20 **Times** 12-3/6.30-9 Closed 25-26 Dec, Mon-Tue, L Wed-Sat, D Sun **Prices** Fixed D 3 course £25-£40, Service optional **Wines** 6 bottles over £30, 28 bottles under £30, 11 by glass **Parking** 100 **Notes** Sunday L £12.50-£15.95, Vegetarian available, Children welcome

CONWY — Map 14 SH77

Castle Hotel Conwy

🏵🏵 British, International

tel: 01492 582800 **High St LL32 8DB**
email: mail@castlewales.co.uk **web:** www.castlewales.co.uk
dir: *A55 junct 18, follow town centre signs, cross estuary (castle on left). Right then left at mini-rdbts onto one-way system. Right at Town Wall Gate, right onto Berry St then High St*

Fine Welsh produce in local landmark

It's a PhD project in the waiting to track the evolution of this hotel through history: suffice to say, built on the site of a Cistercian abbey, with a Victorian bell-gabled façade of local green granite and red Ruabon bricks, and first open for a jug of ale in the 15th century, there's no shortage of character. But this is no museum, with today's hotel positioning itself somewhere on the 'boutique' side of the spectrum and a restaurant, Dawsons, that has a satisfyingly contemporary finish. There's plenty of local flavour on the long menu in the shape of some excellent regional produce – Conwy mussels, for example – and there's attention to detail in the execution. The modish repertoire extends from Thai-style crab and salmon fishcakes with crispy 'seaweed', radish and bean sprout salad and sweet chilli sauce, to

---

main-course fillet of sea bass with a risotto of those excellent mussels, or Welsh lamb hotpot. To finish, warm cherry tart with Amarena cherry ice cream and fresh berry compôte competes with the slate of excellent Welsh cheeses.

Chef Andrew Nelson **Owner** The Lavin family **Seats** 70 **Times** 12-9.30 Closed D 25 Dec All-day dining **Prices** Starter £5.95-£9.95, Main £15.65-£22.95, Dessert £6.50-£9.95 **Wines** 19 bottles over £30, 25 bottles under £30, 16 by glass **Parking** 36 **Notes** Small plates menu spring & summer, Sunday L £14.95-£15.95, Vegetarian available, Children welcome

The Groes Inn

🏵 Traditional British, Welsh

tel: 01492 650545 **Tyn-y-Groes LL32 8TN**
email: reception@groesinn.com **web:** www.groesinn.com
dir: *On B5106, 3m from Conwy*

Historic inn serving simple pub grub

Once a stopping point for weary stagecoach passengers, the 16th-century Groes is said to be Wales's first licensed house. The white-fronted inn has all the expected beamed ceilings and roaring fires, plus some interesting paraphernalia you probably wouldn't expect such as Victorian portraits, a collection of military hats and some historic cooking utensils. Try a pint or bottle of the inn's own Groes ale – a light ale with citrus tones. Food can be taken in the welcoming bar, cosy restaurant, airy conservatory or the garden, which has wonderful views. Fresh pub cooking using classic combinations defines the kitchen's output. Start with a smooth chicken liver pâté with toast and chutney before oven-baked whole rainbow trout, which slides off the bone, served with fennel and king prawns, carrots and roasted new potatoes with lemon and dill butter. Poached pears with cider ice cream provides a satisfying finish.

Chef Lewis Williams, D Kapin **Owner** Dawn & Justin Humphreys **Seats** 100, Pr/dining room 20 **Times** 12-2.15/6.30-9 **Prices** Fixed L 2 course fr £15.95, Starter £5-£8, Main £10-£25, Dessert £5-£7, Service optional **Wines** 16 by glass **Parking** 100 **Notes** Sunday L £12.95-£18.95, Vegetarian available, Children welcome

DEGANWY — Map 14 SH77

Quay Hotel & Spa

🏵🏵 Modern European V

tel: 01492 564100 & 564165 **Deganwy Quay LL31 9DJ**
email: reservations@quayhotel.com **web:** www.quayhotel.com
dir: *M56, A494, A55 junct 18, straight across 2 rdbts. At lights bear left into The Quay. Hotel/Restaurant on right*

Steaks and seafood on the Conwy estuary

A stylish boutique hotel on the Conwy estuary, the Quay is a north Welsh destination for getting away from it all. Within striking distance of Snowdonia, it offers golf and spa treatments in the modern way, and boasts a smart eatery, the Grill Room, upholstered in muted greens and lilacs. Locally-landed fish and seafood are a strong draw, naturally, with oysters in shallots and red wine vinegar, crab croquettes with capers and 'tartare hollandaise', or mussels either Thai-style or marinière to get things going. A charcoal-fired oven ensures more sizzle for the steaks, which come in various cuts, all aged for 28 days, or stay fishy with monkfish medallions with butter-poached langoustines in shellfish bisque. The slapstick kitchen antics depicted on the dessert menu shouldn't be deemed to indicate that any less care has been taken over your hot apple crumble soufflé, served with apple and toffee ripple ice cream. High rollers may opt for the five-course tasting menu with wine flight.

Chef Sue Leacy **Owner** Exclusive Hotels **Seats** 120, Pr/dining room 40 **Times** 12-3/6.30-9.30 **Prices** Prices not confirmed, Service optional **Wines** 18 bottles over £30, 40 bottles under £30, 19 by glass **Parking** 110 **Notes** Sunday L, Children welcome

LLANDUDNO
Map 14 SH78

Bodysgallen Hall and Spa
@@@ – *see below*

Dunoon Hotel
@ Traditional British **NEW** NOTABLE WINE LIST

tel: 01492 860787 **Gloddaeth St LL30 2DW**
email: reservations@dunoonhotel.co.uk **web:** www.dunoonhotel.co.uk
dir: *Exit promenade at War Memorial by pier onto Gloddaeth St. Hotel 200 yds on right*

Local ingredients and unpretentious British cooking

The restaurant here, accessed from the hotel lobby, is full of old-world charm, with oak-panelled walls, brass fittings and chandeliers, and flowers and linen napery on the tables; formally attired staff are relaxed and attentive. The cooking style is more likely to reassure than to startle with modernism, with the kitchen clearly attempting to keep its customer base happy, so dishes are technically accurate and nicely presented without being showy. Among the starters, tarts – perhaps a warm one of pea and parmesan, and smoked fish – maybe locally smoked salmon and trout in silky-smooth risotto, get a decent showing among starters. Main courses have included Conwy Valley pheasant as roast breast and braised leg with pancetta-based gravy, mash and parsnip crisps, venison Wellington and perhaps seared fillet of prosciutto-wrapped monkfish on a bed of creamed leeks. For pudding, look no further than vanilla crème brûlée with plum compôte.

Chef Leighton Thomas **Owner** Rhys & Charlotte Williams **Seats** 80 **Times** 12-2/6.15-8.15 Closed mid Dec-1 Mar **Prices** Service optional **Wines** 8 by glass **Parking** 20 **Notes** ALC menu 5 course £26.50, Pre-theatre D menu available, Sunday L £14.95-£17.95, Vegetarian available, Children welcome

---

Empire Hotel & Spa
@ Modern British

tel: 01492 860555 **Church Walks LL30 2HE**
email: reservations@empirehotel.co.uk **web:** www.empirehotel.co.uk
dir: *From Chester, A55 junct 19 for Llandudno. Follow signs to Promenade, turn right at war memorial & left at rdbt. Hotel 100yds on right*

Traditional brasserie cooking in an impressive Victorian spa hotel

Just off the promenade, the impressive white Victorian hotel building with its portico entrance has been successfully refurbished to blend modern decorative garnishing, including spa facilities, with the 19th-century foundation of the place. The Watkins restaurant is named after a wine business that once flourished on the premises, and is done in clean, stylish fashion with ornate light-fixtures and mirror-panels. The kitchen turns out an essentially traditional bill of fare, with classic brasserie dishes much in evidence. Start with a fishcake of smoked and fresh salmon served with tartare sauce, or smooth chicken liver pâté with Cumberland dressing and crostini, as a prelude to well-seasoned loin of lamb with red cabbage, good roasties and rosemary jus, or perhaps a king prawn curry with basmati. Finish with cherry and almond tart, or Bailey's-laced chocolate cheesecake on raspberry coulis. A short list of reasonably priced wines contains a decent choice by the glass.

Chef Michael Waddy, Larry Mustisya **Owner** Len & Elizabeth Maddocks, Elyse Waddy **Seats** 110 **Times** 12.30-2/6.30-9.30 Closed 22-30 Dec, L Mon-Sat **Prices** Fixed L 3 course £16.50, Fixed D 3 course £23.50, Service optional **Wines** 8 bottles over £30, 39 bottles under £30, 9 by glass **Parking** 54, On street **Notes** Sunday L £16.50, Vegetarian available, Children welcome

---

Bodysgallen Hall and Spa

LLANDUDNO
Map 14 SH78

Modern British v NOTABLE WINE LIST

tel: 01492 584466 **LL30 1RS**
email: info@bodysgallen.com **web:** www.bodysgallen.com
dir: *A55 junct 19, A470 towards Llandudno. Hotel 2m on right*

Classy country-house cooking in a splendid mansion

Despite the fact the hall has been added to by successive generations over the course of 600 hundred years (give or take), the place feels authentic, positively stately in fact. The old stones are now in the hands of the National Trust, so there's no danger the beauty of it all will be tampered with. It is beautiful, a rugged, handsome beast of a building with views to Snowdonia, Conwy Castle and the Isle of Anglesey. The surrounding 200 acres of parkland and gardens includes some amazing features, including a rare 17th-century parterre, various follies, and a walled rose garden. If the grounds and exterior make a fine first impression, the same goes for the interiors of the hotel, which are rich with antiques, oil paintings and dark oak panelling. There are two dining options – the 1620 Bistro (the date of the main hall) and the main event, The Dining Room. The latter is a refined and elegant space, with period details and views over the verdant countryside. Smart dress is preferred, but you don't have to be suited and booted, and the charming service team ensure there's no stuffiness to the experience. The cooking matches the rarefied setting with its ambition and elegance, and there is a finely judged modernity to the kitchen's output. Head chef Michael Cheetham is passionate about the region's produce and it shows. Aberdaron crab with parsnip brittle, truffle powder and chestnut purée is a first course of considerable creativity, followed by an optional sorbet (lemon and thyme, maybe) before the main course. Honey-glazed breast of duck with confit leg roll follows, with stewed cucumber and plum gel, followed by dynamic desserts such as treacle tart parfait with pecan shortbread and an apple sorbet and butterscotch. The wine list does justice to the tremendous cooking.

Chef Michael Cheetham **Owner** The National Trust **Seats** 60, Pr/dining room 40 **Times** 12.30-1.45/7-9.30 Closed 26-26 Dec **Prices** Fixed L 2 course fr £19.50, Fixed D 3 course £39 **Wines** 6 bottles under £30, 8 by glass **Parking** 40 **Notes** Pre-theatre D available, Tasting menu on request, Sunday L £27, Children 6 yrs+

LLANDUDNO *continued*

Imperial Hotel

Modern, Traditional British

tel: 01492 877466 **The Promenade LL30 1AP**
email: reception@theimperial.co.uk **web:** www.theimperial.co.uk
dir: *A470 to Llandudno*

Grand hotel cooking with views of the sea

Where Snowdonia drops away to the sea, Llandudno's promenade basks in the sun, a vision of Victorian leisure in the grand manner, with the flesh-coloured Imperial ruling the roost. Chantrey's Restaurant surveys the maritime scene from panoramic windows, and there are outdoor tables too, for those who want to hear the murmuring surf. The kitchen works within the parameters of what's expected in such a context, but productively and with a few modern touches: smoked haddock mousse is wrapped in smoked salmon and garnished with radishes, capers and lemon, before a little fillet of Welsh beef appears, all tricked out with leek and horseradish rösti, smoked bacon, wild mushrooms, and a sauce lusty with Great Orme ale. Fish might be sea bass with roasted chicory and samphire in sauce vierge, while dessert brings on classic crème brûlée with apple and blueberry compôte, or pecan treacle tart with ginger cake and clotted cream ice cream.

Chef Arwel Jones, Joanne Williams **Owner** Greenclose Ltd **Seats** 150, Pr/dining room 30 **Times** 12.30-3/6-9 **Prices** Starter £6.50-£8.50, Main £19.50-£25.75, Dessert £6.50-£8.50, Service optional **Wines** 37 bottles over £30, 87 bottles under £30, 15 by glass **Parking** 20, Promenade pay & display **Notes** Sunday L £16-£20, Vegetarian available, Children welcome

The Lilly Restaurant with Rooms

Modern Welsh

tel: 01492 876513 **West Pde LL30 2BD**
email: thelilly@live.co.uk **web:** www.thelilly.co.uk
dir: *Just off A546 at Llandudno, follow signs for the Pier, beach front on right*

Modern Welsh cooking overlooking the sea

Parked right on the seafront at the West Shore, the Ashes' family-run restaurant with rooms is quite a looker inside. The dining room is done in ecclesiastical purples, with black-and-white table settings, the many-windowed space capitalising on views of the Llandudno headland and the sea. The bill of fare is modern Welsh cooking, presented cleanly and mobilising plenty of good local materials, such as rump of excellent Elwy lamb on creamed cabbage, served with a little chop and a portion of meaty suet pudding in minty juices. Other dishes are more obviously from the European mainstream, perhaps chicken and chorizo risotto, or truffled wild mushroom tagliatelle with shaved parmesan. The pork taster dish enterprisingly incorporates a Scotch egg along with the expected belly and tenderloin. Finish with passionfruit tart and honeycomb ice cream. Fine home-made breads, appetisers and pre-desserts show this to be a kitchen of serious intent.

Times 12-3/6-9 Closed Mon-Tue, L Wed-Sat, D Sun

Osborne House

Modern British

tel: 01492 860330 **17 North Pde LL30 2LP**
email: sales@osbornehouse.co.uk **web:** www.osbornehouse.co.uk
dir: *A55 at junct 19, follow signs for Llandudno then Promenade, at War Memorial turn right, Osborne House on left opposite entrance to pier*

Relaxed all-day brasserie eating in a Victorian seafront hotel

A Victorian seaside hotel on the prom at Llandudno, Osborne House brings off a tricky stylistic balancing-act between its plethora of period decorative detail, such as brocaded drapes, moulded fireplaces, antique jardinières and oil portraits, and a relaxed modern brasserie approach to all-day dining. Simple dishes with immediate appeal are brought off with a confident flourish, seen in a starter of broccoli, leek and blue cheese risotto, and mains such as slow-roast lamb shank on crushed carrot and swede with redcurrant jus, or sautéed salmon on honey-roast roots in orange and ginger sauce. Fixed-priced menu deals prove popular, but the main menu has such an extravagant variety of choice that it's hard not to delve in. Finish with rhubarb and custard with hazelnut crumble topping, dark chocolate and orange pot with Cointreau cream, or a plate of Celtic cheeses with home-made walnut bread. Alternatively, pitch up in the afternoon and have a champagne tea.

Chef Michael Waddy, Tim McAll **Owner** Len & Elizabeth Maddocks, Elyse Waddy **Seats** 70, Pr/dining room 24 **Times** 10.30am-10pm Closed 22-30 Dec, All-day dining **Prices** Fixed L 2 course £11.50-£12.50, Fixed D 3 course £21.95-£22.95, Starter £4.95-£7.50, Main £10.50-£20.50, Dessert £5.25-£6.25, Service optional **Wines** 9 bottles over £30, 44 bottles under £30, 8 by glass **Parking** 6, On street **Notes** Pre-theatre menu 5pm, Sunday L £15.25-£16.95, Vegetarian available, Children welcome

St George's Hotel

Modern, Traditional, Welsh

tel: 01492 877544 & 862184 **The Promenade LL30 2LG**
email: info@stgeorgeswales.co.uk **web:** www.stgeorgeswales.co.uk
dir: *A55, exit at Glan Conwy for Llandudno. A470 follow signs for seafront (distinctive tower identifies hotel)*

Patriotic Welsh cooking in a grand seafront hotel

Llandudno's prom is the place to be for splendid sunsets and sweeping views across the bay, and St George's Hotel sits centre stage among a grand line-up of seafront buildings. The place is a timeless slice of Victorian wedding cake grandeur, with an irresistible terrace to head for on balmy days, although the floor-to-ceiling windows of the restaurant within allow you to enjoy the same views when the weather isn't playing ball. Balancing trends with tradition, the kitchen brings together excellent local ingredients with confident simplicity: smoked mackerel with horseradish cream, beetroot, and garlic crostini is a typical starter. Lamb is always a good bet in these parts, especially when it is served as a main course of slow-cooked rump and breast with fresh peas, pearl barley and mint sauce jelly, or there may be roast cod loin with mussels, courgette and saffron cream. To finish, the addition of coconut and lemongrass give pannacotta an exotic spin.

Chef Gwyn Roberts **Owner** Anderbury Ltd **Seats** 110, Pr/dining room 12 **Times** 12-2.30/6.30-9.30 **Prices** Fixed L 2 course £14-£22, Fixed D 3 course £21-£38, Starter £6-£9, Main £9-£20, Dessert £6-£9, Service optional **Wines** 10 bottles over £30, 10 bottles under £30, 10 by glass **Parking** 36 **Notes** Pre-theatre menu available, Sunday L £18-£23, Vegetarian available, Children welcome

St Tudno Hotel and Restaurant

◉◉ Modern British, Welsh

tel: 01492 874411 **The Promenade LL30 2LP**
email: sttudnohotel@btinternet.com web: www.st-tudno.co.uk
dir: *On Promenade towards pier, hotel opposite pier entrance*

Modern Welsh cooking overlooking the bay

Sitting snugly in a prime location overlooking the sandy beaches and the bay, the hotel was fashioned from a former convalescent home in the 1970s. It retains something of the style of the seaside hotels of yesteryear, its Terrace Restaurant decorated with a mural depicting the tranquillity of Lake Como, for the enjoyment of those not positioned facing the tranquillity of Llandudno. The cooking is much more in the modern vein, and scores many hits with an unfussy, confident approach to quality Welsh ingredients. Start with seared Anglesey scallops and bacon, garnished with peas, broad beans and shallots, or butternut squash risotto with red onion and Pont Gâr cheese, as a prelude to roast tenderloin and braised cheek of pork with Lyonnaise potatoes, Cos lettuce, roasted apple purée and Madeira jus. A seafood array is generously comprised of plaice, crab, brandade and mussel chowder, with peas, tomato and samphire. The whole show might close with a lemony version of baked Alaska decorated with raspberries, or with Welsh farmhouse cheeses and grape chutney.

Chef Andrew Foster **Owner** Mr Bland **Seats** 60 **Times** 12.30-2/5.30-9.30 **Prices** Fixed L 2 course £15, Starter £6.50-£10.95, Main £17.95-£27.95, Dessert £5.95-£8.95, Service optional **Wines** 91 bottles over £30, 60 bottles under £30, 12 by glass **Parking** 9, On street **Notes** Pre-theatre menu available, Sunday L £14.95-£17.95, Vegetarian available, Children 5 yrs+ D

GWYNEDD

ABERSOCH
Map 14 SH32

Porth Tocyn Hotel

◉◉ Modern British 🍷 NOTABLE WINE LIST

tel: 01758 713303 **Bwlch Tocyn LL53 7BU**
email: bookings@porthtocyn.fsnet.co.uk web: www.porthtocynhotel.co.uk
dir: *2m S of Abersoch, through Sarn Bach & Bwlch Tocyn. Follow brown signs*

Well-established country house with first-class cooking

Three generations of the Fletcher-Brewer family have run Porth Tocyn since 1948, converting a lowly terrace of lead miners' cottages and building the place up into the comfy, relaxed and unstuffy small-scale country house we see today. You can see why they put down such deep roots: who would want to move on from that spectacular view of Cardigan Bay with the peaks of Snowdonia rising in the distance? Inside, all is homely, relaxed and unstuffy, with a lived-in patina in its interconnecting antique-filled lounges. Vast picture windows in the smart restaurant capitalise on that remarkable panorama across the bay, while Louise Fletcher-Brewer oversees the kitchen team as it cooks up an assured repertoire that combines traditional values with more modern sensibilities. Carefully-sourced local, seasonal produce underpins it all, starting with the likes of pan-fried tournedos of hare with black pudding bonbons, sweet potato purée and port jus, followed by pan-fried, herb-crusted cannon of Welsh lamb teamed with carrot and cumin purée, green beans, toasted almonds, crushed potatoes and redcurrant and port jus. Finish with a comfort food classic – warm treacle tart with Chantilly cream.

Chef L Fletcher-Brewer, M Williams **Owner** The Fletcher-Brewer family **Seats** 50 **Times** 12.15-2.30/7.15-9 Closed mid Nov, 2 wks before Etr, occasional low season **Prices** Fixed D 3 course £45.50 **Wines** 26 bottles over £30, 71 bottles under £30, 6 by glass **Parking** 50 **Notes** Light lunches Mon-Sat, Sunday L £13-£25, Vegetarian available, Children 6 yrs+ D

Who are the AA's Restaurants of the Year? See page 14

CAERNARFON

Map 14 SH46

Seiont Manor Hotel

Modern British

tel: 01286 673366 **Llanrug LL55 2AQ**
email: seiontmanor@handpicked.co.uk **web:** www.handpickedhotels.co.uk/seiontmanor
dir: From Bangor follow signs for Caernarfon. Leave Caernarfon on A4086. Hotel 3m on left

Compelling cooking in farmhouse hotel

This charming grey-silver stone building started life in the 18th century as a working farmstead and is now a prestigious country-house hotel. With Snowdonia National Park nearby and Anglesey over the water, there's no shortage of country pursuits; guests can even catch their own fish in the hotel's lake (the River Seiont flows through the 150-acre grounds) and get the chef to cook it. An identifiably Welsh trait runs through the cooking, which is chock-full of appealing ideas. Start with rabbit terrine with watercress purée and pickled carrots, and proceed to roast duck breast with sweet-and-sour walnut compôte, glazed turnips and wilted kale. Good local materials are handled deftly, with seafood given due consideration: Jerusalem artichoke and clam chowder with laverbread, for instance, then fillet of sea trout with a fricassee of mussels, broccoli, potatoes and smoked bacon. Cheeses are as local as can be, and interesting puddings might include pineapple tarte Tatin with pink peppercorn ice cream.

Times 12-2/7-9.30

CRICCIETH

Map 14 SH53

Bron Eifion Country House Hotel

Modern British, Welsh

tel: 01766 522385 **LL52 0SA**
email: enquiries@broneifion.co.uk **web:** www.broneifion.co.uk
dir: A497, between Porthmadog & Pwllheli

Modern Welsh cooking in a Victorian summer residence

The luxuriantly creeper-clad house stands on the Llyn peninsula, and has the dual charm of ravishing gardens and a stone's-throw proximity to the beach at Criccieth. Built as a private summer residence in 1883, it was conceived with rest and relaxation in mind, and retains that reputation today. A majestic staircase, oak panelling and comfortable country-house furniture give the right impression, though the Garden Room restaurant aims for a more contemporary look, with bare tables and windows all around. Modern Welsh cooking is what to expect, with a lengthy rollcall of dishes utilising many of the favoured ingredients of the present. Seared scallops with crisp pancetta, pea purée and tempura-battered quail eggs is a modern classic with a tweak, and could be the prelude to roast duck breast in duck stock and plum sauce with potato gratin, sweet-and-sour cabbage and a white vegetable purée. Refresh the palate at dessert with strawberry cheesecake mousse, served with dried strawberries and sorbet.

Chef Matthew Philips, Richard Williams **Owner** John & Mary Heenan **Seats** 150, Pr/dining room 24 **Times** 12-2/6.30-9 **Prices** Fixed D 2 course fr £5, Starter £6.95-£9.95, Main £14.95-£24.95, Dessert £6.95-£8.95, Service optional **Wines** 20 bottles over £30, 28 bottles under £30, 6 by glass **Parking** 50 **Notes** Gourmand menu 8 course £65, Sunday L £19.95, Vegetarian available, Children welcome

DOLGELLAU

Map 14 SH71

Bwyty Mawddach Restaurant

Modern British

tel: 01341 421752 **Pen Y Garnedd, Llanelltyd LL40 2TA**
email: enquiries@mawddach.com
dir: A470 Llanelltyd to A496 Barmouth, restaurant 0.2m on left after primary school

Confident modern British cooking in barn conversion

When it comes to barn conversions, this one is rather impressive. Ifan Dunn saw the potential in the old granite building on the family farm and turned into a snazzy modern restaurant. The setting is pretty special, too, with views over the Mawddach Estuary and Caderldris (the second highest mountain in Wales), and a glass wall ensures a good view for all inside. The cool, contemporary interior, spread over two floors, has exposed beams vaulted ceiling upstairs and slate floors on the ground floor. The cooking fits the bill amongst all this rustic-chic modernity, with some bright ideas and lots of regional ingredients. Start with celeriac soup with salted almonds, celery and apple, or a linguine rich with slow-cooked local pork. Next up, torched salmon fillet with brown butter and capers, or dry-aged Welsh Black rib-eye steak accompanied by triple-cooked chips, and, for dessert, apple and shot cake crumble with Douglas fir pine ice cream.

Chef Ifan Dunn **Owner** Roger, Will & Ifan Dunn **Seats** 75 **Times** 12-2.30/6-9 Closed 26 Dec, 1 wk Jan, 1 wk Apr, 2 wks Nov, Mon-Tue, D Sun **Prices** Starter £7-£8.50, Main £14-£21, Dessert £7-£8.50, Service optional **Wines** 8 bottles over £30, 19 bottles under £30, 7 by glass **Parking** 20 **Notes** Sunday L £19.95-£21.95, Vegetarian available, Children welcome

Penmaenuchaf Hall Hotel

Modern British NOTABLE WINE LIST

tel: 01341 422129 **Penmaenpool LL40 1YB**
email: relax@penhall.co.uk **web:** www.penhall.co.uk
dir: From A470 take A493 (Tywyn/Fairbourne), entrance 1.5m on left by sign for Penmaenpool

Modern British cooking in a Snowdonia garden room

The setting of this 1860s grey-stone mansion is a treat to savour, embraced by the flanks of lofty Cader Idris, and with the glorious Mawddach Estuary spread before its 21 wooded and landscaped acres. Inside are grand stone fireplaces and all of the oak panelling you would expect of a handsome Victorian pile; dining goes on in the luminous conservatory-style Llygad yr Haul restaurant – a tasteful setting floored with Welsh slate and romantically candlelit at dinner. The kitchen has its heart in French classicism, which it applies to pedigree Welsh produce to deliver essentially modern British cooking driven by flavour and seasonality, and presented with panache. A duo of duck – boudin and smoked – is served with celeriac remoulade and toasted brioche to get things off the blocks, then an unmistakably modern approach at main course stage sees a splendid slab of seared turbot paired robustly with oxtail, braised baby gem lettuce and herb oil. At the end, coffee pannacotta shares a plate with chocolate brownies and Kahlua syrup.

Chef J Pilkington, T Reeve **Owner** Mark Watson, Lorraine Fielding **Seats** 36, Pr/dining room 20 **Times** 12-2/7-9.30 **Prices** Fixed D 3 course fr £25, Starter fr £9, Main fr £27, Dessert fr £9, Service optional **Wines** 53 bottles over £30, 66 bottles under £30, 6 by glass **Parking** 36 **Notes** Sunday L £16.95-£18.95, Vegetarian available, Children 6 yrs+

PORTHMADOG
Map 14 SH53

Royal Sportsman Hotel
◎◎ Modern British, Welsh

tel: 01766 512015 **131 High St LL49 9HB**
email: enquiries@royalsportsman.co.uk **web:** www.royalsportsman.co.uk
dir: At rdbt junct of A497 & A487

Contemporary cooking in a buzzy old coaching inn

The four-square hotel has been holding court on this spot since 1862, when it made its debut as a coaching inn. Today it's very much a 21st-century version of the same, with smart bedrooms, buzzy bar and fireside lounge, plus a restaurant that delivers some rather good stuff. There's a Welsh flavour to the culinary proceedings in the traditionally-decorated dining room, where regional ingredients form the basis of the contemporary cuisine. There's also a 'classics' menu that makes good use of local produce, too. On the main menu, pig's cheek and foie gras terrine sets the standard, with golden raisins flavoured with jasmine to cut though the richness. Main-course rump of Welsh spring lamb is a super piece of meat, with accompanying tapenade, tomatoes and baby courgettes, or there might be pan-fried monkfish with Arborio rice, chorizo, squid and a citrus velouté. There's no shortage of zesty flavours amongst desserts, with the likes of black cherry frozen parfait with green apple sorbet, or dark chocolate fondant with wild blackberries and pistachio.

Chef Russell Croston **Owner** Aby Quddus **Seats** 60 **Times** 12-2.30/6-9 **Prices** Service optional **Wines** 11 by glass **Parking** 17, On street **Notes** Sunday L £10.95-£19.95, Vegetarian available, Children welcome

PORTMEIRION
Map 14 SH53

The Hotel Portmeirion
◎◎ Modern Welsh

tel: 01766 770000 & 772324 **Minffordd LL48 6ET**
email: hotel@portmeirion-village.com **web:** www.portmeirion-village.com
dir: Off A487 at Minffordd

Lively modern Welsh cooking in a fantasy Italianate village

The fantasy Italianate village on the north Wales coast, created by Sir Clough Williams-Ellis over half a century, was conceived around the ruin of what is now the hotel. When the whole place began to materialise in 1926, the hotel, then unlicensed, was its focal point. It's still a gem, with views over the Dwyryd estuary and the hills beyond. A gracefully curving dining room was added in 1931. Fresh, lively, modern Welsh cooking enhances the whole experience no end, in the form of starters such as sautéed langoustines with smoked apple purée, pink grapefruit and celery, before the main business follows on with crisp-skinned sea bass served with crab tortellini and pak choi in a sauce combining the various piquancies of fennel, lemongrass and coriander, or lamb loin with goats'cheese dauphinoise, provençale veg and pesto. Fashionable rhubarb gets a dessert outing in a parfait topped with a little stick of candy-floss, plus a bright pink sorbet and a custard-filled doughnut.

Chef Mark Threadgill **Owner** Portmeirion Ltd **Seats** 100, Pr/dining room 36 **Times** 12-2.30/6.30-9.30 Closed 2 wks Nov **Prices** Fixed L 2 course £18, Fixed D 3 course £30-£38, Starter £8-£12, Main £22-£28, Dessert £8-£10, Service optional **Wines** 45 bottles over £30, 38 bottles under £30, 17 by glass **Parking** 130 **Notes** Concert meal packages available, Sunday L £23.50, Vegetarian available, Children welcome

PWLLHELI
Map 14 SH33

Plas Bodegroes
◎◎ Modern British

tel: 01758 612363 **Nefyn Rd LL53 5TH**
email: gunna@bodegroes.co.uk
dir: On A497, 1m W of Pwllheli

Seasonal cooking in a scene of pastoral contentment

The Chowns' restaurant-with-rooms has been a fixture of the northwest Wales dining scene since the 1980s. A picture of pastoral contentment greets the eye, especially in spring and summer, when lavender scents the air, lambs bleat in the meadows, and jays chase each other amid the rhododendrons. The dining room is no dour oak-panelled retreat, but a fresh, airy space with mint-green walls hung with small artworks, a bare wood floor and elegant high-backed chairs. Chris Chown has always made a virtue of cooking to the seasons, and achieves positive results without recourse to undue complexity or technological boffinry. A fine smoked haddock tart with lemon-dressed fennel and watercress salad is an appealing opener, its pastry excellent, the filling beautifully balanced. Main courses might deliver firm-flavoured local pork loin with a broad bean and bacon fricassee and wild garlic purée, or sea bass in the Asian style, with crab, ginger and pak choi in lemongrass sauce. A satisfying chocolate trio to finish comprises dark mousse, a chocolate-pastried tart and a quenelle of white chocolate ice cream.

Times 12.30-2.30/7-9.30 Closed Dec-Feb, Mon, L Tue-Sat, D Sun

MONMOUTHSHIRE

ABERGAVENNY
Map 9 SO21

Angel Hotel
◎ Modern, Traditional British, International

tel: 01873 857121 **15 Cross St NP7 5EN**
email: mail@angelabergavenny.com **web:** www.angelabergavenny.com
dir: From A40 & A465 junct follow town centre signs, S of Abergavenny, past stations

Old coaching inn with broadly appealing menu

In its heyday a staging post on the Fishguard to London route, this Georgian hotel is still a refuge for travellers, although nowadays a good proportion of its patrons will have come here to dine. Eating in the popular bar is an option, while the menu in the restaurant, with its well-spaced neat tables under the chandeliers, follows a modern brasserie format – even down to moules et frites. Thai fishcake with spicy mayonnaise, followed by seared scallops with chorizo, gnocchi and red pepper sauce, and steak sandwich with chips show the diversity on offer, while desserts can stretch to pannacotta with grilled pineapple, or crème brûlée.

Chef Wesley Hammond **Owner** Caradog Hotels Ltd **Seats** 80, Pr/dining room 120 **Times** 12-2.30/6-9.30 Closed 25 Dec, D 24-30 Dec **Prices** Fixed L 3 course £25, Fixed D 3 course £25, Starter £6.80-£12.80, Main £10.80-£26, Dessert £2-£7.80, Service optional **Wines** 47 bottles over £30, 47 bottles under £30, 10 by glass **Parking** 30 **Notes** Afternoon tea available £19.80, Sunday L £21-£25, Vegetarian available, Children welcome

The Foxhunter
◎◎ Modern British

tel: 01873 881101 **Nantyderry NP7 9DN**
email: info@thefoxhunter.com
dir: Just off A4042 between Usk & Abergavenny

Carefully-sourced ingredients cooked with flair

Matt Tebbutt – he off the telly – practices what he preaches at his pub in a quiet hamlet on the fringes of the Brecon Beacons. It's a one-time stationmaster's house named in honour of an Olympic gold-medal winning horse, and it's been done out

continued

ABERGAVENNY *continued*

with a good deal of charm with wooden and Welsh stone floors, food-related paintings on cream walls, gleaming glassware on smart clothed tables, and a log fire for the chillier months. Tebbutt's food is modern inasmuch as it pays attention to seasonality, provenance (he's an advocate of foraging, too) and flavour, and his menus are a joy to behold. Sautéed scallops come with crisp pork belly, shallot purée and sherry caramel, for example, or there might be a game terrine with toasted brioche and onion jam. This is hearty and unpretentious stuff and it looks good on the plate. Main-course marinated leg of lamb is beautifully tender and served nicely pink, with Jansson's temptation (a Scandinavian potato dish) and purple sprouting broccoli. Red-wine-poached pear and almond Bakewell tart with crème fraîche brings up the rear.

Chef Matt Tebbutt **Owner** Lisa & Matt Tebbutt **Seats** 40, Pr/dining room 30 **Times** 12-2.30/7-9.30 Closed Xmas, 1 Jan, BHs, Mon, D Sun **Prices** Fixed L 2 course fr £22.95, Starter £7.25-£10.95, Main £16.50-£22.50, Dessert £5.95-£7.25, Service optional **Wines** 19 bottles over £30, 38 bottles under £30, 6 by glass **Parking** 25 **Notes** Foraging trip and wild food lunch, Sunday L £23.95-£28.95, Vegetarian available, Children welcome

The Hardwick

◉◉ Modern British 🍷 NOTABLE WINE LIST

tel: 01873 854220 **Old Raglan Rd NP7 9AA**
email: info@thehardwick.co.uk

Compelling modern cooking in revamped country pub

Stephen Terry has set out his stall in a former pub, now extended and with an unpretentious, rustic-chic look. His starting point is his suppliers, all duly name-checked on the menu, and his commitment to using fresh ingredients, along with his love for his craft, shows in every dish. Moist, loosely structured duck liver hash is a great match for confit leg, served with a fried duck egg and leaves in mustardy dressing to start. An alternative might be roast scallops with black pudding, potato purée, and an effective foil of brown butter with shallots, capers and lemon. The same imaginative and confident touch is given to main courses: three ways with rabbit, for instance (poached loin, faggots and burger, with deep-fried polenta and rocket), and pan-fried hake fillet with chorizo, saffron risotto cake, peas and broad beans. Puddings have a high wow factor: perhaps a Kilner jar of lemon crunch — layers of curd, custard, biscuit and caramel topped with meringue.

Chef Stephen Terry **Owner** Stephen & Joanna Terry **Seats** 100, Pr/dining room 50 **Times** 12-3/6.30-10 Closed 25 Dec **Prices** Fixed L 2 course £19, Fixed D 3 course £26, Starter £7-£14, Main £15-£25, Dessert £7-£10, Service optional **Wines** 42 bottles over £30, 30 bottles under £30, 11 by glass **Parking** 50 **Notes** Sunday L £22-£26, Vegetarian available, Children welcome

Llansantffraed Court Hotel

◉◉ Modern British, Welsh 🍷 NOTABLE WINE LIST

tel: 01873 840678 **Old Raglan Rd, Llanvihangel Gobion, Clytha NP7 9BA**
email: reception@llch.co.uk **web:** www.llch.co.uk
dir: M4 junct 24/A449 to Raglan. At rdbt take last exit to Clytha. Hotel on right in 4.5m

Ambitious Welsh modernism in a William and Mary mansion

A handsome brick-built William and Mary house in rural Monmouthshire, LLCH (as the web address has it) stands in 20 acres of trimly kept lawns with mature trees and a walled kitchen garden, within sight of the Tudor church of St Bridget's. Any sudden whirring you might hear will be a copter landing on the helipad. A low-ceilinged raftered dining room, the Court, is elegantly presented, with well-spaced tables dressed in good napery, and the culinary ambition here has entered liftoff with a range of multi-course tasters (five, seven or nine courses with wine

selections) supplementing the principal carte. A page of proudly attributed local suppliers inspires confidence, and the results can be seen in salmon mi-cuit with fennel and orange, or in the well-handled accompaniments of caramelised pear, diced apple, almond sponge and gingerbread purée, the puddings setting for a seared lobe of foie gras. Main courses bring on smoked venison loin with salsify, carrots and a pasty, or sea bass with truffled artichoke, and the finale could be a switched-on tangerine soufflé with citrus ice cream.

Chef Mike Hendry **Owner** Mike Morgan **Seats** 50, Pr/dining room 35 **Times** 12-2/7-9 **Prices** Fixed L 2 course £15, Fixed D 3 course £27.50, Tasting menu £70, Starter £6-£11, Main £14-£22, Dessert £6-£10, Service optional **Wines** 78 bottles over £30, 52 bottles under £30, 130 by glass **Parking** 300 **Notes** Tasting menu 7 course with matched wines, Sunday L £30, Vegetarian available, Children welcome

Restaurant 1861

◉◉ Modern British, European V

tel: 0845 388 1861 & 01873 821297 **Cross Ash NP7 8PB web:** www.18-61.co.uk
dir: On B4521, 9m from Abergavenny, 15m from Ross-on-Wye, on outskirts of Cross Ash

Modern European cooking in a converted Victorian pub

The Kings' converted pub out in the wilds at Cross Ash, a little to the northeast of Abergavenny, was built in the year it's named after. After beginning his career with the Roux brothers, Simon King has gone native in Wales, and 1861 is in many ways a celebration of what the region has to offer, including a constant supply of fine vegetables grown by Kate King's dad. The culinary style applies techniques from the European, notably French, traditions in modern combinations that are unmistakably appealing. Smoked and confit goose with agrodolce cherries, or proper fish soup with saffron rouille and garlic croutons, might kick things off. Mains include good seasonal game such as pheasant fricasséed in grain mustard cream, stuffed trotter in truffled madeira sauce, or richly treated fish like sea bass in red wine, or hake with langoustine fritters in creamy champagne sauce. It's worth the wait for one of the hot desserts, perhaps a banoffee soufflé with chocolate poured in, or go modishly vegetal with acorn pannacotta and pumpkin ice cream.

Chef Simon King **Owner** Simon & Kate King **Seats** 40 **Times** 12-2/7-9 Closed 1st 2 wks Jan, Mon, D Sun **Prices** Fixed L 2 course fr £22, Fixed D 3 course fr £35, Tasting menu £49.50, Starter £8-£13.50, Main £19-£24, Dessert £7.25-£8.50, Service optional **Wines** 30 bottles over £30, 32 bottles under £30, 7 by glass **Parking** 20 **Notes** Tasting menu 7 course, Sunday L £22-£25, Children welcome

Walnut Tree Inn

◉◉◉ – *see opposite*

Walnut Tree Inn

ABERGAVENNY　　　　Map 9 SO21

Modern British NOTABLE WINE LIST

tel: 01873 852797 **Llandewi Skirrid NP7 8AW**
email: mail@thewalnuttreeinn.com
web: www.thewalnuttreeinn.com
dir: *3m NE of Abergavenny on B4521*

Blissfully unfussy and focused cooking by a culinary mastermind

For over 50 years, with the occasional interlude, the Walnut Tree has been a destination for good food. Shaun Hill arrived ten years ago to pick up the mantle, and anyone who knew the place in the days of Franco Taruschio knew from the off that he was the right man for the job. The Walnut Tree of old was all about quality ingredients, simplicity and flavour (Franco didn't mess with the ingredients), and no-one knows that more than Shaun Hill, for he was a regular. Today the whitewashed inn looks dapper and neat, with a couple of cottages available in the grounds if you fancy crashing for the night, and within all is rustic simplicity. There's nothing rough-and-ready about the place – not by a long way – but neither is there any flashiness. The service team are on the ball enough to allow customers room to breathe. Shaun's cooking follows no particular culinary path other than one of good sense and integrity, with the produce centre stage and his acute technical ability bringing the very best out of them. Smoked eel might appear among first courses in the company of a smoked mackerel and pancetta toastie, while another dish delicately balances the flavours of artichoke and saffron in a risotto. Main-course brill with lobster ravioli is a ritzy little combination, or there might be all the earthy robustness of wild duck with morel sauce, and, if extra side dishes are needed, choose from an enticing bunch including spiced root vegetables or sprouts with pomegranate and chestnuts. Desserts are no less well-crafted and appealing: yoghurt and tangerine pannacotta, maybe, or apple parfait with salted caramel sauce and toasted almonds. Like everything at the Walnut Tree, the wine list is put together with intelligence and the customer in mind.

Chef Shaun Hill **Owner** Shaun Hill, William Griffiths **Seats** 70, Pr/dining room 26 **Times** 12-2.30/7-10 Closed 1 wk Xmas, Sun-Mon **Prices** Prices not confirmed, Service optional **Wines** 50 bottles over £30, 40 bottles under £30, 8 by glass **Parking** 30 **Notes** Vegetarian available, Children welcome

LLANGYBI
Map 9 ST39

The White Hart Village Inn
Modern British

tel: 01633 450258 & 07748 114838 **Old Usk Rd NP15 1NP**
email: enquiries@thewhitehartvillageinn.com
dir: *M4 junct 25 onto B4596 Caerleon road, through town centre on High St, straight over rdbt onto Usk Rd continue to Llangybi*

Impressive gastro-pub cooking in a smart village inn

Rich in history and atmosphere, the handsomely revamped 16th-century White Hart is the hub of Llangybi and stands close to the Roman settlement of Caerleon in the beautiful Usk Valley. The traditional bar has low-slung windows, black-painted beams and a blazing fire in the grand inglenook fireplace, while the more contemporary dining areas are the setting for some top-notch gastro-pub food. Regional produce is supplemented by fish deliveries from Brixham, and it all finds its way on to the enticing modern British menus and daily-changing blackboards. Cooking is accurate with good, well-balanced flavours and presentation is simple with no flowery garnishes. Well-seasoned leek and potato soup may get the ball rolling, followed by a moist, well-cooked bream served on an oblong piece of slate with crushed parsnip, sweet-tasting beetroot and orange chicory. A light apple trifle served with refreshing cider granité rounds off the meal nicely. The individual mini-loaves of bread are spot-on – great texture and flavour.

Chef Adam Whittle **Owner** Michael Bates **Seats** 46, Pr/dining room 36
Times 12-3/6-10 Closed Mon (ex BHs), D Sun **Prices** Tasting menu £45, Starter £6.50-£9.75, Main £12.95-£22.50, Dessert £6-£8.50, Service optional **Wines** 4 bottles over £30, 25 bottles under £30, 13 by glass **Parking** 30 **Notes** Fixed L & D Tue-Thu, Tasting menu 6 course Tue-Sat, Sunday L £18.50-£21.50, Vegetarian available, Children welcome

MONMOUTH
Map 10 SO51

Bistro Prego
Modern Italian

tel: 01600 712600 **7 Church St NP25 3BX**
email: enquiries@pregomonmouth.co.uk **web:** www.pregomonmouth.co.uk
dir: *Travelling N A40 at lights left turn, T-junct left turn, 2nd right, hotel at rear of car park*

Buzzy bistro with an Italian edge

This simple and welcoming little bistro with rooms in the heart of Monmouth's old town has cornered a strong local fan base, won over by its no-nonsense approach. The food here is all about sourcing top-class local ingredients and bringing them together without undue fuss or fashionable flim-flam, whether you pop by for a light snack or lunch – perhaps crispy sweetbreads with tartare sauce, followed by slow-roasted pork belly with wild garlic bubble and squeak – or dinner, when the kitchen turns out a more involved bistro offering. As you may have spotted in the name, a strongly Italophile vein courses through it all: the menu skips with flair and imagination from a starter of vincisgrassi – baked pasta with porcini mushrooms and Parma ham – to a local wild boar chop with roasted beetroot, Swiss chard and red wine jus. For pudding, you can't go wrong with rhubarb and apple crumble with vanilla ice cream, or there might be a refreshing finale of pineapple carpaccio with mint, pomegranate and elderflower sorbet.

Chef Stephen Robbins **Owner** Stephen Robbins, Tom David, Sue Howell **Seats** 40
Times 12-2.30/6.30-9.30 Closed 24-26 & 31 Dec, 1 Jan **Prices** Starter £4-£7.50, Main £8.50-£20.50, Dessert £4-£6, Service optional **Wines** 16 bottles over £30, 34 bottles under £30, 16 by glass **Parking** Pay & display at rear of restaurant **Notes** Pre-theatre from 6pm by bkgs only, Sunday L £13.50, Vegetarian available, Children welcome

The Inn at Penallt
Modern British

tel: 01600 772765 **Penallt NP25 4SE**
email: enquiries@theinnatpenallt.co.uk **web:** www.theinnatpenallt.co.uk
dir: *From Monmouth on B4293 towards Trellech. After 2m turn left signed Penallt, at village x-rds turn left, 0.3m on right*

Straightforward, honest cooking in the Wye Valley

There are country views, stone walls, real ales, comfy rooms, good food – it's a classic. The locals know how lucky they are. The diminutive village is home to this 17th-century inn with its robust exterior and slate, wood and roaring fires within. Few rural establishments have the dedication displayed here to sourcing food from both sides of the nearby border. There's a smarter dining room out back if you don't fancy the bonhomie of the bar. Kick things off with a starter of smoked duck breast with poached pear, walnuts and blue cheese sauce, or carpaccio of Welsh beef. Follow on with the blade of that same beef, served with dauphinoise potatoes and a red wine and thyme reduction, or fillet of Anglesey sea bass with a truffle and saffron beurre blanc, and finish with treacle tart with lemon and ginger ice cream.

Chef Peter Hulsmann **Owner** Andrew & Jackie Murphy **Seats** 28, Pr/dining room 28
Times 12-2.30/6-9 Closed Mon, L Tue, D Sun **Prices** Fixed L 2 course £15.95, Starter £5.95-£11.95, Main £13.95-£24.95, Dessert £6.40, Service optional **Wines** 9 bottles over £30, 26 bottles under £30, 9 by glass **Parking** 26 **Notes** Wed evening meal & drink £10.95, Sunday L £16.95-£24.95, Vegetarian available, Children welcome

RAGLAN
Map 9 SO40

The Beaufort Raglan Coaching Inn & Brasserie

Modern British

tel: 01291 690412 **High St NP15 2DY**
email: enquiries@beaufortraglan.co.uk **web:** www.beaufortraglan.co.uk
dir: M4 junct 24 (Newport/Abergavenny), north on A449 2nd junct A40 Raglan/Abergavenny

Historic Welsh Marches inn with modern food

With over 400 years of history behind it, The Beaufort Raglan stands proud in the village, famed for its rather splendid 15th-century castle. The old coaching inn presents a traditional facade to the world, but there's been a bit of a contemporary makeover within, not least in the self-styled Brasserie with its tones of cappuccino, cream and cerise, and designer Lloyd loom chairs at unclothed darkwood tables. There is still plenty of period character on show, though, and a good deal of local ingredients on the menu, which is backed up by daily specials and shows clear-headed, unpretentious thinking. There are steaks cooked on the chargrill, or the likes of sea bass with fennel, asparagus, sauté potatoes and lemon butter sauce among main courses. Start with a goats' cheese and beetroot salad, and finish with a baked egg custard with nutmeg ice cream.

Chef Andrew Taylorson, Eliot Lewis **Owner** Eliot & Jana Lewis **Seats** 100, Pr/dining room 26 **Times** 12-3/6-10 Closed 25 Dec **Prices** Service optional **Wines** 26 bottles over £30, 45 bottles under £30, 12 by glass **Parking** 30 **Notes** Sunday L £12.95-£19.50, Vegetarian available, Children welcome

ROCKFIELD
Map 9 SO41

The Stonemill & Steppes Farm Cottages

Modern British, International

tel: 01600 716273 **NP25 5SW**
email: bookings@thestonemill.co.uk **web:** www.thestonemill.co.uk
dir: A48 to Monmouth, B4233 to Rockfield. 2.6m from Monmouth town centre

Clearly focused European cooking in a 16th-century cider mill

A beautifully converted barn in a 16th-century mill complex with self-catering bed and breakfast cottages, just a few miles west of Monmouth, and within striking distance of the Wye Valley and the Forest of Dean, provides the impressive setting for accomplished ingredients-led cooking. Inside it's a riot of oak beams and vaulted ceilings, with chunky rustic tables around an ancient stone cider press. The kitchen's modern approach makes sound use of fresh regional and Welsh produce to deliver accurately cooked and simply presented modern European ideas. Natural flavours shine through in a starter of mushroom soup with white truffle oil and sea salt. The same straight-up approach to flavour combinations results in an impressively piggy main course of slow-cooked pork belly and roast pork tenderloin with mustard creamed potatoes, spring greens and Calvados sauce. A well-matched pairing of dark chocolate iced parfait with Grand Marnier cream brings things to a close, or you might go for a savoury finish via a slate of Welsh cheeses with oatcakes and apple and plum chutney.

Chef Carl Hammett, Jordan Simons **Owner** Mrs M L Decloedt **Seats** 56, Pr/dining room 12 **Times** 12-2/6-9 Closed 25-26 Dec, 2 wks Jan, Mon, D Sun **Prices** Fixed L 2 course £14.95, Fixed D 3 course £20.95, Starter £6.95-£8.95, Main £16.95-£24.95, Dessert £5.95-£7.95, Service optional **Wines** 10 bottles over £30, 36 bottles under £30, 7 by glass **Parking** 40 **Notes** Sunday L £15.50-£17.50, Vegetarian available, Children welcome

SKENFRITH
Map 9 SO42

The Bell at Skenfrith

Modern British, Welsh NOTABLE WINE LIST

tel: 01600 750235 **NP7 8UH**
email: enquiries@skenfrith.co.uk **web:** www.skenfrith.co.uk
dir: N of Monmouth on A466 for 4m. Left on B4521 towards Abergavenny, 3m on left

Modern Welsh cooking in an isolated country inn

Set amid the wooded slopes and cattle pastures of Monmouthshire, with the river Monnow a stone's throw away, The Bell at Skenfrith is an enticingly isolated 17th-century inn turned restaurant with rooms. It comes with all the period accoutrements we expect of such a place, oak beams and flagged floors included. There's also an organic kitchen garden, the unimpeachable sign of a thoroughgoing commitment to localism. While the ingredients are from here or hereabouts, the kitchen sets its sights rather wider for culinary inspiration, bringing on home-cured salmon mi-cuit dressed in gentle wasabi, venison in a rich chocolate-boosted sauce with croquette potatoes, and sea bass with buttered samphire in shellfish bisque. The vegetarian offering might be something like wild mushroom ravioli in roast garlic and spinach velouté with pea shoots and parmesan. Presentations are neat and tidy, with big glass plates and such, and the imaginative gene sustains the performance through to desserts such as apple mousse with hedgerow berry crumble and cassis jelly, or choose Welsh cheeses with fig chutney.

Chef Damian Hanlon **Owner** The Vaughan family **Seats** 60, Pr/dining room 40 **Times** 12-2.30/7-9.30 Closed Tue (Nov-Mar) **Prices** Service optional **Wines** 47 bottles over £30, 44 bottles under £30, 12 by glass **Parking** 35, Field or village **Notes** Sunday L £22-£26, Vegetarian available, Children 8 yrs+ D

Follow us on facebook
www.facebook.com/TheAAUK

USK

Map 9 SO30

Newbridge on Usk

Traditional British

tel: 01633 451000 & 410262 **Tredunnock NP15 1LY**
email: newbridgeonusk@celtic-manor.com **web:** www.newbridgeonusk.co.uk
dir: *A449 to Usk exit through town & turn left after bridge through Llangibby. After approx 1m Cwrt Bleddyn Hotel on right, turn left opposite hotel up lane. Drive through village of Tredunnock, down hill, inn on banks of River Usk*

Pastoral riverside setting for contemporary cooking

On a bend in the Usk, with views of the river, this restaurant with rooms is in a peaceful spot surrounded by well-tended gardens. The property dates back 200 years, so expect the usual beams, fireplaces and wooden floors, while the two-level restaurant has a rustic charm. The kitchen is assiduous about its sourcing (Welsh lamb and cheeses, fish from Brixham, chicken from the Wye Valley, for instance), and its menu ticks some cosmopolitan boxes. A duo of lamb comes as shoulder in ras el hanout and as seared rump, served with spinach and kale dotted with almonds, and pan-fried wild sea bass fillet is coated in Parma ham and accompanied by globe artichokes and watercress. Flavours are clear: witness starters of glazed belly of pork, nicely sticky, with black pudding and apple salad, and crab risotto with a spicy tomato foam and a parmesan crisp. Puddings like rich dark chocolate mousse with ginger parfait, or banana crème brûlée are followed by petits fours with coffee.

Times 12-2.30/7-10

The Raglan Arms

Modern British

tel: 01291 690800 **Llandenny NP15 1DL**
email: theraglanarms@gmail.com
dir: *M4 junct 24. Turn off A449 towards Usk, then immediately right towards Llandenny*

Unpretentious atmosphere and good, inventive food

In a tiny village consisting of no more than a few houses, a church and this pub, The Raglan Arms has a cheery, welcoming atmosphere, with a log fire, real ales at the bar, and a conservatory extension for dining. The kitchen showcases local produce and has assembled a corker of a menu. The focus might be southern Europe, but ideas are pulled in from further afield to broaden the appeal. Duck spring rolls with plum sauce spiked with chilli, and imam bayildi have appeared

The Crown at Whitebrook

WHITEBROOK

Map 4 SO50

British, French NEW v
tel: 01600 860254 **NP25 4TX**
email: info@crownatwhitebrook.co.uk **web:** www.crownatwhitebrook.co.uk
dir: *From Monmouth take B4293 towards Trellech, in 2.7m left towards Whitebrook, continue for 2m*

Modern metropolitan cooking in the Wye Valley

The setting, in the densely-wooded Wye Valley near to Tintern Abbey, may be Welsh through and through, but The Crown seems to model its modus operandi on the classic upmarket French country auberge. Originally a drovers' inn dating from the 17th century, its venerable beams are the only clue to the building's age once you're inside. A well-drilled team of staff get things off on the right foot with aperitifs served at leather sofas in the cosy lounge area, then it is time to move through to the classy dining room, a modern space of soft-focus coffee and cream hues, with original artwork on the walls. The kitchen here is firing on all cylinders under head chef, Chris Harrod, who has taken The Crown on an ever-upwards trajectory into the top handful of Welsh restaurants. Rock-solid technical abilities are the foundations of a dazzling repertoire of modern ideas, marked by flavour profiles that are never less than fascinating – take grey mullet, which appears in the company of smoked eel wrapped with lemon and crème fraîche in a light cannelloni, avocado purée and a wild leaf salad dressed with shiso. Fresh flavours and razor-sharp timing are to the fore in a main course of poached and roasted sea bass with langoustines, artichoke and butternut squash, while those seeking more robust things might find a nose-to-tail treatment of woodland pork with five spices, date and broccoli. A dessert described tersely as 'rhubarb, vanilla, lemon' delivers rhubarb as a consommé and poached within ravioli parcels, partnered with vanilla cream and lemon crumbs. The cellar is amply stocked with a globe-trotting list that covers all bases.

Chef Chris Harrod **Owner** Chris Harrod **Times** 12-2/7-9 Closed 1st 2 wks Jan, Mon **Prices** Fixed L 2 course fr £19, Fixed D 3 course fr £54, Tasting menu fr £65, Service optional 10% **Wines** 76 bottles over £30, 46 bottles under £30, 17 by glass **Parking** 20 **Notes** Sunday L £34-£65, No children

among starters, and falafel with baked mushrooms, leek gremolata, black truffle, Comté cheese and a poached egg among main courses. Dishes are accurately cooked and attractively presented, and a classic influence is seen in goujons of sole with tartare sauce, followed by veal milanese with meatballs and pasta, while whole megrim sole is roasted and served with beurre blanc and a portion of sautéed potatoes. End with classic glazed lemon tart.

Chef Giles A Cunliffe **Owner** Giles A Cunliffe **Seats** 65 **Times** 12-2.30/7-9.30 Closed 25-26 Dec, Mon, D Sun **Prices** Starter £5.50-£8, Main £11.50-£19.50, Dessert £4.50-£7.50, Service optional **Wines** 15 bottles over £30, 45 bottles under £30, 12 by glass **Parking** 20 **Notes** Sunday L £18-£24, Vegetarian available, Children welcome

The Three Salmons Hotel
◉◉ Modern Welsh 🍷 NOTABLE WINE LIST

tel: 01291 672133 **Bridge St NP15 1RY**
email: general@threesalmons.co.uk **web:** www.threesalmons.co.uk
dir: M4 junct 24/A449, 1st exit signed Usk. On entering town hotel on main road

Smart cooking in a revamped old coaching inn

This old coaching inn has served the community and weary travellers for over 300 years, yet while the Grade II listed building presents a traditional face to the world, inside it has moved with the times (albeit without scaring the horses). The restaurant combines the character of the old building with gently contemporary fixtures and fittings, or you could choose to eat in the less formal bar. It's a flexible kind of place. The menu shows evident passion for the produce of this area, some of which is grown in the hotel's own garden, and there is a welcome egalitarian approach and lack of pretension, too. A starter of smoked eel ravioli with pickled carrot, velouté and fennel seed wafer shows this to be a kitchen of ambition and confidence, but you might opt to follow that with a burger with smoked cheese and chips. Breast of duck with vanilla mash, braised red cabbage and parsnip purée is another way to go, and for dessert, treacle tart with gingerbread ice cream hits the spot.

Chef James Bumpass **Owner** T Strong, B Dean, P Clarke, J Bumpass **Seats** 55, Pr/dining room 22 **Times** 12-2.30/6.30-9.30 **Prices** Tasting menu £39, Starter £5-£7.50, Main £10-£26.50, Dessert £5.50-£7, Service optional **Wines** 39 bottles over £30, 61 bottles under £30, 14 by glass **Parking** 80 **Notes** Afternoon tea £13, Sunday L £12.50-£22.50, Vegetarian available, Children welcome

WHITEBROOK   Map 4 SO50

The Crown at Whitebrook
◉◉◉ – *see opposite*

NEWPORT   Map 9 ST38

Le Patio at the Manor House
◉ Modern French

tel: 01633 413000 **The Celtic Manor Resort, The Manor House, Coldra Woods NP18 1HQ**
email: bookings@celtic-manor.com **web:** www.celtic-manor.com
dir: M4 junct 24, B4237 towards Newport. Hotel 1st on right

French country cooking in a Welsh golf resort

If you're splashing out on a golfing week at the sprawling Celtic Manor Resort, you can ring the changes by eating in a different venue every day you're there. Tucked away in the historic part of the old manor house, Le Patio is the place to head for when you need a hit of hearty French country cooking, served in an informal glass-roofed extension done out with bare blond-wood tables and wicker seats. Starters are as simple as onion soup with croûtons and gruyère, or confit pork terrine with almonds, herbs and sweet garlic served with plum and ginger chutney and onion bread, while mains take in regional classics such as beef bourguignon with mash, bouillabaisse with rouille and toasted garlic bread, and Alsatian chicken slow-cooked in Riesling with cream, lardons, mushrooms and served with sweet potato purée. End with cinnamon and apple bavarois with apple sorbet.

Chef Mikael le Cuziat **Owner** Celtic Manor Resort **Seats** 65, Pr/dining room 20 **Times** 6.30-10 Closed L all week **Prices** Starter £6.50-£9.55, Main £15-£32, Dessert £5.25-£9.95, Service optional **Wines** 15 bottles over £30, 34 bottles under £30, 8 by glass **Parking** 400 **Notes** Vegetarian available, Children welcome

NEWPORT *continued*

Rafters

@ Modern British

tel: 01633 413000 **The Celtic Manor Resort, Coldra Woods NP18 1HQ**
email: bookings@celtic-manor.com web: www.celtic-manor.com
dir: *M4 junct 24, B4237 towards Newport. Hotel 1st on right*

Grill classics at the 19th hole

There are views over the Ryder Cup course from Rafters, a classy grill restaurant on the Celtic Manor Resort. It's within the Twenty Ten Clubhouse (2010 being the year the cup came to town), and with its high beamed ceiling, smart, modern look and those views, there's a lot to like. The kitchen makes a play for Welsh ingredients and, with it being a grill restaurant and all, there are locally-reared steaks aged for 21 days as the star attraction. They come with hickory-infused chips and soused red onion salad, but it you're not in the mood for the red stuff, other main course options might include grilled sea bass with kohlrabi and a pea and spinach velouté, or twice-baked goats' cheese soufflé with roasted chestnuts and butternut squash purée. Kick off with smoked haddock rarebit with crab and sweetcorn fritters, or a classy prawn cocktail, and finish with apple and caramel trifle with cider granité.

Chef Simon Searle **Owner** Celtic Manor Resort **Seats** 80, Pr/dining room 96 **Times** 12-2.30/6-10 Closed D Mon-Wed (Oct-Mar) **Prices** Fixed L 2 course fr £10.95, Starter £6.50-£9.25, Main £15-£36.50, Dessert £5.50-£9.95, Service optional **Wines** 6 by glass **Parking** 115 **Notes** Sunday L £18.50-£22.50, Vegetarian available, Children welcome

Terry M at The Celtic Manor Resort

@ @ @ *– see below*

Terry M at The Celtic Manor Resort

NEWPORT	Map 9 ST38

Modern British
tel: 01633 413000 **Coldra Woods NP18 1HQ**
email: terrym@celtic-manor.com web: www.celtic-manor.com
dir: *From M4 junct 24 take B4237 towards Newport, turn right after 300yds*

Outstanding cooking at a world-class golfing hotel

The slick Celtic Manor Resort has a class act in its midst in the shape of the Terry M restaurant, a fine-dining venue which aims high and hits the spot. It all takes place in an elegant space with a contemporary gloss – think white walls, shimmering modern chandeliers, swanky leather seats and tables dressed in their best whites. It's the kind of space that instils confidence, which is backed up by bang-on formal service and the kitchen's culinary output. Tim McDougall continues to deliver refined dishes which show respect for classical ways and plenty of contemporary va-va-voom. Welsh ingredients figure large on menus that run to full-on tasting version and an excellent value express lunch. It kicks off with an amuse-bouche such as a creamy celeriac soup and excellent bread before a starter such as pressed duck liver with Medjool date compôte and toasted brioche, or white asparagus with a quail's egg and soused mushrooms. Main-course West Country free-range duck comes with hachis parmentier (rather like a posh shepherd's pie) and a sauce rich with Welsh ale, or there might be tenderloin and rump of woodland pork partnered with black pudding and home-cured choucroute. A pre-dessert like honey ice cream with raspberry sauce is next up, before the real deal such as rhubarb soufflé with goats' cheese ice cream and honeyed oats, or chocolate bavarois with blood orange salad and grapefruit mousse.

Chef Tim McDougall **Owner** Celtic Manor Resort **Seats** 50, Pr/dining room 12 **Times** 12-2.30/7-9.30 Closed 1-14 Jan, Mon-Tue **Prices** Fixed L 2 course fr £15.95, Fixed D 3 course fr £49.50, Tasting menu fr £70, Service optional **Wines** 195 bottles over £30, 40 bottles under £30, 12 by glass **Parking** 1000 **Notes** Tasting menu 6 course, Sunday L £28.50, Vegetarian available, No children

PEMBROKESHIRE

HAVERFORDWEST
Map 8 SM91

Wolfscastle Country Hotel
◉ Modern British, Welsh

tel: 01437 741225 **Wolf's Castle SA62 5LZ**
email: info@wolfscastle.com **web:** www.wolfscastle.com
dir: *From Haverfordwest take A40 towards Fishguard. Hotel in centre of Wolf's Castle*

Appealing Wales-meets-Asia menu in peaceful country hotel

The restaurant of this ancient stone-built hotel sports a spiffy brasserie look, with unclothed pale wood tables and sleek grey fabrics, plenty of space for diners and a bright and airy ambience. It goes by the name of Allt-yr-Afon, which translates as 'hill by the river', which pretty much sums up the location, as the place sits on a promontory above the confluence of two rivers in lush Pembrokeshire countryside, making it a hit for weddings and conferences. The kitchen delivers an unfussy repertoire spiced up with a few global influences, a 'Wales-meets-Asia' style that might start with the likes of Thai cod cakes with chilli, coriander, and lime jam. Mains could bring pork, in the form of roast tenderloin and sweet and sour-glazed belly with winter greens and confit potatoes, or sea bass with saffron mashed potatoes, wilted spinach and langoustine cream. Finish with a trio of chocolate fondant, delice, and white chocolate ice cream.

Chef Tom Simmons **Owner** Mr A Stirling **Seats** 55, Pr/dining room 32 **Times** 12-2/6-9 Closed 24-26 Dec **Prices** Starter £5.95-£9.95, Main £12.95-£19.95, Dessert £5.95-£6.95, Service optional **Wines** 6 bottles over £30, 39 bottles under £30, 14 by glass **Parking** 75 **Notes** Sunday L £10.50-£17.50, Vegetarian available, Children welcome

NARBERTH
Map 8 SN11

The Grove
◉◉◉ *– see page 680 and advert below*

the GROVE
NARBERTH
PEMBROKESHIRE

Nestling in the heart of the beautiful Pembrokeshire countryside, The Grove is one of Wales' finest restaurants and a leading small luxury hotel.

The Grove is the perfect setting to unwind and enjoy the best of Welsh cuisine, and a truly memorable time in Pembrokeshire.

T: +44 (0)1834 860915
E: info@thegrove-narberth.co.uk
W: www.thegrove-narberth.co.uk

AA ROSETTE AWARD
FOR CULINARY EXCELLENCE

The Grove

WINNER OF THE AA WINE AWARD FOR WALES 2014–15

Modern British **NOTABLE WINE LIST**

tel: 01834 860915 **Molleston SA67 8BX**
email: info@thegrove-narberth.co.uk
web: www.thegrove-narberth.co.uk
dir: *From A40, take A478 to Narberth. Continue past castle & Herons Brook, turn right bottom of hill*

Contemporary cooking from superlative ingredients in a charming country house

It sounds rather lovely, and it is. The neat, pristine white house, with a fascinating history going all the way back to the 15th century, is surrounded by a gorgeous restored Georgian walled garden, and has stunning views of the Preseli Mountains. Inside it's all rather luxurious, with the period features of the house enhanced through gentle modernisation. The elegant restaurant looks out over the grounds and is sumptuously furnished in warm tones, with soft lighting, works by Welsh artists on the walls, and an open fire in the colder months. In such a setting, you'd hope the food would be up to the mark, and head chef Duncan Barham and his team certainly don't disappoint. The starting point for the seasonally changing menus is tip-top

produce, sourced from the garden and the local environs and brought in fresh every day: you can taste the difference. The brilliant thing about this kitchen is that it knows how to treat these superb ingredients with restraint and respect to produce dishes that sing with natural flavours and are impeccably balanced. So Nant Du Pork to start is a simple but highly effective combination of slow-cooked pork belly with a crispy crackling topping, served with three langoustine tails, sliced baby leeks and a flavour-packed consommé. Brecon red deer is up next, a sublimely tender loin of venison served alongside finely sliced turnip, glazed shallots and a little venison suet pudding for a touch of comfort food indulgence that isn't remotely heavy. Dessert might offer an exercise in textural contrasts with pineapple (roasted, crisp, sorbet, caramel and carpaccio), or all the cocoa delights of a Valrhona dark chocolate terrine with caramelised orange and a yoghurt sorbet.

Chef Duncan Barham **Owner** Neil Kedward, Zoe Agar **Seats** 70, Pr/dining room 25 **Times** 12-2.30/6-9.30 **Prices** Fixed L 2 course £20, Fixed D 3 course £49, Tasting menu £78, Service optional **Wines** 216 bottles over £30, 46 bottles under £30, 18 by glass **Parking** 42 **Notes** Tasting menu 7 course, Sunday L £25, Vegetarian available, Children welcome

Llys Meddyg

◉◉ British

tel: 01239 820008 & 821050 **East St SA42 0SY**
email: contact@llysmeddyg.com web: www.llysmeddyg.com
dir: *A487 to Newport, located on the Main Street, through the centre of town*

Accomplished cooking in a former coaching inn

Llys Meddyg is an attractive package when you want to explore the Pembrokeshire Coast National Park. The handsome Georgian townhouse is easy to spot in the centre of Newport village: converted from a coaching inn, it now earns a crust as a comfortable, smartly-done-out restaurant with rooms. There's a cosy stone-walled cellar bar with flagstones, ceiling beams and a wood-burner, a lovely kitchen garden for pre-dinner drinks, and an elegant restaurant hung with art. The kitchen champions local produce, sustainably sourced whenever possible, and goes foraging to boost the repertoire with nature's seasonal bounty, turning up pennywort to partner home-smoked salmon served with horseradish cream and lemon jelly. Main courses ally precision with a lack of pretension: confit leg and roast breast of pheasant, perhaps, with cannellini bean and vegetable consommé, or pan-fried sea bass accompanied by tomato, pearl onions, crab bisque, nuts and spices. A winter pudding might see mulled pear served with cinnamon doughnut, or a savoury finish with Welsh cheeses is good whatever the season.

Chef Patrick Szenasi **Owner** Ed & Louise Sykes **Seats** 30, Pr/dining room 14 **Times** 6-9 Closed L all week (ex summer L kitchen garden) **Prices** Starter £6.50-£8, Main £14-£25, Dessert £7.50-£9, Service optional **Wines** 4 by glass **Parking** 8, On street **Notes** Vegetarian available, Children welcome

Best Western Lamphey Court Hotel & Spa

◉ Modern British v

tel: 01646 672273 **Lamphey SA71 5NT**
email: info@lampheycourt.co.uk web: www.lampheycourt.co.uk
dir: *M4 then A477 to Pembroke. Left at Milton for Lamphey, hotel on right on entering village*

Homely cooking in a grandiose Georgian mansion

As Georgian mansions go, Lamphey Court is a bit of an eye-popper, a great white whale of an edifice with massive columns fronting a portico entrance that wouldn't have disgraced a Roman temple. Built in 1823, it's now been equipped with a very 21st-century spa and gym, and if you're looking to get plenty of exercise while you're here, the Pembrokeshire Coastal Path isn't far distant, while the national park is all around. Leigh Williams took up the kitchen reins in 2013 with the aim of offering essentially homely food with one or two flourishes of modern Britishism. Start with smoked trout and horseradish cream, or one of the trendy sharing platters of tapas or Italian charcuterie, and then set about confit duck leg on spiced red cabbage in redcurrant jus, or herb-crusted roast salmon in warm dill yoghurt sauce. Favourite puddings include apple and blackberry crumble, or honey and lemon cheesecake.

Chef Leigh Williams **Owner** Tony & France Lain **Seats** 60, Pr/dining room 60 **Times** 12-2.30/6.15-10 **Prices** Fixed L 2 course fr £12.95, Fixed D 3 course fr £25, Starter £3.50-£10.95, Main £9.95-£19.50, Dessert £3.50-£5.50 **Wines** 8 bottles over £30, 26 bottles under £30, 6 by glass **Parking** 40 **Notes** Afternoon tea available, Sunday L £9.95-£15.95, Children welcome

The Shed

◉ Traditional British, Mediterranean

tel: 01348 831518 **SA62 5BN**
email: caroline@theshedporthgain.co.uk web: www.theshedporthgain.co.uk
dir: *7m from St Davids. Off A487*

Fresh seafood and laid-back ambience on the harbour

Seafood fans should beat a path to this simple beach hut-style bistro and wine bar right on the quayside in the adorable fishing village of Porthgain. Formerly a carpenter's workshop and fisherman's storehouse, you couldn't ask for a more authentic venue for tucking into locally-landed and sustainable fish and seafood. Gingham tablecloths, whitewashed walls and fish-related art all work to create a laid-back ambience for unpretentious dishes that gain lustre from the sheer quality and freshness of the raw materials. The simple glory of proper beer-battered fish and chips gets its own menu, or you might go for the three-course format, starting with Penclawdd cockle chowder with bacon and root vegetables in a creamy broth, then progress to pan-fried sea bass with fennel, pomegranate, and dill salad. You can end with a comforting dessert like warm treacle tart with cream and Penderyn whisky and raisin sauce.

Chef Rob & Caroline Jones **Owner** Rob & Caroline Jones **Seats** 60 **Times** 12-3/5.30-9 Closed Nov-Apr (open only wknds except half term & Xmas hols), D Tue (off peak) **Prices** Starter £4.95-£7.95, Main £10.95-£27.95, Dessert £4.95-£6.95, Service optional **Wines** 2 bottles over £30, 24 bottles under £30, 7 by glass **Parking** On village street **Notes** Sunday L, Vegetarian available, Children welcome

Read all about our Wine Award winners on page 17

ST DAVIDS
Map 8 SM72

Cwtch

Modern British

tel: 01437 720491 **22 High St SA62 6SD**
email: info@cwtchrestaurant.co.uk
dir: *A487 St Davids, restaurant on left before Cross Square*

Big taste of Wales in the smallest city

If your Welsh isn't up to scratch, the name is pronounced 'cutsh' and it has all the cosseting connotations of hug, snug, and cosy. The restaurant lives up to its name as far as the ambience goes, with three small dining rooms spread over two floors, and done out with the pared-back simplicity of whitewashed stone walls, sturdy beams and foodie books for diners to leaf through. The cooking takes a similarly restrained approach, leaving peerless Pembrokeshire produce to do the talking. Open with a chunky terrine of ham hock, apricot and pistachio with sourdough toast, followed by a soul-soothing main course of slow-roasted pork belly with onion gravy, apple sauce, black pudding and crackling. Fishy options might run to hake fillet with sweetcorn, smoked pancetta and cockle chowder and red pepper tapenade. Round things off with puddings that fly the Welsh dragon, such as sticky toffee bara brith pudding with vanilla ice cream.

Chef Andy Holcroft **Owner** Jackie & John Hatton-Bell **Seats** 50 **Times** 6-10 Closed 25-26 Dec, Jan, Mon-Tue (Nov-Mar), L Mon-Sat (Oct-Apr), D Sun (Oct-Apr) **Prices** Fixed D 3 course £26-£30, Service optional **Wines** 5 bottles over £30, 24 bottles under £30, 10 by glass **Parking** On street **Notes** Early evening offer 6-6.45pm 2/3 course £22/£26, Vegetarian available, Children welcome

SAUNDERSFOOT
Map 8 SN10

Coast Restaurant

Modern British NEW

tel: 01834 810800 **Coppel Hall Beach SA69 9AJ**
email: reservations@coastsaundersfoot.co.uk
dir:

Emblematic modern structure on the Pembrokeshire shoreline

If you were looking for an emblematic 21st-century restaurant venue, you couldn't go far wrong with Coast. A purpose-built curvaceous wood structure, it stands on the Pembrokeshire shore, with just the sea and sky before it. Huge picture windows allow for relaxed contemplation, and the interior scene is all simple bare tables, banquettes strewn with cushions, and an atmosphere of serenely informal professionalism. The seafood-strong menu construction is exactly of the moment too, built from local materials and with more flexibility than the old three-course format ever allowed. A Nibbles list offers temptations such as tankards of prawns, crispy pigs' ears and apple sauce, or houmous dusted with smoked paprika, before you get into the full starter menu. A broad swathe of heterogeneous choice ranges from crab with mango, wasabi yoghurt and coriander to griddled squid with pink grapefruit and shaved fennel, and mains follow up with the likes of halibut, lentils and cauliflower in garam masala, or 28-day dry-aged rib-eye with peppercorn butter. Finish with marmalade baked Alaska and blood-orange.

Chef Will Holland **Owner** Neil Kedward, Zoe Agar **Seats** 64 **Times** 12-2.30/6-9.30 **Prices** Tasting menu £60, Starter £6-£12, Main £13-£25, Dessert £8-£12 **Wines** 29 bottles over £30, 9 bottles under £30, 17 by glass **Parking** Pay & display before 6pm **Notes** Tasting menu 6 course, Brunch available, Sunday L, Vegetarian available, Children welcome

St Brides Spa Hotel

Modern British

tel: 01834 812304 **St Brides Hill SA69 9NH**
email: reservations@stbridesspahotel.com **web:** www.stbridesspahotel.com
dir: *A478 onto B4310 to Saundersfoot. Hotel above harbour*

Pleasingly unfussy food and fabulous sea views

Perched atop the cliffs looking out across Saundersfoot harbour and Carmarthen Bay, the views alone are reason to pay this spa hotel a visit in fair weather or foul. And if the latter is the case, you can retire to the spa for a spot of pampering to soothe the mind and body before weighing up the dining options. There's the Gallery bar with its own menu of simple classics based on high quality regional produce, and a terrace that is the hot ticket in warmer months. But the Cliff Restaurant kitchen cranks things up a notch to deliver some vibrant, unpretentious cooking. Wherever you choose, the genuinely charming and friendly staff are a big part of the hotel's appeal. You might start with smoked haddock rarebit with tomato carpaccio, before pan-fried tuna with roast garlic mash and red wine jus, finishing with vanilla pannacotta with pistachio ice cream.

Chef Toby Goodwin **Owner** Andrew & Lindsey Evans **Seats** 100, Pr/dining room 50 **Times** 11-6.30 **Prices** Starter £6.50-£8, Main £16-£25, Dessert £6.25-£7.25, Service optional **Wines** 104 bottles over £30, 79 bottles under £30, 14 by glass **Parking** 60 **Notes** All day Gallery menu, L all day from 11am, Sunday L £25-£30, Vegetarian available, Children welcome

POWYS

BRECON
Map 9 SO02

Peterstone Court

Modern British, European

tel: 01874 665387 **Brecon Rd, Llanhamlach LD3 7YB**
email: info@peterstone-court.com **web:** www.peterstone-court.com
dir: *1m from Brecon on A40 to Abergavenny*

Excellent local food on the edge of the Brecon Beacons

With it Georgian proportions and position in the Brecon Beacons National Park (by the River Usk), Peterstone Court has a lot going for it. It's an ideal base for exploring the landscape, but, really and truly, it's the perfect escape for a bit of pampering. There's a suitably contemporary feel to the place on the inside and a classy finish that includes a swish bar and a spa offering treatments and all that jazz (and a seasonal heated outdoor pool). But, best of all, there's the Conservatory Restaurant, which serves up some nifty modern food based on regional ingredients. A starter of beetroot tarte Tatin shows the way, or go for some trendy surf 'n' turf in the shape of crisp pork belly with garlic king prawns. Among main courses, Glaisfer Farm provides lamb, pork and chicken (the former served as a trio of rack, breast and hotpot), or there might be roast wild rabbit with fondant potato and game jus. Finish with white chocolate cheesecake with raspberry coulis and coconut ice cream.

Chef Glyn Bridgeman **Owner** Jessica & Glyn Bridgeman, Sean Gerrard **Seats** 30 **Times** 12-2.30/6-9.30 **Prices** Fixed L 2 course fr £15, Fixed D 3 course fr £19.50, Starter £5.50-£9.95, Main £16-£23, Dessert fr £6.50, Service optional **Wines** 15 bottles over £30, 33 bottles under £30, 9 by glass **Parking** 40 **Notes** Afternoon tea 3-6pm daily, Sunday L £19-£22.50, Vegetarian available, Children welcome

BUILTH WELLS   Map 9 SO05

Caer Beris Manor Hotel
Modern European **NEW**

tel: 01982 552601 **LD2 3NP**
email: caerberis@btinternet.com **web:** www.caerberis.com
dir: *From town centre follow A483/Llandovery signs. Hotel on left on edge of town*

Fusion cooking comes to a Welsh feudal estate

Drenched in a violently colourful history, the Caer Beris estate traces its lineage back to the Welsh feudal kings of late antiquity. Towards the end of the 19th century, a captain in the Hussars remade it into a private sporting estate, but retained such features as the medieval panelling in the dining room. Sitting in 27 acres of parkland bordered by the river Irfon, it's clearly enjoying its present day incarnation as a destination country hotel, the contrasts of time emphasised in the modern seating and tableware that offset the panelling and stone fireplace in the 1896 dining room. Spencer Ralph brings with him a CV overflowing with experience gained in the crucibles of fusion cooking in the southern hemisphere, so expect the likes of pressed duck terrine with poached rhubarb, prune compôte and candied ginger to start, followed by salmon on roast beets and fennel dressed in red wine jus and tarragon oil, or classic Welsh lamb navarin with sweet potato dauphinoise and turnip remoulade. A cockle-warming dessert then turns up in the shape of pear and honey tart with nutmeg ice cream and hot toddy syrup.

Chef Spencer Ralph **Owner** Peter & Katharine Smith **Seats** 40, Pr/dining room 100 **Times** 12-2.30/6.30-9.30 **Prices** Fixed L 2 course fr £12.99, Fixed D 3 course £32, Tasting menu £49 **Wines** 3 bottles over £30, 30 bottles under £30, 7 by glass **Parking** 50 **Notes** Sunday L £9.95-£15.95, Vegetarian available, Children welcome

CRICKHOWELL   Map 9 SO21

The Bear
Modern British, International

tel: 01873 810408 **High St NP8 1BW**
email: bearhotel@aol.com **web:** www.bearhotel.co.uk
dir: *Town centre, off A40 (Brecon road). 6m from Abergavenny*

Vibrant modern Welsh cooking in a medieval pub

The old stagecoach doesn't run past here any more, but an enduring testament to the last time it did is present in the form of a Victorian timetable in the bar. The Bear goes back further than that, though, to the reign of Henry III in the 1430s, when it must have been as much a local beacon as it is now, at the heart of the Brecon Beacons National Park. Its traditional interiors and ancient arched cellar where the beers are kept are all part of the deal, as is vibrant modern food with the emphasis on regionally sourced ingredients. Start with shredded duck à la Peking with plum sauce, sesame seeds and salad, before going on to squid-ink linguine with Cornish crab dressed in coriander and chilli, or confit lamb shoulder cooked for half a day, with pink fir-apples and garlic in rosemary jus. Simple but effective desserts include seasonal baked figs in marsala, with matching ice cream.

Chef Iain Sampson **Owner** Mrs J & Mr S Hindmarsh **Seats** 60, Pr/dining room 30 **Times** 12-2/7-9.30 Closed 25 Dec, L Mon-Sat, D Sun **Prices** Service optional **Wines** 6 bottles over £30, 45 bottles under £30, 10 by glass **Parking** 40 **Notes** Vegetarian available, Children 7 yrs+

Manor Hotel
Modern British

tel: 01873 810212 **Brecon Rd NP8 1SE**
email: info@manorhotel.co.uk **web:** www.manorhotel.co.uk
dir: *On A40, 0.5m from Crickhowell*

Farm-fresh food in a sparkling-white valley hotel

The sparkling-white hotel with handsome portico entrance stands under Table Mountain in a valley of the Brecon Beacons National Park, a thoroughly enthralling spot. Playing its full part in the local community, its kitchen is supplied with the greater part of its prime materials from the family farm seven miles distant in Llangynidr. A pleasantly relaxing dining room with tall plants and elegant furniture has views out towards the hills, and a resourceful menu that incorporates Asian seasonings and French technique. Start perhaps with tempura tiger prawns with chilli jam, moving on to crisp-skinned chicken breast with sweet potato mash, wilted spinach and Perl Las sauce, or salmon fillet with broccoli in béarnaise. A refreshing finisher might be a duo of honeycomb caramel ice cream and mango and passion-fruit sorbet, or there may be lemon tart with strawberry compôte. An Anglo-Welsh cheeseboard comes with tomato and grape chutney.

Chef Glyn Bridgeman **Owner** Glyn & Jessica Bridgeman, Sean Gerrard **Seats** 54, Pr/dining room 26 **Times** 12-2.30/6-9.30 **Prices** Fixed L 2 course £15, Fixed D 3 course £17.50, Starter £4.50-£7, Main £10.50-£17, Dessert £6-£7.50, Service optional **Wines** 2 bottles over £30, 18 bottles under £30, 13 by glass **Parking** 200 **Notes** Simple and Seasonal menu 2/3 course £15/£17.50, Sunday L, Vegetarian available, Children welcome

HAY-ON-WYE   Map 9 SO24

Old Black Lion Inn
Modern British

tel: 01497 820841 **26 Lion St HR3 5AD**
email: info@oldblacklion.co.uk **web:** www.oldblacklion.co.uk
dir: *1m off A438. From TIC car park turn right along Oxford Rd, pass NatWest Bank, next left (Lion St), hotel 20yds on right*

Well-judged, appealing cooking in an historical inn

Dating from the 17th century, the whitewashed inn has bags of character, with beams in low ceilings and stone fireplaces. You can eat in the bar or in the more sedate next-door dining room. The inn has earned something of a local reputation for its fish specials, among them perhaps roast fillet of cod with an interesting sauce of ginger and onion, served with wilted greens and crushed potatoes. Quality shines out of ingredients – roast loin of lamb and mushroom-stuffed breast, for instance, with sherry-glazed vegetables and lamb jus – and dishes are notable for their sensible combinations. A starter of ham hock terrine with mustard and piccalilli sounds straightforward enough, but the kitchen puts thought and effort into all its output, so it may also present seared scallops with crispy speck, broccoli purée, roast almonds and paprika and pimento oil. End with white chocolate parfait partnered by raspberry coulis or delve into the past with jam-topped rice pudding.

Chef Maximillion Evilio **Owner** Dolan Leighton **Seats** 40, Pr/dining room 20 **Times** 12-2/6.30-9 Closed 24-26 Dec **Prices** Starter £4.95-£7.95, Main £12.95-£18.95, Dessert £5.75-£5.95, Service optional **Wines** 10 bottles over £30, 19 bottles under £30, 9 by glass **Parking** 10, On street nearby **Notes** Afternoon tea available, Sunday L £16.95-£19.95, Vegetarian available, Children welcome

HAYE-ON-WYE *continued*

The Swan-at-Hay Hotel

British, French **NEW**

tel: 01497 821188 **Church St HR3 5DQ**
email: stay@swanathay.co.uk **web:** www.swanathay.co.uk
dir: *In town centre, on Brecon Road opposite cinema bookshop*

Alluring menus in a family-run hotel

The Swan is a family-run hotel of grey stone with flower-bordered lawns to the rear, with relaxed and welcoming service in the bistro-style dining room even when it's busy. Local produce is at the core of the kitchen's business, and the concise menu is an appealing slate of contemporary ideas, among them toothsome Gloucester Old Spot and cider rillettes with red onion marmalade, and seasonal roast Craswall partridge (from just a few miles away) with Calvados jus, dauphinoise and honey-roast parsnips. Bresaola is cured in-house and teamed with parmesan and cracked black pepper, and might be followed by one of the fish offerings: perhaps fillet of Loch Duart salmon with rosemary-spiked potatoes, broccoli and orange-flavoured beurre blanc. End with a memorable pudding such as hot chocolate fondant, its centre oozing liquid, with a scoop of vanilla ice cream and raspberry coulis, or a platter of local cheeses.

Chef Harry Mackintosh **Owner** Amy & Harry Mackintosh **Seats** 32, Pr/dining room 6 **Times** 12–3/6.30-9 **Prices** Fixed L 2 course £12.50, Fixed D 3 course £32.50, Tasting menu £55, Starter £5-£9, Main £10-£21, Dessert £6-£9, Service optional **Wines** 7 bottles over £30, 20 bottles under £30, 6 by glass **Parking** 17 **Notes** Sunday L £5, Vegetarian available, Children welcome

---

KNIGHTON   **Map 9 SO27**

Milebrook House Hotel

Modern, Traditional

tel: 01547 528632 **Milebrook LD7 1LT**
email: hotel@milebrookhouse.co.uk **web:** www.milebrookhouse.co.uk
dir: *2m E of Knighton on A4113 (Ludlow)*

Quality British food on the Welsh-English border

Travellers may be fascinated to learn that this rather grand 18th-century stone house in the the embrace of the buxom Marches hills is the former home of legendary explorer Sir Wilfred Thesiger. Milebrook sits in immaculately-tended formal gardens, including a handy kitchen garden which provides a good proportion of the vegetables that end up on your plate. It's a deeply traditional place, much-loved by shooting parties, and with a skilled hand in the kitchen to tailor the menus. The owners have tracked down the best local suppliers and deliver country-house classics cooked with flair and imagination – perhaps smoked haddock and

sorrel risotto cake with spring onion purée and samphire butter, ahead of slow-braised pig cheek with smoked garlic mash, spring greens and caramelised onions. Desserts such as dark chocolate mousse with poached strawberries and honeycomb marshmallow hit the spot, or there are artisan cheeses from both sides of the border.

Times 12–2/6.30-9 Closed L Mon

LLANDRINDOD WELLS   **Map 9 SO06**

The Metropole

Modern British ⓥ

tel: 01597 823700 **Temple St LD1 5DY**
email: info@metropole.co.uk **web:** www.metropole.co.uk
dir: *In centre of town off A483, car park at rear*

Stylish spa hotel with sound modern cooking using regional fare

Run by the same family since Queen Victoria's reign, The Metropole has long been a local landmark with its soaring turrets, opening in the town's heyday as a spa resort. Today's hotel offers 21st-century spa treatments. It also has a couple of dining options, with an informal brasserie, and the Radnor and Miles Restaurant, which takes a slightly more formal approach, with white linen-clad tables and high-backed leather chairs. There's a regional flavour to the menu, with plenty of game in season, and lamb, beef and chicken cooked on the grill. Smoked haddock, shallot and watercress soup with summer truffle oil is a simple enough starter, delivering good flavours, but you might also begin with a pressing of Gressingham duck and foie gras with apples and sloe gin. Next up, grilled sea bass – soft flesh, crispy skin – or Welsh ham hock pot-au-feu with cassoulet, and, for dessert, a riff on rhubarb.

Chef Nick Edwards **Owner** Justin Baird-Murray **Seats** 46, Pr/dining room 250 **Times** 12–2.15/6-9.30 **Prices** Prices not confirmed **Wines** 4 bottles over £30, 29 bottles under £30, 9 by glass **Parking** 150 **Notes** Sunday L, Children welcome

---

LLANFYLLIN   **Map 15 SJ11**

Seeds

Modern British

tel: 01691 648604 **5-6 Penybryn Cottages, High St SY22 5AP**
dir: *In village centre. Take A490 N from Welshpool, follow signs to Llanfyllin*

Accurate cooking in an intimate, relaxed setting

When you don't require your food to push any culinary boundaries or arrive with froths and gels, try Seeds, a superbly relaxing little bistro with an intimate ambience (there are just 20 seats) in a 500-year-old terrace, run by an amiable husband-and-wife-team and their welcoming and unstuffy staff. Mellow jazz floats around the artworks and curios decorating the low-beamed, slate-floored dining room as chef-patron Mark Seager works the stoves of a bijou kitchen, turning out simple, tasty classic bistro dishes. Starters can be as simple as warm black pudding salad with blackcurrant sauce or home-made chicken liver pâté with chutney and toast, while mains take in the likes of rack of Welsh fillet steak with brandy and cream sauce, or grilled sea bass fillet served on roasted cherry tomatoes with balsamic. Desserts follow a similar vein of classic comfort – perhaps bread and butter pudding with cream, or classic crème brûlée.

Chef Mark Seager **Owner** Felicity & Mark Seager **Seats** 20 **Times** 11–2.30/7-9 Closed 25 Dec, 1 wk Feb, 1 wk Aug, 1 wk Oct, Sun-Mon (Sun-Wed winter) **Prices** Fixed D 3 course £27.95-£31.70, Starter £4.50-£6.95, Main £9.50-£18.95, Dessert £4.95-£6.95, Service optional **Wines** 19 bottles over £30, 74 bottles under £30, 3 by glass **Parking** Free town car park, on street **Notes** Pre-music festival menu Jun-Jul, Vegetarian available, Children welcome

LLANGAMMARCH WELLS

Map 9 SN94

The Lake Country House & Spa

◉◉ Modern British

tel: 01591 620202 **LD4 4BS**
email: info@lakecountryhouse.co.uk **web:** www.lakecountryhouse.co.uk
dir: W from Builth Wells on A483 to Garth (approx 6m). Left for Llangammarch Wells, follow hotel signs

Classy modern cooking in a relaxing country house

If you're looking to escape for a few days, The Lake Country House has everything to keep you happy whatever floats your boat. Whether you come for the golf or fishing, to pamper yourself in the spa or simply lose yourself in the gardens for a little while, it's all here. The house has a good deal of period charm – it dates from the 1840s – and the fixtures and fittings give the place an air of understated classical grandeur, not least in the dining room with its smartly dressed tables. The kitchen is not adverse to a touch of modernism, albeit discreetly so, and on a bedrock of sound classical thinking. After canapés in the lounge, you might start with ham hock rillettes with a spiced apple purée, or a terrine filled with Swansea seafood and leeks served with saffron and tomato dressing and caviar. Amongst main courses, fillet of sea bass comes with roasted tomatoes, salsa verde, confit leeks and tempura scallop, and to finish, sticky toffee pudding has accompanying honeycomb, rosemary ice cream and roasted fig.

Chef Darren Tattersall **Owner** Jean Pierre & Jan Mifsud **Seats** 80, Pr/dining room 70 **Times** 12.30-2/7-9 **Prices** Fixed L 2 course £22.50, Fixed D 3 course £45, Service optional **Wines** 120 bottles over £30, 15 bottles under £30, 9 by glass **Parking** 40 **Notes** Sunday L £22.50-£26.50, Vegetarian available, Children 8 yrs+

LLANWDDYN

Map 15 SJ01

Lake Vyrnwy Hotel & Spa

◉ Modern British

tel: 01691 870692 **Lake Vyrnwy SY10 0LY**
email: info@lakevyrnwyhotel.co.uk **web:** www.lakevyrnwy.com
dir: on A4393, 200yds past dam turn sharp right into drive

Interesting menus, breathtaking views

Birdwatching, fishing and hill walking are all possibilities at this stylish Victorian hotel with lovely views over the eponymous lake, and where better to end a day than with dinner in the conservatory restaurant. Local produce is the backbone of the

continued

Llangoed Hall

LLYSWEN

Map 9 SO13

Modern British, European V ◆ NOTABLE WINE LIST
tel: 01874 754525 **LD3 0YP**
email: enquiries@llangoedhall.co.uk **web:** www.llangoedhall.co.uk
dir: On A470, 2m from Llyswen towards Builth Wells

Elegant food in a Brecon country house

Tucked away in the rolling Wye Valley, Llangoed makes a great bolthole for visits to the Brecon Beacons National Park, as well as the literary goings-on at Hay-on-Wye, nine miles off. There are seven acres of fabulous landscaped gardens to roam, or if you're up to the challenge, the nearby Black Mountains offer more testing hikes. It is a grand house with some parts going back to the early Stuart era, and others, such as the sweeping pillared gallery, added by Clough Williams-Ellis (of Portmeirion fame) just before the Great War, all splendidly maintained inside with an emphasis on gracious classicism. Wedgwood blue is the relaxing tone in the dining room, where tables are decorously draped in floor-length linen and artworks by the likes of Whistler and Augustus John adorn the walls. Head chef Nick Brodie brings a similar lightness of touch and attention to detail to the

food, much of it sourced from Llangoed's own organically run kitchen garden. Dinner might take you from a thought-provoking opener of juniper-cured Welsh venison with blueberries, Douglas fir, pickled shallot and wild mushrooms, to a main course featuring turbot poached in red wine and star anise with salsify, watercress foam, truffle, rainbow chard and crosnes. Those seeking meatier satisfaction might find a fillet of Welsh Black beef in the company of cime di rapa greens, onion in various textures, pomme purée, chanterelles and peppercorn sauce. Desserts could bring down the curtain with an ingenious serving of pineapple raviolo with mascarpone cheesecake and coconut sorbet garnished with passionfruit and lychee, while only the finest Valrhona chocolate will do for a dark chocolate crémeux with salted caramel, peanuts and flourless chocolate cake. The weighty, globetrotting wine list offers much to peruse at length.

Chef Nick Brodie **Owner** Llangoed Ltd **Seats** 40, Pr/dining room 96 **Times** 12.30-2/6.30-9.30 **Prices** Prices not confirmed, Service optional 10% **Wines** 7 by glass **Parking** 50 **Notes** Sunday L, Children welcome

LLANWDDYD *continued*

kitchen's output, some from the estate itself: pheasant, for instance, in a fricassee with bacon, button onions, peppers and caramelised apple. Another well-composed main course might see accurately timed pan-fried hake fillet served with crushed new potatoes, brown shrimps, peas and garlic butter, or roast duck breast with braised red cabbage, fondant potato and a date and cherry sauce. Hits among starters include baked pigeon pithivier with lentils and oyster mushrooms and game jus, and smoked halibut rillettes wasabi with pickled onion. Puddings bring a meal to a happy conclusion with orange and lemon curd tart with raspberry sorbet, or limoncello pannacotta.

Chef David Thompson **Owner** The Bisiker family **Seats** 85, Pr/dining room 220 **Times** 12-2/6.45-9.15 **Prices** Prices not confirmed **Wines** 29 bottles over £30, 55 bottles under £30, 10 by glass **Parking** 80 **Notes** Sunday L, Vegetarian available, Children welcome

---

| **LLANWRTYD WELLS** | Map 9 SN84 |

Carlton Riverside
◉◉ Modern British

tel: 01591 610248 **Irfon Crescent LD5 4SP**
email: carltonriverside@hotmail.co.uk web: www.carltonriverside.com
dir: *In town centre beside bridge*

Creative cooking in family-run riverside restaurant

Its name is a bit of a giveaway: this small restaurant is beside the River Irfon running through the village. The restaurant's large windows let in plenty of light, while at night, when the beige-patterned curtains are closed, the lighting level is pitched to create an intimate feel in the elegantly decorated room. An amuse-bouche of leek and potato soup can get things off to a resounding start before chicken and pork terrine with plum chutney, or a plate of charcuterie with a textbook version of celeriac remoulade. The kitchen's clearly well versed in the classical repertory, and technical skills are evident too in a main course of Dover sole with salmon mousse, chive beurre blanc and crushed potatoes. While some dishes can appear busy, a steady nerve keeps them balanced and flavours pull together, not apart, as in partridge breast on cabbage and bacon, served with a venison noisette, and game pie in a ramekin under a pastry lid, all accompanied by port and game jus and dauphinoise. Finish with a trio of rhubarb: jelly, fool and crumble.

Chef Mary Ann Gilchrist **Owner** Dr & Mrs Gilchrist **Seats** 20 **Times** 7-9 Closed Xmas, Sun, L all week **Prices** Starter £6-£12, Main £15.95-£27, Dessert £6-£9, Service optional **Wines** 13 bottles over £30, 35 bottles under £30, 4 by glass **Parking** Car park opposite **Notes** Vegetarian available, Children welcome

Lasswade Country House
◉◉ Modern British

tel: 01591 610515 **Station Rd LD5 4RW**
email: info@lasswadehotel.co.uk web: www.lasswadehotel.co.uk
dir: *Exit A483 into Irfon Terrace, right into Station Rd, 350yds on right*

Organic focus in an Edwardian country house

Run with great charm by owners Roger and Emma Stevens, this grand Edwardian house sits at the edge of the Victorian spa town with 360-degree views of the Cambrian Mountains and Brecon Beacons. It's a soothing spot, and when you add the chef-proprietor's skilled modern British cooking into the deal, the whole package is an inviting prospect. After pre-dinner drinks in the homely lounge, it all takes place in a traditional-style dining room kitted out with burnished mahogany furniture. Driven by a passion for sourcing organic and sustainable produce from Wales and the Marches area, Roger keeps combinations straightforward, timings accurate, and interweaves flavours intelligently. Expect daily-changing dinner menus to get going with home-smoked trout fillets matched with potato and radish

salad, and lemon and thyme oil, followed, perhaps, by a plate of that splendid Cambrian mountain lamb, comprising roast rump, braised breast and sautéed kidneys in grain mustard and tomato sauce with leek soufflé and Madeira wine reduction.

Chef Roger Stevens **Owner** Roger & Emma Stevens **Seats** 20, Pr/dining room 20 **Times** 7.30-9.30 Closed 25-26 Dec, L all week **Prices** Prices not confirmed, Service optional **Wines** 3 bottles over £30, 17 bottles under £30, 4 by glass **Parking** 6 **Notes** Vegetarian available, No children

---

| **LLYSWEN** | Map 9 SO13 |

Llangoed Hall
◉◉◉ – *see page 685*

| **RHONDDA CYNON TAFF** |

| **MISKIN** | Map 9 ST08 |

Miskin Manor Country Hotel
◉◉ Modern, Traditional British **v**

tel: 01443 224204 **Pendoylan Rd CF72 8ND**
email: info@miskin-manor.co.uk web: www.miskin-manor.co.uk
dir: *M4 junct 34, exit onto A4119, signed Llantrisant, hotel 300yds on left*

Inventive modern British cooking in tranquil setting

Buffered from the frenetic M4 and Cardiff's outskirts by 22 acres of grounds with fabulously colourful gardens, Miskin Manor supplies history and contemporary style in equal measure. The romantic Meisgyn Restaurant has an atmospheric Gothic edge, thanks to its curvaceous wrought-iron seats, oak panelling and swagged-back gauzy curtains, but the kitchen team is on-message with modern culinary trends. The brigade takes a serious approach, growing vegetables and herbs in the gardens, and turning out top-notch bread, cakes and desserts from its in-house pastry section. To start, grouse comes in a modish three-way format – confit leg, breast, and mini Scotch egg – while main course might see another trio, lamb this time, served as mini rack, loin, and rolled shoulder, with bubble-and-squeak mash, pumpkin purée, wilted chard, and garden mint sauce. Dessert plays a riff on the rhubarb and custard theme, delivering creamy custard tart with nutmeg and a custard-filled doughnut with a contrasting hit of slightly sharp poached rhubarb.

Chef David Owen **Owner** Mr & Mrs Rosenberg **Seats** 50, Pr/dining room 30 **Times** 12-2.30/6-10 Closed D 25-26 Dec **Prices** Prices not confirmed, Service optional **Wines** 16 bottles over £30, 27 bottles under £30, 12 by glass **Parking** 200 **Notes** Sunday L, Children welcome

---

| **PONTYCLUN** | Map 9 ST08 |

La Luna
◉ Modern International

tel: 01443 239600 **79-81 Talbot Rd, Talbot Green CF72 8AE**
email: info@la-lunarestaurant.com
dir: *M4 junct 34, follow signs for Llantrisant, turn left at 2nd lights*

Relaxed bistro dining near the shops

Describing itself as a brasserie and lounge bar, La Luna is opposite the village's retail park and is not surprisingly a big hit for lunchtime shoppers seeking out the bargain fixed-price offer. There's an excellent value early evening menu, too. The place has an unpretentious, modish vibe on the inside, and a few tables outside for when the sun shines on South Wales. The menu suits the relaxed mood with its unfussy brasserie repertoire; start with chorizo and roasted vegetable risotto, for example, and move on to slow-cooked pork belly with crushed potatoes and rich jus. There are steaks cooked on the grill – sourced from the Usk Valley and matured for 21 days – while a fish main course might be pan-fried sea bass with warm crab

Niçoise and a Spanish-style coriander sauce. When it comes to dessert, how about a chocolate fondant?

Times 12-3/6-10 Closed 24 Dec, 1 Jan & BHs, Mon, D Sun

PONTYPRIDD Map 9 ST08

Llechwen Hall Hotel

Modern Welsh

tel: 01443 742050 **Llanfabon CF37 4HP**
email: reservations@llechwenhall.co.uk **web:** www.llechwen.co.uk
dir: A470 N towards Merthyr Tydfil. 3rd exit at large rdbt then 3rd exit at mini rdbt, hotel signed 0.5m on left

Scenic, historical setting for unfussy cooking

Overlooking four valleys from its hilltop perch, and set in six acres of gorgeous grounds, it's easy to see why Llechwen Hall does such a roaring trade with the wedding parties – there's even a permanent marquee in the grounds. But you don't need to be tying the knot to come here, since the Oak Beam Restaurant is an attractive proposition for a romantic dinner, housed in the traditional 17th-century beamed longhouse, where well-appointed tables are laid with crisp white linen. Taking its cue from carefully-sourced local ingredients, the kitchen deals in a straightforward, modern repertoire that might start with mature Welsh cheese brûlée with asparagus and poppy seed biscuits, before moving on to sautéed cod with crab beignets, celeriac, and dill and lemon remoulade. Whether you go for a savoury or sweet ending, do it on a Welsh note with either a slate of Welsh cheeses, or pice ar y maen baked cheesecake with strawberry compôte.

Chef Paul Trask **Owner** Ramish Gor **Seats** 35, Pr/dining room 300 **Times** 12-2/7-9 **Prices** Starter £4.95-£7.95, Main £11.95-£23.95, Dessert £4.50, Service optional **Wines** 10 bottles over £30, 25 bottles under £30, 4 by glass **Parking** 100 **Notes** Sunday L £9.95-£12.95, Vegetarian available, Children welcome

SWANSEA

REYNOLDSTON Map 8 SS48

Fairyhill

Modern British V NOTABLE WINE LIST

tel: 01792 390139 **SA3 1BS**
email: postbox@fairyhill.net **web:** www.fairyhill.net
dir: M4 junct 47, take A483 then A484 to Llanelli, Gower, Gowerton. At Gowerton follow B4295 for approx 10m

Elegant country-house hotel in lovely setting with real local flavour

This period country house in its hugely tranquil location hits the sweet spot between old-school formality and contemporary good taste. You're in safe hands, and you know it. There are 24 acres of grounds to explore, with streams, waterfalls and woods, and plenty of luxurious spaces within. The restaurant makes excellent use of the produce from the region and delivers a refined experience that doesn't feel in the least bit stuffy. The smart modern British cooking might see you start with Perl Las beignets with walnuts and poached pear, or head off further south for pan-seared stuffed baby squid with tomato fondue, chorizo and capers. Main-course Welsh pork belly comes in a fashionable partnership with Caldey Island lobster, while dessert brings forth iced lemon parfait with blackcurrant and mint. If you're staying the night in one of the stylish bedrooms you'll have good cause to dive into the phenomenally good wine list with gusto.

Chef Paul Davies, David Whitecross **Owner** Mr Hetherington, Mr Davies **Seats** 60, Pr/dining room 40 **Times** 12-2/7-9 Closed 26 Dec, 1-25 Jan **Prices** Fixed L 2 course £20, Fixed D 3 course £45, Service optional **Wines** 120 bottles over £30, 50 bottles under £30, 10 by glass **Parking** 45 **Notes** Sunday L £27.50, Children 8 yrs+

SWANSEA Map 9 SS69

The Dragon Hotel

Modern European

tel: 01792 657100 & 657159 **Kingsway Circle SA1 5LS**
email: enquiries@dragon-hotel.co.uk **web:** www.dragon-hotel.co.uk
dir: M4 junct 42, A483 follow signs for city centre A4067. After lights at Sainsbury's right onto The Strand then left into Kings Ln. Hotel straight ahead

A touch of modern style in the heart of Swansea

The Dragon is breathing fire after a megabucks renovation has brought everything up to full contemporary spec, making the most of its location in the thick of Swansea's town centre action. The buzzy Dragon Brasserie is in pole position for watching the world go by: ringside seats look through floor-to-ceiling windows onto the high street in a thoroughly modern venue with exposed industrial ducting and spotlights above bare darkwood tables and pale wooden floors. The cooking is well-focused and in tune with the setting, offering straightforward modern European dishes built from local produce; keenly-priced two or three-course dinner menus could get going with smooth chicken liver parfait with pear and ginger chutney, then move on to confit belly pork with pork and apple sausage and spring onion mash. Dessert might be saffron and vanilla crème brûlée with chocolate shortbread.

Chef Steve Williams **Owner** Dragon Hotel Ltd **Seats** 65, Pr/dining room 80 **Times** 12-2.30/6-9.30 **Prices** Fixed L 2 course £12.50, Fixed D 3 course £24.95, Starter £5.95-£7.50, Main £12.50-£21.95, Dessert £5.95-£6.95, Service optional **Wines** 6 bottles over £30, 33 bottles under £30, 13 by glass **Parking** 50 **Notes** Tasting menu & pre-theatre menu by reservation only, Sunday L £12.50-£16.95, Vegetarian available, Children welcome

Hanson at the Chelsea Restaurant

Modern Welsh, French

tel: 01792 464068 **17 St Mary St SA1 3LH**
email: andrew_hanson@live.co.uk
dir: In small lane between St Mary Church & Wine St

Appealing bistro cooking in a popular city-centre venue

Andrew Hanson's unassuming-looking restaurant is tucked away down a narrow side-street in the city centre, making it among other things a rather popular lunchtime venue. It looks like a classic modern bistro inside with clothed tables pressed in cheek by jowl, blackboard menus and small framed pictures against a delicate yellow colour-scheme. The service tone is as relaxing and friendly as can be, and the cooking an appealing mix of local produce and French influences, with the emphasis on fish and seafood, but not forgetting fine Welsh lamb. A risotto is often a good test, and the kitchen turns out an exemplary wild mushroom version packed with different varieties, topped with parmesan and moreish herb oil. Fish shines out at main with a sensitively timed piece of cod fillet in beurre blanc topped with leeks and breadcrumbs, while meat-eaters may well be tempted by pork belly cooked for eight hours and served with Pink Lady apple glaze, sage and onion mash and scrumpy sauce. Finish with lemon tart or sticky toffee pudding.

Chef Andrew Hanson, Gareth Sillman, Sam Beddoe **Owner** Andrew & Michelle Hanson **Seats** 50, Pr/dining room 20 **Times** 12-2/7-10 Closed 25-26 Dec, BHs, Sun **Prices** Fixed L 2 course £12.95-£16.95, Fixed D 3 course £19.95, Starter £4.50-£8.95, Main £11.95-£23.50, Dessert £5.75 **Wines** 8 by glass **Notes** Vegetarian available, Children welcome

VALE OF GLAMORGAN

HENSOL
Map 9 ST07

Vale Resort

◉ Modern British

tel: 01443 667800 **Hensol Park CF72 8JY**
email: sales@vale-hotel.com **web:** www.vale-hotel.com
dir: M4 junct 34, exit signed Pendoylan, turn 1st right twice, then 1st left before white house on bend. Hotel on right

Welsh resort hotel with local flavour

This large and luxurious contemporary resort hotel has it all, in spades: a great location near Cardiff and the Glamorgan coast, 650 acres of grounds with a brace of golf courses, and the largest spa complex in Wales. Appetite, therefore, should not be lacking for the kitchen's straightforward modern repertoire, served in the smart bistro-style Vale Grill, a clean-cut space with bare darkwood tables and views of the cheffy action in the open kitchen. Locally-sourced ingredients get a good showing, particularly prime Welsh beef – no, not the Welsh rugby team, who you might meet here after a training session – but a slab of sirloin steak served sizzling from the open grill with béarnaise and triple-cooked chips. On a more delicate note, there could be grey mullet fillet with rocket and pesto risotto, broad beans, salsify, and tapenade dressing, and to finish, apricot bavarois and jelly paired with Earl Grey tea ice cream.

Chef Daniel James **Owner** The Leekes family **Seats** 80, Pr/dining room 50 **Times** 7-11 Closed L all week **Prices** Prices not confirmed **Wines** **Parking** 500 **Notes** Sunday L, Vegetarian available, Children welcome

WREXHAM

LLANARMON DYFFRYN CEIRIOG
Map 15 SJ13

The Hand at Llanarmon

◉ Modern British

tel: 01691 600666 **Ceiriog Valley LL20 7LD**
email: reception@thehandhotel.co.uk **web:** www.thehandhotel.co.uk
dir: Leave A5 at Chirk onto B4500 signed Ceiriog Valley, continue for 11m

Modern European cooking in a whitewashed Ceiriog inn

A whitewashed country inn buried in the sumptuous Ceiriog Valley, the Hand makes a concerted effort to come up to rustic expectations inside, with dozing dogs toasting themselves before the open fires, plenty of chunky furniture and brass ornaments, and a photographic gallery of the area in days gone by. A stuffed fox stands sentinel in the hallway. The kitchen turns out some impressive renditions of modern European food, beginning with braised beef and tomato risotto, or confit duck with Perl Lâs cheese, walnuts and almonds, and continuing with sensitively cooked, crisp-skinned mullet fillet with creamed leeks, peas, gem lettuce and a heap of mash. Welsh lamb is naturally a strong point, especially when it comes with McArdle's black pudding from Chirk, and a fruity redcurrant and red wine sauce. Finish in heartwarming fashion with oat-topped Bramley apple and gooseberry crumble, served with decent custard, or Welsh cheeses and oatcakes.

Times 12-2.20/6.30-8.45 Closed 25 Dec

Northern Ireland

NORTHERN IRELAND
CO ANTRIM

BALLYMENA Map 1 D5

Galgorm Resort & Spa

◉◉ Modern British V ♦ NOTABLE WINE LIST

tel: 028 2588 1001 **136 Fenaghy Rd, Galgorm BT42 1EA**
email: sales@galgorm.com web: www.galgorm.com
dir: *1m from Ballymena on A42, between Galgorm & Cullybackey*

Modish cooking by the river

The River Room Restaurant at the Galgorm Resort delivers on its billing with the fast-flowing River Maine serving up a charming vista. And the floor-to-ceiling windows ensure everyone gets a gander, with the river floodlit at night to create an alluring atmosphere. It all takes place in a swanky resort with three dining options, luxurious rooms, swish spa and posh conference facilities, on a 163-acre estate. The kitchen is the forward-looking, dynamic engine of the place, with a good deal of ambition on show. Things start in style with an amuse-bouche such as pan-fried scallop with wild garlic cream before a first-course ravioli of local rabbit with black pudding purée, apples (caramelised and au naturel), English mustard and watercress sauce. Next up, pan-roasted halibut with a crab rösti, cauliflower, samphire, wild garlic, lobster and fennel shows considered balancing of flavours and textures, and for dessert, liquorice parfait comes with poached rhubarb, rhubarb jelly and sorbet, honeycomb and strawberry.

Chef Chris Rees **Owner** Nicholas & Paul Hill **Seats** 42 **Times** 12-2.30/6.30-9.30 Closed Mon-Tue, L Wed-Sat **Wines** 200 bottles over £30, 54 bottles under £30, 12 by glass **Parking** 200 **Notes** Sunday L £24-£28, Children welcome

BUSHMILLS Map 1 C6

Bushmills Inn Hotel

◉ Modern Irish with a twist V

tel: 028 2073 3000 **9 Dunluce Rd BT57 8QG**
email: mail@bushmillsinn.com web: www.bushmillsinn.com
dir: *2m from Giant's Causeway on A2 in Bushmills after crossing river*

Locally-based cooking near the Giant's Causeway

Whiskey, golf and historic landmarks, Bushmills has proximity to the traveller's holy trinity around these parts: the Old Bushmills Distillery, Royal Portrush Golf Club and the Giant's Causeway. The 17th-century coaching inn is these days a refuge with bags of boutique style and charm. There's a bar done out with lavishly burnished wood, a 30-seater cinema, and a restaurant that keeps pace with the times. There's a good deal of local produce on show, from land and sea, so you might start with Ulster beef carpaccio, or smoked haddock and leek risotto, before moving on to Barbary duck served with spiced red cabbage, celeriac purée and red wine jus, or sea bass fillets with razor clams, buttered spinach and seafood 'essence'. And to finish, chocolate and caramel tart is made with hazelnut and almond pastry, and comes with a Morello cherry sorbet.

Chef Gordon McGladdery, Donna Thompson **Owner** Alan Dunlop **Seats** 120 **Times** 12-5/6-9.30 **Prices** Starter £5.35-£8.95, Main £12.75-£23.50, Dessert £5.95-£7.85, Service optional **Wines** 47 bottles over £30, 39 bottles under £30, 8 by glass **Parking** 70 **Notes** Sunday L £13.85, Children welcome

BELFAST

BELFAST Map 1 D5

Beatrice Kennedy

◉ Modern, Traditional Irish, International V

tel: 028 9020 2290 **44 University Rd BT7 1NJ**
email: reservations@beatricekennedy.co.uk
dir: *Adjacent to Queens University*

Modern bistro food in the university district

The continent never feels far away in this quirky restaurant in the university district, whether you're taken across the Channel by the rich pink and green walls with shelves of books, wooden floors and leather chairs that give off the ambience of a wartime bistro, or the plentiful European references on the eclectic menu. It is a buzzy little venue where all of the front-of-house team pitch in with an unfussy hands-on attitude. Chef-patron Jim McCarthy shows sound talent and avoids complication by concentrating attention on the main ingredients, serving up seared foie gras with gingerbread, apple and cinnamon compôte and a port reduction, followed by rump of wild Irish venison with a croquette of braised shin, squash gnocchi, and parsnip purée. On the fish front, baked Atlantic cod could appear alongside artichoke and salsify risotto, white onion and truffle. For dessert, how about sticky toffee pudding with butterscotch sauce and vanilla ice cream?

Chef Jim McCarthy, Dave O'Callaghan **Owner** Jim McCarthy **Seats** 75, Pr/dining room 25 **Times** 12.30-3/5-10.30 Closed 24-26 Dec, 1 Jan, Etr, Mon, L Tue-Sat **Prices** Fixed D 2 course fr £14.95, Tasting menu fr £35, Starter £4.50-£9.95, Main £15-£20, Dessert £5, Service optional **Wines** 6 bottles over £30, 25 bottles under £30, 4 by glass **Parking** On street **Notes** Pre-theatre menu 5-7pm £14.95, 6 course £40, Sunday L fr £18.50, Children welcome

Café Vaudeville

🏵 French

- -

tel: 028 9043 9160 **25-39 Arthur St BT1 4GQ**
email: info@cafevaudeville.com

Big-flavoured brasserie dishes in a historic city-centre building

In the early 19th century, the premises belonged to an entrepreneur named Dunville, dealer in tea and fine whiskies. After a long incarnation as a bank, the grand city-centre edifice is now a stylish contemporary eatery, its high-ceilinged spaces ringing with swing jazz (with live music on selected evenings). The aptly named Luxebar is one part of the operation, but the modern brasserie menus are a strong attraction too. Dishes are not too precious in their execution, but big on flavour, as in a starter of goats' cheese fritters rolled in crushed walnuts, with beetroot and apple balls in a robust cabernet sauvignon dressing. That could be followed by smoked salmon and cod fishcakes with lemon aïoli, or moistly tender pork belly cooked for 18 hours and served with Pommery mustard mash and garlic sausage in a sauce of the braising juices. Finish with professionally executed chocolate fondant and peanut butter ice cream.

Times 12-3/5-9 Closed Sun

Looking for a restaurant by name?
Use the index on page 751

Deanes at Queens

🏵 Modern British, Irish

- -

tel: 028 9038 2111 **1 College Gardens BT9 6BQ**
email: deanesatqueens@michaeldeane.co.uk
dir: *From city centre go towards Queens University then 1st left onto College Gardens, restaurant 1st on right*

Buzzy brasserie dining near the university

The name Michael Deane needs no introduction in these parts (see entry for EIPIC), and his buzzy bar and grill restaurant in the University Quarter is a hot-ticket in the city. The smart space has large windows to take in the view over the Botanic Gardens and a menu that favours a modish European approach. Start, perhaps, with duck rillettes with celeriac, red onion jam and country bread, or smoked haddock and leek fishcake served with an apple, cabbage and raisin coleslaw. Among main courses, Glenarm salmon is cooked perfectly (deliciously crisp skin) and comes with chorizo orzo pasta, crisp tempura vegetables and gremolata, or go for the 12-hour braised beef in a risotto with leek and parmesan, Serrano ham and Chianti. Finish with all the comfort and joy of a chocolate steamed pudding, with accompanying mint chocolate chip ice cream.

Chef Chris Fearon **Owner** Michael Deane **Seats** 120, Pr/dining room 44
Times 12-3/5.30-10 Closed 25-26 Dec, D Sun **Prices** Fixed L 2 course £12.50, Fixed D 3 course £15-£20, Starter £5-£9, Main £10-£16.50, Dessert £5-£6.50 **Wines** 17 bottles over £30, 24 bottles under £30, 12 by glass **Parking** On street **Notes** Prix Fixe menu 3 course £19.50 Mon-Thu 5.30-7, Sunday L £5-£16.50, Vegetarian available, Children welcome

EIPIC

Rosettes not confirmed at time of going to print – see below

EIPIC

Rosettes not confirmed at time of going to print

BELFAST   Map 1 D5

Modern European ⓥ
tel: 028 9033 1134 **36-40 Howard St BT1 6PF**
email: info@michaeldeane.co.uk **web:** www.michaeldeane.co.uk
dir: *At rear of City Hall. Howard St on left opposite Spires building*

Classy and confident cooking chez Michael Deane

Please note that the Rosette award for this establishment has been suspended due to a change of concept. Reassessment will take place in due course. Michael Deane is an elder statesman of the Northern Irish dining scene, although it's worth pointing out that he's only a shade over 50, and seemingly at the peak of his powers. These days he has a little empire around the city (EIPIC, Meat Locker, Love Fish, Deanes Deli, Deanes at Queens, Deane and Decano) providing the kind of food people want to eat, but here in Howard Street he really shows his culinary chops. It used to be a rather posh gaff, but has mellowed in recent years, remaining serious about the food on the plate, but less so about the other fripperies that come at the high end of eating out. Don't go thinking it is rough-and-ready, though, for this is a smart and classy operation, with neatly laid, linen-dressed tables on a dark-tiled floor and dark-toned walls. The bargain lunch menu is a good entry point for those on a budget, or in a hurry, as well as a la carte offering three courses with a trio of choices at each stage, all built on three components, and, of course, the full-works, seven-course tasting menu with each dish designated by just one ingredient.

Chef Michael Deane, Simon Toye, Danni Barry **Owner** Michael Deane **Seats** 30, Pr/dining room 50 **Times** 12-3/5.30-10 Closed 25 Dec, BHs, Sun-Tue, L Wed-Thu, Sat **Prices** Prices not confirmed **Wines** 76 bottles over £30, 25 bottles under £30, 8 by glass **Parking** On street (after 6pm), car park Clarence St **Notes** Tasting menus available L & D, Children welcome

BELFAST *continued*

James Street South Restaurant & Bar

◉◉ Modern European

tel: 028 9043 4310 **21 James Street South BT2 7GA**
email: info@jamesstreetsouth.co.uk
dir: *Located between Brunswick St & Bedford St*

Confident modern cooking in the city centre

Tucked away behind City Hall, this slick central restaurant has a strong local fan base for all the right reasons. Light floods the bright and spacious dining room through high-arched windows, revealing a pared-back contemporary look involving abstract art on white walls and dark brown leather seats on a blond-wood floor. The man directing the action at the stoves is Niall McKenna, who has built his reputation on solid foundations. Strong bonds with local suppliers are key to sourcing the best local materials, which he subjects to well-honed French techniques in a blend of classical and bright up-to-date ideas. Red gurnard comes with a concasse of tomato, chorizo and capers, and seaweed beurre blanc, ahead of a melt-in-the-mouth veal osso buco with raisin, roasted parsnips, and truffle and ricotta gnocchi, or there might be fillet of Antrim beef teamed with girolles, cauliflower and ox tongue. Dessert hits the spot with an imaginative confection of lemon vacherin with crispy pistachios, curd and fromage frais sorbet.

Chef Niall McKenna **Owner** Niall & Joanne McKenna **Seats** 60, Pr/dining room 40 **Times** 12-2.45/5.45-10.45 Closed 25-26 Dec, 1 Jan, Etr Sun & Mon, 12-15 Jul, Sun **Prices** Prices not confirmed, Service optional **Wines** 35 bottles over £30, 40 bottles under £30, 11 by glass **Parking** On street **Notes** Pre-theatre menu Mon-Sat 2/3 course, Vegetarian available, Children welcome

Malmaison Belfast

◉ Modern French

tel: 028 9022 0200 & 9022 0201 **34-38 Victoria St BT1 3GH**
email: belfast@malmaison.com **web:** www.malmaison.com
dir: *M1 along Westlink to Grosvenor Rd. Follow city centre signs. Pass City Hall on right, turn left onto Victoria St. Hotel on right*

Globally-inspired menu combined with stylish modern decor

The grand industrial proportions and features of this former seed warehouse make the perfect spot for the Mal brand to spread its wings into Belfast. It's got the expected swagger and urban-chic interior, of course, including a pool table in the bar, plus stylish bedrooms and a brasserie that is by turns classy and casual. The menu takes a broad sweep, delivering some perky, modern ideas. There are Asian flavours in starters such as Thai roast pumpkin soup or chicken lollipops, satay, Moroccan-spiced croquette and Thai bonbon, but equally you might go for a classic Caesar salad. Main courses are equally globally-minded, with chicken tikka in a masala sauce sitting alongside smoked haddock fishcake with spinach, poached egg and hollandaise sauce. There are steaks cooked on the grill and burgers, too, and for dessert dishes such as pear tarte Tatin with malt ice cream.

Chef Kyle Greer **Owner** MWB **Seats** 55, Pr/dining room 22 **Times** 12-2.30/6-10.30 **Prices** Fixed L 2 course £15.95, Fixed D 3 course £19.95, Starter £5-£9.50, Main £12-£36, Dessert £6 **Wines** 26 bottles over £30, 16 bottles under £30, 27 by glass **Parking** On street **Notes** Sunday L £19.95, Vegetarian available, Children welcome

The Merchant Hotel

◉◉ Modern European V

tel: 028 9023 4888 **16 Skipper St, Cathedral Quarter BT1 2DZ**
email: thegreatroom@merchanthotel.com **web:** www.themerchanthotel.com
dir: *In city centre, 2nd left at Albert clock onto Waring St. Hotel on left*

Magnificent grand setting for inventive contemporary cooking

The Victorian former headquarters of Ulster Bank is a building on a grand scale – those bankers, hey? – and these days the beneficiaries are those that rock up to eat, drink or sleep at the decidedly swanky Merchant Hotel. There are cool boutique bedrooms, bars (including a happening jazz one), and, in The Great room, a fine-dining restaurant. The latter is a stunning space filled with marble columns and plasterwork under a glass-domed ceiling, with banquettes and chairs upholstered in rich red. The kitchen makes sense of it all with a classical-meets-modern repertoire that sees tip-top regional produce treated with respect. Dundrum crab stars in a first course with fennel and watercress purée and Portavogie prawn beignets, while seared foie gras comes with red-wine poached pear, crispy muesli and pain d'épice. Next up, assiette of squab pigeon (seared breast, confit wing, and foie gras-stuffed leg), or glazed turbot with Castelluccio lentils, guanciale and buttered kale. To finish, try lemon tart with honey clotted cream and raspberries, or French and Irish cheeses with seasonal fruit chutney and crackers.

Chef John Paul Leake **Owner** The Merchant Hotel **Seats** 85, Pr/dining room 18 **Times** 12-2.30/6-10 Closed L Sat **Prices** Prices not confirmed **Wines** 106 bottles over £30, 52 bottles under £30, 13 by glass **Parking** On street **Notes** Pre-theatre 2/3 course £18.50/£22.50, Sunday L, Children welcome

Ramada Encore Belfast City Centre

◉ Modern European NEW

tel: 028 9026 1800 & 9026 1809 **20 Talbot St BT1 2LD**
email: fandb@encorebelfast.co.uk **web:** www.encorebelfast.co.uk
dir: *On Dunbar Link & Talbot St behind St Annes Cathedral*

Vibrant modern setting for casual grill dining

Part of the substantial and prominent Ramada Encore hotel, the SQ Bar & Grill has its own entrance and feels like a stand-alone business. And a popular business it is: the bright and modern open-plan room positively buzzes with life, especially at weekends when there's live music adding to the feel-good vibe. There are cocktails, naturally, and a menu which takes a broad stroke through European cookery and counts Irish beef and Mourne lamb as signature ingredients, the latter as pan-roasted French-style rack – moist, tender and just pink – with roasted courgette and tomato salsa. Start with classic French soup or pan-fried scallops before one of those steaks (14oz rump, maybe, with triple-cooked chips), or go for SQ fish 'n' chips with lemon jelly and tarragon pesto. To finish, Irish cheeses compete for your attention with dark chocolate and chilli brownie with coriander ice cream.

Chef Robert Scott **Owner** Ducales Assets No 1 **Seats** 80, Pr/dining room 100 **Times** 12-10 All-day dining **Prices** Starter £4-£6, Main £11-£18, Dessert £5-£8, Service optional **Wines** 10 bottles under £30, 7 by glass **Parking** 100 **Notes** Sunday L £5-£18, Vegetarian available, Children welcome

Shu

◉◉ Modern Irish

tel: 028 9038 1655 **253-255 Lisburn Rd BT9 7EN**
email: eat@shu-restaurant.com
dir: *From city centre take Lisburn Rd (lower end). Restaurant in 1m, on corner of Lower Windsor Avenue*

Contemporary Irish cooking with a buzz and good service

If the name suggests an Asian influence, think again, for this a thoroughly European kind of restaurant, with classical French thinking as the foundation of the sharp, modern cooking on show. (Shu, by the way, is the ancient Egyptian god of atmosphere). Situated in a Victorian terrace in trendy Lisburn, the airy space with an open-to-view kitchen is served by a smartly turned out team. There is an Asian flavour in one or two dishes on the menu (salt and chilli squid, for example), but a more typical first course might be crispy duck confit with spiced red cabbage purée, or a mushroom risotto flavoured with Madeira and spiked with roast chestnuts. Main-course caramelised pork belly comes with more red cabbage, this time pickled, plus date purée and a sherry-flavoured jus, while a fishy main might be roast fillet of sea bream with a pumpkin and liquorice risotto. Finish with a dessert such as Valrhona chocolate and hazelnut brownie with an Earl Grey-infused chocolate sauce.

Chef Brian McCann **Owner** Alan Reid **Seats** 100, Pr/dining room 24
Times 12-2.30/6-10 Closed 25-26 Dec, 1 Jan, 12-13 Jul, Sun **Prices** Fixed L 2 course £13.25, Fixed D 3 course £28-£31.50, Starter £4.75-£9, Main £14.75-£27, Dessert £5.75, Service optional **Wines** 22 bottles over £30, 43 bottles under £30, 14 by glass **Parking** 4, On street **Notes** Vegetarian available, Children welcome

CO DOWN

CRAWFORDSBURN
Map 1 D5

The Old Inn

◉◉ Modern European

tel: 028 9185 3255 **15 Main St BT19 1JH**
email: info@theoldinn.com **web:** www.theoldinn.com
dir: *From Belfast along A2, past Belfast City Airport. Continue past Holywood & Belfast Folk & Transport museum. 2m after museum left at lights onto B20 for 1.2m*

Revamped restaurant in a historic old inn

As the oldest thatched part of the building dates from the early 17th century, it's fair to say that this sprawling low-slung hotel deserves its title. Over the centuries, an entertaining cast of famous writers and poets as well as the usual motley crew of smugglers has been fed and watered here. Nowadays, guests head for the smartly-refurbished Lewis restaurant, named after author C. S. Lewis who hung out here with his literary pals in the 1950s. The style is that of a contemporary bistro with a modish open-to-view kitchen turning out assured modern European-inflected ideas based on well-sourced Irish meat and game, and spanking-fresh seafood landed in the local ports of Strangford and Portavogie. The result is clear, bold flavours, as seen in a starter of chilled white crab with guacamole. At main course stage, take your pick from rosemary-skewered monkfish and salmon served with chargrilled fennel, smoked paprika, sautéed potatoes and lobster velouté, or a duo of duck breast and confit leg with chicken livers, pommes Anna, and passionfruit and redcurrant jus.

Owner Paul & Garvan Rice **Seats** 134, Pr/dining room 25 **Times** 12-9.30 Closed 25 Dec, All-day dining **Prices** Fixed L 2 course fr £8.95, Fixed D 3 course fr £26.50, Starter £5.50-£10.95, Main £12.95-£25.95, Dessert £4.95-£7, Service optional 10% **Wines** 8 bottles over £30, 38 bottles under £30, 11 by glass **Parking** 80 **Notes** Sizzler menu available £12.50, Sunday L £9.95-£24.50, Vegetarian available, Children welcome

DUNDRUM
Map 1 D5

Mourne Seafood Bar

◉ Seafood

tel: 028 4375 1377 **10 Main St BT33 0LU**
email: bob@mourneseafood.com
dir: *On main road from Belfast to The Mournes, on village main street*

Fresh fish and shellfish at the foot of the Mourne mountains

With a sister establishment in Belfast, the Dundrum branch of Mourne seafood is in a refreshingly peaceful location. At the foot of the Mourne mountains, with a nature reserve close by, it is dedicated of course to fish and shellfish, much of which comes from the proprietors' own seafood beds. The daily-changing menu offers its wares in a broad range of styles, from salt-and-chilli squid with garlic mayo, scallop linguine and wilted greens, or smoked mackerel pâté in lettuce cups to start, and then temptations such as grilled lobster or battered fish and chips with mushy peas following on. Accompaniments are always designed to suit the main items, so expect chorizo, chickpeas and tomato with hake, mustard mash and a poached egg with smoked haddock, or leeks and hollandaise with Glenarm salmon. If you're not of the fish persuasion, there are sirloin steaks with fat chips and béarnaise sauce.

Chef Shea Trainor **Owner** Bob & Joanne McCoubrey **Seats** 75, Pr/dining room 20 **Times** 12.30-9.30 Closed 25 Dec, Mon-Thu (winter) All-day dining **Prices** Starter £4-£6.95, Main £8.95-£17, Dessert £4.50, Service optional **Wines** 6 bottles over £30, 12 bottles under £30, 5 by glass **Parking** On street **Notes** Fixed D menu Sat only, Sunday L £10-£18, Vegetarian available, Children welcome

Read our interview with chef Michael Caines on page 29

NEWTOWNARDS   Map 1 D5

Balloo House

◉ Traditional European

tel: 028 9754 1210 **1 Comber Rd, Killinchy BT23 6PA**
email: info@balloohouse.com **web:** www.balloohouse.com
dir: A22 from Belfast, through Dundonald. 6m from Comber

Lively bistro and serene dining room in a venerable old house

A coaching inn in the Georgian era and a farmhouse in the Victorian, this venerable whitewashed house near Strangford Lough has pretty much seen it all. Stone walls and flagged floors bear witness to its age, and the dining offers two moods – a ground-floor bistro with plenty of happy hubbub, and a more serene evening-only restaurant upstairs, where exposed walls are offset by champagne upholstery and an aura of relaxing civility. A cheery lunch down below might bring on salt and chilli squid with Asian slaw, chilli jam and garlic mayo, Gloucestershire Old Spot pork belly with roast apples, boxty (potato pancakes) and baconed cabbage, with dark chocolate torte and salt caramel ice cream to conclude, all served to a background of REM's greatest hits. Up above, creativity takes wing for Lough Neagh eel teriyaki with smoked eel fritter, apple and radish, duck breast with orange and fennel polenta and sweet-sour cherries, and buttermilk pannacotta with roast peach and raspberries. Certainly one to watch.

Chef Grainne Donnelly **Owner** Danny Millar **Seats** 80, Pr/dining room 30 **Times** 12-9 Closed 25 Dec, All-day dining **Prices** Fixed L 2 course fr £13.95, Fixed D 3 course fr £18.95, Starter £3.25-£6.95, Main £9.95-£21.95, Dessert £5.95-£6.95, Service optional **Wines** 19 bottles over £30, 44 bottles under £30, 7 by glass **Notes** Sunday L fr £22.95, Vegetarian available, Children welcome

CO FERMANAGH

ENNISKILLEN   Map 1 C5

Lough Erne Resort

◉◉ Modern, Traditional

tel: 028 6632 3230 **Belleek Rd BT93 7ED**
email: info@lougherneresort.com **web:** www.lougherneresort.com
dir: A46 from Enniskillen towards Donegal, hotel in 3m

Dynamic modern Irish cooking at a luxury resort hotel

The resort hotel may overlook the tranquil waters of the lough, but it sees more than its fair share of action. A course designed by Nick Faldo keeps golfers in clover, while the hotel hosted the 2013 G8 summit. Inside, the place is loaded with five-star facilities and features, all the way to the Catalina fine-dining restaurant, where smart table linen and swagged drapes create a refined backdrop for Noel McMeel's dynamic modern Irish cooking. Seasonality, localism and traceability are observed assiduously here and the results are stimulating and full of interest. First up might be a crown of locally shot quail alongside a bonbon of the confit leg meat mixed with black pudding, and garnishes of cauliflower purée and caramelised

pear. Dishes look quite busy but every element plays its part, as when Kilkeel cod comes with its own brandade and crayfish in a lemony, capery beurre noisette under parsley foam. Dessert might be intense apple financier with honey and clove custard and a scattering of crystallised seaweed.

Times 1-2.30/6.30-10 Closed L Mon-Sat

Manor House Country Hotel

◉◉ Irish, European

tel: 028 6862 2200 **Killadeas BT94 1NY**
email: info@manorhousecountryhotel.com **web:** www.manorhousecountryhotel.com
dir: On B82, 7m N of Enniskillen

Laudable cooking and loch views

The original manor is a striking building, much modified in the Victorian period when the Italianate tower was added. The Belleek Restaurant is in two parts, one in the old building, the other in a conservatory-style extension with views over Lower Lough Erne. The kitchen deploys the freshest produce from local suppliers and uses them to good effect on a compact menu that manages to encompass modern ideas as well as the more familiar. Roast chicken breast, for instance, served simply in its own juices with Savoy cabbage and mash, preceded by a starter of lobster ravioli stuffed with a generous amount of the crustacean, its flavour enhanced by a sauce of rocket, basil and lemongrass. A degree of complexity can be seen in some main courses – take roast olive-encrusted cannon of lamb, of excellent quality, with braised neck, fennel jam, rosemary jus, swede and broad beans – and a meal can end with a classic version of crème brûlée with cherry compôte.

Chef John Cooke **Owner** Liam & Mary McKenna **Seats** 90, Pr/dining room 350 **Times** 12.30-3/6-10 Closed L Mon-Fri, D Sun **Prices** Fixed L 3 course £19.95, Fixed D 3 course £35, Service optional **Wines** 20 bottles over £30, 40 bottles under £30 **Parking** 300 **Notes** Sunday L £19.95, Vegetarian available, Children welcome

CO LONDONDERRY

LIMAVADY   Map 1 C6

The Lime Tree

◉ Traditional Mediterranean

tel: 028 7776 4300 **60 Catherine St BT49 9DB**
email: info@limetreerest.com
dir: Enter Limavady from Derry side. Restaurant on right on small slip road

Long-running restaurant showcasing the pick of the province

Stanley and Maria Matthews have run their appealing neighbourhood restaurant since 1996 and it's a firmly entrenched presence on the local gastronomic scene. Named after the lime trees planted in Limavady in honour of local lad William Massey landing the top job as PM in New Zealand, the operation is intimate, cosy and impeccably run by Maria out front. Stanley mans the stoves, delivering the best of what Northern Ireland has to offer via Mediterranean-accented menus that continually evolve to take advantage of the splendid, slithering-fresh, locally-landed fish and seafood. The home-made crabcakes are quite rightly a fixture, and could be accompanied by apple salad and a cider and rapeseed oil dressing, while all that fresh fish might find its way into a Spanish-influenced stew laden with tomato and garlic; carnivores can expect chicken tajine with lemon, chilli and coriander. Finish with the deep comfort of steamed Seville orange marmalade sponge with vanilla custard.

Chef Stanley Matthews **Owner** Mr & Mrs S Matthews **Seats** 30 **Times** 12-2/5.30-9 Closed 25-26 Dec, 12 Jul, Sun-Mon, L Sun-Wed **Prices** Fixed L 2 course £11.50-£18, Starter £4.60-£7.95, Main £14.75-£22.50, Dessert £5.50-£6.95, Service optional **Wines** 7 bottles over £30, 29 bottles under £30, 5 by glass **Parking** On street **Notes** Early bird menu 2/3 course Tue-Sat 5.30-7pm, Vegetarian available, Children welcome

Roe Park Resort

@ Modern, Traditional

tel: 028 7772 2222 **BT49 9LB**
email: reservations@roeparkresort.com **web:** www.roeparkresort.com
dir: *On A6 (Londonderry-Limavady road), 0.5m from Limavady. 8m from Derry airport*

Traditional dining in a relaxed resort hotel

Built as a country mansion in the 18th century, surrounded by 150 acres of grounds beside the River Roe, Roe Park has been extended in recent years into a vast modern golfing and leisure resort. Just one of several dining options here, Greens Restaurant is a stylish, split-level space offering mostly traditional cooking with the odd modern twist. Start, perhaps, with confit duck rillette with toasted sourdough, beetroot and orange relish, moving on to fillet of Irish beef with potato croquette, confit garlic, button mushrooms and jus, or grilled salmon supreme with oriental noodles and a ginger and soy dressing. If cheesecake is your thing, there's a daily-changing selection of flavours, or you may want to go down the comfort route with the steamed banana and ginger pudding with fresh cream and sauce anglaise.

Chef Emma Gormley **Owner** Mr Conn, Mr McKeever, Mr Wilton **Seats** 160, Pr/dining room 50 **Times** 12-3/6.30-9 **Prices** Prices not confirmed, Service optional **Wines** 8 by glass **Parking** 250 **Notes** Sunday L, Vegetarian available, Children welcome

---

Browns Restaurant and Champagne Lounge

@ Modern Irish V

tel: 028 7134 5180 **1 Bonds Hill, Waterside BT47 6DW**
email: eat@brownsrestaurant.com
dir: *Phone for directions*

On-the-money modern Irish cooking

Situated on the edge of the city centre by Lough Foyle, Browns has quickly garnered a loyal local following since it opened its doors in 2009. Get in the mood with a glass of bubbly on a squidgy sofa in the champagne lounge, then head for one of the white linen-swathed tables in the dining room, where toffee-hued walls and leather seating, stripy banquettes, and pale wooden floors add up to a sharp contemporary look. Driven by well-sourced local ingredients and unfussy execution, the kitchen turns out an appealing roll-call of modern Irish ideas, with fish and seafood a strong suit. Pan-seared scallops are matched with braised pork cheek, honey and soy sauce, and apple and star anise purée, ahead of roast fillet of monkfish with cauliflower served crispy and in a curried cream sauce. To finish, Turkish Delight, chocolate cookies and ginger cream put a novel spin on crème brûlée.

Chef Ian Orr **Owner** Ian Orr **Seats** 60 **Times** 12-3/5.30-10 Closed 3 days Xmas, Mon, L Sat, D Sun **Prices** Fixed L 2 course £15, Fixed D 3 course £19.95-£21.90, Tasting menu £40, Starter £7.50-£11.95, Main £18.50-£23.50, Dessert £5.95, Service optional **Wines** 35 bottles over £30, 51 bottles under £30, 14 by glass **Parking** On street **Notes** Tasting menu 6 course, Early bird £19.95 Tue-Sat, Children welcome

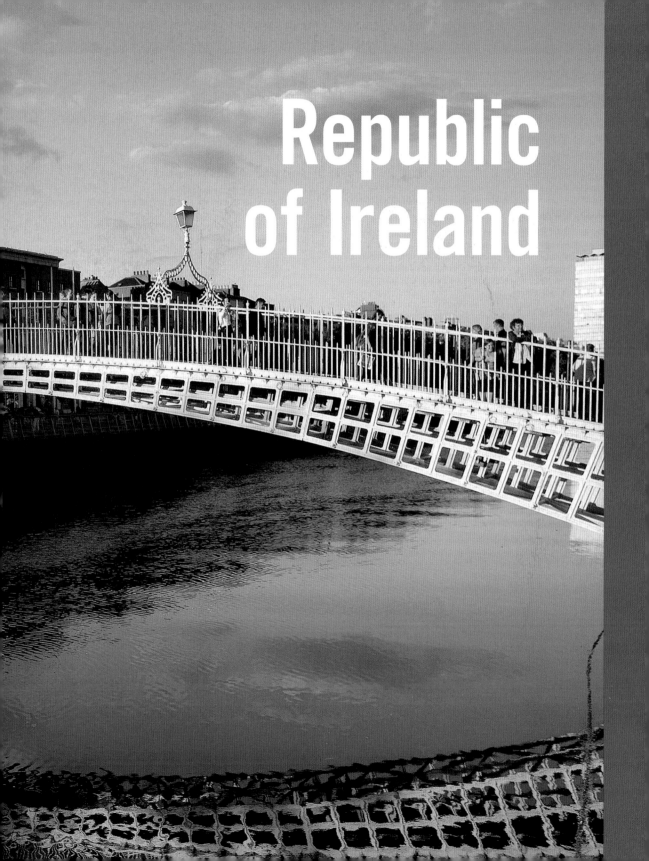

Republic
of Ireland

REPUBLIC OF IRELAND
COUNTY CARLOW

TULLOW
Map 1 C3

Mount Wolseley Hotel, Spa & Country Club
◉ Modern European

tel: 059 9180100 & 9151674
email: info@mountwolseley.ie **web:** www.mountwolseley.ie
dir: N7 from Dublin. In Naas, take N9 towards Carlow. In Castledermot left for Tullow

Modern Irish cooking on an ancestral estate

The Wolseleys of Staffordshire came to Ireland in the 17th century and fought on King William's side in 1690. They remained in possession of this estate until long after independence, but it was redeveloped by new owners the Morrisseys in the 1990s as a sumptuous hotel and country club, with plenty of golf. In keeping with the chic surroundings, the place encompasses a stylish split-level dining room overlooking a garden courtyard, where smartly attired staff attend at equally well turned-out tables. Seafood is a forte, as is demonstrated by a starter of slow-cooked sardines in an emulsified sauce of avocado with cucumber pickle, followed perhaps by fillets of John Dory on beetroot and spinach, pointed up with punchy red pepper purée. For meatier appetites, it might be braised veal shin with beech mushrooms and pearl onions in smoked shallot jus. Finish with unexpectedly rich Prosecco parfait alongside amarena cherries in a spicy compôte.

Times 12.30-2.30/6-9.30 Closed 24-26 Dec, L Mon-Sat

COUNTY CAVAN

CAVAN
Map 1 C4

Radisson Blu Farnham Estate Hotel
◉ European, Modern International V

tel: 049 4377700 **Farnham Estate**
email: info.farnham@radissonblu.com **web:** www.farnhamestate.com
dir: From Dublin take N3 to Cavan. From Cavan take Killeshandra road for 4km

Irish produce, French-influenced cooking

With lakes, rivers and ancient oak forests all around on this massive 1300-acre, 16th-century estate, you're never short of outdoor pursuits to work up a keen appetite at Farnham, a historic stately home that has morphed into an upmarket country hotel offering the full corporate package of spa, golf, wedding and meeting facilities. Clever use of plush drapes and screens helps to soften the capacious space that is the Botanica Restaurant, and a friendly service team is well-versed in the ins and outs of each dish. The kitchen places its faith in local ingredients, bringing it all together with French-inspired flair. Spicy tiger prawns, orange and dill-infused salmon, and smoked mackerel rillettes make up a seafood platter, then roast rack and slow-cooked rump of local lamb is delivered with aubergine caviar and buttery potato mash. Dessert could be a riff on lemon, in the shape of a zesty tart, Madeleines, and jelly.

Chef Philippe Farineau, Gary Stinson **Seats** 117, Pr/dining room 35 **Times** 1-3/7-9.15 Closed L Mon-Sat **Prices** Fixed D 3 course €40, Service optional **Wines** 23 bottles over €30, 22 bottles under €30, 9 by glass **Parking** 600 **Notes** Sunday L fr €24, Children welcome

KINGSCOURT
Map 1 C4

Cabra Castle Hotel
◉ European

tel: 042 9667030 **Cabra Castle**
email: sales@cabracastle.com **web:** www.cabracastle.com
dir: R165 between Kingscourt & Carrickmacross

Grand house with a traditional menu

Making quite a first impression, Cabra Castle cuts a dash in the lush, green landscape. It certainly looks like a castle, but, although its history goes way back to the 17th century, it's not quite as ancient as it seems. That matters not, for today's hotel has splendid proportions and elegant fixtures and fittings, and a first-floor restaurant that affords excellent views over the 100-acre estate. The traditionally decorated room has well-spaced tables dressed in linen cloths and a menu that aims to please in this formal setting. Old-school starters include home-cured gravad lax and pearls of melon with Sauternes jelly and pea shoots, while an earthier option might be hand-made black pudding from Ardee (served with sautéed baby potatoes and tomatoes). Among main courses, fillet of Donegal Angus beef comes with spicy sweet potato wedges and a peppercorn sauce, and salmon is topped with a fresh pesto and toasted almond crust. End with a tangy lemon tart.

Chef Clare Gloukhova **Owner** The Corscadden family **Seats** 80, Pr/dining room 60 **Times** 12.30-2.30/7-9 Closed 24-27 Dec, L Mon-Sat **Wines** 4 by glass **Parking** 120 **Notes** Sunday L €27.95, Vegetarian available, Children welcome

COUNTY CLARE

BALLYVAUGHAN
Map 1 B3

Gregans Castle
◉◉◉ – see opposite

DOOLIN
Map 1 B3

Cullinan's Seafood Restaurant & Guest House
◉◉ Modern French

tel: 065 7074183
email: info@cullinansdoolin.com **web:** www.cullinansdoolin.com
dir: Located in Doolin town centre R479

Artistically presented seafood and meat by the river Aille

The Cullinans' guesthouse in rural Clare overlooks the Aille River meadow, the sumptuous views captured by broad windows on two sides of the dining room. A large seascape mural provides alternative optical diversion. Tables are shoehorned in close enough to encourage happy converse between guests, and James Cullinan's confident, supremely professional knack with seafood is another essential part of the picture. Dishes are presented with a certain artistry and deliver on freshness, flavour and accuracy, as in a starter assembly of salmon, cod, monkfish and langoustine with two sauces, a bisque and a white wine cream. If you're moving on to meat for main, you might encounter superlative Barbary duck breast rubbed with cinnamon and lime zest, served with a ragoût of wild mushrooms and shallots, in an apple and cider sauce, or there could be Black Angus fillet with chorizo and Savoy cabbage in a rich reduction of burgundy. Finish self-indulgently with the likes of milk chocolate tart and raspberry sorbet, or Tia Maria cheesecake with an ice cream made of Ferrero Rocher.

Chef James Cullinan **Owner** James & Carol Cullinan **Seats** 24 **Times** 6-9 Closed Nov-Etr, Wed, Sun, L all week **Prices** Fixed D 3 course €27.50-€30, Starter €6-€9.95, Main €19.50-€28, Dessert €6.95-€8.75, Service optional **Wines** 2 bottles over €30, 24 bottles under €30, 6 by glass **Parking** 20 **Notes** Vegetarian available, Children welcome

ENNIS
Map 1 B3

Temple Gate Hotel
Modern International V

tel: 065 6823300 **The Square**
email: info@templegatehotel.com **web:** www.templegatehotel.com
dir: Exit N18 onto Tulla Rd for 0.25m, hotel on left

Modern bistro cooking in a former convent

The Sisters of Mercy having relocated to a new home nearby in 1995, their Victorian convent not far from the cobbled town centre became a modern hotel, with a pub called Preachers and a dining room named Legends. That latter is a three-part room with big windows and plenty of natural daylight, where modern bistro cooking is the order of the day. Fried garlic mushrooms or a smoked chicken salad start things off, with follow-ups of salmon darne and pea purée in smoked salmon and dill cream sauce, or nutty pork (an escalope coated in nutty breadcrumbs with colcannon in apple and cider sauce). Finish with an ice cream meringue nest and dark chocolate mousse, or lemon cheesecake.

Chef Paul Shortt **Owner** John Madden **Seats** 100, Pr/dining room 60
Times 12.30-2.30/6-9.30 Closed 25-26 Dec **Prices** Fixed L 2 course €16.50-€20, Fixed D 3 course €24.95, Starter €4.75-€8.50, Main €13-€25, Dessert €4.50-€5.50, Service optional **Wines** 7 bottles over €30, 10 bottles under €30, 6 by glass **Parking** 50 **Notes** Early bird menu, Sunday L, Children welcome

LAHINCH
Map 1 B3

Moy House
Modern French V

tel: 065 7082800
email: moyhouse@eircom.net **web:** www.moyhouse.com
dir: Located 1km from Lahinch on the Miltown Malbay road

Seasonal cooking with panoramic views of the bay

The gleaming white hotel on the Clare coast was the ancestral home of the Fitzgerald family, having originally been built for Sir Augustine of that ilk in the mid-Georgian era. Standing proud in 15 acres of grounds overlooking the bay at Lahinch, it's full of period character inside, from the roughcast stone walls of the entrance hall to the country-interiors style of the lounge, though the dining room with its minimalist modern chandeliers and panoramic views from the headland is in more contemporary style. As is the food, which draws on unimpeachable local supply lines for four-course seasonal dinner menus that have much to entice. First up might be potato-filled agnolotti pasta with sauce soubise, garnished with the glorious Burren smoked salmon and shredded spring onion, then locally reared beef with mushroom duxelles, wilted spinach and confit garlic in sauce bordelaise. After a pause for a cheese such as Tipperary's wonderful Cashel Blue with port-poached apple and candied walnuts, things are rounded off with moist almond cake and lemon curd.

Chef Matthew Strefford **Owner** Antoin O'Looney **Seats** 35, Pr/dining room 22
Times 7-8.30 Closed Jan-Mar, Nov-Dec, Sun-Mon (off peak) **Prices** Tasting menu €55, Service optional **Wines** 4 bottles under €30, 4 by glass **Parking** 50 **Notes** Fixed D 5 course €55 (reservation req), Children welcome

Gregans Castle

BALLYVAUGHAN
Map 1 B3

Modern Irish, European
tel: 065 7077005
email: stay@gregans.ie **web:** www.gregans.ie
dir: On N67, 5km S of Ballyvaughan

Outstanding contemporary food at a little house in the Burren

Ireland's smallest National Park, The Burren, is a wild and beautiful landscape that is said to have inspired the fantastical settings in the novels of Tolkien and CS Lewis, who both popped in for a bit of a break from the worlds of hobbits and Narnia in this 18th-century manor turned country-house hotel. Despite the name, it isn't actually a castle – that's over the road and was once the seat of the Princes of the Burren – but let's not quibble over terminology as Gregans is a luxurious hideaway filled with antiques and period Georgian elegance that is unlikely to disappoint. The restaurant is a romantic and refined room where picture windows open onto a view across the gardens to Galway Bay. Candlelight flickers in the evening, and as the summer sun sets, diners are treated to an eerie light show as the dying rays ignite the grey limestone rocks. And if it's a light show you're after, there are some fireworks on the plate too, for this is sharp modern cooking out of the top drawer. The local landscape provides a good deal of the ingredients and the cooking techniques of the team in the kitchen favour modernist culinary thinking. Liscannor Bay lobster stars in a first course with Jerusalem artichoke, sherry and pear combining to form a hugely satisfying whole with well-judged flavours and bags of invention. Next up, roast local lamb might be partnered productively with turnip, carrot, shallot and dill seed jus, or wild turbot served up with potted crab ravioli, peas and black olive crisp. Among desserts, blackcurrant soufflé and sorbet with buttermilk custard is an invigorating combination, or there could be cappuccino parfait with pineapple, coconut and rum. An extremely fine global wine list includes organic and bio-dynamic wines.

Chef David Hurley **Owner** Simon & Frederieke Haden **Seats** 50, Pr/dining room 35
Times 6-9 Closed Nov-Jan, Sun, Wed (ex Sun BHs D), L all week **Prices** Fixed D 2 course €55, Tasting menu €69, Service optional **Wines** 70 bottles over €30, 15 bottles under €30 **Parking** 20 **Notes** D 6 course €69, L menu €35 served in The Corksrew Bar, Vegetarian available, Children welcome

LISDOONVARNA
Map 1 B3

Sheedy's Country House Hotel
◉◉ Modern Irish

tel: 065 7074026
email: info@sheedys.com web: www.sheedys.com
dir: 20m from Ennis on N87

Flavour-led cooking in a small rural hotel

Chef-patron John Sheedy is the latest in a long line of Sheedys who have run the family business since the 18th century. The small-scale country house hotel is the oldest house in the village, which lies on the fringes of the Burren close by the coast, and exudes the sort of family-run, unpretentious tradition that keeps a loyal fan base returning again and again. It goes without saying, then, that John Sheedy has long-established local supply lines to support his passion for authentic ingredients: the kitchen garden provides fresh herbs and vegetables to supplement local organic meat and fish landed at nearby Doolin. Full-on, clearly defined flavours are what to expect in a repertoire of uncomplicated modern dishes, such as rillettes of rabbit with dried plum and brandied chutney, followed by roast rack of Burren lamb with a crisp crust of parsley and mustard, served with confit shoulder, spinach, and a ragoût of broad beans and tomato concasse. A classic lemon posset with raspberry coulis and sorbet and langue de chat biscuits makes a creamy, crunchy and refreshing finish.

Chef John Sheedy Owner John & Martina Sheedy Seats 28 Times 6.30-8.30 Closed mid Oct-mid Mar, 1 day a wk Mar-Apr Prices Starter €6-€10, Main €19-€29, Dessert €8.50-€9.50, Service optional Wines 10 bottles over €30, 15 bottles under €30, 2 by glass Parking 25 Notes Vegetarian available, Children 8 yrs+

Wild Honey Inn
◉◉ Modern Irish

tel: 065 7074300 Kincora
email: info@wildhoneyinn.com web: www.wildhoneyinn.com
dir: N18 from Ennis to Ennistymon. Continue through Ennistymon towards Lisdoonvarna, located on the right at edge of town

Simple cooking done right

The culinary emphasis is on wild, free-range and seasonal produce at this characterful family-run inn. Wild Honey has been around since 1860, and although a makeover in recent years has grafted on a smart contemporary sheen, the place still oozes heaps of cosy character. The bar is utterly unpretentious with its pubby tables and 'first come first served' no bookings policy, so you'd best arrive early to dig into Aidan McGrath's no-nonsense modern bistro cooking. Driven by the splendid produce of the rugged West Coast, his hearty repertoire is simplicity itself, delivered with confidence and well-defined flavours, whether it's a starter of poached Liscannor crab claws with garlic and chilli butter sauce or a posh take on fish and chips, the fish pan-fried in olive oil and butter and served with sauce gribiche and twice-cooked chips. Meatier fare might run to marinated lamb neck fillet with buttered greens, black olives, capers, parsley and garlic, while comforting desserts, such as apple and blueberry crumble or classic vanilla crème brûlée, complete the picture.

Chef Aidan McGrath Owner Aidan McGrath, Kate Sweeney Seats 50, Pr/dining room 40 Times 1-3.30/5-9 Closed Jan-mid Feb, Tue, L Mon, Wed Prices Starter €5-€10.50, Main €18.90-€26.90, Dessert €6.50-€7.50 Wines Notes Restricted opening winter, Sunday L €18.50-€26.90, Vegetarian available, Children 4 yrs+

NEWMARKET-ON-FERGUS
Map 1 B3

Dromoland Castle
◉◉ Traditional Irish, European V

tel: 061 368144
email: sales@dromoland.ie web: www.dromoland.ie
dir: From Ennis take N18, follow signs for Shannon/Limerick. 7m follow Quin. Newmarket-on-Fergus sign. Hotel 0.5m. From Shannon take N18 towards Ennis

Classical haute cuisine in a spectacular castle

It's a castle to be sure. Turrets and ramparts are present and correct at this top-end country-house hotel, with a golf course on the vast estate, a spa within its 15th-century walls, and plenty of good eating to be had. The Fig Tree restaurant is the informal dining option and there's a plush cocktail bar too, but the main deal is the Earl of Thomond restaurant, located in a spectacular room filled with antiques and oak-panelled period character and a resident harpist to soothe the soul. The cooking fits the bill with its unmistakably French accent and top-notch produce drawn from the estate itself and local suppliers. Roast pigeon breasts are served on a grilled polenta cake with pea purée, pickled Jerusalem artichoke and port sauce, followed by pan-fried John Dory fillets matched with saffron remoulade, capers, leeks and cucumber, and chilli and sage butter. Service is formal (expect a cloche or two) and everything looks wonderful on the plate. For dessert, mandarin ice cream is a foil to warm rhubarb crumble tart.

Chef David McCann Owner Dromoland Castle Holdings Ltd Seats 80, Pr/dining room 40 Times 7-10 Closed 24-27 Dec, L all week Prices Fixed L 3 course €40, Starter €15-€19, Main €30-€36, Dessert €10-€15 Wines 210 bottles over €30, 14 bottles under €30, 10 by glass Parking 140 Notes Children welcome

COUNTY CORK

BALLINGEARY
Map 1 B2

Gougane Barra Hotel
◉ Irish, French

tel: 026 47069 Gougane Barra
email: info@gouganebarrahotel.com web: www.gouganebarrahotel.com
dir: Off R584 between N22 at Macroom & N71 at Bantry. Take Keimaneigh junct for hotel

Tried-and-true country cooking in hauntingly beautiful setting

The Cronin family has owned property in hauntingly beautiful Gougane Barra since Victorian times, when its potential as an idyllic retreat was first fully realised, though the present hotel dates back only to the 1930s. Those views over the lake towards the mountains of Cork look especially magnificent from the ample windows of the dining room, where fine seasonal artisan produce takes centre-stage. There are no airs and graces to the cooking, just careful presentation in tried-and-true formulas that never lack for support. Dingle Bay smoked salmon, or a double-act of Clonakilty black and De Róiste white pudding, with bacon and apple sauce, might fire the starting-gun, before grilled cutlets of exemplary West Cork lamb with colcannon and port gravy make their appearance. Fish could be herb-crusted hake with creamed leeks and peas in prawn sauce, with flourless pear frangipane and butterscotch ice cream to round things off in style.

Times 12.30-2.30/6-8.30 Closed 20 Oct-10 Apr, L Mon-Sat (ex group bookings)

BALLYCOTTON
Map 1 C2

Bayview Hotel

 Modern Irish, French

tel: 021 4646746
email: res@thebayviewhotel.com **web:** www.thebayviewhotel.com
dir: *At Castlemartyr on N25 (Cork-Waterford road) turn onto R632 to Garryvoe, then follow signs for Shanagarry & Ballycotton*

Imaginative contemporary cooking and sea views

Bayview Hotel has a prime position above the bay and the harbour, and expansive windows through which you can admire the whole, lovely panorama as you eat. It's a gently contemporary space with muted colour tones, looked over by a charming service team who are pretty much all local. There's a lot of local influence here, in fact, with a passion for the fruits of the countryside and sea around these parts. The seafood is landed down the road, farmers deliver their wares to the door, and the chef and his team know how to make the very best of them in creative, clearly-focused dishes. Start with the humble mackerel, perhaps, which comes three ways on a slate plate – pickled, smoked and pan-fried – with cucumber jelly, wasabi cream, mango mayonnaise and sesame crisps. Next up, roast rack and braised shank of lamb – nice and pink, perfectly rested – comes with spaghetti squash purée, glazed carrots and ras el hanout, and to finish, a well-made lemon tart hits the spot.

Times 1-3/7-9 Closed Nov-Apr, L Mon-Sat

BALLYLICKEY
Map 1 B2

Seaview House Hotel

 Traditional V

tel: 027 50073
email: info@seaviewhousehotel.com **web:** www.seaviewhousehotel.com
dir: *3m N of Bantry towards Glengarriff, 70yds off main road, N71*

Polished cooking in a smart country-house hotel

The grand white-painted Seaview has the promised vista over Bantry Bay, glimpsed through the trees in the pretty gardens, but all the better from the first- and second-floor bedrooms. The restaurant is done out in a traditional manner, traversing three well-proportioned rooms, one of which is a conservatory with lush garden views. There's a good deal of local produce on the menu – crabs out of the bay, perhaps, or lamb from west Cork – and everything is handled with care and attention to detail. Start, perhaps, with a light and flavourful scallop mousse, served with a vermouth sauce and topped with the scallop roe. Next up, a superb piece of sole, grilled on the bone which is removed before service, and partnered

with a caper butter served in a pot, plus mashed potatoes, wilted spinach, broccoli and cauliflower. Chocolate mousse with white chocolate sauce is a typical dessert.

Chef Eleanor O'Donavon **Owner** Kathleen O'Sullivan **Seats** 50
Times 12.30-1.45/7-9.30 Closed Nov-Mar, L Mon-Sat **Prices** Fixed L 2 course €20-€30, Fixed D 3 course €35-€45, Starter €5-€8.50, Main €20-€28.50, Dessert €5.50
Wines 10 by glass **Parking** 32 **Notes** Sunday L €25-€30, Children welcome

BALTIMORE
Map 1 B1

Rolfs Country House

 French, European

tel: 028 20289
email: info@rolfscountryhouse.com **web:** www.rolfscountryhouse.com
dir: *Into Baltimore, sharp left, follow restaurant signs, up hill*

Continental classics in a heavenly spot

Set in beautiful sub-tropical gardens overlooking Baltimore Harbour to Roaringwater Bay and Carbery's 100 islands, it is hardly surprising that the Haffner family have put down roots at their delightful 10-room hotel since 1979. Johannes Haffner is the current incumbent at the stoves, and he runs the culinary side of the operation with his sister Frederica. They bring dedication to ensure that produce is locally grown, reared and caught, organic whenever possible, and pastries and breads are all home baked. The beamed and stone-walled restaurant provides a cosy and informal setting for a classic European repertoire: local mussels come with white wine, garlic and herb cream sauce, while fresh crab arrives with salad leaves from the garden and Marie Rose sauce. At main course, a brace of de-boned

continued

CORK *continued*

quail are flambéed with Cognac and matched with apricots and cream sauce, and to finish, there's caramelised apple tarte Tatin with cream.

Chef Johannes Haffner **Owner** Johannes Haffner **Seats** 50 **Times** 6-9.30 Closed Xmas, Mon-Tue (winter) **Prices** Starter €4.50-€13, Main €22-€29, Dessert €6.50-€8.50 **Wines** 12 by glass **Parking** 45 **Notes** Sunday L, Vegetarian available, Children welcome

---

CORK   Map 1 B2

Maryborough Hotel & Spa

◉ Modern International ∨

tel: 021 4365555 **Maryborough Hill, Douglas**
email: info@maryborough.ie **web:** www.maryborough.com
dir: *From Jack Lynch Tunnel take 2nd exit signed Douglas. Right at 1st rdbt, follow Rochestown road to fingerpost rdbt. Left, hotel on left 0.5m up hill*

Contemporary country-house cooking in a luxury hotel

There's a whiff of glamour at this Georgian country-house hotel, with later additions tacked on, surrounded by 14 acres of well-maintained gardens and woodland. Refurbishment has given a sharp new look to the bar and restaurant, now called Bellini's, giving it a modern glossy sheen. Fresh, locally sourced produce is the kitchen's stock-in-trade, with the long menu a list of bright and modern ideas. Thai-style salmon and cod patties served with lime aïoli and a rice noodle crisp, and terrine of confit duck, with herby pistachio crumble and beetroot and raspberry purée, are the sort of cleverly conceived starters to expect. Quality and accurate timings never fail to impress, seen in intricate main courses of rolled belly pork with spicy ribs, smoked apple, sweet cabbage and apple jus, and roast salmon steak stuffed with fennel mousse served with beetroot and salsify salad. Desserts end assertively with perhaps Baileys parfait with mocha syrup.

Chef Gerry Allen **Owner** Dan O'Sullivan **Seats** 170, Pr/dining room 60 **Times** 12.30-10 Closed 24-26 Dec, All-day dining **Prices** Fixed L 2 course €23-€28, Fixed D 3 course €39-€49, Starter €6-€12, Main €16-€27, Dessert €6-€8, Service optional **Wines** 15 bottles over €30, 13 bottles under €30, 8 by glass **Parking** 300 **Notes** Sunday L €30, Children welcome

---

DURRUS   Map 1 B2

Blairscove House & Restaurant

◉◉ Modern Irish

tel: 027 61127
email: mail@blairscove.ie **web:** www.blairscove.ie
dir: *R591 from Durrus to Crookhaven, in 1.5m restaurant on right through blue gate*

Buffet dining in a converted barn

On a promontory overlooking peaceful Dunmanus Bay, Blairscove is a west Cork country hotel brimming with charm. The main house is Georgian, and the accommodation and restaurant occupy a pretty development facing a lilypond, in what were the piggery, stables and barn. With its soaring ceiling and narrow windows, through which hay was once dispensed to the livestock, the dining room is full of character, not least from striking modern artworks, and so is the catering operation itself. Stroll over to the buffet, cruise-ship fashion, and help yourself to an array of hors d'oeuvres, before ordering from the main menu for the principal dish. That could be a half-rack of new season's lamb with its smoked sweetbreads, served with aubergine gratin in tomatoey sauce choron, or tuna poached in olive oil with toasted pine-nuts and basil, with a vegetarian option of grilled aubergine and spiced chickpeas in walnut dressing, served with labneh. Then it's back to serve-yourself for puddings such as glazed frangipane tart, fruit salad or crème brûlée.

Chef Ronald Klötzer **Owner** P & S De Mey **Seats** 75, Pr/dining room 48 **Times** 6.30-9.30 Closed Nov-17 Mar, Sun-Mon, L all week **Prices** Prices not confirmed, Service optional **Wines** **Parking** 30 **Notes** Vegetarian available, Children welcome

---

GARRYVOE   Map 1 C2

Garryvoe Hotel

◉ Modern Irish

tel: 021 4646718 **Ballycotton Bay, Castlemartyr**
email: res@garryvoehotel.com **web:** www.garryvoehotel.com
dir: *From N25 at Castlemartyr (Cork-Rosslare road) take R632 to Garryvoe*

Modern Irish cooking in a grand seafront hotel

Right on the seafront overlooking Ballycotton Bay, the Garryvoe is something of a local institution, but one that has moved with the times, modernising and aggrandising in the process. The high-ceilinged dining room naturally makes the most of those Cork coastal views, with well-spaced tables set with high-class accoutrements. The cooking might be described as modern Irish, but with no inhibitions about featuring retro dishes too. Start with crab croquette with chilli jam, citrus crab millefeuille and celeriac in wild mushroom bisque, moving onto a classic main course such as roast rump of local lamb with creamed cabbage and root veg in red wine reduction. The finale could be chocolate fondant with pistachio ice cream and raspberry coulis.

Times 1-2.30/6.30-8.45 Closed 24-25 Dec, L Mon-Sat

Follow us on facebook
www.facebook.com/TheAAUK

Get the most out of the AA Restaurant Guide
See page 6

GOLEEN
Map 1 A1

The Heron's Cove
 Traditional Irish

tel: 028 35225 **The Harbour**
email: suehill@eircom.net **web:** www.heronscove.com
dir: In Goleen village, turn left to harbour

Unbroken sea views, super-fresh seafood and more

This delightful restaurant with rooms sits in an idyllic spot on Goleen harbour near to Mizen Head, where the lonely Fastnet Rock lighthouse beams out across the Atlantic at Ireland's most south westerly point. This is an exceptionally easy going, friendly place, where you can eat out to sublime sea views on the balcony overlooking the tiny inlet in summer, and the kitchen takes time to source the best local ingredients that are the backbone of its output. The menu is as straightforward and unfussy as its surroundings; typical starters are moules marinières, or crab cakes with wasabi mayonnaise, while main course could bring a local fish and meat combo of seared Dunmanus Bay scallops with Goleen lamb chops, creamy smoked bacon sauce, rosemary jus and potato cake, or roast leg of duck with Calvados and red cabbage. At the end, apricots and Cointreau add an indulgent note to bread and butter pudding in creamy custard.

Chef Irene Coughlan **Owner** Sue Hill **Seats** 30 **Times** 7-9.30 Closed Xmas, Oct-Apr (only open for pre-bookings), L all week (ex private functions) **Prices** Fixed D 3 course €27.50, Starter €5.50–€13.50, Main €16.75–€35, Dessert €6.95, Service optional **Wines** 25 bottles over €30, 35 bottles under €30, 2 by glass **Parking** 10 **Notes** Vegetarian available, Children welcome

KINSALE
Map 1 B2

Carlton Hotel Kinsale
 Modern European

tel: 021 4706000 **Rathmore Rd**
email: reservations.kinsale@carlton.ie **web:** www.carltonkinsalehotel.com
dir: Before Kinsale turn left signed Charles Fort. 3km, hotel on left

A local flavour in a classy contemporary hotel

With wonderful views over Oysterhaven Bay and the headland, the Carlton Hotel is a modernist vision built of stone, wood and glass. There's a leisure club and spa, conference facilities and the like, but another good reason to visit is to sample the cooking from the new team in the kitchen. The first-floor Rockpool Restaurant gets the great views; a wall of glass keeps out the worst of the weather, the terrace comes into its own when the climate allows. It's all very bright and contemporary, and the cooking has a new focus on regional ingredients, much of it from artisan producers. On the lunch menu, Kinsale seafood stars in a creamy chowder, served with home-made seed bread, and spinach and ricotta is stuffed into tortellini and served with a rocket and pesto crème. The evening menu cranks things up a bit to deliver the likes of polenta-crusted Castletownbere sole with local smoked salmon and shrimp sauce.

Times 12-2.30/6-9.30 Closed Xmas

The White House
Traditional, International

tel: 021 4772125 **Pearse St, The Glen**
email: info@whitehouse-kinsale.ie **web:** www.whitehouse-kinsale.ie
dir: Located in town centre

Broadly appealing menu in a gastronomic hub

The White House has been in the hospitality game since the mid-19th century, and occupies a prime site in the centre of a town that holds a renowned Gourmet Festival every autumn. That means there's plenty to live up to in the gastronomic stakes, and the kitchen here rises to the occasion with a resourceful repertoire of modern Irish dishes that draws inspiration from far and wide, but is also a dab hand at Irish stews, fish pies and the like. Baked cod fillet is coated in Cajun spices for a satisfying main course accompanied by ratatouille topped with melted cheese. Local mussels make a fine starter, with a creamy dressing of white wine, garlic and lemongrass, and favourite puddings take in apple and cinnamon crumble with well-churned vanilla ice cream, or passionfruit and mango cheesecake.

Chef Martin El Sahen **Owner** Michael Frawley **Seats** 45 **Times** 12-10 Closed 25 Dec, All-day dining **Prices** Prices not confirmed, Service optional **Wines** 9 by glass **Parking** Car park at rear of building **Notes** Vegetarian available, Children welcome

MALLOW
Map 1 B2

Springfort Hall Country House Hotel
Modern, Irish

tel: 022 21278 & 30620
email: stay@springfort-hall.com **web:** www.springfort-hall.com
dir: N20 onto R581 at Two Pot House, hotel 500mtrs on right

Modern dining in a Georgian country house

The kitchen team in this immaculately-preserved Georgian country house certainly aren't scared of a bit of domestic hard graft: no corners are cut here – meat and fish is smoked in-house and everything is made from scratch from fresh, judiciously-sourced local produce. The setting for all of this laudable culinary endeavour is the palatial Lime Tree Restaurant, where all the detail of the original ornate plasterwork is picked out in gold paint and a crystal chandelier hangs above pristine white linen-clothed tables on polished timber flooring. The kitchen deals in a broadly modern Irish style of cookery, sending out ideas such as black pudding and glazed pork belly with pickled leeks, apple purée and cider jelly, followed by seared wild venison with butternut squash purée, Savoy cabbage, pickled mushrooms and candied pumpkin seeds.

Times 12-9.30 Closed 25-26 Dec, All-day dining

SHANAGARRY
Map 1 C2

Ballymaloe House
Traditional Irish **NOTABLE WINE LIST**

tel: 021 4652531
email: res@ballymaloe.ie **web:** www.ballymaloe.com
dir: From R630 at Lakeview rdbt, left onto R631, left onto Cloyne. Continue for 2m on Ballycotton Rd

Fabulous food in a classic country-house setting

Ivan and Myrtle Allen were way, way ahead of the curve some 50 years ago when they opened a restaurant in their farmhouse. No-one had heard the term 'farm to fork', nobody was doing anything quite like it. Fast forward to 2014 and there is a cookery school and hotel accommodation, and the idea of fresh produce brought to the table in double-quick time and served simply just seems normal. The place is still run by the Allen family (sadly, Ivan died in 1998) and its reputation has spread internationally. The restaurant is supplied by the farm and walled garden and the two chefs (Jason Fahey and Gillian Hegarty) have a wealth of superb foodstuffs to work with. The four dining rooms are traditional and comfortable. Cod landed at nearby Ballycotton might appear in a first course with salsa verde, while another starter combines a salad of garden leaves with Crozier blue cheese, pear and walnuts. Main-course Gubbeen ham is baked with Saint-Véran (a white Burgundy) and comes with pommes boulangère and spinach, and there's a pre-theatre menu, too.

Chef Jason Fahey, Gillian Hegarty **Owner** The Allen family **Seats** 110, Pr/dining room 50 **Times** 1-1.30/7-9.30 Closed Xmas, 6 Jan-6 Feb, Mon-Tue in Feb, L Wed in Feb, D Sun in Feb **Prices** Fixed L 3 course €40-€45, Fixed D 3 course €50, Tasting menu €45, Service optional **Wines** 300 bottles over €30, 20 bottles under €30, 18 by glass **Parking** 100 **Notes** Fixed D 5 course €70, Sunday L, Vegetarian available, Children 7yrs+ D

COUNTY DONEGAL

DONEGAL
Map 1 B5

Harvey's Point Hotel

Modern, Irish

tel: 074 9722208 **Lough Eske**
email: stay@harveyspoint.com **web:** www.harveyspoint.com
dir: *From Donegal 2m towards Lifford, left at Harvey's Point sign, follow signs, take 3 right turns to hotel gates*

Contemporary European cooking overlooking Lough Eske

The Swiss family Gysling have run this luxurious retreat in the wilds of Donegal since the late 1980s. Perched on the shore of Lough Eske, it's the very image of a remote country hotel. The split-level Lakeside dining room democratically allows everyone to drink in the uplifting views of the lough, and there is also a new Seafood Bar and Grill. Gavin O'Rourke's menus are firmly in the contemporary vein, with thought-provoking combinations and multitudinous textures on display in dishes such as fennel six ways (custard, jam, confit, purée, crisp and powder) seasoned with star-anise salt, against which lobster tortellini with black truffle shavings and parmesan sounds positively trad. Fish is a strong point, as in a main dish of grilled sea-trout with a crab croquette in pearl barley emulsion sauce, or there may be chocolate-glazed venison loin with pistachio crumble and a poached plum. That dish feels halfway to a dessert in itself, should you not find room for white chocolate and ginger cheesecake with roasted figs and almond brittle.

Times 6.30-9.30 Closed Sun-Thu (Nov-Apr), Sun, Wed (Jun-Oct), L all week

The Red Door Country House

Modern/Traditional European **NEW**

tel: 074 9360289 **Fahan, Inishowen**
email: info@thereddoor.ie **web:** www.thereddoor.ie
dir: *In Fahan village, church on right, The Red Door signed on left*

Confident modern Irish cooking by a lough

If it's a deal breaker, rest assured the front door is indeed red. With views over Lough Swilly, this country house is popular for weddings and business meetings, but also has a restaurant run by a hands-on team who bake their own bread and do a good deal of the meat butchery themselves. The series of dining rooms – including a sun room – have traditional finishes, with polished teak tables and smart linen napery. The menu shows a passion for the produce of this part of the world, along with sound classical training and some bright modern thinking. Seared scallops with Haven Smokehouse salmon comes with pickled cucumber, cumin-scented beetroot and courgette jelly in a smart first course, followed perhaps by rack of Donegal lamb with ratatouille and boulangère potatoes, or roast wild Irish hake served on the bone. To finish, strawberry and white chocolate mousse, or tarte Tatin with apple parfait and crème anglaise.

Chef Sean Clifford **Owner** Shay McCallion **Seats** 120 **Times** 12-4/5-close Closed Mon-Wed, L Thu-Fri **Prices** Fixed L 3 course €27, Fixed D 3 course €32, Starter €6-€10.50, Main €19.50-€28, Dessert €6.50-€9 **Wines** **Notes** Early blrd menu available (subject to availability), Sunday L €21-€25, Vegetarian available, Children welcome

DUNFANAGHY
Map 1 C6

Arnolds Hotel

Traditional

tel: 074 9136208 **Main St**
email: enquiries@arnoldshotel.com **web:** www.arnoldshotel.com
dir: *On N56 from Letterkenny, hotel on left on entering the village*

Good Irish cooking on the coast

In a village overlooking Sheephaven Bay, with Killahoey Beach a stroll away, Arnolds Hotel has been welcoming guests since 1922. It's a friendly, comfortable and comforting place, with open fires in the winter, and a restaurant capitalising on those coastal views. The kitchen takes a fuss-free approach, relying on quality raw materials and sound technique to make the most of flavours. To start there may be steamed mussels in garlic and dill cream, or balls of mushroom risotto coated in oatmeal, fried and dressed with white truffle and parmesan. Fish is well handled, seen in baked fillet of turbot served simply on pea purée with red pesto, or there might be honey-glazed roast duckling on rösti with a rich orange sauce, or fillet steak with grilled mushrooms, mustard mash and a bourbon and pepper cream. Desserts are of the home-baked, comfort food variety, such as Arnolds Hotel Pavlova, apple pie and rhubarb crumble.

Chef John Corcoran **Owner** The Arnold family **Seats** 60 **Times** 6-9.30 Closed Nov-Apr (excl New Year) **Prices** Prices not confirmed, Service optional **Wines** **Parking** 40 **Notes** Sunday L, Vegetarian available, Children welcome

LETTERKENNY
Map 1 C5

Radisson Blu Hotel Letterkenny

Modern Irish

tel: 074 9194444 **Paddy Harte Rd**
email: info.letterkenny@radissonblu.com **web:** www.radissonblu.ie/hotel-letterkenny
dir: *N14 into Letterkenny. At Polestar Rdbt take 1st exit, to hotel*

Unpretentious cooking in a modern hotel

Donegal's timeless attractions are on the doorstep of this contemporary-styled hotel. The building is bright and airy thanks to the liberal use of glass, wood and steel in its construction, a style which is used to good effect in the clean-cut TriBeCa Brasserie. Done out with plenty of light wood, warm tones, unclothed tables and a large screen showing the action in the kitchen, the place certainly looks the part, and if the buzz of contented diners is anything to go by, the formula works a treat. The kitchen builds its crowd-pleasing repertoire of modern brasserie dishes on well-sourced ingredients. A starter of pan-seared sea trout with roasted asparagus and prosciutto and red pepper dressing sets the tone, ahead of roast glazed rump of Slaney Valley lamb with fondant potato, carrots and wild mushroom sauce. At the end, rice krispies make a quirky base for a lime and chocolate pie with lime sorbet.

Chef Collette Langan **Owner** Paul Byrne **Seats** 120, Pr/dining room 320 **Times** 12.30-3.30/6-9.30 Closed L Mon-Sat **Prices** Fixed L 2 course €14.95-€18.95, Fixed D 3 course €19.95, Starter €4.50-€9.95, Main €13.95-€23.95, Dessert €5.95-€10.95, Service optional **Wines** 20 bottles under €30, 5 by glass **Parking** 150 **Notes** Early bird menu 6-7pm €19.95, Fixed L 2/3 course Sun only, Sunday L €18.95-€20.95, Vegetarian available, Children welcome

MOVILLE
Map 1 C6

Redcastle Hotel, Golf & Spa Resort

Modern, International

tel: 074 9385555 **Inishowen Peninsula**
email: info@redcastlehotel.com **web:** www.redcastlehotel.com
dir: On R238 between Derby & Greencastle

Traditionally based Irish cooking with loughside views

The Redcastle estate can trace its lineage all the way back to a 16th-century proprietor called Cathal O Doherty. At one point, it was owned by a Pennsylvania farming family, but today it makes a superbly located northwestern seafront hotel in the modern boutique style. A terrace overlooking Lough Foyle is a covetable place for a sundowner, informal eating is offered in the Captain's Bar, or repair to the Edge dining room for some traditionally based Irish cooking with modern flourishes. Start with a tartlet of Cooleeney Camembert and fennel marmalade with crispy bacon, cranberries and tarragon, or smoked chicken Caesar with all the trimmings. Mains might take an oriental theme for roast cod with pak choi, mussels and ginger, and lemongrass jelly, or else aim to fortify by means of slow-braised lamb shank with roast celeriac and champ on tomato fondue. Conclude with Irish cheeses, or blackberry Bakewell sponge with cardamom custard and blackberry sorbet.

Chef Gordon Smyth **Owner** Pisona Developments **Seats** 120 **Times** 12-4/6-9.30 Closed 25 Dec **Prices** Prices not confirmed, Service optional **Wines** 16 bottles over €30, 11 bottles under €30, 6 by glass **Parking** 360 **Notes** Early bird offer off peak, Sunday L, Vegetarian available, Children welcome

RATHMULLAN
Map 1 C6

Rathmullan House

Modern Irish

tel: 074 9158188
email: info@rathmullanhouse.com **web:** www.rathmullanhouse.com
dir: R245 Letterkenny to Ramelton, over bridge right onto R247 to Rathmullan. On entering village turn at Mace shop through village gates. Hotel on right

Regional Irish cooking at a loughside country house

Rathmullan, built in the late Georgian period for an army officer, was soon acquired by the Batts, an Irish banking dynasty in whose honour today's hotel bar is named. The house began its hotel career in the 1960s, and has since been a favoured destination for its peaceful location overlooking Lough Swilly in the far northwest. Start with a drink in front of the Drawing Room fire before progressing to the singularly characterful Weeping Elm restaurant, with its tented ceiling, bare wood floors and lough views. Here, Michael Harley offers regionally sourced modern Irish food, with some coming from the hotel's own walled garden. It's all fresh as can be, from vegetables and salads to seafood such as Mulroy mussels and Lissadell clams in garlicky white wine sauce. Move on to dry-aged 30-day ribeye and sirloin steaks with potato gratin in red wine jus, or Parma-hammed chicken breast with spinach and champ. Fish landed at Greencastle turn up in shoals in a leek velouté, and the finisher could be baked lemon cheesecake with berry compôte and ice cream laced with Kilbeggan whiskey.

Chef Michael Harley **Owner** The Wheeler family **Seats** 70, Pr/dining room 30 **Times** 1-2.30/7-8.45 Closed Jan-mid Feb, Xmas **Prices** Fixed D 3 course €45-€55, Starter €8-€14, Main €17.50-€30, Dessert €7.50-€12 **Wines** 20 bottles over €30, 15 bottles under €30, 10 by glass **Parking** 40 **Notes** Vegetarian available, Children welcome

DUBLIN

DUBLIN
Map 1 D4

Ashling Hotel, Dublin

Irish, European **NEW**

tel: 01 6772324 **Parkgate St**
email: info@ashlinghotel.ie **web:** www.ashlinghotel.ie
dir: Close to River Liffey, opposite Heuston Station

Successful modern skilfully turned-out cooking near Dublin Zoo

The Ashling is a large, modern and glitzy hotel near Phoenix Park and Dublin Zoo, where Chesterfields Restaurant occupies a spacious, softly lit room with plushly upholstered dining chairs and a busily patterned carpet. The kitchen has some success with its combinations of flavours and textures, and dishes are noted for their accurate timings. This is shown in seared scallops with pancetta crisps, cauliflower purée and hollandaise, for instance, then roast breast of guinea fowl with crisp gnocchi, sautéed curly kale and Madeira jus. Prime native produce is the stock-in-trade, among it carpaccio of wild Wicklow venison with raspberry vinaigrette and a pomegranate and pine nut salsa, and line-caught fillet of cod in Parma ham served with spinach and brown shrimp ravioli, fine beans and lemon cream. Irish farmhouse cheeses bring up the rear along with puddings along the lines of autumn berry Eton Mess and classic crème brûlée.

Chef Gary Costello **Owner** Foxfield Inns Ltd **Seats** 180 **Times** 12.30-2.30/6-9.30 Closed 24-26 Dec **Prices** Fixed L 2 course €14.50-€17.95, Fixed D 3 course €29.50-€34.50, Starter €6.50-€12, Main €14.50-€29, Dessert €6-€7.50 **Wines** 8 bottles over €30, 8 bottles under €30, 6 by glass **Parking** 80 **Notes** Sunday L €10.50-€13, Vegetarian available, Children welcome

Castleknock Hotel & Country Club

European, International

tel: 01 6406300 **Porterstown Rd, Castleknock**
email: info@chcc.ie **web:** www.castleknockhotel.com
dir: M50 from airport. Exit at junct 6 (signed Navan, Cavan & M3) onto N3, becomes M3. Exit at junct 3. At top of slip road 1st left signed Consilla (R121). At T-junct left. 1km to hotel

Contemporary dining in a country club setting

Just 15 minutes from the centre of Dublin, Castleknock is a country club with plenty of pizazz. The green fairways of the 18-hole golf course blanket the grounds, while inside it is classy and pristine, with all the spa facilities you can imagine. There are several eating and drinking options, the pick of the bunch being the Park Restaurant, with its elegant finish. There are floor-to-ceiling windows with swagged curtains, richly-coloured walls and large artworks, plus burnished darkwood tables. Steak has long been the mainstay of the kitchen's output, but there is a lot more going on besides, and a heap of regional produce to ensure a local flavour. Confit of wild Wicklow rabbit with apple gel, hazelnuts, Granny Smith apple and watercress is a creative first course, followed perhaps by roast rump of Cooley lamb – a fine piece of meat, soft and tender – and served with broad beans, feta and a warm potato salad.

Chef Neil Kearns **Owner** FBD Group **Seats** 65, Pr/dining room 400 **Times** 12.30-3/5.30-10 Closed 24-26 Dec **Prices** Fixed L 2 course €20.95-€32, Fixed D 3 course €25-€40, Starter €5.50-€13.50, Main €16.50-€24.50, Dessert €6.25-€7.50 **Wines** 12 by glass **Parking** 200 **Notes** Fixed 4 course D 2 people & wine €69, Sunday L, Vegetarian available, Children welcome

DUBLIN *continued*

The Cellar Restaurant

◉◉ Modern Irish

tel: 01 6030600 & 6030630 **Merrion Hotel, Upper Merrion St**
email: info@merrionhotel.com
dir: *Top Upper Merrion Street, opp Government buildings*

Smart cooking of fine local produce

The Merrion Hotel's Cellar Restaurant (see also Restaurant Patrick Guilbaud) may have no natural light, but it's a bright room under its vaulted ceiling, with lots of nooks and crannies and top-end fittings and furnishings. The kitchen bases its cooking on indigenous ingredients and promotes local and artisan producers whenever possible, seen in imaginative starters like confit of Galway salmon with horseradish and potato salad, pickled cucumber and cucumber gel, and saddleback pork and pistachio terrine with fig chutney, a cherry and balsamic treacle adding another flavour dimension. Main courses pull some punches too, without being overwrought or fussy: meltingly tender veal liver with rich onion gravy laced with red wine accompanied by bacon and buttery mash, say, or roast skate wing with lemon and brown shrimp beurre noisette and garlicky spinach. Cheeses are Irish, with ingredients in some puddings coming from wilder shores: a smooth light soufflé of exotic fruits, for instance, with mango ice cream and coconut liqueur-infused custard.

Times 12.30-2/6-10 Closed L Sat

Crowne Plaza Dublin Northwood

◉ Asian Fusion, International

tel: 01 8628888 **Northwood Park, Santry Demesne, Santry**
email: info@crowneplazadublin.ie web: www.cpdublin.crowneplaza.com
dir: *M50 junct 4, left into Northwood Park, 1km, hotel on left*

Fusion food and more in a modern hotel

In a quiet location on the edge of Northwood Park, 10 minutes from the airport, the Crowne Plaza is a modern hotel, its restaurant a bright and airy space overlooking the courtyard gardens. The kitchen takes its inspiration from the techniques and flavours of Asia and the Pacific Rim, with crisp duck spring roll with an Asian-style salad and yoghurt and chilli dressing to start, followed by chicken stir-fried with noodles and vegetables sauced with coconut green curry. But this is no style slave, so asparagus and Parma ham with a poached egg and hollandaise may appear before roast halibut fillet with tapenade and a casserole of haricot beans, chorizo and red peppers, with lemon tart for pudding.

Chef Logan Irwin **Owner** Tifco Ltd **Seats** 156, Pr/dining room 15 **Times** 5.30-10 Closed 25 Dec, L all week **Prices** Fixed L 2 course €12.50-€30, Fixed D 3 course €24.95-€34.95, Starter €5.95-€14, Main €11.65-€26, Dessert €5.95-€11 **Wines** 34 bottles over €30, 17 bottles under €30, 15 by glass **Parking** 360 **Notes** Vegetarian available, Children welcome

Crowne Plaza Hotel Dublin – Blanchardstown

◉ Italian, European, International

tel: 01 8977777 **The Blanchardstown Centre**
email: info@cpireland.crowneplaza.com web: www.cpireland.ie
dir: *M50 junct 6 (Blanchardstown)*

Italian dining in a funky modern venue

The Blanchardstown branch of the Crowne Plaza empire fits the bill, whether you're suited and booted for business, or dropping by to refuel after a hit of retail therapy in the shops and boutiques of the nearby Blanchardstown Centre. The Forchetta restaurant works a loud and proud contemporary look with bold floral wallpaper and bare dark wood tables – it's a buzzy, breezy setting that suits the crowd-pleasing modern Italian menu. The usual suspects from the world of pizza and pasta are all

present and correct, or you might ignore convention and start with a fish soup involving mussels, clams, prawns, salmon and cod in a tomato and white wine broth, and follow with a chargrilled Irish steak, or lamb shank roasted in red wine, garlic and rosemary. Puddings are Italian classics – pannacotta or tiramisù, for example.

Chef Jason Hayde **Owner** Tifco Hotels **Seats** 100, Pr/dining room 45 **Times** 12-2.30/6-9.30 Closed 24-25 Dec **Prices** Fixed L 2 course €20-€35, Fixed D 3 course €24.95-€55, Starter €7-€15, Main €10.50-€29.95, Dessert €6-€8.50, Service optional **Wines** 20 bottles over €30, 27 bottles under €30, 6 by glass **Parking** 200 **Notes** Carvery L served Sanctuary Bar, Bar food daily noon-10, Vegetarian available, Children welcome

Fahrenheit Restaurant

◉ Modern Irish NEW

tel: 01 8332321 & 8523263 **Castle Av, Clontarf**
email: mwoods@clontarfcastle.ie web: www.clontarfcastle.ie
dir: *From Dublin city. O'Connell St, head south onto O'Connell St lower, left onto Abbey St lower, continue onto R105 at Clontarf Rd left onto Castle Ave, left after 500m*

Modern Irish cookery in a boutique castle

Ten minutes out of the city centre, Dublin's Clontarf Castle Hotel is a beguiling mix of ancient structure and modern boutique luxiness. Dating from the 12th century, it served as headquarters for the English army's quartermaster-general during Cromwell's rampages, but achieved its present apogee on reopening as an upmarket hotel in 1998. The Fahrenheit Grill is the destination restaurant, a dramatic showcase room for some striking modern Irish cookery. Kick off with a breakfast salad of crisp-fried egg, bacon and Clonakilty black pudding, or scallops and pork belly with sweet potato purée. Move on to substantial main courses such as breast and confit leg of duck with carrot purée in vanilla and cardamom jus, or cod with a cassoulet of chorizo, white beans and tomato, and saffron mash. It all concludes with Bramley apple crumble and salted caramel ice cream, wild honey parfait with macerated figs, or lemon pannacotta with blackberry compôte.

Chef Stuart Heeney **Owner** Gerry Houlihan **Seats** 90 **Times** 5.30-10 Closed L all week (private pre-booked only) **Prices** Starter €5.95-€8.25, Main €14.95-€27.95, Dessert €6.50-€7, Service optional **Wines** 15 bottles over €30, 38 bottles under €30, 13 by glass **Parking** 200 **Notes** Early bird 2/3 course €19.20/€24, Table D'hôte menu 3 course, Vegetarian available, Children welcome

Radisson Blu St Helens Hotel

◉ Traditional Italian, International NEW

tel: 01 218 6000 & 218 6032 **Stillorgan Rd**
email: talavera@radissonblu.com web: radissonblu.ie/sthelenshotel-dublin
dir: *On N11 Stillorgan dual carriageway*

Regional and classic Italian cooking in a grand house

This grand old house dates from the middle of the 17th century but has all the expected 21st-century mod cons of a Radisson Blu. There's a restaurant called talavera, which serves up smart Italian food in a series of rooms with either traditional country-house decor or rather more contemporary chic. There's also an all-day Orangery Bar for a cocktail or afternoon tea. The main restaurant focuses on the cooking of Lombardy, from whence the chef hails, and there's a tasting menu which includes a risotto – of course – and maybe osso buco as the star attraction. Otherwise you might start with a classic carpaccio, or spaghetti with tomato sauce and a generous amount of seafood (mussels, squid and prawns). Move on to noisettes of lamb with a fresh mint dressing and chorizo-flavoured mash, or pan-fried brill with asparagus confit, tomatoes and capers. Finish with rhubarb tart or tiramisù.

Chef Giancarlo Anselmi **Owner** Cosgrave Developments **Seats** 120, Pr/dining room 96 **Times** 5.30-9.30 **Prices** Fixed L 2 course €24.95-€29.95, Fixed D 3 course €29.95, Starter €8.95-€18.45, Main €18.50-€30.95, Dessert €6.95-€10.50, Service optional **Wines** 12 bottles over €30, 3 bottles under €30, 11 by glass **Parking** 220 **Notes** Sunday L, Vegetarian available, Children welcome

Restaurant Patrick Guilbaud

Modern French V

tel: 01 6764192 **Merrion Hotel, 21 Upper Merrion St**
email: info@restaurantpatrickguilbaud.ie
web: www.restaurantpatrickguilbaud.ie
dir: *Opposite government buildings, next to Merrion Hotel*

Outstanding French cooking at the pre-eminent Dublin address

The elite strike force of proprietor Patrick Guilbaud and chef Guillaume Lebrun lead the line in Dublin's culinary premier league. Monsieur Guilbaud's vision to serve up haute cuisine in the city began back in 1981, and for many years his restaurant has remained at the top of the table, as the top table. It all takes place in the luxe Merrion Hotel, occupying a Georgian townhouse, but it feels like a stand-alone restaurant to all intents and purposes. There's nothing stuffy about the place, with a bright, contemporary finish that combines colourful artworks with soothingly neutral colour tones, watched over by a service team who know their onions. French culinary traditions lie at the heart of the menu, but this is modern stuff, too, with creativity running through from top to bottom. Irish produce gets a good run-out of course, with equal importance on provenance and seasonality. The technical skill in the kitchen is evident from the off, with dishes delivering interesting combinations, compelling flavours, and visual impact. Take a first-course dish of suckling pig croquettes, for example, which comes with fried quail's egg, foie gras and red pepper mostarda, or another where pan-roasted duck foie gras is served with iced red miso, cocoa and peanut croquant. The thrills continue into main courses. 'Mellow' spiced Wicklow lamb stars in a main course with black garlic, piquillo peppers and olive crumble, while another partners fillet of Irish beef with roast foie gras, Madeira and truffle jus. The kitchen can also produce some stellar vegetarian courses such as a delicate Cévennes onion tart, maybe, with vacche rossa (red cow) parmesan and truffle vinaigrette. Desserts continue in the same vein, delivering well-judged flavours and showing real skill in the making. Green apple parfait comes with pistachio ice cream, delicate meringue and vanilla espuma, and another partners pear and walnut soufflé with a Poire William sorbet. Saving room for a cheese course is a good idea, what with the great selection of Irish and French options to choose from, while the wine list, perhaps unsurprisingly, remains faithful to France without ignoring the rest of the world.

Chef Guillaume Lebrun **Owner** Patrick Guilbaud, Guillaume Lebrun, Stéphane Robin **Seats** 80, Pr/dining room 25 **Times** 12.30-2.15/7.30-10.15 Closed 25 Dec, 1st wk Jan, Sun-Mon **Prices** Fixed L 2 course fr €40, Fixed D 3 course fr €105, Tasting menu €90-€180, Service optional **Wines** 12 by glass **Parking** Parking in square **Notes** A la carte menu 2/3/4 course €85/€105/€130, Children welcome

DUBLIN *continued*

Restaurant Patrick Guilbaud

◉◉◉◉ – *see opposite*

Roganstown Hotel and Country Club

◉ European

tel: 01 843 3118 **Naul Rd, Sword**
email: info@roganstown.com **web:** www.roganstown.com

Modern cooking in a golfing resort

A sprawling resort with golf, spa and conference facilities, Roganstown is also home to the impressive McLoughlins Restaurant. Located in a wood-panelled room within the hotel (the original part of the structure was a farmhouse in a former life), there's plenty of room between well-dressed tables. The kitchen seeks out first-class ingredients and delivers a menu that has ambition and a contemporary feel. A first course dish of lightly smoked scallops (nicely seared) arrive under a cloche to make an impression, served with a silky purée of minted peas and some pickled vegetables. Next up, among main courses, suckling pig cutlets are tender and moist, coming with a 'Pomme William', braised red cabbage and sweet potato purée, while a fishy main might be pan-fried salmon with a shellfish velouté. There are modern cooking techniques on show, not least in a dessert of saffron-poached pear with textures of raspberry.

Chef Jason Lelièvre, Luke Philipps **Owner** Ian McGuiness **Seats** 100, Pr/dining room 30 **Times** 12.30-4.30/5-10 Closed Xmas, Mon-Tue, L Wed-Sat **Prices** Fixed D 3 course €23.95-€38.95, Starter €7.95, Main €23.95-€28.95, Dessert €7.50-€12, Service optional **Wines** 3 bottles over €30, 20 bottles under €30, 8 by glass **Notes** Sunday L €19.95-€24.95, Vegetarian available, Children welcome

The Shelbourne Dublin, a Renaissance Hotel

◉◉ Traditional Irish, European

tel: 01 6634500 **27 St Stephen's Green**
email: rhi.dubbr.dts@renaissancehotels.com **web:** www.theshelbourne.ie
dir: *M1 to city centre, along Parnell St to O'Connell St towards Trinity College, 3rd right into Kildare St, hotel on left*

Grand modern hotel with seafood, steaks and modernist dishes too

In a sign that all bases are covered, the Shelbourne retains a 'genealogy butler', to research your family background, should you decide to delve into who you think you are. This grand modern hotel is in a prime location on St Stephen's Green, the expansive garden square at the heart of the capital, offering a range of eating and drinking options culminating in the tip-top Saddle Room. Here a menu of modern brasserie dishes specialises in seafood (including generously loaded platters) and majestic 32-day-aged beef (two of you might set about a pound of Chateaubriand). Modernists might look further afield to the likes of seared foie gras in Banyuls with fig compôte, or Knockdrinna goats' cheese with pickled courgette in beetroot emulsion. Mains might include rabbit loin wrapped in Alsace bacon with kale and puréed carrots, or roast halibut with baby leeks in chilled oyster cream. A five-course taster offers a tour of the more adventurous dishes, while puddings take a traditional line for rhubarb crumble, or blackberry mousse with caramelised apple.

Chef Garry Hughes **Owner** Renaissance Hotels **Seats** 120, Pr/dining room 20 **Times** 12.30-2.30/5.45-10.30 **Prices** Fixed L 2 course fr €21.95, Fixed D 3 course fr €42, Tasting menu fr €70, Starter €7.95-€19, Main €16.95-€38.95, Dessert €8.95-€15 **Wines** 100 bottles over €30, 10 bottles under €30, 12 by glass **Parking** Valet parking **Notes** Daily pre-theatre menu 2/3 course available 6-7pm, Sunday L €24.95-€28.95, Vegetarian available, Children welcome

Stillorgan Park Hotel

◉ Traditional Mediterranean, International

tel: 01 2001800 **Stillorgan Rd**
email: info@stillorganpark.com **web:** www.stillorganpark.com
dir: *On N11 follow signs for Wexford, pass RTE studios on left, through next 5 sets of lights. Hotel on left*

Gently modern cooking in a spa hotel

A hotel with a spa and wedding packages among its attractions, Stillorgan Park is also home to the Purple Sage restaurant, with its breezy vibe and contemporary finish. There are plenty of nooks and crannies in the split-level room if you're after a bit of privacy. The menu takes a gently modern tack, nothing too wacky, and with classic combinations at the heart of the action. Pan-fried venison sausage, for example, might turn up with root vegetable purée and cranberry compôte, or a smoked trout and prawn mousse. Grilled breast of pheasant with a chestnut and apricot stuffing is a wintery main course, or go for roasted monkfish with black truffle and a fresh herb risotto. For dessert, lemon and lime frangipane tart served with vanilla ice cream has a satisfying tartness, and there are Irish cheeses, too.

Chef Enda Dunne **Owner** Des Pettitt **Seats** 140, Pr/dining room 60 **Times** 12-3/5.45-10.15 Closed 25 Dec, L Sat, D Sun **Prices** Starter €5.70-€9, Main €17-€24, Dessert €6.50-€8.75, Service optional **Wines** 5 bottles over €30, 20 bottles under €30, 14 by glass **Parking** 300 **Notes** Early bird menu 2/3 course €21/ €25, Sunday L, Vegetarian available, Children welcome

The Westbury Hotel

◉◉ Modern Irish

tel: 01 6791122 **Grafton St**
email: westbury@doylecollection.com **web:** www.doylecollection.com
dir: *Adjacent to Grafton St, half way between Trinity College & St Stephen's Green*

Refined modern cooking in a city-centre hotel

The restaurant at this city centre hotel is a swishly decorated and furnished room dedicated to Oscar Wilde. The kitchen picks the cream of Ireland's produce and showcases it to good effect on a menu that's a beguiling mix of modern ideas. Prawn and crab cocktail with Marie Rose sauce sounds familiar enough, but here it's an exemplary example of the beast, and jostles for attention with foie gras crusted in pain d'épice, served with pear salad and caramelised walnuts. Among main courses, spicy duck has been given the Eastern treatment, served with honey and soy sauce, a spring roll and squash purée spiked with chilli. Alternatively you might go for a daily fish dish – say, properly timed fillet of halibut with smoked bacon essence, Jerusalem artichokes and roast salsify. Puddings are a strong suit too, among them perhaps red berry vacherin with blackberry sorbet.

Chef Sandeep Singh **Owner** The Doyle Collection **Seats** 95 **Times** 6.30-10.30 Closed Sun-Mon, L all week **Prices** Prices not confirmed, Service optional **Wines** 56 bottles over €30, 14 bottles under €30, 10 by glass **Notes** Pre-theatre available, Vegetarian available, Children welcome

Read all about our Wine Award winners on page 17

COUNTY DUBLIN

DONABATE
Map 1 D4

The Waterside House Hotel
◎ Modern French **NEW**

tel: 01 8436153
email: info@watersidehousehotel.ie **web:** www.samphire.ie
dir: *Exit M1 junct 4 (Donabate/Portrane), 3rd exit at rdbt, pass Newbridge House Demesne on left, continue over rail bridge, right at sign for golf courses & hotel. Hotel on left*

Local seafood in Irish/French menu plus lovely sea views

The hotel's name drops a large hint as to its location (the waves practically lap at the foundations), and its Samphire Restaurant is named for the wild vegetable that grows literally its doorstep. Splendid sea views are the backdrop here, and in such a spot, you expect locally-landed seafood to plays its part. It turns up in the shape of pan-seared hake fillet with cauliflower purée, asparagus and lemon beurre blanc, or wild sea bass with potato and crab salad, baby vegetables and sauce Nero. Meat eaters get a fair crack of the whip too, as the Ireland-meets-France menu encompasses the likes of confit duck leg with chorizo and cannelini beans, and there's plenty of local terroir in a plate of roast Tipperary pork loin with confit belly, Clonakilty black pudding beignet, pickled carrot, and carrot and aniseed purée.

Chef Tom Walsh **Owner** Chris & Thelma Slattery **Seats** 40, Pr/dining room 35 **Times** 12-3.30/5-9.45 Closed Mon-Tue (winter), L Mon-Thu, D Mon-Tue **Prices** Fixed L 2 course €23.95-€26.95, Fixed D 3 course €26.95-€39.95, Tasting menu €45-€75, Starter €5.95-€15, Main €21.50-€32, Dessert €6.95-€10, Service optional **Wines** 32 bottles over €30, 5 bottles under €30, 10 by glass **Parking** 110 **Notes** Sunday L €23.95-€26.95, Vegetarian available

KILLINEY
Map 1 D4

Fitzpatrick Castle Hotel
◎ Modern European

tel: 01 2305400
email: info@fitzpatricks.com **web:** www.fitzpatrickcastle.com
dir: *From Dun Laoghaire port turn left, on coast road right at lights, left at next lights. Follow to Dalkey, right at Ivory pub, immediate left, up hill, hotel at top*

Country-house cooking with views over Dublin Bay

The castellated house was built in the 18th century, and has had something of a martial career, being successively owned by a parade of army officers, the scene of fighting during the Easter Rising, and having troops stationed here during the second world war. Things are rather calmer now, as befits the tranquil prospect of its perch overlooking Dublin Bay. A range of hospitable dining venues culminates in the elegant PJ's restaurant, where brocade-upholstered chairs and smart table settings are the background for a menu of well-wrought country-house cooking. There's no wild experimentation here, just good honest preparations of prime materials. Expect Dublin Bay prawns in provençal sauce or garlic butter, as the prelude to grilled lamb cutlets with minted pea and potato cake and redcurrant jelly, or plaice with apple pie, or a chocolate brownie served with berry compôte and vanilla ice cream.

Chef Phil Whittal **Owner** Eithne Fitzpatrick **Seats** 75 **Times** 3-5.30/6-9.30 Closed 25 Dec, L Mon-Sat **Prices** Fixed L 2 course €25-€33, Fixed D 3 course €30-€38, Starter €6-€13.75, Main €16-€28, Dessert €7, Service optional **Wines** 7 bottles over €30, 156 bottles under €30, 11 by glass **Parking** 200 **Notes** Sunday L €25-€38, Vegetarian available, Children welcome

LUCAN
Map 1 D4

Finnstown Country House Hotel
◎ Traditional European

tel: 01 6010700 **Newcastle Rd**
email: edwina@finnstown-hotel.ie **web:** www.finnstown.com
dir: *N4 S/bound exit 4, left on slip road straight across rdbt & lights. Hotel on left*

Accomplished cooking in an 18th-century manor hotel

This creeper-hung 18th-century hotel, a portico over the front door, is on a 45-acre estate but is only a half-hour from the city centre. Its Peacock restaurant is a handsome room for dining, offering honest-to-goodness cooking of fine ingredients from a menu that doesn't try to change the world. Mango and chilli salsa, for grilled duck and spring roll sausage, is about as exotic as things get with tian of crab and prawns Marie Rose more typical. Crabmeat may turn up again in a main course as a partner for baked fillet of sea trout in a herb crust with shellfish and brandy bisque, an alternative to seared peppered duck breast with mushroom and basil cream and sautéed spinach. End with a straightforward dessert, such as lemon tart or chocolate mousse.

Times 12.30-2.30/7-9 Closed 24-26 Dec, D Sun

COUNTY GALWAY

BARNA
Map 1 B3

The Pins at The Twelve
◎ International, Italian

tel: 091 597000 **Barna Village**
email: enquire@thetwelvehotel.ie
dir: *Coast road Barna village, 10 mins from Galway*

Eclectic dining in a design-led venue

Part of the boutique-style Twelve Hotel, gastronomes will be pleased to learn that The Pins is actually an unusual amalgam of bar, bakery, bistro and pizzeria: the on-site Pins Bakery means that bread and pastries are as fresh as it gets, and if you want to keep things simple, the Dozzina pizzeria turns out traditional artisan pizzas made in an oven hewn from Vesuvian stone. But if you want to put the kitchen through its paces, there's also a menu of 'casual, local' food that champions regional suppliers in uncomplicated ideas along the lines of seared venison steak with venison sausage roll, braised red cabbage, root vegetables, and truffle mash and jus. If you're in the mood for fish, organic Connemara sea trout might be served with white beans, chorizo and chard in a mussel and wine broth. For more ambitious modern fare, head up to the first-floor West Restaurant (see separate entry under The Twelve).

Chef Martin O'Donnell **Owner** Fergus O'Halloran **Seats** 140, Pr/dining room 20 **Times** breakfast-10 All-day dining **Prices** Prices not confirmed, Service optional **Wines** 300 bottles over €30, 60 bottles under €30, 35 by glass **Parking** 120 **Notes** BBQ menu options private functions, Sunday L, Vegetarian available, Children welcome

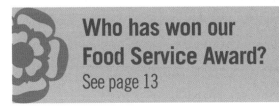

Who has won our Food Service Award?
See page 13

BARNA *continued*

Upstairs@West, The Twelve

Modern Irish NOTABLE WINE LIST

tel: 091 597000 **Barna Village**
email: west@thetwelvehotel.ie **web:** www.thetwelvehotel.ie
dir: Coast road Barna village, 10 mins from Galway

Well-conceived modern dishes in a seaside hotel

A boutique hotel with bags of contemporary swagger, The Twelve is in a coastal area just a short distance from the centre of Galway. There's a lot going on: a cool bar, a bakery selling artisan breads and cakes, a pizza place, and not forgetting the stylish bedrooms. The main dining action takes place in the Upstairs restaurant, which is focused on seasonal regional produce and wines from around the world. Billed as 'small plates' or 'large plates', kick off with Marty's Killarly harbour mussels in a Pernod and shallot reduction, served with a homemade seaweed soda farl, or go for the crisp pork belly with Connemara scallops, apple purée and cider reduction. Those larger plates follow the same path, delivering appealing plates with bang-on flavours and a contemporary flourish; Glin Valley chicken, maybe, with Colcannon gnocchi and chicken foam, or a côte de boeuf for two to share, with triple-cooked chips and Cashel Blue béarnaise. Finish with a lemon and lavender pudding with whiskey wine gums and lemon sherbet, and the artisan Irish cheeses are well worth checking out.

Chef Martin O'Donnell **Owner** Fergus O'Halloran **Seats** 94, Pr/dining room 100 **Times** 1-4/6-10 Closed Mon-Tue, L Wed-Fri **Prices** Prices not confirmed, Service optional **Wines** 300 bottles over €30, 60 bottles under €30, 35 by glass **Parking** 120 **Notes** Gourmet menu 5 course with wine, Wine tutorials, Sunday L, Vegetarian available, Children welcome

CASHEL
Map 1 A4

Cashel House

Traditional, International V

tel: 095 31001
email: res@cashel-house-hotel.com **web:** www.cashel-house-hotel.com
dir: S of N59. 1m W of Recess

A heavenly location and top-notch regional produce

Standing at the head of Cashel Bay in 50 acres of delightful, gardens, Cashel House is a gracious 19th-century country house that has been in the hands of the McEvilly family since 1968. When you have worked up a serious appetite on the local golf courses and woodland walks, the restaurant offers a repertoire of French-accented classics, served in either an airy conservatory extension, or a polished traditional setting amid antiques and artworks. Connemara's lakes, rivers, hillsides and the fishermen out in the bay supply the kitchen with the finest produce it could wish for, which is handled simply and with the confidence to let the flavours do the talking. A puff pastry parcel containing quail breast wrapped in ham with a creamy brandy sauce sets the ball rolling, before a sorbet (champagne, perhaps), then pan-fried monkfish comes with tomato, saffron and coriander concasse, or there could be roast rack of Connemara lamb with Guinness and honey sauce. White and dark chocolate terrine with orange liqueur sauce makes a fine finale.

Chef Arturo Tillo **Owner** Kay McEvilly & family **Seats** 70, Pr/dining room 20 **Times** 12.30-2.30/6.30-9 Closed 2 Jan-12 Feb **Prices** Fixed L 2 course €20-€25, Fixed D 2 course €25-€30, Starter €8-€12.75, Main €16.50-€32, Dessert €7.50 **Wines** 5 by glass **Parking** 30 **Notes** 5 course D €58, Sunday L €25-€30, Children welcome

CLIFDEN
Map 1 A4

Abbeyglen Castle Hotel

French, International

tel: 095 21201 **Sky Rd**
email: info@abbeyglen.ie **web:** www.abbeyglen.ie
dir: N59 from Galway towards Clifden. Hotel 1km from Clifden on Sky Rd

Fresh local produce in a charming old property

The crenallated Victorian fantasy of Abbeyglen Castle basks in views sweeping from Connemara's Twelve Bens mountains to the shores of Clifden Bay. Ensconced in 12 acres of lovely grounds, it is just a five-minute walk from the bustle and cosy pubs of Clifden village, but you might find it hard to drag yourself away from its classic country-house comforts. In the restaurant at dinner, the decor is bold and bright with artworks on cherry-red walls, crystal chandeliers, and a pianist tinkles away on a grand piano. Expect classic cooking built on excellent local materials. As you'd hope, given the closeness to the briny, fish and seafood makes a good showing – fresh oysters, seafood chowder, or poached salmon with hollandaise – while meat could turn up as slow-roasted suckling pig teamed with braised belly pork, apple chutney, celeriac crisps and a grain mustard reduction. Puddings finish slap in the comfort zone with the likes of chocolate bread-and-butter pudding or rhubarb crumble with crème anglaise.

Times 7-9 Closed 6-31 Jan, L all week

GALWAY
Map 1 B3/4

Ardilaun Hotel & Leisure Club

Modern International

tel: 091 521433 **Taylor's Hill**
email: info@theardilaunhotel.ie **web:** www.theardilaunhotel.ie
dir: 1m from city centre, towards Salthill on west side of city, near Galway Bay

Contemporary cooking in a quietly set hotel

In a quiet spot on the outskirts of the city towards Galway Bay, the Ardilaun Hotel has been built up around a 19th-century property, with the restaurant looking out on its five acres of grounds. The kitchen takes a European-wide stance, with starters along the lines of smoked haddock and potato cake on spinach with sauce vierge and pickled cucumber, and a salad of crisp pancetta, radish, peas and mozzarella with coriander and green pepper dressing. Well-chosen ingredients go into main courses too: a medley of Galway Bay seafood with a ragoût of sweetcorn, fennel and spring onions and truffle and chive cream, and roast bacon-wrapped chicken breast stuffed with sage and onions on cauliflower purée with mushroom sauce. Lemon meringue pie with berry compôte is a good way to end.

Chef David O'Donnell **Owner** John Ryan & family **Seats** 180, Pr/dining room 380 **Times** 1-2.30/6.30-9.15 Closed 23-26 Dec, L Mon-Sat **Prices** Fixed L 2 course €14.50, Fixed D 3 course €28, Starter €8.75-€10.50, Main €17.25-€52, Dessert €6.95-€7.95 **Wines** 62 bottles over €30, 9 bottles under €30, 9 by glass **Parking** 300 **Notes** Meal deal in Bistro 2/3 course €24/€27.50, Sunday L €9.95-€23, Vegetarian available, Children welcome

Follow the AA on twitter @TheAA_Lifestyle

The G Hotel

◉◉ Modern Irish V

tel: 091 865200 **Wellpark, Dublin Rd**
email: info@theg.ie **web:** www.theghotel.ie
dir: *Telephone for detailed directions*

Modern Irish brasserie cooking in a postmodern experience hotel

That gnomic initial is the clue to the style – a Force 10 postmodern experience hotel with interiors by avant-garde milliner Philip Treacy. Gendered lounges are in blue for boys, and screaming pink with black-and-white concentric circles for girls. Hard reflective surfaces are offset by pillbox views of the wild western coast, while Gigi's restaurant is done in full-throttle collisions of purple and pink, leafy green and sky blue, and then some. You might think Pauline Reilly's contemporary Irish brasserie cooking would struggle to keep up, but there's plenty of vivacity here too, from laden sharing boards of charcuterie or seafood, or starters such as king scallops with smoked bacon and caper noisette, to outstanding main-course proteins like Wexford beef ribeye with oxtail cannelloni, or roast sea bass in clam and mussel broth with saffron whipped potatoes. Sign up for Dinner and A Movie, and as soon as you've finished your cookies-and-cream cheesecake with winter berry and star-anise compôte, you can glide through to the EYE cinema for a 3D treat.

Chef Pauline Reilly **Owner** Edward Hotels **Seats** 90 **Times** 12.30-3/5.30-10 Closed 23-26 Dec, L Mon-Sat **Prices** Fixed D 3 course €25-€55, Service optional **Wines** 26 bottles over €30, 16 bottles under €30, 15 by glass **Parking** 200 **Notes** Seasonal menu Sun-Fri 6-7.30pm 2/3 course €29.50/€36, Sunday L €25-€29, Children welcome

Park House Hotel & Restaurant

◉ Modern Irish, International

tel: 091 564924 **Forster St, Eyre Square**
email: parkhousehotel@eircom.net **web:** www.parkhousehotel.ie
dir: *In city centre/Eyre Sq*

Appealing menu in bustling city-centre hotel

Standing just off the city's Eyre Square and built of striking pink granite, Park House has been offering high standards of food and accommodation for well over 35 years. Its celebrated Park Restaurant – where paintings of old Galway help keep the past alive – fairly bustles at lunchtime and mellows in the evening. Endearing classical design – in reds and golds with banquette seating and chairs and closely-set tables – suits the surroundings, likewise the traditional-inspired cooking is classically underpinned, while making good use of traceable local ingredients on a menu with broad appeal. Orange- and honey-glazed breast of duckling with a peppercorn sauce, for instance, or prime fillet steak au poivre to Dublin Bay prawns thermidor. Finish with profiteroles, apple pie or Pavlova.

Chef Robert O'Keefe, Martin Keane **Owner** Eamon Doyle, Kitty Carr **Seats** 145, Pr/dining room 45 **Times** 12-3/6-10 Closed 24-26 Dec **Prices** Prices not confirmed, Service optional **Wines** 4 by glass **Parking** 40, Adjacent to hotel **Notes** Early evening menu €33.95, Sunday L, Vegetarian available, Children welcome

---

Lough Inagh Lodge

◉◉ Irish, French

tel: 095 34706 & 34694 **Inagh Valley**
email: inagh@iol.ie **web:** www.loughinaghlodgehotel.ie
dir: *From Galway take N344. After 3.5m hotel on right*

Spectacular scenery and Irish country-house cooking

Dating from 1880, when it was built as a fishing lodge, this boutique hotel is in a lovely spot on the shore of Lough Inagh surrounded by wild mountains. There's an oak-panelled bar, a library with a log fire, and a restaurant where silver and glassware reflect candlelight and an oval window gives wonderful views. Chatty and attentive staff are happy to make recommendations about the set-price dinner menu, which might open with air-dried lamb and beef with a warm chickpea croquette and red onion marmalade, or mussels steamed with white wine and garlic. A modern spin is given to traditional Irish cuisine, along with the more classical, and fresh native produce is evident. Main courses are commendably free of frills and flounces. Precisely cooked duck breast, sliced and fanned on the plate, in a sauce of plum purée hinting at star anise, for instance, is served with fondant potato and well-timed seasonal vegetables, or baked lobster with a simple lemon butter. End with luscious chocolate pudding with raspberry sorbet and slices of poached orange.

Times 7-8.45 Closed mid Dec-mid Mar

Coastguard Restaurant

◉ Modern Irish NEW

tel: (066) 9150200
email: reservations@dingleskellig.com **web:** www.dingleskellig.com
dir: *N86 from Tralee (30km). Hotel on harbourside on L*

Modern Irish cooking and Dingle Bay views

It isn't possible to get much further west on the European continent than this spot. The Dingle Skellig Hotel is a sprawling establishment right on the coast with glorious views all round. A family-friendly sort of place, there's a kids' club, leisure facilities, a room for teenagers to hang out, plus a spa for the grown-ups. The main dining option is the Coastguard Restaurant (food is also available in the bar, bistro and cocktail lounge), with its stunning view over the bay through capacious picture windows. The kitchen works with the excellent produce around these parts, with locally landed fish and West Kerry lamb stealing the show. The modern Irish repertoire runs to a classic combination of pan-fried scallops with local black pudding, pea purée and Parma ham crisps, each element cooked correctly, followed by seared breast of duckling with a confit fig and sautéed fennel. Finish with orange and rhubarb crème brûlée.

Chef John Ryan **Owner** Tomas Garvey **Seats** 120, Pr/dining room **Times** 6.30-9.15 Closed Jan **Prices** Fixed D 3 course €24-€39, Service optional **Wines** 35 bottles over €30, 14 bottles under €30, 10 by glass **Notes** Vegetarian available, Children welcome

Follow us on facebook
www.facebook.com/TheAAUK

DINGLE (AN DAINGEAN) *continued*

Gormans Clifftop House & Restaurant

◉ Modern, Traditional

tel: 066 9155162 & 083 0033133 **Glaise Bheag, Ballydavid (Baile na nGall)**
email: info@gormans-clifftophouse.com **web:** www.gormans-clifftophouse.com
dir: *R559 to An Mhuirioch, turn right at T-junct, N for 3km*

Clifftop cracker with splendid local produce

The stone-built house perching on the clifftops above Smerwick harbour on the northwestern tip of the Dingle Peninsula has been owned by the Gorman family since the 18th century, which might explain why chef-proprietor Vincent Gorman has a passion for sourcing as much as possible of his materials from the local farms and ports. Simplicity is the key to this delightful restaurant with rooms: there's nothing to get in the way of the dining room's sweeping views across the Atlantic, produce is spanking fresh and the concise menu offers five choices at each stage. You might start with locally smoked organic salmon served with a simple salad and horseradish cream, and follow with a hearty Kerry lamb stew with root vegetables and potatoes, or pan-fried hake fillet with roasted cherry tomatoes, lemon butter and fresh herbs. To finish, there could be mango parfait with passionfruit and mango syrup.

Chef Vincent Gorman **Owner** Sile & Vincent Gorman **Seats** 30 **Times** 7-8 Closed Oct-Mar, Sun, L all week **Prices** Fixed D 3 course €35-€45, Starter €6.50-€14.50, Main €18.50-€26.50, Dessert €6.50-€9.50, Service optional **Wines** 10 bottles over €30, 17 bottles under €30, 6 by glass **Parking** 25 **Notes** Vegetarian available, Children welcome

KENMARE   Map 1 B2

Sheen Falls Lodge

◉◉ Modern European V

tel: 064 6641600 **Sheen Falls Lodge**
email: info@sheenfallslodge.ie **web:** www.sheenfallslodge.ie
dir: *From Kenmare take N71 to Glengarriff. Take 1st left after suspension bridge. 1m from Kenmare*

Memorable cooking and waterfall views

High on a promontory in woodland and gardens, this modern building has views of Kenmare Bay to one side and of Sheen Falls on the other. La Cascade restaurant has views of the falls too — floodlit after dark — although attention is likely to be diverted to the enticements on the menu. The cooking is based on a contemporary European repertory, with the kitchen applying its own creative spin on things, adding confit pork belly ravioli to green pea soup, for instance, and making another starter of veal carpaccio and pan-fried sweetbreads and serving them with a 'dust' of aged balsamic, and watermelon and samphire marinated in salted olive oil. Main courses are intelligently composed, offering much to interest, with fillet of local hake paired with a crab beignet and served with thyme risotto, bell pepper jus and seasonal vegetables, and pan-fried smoked duck breast accompanied by confit drumstick, dandelion leaves, sage butter and gnocchi. A touch of novelty is seen in puddings like mojito sponge with pineapple sorbet and pineapple and chilli kebab.

Chef Philip Brazil **Owner** Palladium Hotels & Resorts **Seats** 120, Pr/dining room 40 **Times** 7-9.30 Closed 2 Jan-1 Feb, L all week **Prices** Fixed D 3 course fr €65, Service optional **Wines** 16 by glass **Parking** 75 **Notes** Children welcome

KILLARNEY   Map 1 B2

Cahernane House Hotel

◉◉ Modern European, International

tel: 064 6631895 **Muckross Rd**
email: info@cahernane.com **web:** www.cahernane.com
dir: *From Killarney follow signs for Kenmare, then from Muckross Rd over bridge. Hotel signed on right. Hotel 1m from town centre*

Modern country-house cooking in a tranquil setting

Ringed by peaks in the heart of the Killarney National Park, Cahernane was once the seat of the Earls of Pembroke, and sits in a peaceful private estate just a short stroll from the shores of Lough Leane. Reached via an impressive avenue of mature trees, the 17th-century house is a deeply traditional place replete with original fireplaces, intricate ceilings and ancestral oil portraits — a style that makes for a sense of occasion when dining in the Herbert Room Restaurant to a backdrop of the lake and immaculately kept grounds. The food is weighted towards classical and traditional themes enlivened with flashes of modern flair, so things kick off with pan-fried quail with date and orange purée, citrus emulsion and home-made chutney, while a well-thought-out main course sees roast saddle of venison partnered with celeriac remoulade, butternut squash purée and a juniper-infused jus. To finish, natural yoghurt sorbet makes an intelligent counterpoint to the richness of praline crème brûlée. For a more casual mood, there's bistro fare in the old wine cellar bar.

Times 12-2.30/7-9.30 Closed Jan-Feb, L all week (ex by arrangement), D Sun

The Lake Hotel

◉ Traditional European V

tel: 064 6631035 **On the Shore, Muckross Rd**
email: info@lakehotel.com **web:** www.lakehotelkillarney.com
dir: *2km from town centre on N71 Muckross Rd*

Lough views and successful modern cooking

The Lake Hotel earns its name, as it's bang on the shore of Lough Lein, with glorious views over water and mountains. The hotel has been much extended over the years, and The Castlelough Restaurant, built as part of the original 1820 house, has itself seen total refurbishment while retaining its high ceilings, cornicing and vast windows catching those views. The kitchen works around a slate of modern ideas based on classical traditions, using the area's tip-top ingredients. An assiette of duck, for instance, comes as terrine, smoked, with hazelnuts and orange, and warm pithivier, and a plate of smoked fish as salmon blini, sea trout with lemon and caviar dressing, and haddock fishcake with caper aïoli. Main courses can seem more mainstream, as in chicken breast with fondant potato, pea purée, and leek and mushroom ragout, although roast saddle of rabbit partnered by monkfish and served with black pudding, carrots and a savoury jus brings an interesting interpretation of surf 'n' turf.

Chef Noel Enright **Owner** The Huggard family **Seats** 100, Pr/dining room 65 **Times** 12-4.30/6.30-9 Closed Dec-Jan, L all week **Prices** Fixed L 2 course €15-€25, Fixed D 3 course €38, Starter €5-€10, Main €18-€30, Dessert €6-€9, Service optional **Wines** 37 bottles over €30, 12 bottles under €30, 6 by glass **Parking** 150 **Notes** Signature tasting menu available, Sunday L, Children welcome

Muckross Park Hotel & Cloisters Spa

◉ Modern Irish v

tel: 064 6623400 **Lakes of Killarney**
email: info@muckrosspark.com **web:** www.muckrosspark.com
dir: *From Killarney take N71 towards Kenmare. Hotel on left before entrance to Muckross House*

Modern food in a characterful country house

This upmarket hotel and spa occupies a venerable old house that first opened its doors as the Herbert Arms in 1795. The location overlooking the Killarney National Park, with the Blue Pool River running through the grounds, is a dream, and there's history too: Queen Victoria stayed here, and George Bernard Shaw holed up in the summer of 1923 to write *Pygmalion*; his sojourn is referenced in the fine-dining GB Shaw's Restaurant. The venue sports a smart contemporary sheen, and local produce is the name of the game, appearing in appealing modern European-accented dishes. Duck foie gras with apple membrillo and truffled brioche might be one way to start, while the main course could see venison partnered by celeriac purée, pear, and chocolate jus; fish turns up in the shape of monkfish with aubergine purée, pancetta and tomato. To end, blood orange jelly and sorbet add an up-to-date edge to vanilla rice pudding.

Chef Paul O'Connor **Owner** Muckross Park Hotel Ltd **Seats** 70, Pr/dining room 60 **Times** 6.30-9.30 Closed midwk Nov-Feb, Mon, L all week **Prices** Fixed L 2 course €20-€32, Fixed D 3 course €45-€55, Starter €7-€16, Main €18-€32, Dessert €8-€14, Service optional **Wines** 38 bottles over €30, 31 bottles under €30, 10 by glass **Parking** 150 **Notes** Children welcome

---

KILLORGLIN   Map 1 A2

Carrig House Country House & Restaurant

◉ Modern Irish, European

tel: 066 9769100 **Caragh Lake**
email: info@carrighouse.com **web:** www.carrighouse.com
dir: *N70 to Killorglin*

Fine dining with expansive lough views

Carrig is a lovingly restored Victorian country manor in acres of colourful woodland gardens with views across Caragh Lake to the Kerry Mountains. Inside, the genteel house is done out in period style, with turf fires sizzling in cosy, chintzy lounges, while the dining room is the very image of 19th-century chic; all William Morris wallpapers, swagged curtains, polished floorboards, and formally laid tables. The cooking, on the other hand, takes a more up-to-date approach, lining up superb local ingredients and sending them to finishing school: crab could get a modish three-way treatment as ravioli, soup and pasty, and might be followed by Skeganore duck breast with vanilla and lime potato purée, and sweet port and brandy jus. For dessert, maybe prune and Armagnac crème brûlée.

Times 7-9

TRALEE   Map 1 A2

Ballygarry House Hotel and Spa

◉ Modern Irish

tel: 066 7123322 **Leebrook**
email: info@ballygarryhouse.com **web:** www.ballygarryhouse.com
dir: *1.5km from Tralee, on N21*

Excellent Irish ingredients in a well-established family-run hotel

After 50 years in the hands of the same family, you might expect service at this upmarket country house hotel with a delicious pampering spa to run like a well-oiled clock, and you'd be right. The location, too, is a big plus: set in six acres of gorgeous gardens at the foot of the Kerry Mountains. Landscapes hereabouts run the gamut from mountains to lakes, woodland, and ocean – a perfect environment,

then, for the kitchen to get its hands on the finest local materials from land and sea, so on the food front you can expect well-executed Irish cooking served in the bright and cheerful surroundings of the Brooks Restaurant. Start with heartwarming seafood chowder served with home-made brown soda bread, and go on with roast rack of lamb with wild mushrooms and sherry jus, or baked sea bass with potato rösti, crab meat, and fresh pea cream.

Chef John O'Sullivan **Owner** Padraig McGillicudy **Seats** 90 **Times** 12.30-2.30/6.30-9.30 Closed 22-26 Dec **Prices** Fixed L 3 course €25, Fixed D 3 course €35, Starter €5.95-€10.95, Main €19.95-€28.95, Service optional **Wines** 14 bottles over €30, 20 bottles under €30, 6 by glass **Parking** 200 **Notes** Sunday L €25, Vegetarian available, Children welcome

---

Ballyseede Castle

◉◉ Traditional European

tel: 066 7125799
email: info@ballyseedecastle.com **web:** www.ballyseedecastle.com
dir: *On N21 just after N21/N22 junct*

Appealing well-conceived food in a castle hotel

The castle is indeed that, crenellated and turreted, dating from the late 16th century, surrounded by 30 acres of woodland. It's now a deluxe hotel offering the full-on country-house experience (weddings are also popular). The O'Connell Restaurant looks like something in a stately home, a gracefully curved room with luxurious drapes at the windows, columns, oil paintings and a chandelier. 'Resplendent grandeur' heads the menu, but the cooking is more down-to-earth than that might suggest, the kitchen clearly taking a contemporary outlook on matters culinary. Starters make an impact, from breaded monkfish cheeks and prawns with home-made tomato and caraway seed ketchup and tartare sauce, to braised belly pork with a black pudding croquette, crackling, fried apple and a sticky jus. Top-quality native produce is used throughout, evident in well-conceived, unfussy main courses: perhaps pan-fried salmon fillet with a creamy sauce of leeks, peas, dill and saffron, or roast duck confit glazed in honey and orange with a jus of port, grapes and orange. End with something like chocolate parfait and butterscotch sauce.

Times 12.30-2.30/7-9 Closed Jan-3 Mar, L Mon-Sat

COUNTY KILDARE

STRAFFAN   Map 1 C/D4

Barberstown Castle

◉◉ Irish, French

tel: 01 6288157
email: info@barberstowncastle.ie **web:** www.barberstowncastle.ie
dir: *R406, follow signs for Barberstown*

Classic cooking in a 13th-century castle

Close to Dublin city centre and the airport, Barberstown Castle presents a fascinating timeline running through eight centuries of history from its 13th-century crenallated tower to wings added by Elizabethan and Victorian inhabitants, which now house the elegant dining rooms. You can take oodles of period character as read: amid walls hung with tapestries, wooden and flagstoned floors, and throne-like wooden chairs at candlelit, linen-clad tables, dinner is always a bit special, and staff make sure it all ticks along in a smooth and professional manner. Classical country-house influences are to the fore – the man directing the culinary action is French, after all – in a repertoire built on prime local materials and a pitch-perfect grasp of how flavours and textures work together. Expect main courses such as chargrilled Irish beef fillet with fondant potato, baby spinach, celeriac purée and foie gras sauce, or wild sea bass matched with scallops, fennel compôte, vine tomatoes, and star anise cream. Bringing up the rear are desserts that might include buttermilk pannacotta with Irish rhubarb compôte and jelly.

Times 7.30-10 Closed 24-26 Dec, Jan, Sun-Thu, L all week

STRAFFEN *continued*

The K Club

◉◉ Traditional French **NEW**

tel: 01 6017200 **River Room**
email: sales@kclub.ie **web:** www.kclub.ie
dir: *From Dublin take N4, exit for R406, hotel on right in Straffan*

Classy, contemporary food in a five-star hotel

The architect was aiming for the French château look, and by jove he got it! That was back in 1832, and today his vision performs as a five-star hotel as if built for the job. It is a luxurious place with a swanky spa, golf course and no stone left unturned in the pursuit of indulgence. There are dining options aplenty, not least of which is the River Restaurant, with its commanding views of the Liffey and the hotel's formal gardens. Tables are generously spaced and smartly laid, with grand floral displays making a statement in their own right. The cooking is classically minded and built on solid regional foundations. Roast breast of wood pigeon in the company of its confit leg shows sound technique, served with artichoke purée and a jus rich with Madeira. For mains, loin of Wicklow venison is no less impressive, with red rhubarb compôte, ceps and an oozing chunk of local honeycomb. Warm poached Comice pear filled with a chocolate frangipane, plus a chocolate sauce and pear as sorbet and foam, is a satisfying finale.

Chef Finbar Higgins **Owner** Dr Michael Smurfit **Seats** 110, Pr/dining room 30
Times 1-3/7-9.15 **Prices** Fixed L 3 course €45, Fixed D 3 course €63, Tasting menu €53-€83, Starter €18-€30, Main €35-€53, Dessert €10-€12, Service optional **Wines** 250 bottles over €30, 10 by glass **Parking** 300 **Notes** Sunday L €45, Vegetarian available, Children welcome

COUNTY KILKENNY

KILKENNY   Map 1 C3

Kilkenny River Court Hotel

◉ Modern, Traditional

tel: 056 7723388 **The Bridge, John St**
email: info@rivercourthotel.com **web:** www.rivercourthotel.com
dir: *In town centre, opposite castle*

Historic castle setting for ambitious cooking

This contemporary hotel has a clear line of sight across the battlements of 12th-century Kilkenny Castle and the free-flowing River Nore. It's a treat day or night as the castle is lit up in the evening and floor-to-ceiling windows mean you get the best view in town. The restaurant is done out in a smart modish manner with well-dressed tables, high-backed leather seats and moody lighting to set the upmarket tone. The menu matches the contemporary disposition with some well-crafted, well-presented food. Start with teriyaki-flavoured flaked salmon with buffalo mozzarella, curly endive and plum tomato salad, before moving on to fillet of hake with a fricassee of fennel, garden peas, capers and a herby beurre blanc, or cider-braised pork belly with creamed leeks, Savoy cabbage and champ. There's good cooking at dessert stage, too: a trio of Cox's Orange Pippin (strudel, parfait and jelly), for example.

Chef Nicholas Codoul **Owner** Rubyside Ltd **Seats** 80 **Times** 1-2.30/6-9.30 Closed Xmas, L Mon-Sat, D Sun **Prices** Fixed L 2 course fr €21.95, Fixed D 3 course fr €29.95, Service optional **Wines** 20 bottles over €30, 10 bottles under €30, 4 by glass **Parking** 120 **Notes** Early bird from €24.95, Sunday L €21.95-€24.95, Vegetarian available, Children welcome

THOMASTOWN   Map 1 C3

Kendals Brasserie

◉ French, European

tel: 056 7773000 **Mount Juliet Hotel**
email: info@mountjuliet.ie
dir: *M7 from Dublin, N9 towards Waterford, exit at junct 9/Danesfort for hotel*

A taste of France beside the golf course

The name might not have a cross-Channel ring to it, but French brasserie classics are the name of the game at Kendals, which is the more casual venue at the swanky 18th-century Mount Juliet Hotel. Housed in the estate's converted stables – now the golf clubhouse – the setting is light and airy in the day, looking over the fairways through large windows, and more romantic when it is candlelit for dinner. Top-class local ingredients underpin the repertoire of French brasserie classics, which could kick off with salade Lyonnaise, beef carpaccio, or salt-cod brandade with marinated cherry tomatoes and curly endive, ahead of local Slaney lamb, slow-cooked for 15 hours and served with pommes Anna, Chantenay carrots and peas, and thyme jus. Finish with banana tarte Tatin with home-made rum and raisin ice cream. If you want to trade up on another visit, the posh option is the Lady Helen Restaurant (see entry below).

Chef Cormac Rowe **Owner** Mount Juliet **Seats** 70 **Times** 6-9.30 Closed Mon & Wed (seasonal) **Prices** Starter €6-€9.50, Main €17.50-€28, Dessert €3.50-€11 **Wines** 38 bottles over €30, 25 bottles under €30, 10 by glass **Parking** 200 **Notes** Early bird menu 6-7pm 3 course €25, Vegetarian available, Children welcome

The Lady Helen Restaurant

◉◉◉ – *see opposite*

COUNTY LEITRIM

MOHILL   Map 1 C4

Lough Rynn Castle

◉◉ Modern, Traditional Irish

tel: 071 9632700
email: enquiries@loughrynn.ie **web:** www.loughrynn.ie
dir: *N4 (Dublin to Sligo), hotel 8km off N4 & 2km from Mohill*

Contemporary flavours in a peaceful location

The 200-year-old ancestral home of Lord Leitrim was built to impress: Lough Rynn Castle sits in 300 acres of idyllic Ireland beside the eponymous lough, complete with its own championship golf course. The Sandstone Restaurant is an intimate space in the converted stables that makes a feature of its bare stone walls (hence the name), and comes plushly furnished with well-upholstered high-backed chairs and linen-clothed tables. The kitchen lives up to the fine-dining expectations of the setting, taking care in sourcing the finest County Leitrim ingredients, and putting it all together with skill and imagination in an ambitious repertoire of contemporary European-accented dishes. Crab cannelloni arrives with seared scallops, the crunch of samphire, a scallop and watermelon gel, and seafood foam, followed by a two-way serving of lamb -seared loin with basil jus, and braised knuckle in filo pastry – with celeriac purée, sautéed courgettes and potato croquettes. The curtain comes down with an apple and olive oil timbale with iced beetroot parfait, violet and beetroot foam, olive oil jelly and pistachio cream.

Times 12-2.30/7-9 Closed L Mon-Sat

COUNTY LIMERICK

LIMERICK
Map 1 B3

Limerick Strand Hotel
Modern International

tel: 061 421800 **Ennis St**
email: info@strandlimerick.ie **web:** www.strandlimerick.ie
dir: On the Shannon side of Sarsfield Bridge, on River Shannon

River views and comforting food

The aptly-named River Restaurant of the spanking-new contemporary Limerick Strand Hotel is the place to head to for dining with the best views in town. Floor-to-ceiling glass walls mean everyone gets a view of the Shannon flowing by to go with a well-prepared and presented repertoire of straightforward modern European food. There's an abundance of splendid raw materials in these parts, and they find their way into dishes such as beef carpaccio with rocket, parmesan, horseradish crisp and citrus vinaigrette, while mains run to mixed grills, steaks or herb-crusted rack of new season Kerry lamb with fondant potato, carrot gratin, and red wine jus. For pudding, perhaps a refreshing lemon vacherin with raspberry sauce.

Chef Tom Flavin **Seats** 120, Pr/dining room 450 **Times** 6-10 **Prices** Fixed D 3 course €29.95-€34.95, Starter €4.95-€9.95, Main €14.95-€24.95, Dessert €4.95-€8, Service optional **Wines Parking** 200 **Notes** Sunday L €23.95, Children welcome

COUNTY LOUTH

CARLINGFORD
Map 1 D4

Ghan House
Modern Irish

tel: 042 9373682
email: info@ghanhouse.com **web:** www.ghanhouse.com
dir: M1 junct 18 signed Carlingford, 5mtrs on left after 50kph speed sign

Wide-ranging menus on the lough

On the shore of Carlingford Lough in a walled garden, Ghan House is a family-run hotel and restaurant with views over the water. The kitchen's a busy place, making everything in-house, from bread to ice cream; herbs, fruit and vegetables come from the hotel's garden and shellfish from the lough. The eclectic menu picks up ideas from international cuisines, so to start might come seafood chowder, confit duck leg with cassoulet and thyme jus, and mackerel escabèche with black onion seed crackers, potato salad and smoked haddock cream. The menu name-checks sources — Cooley lamb and beef, fish landed at Kilkeel harbour — so quality and freshness are guaranteed. Fillet of cod is marinated in Indian spices, accurately fried and served with fennel compôte, curried yoghurt and pineapple salsa, and pink-seared duck breast is accompanied by beetroot ketchup, candied parsnips and parsnip purée. Puddings seem to be rooted in a more familiar repertoire, among them vanilla crème brûlée, and dark chocolate fondant with vanilla ice cream.

Times 1-3/6-11 Closed 24-26 & 31 Dec, 1-2 Jan, 1 day a wk (varies), L Mon-Sat (open most Sun or by arrangement), D 1 day a wk (varies)

The Lady Helen Restaurant

THOMASTOWN
Map 1 C3

Modern Irish V
tel: 056 7773000 **Mount Juliet Hotel**
email: info@mountjuliet.ie **web:** www.mountjuliet.com
dir: M7 from Dublin, N9 towards Waterford, exit at junct 9/Danesfort for hotel

Cooking of artistry and impact in a manor-house hotel

Standing in the midst of the lush sprawl of a country estate not far from Kilkenny, the Mount Juliet is a Georgian manor-house hotel out of the top drawer. Its various magnificences include river and lake fishing, woodland for strolling in, a golf-course designed by Jack Nicklaus, shooting, archery and spa treatments, but there is still an endearingly family-friendly feel to the place, as members of the Little Rascals kids' club will no doubt attest. Panoramic views over the grounds and the river are just one of the attractions of the Lady Helen dining room, a gracious space done in fashionably muted beige, where any bedazzlement properly arrives on the plate, courtesy of chef Ken Harker, under the executive tutelage of Cormac Rowe. The tone of service is gently formal, but staff are friendly and keen, and have a good knowledge of what's on those menus.

Suppliers and sources are credited in the preamble, from Wexford seafood to wild game, with the option of choosing from the carte or signing up to a six-course tasting menu with wine suggestions. Dishes combine obvious artistry with directness of impact, so that a starter might comprise quail leg confit cromesquis with red chicory and apple salad dually dressed with truffled aioli and hazelnut velouté. Mains might offer a meaty treatment for fish, so that turbot arrives in the company of foie gras, lentils and carrots, or there may be a north African note, as when Challans duck breast is dusted in spicy ras el hanout, served with spiced bulgar wheat, poached rhubarb, ribbons of mooli and yoghurt blobs. The multi-faceted approach continues into dessert plates that might juxtapose classic lemon tart with goats' curd parfait, raspberry sorbet and yuzu jelly. Incidentals such as breads and petits fours emphasise the consistent attention to detail.

Chef Cormac Rowe **Owner** Kileen Investments **Seats** 60, Pr/dining room 80 **Times** 6.30-9.45 Closed L all week, D Sun, Tue **Prices** Fixed D 3 course €65, Tasting menu €55-€75, Service optional **Wines** 10 by glass **Parking** 200 **Notes** Fixed D 4 course, Tasting menu 8 course, Children welcome

COUNTY MAYO

BALLINA
Map 1 B4

Belleek Castle

@ @ Modern Irish

tel: 096 22400 & 21878 **Belleek**
email: info@belleekcastle.com **web:** www.belleekcastle.com
dir: In Belleek woods N of Ballina

Special occasion dining in historic castle

Belleek may call itself a castle and even look like one, but this pocket-sized stately home in a thousand-acre forested estate on the banks of the River Moy is actually a Victorian folly whose dainty 19th-century Gothic gables and skinny turrets wouldn't put up much of a fight if shots were fired in anger. In fact, the only popping noises to be heard are caused by the opening of champagne bottles at one of the many weddings taking place. Inside, oak panelling, coffered ceilings, chandeliers, and crimson walls hung with tapestries make for a suitably faux-medieval baronial setting in the dining room, which was originally the library of the manor house. The kitchen takes well-sourced local ingredients — some foraged seasonally in the surrounding grounds and woodlands — as the eminently solid building blocks of a straightforward country-house menu. Fresh hot-smoked salmon makes for a deliciously simple starter, ahead of a duo of duck (pan-roasted breast, and braised leg in pastry) served with potato and swede gratin and light veal jus.

Times 1-5.30/6-9.30 Closed Xmas & Jan

Mount Falcon Estate

@ @ Traditional French

tel: 096 74472 **Foxford Rd**
email: info@mountfalcon.com **web:** www.mountfalcon.com
dir: On N26, 6m from Foxford & 3m from Ballina. Hotel on left

Polished cooking using exemplary local materials

The grand baronial-style house stands in 100 acres of grounds, with pristine lawns and woodland, and a helipad if you plan to arrive in style. The hotel on the banks of River Moy is popular with golfers, who are drawn to the top courses that pepper the landscape in these parts. The dining option is the Kitchen Restaurant, so named as it takes up the kitchen and pantry area of this splendid old house, and it looks good with its linen-clad tables and food-related prints on the walls. The chef hails from Paris and there's a definite French classicism to his output, as well as a genuine appreciation of the top-quality produce available in this part of Ireland. The 100-acre estate makes a contribution to the menu, too. Start perhaps with a winning combo of Wicklow pigeon and 'Kelly's' black pudding, the pigeon marinated in cocoa liqueur, the black pudding in a crisp croquette, plus root parsley purée, parsley steam cake, cocoa jelly and a grand veneur sauce — refined and complex stuff. Main course might deliver corn-fed chicken cooked sous-vide with truffle spätzle, confit black lard and lavender jus.

Chef Philippe Farineau **Owner** Alan Maloney **Seats** 70, Pr/dining room 30
Times 6.30-9 Closed 25 Dec, L Mon-Sat **Prices** Prices not confirmed, Service optional
Wines 12 by glass **Parking** 100 **Notes** Fixed L 5 course €55-€65, Sunday L, Vegetarian available, Children welcome

BELMULLET
Map 1 A5

The Talbot Hotel

@ Modern Irish **NEW**

tel: 097 20484 **Barrack St**
email: info@thetalbothotel.ie **web:** www.thetalbothotel.ie

Contemporary cooking amid boutique glamour

Sprinkled with boutique fairy dust, The Talbot has a stylish look and a friendly attitude. The bar still functions as such with live music at weekends ensuring the place still has lots of energy to go with all the style. The main dining option — The Barony Restaurant — looks plush and glam with its colourful fabrics and sparkling chandeliers, and there's a small terrace for an alfresco lunch or early dinner. The kitchen seeks out good regional ingredients and delivers a menu that matches the tone of the place for contemporary attitude. Start with smoked duck breast in a salad with seasonal leaves, roasted walnuts and orange segments dressed in a walnut vinaigrette, and move on to pan-seared sea bass (with a nicely crispy skin) served on a cassoulet flavoured with a mild chorizo. For dessert, rum crème brûlée comes with a caramelised banana.

Chef Brendon Conmy **Owner** Tom & Orla Talbot **Seats** 60, Pr/dining room 12
Times 6.30-9 Closed Reduced hrs out of season **Prices** Fixed D 3 course €30-€35, Starter €5.90-€9.90, Main €15.90-€24.90, Dessert €6.50-€8.50, Service optional
Wines **Parking** On street **Notes** Vegetarian available, Children welcome

CONG
Map 1 B4

The George V Dining Room

@ @ Traditional European, International

Ashford Castle
email: ashford@ashford.ie **web:** www.ashford.ie
dir: In Cross, turn left at church onto R345 signed Cong. Turn left at hotel sign & continue through castle gates

Classy cooking in a magnificent castle

There need be no quibbling about castle credentials here, for it's a castle and no mistake. Once the Guinness family summer retreat, it's a magnificent building with parts that date back to the 13th century. With its position by a lough, surrounded by the beautiful estate, Ashford Castle is a luxurious escape from the real world. The magnificence outside is matched within, not least in the George V Dining Room with its opulent fixtures and fittings and grand proportions — chandeliers, panelled walls, rich fabrics and well-dressed tables generously spaced around the room. There's a good deal of fine Irish produce on the classically-minded menu, and a roast of the day is carved at the table. Start, perhaps, with butter-seared Irish scallops served with crisp risotto cakes, pesto foam and raspberry coulis, followed by roast loin of local venison accompanied by a crisp samosa filled with venison and girolle mousse, plus a cheddar potato, carrot purée and blackberry jus. Finish with a well-crafted dessert of white chocolate and blackberries that shows sharp technical skills.

Times 7-9.30 Closed L all week

Get the most out of the AA Restaurant Guide
See page 6

MULRANNY

Map 1 A4

Mulranny Park Hotel

@@ Modern

tel: 098 36000
email: info@mulrannyparkhotel.ie **web:** www.mulrannyparkhotel.ie
dir: R311 from Castlebar to Newport onto N59. Hotel on right

Local produce and dramatic Atlantic views

This smart modern restaurant in a refurbished Victorian railway hotel benefits from breathtaking views across Clew Bay and out to sea. Unsurprisingly window tables are worth their weight in gold while professional service is underpinned by a genuine friendliness. Classically-based cooking lets its hair down in the presentation stakes but make no mistake, this is sound cooking using well-sourced, local ingredients. You might be offered chilled Irish Cashel Blue cheese and Guinness parfait, tomato and mint chutney and pickled pear, followed by a perfectly cooked baked suprême of organic Clare Island salmon, crab and chive orzo, aubergine caviar and cep jus. Honey and yoghurt pannacotta is a delicate finale.

Chef Ollie O'Regan **Owner** Tom Bohan, Tom Duggan **Seats** 100, Pr/dining room 50 **Times** 6.30-9 Closed Jan **Prices** Prices not confirmed, Service optional **Wines** 6 bottles over €30, 14 bottles under €30, 3 by glass **Parking** 200 **Notes** Vegetarian available, Children welcome

WESTPORT

Map 1 B4

Hotel Westport Leisure, Spa & Conference

@ Irish, British, European

tel: 098 25122 **Newport Rd**
email: reservations@hotelwestport.ie **web:** www.hotelwestport.ie
dir: N5 to Westport. Right at end of Castlebar St, 1st right before bridge, right at lights, left before church. Follow to end of street

Exemplary local produce at a riverside hotel

Heavenly scenery frames this expansive family-run hotel and spa set in seven acres of mature woodland. And with miles of walking and cycling on the Great Western Greenway close to hand, there's no excuse for failing to bring a keen appetite to table. After a recent top-to-tail refurbishment, the place is looking pretty nifty, with plush carpets and seating beneath an ornate ceiling, while views overlooking the Carrowbeg River are timeless. Expect a bedrock of straightforward modern ideas built on the finest local, seasonal materials – perhaps home-cured organic Clare Island salmon with cucumber jelly, shaved fennel and lemon oil, followed by the simplicity of roast rib of beef with horseradish jus and pan juices, or grilled fillet of wild Atlantic hake matched with roast vegetables and salsa verde. Finish with rich chocolate fondant with pistachio ice cream, or bow out on a savoury note with Irish artisan cheeses.

Chef Stephen Fitzmaurice **Owner** Cathal Hughes **Seats** 120, Pr/dining room 45 **Times** 1-2.30/6-9.30 **Prices** Fixed L 2 course €21.50-€23.50, Fixed D 3 course €35-€36, Tasting menu €35-€36, Service optional **Wines** 20 bottles over €30, 31 bottles under €30, 10 by glass **Parking** 220 **Notes** Afternoon tea available daily, Sunday L €21.50-€25, Vegetarian available, Children welcome

Knockranny House Hotel

@@ Modern International

tel: 098 28600
email: info@khh.ie **web:** www.knockrannyhousehotel.ie
dir: On N5 (Dublin to Castlebar road), hotel on left before entering Westport

Inventive modern Irish cooking in the tranquil west

The Noonans' tranquil spa hotel makes the most of its Mayo situation, with stunning views every which way, but none more calming to the senses than over Clew Bay. Inside comes with all the accoutrements of an upscale hotel, including a full-dress dining room, La Fougère, which eschews modern minimalism in favour of immaculate table linen and glassware. The kitchen draws on thoroughbred west Irish produce, including saladings from Knockranny's own organic garden, and Seamus Commons is a dab hand at the art of combining tastes and textures. That may be seen in a first course pairing of rare-breed pork belly with a seared langoustine, hazelnuts and lime-spiked squash purée. Mains offer the choice of extravagantly worked fish dishes such as John Dory in lobster velouté with lemon and dill gnocchi, smoked eel and puréed fennel, or pedigree meats like loin and shoulder of rose veal with smoked pommes Anna in sauce chasseur. Nor does the invention flag at dessert, in complex creations such as spiced pineapple with lime parfait, minted lime sponge, mango sorbet and passion-fruit jelly.

Chef Seamus Commons **Owner** Adrian & Geraldine Noonan **Seats** 90, Pr/dining room 120 **Times** 6.30-9.30 Closed Xmas, L Mon-Sat (open selected Sun) **Prices** Prices not confirmed, Service optional **Wines** 196 bottles over €30, 30 bottles under €30, 6 by glass **Parking** 200 **Notes** Table d'hôte menu €52, Sunday L, Vegetarian available, Children welcome

COUNTY MEATH

DUNBOYNE

Map 1 D4

Dunboyne Castle Hotel & Spa

@@ Traditional NEW

tel: 01 8013500
email: ediaz@dunboynecastlehotel.com **web:** www.dunboynecastlehotel.com
dir: In Dunboyne take R157 towards Maynooth. Hotel on left

Classy contemporary Irish cooking in a regal setting

The main structure was built in the mid-1800s and looks suitably regal, with later tasteful development extending the space to the sprawling property seen today. It's all very contemporary on the inside, with a swish spa and modern meeting rooms, while the business of eating takes place in The Ivy restaurant. The modern Irish cooking is based on high-quality produce sourced with due diligence and cooked with skill. Pan-seared scallops with cauliflower purée, shards of crisp pancetta and black pudding powder is a fine version of a modern classic, or there might be brown crab salad with avocado purée and Granny Smith apples. Everything looks good on the plate and flavour combinations are well considered, not least in a main course of rack of new season lamb with braised neck and a glossy veal jus. Turbot might star in a main course, poached in red wine and partnered with samphire and bok choy, plus girolles and a garlicky pommes purée. A dessert of lemon and pink praline meringue pie with Earl grey and lemon sorbet brings down the curtain in style.

Chef John Nagle **Owner** The Fylan Collection **Seats** 154, Pr/dining room 120 **Times** 1-3/6.30-9.30 Closed L Mon-Sat **Prices** Fixed D 3 course €26.95-€29.95, Tasting menu €65-€90, Starter €7-€12, Main €17-€30, Dessert €6.50-€10 **Wines** 19 bottles over €30, 18 bottles under €30, 10 by glass **Parking** 360 **Notes** Sunday L €20-€23, Vegetarian available, Children welcome

KILMESSAN
Map 1 D5

The Station House Hotel

European, Mediterranean V

tel: 046 9025239 & 9025565
email: info@stationhousehotel.ie web: www.stationhousehotel.ie
dir: *From Dublin N3 junct 6 to Dunshaughlin, R125 to Kilmessan*

Extensive menu in converted railway station

The last train rumbled past in the 1960s and the former station house has found a new lease of life as a country-house hotel. These days there are traditionally decorated bedrooms – even a suite in the old signal box – and a restaurant occupying the one-time waiting room. The Signal Restaurant has smart, linen-clad tables and a broad menu that keeps things relatively simple and classical. A starter, for example, of wild mushroom and garlic risotto might kick things off, or go for roasted quail, scented with rosemary, de-boned and served with roast chestnuts and red wine sauce. Next up, there are main courses such as baked fillet of salmon with a tomato and basil sauce, or a grilled Irish fillet steak with peppercorn sauce. Desserts run to caramel mousse with toffee sauce or baked apple strudel with crème anglaise.

Chef David Mulvihill Owner Chris & Thelma Slattery Seats 90, Pr/dining room 180 Times 12.30-4.30/5-10.30 Prices Fixed L 2 course €19.95-€22.95, Fixed D 3 course €26.95, Tasting menu €39.95, Starter €5.95-€8.95, Main €17.95-€28.95, Dessert €5.95-€6.95, Service optional Wines 20 bottles over €30, 20 bottles under €30, 6 by glass Parking 200 Notes Fixed D 4 course €29.95, Sunday L, Children welcome

SLANE
Map 1 D4

Tankardstown

Modern Irish

tel: 041 9824621
email: info@tankardstown.ie web: www.tankardstowne.ie
dir: *M1 exit 10, N51 (Navan-Slane road), take turn directly opposite main entrance to Slane Castle, signed Kells. Continue for 5km*

Modern Irish cooking in a classy rustic setting

There's a fine Georgian manor house at the heart of the Tankardstown estate, but much more besides. It's a big hit on the wedding scene, not surprisingly given the charm of the place and its superb setting, whilst its Brabazon restaurant puts the place on the culinary map. Housed in a one-time cow house, the restaurant has plenty of charm of its own and a lavender-scented garden terrace which is a real boon in the warmer months. The kitchen – headed up by Richard Luckey – gets a good amount of its ingredients from the walled organic gardens and the estate's flock of hens, as well as top-class local and seasonal materials from a trusty network of suppliers, and the cooking is modern and precise. Pressed ham hock with apple and elderflower purée, pain d'épice crumbs, quail's egg and pea soup is a first-course with well-judged flavours. Next up, perhaps fillet of turbot poached in red wine and served with palourde clams, oxtail, ratte potatoes and a chicken and tomato consommé, and to finish, raspberry soufflé with raspberry sauce.

Chef Richard Luckey Owner Patricia & Brian Conroy Seats 70, Pr/dining room 50 Times 12-4/6-9 Closed 3 days Xmas, Mon-Tue (seasonal), L Mon-Thu (seasonal) Prices Fixed L 2 course €25, Fixed D 3 course €40, Service optional Wines 20 bottles over €30, 9 bottles under €30, 9 by glass Notes Fixed 3 course menu available for groups over 10 €35, Sunday L €25-€30, Vegetarian available, Children welcome

COUNTY MONAGHAN

CARRICKMACROSS
Map 1 C4

Shirley Arms Hotel

Modern

tel: 042 9673100 Main St
email: reception@shirleyarmshotel.ie web: www.shirleyarmshotel.ie
dir: *N2 to Derry, take Ardee Rd to Carrickmacross*

Appealing food in modernised Georgian coaching inn

An easy hour's drive from both Dublin and Belfast, the Shirley Arms is a handsome, honey-hued, stone-built Georgian coaching house transformed into a stylish modern hotel and restaurant. White's Restaurant takes its name from the hotel's original title, and goes for a smart contemporary look with high ceilings, large windows and timber dividers to break up the space. The kitchen turns out a please-all repertoire of easygoing modern dishes that dips into an eclectic bag of global influences, as in a well-made seafood risotto starter which gets a kick of Asian fire from chilli sambal, and Mediterranean warmth from lemon zest, mascarpone and parmesan shavings. Main course takes refuge in a straightforward modern serving of duck – honey-roasted suprême and confit leg – partnered by braised red cabbage and a tart redcurrant jus. Awaiting at the end, vanilla crème brûlée comes with raspberry sorbet, lemon curd and shortbread.

Times 12-3/5-9.30 Closed Good Fri, 25-26 Dec

GLASLOUGH
Map 1 C5

The Lodge at Castle Leslie Estate

Traditional Irish, International

tel: 047 88100 The Lodge, Castle Leslie Estate
email: info@castleleslie.com web: www.castleleslie.com
dir: *M1 junct 14 N Belfast signed Ardee/Derry. Follow N2 Derry Monaghan bypass, then N12 to Armagh for 2m, left N185 to Glaslough*

Modern country-house cooking in splendid isolation

The Castle Leslie Estate extends over 1,000 acres, sprinkled with ancient woodlands and lakes, and boasts two plush boltholes – the Castle and The Lodge – operating as separate country-house hotels, each with a distinct identity. The boutique-style lodge comes with a luxury spa, and Snaffles, a large, stylish contemporary restaurant with a hand-carved ceiling, oak beams, a glass wall opening the space up to country views, and a baby grand piano to add to the refined atmosphere. The kitchen keeps its finger on the pulse of culinary trends, turning out up-to-date country house cooking. Lough Neagh smoked eel gets things under way, matched intelligently with beetroot risotto, foam and crème fraîche. Then Fermanagh Saddleback pork gets a workout, arriving as rolled roasted fillet and slow-cooked belly with black pudding soufflé, apple, red cabbage, and caramelised onion mash. If you're up for fish, there might be pan-fried turbot with carrot gratin Muscat butter sauce. Finish with coffee and caramel macaroon with praline sauce and vanilla ice cream.

Chef Andrew Bradley Owner Samantha Leslie Seats 110, Pr/dining room 50 Times 6-9.30 Closed 24-27 Dec, L all week Prices Prices not confirmed, Service optional Wines 27 bottles over €30, 37 bottles under €30, 14 by glass Parking 200 Notes Tasting menu available, Vegetarian available, Children welcome

COUNTY ROSCOMMON

ROSCOMMON
Map 1 B4

Kilronan Castle Estate & Spa
Modern French v

tel: 071 9618000 & 086 0210542 **Ballyfarnon**
email: enquiries@kilronancastle.ie **web:** www.kilronancastle.ie
dir: *M4 to N4, exit R299 towards R207 Droim ar Snámh/Drumsna/Droim. Exit R207 for R280, turn left Keadue Road R284*

Country house classics amid Victorian Gothic grandeur

Kilronan certainly looks like a real castle complete with a foursquare crenellated turret, but it is actually a mere stripling, dating from the early 19th century, and after a thorough restoration as recently as 2006, it now trades as an upmarket hotel with luxurious spa and leisure facilities. The interior sports the full-dress Victorian Gothic look, a style which works to particularly impressive effect in the Douglas Hyde restaurant, where oak panelling galore and a magnificent carved fireplace combine with crystal chandeliers and heavy swagged drapes. Perhaps unsurprisingly, given the grand setting, the kitchen looks to French classicism for its inspiration, spiked here and there with oriental notes. Seasonal wild garlic is used together with ginger and chilli to lift a tian of crabmeat, while main course sees loin of venison glazed with honey, crushed pepper and herbs and served with roast squash and red wine sauce.

Chef Suchil Kumar **Owner** Hanly Group **Seats** 80, Pr/dining room 80 **Times** 1-3.30/6-10 Closed L Mon-Sat (ex group requests) **Prices** Fixed L 2 course €23, Fixed D 3 course €45, Tasting menu €79, Starter €6.75-€11.95, Main €21.50-€36.50, Dessert €7.95-€11.95 **Wines** 48 bottles over €30, 22 bottles under €30, 18 by glass **Parking** 200 **Notes** ALC menu available, Sunday L €29.50, Children welcome

COUNTY SLIGO

SLIGO
Map 1 B5

The Glasshouse
Modern NEW v

tel: 071 9194300 **Swan Point**
email: info@theglasshouse.ie **web:** www.theglasshouse.ie
dir: *N4 to Sligo town. Continue through rdbt, on entering relief road take 2nd turning on right, continue to Wine Street, Hotel on left on Hyde Bridge*

Modern Irish cooking in a glass city-centre hotel

A contemporary boutique hotel in downtown Sligo, the great glass edifice gives the impression that an ocean liner somehow sailed up the Garavogue river and ran aground. That dramatic setting is complemented by stylish interiors that make a virtue of open, uncluttered spaces enlivened throughout with strategic dashes of colour. The principal dining room is The Kitchen, and combines cheering contrasting red and golden shades in the seating with diverting views over the river. Alan Fitzmaurice cooks in unmistakable modern Irish mode, marshalling fine regional produce into dishes such as Donegal crab with pickled pineapple and pea purée in spiced mango dressing, to be followed by chicken breast stuffed with leeks, applewood-smoked cheese and lemon in red wine 'paint', or hake with a bean and chorizo stew and saffron cream. Finish on a light note with lemon posset, lemon pistachio shortbread and mixed berry jelly, or else with artisan Irish cheeses.

Chef Enda Delaney **Owner** Michael O'Heir, Ronnie Grenoey **Seats** 108, Pr/dining room 140 **Times** 12-5/6.30-9.30 Closed 25 Dec **Prices** Prices not confirmed **Wines** 8 by glass **Parking** 160 **Notes** Sunday L, Children welcome

Radisson Blu Hotel & Spa Sligo
Modern Irish, Mediterranean

tel: 071 9140008 & 9192400 **Rosses Point Rd, Ballincar**
email: info.sligo@radissonblu.com **web:** www.radissonblu.ie/sligo
dir: *From N4 into Sligo to main bridge. Take R291 on left. Hotel 1.5m on right*

Classy hotel serving top-grade local produce

Named after a castle once owned by Lord Mountbatten, the Classiebawn Restaurant is the culinary focus of this clean-cut modern hotel. Although the decor is faultlessly upmarket, it is the breathtaking views of Sligo Bay and Knockhaven Mountain that immediately grab your attention. The kitchen stays abreast of modern trends and serves up contemporary, internationally-inspired food made with fresh, seasonal, locally-sourced ingredients. Fussy embellishments are kicked into touch here in tried-and-tested stalwarts such as seared scallops with Clonakilty black pudding, creamed potatoes and chive butter sauce, or rump of Connemara lamb with braised Puy lentils teamed with confit garlic and thyme jus. Flavours are on the money to the end – a Classiebawn lemon tart made with an unstinting hand on the lemon zest, served with lime curd.

Chef Joe Shannon **Owner** Radisson Blu **Seats** 120, Pr/dining room 60 **Times** 6-10 **Prices** Prices not confirmed **Wines** 6 bottles over €30, 6 bottles under €30, 7 by glass **Parking** 600 **Notes** Seasonal early bird menu, Vegetarian available, Children welcome

COUNTY TIPPERARY

CLONMEL
Map 1 C3

Hotel Minella
Traditional NEW v

tel: 052 612 2388
email: reservations@hotelminella.ie **web:** www.hotelminella.com
dir: *S of river in town*

Country cooking in an extended Georgian hotel

The garden runs down to the banks of the River Suir and those are the Comeragh Mountains looming in the background – a charming spot. The hotel has extended out from an original Georgian mansion and doesn't lack for facilities. The restaurant is at ground-floor level in the original house, so has plenty of character and a traditional, period feel, as well as views across the garden to the river. The kitchen team keep things simple with a good choice of unchallenging fare with a local flavour. Two crisp and golden fishcakes might get the ball rolling, packed with a decent amount of fish and herbs, and served with home-made tartare sauce and dressed salad leaves. Next up, roast rack of lamb comes nicely pink and in the company of a redcurrant and rosemary sauce, plus accurately cooked vegetables. For dessert, a wobbly pannacotta is flavoured with a mix of berries.

Chef Christopher Bray **Owner** John & Elizabeth Nallen **Seats** 120, Pr/dining room 60 **Times** 12.30-3/6.30-9.30 **Prices** Fixed L 3 course €28, Fixed D 3 course €35-€45 **Wines** **Notes** Sunday L €28-€35, Children welcome

Who has made the top ten per cent this year?
See page 34

THURLES — Map 1 C3

Inch House Country House & Restaurant

⚜ Irish

tel: 050 451348
email: mairin@inchhouse.ie **web:** www.inchhouse.ie
dir: 6.5km NE of Thurles on R498

Splendid ingredients cooked simply in a Georgian manor

Quite the enterprise, Inch House is the hub of a working farm run by the Egan family, which is not only a rather lovely country house hotel, but a hive of activity. They run the hotel and farm the land, but they also make preserves and chutneys which you can enjoy at home. There's plenty of comfort to be had at Inch House, though, with swish bedrooms and a relaxed service style that makes you feel like part of the family (almost). Needless to say the land provides a lot of the ingredients – they make their own black pudding, too – and what isn't home-grown won't have travelled very far. This is country-house cooking. Warm Gortnamona goats' cheese with a walnut and crumb crust is a simple enough starter, the cheese gently warmed through and served with salad from the garden and the house's red onion marmalade. Next up, suprême of chicken wrapped in bacon with a mushroom sauce, and for dessert, a berry crème brûlée.

Chef John Barry **Owner** John & Nora Egan **Seats** 50 **Times** 6-9.15 Closed Xmas, Sun-Mon, L all week **Prices** Fixed D 3 course fr €35, Starter €7-€12, Main €18-€32, Dessert €7-€10, Service optional **Wines** 2 by glass **Parking** 50 **Notes** ALC available Sat only, Vegetarian available, Children 3 yrs+

COUNTY WATERFORD

ARDMORE — Map 1 C2

Cliff House Hotel

⚜⚜⚜⚜ – *see opposite*

BALLYMACARBRY — Map 1 C2

Hanora's Cottage

⚜ Modern Traditional v

tel: 052 6136134 & 6136442 **Nire Valley**
email: hanorascottage@eircom.net **web:** www.hanorascottage.com
dir: *From Clonmel or Dungarvan to Ballymacarbry. Exit by pub, 3m, establishment by Nire Church*

Charming country hotel with good honest cooking

With its glorious setting in the lush Nire Valley, forays into nature's beauty are very much on the agenda for walkers, twitchers and nature lovers of all shades at this small-scale country house hotel beside the church and river. The smart restaurant is as classic and unpretentious as the cooking, which is built on solid foundations of carefully-sourced local materials treated with the respect they deserve. Husband and wife team Eoin and Judith Wall run a kitchen that cuts no corners, making everything in-house and delivering honest, full-flavoured and accurately cooked dishes. Pan-fried lamb's kidneys with blue cheese and cream are served with a Cashel Blue cheese muffin to soak up the sauce, while a simple grilled fillet of spanking fresh hake is matched with tomato confit, buttery mash, braised red cabbage and sauced with Bay Lough cheese, which is made just five kilometres away, for those interested in food mileage. For pudding, there's pear and meringue roulade with crunchy toasted walnuts and decadent fudge sauce.

Chef Eoin and Judith Wall **Owner** Mary & Eoin Wall **Seats** 40 **Times** 6.30-9 Closed 25-28 Dec, Sun **Prices** Prices not confirmed, Service optional **Wines** **Parking** 20 **Notes** No children

WATERFORD — Map 1 C2

Bistro at the Tower

⚜ Modern Irish with European influences NEW

tel: 051 862300 **The Mall**
email: events@thw.ie **web:** www.towerhotelwaterford.com
dir: *City centre, main N25. Located at end of Merchants Quay*

Seafood-led menu at a smart city-centre hotel

Part of an Irish-Spanish group of upmarket venues, the Tower is a smart hotel and leisure centre on the Mall in Waterford, a comfortable haven of mod cons with an ancient turret. Its principal dining room, the Bistro, has recently been relaunched with an inspired, vividly colourful new design influenced by the pacific calm of the nearby Marina. With so many fishing villages hereabouts, it comes as no surprise to find that fish and seafood are strong suits. A meal might begin with seafood chowder, or fishcakes in Thai sweet chilli sauce, as a means of whetting the appetite for salmon fillet with egg noodles and stir-fried veg, or a mixed grill of seafood with chorizo in lemon butter. Meatheads need look no further than grilled Irish Angus steak of impeccable pedigree, with garlic potatoes in Jameson's and peppercorn sauce. Finish with chocolate fondant, served with fudge sauce and honeycomb ice cream.

Chef John Moore, Ray Kelly **Owner** FBD Hotels & Resorts **Seats** 80, Pr/dining room 70 **Times** 12.30-2.30/6.30-9.30 Closed 24-26 Dec, L Mon-Sat (open on request) **Prices** Fixed L 2 course €16.50-€23.50, Fixed D 3 course €20-€25, Starter €5-€7, Main €17-€23, Dessert €5.95-€6.95, Service optional **Wines** 12 bottles over €30, 26 bottles under €30, 4 by glass **Parking** 90 **Notes** Pre-theatre menu wine & dine 2 people €59, Sunday L €12.50-€23.50, Vegetarian available, Children welcome

Faithlegg House Hotel & Golf Resort

⚜ Modern Irish, French

tel: 051 382000 **Faithlegg**
email: liammoran@fhh.ie **web:** www.faithlegg.com
dir: *From Waterford follow Dunmore East Rd then Cheekpoint Rd*

Modern country-house cooking in an 18th-century hotel

The original mansion, built in the 1780s, opened as a country-house hotel in 1998 after immaculate restoration. It has its own 18-hole golf course and leisure centre, while the high-ceilinged restaurant looks over the garden from what was a pair of drawing rooms. The cooking makes an impact, based as it is on native produce and a range of neat ideas. Boudin of black pudding with blue cheese foam, perry sorbet and Irish stout jus is a novel but effective starter. Move on to tea-smoked salmon fillet on mussel and saffron stew with pickled red onion flavoured with dill, or grilled loin and roast haunch steak of venison with roast celeriac and curly kale cream. End loyally with Irish artisan cheeses or Baileys crème brûlée.

Chef Jenny Flynn **Owner** FBD Hotel Group **Seats** 86, Pr/dining room 50 **Times** 1-2.30/6-9.30 Closed 25 Dec, L pre-book only **Prices** Fixed L 2 course €11.95-€19.50, Fixed D 3 course €25-€37, Starter €8-€13, Main €22-€32, Dessert €7.90-€18.50, Service optional **Wines** 36 bottles over €30, 17 bottles under €30, 8 by glass **Parking** 120 **Notes** Twilight menu 6-7.30 wine & dine €79 per couple, Sunday L €13.95-€28.50, Vegetarian available, Children welcome

Cliff House Hotel

ARDMORE   Map 1 C2

Modern Irish V
tel: 024 87800 & 87803
email: info@thecliffhousehotel.com
web: www.thecliffhousehotel.com
dir: *N25 to Ardmore. Hotel at the end of village via The Middle Road*

Dutch master's dazzling contemporary cooking on a Waterford cliff

About an hour's drive (but who's counting?) from the airports at Cork and Waterford, and about the same from the car ferry at Rosslare, the stunningly located boutique hotel stands on a low cliff at Ardmore. It's an area of Ireland rich in historic houses, gardens and fine walking, and the ancient fishing village of Ardmore itself is worth a wander too. The interiors have been laid out according to best contemporary design practice, with plenty of daylight flooding in from the ocean. Sunrises and sunsets, not to mention the stormy weather for which Ireland is famous, might have been laid on as part of the amenities, with the bar, terrace and principal restaurant all getting in on the action. Dutch-born Martijn Kajuiter is in charge of the last, ably supported by his right-hand man at the stoves, Kwanghi Chan. Having grown up in his parents' bistro in Groningen, you could say he had a head start, but since his arrival here in 2007, he has spread his culinary wings. The ingredients (some of them supplied from a kitchen garden in Youghal set up by Kajuiter) are exceptional in every sense, and the cooking achieves an extraordinary harmony between traditional Irish modes and the kind of technical daring that has jaws dropping. The menu evolves to keep pace with the kitchen team's explorations, which is to say pretty fast, although certain dishes remain as constants: an exquisite presentation of Bantry Bay salmon (cured, marinated, iced and ballotine) with cucumber, beetroot and horseradish;

grilled Angus beef fillet in Kilbeggan whiskey and beef tea; the 80% chocolate mousse with olive oil crumbs, Maldon salt and white coffee ice cream. It's on the eight-course taster menus, though, that the fireworks dazzle. A truffled egg comes with romanesco, hazelnuts and Cheddar, while the perfectly timed halibut with grilled shrimp and black quinoa in chicken-stock jus is a triumph of contrasting flavours. Dishes are presented as carefully arranged individual components in the modern way, but the components pull together to make a seamless whole, as when broad beans, spring onions, morels and gnocchi all do their collaborative bits for a serving of superb Irish rose veal. Prior to dessert variations of chocolate or apple, Kajuiter gets to celebrate his twin heritages with a plate of Dutch and Irish cheeses, accompanied by spelt, Alexanders and honey.

Chef Martijn Kajuiter **Owner** Valshan Ltd **Seats** 64, Pr/ dining room 20 **Times** 6.30-10 Closed Xmas, Sun-Mon (occasional Tue), L all week **Prices** Fixed L 2 course €25.50-€37, Fixed D 3 course fr €70, Tasting menu fr €95, Starter €12.50-€24.50, Main €40-€45, Dessert €12.50-€21.50 **Wines** 100 bottles over €30, 3 bottles under €30, 12 by glass **Parking** 30 **Notes** 3 course ALC €68, Sunday L €29.50-€32.50, Children welcome

COUNTY WEXFORD

GOREY — Map 1 D3

Amber Springs Hotel

Modern European

tel: 053 9484000 **Wexford Rd**
email: info@ambersprings.ie **web:** www.ambersprings.ie
dir: N11 junct 23, 500mtrs from Gorey by-pass at junct 23

Modern hotel with food to match

This spanking-new contemporary hotel in historic Gorey opened in 2006 and has something for everyone, whether you're tying the knot, planning a spot of down time in the spa, setting up a corporate team building session, or just looking to de-stress by the coast and eat well. The latter is taken care of by Kelby's Bistro, a clean-cut, neutral modern space up on the first floor, where sweeping picture windows open up views across the gardens to fields beyond. Straightforward, easygoing comfort food is the deal here, with much of the seasonal produce — particularly beef — provided by the owners' farm, as in a main course of dry-aged Angus sirloin steak served with onion and truffle purée, smoked butter hollandaise, and cherry tomatoes. This might come book-ended by crispy deep-fried lemon and pepper-coated calamari with a spicy kick from mango and chilli purée, and glazed chocolate mousse with pistachio ice cream to finish.

Chef Conor Spacey **Seats** 138, Pr/dining room 120 **Times** 1-3/6-9 Closed 25-26 Dec, L Mon-Sat **Prices** Fixed L 2 course €25, Fixed D 3 course €30 **Wines Parking** 178 **Notes** Sunday L €25, Vegetarian available, Children welcome

Ashdown Park Hotel

Mediterranean, European

tel: 053 9480500 **Station Rd**
email: info@ashdownparkhotel.com **web:** www.ashdownparkhotel.com
dir: On approach to Gorey town take N11 from Dublin. Take left signed for Courtown. Hotel on left

Crowd-pleasing menu in an elegant setting

With sandy beaches and golf courses nearby, this modern hotel on a grand scale, within walking distance of the centre of Gorey, has plenty of attractions of its own. There's a spa and conference facilities, for a start, plus some 22 acres of grounds to explore. It is also home to the Rowan Tree Restaurant, where tables are dressed up in crisp white linen, and the kitchen turns out some pleasingly straightforward dishes based on good local ingredients, including some things from the grounds. Start with a Caesar salad with croûtons, smoked bacon and parmesan, or prawn and pineapple skewers with an Asian dressing. Next up, rump of Wexford lamb is roasted and served with buttered cabbage and thyme jus, or there might be a duo of cod and rainbow trout with braised leeks and almond and dill butter, and for dessert, something like mango cheesecake with blackcurrant coulis.

Times 12.30-3/5.30-9 Closed 24-26 Dec, L Mon-Fri

Marlfield House

Classical

tel: 053 9421124 **Courtown Rd**
email: info@marlfieldhouse.ie **web:** www.marlfieldhouse.com
dir: N11 junct 23, follow signs to Courtown. Turn left for Gorey at Courtown Road Rdbt, hotel 1m on the left

Grand hotel dining in the heart of Wexford

If you hanker after a touch of country-house luxury and you're in the southeast of Ireland, head on over to Marlfield House. It's been a while since the Earls of Courtown held grand house parties in this opulent Regency era home, but you can get a taste of it in today's smart and luxurious hotel. The dining room consists of more than one handsomely decorated space, leading into an impressive conservatory, whilst murals and mirrors are interspersed with huge windows which open onto the immaculate garden. The kitchen garden plays its part in delivering first-rate seasonal produce, and the chefs do the rest. The contemporary Mediterranean-inflected menu might see you starting with crab and lemon crumble with roast beetroot salad, or pan-roasted quail with ragoût of fennel peppers and thyme jus. Next up, seared North Atlantic monkish with a cassoulet of saffron potatoes, or pan-fried rib-eye of Wexford beef, and for dessert, buttermilk pannacotta with Wexford berries, sesame seed tuile and toasted almond flakes.

Times 12.30-2.30/7-9 Closed Xmas, Jan-Feb, Mon-Tue (Mar-Apr, Nov-Dec), L Mon-Sat

Seafield Golf & Spa Hotel

Modern Irish, French

tel: 053 942 4000 **Ballymoney**
email: reservations@seafieldhotel.com **web:** www.seafieldhotel.com
dir: M11 exit 22

Smart contemporary cooking in a modern spa hotel

We've Italian designers to thank for the super-cool finish within this luxe spa and golf hotel on the cliffs above the sea, with not a hint of old-school formality or corporate banality. This place is glamorous and no mistake. The high-end finish extends to the restaurant, which has not an iota of stuffiness. A huge bronze female centaur keeps watch over the dining room, where lighting and music levels are kept soft, and the decor is in cool black, from the marble walls to the chandeliers. The food matches the venue for modernity and creativity, but keeps true to the spirit of its locale with a good showing of regional ingredients. There's real technical proficiency on show, and plenty of creative thinking. Take a starter of jasmine-cured monkfish, for example, with octopus carpaccio and smoked mint jelly, or a main-course fillet of Tipperary beef with an oxtail terrine, warm parsley jelly and wild mushroom gratin. Everything looks beautiful on the plate, not least a dessert such as orange-infused crème brûlée with a few extra surprises.

Chef Malek Hamidouche **Owner** Seafield Hotel Ltd **Seats** 90, Pr/dining room 40 **Times** 6.30-9.30 Closed L all week **Prices** Tasting menu fr €65, Starter €10.95-€11.95, Main €22.95-€28.95, Dessert €9.50-€11.50 **Wines** 36 bottles over €30, 6 bottles under €30, 12 by glass **Notes** Vegetarian available, Children welcome

ROSSLARE
Map 1 D2

Beaches Restaurant at Kelly's Resort Hotel

Traditional European

tel: 053 9132114
email: info@kellys.ie **web:** www.kellys.ie
dir: From N25 take Rosslare/Wexford road signed Rosslare Strand

Beachside resort hotel with modern cooking

The Beaches restaurant is aptly named, as it sits on five miles of golden sands in Rosslare. The Kelly family have run their resort hotel since 1895 – why move when you can work in a setting like this? – and the venue is set up to capitalise on the views, bathed in light through good-sized windows, and with restful pastel hues, white linen on the tables, and a mini gallery of original artworks on the walls. Local produce is as good as it gets, and the kitchen has the experience and confidence to treat it all simply and let the sheer quality do the talking in simple contemporary dishes. Confit duck arrives in an unfussy combo with spiced pears and baked plums with five spice, while local goose from an artisan producer is roasted and pointed up with chestnut stuffing, braised ham, caramelised pear and glazed pearl onions. Yoghurt and lime pannacotta with raspberry sorbet provides a refreshing finale.

Times 1-2/7.30-9 Closed mid Dec-mid Feb

La Marine Bistro

Modern

tel: 053 9132114 **Kelly's Resort Hotel & Spa**
email: info@kellys.ie
dir: From N25 take Rosslare/Wexford road signed Rosslare Strand

Bistro-style cooking at a smart seaside resort hotel

The more casual stand-alone restaurant of Kelly's Resort Hotel is an easygoing venue with views of the chefs at work in the open kitchen. The shipshape French bistro theme suits the beachside setting to a T, as does its menu of classic Gallic bistro fare, which is all built on the eminently solid foundations of spanking fresh local produce. Top-class fish and seafood comes but a short way from Kilmore Quay to be treated simply and sent out in ideas such as monkfish medallions with warm saffron and garlic mayonnaise, or scallops with creamy spiced Puy lentils and coconut crème fraîche. Meat eaters are not sent home hungry either – there may be roast rack of lamb with gratin dauphinoise and redcurrant sauce, and to finish, pear, chocolate and almond pithivier or well-chosen local cheeses.

Times 12.30-2/6.30-9 Closed mid Dec-Feb

Who are the AA's Restaurants of the Year? See page 14

WEXFORD
Map 1 D3

Whitford House Hotel Health & Leisure Club

Traditonal European

tel: 053 9143444 **New Line Rd**
email: info@whitford.ie **web:** www.whitford.ie
dir: From Rosslare ferry port take N25. At Duncannon Rd rdbt right onto R733, hotel immediately on left. 1.5m from Wexford

Traditionally based cooking in a family-run hotel

A family-run boutique hotel since the 1960s, not far from the town centre and within reach of the Rosslare ferry, Whitford House is a haven of contemporary creature comforts. State-of-the-art spa facilities and a little cocktail bar are among the various ways to indulge yourself, but best of all is the Seasons dining room. Primrose-coloured walls and gaily striped upholstery make an uplifting impression, and the cooking sticks to a traditionally based route, but with plenty of style. Start in Mediterranean fashion with a puff pastry tart piled with roasted tomatoes, mozzarella and basil, served with a balsamic-dressed salad of rocket, pine nuts and parmesan, before going on to slow-roast lamb rump in its own juices, or steamed salmon on spinach, sauced with white wine. Comforting pudding options include strawberry pavlova, sherry trifle or sticky toffee pudding and butterscotch sauce, and there are great Irish cheeses, served with Gubbeen cheese crackers.

Chef Siobhan Devereux **Owner** The Whitty family **Seats** 100 **Times** 12.30-3/7-9 Closed 24-27 Dec, L Mon-Sat, D Mon-Thu (out of season) **Prices** Service optional **Wines** 2 bottles over €30, 22 bottles under €30, 4 by glass **Parking** 220 **Notes** Vintage tea mornings, Sunday L €10.95-€17.95, Vegetarian available, Children welcome

COUNTY WICKLOW

DELGANY
Map 1 D3

Glenview Hotel

European NEW v

tel: 01 2873399 **Glen O' the Downs**
email: sales@glenviewhotel.com **web:** www.glenviewhotel.ie
dir: From Dublin city centre follow signs for N11, past Bray on N11 S'bound, exit 9

Imaginative seasonal cooking and lush valley views

The Woodlands Restaurant at this hotel is up on the first floor to maximise the view over the Glen o' the Downs, and it is an impressive vista. There are large arched windows to make the best of the views over the treetops and down the valley, and inside all is soothing pastel shades and sparkling glassware. The chef has Indian heritage and there are one or two Asian touches on the menu, but the food is mostly what is loosely termed modern Irish cooking. A starter of pan-fried scallops with shellfish bisque is a winning combination, or there might be confit duck leg croquettes served with a spiced apple purée. To follow, Wicklow lamb comes in a fashionable three-way construction, with an array of vegetables, and Kilmore Quay cod is flavoured with Goan spices and served with quail's egg and red onion chutney. For dessert, pannacotta with fresh strawberries is a summer treat.

Chef Sandeep Pandy **Owner** Paddy Crean **Seats** Pr/dining room 36 **Times** 12.30-2.30/5.30-9.30 Closed L Mon-Sat **Prices** Fixed L 2 course €24.95, Starter €6.95-€11, Main €16.50-€26.95, Dessert €7.25-€10 **Wines** 20 bottles over €30, 19 bottles under €30, 13 by glass **Notes** Sunday L €24.95-€29, Children welcome

Map 1 D3

ENNISKERRY

Powerscourt Hotel

◉◉ Modern European V

tel: 01 2748888 **Powerscourt Estate**
email: info@powerscourthotel.com **web:** www.powerscourthotel.com
dir: N11 to R117 Enniskerry, follow signs for Powerscourt Gardens

Upscale dining in a Palladian hotel

With a sweeping Palladian mansion at its heart, the Powerscourt resort has a couple of golf courses, a luxurious spa and classy bedrooms. There's also an Irish pub called McGills, but the main event food-wise is the swish and glamorous Sika Restaurant. There are glorious mountain views from its third-floor dining room, a space decorated with an upscale finish while maintaining plenty of the room's original character. There's a chef's table, too. The food is contemporary Irish inasmuch as it takes first-class regional produce and applies both modern and classical techniques. Take a starter of pan-fried scallops, for example, with Jerusalem artichokes, pancetta and apple balsamic jus, or a main course dish of Atlantic halibut with parsnip purée, brown shrimps and a vermouth cream. A meaty main course might be Challans duck breast served with its confit leg, plus Savoy cabbage, black pudding and a pickled garlic jus. Desserts are no less creative and well crafted; lemon tart with toasted almond ice cream, for example, or apple fondant with a Granny Smith sorbet.

Chef Peter Byrne **Owner** Sugar Loaf Ventures **Seats** 140, Pr/dining room 24 **Times** 1-2.30/6-10 Closed L Mon-Sat **Prices** Fixed L 2 course €22-€26, Tasting menu €62-€82, Starter €10-€18, Main €28-€38, Dessert €9-€14, Service optional **Wines** 60 bottles over €30, 5 bottles under €30, 10 by glass **Parking** 214 **Notes** Children welcome

Map 1 D3

MACREDDIN

BrookLodge Hotel & Macreddin Village

◉◉ Modern Irish

tel: 0402 36444
email: info@brooklodge.com **web:** www.brooklodge.com
dir: N11 to Rathnew, R752 to Rathdrum, R753 to Aughrim, follow signs to Macreddin Village

Dramatic dining venue, organic and wild food

Looking every inch the luxurious country-house retreat, the BrookLodge hotel is the heart of the purpose-built Macreddin Village. The upmarket operation comprises an 18-hole golf course and spa, a pub and brewery, café, bakery, smokehouse, and Italian restaurant. The Strawberry Tree (dinner-only) is the top foodie option of the whole set-up, a strikingly opulent setting, spreading through three grand rooms with mirrored ceilings reflecting twinkling modern chandeliers, bare burnished mahogany tables, and gilt-framed mirrors on midnight-blue walls. Given its status as Ireland's first certified organic restaurant, provenance of seasonal ingredients is king, so if it's not wild or foraged, it's sourced from certified organic producers, with herbs and soft fruit grown in the estate's own walled garden. The kitchen brings all of this peerless produce together creatively, showing its skill in simple dishes such as wild wood pigeon terrine with strawberry and green pepper jam, followed by guinea fowl with dried fruit compote, or organic Irish Angus beef roasted in a crust of Irish turf for that true touch of terroir.

Chef Tim Daly, Evan Doyle **Owner** The Doyle family **Seats** 120, Pr/dining room 50 **Times** 7-9.30 Closed 24-26 Dec, Mon, L all week **Prices** Prices not confirmed **Wines** 94 bottles over €30, 32 bottles under €30, 21 by glass **Parking** 200 **Notes** Fixed D 5 course €65-€95, Vegetarian available, Children welcome

Map 1 D3

NEWTOWN MOUNT KENNEDY

Druids Glen Resort

◉ **NEW** V

tel: 01 2870800
email: reservations@druidsglenresort.com **web:** www.druidsglenresort.com
dir: Follow M50 south from airport. Follow M11/N11 through Kilmacanogue, junct 12 signed Newtown Mount Kennedy, follow signs

Simple brasserie dishes and two golf courses

They don't do things by halves here at Druids Glen: the place boasts not just one, but two championship golf courses, plus the full package of spa pampering and leisure facilities in its acreages of landscaped grounds, with the Wicklow hills thrown in as a backdrop. Naturally, the place does a brisk trade in weddings and conferences, and when you have finished tying the knot, team building or whacking balls around, there's straightforward modern cooking built on top-notch local materials in the Druids Brasserie. To views over the famous Druid Glen course, you might tee off with duck liver pâté with chutney (made with apples from the hotel's orchards) and toasted sourdough, then follow on with cutlet, loin and liver of local lamb with fondant potato, caramelised pearl onions, pea and mint purée and port sauce. Finish with apple tart Tatin with clotted cream or a platter of Irish cheeses.

Seats 170, Pr/dining room 22 **Times** 1-2.30/5.30-10 **Prices** Fixed L 2 course €22-€26, Fixed D 3 course €35-€42.50, Starter €7-€13.75, Main €19.75-€29.50, Dessert €6.50-€8.50, Service optional **Wines** 28 bottles over €30, 15 bottles under €30, 11 by glass **Parking** 400 **Notes** Sunday L €26-€32, Children welcome

Follow us on facebook
www.facebook.com/TheAAUK

What makes a 5-Rosette restaurant?
See page 9

RATHNEW | Map 1 D3

Hunter's Hotel

 Traditional French

tel: 0404 40106 **Newrath Bridge**
email: reception@hunters.ie **web:** www.hunters.ie
dir: *N11 exit at Wicklow/Rathnew junct. 1st left onto R761. Restaurant 0.25m before village*

Classical Irish cooking in an ancestral family hotel

Great venerability resides not just in the stones of Hunter's, Ireland's oldest coaching inn, but in the ownership, which has passed through generations of the Gelletlie family since 1825. Barely half-an-hour from the Dun Laoghaire ferry, it sits in riotously colourful gardens, its dining room a vision of crisp linen, mahogany and fine living. A small team of dedicated, volubly friendly staff runs the show. Expect daily-changing menus of classically informed Irish cooking, starting with spanking-fresh crab tian in dill mayonnaise, and progressing via an intermediate course (perhaps leek and potato soup or lime and ginger sorbet) to the likes of crisply roasted breast and leg of duckling with blueberry sauce and pomme purée, or a loaded seafood brochette in curry dressing. Strawberry pannacotta to finish comes in a cocktail glass, lifted with a portion of balsamic-marinated strawberries, or you might be tempted by a selection of Ireland's new generation of artisan cheeses.

Times 12.45-3/7.30-9 Closed 3 days Xmas

Tinakilly Country House & Restaurant

◉◉ Modern Irish

tel: 0404 69274
email: reservations@tinakilly.ie **web:** www.tinakilly.ie
dir: *From Dublin Airport follow N11/M11 to Rathnew. Continue on R750 towards Wicklow. Hotel entrance approx 500mtrs from village on left*

Modernised country-house cooking overlooking the Irish Sea

The distinguished grey Italianate Victorian mansion was built in 1883 for an engineer who pioneered the laying of the undersea telegraph connecting the British Isles to north America. Clad in climbing foliage, it gazes fondly out over the Irish Sea. An L-shaped dining room with high ceilings and vibrant green walls contains a mix of antique and modern furniture as well as bare and clothed tables, and makes a diverting setting for Eddie McCormick's modernised country-house cooking. Ingredients are well-chosen and the timing and seasoning of dishes does them justice, as for an opening pairing of scallops and the famous Clonakilty black pudding of County Cork, with butternut purée and pea-shoots. Mains offer fine local meats such as herb-crusted Wicklow lamb rack in a provençal medium of chargrilled ratatouille veg and tomato fondue, or freshest fish such as Parma ham-wrapped cod with braised fennel, baby leeks and champ. A tarte Tatin variant made with pineapple is a success, the triumph ratified by its unabashedly boozy rum and raisin ice cream.

Times 12.30-4/6.30-8.30 Closed 24-26 & 31 Dec, 1-2 Jan, L Mon-Sat

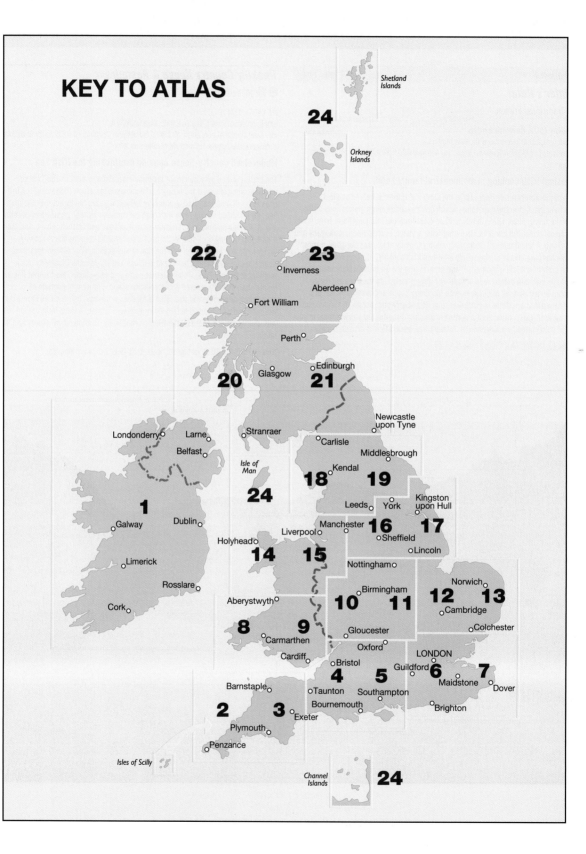

KEY TO ATLAS

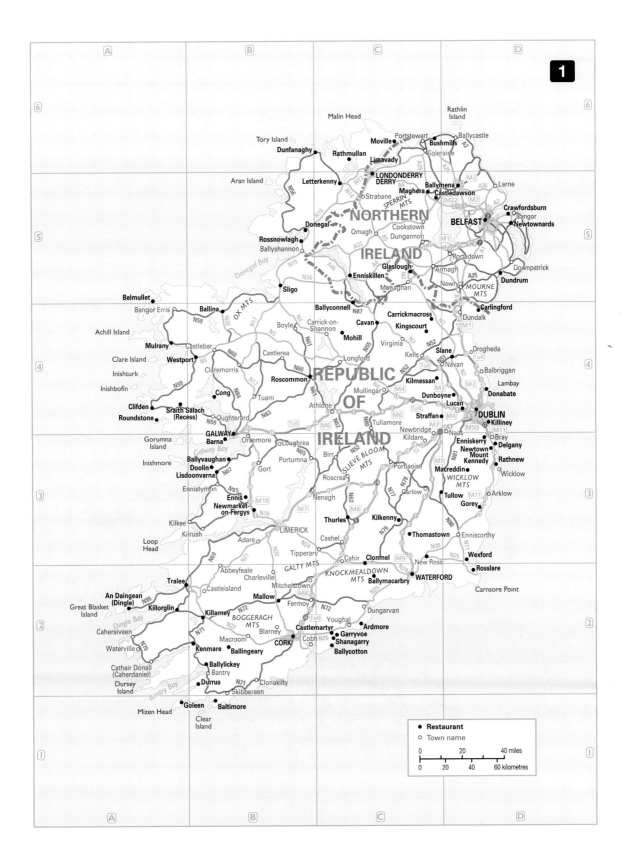

2

	Motorway/toll motorway	● **Oundle**	Restaurant
	Motorway junction full/restricted. Service area	○ Cardiff	AA Restaurant of the Year
	Primary route single/dual carriageway	○ Spalding	Town/Village name
A34	Other A road single/dual carriageway		National boundary
B3400	B road	**ESSEX**	English county name & boundary
	Unclassified road	**CONWY**	Welsh county name & boundary
ⓥ	Vehicle ferry	**MORAY**	Scottish county name & boundary
ⓒ	Fast vehicle ferry or catamaran		National Park

ISLES OF SCILLY

Bryher · Tresco · St Martin's · Higher Town · New Grimsby · Hugh Town · St Mary's · ISLES OF SCILLY TRI MARY'S? · Old Town · Middle Town · St Agnes

SV

Lundy

Hartland Point
Hartland

Morwenstow

Kilkhampton

Bude
Bay
Bude · Stratton

Widemouth Bay

Crackington Haven · Week St Mary

Boscastle

Tintagel

Lau

Delabole · Camelford

Port Isaac

Polzeath · Pendoggett · St Tudy · Bolventor · BODMIN MOOR · Blisland

Harlyn · **Rock** · **Padstow**

Porthcothan · **Wadebridge** · **Bodmin**

SW

Mawgan Porth · St Mawgan · C O R N W A L L · St Cleer

Watergate Bay · St Columb Major · Lanivet · Dobwalls

Newquay · St Columb Major · Roche · St Blazey · Bugle · **Lostwithiel** · **Liskeard** · St Keyne

West Pentire · Summercourt · **St Austell** · **Golant** · Pelynt · Wide

Perranporth · Ladock · St Stephen · **Fowey** · Polperro · **Looe** · Polruan · **Talland Bay**

St Agnes · Marazanvose · Grampound · Pentewan · **Mevagissey**

Porthtowan · Tregony · Gorran Haven

Portreath · St Day · Carnon Downs · **Truro** · **Portloe**

St Ives Bay · Gwithian · **Redruth** · **Veryan**

St Ives · Zennor · Lelant · **Camborne** · St Just-in-Roseland · **Portscatho**

Hayle · Penryn · **Falmouth** · **St Mawes**

St Just · Marazion · Constantine · **Mawnan Smith**

Penzance · **Perranuthnoe** · **Helston** · Gweek

Land's End · Newlyn · Praa Sands · **Porthleven** · Manaccan · St Keverne

Sennen · St Buryan · Mousehole · Coverack

Porthcurno · Treen · Mount's Bay · **Mullion**

Lizard
Lizard Point · Cadgwith

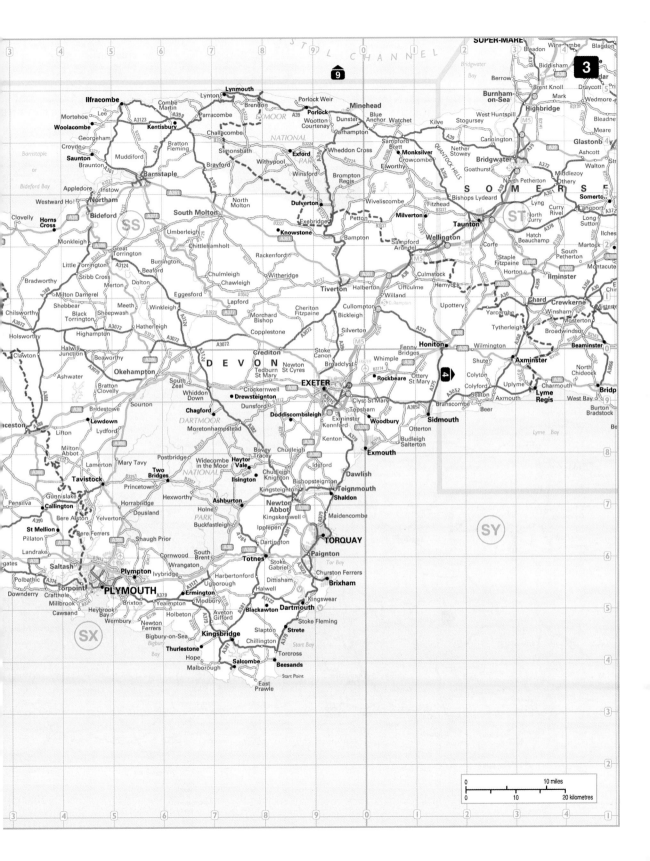

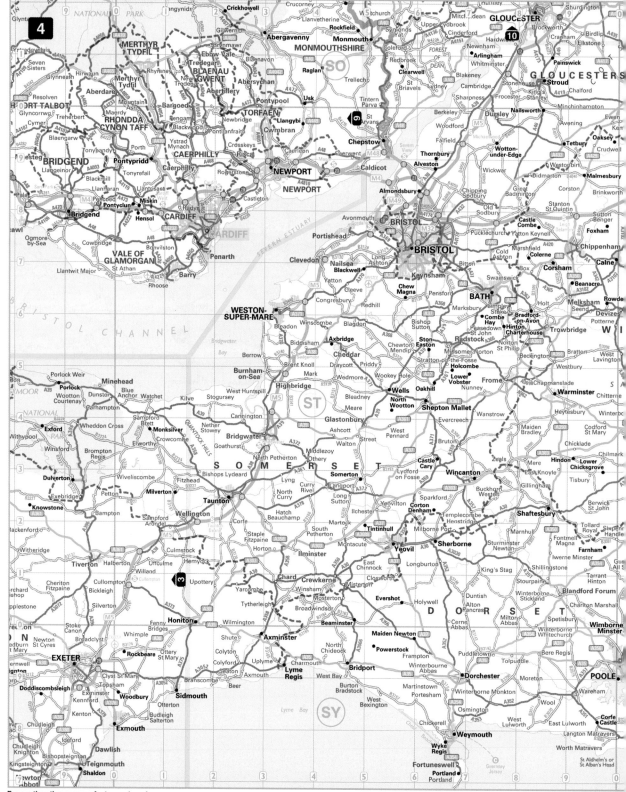

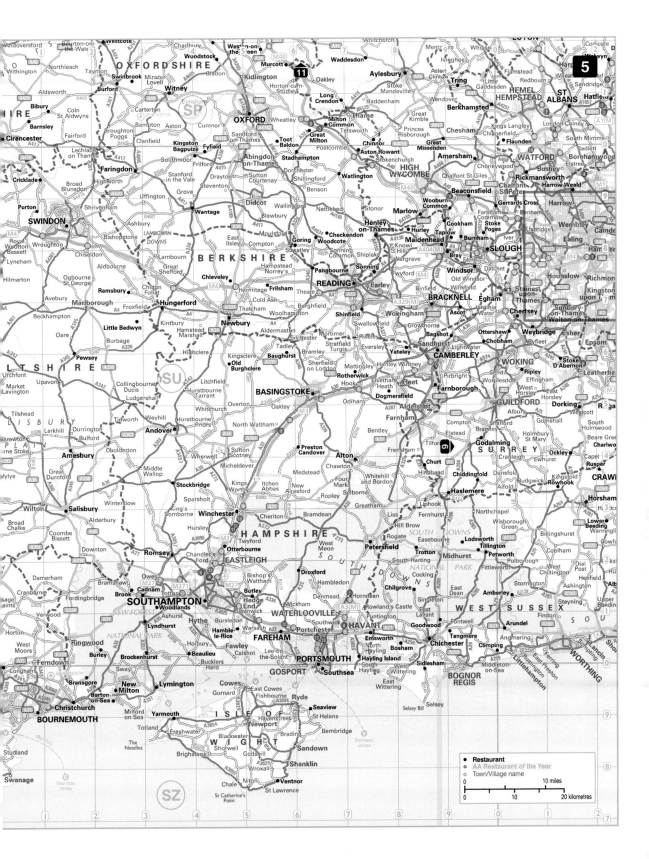

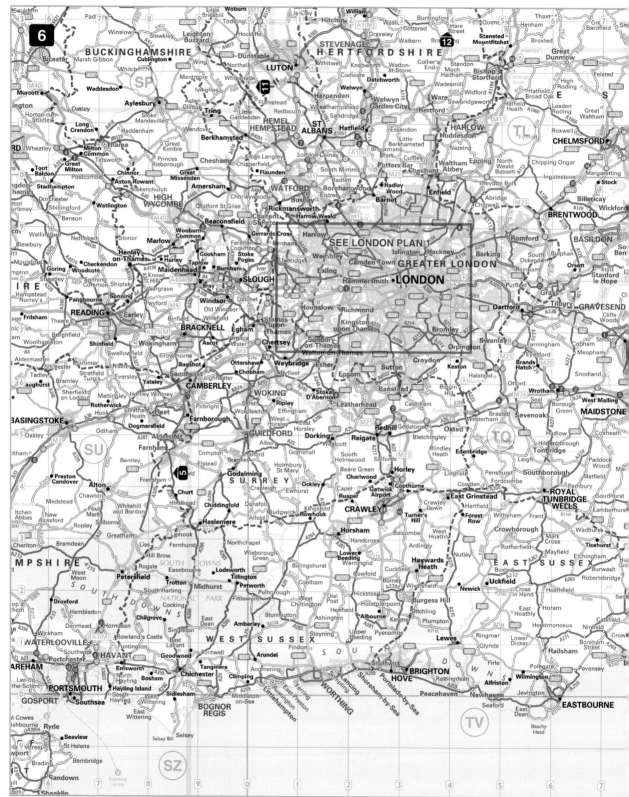

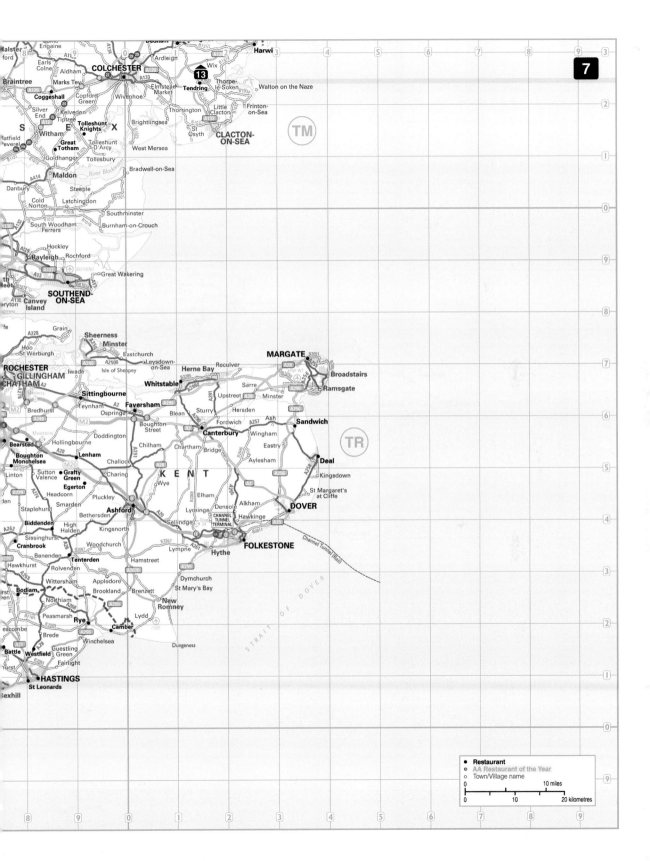

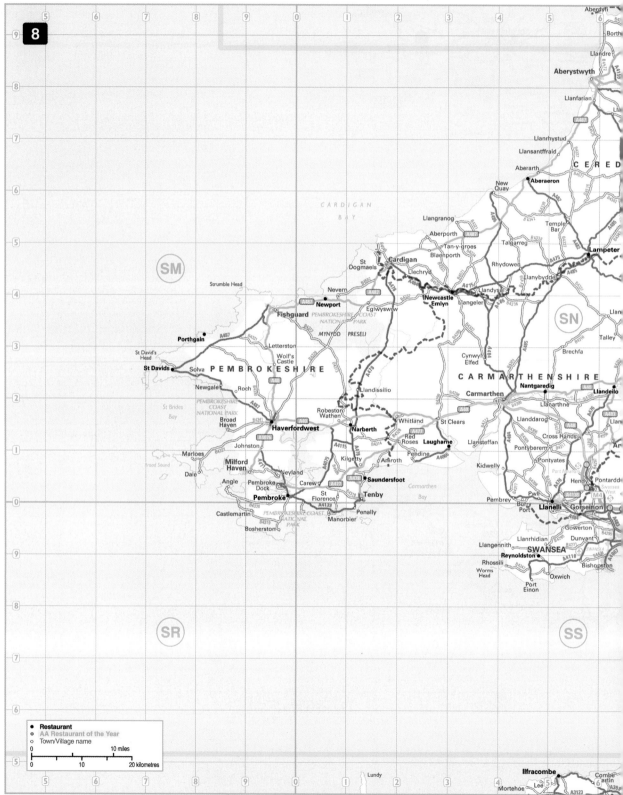

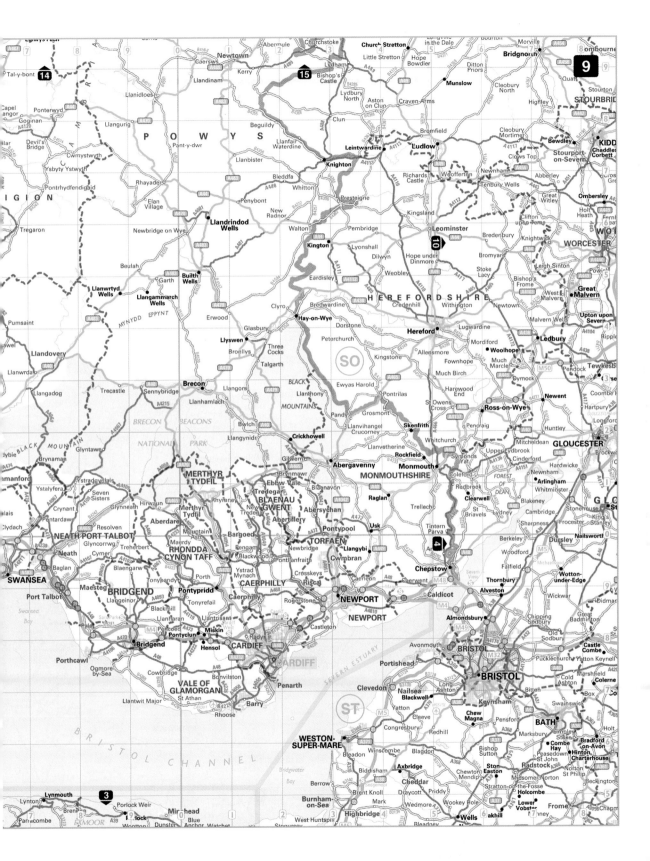

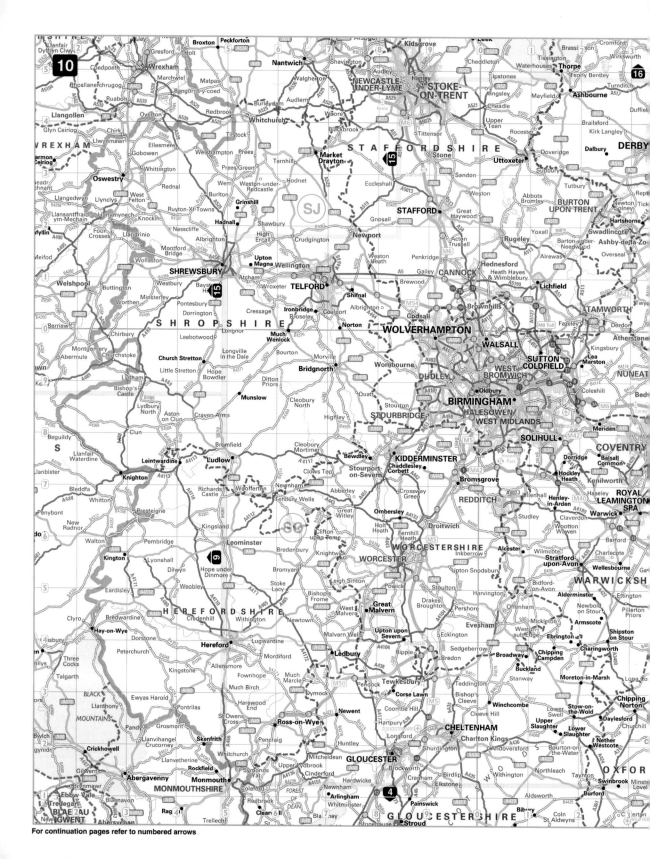

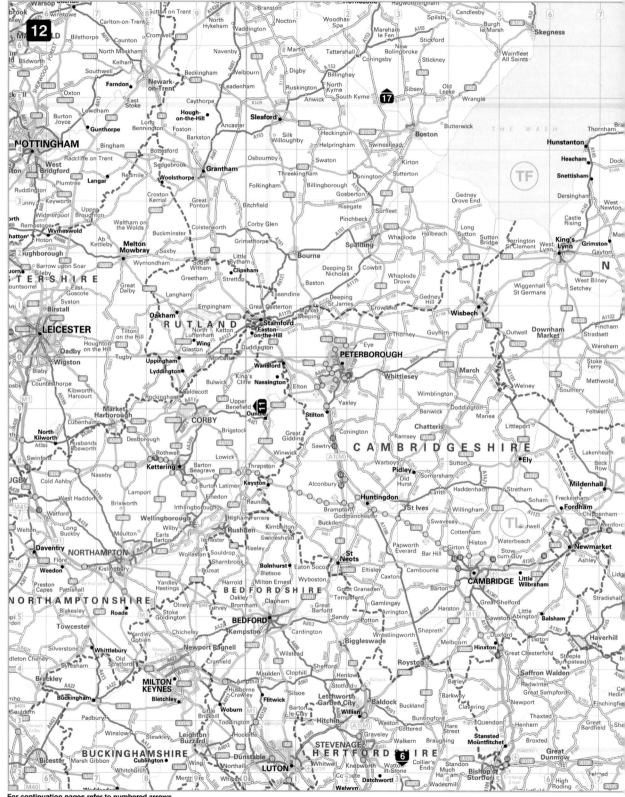

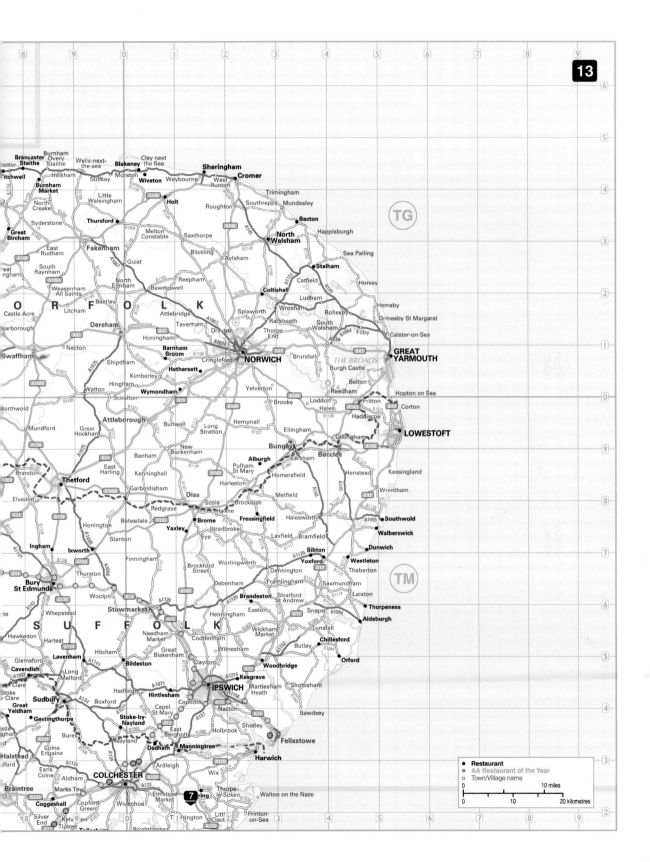

ISLE OF
ANGLESEY

Holyhead

Trearddur Bay

Holy
Island

Rhosneigr

A
N
G
L
E
S
E
Y

Cemaes

Amlwch

Llanerchymedd

Llanfachraeth

Benllech

Red
Wharf Bay

Llangoed

Pentraeth

Menai
Bridge

Llanfair
P G

Beaumaris

Bangor

Aberffraw

Y Felinheli

Newborough

Caernarfón

Bontnewydd

Caernarfon
Bay

Llanrug

Llanberis

Llandwrog

Llanwnda

Penygroes

Rhyd Ddu

Clynnog-fawr

Llanaelhaearn

Morfa Nefyn

Nefyn

Bodfuan

PENINSULA

Llanystumdwy

Prenteg

Tremadog

Maentwrog

Criccieth

Porthmadog

Portmeirion

LLEYN

Sarn

Borth-y-Gest

Talsarnau

Trawsfynydd

Pwllheli

Aberdaron

Y Rhiw

Llanbedrog

Abersoch

Harlech

Bardsey
Island

Llanbedr

Dyffryn Ardudwy

Ganllwyd

Tal-y-bont

Barmouth

Fairbourne

Dolgellau

Llwyngwril

Corris

Llandudno

Deganwy

Rhôs-
on-Sea

Colwyn Bay

Rhyl

Conwy

Abergele

Llandulas

Penmaenmawr

Llansanffraid
Glan Conwy

Betws-yn-Rhos

Llanfairfechan

Tal-y-Cafn

Llanllechid

Bethesda

Tal-y-Bont

Trefriw

Llanrwst

Llangernyw

Llanfair
Talhaiarn

Llansannan

Bylchau

Capel Curig

CONWY

Betws-y-Coed

Dolwyddelan

Penmachno

Pentrefoelas

Cerrigydrudion

Y Maerd

Beddgelert

Blaenau Ffestiniog

Ffestiniog

SNOWDONIA

NATIONAL

PARK

Llanuwchllyn

Bala

G W Y N E D D

M
O
U
N
T
A
I
N
S

Dinas-Mawddwy

Mallwyd

Llangadfan

Cemmaes
Road

Llanbrynmair

Carno

Tywyn

Bryncrug

Pennal

Machynlleth

Aberdyfi

Eglwys Fach

SN

Borth

Tal-y-bont

Llandre

Aberystwyth

Capel
Bangor

Ponterwyd

Llanidloes

Restaurant
AA Restaurant of the Year
Town/Village name

0		10 miles
0	10	20 kilometres

For continuation pages refer to numbered arrows

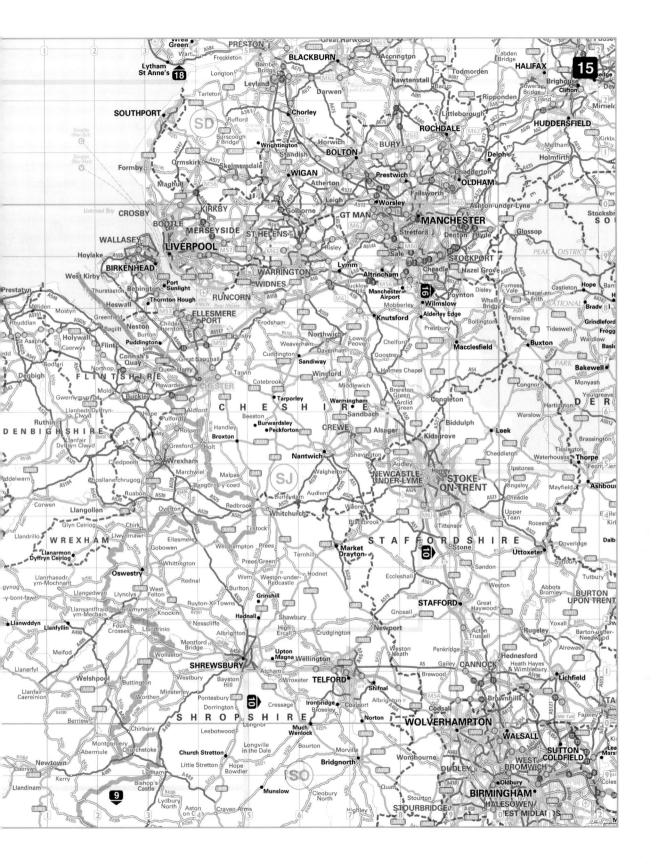

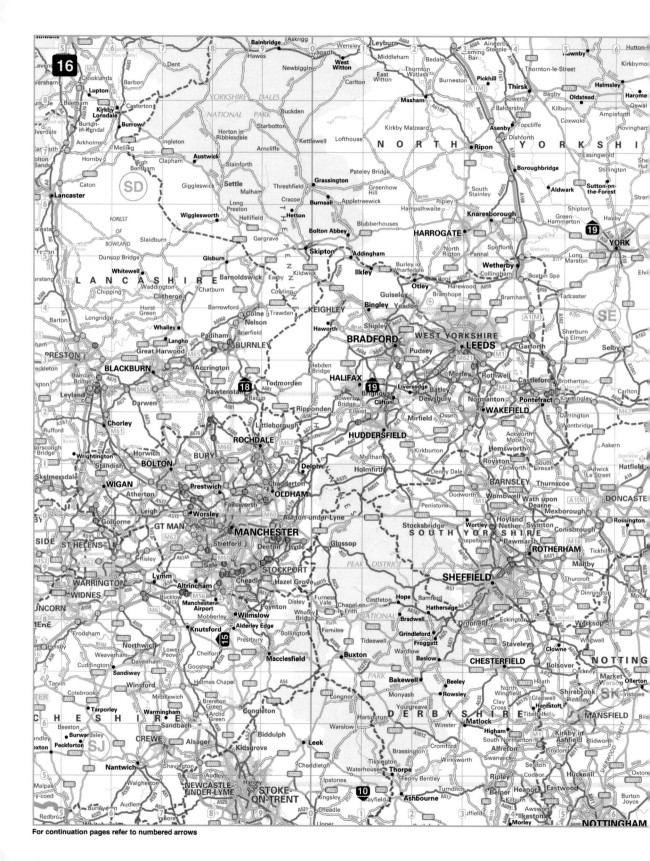

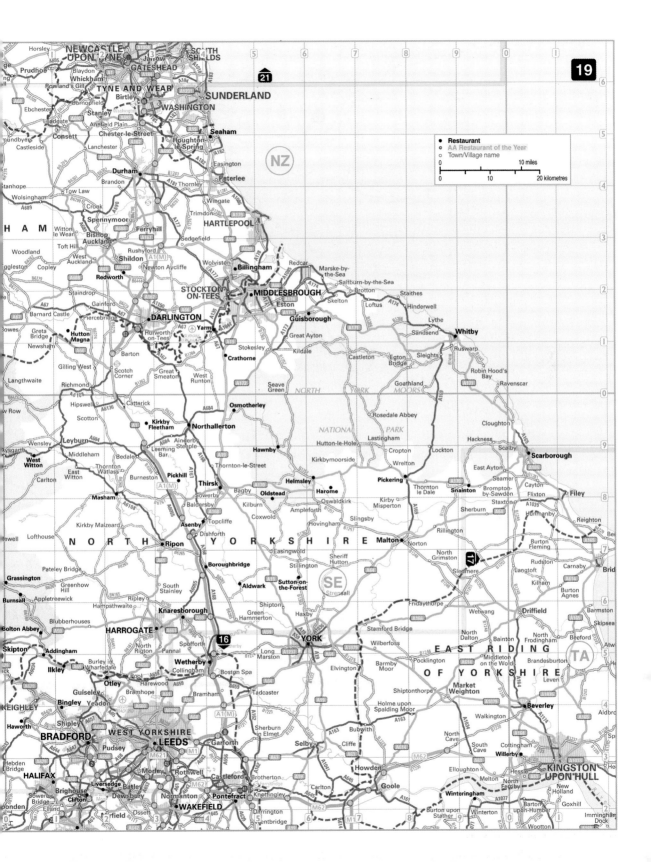

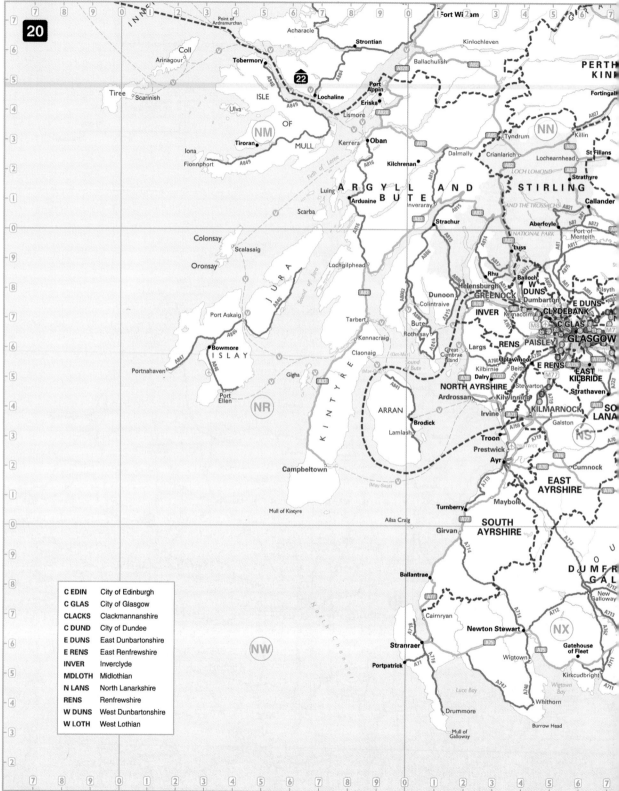

20

C EDIN   City of Edinburgh
C GLAS   City of Glasgow
CLACKS   Clackmannanshire
C DUND   City of Dundee
E DUNS   East Dunbartonshire
E RENS   East Renfrewshire
INVER   Inverclyde
MDLOTH   Midlothian
N LANS   North Lanarkshire
RENS   Renfrewshire
W DUNS   West Dunbartonshire
W LOTH   West Lothian

NA H-EILEANAN AN IAR

ISLE OF LEWIS

Rudha Rhobhanais
(Butt of Lewis)
Port Nis
(Port of Ness)

Cellar Head

Cape Wrath

Scourie

Lochinver

Inchnadamph

Lochinver

Achiltibuie

Great Bernera

Carlabhagh
(Carloway)

Tiumpan Head

Steornabhagh
(Stornoway)

OUTER HEBRIDES

Scarp

Scalpay

Taransay

Tairbeart
(Tarbert)

HARRIS

Pabbay

Berneray

Boreray

Ullapool

Gruinord Bay

Gairloch

Kinlochewe

Achnasheen

NORTH UIST

Loch nam Madadh
(Lochmaddy)

Benbecula

Ronay

Wiay

Stein

Colbost

Dunvegan

Staffin

Uig

ISLE OF SKYE

Portree

Struan

Drynoch

Torridon

NORTH WEST HIGHLANDS

SOUTH UIST

Loch Baghasdail
(Lochboisdale)

Eriskay

Canna

Soay

Scalpay

Raasay

Inner Sound

Kyle of Lochalsh

Cannich

Shiel Bridge

BARRA

Bagh a Chaisteil
(Castlebay)

Sandray

Mingulay

INNER HEBRIDES

Rùm

Eigg

Muck

Point of Ardnamurchan

Isleornsay

Ardvasar

Mallaig

Sound of Sleat

Invergarry

NL

Coll

Arinagour

Glenfinnan

Fort William

Kinlochleven

Spean Bridge

Tobermory

Strontian

Ballachulish

Tiree

Scarinish

ISLE OF MULL

Lochaline

Port Appin

Eriska

Lismore

Ulva

Iona

Fionnphort

Tiroran

Kerrera

Oban

Dalmally

Crianlaric

Kilchrenan

Tyn

For continuation pages refer to numbered arrows

Restaurant
AA Restaurant of the Year
Town/Village name

| 0 | | 10 | | 20 miles |
| 0 | 10 | 20 | 30 kilometres |

Durness
Strathy Point
Bettyhill
Tongue
Melvich
Thurso
Scrabster
Gills
Dunnet Head
Duncansby Head
John o' Groats
St Margaret's Hope
Stromness
PENTLAND FIRTH

NC
Altnaharra
Wick
ND
Lybster
Dunbeath

Helmsdale

Lairg
Golspie
Brora
Bonar Bridge
Dornoch
Tain

HIGHLAND

Alness
Invergordon
Cromarty
NH
Dingwall
Fortrose
Nairn
Forres
Lossiemouth
Elgin
Buckie
Cullen
Portsoy
Banff
Fraserburgh
Muir of Ord
INVERNESS
MORAY
Rothes
Keith
Aberchirder
Turriff
NJ
Aberlour
Huntly
Peterhead
Dufftown
NK
Drumnadrochit
Grantown-on-Spey
Oldmeldrum
Ellon
Carrbridge
Tomintoul
Alford
Kintore
Balmedie
Dyce
Inverurie
Invermoriston
Aviemore
CAIRNGORMS
ABERDEENSHIRE
CITY OF ABERDEEN
Fort Augustus
Monadhliath Mountains
CAIRNGORM MOUNTAINS
ABERDEEN
Kingussie
NATIONAL
Peterculter
Newtonmore
Braemar
Ballater
Aboyne
Banchory
Crathes
PARK
Stonehaven
GRAMPIAN MOUNTAINS
Laurencekirk
Inverbervie
Blair Atholl
NO
Killiecrankie
Pitlochry
ANGUS
Brechin
Montrose
NN
Kirriemuir
Inverkeilor
PERTH AND KINROSS
Aberfeldy
Blairgowrie
Forfar
21
Fortingall
Kenmore
Dunkeld
Coupar Angus
Arbroath
Kinclaven
SIDLAW HILLS
Carnoustie
Killin
DUNDEE
Newport-on-Tay
Loch Earnhead
St Fillans
Perth
St Andrews Bay
Camrie
Crieff

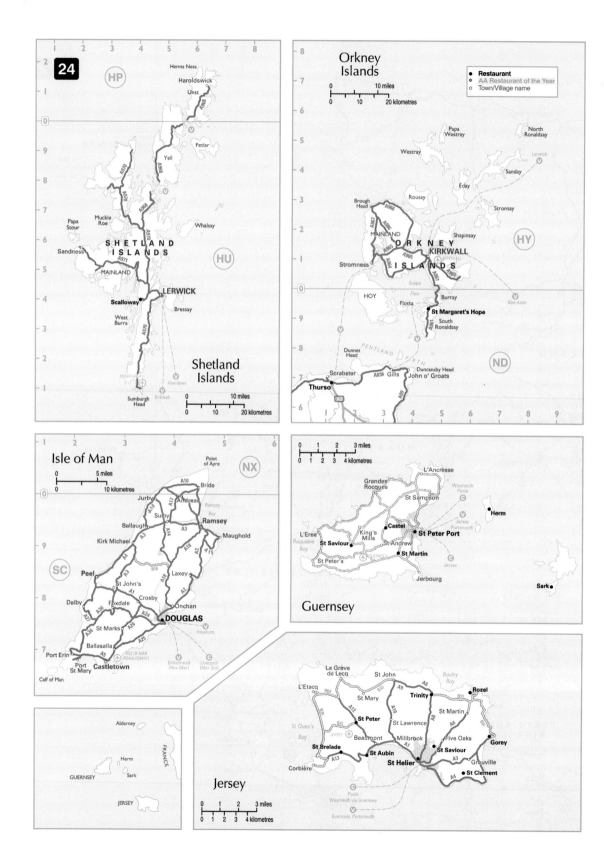

24

Shetland Islands

Herma Ness
Haroldswick
Unst
A968

HP

HU

Fetlar

Yell
A968

A970

Whalsay

Muckle Roe

Papa Stour

SHETLAND
ISLANDS

Sandness
A971
MAINLAND

LERWICK
Scalloway
Bressay

West Burra

A970

Sumburgh Head
Kirkwall
Aberdeen

Orkney Islands

● Restaurant
◉ AA Restaurant of the Year
○ Town/Village name

0   10 miles
0   10   20 kilometres

Papa Westray

North Ronaldsay

Westray

Sanday

Lerwick

Éday

Rousay

Stronsay

Brough Head
A966

MAINLAND

ORKNEY
A965

KIRKWALL

Shapinsay

HY

Stromness
A964
ISLANDS

Scapa Flow

HOY

Flotta

Burray

Aberdeen

St Margaret's Hope
South Ronaldsay

A961

Dunnet Head

PENTLAND FIRTH

ND

Scrabster
A836 Gills
Duncansby Head
John o' Groats

Thurso

A9

Isle of Man

Point of Ayre

NX

0   5 miles
0   10 kilometres

Bride
A10

Jurby
Sulby
A17
Andreas

A3
Ballaugh
A14
Ramsey Bay
Ramsey

Kirk Michael

Maughold

A18
A2
A15

SC

Peel
A3
A1
St John's
Crosby
A18
Laxey

Dalby

Foxdale
A24
Onchan

A36
St Marks
A26
DOUGLAS

Ballasalla
A25

Port Erin
A5
Heysham

Port St Mary
Castletown
ISLE OF MAN (RONALDSWAY)

Birkenhead (Nov–Mar)
Liverpool (Mar–Oct)

Calf of Man

Guernsey

0   1   2   3 miles
0 1 2 3 4 kilometres

L'Ancresse

Grandes Rocques
Weymouth Poole

St Sampson

Herm

L'Eree
Castel
St Saviour
King's Mills
St Peter Port
St Andrew
Jersey Portsmouth

L'Eree
Roquaine Bay

St Peter's
St Martin

Jerbourg

Sark

Jersey

GUERNSEY

Alderney

Herm

FRANCE

Sark

JERSEY

La Grève de Lecq
St John
Bouley Bay

L'Etacq
St Mary
Rozel
Trinity

St Ouen's Bay
St Peter
St Martin

Beaumont
St Lawrence
Five Oaks
Gorey

St Brelade
Millbrook
St Saviour

Corbière
St Aubin
St Helier
Grouville

St Clement

0   1   2   3 miles
0 1 2 3 4 kilometres

Index of Restaurants

N

Acknowledgments

The Automobile Association wishes to thank the following photographers and organisations for their assistance in the preparation of this book.

Abbreviations for the picture credits are as follows – (t) top; (b) bottom; (l) left; (r) right; (c) centre; (AA) AA World Travel Library

Front Cover: © A. Astes / Alamy

England Opener AA/Adam Burton;
London Opener AA/James Tims;
Scotland Opener AA/Sue Anderson;
Wales Opener AA/Mark Bauer;
Republic of Ireland Opener AA/Karl Blackwell

003 Courtesy of Paul Sanders Photography; 004 Courtesy of Olive Tree Restaurant at the Queensbury Hotel, Wiltshire; 008 © Sandy Young / Alamy; 010 Courtesy of David Griffin Photography; 011 Courtesy of Rob Whitrow Photography; 012 Courtesy of The River Café, London; 013t Courtesy of Hilton, Galvin at Windows, London; 014-015 AA/James Tims; 014l Courtesy of The Sticky Walnut, Cheshire; 014r Courtesy of London Berners Tavern; 015l Courtesy of Timberyard, Edinburgh; 015r Courtesy of Bully's, South Glamorgan; 016 © Don B. Stevenson / Alamy; 17 AA/James Tims; 018-019 AA/James Tims; 018 Courtesy of Olive Tree Restaurant at the Queensbury Hotel, Wiltshire; 019l Courtesy of The Peat Inn, Glasgow; 019r Courtesy of The Grove, Hertfordshire; 020-021 © Images of Birmingham Premium / Alamy; 023 © Images of Birmingham / Alamy; 024-025 © Neil Setchfield / Alamy; 027 Courtesy of Paul Sanders Photography; 028-029 Courtesy of Andrew Brownsword Hotels; 030-031 Courtesy of Andrew Brownsword Hotels; 251 AA/Tom Mackie; 345 AA/ Sarah Montgomery; 583 © Christopher smith / Alamy; 598 AA/Peter Sharpe; 657 AA/Jim Henderson; 677 AA/Colin Molyneux; 688 © Billy Stock / Alamy; 689 AA/ Christopher Hill; 695 AA/Christopher Hill; 725 AA/Caroline Jones.

Every effort has been made to trace the copyright holders, and we apologise in advance for any unintentional omissions or errors. We would be pleased to apply any corrections in a following edition of this publication.